THOMSON LEAR

CERTIFIED BUSINESS MANAGER

CBM Examination Preparation Guide

Helping Business Specialists Become Business Generalists

P2

volume three
theory for functional areas

Australia · Canada · Mexico · Singapore · Spain · United Kingdom · United States

Certified Business Manager (CBM) Examination Preparation Guide

Part 2, Volume 3: Theory for Functional Areas

VP/Executive Publisher:
Dave Shaut

Sr. Acquisition Editor:
Scott Person

Developmental Editor:
Sara Froelicher

Sr. Production Editor:
Deanna Quinn

Marketing Manager:
Mark Linton

Manufacturing Coordinator:
Charlene Taylor

Internal Designer:
Chris Miller

Cover Designer:
Chris Miller

Production House and Compositor:
Carlisle Publisher Services

Printer:
West Group

COPYRIGHT © 2004
by South-Western, a division of Thomson Learning. Thomson Learning™ is a trademark used herein under license.

Printed in the United States of America
1 2 3 4 5 05 04 03 02

For more information
contact South-Western,
5191 Natorp Boulevard,
Mason, Ohio 45040.
Or you can visit our Internet site at:
http://www.swlearning.com

ALL RIGHTS RESERVED.
No part of this work covered by the copyright hereon may be reproduced or used in any form or by any means—graphic, electronic, or mechanical, including photocopying, recording, taping, Web distribution or information storage and retrieval systems—without the written permission of the publisher.

For permission to use material from this text or product, contact us by
Tel (800) 730-2214
Fax (800) 730-2215
http://www.thomsonrights.com

Library of Congress Control Number: 2003103961

ISBN 0-324-27327-4

Contents

Preface	ix

Accounting — Module 600

601	Accounting Strategies	2
603	Role of Accounting and Controller	3
605	The Accounting Process	8
610	Assets, Liabilities, and Owner's Equity	9
620	Analysis and Use of Financial Statements	27
630	Cost Behavior, Control, and Decision Making	43
640	Product and Service Costs	57
650	Operating Budgets and Performance Evaluation	68
660	Decision Making and Accounting	98
665	Accounting and Reporting	120
670	Information Systems and Accounting	122
675	Auditing and Accounting	123
680	Control and Accounting	127
685	Ethics and Accounting	140
690	Economics and Accounting	142
695	Law and Accounting	142
699	International Issues	143

Module 600 Glossary ... 172
Module 600 Endnotes ... 188

Finance — Module 700

701 Finance Strategies ... 191
703 Role of Finance and Chief Financial Officer ... 196
704 Working Capital Policy ... 199
705 Managing Short-Term Assets ... 208
710 Managing Short-Term Financing ... 220
715 Managing Long-Term Financing ... 232
720 Financial Forecasting, Planning, and Control ... 266
725 Cost of Capital, Capital Structure, and Dividend Policy ... 292
735 Capital Budgeting ... 315
745 Financial Markets, Instruments, and Institutions ... 335
755 Financial Risk Management ... 346
760 Mergers, Acquisitions, and Business Valuations ... 335
765 Operations, Marketing, and Finance ... 365
770 Quantitative Techniques and Finance ... 367
775 Economics and Finance ... 381
780 Accounting and Finance ... 386
785 Quality and Finance ... 387
790 Law and Finance ... 388
795 Ethics and Finance ... 391
799 International Issues ... 392
Module 700 Appendix ... 442
Module 700 Glossary ... 450
Module 700 Endnotes ... 479

Information Technology — Module 800

801	Information Technology Strategies	481
803	Role of Information Technology and Chief Information Officer	487
805	Information Systems Planning	488
810	Information Technology Control and Governance	496
815	Information Technology Risk Management	497
820	Managing Information and Technology	503
825	Decision Making and Information Technology	511
830	Value Creation with Information Technology	519
835	Quality and Information Technology	525
840	Best Practices in Information Technology	526
845	Data and Knowledge Management	530
850	Systems Development and Acquisition	530
855	Managing Information Technology Resources	578
860	Telecommunications and Networks	589
865	Business Information Systems	608
870	Information Technology Security and Controls	621
875	Electronic Commerce and Information Technology	630
880	Information Technology Contingency Plans	641
885	Auditing and Information Technology	643
890	Ethics and Information Technology	644
895	Law and Information Technology	647
899	International Issues	653
Module 800 Glossary		659
Module 800 Endnotes		673

Corporate Control and Governance — Module 900

901 Corporate Control Strategies	675
910 Internal Control Framework and Control Models	677
920 Best Practices in Internal Control	684
930 Corporate Fraud	685
940 Corporate Risk Management	726
950 Corporate Citizenship and Accountability	745
960 Corporate Public Policy and Affairs	756
970 Issues Management and Crisis Management	761
980 Corporate Ethics and Management Assurance	771
990 Corporate Governance	782
999 International Issues	792
Module 900 Glossary	802
Module 900 Endnotes	810

International Business — Module 1000

1001 Global Business Strategies	818
1010 Forms of International Business and Marketing Strategies	823
1020 International Risks	836
1030 Global Organization Structure and Control	838
1040 International Trade and Investment	855
1050 International Payments	866
1060 International Cultures and Protocols	871
1070 Economics and International Business	880
1075 International Banking	901
1080 Law and International Business	908
1090 Ethics and International Business	919

1099 International Issues ... 924
Module 1000 Glossary ... 931
Module 1000 Endnotes ... 948

Subject Index 953

Preface

Helping Business Specialists Become Business Generalists

Here is the best source to help streamline your CBM Exam preparation efforts.

The ***Certified Business Manager (CBM) Examination Preparation Guide: Part 2, Volume 3: Theory for Functional Areas*** is one of a six-volume series developed solely to help you prepare for the CBM Exam. Designed with flexibility in mind, each guide can be used either in a self-study or group-study environment. Third-party review course providers such as professional associations, universities, and private organizations can also use this series to conduct review classes for CBM Exam candidates.

Developed by the best minds in the business management field, this series is a compilation of information from subject matter experts who are highly trained and experienced in the business management field. For a complete listing of these experts, see the acknowledgements section.

The goal of the CBM program is to help business specialists become business generalists. The CBM is to a business manager as the CPA is to an accountant, as the PE is to an engineer, and as the CFA is to an investment analyst.

The CBM Exam consists of three parts:

Part 1: Core Areas
Part 2: Functional Areas
Part 3: Integrated Areas

Designed specifically with these three parts in mind, this Study Guide series addresses all of these parts to make exam preparation both comprehensive and easy as possible.

Part 1, Volume 1: Theory for Core Areas
Part 1, Volume 2: Practice for Core Areas
Part 2, Volume 3: Theory for Functional Areas
Part 2, Volume 4: Practice for Functional Areas
Part 3, Volume 5: Theory for Integrated Areas
Part 3, Volume 6: Practice for Integrated Areas

Each part requires two volumes to study from: Theory and Practice Guides. Theory Guides (Volumes 1, 3, and 5) cover the subject matter as defined in the Common Body of Knowledge for Business (CBKB), which is the basis for the CBM Exam. The CBKB is a blend of undergraduate and graduate studies in business spread over ten modules. Practice Guides (Volumes 2, 4, and 6) contain multiple-choice questions, answers, and explanations in line with the CBKB. The three-part CBM Exam contains multiple-choice questions only.

The best way to study the Theory Guides is to review the module glossary prior to reading the corresponding text. Due to the comprehensive nature of the Theory Guides, the CBM practitioner can also use them as desk reference resources. The best way to study the Practice Guides is to self-test the questions prior to reading the study questions, answers, and explanations. When reading the Theory and Practice Guides together, read the Theory Guides first followed by the Practice Guides.

The CBM program is sponsored and administered by the Association of Professionals in Business Management (APBM) who can be reached at the following address.

Association of Professionals in Business Management
4929 Wilshire Boulevard, Suite 930, Los Angeles, California, 90010-3835 USA
Phone: 323-936-6757   Fax: 323-936-6171
e-mail: info@cbmexam.com   Web site: *www.cbmexam.com*

Questions related to application materials, eligibility requirements, examination sites and dates, fees, and other administrative matters should be directed to *info@cbmexam.com* or visit *www.cbmexam.com*.

To purchase this series, or individual guides, contact either South-Western, a division of Thomson Learning, *www.swlearning.com/cbm.html*, *www.cbmexam.com*, or SRV Professional Publications *www.srvbooks.com*. Volume purchases can be made through South-Western for university, corporate, government, and professional association purchases by contacting *www.swlearning.com/cbm.html* or 1-800-842-3636.

Acknowledgments

A special thanks to the following South-Western authors for allowing the use of their information in developing comprehensive and high-quality study guides to prepare for the CBM Exam.

Accounting, Module 600

Financial and Managerial Accounting by Warren/Reeve/Fess, 7th edition, © 2002, 0-324-02540-8
International Accounting by Iqbal, 2nd edition, © 2002, 0-324-02350-2

Finance, Module 700

Essentials of Managerial Finance by Besley/Brigham, 12th edition, © 2000, 0-030-25872-3
International Financial Management by Madura, 7th edition, © 2003, 0-324-16551-X
Short-Term Financial Management by Maness/Zietlow, 2nd edition, © 2002, 0-030-31513-1

Information Technology, Module 800

Management Information Systems by Oz, 3rd edition, © 2002, 0-619-06250-9

Corporate Control and Governance, Module 900

Fraud Examination by Albrecht, 1st edition, © 2003, 0-324-16296-0
Business and Society by Carroll/Buchholtz, 5th edition, © 2003, 0-324-11495-8
Risk Management and Insurance by Trieschmann, 11th edition, © 2001, 0-324-01663-8

International Business, Module 1000

International Economics by Carbaugh, 8th edition, © 2002, 0-324-05589-7
International Business by Czinkota, 6th edition, © 2003, 0-324-17660-0
Essentials of Business Law and the Legal Environment by Mann/Roberts, 7th edition, © 2001, 0-324-04052-0
International Management by Rodrigues, 2nd edition, © 2001, 0-324-04150-0
International Business Law and Its Environment by Schaffer/Earle/Agusti, 5th edition, © 2002, 0-324-06098-X

About South-Western (A part of The THOMSON Corporation)

South-Western, a part of The Thomson Corporation, is the leading educational provider of business and economics materials worldwide. South-Western offers the most extensive selection of business education products and services on the market today for higher education, secondary education, as well as corporate and retail business environments. Integrating the latest technologies with many of its products, South-Western also delivers interactive learning solutions that engage learners, enhance retention and provide results.

The Professional Portfolio

South-Western is pleased to add the *CBM Examination Preparation Guide* to its Professional Portfolio. This rapidly expanding, topic-specific collection includes corporate strategy, business and technology, finance, global business, marketing, and other significant business titles.

MODULE 600

Accounting

601 Accounting Strategies, 2

603 Role of Accounting and Controller, 3

605 The Accounting Process, 8

610 Assets, Liabilities, and Owner's Equity, 9

620 Analysis and Use of Financial Statements, 27

630 Cost Behavior, Control, and Decision Making, 43

640 Product and Service Costs, 57

650 Operating Budgets and Performance Evaluation, 68

660 Decision Making and Accounting, 98

665 Accounting and Reporting, 120

670 Information Systems and Accounting, 122

675 Auditing and Accounting, 123

680 Control and Accounting, 127

685 Ethics and Accounting, 140

690 Economics and Accounting, 142

695 Law and Accounting, 142

699 International Issues, 143

Module 600 Glossary, 172

Module 600 Endnotes, 188

Accounting Strategies

The Accounting Function

The accounting function in a firm is a service activity. Its objective is to provide quantitative information, primarily financial in nature, about economic entities that is intended to be useful in making economic decisions. The economic decision makers, whether they are external or internal to a firm, must recognize that the information they receive from the accounting function of a firm constitute only a part of the information they need to make sound decisions. Examples of external decision makers include investors, creditors, and regulators. Examples of internal decision makers are managers, owners, and employees.

The reports generated from accounting information can be thought of as the tools of the accounting trade. Those attempting to use the accounting reports must have a thorough and clear understanding of what these tools can do and what they cannot do. The decision makers should be aware of the limitations of the accounting tools and imperfections of the accounting information due to estimations and judgments involved.

Both internal and external decision makers are attempting to predict the future and timing of cash flows of the firm in terms of determining whether they will be paid, when they will be paid, and how much they will be paid. Here cash is the ultimate measuring criterion in evaluating a firm's success or failure.

The accounting function collects the raw data from business transactions and converts them into information useful to the decision maker. In this regard, the accounting information should contain two qualitative characteristics: primary and secondary qualities. See Exhibit 600.1 for qualities of accounting information.

The challenge to the accounting management, as well as to the senior management of a firm, is to develop strategies to achieve the primary and secondary qualitative characteristics of useful accounting information. When accounting information has these qualitative characteristics, the firm can provide the useful and needed quantitative information to decision makers.

Primary Qualities

The two primary qualities that distinguish useful accounting information are relevance and reliability. If either of these qualities is missing, accounting information will not be useful. Relevance means the information must have a bearing on a particular decision situation. Relevant accounting information possesses at least two characteristics: timeliness and predictive value or feedback value. Timeliness means accounting information must be provided in time to influence a particular decision. Predictive value means accounting information can be used to predict the future and timing of cash flows. Feedback value means the accounting function must provide decision makers with information that allows them to assess the progress or economic worth of an investment.

To be considered reliable, accounting information must possess three qualities: verifiability, representational faithfulness, and neutrality. Information is considered verifiable if several individuals, working independently, would arrive at similar conclusions using the same data. Representational faithfulness means accounting information must report what actually happened. Neutrality means accounting information must be free of bias or distortion.

Exhibit 600.1 *Qualities of Accounting Information*

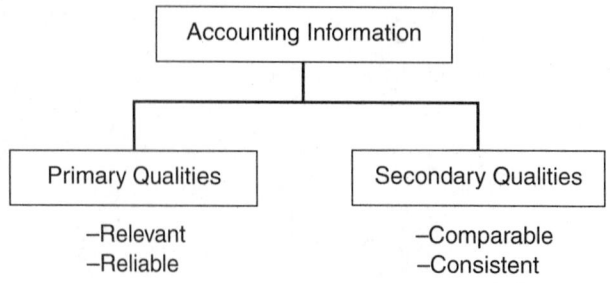

Secondary Qualities

"Secondary qualities" does not mean that these characteristics are of lesser importance than the primary qualities. If a secondary characteristic is missing, the accounting information is not necessarily useless. The secondary qualities of useful information are comparability and consistency. Comparability means accounting reports generated for one firm may be easily and usefully compared with the accounting reports generated for other firms. If the two firms use totally different accounting methods, it would be very difficult to make a useful comparison of their data and information. Consistency means that a firm systematically uses the same accounting methods and procedures from one accounting period to the next accounting period.

In addition to the primary and secondary qualities, the accounting information must be understandable to economic decision makers. "Earnings management" strategy can destroy the primary and secondary qualities of accounting information.

Role of Accounting and Controller

The Role of Accounting in Business

What is the role of accounting in business? The simplest answer to this question is that accounting provides information for managers to use in operating the business. In addition, accounting provides information to other stakeholders to use in assessing the economic performance and condition of the business.

In a general sense, accounting can be defined as an information system that provides reports to stakeholders about the economic activities and condition of a business. You may think of accounting as the "language of business." This is because accounting is the means by which business information is communicated to the stakeholders. For example, accounting reports summarizing the profitability of a new product help **Coca-Cola's** management decide whether to continue selling the product. Likewise, financial analysts use accounting reports in deciding whether to recommend the purchase of Coca-Cola's stock. Banks use accounting reports in determining the amount of credit to extend to Coca-Cola. Suppliers use accounting reports in deciding whether to offer credit for Coca-Cola's purchases of supplies and raw materials. State and federal governments use accounting reports as a basis for assessing taxes on Coca-Cola.

> Accounting is an information system that provides reports to stakeholders about the economic activities and condition of a business.

Accrual accounting, which matches revenues against expenses, provides most useful information for decision makers. The process by which accounting provides information to business stakeholders is illustrated in Exhibit 600.2.

Exhibit 600.2 *Accounting Information and the Stakeholders of a Business*

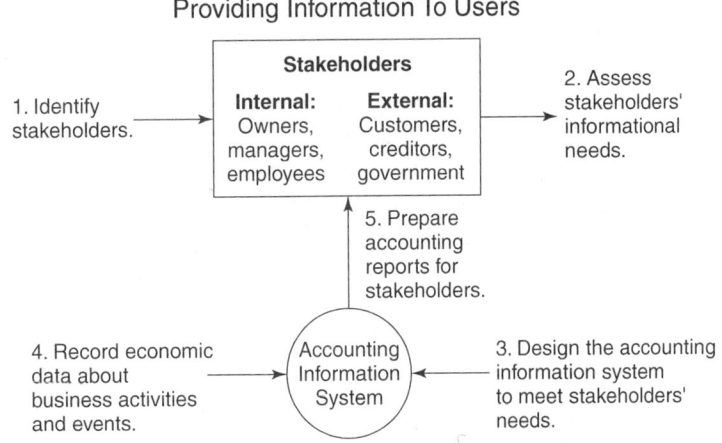

A business must first identify its stakeholders. It must then assess the various informational needs of those stakeholders and design its accounting system to meet those needs. Finally, the accounting system records the economic data about business activities and events, which the business reports to the stakeholders according to their informational needs.

Stakeholders use accounting reports as a primary source of information on which they base their decisions. They use other information as well. For example, in deciding whether to extend credit to an appliance store, a banker might use economic forecasts to assess the future demand for the store's products. During periods of economic downturn, the demand for consumer appliances normally declines. The banker might inquire about the ability and reputation of the managers of the business. For small corporations, bankers may require major stockholders to personally guarantee the loans of the business. Finally, bankers might consult industry publications that rank similar businesses as to their quality of products, customer satisfaction, and future prospects for growth.

Profession of Accounting

Accountants engage in either private accounting or public accounting. Accountants employed by a business firm or a not-for-profit organization are said to be engaged in **private accounting.** Accountants and their staff who provide services on a fee basis are said to be employed in **public accounting.**

Because all functions within a business use accounting information, experience in private or public accounting provides a solid foundation for a career. Many positions in industry and in government agencies are held by individuals with accounting backgrounds.

Private Accounting

The scope of activities and duties of private accountants varies widely. Private accountants are frequently called *management accountants*. If they are employed by a manufacturer, they may be referred to as *industrial* or *cost accountants*. The chief accountant in a business may be called the **controller.** Various state and federal agencies and other not-for-profit agencies also employ accountants.

Public Accounting

In public accounting, an accountant may practice as an individual or as a member of a public accounting firm. Public accountants who have met a state's education, experience, and examination requirements may become **certified public accountants (CPAs).**

Most states do not permit individuals to practice as CPAs until they have had from one to three years' experience in public accounting. Some states, however, accept similar employment in private accounting as equivalent experience. All states require continuing professional education and adherence to standards of ethical conduct.[1]

Specialized Accounting Fields

You may think that all accounting is the same. However, you will find several specialized fields of accounting in practice. The two most common are financial accounting and managerial accounting. Other fields include cost accounting, environmental accounting, tax accounting, accounting systems, international accounting, not-for-profit accounting, and social accounting.

Financial accounting is primarily concerned with the recording and reporting of economic data and activities for a business. Although such reports provide useful information for managers, they are the primary reports for owners, creditors, governmental agencies, and the public. For example, if you wanted to buy some stock in **PepsiCo, American Airlines,** or **McDonald's,** how would you know in which company to invest? One way is to review financial reports and compare the financial performance and condition of each company. The purpose of financial accounting is to provide such reports. We address this topic in greater detail later.

Managerial accounting, or **management accounting,** uses both financial accounting and estimated data to aid management in running day-to-day operations and in planning future operations. Management accountants gather and report information that is relevant and timely to the decision-making needs of management. For example, management might need information on alternative ways to finance the construction of a new building. Alternatively, management might need information on whether to expand its operations into a new product line. Thus, reports to management can differ widely in form and content. We provide additional discussion of this topic later.

Generally Accepted Accounting Principles

If the management of a company could record and report financial data as it saw fit, comparisons among companies would be difficult, if not impossible. Thus, financial accountants follow **generally accepted accounting principles (GAAP)** in preparing reports. These reports allow investors and other stakeholders to compare one company to another.

Accounting principles and concepts develop from research, accepted accounting practices, and pronouncements of authoritative bodies. Currently, the **Financial Accounting Standards Board (FASB)** is the authoritative body having the primary responsibility for developing accounting principles. The FASB publishes *Statements of Financial Accounting Standards* and *Interpretations* to these Standards.

Because generally accepted accounting principles impact how companies report and what they report, all stakeholders are interested in the setting of these principles. For example, the FASB proposed a standard on how to account for options granted employees and managers to purchase shares of ownership in the company. The proposal was opposed by managers because it would negatively impact the financial results of many companies. Managers and others, including the U. S. Senate, urged the FASB to revise or drop the proposal.[2] In response to these comments, the FASB significantly revised the proposed standard.

Next, we emphasize accounting principles and concepts. It is through this emphasis on the "why" of accounting as well as the "how" that you will gain an understanding of the full significance of accounting. In the following paragraphs, we discuss the business entity concept, the cost concept, and the matching concept.

The Business Entity Concept

The individual business unit is the business entity for which economic data are needed. This entity could be an automobile dealer, a department store, or a grocery store. The business entity must be identified, so that the accountant can determine which economic data should be analyzed, recorded, and summarized in reports.

The **business entity concept** is important because it limits the economic data in the accounting system to data related directly to the activities of the business. In other words, the business is viewed as an entity separate from its owners, creditors, or other stakeholders. For example, the accountant for a business with one owner (a proprietorship) would record the activities of the business only, not the personal activities, property, or debts of the owner.

> Under the business entity concept, the activities of a business are recorded separately from the activities of the stakeholders.

The Cost Concept

If a building is bought for $150,000, that amount should be entered into the buyer's accounting records. The seller may have been asking $170,000 for the building up to the time of the sale. The buyer may have initially offered $130,000 for the building. The building may have been assessed at $125,000 for property tax purposes. The buyer may have received an offer of $175,000 for the building the day after it was acquired. These latter amounts have no effect on the accounting records because they did not result in an exchange of the building from the seller to the buyer. The **cost concept** is the basis for entering the *exchange price, or cost, of $150,000* into the accounting records for the building.

Continuing the illustration, the $175,000 offer received by the buyer the day after the building was acquired indicates that it was a bargain purchase at $150,000. To use $175,000 in the accounting records, however, would record an illusory or unrealized profit. If, after buying the building, the buyer accepts the offer and sells the building for $175,000, a profit of $25,000 is then realized and recorded. The new owner would record $175,000 as the cost of the building.

Using the cost concept involves two other important accounting concepts—objectivity and the unit of measure. The **objectivity concept** requires that the accounting records and reports be based upon objective evidence. In exchanges between a buyer and a seller, both try to get the best price. Only the final agreed-upon amount is objective enough for accounting purposes. If the amounts at which properties were recorded were constantly being revised upward and downward based on offers, appraisals, and opinions, accounting reports would soon become unstable and unreliable.

The **unit of measure concept** requires that economic data be recorded in dollars. Money is a common unit of measurement for reporting uniform financial data and reports.

The Matching Concept

Matching concept refers to the matching of expenses and revenues (hence net income) for an accounting period.

Exhibit 600.3 *Financial Accounting and Managerial Accounting*

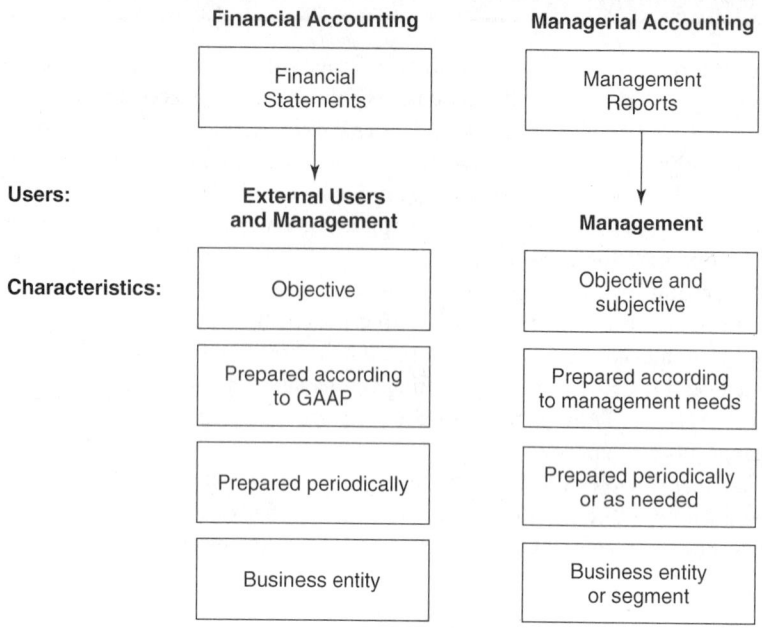

The Differences Between Managerial and Financial Accounting

Although economic information can be classified in many ways, accountants often divide accounting information into two types: financial and managerial. The diagram in Exhibit 600.3 illustrates the relationship between financial accounting and managerial accounting. Understanding this relationship is useful in understanding the information needs of management.

Financial accounting information is reported in statements that are useful for persons or institutions who are "outside" or external to the organization. Examples of such users include shareholders, creditors, government agencies, and the general public. To the extent that management uses the financial statements in directing current operations and planning future operations, the two areas of accounting overlap. For example, in planning future operations, management often begins by evaluating the results of past activities as reported in the financial statements. The financial statements objectively and periodically report the results of past operations and the financial condition of the business according to generally accepted accounting principles (GAAP).

Managerial accounting information includes both historical and estimated data used by management in conducting daily operations, planning future operations, and developing overall business strategies. The characteristics of managerial accounting are influenced by the varying needs of management. First, managerial accounting reports provide both objective measures of past operations and subjective estimates about future decisions. Using subjective estimates in managerial accounting reports assists management in responding to business opportunities. Second, managerial reports need not be prepared according to generally accepted accounting principles. Because only management uses managerial accounting information, the accountant can provide the information according to management's needs. Third, managerial accounting reports may be provided periodically, as with financial accounting, or at any time management needs information. For example, if senior management is deciding on a geographical expansion, a managerial accounting report can be developed in a format and within a time frame to assist management in the decision. Lastly, managerial accounting reports can be prepared to report information for the business entity or a segment of the entity, such as a division, product, project, or territory.

Exhibit 600.4 *Partial Organization Chart for Callaway Golf Company*

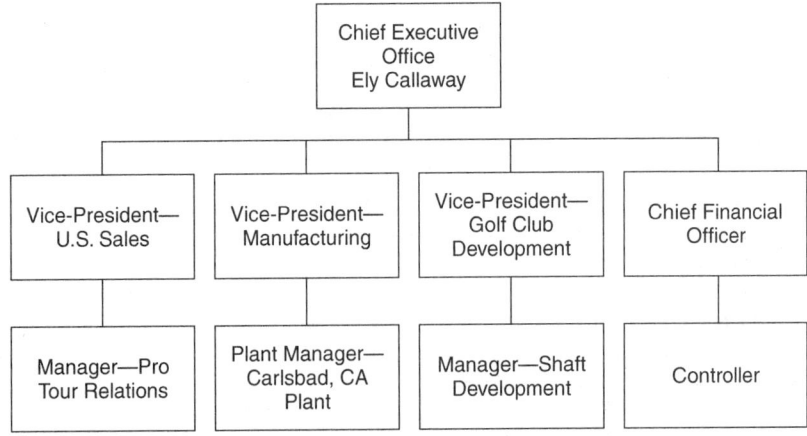

The Management Accountant (Controller) in the Organization

In most large organizations, departments or similar units are assigned responsibilities for specific functions or activities. This operating structure of an organization can be diagrammed in an organization chart. Exhibit 600.4 is a partial organization chart for **Callaway Golf Company,** the manufacturer and distributor of Big Bertha® woods and irons.

The individual reporting units in an organization can be viewed as having either (1) line responsibilities or (2) staff responsibilities. A **line** department or unit is one directly involved in the basic objectives of the organization. For Callaway Golf, the vice-president of manufacturing and the manager of the Carlsbad plant occupy line positions because they are responsible for manufacturing Callaway's products. Likewise, the vice-president of U.S. sales and other sales managers are in line positions because they are directly responsible for generating revenues.

> *The responsibilities of a controller include financial accounting, cost accounting, public reporting, government reporting, accounting information systems, and internal control.*

A **staff** department or unit is one that provides services, assistance, and advice to the departments with line or other staff responsibilities. A staff department has no direct authority over a line department. For example, the manager of pro tour relations is a staff position supporting the sales organization. In addition, the vice-president of golf club development occupies a staff position because new products are developed to support sales and manufacturing. Likewise, the vice-president of finance (sometimes called the *chief financial officer*) occupies a staff position to which the controller reports. In most business organizations, the **controller** is the chief management accountant.

The controller's staff often consists of several management accountants. Each accountant is responsible for a specialized accounting function, such as systems and procedures, general accounting, budgets and budget analysis, special reports and analysis, taxes, and cost accounting.

Experience in managerial accounting is often an excellent training ground for senior management positions. One poll indicated that over 21% of the chief executive officers (CEOs) of the largest 1,000 companies in the United States have career paths that began with accounting or finance. More CEOs started out in these areas than in any other functional business area.[3] This is not surprising, as accounting and finance bring an individual into contact with all phases of operations.

603. ROLE OF ACCOUNTING AND CONTROLLER

Exhibit 600.5 *Accounting Cycle*

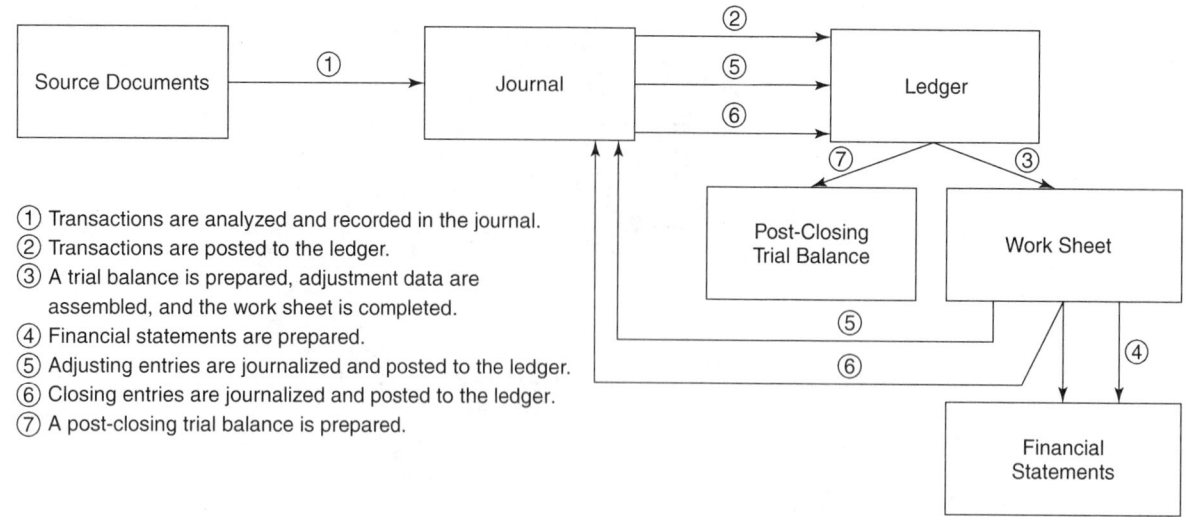

① Transactions are analyzed and recorded in the journal.
② Transactions are posted to the ledger.
③ A trial balance is prepared, adjustment data are assembled, and the work sheet is completed.
④ Financial statements are prepared.
⑤ Adjusting entries are journalized and posted to the ledger.
⑥ Closing entries are journalized and posted to the ledger.
⑦ A post-closing trial balance is prepared.

The Accounting Process

Accounting Cycle

In a computerized accounting system, the software automatically records and posts transactions. The ledger and supporting records are maintained in computerized master files. In addtion, a work sheet is normally not prepared.

The process that begins with analyzing and journalizing transactions and ends with the post-closing trial balance is called the *accounting cycle*. The most important output of the accounting cycle is the financial statements, such as income statement, balance sheet, retained earning statement, and statement of cash flows.

Understanding the steps of the accounting cycle is essential for further study of accounting. The basic steps of the cycle are shown, by number, in the flowchart in Exhibit 600.5.

Fiscal Year

The annual accounting period adopted by a business is known as its **fiscal year.** Fiscal years begin with the first day of the month selected and end on the last day of the following twelfth month. The period most commonly used is the calendar year. Other periods are not unusual, especially for businesses organized as corporations. For example, a corporation may adopt a fiscal year that ends when business activities have reached the lowest point in its annual operating cycle. Such a fiscal year is called the **natural business year.** At the low point in its operating cycle, a business has more time to analyze the results of operations and to prepare financial statements.

Because companies with fiscal years often have highly seasonal operations, investors and others should be careful in interpreting partial year reports for such companies. That is, you should expect the results of operations for these companies to vary significantly throughout the fiscal year.

The financial history of a business may be shown by a series of balance sheets and income statements for several fiscal years. If the life of a business is expressed by a line moving from left to right, the series of balance sheets and income statements may be graphed as follows.

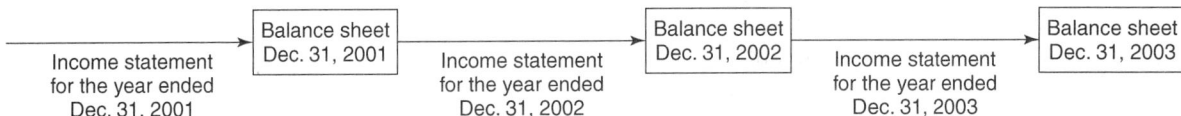

Financial History of a Business

You may think of the income statements, balance sheets, and financial history of a business as similar to the record of a college football team. The final score of each football game is similar to the net income reported on the income statement of a business. The team's season record after each game is similar to the balance sheet. At the end of the season, the final record of the team measures its success or failure. Likewise, at the end of a life of a business, its final balance sheet is a measure of its financial success or failure.

Assets, Liabilities, and Owner's Equity

The Accounting Equation

The resources owned by a business are its assets. Examples of assets include cash, land, buildings, and equipment. The rights or claims to the assets are normally divided into two principal types: (1) the rights of creditors and (2) the rights of owners. The rights of creditors represent debts of the business and are called **liabilities**. The rights of the owners are called **owner's equity**. The relationship between the two may be stated in the form of an equation, as follows.

$$\text{Assets} = \text{Liability} + \text{Owner's Equity}$$

This equation is known as the **accounting equation**. It is usual to place liabilities before owner's equity in the accounting equation because creditors have first rights to the assets. The claim of the owners is sometimes given greater emphasis by transposing liabilities to the other side of the equation, which yields:

$$\text{Assets} - \text{Liabilities} = \text{Owner's Equity}$$

To illustrate, if the assets owned by a business amount to $100,000 and the liabilities amount to $30,000, the owner's equity is equal to $70,000, as shown below.

Assets	−	Liabilities	=	Owner's Equity
$100,000	−	$30,000	=	$70,000

Example 1 *If a company's assets increase by $20,000 and its liabilities decrease by $5,000, how much did the owner's equity increase or decrease?*

Change in Assets	=	Change in Liabilities	+	Change in Owner's Equity
+$20,000	=	−$5,000	+	X
+$25,000	=			X

Business Transactions and the Accounting Equation

For example, paying a monthly telephone bill of $168 affects a business's financial condition because it now has less cash on hand. Such an economic event or condition that directly changes an entity's financial condition or directly affects its results of operations is a business transaction. For example, purchasing land for $50,000 is a business transaction. In contrast, a change in a business's credit rating does not directly affect cash or any other element of its financial condition.

All business transactions can be stated in terms of changes in the elements of the accounting equation. You will see how business transactions affect the accounting equation by studying some typical transactions. As a basis for illustration, we will use a business organized by Chris Clark.

All business transactions can be stated in terms of changes in the elements of the accounting equation.

Assume that on November 1, 2002, Chris Clark organizes a corporation that will be known as NetSolutions. The first phase of Chris's business plan is to operate NetSolutions as a service business that provides assistance to individuals and small businesses in developing Web pages and in configuring and installing application software. Chris expects this initial phase of the business to last one to two years. During this period, Chris will gather information on the software and hardware needs of customers. During the second phase of the business plan, Chris plans to expand NetSolutions into an Internet-based retailer of software and hardware for individuals and small businesses.

Each transaction or group of similar transactions during NetSolutions' first month of operations is described in the following paragraphs. The effect of each transaction on the accounting equation is then shown.

TRANSACTION a Chris Clark deposits $25,000 in a bank account in the name of NetSolutions in return for shares of stock in the corporation. Stock issued to owners (stockholders), such as Chris Clark, is referred to as **capital stock**. The effect of this transaction is to increase the asset (cash), on the left side of the equation, by $25,000. To balance the equation, the owner's equity (capital stock), on the right side of the equation, is increased by the same amount. The effect of this transaction on NetSolutions' accounting equation is shown below.

	Assets	=	Owner's Equity
	Cash		Capital Stock
a.	25,000	=	25,000 Investment by stockholder

Note that the accounting equation shown above relates only to the business, NetSolutions. Under the business entity concept, Chris Clark's personal assets, such as a home or personal bank account, and personal liabilities are excluded from the equation.

TRANSACTION b If you purchased this textbook by paying cash, you entered into a transaction in which you exchanged one asset for another. That is, you exchanged cash for the textbook. Businesses often enter into similar transactions. NetSolutions, for example, exchanged $20,000 cash for land. The land is located in a new business park with convenient access to transportation facilities. Chris Clark plans to rent office space and equipment during the first phase of the business plan. During the second phase, Chris plans to build an office and warehouse on the land.

The purchase of the land changes the makeup of the assets but does not change the total assets. The items in the equation prior to this transaction and the effect of the transaction are shown next, as well as the new amounts, or *balances*, of the items.

	Assets			=	Owner's Equity
	Cash	+	Land		Capital Stock
Bal.	25,000			=	25,000
b.	−20,000		+20,000		
Bal.	5,000		20,000		25,000

Example 2 If NetSolutions had purchased a van for $28,000, paying $8,000 cash and signing a loan agreement (note payable) for $20,000, how would the transaction be recorded using the accounting equation?

Cash	+	Van	=	Notes Payable
−8,000	+	28,000		+20,000

TRANSACTION c You have probably used a credit card at one time or another to buy clothing or other merchandise. In this type of transaction, you received clothing for a promise to pay your credit card bill in the future. That is, you received an asset and incurred a liability to pay a future bill. During the month, NetSolutions entered into a similar transaction, buying supplies for $1,350 and agreeing to pay the supplier in the near future. This type of transaction is called a purchase *on account.* The liability created is called an **account payable.** Items such as supplies that will be used in the business in the future are called **prepaid expenses,** which are assets. The effect of this transaction is to increase assets and liabilities by $1,350, as follows.

	Assets			=	Liabilities	+	Owner's Equity
	Cash	+ Supplies	+ Land		Accounts Payable	+	Capital Stock
Bal.	5,000		20,000				25,000
c.		+1,350			+1,350		
Bal.	5,000	1,350	20,000		1,350		25,000

TRANSACTION d You may have earned money by painting houses. If so, you received money for rendering services to a customer. Likewise, a business earns money by selling goods or services to its customers. This amount is called **revenue.**

During its first month of operations, NetSolutions provided services to customers, earning fees of $7,500 and receiving the amount in cash. This transaction increased cash and the owner's equity by $7,500, as shown here.

	Assets			=	Liabilities	+	Owner's Equity	
	Cash	+ Supplies	+ Land		Accounts Payable	+	Capital Stock	+ Retained Earnings
Bal.	5,000	1,350	20,000		1,350		25,000	
d.	+ 7,500							+ 7,500 Fees earned
Bal.	12,500	1,350	20,000		1,350		25,000	7,500

You should note that the increase in owner's equity from earning revenue is listed in the equation under "Retained Earnings." **Retained earnings** is the owner's equity created by the business operations (revenues less expenses). Transactions affecting earnings are kept separate from transactions related to owner's investments (capital stock). This is useful in preparing reports to owners and creditors and in satisfying legal requirements.

Special terms may be used to describe certain kinds of revenue, such as **sales** for the sale of merchandise. Revenue from providing services is called **fees earned.** For example, a physician would record fees earned for services to patients. Other examples include **rent revenue** (money received for rent) and **interest revenue** (money received for interest).

Instead of requiring the payment of cash at the time services are provided or goods are sold, a business may accept payment at a later date. Such revenues are called *fees on account* or *sales on account.* In such cases, the firm has an **account receivable,** which is a claim against the customer. An account receivable is an asset, and the revenue is earned as if cash had been received. When customers pay their accounts, there is an exchange of one asset for another. Cash increases, while accounts receivable decreases.

TRANSACTION e If you painted houses to earn money, you probably used your own ladders and brushes. NetSolutions also spent cash or used up other assets in earning revenue. The amounts used in this process of earning revenue are called **expenses.** Expenses include supplies used, wages of employees, and other assets and services used in operating the business.

For NetSolutions, the expenses paid during the month were as follows: wages, $2,125; rent, $800; utilities, $450; and miscellaneous, $275. Miscellaneous expenses include small amounts paid for such items as postage, coffee, and magazine subscriptions. The effect of this group of transactions is the opposite of the effect of revenues. These transactions reduce cash and owner's equity, as shown here.

	Assets			=	Liabilities	+	Owner's Equity		
	Cash	+ Supplies	+ Land		Accounts Payable	+	Capital Stock	+ Retained Earnings	
Bal.	12,500	1,350	20,000		1,350		25,000	7,500	
e.	− 3,650							− 2,125	Wages expense
								− 800	Rent expense
								− 450	Utilities expense
								− 275	Misc. expense
Bal.	8,850	1,350	20,000		1,350		25,000	3,850	

Businesses usually record each revenue and expense transaction separately as it occurs. However, to simplify this illustration, we have summarized NetSolutions' revenues and expenses for the month in transactions (d) and (e).

TRANSACTION f   When you pay your monthly credit card bill, you decrease the cash in your checking account and also decrease the amount you owe to the credit card company. Likewise, when NetSolutions pays $950 to creditors during the month, it reduces both assets and liabilities, as shown below.

	Assets			=	Liabilities	+	Owner's Equity	
	Cash	+ Supplies	+ Land		Accounts Payable	+ Capital Stock	+ Retained Earnings	
Bal.	8,850	1,350	20,000		1,350	25,000	3,850	
f.	−950				−950			
Bal.	7,900	1,350	20,000		400	25,000	3,850	

You should note that paying an amount on account is different from paying an amount for an expense. The payment of an expense reduces owner's equity, as illustrated in transaction (e). Paying an amount on account reduces the amount owed on a liability.

TRANSACTION g   At the end of the month, the cost of the supplies on hand (not yet used) is $550. The remainder of the supplies ($1,350 − $550) was used in the operations of the business and is treated as an expense. This decrease of $800 in supplies and owner's equity is shown as follows.

	Assets			=	Liabilities	+	Owner's Equity	
	Cash	+ Supplies	+ Land		Accounts Payable	+ Capital Stock	+ Retained Earnings	
Bal.	7,900	1,350	20,000		400	25,000	3,850	
g.		−800					−800 Supplies expense	
Bal.	7,900	550	20,000		400	25,000	3,050	

TRANSACTION h   At the end of the month, NetSolutions pays $2,000 to stockholders (Chris Clark) as dividends. **Dividends** are distributions of earnings to stockholders. The payment of the dividends reduces both cash and owner's equity. The effect of this transaction is shown as follows.

	Assets			=	Liabilities	+	Owner's Equity	
	Cash	+ Supplies	+ Land		Accounts Payable	+ Capital Stock	+ Retained Earnings	
Bal.	7,900	550	20,000		400	25,000	3,050	
h.	−2,000						−2,000 Dividends	
Bal.	5,900	550	20,000		400	25,000	1,050	

You should be careful not to confuse dividends with expenses. Dividends *do not* represent assets or services used in the process of earning revenues. The owner's equity decrease from dividends is listed in the equation under Retained Earnings. This is because dividends are considered a distribution of earnings to stockholders.

Example 3 *If supplies of $2,500 were purchased during the month and supplies of $350 are on hand at the end of the month, how much is supplies expense for the month?*

$2,150 ($2,500 supplies purchased − $350 on hand)

SUMMARY   The transactions of NetSolutions (a through h) are summarized as follows. They are identified by letter, and the balance of each item is shown after each transaction.

	Assets				=	Liabilities	+	Owner's Equity		
	Cash	+	Supplies	+	Land	=	Accounts Payable	+	Capital Stock	+	Retained Earnings	
a.	+25,000								25,000			Investment by stockholder
b.	−20,000				+20,000						
Bal.| 5,000				20,000				25,000		
c.			+1,350				+1,350				
Bal.| 5,000		1,350		20,000		1,350		25,000		
d.	+7,500										+7,500 Fees earned
Bal.| 12,500		1,350		20,000		1,350		25,000		7,500
e.	−3,650										−2,125 Wages expense
											− 800 Rent expense
											− 450 Utilities expense
											− 275 Misc. expense
Bal.| 8,850		1,350		20,000		1,350		25,000		3,850
f.	− 950						− 950				
Bal.| 7,900		1,350		20,000		400				3,850
g.			− 800								− 800 Supplies expense
Bal.| 7,900		550		20,000		400		25,000		3,050
h.	− 2,000										−2,000 Dividends
Bal.| 5,900		550		20,000		400		25,000		1,050

In reviewing the preceding summary, you should note the following, which apply to all types of businesses.

1. The effect of every transaction is *an increase or a decrease in one or more of the accounting equation elements.*
2. The two sides of the accounting equation are *always equal.*
3. The owner's equity is *increased by amounts invested by stockholders (capital stock)* and is *decreased by dividends to stockholders (retained earnings).* In addition, the owner's equity (retained earnings) is *increased by revenues* and is *decreased by expenses.* The effects of these four types of transactions on owner's equity are illustrated in Exhibit 600.6.

Financial Statements

After transactions have been recorded and summarized, reports are prepared for users. The accounting reports that provide this information are called **financial statements.** The principal financial statements of a corporation are the income

Exhibit 600.6   *Effects of Transactions on Owner's Equity*

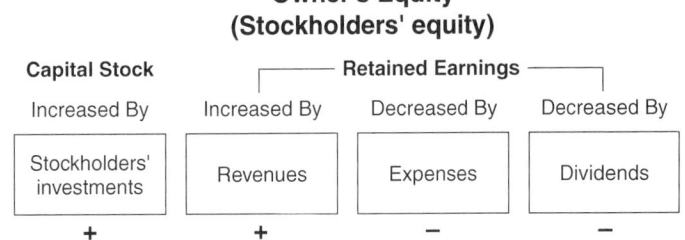

610. ASSETS, LIABILITIES, AND OWNERS' EQUITY

statement, the retained earnings statement, the balance sheet, and the statement of cash flows. The order in which the statements are normally prepared and the nature of the data presented in each statement are as follows.

- **Income statement**—A summary of the revenue and expenses *for a specific period of time,* such as a month or a year.
- **Retained earnings statement**—A summary of the changes in the earnings retained in the corporation for *a specific period of time,* such as a month or a year.
- **Balance sheet**—A list of the assets, liabilities, and owner's equity *as of a specific date,* usually at the close of the last day of a month or a year.
- **Statement of cash flows**—A summary of the cash receipts and cash payments *for a specific period of time,* such as a month or a year.

The basic features of the four statements and their interrelationships are illustrated in Exhibit 600.7. The data for the statements were taken from the summary of transactions of NetSolutions.

All financial statements should be identified by the name of the business, the title of the statement, and the *date* or *period of time.* The data presented in the income statement, the retained earnings statement, and the statement of cash flows are for a period of time. The data presented in the balance sheet are for a specific date.

Income Statement

The income statement reports the revenues and expenses for a period of time, based on the **matching concept.** This concept is applied by *matching* the expenses with the revenue generated during a period by those expenses.

Net income—the excess of revenue over expenses—increases owner's equity.

Revenues are recognized when the earning process is completed and an exchange has taken place. The income statement also reports the excess of the revenue over the expenses incurred. This excess of the revenue over the expenses is called **net income** or **net profit.**

If the expenses exceed the revenue, the excess is a **net loss.**

The effects of revenue earned and expenses incurred during the month for NetSolutions were shown in the equation as increases and decreases in owner's equity (retained earnings). Net income for a period has the effect of increasing owner's equity (retained earnings) for the period, whereas a net loss has the effect of decreasing owner's equity (retained earnings) for the period.

The revenue, expenses, and the net income of $3,050 for NetSolutions are reported in the income statement in Exhibit 600.7. The order in which the expenses are listed in the income statement varies among businesses. One method is to list them in order of size, beginning with the larger items. Miscellaneous expense is usually shown as the last item, regardless of the amount. Exhibit 600.8 shows various accounts that go into the preparation of the income statement.

Retained Earnings Statement

The primary statement for analyzing changes in the owner's equity of a corporation is the retained earnings statement. The retained earnings statement is a connecting link between the income statement and the balance sheet.

Financial statements are used to evaluate the current financial condition of a business and to predict its future operating results and cash flows. For example, bank loan officers use a business's financial statements in deciding whether to grant a loan to the business. Once the loan is granted, the borrower may be required to maintain a certain level of assets in excess of liabilities. The business's financial statements are used to monitor this level.

Two types of transactions affect the retained earnings during the month: (1) the revenues and expenses that resulted in net income of $3,050 for the month and (2) dividends of $2,000 paid to stockholders. These transactions are summarized in the retained earnings statement for NetSolutions shown in Exhibit 600.7.

Because NetSolutions has been in operation for only one month, it has no retained earnings at the beginning of November. For December, however, there is a beginning balance—the balance at the end of November

Exhibit 600.7 *Financial Statements for NetSolutions*

NetSolutions
Income Statement
for the Month Ended November 30, 2002

Fees earned		$7,500.00
Operating expenses:		
Wages expense	$2,125.00	
Rent expense	800.00	
Supplies expense	800.00	
Utilities expense	450.00	
Miscellaneous expense	275.00	
Total operating expenses		4,450.00
Net income		$3,050.00

NetSolutions
Retained Earnings Statement
for the Month Ended November 30, 2002

Net income for November 2002	$3,050.00
Less dividends	2,000.00
Retained earnings, November 30, 2002	$1,050.00

NetSolutions
Balance Sheet
November 30, 2002

Assets		Liabilities	
Cash	$5,900.00	Accounts payable	$400.00
Supplies	550.00	**Stockholders' Equity**	
Land	2,000.00	Capital stock $25,000	
		Retained earnings 1,050	26,050.00
		Total liabilities and	
Total assets	$26,450.00	stockholders' equity	$26,450.00

NetSolutions
Statement of Cash Flows
for the Month Ended November 30, 2002

Cash flows from operating activities:		
Cash received from customers	$7,500.00	
Deduct cash payments for expenses and		
payments to creditors	4,600.00	
Net cash flow from operating activities		$2,900.00
Cash flows from investing activities:		
Cash payments for acquisition of land		(2,000.00)
Cash flows from financing activities:		
Cash received from sale of stock	$25,000.00	
Deduct cash dividends	2,000.00	
Net cash flow from financing activities		23,000.00
Net cash flow and November 30, 2002 cash balance		$5,900.00

2002. This balance of $1,050 is reported on the retained earnings statement. To illustrate, assume that NetSolutions earned net income of $4,155 and paid dividends of $2,000 during December 2002. The retained earnings statement for NetSolutions for December 2002 is shown in Exhibit 600.9. Exhibit 600.10 shows various accounts that go into the preparation of a retained earnings statement.

610. ASSETS, LIABILITIES, AND OWNERS' EQUITY

Exhibit 600.8 *Income Statement Accounts*

Account Title	Account Classification
Advertising Expense	Operating expense
Amortization Expense	Operating expense
Cost of Merchandise (Goods) Sold	Cost of merchandise (goods sold)
Depletion Expense	Operating expense
Dividend Revenue	Other income
Exchange Gain	Other income
Exchange Loss	Other expense
Fees Earned	Revenue
Gain on Disposal of Fixed Assets	Other income
Gain on Redemption of Bonds	Extraordinary item
Gain on Sale of Investments	Other income
Income Tax Expense	Income tax
Insurance Expense	Operating expense
Interest Expense	Other expense
Interest Revenue	Other income
Loss on Disposal of Fixed Assets	Other expense
Loss on Redemption of Bonds	Extraordinary item
Loss on Sale of Investments	Other expense
Merchandise Inventory	Cost of merchandise sold
Miscellaneous Expense	Operating expense
Payroll Tax Expense	Operating expense
Pension Expense	Operating expense
Purchases	Cost of merchandise sold
Purchases Discounts	Cost of merchandise sold
Purchases Returns and Allowances	Cost of merchandise sold
Rent Expense	Operating expense
Rent Revenue	Other income
Salaries Expense	Operating expense
Sales	Revenue from sales
Sales Discounts	Revenue from sales
Sales Returns and Allowances	Revenue from sales
Supplies Expense	Operating expense
Transportation In	Cost of merchandise sold
Transportation Out	Operating expense
Uncollectible Accounts Expense	Operating expense
Utilities Expense	Operating expense
Vacation Pay Expense	Operating expense
Wages expense	Operating expense

Exhibit 600.9 *Retained Earnings Statement for NetSolutions*

NetSolutions
Retained Earnings Statement
for the Month Ended December 30, 2002

Retained earnings, December 1, 2002		$10,500
Net income for the month	$4,155	
Less dividends	2,000	
Increase in retained earnings		2,155
Retained earnings, December 31, 2002		$3,205

Exhibit 600.10 *Retained Earnings Statement Accounts*

Account Title	Account Classification
Cash Dividends	Stockholders' equity
Prior Period Adjustments	Retained earnings
Property Dividends	Stockholders' equity
Reserves	Retained earnings
Restricted Earnings	Retained earnings
Retained Earnings	Stockholders' equity
Stock Dividends	Stockholders' equity
Transfers to Capital	Retained earnings
Unrestricted Earnings	Retained earnings

Balance Sheet

The balance sheet in Exhibit 600.7 reports the amounts of NetSolutions' assets, liabilities, and owner's equity at the end of November. These amounts are taken from the last line of the summary of transactions presented earlier. The form of balance sheet shown in Exhibit 600.7 is called the **account form** because it resembles the basic format of the accounting equation, with assets on the left side and the liabilities and owner's equity sections on the right side. An alternative form of balance sheet called the **report form** presents the liabilities and owner's equity sections below the assets section.

The assets section of the balance sheet normally presents assets in the order that they will be converted into cash or used in operations. Cash is presented first, followed by receivables, supplies, prepaid insurance, and other assets. The assets of a more permanent nature are shown next, such as land, buildings, and equipment.

Assets

Assets are commonly divided into classes for presentation on the balance sheet. Two of these classes are (1) current assets and (2) noncurrent assets (for example, property, plant, and equipment). Most assets are listed at historical cost.

CURRENT ASSETS Cash and other assets that are expected to be converted to cash or sold or used up usually within one year or less, through the normal operations of the business, are called **current assets.** In addition to cash, the current assets usually owned by a service business are notes receivable, accounts receivable, supplies, and other prepaid expenses.

Two common classes of assets are current assets and noncurrent or long-term assets (e.g., property, plant, and equipment).

Notes receivable are amounts customers owe. They are written promises to pay the amount of the note and possibly interest at an agreed upon rate. Accounts receivable are also amounts customers owe, but they are less formal than notes and do not provide for interest. Accounts receivable normally result from providing services or selling merchandise on account. Notes receivable and accounts receivable are current assets because they will usually be converted to cash within one year or less.

NONCURRENT ASSETS The property, plant, and equipment section may also be described as **noncurrent** or **long-term assets, fixed assets,** or **plant assets**. These assets, include equipment, machinery, buildings, and land. With the exception of land, fixed assets depreciate over a period of time. Depreciation is a noncash item. The cost, accumulated depreciation, and book value of each major type of fixed asset is normally reported on the balance sheet or in accompanying notes. The book value of a fixed asset is historical cost minus accumulated depreciation.

Liabilities

Liabilities are the amounts the business owes to creditors. The two most common classes of liabilities are (1) current liabilities and (2) long-term liabilities.

Two common classes of liabilities are current liabilities and long-term liabilities.

CURRENT LIABILITIES Liabilities that will be due within a short time (usually one year or less) and that are to be paid out of current assets are called **current liabilities.** The most common liabilities in this group are notes payable and

610. ASSETS, LIABILITIES, AND OWNERS' EQUITY

accounts payable. Other current liability accounts commonly found in the ledger are Wages Payable, Interest Payable, Taxes Payable, and Unearned Fees.

LONG-TERM LIABILITIES Liabilities that will not be due for a long time (usually more than one year) are called **long-term liabilities.** If NetSolutions had long-term liabilities, they would be reported below the current liabilities. As long-term liabilities come due and are to be paid within one year, they are classified as current liabilities. If they are to be renewed rather than paid, they would continue to be classified as long-term. When an asset is pledged as security for a liability, the obligation may be called a *mortgage note payable* or a *mortgage payable*.

Stockholders' Equity

The stockholders' right to the assets of the business is presented on the balance sheet below the liabilities section. The stockholders' equity is added to the total liabilities, and this total must be equal to the total assets. The equity includes capital stock, additional paid-in-capital, and retained earnings. Exhibit 600.11 shows various accounts that go into the preparation of a balance sheet.

Statement of Cash Flows

The **statement of cash flows** reports a firm's major cash inflows and outflows for a period. It provides useful information about a firm's ability to generate cash from operations, maintain and expand its operating capacity, meet its financial obligations, and pay dividends. *Cash* refers to cash and cash equivalents. Examples of cash equivalents include marketable securities, certificates of deposit, U.S. Treasury bills, and money market funds.

The statement of cash flows is one of the basic financial statements. It is useful to managers in evaluating past operations and in planning future investing and financing activities. It is useful to investors, creditors, and others in assessing a firm's profit potential. In addition, it is a basis for assessing the firm's ability to pay its maturing debt.

The statement of cash flows reports cash flows by three types of activities.

1. **Cash flows from operating activities** are cash flows from transactions that affect net income. It shows a summary of cash receipts and cash payments from operations. Examples of such transactions include the purchase and sale of merchandise by a retailer. The net cash flow operating activities ($2,900 in Exhibit 600.7) will normally differ from the amount of net income for the period ($3,050 in Exhibit 600.7). The difference occurs because revenues and expenses may not be recorded at the same time that cash is received from customers or paid to creditors.
2. **Cash flows from investing activities** are cash flows from transactions that affect the investments in noncurrent assets. Examples of such transactions include the sale and purchase of fixed assets, such as equipment, land, and buildings.
3. **Cash flows from financing activities** are cash flows from transactions that affect the equity and debt of the business. Examples of such transactions include issuing or retiring equity and debt securities, and cash dividends.

The statement of cash flows reports cash flows from operating, investing, and financing activities.

The cash flows from operating activities is normally presented first, followed by the cash flows from investing activities and financing activities. The total of the net cash flow from these activities is the net increase or decrease in cash for the period. The cash balance at the beginning of the period is added to the net increase or decrease in cash, resulting in the cash balance at the end of the period. The ending cash balance on the statement of cash flows equals the cash reported on the balance sheet.

Exhibit 600.12 shows common cash flow transactions reported in each of the three sections of the statement of cash flows. By reporting cash flows by operating, investing, and financing activities, significant relationships within and among the activities can be evaluated. For example, the cash receipts from issuing bonds can be related to repayments of borrowings when both are reported as financing activities. Also, the impact of each of the three activities (operating, investing, and financing) on cash flows can be identified. This allows investors and creditors to evaluate the effects of cash flows on a firm's profits and ability to pay debt.

Exhibit 600.11 *Balance Sheet Accounts*

Account Title	Account Classification
Accounts Payable	Current liability
Accounts Receivable	Current asset
Accumulated Depreciation	Fixed asset
Accumulated Depletion	Fixed asset
Allowance for Doubtful Accounts	Current asset
Bonds Payable	Long-term liability
Building	Fixed asset
Capital Stock	Stockholders' equity
Cash	Current asset
Cash Dividends Payable	Current liability
Common Stock	Stockholders' equity
Deferred Income Tax Payable	Current liability/Long-term liability
Discount on Bonds Payable	Long-term liability
Donated Capital	Stockholders' equity
Employees Federal Income Tax Payable	Current liability
Equipment	Fixed asset
Factory Overhead (Overapplied)	Deferred credit
Factory Overhead (Underapplied)	Deferred debit
Federal Income Tax Payable	Current liability
Federal Unemployment Tax Payable	Current liability
Finished Goods	Current asset
Goodwill	Intangible asset
Income Tax Payable	Current liability
Interest Receivable	Current asset
Investment in Bonds	Investment
Investment in Stocks	Investment
Investment in Subsidiary	Investment
Land	Fixed asset
Marketable Securities	Current asset
Materials	Current asset
Medicare Tax Payable	Current liability
Merchandise Inventory	Current asset
Notes Payable	Current liability/Long-term liability
Notes Receivable	Current asset/Investment
Organization Costs	Intangible asset
Patents	Intangible asset
Paid-In Capital from Sale of Treasury Stock	Stockholders' equity
Paid-In Capital in Excess of Par (Stated Value)	Stockholders' equity
Petty Cash	Current asset
Premium on Bonds Payable	Long-term liability
Prepaid Insurance	Current asset
Prepaid Rent	Current asset
Preferred Stock	Stockholders' equity
Prior Period Adjustments	Stockholders' equity
Retained Earnings	Stockholders' equity
Salaries Payable	Current liability
Sales Tax Payable	Current liability
Sinking Fund Cash	Investment
Sinking Fund Investments	Investment
Social Security Tax Payable	Current liability
State Unemployment Tax Payable	Current liability
Stock Dividends Distributable	Stockholders' equity
Supplies	Current asset
Treasury Stock	Stockholders' equity
Unearned Rent	Current liability
Vacation Pay Payable	Current liability/Long-term liability
Work in Process	Current asset

610. ASSETS, LIABILITIES, AND OWNERS' EQUITY

Exhibit 600.12 *Cash Flows*

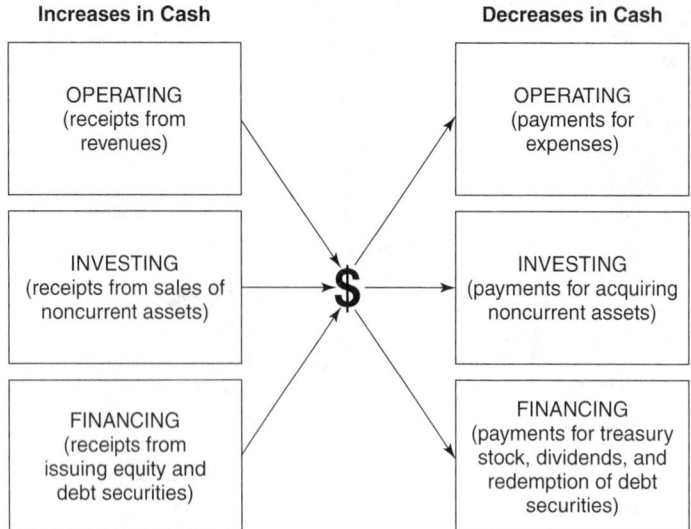

Cash Flows From Operating Activities

The most important cash flows of a business often relate to operating activities. There are two alternative methods for reporting cash flows from operating activities in the statement of cash flows. These methods are (1) the direct method and (2) the indirect method as shown in Exhibit 600.13.

The **direct method** reports the sources of operating cash and the uses of operating cash. The major source of operating cash is cash received from customers. The major uses of operating cash include cash paid to suppliers for merchandise and services and cash paid to employees for wages. The difference between these operating cash receipts and cash payments is the net cash flow from operating activities.

The primary advantage of the direct method is that it reports the sources and uses of cash in the statement of cash flows. Its primary disadvantage is that the necessary data may not be readily available and may be costly to gather.

The **indirect method** reports the operating cash flows by beginning with net income and adjusting it for revenues and expenses that do not involve the receipt or payment of cash. In other words, accrual net income is adjusted to determine the net amount of cash flows from operating activities.

A major advantage of the indirect method is that it focuses on the differences between net income and cash flows from operations. In this sense, it shows the relationship between the income statement, the balance sheet, and the statement of cash flows. Because the data are readily available, the indirect method is normally less costly to use than the direct method. Because of these advantages, most firms use the indirect method to report cash flows from operations.

Exhibit 600.14 illustrates the cash flow from operating activities section of the statement of cash flows under the direct and indirect methods. Both statements are for NetSolutions for the month ended November 2002. Both methods show the same amount of net cash flow from operating activities, regardless of the method.

Example 4 Net income was $45,000 for the year. The accumulated depreciation balance increased by $15,000 over the year. There were no sales of fixed assets or changes in noncash current assets or liabilities. What is the cash flow from operations?

$60,000 ($45,000 + $15,000)

Example 5 Net income was $36,000 for the year. Accounts receivable increased $3,000, and accounts payable increased $5,000. What is the cash flow from operations?

$38,000 ($36,000 − $3,000 + $5,000)

Exhibit 600.13 *Methods to Report Cash Flows From Operating Activities*

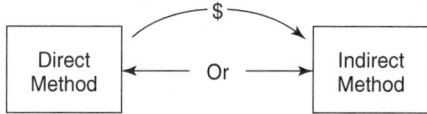

Exhibit 600.14 *Cash Flows From Operations: Direct and Indirect Methods for NetSolutions*

Direct Method		Indirect Method	
Cash flows from operating activities:		Cash flows from operating activities:	
Cash received from customers	$7,500	Net income, per income statement	$3,050
Deduct cash payments for expenses and payments to creditors	4,600	Add increase in accounts payable	400
			$3,450
		Deduct increase in supplies	550
Net cash flow from operating activities	$2,900	Net cash flow from operating activities	$2,900

Cash Flows From Investing Activities

Cash inflows from investing activities normally arise from selling fixed assets, investments, and intangible assets. Cash outflows normally include payments to acquire fixed assets, investments, and intangible assets. NetSolutions paid $20,000 to acquire land.

Cash flows from investing activities are reported on the statement of cash flows by first listing the cash inflows. The cash outflows are then presented. If the inflows are greater than the outflows, **net cash flow provided by investing activities** is reported. If the inflows are less than the outflows, **net cash flow used for investing activities** is reported.

Example 6 *A building with a cost of $145,000 and accumulated depreciation of $35,000 was sold for a $10,000 gain. How much cash was generated from this investing activity?*

$120,000 ($145,000 − $35,000 + $10,000)

Cash Flows From Financing Activities

Cash inflows from financing activities normally arise from issuing debt or equity securities. Examples of such inflows include issuing bonds, notes payable, and preferred and common stocks. Cash outflows from financing activities include paying cash dividends, repaying debt, and acquiring treasury stock.

Cash flows from financing activities are reported on the statement of cash flows by first listing the cash inflows. The cash outflows are then presented. If the inflows are greater than the outflows, **net cash flow provided by financing activities** is reported. If the inflows are less than the outflows, **net cash flow used for financing activities** is reported.

The cash flows from financing activities section in the statement of cash flows for NetSolutions is shown below.

Cash flows from financing activities:	
Cash received from sale of stock	$25,000
Deduct cash dividends	2,000
Net cash flow from financing activities	$23,000

610. ASSETS, LIABILITIES, AND OWNERS' EQUITY

> **Example 7** Sales reported on the income statement were $350,000. The accounts receivable balance declined $8,000 over the year. What was the amount of cash received from customers?
>
> $358,000 ($350,000 + $8,000)

Following is a summary of statement of cash flows for NetSolutions as of November 30, 2002:

Net cash flow from operating activities	$ 2,900
Plus net cash flow from investing activities	(20,000)
Plus net cash flow from financing activities	23,000
Equal net increase (decrease) in cash	$ 5,900
Plus cash at beginning of year	0
Equal cash at end of year	$ 5,900*

*This amount is the same as the cash account in the balance sheet as of November 30, 2002. (Exhibit 600.7)

Exhibit 600.15 shows various accounts that go into the preparation of statement of cash flows.

Noncash Investing and Financing Activities

A business may enter into investing and financing activities that do not directly involve cash. For example, it may issue common stock to retire long-term debt. Such a transaction does not have a direct effect on cash. However, the transaction does eliminate the need for future cash payments to pay interest and retire the bonds. Thus, because of their future effect on cash flows, such transactions should be reported to readers of the financial statements.

When noncash investing and financing transactions occur during a period, their effect is reported in a separate schedule. This schedule usually appears at the bottom of the statement of cash flows. For example, in such a schedule, **Amazon.com** disclosed the issuance of $217 million in common stock for Internet acquisitions. Other examples of noncash investing and financing transactions include acquiring fixed assets by issuing bonds or capital stock and issuing common stock in exchange for convertible preferred stock.

Cash Flow per Share

The term *cash flow per share* is sometimes reported in the financial press. Often, the term is used to mean "cash flow from operations per share." Such reporting may be misleading to users of the financial statements. For example, users might interpret cash flow per share as the amount available for dividends. This would not be the case if most of the cash generated by operations is required for repaying loans or for reinvesting in the business. Users might also think that cash flow per share is equivalent or perhaps superior to earnings per share. For these reasons, the financial statements, including the statement of cash flows, should not report cash flow per share.

Free Cash Flow

A valuable tool for evaluating the cash position of a business is free cash flow. **Free cash flow** is a measure of operating cash flow available for corporate purposes after providing sufficient fixed asset additions to maintain current productive capacity and dividends. Thus, free cash flow can be calculated as follows.

	Cash flow from operating activities
Less:	Cash used to purchase fixed assets to maintain productive capacity used up in producing income during the period
Less:	Cash used for dividends
	Free cash flow

Exhibit 600.15 *Statement of Cash Flow Accounts*

Account Title	Account Classification
Cash received from customers for sale of goods or services	Cash flows from operating activities
Cash received from interest on loans	Cash flows from operating activities
Cash received from dividends on investments	Cash flows from operating activities
Cash received from sale of trading securities	Cash flows from operating activities
Cash payments for operating expenses	Cash flows from operating activities
Cash payments for merchandise	Cash flows from operating activities
Cash payments for materials	Cash flows from operating activities
Cash payments for wages	Cash flows from operating activities
Cash payments for interest	Cash flows from operating activities
Cash payments for taxes	Cash flows from operating activities
Cash payments to purchase trading securities	Cash flows from operating activities
Depreciation (added to net income)	Cash flows from operating activities
Gain on sale of fixed assets (subtracted from net income)	Cash flows from operating activities
Loss on sale of fixed assets (added to net income)	Cash flows from operating activities
Net Income (starting point)	Cash flows from operating activities
Cash receipts from sale of property (e.g., land, plant, equipment, buildings)	Cash flows from investing activities
Cash receipts from collection of loans	Cash flows from investing activities
Cash receipts from sale of Investments	Cash flows from investing activities
Cash payments for acquisition of property (e.g., land, plant, equipment, buildings)	Cash flows from investing activities
Cash payments to make loans	Cash flows from investing activities
Cash received from sale of stock (e.g., preferred or common)	Cash flows from financing activities
Cash received from issuing of debt	Cash flows from financing activities
Cash paid for dividends	Cash flows from financing activities
Cash paid to retire bonds payable	Cash flows from financing activities
Cash paid to repay debt	Cash flows from financing activities
Cash paid to reacquire stock (e.g., preferred or common)	Cash flows from financing activities

A company that has free cash flow is able to fund internal growth, retire debt, and enjoy financial flexibility. A company with no free cash flow is unable to maintain current productive capacity or dividend payouts to stockholders. Lack of free cash flow can be an early indicator of liquidity problems. Indeed, as stated by one analyst, "Free cash flow gives the company firepower to reduce debt and ultimately generate consistent, actual income."[4]

Example 8 Assume that O'Brien Company had cash flow from operating activities of $1,400,000. O'Brien Company invested $450,000 in fixed assets to maintain productive capacity, and another $300,000 to expand capacity. Dividends were $100,000. What is free cash flow for O'Brien Company?

Cash flow from operating activities		$1,400,000
Less: Cash invested in fixed assets to maintain productive capacity	$450,000	
Less: Cash for dividends	100,000	550,000
Free cash flow		$ 850,000

A General Model for the Statement of Cash Flows

Until now, we focused on the financial data for NetSolutions. Now we present a general model of the statement of cash flows for XYZ Company that is more inclusive than that of NetSolutions.

Sources and Uses of Cash

The analysis of sources and uses of cash will help managers to see the "big picture" of cash activities regardless of their sources and uses. This analysis does not break down in a manner similar to the Statement of Cash Flows into operating, investing, and financing activities. Rather, it lists all sources of cash together in one place and all uses of cash together in one place. Cash activities of a firm could be summarized as follows.

$$\text{Cash flows from assets} = \text{Cash flows to creditors} + \text{Cash flows to owners}$$

Cash flow to creditors is computed from the interest paid minus net new borrowings. Cash flow to owners (shareholders) is computed from the dividends paid minus net new equity. Those activities that bring cash in to the firm are called *sources of cash*. Those activities that involve spending cash are called *uses* (or *applications*) of cash. Remember the accounting equation:

$$\text{Assets} = \text{Liabilities} + \text{Owner's equity}$$

An increase in the asset account or a decrease in the liability or equity account is a use of cash. Similarly, a decrease in the asset account or an increase in the liability or equity account is a source of cash. This can be represented in a table as follows.

Item	Use of Cash	Source of Cash
Asset	Increase	Decrease
Liability or Equity	Decrease	Increase

For example:

1. Buying more inventory or fixed assets increases the asset account and uses cash.
2. Paying off a loan or buying back the company stock (treasury stock) decreases the liability or equity account and uses cash.
3. Selling inventory or collecting receivables from customers decreases the asset account and provides cash.
4. Borrowing funds or selling stock increases the liability or equity account and provides cash.

Note that all "uses of cash" are deducted from net income and all "sources of cash" are added to net income when computing cash flows from operating activities.

The net addition to cash account is the difference between sources and uses of cash, and it should agree with the change in the cash account on the current balance sheet. What we need to do is trace the changes in the firm's two balance sheets (i.e., previous period and current period) to see how the firm obtained its cash and how the firm spent its cash.

Examples of sources of cash include the following.

- Decrease in accounts receivable
- Decrease in inventory
- Decrease in fixed assets
- Increase in accounts payable
- Increase in notes payable
- Increase in long-term debt
- Increase in common stock
- Increase in retained earnings

Examples of uses of cash include the following.

- Increase in accounts receivable
- Increase in inventory
- Increase in fixed assets
- Decrease in accounts payable
- Decrease in notes payable
- Decrease in long-term debt
- Decrease in common stock
- Decrease in retained earnings

Example 9 *The difference between two balance sheet accounts (in thousands) for a firm is shown below.*

Increase in accounts receivable	$35
Decrease in inventory	5
Increase in fixed assets	20
Increase in accounts payable	22
Decrease in long-term debt	30
Decrease in notes payable	15
Increase in common stock	50
Increase in retained earnings	40

What is the net addition to the cash account for the firm?

Sources of cash = $5 + $22 + $50 + $40 = $117

Uses of cash = $35 + $20 + $30 + $15 = $100

Net addition to cash = Sources of cash − Uses of cash = $117 − $100 = $17

Exhibit 600.16 shows the Statement of Cash Sources and Uses for the XYZ Company, where total sources ($199 million) are equal to total uses ($199 million). Exhibit 600.17 presents a Statement of Cash Flows for the XYZ Company, where it shows the cash at the end of the year 2003 as $15 million. This is the same balance in cash and marketable securities account of $15 million in the Statement of Cash Sources and Uses. The Statement of Cash Sources and Uses is an intermediate schedule to facilitate accounting of all sources and uses of cash, and is tied to the Statement of Cash flows.

Exhibit 600.16 *XYZ Company: Statement of Cash Sources and Uses During 2003 (millions of dollars)*

			Change	
	12/31/03	12/31/02	Sources	Uses
Balance Sheet Changes				
Cash and marketable securities	$ 15.0	$ 40.0	$ 25.0	
Accounts receivable	180.0	160.0		$ 20.0
Inventory	270.0	200.0		70.0
Gross plant and equipment	680.0	600.0		80.0
Accounts payable	30.0	15.0	15.0	
Accruals	60.0	55.0	5.0	
Notes payable	40.0	35.0	5.0	
Long-term bonds	300.0	255.0	45.0	
Common stock (25 million shares)	130.0	130.0		
Income Statement Information				
Net income		$ 54.0		
Add: Depreciation		50.0		
Gross cash flow from operations		$104.0	104.0	
Dividend payment		29.0	—	29.0
Totals			$199.0	$199.0

Exhibit 600.17 XYZ Company: Statement of Cash Flows for the Period Ending December 31, 2003 (millions of dollars)

Cash Flows from Operating Activities		
Net income		$ 54.0
Additions to net income		
Depreciation[a]	50.0	
Increase in accounts payable	15.0	
Increase in accruals	5.0	
Subtractions from net income		
Increase in accounts receivable	(20.0)	
Increase in inventory	(70.0)	
Net cash flow from operations		$ 34.0
Cash Flows from Investing Activities		
Acquisition of fixed assets		$(80.0)
Cash Flows from Financing Activities		
Increase in notes payable	$ 5.0	
Increase in bonds	45.0	
Dividend payment	(29.0)	
Net cash flow from financing		$ 21.0
Net change in cash		$(25.0)
Cash at the beginning of the year		40.0
Cash at the end of the year		$ 15.0

[a]Depreciation is a noncash expense that was deducted when calculating net income. It must be added back to show the correct cash flow from operations.

Example 10 The net income reported for Firm A for the current year on its income statement was $60,000. Depreciation on fixed assets for the year was $20,000. Balances of the current assets and current liability accounts at the end and beginning of the year are listed below.

	End	Beginning
Cash	$55,000	$60,000
Net accounts receivable	62,000	48,000
Inventories	80,000	90,000
Prepaid expense	4,000	5,000
Accounts payable	71,000	81,000
Cash dividends payable	5,000	6,000
Salaries payable	8,000	9,000

What is the cash flows from operating activities section of a statement of cash flows using the indirect method?

Cash flows from operating activities:			
Net income, per income statement			$60,000
Add:	Depreciation	$20,000	
	Decrease in inventories	10,000	
	Decrease in prepaid expense	1,000	$31,000
Deduct:	Increase in net accounts receivable	$14,000	
	Decrease in accounts payable	10,000	
	Decrease in salaries payable	1,000	$25,000
Net cash flow from operating activities			$66,000

Analysis and Use of Financial Statements

Financial Statement Analysis

How does one decide on the companies in which to invest? This section describes and illustrates common financial data that can be analyzed to assist you in making investment decisions.

Basic Analytical Procedures

The basic financial statements provide much of the information users need to make economic decisions about businesses. In this section, we illustrate how to perform a complete analysis of these statements by integrating individual analytical measures.

Analytical procedures may be used to compare items on a current statement with related items on earlier statements. For example, cash of $150,000 on the current balance sheet may be compared with cash of $100,000 on the balance sheet of a year earlier. The current year's cash may be expressed as 1.5 or 150% of the earlier amount, or as an increase of 50% or $50,000.

Analytical procedures are also widely used to examine relationships within a financial statement. To illustrate, assume that cash of $50,000 and inventories of $250,000 are included in the total assets of $1,000,000 on a balance sheet. In relative terms, the cash balance is 5% of the total assets, and the inventories are 25% of the total assets.

In this section, we will illustrate a number of common analytical measures such as horizontal analysis, vertical analysis, and common-size statement analysis. The measures are not ends in themselves. They are only guides in evaluating financial and operating data. Many other factors, such as trends in the industry and general economic conditions, should also be considered.

Horizontal Analysis

The percentage analysis of increases and decreases in related items in comparative financial statements is called **horizontal analysis.** The amount of each item on the most recent statement is compared with the related item on one or more earlier statements. The amount of increase or decrease in the item is listed, along with the percent of increase or decrease.

Horizontal analysis may compare two statements. In this case, the earlier statement is used as the base. Horizontal analysis may also compare three or more statements. In this case, the earliest date or period may be used as the base for comparing all later dates or periods. Alternatively, each statement may be compared to the immediately preceding statement. Exhibit 600.18 is a condensed comparative balance sheet for two years for Lincoln Company, with horizontal analysis.

We cannot fully evaluate the significance of the various increases and decreases in the items shown in Exhibit 600.18 without additional information. Although total assets at the end of 2003 were $91,000 (7.4%) less than at the beginning of the year, liabilities were reduced by $133,000 (30%), and stockholders' equity increased $42,000 (5.3%). It appears that the reduction of $100,000 in long-term liabilities was achieved mostly through the sale of long-term investments.

> **Example 11** Accounts Payable was $600,000 in the current year and $500,000 in the preceding year. What is the amount and the percentage of increase or decrease that would be shown in a balance sheet with horizontal analysis?
>
> $100,000 or 20% ($100,000/$500,000) increase

The balance sheet in Exhibit 600.18 may be expanded to include the details of the various categories of assets and liabilities. An alternative is to present the details in separate schedules. Exhibit 600.19 is a supporting schedule with horizontal analysis.

Exhibit 600.18 *Comparative Balance Sheet—Horizontal Analysis*

Lincoln Company
Comparative Balance Sheet
December 31, 2003 and 2002

	2003	2002	Increase (Decrease) Amount	Percent
Assets				
Current assets	$ 550,000	$ 533,000	$ 17,000	3.2%
Long-term investments	95,000	177,500	(82,500)	(46.5%)
Property, plant, and equipment (net)	444,500	470,000	(25,500)	(5.4%)
Intangible assets	50,000	50,000	—	—
Total assets	$1,139,500	$1,230,500	$ (91,000)	(7.4%)
Liabilities				
Current liabilities	$ 210,000	$ 243,000	$ (33,000)	(13.6%)
Long-term liabilities	100,000	200,000	(100,000)	(50.0%)
Total liabilities	$310,000	$ 443,000	$(133,000)	(30.0%)
Stockholders' Equity				
Preferred 6% stock, $100 par	$ 150,000	$ 150,000	—	—
Common stock, $10 par	500,000	500,000	—	—
Retained earnings	179,500	137,500	$ 42,000	30.5%
Total stockholders' equity	$ 829,500	$ 787,500	$ 42,000	5.3%
Total liabilities and stockholders' equity	$1,139,500	$1,230,500	$ (91,000)	(7.4%)

Exhibit 600.19 *Comparative Schedule of Current Assets—Horizontal Analysis*

Lincoln Company
Comparative Schedule of Current Assets
December 31, 2003 and 2002

	2003	2002	Increase (Decrease) Amount	Percent
Cash	$ 90,500	$ 64,700	$25,800	39.9%
Marketable securities	75,000	60,000	15,000	25.0%
Accounts receivable (net)	115,000	120,000	(5,000)	(4.2%)
Inventories	264,000	283,000	(19,000)	(6.7%)
Prepaid expenses	5,500	5,300	200	3.8%
Total current assets	$550,000	$533,000	$17,000	3.2%

The decrease in accounts receivable may be due to changes in credit terms or improved collection policies. Likewise, a decrease in inventories during a period of increased sales may indicate an improvement in the management of inventories.

The changes in the current assets in Exhibit 600.19 appear favorable. This assessment is supported by the 24.8% increase in net sales shown in Exhibit 600.20.

An increase in net sales may not have a favorable effect on operating performance. The percentage increase in Lincoln Company's net sales is accompanied by a greater percentage increase in the cost of goods (merchandise) sold. This has the effect of reducing gross profit. Selling expenses increased significantly, and administrative expenses increased slightly. Overall, operating expenses increased by 20.7%, whereas gross profit increased by only 19.7%.

The increase in income from operations and in net income is favorable. However, a study of the expenses and additional analyses and comparisons should be made before reaching a conclusion as to the cause.

Exhibit 600.20 *Comparative Income Statement—Horizontal Analysis*

Lincoln Company
Comparative Income Statement
For the Years Ended December 31, 2003 and 2002

	2003	2002	Increase (Decrease) Amount	Percent
Sales	$1,530,500	$1,234,000	$296,500	24.0%
Sales returns and allowances	32,500	34,000	(1,500)	(4.4%)
Net sales	$1,498,000	$1,200,000	$298,000	24.8%
Cost of goods sold	1,043,000	820,000	223,000	27.2%
Gross profit	$ 455,000	$ 380,000	$ 75,000	19.7%
Selling expenses	$ 191,000	$ 147,000	$ 44,000	29.9%
Administrative expenses	104,000	97,400	6,600	6.8%
Total operating expenses	$ 295,000	$ 244,400	$ 50,600	20.7%
Income from operations	$ 160,000	$ 135,600	$ 24,400	18.0%
Other income	8,500	11,000	(2,500)	(22.7%)
	$ 168,500	$ 146,600	$ 21,900	14.9%
Other expense	6,000	12,000	(6,000)	(50.0%)
Income before income tax	$ 162,500	$ 134,600	$ 27,900	20.7%
Income tax expense	71,500	58,100	13,400	23.1%
Net income	$ 91,000	$ 76,500	$ 14,500	19.0%

Exhibit 600.21 *Comparative Retained Earnings Statement—Horizontal Analysis*

Lincoln Company
Comparative Retained Earnings Statement
December 31, 2003 and 2002

	2003	2002	Increase (Decrease) Amount	Percent
Retained earnings, January 1	$137,500	$100,000	$37,500	37.5%
Net income for the year	91,000	76,500	14,500	19.0%
Total	$228,500	$176,500	$52,000	29.5%
Dividends:				
On preferred stock	$ 9,000	$ 9,000	—	—
On common stock	40,000	30,000	$10,000	33.3%
Total	$ 49,000	$ 39,000	$10,000	25.6%
Retained earnings, December 31	$179,500	$137,500	$42,000	30.5%

Exhibit 600.21 illustrates a comparative retained earnings statement with horizontal analysis. It reveals that retained earnings increased 30.5% for the year. The increase is due to net income of $91,000 for the year, less dividends of $49,000.

Vertical Analysis

A percentage analysis may also be used to show the relationship of each component to the total within a single statement. This type of analysis is called **vertical analysis.** Like horizontal analysis, the statements may be prepared in either detailed or condensed form. In the latter case, additional details of the changes in individual items may be presented in supporting schedules. In such schedules, the percentage analysis may be based on either the total of the schedule or the

Exhibit 600.22 *Comparative Balance Sheet—Vertical Analysis*

Lincoln Company
Comparative Balance Sheet
December 31, 2003 and 2002

	2003 Amount	2003 Percent	2002 Amount	2002 Percent
Assets				
Current assets	$ 550,000	48.3%	$ 533,000	43.3%
Long-term investments	95,000	8.3	177,500	14.4
Property, plant, and equipment (net)	444,500	39.0	470,000	38.2
Intangible assets	50,000	4.4	50,000	4.1
Total assets	$1,139,500	100.0%	$1,230,500	100.0%
Liabilities				
Current liabilities	$ 210,000	18.4%	$ 243,000	19.7%
Long-term liabilities	100,000	8.8	200,000	16.3
Total liabilities	$ 310,000	27.2%	$ 443,000	36.0%
Stockholders' Equity				
Preferred 6% stock, $100 par	$ 150,000	13.2%	$ 150,000	12.2%
Common stock, $10 par	500,000	43.9	500,000	40.6
Retained earnings	179,500	15.7	137,500	11.2
Total stockholders' equity	$ 829,500	72.8%	$ 787,500	64.0%
Total liabilities and stockholders' equity	$1,139,500	100.0%	$1,230,500	100.0%

statement total. Although vertical analysis is limited to an individual statement, its significance may be improved by preparing comparative statements.

In vertical analysis of the balance sheet, each asset item is stated as a percent of the total assets. Each liability and stockholders' equity item is stated as a percent of the total liabilities and stockholders' equity. Exhibit 600.22 is a condensed comparative balance sheet with vertical analysis for Lincoln Company.

The major percentage changes in Lincoln Company's assets are in the current asset and long-term investment categories. In the Liabilities and Stockholders' Equity sections of the balance sheet, the greatest percentage changes are in long-term liabilities and retained earnings. Stockholders' equity increased from 64% to 72.8% of total liabilities and stockholders' equity in 2003. There is a comparable decrease in liabilities.

In a vertical analysis of the income statement, each item is stated as a percent of net sales. Exhibit 600.23 is a condensed comparative income statement with vertical analysis for Lincoln Company.

We must be careful when judging the significance of differences between percentages for the two years. For example, the decline of the gross profit rate from 31.7% in 2002 to 30.4% in 2003 is only 1.3 percentage points. In terms of dollars of potential gross profit, however, it represents a decline of approximately $19,500 (1.3% × $1,498,000).

> **Example 12** At the end of the current year, Accounts Payable was $600,000 and total liabilities and stockholders' equity was $1,200,000. What percent would be shown for Accounts Payable in a balance sheet with vertical analysis?
>
> 50% ($600,000/$1,200,000)

Common-Size Statement Analysis

Horizontal and vertical analyses with both dollar and percentage amounts are useful in assessing relationships and trends in financial conditions and operations of a business. Vertical analysis with both dollar and percentage amounts is also useful in comparing one company with another or with industry averages. Such comparisons are easier to make with the use of common-size statements. In a **common-size statement analysis,** all items are expressed in percentages.

Exhibit 600.23 *Comparative Income Statement—Vertical Analysis*

Lincoln Company
Comparative Income Statement
For the Years Ended December 31, 2003 and 2002

	2003 Amount	2003 Percent	2002 Amount	2002 Percent
Sales	$1,530,500	102.2%	$1,234,000	102.8%
Sales returns and allowances	32,500	2.2	34,000	2.8
Net sales	$1,498,000	100.0%	$1,200,000	100.0%
Cost of goods sold	1,043,000	69.6	820,000	68.3
Gross profit	$ 455,000	30.4%	$ 380,000	31.7%
Selling expenses	$ 191,000	12.8%	$ 147,000	12.3%
Administrative expenses	104,000	6.9	97,400	8.1
Total operating expenses	$ 295,000	19.7%	$ 244,400	20.4%
Income from operations	$ 160,000	10.7%	$ 135,600	11.3%
Other income	8,500	0.6	11,000	0.9
	$ 168,500	11.3%	$ 146,600	12.2%
Other expense	6,000	0.4	12,000	1.0
Income before income tax	$ 162,500	10.9%	$ 134,600	11.2%
Income tax expense	71,500	4.8	58,100	4.8
Net income	$91,000	6.1%	$ 76,500	6.4%

Common-size statements are useful in comparing the current period with prior periods, individual businesses, or one business with industry percentages. Industry data are often available from trade associations and financial information services. Exhibit 600.24 is a comparative common-size income statement for two businesses.

Exhibit 600.24 indicates that Lincoln Company has a slightly higher rate of gross profit than Madison Corporation. However, this advantage is more than offset by Lincoln Company's higher percentage of selling and administrative expenses. As a result, the income from operations of Lincoln Company is 10.7% of net sales, compared with 14.4% for Madison Corporation—an unfavorable difference of 3.7 percentage points.

Other Analytical Measures

In addition to the preceding analyses, other relationships may be expressed in simple ratios and percentages. Often, these items are taken from the financial statements and thus are a type of vertical analysis. Comparing these items with items from earlier periods is a type of horizontal analysis.

Example 13 *The percentages of gross profit and net income to sales for fiscal year-end 1999 for **Kmart Corp.** and **Wal-Mart Stores Inc.** are shown below.*

	Kmart Corp.	Wal-Mart Stores Inc.
Gross profit to sales	21.8%	21.0%
Net income to sales	1.5%	3.3%

Wal-Mart has a slightly lower gross profit margin than Kmart, which is likely due to lower prices. However, Wal-Mart has a much leaner operating expense structure, so it is able to earn an overall higher percentage of net income to sales.

Exhibit 600.24 *Common-Size Income Statement*

Lincoln Company and Madison Corporation
Condensed Common-Size Income Statement
For the Year Ended December 31, 2003

	Lincoln Company	Madison Corporation
Sales	102.2%	102.3%
Sales returns and allowances	2.2	2.3
Net sales	100.0%	100.0%
Cost of goods sold	69.6	70.0
Gross profit	30.4%	30.0%
Selling expenses	12.8%	11.5%
Administrative expenses	6.9	4.1
Total operating expenses	19.7%	15.6%
Income from operations	10.7%	14.4%
Other income	0.6	0.6
	11.3%	15.0%
Other expense	0.4	0.5
Income before income tax	10.9%	14.5%
Income tax expense	4.8	5.5
Net income	6.1%	9.0%

Solvency Analysis

Some aspects of a business's financial condition and operations are of greater importance to some users than others. However, all users are interested in the ability of a business to pay its debts as they are due and to earn income. The ability of a business to meet its financial obligations (debts) is called **solvency** or **liquidity**. The ability of a business to earn income is called **profitability**.

The factors of solvency and profitability are interrelated. A business that cannot pay its debts on a timely basis may experience difficulty in obtaining credit. A lack of available credit may, in turn, lead to a decline in the business's profitability. Eventually, the business may be forced into bankruptcy. Likewise, a business that is less profitable than its competitors is likely to be at a disadvantage in obtaining credit or new capital from stockholders.

> *Solvency analysis focuses on the ability of a business to pay or otherwise satisfy its current and noncurrent liabilites.*

In the following paragraphs, we discuss various types of financial analyses that are useful in evaluating the solvency of a business. In the next section, we discuss various types of profitability analyses. The examples in both sections are based on Lincoln Company's financial statements presented earlier. In some cases, data from Lincoln Company's financial statements of the preceding year and from other sources are also used. These historical data are useful in assessing the past performance of a business and in forecasting its future performance. The results of financial analyses may be even more useful when they are compared with those of competing businesses and with industry averages.

Solvency analysis focuses on the ability of a business to pay or otherwise satisfy its current and noncurrent liabilities. It is normally assessed by examining balance sheet relationships, using the following major analyses:

1. Current position analysis
2. Accounts receivable analysis
3. Inventory analysis
4. The ratio of fixed assets to long-term liabilities
5. The ratio of liabilities to stockholders' equity
6. The number of times interest charges are earned

1. Current Position Analysis

To be useful in assessing solvency, a ratio or other financial measure must relate to a business's ability to pay or otherwise satisfy its liabilities. Using measures to assess a business's ability to pay its current liabilities is called **current position analysis.** Such analysis is of special interest to short-term creditors.

An analysis of a firm's current position normally includes determining the working capital, the current ratio, and the acid-test ratio. The current and acid-test ratios are most useful when analyzed together and compared to previous periods and other firms in the industry.

WORKING CAPITAL The excess of the current assets of a business over its current liabilities is called **working capital.** The working capital is often used in evaluating a company's ability to meet currently maturing debts. It is especially useful in making monthly or other period-to-period comparisons for a company. However, amounts of working capital are difficult to assess when comparing companies of different sizes or in comparing such amounts with industry figures. For example, working capital of $250,000 may be adequate for a small local hardware store, but it would be inadequate for all of **Home Depot.**

CURRENT RATIO Another means of expressing the relationship between current assets and current liabilities is the **current ratio.** This ratio is sometimes called the **working capital ratio** or **bankers' ratio.** The ratio is computed by dividing the total current assets by the total current liabilities. For Lincoln Company, working capital and the current ratio for 2003 and 2002 are as follows.

	2003	2002
Current assets	$550,000	$533,000
Current liabilities	210,000	243,000
Working capital	$340,000	$290,000
Current ratio	2.6	2.2

The current ratio is a more reliable indicator of solvency than is working capital. To illustrate, assume that as of December 31, 2003, the working capital of a competitor is much greater than $340,000, but its current ratio is only 1.3. Considering these facts alone, Lincoln Company, with its current ratio of 2.6, is in a more favorable position to obtain short-term credit than the competitor, which has the greater amount of working capital.

ACID-TEST RATIO The working capital and the current ratio do not consider the makeup of the current assets. To illustrate the importance of this consideration, the current position data for Lincoln Company and Jefferson Corporation as of December 31, 2003, are as follows.

	Lincoln Company	Jefferson Corporation
Current assets:		
Cash	$ 90,500	$ 45,500
Marketable securities	75,000	25,000
Accounts receivable (net)	115,000	90,000
Inventories	264,000	380,000
Prepaid expenses	5,500	9,500
Total current assets	$550,000	$550,000
Current liabilities	210,000	210,000
Working capital	$340,000	$340,000
Current ratio	2.6	2.6

Both companies have a working capital of $340,000 and a current ratio of 2.6. But the ability of each company to pay its current debts is significantly different. Jefferson Corporation has more of its current assets in inventories. Some of these inventories must be sold and the receivables collected before the current liabilities can be paid in full. Thus, a large amount of time may be necessary to convert these inventories into cash. Declines in market prices and a reduction in demand could also impair its ability to pay current liabilities. In contrast, Lincoln Company has cash and current assets (marketable securities and accounts receivable) that can generally be converted to cash rather quickly to meet its current liabilities.

A ratio that measures the "instant" debt-paying ability of a company is called the **acid-test ratio** or **quick ratio**. It is the ratio of the total quick assets to the total current liabilities. **Quick assets** are cash and other current assets that can be quickly converted to cash. Quick assets normally include cash, marketable securities, and receivables. The acid-test ratio data for Lincoln Company are as follows.

> The **Wm. Wrigley Company** maintains a high current ratio—3.9 for a recent year. Wrigley's stable and profitable chewing gum business has allowed it to develop a strong cash position coupled with no short-term notes payable.

	2003	2002
Quick assets:		
Cash	$ 90,500	$ 64,700
Marketable equity securities	75,000	60,000
Accounts receivable (net)	115,000	120,000
Total quick assets	$280,500	$244,700
Current liabilities	$210,000	$243,000
Acid-test ratio (Quick Ratio)	1.3	1.0

Example 14 *A balance sheet shows $300,000 of cash, marketable securities, and receivables, and $250,000 of inventories. Current liabilities are $200,000. What are (a) the current ratio and (b) the acid-test ratio?*

(a) 2.75 ($550,000/$200,000);   (b) 1.5 ($300,000/$200,000)

2. Accounts Receivable Analysis

The size and makeup of accounts receivable change constantly during business operations. Sales on account increase accounts receivable, whereas collections from customers decrease accounts receivable. Firms that grant long credit terms usually have larger accounts receivable balances than those granting short credit terms. Increases or decreases in the volume of sales also affect the balance of accounts receivable.

It is desirable to collect receivables as promptly as possible. The cash collected from receivables improves solvency. In addition, the cash generated by prompt collections from customers may be used in operations for such purposes as purchasing merchandise in large quantities at lower prices. The cash may also be used for payment of dividends to stockholders or for other investing or financing purposes. Prompt collection also lessens the risk of loss from uncollectible accounts.

ACCOUNTS RECEIVABLE TURNOVER The relationship between credit sales and accounts receivable may be stated as the **accounts receivable turnover**. This ratio is computed by dividing net sales on account by the average net accounts receivable. It is desirable to base the average on monthly balances, which allows for seasonal changes in sales. When such data are not available, it may be necessary to use the average of the accounts receivable balance at the beginning and the end of the year. If there are trade notes receivable as well as accounts, the two may be combined. The accounts receivable turnover data for Lincoln Company are as follows. All sales were made on account.

	2003	2002
Net sales on account	$1,498,000	$1,200,000
Accounts receivable (net):		
Beginning of year	$ 120,000	$ 140,000
End of year	115,000	120,000
Total	$ 235,000	$ 260,000
Average (Total ÷ 2)	$ 117,500	$ 130,000
Accounts receivable turnover	12.7	9.2

The increase in the accounts receivable turnover for 2003 indicates that there has been an improvement in the collection of receivables. This may be due to a change in the granting of credit, in collection practices, or in both.

NUMBER OF DAYS' SALES IN RECEIVABLES Another measure of the relationship between credit sales and accounts receivable is the **number of days' sales in receivables.** This ratio is computed by dividing the net accounts receivable at the end of the year by the average daily sales on account. Average daily sales on account is determined by dividing net sales on account by 365 days. The number of days' sales in receivables is computed for Lincoln Company as follows.

	2003	2002
Accounts receivable (net), end of year	$ 115,000	$ 120,000
Net sales on account	$1,498,000	$1,200,000
Average daily sales on account (sales ÷ 365)	$ 4,104	$ 3,288
Number of days' sales in receivables	28.0*	36.5*
*Accounts receivable ÷ Average daily sales on account		

The number of days' sales in receivables is an estimate of the length of time (in days) the accounts receivable have been outstanding. Comparing this measure with the credit terms provides information on the efficiency in collecting receivables. For example, assume that the number of days' sales in receivables for Grant Inc. is 40. If Grant Inc.'s credit terms are n/45, then its collection process appears to be efficient. On the other hand, if Grant Inc.'s credit terms are n/30, its collection process does not appear to be efficient. A comparison with other firms in the same industry and with prior years also provides useful information. Such comparisons may indicate efficiency of collection procedures and trends in credit management.

> **Example 15** Sales were $1,200,000, of which 80% were on account. The accounts receivable balance at the beginning of the year was $56,000, and at the end of the year it was $40,000. What are (a) the accounts receivable turnover and (b) the number of days' sales in receivables?
>
> (a) 20 [(0.80 × $1,200,000)/($56,000 + $40,000)/2]; (b) 15.2 days [$40,000/($960,000/365)]

3. Inventory Analysis

A business should keep enough inventory on hand to meet the needs of its customers and its operations. At the same time, however, an excessive amount of inventory reduces solvency by tying up funds. Excess inventories also increase insurance expense, property taxes, storage costs, and other related expenses. These expenses further reduce funds that could be used elsewhere to improve operations. Finally, excess inventory also increases the risk of losses because of price declines or obsolescence of the inventory. Two measures that are useful for evaluating the management of inventory are the inventory turnover and the number of days' sales in inventory.

INVENTORY TURNOVER The relationship between the volume of goods (merchandise) sold and inventory may be stated as the **inventory turnover.** It is computed by dividing the cost of goods sold by the average inventory. If monthly data are not available, the average of the inventories at the beginning and the end of the year may be used. The inventory turnover for Lincoln Company is computed as follows.

	2003	2002
Cost of goods sold	$1,043,000	$820,000
Inventories:		
Beginning of year	$ 283,000	$311,000
End of year	264,000	283,000
Total	$ 547,000	$594,000
Average (Total ÷ 2)	$ 273,500	$297,000
Inventory turnover	3.8	2.8

The inventory turnover improved for Lincoln Company because of an increase in the cost of goods sold and a decrease in the average inventories. Differences across inventories, companies, and industries are too great to allow a general statement on what is a good inventory turnover. For example, a firm selling food should have a higher turnover than a firm selling furniture or jewelry. Likewise, the perishable foods department of a supermarket should have a higher turnover than the soaps and cleansers department. However, for each business or each department within a business, there is a reasonable turnover rate. A turnover lower than this rate could mean that inventory is not being managed properly.

*The inventory turnover of McDonald's Corporation for a recent year was 39, while for **Toys "R" Us Inc.**, it was 4.3. McDonald's inventory turnover is higher because it sells perishable food products, while toys can sit on the shelf longer without "spoiling."*

NUMBER OF DAYS' SALES IN INVENTORY Another measure of the relationship between the cost of goods sold and inventory is the **number of days' sales in inventory.** This measure is computed by dividing the inventory at the end of the year by the average daily cost of goods sold (cost of goods sold divided by 365). The number of days' sales in inventory for Lincoln Company is computed as follows.

	2003	2002
Inventories, end of year	$ 264,000	$283,000
Cost of goods sold	$1,043,000	$820,000
Average daily cost of goods sold (COGS ÷ 365 days)	$ 2,858	$ 2,247
Number of days' sales in inventory	92.4	125.9

The number of days' sales in inventory is a rough measure of the length of time it takes to acquire, sell, and replace the inventory. For Lincoln Company, there is a major improvement in the number of days' sales in inventory during 2003. However, a comparison with earlier years and similar firms would be useful in assessing Lincoln Company's overall inventory management.

4. Ratio of Fixed Assets to Long-Term Liabilities

Long-term notes and bonds are often secured by mortgages on fixed assets. The **ratio of fixed assets to long-term liabilities** is a solvency measure that indicates the margin of safety of the noteholders or bondholders. It also indicates the ability of the business to borrow additional funds on a long-term basis. The ratio of fixed assets to long-term liabilities for Lincoln Company is as follows.

	2003	2002
Fixed assets (net)	$444,500	$470,000
Long-term liabilities	$100,000	$200,000
Ratio of fixed assets to long-term liabilities	4.4	2.4

The major increase in this ratio at the end of 2003 is mainly due to liquidating one-half of Lincoln Company's long-term liabilities. If the company needs to borrow additional funds on a long-term basis in the future, it is in a strong position to do so.

5. Ratio of Liabilities to Stockholders' Equity

Claims against the total assets of a business are divided into two groups: (1) claims of creditors and (2) claims of owners. The relationship between the total claims of the creditors and owners—the **ratio of liabilities to stockholders' equity**—is a solvency measure that indicates the margin of safety for creditors. It also indicates the ability of the business to withstand adverse business conditions. When the claims of creditors are large in relation to the equity of the stockholders, there are usually significant interest payments. If earnings decline to the point where the company is unable to meet its interest payments, the business may be taken over by the creditors.

The relationship between creditor and stockholder equity is shown in the vertical analysis of the balance sheet. For example, the balance sheet of Lincoln Company in Exhibit 600.22 indicates that on December 31, 2003, liabilities represented

27.2% and stockholders' equity represented 72.8% of the total liabilities and stockholders' equity (100.0%). Instead of expressing each item as a percent of the total, this relationship may be expressed as a ratio of one to the other, as follows.

	2003	2002
Total liabilities	$310,000	$443,000
Total stockholders' equity	$829,500	$787,500
Ratio of liabilities to stockholders' equity	0.37	0.56

The ratio of liabilities to stockholders' equity varies across industries. For example, recent annual reports of some selected companies showed the following ratio of liabilities to stockholders' equity

Continental Airlines	4.31
Procter & Gamble	1.85
Circuit City Stores	0.93

The airline industry generally uses more debt financing than the consumer product or retail industries. Thus, the airline industry is generally considered more risky.

The balance sheet of Lincoln Company shows that the major factor affecting the change in the ratio was the $100,000 decrease in long-term liabilities during 2003. The ratio at the end of both years shows a large margin of safety for the creditors.

6. Number of Times Interest Charges Are Earned

Corporations in some industries, such as airlines, normally have high ratios of debt to stockholders' equity. For such corporations, the relative risk of the debtholders is normally measured as the **number of times interest charges are earned** during the year. The higher the ratio, the lower the risk that interest payments will not be made if earnings decrease. In other words, the higher the ratio, the greater the assurance that interest payments will be made on a continuing basis. This measure also indicates the general financial strength of the business, which is of interest to stockholders and employees as well as creditors.

The amount available to meet interest charges is not affected by taxes on income. This is because interest is deductible in determining taxable income. Thus, the number of times interest charges are earned is computed as shown below.

	2003	2002
Income before income tax	$ 900,000	$ 800,000
Add interest expense	300,000	250,000
Amount available to meet interest charges	$1,200,000	$1,050,000
Number of times interest charges earned	4	4.2

Analysis such as this can also be applied to dividends on preferred stock. In such a case, net income is divided by the amount of preferred dividends to yield the **number of times preferred dividends are earned.** This measure indicates the risk that dividends to preferred stockholders may not be paid.

Example 16 *What would be the number of times interest charges are earned for a company with $1,500,000, 10% debt; net income of $120,000; and a corporate tax rate of 40%?*

$$\frac{[\$120,000/(1.0 - 0.4)] + \$150,000}{\$150,000} = 2.33$$

Profitability Analysis

The ability of a business to earn profits depends on the effectiveness and efficiency of its operations as well as the resources available to it. Profitability analysis, therefore, focuses primarily on the relationship between operating results as reported in the income statement and resources available to the business as reported in the balance sheet. Major analyses used in assessing profitability include the following.

1. Ratio of net sales to assets
2. Rate earned on total assets
3. Rate earned on total stockholders' equity
4. Rate earned on common stockholders' equity
5. Earnings per share on common stock
6. Price-earnings ratio
7. Dividends per share of common stock
8. Dividend yield of common stock

Profitability analysis focuses on the relationship between operating results and the resources available to a business.

1. Ratio of Net Sales to Assets

The **ratio of net sales to assets** is a profitability measure that shows how effectively a firm utilizes its assets. For example, two competing businesses have equal amounts of assets. If the sales of one are twice the sales of the other, the business with the higher sales is making better use of its assets.

In computing the ratio of net sales to assets, any long-term investments are excluded from total assets, because such investments are unrelated to normal operations involving the sale of goods or services. Assets may be measured as the total at the end of the year, the average at the beginning and end of the year, or the average of monthly totals. The basic data and the computation of this ratio for Lincoln Company are as follows.

	2003	2002
Net sales	$1,498,000	$1,200,000
Total assets (excluding long-term investments):		
Beginning of year	$1,053,000	$1,010,000
End of year	1,044,500	1,053,000
Total	$2,097,500	$2,063,000
Average (Total ÷ 2)	$1,048,750	$1,031,500
Ratio of net sales to assets	1.4	1.2

This ratio improved during 2003, primarily due to an increase in sales volume. A comparison with similar companies or industry averages would be helpful in assessing the effectiveness of Lincoln Company's use of its assets.

2. Rate Earned on Total Assets

The **rate earned on total assets** measures the profitability of total assets, without considering how the assets are financed. This rate is therefore not affected by whether the assets are financed primarily by creditors or stockholders.

The rate earned on total assets is computed by adding interest expense to net income and dividing this sum by the average total assets. Adding interest expense to net income eliminates the effect of whether the assets are financed by debt or equity. The rate earned by Lincoln Company on total assets is computed as follows.

	2003	2002
Net income	$ 91,000	$ 76,500
Plus interest expense	6,000	12,000
Total	$ 97,000	$ 88,500
Total assets:		
Beginning of year	$1,230,500	$1,187,500
End of year	1,139,500	1,230,500
Total	$2,370,000	$2,418,000
Average (Total ÷ 2)	$1,185,000	$1,209,000
Rate earned on total assets	8.2%	7.3%

The rate earned on total assets of Lincoln Company during 2003 improved over that of 2002. A comparison with similar companies and industry averages would be useful in evaluating Lincoln Company's profitability on total assets.

Sometimes it may be desirable to compute the **rate of income from operations to total assets.** This is especially true if significant amounts of nonoperating income and expense are reported on the income statement. In this case, any assets related to the nonoperating income and expense items should be excluded from total assets in computing the rate. In addition, using income from operations (which is before tax) has the advantage of eliminating the effects of any changes in the tax structure on the rate of earnings. When evaluating published data on rates earned on total assets, you should be careful to determine the exact nature of the measure that is reported.

3. Rate Earned on Total Stockholders' Equity

Another measure of profitability is the **rate earned on total stockholders' equity.** It is computed by dividing net income by average total stockholders' equity. In contrast to the rate earned on total assets, this measure emphasizes the rate of income earned on the amount invested by the stockholders.

The total stockholders' equity may vary throughout a period. For example, a business may issue or retire stock, pay dividends, and earn net income. If monthly amounts are not available, the average of the stockholders' equity at the beginning and the end of the year is normally used to compute this rate. For Lincoln Company, the rate earned on total stockholders' equity is computed as follows.

	2003	2002
Net income	$ 91,000	$ 76,500
Stockholders' equity:		
Beginning of year	$ 787,500	$ 750,000
End of year	829,500	787,500
Total	$1,617,000	$1,537,500
Average (Total ÷ 2)	$ 808,500	$ 768,750
Rate earned on total stockholders' equity	11.3%	10.0%

The rate earned by a business on the equity of its stockholders is usually higher than the rate earned on total assets. This occurs when the amount earned on assets acquired with creditors' funds is more than the interest paid to creditors. This difference in the rate on stockholders' equity and the rate on total assets is called **leverage.**

Lincoln Company's rate earned on stockholders' equity for 2003, 11.3%, is greater than the rate of 8.2% earned on total assets. The leverage of 3.1% (11.3% − 8.2%) for 2003 compares favorably with the 2.7% (10.0% − 7.3%) leverage for 2002. Exhibit 600.25 shows the 2003 and 2002 leverages for Lincoln Company.

4. Rate Earned on Common Stockholders' Equity

A corporation may have both preferred and common stock outstanding. In this case, the common stockholders have the residual claim on earnings. The **rate earned on common stockholders' equity** focuses only on the rate of profits earned on the amount invested by the common stockholders. It is computed by subtracting preferred dividend requirements from the net income and dividing by the average common stockholders' equity.

Lincoln Company has $150,000 of 6% nonparticipating preferred stock outstanding on December 31, 2003 and 2002. Thus, the annual preferred dividend requirement is $9,000 ($150,000 × 6%). The common stockholders' equity

Exhibit 600.25 *Leverages for Lincoln Company*

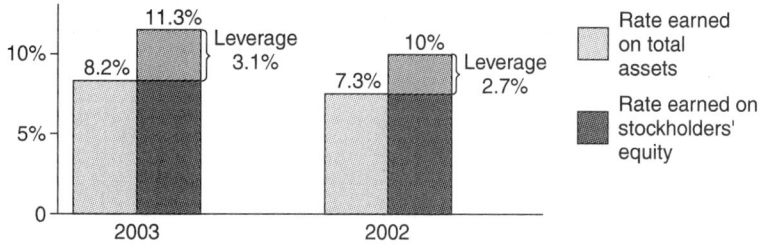

equals the total stockholders' equity, including retained earnings, less the par of the preferred stock ($150,000). The basic data and the rate earned on common stockholders' equity for Lincoln Company are as follows.

	2003	2002
Net income	$ 91,000	$ 76,500
Preferred dividends	9,000	9,000
Remainder—identified with common stock	$ 82,000	$ 67,500
Common stockholders' equity:		
Beginning of year	$ 637,500	$ 600,000
End of year	679,500	637,500
Total	$1,317,000	$1,237,500
Average (Total ÷ 2)	$ 658,500	$ 618,750
Rate earned on common stockholders' equity	12.5%	10.9%

The rate earned on common stockholders' equity differs from the rates earned by Lincoln Company on total assets and total stockholders' equity. This occurs if there are borrowed funds and also preferred stock outstanding, which rank ahead of the common shares in their claim on earnings. Thus, the concept of leverage, as we discussed in the preceding section, can also be applied to the use of funds from the sale of preferred stock as well as borrowing. Funds from both sources can be used in an attempt to increase the return on common stockholders' equity.

Example 17 *The approximate rates earned on assets and stockholders' equity for Adolph Coors Company and Anheuser-Busch Companies for a recent fiscal year are shown below.*

	Adolph Coors	Anheuser-Busch
Rate earned on assets	5%	13%
Rate earned on stockholders' equity	9%	30%

Anheuser-Busch has been more profitable and has benefited from a greater use of leverage than has Adolph Coors.

5. Earnings per Share on Common Stock

One of the profitability measures often quoted by the financial press is **earnings per share (EPS) on common stock.** It is also normally reported in the income statement in corporate annual reports. If a company has issued only one class of stock, the earnings per share is computed by dividing net income by the number of shares of stock outstanding. If preferred and common stock are outstanding, the net income is first reduced by the amount of preferred dividend requirements. The data on the earnings per share of common stock for Lincoln Company are as follows.

	2003	2002
Net income	$91,000	$76,500
Preferred dividends	9,000	9,000
Remainder—identified with common stock	$82,000	$67,500
Shares of common stock outstanding	50,000	50,000
Earnings per share on common stock	$1.64	$1.35

6. Price-Earnings Ratio

Another profitability measure quoted by the financial press is the **price-earnings (P/E) ratio** on common stock. The price-earnings ratio is an indicator of a firm's future earnings prospects. It is computed by dividing the market price per share of common stock at a specific date by the annual earnings per share. To illustrate, assume that the market prices per common share are 41 at the end of 2003 and 27 at the end of 2002. The price-earnings ratio on common stock of Lincoln Company is computed as follows.

Price-earnings (P/E) ratios that are much higher than the market averages are generally associated with companies with fast-growing profits. P/E ratios that are much lower than the market averages are generally associated with "out of favor" or declining profit companies.

	2003	2002
Market price per share of common stock	$41.00	$27.00
Earnings per share on common stock	÷1.64	÷1.35
Price-earnings ratio on common stock	25	20

The price-earnings ratio indicates that a share of common stock of Lincoln Company was selling for 20 times the amount of earnings per share at the end of 2002. At the end of 2003, the common stock was selling for 25 times the amount of earnings per share.

7. Dividends per Share of Common Stock

Because the primary basis for dividends is earnings, **dividends per share** and earnings per share on common stock are commonly used by investors in assessing alternative stock investments. The dividends per share for Lincoln Company were $0.80 ($40,000 ÷ 50,000 shares) for 2003 and $0.60 ($30,000 ÷ 50,000 shares) for 2002.

The dividend per share, dividend yield, and P/E ratio of a common stock are normally quoted on the daily listing of stock prices in The Wall Street Journal and other financial publications.

Dividends per share can be reported with earnings per share to indicate the relationship between dividends and earnings. Comparing these two per share amounts indicates the extent to which the corporation is retaining its earnings for use in operations. Exhibit 600.26 shows these relationships for Lincoln Company.

8. Dividend Yield of Common Stock

The **dividend yield** on common stock is a profitability measure that shows the rate of return to common stockholders in terms of cash dividends. It is of special interest to investors whose main investment objective is to receive current returns (dividends) on an investment rather than an increase in the market price of the investment. The dividend yield is computed by dividing the annual dividends paid per share of common stock by the market price per share on

Exhibit 600.26 *Dividends and Earnings per Share of Common Stock*

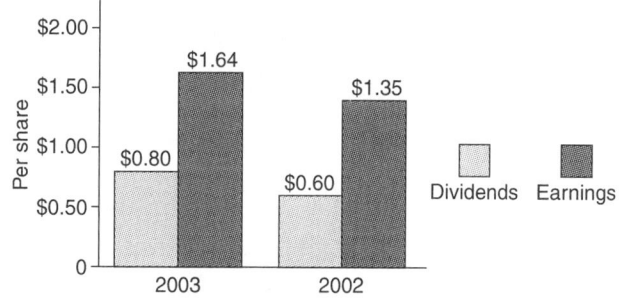

a specific date. To illustrate, assume that the market price was 41 at the end of 2003 and 27 at the end of 2002. The dividend yield on common stock of Lincoln Company is as follows.

	2003	2002
Dividends per share of common stock	$0.80	$0.60
Market price per share of common stock	÷41.00	÷27.00
Dividend yield on common stock	1.95%	2.22%

Summary of Analytical Measures

Exhibit 600.27 presents a summary of the analytical measures that we have discussed. These measures can be computed for most medium-size businesses. Depending on the specific business being analyzed, some measures might be omitted or additional measures could be developed. The type of industry, the capital structure, and the diversity of the business's operations usually affect the measures used. For example, analysis for an airline might include revenue per passenger mile and cost per available seat as measures. Likewise, analysis for a hotel might focus on occupancy rates.

Percentage analyses, ratios, turnovers, and other measures of financial position and operating results are useful analytical measures. They are helpful in assessing a business's past performance and predicting its future. They are not, however, a substitute for sound judgment. In selecting and interpreting analytical measures, conditions peculiar to a business or its industry should be considered. In addition, the influence of the general economic and business environment should be considered.

Exhibit 600.27 *Summary of Analytical Measures*

	Method of Computation	Use
Solvency measures:		
Working capital	Current assets − Current liabilities	To indicate the ability to meet currently maturing obligations
Current ratio	Current assets / Current liabilities	To indicate the ability to meet currently maturing obligations
Acid-test ratio	Quick assets / Current liabilities	To indicate instant debt-paying ability
Accounts receivable turnover	Net sales on account / Average accounts receivable	To assess the efficiency in collecting receivables and in the management of credit
Numbers of days' sales in receivables	Accounts receivable, end of year / Average daily sales on account	To assess the efficiency in collecting receivables and in the management of credit
Inventory turnover	Cost of goods sold / Average inventory	To assess the efficiency in the management of inventory
Number of days' sales in inventory	Inventory, end of year / Average daily cost of goods sold	To assess the efficiency in the management of inventory
Ratio of fixed assets to long-term liabilities	Fixed assets (net) / Long-term liabilities	To indicate the margin of safety to long-term creditors
Ratio of liabilities to stockholders' equity	Total liabilities / Total stockholders' equity	To indicate the margin of safety to creditors
Number of times interest charges are earned	(Income before income tax + Interest expense) / Interest expense	To assess the risk to debtholders in terms of number of times interest charges were earned

Exhibit 600.27 *Continued*

	Method of Computation	Use
Profitability measures:		
Ratio of net sales to assets	$\dfrac{\text{Net sales}}{\text{Average total assets (excluding long-term investments)}}$	To assess the effectiveness in the use of assets
Rate earned on total assets	$\dfrac{\text{Net income + Interest expense}}{\text{Average total assets}}$	To assess the profitability of the assets
Rate earned on total stockholders' equity	$\dfrac{\text{Net income}}{\text{Average total stockholders' equity}}$	To assess the profitability of the investment by stockholders
Rate earned on common stockholders' equity	$\dfrac{\text{Net income} - \text{Preferred dividends}}{\text{Average common stockholders' equity}}$	To assess the profitability of the investment by common stockholders
Earnings per share on common stock	$\dfrac{\text{Net income} - \text{Preferred dividends}}{\text{Shares of common stock outstanding}}$	
Price-earnings ratio	$\dfrac{\text{Market price per share of common stock}}{\text{Earnings per share of common stock}}$	To indicate future earnings prospects, based on the relationship between market value of common stock and earnings
Dividends per share of common stock	$\dfrac{\text{Dividends}}{\text{Shares of common stock outstanding}}$	To indicate the extent to which earnings are being distributed to common stockholders
Dividend yield on common stock	$\dfrac{\text{Dividends per share of common stock}}{\text{Market price per share of common stock}}$	To indicate the rate of return to common stockholders in terms of dividends

In determining trends, the interrelationship of the measures used in assessing a business should be carefully studied. Comparable indexes of earlier periods should also be studied. Data from competing businesses may be useful in assessing the efficiency of operations for the firm under analysis. In making such comparisons, however, the effects of differences in the accounting methods used by the businesses should be considered.

Cost Behavior, Control, and Decision Making

In this section, we discuss commonly used methods for classifying costs according to how they change. We also discuss how management uses cost-volume-profit analysis as a tool in making business decisions.

Cost Behavior

Knowing how costs behave is useful to management for a variety of purposes. For example, knowing how costs behave allows managers to predict profits as sales and production volumes change. Knowing how costs behave is also useful for estimating costs. Estimated costs, in turn, affect a variety of management decisions, such as whether to use excess machine capacity to produce and sell a product at a reduced price.

Cost behavior refers to the manner in which a cost changes as a related activity changes. To understand cost behavior, two factors must be considered. First, we must identify the activities that are thought to cause the cost to be incurred. Such activities are called **activity bases** (or **activity drivers**). Second, we must specify the range of activity over which the changes in the cost are of interest. This range of activity is called the **relevant range.**

To illustrate, hospital administrators must plan and control hospital food costs. To fully understand why food costs change, the activity that causes cost to be incurred must be identified. In the case of food costs, the feeding of patients is a major cause of these costs. The number of patients *treated* by the hospital would not be a good activity base because some patients are outpatients who do not stay in the hospital. The number of patients who *stay* in the hospital, however, is a good activity base for studying food costs. Once the proper activity base is identified, food costs can then be analyzed over the range of the number of patients who normally stay in the hospital (the relevant range).

Three of the most common classifications of cost behavior are variable costs, fixed costs, and mixed costs.

Variable Costs

When the level of activity is measured in units produced, direct materials and direct labor costs are generally classified as variable costs. **Variable costs** are costs that vary in proportion to changes in the level of activity. For example, assume that Jason Inc. produces stereo sound systems under the brand name of J-Sound. The parts for the stereo systems are purchased from outside suppliers for $10 per unit and are assembled in Jason Inc.'s Waterloo plant. The direct materials costs for Model JS-12 for the relevant range of 5,000 to 30,000 units of production are shown below.

Number of Units of Model JS-12 Produced	Direct Materials Cost per Unit	Total Direct Materials Cost
5,000 units	$10	$ 50,000
10,000	10	100,000
15,000	10	150,000
20,000	10	200,000
25,000	10	250,000
30,000	10	300,000

Variable costs are the same per unit, while the total variable cost changes in proportion to changes in the activity base. For Model JS-12, for example, the direct materials cost for 10,000 units ($100,000) is twice the direct materials cost for 5,000 units ($50,000). The total direct materials cost varies in proportion to the number of units produced because the direct materials cost per unit ($10) is the same for all levels of production. Thus, producing 20,000 additional units of JS-12 will increase the direct materials cost by $200,000 (20,000 × $10), producing 25,000 additional units will increase the materials cost by $250,000, and so on.

Exhibit 600.28 illustrates how the variable costs for direct materials for Model JS-12 behave in total and on a per-unit basis as production changes.

Exhibit 600.28 *Variable Cost Graphs*

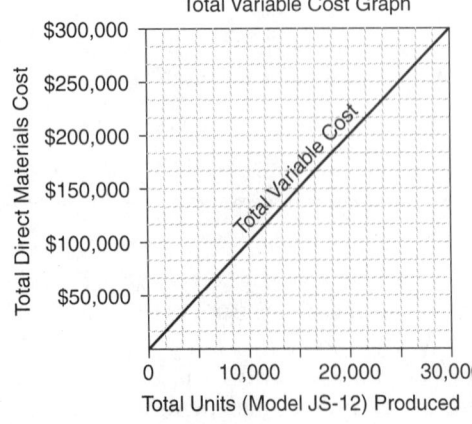
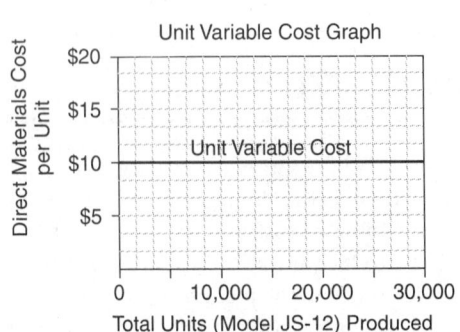

There are a variety of activity bases used by managers for evaluating cost behavior. The following list provides some examples of variable costs, along with their related activity bases for various types of businesses.

Type of Business	Cost	Activity Base
University	Instructor salaries	Number of classes
Passenger airline	Fuel	Number of miles flown
Manufacturing	Direct materials	Number of units produced
Hospital	Nurse wages	Number of patients
Hotel	Maid wages	Number of guests
Bank	Teller wages	Number of banking transactions
Insurance	Claim processing salaries	Number of claims

Fixed Costs

Fixed costs are costs that remain the same in total dollar amount as the level of activity changes. To illustrate, assume that Minton Inc. manufactures, bottles, and distributes La Fleur Perfume at its Los Angeles plant. The production supervisor at the Los Angeles plant is Jane Sovissi, who is paid a salary of $75,000 per year. The relevant range of activity for a year is 50,000 to 300,000 bottles of perfume. Sovissi's salary is a fixed cost that does not vary with the number of units produced. Regardless of the number of bottles produced within the range of 50,000 to 300,000 bottles, Sovissi receives a salary of $75,000.

Although the total fixed cost remains the same as the number of bottles produced changes, the fixed cost per bottle changes. As more bottles are produced, the total fixed costs are spread over a larger number of bottles, and thus the fixed cost per bottle decreases. This relationship is shown below for Jane Sovissi's $75,000 salary.

Number of Bottles of Perfume Produced	Total Salary for Jane Sovissi	Salary per Bottle of Perfume Produced
50,000 bottles	$75,000	$1.500
100,000	75,000	0.750
150,000	75,000	0.500
200,000	75,000	0.375
250,000	75,000	0.300
300,000	75,000	0.250

Exhibit 600.29 illustrates how the fixed cost of Jane Sovissi's salary behaves in total and on a per-unit basis as production changes. When units produced is the measure of activity, examples of fixed costs include straight-line depreciation of factory equipment, insurance on factory plant and equipment, and salaries of factory supervisors. Other examples of fixed costs and their activity bases for a variety of businesses are as follows.

Type of Business	Fixed Cost	Activity Base
University	Building depreciation	Number of students
Passenger airline	Airplane depreciation	Number of passengers
Manufacturing	Plant manager salary	Number of units produced
Hospital	Property insurance	Number of patients
Hotel	Property taxes	Number of guests
Bank	Branch manager salary	Number of customer accounts
Insurance	Computer depreciation	Number of insurance policies

Exhibit 600.29 *Fixed Cost Graphs*

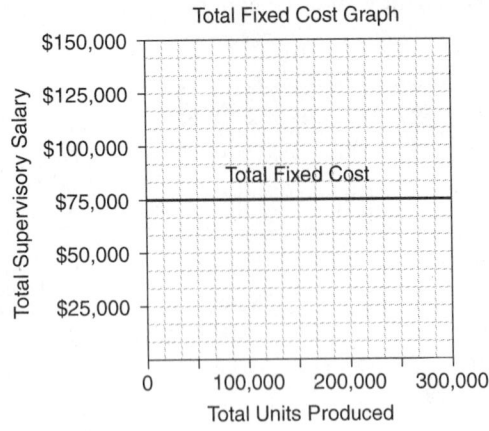
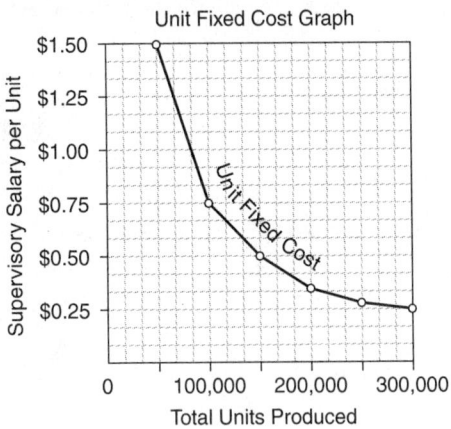

Exhibit 600.30 *Mixed Costs Graph*

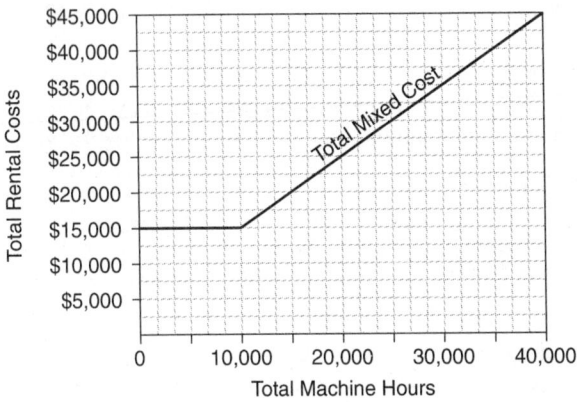

Mixed Costs

A **mixed cost** has characteristics of both a variable and a fixed cost. For example, over one range of activity, the total mixed cost may remain the same. It thus behaves as a fixed cost. Over another range of activity, the mixed cost may change in proportion to changes in the level of activity. It thus behaves as a variable cost. Mixed costs are sometimes called *semivariable* or *semifixed* costs.

To illustrate, assume that Simpson Inc. manufactures sails, using rented machinery. The rental charges are $15,000 per year, plus $1 for each machine hour used over 10,000 hours. If the machinery is used 8,000 hours, the total rental charge is $15,000. If the machinery is used 20,000 hours, the total rental charge is $25,000 [$15,000 + (10,000 hours × $1)], and so on. Thus, if the level of activity is measured in machine hours and the relevant range is 0 to 40,000 hours, the rental charges are a fixed cost up to 10,000 hours and a variable cost thereafter. This mixed cost behavior is shown graphically in Exhibit 600.30.

In analyses, mixed costs are usually separated into their fixed and variable components. The **high-low method** is a cost estimation technique that may be used for this purpose. Other methods of separating mixed costs include the scattergraph method, the least squares method, the account analysis method, and engineering methods. The high-low method uses the highest and lowest activity levels and their related costs to estimate the variable cost per unit and the fixed cost component of mixed costs.

To illustrate, assume that the Equipment Maintenance Department of Kason Inc. incurred the following costs during the past five months.

	Production	Total Cost
June	1,000 units	$45,550
July	1,500	52,000
August	2,100	61,500
September	1,800	57,500
October	750	41,250

The number of units produced is the measure of activity, and the number of units produced between June and October is the relevant range of production. For Kason Inc., the difference between the number of units produced and the difference between the total cost at the highest and lowest levels of production are as follows.

	Production	Total Cost
Highest level	2,100 units	$61,500
Lowest level	750	41,250
Difference	1,350 units	$20,250

Because the total fixed cost does not change with changes in volume of production, the $20,250 difference in the total cost is the change in the total variable cost. Hence, dividing the difference in the total cost by the difference in production provides an estimate of the variable cost per unit. For Kason Inc., this estimate is $15, as shown below.

$$\text{Variable cost per unit} = \frac{\text{Difference in total cost}}{\text{Difference in production}}$$

$$\text{Variable cost per unit} = \frac{\$20,250}{1,350 \text{ units}} = \$15$$

The fixed cost will be the same at both the highest and the lowest levels of production. Thus, the fixed cost can be estimated at either of these levels. This is done by subtracting the estimated total variable cost from the total cost, using the following total cost equation.

Total cost = (Variable cost per unit × Units of production) + Fixed cost

Highest level:
$61,500 = ($15 × 2,100 units) + Fixed cost
$61,500 = $31,500 + Fixed cost
$30,000 = Fixed cost

Lowest level:
$41,250 = ($15 × 750 units) + Fixed cost
$41,250 = $11,250 + Fixed cost
$30,000 = Fixed cost

The total equipment maintenance cost for Kason Inc. can thus be analyzed as a $30,000 fixed cost and a $15 per-unit variable cost. Using these amounts in the total cost equation, the total equipment maintenance cost at other levels of production can be estimated.

Example 18 The manufacturing cost at the highest production level of 2,500 units is $125,000. The manufacturing cost at the lowest production level of 1,000 units is $80,000. Using the high-low method, what are (a) the variable cost per unit and (b) the total fixed cost?

(a) $30 per unit [($125,000 2 $80,000) 4 (2,500 2 1,000)];   (b) $50,000 [$125,000 2 ($30 3 2,500)]

Summary of Cost Behavior Concepts

Examples of common variable, fixed, and mixed costs when the number of units produced is the activity base are:

Variable Cost	Fixed Cost	Mixed Cost
Direct materials	Depreciation expense	Quality Control Department salaries
Direct labor	Property taxes	Purchasing Department salaries
Electricity expense	Officer salaries	Maintenance expenses
Sales commissions	Insurance expense	Warehouse expenses

Mixed costs contain a fixed cost component that is incurred even if nothing is produced. For analyses, the fixed and variable cost components of mixed costs should be separated using the high-low method or other.

The following table summarizes the cost behavior attributes of variable costs and fixed costs.

Cost	Effect of Changing Activity Level — Total Amount	Effect of Changing Activity Level — Per-Unit Amount
Variable	Increases and decreases proportionately with activity level.	Remains the same regardless of activity level.
Fixed	Remains the same regardless of activity level.	Increases and decreases inversely with activity level.

Reporting Variable and Fixed Costs for Decision Making

Separating costs into their variable and fixed components for reporting purposes can be useful for decision making. One method of reporting variable and fixed costs is called **variable costing** or **direct costing** which is discussed in Section 660. Under variable costing, only the variable manufacturing costs (direct materials, direct labor, and variable factory overhead) are included in the product cost. The fixed factory overhead is an expense of the period in which it is incurred.

Cost-Volume-Profit Relationships

After costs have been classified as fixed and variable, their effect on revenues, volume, and profits can be studied by using cost-volume-profit analysis. **Cost-volume profit analysis** is the systematic examination of the relationships among selling prices, sales and production volume, costs, expenses, and profits.

Cost-volume-profit analysis provides management with useful information for decision making. For example, cost-volume-profit analysis may be used in setting selling prices, selecting the mix of products to sell, choosing among marketing strategies, and analyzing the effects of changes in costs on profits. In today's business environment, management must make such decisions quickly and accurately. As a result, the importance of cost-volume-profit analysis has increased in recent years.

Contribution Margin Concept

One relationship among cost, volume, and profit is the contribution margin. The **contribution margin** is the excess of sales revenues over variable costs. The contribution margin concept is especially useful in business planning because it gives insight into the profit potential of a firm. To illustrate, the income statement of Lambert Inc. in Exhibit 600.31 has been prepared in a contribution margin format.

The contribution margin of $400,000 is available to cover the fixed costs of $300,000. Once the fixed costs are covered, any remaining amount adds directly to the income from operations of the company. Think of the fixed costs as a bucket and the contribution margin as water filling the bucket. Once the bucket is filled, the overflow represents income from operations. Up until the point of overflow, however, the contribution margin contributes to fixed costs (filling the bucket).

Exhibit 600.31 *Contribution Margin Income Statement*

Sales	$1,000,000
Variable costs	600,000
Contribution margin	$ 400,000
Fixed costs	300,000
Income from operations	$ 100,000

CONTRIBUTION MARGIN RATIO The contribution margin can also be expressed as a percentage. The **contribution margin ratio,** sometimes called the **profit-volume ratio,** indicates the percentage of each sales dollar available to cover the fixed costs and to provide income from operations. For Lambert Inc., the contribution margin ratio is 40%, as computed below.

$$\text{Contribution margin ratio} = \frac{\text{Sales} - \text{Variable costs}}{\text{Sales}}$$

$$\text{Contribution margin ratio} = \frac{\$1,000,000 - \$600,000}{\$1,000,000} = 40\%$$

The contribution margin ratio measures the effect on income from operations of an increase or a decrease in sales volume. For example, assume that the management of Lambert Inc. is studying the effect of adding $80,000 in sales orders. Multiplying the contribution margin ratio (40%) by the change in sales volume ($80,000) indicates that income from operations will increase $32,000 if the additional orders are obtained. The validity of this analysis is illustrated by the following contribution margin income statement of Lambert Inc.

Sales	$1,080,000
Variable costs ($1,080,000 × 60%)	648,000
Contribution margin ($1,080,000 × 40%)	$ 432,000
Fixed costs	300,000
Income from operations	$ 132,000

Variable costs as a percentage of sales are equal to 100% minus the contribution margin ratio. Thus, in the above income statement, the variable costs are 60% (100% − 40%) of sales, or $648,000 ($1,080,000 × 60%). The total contribution margin, $432,000, can also be computed directly by multiplying the sales by the contribution margin ratio ($1,080,000 × 40%).

In using the contribution margin ratio in analysis, factors other than sales volume, such as variable cost per unit and sales price, are assumed to remain constant. If such factors change, their effect must be considered.

The contribution margin ratio is also useful in setting business policy. For example, if the contribution margin ratio of a firm is large and production is at a level below 100% capacity, a large increase in income from operations can be expected from an increase in sales volume. A firm in such a position might decide to devote more effort to sales promotion because of the large change in income from operations that will result from changes in sales volume. In contrast, a firm with a small contribution margin ratio will probably want to give more attention to reducing costs before attempting to promote sales.

UNIT CONTRIBUTION MARGIN The unit contribution margin is also useful for analyzing the profit potential of proposed projects. The **unit contribution margin** is the dollars from each unit of sales available to cover fixed costs and provide income from operations. For example, if Lambert Inc.'s unit selling price is $20 and its unit variable cost is $12, the unit contribution margin is $8 ($20 − $12).

The *contribution margin ratio* is most useful when the increase or decrease in sales volume is measured in sales dollars. The *unit contribution margin* is most useful when the increase or decrease in sales volume is measured in sales units (quantities). To illustrate, assume that Lambert Inc. sold 50,000 units. Its income from operations is $100,000, as shown in the following contribution margin income statement.

Sales (50,000 units × $20)	$1,000,000
Variable costs (50,000 units × $12)	600,000
Contribution margin (50,000 units × $8)	$ 400,000
Fixed costs	300,000
Income from operations	$ 100,000

If Lambert Inc.'s sales could be increased by 15,000 units, from 50,000 units to 65,000 units, its income from operations would increase by $120,000 (15,000 units × $8), as shown below.

Sales (65,000 units × $20)	$1,300,000
Variable costs (65,000 units × $12)	780,000
Contribution margin (65,000 units × $8)	$ 520,000
Fixed costs	300,000
Income from operations	$ 220,000

Unit contribution margin analyses can provide useful information for managers. The preceding illustration indicates, for example, that Lambert could spend up to $120,000 for special advertising or other product promotions to increase sales by 15,000 units.

Example 19 *Sales are 20,000 units at $12 per unit, variable costs are $9 per unit, and fixed costs are $25,000. What are (a) the contribution margin ratio, (b) the unit contribution margin, and (c) the income from operations?*

(a) 25% [($240,000 − $180,000) ÷ $240,000];
(b) $3 per unit ($12 − $9);
(c) $35,000 ($240,000 − $180,000 − $25,000)

Mathematical Approach to Cost-Volume-Profit Analysis

Accountants use various approaches for expressing the relationship of costs, sales (volume), and income from operations (operating profit). The mathematical approach is one method that is used often in practice, while the graphic approach is another method.

The mathematical approach to cost-volume-profit analysis uses equations (1) to determine the units of sales necessary to achieve the break-even point in operations or (2) to determine the units of sales necessary to achieve a target or desired profit. We will next describe and illustrate these equations and their use by management in profit planning.

Break-Even Point

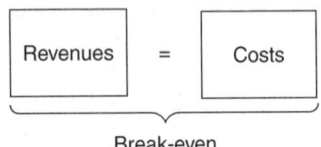

The **break-even point** is the level of operations at which a business's revenues and expired costs are exactly equal. At break-even, a business will have neither an income nor a loss from operations. The break-even point is useful in business planning, especially when expanding or decreasing operations.

To illustrate the computation of the break-even point, assume that the fixed costs for Barker Corporation are estimated to be $90,000. The unit selling price is $25, unit variable cost is $15, and unit contribution margin is $10 for Barker Corporation.

The break-even point is 9,000 units, which can be computed by using the following equation

$$\text{Break-even sales (units)} = \frac{\text{Fixed costs}}{\text{Unit contribution margin}}$$

$$\text{Break-even sales (units)} = \frac{\$90,000}{\$10} = 9,000 \text{ units}$$

The following income statement verifies the preceding computation.

Sales (9,000 units × $25)	$225,000
Variable costs (9,000 units × $15)	135,000
Contribution margin	$ 90,000
Fixed costs	90,000
Income from operations	$ 0

The break-even point is affected by changes in the fixed costs, unit variable costs, and the unit selling price. Next, we will briefly describe the effect of each of these factors on the break-even point.

EFFECT OF CHANGES IN FIXED COSTS Although fixed costs do not change in total with changes in the level of activity, they may change because of other factors. For example, changes in property tax rates or factory supervisors' salaries change fixed costs. Increases in fixed costs will raise the break-even point. Likewise, decreases in fixed costs will lower the break-even point. For example, **General Motors** closed 21 plants and eliminated 74,000 jobs to lower its break-even from approximately 7 million to 5 million automobiles through the 1990s.

To illustrate, assume that Bishop Co. is evaluating a proposal to budget an additional $100,000 for advertising. Fixed costs before the additional advertising are estimated at $600,000, and the unit contribution margin is $20. The break-even point before the additional expense is 30,000 units, computed as follows.

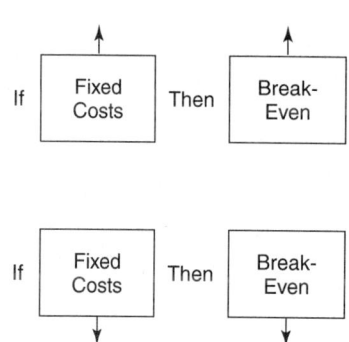

$$\text{Break-even sales (units)} = \frac{\text{Fixed costs}}{\text{Unit contribution margin}}$$

$$\text{Break-even sales (units)} = \frac{\$600,000}{\$20} = 30,000 \text{ units}$$

If the additional amount is spent, the fixed costs will increase by $100,000 and the break-even point will increase to 35,000 units, computed as follows

$$\text{Break-even sales (units)} = \frac{\text{Fixed costs}}{\text{Unit contribution margin}}$$

$$\text{Break-even sales (units)} = \frac{\$700,000}{\$20} = 35,000 \text{ units}$$

The $100,000 increase in the fixed costs requires an additional 5,000 units ($100,000 ÷ $20) of sales to break even. In other words, an increase in sales of 5,000 units is required in order to generate an additional $100,000 of total contribution margin (5,000 units × $20) to cover the increased fixed costs.

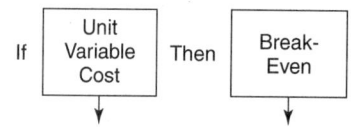

EFFECT OF CHANGES IN UNIT VARIABLE COSTS Although unit variable costs are not affected by changes in volume of activity, they may be affected by other factors. For example, changes in the price of direct materials and the wages for factory workers providing direct labor change unit variable costs. Increases in unit variable costs will raise the break-even point. Likewise, decreases in unit variable costs will lower the break-even point. For example, when fuel prices rise or decline, there is a direct impact on the break-even passenger load for **American Airlines**.

To illustrate, assume that Park Co. is evaluating a proposal to pay an additional 2% commission on sales to its salespeople as an incentive to increase sales. Fixed costs are estimated at $840,000, and the unit selling price, unit variable cost, and unit contribution margin before the additional 2% commission are as follows.

Unit selling price	$250
Unit variable cost	145
Unit contribution margin	$105

The break-even point is 8,000 units, computed as follows.

$$\text{Break-even sales (units)} = \frac{\text{Fixed costs}}{\text{Unit contribution margin}}$$

$$\text{Break-even sales (units)} = \frac{\$840,000}{\$105} = 8,000 \text{ units}$$

If the sales commission proposal is adopted, variable costs will increase by $5 per unit ($250 × 2%). This increase in the variable costs will decrease the unit contribution margin by $5 (from $105 to $100). Thus, the break-even point is raised to 8,400 units, computed as follows

$$\text{Break-even sales (units)} = \frac{\text{Fixed costs}}{\text{Unit contribution margin}}$$

$$\text{Break-even sales (units)} = \frac{\$840,000}{\$100} = 8,400 \text{ units}$$

At the original break-even point of 8,000 units, the new unit contribution margin of $100 would provide only $800,000 to cover fixed costs of $840,000. Thus, an additional 400 units of sales will be required in order to provide the additional $40,000 (400 units × $100) contribution margin necessary to break even.

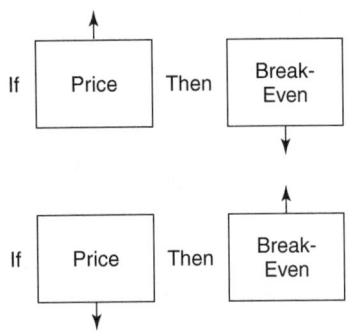

EFFECT OF CHANGES IN THE UNIT SELLING PRICE Increases in the unit selling price will lower the break-even point, while decreases in the unit selling price will raise the break-even point. For example, when **The Golf Channel** went from a premium cable service price of $6.95 per month to a much lower basic cable price, its break-even point increased from 6 million to 19 million subscribers.

To illustrate, assume that Graham Co. is evaluating a proposal to increase the unit selling price of its product from $50 to $60. The following data have been gathered.

	Current	Proposed
Unit selling price	$50	$60
Unit variable cost	30	30
Unit contribution margin	$20	$30
Total fixed costs	$600,000	$600,000

The break-even point based on the current selling price is 30,000 units, computed as follows:

$$\text{Break-even sales (units)} = \frac{\text{Fixed costs}}{\text{Unit contribution margin}}$$

$$\text{Break-even sales (units)} = \frac{\$600,000}{\$20} = 30,000 \text{ units}$$

If the selling price is increased by $10 per unit, the break-even point is decreased to 20,000 units, computed as follows:

$$\text{Break-even sales (units)} = \frac{\text{Fixed costs}}{\text{Unit contribution margin}}$$

$$\text{Break-even sales (units)} = \frac{\$600{,}000}{\$30} = 20{,}000 \text{ units}$$

The increase of $10 per unit in the selling price increases the unit contribution margin by $10. Thus, the break-even point decreases by 10,000 units (from 30,000 units to 20,000 units).

Example 20 *The selling price for a product is $60 per unit. The variable cost is $35 per unit, while fixed costs are $80,000. What are the following amounts: (a) the break-even point in sales units and (b) the break-even point if the selling price were increased to $67 per unit?*

(a) 3,200 units [$80,000 ÷ ($60 − $35)];
(b) 2,500 units [$80,000 ÷ ($67 − $35)]

SUMMARY OF EFFECTS OF CHANGES ON BREAK-EVEN POINT The break-even point in sales (units) moves in the same direction as changes in the variable cost per unit and fixed costs. In contrast, the break-even point in sales (units) moves in the opposite direction to changes in the sales price per unit. A summary of the impact of these changes on the break-even point in sales (units) is shown below.

Type of Change	Direction of Change	Effect of Change on Break-Even Sales (Units)
Fixed cost	Increase	Increase
	Decrease	Decrease
Variable cost per unit	Increase	Increase
	Decrease	Decrease
Unit sales price	Increase	Decrease
	Decrease	Increase

Target Profit

At the break-even point, sales and costs are exactly equal. However, the break-even point is not the goal of most businesses. Rather, managers seek to maximize profits. By modifying the break-even equation, the sales volume required to earn a target or desired amount of profit may be estimated. For this purpose, target profit is added to the break-even equation as shown below.

$$\text{Sales (units)} = \frac{\text{Fixed costs} + \text{Target profit}}{\text{Unit contribution margin}}$$

To illustrate, assume that fixed costs are estimated at $200,000, and the desired profit is $100,000. The unit selling price, unit variable cost, and unit contribution margin are as follows.

Unit selling price	$75
Unit variable cost	45
Unit contribution margin	$30

The sales volume necessary to earn the target profit of $100,000 is 10,000 units, computed as follows

$$\text{Sales (units)} = \frac{\text{Fixed costs} + \text{Target profit}}{\text{Unit contribution margin}}$$

$$\text{Sales (units)} = \frac{\$200{,}000 + \$100{,}000}{\$30} = 10{,}000 \text{ units}$$

630. COST BEHAVIOR, CONTROL, AND DECISION MAKING

The following income statement verifies this computation.

Sales (10,000 units × $75)	$750,000
Variable costs (10,000 units × $45)	450,000
Contribution margin (10,000 units × $30)	$300,000
Fixed costs	200,000
Income from operations	$100,000 ← Target profit

Example 21 The sales price is $140 per unit, variable costs are $60 per unit, and fixed costs are $240,000. What would be (a) the break-even point in sales units and (b) the break/even point in sales units if a target profit of $50,000 is desired?

(a) 3,000 units [$240,000 ÷ ($140 − $60)];
(b) 3,625 units [($240,000 + $50,000) ÷ ($140 − $60)]

Use of Computers in Cost-Volume-Profit Analysis

With computers, the graphic approach and the mathematical approach to cost-volume profit analysis are easy to use. Managers can vary assumptions regarding selling prices, costs, and volume and can immediately see the effects of each change on the break-even point and profit. Such an analysis is called a **"what if" analysis** or **sensitivity analysis**.

Sales Mix Considerations

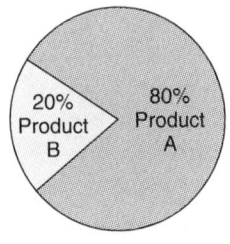

Sales Mix

In most businesses, more than one product is sold at varying selling prices. In addition, the products often have different unit variable costs, and each product makes a different contribution to profits. Thus, the sales volume necessary to break even or to earn a target profit for a business selling two or more products depends upon the sales mix. The **sales mix** is the relative distribution of sales among the various products sold by a business.

To illustrate the calculation of the break-even point for a company that sells more than one product, assume that Cascade Company sold 8,000 units of Product A and 2,000 units of Product B during the past year. The sales mix for products A and B can be expressed as percentages (80% and 20%) or as a ratio (80:20).

Cascade Company's fixed costs are $200,000. The unit selling prices, unit variable costs, and unit contribution margins for products A and B and their sales mix are as follows.

Product	Unit Selling Price	Unit Variable Cost	Unit Contribution Margin	Sales Mix
A	$ 90	$70	$20	80%
B	140	95	45	20%

In computing the break-even point, it is useful to think of the individual products as components of one overall enterprise product. For Cascade Company, this overall enterprise product is called E. We can think of the unit selling price of E as equal to the total of the unit selling prices of products A and B, multiplied by their sales mix percentages. Likewise, we can think of the unit variable cost and unit contribution margin of E as equal to the total of the unit variable costs and unit contribution margins of products A and B, multiplied by the sales mix percentages. These computations are as follows.

Unit selling price of E:	($90 × 0.8) + ($140 × 0.2) = $100
Unit variable cost of E:	($70 × 0.8) + ($ 95 × 0.2) = $ 75
Unit contribution margin of E:	($20 × 0.8) + ($ 45 × 0.2) = $ 25

The break-even point of 8,000 units of E can be determined in the normal manner as follows.

$$\text{Break-even sales (units)} = \frac{\text{Fixed costs}}{\text{Unit contribution margin}}$$

$$\text{Break-even sales (units)} = \frac{\$200,000}{\$25} = 8,000 \text{ units}$$

Since the sales mix for products A and B is 80% and 20%, the break-even quantity of A is 6,400 units (8,000 units × 80%) and B is 1,600 units (8,000 units × 20%). This analysis can be verified in the following income statement.

	Product A	Product B	Total
Sales:			
6,400 units × $90	$576,000		$576,000
1,600 units × $140		$224,000	224,000
Total sales	$576,000	$224,000	$800,000
Variable costs:			
6,400 units × $70	$448,000		$448,000
1,600 units × $95		$152,000	152,000
Total variable costs	$448,000	$152,000	$600,000
Contribution margin	$128,000	$72,000	$200,000
Fixed costs			200,000
Income from operations			$ 0 ← Break-even point

The effects of changes in the sales mix on the break-even point can be determined by repeating this analysis, assuming a different sales mix.

Special Cost-Volume-Profit Relationships

Some additional relationships useful to managers can be developed from cost-volume-profit data. Two of these relationships are the margin of safety and operating leverage.

Margin of Safety

The difference between the current sales revenue and the sales at the break-even point is called the **margin of safety.** It indicates the possible decrease in sales that may occur before an operating loss results. For example, if the margin of safety is low, even a small decline in sales revenue may result in an operating loss.

If sales are $250,000, the unit selling price is $25, and sales at the break-even point are $200,000, the margin of safety is 20%, computed as follows.

$$\text{Margin of safety} = \frac{\text{Sales} - \text{Sales at break-even point}}{\text{Sales}}$$

$$\text{Margin of safety} = \frac{\$250,000 - \$200,000}{\$250,000} = 20\%$$

The margin of safety may also be stated in terms of units. In this illustration, for example, the margin of safety of 20% is equivalent to $50,000 ($250,000 × 20%). In units, the margin of safety is 2,000 units ($50,000 ÷ $25). Thus, the current sales of $250,000 may decline $50,000 or 2,000 units before an operating loss occurs.

Operating Leverage

The relative mix of a business's variable costs and fixed costs is measured by the **operating leverage**. It is computed as follows.

$$\text{Operating leverage} = \frac{\text{Contribution margin}}{\text{Income from operations}}$$

Because the difference between contribution margin and income from operations is fixed costs, companies with large amounts of fixed costs will generally have a high operating leverage. Thus, companies in capital-intensive industries, such as the airline and automotive industries, will generally have a high operating leverage. A low operating leverage is normal for companies in industries that are labor-intensive, such as professional services.

Managers can use operating leverage to measure the impact of changes in sales on income from operations. A high operating leverage indicates that a small increase in sales will yield a large percentage increase in income from operations. In contrast, a low operating leverage indicates that a large increase in sales is necessary to significantly increase income from operations. To illustrate, assume the following operating data for Jones Inc. and Wilson Inc.

	Jones Inc.	Wilson Inc.
Sales	$400,000	$400,000
Variable costs	300,000	300,000
Contribution margin	$100,000	$100,000
Fixed costs	80,000	50,000
Income from operations	$ 20,000	$ 50,000

Both companies have the same sales, the same variable costs, and the same contribution margin. Jones Inc. has larger fixed costs than Wilson Inc. and, as a result, a lower income from operations and a higher operating leverage. The operating leverage for each company is computed as follows.

Jones Inc.

$$\text{Operating leverage} = \frac{\$100,000}{\$ 20,000} = 5$$

Wilson Inc.

$$\text{Operating leverage} = \frac{\$100,000}{\$ 50,000} = 2$$

Jones Inc.'s operating leverage indicates that, for each percentage point change in sales, income from operations will change five times that percentage. In contrast, for each percentage point change in sales, the income from operations of Wilson Inc. will change only two times that percentage. For example, if sales increased by 10% ($40,000) for each company, income from operations will increase by 50% (10% × 5), or $10,000 (50% × $20,000), for Jones Inc. The sales increase of $40,000 will increase income from operations by only 20% (10% × 2), or $10,000 (20% × $50,000), for Wilson Inc. The validity of this analysis is shown as follows.

	Jones Inc.	Wilson Inc.
Sales	$440,000	$440,000
Variable costs	330,000	330,000
Contribution margin	$110,000	$110,000
Fixed costs	80,000	50,000
Income from operations	$ 30,000	$ 60,000

For Jones Inc., even a small increase in sales will generate a large percentage increase in income from operations. Thus, Jones's managers may be motivated to think of ways to increase sales. In contrast, Wilson's managers might attempt to increase operating leverage by reducing variable costs and thereby change the cost structure.

Example 22 *What is the operating leverage for a company with sales of $410,000, variable costs of $250,000, and fixed costs of $80,000?*

2.0 [($410,000 − $250,000) ÷ ($410,000 − $250,000 − $80,000)]

Assumptions of Cost-Volume-Profit Analysis

The reliability of cost-volume-profit analysis depends upon the validity of several assumptions. The primary assumptions are as follows.

1. Total sales and total costs can be represented by straight lines.
2. Within the relevant range of operating activity, the efficiency of operations does not change.
3. Costs can be accurately divided into fixed and variable components.
4. The sales mix is constant.
5. There is no change in the inventory quantities during the period.

These assumptions simplify cost-volume-profit analysis. Because they are often valid for the relevant range of operations, cost-volume-profit analysis is useful to decision making.

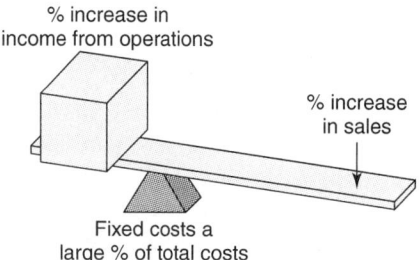

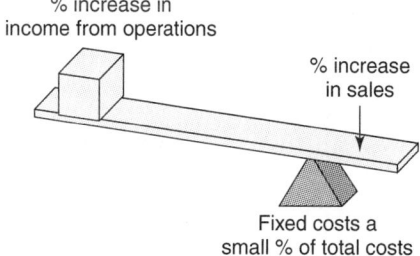

Product and Service Costs

Manufacturing Cost Terms

Managers rely on managerial accountants to provide useful *cost* information to support decision making. What is a cost? A **cost** is a payment of cash or its equivalent or the commitment to pay cash in the future for the purpose of generating revenues. A cost provides a benefit that is used immediately or deferred to a future period of time. If the benefit is used immediately, then the cost is an expense, such as salary expense. If the benefit is deferred, then the cost is an asset, such as equipment. As the asset is used, an expense, such as depreciation expense, is recognized.

In this section, we will illustrate manufacturing costs for Goodwell Printers, a manufacturing firm. A **manufacturing business** converts materials into a finished product through the use of machinery and labor. Goodwell Printers prints textbooks, like the one you are using now. Exhibit 600.32 provides an overview of Goodwell Printers' textbook printing operations. The Printing Department feeds large rolls of paper into printing presses. The printing presses use electricity and ink. From the Printing

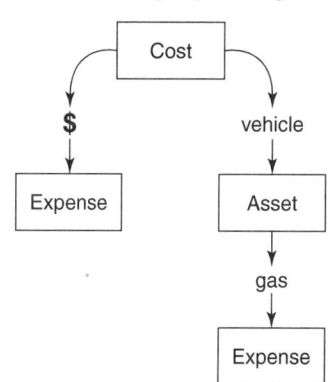

Department, the printed pages are stacked and moved to the Binding Department. In the Binding Department, the pages are cut, separated, stacked, and bound to book covers. A finished book is the final output of the Binding Department.

Materials

Some service companies also have direct materials costs. For example, fuel is a direct materials cost to a flight for an airline, while medicines are a direct materials cost to a patient in a hospital.

The cost of materials that are an integral part of the product is classified as **direct materials cost.** For example, the direct materials cost for Goodwell Printers would include paper and book covers.

As a practical matter, a direct materials cost must not only be an integral part of the finished product, but it must also be a significant portion of the total cost of the product. Other examples of direct materials costs are the cost of electronic components for a TV manufacturer and tires for an automobile manufacturer.

The costs of materials that are not a significant portion of the total product cost are termed **indirect materials.** Indirect materials are considered a part of factory overhead, which we discuss later. For Goodwell Printers, the costs of ink and binding glue are classified as indirect materials.

Factory Labor

The cost of wages of employees who are directly involved in converting materials into the manufactured product is classified as **direct labor cost.** The direct labor cost of Goodwell Printers includes the wages of the employees who operate the printing presses. Other examples of direct labor costs are carpenters' wages for a construction contractor, mechanics' wages in an automotive repair shop, machine operators' wages in a tool manufacturing plant, and assemblers' wages in a microcomputer assembly plant.

As a practical matter, a direct labor cost must not only be an integral part of the finished product, but it must also be a significant portion of the total cost of the product. For Goodwell Printers, the printing press operators' wages are

Exhibit 600.32 *Textbook Printing Operations of Goodwell Printers*

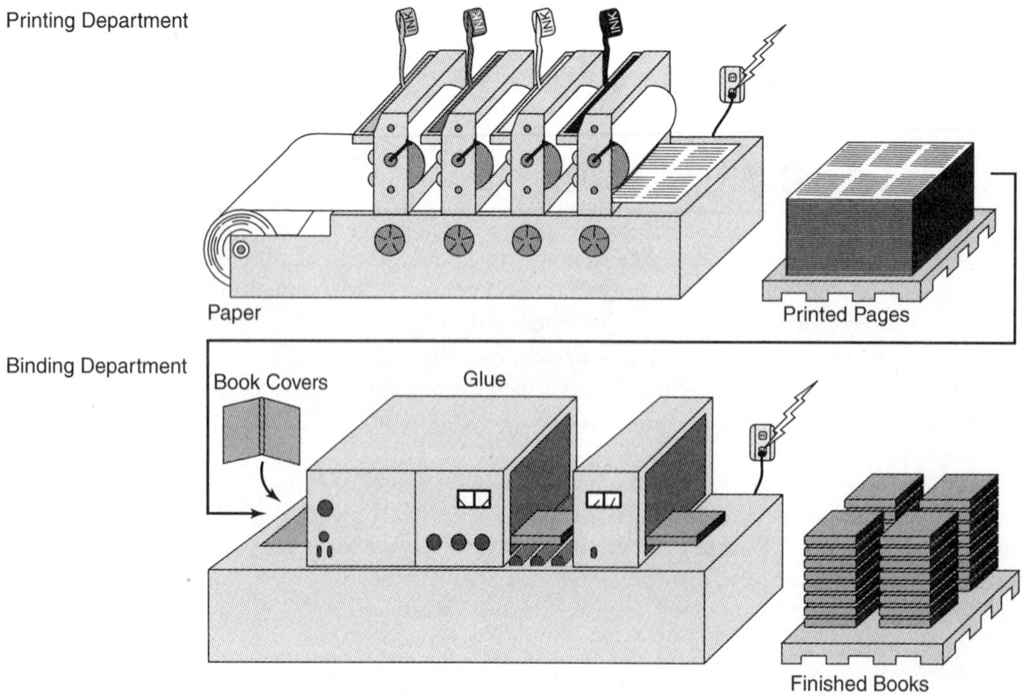

a significant portion of the total cost of each book. Labor costs that do not enter directly into the manufacture of a product are termed **indirect labor** and are recorded as factory overhead. Indirect labor for Goodwell Printers might include the salaries of maintenance, plant management, and quality control personnel.

Factory Overhead Cost

Costs other than direct materials cost and direct labor cost incurred in the manufacturing process are classified as **factory overhead cost.** Factory overhead is sometimes called **manufacturing overhead** or **factory burden.** Examples of factory overhead costs, in addition to indirect materials and indirect labor, are machine depreciation, factory utilities, factory supplies, and factory insurance. In addition, payments to employees for overtime and nonproductive time (such as idle time) are considered factory overhead. For many industries, factory overhead costs are becoming a larger portion of the costs of a product as manufacturing processes become more automated.

Direct materials, direct labor, and factory overhead costs are product costs.

The direct materials, direct labor, and factory overhead costs are considered **product costs** because they are associated with making a product. The costs of converting the materials into finished products consist of direct labor and factory overhead costs, which are commonly called **conversion costs.**

Example 23 *Identify whether the following costs are direct materials, direct labor, or factory overhead for an automobile assembler: tires, quality engineering salaries, assembly wages, coil steel, painter wages, plant manager salary, cleaning fluids.*

Tires and coil steel—direct materials; assembly wages and painter wages—direct labor; quality engineering salaries, plant manager's salary, and cleaning fluids—factory overhead.

Cost Accounting System Overview

An objective of a **cost accounting system** is to accumulate product costs. Product cost information is used by managers to establish product prices, control operations, and develop financial statements. In addition, the cost accounting system improves control by supplying data on the costs incurred by each manufacturing department or process.

There are two main types of cost accounting systems for manufacturing operations: job order cost systems and process cost systems. Each of the two systems is widely used, and any one manufacturer may use more than one type.

A **job order cost system** provides a separate record for the cost of each quantity of product that passes through the factory. A particular quantity of product is termed a *job.* A job order cost system is best suited to industries that manufacture custom goods to fill special orders from customers or that produce a high variety of products for stock. Manufacturers that use a job order cost system are sometimes called **job shops.** An example of a job shop would be an apparel manufacturer, such as **Levi Strauss.**

Many service firms also use job order cost systems to accumulate the costs associated with providing client services. For example, an accounting firm will accumulate all of the costs associated with a particular client engagement, such as accountant time, copying charges, and travel costs. Recording costs in this manner helps the accounting firm control costs during a client engagement and determines client billing and profitability.

Under a **process cost system,** costs are accumulated for each of the departments or processes within the factory. A process system is best suited for manufacturers of units of product that are not distinguishable from each other during a continuous production process. An example would be an oil refinery.

Example 24 *Name two types of cost systems and a typical user of each system.*

Job order cost system: cabinet manufacturer, law practice, movie studio.
Process cost system: food processing, paper processing, metal processing, petroleum refining.

Job Order Cost Systems for Manufacturing Businesses

In this section, we will illustrate the job order cost system for a manufacturing firm, Goodwell Printers. The job order system accumulates manufacturing costs by job, as shown in Exhibit 600.33. The **materials inventory,** sometimes called **raw materials inventory,** consists of the costs of the direct and indirect materials that have not yet entered the manufacturing process. For Goodwell Printers, the materials inventory would consist of paper, ink, glue, and book covers. The **work in process inventory** consists of direct materials costs, direct labor costs, and factory overhead costs that have entered the manufacturing process but are associated with products that have not been completed. Examples are the costs of Jobs 71 and 72 that are still in the printing process in Exhibit 600.33. Completed jobs that have not been sold are termed **finished goods inventory.** Examples are completed printed books from Jobs 69 and 70 shown in Exhibit 600.33. Upon sale, a manufacturer will record the cost of the sale as **cost of goods sold.** An example is the case of *Physics* books sold to the bookstore in Exhibit 600.33. The *cost of goods sold* for a manufacturer is comparable to the *cost of merchandise sold* for a merchandising business.

The work in process inventory consists of direct materials, direct labor, and factory overhead costs of products not yet completed.

In a job order cost accounting system, perpetual inventory controlling accounts and subsidiary ledgers are maintained for materials, work in process, and finished goods inventories. Each inventory account is debited for all additions and is credited for all deductions. The balance of each account thus represents the balance on hand.

As with recording materials, many organizations are automating the labor recording process. For example, in companies that build very large products, such as submarines, jet aircraft, or space vehicles, direct labor employees can be given magnetic cards, much like credit cards. These cards can be used to log in and log out of particular work assignments on particular jobs by running the card through a magnetic reader at any number of remote computer terminals.

ALLOCATING FACTORY OVERHEAD   Factory overhead includes all manufacturing costs except direct materials and direct labor. Factory overhead is much different from direct labor and direct materials because it is indirectly related to the jobs. How, then, do the jobs get assigned a portion of overhead costs? The answer is through cost allocation. **Cost allocation** is the process of assigning factory overhead costs to a cost object, such as a job. The factory overhead costs are assigned to the jobs on the basis of some known measure about each job. The measure used to allocate factory overhead is frequently called an **activity base, allocation base,** or **activity driver.** The estimated activity base should be a measure that reflects the consumption or use of factory overhead cost. For example, the direct labor is recorded for each job using time tickets. Thus, direct labor could be used to allocate production-related factory overhead costs to each job. Likewise, direct materials costs are known about each job through the materials requisitions. Thus, materials-related factory overhead, such as Purchasing Department salaries, could logically be allocated to the job on the basis of direct materials cost.

PREDETERMINED FACTORY OVERHEAD RATE   In order that job costs may be currently available, factory overhead may be allocated or applied to production using a **predetermined factory overhead rate.** The predetermined factory overhead rate is calculated by dividing the estimated amount of factory overhead for the forthcoming year by the estimated activity base, such as machine hours, direct materials costs, direct labor costs, or direct labor hours.

Exhibit 600.33   *Manufacturing Costs and Jobs*

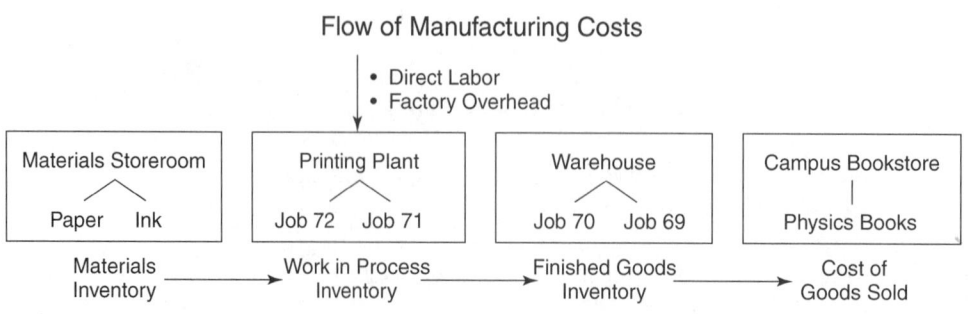

To illustrate calculating a predetermined overhead rate, assume that Goodwell Printers estimates the total factory overhead cost to be $50,000 for the year and the activity base to be 10,000 direct labor hours. The predetermined factory overhead rate would be calculated as $5 per direct labor hour, as follows.

$$\text{Predetermined factory overhead rate} = \frac{\text{Estimated total factory overhead costs}}{\text{Estimated activity base}}$$

$$\text{Predetermined factory overhead rate} = \frac{\$50,000}{10,000 \text{ direct labor hours}} = \$5 \text{ per direct labor hour}$$

Why is the predetermined overhead rate calculated from estimated numbers at the beginning of the period? The answer is to ensure timely information. If a company waited until the end of an accounting period when all overhead costs are known, the allocated factory overhead would be accurate but not timely. If the cost system is to have maximum usefulness, cost data should be available as each job is completed, even though there may be a small sacrifice in accuracy. Only through timely reporting can management make needed adjustments in pricing or in manufacturing methods and achieve the best possible combination of revenue and cost on future jobs.

A number of companies are using a new product-costing approach called activity-based costing. **Activity-based costing** is a method of accumulating and allocating factory overhead costs to products using many overhead rates. Each rate is related to separate factory activities, such as inspecting, moving, and machining.

Example 25 *Factory overhead costs are estimated to be $120,000. Direct labor hours are estimated to be 20,000 hours. Determine (a) the predetermined factory overhead rate and (b) the amount of factory overhead applied to a job with 30 direct labor hours.*

(a) $6 per hour ($120,000/20,000); (b) $180 ($6 × 30 hours)

APPLYING FACTORY OVERHEAD The factory overhead costs applied and the actual factory overhead costs incurred during a period will usually differ. If the amount applied exceeds the actual costs incurred, the factory overhead account will have a credit balance. This credit is described as **overapplied** or **overabsorbed factory overhead.** If the amount applied is less than the actual costs incurred, the account will have a debit balance.

If the underapplied or overapplied balance increases in only one direction and it becomes large, the balance and the overhead rate should be investigated. For example, if a large balance is caused by changes in manufacturing methods or in production goals, the factory overhead rate should be revised. On the other hand, a large underapplied balance may indicate a serious control problem caused by inefficiencies in production methods, excessive costs, or a combination of factors.

DISPOSAL OF FACTORY OVERHEAD BALANCE The balance in the factory overhead account is carried forward from month to month. It is reported on interim balance sheets as a deferred debit or credit. This balance should not be carried over to the next year, however, since it applies to the operations of the year just ended.

One approach for disposing of the balance of factory overhead at the end of the year is to transfer the entire balance to the cost of goods sold account. A more complex approach involves disposing of the balance among the work in process, finished goods, and cost of goods sold accounts.

Cost of Goods Sold

Just as there are various methods of costing materials entering into production, there are various methods of determining the cost of the finished goods sold. Examples include first-in, first-out (FIFO) method and last-in, first-out (LIFO) method.

Example 26 *Boxer Company completed 80,000 units at a cost of $680,000. The beginning finished goods inventory was 10,000 units at $80,000. What is the cost of goods sold for 60,000 units, assuming a FIFO cost flow?*

$505,000 [$80,000 + (50,000 × $8.50)]

Exhibit 600.34 *Income Statement of Goodwell Printers*

Goodwell Printers Income Statement for the Month Ended December 31, 2003		
Sales		$28,000
Cost of goods sold		20,150
Gross profit		$ 7,850
Selling and administrative expenses:		
Sales salaries expense	$2,000	
Office salaries expense	1,500	
Total selling and administrative expenses		3,500
Income from operations		$ 4,350

Period Costs

In addition to product costs (direct materials, direct labor, and factory overhead), businesses also have period costs. **Period costs** are expenses that are used in generating revenue during the current period and are not involved in the manufacturing process. Period costs are generally classified into two categories: selling and administrative. **Selling expenses** are incurred in marketing the product and delivering the sold product to customers. **Administrative expenses** are incurred in the administration of the business and are not related to the manufacturing or selling functions. The income statement for Goodwell Printers would be as shown in Exhibit 600.34. Assume that Goodwell Printers sold 2,000 American history textbooks during December for $14 per unit, giving a total of $28,000 sales.

The cost of goods sold is $20,150, which includes $20,000 for direct materials, direct labor, and factory overhead cost computed at $10/unit. The cost of goods sold also includes $150 underapplied factory overhead.

Two items of period costs include $2,000 for sales salaries expense and $1,500 for office salaries expense.

Service companies, such as telecommunications, insurance, banking, broadcasting, and hospitality, typically have a large portion of their total costs as period costs. This is because most service companies do not have products that can be inventoried, and hence, they do not have product costs.

Examples of Period Costs

Selling Expenses
- Advertising expenses
- Sales salaries expenses
- Commission expenses

Administrative Expenses
- Office salaries expenses
- Office supplies expenses
- Depreciation expense– office buildings and equipment

Job Order Costing for Decision Making

The job order cost system that we developed in the previous sections can be used to evaluate an organization's cost performance. The unit costs for similar jobs can be compared over time to determine if costs are staying within expected ranges. If costs increase for some unexpected reason, the details in the job cost sheets can help discover the reasons.

To illustrate, Exhibit 600.35 shows the direct materials on the job cost sheets for Jobs 144 and 163 for a furniture company. Since both job cost sheets refer to the same type and number of chairs, the direct materials cost per unit should be about the same. However, the materials cost per chair for Job 144 is $28, while for Job 163 it is $35. For some reason, materials costs have increased since the folding chairs were produced for Job 144.

Job cost sheets can be used to investigate possible reasons for the increased cost. First, you should note that the rate for direct materials did not change. Thus, the cost increase is not related to increasing prices. What about the wood consumption? This tells us a different story. The quantity of wood used to produce 200 chairs in Job 144 is 1,600 board feet. However, Job 163 required 2,000 board feet. How can this be explained? Any one of the following explanations is possible and could be investigated further.

Exhibit 600.35 *Comparing Data from Job Cost Sheets*

Job 144
Item: 200 folding chairs

	Materials Quantity (board feet)	Materials Price	Materials Amount
Direct materials:			
Wood	1,600	$3.50	$5,600
Direct materials per chair			$28

Job 163
Item: 200 folding chairs

	Materials Quantity (board feet)	Materials Price	Materials Amount
Direct materials:			
Wood	2,000	$3.50	$7,000
Direct materials per chair			$35

1. There was a new employee who was not adequately trained for cutting the wood for chairs. As a result, the employee improperly cut and scrapped many pieces.
2. The lumber was of poor quality. As a result, the cutting operator ended up using and scrapping additional pieces of lumber.
3. The cutting tools were in need of repair. As a result, the cutting operators miscut and scrapped many pieces of wood.
4. The operator was careless. As a result of poor work, many pieces of cut wood had to be scrapped.
5. The instructions attached to the job were incorrect. The operator cut wood according to the instructions but discovered that the pieces would not fit. As a result, many pieces had to be scrapped.

You should note that many of these explanations are not necessarily related to operator error. Poor cost performance may be the result of root causes that are outside the control of the operator.

Job Order Cost Systems for Professional Service Businesses

A job order cost accounting system may be useful to the management of a professional service business in planning and controlling operations. For example, an advertising agency, an attorney, and a physician all share the common characteristic of providing services to individual customers, clients, or patients. In such cases, the customer, client, or patient can be viewed as an individual job for which costs are accumulated.

Because the "product" of a service business is service, management's focus is on direct labor and overhead costs. The cost of any materials or supplies used in rendering services for a client is usually small and is normally included as part of the overhead.

The direct labor and overhead costs of rendering services to clients are accumulated in a work in process account. This account is supported by a cost ledger. A job cost sheet is used to accumulate the costs for each client's job. When a job is completed and the client is billed, the costs are transferred to a cost of services account. This account is similar to the cost of merchandise sold account for a merchandising business or the cost of goods sold account for a manufacturing business. A finished goods account and related finished goods ledger are not necessary, since the revenues associated with the services are recorded after the services have been provided. The flow of costs through a service business using a job order cost accounting system is shown in Exhibit 600.36.

In practice, additional accounting considerations unique to service businesses may need to be considered. For example, a service business may bill clients on a weekly or monthly basis rather than waiting until a job is completed. In these situations, a portion of the costs related to each billing should be transferred from the work in process account to the cost of services account. A service business may also have advance billings that would be accounted for as deferred revenue until the services have been completed.

Exhibit 600.36 *Flow of Costs Through a Service Business*

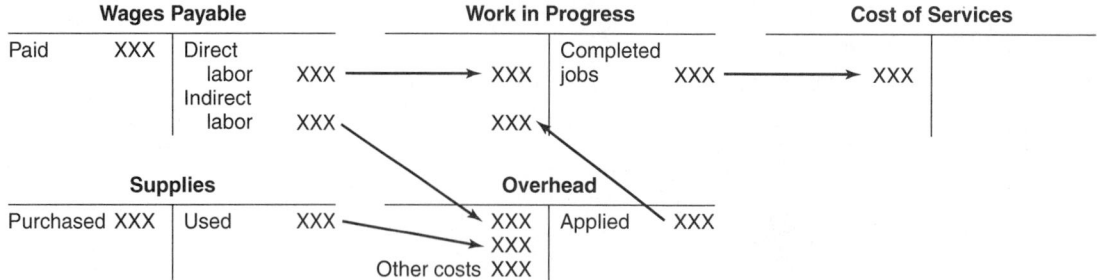

Process Cost Systems

If you bake cookies, the ingredients would include flour, sugar, and shortening. These ingredients would all be added at the beginning of the baking process by mixing them in a bowl. After mixing, do you have cookies? No. Why? Because they aren't baked (converted). But are they 100% complete with respect to materials? Yes, all the materials have been added to the baking process. When will they be cookies? When they are 100% complete with respect to materials *and* baking.

Now, assume that you ask the question, "How much cost have I incurred in baking cookies after 15 minutes (out of 30 minutes) of baking time?" The answer would require that you separate the ingredients and the electricity costs. These two costs are incurred in the baking process at different rates, and so it is convenient to identify them separately. The ingredient costs have all been incurred, since they were all introduced at the beginning of the process. The electricity costs, however, are a different story. Since the baking is only 50% complete, only 50% of the electricity costs (for the oven) have been incurred in the baking process. Therefore, the answer to the question is that all the materials costs and half the electricity costs have been incurred in the baking process after 15 minutes of baking.

In this section, we apply these concepts to manufacturers that use a process cost system. After introducing process costing, we discuss decision making with process cost system reports. We conclude the section with a brief discussion of just-in-time cost systems.

Comparing Job Order Costing and Process Costing

The job order cost system is best suited to industries that make special orders for customers or manufacture different products in groups. Industries that may use job order cost systems include special-order printing, custom-made tailoring, furniture manufacturing, shipbuilding, aircraft building, and construction. Process manufacturing is different from job-order manufacturing. **Process manufacturers** typically use large machines to process a flow of raw materials into a finished state. For example, a petrochemical business processes crude oil through numerous refining steps to produce higher grades of oil until gasoline is produced. The cost accounting system used by process manufacturers is called the **process cost system.**

In some ways, the process cost and job order cost systems are similar. Both systems accumulate product costs—direct materials, direct labor, and factory overhead—and allocate these costs to the units produced. Both systems maintain perpetual inventory accounts with subsidiary ledgers for materials, work in process, and finished goods. Both systems also provide product cost data to management for planning, directing, improving, controlling, and decision making. The main difference between the two systems is the form in which the product costs are accumulated and reported.

Exhibit 600.37 illustrates the main differences between the job order and process cost systems. In a job order cost system, product costs are accumulated by job and are summarized on job cost sheets. The job cost sheets provide unit cost information and can be used by management for product pricing, cost control, and inventory valuation. The process manufacturer does not manufacture according to "jobs." Thus, costs are accumulated by department. Each unit of product that passes through the department is similar. Thus, the production costs reported by each department provide unit cost information that can be used by management for cost control. In a job order cost system, the work in process inventory at the end of the accounting period is the sum of the job cost sheets for partially completed jobs. In a process cost system, the amount of work in process inventory is determined by allocating costs between completed and partially completed units within a department.

Process manufacturers accumulate costs by department.

Exhibit 600.37 *Job Order and Process Cost Systems Compared*

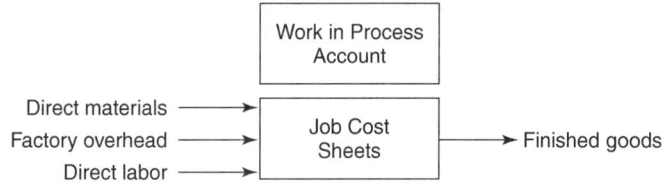

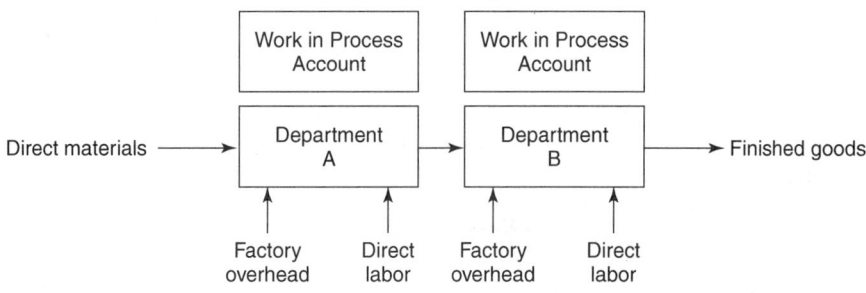

Exhibit 600.38 *Physical Flows for a Process Manufacturer*

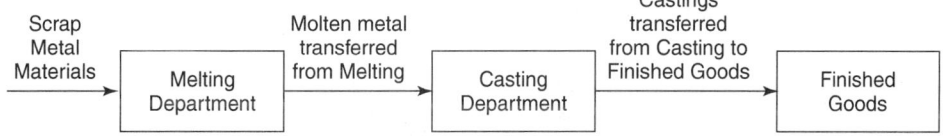

Physical Flows and Cost Flows for a Process Manufacturer

Materials costs are a large portion of the costs for most process manufacturers. Often, the materials costs can be as high as 70% of the total manufacturing costs. Thus, accounting for materials costs is very important for process operations.

Exhibit 600.38 illustrates the physical flow of materials for a steel processor. Direct materials in the form of scrap metal are placed into a furnace in the Melting Department. The Melting Department uses conversion costs (direct labor and factory overhead) during the melting process. The molten metal is then transferred to the Casting Department, where it is poured into an ingot casting. The Casting Department also uses conversion costs during the casting process. The ingot castings are transferred to the finished goods inventory for shipment to customers.

The cost flows in a process cost system reflect the physical materials flows.

The First-In, First-Out [FIFO] Method

In a process cost system, the accountant determines the cost transferred out and thus the amount remaining in inventory for each department. For many manufacturing processes, materials are added at the beginning of production, and the units are moved through the production processes in a **first-in, first-out (FIFO)** flow. That is, the first units entering the production process are the first to be completed.

We assume that all materials used in the department are added at the beginning of the process, and conversion costs (direct labor and factory overhead) are incurred evenly throughout the melting process. The objective is to determine the cost of goods completed and the ending inventory valuation, which are represented by the question marks. We determine these amounts by using the following four steps.

1. Determine the units to be assigned costs.
2. Calculate equivalent units of production.
3. Determine the cost per equivalent unit.
4. Allocate costs to transferred and partially completed units.

Bringing It All Together: The Cost of Production Report

A **cost of production report** is normally prepared for each processing department at periodic intervals.
The report summarizes the four previous steps by providing the following production quantity and cost data.

1. The units for which the department is accountable and the disposition of those units
2. The production costs incurred by the department and the allocation of those costs between completed and partially completed units

The cost of production report is also used to control costs. Each department manager is responsible for the units entering production and the costs incurred in the department. Any failure to account for all costs and any significant differences in unit product costs from one month to another should be investigated.

Using the Cost of Production Report for Decision Making

The cost of production report is one source of information that may be used by managers to control and improve operations. This greater detail helps management isolate problems and opportunities. To illustrate, assume that the Blending Department of Holland Beverage Company prepared cost of production reports for April and May. In addition, assume that the Blending Department had no beginning or ending work in process inventory either month. Thus, in this simple case, there is no need to determine equivalent units of production for allocating costs between completed and partially completed units. The cost of production reports for April and May in the Blending Department are as follows.

Cost of Production Reports
Holland Beverage Company—Blending Department
for the Months Ended April 30 and May 31, 2003

	April	May
Direct materials	$ 20,000	$ 40,600
Direct labor	15,000	29,400
Energy	8,000	20,000
Repairs	4,000	8,000
Tank cleaning	3,000	8,000
Total	$ 50,000	$106,000
Units completed	÷ 100,000	÷ 200,000
Cost per unit	$ 0.50	$ 0.53

Note that the preceding reports provide more cost detail than simply reporting direct materials and conversion costs. The May results indicate that total unit costs have increased from $0.50 to $0.53, or 6% from the previous month. What caused this increase? To determine the possible causes for this increase, the cost of production report may be restated in per-unit terms, as shown on the next page.

	Blending Department Per-Unit Expense Comparisons		
	April	May	% Change
Direct materials	$0.200	$0.203	1.50%
Direct labor	0.150	0.147	−2.00%
Energy	0.080	0.100	25.00%
Repairs	0.040	0.040	0.00%
Tank cleaning	0.030	0.040	33.33%
Total	$0.500	$0.530	6.00%

Both energy and tank cleaning per-unit costs have increased dramatically in May. Further investigation should focus on these costs. For example, an increasing trend in energy may indicate that the machines are losing fuel efficiency, thereby requiring the company to purchase an increasing amount of fuel. This unfavorable trend could motivate management to repair the machines. The tank cleaning costs could be investigated in a similar fashion.

In addition to unit production cost trends, managers of process manufacturers are also concerned about yield trends. **Yield** is the ratio of the materials output quantity to the input quantity. A yield less than one occurs when the output quantity is less than the input quantity due to materials losses during the process. For example, if 1,000 pounds of sugar entered the packing operation, and only 980 pounds of sugar were packed, the yield would be 98%. Two percent or 20 pounds of sugar were lost or spilled during the packing process.

Just-in-Time Processing

The objective of many companies is to produce products with high quality, low cost, and instant availability. One approach to achieving this objective is to implement just-in-time processing. **Just-in-time processing (JIT)** is a philosophy that focuses on reducing time and cost and eliminating poor quality. A JIT system achieves production efficiencies and flexibility by reorganizing the traditional production process.

In a traditional production process (illustrated in Exhibit 600.39), a product moves from process to process as each function or step is completed. Each worker is assigned a specific job, which is performed repeatedly as unfinished products are received from the preceding department. For example, a furniture manufacturer might use seven production departments to perform the operating functions necessary to manufacture furniture, as shown in the diagram in Exhibit 600.39.

For the furniture maker in the illustration, manufacturing would begin in the Cutting Department, where the wood would be cut to design specifications. Next, the Drilling Department would perform the drilling function, after which the Sanding Department would sand the wood, the Staining Department would stain the furniture, and the Varnishing Department would apply varnish and other protective coatings. Then, the Upholstery Department would add fabric and other materials. Finally, the Assembly Department would assemble the furniture to complete the process.

In the traditional production process, production supervisors attempt to enter enough materials into the process to keep all the manufacturing departments operating. Some departments, however, may process materials more rapidly than others. In addition, if one department stops production because of machine breakdowns, for example, the preceding departments usually continue production in order to avoid idle time. This may result in a build-up of work in process inventories in some departments.

In a just-in-time system, processing functions are combined into work centers, sometimes called **manufacturing cells.** For example, the seven departments just illustrated for the furniture manufacturer might be reorganized into

Exhibit 600.39 *Traditional Production Line—Furniture Manufacturer*

Exhibit 600.40 *Just-in-Time Production Line—Furniture Manufacturer*

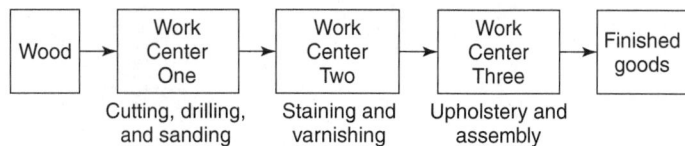

three work centers. As shown in the diagram in Exhibit 600.40, Work Center One would perform the cutting, drilling, and sanding functions; Work Center Two would perform the staining and varnishing functions; Work Center Three would perform the upholstery and assembly functions.

In the traditional production line, a worker typically performs only one function. However, in a work center in which several functions take place, the workers are often cross-trained to perform more than one function. Research has indicated that workers who perform several manufacturing functions identify better with the end product. This creates pride in the product and improves quality and productivity.

Implementing JIT may also result in reorganizing service activities. Specifically, the service activities may be assigned to individual work centers, rather than to centralized service departments. For example, each work center may be assigned the responsibility for the repair and maintenance of its machinery and equipment. Accepting this responsibility creates an environment in which workers gain a better understanding of the production process and the machinery. In turn, workers tend to take better care of the machinery, which decreases repairs and maintenance costs, reduces machine downtime, and improves product quality.

In a JIT system, wasted motion from moving the product and materials is reduced. The product is often placed on a movable carrier that is centrally located in the work center. After the workers in a work center have completed their activities with the product, the entire carrier and any additional materials are moved just in time to satisfy the demand or need of the next work center. In this sense, the product is said to be "pulled through." Each work center is connected to other work centers through information contained on *Kanbans*, which is a Japanese term for "cards."

The experience of **Caterpillar Inc.** illustrates the impact of JIT. Before implementing JIT, an average transmission would travel 10 miles through the factory and require 1,000 pieces of paper for materials, labor, and movement transactions. After implementing JIT, Caterpillar improved manufacturing so that an average transmission traveled only 200 feet and required only 10 pieces of paper.

In summary, the primary benefit of JIT systems is the increased efficiency of operations, which is achieved by eliminating waste, removing non-value-added activities and simplifying the production process. At the same time, JIT systems emphasize continuous improvement in the manufacturing process and the improvement of product quality.

650 Operating Budgets and Performance Evaluation

Operating Budgets

You may have financial goals for your life. To achieve these goals, it is necessary to plan for future expenses. For example, you may consider taking a part-time job to save money for school expenses for the coming school year. How much money would you need to earn and save in order to pay these expenses? One way to answer this question would be to prepare a budget. For example, a budget would show an estimate of your expenses associated with school, such as tuition, fees, and books. In addition, you would have expenses for day-to-day living, such as rent, food, and clothing. You might also have expenses for travel and entertainment. Once the school year begins, you can use the budget as a tool for guiding your spending priorities during the year.

The budget is used in businesses in much the same way as it can be used in personal life. For example, **DaimlerChrysler** uses budgeting to determine the number of cars to be produced, number of shifts to operate, number of people to be employed, and amount of material to be purchased. The budget provides the company a "game plan" for the year. In this section, you will see how budgets can be used for financial planning and control.

Nature and Objectives of Budgeting

If you were driving across the country, you might plan your trip with the aid of a road map. The road map would lay out your route across the country, identify stopovers, and reduce your chances of getting lost. In the same way, a **budget** charts a course for a business by outlining the plans of the business in financial terms. Like the road map, the budget can help a company navigate through the year and reduce negative outcomes.

Although budgets are normally associated with profit-making businesses, they also play an important role in operating most units of government. For example, budgets are important in managing rural school districts and small villages as well as agencies of the federal government. Budgets are also important for managing the operations of churches, hospitals, and other nonprofit institutions. Individuals and families also use budgeting techniques in managing their financial affairs. In this chapter, we discuss the principles of budgeting in the context of a business organized for profit.

Objectives of Budgeting

Budgeting involves (1) establishing specific goals, (2) executing plans to achieve the goals, and (3) periodically comparing actual results with the goals. These goals include both the overall business goals as well as the specific goals for the individual units within the business. Establishing specific goals for future operations is part of the *planning* function of management, while executing actions to meet the goals is the *directing* function of management. Periodically comparing actual results with these goals and taking appropriate action is the *controlling* function of management. The relationships of these functions are illustrated in Exhibit 600.41.

PLANNING A set of goals is often necessary to guide and focus individual and group actions. For example, students set academic goals, athletes set athletic goals, employees set career goals, and businesses set financial goals. In the same way, budgeting supports the planning process by requiring all organizational units to establish their goals for the upcoming period. These goals, in turn, motivate individuals and groups to perform at high levels. For example, **Florida Power and Light (FP&L),** an electric utility, announced plans to reduce costs by 8% of its total budget in order to maintain its target profitability. Using the budget to communicate these expectations throughout the organization helped FP&L to reach its target. Without the budget establishing this clear expectation, these results would have been very difficult to achieve.

Planning not only motivates employees to attain goals but also improves overall decision making. During the planning phase of the budget process, all viewpoints are considered, options identified, and cost reduction opportunities assessed. This effort leads to better decision making for the organization. As a result, the budget process may reveal opportunities or threats that were not known prior to the budget planning process. For example, the financial planning process helped **General Motors** identify the high costs associated with its far-flung parts operations. As a result, GM decided to sell over 45 lines of businesses (radiator caps, vacuum pumps, electric motors, etc.) in order to focus on its core auto-making business.

DIRECTING Once the budget plans are in place, they can be used to direct and coordinate operations in order to achieve the stated goals. For example, your goal to receive an "A" in a course would result in certain activities, such as reading the book, completing assignments, participating in class, and studying for exams. Such actions are fairly easy to direct and coordinate. A business, however, is much more complex and requires more formal direction and coordination. The budget is one way to direct and coordinate business activities and units to achieve stated goals. The budgetary units of an organization are called **responsibility centers.** Each responsibility center is led by a manager who has the authority over and responsibility for the unit's performance.

Exhibit 600.41 *Planning, Directing, and Controlling*

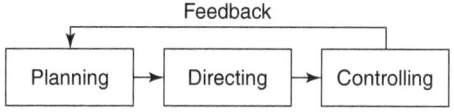

If there is a change in the external environment, the budget process can also be used by unit managers to readjust the operations. For example, **SKI Ltd.** uses weather information to plan expenditures at its Killington and Mt. Snow ski resorts in Vermont. When the weather is forecasted to turn cold and dry, the company increases expenditures in snow-making activities and adds to the staff in order to serve a greater number of skiers.

CONTROLLING   As time passes, the actual performance of an operation can be compared against the planned goals. This provides prompt feedback to employees about their performance. If necessary, employees can use such **feedback** to adjust their activities in the future. For example, a salesperson may be given a quota to achieve $100,000 in sales for the period. If the actual sales are only $75,000, the salesperson can use this feedback about underperformance to change sales tactics and improve future sales. Feedback is not only helpful to individuals, but it can also redirect a complete organization. For example, **The Coca-Cola Company** slashed its workforce by 20%, or 6,000 employees, as a result of the company reporting its first quarterly earnings loss in a decade.

Comparing actual results to the plan also helps prevent unplanned expenditures. The budget encourages employees to establish their spending priorities. For example, departments in universities have budgets to support faculty travel to conferences and meetings. The travel budget communicates to the faculty the upper limit on travel. Often, desired travel exceeds the budget. Thus, the budget requires the faculty to prioritize travel-related opportunities. Later in this module, we will discuss comparing actual costs with budgeted costs in greater detail.

Human Behavior and Budgeting

In the budgeting process, business, team, and individual goals are established. Human behavior problems can arise if (1) the budget goal is unachievable (too tight), (2) the budget goal is very easy to achieve (too loose), or (3) the budget goals of the business conflict with the objectives of employees (goal conflict).

SETTING BUDGET GOALS TOO TIGHTLY   People can become discouraged if performance expectations are set too high. For example, would you be inspired or discouraged by a guitar instructor expecting you to play like Eric Clapton after only a few lessons? You'd probably be discouraged. This same kind of problem can occur in businesses if employees view budget goals as unrealistic or unachievable. In such a case, the budget discourages employees from achieving the goals. On the other hand, aggressive but attainable goals are likely to inspire employees to achieve the goals. Therefore, it is important that employees (managers and nonmanagers) be involved in establishing reasonable budget estimates.

Involving all employees encourages cooperation both within and among departments. It also increases awareness of each department's importance to the overall objectives of the company. Employees view budgeting more positively when they have an opportunity to participate in the budget-setting process. This is because employees with a greater sense of control over the budget process will have a greater commitment to achieving its goals. In such cases, budgets are valuable planning tools that increase the possibility of achieving business goals.

There is strong evidence that loose budgets may be appropriate in settings involving high uncertainty, such as research and development. The loose budget acts as a sort of "shock absorber," giving managers maneuvering room to minimize work disruptions.

SETTING BUDGET GOALS TOO LOOSELY   Although it is desirable to establish attainable goals, it is undesirable to plan lower goals than may be possible. Such budget "padding" is termed **budgetary slack.** An example of budgetary slack is including spare employees in the plan. Managers may plan slack in the budget in order to provide a "cushion" for unexpected events or improve the appearance of operations. Budgetary slack can be avoided if lower- and mid-level managers are required to support their spending requirements with operational plans.

Slack budgets can cause employees to develop a "spend it or lose it" mentality. This often occurs at the end of the budget period when actual spending is much less than the budget. Employees may attempt to spend the remaining budget (purchase equipment, hire consultants, purchase supplies) in order to avoid having the budget cut next period.

SETTING CONFLICTING BUDGET GOALS   **Goal conflict** occurs when individual self-interest differs from business objectives. To illustrate, the manager of the Transportation Department of one company was instructed to stay within the department's budget. To meet the budget goal, the manager stopped transporting all shipments for the last two weeks of the period. Though the Transportation Department budget was met, customers were upset because they did not receive their orders. As a result, many customers stopped doing business with the company or demanded price discounts that far exceeded the additional transportation costs that should have been spent. In this example, the budget pressure caused the Transportation Department manager to make a decision that appeared correct from the department's view but was harmful to the business. Goal conflict can be avoided if budget goals are carefully designed for consistency across all areas of the organization.

Budgeting Systems

Budgeting systems vary among businesses because of such factors as organizational structure, complexity of operations, and management philosophy. Differences in budget systems are even more significant among different types of businesses, such as manufacturers and service businesses. The details of a budgeting system used by an automobile manufacturer such as **Ford** would obviously differ from a service company such as **American Airlines.** However, the basic budgeting concepts illustrated in the following paragraphs apply to all types of businesses and organizations.

The budgetary period for operating activities normally includes the fiscal year of a business. A year is short enough that future operations can be estimated fairly accurately, yet long enough that the future can be viewed in a broad context. However, to achieve effective control, the annual budgets are usually subdivided into shorter time periods, such as quarters of the year, months, or weeks.

A variation of fiscal-year budgeting, called **continuous budgeting,** maintains a twelve-month projection into the future. The twelve-month budget is continually revised by removing the data for the period just ended and adding estimated budget data for the same period next year, as shown in Exhibit 600.42.

Developing budgets for the next fiscal year usually begins several months prior to the end of the current year. This responsibility is normally assigned to a budget committee. Such a committee often consists of the budget director and such high-level executives as the controller, the treasurer, the production manager, and the sales manager. Once the budget has been approved, the budget process is monitored and summarized by the Accounting Department, which reports to the committee.

There are several methods of developing budget estimates. One method, termed **zero-based budgeting,** requires managers to estimate sales, production, and other operating data as though operations are being started for the first time. This approach has the benefit of taking a fresh view of operations each year. A more common approach is to start with last year's budget and revise it for actual results and expected changes for the coming year. Two major budgets using this approach are the static budget and the flexible budget.

Static Budget

A **static budget** shows the expected results of a responsibility center for only one activity level. Once the budget has been determined, it is not changed, even if the activity changes. Static budgeting is used by many service companies and for some administrative functions of manufacturing companies, such as purchasing, engineering, and accounting. For example, the Assembly Department manager for Colter Manufacturing Company prepared the static budget for the upcoming year, shown in Exhibit 600.43.

A disadvantage of static budgets is that they do not adjust for changes in activity levels. For example, assume that the actual amounts spent by the Assembly Department of Colter Manufacturing totaled $72,000, which is $12,000 or 20% ($12,000 ÷ $60,000) more than budgeted. Is this good news or bad news? At first you might think that this is a bad result. However, this conclusion may not be valid, as static budget results may be difficult to interpret. To illustrate, assume that the assembly manager constructed the budget based on plans to assemble *8,000* units during the year. However, *10,000* units were actually produced, which represents 25% (2,000 ÷ 8,000) more work than expected. Should the additional $12,000 in spending in excess of the budget be considered "bad news"? Maybe not. The Assembly Department provided 25% more output for only 20% additional cost.

Exhibit 600.42   *Continuous Budgeting*

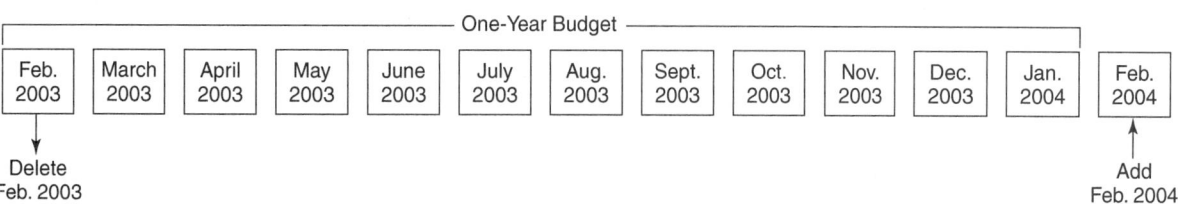

Exhibit 600.43 *Static Budget*

Colter Manufacturing Company
Assembly Department Budget
for the Year Ending July 31, 2003

Direct labor	$40,000
Electric power	5,000
Supervisor salaries	15,000
Total department costs	$60,000

Exhibit 600.44 *Flexible Budget*

Colter Manufacturing Company
Assembly Department Budget
for the Year Ending July 31, 2003

Units of production	8,000	9,000	10,000
Variable cost:			
Direct labor ($5 per unit)	$40,000	$45,000	$50,000
Electric power ($0.50 per unit)	4,000	4,500	5,000
Total variable cost	$44,000	$49,500	$55,000
Fixed cost:			
Electric power	$ 1,000	$ 1,000	$ 1,000
Supervisor salaries	15,000	15,000	15,000
Total fixed cost	$16,000	$16,000	$16,000
Total department costs	$60,000	$65,500	$71,000

Flexible Budget

Unlike static budgets, **flexible budgets** show the expected results of a responsibility center for several activity levels. You can think of a flexible budget as a series of static budgets for different levels of activity. Such budgets are especially useful in estimating and controlling factory costs and operating expenses. Exhibit 600.44 is a flexible budget for the annual manufacturing expense in the Assembly Department of Colter Manufacturing Company.

Flexible budgets show expected results for several activity levels.

When constructing a flexible budget, we first identify the relevant activity levels. In Exhibit 600.44, there are 8,000, 9,000, and 10,000 units of production. Alternative activity bases, such as machine hours or direct labor hours, may be used in measuring the volume of activity. Second, we identify the fixed and variable cost components of the costs being budgeted. For example, in Exhibit 600.44, the electric power cost is separated into its fixed cost ($1,000 per month) and variable cost ($0.50 per unit). Lastly, we prepare the budget for each activity level by multiplying the variable cost per unit by the activity level and then adding the monthly fixed cost.

With a flexible budget, the department manager can be evaluated by comparing actual expenses to the budgeted amount for actual activity. For example, if Colter Manufacturing Company's Assembly Department actually spent $72,000 to produce 10,000 units, the manager would be considered over budget by $1,000 ($72,000 − $71,000). Under the static budget in Exhibit 600.43, the department was $12,000 over budget. This comparison is illustrated in Exhibit 600.45. The flexible budget for the Assembly Department is much more accurate than the static budget, because budget amounts adjust for changes in activity.

> **Example 27** At the beginning of the period, the Assembly Department budgeted direct labor of $45,000 and supervisor salaries of $30,000 for 5,000 hours of production. The department actually completed 6,000 hours of production. What is the appropriate total budget for the department, assuming that it uses flexible budgeting?
>
> $84,000 [($9 × 6,000) + $30,000]

Exhibit 600.45 *Static and Flexible Budgets*

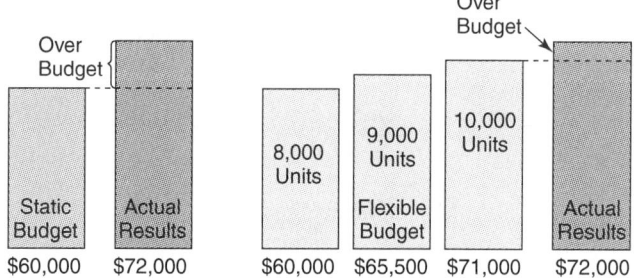

Computerized Budgeting Systems

In developing budgets, many firms use computerized budgeting systems. Such systems speed up and reduce the cost of preparing the budget. This is especially true when large quantities of data need to be processed. Computers are also useful in continuous budgeting. Reports that compare actual results with amounts budgeted can also be prepared on a timely basis through the use of computerized systems. For example, **Fujitsu** used Enterprise Resource Planning (ERP) software to streamline its budgeting process from 6 to 8 weeks down to 10 to 15 days.

Managers often use computer spreadsheets or simulation models to represent the operating and budget relationships. By using computer simulation models, the impact of various operating alternatives on the budget can be assessed. For example, the budget can be revised to show the impact of a proposed change in indirect labor wage rates. Likewise, the budgetary effect of a proposed product line can be determined.

A common objective of using computer-based budgeting is to tie all the budgets of the organization together. In the next section, we will illustrate how a company ties its budgets together to develop a complete plan.

Master Budget

Manufacturing operations require a series of budgets that are linked together in a **master budget.** The major parts of the master budget are as follows.

Budgeted Income Statement	Budgeted Balance Sheet
Sales budget	Cash budget
Cost of goods sold budget:	Capital expenditures budget
Production budget	
Direct materials purchases budget	
Direct labor cost budget	
Factory overhead cost budget	
Selling and administrative expenses budget	

Exhibit 600.46 shows the relationship among the income statement budgets. The budget process begins by estimating sales. The sales information is then provided to the various units for estimating the production and selling and administrative expenses budgets. The production budgets are used to prepare the direct materials purchases, direct labor cost, and factory overhead cost budgets. These three budgets are used to develop the cost of goods sold budget. Once these budgets and the selling and administrative expenses budget have been completed, the budgeted income statement can be prepared.

After the budgeted income statement has been developed, the budgeted balance sheet can be prepared. Two major budgets comprising the budgeted balance sheet are the cash budget and the capital expenditures budget.

Exhibit 600.46 *Income Statement Budgets*

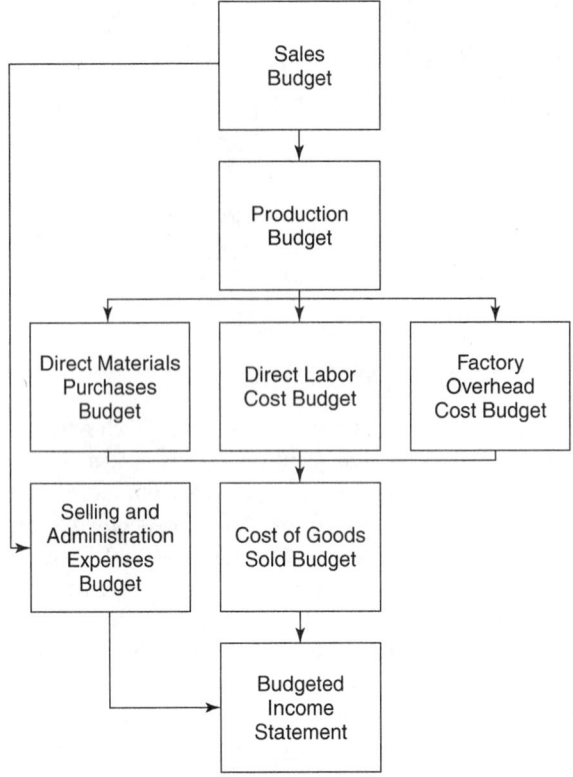

Income Statement Budgets

In the following sections, we will illustrate the major elements of the income statement budget. We will use a small manufacturing business, Elite Accessories Inc., as the basis for our illustration.

Sales Budget

The **sales budget** normally indicates for each product (1) the quantity of estimated sales and (2) the expected unit selling price. These data are often reported by regions or by sales representatives.

In estimating the quantity of sales for each product, past sales volumes are often used as a starting point. These amounts are revised for factors that are expected to affect future sales, such as the factors listed below.

- backlog of unfilled sales orders
- planned advertising and promotion
- expected industry and general economic conditions
- productive capacity
- projected pricing policy
- findings of market research studies

Once an estimate of the sales volume is obtained, the expected sales revenue can be determined by multiplying the volume by the expected unit sales price. Exhibit 600.47 is the sales budget for Elite Accessories Inc.

For control purposes, management can compare actual sales and budgeted sales by product, region, or sales representative. Management would investigate any significant differences and take possible corrective actions.

Exhibit 600.47 *Sales Budget*

<table>
<tr><th colspan="4">Elite Accessories Inc.
Sales Budget
for the Year Ending December 31, 2003</th></tr>
<tr><th>Product and Region</th><th>Unit Sales Volume</th><th>Unit Selling Price</th><th>Total Sales</th></tr>
<tr><td>Wallet:</td><td></td><td></td><td></td></tr>
<tr><td>East</td><td>287,000</td><td>$12.00</td><td>$ 3,444,000</td></tr>
<tr><td>West</td><td>241,000</td><td>12.00</td><td>2,892,000</td></tr>
<tr><td>Total</td><td>528,000</td><td></td><td>$ 6,336,000</td></tr>
<tr><td>Handbag:</td><td></td><td></td><td></td></tr>
<tr><td>East</td><td>156,400</td><td>$25.00</td><td>$ 3,910,000</td></tr>
<tr><td>West</td><td>123,600</td><td>25.00</td><td>3,090,000</td></tr>
<tr><td>Total</td><td>280,000</td><td></td><td>$ 7,000,000</td></tr>
<tr><td>Total revenue from sales</td><td></td><td></td><td>$13,336,000</td></tr>
</table>

Production Budget

Production should be carefully coordinated with the sales budget to ensure that production and sales are kept in balance during the period. The number of units to be manufactured to meet budgeted sales and inventory needs for each product is set forth in the **production budget.** The budgeted volume of production is determined as follows.

```
    Expected units to be sold
  + Desired units in ending inventory
  − Estimated units in beginning inventory
    Total units to be produced
```

Exhibit 600.48 is the production budget for Elite Accessories Inc.

Exhibit 600.48 *Production Budget*

<table>
<tr><th colspan="3">Elite Accessories Inc.
Production Budget
for the Year Ending December 31, 2003</th></tr>
<tr><th></th><th colspan="2">Units</th></tr>
<tr><th></th><th>Wallet</th><th>Handbag</th></tr>
<tr><td>Expected units to be sold (from Exhibit 600.47)</td><td>528,000</td><td>280,000</td></tr>
<tr><td>Plus desired ending inventory, December 31, 2003</td><td>80,000</td><td>60,000</td></tr>
<tr><td>Total</td><td>608,000</td><td>340,000</td></tr>
<tr><td>Less estimated beginning inventory, January 1, 2003</td><td>88,000</td><td>48,000</td></tr>
<tr><td>Total units to be produced</td><td>520,000</td><td>292,000</td></tr>
</table>

Example 28 Sales of 45,000 units are budgeted for the period. The estimated beginning inventory is 3,000 units, and the desired ending inventory is 5,000 units. What is the budgeted production (in units) for the period?

47,000 units (45,000 units + 5,000 units − 3,000 units)

Direct Materials Purchases Budget

The production budget is the starting point for determining the estimated quantities of direct materials to be purchased. Multiplying these quantities by the expected unit purchase price determines the total cost of direct materials to be purchased.

> Materials required for production
> \+ Desired ending materials inventory
> − Estimated beginning materials inventory
> ──────────────────────
> Direct materials to be purchased

In Elite Accessories Inc.'s production operations, leather and lining are required for wallets and handbags. The quantity of direct materials expected to be used for each unit of product is as follows.

Wallet:	Handbag:
Leather: 0.30 square yard per unit	Leather: 1.25 square yards per unit
Lining: 0.10 square yard per unit	Lining: 0.50 square yard per unit

Based on these data and the production budget, the **direct materials purchases budget** is prepared. As shown in the budget in Exhibit 600.49, for Elite Accessories Inc. to produce 520,000 wallets, 156,000 square yards (520,000 units × 0.30 square yard per unit) of leather are needed. Likewise, to produce 292,000 handbags, 365,000 square yards (292,000 units × 1.25 square yards per unit) of leather are needed. We can compute the needs for lining in a similar manner. Then adding the desired ending inventory for each material and deducting the estimated beginning inventory determines the amount of each material to be purchased. Multiplying these amounts by the estimated cost per square yard yields the total materials purchase cost.

The direct materials purchases budget helps management maintain inventory levels within reasonable limits. For this purpose, the timing of the direct materials purchases should be coordinated between the purchasing and production departments.

Exhibit 600.49 *Direct Materials Purchases Budget*

Elite Accessories Inc.
Direct Materials Purchases Budget
for the Year Ending December 31, 2003

	Direct Materials		
	Leather	Lining	Total
Square yards required for production:			
Wallet (Note A)	156,000	52,000	
Handbag (Note B)	365,000	146,000	
Plus desired inventory, December 31, 2003	20,000	12,000	
Total	541,000	210,000	
Less estimated inventory, January 1, 2003	18,000	15,000	
Total square yards to be purchased	523,000	195,000	
Unit price (per square yard)	× $4.50	× $1.20	
Total direct materials to be purchased	$2,353,500	$234,000	$2,587,500

Note A: Leather: 520,000 units × 0.30 sq. yd. per unit = 156,000 sq. yds.
           Lining: 520,000 units × 0.10 sq. yd. per unit = 52,000 sq. yds.
Note B: Leather: 292,000 units × 1.25 sq. yd. per unit = 365,000 sq. yds.
           Lining: 292,000 units × 0.50 sq. yd. per unit = 146,000 sq. yds.

Direct Labor Cost Budget

The production budget also provides the starting point for preparing the direct labor cost budget. For Elite Accessories Inc., the labor requirements for each unit of product are estimated as follows.

Wallet:	Handbag:
Cutting Department: 0.10 hour per unit	Cutting Department: 0.15 hour per unit
Sewing Department: 0.25 hour per unit	Sewing Department: 0.40 hour per unit

Based on these data and the production budget, Elite Accessories Inc. prepares the direct labor budget. As shown in the budget in Exhibit 600.50, for Elite Accessories Inc. to produce 520,000 wallets, 52,000 hours (520,000 units × 0.10 hour per unit) of labor in the Cutting Department are required. Likewise, to produce 292,000 handbags, 43,800 hours (292,000 units × 0.15 hour per unit) of labor in the Cutting Department are required. In a similar manner, we can determine the direct labor hours needed in the Sewing Department to meet the budgeted production. Multiplying the direct labor hours for each department by the estimated department hourly rate yields the total direct labor cost for each department.

The direct labor needs should be coordinated between the production and personnel departments. This ensures that there will be enough labor available for production.

Example 29 Budgeted production is 22,000 units. Each unit requires 0.70 pound of steel and 0.20 direct labor hour. Steel is purchased for $45 per pound, and direct labor is $18 per hour. Steel has an estimated beginning inventory of 700 units and a desired ending inventory of 200 units. For the period, what is the budgeted (a) direct materials purchases and (b) direct labor cost?

(a) $670,500 {[(22,000 units × 0.70 lb.) + 200 lbs. − 700 lbs.] × $45};
(b) $79,200 (22,000 units × 0.20 hr. × $18)

Exhibit 600.50 *Direct Labor Cost Budget*

Elite Accessories Inc.
Direct Labor Cost Budget
for the Year Ending December 31, 2003

	Cutting	Sewing	Total
Hours required for production:			
Wallet (Note A)	52,000	130,000	
Handbag (Note B)	43,800	116,800	
Total	95,800	246,800	
Hourly rate	× $12.00	× $15.00	
Total direct labor cost	$1,149,600	$3,702,000	$4,851,600

Note A: Cutting Department: 520,000 units × 0.10 hour per unit = 52,000 hours
Sewing Department: 520,000 units × 0.25 hour per unit = 130,000 hours
Note B: Cutting Department: 292,000 units × 0.15 hour per unit = 43,800 hours
Sewing Department: 292,000 units × 0.40 hour per unit = 116,800 hours

Exhibit 600.51 *Factory Overhead Cost Budget*

Elite Accessories Inc.
Factory Overhead Cost Budget
for the Year Ending December 31, 2003

Indirect factory wages	$ 732,800
Supervisor salaries	360,000
Power and light	306,000
Depreciation of plant and equipment	288,000
Indirect materials	182,800
Maintenance	140,280
Insurance and property taxes	79,200
Total factory overhead cost	$2,089,080

Factory Overhead Cost Budget

The estimated factory overhead costs necessary for production make up the factory overhead cost budget. This budget usually includes the total estimated cost for each item of factory overhead, as shown in Exhibit 600.51.

A business may prepare supporting departmental schedules, in which the factory overhead costs are separated into their fixed and variable cost elements. Such schedules enable department managers to direct their attention to those costs for which they are responsible and to evaluate performance.

Cost of Goods Sold Budget

The direct materials purchases budget, direct labor cost budget, and factory overhead cost budget are the starting point for preparing the **cost of goods sold budget.** To illustrate, these data are combined with the desired ending inventory and the estimated beginning inventory data below to determine the budgeted cost of goods sold shown in Exhibit 600.52.

Estimated inventories on January 1, 2003:		Desired inventories on December 31, 2003:	
Finished goods	$1,095,600	Finished goods	$1,565,000
Work in process	214,400	Work in process	220,000

Selling and Administrative Expenses Budget

The sales budget is often used as the starting point for estimating the selling and administrative expenses. For example, a budgeted increase in sales may require more advertising. Exhibit 600.53 is a selling and administrative expenses budget for Elite Accessories Inc.

Detailed supporting schedules are often prepared for major items in the selling and administrative expenses budget. For example, an advertising expense schedule for the Marketing Department should include the advertising media to be used (newspaper, direct mail, television), quantities (column inches, number of pieces, minutes), and the cost per unit. Attention to such details results in realistic budgets. Effective control results from assigning responsibility for achieving the budget to department supervisors.

Budgeted Income Statement

The budgets for sales, cost of goods sold, and selling and administrative expenses, combined with the data on other income, other expense, and income tax, are used to prepare the budgeted income statement. Exhibit 600.54 is a budgeted income statement for Elite Accessories Inc.

The budgeted income statement summarizes the estimates of all phases of operations. This allows management to assess the effects of the individual budgets on profits for the year. If the budgeted net income is too low, management could review and revise operating plans in an attempt to improve income.

Exhibit 600.52 *Cost of Goods Sold Budget*

Elite Accessories Inc.
Cost of Goods Sold Budget
for the Year Ending December 31, 2003

Finished goods inventory, January 1, 2003		$1,095,600
Work in process inventory, January 1, 2003	$214,400	
Direct materials:		
Direct materials inventory, January 1, 2003 (Note A)	$99,000	
Direct materials purchases (from Exhibit 600.49)	2,587,500	← Direct materials purchases budget
Cost of direct materials available for use	$2,686,500	
Less direct materials inventory, December 31, 2003 (Note B)	104,400	
Cost of direct materials placed in production	$2,582,100	
Direct labor (from Exhibit 600.50)	4,851,600	← Direct labor cost budget
Factory overhead (from Exhibit 600.51)	2,089,080	← Factory overhead cost budget
Total manufacturing costs		9,522,780
Total work in process during period		$9,737,180
Less work in process inventory, December 31, 2003		220,000
Cost of goods manufactured		9,517,180
Cost of finished goods available for sale		$10,612,780
Less finished goods inventory, December 31, 2003		1,565,000
Cost of goods sold		$9,047,780

Note A:	Leather:	18,000 sq. yds. × $4.50 per sq. yd.	$81,000
	Lining:	15,000 sq. yds. × $1.20 per sq. yd.	18,000
	Direct materials inventory, January 1, 2003		$99,000
Note B:	Leather:	20,000 sq. yds. × $4.50 per sq. yd.	$90,000
	Lining:	12,000 sq. yds. × $1.20 per sq. yd.	14,400
	Direct materials inventory, December 31, 2003		$104,400

Exhibit 600.53 *Selling and Administrative Expenses Budget*

Elite Accessories Inc.
Selling and Administrative Expenses Budget
for the Year Ending December 31, 2003

Selling expenses:		
Sales salaries expense	$715,000	
Advertising expense	360,000	
Travel expense	115,000	
Total selling expenses		$1,190,000
Administrative expenses:		
Officers' salaries expense	$360,000	
Office salaries expense	258,000	
Office rent expense	34,500	
Office supplies expense	17,500	
Miscellaneous administrative expenses	25,000	
Total administrative expenses		695,000
Total selling and administrative expenses		$1,885,000

Exhibit 600.54 *Budgeted Income Statement*

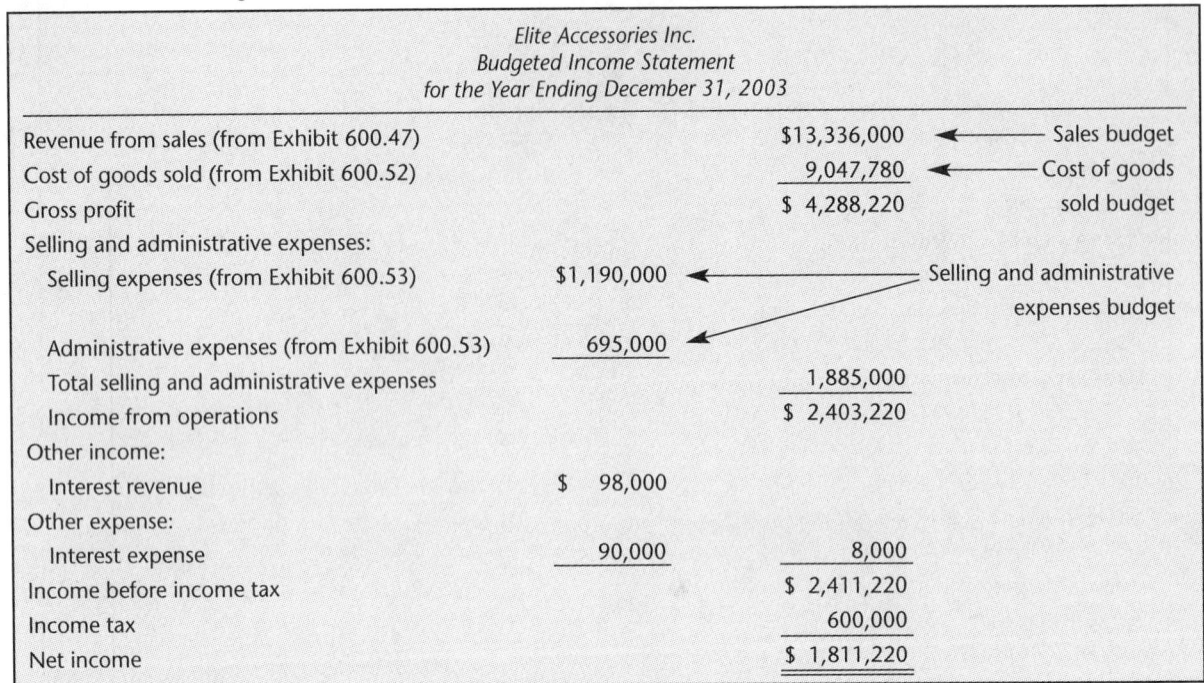

Elite Accessories Inc.
Budgeted Income Statement
for the Year Ending December 31, 2003

Revenue from sales (from Exhibit 600.47)		$13,336,000	← Sales budget
Cost of goods sold (from Exhibit 600.52)		9,047,780	← Cost of goods sold budget
Gross profit		$ 4,288,220	
Selling and administrative expenses:			
Selling expenses (from Exhibit 600.53)	$1,190,000		← Selling and administrative expenses budget
Administrative expenses (from Exhibit 600.53)	695,000		
Total selling and administrative expenses		1,885,000	
Income from operations		$ 2,403,220	
Other income:			
Interest revenue	$ 98,000		
Other expense:			
Interest expense	90,000	8,000	
Income before income tax		$ 2,411,220	
Income tax		600,000	
Net income		$ 1,811,220	

Balance Sheet Budgets

Balance sheet budgets are used by managers to plan financing, investing, and cash objectives for the firm. The balance sheet budgets illustrated for Elite Accessories Inc. in the following sections are the cash budget and the capital expenditures budget.

Cash Budget

The **cash budget** is one of the most important elements of the budgeted balance sheet. The cash budget presents the expected receipts (inflows) and payments (outflows) of cash for a period of time.

The cash budget presents the expected receipts and payments of cash for a period of time.

Information from the various operating budgets, such as the sales budget, the direct materials purchases budget, and the selling and administrative expenses budget, affects the cash budget. In addition, the capital expenditures budget, dividend policies, and plans for equity or long-term debt financing also affect the cash budget.

We illustrate the monthly cash budget for January, February, and March 2003, for Elite Accessories Inc. We begin by developing the estimated cash receipts and estimated cash payments portion of the cash budget.

ESTIMATED CASH RECEIPTS Estimated cash receipts are planned additions to cash from sales and other sources, such as issuing securities or collecting interest. A supporting schedule can be used in determining the collections from sales. To illustrate this schedule, assume the following information for Elite Accessories Inc.

Accounts receivable, January 1, 2003				$370,000
	January	February	March	
Budgeted sales	$1,080,000	$1,240,000	$970,000	

Elite Accessories Inc. expects to sell 10% of its merchandise for cash. Of the remaining 90% of the sales on account, 60% are expected to be collected in the month of the sale and the remainder in the next month.

MODULE 600. ACCOUNTING

Exhibit 600.55 *Schedule of Collections from Sales*

Elite Accessories Inc.
Schedule of Collections from Sales
for the Three Months Ending March 31, 2003

	January	February	March
Receipts from cash sales:			
Cash sales (10% × current month's sales—Note A)	$108,000	$ 124,000	$ 97,000
Receipts from sales on account:			
Collections from prior month's sales (40% of previous month's credit sales—Note B)	$370,000	$ 388,800	$446,400
Collections from current month's sales (60% of current month's credit sales—Note C)	583,200	669,600	523,800
Total receipts from sales on account	$953,200	$1,058,400	$970,200

Note A: $108,000 = $1,080,000 × 10%
$124,000 = $1,240,000 × 10%
$ 97,000 = $ 970,000 × 10%

Note B: $370,000, given as January 1, 2003 Accounts Receivable balance
$388,800 = $1,080,000 × 90% × 40%
$446,400 = $1,240,000 × 90% × 40%

Note C: $583,200 = $1,080,000 × 90% × 60%
$669,600 = $1,240,000 × 90% × 60%
$523,800 = $ 970,000 × 90% × 60%

Using this information, we prepare the schedule of collections from sales, shown in Exhibit 600.55. The cash receipts from sales on account are determined by adding the amounts collected from credit sales earned in the current period (60%) and the amounts accrued from sales in the previous period as accounts receivable (40%).

Example 30 A company collects 25% of its sales in the month of the sale and 75% in the month following the sale. If sales are budgeted to be $750,000 for March and $900,000 for April, what are the budgeted cash receipts for April?

$787,500 [($750,000 × 0.75) + ($900,000 × 0.25)]

ESTIMATED CASH PAYMENTS Estimated cash payments are planned reductions in cash from manufacturing costs, selling and administrative expenses, capital expenditures, and other sources, such as buying securities or paying interest or dividends. A supporting schedule can be used in estimating the cash payments for manufacturing costs. To illustrate, assume the following information for Elite Accessories Inc.

Accounts payable, January 1, 2003 $190,000

	January	February	March
Manufacturing costs	$840,000	$780,000	$812,000

Depreciation expense on machines is estimated to be $24,000 per month and is included in the manufacturing costs. The accounts payable were incurred for manufacturing costs. Elite Accessories Inc. expects to pay 75% of the manufacturing costs in the month in which they are incurred and the balance in the next month.

Using this information, we can prepare the schedule of payments for manufacturing costs, as shown in Exhibit 600.56.

650. OPERATING BUDGETS AND PERFORMANCE EVALUATION

Exhibit 600.56 *Schedule of Payments for Manufacturing Costs*

Elite Accessories Inc.
Schedule of Payments for Manufacturing Costs
for the Three Months Ending March 31, 2003

	January	February	March
Payments of prior month's manufacturing costs			
{[25% × previous month's manufacturing costs (less depreciation)]—Note A}	$190,000	$204,000	$189,000
Payments of current month's manufacturing costs			
{[75% × current month's manufacturing costs (less depreciation)]—Note B}	612,000	567,000	591,000
Total payments	$802,000	$771,000	$780,000

Note A: $190,000, given as January 1, 2003 Accounts Payable balance
$204,000 = ($840,000 − $24,000) × 25%
$189,000 = ($780,000 − $24,000) × 25%

Note B: $612,000 = ($840,000 − $24,000) × 75%
$567,000 = ($780,000 − $24,000) × 75%
$591,000 = ($812,000 − $24,000) × 75%

In Exhibit 600.56, the cash payments are determined by adding the amounts paid from costs incurred in the current period (75%) and the amounts accrued as a liability from costs in the previous period (25%). The $24,000 of depreciation must be excluded from all calculations, since depreciation is a noncash expense that should not be included in the cash budget.

COMPLETING THE CASH BUDGET   To complete the cash budget for Elite Accessories Inc., as shown in Exhibit 600.57, assume that Elite Accessories Inc. is expecting the following.

Cash balance on January 1	$280,000
Quarterly taxes paid on March 31	150,000
Quarterly interest expense paid on January 10	22,500
Quarterly interest revenue received on March 21	24,500
Sewing equipment purchased in February	274,000

In addition, monthly selling and administrative expenses, which are paid in the month incurred, are estimated as follows.

	January	February	March
Selling and administrative expenses	$160,000	$165,000	$145,000

We can compare the estimated cash balance at the end of the period with the minimum balance required by operations. Assuming that the minimum cash balance for Elite Accessories Inc. is $340,000, we can determine any expected excess or deficiency.

The minimum cash balance protects against variations in estimates and for unexpected cash emergencies. For effective cash management, much of the minimum cash balance should be deposited in income-producing securities that can be readily converted to cash. U.S. Treasury Bills or Notes are examples of such securities.

Capital Expenditures Budget

The **capital expenditures budget** summarizes plans for acquiring fixed assets. Such expenditures are necessary as machinery and other fixed assets wear out, become obsolete, or for other reasons need to be replaced. In addition, expanding plant facilities may be necessary to meet increasing demand for a company's product.

Exhibit 600.57 *Cash Budget*

<table>
<tr><th colspan="4">Elite Accessories Inc.
Cash Budget
for the Three Months Ending March 31, 2003</th></tr>
<tr><th></th><th>January</th><th>February</th><th>March</th></tr>
<tr><td>Estimated cash receipts from:</td><td></td><td></td><td></td></tr>
<tr><td> Cash sales (from Exhibit 600.55)</td><td>$ 108,000</td><td>$ 124,000</td><td>$ 97,000</td></tr>
<tr><td> Collections of accounts receivable (from Exhibit 600.55)</td><td>953,200</td><td>1,058,400</td><td>970,200</td></tr>
<tr><td> Interest revenue</td><td></td><td></td><td>24,500</td></tr>
<tr><td> Total cash receipts</td><td>$1,061,200</td><td>$1,182,400</td><td>$1,091,700</td></tr>
<tr><td>Estimated cash payments for:</td><td></td><td></td><td></td></tr>
<tr><td> Manufacturing costs (from Exhibit 600.56)</td><td>$ 802,000</td><td>$ 771,000</td><td>$ 780,000</td></tr>
<tr><td> Selling and administrative expenses</td><td>160,000</td><td>165,000</td><td>145,000</td></tr>
<tr><td> Capital additions</td><td></td><td>274,000</td><td></td></tr>
<tr><td> Interest expense</td><td>22,500</td><td></td><td></td></tr>
<tr><td> Income taxes</td><td></td><td></td><td>150,000</td></tr>
<tr><td> Total cash payments</td><td>$ 984,500</td><td>$1,210,000</td><td>$1,075,000</td></tr>
<tr><td>Cash increase (decrease)</td><td>$ 76,700</td><td>$ (27,600)</td><td>$ 16,700</td></tr>
<tr><td>Cash balance at beginning of month</td><td>280,000</td><td>356,700</td><td>329,100</td></tr>
<tr><td>Cash balance at end of month</td><td>$ 356,700</td><td>$ 329,100</td><td>$ 345,800</td></tr>
<tr><td>Minimum cash balance</td><td>340,000</td><td>340,000</td><td>340,000</td></tr>
<tr><td>Excess (deficiency)</td><td>$ 16,700</td><td>$ (10,900)</td><td>$ 5,800</td></tr>
</table>

Schedule of collections from sales

Schedule of cash payments for manufacturing costs

Exhibit 600.58 *Capital Expenditures Budget*

<table>
<tr><th colspan="6">Elite Accessories Inc.
Capital Expenditures Budget
for the Five Years Ending December 31, 2007</th></tr>
<tr><th>Item</th><th>2003</th><th>2004</th><th>2005</th><th>2006</th><th>2007</th></tr>
<tr><td>Machinery—Cutting Department</td><td>$400,000</td><td></td><td></td><td>$280,000</td><td>$360,000</td></tr>
<tr><td>Machinery—Sewing Department</td><td>274,000</td><td>$260,000</td><td>$560,000</td><td>200,000</td><td></td></tr>
<tr><td>Office equipment</td><td></td><td>90,000</td><td></td><td></td><td>60,000</td></tr>
<tr><td>Total</td><td>$674,000</td><td>$350,000</td><td>$560,000</td><td>$480,000</td><td>$420,000</td></tr>
</table>

The useful life of many fixed assets extends over long periods of time. In addition, the amount of the expenditures for such assets may vary from year to year. It is normal to project the plans for a number of periods into the future in preparing the capital expenditures budget. Exhibit 600.58 is a five-year capital expenditures budget for Elite Accessories Inc.

The capital expenditures budget should be considered in preparing the other operating budgets. For example, the estimated depreciation of new equipment affects the factory overhead cost budget and the selling and administrative expenses budget. The plans for financing the capital expenditures may also affect the cash budget.

Budgeted Balance Sheet

The budgeted balance sheet estimates the financial condition at the end of a budget period. The budgeted balance sheet assumes that all operating budgets and financing plans are met. It is similar to a balance sheet based on actual data in the accounts. For this reason, we do not illustrate a budgeted balance sheet for Elite Accessories Inc. If the budgeted balance sheet indicates a weakness in financial position, revising the financing plans or other plans may be necessary. For example, a large amount of long-term debt in relation to stockholders' equity might require revising financing plans for capital expenditures. Such revisions might include issuing equity rather than debt.

650. OPERATING BUDGETS AND PERFORMANCE EVALUATION

Performance Evaluation

Have you ever wondered if there is an economic reason why large retail stores, such as **JCPenney Co.** and **Sears,** are divided into departments? Typically, these stores include a Men's Department, Women's Department, Appliances Department, Home Entertainment Department, and Sporting Goods Department. Each department usually has a manager who is responsible for the financial performance of the department. The store may be the responsibility of a store manager, and a group of stores within a particular geographic area may be the responsibility of a division or district manager. If you were to be hired by a department store chain, you would probably begin your career in a department. Running a department would be a valuable experience before becoming responsible for a complete store. Likewise, responsibility for a complete store provides excellent training for other management positions.

In this section, we will focus on the role of accounting in assisting managers in planning and controlling organizational units, such as divisions, stores, and departments.

Centralized and Decentralized Operations

A **centralized** business is one in which all major planning and operating decisions are made by top management. For example, a one-person, owner/manager-operated business is centralized because all plans and decisions are made by one person. In a small owner/manager-operated business, centralization may be desirable. This is because the owner/manager's close supervision ensures that the business will be operated in the way the owner/manager wishes.

Separating a business into **divisions** or operating units and delegating responsibility to unit managers is called **decentralization.** In a decentralized business, the unit managers are responsible for planning and controlling the operations of their units.

Divisions are often structured around common functions, products, customers, or regions. For example, **Delta Air Lines** is organized around *functions,* such as the Flight Operations Division. The **Procter & Gamble Company** is organized around common *products,* such as the Soap Division, which sells a wide array of cleaning products.

There is no one best amount of decentralization for all businesses. In some companies, division managers have authority over all operations, including fixed asset acquisitions and retirements. In other companies, division managers have authority over profits but not fixed asset acquisitions and retirements. The proper amount of decentralization for a company depends on its advantages and disadvantages for the company's unique circumstances.

Advantages of Decentralization

As a business grows, it becomes more difficult for top management to maintain close daily contact with all operations. In such cases, delegating authority to managers closest to the operations usually results in better decisions. These managers often anticipate and react to operating data more quickly than could top management. In addition, as a company expands into a wide range of products and services, it becomes more difficult for top management to maintain operating expertise in all product lines and services. Decentralization allows managers to focus on acquiring expertise in their areas of responsibility. For example, in a company that maintains operations in insurance, banking, and health care, managers could become "experts" in their area of operation and responsibility.

Decentralized decision making also provides excellent training for managers. This may be a factor in helping a company retain quality managers. Since the art of management is best acquired through experience, delegating responsibility allows managers to acquire and develop managerial expertise early in their careers.

Businesses that work closely with customers, such as hotels, are often decentralized. This helps managers create good customer relations by responding quickly to customers' needs. In addition, because managers of decentralized operations tend to identify with customers and with operations, they are often more creative in suggesting operating and product improvements.

Disadvantages of Decentralization

A primary disadvantage of decentralized operations is that decisions made by one manager may negatively affect the profitability of the entire company. For example, the Pizza Hut chain added chicken to its menu and ended up taking business away from KFC. Then KFC retaliated with a blistering ad campaign against Pizza Hut. This happened even though both chains are part of the same company, **Tricon Global Restaurants**!

Another potential disadvantage of decentralized operations is duplicating assets and costs in operating divisions. For example, each manager of a product line might have a separate sales force and administrative office staff. Centralizing these personnel could save money.

Responsibility Accounting

In a decentralized business, an important function of accounting is to assist unit managers in evaluating and controlling their areas of responsibility, called **responsibility centers**. **Responsibility accounting** is the process of measuring and reporting operating data by responsibility center. Three common types of responsibility centers are cost centers, profit centers, and investment centers. These three responsibility centers differ in their scope of responsibility, as shown below.

Cost Center	Profit Center	Investment Center
Cost	Revenue − Cost Profit	Revenue −Cost Profit Investment in assets

Responsibility Accounting for Cost Centers

In a **cost center,** the unit manager has responsibility and authority for controlling the costs incurred. For example, the supervisor of the Power Department has responsibility for the costs incurred in providing power. A cost center manager does not make decisions concerning sales or the amount of fixed assets invested in the center. Cost centers may vary in size from a small department to an entire manufacturing plant. In addition, cost centers may exist within other cost centers. For example, we could view an entire university as a cost center, and each college and department within the university could also be a cost center, as shown in Exhibit 600.59.

Because managers of cost centers have responsibility and authority over costs, responsibility accounting for cost centers focuses on costs. To illustrate, the budget performance reports in Exhibit 600.60 are part of a responsibility accounting system. These reports aid the managers in controlling costs.

In Exhibit 600.60, the reports prepared for the department supervisors show the budgeted and actual manufacturing costs for their departments. The supervisors can use these reports to focus on areas of significant difference, such as the difference between the budgeted and actual materials cost. The supervisor of Department 1 in Plant A may use additional information from a scrap report to determine why materials are over budget. Such a report might show that materials were scrapped as a result of machine malfunctions, improper use of machines by employees, or low quality materials.

For higher levels of management, responsibility accounting reports are usually more summarized than for lower levels of management. In Exhibit 600.60, for example, the budget performance report for the plant manager summarizes

Exhibit 600.59 *Cost Centers in a University*

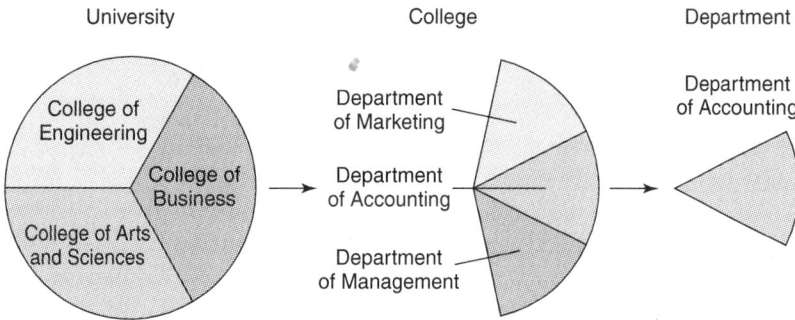

650. OPERATING BUDGETS AND PERFORMANCE EVALUATION

Exhibit 600.60 *Responsibility Accounting Reports for Cost Centers*

Budget Performance Report
Vice-President, Production
for the Month Ended October 31, 2003

	Budget	Actual	Over Budget	Under Budget
Administration	$ 19,500	$ 19,700	$ 200	
Plant A	467,475	470,330	2,855	
Plant B	395,225	394,300		$925
	$882,200	$884,330	$3,055	$925

Budget Performance Report
Manager, Plant A
for the Month Ended October 31, 2003

	Budget	Actual	Over Budget	Under Budget
Administration	$ 17,500	$ 17,350		$150
Department 1	109,725	111,280	$ 1,555	
Department 2	190,500	192,600	2,100	
Department 3	149,475	149,100		650
	$467,475	$470,330	$ 3,655	$800

Budget Performance Report
Supervisor, Department I—Plant A
for the Month Ended October 31, 2003

	Budget	Actual	Over Budget	Under Budget
Factory wages	$ 58,100	$ 58,000		$100
Materials	32,500	34,225	$1,725	
Supervisory salaries	6,400	6,400		
Power and light	5,750	5,690		60
Depreciation of plant and equipment	4,000	4,000		
Maintenance	2,000	1,990		
Insurance and property taxes	975	975		10
	$109,725	$111,280	$1,725	$170

budget and actual cost data for the departments under the manager's supervision. This report enables the plant manager to identify the department supervisors responsible for major differences. Likewise, the report for the vice-president of production summarizes the cost data for each plant. The plant managers can thus be held responsible for major differences in budgeted and actual costs in their plants.

Responsibility Accounting for Profit Centers

In a **profit center,** the unit manager has the responsibility and the authority to make decisions that affect both costs and revenues (and thus profits). Profit centers may be divisions, departments, or products. For example, a consumer products company might organize its brands (product lines) as divisional profit centers. The manager of each brand could have responsibility for product cost and decisions regarding revenues, such as setting sales prices. The manager of a profit center does not make decisions concerning the fixed assets invested in the center. For example, the brand manager of a consumer products company does not make the decision to expand the plant capacity for the brand.

Profit centers are often viewed as an excellent training assignment for new managers. For example, Lester B. Korn, Chairman and Chief Executive Officer of **Korn/Ferry International,** offered the following strategy for young executives en route to top management positions.

Profit centers may be divisions, departments, or products.

Get Profit-Center Responsibility—Obtain a position where you can prove yourself as both a specialist with particular expertise and a generalist who can exercise leadership, authority, and inspire enthusiasm among colleagues and subordinates.

Responsibility accounting reports usually show the revenues, expenses, and income from operations for the profit center. The profit center income statement should include only revenues and expenses that are controlled by the manager. **Controllable revenues** are revenues earned by the profit center. **Controllable expenses** are costs that can be influenced (controlled) by the decisions of profit center managers. For example, the manager of the Men's Department at **Nordstrom** most likely controls the salaries of department personnel but does not control the property taxes of the store.

Service Department Charges

We will illustrate profit center income reporting for the Nova Entertainment Group (NEG). Assume that NEG is a diversified entertainment company with two operating divisions organized as profit centers: the Theme Park Division and the Movie Production Division. The revenues and operating expenses for the two divisions are shown on the following page. The operating expenses consist of the direct expenses, such as the wages and salaries of a division's employees.

	Theme Park Division	Movie Production Division
Revenues	$6,000,000	$2,500,000
Operating expenses	2,495,000	405,000

In addition to direct expenses, divisions may also have expenses for services provided by internal centralized **service departments.** These service departments are often more efficient at providing service than are outside service providers. Examples of such service departments include the following.

- Research and Development
- Government Relations
- Telecommunications
- Publications and Graphics
- Facilities Management
- Purchasing
- Information Systems
- Payroll Accounting
- Transportation
- Personnel Administration

A profit center's income from operations should reflect the cost of any internal services used by the center. To illustrate, assume that NEG established a Payroll Accounting Department. The costs of the payroll services, called **service department charges,** are charged to NEG's profit centers, as shown in Exhibit 600.61.

Exhibit 600.61 *Payroll Accounting Department Charges to NEG's Theme Park and Movie Production Divisions*

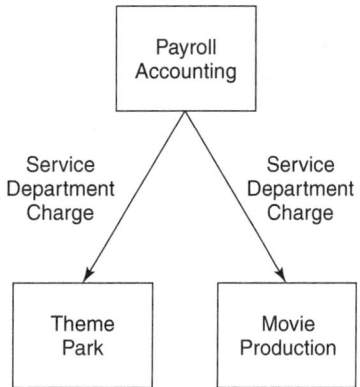

Service department charges are *indirect expenses* to a profit center. They are similar to the expenses that would be incurred if the profit center had purchased the services from a source outside the company. A profit center manager has control over such expenses if the manager is free to choose *how much* service is used from the service department.

To illustrate service department charges, assume that NEG has two other service departments—Purchasing and Legal, in addition to Payroll Accounting. The expenses for the year ended December 31, 2003, for each service department are as follows.

Purchasing	$400,000
Payroll Accounting	255,000
Legal	250,000
Total	$905,000

An **activity base** for each service department is used to charge service department expenses to the Theme Park and Movie Production Divisions. The activity base for each service department is a measure of the services performed. For NEG, the service department activity bases are as follows.

Department	Activity Base
Purchasing	Number of purchase requisitions
Payroll Accounting	Number of payroll checks
Legal	Number of billed hours

The use of services by the Theme Park and Movie Production Divisions is as follows.

	Service Usage		
	Purchasing	Payroll Accounting	Legal
Theme Park Division	25,000 purchase requisitions	12,000 payroll checks	100 billed hours
Movie Production Division	15,000	3,000	900
Total	40,000 purchase requisitions	15,000 payroll checks	1,000 billed hours

The rates at which services are charged to each division are called **service department charge rates.** These rates are determined by dividing each service department's expenses by the total service usage as follows.

$$\text{Purchasing: } \frac{\$400,000}{40,000 \text{ purchase requisitions}} = \$10 \text{ per purchase requisition}$$

$$\text{Payroll Accounting: } \frac{\$255,000}{15,000 \text{ payroll checks}} = \$17 \text{ per payroll check}$$

$$\text{Legal: } \frac{\$250,000}{1,000 \text{ hours}} = \$250 \text{ per hour}$$

Example 31 *The centralized payroll department has expenses of $120,000. The department processed a total of 25,000 payroll checks for the period. If the Eastern Division has 6,000 payroll checks for the period, how much should it be charged for payroll services?*

$28,800 [($120,000/25,000) × 6,000]

The use of services by the Theme Park and Movie Production Divisions is multiplied by the service department charge rates to determine the charges to each division, as shown in Exhibit 600.62.

The Theme Park Division employs many temporary and part-time employees who are paid weekly. This is in contrast to the Movie Production Division, which has a more permanent payroll that is paid on a monthly basis. As a re-

Exhibit 600.62 *Service Department Charges to NEG Divisions*

Nova Entertainment Group
Service Department Charges to NEG Divisions
for the Year Ended December 31, 2003

Service Department	Theme Park Division	Movie Production Division
Purchasing (Note A)	$250,000	$150,000
Payroll Accounting (Note B)	204,000	51,000
Legal (Note C)	25,000	225,000
Total service department charges	$479,000	$426,000

Note A:
25,000 purchase requisitions × $10 per purchase requisition = $250,000
15,000 purchase requisitions × $10 per purchase requisition = $150,000

Note B:
12,000 payroll checks × $17 per check = $204,000
3,000 payroll checks × $17 per check = $51,000

Note C:
100 hours × $250 per hour = $25,000
900 hours × $250 per hour = $225,000

Exhibit 600.63 *Divisional Income Statements—NEG*

Nova Entertainment Group
Divisional Income Statements
for the Year Ended December 31, 2003

	Theme Park Division	Movie Production Division
Revenues*	$6,000,000	$2,500,000
Operating expenses	2,495,000	405,000
Income from operations before service department charges	$3,505,000	$2,095,000
Less service department charges:		
Purchasing	$ 250,000	$ 150,000
Payroll Accounting	204,000	51,000
Legal	25,000	225,000
Total service department charges	$ 479,000	$ 426,000
Income from operations	$3,026,000	$1,669,000

*For a profit center that sells products, the income statement would show: Net sales − Cost of goods sold = Gross profit. The operating expenses would be deducted from the gross profit to get the income from operations before service department charges.

sult, the Theme Park Division requires 12,000 payroll checks. This results in a large service charge from Payroll Accounting to the Theme Park Division. In contrast, the Movie Production Division uses many legal services for contract negotiations. Thus, there is a large service charge from Legal to the Movie Production Division.

Profit Center Reporting

The divisional income statements for NEG are presented in Exhibit 600.63. These statements show the service department charges to the divisions.

The **income from operations** is a measure of a manager's performance. In evaluating the profit center manager, the income from operations should be compared over time to a budget. It should not be compared across profit centers, since the profit centers are usually different in terms of size, products, and customers.

Example 32 *If sales are $500,000, the cost of goods sold is $285,000, selling expenses are $85,000, and service department charges are $53,000, what is the income from operations?*

$77,000 ($500,000 − $285,000 − $85,000 − $53,000)

Responsibility Accounting for Investment Centers

In an **investment center,** the unit manager has the responsibility and the authority to make decisions that affect not only costs and revenues but also the assets invested in the center. Investment centers are widely used in highly diversified companies organized by divisions.

The manager of an investment center has more authority and responsibility than the manager of a cost center or a profit center. The manager of an investment center occupies a position similar to that of a chief operating officer or president of a company and is evaluated in much the same way.

Because investment center managers have responsibility for revenues and expenses, income from operations is an important part of investment center reporting. In addition, because the manager has responsibility for the assets invested in the center, two additional measures of performance are often used. These measures are the rate of return on investment and residual income. Top management often compares these measures across investment centers to reward performance and assess investment in the centers.

To illustrate, assume that DataLink Inc. is a cellular phone company that has three regional divisions, Northern, Central, and Southern. Condensed divisional income statements for the investment centers are shown in Exhibit 600.64.

Using only income from operations, the Central Division is the most profitable division. However, income from operations does not reflect the amount of assets invested in each center. For example, if the amount of assets invested in the Central Division is twice that of the other divisions, then the Central Division would be the least profitable in terms of the rate of return on these assets.

Rate of Return on Investment

Because investment center managers also control the amount of assets invested in their centers, they should be held accountable for the use of these assets. One measure that considers the amount of assets invested is the **rate of return on investment** (ROI) or **rate of return on assets.** It is one of the most widely used measures for investment centers and is computed as follows.

$$\text{Rate of return on investment ROI} = \frac{\text{Income from operations}}{\text{Invested assets}}$$

Exhibit 600.64 *Divisional Income Statements—DataLink Inc.*

DataLink Inc.
Divisional Income Statements
for the Year Ended December 31, 2003

	Northern Division	Central Division	Southern Division
Revenues	$560,000	$672,000	$750,000
Operating expenses	336,000	470,400	562,500
Income from operations before service department charges	$224,000	$201,600	$187,500
Service department charges	154,000	117,600	112,500
Income from operations	$ 70,000	$ 84,000	$ 75,000

The rate of return on investment is useful because the three factors subject to control by divisional managers (revenues, expenses, and invested assets) are used in its computation. By measuring profitability relative to the amount of assets invested in each division, the rate of return on investment can be used to compare divisions. The higher the rate of return on investment, the better the division utilizes its assets to generate income. To illustrate, the rate of return on investment for each division of DataLink Inc., based on the book value of invested assets, is as follows.

	Northern Division	Central Division	Southern Division
Income from operations	$ 70,000	$ 84,000	$ 75,000
Invested assets	$350,000	$700,000	$500,000
Rate of return on investment	20%	12%	15%

Although the Central Division generated the largest income from operations, its rate of return on investment (12%) is the lowest. Hence, relative to the assets invested, the Central Division is the least profitable division. In comparison, the rate of return on investment of the Northern Division is 20% and the Southern Division is 15%. These differences in the rates of return on investment can be further analyzed using an expanded formula for the rate of return on investment.

In the expanded formula, the rate of return on investment is the product of two factors. The first factor is the ratio of income from operations to sales, often called the **profit margin.** The second factor is the ratio of sales to invested assets, often called the **investment turnover.** In the illustration at the left, profits can be earned by either increasing the investment turnover (turning the crank faster), by increasing the profit margin (increasing the size of the opening), or both.

Using the expanded expression yields the same rate of return on investment for the Northern Division, 20%, as computed previously.

Rate of return on investment (ROI) = Profit margin × Investment turnover

$$\text{Rate of return on investment (ROI)} = \frac{\text{Income from operations}}{\text{Sales}} \times \frac{\text{Sales}}{\text{Invested assets}}$$

$$\text{ROI} = \frac{\$70,000}{\$560,000} \times \frac{\$560,000}{\$350,000}$$

$$\text{ROI} = 12.5\% \times 1.6$$

$$\text{ROI} = 20\%$$

The expanded expression for the rate of return on investment is useful in evaluating and controlling divisions. This is because the profit margin and the investment turnover focus on the underlying operating relationships of each division.

The profit margin component focuses on profitability by indicating the rate of profit earned on each sales dollar. If a division's profit margin increases, and all other factors remain the same, the division's rate of return on investment will increase. For example, a division might add more profitable products to its sales mix and thereby increase its overall profit margin and rate of return on investment.

The profit margin indicates the rate of profit on each sales dollar, while the investment turnover indicates the rate of sales on each dollar of invested assets.

The investment turnover component focuses on efficiency in using assets and indicates the rate at which sales are generated for each dollar of invested assets. The more sales per dollar invested, the greater the efficiency in using the assets. If a division's investment turnover increases, and all other factors remain the same, the division's rate of return on investment will increase. For example, a division might attempt to increase sales through special sales promotions or reduce inventory assets by using just-in-time principles, either of which would increase investment turnover.

The rate of return on investment, using the expanded expression for each division of DataLink Inc., is summarized as follows.

$$\text{Rate of return on investment (ROI)} = \frac{\text{Income from operations}}{\text{Sales}} \times \frac{\text{Sales}}{\text{Invested assets}}$$

$$\text{Northern Division (ROI)} = \frac{\$70,000}{\$560,000} \times \frac{\$560,000}{\$350,000}$$

$$\text{ROI} = 12.5\% \times 1.6$$
$$\text{ROI} = 20\%$$

$$\text{Central Division (ROI)} = \frac{\$84,000}{\$672,000} \times \frac{\$672,000}{\$700,000}$$

$$\text{ROI} = 12.5\% \times 0.96$$
$$\text{ROI} = 12\%$$

$$\text{Southern Division (ROI)} = \frac{\$75,000}{\$750,000} \times \frac{\$750,000}{\$500,000}$$

$$\text{ROI} = 10\% \times 1.5$$
$$\text{ROI} = 15\%$$

Although the Northern and Central Divisions have the same profit margins, the Northern Division investment turnover (1.6) is larger than that of the Central Division (0.96). Thus, by using its invested assets more efficiently, the Northern Division's rate of return on investment is higher than the Central Division's. The Southern Division's profit margin of 10% and investment turnover of 1.5 are lower than those of the Northern Division. The product of these factors results in a return on investment of 15% for the Southern Division, compared to 20% for the Northern Division.

To determine possible ways of increasing the rate of return on investment, the profit margin and investment turnover for a division may be analyzed. For example, if the Northern Division is in a highly competitive industry in which the profit margin cannot be easily increased, the division manager might focus on increasing the investment turnover. To illustrate, assume that the revenues of the Northern Division could be increased by $56,000 through increasing operating expenses, such as advertising, to $385,000. The Northern Division's income from operations will increase from $70,000 to $77,000, as shown below.

Revenues ($560,000 + $56,000)	$616,000
Operating expenses	385,000
Income from operations before service department charges	$231,000
Service department charges	154,000
Income from operations	$77,000

The rate of return on investment for the Northern Division, using the expanded expression, is recomputed as follows

$$\text{Rate of return on investment (ROI)} = \frac{\text{Income from operations}}{\text{Sales}} \times \frac{\text{Sales}}{\text{Invested assets}}$$

$$\text{Northern Division revised (ROI)} = \frac{\$77,000}{\$616,000} \times \frac{\$616,000}{\$350,000}$$

$$\text{ROI} = 12.5\% \times 1.76$$
$$\text{ROI} = 22\%$$

Although the Northern Division's profit margin remains the same (12.5%), the investment turnover has increased from 1.6 to 1.76, an increase of 10% (0.16 ÷ 1.6). The 10% increase in investment turnover also increases the rate of return on investment by 10% (from 20% to 22%).

In addition to using it as a performance measure, the rate of return on investment may assist management in other ways. For example, in considering a decision to expand the operations of DataLink Inc., management might consider giving priority to the Northern Division because it earns the highest rate of return on investment. If the current rates of return on investment are maintained in the future, an investment in the Northern Division will return 20 cents

(20%) on each dollar invested. In contrast, investments in the Central Division will earn only 12 cents per dollar invested, and investments in the Southern Division will return only 15 cents per dollar.

A disadvantage of the rate of return on investment as a performance measure is that it may lead divisional managers to reject new investments that could be profitable for the company as a whole. For example, the Northern Division of DataLink Inc. has an overall rate of return on investment of 20%. The minimum acceptable rate of return on investment for DataLink Inc. is 10%. The manager of the Northern Division has the opportunity of investing in a new project that is estimated will earn a 17% rate of return. If the manager of the Northern Division invests in the project, however, the Northern Division's overall rate of return will decrease from 20%. Thus, the division manager might decide to reject the project, even though the investment would exceed DataLink's minimum acceptable rate of return on investment. The CFO of **Millennium Chemicals Inc.** referred to a similar situation by stating: "We had too many divisional executives who failed to spend money on capital projects with more than satisfactory returns because those projects would have lowered the average return on assets of their particular business."

Example 33 Income from operations is $35,000, invested assets are $140,000, and sales are $437,500. What is the (a) profit margin, (b) investment turnover, and (c) rate of return on investment?

(a) 8% ($35,000/$437,500);
(b) 3.125 ($437,500/$140,000);
(c) 25% (8% × 3.125, or $35,000/$140,000)

Residual Income

An additional measure of evaluating divisional performance—residual income—is useful in overcoming some of the disadvantages associated with the rate of return on investment. **Residual income** is the excess of income from operations over a minimum acceptable income from operations, as illustrated below.

Income from Operations − Minimum Acceptable Rate of Return on Assets = Residual Income

The minimum acceptable income from operations is normally computed by multiplying a minimum rate of return by the amount of divisional assets. The minimum rate is set by top management, based on such factors as the cost of financing the business operations. To illustrate, assume that DataLink Inc. has established 10% as the minimum acceptable rate of return on divisional assets. The residual incomes for the three divisions are as follows.

	Northern Division	Central Division	Southern Division
Income from operations	$70,000	$84,000	$75,000
Minimum acceptable income from operations as a percent of assets:			
$350,000 × 10%	35,000		
$700,000 × 10%		70,000	
$500,000 × 10%			50,000
Residual income	$35,000	$14,000	$25,000

The Northern Division has more residual income than the other divisions, even though it has the least amount of income from operations. This is because the assets on which to earn a minimum acceptable rate of return are less for the Northern Division than for the other divisions.

The major advantage of residual income as a performance measure is that it considers both the minimum acceptable rate of return and the total amount of the income from operations earned by each division. Residual income encourages division managers to maximize income from operations in excess of the minimum. This provides an incentive to accept any project that is expected to have a rate of return in excess of the minimum. Thus, the residual income number supports both divisional and overall company objectives.

Example 34 *The International Division has income from operations of $87,000 and assets of $240,000. The minimum acceptable rate of return on assets is 12%. What is the residual income for the division?*

$58,200 [$87,000 − ($240,000 × 12%)]

The Balanced Scorecard

In addition to financial divisional performance measures, many companies are also relying on nonfinancial divisional measures. One popular evaluation approach is the **balanced scorecard.** The balanced scorecard is a set of financial and nonfinancial measures that reflect multiple performance dimensions of a business. A common balanced scorecard design measures performance in the innovation and learning, customer, internal, and financial dimensions of a business. These four areas can be diagrammed as shown in Exhibit 600.65.

The innovation and learning perspective measures the amount of innovation in an organization. For example, a drug company, such as **Merck,** would measure the number of drugs in its FDA (Food and Drug Administration) approval pipeline, the amount of research and development (R&D) spending per period, and the length of time it takes to turn ideas into marketable products. Managing the performance of its R&D processes is critical to Merck's longer-term prospects and thus would be an additional performance perspective beyond the financial numbers. The customer perspective would measure customer satisfaction, loyalty, and perceptions. For example, **Amazon.com** measures the number of repeat visitors to its Web site as a measure of customer loyalty. Amazon.com needs repeat business because the costs to acquire a new customer are very high. The internal process perspective measures the effectiveness and efficiency of internal business processes. For example, **DaimlerChrysler** measures quality by the average warranty claims per automobile, measures efficiency by the average labor hours per automobile, and measures the average time to assemble each automobile. The financial perspective measures the economic performance of the responsibility center as we have illustrated in the previous sections of this chapter. All companies will use financial measures. For example, one survey found that over 70% of companies use income from operations as a percent of sales, 62% use rate of return on investment, and 13% use residual income as financial performance measures.

Exhibit 600.65 *The Balanced Scorecard*

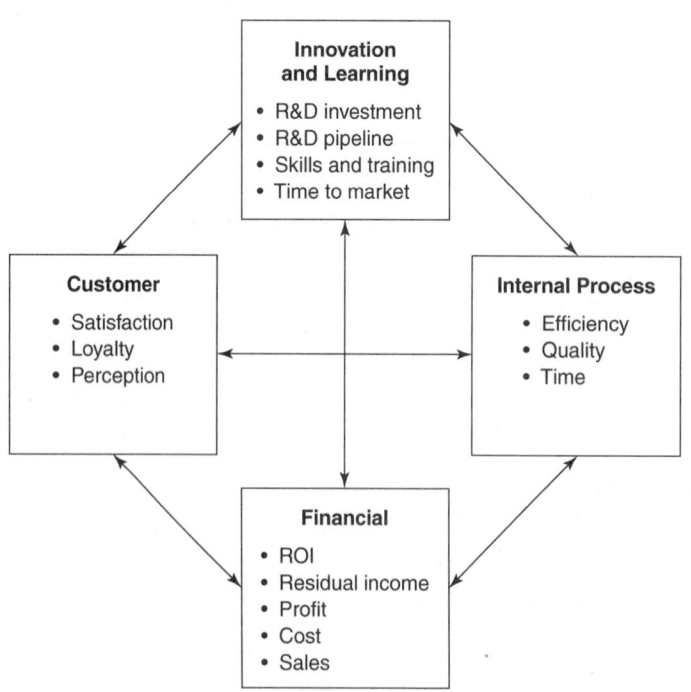

The balanced scorecard is designed to reveal the underlying nonfinancial drivers, or causes, of financial performance. For example, if a business improves customer satisfaction, this will likely lead to improved financial performance. In addition, the balanced scorecard helps managers consider trade-offs between short- and long-term performance. For example, additional investment in research and development (R&D) would penalize the short-term financial perspective, because R&D is an expense that reduces income from operations. However, the innovation perspective would measure additional R&D expenditures favorably, because current R&D expenditures will lead to future profits from new products. The balanced scorecard will motivate the manager to invest in new R&D, even though it is recognized as a current period expense. A recent survey has indicated that 40% of the companies use or are planning to use the balanced scorecard. Thus, the balanced scorecard is gaining acceptance because of its ability to reveal the underlying causes of financial performance, while helping managers consider the short- and long-term implications of their decisions.

Transfer Pricing

When divisions transfer products or render services to each other, a **transfer price** is used to charge for the products or services. Because transfer prices affect the goals for both divisions, setting these prices is a sensitive matter for division managers.

Transfer prices should be set so that overall company income is increased when goods are transferred between divisions. As we will illustrate, however, transfer prices may be misused in such a way that overall company income suffers.

In the following paragraphs, we discuss various approaches to setting transfer prices. Exhibit 600.66 shows the range of prices that results from common approaches to setting transfer prices. Transfer prices can be set as low as the variable cost per unit or as high as the market price. Often, transfer prices are negotiated at some point between variable cost per unit and market price.

A survey of transfer pricing practices has reported the following usage.

Cost price (variable or full)	46%
Market price	37
Negotiated price	17

Source: Roger Y. W. Tang, "Transfer Pricing in the 1990's," *Management Accounting,* February 1992, pp. 22–26.

Transfer prices may be used when decentralized units are organized as cost, profit, or investment centers. To illustrate, we will use a packaged snack food company (Wilson Company) with no service departments and two operating divisions (Eastern and Western) organized as investment centers. Condensed divisional income statements for Wilson Company, assuming no transfers between divisions, are shown in Exhibit 600.67.

Exhibit 600.66 *Commonly Used Transfer Prices*

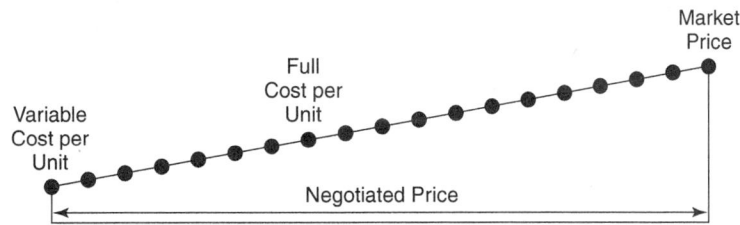

Exhibit 600.67 *Wilson Company Income Statement —No Transfers Between Divisions*

<table>
<tr><td colspan="4" align="center">Wilson Company
Divisional Income Statements
for the Year Ended December 31, 2003</td></tr>
<tr><td></td><td>Eastern Division</td><td>Western Division</td><td>Total</td></tr>
<tr><td>Sales:</td><td></td><td></td><td></td></tr>
<tr><td>50,000 units × $20 per unit</td><td>$1,000,000</td><td></td><td>$1,000,000</td></tr>
<tr><td>20,000 units × $40 per unit</td><td></td><td>$800,000</td><td>800,000</td></tr>
<tr><td></td><td></td><td></td><td>$1,800,000</td></tr>
<tr><td>Expenses:</td><td></td><td></td><td></td></tr>
<tr><td>Variable:</td><td></td><td></td><td></td></tr>
<tr><td>50,000 units × $10 per unit</td><td>$500,000</td><td></td><td>$500,000</td></tr>
<tr><td>20,000 units × $30* per unit</td><td></td><td>$600,000</td><td>600,000</td></tr>
<tr><td>Fixed</td><td>300,000</td><td>100,000</td><td>400,000</td></tr>
<tr><td>Total expenses</td><td>$800,000</td><td>$700,000</td><td>$1,500,000</td></tr>
<tr><td>Income from operations</td><td>$200,000</td><td>$100,000</td><td>$300,000</td></tr>
</table>

*$20 of the $30 per unit represents materials costs, and the remaining $10 per unit represents other variable conversion expenses incurred within the Western Division.

Market Price Approach

Using the **market price approach,** the transfer price is the price at which the product or service transferred could be sold to outside buyers. If an outside market exists for the product or service transferred, the current market price may be a proper transfer price.

To illustrate, assume that materials used by Wilson Company in producing snack food in the Western Division are currently purchased from an outside supplier at $20 per unit. The same materials are produced by the Eastern Division. The Eastern Division is operating at full capacity of 50,000 units and can sell all it produces to either the Western Division or to outside buyers. A transfer price of $20 per unit (the market price) has no effect on the Eastern Division's income or total company income. The Eastern Division will earn revenues of $20 per unit on all its production and sales, regardless of who buys its product. Likewise, the Western Division will pay $20 per unit for materials (the market price). Thus, the use of the market price as the transfer price has no effect on the Eastern Division's income or total company income. In this situation, the use of the market price as the transfer price is proper. The condensed divisional income statements for Wilson Company in this case are also shown in Exhibit 600.67.

Negotiated Price Approach

If unused or excess capacity exists in the supplying division (the Eastern Division), and the transfer price is equal to the market price, total company profit may not be maximized. This is because the manager of the Western Division will be indifferent toward purchasing materials from the Eastern Division or from outside suppliers. Thus, the Western Division may purchase the materials from outside suppliers. If, however, the Western Division purchases the materials from the Eastern Division, the difference between the market price of $20 and the variable costs of the Eastern Division can cover fixed costs and contribute to company profits. When the negotiated price approach is used in this situation, the manager of the Western Division is encouraged to purchase the materials from the Eastern Division.

The **negotiated price approach** allows the managers of decentralized units to agree (negotiate) among themselves as to the transfer price. The only constraint on the negotiations is that the transfer price be less than the market price but greater than the supplying division's variable costs per unit.

To illustrate the use of the negotiated price approach, assume that instead of a capacity of 50,000 units, the Eastern Division's capacity is 70,000 units. In addition, assume that the Eastern Division can continue to sell only 50,000 units to outside buyers. A transfer price less than $20 would encourage the manager of the Western Division to purchase from the Eastern Division. This is because the Western Division's materials cost per unit would decrease, and its income from operations would increase. At the same time, a transfer price above the Eastern Division's variable costs per unit of $10 (from Exhibit 600.67) would encourage the manager of the Eastern Division to use the excess capacity to supply materials to the Western Division. In doing so, the Eastern Division's income from operations would increase.

Exhibit 600.68 *Wilson Company Income Statements —Negotiated Transfer Price*

Wilson Company
Divisional Income Statements
For the Year Ended December 31, 2003

	Eastern Division	Western Division	Total
Sales:			
50,000 units × $20 per unit	$1,000,000		$1,000,000
20,000 units × $15 per unit	300,000		300,000
20,000 units × $40 per unit		$800,000	800,000
	$1,300,000	$800,000	$2,100,000
Expenses:			
Variable:			
70,000 units × $10 per unit	$700,000		$700,000
20,000 units × $25* per unit		$500,000	500,000
Fixed	300,000	100,000	400,000
Total expenses	$1,000,000	$600,000	$1,600,000
Income from operations	$300,000	$200,000	$500,000

*$10 of the $25 are variable conversion expenses incurred solely within the Western Division, and $15 per unit represents the transfer price per unit from the Eastern Division.

We continue the illustration with the aid of Exhibit 600.68, assuming that Wilson Company's division managers agree to a transfer price of $15 for the Eastern Division's product. By purchasing from the Eastern Division, the Western Division's materials cost would be $5 per unit less. At the same time, the Eastern Division would increase its sales by $300,000 (20,000 units × $15 per unit) and increase its income by $100,000 ($300,000 sales − $200,000 variable costs). The effect of reducing the Western Division's materials cost by $100,000 (20,000 units × $5 per unit) is to increase its income by $100,000. Therefore, Wilson Company's income is increased by $200,000 ($100,000 reported by the Eastern Division and $100,000 reported by the Western Division), as shown in the condensed income statements in Exhibit 600.68.

In this illustration, any transfer price less than the market price of $20 but greater than the Eastern Division's unit variable costs of $10 would increase each division's income. In addition, overall company profit would increase by $200,000. By establishing a range of $20 to $10 for the transfer price, each division manager has an incentive to negotiate the transfer of the materials.

Cost Price Approach

Under the **cost price approach,** cost is used to set transfer prices. With this approach, a variety of cost concepts may be used. For example, cost may refer to either total product cost per unit or variable product cost per unit. If total product cost per unit is used, direct materials, direct labor, and factory overhead are included in the transfer price. If variable product cost per unit is used, the fixed factory overhead component of total product cost is excluded from the transfer price.

Either actual costs or standard (budgeted) costs may be used in applying the cost price approach. If actual costs are used, inefficiencies of the producing division are transferred to the purchasing division. Thus, there is little incentive for the producing division to control costs carefully. For this reason, most companies use standard costs in the cost price approach. In this way, differences between actual and standard costs remain with the producing division for cost control purposes.

When division managers have responsibility for cost centers, the cost price approach to transfer pricing is proper and is often used. The cost price approach may not be proper, however, for decentralized operations organized as profit or investment centers. In profit and investment centers, division managers have responsibility for both revenues and expenses. The use of cost as a transfer price ignores the supplying division manager's responsibility for revenues. When a supplying division's sales are all intracompany transfers, for example, using the cost price approach prevents the supplying division from reporting any income from operations. A cost-based transfer price may therefore not motivate the division manager to make intracompany transfers, even though they are in the best interests of the company.

Decision Making and Accounting

Decision Models in Accounting

Managers must consider the effects of alternative decisions on their businesses. In this section, we discuss differential analysis, which reports the effects of alternative decisions on total revenues and costs. We describe and illustrate practical approaches to setting product prices. We discuss how production bottlenecks influence product mix and pricing decisions. Finally, we show two income models and describe how management uses them in decision making.

Differential Analysis

Planning for future operations involves decision making. For some decisions, revenue and cost data from the accounting records may be useful. However, the revenue and cost data for use in evaluating courses of future operations or choosing among competing alternatives are often not available in the accounting records and must be estimated.
Consider:

- The decision by **General Motors** to purchase on-board communications products from **Delphi Automotive Systems** instead of making them internally.
- The decision by **Marriott** hotels to accept a special price from a bid placed on **priceline.com**.
- The decision by **TWA** to discontinue service to Rome, Madrid, and Barcelona.

In each of these decisions, the estimated revenues and costs were **relevant.** The relevant revenues and costs focus on the differences between each alternative. Costs that have been incurred in the past are not relevant to the decision. These costs are called **sunk costs.**

Differential revenue is the amount of increase or decrease in revenue expected from a course of action as compared with an alternative. To illustrate, assume that certain equipment is being used to manufacture calculators, which are expected to generate revenue of $150,000. If the equipment could be used to make digital clocks, which would generate revenue of $175,000, the differential revenue from making and selling digital clocks is $25,000.

Differential cost is the amount of increase or decrease in cost that is expected from a course of action as compared with an alternative. For example, if an increase in advertising expenditures from $100,000 to $150,000 is being considered, the differential cost of the action is $50,000.

Differential income or loss is the difference between the differential revenue and the differential costs. Differential income indicates that a particular decision is expected to be profitable, while a differential loss indicates the opposite.

Differential analysis focuses on the effect of alternative courses of action on the relevant revenues and costs. For example, if a manager must decide between two alternatives, differential analysis would involve comparing the differential revenues of the two alternatives with the differential costs.

Decision	Differential Analysis
Alternative A	
	Differential revenue
or	− Differential costs
	Differential income or loss
Alternative B	

In this section, we will discuss the use of differential analysis in analyzing the following alternatives.

1. Leasing or selling equipment
2. Discontinuing an unprofitable segment
3. Manufacturing or purchasing a needed part

4. Replacing usable fixed assets
5. Processing further or selling an intermediate product
6. Accepting additional business at a special price

1. Lease or Sell Equipment

Management may have a choice between leasing or selling a piece of equipment that is no longer needed in the business. In deciding which option is best, management may use differential analysis. To illustrate, assume that Marcus Company is considering disposing of equipment that cost $200,000 and has $120,000 of accumulated depreciation to date. Marcus Company can sell the equipment through a broker for $100,000 less a 6% commission. Alternatively, Potamkin Company (the lessee) has offered to lease the equipment for five years for a total of $160,000. At the end of the fifth year of the lease, the equipment is expected to have no residual value. During the period of the lease, Marcus Company (the lessor) will incur repair, insurance, and property tax expenses estimated at $35,000. Exhibit 600.69 shows Marcus Company's analysis of whether to lease or sell the equipment.

Note that in Exhibit 600.69, the $80,000 book value ($200,000 − $120,000) of the equipment is a sunk cost and is not considered in the analysis. The $80,000 is a cost that resulted from a previous decision. It is not affected by the alternatives now being considered in leasing or selling the equipment. The relevant factors to be considered are the differential revenues and differential costs associated with the lease or sell decision. This analysis is verified by the traditional analysis in Exhibit 600.70.

The alternatives presented in Exhibits 600.69 and 600.70 were relatively simple. However, regardless of the complexity, the approach to differential analysis is basically the same. Two additional factors that often need to be considered are (1) differential revenue from investing the funds generated by the alternatives and (2) any income tax

Exhibit 600.69 *Differential Analysis Report—Lease or Sell Equipment*

Proposal to Lease or Sell Equipment June 22, 2003		
Differential revenue from alternatives:		
Revenue from lease	$160,000	
Revenue from sale	100,000	
Differential revenue from lease		$60,000
Differential cost of alternatives:		
Repair, insurance, and property tax expenses	$ 35,000	
Commission expense on sale	6,000	
Differential cost of lease		29,000
Net differential income from the lease alternative		**$31,000**

Exhibit 600.70 *Traditional Analysis*

Lease or Sell			
Lease alternative:			
Revenue from lease		$160,000	
Depreciation expense for remaining five years	$80,000		
Repair, insurance, and property tax expenses	35,000	115,000	
Net gain			$45,000
Sell alternative:			
Sales price		$100,000	
Book value of equipment	$80,000		
Commission expense	6,000	86,000	
Net gain			14,000
Net differential income from the lease alternative			**$31,000**

differential. In Exhibit 600.69, there could be differential interest revenue related to investing the cash flows from the two alternatives. Any income tax differential would be related to the differences in the timing of the income from the alternatives and the differences in the amount of investment income.

2. Discontinue a Segment or Product

When a product or a department, branch, territory, or other segment of a business is generating losses, management may consider eliminating the product or segment. It is often assumed, sometimes in error, that the total income from operations of a business would be increased if the operating loss could be eliminated. Discontinuing the product or segment usually eliminates all of the product or segment's variable costs (direct materials, direct labor, sales commissions, and so on). However, if the product or segment is a relatively small part of the business, the fixed costs (depreciation, insurance, property taxes, and so on) may not be decreased by discontinuing it. It is possible in this case for the total operating income of a company to decrease rather than increase by eliminating the product or segment. To illustrate, the income statement for **Battle Creek Cereal Co.** presented in Exhibit 600.71 is for a normal year ending August 31, 2003.

Because Bran Flakes incurs annual losses, management is considering discontinuing it. Total annual operating income of $80,000 ($40,000 Toasted Oats + $40,000 Corn Flakes) might seem to be indicated by the income statement in Exhibit 600.71 if Bran Flakes is discontinued.

Discontinuing Bran Flakes, however, would actually decrease operating income by $15,000, to $54,000 ($69,000 − $15,000). This is shown by the differential analysis report in Exhibit 600.72, in which we assume that discontinuing Bran Flakes would have no effect on fixed costs and expenses.

Exhibit 600.71 *Income (Loss) by Product*

<table>
<tr><td colspan="5" align="center">Battle Creek Cereal Co.
Condensed Income Statement
for the Year Ended August 31, 2003</td></tr>
<tr><td></td><td>Corn Flakes</td><td>Toasted Oats</td><td>Bran Flakes</td><td>Total</td></tr>
<tr><td>Sales</td><td>$500,000</td><td>$400,000</td><td>$100,000</td><td>$1,000,000</td></tr>
<tr><td>Cost of goods sold:</td><td></td><td></td><td></td><td></td></tr>
<tr><td> Variable costs</td><td>$220,000</td><td>$200,000</td><td>$ 60,000</td><td>$ 480,000</td></tr>
<tr><td> Fixed costs</td><td>120,000</td><td>80,000</td><td>20,000</td><td>220,000</td></tr>
<tr><td> Total cost of goods sold</td><td>$340,000</td><td>$280,000</td><td>$ 80,000</td><td>$ 700,000</td></tr>
<tr><td>Gross profit</td><td>$160,000</td><td>$120,000</td><td>$ 20,000</td><td>$ 300,000</td></tr>
<tr><td>Operating expenses:</td><td></td><td></td><td></td><td></td></tr>
<tr><td> Variable expenses</td><td>$ 95,000</td><td>$ 60,000</td><td>$ 25,000</td><td>$ 180,000</td></tr>
<tr><td> Fixed expenses</td><td>25,000</td><td>20,000</td><td>6,000</td><td>51,000</td></tr>
<tr><td> Total operating expenses</td><td>$120,000</td><td>$ 80,000</td><td>$ 31,000</td><td>$ 231,000</td></tr>
<tr><td>Income (loss) from operations</td><td>$ 40,000</td><td>$ 40,000</td><td>$(11,000)</td><td>$ 69,000</td></tr>
</table>

Exhibit 600.72 *Differential Analysis Report—Discontinue an Unprofitable Segment*

<table>
<tr><td colspan="3" align="center">Proposal to Discontinue Bran Flakes
September 29, 2003</td></tr>
<tr><td colspan="3">Differential revenue from annual sales of Bran Flakes:</td></tr>
<tr><td> Revenue from sales</td><td></td><td>$100,000</td></tr>
<tr><td colspan="3">Differential cost of annual sales of Bran Flakes:</td></tr>
<tr><td> Variable cost of goods sold</td><td>$60,000</td><td></td></tr>
<tr><td> Variable operating expenses</td><td>25,000</td><td>85,000</td></tr>
<tr><td>**Annual differential income from sales of Bran Flakes**</td><td></td><td>**$ 15,000**</td></tr>
</table>

Exhibit 600.73 *Traditional Analysis*

	Proposal to Discontinue Bran Flakes September 29, 2003		
	Bran Flakes, Toasted Oats, and Corn Flakes	Discontinue Bran Flakes*	Toasted Oats and Corn Flakes
Sales	$1,000,000	$100,000	$900,000
Cost of goods sold:			
Variable costs	$ 480,000	$ 60,000	$420,000
Fixed costs	220,000	—	220,000
Total cost of goods sold	$ 700,000	$ 60,000	$640,000
Gross profit	$ 300,000	$ 40,000	$260,000
Operating expenses:			
Variable expenses	$ 180,000	$ 25,000	$155,000
Fixed expenses	51,000	—	51,000
Total operating expenses	$ 231,000	$ 25,000	$206,000
Income (loss) from operations	$ 69,000	$ 15,000	$ 54,000

*Fixed costs do not decline with the discontinuance of Bran Flakes.

The traditional analysis in Exhibit 600.73 verifies the preceding differential analysis. In Exhibit 600.73, only the short-term (one year) effects of discontinuing Bran Flakes are considered. When eliminating a product or segment, management may also consider the long-term effects. For example, the plant capacity made available by discontinuing Bran Flakes might be eliminated. This could reduce fixed costs. Some employees may have to be laid off, and others may have to be relocated and retrained. Further, there may be a related decrease in sales of more profitable products to those customers who were attracted by the discontinued product.

Example 35 *Product A has a loss from operations of $18,000 and fixed costs of $25,000. Product B has a loss from operations of $12,000 and fixed costs of $8,000. All remaining products have income from operations of $75,000 and fixed costs of $30,000. (1) Which product(s) should be discontinued, and (2) what would be the estimated income from operations if the action in (1) is taken?*

(1) Product B; (2) $49,000 ($75,000 − $18,000 − $8,000)

---

3. Make or Buy a Part

The assembly of many parts is often a major element in manufacturing some products, such as automobiles. These parts may be made by the product's manufacturer, or they may be purchased. For example, some of the parts for an automobile, such as the motor, may be produced by the automobile manufacturer. Other parts, such as tires, may be purchased from other manufacturers. In addition, in manufacturing motors, such items as spark plugs and nuts and bolts may be acquired from suppliers.

Management uses differential costs to decide whether to make or buy a part. For example, if a part is purchased, management has concluded that it is less costly to buy the part than to manufacture it. Make or buy options often arise when a manufacturer has excess productive capacity in the form of unused equipment, space, and labor.

The differential analysis is similar, whether management is considering making a part that is currently being purchased or purchasing a part that is currently being made. To illustrate, assume that an automobile manufacturer has been purchasing instrument panels for $240 a unit. The factory is currently operating at 80% of capacity, and no major increase in production is expected in the near future. The cost per unit of manufacturing an instrument panel internally, including fixed costs, is estimated as follows.

Direct materials	$ 80
Direct labor	80
Variable factory overhead	52
Fixed factory overhead	68
Total cost per unit	$280

If the *make* price of $280 is simply compared with the *buy* price of $240, the decision is to buy the instrument panel. However, if unused capacity could be used in manufacturing the part, there would be no increase in the total amount of fixed factory overhead costs. Thus, only the variable factory overhead costs need to be considered. The relevant costs are summarized in the differential report in Exhibit 600.74.

Exhibit 600.74 *Differential Analysis Report—Make or Buy*

Proposal to Manufacture Instrument Panels
February 15, 2003

Purchase price of an instrument panel		$240.00
Differential cost to manufacture:		
Direct materials	$80.00	
Direct labor	80.00	
Variable factory overhead	52.00	212.00
Cost savings from manufacturing an instrument panel		**$ 28.00**

Other possible effects of a decision to manufacture the instrument panel should also be considered. For example, increasing production in the future might require using the currently idle capacity. This decision may affect employees. It may also affect future business relations with the instrument panel supplier, who may provide other essential parts. The company's decision to manufacture instrument panels might jeopardize the timely delivery of these other parts.

Example 36 Part K can be purchased for $30 per unit. Part K can be manufactured internally using $7.50 of direct materials and 0.75 hour of direct labor at $12 per direct labor hour (dlh). Factory overhead is applied at a rate of $20 per direct labor hour. ($7 per dlh is fixed.) What is the cost savings or penalty from manufacturing the part internally?

$3.75 cost savings {$30 − [$7.50 + (0.75 × $12) + (0.75 × $13)]}

---

4. Replace Equipment

The usefulness of fixed assets may be reduced long before they are considered to be worn out. For example, equipment may no longer be efficient for the purpose for which it is used. On the other hand, the equipment may not have reached the point of complete inadequacy. Decisions to replace usable fixed assets should be based on relevant costs. The relevant costs are the future costs of continuing to use the equipment versus replacement. The book values of the fixed assets being replaced are sunk costs and are irrelevant.

To illustrate, assume that a business is considering the disposal of several identical machines having a total book value of $100,000 and an estimated remaining life of five years. The old machines can be sold for $25,000. They can be replaced by a single high-speed machine at a cost of $250,000. The new machine has an estimated useful life of five years and no residual value. Analyses indicate an estimated annual reduction in variable manufacturing costs from $225,000 with the old machine to $150,000 with the new machine. No other changes in the manufacturing costs or the operating expenses are expected. The relevant costs are summarized in the differential report in Exhibit 600.75.

Exhibit 600.75 *Differential Analysis Report—Replace Equipment*

	Proposal to Replace Equipment November 28, 2003	
Annual variable costs—present equipment	$225,000	
Annual variable costs—new equipment	150,000	
Annual differential decrease in cost	$ 75,000	
Number of years applicable	× 5	
Total differential decrease in cost	$375,000	
Proceeds from sale of present equipment	25,000	$400,000
Cost of new equipment		250,000
Net differential decrease in cost, 5-year total		$150,000
Annual net differential decrease in cost—new equipment		**$ 30,000**

Other factors are often important in equipment replacement decisions. For example, differences between the remaining useful life of the old equipment and the estimated life of the new equipment could exist. In addition, the new equipment might improve the overall quality of the product, resulting in an increase in sales volume. Additional factors could include the time value of money and other uses for the cash needed to purchase the new equipment.

The amount of income that is forgone from an alternative use of an asset, such as cash, is called an **opportunity cost.** For example, your opportunity cost of attending school is the income forgone from lost work hours. Although the opportunity cost does not appear as a part of historical accounting data, it is useful in analyzing alternative courses of action. To illustrate, assume that the cash outlay of $250,000 for the new equipment, less the $25,000 proceeds from the sale of the present equipment, could be invested to yield a 10% return. Thus, the annual opportunity cost related to the purchase of the new equipment is $22,500 (10% × $225,000).

5. Process Further or Sell a Product

When a product is manufactured, it progresses through various stages of production. Often a product can be sold at an intermediate stage of production, or it can be processed further and then sold. In deciding whether to sell a product at an intermediate stage or to process it further, differential analysis is useful. The differential revenues from further processing are compared to the differential costs of further processing. The costs of producing the intermediate product do not change, regardless of whether the intermediate product is sold or processed further. Thus, these costs are not differential costs and are irrelevant to the decision to process further.

To illustrate, assume that a business produces kerosene in batches of 4,000 gallons. Standard quantities of 4,000 gallons of direct materials are processed, which cost $0.60 per gallon. Kerosene can be sold without further processing for $0.80 per gallon. It can be processed further to yield gasoline, which can be sold for $1.25 per gallon. Gasoline requires additional processing costs of $650 per batch, and 20% of the gallons of kerosene will evaporate during production. Exhibit 600.76 summarizes the differential revenues and costs in deciding whether to process kerosene to produce gasoline.

After initial release, film studios "process" movies further by releasing them in DVD format for the home market. Items that are relevant to making this decision are the copying and packaging costs for the disk, marketing costs associated with promoting the disk, and anticipated revenues from selling the disk. The original movie production costs are not relevant to the decision.

The differential income from further processing kerosene into gasoline is $150 per batch. The initial cost of producing the intermediate kerosene, $2,400 (4,000 gallons × $0.60), is not considered in deciding whether to process kerosene further. This initial cost will be incurred, regardless of whether gasoline is produced.

Exhibit 600.76 *Differential Analysis Report—Process Further or Sell*

Proposal to Process Kerosene Further October 1, 2003		
Differential revenue from further processing per batch:		
Revenue from sale of gasoline [(4,000 gallons − 800 gallons evaporation) × $1.25]	$4,000	
Revenue from sale of kerosene (4,000 gallons × $0.80)	3,200	
Differential revenue		$800
Differential cost per batch:		
Additional cost of producing gasoline		650
Differential income from further processing gasoline per batch		**$150**

Example 37 Product T is produced for $2.50 per gallon ($1.00 fixed cost) and can be sold without additional processing for $3.50 per gallon. Product T can be processed further into Product V at a cost of $1.60 per gallon ($0.90 fixed). Product V can be sold for $4.00 per gallon. What is the differential income or loss per gallon from processing Product T into Product V?

$0.20 loss [$4.00 − $3.50 − $1.60 + $0.90]

---

6. Accept Business at a Special Price

Differential analysis is also useful in deciding whether to accept additional business at a special price. The differential revenue that would be provided from the additional business is compared to the differential costs of producing and delivering the product to the customer. If the company is operating at full capacity, any additional production will increase both fixed and variable production costs. If, however, the normal production of the company is below full capacity, additional business may be undertaken without increasing fixed production costs. In this case, the differential costs of the additional production are the variable manufacturing costs. If operating expenses increase because of the additional business, these expenses should also be considered.

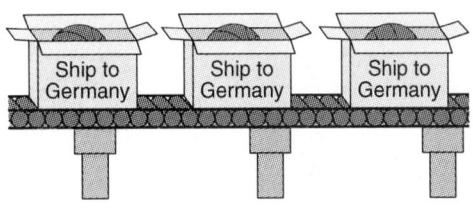

To illustrate, assume that the monthly capacity of a sporting goods business is 12,500 basketballs. Current sales and production are averaging 10,000 basketballs per month. The current manufacturing cost of $20 per unit consists of variable costs of $12.50 and fixed costs of $7.50. The normal selling price of the product in the domestic market is $30. The manufacturer receives from an exporter an offer for 5,000 basketballs at $18 each. Production can be spread over a three-month period without interfering with normal production or incurring overtime costs. Pricing policies in the domestic market will not be affected. Simply comparing the sales price of $18 with the present unit manufacturing cost of $20 indicates that the offer should be rejected. However, by focusing only on the differential cost, which in this case is the variable cost, the decision is different. Exhibit 600.77 shows the differential analysis report for this decision.

Exhibit 600.77 *Differential Analysis Report—Sell at Special Price*

Proposal to Sell Basketballs to Exporter March 10, 2003	
Differential revenue from accepting offer:	
Revenue from sale of 5,000 additional units at $18	$90,000
Differential cost of accepting offer:	
Variable costs of 5,000 additional units at $12.50	62,500
Differential income from accepting offer	**$27,500**

Proposals to sell a product in the domestic market at prices lower than the normal price may require additional considerations. For example, it may be unwise to increase sales volume in one territory by price reductions if sales volume is lost in other areas. Manufacturers must also conform to the Robinson-Patman Act, which prohibits price discrimination within the United States unless differences in prices can be justified by different costs of serving different customers.

> **Example 38** *Product D is normally sold for $4.40 per unit. A special price of $3.60 is offered for the export market. The variable production cost is $3.00 per unit. An additional export tariff of 10% of revenue will be required for all export products. What is the differential income or loss per unit from selling Product D for export?*
>
> $0.24 income [$3.60 − $3.00 − (0.10 × $3.60)]

Setting Normal Product Selling Prices

Differential analysis may be useful in deciding to lower selling prices for special short-run decisions, such as whether to accept business at a price lower than the normal price. In such cases, the minimum short-run price is set high enough to cover all variable costs. Any price above this minimum price will improve profits in the short run. In the long run, however, the normal selling price must be set high enough to cover all costs and expenses (both fixed and variable) and provide a reasonable profit. Otherwise, the business may not survive.

The normal selling price can be viewed as the target selling price to be achieved in the long run. The basic approaches to setting this price are as follows.

Market Methods	Cost-Plus Methods
1. Demand-based methods	1. Total cost concept
2. Competition-based methods	2. Product cost concept
	3. Variable cost concept

Managers using the market methods refer to the external market to determine the price. Demand-based methods set the price according to the demand for the product. If there is high demand for the product, then the price may be set high, while lower demand may require the price to be set low. An example of setting different prices according to the demand for the product is found in the telecommunications industry, with low weekend rates and high business day rates for long-distance telephone calls.

Competition-based methods set the price according to the price offered by competitors. For example, if a competitor reduces the price, then management may be required to adjust the price to meet the competition. The market-based pricing approaches are discussed in greater detail in marketing courses, so we will not expand upon them here.

Managers using the cost-plus methods price the product in order to achieve a target profit. Managers add to the cost an amount called a **markup,** so that all costs plus a profit are included in the selling price. In the following paragraphs, we describe and illustrate the three cost concepts often used in applying the cost-plus approach: (1) total cost, (2) product cost, and (3) variable cost.

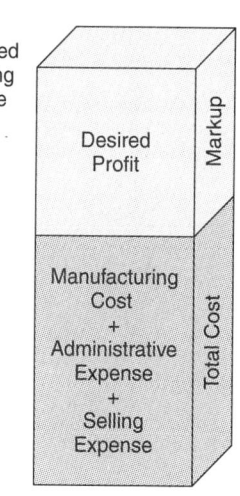

Total Cost Concept

Using the **total cost concept,** all costs of manufacturing a product plus the selling and administrative expenses are included in the cost amount to which the markup is added. Since all costs and expenses are included in the cost amount, the dollar amount of the markup equals the desired profit.

The first step in applying the total cost concept is to determine the total cost of manufacturing the product. This cost includes the costs of direct materials, direct labor, and factory overhead and should be available from the accounting records. The next step is to add the estimated selling and administrative expenses to the total cost of manufacturing the product. The cost amount per unit is then computed by dividing the total costs by the total units expected to be produced and sold.

After the cost amount per unit has been determined, the dollar amount of the markup is determined. For this purpose, the markup is expressed as a percentage of cost. This percentage is then multiplied by the cost amount per unit. The dollar amount of the markup is then added to the cost amount per unit to arrive at the selling price.

The markup percentage for the total cost concept is determined by applying the following formula.

$$\text{Markup percentage} = \frac{\text{Desired profit}}{\text{Total costs}}$$

The numerator of the formula is only the desired profit. This is because all costs and expenses are included in the cost amount to which the markup is added. The denominator of the formula is the total costs.

To illustrate, assume that the costs for calculators of Digital Solutions Inc. are as follows.

Variable costs:	
Direct materials	$ 3.00 per unit
Direct labor	10.00
Factory overhead	1.50
Selling and administrative expenses	1.50
Total	$16.00 per unit
Fixed costs:	
Factory overhead	$50,000
Selling and administrative expenses	20,000

Digital Solutions Inc. desires a profit equal to a 20% rate of return on assets, $800,000 of assets are devoted to producing calculators, and 100,000 units are expected to be produced and sold. The calculators' total cost is $1,670,000, or $16.70 per unit, computed as follows.

Variable costs ($16.00 × 100,000 units)			$1,600,000
Fixed costs:			
Factory overhead		$50,000	
Selling and administrative expenses		20,000	70,000
Total costs			$1,670,000
Total cost per calculator ($1,670,000 ÷ 100,000 units)			$ 16.70

The desired profit is $160,000 (20% × $800,000), and the markup percentage for a calculator is 9.6%, computed as follows.

$$\text{Markup percentage} = \frac{\text{Desired profits}}{\text{Total costs}}$$

$$\text{Markup percentage} = \frac{\$160,000}{\$1,670,000} = 9.6\%$$

Based on the total cost per unit and the markup percentage for a calculator, Digital Solutions Inc. would price each calculator at $18.30 per unit, as shown below.

Total cost per calculator	$16.70
Markup ($16.70 × 9.6%)	1.60
Selling price	$18.30

The ability of the selling price of $18.30 to generate the desired profit of $160,000 is shown by the following income statement.

Digital Solutions Inc.
Income Statement
for the Year Ended December 31, 2003

Sales (100,000 units × $18.30)		$1,830,000
Expenses:		
Variable (100,000 units × $16.00)	$1,600,000	
Fixed ($50,000 + $20,000)	70,000	1,670,000
Income from operations		$ 160,000

The total cost concept of applying the cost-plus approach to product pricing is often used by contractors who sell products to government agencies. In many cases, government contractors are required by law to be reimbursed for their products on a total-cost-plus-profit basis.

Example 39 The microcomputer industry is developing products that can be sold to consumers for under $1,000. By using the total cost concept, the following price can be determined:

Motherboard	$140
Memory	50
Processor	90
Disk drive	198
Peripherals	265
Factory overhead and assembly	48
Product cost	$791
Administrative expenses	26
Total cost	$817
Manufacturer markup	91
Manufacturer's price to retailer	$908
Retailer markup	91
Retail price to final consumer	$999

Notice that there are two markups included in the final price—one for the manufacturer and one for the retailer.

Product Cost Concept

Using the **product cost concept,** only the costs of manufacturing the product, termed the product cost, are included in the cost amount to which the markup is added. Estimated selling expenses, administrative expenses, and profit are included in the markup. The markup percentage is determined by applying the following formula.

$$\text{Markup percentage} = \frac{\text{Desired profit} + \text{Total selling and administrative expenses}}{\text{Total manufacturing costs}}$$

The numerator of the markup percentage formula is the desired profit plus the total selling and administrative expenses. These expenses must be included in the markup, since they are not included in the cost amount to which the markup is added. The denominator of the formula includes the costs of direct materials, direct labor, and factory overhead.

To illustrate, assume the same data used in the preceding illustration. The manufacturing cost for Digital Solutions Inc.'s calculator is $1,500,000, or $15 per unit, computed as follows.

Direct materials ($3 × 100,000 units)		$ 300,000
Direct labor ($10 × 100,000 units)		1,000,000
Factory overhead:		
Variable ($1.50 × 100,000 units)	$150,000	
Fixed	50,000	200,000
Total manufacturing costs		$1,500,000
Manufacturing cost per calculator ($1,500,000 ÷ 100,000 units)		$ 15

The desired profit is $160,000 (20% × $800,000), and the total selling and administrative expenses are $170,000 [(100,000 units × $1.50 per unit) + $20,000]. The markup percentage for a calculator is 22%, computed as follows.

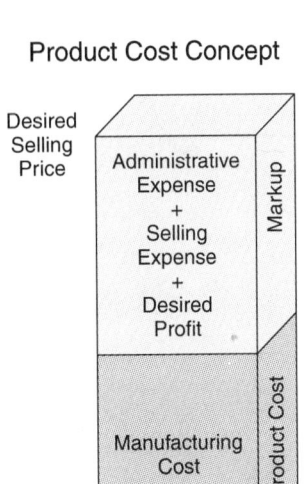

Product Cost Concept

$$\text{Markup percentage} = \frac{\text{Desired profit} + \text{Total selling and administrative expenses}}{\text{Total manufacturing costs}}$$

$$\text{Markup percentage} = \frac{\$160,000 + \$170,000}{\$1,500,000}$$

$$\text{Markup percentage} = \frac{\$330,000}{\$1,500,000} = 22\%$$

Based on the manufacturing cost per calculator and the markup percentage, Digital Solutions Inc. would price each calculator at $18.30 per unit, as shown below.

Manufacturing cost per calculator	$15.00
Markup ($15 × 22%)	3.30
Selling price	$18.30

Variable Cost Concept

The **variable cost concept** emphasizes the distinction between variable and fixed costs in product pricing. Using the variable cost concept, only variable costs are included in the cost amount to which the markup is added. All variable manufacturing costs, as well as variable selling and administrative expenses, are included in the cost amount. Fixed manufacturing costs, fixed selling and administrative expenses, and profit are included in the markup.

The markup percentage is determined by applying the following formula.

$$\text{Markup percentage} = \frac{\text{Desired profit} + \text{Total fixed costs}}{\text{Total variable costs}}$$

The numerator of the markup percentage formula is the desired profit plus the total fixed manufacturing costs and the total fixed selling and administrative expenses. These costs and expenses must be included in the markup, since they are not included in the cost amount to which the markup is added. The denominator of the formula includes the total variable costs.

To illustrate, assume the same data used in the two preceding illustrations. The calculator variable cost is $1,600,000, or $16.00 per unit, computed as follows.

Variable costs:	
Direct materials ($3 × 100,000 units)	$ 300,000
Direct labor ($10 × 100,000 units)	1,000,000
Factory overhead ($1.50 × 100,000 units)	150,000
Selling and administrative expenses ($1.50 × 100,000 units)	150,000
Total variable costs	$1,600,000
Variable cost per calculator ($1,600,000 ÷ 100,000 units)	$ 16

The desired profit is $160,000 (20% × $800,000), the total fixed manufacturing costs are $50,000, and the total fixed selling and administrative expenses are $20,000. The markup percentage for a calculator is 14.4%, computed as follows.

Variable Cost Concept

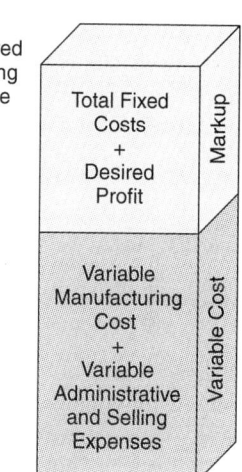

$$\text{Markup percentage} = \frac{\text{Desired profit} + \text{Total fixed costs}}{\text{Total variable costs}}$$

$$\text{Markup percentage} = \frac{\$160,000 + \$50,000 + \$20,000}{\$1,600,000}$$

$$\text{Markup percentage} = \frac{\$230,000}{\$1,600,000} = 14.4\%$$

Based on the variable cost per calculator and the markup percentage, Digital Solutions Inc. would price each calculator at $18.30 per unit, as shown below.

Variable cost per calculator	$16.00
Markup ($16.00 × 14.4%)	2.30
Selling price	$18.30

Example 40 *Product Z has a total cost of $30 per unit. Of this amount, $10 per unit is selling and administrative costs. The total variable cost is $18 per unit. The desired profit is $3 per unit. Determine the markup percentage on (1) total cost, (2) product cost, and (3) variable cost.*

(1) 10% ($3 ÷ $30);
(2) 65% [($10 + $3) ÷ $20];
(3) 83.3% [($12 + $3) ÷ $18]

Choosing a Cost-Plus Approach Cost Concept

All three cost concepts produced the same selling price ($18.30) for Digital Solutions Inc. In practice, however, the three cost concepts are usually not viewed as alternatives. Each cost concept requires different estimates of costs and expenses. This difficulty and the complexity of the manufacturing operations should be considered in choosing a cost concept.

To reduce the costs of gathering data, estimated (standard) costs rather than actual costs may be used with any of the three cost concepts. However, management should exercise caution when using estimated costs in applying the cost-plus approach. The estimates should be based on normal (attainable) operating levels and not theoretical (ideal) levels of performance. In product pricing, the use of estimates based on ideal- or maximum-capacity operating levels might lead to setting product prices too low. In this case, the costs of such factors as normal spoilage or normal periods of idle time might not be considered.

The decision-making needs of management are also an important factor in selecting a cost concept for product pricing. For example, managers who often make special pricing decisions are more likely to use the variable cost concept. In contrast, a government defense contractor would be more likely to use the total cost concept.

A variation of the cost concepts discussed in the preceding paragraphs is the **target cost concept.** Under this concept, which was first used by the Japanese, the selling price is assumed to be set by the marketplace. The target cost is determined by *subtracting* a desired profit from the selling price. Thus, managers must design and manufacture the product to achieve its target cost. In contrast, the three cost concepts discussed previously start with a given product cost and *add* a markup to determine the selling price. Some argue that the target cost concept may be better than the cost-plus approaches in highly competitive markets that require continual product cost reductions to remain competitive.

Activity-Based Costing

As illustrated in the preceding paragraphs, costs are an important consideration in setting product prices. To more accurately measure the costs of producing and selling products, some companies use activity-based costing. **Activity-based costing (ABC)** identifies and traces activities to specific products.

Activity-based costing may be useful in making product pricing decisions where manufacturing operations involve large amounts of factory overhead. In such cases, traditional overhead allocation using activity bases such as units produced or machine hours may yield inaccurate cost allocations. This, in turn, may result in distorted product costs and product prices. By providing more accurate product cost allocations, activity-based costing aids in setting product prices that will cover costs and expenses.

Product Profitability and Pricing Under Production Bottlenecks

An important consideration influencing production volumes and prices is production bottlenecks. A production **bottleneck (or constraint)** occurs at the point in the process where the demand for the company's product exceeds the ability to produce the product. The **theory of constraints (TOC)** is a manufacturing strategy that focuses on reducing the influence of bottlenecks on a process.

Product Profitability Under Production Bottlenecks

When a company has a bottleneck in its production process, it should attempt to maximize its profitability, subject to the influence of the bottleneck. To illustrate, assume that Snapp-Off Tool Company makes three types of wrenches: small, medium, and large. All three products are processed through a heat treatment operation, which hardens the steel tools. Snapp-Off Tool's heat treatment process is operating at full capacity and is a production bottleneck. The product contribution margin per unit and the number of hours of heat treatment used by each type of wrench are as follows.

	Small Wrench	Medium Wrench	Large Wrench
Sales price per unit	$130	$140	$160
Variable cost per unit	40	40	40
Contribution margin per unit	$ 90	$100	$120
Heat treatment hours per unit	1	4	8

The large wrench appears to be the most profitable product because its contribution margin per unit is the greatest. However, the contribution margin per unit can be a misleading indicator of profitability in a bottleneck operation. The correct measure of performance is the value of each bottleneck hour, or the contribution margin per bottleneck hour. Using this measure, each product has a much different profitability when compared to the contribution margin per unit information, as shown in Exhibit 600.78.

Exhibit 600.78 *Contribution Margin per Bottleneck Hour*

	Small Wrench	Medium Wrench	Large Wrench
Sales price	$130	$140	$160
Variable cost per unit	40	40	40
Contribution margin per unit	$ 90	$100	$120
Bottleneck (heat treatment) hours per unit	÷ 1	÷ 4	÷ 8
Contribution margin per bottleneck hour	$ 90	$ 25	$ 15

The small wrench produces the most contribution margin per bottleneck (heat treatment) hour used, while the large wrench produces the smallest profit per bottleneck hour. Thus, the small wrench is the most profitable product. This information is the opposite of that implied by the unit contribution margin profit.

Example 41 *Product A has a contribution margin of $15 per unit. Product B has a contribution margin of $20 per unit. Product A requires 3 furnace hours, while Product B requires 5 furnace hours. Determine the most profitable product, assuming that the furnace is a bottleneck.*

Product A ($15 ÷ 3 hours = $5 per hour, which is greater than $20 ÷ 5 hours, or $4 per hour)

Product Pricing Under Production Bottlenecks

Each hour of a bottleneck delivers profit to the company. When a company has a production bottleneck, the contribution margin per hour of bottleneck provides a measure of the product's relative profitability. This information can also be used to adjust the product price to better reflect the value of the product's use of a bottleneck. Products that use a large number of bottleneck hours per unit require more contribution margin than products that use few bottleneck hours per unit. For example, Snapp-Off Tool Company should increase the price of the large wrench in order to deliver more contribution margin per bottleneck hour.

To determine the price of the large wrench that would equate its profitability to the small wrench, we need to solve the following equation.

$$\text{Contribution margin per bottleneck hour per small wrench} = \frac{\text{Revised price of large wrench} - \text{Variable cost per large wrench}}{\text{Bottleneck hours per large wrench}}$$

$$\$90 = \frac{\text{Revised price of large wrench} - \$40}{8}$$

$720 = Revised price of large wrench − $40
$760 = Revised price of large wrench

The large wrench's price would need to be increased to $760 in order to deliver the same contribution margin per bottleneck hour as does the small wrench, as verified below.

Revised price of large wrench	$760
Less: Variable cost per unit of large wrench	40
Contribution margin per unit of large wrench	$720
Bottleneck hours per unit of large wrench	÷ 8
Revised contribution margin per bottleneck hour	$ 90

At a price of $760, the company would be indifferent between producing and selling the small wrench or the large wrench, all else being equal. This analysis assumes that there is unlimited demand for the products. If the market were unwilling to purchase the large wrench at this price, then the company should produce the small wrench.

Income Models and Decision Making

Just as you should evaluate the relative financial impact of various choices, so must a business evaluate the financial impact of its choices. In this section we will discuss how businesses measure profitability, using absorption costing and variable costing. After illustrating and comparing these concepts, we discuss how businesses use them for controlling costs, pricing products, planning production, analyzing market segments, and analyzing contribution margins.

The Income Statement Under Variable Costing and Absorption Costing

Absorption Costing

Inventory:
Cost of Goods Manufactured
- Direct materials
- Direct labor
- Variable factory overhead
- Fixed factory overhead

Variable Costing

Inventory:
Cost of Goods Manufactured
- Direct materials
- Direct labor
- Variable factory overhead

Period Expense → Fixed factory overhead

One of the most important items affecting a business's net income is the cost of goods sold. In many cases, the cost of goods sold is larger than all of the other expenses combined. The cost of goods sold can be determined under either the absorption costing or variable costing concept.

Under **absorption costing,** all manufacturing costs are included in finished goods and remain there as an asset until the goods are sold. Absorption costing is necessary in determining historical costs for financial reporting to external users and for tax reporting.

Variable costing may be more useful to management in making decisions. In **variable costing,** which is also called **direct costing,** the cost of goods manufactured is composed only of *variable* manufacturing costs—costs that increase or decrease as the volume of production rises or falls. These costs are the direct materials, direct labor, and only those factory overhead costs that vary with the rate of production. The remaining factory overhead costs, which are fixed or nonvariable costs, are generally related to the productive capacity of the manufacturing plant and are not affected by changes in the quantity of product manufactured. Thus, the fixed factory overhead does not become a part of the cost of goods manufactured but is treated as an expense of the period in which it is incurred.

To illustrate the difference between the variable costing income statement and the absorption costing income statement, assume that Belling Co. manufactured 15,000 units at the following costs.

	Total Cost	Number of Units	Unit Cost
Manufacturing costs:			
Variable	$375,000	15,000	$25
Fixed	150,000	15,000	10
Total	$525,000		$35
Selling and administrative expenses:			
Variable ($5 per unit sold)	$ 75,000		
Fixed	50,000		
Total	$125,000		

The variable costing income statement includes only variable manufacturing costs in the cost of goods sold.

The units sell at a price of $50, as shown in the variable costing income statement for Belling Co. in Exhibit 600.79. In this income statement, variable costs are separated from fixed costs. The variable cost of goods sold, which includes the variable manufacturing costs, is deducted from sales to yield the **manufacturing margin** of $375,000. The variable selling and administrative expenses of $75,000 are deducted from the manufacturing margin to yield the contribution margin of $300,000. Thus, the **contribution margin** is sales less variable

MODULE 600. ACCOUNTING

Exhibit 600.79 *Variable Costing Income Statement*

Sales (15,000 × $50)		$750,000
Variable cost of goods sold (15,000 × $25)		375,000
Manufacturing margin		$375,000
Variable selling and administrative expenses		75,000
Contribution margin		$300,000
Fixed costs:		
Fixed manufacturing costs	$150,000	
Fixed selling and administrative expenses	50,000	200,000
Income from operations		$100,000

Exhibit 600.80 *Absorption Costing Income Statement*

Sales (15,000 × $50)	$750,000
Cost of goods sold (15,000 × $35)	525,000
Gross profit	$225,000
Selling and administrative expenses ($75,000 + $50,000)	125,000
Income from operations	$100,000

costs. The income from operations of $100,000 is then determined by deducting fixed costs of $200,000 from the contribution margin.

Exhibit 600.80 shows the absorption costing income statement prepared for Belling Co. The absorption costing income statement does not distinguish between variable and fixed costs. All manufacturing costs are included in the cost of goods sold. Deducting cost of goods sold from sales yields the $225,000 gross profit. Deducting selling and administrative expenses then yields income from operations of $100,000.

> **Example 42** A company has sales of $450,000, cost of goods sold of $300,000, variable cost of goods sold of $220,000, and variable selling expenses of $50,000. What are (a) its manufacturing margin and (b) its contribution margin?
>
> (a) $230,000 ($450,000 − $220,000);   (b) $180,000 ($230,000 − $50,000)

Income Analysis Under Variable Costing and Absorption Costing

As we have illustrated, the income from operations under variable costing can differ from the income from operations under absorption costing. This difference results from change in the quantity of the finished goods inventory, which are caused by differences in the levels of sales and production. In analyzing and evaluating operations, management should be aware of the possible effects of changing inventory levels under the two concepts.

As illustrated, if absorption costing is used, management should be careful in analyzing income from operations when large changes in inventory levels occur. Managers could misinterpret increases or decreases in income from operations, due to mere changes in inventory levels, to be the result of business events, such as changes in sales volume, prices, or costs.

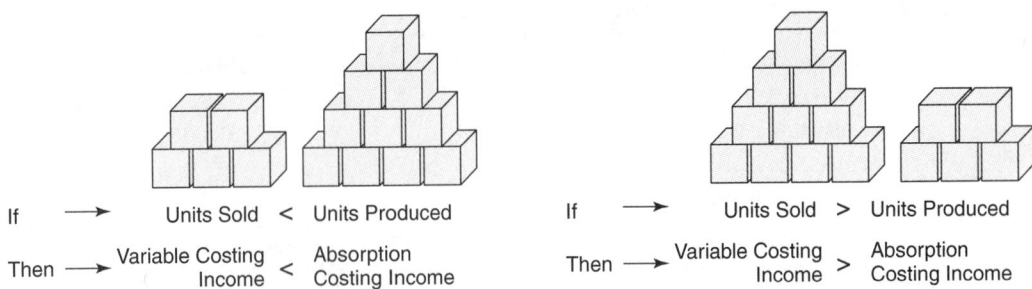

Many accountants believe that variable costing should be used for evaluating operating performance because absorption costing encourages management to produce inventory. This is because producing inventory absorbs fixed costs and causes the income from operations to appear higher, as we have illustrated above. In the long run, building inventory without the promise of future sales may lead to higher handling, storage, financing, and obsolescence costs.

Example 43 *Fixed costs are $40 per unit and variable costs are $120 per unit. Production exceeded sales by 5,000 units. What is the difference in the variable costing and absorption costing income from operations?*

Variable costing income from operations will be $200,000 ($40 per unit × 5,000) less than absorption costing income from operations.

Example 44 *The beginning inventory is 8,000 units, all of which are sold during the period. The beginning inventory fixed costs are $60 per unit, and variable costs are $300 per unit. What is the difference in the variable costing and absorption costing income from operations, assuming no ending inventory?*

Variable costing income from operations will be $480,000 ($60 per unit × 8,000) greater than absorption costing income from operations.

Example 45 *Variable costs are $100 per unit, and fixed costs are $50,000. Sales are estimated to be 4,000 units. (a) How much would absorption costing income from operations differ between a plan to produce 4,000 units and 5,000 units? (b) How much would variable costing income from operations differ between the two production plans?*

(a) $10,000 greater for 5,000 units of production
 [1,000 units × ($50,000 ÷ 5,000), or 4,000 units × ($12.50 − $10.00)];
(b) There would be no difference in income from operations.

Management's Use of Variable Costing and Absorption Costing

Managerial accountants should carefully analyze each situation in evaluating whether variable costing or absorption costing reports would be more useful to management. In many situations, preparing reports under both concepts provides useful insights. In the following paragraphs, we discuss such reports and their advantages and disadvantages to management in making decisions related to the items identified in Exhibit 600.81.

Controlling Costs

All costs are controllable in the long run by someone within a business, but they are not all controllable at the same level of management. For example, plant supervisors, as members of operating management, are responsible for controlling the use of direct materials in their departments. They have no control, however, of insurance costs related to the buildings housing their departments. For a specific level of management, **controllable costs** are costs that can be influenced by management at that level, and **noncontrollable costs** are costs that another level of management controls. This distinction is useful in fixing the responsibility for incurring costs and for reporting costs to those responsible for their control.

Exhibit 600.81 *Accounting Reports and Management Decisions*

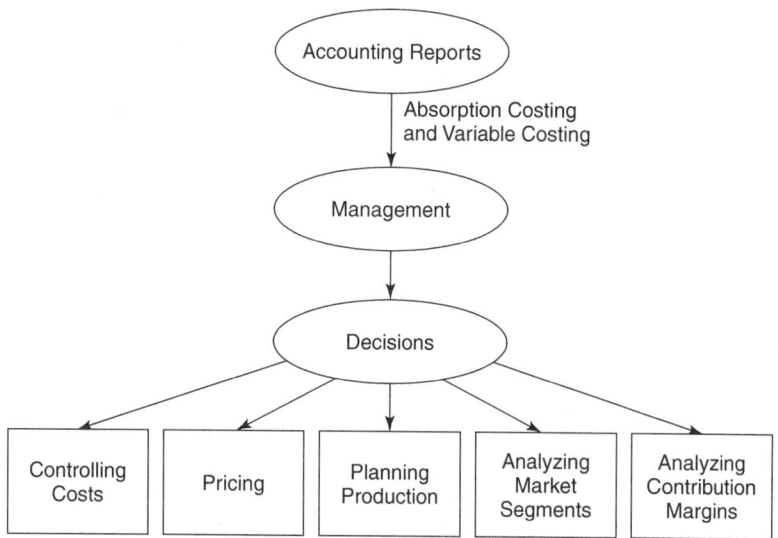

Variable manufacturing costs are controlled at the operating level. If the product's cost includes only variable manufacturing costs, the cost can be controlled by operating management. The fixed factory overhead costs are normally the responsibility of a higher level of management. When the fixed factory overhead costs are reported as a separate item in the variable costing income statement, they are easier to identify and control than when they are spread among units of product, as they are under absorption costing.

As in the case with the fixed and variable manufacturing costs, the control of the variable and fixed operating expenses is usually the responsibility of different levels of management. Under variable costing, the variable selling and administrative expenses are reported separately from the fixed selling and administrative expenses. Because they are reported in this manner, both types of operating expenses are easier to identify and control than is the case under absorption costing.

Pricing Products

Many factors enter into determining the selling price of a product. The cost of making the product is clearly significant. Microeconomic theory states that income is maximized by expanding output to the volume where the revenue realized by the sale of an additional unit (marginal revenue) equals the cost of that unit (marginal cost). Although the degree of accuracy assumed in economic theory is rarely achieved, the concepts of marginal revenue and marginal cost are useful in setting selling prices.

In the short run, a business is committed to its existing manufacturing facilities. The pricing decision should be based upon making the best use of such capacity. The fixed costs cannot be avoided, but the variable costs can be eliminated if the company does not manufacture the product. The selling price of a product, therefore, should at least be equal to the variable costs of making and selling it. Any price above this minimum selling price contributes an amount toward covering fixed costs and providing income. Variable costing procedures yield data that emphasize these relationships.

In the long run, plant capacity can be increased or decreased. If a business is to continue operating, the selling prices of its products must cover all costs and provide a reasonable income. Hence, in establishing pricing policies for the long run, information provided by absorption costing procedures is needed.

The results of a research study indicated that the companies studied used absorption costing in making routine pricing decisions. However, these companies regularly used variable costing as a basis for setting prices in many short-run situations.

There are no simple solutions to most pricing problems. Consideration must be given to many factors of varying importance. Accounting can contribute by preparing analyses of various pricing plans for both the short run and the long run. Additional analyses useful for product pricing are further described and illustrated in a later section.

Planning Production

Planning production also has both short-run and long-run implications. In the short run, production is limited to existing capacity. Operating decisions must be made quickly before opportunities are lost. For example, a company manufacturing products with a seasonal demand may have an opportunity to obtain an off-season order that will not interfere with its production schedule nor reduce the sales of its other products. The relevant factors for such a short-run decision are the additional revenues and the additional variable costs associated with the off-season order. If the revenues from the special order will provide a contribution margin, the order should be accepted because it will increase the company's income from operations. For long-run planning, management must also consider the fixed costs.

Analyzing Market Segments

Market analysis is performed by the sales and marketing function in order to determine the profit contributed by market segments. A **market segment** is a portion of business that can be assigned to a manager for profit responsibility. Examples of market segments include sales territories, products, salespersons, and customer distribution channels. Variable costing can provide significant insight to decision making regarding such segments.

To illustrate, assume the following data for the month of March 2003 for Camelot Fragrance Company. Camelot Fragrance Company manufactures and markets the Gwenevere perfume line for women and the Lancelot cologne line for men.

	Northern Territory	Southern Territory	Total
Sales:			
Gwenevere	$60,000	$30,000	$ 90,000
Lancelot	20,000	50,000	70,000
Total territory sales	$80,000	$80,000	$160,000
Variable production costs:			
Gwenevere (12% of sales)	$ 7,200	$ 3,600	$ 10,800
Lancelot (12% of sales)	2,400	6,000	8,400
Total variable production cost by territory	$ 9,600	$ 9,600	$ 19,200
Promotion costs:			
Gwenevere (variable at 30% of sales)	$18,000	$ 9,000	$ 27,000
Lancelot (variable at 20% of sales)	4,000	10,000	14,000
Total promotion cost by territory	$22,000	$19,000	$ 41,000
Sales commissions:			
Gwenevere (variable at 20% of sales)	$12,000	$ 6,000	$ 18,000
Lancelot (variable at 10% of sales)	2,000	5,000	7,000
Total sales commissions by territory	$14,000	$11,000	$ 25,000

This information can be used by Camelot Fragrance Company to prepare a sales territory, product, and salesperson profitability analysis. Each of these is discussed on the following pages.

SALES TERRITORY PROFITABILITY ANALYSIS An income statement presenting the contribution margin by sales territories is often useful to management in evaluating past performance and in directing future sales efforts. Sales territory profitability analysis may lead management to reduce costs in lower-profit sales territories or to increase sales effort in higher-profit territories. For example, the **Coca-Cola Company** earns over 75% of its total corporate profits outside of the United States. This information motivates the Coca-Cola management to continue expanding operations and sales efforts around the world.

There are many possible explanations for profit differences between territories, including differences in pricing, sales unit volumes, media rates, selling costs, and the types of products sold. To illustrate the analysis of profit differences by sales territory, Exhibit 600.82 shows the contribution margin by sales territory for Camelot Fragrance Company.

The contribution margin for each territory consists of the sales less the variable costs associated with producing and selling products in each territory. In addition to the contribution margin, the contribution margin ratio (contribution margin divided by sales) for each territory is useful in evaluating sales territories and directing operations toward more profitable activities. For the Northern Territory, the contribution margin ratio is 43% ($34,400 ÷ $80,000), and for the Southern Territory the ratio is 50.5% ($40,400 ÷ $80,000). Although each territory had the same sales, the contribution margin ratios are different. Why is this?

Exhibit 600.82 *Contribution Margin by Sales Territory Report*

Camelot Fragrance Company
Contribution Margin by Sales Territory
for the Month Ended March 31, 2003

		Northern Territory		Southern Territory
Sales		$80,000		$80,000
Variable cost of goods sold		9,600		9,600
Manufacturing margin		$70,400		$70,400
Variable selling expenses:				
Promotion costs	$22,000		$19,000	
Sales commissions	14,000	36,000	11,000	30,000
Contribution margin		$34,400		$40,400
Contribution margin ratio		43%		50.5%

In this case, the difference in territory profit performance can be explained by the difference in sales mix between the two territories. **Sales mix,** sometimes referred to as *product mix,* is defined as the relative distribution of sales among the various products sold. From the assumed information, the Southern Territory had a higher relative proportion of Lancelot sales than did the Northern Territory. If the Lancelot line is more profitable than the Gwenevere line, then we would expect the Southern Territory's overall profitability to be higher than the Northern Territory's, as shown in Exhibit 600.82. To verify the difference between the profitabilities of the two products, product profitability analysis may be performed.

PRODUCT PROFITABILITY ANALYSIS   Management should focus its sales efforts on those products that will provide the maximum total contribution margin. An income statement presenting the contribution margin by products is often used by management to guide product-related sales and promotional efforts. For example, **Ford's** *Explorer* sport utility vehicle is one of its most profitable models. Ford uses this information to motivate higher production levels and promotion effort for this brand.

Some products are more profitable than others due to differences with respect to pricing, manufacturing costs, advertising support, or salesperson support. To illustrate the analysis of these differences, Exhibit 600.83 shows the contribution margin by product line for Camelot Fragrance Company.

As you can see, Lancelot's contribution margin ratio is greater than Gwenevere's, even though both product lines have the same manufacturing margin as a percent of sales. The higher contribution margin ratio is the result of Lancelot's lower promotion costs and sales commissions

> Customer, territory, product, and salesperson profit analysis is done by using a "data warehouse." A data warehouse is a relational database of revenue and cost information that can be divided into many different profit views. For example, **Johnson and Johnson's** data warehouse, called Darwin, enables managers from fifty countries around the world to see various profit views at the click of a mouse.

Exhibit 600.83 *Contribution Margin by Product Line Report*

Camelot Fragrance Company
Contribution Margin by Product Line
for the Month Ended March 31, 2003

		Gwenevere		Lancelot
Sales		$90,000		$70,000
Variable cost of goods sold		10,800		8,400
Manufacturing margin		$79,200		$61,600
Variable selling expenses:				
Promotion costs	$27,000		$14,000	
Sales commissions	18,000	45,000	7,000	21,000
Contribution margin		$34,200		$40,600
Contribution margin ratio		38%		58%

660. DECISION MAKING AND ACCOUNTING

as a percent of sales. The sales territory profitability analysis and the product profitability analysis both indicate the superior profit performance of the Lancelot line. Thus, management should emphasize the Lancelot product line in its marketing plans, try to reduce the promotion and sales commission expenses associated with Gwenevere sales, or increase the price of Gwenevere.

SALESPERSON PROFITABILITY ANALYSIS In addition to the sales territory and product profitability analyses, sales managers may wish to evaluate the performance of salespersons. This may be done with a salesperson profitability analysis.

A report to management for use in evaluating the sales performance of each salesperson could include total sales, variable cost of goods sold, variable selling expenses, contribution margin, and contribution margin ratio. Exhibit 600.84 illustrates such a report for three salespersons in the Northern Territory of Camelot Fragrance Company.

The total sales and costs of all three salespersons agree with the sales and costs for the Northern Territory in Exhibit 600.82. Thus, this report provides the Northern Territory manager with a more detailed analysis of the territory's performance. The report indicates that Beth Williams produced the greatest contribution margin for the company but had the lowest contribution margin ratio. Beth Williams sold $40,000 of product, which is twice as much product as the other two salespersons. However, Beth Williams sold only the Gwenevere product line, which has the lowest contribution margin ratio (from Exhibit 600.83). The other two salespersons sold equal amounts of Gwenevere and Lancelot. These two salespersons had higher contribution margin ratios because of the sales of the higher-margin Lancelot line. The territory manager could use this report to encourage Rodriguez and Ginger to sell more total product, while encouraging Williams to place more selling effort on the Lancelot line.

Other factors should also be considered in evaluating the performance of salespersons. For example, sales growth rates, years of experience, customer service, size of the territory, and actual performance compared to budgeted performance may also be important.

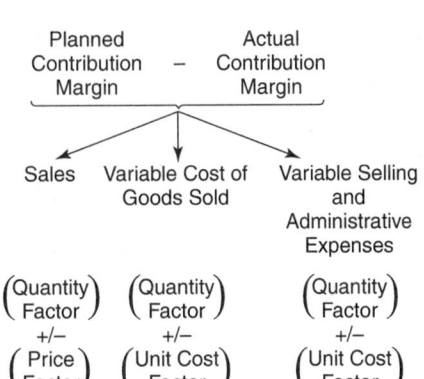

Analyzing Contribution Margins

Another use of the contribution margin concept to assist management in planning and controlling operations focuses on differences between planned and actual contribution margins. However, mere knowledge of the differences is insufficient. Management needs information about the causes of the differences. The systematic examination of the differences between planned and actual contribution margins is termed **contribution margin analysis**.

Exhibit 600.84 *Contribution Margin by Salesperson Report*

	Inez Rodriguez	Tom Ginger	Beth Williams	Northern Territory—Total
Sales	$20,000	$20,000	$40,000	$80,000
Variable cost of goods sold	2,400	2,400	4,800	9,600
Manufacturing margin	$17,600	$17,600	$35,200	$70,400
Variable selling expenses:				
Promotion costs	$ 5,000	$ 5,000	$12,000	$22,000
Sales commissions	3,000	3,000	8,000	14,000
	$ 8,000	$ 8,000	$20,000	$36,000
Contribution margin	$ 9,600	$ 9,600	$15,200	$34,400
Contribution margin ratio	48%	48%	38%	43%
Sales mix (% Lancelot sales)	50%	50%	0	25%

Camelot Fragrance Company
Contribution Margin by Salesperson—Northern Territory
for the Month Ended March 31, 2003

Since contribution margin is the excess of sales over variable costs, a difference between the planned and actual contribution margin can be caused by (1) an increase or decrease in the amount of sales or (2) an increase or decrease in the amount of variable costs. An increase or decrease in either element may in turn be due to (1) an increase or decrease in the number of units sold or (2) an increase or decrease in the unit sales price or unit cost. The effect of these two factors on either sales or variable costs may be stated as follows.

1. **Quantity factor**—the effect of a difference in the number of units sold, assuming no change in unit sales price or unit cost. The quantity factor is the difference between the actual quantity sold and the planned quantity sold, multiplied by the planned unit sales price or unit cost.
2. **Unit price factor** or **unit cost factor**—the effect of a difference in unit sales price or unit cost on the number of units sold. The unit price or unit cost factor is the difference between the actual unit price or unit cost and the planned unit price or unit cost, multiplied by the actual quantity sold.

We will use Exhibit 600.85 for Noble Inc. for the year ended December 31, 2003, as a basis for illustrating contribution margin analysis. For the sake of simplicity, we will assume a single commodity. The analysis would be more complex if several different commodities were sold, but the basic principles would not be affected.

The analysis of these data in Exhibit 600.86 shows that the favorable increase of $25,000 in the contribution margin was due in large part to an increase in the number of units sold. This increase was partially offset by a decrease in the unit sales price and an increase in the unit cost for variable selling and administrative expenses. The decrease in the unit cost for the variable cost of goods sold was an additional favorable result of 2003 operations.

The information presented in the contribution margin analysis report is useful to management in evaluating past performance and in planning future operations. For example, the impact of the $0.50 reduction in the unit sales price on the number of units sold and on the total sales for the year is useful information that management can use in determining whether further price reductions might be desirable. The contribution margin analysis report also highlights the impact of changes in unit variable costs and expenses. For example, the $0.05 increase in the unit variable selling and administrative expenses might be a result of increased advertising expenditures. If so, the increase in the number of units sold in 2003 could be attributed to both the $0.50 price reduction and the increased advertising.

Example 46 *If the actual price was $48 per unit, the planned price was $40 per unit, and the volume sold increased by 5,000 units, to a total of 60,000 units, what would be (a) the quantity factor and (b) the unit price factor for sales?*

(a) $200,000 (5,000 units × $40 per unit);   (b) $480,000 ($8 × 60,000 units)

Exhibit 600.85   *Data Table for Noble Inc.*

	Actual	Planned	Increase or (Decrease)
Sales	$937,500	$800,000	$137,500
Less: Variable cost of goods sold	$425,000	$350,000	$ 75,000
Variable selling and administrative expenses	162,500	125,000	37,500
Total	$587,500	$475,000	$112,500
Contribution margin	$350,000	$325,000	$ 25,000
Number of units sold	125,000	100,000	
Per unit:			
Sales price	$7.50	$8.00	
Variable cost of goods sold	$3.40	$3.50	
Variable selling and administrative expenses	$1.30	$1.25	

Exhibit 600.86 *Contribution Margin Analysis Report for Noble Inc.*

Noble Inc.
Contribution Margin Analysis
for the Year Ended December 31, 2003

Increase in amount of sales attributed to:			
Quantity factor:			
Increase in number of units sold in 2003		25,000	
Planned sales price in 2003		× $8.00	$200,000
Price factor:			
Decrease in unit sales price in 2003		$(0.50)	
Number of units sold in 2003		× 125,000	(62,500)
Net increase in amount of sales			$137,500
Increase in amount of variable cost of goods sold attributed to:			
Quantity factor:			
Increase in number of units sold in 2003	25,000		
Planned unit cost in 2003	× $3.50	$ 87,500	
Unit cost factor:			
Decrease in unit cost in 2003	$ (0.10)		
Number of units sold in 2003	× 125,000	(12,500)	
Net increase in amount of variable cost of goods sold		$ 75,000	
Increase in amount of variable selling and administrative expenses attributed to:			
Quantity factor:			
Increase in number of units sold in 2003	25,000		
Planned unit cost in 2003	× $1.25	$ 31,250	
Unit cost factor:			
Increase in unit cost in 2003	$ 0.05		
Number of units sold in 2003	× 125,000	6,250	
Net increase in the amount of variable selling and administrative expenses		$ 37,500	
Net increase in amount of variable costs			112,500
Increase in contribution margin			$ 25,000

Accounting and Reporting

Corporate Annual Reports

Corporations normally issue annual reports to their stockholders and other interested parties. Such reports summarize the corporation's operating activities for the past year and plans for the future. There are many variations in the order and form for presenting the major sections of annual reports. However, one section of the annual report is devoted to the financial statements, including the accompanying notes. In addition, annual reports usually include the following sections.

1. Financial Highlights
2. President's Letter to the Stockholders
3. Management Discussion and Analysis
4. Independent Auditors' Report
5. Historical Summary

1. Financial Highlights

The Financial Highlights section summarizes the operating results for the last year or two. It is sometimes called *Results in Brief*. It is usually presented on the first one or two pages of the annual report.

There are many variations in the format and content of the Financial Highlights section. Such items as sales, net income, net income per common share, cash dividends paid, cash dividends per common share, and the amount of capital expenditures are typically presented. In addition to these data, information about the financial position at the end of the year may be presented.

2. President's Letter to the Stockholders

A letter from the company president to the stockholders is also presented in most annual reports. These letters usually discuss such items as reasons for an increase or decrease in net income, changes in existing plants, purchase or construction of new plants, significant new financing commitments, social responsibility issues, and future plans.

3. Management Discussion and Analysis

A required disclosure in the annual report filed with the Securities and Exchange Commission is the **Management Discussion and Analysis (MDA).** The MDA provides critical information in interpreting the financial statements and assessing the future of the company.

The MDA includes an analysis of the results of operations and discusses management's opinion about future performance. It compares the prior year's income statement with the current year's to explain changes in sales, significant expenses, gross profit, and income from operations. For example, an increase in sales may be explained by referring to higher shipment volume or stronger prices.

The MDA also includes an analysis of the company's financial condition. It compares significant balance sheet items between successive years to explain changes in liquidity and capital resources. In addition, the MDA discusses significant risk exposure, such as fluctuations in foreign currencies, credit risk, and worldwide economic conditions.

4. Independent Auditors' Report

Before issuing annual statements, all publicly held corporations are required to have an independent audit (examination) of their financial statements. For the financial statements of most companies, the CPAs who conduct the audit render an opinion on the fairness of the statements.

5. Historical Summary

The Historical Summary section reports selected financial and operating data of past periods, usually for five or ten years. It is usually presented near the financial statements for the current year. There are wide variations in the types of data reported and the title of this section.

New Business Reporting Model

The American Institute Certified Public Accountants (AICPA) is proposing a new business reporting model for accountants and corporations.[5] It is based on the premise that the highest quality auditing will be of declining value if the underlying information is outdated or exclude relevant factors.

The new business reporting model would encompass five fundamental elements: (1) reliable systems to collect and analyze information, (2) industry-specific financial and nonfinancial performance measures, (3) better quality disclosures written in "plain English," (4) corporate accountability, and (5) real-time distribution of information. These fundamentals must integrate within an organization as the organization moves toward online, real-time reporting. Achieving the online, real-time goal is the only way to truly meet market-place demands for more relevant, up-to-date minute information.

By supplying a broader "bandwidth" of information that addresses such issues as off-balance-sheet activity, liquidity, nonfinancial performance indicators, and unreported intangibles, financial reporting can begin to address the complexities of today's corporations.

The goal is to improve the timeliness, reliability, and transparency of financial information reported to investors, creditors, and others.

Financial Quality

A manufacturing firm is mostly concerned about its product quality. Similarly, financial quality should be of concern to any organization, whether manufacturing or not. Financial quality means a firm's ability to produce a continuous stream of earnings that are supported by renewable sources of cash flow. The issue here is whether the cash flows are coming from recurring events or from nonrecurring events, where the former is preferred. *In a way, a continuous stream of earnings provides a renewable source of cash flows.*

Why assess financial quality? Financial statements of corporations are complex and difficult to read and understand because of the vast amounts of data in them and many disclosures and footnotes contained in them. Two user groups watch financial statements very closely in an effort to understand them prior to making decisions. These groups include (1) equity holders and equity analysts and (2) credit holders and credit analysts.

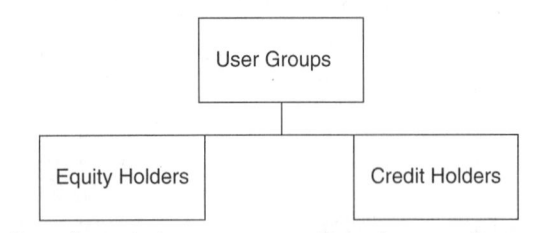

- Focus is on stock "buy" decision
- Focus is on stock "sell" decision
- Focus is on earning power

- Focus is on granting credit
- Focus is on extending credit
- Focus is on earning power

Both user groups are interested in a firm's ability to generate cash flows and its earning power. For equity holders, cash flow can be used for reinvestment to produce capital gains, for dividend payments, and for stock buyback. For credit holders, the cash flow can be used for the payment of interest and principal on loans. The sooner the cash flow is generated, the better. Current financial statements that show historical data can be used to assess financial quality. Financial quality can be expressed in terms of an equation, as follows:

Financial Quality = Income Statement Quality + Balance Sheet Quality

Authors Comiskey and Mulford in their book *Guide to Financial Reporting and Analysis* label the income statement quality as "earnings quality" and the balance sheet quality as "position quality."[6] Earnings quality focuses on reported income that is sustainable and backed by cash flows. Examples of earnings quality include (1) nonrecurring revenue or gain that impairs the earnings quality and (2) nonrecurring expense or loss that enhance the earnings quality. Position quality is a measurement of differences in liquidation values and book values for on-balance-sheet items and the amount of liquidation values for off-balance-sheet items. Examples of position quality that affects on-balance-sheet items include (1) liquidation value of asset exceeding book value resulting in enhancing the position quality and (2) book value of asset exceeding liquidation value resulting in impairing the position quality. Examples of position quality that affects off-balance-sheet items include (1) off-balance-sheet assets that enhance the position quality and (2) off-balance-sheet liabilities that impair the position quality.

A financial statement item is said to be of high financial quality when it sends a positive signal of earnings power. Similarly, low financial quality results from an item that sends a negative signal of earnings power. Financial quality leads to financial flexibility in that it provides the ability to deal with unexpected events while sustaining earning power. Financial flexibility protects against financial setbacks, and it mainly comes from the balance sheet (position) quality. When a firm attains financial flexibility, it can raise money in less time with low cost and from several sources.

Information Systems and Accounting

Basic Accounting Systems

An **accounting system** is the methods and procedures for collecting, classifying, summarizing, and reporting a business's financial and operating information. The accounting system for most businesses, however, is more complex than NetSolutions'. Accounting systems for large businesses must be able to collect, accumulate, and report many types of transactions. For example, **United Airlines'** accounting system collects and maintains information on ticket reservations, credit card collections, aircraft maintenance, employee hours, frequent-flier mileage balances, fuel consumption, and travel agent commissions, just to name a few. As you might expect, United Airlines' accounting system has evolved as the company has grown.

Accounting systems evolve through a three-step process as a business grows and changes. The first step in this process is **analysis,** which consists of (1) identifying the needs of those who use the business's financial information and (2) determining how the system should provide this information. For NetSolutions, we determined that Chris Clark would need financial statements for the new business. In the second step, the system is **designed** so that it will meet the users' needs. For NetSolutions, a very basic manual system was designed. This system included a chart of accounts, a two-column journal, and a general ledger. Finally, the system is **implemented** and used. For NetSolutions, the system was used to record transactions and prepare financial statements.

Hershey Foods learned the hard way about the importance of careful analysis and design prior to implementing a complex information system. Hershey implemented a $112 million computer system by using a "big-bang" start-up, rather than using a gradual implementation strategy. When the switch was thrown, the company ran into immediate problems shipping orders to customers. As a result, profits were cut by 20%, and product shipments during the all-important Halloween selling season were delayed.

An accounting system must be able to adapt to changing information needs. Thus, once a system has been implemented, **feedback,** or input, from the users of the information can be used to analyze and improve the system.

Internal controls and information processing methods are essential in an accounting system. **Internal controls** are the policies and procedures that protect assets from misuse, ensure that business information is accurate, and ensure that laws and regulations are being followed. **Processing methods** are the means by which the system collects, summarizes, and reports accounting information. These methods may be either *manual* or *computerized*.

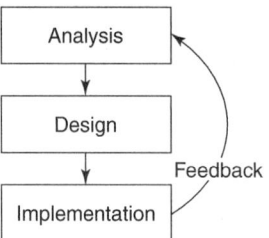

Understanding manual systems helps you understand how computerized systems function. Computerized accounting systems use electronic technology and media to perform more rapidly the same processing functions as manual accounting systems.

Auditing and Accounting

Nature of Auditing

Basically speaking, accounting is collection of data and information while auditing is verification of such data and information. As stated in Section 603, accounting can be divided into financial accounting and managerial accounting. Similarly, auditing can be divided into external auditing and internal auditing.

External Auditing

External auditing is defined as a systematic process of objectively obtaining and evaluating evidence regarding assertions about economic actions and events to ascertain the degree of correspondence between those assertions and established criteria, and communicating the audit results to interested parties.

External auditing work is conducted by independent, public accountants working for a private organization, using professional standards and complying with generally accepted auditing standards. Basically, external auditors perform financial audit work. The audit report is the auditor's formal means of communicating to interested parties a conclusion about the audited financial statements. In issuing an audit report, the auditor must meet the four generally accepted auditing standards of reporting.

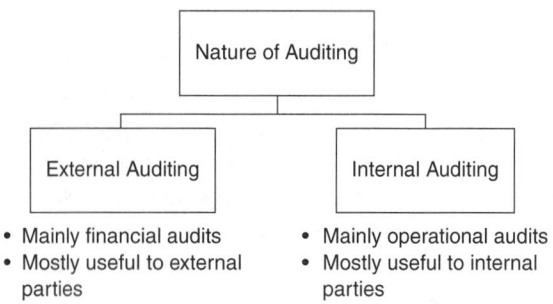

The Standard Audit Report

The standard report is the most common report issued. It contains an "unqualified opinion" stating that the financial statements present fairly, in all material respects, the financial position, results of operations, and cash flows of the entity in conformity with generally accepted accounting principles. This conclusion may be expressed only when the auditor has formed such an opinion on the basis of an audit performed in accordance with generally accepted auditing standards.

Departures From the Standard Audit Report

There are two categories of departure from the unqualified opinion. The first category of departure report is that the opinion paragraph continues to express an unqualified opinion because the financial statements are in conformity with generally accepted accounting principles. However, some circumstances exist that require the auditor to add an explanatory paragraph to the standard report.

The second category of departure results when either of the following circumstances occurs.

- The financial statements contain a material departure from generally accepted accounting principles.
- The auditor has been unable to obtain sufficient competent evidence regarding one or more of management's assertions, and as a result does not have a reasonable basis for an unqualified opinion on the financial statements as a whole.

In case of departures, the auditor will express one of the following types of opinions.

- A "qualified opinion," which states that, except for the effects of the matter(s) to which the qualification relates, the financial statements present fairly and in conformity with generally accepted accounting principles
- An "adverse opinion," which states that the financial statements do not present fairly and in conformity with generally accepted accounting principles
- A "disclaimer of opinion," which states that the auditor does not express an opinion on the financial statements

Of all the possible audit opinions, management of a firm prefers an unqualified opinion.

Need for a Financial Statement Audit

Why audit financial statements? Public companies in the United States are required to submit their audited financial statements in order to be registered, listed, and traded in the securities markets. Without audits, companies would be denied access to capital markets. Banks need audited financial statements before lending money.

Users of financial statements (e.g., investors, creditors, and others) use the audited financial statements to make investment, lending, and other decisions. They look to the independent auditor's report for assurance that the statements are relevant and reliable. Users seek assurance from outside independent auditors that the information in the financial statements is both free from the firm's management bias and that it is neutral (i.e., the information is not presented in a way that favors one user group over another).

Decisions made by users of the financial statements have significant economic and social consequences. Therefore, users look to the independent auditor for assurance that the financial statements have been prepared in conformity with generally accepted accounting principles and that they include all the required and appropriate disclosures for informed decision making.

Users want to make sure that the auditors verify management assertions to minimize misrepresentations and errors, and to assure that the statements are correct, complete, and unbiased. In this regard, audit reports will provide the credibility of financial statements.

Benefits of a Financial Statement Audit

The economic benefits of financial statements audits include the following.

- Large companies will have access to capital markets to raise money by issuing stock or bonds.
- Small companies can obtain loan from banks at a lower interest rate than otherwise.
- Both employees and management will be more careful before misappropriating company assets due to the audit process. The audit can act as a deterrent to fraudulent activities (e.g., embezzlements, theft, and other irregularities).
- Auditors usually make recommendations to increase the efficiency and effectiveness of business operations based on the work performed during the audit process.

Limitations of a Financial Statement Audit

Similar to accounting, audit work is not an exact science. It is a human endeavor, and subject to time and cost limitations. The time constraint can affect the amount of evidence collected while the cost constraint imposes selective testing or sampling of business records and supporting data. The relatively short period available for the auditor can cause some audit issues to remain unresolved before the publication of the auditor's report.

Another significant limitation is the established accounting framework for the preparation of financial statements. Accounting standards allow for alternative use of accounting principles and methods. Estimates and judgment are inherent parts of the accounting process. Both auditors and management of the audited organization cannot foresee the outcome of uncertainties inherent in business activities. Because of these limitations and constraints, the audit work does not or cannot guarantee the exactness of and cannot add certainty to financial statements. Despite these limitations, a financial statement audit can add credibility to the financial statement.

Comparison of Financial Accounting With External Auditing

Financial Accounting	External Auditing
It is the responsibility of an organization's management.	It is the responsibility of an independent auditor working for a public accounting firm.
It is guided by generally accepted accounting principles and business ethics.	It is guided by generally accepted auditing standards and professional ethics.
Its focus is to analyze business events; measure, collect, and record transaction data; and classify and summarize such recorded data.	Its focus is to obtain and evaluate evidence, verify data in financial statements, and assure conformity with generally accepted accounting principles.
Its output is to prepare and distribute financial statements along with auditor's report to stockholders in annual report.	Its output is to express a professional opinion on the financial statements and issue an audit report to client.

Internal Auditing

Internal auditing is defined as an independent, objective assurance and consulting activity designed to add value and improve an organization's operations. It helps an organization accomplish its objectives by bringing a systematic, disciplined approach to evaluate and improve the effectiveness of risk management, control, and governance processes.

Internal auditing work is conducted by internal auditors working for an organization, using the standards established for the professional practice of internal auditing by the Institute of Internal Auditors (IIA). Basically, internal auditors perform operational audit work.

The IIA's performance standards define the nature of internal audit work as follows.

- **Risk Management.** The internal audit activity should assist the organization by identifying and evaluating significant exposures to risk and contributing to the improvement of risk-management and control systems.
- **Control.** The internal audit activity should assist the organization in maintaining effective controls by evaluating their effectiveness and efficiency and by promoting continuous improvement.
- **Governance.** The internal audit activity should contribute to the organization's governance process by evaluating and improving the process through which (1) values and goals are established and communicated, (2) the accomplishment of goals is monitored, (3) accountability is ensured, and (4) values are preserved.

The IIA's attribute standards define the internal audit's purpose, authority, and responsibility, independence and objectivity, proficiency and due professional care, and quality assurance and improvement program as follows.

- The purpose, authority, and responsibility of the internal audit activity should be formally defined in a charter, consistent with the Standards, and approved by the board. Here, "the board" means board of directors, audit committee of such boards, head of an agency or legislative body to whom internal auditors report, board of governors or trustees of a nonprofit organization, or any other designated governing bodies of an organization.
- The internal audit activity should be independent, and internal auditors should be objective in performing their work.
- Internal audit engagement should be performed with proficiency and due professional care.
- The chief audit executive should develop and maintain a quality assurance and improvement program that covers all aspects of the internal audit activity and continuously monitors its effectiveness.

Types of Audits Performed

In general, there are six types of audits performed by either external or internal auditors. In a way, audits can be divided into two categories: financial and nonfinancial. The different types of nonfinancial audits include: (1) operational auditing, (2) compliance auditing, (3) IT auditing, (4) performance auditing, and (5) program auditing. Each type is presented next.

Types of Audits
Financial auditing (focus is on balance sheet and income statement)
Operational auditing (focus is on resource utilization, accomplishment of operational goals)
Compliance auditing (focus is on adherence to laws and regulations)
IT auditing (focus is on integrity and security of computer systems)
Performance auditing (focus is on effectiveness, economy, and efficient use of resources)
Program auditing (focus is on achieving program goals)

Basically, **financial auditing** focuses on balance sheets and income statements. Balance sheets and income statements are the two primary outputs of the financial reporting process. The statement of cash flows and retained earnings are also produced during the financial audit process.

Operational auditing is defined as determining whether the entity is managing and utilizing its resources economically and efficiently. To gain the auditee's cooperation, it is good to allow the auditee to participate in the development of recommendations for improvement. General audit objectives for an operational review include the following.

- To ensure the reliability and integrity of information
- To ensure compliance with policies, plans, procedures, laws, and regulations
- To ensure the safeguarding of assets (e.g., inventories)
- To ensure the economical and efficient use of resources
- To ensure the accomplishment of established objectives and goals for operations or programs

A determination of cost savings is most likely to be an objective of operational auditing. Some specific examples of operational auditing objectives include: (1) determining if purchasing management procures the right materials at the right time in the right quantities at the right price, (2) determining that proper measures of performance are used for a governmental agency providing service to the citizens, and (3) determining if the marketing department has the organizational status needed to accomplish its objectives and operations in a manner that is cost-beneficial to the company.

Compliance auditing is defined as determining whether the entity complies with laws and regulations. Examples of compliance audit objectives include: (1) determination of approval for expenditure of restricted funds at a government-supported university, (2) evaluating the propriety of the accounting for and use of customer deposits at a public utility, (3) determining if purchases are approved at the proper level of authorization on the basis of dollar amount, as designated by company policy, and (4) determining whether employee benefit programs are operating in accordance with corporate policy and government regulations.

Information Technology (IT) auditing is defined as determining the integrity and security of electronic data processing systems and the data they generate along with computer operations.

Performance auditing and **program auditing** are conducted by government auditors. Performance audits are similar to operational audits conducted by auditors in the private sector. According to the 1994 U.S. General Accounting Office (GAO) Government Auditing Standards, a performance audit is an objective and systematic examination of evidence for the purpose of providing an independent assessment of the performance of an existing or proposed government organization, program, or activity in order to provide useful information to improve public accountability and decision making. Performance audits generally focus on efficiency and effectiveness, with emphasis on effectiveness. Program audits focus on achieving program goals.

Control and Accounting

Control Procedures

Control procedures are established to provide reasonable assurance that business goals will be achieved, including the prevention of fraud. In the following paragraphs, we will briefly discuss control procedures that can be integrated throughout the accounting system. These procedures are listed in Exhibit 600.87.

An accounting clerk for the Grant County (Washington) Alcoholism Program was in charge of collecting money, making deposits, and keeping the records. While the clerk was away on maternity leave, the replacement clerk discovered a fraud: $17,800 in fees had been collected but had been hidden for personal gain.

COMPETENT PERSONNEL, ROTATING DUTIES, AND MANDATORY VACATIONS The successful operation of an accounting system requires procedures to ensure that people are able to perform the duties to which they are assigned. Hence, it is necessary that all accounting employees be adequately trained and supervised in performing their jobs. It may also be advisable to rotate duties of clerical personnel and mandate vacations for nonclerical personnel. These policies encourage employees to adhere to prescribed procedures. In addition, existing errors or fraud may be detected.

Exhibit 600.87 *Internal Control Procedures*

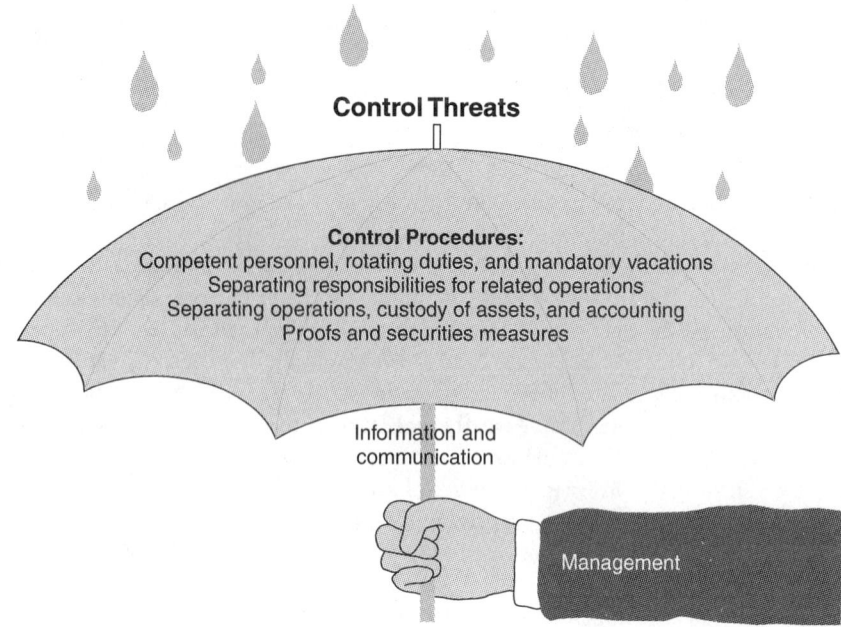

SEPARATING RESPONSIBILITIES FOR RELATED OPERATIONS To decrease the possibility of inefficiency, errors, and fraud, the responsibility for related operations should be divided among two or more persons. For example, the responsibilities for purchasing, receiving, and paying for computer supplies should be divided among three persons or departments. If the same person orders supplies, verifies the receipt of the supplies, and pays the supplier, the following abuses are possible.

1. Orders may be placed on the basis of friendship with a supplier, rather than on price, quality, and other objective factors.
2. The quantity and quality of supplies received may not be verified, thus causing payment for supplies not received or poor-quality supplies.
3. Supplies may be stolen by the employee.
4. The validity and accuracy of invoices may be verified carelessly, thus causing the payment of false or inaccurate invoices.

The "checks and balances" provided by dividing responsibilities among various departments requires no duplication of effort. The business documents prepared by one department are designed to coordinate with and support those prepared by other departments.

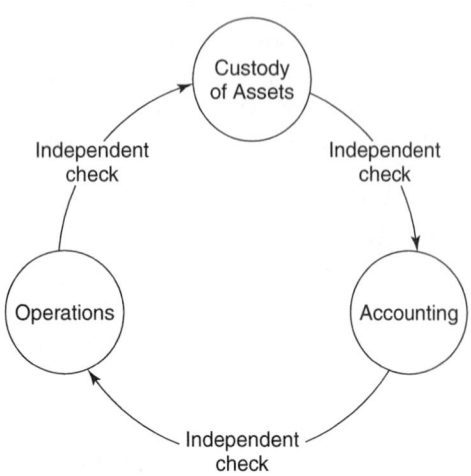

SEPARATING OPERATIONS, CUSTODY OF ASSETS, AND ACCOUNTING Control policies should establish the responsibilities for various business activities. To reduce the possibility of errors and fraud, the responsibilities for operations, custody of assets, and accounting should be separated. The accounting records then serve as an independent check on the individuals who have custody of the assets and who engage in the business operations. For example, the employees entrusted with handling cash receipts from credit customers should not record cash receipts in the accounting records. To do so would allow employees to borrow or steal cash and hide the theft in the records. Likewise, if those engaged in operating activities also record the results of operations, they could distort the accounting reports to show favorable results. For example, a store manager whose year-end bonus is based upon operating profits might be tempted to record fictitious sales in order to receive a larger bonus.

PROOFS AND SECURITY MEASURES Proofs and security measures should be used to safeguard assets and ensure reliable accounting data. This control procedure applies to many different techniques, such as authorization, approval, and reconciliation procedures. For example, employees who travel on company business may be required to obtain a department manager's approval on a travel request form.

Other examples of control procedures include the use of bank accounts and other measures to ensure the safety of cash and valuable documents. A cash register that displays the amount recorded for each sale and provides the customer a printed receipt can be an effective part of the internal control structure. An all-night convenience store could use the following security measures to deter robberies.

Over $700,000 of child support money disappeared over seven years due to the alleged falsification of checks by an accountant in Indiana's Family and Social Services Administration. The fraud could have been discovered, according to the State Examiner, if the agency reconciled its books, controlled access to blank checks, and used receipts.

1. Locate the cash register near the door, so that it is fully visible from outside the store; have two employees work late hours; employ a security guard.
2. Deposit cash in the bank daily, before 5 P.M.
3. Keep only small amounts of cash on hand after 5 P.M. by depositing excess cash in a store safe that can't be opened by employees on duty.
4. Install cameras and alarm systems.

Example 47 *Why is separation of duties considered a control procedure?*

Internal control is enhanced by separating the control of a transaction from the recordkeeping function. Fraud is more easily committed when a single individual controls both the transaction and the accounting for the transaction.

Monitoring

Monitoring the internal control system locates weaknesses and improves control effectiveness. The internal control system can be monitored through either ongoing efforts by management or by separate evaluations. Ongoing monitoring efforts may include observing both employee behavior and warning signs from the accounting system. The indicators shown in Exhibit 600.88 may be clues to internal control problems.

Separate monitoring evaluations are generally performed when there are major changes in strategy, senior management, business structure, or operations. In large businesses, internal auditors who are independent of operations normally are responsible for monitoring the internal control system. Internal auditors can report issues and concerns to an audit committee of the board of directors, who are independent of management. In addition, external auditors also evaluate internal control as a normal part of their annual financial statement audit.[7]

Information and Communication

Information and communication are essential elements of internal control. Information about the control environment, risk assessment, control procedures, and monitoring are needed by management to guide operations and ensure compliance with reporting, legal, and regulatory requirements.

Management can also use external information to assess events and conditions that impact decision making and external reporting. For example, management uses information from the Financial Accounting Standards Board (FASB) to assess the impact of possible changes in reporting standards.

*In one of the largest frauds ever committed against a university, a former financial aid officer for **New York University** was charged with stealing $4.1 million from the state of New York. The aid officer allegedly falsified over a thousand tuition assistance checks to students who were not entitled to receive aid and who did not know about the checks. The aid officer deposited the bogus checks for personal use. The initial evidence of the fraud was the officer's spending of $785,000 on expensive jewelry.*

Exhibit 600.88 *Indicators of Internal Control Problems*

Clues To Potential Problems

Warning signs with regard to people	Warning signs from the accounting system
1. Abrupt change in lifestyle (without winning the lottery). 2. Close social relationships with suppliers. 3. Refusing to take a vacation. 4. Frequent borrowing from other employees. 5. Excessive use of alcohol or drugs.	1. Missing documents or gaps in transaction numbers (could mean documents are being used for fraudulent transactions). 2. An unusual increase in customer refunds (refunds may be phony). 3. Differences between daily cash receipts and bank deposits (could mean receipts are pocketed before being deposited). 4. Sudden increase in slow payments (employee may be pocketing the payment). 5. Backlog in recording transactions (possibly an attempt to delay detection of fraud).

Nature of Cash and the Importance of Controls Over Cash

Cash includes coins, currency (paper money), checks, money orders, and money on deposit that is available for unrestricted withdrawal from banks and other financial institutions. Normally, you can think of cash as anything that a bank would accept for deposit in your account. For example, a check made payable to you could normally be deposited in a bank and thus is considered cash.

We will assume in this section that a business maintains only *one* bank account, represented in the ledger as *Cash*. In practice, however, a business may have several bank accounts, such as one for general cash payments and another for payroll. For each of its bank accounts, the business will maintain a ledger account, one of which may be called *Cash in Bank—First Bank,* for example. It will also maintain separate ledger accounts for cash that it does not keep in the bank, such as cash for small payments, and cash used for special purposes, such as travel reimbursements. We will introduce some of these other cash accounts in the section.

Because of the ease with which money can be transferred, cash is the asset most likely to be diverted and used improperly by employees. In addition, many transactions either directly or indirectly affect the receipt or the payment of cash. Businesses must therefore design and use controls that safeguard cash and control the authorization of cash transactions. In the following paragraphs, we will discuss these controls.

Control of Cash Receipts

To protect cash from theft and misuse, a business must control cash from the time it is received until it is deposited in a bank. Such procedures are called preventive controls. Procedures that are designed to detect theft or misuse of cash are called detective controls. In a sense, detective controls are also preventive in nature, since employees are less likely to steal or misuse cash if they know there is a good chance they will be discovered.

Retail businesses normally receive cash from two main sources: (1) cash receipts from customers and (2) mail receipts from customers making payments on account. These two sources of cash are shown in Exhibit 600.89.

Controlling Cash Received From Cash Sales

Regardless of the source of cash receipts, every business must properly safeguard and record its cash receipts. One of the most important controls to protect cash received in over-the-counter sales is a cash register. You may have noticed that when a clerk (cashier) enters the amount of a sale, the cash register normally displays the amount. This is a control to ensure that the clerk has charged you the correct amount. You also receive a receipt to verify the accuracy of the amount.

At the beginning of a work shift, each cash register clerk is given a cash drawer that contains a predetermined amount of cash for making change for customers. The amount in each drawer is sometimes called a change fund. At the end of the work shift, each clerk and the supervisor count the cash in the clerk's cash drawer. The amount of cash

Exhibit 600.89 *Retailers' Sources of Cash*

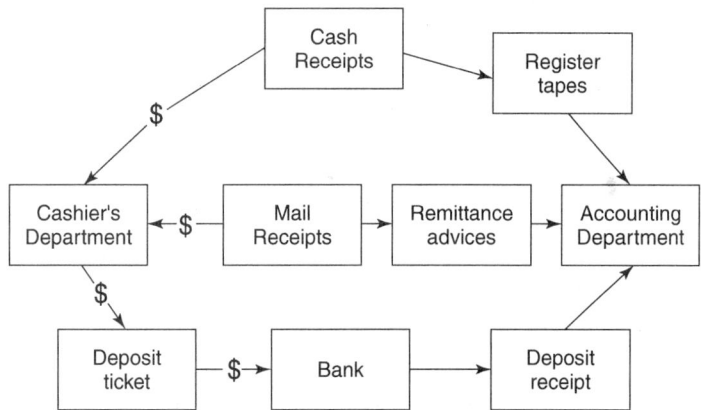

in each drawer should equal the beginning amount of cash plus the cash sales for the day. However, errors in recording cash sales or errors in making change cause the amount of actual cash on hand to differ from this amount. Such differences are recorded in a cash short and over account.

At the end of the accounting period, a debit balance in the cash short and over account is included in Miscellaneous Administrative Expense in the income statement. A credit balance is included in the Other Income section. If a clerk consistently has significant cash short and over amounts, the supervisor may require the clerk to take additional training.

After a cash register clerk's cash has been counted and recorded on a memorandum form, the cash is then placed in a store safe in the Cashier's Department until it can be deposited in the bank. The supervisor forwards the clerk's cash register tapes to the Accounting Department, where they become the basis for recording the transactions for the day.

Controlling Cash Received in the Mail

Cash is received in the mail when customers pay their bills. This cash is usually in the form of checks and money orders. Most companies' invoices are designed so that customers return a portion of the invoice, called a remittance advice, with their payment. The employee who opens the incoming mail should initially compare the amount of cash received with the amount shown on the remittance advice. If a customer does not return a remittance advice, an employee prepares one. Like the cash register, the remittance advice serves as a record of cash initially received. It also helps ensure that the posting to the customer's account is accurate. Finally, as a preventive control, the employee opening the mail normally also stamps checks and money orders "For Deposit Only" in the bank account of the business.

Some retail companies use debit card systems to transfer and record the receipt of cash. In a debit card system, a customer pays for goods at the time of purchase by presenting a plastic card. The card authorizes the electronic transfer of cash from the customer's checking account to the retailer's bank account at the time of the sale.

All cash received in the mail is sent to the Cashier's Department. An employee there combines it with the receipts from cash sales and prepares a bank deposit ticket. The remittance advices and their summary totals are delivered to the Accounting Department. An accounting clerk then prepares the records of the transactions and posts them to the customer accounts.

When cash is deposited in the bank, the bank normally stamps a duplicate copy of the deposit ticket with the amount received. This bank receipt is returned to the Accounting Department, where a clerk then compares the receipt with the total amount that should have been deposited. This control helps ensure that all the cash is deposited and that no cash is lost or stolen on the way to the bank. Any shortages are thus promptly detected.

The separation of the duties of the Cashier's Department, which handles cash, and the Accounting Department, which records cash, is a preventive control. If Accounting Department employees both handled and recorded cash, an employee could steal cash and change the accounting records to hide the theft.

Internal Control of Cash Payments

Internal control of cash payments should provide reasonable assurance that payments are made for only authorized transactions. In addition, controls should ensure that cash is used efficiently. For example, controls should ensure that all available discounts, such as purchase and trade discounts, are taken.

In a small business, an owner/manager may sign all checks, based upon personal knowledge of goods and services purchased. In a large business, however, checks are often prepared by employees who do not have such a complete knowledge of the transactions. In a large business, for example, the duties of purchasing goods, inspecting the goods received, and verifying the invoices are usually performed by different employees. These duties must be coordinated to ensure that checks for proper amounts are issued to creditors. One system used for this purpose is the voucher system.

Basic Features of the Voucher System

A **voucher system** is a set of procedures for authorizing and recording liabilities and cash payments. A voucher system normally uses (1) vouchers, (2) a file for unpaid vouchers, and (3) a file for paid vouchers. Generally, a voucher is any document that serves as proof of authority to pay cash. For example, an invoice properly approved for payment could be considered a voucher. In many businesses, however, a **voucher** is a special form for recording relevant data about a liability and the details of its payment.

Each voucher includes the creditor's invoice number and the amount and terms of the invoice. The accounts used in recording the purchase (or transaction) are listed in the *account distribution*.

A voucher is normally prepared in the Accounting Department, after all necessary supporting documents have been received. For example, when a voucher is prepared for the purchase of goods, the voucher should be supported by the supplier's invoice, a purchase order, and a receiving report. In preparing the voucher, an accounts payable clerk verifies the quantity, price, and mathematical accuracy of the supporting documents. This provides assurance that the payment is for goods that were properly ordered and received.

After a voucher is prepared, the voucher and its supporting documents are given to the proper official for approval. After it has been approved, the voucher is returned to the Accounting Department, where it is recorded in the accounts. It is then filed in an unpaid voucher file by its due date so that all available purchase discounts are taken.

On its due date, the voucher is removed from the unpaid voucher file. The date, the number, and the amount of the check written in payment are listed on the back of the voucher. The payment of the voucher is recorded in the same manner as the payment of an account payable.

After payment, vouchers are marked "Paid" and are usually filed in numerical order in a paid voucher file. They are then readily available for examination by employees needing information about past payments.

A voucher system may be either manual or computerized. In a computerized system, properly approved supporting documents (such as purchase orders and receiving reports) would be entered directly into computer files. At the due date, the checks would be automatically generated and mailed to creditors. At that time, the voucher would be automatically transferred to a paid voucher file. In some cases, payments may be made electronically rather than by check.

Electronic Funds Transfer

With rapidly changing technology, new systems are being devised to more efficiently record and transfer cash among companies. Such systems often use **electronic funds transfer (EFT)**. In an EFT system, computers rather than paper (money, checks, etc.) are used to effect cash transactions. For example, a business may pay its employees by means of EFT. Under such a system, employees may authorize the deposit of their payroll checks directly into checking accounts. Each pay period, the business electronically transfers the employees' net pay to their checking accounts through the use of computer systems and telephone lines. Likewise, many companies are using EFT systems to pay their suppliers and other vendors.

Bank Accounts: Their Nature and Use as a Control Over Cash

Most of you are already familiar with bank accounts. You have a checking account at a local bank, credit union, savings and loan association, or other financial institution. In this section, we discuss the nature of a bank account used by a business. The features of such accounts will be similar to your own bank account. We then discuss the use of bank accounts as an additional control over cash.

Business Bank Accounts

A business often maintains several bank accounts. The forms used with each bank account are a signature card, deposit ticket, check, and record of checks drawn.

When you open a checking account, you sign a **signature card.** This card is used by the bank to verify the signature on checks that are submitted for payment. Also, when you open an account, the bank assigns an identifying number to the account.

The details of a deposit are listed by the depositor on a printed **deposit ticket** supplied by the bank. These forms are often prepared in duplicate. The bank teller stamps or initials a copy of the deposit ticket and gives it to the depositor as a receipt. Other types of receipts may also be used to give the depositor written proof of the date and the total amount of the deposit.

A **check** is a written document signed by the depositor, ordering the bank to pay a sum of money to an individual or entity. There are three parties to a check— the drawer, the drawee, and the payee. The **drawer** is the one who signs the check, ordering payment by the bank. The **drawee** is the bank on which the check is drawn. The **payee** is the party to whom payment is to be made.

The name and address of the depositor are usually printed on each check. In addition, checks are prenumbered, so that they can easily be kept track of by both the issuer and the bank. Banks encode their identification number and the depositor's account

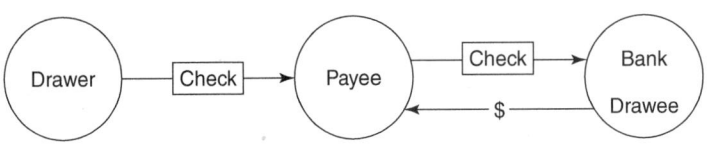

number in magnetic ink on each check. These numbers make it possible for the bank to sort and post checks automatically. When a check is presented for payment, the amount for which it is drawn is inserted, next to the account number, in magnetic ink. The processed check shown at the beginning of this chapter illustrated these features.

A record of each check should be prepared at the time a check is written. A small booklet called a **transactions register** is often used by both businesses and individuals for this purpose.

The purpose of a check may be written in space provided on the check or on an attachment to the check. Normally, checks issued to a creditor on account are sent with a form that identifies the specific invoice that is being paid. The purpose of this **remittance advice** is to make sure that proper credit is recorded in the accounts of the creditor. In this way, mistakes are less likely to occur.

Before depositing the check, the payee removes the remittance advice. The payee may then use the remittance advice as written proof of the details of the cash receipt.

Bank Statement

Banks usually maintain a record of all checking account transactions. A summary of all transactions, called a **statement of account,** is mailed to the depositor, usually each month. Like any account with a customer or a creditor, the bank statement shows the beginning balance, additions, deductions, and the balance at the end of the period.

The depositor's checks received by the bank during the period may accompany the bank statement, arranged in the order of payment. The paid checks are stamped "Paid," together with the date of payment. Other entries that the bank has made in the depositor's account may be described in debit or credit memorandums enclosed with the statement.

You should note that a depositor's checking account balance *in the bank's records* is a liability with a credit balance. Debit memorandums issued by the bank on a depositor's account therefore decrease the depositor's balance. Likewise, credit memorandums increase the depositor's balance. A bank issues a debit memorandum to charge (decrease) a depositor's account for service charges or for deposited checks returned because of insufficient funds. Likewise, a bank issues a credit memorandum when it increases the depositor's account for collecting a note receivable for the depositor, making a loan to the depositor, receiving a wire deposit, or adding interest to the depositor's account.

Bank Accounts as a Control Over Cash

A bank account is one of the primary tools a business uses to control cash. For example, businesses often require that all cash receipts be initially deposited in a bank account. Likewise, businesses usually use checks to make all cash payments, except for very small amounts. When such a system is used, there is a double record of cash transactions—one by the business and the other by the bank.

A bank account and a business's records provide a double record of cash transactions.

Exhibit 600.90 *Power Networking's Records and Bank Statement*

	Bank Statement		Power Networking Records	
Beginning Balance		$ 4,218.60	Beginning Balance	$ 4,227.60
Additions:				
Deposits		13,749.75	Deposits	14,565.95
Miscellaneous		408.00		
Deductions:				
Checks		14,698.57	Checks	16,243.56
NSF Check	$300			
Service Charge	18	318.00		
Ending Balance		$ 3,359.78	Ending Balance	$ 2,549.99

Power Networking should determine the reason for the difference in these two amounts.

A business can use a bank statement to compare the cash transactions recorded in its accounting records to those recorded by the bank. The cash balance shown by a bank statement is usually different from the cash balance shown in the accounting records of the business, as shown in Exhibit 600.90.

This difference may be the result of a delay by either party in recording transactions. For example, there is a time lag of one day or more between the date a check is written and the date that it is presented to the bank for payment. If the depositor mails deposits to the bank or uses the night depository, a time lag between the date of the deposit and the date that it is recorded by the bank is also probable. The bank may also debit or credit the depositor's account for transactions about which the depositor will not be informed until later.

The difference may be the result of errors made by either the business or the bank in recording transactions. For example, the business may incorrectly post to Cash a check written for $4,500 as $450. Likewise, a bank may incorrectly record the amount of a check.

Bank Reconciliation

For effective control, the reasons for the difference between the cash balance on the bank statement and the cash balance in the accounting records should be determined by preparing a bank reconciliation. A **bank reconciliation** is a listing of the items and amounts that cause the cash balance reported in the bank statement to differ from the balance of the cash account in the ledger.

A bank reconciliation is usually divided into two sections. The first section begins with the cash balance according to the bank statement and ends with the adjusted balance. The second section begins with the cash balance according to the depositor's records and ends with the adjusted balance. The two amounts designated as the adjusted balance must be equal. The content of the bank reconciliation is shown below.

Cash balance according to bank statement			$XXX	Cash balance according to depositor's records			$XXX
Add: Additions by depositor not on bank statement		$XX		Add: Additions by bank not recorded by depositor		$XX	
Bank errors		XX	XX	Depositor errors		XX	XX
			$XXX				$XXX
Deduct: Deductions by depositor not on bank statement		$XX		Deduct: Deductions by bank not recorded by depositor		$XX	
Bank errors		XX	XX	Depositor errors		XX	XX
Adjusted balance			$XXX	Adjusted balance			$XXX

must be equal

The following steps are useful in finding the reconciling items and determining the adjusted balance of Cash.

1. Compare each deposit listed on the bank statement with unrecorded deposits appearing in the preceding period's reconciliation and with deposit receipts or other records of deposits. *Add deposits not recorded by the bank to the balance according to the bank statement.*
2. Compare paid checks with outstanding checks appearing on the preceding period's reconciliation and with recorded checks. *Deduct checks outstanding that have not been paid by the bank from the balance according to the bank statement.*
3. Compare bank credit memorandums to entries in the journal. For example, a bank would issue a credit memorandum for a note receivable and interest that it collected for a depositor. *Add credit memorandums that have not been recorded to the balance according to the depositor's records.*
4. Compare bank debit memorandums to entries recording cash payments. For example, a bank normally issues debit memorandums for service charges and check printing charges. A bank also issues debit memorandums for not-sufficient-funds checks. A *not-sufficient-funds (NSF) check* is a customer's check that was recorded and deposited but was not paid when it was presented to the customer's bank for payment. NSF checks are normally charged back to the customer as an account receivable. *Deduct debit memorandums that have not been recorded from the balance according to the depositor's records.*
5. List any errors discovered during the preceding steps. For example, if an amount has been recorded incorrectly by the depositor, the amount of the error should be added to or deducted from the cash balance according to the depositor's records. Similarly, errors by the bank should be added to or deducted from the cash balance according to the bank statement.

Presentation of Cash on the Balance Sheet

Cash is the most liquid asset, and therefore it is listed as the first asset in the Current Assets section of the balance sheet. Most companies present only a single cash amount on the balance sheet by combining all their bank and cash fund accounts.

A company may have cash in excess of its operating needs. In such cases, the company normally invests in highly liquid investments in order to earn interest. These investments are called **cash equivalents.** To be classified as a cash equivalent, the investment is expected to be converted to cash within 90 days. Examples of cash equivalents include U.S. Treasury Bills, notes issued by major corporations (referred to as *commercial paper*), and money market funds. Companies that have invested excess cash in cash equivalents usually report *Cash and cash equivalents* as one amount on the balance sheet.

Banks may require depositors to maintain minimum cash balances in their bank accounts. Such a balance is called a **compensating balance.** This requirement is often imposed by the bank as a part of a loan agreement or line of credit. A *line of credit* is a preapproved amount the bank is willing to lend to a customer upon request. Compensating balance requirements should be disclosed in notes to the financial statements.

Internal Control of Receivables

The principles of internal control that we discussed in prior sections can be used to establish controls to safeguard receivables. For example, the four functions of credit approval, sales, accounting, and collections should be separated, as shown in Exhibit 600.91.

The individuals responsible for sales should be separate from the individuals accounting for the receivables and approving credit. By doing so, the accounting and credit approval functions serve as independent checks on sales. The employee who handles the accounting for receivables should not be involved with collecting receivables. Separating these functions reduces the possibility of errors and misuse of funds.

To illustrate the need to separate functions, assume that the accounts receivable billing clerk has access to cash receipts from customer collections. The clerk can steal a customer's cash payment and then alter the customer's monthly statement to indicate that the payment was received. The customer would not complain and the theft could go undetected.

To further illustrate the need for internal control of receivables, assume that salespersons have authority to approve credit. If the salespersons are paid commissions, say 10% of sales, they can increase their commissions by approving poor credit risks. Thus, the credit approval function is normally assigned to individuals outside the sales area.

Exhibit 600.91 *Separating the Receivable Functions*

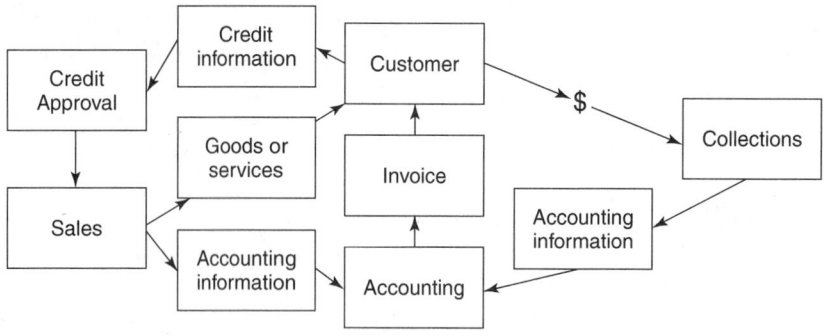

Internal Control of Inventories

The cost of inventory is a significant item in many businesses' financial statements. What do we mean by the term *inventory*? **Inventory** is used to indicate (1) merchandise held for sale in the normal course of business and (2) materials in the process of production or held for production. In this section, we focus primarily on inventory of merchandise purchased for resale.

What costs should be included in inventory? As we have illustrated in earlier sections, the cost of merchandise is its purchase price, less any purchases discounts. These costs are usually the largest portion of the inventory cost. Merchandise inventory also includes other costs, such as transportation, import duties, and insurance against losses in transit.

For companies such as **Circuit City,** good internal control over inventory must be maintained. Two primary objectives of internal control over inventory are safeguarding the inventory and properly reporting it in the financial statements. These internal controls can be either preventive or detective in nature. A preventive control is designed to prevent errors or misstatements from occurring. A detective control is designed to detect an error or misstatement after it has occurred.

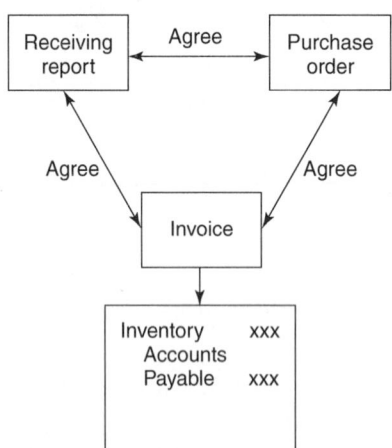

Control over inventory should begin as soon as the inventory is received. Prenumbered receiving reports should be completed by the company's receiving department in order to establish the initial accountability for the inventory. To make sure the inventory received is what was ordered, each receiving report should agree with the company's original purchase order for the merchandise. Likewise, the price at which the inventory was ordered, as shown on the purchase order, should be compared to the price at which the vendor billed the company, as shown on the vendor's invoice. After the receiving report, purchase order, and vendor's invoice have been reconciled, the company should record the inventory and related account payable in the accounting records.

Controls for safeguarding inventory include developing and using security measures to prevent inventory damage or employee theft. For example, inventory should be stored in a warehouse or other area to which access is restricted to authorized employees. The removal of merchandise from the warehouse should be controlled by using requisition forms, which should be properly authorized. The storage area should also be climate controlled to prevent damage from heat or cold. Further, when the business is not operating or is not open, the storage area should be locked.

When shopping, you may have noticed how retail stores protect inventory from customer theft. Retail stores often use such devices as two-way mirrors, cameras, and security guards. Highpriced items are often displayed in locked cabinets. Retail clothing stores often place plastic alarm tags on valuable items such as leather coats. Sensors at the exit doors set off alarms if the tags have not been removed by the clerk. These controls are designed to prevent customers from shoplifting.

Using a perpetual inventory system for merchandise also provides an effective means of control over inventory. The amount of each type of merchandise is always readily available in a subsidiary **inventory ledger.** In addition, the subsidiary ledger can be an aid in maintaining inventory quantities at proper levels. Frequently comparing balances with predetermined maximum and minimum levels allows for the timely reordering of merchandise and prevents the ordering of excess inventory.

All merchandise <u>owned</u> by a business should be included in the business's inventory.

To ensure the accuracy of the amount of inventory reported in the financial statements, a merchandising business should take a **physical inventory** (i.e., count the merchandise). In a perpetual inventory system, the physical inventory is compared to the recorded inventory in order to determine the amount of shrinkage or shortage. If the inventory shrinkage is unusually large, management can investigate further and take any necessary corrective action. Knowledge that a physical inventory will be taken also helps prevent employee thefts or misuses of inventory.

How does a business "take" a physical inventory? The first step in this process is to determine the quantity of each kind of merchandise owned by the business. A common practice is to use teams of two persons. One person determines the quantity, and the other lists the quantity and description on inventory count sheets. Quantities of high-cost items are usually verified by supervisors or a second count team.

What merchandise should be included in inventory? All the merchandise *owned* by the business on the inventory date should be included. For merchandise in transit, the party (the seller or the buyer) who has title to the merchandise on the inventory date is the owner. To determine who has title, it may be necessary to examine purchases and sales invoices of the last few days of the current period and the first few days of the following period.

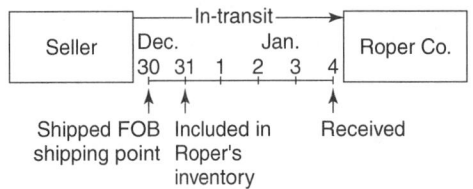

As we discussed in an earlier section, shipping terms determine when title passes. When goods are purchased or sold **FOB shipping point,** title passes to the buyer when the goods are shipped. When the terms are **FOB destination,** title passes to the buyer when the goods are delivered.

To illustrate, assume that Roper Co. orders $25,000 of merchandise on December 28, 2003. The merchandise is shipped FOB shipping point by the seller on December 30 and arrives at Roper Co.'s warehouse on January 4, 2004. As a result, the merchandise is not counted by the inventory crew on December 31, the end of Roper Co.'s fiscal year. However, the $25,000 of merchandise should be included in Roper's inventory because title has passed. Roper Co. should record the merchandise in transit on December 31, debiting Merchandise Inventory and crediting Accounts Payable for $25,000.

Manufacturers sometimes ship merchandise to retailers who act as the manufacturer's agent when selling the merchandise. The manufacturer retains title until the goods are sold. Such merchandise is said to be shipped *on consignment* to the retailers. The unsold merchandise is a part of the manufacturer's (consignor's) inventory, even though the merchandise is in the hands of the retailers. The consigned merchandise should not be included in the retailer's (consignee's) inventory.

Effect of Inventory Errors on Financial Statements

Any errors in the inventory count will affect both the balance sheet and the income statement. For example, an error in the physical inventory will misstate the ending inventory, current assets, and total assets on the balance sheet. This is because the physical inventory is the basis for recording the adjusting entry for inventory shrinkage. Also, an error in taking the physical inventory misstates the cost of goods sold, gross profit, and net income on the income statement. In addition, because net income is closed to retained earnings at the end of the period, total stockholders' equity will also be misstated on the balance sheet. This misstatement of stockholders' equity (retained earnings) will equal the misstatement of the ending inventory, current assets, and total assets.

To illustrate, assume that in taking the physical inventory on December 31, 2003, Sapra Company incorrectly recorded its physical inventory as $115,000 instead of the correct amount of $125,000. As a result, the merchandise inventory, current assets, and total assets reported on the December 31, 2003, balance sheet would be understated by $10,000 ($125,000 − $115,000). Because the ending physical inventory is understated, the inventory shrinkage and the cost of merchandise sold will be overstated by $10,000. Thus, the gross profit and the net income for the year will be understated by $10,000. Because the net income is closed to retained earnings at the end of the period, the total stockholders' equity on the December 31, 2003, balance sheet will also be understated by $10,000. The effects on Sapra Company's financial statements are summarized as follows

	Amount of Misstatement
Balance Sheet:	
Merchandise inventory understated	$(10,000)
Current assets understated	(10,000)
Total assets understated	(10,000)
Total stockholders' equity understated	(10,000)
Income Statement:	
Cost of merchandise sold overstated	$10,000
Gross profit understated	(10,000)
Net income understated	(10,000)

Now assume that in the preceding example the physical inventory had been *overstated* on December 31, 2003, by $10,000. That is, Sapra Company erroneously recorded its inventory as $135,000. In this case, the effects on the balance sheet and income statement would be just the *opposite* of those indicated above.

Errors in the physical inventory are normally detected in the period after they occur. In such cases, the financial statements of the prior year must be corrected.

Example 48 At the end of 2003, the physical ending inventory of Melchor Co. was overstated by $25,000. What is the effect of this error on the financial statements?

On the 2003 balance sheet, the merchandise inventory, current assets, total assets, and total stockholders' equity are overstated by $25,000. On the income statement, the cost of merchandise sold is understated by $25,000, and the gross profit and net income are overstated by $25,000.

Internal Control of Fixed Assets

Because of their dollar value and long-term nature, it is important to design and apply effective internal controls over fixed assets. Such controls should begin with authorization and approval procedures for the purchase of fixed assets. Controls should also exist to ensure that fixed assets are acquired at the lowest possible costs. One procedure to achieve this objective is to require competitive bids from preapproved vendors.

As soon as a fixed asset is received, it should be inspected and tagged for control purposes and recorded in a subsidiary ledger. This establishes the initial accountability for the asset. Subsidiary ledgers for fixed assets are also useful in determining depreciation expense and recording disposals. Operating data that may be recorded in the subsidiary ledger, such as number of breakdowns, length of time out of service, and cost of repairs, are useful in deciding whether to replace the asset. A company that maintains a computerized subsidiary ledger may use bar-coded tags so that fixed asset data can be directly scanned into computer records.

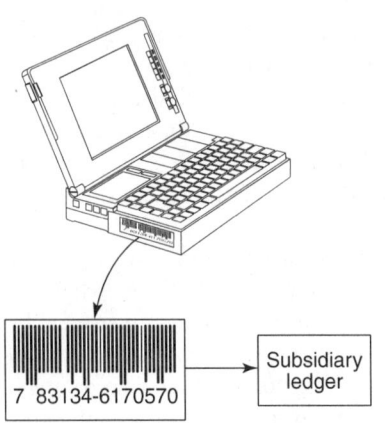

Fixed assets should be insured against theft, fire, flooding, or other disasters. They should also be safeguarded from theft, misuse, or other damage. For example, fixed assets that are highly open to theft, such as computers, should be locked or otherwise protected when not in use. For computers, safeguarding also includes climate controls and special fire-extinguishing equipment. Procedures should also exist for training employees to properly operate fixed assets such as equipment and machinery.

A physical inventory of fixed assets should be taken periodically in order to verify the accuracy of the accounting records. Such an inventory would detect missing, obsolete, or idle fixed assets. In addition, fixed assets should be inspected periodically in order to determine their condition.

Careful control should also be exercised over the disposal of fixed assets. All disposals should be properly authorized and approved. Fully depreciated assets should be retained in the accounting records until disposal has been authorized and they are removed from service.

Natural Resources

The fixed assets of some businesses include timber, metal ores, minerals, or other natural resources. As these businesses harvest or mine and then sell these resources, a portion of the cost of acquiring them must be debited to an expense account. This process of transferring the cost of natural resources to an expense account is called **depletion.** The amount of depletion is determined by multiplying the quantity extracted during the period by the depletion rate. This rate is computed by dividing the cost of the mineral deposit by its estimated size.

Computing depletion is similar to computing units-of-production depreciation. To illustrate, assume that a business paid $400,000 for the mining rights to a mineral deposit estimated at 1,000,000 tons of ore. The depletion rate is $0.40 per ton ($400,000/1,000,000 tons). If 90,000 tons are mined during the year, the periodic depletion is $36,000 (90,000 tons × $0.40).

> **Example 49** A business purchased mineral rights to 250,000 tons of ore for $1,500,000. If 35,000 tons of ore were mined in the first year, what are (a) the depletion rate per ton and (2) the depletion expense for the first year?
>
> (a) $6 per ton ($1,500,000/250,000 tons);   (b) $210,000 (35,000 tons × $6)

Like the accumulated depreciation account, Accumulated Depletion is a *contra asset* account. It is reported on the balance sheet as a deduction from the cost of the mineral deposit.

Internal Controls for Payroll Systems

Payroll processing requires the input of a large amount of data, along with numerous and sometimes complex computations. These factors, combined with the large dollar amounts involved, require controls to ensure that payroll payments are timely and accurate. In addition, the system must also provide adequate safeguards against theft or other misuse of funds.

The cash payment controls also apply to payrolls. Thus, it is normally desirable to use a system that includes procedures for proper authorization and approval of payroll. When a check-signing machine is used, it is important that blank payroll checks and access to the machine be carefully controlled to prevent the theft or misuse of payroll funds.

It is especially important to authorize and approve in writing employee additions and deletions and changes in pay rates. For example, numerous payroll frauds have involved a supervisor adding fictitious employees to the payroll. The supervisor then cashes the fictitious employees' checks. Similar frauds have occurred where employees have been fired but the Payroll Department is not notified. As a result, payroll checks to the fired employees are prepared and cashed by a supervisor.

To prevent or detect frauds such as those we described above, employees' attendance records should be controlled. For example, you may have used an "In and Out" card on which your time of arrival to and departure from work was recorded when you inserted the card into a time clock. A Payroll Department employee may be stationed near the time clock during normal arrival and departure times in order to verify that employees "clock in" only once and only for themselves. Employee identification cards or badges may also be used to verify that only authorized employees are clocking in and are permitted to enter work areas. When payroll checks are distributed, employee identification cards may be used to deter one employee from picking up another's check.

Other controls include verifying and approving all payroll rate changes. In addition, in a computerized system, all program changes should be properly approved and tested by employees who are independent of the payroll system. The use of a special payroll bank account, also enhances control over payroll. Exhibit 600.92 shows flow of data in a payroll system.

Exhibit 600.92 *Flow of Data in a Payroll System*

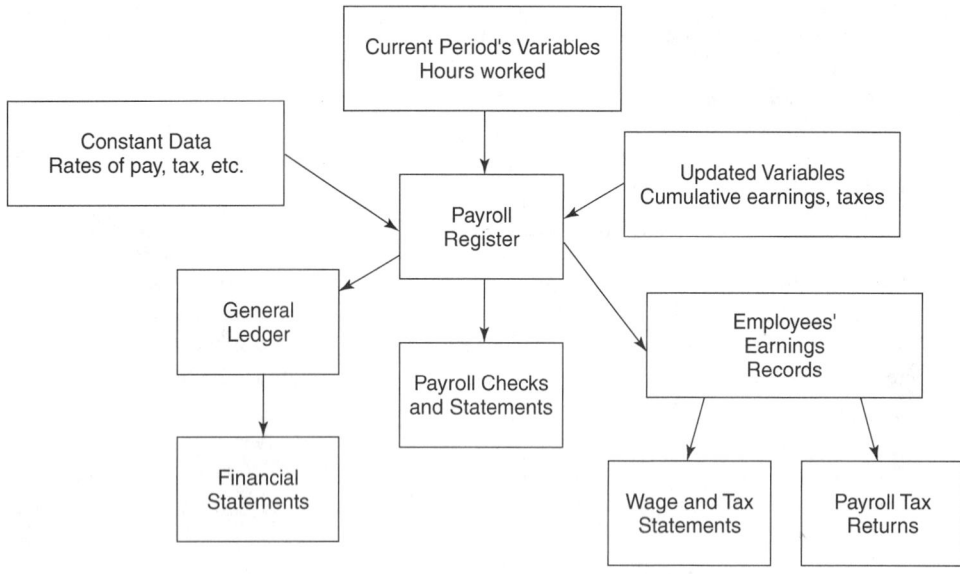

Ethics and Accounting

Business Ethics

The moral principles that guide the conduct of individuals are called **ethics.** Regardless of differences among individuals, proper ethical conduct implies a behavior that considers the impact of one's actions on society and others. In other words, proper ethical conduct implies that you not only consider what's in your best interest, but also what's in the best interests of others.

Ethical conduct is good business. For example, an automobile manufacturer that fails to correct a safety defect to save costs may later lose sales due to lack of consumer confidence. Likewise, a business that pollutes the environment may find itself the target of lawsuits and customer boycotts.

Businesspeople should work within an ethical framework. Although an ethical framework is based on individual experiences and training, there are a number of sound principles that form the foundation for ethical behavior:

1. *Avoid small ethical lapses.* Small ethical lapses may appear harmless in and of themselves. Unfortunately, such lapses can compromise your work. Small ethical lapses can build up and lead to larger consequences later.

2. *Focus on your long-term reputation.* One characteristic of an ethical dilemma is that it places you under severe short-term pressure. The ethical dilemma is created by the stated or unstated threat that failure to "go along" may result in undesirable consequences. You should respond to ethical dilemmas by minimizing the short-term pressures and focusing on long-term reputation instead. Your reputation is very valuable. You will lose your effectiveness if your reputation becomes tarnished.

3. *Expect to suffer adverse personal consequences for holding to an ethical position.* In some unethical organizations, managers have endured career setbacks for not budging from their ethical positions. Some managers have resigned because they were unable to support management in what they perceived as unethical behavior. Thus, in the short term, ethical behavior can sometimes adversely affect your career.

Code of Ethics

Similar to law, medicine, and engineering, accounting is a profession. Each of these fields has a code of ethics, and penalties for violating the code of ethics may include loss of the license to practice. In addition, many business organizations have developed their own ethics policies and codes of conduct for their employees to follow.

Accountants provide information about costs and benefits to management for decision making. Accountants should use professional judgment during the compilation of such costs and benefits because this information could affect sensitive areas such as healthcare and environment. In the last two areas, it is difficult to evaluate and assess such information objectively.

Ethics for Accountants

Next, we provide some examples of ethical and unethical scenarios for accountants.

- It is ethical when the auditor and several members of management of a company (the auditor's client) go out to lunch on the last day of the audit work and the company pays for the entire lunch. Acceptance of a free lunch would not normally be considered unethical because the auditor did not receive any special treatment.
- It is unethical when the audit partner in charge of a bank that he is auditing finances a $300,000 home mortgage loan with the bank at a lower interest rate than that offered to other customers of the bank. Acceptance of this special financing arrangement would be considered unethical because it could jeopardize the auditor's independence and objectivity required during the audit.

Of course, not all situations are as clear cut as above. Ethical dilemmas sometimes arise, and their resolution may not be easy. In some situations, the right course of action is clear even though it may have a negative effect. In other cases, the issues may be so complex and conflicting that the right course of action is not clear.

Ethics for Management

In accounting, unethical decisions may be made jointly between accountants and management of the organization. Management may be subject to the financial numbers game (1) to increase market price for their stock, (2) to improve credit quality and receive higher debt rating in order to lower borrowing cost from banks, and (3) to increase profit-based bonuses and stock options. During this game, management may resort to unethical activities such as (1) recognizing premature or fictitious revenue, (2) aggressive capitalization policies, (3) over/under reported assets and liabilities, and (4) manipulating components of income statement, balance sheet, and cash flow statements.

Authors Charles W. Mulford and Eugene E. Comiskey, in their book *The Financial Numbers Game: Detecting Creative Accounting Practices,* define the financial numbers game in several ways.[8]

- *Aggressive Accounting.* A forceful and intentional choice and application of accounting principles done in an effort to achieve desired results, typically higher current earnings, whether the practices followed are in accordance with generally accepted accounting principles (GAAP) or not.
- *Earnings Management.* The active manipulation of earnings toward a predetermined target, which may be set by management, a forecast made by stock market financial analysts, or an amount that is consistent with a smoother, more sustainable earnings stream.
- *Income Smoothing.* A form of earnings management designed to remove peaks and valleys from a normal earnings series, including steps to reduce and "store" profits during good years for use during bad (slower) years. Equity reserves, discussed in Section 699, can be used for income smoothing.
- *Fraudulent Financial Reporting.* Intentional misstatements or omissions of amounts or disclosures in financial statements, done to deceive financial statement users, that are determined to be fraudulent by an administrative, civil, or criminal proceeding.
- *Creative Accounting Practices.* Any and all steps used to play the financial numbers game, including the aggressive choice and application of accounting principles, fraudulent financial reporting, and any steps taken toward earnings management or income smoothing.

690 Economics and Accounting

Differences Between Economics and Accounting

The best way to learn economics is to compare and contrast it with accounting. Economics is the study of how individuals and organizations choose to use limited resources such as land, materials, money, machines, energy, and people. Accounting is the study of how good an individual or organization actually used such scarce resources. In doing so, it maintains books to record revenues and costs, and to measure income.

Economic Profits Versus Accounting Profits

Economic profits are different from accounting profits (income). Economic profits are the profits over and above the normal rate of return on investment; anything greater than the normal opportunity cost of capital. Economic theory explicitly considers the opportunity cost, which is the cost of a foregone decision.

$$\text{Economic Profits} = \text{Normal Accounting Profits} - \text{Opportunity Cost of Capital}$$

Accounting profits are defined as the difference between total revenues and total costs. Accounting theory does not explicitly consider the opportunity cost.

$$\text{Accounting Profit} = \text{Total Revenues} - \text{Total Costs}$$

Economic Income Versus Accounting Income

Economic income is the amount of money a household can spend during a given time period without increasing or decreasing in net assets. Sources of economic income include wages, salaries, dividends, interest income, rents, and government-initiated transfer payments. Accounting income is the same as the accounting profits.

Economic Costs Versus Accounting Costs

Economic costs are the full costs of production including (1) a normal rate of return on investment and (2) the opportunity cost of each factor of production. Land, labor, and capital are the three key factors of production, which are the inputs into the production process. Accounting costs include product costs and period costs to produce a product or to render a service.

Economic Growth Versus Accounting Growth

Economic growth is an increase in the total output of an economy. It occurs when a society acquires new resources or when it learns to produce more goods and services using existing resources or less resources at least possible cost. This means the economic growth occurs when a society is more efficient. Accounting growth includes estimations and projections of revenues and costs based on historical data and/or human judgment.

695 Law and Accounting

Impact of Law on Accounting

Although various laws govern accounting policies and procedures, we discuss three laws that are of importance to a business manager. These include the Foreign Corrupt Practices Act (FCPA), the Private Securities Litigation Reform Act (the "Reform Act"), and the Federal Sentencing Guidelines.

Foreign Corrupt Practices Act

The Foreign Corrupt Practices Act (FCPA) imposes internal control requirements on companies with securities registered under the Securities Act of 1934. The accounting requirements of the FCPA reflect the ideas that accurate record-keeping is essential to managerial responsibility and that investors should be able to rely on the financial reports they receive. Accordingly, the accounting requirements were enacted (1) to ensure that an issuer's books accurately reflect financial transactions, (2) to protect the integrity of independent audits of financial statements, and (3) to promote the reliability of financial information required by the 1934 Act.

The main thrust of the FCPA is to prohibit all U.S. domestic concerns from bribing foreign governmental or political officials. In this regard, the FCPA requires that SEC-regulated companies keep accurate books and records, and have sufficient internal control to assure that "access to assets is permitted only in accordance with management's authorizations" to prevent slush funds and bribe payments.

Private Securities Litigation Reform Act of 1995

The Reform Act focuses on protecting companies from unwarranted class actions and other private actions based on claims of material misstatements or omissions in financial statements issued by public companies. The Act imposes statutory requirements for auditors to disclose illegal corporate activity.

The Reform Act requires that audits of public companies include procedures designed to do the following.

- Provide reasonable assurance of detecting illegal acts that may have a direct and material effect on the determination of financial statement amounts
- Identify related-party transactions that are material to financial statements or related disclosures
- Evaluate the ability of the company to continue as a going concern during the ensuing fiscal year

The Act also requires auditor notification to management, board, and SEC when an illegal act may have occurred.

Federal Sentencing Guidelines

The Federal Sentencing Guidelines state that a company can reduce its applicable fine by setting up an effective compliance program that may be reasonably expected to prevent illegal activity through prevention and detection. The guidelines look at aggravating and mitigating factors in determining the appropriate sentence imposed.

Examples of aggravating factors include lack of a control system, gross negligence, and lack of integrity and honesty. Examples of mitigating factors include (1) the presence of an effective program to prevent and detect violation of law where the company exercises due diligence in seeking to prevent and detect criminal conduct by its employees, (2) the amount of cooperation provided to authorities during investigation of an illegal activity, and (3) timely reporting of illegal activity, known or suspected. The due diligence must be designed to fit the characteristics of the company, such as the size and nature of the business, and the likelihood that certain illegal acts may occur.

From the schedule of fines, aggravating factors can increase a fine fourfold; mitigating factors can reduce it by 95%. In addition to paying fines, companies can be ordered to make restitution to victims and may be subject to supervised probation.

International Issues

Cultural Influences on Accounting

By the year 2010, more than half of the world's corporations will operate on a seamless, global basis. The companies that become multicultural entities will be rewarded.[9] The globalization of the economy requires many new skills in professional accountants that were previously not critical or even necessary. They include an appreciation of cultural diversity and cultural sensitivity. To be professionally successful, accountants must possess a global perspective.[10]

Cultures vary from country to country and exercise heavy influence on business practices. In some countries, such as Japan, the source of financing is mostly debt, while in other countries, such as the United Kingdom, it is from investment by equity holders. How may the debt to equity ratio of a Japanese operation be compared with a British operation? Would such a comparison provide any useful insights to the analyst? This example gives some idea of the challenges faced by accounting in the international arena. The decision-making process for resolution of operational and conceptual issues must, therefore, take into account cultural influences on accounting.

Culture and Environmental Influences

One of the major objectives of financial reporting is to provide information to users for making economic decisions. Since environments differ from country to country, the types of decisions that need to be made and their information requirements are also different. This explains why there are different accounting systems in different countries: Accounting provides information for making economic decisions in the *unique* environment of each country, therefore, the accounting systems are necessarily *environment-specific*. There are five major environmental influences that collectively formulate cultural or societal values.

1. The economic system
2. The political system
3. The legal system
4. The educational system
5. Religion

The economic, political, and legal systems are closely intertwined. The educational system can be a force to counter, reinforce, or modify influences of the economic, political, and legal systems. Since religion is a matter of faith, it is shown separately. The degree of influence of religion, as an environmental factor, varies from country to country. In many parts of the world, especially in some Muslim countries, it is perhaps the most powerful of the environmental influences. These major environmental influences collectively play a key role in the formation of cultural values. The cultural values affect, among others, the accounting profession's values. The shared values of the accounting professionals influence the accounting system of a country. In turn, information from the accounting system affects the economic, political, legal, and educational systems. These relationships are illustrated in Exhibit 600.93.

We will now take a closer look at these environmental influences, and also discuss some major issues related to each of them.

The Economic System

The *degree of economic development and the level of technology* in a country determine, to a great extent, the level of complexity of its accounting system. The accounting system of an economically developed country with a high-technology

Exhibit 600.93 *Environmental Influences on Accounting*

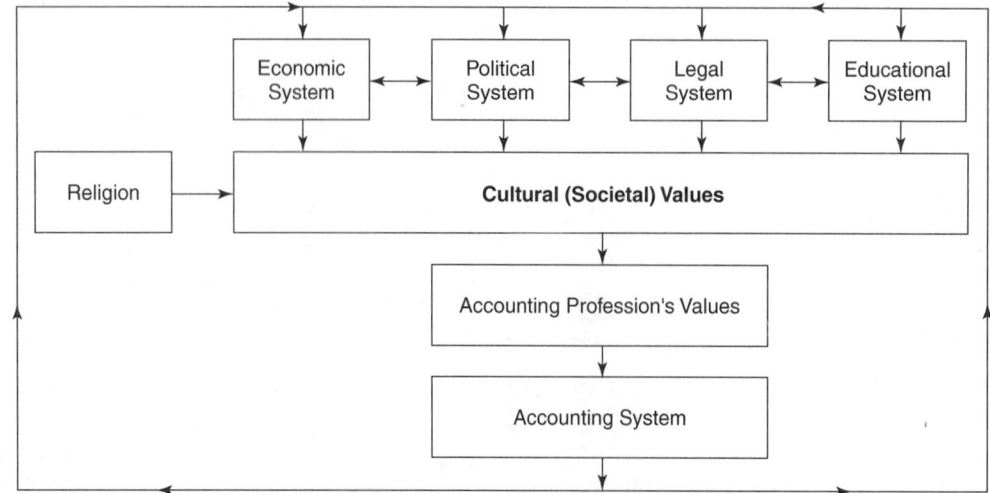

economy would be different from the accounting system of a country with primarily an agrarian economy. Intangibles (e.g., patents and copyrights) have significantly greater importance in a country that has a high-technology economy than one that has a subsistence-level economy.

The degree of the *concentration of ownership* of business in a society influences the need for and extent of disclosures. If business ownerships are dispersed in a country, there would likely be greater and varied disclosures to meet the needs of the many investors.

The *source of business financing* is an important consideration for the orientation of accounting reports and disclosures. If debt is the major source of financing, then much of the information can be furnished directly to the lenders, instead of being disclosed to the public at large. Financial reports, as a result, would be creditor-oriented, and their content would primarily address the information needs of the lenders. In case equity capital is the major source of financing, the financial reports would be mainly geared toward equity holders.

To varying degrees, the *tax laws* of a country have an impact on income measurement. In many countries, e.g., Japan, Germany, and France, income for taxation is the same as for financial reporting. In such cases the accounting system is synchronized with the tax laws. In other countries, e.g., the United States and the United Kingdom, income for taxation is computed differently from the income for financial reporting. The accounting systems in such countries are hence relatively independent of the provisions of the tax laws.

If a country has a *highly inflationary economy,* the accounting system would require restatement of the historical-cost-based financial statements to reflect the impact of inflation. In extreme cases, there may be a departure to a non-historical-cost-based, i.e., current value-based measurement, especially if the price-level volatility is either a combination of general and specific or is mainly specific.

ECONOMIC STABILITY AND ECONOMIC RISK EXPOSURE The degree of economic risk exposure to the investors and creditors in a country is directly related to the degree of economic instability of the country. A highly unstable economy makes it very difficult to formulate reasonably reliable forecasts. It also necessitates a frequent, and sometimes drastic, changing of plans. Economic stability of a country, among others, facilitates the development and continuous improvement of a conceptually sound accounting system.

The Political System

The political system of a country, its philosophy, and its objectives determine broad economic policies such as centrally planned versus market-driven economies, and private ownership versus public ownership of property.

POLITICAL STABILITY AND ECONOMIC STABILITY There is a close link between political stability and economic stability. They usually go hand in hand. As discussed in the previous section, economic stability is necessary for the development and continuous improvement of a cogent and responsive accounting system. Due to the relationship between economic stability and political stability, it can be inferred that the development of an accounting system is facilitated when the country has political stability. An Ernst & Young survey of the Global 1000 companies identified political instability to be *the major barrier* to investment in a country. Fifty-three percent of the respondents cited political instability as a major barrier while 36 percent stated it is somewhat of a barrier. Next in line are financial risk, legal infrastructure, bureaucracy, exchange controls, and commercial infrastructure.[11]

The concern of the Global 1000 companies regarding political instability as the major barrier to investment is understandable. Evidence exists that a successive government may not honor a contract entered into by the previous government. In 1997, the new Pakistani government refused to accept terms of a $1.6 billion contract that the previous government had entered into with **The Hub Power Company**. Interestingly, this was the biggest direct investment project in the country made by a foreign investor.[12] An editorial in one of the major Pakistani newspapers summed up the impact of the 3-year-old dispute as follows:

> Since efforts are underway to encourage investment inflows, the country can ill-afford such image-denting issues...
> The controversy has attracted much international attention and important world capitals have asked Pakistan to settle it quickly...
> Pakistan's efforts to attract new investment cannot bring the desired results without burying this hatchet. Fresh capital inflows are critical for economic recovery and revival of its growth momentum. The government should know which side of its economy's bread needs to be buttered.[13]

During the same year, 1997, South Korea's **LG Electronics Inc.** canceled a plan to build a consumer electronics plant in Russia due to "political instability."[14] Political instability of a country scares off foreign investors because it is generally due to the mismanagement of the economy, corruption, lack of accountability, lengthy delays in decision making, and political interference in economic and business affairs. *In sum, political instability of a country is often a result of the deterioration of economic conditions. The development of a comprehensive and sophisticated accounting system is difficult under such a set of circumstances.*

BUREAUCRATIC HURDLES   A political system that is supported by a complex bureaucracy often leads to long delays due to indecisions or untimely decisions. Sometimes the delays are too long for the investors, resulting in the termination of the projects. In December 1999, U.S.-based **Cogentrix Energy Inc.** decided to stop development of a $1.3 billion power plant in India. In 1992, India had invited Cogentrix to make the investment, and designated the project "fast-track." Cogentrix lost patience and decided to terminate the project in 1999 due to lengthy delays in obtaining government approvals. After seven years, the so-called "fast track" project had not even broken ground.[15] Often the delays result from complex rules, procedures, and obligations developed by the bureaucracy, a byproduct of the political system.

POLITICAL CORRUPTION   A corrupt political system contributes to the economic deterioration of a country because the policy formulation and the decisions of those in power leads to inefficient allocation of scarce economic resources. Their objective is to amass personal wealth, create family fiefdoms, and practice cronyism. The *modus operandi* is political favors and financial kickbacks, rather than adhering to laws and principles and allocating resources for the common good.

It is encouraging to note that recently societal pressure in some countries is successful in curtailing widespread corruption. In March 2000, Thailand's politically powerful interior minister resigned after an anti-corruption organization, formed in 1997, accused him of concealing his assets by falsely claiming that he had borrowed $1.21 million from a private company. The National Counter-Corruption Commission, an independent body, thus toppled one of the most influential figures in Thailand politics. It is a sign that the "landscape of the nation's deeply corrupt political system has begun to shift."[16] The corruption case against the interior minister next goes before a special Constitutional Court.

In Indonesia, also during March 2000, state prosecutors for the first time arrested a key member of former President Suharto's inner circle, Mohamad "Bob" Hasan, after a corruption investigation. Hasan had served as the minister of trade and industry in Suharto's last government. He also looked after business interests of the Suharto family. The arrest raised hopes "the new government is getting serious about probing the financial dealings of the onetime ruler."[17]

The Legal System

In many countries, including some Western European countries, the legal system has a direct impact on accounting. Laws contain detailed accounting regulations specifying comprehensive accounting rules and procedures. In such countries, accounting rules are based on legislative requirements. The government, therefore, determines and enforces these requirements through accounting rules.

The comprehensive body of statute and case law was a concept that the Romans borrowed from the Greeks. Romans put the idea into practice and many countries in the world have adopted the ideal of written law to protect individuals from other individuals and from the power of the state.

> The rule of law is so central to Western civilization that most of us take it for granted. Of course we are governed by laws, we say—it's natural. In fact, though, the rule of law is not a necessary aspect of the human condition. Another great ancient empire, China, arranged things precisely the opposite of the Roman way. Confucius and his disciples down through the centuries distrusted written laws. A dusty statute book was too inflexible to handle the infinite variety of human experience, the Chinese sages felt. They chose to trust people, not laws—to rely on innate human goodness as the best guarantee of a civil society. Even today the concept of written law and written contract is fairly weak in China and other East Asian nations within its cultural ambit.[18]

Legal systems of most non-Western countries are quite different from the legal systems common in Western countries. The sanctity of contract is fundamental to business dealings in the West. However, in many countries, including China, the concept of written contract is literally foreign. Since global economy involves cross-border transactions, it is essential that a common commitment to the sanctity of contract and rule of law by all parties to the transaction be understood and accepted. In 1999, the Chinese government sent 35 lawyers, judges, government officials, and law professors to a program on U.S. law at Temple University. In China it is common for a court to try a criminal suspect who does not have legal counsel. One of the participants in the Temple University program stated, "It is true, our legal system is still developing. We can learn from the American legal system how to move forward our own Chinese legal system."[19]

Besides the underdevelopment of a legal system that can handle transactions in a global economy, there are two other issues that are noteworthy: Lengthy trials and judicial corruption.

LENGTHY TRIALS In some countries a civil litigation may last for several decades. For example, in India a legal case may take 30 years. The same is true of India's neighboring country Pakistan. A case that had been pending in the Supreme Court of Pakistan for 26 years was finally settled out of court by descendants of the parties involved:

> Interestingly, the majority of the characters in the case have died. Lal Din, the petitioner, and Haji Abdul Waheed, the respondent, died during the pendency of the case in the Supreme Court. Two out of three members of the Supreme Court bench, which had decided the case, have died. Both the counsels for the appellant, and Shaikh Saeed Akhtar, have died. Advocate Gul Mohammad was later made a judge of the Lahore High Court. Subsequently, he became the chief justice of the Federal Shariat Court. He is also no more in this world.[20]

There are some encouraging signs that the situation could possibly improve in the future. Several countries are considering different options to alleviate the problem of long delays. India had a backlog of more than three million cases in 1997, and the options considered included adopting the U.S.-style plea bargaining system. The Federal Law and Justice Minister of India stated that the ultimate objective is to limit the duration of a trial to possibly less than one year.[21] In Pakistan the Chief Justice of Pakistan has directed that cases pending since 1990 be declared "old cases" and scheduled for daily hearing. He also directed the chief justices of provincial high courts to monitor progress in the speedy disposal of long-pending cases and compile the data relating to their disposal.[22] The lengthy delays can be attributed to the Asian legal framework that is completely different from that of Western countries.[23]

JUDICIAL CORRUPTION In some countries judicial corruption is rampant. The majority or a sizeable minority of judges willingly accept and sometimes even solicit bribes. In cases when a party to a case pays a bribe to the presiding judge, it clearly makes the judge unfit for rendering an impartial verdict. In 1999, a constitutional assembly in Venezuela declared a judicial emergency because of an accusation of corruption and other irregularities against nearly half of Venezuela's 4,700 judges.[24]

The Educational System

The educational system and the level of literacy in a country impact the country's accounting system in two ways:

- Well-educated users of accounting information can understand sophisticated accounting information.
- The accountants in a country that has high educational standards are usually better trained and possess the necessary competencies and skills to satisfactorily complete their professional assignments.

In sum, educational backgrounds of both users and preparers of accounting information strongly affect the degree of development and level of sophistication of a country's accounting system.

Sometimes changes in the environment of a country make the country's accounting system obsolete. Some local authorities in Russia still require use of the accounting system that was developed and practiced during the era of the Soviet-planned economy. Obviously, the old accounting system is unable to meet the requirements of the current economy that is no longer centrally planned. Consequently, some Western firms keep two sets of accounting books: one to meet the local authorities' requirements and the other to meet their own information needs.

Religion

Religion, in the broad sense of the term, affects basic accounting concepts. In many Muslim countries, e.g., Pakistan, the idea of interest on loans is contrary to widely held religious beliefs. In December 1999, Pakistan's Supreme Court declared that both paying and receiving interest are unacceptable in Islam. The court ordered the government to introduce an interest-free economic system by 2001.[25] The likely result is to find different ways of presenting and communicating accounting information related to credit transactions.

It should be understood that some religious requirements might be interpreted differently in different countries. Take the separation of sexes, for example. Laws in Saudi Arabia prohibit mixing of the sexes. This requires that Saudi businesswomen must have a male sponsor to represent them in dealings with the governmental departments and business organizations. The female owner of a business cannot deal directly even with her own male employees. Not surprisingly, a survey of Saudi Arabian businesswomen showed that the difficulty of dealing directly with other parties was the most common complaint among them.[26] In contrast, businesswomen and female workers in many other Muslim countries such as Indonesia, Egypt, and Oman can deal directly with their male employees, co-workers, and the government employees.

699. INTERNATIONAL ISSUES

Culture's Impact on Financial Reporting

Culture's deep imprint on financial reporting can be illustrated by the secondary statement approach. The **secondary statement approach** uses the accounting principles of another country for the preparation of financial statements. Secondary financial statements are also audited according to auditing standards of the same country. The objective is to enhance the understandability and usefulness of the financial statements for the target audience, i.e., the users in that country.

The approach, however, cannot compensate for the differences in cultural environments. The interpretation of secondary financial statements is difficult because business customs based on local culture differ from country to country. *National business customs leave an imprint on the primary financial statements that cannot be duplicated in the secondary financial statements.* Howard Lowe has eloquently stated this in discussing Japanese consolidated financial statements using U.S. accounting principles.

> The notion of control through direct or indirect majority share ownership and the presence of a holding company or a dominant parent company are foreign concepts to the typical Japanese executive. Share ownership is generally regarded as of major significance in the forming and maintaining of corporate groups. Consequently, American practices of consolidation tend to group Japanese corporations in a manner contrary to their normal functioning. Such practices tend to break up the complex and dynamic reality of the natural groups into American-type corporate groups attempting to portray an American perspective to something uniquely Japanese.
>
> Japanese consolidated statements patterned after American standards have survived only because foreign users have been largely unaware of their inappropriate focus and innocent misrepresentation. Many of the most important firms affecting the future fortunes of the group are not even represented in these statements.
>
> Consequently, its [Japan's] unique business organizational environment often makes its consolidated financial reports less rather than more useful to readers.[27]

This reminds us again that the global economy is making it increasingly important to be knowledgeable in other cultures to do our jobs effectively.

Cultural Considerations in Control Systems

This section presents control concepts and considerations for designing an effective control system in multinational operations. A **control system** compares the actual performance (results) with the planned performance (goals) so that management may take appropriate action when necessary. A control system includes information that is internal, external, financial, and nonfinancial.

In addition to formal control systems, informal control methods play an important role in multinational companies. The main informal control method is to transfer an executive from one international operation to another with explicit or implicit understanding about expected performance. Another informal control method is to hold meetings between parent company executives and subsidiary executives, usually at a subsidiary's location. Annual meetings of executives from international operations also provide an opportunity to informally assess performance and to exchange information.

Cultural differences necessitate adaptation of control measures to each country's cultural environment. Different languages and communication styles are but a couple of the issues facing multinational corporations while designing and implementing control measures across national boundaries.

A subsidiary organized in a new country might mean another language in which strategic plans, budgets, and reports are written. In many countries, there are different languages and each has many dialects. Some technical words may be difficult or impossible to translate into the local language.

Cultural Considerations for Motivation

An information system provides control measures that attempt to motivate—and motivation has to do with human behavior. Because companies in a global economy operate in multiple societies, each with its own culture, designing a system that will influence human behavior in the desired manner requires cultural awareness. This is a prerequisite for a successful system. Otherwise, there may be undesirable consequences.

> If the damage to cultural values is substantial, the members of the culture will find ways to retaliate. They withhold their cooperation, resort to foot-dragging, and use other subtle ways to make the changes not worth having. The

resulting lowered morale is one of the prices paid by managers who choose to ignore the social consequences of the intended changes.[28]

Policy Formulation in Different Cultures

Cultural realities must be confronted and issues resolved to ensure that corporate policies are well thought out and well articulated. This requires taking into account not only organizational goals but also cultural differences, different business practices, and business ethics. Some issues are easy to resolve. In a company function, pork should not be served in Israel or in Muslim countries. Other issues are more complex. They can be addressed only after first thoroughly analyzing them and then articulating a clear corporate policy. It is important to always remember that MNC operations are not confined to one part of the world. *MNCs are inherently corporate citizens of the base country as well as of the world.*

Business Ethics

Some assert that cultural differences preclude applying one set of ethical standards worldwide. Research findings, however, indicate that despite cultural differences, standards of moral judgment do not vary significantly among countries.[29] Therefore, ethical considerations become critically important variables in the long-run decision process.

There are also side benefits. Instituting formal ethical policies in a company leads to lower internal control costs for the company.[30] In 1999, a Conference Board survey of 124 companies in 22 countries found that 78% of boards of directors are setting ethics standards, up from 41% in 1991 and 21% in 1987. Business leaders see the self-regulation as a way to avoid legislative or judicial intrusions into their operations. Ethics codes also help promote tolerance of diverse practices and customs while doing business abroad.[31]

The previous discussion is not to imply that all ethical issues are easily resolved and the situations involving ethical dilemmas do not exist. However, proper focus does help. *Formulation of corporate policy should focus on long-run results rather than short-term expediency.* The leadership and attitude of top management coupled with a proactive management style can go a long way toward cultivation of a corporate culture in which all constructive ideas are accepted, nourished, and given a chance to flourish. A performance evaluation system that takes into account performance in the areas of cultural sensitivity and long-run perspective provides incentives that motivate managers and employees to behave in an ethical manner consistent with corporate policies.

Because of familiarity with local culture and business customs, a local staff can be invaluable during the corporate policy formulation process to ensure that the policies are consistently local-culture-sensitive as well as motivators for ethical behavior.

Accounting Measurement and Disclosures

In this section, we will discuss a variety of issues relating to financial reporting disclosures and current disclosure practices and trends. Recording economic transactions and events in the accounting system (**measurement**) precedes preparation of the financial statements (**disclosure**). At the time of recording, monetary values are assigned to economic transactions and events. The accounting standards of a country provide the rules for assigning those monetary values. Since accounting standards differ from country to country, consequently recording (measurement) of the same type of economic transactions and events differs. Thus financial reports (disclosures) are directly affected by accounting measurement. *Note: Accounting measurement and disclosure are interconnected.*

The term **financial reporting disclosures** includes the disclosures from the accounting system as well as outside the accounting system. For example, a contingent loss that is probable but cannot be estimated reasonably is disclosed even though it cannot be recorded in the accounting system. Different types of financial reporting disclosures include

- Disclosures within the financial statements
- Disclosures supplementary to the financial statements
- Required disclosures
- Voluntary disclosures
- Disclosures in monetary terms
- Disclosures in nonmonetary terms
- Quantitative disclosures
- Nonquantitative (narrative) disclosures

Both the scope and the extent of financial reporting disclosures have widened considerably in recent years. The trend is expected to continue because of the rapid pace of globalization. Varied international environments in which a multinational company operates contribute to varied disclosures. For example, intense environmental concerns or powerful labor unions have a direct impact on the scope and the extent of disclosures made by a company about its performance in those areas.

The Evolving Disclosure Process

It is widely acknowledged that a corporation's accountability extends beyond its investors and creditors, which is due to two reasons. First, a society entrusts a corporation with the management of its scarce resources, which makes the corporation accountable to the society. A corporation needs to provide information to members of the society so that they can assess whether scarce resources are used efficiently and effectively. Second, the corporation's activities affect quality of life and standard of living of the individuals who may be neither its investors nor its creditors. Such individuals need information to be able to form an opinion about corporate performance in their areas of concern. Depending on their perceptions, they may wish to take some appropriate actions to influence activities of the corporation. This wider concept of corporate disclosure responsibility has been recognized and accepted for decades. It is evidenced by the statement, "We maximize shareholder value over the long term by harmonizing the interests of *all* our stakeholders: customers, suppliers, employees, and members of the community at large, as well as shareholders."[32] The users of financial reports include various groups of people collectively known as **stakeholders**.

The area of accounting disclosures is still evolving. At least two issues remain unresolved. First, no commonly accepted framework exists for providing information to the users who are neither investors nor creditors. Such users are hard to identify and their number and demands for disclosures are apparently increasing. The second issue is that the benefits of disclosures, unlike most of their costs, are often difficult or impossible to trace. The diversity of user groups and how each user group benefits from the disclosures pose monumental problems in identifying the relationship between cause (costs) and effect (benefits).

Reasons for Financial Reporting Disclosures

Conceptually, there are two major socio-economic reasons for disclosures.

- To reduce uncertainty to capital providers (investors and creditors) so that they can use the information to weigh the predicted returns of each alternative against the associated risk level.
- To provide relevant information to the individuals and groups who are affected by the operating activities of corporations in their quality of life and standard of living.

Broadly, disclosures are made to provide information so that decision makers can make informed decisions, to satisfy externally imposed requirements, and to meet certain self-interest objectives.

Internationalization of Financial Markets

Global financial markets are a reality. Corporations can now raise capital from sources in different parts of the world. Global financial markets have become such powerful sources of capital that many companies are now listing on security exchanges of other countries.

A country's regulatory agency sets the minimum disclosure requirements for listing on its security markets. Globalization of financial markets has created an acute awareness among the securities regulators in many countries that their regulatory disclosure requirements need to be strengthened.

Statutory and Legal Requirements

In some countries, e.g., Germany and Japan, statutory and legal requirements prescribe the accounting treatment of transactions. In such countries, company law and taxation systems are the most important influences on accounting practice and financial reporting.

Significant impact of multinational enterprises on a nation's social, economic, and ecological environments has resulted in the enactment of many new statutes and laws requiring additional disclosures in recent years.

Accounting Profession

In many countries where the accounting profession has advanced to a mature state, for example, the United States and the United Kingdom financial reporting disclosure requirements are determined by the profession. The accounting profession in such countries is typically quite influential. The standard-setting process includes open deliberations. Diverse interest groups are given opportunities to provide their input before a standard is promulgated. Internationalization has compelled the accounting profession in such countries to address the issues related to those topics that have become significantly more important. Segment reporting, consolidation, foreign currency transactions, and foreign currency translation are just a few examples.

Additional disclosures are also being required to enhance the comparability of financial statements that are prepared using accounting standards of different countries.

Influential Special Interest Groups

Some groups are so influential that a corporation makes special disclosures directed to their information needs. For example, a labor union may successfully negotiate special disclosures on matters such as safe working conditions, number of work-related injuries, and classification of employees by age, sex, and so on. The nature and emphasis of special interest disclosures varies across nations.

Voluntary Disclosures

Corporations make voluntary disclosures for a variety of reasons.

- *Educating the users of financial reports.* This may be on a variety of topics such as operating conditions, future prospects, reasons for certain corporate actions, and so on.
- *Image building.* Disclosure about socially responsible actions generate goodwill for future economic benefits. Examples include disclosures of the expenditures made for environmental protection, safe working conditions, scholarship funds for college students, and training programs for underrepresented segments of the population.
- *Avoidance of potential governmental regulation or control.* A corporation may make voluntary disclosures if there is a risk that nondisclosures may result in governmental regulations or control. The objective is to forestall any potential governmental action that would have adverse effects. The timing, nature, and extent of such disclosures require managerial judgment.
- *Lower cost of capital.* Voluntary disclosures are inherently above and beyond what is required by regulators. A corporation competing with other enterprises in global capital markets may find it advantageous to voluntarily provide additional disclosures. Everything else being equal, capital providers would choose Company A over Company B if they perceive Company A to carry lower risk. Disclosures remove or reduce uncertainties about the future, thus reducing the perceived level of risk.

Firms participating in global capital markets generally tend to voluntarily disclose more information than is required by regulators. The competition for investment funds is propelling this practice. *A number of the disclosures made in annual reports are, therefore, driven by market rather than regulatory requirements.* While formulating their disclosure policies companies may find it in their best interest to go beyond the minimum requirements.[33]

Costs Versus Benefits Criterion

As mentioned earlier, identifying the users and their information needs are necessary for deciding on the types of disclosure to be made and the extent of detail provided. We have noted earlier that the identity of user groups is not always clear. Due to the existence of multiple users with varied information needs for a variety of decisions, there is always a question regarding the "right balance" for providing information. Due to multiplicity of the variables in a given situation, it is not surprising that no consensus on what constitutes the right balance exists.

Accounting information is not free; accounting systems cost money. Using the cost versus benefits criterion while choosing an accounting system requires that the expected benefits exceed the expected costs of the system.[34] The difficulty, or impossibility, of establishing cause (costs of disclosures) and effect (benefits to the users of information) relationship in the situations involving noninvestors and noncreditors poses a daunting challenge in attempting to use the costs versus benefits criterion.

The costs of financial reporting disclosures, however, are not limited to the monetary amounts for installing and maintaining an accounting system. They also include other costs that are difficult, if not impossible, to quantify. *The common thread among this group of costs is that the information obtained through disclosures may be used for purposes that are against the best interest of the company providing the information.* For example:

- Competitors may obtain competitive advantage.
- Workers' unions may make costly demands.
- Regulatory agencies may increase regulation.
- Plaintiffs may find the information helpful in their legal claims against the corporation.

Competitive Advantage

One of the costs of disclosures listed previously merits discussion. It is often claimed by corporate executives that extensive disclosures erode their ability to compete. Interestingly, there is no evidence to support this assertion. Efficient flow of information is a prerequisite to a free market economy. It is difficult to visualize the existence of an efficient, free market economy in the absence of extensive information flow.

Disclosures stimulate and encourage competition, which leads to streamlining operations. Without streamlining, it would be impossible to survive, let alone grow, in an intense competitive environment. Internationalization of trade and investments has increased competition as well as the need for information. The ultimate beneficiaries are the consumers.

Worldwide Diversity in Measurement and Reporting

Now we will look at some examples of worldwide diversity in measurement and reporting. Our objective is to develop an appreciation of how the same type of economic transaction or event may be recorded differently because of different accounting principles worldwide.

The accounting standards of a country provide guidelines for recording economic transactions and events. Within the framework, they provide an answer to the question: What accounts are to be debited and credited, and for what amounts? We will illustrate the diversity by focusing on certain accounting aspects of inventories. The information for selected countries is shown in Exhibit 600.94.

We will use two examples to illustrate how the measurement of information affects disclosures in financial reports.

Example 50 *Foster Company, based in Australia, uses the first-in, first-out (FIFO) cost flow assumption. The following information is pertinent regarding Foster's inventory.*

	(000) Units	Unit Cost	(000) Total Cost
Beginning inventory	100	$10	$ 1,000
Purchases	1,000	12	12,000
Goods available for sale	1,100		$13,000
Ending inventory, 50 units:			
Net realizable value		$550	
Replacement cost		$650	

Using the Australian accounting principles, as shown in Exhibit 600.94, "market" is generally considered to be net realizable value while applying the lower of cost or market.

The cost basis of ending inventory for financial reporting is determined as follows.

Historical cost using FIFO (50 × $12)	$600
Net realizable value (given)	$550

The ending inventory in the balance sheet will be shown in the amount of $550, the lower of historical cost using FIFO ($600) and net

Exhibit 600.94   *Accounting Differences—Inventories*

Country	"Market" in Lower of Cost or Market	LIFO Allowed	LIFO Common In Usage
Australia	Net realizable value	No	N/A*
Austria	Replacement cost or net realizable value	Yes	No
Brazil	Replacement cost or net realizable value, whichever is lower	Yes	No
Canada	Replacement cost or net realizable value	Yes	No
Czech Republic	N/A	No	N/A
Denmark	Net realizable value	No	N/A
Finland	Replacement cost or net realizable value	Yes	No
France	Net realizable value	No	N/A
Germany	Replacement cost or net realizable value minus normal profit	Yes	No
India	Net realizable value	Yes	No
Japan	Replacement cost	Yes	Yes
Mexico	Realizable value	Yes	Yes
Netherlands	Net realizable value	Yes	Yes
New Zealand	Net realizable value	No	N/A
Spain	Net realizable value	Yes	No
Sweden	Net realizable value	No	N/A
Switzerland	Net realizable value	Yes	No
United Kingdom	Net realizable value	Yes	No
United States	Middle amount from replacement cost, net realizable value, and net realizable value minus normal profit	Yes	Yes

N/A: Not applicable

realizable value ($550). The income statement will reflect an additional $50 expense resulting from writing down inventory from $600 to $550.

Example 51 *Using the same information as in the previous example, except assuming that the accounting standards define "market" as replacement cost, the value of ending inventory would be:*

Historical cost basis using FIFO (50 × $12)	$600
Replacement cost (given)	$650

The ending inventory in the balance sheet will be shown in the amount of $600, which is the lower of the two amounts. In this case, application of the lower of cost or market principle will have no impact on the income statement.

Role of Reserves

Reserves are commonly used in many countries for a variety of reasons. In many countries, for example, Japan, France, and Italy, financial reports are creditor-oriented. Banks are the primary users of financial reports since they are the major source of funds for enterprises—rather than the stockholders. Naturally, accounting standards in those countries were established to ensure that creditors' interests would be protected. This has resulted in a conservative accounting practice called the **prudence concept.** Laws in many countries permit undervaluation of assets and overstatement of expenses and liabilities. For example, in Germany, if a loss is *reasonably possible,* it must be recorded. This contrasts with the U.S. practice of recognizing a contingent loss only if it is *probable* (likely to occur) and reasonably estimable.

We now discuss the role of reserves in accomplishing various objectives. All of the reserves in the following discussion are **equity reserves.** They appear in the stockholders' equity section of the balance sheet.

EXPENSE LIABILITY RESERVE One of the many purposes for using reserves is to achieve income smoothing, that is, to show a steady growth in income from one year to the next. Reserves used for this purpose are generally called **expense liability reserves.** In a highly profitable year, the company transfers a portion of its actual income into an expense liability reserve, thus understanding reported income for that year. The firm moves an amount from the reserve to the reported income in a later year when actual income is low, thereby overstating reported income for the year. This phenomenon has been called **income smoothing, income leveling,** and **managed earnings.** The use of reserves to transfer income between periods is done by a majority of firms in Austria, Spain, South Korea, Australia, and Switzerland.[35]

Clearly, in countries where income smoothing is practiced to a significant degree, the income statements of the firm are less meaningful for financial analysis, particularly when the movement of funds into and out of reserves is not disclosed. In fact, in a number of countries the actual existence of reserves is not even disclosed. These undisclosed reserves are called "hidden" or "silent" reserves.[36] In 1993, when **Daimler-Benz** applied for listing on the New York Stock Exchange, it disclosed 4 billion Deutsche marks ($2.45 billion) in hidden reserves.[37]

LEGAL (STATUTORY) RESERVE Several countries legally require that companies maintain legal (statutory) reserves. The purpose is to provide additional protection to creditors. The amounts transferred to the legal reserve are not available for dividends. Usually, the legal requirements specify that a certain percentage of income (sometimes dividends) be credited to a legal reserve. For example, in Oman 10% of the annual net profit is transferred to the legal reserve until the reserve balance equals one third of share capital. In France the requirement calls for an annual transfer of 5% of the net income to the legal reserve until the reserve equals 10% of legal capital.

GENERAL RESERVE Another commonly used reserve is called a general reserve. This reserve normally serves the same purpose as an appropriation of retained earning, that is, it restricts the maximum amount that can be declared for dividends.

In some countries a general reserve is also used for income soothing. Accounting procedures to accomplish this are similar to those discussed earlier for the expense liability reserve.

REVALUATION RESERVE In some countries, notably Denmark, Portugal, Sweden, the Netherlands, and the United Kingdom, valuing fixed assets at a higher current value is acceptable. This is accomplished by recording an upward adjustment of the asset and correspondingly crediting the revaluation reserve for an equal amount. In subsequent periods, the asset is depreciated at the adjusted value, thus resulting in a higher depreciation expense. The incremental depreciation may be charged either directly to the revaluation reserve or to income, depending on accounting standards and tax laws of the country.

Perceptions Based on the Method of Disclosure

Research suggests that different disclosure methods result in different user perceptions. A study compared the effects of two methods of disclosing an obligation: **balance sheet recognition** versus **footnote disclosure.** Commercial lenders were surveyed to determine whether the disclosure method affected their perceptions of the item. It was discovered that the commercial lenders were more likely to perceive the obligation as a form of debt when it was recognized as a balance sheet liability than when disclosed in the footnotes accompanying the financial statements. The researchers concluded that the method of disclosing is an important issue that must be considered in formulation of accounting standards.[38]

It is erroneous to conclude that uniform accounting standards lead to uniform disclosures. Accounting standards normally provide a range of acceptability, as opposed to prescribing one "right" disclosure method. Empirical evidence suggests that while using accounting standards of the same country, there can be a variety of ways companies make disclosures. A study comparing goodwill disclosures by 621 publicly traded firms in the United States demonstrated that the firms varied substantially in their goodwill-related asset and expense disclosures. The authors of the study concluded that due to this reason investors cannot easily identify the financial statement effects of existing goodwill accounting rules for a substantial number of firms with material goodwill.[39]

Reporting Approaches of Multinational Companies

A multinational company (MNC) has to decide on its disclosure mode for reporting in different countries. Since no required international reporting standards exist that provide the guidance, MNCs have tried a variety of approaches to communicate information to the target audiences abroad. We will discuss six of these approaches.

1. **Compliance with base country's requirements.** Most countries in the world (the United States being a notable exception) accept financial reports prepared according to accounting principles of a reporting entity's base country. This is the most convenient and the least costly way for MNCs to fulfill their legal reporting requirements. No special effort is made to assist the users in other countries in understanding and interpreting the financial reports.
2. **Translation into the local language.** A slight improvement over the first approach is to translate the text part of financial reports into the local language. It is common for many MNCs to publish their reports in several languages in addition to the languages of their base countries. **Bayer** publishes its complete annual report in English and German and a shorter version in English, German, French, Italian, Japanese, and Spanish.
3. **Translations into the local language and currency.** Besides translating the text portion of the financial reports into the local language, many companies also translate the monetary amounts into the local currency. Commonly the exchange rate on the balance sheet date is used to translate all of the monetary amounts. For example, **Toyota** uses this approach for its U.S. audience using the Tokyo Foreign Exchange market's exchange rate for yen to the U.S. dollar on the balance sheet date.
4. **Provision of information on the base country's accounting standards used.** A few multinational companies provide information on the accounting principles of their base country used in preparation of the financial reports. This approach recognizes the reality of different accounting standards in the world and attempts to help the users by providing an explanation of the accounting standards on which financial reports are based.

    Philips N.V., based in the Netherlands, lists all the relevant differences between U.S. GAAP and Dutch GAAP in the annual report targeted to the U.S. audience. It provides an item-by-item narrative explanation of the differences between the two sets of GAAP as well as the resulting monetary differences in its annual report.
5. **Selective restatements.** A few companies provide partial restatements of their financial statements using the GAAP of the target audience country. For example, a Sweden-based multinational may restate its income amount according to Australian accounting principles. The Australian users can correctly assume that the restated income amount is comparable to income amounts of other companies using Australian accounting standards.

    Selective restatements partially solve the problems created by worldwide diversity in accounting standards. **Philips** and **BP Amoco** restate their net income from their base country GAAP to U.S. GAAP.
6. **Secondary statements.** Secondary statements are a complete set of financial statements (including accompanying notes) prepared according to accounting standards of another country. In addition, the independent auditors express an opinion on the secondary statements using auditing standards of the other country. These statements, prepared specifically for users in another country, attempt to enhance their understanding and usefulness to the target audience. **Honda**, **Sony**, and **DaimlerChrysler** issue secondary statements for U.S. users.

Disclosure Issues for Multinationals

In the absence of required worldwide disclosure standards, the type and quality of disclosures made by companies vary from country to country and from company to company. To appreciate the complexity of the problem faced by an MNC in deciding the nature and extent of disclosure, let us note these issues.

- There are multiple users with varied information needs.
- Users in different countries have varying levels of education. It directly affects their ability to comprehend and interpret sophisticated financial information. Conscious efforts need to be made so that the information is interpreted correctly by the users.
- The sheer size of a typical MNC generates information of mind-boggling volume. A decision must be made regarding what and how much should be disclosed from the great mass of data.
- Information originates from different parts of the world with different cultures that result in different operating environments. Some types of disclosures may embarrass or even anger the local government or general population, leading to adverse effects on the MNC. Balancing of local sensitivities against the need for adequate disclosures is necessary.
- A balance must be struck between legitimate information needs of users for decision making against the possibility that disclosures may be misused by others to harm the company.
- Cost effectiveness of disclosure when many user groups cannot be identified and benefits to the user groups cannot be traced requires exercise of a high degree of professional judgment.

It should be clear from the previous issues that deciding on what to disclose, how much to disclose, and how to disclose it are complex questions. Responses require weighing and balancing many opposing factors. In the end, the manager can only hope that the final mix will serve the appropriate needs of users in a cost-effective manner.

Selected Social Impact Disclosure Practices

Social impact disclosures are of many different types. They may be *required* disclosures, to hold the management accountable for effective and efficient use of scarce economic resources. On the other hand, many companies make voluntary disclosures for the reasons already discussed. The orientation of social impact disclosures is heavily influenced by specific societal concerns in a country. We will focus on disclosures in three categories: employees, value-added statements, and environmental protection.

Employees

Human resource disclosure requirements have received the greatest attention in the social impact reporting area. Annual reports of companies from most countries routinely contain information on employees. The level of specificity and detail, however, varies considerably. As mentioned earlier, this is explained by the societal conditions and environmental pressures in a country. For example, in the United States, the disclosures may include equal employment opportunities for underrepresented groups, while in Germany the disclosures may emphasize working conditions and employee training. Even though this area has received more attention than any other area of social impact reporting, the disclosure requirements are still quite limited.

At the international level, perhaps the United Nations (U.N.) has been in the forefront in recommending extensive disclosures in this area. The U.N. recommends disclosures of the number of employees for the company and by segments (geographic and line of business). It also recommends that corporate policies regarding the recognition of labor unions and labor relations be disclosed.[40] The European Union's Fourth Directive and Seventh Directive require information on the average number of employees, a breakdown of the number of employees by category, and a breakdown of employee costs. Interestingly, the Directives do not define what constitutes a "category."

At the national level, perhaps the most extensive disclosures are required in France. **Bilan Social** (social report) contains mainly employee-related information covering topics such as pay structure, hiring policies, health and safety conditions, training, and industrial relations. The most common disclosure to be found in practice at the national level is the number of employees. Reporting in this area is still at an early stage of development as evidenced by the existing diversity in practice.

Value-Added Statements

The purpose of a company's value-added statement is to show, in financial terms, the contributions made by all participating groups in the creation of wealth. Value-added statements show the value added to acquired materials and services by a company, and the beneficiaries to whom the created value was distributed.

Value added = Total revenue − Cost of goods, materials, and services purchased externally

Value-added statements are prepared primarily in Western European countries, especially Germany, the United Kingdom, France (where they are required as part of *Bilan Social*), the Netherlands, and Sweden. They are also found in South Africa, Australia, and New Zealand.

At the international level, there are no formal requirements regarding value-added statements. In the absence of any requirements at the international or national level (except in France), there is a lack of uniformity in value-added disclosures.

Environmental Performance

Environmental concerns have been receiving considerable attention for many reasons, including heightened public awareness, tougher governmental laws and regulations, and well-publicized major environmental disasters in the recent past. For example, **Union Carbide's** chemical leak in Bhopal (India) in 1984 caused approximately 4,000 deaths and 200,000 injuries. The investors are especially interested in this disclosure area because the costs for environmental cleanup, legal claims paid for damages, and fines imposed on a company for noncompliance with environmental laws and regulations have an adverse effect on current and future corporate earnings.

In spite of the acknowledged importance of this disclosure area, only a few requirements exist worldwide. When disclosures are made, they generally tend to be narrative in form. At the international level, the U.N. recommends disclosure of the measures undertaken by a company to promote a cleaner environment and to reduce risks of harm to the environment. Interestingly, the U.N. guidelines also recommend environmental audits and risk assessments by companies.[41]

At the regional level, the European Union has a policy for environmental protection. The policy includes setting up requirements in the future on corporate disclosures on environmental impacts. The North American Free Trade Agreement among the United States, Canada, and Mexico includes side agreements for environmental protection.

The countries requiring environmental disclosures include Norway, the United States, and France. Norway requires that the board of directors report to include information on emission levels and the measures taken or planned to clean up the environment. The Securities and Exchange Commission (SEC) of the United States requires disclosure of contingent environmental liabilities. The SEC staff has been looking closely over the past several years at the adequacy of environmental disclosures. The SEC regularly receives information from the U.S. Environmental Protection Agency on companies that have past, present, or potential problems in compliance with environmental laws.[42] France's revised penal code, effective March 1, 1994, makes corporations accountable for endangering others. The code includes provisions dealing with "environmental terrorism," including willful pollution.

President Vicente Fox of Mexico has repeatedly expressed his commitment to include ecological considerations at every stage of his government. He has adopted the following environmental stance.

- A sharp reduction in commercial logging
- Inclusion of pollution as an offsetting cost (negative factor) when calculating economic growth
- Special tax breaks to industry for installing environmental controls
- A substantial funding increase and added policing authority for the governmental agency that enforces pollution laws and investigates their violations

Soon after his election, Fox stated, "We will make Mexico's environment, its water and forests, a national-security issue." He added, "We will turn around the concept of development to include the environment as a factor in economic and social decisions—not as a separate sector, but as an essential element in creating sustainable economic and social progress."[43]

In order to strengthen compliance with environmental laws and to instill sensitivity to the protection of the environment among corporate personnel, top management can take the following steps.

- The mission statement includes a firm commitment to environmentally responsible operations and activities.
- A detailed policy document developed for employees on how to prevent, detect, and correct environmental problems.
- Environmental audits performed periodically to ensure compliance with corporate policies.
- Performance in the environmental area included among the criteria used to evaluate managers. This can be a powerful incentive to managers.
- Corporate support to the organizations engaged in environmental cleanup, renewal of natural resources, and development of cleaner technologies.

A growing number of corporations such as **General Motors** and **Imperial Chemical Industries** are making extensive voluntary environmental disclosures. The disclosures in this area are becoming increasingly detailed.

Worldwide Disclosures Diversity and Harmonization

Though accounting is called the language of business, its meaning varies from country to country. Accounting standards reflect its role in a nation's culture, especially its economy. Whereas a public accountant in Mexico City considers the stockholders the primary users of financial statements, an accountant in Frankfurt gears financial statements toward tax authorities. How are accounting standards developed in different countries? What are the implications of different accounting standards? What efforts are being made to achieve harmonization? These are some of the topics discussed in this section.

The global economy is making nations increasingly interdependent. Businesses that aspire to profit from international trade and investments must understand the impact of varying accounting standards on financial statements. Today's international accountants have the expertise for assisting businesses in becoming active participants in the global economy.

Exhibit 600.95 *Government Involvement in Economy*

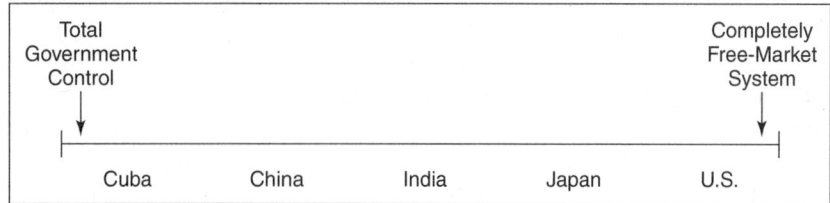

Disclosure Diversity

Accounting standards are heavily influenced by a nation's culture. An important cultural factor is the degree of government involvement in the economy. All economies lie somewhere between the two extremes of total state control and a completely free-market system as illustrated in Exhibit 600.95.

In countries with relatively few publicly-owned enterprises and mostly state-controlled markets, the government usually takes a decisive role in promulgating accounting standards. In contrast, in the countries with large corporations that have widely dispersed ownership, the responsibility for accounting standard setting is often assumed by the profession itself.

Because different approaches to standard setting arise from different perceptions of what constitutes useful financial information, the diversity of approaches yields dramatically different accounting standards worldwide.

The Balance Sheet Emphasis Versus the Income Statement Emphasis

Accounting standards tend to be oriented toward users of financial reports. From among all the users, capital providers exercise the greatest influence over their orientation. If banks are the main capital providers, then standards typically emphasize the balance sheet. Bank authorities focus on the information that helps them evaluate the short-term and long-term liquidity position of a borrower. An entity's financial position helps the lending bank to assess its ability to pay back its debts.

In contrast, where stockholders are the main source of funds, a corporation's earnings are perceived as an important predictor of its future success. Therefore, the income statement receives greater attention from the standard setters. Any change in accounting principles affecting reported income often generates tremendous interest and sometimes great controversy. Some years ago, the U.S. Financial Accounting Standards Board (FASB) attempted to promulgate a financial accounting standard that would have required companies to show employee stock options as an expense in the income statement. The reaction from large, powerful corporations against the proposed standard was so strong that, according to many observers, the FASB was left with little choice but to drop the idea.

Accounting Standard Setting and Financial Reporting in Selected Countries

In this section we will take a close look at the accounting standard-setting process and financial reporting practices of five countries: Brazil, the Netherlands Germany, Japan, and the United States. We will review the accounting and reporting differences among the five countries and the cultural influences contributing to those differences. Cultural values of a country and its accounting system influence each other. The natural outcome is the worldwide diversity of accounting and reporting differences. Earlier, through comparative analyses, we obtained an overview of the diversity among many countries in the areas selected. In this section, a closer look at each of the five countries will enhance our appreciation of the relationship between accounting and its environments.

Brazil

Brazil is a Latin country. The government, Corporation Law, and tax regulations have a strong influence on accounting and financial reporting practices. Though the government has adopted liberal trade policies and privatization of some government-controlled industries in recent years, Brazilian stock markets are relatively small when compared with those of industrialized countries of Western Europe, North America, and the Asia-Pacific region. Financial statements disclosures in Brazil are oriented mostly toward creditors, who are the major source of funds, and tax authorities. The disclosures geared toward equity investors are relatively minor.

STANDARD SETTING   The Corporation Law of 1976, amended in 1997, is the primary source of accounting principles and practices applicable to Brazilian corporations. The Brazilian Institute of Accountants—*Instituto Brasileiro de Contadores* (IBRACON)—and the Federal Council of Accounting, *Conselho Federal de Contabilidade*, are accounting professional organizations. They also provide guidance on accounting principles, preparation of financial statements, and auditing standards. The Securities Exchange Commission—*Commissao de Valores Mobiliarios* (CVM)—is responsible for accounting standards for the companies that are publicly traded. If IBRACON standards are approved by the CVM, they are binding on all publicly traded companies.

FINANCIAL STATEMENTS   Comparative financial statements must be prepared annually. They include the following.

- Balance sheet
- Income statement
- Statement of changes in stockholders' equity
- Statement of changes in financial position
- Notes to the financial statements

Financial statements are accompanied by a report by the board of directors. The basis for measurement is historical cost. Financial statements are prepared on the accrual basis. The principles of conservatism, materiality, and consistency are considered important in the preparation of financial statements.

REVALUATION OF ASSETS   Corporation Law permits the upward revaluation of assets, but tax regulations permit the revaluation of long-term assets only. In practice only property, plant, and equipment are revalued for both accounting and tax purposes.

FINANCE LEASES   Finance leases are not capitalized in practice, even though their capitalization is allowed.

CAPITALIZATION OF INTEREST   Normally all interest costs must be expensed. An exception exists for enterprises at the developmental stage.

INVENTORY VALUATION   Inventories are valued at the lower of cost or market. Market value is considered to be the lower of replacement cost and net realizable value. The first-in, first-out (FIFO) and average cost are commonly used methods for determining inventory cost. The last-in, first-out (LIFO) method is not commonly used since it is unacceptable for tax purposes.

RESEARCH AND DEVELOPMENT COSTS   Research and development costs that are expected to benefit future years may be capitalized and amortized over their useful life. For tax purposes, the minimum amortization period is five years.

SEGMENT REPORTING   Segment reporting is not required.

CONSOLIDATION   Normally the purchase method is required. The pooling of interests method is allowed only under rare circumstances.

The Netherlands

STANDARD SETTING   Title 9 of the Civil Code, updated in 1997, sets the accounting and financial reporting requirements. Title 9 also provides flexibility to comply with the European Union's Fourth Company Law Directive and Seventh Company Law Directive dealing with financial statement contents and consolidation, respectively.

FINANCIAL STATEMENTS   Required financial statements are the following.

- Balance sheet
- Income statement
- Notes to the financial statements

The annual report includes a report by the supervisory board. Civil Code requires an accrual basis. The required concepts include matching, going concern, and prudence concepts. The historical cost basis is allowed for valuation purposes. However, for inventories, tangible, financial, and fixed assets, current value is also allowed. Financial reporting and tax reporting are independent of each other.

REVALUATION OF ASSETS   The law permits the upward revaluation of assets using a current cost convention with the exception of intangible assets. Depreciation expense for tax purposes is on an historical-cost basis only. For financial reporting, depreciation can be on a current value basis.

FINANCE LEASES   The lessee holding assets on a finance lease is required to capitalize such assets, and the related lease commitment is included in liabilities.

CAPITALIZATION OF INTEREST   Interest costs on the borrowings that are directly attributable to manufacturing or construction of assets can be capitalized as part of the total cost of the asset during the manufacturing or construction period.

INVENTORY VALUATION   Inventories are valued at the lower of cost or net realizable value. The cost in this context is actual historical cost or current cost. To arrive at cost, weighted average, FIFO, and LIFO are commonly used methods.

RESEARCH AND DEVELOPMENT COSTS   Costs for research and development are commonly written off as an expense during the period when incurred in practice. They may, however, be capitalized. If capitalized, they should be disclosed separately as an intangible asset.

SEGMENT REPORTING   Segment disclosures are required if sales of a business or a geographical segment exceed 10% of the total net sales.

CONSOLIDATION   Title 9 requires that all group companies and the parent company should be consolidated. Group companies are defined as subsidiaries plus other entities. The other entities include partnerships and entities with 50% or less ownership, provided they are controlled. Subsidiaries not operated by the parent company and economically independent are excluded from consolidation. Normally, only the purchase method is allowed for consolidation. The pooling of interests method is allowed only if neither entity can be identified as the acquirer. As a result, the pooling of interests method is not used in practice.

Germany

STANDARD SETTING   The Commercial Code, as amended in 1994, is the primary source of standards for financial reporting. The strongest influence on generally accepted accounting principles in Germany is the German Stock Corporation Law of 1965, as amended in 1993, and the Limited Liability Companies Law of 1892, which contain accounting standards specific to those entities. Generally, tax benefits can be claimed only if the items are treated in the same manner for financial reporting and tax reporting. Consequently, German companies tend to understate assets and overstate liability, to the extent possible, for minimizing their tax liability.

FINANCIAL STATEMENTS   Companies are required to present the following.

- Balance sheet
- Income statement
- Statement of cash flows
- Notes to the financial statements

Relatively very few companies are listed on stock exchanges. Debt financing is considered preferable to equity financing due to tax regulations. The Commercial Code requires corporations to supplement financial statements with a management report. Banks are the major source of business financing.

Basic accounting concepts include going concern, matching, the historical-cost basis, and the accrual basis. In addition, the prudence concept must also be followed. The prudence concept provides for the recognition of all anticipated risks and losses up to the balance sheet date. Recognition of unrealized profits is prohibited. Netting of assets against liabilities or income against expenses is not allowed. Accounting principles must be applied consistently across periods.

REVALUATION OF ASSETS The historical-cost basis is strictly followed. The Commercial Code does not permit the revaluation of an individual asset above its historical acquisition cost.

FINANCE LEASES Finance leases are required to be capitalized by the lessor and the lessee.

CAPITALIZATION OF INTEREST The interest cost on a loan used to finance the production of an asset may be capitalized and included in its costs. The interest to be capitalized in this manner is limited to the amount incurred during the production period. In case of interest capitalization, disclosure is required in the notes to the financial statements.

INVENTORY VALUATION Inventories are valued at the lower of cost or market. For cost determination, specific identification, average cost, FIFO, and LIFO inventory methods are acceptable. For the application of the lower of cost or market concept to inventories, market value can be either replacement cost or net realizable value. When both replacement cost and net realizable value are available, the lower of the two is considered to be market value. If replacement cost information is not available, then net realizable value is considered market value. Since the tax laws allow the deduction of normal profit to arrive at the net realizable value amount, the same practice is followed for financial reporting. The net realizable value, as a result, often means net realizable value minus normal profit.

RESEARCH AND DEVELOPMENT COSTS Expenditures related to research and development must be expensed as incurred.

SEGMENT REPORTING The Commercial Code requires disclosures of sales by industry and by geographically defined markets in the notes to the financial statements.

CONSOLIDATION A company is required to prepare consolidated financial statements and a group management report. The entities included in the consolidated financial statements are subsidiaries as well as the companies that are under control even though a majority of the voting shares are not owned. Consolidated statements are generally prepared according to the purchase method. The pooling of interests method is allowed only in certain circumstances.

Japan

STANDARD SETTING The primary source of standards for financial reporting is the Commercial Code of Japan. In addition, the Income Tax Law and the Securities and Exchange Law are important influences on financial reporting practices of major Japanese companies. The Income Tax Law is very influential because financial reporting and taxation reporting in Japan are the same. In essence, the Income Tax Law prescribes what revenues and expenses can be recognized. Interestingly, the Commercial Code has creditor (balance sheet) orientation, while the Securities and Exchange Law has investor (income statement) orientation.

FINANCIAL STATEMENTS The Commercial Code requires the preparation of five financial statements.

- Balance sheet
- Income statement
- Notes to the financial statements
- Business report
- Proposal for retained earnings appropriations

The Securities and Exchange Law also requires cash flow statements for publicly traded companies.

The objective of financial statements in Japan is to protect the interest of both the creditors and the investors. Thus, disclosures dealing with dividend availability, creditworthiness, and earnings per share are of paramount importance. The accrual basis of accounting is employed.

The **business report** covers many of the matters typically found in the Management Discussion and Analysis part of companies' annual reports in North America. An example of the topics include a description of the business; financial summary data for the year and the past three years; and disclosures relating to capital, employees, names of major shareholders, names of major creditors, and names of directors and statutory auditors. It also includes significant events after the balance sheet date.

The **proposal for appropriation of retained earnings** is prepared for approval at the stockholders' meeting for dividend payments and bonus payments to members of the board of directors and statutory auditors.

REVALUATION OF ASSETS   Revaluation of assets is not permitted.

FINANCE LEASES   Tax regulations stipulate conditions under which a lease can be capitalized. Financial statements follow the tax treatment for leases. Capitalization of leases is rare in practice.

CAPITALIZATION OF INTEREST   A corporation has the option to capitalize interest costs during the construction period for the assets constructed for its own use.

INVENTORY VALUATION   The tax regulation allows a corporation to value inventory at the lower of cost or market value. Market value is defined as the replacement cost. The cost determination may be made by using specific identification, FIFO, LIFO, average, most recent purchase, or retail inventory methods. A change in inventory method can be made only after obtaining approval from the tax office. The method of inventory valuation adopted for tax purposes must be used for financial reporting purposes.

RESEARCH AND DEVELOPMENT COSTS   Expenditures for research and development are expensed as incurred.

SEGMENT REPORTING   Listed companies that file consolidated financial statements must provide segment information on their industry segments and geographic segments. The disclosures required are sales and operating profit by segment. The criterion for an industry segment is that its sales or its operating profit exceeds 10% of total sales or 10% of total operating profit. The criterion for a geographic segment is that its sales exceed 20% of total sales.

CONSOLIDATION   Only listed companies are required to prepare consolidated financial statements. The parent company must own, directly or indirectly, majority ownership in the other entities for consolidation purposes. Consolidated financial statements are prepared according to the purchase method. The pooling of interests method is allowed but rarely used.

United States

STANDARD SETTING   The U.S. Congress has given the Securities and Exchange Commission (SEC) responsibility for establishing generally accepted accounting principles (GAAP) for companies whose stock is publicly traded. The SEC has, in turn, largely delegated this responsibility to the accounting profession.

1. The Financial Accounting Standards Board (FASB)—**http://www.fasb.org**—is the main body responsible for promulgating accounting standards in the United States. Established in 1973, the FASB is composed of seven members. The Financial Accounting Foundation oversees the FASB's operations and provides its funding. The FASB follows due process procedures in establishing accounting principles.

   Pronouncements of the FASB include:
   - *Statements of Financial Accounting Concepts.* These are fundamental concepts on which accounting and reporting standards are based.
   - *Statements of Financial Accounting Standards.* These are the major pronouncements issued by the FASB and are the primary basis for GAAP.

2. The Governmental Accounting Standards Board (GASB) was created in 1984. GASB's responsibility is to establish accounting principles for municipal and state government bodies, hospitals, universities, and other not-for-profit entities. The Financial Accounting Foundation oversees the operations and financing of the GASB.

3. The American Institute of Certified Public Accountants (AICPA) is an organization of certified public accountants. It is influential in the development of accounting principles and practices. The AICPA has formed the Accounting Standards Executive Committee (AcSEC) which issues *Statements of Position* on accounting issues not covered by the FASB.

FINANCIAL STATEMENTS The required set of financial statements consists of the following.

- Balance sheet
- Statement of comprehensive income
- Statement of cash flows
- Statement of changes in stockholders' equity
- Notes to the statements

The concepts used in financial statements include going concern, matching, consistency in the application of accounting principles across periods, and accrual basis.

REVALUATION OF ASSETS The historical-cost basis is used for the valuation of most assets. Certain types of investments and all derivatives are required to be revalued at their fair (market) value.

FINANCE LEASES Finance leases are required to be capitalized.

CAPITALIZATION OF INTEREST Interest costs must be capitalized for self-constructed property or equipment. The amount to be capitalized is the interest costs that could have been avoided if construction costs for the asset had not been incurred.

INVENTORY VALUATION The application of the lower of cost or market principle is required. Cost may be determined by using FIFO, LIFO, average cost, and specific identification. If LIFO is used for taxation, it must also be used for financial reporting. In the application of lower of cost or market, market is the middle amount from among replacement cost, net realizable value, and net realizable value minus normal profit.

RESEARCH AND DEVELOPMENT COSTS Research and development costs are expensed immediately.

SEGMENT REPORTING Segment reporting is required of all companies whose securities are publicly traded. A segment is reportable if it meets any one of the following three criteria.

- *Revenue.* A segment's total revenue is 10% or more of the total revenue of the company.
- *Profit or loss.* The operating profit is greater than 10% of the total operating profit of all segments that reported operating profits (or greater than 10% of the total operating loss of all segments that reported operating losses).
- *Assets.* The assets are 10% or more of the combined assets of all operating segments.

The following information is required to be disclosed for a reportable segment.

- Operating profit or loss
- Specified income statement items such as operating revenues, depreciation, and noncash expenses
- Total assets
- Total capital expenditures
- Reconciliation of the sum of segment totals to the company total for each of the following three items
    1. Revenues
    2. Operating profit
    3. Assets

The company is required to disclose how reportable segments are identified. The criteria for the identification of segments for external reports should be the same as those used by the management to distinguish business segments for internal reporting purposes.

CONSOLIDATION Consolidated financial statements are required when a parent has a controlling interest in the voting stock of other entities. Exceptions to the requirement for consolidated statements occur when control is temporary or when restrictions cast doubt on the parent's ability to control a subsidiary, for example, the subsidiary is in bankruptcy. Currently, either the purchase method or the pooling of interests method is required to be used based on the application of the criteria in a given business combination situation. The FASB has published a proposed statement of financial accounting standards. If adopted, only the purchase method will be acceptable.

Exhibit 600.96 *Elements of Financial Statements*

Country	Balance Sheet	Income Statement	Statement of Funds/Cash Flow
Brazil	R	R	R
Germany	R	R	O
Japan	R	R	P
Netherlands	R	R	O
United States	R	R	R

R = Required
P = Required for publicly traded companies
O = Optional

Exhibit 600.97 *Basic Accounting Concepts and Conventions*

Country	Cost Basis	Accrual Basis	Going Concern	Legal Form versus Substance
Brazil	HP, HR	Required	Required	Legal
Germany	HC	Required	Required	Legal
Japan	HC	Required	Required	Legal
Netherlands	CC, HC, HR	Required	Required	Substance
United States	MA	Required	Required	Substance

CC = Current cost
HC = Historical cost
HP = Historical cost with price-level adjustments
HR = Historical cost with revaluation option
MA = Mixed attributes (a blend of historical cost and current cost)

Exhibit 600.98 *Segment Disclosure Requirements*

	Required Segment Disclosures	
Country	Geographical	Industrial
Brazil	O	O
Germany	R	R
Japan	R	R
Netherlands	R	R
United States	I	I

R = Required
O = Optional
I = Segments identified by using the same criteria that were used for internal reporting purposes

Exhibits 600.96, 600.97, and 600.98 summarize the elements of financial statements, the basic accounting concepts and conventions, and the segment disclosure requirements, respectively, for the five countries we have discussed previously.

Standardization Versus Harmonization

The efficient flow of goods, capital, and resources across national boundaries and the location of financial and business operations in more than one country require that accounting standards not be country-specific. Many factors, for example, foreign currencies, different inflation rates, and the need for consolidated financial statements are promoting internationalization of accounting standards.

One of the early calls to internationalize accounting standards came from a prominent European executive, the president of Royal Dutch Petroleum Company, in 1979:

> Financial information is a form of a language. And if the language of financial information is to be put to use, so that investment and credit decisions can more readily be taken, it should not only be intelligible, it should also be comparable. International differences in accounting standards should be narrowed. Although this may seem to be an impossible chasm, it can be achieved—if enough countries are willing.[44]

Different accounting treatment of the same type of transactions and events makes it difficult to analyze and compare financial statements. This explains why there is growing support for international accounting standards.

> An international set of accounting standards would allow a more level playing field because income statements and balance sheet ratios would become more consistent between competing companies.[45]

According to Wyatt, "The linkage of worldwide capital markets is one of the driving forces behind the movement toward a single set of accounting rules."[46]

Comparability of accounting information is vital to international trade and investment. The question is how to achieve comparability. **Standardization** means requiring the same accounting standards worldwide. Standardization would ensure full comparability.

Many, however, doubt the feasibility of complete standardization of accounting rules. Specific needs linked with national cultural needs make national accounting standards necessary. As a solution, the concept of *harmonization* has gained widespread popularity. **Harmonization** means that the differences among national accounting standards should be kept to a minimum. Harmonization accommodates the existence of alternative accounting rules or practices in different countries as long as they are *in harmony* with each other and can be reconciled.

Auditing Issues for Global Operations

Internal auditing and external auditing are two separate but related functions. The two audit functions share a common objective—to determine reliability of accounting information. In this section we first discuss the issues related to internal auditing and then the issues related to external auditing.

Internal Auditing

Internal auditing is an independent evaluation of the operations and internal control system of an organization to determine whether management's policies and prescribed procedures are being followed, and also whether the resources are safeguarded and used efficiently to achieve organizational objectives. The major objectives of internal auditing are the following.

- To determine whether financial and operating information has reliability and integrity.
- To determine whether management and accounting controls are in place and are effective.
- To determine whether assets are safeguarded and used efficiently.

Internal auditing deals with the areas that are important to the management of a company: Accuracy of financial and operating reports, compliance with policies, and the safeguarding of assets and their efficient usage.

Global Trends in Internal Auditing

The importance of an internal audit function increases as operations of an organization become geographically dispersed. The practice of internal auditing is increasing worldwide. In many countries, internal auditing is required by law.

An important factor contributing to the establishment of audit committees has been the Foreign Corrupt Practices Act (FCPA). The impact of the FCPA has been felt worldwide due to its broad scope and its penalty provisions. In the United States, the New York Stock Exchange and the National Association of Securities Dealers Automated Quotations (NASDAQ) both require that all companies listed on those security markets have audit committees. The New York Stock Exchange mandates that the audit committees consist of nonmanagement directors only, while NASDAQ requires that the majority be nonmanagement directors. The Committee of Sponsoring Organizations (COSO) of the Treadway Commission in the United Kingdom considers an effective internal audit function to be important for the reliability and integrity of financial and operational information. COSO has also stated that an enlightened and proactive audit committee is a powerful agent for corporate self-regulation.

TECHNOLOGICAL ADVANCES   Instantaneous electronic transfers and computerized information systems have raised new concerns about both asset security and data security. It makes the role of internal auditing significantly more important. The new technologies enable the internal auditor to perform audit tests and analyses faster and more economically.

RELIANCE OF EXTERNAL AUDITORS ON INTERNAL AUDIT REPORTS   For cost savings and avoidance of unnecessary duplication, it is common for external auditors to rely on internal audit reports. This further enhances the importance of the internal audit function.

INTERNATIONAL OPERATIONS   Conceptually, there is no difference between internal audits of domestic operations and internal audits of international operations. However, international operations add certain *practical* complexities that necessitate adaptations and adjustments.

- *Geographic distances.* Long geographic distances make it impossible to personally oversee operations through physical observation and visual inspection.
- *Local laws.* To ensure compliance with local laws, it is a prerequisite to be knowledgeable about them. Local laws apply to a multitude of operational areas: environmental protection, product safety, and working conditions, to name a few. In France, for example, a penal code that took effect in 1994 makes corporations, small companies, and nonprofit organizations accountable for endangering others. The code contains penalty provisions for "environmental terrorism," including willful pollution.
- *Business customs.* Business practices are different worldwide. In some countries (for example, Japan) banks typically do not return canceled checks. In other countries, confirmation of receivables and payables is not a customary practice.
- *National currencies.* With very few exceptions, most countries have their own national monetary unit. This requires that the internal auditors be familiar with the monetary unit of the country where an international operation is located.
- *Local records in the local language.* In most cases, local records are kept in the local language. This requires that either the internal auditor be proficient in the local language, or the records must be translated. Translation creates potential problems arising from differences in accounting terminology. Even when the language is the same, accounting terms may have different meanings. For example, the term turnover has an entirely different meaning in the United Kingdom than it does in the United States.
- *Infrastructure.* The degree to which the infrastructure of a country is developed has a direct impact on the design of the internal control system and internal audit function.
- *Availability of internal auditors.* Lack of availability of well-trained, skilled internal auditors is a problem in many countries.

The previous factors often require top management to make decisions for balancing conflicting factors. Many tradeoffs required for making such decisions make them more complex than those made for domestic operations. Internal auditors can provide in-house consulting expertise in such a complex decision-making environment.

Internal Auditing in the International Environment

International operations add certain practical complexities to the internal auditing function. Fortunately, some of those complexities are decreasing primarily due to three reasons.

1. *Business Practices.* The ever-increasing magnitude and importance of international business has resulted in a greater uniformity in business practices worldwide. Differences in business practices in different parts of the world are not as pronounced as they used to be. For example, written agreements are commonly accepted now in most of those countries where local customs previously dictated otherwise.
2. *Technology.* Advancements in technology such as the Internet and fax machines have alleviated many problems previously posed either by geographic distance or the lack of a well-developed infrastructure within a country. Communication systems are now very efficient and less costly than they were only a few years ago. A country's poor postal system, for example, does not pose as much of a problem now as it did a few years ago.

3. *Currencies.* Some currency-related issues have become relatively simple for a variety of reasons. Examples include adoption of a common currency by many countries (the euro); adoption of another country's currency as the national currency (U.S. dollar's adoption as the national currency in Ecuador and Panama); and stabilization of the national currencies in some countries (Brazil).

Coordination of Internal Audits With External Audits

Coordination of the internal audit and external audit functions is desirable to ensure that the audit scope is adequate and there is minimal duplication of efforts. The Institute of Internal Auditors specifies that the director of internal auditing should coordinate internal and external audit work. This requires support of the board of directors to achieve effective coordination.[47] The International Federation of Accountants (IFAC) has also addressed the issue. The IFAC requires the external auditor to evaluate the internal audit function when it appears that internal auditing work is relevant to the external audit in specific areas. This assessment of the internal audit function will influence the decision about the extent of using internal auditing work.[48] The standard also contains guidance regarding the procedures that should be considered by the external auditor in evaluating and testing the work of an internal auditor for the purpose of using that work.[49]

Even though external auditors cannot substitute the work of internal auditors for their own work, the scope of work for an external audit may be affected by internal auditing work. The extent to which this happens depends primarily on the assessment of external auditors regarding the competence and objectivity of internal auditors. All large international public accounting firms have policies on relations with a client's internal auditors. U.S. generally accepted auditing standards permit the external auditors to use the internal auditors for direct assistance on the external audit. In such cases, the U.S. auditing standards require the external auditors to assess the internal auditors' competency and objectivity. When internal auditors provide direct assistance in an external audit, external auditors should supervise and assess the internal auditors' work. The fee reduction for the external auditors is usually substantial when there is a highly regarded internal audit function. Additionally, the external audit may be completed in less time.[50]

Since the internal audit function is an important aspect of an internal control system, an understanding of the internal audit function by external auditors also contributes to their evaluation of the overall internal control system of the client company.

External Auditing

External audits are performed by public accountants. During the audit, external auditors perform the necessary audit procedures to the financial statements and supporting evidence to determine whether the financial statements are in conformity with generally accepted accounting standards. If the auditor's opinion states that the statements conform to the standards, it lends credibility to the representations contained in the financial statements. The external auditor's opinion is especially important for the parent company, investors, and creditors. The parent company can rely on the financial statements of international operations for preparing the consolidated financial statements and for internal decision making. The investors and creditors use financial statements audited by the external auditors to make their decisions. It is critical for a multinational company to make its audited financial statements available to regulatory agencies, investors, creditors, and security analysts for the purposes of listing its securities on international securities markets and for actively participating in international capital markets.

External Audit Objective

The basic objective of the external audit is the same in all countries—to determine if the financial statements are properly prepared. The external auditors audit financial statements and supporting evidence by applying the auditing standards. *Though the objective is the same, external audits are performed differently in different countries since accounting standards as well as auditing standards differ from country to country.*

ACCOUNTING STANDARDS A prerequisite for conducting an external audit is that the external auditor must be knowledgeable of a country's accounting standards and also possess the expertise in their application. Accounting standards differ worldwide. Therefore, financial statements prepared in conformity with the accounting standards of one country are not comparable to financial statements prepared in accordance with the accounting standards of another country. For example, in some countries plant assets can be written-up subsequent to their acquisition, a practice that is not acceptable in other countries. The representations made by the financial statements in conformity with different accounting standards require different auditing standards and procedures.

AUDITING STANDARDS The auditing standard-setting process differs from country to country. In some countries, auditing standards are set by the public accounting profession. In other countries, auditing standards are based on government requirements as mandated in the countries' laws and regulations. Then there are countries where both the public accounting profession and the government participate in the auditing standard-setting process.

In countries where statutory audit requirements exist, for example, Germany, the purpose of the external audit is primarily to ensure that the financial records are kept and the financial statements are prepared according to legal requirements. In countries where the public accounting profession assumes the primary responsibility to set auditing standards, for example, the United States, an external audit is conducted using generally accepted auditing standards. In such cases, auditing standards are set by the profession to determine whether the financial statements are in conformity with generally accepted accounting principles.

Regardless of who sets auditing standards, the standards and audit procedure requirements vary from country to country. For example, independent confirmation of accounts receivable and physical observation of inventory are required in some countries, while such requirements do not exist in other countries.

External Auditing in the International Environment

The objective of an external audit is the same throughout the world: to determine the conformity of financial statements to applicable accounting standards. As we noted earlier, accounting standards as well as auditing standards differ from country to country. These factors add extra dimensions to the audits conducted in an international setting.

For a multinational company with operations in many different parts of the world, it is not usually feasible to send external auditors from the base country to each of the locations of international operations for several reasons

- Geographic distance makes travel costly and usually has an adverse effect on the performance of the auditor due to unfamiliar surroundings, fatigue, jet lag, and travel-related stress.
- Thorough knowledge of applicable accounting standards and the expertise in auditing standards of a country can only be acquired through training and practical experience in that country.
- In many countries, legal requirements have a direct and significant impact on the external audit. This requires an orientation that is different from the orientation in countries with few legal implications for an external audit.
- Business customs differ among countries. Familiarity with business customs of a country may be necessary to collect and test the supporting evidence for successfully completing the audit.

The previous points favor using an external auditor who practices in the country where an international operation is located. However, there is a need to have a coordination mechanism with the parent company. The quality of an external audit in an international setting depends heavily on the qualifications of an external auditor.

QUALIFICATIONS Education, experience, and certification requirements for external auditors vary in different parts of the world. For example, in some countries, an external auditor is not required to have any formal education and training in the audit function. This is especially the case in several countries with statutory audit requirements. Coordination is necessary to ensure that the qualifications of the external auditor are satisfactory to meet the parent company's needs for reliable information.

Independent Auditing Environment in Selected Countries

In this section, we will look at auditing practices in five countries and observe some notable trends.

1. BRAZIL Public companies and financial institutions are required to publish financial statements audited by independent auditors registered with the Securities Commission. The required annual financial statements include a balance sheet, an income statement (profit and loss accounts), a statement of retained earnings, a statement of changes in financial position, a statement of sources and use of funds, and notes to the financial statements. The board of directors of a company selects independent auditors. The Corporate Law requires that the financial statements must be published within a specified time range before the general annual meeting of shareholders.

An independent auditor's qualifications in Brazil include membership in a professional organization in Brazil. This means meeting education and practical experience requirements for admission as a member of the professional organization.

Auditing standards in Brazil are set primarily by the Federal Council for Accounting. On a smaller scale, the Brazilian Institute of Accountants and the Securities Commission are also involved in the auditing standard-setting process.

The Brazilian Institute of Accountants is a member of the International Federation of Accountants. Its auditing pronouncements generally conform to the IFAC guidelines.[51]

2. THE NETHERLANDS   Financial statements of all companies except qualifying small companies require statutory audit by independent auditors appointed by shareholders in a general meeting. The required financial statements are the balance sheet, the income statement, and notes to the financial statements. Large companies (according to the specified criteria) must also prepare a cash flow statement. The required annual financial statements are on two bases: a parent company only basis and the consolidated basis.

Legally, the only enforceable provisions dealing with accounting and auditing are those from the Civil Code. Therefore, both the EU Fourth Directive and EU Seventh Directive have been incorporated in the Civil Code. Though auditing rules come from the Civil Code, the auditing profession is self-regulated. Independent audits are performed by the registered accountants. Registered accountants must be members of the Royal Netherlands Institute of Registered Accountants. An auditor must be independent of the client company to be audited. This means not having any financial interest in the company.

In addition to an opinion on the financial statements, the independent auditor is required to ascertain whether the directors' report meets the legal requirements and is consistent with the financial statements. Independent auditors are also required to determine if all of the required disclosures have been made. The disclosure requirements in the Netherlands depend on the size of the company.

There is no explicit requirement for Dutch auditors to follow the IFAC guidelines. However, the Royal Netherlands Institute of Registered Accountants is a member of the IFAC and has issued statements on auditing practice that are largely based on IFAC guidelines. For all practical purposes, IFAC audit standards are complied with in the Netherlands.[52]

3. GERMANY   The German Commercial Code requires a statutory audit of the annual financial statements of all companies (except very small companies specified in the code). The financial statements required by law are the balance sheet, the income statement, and notes. All corporations listed on the stock exchange regardless of size are required to be audited. EU accounting and audit regulations are incorporated into German law.

Auditors are appointed by shareholders each year. The auditor conducting a statutory audit, whether an individual or a firm, must hold German professional qualifications. Statutory auditors must be independent of the client. They must not own shares in the companies they audit and may not be employees or members of the board of directors.

There are two professional organizations for auditors: the Chamber of Certified Public Accountants and the Institute of Public Accountants. Auditors are required by statutes to be members of the Chamber of Certified Public Accountants, which specifies duties and professional ethics requirements (to a large extent) of public accountants. The Institute of Public Accountants issues recommendations on audit standards within the legal framework. Compliance with the IFAC audit guidelines depends on whether they are incorporated in German audit standards.

The German Commercial Code requires the independent auditors to report whether the financial statements comply with legal provisions, give a *true and fair view* of financial position and results of operations, and are in conformity with required accounting standards that are incorporated in German law. Because German auditors are required to conduct a full-scope audit, an extensive information base of the audit client's operating environment and accounting system is accumulated.[53]

4. JAPAN   The Commercial Code requires stockholders of all corporations to elect statutory auditors. In addition, large corporations (discussed later) and corporations subject to the Securities and Exchange Law must appoint an independent auditor. The Commercial Code requires four basic financial statements: the balance sheet, income statement, business report, and proposal for appropriations of retained earnings. The business report covers a multitude of informational items such as a description of the business, important data for more than the past three years, names of directors and statutory auditors, names of major stockholders and their equity percentages, and names of major lenders, to name a few. The proposal for appropriations of retained earnings is prepared for approval by shareholders at the annual meeting. The appropriations proposed are for dividend payments and bonuses for directors and statutory auditors.

Statutory Auditors   There are no established professional qualifications for statutory auditors, and typically they are not professional accountants. The statutory auditor expresses an opinion as to whether the performance of the company's directors is in conformity with requirements of the Commercial Code. A statutory auditor may receive a portion of the corporation's profits as a bonus. Though usually not independent, the statutory auditor cannot be an employee or a director of the corporation.

Large Corporations   Large corporations (defined in terms of the size of share capital or total liabilities) must have a board of statutory auditors with at least three statutory auditors. Financial statements of every large corporation are subject to both an independent audit and a statutory audit. Statutory auditors of large corporations must report on the appropriateness of the financial statements and express an opinion on the independent auditor's report.

Independent Auditors   Independent auditors are either Japanese CPAs or an audit corporation. The Securities and Exchange Law and the Commercial Code have different requirements regarding the professional duties of independent auditors.

- The Securities and Exchange Law requires an independent auditor to express an opinion as to whether the financial statements are a fair representation of the financial position and results of operations of the company.
- The Commercial Code requires that the independent auditor express an opinion as to whether financial statements are in compliance with the Commercial Code and the company's articles of incorporation.

The appointment procedures prescribed for independent auditors differ between the Commercial Code and the Securities and Exchange Law.

- For Commercial Code purposes, the appointment is in two steps. First, the candidates for appointment are approved by the statutory auditors. Subsequently, shareholders appoint the independent auditors.
- Under the Securities and Exchange Law, the independent auditors are appointed by the board of directors. They are initially appointed for a one-year term but are eligible for automatic reappointment.

The independent auditors of a corporation submit their report on financial statements to the statutory auditors. The statutory auditors present their report to the board of directors. Guidelines for submission of reports from one level to the next include a specified time frame that varies according to the size of the corporation.

Auditing Profession   The Japanese Institute of Certified Public Accountants (JICPA) is the only professional accounting and auditing organization in Japan. Its Audit Committee is involved in establishing professional standards and standards for ethics. There are relatively few Certified Public Accountants in Japan when compared with other industrialized countries. This is attributable to rigorous examination standards and experience requirements.

Auditing standards are incorporated into Japanese law. Therefore, the degree of consistency of Japanese audit standards with the IFAC standards depends on the extent to which the IFAC standards are incorporated into laws. The financial statements subject to independent audit are the balance sheet and the income statement. The corporations that are subject to the Securities and Exchange Law, financial statements of the parent company, as well as the consolidated financial statements receive independent audit.[54]

The Japanese Institute of Certified Public Accountants and the Japan Federation of Economic Organizations are leading the efforts for formation of a private organization that will spearhead the development of Japanese accounting standards.

By establishing a private organization independent of the political sphere, The Japanese Institute of Certified Public Accountants and the Japan Federation of Economic Organizations aim to increase the transparency of the standard-setting process to boost international confidence in Japan's accounting standards.

The Finance Ministry has agreed in principle to transfer its authority in this area to the new entity. The new entity will be structured as a foundation that will draw members from the business community, the accounting profession, academia, and security dealers.

5. UNITED STATES   Corporate laws of various states in the United States typically do not require appointment of an independent auditor. The Securities and Exchange Commission and the national securities exchanges, however, generally require audited financial statements for filing purposes. Independent auditors are usually appointed by the board of directors of nonpublic companies and by stockholders' approval for public companies.

Generally accepted auditing standards are issued by the Auditing Standards Board of the American Institute of Certified Public Accountants (AICPA) in the form of *Statements on Auditing Standards* (SASs). The generally accepted auditing standards, provide a framework to the independent auditor. Independent auditors are required to comply with these ten standards *and* all other SASs while performing an audit. Though the standards are formulated by the Auditing Standards Board, their requirements are often influenced directly by the Securities and Exchange Commission and court decisions, and indirectly by pressure from the U.S. Congress. In most material respects, the auditing standards are consistent with IFAC's International Standards on Auditing.

Each state has its own board of accountancy to regulate the practice of public accounting within the state. All states have licensing requirements for the practice of public accounting. A public accountant can be licensed without being a member of the AICPA. In almost all states, only licensed certified public accountants (CPAs) can perform independent (external) audits. The annual financial statements filed with the SEC are required to be audited by, and the auditor's report is required to be signed by, licensed certified public accountants. All state boards of accountancy are state governmental agencies. There is no federal agency that grants licenses to practice public accounting nationwide in the United States.

Though specific requirements vary from state to state, generally all states require that an individual meet three requirements to become a licensed certified public accountant in the state.

- *Achieve a minimum level of higher education.* Most states require a baccalaureate degree with the equivalent of a major in accounting. Many states require education equivalent to a master's degree.
- *Pass the CPA examination.*
- *Obtain minimum acceptable professional experience.* States vary in their experience requirements both in type and length. Most states require two to three years of experience in public accounting before a license to practice as a certified public accountant is granted.

Reciprocity among states—allowing a licensed CPA from another state to practice in the state without requiring him or her to obtain a license—depends on the laws of each state.

Independent auditors in the United States are required to consider "inherent risk" brought about by economic conditions while planning an audit. *The auditors should include global risks among the risk factors.*[55] In their reports on financial statements, the U.S. auditors express an opinion as to whether the financial statements present fairly the corporation's financial position, results of operations, and cash flows in accordance with generally accepted accounting principles.

Report on Financial Statements Prepared for Use in Other Countries With the internationalization of business, auditors in the United States may be appointed to audit and report on financial statements of a U.S. entity that are prepared in conformity with accounting principles of another country, for use outside the United States.

If the financial statements (in conformity with generally accepted accounting principles of another country) are prepared for use *only* outside the United States, the auditor may issue either one of the two forms of report.

1. A United States-style report modified to report on the accounting principles of another country
2. The report form of the other country, whose accounting principles were used for preparation of the financial statements

Opinions Based on Another Auditor's Report An independent auditor may report on consolidated or combined financial statements, even if the auditor did not audit every entity in the consolidated or combined group. This happens when the principal auditor does not have an office in the country where the client has significant operations. Let us assume that the U.S.-based parent, Schoenen Company, has three subsidiaries: Sohail Company in Singapore, Younas Company in Pakistan, and Sajid Company in Abu Dhabi. Only Schoenen Company and Younas Company were audited by the principal auditor, while Sohail Company and Sajid Company were audited by local auditing firms. This is shown in Exhibit 600.99.

Exhibit 600.99 *Example of Parent and Affiliates Audited by Principal and Other Auditors*

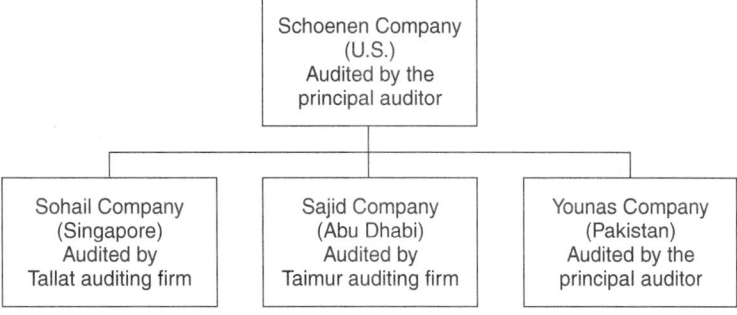

The principal auditor must decide whether to refer to other auditors' reports. If the principal auditor decides not to refer to other auditors' reports, there is no modification in the report on financial statements of the consolidated or combined entity. *In such cases, the principal auditor is assuming responsibility for the other auditors' work.*

If the principal auditor decides, instead, to refer to the reports of other auditors, the scope of the work done by the other auditors must be described in the principal auditor's report. *By making reference to other auditors' reports, the principal auditor is indicating the degree of responsibility each auditor is assuming in the report.*

Note: *The purpose of reference to other auditors' reports is only to clearly divide the extent of responsibility assumed by each auditor. Such a reference is not considered a qualified opinion.*

Audit Considerations for the SEC The SEC generally finds only unqualified opinions acceptable. Thus companies that file their financial statements with the SEC have the *de facto* requirement of resolving any issues regarding the acceptability of their financial statements.

A CPA firm that has been the auditor for an SEC registrant and either has resigned, has declined to stand for reelection, or has been dismissed is required to report that fact directly in writing to the former SEC client, with a simultaneous copy sent directly by the firm to the chief accountant of the SEC. This letter must be sent by the end of the fifth business day following the CPA firm's determination that the client-auditor relationship has ended.

Module 600 Glossary

A

Absorption costing A product costing approach that assigns all fixed and variable manufacturing costs to the units produced.

Accelerated depreciation method A depreciation method that provides for a high depreciation expense in the first year of use of an asset and a gradually declining expense thereafter.

Account The form used to record additions and deductions for each individual asset, liability, owner's equity, revenue, and expense.

Account form The form of balance sheet with the assets section presented on the left-hand side and the liabili- ties and owner's equity sections presented on the right-hand side.

Accounting The process of identifying, measuring, and communicating economic information to permit informed judgments and decisions by users of the information.

Accounting cycle The sequence of basic accounting procedures during a fiscal period.

Accounting equation The expression of the relationship between assets, liabilities, and owner's equity; it is most commonly stated as Assets = Liabilities + Owner's Equity.

Accounting exposures The transaction and translation risk exposures.

Accounting period concept An accounting principle that requires accounting reports be prepared at periodic intervals.

Accounting principles See Accounting standards.

Accounting Principles Board Opinion No. 15 A standard issued by the Accounting Principles Board in the United States that outlines all the factors pertinent to the computation of earnings per common share.

Accounting standards The rules that govern the measuring and recording of economic activities and the reporting of accounting information to external users.

Accounting system The methods and procedures used by a business to record and report financial data for use by management and external users.

Account payable A liability created by a purchase made on credit.

Account receivable A claim against a customer for services rendered or goods sold on credit.

Accounts receivable turnover A measure used to determine a company's average collection period for receivables; computed by dividing net sales (or net credit sales) by average accounts receivable.

Accrual accounting rate of return (AARR) method A capital budgeting method that reports accounting income using the accrual basis.

Accrual basis A basis of accounting in which revenues are recognized in the period earned, and expenses are recognized in the period incurred in the process of generating revenues.

Accrued expenses Expenses that have been incurred but not paid. Sometimes called *accrued liabilities*.

Accrued revenues Revenues that have been earned but not collected Sometimes called *accrued assets*.

Accumulated depreciation account The contra asset account used to accumulate the depreciation recognized to date on plant assets.

Acid-test ratio A ratio that measures the "instant" debt-paying ability of a company. Also known as *quick ratio*.

Activity analysis The study of employee effort and other business records to determine the cost of activities.

Activity base The measure used to allocate factory overhead. Also known as *allocation base,* or *activity driver.*

Activity-based costing (ABC) An accounting framework based on determining the cost of activities and allocating these costs to products, using activity rates. An approach to costing that focuses on activities as the fundamental cost objects. It uses the cost of these activities as the basis for assigning costs to other cost objects such as products, services, or customers. It provides more accurate allocation of indirect costs than traditional methods.

Activity-based management (ABM) A discipline that focuses on the management of activities for improving the value received by the customer and the profit achieved by providing this value.

Activity base usage The amount of activity base used by a particular product.

Activity cost pools Cost accumulations that are associated with a given activity, such as machine usage, inspections, moving, and production setups.

Activity rates The cost of an activity per unit of activity base, determined by dividing the activity cost pool by the activity base.

Activity ratios See Efficiency ratios.

Adjusted trial balance The trial balance which is prepared after all the adjusting entries have been posted. Used to verify the equality of the total debit balances and total credit balances before preparing the financial statements.

Adjusting entries Entries required at the end of an accounting period to bring the ledger up to date.

Adjusting process The process of updating the accounts at the end of a period.

Administrative expenses (general expenses) Expenses incurred in the administration or general operations of a business.

Advanced determination ruling (ADR) A transfer pricing guideline in the United States that allows a company to get approval for a parent-subsidiary specific product pricing.

Advance pricing agreement An agreement between a company and tax authorities that gives the company approval for using certain transfer pricing methods and the procedures for its application.

Aging the receivables The process of analyzing the accounts receivable and classifying them according to various age groupings, with the due date being the base point for determining age.

Allowance method A method of accounting for uncollectible receivables, whereby advance provision for the uncollectibles is made.

Allowances for deferred income tax assets A contra account to the deferred income tax assets account.

American Institute of Certified Public Accountants (AICPA) An organization that issues the generally accepted auditing standards in the form of Statements on Auditing Standards in the United States.

Amortization The periodic expense attributed to the decline in usefulness of an intangible asset.

Annuity A series of equal cash flows at fixed intervals.

Appraisal costs Costs to detect, measure, evaluate, and audit products and processes to ensure that they conform to customer requirements and performance standards.

Appropriation The amount of a corporation's retained earnings that has been restricted and therefore is not available for distribution to shareholders as dividends.

Arbitrage An activity done to take advantage of rate discrepancies by buying the currency in the low-cost markets and selling in the high-cost markets.

Asia-Pacific Economic Cooperation (APEC) An organization committed to the trade and investment concept of open regionalism. Its 20-member countries include Australia, Brunei, Canada, Chile, China (including Hong Kong), Indonesia, Japan, Korea, Malaysia, Mexico, New Zealand, Papua New Guinea, Peru, Philippines, Russia, Singapore, Chinese Taipei, Thailand, the United States, and Vietnam.

Asset-and-liability approach The recognition of deferred tax liabilities or deferred tax assets for the income tax that will be levied or recovered on temporary timing differences between the taxable income amount and the pretax financial income amount.

Assets Physical items (tangible) or rights (intangible) that have value and that are owned by the business entity.

Associated firms. See Representative firms.

Association of Southeast Asian Nations (ASEAN) The most important trading bloc in Southeast Asia. The member countries include Brunei, Cambodia, Indonesia, Laos, Malaysia, Myanmar, the Philippines, Singapore, Thailand, and Vietnam. The member countries plan to establish a free-trade area by 2003.

Auditor's report A report that communicates the results of the external audit, and the format of the report is necessarily mandated by the nature of the audit. Because there are no worldwide uniform accounting and auditing standards, there is no worldwide uniform format of an auditor's report.

Available-for-sale security A debt or equity security that is not classified as either a held-to-maturity or a trading security.

Average cost method The method of inventory costing that is based on the assumption that costs should be charged against revenue in accordance with the weighted average unit costs of the items sold.

Average rate of return A method of evaluating capital investment proposals that focuses on the expected profitability of the investment.

B

Balance of payments deficit When a country's cumulative imports exceed its cumulative exports.

Balance of payments surplus When a country's cumulative exports exceed its cumulative imports.

Balance of the account The amount of difference between the debits and the credits that have been entered into an account.

Balance sheet A financial statement listing the assets, liabilities, and owner's equity of a business entity as of a specific date.

Balance sheet recognition Information presented within the balance sheet.

Balanced scorecard A set of financial and nonfinancial measures that reflect multiple performance dimensions of a business.

Balassa-Samuelson Theory A theory that states inflation is difficult to get rid of in a fast-growing economy.

Bank reconciliation The analysis that details the items responsible for the difference between the cash balance reported in the bank statement and the balance of the cash account in the ledger.

Betterment An expenditure that increases operating efficiency or capacity for the remaining useful life of a plant asset.

Big Five Public accounting firms that have the capability to perform external audits in different parts of the world. The Big Five accounting firms include Andersen, KPMG Peat Marwick, Deloitte Touche Tohmatsu, Ernst & Young, and PricewaterhouseCoopers.

Bilan Social (social report) A required report in France. It contains mainly employee-related information covering topics such as pay structure, hiring policies, health and safety conditions, training, and industrial relations.

Bilateral advance pricing agreement When the multinational company receives the approval of proposed transfer pricing approaches from tax authorities of two countries.

Bond A form of interest-bearing note employed by corporations to borrow on a long-term basis.

Bond indenture The contract between a corporation issuing bonds and the bondholders.

Book value The amount at which an asset or liability is reported on the balance sheet. Also called *basis* or *carrying value*.

Book value of the asset The difference between the balance of a fixed asset account and its related accumulated depreciation account.

Boot The cash balance owed the seller when an old asset is traded for a new asset.

Break-even point The level of business operations at which revenues and expired costs are equal.

Budget An outline of a business's future plans, stated in financial terms. A budget is used to plan and control operational departments and divisions.

Budget performance report A report comparing actual results with budget figures.

Business An organization in which basic resources (inputs), such as materials and labor, are assembled and processed to provide goods or services (outputs) to customers.

Business entity concept The concept that accounting applies to individual economic units and that each unit is separate from the persons who supply its assets.

Business report A report that covers many of the matters typically found in the Management Discussion and Analysis part of companies' annual reports in North America.

Business stakeholder A person or entity that has an interest in the economic performance of the business.

Business transaction The occurrence of an economic event or a condition that must be recorded in the accounting records.

C

Capital budgeting The process of identifying, evaluating, and planning long-term investment decisions.

Capital expenditures Costs that add to the usefulness of assets for more than one accounting period.

Capital expenditures budget The budget summarizing future plans for acquiring fixed assets.

Capital investment analysis The process by which management plans, evaluates, and controls long-term capital investments involving property, plant, and equipment.

Capital lease A lease treated as a purchase of property by the lessee. Leases that treat the leased assets as purchased assets in the accounts.

Capital rationing The process by which management allocates available investment funds among competing capital investment proposals.

Capital stock The portion of a corporation's owner's equity contributed by investors (owners) in exchange for shares of stock.

Capital structure ratios *See* Coverage ratios.

Carrying amount The amount at which a long-term investment or a long-term liability is reported on the balance sheet.

Cash Coins, currency (paper money), checks, money orders, and money on deposit that is available for unrestricted withdrawal from banks or other financial institutions.

Cash basis A basis of accounting in which revenue is recognized in the period cash is received, and expenses are recognized in the period cash is paid.

Cash budget One of the most important elements of the budgeted balance sheet. It presents the expected receipts (inflows) and payments (outflows) of cash for a period of time.

Cash dividend A cash distribution of earnings by a corporation to its shareholders.

Cash equivalents Highly liquid investments that are usually reported on the balance sheet with cash.

Cash flows from financing activities The section of the statement of cash flows that reports cash flows from transactions affecting the equity and debt of the entity.

Cash flows from investing activities The section of the statement of cash flows that reports cash flows from transactions affecting investments in noncurrent assets.

Cash flows from operating activities The section of the statement of cash flows that reports the cash transactions affecting the determination of net income.

Cash payback period The expected period of time that will elapse between the date of a capital expenditure and the complete recovery in cash (or equivalent) of the amount invested.

Cash short and over account An account which has recorded errors in cash sales or errors in making change causing the amount of actual cash on hand to differ from the beginning amount of cash plus the cash sales for the day.

Centralized internal audit model In this type of organization, there is only one central internal audit organization that is located at the headquarters of the parent company. The internal auditors travel to various parts of the world where operations are located to perform internal audits, and to perform other functions such as quality control, audit research, liaison with external auditors, training, and technical support.

Centralized multinational organizations Organizations that retain to a great extent the authority to make decisions at parent company headquarters.

Certified internal auditor (CIA) A certification program sponsored by the Institute of Internal Auditors consisting of an examination and a mandatory two years of practical experience in internal auditing before certification.

Certified public accountant (CPA) The professional designation for public accountants and independent (external) auditors in the United States and some other countries.

Chart of accounts The system of accounts that make up the ledger for a business.

Classic system A national tax system that subjects income to taxes when income is received by the taxable entity.

Closing entries Entries necessary to eliminate the balances of temporary accounts in preparation for the following accounting period.

Collectivism The belief that interests of the organization should have top priority.

Comarketing agreement Two or more companies who share the risks and rewards of long-term marketing programs.

Common-size statement A financial statement in which all items are expressed only in relative terms.

Common stock The basic ownership class of corporate stock.

Comprehensive income All changes in stockholders' equity during a period, except those resulting from dividends and stockholders' investments.

Consistency principle A requirement that accounting methods be used consistently from one period to the next unless conditions have changed that make it appropriate to switch to another method to provide more useful information.

Consolidated financial statements Financial statements resulting from combining parent and subsidiary company statements. The statements prepared by the parent company that essentially portray the financial position and results of operations of the parent and its subsidiaries as though they were one economic unit.

Consolidation The creation of a new corporation by the transfer of assets and liabilities from two or more existing corporations.

Constant dollar accounting See Constant monetary unit restatement.

Constant monetary unit restatement A general term for restating historical cost basis financial statements for changes in general purchasing power of the monetary unit.

Continuous budgeting A method of budgeting that provides for maintaining a twelve-month projection into the future.

Contra accounts Accounts that are offset against other accounts.

Contra asset An account that affects an asset account, such as the allowance for uncollectible accounts receivable or accumulated depreciation.

Contract rate The interest rate specified on a bond; sometimes called the coupon rate of interest.

Contribution margin Sales less variable costs and variable selling and administrative expenses.

Contribution margin analysis The systematic examination of the differences between planned and actual contribution margins.

Contribution margin ratio The percentage of each sales dollar that is available to cover the fixed costs and provide an operating income.

Control system A system that compares the actual performance (results) with planned performance (goals) so that management may take appropriate action as necessary.

Controllable costs Cost that can be influenced (increased, decreased, or eliminated) by someone such as a manager or factory worker.

Controllable expenses Costs that can be influenced by the decisions of a manager.

Controllable variance The difference between the actual amount of variable factory overhead cost incurred and the amount of variable factory overhead budgeted for the standard product.

Controller The chief management accountant of a business.

Controlling account The account in the general ledger that summarizes the balances of the accounts in a subsidiary ledger.

Convenience translation Translation of currency using the year-end exchange rates.

Conversion costs The combination of direct labor and factory overhead costs.

Conversion value The equivalent amount of another currency at a given exchange rate.

Copromotion agreement A product that is promoted jointly by two companies under the same brand name and marketing plan. Generally the manufacturing company handles receivables, inventory, and so on and pays a commission to the copromotor. Compensation is almost always based on the product sales level.

Copyright The exclusive right to publish and sell a literary, artistic, or musical composition.

Corporation A separate legal entity that is organized in accordance with state or federal statutes and in which ownership is divided into shares of stock.

Correspondent firms See Representative firms.

Cost A disbursement of cash (or a commitment to pay cash in the future) for the purpose of generating revenues.

Cost accounting system A system used to accumulate manufacturing costs for financial reporting and decision-making purposes.

Cost allocation The process of assigning indirect cost to a cost object, such as a job.

Cost-based transfer pricing The price one segment of a company charges another segment of the same company for the transfer of a good or a service based on some type of cost. Examples include variable manufacturing costs, full manufacturing (absorption) costs, and full product costs.

Cost behavior The manner in which a cost changes in relation to its activity base (driver).

Cost center A responsibility center in which a manager is accountable for costs only. A decentralized unit in which the department or division manager has responsibility for the control of costs incurred and the authority to make decisions that affect these costs.

Cost concept The basis for entering the exchange price, or cost, into the accounting records.

Cost distortion Inaccurate product costs that are the result of applying a cost allocation method that is inappropriate for the situation.

Cost driver Any factor that causes a change in the cost of an activity.

Cost method A method of accounting for an investment in common stock, by which the investor recognizes as income its share of cash dividends of the investee.

Cost object Any customer, product, service, project, or other work unit for which a separate cost measurement is desired.

Cost of goods sold The cost of the manufactured product sold.

Cost of goods sold budget A budget in which the desired ending inventory and the estimated beginning inventory data are combined with data from direct materials budget, direct labor budget, and factory overhead cost budget.

Cost of merchandise sold The cost of merchandise purchased by a merchandise business and sold.

Cost of production report A report prepared periodically by a processing department, summarizing (1) the units for which the department is accountable and the disposition of those units and (2) the costs incurred by the department and the allocation of those costs between completed and incomplete production.

Cost of quality report A report summarizing the costs, percent of total, and percent of sales by appraisal, prevention, internal failure, and external failure cost of quality categories.

Cost per equivalent unit The rate used to allocate costs between completed and partially completed production in a process costing system.

Cost price approach An approach to transfer pricing that uses cost as the basis for setting the transfer price.

Costs of quality The cost associated with controlling quality (prevention and appraisal) and failing to control quality (internal and external failure).

Cost variance The difference between actual cost and the flexible budget at actual volumes.

Cost-volume-profit analysis The systematic examination of the relationships among selling prices, volume of sales and production, costs, expenses, and profits.

Cost-volume-profit chart A chart used to assist management in understanding the relationships among costs, expenses, sales, and operating profit or loss.

Coverage ratios Ratios that measure the degree of protection for long-term creditors and investors.

Credit The right side of an account; the amount entered on the right side of an account; to enter an amount on the right side of an account.

Credit memorandum The form issued by a seller to inform a buyer that a credit has been posted to the buyer's account receivable.

Cross-currency swap An agreement by two parties to exchange their liabilities or assets in different currencies.

Cumulative preferred stock Preferred stock that is entitled to current and past dividends before dividends may be paid on common stock.

Currency exchange rate The rates at which currency in another country can be exchanged for U.S. dollars.

Currency options contract A contract giving one of the parties the right to decide in the future whether an exchange will actually take place at a certain price.

Currency swap An agreement to exchange two different currencies at an agreed exchange rate.

Current assets Cash or other assets that are expected to be converted to cash or sold or used up, usually within a year or less, through the normal operations of a business.

Current cost accounting See Current value accounting.

Current exchange rate The exchange rate on the balance sheet date.

Current liabilities Liabilities that will be due within a short time (usually one year or less) and that are to be paid out of current assets.

Currently attainable standards Standards that represent levels of operation that can be attained with reasonable effort.

Current-noncurrent method A translation method in which balance sheet items classified as "current" are translated at the current exchange rate on the balance sheet date, and items classified as "noncurrent" are translated at appropriate historical rates.

Current purchasing power accounting See Constant monetary unit restatement.

Current rate method A translation method that translates all assets and all liabilities at the current exchange rate—the rate on the balance sheet date. Paid-in capital accounts are translated at the applicable historical rates, dividends at the exchange rate on the date of declaration and on the income statement, and all revenue and expense items at the weighted average exchange rate for the period.

Current ratio A financial ratio that is computed by dividing current assets by current liabilities.

Current value accounting Valuation systems designed to show the effects of changes in prices of individual items on financial statements.

Customer-centric companies Companies that set explicit targets for retaining customers and make extraordinary efforts to exceed their customer loyalty goals.

D

Debit (1) The left side of an account. (2) the amount entered on the left side of an account. (3) to enter an amount on the left side of an account.

Debit memorandum The form issued by a buyer to inform a seller that a debit has been posted to the seller's account payable.

Debt capital Capital that is financed by borrowing.

Decentralization The separation of a business into more manageable operating units.

Decentralized internal audit model In this type of organization, the internal auditors are on locations throughout the world, wherever international operations are located. Each international operation has its own internal audit organization.

Decentralized multinational organizations Organizations that give managements of the subsidiaries considerable independence of action.

Declining-balance depreciation method A method of depreciation that provides declining periodic depreciation expense over the estimated life of an asset.

Deferred expenses Items that are initially recorded as assets but are expected to become expenses over time or through the normal operations of the business. Sometimes called prepaid expenses.

Deferred income tax asset The future tax benefits from earnings that have already been taxed but have not been reported in the income statement yet.

Deferred income tax liability The future tax liability that results from current or past periods' earnings that have already been reported in the financial statements but have not been taxed yet.

Deferred revenues Items that are initially recorded as liabilities but are expected to become revenues over time or through the normal operations of the business. Sometimes called unearned revenues.

Defined benefit plan A pension plan that promises employees a fixed annual pension benefit at retirement, based on years of service and compensation levels.

Defined contribution plan A pension plan that requires a fixed amount of money to be invested for the employee's behalf during the employee's working years.

Depletion The cost of metal ores and other minerals removed from the earth.

Depreciation In a general sense, the decrease in usefulness of plant assets other than land. In accounting, refers to the systematic allocation of a fixed asset's cost to expense.

Depreciation expense The portion of the cost of a fixed asset that is recorded as an expense each year of its useful life.

Derivative A contract whose market value fluctuates in direct proportion to fluctuations in the market value of a commodity or a financial instrument or a foreign currency.

Differential analysis The area of accounting concerned with the effect of alternative courses of action on revenues and costs.

Differential cost The amount of increase or decrease in cost expected from a particular course of action as compared with an alternative.

Differential revenue The amount of increase or decrease in revenue expected from a particular course of action as compared with an alternative.

Direct-financing lease A lease where the lessor provides financing only, and assumes financial risks but does not assume inventory risk.

Direct investment Establishing operations in a country.

Direct labor cost Wages of factory workers who are directly involved in converting materials into a finished product.

Direct labor rate variance The cost associated with the difference between the standard rate and the actual rate paid for direct labor used in producing a commodity.

Direct labor time variance The cost associated with the difference between the standard hours and the actual hours of direct labor spent producing a commodity.

Direct materials cost The cost of materials that are an integral part of the finished product.

Direct materials price variance The cost associated with the difference between the standard price and the actual price of direct materials used in producing a commodity.

Direct materials quantity variance The cost associated with the difference between the standard quantity and the actual quantity of direct materials used in producing a commodity.

Direct method A method of reporting the cash flows from operating activities as the net income from operations adjusted for all deferrals of past cash receipts and payments and all accruals of expected future cash receipts and payments.

Direct write-off method A method of accounting for uncollectible receivables, whereby an expense is recognized only when specific accounts are judged to be uncollectible.

Disclosure Financial statements.

Discontinued operations The operations of a business segment that has been disposed of.

Discount The interest deducted from the maturity value of a note. The excess of the face amount of bonds over their issue price. The excess of par value of stock over its sales price.

Discount rate The rate used in computing the interest to be deducted from the maturity value of a note.

Dishonored note receivable A note that the maker fails to pay on its due date.

Dividends Distributions to the owners (stockholders) of a corporation.

Dividends per share The cash dividends per common shares commonly used by investors in assessing alternative stock investments, computed by dividing dividends by the number of shares of stock outstanding.

Dividend yield The rate of return to stockholders in terms of cash dividend distributions.

Division A decentralized organizational unit that is structured around a common function, product, customer, or geographical territory. Divisions can be cost, profit, or investment centers.

Doomsday ratio The ratio of cash and cash equivalents to current liabilities.

Double-entry accounting A system for recording transactions, based on recording increases and decreases in accounts so that debits always equal credits.

Downsizing The elimination of jobs due to reengineering.

E

Earnings flexibility *See* Income smoothing.

Earnings per share (EPS) on common stock The profitability ratio of net income available to common shareholders to the number of common shares outstanding.

Economic exposure A condition that results from the impact of changes in exchange rates on future cash flows.

Economic risk The uncertainty surrounding key elements of the investment process.

Effective interest rate method One method of amortizing a bond discount. Also known as the interest method.

Effective rate of interest The market rate of interest when bonds are issued.

Efficiency ratios Ratios that measure how effectively the enterprise is using the assets employed.

Electronic data interchange (EDI) An information technology that allows different business organizations to use computers to communicate orders, relay information, and make or receive payments.

Electronic funds transfer (EFT) A payment system that uses computerized information rather than paper (money, checks, etc.) to effect a cash transaction.

Elements of internal control The control environment, risk assessment, control activities, information and communication, and monitoring.

Employee fraud The intentional act of deceiving an employer for personal gain.

Employee involvement A philosophy that grants employees the responsibility and authority to make their own decisions about their operations.

Employee's earnings record A detailed record of each employee's earnings.

Engineering change order A document that initiates a change in the specification of a product or process.

Environment-specific An accounting system designed to provide information for making decisions in a given environment. Five major environmental influences on accounting consist of the economic system, political system, legal system, educational system, and religion.

Equity capital Capital that is financed by shares (stocks).

Equity method A method of accounting for investments in common stock, by which the investment account is adjusted for the investor's share of periodic net income and dividends of the investee. A method in which income of a subsidiary is recognized by the parent company according to ownership percentage. The investment in the subsidiary account balance is adjusted accordingly.

Equity reserves A general term to describe many different types of reserves that serve different purposes.

Equity security A security that represents ownership in a business, such as stock in a corporation.

Equivalent units of production The number of units that could have been completed within a given accounting period with respect to direct materials and conversion costs. Equivalent units are used to allocate departmental costs incurred during the period between completed units and in-process units at the end of the period.

Ethics The moral principles that guide the conduct of individuals.

European Confederation of Institutes of Internal Auditing This organization, comprised of 17 internal audit organizations representing 18 European nations plus Israel, helps in the development of internal auditing standards.

European Union (EU) A single trading block currently linking 15 European nations into a single market in order to eliminate tariff and custom restrictions. The 15 nations include Austria, Belgium, Denmark, Finland, France, Germany, Great Britain, Greece, Ireland, Italy, Luxembourg, Netherlands, Portugal, Spain, and Sweden.

European Union directives Rules issued by the European Union. These are binding on member countries.

Exchange rate The amount of one currency needed to obtain one unit of another currency.

Exit measurement *See* Output price measurement.

Expense liability reserves An equity reserve used to achieve income smoothing or to show a steady growth in income from year to year.

Expenses Assets used up or services consumed in the process of generating revenues.

External failure costs The costs incurred after defective units or services have been delivered to consumers.

Extraordinary items Events or transactions that are unusual and infrequent.

Extraordinary repair An expenditure that increases the useful life of an asset beyond the original estimate.

F

Facilitating payments Payments made to influence an official to take an action that the official must take anyway.

Factors of production A firm's inputs, such as costs for labor, materials, machines, and buildings that are necessary for bringing the good to the market.

Factory overhead cost All of the costs of operating the factory except for direct materials and direct labor.

Femininity The quality of life, nurturing, and relationships.

FICA tax Federal Insurance Contributions Act tax used to finance federal programs for old-age and disability benefits (social security) and health insurance for the aged (Medicare).

Finance lease *See* Capital lease.

Financial accounting A component of an organization's internal accounting system that provides information primarily for users outside the organization. The branch of accounting that is concerned with the recording of transactions using generally accepted accounting principles (GAAP) for a business or other economic unit and with a periodic preparation of various statements from such records.

Financial Accounting Standards Board (FASB) The main body responsible for promulgating accounting standards in the United States.

Financial ratio analysis An evaluation of financial performance and financial position between two or more firms.

Financial reporting disclosures The information presented in financial statements. Such disclosures may be either within the statements or in the accompanying notes.

Financial statement analysis The conversion of the data in financial statements into useful information.

Finished goods inventory The cost of finished products on hand that have not been sold.

Finished goods ledger The subsidiary ledger that contains the individual accounts for each kind of commodity or product produced.

First-in, first-out (FIFO) method A method of inventory costing based on the assumption that the costs of merchandise sold should be charged against revenue in the order in which the costs were incurred.

Fiscal year The annual accounting period adopted by a business.

Fixed assets Physical resources that are owned and used by a business and are permanent or have a long life.

Fixed costs Costs that tend to remain the same in amount, regardless of variations in the level of activity.

Fixed rate currency Currency with a fixed rate of exchange within narrow limits against a major currency, such as the U.S. dollar or the British pound.

Flexible budget A budget that adjusts for varying rates of activity.

Floating rate currency Currency whose exchange rate is determined by market forces.

FOB (free on board) destination Terms of agreement between buyer and seller whereby ownership passes when merchandise is received by the buyer and the seller pays the transportation costs.

FOB (free on board) shipping point Terms of agreement between buyer and seller whereby ownership passes when merchandise is delivered to the freight carrier and the buyer pays the transportation costs.

Footnote disclosure Information contained in a note accompanying the financial statements.

Foreign Corrupt Practices Act (FCPA) An act passed by the U.S. Congress in 1977 and revised in 1988 intended to curb influence peddling.

Foreign currency forward contract An agreement with a currency trader, for example, a bank, to deliver in the future one currency for another at an agreed-upon "forward" exchange rate.

Foreign currency transactions Transactions denominated in a currency other than the reporting currency of the entity.

Foreign currency translation A conversion of amounts in accounts of international subsidiaries (recorded in a foreign currency) to the currency used for consolidated financial statements.

Foreign exchange risk management The management of the risk of loss from currency exchange rate movements on transactions, translation, or remeasurement involving foreign currency.

Forward exchange contract An agreement to buy (or sell) a foreign currency in the future at a fixed rate called a forward rate.

Forward rate The fixed future rate used in a forward exchange contract.

Free cash flow The amount of operating cash flow remaining after replacing current productive capacity and maintaining current dividends.

Free market economic system An economic concept used to denote the economic system of a country unimpeded by government restrictions, and ideally subject to the laws of supply and demand of the market.

Fringe benefits A variety of employee benefits that may take many forms, including vacations, pension plans, and health, life, and disability insurance.

Functional currency The currency of the primary environment in which the international subsidiary operates.

Future value The estimated worth in the future of an amount of cash on hand today invested at a fixed rate of interest.

G

Gearing adjustment A gearing adjustment equals the average borrowing divided by average operating assets multiplied by total current value adjustments for cost of goods sold, depreciation, and so on. It shows the benefit (or disadvantage) to shareholders from debt financing during a period of changing prices. The amount of gearing adjustment is added (deducted) to current cost income.

General ledger The primary ledger, when used in conjunction with subsidiary ledgers, that contains all of the balance sheet and income statement accounts.

Generally accepted accounting principles (GAAP) Accounting principles in the United States that are recognized by a standard-setting body or by authoritative support for the preparation of financial statements.

General price index An index used to estimate the amount of inflation or deflation in an economy.

General price-level accounting *See* Constant monetary unit restatement.

General reserve An equity reserve that normally serves the same purpose as an appropriation of retained earnings, that is, it temporarily restricts the maximum amount that can be declared for dividends.

Global International or worldwide.

Global capital markets Capital markets in a global economy that attract investors and investees from throughout the world.

Goal conflict Occurs when an employee's self-interest differs from business objectives.

Going concern concept The accounting concept that an economic entity will continue in operation for the foreseeable future.

Goodwill The amount paid by the buyer of a business for above-normal profits. An intangible asset of a business due to such favorable factors as location, product superiority, reputation, and managerial skill.

Gross pay The total earnings of an employee for a payroll period.

Gross profit The excess of net sales over the cost of merchandise sold.

Gross profit method A means of estimating inventory based on the relationship of gross profit to sales.

H

Harmonization Keeping the differences among national accounting standards to a minimum. Alternative accounting rules or practices may exist in different countries as long as they are "in harmony" with one another and can be reconciled.

Hedging Measures taken to protect against risks associated with foreign exchange fluctuations.

Held-to-maturity securities Investments in bonds or other debt securities that management intends to hold to their maturity.

High-low method A technique that uses the highest and lowest total costs as a basis for estimating the variable cost per unit and the fixed cost component of a mixed cost.

High power distance culture A state in which a person at a higher position in the organizational hierarchy makes the decision and the employees at the lower levels simply follow the instructions.

Historical cost convention A method of accounting using data in terms of the units of currency in which a transaction originally took place.

Horizontal analysis Financial analysis that compares an item in a current statement with the same item in prior statements.

I

Idle capacity The unused capacity of a selling segment that is not needed for producing products or services to meet demand from the external market.

Imperfect market A market where factors of production are somewhat immobile.

Imperfect market theory A firm engages in international trade to gain access to factors of production.

Income from operations (operating income) The excess of gross profit over total operating expenses.

Income leveling *See* Income smoothing.

Income smoothing Use of reserves to transfer income between periods.

Income statement A summary of the revenues and expenses of a business entity for a specific period of time.

Income summary The account used in the closing process for transferring the revenue and expense account balances to the retained earnings account at the end of the period.

Indirect investment Buying equity or debt securities originating from a country as investments.

Indirect method A method of reporting the cash flows from operating activities as the net income from operations adjusted for all deferrals of past cash receipts and payments and all accruals of expected future cash receipts and payments.

Individualism The trait in which the employee attaches higher importance to personal and family interests than to the organization.

Inflation A period when prices in general are rising and the purchasing power of money is declining.

Inflation accounting Accounting to cope with changing price levels.

Influence peddling Providing monetary or nonmonetary benefits to a person in a position of authority in exchange for an action by that person that benefits the company—normally an action that would not have been taken without the monetary or nonmonetary benefit.

Input price measurement A current value is assigned to an item on the basis of its replacement cost.

Institute of Internal Auditors (IIA) The most influential international organization in the development of internal auditing standards. It was established in 1941.

Intangible assets Long-lived assets that are useful in the operations of a business, are not held for sale, and are without physical qualities.

Integrated international operation A foreign operation whose economic activities have a direct impact on the reporting (parent) entity.

Integrated system A national tax system that attempts to eliminate double taxation by taxing corporate income differently depending on whether it is distributed to shareholders.

Internal auditing An objective evaluation of operations and control systems of an organization to determine whether its policies and procedures are being followed, and also whether its resources are safeguarded and used efficiently to achieve organizational objectives.

Internal controls The detailed policies and procedures used to direct operations, ensure accurate reports, and ensure compliance with laws and regulations.

Internal failure costs The costs associated with defects that are discovered by the organization before the product or service is delivered to the consumer.

Internal rate of return method A method of analysis of proposed capital investments that focuses on using present value concepts to compute the rate of return from the net cash flows expected from the investment.

International See Global.

International accounting Accounting for international transactions, comparisons of accounting principles in different countries, harmonization of diverse accounting standards worldwide, and accounting information for the management and control of global operations.

International Accounting Standard (IAS) An accounted rule developed by the International Accounting Standards Committee in order to harmonize accounting standards worldwide.

International corporation A company that exports its products overseas.

International Federation of Accountants (IFAC) An organization engaged in efforts to harmonize auditing standards worldwide.

International Organization of Securities Commission (IOSCO) A private organization of securities market regulators that promotes the integration of securities markets worldwide.

International Standards on Auditing (ISA) A comprehensive set of auditing standards issued by the International Federation of Accountants. Audits conducted in accordance with these standards can be relied on by securities regulatory authorities for multinational reporting purposes.

Intervention An action taken by the central bank of a country to influence the exchange rate of its currency in the market.

Inventory shrinkage Loss of inventory due to shoplifting, employee theft, or errors in recording or counting inventory.

Inventory turnover A ratio that measures the relationship between the volume of goods (merchandise) sold and the amount of inventory carried during the period.

Investment center A responsibility center where the manager is responsible for costs, revenues, profits, and investment in assets. A decentralized unit in which the manager has the responsibility and authority to make decisions that affect not only costs and revenues but also the plant assets available to the center.

Investments The balance sheet caption used to report long-term investments in stocks or bonds not intended as a source of cash in the normal operations of the business.

Investment turnover A component of the rate of return on investment, computed as the ratio of sales to invested assets.

Invoice The bill provided by the seller (who refers to it as a sales invoice) to a buyer (who refers to it as a purchase invoice) for items purchased.

J

Job cost sheet An account in the work in process subsidiary ledger in which the costs charged to a particular job order are recorded.

Job order cost system A type of cost accounting system that provides for a separate record of the cost of each particular quantity of product that passes through the factory.

Journal The initial record in which the effects of a transaction on accounts are recorded.

Journal entry The form of recording a transaction in a journal.

Journalizing The process of recording a transaction in a journal.

Just-in-time (JIT) manufacturing A business philosophy that focuses on eliminating time, cost, and poor quality within manufacturing processes.

Just-in-time processing A processing approach that focuses on eliminating time, cost, and poor quality within manufacturing and nonmanufacturing processes.

L

Labor productivity A measure of the relationship between workers' hours and the actual output produced.

Large power distance culture The culture where a person at a higher position in the organizational hierarchy makes the decisions, and the employees at the lower levels simply follow the instructions.

Last-in, first-out (LIFO) method A method of inventory costing based on the assumption that the most recent merchandise costs incurred should be charged against revenue.

Lead time The elapsed time between starting a unit of product into the beginning of a process and its completion.

Lease A contract between a lessor and a lessee that gives the lessee the right to use specific property owned by the lessor, for a given time period, in exchange for cash or other consideration—typically a commitment to make future cash payments.

Ledger The group of accounts used by a business.

Leverage The tendency of the rate earned on stockholders' equity to vary from the rate earned on total assets because the amount earned on assets acquired through the use of funds provided by creditors varies from the interest paid to these creditors.

Leverage ratios See Coverage ratios.

Liabilities Debts owed to outsiders (creditors).

Licensing program Proprietary information, such as patent rights or expertise, that is licensed by the owner (licenser) to another party (licensee). Compensation paid to the licenser usually includes license issuance fees, milestone payments, and/or royalties.

Liquidity ratios Ratios that measure the enterprise's short-run ability to pay its maturing obligations.

Long-term liabilities Liabilities that are not due for a long time (usually more than one year).

Long-term orientation The adaptation of traditions to meet current needs.

Loss from operations The excess of operating expenses over gross profit.

Lower-of-cost-or-market (LCM) method A method of valuing inventory that reports the inventory at the lower of its cost or current market value (replacement cost).

Low power distance culture A state in which employees perceive few power differences and follow a superior's instructions only when either they agree or feel threatened.

M

Managed earnings *See* Income smoothing.

Management Discussion and Analysis (MDA) A required disclosure in the annual report filed with the Securities and Exchange Commission; it provides critical information in interpreting financial statements.

Managerial accounting The branch of accounting that uses both historical and estimated data in providing information that management uses in conducting daily operations, in planning future operations, and in developing overall business strategies.

Managerial accounting (or management accounting) A component of an organization's internal accounting system that provides financial and nonfinancial information used by managers and others within the organization for use in planning, controlling, and decision making.

Managers Individuals who the owners have authorized to operate the business.

Manufacturing businesses A type of business that changes basic inputs into products that are sold to individual customers.

Manufacturing cells A grouping of production processes where employees are cross-trained to perform more than one function.

Manufacturing margin The variable cost of goods sold deducted from sales.

Margin of safety The difference between current sales revenue and the sales at the break-even point.

Market-based transfer pricing The price one segment of a company charges another segment of the same company for the transfer of a good or a service based on its current market price.

Market price approach An approach to transfer pricing that uses the price at which the product or service transferred could be sold to outside buyers as the transfer price.

Market segment A portion of business that can be assigned to a manager for profit responsibility.

Markup An amount that is added to a "cost" amount to determine product price.

Masculinity The relative importance of the qualities associated with men, such as assertiveness and materialism.

Master budget The comprehensive budget plan encompassing all the individual budgets related to sales, cost of goods sold, operating expenses, capital expenditures, and cash.

Master operating budget A plan for achieving the corporate goals for a period of time (normally one year).

Matching concept The concept that expenses incurred in generating revenue should be matched against the revenue in determining the net income or net loss for the period.

Materiality concept A concept of accounting that accounts for items that are deemed significant for a given size of operations. This concept, requiring use of professional judgment, describes information that must be included or disclosed to prevent financial statements from misleading their users.

Materials inventory The cost of materials that have not yet entered into the manufacturing process.

Materials ledger The subsidiary ledger that contains the individual accounts for each type of material.

Materials requisitions The form or electronic transmission used by a manufacturing department to authorize materials issuances from the storeroom.

Maturity value The amount due (face value plus interest) at the maturity or due date of a note.

Measurement Recording economic transactions in the accounting system.

Merchandise inventory Merchandise on hand and available for sale to customers.

Merchandising businesses A type of business that purchases products from other businesses and sells them to customers.

Merger The combining of two corporations by the acquisition of the properties of one corporation by another, with the dissolution of one of the corporations.

Minority interest The portion of a subsidiary corporation's stock that is not owned by the parent corporation.

Mixed cost A cost with both variable and fixed characteristics, sometimes called a semivariable or semifixed cost.

Monetary items All assets and liabilities expressed in fixed amounts of currency.

Monetary-nonmonetary method A translation method that restates monetary items on the balance sheet at the current exchange rate on the balance sheet date and nonmonetary items at their historical exchange rates.

Multinational corporation (MNC) A company that considers the globe as a single marketplace.

Multinational enterprise (MNE) *See* Multinational corporation.

Multiple production department factory overhead rate method A method that allocates factory overhead to products by using factory overhead rates for each production department.

Multiple-step income statement An income statement with several sections, subsections, and subtotals.

N

Natural business year A year that ends when a business's activities have reached the lowest point in its annual operating cycle.

Negative exposure A condition that exists when a foreign subsidiary has more current liabilities than current assets.

Negotiated price approach An approach to transfer pricing that allows managers of decentralized units to agree (negotiate) among themselves as to the transfer price.

Negotiated transfer pricing A system that requires managers of selling and buying divisions to negotiate a mutually acceptable transfer price.

Nepotism Relatives of those in power tend to easily obtain business licenses, lucrative government contracts, real estate deals, and so on.

Net income The amount by which revenues exceed expenses.

Net loss The amount by which expenses exceed revenues.

Net pay Gross pay less payroll deductions; the amount the employer is obligated to pay the employee.

Net present value (NPV) The difference between the initial investment and the net present value of expected future net cash inflows.

Net present value method A method of analysis of proposed capital investments that focuses on the present value of the cash flows expected from the investments.

Net realizable value The valuation of an asset at an amount equal to the estimated selling price less any direct cost of disposal.

New economy High productivity and low inflation.

Noncontrollable costs Costs that cannot be influenced (increased, decreased, or eliminated) by someone such as a manager or factory worker.

Nonfinancial measure A performance measure that has not been stated in dollar terms.

Nonmonetary item An item that does not represent a claim to, or for, a specified number of monetary units.

Nonparticipating preferred stock Preferred stock with a limited dividend preference.

Nonroutine reports Reports prepared for the purpose of providing information to managers to assist them in formulating policies, preparing strategic plans, and preparing tactical (operational) plans.

Nonvalue-added activities The cost of activities that are perceived as unnecessary from the customer's perspective and are thus candidates for elimination.

Nonvalue-added lead time The time that units wait in inventories, move unnecessarily, and wait during machine breakdowns.

North American Free Trade Agreement (NAFTA) A trade agreement among Canada, Mexico, and the United States with the objective of creating a single market with no trade barriers.

Notes receivable A written promise to pay by the maker, representing an amount to be received by the payee.

Number of days' sales in inventory A measure of the length of time it takes to acquire, sell, and replace the inventory.

Number of days' sales in receivables An estimate of the length of time the accounts receivable have been outstanding.

Number of times the interest charges are earned A ratio that measures the risk that interest payments to debtholders will continue to be made if earnings decrease.

O

Objectivity concept Requires that the accounting records and reports be based upon objective evidence.

One-transaction approach An approach used to translate foreign currency where the transaction is not considered to be completed until the final settlement. Any transaction gain or loss will be reflected on the settlement date in an adjustment to the value of the resource acquired.

Open regionalism The use of declarations instead of treaties to combine an informal regional trading strategy with a commitment to global openness.

Operating leases A lease where the lessor retains most of the risks and rewards of ownership; commonly referred to as rentals. Leases that do not meet the criteria for capital leases and thus are accounted for as operating expenses.

Operating leverage A measure of the relative mix of a business's variable costs and fixed costs, computed as contribution margin divided by operating income.

Operational plans Nonroutine plans that are designed to implement strategic plans.

Opportunity cost The amount of income forgone from an alternative use of cash or its equivalent.

Opportunity costs per unit The contribution margin per unit sacrificed by the selling segment due to the internal transfer of one unit of the good or service, rather than selling it in the external market.

Organization for Economic Cooperation and Development (OECD) An organization that promotes worldwide economic development in general, and economic growth and stability of its member countries in particular. Its work focuses primarily on providing financial accounting and reporting guidelines to multinational corporations for disclosures to host countries.

Other expense An expense that cannot be traced directly to operations.

Other income Revenue from sources other than the primary operating activity of a business.

Output price measurement The current value of an item equals its net realizable value.

Outstanding stock The stock that is in the hands of stockholders.

Overapplied factory overhead The amount of factory overhead applied in excess of the actual factory overhead costs incurred for production during a period.

Owner's equity The owner's right to the assets of the business after the total liabilities are deducted.

P

Par The monetary amount printed on a stock certificate.

Parent The company acquiring the stock of a subsidiary.

Parent company The company owning a majority of the voting stock of another corporation.

Parent/subsidiary relationship A combination of companies where control of other companies, known as subsidiaries, is achieved by a company, known as the parent, through acquisition of voting stock.

Pareto chart A bar chart that shows the totals of a particular attribute for a number of categories, ranked left to right from the largest to smallest totals.

Participatory design approach The design of the information system where all users must be actively involved.

Partnership An unincorporated business owned by two or more individuals.

Patents Exclusive rights to produce and sell goods with one or more unique features.

Payback period (PBP) method A capital budgeting method that measures the time it will take to recoup, in the form of net cash inflows, the net dollars invested in a project.

Payroll The total amount paid to employees for a certain period.

Payroll register A multicolumn form used to assemble and summarize payroll data at the end of each payroll period.

Performance report A routine report that compares actual performance against budgetary goals.

Period costs Those costs that are used up in generating revenue during the current period and that are not involved in the manufacturing process These costs are recognized as expenses on the current period's income statement.

Periodic inventory system A system of inventory accounting in which only the revenue from sales is recorded each time a sale is made. The cost of merchandise on hand at the end of a period is determined by a detailed listing (physical inventory) of the merchandise on hand.

Permanent differences Differences that are caused by certain types of revenues that are exempted from taxation and certain types of expenses that are not deductible for tax purposes.

Perpetual inventory system A system of inventory accounting in which both the revenue from sales and the cost of merchandise sold are recorded each time a sale is made, so that the records continually disclose the amount of the inventory on hand.

Petty cash fund A special cash fund used to pay relatively small amounts.

Physical inventory The detailed listing of merchandise on hand.

Political risk The actions and activities of foreign (host) governments directed at multinational corporations.

Pooling-of-interests method An accounting method used for a business combination where the acquired entity's assets and equities are combined at book value. No goodwill is created in a pooling of interests. A method of accounting for an affiliation of two corporations resulting from an exchange of voting stock of one corporation for substantially all the voting stock of the other corporation.

Portfolio approach A method used to manage economic exposure of a company by offsetting negative exposure in one country with positive exposure in another.

Positive exposure A condition that exists when a foreign subsidiary has more current assets than current liabilities.

Post-closing trial balance A trial balance prepared after all of the temporary accounts have been closed.

Posting The process of transferring debits and credits from a journal to the accounts.

Post-retirement benefits Rights to benefits that employees earn during their term of employment for themselves and their dependents after they retire.

Power distance The extent of inequality between superiors and subordinates.

Predetermined factory overhead rate The rate used to apply factory overhead costs to the goods manufactured. It is determined by dividing the budgeted overhead cost by the estimated activity usage at the beginning of the fiscal period.

Preferred stock A class of stock with preferential rights over common stock.

Premium The excess of the issue price of bonds over the face amount. The excess of the sales price of stock over its par amount.

Prepaid expenses Purchased commodities or services that have not been used up at the end of an accounting period.

Present value The estimated worth today of an amount of cash to be received (or paid) in the future.

Present value concept A concept in which cash to be received (or paid) in the future is worth less than the same amount of money held today.

Present value index An index computed by dividing the total present value of the net cash flow to be received from a proposed capital investment by the amount to be invested.

Present value of an annuity The sum of the present values of a series of equal cash flows to be received at fixed intervals.

Prevention costs Costs incurred to prevent defects from occurring during the design and delivery of products or services.

Price-earnings ratio The ratio, often called the P/E ratio, computed by dividing the market price per share of common stock at a specific date by the company's earnings per share on common stock.

Price factor The effect of a difference in unit sales price or unit cost on the number of units sold.

Prior-period adjustments Corrections of material errors related to a prior period or periods, excluded from the determination of net income.

Privatization The transfer of property from the state to individuals and private enterprises.

Proceeds The net amount available from discounting a note.

Process cost system A type of cost accounting system that accumulates costs for each of the various departments or processes within a manufacturing facility.

Process manufacturers Manufacturers that use machines to process a continuous flow of raw materials through various stages of completion into a finished state.

Process-oriented layout Organizing work in a plant or administrative function around processes (tasks).

Product cost concept A concept used in applying the cost-plus approach to product pricing in which only the costs of manufacturing the product, termed the product cost, are included in the cost amount to which the markup is added.

Product costing Determining the cost of a product.

Product costs The three components of manufacturing cost: direct materials, direct labor, and factory overhead costs.

Product cycle theory A firm's progression from its domestic markets to international markets with exports being the entry point in international trade.

Production bottleneck A condition that occurs when product demand exceeds production capacity The bottleneck resource is a portion of the production process that is operating at 100% of capacity and is unable to meet product demand.

Production budget A budget of estimated production.

Productivity The output per hour of workers' time.

Product-oriented layout Organizing work in a plant or administrative function around products; sometimes referred to as product cells.

Profitability The ability of a firm to earn income.

Profitability ratios Ratios that measure the degree of success or failure of an enterprise or division for a given period of time.

Profit center A responsibility center where the manager is responsible for both revenues and costs. A decentralized unit in which the manager has the responsibility and the authority to make decisions that affect both costs and revenues (and thus profits).

Profit margin A component of the rate of return on investment, computed as the ratio of income from operations to sales.

Profit-volume chart A chart used to assist management in understanding the relationship between profit and volume.

Promissory note A written promise to pay a sum in money on demand or at a definite time.

Proposal for appropriation of retained earnings A report prepared for approval at the stockholders' meeting for dividend payments and bonus payments to members of the board of directors and statutory auditors.

Proprietorship A business owned by one individual.

Prudence concept The concept that provision be made for all known liabilities and losses whether the amount is known with certainty or not.

Pull manufacturing A just-in-time method wherein customer orders trigger the release of finished goods, which trigger production, which trigger release of materials from suppliers.

Purchase method An accounting method used for a business combination where the acquired entity's assets and equities are combined at fair market value. Goodwill is created to the extent that cost exceeds the fair market value of the identifiable assets of the unit acquired. The accounting method employed when a parent company acquires a controlling share of the voting stock of a subsidiary other than by the exchange of voting common stock.

Purchases discounts An available discount taken by a buyer for early payment of an invoice.

Purchases returns and allowances Reductions in purchases resulting from merchandise being returned to the seller or from the seller's reduction in the original purchase price.

Purchasing power gain A gain that arises from holding monetary items during times when the general purchasing power of the monetary unit changes.

Purchasing power loss A loss that arises from holding monetary items during times when the general purchasing power of the monetary unit changes.

Push manufacturing Materials are released into production and work in process is released into finished goods in anticipation of future sales.

Q

Quantity factor The effect of a difference in the number of units sold, assuming no change in unit sales price or unit cost.

Quick assets The sum of cash, receivables, and marketable securities.

Quick ratio A financial ratio that measures the ability to pay current liabilities within a short period of time.

R

Rate earned on common stockholders' equity A measure of profitability computed by dividing net income, reduced by preferred dividend requirements, by common stockholders' equity.

Rate earned on stockholders' equity A measure of profitability computed by dividing net income by total stockholders' equity.

Rate earned on total assets A measure of the profitability of assets, computed as net income plus interest expense divided by total average assets.

Rate of return on investment (ROI) A measure of managerial efficiency in the use of investments in assets, computed as income from operations divided by invested assets.

Ratio of fixed assets to long-term liabilities A financial ratio that provides a measure indicating the margin of safety to creditors.

Ratio of liabilities to stockholders' equity The relationship between the total claims of the creditors and owners.

Ratio of net sales to assets A profitability measure that shows how effectively a firm utilizes its assets.

Raw and in process inventory The capitalized cost of direct materials purchases, labor, and overhead charged to the production cell.

Real accounts Balance sheet accounts.

Realized gains Gains that are actually incurred.

Realized losses Losses that are actually incurred.

Receivables All money claims against other entities, including people, business firms, and other organizations.

Receiving report The form or electronic transmission used by the receiving personnel to indicate that materials have been received and inspected.

Reengineering The configuration of the internal processes, products, and employees so that essential operating activities are performed effectively and efficiently. All nonessential activities and tasks are eliminated, thereby reducing costs.

Regional audit staff internal audit model In this type of organization, the regional staff is responsible for performing audits in all of the operations in the region. This model has recently been gaining popularity among many multinationals.

Regular reports Reports that assist managers in planning activities and controlling operations.

Relevant range The range of activity over which changes in cost are of interest to management.

Rental A type of lease in which the lessor retains not only legal title, but most of the risks and rewards of ownership.

Replacement cost The total cost to acquire another item that would perform the functions identical to those performed by an existing item.

Report form The form of balance sheet with the liabilities and owner's equity sections presented below the assets section.

Representative firms Locally owned accounting firms that have agreements with a Big Five or some other accounting firm. The agreement covers areas such as standards of performance and standards of conduct.

Research and development costs The direct and indirect outlays for exploring potential new products and developing new products.

Research collaboration Two or more companies that participate in a defined research program and benefit from the results. Research costs can be funded entirely by one of the parties, shared equally by the parties, or shared according to some other agreed-upon proportion.

Resident staff and central reviewers internal audit model In this type of organization, the resident internal auditors located on site perform the audit work. Their work is periodically reviewed by the traveling members of the parent company's central internal audit staff.

Resident staff and regional and central reviewers internal auditing model In this type of organization, the resident staff conducts the internal audits. Regional reviewers, responsible for certain geographical areas, oversee their work to ensure compliance with the parent company policies. The central staff from headquarters makes periodic reviews to ensure reporting uniformity throughout all the regions.

Resident staff and regional reviewers internal audit model In this type of organization, the work of the resident internal auditors is reviewed by the regional reviewers to ensure uniformity. Independent review from regional staff also enhances the degree of reliability of the reports.

Residual income (RI) RI expresses performance in the form of a profit amount that is left after the cost of invested capital has been subtracted. The excess of income from operations over a "minimum" amount of desired income from operations.

Residual value The estimated recoverable cost of a depreciable asset as of the time of its removal from service.

Responsibility accounting The process of measuring and reporting operating data by areas of responsibility.

Responsibility center An organizational unit for which a manager is assigned responsibility for the unit's performance.

Retail inventory method A means of estimating inventory based on the relationship of the cost and the retail price of merchandise.

Retained earnings Net income retained in a corporation.

Retained earnings statement A summary of the changes in the earnings retained in the corporation for a specific period of time.

Return on assets (ROA) ROA equals net income divided by total assets.

Return on investment (ROI) ROI incorporates the investment base and profits to assess performance.

Revaluation reserve An equity reserve used to value fixed assets at an appraised value or a replacement value. This is done by upward adjustment of the asset and correspondingly recording an equal amount in a revaluation reserve.

Revenue The gross increase in owner's equity as a result of business and professional activities that earn income.

Revenue center A responsibility center in which a manager is accountable for revenues only.

Revenue expenditures Expenditures that benefit only the current period.

Revenue recognition concept The principle by which revenues are recognized in the period in which they are earned.

Rightsizing See Downsizing.

Risk management The identification of threats and the design of an approach to their containment.

Routine reporting Reports that enable managers to plan activities and control operations.

Rules of Professional Conduct A section in the American Institute of Certified Public Accountants' Code of Professional Conduct that contains rules that govern the performance of professional services and identify both acceptable and unacceptable behavior.

S

Sales budget One of the major elements of the income statement budget that indicates the quantity of estimated sales and the expected unit selling price.

Sales discounts An available discount granted by a seller for early payment of an invoice; a contra account to Sales.

Sales mix The relative distribution of sales among the various products available for sale.

Sales returns and allowances Reductions in sales resulting from merchandise being returned by customers or from the seller's reduction in the original sales price; a contra account to Sales.

Sales-type lease In the United States, a type of capital lease where a dealer's or manufacturer's profit or loss is a basic part of the transaction for the lessor.

Secondary statement approach A complete set of financial statements including accompanying notes prepared according to the accounting standards of another country. Independent auditors express an opinion on secondary statements using the auditing standards of that country.

Selective restatements Partial restatements of companies' reports used to help resolve the problems created by diversity in accounting standards throughout the world.

Self-sustaining international operation A foreign operation whose activities generally have no direct impact on the reporting entity's operations.

Selling expenses Expenses incurred directly in the sale of merchandise.

Service department charges The costs of services provided by an internal service department and transferred to a responsibility center.

Services businesses A business providing services rather than products to customers.

Settlement date The date when payment of funds is made on the maturity of a foreign exchange contract.

Setup Changing the characteristics of a machine to produce a different product.

Short-term orientation Values that respect tradition, personal stability, quick results from the efforts made, and concern with appearances.

Single plantwide factory overhead rate method A method that allocates all factory overhead to products by using a single factory overhead rate.

Single-step income statement An income statement in which the total of all expenses is deducted in one step from the total of all revenues.

Sinking fund Assets set aside in a special fund to be used for a specific purpose.

Six sigma quality 3.4 defects per million units processed.

Slide The erroneous movement of all digits in a number, one or more spaces to the right or the left, such as writing $542 as $5,420.

Small power distance culture A culture where employees perceive few power differences and follow a superior's instructions only when they either agree or feel threatened.

Solvency The ability of a business to pay its debts.

Solvency ratios See Liquidity ratios.

Special reports Reports that help managers formulate policies, prepare strategic plans, and prepare operational plans.

Specific price index An index that shows the price changes for a specific good or service over time.

Spot rate The rate quoted for current currency transactions.

Stakeholders The users of financial reports.

Standard cost A detailed estimate of what a product should cost.

Standard cost systems Accounting systems that use standards for each element of manufacturing cost entering into the finished product.

Standardization Full comparability of accounting information.

Stated value A value approved by the board of directors of a corporation for no-par stock. Similar to par value.

Statement of cash flows A summary of the major cash receipts and cash payments for a period.

Statement of Financial Accounting Standards No. 52 A U.S. foreign currency standard issued by the Financial Accounting Standards Board acknowledging that the functional currency of an entity is the currency of the primary environment in which the entity operates.

Statement of stockholders' equity A summary of the changes in the stockholders' equity of a corporation that have occurred during a specific period of time.

Statements on Auditing Standards (SAS) Standards issued by the American Institute of Certified Public Accountants in the United States concerning generally accepted auditing standards.

Static budget A budget that does not adjust to changes in activity levels.

Statutory (legal) reserve An equity reserve required by several countries to provide additional protection to creditors.

Statutory merger One company acquires the net assets of another company or companies.

Stock Shares of ownership of a corporation.

Stock dividend Distribution of a company's own stock to its shareholders.

Stockholders The owners of a corporation.

Stock split A reduction in the par or stated value of a share of common stock and the issuance of a proportionate number of additional shares.

Straight-line depreciation method A method of depreciation that provides for equal periodic depreciation expense over the estimated life of an asset.

Strategic alliance A firm's collaboration with companies in other countries to share rights and responsibilities as well as revenues and expenses as defined in a written agreement. Some common types of strategic alliances include research collaboration, a licensing program, and a copromotion deal.

Strategic plan A plan that integrates an organization's major goals, policies, and action sequences into a cohesive whole.

Strategic planning The process of deciding on the goals of the organization and the strategies for attaining these goals.

Subsidiary The company whose voting stock is acquired by a parent company to exercise control over it.

Subsidiary company The corporation that is controlled by a parent company.

Subsidiary ledger A ledger containing individual accounts with a common characteristic.

Sum-of-the-years-digits depreciation method A method of depreciation that provides for declining periodic depreciation expense over the estimated life of an asset.

Sunk cost A cost that is not affected by subsequent decisions.

Supplier partnering A just-in-time method that views suppliers as a valuable contributor to the overall success of the business.

T

T account A form of account resembling the letter T, showing debits on the left and credits on the right.

Target cost concept A concept used to design and manufacture a product at a cost that will deliver a target profit for a given market-determined price.

Target costing A costing method that sets cost targets for new products based on market price.

Taxable income The base on which the amount of income tax is determined.

Taxable income The income amount on which tax is levied.

Tax credit The reduction of a tax liability by an amount equal to the amount of the tax credit.

Tax holiday The period of time during which a foreign investor is exempted from taxes.

Temporal method A currency translation method in which translation is viewed as a restatement of the financial statements. The foreign currency amounts are translated at the exchange rates in effect at the dates when those items were measured in the foreign currency.

Temporary accounts Revenue, expense, or income summary accounts that are periodically closed; nominal accounts.

Temporary differences Differences between income before income tax and taxable income created by items that are recognized in one period for income statement purposes and in another period for tax purposes. Such differences reverse, or turn around, in later years.

Temporary investments Investments in securities that can be readily sold when cash is needed.

Territorial approach A national tax system that only taxes domestic income.

The Eighth Directive The EU Eighth Directive deals with auditing of financial statements of companies in EU countries, and specifies that they be consistent with EU law. It also sets qualifications for auditors and the firms conducting audits, including education and experience requirements. In addition, the Directive deals with ethical matters such as independence, and includes sanctions for cases in which audits are not conducted as prescribed by statute.

The Fourth Directive The EU Fourth Directive contains comprehensive accounting rules relevant to corporate accounting. It covers financial statements, their contents, methods of presentation, valuation methods, and disclosure of information.

The Seventh Directive The EU Seventh Directive addresses consolidated financial statement issues.

Theoretical standards Standards that represent levels of performance that can be achieved only under perfect operating conditions.

Theory of comparative advantage Each country should produce only those goods and services that it can produce with relative efficiency.

Theory of constraints (TOC) A manufacturing strategy that attempts to remove the influence of bottlenecks (constraints) on a process.

Thin capitalization The set of taxation issues from a host government's perspective, arising from the perceived imbalance between debt capital and equity capital when a foreign investor is financing a business operation in the country.

Time tickets The form on which the amount of time spent by each employee and the labor cost incurred for each individual job, or for factory overhead, are recorded.

Time value of money concept The concept that money invested today will earn income.

Total cost concept A concept used in applying the cost-plus approach to product pricing in which all the costs of manufacturing the product plus the selling and administrative expenses are included in the cost amount to which the markup is added.

Trade discounts Special discounts from published list prices offered by sellers to certain classes of buyers.

Trade-in allowance The amount a seller grants a buyer for a fixed asset that is traded in for a similar asset.

Trademark A name, term, or symbol used to identify a business and its products.

Trading blocs Free trade zones created by member countries through mutual agreements.

Trading security A debt or equity security that management intends to actively trade for profit.

Transaction risk exposure A condition that is caused by the changes in the exchange rate between the transaction date and the settlement date.

Transfer price The price one segment of a company charges another segment of the same company for the transfer of a good or a service.

Transnational corporation (TNC) The term favored by the United Nations as an alternative to the term multinational corporation.

Transposition The erroneous arrangement of digits in a number, such as writing $542 as $524.

Treasury stock A corporation's issued stock that has been reacquired.

Trend analysis A financial analysis that provides intrafirm as well as interfirm comparisons for two or more periods or dates.

Trial balance A summary listing of the titles and balances of the accounts in the ledger.

True and fair view A British concept of what financial statements ought to convey and an important feature of the Fourth Directive. The implementation of this concept means that companies may be required to disclose additional or different information. Each country determines, based on its own circumstances, how its corporations should comply with the true and fair view concept.

Turnover ratios See Efficiency ratios.

Two-column journal An all-purpose journal.

Two-transaction approach An approach used to translate foreign currency where any gains or losses are separately recorded as gains or losses from exchange rate exchanges.

U

Uncertainty acceptance The extent to which uncertainty is considered a normal part of life; feeling comfortable with ambiguity and unfamiliar risks.

Uncertainty avoidance The extent to which uncertainty is avoided in a culture.

Uncollectible accounts expense The operating expense incurred because of the failure to collect receivables.

Underapplied factory overhead The amount of actual factory overhead in excess of the factory overhead applied to production during a period.

Unearned revenue The liability created by receiving cash in advance of providing goods or services.

Unit contribution margin The dollars available from each unit of sales to cover fixed costs and provide operating profits.

United Nations (UN) An organization representing governments of all countries in the world.

Unit of measure concept A concept of accounting that requires that economic data be recorded in dollars.

Units-of-production depreciation method A method of depreciation that provides for depreciation expense based on the expected productive capacity of an asset.

Universal See Global.

Unrealized holding gain or loss The difference between the fair market values of the securities and their cost.

Unrealized (holding) gains Gains that are not yet actually incurred, for example, as a result of a foreign currency translation.

Unrealized (holding) losses Losses that are not yet actually incurred, for example, as a result of a foreign currency translation.

V

Value added Value added equals total revenue minus the cost of goods, materials, and services purchased externally.

Value added statements Primarily used in European countries for the purpose of showing, in financial terms, the contributions made by many participating groups in the creation of wealth in a company.

Value-added activities Activities that customers perceive as increasing the utility (usefulness) of the products or services they purchase.

Value-added activities The cost of activities that are needed to meet customer requirements.

Value-added lead time The time required to manufacture a unit of product or other output.

Value-added tax (VAT) A tax based on consumer spending.

Variable cost concept A concept used in applying the cost-plus approach to product pricing in which only the variable costs are included in the cost amount to which the markup is added.

Variable costing The concept that considers the cost of products manufactured to be composed only of those manufacturing costs that increase or decrease as the volume of production rises or falls (direct materials, direct labor, and variable factory overhead).

Variable costs Costs that vary in total dollar amount as the level of activity changes.

Variance The difference between actual performance and planned performance.

VAT concept A concept based on taxing each production activity or business activity that adds value to materials or goods purchased from other businesses.

Vertical analysis An analysis that compares each item in a current statement with a total amount within the same statements.

Volume variance The difference between the budgeted fixed overhead at 100% of normal capacity and the standard fixed overhead for the actual production achieved during the period.

Voucher A document that serves as evidence of authority to pay cash.

Voucher system Records, methods, and procedures used in verifying and recording liabilities and paying and recording cash payments.

W

Working capital The excess of the current assets of a business over its current liabilities.

Work in process inventory The direct materials costs, the direct labor costs, and the factory overhead costs that have entered into the manufacturing process, but are associated with products that have not been finished.

Work sheet A working paper used to summarize adjusting entries and assist in the preparation of financial statements.

Worldwide approach A national tax system that subjects both domestic source and foreign source income to taxes.

Y

Yield A measure of materials usage efficiency; it measures the ratio of the materials output quantity to the materials input quantity. Yields less than 1.0 are the result of materials losses in the process.

Z

Zero-based budgeting A concept of budgeting that requires all levels of management to start from zero and estimate budget data as if there had been no previous activities in their unit.

Module 600 Endnotes

1. The text of the *Code of Professional Conduct* of the American Institute of Certified Public Accountants is reproduced in Appendix B.
2. Glenn Alan Cheney, "Senate Rips FASB on Stock Options," *Accounting Today* (May 23, 1994).
3. "Corporate Elite Career Path," *Business Week,* October 11, 1993, p. 65.
4. Jill Krutick, *Fortune,* March 30, 1998, p. 106.
5. *The CPA Letter,* AICPA, December 2002, Vol. 82, No. 10.
6. Eugene E. Comiskey and Charles W. Mulford, *Guide to Financial Reporting and Analysis,* John Wiley & Sons, Inc., 2000.
7. Edwin C. Bliss, "Employee Theft," *Boardroom Reports,* July 15, 1994, pp. 5–6.
8. Charles W. Mulford and Eugene E. Comiskey, *The Financial Numbers Game: Detecting Creative Accounting Practices,* John Wiley & Sons, Inc., New York, 2000.
9. Deloitte & Touche. "Deloitte & Touche Analyses Key Business Issues." *Deloitte & Touche Review,* 2 February 1998, p. 4.
10. American Institute of Certified Public Accountants. "CPA Vision Project Identifies Top Five Issues for Profession." *The CPA Letter,* April 1998, pp. 1 and 12.
11. "What's Ahead with Global Investors?" *Management Accounting,* January 1995, p. 21.
12. Scott McDonald. "Power Feud Casts Harsh Spotlight on Pak Woes." *India-West,* 10 September 1999, p. B25.
13. "The Power-tariff Row." *The News International,* 25 March 2000, p. 7.
14. "LG Drops Russia Plant." *Gulf News,* 4 January 1997, p. 20.
15. Jonathan Karp. "Cogentrix, CLP Halt Development of India Power Plant." *The Wall Street Journal,* 10 December 1999, p. A12.
16. Seth Mydans. "A Top Thai Official Resigns in Scandal." *San Francisco Chronicle,* 30 March 2000, p. A18.
17. Jay Solomon and Puspa Madni. "Indonesia Arrests Big Crony of Suharto, Raising Hopes for Full Corruption Probe." *The Wall Street Journal,* 29 March 2000, p. A19.
18. T.R. Reid. "The World According to Rome." *National Geographic,* August 1997, pp. 63–64.
19. Jennifer Lin. "Chinese Lawyers, Judges Studying Law, American-Style." *The Tribune,* 25 September 1999, p. C8.
20. "Case Settled After 26 Years." *Dawn,* 13 June 1997, p. 3.
21. "India Seeks to Clear Court Backlog." *Gulf News,* 3 July 1997, p. 20.
22. "CJ Satisfied With Court's Disposal of Cases." *The Nation,* 25 March 2000, p. 14.
23. Alan Gersten. "Eastern Exposure." *Journal of Accountancy,* August 1999, p. 53.
24. "Judicial Emergency Declared in Venezuela." *San Francisco Chronicle,* 20 August 1999, p. D3.
25. Raja Asghar. "Pakistan Top Court Rules Bank Interest is Un-Islamic." *India-West,* 31 December 1999, p. A44.
26. "Businesswomen Try to Overcome Obstacles in Saudi Arabia." *Gulf News,* 3 July 1998, p. 18.
27. Howard D. Lowe. "Shortcomings of Japanese Consolidated Financial Statements." *Accounting Horizons,* September 1990, pp. 8–9.

28. Joseph M. Juran. *Juran on Quality by Design: The New Steps for Planning Quality into Goods and Services.* New York: The Free Press, 1992, p. 433.
29. Robert B. Sweeney. "Ethics in an International Environment." *Management Accounting,* February 1991, p. 27.
30. "Ethics Policies Help Reduce Internal Control Costs." *Journal of Accountancy,* April 1994, p. 14.
31. "Global Ethics Codes." *The Wall Street Journal,* 19 August 1999, p. A1.
32. Toyota. "To Our Fellow Toyota Stakeholders." *Toyota Annual Report 1998,* p. 1.
33. C.A. Frost, and K.P. Ramin. "Corporate Financial Disclosure: A Global Assessment." in F. Choi (ed.), *International Accounting and Finance Handbook,* 2nd ed. New York: John Wiley & Sons, Inc., 1997, p. 18.31.
34. Charles T. Horngren, George Foster, and Srikant M. Datar. *Cost Accounting: A Managerial Emphasis,* 10th ed. Upper Saddle River, N.J.: Prentice Hall, 2000, p. 11.
35. Dhia D. AlHashim, and J.S. Arpan. *International Dimensions of Accounting,* 3d ed. Boston: PWSKent Company, 1992, pp. 86–87.
36. *Ibid.,* p. 87.
37. *Annual Report 1993* (Stuttgart, Germany: Daimler-Benz, 1994), p. 73.
38. R.M. Harper Jr., W.G. Mister, and J.R. Strawser. "The Effect of Recognition versus Disclosure of Unfunded Postretirement Benefits on Lenders' Perceptions of Debt." *Accounting Horizons,* September 1991, pp. 50–56.
39. L. Duvall, R. Jennings, J. Robinson, and R. Thompson II. "Can Investors Unravel the Effects of Goodwill Accounting?" *Accounting Horizons,* June 1992, pp. 1–14.
40. United Nations Center on Transnational Corporations. *Conclusions on Accounting and Reporting by Transnational Corporations.* New York: United Nations, 1988.
41. United Nations Commission on Transnational Corporations. *Information Disclosure Relating to Environmental Measures.* New York: United Nations, 1990, p. 6.
42. "Environmental Disclosure: Recent Developments." *Deloitte & Touche Review,* 13 July 1992, pp. 1–2.
43. Robert Collier. "Helping Fox Paint a Greener Mexico." *San Francisco Chronicle,* 6 July 2000, pp. A1 and A15.
44. D. De Bryjne. "Global Standards: A Tower of Babel?" *Financial Executive,* February 1980, pp. 30–39.
45. Nancy Anderson. "The Globalization of GAAP." *Management Accounting,* August 1993, pp. 52–54.
46. Arthur R. Wyatt and Joseph F. Yospe. "Wake-up Call to American Business: International Accounting Standards Are on the Way." *Journal of Accountancy,* July 1993, pp. 80–85.
47. Institute of Internal Auditors. *Codification of Standards for the Professional Practice of Internal Auditing.* Altamonte Springs, Fla.: The Institute of Internal Auditors, 1993, pp. 75–76.
48. International Federation of Accountants. *IFAC Handbook 1999: Technical Pronouncements.* New York: International Federation of Accountants, 1999, pp. 224–225.
49. *Ibid.,* pp. 226–227.
50. Alvin A. Arens and James K. Loebbecke. *Auditing: An Integrated Approach,* 8th ed. Upper Saddle River, N.J.: Prentice-Hall, 2000, p. 794.
51. Deloitte Touche Tohmatsu. *Brazil: International Tax and Business Guide.* New York: Deloitte Touche Tohmatsu International, 1997, pp. 45–49.
52. Deloitte Touche Tohmatsu. *Netherlands: International Tax and Business Guide.* New York: Deloitte Touche Tohmatsu International, 1998, pp. 58–59.
53. Price Waterhouse. *Doing Business In Germany: Information Guide.* New York: Price Waterhouse, 1996, pp. 90–94.
54. Deloitte Touche Tohmatsu. *Japan: International Tax and Business Guide.* New York: Deloitte Touche Tohmatsu International, 1997, pp. 41–51.
55. Donald H. Taylor and G. William Glezen. *Auditing: Integrated Concepts and Procedures*, 6th ed. New York: John Wiley & Sons, Inc., 1994, pp. 299–300.

MODULE 700

Finance

701 Finance Strategies, 191

703 Role of Finance and Chief Financial Officer, 196

704 Working Capital Policy, 199

705 Managing Short-Term Assets, 208

710 Managing Short-Term Financing, 220

715 Managing Long-Term Financing, 232

720 Financial Forecasting, Planning, and Control, 266

725 Cost of Capital, Capital Structure, and Dividend Policy, 292

735 Capital Budgeting, 315

745 Financial Markets, Instruments, and Institutions, 335

755 Financial Risk Management, 346

760 Mergers, Acquisitions, and Business Valuations, 355

765 Operations, Marketing, and Finance, 365

770 Quantitative Techniques and Finance, 367

775 Economics and Finance, 381

780 Accounting and Finance, 386

785 Quality and Finance, 387

790 Law and Finance, 388

795 Ethics and Finance, 391

799 International Issues, 392

Module 700 Appendix, 442

Module 700 Glossary, 450

Module 700 Endnotes, 479

Finance Strategies

The Goals of the Corporation

Business decisions are not made in a vacuum—decision makers have some objective in mind. *We operate on the assumption that management's primary goal is* **stockholder wealth maximization,** which, as we will see, translates into *maximizing the value of the firm as measured by the price of the firm's common stock.* Firms do, of course, have other objectives—in particular, managers, who make the actual decisions, are interested in their own personal satisfaction, in their employees' welfare, and in the good of the community and of society at large. Still, for the reasons set forth in the following sections, *stock price maximization is the most important goal of most corporations.*

Managerial Incentives to Maximize Shareholder Wealth

It is the stockholders who own the firm and elect the management team. Management, in turn, is supposed to operate in the best interests of the stockholders. As a stockholder of a company, you probably would want the managers to make decisions that would maximize the value of the stock you own, including dividends. We know, however, that because the stock of most large corporations is widely held, the managers of such organizations have a great deal of latitude in making business decisions. This being the case, might not managers pursue goals other than stock price maximization? For example, some have argued that the managers of a large, well-entrenched corporation could work just hard enough to keep stockholder returns at a "reasonable" level and then devote the remainder of their efforts and resources to public service activities, to employee benefits, to higher executive salaries, or to golf.

It is almost impossible to determine whether a particular management team is trying to maximize shareholder wealth or is merely attempting to keep stockholders satisfied while pursuing other goals. For example, how can we tell whether employee or community benefit programs are in the long-run best interests of the stockholders? Similarly, are relatively high executive salaries really necessary to attract and retain excellent managers, or are they just another example of managers taking advantage of stockholders?

It is impossible to give definitive answers to these questions. However, we do know that the managers of a firm operating in a competitive market will be forced to undertake actions that are reasonably consistent with shareholder wealth maximization. If they depart from this goal, they run the risk of being removed from their jobs. We will have more to say about the conflict between managers and shareholders later in the section.

Social Responsibility

Another issue that deserves consideration is **social responsibility:** Should businesses operate strictly in their stockholders' best interests, or are firms also responsible for the welfare of their employees, customers, and the communities in which they operate? Certainly firms have an ethical responsibility to provide a safe working environment, to avoid polluting the air or water, and to produce safe products. However, socially responsible actions have costs, and it is questionable whether businesses would incur these costs voluntarily. If some firms do act in a socially responsible manner while others do not, then the socially responsible firms will be at a disadvantage in attracting funds. To illustrate, suppose the firms in a given industry have **profits** and **rates of return on investment** that are close to **normal**—that is, close to the average for all firms and just sufficient to attract capital. If one company attempts to exercise social responsibility, it will have to raise prices to cover the added costs. If the other businesses in its industry do not follow suit, their costs and prices will be lower. The socially responsible firm will not be able to compete, and it will be forced to abandon its efforts. Thus, any voluntary socially responsible acts that raise costs will be difficult, if not impossible, in industries that are subject to keen competition.

What about oligopolistic firms with profits above normal levels? Cannot such firms devote resources to social projects? Undoubtedly they can, and many large, successful firms do engage in community projects, employee benefit programs, and the like, to a greater degree than would appear to be called for by pure profit or wealth maximization goals. Still, publicly-owned firms are constrained in such actions by capital market factors. To illustrate, suppose a saver who has funds to invest is considering two alternative firms. One firm devotes a substantial part of its resources to social

701. FINANCE STRATEGIES

actions, while the other concentrates on profits and stock prices. Most investors are likely to shun the socially-oriented firm, thus putting it at a disadvantage in the capital market. After all, why should the stockholders of one corporation subsidize society to a greater extent than those of other businesses? For this reason, even highly profitable firms (unless they are closely held rather than publicly owned) generally are constrained against taking unilateral cost-increasing social actions.

Does all this mean that firms should not exercise social responsibility? Not at all, but it does mean that most significant cost-increasing actions associated with social responsibility will have to be put on a *mandatory* rather than a voluntary basis, at least initially, to ensure that the burden falls uniformly on all businesses.

Stock Price Maximization and Social Welfare

If a firm attempts to maximize its stock price, is this good or bad for society? In general, it is good. Aside from such illegal actions as attempting to form monopolies, violating safety codes, and failing to meet pollution control requirements, *the same actions that maximize stock prices also benefit society*. First, note that stock price maximization requires efficient, low-cost plants that produce high-quality goods and services at the lowest possible cost. Second, stock price maximization requires the development of products that consumers want and need, so the profit motive leads to new technology, to new products, and to new jobs. Finally, stock price maximization necessitates efficient and courteous service, adequate stocks of merchandise, and well-located business establishments—these factors all are necessary to maintain a customer base that is necessary for producing sales, and thus profits. Therefore, actions that help a firm increase the price of its stock also are beneficial to society at large. This is why profit-motivated, free-enterprise economies have been so much more successful than socialistic and communistic economic systems. Because managerial finance plays a crucial role in the operation of successful firms, and because successful firms are absolutely necessary for a healthy, productive economy, it is easy to see why finance is important from a social standpoint.

Managerial Actions to Maximize Shareholder Wealth

To maximize the price of a firm's stock, what types of actions should its management take? First, consider the question of stock prices versus profits: Will **profit maximization** also result in stock price maximization? In answering this question, we must consider the matter of total corporate profits versus **earnings per share (EPS).**

For example, suppose Xerox had 300 million shares outstanding and earned $1,200 million, or $4 per share. If you owned 100 shares of the stock, your share of the total profits would be $400. Now suppose Xerox sold another 300 million shares and invested the funds received in assets that produced $300 million of income. Total income would rise to $1,500 million, but earnings per share would decline from $4 to $2.50 = $1,500/600. Now your share of the firm's earnings would be only $250, down from $400. You (and other existing stockholders) would have suffered an earnings dilution, even though total corporate profits had risen. Therefore, other things held constant, *if management is interested in the well-being of its current stockholders, it should concentrate on earnings per share rather than on total corporate profits.*

Will maximization of expected earnings per share always maximize stockholder welfare, or should other factors be considered? Think about the *timing of the earnings*. Suppose Xerox had one project that would cause earnings per share to rise by $0.20 per year for five years, or $1 in total, while another project would have no effect on earnings for four years but would increase earnings by $1.25 in the fifth year. Which project is better—in other words, is $0.20 per year for five years better or worse than $1.25 in Year 5? The answer depends on which project adds the most to the value of the stock, which in turn depends on the time value of money to investors. Thus, timing is an important reason to concentrate on wealth as measured by the price of the stock rather than on earnings alone.

Another issue relates to *risk*. Suppose one project is expected to increase earnings per share by $1, while another is expected to raise earnings by $1.20 per share. The first project is not very risky—if it is undertaken, earnings will almost certainly rise by about $1 per share. However, the other project is quite risky, so, although our best guess is that earnings will rise by $1.20 per share, we must recognize the possibility that there might be no increase whatsoever, or even a loss. Depending on how averse stockholders are to risk, the first project might be preferable to the second.

The riskiness inherent in projected earnings per share (EPS) also depends on *how the firm is financed*. As we shall see, many firms go bankrupt every year, and the greater the use of debt, the greater the threat of bankruptcy. *Consequently, while the use of debt financing might increase projected EPS, debt also increases the riskiness of projected future earnings.*

Another issue is the matter of paying dividends to stockholders versus retaining earnings and reinvesting them in the firm, thereby causing the earnings stream to grow over time. Stockholders like cash dividends, but they also like the growth in EPS that results from plowing earnings back into the business. The financial manager must decide exactly how much of the current earnings to pay out as dividends rather than to retain and reinvest—this is called the **dividend policy decision.** The optimal dividend policy is the one that maximizes the firm's stock price.

We see, then, that the firm's stock price is dependent on the following factors.

1. Projected earnings per share.
2. Timing of the earnings stream.
3. Riskiness of the projected earnings.
4. Use of debt.
5. Dividend policy.

Every significant corporate decision should be analyzed in terms of its effect on these factors and hence on the price of the firm's stock. For example, suppose Occidental Petroleum's coal division is considering opening a new mine. If this is done, can it be expected to increase EPS? Is there a chance that costs will exceed estimates, that prices and output will fall below projections, and that EPS will be reduced because the new mine was opened? How long will it take for the new mine to show a profit? How should the capital required to open the mine be raised? If debt is used, by how much will this increase Occidental's riskiness? Should Occidental reduce its current dividends and use the cash thus saved to finance the project, or should it maintain its dividends and finance the mine with external capital? Managerial finance is designed to help answer questions like these, plus many more.

Agency Relationships

An *agency relationship* exists when one or more people (the principals) hire another person (the agent) to perform a service and then delegate decision-making authority to that agent. Important agency relationships exist (1) between stockholders and managers and (2) between stockholders and creditors (debtholders).

Stockholders Versus Managers

A potential **agency problem** arises whenever the manager of a firm owns less than 100% of the firm's common stock. If a firm is a proprietorship managed by the owner, the owner-manager will presumably operate the business in a fashion that will improve his or her own welfare, with welfare measured in the form of increased personal wealth, more leisure, or perquisites. However, if the owner-manager incorporates and sells some of the firm's stock to outsiders, a potential conflict of interests immediately arises. For example, the owner-manager might now decide not to work as hard to maximize shareholder wealth because less of this wealth will go to him or her, or decide to take a higher salary or enjoy more perquisites because part of those costs will fall on the outside stockholders. This potential conflict between two parties, the principals (outside shareholders) and the agent (manager), is an agency problem.

In general, if a conflict of interest exists, what can be done to ensure that management treats the outside stockholders fairly? Several mechanisms are used to motivate managers to act in the shareholders' best interests. These include (1) the threat of firing, (2) the threat of takeover, and (3) managerial compensation plans.

1. **The threat of firing.** It wasn't long ago that the management teams of large firms felt secure in their positions, because the chances of being ousted by stockholders were so remote that managers rarely felt their jobs were in jeopardy. This situation existed because ownership of most firms was so widely distributed, and management's control over the proxy (voting) mechanism was so strong, that it was almost impossible for dissident stockholders to gain enough votes to overthrow the managers. However, today much of the stock of an average large corporation is owned by a relatively few large institutions rather than by thousands of individual investors, and the institutional money managers have the clout to influence a firm's operations. Examples of major corporations whose managements have been ousted include **United Airlines**, **Disney**, and **IBM**.

2. **The threat of takeover. Hostile takeovers** (instances in which management does not want the firm to be taken over) are most likely to occur when a firm's stock is undervalued relative to its potential. In a hostile takeover, the managers of the acquired firm generally are fired, and any who are able to stay on lose the power they had prior to the acquisition. Thus, managers have a strong incentive to take actions that maximize stock prices. In the words of one company president, "If you want to keep control, don't let your company's stock sell at a bargain price."

   Actions to increase the firm's stock price and to keep it from being a bargain obviously are good from the standpoint of the stockholders, but other tactics that managers can use to ward off a hostile takeover might not be. Two examples of questionable tactics are *poison pills* and *greenmail*. A **poison pill** is an action a firm can take that practically kills it and thus makes it unattractive to potential suitors. Examples include Disney's plan to sell large blocks of its stock at low prices to "friendly" parties, **Scott Industries'** decision to make all of its debt immediately payable if its management changed, and **Carleton Corporation's** decision to give huge retirement bonuses, which represented a large part of the company's wealth, to its managers if the firm was taken over (such payments are called *golden parachutes*). **Greenmail,** which is like blackmail, occurs when (a) a potential acquirer (firm or individual) buys a block of stock in a company, (b) the target company's management becomes frightened that the acquirer will make a tender offer and gain control of the company, and (c) to head off a possible takeover, management offers to pay greenmail, buying the stock owned by the potential raider at a price above the existing market price without offering the same deal to other stockholders. A good example of greenmail was Disney's buyback of 11.1% of its stock from Saul Steinberg's Reliance Group in 1984, which gave Steinberg a quick $60 million profit (he held the stock only a few months). The day the buyback was announced, the price of Disney's stock dropped approximately 10%. A group of stockholders sued, and Steinberg and the Disney directors were forced to pay $45 million to Disney stockholders.

3. **Managerial compensation plans.** Increasingly, firms are tying managers' compensation to the company's performance, and this motivates managers to operate in a manner consistent with stock price maximization.

   In the 1950s and 1960s, most performance-based incentive plans involved **executive stock options,** which allowed managers to purchase stock at some future time at a given price. Because the value of the options was tied directly to the price of the stock, it was assumed that granting options would provide an incentive for managers to take actions that would maximize the stock's price. This type of managerial incentive lost favor in the 1970s, however, because the general stock market declined, and stock prices did not necessarily reflect companies' earnings growth. Incentive plans should be based on those factors over which managers have control, and because they cannot control the general stock market, stock option plans were not good incentive devices. Therefore, while 61 of the 100 largest U.S. firms used stock options as their sole incentive compensation in 1970, not even one of the largest 100 companies relied exclusively on such plans in 1999.

   An important incentive plan now is **performance shares,** which are shares of stock given to executives on the basis of performance as measured by earnings per share, return on assets, return on equity, and so on. For example, **Honeywell** uses growth in earnings per share as its primary performance measure. If the company achieves a targeted average growth in earnings per share, the managers will earn 100% of their shares. If the corporate performance is above the target, Honeywell's managers can earn even more shares. But if growth is below the target, they get less than 100% of the shares.

   All incentive compensation plans—executive stock options, performance shares, profit-based bonuses, and so forth—are designed to accomplish two things. First, these plans provide inducements to executives to act on those factors under their control in a manner that will contribute to stock price maximization. Second, the existence of such performance plans helps companies attract and retain top-level executives. Well-designed plans can accomplish both goals.

Stockholders Versus Creditors

A second agency problem involves conflicts between stockholders and creditors (debtholders). Creditors lend funds to the firm at rates that are based on (1) the riskiness of the firm's existing assets, (2) expectations concerning the riskiness of future asset additions, (3) the firm's existing capital structure (that is, the amount of debt financing it uses), and (4) expectations concerning future capital structure changes. These are the factors that determine the riskiness of the firm's debt, so creditors base the interest rate they charge on expectations regarding these factors.

Now suppose the stockholders, acting through management, cause the firm to take on new ventures that have much greater risk than was anticipated by the creditors. This increased risk will cause the value of the outstanding debt to fall. If the risky ventures turn out to be successful, all of the benefits will go to the stockholders because the creditors only get a fixed return. However, if things go sour, the bondholders will have to share the losses. What this amounts to, from the stockholders' point of view, is a game of "heads I win, tails you lose," which obviously is not a good game for the bondholders.

Similarly, if the firm increases its use of debt in an effort to boost the return to stockholders, the value of the old debt will decrease, so we have another "heads I win, tails you lose" situation. To illustrate, consider what happened to **RJR Nabisco's** bondholders when, in 1988, RJR's chief executive officer announced his plan to take the company private with funds the company would borrow (termed a *leverage buyout*). Stockholders saw their shares jump in value from $56 to over $90 in just a few days, but RJR's bondholders suffered losses of approximately 20%. Investors immediately realized that taking RJR Nabisco private would cause the amount of its debt to rise dramatically, and thus its riskiness would soar. This, in turn, led to a huge decline in the price of RJR's outstanding bonds. Ultimately, RJR's management was not successful in its buyout attempt. But Nabisco was purchased by another company for more than $100 per share—what a gain for the stockholders!

Can and should stockholders, through their managers/agents, try to expropriate wealth from the firm's creditors? In general, the answer is no. First, because such attempts have been made in the past, creditors today protect themselves reasonably well against stockholder actions through restrictions in credit agreements. Second, if potential creditors perceive that a firm will try to take advantage of them in unethical ways, they will either refuse to deal with the firm or else will require a much higher than normal rate of interest to compensate for the risks of such "sneaky" actions. Thus, firms that try to deal unfairly with creditors either lose access to the debt markets or are saddled with higher interest rates, both of which decrease the long-run value of the stock.

In view of these constraints, it follows that the goal of maximizing shareholder wealth requires fair play with creditors: Stockholder wealth depends on continued access to capital markets, and access depends on fair play and abiding by both the letter and the spirit of credit agreements. Managers, as agents of both the creditors and the stockholders, must act in a manner that is fairly balanced between the interests of these two classes of security holders. Similarly, because of other constraints and sanctions, management actions that would expropriate wealth from any of the firm's **stakeholders** (employees, customers, suppliers, and so on) will ultimately be to the detriment of shareholders. Therefore, maximizing shareholder wealth requires the fair treatment of all stakeholders.

The External Environment

Although managerial actions affect the value of a firm's stock, external factors also influence stock prices. Included among these factors are legal constraints, the general level of economic activity, the tax laws, and conditions in the stock market. Exhibit 700.1 diagrams these general relationships. Working within the set of external constraints shown in the box at the extreme left, management makes a set of long-run strategic policy decisions that chart a future course for the firm. These policy decisions, along with the general level of economic activity and the level of corporate income taxes, influence the firm's expected profitability, the timing of its cash flows, their eventual transfer to stockholders in the form

Exhibit 700.1 *Summary of Major Factors Affecting Stock Prices*

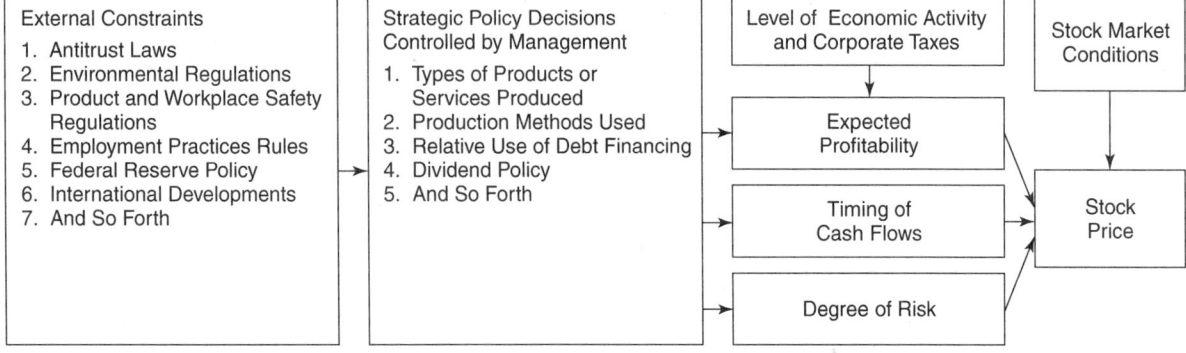

of dividends, and the degree of risk inherent in projected earnings and dividends. Profitability, timing, and risk all affect the price of the firm's stock, but so does another factor, conditions in the stock market as a whole, because all stock prices tend to move up and down together to some extent.

Role of Finance and Chief Financial Officer

The Financial Manager's Responsibilities

The financial manager's task is to make decisions concerning the acquisition and use of funds for the greatest benefit of the firm. Here are some specific activities that are involved.

1. **Forecasting and planning.** The financial manager must interact with other executives as they look ahead and lay the plans that will shape the firm's future position.
2. **Major investment and financing decisions.** A successful firm generally has rapid growth in sales, which requires investments in plant, equipment, and inventory. The financial manager must help determine the optimal sales growth rate, and he or she must help decide on the specific assets to acquire and the best way to finance those assets. For example, should the firm raise funds by borrowing (debt) or by selling stock (equity)? If the firm uses debt (borrows), should it be long term or short term?
3. **Coordination and control.** The financial manager must interact with other executives to ensure that the firm is operated as efficiently as possible. All business decisions have financial implications, and all managers—financial and otherwise—need to take this into account. For example, marketing decisions affect sales growth, which, in turn, influences investment requirements. Thus, marketing decision makers must consider how their actions affect (and are affected by) such factors as the availability of funds, inventory policies, and plant capacity utilization.
4. **Dealing with the financial markets.** The financial manager must deal with the money and capital markets. Each firm affects and is affected by the general financial markets where funds are raised, where the firm's securities are traded, and where its investors are either rewarded or penalized.

In summary, *financial managers make decisions regarding which assets their firms should acquire, how those assets should be financed, and how to manage their firms' existing resources.* If these responsibilities are performed optimally, financial managers will help to maximize the values of their firms, and this will also maximize the long-term welfare of those who buy from or work for the company, as well as the community where the firm is located.

Both controller and treasurer report to the vice president of finance or chief financial officer (CFO). The duties and responsibilities of the controller were presented in Module 600 Accounting, Section 603. The duties and responsibilities of the treasurer include short-term and long-term financing, banking arrangements, credit and collections, cash management and investments, risk management, and investor relations.

Finance in the Organizational Structure of the Firm

Organizational structures vary from firm to firm, but Exhibit 700.2 presents a fairly typical picture of the role of finance within a corporation. The chief financial officer—who has the title of vice president of finance—reports to the president. The financial vice president's key subordinates are the treasurer and the controller. In most firms the treasurer has direct responsibility for managing the firm's cash and marketable securities, for planning how funds are raised, for selling stocks and bonds to raise funds, and for overseeing the corporate pension fund. The treasurer also supervises the credit manager, the inventory manager, and the director of capital budgeting (who analyzes decisions related to investments in fixed assets). The controller is responsible for the activities of the accounting and tax departments.

Exhibit 700.2 *Place of Finance in a Typical Business Organization*

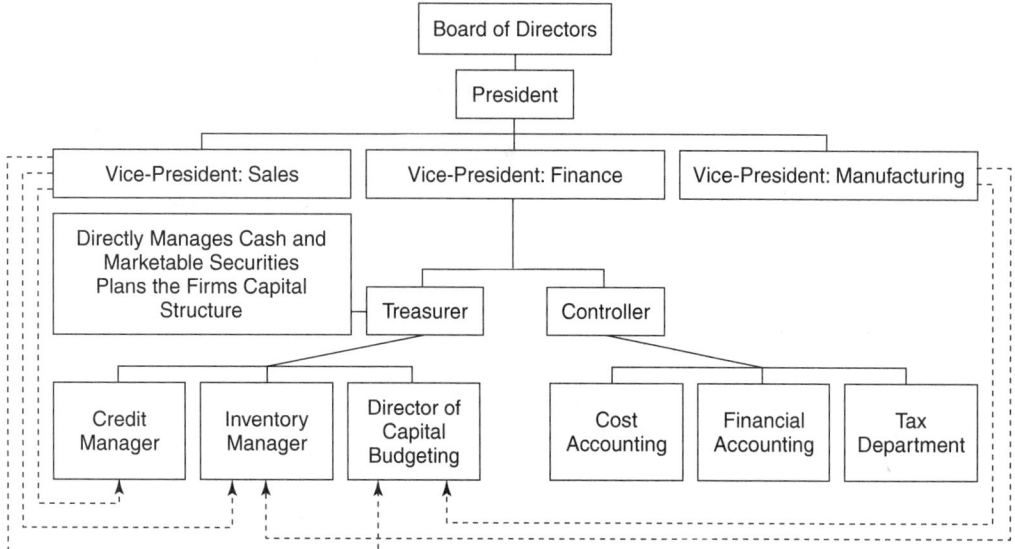

Alternative Forms of Business Organization

There are three main forms of business organization: (1) proprietorships, (2) partnerships, and (3) corporations. In terms of numbers, about 75% of businesses are operated as proprietorships, nearly 7% are partnerships, and the remaining 18% are corporations. Based on dollar value of sales, however, almost 90% of all business is conducted by corporations, while the remaining 10% is generated by both proprietorships and partnerships. Because most business is conducted by corporations, we will concentrate on them in this section. However, it is important to understand the differences among the three forms of business organizations.

Proprietorship

A **proprietorship** is an unincorporated business owned by one individual. Starting a proprietorship is fairly easy—just begin business operations. However, in most cases, even the smallest business must be licensed by the municipality (city, county, or state) in which it operates.

The proprietorship has three important *advantages*.

1. It is easily and inexpensively formed.
2. It is subject to few government regulations.
3. It is taxed like an individual, not a corporation.

The proprietorship also has four important *limitations*.

1. The proprietor has *unlimited personal liability* for business debts, which can result in losses that exceed the money he or she has invested in the company.
2. The life of a business organized as a proprietorship is limited to the life of the individual who created it.
3. Transferring ownership is somewhat difficult—disposing of the business is similar to selling a house in that the proprietor has to seek out and negotiate with a potential buyer.
4. It is difficult for a proprietorship to obtain large sums of capital, because the firm's financial strength generally is based on the financial strength of the sole owner.

For these reasons, individual proprietorships are confined primarily to small business operations. In fact, only about 1% of all proprietorships have assets that are valued at $1 million or greater, while nearly 90% have assets valued at $100,000 or less. However, businesses frequently are started as proprietorships and then converted to corporations when their growth causes the disadvantages of being a proprietorship to outweigh the advantages.

703. ROLE OF FINANCE AND CHIEF FINANCIAL OFFICER

Partnership

A **partnership** is like a proprietorship, except there are two or more owners. Partnerships can operate under different degrees of formality, ranging from informal, oral understandings to formal agreements filed with the secretary of the state in which the partnership does business. Most legal experts would recommend the partnership agreement be put in writing.

The *advantages* of a partnership are the same as for a proprietorship.

1. Formation is easy and relatively inexpensive.
2. It is subject to few government regulations.
3. It is taxed like an individual, not a corporation.

The *disadvantages* are also similar to those associated with proprietorships.

1. Unlimited liability
2. Limited life of the organization
3. Difficulty of transferring ownership
4. Difficulty of raising large amounts of capital

Regarding liability, the partners can potentially lose all of their personal assets, even those assets not invested in the business, because under partnership law each partner is liable for the business's debts. Therefore, if any partner is unable to meet his or her pro rata claim in the event the partnership goes bankrupt, the remaining partners must make good on the unsatisfied claims, drawing on their personal assets if necessary. Thus, the business-related activities of any of the firm's partners can bring ruin to the other partners, even though those partners were not a direct party to such activities. For example, the partners of the national accounting firm **Laventhol and Horwath**, a huge partnership that went bankrupt at the end of 1992 as a result of suits filed by investors who relied on faulty audit statements, learned all about the perils of doing business as a partnership—they discovered that a Texas partner who audits a savings and loan that goes under can bring ruin to a millionaire New York partner who never went near the S&L.

However, it is possible to limit the liabilities of some of the partners by establishing a *limited partnership*, wherein one (or more) partner is designated the *general partner* and the others *limited partners*. Limited partnerships are quite common in the area of real estate investment, but they do not work well with most types of businesses, including accounting firms, because one partner rarely is willing to assume all of the business's risk. Not long ago, the national accounting firms reorganized themselves as limited liability partnerships, which are partnerships in which only the assets of the partnership and the "engagement" partner (partner in charge of the situation) are at risk.

The first three disadvantages—unlimited liability, impermanence of the organization, and difficulty of transferring ownership—lead to the fourth, the difficulty partnerships have in attracting substantial amounts of funds. This is no particular problem for a slow-growing business, but if a business's products really catch on, and if it needs to raise large amounts of funds to capitalize on its opportunities, the difficulty in attracting funds becomes a real drawback. Thus, growth companies such as **Microsoft** and **Dell Computer** generally begin life as a proprietorship or partnership, but at some point they find it necessary to convert to a corporation.

Corporation

A **corporation** is a legal entity created by a state. It is separate and distinct from its owners and managers. This separateness gives the corporation three major *advantages*.

1. A corporation can continue after its original owners and managers are deceased; thus it is said to have *unlimited life*.
2. Ownership interests can be divided into shares of stock, which in turn can be *transferred far more easily* than can proprietorship or partnership interests.
3. A corporation offers its owners *limited liability*. To illustrate the concept of limited liability, suppose you invested $10,000 to become a partner in a business that subsequently went bankrupt, owing creditors $1 million. Because the owners are liable for the debts of a partnership, you could be assessed for a share of the company's debt, and you could be held liable for the entire $1 million if your partners could not pay their shares—this is what we mean by unlimited liability. On the other hand, if you invested $10,000 in the stock of a corporation that then went bankrupt, your potential loss on the investment would be limited to your $10,000 investment.

In the case of small corporations, the limited liability feature is often a fiction, because bankers and credit managers frequently require personal guarantees from the stockholders of small, weak businesses.

These three factors—unlimited life, easy transferability of ownership interest, and limited liability—make it much easier for corporations than for proprietorships or partnerships to raise money in the financial markets.

The corporate form of business offers significant advantages over proprietorships and partnerships, but it does have two primary disadvantages.

1. Corporate *earnings are subject to double taxation*—the earnings of the corporation are taxed, and then any earnings paid out as dividends are taxed again as income to the stockholders.
2. Setting up a corporation, and filing required state and federal reports, is more complex and time-consuming than for a proprietorship or a partnership.

Although a proprietorship or a partnership can commence operations without much paperwork, setting up a corporation requires that the incorporators hire a lawyer to prepare a charter and a set of bylaws. The **corporate charter** includes the (1) name of the proposed corporation, (2) types of activities it will pursue, (3) amount of capital stock, (4) number of directors, and (5) names and addresses of directors. The charter is filed with the secretary of the state in which the firm will be incorporated, and, when it is approved, the corporation is officially in existence. Then, after the corporation is in operation, quarterly and annual financial statements and tax reports must be filed with state and federal authorities.

A majority of major U.S. corporations are chartered in Delaware, which has, over the years, provided a favorable legal environment for corporations. It is not necessary for a firm to be headquartered, or even to conduct operations, in its state of incorporation.

The **bylaws** are a set of rules drawn up by the founders of the corporation to aid in governing the internal management of the company. Included are such points as (1) how directors are to be elected (all elected each year, or perhaps one-third each year for three-year terms); (2) whether the existing stockholders will have the first right to buy any new shares the firm issues (the preemptive right); and (3) procedures for changing the bylaws themselves, should conditions require it.

The value of any business other than a very small one probably will be maximized if it is organized as a corporation for these reasons.

1. Limited liability reduces the risks borne by investors, and, other things held constant, *lower risk means higher value*.
2. Corporations can attract funds more easily than can unincorporated businesses, and these funds can be invested in *growth opportunities* that help increase the firm's value.
3. Corporate ownership can be transferred more easily than ownership of either a proprietorship or a partnership. Therefore, all else equal, *investors would be willing to pay more* for a corporation than a proprietorship or partnership—this means that the corporate form of organization can enhance the value of a business.
4. Corporations are taxed differently than proprietorships and partnerships, and some of the *tax differences are beneficial* for corporations.

Most firms are managed with value maximization in mind, and this, in turn, has caused most large businesses to be organized as corporations.

Working Capital Policy

Working Capital Management

Generally we divide financial management decisions into the management of assets (investments) and liabilities (sources of financing) in (1) the *long term* and (2) the *short term*. In this section, we discuss *short-term financial management*, also termed **working capital management**, which involves management of the current assets and the current liabilities of a firm. You will realize that a firm's value cannot be maximized in the long run unless it survives the short run. In fact, the principal reason firms fail is because they are unable to meet their working capital needs. Thus, *sound working capital management is a requisite for firm survival*. Much of a financial manager's or treasurer's time is devoted to working capital management.

Working Capital Terminology

It is useful to begin the discussion of working capital policy by reviewing some basic definitions and concepts.

1. The term **working capital,** sometimes called *gross working capital,* generally refers to current assets.
2. **Net working capital** is defined as current assets minus current liabilities.
3. The *current ratio,* is calculated by dividing current assets by current liabilities, and it is intended to measure a firm's liquidity. However, a high current ratio does not insure that a firm will have the cash required to meet its needs. If inventories cannot be sold, or if receivables cannot be collected in a timely manner, then the apparent safety reflected in a high current ratio could be illusory.
4. The best and most comprehensive picture of a firm's liquidity position is obtained by examining its *cash budget.* The cash budget, which forecasts cash inflows and outflows, focuses on what really counts, the firm's ability to generate sufficient cash inflows to meet its required cash outflows. Cash budgeting will be discussed in Section 705.
5. **Working capital policy** refers to the firm's basic policies regarding (a) target levels for each category of current assets and (b) how current assets will be financed.

We must distinguish between those current liabilities that are specifically used to finance current assets and those current liabilities that represent (1) current maturities of long-term debt; (2) financing associated with a construction program that, after the project is completed, will be funded with the proceeds of a long-term security issue; or (3) the use of short-term debt to finance fixed assets.

Exhibit 700.3 contains balance sheets for Unilate Textiles constructed at three different dates. According to the definitions given, Unilate's December 31, 2000, working capital (current assets) was $465.0 million, and its net working capital was $335.0 million = $465.0 million − $130.0 million. Also, Unilate's year-end 2000 current ratio was 3.6.

What if the total current liabilities of $130 million at the end of 2000 included the current portion of long-term debt, say $10 million? This account is unaffected by changes in working capital policy because it is a function of past long-term debt financing decisions. Thus, even though we define long-term debt coming due in the next accounting period as a current liability, it is not a working capital decision variable in the current period. Similarly, if Unilate were building a new factory and initially financed the construction with a short-term loan that would be replaced later with

Exhibit 700.3 *Unilate Textiles: Historical and Projected Balance Sheets (millions of dollars)*

	12/31/00 (Historical)	9/30/01 (Projected)	12/31/01 (Projected)
Cash and marketable securities	$ 15.0	$ 30.0	$ 16.5
Accounts receivable	180.0	251.5	198.0
Inventories	270.0	410.0	297.0
Total current assets	$465.0	$ 691.5	$511.5
Net plant and equipment	380.0	408.5	418.0
Total assets	$845.0	$1,100.0	$929.5
Accounts payable	$30.0	$90.0	$ 33.0
Accruals	60.0	100.0	66.0
Notes payable	40.0	129.0	46.8
Total current liabilities	$130.0	$ 319.0	$145.8
Long-term bonds	300.0	309.0	309.0
Total liabilities	$430.0	$ 628.0	$454.8
Common stock	130.0	159.3	159.3
Retained earnings	285.0	312.7	315.4
Total owner's equity	$415.0	$ 472.0	$474.7
Total liabilities and equity	$845.0	$1,100.0	$929.5
Net working capital	$335.0	$ 372.5	$365.7
Current ratio	3.6	2.2	3.5

mortgage bonds, the construction loan would not be considered part of working capital management. Although such accounts are not part of Unilate's working capital decision process, they cannot be ignored because they are *due* in the current period, and they must be taken into account when Unilate's managers construct the cash budget and assess the firm's ability to meet its current obligations (its liquidity position).

The Requirement for External Working Capital Financing

Unilate's operations and the sale of textile products are very seasonal, typically peaking in September and October. Thus, at the end of September, Unilate's inventories are significantly higher than they are at the end of the calendar year. Unilate offers significant sales incentives to wholesalers during August and September in an effort to move inventories out of its warehouses and into those of its customers; otherwise, inventories would be even higher than shown in Exhibit 700.3. Because of this sales surge, Unilate's receivables also are much higher at the end of September than at the end of December.

Consider what is expected to happen to Unilate's current assets and current liabilities from December 31, 2000, to September 30, 2001. Current assets are expected to increase from $465.0 million to $691.5 million, or by $226.5 million. Because increases on the asset side of the balance sheet must be financed by identical increases on the liabilities and equity side, the firm must raise $226.5 million to meet the expected increase in working capital over the period. However, the higher volume of purchases, plus labor expenditures associated with increased production, will cause accounts payable and accruals to increase spontaneously by only $100 million—from $90.0 million ($30.0 million in payables plus $60.0 million in accruals) to $190.0 million ($90.0 million in payables plus $100.0 million in accruals)—during the first nine months of 2001. This leaves a projected $126.5 million = $226.5 million − $100.0 million current asset financing requirement, which Unilate expects to finance primarily by an $89.0 million increase in notes payable. Therefore, for September 30, 2001, notes payable are projected to rise to $129.0 million. Notice that from December 2000 to September 2001, Unilate's net working capital is expected to increase from $335.0 million to $372.5 million, but its current ratio is expected to fall from 3.6 to 2.2. This occurs because most, but not all, of the funds invested in current assets are expected to come from current liabilities.

The fluctuations in Unilate's working capital position shown in Exhibit 700.3 result from seasonal variations. Similar fluctuations in working capital requirements, and hence in financing needs, also occur during business cycles—working capital needs typically decline during recessions but increase during booms. For some companies, such as those involved in agricultural products, seasonal fluctuations are much greater than business cycle fluctuations, but for other companies, such as appliance or automobile manufacturers, cyclical fluctuations are larger. In the following sections we look in more detail at the requirement for working capital financing, and we examine some alternative working capital policies.

The Cash Conversion Cycle

The concept of working capital management starts with borrowing money from a bank to buy inventory, sell the inventory to pay off the bank loan, and then repeat the cycle. The working capital management process that Unilate Textiles faces can be summarized as follows.

1. Unilate orders and then receives the materials it needs to produce the textile products its sells. Unilate purchases from its suppliers on credit, so an account payable is created for credit purchases. Such purchases have no immediate cash flow effect because payment is not made until some later date (perhaps 20 to 30 days after purchase).
2. Labor is used to convert the materials (cotton and wool) into finished goods (cloth products, thread, etc.). However, wages are not fully paid at the time the work is done, so accrued wages build up (maybe for a period of one or two weeks).
3. The finished products are sold, but on credit; so sales create receivables, not immediate cash inflows.
4. At some point during the cycle, Unilate must pay off its accounts payable and accrued wages. *If* these payments are made before Unilate has collected cash from its receivables, a net cash outflow occurs and this outflow must be financed.

5. The cycle is completed when Unilate's receivables are collected (perhaps in 30 to 40 days). At that time, the company is in a position to pay off the credit that was used to finance production of the product, and it can then repeat the cycle.

The preceding steps are formalized with the **cash conversion cycle** model, which focuses on the length of time between when the company makes payments, or invests in the manufacture of inventory, and when it receives cash inflows, or realizes a cash return from its investment in production.[1] The following terms are used in the model.

1. The *inventory conversion period* is the average length of time required to convert materials into finished goods and then to sell those goods; it is the amount of time the product remains in inventory in various stages of completion. The inventory conversion period is calculated by dividing inventory by the cost of goods sold per day. For example, we can compute the inventory conversion period for Unilate Textiles using the 2000 balance sheet figures shown in Exhibit 700.3. In 2000, Unilate sold $1,500 million of its product with a cost of goods sold equal to $1,230 million, so the inventory conversion period would be:

$$\text{Inventory conversion period} = \frac{\text{Inventory}}{\text{Cost of goods sold per day}} = \frac{\text{Inventory}}{\left(\frac{\text{Cost of goods sold}}{360}\right)} \quad (7.1)$$

$$= \frac{\$270 \text{ million}}{\left(\frac{\$1,230 \text{ million}}{360}\right)} = \frac{\$270}{\$3.417}$$

$$= 79.0 \text{ days}$$

Thus, according to its 2000 operations, it takes Unilate 79.0 days to convert materials into finished goods and then to sell those goods.

2. The *receivables collection period* is the average length of time required to convert the firm's receivables into cash—that is, to collect cash following a sale. The receivables collection period also is called the days sales outstanding (DSO), and it is calculated by dividing accounts receivable by the average credit sales per day. Because sales in 2000 equaled $1,500 million, Unilate's receivables collection period (DSO) is:

$$\text{Receivables collection period} = \text{DSO} = \frac{\text{Receivables}}{\text{Daily credit sales}} = \frac{\text{Receivable}}{\left(\frac{\text{Credit sales}}{360}\right)} \quad (7.2)$$

$$= \frac{\$180 \text{ million}}{\left(\frac{\$1,500 \text{ million}}{360}\right)} = \frac{\$180}{\$4.167}$$

$$= 43.2 \text{ days}$$

Thus, the cash payments associated with credit sales are not collected until 43.2 days after the sales.

3. The *payables deferral period* is the average length of time between the purchase of raw materials and labor and the payment of cash for them. It is computed by dividing accounts payable by the daily credit purchases. Unilate's daily cost of goods sold is $3.417 million, so the payables deferral period for Unilate would be:

$$\text{Payables deferral period} = \text{DPO} = \frac{\text{Accounts payable}}{\text{Credit purchases per day}} = \frac{\text{Accounts payable}}{\left(\frac{\text{Cost of goods sold}}{360}\right)} \quad (7.3)$$

$$= \frac{\$30 \text{ million}}{\left(\frac{\$1,230 \text{ million}}{360}\right)} = \frac{\$30}{\$3.417}$$

$$= 8.8 \text{ days}$$

So Unilate pays its suppliers an average of 8.8 days after materials are purchased.

4. The *cash conversion cycle* computation nets out the three periods just defined, resulting in a value that equals the length of time between the firm's actual cash expenditures to pay for (invest in) productive resources (ma-

Exhibit 700.4 *The Cash Conversion Cycle*

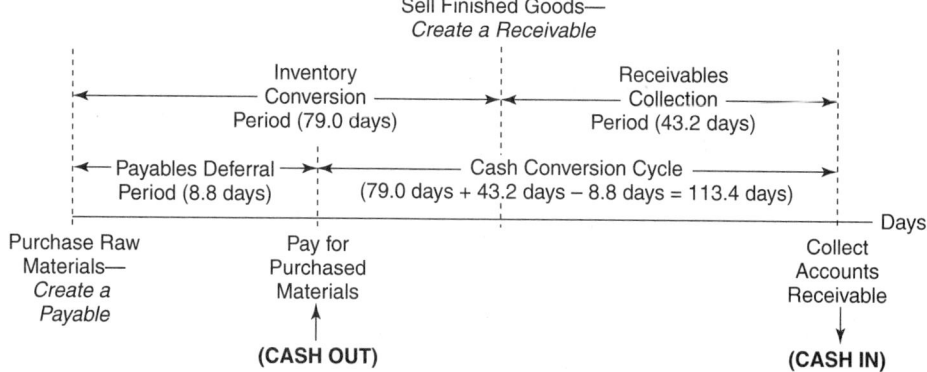

terials and labor) and its own cash receipts from the sale of products (that is, the length of time between paying for labor and materials and collecting on receivables). The cash conversion cycle thus equals the average length of time a dollar is tied up in current assets.

We can now use these definitions to analyze Unilate's cash conversion cycle. First, the concept is diagrammed in Exhibit 700.4. Thus, the cash conversion cycle can be expressed by this equation:

$$\begin{matrix} \text{Cash} \\ \text{conversion} \\ \text{cycle} \end{matrix} = \begin{pmatrix} \text{Inventory} \\ \text{conversion} \\ \text{period} \end{pmatrix} + \begin{pmatrix} \text{Receivables} \\ \text{collection} \\ \text{period} \end{pmatrix} - \begin{pmatrix} \text{Payables} \\ \text{deferral} \\ \text{period} \end{pmatrix} \quad (7.4)$$

$$= 79.0 \text{ days} + 43.2 \text{ days} - 8.8 \text{ days}$$

$$= 113.4 \text{ days}$$

To illustrate, according to Unilate's 2000 operations, it takes an average of 79.0 days to convert raw materials (cotton, wool, and so on) into finished goods (cloth, thread, and so on) and then sell them, and then it takes another 43.2 days to collect on receivables. However, 8.8 days normally elapse between receipt of raw materials and payment for them. In this case, the cash conversion cycle is 113.4 days. The *receipt* of cash from manufacturing and selling the products will be delayed by about 122 days because (1) the product will be "tied up" in inventory for 79 days, and (2) the cash from the sale will not be received until about 43 days after the selling date. But the *disbursement* of cash for the raw materials purchased will be delayed by nearly 9 days because Unilate does not pay cash for the raw materials when they are purchased. So for Unilate, the net delay in cash receipts associated with an investment (cash disbursement) in inventory is 113.4 days. What does this mean to Unilate?

Given its cash conversion cycle, Unilate knows when it starts processing its textile products that it will have to finance the manufacturing and other operating costs for a 113-day period, which is nearly one-third of a year. The firm's goal should be to shorten its cash conversion cycle as much as possible without harming operations. This would improve profits because the longer the cash conversion cycle, the greater the need for external, or nonspontaneous, financing, and such financing has a cost.

The cash conversion cycle can be shortened (1) by reducing the inventory conversion period by processing and selling goods more quickly, (2) by reducing the receivables collection period by speeding up collections, or (3) by lengthening the payables deferral period by slowing down its own payments. To the extent that these actions can be taken *without harming the return* associated with the management of these accounts, they should be carried out. So when taking actions to reduce the inventory conversion period, a firm should be careful to *avoid inventory shortages that could cause "good" customers to buy from competitors;* when taking actions to speed up the collection of receivables, a firm should be careful to *maintain good relations with its "good" credit customers;* and when taking actions to lengthen the payables deferral period, a firm should be careful *not to harm its own credit reputation.*

We can illustrate the benefits of shortening the cash conversion cycle by looking again at Unilate Textiles. Suppose Unilate must spend an average of $12.30 on materials and labor to manufacture its products, which are sold for $15.00 per unit. To generate the $1,500 million sales realized in 2000, Unilate turned out 277,778 items per day. At this rate of production, it must invest $3.417 million = $12.30 × 277,778 units each day to support the manufacturing process. This investment must be financed for 113.4 days—the length of the cash conversion cycle—so the company's working capital financing needs will be $387.5 million = 113.4 × $3.417 million. If Unilate could reduce the cash conversion cycle to 93.4 days—say, by deferring payment of its accounts payable an additional 20 days or by speeding up either the production process or the collection of its receivables—it could reduce its working capital financing requirements by $68.3 million = 20 days × $3.417 million. We see, then, that actions that affect the inventory conversion period, the receivables collection period, and the payables deferral period all affect the cash conversion cycle; hence they influence the firm's need for current assets and current asset financing.

Working Capital Investment and Financing Policies

Working capital policy involves two basic questions: (1) What is the appropriate level for current assets, both in total and by specific accounts? and (2) How should current assets be financed?

Alternative Current Asset Investment Policies

Exhibit 700.5 shows three alternative policies regarding the total amount of current assets carried. Essentially, these policies differ in that different amounts of current assets are carried to support any given level of sales. The line with the steepest slope represents a **relaxed current asset investment** (or "fat cat") **policy**, where relatively large amounts of cash, marketable securities, and inventories are carried and where sales are stimulated by the use of a credit policy that provides liberal financing to customers and a corresponding high level of receivables. Conversely, with the **restricted current asset investment** (or "lean-and-mean") **policy**, the holdings of cash, securities, inventories, and receivables are minimized. The **moderate current asset investment policy** is between the two extremes.

Under conditions of certainty—when sales, costs, lead times, payment periods, and so on, are known for sure—all firms would hold only minimal levels of current assets. Any larger amounts would increase the need for external funding without a corresponding increase in profits, while any smaller holdings would involve late payments to labor and suppliers and lost sales due to inventory shortages and an overly restrictive credit policy.

However, the picture changes when uncertainty is introduced. Here the firm requires some minimum amount of cash and inventories based on expected payments, expected sales, expected order lead times, and so on, plus additional

Exhibit 700.5 *Alternative Current Asset Investment Policies (millions of dollars)*

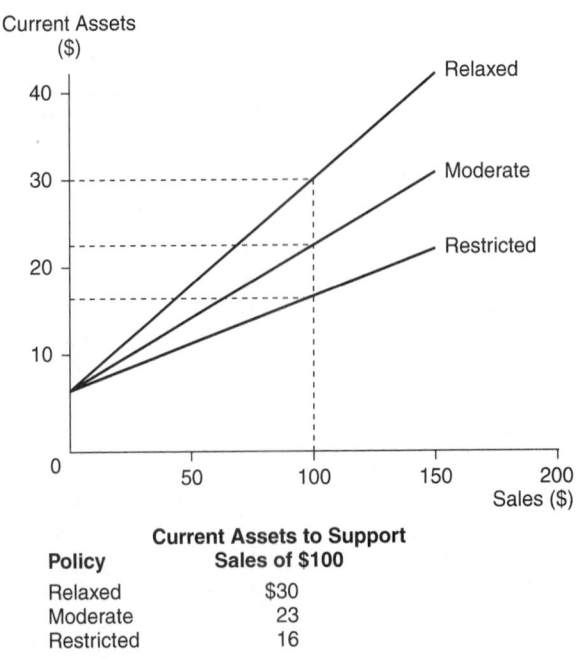

amounts, or *safety stocks,* which enable it to deal with departures from the expected values. Similarly, accounts receivable levels are determined by credit terms, and the tougher the credit terms, the lower the receivables for any given level of sales. With a restricted current asset investment policy, the firm would hold minimal levels of safety stocks for cash and inventories, and it would have a tight credit policy even though this would mean running the risk of losing sales. A restricted, lean-and-mean current asset investment policy generally provides the highest expected return on investment, but it entails the greatest risk, while the reverse is true under a relaxed policy. The moderate policy falls in between the two extremes in terms of both expected risk and return.

In terms of the cash conversion cycle, a restricted investment policy would tend to reduce the inventory conversion and receivables collection periods, which would result in a relatively short cash conversion cycle. Conversely, a relaxed policy would create higher levels of inventories and receivables, longer inventory conversion and receivables collection periods, and a relatively long cash conversion cycle. A moderate policy would produce a cash conversion cycle somewhere between the two extremes.

Alternative Current Asset Financing Policies

Most businesses experience seasonal fluctuations, cyclical fluctuations, or both. For example, construction firms have peaks in the spring and summer, retailers peak around Christmas, and the manufacturers who supply both construction companies and retailers follow similar patterns. Similarly, virtually all businesses must build up current assets when the economy is strong, but they then sell off inventories and have net reductions of receivables when the economy slacks off. Still, current assets rarely drop to zero, and this realization has led to the development of the idea that some current assets should be considered **permanent current assets** because their levels remain stable no matter the seasonal or economic conditions. Applying this idea to Unilate Textiles, Exhibit 700.3 (presented earlier) suggests that, at this stage in its life, Unilate's total assets are growing at a 10% rate, from $845.0 million at the end of 2000 to a projected $929.5 million by the end of 2001, but seasonal fluctuations are expected to push total assets up to $1,100.0 million during the firm's peak season in 2001. Assuming Unilate's permanent assets grow continuously, and at the *same rate,* throughout the year, then 9/12ths (75%) of the 10% growth in assets will accrue by the end of September and permanent assets would equal $908.4 million = $845.0 million + (9/12)($929.5 million − $845.0 million). But the actual level of assets is expected to be $1,100.0 million because this is Unilate's peak season. So at the end of September, Unilate's total assets of $1,100.0 million consist of $908.4 million of permanent assets and $191.6 million = $1,100.0 million − $908.4 million of seasonal, or **temporary, current assets.** Unilate's temporary current assets fluctuate from zero during the slow season in December to nearly $192 million during the peak season in September. Therefore, temporary current assets are those amounts of current assets that vary with respect to the seasonal or economic conditions of a firm. The manner in which the permanent and temporary current assets are financed is called the firm's *current asset financing policy.* Three approaches are described next, including the maturity matching approach, aggressive approach, and conservative approach.

Maturity Matching, or "Self-Liquidating," Approach

The **maturity matching, or "self-liquidating," approach** calls for matching asset and liability maturities as shown in Panel a of Exhibit 700.6. This strategy minimizes the risk that the firm will be unable to pay off its maturing obligations *if* the liquidations of the assets can be controlled to occur on or before the maturities of the obligations. To illustrate, suppose Unilate borrows on a one-year basis and uses the funds obtained to build and equip a plant. Cash flows from the plant (profits plus depreciation) would not be sufficient to pay off the loan at the end of only one year, so the loan would have to be renewed. If for some reason the lender refused to renew the loan, then Unilate would have problems. If the plant is financed with long-term debt, however, the required loan payments are better matched with cash flows from operations, and the problem of renewal will not arise.

At the limit, a firm could attempt to match exactly the maturity structure of its assets and liabilities. Inventory expected to be sold in 30 days could be financed with a 30-day bank loan; a machine expected to last for five years could be financed by a five-year loan; a 20-year building could be financed by a 20-year mortgage bond; and so forth. Actually, of course, two factors prevent this exact maturity matching: (1) there is uncertainty about the lives of assets, and (2) some common equity must be used, and common equity has no maturity. To illustrate the uncertainty factor, Unilate might finance inventories with a 30-day loan, expecting to sell the inventories and to use the cash generated to retire the loan. But if sales were slow, the cash would not be forthcoming, and the use of short-term credit could end up causing a problem (for example, look at the cash conversion cycle computed for Unilate in the previous section). Still, if Unilate makes an attempt to match asset and liability maturities, we would define this as a *moderate current asset financing policy.*

Exhibit 700.6 *Alternative Current Asset Financing Policies*

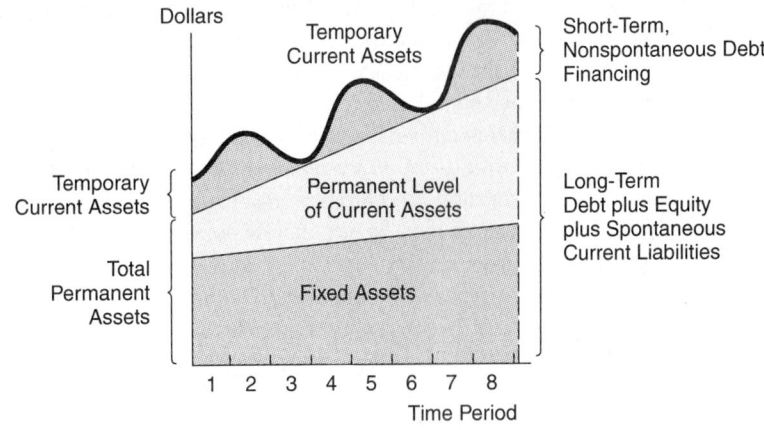

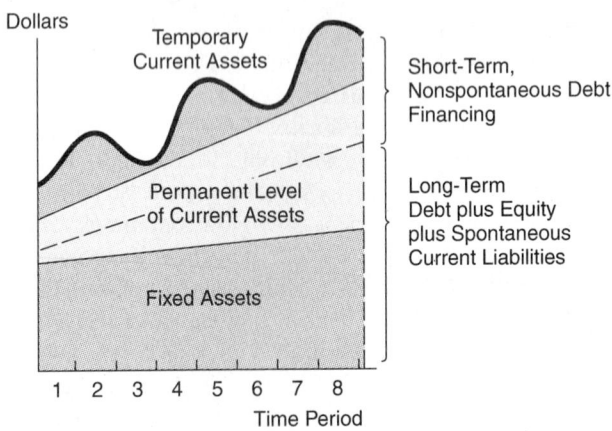

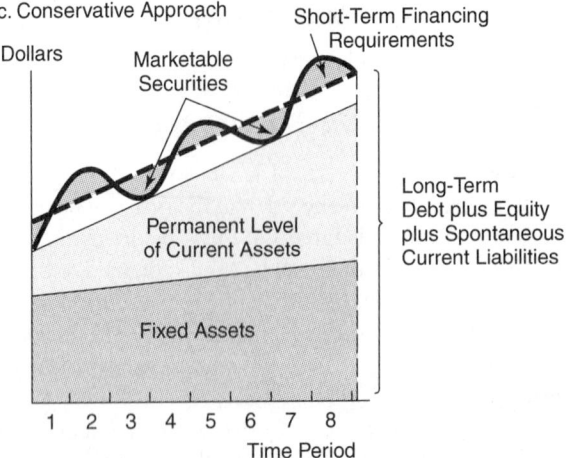

Aggressive Approach

Panel b of Exhibit 700.6 illustrates the **aggressive approach,** used by a firm that (1) finances all of its temporary assets with short-term, nonspontaneous debt and (2) finances its fixed assets with long-term capital, but some of the remainder of its permanent current assets is financed with short-term, nonspontaneous credit. A look back at Exhibit 700.3 shows that Unilate actually follows this strategy. Unilate has $499.9 million in permanent current assets ($908.4 million in permanent assets less $408.5 million fixed assets) projected for September 2001, so its temporary current assets must be $191.6 million = $691.5 million − $499.9 million. However, the firm is projected to have $129.0 million in notes payable as well as temporary financing equal to about $100.0 million from peak levels of accounts payable and accruals (payables are projected to be $60.0 million higher than at the end of 2000, and accruals are projected to be $40.0 million higher). Thus, Unilate's level of temporary financing, which is $229.0 million, exceeds its level of temporary current assets, which is $191.6 million, so some part of its permanent assets is financed with temporary capital.

Returning to Exhibit 700.6, note that we used the term *relatively* in the title for Panel b because there can be different *degrees* of aggressiveness. For example, the dashed line in Panel b could have been drawn *below* the line designating fixed assets, indicating that all of the permanent current assets and part of the fixed assets were financed with short-term credit; this would be a highly aggressive, extremely nonconservative position, and the firm would be very much subject to dangers from rising interest rates as well as to loan renewal problems. However, short-term debt often is cheaper than long-term debt, and some firms are willing to sacrifice safety for the chance of higher profits.

Conservative Approach

As shown in Panel c of Exhibit 700.6, the dashed line could also be drawn *above* the line designating permanent current assets, indicating that permanent capital is being used to finance all permanent asset requirements and also to meet some or all of the seasonal, temporary demands. In the situation depicted in our graph, the firm uses a small amount of short-term, nonspontaneous credit to meet its peak requirements, but it also meets a part of its seasonal needs by "storing liquidity" in the form of marketable securities during the off-season. The humps above the dashed line represent short-term financing; the troughs below the dashed line represent short-term security holdings. Panel c represents the **conservative approach,** which is a very safe current asset financing policy that generally is not as profitable as the other two approaches.

Advantages and Disadvantages of Short-Term Financing

The three possible financing policies or approaches described in the previous section were distinguished by the relative amounts of short-term debt used under each policy. The aggressive policy calls for the greatest use of short-term debt, while the conservative policy requires the least; maturity matching falls in between. Although using short-term credit generally is riskier than using long-term credit, short-term credit does have some significant advantages. The pros and cons of short-term financing are considered in this section.

Speed

A short-term loan can be obtained much faster than long-term credit. Lenders will insist on a more thorough financial examination before extending long-term credit, and the loan agreement will have to be spelled out in considerable detail because much can happen during the life of a 10- or 20-year loan. Therefore, if funds are needed in a hurry, the firm should look to short-term sources.

Flexibility

If the needs for funds are seasonal or cyclical, a firm might not want to commit itself to long-term debt for three reasons. First, the costs associated with issuing long-term debt are significantly greater than the costs of getting short-term credit. Second, some long-term debts carry expensive penalties for prepayments (paying prior to maturity). Accordingly, if a firm thinks its need for funds will diminish in the near future, it should choose short-term debt for the flexibility it provides. Third, long-term loan agreements always contain provisions, or covenants, that constrain the firm's future actions. Short-term credit agreements generally are much less onerous in this regard.

Cost of Long-Term Versus Short-Term Debt

The yield curve normally is upward sloping, indicating that interest rates generally are lower on short-term than on long-term debt. Thus, under normal conditions, interest costs at the time the funds are obtained will be lower if the firm borrows on a short-term rather than on a long-term basis.

Risk of Long-Term Versus Short-Term Debt

Even though short-term debt is often less expensive than long-term debt, short-term credit subjects the firm to more risk than does long-term financing. This occurs for two reasons: (1) If a firm borrows on a long-term basis, its interest costs will be relatively stable, perhaps even fixed, over time, but if it uses short-term credit, its interest expense will fluctuate widely, at times reaching quite high levels. For example, the rate banks charge large corporations for short-term debt more than tripled over a two-year period in the early 1980s, rising from 6.25 to 21%. Many firms that had borrowed heavily on a short-term basis simply could not meet their rising interest costs, and as a result bankruptcies hit record levels during that period. Similarly, in 1994, because the Federal Reserve increased rates six times during the year, short-term rates increased by more than 3%, which created a significant burden for many firms. (2) If a firm borrows heavily on a short-term basis, it could find itself unable to repay this debt, and it might be in such a weak financial position that the lender will not extend the loan; this too could force the firm into bankruptcy. **Braniff Airlines** failed during a credit crunch in the 1980s for this very reason.

Multinational Working Capital Management

For the most part, the techniques used to manage short-term assets and liabilities in multinational corporations are the same as those used in purely domestic corporations. But multinational corporations face a far more complex task because they operate in many different business cultures, political environments, economic conditions, and so forth. Six factors complicate managerial finance in general in the international business arena: (1) different currency denominations, (2) differences in economic and legal environments, (3) language differences, (4) cultural differences, (5) governmental role, and (6) political risk. Difficulties with each of these factors are more acute when managing working capital internationally because decisions made in the short run can have significant consequences on the long-run survival of the firm and such decisions are more difficult to adjust or reverse when rules and regulations and business cultures differ significantly from one business setting to another.

The results of a recent study provide some indication of how working capital policies of U.S. firms and European firms differ.[2] First, the average cash conversion cycle of European firms (about 263 days) was more than twice the average cash conversion cycle of U.S. firms (about 116 days). A possible explanation for this disparity is that European firms had much higher growth rates than their U.S. counterparts. Second, it appears from the results of the study that U.S. firms follow much more conservative working capital policies than European firms. The average current ratio and the average quick ratio proved to be significantly greater for U.S. firms than for European firms, which suggests that corporations in the United States use significantly more long-term financing alternatives than corporations in Europe (remember that when the current ratio equals to 1.0, current assets equal current liabilities). Although a more in-depth study is needed to determine why U.S. firms seem to follow more conservative working capital policies than European firms, one possible explanation might be found in the differences that are apparent in the banking systems in Europe and in the United States. U.S. financial institutions generally are at a competitive disadvantage in the global arena because they are subject to more restrictions and regulations than banking organizations in other countries. Foreign banks generally can branch with little or no restrictions and are allowed, in many cases, to own corporations to which they also lend funds. For these reasons, European banks often have close relationships with their debtor corporations; thus, they tend to be more willing to provide short-term, risky debt than we observe in U.S. banking organizations.

Managing Short-Term Assets

Working Capital Management Policies

All else equal, the riskiness of the portfolio of assets held by a firm is based on the combination of short- and long-term investments (assets) the firm makes. The relative amount that is invested in short-term assets is a function of decisions that are made concerning the management of cash and marketable securities, accounts receivable, and inventories. Of these three assets, we generally consider cash and marketable securities to be least risky, or most *liquid*. But the degree of risk can vary for either accounts receivable or inventories, depending on the general characteristics of the firm's working capital policy. For example, we generally view receivables as relatively safe assets because they represent sales the firm expects to collect in the future. But a firm with an overly aggressive, or relaxed, credit policy might have many slow payers or bad-debt customers that make its receivables extremely risky, thus fairly *illiquid*.

In this section, we discuss working capital management policies with respect to the current (short-term) assets of the firm. Keep in mind that, although short-term assets generally are safer than long-term assets, they earn a lower rate of return. Thus, all else equal, firms that hold greater amounts of short-term assets are considered less risky than firms that hold greater amounts of long-term assets; at the same time, firms with more short-term assets earn lower returns than firms with more long-term assets. Consequently, financial managers are faced with a dilemma of whether to forgo higher returns to attain lower risk or to forgo lower risk to achieve higher returns. In general, however, we will see that some amount of short-term assets is required to maintain normal operations.

Cash Management

Maximizing shareholders' value is based on cash flows. Thus, managing cash flows is an extremely important task for a financial manager. Part of this task is determining how much cash a firm should have on hand at any time to ensure normal business operations continue uninterrupted. In this section, we discuss some of the factors that affect the amount of cash firms hold, and we describe some of the cash management techniques currently used by businesses.

For the purposes of our discussion, the term *cash* refers to the funds a firm holds that can be used for immediate disbursement—this includes the amount a firm holds in its checking account as well as the amount of actual coin and currency it holds. Cash is a "nonearning, or idle, asset" that is required to pay bills. When possible, cash should be "put to work" by investing in assets that have positive expected returns. Thus, the goal of the cash manager is to minimize the amount of cash the firm must hold for use in conducting its normal business activities, yet, at the same time, to have sufficient cash to (1) pay suppliers, (2) maintain the firm's credit rating, and (3) meet unexpected cash needs.

Firms hold cash for the following reasons.

1. Cash balances are necessary in business operations because payments must be made in cash, and receipts are deposited in a cash account. Cash balances associated with routine payments and collections are known as **transactions balances.**

2. A bank often requires a firm to maintain a **compensating balance** on deposit to help offset the costs of providing services such as check clearing and cash management advice.

3. Because cash inflows and cash outflows are somewhat unpredictable, firms generally hold some cash in reserve for random, unforeseen fluctuations in cash flows. These *safety stocks* are called **precautionary balances**—the less predictable the firm's cash flows, the larger such balances should be. However, if the firm has easy access to borrowed funds—that is, if it can borrow on short notice (for example, via a line of credit at the bank)—its need for precautionary balances is reduced.

4. Sometimes cash balances are held to enable the firm to take advantage of bargain purchases that might arise. These funds are called **speculative balances.** As with precautionary balances, though, firms that have easy access to borrowed funds are likely to rely on their ability to borrow quickly rather than to rely on cash balances for speculative purposes.

Although the cash accounts of most firms can be thought of as consisting of transactions, compensating, precautionary, and speculative balances, we cannot calculate the amount needed for each purpose, sum them, and produce a total desired cash balance because the same money often serves more than one purpose. For instance, precautionary and speculative balances can also be used to satisfy compensating balance requirements. Firms do, however, consider all four factors when establishing their target cash positions. Section 770 presents quantitative techniques in cash management.

In addition to the four motives above, a firm maintains cash balances to preserve its credit rating by keeping its liquidity position in line with those of other firms in the industry. A strong credit rating enables the firm both to purchase goods from suppliers on favorable terms and to maintain an ample line of credit with its bank.

The Cash Budget

Perhaps the most critical ingredient to proper cash management is the ability to estimate the cash flows of the firm so the firm can make plans to borrow when cash is deficient or to invest when cash is in excess of what is needed. Without a doubt, financial managers will agree that the most important tool for managing cash is the cash budget (forecast). The cash budget helps management plan investment and borrowing strategies, and it also is used to provide feedback and control to improve the efficiency of cash management in the future.

The firm estimates its general needs for cash as a part of its overall budgeting, or forecasting, process. First, the firm forecasts its operating activities such as expenses and revenues for the period in question. Then, the financing and investment activities necessary to attain that level of operations must be forecasted. Such forecasts entail the construction of *pro forma* financial statements. The information provided from the *pro forma* balance sheet and income statement is combined with projections about the delay in collecting accounts receivable, the delay in paying suppliers and employees, tax payment dates, dividend and interest payment dates, and so on. All of this information is summarized in the **cash budget**, which shows the firm's projected cash inflows and cash outflows over some specified period. Generally, firms use a monthly cash budget forecasted over the next year plus a more detailed daily or weekly cash budget for the coming month. The monthly cash budgets are used for planning purposes and the daily or weekly budgets are used for actual cash control. Cash budget was fully discussed in Module 600 Accounting, Section 650.

Cash Management Techniques

Most cash management activities are performed jointly by the firm and its primary bank, but the financial manager ultimately is responsible for the effectiveness of the cash management program. Effective cash management encompasses proper management of both the cash inflows and the cash outflows of a firm, which entails consideration of the factors discussed next.

Cash Flow Synchronization

It would be ideal if the receipt of a cash payment from a customer occurred at exactly the same time a bill needs to be paid; that portion paid out would never be idle and any excess could be invested quickly to reduce the time it is idle. Recognizing this point, companies try to arrange it so that cash inflows and cash outflows are matched as well as possible—customers are billed so their billing cycles coordinate with when the firm pays its own bills. Having **synchronized cash flows** enables a firm to reduce its cash balances, decrease its bank loans, lower interest expenses, and boost profits. The more predictable the timing of the cash flows, the greater the synchronization that can be attained—utilities and credit card companies generally have a high degree of cash flow synchronization.

Check-Clearing Process

When a customer writes and mails a check, this does *not* mean that the funds are immediately available to the receiving firm. Most of us have been told by someone that "the check is in the mail," and we also have deposited a check in an account and then been told that we cannot write checks against the deposit until the **check-clearing process** has been completed. Our bank must first make sure that the deposited check is good and then receive funds itself from the customer's bank before it will give us cash.

A check must first be delivered through the mail and then be cleared through the banking system before the money can be put to use. Checks received from customers in distant cities are especially subject to delays because of mail time and also because more parties are involved in the check-clearing process. For example, assume that you receive a check and deposit it in your bank. Your bank must send the check to the bank on which it was drawn. Only when this latter bank transfers funds to your bank are the funds available for you to use. If a check is deposited in the same bank on which it was drawn, that bank merely transfers funds by bookkeeping entries from one of its depositors to another. But most deposited checks are drawn from outside banks, so the verification, or clearing process, generally is handled by a check-clearing system, termed a *clearinghouse,* set up by the Federal Reserve or a network of banks in a particular region. The length of time required for checks to clear is a function of the distance between the payer's (check writer) bank and the payee's (depositor) bank. In the case of private clearinghouses, it can range from one to three days. The maximum time required for checks to clear through the Federal Reserve System is two days, but mail delays can slow down things on each end of the Fed's involvement in the process.

Using Float

Float is defined as the difference between the balance shown in a firm's (or individual's) checkbook and the balance on the bank's records. Suppose a firm writes, on average, checks in the amount of $5,000 each day, and it normally takes six days from the time the check is mailed until it is cleared and deducted from the firm's bank account. This will cause the firm's own checkbook to show a balance equal to $30,000 = $5,000 × 6 days smaller than the balance on the bank's records; this difference is called **disbursement float.** Now suppose the firm also receives checks in the amount of $5,000 daily, but it loses four days while they are being deposited and cleared. This will result in $20,000 of **collections float.** In total, the firm's **net float**—the difference between $30,000 positive disbursement float and the $20,000 negative collections float—will be $10,000, which means the balance the bank shows in the firm's checking account is $10,000 greater than the balance the firm shows in its own checkbook.

Delays that cause float arise because it takes time for checks (1) to travel through the mail (*mail delay*), (2) to be processed by the receiving firm (*processing delay*), and (3) to clear through the banking system (*clearing, or availability, delay*). Basically, the size of a firm's net float is a function of its ability to speed up collections on checks received and to slow down collections on checks written. Efficient firms go to great lengths to speed up the processing of incoming checks, thus putting the funds to work faster, and they try to delay their own payments as long as possible.

Acceleration of Receipts

A firm cannot use customers' payments until they are received *and* converted into a spendable form, such as cash or an increase in a checking account balance. Thus, it would benefit the firm to accelerate the collection of customers' payments and conversion of those payments into cash. Although some of the delays that cause float cannot be controlled directly, the techniques described next are used to manage collections:

LOCKBOXES   A **lockbox arrangement** requires customers to send their payments to a post office box located in the area near where they live rather than directly to the firm. The firm arranges for a local bank to collect the checks from the post office box, perhaps several times a day, and to immediately deposit them into the company's checking account. By having lockboxes close to the customers, a firm can reduce float because, at the very least, (1) the mail delay is less than if the payment had to travel farther and (2) checks are cleared faster because the banks the checks are written on are in the same Federal Reserve district; thus, fewer parties are involved in the clearing process.

PREAUTHORIZED DEBITS   If a firm receives regular, repetitious payments from its customers, it might want to establish a **preauthorized debit system** (sometimes called preauthorized payments). With this arrangement, the collecting firm and its customer (paying firm) enter into an agreement whereby the paying firm's bank periodically transfers funds from the paying firm's account to the collecting firm's account, even if that account is located at another bank. Preauthorized debiting accelerates the transfer of funds because mail and check-clearing delays are completely eliminated, and the processing delay is reduced substantially.

CONCENTRATION BANKING   **Concentration banking** is a cash management arrangement used to mobilize funds from decentralized receiving locations, whether they are lockboxes or decentralized company locations, into one or more central cash pools. The cash manager then uses these pools for short-term investing or reallocation among the firm's various bank accounts. By pooling its cash, the firm is able to take maximum advantage of economies of scale in cash management and investment. Often commissions are less per dollar on large investments, and there are instances where investments of larger dollar amounts earn higher returns than smaller investments.

Disbursement Control

Accelerating collections represents one side of cash management, and controlling funds outflows, or disbursements, represents the other side. Three methods commonly used to control disbursements include the following.

PAYABLES CONCENTRATION   Centralizing the processing of payables permits the financial manager to evaluate the payments coming due for the entire firm and to schedule the availability of funds to meet these needs on a company-wide basis, and it also permits more efficient monitoring of payables and the effects of float. A disadvantage to a centralized disbursement system is that regional offices might not be able to make prompt payment for services rendered, which can create ill will and raise the company's operating costs. But as firms become more electronically proficient, the centralization of disbursements can be coordinated more effectively and such situations should be reduced substantially.

ZERO-BALANCE ACCOUNTS   A **zero-balance account (ZBA)** is a special disbursement account that has a balance equal to zero when there is no disbursement activity. Typically, a firm establishes several ZBAs in its concentration bank and funds them from a master account. As checks are presented to a ZBA for payment, funds are automatically transferred from the master account.

CONTROLLED DISBURSEMENT ACCOUNTS Whereas ZBAs typically are established at concentration banks, **controlled disbursement accounts (CDA)** can be set up at any bank. Such accounts are not funded until the day's checks are presented against the account. The firm relies on the bank that maintains the CDA to provide information in the morning (before 11 A.M. New York time) concerning the total amount of the checks that will be presented for payment that day. This permits the financial manager (1) to transfer funds to the controlled disbursement account to cover the checks presented for payment or (2) to invest excess cash at midday, when money market trading is at a peak.

Marketable Securities

Realistically, the management of cash and marketable securities cannot be separated—management of one implies management of the other because the amount of marketable securities held by a firm depends on its short-term cash needs.

Rationale for Holding Marketable Securities

Near-cash assets include U.S. treasury bills, commercial paper, negotiable CDs, money market mutual funds, and eurodollar time deposits.

Marketable securities, or *near-cash* assets, are extremely liquid, short-term investments that permit the firm to earn positive returns on cash that is not needed to pay bills immediately but will be needed sometime in the near term, perhaps in a few days, weeks, or months. Although such investments typically provide much lower yields than operating assets, nearly every large firm has them. The two basic reasons for owning marketable securities are as follows.

1. Marketable securities serve as a *substitute for cash balances*. Firms often hold portfolios of marketable securities, liquidating part of the portfolio to increase the cash account when cash is needed because the *marketable securities offer a place to temporarily put cash balances to work earning a positive return*. In such situations, the marketable securities could be used as a substitute for transactions balances, for precautionary balances, for speculative balances, or for all three.
2. Marketable securities are also used as a *temporary investment* (a) to finance seasonal or cyclical operations and (b) to amass funds to meet financial requirements in the near future. For example, if the firm has a conservative financing policy, then its long-term capital will exceed its permanent assets, and marketable securities will be held when inventories and receivables are low.

Characteristics of Marketable Securities

A wide variety of securities is available to firms that choose to hold marketable securities. But the characteristics generally associated with marketable securities are as follows.

1. **Maturity.** Firms hold marketable securities in order to *temporarily* invest cash that otherwise would be idle in the short run. Therefore, marketable securities are short-term investments; often they are held only for a few days or weeks. If the cash budget indicates the funds are not needed in the foreseeable future, then longer-term investments, which generally earn higher returns, should be used.
2. **Risk.** An equation for determining the nominal interest rate is:

$$k_{Nom} = k^* + IP + DRP + LP + MRP$$

Here k^* is the real risk-free rate, IP is a premium for expected inflation, DRP is the default risk premium, LP is the liquidity (or marketability) risk premium, and MRP is the maturity (or interest rate) risk premium. Also, remember that the risk-free rate, k_{RF}, is equal to $k^* + IP$, and a U.S. Treasury bill comes closest to the risk-free rate. For other instruments considered appropriate as marketable securities, the default and liquidity risks are small, and the interest-rate risk is negligible. These risks are small because marketable securities mature in the short term, and the short run is less uncertain than the long run. Also, recall that prices of long-term investments, such as bonds, are much more sensitive to changes in interest rates than are prices of short-term investments. In general, then, the total risk associated with a portfolio of marketable securities (short term) is less than the total risk associated with a portfolio of long-term investments.

3. **Liquidity.** We generally judge an asset's *marketability* according to how quickly and easily it can be bought and sold in the financial markets. If an asset can be sold easily on short notice for close to its original purchase price, it is said to be *liquid*. Because marketable securities are held as a *substitute* for cash and as a *temporary* investment, such instruments should be very liquid.
4. **Return (Yield).** Because the marketable securities portfolio generally is composed of highly liquid, short-term securities with low risks, the returns associated with such investments are relatively low when compared to other investments. But given the purpose of the marketable securities portfolio, treasurers should not sacrifice safety for higher rates of return.

Credit Management

If you ask financial managers whether they would prefer to sell their products for cash or for credit, you would expect them to respond by saying something like this: "*If sales levels are not affected,* cash sales are preferred because payment is certain and immediate and because the costs of granting credit and maintaining accounts receivable would be eliminated." *Ideally,* then, firms would prefer to sell for cash only. So why do firms sell for credit? The primary reason most firms offer credit sales is because their competitors offer credit. Consider what you would do if you had the opportunity to purchase the same product for the same price from two different firms, but one firm required cash payment at the time of the purchase while the other firm allowed you to pay for the product one month after the purchase without any additional cost. From which firm would you purchase? Like you, firms prefer to delay their payments, especially if there are no additional costs associated with the delay.

Effective credit management is extremely important because too much credit is very costly in terms of the investment in, and maintenance of, accounts receivables, while too little credit could result in the loss of profitable sales. Carrying receivables has both direct and indirect costs, but it also has an important benefit—granting credit should increase profits. Thus, to maximize shareholders' wealth, a financial manager needs to understand how to effectively manage the firm's credit activities.

In this section, we discuss (1) the factors considered important when determining the appropriate credit policy for a firm, (2) procedures for monitoring the credit policy to ensure it is being administered properly, and (3) how to evaluate whether credit policy changes will be beneficial to the firm.

Credit Policy

The major controllable variables that affect demand for a company's products are sales prices, product quality, advertising, and the firm's **credit policy.** The firm's credit policy, in turn, includes the factors we discuss next.

1. **Credit standards** refer to the strength and creditworthiness a customer must exhibit in order to qualify for credit. The firm's credit standards are applied to determine which customers qualify for the regular credit terms and how much credit each customer should receive. The major factors considered when setting credit standards relate to the likelihood that a given customer will pay slowly or perhaps even end up as a bad debt loss. Determining the credit quality, or creditworthiness, of a customer probably is the most difficult part of credit management. But credit evaluation is a well-established practice and a good credit manager can make reasonably accurate judgments of the probability of default exhibited by different classes of customers by examining a firm's current financial position and evaluating factors that might affect the financial position in the future.
2. **Terms of credit** are the conditions of the credit sale, especially with regard to the payment arrangements. Firms need to determine when the **credit period** begins, how long the customer has to pay for credit purchases before the account is considered delinquent, and whether a cash discount for early payment should be offered. An examination of the credit terms offered by firms in the United States would show great variety across industries—credit terms range from cash before delivery (CBD) and cash on delivery (COD) to offering **cash discounts** for early payment. For example, a firm that offers terms of 2/10 net 30 gives its customers a 2% discount from the purchase price if the bill is paid on or before the tenth day of the billing cycle; otherwise the entire bill (the net amount) is due by Day 30. Due to the competitive nature of trade credit, most financial managers follow the norm of the industry in which they operate when setting credit terms.

3. **Collection policy** refers to the procedures the firm follows to collect its credit accounts. The firm needs to determine when and how notification of the credit sale will be conveyed to the buyer. The quicker a customer receives an invoice, the sooner the bill *can* be paid. In today's world, firms have turned more to the use of electronics to "send" invoices to customers. One of the most important collection policy decisions is how the past-due accounts should be handled. For example, notification might be sent to customers when a bill is 10 days past due; a more severe notice, followed by a telephone call, might be used if payment is not received within 30 days; and the account might be turned over to a collection agency after 90 days.

Receivables Monitoring

Once a firm sets its credit policy, it wants to operate within the policy's limits. Thus, it is important that a firm examine its receivables periodically to determine whether customers' payment patterns have changed such that credit operations are outside the credit policy limits. For instance, if the balance in receivables increases either because the amount of "bad," or uncollectible, sales increases or because the average time it takes to collect existing credit sales increases, the firm should consider making changes in its credit policy. **Receivables monitoring** refers to the process of evaluating the credit policy to determine if a shift in the customers' payment patterns has occurred.

Traditionally, firms have monitored accounts receivables by using methods that measure the amount of time credit remains outstanding. Two such methods are the *days sales outstanding (DSO)* and the *aging schedule*:

Days Sales Outstanding (DSO)

Days sales outstanding (DSO), which is sometimes called the *average collection period*, represents the average time it takes to collect credit accounts. DSO is computed by dividing *annual* credit sales by *daily* credit sales. For example, we found the receivables collection period, or DSO, for Unilate was 43.2 days in 2000. The DSO of 43.2 days can be compared with the credit terms offered by Unilate. If Unilate's credit terms are 2/10 net 30, then we know there are customers that are delinquent when paying their accounts. In fact, if many customers are paying within 10 days to take advantage of the discount, the others would, on average, have to be taking much longer than 43.2 days. One way to check this possibility is to use an aging schedule as described next.

Aging Schedule

An **aging schedule** is a breakdown of a firm's receivables by age of account. Exhibit 700.7 contains the December 31, 2000, aging schedule for Unilate Textiles. The standard format for aging schedules generally includes age categories broken down by month because banks and financial analysts usually want companies to report their receivables ages in this form. However, more precision, thus better monitoring information, can be attained by using narrower age categories (for example, one or two weeks).

According to Unilate's aging schedule, only 40% of the credit sales in December 2000 were collected within the credit period of 30 days; thus, 60% of the credit sales collections were delinquent. Some of the payments were delinquent by only a few days, while others were delinquent by three to four times the 30-day credit period.

Management should constantly monitor the days sales outstanding and the aging schedule to detect trends, to see how the firm's collection experience compares with its credit terms, and to see how effectively the credit department

Exhibit 700.7 *Unilate Textiles: Receivables Aging Schedule for 2000*

Age of Account (in days)	Net Amount Outstanding	Fraction of Total Receivables	Average Days
0–30	$ 72,000	40%	18
31–60	90,000	50	55
61–90	10,800	6	77
More than 90	7,200	4	97
	$180,000	100%	

DSO = 0.40(18 days) + 0.50(55 days) + 0.06(77 days) + 0.04(97 days)
= 43.2 days

is operating in comparison with other firms in the industry. If the DSO starts to lengthen or if the aging schedule begins to show an increasing percentage of past-due accounts, then the firm's credit policy might need to be tightened.

We must be careful when interpreting changes in DSO or the aging schedule, however, because if a firm experiences sharp seasonal variations, or if it is growing rapidly, then both measures could be distorted. Therefore, *a change in either the DSO or the aging schedule should be taken as a signal to investigate further, but not necessarily as a sign that the firm's credit policy has weakened.* If a firm generally experiences widely fluctuating sales patterns, some type of modified aging schedule should be used to correctly account for these fluctuations.[3] Still, days sales outstanding and the aging schedule are useful tools for reviewing the credit department's performance.

Analyzing Proposed Changes in Credit Policy

The key question when deciding on a proposed credit policy change is this: Will the firm realize a net benefit? Unless the added benefits expected from a credit policy change exceed the added costs, the policy change should *not* be made.

To illustrate how we can evaluate whether a proposed change in a firm's credit policy is appropriate, let's examine what would happen if Unilate Textiles makes changes to reduce its average collection period. Assume that Unilate's financial manager has proposed that this task be accomplished in 2001 by (1) billing customers sooner, and exerting more pressure on delinquent customers to pay their bills, and (2) tightening existing credit standards slightly—the credit department will more closely examine the financial positions of credit customers and suspend the credit of customers who are considered "habitually delinquent." It is apparent that both of these actions will result in a direct increase in the costs associated with Unilate's credit policy; in fact, credit evaluation and collection costs are expected to increase from $16 million to $17 million. At the same time, even though Unilate has an extremely loyal customer base, it is expected that $2 million in annual sales will be lost to competitors because some customers will have their credit decreased or even eliminated. But because the credit policy changes will have little, if any, effect on the "good" credit customers, the financial manager does not expect there to be a change in the proportion of customers (20%) who currently take advantage of the cash discount. If the proposed credit policy changes are approved, the financial manager believes the average collection period, or DSO, for receivables can be reduced from 43.2 days to 35.6 days—this is more in line with the credit terms offered by Unilate (2/10 net 30), and it is closer to the industry average of 32.1 days. Also, if the average collection period is reduced, the amount "carried" in accounts receivable is reduced, which means less funds are "tied up" in receivables. Exhibit 700.8 summarizes the information about Unilate's existing credit policy and the financial manager's proposed changes.

Should Unilate adopt the financial manager's proposal? To answer this question, we need to compute the marginal costs and benefits associated with changing the existing credit policy to determine if the proposal is more advantageous than the current policy. The obvious costs to the firm include the $2 million decrease in sales and the $1 million increase

Exhibit 700.8 Unilate Textiles: Existing and Proposed Credit Policies (millions of dollars)—Expected for 2001

Policy	Existing Policy	Proposed Policy
Credit terms	2/10 net 30	2/10 net 30
Gross credit sales[a]	$1,656.6	$1,654.6
Net credit sales (S)	$1,650.0	$1,648.0
Cash discount[b]	$6.6	$6.6
Variable cost ratio[c] (V)	82%	82%
Bad debts	$ 0	$ 0
Credit evaluation and collection costs	$ 16	$ 17
Days sales outstanding (DSO)	43.2 days	35.6 days

[a]We determined that Unilate's 2001 *net* forecasted sales is $1,650 million, which represents what the firm expects to collect from credit sales, net of cash discounts. The gross sales, which includes cash discounts, can be computed as follows:

Net sales = 0.80 (Gross sales) + (0.20) (1 − 0.02) (Gross sales)

= (Gross sales) [0.80 + (0.20) (0.98)] = $1,650 million

Gross sales = $\dfrac{\$1{,}650 \text{ million}}{0.996}$ = $1,656.6 million

[b]Unilate offers credit terms of 2/10 net 30, and 20% of its customers take advantage of the cash discount; thus, the total cash discount is $6.6 million = (0.20) (0.02) ($1,656.6 million). This value will be the same with both credit policies.

[c]We have assumed that the variable cost of goods sold for Unilate is 82% of *net* sales. We use the same assumption here.

in credit and collection costs, which, in combination, will decrease taxable earnings by $3 million. But the decline in sales will also reduce variable operating costs by $1.6 million = $2 million × 0.82. In addition, decreases in both credit sales and the average collection period mean less funds will be "tied up" in receivables, thus the opportunity, or carrying, cost of receivables will also be less.

To compute the carrying cost, we need to determine how much Unilate has invested in receivables and the "cost" of this investment. The amount invested in receivables can be computed by determining the amount Unilate paid for the products that were sold on credit, but for which cash payment has not been received.

$$\frac{\text{Receivables}}{\text{investment}} = \frac{\text{Average accounts}}{\text{receivable balance}} \times \frac{\text{Variable}}{\text{cost ratio}}$$

$$= [\text{DSO} \times (\text{Sales per day})] \times \text{Variable cost ratio} \qquad (7.5)$$

$$= \left[\text{DSO} \times \left(\frac{S}{360}\right)\right] \times v$$

Variable cost ratio is "v". Only variable costs enter the calculation because it is this amount that represents the funds the firm has "tied up" in receivables, which is the amount that must be financed. For Unilate, the receivables investments associated with the existing and the proposed credit policies are as follows.

$$\text{Receivables investment}_{\text{Current}} = \left[43.2 \text{ days} \times \left(\frac{\$1,656.6 \text{ million}}{360}\right)\right] \times (0.82)$$

$$= \$198.8 \text{ million} \times 0.82$$

$$= 163.0 \text{ million}$$

$$\text{Receivables investment}_{\text{Proposal}} = \left[35.6 \text{ days} \times \left(\frac{\$1,654.6 \text{ million}}{360}\right)\right] \times (0.82)$$

$$= \$163.6 \text{ million} \times (0.82)$$

$$= \$134.2 \text{ million}$$

Once the investment in receivables is computed, the receivables carrying (opportunity) cost can be computed by determining how much return these funds would have earned if they were invested elsewhere.

$$\frac{\text{Receivables}}{\text{carrying cost}} = \frac{\text{Receivables}}{\text{investment}} \times \frac{\text{Opportunity}}{\text{cost of funds}} \qquad (7.6)$$

$$= \left[\text{DSO} \times \left(\frac{S}{360}\right)\right] \times v \times k_{AR}$$

where k_{AR} represents the opportunity cost associated with the funds "tied up" in accounts receivable. Therefore, if Unilate's opportunity cost for funds invested in receivables is 10%, the cost of carrying receivables with the existing policy and with the proposal would be as follows.

$$\text{Receivables carrying cost}_{\text{Current}} = \$163.0 \text{ million} \times 0.10 = \$16.3 \text{ million}$$
$$\text{Receivables carrying cost}_{\text{Proposal}} = \$134.2 \text{ million} \times 0.10 = \$13.4 \text{ million}$$

If the proposed credit policy changes are adopted, then the required investment in receivables will decrease by $28.8 million = $163.0 million − $134.2 million, which will decrease the cost of carrying receivables by $2.9 million, from $16.3 million to $13.4 million.

Exhibit 700.9 summarizes the results of the analysis we just described, and it illustrates the general idea behind credit policy analysis. The combined effect of all the changes in credit policy is a projected $900,000 annual increase in after-tax revenues, which suggests the credit policy changes would be beneficial for Unilate. There might, of course, be corresponding changes on the projected balance sheet—the lower sales might necessitate somewhat less cash and inventories. These changes, as well as any other changes, also would have to be considered in the analysis. For simplicity, we assume the only changes relevant to the decision to change the credit policy are those discussed here and contained in Exhibit 700.9.

The analysis in Exhibit 700.9 provides Unilate's managers with a vehicle for considering the impact of credit policy changes on the firm's income statement and balance sheet variables. However, a great deal of judgment must

Exhibit 700.9 Unilate Textiles: Analysis of Changing Credit Policy (millions of dollars)

	Projected 2001 Revenues/Costs under Current Credit Policy	Projected 2001 Revenues/Costs under Proposed Credit Policy	Income Effect of Credit Policy Change
Gross sales[a]	$1,656.6	$1,654.6	($2.0)
Less: Cash discounts[a]	(6.6)	(6.6)	0.0
Net sales	1,650.0	1,648.0	(2.0)
Variable cost of goods sold[a]	(1,353.0)	(1,351.4)	1.6
Bad debts	(0.0)	(0.0)	0.0
Credit evaluation and collection costs	(16.0)	(17.0)	(1.0)
Receivables carrying cost	(16.3)	(13.4)	2.9
Revenues net of variable production costs and credit costs	$ 264.7	$ 266.2	$1.5
Tax impact (40%)[b]	(105.9)	(106.5)	(0.6)
After-tax revenues	$ 158.8	$ 159.7	$0.9

[a]See footnotes in Exhibit 700.8.
[b]For this example, it is not necessary to include the tax impact because the marginal tax rate will not change under the proposed credit policy changes. Therefore, if the proposal is acceptable before taxes, it is also acceptable after taxes. This might not be the case if the marginal tax rate that applies to the proposal differs from the existing rate.

be applied to the decision because both customers' and competitors' responses to credit policy changes are very difficult to estimate. Nevertheless, this type of numerical analysis can provide a good starting point for credit policy decisions.

Multinational Working Capital Management

As we mentioned earlier, the methods used to manage short-term assets in multinational corporations are essentially the same as those used in purely domestic corporations. But there are some differences, which we discuss in this section.

Cash Management

Like a purely domestic company, a multinational corporation wants (1) to speed up collections and to slow down disbursements where possible, (2) to shift cash as rapidly as possible to those areas where it is needed, and (3) to try to put temporary cash balances to work earning positive returns. Multinational companies use the same general procedures for achieving these goals as domestic firms, but because of longer distances and more serious mail delays, lockbox systems and electronic funds transfers are even more important.

One potential problem a multinational company faces that a purely domestic company does not is the chance that a foreign government will restrict transfers of funds out of the country. Foreign governments sometimes limit the amount of cash that can be taken out of their countries because they want to encourage investment domestically. Even if funds can be transferred without limitation, deteriorating exchange rates might make it unattractive for a multinational firm to move funds to its operations in other countries.

Once it has been determined what funds can be transferred out of the various nations in which a multinational corporation operates, it is important to get those funds to locations where they will earn the highest returns. Whereas domestic corporations tend to think in terms of domestic securities, multinationals are more likely to be aware of investment opportunities all around the world. Most multinational corporations use one or more global concentration banks, located in money centers such as London, New York, Tokyo, Zurich, or Singapore; and their staffs in those cities, working with international bankers, are able to take advantage of the best rates available anywhere in the world.

Credit Management

Credit policy generally is more important for a multinational corporation than for a purely domestic firm for two reasons. First, much U.S. trade is with poorer, less-developed nations, and in such situations granting credit generally is a necessary condition for doing business. Second, and in large part as a result of the first point, developed nations whose economic health depends on exports often help their manufacturing firms compete internationally by granting credit to foreign countries. In Japan, for example, government agencies help firms identify potential export markets and also help potential customers arrange credit for purchases from Japanese firms. The U.S. government has programs that help domestic firms to export products, but it does not provide the degree of financial assistance that local governments offer many multinationals based in other countries.

When granting credit, the multinational firm faces a riskier situation than purely domestic firms because, in addition to the normal risks of default, (1) political and legal environments often make it more difficult to collect defaulted accounts, and (2) the multinational corporations must worry about exchange rate changes between the time a sale is made and the time a receivable is collected. We know, though, that hedging can reduce this type of risk, but at a cost.

By pointing out the risks in granting credit internationally, we are not suggesting that such credit is bad. Quite the contrary—the potential gains from international operations far outweigh the risks, at least for companies (and banks) that have the necessary expertise.

Inventory Management

Inventory management in a multinational setting is more complex than in a purely domestic setting because of logistical problems that arise with handling inventories. For example, should a firm concentrate its inventories in a few strategic centers located worldwide? Such a strategy might minimize the total amount of, thus the investment in, inventories needed to operate the global business; but it also might cause delays in getting goods from central storage locations to user locations all around the world. It is clear, however, that both working stocks and safety stocks will have to be maintained at each user location, as well as at the strategic storage centers.

Exchange rates can significantly influence inventory policy. For example, if a local currency was expected to increase in value against the dollar, a U.S. company operating in that country would want to increase stocks of local products before the rise in the currency, and vice versa. Another factor that must be considered is the possibility of import or export quotas or tariffs. Quotas restrict the quantities of products firms can bring into a country, while tariffs, like taxes, increase the prices of products that are allowed to be imported. Both quotas and tariffs are designed to restrict the ability of foreign corporations to compete with domestic companies; at the extreme, foreign products are excluded altogether.

Another danger in certain countries is the threat of expropriation, or government takeover of the firm's local operations. If the threat of expropriation is large, inventory holdings will be minimized, and goods will be brought in only as needed. Similarly, if the operation involves extraction of raw material, processing plants might be moved offshore rather than located close to the production site.

Taxes also must be considered, and they have two effects on multinational inventory management. First, countries often impose property taxes on assets, including inventories, and when this is done, the tax is based on holdings as of a specific date, say, January 1 or March 1. Such rules make it advantageous for a multinational firm (1) to schedule production so that inventories are low on the assessment date and (2) if assessment dates vary among countries in a region, to hold safety stocks in different countries at different times during the year.

In general, then, multinational firms use techniques similar to those described in this chapter to manage current assets, but their job is more complex because business, legal, and economic environments can differ significantly from one country to another.

Short-Term Investment Strategies

There are many possible investment strategies that can be used. Generically, we divide them into passive strategies and active strategies. A **passive investment strategy** involves a minimal amount of oversight and very few transactions once the portfolio has been selected.

An **active investment strategy** involves more trading and active monitoring of the portfolio and may be motivated by a philosophy that the investor can "beat the market." In the money markets, this generally means earning higher-than-normal yield spreads and/or capital gains as a result of accurate anticipation of interest rate movements.

Passive Strategies

A popular passive strategy is the **buy-and-hold strategy.** Quite often, this is part of a "maturity matching" approach to investing that prescribes investing in a security that will mature at the end of the investment horizon. The horizon is based on how long the company can tie up the investable funds. This eliminates interest rate risk if the company does hold the security to maturity as planned, because it will receive the face value of the security at that time. The buy-and-hold strategy may be implemented by investing part or all of the portfolio in an index fund, which is a managed portfolio assembled to mirror a particular money market composite. The composite serves as an index because it is calculated by averaging the yields of a broadly based basket of securities. A **modified buy-and-hold strategy** might be used when the investor wishes to take advantage of favorable interest rate movements, should they occur. If rates come down and the portfolio report shows a paper capital gain, the investor may sell or swap for another security to capture the gain.

Active Strategies

There are numerous active strategies. One strategy is to try to spot inefficiencies in the way securities are priced at present and to buy those that are underpriced (have higher yields than warranted by their level of risk). These are then held to maturity or sold at a capital gain when the market recognizes the mispricing and corrects it by bidding up the price. One way of implementing this strategy is to study yield spreads.

Historical yield spread analysis suggests other profitable trading strategies. For temporarily underpriced securities, the yield offered will be higher than warranted by the underlying risks. Market overreactions to events such as credit rating changes (part of the event risk phenomenon) may open up some attractive yield opportunities. The historical yield spreads, computed as the difference between a given security and short-term Treasury bills on the top-quality securities for each instrument are available. The analyst compares the current yield spread for the instrument type (or given rating class) or for an individual security within that type to see if abnormally large spreads exist.[17] An aggressive investor might research the largest spreads available, seeking to determine why they exist, and if there is no exceptional default, liquidity, or event risk associated to account for the spread, a purchase would be made.

A second, and also a very popular, active strategy is **riding the yield curve.** This involves buying securities with maturities longer than the investment horizon, fully intending to liquidate the position early. If the yield curve is stable, meaning it neither shifts nor changes slope during the holding period, the investor can generally outperform a maturity matching strategy. This occurs because the normal yield curve is upward-sloping, giving higher interest rates for longer-maturity instruments.

Aggregate Investment in Cash and Securities

The manager may select from three generic strategies when deciding what quantity of total assets to hold in the form of cash and securities: a low-liquidity, moderate-liquidity, or high-liquidity strategy. The lower the liquidity, the riskier the strategy, and the higher the strategy's expected profitability.

The **low-liquidity strategy** entails driving the investment in cash and securities to a minimum. Therefore, cash and securities are a very small proportion of total assets. Assuming that the company does not subsequently overinvest in inventories and receivables, this approach should enhance profitability while also increasing business risk. Lesser amounts invested in cash and securities implies larger amounts invested in receivables, inventories, and higher-return fixed assets. This comes at the expense of greater default and bankruptcy risk, however, because the company has a smaller liquidity cushion with which to weather unexpected and business cycle–related downturns in operating revenues. Obviously, other sources of liquidity—salability of inventories and receivables (or the ability to secure these), available credit lines, and other sources of untapped debt capacity—affect the risk (and therefore the advisability) of the low-liquidity strategy. Companies following the low-liquidity strategy justify it on the basis of untapped credit lines, which we included in the definition of the liquid reserve.

The **moderate-liquidity strategy** implies a somewhat greater investment in cash and securities, with correspondingly less risk. This strategy may be premised on a matching philosophy: the higher the level of near-term current liability obligations, the greater the proportion of assets the company should hold in cash and securities. The many defunct savings and loan associations are sober reminders of what can happen to organizations whose assets and liabilities are substantially mismatched ("duration gap").

Fixed asset investments are generally property, plant, and equipment expenditures made in support of new products and market expansion, which presumably have positive net present value, thus enhancing shareholder value.

The **high-liquidity strategy** prescribes a higher proportion of assets to be held in cash and securities. Risk of default on securities and the risk of bankruptcy are reduced because of the greater liquidity cushion, but profitability is lower as well. Companies with significant business risk or financial risk might implement this strategy. Automakers and **Microsoft** justify their high-liquidity strategies because of unknown future capital investment opportunities, such as newly-developed technologies. Again, the company's posture toward risk and the availability of other potential sources of liquidity should be analyzed before adopting a particular cash and securities strategy.

The company's present financial situation may lead it to temporarily deviate from its chosen strategy. It may invest either more or less in cash and securities than the chosen strategy indicates. The current cash-flow forecast, in connection with the amount of borrowing, the amount of untapped short-term credit lines, and the financial position of the company, might be taken into consideration. The cash and securities balance might be augmented if the cash forecast shows net cash outflows or increased uncertainty in the cash forecast and a lack of alternate sources of liquidity. The treasurer also may take other precautions, such as engaging in hedging transactions if the cash-flow uncertainty stems from future movements in interest rates or commodity input prices. Finally, the decision maker should consider what fraction of the total will be held in cash and what fraction will be held in securities when determining the company's aggregate investment in cash and securities.

Managing Short-Term Financing

Managing Short-Term Liabilities

We discussed the decisions the financial manager must make concerning alternative current asset financing policies. We also showed how debt maturities can affect both risk and expected returns: While short-term debt generally is riskier than long-term debt, it generally is also less expensive, and it can be obtained faster and under more flexible terms. The primary purpose of this section is to examine the different types of short-term credit that are available to the financial manager. We also examine the types of issues the financial manager must consider when selecting among the various types of short-term credit—that is, short-term, or current, liabilities. We then present strategies for short-term financing.

Sources of Short-Term Financing

Statements about the flexibility, cost, and riskiness of short-term debt versus long-term debt depend, to a large extent, on the type of short-term credit that actually is used. **Short-term credit** is defined as any liability *originally* scheduled for payment within one year. There are numerous sources of short-term funds, and in the following sections we describe seven major types: (1) accruals, (2) accounts payable (trade credit), (3) short-term bank loans, (4) commercial paper, (5) letter of credit, (6) banker's acceptance, and (7) reverse repurchase agreement. The cost of bank loans is presented.

Accruals

Firms generally pay employees on a weekly, biweekly, or monthly basis, so the balance sheet typically will show some accrued wages. Similarly, the firm's own estimated income taxes, the social security and income taxes withheld from employee payrolls, and the sales taxes collected generally are paid on a weekly, monthly, or quarterly basis, so the balance sheet typically will show some accrued taxes along with accrued wages.

Accruals increase automatically, or spontaneously, as a firm's operations expand. Further, this type of debt generally is considered "free" in the sense that no explicit interest is paid on funds raised through accruals. However, a firm ordinarily cannot control its accruals: The timing of wage payments is set by economic forces and industry custom, while tax payment dates are established by law. Thus, firms use all the accruals they can, but they have little control over the levels of these accounts.

Accounts Payable (Trade Credit)

Firms generally make purchases from other firms on credit, recording the debt as an *account payable*. This type of financing, which is called **trade credit,** is the largest single category of short-term debt, representing about 40% of the current liabilities for the average nonfinancial corporation. The percentage is somewhat larger for smaller firms: Because small companies often do not qualify for financing from other sources, they rely most heavily on trade credit.

Trade credit is a *spontaneous* source of financing in the sense that it arises from ordinary business transactions. For example, suppose a firm makes average purchases of $2,000 a day on terms of net 30, meaning that it must pay for goods 30 days after the invoice date. On average, it will owe 30 times $2,000, or $60,000, to its suppliers. If its sales, and consequently its purchases, were to double, then its accounts payable also would double, to $120,000. So simply by growing, the firm would have spontaneously generated an additional $60,000 of financing. Similarly, if the terms under which it bought were extended from 30 to 40 days, its accounts payable would expand from $60,000 to $80,000. Thus, lengthening the credit period, as well as expanding sales and purchases, generates additional financing.

THE COST OF TRADE CREDIT Firms that sell on credit have a *credit policy* that includes certain *terms of credit*. For example, Microchip Electronics sells on credit with terms of 2/10, net 30, which means that Microchip gives its customers a 2% discount from the invoice price if payment is made within ten days of the billing date; otherwise, if the discount is not taken, the full invoice amount is due and must be paid within 30 days of the billing date.

Note that the *true* price of the products Microchip offers is the net price, which is 98% of the list price, because any customer can purchase an item at a 2% "discount" as long as payment is made within ten days. Consider Personal Computer Company (PCC), which buys its memory chips from Microchip. One commonly used memory chip is listed at $100, so the true cost to PCC is $98. Now if PCC wants an additional 20 days of credit beyond the ten-day discount period, it will incur a finance charge of $2 per chip for that credit. Thus, the $100 list price can be thought of as follows.

$$\text{List price} = \$98 \text{ true price} + \$2 \text{ finance charge}$$

The question that PCC must ask before it takes the additional 20 days of credit from Microchip is whether the firm could obtain similar credit with better terms from some other lender, say a bank. In other words, could 20 days of credit be obtained for less than $2 per item?

PCC buys an average of 44,100 memory chips from Microchip each year (assume 360 days), which, at the net or true price, amounts to an average annual purchase equal to $4,321,800, or $12,005 per day. For simplicity, assume that Microchip is PCC's only supplier. If PCC pays on the 10th day and takes the discount, its payables will average 10 × $12,005 = $120,050. Thus, PCC will receive $120,050 of credit from its only supplier, Microchip Electronics.

Now suppose PCC decides to take the additional 20 days' credit and thus must pay the finance charge. Because PCC now will pay on the 30th day, its accounts payable will increase to 30 × $12,005 = $360,150. Under these circumstances, Microchip will be supplying PCC with an additional $240,100 = $360,150 − $120,050 of credit, which PCC could use to build up its cash account, to pay off debt, to expand inventories, or even to extend more credit to its own customers and hence to increase its own accounts receivable. So it should be apparent that a firm's policy with regard to taking or not taking cash discounts can have a significant effect on its financial statements. If PCC does not take the cash discount, its accounts payable balance will be $240,100 greater than if it does take the discount ($360,150 compared to $120,050).

The additional credit offered by Microchip has a cost—PCC must pay the finance charge by forgoing the 2% discount on its purchases from Microchip. By forgoing the discount, PCC actually will pay $100 rather than $98 per chip, so its annual cost for the chips will be $100 × 44,100 = $4,410,000 instead of $98 × 44,100 = $4,321,800. The additional cost should be considered a finance charge for being able to keep the funds an additional 20 days. So the annual financing cost is $4,410,000 − $4,321,800 = $88,200. Dividing the $88,200 financing cost by the $240,100 in *average* annual *additional* credit, we find the implicit cost of the additional trade credit to be 36.7%.

$$\text{Approximate percentage cost} = \frac{\$88,200}{\$240,100} = 36.7\%$$

Should PCC take the discount, or should it wait 20 days and pay the full invoice price? If PCC can borrow from its bank (or from other sources) at an interest rate less than 36.7%, it should take the discount by borrowing from its bank to obtain any additional funds it needs—PCC should *not* obtain credit in the form of accounts payable by forgoing discounts if cheaper sources, such as the bank, are available.

The following equation can be used to calculate the *approximate* percentage cost, on an annual basis, of not taking cash discounts—that is, the cost of forgoing discounts.

$$\begin{pmatrix}\text{Approximate cost}\\ \text{of forgoing a}\\ \text{cash discount (\%)}\end{pmatrix} = \frac{\text{Discount percent}}{100 - \begin{pmatrix}\text{Discount}\\ \text{percent}\end{pmatrix}} \times \frac{360 \text{ days}}{\begin{pmatrix}\text{Total days net}\\ \text{credit is available}\end{pmatrix} - \begin{pmatrix}\text{Discount}\\ \text{period}\end{pmatrix}} \quad (7.7)$$

The numerator of the first term, Discount percent, is the dollar cost per $100 invoice value of forgoing (not taking) the discount, while the denominator in this term, (100 − Discount percent), represents the funds the firm has available by forgoing the discount. Thus, the first term in Equation 7.7 is the percent cost of using trade credit as a source of financing for the number of days in the credit period beyond the discount period. The denominator of the second term is the number of days of extra credit obtained by forgoing the discount; so the entire second term shows how many times each year the percent cost of the trade credit would be incurred if the firm continues this practice. To illustrate the equation, the approximate cost of not taking a discount when the terms are 2/10, net 30, is calculated as follows.

$$\begin{pmatrix}\text{Approximate cost}\\ \text{of forgoing a}\\ \text{cash discount}\end{pmatrix} = \frac{2}{100 - 2} \times \frac{360}{30 - 10} = \frac{2}{98} \times \frac{360}{20}$$

$$= 0.02041 \times 18 = 0.367 = 36.7\%$$

Notice, that, according to Equation 7.7, the cost of trade credit *per credit period* is always the same as long as the terms of credit do not change—in our example, the cost is 2/98 = 0.0204. Therefore, the cost of using trade credit for financing can be reduced by delaying payment of accounts payable. For example, if PCC could get away with paying in 50 days rather than in the specified 30 days, then the effective credit period would become 40 days (50 days minus 10 days), the number of times during the year the discount would be lost would fall from 18 to 360/40 = 9, and the approximate cost would drop from 36.7% to 18.4%. Similarly, the effective annual rate would drop from 43.9% to 19.9%.

The practice of paying trade credit beyond the credit period, or deliberately becoming a delinquent account, is called **stretching accounts payable.** In periods of excess capacity, firms might be able to get away with *stretching* because suppliers need the business. But there are consequences associated with credit delinquency, such as being branded a "slow payer"—the most serious is that credit might be cut off all together.

Short-Term Bank Loans

Commercial banks, whose loans generally appear on firms' balance sheets as notes payable, are second in importance to trade credit as a source of short-term financing. The influence of banks actually is greater than it appears from the dollar amounts they lend because banks provide *nonspontaneous* funds. As a firm's financing needs increase, it specifically requests additional funds from its bank. If the request is denied, the firm might be forced to abandon attractive growth opportunities. The key features of bank loans are discussed in the following paragraphs.

MATURITY Although banks do make longer-term loans, *the bulk of their lending is on a short-term basis.* Bank loans to businesses frequently are written as 90-day notes, so the loan must be repaid or renewed at the end of 90 days. Of course, if a borrower's financial position has deteriorated, the bank might refuse to renew the loan. This can mean serious trouble for the borrower.

PROMISSORY NOTE When a bank loan is approved, the agreement is executed by signing a **promissory note.** The note specifies (1) the amount borrowed; (2) the percentage interest rate; (3) the repayment schedule, which can call for payment either as a lump sum or as a series of installments; (4) any collateral that has to be put up as security for the loan; and (5) any other terms and conditions to which the bank and the borrower have agreed. When the note is signed, the bank credits the borrower's checking account with the amount of the loan, so on the borrower's balance sheet both cash and notes payable increase equally.

COMPENSATING BALANCES Banks sometimes require borrowers to maintain an average demand deposit (checking account) balance equal to from 10% to 20% of the amount borrowed. This is called a **compensating balance (CB).** In effect, the bank charges borrowers for *servicing* the loans (bookkeeping, maintaining a line of credit, and so on) by requiring compensating balances, and such balances might increase the effective interest rate on the loans.

LINE OF CREDIT A **line of credit** is an agreement between a bank and a borrower indicating the maximum credit the bank will extend to the borrower. For example, on December 31 a bank loan officer might indicate to a financial manager that the bank regards the firm as being "good" for up to $200,000 during the forthcoming year. If on January 10 the financial manager signs a 90-day promissory note for $60,000, this would be called "drawing, or taking, down" $60,000 of the total line of credit. This amount would be credited to the firm's checking account at the bank, and before repayment of the $60,000, the firm could borrow additional amounts up to a *total* of $200,000 outstanding at any one time.

When a line of credit is *guaranteed,* it is called a **revolving credit agreement.** A revolving credit agreement is similar to a regular, or general, line of credit, except the bank has a *legal obligation* to provide the funds when requested by the borrower. The bank generally charges a **commitment fee** on the unused balance (sometimes on the total credit commitment) of the credit line for guaranteeing the availability of the funds.

Note that an important feature distinguishes a revolving credit agreement from a general line of credit: The bank has a *legal obligation* to honor a revolving credit agreement, and it receives a commitment fee for guaranteeing the funds will be available when requested by the borrower. Neither the legal obligation nor the fee exists under the general line of credit.

Commercial Paper

Commercial paper is a type of unsecured promissory note issued by large, strong firms, and it is sold primarily to other businesses, to insurance companies, to pension funds, to money market mutual funds, and to banks. This form of financing has grown rapidly in recent years—in 1999, the amount of commercial paper outstanding was about the same as the amount of regular business loans.

USE OF COMMERCIAL PAPER The use of commercial paper is restricted to a comparatively small number of firms that are *exceptionally* good credit risks. Dealers prefer to handle the "paper" of firms whose net worth is $100 million or more and whose annual borrowing exceeds $10 million. One potential problem with commercial paper is that a debtor who is in temporary financial difficulty might receive little help because commercial paper dealings generally are less personal than are bank relationships. Thus, banks generally are more able and willing to help a good customer weather a temporary storm than is a commercial paper dealer. On the other hand, using commercial paper permits a corporation to tap a wider range of credit sources, including financial institutions outside its own area and industrial corporations across the country, and this can reduce interest costs.

The maximum maturity for commercial paper without SEC registration is 270 days. Also, commercial paper can only be sold to "sophisticated" investors; otherwise, SEC registration would be required even for maturities of 270 days or less.

MATURITY AND COST Generally, commercial paper is issued in denominations of $100,000 or more, so few individuals can afford to *directly* invest in the commercial paper market. Maturities of commercial paper vary from one to nine months, with an average of about five months. The rate on commercial paper fluctuates with supply and demand conditions—it is determined in the marketplace, varying daily as conditions change. Generally, the rates on commercial paper are lower than the stated prime rate of interest. For example, in August 1999, the average rate on 90-day commercial paper was about 5.3%, which was about 1.7% less than the prime rate but nearly 0.7% greater than 90-day Treasury bill rates.

Commercial paper is called a discount instrument because it is sold at a price below its face, or maturity, value. So the cost of using commercial paper as a source of financing is computed the same as for a discount interest loan.

Letter of Credit

A **letter of credit** (LOC) is a promise, generally by a bank, to make payment to a party on presentation of a draft provided that the party complies with certain documentary requirements as stated in the LOC agreement. The net effect of the LOC is to trade the credit of a well-known bank for that of a perhaps lesser-known corporate borrower. LOCs are generally a required feature of international borrowing.

710. MANAGING SHORT-TERM FINANCING

Banker's Acceptance

A **banker's acceptance** is a time draft drawn against a deposit in a commercial bank but with payment at maturity guaranteed by the bank. The original time draft usually is a result of international transactions between importers and exporters.

For example, a U.S. importer wishing to import goods from abroad may request its bank to issue a letter of credit on its behalf in favor of the foreign seller. If the bank finds the importer's credit standing satisfactory, it will issue such a letter, authorizing the foreign exporter to draw a time draft on it in payment for the goods delivered. Equipped with this authorization, the exporter can discount the time draft with its bank when it ships the goods, thereby receiving payment immediately; the foreign bank then forwards the time draft, along with the shipping documents, to its correspondent bank in the United States. Generally, the U.S. correspondent bank will present the time draft for "acceptance" at the importer's bank, which forwards the shipping documents to the importer, who now may claim the shipment. Once accepted by the importer's bank, the time draft becomes a negotiable money market security, referred to as a bankers acceptance that trades in the money market until the maturity date of the time draft.

Reverse Repurchase Agreement

Repurchase agreements are used as a short-term investment alternative. In essence, a **reverse repurchase agreement** (a reverse repo) is the other side of the repurchase agreement transaction. In this case, a corporate investment manager may negotiate with its bank to sell to the bank a specific dollar amount of marketable securities currently held in the firm's investment portfolio at a specified price. Thus the party currently holding the securities initiates reverse repos. In addition, the contract stipulates that the selling corporation agrees to repurchase the designated securities at the same price plus a stipulated amount of interest in an agreed on number of days in the future. Most repos or reverse repos are overnight or 1-day contracts.

Such an agreement might be used to obtain a quick infusion of cash to offset the delay of forecasted cash receipts without actually liquidating a portion of the firm's investment portfolio. Such transactions can also be useful for end-of-year financial statement window dressing.

The Cost of Bank Loans

The cost of bank loans varies for different types of borrowers at any given point in time and for all borrowers over time. Interest rates are higher for riskier borrowers, and rates also are higher on smaller loans because of the fixed costs involved in making and servicing loans. If a firm can qualify as a "prime credit" because of its size and financial strength, it might be able to borrow at the **prime rate,** which traditionally has been the lowest rate banks charge. Rates on other loans generally are scaled up from the prime rate.

Bank rates vary widely over time depending on economic conditions and Federal Reserve policy. When the economy is weak, then (1) loan demand usually is slack, (2) inflation is low, and (3) the Fed also makes plenty of money available to the system. As a result, rates on all types of loans are relatively low. Conversely, when the economy is booming, loan demand typically is strong and the Fed restricts the money supply; the result is high interest rates. Interest rates on other bank loans also vary, generally moving with the prime rate.

Interest paid on a bank loan generally is calculated in one of three ways: (1) *simple interest,* (2) *discount interest,* and (3) *add-on interest.*

Use of Security in Short-Term Financing

The term asset-based financing *is often used as a synonym for* secured financing. *In recent years accounts receivable have been used as security for long-term bonds, and this permits corporations to borrow from lenders such as pension funds rather than being restricted to banks and other traditional short-term lenders.*

Thus far we have not addressed the question of whether loans should be secured. Commercial paper is never secured, but all other types of loans can be secured if this is deemed necessary or desirable. Given a choice, it ordinarily is better to borrow on an unsecured basis because the bookkeeping costs of **secured loans** often are high. However, weak firms might find that they can borrow only if they put up some type of security or that by using security they can borrow at a lower rate.

Several different kinds of security, or collateral, can be employed, including marketable securities, land or buildings, equipment, inventory, and accounts receivable.

Marketable securities make excellent collateral, but few firms that need loans also hold such portfolios. Similarly, real property (land and buildings) and equipment are good forms of collateral, but they generally are used as security for long-term loans rather than for working capital loans. Therefore, most secured short-term business borrowing involves the use of accounts receivable and inventories as collateral.

To understand the use of security, consider the case of a Chicago hardware dealer who wanted to modernize and expand his store. He requested a $200,000 bank loan. After examining his business's financial statements, the bank indicated that it would lend him a maximum of $100,000 and that the interest rate would be 12%, discount interest, for an effective rate of 13.6%. The owner had a substantial personal portfolio of stocks, and he offered to put up $300,000 of high-quality stocks to support the $200,000 loan. The bank then granted the full $200,000 loan, and at a rate of only 11%, simple interest. The store owner also might have used his inventories or receivables as security for the loan, but processing costs would have been high.

In the past, state laws have varied greatly with regard to the use of security in financing. Today, however, nearly every secured loan is established under the **Uniform Commercial Code,** which has standardized and simplified the procedures for establishing loan security. The heart of the Uniform Commercial Code is the *Security Agreement,* a standardized document on which the specific pledged assets are listed. The assets can be items of equipment, accounts receivable, or inventories. Procedures under the Uniform Commercial Code for using accounts receivable and inventories as security for short-term credit are described in the following sections.

Accounts Receivable Financing

Accounts receivable financing involves either the pledging of receivables or the selling of receivables (called *factoring*). The **pledging** of accounts receivable is characterized by the fact that the lender not only has a claim against the receivables but also has **recourse** to the borrower: If the person or firm that bought the goods does not pay, the selling firm (borrower) rather than the lender must take the loss. Therefore, the risk of default on the pledged accounts receivable remains with the borrower. The buyer of the goods ordinarily is not notified about the pledging of the receivables, and the financial institution that lends on the security of accounts receivable generally is either a commercial bank or one of the large industrial finance companies.

Factoring, or *selling accounts receivable,* involves the purchase of accounts receivable by the lender (called a factor), generally without recourse to the borrower, which means that if the purchaser of the goods does not pay for them, the lender rather than the seller of the goods (borrower) takes the loss. Under factoring, the buyer of the goods typically is notified of the transfer and is asked to make payment directly to the lending institution. Because the factor assumes the risk of default on bad accounts, it generally carries out the credit investigation. Accordingly, factors provide not only money but also a credit department for the borrower. Incidentally, the same financial institutions that make loans against pledged receivables also serve as factors. Thus, depending on the circumstances and the wishes of the borrower, a financial institution will provide either type of receivables financing.

Procedure for Pledging Accounts Receivable

The financing of accounts receivable is initiated by a legally binding agreement between the seller of the goods and the financing institution. The agreement sets forth in detail the procedures to be followed and the legal obligations of both parties. Once the working relationship has been established, the seller periodically takes a batch of invoices to the financing institution. The lender reviews the invoices and makes credit appraisals of the buyers. Invoices of companies that do not meet the lender's credit standards are not accepted for pledging.

The financial institution seeks to protect itself at every phase of the operation. First, selection of sound invoices is one way the lender safeguards itself. Second, if the buyer of the goods does not pay the invoice, the lender still has recourse against the seller (the borrowing firm). Third, additional protection is afforded the lender because the loan generally will be less than 100% of the pledged receivables; for example, the lender might advance the selling firm only 75% of the amount of the pledged invoices. The percent advanced depends on the quality of the accounts pledged.

Procedure for Factoring Accounts Receivable

The procedures used in factoring are somewhat different from those for pledging. Again, an agreement between the seller and the factor specifies legal obligations and procedural arrangements. When the seller receives an order from a buyer, a credit approval slip is written and immediately sent to the factoring company for a credit check. If the factor approves the credit, shipment is made and the invoice is stamped to notify the buyer to make payment directly to the factoring company. If the factor does not approve the sale, the seller generally refuses to fill the order; if the sale is made anyway, the factor will not buy the account.

The factor normally performs three functions: (1) credit checking, (2) lending, and (3) risk bearing. Consider a typical factoring situation: The goods are shipped, and even though payment is not due for 30 days, the factor immediately makes funds available to the borrower (the seller of the goods). Suppose $10,000 worth of goods are shipped. Further, assume that the factoring commission for credit checking and risk bearing is 2½% of the invoice price, or $250, and that the interest expense is computed at a 9% annual rate on the invoice balance, or $75 = $10,000 × (0.09/360) × 30 days. The selling firm's accounting entry is as follows.

Cash	$ 9,175
Interest expense	75
Factoring commission	250
Reserve due from factor on collection account	500
Accounts receivable	$ 10,000

The $500 due from the factor upon collection of the account is a reserve established by the factor to cover disputes between the seller and customers over damaged goods, goods returned by customers to the seller, and the failure to make an outright sale of goods. The reserve is paid to the selling firm when the factor collects on the account.

Factoring normally is a continuous process instead of the single cycle just described. The firm that sells the goods receives an order; it transmits this order to the factor for approval; upon approval, the firm ships the goods; the factor advances the invoice amount minus withholdings to the seller; the buyer (customer) pays the factor when payment is due; and the factor periodically remits any excess in the reserve to the seller of the goods. Once a routine has been established, a continuous circular flow of goods and funds takes place between the seller, the buyers of the goods, and the factor. Thus, once the factoring agreement is in force, funds from this source are *spontaneous* in the sense that an increase in sales will automatically generate additional credit.

Visa and MasterCard represent a prime example of nonrecourse factoring. When you purchase from a retailer such as **Wal-Mart** using Visa or MasterCard, the retailer is paid only 95 to 97% of the invoice by these credit companies. The reason the three to 5% discount is charged by Visa and MasterCard is because they provide credit checking services and suffer any losses due to customer nonpayment—the retailer does not incur these costs.

Cost of Receivables Financing

Both accounts receivable pledging and factoring are convenient and advantageous, but they can be costly. The credit-checking and risk-bearing fee is 1% to 5% of the amount of invoices accepted by the factor, and it could be even more if the buyers are poor credit risks. The cost of money is reflected in the interest rate (usually two to three percentage points over the prime rate) charged on the unpaid balance of the funds advanced by the factor.

Evaluation of Receivables Financing

It cannot be said categorically that accounts receivable financing is either a good or a bad way to raise funds. Among the advantages is, first, the flexibility of this source of financing. As the firm's sales expand, more financing is needed, but a larger volume of invoices, and hence a larger amount of receivables financing, is generated automatically. Second, receivables can be used as security for loans that otherwise would not be granted. Third, factoring can provide the services of a credit department that otherwise might be available only at a higher cost.

Accounts receivable financing also has disadvantages. First, when invoices are numerous and relatively small in dollar amount, the administrative costs involved might be excessive. Second, because receivables represent the firm's most liquid noncash assets, some trade creditors might refuse to sell on credit to a firm that factors or pledges its receivables on the grounds that this practice weakens the firm's financial strength.

Future Use of Receivables Financing

It is easy to make a prediction at this point: In the future, accounts receivable financing will increase in relative importance. Computer technology is advancing rapidly toward the point where credit records of individuals and firms can be kept on electronic media. For example, one device used by retailers consists of a box which, when an individual's magnetic credit card is inserted, gives a signal that the credit is "good" and that a bank is willing to "buy" the receivable created as soon as the store completes the sale. The cost of handling invoices will be reduced greatly over present-day costs because the new systems will be so highly automated. This will make it possible to use accounts receivable financing for very small sales, and it will reduce the cost of all receivables financing. The net result will be a marked expansion of accounts receivable financing. In fact, when consumers use credit cards such as MasterCard or Visa, the seller is in effect factoring receivables. The seller receives the amount of the purchase, minus a percentage fee, the next working day. The credit card user (buyer) receives 30 days' (or so) credit, at which time he or she remits payment directly to the credit card company or sponsoring bank.

Inventory Financing

A substantial amount of credit is secured by business inventories. If a firm is a relatively good credit risk, the mere existence of the inventory might be a sufficient basis for receiving an unsecured loan. However, if the firm is a relatively poor risk, the lending institution might insist on security in the form of a *lien*, or legal claim, against the inventory. Methods for using inventories as security are discussed in this section.

Blanket Liens

The *inventory blanket lien* gives the lending institution a lien against all of the borrower's inventories. However, the borrower is free to sell inventories, and thus the value of the collateral can be reduced below the level that existed when the loan was granted. A blanket lien generally is used when the inventory put up as collateral is relatively low priced, fast moving, and difficult to identify individually. A blanket lien is also called a floating lien.

Trust Receipts

Because of the inherent weakness of the blanket lien, another procedure for inventory financing has been developed—the *trust receipt*, which is an instrument acknowledging that the goods are held in trust for the lender. Under this method, the borrowing firm, as a condition for receiving funds from the lender, signs and delivers a trust receipt for the goods. The goods can be stored in a public warehouse or held on the premises of the borrower. The trust receipt states that the goods are held in trust for the lender or are segregated on the borrower's premises on the lender's behalf and that any proceeds from the sale of the goods must be transmitted to the lender at the end of each day. Automobile dealer financing is one of the best examples of trust receipt financing.

One defect of trust receipt financing is the requirement that a trust receipt be issued for specific goods. For example, if the security is automobiles in a dealer's inventory, the trust receipts must indicate the cars by registration number. To validate its trust receipts, the lending institution must send someone to the borrower's premises periodically to see that the auto numbers are listed correctly, because auto dealers who are in financial difficulty have been known to sell cars backing trust receipts and then use the funds for other operations rather than to repay the bank. Problems are compounded if the borrower has a number of different locations, especially if they are separated geographically from the lender. To offset these inconveniences, warehouse receipt financing has come into wide use as a method of securing loans with inventory.

Warehouse Receipts

Warehouse receipt financing is another way to use inventory as security. A *public warehouse* is an independent third-party operation engaged in the business of storing goods. Items that require aging, such as tobacco and liquor, are often financed and stored in public warehouses. When the inventory products used as collateral are moved to public warehouses, the financing arrangement is termed *terminal warehousing*. Sometimes terminal warehousing is not practical because of the bulkiness of goods and the expense of transporting them to and from the borrower's premises. In such cases, a *field warehouse* might be established on the borrower's grounds. To provide inventory supervision, the lending institution employs a third party in the arrangement, the field warehousing company, which acts as its agent.

Field warehousing can be illustrated by a simple example. Suppose a firm that has iron stacked in an open yard on its premises needs a loan. A field warehousing concern can place a temporary fence around the iron, erecting a sign stating, "This is a field warehouse supervised by the Smith Field Warehousing Corporation," and then assign an employee to supervise and control the fenced-in inventory.

This example illustrates the three essential elements for the establishment of a field warehouse: (1) public notification, (2) physical control of the inventory, and (3) supervision by a custodian of the field warehousing concern. When the field warehousing operation is relatively small, the third condition is sometimes violated by hiring an employee of the borrower to supervise the inventory. This practice is viewed as undesirable by most lenders because there is no control over the collateral by a person independent of the borrowing firm.

Acceptable Products

Canned foods account for nearly 20% of all field warehouse loans. In addition, many other types of products provide a basis for field warehouse financing. Some of these are miscellaneous groceries, which represent nearly 15%; lumber products, about 10%; and coal and coke, about 5%. These products are relatively nonperishable and are sold in well-developed, organized markets. Nonperishability protects the lender if it should have to take over the security. For this reason, a bank would not make a field warehousing loan on perishables such as fresh fish; but frozen fish, which can be stored for a long time, can be field warehoused.

Cost of Financing

The fixed costs of a field warehousing arrangement are relatively high; such financing therefore is not suitable for a very small firm. If a field warehousing company sets up a field warehouse, it typically will set a minimum charge of about $25,000 per year, plus about 1 to 2% of the amount of credit extended to the borrower. Furthermore, the financing institution will charge an interest rate of two to three percentage points over the prime rate. An efficient field warehousing operation requires an inventory of at least $1 million.

Evaluation of Inventory Financing

The use of inventory financing, especially field warehouse financing, as a source of funds has many advantages. First, the amount of funds available is flexible because the financing is tied to the growth of inventories, which in turn is related directly to financing needs. Second, the field warehousing arrangement increases the acceptability of inventories as loan collateral; some inventories simply would not be accepted by a bank as security without such an arrangement. Third, the necessity for inventory control and safekeeping as well as the use of specialists in warehousing often results in improved warehouse practices, which in turn save handling costs, insurance charges, theft losses, and so on. Thus, field warehousing companies often save money for firms in spite of the costs of financing that we have discussed. The major disadvantages of field warehousing include the paperwork, physical separation requirements, and, for small firms, the fixed-cost element.

Short-Term Financing Strategies

Financing and the Cash Flow Timeline

At this point, we have reached a position on the company's cash flow timeline at which cash has been collected and cash has been disbursed, resulting in a daily ending cash position that may be positive or negative. If the daily cash position is positive, then the cash manager faces an investment opportunity. If the daily cash position is negative, the cash manager faces a dilemma on how to fund the cash deficit.

A deficit cash position may be the result of inefficient or inappropriate working capital policies. Excess accumulation of inventory, slow collections, and/or quick disbursements may lead to cash being disbursed prior to cash collection. Thus the financial manager should reevaluate the company's working capital policies to ensure the most efficient stream of cash flow resulting from operations.

Even the most efficient working capital policies, however, may result in a deficit cash position at different times during the working capital cycle. This is especially true during periods of rapid growth and during the early phase of the working capital cycle. At this point the manager must have a well-developed plan for financing short-term cash deficit positions.

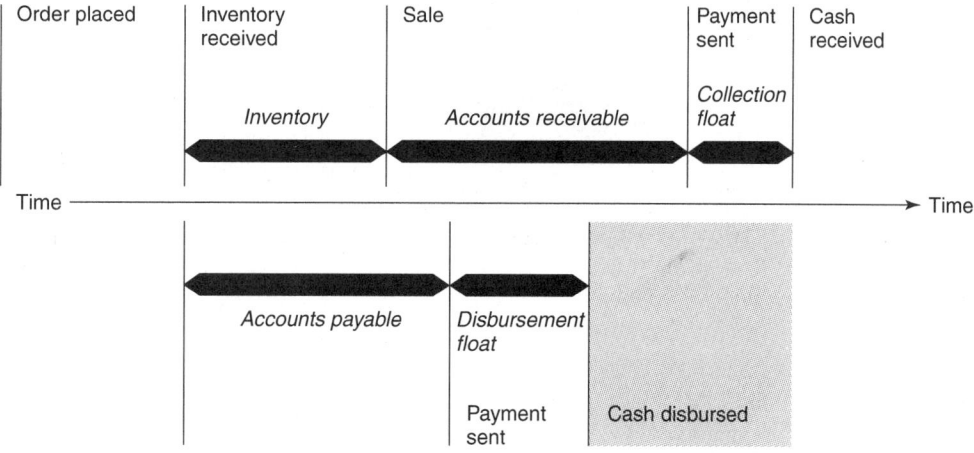

Specific Financing Strategies

Over the course of its operating cycle, a firm's assets tend to fluctuate, rising as operations gear up for seasonal peak sales and then subsiding as sales fall. Exhibit 700.10 demonstrates this trend for a firm that is growing and adding to its fixed asset base. In the exhibit, assets begin to grow as time moves from the left to the right with inventory build up in anticipation of future sales. As sales pick up, inventory is maintained for a time by increased production, and receivables begin to accumulate as inventory is sold. As sales level off, production is reduced, resulting in a drop in inventory. Receivables also begin to fall as collections exceed the creation of new receivables. As receivables are collected, the cash received is used to pay off accounts payable and other short-term loans used to finance the earlier accumulation of inventory and receivables. This cycle then repeats itself as the firm approaches a new operating period.

In Exhibit 700.10, you may have noticed the decomposition of total current assets into two parts, a level of **permanent current assets** and a level of **temporary current assets.** It may seem strange to refer to current assets as permanent but a firm always has some minimum or permanent amount of inventory and receivables on its books. Although the products in inventory and the specific accounts held as receivables do turn over, there is always a minimum amount of resources invested in these accounts. This minimum level of ongoing inventory and receivables is what is referred to as permanent current assets.

The temporary component of total current assets, then, represents the accumulation of inventory in anticipation of the peak selling season and the resulting receivables generated by the increasing sales. This bulge in inventory and receivables then subsides as the firm passes through its peak-selling season.

Exhibit 700.10 *The Firm's Fluctuating Assets Over Its Operating Cycle*

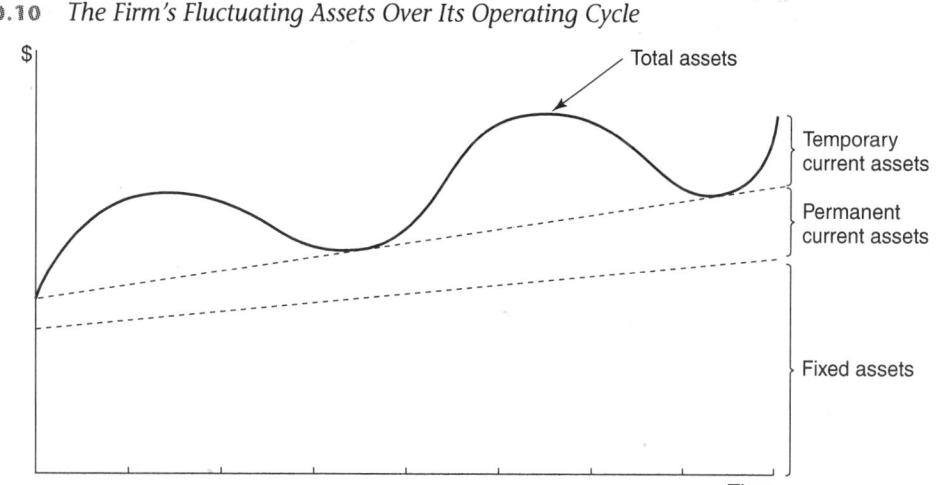

710. MANAGING SHORT-TERM FINANCING

Exhibit 700.11 *Short-Term Financing Strategies*

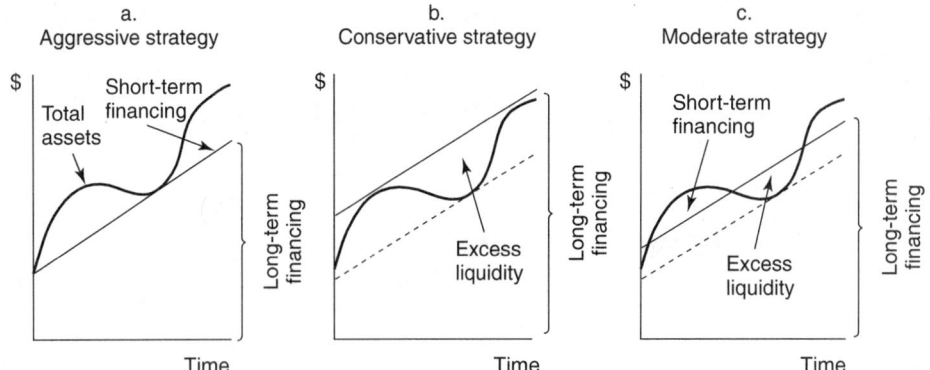

There are three basic strategies from which the financial manager can choose as financing is sought to support the firm's asset needs over its operating cycle. The three strategies include the aggressive strategy, the conservative strategy, and the moderate strategy. These three financing strategies are illustrated in Exhibit 700.11. You may wish to refer to this exhibit as each of the strategies is discussed below.

Aggressive Strategy

Aggressive strategy versus conservative strategy versus moderate strategy

- With aggressive financing strategy, a firm uses more short-term sources, its debt costs are low, profits are high, and solvency (liquidity) is low.
- With conservative financing strategy, a firm uses more long-term sources, its debt costs are high, profits are low, and solvency (liquidity) is high.
- With moderate financing strategy, a firm operates in between the aggressive and conservative strategies.

The **aggressive financing strategy** is basically a maturity matching strategy. Using this strategy, the financial manager chooses to match the maturity of the source of financing with the duration of the need of cash. In the exhibit, the wavy line represents the total assets of the firm over time. Over the course of the firm's operating activities, total assets rise and fall primarily because of the fluctuations in receivables, inventory, and payables over the working capital cycle. The wavy line will exhibit an upward trend if the firm is growing and adding to its fixed asset base. In Panel a of Exhibit 700.11, the firm is maximizing its reliance on short-term financing and minimizing its reliance on permanent or long-term financing. The corporation's net working capital position, as a result, is minimal because of the heavy reliance on short-term financing, and therefore the solvency position of the firm, as measured by the current ratio, will suffer. This strategy has an advantage in that during normal financial conditions, short-term sources of financing cost less than longer-term sources. For example, on April 14, 2000, 90-day Treasury bills yielded 5.67% while 5-year Treasury notes yielded 6.18%. Thus there is normally a trade-off of a lower financing cost at the expense of a reduced solvency level.

There is some evidence that firms use a maturity matching strategy as reported by Beranek, Cornwell, and Choi. In their research, they found that firms do not emphasize external short-term sources in the financing of capital expenditures, nor do they use the bulk of long-term external financing in a given period to finance the acquisition of short-lived assets. Thus firms generally act as if they seek to match the maturity of their external financing with the life of their acquired assets.

Conservative Strategy

The **conservative financing strategy** uses only long-term sources to fulfill all the corporation's financing needs as demonstrated in Panel b of Exhibit 700.11. As total assets increase as a result of a build up of inventory and receivables, the firm draws down its excess liquidity stored in short-term investments. Then as inventory is sold and receivables collected, excess cash is reinvested in short-term investments. Thus over a part of its working capital cycle, the corporation has an excess solvency position, as indicated by a relatively high current ratio. Because the corporation uses no short-term financing, it will have substantial financing flexibility in acquiring new short-term sources of financing if it underestimates its actual future cash needs. Under normal financial market conditions, this strategy is relatively expensive because long-term financing sources are generally more expensive than short-term sources. However, the reliance on longer-term sources does provide a greater solvency position as measured by the current ratio.

Moderate Strategy

The **moderate financing strategy,** Panel c of Exhibit 700.11, is a blend of the extreme strategies represented by the aggressive and conservative strategies discussed previously. The exact blend of short- and long-term sources depends on the risk preferences of the corporation as well as the current financial market conditions.

The Effective Cost of Short-Term Financing

Short-term financing arrangements have several features that cause the stated interest rate on the financing to be different from the **effective interest rate.** A very general formula that forms the basis for our discussion is shown in Equation 7.8.

$$\text{Effective rate} = \frac{\text{Out-of-pocket expenses}}{\text{Usable funds}} \times \frac{365}{M} \tag{7.8}$$

Out-of-pocket expenses include interest expense and fees. Interest expense is based on the stated interest rate and the amount borrowed over the funding period. Fees include commitment fees charged by the bank for the total amount of funds the bank stands ready to lend to the firm through a line of credit or a letter of credit facility, letter of credit fees, or commercial paper dealer fees. **Usable funds** represent the net proceeds the firm receives from the financing vehicle. If funds are received through a credit line, the amount received may be less than the amount borrowed if the bank requires the firm to leave compensating balances as a percent of the amount borrowed. If funds are received through an issue of commercial paper, then the amount received is reduced by the discounted interest paid.

The final part of Equation 7.8 annualizes the length of the borrowing period, M, assuming that it is one year or less. The effective rate thus calculated is the annualized effective simple interest rate on the financing arrangement. This equation is applied to commercial paper and a bank credit line facility in the following sections.

Effective Cost of Commercial Paper

The treasurer at Consolidated Trailways, Inc., is preparing a new issue of commercial paper through a dealer network. Commercial paper is a typical source of financing for Consolidated and the firm generally has several million dollars of paper outstanding throughout the year. In discussing the new issue with its commercial paper dealer, Consolidated has learned that new 30-day issues in the range of $1 to $5 million can be priced to sell at a 9% discount rate. The dealer's fee will be an annual rate of 1/8 of 1% and the commitment fee on a back-up line of credit will be an annual rate of .25%. The treasurer wants to know what the effective rate of issuing $3 million 30-day commercial paper will be.

Out-of-Pocket Costs

To apply Equation 7.8, the treasurer needs to determine the value of two variables: out-of-pocket costs and usable funds. Let's start with out-of-pocket costs. First, the major component of out-of-pocket costs is the interest that Consolidated will have to pay. The commercial paper will be issued on a discount basis; the difference between the face amount and the discounted price is the interest that the firm pays. The face amount is the $3 million stated earlier. The discounted price is the face amount minus 30 days interest, 30 days being the maturity of the paper. The discount price is $2,977,500 = $3 million − (.09 × (30/360) × $3 million). The interest paid is thus $22,500. Note that the interest computation uses a 360-day year, which is the convention with discount rates. The dealer's fee is .125%, which costs the firm $312.50 = $3 million × .00125 × (30/360). The commitment fee for the back-up line of credit is $625 = $3 million × (.0025 × (30/360)). The total out-of-pocket cost is the sum of the interest expense, dealer fee, and bank commitment fee, which totals $23,437.50 = $22,500 + $312.50 + $625.

Usable Funds

Next, the dollar amount of usable funds must be determined. The treasurer has determined that the discount price of the $3 million issue will result in proceeds of $2,977,500, which is equal to the face value minus the discount interest at the asked rate.

Effective Interest Rate

Plugging the values for the out-of-pocket costs and usable funds into Equation 7.8 results in the effective annualized interest rate for the 30-day commercial paper.

$$\text{Effective rate} = \frac{\$23,473.50}{\$2,977,500} \times \frac{365}{30}$$

$$\text{Effective rate} = .0958 \text{ or } 9.58\%$$

The effective cost of the paper is 58 basis points above the stated asked discount rate of 9%. Note the money market convention that effective rates are based on a 365-day year rather than a 360-day year.

Had Consolidated not been a regular issuer of commercial paper, using a line of credit as a back-up facility might not be appropriate. Credit lines are not generally set up for periods less than one year. Therefore the annual cost of the credit line will have to be allocated to the 30-day financing period and then annualized. This will result in an out-of-pocket cost of $30,312.50 = $22,500 + $312.50 + $7,500. The $7,500 is the annual cost of the credit line commitment fee and must now be allocated in total to the 30-day financing period. Usable funds will remain unchanged. The effective rate then becomes 12.39%. In this case, the use of a letter of credit rather than a line of credit as a back-up facility is more appropriate. A letter of credit can be designed to be in effect for any length of period necessary.

Managing Long-Term Financing

Traditional sources of long-term financing include common stock (equity) and bonds, term loans, and notes (debt). Alternative sources of long-term financing include preferred stocks, leases, options, warrants, and convertibles. Another possible source is treasury stock, which is company stock repurchased by the company from the open market. The treasury stock, which is taken out of circulation after its repurchase, can be resold to investors in the open market.

Common Stock

Balance Sheet Accounts and Definitions

An understanding of legal and accounting terminology is vital to both investors and financial managers if they are to avoid misinterpretations and possibly costly mistakes. Therefore, we begin our analysis of common stock with a discussion of accounting and legal issues. Consider first Exhibit 700.12 which shows the **common equity** section of Unilate Textiles' balance sheet. Unilate's owners—its stockholders—have authorized management to issue a total of 40 million shares, and management has thus far actually issued (or sold) 25 million shares. Each share has a **par value** of $1; this is the minimum amount for which new shares can be issued. A stock's par value is an arbitrary figure that originally indicated the minimum amount of money stockholders had put up. Today, firms generally are not required to establish a par value for their stock. Thus, Unilate Textiles could have elected to use *no-par* stock, in which case the common stock and additional paid-in capital accounts would have been consolidated under one account called *common stock*, which would show a 2000 balance of $130 million. During 2000, Unilate earned $54 million, paid $29 million in dividends, and retained $25 million. The $25 million was added to the $260 million accumulated **retained earnings** shown on the year-end 1999 balance sheet to produce the $285 million retained earnings at year-end 2000. Thus, since its inception, Unilate has retained, or plowed back, a total of $285 million. This is money that belongs to the stockholders that they could have received in the form of dividends. Instead, the stockholders chose to let management reinvest the $285 million in the business so growth could be achieved.

Exhibit 700.12 *Unilate Textiles Balance Sheet: Common Equity Accounts as of December 31 (millions of dollars, except per share data)*

	2000	1999
Common stock (40 million shares authorized, 25 million shares outstanding, $1 par)	$ 25.0	$ 25.0
Additional paid-in capital	105.0	105.0
Retained earnings	285.0	260.0
Total common stockholders' equity (net worth)	$415.0	$390.0
Book value per share	$16.60	$15.60

Now consider the $105 million **additional paid-in capital.** This account shows the difference between the stock's par value and what new stockholders paid when they bought newly issued shares. For example, in 1980, when Unilate was formed, 15 million shares were issued at par value; thus, the first balance sheet showed a zero for paid-in capital and $15 million for the common stock account. However, in 1983, to raise funds for expansion projects, Unilate issued 10 million shares at a market price of $11.50 per share—total value of the issue was $115 million. At that time, the common stock account was increased by $10 million ($1 par value for the 10 million shares issued), and the remainder of the $115 million issue value, $105 million, was added to additional paid-in capital. Unilate has not issued any more stock since 1983, so the only change in the common equity section since that time has been in retained earnings.

The **book value per share** shown in Exhibit 700.12 is computed by dividing the amount of total stockholders' equity, which also is called *net worth*, by the number of shares outstanding. Unilate's book value per share increased in 2000 to $16.60, from $15.60 in 1999. Whenever stock is sold at a price above book value or the change in retained earnings is positive, book value will increase, and vice versa. Because book value is a historical cost amount, investors prefer that the market value of stock be greater than its book value; a stock that is selling below its book value might suggest the company is experiencing financial difficulty.

Legal Rights and Privileges of Common Stockholders

The common stockholders are the owners of a corporation, and as such they have certain rights and privileges. The most important rights are discussed in this section. They include control of the firm and the preemptive right.

Control of the Firm

The stockholders have the right to elect the firm's directors, who in turn elect the officers who manage the business. In a small firm, the major stockholder typically assumes the positions of president and chairperson of the board of directors. In a large, publicly-owned firm, the managers typically have some stock, but their personal holdings are insufficient to provide voting control. Thus, the managements of most publicly-owned firms can be removed by the stockholders if they decide a management team is not effective.

Various state and federal laws stipulate how stockholder control is to be exercised. First, corporations must hold an election of directors periodically, usually once a year, with the vote taken at the annual meeting. Frequently, one-third of the directors are elected each year for a three-year term. Each share of stock normally has one vote; thus, the owner of 1,000 shares has 1,000 votes. Stockholders can appear at the annual meeting and vote in person, but typically they transfer their right to vote to a second party by means of an instrument known as a **proxy.** Management always solicits stockholders' proxies and usually gets them. However, if earnings are poor and stockholders are dissatisfied, an outside group might solicit the proxies in an effort to overthrow management and take control of the business. This is known as a **proxy fight.**

Managers who do not have majority control (more than 50% of their firms' stock) are very much concerned about proxy fights and takeovers, and many attempt to get stockholder approval for changes in their corporate charters that would make takeovers more difficult. For example, a number of companies have gotten their stockholders to agree (1) to elect only one-third of the directors each year (rather than electing all directors each year); (2) to require 75% of the stockholders (rather than 50%) to approve a merger; and (3) to vote in a "poison pill" provision that would allow the stockholders of a firm that is taken over by another firm to buy shares in the second firm at a reduced price. The third provision makes the acquisition unattractive and, thus, wards off hostile takeover attempts. Managements seeking such changes generally cite a fear that the firm will be picked up at a bargain price, but it often appears that managers' concerns about their own positions might be an even more important consideration.

The Preemptive Right

Common stockholders often have the right, called the **preemptive right,** to purchase any additional shares sold by the firm. In some states the preemptive right is automatically included in every corporate charter; in others it is necessary to insert it specifically into the charter.

The purpose of the preemptive right is twofold. First, it protects the power of control of current stockholders. If it were not for this safeguard, the management of a corporation under criticism from stockholders could prevent stockholders from removing it from office by issuing a large number of additional shares and purchasing these shares itself. Management could thereby secure control of the corporation and frustrate the will of the current stockholders.

The second, and more important, reason for the preemptive right is that it protects stockholders against a dilution of value. For example, suppose 1,000 shares of common stock, each with a price of $100, were outstanding, making the total market value of the firm $100,000. If an additional 1,000 shares were sold at $50 a share, or for $50,000, this would raise the total market value of the firm to $150,000. When the total market value is divided by the new total shares outstanding, a value of $75 a share is obtained. The old stockholders thus lose $25 per share, and the new stockholders have an instant profit of $25 per share. Thus, selling common stock at a price below the market value would dilute its price and would transfer wealth from the present stockholders to those who were allowed to purchase the new shares. The preemptive right prevents such occurrences.

Types of Common Stock

Although most firms have only one type of common stock, in some instances **classified stock** is used to meet the special needs of the company. Generally, when special classifications of stock are used, one type is designated Class A, another Class B, and so on. Small, new companies seeking to obtain funds from outside sources frequently use different types of common stock. For example, when **Genetic Concepts** went public, its Class A stock was sold to the public and paid a dividend, but this stock did not have voting rights until five years after its issue. Its Class B stock, which was retained by the organizers of the company, had full voting rights for five years, but the legal terms stated that dividends could not be paid on the Class B stock until the company had established its earning power by building up retained earnings to a designated level. The use of classified stock thus enabled the public to take a position in a conservatively financed growth company without

Another type of common stock is target stock *which represents a claim on a specific, usually new, part of a firm such as when starting a new business, division, branch office, warehouse, subsidiary, or a new product line.*

sacrificing income, while the founders retained absolute control during the crucial early stages of the firm's development. At the same time, outside investors were protected against excessive withdrawals of funds by the original owners. As is often the case in such situations, the Class B stock was called **founders' shares.**

Note that "Class A," "Class B," and so on, have no standard meanings—one firm could designate its Class B shares as founders' shares and its Class A shares as those sold to the public, while another could reverse these designations. Still other firms could use stock classifications for entirely different purposes.

Evaluation of Common Stock as a Source of Funds

Thus far the section has covered the main characteristics of common stock. Now we will appraise stock financing both from the viewpoint of the corporation and from a social perspective.

From the Corporation's Viewpoint

The advantages and disadvantages of using common stock as a financing source are listed in this section.

ADVANTAGES   Common stock offers several advantages to the corporation.

1. Common stock does not legally obligate the firm to make payments to stockholders: Only if the company generates earnings and has no pressing internal needs for them will it pay dividends.

2. Common stock carries no fixed maturity date—it never has to be "repaid" as would a debt issue.
3. Because common stock cushions creditors against losses, the sale of common stock generally increases the creditworthiness of the firm. This in turn raises its bond rating, lowers its cost of debt, and increases its future ability to use debt.
4. If a company's prospects look bright, then common stock often can be sold on better terms than debt. Stock appeals to certain groups of investors because (a) it typically carries a higher expected total return (dividends plus capital gains) than does preferred stock or debt; and (b) as a representation of the ownership of the firm, stock provides the investor with a better hedge against unanticipated inflation because common dividends tend to rise during inflationary periods.

DISADVANTAGES Disadvantages associated with issuing common stock include the following.

1. The sale of common stock gives some voting rights, and perhaps even control, to new stockholders. For this reason, additional equity financing often is avoided by managers who are concerned about maintaining control. The use of founders' shares and other classes of common stock can mitigate this problem.
2. Common stock gives new owners the right to share in the income of the firm; if profits soar, then new stockholders will share in this bonanza, whereas if debt had been used, new investors (creditors in this case) would have received only a fixed return, no matter how profitable the company had been, and existing stockholders would have received the rest. This point has given rise to an important theory: "If a firm sells a large issue of bonds, this is a signal that management expects the company to earn high profits on investments financed by the new capital and that it does not wish to share these profits with new stockholders. On the other hand, if the firm issues stock, this is a signal that its prospects are not so bright."
3. As we shall see, the costs of underwriting and distributing common stock usually are higher than those for debt or preferred stock. Flotation costs for common stock characteristically are higher because (a) the costs of investigating an equity security investment are higher than those for a comparable debt security; and (b) stocks are riskier than debt, meaning that investors must diversify their equity holdings, so a given dollar amount of new stock must be sold to a larger number of purchasers than the same amount of debt.
4. If the firm has more equity than is called for in its optimal capital structure, the average cost of capital will be higher than necessary. Therefore, a firm would not want to sell stock if the sale caused its equity ratio (1.0 minus the debt ratio) to exceed the optimal level.
5. Under current tax laws, common stock dividends are not deductible as an expense for tax purposes, but bond interest is deductible. Taxes raise the relative cost of equity as compared with debt.

From a Social Viewpoint

From a social viewpoint, common stock is a desirable form of financing because it makes businesses less vulnerable to the consequences of declines in sales and earnings. Common stock financing involves no fixed charge payments that might force a faltering firm into bankruptcy. From the standpoint of the economy as a whole, if too many firms used too much debt, business fluctuations would be amplified, and minor recessions could turn into major ones. Not long ago, when the level of leveraged mergers and buyouts was raising the aggregate debt ratio (the average debt ratio of all firms), the Federal Reserve and other authorities voiced concern over the possible dangers created by the situation, and congressional leaders debated the wisdom of social controls over corporations' use of debt. Like most important issues, this one is debatable, and the debate centers around who can better determine "appropriate" capital structures—corporate managers or government officials.

Long-Term Debt

Different groups of investors prefer different types of securities, and investors' tastes change over time. Thus, astute financial managers offer a variety of securities, and they package their new security offerings at each point in time to appeal to the greatest possible number of potential investors. In this section, we consider the various types of long-term debt available to financial managers.

Long-term debt is often called **funded debt.** When a firm "funds" its short-term debt, this means that it replaces short-term debt with securities of longer maturity. Funding does not imply that the firm places money with a trustee or other repository; and it means that the firm replaces short-term debt with long-term debt or equity. **Pacific Gas & Electric Company (PG&E)** provides a good example of funding. PG&E has a continuous construction program, and it typically uses short-term debt to finance construction expenditures. However, once short-term debt has built up to about $100 million, the company sells a stock or bond issue, uses the proceeds to pay off (or fund) its bank loans, and starts the cycle again. There is a fixed cost involved in selling stocks or bonds that makes it quite expensive to issue small amounts of these securities. Therefore, the process used by PG&E and other companies is quite logical.

Traditional Debt Instruments

There are many types of long-term debt instruments: term loans, bonds, secured and unsecured notes, marketable and nonmarketable debt, and so on. In this section, we briefly discuss the traditional long-term debt instruments, after which we examine some important features of debt contracts and some innovations in long-term debt financing.

Term Loans

A **term loan** is a contract under which a borrower agrees to make a series of interest and principal payments on specific dates to the lender. Term loans usually are negotiated directly between the borrowing firm and a financial institution—generally a bank, an insurance company, or a pension fund. Although term loans' maturities vary from two to 30 years, most are for periods in the 3-year to 15-year range.

Most term loans are amortized, which means they are paid off in equal installments over the life of the loan. Amortization protects the lender against the possibility that the borrower will not make adequate provisions for the loan's retirement during the life of the loan. Also, if the interest and principal payments required under a term loan agreement are not met on schedule, the borrowing firm is said to have defaulted, and it can then be forced into bankruptcy.

Term loans have three major advantages over public offerings—*speed, flexibility,* and *low issuance costs*. Because they are negotiated directly between the lender and the borrower, formal documentation is minimized. The key provisions of a term loan can be worked out much more quickly than those for a public issue, and it is not necessary for the loan to go through the Securities and Exchange Commission registration process. A further advantage of term loans has to do with future flexibility. If a bond issue is held by many different bondholders, it is virtually impossible to obtain permission to alter the terms of the agreement, even though new economic conditions might make such changes desirable. With a term loan, the borrower generally can sit down with the lender and work out mutually agreeable modifications to the contract.

The interest rate on a term loan can be either fixed for the life of the loan or variable. If a fixed rate is used, generally it will be set close to the rate on bonds of equivalent maturity and risk. If the rate is variable, it usually will be set at a certain number of percentage points over either the prime rate, the commercial paper rate, rates on Treasury securities, or the London InterBank Offered Rate (LIBOR), which is the rate of interest offered by the largest and strongest London banks on deposits of other large banks of the highest credit standing. Then, when the index rate goes up or down, so does the rate charged on the outstanding balance of the term loan. Rates might be adjusted annually, semiannually, quarterly, monthly, or on some other basis, depending on what the contract specifies. Today, most term loans made by banks have floating rates; in 1970, there were very few floating-rate term notes. With the increased volatility of interest rates in recent years, banks and other lenders have become increasingly reluctant to make long-term, fixed-rate loans.

Bonds

A **bond** is a long-term contract under which a borrower agrees to make payments of interest and principal on specific dates to the holder of the bond. Although bonds traditionally have been issued with maturities of between 20 and 30 years, in recent years shorter maturities, such as 7 to 10 years, have been used to an increasing extent. Bonds are similar to term loans, but a bond issue generally is advertised, offered to the public, and actually sold to many different investors. Indeed, thousands of individual and institutional investors might purchase bonds when a firm sells a bond issue, whereas there usually is only one lender in the case of a term loan.

However, for very large term loans, 20 or more financial institutions might form a syndicate to grant the credit. Also, it should be noted that a bond issue can be sold to one lender (or to just a few); in this case, the issue is said to be "privately placed." Companies that place bonds privately do so for the same reasons that they use term loans—speed, flexibility, and low issuance costs. With bonds the interest rate generally is fixed, although in recent years there has been an increase in the use of various types of floating rate bonds. There also are a number of different types of bonds, the more important of which are discussed next.

MORTGAGE BONDS With a **mortgage bond,** the corporation pledges certain assets as security for the bond. To illustrate, in 2000 **Scobes Corporation** needed $10 million to build a major regional distribution center. Bonds in the amount of $4 million, secured by a mortgage on the property, were issued. (The remaining $6 million was financed with equity capital.) If Scobes defaults on the bonds, the bondholders can foreclose on the property and sell it to satisfy their claims.

If Scobes chooses to, it can issue *second mortgage bonds* secured by the same $10 million plant. In the event of liquidation, the holders of these second mortgage bonds would have a claim against the property, but only after the first mortgage bondholders had been paid off in full. Thus, second mortgages are sometimes called *junior mortgages* because they are junior in priority to the claims of *senior mortgages,* or *first mortgage bonds.*

All mortgage bonds are written subject to an *indenture,* which is a legal document that spells out in detail the rights of both the bondholders and the corporation (bond issuer). Indentures generally are "open ended," meaning that new bonds might be issued from time to time under the existing indenture. However, the amount of new bonds that can be issued almost always is limited to a specified percentage of the firm's total "bondable property," which generally includes all plant and equipment. For example, **Savannah Electric Company** can issue first mortgage bonds totaling up to 60% of its fixed assets. If its fixed assets totaled $1 billion, and if it had $500 million of first mortgage bonds outstanding, it could, by the property test, issue another $100 million of bonds (60% of $1 billion = $600 million).

DEBENTURES A **debenture** is an unsecured bond, and as such it provides no lien against specific property as security for the obligation. Therefore, debenture holders are general creditors whose claims are protected by property not otherwise pledged. In practice, the use of debentures depends both on the nature of the firm's assets and on its general credit strength. An extremely strong company, such as **IBM**, will tend to use debentures; it simply does not need to put up property as security for its debt. Debentures also are issued by companies in industries in which it would not be practical to provide security through a mortgage on fixed assets. Examples of such industries are the large mail-order houses and commercial banks, which characteristically hold most of their assets in the form of inventory or loans, neither of which is satisfactory security for a mortgage bond.

SUBORDINATED DEBENTURES The term *subordinate* means "below," or "inferior to," and, in the event of bankruptcy, subordinated debt has claims on assets only after senior debt has been paid off. **Subordinated debentures** might be subordinated either to designated notes payable (usually bank loans) or to all other debt. In the event of liquidation or reorganization, holders of subordinated debentures cannot be paid until all senior debt, as named in the debentures' indenture, has been paid.

OTHER TYPES OF BONDS Several other types of bonds are used sufficiently often to warrant mention. First, **convertible bonds** are securities that are convertible into shares of common stock, at a fixed price, at the option of the bondholder. Convertibles have a lower coupon rate than nonconvertible debt, but they offer investors a chance for capital gains in exchange for the lower coupon rate. Bonds issued with **warrants** are similar to convertibles. Warrants are options that permit the holder to buy stock for a stated price, thereby providing a capital gain if the price of the stock rises. Bonds that are issued with warrants, like convertibles, carry lower coupon rates than straight bonds. **Income bonds** pay interest only when the firm has sufficient income to cover the interest payments. Thus, these securities cannot bankrupt a company, but from an investor's standpoint they are riskier than "regular" bonds. **Putable bonds** are bonds that can be turned in and exchanged for cash at the bondholder's option; generally, the option to turn in the bond can be exercised only if the firm takes some specified action, such as being acquired by a weaker company or increasing its outstanding debt by a large amount. With an **indexed,** or **purchasing power, bond,** which is popular in countries plagued by high rates of inflation, the interest rate payment is based on an inflation index such as the consumer price index; so the interest paid rises automatically when the inflation rate rises, thus protecting the bondholders against inflation.

Specific Debt Contract Features

A firm's managers are concerned with both the effective cost of debt and any restrictions in debt contracts that might limit the firm's future actions. In this section, we discuss features that could affect either the cost of the firm's debt or the firm's future flexibility.

Bond Indentures

Earlier we discussed *agency problems*, which relate to conflicts of interest among corporate stakeholders—stockholders, bondholders, and managers. Bondholders have a legitimate fear that once they lend money to a company and are "locked in" for up to 30 years, the company will take some action that is designed to benefit stockholders but that harms bondholders. For example, **RJR Nabisco**, when it was highly rated, sold 30-year bonds with a low coupon rate, and investors bought those bonds in spite of the low yield because of their low risk. Then, after the bonds had been sold, the company announced plans to issue a great deal more debt, increasing the expected rate of return to stockholders but also increasing the riskiness of the bonds. RJR's bonds fell 20% the week the announcement was made. **Safeway Stores** and a number of other companies have done the same thing, and their bondholders also lost heavily as the market yield on the bonds rose and drove the prices of the bonds down.

Investors attempt to reduce agency problems by use of legal restrictions designed to ensure, insofar as possible, that the company does nothing to cause the quality of its bonds to deteriorate after they have been issued. The **indenture** is the legal document that spells out the rights of the bondholders and the corporation. A **trustee,** usually a bank, is assigned to represent the bondholders and to make sure that the terms of the indenture are carried out. The indenture might be several hundred pages in length, and it will include **restrictive covenants** that cover such points as the conditions under which the issuer can pay off the bonds prior to maturity, the level at which the issuer's times-interest-earned ratio must be maintained if the company is to sell additional bonds, and restrictions against the payment of dividends when earnings do not meet certain specifications.

A firm will have different indentures for each major type of bond it issues, including its first mortgage bonds, its debentures, its convertibles, and so on.

The trustee is responsible both for making sure the covenants are not violated and for taking appropriate action if they are. What constitutes "appropriate action" varies with the circumstances. It might be that to insist on immediate compliance would result in bankruptcy, which in turn might lead to large losses on the bonds. In such a case, the trustee might decide that the bondholders would be better served by giving the company a chance to work out its problems rather than by forcing it into bankruptcy.

The Securities and Exchange Commission (SEC) approves indentures for publicly traded bonds and makes sure that all indenture provisions are met before allowing a company to sell new securities to the public. The indentures of many larger corporations were written back in the 1930s or 1940s, and many issues of new bonds, all covered by the same indenture, have been sold down through the years. The interest rates on the bonds, and perhaps also the maturities, will change from issue to issue, but bondholders' protection as spelled out in the indenture will be the same for all bonds of a given type.

Call Provisions

Most bonds contain a **call provision,** which gives the issuing corporation the right to call the bonds for redemption. The call provision generally states that the company must pay the bondholders an amount greater than the par value for the bonds when they are called. The additional sum, which is termed a *call premium,* typically is set equal to one year's interest if the bonds are called during the first year, and the premium declines at a constant rate of INT/N each year thereafter, where INT = annual interest and N = original maturity in years. For example, the call premium on a $1,000 par value, ten-year, 10% bond would generally be $100 if it were called during the first year, $90 during the second year (calculated by reducing the $100, or 10%, premium by one-tenth), and so on. However, bonds usually are not callable until several years (generally five to ten) after they are issued; bonds with these *deferred calls* are said to have *call protection*.

Suppose a company sold bonds when interest rates were relatively high. Provided the issue is callable, the company could sell a new issue of low-yielding bonds if and when interest rates drop. It could then use the proceeds to retire the high-rate issue and thus reduce its interest expense. This process is called **bond refunding**.

Sinking Funds

A **sinking fund** is a provision that facilitates the orderly retirement of a bond issue. Typically, the sinking fund provision requires the firm to retire a portion of the bond issue each year. On rare occasions the firm might be required to deposit money with a trustee, which invests the funds and then uses the accumulated sum to retire the bonds when they mature. A failure to meet the sinking fund requirement causes the bond issue to be thrown into default, which might force the company into bankruptcy. Obviously, a sinking fund can constitute a dangerous cash drain on the firm.

In most cases, the firm is given the right to handle the sinking fund in either of two ways.

1. The company can call in for redemption (at par value) a certain percentage of the bonds each year; for example, it might be able to call 2% of the total original amount of the issue at a price of $1,000 per bond. The bonds are numbered serially, and those called for redemption are determined by a lottery administered by the trustee.
2. The company might buy the required amount of bonds on the open market.

The firm will choose the least-cost method. If interest rates have risen, causing bond prices to fall, it will buy bonds in the open market at a discount; if interest rates have fallen, it will call the bonds. Note that a call for sinking fund purposes is quite different from a refunding call. A sinking fund call requires no call premium, but only a small percentage of the issue normally is callable in any one year.

Bond Innovations in the Past Few Decades

Zero (or Very Low) Coupon Bonds

Some bonds pay no interest but are offered at a substantial discount below their par values and hence provide capital appreciation rather than interest income. These securities are called **zero coupon bonds** ("*zeros*"), or *original issue discount bonds (OIDs)*. Corporations first used zeros in a major way in 1981. More recently, many large companies like **IBM** and **JCPenney** have used them to raise billions of dollars. Municipal governments also sell "zero munis," and investment bankers have in effect created zero coupon Treasury bonds by "stripping" the interest payments and selling only the right to receive principal repayment at maturity.

Not all OIDs have zero coupons. For example, a company might sell an issue of five-year bonds with a 3% coupon at a time when other bonds with similar ratings and maturities are yielding 9%. If an investor purchases these bonds at a price of $762.62, the yield to maturity would be 9%. The discount of $1,000 − $762.62 = $237.38 represents the capital appreciation the bondholder receives for holding the bond for five years. Thus, zero coupon bonds are just one type of original issue discount bond. Any nonconvertible bond whose coupon rate is set below the going market rate at the time of its issue will sell at a discount, and it will be classified as an OID bond.

OID bonds have lost favor with many individual investors in recent years. The primary reason is because the interest income that must be reported each year for tax purposes includes the dollar amount of interest actually received, which is $0 for zero coupons, plus the annual *prorated* capital appreciation. For example, the purchaser of the 3% coupon bond just mentioned actually would receive $30 interest each year. But the interest income reported for tax purposes would be $30 + ($237.38/5) = $77.48. Thus, taxes would have to be paid on prorated capital gains that would not be received for five years ($47.48 each year). For this reason, most OID bonds currently are held by institutional investors, such as insurance companies and pension funds, rather than individual investors.

Shortly after corporations began to issue zeros, investment bankers figured out a way to create zeros from U.S. Treasury bonds, which are issued only in coupon form. In 1982 **Salomon Brothers** (now **Salomon Smith Barney**) bought $1 billion of 12%, 30-year Treasuries. Each bond had 60 coupons worth $60 each, which represented the interest payments due every six months. Salomon then in effect clipped the coupons and placed them in 60 piles; the last pile also contained the now "stripped" bond itself, which represented a promise of $1,000 in the year 2012. These 60 piles of U.S. Treasury promises were then placed with the trust department of a bank and used as collateral for "zero coupon U.S. Treasury Trust Certificates," which are, in essence, zero coupon Treasury bonds. A pension fund that expected to need money in 2002 could have bought 20-year certificates backed by the interest the Treasury will pay in 2002. Treasury zeros are, of course, safer than corporate zeros, so they are very popular with pension fund managers.

Corporate (and municipal) zeros generally are callable at the option of the issuer, just like coupon bonds, after some stated call protection period. The call price is set at a premium over the accrued value at the time of the call.

Stripped U.S. Treasury bonds (Treasury zeros) generally are not callable because the Treasury normally sells non-callable bonds. Thus, Treasury zeros are completely protected against reinvestment risk (the risk of having to invest cash flows from a bond at a lower rate because of a decline in interest rates).

Floating Rate Debt

In the early 1980s, inflation pushed interest rates up to unprecedented levels, causing sharp declines in the prices of long-term bonds. Even some supposedly "risk-free" U.S. Treasury bonds lost fully half their value, and a similar situation occurred with corporate bonds, mortgages, and other fixed-rate, long-term securities. As a result, many lenders became reluctant to lend money at fixed rates on a long-term basis, and they would do so only at extraordinarily high rates.

There normally is a *maturity risk premium* embodied in long-term interest rates; this premium is designed to offset the risk of declining bond prices if interest rates rise. Prior to the 1970s, the maturity risk premium on 30-year bonds was about one percentage point, meaning that under normal conditions, a firm might expect to pay about one percentage point more to borrow on a long-term than on a short-term basis. However, in the early 1980s, the maturity risk premium is estimated to have jumped to about three percentage points, which made long-term debt very expensive relative to short-term debt. Lenders were able and willing to lend on a short-term basis, but corporations were correctly reluctant to borrow on a short-term basis to finance long-term assets—such action is extremely dangerous. Therefore, there was a situation in which lenders did not want to lend on a long-term basis, but corporations needed long-term money. The problem was solved by the introduction of long-term, *floating rate debt*.

A typical **floating rate bond** works as follows. The coupon rate is set for, say, the initial six-month period, after which it is adjusted every six months based on some market rate. Some corporate issues have been tied to the Treasury bond rate, while other issues have been tied to short-term rates. Many additional provisions can be included in floating rate issues; for example, some are convertible to fixed rate debt, whereas others have upper and lower limits ("caps" and "collars") on how high or low the yield can go.

Floating rate debt is advantageous to investors because the interest rate moves up if market rates rise. This causes the market value of the debt to be stabilized, and it also provides lenders such as banks with income that is better geared to their own obligations. Moreover, floating rate debt is advantageous to corporations because by using it, firms can issue debt with a long maturity without committing themselves to paying a historically high rate of interest for the entire life of the loan. Of course, if interest rates were to move even higher after a floating rate note had been signed, the borrower would have been better off issuing conventional, fixed rate debt.

Junk Bonds

Prior to the 1980s, fixed income investors such as pension funds and insurance companies generally were unwilling to buy risky bonds, so it was almost impossible for risky companies to raise capital in the public bond markets. These companies, if they could raise debt capital at all, had to do so in the term loan market, where the loan could be tailored to satisfy the lender. Then, in the late 1970s, Michael Milken of the investment banking firm **Drexel Burnham Lambert**, relying on historical studies that showed risky bonds yielded more than enough to compensate for their risk, began to convince certain institutional investors of the merits of purchasing risky debt. Thus was born the **junk bond**, a high-risk, high-yield bond issued to finance a leveraged buyout, a merger, or a troubled company. For example, when Ted Turner attempted to buy **CBS**, he planned to finance the acquisition by issuing junk bonds to CBS's stockholders in exchange for their shares. Similarly, **Public Service of New Hampshire** financed construction of its troubled Seabrook nuclear plant with junk bonds, and junk bonds were used in the **RJR Nabisco** leveraged buyout (LBOs). In junk bond deals, the debt ratio generally is extremely high, so the bondholders must bear as much risk as stockholders normally would. The bonds' yields reflect this fact—a coupon rate of 25% per annum was required to sell the Public Service of New Hampshire bonds.

The phenomenal growth of the junk bond market was impressive but controversial. Significant risk, combined with unscrupulous dealings, created significant losses for investors. Recently, however, the junk bond market has begun to grow once again.

Bond Ratings

Since the early 1900s, bonds have been assigned quality ratings that reflect their probability of going into default. The two major rating agencies are **Moody's Investors Service (Moody's)** and **Standard & Poor's Corporation (S&P)**. These

Exhibit 700.13 *Moody's and S&P Bond Ratings*

	High Quality		Investment Grade		Junk Bonds			
					Substandard		Speculative	
Moody's	Aaa	Aa	A	Baa	Ba	B	Caa	C
S&P	AAA	AA	A	BBB	BB	B	CCC	D

NOTE: Both Moody's and S&P use "modifiers" for bonds rated below triple A. S&P uses a plus and minus system; thus, A+ designates the strongest A-rated bonds and A− the weakest. Moody's uses a 1, 2, or 3 designation, with 1 denoting the strongest and 3 the weakest; thus, within the double-A category, Aa1 is the best, Aa2 is average, and Aa3 is the weakest.

agencies' rating designations are shown in Exhibit 700.13. The triple- and double-A bonds are extremely safe. Single-A and triple-B bonds are strong enough to be called **investment grade bonds,** and they are the lowest-rated bonds that many banks and other institutional investors are permitted by law to hold. Double-B and lower bonds are speculative, or junk bonds; they have a significant probability of going into default, and many financial institutions are prohibited from buying them.

Bond Rating Criteria

Bond ratings are based on both qualitative and quantitative factors. Some of the factors considered by the bond rating agencies include the financial strength of the company as measured by various ratios, collateral provisions, seniority of the debt, restrictive covenants, provisions such as a sinking fund or a deferred call, litigation possibilities, regulation, and so on. Representatives of the rating agencies have consistently stated that no precise formula is used to set a firm's rating; all the factors listed, plus others, are taken into account, but not in a mathematically precise manner. Statistical studies have borne out this contention—researchers who have tried to predict bond ratings on the basis of quantitative data have had only limited success, indicating that the agencies use subjective judgment when establishing a firm's rating.

Importance of Bond Ratings

Bond ratings are important both to firms and to investors. First, because a bond's rating is an indicator of its default risk, the rating has a direct, measurable influence on the bond's interest rate and the firm's cost of debt. Second, most bonds are purchased by institutional investors rather than individuals, and many institutions are restricted to investment-grade securities. Thus, if a firm's bonds fall below BBB, it will have a difficult time selling new bonds because many potential purchasers will not be allowed to buy them.

Changes in Ratings

Changes in a firm's bond rating affect both its ability to borrow long-term capital and the cost of that capital. Rating agencies review outstanding bonds on a periodic basis, occasionally upgrading or downgrading a bond as a result of its issuer's changed circumstances.

Rationale for Using Different Types of Securities

Why are there so many different types of long-term securities? At least a partial answer to this question might be seen in Exhibit 700.14 which depicts the now familiar risk/return trade-off function drawn to show the risk and the expected after-personal-tax returns for the various securities of Allied Air Products. First, U.S. Treasury bills, which represent the risk-free rate, are shown for reference. The lowest-risk long-term securities offered by Allied are its floating rate notes; these securities are free of interest rate risk, but they are exposed to some risk of default. The first mortgage bonds are somewhat riskier than the notes (because the bonds are exposed to interest rate risk), and they sell at a somewhat higher required and expected after-tax return. The second mortgage bonds are even riskier, so they have a still higher expected return. Subordinated debentures, income bonds, and preferred stocks are all increasingly risky, and their expected returns increase accordingly.

Why does Allied issue so many different classes of securities? Why not offer just one type of bond, plus common stock? The answer lies in the fact that different investors have different risk/return trade-off preferences, so to appeal

Exhibit 700.14 *Allied Air Products: Risks and Returns on Different Classes of Securities*

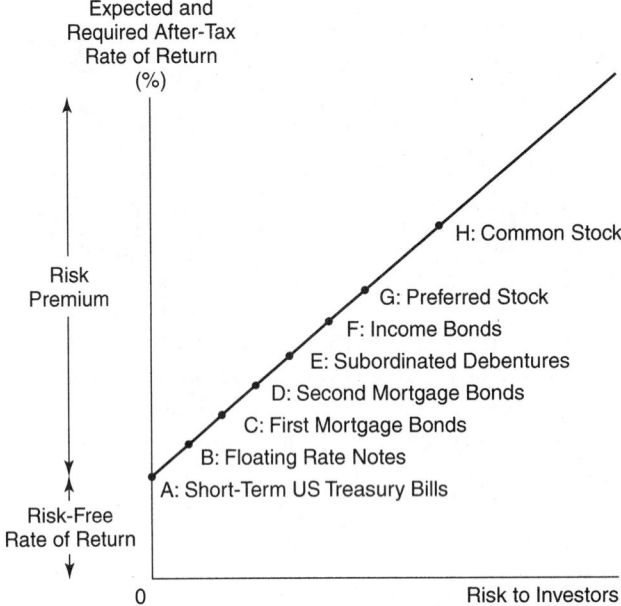

to the broadest possible market, Allied must offer securities that attract as many different types of investors as possible. Also, different securities are more popular at different points in time, and firms tend to issue whatever is popular at the time they need money. Used wisely, a policy of selling differentiated securities to take advantage of market conditions can lower a firm's overall cost of capital below what it would be if the firm used only one class of debt.

Factors Influencing Long-Term Financing Decisions

As we show in this section, many factors influence a firm's long-term financing decisions. Each factor's relative importance varies among firms at any point in time and for any given firm over time, but any company planning to raise new long-term capital should consider each of these points.

Target Capital Structure

Firms typically establish target capital structures, and one of the most important considerations in any financing decision is how the firm's actual capital structure compares to its target structure. However, few firms finance each year exactly in accordance with their target capital structures, primarily because exact adherence would increase their flotation costs. Because smaller issues of new securities have proportionally larger flotation costs, firms tend to use debt one year and stock the next.

Making fewer but larger security offerings would cause a firm's capital structure to fluctuate above and below its optimal level rather than stay right on target. However, small fluctuations about the optimal capital structure have little effect either on a firm's cost of debt and equity or on its overall cost of capital. Also, investors would recognize that its actions were prudent and that the firm would save substantial amounts of flotation costs by financing in this manner. Therefore, even though firms do tend to finance over the long haul in accordance with their target capital structures, flotation costs have a definite influence on the specific financing decisions in any given year.

Maturity Matching

Assume that Unilate Textiles decides to float a single $13.5 million nonconvertible bond issue with a sinking fund. It must next choose a maturity for the issue, taking into consideration the shape of the yield curve, management's own expectations about future interest rates, and the maturity of the assets being financed. In the case at hand, Unilate's capital projects during the next two years consist primarily of new, automated manufacturing equipment. This equipment has an expected economic life of ten years (even though it falls into the MACRS five-year class life). Should Unilate finance the debt portion of the capital raised for this equipment with 1-year, 10-year, 20-year, or 30-year debt, or with debt of some other maturity? *One approach is to match the maturity of the liabilities with the maturity of the assets being financed.*

Note that some of the new capital for the machinery will come from common stock, which generally is considered to be a perpetual security with an infinite maturity. Of course, common stock can always be repurchased on the open market or by other means, so its effective maturity can be reduced significantly, but generally it has no maturity.

Debt maturities, however, are specified at the time of issue. If Unilate financed its capital budgets over the next two years with ten-year sinking fund bonds, it would be matching its asset and liability maturities. The cash flows resulting from the new machinery should be sufficient to make the interest and sinking fund payments on the issue, and the bonds would be retired as the machinery wore out. If Unilate used one-year debt, it would have to pay off the loan with cash flows derived from assets other than the machinery in question. If its operations were stable, the company probably could roll over the one-year debt, but if interest rates rose, then it would have to pay a higher rate. If Unilate subsequently experienced difficulties, its lenders might be hesitant to extend the loan, and the company might be unable to obtain new short-term debt at any reasonable rate. At the other extreme, if it used 20-year or 30-year debt, Unilate would still have to service the debt long after the assets purchased with the debt had been scrapped and had ceased providing cash flows, and this would worry potential lenders.

For all these reasons, one commonly used financing strategy is to match debt maturities with asset maturities. In recognition of this fact, firms do consider maturity relationships, and this factor has a major influence on the type of debt securities used.

Interest Rate Levels

Financial managers also consider interest rate levels, both absolute and relative, when making financing decisions. For example, long-term interest rates were high by historic standards in 1981 and 1982, so many managers were reluctant to issue long-term debt and thus lock in those high costs for long periods. We already know that one solution to this problem is to use long-term debt with a call provision. Callability permits the company to refund the issue should interest rates drop, as they did in 1993. But there is a cost, because firms must pay more if they make their debt callable. Alternatively, a firm might finance with short-term debt whenever long-term rates are historically high, and then, assuming that interest rates subsequently fall, sell a long-term issue to replace the short-term debt. Of course, this strategy has its risks. If interest rates climb even higher, the firm will be forced to renew the short-term debt at higher and higher rates, or to replace the short-term debt with a long-term bond that costs more than it would have cost earlier.

Expectations About Future Interest Rates

At a time when the interest rate on AAA corporate bonds was over 12%, which was high by historical standards, **Exxon's** investment bankers advised the company to tap the Eurodollar bond market for relatively cheap fixed rate financing. A *Eurodollar bond* is a bond sold outside of the United States but denominated in U.S. dollars. At the time, Exxon could have issued its bonds in London at 0.4 percentage points *below* comparable-maturity Treasury bonds. However, one Exxon officer was quoted as cautioning, "I say so what. The absolute level of rates is too high. We would rather wait." The managers of Exxon, as well as those of many other companies, were betting that the next move in interest rates would be down.

This example illustrates that firms do base their financing decisions on expectations about future interest rates. In Exxon's case, the financial staff turned out to be correct. However, the success of such a strategy requires interest rate forecasts to be right more often than they are wrong, and it is very difficult to find someone with a long-term forecasting record better than 50–50.

The Firm's Current and Forecasted Financial Conditions

If a firm's current financial condition is poor, its managers might be reluctant to issue new long-term debt because (1) a new bond issue probably would trigger a review by the rating agencies, and (2) long-term debt issued when a firm is in poor financial condition costs more and is subject to more severe restrictive covenants than debt issued from a strong position. Thus, a firm that is in a weakened condition but that is forecasting an improvement would be inclined to delay permanent financing until things improved. Conversely, a firm that is strong now but whose forecasts indicate a potentially bad time just ahead would be motivated to finance long term now rather than to wait. These scenarios imply that the capital markets are inefficient in the sense that investors do not have as much information about the firm's future as does its management. This situation undoubtedly is true at times.

The firm's earnings outlook, and the extent to which forecasted higher earnings per share are reflected in stock prices, also has an effect on the choice of securities. If a successful research and development program has just been concluded, and, consequently, management forecasts higher earnings than do most investors, the firm would not want to issue common stock. It would use debt, and then, after earnings had risen and pushed up the stock price, it would sell common stock to restore the capital structure to its target level.

Restrictions in Existing Debt Contracts

Earlier we discussed the fact that Savannah Electric Company has at times been restricted from issuing new first mortgage bonds by its indenture coverage requirements. This is just one example of how indenture covenants can influence a firm's financing decisions. Restrictions on the current ratio, the debt ratio, and so on, can also restrict a firm's ability to use different types of financing at a given time.

Availability of Collateral

Generally, for a particular firm, secured long-term debt will be less costly than unsecured debt. Thus, firms with large amounts of general-purpose (as opposed to specialized) fixed assets are likely to use a relatively large amount of debt, especially mortgage bonds. Additionally, each year's financing decision will be influenced by the amount of newly acquired assets that are available as security for new bonds.

Bond Refunding Operations

Bond refunding analysis is similar to capital budgeting analysis. Also, bond refunding can be compared to the process individuals go through to refinance a house—an existing debt (mortgage) with a high interest rate is replaced by a new debt (mortgage) with a lower interest rate.

The refunding decision actually involves two separate questions: (1) Would it be profitable to call an outstanding issue now and to replace it with a new issue? (2) Even if refunding currently is profitable, would it be better to call now or to postpone the refunding to a later date?

As we noted, refunding decisions are similar to capital budgeting decisions, and the net present value method is the primary tool. In essence, the costs of undertaking the refunding operation (the investment outlay) are compared to the present value of the interest that will be saved if the high-interest rate bond is called and replaced with a new, low-interest rate bond. If the net present value of refunding is positive, then the refunding should take place. The costs of the refunding operation consist primarily of the call premium on the old bond issue and the flotation costs associated with selling the new issue. The cash flow benefits consist primarily of the interest expenses that will be saved if the company replaces high-cost debt with low-cost debt. The discount rate used to find the present value of the interest savings is the after-tax cost of new debt—the interest saved is the difference between two relatively certain cash flow streams, so the difference essentially is riskless. Therefore, a low discount rate should be used, and that rate is today's after-tax cost of new debt in the market.

To illustrate the refunding decision, consider the Strasburg Communications Corporation, which has a $100 million, 13%, semiannual coupon bond outstanding with ten years remaining to maturity. The bond has a call provision that permits the company to retire the issue by calling in the bonds at an 8% call premium. Investment bankers have assured Strasburg that it could issue an additional $100 million of new 10% coupon, ten-year bonds that pay interest semiannually. Flotation costs on the new refunding issue will amount to $4,000,000. Predictions are that long-term interest rates are unlikely to fall below 10%. Strasburg's marginal tax rate is 40%. Should the company refund the $100 million of 13% semiannual coupon bonds?

Strasburg's refunding analysis is presented in Exhibit 700.15. Because the marginal tax rate is 40%, the company's after-tax cost of new debt is equal to 6%, or 3% per six-month period. And because the bonds have semiannual coupons, there will be 20 semiannual periods in the analysis.

Exhibit 700.15 *NPV Refunding Analysis for Strasburg Communications Corporation*

Cost of Refunding at t = 0	
Call premium on old bond (0.08 × $100 million)	$ 8,000,000
Flotation costs on new issue	4,000,000
Total initial outlay	$12,000,000
Semiannual Interest Savings Due to Refunding: t = 1 to 20	
(10 years of payments twice a year)	
Interest on old bond (0.065 × $100 million)	$6,500,000
Interest on new bond (0.050 × $100 million)	5,000,000
Interest savings per period	$1,500,000
Increased taxes due to lower interest payment[a] (0.40 × $1,500,000)	$ (600,000)
Net interest savings	$ 900,000

Refunding Cash Flow Timeline

Interest period	0	k = 3%	1	2	...	10 Year / 20
Initial outlay	(12,000,000)					
Interest savings	0		900,000	900,000	...	900,000
Net cash flow	(12,000,000)		900,000	900,000	...	900,000

NPV of refunding at $k_{dT}/2$ = 3% is $1,389,727

[a] Strasburg's interest expense will decrease by $1,500,000, thus taxable income will increase by $1,500,000, if the new bond is issued. Strasburg will have to pay 0.40 × $1,500,000 = $600,000 additional taxes on this increased taxable income.

The net present value of refunding is positive, so Strasburg should refund the old bond issue—the firm's value will be increased by $1,389,727 if the old bond is retired.

Foreign Debt Instruments

Like the U.S. debt markets, the international debt markets offer a variety of instruments with many different features. In this section, we discuss a few of the more familiar types of debt that are traded internationally.

Any debt sold outside the country of the borrower is called an international debt. However, there are two important types of international debt: foreign debt and Eurodebt. **Foreign debt** is debt sold by a foreign borrower but denominated in the currency of the country in which the issue is sold. For instance, **Bell Canada** might need U.S. dollars to finance the operations of its subsidiaries in the United States. If it decides to raise the needed capital in the domestic U.S. bond market, the bond will be underwritten by a syndicate of U.S. investment bankers, denominated in U.S. dollars, and sold to U.S. investors in accordance with SEC and applicable state regulations. Except for the foreign origin of the borrower (Canada), this bond will be indistinguishable from those issued by equivalent U.S. corporations. Because Bell Canada is a foreign corporation, however, the bond will be called a *foreign bond*. Foreign bonds generally are labeled according to the country in which they are issued. For example, if foreign bonds are issued in the United States they are called *Yankee bonds*, if they are issued in Japan they are called *Samurai bonds*, and if they are issued in England they are called *Bulldog bonds*.

The term **Eurodebt** is used to designate any debt sold in a country other than the one in whose currency the debt is denominated. Examples include *Eurobonds*, such as a British firm's issue of pound bonds sold in France or a **Ford Motor Company** issue denominated in dollars and sold in Germany. The institutional arrangements by which Eurobonds are marketed are different than those for most other bond issues, with the most important distinction being a far lower level of required disclosure than normally is found for bonds issued in domestic markets, particularly in the United States. Governments tend to be less strict when regulating securities denominated in foreign currencies than they are on home-currency securities because the bonds' purchasers generally are more "sophisticated." The lower disclosure requirements result in lower total transaction costs for Eurobonds.

Eurobonds appeal to investors for several reasons. Generally, they are issued in bearer form rather than as registered bonds, so the names and nationalities of investors are not recorded. Individuals who desire anonymity, whether for privacy reasons or for tax avoidance, find Eurobonds to their liking. Similarly, most governments do not withhold taxes on interest payments associated with Eurobonds.

More than half of all Eurobonds are denominated in dollars; bonds in Japanese yen, German marks, and Dutch guilders account for most of the rest. Although centered in Europe, Eurobonds truly are international. Their underwriting syndicates include investment bankers from all parts of the world, and the bonds are sold to investors not only in Europe but also in such faraway places as Bahrain and Singapore. Until recently, Eurobonds were issued solely by multinational firms, by international financial institutions, or by national governments. Today, however, the Eurobond market also is being tapped by purely domestic U.S. firms such as electric utilities, which find that by borrowing overseas they can lower their debt costs.

Some other types of Eurodebt include the following.

1. **Eurocredits.** Eurocredits are bank loans that are denominated in the currency of a country other than where the lending bank is located. Many of these loans are very large, so the lending bank often forms a loan syndicate to help raise the needed funds and to spread out some of the risks associated with the loan.

    Interest rates on Eurocredits, as well as other short-term Eurodebt, typically are tied to a standard rate known by the acronym **LIBOR,** which stands for *London InterBank Offer Rate*. LIBOR is the rate of interest offered by the largest and strongest London banks on deposits of other large banks of the highest credit standing. In September 1999, LIBOR rates were about 1/2 percentage point above domestic U.S. bank rates on time deposits of the same maturity—5.04% for three-month CDs versus 5.53% for three-month LIBOR CDs.

2. **Euro-commercial paper (Euro-CP).** Euro-CP is similar to commercial paper issued in the United States. It is a short-term debt instrument issued by corporations, and it has typical maturities of one, three, and six months. The principal difference between Euro-CP and U.S. commercial paper is that there is not as much concern about the credit quality of Euro-CP issuers.

3. **Euronotes.** Euronotes, which represent medium-term debt, typically have maturities from one year to ten years. The general features of Euronotes are much like those of longer-term debt instruments like bonds. The principal amount is repaid at maturity and interest often is paid semiannually. Most foreign companies use Euronotes like they would a line of credit, continuously issuing notes to finance medium-term needs.

Preferred Stock, Leases, Options, Warrants, and Convertibles

Alternative long-term financing arrangements include preferred stock, leases, options, warrants, and convertibles. They are alternative to traditional financing sources such as the use of common stock and various types of long-term debt.

Preferred Stock

Preferred stock is a *hybrid* security—it is similar to bonds in some respects and to common stock in others. The hybrid nature of preferred stock becomes apparent when we try to classify it in relation to bonds and common stock. Like bonds, preferred stock has a par value. Preferred dividends also are similar to interest payments in that they generally are fixed in amount and must be paid before common stock dividends can be paid. However, if the preferred dividend is not earned, the directors can omit (or "pass") it without throwing the company into bankruptcy. So although preferred stock has a fixed payment like bonds, a failure to make this payment will not lead to bankruptcy.

Accountants classify preferred stock as equity and report it in the equity portion of the balance sheet under "preferred stock" or "preferred equity." However, financial analysts sometimes treat preferred stock as debt and sometimes as equity, depending on the type of analysis being made. If the analysis is being made by a common stockholder, the key consideration is the fact that the preferred dividend is a fixed charge that reduces the amount that can be distributed to common shareholders, so from the common stockholder's point of view preferred stock is similar to debt. Suppose, however, that the analysis is being made by a bondholder studying the firm's vulnerability to failure in the event of a decline in sales and income. If the firm's income declines, the debtholders have a prior claim to the available income ahead of preferred stockholders, and if the firm fails, debtholders have a prior claim to assets when the firm is liquidated. Thus, to a bondholder, preferred stock is similar to common equity.

From management's perspective, preferred stock lies between debt and common equity. Because failure to pay dividends on preferred stock will not force the firm into bankruptcy, preferred stock is safer to use than debt. At the same time, if the firm is highly successful, the common stockholders will not have to share that success with the preferred stockholders because preferred dividends are fixed. Remember, however, that the preferred stockholders do have a higher priority claim than the common stockholders. We see, then, that preferred stock has some of the characteristics of debt and some of the characteristics of common stock, and it is used in situations in which conditions are such that neither debt nor common stock is entirely appropriate.

Major Provisions of Preferred Stock Issues

Preferred stock has a number of features, the most important of which are discussed in the following sections. As you will see, some of the features we discuss here are also features included in debt instruments, which we discussed earlier in this section.

PRIORITY TO ASSETS AND EARNINGS Preferred stockholders have priority over common stockholders with regard to earnings and assets. Thus, dividends must be paid on preferred stock before they can be paid on the common stock, and, in the event of bankruptcy, the claims of the preferred shareholders must be satisfied before the common stockholders receive anything. To reinforce these features, most preferred stocks have coverage requirements similar to those on bonds. These restrictions limit the amount of preferred stock a company can use, and they also require a minimum level of retained earnings before common dividends can be paid.

PAR VALUE Unlike common stock, preferred stock always has a par value (or its equivalent under some other name), and this value is important. First, the par value establishes the amount due the preferred stockholders in the event of liquidation. Second, the preferred dividend frequently is stated as a percentage of the par value. For example, an issue of Duke Power's preferred stock has a par value of $100 and a stated dividend of 7.8% of par. The same results would, of course, be produced if this issue of Duke's preferred stock simply called for an annual dividend of $7.80.

CUMULATIVE DIVIDENDS Most preferred stock provides for **cumulative dividends;** that is, any preferred dividends not paid in previous periods must be paid before common dividends can be paid. The cumulative feature is a protective device because if the preferred stock dividends were not cumulative, a firm could avoid paying preferred and common stock dividends for, say, ten years, plowing back all its earnings, and then pay a huge common stock dividend but pay only the stipulated annual dividend to the preferred stockholders. Obviously, such an action effectively would void the preferred position the preferred stockholders are supposed to have. The cumulative feature helps prevent such abuses.

CONVERTIBILITY Approximately 40% of the preferred stock that has been issued in recent years is convertible into common stock. For example, on March 25, 1999, **Global Maintech** issued 1,600 shares of Series C convertible preferred that can be converted into a minimum of 400 shares of common stock at the option of the preferred shareholder.

OTHER PROVISIONS Some other provisions occasionally found in preferred stocks include the following.

1. **Voting rights.** Although preferred stock is not voting stock, preferred stockholders generally are given the right to vote for directors if the company has not paid the preferred dividend for a specified period, such as ten quarters. This feature motivates management to make every effort to pay preferred dividends.

2. **Participating.** A rare type of preferred stock is one that participates with the common stock in sharing the firm's earnings. Participating preferred stocks generally work as follows: (a) the stated preferred dividend is paid—for example, $5 a share; (b) the common stock is then entitled to a dividend in an amount up to the preferred dividend; (c) if the common dividend is raised, say to $5.50, the preferred dividend must likewise be raised to $5.50.

3. **Sinking fund.** In the past (before the mid-1970s), few preferred issues had sinking funds. Today, however, most newly issued preferred stocks have sinking funds that call for the purchase and retirement of a given percentage of the preferred stock each year. If the amount is 2%, which frequently is used, the preferred issue will have an average life of 25 years and a maximum life of 50 years.

4. **Call provision.** A call provision gives the issuing corporation the right to call in the preferred stock for redemption. As in the case of bonds, call provisions generally state that the company must pay an amount greater than the par value of the preferred stock, the additional sum being termed a **call premium.** For example, **Bangor Hydro-Electric Company** has various issues of preferred stock outstanding, two of which are callable. The

call prices on the two issues are $100 and $110. Before it was called in December 1997, Bangor had another callable preferred issue that included a sinking fund provision.

5. **Maturity.** Before the mid-1970s, most preferred stock was perpetual—it had no maturity and never needed to be paid off. Today, however, most new preferred stock has a sinking fund and thus an effective maturity date.

Pros and Cons of Preferred Stock

As noted here, there are both advantages and disadvantages to financing with preferred stock.

ISSUER'S (FIRM'S) VIEWPOINT By using preferred stock, a firm can fix its financial costs and thus keep more of the potential future profits for its existing set of common stockholders, yet still avoid the danger of bankruptcy if earnings are too low to meet these fixed charges. Also, by selling preferred stock rather than common stock, the firm avoids sharing control with new investors.

However, preferred stock does have a major disadvantage from the issuer's standpoint: It has a higher after-tax cost of capital than debt. The major reason for this higher cost is taxes: Preferred dividends are not deductible as a tax expense, whereas interest expense is deductible. This makes the component cost of preferred stock much greater than that of bonds—the after-tax cost of debt is approximately two-thirds of the stated coupon rate for profitable firms, whereas the cost of preferred stock is the full percentage amount of the preferred dividend. Of course, the deductibility differential is most important for issuers that are in relatively high tax brackets. If a company pays little or no taxes because it is unprofitable or because it has a great deal of accelerated depreciation, the deductibility of interest does not make much difference. Thus, the lower a company's tax bracket, the more likely it is to issue preferred stock.

BONDHOLDER'S (INVESTOR'S) VIEWPOINT In designing securities, the financial manager must consider the investor's point of view. It is sometimes asserted that preferred stock has so many disadvantages to both the issuer and the investor that it should never be issued. Nevertheless, preferred stock is being issued in substantial amounts. It provides investors with a steadier and more assured income than common stock, and it has a preference over common stock in the event of liquidation. In addition, 70% of the preferred dividends received by corporations are not taxable. For this reason, most preferred stock is owned by corporations.

The principal disadvantage of preferred stock from an investor's standpoint is that although preferred stockholders bear some of the ownership risks, their returns are limited. Other disadvantages are that (1) preferred stockholders have no legally enforceable right to dividends, even if a company earns a profit; and (2) *for individual as opposed to corporate investors,* after-tax bond yields generally are higher than those on preferred stock, even though the preferred is riskier.

Leases

Firms generally own fixed assets and report them on their balance sheets, but it is the *use* of buildings and equipment that is important, not their ownership per se. One way of obtaining the use of assets is to buy them, but an alternative is to lease them. Prior to the 1950s, leasing generally was associated with real estate—land and buildings. Today, however, it is possible to lease virtually any kind of fixed asset, and in 1999 more than 25% of all new capital equipment acquired by businesses was leased. In fact, it is estimated that 70% of firms listed in the *Fortune 1000* lease some equipment.

Types of Leases

Leasing takes three different forms: (1) sale-and-leaseback arrangements, (2) operating or service leases, and (3) financial or capital leases.

SALE AND LEASEBACK Under a **sale and leaseback,** a firm that owns land, buildings, or equipment sells the property and simultaneously executes an agreement to lease the property back for a particular period under specific terms. The purchaser could be an insurance company, a commercial bank, a specialized leasing company, or even an individual investor. The sale-and-leaseback plan is an alternative to taking out a mortgage loan. The firm that sells the property, or the **lessee,** immediately receives the purchase price from the buyer, or the **lessor.** At the same time, the seller-lessee firm retains the use of the property just as if it had borrowed and mortgaged the property to secure the loan. Note that under a mortgage loan arrangement, the financial institution normally would receive a series of equal payments just sufficient to amortize the loan while providing a specified rate of return to the lender on the outstanding balance. Under a sale-and-leaseback arrangement, the lease payments are set up in exactly the same way; the payments are set so the investor-lessor recoups the purchase price and earns a specified rate of return on the investment.

OPERATING, OR SERVICE, LEASES Operating leases, sometimes called *service leases,* provide for both *financing* and *maintenance.* IBM is one of the pioneers of the operating lease contract, and computers and office copying machines, together with automobiles and trucks, are the primary types of equipment involved. Ordinarily, these leases call for the lessor to maintain and service the leased equipment, and the cost of providing maintenance is built into the lease payments.

Another important characteristic of operating leases is the fact that they frequently are *not fully amortized;* in other words, the payments required under the lease contract are not sufficient to recover the full cost of the equipment. However, the lease contract is written for a period considerably shorter than the expected economic life of the leased equipment, and the lessor expects to recover all investment costs through subsequent renewal payments, through subsequent leases to other companies (lessees), or by selling the leased equipment.

A final feature of operating leases is that they frequently contain a *cancellation clause,* which gives the lessee the right to cancel the lease before the expiration of the basic agreement. This is an important consideration for the lessee, because it means that the equipment can be returned if it is rendered obsolete by technological developments or if it no longer is needed because of a decline in the lessee's business.

FINANCIAL, OR CAPITAL, LEASES Financial leases, sometimes called *capital leases,* are differentiated from operating leases in three respects: (1) they do *not* provide for maintenance services, (2) they are *not* cancelable, and (3) they are *fully amortized*—that is, the lessor receives rental payments that are equal to the full price of the leased equipment plus a return on the investment. In a typical financial lease arrangement, the firm that will use the equipment (the lessee) selects the specific items it requires and negotiates the price and delivery terms with the manufacturer. The user firm then negotiates terms with a leasing company and, once the lease terms are set, arranges to have the lessor buy the equipment from the manufacturer or the distributor. When the equipment is purchased, the user firm simultaneously executes the lease agreement.

Financial leases are similar to sale-and-leaseback arrangements, except that the leased equipment is new and the lessor buys it from a manufacturer or a distributor instead of from the user-lessee. A sale and leaseback might thus be thought of as a special type of financial lease, and both sale-and-leaseback leases and financial leases are analyzed in the same manner.

Financial Statement Effects of Leases

Lease payments are shown as operating expenses on a firm's income statement, but under certain conditions, neither the leased assets nor the liabilities under the lease contract appear on the firm's balance sheet. For this reason, leasing is often called **off-balance-sheet financing.** This point is illustrated in Exhibit 700.16 by the balance sheets of two hypothetical firms, B (for Buy) and L (for Lease). Initially, the balance sheets of both firms are identical, and both have debt ratios of 50%. Each firm then decides to acquire fixed assets that cost $100. Firm B borrows $100 to make the purchase, so both an asset and a liability are recorded on its balance sheet, and its debt ratio is increased to 75%. Firm L leases the equipment, so its balance sheet is unchanged. The lease might call for fixed charges as high as or even higher than those on the loan, and the obligations assumed under the lease might be equally or more dangerous from the standpoint of financial safety, but the firm's debt ratio remains at 50%.

Exhibit 700.16 *Balance Sheet Effects of Leasing*

Before Asset Increase				After Asset Increase							
Firms B and L				Firm B—Purchases Asset				Firm L—Leases Asset			
Current assets	$ 50	Debt	$ 50	Current assets	$ 50	Debt	$150	Current assets	$ 50	Debt	$ 50
Fixed assets	50	Equity	50	Fixed assets	150	Equity	50	Fixed assets	50	Equity	50
Total	$100		$100	Total	$200		$200	Total	$100		$100
	Debt ratio = 50%				Debt ratio = 75%				Debt ratio = 50%		

715. MANAGING LONG-TERM FINANCING

To correct this problem, the Financial Accounting Standards Board (FASB) issued **FASB #13,** which requires that for an unqualified audit report, firms that enter into financial (or capital) leases must restate their balance sheets to report leased assets as fixed assets and the present value of future lease payments as a debt. This process is called *capitalizing the lease,* and its net effect is to cause Firms B and L to have similar balance sheets, both of which will resemble the one shown for Firm B after the asset increase.

The logic behind FASB #13 is as follows. If a firm signs a lease contract, its obligation to make lease payments is just as binding as if it had signed a loan agreement. The failure to make lease payments can bankrupt a firm just as surely as can the failure to make principal and interest payments on a loan. Therefore, for all intents and purposes, a financial lease is identical to a loan. There are, however, certain legal differences between loans and leases. For example, in a bankruptcy liquidation, the lessor is entitled to take possession of the leased asset, and, if the value of the asset is less than the required payments under the lease, the lessor can enter a claim (as a general creditor) for one year's lease payments. In a bankruptcy reorganization, the lessor receives the asset plus three years' lease payments if needed to bring the value of the asset up to the remaining investment in the lease. This being the case, when a firm signs a lease agreement, it has, in effect, raised its "true" debt ratio and thereby changed its "true" capital structure. Accordingly, if the firm previously had established a target capital structure, and if there is no reason to think that the optimal capital structure has changed, then using lease financing requires additional equity backing in exactly the same manner as does the use of debt financing.

If a disclosure of the lease in the Exhibit 700.16 example were not made, then investors could be deceived into thinking that Firm L's financial position is stronger than it actually is. Even if the lease were disclosed in a footnote, investors might not fully recognize its impact and might not see that Firms B and L essentially are in the same financial position. If this were the case, Firm L would have increased its true amount of debt through a lease arrangement, but its required return on debt, k_d, its required return on equity, k_s, and consequently its weighted average cost of capital would have increased less than those of Firm B, which borrowed directly. Thus, investors would be willing to accept a lower return from Firm L because they would view it as being in a stronger financial position than Firm B. These benefits of leasing would accrue to stockholders at the expense of new investors, who were, in effect, being deceived by the fact that the firm's balance sheet did not fully reflect its true liability situation. This is why FASB #13 was issued.

A lease will be classified as a capital lease, and hence be capitalized and shown directly on the balance sheet, if any one of the following conditions exists.

1. Under the terms of the lease, ownership of the property effectively is transferred from the lessor to the lessee.
2. The lessee can purchase the property or renew the lease at less than a fair market price when the lease expires.
3. The lease runs for a period equal to or greater than 75% of the asset's life. Thus, if an asset has a 10-year life and if the lease is written for more than 7.5 years, the lease must be capitalized.
4. The present value of the lease payments is equal to or greater than 90% of the initial value of the asset.

These rules, together with strong footnote disclosures for operating leases, are sufficient to ensure that no one will be fooled by lease financing. Thus, leases are recognized to be essentially the same as debt, and they have the same effects as debt on the firm's required rate of return. Therefore, leasing generally will not permit a firm to use more financial leverage than could be obtained with conventional debt.

Options

An **option** is a contract that gives its holder the right to buy (or sell) an asset at some predetermined price within a specified period of time. "Pure options" are instruments that are created by outsiders (generally investment banking firms) rather than by the firm itself; they are bought and sold primarily by investors (or speculators). However, financial managers should understand the nature of options because this will help them structure warrant and convertible financings, both of which have similar characteristics.

Option Types and Markets

There are many types of options and option markets. To understand how options work, suppose you owned 100 shares of **IBM** stock that, on September 1, 1999, sold for $127.25 per share. You could sell to someone else the right to buy your 100 shares at any time during the next five months at a price of, say, $140 per share. The $140 is called the **striking,** or **exercise, price.** Such options exist, and they are traded on a number of exchanges, with the Chicago Board Options Exchange (CBOE) being the oldest and largest. This type of option is known as a **call option** because the option holder can "call" in 100 shares of stock for purchase any time during the option period. The seller of a call option is known as an option writer. An investor who writes a call option against stock held in his or her portfolio is said to be selling *covered options;* options sold without the stock to back them up are called *naked options.*

On September 1, 1999, IBM's five-month, $140 call options sold on the CBOE for $7.50 each. Thus, for ($7.50)(100) = $750, you could buy an option contract that would give you the right to purchase 100 shares of IBM at a price of $140 per share at any time during the following five months. If the stock stayed below $140 during that period, you would lose your $750, but if the stock's price rose to $150, your $750 investment would be worth ($150 − $140)(100) = $1,000. That translates into a very healthy rate of return on your $750 investment. Incidentally, if the stock price did go up, you probably would not actually exercise your options to buy the stock; rather, you would sell the options to another option buyer, at a price greater than or equal to $10 per option—you originally paid only $7.50.

You also can buy an option that gives you the right to sell a stock at a specified price during some period in the future—this is called a **put option.** For example, suppose you expect IBM's stock price to decline from its current level sometime during the next five months. For $687.50 = $6.875 × 100 you could buy a five-month put option giving you the right to sell 100 shares (which you would not necessarily own) at a price of $120 per share ($120 is the put option striking price). If you bought a 100-share put contract for $687.50 and IBM's stock price actually fell to $110, you would make ($120 − $110)(100) = $1,000 minus the $687.50 you paid for the put option, for a net profit (before taxes and commissions) of $312.50.

Options trading is one of the hottest financial activities in the United States today. The leverage involved makes it possible for speculators with just a few dollars to make a fortune almost overnight. Also, investors with sizable portfolios can sell options against their stocks and earn the value of the options (minus brokerage commissions) even if the stocks' prices remain constant. Still, those who have profited most from the development of options trading are security firms, which earn very healthy commissions on such trades.

The corporations on whose stocks options are written, such as IBM, have nothing to do with the options market. They neither raise money in that market nor have any direct transactions in it, and option holders neither receive dividends nor vote for corporate directors (unless they exercise their options to purchase the stock, which few actually do). There have been studies by the Securities and Exchange Commission (SEC) and others as to whether options trading stabilizes or destabilizes the stock market and whether it helps or hinders corporations seeking to raise new capital. The studies have not been conclusive, but options trading is here to stay, and many regard it as the most exciting game in town.

Option Values

The value of an option is closely related to the value of the *underlying* stock, which is the stock on which the option is written, and the striking price. For example, an investor who purchases call options hopes that the value of the underlying stock goes above the striking price during the option period, because then the option could be exercised at a gross profit equal to the market value of the stock less the striking price. In this case, the investor is said to have an **in-the-money option** because he or she can exercise the call option by purchasing the stock at the striking price and then can immediately sell the stock for its market value, which is greater than the striking price. For example, if IBM's stock sells for $150 at the beginning of 2000, call options with a striking price of $140 would be in the money because the option holder could exercise the options by paying the option seller $14,000 for 100 shares of IBM stock, and then the stock could be sold on the NYSE for $15,000—the financial benefit of exercising to the option holder would be $1,000 before commissions and taxes. If the market value of IBM's stock is $130, or any other amount below the striking price, the call is said to be an **out-of-the-money option** because it would not be favorable for the option holder to exercise the call—if the investor were to exercise the call option, there would be a financial loss because the stock would be purchased at a value (the $140 striking price) greater than it could be sold (the $130 market value). The opposite relationship holds for put options because the striking price represents the price at which an investor can *sell* the stock to the put option writer (seller). To be able to sell to the put option writer, the investor first must *buy* the stock in the market (for example, on the NYSE). Thus, for a put option to be in-the-money, the striking price must be above the market value of the underlying stock.

As you can see, both the value of the underlying stock and the striking price of the option are very important in determining whether an option is in-the-money or out-of-the-money. If an option is out-of-the-money on its expiration date, it is worthless. Therefore, the stock price and the striking price are important for determining the market value of an option. In fact, options are called *derivative securities* because their values are dependent on, or derived from, the value of the underlying asset and the striking price.

In addition to the stock price and the striking price, the value of an option also depends on (1) the option's time to maturity and (2) the variability of the underlying stock's price, as explained here.

1. The longer an option has to run, the greater its value. If a call option expires at 4 P.M. today, there is not much chance that the stock price will go way up. Therefore, the option will sell at close to the difference between the stock price and the striking price (P_s − striking price), or zero if this difference is negative. On the other hand, if it has a year to go, the stock price could rise sharply, pulling the option's value up with it.

2. An option on an extremely volatile stock will be worth more than one on a very stable stock. We know that an option on a stock whose price rarely moves will not offer much chance for a large gain. On the other hand, an option on a stock that is highly volatile could provide a large gain, so such an option will be valuable. Note also that because losses on options are limited, large declines in a stock's price do not have a corresponding bad effect on call option holders. Therefore, stock price volatility can only enhance the value of an option.

If everything else were held constant, then the longer an option's life, the higher its market price would be, no matter the type of option. Also, the more volatile the price of the underlying stock, the higher the option's market price, regardless of the option type.

Suppose that for $2 you could buy a call option on a stock now selling for $20. The striking price is also $20. Now suppose the stock is highly volatile, and you think it has a 50% probability of selling for either $10 or $30 when the option expires in one month. What is the expected value of the option? If the stock sells for $30, the option will be worth $30 − $20 = $10. Because there is a 50–50 chance that the stock will be worth $10 or $30, the expected value of the option is $5:

$$\text{Expected value of option} = 0.5(0) + 0.5(\$10) = \$5$$

To be exactly correct, we would have to discount the $5 back for one month.

Now suppose the stock was more volatile, with a 50–50 chance of being worth zero or $20. Here the option would be worth

$$\text{Expected value of option} = 0.5(0) + 0.5(\$20) = \$10$$

This demonstrates that the greater the volatility of the stock, the greater the value of the option. The reason this result occurs is because the large loss on the stock ($20) had no more of an adverse effect on the option holder than the small loss ($10). Thus, option holders benefit greatly if a stock goes way up, but they do not lose too badly if it drops all the way to zero. These concepts have been used to develop formulas for pricing options, with the most widely used formula being the Black-Scholes model.

Warrants

A **warrant** is an option *issued by a company* that gives the holder the right to buy a stated number of shares of the company's stock at a specified price. Generally, warrants are distributed along with debt, and they are used to induce investors to buy a firm's long-term debt at a lower interest rate than otherwise would be required. For example, when **Pac-Atlantic Air (PAA)** wanted to sell $100 million of 20-year bonds in 1998, the company's investment bankers informed the financial vice president that straight bonds would be difficult to sell and that an interest rate of 11% would be required. However, the investment bankers suggested as an alternative that investors would be willing to buy bonds with an annual coupon rate as low as 8% if the company would offer 30 warrants with each $1,000 bond, each warrant entitling the holder to buy one share of common stock at a price of $12 per share. The stock was selling for $10 per share at the time, and the warrants would expire in 2005 if they had not been exercised previously.

Why would investors be willing to buy Pac-Atlantic's bonds at a yield of only 8% in an 11% market just because warrants were offered as part of the package? The answer is that warrants are long-term options, and they have a value for the reasons set forth in the previous section. In the PAA case, this value offset the low interest rate on the bonds and made the entire package of low interest bonds plus warrants attractive to investors.

Use of Warrants in Financing

Warrants generally are used by small, rapidly growing firms as "sweeteners" to help sell either debt or preferred stock. Such firms frequently are regarded as being very risky, and their bonds can be sold only if the firms are willing to pay extremely high rates of interest and to accept very restrictive indenture provisions. To avoid this, firms such as Pac-Atlantic often offer warrants along with their bonds. However, some strong firms also have used warrants. In one of the largest financings of any type ever undertaken by a business firm at the time, **AT&T** raised $1.57 billion by selling bonds with warrants. This marked the first use ever of warrants by a large, strong corporation.

Getting warrants along with bonds enables investors to share in a company's growth if that firm does in fact grow and prosper; therefore, investors are willing to accept a lower bond interest rate and less restrictive indenture provisions. A bond with warrants has some characteristics of debt and some of equity. It is a hybrid security that provides the financial manager with an opportunity to expand the firm's mix of securities and to appeal to a broader group of investors, thus lowering the firm's cost of capital. Virtually all warrants today are **detachable warrants,** meaning that after a bond with attached warrants has been sold, the warrants can be detached and traded separately from the bond. Further, when these warrants are exercised, the bonds themselves (with their low coupon rate) will remain outstanding. Thus, the warrants will bring in additional equity capital while leaving low interest rate debt on the issuer's books.

The warrants' exercise price generally is set at from 10% to 30% above the market price of the stock on the date the bond is issued. For example, if the stock sells for $10, the exercise price will probably be set in the $11 to $13 range. If the firm does grow and prosper, and if its stock price rises above the exercise price at which shares can be purchased, warrant holders will turn in their warrants, along with cash equal to the stated exercise price, in exchange for stock. Without some incentive, however, many warrants would never be exercised until just before expiration. Their value in the market would be greater than their exercise value; thus holders would sell warrants rather than exercise them.

There are three conditions that encourage holders to exercise their warrants.

1. Warrant holders surely will exercise warrants and buy stock if the warrants are about to expire with the market price of the stock above the exercise price. This means that if a firm wants its warrants exercised soon in order to raise capital, it should set a relatively short expiration date.
2. Warrant holders will tend to exercise voluntarily and buy stock if the company raises the dividend on the common stock by a sufficient amount. Because no dividend is paid on the warrant, it provides no current income. However, if the common stock pays a high dividend, it provides an attractive dividend yield. Therefore, the higher the stock's dividend, the greater the opportunity cost of holding the warrant rather than exercising it. Thus, if a firm wants its warrants exercised, it can raise the common stock's dividend.
3. Warrants sometimes have **stepped-up exercise prices,** which prod owners into exercising them. For example, the Mills Agricorp has warrants outstanding with an exercise price of $25 until December 31, 2002, at which time the exercise price will rise to $30. If the price of the common stock is over $25 just before December 31, 2002, many warrant holders will exercise their options before the stepped-up price takes effect.

Another useful feature of warrants is that they generally bring in funds only if such funds are needed. If the company grows, it probably will need new equity capital. At the same time, this growth will cause the price of the stock to rise and the warrants to be exercised, thereby allowing the firm to obtain additional cash. If the company is not successful and cannot profitably employ additional money, the price of its stock probably will not rise sufficiently to induce exercise of the options.

Convertibles

Convertible securities are bonds or preferred stocks that can be exchanged for common stock at the option of the holder. Unlike the exercise of warrants, which provides the firm with additional funds, conversion does not bring in additional capital—debt or preferred stock simply is replaced by common stock. Of course, this reduction of debt or preferred stock will strengthen the firm's balance sheet and make it easier to raise additional capital, but this is a separate action.

Conversion Ratio and Conversion Price

One of the most important provisions of a convertible security is the **conversion ratio, CR,** defined as the number of shares of stock the convertible holder receives upon conversion. Related to the conversion ratio is the conversion price, P_c, which is the effective price paid for the common stock obtained by converting a convertible security. The relationship between the conversion ratio and the conversion price can be illustrated by the convertible debentures issued at par value by Bee TV Inc. in 2000. At any time prior to maturity on July 1, 2020, a debenture holder can exchange a bond for 20 shares of common stock; therefore, CR = 20. The bond has a par value of $1,000, so the holder would be relinquishing this amount upon conversion. Dividing the $1,000 par value by the 20 shares received gives a conversion price of P_c = $50 a share:

$$\text{Conversion price} = \frac{\text{Par value of bond}}{\text{Conversion ratio}} \quad (7.9)$$

$$= \frac{\$1,000}{20} = \$50$$

Like a warrant's exercise price, the conversion price usually is set at from 10% to 30% above the prevailing market price of the common stock at the time the convertible issue is sold. Generally, the conversion price and ratio are fixed for the life of the bond, although sometimes a stepped-up conversion price is used.

Another factor that might cause a change in the conversion price and ratio is a standard feature of almost all convertibles—the clause protecting the convertible against dilution from stock splits, stock dividends, and the sale of common stock at prices below the conversion price. The typical provision states that if common stock is sold at a price below the conversion price, the conversion price must be lowered (and the conversion ratio raised) to the price at which the new stock was issued. Also, if the stock is split (or if a stock dividend is declared), the conversion price must be lowered by the percentage of the stock split (or stock dividend). If this protection were not contained in the contract, a company could completely thwart conversion by the use of stock splits. Warrants are similarly protected against such dilution.

Use of Convertibles in Financing

Convertibles offer three important advantages from the *issuer's* standpoint. First, convertibles, like bonds with warrants, permit a company to sell debt with a lower interest rate and with less restrictive covenants than straight bonds. Second, convertibles generally are subordinated to mortgage bonds, bank loans, and other senior debt, so financing with convertibles leaves the company's access to "regular" debt unimpaired. Third, convertibles provide a way of selling common stock at prices higher than those currently prevailing. Many companies actually want to sell common stock and not debt, but they believe that the price of their stock is temporarily depressed. The financial manager might know, for example, that earnings are depressed because of start-up costs associated with a new project, but he or she might expect earnings to rise sharply during the next year or so, pulling the price of the stock along. In this case, if the company sold stock now it would be giving up too many shares to raise a given amount of money. However, if it sets the conversion price at 20% to 30% above the present market price of the stock, then 20% to 30% fewer shares will have to be given up when the bonds are converted. Notice, however, that management is counting on the stock's price rising sufficiently above the conversion price to make the bonds attractive in conversion. If earnings do not rise and pull the stock price up, and hence if conversion does not occur, the company could be saddled with debt in the face of low earnings, which could be disastrous.

How can the company be sure that conversion will occur if the price of the stock rises above the conversion price? Typically, convertibles contain a call provision that enables the issuing firm to force bondholders to convert. Suppose the conversion price is $50, the conversion ratio is 20, the market price of the common stock has risen to $60, and the call price on the convertible bond is $1,050. If the company calls the bond, bondholders could either convert into common stock with a market value of $1,200 or allow the company to redeem the bond for $1,050. Naturally, bondholders prefer $1,200 to $1,050, so conversion will occur. The call provision therefore gives the company a means of *forcing* conversion, but only if the market price of the stock is greater than the conversion price.

Convertibles are useful, but they do have three important disadvantages.

1. The use of a convertible security might, in effect, give the issuer the opportunity to sell common stock at a price higher than it could sell stock otherwise. However, if the common stock increases greatly in price, the company probably would have been better off if it had used straight debt in spite of its higher interest rate and then later sold common stock to refund the debt.
2. If the company truly wants to raise equity capital, and if the price of the stock does not rise sufficiently after the bond is issued, then the firm will be stuck with debt.
3. Convertibles typically have a low coupon interest rate, an advantage that will be lost when conversion occurs. Warrant financings, on the other hand, permit the company to continue to use the low-coupon debt for a longer period.

Reporting Earnings When Warrants or Convertibles Are Outstanding

If warrants or convertibles are outstanding, a firm theoretically can report earnings per share (EPS) in one of three ways.

1. **Simple EPS.** The earnings available to common stockholders are divided by the average number of shares *actually* outstanding during the period.
2. **Primary EPS.** The earnings available are divided by the average number of shares that would have been outstanding if warrants and convertibles *likely to be converted* in the near future had actually been exercised or converted.
3. **Fully diluted EPS.** This is similar to primary EPS except that all warrants and convertibles are *assumed to be exercised or converted*, regardless of the likelihood of either occurring.

Simple EPS is virtually never reported by firms that have warrants or convertibles likely to be exercised or converted; the SEC prohibits use of this figure, and it requires that primary and fully diluted earnings be shown on the income statement.

Valuation of Financial Assets—Bonds

Corporations raise capital in two forms—debt and equity. We will examine the valuation process for bonds (the principal type of long-term debt), and for stock (equity) and tangible assets.

A **bond** is a long-term promissory note issued by a business or governmental unit. For example, suppose on January 3, 2000, Unilate Textiles borrowed $25 million by selling 25,000 individual bonds for $1,000 each. Unilate received the $25 million, and it promised to pay the bondholders annual interest and to repay the $25 million on a specified date. The lenders were willing to give Unilate $25 million, so the value of the bond issue was $25 million. But how did the investors decide that the issue was worth $25 million? As a first step in explaining how the values of this and other bonds are determined, we need to define some terms.

1. **Principal amount, face value, maturity value, and par value.** The **principal amount** of debt generally represents the amount of money the firm borrows and promises to repay at some future date. For much debt issued by corporations, including bonds, the principal amount is repaid at maturity, so we often refer to the principal value as the **maturity value.** In addition, the principal value generally is written on the "face" of the debt instrument, or certificate, so it is also called the **face value.** Further, when the market value of debt is the same as its face value, it is said to be selling at *par*; thus the principal amount is also referred to as the **par value.** For most debt, then, *the terms principal amount, face value, maturity value, and par value refer to the same value—the amount that must be repaid by the borrower.* We use the terms interchangeably throughout the book. The face value of a corporate bond is usually set at $1,000, although multiples of $1,000 (for example, $5,000) are also used.
2. **Coupon interest rate.** The bond requires the issuer to pay a specified number of dollars of interest each year (or, more typically, each six months). When this **coupon payment,** as it is called, is divided by the par value, the result is the **coupon interest rate.** For example, Unilate's bonds have a $1,000 par value, and they pay $150 in interest each year. The bond's coupon interest is $150, so its coupon interest rate is $150/$1,000 = 15%. The $150 is the yearly "rent" on the $1,000 loan. This payment, which is fixed at the time the bond is issued, remains in force, by contract, during the life of the bond.
3. **Maturity date.** Bonds generally have a specified **maturity date** on which the par value must be repaid. Unilate's bonds, which were issued on January 3, 2000, will mature on January 2, 2015; thus, they had a 15-year maturity at the time they were issued. Most bonds have **original maturities** (the maturity at the time the bond is issued) of from 10 to 40 years, but any maturity is legally permissible. Of course, the effective maturity of a bond declines each year after it has been issued. Thus, Unilate's bonds had a 15-year original maturity, but in 2001 they had a 14-year maturity, and so on.
4. **Call provisions.** Often, bonds have a provision whereby the issuer can pay them off prior to maturity by "calling them in" from the investors. This feature is known as a **call provision.** If a bond is callable, and if interest rates in the economy decline, then the company can sell a new issue of low-interest-rate bonds and use the proceeds to retire the old, high-interest-rate issue, just as a homeowner can refinance a home mortgage.

5. **New issues versus outstanding bonds.** As we shall see, a bond's market price is determined primarily by the cash flows it generates, or the dollar interest it pays, which depends on the coupon interest rate—the higher the coupon, other things held constant, the higher the market price of the bond. At the time a bond is issued, the coupon generally is set at a level that will cause the market price of the bond to equal its par value. If a lower coupon were set, investors simply would not be willing to pay $1,000 for the bond, while if a higher coupon were set, investors would clamor for the bond and bid its price up over $1,000. Investment bankers can judge quite precisely the coupon rate that will cause a bond to sell at its $1,000 par value.

A bond that has just been issued is known as a *new issue.* (*The Wall Street Journal* classifies a bond as a new issue for about one month after it has first been issued.) Once the bond has been on the market for a while, it is classified as an *outstanding bond,* also called a *seasoned issue.* Newly issued bonds generally sell very close to par, but the prices of outstanding bonds can vary widely from par. Coupon interest payments are constant, so when economic conditions change, a bond with a $150 coupon that sold at par when it was issued can sell for more or less than $1,000 thereafter.

The Basic Bond Valuation Model

The value of any asset can be expressed in general form as follows.

$$\text{Asset value} = V = \frac{\hat{CF}_1}{(1+k)^1} + \frac{\hat{CF}_2}{(1+k)^2} + \cdots + \frac{\hat{CF}_n}{(1+k)^n} \qquad (7.10)$$

Here

$\hat{CF}_t$ = The cash flow expected to be generated by the asset in period t.

k = The return investors consider appropriate for holding such an asset. This return is usually termed the *required return,* and it is based on both economic conditions and the riskiness of the asset.

According to Equation 7.10, the value of an asset is affected by the cash flows it is expected to generate, $\hat{CF}$ and the return required by investors, k. As you can see, *the higher the expected cash flows, the greater the asset's value; also, the lower the required return, the greater the asset's value.* In the remainder of this section, we discuss how this general valuation concept can be applied to determine the value of various types of assets. First, we examine the valuation process for financial assets, and then we apply the process to value real assets.

Equation 7.10 shows that the value of a financial asset is based on the cash flows expected to be generated by the asset in the future. In the case of a bond, the cash flows consist of interest payments during the life of the bond plus a return of the principal amount borrowed when the bond matures. In a cash flow time line format, here is the situation.

```
0   k_d%   1        2       N-1      N
    |      |        |        |       |
           INT      INT      INT     INT
PV of INT ←┘        │        │       M
PV of M ←───────────┴────────┴───────┘
Bond Value = V_d
```

Here

k_d = The average rate of return investors require to invest in the bond. So, for the Unilate Textiles bond issue k_d = 15%.

N = The number of years before the bond matures. For the Unilate bonds, N = 15. Note that N declines each year after the bond has been issued, so a bond that had a maturity of 15 years when it was issued (original maturity = 15) will have N = 14 after one year, N = 13 after two years, and so on. Note also that at this point we assume that the bond pays interest once a year, or annually, so N is measured in years.

INT = Dollars of interest paid each period = Coupon rate × Par value. In our example, INT = 0.15 × $1,000 = $150.

M = The par, or face, value of the bond = $1,000. This amount must be paid off at maturity. In calculator terminology, FV = M = 1000.

We can now redraw the cash flow time line to show the numerical values for all variables except the bond's value.

```
0    15%   1       2        14       15
|----------|-------|---...---|--------|
Value      150     150       150      150
                                     1,000
                                     -----
                                     1,150
```

Now the following general equation can be solved to find the value of any bond.

$$\text{Bond value} = V_d = \frac{INT}{(1+k_d)^1} + \frac{INT}{(1+k_d)^2} + \cdots + \frac{INT}{(1+k_d)^N} + \frac{M}{(1+k_d)^N} \quad (7.11)$$

$$= \sum_{t=1}^{n} \frac{INT}{(1+k_d)^t} + \frac{M}{(a+k_d)^N}$$

Notice the interest payments represent an annuity, and repayment of the par value at maturity represents a single, or lump-sum, payment. Thus, Equation 7.11 can be rewritten for use with the tables.

$$V_d = INT(PVIFA_{k_d,N}) + M(PVIF_{k_d,N}) \quad (7.11a)$$

Inserting values for our particular bond, we have

$$V_d = \sum_{t=1}^{15} \frac{\$150}{(1.15)^t} + \frac{\$1,000}{(1.15)}$$

$$= \$150(\hat{P}VIFA_{15\%,15}) + \$1,000(PVIF_{15\%,15})$$

The value of the bond can be computed by using three procedures: (1) numerically, (2) using the tables, and (3) with a financial calculator. We will show the first two procedures.

1. NUMERICAL SOLUTION Simply discount each cash flow back to the present and sum these PVs to find the value of the bond. This procedure is not efficient. Alternatively, we can use the following equation to find the solution.

$$V_d = \text{PV of the interest payment (an annuity)} + \text{PV of the face value (a lump-sum amount)}$$

$$= \$150\left[\frac{1 - \frac{1}{(1.15)^{15}}}{0.15}\right] + \$1,000\left[\frac{1}{(1.15)^{15}}\right]$$

$$= \$150(5.84737) + \$1,000(0.12289)$$
$$= \$877.11 + \$122.89$$
$$= \$1,000$$

2. TABULAR SOLUTION Simply look up the appropriate PVIF and PVIFA values in Tables A.1 and A.2 of Module 700 Appendix, insert them into the equation, and complete the arithmetic.

$$V_d = \$150(5.8474) + \$1,000(0.1229)$$
$$= \$877.11 + \$122.90$$
$$= \$1000.01 \approx \$1,000 \text{ (rounding error)}$$

Finding the Interest Rate on a Bond: Yield to Maturity

Suppose you were offered a 14-year, 15% coupon, $1,000 par value bond at a price of $1,368.31. What rate of interest would you earn on your investment if you bought the bond and held it to maturity? This rate is called the bond's **yield** to maturity (YTM), and it is the interest rate discussed by bond traders when they talk about rates of return. To find the yield to maturity, you could solve Equation 7.11 or 7.11a for k_d:

$$V_d = \$1,368.31 = \frac{\$150}{(1+k_d)^1} + \cdots + \frac{\$150}{(1+k_d)^{14}} + \frac{\$1,000}{(1+k_d)^{14}}$$

$$= \$150(\text{PVIFA}_{k_d,14}) + \$1,000(\text{PVIF}_{k_d,14})$$

If you have a financial calculator, you would simply enter N = 14, PMT = 150, FV = 1000, and PV = −1368.31, and then press the I key. The calculator will blink (or perhaps go blank) for a few seconds, and then the answer, 10%, will appear.

If you do not have a financial calculator, you can substitute values for PVIFA and PVIF at different interest rates until you find a pair that "works" so that the present value of the interest payments combined with the present value of the repayment of the face value at maturity equals the current price of the bond. But what would be a good interest rate to use as a starting point? First, you know that the bond is selling at a premium over its par value ($1,368.31 versus $1,000), so the bond's yield to maturity must be below its 15% coupon rate. Therefore, you might start by trying rates below 15%. It could take you a while to "zero in" on the appropriate rate. It probably would be better to get an estimate of the rate by computing the *approximate* yield to maturity, which can be found with the following equation.

$$\text{Approximate yield to maturity} = \frac{\text{Annual interest} + \text{Accrued capital gains}}{\text{Average value of bond}} \quad (7.12)$$

$$= \frac{\text{INT} + \left(\dfrac{M - V_d}{N}\right)}{\left[\dfrac{2(V_d) + M}{3}\right]}$$

Equation 7.12 is based on computations of approximate yields in the past and it does not consider the time value of money, so it should be used only to approximate a bond's yield to maturity. For the bond we are examining, the approximate yield to maturity is

$$\text{Yield to maturity} = k_d \approx \frac{\$150 + \left(\dfrac{\$1,000 - \$1,368.31}{14}\right)}{\left[\dfrac{2(\$1,368.31) + \$1,000}{3}\right]}$$

$$= \frac{\$150 + (-\$26.31)}{\$1,245.54} = 0.0993 \approx 10\%$$

Inserting interest factors for 10%, you obtain a value equal to

$$V_d = \$150(7.3667) + \$1,000(0.2633)$$
$$= \$1,105.01 + \$263.30$$
$$= \$1,368.31$$

This calculated value is equal to the market price of the bond, so 10% is the bond's actual yield to maturity: k_d = YTM = 10.0%.

The yield to maturity is identical to the total annual rate of return discussed in the preceding section. The YTM for a bond that sells at par consists entirely of an interest yield, but if the bond sells at a price other than its par value, the YTM consists of the interest yield plus a positive or negative capital gains yield. Note also that a bond's yield to maturity changes whenever interest rates in the economy change, and this is almost daily. One who purchases a bond and holds it until it matures will receive the YTM that existed on the purchase date, but the bond's calculated YTM will change frequently between the purchase date and the maturity date.

Valuation of Financial Assets—Equity (Stock)

Each corporation issues at least one type of stock, or equity, called *common stock*. Some corporations issue more than one type of common stock, and some issue *preferred stock* in addition to common stock. As the names imply, most equity is in the form of common stock, and preferred shareholders have preference over common shareholders when a firm distributes funds to stockholders. Dividends, as well as liquidation proceeds resulting from bankruptcy, are paid to preferred stockholders before common stockholders. But preferred stockholders generally are paid the same dividend each year, while the dividends paid to common stockholders can vary and are often dependent on current and previous earnings levels and the future growth plans of the firm. For the purposes of our discussion in this section, you need to be aware that the cash flows generated by investing in preferred stock are normally constant, while the cash flows generated by common stock can be constant, but often vary from year to year.

In this section, we examine the process to value stock, both preferred and common. We begin by introducing a general stock valuation model. Then, we apply the model to three scenarios: (1) when there is no growth in dividends so the amount paid each year remains constant (like preferred dividends), (2) when dividends increase at a constant rate each year, and (3) when dividends grow at different rates (nonconstant growth).

Definitions of Terms Used in the Stock Valuation Models

Stocks provide an expected future cash flow stream, and a stock's value is found in the same manner as the values of other assets—namely, as the present value of the expected future cash flow stream. The expected cash flows consist of two elements: (1) the dividends expected in each year and (2) the price investors expect to receive when they sell the stock, which includes the return of the original investment plus a capital gain or loss.

Before we present the general stock valuation model, we define some terms and notations we will use throughout this section.

$\hat{D}_t$ = Dividend the stockholder expects to receive at the end of Year t (pronounced "D hat t"). D_0 is the most recent dividend, which has already been paid; $\hat{D}_1$ is the next dividend expected to be paid, and it will be paid at the end of this year; $\hat{D}_2$ is the dividend expected at the end of two years; and so forth. $\hat{D}_1$ represents the first cash flow a new purchaser of the stock will receive. Note that D_0, the dividend that has just been paid, is known with certainty (thus, there is no "hat" over the D). However, all future dividends are *expected* values, so the estimate of $\hat{D}_t$ might differ among investors for some stocks.

P_0 = Actual **market price** of the stock today.

$\hat{P}_t$ = Expected price of the stock at the end of Year t. $\hat{P}_0$ is the **intrinsic**, or *theoretical*, **value** of the stock today as seen by the particular investor doing the analysis; $\hat{P}_1$ is the price *expected* at the end of one year; and so on. Note that $\hat{P}_0$ is the intrinsic value of the stock today based on a particular investors estimate of the stock's expected dividend stream and the riskiness of that stream. Hence, whereas P_0 is fixed and is identical for all investors because it represents the price at which the stock currently can be purchased in the stock market, $\hat{P}_0$ could differ among investors depending on what they feel the firm actually is worth. The caret, or "hat", is used to indicate that $\hat{P}_t$ is an estimated value. $\hat{P}_0$, the individual investor's estimate of the intrinsic value today, could be above or below P_0, the current stock price, but an investor would buy the stock only if his or her estimate of $\hat{P}_0$ were equal to or greater than P_0.

Because there are many investors in the market, there can be many values for $\hat{P}_0$. However, we can think of a group of "average," or "marginal," investors whose actions actually determine the market price. For these marginal investors, P_0 must equal $\hat{P}_0$; otherwise, a disequilibrium would exist, and buying and selling in the market would change P_0 until $P_0 = \hat{P}_0$.

g = Expected **growth rate** in dividends as predicted by a marginal, or average, investor. (If we assume that dividends are expected to grow at a constant rate, g is also equal to the expected rate of growth in the stock's price.) Different investors might use different g's to evaluate a firm's stock, but the market price, P_0, is set on the basis of the g estimated by marginal investors.

k_s = Minimum acceptable, or **required, rate of return** on the stock, considering both its riskiness and the returns available on other investments. Again, this term generally relates to average investors.

$\dfrac{\hat{D}_1}{P_0}$ = Expected **dividend yield** on the stock during the coming year. If the stock is expected to pay a dividend of $1 during the next 12 months, and if its current price is $10, then the expected dividend yield is $1/$10 = 0.10 = 10%.

$\dfrac{\hat{P}_1 - P_0}{P_0}$ = Expected **capital gains yield** on the stock during the coming year. If the stock sells for $10 today, and if it is expected to rise to $10.50 at the end of one year, then the expected capital gain is $\hat{P}_1 - P_0$ = $10.50 − $10.00 = $0.50, and the expected capital gains yield is $0.50/$10 = 0.05 = 5%.

715. MANAGING LONG-TERM FINANCING

$\hat{k}_s$ = **Expected rate of return** that an investor who buys the stock anticipates, or expects to receive. $\hat{k}_s$ could be above or below k_s, but one would buy the stock only if $\hat{k}_s$ was equal to or greater than k_s. $\hat{k}_s$ = expected dividend yield plus expected capital gains yield; in other words,

$$\hat{k}_s = \frac{\hat{D}_1}{P_0} + \frac{\hat{P}_1 - P_0}{P_0}$$

In our example, the expected total return = $\hat{k}_s$ = 10% + 5% = 15%.

$\bar{k}_s$ = **Actual**, or **realized**, *after the fact* **rate of return** (pronounced "k bar s"). You might expect to obtain a return of $\hat{k}_s$ = 14% if you buy **IBM** stock today, but if the market goes down, you might end up next year with an actual realized return that is much lower, perhaps even negative (for example, $\bar{k}_s$ = 8%).

Expected Dividends as the Basis for Stock Values

Remember that according to Equation 7.10 the value of any asset is the present value of the cash flows expected to be generated by the asset in the future. In our discussion of bonds, we found that the value of a bond is the present value of the interest payments over the life of the bond plus the present value of the bond's maturity (or par) value. Stock prices are likewise determined as the present value of a stream of cash flows, and the basic stock valuation equation is similar to the bond valuation equation (Equation 7.11). What are the cash flows that corporations provide to their stockholders? First, think of yourself as an investor who buys a stock with the intention of holding it (in your family) forever. In this case, all that you (and your heirs) will receive is a stream of dividends, and the value of the stock today is calculated as the present value of an infinite stream of dividends, which is depicted on a cash flow timeline as follows:

Thus, to compute the value of the stock, we must solve the following equation.

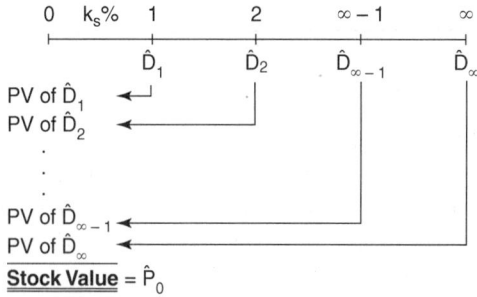

Value of stock $V_s = \hat{P}_0$ = PV of expected future dividends

$$= \frac{\hat{D}_1}{(1+k_s)^1} + \frac{\hat{D}_2}{(1+k_s)^2} + \cdots + \frac{\hat{D}_\infty}{(1+k_s)^\infty} \qquad (7.13)$$

$$= \sum_{t=1}^{\infty} \frac{\hat{D}_t}{(1+k_s)^t}$$

What about the more typical case, where you expect to hold the stock for a specific (finite) period and then sell it—what will be the value of $\hat{P}_0$ in this case? Unless the company is likely to be liquidated and thus to disappear, *the value of the stock is still determined by Equation 7.13.* To see this, recognize that for any individual investor, the expected cash flows consist of expected dividends plus the expected sale price of the stock. However, the sale price the current investor receives will depend on the dividends the future investor expects. Therefore, for all present and future investors in total, expected cash flows must be based on all of the expected future dividends. To put it another way, unless a firm is liquidated or sold to another concern, the cash flows it provides to its stockholders will consist only of a stream of dividends; therefore, the value of a share of its stock must be established as the present value of that expected dividend stream that will be paid throughout the life of the company.

The general validity of Equation 7.13 also can be confirmed by asking the following question: Suppose I buy a stock and expect to hold it for one year. I will receive dividends during the year plus the value $\hat{P}_1$ when I sell the stock at the end of the year. But what will determine the value of $\hat{P}_1$? The answer is that it will be determined as the present value of the dividends during Year 2 plus the stock price at the end of that year, which in turn will be determined as the present value of another set of future dividends and an even more distant stock price. This process can be continued forever, and the ultimate result is Equation 7.13.

Equation 7.13 is a generalized stock valuation model in the sense that the time pattern of $\hat{D}_t$ can be anything: $\hat{D}_t$ can be rising, falling, or constant, or it can even be fluctuating randomly, and Equation 7.13 still will hold. Often, however, the projected stream of dividends follows a systematic pattern, in which case we can develop a simplified (that is, easier to apply) version of the stock valuation model expressed in Equation 7.13. In the following sections we consider the scenarios of zero growth, constant growth, and nonconstant growth.

Scenario 1: Valuing Stocks With Zero Growth

Suppose dividends are not expected to grow at all; instead they are expected to stay the same every year. Here we have a **zero-growth stock,** for which the dividends expected in future years are equal to some constant amount—the current dividend. That is, $\hat{D}_1 = \hat{D}_2 = \cdots = \hat{D}_\infty$. Therefore, we can drop the subscripts and the "hats" on D and rewrite Equation 7.13 as follows.

$$\hat{P}_0 = \frac{D}{(1 + k_s)^1} + \frac{D}{(1 + k_s)^2} + \cdots + \frac{D}{(1 + k_s)^\infty} \tag{7.13a}$$

A security that is expected to pay a constant amount each year forever is called a perpetuity. Therefore, a *zero-growth stock is a perpetuity.*

Remember the value of any perpetuity is simply the payment amount divided by the discount rate, so the value of a zero-growth stock reduces to this formula.

$$\text{Value of zero-growth stock: } \hat{P}_0 = \frac{D}{k_s} \tag{7.14}$$

For example, if we have a stock that is expected to always pay a dividend equal to $1.20, and the required rate of return associated with such an investment is 12%, the stock's value should be

$$\hat{P}_0 = \frac{\$1.20}{0.12} = \$10.00$$

Generally, we can find the price of a stock and the most recent dividend paid to the stockholders by looking in a financial newspaper such as *The Wall Street Journal.* Therefore, if we have a stock with constant dividends, we can solve for the expected rate of return by rearranging Equation 7.14 to produce

$$\hat{k}_s = \frac{D}{P_0} \tag{7.14a}$$

Because we are dealing with an *expected rate of return,* we put a "hat" on the k value. Thus, if we bought a stock at a price of $10 and expected to receive a constant dividend of $1.20, our expected rate of return would be

$$\hat{k}_s = \frac{\$1.20}{\$10.00} = 0.12 = 12.0\%$$

By now, you probably have recognized that Equation 7.14 can be used to value preferred stock. Recall that preferred stocks entitle their owners to regular, or fixed, dividend payments. And, if the payments last forever, the issue is a *perpetuity* whose value is defined by Equation 7.14. To generalize, we can use Equation 7.14 to value any asset, including common stock, with expected future cash flows that exhibit the properties of a perpetuity—constant cash flows forever.

Scenario 2: Valuing Stocks With Constant Growth

In general, investors expect the earnings and common stock dividends of most companies to increase each year. Even though expected growth rates vary from company to company, it is not uncommon for investors to expect dividend growth to continue in the foreseeable future at about the same rate as that of the nominal gross national product (real GNP plus inflation). On this basis, we might expect the dividend of an average, or "normal," company to grow at a rate of 3 to 6% a year. Thus, if a **normal, or constant, growth** company's last dividend, which has already been paid, was D_0, its dividend in any future year can be forecasted as $\hat{D}_t = D_0(1 + g)^t$, where g is the constant expected rate of growth and t represents the year of the dividend forecast. For example, if a firm just paid a dividend of $1.20 (that is, $D_0 = \$1.20$), and if investors expect a 5% growth rate, then the estimated dividend one year hence would be $\hat{D}_1 = \$1.20(1.05) = \$1.26$; $\hat{D}_2$ would be $1.323; and the estimated dividend five years hence would be:

$$\hat{D}_5 = D_0(1 + g)^5 = \$1.20(1.05)^5 = \$1.532$$

Using this method for estimating future dividends, we can determine the current stock value, $\hat{P}_0$, using Equation 7.13 as set forth previously—in other words, we can find the expected future cash flow stream (the dividends), then calculate the present value of each dividend payment, and finally sum these present values to find the value of the stock. Thus, the intrinsic value of the stock is equal to the present value of its expected future dividends.

If g is constant, however, Equation 7.13 can be rewritten as follows.

$$\hat{P}_0 = \frac{D_0(1+g)^1}{(1+k_s)^1} + \frac{D_0(1+g)^2}{(1+k_s)^2} + \cdots + \frac{D_0(1+g)^\infty}{(1+k_s)^\infty} \quad (7.15)$$

$$= \frac{D_0(1+g)}{k_s - g} = \frac{\hat{D}_1}{k_s - g}$$

Inserting values into the last version of Equation 7.15, we find the value of our illustrative stock is $18.00.

$$\hat{P}_0 = \frac{\$1.20(1.05)}{0.12 - 0.05} = \frac{\$1.26}{0.07} = \$18.00$$

The **constant growth model** as set forth in the last term of Equation 7.15 is often called the Gordon Model, after Myron J. Gordon, who did much to develop and popularize it.

Note that Equation 7.15 is sufficiently general to encompass the zero growth case described earlier. If growth is zero, this is simply a special case of constant growth, and Equation 7.15 becomes Equation 7.14. Note also that a necessary condition for the derivation of the simplified form of Equation 7.15 is that k_s be greater than g. If the equation is used in situations where k_s is not greater than g, the results will be meaningless.

Growth in dividends occurs primarily as a result of growth in *earnings per share (EPS)*. Earnings growth, in turn, results from a number of factors, including (1) inflation, (2) the amount of earnings the company retains and reinvests, and (3) the rate of return the company earns on its equity (ROE). Regarding inflation, if output (in units) is stable and if both sales prices and input costs rise at the inflation rate, then EPS will also grow at the inflation rate. EPS also will grow as a result of the reinvestment, or plowback, of earnings. If the firm's earnings are not all paid out as dividends (that is, if some fraction of earnings is retained), the dollars of investment behind each share will rise over time, which should lead to growth in future earnings and dividends.

Expected Rate of Return on a Constant Growth Stock

We can solve Equation 7.15 for $\hat{k}_s$, again using the hat to denote that we are dealing with an expected rate of return.

$$\begin{array}{c}\text{Expected rate}\\ \text{of return}\end{array} = \begin{array}{c}\text{Expected}\\ \text{dividend yield}\end{array} + \begin{array}{c}\text{Expected growth rate,}\\ \text{or capital gains yield}\end{array} \quad (7.16)$$

$$\hat{k}_s = \frac{\hat{D}_1}{P_0} + g$$

Thus, if you buy a stock for a price $P_0 = \$18$, and if you expect the stock to pay a dividend $\hat{D}_1 = \$1.26$ one year from now and to grow at a constant rate g = 5% in the future, then your expected rate of return will be 12%.

$$\hat{k}_s = \frac{\$1.26}{\$18} + 0.05 = 0.07 + 0.05 = 0.12 = 12.0\%$$

In this form, we see that $\hat{k}_s$ is the *expected total return* and that it consists of an *expected dividend yield*, $\hat{D}_1/P_0 = 7\%$, plus an *expected growth rate or capital gains yield*, g = 5%.

Suppose this analysis had been conducted on January 1, 2000, so $P_0 = \$18$ is the January 1, 2000 stock price and $\hat{D}_1 = \$1.26$ is the dividend expected at the end of 2000 (December 31). What is the expected stock price at the end of 2000 (or the beginning of 2001)? We would again apply Equation 7.15, but this time we would use the expected 2001 dividend, $\hat{D}_{2001} = \hat{D}_2 = \hat{D}_1(1 + g) = \$1.26(1.05) = \$1.323$.

$$P_1 = \frac{\hat{D}_2}{k_s - g} = \hat{P}_{1/1/01} = \frac{\hat{D}_{12/31/01}}{k_s - g} = \frac{\$1.323}{0.12 - 0.05} = \$18.90$$

Now notice that $18.90 is 5% greater than P_0, the $18 price on January 1, 2000.

$$\hat{P}_{1/1/00} = \$18.00(1.05) = \$18.90$$

Thus, we would expect to make a capital gain of $18,90 − $180.00 = $0.90 during the year, which is a capital gains yield of 5%.

$$\text{Capital gains yield} = \frac{\text{Capital gain}}{\text{Beginning price}} = \frac{\text{Ending price} - \text{Beginning price}}{\text{Beginning price}}$$

$$= \frac{\$18.90 - \$18.00}{\$18.00} = \frac{\$0.90}{\$18.00} = 0.05 = 5.0\%$$

We could extend the analysis on out, and in each future year the expected capital gains yield would equal g = 5%, the expected dividend growth rate.

Continuing, the dividend yield in 2001 could be estimated as follows.

$$\text{Dividend yield}_{2001} = \frac{\hat{D}_{12/31/01}}{P_{1/1/01}} = \frac{\$1.323}{\$18.90} = 0.07 = 7.0\%$$

The dividend yield for 2002 could also be calculated, and again it would be 7%. Thus, for a constant growth stock, the following conditions must hold.

1. The dividend is expected to grow forever at a constant rate, g.
2. The stock price is expected to grow at this same rate.
3. The expected dividend yield is a constant.
4. The expected capital gains yield is also a constant, and it is equal to g.
5. The expected total rate of return, $\hat{k}_s$, is equal to the expected dividend yield plus the expected growth rate: $\hat{k}_s$ = dividend yield + g.

The term *expected* should be clarified—it means expected in a probabilistic sense, as the statistically expected outcome. Thus, if we say the growth rate is expected to remain constant at 5%, we mean that the best prediction for the growth rate in any future year is 5%, not that we literally expect the growth rate to be exactly equal to 5% in each future year. In this sense, the constant growth assumption is a reasonable one for many large, mature companies.

Scenario 3: Valuing Stocks With Nonconstant Growth

Firms typically go through *life cycles*. During the early part of their lives, their growth is much faster than that of the economy as a whole; then they match the economy's growth; and finally their growth is slower than that of the economy. Automobile manufacturers in the 1920s and computer software firms such as Microsoft in the 1990s are examples of firms in the early part of the cycle. Other firms, such as the those in the tobacco industry or coal industry, are currently in the waning stages of their life cycles, so their growth is not keeping pace with the general economic growth (in some cases growth is negative). Firms whose growths are not about the same as the economy's growth are called **nonconstant growth** firms.

Stock Market Equilibrium

The required return on a stock, k_s, can be found using the Security Market Line (SML) equation as it was developed in our discussion of the Capital Asset Pricing Model (CAPM).

$$k_s = k_{RF} + (k_M - k_{RF})b_s$$

If the risk-free rate of return is 8%, if the market risk premium is 4%, and if Stock X has a beta of 2, then the marginal investor will require a return of 16% on Stock X, calculated as follows.

$$k_x = 8\% + (12\% - 8\%)2.0 = 16\%$$

This 16% required return is shown as a point on the SML in Exhibit 700.17.

The average investor will want to buy Stock X if the expected rate of return is more than 16%, will want to sell it if the expected rate of return is less than 16%, and will be indifferent, hence will hold but not buy or sell, if the expected rate of return is exactly 16%. Now suppose the investor's portfolio contains Stock X, and he or she analyzes the stock's prospects and concludes that its earnings, dividends, and price can be expected to grow at a constant rate of 5% per year. The last dividend was $D_0 = \$2.86$, so the next expected dividend is

$$\hat{D}_1 = \$2.86(1.05) = \$3.00$$

Our average investor observes that the present price of the stock, P_0, is $30. Should he or she purchase more of Stock X, sell the present holdings, or maintain the present position?

The investor can calculate Stock X's *expected rate of return* as follows.

$$\hat{k}_x = \frac{\hat{D}_1}{P_0} + g = \frac{\$3.00}{\$30.00} + 0.05 = 0.15 = 15\%$$

This value is plotted on Exhibit 700.17 as Point X, which is below the SML. Because the expected rate of return is less than the required return, this marginal investor would want to sell the stock, as would other holders. However, few people would want to buy at the $30 price, so the present owners would be unable to find buyers unless they cut the price of the stock. Thus, the price would decline, and this decline would continue until the stock's price reached $27.27, at which point the market for this security would be in **equilibrium,** because the expected rate of return, 16%, would be equal to the required rate of return.

$$\hat{k}_x = \frac{\$3.00}{\$27.27} + 0.05 = 0.11 + 0.05 = 0.16 = 16\% = k_x$$

Had the stock initially sold for less than $27.27, say at $25, events would have been reversed. Investors would have wanted to buy the stock because its expected rate of return would have exceeded its required rate of return, and buy orders would have driven the stock's price up to $27.27.

Exhibit 700.17 *Expected and Required Returns on Stock X*

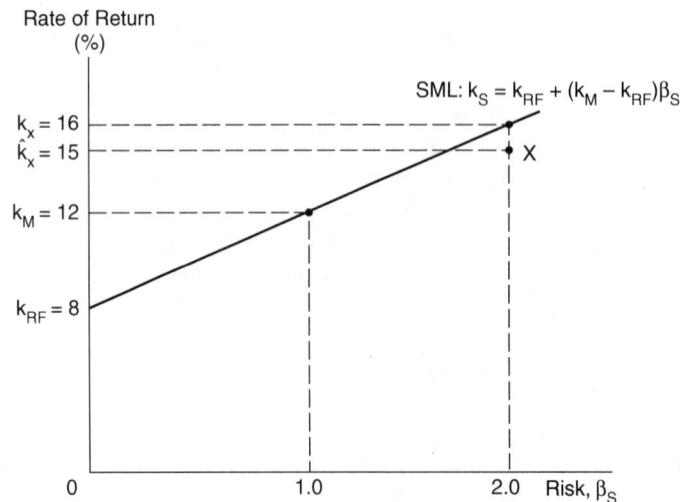

To summarize, in equilibrium these two conditions must hold.

1. The expected rate of return as seen by the marginal investor must equal the required rate of return: $\hat{k}_x = k_x$.
2. The actual market price of the stock must equal its intrinsic value as estimated by the marginal investor: $P_0 = \hat{P}_0$.

Of course, some individual investors might believe that $\hat{k}_x > k_x$ and $P_0 < \hat{P}_0$, and hence they would invest most of their funds in the stock, while other investors might have an opposite view and would sell all of their shares. However, it is the marginal investor who establishes the actual market price, and for this investor, $\hat{k}_x = k_x$ and $P_0 = \hat{P}_0$. If these conditions do not hold, trading will occur until they do hold.

The Efficient Markets Hypothesis

A body of theory called the **Efficient Markets Hypothesis (EMH)** holds (1) that stocks are always in equilibrium and (2) that it is impossible for an investor to *consistently* "beat the market." Because there are hundreds of stock market analysts, the prices of the stock adjusts almost immediately to reflect any new developments.

Financial theorists generally define three forms, or levels, of information efficiency in the market.

1. The *weak form* of the EMH states that all information contained in past price movements is fully reflected in current market prices. Therefore, information about recent, or past, trends in stock prices is of no use in selecting stocks—the fact that a stock has risen for the past three days, for example, gives us no useful clues as to what it will do today or tomorrow. People who believe that weak-form efficiency exists also believe that "tape watchers" and "chartists" are wasting their time.
2. The *semistrong form* of the EMH states that current market prices reflect all *publicly available* information. If this is true, no abnormal returns can be earned by analyzing stocks. Thus, if semistrong-form efficiency exists, it does no good to pore over annual reports or other published data because market prices will have adjusted to any good or bad news contained in such reports as soon as they came out. However, insiders (say, the presidents of companies), even under semistrong-form efficiency, can still make abnormal returns on their own companies' stocks.
3. The *strong form* of the EMH states that current market prices reflect all pertinent information, whether publicly available or privately held. If this form holds, even insiders would find it impossible to earn abnormal returns in the stock market.

Many empirical studies have been conducted to test for the three forms of market efficiency. Most of these studies suggest that the stock market is indeed highly efficient in the weak form and reasonably efficient in the semistrong form, at least for the larger and more widely followed stocks. However, the strong-form EMH does not hold, so abnormal profits can be made by those who possess inside information.

What bearing does the EMH have on financial decisions? Because stock prices do seem to reflect public information, most stocks appear to be fairly valued. This does not mean that new developments could not cause a stock's price to soar or to plummet, but it does mean that stocks, in general, are fairly priced, and the prices probably are in equilibrium—it is safe to assume $\hat{k} = k$ and $P = \hat{P}$. However, there are certainly cases in which corporate insiders have information not known to outsiders.

Valuation of Real (Tangible) Assets

In the previous sections, we found that the values of financial assets, bonds and stocks, are based on the present value of the future cash flows expected from the assets. Valuing real assets is no different. We need to compute the present value of the expected cash flows associated with the asset. For example, suppose Unilate Textiles is considering purchasing a machine so that it can manufacture a new line of products. After five years, the machine will be worthless because it will be used up. But during the five years Unilate uses the machine, the firm will be able to increase its net cash flows by the following amounts.

Year	Expected Cash Flow, $\hat{CF}_t$
1	$120,000
2	100,000
3	150,000
4	80,000
5	50,000

If Unilate wants to earn a 14% return on investments like this machine, what is the value of the machine to the company? To find the answer, we need to solve for the present value of the uneven cash flow stream produced by the machine. Thus, the value of this machine can be depicted as follows.

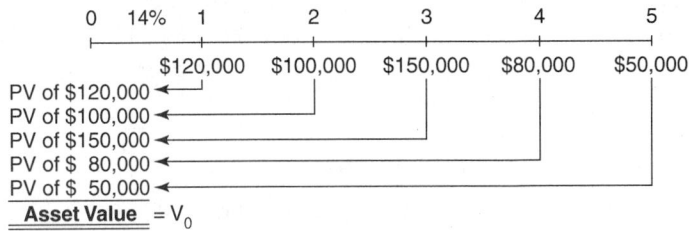

To compute the value of the machine, we simply apply Equation 7.10.

$$V_0 + \text{Present value of future CF} = \frac{\$120{,}000}{(1.14)^1} + \frac{\$100{,}000}{(1.14)^2} + \frac{\$150{,}000}{(1.14)^3} + \frac{\$80{,}000}{(1.14)^4} + \frac{\$50{,}000}{(1.14)^5}$$

The value of the machine can be computed by using three procedures: (1) numerically, (2) using the tables, and (3) with a financial calculator. We will show the first two procedures.

1. NUMERICAL SOLUTION Because the stream of cash flows is uneven (that is, it is not an annuity), we must discount each cash flow back to the present and sum these PVs to find the machine's value.

$$V_0 = \$120{,}000 \times \left[\frac{1}{(1.14)^1}\right] + \$100{,}000 \times \left[\frac{1}{(1.14)^2}\right] + \$150{,}000 \times \left[\frac{1}{(1.14)^3}\right]$$

$$+ \$80{,}000 \times \left[\frac{1}{(1.14)^4}\right] + \$50{,}000 \times \left[\frac{1}{(1.14)^5}\right]$$

$$= \$105{,}263.16 + \$76{,}946.75 + \$101{,}245.73 + \$47{,}366.42 + \$25{,}968.43$$

$$= \$356{,}790.46$$

2. TABULAR SOLUTION Simply look up the appropriate PVIF values in Table A-1 of Module 700 Appendix, insert them into the equation, and complete the arithmetic.

$$V_0 = \$120{,}000(\text{PVIF}_{14\%,1}) + \$100{,}000(\text{PVIF}_{14\%,2}) + \$150{,}000(\text{PVIF}_{14\%,3})$$
$$+ \$80{,}000(\text{PVIF}_{14\%,4}) + \$50{,}000(\text{PVIF}_{14\%,5})$$
$$= \$120{,}000(0.8772) + \$100{,}000(0.7695) + \$150{,}000(0.6750)$$
$$+ \$80{,}000(0.5921) + \$50{,}000(0.5194) = \$356{,}802 \text{ (Rounding Difference)}$$

The present value of the machine to the company is $356,802 and this is compared to the initial cash outlay to purchase the machine.

Financial Forecasting, Planning, and Control

Financial Planning and Control

In this section, we will see how a financial manager can use some of the information obtained through financial statement analysis for financial planning and control of the firm's future operations. Well-run companies generally base their operating plans on a set of forecasted financial statements. The **financial planning** process begins with a sales forecast for the next few years. Then the assets required to meet the sales targets are determined, and a decision is made concerning how to finance the required assets. At that point, income statements and balance sheets can be projected, and earnings and dividends per share, as well as the key ratios, can be forecasted.

Once the "base case" forecasted financial statements and ratios have been prepared, top managers want to know (1) how realistic the results are, (2) how to attain the results, and (3) what impact changes in operations would have on the forecasts. At this stage, which is the **financial control** phase, the firm is concerned with implementing the financial plans, or forecasts, and dealing with the feedback and adjustment process that is necessary to ensure the goals of the firm are pursued appropriately.

The first part of the section is devoted to financial planning using projected financial statements, or forecasts, and the second part of the section focuses on financial control using budgeting and the analysis of leverage to determine how changes in operations affect financial forecasts.

Financial Planning and Forecasting

Sales Forecasts

Forecasting is an essential part of the planning process, and a **sales forecast** is the most important ingredient of financial forecasting. The sales forecast generally starts with a review of sales during the past five to ten years, which can be expressed in a graph.

Based on its historical sales trend, plans for new product and market introductions, and Unilate's forecast for the economy, the firm's planning committee has projected a 10% growth rate for sales during 2001. So 2001 sales are expected to be $1,650 million, which is 10% higher than 2000 sales of $1,500 million.

If the sales forecast is inaccurate, the consequences can be serious. First, if the market expands significantly *more* than Unilate has geared up for, the company probably will not be able to meet demand. Customers will buy competitors' products, and Unilate will lose market share, which will be hard to regain. On the other hand, if the projections are overly optimistic, Unilate could end up with too much plant, equipment, and inventory. This would mean low turnover ratios, high costs for depreciation and storage, and, possibly, write-offs of obsolete or unusable inventory. All of this would result in a low rate of return on equity, which in turn would depress the company's stock price. If Unilate had financed an unnecessary expansion with debt, its problems would, of course, be compounded. Remember from our analysis of its 2000 financial statements in the previous sections that Unilate's current financial position is considered poor. Thus, an accurate sales forecast is critical to the well-being of the firm.

Projected (Pro Forma) Financial Statements

Any forecast of financial requirements involves (1) determining how much money the firm will need during a given period, (2) determining how much money the firm will generate internally during the same period, and (3) subtracting the funds generated from the funds required to determine the external financial requirements. One method used to estimate external requirements is the *projected, or pro forma, balance sheet method,* which is discussed in this section.

The projected balance sheet method is straightforward—simply project the asset requirements for the coming period, then project the liabilities and equity that will be generated under normal operations, and subtract the projected liabilities and equity from the required assets to estimate the **additional funds needed (AFN)** to support the level of forecasted operations. The steps in the procedure are explained next.

STEP 1. FORECAST THE 2001 INCOME STATEMENT The **projected (pro forma) balance sheet method** begins with a forecast of sales. Next, the income statement for the coming year is forecasted to obtain an initial estimate of the amount of retained earnings the company will generate during the year. This requires assumptions about the operating cost ratio, the tax rate, interest charges, and the dividends paid. In the simplest case, the assumption is made that costs will increase at the same rate as sales; in more complicated situations, cost changes are forecasted separately. Still, the objective of this part of the analysis is to determine how much income the company will earn and then retain for reinvestment in the business during the forecasted year.

Exhibit 700.18 shows Unilate's actual 2000 income statement and the initial forecast of the 2001 income statement if the conditions just mentioned exist. To create the 2001 income forecast, we assume that sales and variable operating costs will be 10% greater in 2001 than in 2000. In addition, it is assumed that Unilate currently operates at full capacity, so it will need to expand its plant capacity in 2001 to handle the additional operations. Therefore, in Exhibit 700.18, the 2001 forecasts of sales, *all* operating costs, and depreciation are 10% greater than their 2000 levels. The result is that earnings before interest and taxes (EBIT) is forecasted to be $143 million in 2001.

Exhibit 700.18 Unilate Textiles: Actual 2000 and Projected 2001 Income Statements (millions of dollars, except per share data)

	2000 Results	2001 Forecast Basis	2001 Initial Forecast
Net sales	$1,500.0	× 1.10	$1,650.0
Cost of goods sold	(1,230.0)	× 1.10	(1,353.0)
Gross profit	$ 270.0		$ 297.0
Fixed operating costs except depreciation	(90.0)	× 1.10	(99.0)
Depreciation	(50.0)	× 1.10	(55.0)
Earnings before interest and taxes (EBIT)	$ 130.0		143.0
Less interest	(40.0)		(40.0)
Earnings before taxes (EBT)	$ 90.0		$ 103.0
Taxes (40%)	(36.0)		(41.2)
Net income	$ 54.0		$ 61.8
Common dividends	(29.0)		(29.0)
Addition to retained earnings	$ 25.0		$ 32.8
Earnings per share	$ 2.16		$ 2.47
Dividends per share	$ 1.16		$ 1.16
Number of common shares (millions)	25.00		25.00

To complete the initial forecast of 2001 income, we assume no change in the financing of the firm because, at this point, it is not known if additional financing is needed. But it is apparent that the 2001 interest expense will change if the amount of debt (borrowing) the firm needs to support the forecasted increase in operations changes. To forecast the 2001 dividends, we simply assume the dividend per share will be the same as it was in 2000, $1.16; so the total common dividends forecasted for 2001 would be $29.0 million if no additional common stock is issued. Like the interest expense amount, however, the amount of total dividends used to create this initial forecast will change if Unilate decides to sell new stock to raise any additional financing necessary to support the new operations or to raise the dividends per share paid to existing shareholders.

From the initial forecast of 2001 income contained in Exhibit 700.18, we can see that $32.8 million dollars is expected to be added to retained earnings in 2001. As it turns out, this addition to retained earnings represents the amount Unilate is expected to invest in itself (internally generated funds) to support the increase in operations in 2001. So the next step is to determine what impact this level of investment will have on the Unilate's forecasted 2001 balance sheet.

STEP 2. FORECAST THE 2001 BALANCE SHEET If we assume the 2000 end-of-year asset levels were just sufficient to support 2000 operations, then in order for Unilate's sales to increase in 2001, its assets must also grow. Because the company was operating at full capacity in 2000, *each* asset account must increase if the higher sales level is to be attained: More cash will be needed for transactions, higher sales will lead to higher receivables, additional inventory will have to be stocked, and new plant and equipment must be added for production.

Further, if Unilate's assets are to increase, its liabilities and equity must also increase—the additional assets must be financed in some manner. Some liabilities will increase *spontaneously* due to normal business relationships. For example, as sales increase, so will Unilate's purchases of raw materials, and these larger purchases will spontaneously lead to higher levels of accounts payable. Similarly, a higher level of operations will require more labor, while higher sales will result in higher taxable income. Therefore, both accrued wages and accrued taxes will increase. In general, these current liability accounts, which provide **spontaneously generated funds,** will increase at the same rate as sales.

Notes payable, long-term bonds, and common stock will not rise spontaneously with sales—rather, the projected levels of these accounts will depend on conscious financing decisions that will be made later. Therefore, for the initial forecast, it is assumed these account balances remain unchanged from their 2000 levels.

Exhibit 700.19 contains Unilate's 2000 actual balance sheet and an initial forecast of its 2001 balance sheet. The mechanics of the balance sheet forecast are similar to those used to develop the forecasted income statement. First, those balance sheet accounts that are expected to increase directly with sales are multiplied by 1.10 to obtain the initial 2001 forecasts. Thus, 2001 cash is projected to be $15.0 × 1.10 = $16.5 million, accounts receivable are projected to be $180.0 × 1.10 = $198.0 million, and so on. In our example, all assets increase with sales, so once the individual assets have been forecasted, they can be summed to complete the asset side of the forecasted balance sheet.

Exhibit 700.19 *Unilate Textiles: Actual 2000 and Projected 2001 Balance Sheets (millions of dollars)*

	2000 Balances	2001 Forecast Basis[a]	2001 Initial Forecast
Cash	$ 15.0	× 1.10	$ 16.5
Accounts receivable	180.0	× 1.10	198.0
Inventories	270.0	× 1.10	297.0
Total current assets	$465.0		$511.5
Net plant and equipment	380.0	× 1.10	418.0
Total assets	$845.0		$929.5
Accounts payable	$ 30.0	× 1.10	$ 33.0
Accruals	60.0	× 1.10	66.0
Notes payable	40.0		40.0[b]
Total current liabilities	$130.0		$139.0
Long-term bonds	300.0		300.0[b]
Total liabilities	$430.0		$439.0
Common stock	130.0		130.0[b]
Retained earnings	285.0	+$32.8[d]	317.8
Total owner's equity	$415.0		$447.8
Total liabilities and equity	$845.0		$886.8
Additional funds needed (AFN)			$ 42.7[c]

[a] × 1.10 indicates "times (1 + g)"; used for items which grow proportionally with sales.

[b] Indicates a 2000 figure carried over for the initial forecast.

[c] The "additional funds needed (AFN)" is computed by subtracting the amount of total liabilities and equity from the amount of total assets.

[d] The $32.8 million represents the "addition to retained earnings" from the 2001 Projected Income Statement given in 700.18.

Next, the spontaneously increasing liabilities (accounts payable and accruals) are forecasted. Then those liability and equity accounts whose values reflect conscious management decisions—notes payable, long-term bonds, and stock—*initially are forecasted* to remain at their 2000 levels. Thus, the amount of 2001 notes payable initially is set at $40.0 million, the long-term bond account is forecasted at $300.0 million, and so forth. The forecasted 2001 level of retained earnings will be the 2000 level plus the forecasted addition to retained earnings, which was computed as $32.8 million in the projected income statement we created in Step 1 (Exhibit 700.18).

The forecast of total assets in Exhibit 700.19 is $929.5 million, which indicates that Unilate must add $84.5 million of new assets (compared to 2000 assets) to support the higher sales level expected in 2001. However, according to the initial forecast of the 2001 balance sheet, the total liabilities and equity sum to only $886.8 million, which is an increase of only $41.8 million. So the amount of total assets exceeds the amount of total liabilities and equity by $42.7 million = $929.5 million − $886.8 million. This indicates $42.7 million of the forecasted increase in total assets will not be financed by liabilities that spontaneously increase with sales (accounts payable and accruals) or by an increase in retained earnings. Unilate can raise the additional $42.7 million, which we designate *additional funds needed (AFN)*, by borrowing from the bank as notes payable, by issuing long-term bonds, by selling new common stock, or by some combination of these actions.

The initial forecast of Unilate's financial statements has shown us that (1) higher sales must be supported by higher asset levels, (2) some of the asset increases can be financed by spontaneous increases in accounts payable and accruals and by retained earnings, and (3) any shortfall must be financed from external sources, either by borrowing or by selling new stock.

STEP 3. RAISING THE ADDITIONAL FUNDS NEEDED Unilate's financial manager will base the decision of exactly how to raise the $42.7 million additional funds needed on several factors, including its ability to handle additional debt, conditions in the financial markets, and restrictions imposed by existing debt agreements. At this point, it is important to understand that, regardless of how Unilate raises the $42.7 million AFN, the initial forecasts of both the income statement and the balance sheet will be affected. If Unilate takes on new debt, its interest expenses will rise; and if additional shares of common stock are sold, *total* dividend payments will increase if the *same dividend per share* is paid to all common stockholders. Each of these changes, which we term financing feedbacks, will affect the amount of additional retained earnings originally forecasted, which in turn will affect the amount of additional funds needed.

STEP 4. FINANCING FEEDBACKS As mentioned in Step 3, one complexity that arises in financial forecasting relates to **financing feedbacks.** The external funds raised to pay for new assets create additional expenses that must be reflected in the income statement and that lower the initially forecasted addition to retained earnings, which means more external funds are needed to make up for the lower amount added to retained earnings. In other words, if Unilate raised the $42.7 million AFN by issuing new debt and new common stock, it would find both the interest expense and the total dividend payments would be higher than the amounts contained in the forecasted income statement shown in Exhibit 700.18. Consequently, after adjusting for the higher interest and dividend payments, the forecasted addition to retained earnings would be lower than the initial forecast of $32.8 million. Because the retained earnings will be lower than projected, a financing shortfall will exist even after the original AFN of $42.7 million is considered. So in reality, Unilate must raise more than $42.7 million to account for the financing feedbacks that affect the amount of internal financing expected to be generated from the increase in operations. To determine the amount of external financing actually needed, we have to adjust the initial forecasts of both the income statement (Step 1) and the balance sheet (Step 2) to reflect the impact of raising the additional external financing. This process has to be repeated until AFN = 0 in Exhibit 700.19, which means Step 1 and Step 2 might have to be repeated several times to fully account for the financing feedbacks.

Exhibit 700.20 contains the adjusted 2001 preliminary forecasts for the income statement and the balance sheet of Unilate Textiles after all of the financing effects are considered. To generate the adjusted forecasts, it is assumed that of the total external funds needed, 65% will be raised by selling new common stock at $23 per share, 15% will be borrowed from the bank at an interest rate of 7%, and 20% will be raised by selling long-term bonds with a coupon interest of 10%. Under these conditions, it can be seen from Exhibit 700.20 that Unilate actually needs $45.0 million to support the forecasted increase in operations, not the $42.7 million contained in the initial forecast. The additional $2.3 million is needed because the added amounts of debt and common stock will cause interest and dividend payments to increase, which will decrease the contribution to retained earnings by $2.3 million.

ANALYSIS OF THE FORECAST The 2001 forecast as developed here represents a preliminary forecast, because we have completed only the first stage of the entire forecasting process. Next, the projected statements must be analyzed to determine whether the forecast meets the firm's financial targets. If the statements do not meet the targets, then elements of the forecast must be changed.

Exhibit 700.21 shows Unilate's 2000 ratios plus the projected 2001 ratios based on the preliminary forecast and the industry average ratios. The firm's financial condition at the close of 2000 was weak, with many ratios being well below the industry averages. The preliminary final forecast for 2001 (after financing feedbacks are considered), which assumes that Unilate's past practices will continue into the future, shows an improved debt position. But the overall financial position still is somewhat weak, and this condition will persist unless management takes some actions to improve things.

Unilate's management actually plans to take steps to improve its financial condition. The plans are to (1) close down certain operations, (2) modify the credit policy to reduce the collection period for receivables, and (3) better manage inventory so that products are turned over more often. These proposed operational changes will affect both the income statement and the balance sheet, so the preliminary forecast will have to be revised again to reflect the impact of such changes. When this process is complete, management will have its final forecast. To keep things simple, we do not show the final forecast here; instead, for the remaining discussions we assume the preliminary forecast is not substantially different and use it as the final forecast for Unilate's 2001 operations.

As we have shown, forecasting is an iterative process, both in the way the financial statements are generated and in the way the financial plan is developed. For planning purposes, the financial staff develops a preliminary forecast based on a continuation of past policies and trends. This provides the executives with a starting point, or "straw man" forecast. Next, the model is modified to see what effects alternative operating plans would have on the firm's earnings and financial condition. This results in a revised forecast.

Other Considerations in Forecasting

We have presented a very simple method for constructing pro forma financial statements under rather restrictive conditions. In this section, we describe some other conditions that should be considered when creating forecasts.

EXCESS CAPACITY The construction of the 2001 forecasts for Unilate was based on the assumption that the firm's 2000 operations were at full capacity, so any increase in sales would require additional assets, especially plant and equipment. If Unilate did *not* operate at full capacity in 2000, then plant and equipment would only have to be increased if

Exhibit 700.20 Unilate Textiles: 2001 Adjusted Forecast of Financial Statements (millions of dollars)

Income Statement	Initial Forecast	Adjusted Forecast	Financing Adjustment
Net sales	$1,650.0	$1,650.0	
Cost of goods sold	(1,353.0)	(1,353.0)	
Gross profit	$ 297.0	$ 297.0	
Fixed operating costs except depreciation	(99.0)	(99.0)	
Depreciation	(55.0)	(55.0)	
Earnings before interest and taxes (EBIT)	$ 143.0	$ 143.0	
Less interest	(40.0)	(41.4)	(1.4)
Earnings before taxes (EBT)	$ 103.0	$ 101.6	(1.4)
Taxes (40%)	(41.2)	(40.7)	0.5
Net Income	$ 61.8	$ 61.0	(0.8)[b]
Common dividends	(29.0)	(30.5)	(1.5)
Addition to retained earnings	$ 32.8	$ 30.5	(2.3)[a]
Earnings per share	$ 2.47	$ 2.32	
Dividends per share	$ 1.16	$ 1.16	
Number of common shares (millions)	25.00	26.27	

Balance Sheet			
Cash	$ 16.5	$ 16.5	
Accounts receivable	198.0	198.0	
Inventories	297.0	297.0	
Total current assets	$511.5	$511.5	
Net plant and equipment	418.0	418.0	
Total assets	$929.5	$929.5	
Accounts payable	$ 33.0	$ 33.0	
Accruals	66.0	66.0	
Notes payable	40.0	46.8	$6.8
Total current liabilities	$139.0	$145.8	
Long-term bonds	300.0	309.0	$9.0
Total liabilities	$439.0	$454.8	
Common stock	130.0	159.3	$29.3
Retained earnings	317.8	315.5	$ (2.3)[a]
Total owner's equity	$447.8	$474.8	
Total Liabilities and Equity	$886.8	$929.5	
Additional Funds Needed (AFN)	$42.7	$0.0	$42.8 [b,c]

[a] The financing adjustment for the addition to retained earnings in the income statement is the same as the financing adjustment for retained earnings in the balance sheet.

[b] Rounding difference.

[c] The total AFN, or external funding needs, equal $42.7 million plus the $2.3 million decrease in the change in retained earnings from the initial forecast; thus, total funds needed equal $45.0 million—$6.8 million will be from new bank notes, $9.0 million will come from issuing new bonds, and $29.3 million will be raised by issuing new common stock.

Exhibit 700.21 *Unilate Textiles: Key Ratios*

	2000	Adjusted Preliminary 2001	Industry Average
Current ratio	3.6×	3.5×	4.1×
Inventory turnover	4.6×	5.6×	7.4×
Days sales outstanding	43.2 days	43.2 days	32.1 days
Total assets turnover	1.8×	1.8×	2.1×
Debt ratio	50.9%	48.9%	45.0%
Times interest earned	3.3×	3.5×	6.5×
Profit margin	3.6%	3.7%	4.7%
Return on assets	6.4%	6.6%	12.6%
Return on equity	13.0%	12.8%	17.2%

the additional sales (operations) forecasted in 2001 exceeded the unused capacity of the existing assets. For example, if Unilate actually utilized only 80% of its fixed assets' capacity to produce 2000 sales of $1,500 million, then

$$\$1,500.0 \text{ million} = 0.80 \times (\text{Plant capacity})$$

$$\text{Plant capacity} = \frac{\$1,500.0 \text{ million}}{0.80} = \$1,875 \text{ million}$$

In this case, then, Unilate could increase sales to $1,875 million, or by 25% of 2000 sales, before full capacity is reached and plant and equipment would have to be increased. In general, we can compute the sales capacity of the firm if it is known what percent of assets are utilized to produce a particular level of sales.

$$\text{Full capacity sales} = \frac{\text{Sales level}}{(\text{Percent of capacity used to generate sales level})}$$

If Unilate does not have to increase plant and equipment, fixed assets would remain at the 2000 level of $380 million, so the amount of AFN would be $4.7 million, which is $38 million (10% of $380 million fixed assets) less than the initial forecast reported in Exhibit 700.19.

In addition to the excess capacity of fixed assets, the firm could have excesses in other assets that can be used for increases in operations. For instance, we concluded that Unilate's inventory level at the end of 2000 probably was greater than it should have been. If true, some increase in 2001 forecasted sales can be absorbed by the above-normal inventory and production would not have to be increased until inventory levels are reduced to normal—this requires no additional financing.

In general, excess capacity means less external financing is required to support increases in operations than would be needed if the firm previously operated at full capacity.

ECONOMIES OF SCALE There are economies of scale in the use of many types of assets, and when such economies occur, a firm's variable cost of goods sold ratio is likely to change as the size of the firm changes (either increases or decreases) substantially. Currently, Unilate's variable cost ratio is 82% of sales; but the ratio might decrease to 80% of sales if operations increase significantly. If everything else is the same, changes in the variable cost ratio affect the addition to retained earnings, which in turn affects the amount of AFN.

LUMPY ASSETS In many industries, technological considerations dictate that if a firm is to be competitive, it must add fixed assets in large, discrete units; such assets often are referred to as **lumpy assets.** For example, in the paper industry, there are strong economies of scale in basic paper mill equipment, so when a paper company expands capacity, it must do so in large, lumpy increments. Lumpy assets primarily affect the turnover of fixed assets and, consequently, the financial requirements associated with expanding. For instance, if instead of $38 million Unilate needed an additional $50 million in fixed assets to increase operations 10%, the AFN would be much greater. With *lumpy assets,* it is possible that a small projected increase in sales would require a significant increase in plant and equipment, which would require a very large financial requirement.

Financial Control

In the previous section, we focused on financial forecasting, emphasizing how growth in sales requires additional investment in assets, which in turn generally requires the firm to raise new funds externally. In the sections that follow, we consider the planning and control systems used by financial managers when implementing the forecasts. First, we look at the relationship between sales volume and profitability under different operating conditions. These relationships provide information that is used by managers to plan for changes in the firm's level of operations, financing needs, and profitability. Later, we examine the control phase of the planning and control process, because a good control system is essential both to ensure that plans are executed properly and to facilitate a timely modification of plans if the assumptions on which the initial plans were based turn out to be different than expected.

The planning process can be enhanced by examining the effects of changing operations on the firm's profitability, both from the standpoint of profits from operations and from the standpoint of profitability after financing effects are considered.

Operating Break-even Analysis

The relationship between sales volume and operating profitability is explored in cost-volume-profit planning, or operating break-even analysis. **Operating break-even analysis** is a method of determining the point at which sales will just cover operating costs—that is, the point at which the firm's operations will break even. It also shows the magnitude of the firm's operating profits or losses if sales exceed or fall below that point. Break-even analysis is important in the planning and control process because the cost-volume-profit relationship can be influenced greatly by the proportion of the firm's investment in assets that are fixed. A sufficient volume of sales must be anticipated and achieved if fixed and variable costs are to be covered, or else the firm will incur losses from operations. In other words, if a firm is to avoid accounting losses, its sales must cover all costs—those that vary directly with production and those that remain constant even when production levels change. Costs that vary directly with the level of production generally include the labor and materials needed to produce and sell the product, while the fixed operating costs generally include costs such as depreciation, rent, and insurance expenses that are incurred regardless of the firm's production level.

Operating break-even analysis deals only with the upper portion of the income statement—the portion from sales to net operating income (NOI), which is also termed earnings before interest and taxes (EBIT). This portion generally is referred to as the *operating section*, because it contains only the revenues and expenses associated with the normal production and selling operations of the firm. Exhibit 700.22 gives the operating section of Unilate's forecasted 2001 income statement, which was shown in Exhibit 700.20. For the discussion that follows, we have assumed that all of Unilate's products sell for $15.00 each and the variable cost of goods sold per unit is $12.30, which is 82% of the selling price.

Exhibit 700.22 *Unilate Textiles: 2001 Forecasted Operating Income (millions of dollars)*

Sales (S)	$1,650.0
Variable cost of goods sold (VC)	(1,353.0)
Gross profit (GP)	$ 297.0
Fixed operating costs (F)	(154.0)
Net operating income (NOI) = EBIT	$ 143.0

NOTES:

Sales in units = 110 million units.

Selling price per unit = $15.00.

Variable costs per unit = $1,353/110 = $12.30.

Fixed operating costs = $154 million, which includes $55 million depreciation and $99 million in other fixed costs such as rent, insurance, and general office expenses.

EBIT = Earnings Before Interest and Taxes

Break-even Chart

Exhibit 700.22 shows the net operating income for Unilate if 110 million units are produced and sold during the year. But what if Unilate doesn't sell 110 million units? Certainly, the firm's net operating income will be something other than $143 million. Exhibit 700.23 shows the total revenues and total operating costs for Unilate at various levels of sales, beginning with zero. According to the information given in Exhibit 700.22, Unilate has fixed costs, which include depreciation, rent, insurance, and so on, equal to $154 million. This amount must be paid even if the firm produces and sells nothing, so the $154 million fixed cost is represented by a horizontal line. If Unilate produces and sells nothing, its sales revenues will be zero; but *for each unit sold,* the firm's sales will increase by $15. Therefore, the total revenue line starts at the origin of the X and Y axes, and it has a slope equal to $15.00 to account for the dollar increase in sales for each additional unit sold. On the other hand, the line representing the total operating costs intersects the Y axis at $154 million, which represents the fixed costs incurred even when no products are sold, and it has a slope equal to $12.30, which is the cost directly associated with the production of each additional unit sold. The point at which the total revenue line intersects the total cost line is the **operating break-even point,** because this is where the revenues generated from sales just cover the *total operating costs* of the firm. Notice that prior to the break-even point, the total cost line is above the total revenue line, which shows Unilate will suffer operating losses because the total costs cannot be covered by the sales revenues. And, after the break-even point, the total revenue line is above the total cost line because revenues are more than sufficient to cover total operating costs, so Unilate will realize operating profits. Total costs include fixed costs and variable costs.

Break-even Computation

Exhibit 700.23 shows that Unilate must sell 57 million units to be at the operating break-even point. If Unilate sells 57 million products, it will generate $855 million in sales revenues, which will be just enough to cover the $855 million total operating costs—$154 million fixed costs and $701 million variable costs (57 million units at $12.30 per

Exhibit 700.23 *Unilate Textiles: Operating Break-even Chart*

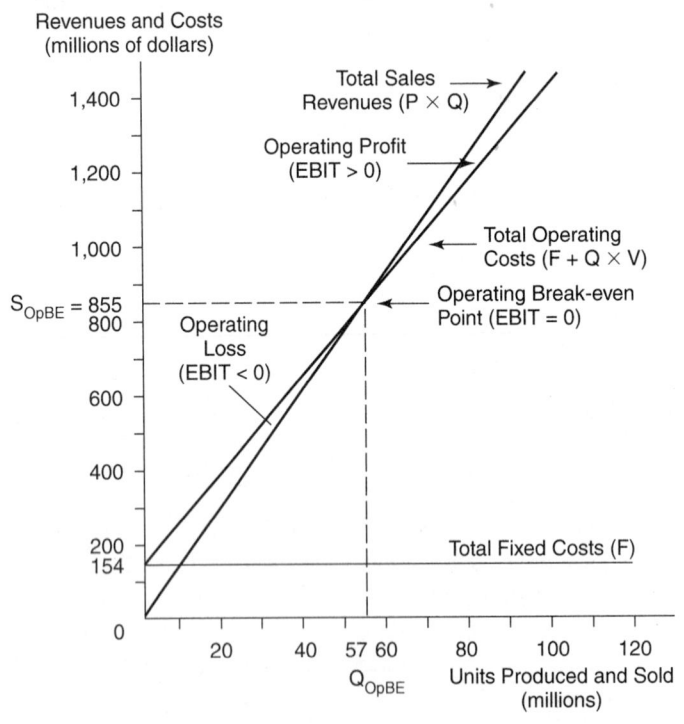

NOTES:

S_{OpBE} = operating break even in dollars
Q = sales in units: Q_{OpBE} = operating break even in units
F = fixed costs = $154 million
V = variable costs per unit = $12.30
P = price per unit = $15.00

unit). If we do not have a graph like Exhibit 700.23, how can the operating break-even point be computed? Actually, it is rather simple. Remember, the operating break-even point is where the revenues generated from sales just cover the total operating costs, which include both the costs directly attributable to producing each unit and the fixed operating costs that remain constant regardless of the production level. As long as the selling price of each unit (the slope of the total revenue line) is greater than the variable operating cost of each unit (the slope of the total operating cost line), each unit sold will generate revenues that contribute to covering the fixed operating costs. For Unilate, this contribution (termed the *contribution margin*) is $2.70, which is the difference between the $15.00 selling price and the $12.30 variable cost of each unit. To compute the operating break even for Unilate then, we have to determine how many units need to be sold to cover the fixed operating cost of $154 million if each unit has a contribution margin equal to $2.70. Just divide the $154 million fixed cost by the $2.70 contribution margin and you will discover the break-even point is 57 million units, which equates to $855 million in sales revenues.

More formally, the operating break-even point can be found by setting the total revenues equal to the total operating costs so that net operating income (NOI) is zero. In equation form, NOI = 0 if

$$\text{Sales revenues} = \text{Total operating costs} = \text{Total variable costs} + \text{Total fixed costs}$$
$$(P \times Q) = \text{TOC} = (V \times Q) + F$$

where P is the sales price per unit, Q is the number of units produced and sold, V is the variable operating cost per unit, and F is the total fixed operating costs. Solving for the quantity that needs to be sold, Q, produces a formula that can be used to find the number of units that needs to be sold to achieve operating break even.

$$Q_{\text{OpBE}} = \frac{F}{P - V} = \frac{F}{\text{Contribution margin}} \qquad (7.17)$$

Thus, the operating break-even point for Unilate is

$$Q_{\text{OpBE}} = \frac{\$154.0 \text{ million}}{\$15.00 - \$12.30} = \frac{\$154.0 \text{ million}}{\$2.70} = 57.0 \text{ million units.}$$

In the remainder of the section, we omit the word *million* in the computations and include it only in the final answer.

From Equation 7.17, we can see that the operating break-even point is lower (higher) if the numerator is lower (higher) or if the denominator is higher (lower). Therefore, all else equal, one firm will have a lower operating break-even point than another firm if its fixed costs are lower, if selling price of its product is higher, if its variable operating cost per unit is lower, or if some combination of these exists. For instance, if Unilate could increase the sales price per unit from $15.00 to $15.80 without affecting either its fixed operating costs ($154 million) or its variable operating cost per unit ($12.30), then its operating break-even point would fall to 44 million units.

The operating break-even point also can be stated in terms of the total sales revenues needed to cover total operating costs. At this point, we just need to multiply the sales price per unit by the break-even quantity we found using Equation 7.17, which yields $855 million for Unilate. Or we can restate the contribution margin as a percent of the sales price per unit (this is called the *gross profit margin*) and then apply Equation 7.17. In other words,

$$S_{\text{OpBE}} = \frac{F}{1 - \left(\dfrac{V}{P}\right)} = \frac{F}{\text{Gross profit margin}} \qquad (7.18)$$

Solving Equation 7.18 for Unilate, the operating break even based on dollar sales is

$$S_{\text{OpBE}} = \frac{\$154.0}{1 - \left(\dfrac{\$12.30}{\$15.00}\right)} = \frac{\$154.0}{1 - 0.82} = \frac{\$154.0}{0.18} = \$855.6 \text{ million}$$

Equation 7.18 shows that 18¢ of every $1 sales revenues goes to cover the fixed operating costs, so about $855 million worth of the product must be sold to break even. (If we use Equation 7.17 to compute the operating break even rounded to two decimal places, the result is 57.04 million units; thus the dollar sales needed to break even is 57.04 × $15 = $855.6 million.)

Break-even analysis based on dollar sales rather than on units of output is useful in determining the break-even volume for a firm that sells many products at varying prices. This analysis requires only that total sales, total fixed costs, and total variable costs at a given level are known.

Using Operating Break-even Analysis

Operating break-even analysis can shed light on three important types of business decisions: (1) When making new product decisions, break-even analysis can help determine how large the sales of a new product must be for the firm to achieve profitability. (2) Break-even analysis can be used to study the effects of a general expansion in the level of the firm's operations; an expansion would cause the levels of both fixed and variable costs to rise, but it would also increase expected sales. (3) When considering modernization and automation projects, where the fixed investment in equipment is increased in order to lower variable costs, particularly the cost of labor, break-even analysis can help management analyze the consequences of purchasing these projects.

However, care must be taken when using operating break-even analysis. To apply break-even analysis as we have discussed here requires that the sales price *per unit,* the variable cost *per unit,* and the *total* fixed operating costs do not change with the level of the firm's production and sales. Within a narrow range of production and sales, this assumption probably is not a major issue. But what if the firm expects either to produce a much greater (or fewer) number of products than normal or to expand (reduce) its plant and equipment significantly? Will the numbers change? Most likely the answer is yes. Therefore, use of a single break-even chart like the one presented in Exhibit 700.23 is impractical—such a chart provides useful information, but the fact that it cannot deal with changes in the price of the product, with changing variable cost rates, and with changes in fixed cost levels suggests the need for a more flexible type of analysis. Today, such analysis is provided by computer simulation. Functions such as those expressed in Equations 7.17 and 7.18 (or more complicated versions of them) can be put into a spreadsheet or similarly modeled with other computer software, and then variables such as sales price, P, the variable cost per unit, V, and the level of fixed costs, F can be changed. The model can instantaneously produce new versions of Exhibit 700.23, or a whole set of such graphs, to show what the operating break-even point would be under different production setups and price-cost situations.

Operating Leverage

If a high percentage of a firm's total operating costs are fixed, the firm is said to have a high degree of **operating leverage.** In physics, leverage implies the use of a lever to raise a heavy object with a small amount of force. In politics, people who have leverage can accomplish a great deal with their smallest word or action. *In business terminology, a high degree of operating leverage, other things held constant, means that a relatively small change in sales will result in a large change in operating income.*

Operating leverage arises because the firm has fixed operating costs that must be covered no matter the level of production. The impact of the leverage, however, depends on the actual operating level of the firm. For example, Unilate has $154.0 million in fixed operating costs, which are covered rather easily because the firm currently sells 110 million products; thus, it is well above its operating break-even point of 57 million units. But what would happen to the operating income if Unilate sold more or less than forecasted? To answer this question we need to determine the **degree of operating leverage (DOL)** associated with Unilate's forecasted 2001 operations.

Operating leverage can be defined more precisely in terms of the way a given change in sales volume affects operating income (NOI). To measure the effect of a change in sales volume on NOI, we calculate the degree of operating leverage, which is defined as the percentage change in NOI (or EBIT) associated with a given percentage change in sales.

$$\text{DOL} = \frac{\text{Percentage change in NOI}}{\text{Percentage change in sales}} = \frac{\left(\frac{\Delta \text{NOI}}{\text{NOI}}\right)}{\left(\frac{\Delta \text{Sales}}{\text{Sales}}\right)} = \frac{\left(\frac{\Delta \text{EBIT}}{\text{EBIT}}\right)}{\left(\frac{\Delta \text{Sales}}{\text{Sales}}\right)} = \frac{\left(\frac{\Delta \text{EBIT}}{\text{EBIT}}\right)}{\left(\frac{\Delta Q}{Q}\right)} \qquad (7.19)$$

In effect, the DOL is an index number that measures the effect of a change in sales on operating income or Earnings Before Interest and Taxes (EBIT).

Exhibit 700.22 shows that the NOI for Unilate is $143.0 million at production and sales equal to 110 million units. If the number of units produced and sold increases to 121 million, the operating income (in millions of dollars) would be

$$\text{NOI} = 121(\$15.00 - \$12.30) - \$154.0 = \$172.7$$

So the degree of operating leverage associated with this change is 2.08.

$$\text{DOL} = \frac{\left[\dfrac{\$172.7 - \$143.0}{\$143.0}\right]}{\left[\dfrac{\$15.00(121-110)}{\$15.00(110)}\right]} = \frac{\left(\dfrac{\$29.7}{\$143.0}\right)}{\left(\dfrac{11}{110}\right)} = \frac{0.208}{0.100} = \frac{20.8\%}{10.0\%} = 2.08\times$$

Exhibit 700.24 *Unilate Textiles: Operating Income at Sales Levels of 110 Million Units and 121 Million Units (millions of dollars)*

	2001 Forecasted Operations	Sales Increase	Unit Change	Percent Change
Sales in units (millions)	110	121	11	+10.0%
Sales revenues	$1,650.0	$1,815.0	$165.0	+10.0%
Variable cost of goods sold	(1,353.0)	(1,488.3)	(135.3)	+10.0%
Gross profit	$ 297.0	$ 326.7	$ 29.7	+10.0%
Fixed operating costs	(154.0)	(154.0)	(0.0)	0.0%
Net operating income (EBIT)	$ 143.0	$ 172.7	$ 29.7	+20.8%

To interpret the meaning of the value of the degree of operating leverage, remember we computed the percent change in operating income and then divided the result by the percent change in sales. Taken literally then, Unilate's DOL of 2.08× indicates that the percent change in operating income will be 2.08 times the percent change in sales from the current 110 million units ($1,650.0 million). So if the number of units sold increases from 110 million to 121 million, or by 10%, Unilate's operating income should increase by 2.08 × 10% = 20.8%—at 121 million units, *operating income* should be 20.8% greater than the $143.0 million generated at 110 million units of sales; the new operating income should be $172.7 million = 1.208 × $143 million. Exhibit 700.24 shows a comparison of the operating incomes generated at the two different sales levels.

The results contained in Exhibit 700.24 show that Unilate's *gross profit* would increase by $29.7 million, or by 10%, if sales increase 10%. The fixed operating costs remain constant at $154.0 million, so EBIT also increases by $29.7 million, and the total impact of a 10% increase in sales is a 20.8% increase in operating income. If the fixed operating costs were to increase in proportion to the increase in sales—that is 10%—then the net operating income would also increase by 10% because all revenues and costs would have changed by the same proportion. But in reality, fixed operating costs will not change (a 0% increase); thus, a 10% increase in Unilate's forecasted 2001 sales will result in an *additional* 10.8% increase in operating income. The total increase is 20.8%, which results because operating leverage exists.

Equation 7.19 can be simplified so that the degree of operating leverage at a particular level of operations can be calculated as follows.

$$DOL_Q = \frac{Q1P - V2}{Q1P - V2 - F} \quad (7.20)$$

Or, rearranging the terms, DOL can be stated in terms of sales revenues as follows:

$$DOL_S = \frac{(Q \times P) - (Q \times V)}{(Q \times P) - (Q \times V) - F} = \frac{S - VC}{S - VC - F} = \frac{\text{Gross profit}}{\text{EBIT}} \quad (7.20a)$$

To solve Equation 7.20 or Equation 7.20a, we only need information from Unilate's forecasted operations; we do not need information about the possible change in forecasted operations. So Q represents the forecasted 2001 level of production and sales, and S and VC are the sales and variable operating costs, respectively, at that level of operations. For Unilate, the equation solution for DOL would be

$$DOL_{S4} = \frac{110(\$15.00 - \$12.30)}{110(\$15.00 - \$12.30) - \$154} = \frac{\$1,650 - \$1,353}{\$1,650 - \$1,353 - \$154}$$

$$= \frac{\$297}{\$143} = 2.08\times$$

Equation 7.20 normally is used to analyze a single product, such as **GM's** Chevrolet Cavalier, whereas Equation 7.20a is used to evaluate an entire firm with many types of products and, hence, for which "quantity in units" and "sales price" are not meaningful.

The DOL of 2.08× indicates that *each* 1% *change* in sales will result in a 2.08% *change* in operating income. What would happen if Unilate's sales decrease, say, by 10%? According to the interpretation of the DOL figure, Unilate's operating income would be expected to decrease by 20.8%. Exhibit 700.25 shows that this actually

Exhibit 700.25 Unilate Textiles: Operating Income at Sales Levels of 110 Million Units and 99 Million Units (millions of dollars)

	2001 Forecasted Operations	Sales Decrease	Unit Change	Percent Change
Sales in units (millions)	110	99	(11)	−10.0%
Sales revenues	$1,650.0	$1,485.0	$(165.0)	−10.0%
Variable cost of goods sold	(1,353.0)	(1,217.7)	135.3	−10.0%
Gross profit	$ 297.0	$ 267.3	$(29.7)	−10.0%
Fixed operating costs	(154.0)	(154.0)	(0.0)	0.0%
Net operating income (EBIT)	$ 143.0	$ 113.3	$(29.7)	−20.8%

would be the case. Therefore, the DOL value indicates the *change* (increase or decrease) in operating income resulting from a *change* (increase or decrease) in the level of operations. It should be apparent that the greater the DOL, the greater the impact of a change in operations on operating income, whether the change is an increase or a decrease.

The DOL value found by using Equation 7.20a is the degree of operating leverage only for a specific initial sales level. For Unilate, that sales level is 110 million units, or $1,650 million. The DOL value would differ if the initial (existing) level of operations differed. For example, if Unilate's operating cost structure was the same, but only 65 million units were produced and sold, the DOL would have been

$$DOL_{65} = \frac{(65)(\$15.00 - \$12.30)}{[(65)(\$15.00 - \$12.30)] - \$154.0} = \frac{\$175.5}{\$21.5} = 8.19\times$$

The DOL at 65 million units produced and sold is nearly four times greater than the DOL at 110 million units. Thus, from a base sales of 65 million units, a 10% increase in sales, from 65 million units to 71.5 million units, would result in a 8.16 × 10% = 81.6% increase in operating income, from $21.5 million to $39.05 million. This shows that when Unilate's operations are closer to its operating break-even point of 57 million units, its degree of operating leverage is higher.

In general, given the same operating cost structure, if a firm's level of operations is decreased, its DOL increases; or, stated differently, the closer a firm is to its operating break-even point, the greater is its degree of operating leverage. This occurs because, as Exhibit 700.23 indicates, the closer a firm is to its operating break-even point, the more likely it is to incur an operating loss due to a decrease in sales—there is not a very large buffer in operating income to absorb a decrease in sales and still be able to cover the fixed operating costs. Similarly, at the same level of production and sales, a firm's degree of operating leverage will be higher the lower the contribution margin for its products—the lower the contribution margin, the less each product sold is able to help cover the fixed operating costs, and the closer the firm is to its operating break-even point. Therefore, the higher the DOL for a particular firm, it generally can be concluded the closer the firm is to its operating break-even point, and the more sensitive its operating income is to a change in sales volume. *Greater sensitivity generally implies greater risk; thus, it can be stated that firms with higher DOLs generally are considered to have riskier operations than firms with lower DOLs.*

Operating Leverage and Operating Break-even Point

The relationship between operating leverage and the operating break-even point is illustrated in Exhibit 700.26, where various levels of operations are compared for Unilate and two other textile manufacturers. One firm has a higher contribution margin than Unilate and the other firm has lower fixed operating costs, so we know the other two firms have operating break-even points that are less than Unilate's. Allied Cloth has the lowest operating break-even point, because it has the highest contribution margin relative to its fixed costs. Unilate has the highest operating break-even point because it uses the greatest relative amount of operating leverage of the three firms. Consequently, all else equal, of the three textile manufacturers, Unilate's operating income would be magnified the most if actual sales turned out to be greater than forecasted; but it also would experience the greatest decrease in operating income if actual sales turned out to be less than expected.

Exhibit 700.26 *Relationship Between Operating Leverage and Operating Break-even Point*

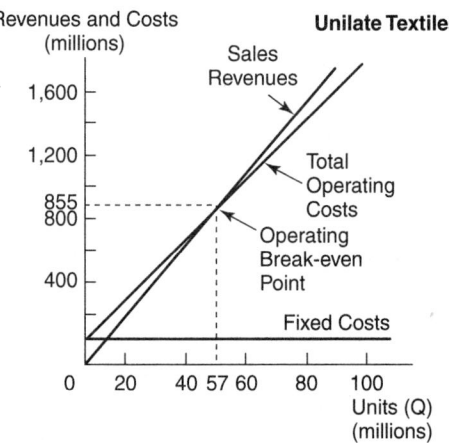

Unilate Textiles

Selling price = $15.00
Variable cost per unit = $12.30
Fixed costs = $154 million
Operating break even = 57 million units
= $855 million

Sales Level Units (Q)	Revenues ($)	Total Operating Costs	Operating Profit (EBIT)	DOL
30	$ 450	$ 523	$(73)	
60	900	892	8	20.3
110	1,650	1,507	143	2.1
150	2,250	1,999	251	1.6

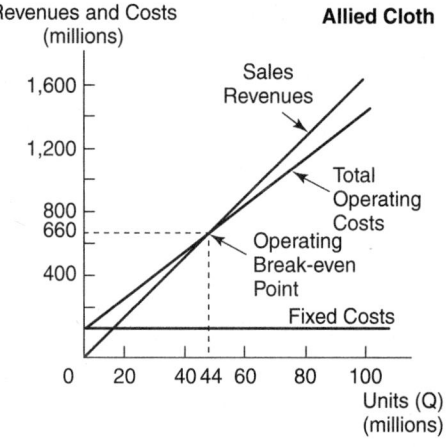

Allied Cloth

Selling price = $15.00
Variable cost per unit = $11.50
Fixed costs = $154 million
Operating break even = 44 million units
= $660 million

Sales Level Units (Q)	Revenues ($)	Total Operating Costs	Operating Profit (EBIT)	DOL
30	$ 450	$ 499	$(49)	
60	900	844	56	3.8
110	1,650	1,419	231	1.7
150	2,250	1,879	371	1.4

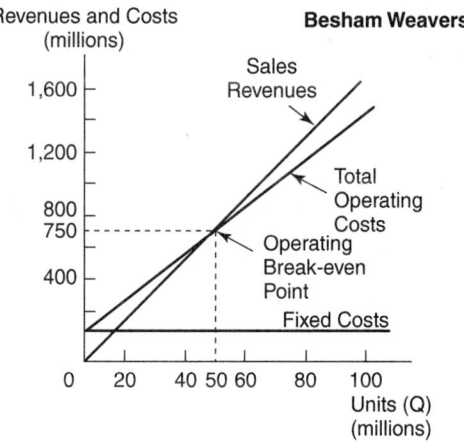

Besham Weavers

Selling price = $15.00
Variable cost per unit = $12.30
Fixed costs = $135 million
Operating break even = 50 million units
= $750 million

Sales Level Units (Q)	Revenues ($)	Total Operating Costs	Operating Profit (EBIT)	DOL
30	$ 450	$ 504	$(54)	
60	900	873	27	6.0
110	1,650	1,488	162	1.8
150	2,250	1,980	270	1.5

Financial Break-even Analysis

Operating break-even analysis deals with evaluation of production and sales to determine at what level the firm's sales revenues will just cover its operating costs; the point where the operating income is zero. **Financial break-even analysis** is a method of determining the operating income, or EBIT, the firm needs to just cover all of its *financing costs* and produce earnings per share equal to zero. Typically, the financing costs involved in financial break-even analysis consist of the interest payments to bondholders and the dividend payments to preferred stockholders. Usually these financing costs are fixed, and, in every case, they must be paid before dividends can be paid to common stockholders.

Exhibit 700.27 *Unilate Textiles: 2001 Forecasted Earnings per Share (millions of dollars)*

Earnings before interest and taxes (EBIT)	$143.0
Interest	(41.4)
Earnings before taxes (EBT)	$101.6
Taxes (40%)	(40.6)
Net income	$ 61.0
Preferred dividends	(0.0)
Earnings available to common stockholders	$ 61.0

NOTES:

$Shrs_C$ = Number of common shares outstanding = 26.3 million
EPS = Earnings per share = $61.0/26.3 = $2.32

Exhibit 700.28 *Unilate Textiles: Financial Break-even Chart*

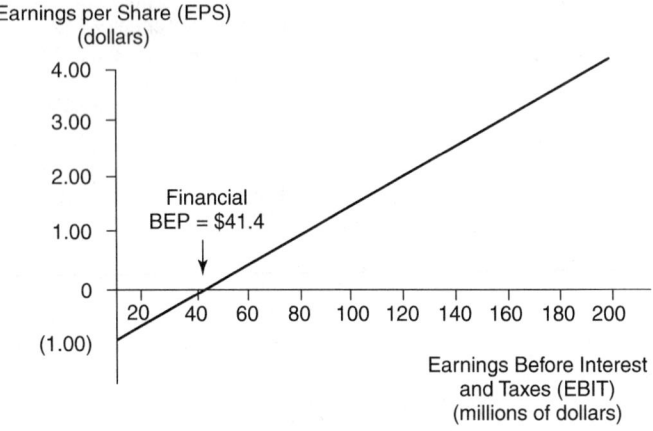

Financial break-even analysis deals with the lower portion of the income statement—the portion from operating income (EBIT) to earnings available to common stockholders. This portion of the income statement generally is referred to as the *financing section,* because it contains the expenses associated with the financing arrangements of the firm. The financing section of Unilate's forecasted 2001 income statement is contained in Exhibit 700.27.

BREAK-EVEN GRAPH Exhibit 700.28 shows the earnings per share (EPS) for Unilate at various levels of EBIT. The point at which EPS equals zero is referred to as the **financial break-even point.** As the graph indicates, the financial break-even point for Unilate is where EBIT equals $41.4 million. At this EBIT level, the income generated from operations is just sufficient to cover the financing costs, including income taxes; thus, EPS equals zero. To see this, we can compute the EPS when EBIT is $41.4 million.

Earnings before interest and taxes (EBIT)	$41.4
Interest	(41.4)
Earnings before taxes (EBT)	0.0
Taxes (40%)	(0.0)
Net income	0.0
Earnings available to common stockholders (EAC)	$ 0.0
EPS = $0/26.3 = $0	

MODULE 700. FINANCE

BREAK-EVEN COMPUTATION The results obtained from Exhibit 700.28 can be translated algebraically to produce a relatively simple equation that can be used to compute the financial break-even point of any firm. First, remember the financial break-even point is defined as the level of EBIT that generates EPS equal to zero. Therefore, at the financial break-even point,

$$\text{EPS} = \frac{\text{Earnings available to common stockholders}}{\text{Number of common shares outstanding}} = 0 \qquad (7.21)$$

$$= \frac{(\text{EBIT} - I)(1 - T) - D_{ps}}{\text{Shrs}_c} = 0$$

where EBIT is the earnings before interest and taxes, I represents the interest payments on debt, T is the marginal tax rate, D_{ps} is the amount of dividends paid to preferred stockholders, and Shrs_c is the number of common shares outstanding. Notice that EPS equals zero if the numerator in Equation 7.21, which is the earnings available to common stockholders, equals zero; so the financial break-even point also can be stated as follows.

$$(\text{EBIT} - I)(1 - T) - D_{ps} = 0$$

Rearranging this equation to solve for EBIT gives the solution for the level of EBIT needed to produce EPS equal to zero. Therefore, the computation for a firm's financial break-even point is

$$\text{EBIT}_{\text{FinBE}} = I + \frac{D_{ps}}{(1 - T)} \qquad (7.22)$$

Using Equation 7.22, the financial break-even point for Unilate Textiles in 2001 is

$$\text{EBIT}_{\text{FinBE}} = \$41.4 + \frac{\$0}{1 - 0.4} = \$41.4$$

which is the same result shown in Exhibit 700.28.

According to Equation 7.22, the amount of preferred stock dividends must be stated on a before-tax basis to determine the financial break-even point. If a firm has no preferred stock though, the firm only needs to cover its interest payments, so the financial break-even point simply equals the interest expense. This is the case for Unilate, because it has no preferred stock. Because most corporations in the United States do not have preferred stock outstanding, we will not include preferred dividends in the discussions that follow.

USING FINANCIAL BREAK-EVEN ANALYSIS Financial break-even analysis can be used to help determine the impact of the firm's financing mix on the earnings available to common stockholders. When the firm uses financing alternatives that require fixed financing costs such as interest, financial leverage exists. Financial leverage affects the financing section of the income statement like operating leverage affects the operating section. This point is discussed next.

Financial Leverage

While operating leverage considers how changing sales volume affects operating income, **financial leverage** considers the impact changing operating income has on earnings per share, or earnings available to common stockholders. So operating leverage affects the operating section of the income statement, whereas financial leverage affects the financing section of the income statement. *Financial leverage takes over where operating leverage leaves off, further magnifying the effects on earnings per share of changes in the level of sales.* For this reason, operating leverage sometimes is referred to as *first-stage leverage* and financial leverage as *second-stage leverage*.

Like operating leverage, financial leverage arises because fixed costs exist; in this case, the fixed costs are associated with how the firm is financed. The **degree of financial leverage (DFL)** is defined as the percent change in earnings per share (EPS) that results from a given percent change in earnings before interest and taxes (EBIT), and it is computed as follows.

$$\text{DFL} = \frac{\text{Percent change in EPS}}{\text{Percent change in EBIT}} = \frac{\left(\dfrac{\Delta \text{EPS}}{\text{EPS}}\right)}{\left(\dfrac{\Delta \text{EBIT}}{\text{EBIT}}\right)} \qquad (7.23)$$

Exhibit 700.29 *Unilate Textiles: Earnings per Share at Sales Levels of 110 Million Units and 121 Million Units (millions of dollars, except per share data)[a]*

	2001 Forecasted Operations	Sales Increase	Dollar Change	Percent Change
Sales in units (millions)	110	121		+10.0%
Earnings before interest and taxes (EBIT)	$143.0	$172.7	$29.7	+20.8%
Interest (I)	(41.4)	(41.4)	(0.0)	+ 0.0%
Earnings before taxes (EBT)	$101.6	$131.3	$29.7	+29.2%
Taxes (40%)	(40.6)	(52.5)	(11.9)	+29.2%
Net income	$ 61.0	$78.8	$17.8	+29.2%
Earning per share (26.3 million shares)	$ 2.32	$ 3.00	$0.68	+29.2%

Exhibit 700.29 shows the results of increasing Unilate's EBIT 20.8%. The increase in EPS is 29.2%, which is 1.40 times the change in EBIT; so the DFL for Unilate equals 1.40.

The degree of financial leverage at a particular level of EBIT can be computed easily by using the following equation:

$$\text{DFL} = \frac{\text{EBIT}}{\text{EBIT} - \text{I}} = \frac{\text{EBIT}}{\text{EBIT} - [\text{Financial BEP}]} \tag{7.24}$$

Using Equation 7.24, the DFL for Unilate Textiles at EBIT equal to $143.0 million (sales of 110 million units) is

$$\text{DFL}_{110} = \frac{\$143.0}{\$143.0 - \$41.4} = \frac{\$143.0}{\$101.6} = 1.40 \times$$

The interpretation of the DFL value is the same as for the degree of operating leverage, except the starting point for evaluating financial leverage is the earnings before interest and taxes (EBIT) and the ending point is earnings per share (EPS). So because the DFL for Unilate is 1.40×, the company can expect a 1.40% change in EPS for every 1% change in EBIT; a 20.8% increase in EBIT results in approximately a 29.2% (20.8% × 1.40) increase in earnings available to common stockholders, thus the same percent increase in EPS (the number of common shares outstanding does not change). Unfortunately, the opposite also is true—if Unilate's 2001 EBIT is 20.8% below expectations, its EPS will be 29.2% below the forecast of $2.32, or $1.64. To prove this result is correct, construct the financing section of Unilate's income statement when EBIT equals $113.3 million = (1 − 0.208) × $143.0 million.

The value of the degree of financial leverage found using Equation 7.24 pertains to one specific initial EBIT level. If the level of sales changes, and thus the EBIT changes, so does the value computed for DFL. For example, at sales equal to 80 million units, Unilate's EBIT would be $62 million = [80 million ($15.00 − $12.30)] − $154.0 million, and the DFL value would be

$$\text{DFL}_{80} = \frac{\$62.0}{\$62.0 - \$41.4} = \frac{\$62.0}{\$20.6} = 3.01 \times$$

Compared to sales equal to 110 million units, at sales equal to 80 million units Unilate would have greater difficulty covering the fixed financing costs, so its DFL is much greater. At EBIT equal to $62.0 million, Unilate is close to its financial break-even point—EBIT equal to $41.4 million—and its degree of financial leverage is high. So the more difficulty a firm has covering its fixed financing costs with operating income, the greater its degree of financial leverage. In general then, the higher the DFL for a particular firm, it generally can be concluded the closer the firm is to its financial break-even point, and the more sensitive its earnings per share is to a change in operating income. *Greater sensitivity implies greater risk; thus it can be stated that firms with higher DFLs generally are considered to have greater financial risk than firms with lower DFLs.*

Combining Operating and Financial Leverage (DTL)

Our analysis of operating leverage and financial leverage has shown that *(1) the greater the degree of operating leverage, or fixed operating costs for a particular level of operations, the more sensitive EBIT will be to changes in sales volume, and (2) the greater the degree of financial leverage, or fixed financial costs for a particular level of operations, the more sensitive*

EPS will be to changes in EBIT. Therefore, if a firm has a considerable amount of both operating and financial leverage, then even small changes in sales will lead to wide fluctuations in EPS. Look at the impact leverage has on Unilate's forecasted 2001 operations. We found that if the sales volume increases by 10%, Unilate's EBIT would increase by 20.8%; and if EBIT increases by 20.8%, its EPS would increase by 29.2%. So in combination, a 10% increase in sales volume would result in a 29.2% increase in EPS. This shows the impact of total leverage, which is the combination of both operating leverage and financial leverage, with respect to Unilate's current operations.

The degree of total leverage (DTL) is defined as the percent change in EPS resulting from a change in sales volume. This relationship can be written as follows.

$$\text{Degree of total leverage} = \text{DTL} = \frac{\left(\frac{\Delta \text{EPS}}{\text{EPS}}\right)}{\left(\frac{\Delta \text{Sales}}{\text{Sales}}\right)} = \frac{\left(\frac{\Delta \text{EBIT}}{\text{EBIT}}\right)}{\left(\frac{\Delta \text{Sales}}{\text{Sales}}\right)} \times \frac{\left(\frac{\Delta \text{EPS}}{\text{EPS}}\right)}{\left(\frac{\Delta \text{EBIT}}{\text{EBIT}}\right)} = \text{DOL} \times \text{DFL} \quad (7.25)$$

Combining the equations for DOL (Equations 7.20 and 7.20a) and for DFL (Equation 7.24), Equation 7.25 can be restated as follows.

$$\text{DTL} = \frac{\text{Gross profit}}{\text{EBIT}} \times \frac{\text{EBIT}}{\text{EBIT} - [\text{Financial BEP}]} = \frac{\text{Gross profit}}{\text{EBIT} - [\text{Financial BEP}]} \quad (7.26)$$

$$= \frac{S - VC}{\text{EBIT} - I} = \frac{Q(P - V)}{[Q(P - V) - F] - I}$$

Using Equation 7.26, the degree of total leverage (DTL) for Unilate would be

$$\text{DTL}_{110} = \frac{110(\$15.00 - \$12.30)}{[110(\$15.00 - \$12.30) - \$154.0] - \$41.4}$$

$$= \frac{\$297.0}{\$143.0 - \$41.4} = \frac{\$297.0}{\$101.6}$$

$$= 2.92\times$$

According to Equation 7.25, we could have arrived at the same result for DTL by multiplying the degree of operating leverage by the degree of financial leverage, so the DTL for Unilate would be 2.08 × 1.40 ≈ 2.92. This value indicates that for every 1% change in sales volume, Unilate's EPS will change by 2.92%; a 10% increase in sales will result in a 29.2% increase in EPS. This is exactly the impact expected.

The value of DTL can be used to compute the new earnings per share (EPS*) after a change in sales volume. We already know that Unilate's EPS will change by 2.92% for every 1% change in sales. So EPS* resulting from a 10% increase in sales can be computed as follows.

$$\text{EPS*} = \text{EPS}[1 + (.10)(2.92)] = \$2.32 \times (1 + 0.292) = \$3.00$$

which is the same result given in Exhibit 700.29.

The degree of combined (total) leverage concept is useful primarily for the insights it provides regarding the joint effects of operating and financial leverage on earnings per share. The concept can be used to show management, for example, that a decision to automate a plant and to finance the new equipment with debt would result in a situation in which a 10% decline in sales would result in a nearly 50% decline in earnings, whereas with a different operating and financial package, a 10% sales decline would cause earnings to decline only by 15%. Having the alternatives stated in this manner gives decision makers a better idea of the ramifications of alternative actions with respect to the firm's level of operations and how those operations are financed.

Using Leverage and Forecasting for Control

From the discussion in the previous sections, it should be clear what the impact on income would be if the 2001 sales forecast for Unilate Textiles is different than expected. If sales are greater than expected, both operating and financial leverage will magnify the "bottom line" impact on EPS (DTL = 2.92). But the opposite also holds. Consequently, if Unilate does not meet its forecasted sales level, leverage will result in a magnified loss in income compared to what is expected. This will occur because production facilities might have been expanded too greatly, inventories might be built up too quickly, and so on; the end result might be that the firm suffers a significant income loss. This loss will result in a lower than expected addition to retained earnings, which means the plans for additional external funds needed to support the firm's operations will be inadequate. Likewise, if the sales forecast is too low, then, if the firm is at full capacity, it will not be able to meet the additional demand, and sales opportunities will be lost—perhaps forever. In the previous sections, we showed only how changes in operations (2001 forecasts) affect the income generated by the firm; we did not continue the process to show the impact on the balance sheet and the financing needs of the firm. To determine the impact on the financial statements, the financial manager needs to repeat the steps discussed in the first part of this section. It is at this stage the financial manager needs to evaluate and act on the feedback received from the forecasting and budgeting processes. In effect, then, the forecasting (planning) and control of the firm is an ongoing activity, a vital function to the long-run survival of any firm.

The forecasting and control functions described in this section are important for several reasons. First, if the projected operating results are unsatisfactory, management can "go back to the drawing board," reformulate its plans, and develop more reasonable targets for the coming year. Second, it is possible that the funds required to meet the sales forecast simply cannot be obtained; if so, it obviously is better to know this in advance and to scale back the projected level of operations than to suddenly run out of cash and have operations grind to a halt. Third, even if the required funds can be raised, it is desirable to plan for their acquisition well in advance. Finally, any deviation from the projections needs to be dealt with to improve future forecasts and the predictability of the firm's operations to ensure the goals of the firm are being pursued appropriately.

Short-Term Financial Planning

This section demonstrates how to develop a short-term financial planning model so that the financial manager can better ascertain the overall impact that short-term financial management decisions have on the net operating cash flows of the company. With such a forecast in hand, the financial manager can better plan the firm's short-term investment and financing strategies.

A Simple Percent-of-Sales Forecasting Model

We first apply the modeling principles by developing a relatively simple financial forecasting model. The example model estimates the needed external funds required for a given sales growth estimate.

The heart of this relatively simple forecasting technique lies in the assumption that current assets and possibly noncurrent or fixed assets as well as current liabilities fluctuate proportionately with sales. For example, if total assets are currently 45% of sales and if it can be assumed that this relationship will remain roughly the same over the next year or two, then for every additional $1,000 of sales over the current sales level, total assets must increase by $450. This increase in assets must be financed by a source of funds, such as an increase in liabilities or an increase in equity.

One readily available financing source, often referred to as a spontaneous source, is current liabilities. Accounts payable and accrued wages vary with the level of sales. If current liabilities traditionally amount to about 25% of sales, then for every $1,000 of sales above the current level, current liabilities (a source of funds) will increase by $1,000 × .25, or $250.

We still have an excess of uses of funds (an increase in assets) over sources of funds (an increase in liabilities) in the amount of $200 = $450 − $250. The final source of funds considered is retained earnings. This internal source can be calculated by multiplying the firm's net profit margin m by the forecasted sales level S over the planning period multiplied by the fraction 1 minus the dividend payout ratio (dpo). This final figure represents the funds from operations that will be retained for internal investment purposes. Note that depreciation is not added back because the asset figure is net of depreciation. At this point, if uses of funds still exceed sources of funds, new external financing will be required during the planning period. This forecasting model for needed external funds (NEF) can be reduced to the relatively simple formula shown below.

$$\begin{aligned} \text{NEF} =\ & (\text{Total assets/Sales}) \times \text{Change in sales} \\ & - (\text{Current liabilities/Sales}) \times \text{Change in sales} \\ & - \text{Sales} \times \text{Net profit margin} \times [1 + (\text{Dividends/Net profit})] \\ \text{NEF} =\ & (\text{TA/S}) \times \Delta S - (\text{CL/S}) \times \Delta S - [S \times m \times (1 - \text{dpo})] \end{aligned}$$

In this equation, ΔS represents the expected change in sales over the planning period.

We now use an example to show how this forecasting model works. Assume the following data are representative of a company's financial position. Furthermore, assume that management expects sales to increase by $2.75 million during the coming year, 2002. Plugging these values into the forecasting model yields the following estimate of NEF.

Balance Sheet for 2001			
Total assets	$15,580,000	Current liabilities	$4,261,000
		Long-term debt	3,638,000
		Net worth	7,681,000

Income Statement for 2001	
Net sales	$12,250,000
Net profit	692,000
Dividends	429,000

Thus

$$TA/S = 1.272$$
$$CL/S = .348$$
$$m = .056$$
$$dpo = .62$$

$$NEF = (1.272 \times \$2.75) - (.348 \times \$2.75) - (\$15 \times .056 \times (1 - .62))$$
$$= \$3.498 - \$.957 - \$.319 = \$2.222$$

If sales increase by $2.75 million, then total assets will expand by $3.498 million, current liabilities will expand by $.957 million, and retained profits will expand by $.319 million. The company's 2002 balance sheet will look like the following.

2002 Total assets	= $19,078,000	= $15,580,000 + $3,498,000
2002 Current liabilities	= $5,218,000	= $4,261,000 + $957,000
2002 Long-term debt	= $3,638,000	= Assumed held constant
2002 Net worth	= $8,000,000	= $7,681,000 + $319,000

Summing up the current liabilities, long-term debt, and net worth, we arrive at a total of $16,856,000. We can see above that total assets are forecasted to be $19,078,000. Thus the financing side of the balance sheet is $2,222,000 short of the funds needed to finance the asset side of the balance sheet as predicted by the NEF equation.

The financial manager now knows that if sales grow as predicted and if the financial and operating policies are such that there should be $1.272 of assets for each dollar of sales, $.348 of current liabilities per dollar of sales, a profit margin of 5.6%, and 62% of the profits paid as dividends, then the firm must obtain $2.222 million of outside financing. This new financing may be obtained through either new debt or through new equity sources, but that level of funding must be acquired to finance the forecasted growth in assets.

Understanding the Financial Planning Model

As a company begins producing and selling a product or service, it generates revenues and expenses represented by the income statement. Our financial planning model then transforms the income statement into a cash flow statement by converting revenues into cash receipts based on collections fractions and converting expenses into cash disbursement based on payment fractions. The projected income statement and resulting cash flow statement then impact the balance sheet by changing the level of current assets (cash, receivables, and inventory), current liabilities (accounts payable), accumulated depreciation, and retained earnings. If spontaneous assets grow faster than spontaneous liabilities and equity, then additional financing is required to improve the company's financial position. The financial manager is then faced with choosing the type, amount, and maturity of financing that enhances the value of the firm. If spontaneous liabilities and equity grow faster than spontaneous assets, then excess liquidity is generated and the financial manager can either retire debt, pay a dividend, or invest in financial assets. Again, the choice made should be the one that enhances the value of the firm.

Cash Forecasting

Four factors account for corporate emphasis on short-term cash forecasts. First, cash forecasts drive the short-term investing and borrowing strategies. Selecting the maturity of a short-term investment, when to repay borrowings, or the size of a credit line to request all depend critically on the forecasted cash position. Alternating cash surpluses and shortages occur because cash receipts and disbursements are not synchronized.

Second, the forecast is an important input into short-term financial policy decisions, including disbursement policies, credit terms, and bank selection; *making decisions along the cash flow timeline requires accurate estimation of flow size and timing*. Accurate anticipation of cash balances might be less important if the company has a controlled disbursement account (particularly when funding is automated) or has sufficient balances (for example, to compensate for credit and/or noncredit services) to absorb uncertainties.

Third, cash forecasts function as a control device. Before the beginning of each year, the forecasting staff develops a cash budget, which is a forecast of cash flows and the cash balance for each month. As the year progresses, deviations of actual cash balances from cash budget projections signal the cash manager to investigate and take corrective action. Sales and marketing managers may use the cash balance variances as an early warning system when declining cash receipts are found to be the cause of the variance. Accurate forecasts can provide added value when they signal a cash shortage and the need for action before problems emerge, or corrective action as actual data become available. Sagner (2000) estimates that a $15 million portfolio will earn an added 1/5 to 1/4 of 1% (equal to $37,500 per year) and save an additional $5,500 in transactions costs when moving from overnight (sweep account) investing to one-month maturities.

Fourth, effective risk management is possible with forecasts of the cash-flow effects of interest rate changes, commodity price changes, and foreign exchange rate changes.

Forecasting Monthly Cash Flows

The most important cash forecast from a top management perspective is the monthly cash forecast. This forecast shows cash receipts and disbursements on a monthly basis for a minimum horizon of one year; when done before the beginning of a new fiscal year, it is called the cash budget. The cash budget is a document showing anticipated cash receipts and disbursements for a future period, usually one year. This cash budget is formulated to be consistent with the company's operating budget, which specifies planned sales and operating expenses. Many companies extend the monthly forecast out to a 5-year horizon to correspond with the company's long-range financial plan. The level of detail and anticipated accuracy diminishes with longer forecast horizons, however. The three commonly used cash forecasting approaches are the receipts and disbursements method (sometimes referred to as cash scheduling), the modified accrual method, and the pro forma balance sheet approach.

Approach 1: The Receipts and Disbursements Method

The **receipts and disbursements method** involves looking up most of the data variables in company sources and estimating cash effect timing of noncash events. The major noncash events are product sales and material purchases. Usually, receipts are listed separately on a receipts schedule and disbursements on a separate disbursements schedule. The forecaster then combines the receipts and disbursements on a projected schedule (think of it as a projected cash flow timeline) according to anticipated cash flow dates. The layout used may vary from a desk calendar to a fancy computer spreadsheet that is linked to numerous other corporate spreadsheets. Periodic and accurate intracompany communications are critical to the accuracy of the approach. Accuracy suffers when the horizon extends beyond one month, however, and earlier inaccuracies compound into large errors for longer horizons.

Format of the Receipts and Disbursements Forecast

A template that might be used for receipts and disbursements is shown in Exhibit 700.30. Note that this format takes into account beginning and ending cash (both calculated by assuming no short-term investments or borrowings), the period's cash flows, and required minimal cash levels. The ending cash for one month serves as the beginning cash for the following month. The minimum cash balance is a function of management policy that a certain emergency cash stock be held and/or a compensating balance be kept at deposit banks. The bottom line, excess cash or required total financing, is a cumulative total. It represents the account balance of the amount invested or borrowed as of the end of the period. The net cash flow indicates how much additional money is invested or paid back (on outstanding loans), if positive, or the dollar figure of investments liquidated or additional lending, if negative.

Exhibit 700.30 *Template for Receipts and Disbursements Method for World Communications*

World Communications Corp.
Cash Receipts and Disbursements

	January 2001	February 2001	March 2001
BEGINNING CASH BALANCE	$ 1,500,000	$ 2,612,050	($ 1,552,238)
CASH RECEIPTS:			
Cash sales	$ 5,600,000	$ 3,500,000	$ 3,125,000
Cash collection of prior month's credit sales	$10,200,000	$ 8,400,000	$ 5,250,000
Cash collection of credit sales made 2 months ago	$ 5,750,000	$ 3,187,500	$ 2,625,000
Interest income received	$ 9,675	$ 2,535	$ 0
Cash dividends received	$ 375	$ 245	$ 165
Cash from asset sales	$ 0	$ 15	$ 0
Cash proceeds from long term borrowings	$ 4,500	$ 0	$ 0
Cash proceeds from equity issuance	$ 0	$ 0	$ 0
TOTAL CASH RECEIPTS:	$21,564,550	$15,090,295	$11,000,165
CASH DISBURSEMENTS:			
Cash purchases	$ 6,750,000	$ 2,720,000	$ 2,500,000
Cash payment for prior month credit purchases	$11,250,000	$ 4,533,333	$ 4,166,667
Cash payment for credit purchases made 2 months ago	$ 0	$ 0	$0
Interest payments	$ 250	$ 250	$ 250
Principal repayments	$ 1,000	$ 1,000	$ 1,000
Cash dividends paid	0	$12,000,000	$ 0
Tax payments	$ 1,250	$ 0	$ 0
Asset acquisitions	$ 2,450,000	$ 0	$ 1,250,000
TOTAL CASH DISBURSEMENTS:	$20,452,500	$19,254,583	$ 7,917,917
CASH FLOW (RECEIPTS − DISBURSEMENTS)	$ 1,112,050	$ 4,164,288	$ 3,082,248
ENDING CASH (BEG CASH + CASH FLOW)	$ 2,612,050	$ 1,552,238	$ 1,530,010
LESS: Minimum cash balance	$ 1,000,000	$ 1,000,000	$ 1,000,000
CASH SURPLUS (IF POSITIVE)	$ 1,612,050	0	$ 530,010
CASH SHORTFALL (IF NEGATIVE)	0	$ 2,552,238	0

An alternative format is to use the Statement of Cash Flows format for the receipts and disbursements, thereby classifying sources and uses of cash according to whether they are operating, investing, or financing cash flows. Because businesses must include the cash flow statement as part of their reporting, monitoring forecast accuracy is simple.

Interpreting the Receipts and Disbursements Forecast

Take a closer look at Exhibit 700.30 to see how the treasury analyst can use it to make investing and borrowing decisions. The company starts the quarter with $1.5 million in cash and cash equivalents. Everything looks fine after January, with an ending cash position of $2.6 million. Even after subtracting the minimum cash balance of $1 million, there is a large cash surplus. This represents an investable balance, which usually is invested in short-term securities.

The large net cash outflow in February, mainly resulting from the dividend payment, causes the company to liquidate the short-term securities but still run short of cash. Even before considering the required minimum of $1 million, the company is unable to cover the cash outflow. The company will have to borrow more than $1 million to maintain the necessary minimum cash. March brings a net cash inflow, large enough to not only pay off the $1 million-plus credit line borrowing but also to invest in $530,010 of short-term securities.

Notice three uses for the monthly cash forecast. First, we are able to anticipate the need for credit and the amount of borrowing that should be prearranged to cover anticipated deficits. In World Communication's case, the company will likely arrange a credit line of at least $3 million because forecasts are never perfect and there might be a smaller receipt total or larger disbursement total in any given month. Or the company may allow the $1 million minimum liquidity to act as a buffer against unforeseen cash needs and only borrow $1 million. Of course, the analyst looks at least one year ahead, not merely the three months we show here. Second, we are able to project short-term investment amounts and, based on how long cash surpluses will persist, the allowable maturity of those securities. Normally, longer maturities bring higher yields, and the analyst will study the forecast for 6 or 12 months ahead to see how long projected cash surpluses will last. Third, the analyst might use such projections to help establish the company's target cash balance. The company might arrange more long-term borrowing to increase the year-beginning cash position and avoid short-term borrowing altogether. One caution when using monthly cash budgets: This forecast is giving us anticipated *end-of-month* cash balances. These could well mask larger intramonth receipt and disbursement mismatches, and the analyst will look at the historical pattern of cash flows to determine if these have occurred. This provides further motivation to arrange credit lines larger than the largest cumulative month-end cash shortage recorded in the cash forecast.

Developing the Receipts and Disbursements Forecast

The steps involved in generating the cash forecast using the receipts and disbursements method are straightforward. First, the analyst must develop or look up the company's sales forecast. Preferably, a range of sales forecasts can be developed, linked to likely scenarios for the horizon period. This enables the forecaster to incorporate the uncertainty inherent in the sales forecast through techniques such as simulation. To aid in the sales projection, the analyst may break down the sales revenue forecast into its components, unit sales and selling prices.

Second, the analyst lays out the incoming cash from cash sales, cash collections, asset sales, and other sources. But what if the company offers credit terms, and a given month's sales generates cash across several subsequent months? The historical or anticipated payment pattern for the company's customers is used to project the cash receipts from sales. Returning to the receipts and disbursement illustration (Exhibit 700.30) helps.

World Communications first projects sales for its product lines, which we show as a memo item at the top of Exhibit 700.31. Next, it studies historical collection patterns, to determine the uncollected balance fractions shown in the second column (these may already be available if the credit department is using them to monitor collection efficiency. The key is to determine when cash is received from customers—when does the customer actually make payment? A few months of actual sales will also be included in our data, because of the lag in collections. Here, the analyst is making a projection in early January, so we have actual data from October, November, and December, in case there is a three-month lag in collections. In World Communications' case, October's sales are not used, because 95% of sales are collected within two months, and the remaining 5% are uncollectible. World receives 32% in the month of sale, 48% in the next month (lag one month), and 15% in the second following month (lag two months). These proportions add to 100% only if World experienced negligible bad debt losses. Here, as noted, World fails to collect 5% of sales (100%-32%-48%-15%). To calculate January's cash receipts from sales, we take 32% of January's projected sales of $17.5 million, plus 48% of December's sales of $21.25 million, plus 15% of November's sales of 38.33 million. The sum is $21.55 million of cash receipts, which constitutes most of January's total cash receipts in Exhibit 700.30.

Third, cash disbursements, including payments to suppliers, employees, governments, and funds providers are arrayed. The difference in the cash receipts and disbursements gives the period's net cash flow. Many forecasters stop

Exhibit 700.31 *Cash Receipts From Sales Worksheet for World Communications*

		\multicolumn{6}{c}{Projecting Cash Collections From Earlier Sales}
		\multicolumn{6}{c}{Month Sales}
Item	Proportion	Oct 2000	Nov 2000	Dec 2000	Jan 2001	Feb 2001	Mar 2001
MEMO: Actual (Forecast) Sales:		$20,000,000	$38,333,333	$21,250,000	$17,500,000	$10,937,500	$9,765,625
Cash sales	32%				$ 5,600,000	$ 3,500,000	$3,125,000
Collections of credit sales:							
Lagged 1 month	48%				10,200,000	8,400,000	5,250,000
Lagged 2 months	15%				5,750,000	3,187,500	2,625,000
Lagged 3 months*	0%				0	0	0
Total cash receipts from sales					$21,550,000	$15,087,500	$11,000,000

*Bad debt loss rate is 5% (=100% − 32% − 48% − 15%).

here, but, as shown in Exhibit 700.30, it is valuable to go beyond this to add beginning cash, arriving at ending cash. Financing and investments can be handled in two different ways. They can be treated as a residual: If ending cash is negative, arrange this amount of financing; if positive, plan to invest the surplus amount. Or the financing and investing can be built into the forecast to reflect planned financing and investing. Regardless, asset sales and capital investments should be included as separate categories under receipts and disbursements. Strengths of the receipts and disbursements method include simplicity, accuracy for near-term forecasts, and attractiveness as a monitoring and control tool. Weaknesses include the inaccuracy for forecast horizons greater than three months (largely resulting from the cumulation of early errors) and the over-reliance on the forecaster's judgment that typifies real-life applications of the technique.

Approach 2: The Modified Accrual Method

Modified Accrual Method

A second technique useful for monthly forecasts is the modified accrual method. Sometimes called the accrual addback technique or adjusted net income technique, the approach begins with accounting reports or the operating budget and then adjusts these numbers to reflect the timing of cash flows related to these transactions. For small businesses and nonprofit organizations doing their income statements on a cash basis, very few adjustments to the operating budget or projected income statement are necessary. The only problem encountered in that case is if the historical tracker used to develop a forecast is invalidated because of faster or slower processing of invoices, checks received, and so on. In its simplest form, the modified accrual forecast is easily determined, as shown in Equation 7.27.

$$CF_t = NI_t + NC_t - CA_t + CL_t \tag{7.27}$$

when for period t:

CF_t = cash flow
NI_t = net income
NC_t = noncash charges
CA_t = current asset change
CL_t = current liability change

Example of the Modified Accrual Technique

AMAX Coal has assembled the following pro forma income statement and parts of its present and pro forma balance sheets, which are shown in highly condensed form.

Pro Forma Income Statement ($ mils.)	
Sales	$10,000
− COGS	$ 6,000
Gross margin	$ 4,000
− operating exps.	$ 3,150*
Operating profit	$ 850
− interest exp.	$ 25
Pretax income	$ 800
− taxes	$ 300
Net income	$ 500

*Includes depreciation and other noncash charges of $145 million.

	Present Balance Sheet ($ mils.)	Pro Forma Balance Sheet ($ mils.)
Current Assets:		
Cash	$ 10	Uncertain; assume to be unchanged.
Accts. receivable	$ 970	$ 960
Inventories	$ 835	$ 820
Long-term Assets		
Property, plant, and equip.	$12,000	$11,700
Current Liabilities:		
Accounts payable	$ 745	$ 730
Notes payable	$ 500	$ 500
Long-term debt	$ 7,000	$ 8,000

Forecast Solution:
Net income and the noncash charges are taken from the projected income statement. Changes in current assets and current liabilities are calculated as (Projected Balance Sheet Amount − Present Balance Sheet Amount). If AMAX Coal, Inc., projects net income of $500 million, noncash charges of $145 million, decreases in current assets of $25 million (in this case, the change in accounts receivable plus change in inventories), and decreases in current liabilities of $15 million (here, the change in accounts payable), cash flow for the period using our simple equation is:

$$CF_t = \$500 + \$145 - (-\$25) + (-\$15) = \$655 \text{ million}$$

Current asset changes are subtracted because increases in items such as inventories drain cash flow, and current liability changes are added because they represent sources of cash flow. Typical noncash charges are depreciation, amortization of intangibles, and gains or losses on asset sales. Notice that the cash flow formula presented is an operating cash flow forecast. The change, if any, in long-term assets, long-term liabilities, and equity will not affect the forecasted cash flow. If desired, Equation 7.27 easily can be expanded to include anticipated dividends, loan interest or principal payments, acquisitions, and other episodic cash flows. At that point, however, it might be easier to simply change to a projected statement of cash flow format.

The major strength of the modified accrual technique is ease of implementation: The data are already available, in most cases, in the form of a budget or projected income statement. The adjustments to net income to arrive at cash flow are easily made, as shown above. The technique is also relatively accurate for intermediate-term forecasting, when compared with other techniques. However, it suffers from inaccuracy in the short-run horizons and may lack sufficient detail to ensure accuracy.

Approach 3: The Pro Forma Balance Sheet Method

Pro Forma Balance Sheet Method

The pro forma balance sheet approach to generating a cash forecast involves determination of the amount of cash and marketable securities by computing the difference between projected assets (excluding cash and marketable securities) and the sum of projected liabilities and owner's equity. This approach, very popular for medium-term and long-term forecasting, is illustrated in Exhibit 700.32.

In projecting the balance sheet, current liabilities and noncash assets might be predicted as a percentage of anticipated sales, and the long-term liabilities and common stock assumed to remain constant. The change in retained earnings is based on anticipated net income less planned cash dividends. If we subtract the sum of liabilities and owner's equity from noncash assets, we get a residual amount labeled "cash and marketable securities," which is our cash forecast. If this amount is negative, additional financing will have to be arranged. Then the new financing amount is plugged into the liability section; interest expense, net income, and additions to retained earnings recomputed and a new cash amount calculated. In other cases, the figure may be a large positive amount, in which case some previous borrowings may be paid down, stock repurchased, or greater expansion in fixed assets arranged. The fact that the forecast leads naturally to financial planning demonstrates the value of longer-term cash forecasts. The pro forma balance sheet approach is well suited for these longer-range cash forecasts.

Exhibit 700.32 *Pro Forma Balance Sheet Method*

BALANCE SHEET PROJECTION FORECASTING METHOD
Cash and Marketable Securities Residual of Balance Sheet Projection

Month Account	Jan	Feb	Mar
Cash and M.S.*	Plug	Plug	Plug
Accts. receivable	$ 35	$ 36	$ 36
Inventories	$ 65	$ 66	$ 68
Prepaid expenses	$ 15	$ 15	$ 16
Current assets	$115	$117	$120
Prop., plant, equipment	$210	$223	$227
TOTAL ASSETS	$325	$340	$347
Accts. payable	$ 30	$ 31	$ 31
Notes payable	$ 25	$ 26	$ 26
Accrued expenses	$ 10	$ 10	$ 10
Current liabilities	$ 65	$ 67	$ 67
Long-term liabilities	$ 45	$ 46	$ 47
TOTAL LIABILITIES	$110	$113	$114
Stockholders' equity			
Common stock	$ 5	$ 5	$ 5
Paid-in capital	$ 20	$ 20	$ 20
Retained earnings	$205	$220	$235
EQUITY	$230	$245	$260
TOTAL LIABS. and EQUITY	$340	$358	$374

*Calculation of Cash & Marketable Securities Plug Amount
Cash and M.S.
   = (Totals Liabs.
   + Stockholders' Equity)
   − Total Assets: 340 − 325 = 15   358 − 340 = 18   374 − 347 = 27

Basically, the pro forma balance sheet represents a crude approximation of sources and uses of funds, with funds defined as cash and marketable securities. Liability and equity accounts represent sources of funds; asset amounts represent uses of funds. The major strength of this forecasting approach is its ease of implementation. The major weakness is the difficulty in making accurate monthly forecasts by using balance sheet projections. For annual totals, the technique is acceptable, but for monthly forecasts, the failure to adjust for differences between accrual-based net income (which drives the retained earnings projection) and cash flows arising from that income stream hurts forecast accuracy.

Cost of Capital, Capital Structure, and Dividend Policy

The Cost of Capital

It is vitally important that a firm knows how much it pays for the funds used to purchase assets. The average return required by the firm's investors determines how much must be paid to attract funds—it is the firm's average cost of funds, which more commonly is termed the *cost of capital*. The firm's cost of capital is very important because it represents the minimum rate of return that must be earned from investments, such as capital budgeting projects, to ensure the value of the firm does not decrease—the cost of capital is the firm's *required rate of return*. For example, if investors provide funds to a firm for an average cost of 15%, wealth will decrease if the funds are used to generate returns less than 15%, wealth will not change if exactly 15% is earned, and wealth will increase if returns greater than 15% can be generated.

In this section, we discuss the concept of cost of capital, how the average cost of capital is determined, and how the cost of capital is used in financial decision making. How much it costs a firm for its funds is based on the return demanded by investors—if the return offered by the firm is not high enough, then investors will not provide sufficient funds. In other words, the rate of return an investor earns on a corporate security effectively is a cost to the firm of using those funds, so the same models are used by investors and by corporate treasurers to determine required rates of return.

Our first topic in this section is the logic of the weighted average cost of capital. Next, we consider the costs of the major types of capital, after which we see how the costs of the individual components of the capital structure are brought together to form a weighted average cost of capital (WACC).

The Logic of the Weighted Average Cost of Capital

It is possible to finance a firm entirely with equity funds by issuing only stock. In that case, the cost of capital used to analyze capital budgeting decisions should be the company's required return on equity. However, most firms raise a substantial portion of their funds as long-term debt, and some also use preferred stock. For these firms, their cost of capital must reflect the average cost of the various sources of long-term funds used, not just the firms' costs of equity.

Assume that Unilate Textiles has a 10% cost of debt and a 13.7% cost of equity. Further, assume that Unilate has made the decision to finance next year's projects by selling debt only. The argument is sometimes made that the cost of capital for these projects is 10% because only debt will be used to finance them. However, this position is incorrect. If Unilate finances a particular set of projects with debt, the firm will be using up some of its potential for obtaining new debt in the future. As expansion occurs in subsequent years, Unilate will at some point find it necessary to raise additional equity to prevent the debt ratio from becoming too large.

To illustrate, suppose Unilate borrows heavily at 10% during 2001, using up its debt capacity in the process, to finance projects yielding 11.5%. In 2002 it has new projects available that yield 13%, well above the return on 2001 projects, but it cannot accept them because they would have to be financed with 13.7% equity money. To avoid this problem, Unilate should be viewed as an ongoing concern, and *the cost of capital used in capital budgeting should be calculated as a weighted average, or combination, of the various types of funds generally used, regardless of the specific financing used to fund a particular project.*

Basic Definitions of Cost Capital Components

The items on the right side of a firm's balance sheet—various types of debt, preferred stock, and common equity—are its **capital components.** Any increase in total assets must be financed by an increase in one or more of these capital components.

Capital is a necessary factor of production, and, like any other factor, it has a cost. The cost of each component is called the *component cost* of that particular type of capital; for example, if Unilate can borrow money at 10%, its component cost of debt is 10%. Throughout this section we concentrate on debt, preferred stock, retained earnings, and new issues of common stock, which are the four major capital structure components. We will use the following symbols to designate specific component costs of capital.

- k_d = Interest rate on the firm's debt = before-tax component cost of debt. For Unilate, k_d = 10.0%.
- k_{dT} = $k_d(1 - T)$ = After-tax component cost of debt, where T is the firm's marginal tax rate. k_{dT} is the debt cost used to calculate the weighted average cost of capital. For Unilate, T = 40%, so k_{dT} = $k_d(1 - T)$ = 10.0%(1 − 0.4) = 10.0%(0.6) = 6.0%.
- k_{ps} = Component cost of preferred stock. Unilate has no preferred stock at this time, but, as new funds are raised, the company plans to issue preferred stock. The cost of preferred stock, k_{ps}, will be 10.3%.
- k_s = Component cost of retained earnings (or internal equity). For Unilate, $k_s \approx$ 13.7%.
- k_e = Component cost of external equity obtained by issuing new common stock as opposed to retaining earnings. As we shall see, it is necessary to distinguish between common equity needs that can be satisfied by retained earnings and the common equity needs that are satisfied by selling new stock. This is why we distinguish between internal and external equity, k_s and k_e. Further, k_e is always greater than k_s. For Unilate, $k_e \approx$ 14.3%.
- WACC = The weighted average cost of capital. In the future, when Unilate needs *new* capital to finance asset expansion, it will raise part of the new funds as debt, part as preferred stock, and part as common equity (with common equity coming either from retained earnings or from the issuance of new common stock). We will calculate WACC for Unilate Textiles shortly.

Cost of Debt, k_{dT}

The after-tax cost of debt, k_{dT}, is the interest rate on debt, k_d, less the tax saving that results because interest is deductible. This is the same as k_d multiplied by $(1 - T)$, where T is the firm's marginal tax rate.

$$\text{After-tax component cost of debt} = k_{dT} = \text{(Bondholders' required rate of return)} - \text{(Tax savings)} \quad (7.28)$$
$$= k_d - k_d \times T$$
$$= k_d(1 - T)$$

In effect, the government pays part of the cost of debt because interest is deductible. Therefore, if Unilate can borrow at an interest rate of 10%, and if it has a marginal tax rate of 40%, then its after-tax cost of debt is 6%.

$$k_{dT} = k_d(1 - T) = 10.0\%(1.0 - 0.4)$$
$$= 10.0\%(0.6)$$
$$= 6.0\%$$

We use the after-tax cost of debt because the value of the firm's stock, which we want to maximize, depends on *after-tax* cash flows. Because interest is a deductible expense, it produces tax savings that reduce the net cost of debt, making the after-tax cost of debt less than the before-tax cost. We are concerned with after-tax cash flows, so after-tax rates of return are appropriate.

Cost of Preferred Stock, k_{ps}

In Section 715, we found that the dividend associated with preferred stock is constant and that preferred stock has no stated maturity. Thus, a preferred dividend, which we designate D_{ps}, represents a perpetuity, and the component **cost of preferred stock, k_{ps},** is the preferred dividend, D_{ps}, divided by the net issuing price, NP, or the price the firm receives after deducting the costs of issuing the stock, which are called *flotation costs*.

$$\text{Component cost of preferred stock} = k_{ps} = \frac{D_{ps}}{NP} = \frac{D_{ps}}{P_0 - \text{Flotation costs}} \quad (7.29)$$

For example, in the future, Unilate is going to issue preferred stock that pays a $10 dividend per share and sells for $100 per share in the market. It will cost 3%, or $3 per share, to issue the new preferred stock, so Unilate will net $97 per share. Therefore, Unilate's cost of preferred stock is 10.3%.

$$k_{ps} = \frac{\$10}{\$97}$$
$$= 0.103 = 10.3\%$$

No tax adjustments are made when calculating k_{ps} because preferred dividends, unlike interest expense on debt, are not tax deductible, so there are no tax savings associated with the use of preferred stock.

Cost of Retained Earnings, ks

The costs of debt and preferred stock are based on the returns investors require on these securities. Similarly, the **cost of retained earnings, k_s,** is the rate of return stockholders require on equity capital the firm obtains by retaining earnings that otherwise could be distributed to common stockholders as dividends.

The reason we must assign a cost of capital to retained earnings involves the *opportunity cost principle*. The firm's after-tax earnings literally belong to its stockholders. Bondholders are compensated by interest payments, and preferred stockholders by preferred dividends, but the earnings remaining after interest and preferred dividends belong to the common stockholders, and these earnings help compensate stockholders for the use of their capital. Management can either pay out the earnings in the form of dividends or retain earnings and reinvest them in the business. If management decides to retain earnings, there is an opportunity cost involved—stockholders could have received the earnings as dividends and invested this money in other stocks, in bonds, in real estate, or in anything else. Thus, the firm should earn a return on earnings it retains that is at least as great as the return stockholders themselves could earn on alternative investments of comparable risk.

What rate of return can stockholders expect to earn on equivalent-risk investments? First, recall that stocks normally are in equilibrium, with the expected and required rates of return being equal: $\hat{k}_s = k_s$. Therefore, we can assume that Unilate's stockholders expect to earn a return of k_s on their money. *If the firm cannot invest retained earnings and earn at least k_s, it should pay these funds to its stockholders and let them invest directly in other assets that do provide this return.*

Whereas debt and preferred stocks are contractual obligations that have easily determined costs, it is not as easy to measure k_s. However, we can employ the principles applied in asset valuation to produce reasonably good cost of equity estimates. To begin, we know that if a stock is in equilibrium (which is the typical situation), then its required rate of return, k_s, is also equal to its expected rate of return, $\hat{k}_s$. Further, its required return is equal to a risk-free rate, k_{RF}, plus a risk premium, RP, whereas the expected return on a constant growth stock is equal to the stock's dividend yield, $\hat{D}_1/P_0$, plus its expected growth rate, g:

Required rate of return = Expected rate of return

$$k_s = k_{RF} + RP = \frac{\hat{D}_1}{P_0} + g = \hat{k}_s \quad (7.30)$$

Because the two must be equal, we can estimate k_s either as $k_s = k_{RF} + RP$ or as $\hat{k}_s = \hat{D}_1/P_0 + g$. Actually, three methods are commonly used for finding the cost of retained earnings: (1) the capital asset pricing model (CAPM) approach, (2) the bond-yield-plus-risk-premium approach, and (3) constant growth model using the discounted cash flow (DCF) approach. These three approaches are discussed next.

The CAPM Approach

The Capital Asset Pricing Model (CAPM) is as follows.

$$k_s = k_{RF} + (k_M - k_{RF})\beta_s \quad (7.31)$$

Equation 7.31 shows that the CAPM estimate of k_s begins with the risk-free rate, k_{RF}, to which is added a risk premium that is based on the stock's relation to the market as measured by its beta, β_s, and the magnitude of the market risk premium, which is the difference between the market return, k_M, and the risk-free rate, k_{RF}.

To illustrate the CAPM approach, assume that $k_{RF} = 7\%$, $k_M = 11\%$, and $\beta_s = 1.6$ for Unilate's common stock. Using the CAPM approach, Unilate's cost of retained earnings, k_s, is calculated as follows:

$$k_s = 7.0\% + (11.0\% - 7.0\%)(1.6)$$
$$= 7.0\% + 6.4\%$$
$$= 13.4\%$$

It should be noted that although the CAPM approach appears to yield an accurate, precise estimate of k_s, there actually are several problems with it. First, if a firm's stockholders are not well diversified, they might be concerned with total risk rather than with market risk only (measured by β); in this case the firm's true investment risk will not be measured by its beta, and the CAPM procedure will understate the correct value of k_s. Further, even if the CAPM method is valid, it is difficult to obtain correct estimates of the inputs required to make it operational because: (1) there is controversy about whether to use long-term or short-term Treasury yields for k_{RF}; and (2) both β_s and k_M should be estimated values, which often are difficult to obtain.

Bond-Yield-Plus-Risk-Premium Approach

Although it is a subjective procedure, analysts often estimate a firm's cost of common equity by adding a risk premium of three to five percentage points to the interest rate on the firm's own long-term debt. It is logical to think that firms with risky, low-rated, and consequently high-interest-rate debt will also have risky, high-cost equity. Using this logic to estimate the cost of common stock is relatively easy, because all we have to do is add a risk premium to a readily observable debt cost. For example, Unilate's cost of equity might be estimated as follows:

$$k_s = \text{Bond yield} + \text{Risk premium}$$
$$= 10.0\% + 4.0\%$$
$$= 14.0\%$$

Because the 4% risk premium is a judgmental estimate, the estimated value of k_s also is judgmental. Empirical work suggests that the risk premium over a firm's own bond yield generally has ranged from three to five percentage points, so this method is not likely to produce a precise cost of equity—about all it can do is get us into the right ballpark.

Constant Growth Model Using the DCF Approach

We learned that both the price and the expected rate of return on a share of common stock depend, ultimately, on the dividends expected on the stock, and the value of a share of stock can be written as follows:

$$P_0 = \frac{\hat{D}_1}{(1 + k_s)^1} + \frac{\hat{D}_2}{(1 + k_s)^2} + \cdots + \frac{\hat{D}_\infty}{(1 + k_s)^\infty} \qquad (7.32)$$

$$= \sum_{t=1}^{\infty} \frac{\hat{D}_t}{(1 + k_s)^t}$$

Here P_0 is the current price of the stock; $\hat{D}_t$ is the dividend *expected* to be paid at the end of Year t; and k_s is the required rate of return. If dividends are expected to grow at a constant rate, then, Equation 7.32 reduces to

$$P_0 = \frac{\hat{D}_1}{k_s - g} \qquad (7.32a)$$

We can solve Equation 7.32a for k_s to estimate the required rate of return on common equity, which for the marginal investor is also equal to the expected rate of return.

$$k_s = \hat{k}_s = \frac{\hat{D}_1}{P_0} + g \qquad (7.33)$$

Thus, investors expect to receive a dividend yield, $\hat{D}_1/P_0$, plus a capital gain, g, for a total expected return of $\hat{D}/\hat{k}_s$, and in equilibrium this expected return is also equal to the required return, k_s. From this point on, we will assume that equilibrium exists, and we will use the terms k_s and $\hat{k}_s$ interchangeably, so we will drop the "hat," ^, above k_s.

To illustrate the DCF approach, suppose Unilate's stock sells for $23; the common stock dividend expected to be paid in 2001 is $1.31, which is 15¢ higher than the dividend paid in 2000; and its expected long-term growth rate is 8%. Unilate's expected and required rate of return, and hence its cost of retained earnings, is 13.7%.

$$\hat{k}_s = k_s = \frac{\$1.31}{\$23.00} + 0.08$$
$$= 0.057 + 0.08$$
$$= 0.137 = 13.7\%$$

This 13.7% is the minimum rate of return that management must expect to earn to justify retaining earnings and plowing them back into the business rather than paying them out to stockholders as dividends.

We have used three methods to estimate the cost of retained earnings, which actually is a single number. To summarize, we found the cost of common equity to be (1) 13.4% using the CAPM method; (2) 14.0% with the bond-yield-plus-risk-premium approach; and (3) 13.7% using the constant growth model, the DCF approach. It is not unusual to get different estimates, because each of the approaches is based on different assumptions—the CAPM assumes investors are well diversified, the bond-yield-plus-risk-premium approach assumes the cost of equity is closely related to the firm's cost of debt, and the constant growth model assumes the firm's dividends and earnings will grow at a constant rate far into the future. So which estimate should be used? Probably all of them. Many analysts use multiple approaches to estimate a single value, then average the results. For Unilate, then, the average of the estimates is 13.7% = (13.4% + 14.0% + 13.7%)/3.

People experienced in estimating equity capital costs recognize that both careful analysis and sound judgment are required. It would be nice to pretend that judgment is unnecessary and to specify an easy, precise way of determining the exact cost of equity capital. Unfortunately, this is not possible—finance is in large part a matter of judgment.

Cost of Newly Issued Common Stock, or External Equity, k_e

The **cost of new common equity, k_e,** or external equity capital, is similar to the cost of retained earnings, k_s, except it is higher because there is a cost to issuing new stock. Because the firm incurs costs when selling new securities, called **flotation costs,** the full market value of the stock cannot be used for investments—only the amount left after paying flotation costs is available. Thus, the cost of issuing new common stock (external equity), k_e, must be greater than the cost of retained earnings (internal equity), k_s, because there are no flotation costs associated with retained earnings.

In general, the cost of issuing new equity, k_e, can be found by modifying the DCF formula used to compute the cost of retained earnings, k_s, to obtain the following equation.

$$k_e = \frac{\hat{D}_1}{NP} + g = \frac{\hat{D}_1}{P_0(1 - F)} + g \qquad (7.34)$$

Here F is the percentage flotation cost (in decimal form) incurred in selling the new stock issue, so $P_0(1 - F)$ is the net price per share received by the company.

If Unilate can issue new common stock at a flotation cost of 10%, k_e is computed as follows.

$$k_e = \frac{\$1.31}{\$23.00(1 - 0.10)} + 0.08$$
$$= \frac{\$1.31}{\$20.70} + 0.08$$
$$= 0.143 = 14.3\%$$

Using the DCF approach to estimate the cost of retained earnings, we found that investors require a return of $k_s = 13.7\%$ on the stock. However, because of flotation costs, the company must earn more than 13.7% on funds obtained by selling stock if it is to provide a 13.7% return. Specifically, if the firm earns 14.3% on funds obtained from new stock, then earnings per share will not fall below previously expected earnings, the firm's expected dividend can be maintained, and, as a result, the price per share will not decline. If the firm earns less than 14.3%, then earnings, dividends, and growth will fall below expectations, causing the price of the stock to decline. If it earns more than 14.3%, the price of the stock will rise.

Weighted Average Cost of Capital, WACC

Each firm has an optimal capital structure, or mix of debt, preferred stock, and common equity, that causes its stock price to be maximized. Therefore, a rational, value-maximizing firm will establish a **target (optimal) capital structure** and then raise new capital in a manner that will keep the actual capital structure on target over time. In this section we assume that the firm has identified its optimal capital structure, it uses this optimum as the target, and it raises funds so it constantly remains on target.

The target proportions of debt, preferred stock, and common equity, along with the component costs of capital, are used to calculate the firm's **weighted average cost of capital (WACC)**. To illustrate, suppose Unilate Textiles has determined that in the future it will raise new capital according to the following proportions: 45% debt, 5% preferred stock, and 50% common equity (retained earnings plus common stock). In the preceding sections, we found that its before-tax cost of debt, k_d, is 10%, so its *after-tax* cost of debt, k_{dT}, is 6%; its cost of preferred stock, k_{ps}, is 10.3%; and its cost of common equity from retained earnings, k_s, is 13.7% if all of its equity financing comes from retained earnings. Now we can calculate Unilate's weighted average cost of capital (WACC) as follows.

$$\begin{aligned} \text{WACC} &= \left[\begin{pmatrix}\text{Proportion}\\\text{of}\\\text{debt}\end{pmatrix} \times \begin{pmatrix}\text{After-tax}\\\text{cost of}\\\text{debt}\end{pmatrix}\right] + \left[\begin{pmatrix}\text{Proportion}\\\text{of preferred}\\\text{stock}\end{pmatrix} \times \begin{pmatrix}\text{Cost of}\\\text{preferred}\\\text{stock}\end{pmatrix}\right] + \left[\begin{pmatrix}\text{Proportion}\\\text{of common}\\\text{equity}\end{pmatrix} \times \begin{pmatrix}\text{Cost of}\\\text{common}\\\text{equity}\end{pmatrix}\right] \\ &= w_d k_{dT} + w_{ps} k_{ps} + w_s k_s \\ &= 0.45(6.0\%) + 0.05(10.3\%) + 0.50(13.7\%) \\ &\approx 10.1\% \end{aligned} \quad (7.35)$$

Here w_d, w_{ps}, and w_s are the weights used for debt, preferred stock, and common equity, respectively.

Every dollar of new capital that Unilate obtains consists of 45¢ of debt with an after-tax cost of 6%, 5¢ of preferred stock with a cost of 10.3%, and 50¢ of common equity (all from additions to retained earnings) with a cost of 13.7%. The average cost of each whole dollar, WACC, is 10.1% as long as these conditions continue. If the component costs of capital change when new funds are raised in the future, then WACC changes. We discuss changes in the component costs of capital in the next section.

The Marginal Cost of Capital, MCC

The marginal cost of any item is the cost of another unit of that item; for example, the marginal cost of labor is the cost of adding one additional worker. The marginal cost of labor might be $25 per person if ten workers are added but $35 per person if the firm tries to hire 100 new workers because it will be harder to find that many people willing and able to do the work. The same concept applies to capital. As the firm tries to attract more new dollars, at some point, the cost of each dollar will increase. Thus, the **marginal cost of capital (MCC)** *is defined as the cost of the last dollar of new capital that the firm raises, and the marginal cost rises as more and more capital is raised during a given period.*

In the preceding section, we computed Unilate's WACC to be 10.1%. As long as Unilate keeps its capital structure on target, and as long as its debt has an after-tax cost of 6%, its preferred stock a cost of 10.3%, and its common equity a cost of 13.7%, then its weighted average cost of capital will be 10.1%. Each dollar the firm raises will consist of some long-term debt, some preferred stock, and some common equity, and the cost of the whole dollar will be 10.1%—its marginal cost of capital (MCC) will be 10.1%.

The MCC Schedule

A graph that shows how the WACC changes as more and more new capital is raised by the firm is called the **marginal cost of capital schedule.** Exhibit 700.33 shows Unilate's MCC schedule if the cost of debt, cost of preferred stock, and cost of common equity *never change*. Here the dots represent dollars raised, and because each dollar of new capital will have an average cost equal to 10.1%, the marginal cost of capital (MCC) for Unilate is constant at 10.1% under the assumptions we have used to this point.

Do you think Unilate actually could raise an unlimited amount of new capital at the 10.1% cost? Probably not, because, as a practical matter, as a company raises larger and larger amounts of funds during a given time period, the costs of those funds begin to rise, and as this occurs, the weighted average cost of each new dollar also rises.

Exhibit 700.33 *Marginal Cost of Capital (MCC) Schedule for Unilate Textiles*

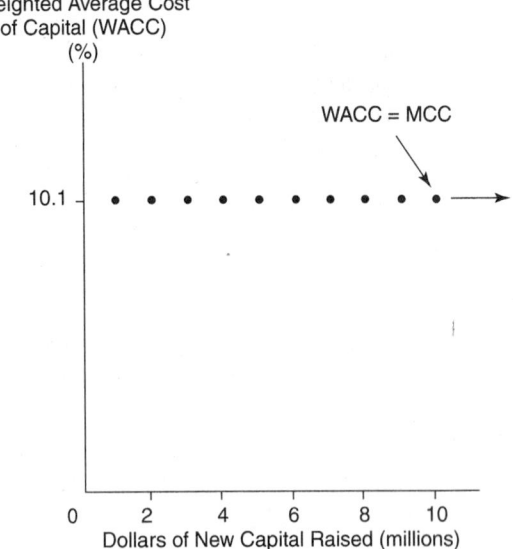

Thus, companies cannot raise unlimited amounts of capital at a constant cost—at some point, the cost of each new dollar will increase, no matter what its source (debt, preferred stock, or common equity).

How much new capital can Unilate raise before it exhausts its retained earnings and is forced to sell new common stock? In other words, where will an increase in the MCC schedule occur?

We forecast that Unilate's 2001 net income would be $61 million and that $30.5 million would be paid out as dividends so that $30.5 million will be added to retained earnings (the payout ratio is 50%). Thus, Unilate can invest in capital projects to the point where the common equity needs equal $30.5 million before new common stock has to be issued. Remember, though, that when Unilate needs new funds, the target capital structure indicates only 50% of the total should be common equity; the remainder of the funds should come from issues of bonds (45%) and preferred stock (5%). Thus, we know:

$$\text{Common equity} = 0.50 \, (\text{Total new capital raised})$$

We can use this relationship to determine how much *total new capital*—debt, preferred stock, and retained earnings—can be raised before the $30.5 million of retained earnings is exhausted and Unilate is forced to sell new common stock. Just set the common equity needs equal to the retained earnings amount, and solve for the total new capital amount.

$$\text{Common equity} = \text{Retained earnings} = \$30.5 \text{ million} = 0.50 \left(\begin{array}{c} \text{Total new} \\ \text{capital raised} \end{array} \right)$$

$$\left(\begin{array}{c} \text{Total new} \\ \text{capital raised} \end{array} \right) = \frac{\$30.5 \text{ million}}{0.50} = \$61.0 \text{ million}$$

Thus, Unilate can raise a total of $61 million before it has to sell new common stock to finance its capital projects.

If Unilate needs exactly $61 million in new capital, the breakdown of the amount that would come from each source of capital and the computation for the weighted average cost of capital (WACC) would be as follows.

Capital Source	Weight	Amount in Millions	After-Tax Component Cost	WACC
Debt	0.45	$27.45	6.0%	2.7%
Preferred stock	0.05	3.05	10.3	0.5
Common equity	0.50	30.50	13.7	6.9
	1.00	$61.00		$WACC_1 = 10.1\%$

MODULE 700. FINANCE

Therefore, if Unilate needs *exactly* $61 million in new capital in 2001, retained earnings will be just enough to satisfy the common equity requirement, so the firm will not need to sell new common stock and its weighted average cost of capital (WACC) will be 10.1%. But what will happen if Unilate needs more than $61 million in new capital? If Unilate needs $64 million, for example, retained earnings will not be sufficient to cover the $32 million common equity requirements (50% of the total funds), so new common stock will have to be sold. The cost of issuing new common stock, k_e, is greater than the cost of retained earnings, k_s; hence, the WACC will be greater. If Unilate raises $64 million in new capital, the breakdown of the amount that would come from each source of capital and the computation for the weighted average cost of capital (WACC) would be as follows.

Capital Source	Weight	Amount in Millions	After-Tax Component Cost	WACC
Debt	0.45	$28.80	6.0%	2.7%
Preferred stock	0.05	3.20	10.3	0.5
Common equity	0.50	32.00	14.3	7.2
	1.00	$64.00		$WACC_2 = 10.4\%$

The WACC will be greater because Unilate will have to sell new common stock, which has a higher component cost than retained earnings (14.3% versus 13.7%). Consequently, if Unilate's capital budgeting needs are greater than $61 million, new common stock will need to be sold, and its WACC will increase. The $61 million in total new capital is defined as the *retained earnings break point,* because above this amount of total capital, a break, or jump, in Unilate's MCC schedule occurs. In general, a **break point (BP)** is defined as the dollar of *new total capital* that can be raised before an increase in the firm's weighted average cost of capital occurs.

Exhibit 700.34 graphs Unilate's marginal cost of capital schedule with the retained earnings break point. Each dollar has a weighted average cost of 10.1% until the company has raised a total of $61 million. This $61 million will consist of $27.45 million of new debt with an after-tax cost of 6%, $3.05 million of preferred stock with a cost of 10.3%, and $30.50 million of retained earnings with a cost of 13.7%. However, if Unilate raises one dollar over $61 million, each new dollar will contain 50¢ of equity *obtained by selling new common equity at a cost of 14.3%;* therefore, WACC jumps from 10.1% to 10.4%, as calculated above and shown in Exhibit 700.35.

Note that we really don't think the MCC jumps by precisely 0.3% when we raise $1 over $61 million. Thus, Exhibit 700.34 should be regarded as an approximation rather than as a precise representation of reality.

Exhibit 700.34 *Marginal Cost of Capital Schedule for Unilate Textiles Using Both Retained Earnings and New Common Stock*

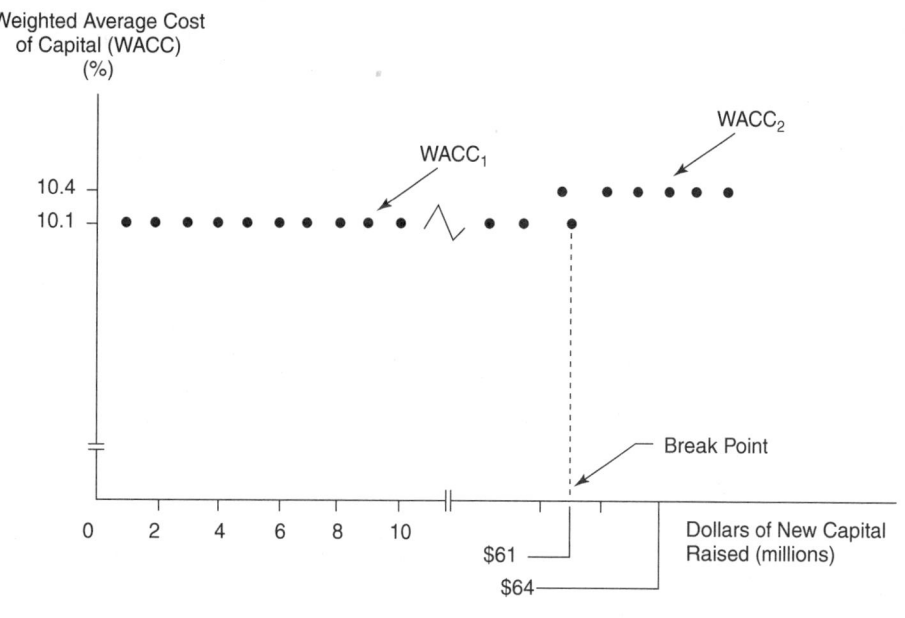

Exhibit 700.35 *WACC and Break Points for Unilate's MCC Schedule*

I. Break Points
1. $BP_{Retained\ earnings} = \$30,500,000/0.50 = \$61,000,000$
2. $BP_{Debt} = 54,000,000/0.45 = \$120,000,000$

II. Weighted Average Cost of Capital (WACC)

1. New Capital Needs: $0–$61,000,000

	Breakdown of Funds at $61,000,000	Weight ×	After-Tax Component Cost	= WACC
Debt (10%)	$ 27,450,000	0.45	6.0%	2.7%
Preferred stock	3,050,000	0.05	10.3	0.5
Common equity (Retained earnings)	30,500,000	0.50	13.7	6.9
	$ 61,000,000	1.00	$WACC_1 =$	10.1%

2. New Capital Needs: $61,000,001–$120,000,000

	Breakdown of Funds at $120,000,000	Weight ×	After-Tax Component Cost	= WACC
Debt (10%)	$ 54,000,000	0.45	6.0%	2.7%
Preferred stock	6,000,000	0.05	10.3	0.5
Common equity (New stock issue)	$ 60,000,000	0.50	14.3	7.2
	$120,000,000	1.00	$WACC_2 =$	10.4%

3. New Capital Needs: Above $120,000,000

	Breakdown of Funds at $130,000,000	Weight ×	After-Tax Component Cost	= WACC
Debt (12%)	$ 58,500,000	0.45	7.2%	3.2%
Preferred stock	6,500,000	0.05	10.3	0.5
Common equity (New stock issue)	65,000,000	0.50	14.3	7.2
	$130,000,000	1.00	$WACC_3 =$	10.9%

In general, a break point will occur whenever the cost of one of the capital components increases, and the break point can be determined by the following equation.

$$\text{Break point} = \frac{\text{Total amount of lower cost capital of a given type}}{\text{Proportion of this type of capital in the capital structure}} \quad (7.36)$$

We see, then, that numerous break points can occur. At the limit, we can even think of an MCC schedule with so many break points that it rises almost continuously beyond some given level of new financing.

The easiest sequence for calculating MCC schedules is as follows.

1. Use Equation 7.36 to determine each point at which a break occurs. A break will occur any time the cost of one of the capital components rises. (It is possible, however, that two capital components could both increase at the same point.) After determining the exact break points, make a list of them.
2. Determine the cost of capital for each component in the intervals between breaks.
3. Calculate the weighted averages of these component costs to obtain the WACCs in each interval, as we did in Exhibit 700.35. The WACC is constant within each interval, but it rises at each break point.

Notice that if there are n separate breaks, there will be n + 1 different WACCs. For example, two breaks means there will be three different WACCs. Also, we should note again that a different MCC schedule would result if a different capital structure is used.

Example 1 *The first break point is not necessarily the point at which retained earnings are used up; it is possible for low-cost debt to be exhausted before retained earnings have been used up. For example, if Unilate had available only $22.5 million of 10% debt, BP_{Debt} would occur at $50 million:*

$$BP_{Debt} = \frac{\$22.5 \text{ million}}{0.45} = \$50 \text{ million}$$

Thus, the break point for debt would occur before the break point for retained earnings, which occurs at $61 million.

Capital Structure

Earlier, when we calculated the weighted average cost of capital for use in capital budgeting, we took the capital structure weights, or the mix of securities the firm uses to finance its assets, as a given. However, if the weights are changed, the calculated cost of capital, and thus the set of acceptable projects, will also change. Further, changing the capital structure will affect the riskiness inherent in the firm's common stock, and this will affect the return demanded by stockholders, k_s, and the stock's price, P_0. Therefore, the choice of a capital structure is an important decision. In this section, we discuss concepts relating to capital structure decisions.

The Target Capital Structure

Firms can choose whatever mix of debt and equity they desire to finance their assets, subject to the willingness of investors to provide such funds. And, as we shall see, many different mixes of debt and equity, or **capital structures,** exist. In some firms, such as **Chrysler Corporation**, debt accounts for more than 70% of the financing, while other firms, like **Microsoft**, have little or no debt. In the next few sections, we will discuss factors that affect a firm's capital structure, and we will conclude a firm should attempt to determine what its optimal, or best, mix of financing should be. But it will become apparent that determining the exact optimal capital structure is not a science, so after analyzing a number of factors, a firm establishes a **target capital structure** it believes is optimal, and which it uses as guidance for raising funds in the future. This target might change over time as conditions vary, but at any given moment the firm's management has a specific capital structure in mind, and individual financing decisions should be consistent with this target. If the actual proportion of debt is below the target level, new funds probably will be raised by issuing debt, whereas if the proportion of debt is above the target, stock probably will be sold to bring the firm back in line with the target ratio.

Capital structure policy involves a trade-off between risk and return. Using more debt raises the riskiness of the firm's earnings stream, but a higher proportion of debt generally leads to a higher expected rate of return; and, we know that the higher risk associated with greater debt tends to lower the stock's price. At the same time, however, the higher expected rate of return makes the stock more attractive to investors, which, in turn, ultimately increases the stock's price. Therefore, *the optimal capital structure is the one that strikes a balance between risk and return to achieve our ultimate goal of maximizing the price of the stock.*

Four primary factors influence capital structure decisions.

1. The first is the firm's *business risk,* or the riskiness that would be inherent in the firm's operations if it used no debt. The greater the firm's business risk, the lower the amount of debt that is optimal.

2. The second key factor is the firm's *tax position.* A major reason for using debt is that interest is tax deductible, which lowers the effective cost of debt. However, if much of a firm's income is already sheltered from taxes by accelerated depreciation or tax loss carryovers, its tax rate will be low, and debt will not be as advantageous as it would be to a firm with a higher effective tax rate.

3. The third important consideration is *financial flexibility,* or the ability to raise capital on reasonable terms under adverse conditions. Corporate treasurers know that a steady supply of capital is necessary for stable operations, which in turn are vital for long-run success. They also know that when money is tight in the economy, or when a firm is experiencing operating difficulties, a strong balance sheet is needed to obtain funds from suppliers of capital. Thus, it might be advantageous to issue equity to strengthen the firm's capital base and financial stability.

4. The fourth debt-determining factor has to do with *managerial attitude (conservatism or aggressiveness)* with regard to borrowing. Some managers are more aggressive than others; hence, some firms are more inclined to use debt in an effort to boost profits. This factor does not affect the optimal, or value-maximizing, capital structure, but it does influence the target capital structure a firm actually establishes.

These four points largely determine the target capital structure, but, as we shall see, operating conditions can cause the actual capital structure to vary from the target at any given time. For example, the debt/assets ratio of **Unisys** clearly has been much higher than its target, and the company has taken some significant corrective actions in recent years to improve its financial position.

Determining the Optimal Capital Structure

We can illustrate the effects of financial leverage using the data shown in Exhibit 700.36 for an illustrative company, which we will call OptiCap. As shown in the top section of the table, the company has no debt. Should it continue the policy of using no debt, or should it start using financial leverage? If it does decide to substitute debt for equity, how far should it go? As in all such decisions, the correct answer is that it should *choose the combination of debt and equity, or a capital structure, that will maximize the price of the firm's stock.*

EBIT/EPS Analysis of the Effects of Financial Leverage

Changes in the use of debt will cause changes in earnings per share and, consequently, in the stock price. To understand the relationship between financial leverage and earnings per share (EPS), first consider Exhibit 700.37, which shows how OptiCap's cost of debt would vary if it used different percentages of debt in its capital structure. Naturally, the higher the percentage of debt, the riskier the debt, hence the higher the interest rate lenders will charge.

Now consider Exhibit 700.38, which shows how expected EPS varies with changes in financial leverage. Section I of Exhibit 700.38 begins with a probability distribution of sales; we assume for simplicity that sales can take on only three values, $100,000, $200,000, or $300,000. In the remainder of Section I, we calculate earnings before interest and taxes (EBIT) at each of the three sales levels. Note that we assume both sales and operating costs are independent of financial leverage. Therefore, the three EBIT figures ($0, $40,000, and $80,000) will always remain the same, no matter how much debt OptiCap uses.

Exhibit 700.36 *Data on OptiCap*

I. Balance Sheet on 12/31/00

Current assets	$100,000	Debt	$ 0
Net fixed assets	100,000	Common equity (10,000 shares)	200,000
Total assets	$200,000	Total liabilities and equity	$200,000

II. Income Statement for 2000

Sales		$200,000
Fixed operating costs	$(40,000)	
Variable operating costs (60%)	(120,000)	(160,000)
Earnings before interest and taxes (EBIT)		$ 40,000
Interest		0
Taxable income		$ 40,000
Taxes (40%)		(16,000)
Net income		$ 24,000

Other Data

1. Earnings per share = EPS = $24,000/10,000 shares = $2.40.
2. Dividends per share = DPS = $24,000/10,000 shares = $2.40. Thus, OptiCap pays out all its earnings as dividends.
3. Book value per share = $200,000/10,000 shares = $20.
4. Market price per share = P_0 = $20. Thus, the stock sells at its book value, so (Market price)/(Book price) = M/B = 1.0.
5. Price/earnings ratio = P/E = $20/$2.40 = 8.33 times.

Exhibit 700.37 *Interest Rates for OptiCap With Different Debt/Asset Ratios*

Amount Borrowed[a]	Debt/Assets Ratio	Interest Rate, k_d, on All Debt
$ 20,000	10%	8.0%
40,000	20	8.3
60,000	30	9.0
80,000	40	10.0
100,000	50	12.0
120,000	60	15.0

[a]We assume that the firm must borrow in increments of $20,000. We also assume that OptiCap is unable to borrow more than $120,000, or 60% of assets, because of restrictions in its corporate charter.

Section II of Exhibit 700.38, the zero-debt case, calculates OptiCap's earnings per share at each sales level under the assumption that the company continues to use no debt. Net income is divided by the 10,000 shares outstanding to obtain EPS (remember there is no preferred stock). If sales are as low as $100,000, EPS will be zero, but it will rise to $4.80 at a sales level of $300,000. The EPS at each sales level then is multiplied by the probability of that sales level and summed to calculate the expected EPS, which is $2.40. We also calculate the standard deviation of EPS and the coefficient of variation as indicators of the firm's risk at a zero debt/assets ratio: $\sigma_{EPS} = \$1.52$, and $CV_{EPS} = 0.63$.

Section III of Exhibit 700.38 shows the financial results that could be expected if OptiCap were financed with a debt/assets ratio of 50%. In this situation, $100,000 of the $200,000 total capital would be debt. The interest rate on the debt, 12%, is taken from Exhibit 700.37. With $100,000 of 12% debt outstanding, the company's interest expense in Exhibit 700.38 would be $12,000 per year. This is a fixed cost—it is the same regardless of the level of sales—and it is deducted from the EBIT values as calculated in the top section. With debt = 0, there would be 10,000 shares outstanding. However, if half of the equity were replaced by debt so that debt = $100,000, there would be only 5,000 shares outstanding, and we must use this fact to determine the EPS figures that would result at each of the three possible sales levels. With a debt/assets ratio of 50%, the EPS figure would be −$1.44 if sales were as low as $100,000; it would rise to $3.36 if sales were $200,000; and it would soar to $8.16 if sales were as high as $300,000.

We see, then, that using leverage has both good and bad effects: higher leverage increases expected earnings per share (in this example, until the debt/assets [D/A] ratio equals 50%), but it also increases the firm's risk. Clearly, the debt/assets ratio should not exceed 50%, but where, in the range of 0 to 50%, should it be set? This issue is discussed in the following sections.

EPS Indifference Analysis

Another way of considering the data on OptiCap's two financing methods is through the use of **EPS indifference point**—that is, the point at which EPS is the same regardless of whether the firm uses debt or common stock. At a low level of sales, EPS is much higher if stock rather than debt is used. However, the debt line has a steeper slope, showing that earnings per share will go up faster with increases in sales if debt is used. The two lines cross at sales of $160,000. Below that level, EPS would be higher if the firm uses more common stock; above it, debt financing would produce higher earnings per share.

Degree of Leverage

In Section 720, we showed that leverage, whether operating or financial, is created when a firm has fixed costs associated either with its sales and production operations or with the types of financing it uses. We also found that the two types of leverage, operating and financial, are interrelated. Therefore, if OptiCap *reduced* its operating leverage, this probably would lead to an *increase* in its optimal use of financial leverage. On the other hand, if the firm decided to *increase* its operating leverage, its optimal capital structure probably would call for *less* debt.

Exhibit 700.38 *OptiCap: EPS With Different Amounts of Financial Leverage (thousands of dollars, except per-share figures)*

I. Calculation of EBIT			
Probability of indicated sales	0.2	0.6	0.2
Sales	$ 100.0	$ 200.0	$ 300.0
Fixed costs	(40.0)	(40.0)	(40.0)
Variable costs (60% of sales)	(60.0)	(120.0)	(180.0)
Total costs (except interest)	$(100.0)	$(160.0)	$(220.0)
Earnings before interest and taxes (EBIT)	$ 0.0	$ 40.0	$ 80.0
II. Situation If Debt/Assets (D/A) = 0%			
EBIT (from Section I)	$ 0.0	$ 40.0	$ 80.0
Less interest	(0.0)	(0.0)	(0.0)
Earnings before taxes (EBT)	$0.0	$ 40.0	$ 80.0
Taxes (40%)	(0.0)	(16.0)	(32.0)
Net income	$ 0.0	$ 24.0	$ 48.0
Earnings per share (EPS) on 10,000 shares[a]	$ 0.0	$ 2.40	$ 4.80
Expected EPS		$ 2.40	
Standard deviation of EPS		$ 1.52	
Coefficient of variation		0.63	
III. Situation If Debt/Assets (D/A) = 50%			
EBIT (from Section I)	$ 0.0	$ 40.0	$ 80.0
Less interest (0.12 × $100,000)	(12.0)	(12.0)	(12.0)
Earnings before taxes (EBT)	$(12.0)	$ 28.0	$ 68.0
Taxes (40%; tax credit on losses)	4.8	(11.2)	(27.2)
Net income	$(7.2)	$ 16.8	$ 40.8
Earnings per share (EPS) on 5,000 shares[a]	$(1.44)	$ 3.36	$ 8.16
Expected EPS		$ 3.36	
Standard deviation of EPS		$ 3.04	
Coefficient of variation		0.90	

[a]The EPS figures can also be obtained using the following formula, in which the numerator amounts to an income statement at a given sales level laid out horizontally:

$$EPS = \frac{(Sales - Fixed\ costs - Variable\ costs - Interest)(1 - Tax\ rate)}{Shares\ outstanding} = \frac{(EBIT - I)(1 - T)}{Shares\ outstanding}$$

For example, with zero debt and Sales = $200,000, EPS is $2.40:

$$EPS_{D/A=0} = \frac{\$200{,}000 - \$40{,}000 - \$120{,}000 - 0)(0.6)}{10{,}000} = \$2.40$$

With 50% debt and Sales = $200,000, EPS is $3.36:

$$EPS_{D/A=0.5} = \frac{(\$200{,}000 - \$40{,}000 - \$120{,}000 - \$12{,}000)(0.6)}{5{,}000} = \$3.36$$

The sales level at which EPS will be equal under the two financing policies, or the indifference level of sales, S_I, can be found by setting $EPS_{D/A=0}$ equal to $EPS_{D/A=0.5}$ and solving for S_I:

$$EPS_{D/A=0} = \frac{S_I - \$40{,}000 - 0.6S_I - 0)(0.6)}{10{,}000} = \frac{S_I - \$400{,}000 - 0.6S_I - \$12{,}000)(0.6)}{5{,}000} = EPS_{D/A=0.5}$$

$S_I = \$160{,}000$

By substituting this value of sales into either equation, we can find EP_{S_I}, the earnings per share at this indifference point. In our example, $EPS_I = \$1.44$.

The theory of finance has not been developed to the point where we can actually specify simultaneously the optimal levels of operating and financial leverage. However, we can see how operating and financial leverage interact through an analysis of the *degree of leverage concept* we introduced in Section 720.

Degree of Operating Leverage (DOL)

The **degree of operating leverage (DOL)** is defined as the percentage change in operating income (that is, earnings before interest and taxes, or EBIT) associated with a given percentage change in sales. Thus, the degree of operating leverage is

$$\text{DOL} = \frac{\text{Percentage change in NOI}}{\text{Percentage change in sales}} = \frac{\left(\frac{\Delta \text{EBIT}}{\text{EBIT}}\right)}{\left(\frac{\Delta \text{Sales}}{\text{Sales}}\right)} = \frac{\left(\frac{\Delta \text{EBIT}}{\text{EBIT}}\right)}{\left(\frac{\Delta Q}{Q}\right)} \tag{7.37}$$

According to Equation 7.37, the DOL is an index number that measures the effect of a change in sales on operating income, or EBIT.

DOL for a particular level of production and sales, Q, can be computed using the following equation.

$$\text{DOL}_Q = \frac{Q(P - V)}{Q(P - V) - F} \tag{7.38}$$

or based on dollar sales rather than units:

$$\text{DOL}_S = \frac{S - VC}{S - VC - F} = \frac{\text{Gross profit}}{\text{EBIT}} \tag{7.38a}$$

Here, Q is the initial units of output, P is the average sales price per unit of output, V is the variable cost per unit, F is fixed operating costs, S is initial sales in dollars, and VC is total variable costs. Equation 7.38 normally is used to analyze a single product, such as **IBM's** PC, whereas Equation 7.38a is used to evaluate an entire firm with many types of products for which "quantity in units" and "sales price" are not meaningful.

Applying Equation 7.38a to data for OptiCap at a sales level of $200,000 as shown back in Exhibit 700.38, we find its degree of operating leverage to be 2.0.

$$\text{DOL}_{\$200,000} = \frac{\$200,000 - \$120,000}{\$200,000 - \$120,000 - \$40,000} = \frac{\$80,000}{\$40,000} = 2.0\times$$

Thus, for every 1% change (increase or decrease) in sales there will be a 2% change (increase or decrease) in EBIT. This situation is confirmed by examining Section I of Exhibit 700.38, where we see that a 50% increase in sales, from $200,000 to $300,000, causes EBIT to double. Note, however, that if sales decrease by 50%, then EBIT will decrease by 100%; according to Exhibit 700.38, EBIT decreases to $0 if sales decrease to $100,000.

Note also that the DOL is specific to the initial sales level; thus, if we evaluated OptiCap from a sales base of $300,000, there would be a different DOL.

$$\text{DOL}_{\$300,000} = \frac{\$300,000 - \$180,000}{\$300,000 - \$180,000 - \$40,000} = \frac{\$120,000}{\$80,000} = 1.5\times$$

In general, if a firm is operating at close to its breakeven level, the degree of operating leverage will be high, but DOL declines the higher the base level of sales is above breakeven sales.

Degree of Financial Leverage (DFL)

Operating leverage affects earnings before interest and taxes (EBIT), whereas financial leverage affects earnings after interest and taxes, or the earnings available to common stockholders. In terms of Exhibit 700.38, operating leverage affects the top section, whereas financial leverage affects the lower sections. *Financial leverage takes over where operating leverage leaves off, further magnifying the effects on earnings per share of changes in the level of sales.*

The **degree of financial leverage (DFL)** is defined as the percentage change in earnings per share that results from a given percentage change in earnings before interest and taxes (EBIT), and it is calculated as follows.

$$\text{DFL} = \frac{\text{Percent change in EPS}}{\text{Percentage change in EBIT}} = \frac{\left(\frac{\Delta \text{EPS}}{\text{EPS}}\right)}{\left(\frac{\Delta \text{EBIT}}{\text{EBIT}}\right)} = \frac{\text{EBIT}}{\text{EBIT} - I} \quad (7.39)$$

At sales of \$200,000 and an EBIT of \$40,000, the degree of financial leverage when OptiCap has a 50% debt/assets ratio is

$$\text{DFL}_{S=\$200{,}000,\ \text{Debt/TA}=50\%} = \frac{\$40{,}000}{\$40{,}000 - \$12{,}000} = 1.43\times$$

Therefore, a 100% change (increase or decrease) in EBIT would result in a 100(1.43) = 143% change (increase or decrease) in earnings per share. This can be confirmed by referring to the lower section of Exhibit 700.38, where we see that a 100% increase in EBIT, from \$40,000 to \$80,000, produces a 143% increase in EPS.

$$\%\Delta \text{EPS} = \frac{\Delta \text{EPS}}{\text{EPS}_0} = \frac{\$8.16 - \$3.36}{\$3.36} = \frac{\$4.80}{\$3.36} = 1.43 = 143\%$$

If no debt were used, the degree of financial leverage would by definition be 1.0, so a 100% increase in EBIT would produce exactly a 100% increase in EPS. This can be confirmed from the data in Section II of Exhibit 700.38.

Degree of Total Leverage (DTL)

We have seen that (1) the greater the degree of operating leverage (or fixed operating costs), the more sensitive EBIT will be to changes in sales, and (2) the greater the degree of financial leverage (fixed financial costs), the more sensitive EPS will be to changes in EBIT. Therefore, if a firm uses a considerable amount of both operating and financial leverage, then even small changes in sales will lead to wide fluctuations in EPS.

Equation 7.38 for the degree of operating leverage can be combined with Equation 7.39 for the degree of financial leverage to produce the equation for the **degree of total leverage (DTL),** which shows how a given change in sales will affect earnings per share. Here are three equivalent equations for DTL.

$$\text{DTL} = (\text{DOL}) \times (\text{DFL})$$

$$\text{DTL} = \frac{Q(P - V)}{A(P - V) - F - I}$$

$$\text{DTL} = \frac{S - VC}{S - VC - F - I} = \frac{\text{Gross profit}}{\text{EBIT} - I} \quad (7.40)$$

For OptiCap at sales of \$200,000, we can substitute data from Exhibit 700.37 into Equation 7.40 to find the degree of total leverage if the debt ratio is 50%.

$$\text{DTL}_{S=\$200{,}000,\ \text{Debt/TA}=50\%} = \frac{\$200{,}000 - \$120{,}000}{\$200{,}000 - \$120{,}000 - \$40{,}000 - \$12{,}000} = \frac{\$80{,}000}{\$28{,}000}$$
$$= 2.00 \times 1.43 = 2.86\times$$

We can use the degree of total leverage (DTL) to find the new earnings per share (EPS1) for any given percentage increase in sales, proceeding as follows.

$$\begin{aligned}\text{EPS}_1 &= \text{EPS}_0 + \text{EPS}_0[(\text{DTL}) \times (\%\Delta \text{Sales})] \\ &= \text{EPS}_0[1.0 + (\text{DTL}) \times (\%\Delta \text{Sales})]\end{aligned} \quad (7.41)$$

For example, a 50% (or 0.5) increase in sales, from \$200,000 to \$300,000, would cause EPS$_0$ (\$3.36 as shown in Section III of Exhibit 700.38) to increase to \$8.16.

$$\text{EPS}_1 = \$3.36[1.0 + (2.86)(0.5)] = \$3.36(2.43) = \$8.16.$$

This figure agrees with the one for EPS shown in Exhibit 700.38.

The degree of leverage concept is useful primarily for the insights it provides regarding the joint effects of operating and financial leverage on earnings per share. The concept can be used to show management the impact of financing the firm with debt versus common stock. For example, management might find that the current capital structure is such that a 10% decline in sales would produce a 50% decline in earnings, whereas with a different financing package, thus a different degree of total leverage, a 10% sales decline would cause earnings to decline by only 20%. Having the alternatives stated in this manner gives decision makers a better idea of the ramifications of alternative financing plans, hence different capital structures.

Liquidity and Capital Structure

There are some practical difficulties with the type of analysis described in the previous section, including the following.

1. It is virtually impossible to determine exactly how either P/E ratios or equity capitalization rates (k_s values) are affected by different degrees of financial leverage. The best we can do is make educated guesses about these relationships.
2. The managers might be more or less conservative than the average stockholder, so management might set a somewhat different target capital structure than the one that would maximize the stock price. The managers of a publicly owned firm never would admit this because, unless they owned voting control, they would be removed from office very quickly. However, in view of the uncertainties about what constitutes the value-maximizing capital structure, management could always say that the target capital structure employed is, in its judgment, the value-maximizing structure, and it would be difficult to prove otherwise. Still, if management is far off target, especially on the low side, then chances are very high that some other firm or management group will take over the company, increase its leverage, and thereby raise its value.
3. Managers of large firms, especially those that provide vital services such as electricity or telephones, have a responsibility to provide continuous service; therefore, they must refrain from using leverage to the point where the firms' long-run survivals are endangered. Long-run viability might conflict with short-run stock price maximization and capital cost minimization.

For all these reasons, managers are concerned about the effects of financial leverage on the risk of bankruptcy, and an analysis of this factor is therefore an important input in all capital structure decisions. Accordingly, managers give considerable weight to financial strength indicators such as the **times-interest-earned (TIE) ratio,** which is computed by dividing earnings before interest and taxes by interest expense. Remember that the TIE ratio provides an indication of how well the firm can cover its interest payments with operating income (EBIT)—the lower this ratio, the higher the probability that a firm will default on its debt and be forced into bankruptcy.

Particular attention should be given to the times-interest-earned (TIE) ratio because it gives a measure of how safe the debt is and how vulnerable the company is to financial distress. The TIE ratio depends on three factors: (1) the percentage of debt, (2) the interest rate on the debt, and (3) the company's profitability. Generally, the least leveraged industries, such as the drug and electronics industries, have the highest coverage ratios, whereas the utility industry, which finances heavily with debt, has a low average coverage ratio.

Capital Structure Theory

Over the years, researchers have proposed numerous theories to explain what firms' capital structures should be and why firms have different capital structures. The general theories of capital structure have been developed along two main lines: (1) tax benefit/bankruptcy cost trade-off theory and (2) signaling theory. These two theories are discussed in this section.

Tax Benefit/Bankruptcy Cost Trade-Off Theory

Modern capital structure theory began in 1958, when Professors Franco Modigliani and Merton Miller (hereafter MM) published what is considered by many to be the most influential finance article ever written.[4] MM proved—under a very restrictive set of assumptions, including that there exist no personal income taxes, no brokerage costs, and no bankruptcy—that due to the tax deductibility of interest on corporate debt, a firm's value rises continuously as more debt is used, and hence its value will be maximized by financing almost entirely with debt.

Because several of the assumptions outlined by MM obviously were, and are, unrealistic, MM's position was only the beginning of capital structure research. Subsequent researchers, and MM themselves, extended the basic theory by relaxing the assumptions. Other researchers attempted to test the various theoretical models with actual data to see exactly how stock prices and capital costs are affected by capital structure. Both the theoretical and the empirical results have added to our understanding of capital structure, but none of these studies has produced results that can be used to precisely identify a firm's optimal capital structure.

Signaling Theory

MM assumed that investors have the same information about a firm's prospects as its managers—this is called **symmetric information** because both those who are inside the firm (managers and employees) and those who are outside the firm (investors) have identical information. However, we know that in fact managers generally have better information about their firms than do outside investors. This is called **asymmetric information,** and it has an important effect on decisions to use either debt or equity to finance capital projects.

The conclusions are that firms with extremely bright prospects prefer not to finance through new stock offerings, whereas firms with poor prospects do like to finance with outside equity. How would you, as an investor, react to these conclusions? You ought to say, "If I see that a company plans to issue new stock, this should worry me because I know that management would not want to issue stock if future prospects looked good, but it would want to issue stock if things looked bad. Therefore, I should lower my estimate of the firm's value, other things held constant, if I read an announcement of a new stock offering." Of course, the negative reaction would be stronger if the stock sale was by a large, established company such as **GM** or **IBM**, which surely would have many financing options, than if it was by a small company such as **USR Industries**. For USR, a stock sale might mean truly extraordinary investment opportunities that were so large that they just could not be financed without a stock sale.

If you gave the preceding answer, your views are completely consistent with those of many sophisticated portfolio managers of institutions such as **Morgan Guaranty Trust**. *So, simply stated, the announcement of a stock offering by a mature firm that seems to have multiple financing alternatives is taken as a* **signal** *that the firm's prospects as seen by its management are not bright*. This, in turn, suggests that when a mature firm announces a new stock offering, the price of its stock should decline. Empirical studies have shown that this situation does indeed exist.

What are the implications of all this for capital structure decisions? The answer is that firms should, in normal times, maintain a **reserve borrowing capacity** that can be used in the event that some especially good investment opportunities come along. *This means that firms should generally use less debt than would be suggested by the tax benefit/bankruptcy cost trade-off.*

If you find our discussion of capital structure theory somewhat inexact, you are not alone. In truth, no one knows how to identify precisely the optimal capital structure for a firm or how to measure precisely the effect of the firm's capital structure on either its value or its cost of capital. In real life, capital structure decisions must be made more on the basis of judgment than numerical analysis. Still, an understanding of the theoretical issues as presented here is essential to making sound judgments on capital structure issues.

Dividend Policy

We refer to the cash payments, or distributions, made to stockholders from the firm's earnings, whether those earnings were generated in the current period or in previous periods, as **dividends.** Consequently, a firm's *dividend policy* involves the decision to pay out earnings or to retain them for reinvestment in the firm. Remember that, according to the constant dividend growth model, the value of common stock can be computed as $P_0 = \hat{D}_1/(k_s - g)$. This equation shows that if the firm adopts a policy of paying out more cash dividends, $\hat{D}_1$ will rise, which will tend to increase the price of the stock. However, if cash dividends are increased, then less money will be available for reinvestment and the expected future growth rate, g, will be lowered, which will depress the price of the stock. Thus, changing the dividend has two opposing effects. *The* **optimal dividend policy** *for a firm strikes that balance between current dividends and future growth that maximizes the price of the stock.*

In this section, we first examine factors that affect the optimal dividend policy and the types of dividend policies generally used by firms.

Dividend Policy and Stock Value

How do dividend policy decisions affect a firm's stock price? Academic researchers have studied this question extensively for many years, and they have yet to reach definitive conclusions. On the one hand, there are those who suggest that dividend policy is *irrelevant* because they argue a firm's value should be determined by the basic earning power and business risk of the firm, in which case value depends only on the income (cash) produced, not on how the income is split between dividends and retained earnings (and hence growth).

Proponents of this line of reasoning, called the **dividend irrelevance theory,** would contend that investors care *only* about the *total returns* they receive, not whether they receive those returns in the form of dividends or capital gains. Thus, *if the dividend irrelevance theory is correct, there exists no optimal dividend policy because dividend policy does not affect the value of the firm.*

On the other hand, it is quite possible that investors prefer one dividend policy over another; if so, a firm's dividend policy is *relevant*. For example, it has been argued that investors prefer to receive dividends "today" because current dividend payments are more certain than the future capital gains that *might* result from investing retained earnings in growth opportunities, so k_s should decrease as the dividend payout is increased.[5]

Another factor that might cause investors to prefer a particular dividend policy is the tax effect of dividend receipts. Investors must pay taxes at the time dividends and capital gains are received. Thus, depending on his or her tax situation, an investor might prefer either a payout of current earnings as dividends, which would be taxed in the current period, or capital gains associated with growth in stock value, which would be taxed when the stock is sold, perhaps many years in the future and perhaps at different rates than dividends. Investors who prefer to delay the impact of taxes would be willing to pay more for low payout companies than for otherwise similar high payout companies, and vice versa.

Those who believe the firm's dividend policy is relevant are proponents of the **dividend relevance theory,** which asserts dividend policy can affect the value of a firm through investors' preferences.

Investors and Dividend Policy

Although academic researchers have studied the dividend policy issue extensively, the issue remains unresolved; researchers at this time simply cannot tell corporate decision makers exactly how dividend policy affects stock prices and capital costs. But from the research, some views have been presented concerning investors' reactions to dividend policy changes and why firms have particular dividend policies. Three of these views are discussed in this section.

Information Content, or Signaling, Hypothesis

If investors expect a company's dividend to increase by 5% per year, and if, in fact, the dividend is increased by 5%, then the stock price generally will not change significantly on the day the dividend increase is announced. In Wall Street parlance, such a dividend increase would be "discounted," or *anticipated,* by the market. However, if investors expect a 5% increase, but the company actually increases the dividend by 25%—say from $2 to $2.50—this generally would be accompanied by an increase in the price of the stock. Conversely, a less-than-expected dividend increase, or a reduction, generally would result in a price decline.

It is a well-known fact that corporations are extremely reluctant to cut dividends and, therefore, *managers do not raise dividends unless they anticipate higher, or at least stable, earnings in the future to sustain the higher dividends.* This means that a larger-than-expected dividend increase is taken by investors as a *signal* that the firm's management forecasts improved future earnings, whereas a dividend reduction signals a forecast of poor earnings. Thus, it can be argued investors' reactions to changes in dividend payments do not show that investors prefer dividends to retained earnings; rather, the stock price changes simply indicate important information is contained in dividend announcements—in effect, dividend announcements provide investors with information previously known only to management. This theory is referred to as the **information content,** or **signaling, hypothesis.**

Clientele Effect

It also has been shown that it is very possible that a firm sets a particular dividend payout policy, which then attracts a *clientele* consisting of those investors who like the firm's dividend policy. For example, some stockholders, such as retired individuals, prefer current income to future capital gains, so they want the firm to pay out a higher percentage of its earnings. Other stockholders have no need for current investment income, so they favor a low payout ratio. If investors could not invest in companies with different dividend policies, it might be very expensive for them to achieve their investment goals—investors that prefer capital gains could reinvest any dividends they receive, but they first would have to pay taxes on the income. In essence, then, a **clientele effect** might exist if stockholders are attracted to companies because they have particular dividend policies. Those investors who desire current investment income can purchase shares in high-dividend-payout firms, whereas those who do not need current cash income can invest in low-payout firms. Consequently, we would expect the stock price of a firm to change if the firm changes its dividend policy, because investors will adjust their portfolios to include firms with the desired dividend policy.

Free Cash Flow Hypothesis

If it is the intent of the financial manager to maximize the value of the firm, then investors should prefer that firms pay dividends only if acceptable capital budgeting opportunities do not exist. We know that acceptable capital budgeting projects increase the value of the firm. We also know that, because flotation costs are incurred when issuing new stock, it costs a firm more to raise funds using new common equity than it does using retained earnings. So to maximize value, wherever possible a firm should use retained earnings rather than issue new common stock to finance capital budgeting projects. Thus, dividends should be paid only when *free cash flows* in excess of capital budgeting needs exist. If management does otherwise, the firm's value will not be maximized. According to the **free cash flow hypothesis,** the firm should distribute any earnings that cannot be reinvested at a rate at least as great as the investors' required rate of return, k_s (that is, the free cash flows). Everything else equal, firms that retain *free cash flows* will have lower values than firms that distribute *free cash flows* because the firms that retain free cash flows actually decrease investors' wealth by investing in projects with IRR $<$ k_s.

The free cash flow hypothesis might help to explain why investors react differently to identical dividend changes made by similar firms. For example, a firm's stock price should not change dramatically if it reduces its dividend for the purposes of investing in capital budgeting projects with positive NPVs. On the other hand, a company that reduces its dividend simply to increase free cash flows should experience a significant decline in the market value of its stock because the dividend reduction is not in the best interests of the stockholders—in this case, an agency problem exists. Thus, the free cash flow hypothesis suggests the dividend policy can provide information about the firm's behavior with respect to wealth maximization.

Dividend Policy in Practice

We have provided some insights concerning the relevance of dividend policy and how investors might view dividend payments from firms. However, no one has been able to develop a formula that can be used to tell management specifically how a given dividend policy will affect a firm's stock price. Even so, managements still must establish dividend policies. This section discusses several alternative policies and procedures that are used in practice.

Types of Dividend Payments

The dollar amounts of dividends paid by firms follow a variety of patterns. In general, though, firms pay dividends using one of the four payout policies discussed next.

RESIDUAL DIVIDEND POLICY In practice, dividend policy is very much influenced by investment opportunities and by the availability of funds with which to finance new investments. This fact has led to the development of a **residual dividend policy,** which states that a firm should follow these steps when deciding how much earnings should be paid out as dividends: (1) determine the optimal capital budget for the year, (2) determine the amount of capital needed to finance that budget, (3) use retained earnings to supply the equity component to the extent possible, and (4) pay dividends only if more earnings are available than are needed to support the optimal capital budget. The word *residual* means "left over," and the residual policy implies that dividends should be paid only out of "leftover" earnings.

The basis of the residual policy is the fact that *investors prefer to have the firm retain and reinvest earnings rather than pay them out in dividends if the rate of return the firm can earn on reinvested earnings exceeds the rate investors, on average, can themselves obtain on other investments of comparable risk*. For example, if the corporation can reinvest retained earnings at a 14% rate of return, whereas the best rate the average stockholder can obtain if the earnings are passed on in the form of dividends is 12%, then stockholders should prefer to have the firm retain the profits.

To continue, we saw that the cost of retained earnings is an *opportunity cost* that reflects rates of return available to equity investors. If a firm's stockholders can buy other stocks of equal risk and obtain a 12% dividend-plus-capital-gains yield, then 12% is the firm's cost of retained earnings. The cost of new outside equity raised by selling common stock will be higher than 12% because of the costs associated with the issue.

Most firms have a target capital structure that calls for at least some debt, so new financing is done partly with debt and partly with equity. As long as the firm finances with the optimal mix of debt and equity, and as long as it uses only internally generated equity (retained earnings), its marginal cost of each new dollar of capital will be minimized. Internally generated equity is available for financing a certain amount of new investment, but beyond that amount the firm must turn to more expensive new common stock. At the point where new stock must be sold, the cost of equity, and consequently the marginal cost of capital, rises.

According to the residual dividend policy, a firm that has to issue new common stock to finance capital budgeting needs does not have residual earnings, and dividends will be zero.

Because both the earnings level and the capital budgeting needs of a firm vary from year to year, strict adherence to the residual dividend policy would result in dividend variability—one year the firm might declare zero dividends because investment opportunities are good, but the next year it might pay a large dividend because investment opportunities are poor. Similarly, fluctuating earnings would also lead to variable dividends even if investment opportunities were stable over time. Thus, following the residual dividend policy would be optimal only if investors were not bothered by fluctuating dividends. However, if investors prefer stable, dependable dividends, k_s would be higher, and the stock price lower, if the firm followed the residual theory in a strict sense rather than attempting to stabilize its dividends over time.

STABLE, PREDICTABLE DIVIDENDS In the past, many firms set a specific annual dollar dividend per share and then maintained it, increasing the annual dividend only if it seemed clear that future earnings would be sufficient to allow the new dividend to be maintained. A corollary of that policy was this rule: *Never reduce the annual dividend.*

When the economy expands quickly, inflationary pressures plus reinvested earnings generally tend to push earnings up, so many firms that would otherwise follow the stable dollar dividend payment policy switch to a "stable growth rate" policy. Here the firm sets a target growth rate for dividends (for example, 6% per year) and strives to increase dividends by this amount each year. Obviously, earnings must be growing at a reasonably steady rate for this policy to be feasible, but where it can be followed, such a policy provides investors with a stable real income.

There are two good reasons for paying **stable, predictable dividends** rather than following the residual dividend policy. First, given the existence of the information content, or signaling, idea, a fluctuating payment policy would lead to greater uncertainty, hence to a higher k_s and a lower stock price, than would exist under a stable policy. Second, many stockholders use dividends for current consumption, and they would be put to trouble and expense if they had to sell part of their shares to obtain cash if the company cut the dividend.

As a rule, stable, predictable dividends imply more certainty than variable dividends, thus a lower k_s and a higher firm value. So it is this dividend policy most firms favor. Even though the optimal dividend as prescribed by the residual policy might vary somewhat from year to year, a firm might delay some investment projects, depart from its target capital structure during a particular year, or even issue new common stock to avoid the problems associated with unstable dividends, and thus provide a lower k_s and a higher firm value.

CONSTANT PAYOUT RATIO It would be possible for a firm to pay out a constant *percentage* of earnings (dividends per share divided by earnings per share), but because earnings surely will fluctuate, this policy would mean that the dollar amount of dividends would vary. For example, if **Eastman Kodak** had followed the policy of paying a constant percentage of earnings per share, say 40%, the dividends per share paid since 1978 would have fluctuated exactly the same as earnings per share and thus the company would have had to cut its dividend in several different years. Therefore, with the **constant payout ratio** dividend policy, if earnings fluctuate, investors would have had much greater uncertainty concerning the expected dividends each year, and chances are k_s also would be greater; hence, its stock price would be lower. Although Kodak's stock price has fluctuated somewhat, it has shown a general upward trend since the 1980s, in spite of the substantial earnings fluctuations. Had it cut the dividend to keep the payout ratio constant, Kodak's stock price would have "fallen out of bed" several times if investors interpreted the dividend reduction as a signal that management thought the earnings declines were permanent.

LOW REGULAR DIVIDEND PLUS EXTRAS A policy of paying a low regular dividend plus a year-end extra in good years is a compromise between a stable dividend (or stable growth rate) and a constant payout rate. Such a policy gives the firm flexibility, yet investors can count on receiving at least a minimum dividend. Therefore, if a firm's earnings and cash flows are quite volatile, this policy might be its best choice. The directors can set a relatively low regular dividend—low enough so that it can be maintained even in low-profit years or in years when a considerable amount of retained earnings is needed for investments—and then supplement it with an **extra dividend** in years when excess funds are available. **Ford**, **General Motors**, and other auto companies, whose earnings fluctuate widely from year to year, formerly followed such a policy, but in recent years they have joined the crowd and now follow our first choice, a stable dividend policy.

Payment Procedures

Dividends normally are paid quarterly, and, when conditions permit, the dividend is increased. For example, on April 9, 1999, the board of directors of Eastman Kodak declared a 44¢ quarterly common stock dividend. Earlier in the year, Kodak's board indicated that it anticipated the annual dividend to be $1.76, which was the same as the dividend paid in 1998. So Kodak's stockholders were not surprised when the 44¢ quarterly dividend was announced; they would have been *shocked* if the dividend had been eliminated, because Kodak has paid a dividend for more than 40 years.

When Kodak declared the dividend, it issued the following statement (www.kodak.com).

> Rochester, NY, April 9—Eastman Kodak Company's Board of Directors voted a quarterly cash dividend of 44 cents a share on the outstanding common stock of the company.
>
> The dividend is payable July 1, 1999, to shareholders of record at the close of business, June 1, 1999.

The three dates included in this announcement are important to current stockholders. These dates, as well as the ex-dividend date, are defined as follows.

1. **Declaration date.** On the *declaration date,* April 9, 1999 in Kodak's case, the board of directors meets and declares the regular dividend. For accounting purposes, the declared dividend becomes an actual liability on the declaration date, and if a balance sheet were constructed, the amount ($0.44) × (Number of shares outstanding) would appear as a current liability, and retained earnings would be reduced by a like amount.

2. **Holder-of-record date.** At the close of business on the **holder-of-record date,** or **date of record,** the company closes its stock transfer books and produces a list of shareholders as of that date. Thus, if Kodak was notified of the sale and transfer of some stock before 5 P.M. on Tuesday, June 1, 1999, then the new owner received the dividend. However, if notification was received after June 1, the previous owner of the stock got the dividend check because his or her name appeared on the company's ownership records.

3. **Ex-dividend date.** The securities industry has set up a convention of declaring that the right to the dividend remains with the stock until two business days *prior* to the holder-of-record date. This is to ensure the company is notified of the transfer in time to record the new owner and thus pay the dividend to him or her. The date when the right to receive the next dividend payment no longer goes with the stock—new purchasers will not receive the next dividend—is called the **ex-dividend date.** In the case of Kodak, the *ex-dividend* date was Friday, May 28, 1999, which is two *business days* before the *holder-of-record* date, Tuesday, June 1, 1999. Therefore, any investor who purchased the stock on or after that date did not receive the next dividend payment associated with the stock. All else equal, then, we would expect that the price of Kodak's stock dropped on the ex-dividend date approximately by the amount of the dividend—assuming no other price fluctuations, the price at which Kodak's stock opened on Friday, May 28, should have been about 44 cents less than the close on Thursday, May 27. The price of the stock actually decreased by a little more than 44 cents due to other factors, including a general market decline on that day.

4. **Payment date.** Kodak paid the common stock dividends on July 1, 1999—this is the *payment date.* Recently, many firms have started paying dividends electronically.

Factors Influencing Dividend Policy

In addition to managements' beliefs concerning which dividend theory is most correct, a number of other factors are considered when a particular dividend policy is chosen. The factors firms take into account can be grouped into these four broad categories.

1. **Constraints on dividend payments.** The amount of dividends a firm can pay might be limited due to (1) debt contract restrictions, which often stipulate that no dividends can be paid unless certain financial measures, such as the times-interest-earned ratio, exceed stated minimums; (2) the fact that dividend payments cannot exceed the balance sheet item "retained earnings" (this is known as the *impairment of capital rule,* which is designed to protect creditors by prohibiting the company from distributing assets to stockholders before debtholders are paid); (3) cash availability, because cash dividends can be paid only with cash; and (4) restrictions imposed by the Internal Revenue Service (IRS) on improperly accumulated retained earnings. If the IRS can demonstrate that a firm's dividend payout ratio is being held down deliberately to help its stockholders avoid personal taxes, the firm is subject to heavy tax penalties. But this factor generally is relevant only to privately-owned firms.

2. **Investment opportunities.** Firms that have large numbers of acceptable capital budgeting projects generally have low dividend payout ratios, and vice versa. But if a firm can accelerate or postpone projects (flexibility), then it can adhere more closely to a target dividend policy.

3. **Alternative sources of capital.** When a firm needs to finance a given level of investment and flotation costs are high, k_e will be well above k_s, making it better to set a low payout ratio and to finance through retention rather than through sale of new common stock. Also, if the firm can adjust its debt/assets ratio without raising capital costs sharply, it can maintain a stable dollar dividend, even if earnings fluctuate, by using a variable debt/assets ratio. Another factor considered by management when making financing decisions is ownership dilution—if management is concerned about maintaining control, it might be reluctant to sell new stock; hence, the company might retain more earnings than it otherwise would.
4. **Effects of dividend policy on k_s.** The effects of dividend policy on k_s might be considered in terms of four factors: (a) stockholders' desire for current versus future income, (b) the perceived riskiness of dividends versus capital gains, (c) the tax advantage of capital gains over dividends, and (d) the information content of dividends (signaling). Because we discussed each of these factors earlier, we need only note here that the importance of each factor in terms of its effect on k_s varies from firm to firm depending on the makeup of its current and possible future stockholders.

It should be apparent from our discussions that dividend policy decisions truly are exercises in informed judgment, not decisions that can be quantified precisely. Even so, to make rational dividend decisions, financial managers must consider all of the points discussed in the preceding sections.

Stock Dividends and Stock Splits

Stock dividends and stock splits are related to the firm's cash dividend policy. The rationale for stock dividends and splits can best be explained through an example. We will use Porter Electronic Controls Inc., a $700 million electronic components manufacturer, for this purpose. Since its inception, Porter's markets have been expanding, and the company has enjoyed growth in sales and earnings. Some of its earnings have been paid out in dividends, but some are also retained each year, causing earnings per share and market price per share to grow. The company began its life with only a few thousand shares outstanding, and, after some years of growth, each of Porter's shares had a very high earnings per share (EPS) and dividends per share (DPS). When a "normal" price/earnings (P/E) ratio was applied, the derived market price was so high that few people could afford to buy a "round lot" of 100 shares. This limited the demand for the stock and thus kept the total market value of the firm below what it would have been if more shares, at a lower price, had been outstanding. To correct this situation, Porter "split its stock," as described next.

Stock Splits

Although there is little empirical evidence to support the contention, there is nevertheless a widespread belief in financial circles that an *optimal, or psychological, price range* exists for stocks. "Optimal" means that if the price is within this range, the P/E ratio, hence the value of the firm, will be maximized. Many observers, including Porter's management, believe that the best range for most stocks is from $20 to $80 per share. Accordingly, if the price of Porter's stock rose to $80, management probably would declare a two-for-one **stock split,** thus doubling the number of shares outstanding, halving the earnings and dividends per share, and thereby lowering the price of the stock. Each stockholder would have more shares, but each share would be worth less. If the post-split price were $40, Porter's stockholders would be exactly as well off as they were before the split because they would have twice as many shares at half the price as before the split. However, if the price of the stock were to stabilize above $40, stockholders would be better off. Stock splits can be of any size—for example, the stock could be split 2-for-1, 3-for-1, $1\frac{1}{2}$-for-1, or in any other way.

Reverse splits, which reduce the shares outstanding and increase the stock price, can even be used. For instance, a company whose stock sells for $5 might employ a 1-for-5 reverse split, exchanging one new share for five old ones and raising the value of the shares to about $25, which is within the optimal range. On February 11, 1999, for example, **Galaxy Foods** initiated a 1-for-7 reverse split to avoid being delisted from the NASDAQ SmallCap Market.

Stock Dividends

Stock dividends are similar to stock splits in that they "divide the pie into smaller slices" without affecting the fundamental position of the current stockholders. On a 5% stock dividend, the holder of 100 shares would receive an additional five shares (without cost); on a 20% stock dividend, the same holder would receive 20 new shares; and so on. Again, the total number of shares is increased, so earnings, dividends, and price per share all decline.

If a firm wants to reduce the price of its stock, should it use a stock split or a stock dividend? Stock splits generally are used after a sharp price run-up to produce a large price reduction. Stock dividends typically are used on a regular annual basis to keep the stock price more or less constrained. For example, if a firm's earnings and dividends were growing at about 10% per year, its stock price would tend to go up at about that same rate, and it would soon be outside the desired trading range. A 10% annual stock dividend would maintain the stock price within the optimal trading range.

Balance Sheet Effects

Although the economic effects of stock splits and stock dividends are virtually identical, accountants treat them somewhat differently. On a 2-for-1 split, the shares outstanding are doubled, and the stock's par value is halved. This treatment is shown in Section II of Exhibit 700.39 for Porter Electronic Controls, using a pro forma 2001 balance sheet.

Section III of Exhibit 700.39 shows the effect of a 20% stock dividend. With a stock dividend, the par value is not reduced, but an accounting entry is made transferring capital from the retained earnings account to the common stock and paid-in capital accounts. The transfer from retained earnings is calculated as follows.

$$\begin{pmatrix} \text{Dollars transferred} \\ \text{from retained} \\ \text{earnings} \end{pmatrix} = \left[\begin{pmatrix} \text{Number of shares} \\ \text{outstanding} \end{pmatrix} \times \begin{pmatrix} \text{Stock dividend} \\ \text{as a percent} \end{pmatrix} \right] \times \begin{pmatrix} \text{Market price} \\ \text{of the stock} \end{pmatrix} \quad (7.42)$$

Porter has 5 million shares outstanding, and they sell for $80 each, so a 20% stock dividend would require the transfer of $80 million.

$$\text{Dollars transferred} = [(5,000,000)(0.2)](\$80) = \$80,000,000$$

As shown in the exhibit, $1 million of this $80 million is added to the common stock account and $79 million is added to the additional paid-in capital account. The retained earnings account is reduced from $285 million to $205 million.

Exhibit 700.39 *Porter Electronic Controls Inc.: Stockholders' Equity Accounts, Pro Forma, December 31, 2001 (millions of dollars, except per share values)*

I. Before a Stock Split or Stock Dividend	
Common stock (5 million shares outstanding, $1 par)	$ 5.0
Additional paid-in capital	10.0
Retained earnings	285.0
Total common stockholders' equity	$300.0
Book value per share	$ 60.0
II. After a Two-for-One Stock Split	
Common stock (10 million shares outstanding, $0.50 par)	$ 5.0
Additional paid-in capital	10.0
Retained earnings	285.0
Total common stockholders' equity	$300.0
Book value per share	$ 30.0
III. After a 20% Stock Dividend	
Common stock (6 million shares outstanding, $1 par)[a]	$ 6.0
Additional paid-in capital[b]	89.0
Retained earnings[b]	205.0
Total common stockholders' equity	$300.0
Book value per share	$ 50.0

[a] Shares outstanding are increased by 20%, from 5 million to 6 million.

[b] A transfer equal to the market value of the new shares is made from the retained earnings account to the additional paid-in capital and common stock accounts:

Transfer = [(5,000,000 shares)(0.2)]($80) = $80,000,000.

Of this $80 million, ($1 par)(1,000,000 shares) = $1,000,000 goes to common stock and the remaining $79 million to paid-in capital.

Price Effects

Several empirical studies have examined the effects of stock splits and stock dividends on stock prices. These studies suggest that investors see stock splits and stock dividends for what they are—*simply additional pieces of paper*. If stock dividends and splits are accompanied by higher earnings and cash dividends, then investors will bid up the price of the stock. However, if stock dividends are not accompanied by increases in earnings and cash dividends, the dilution of earnings and dividends per share causes the price of the stock to drop by the same percentage as the stock dividend. Thus, the fundamental determinants of price are the underlying earnings and cash dividends per share, and stock splits and stock dividends merely cut the pie into thinner slices.

Dividend Policies Around the World

The dividend policies of companies around the world vary considerably. A recent study found the dividend payout ratios of companies range from 10.5% in the Philippines to nearly 70% in Taiwan.[6] As a percent of earnings, the dividends paid out in Canada, France, Italy, and the United States range from about 20% to 25%, in Spain and the United Kingdom the range is from 30% to 40%, in Germany and Mexico the rate is between 40% and 50%, and it is more than 50% for companies in Japan and Southeast Asian countries.

Why do international differences in dividend policies exist? It seems logical to attribute the differences to dissimilar tax structures because both dividends and capital gains are taxed differently around the world. The tax codes in most developed countries encourage personal investing and savings more than the U.S. Tax Code. For example, Germany, Italy, and many other European countries do not tax capital gains, and in most other developed countries, including Japan, France, and Canada, capital gains are not taxed unless they exceed some minimum amount. Further, in Germany and Italy, dividends are not taxed as income, and in most other countries some amount of dividends is tax-exempt. The general conclusion we can make, then, is that in countries where capital gains are not taxed, investors should show a preference for companies that retain earnings rather than pay dividends. But it has been found that differences in taxes do not explain the differences in dividend payout ratios among the countries.

A study by Rafael La Porta, Florencio Lopez-de-Silanes, Andrei Shleifer, and Robert W. Vishny offers some insight into the dividend policy differences that exist around the world. They suggest that, all else equal, companies pay out greater amounts of earnings as dividends in countries that have measures that help protect the rights of minority stockholders. In such countries, though, firms with many growth opportunities tend to pay lower dividends, which is to be expected because the funds are needed to finance the growth and shareholders are willing to forgo current income in hopes of greater future benefits. On the other hand, in countries where shareholders' rights are not well protected, investors prefer dividends because there is great uncertainty about whether management will use earnings for self-gratification rather than for the benefit of the firm. Investors in these countries accept any dividends they can get—that is, they prefer a "bird in the hand." Some countries, including Brazil, Chile, Colombia, Greece, and Venezuela, have regulations that mandate firms pay dividends. In these countries, minority shareholders have few, if any, legally protected rights.

In summary, it appears the most important factor that determines whether stockholders prefer earnings be retained or paid out as dividends is the level of risk associated with future expected dividends, which is mitigated to some degree by regulations that protect minority shareholders' rights.

Capital Budgeting

Importance of Capital Budgeting

In this section, we apply asset valuation concepts to investment decisions involving the fixed assets of a firm, or *capital budgeting*. Here the term *capital* refers to fixed assets used in production, while a *budget* is a plan that details projected inflows and outflows during some future period. Thus, the capital budget is an outlay of planned expenditures on fixed assets, and **capital budgeting** is the process of analyzing projects and deciding which are acceptable investments and which actually should be purchased.

A number of factors combine to make capital budgeting decisions perhaps the most important ones financial managers must make. First, the impact of capital budgeting is long term; thus, the firm loses some decision-making flexibility when capital projects are purchased. For example, when a firm invests in an asset with a ten-year economic life, its operations are affected for ten years—the firm is "locked in" by the capital budgeting decision. Further, because asset expansion is fundamentally related to expected future sales, a decision to buy a fixed asset that is expected to last ten years involves an implicit ten-year sales forecast.

An error in the forecast of asset requirements can have serious consequences. If the firm invests too much in assets, it will incur unnecessarily heavy expenses. But if it does not spend enough on fixed assets, it might find that inefficient production and inadequate capacity lead to lost sales that are difficult, if not impossible, to recover. Timing is also important in capital budgeting—capital assets must be ready to come "on line" when they are needed; otherwise, opportunities might be lost.

Effective capital budgeting can improve both the timing of asset acquisitions and the quality of assets purchased. A firm that forecasts its needs for capital assets in advance will have an opportunity to purchase and install the assets before they are needed. Unfortunately, many firms do not order capital goods until they approach full capacity or are forced to replace worn-out equipment. If many firms order capital goods at the same time, backlogs result, prices increase, and firms are forced to wait for the delivery of machinery; in general, the quality of the capital goods deteriorates. If a firm foresees its needs and purchases capital assets early, it can avoid these problems.

Finally, capital budgeting is also important because the acquisition of fixed assets typically involves substantial expenditures, and before a firm can spend a large amount of money, it must have the funds available—large amounts of money are not available automatically. Therefore, a firm contemplating a major capital expenditure program must arrange its financing well in advance to be sure the funds required are available.

Generating Ideas for Capital Projects

The same general concepts that we developed for valuing financial assets are involved in capital budgeting. However, whereas a set of stocks and bonds exists in the financial markets, and investors select from this set, capital budgeting projects are created by the firm. For example, a sales representative might report that customers frequently ask for a particular product that the company does not currently produce. The sales manager then discusses the idea with the marketing research group to determine the size of the market for the proposed product. If it appears likely that a significant market does exist, cost accountants and engineers will be asked to estimate production costs. And then if it appears the product can be produced and sold at a sufficient profit, the project will be undertaken.

A firm's growth, and even its ability to remain competitive and to survive, depends on a constant flow of ideas for new products, ways to make existing products better, and ways to produce output at a lower cost. Accordingly, a well-managed firm will go to great lengths to develop good capital budgeting proposals. Some firms even provide incentives to employees to encourage suggestions that lead to beneficial investment proposals. If a firm has capable and imaginative executives and employees, and if its incentive system works properly, many ideas for capital investment will be advanced.

Because some capital investment ideas will be good and others will not, procedures must be established for evaluating the worth of such projects to the firm. Our topic in the remainder of this section is the evaluation of the acceptability of capital projects.

Project Classifications

Capital budgeting decisions generally are termed either *replacement decisions* or *expansion decisions*. **Replacement decisions** involve determining whether capital projects should be purchased to take the place of (replace) existing assets that might be worn out, damaged, or obsolete. Usually the replacement projects are necessary to maintain or improve profitable operations using the existing production levels. On the other hand, if a firm is considering whether to *increase* operations by adding capital projects to existing assets that will help produce either more of its existing products or entirely new products, **expansion decisions** are made.

Some of the capital budgeting decisions involve *independent projects,* while others will involve *mutually exclusive projects*. **Independent projects** are projects whose cash flows are not affected by one another, so the acceptance of one project does not affect the acceptance of the other project(s)—*all independent projects can be purchased if they all are acceptable.* For example, if **Microsoft** decided to purchase the **NBC** television network, it still could produce its computer software. On the other hand, if a capital budgeting decision involves **mutually exclusive projects,** then when one project is taken on, the others must be rejected—*only one mutually exclusive project can be purchased, even if they* *all are acceptable.* For example, **Global Sports and Entertainment, Ltd.** has a parcel of land on which it wants to build either an amusement park or a domed sports arena. The land is not large enough for both alternatives, so if Global chooses to build the amusement park, it could not build the arena, and vice versa.

In general, relatively simple calculations, and only a few supporting documents, are required for replacement decisions, especially maintenance-type investments in profitable plants. More detailed analysis is required for cost-reduction replacements, for expansion of existing product lines, and especially for investments in new products or areas. Also, within each category projects are broken down by their dollar costs: Larger investments require both more detailed analysis and approval at a higher level within the firm. Thus, although a plant manager might be authorized to approve maintenance expenditures up to $10,000 on the basis of a relatively unsophisticated analysis, the full board of directors might have to approve decisions that involve either amounts greater than $1 million or expansions into new products or markets. Statistical data generally are lacking for new product decisions, so here judgments, as opposed to detailed cost data, are especially important.

Similarities Between Capital Budgeting and Asset Valuation

Capital budgeting decisions involve valuation of assets, or projects. Therefore, capital budgeting involves exactly the same steps used in general asset valuation.

1. Determine the cost, or purchase price, of the asset.
2. Estimate the cash flows expected from the project, including the salvage value of the asset at the end of its expected life. This is similar to estimating the future dividend or interest payment stream on a stock or bond, along with the stock's expected selling price or the bond's maturity value.
3. Evaluate the riskiness of the projected cash flows to determine the appropriate rate of return to use for computing the present value of the estimated cash flows. For this assessment, management needs information about the probability distributions of the cash flows.
4. Compute the present value of the expected cash flows to obtain an estimate of the asset's value to the firm. This is equivalent to finding the present value of a stock's expected future dividends.
5. Compare the present value of the future expected cash flows with the initial investment, or cost, required to acquire the asset. Alternatively, the expected rate of return on the project can be calculated and compared with the rate of return considered appropriate for the project.

If an individual investor identifies and invests in a stock or bond whose true value is greater than its market price, the value of the investor's portfolio will increase. Similarly, if a firm identifies (or creates) an investment opportunity with a present value greater than its cost, the value of the firm will increase. Thus, there is a very direct link between capital budgeting and stock values: The more effective the firm's capital budgeting procedures, the higher the price of its stock.

Capital Budgeting Evaluation Techniques

The basic methods used by businesses to evaluate projects and to decide whether they should be accepted for inclusion in the capital budget are (1) payback (PB), (2) net present value (NPV), and (3) internal rate of return (IRR). As you will see, to determine a project's acceptability using any of these three techniques, its expected cash flows are needed. However, unlike the other two, the payback method does not consider the time value of money—so we call payback a *nondiscounting technique* and NPV and IRR *discounting techniques*. We will explain how each evaluation criterion is calculated, and then we will determine how well each performs in terms of identifying those projects that will maximize the firm's stock price.

We use the tabular and time line cash flow data shown in Exhibit 700.40 for Project S and Project L to illustrate all the methods, and throughout this section we assume that the projects are equally risky. Note that the cash flows, $\hat{CF}_t$, are expected values and that they have been adjusted to reflect taxes, depreciation, salvage values, and any other changes in cash flows associated with the capital projects. Also, we assume that all cash flows occur at the end of the designated year. Incidentally, the S stands for *short* and the L for *long:* Project S is a short-term project in the sense that its cash inflows tend to come in sooner than Project L's.

Exhibit 700.40 Net Cash Flows for Project S and Project L

	Expected After-Tax Net Cash Flows, $\hat{CF}_t$	
Year (t)	Project S	Project L
0[a]	$(3,000)	$(3,000)
1	1,500	400
2	1,200	900
3	800	1,300
4	300	1,500

Project S:

0	1	2	3	4
−3,000	1,500	1,200	800	300

Project L:

0	1	2	3	4
−3,000	400	900	1,300	1,500

[a]$\hat{CF}_0$ represents the initial investment, or net cost of the project.

Exhibit 700.41 Payback Period for Project S and Project L

Project S:

	0	1	2	PB$_S$ 3	4
Net cash flow	−3,000	1,500	1,200	800	300
Cumulative net cash flow	−3,000	−1,500	−300	500	800

Project L:

	0	1	2	3	PB$_L$ 4
Net cash flow	−3,000	400	900	1,300	1,500
Cumulative net cash flow	−3,000	−2,600	−1,700	−400	1,100

Payback Period

The **payback period,** defined as the expected number of years required to recover the original investment (the cost of the asset), is the simplest and, as far as we know, the oldest *formal* method used to evaluate capital budgeting projects. To compute a project's payback period, simply add up the expected cash flows for each year until the amount initially invested in the project is recovered. The total amount of time, including the fraction of a year if appropriate, that it takes to recapture the original amount invested is the payback period. The payback calculation process for both Project S and Project L is diagrammed in Exhibit 700.41.

The exact payback period can be found using the following formula.

$$\text{Payback} = \text{PB} = \begin{pmatrix} \text{Number of years before} \\ \text{full recovery of} \\ \text{original investment} \end{pmatrix} + \begin{pmatrix} \dfrac{\text{Uncovered cost at start}}{\text{of full-recovery year}} \\ \dfrac{}{\text{Total cash flow during}} \\ \text{full-recovery year} \end{pmatrix} \quad (7.43)$$

The diagram in Exhibit 700.41 shows that the payback period for Project S is between two years and three years, so, using Equation 7.43, the exact payback period is

$$\text{PB}_S = 2 + \frac{300}{800} = 2.4 \text{ years}$$

Applying the same procedure to Project L, we find Payback$_L$ = 3.3 years.

Using payback to make capital budgeting decisions is based on the concept that it is better to recover the cost of (investment in) a project sooner rather than later. Therefore, Project S is considered better than Project L because it has a lower payback. *As a general rule, a project is considered acceptable if its payback is less than the maximum cost re-*

covery time established by the firm. For example, if the firm requires projects to have a payback of three years or less, Project S would be acceptable but Project L would not.

The payback method is very simple, which explains why payback traditionally has been one of the most popular capital budgeting techniques. But payback ignores the time value of money, so relying solely on this method could lead to incorrect decisions—at least if our goal is to maximize value. If a project has a payback of three years, we know how quickly the initial investment will be covered by the expected cash flows, but this information does not provide any indication of whether the return on the project is sufficient to cover the cost of the funds invested. In addition, when payback is used, the cash flows beyond the payback period are ignored. For example, even if Project L had a fifth year of cash flows equal to $50,000, its payback would remain 3.3 years, which is less desirable than the payback of 2.4 years for Project S. But, with the additional $50,000 cash flow, Project L most likely would be preferred.

Net Present Value (NPV)

To correct for the major defect of any *nondiscounting* technique—ignoring the time value of money—methods were developed to include consideration of the time value of money. One such method is the **net present value (NPV) method,** which relies on **discounted cash flow (DCF) techniques.** To implement this approach, we simply find the present value of all the future cash flows a project is expected to generate and then subtract (add a negative cash flow) its initial investment (original cost) to find the *net* benefit the firm will realize from investing in the project. *If the net benefit computed on a present value basis (that is, NPV) is positive, then the project is considered an acceptable investment.* NPV is computed using the following equation.

$$\text{NPV} = \hat{CF}_0 + \frac{\hat{CF}_1}{(1+k)^1} + \frac{\hat{CF}_2}{(1+k)^2} + \cdots + \frac{\hat{CR}_n}{(1+k)^n} \quad (7.44)$$

$$= \sum_{t=0}^{n} \frac{\hat{CF}_t}{(1+k)^t}$$

Here $\hat{CF}_t$ is the expected net cash flow at Period t, and k is the rate of return required by the firm to invest in this project. The rate of return required by the firm generally is termed the firm's cost of capital, because it is the average rate the firm must pay for the funds used to purchase capital projects. Cash outflows (expenditures on the project, such as the cost of buying equipment or building factories) are treated as negative cash flows. For Project S and Project L, only $\hat{CF}_0$ is negative, but for many large projects such as the Alaska Pipeline, an electric generating plant, or **Chrysler's** Neon project, outflows occur for several years before operations begin and cash flows turn positive.

At a 10% required rate of return, Project S's NPV is $161.33:

CASH FLOW TIMELINE FOR PROJECT S:

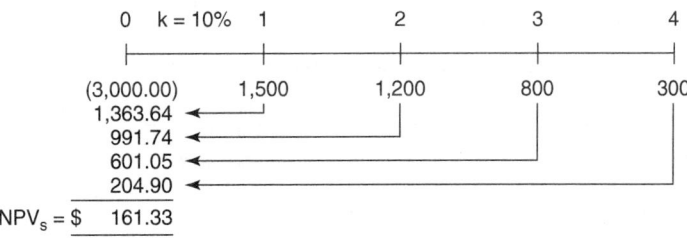

We show the regular cash flow time line as the top portion of the diagram, and then we show the solution in the bottom left portion of the diagram.

1. NUMERICAL SOLUTION As the lower section of the cash flow time line shows, to find the NPV, we compute the present value of each cash flow and sum the results. Using Equation 7.44, the numerical solution for the NPV for Project S is

$$PV_S = \$(3{,}000) + \frac{\$1{,}500}{(1.10)^1} + \frac{\$1{,}200}{(1.10)^2} + \frac{\$800}{(1.10)^3} + \frac{\$300}{(1.10)^4}$$
$$= \$(3{,}000) + \$1{,}500(0.90909) + \$1{,}200(0.82645) + \$800(0.75131) + \$300(0.68301)$$
$$= \$(3{,}000) + \$1{,}363.64 + \$991.74 + \$601.05 + 204.90$$
$$= \$161.33$$

Of course, if the stream of future cash flows was constant rather than nonconstant, then the future cash flow stream would represent an annuity, and our computations would be simplified.

2. TABULAR SOLUTION We can also write Equation 7.44 in the following form.

$$NPV = \hat{CF}_0 + \hat{CF}_1(PVIF_{k,1}) + \hat{CF}_2(PVIF_{k,2}) + \cdots + \hat{CF}_n(PVIF_{k,n})$$
$$= \hat{CF}_0 + \sum_{t=1}^{n} \hat{CF}_t(PVIF_{k,t}) \tag{7.44a}$$

Looking up the interest factors in Table A-1 of Module 700 Appendix, we compute NPV_S as follows.

$$\begin{aligned}
NPV_S &= \$(3,000) + \$1,500(0.9091) + \$1,200(0.8264) + \$800(0.7513) + \$300(0.6830) \\
&= \$(3,000) + \$1,363.65 + \$991.68 + \$601.04 + \$204.90 \\
&= \$161.27 \text{ (rounding difference)}
\end{aligned}$$

Using the same process for Project L, we find $NPV_L = \$108.67$. On this basis, both projects should be accepted if they are independent, but Project S should be the one chosen if they are mutually exclusive.

If you look at the cash flow time line for Project S, you can see the reason it has a positive NPV is because the initial investment of \$3,000 is recovered on a present value basis prior to the end of the project's life. In fact, if we use the payback concept developed in the previous section, we can compute how long it would take to recapture the initial outlay of \$3,000 using the discounted cash flows given in the cash flow time line—the sum of the present values of the cash flows for the first three years is \$2,956.43, so all of the \$3,000 cost is not recovered until 3.2 years = 3 years + [(\$3,000 − \$2,956.43)/\$204.90] years. Therefore, on a present value basis, it takes 3.2 years for Project S to recover, or pay back, its original cost. This is called the **discounted payback** of Project S—it is the length of time it takes for a project's *discounted* cash flows to repay the cost of the investment. The discounted payback for Project L is 3.90 years, so Project S is more acceptable. Unlike the traditional payback computation discussed in the previous section, the discounted payback computation does consider the time value of money. *Using the discounted payback method, a project should be accepted when its discounted payback is less than its expected life* because, in such cases, the present value of the future cash flows the project is expected to generate exceeds the initial cost of the asset (initial investment)—that is, NPV > 0.

Rationale for the NPV Method

The rationale for the NPV method is straightforward. An NPV of zero signifies that the project's cash flows are just sufficient to repay the invested capital and to provide the required rate of return on that capital. If a project has a positive NPV, then it generates a return that is greater than is needed to pay for funds provided by investors, and this excess return accrues solely to the firm's stockholders. Therefore, if a firm takes on a project with a positive NPV, the position of the stockholders is improved because the firm's value is greater. In our example, shareholders' wealth would increase by \$161.33 if the firm takes on Project S but by only \$108.67 if it takes on Project L. Viewed in this manner, it is easy to see why Project S is preferred to Project L, and it also is easy to see the logic of the NPV approach.

This description of the process is somewhat oversimplified. Both analysts and investors anticipate that firms will identify and accept positive NPV projects, and current stock prices reflect these expectations. Thus, stock prices react to announcements of new capital projects only to the extent that such projects were not already expected. In this sense, we can think of a firm's value as consisting of two parts: (1) the value of its existing assets and (2) the value of its "growth opportunities," or projects with positive NPVs. **AT&T** is a good example of this: The company has the world's largest long-distance network plus telephone manufacturing facilities, both of which provide current earnings and cash flows, and it has **Bell Labs**, which has the *potential* for coming up with new products in the computer/telecommunications area that could be extremely profitable. Security analysts (and investors) thus analyze AT&T as a company with a set of cash-producing assets plus a set of growth opportunities that will materialize if and only if the company can come up with a number of positive NPV projects through its capital budgeting process.

Internal Rate of Return (IRR)

In Section 715, we presented procedures for finding the yield to maturity (YTM), or rate of return, on a bond—if you invest in the bond and hold it to maturity, you can expect to earn the YTM on the money you invested. Exactly the same concepts are employed in capital budgeting when the *internal rate of return method* is used. The **internal rate of return (IRR)** is the rate of return the firm expects to earn if the project is purchased; thus it is defined as the discount rate that equates the present value of a project's expected cash flows to the investment outlay, or initial cost. *As long as the project's IRR, which is its expected return, is greater than the rate of return required by the firm for such an investment, the project is acceptable.*

We can use the following equation to solve for a project's IRR.

$$\hat{CF}_0 + \frac{\hat{CF}_1}{(1+IRR)^1} + \frac{\hat{CF}_2}{(1+IRR)^2} + \cdots + \frac{\hat{CF}_n}{(1+IRR)^n} = 0$$

$$= \sum_{t=0}^{n} \frac{\hat{CF}_t}{(1+IRR)^t} = 0 \qquad (7.45)$$

For Project S, the cash flow time line for the IRR computation is as follows.

CASH FLOW TIMELINE FOR PROJECT S:
Using Equation 7.45, here is the setup for computing IRR_S.

$$-3{,}000 + \frac{1{,}500}{(1+IRR)^1} + \frac{1{,}200}{(1+IRR)^2} + \frac{800}{(1+IRR)^3} + \frac{300}{(1+IRR)^4} = 0$$

```
      0    IRR = ?   1          2          3          4
      ├──────────────┼──────────┼──────────┼──────────┤
   (3,000)         1,500      1,200       800        300

Sum of PVs for CF₁₋₄ = 3,000

       NPV =    0
```

1 AND 2. NUMERICAL AND TABULAR SOLUTION   Although it is easy to find the NPV without a financial calculator, this is *not* true of the IRR. If the cash flows are constant from year to year, then we have an annuity, and we can use annuity factors presented in Appendix A to find the IRR. However, if the cash flows are not constant, as is generally the case in capital budgeting, then it is difficult to find the IRR without a financial calculator. Without a financial calculator, you basically have to solve Equation 7.45 by trial and error—try some discount rate (or corresponding PVIF factors), and see if the equation solves to zero, and if it does not, try a different discount rate until you find one that forces the equation to equal zero. The discount rate that causes the equation to equal zero is defined as the IRR. For a realistic project with a fairly long life, the trial and error approach is a tedious, time-consuming task.

Here are the IRRs for Project S and Project L.

$$IRR_S = 13.1\%$$
$$IRR_L = 11.4\%$$

Projects that have IRRs greater than their **required rates of return**, *or* **hurdle rates** *are acceptable investments.* For example, if the hurdle rate required by the firm is 10%, then both Project S and Project L are acceptable. If they are mutually exclusive, Project S is more acceptable than Project L because $IRR_S > IRR_L$.

Rationale for the IRR Method

Why is a project acceptable if its IRR is greater than its required rate of return? Because the IRR on a project is its expected rate of return, and if this return exceeds the cost of the funds used to finance the project, a surplus remains after paying for the funds—this surplus accrues to the firm's stockholders. Therefore, *taking on a project whose IRR exceeds its required rate of return, or cost of funds, increases shareholders' wealth.* On the other hand, if the internal rate of return is less than the cost of funds, then taking on the project imposes a cost on current stockholders. Consider what would happen if you borrowed funds at a 15% interest rate to invest in the stock market, and the stocks you picked earned only 13%. You still have to pay the 15% interest, so you end up losing 2% on the investment. On the other hand, anything you earn in excess of 15% is yours to keep, because only 15% interest has to be paid to the lender. So 15% is your *cost of funds,* which is what you must *require* your investments to earn to break even. It is this "breakeven" characteristic that makes the IRR useful in evaluating capital projects.

Comparison of the NPV and IRR Methods

We found the NPV for Project S is $161.33—this means that if the project is purchased, the value of the firm will increase by $161.33. The IRR for Project S is 13.1%—this means that if the firm purchases Project S, it will earn a 13.1% rate of return on its investment. We generally measure wealth in dollars, so the NPV method should be used to accomplish the goal of maximizing shareholders' wealth. In reality, using the IRR method could lead to investment decisions that increase, but do not maximize wealth. We choose to discuss the IRR method and compare it to the NPV method because many corporate executives are familiar with the meaning of IRR, it is entrenched in the corporate world, and it does have some virtues. Therefore, it is important that business managers understand the IRR method and be prepared to explain why, at times, a project with a lower IRR might be preferable to one with a higher IRR.

NPV Profiles

A graph that shows a project's NPV at various discount rates (required rates of return) is termed the project's **net present value (NPV) profile.** To construct the profiles, we calculate the projects' NPVs at various discount rates, say, 0, 5, 10, 15, and 20%, and plot these values on a graph.

Because the IRR is defined as the discount rate at which a project's NPV equals zero, the point where its *NPV profile crosses the X axis indicates a project's internal rate of return.* NPV profiles can be very useful in project analysis. The **crossover rate** is the discount rate at which the NPV profiles of two projects cross and, thus, at which the projects' NPVs are equal.

Independent Projects

Note that the internal rate of return formula, Equation 7.45, is simply the NPV formula, Equation 7.44, solved for the particular discount rate that forces the NPV to equal zero. Thus, the same basic equation is used for both methods, but in the NPV method the discount rate, k, is specified and the NPV is found, whereas in the IRR method the NPV is set equal to zero, and the interest rate that forces this equality (the IRR) is determined. Mathematically, therefore, the NPV and IRR methods will always lead to the same accept/reject decisions for independent projects: *If a project's NPV is positive, its IRR will exceed k, while if NPV is negative, k will exceed the IRR. In every case, if a project is acceptable using the IRR method, then the NPV method also will show it is acceptable.*

Mutually Exclusive Projects

If we assume that Project S and Project L are *mutually exclusive* rather than independent, then we can choose either Project S or Project L, or we can reject both, but we cannot invest in both. *A conflict exists* if the required rate of return is less than the crossover rate: NPV says choose Project L over Project S, while IRR says the opposite. Which answer is correct? Logic suggests that the NPV method is better because it selects the project that adds the most to shareholder wealth.

Two basic conditions can cause NPV profiles to cross and thus lead to conflicts between NPV and IRR: (1) when *project size (or scale) differences* exist, meaning that the cost of one project is larger than that of the other, or (2) when *timing differences* exist, meaning that the timing of cash flows from the two projects differs such that most of the cash flows from one project come in the early years and most of the cash flows from the other project come in the later years, as occurs with Projects L and S.

When either size or timing differences occur, the firm will have different amounts of funds to invest in the various years, depending on which of the two mutually exclusive projects it chooses. For example, if one project costs more than the other, then the firm will have more money at t = 0 to invest elsewhere if it selects the smaller project. Similarly, for projects of equal size, the one with the larger early cash inflows provides more funds for reinvestment in the early years. Given this situation, the rate of return at which differential cash flows can be invested is an important consideration.

The critical issue in resolving conflicts between mutually exclusive projects is this: How useful is it to generate cash flows earlier rather than later? The value of early cash flows depends on the rate at which we can reinvest these cash flows. *The NPV method implicitly assumes that the rate at which cash flows can be reinvested is the required rate of return, whereas the IRR method implies that the firm has the opportunity to reinvest at the project's IRR.* These assumptions are inherent in the mathematics of the discounting process. The cash flows can actually be withdrawn as dividends by the stockholders and spent on pizza, but the NPV method still assumes that cash flows can be reinvested at the required rate of return, while the IRR method assumes reinvestment at the project's IRR.

Which is the better assumption—that cash flows can be reinvested at the required rate of return or that they can be reinvested at the project's IRR? To reinvest at the IRR associated with a capital project, the firm would have to be able to reinvest the project's cash flows in another project with an identical IRR—such projects generally do not continue to exist, or it is not feasible to reinvest in such projects, because competition in the investment markets drives their prices up and their IRRs down. On the other hand, at the very least, a firm could repurchase the bonds and stock it has issued to raise capital budgeting funds and thus repay some of its investors, which would be the same as investing at its required rate of return. Thus, we conclude that the *more realistic* **reinvestment rate assumption** *is the required rate of return, which is implicit in the NPV method*. This, in turn, leads us to prefer the NPV method, at least for firms willing and able to obtain capital at a cost reasonably close to their current cost of capital.

We should reiterate that *when projects are independent, the NPV and IRR methods both provide exactly the same accept/reject decision*. However, *when evaluating mutually exclusive projects*, especially those that differ in scale or timing, *the NPV method should be used to determine which project should be purchased*.

Multiple IRRs

There is one other situation in which the IRR approach might not be usable—this is when projects have unconventional cash flow patterns. A project has a *conventional* cash flow pattern if it has cash outflows (costs) in one or more periods at the beginning of its life followed by a series of cash inflows. If, however, a project has a large cash outflow either sometime during or at the end of its life, then it has an *unconventional* cash flow pattern. Projects with unconventional cash flow patterns present unique difficulties when the IRR method is used, including the possibility of **multiple IRRs.**

There exists an IRR solution for each time the *direction* of the cash flows associated with a project is interrupted (that is, inflows change to outflows, and vice versa). For example, a conventional cash flow pattern only has one net cash outflow at the beginning of the project's life, so the direction of the cash flows changes (is interrupted) once from negative (outflow) to positive (inflow), and there is only one IRR solution. A project with a ten-year life that has cash inflows every year except that $\hat{CF}_0 < 0$ and $\hat{CF}_5 < 0$ will have two IRR solutions because the cash flow pattern has two direction changes, or interruptions—one after the initial cost is paid and another five years later.

Other Evaluation Methods Used in Capital Budgeting Analysis

There are two other methods worth mentioning here. These include accounting rate of return (ARR) method and profitability index (PI) method.

The ARR method is based on accounting data and is computed as the average annual profits after taxes divided by the initial cash outlay in the project. This accounting rate of return is then compared to the required rate of return to determine if a particular project should be accepted or rejected. Strengths of the ARR method include that it is simple and that accounting data is readily available. Drawbacks of the ARR method include that it does not consider the project's cash flows and that it ignores the time value of money.

The PI method is a benefit/cost ratio and is computed as the present value of future net cash flows divided by the initial cash outlay in the project. As long as the PI is 1.00 or greater, the project is acceptable. For any given project, the NPV method and the PI method give the same accept-reject answer. When choosing between mutually exclusive projects, the NPV method is preferred because the project's benefits are expressed in absolute terms. In contrast, the PI method expresses in relative terms.

Conclusions on the Capital Budgeting Decision Methods

In the previous section, we compared the NPV and IRR methods to highlight their relative strengths and weaknesses for evaluating capital projects, and in the process we probably created the impression that "sophisticated" firms should use only one method in the decision process—NPV. However, virtually all capital budgeting decisions are analyzed by computer, so it is easy to calculate and list all the decision measures: payback, discounted payback, NPV, and IRR. In making the accept/reject decision, most large, sophisticated firms such as **IBM**, **General Electric**, and **General Motors** calculate and consider multiple measures because each provides decision makers with a somewhat different piece of relevant information.

Payback and discounted payback provide information about both the risk and the *liquidity* of a project—a long payback means (1) that the investment dollars will be locked up for many years, hence the project is relatively illiquid, and (2) that the project's cash flows must be forecast far out into the future, hence the project is probably quite risky. We generally define liquidity as the ability to convert an asset into cash quickly without loss of the original investment. Thus, in most cases, short-term assets are considered more liquid than long-term assets. A good analogy for this is the bond valuation process. An investor should never compare the yields to maturity on two bonds without considering their terms to maturity because a bond's riskiness is significantly influenced by its maturity.

NPV is important because it gives a direct measure of the dollar benefit (on a present value basis) to the firm's shareholders, so we regard NPV as the best single measure of *profitability*. IRR also measures profitability, but here it is expressed as a percentage rate of return, which many decision makers, especially nonfinancial managers, seem to prefer. Further, IRR contains information concerning a project's "safety margin," which is not inherent in NPV. To illustrate, consider the following two projects: Project T costs $10,000 at t = 0 and is expected to return $16,500 at the end of one year, while Project B costs $100,000 and has an expected payoff of $115,500 after one year. At a 10% required rate of return, both projects have an NPV of $5,000, so by the NPV rule we should be indifferent between the two. However, Project T actually provides a much larger margin for error. Even if its realized cash inflow were almost 40% below the $16,500 forecast, the firm would still recover its $10,000 investment. On the other hand, if Project B's inflows fell by only 14% from the forecasted $115,500, the firm would not recover its investment. Further, if no inflows were generated at all, the firm would lose only $10,000 with Project T but $100,000 if it took on Project B.

The NPV contains no information about either the "safety margin" inherent in a project's cash flow forecasts or the amount of capital at risk, but the IRR does provide "safety margin" information—Project T's IRR is a whopping 65.0%, while Project B's IRR is only 15.5%. As a result, the realized return could fall substantially for Project T, and it would still make money. Note, though, that the IRR method has a reinvestment assumption that probably is unrealistic, and it is possible for projects to have multiple IRRs.

In summary, the different methods provide different types of information to decision makers. Because it is easy to calculate them, all should be considered in the decision process. For any specific decision, more weight might be given to one method than another, but it would be foolish to ignore the information provided by any of the methods.

At this point, we should note that multinational corporations use essentially the same capital budgeting techniques that we described in this section. However, foreign governments, international regulatory environments, and financial and product markets in other countries pose certain challenges to U.S. firms that must make capital budgeting decisions for their foreign operations.

The Post-Audit

An important aspect of the capital budgeting process is the **post-audit,** which involves (1) comparing actual results with those predicted by the project's sponsors and (2) explaining why any differences occurred. For example, many firms require that the operating divisions send monthly reports for the first six months after a project goes into operation and quarterly reports thereafter, until the project's results are up to expectations. From then on, reports on the project are handled like those of other operations.

The post-audit has two main purposes.

1. **Improve forecasts.** When decision makers are forced to compare their projections to actual outcomes, there is a tendency for estimates to improve. Conscious or unconscious biases are observed and eliminated; new forecasting methods are sought as the need for them becomes apparent; and people simply tend to do everything better, including forecasting, if they know that their actions are being monitored.

2. **Improve operations.** Businesses are run by people, and people can perform at higher or lower levels of efficiency. When a divisional team has made a forecast about an investment, its members are, in a sense, putting their reputations on the line. If costs are above predicted levels, sales below expectations, and so on, executives in production, marketing, and other areas will strive to improve operations and to bring results in line with forecasts. In a discussion related to this point, an **IBM** executive made this statement: "You academicians worry only about making good decisions. In business, we also worry about making decisions good."

The post-audit is not a simple process—a number of factors can cause complications. First, we must recognize that each element of the cash flow forecast is subject to uncertainty, so a percentage of all projects undertaken by any reasonably venturesome firm will necessarily go awry. This fact must be considered when appraising the performances of the operating executives who submit capital expenditure requests. Second, projects sometimes fail to meet expectations for reasons beyond the control of the operating executives and for reasons that no one could realistically be expected to anticipate. For example, the 1991–1992 recession adversely affected many projects. Third, it is often difficult to separate the operating results of one investment from those of a larger system. Although some projects stand alone and permit ready identification of costs and revenues, the actual cost savings that result from a new computer system, for example, might be very hard to measure. Fourth, it is often hard to hand out blame or praise because the executives who were actually responsible for a given decision might have moved on by the time the results of a long-term investment are known.

Because of these difficulties, some firms tend to play down the importance of the post-audit. However, observations of both businesses and governmental units suggest that the best-run and most successful organizations are the ones that put the greatest emphasis on post-audits. Accordingly, we regard the post-audit as being an extremely important element in a good capital budgeting system.

Cash Flow Estimation and Risks

The most important, but also the most difficult, step in the analysis of a capital project is estimating its **cash flows**—the investment outlays and the net cash flows expected after the project is purchased. Many variables are involved in cash flow estimation, and many individuals and departments participate in the process. For example, the forecasts of unit sales and sales prices normally are made by the marketing group based on its knowledge of advertising effects, the state of the economy, competitors' reactions, and trends in consumers' tastes. Similarly, the capital outlays associated with a new product generally are determined by the engineering and product development staffs, while operating costs are estimated by cost accountants, production experts, personnel specialists, purchasing agents, and so forth. Because it is difficult to make accurate forecasts of the costs and revenues associated with a large, complex project, forecast errors can be quite large.

The financial staff's role in the forecasting process includes (1) coordinating the efforts of the other departments, such as engineering and marketing, (2) ensuring that everyone involved with the forecast uses a consistent set of economic assumptions, and (3) making sure that no biases are inherent in the forecasts. This last point is extremely important, because division managers often become emotionally involved with pet projects or develop empire-building complexes, both of which can lead to cash flow forecasting biases that make bad projects look good—on paper.

It is almost impossible to overstate the difficulties one can encounter with cash flow forecasts. Also, it is difficult to overstate the importance of these forecasts. In this section, we will give you a sense of some of the inputs that are involved in forecasting the cash flows associated with a capital project and in minimizing forecasting errors.

Relevant Cash Flows

One important element in cash flow estimation is the determination of **relevant cash flows,** which are defined as the specific set of cash flows that should be considered in the capital budgeting decision. This process can be rather difficult, but two cardinal rules can help financial analysts avoid mistakes: (1) Capital budgeting decisions must be based on *cash flows after taxes,* not accounting income, and (2) only *incremental cash flows* are relevant to the accept/reject decision. These two rules are discussed in detail in the following sections.

Cash Flow Versus Accounting Income

In capital budgeting analysis, *after-tax cash flows, not accounting profits,* are used—it is cash that pays the bills and can be invested in capital projects, not profits. Cash flows and accounting profits can be very different. To illustrate, consider Exhibit 700.42, which shows how accounting profits and cash flows are related to one another. We assume that Unilate Textiles is planning to start a new division at the end of 2000; that sales and all costs, except depreciation, represent actual cash flows and are projected to be constant over time; and that the division will use accelerated depreciation, which will cause its reported depreciation charges to decline over time.

The top section of the table shows the situation in the first year of operations, 2001. Accounting profits are $7 million, but the division's net cash flow—money that is available to Unilate—is $22 million. The $7 million profit is the *return on the funds* originally invested, while the $15 million of depreciation is a *return of part of the funds* originally invested, so the $22 million cash flow consists of both a return *on* and a return *of* part of the invested capital.

The bottom part of the table shows the situation projected for 2006. Here reported profits have doubled because of the decline in depreciation, but net cash flow is down sharply because taxes have doubled. The amount of money received by the firm is represented by the cash flow figure, not the net income figure. And although accounting profits are important for some purposes, it is cash flows that are relevant for the purposes of setting a value on a project

Exhibit 700.42 *Accounting Profits Versus Net Cash Flow (thousands of dollars)*

	Accounting Profits	Cash Flows
I. 2001 Situation		
Sales	$50,000	$50,000
Costs except depreciation	(25,000)	(25,000)
Depreciation	(15,000)	—
Net operating income or cash flow	$10,000	$25,000
Taxes based on operating income (30%)	(3,000)	(3,000)
Net income or net cash flow	$ 7,000	$22,000
Net cash flow = Net income plus depreciation = $ 7,000 + $15,000 = $22,000		
II. 2006 Situation		
Sales	$50,000	$50,000
Costs except depreciation	(25,000)	(25,000)
Depreciation	(5,000)	—
Net operating income or cash flow	$20,000	$25,000
Taxes based on operating income (30%)	(6,000)	(6,000)
Net income or net cash flow	$14,000	$19,000
Net cash flow = Net income plus depreciation = $14,000 + $5,000 = $19,000		

using discounted cash flow (DCF) techniques—cash flows can be reinvested to create value, profits cannot. Therefore, in capital budgeting, we are interested in net cash flows, which, in most cases, we can define as

$$\text{Net cash flow} = \text{Net income} + \text{Depreciation}$$
$$= \text{Return } on \text{ capital} + \text{Return } of \text{ capital}$$

not in accounting profits per se. Actually, net cash flow should be adjusted to reflect all noncash charges, not just depreciation. However, for most projects, depreciation is by far the largest noncash charge. Also, note that Exhibit 700.42 ignores interest charges, which would be present if the firm used debt. Most firms do use debt and hence finance part of their capital budgets with debt. Therefore, the question has been raised as to whether interest charges should be reflected in capital budgeting cash flow analysis. The consensus is that interest charges should not be dealt with explicitly in capital budgeting—rather, the effects of debt financing are reflected in the cost of capital, which is used to discount the cash flows. If interest were subtracted and cash flows were then discounted, we would be double counting the cost of debt.

Incremental Cash Flows

In evaluating a capital project, we are concerned only with those cash flows that result directly from the decision to accept the project. These cash flows, called **incremental cash flows,** represent the changes in the firm's total cash flows that occur as a direct result of accepting the project. To determine if a specific cash flow is considered incremental, we need to find out whether it is affected by the purchase of the project. Cash flows that will change because the project is purchased are *incremental cash flows* that need to be included in the capital budgeting evaluation; cash flows that are not affected by the purchase of the project are not relevant to the capital budgeting decision. Unfortunately, identifying the relevant cash flows for a project is not always as simple as it seems. Some special problems in determining incremental cash flows are discussed next.

SUNK COSTS   Sunk costs are not incremental costs, and they should not be included in the analysis. A **sunk cost** is an outlay that has already been committed or that has already occurred and hence is not affected by the accept/reject decision under consideration. To illustrate, in 1999 Unilate Textiles considered building a distribution center in New England in an effort to increase sales in that area of the country. To help with its evaluation, Unilate hired a consulting firm to perform a site analysis and provide a feasibility study for the project; the cost was $100,000, and this amount was expensed for tax purposes. This expenditure is *not* a relevant cost that should be included in the capital budgeting evaluation of the prospective distribution center because Unilate cannot recover this money, regardless of whether the new distribution center is built.

OPPORTUNITY COSTS The second potential problem relates to **opportunity costs,** which are defined as the cash flows that could be generated from assets the firm already owns provided they are not used for the project in question. To illustrate, Unilate already owns a piece of land that is suitable for a distribution center. When evaluating the prospective center in New England, should the cost of the land be disregarded because no additional cash outlay would be required? The answer is no, because there is an opportunity cost inherent in the use of the property. In this case, the land could be sold to yield $150,000 after taxes. Use of the site for the distribution center would require forgoing this inflow, so the $150,000 must be charged as an opportunity cost against the project. Note that the proper land cost in this example is the $150,000 market-determined value, irrespective of whether Unilate originally paid $50,000 or $500,000 for the property. (What Unilate paid would, of course, have an effect on taxes and hence on the after-tax opportunity cost.)

EXTERNALITIES: EFFECTS ON OTHER PARTS OF THE FIRM The third potential problem involves the effects of a project on other parts of the firm; economists call these effects **externalities.** For example, Unilate does have some existing customers in New England who would use the new distribution center because its location would be more convenient than the North Carolina distribution center they have been using. The sales, and hence profits, generated by these customers would not be new to Unilate; rather, they would represent a transfer from one distribution center to another. Thus, the net revenues produced by these customers should not be treated as incremental income in the capital budgeting decision. Although they often are difficult to quantify, externalities such as these should be considered.

SHIPPING AND INSTALLATION COSTS When a firm acquires fixed assets, it often must incur substantial costs for shipping and installing the equipment. These charges are added to the invoice price of the equipment when the total cost of the project is being determined. Also, for depreciation purposes, the *depreciable basis* of an asset, which is the total amount that can be depreciated, includes the purchase price and any additional expenditures required to make the asset operational, including shipping and installation. Therefore, the full cost of the equipment, including shipping and installation costs, is used as the depreciable basis when depreciation charges are calculated. So if Unilate Textiles bought a computer with an invoice price of $100,000 and paid another $10,000 for shipping and installation, then the full cost of the computer, and its depreciable basis, would be $110,000.

Keep in mind that *depreciation is a noncash expense, so there is not a cash outflow associated with the recognition of depreciation expense each year.* But because depreciation is an expense, *it affects the taxable income of a firm, thus the amount of taxes paid by the firm, which is a cash flow.*

INFLATION Inflation is a fact of life, and it should be recognized in capital budgeting decisions. If expected inflation is not built into the determination of expected cash flows, then the calculated net present value and internal rate of return will be incorrect—both will be artificially low. It is easy to avoid inflation bias—simply build inflationary expectations into the cash flows used in the capital budgeting analysis. Expected inflation should be reflected in the revenue and cost figures, thus the annual net cash flow forecasts. The required rate of return does not have to be adjusted by the firm for inflation expectations because investors include such expectations when establishing the rate at which they are willing to permit the firm to use their funds. Investors decide at what rates a firm can raise funds in the capital markets, and they include an adjustment for inflation when determining the rate that is appropriate.

Identifying Incremental Cash Flows

Generally, when we identify the incremental cash flows associated with a capital project, we separate them according to when they occur during the life of the project. In most cases, we can classify a project's incremental cash flows as (1) cash flows that occur *only at the start* of the project's life—time period 0, (2) cash flows that *continue throughout* the project's life—time periods 1 through n, and (3) cash flows that occur *only at the end,* or the termination, of the project—time period n. We discuss these three incremental cash flow classifications and identify some of the relevant cash flows next. But keep in mind, when identifying the incremental cash flows for capital budgeting, the primary question is which cash flows will be affected by purchasing the project—if a cash flow does not change, it is not relevant for the capital budgeting analysis.

Initial Investment Outlay

The **initial investment outlay** refers to the incremental cash flows that *occur only at the start of a project's life*, $\hat{CF}_0$. The initial investment includes such cash flows as the purchase price of the new project and shipping and installation costs. If the capital budgeting decision is a *replacement decision,* the initial investment must also take into account the cash flows associated with the disposal of the old, or replaced, asset, which include any cash received or paid to scrap the old asset and any tax effects associated with the disposal.

In many cases, the addition or replacement of a capital asset has an impact on the net working capital of the firm. For example, normally, additional inventories are required to support a new operation, and expanded sales also lead to additional accounts receivable.

We should note that there are instances in which the change in net working capital associated with a capital project actually results in a decrease in the firm's current funding requirements, which frees up cash flows for investment. Usually this occurs if the project being considered is much more efficient than the existing asset(s). In any event, *the change in net working capital that results from the acceptance of a project is an incremental cash flow that must be considered in the capital budgeting analysis.* And because the changes in net working capital requirements occur at the start of the project's life, this cash flow impact is an incremental cash flow that is included as a part of the initial investment outlay.

Incremental Operating Cash Flows

Most capital projects also affect the day-to-day cash flows generated by the firm. For example, Unilate has discovered that it can reduce its total operating costs by $10 million by purchasing a new weaving machine to replace a machine it has been using for ten years. The cost reduction would result because the technological advancements of the new machine would allow Unilate to use less electricity and fewer raw materials (wool, cotton, and so on) in its manufacturing process. These cost savings, as well as any changes in depreciation expense, will affect the taxes paid by Unilate each year the new machine is in service. Thus, Unilate's normal *operating cash flows* will change if the project is accepted. We define **incremental operating cash flows** as the changes in day-to-day cash flows that result from the purchase of a capital project. The impact of incremental operating cash flows continues until the firm disposes of the asset.

In most cases, the *incremental operating cash flows* for each year can be computed directly by using the following equation.

$$\text{Incremental operating cash flow}_t = \Delta\text{Cash revenues}_t - \Delta\text{Cash expenses}_t - \Delta\text{Taxes}_t \quad (7.46)$$

The symbols in Equation 7.46 are defined as follows.

where Δ = The Greek symbol delta, which represents the change in something.

We have emphasized that depreciation is a *noncash* expense. So why is the change in depreciation expense included in the computation of incremental operating cash flow shown in Equation 7.46? The change in depreciation expense needs to be computed because, when depreciation changes, taxable income changes and so does the amount of income taxes paid; and the amount of taxes paid is a cash flow.

Terminal Cash Flow

The **terminal cash flow** occurs at the end of the life of the project, and it is associated with the final disposal of the project and returning the firm's operations to where they were before the project was accepted. Consequently, the terminal cash flow includes the salvage value, which could be either positive (selling the asset) or negative (paying for removal), and the tax impact of the disposition of the project. In addition, we generally assume the firm returns to the operating level that existed prior to the acceptance of the project; thus, any working capital accounts changes that occurred at the beginning of the project's life will be reversed at the end of its life. For example, as an expansion project's life approaches termination, inventories will be sold off and not replaced, and receivables will also be converted to cash. As these changes occur, the firm will receive an end-of-project cash flow equal to the net working capital requirement that occurred when the project was begun. Unilate expects the life of the New England distribution center to be ten years, so the inventories at that location will be reduced to zero in the tenth year. Because inventories will not have to be replenished during the last sales period, cash flows in Year 10 will increase by $5 million.

Incorporating Risk in Capital Budgeting Analysis

To this point, we have assumed the projects being evaluated have the same risk as the projects that the firm currently possesses. However, there are three separate and distinct types of project risk that need to be examined to determine if the required rate of return used to evaluate a project should be different than the *average* required rate of the firm. The three risks are (1) the project's own **stand-alone risk,** or the risk it exhibits when evaluated alone rather than as part of a combination, or portfolio, of assets—the effect of the project on the other assets of the firm is disregarded; (2) **corporate,** or **within-firm, risk,** which is the effect a project has on the total, or overall, riskiness of the company, without considering which risk component, systematic or unsystematic, is affected—the effect the project has on the stockholders' own personal diversification is disregarded; and (3) **beta,** or **market, risk,** which is project risk assessed from the standpoint of a stockholder who holds a well-diversified portfolio. As we shall see, a particular project might have high stand-alone risk, yet taking it on might not have much effect on either the firm's risk or that of its owners because of portfolio, or diversification, effects.

As we shall see shortly, a project's stand-alone risk is measured by the variability of the project's expected returns; its corporate risk is measured by the project's impact on the firm's earnings variability; and its beta risk is measured by the project's effect on the firm's beta coefficient. Taking on a project with a high degree of either stand-alone risk or corporate risk will not necessarily affect the firm's beta to any great extent. However, if the project has highly uncertain returns, and if those returns are highly correlated with returns on the firm's other assets and also with most other assets in the economy, the project will exhibit a high degree of all three types of risk. For example, suppose **General Motors** decides to undertake a major expansion to build solar-powered autos. GM is not sure how its technology will work on a mass production basis, so there are great risks in the venture—its stand-alone risk is high. Management also estimates that the project will have a higher probability of success if the economy is strong, because people will have more money to spend on the new autos. This means that the project will tend to do well if GM's other divisions also do well and to do badly if other divisions do badly. This being the case, the project will also have high corporate risk. Finally, because GM's profits are highly correlated with those of most other firms, the project's beta coefficient will also be high. Thus, this project will be risky under all three definitions of risk.

Stand-Alone Risk

What about a project's stand-alone risk—is it of any importance to anyone? In theory, stand-alone risk should be of little or no concern, because we know diversification can eliminate some of this type of risk. However, it is of great importance for the following reasons.

1. It is easier to estimate a project's stand-alone risk than its corporate risk, and it is far easier to measure stand-alone risk than beta risk.
2. In the vast majority of cases, all three types of risk are highly correlated—if the general economy does well, so will the firm, and if the firm does well, so will most of its projects. Thus, stand-alone risk generally is a good proxy for hard-to-measure corporate and beta risk.
3. Because of points 1 and 2, if management wants a reasonably accurate assessment of a project's riskiness, it should spend considerable effort on determining the riskiness of the project's own cash flows—that is, its stand-alone risk.

The starting point for analyzing a project's stand-alone risk involves determining the uncertainty inherent in the project's cash flows. This analysis can be handled in a number of ways, ranging from informal judgments to complex economic and statistical analyses involving large-scale computer models. To illustrate, many of the individual cash flows in a project are subject to uncertainty. For example, sales for each year were projected at 15,000 units to be sold at a net price of $2,000 per unit, or $30 million in total. Actual unit sales almost certainly would be somewhat higher or lower than 15,000, however, and also the sales price might turn out to be different from the projected $2,000 per unit. In effect, the sales quantity and the sales price estimates are expected values taken from probability distributions. The distributions could be relatively "tight," reflecting small standard deviations and low risk, or they could be "flat," denoting a great deal of uncertainty about the final value of the variable in question and hence a high degree of stand-alone risk.

The nature of the individual cash flow distributions, and their correlations with one another, determine the nature of the NPV distribution and, thus, the project's stand-alone risk. We next discuss three techniques for assessing a project's stand-alone risk: (1) sensitivity analysis, (2) scenario analysis, and (3) Monte Carlo simulation.

Exhibit 700.43 *Sensitivity Analysis (thousands of dollars)*

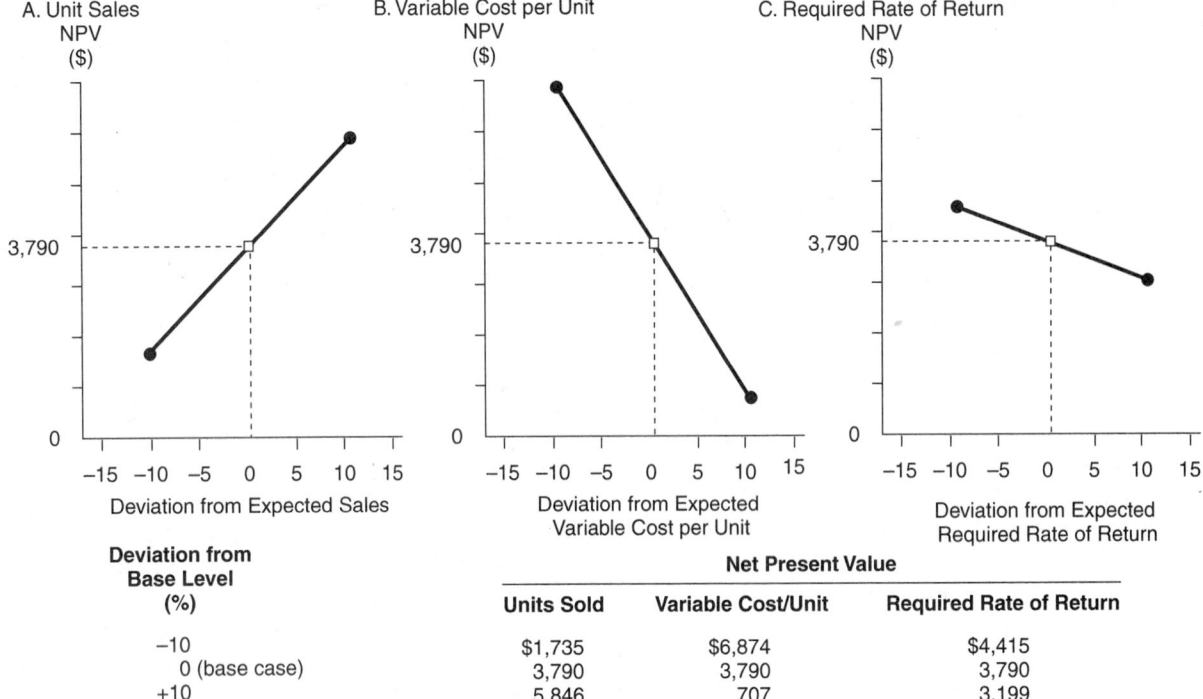

Sensitivity Analysis

The cash flows used to determine the acceptability of a project result from forecasts of uncertain events, such as economic conditions in the future and expected demand for a product. Intuitively, then, we know the cash flow amounts used to determine the net present value of a project might be significantly different from what actually happens in the future; but those numbers represent our best, and most confident, prediction concerning the expected cash flows associated with a project. We also know that if a key input variable, such as units sold, changes, the project's NPV also will change. **Sensitivity analysis** is a technique that shows exactly how much the NPV will change in response to a given change in an input variable, other things held constant.

In a sensitivity analysis, we begin with the base case situation that was developed using the expected values for each input; next each variable is changed by specific percentage points above and below the expected value, holding other things constant; then a new NPV is calculated for each of these values; and, finally, the set of NPVs is plotted against the variable that was changed. Exhibit 700.43 shows the computer project's sensitivity graphs for three of the key input variables. The table below the graphs gives the NPVs that were used to construct the graphs. The slopes of the lines in the graphs show how sensitive NPV is to changes in each of the inputs: *the steeper the slope, the more sensitive the NPV is to a change in the variable.* In the figure we see that the project's NPV is very sensitive to changes in variable costs, less sensitive to changes in unit sales, and not very sensitive at all to changes in the required rate of return. So when estimating these variables' values, HEP should take extra care to ensure the accuracy of the forecast for variable costs per unit.

If we were comparing two projects, the one with the steeper sensitivity lines would be regarded as riskier because for that project a relatively small error in estimating a variable such as unit sales would produce a large error in the project's expected NPV. Thus, sensitivity analysis can provide useful insights into the riskiness of a project.

Scenario Analysis

Although sensitivity analysis probably is the most widely used risk analysis technique, it does have limitations. Consider, for example, a proposed coal mine project whose NPV is highly sensitive to changes in output, in variable costs, and in sales price. However, if a utility company has contracted to buy a fixed amount of coal at an inflation-adjusted price per ton, the mining venture might be quite safe in spite of its steep sensitivity lines. *In general, a project's stand-alone risk depends on both (1) the sensitivity of its NPV to changes in key variables and (2) the range of likely values of these variables as reflected in their probability distributions.* Because sensitivity analysis considers only the first factor, it is incomplete.

Exhibit 700.44 *Scenario Analysis (dollars are in thousands, except sales price)*

Scenario	Sales Volume (units)	Sales Price	NPV	Probability of Outcome (Pr_i)	$NPV \times Pr_i$
Best case	20,000	$2,500	$17,494	0.20	$3,499
Most likely case	15,000	2,000	3,790	0.60	2,274
Worst case	10,000	1,500	(6,487)	0.20	(1,297)
				1.00	Expected NPV = $4,475
					σ_{NPV} = $7,630
					CV_{NPV} = 1.7

$$\text{Expected NPV} = \sum_{i=1}^{n} PR_i(NPV_i) = 0.20(\$17,494) + 0.60(\$3,790) + 0.20(-\$6,487) = \$4,475$$

$$\sigma_{NPV} = \sqrt{\sum_{i=1}^{n} Pr_i(NPV_i - \text{Expected NPV})^2}$$

$$= \sqrt{0.20(17,494 - \$4,475)^2 + 0.60(\$3,790 - \$4,475)^2 + 0.20(-\$6,487 - \$4,475)^2} = \$7,630$$

$$CV_{NPV} = \frac{\sigma_{NPV}}{\text{Expected NPV}} = \frac{\$7,630}{\$4,475} = 1.7$$

Scenario analysis is a risk analysis technique that considers both the sensitivity of NPV to changes in key variables and the likely range of variable values. In a scenario analysis, the financial analyst asks operating managers to pick a "bad" set of circumstances (low unit sales, low sales price, high variable cost per unit, high construction cost, and so on) and a "good" set. The NPVs under the bad and good conditions are then calculated and compared to the expected, or base case, NPV.

As an example, let us return to the appliance control computer project. Assume that HEP's managers are fairly confident of their estimates of all the project's cash flow variables except price and unit sales. Further, they regard a drop in sales below 10,000 units or a rise above 20,000 units as being extremely unlikely. Similarly, they expect the sales price as set in the marketplace to fall within the range of $1,500 to $2,500. Thus, 10,000 units at a price of $1,500 defines the lower bound, or the **worst-case scenario,** whereas 20,000 units at a price of $2,500 defines the upper bound, or the **best-case scenario.** Remember that the **base case** values are 15,000 units and a price of $2,000.

To carry out the scenario analysis, we use the worst-case variable values to obtain the worst-case NPV and the best-case variable values to obtain the best-case NPV. We then use the result of the scenario analysis to determine the *expected* NPV, standard deviation of NPV, and the coefficient of variation. To complete these computations, we need an estimate of the probabilities of occurrence of the three scenarios, the Pr_i values. Suppose management estimates that there is a 20% probability of the worst case scenario occurring, a 60% probability of the base case, and a 20% probability of the best case. Of course, it is *very difficult* to estimate scenario probabilities accurately. The scenario probabilities and NPVs constitute a probability distribution of returns just like those we dealt with earlier, except that the returns are measured in dollars instead of in percentages, or rates of return.

We performed the scenario analysis using a spreadsheet model, and Exhibit 700.44 summarizes the results of this analysis. We see that the base case (or most likely case) forecasts a positive NPV result; the worst case produces a negative NPV; and the best case results in a very large positive NPV. But the expected NPV for the project is $4.5 million and the project's coefficient of variation is 1.7. Now we can compare the project's coefficient of variation with the coefficient of variation of HEP's average project to get an idea of the relative riskiness of the appliance control computer project. HEP's existing projects, on average, have a coefficient of variation of about 1.0, so, on the basis of this stand-alone risk measure, HEP's managers would conclude that the appliance computer project is riskier than the firm's "average" project.

Monte Carlo Simulation

Scenario analysis provides useful information about a project's stand-alone risk. However, it is limited in that it only considers a few discrete outcomes (NPVs) for the project, even though there really are many more possibilities. **Monte Carlo simulation,** so named because this type of analysis grew out of work on the mathematics of casino gambling, ties together sensitivities and input variable probability distributions.

Simulation is more complicated than scenario analysis because the probability distribution of each uncertain cash flow variable has to be specified. Once this has been done, a value from the probability distribution for each variable is randomly chosen to compute the project's cash flows, and then these values are used to determine the project's NPV. Simulation is usually completed using a computer because the process just described is repeated again and again, say, for 500 times, which results in 500 NPVs and a probability distribution for the project's NPV values. Thus, the output produced by simulation is a probability distribution that can be used to determine the most likely range of outcomes to be expected from a project. This provides the decision maker with a better idea of the various outcomes that are possible than is available from a point estimate of the NPV. In addition, simulation software packages can be used to estimate the probability of NPV > 0, of IRR > k, and so on. This additional information can be quite helpful in assessing the riskiness of a project.

Unfortunately, Monte Carlo simulation is not easy to apply because it is often difficult to specify the relationships, or correlations, among the uncertain cash flow variables. The problem is not insurmountable, but it is important not to underestimate the difficulty of obtaining valid estimates of probability distributions and correlations among variables. Such problems have been cited as reasons Monte Carlo simulation has not been widely used in industry.

Corporate (Within-Firm) Risk

To measure corporate, or within-firm, risk, we need to determine how the capital budgeting project is related to the firm's existing assets. Remember that two assets can be combined to reduce risk if their payoffs move in opposite directions—when the payoff from one asset falls, the payoff from the other asset rises. In reality, it is not easy to find assets with payoffs that move opposite each other. As long as assets are *not* perfectly positively related (r = +1.0), some diversification, or risk reduction, can still be achieved. Many firms use this principle to reduce the risk associated with their operations—adding new projects that are not highly related to existing assets can help reduce corporate risk and reduce fluctuations associated with sales.

Corporate risk is important for three primary reasons.

1. Undiversified stockholders, including the owners of small businesses, are more concerned about corporate risk than about beta risk.
2. Empirical studies of the determinants of required rates of return (k) generally find that both beta and corporate risk affect stock prices. This suggests that investors, even those who are well diversified, consider factors other than beta risk when they establish required returns.
3. The firm's stability is important to its managers, workers, customers, suppliers, and creditors, as well as to the community in which it operates. Firms that are in serious danger of bankruptcy, or even of suffering low profits and reduced output, have difficulty attracting and retaining good managers and workers. Also, both suppliers and customers are reluctant to depend on weak firms, and such firms have difficulty borrowing money at reasonable interest rates. These factors tend to reduce risky firms' profitability and hence the prices of their stocks; thus they also make corporate risk significant.

Therefore, corporate risk is important even if a firm's stockholders are well diversified.

Beta (Market) Risk

The types of risk analysis discussed thus far in the section provide insights into a project's risk and thus help managers make better accept/reject decisions. However, these risk measures do not take account of portfolio risk, and they do not specify whether a project should be accepted or rejected. In this section, we show how the capital asset pricing model (CAPM) can be used to help overcome those shortcomings. Of course, the CAPM has shortcomings of its own, but it nevertheless offers useful insights into risk analysis in capital budgeting.

Beta (or Market) Risk and Required Rate of Return for a Project

In Section 755, we developed the concept of beta, β, as a risk measure for individual stocks. From our discussion, we concluded systematic risk is the relevant risk of a stock because unsystematic, or firm-specific, risk can be reduced significantly or eliminated through diversification. This same concept can be applied to capital budgeting projects because the firm can be thought of as a composite of all the projects it has undertaken. Thus, the relevant risk of a project can be viewed as the impact it has on the firm's systematic risk. This line of reasoning leads to the conclusion that if the beta coefficient for a project, β_{proj}, can be determined, then the **project required rate of return, k_{proj},** can be found using the following form of the CAPM equation.

$$k_{proj} = k_{RF} + (k_M - k_{RF})\beta_{proj}$$

Measuring Beta Risk for a Project

The estimation of project betas is even more difficult than for stocks and more fraught with uncertainty. One way a firm can try to measure the beta risk of a project is to find *single-product* companies in the same line of business as the project being evaluated and then use the betas of those companies to determine the required rate of return for the project being evaluated. This technique is termed the **pure play method,** and the single-product companies that are used for comparisons are called *pure play firms*. For example, if Erie could find three existing single-product firms that operate barges, it could use the average of the betas of those firms as a proxy for the barge project's beta.

The pure play approach can only be used for major assets such as whole divisions, and even then it is frequently difficult to implement because it is often impossible to find pure play proxy firms. However, when **IBM** was considering going into personal computers, it was able to obtain data on **Apple Computer** and several other essentially pure play personal computer companies. This is often the case when a firm considers a major investment outside its primary field.

Project Risk Conclusions

We have discussed the three types of risk normally considered in capital budgeting analysis—the project's stand-alone risk, within-firm (or corporate) risk, and beta (or market) risk—and we have discussed ways of assessing each. However, two important questions remain: (1) Should a firm be concerned with stand-alone and corporate risk in its capital budgeting decisions, and (2) What do we do when the stand-alone or within-firm risk assessments and the beta risk assessment lead to different conclusions?

These questions do not have easy answers. From a theoretical standpoint, well-diversified investors should be concerned only with beta risk, managers should be concerned only with stock price maximization, and these two factors should lead to the conclusion that beta risk should be given virtually all the weight in capital budgeting decisions. However, if investors are not well diversified, if the CAPM does not operate exactly as theory says it should, or if measurement problems keep managers from having confidence in the CAPM approach in capital budgeting, it might be appropriate to give stand-alone and corporate risk more weight than financial theorists suggest. Note also that the CAPM ignores bankruptcy costs, even though such costs can be substantial, and that the probability of bankruptcy depends on a firm's corporate risk, not on its beta risk. Therefore, one can easily conclude that even well-diversified investors should want a firm's management to give at least some consideration to a project's corporate risk instead of concentrating entirely on beta risk.

Although it would be desirable to reconcile these problems and to measure project risk on some absolute scale, the best we can do in practice is to determine project risk in a somewhat nebulous, relative sense. For example, we can generally say with a fair degree of confidence that a particular project has more or less stand-alone risk than the firm's average project. Then, assuming that stand-alone and corporate risk are highly correlated (which is typical), the project's stand-alone risk will be a good measure of its corporate risk. Finally, assuming that beta risk and corporate risk are highly correlated (as is true for most companies), a project with more corporate risk than average will also have more beta risk, and vice versa for projects with low corporate risk.

How Project Risk Is Considered in Capital Budgeting Decisions

Thus far, we have seen that purchasing a capital project can affect a firm's beta risk, its corporate risk, or both. We also have seen that it is extremely difficult to quantify either type of risk. In other words, although it might be possible to reach the general conclusion that one project is riskier than another, it is difficult to develop a really good *measure* of project risk. This lack of precision in measuring project risk makes it difficult to incorporate differential risk into capital budgeting decisions.

Exhibit 700.45 *Capital Budgeting Decisions Using Risk-Adjusted Discount Rates*

Project	Project Risk	Required Return	Estimated Life	Initial Investment Outlay—CF0	Incremental Operating Cash Flows—$CF_1 - CF_5$	NPV	IRR
A	Low	12%	5	$(10,000)	$2,850	$273.61	13.1%
B	Average	15	5	(11,000)	3,210	(239.58)	14.1
C	Average	15	5	(9,000)	2,750	218.43	16.0
D	High	20	5	(12,000)	3,825	(560.91)	17.9

Project Risk Classification	Required Rate of Return
Low	12%
Average	15
High	20

In reality, most firms incorporate project risk in capital budgeting decisions using the **risk-adjusted discount rate** approach. With this approach, the required rate of return, which is the rate at which the expected cash flows are discounted, is adjusted if the project's risk is substantially different from the average risk associated with the firm's existing assets. Therefore, average-risk projects would be discounted at the rate of return required of projects that are considered "average," or normal for the firm; above-average risk projects would be discounted at a higher-than-average rate; and below-average risk projects would be discounted at a rate below the firm's average rate of return. Unfortunately, because risk cannot be measured precisely, there is no accurate way of specifying exactly how much higher or lower these discount rates should be; given the present state of the art, *risk adjustments are necessarily judgmental and somewhat arbitrary.*

Although the process is not exact, many companies use a two-step procedure to develop risk-adjusted discount rates for use in capital budgeting. First, the overall required rate of return is established for the firm's existing assets. This process is completed on a division-by-division basis for very large firms, perhaps using the CAPM. Second, all projects generally are classified into three categories—high risk, average risk, and low risk. Then, the firm or division uses the average required rate of return as the discount rate for average-risk projects, reduces the average rate by one or two percentage points when evaluating low-risk projects, and raises the average rate by several percentage points for high-risk projects. For example, if a firm's basic required rate of return is estimated to be 12%, an 18% discount rate might be used for a high-risk project and a 9% rate for a low-risk project. Average-risk projects, which constitute about 80% of most capital budgets, would be evaluated at the 12% rate of return. Exhibit 700.45 contains an example of the application of risk-adjusted discount rates for the evaluation of four projects. Each of the four projects has a five-year life, and each is expected to generate a constant cash flow stream during its life; therefore, each project's future cash flow pattern represents an annuity. The analysis shows that only Project A and Project C are acceptable when risk is considered. Note, though, that if the average required rate of return is used to evaluate all the projects, Project C and Project D would be considered acceptable because their IRRs are greater than 12%. Using the average required rate of return would lead to an incorrect decision. Thus, *if project risk is not considered in capital budgeting analysis, incorrect decisions are possible.*

Although the risk-adjusted discount rate approach is far from precise, it does at least recognize that different projects have different risks, and projects with different risks should be evaluated using different required rates of return.

Capital Rationing

Independent projects are accepted if their NPVs are positive, and choices among mutually exclusive projects are made by selecting the one with the highest NPV. In this analysis, it is assumed that if in a particular year the firm has an especially large number of good projects, management simply will go into the financial markets and raise whatever funds are required to finance all of the acceptable projects. However, some firms do set limits on the amount of funds they are willing to raise, and, if this is done, the capital budget must also be limited. This situation is known as **capital rationing.**

Elaborate and mathematically sophisticated models have been developed to help firms maximize their values when they are subject to capital rationing. However, a firm that subjects itself to capital rationing is deliberately forgoing profitable projects, and hence it is

Capital rationing is of two types: soft and hard. Soft capital rationing occurs when a business unit or project is allocated a certain amount of financing while hard capital rationing occurs when the entire company cannot raise financing due to financial distress or preexisting contractual agreement.

not truly maximizing its value. This point is well known, so few large, sophisticated firms ration capital today.

Financial Markets, Instruments, and Institutions

The Financial Environment

Financial managers must understand the environment and markets within which businesses operate. Therefore, in this section, we examine the markets where firms raise funds, securities are traded, and stock prices are established, as well as the institutions that operate in these markets. In the process, we will explore the principal factors that determine money costs in the economy.

The Financial Markets

Businesses, individuals, and government units often need to raise capital to fund investments. For example, suppose **Carolina Power & Light (CP&L)** forecasts an increase in the demand for electricity in North Carolina, and the company decides to build a new power plant. Because CP&L almost certainly will not have the hundreds of millions or billions of dollars needed to pay for the plant, the company will have to raise these funds in the financial markets. Or suppose you want to buy a home that costs $100,000, but you only have $20,000 in savings. How can you raise the additional $80,000? At the same time, some individuals and firms have incomes that are greater than their current expenditures, so they have funds available to invest. For example, Carol Hawk has an income of $36,000, but her expenses are only $30,000, while **Reliant Energy** recently agreed to invest nearly $2.5 billion over the next seven years to purchase power companies in Europe.

People and organizations wanting to borrow money are brought together with those having surplus funds in the *financial markets*. Unlike *physical (real) asset markets*, which are those for such products as wheat, autos, real estate, computers, and machinery, *financial asset markets* deal with stocks, bonds, mortgages, and other *claims on real assets* with respect to the distribution of future cash flows.

In a general sense, the term financial market refers to a conceptual "mechanism" rather than a physical location or a specific type of organization or structure. We usually describe the **financial markets** as being a system comprised of individuals and institutions, instruments, and procedures that bring together borrowers and savers, no matter the location. Note that "markets" is plural—there are a great many different financial markets, each one consisting of many institutions, in a developed economy such as the United States. Each market deals with a somewhat different type of instrument in terms of the instrument's maturity and the assets backing it. Also, different markets serve different types of customers, or operate in different parts of the country. Here are some of the major types of markets.

1. *Debt markets* are the markets where loans are traded, while *equity markets* are the markets where stocks of corporations are traded. A debt instrument is a contract that specifies the amounts, as well as the times, a borrower must repay funds provided by a lender. The borrower can be an individual, a government, or a business. On the other hand, equity represents "ownership" in a corporation and entitles stockholders to share in any cash distribution generated from income (dividends) and from liquidation of the firm.

2. *Money markets* are the markets for debt securities with maturities of one year or less, while *capital markets* are the markets for long-term debt and corporate stocks. The primary function of the money markets is to provide liquidity to businesses, governments, and individuals to meet short-term needs for cash, because, in most cases, the timings of cash inflows and cash outflows do not coincide exactly. For example, if you had funds that you do not need for tuition payments until six months from now, you can invest those funds in a money market security and earn a greater return than if the funds were left in a checking account. The primary function of the capital market is to provide the opportunity to transfer cash surpluses or deficits to future years. For example, without the availability of mortgages, most individuals could not afford to buy houses when they are young and just starting their careers.

3. *Mortgage markets* deal with loans on residential, commercial, and industrial real estate, and on farmland, while *consumer credit markets* involve loans on autos and appliances, as well as loans for education, vacations, and so forth.

4. *World, national, regional, and local markets* also exist. Thus, depending on an organization's size and scope of operations, it might be able to borrow all around the world, or it might be confined to a strictly local, even neighborhood, market.

5. *Primary markets* are the markets in which corporations (and governments) raise new capital. If **General Electric (GE)** were to sell a new issue of common stock to raise capital, this would be a primary market transaction. The corporation selling the newly created stock receives the proceeds from the sale in a primary market transaction. *Secondary markets* are markets in which existing, previously issued (already outstanding) securities are traded among investors. Thus, if Edgar Rice decided to buy 1,000 shares of **IBM** stock, the purchase would occur in the secondary market. The New York Stock Exchange is a secondary market, because it deals in outstanding, as opposed to newly issued stocks and bonds. Secondary markets also exist for mortgages, various other types of loans, and other financial assets. The corporation (or government) whose securities are being traded is not involved in a secondary market transaction and, thus, does not receive any funds from such a sale.

6. *Spot markets* and *futures markets* are terms that refer to whether the assets are being bought or sold for "on the spot" delivery (immediately or within a few days) or for delivery at some later date, such as six months or a year into the future. Futures markets have grown in importance in recent years.

A healthy economy is dependent on efficient transfers of funds from people who are net savers to firms, governments, and individuals who need funds. Without efficient transfers, the economy simply could not function: Carolina Power & Light could not raise capital, so Raleigh's citizens would have no electricity; you would not be able to buy the house you want; Carol Hawk would have no place to invest her savings; and so on. Clearly, without financial markets, the level of employment and productivity, hence our standard of living, would be much lower. Therefore, it is essential that our financial markets function efficiently—not only quickly, but also at a low cost.

Financial Institutions

Funds are transferred between those who have funds to invest (savers) and those who need the funds (borrowers) by the three different processes diagrammed in Exhibit 700.46.

1. A *direct transfer* of money and securities, as shown in the top section, occurs when a business sells its stocks or bonds directly to savers (investors), without going through any type of financial institution. The business delivers its securities to savers, who in turn give the firm the money it needs.

2. As shown in the middle section, a transfer also can go through an *investment banking house* such as **Morgan Stanley Dean Witter**, which serves as a middleman and facilitates the issuance of securities. The company sells its stocks or bonds to the investment bank, which in turn sells these same securities to investors. The business's securities and the savers' money merely "pass through" the investment banking house. However, the investment bank does buy and hold the securities for a period of time, so it is taking a chance—it might not be able to resell them to savers for as much as it paid. Because new securities are involved and the corporation receives money from the sale, this is a primary market transaction. It should be noted that investment banking has nothing to do with the traditional banking process as we know it—investment banking deals with the issuance of new securities, not deposits and loans.

3. Transfers can also be made through a *financial intermediary* such as a bank or a mutual fund. Here the intermediary obtains funds from savers, issuing its own securities or liabilities in exchange, and then it uses the

Exhibit 700.46 *Diagram of the Capital Formation Process*

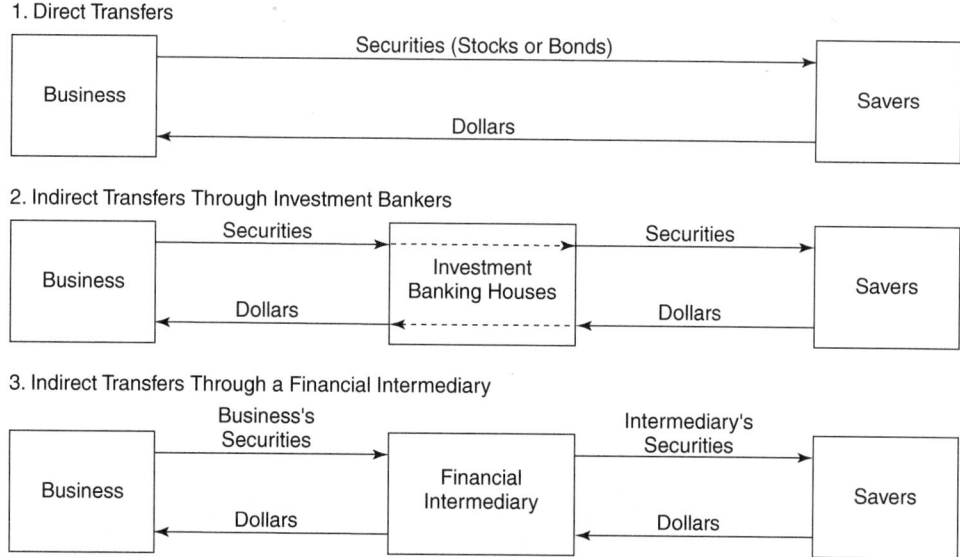

money to lend out or to purchase another business's securities. For example, a saver might give dollars to a bank, receiving from it a certificate of deposit, and then the bank might lend the money to a small business in the form of a mortgage loan. Thus, intermediaries literally create new forms of capital—in this case, certificates of deposit, which are both safer and more liquid than mortgages and thus are better securities for most savers to hold. The existence of intermediaries greatly increases the efficiency of the financial markets because, without them, savers would have to provide funds *directly* to borrowers, which would be a much costlier process.

Direct transfers of funds from savers to businesses are possible and do occur on occasion, but it is generally more efficient for a business to enlist the services of an **investment banker. Merrill Lynch, Morgan Stanley Dean Witter,** and **Goldman Sachs** are examples of financial service corporations that offer investment banking services. Such organizations (1) help corporations design securities with the features that currently are most attractive to investors, (2) buy these securities from the corporation, and (3) then resell them to savers. Although the securities are sold twice, this process really is one primary market transaction, with the investment banker acting as a middleman as funds are transferred from savers to businesses.

The **financial intermediaries** shown in the third section of Exhibit 700.46 do more than simply transfer money and securities between borrowers and savers—they literally create new financial products. Because the intermediaries generally are large, they gain economies of scale in analyzing the creditworthiness of potential borrowers, in processing and collecting loans, in pooling risks, and thus helping individual savers diversify—that is, "not put all their financial eggs in one basket." Further, a system of specialized intermediaries can enable savings to do more than just draw interest. For example, individuals can put money into banks and get both interest income and a convenient way of making payments (checking), or put money into life insurance companies and get both interest income and financial protection for their beneficiaries.

In the United States and other developed nations, a large set of specialized, highly efficient financial intermediaries has evolved. Competition and government policy have created a rapidly changing arena, however, such that different types of institutions currently perform services that formerly were reserved for others. This trend, which most certainly will continue into the future, has caused institutional distinctions to become blurred. Still, there remains a degree of institutional identity, and here are the major classes of financial intermediaries.

1. *Commercial banks,* which are the traditional "department stores of finance," serve a wide variety of customers. Historically, the commercial banks were the major institutions that handled checking accounts and through which the Federal Reserve System expanded or contracted the money supply. Today, however, other institutions also provide checking services and significantly influence the effective money supply. Conversely, commercial banking organizations provide an ever-widening range of services, including trust operations, stock brokerage services, and insurance.

    Note that commercial banking organizations are quite different from investment banks. Commercial banks lend money, whereas investment banks help companies raise capital from other parties.

Banks have different basic policies toward risk. Some banks are inclined to follow relatively conservative lending practices, while others engage in what are properly termed "creative banking practices." These policies reflect partly the personalities of officers of the bank and partly the characteristics of the bank's deposit liabilities. Thus, a bank with fluctuating deposit liabilities in a static community will tend to be a conservative lender, while a bank whose deposits are growing with little interruption might follow more liberal credit policies. Similarly, a large bank with broad diversification over geographic regions or across industries can obtain the benefit of combining and averaging risks. Thus, marginal credit risks that might be unacceptable to a small bank or a specialized bank can be pooled by a large branch banking system to reduce the overall risk of a group of marginal accounts.

Some bank loan officers are active in providing counsel and in stimulating development loans to firms in their early and formative years. Certain banks have specialized departments that make loans to firms expected to grow and thus to become more important customers. The personnel of these departments can provide valuable counseling to customers.

Banks differ in the extent to which they will support the activities of borrowers in bad times. This characteristic is referred to as the degree of *loyalty* of the bank. Some banks might put great pressure on a business to liquidate its loans when the firm's outlook becomes clouded, whereas others will stand by the firm and work diligently to help it get back on its feet.

Banks differ greatly in their degrees of loan specialization. Larger banks have separate departments that specialize in different kinds of loans—for example, real estate loans, farm loans, and commercial loans. Within these broad categories, there might be a specialization by line of business, such as steel, machinery, cattle, or textiles. The strengths of banks also are likely to reflect the nature of the business and the economic environment in which the banks operate. For example, some California banks have become specialists in lending to technology companies, while many Midwestern banks are agricultural specialists. A sound firm can obtain more creative cooperation and more active support by going to a bank that has experience and familiarity with its particular type of business. Therefore, a bank that is excellent for one firm might be unsatisfactory for another.

The size of a bank can be an important factor. Because the maximum loan a bank can make to any one customer is limited to 15% of the bank's capital accounts (capital stock plus retained earnings), it generally is not appropriate for large firms to develop borrowing relationships with small banks.

The term "merchant bank" originally was applied to banks that not only loaned depositors' money but also provided customers with equity capital and financial advice. Prior to 1933, U.S. commercial banks performed all types of merchant banking functions. However, about one-third of the U.S. banks failed during the Great Depression, in part because of these activities, so in 1933 the Glass-Steagall Act was passed in an effort to reduce banks' exposure to risk. In recent years, commercial banks have tried to get back into merchant banking, in part because their foreign competitors offer such services, and U.S. banks need to be able to compete with their foreign counterparts for multinational corporations' business. Currently, the larger banks, often through holding companies, do offer merchant banking, at least to a limited extent. This trend should continue, and, if it does, corporations will need to consider a bank's ability to provide a full range of commercial and merchant banking services when choosing a bank.

Some banks also provide cash management services, assist with electronic funds transfers, help firms obtain foreign exchange, and the like; and the availability of such services should be taken into account when selecting a bank. Also, if the firm is a small business whose manager owns most of its stock, the bank's willingness and ability to provide trust and estate services also should be considered.

2. *Savings and loan associations (S&Ls),* which have traditionally served individual savers and residential and commercial mortgage borrowers, take the funds of many small savers and then lend this money to home buyers and other types of borrowers. Because the savers obtain a degree of liquidity that would be absent if they bought the mortgages or other securities directly, perhaps the most significant economic function of the S&Ls is to "create liquidity" that otherwise would be lacking. Savers benefit by being able to invest their savings in more liquid, better managed, and less risky accounts (investments), whereas borrowers benefit from the economies of scale that allow them to obtain more capital at lower costs than would otherwise be possible.

3. *Credit unions* are cooperative associations whose members have a common bond, such as being employees of the same occupation or firm. Members' savings are loaned only to other members, generally for auto purchases, home improvements, and the like. Credit unions often are the cheapest source of funds available to individual borrowers.

4. *Pension funds* are retirement plans funded by corporations or government agencies for their workers and administered primarily by the trust departments of commercial banks or by life insurance companies. Pension funds invest primarily in long-term financial instruments, such as bonds, stocks, mortgages, and real estate.

5. *Life insurance companies* take savings in the form of annual premiums, then invest these funds in stocks, bonds, real estate, and mortgages, and finally make payments to the beneficiaries of the insured parties. In recent years life insurance companies have also offered a variety of tax-deferred savings plans designed to provide benefits to the participants when they retire.

6. *Mutual funds* are investment companies that accept money from savers and then use these funds to buy various types of financial assets such as stocks, long-term bonds, short-term debt instruments, and so on. These organizations pool funds and thus reduce risks through diversification. Different funds are designed to meet the objectives of different types of savers. Hence, there are income funds for those who prefer current income, growth funds for savers who are willing to accept significant risks in the hopes of higher returns, and still other funds that are used as interest-bearing checking accounts (**money market funds**). There are literally hundreds of different types of mutual funds with dozens of different goals and purposes.

Financial institutions historically have been heavily regulated in the United States, with the primary purpose of this regulation being to ensure the safety of the institutions and thus to protect depositors. However, these regulations—which have taken the form of prohibitions on nationwide branch banking, restrictions on the types of assets the institutions can buy and sell, ceilings on the interest rates they can pay, and limitations on the types of services they can provide—have tended to impede the free flow of funds from surplus to deficit areas and thus have hurt the efficiency of our financial markets. Also, for the most part, U.S. financial institutions are at a competitive disadvantage in the international financial markets because most foreign financial institutions, including banks, are not as restricted with respect to organizational structure, ability to branch, nonbanking activities, and so forth. Recognizing this fact, Congress has authorized some major changes recently, and more will be forthcoming.

The result of the ongoing regulatory changes has been a blurring of the distinctions among the different types of institutions. Indeed, the trend in the United States today is toward huge financial service organizations, which own banks, S&Ls, investment banking houses, insurance companies, pension plan operations, and mutual funds, and which have branches across the country and even around the world. In recent years, for example, **Citigroup** was formed by combining (1) **Travelers Group**, which included an insurance company (Travelers) and an investment organization (Smith Barney); (2) **Salomon Brothers**, which was an investment organization that included an investment banking operation; and (3) **Citicorp**, which was one of the largest banking organizations in the United States. During the same period, **BankAmerica Corporation** and **NationsBank Corporation** combined forces to form the nation's largest bank, **Bank of America**, which boasts that it serves about one-third of U.S. households and that two-thirds of large U.S. corporations use its cash management services. In general, the direction of recent mergers and acquisitions in the financial services industry is to form larger, more diversified companies that can better compete internationally.

The Stock Market

As noted earlier, secondary markets are those in which outstanding, previously issued securities are traded. By far the most active secondary market, and the most important one to financial managers, is the stock market. It is here that the prices of firms' stocks are established, and, because the primary goal of managerial finance is to maximize the firm's stock price, a knowledge of this market is essential for anyone involved in managing a business.

When we differentiate stock markets, we have traditionally divided them into two basic types: (1) *organized exchanges*, which include the New York Stock Exchange (NYSE), the American Stock Exchange (AMEX), and several regional exchanges and (2) the less formal *over-the-counter market*. But, as we shall see shortly, these lines of demarcation are much less precise today than in past years due to market mergers. Because the organized exchanges have actual physical market locations and are easier to describe and understand, we will consider them first.

The Stock Exchanges

The **organized security exchanges** are tangible physical entities. Each of the larger ones occupies its own building, has specifically designated members, and has an elected governing body—its board of governors. Members are said to have "seats" on the exchange, although everybody stands up. These seats, which are bought and sold, give the holder the right to trade on the exchange. For example, there are 1,366 seats on the New York Stock Exchange (NYSE); and, in August 1999, a seat on the NYSE sold for $2.65 million, which is an all-time high. Most of the larger investment banking houses operate *brokerage departments* that own seats on the exchanges and designate one or more of their officers as members.

Like other markets, security exchanges facilitate communication between buyers and sellers. For example, **Merrill Lynch** might receive an order in its Atlanta office from a customer who wants to buy 100 shares of **IBM** stock. Simultaneously, **Morgan Stanley Dean Witter's** Denver office might receive an order from a customer wishing to sell 100 shares of IBM. Each broker communicates by wire with the firm's representative on the NYSE. Other brokers throughout the country are also communicating with their own exchange members. The exchange members with *sell orders* offer the shares for sale, and they are bid for by the members with *buy orders*. Thus, the exchanges operate as *auction markets*.

The Over-the-Counter (OTC) Market

If a security is not traded on an organized exchange, it is customary to say it is traded *over the counter*. In contrast to the organized security exchanges, the **over-the-counter market** is an intangible organization that consists of a network of brokers and dealers around the country. An explanation of the term "over-the-counter" will help clarify exactly what this market is. The exchanges operate as auction markets—buy and sell orders come in more or less simultaneously, and exchange members match these orders. If a stock is traded less frequently, perhaps because it is the stock of a new or a small firm, few buy and sell orders come in, and matching them within a reasonable length of time would be difficult. To avoid this problem, some brokerage firms maintain an inventory of such stocks—they buy when individual investors want to sell and sell when investors want to buy. At one time the inventory of securities was kept in a safe, and the stocks, when bought and sold, literally were passed over the counter.

Traditionally the over-the-counter market has been defined to include all facilities that are needed to conduct security transactions not conducted on the organized exchanges. These facilities consist of (1) the relatively few *dealers* who hold inventories of over-the-counter securities and who are said to "make a market" in these securities, (2) the thousands of *brokers* who act as *agents* in bringing these dealers together with investors, and (3) the computers, terminals, and *electronic networks* that provide a communications link between dealers and brokers. Unlike the organized exchanges, the OTC does not operate as an auction market. The dealers who make a market in a particular stock continuously quote a price at which they are willing to buy the stock (the *bid price*) and a price at which they will sell shares (the *asked price*). Each dealer's prices, which are adjusted as supply and demand conditions change, can be read off computer screens all across the country. The spread between bid and asked prices represents the dealer's markup, or profit.

Most of the brokers and dealers who make up the over-the-counter market are members of a self-regulating body known as the *National Association of Security Dealers* (NASD), which licenses brokers and oversees trading practices. The computerized trading network used by NASD is known as the NASD Automated Quotation System (NASDAQ), and *The Wall Street Journal* and other newspapers contain information on NASDAQ transactions. Today, the NASDAQ is considered a sophisticated market of its own, separate from the OTC. In fact, unlike the OTC, the NASDAQ has *market makers* who continuously monitor activities in various stocks to ensure they are available to traders who want to buy or sell. And, in an effort to become more competitive with the NYSE and with international markets, the NASDAQ, the AMEX, and the Philadelphia Stock Exchange merged in 1998 to form the Nasdaq-Amex Market Group, which might best be referred to as an *organized investment network*. Increased competition among global stock markets assuredly will result in similar alliances among various exchanges/markets in the future.

In terms of numbers of issues, the majority of stocks are traded over the counter. However, because the stocks of larger companies are listed on the organized exchanges, about two-thirds of the dollar volume of stock trading takes place on those exchanges.

The Market for Common Stock

Some companies are so small that their common stocks are not actively traded; they are owned by only a few people, usually the companies' managers. Such firms are said to be *privately owned,* or **closely held, corporations,** and their stock is called *closely held stock.* In contrast, the stocks of most larger companies are owned by a large number of investors, most of whom are not active in management. Such companies are said to be **publicly owned corporations,** and their stock is called *publicly held stock.*

Institutional investors such as pension trusts, insurance companies, and mutual funds own 45 to 50% of all common stocks. These institutions buy and sell fairly actively, however, so they account for more than 75% of all transactions. Thus, the institutional investors have a heavy influence on the prices of individual stocks.

Types of Stock Market Transactions

We can classify stock market transactions into three distinct types.

1. **Trading in the outstanding shares of established, publicly-owned companies: the secondary market.** Unilate Textiles has 25 million shares of stock outstanding. If the owner of 100 shares sells his or her stock, the trade is said to have occurred in the **secondary market.** Thus, the market for outstanding shares, or used shares, is the secondary market. The company receives no new money when sales occur in this market.

2. **Additional shares sold by established, publicly-owned companies: the primary market.** If Unilate decides to sell (or issue) an additional one million shares to raise new equity capital, this transaction is said to occur in the **primary market.** Recall that Unilate has 40 million shares authorized but only 25 million outstanding; thus, it has 15 million authorized but unissued shares. If it had no authorized but unissued shares, management could increase the authorized shares by obtaining stockholders' approval, which would generally be granted without any arguments.

3. **New public offerings by privately-held firms: the primary market.** When **Coors Brewing Company,** which was owned by the Coors family at the time, decided to sell some stock to raise capital needed for a major expansion program, it took its stock public. Whenever stock in a closely held corporation is offered to the public for the first time, the company is said to be **going public.** The market for stock that has recently gone public normally is called the **initial public offering (IPO) market.**

    Firms can go public without raising any additional capital. Or sometimes a firm goes *public* when growth opportunities no longer can be financed solely by debt and the existing stockholder base, which generally consists of the original owners and current managers of the corporation and a few investors not actively involved in the company's management. The purpose of going public is to increase the ownership base and the funding sources available to the company so that growth opportunities can be better financed and the firm's value can be increased more than otherwise would be possible. Thus, as a firm experiences greater and greater growth and its size expands significantly, there generally is pressure to go public. Unfortunately, when a firm does go public, the red tape increases, because financial reporting and disclosure guidelines and security regulations are more restrictive for public firms than for private firms.

The Decision to List the Stock

To have its stock listed, a company must apply to an exchange, pay a relatively small fee, and meet the exchange's minimum requirements. These requirements relate to the size of the company's net income as well as to the number of shares outstanding and in the hands of outsiders (as opposed to the number held by insiders, who generally do not trade their stock very actively). The company also must agree to disclose certain information to the exchange; this information is designed to help the exchange track trading patterns and thus try to prevent manipulation of the stock's price. The size qualifications increase as one moves from the regional exchanges to the AMEX and on to the NYSE.

Assuming that a company qualifies, many people believe that listing is beneficial both to the company and to its stockholders. Listed companies receive a certain amount of free advertising and publicity, and the status as a listed company enhances their prestige and reputation. This might have a beneficial effect on the sales of the firm's products, and it probably is advantageous in terms of lowering the required rate of return on its common stock. Investors respond favorably to increased information, increased liquidity, and confidence that the quoted price is not being manipulated. By providing investors with these benefits in the form of listing their companies' stock, financial managers might lower their firms' costs of capital and increase the value of their stocks.

Regulation of Securities Markets

Sales of new securities, as well as operations in the secondary markets, are regulated by the **Securities and Exchange Commission (SEC)** and, to a lesser extent, by each of the 50 states. For the most part, the SEC regulations are intended to (1) ensure investors receive fair financial disclosure from publicly traded companies and (2) discourage fraudulent and misleading behavior by firms' investors, owners, and employees to manipulate stock prices. The primary elements of SEC regulation follow.

1. The SEC has jurisdiction over all interstate offerings of new securities to the general public in amounts of $1.5 million or more. A company wishing to issue new stock must file a **registration statement** that provides financial, legal, and technical information about the company. A **prospectus** that summarizes the information

in the registration statement generally is provided to prospective investors for use in selling the securities. SEC lawyers and accountants analyze both the registration statement and the prospectus; if the information is inadequate or misleading, the SEC will delay or stop the public offering.

2. The SEC also regulates all national securities exchanges, and companies whose securities are listed on an exchange must file annual reports similar to the registration statement with both the SEC and the exchange.
3. The SEC has control over stock trades by corporate **insiders.** Officers, directors, and major stockholders must file monthly reports of changes in their holdings of the corporation's stock. Any *short-term* profits from such transactions must be handed over to the corporation.
4. The SEC has the power to prohibit manipulation by such devices as pools (aggregations of funds used to affect prices artificially) or wash sales (sales between members of the same group to record artificial transaction prices).
5. The SEC has control over the form of the proxy and the way the company uses it to solicit votes.

Control over the flow of credit into securities transactions is exercised by the Board of Governors of the Federal Reserve System. The Fed exercises this control through **margin requirements,** which represent the percentage of the purchase price that must be deposited (invested) by investors—the percentage that can be borrowed is equal to 100% less the margin requirement set by the Fed. If a great deal of margin borrowing has been going on, a decline in stock prices can result in inadequate loan coverages, which would force stock brokers to issue **margin calls,** which in turn would require investors either to put up more money or to have their margined stock sold to pay off their loans. Such forced sales would further depress the stock market and could set off a downward spiral, such as the events that took place in October 1987. The margin requirement currently is 50%.

States also have some control over the issuance of new securities within their boundaries. This control usually is exercised by a "corporation commissioner" or someone with a similar title. State laws relating to securities sales are called **blue sky laws** because they were put into effect to keep unscrupulous promoters from selling securities that offered the "blue sky" but that actually had little or no asset backing.

The securities industry itself realizes the importance of stable markets, sound brokerage firms, and no perception of stock manipulation. Therefore, the various exchanges work closely with the SEC to police transactions on the exchanges and to maintain the integrity and credibility of the system. Similarly, the National Association of Securities Dealers (NASD) cooperates with the SEC to police trading in the OTC market. These industry groups also cooperate with regulatory authorities to set net worth and other standards for securities firms, to develop insurance programs to protect the customers of brokerage houses, and the like.

In general, government regulation of securities trading, as well as industry self-regulation, is designed to ensure that investors receive information that is as accurate as possible, that no one artificially manipulates the market price of a given stock, and that corporate insiders do not take advantage of their position to profit in their companies' stocks at the expense of other stockholders. Neither the SEC, the state regulators, nor the industry itself can prevent investors from making foolish decisions or from having bad luck, but regulators can and do help investors obtain the best data possible for making sound investment decisions.

Financial Instruments in International Markets

For the most part, the financial securities of companies and institutions in other countries are similar to those in the United States. There are some differences, however, which we discuss in this section. Also, financial securities exist that have been created to permit investors easier access to international investments, such as *American Depository Receipts*.

American Depository Receipts

Foreign companies can be traded internationally through *depository receipts,* which represent shares of the underlying stocks of foreign companies. In the United States, most foreign stock is traded through **American Depository Receipts (ADRs).** ADRs are not foreign stocks; rather they are certificates created by such organizations as banks. The certificates represent ownership in stocks of foreign companies that are held in trust by a bank located in the country where the stock is traded. ADRs provide Americans the ability to invest in foreign companies with less complexity and difficulty than might otherwise be possible. Each ADR certificate represents a certain number of shares of stock of a foreign company, and it entitles the owner to receive any dividends paid by the company in U.S. dollars. In addition, ADRs are traded in the stock markets in the United States, which often are more liquid than foreign markets. All financial information, including values, is denominated in dollars and stated in English; thus, there are no problems with exchange rates and language translations.

In many cases, investors can purchase foreign securities directly. But such investments might be complicated by legal issues, the ability to take funds such as dividends out of the country, and interpretation into domestic terms. Thus, ADRs provide investors the ability to participate in the international financial markets without having to bear risks greater than those associated with the corporations in which the investments are made. The market values of ADRs move in tandem with the market values of the underlying stocks that are held in trust.

Foreign Equity Instruments

The equities of foreign companies are like those of U.S. corporations. The primary difference between stocks of foreign companies and those of American companies is that U.S. regulations provide greater protection of stockholders' rights than those of most other countries. In the international markets, equity generally is referred to as *Euro stock* or *Yankee stock.*

1. *Euro stock* refers to stock that is traded in countries other than the home country of the company, not including the United States. Thus, if the stock of a Japanese company is sold in Germany, it would be considered a Euro stock.
2. *Yankee stock* is stock issued by foreign companies that is traded in the United States. If a Japanese company sold its stock in the United States, it would be called Yankee stock in the international markets.

As the financial markets become more global and more sophisticated, the financial instruments offered both domestically and internationally will change. Already, foreign companies and governments have discovered that financial markets in the United States provide excellent sources of funds because a great variety of financial outlets exist. As technology improves and regulations that bar or discourage foreign investing are repealed, the financial markets of other developed countries will become more prominent and new, innovative financial products will emerge.

The Investment Banking Process

When a business (or government unit) needs to raise funds in the financial markets, it generally enlists the services of an **investment banker** (see Panel 2 in Exhibit 700.46). **Merrill Lynch**, **Morgan Stanley Dean Witter**, and **Goldman Sachs** are examples of companies that offer investment banking services. Such organizations (1) help corporations design securities with the features that are most attractive to investors given existing market conditions, (2) buy these securities from the corporations, and (3) then resell them to investors (savers). Although the securities are sold twice, this process really is one primary market transaction, with the investment banker acting as an intermediary (agent) as funds are transferred from savers to businesses.

We should note that investment banking has nothing to do with the traditional banking process as we know it—investment banking deals with the issuance of new securities, not deposits and loans. The major investment banking houses often are divisions of large financial service corporations engaged in a wide range of activities. For example, Merrill Lynch has a brokerage department that operates thousands of offices worldwide, as well as an investment banking department that helps companies issue securities, take over other companies, and the like. Merrill Lynch's brokers sell previously issued stocks as well as stocks that are issued through their investment banking departments. Thus, financial service organizations such as Merrill Lynch sell securities in both the secondary markets and the primary markets.

In this section we describe how securities are issued in the financial markets, and we explain the role of investment bankers in this process. Two stages are involved in raising capital where Stage I deals with the firm itself and Stage II deals with the firm and its selected investment banker.

Raising Capital: Stage I Decisions

The firm itself makes some preliminary decisions on its own, including the following.

1. **Dollars to be raised.** How much new capital do we need?
2. **Type of securities used.** Should stock, bonds, or a combination be used? Further, if stock is to be issued, should it be offered to existing stockholders or sold directly to the general public?
3. **Competitive bid versus negotiated deal.** Should the company simply offer a block of its securities for sale to the highest bidder, or should it sit down with an investment banker and negotiate a deal? These two procedures are called *competitive bids* and *negotiated deals*. Only a handful of the largest firms on the NYSE, whose securities are already well known to the investment banking community, are in a position to use the competitive bid

process. The investment banks would have to do a large amount of investigative work in order to bid on an issue unless they were already quite familiar with the firm, and the costs involved would be too high to make it worthwhile unless the investment bank was sure of getting the deal. Therefore, the vast majority of offerings of stocks or bonds are made on a negotiated basis.

4. **Selection of an investment banker.** Assuming the issue is to be negotiated, which investment banker should the firm use? Older firms that have "been to market" before will already have established a relationship with an investment banker, although it is easy enough to change investment bankers if the firm is dissatisfied. However, a firm that is just going public will have to choose an investment bank, and different investment banking houses are better suited for different companies. The older, larger "establishment houses" like Morgan Stanley Dean Witter deal mainly with large companies like **AT&T**, **IBM**, and **Exxon**. Other investment bankers specialize in more speculative issues like initial public offerings.

Raising Capital: Stage II Decisions

Stage II decisions, which are made jointly by the firm and its selected investment banker, include the following.

1. **Reevaluating the initial decisions.** The firm and its investment banker will reevaluate the initial decisions about the size of the issue and the type of securities to use. For example, the firm initially might have decided to raise $50 million by selling common stock, but the investment banker might convince management that it would be better off, in view of current market conditions, to limit the stock issue to $25 million and to raise the other $25 million as debt.

2. **Best efforts or underwritten issues.** The firm and its investment banker must decide whether the investment banker will work on a best efforts basis or underwrite the issue. In an **underwritten arrangement,** the investment banker generally assures the company that the entire issue will be sold, so the investment banker bears significant risks in such an offering. With this type of arrangement, the investment banking firm typically buys the securities from the issuing firm and then sells the securities in the primary markets, hoping to make a profit. In a **best efforts arrangement,** the investment banker does not guarantee that the securities will be sold or that the company will get the cash it needs. With this type of arrangement, the investment banker does not buy the securities from the issuing firm; rather the securities are handled on a contingency basis, and the investment banker is paid a commission based on the amount of the issue that is sold. The investment banker essentially promises to exert its *best efforts* when selling the securities. With a *best efforts arrangement,* the issuing firm takes the chance the entire issue will not be sold and that all the needed funds will not be raised. For example, the very day IBM signed an *underwritten* agreement to sell $1 billion of bonds in 1979, interest rates rose sharply, and bond prices fell. IBM's investment bankers lost somewhere between $10 million and $20 million. Had the offering been on a best efforts basis, IBM would have been the loser.

3. **Issuance costs.** The investment banker's fee must be negotiated, and the firm also must estimate the other expenses it will incur in connection with the issue—lawyers' fees, accountants' costs, printing and engraving, and so on. Usually, the investment banker will buy the issue from the company at a discount below the price at which the securities are to be offered to the public, and this **underwriter's spread** covers the investment banker's costs and provides a profit.

    Flotation costs as a percentage of the proceeds are higher for stocks than for bonds, and costs are also higher for small issues than for large issues. The relationship between size of issue and flotation costs is primarily due to the existence of fixed costs: certain costs must be incurred regardless of the size of the issue, so the percentage flotation cost is quite high for small issues.

4. **Setting the offering price.** If the company already is publicly owned, the **offering price** will be based on the existing market price of the stock or the yield on the bonds. For common stock, the most typical arrangement calls for the investment banker to buy the securities at a prescribed number of points below the closing price on the last day of registration. For example, on July 1, 2000, the stock of Unilate Textiles had a current price of $23, and it had traded between $20 and $25 a share during the previous three months. Unilate and its underwriter agreed that the investment banker would buy 5 million new shares at $1 below the closing price on the last day of registration, which was expected to be in early October. The stock actually closed at $20.50 on the day the SEC released the issue, so the company received $19.50 a share. The shares then were sold to the public at a price of $20.50. As is typical, Unilate's agreement had an escape clause that provided for the contract to be voided if the price of the stock had fallen below a predetermined figure. In the Unilate case, this "upset" price was set at $18.50 a share. Thus, if the closing price of the shares on the last day of registration had been $18, Unilate would have had the option of withdrawing from the agreement.

Investment bankers have an easier job if an issue is priced relatively low, but the issuer of the securities naturally wants as high a price as possible. Therefore, an inherent conflict of interest on price exists between the investment banker and the issuer. However, if the issuer is financially sophisticated and makes comparisons with similar security issues, the investment banker will be forced to price close to the market.

It is important to note that *if pressure from the new shares drives down the price of the stock, all shares outstanding, not just the new shares, will be affected.* Thus, if Unilate's stock fell from $23 to $20.50 as a result of the financing, and if the price remained at that new level, the company would incur a loss of $2.50 on each of the 25 million shares previously outstanding, or a total market value loss of $62.5 million. In a sense, that loss would be a *flotation cost* because it would be a cost associated with the new issue. However, if the company's prospects really were poorer than investors had thought, then most of the price decline eventually would have occurred anyway. On the other hand, if the company's prospects are not really all that bad (if the signal was incorrect), then over time Unilate's stock price would increase, and the company would not suffer a permanent loss of $62.5 million.

If the company is going public for the first time, it will have no established price (or demand curve), so the investment bankers will have to estimate the equilibrium price at which the stock will sell after issue. If the offering price is set below the true equilibrium price, the stock will rise sharply after issue, and the company and its original stockholders will have given away too many shares to raise the required capital. If the offering price is set above the true equilibrium price, either the issue will fail or, if the investment bankers succeed in selling the stock, their investment clients will be unhappy when the stock subsequently falls to its equilibrium level. Therefore, it is important that the equilibrium price be approximated as closely as possible.

Selling Procedures

Once the company and its investment bankers have decided how much money to raise, the type of securities to issue, and the basis for pricing the issue, they will prepare and file a registration statement and prospectus with the SEC. It generally takes about 20 days for the issue to be approved by the SEC. The final price of the stock (or the interest rate on a bond issue) is set at the close of business the day the issue clears the SEC, and the securities are then offered to the public the following day.

Investment bankers must pay the issuing firm within four days of the time the offering officially begins, so, typically, the investment bankers sell the stock within a day or two after the offering begins. But, on occasion investment bankers miscalculate, set the offering price too high, and are unable to move the issue. Similarly, the market might decline during the offering period, which again would force the investment bankers to reduce the price of the stock. In either instance, on an underwritten offering the firm would still receive the price that was agreed upon, and the investment bankers would have to absorb any losses that were incurred.

Because they are exposed to large potential losses, investment bankers typically do not handle the purchase and distribution of an issue single-handedly unless it is a very small one. If the amount of money involved is large and the risk of price fluctuations substantial, an investment banker forms an **underwriting syndicate** in an effort to minimize the amount of risk each one carries. The investment banking house that sets up the deal is called the **lead, or managing, underwriter.**

In addition to the underwriting syndicate, on larger offerings still more investment bankers are included in a **selling group,** which handles the distribution of securities to individual investors. The selling group includes all members of the underwriting syndicate plus additional dealers who take relatively small participations (or shares of the total issue) from the syndicate members. Members of the selling group act as selling agents and receive commissions for their efforts—they do not purchase the securities, so they do not bear the same risks the underwriting syndicate does. Thus, the underwriters act as wholesalers and bear the risks associated with the issue, whereas members of the selling group act as retailers. The number of investment banking houses in a selling group depends partly on the size of the issue; for example, the one set up when Communications Satellite Corporation (Comsat) went public consisted of 385 members.

Shelf Registrations

The selling procedures described previously, including the 20-day minimum waiting period between registration with the SEC and sale of the issue, apply to most security sales. However, large, well-known public companies that issue securities frequently might file a master registration statement with the SEC and then update it with a short-form statement just prior to each individual offering. In such a case, a company could decide at 10 A.M. to sell registered securities and have the sale completed before noon. This procedure is known as **shelf registration** because in effect the company puts its new securities "on the shelf" and then sells them to investors when it thinks the market is right.

Maintenance of the Secondary Market

In the case of a large, established firm like **General Motors**, the investment banking firm's job is finished once it has disposed of the stock and turned the net proceeds over to the company. However, when a company is going public for the first time, the investment banker is under an obligation to maintain a market for the shares after the issue has been completed. Such stocks typically are traded in the over-the-counter market, and the lead underwriter generally agrees to "make a market" in the stock and to keep it reasonably liquid. The company wants a good market to exist for its stock, as do its stockholders. Therefore, if the investment banking house wants to do business with the company in the future, to keep its own brokerage customers happy, and to have future referral business, it will hold an inventory of the shares and help to maintain an active secondary market in the stock.

Financial Risk Management

Investment Risk

In this section, we take an in-depth look at how investment risk should be measured and how it affects assets' values and rates of return. When we examined the determinants of interest rates, we defined the real risk-free rate, k^*, to be the rate of interest on a risk-free security in the absence of inflation. The actual interest rate on a particular debt security was shown to be equal to the real risk-free rate plus several premiums that reflect both inflation and the riskiness of the security in question. In this section we define more precisely what the term *risk* means as it relates to investments, we examine procedures used to measure risk, and we discuss the relationship between risk and return. It is important for both investors and financial managers to understand these concepts and use them when considering investment decisions, whether the decisions concern financial assets or real assets.

We will demonstrate in this section that each investment—each stock, bond, or physical asset—has two different types of risk: (1) diversifiable risk and (2) nondiversifiable risk. The sum of these two components is the investment's total risk. Diversifiable risk is not important to rational, informed investors because they will eliminate its effects by "diversifying" it away. The really significant risk is nondiversifiable risk—this risk is bad in the sense that it cannot be eliminated, and if you invest in anything other than riskless assets, such as short-term Treasury bills, you will be exposed to it. In the balance of the section we will explain these risk concepts and show you how risk enters into the investment decision process.

Defining and Measuring Risk

Risk is defined in *Webster's Collegiate Dictionary* as "possibility of loss or injury: *peril*." Thus, we generally use the term *risk* to refer to the chance that some unfavorable event will occur. For example, if you engage in skydiving, you are taking a chance with your life—skydiving is risky. If you bet on the horses, you are risking your money. If you invest in speculative stocks (or, really, *any* stock), you are taking a risk in the hope of making an appreciable return.

Most people view risk in the manner we just described—a chance of loss. But in reality, *risk* occurs when we cannot be certain about the outcome of a particular activity or event, so we are not sure what will occur in the future. Consequently, *risk* results from the fact that an action such as investing can produce more than one outcome in the future.

To illustrate the riskiness of financial assets, suppose you have a large amount of money to invest for one year. You could buy a Treasury security that has an expected return equal to 6%. The rate of return expected from this investment can be determined quite precisely because the chance of the government defaulting on Treasury securities is negligible; the outcome essentially is guaranteed, which means this is a risk-free investment. On the other hand, you could buy the common stock of a newly formed company that has developed technology that can be used to extract petroleum from the mountains in South America without defacing the landscape and without harming the ecology. The technology has yet to be proven economically feasible, so it is not known what returns the common stockholders will receive in the future. Experts who have analyzed the common stock of the company have determined that the *expected*, or average long-run, return for such an investment is 30%; each year the investment could yield a positive return as high as 900%, but there also is the possibility the company will not survive, in which case, the entire investment will be lost and the return will be —100%. The return investors receive each year cannot be determined precisely because more than one outcome is possible—this is a risky investment. Because there is a significant danger of actually earning considerably less than the expected return, investors probably would consider the stock to be quite risky. But there also is a very good chance the actual return will be greater than expected, which, of course, is an outcome we gladly accept. So, when we think of investment risk, along with the chance of actually receiving less than expected, we should consider the chance of actually receiving more than expected. If we consider investment risk from this perspective, we can define **risk** as the chance of receiving an actual return other than expected, which simply means there is *variability in the returns,* or outcomes, from the investment. Therefore, investment risk can be measured by the variability of the investment's returns.

Investment risk, then, is related to the possibility of actually earning a return other than expected—the greater the variability of the possible outcomes, the riskier the investment. And as we will soon discover, *the return expected from an investment is positively related to the investment's risk—a higher expected return represents an investor's compensation for taking on greater risk.* But this relationship is not quite as clear-cut as it sounds, because we generally define and evaluate risk on two different bases: (1) **stand-alone risk,** which is the risk associated with an investment when it is held by itself, not in combination with other assets, and (2) **portfolio risk,** which is the risk associated with an investment when it is held in combination with other assets, not by itself. In the remainder of the section, we define risk more precisely and differentiate between stand-alone risk and portfolio risk when determining the appropriate expected rate of return for an investment.

Measuring Stand-Alone Risk: The Standard Deviation

Because we have defined risk as the variability of returns, we can measure risk by examining the tightness of the probability distribution associated with the possible outcomes. In general, the width of a probability distribution indicates the amount of scatter, or variability, of the possible outcomes. Therefore, *the tighter the probability distribution of expected returns, the less its variability—thus the smaller the risk associated with the investment.* According to this definition, U.S. Electric is much less risky than Martin Products because the actual payoffs that are possible are closer to the expected return for U.S. Electric than for Martin Products.

To be most useful, any measure of risk should have a definite value—we need a measure of the tightness of the probability distribution. The measure we use most often is the **standard deviation,** the symbol for which is σ, pronounced "sigma." The smaller the standard deviation, the tighter the probability distribution, and, accordingly, the lower the riskiness of the investment. To calculate the standard deviation, we proceed as shown in Exhibit 700.47, taking the following steps.

1. We calculate the expected rate of return using Equation 7.47. For Martin, we previously found $\hat{k} = 15\%$.

$$\text{Expected rate of return} = \hat{k} = Pr_1 k_1 + Pr_2 k_2 + \cdots + P$$

$$= \sum_{i=1}^{n} Pr_i k_i \qquad (7.47)$$

2. Subtract the expected rate of return ($\hat{k}$) from each possible outcome (k_i) to obtain a set of deviations from $\hat{k}$.

$$\text{Deviation}_i = k_i - \hat{k}.$$

The deviations are shown in Column 3 of Exhibit 700.47.

Exhibit 700.47 *Calculating Martin Products' Standard Deviation*

Payoff k_i (1)		Expected Return $\hat{k}$ (2)		$k_i - \hat{k}$ (3)	$(k_i - \hat{k})^2$ (4)	Probability (5)	$(k_i - \hat{k})^2 Pr_i$ (4) × (5) = (6)
110%	−	15%	=	95	9,025	0.2	(9,025)(0.2) = 1,805.0
22	−	15	=	7	49	0.5	(49)(0.5) = 24.5
(60)	−	15	=	−75	5,625	0.3	(5,625)(0.3) = 1,687.5
							Variance = σ^2 = 3,517.0
							Standard deviation = $\sigma = \sqrt{\sigma^2} = \sqrt{3,517.0} = 59.3\%$

755. FINANCIAL RISK MANAGEMENT

3. Square each deviation (shown in Column 4), multiply the result by the probability of occurrence for its related outcome (Column 5), and then sum these products to obtain the **variance** of the probability distribution, which is shown in Column 6. Thus, variance is defined as

$$\text{Variance} = \sigma^2 = \sum_{i=1}^{n} (k_i - \hat{k})^2 Pr_i$$

4. Finally, we take the square root of the variance to obtain the standard deviation shown at the bottom of Column 6.

$$\text{Standard deviation} = \sigma\sqrt{\sigma^2} = \sqrt{\sum_{i=1}^{n} (k_i - \hat{k})^2 Pr_i} \qquad (7.48)$$

Thus, the standard deviation is a weighted average deviation from the expected value, and it gives an idea of how far above or below the expected value the actual value is likely to be. Martin's standard deviation is seen in Exhibit 700.47 to be 59.3%, and, using these same procedures, we find U.S. Electric's standard deviation to be 3.6%. The larger standard deviation of Martin Products indicates a greater variation of returns, thus a greater chance that the expected return will not be realized; therefore, Martin Products would be considered a riskier investment than U.S. Electric, according to this measure of risk.

Coefficient of Variation

Another useful measure to evaluate risky investments is the **coefficient of variation (CV),** which is the standard deviation divided by the expected return:

$$\text{Coefficient of variation} = CV = \frac{\text{Risk}}{\text{Return}} = \frac{\sigma}{\hat{k}} \qquad (7.49)$$

The coefficient of variation shows the risk per unit of return, and it provides a more meaningful basis for comparison when the expected returns on two alternatives are not the same.

Measuring Portfolio Risk— Holding Combinations of Assets

In the preceding section, we considered the riskiness of investments held in isolation. Now we analyze the riskiness of investments held in portfolios. As we shall see, holding an investment, whether a stock, bond, or other asset, as part of a portfolio generally is less risky than holding the same investment all by itself. In fact, most financial assets are not held in isolation; rather, they are held as parts of portfolios. Banks, pension funds, insurance companies, mutual funds, and other financial institutions are required by law to hold diversified portfolios. Even individual investors—at least those whose security holdings constitute a significant part of their total wealth—generally hold stock portfolios, not the stock of only one firm. This being the case, from an investor's standpoint the fact that a particular stock goes up or down is not very important; what is important is the return on his or her portfolio, and the risk associated with the entire portfolio. Logically, then, *the risk and return characteristics of an investment should not be evaluated in isolation; rather, the risk and return of an individual security should be analyzed in terms of how that security affects the risk and return of the portfolio in which it is held.*

*A portfolio is a collection of investment securities or assets. If you owned some **General Motors** stock, some **Exxon** stock, and some **IBM** stock, you would hold a three-stock portfolio.*

Portfolio Returns

The **expected return on a portfolio,** $\hat{k}_P$, is simply the weighted average of the expected returns on the individual stocks in the portfolio, with the weights being the fraction of the total portfolio invested in each stock.

$$\hat{k}_P = w_1 \hat{k}_1 + w \hat{k} + \ldots + w_N \hat{k}_N$$

$$= \sum_{j=1}^{N} w^j \hat{k}^j \qquad (7.50)$$

Here the $\hat{k}_j$'s are the expected returns on the individual stocks, the w_j's are the weights, and there are N stocks in the portfolio. Note that (1) w_j is the proportion of the portfolio's dollar value invested in Stock j (that is, the value of the investment in Stock j divided by the total value of the portfolio), and (2) the w_j's must sum to 1.0.

In January 2000, a security analyst estimated that the following returns could be expected on four large companies.

	Expected Return
AT&T	10%
General Electric	13%
Microsoft	30%
Citigroup	16%

If we formed a $100,000 portfolio, investing $25,000 in each stock, the expected portfolio return would be 17.25%.

$$k_P = w_1\hat{k}_1 + w_2\hat{k}_2 + w_3\hat{k}_3 + w_4\hat{k}_4$$
$$= 0.25(10\%) + 0.25(13\%) + 0.25(30\%) + 0.25(16\%)$$
$$= 17.25\%$$

Of course, after the fact and a year later, the actual **realized rates of return, $\bar{k}$,** on the individual stocks—the $\bar{k}_j$, or "k-bar," values—will almost certainly be different from their expected values, so $\bar{k}_P$ will be somewhat different from $\hat{k}_P = 17.25\%$. For example, **General Electric** stock might double in price and provide a return of $+100\%$, whereas **Citigroup** stock might have a terrible year, fall sharply, and have a return of -75%. Note, though, that those two events would be somewhat offsetting, so the portfolio's return might still be close to its expected return, even though the individual stocks' actual returns were far from their expected returns.

Portfolio Risk

As we just saw, the expected return of a portfolio is simply a weighted average of the expected returns of the individual stocks in the portfolio. However, unlike returns, the riskiness of a portfolio, σ_P, generally is *not* a weighted average of the standard deviations of the individual securities in the portfolio; the portfolio's risk usually is *smaller* than the weighted average of the stocks' σ's. In fact, at least theoretically, it is possible to combine two stocks that by themselves are quite risky as measured by their standard deviations and to form a portfolio that is completely riskless, or risk-free, with $\sigma_P = 0$.

What would happen if we included more than two stocks in the portfolio? *As a rule, the riskiness of a portfolio will be reduced as the number of stocks in the portfolio increases.* If we added enough stocks, could we completely eliminate risk? In general, the answer is no, but the extent to which adding stocks to a portfolio reduces its risk depends on the *degree of correlation* among the stocks: *The smaller the positive correlation coefficient, the greater the diversification effect of adding a stock to a portfolio.* If we could find a set of stocks whose correlations were negative, all risk could be eliminated. *In the typical case, where the correlations among the individual stocks are positive but less than $+1.0$, some, but not all, risk can be eliminated.*

Firm-Specific Risk Versus Market Risk

As noted earlier, it is very difficult, if not impossible, to find stocks whose expected returns are not positively correlated—most stocks tend to do well when the economy is strong and do poorly when it is weak. Thus, even very large portfolios end up with a substantial amount of risk, but the risk generally is less than if all of the money was invested in only one stock. Some risk always remains, however, so it is virtually impossible to diversify away the effects of broad stock market movements that affect almost all stocks.

The part of a stock's risk that can be eliminated is called *diversifiable,* or *firm-specific* or *unsystematic, risk;* the part that cannot be eliminated is called *nondiversifiable,* or *market* or *systematic, risk.* The name is not especially important, but the fact that a large part of the riskiness of any individual stock can be eliminated through portfolio diversification is vitally important.

Firm-specific, or **diversifiable, risk** is caused by such things as lawsuits, strikes, successful and unsuccessful marketing programs, the winning and losing of major contracts, and other events that are unique to a particular firm. Because the actual outcomes of these events are essentially random, their effects on a portfolio can be eliminated by diversification—bad events in one firm will be offset by good events in another. **Market,** or **nondiversifiable, risk,** on the other hand, stems from factors that *systematically* affect most firms, such as war, inflation, recessions, and high interest rates. Because most stocks tend to be affected similarly (negatively) by these *market* conditions, systematic risk cannot be eliminated by portfolio diversification.

We know that investors demand a premium for bearing risk; that is, the higher the riskiness of a security, the higher the expected return required to induce investors to buy (or to hold) it. However, if investors are primarily concerned with *portfolio risk* rather than the risk of the individual securities in the portfolio, how should the riskiness of an individual stock be measured? The answer, as provided by the **Capital Asset Pricing Model (CAPM),** is this: *The relevant riskiness of an individual stock is its contribution to the riskiness of a well-diversified portfolio.* In other words, the riskiness of General Electric's stock to a doctor who has a portfolio of 40 stocks or to a trust officer managing a 150-stock portfolio is the contribution that the GE stock makes to the portfolio's riskiness. The stock might be quite risky if held by itself, but if most of this stand-alone risk can be eliminated by diversification, then its **relevant risk,** which is its *contribution to the portfolio's risk,* is much smaller than its total, or stand-alone, risk.

Are all stocks equally risky in the sense that adding them to a well-diversified portfolio would have the same effect on the portfolio's riskiness? The answer is no. Different stocks will affect the portfolio differently, so different securities have different degrees of relevant risk. How can the relevant risk of an individual stock be measured? As we have seen, all risk except that related to broad market movements can, and presumably will, be diversified away. After all, why accept risk that can be easily eliminated? *The risk that remains after diversifying is market risk, or risk that is inherent in the market, and it can be measured by evaluating the degree to which a given stock tends to move up and down with the market.*

The Concept of Beta

Remember the relevant risk associated with an individual stock is based on its systematic risk, which depends on how sensitive the firm's operations are to economic events such as interest rate changes and inflationary pressures. Because the general movements in the financial markets reflect movements in the economy, the market risk of a stock can be measured by observing its tendency to move with the market, or with an average stock that has the same characteristics as the market. The measure of a stock's sensitivity to market fluctuations is called its **beta coefficient,** and it generally is designated with the Greek symbol for beta, β. Beta is a key element of the CAPM.

Types of Risks

Earlier, we distinguished between *market risk,* which is measured by the firm's beta coefficient, and *total risk,* which includes both beta risk and a type of risk that can be eliminated by diversification (*firm-specific risk*). In Section 735 we considered how capital budgeting decisions affect the riskiness of the firm. There again we distinguished between beta risk (the effect of a project on the firm's beta) and corporate risk (the effect of the project on the firm's total risk).

Now we introduce three new dimensions of risk:

1. **Business risk** is defined as the uncertainty inherent in projections of future returns, either on assets (ROA) or on equity (ROE), if the firm uses no debt, or debt-like financing (that is, preferred stock)—it is the risk associated with the firm's operations.
2. **Financial risk** is defined as the additional risk, over and above basic business risk, placed on common stockholders that results from using financing alternatives with fixed periodic payments, such as debt and preferred stock—it is the risk associated with using debt or preferred stock.
3. **Country risk** is defined as the adverse impact of a country's environment on an MNC's cash flows.

Conceptually, the firm has a certain amount of risk inherent in its production and sales operations; this is its business risk. When it uses debt, it partitions this risk and concentrates most of it on one class of investors—the common stockholders—this is its financial risk. Use of preferred stock also adds to financial risk. Both business risk and financial risk affect the capital structure of a firm.

Business Risk

Business risk is the single most important determinant of capital structure. Smaller companies, especially single-product firms, also have a relatively high degree of business risk. Business risk varies from one industry to another and also among firms in a given industry. Further, business risk can change over time. Business risk depends on a number of factors, the more important of which include the following.

1. Sales variability (volume and price). The more stable the unit sales (volume) and prices of a firm's products, other things held constant, the lower its business risk.
2. Input price variability. A firm whose input prices (labor, product costs, and so forth) are highly uncertain is exposed to a high degree of business risk.
3. Ability to adjust output prices for changes in input prices. Some firms have little difficulty in raising the prices of their products when input costs rise, and the greater the ability to adjust selling prices, the lower the degree of business risk. This factor is especially important during periods of high inflation.
4. The extent to which costs are fixed: operating leverage. If a high percentage of a firm's operating costs are fixed and hence do not decline when demand falls off, this increases the company's business risk. This factor is called *operating leverage*.

Each of these factors is determined partly by the firm's industry characteristics, but each also is controllable to some extent by management. For example, most firms can, through their marketing policies, take actions to stabilize both unit sales and sales prices. However, this stabilization might require either large expenditures on advertising or price concessions to induce customers to commit to purchasing fixed quantities at fixed prices in the future. Similarly, firms can reduce the volatility of future input costs by negotiating long-term labor and materials supply contracts, but they might have to agree to pay prices somewhat above the current market price to obtain these contracts.

Financial Risk

Financial risk results from using **financial leverage,** which exists when a firm uses fixed income securities, such as debt and preferred stock, to raise capital. When financial leverage is created, a firm intensifies the business risk borne by the common stockholders. To illustrate, suppose ten people decide to form a corporation to produce operating systems for personal computers. There is a certain amount of business risk in the operation. If the firm is capitalized only with common equity, and if each person buys 10% of the stock, then each investor will bear an equal share of the business risk. However, suppose the firm is capitalized with 50% debt and 50% equity, with five of the investors putting up their capital as debt and the other five putting up their money as equity. In this case, the cash flows received by the debtholders are based on a contractual agreement, so the investors who put up the equity will have to bear essentially all of the business risk, and their position will be twice as risky as it would have been had the firm been financed only with equity. Thus, *the use of debt intensifies the firm's business risk borne by the common stockholders.*

Country Risk

An MNC conducts country risk analysis when assessing whether to continue conducting business in a particular country. The analysis can also be used when determining whether to implement new projects in foreign countries. Country risk can be partitioned into the country's political risk and its financial risk. Financial managers must understand how to measure country risk so that they can make investment decisions that maximize their MNC's value.

Why Country Risk Analysis Is Important

Country risk is the potentially adverse impact of a country's environment on an MNC's cash flows. Country risk analysis can be used to monitor countries where the MNC is currently doing business. If the country risk level of a particular country begins to increase, the MNC may consider divesting its subsidiaries located there. Country risk analysis can also be used by MNCs as a screening device to avoid conducting business in countries with excessive risk. Events that heighten country risk tend to discourage U.S. direct foreign investment in that particular country.

Country risk analysis is not restricted to predicting major crises. It is also used by an MNC to revise its investment or financing decisions in light of recent events.

Political Risk Factors

As one might expect, many country characteristics related to the political environment can influence an MNC. An extreme form of political risk is the possibility that the host country will take over a subsidiary. In some cases of expropriation, some compensation (the amount decided by the host country government) is awarded. In other cases, the assets are confiscated and no compensation is provided. Expropriation can take place peacefully or by force. The following are some of the more common forms of political risk.

- Attitude of consumers in the host country
- Actions of host government
- Blockage of fund transfers
- Currency inconvertibility
- War
- Bureaucracy
- Corruption

Financial Risk Factors

Along with political factors, financial factors should be considered when assessing country risk. One of the most obvious financial factors is the current and potential state of the country's economy. An MNC that exports to a country or develops a subsidiary in a country is highly concerned about that country's demand for its products. This demand is, of course, strongly influenced by the country's economy. A recession in the country could severely reduce demand for the MNC's exports or products sold by the MNC's local subsidiary.

A country's economic growth is dependent on several financial factors, which are identified here.

- *Interest rates.* Higher interest rates tend to slow the growth of an economy and reduce demand for the MNC's products. Lower interest rates often stimulate the economy and increase demand for the MNC's products.
- *Exchange rates.* Exchange rates can influence the demand for the country's exports, which in turn affects the country's production and income level. A strong currency may reduce demand for the country's exports, increase the volume of products imported by the country, and therefore reduce the country's production and national income. A very weak currency can cause speculative outflows and reduce the amount of funds available to finance growth by businesses.
- *Inflation.* Inflation can affect consumers' purchasing power and therefore their demand for an MNC's goods. It also indirectly affects a country's financial condition by influencing the country's interest rates and currency value. A high level of inflation may also lead to a decline in economic growth.

Most financial factors that affect a country's economic conditions are difficult to forecast. Thus, even if an MNC considers them in its country risk assessment, it may still make poor decisions because of an improper forecast of the country's financial factors.

Some financial conditions may be caused by political risk. For example, the September 11, 2001, terrorist attack on the United States affected U.S.-based MNCs because of political risk and financial risk. Political uncertainty caused uncertainty about economic conditions, which resulted in a reduction in spending by consumers, and therefore, a reduction in cash flows of MNCs.

Types of Country Risk Assessment

Although there is no consensus as to how country risk can best be assessed, some guidelines have been developed. The first step is to recognize the difference between (1) an overall risk assessment of a country without consideration of the MNC's business and (2) the risk assessment of a country as it relates to the MNC's type of business. The first type can be referred to as **macroassessment** of country risk and the latter type as a **microassessment.** Each type is discussed in turn.

It is important to know how an appropriate country risk assessment varies with the firm, industry, and project of concern and therefore why a macroassessment of country risk has its limitations. A microassessment is also necessary when evaluating the country risk related to a particular project proposed by a particular firm.

In addition to political variables, financial variables are also necessary for microassessment of country risk. Microfactors include the sensitivity of the firm's business to real GDP growth, inflation trends, interest rates, and other factors. Due to differences in business characteristics, some firms are more susceptible to the host country's economy than others.

In summary, the overall assessment of country risk consists of four parts.

1. Macropolitical risk
2. Macrofinancial risk
3. Micropolitical risk
4. Microfinancial risk

Although these parts can be consolidated to generate a single country risk rating, it may be useful to keep them separate so that an MNC can identify the various ways its direct foreign investment or exporting operations are exposed to country risk.

Techniques to Assess Country Risk

Once a firm identifies all the macro- and microfactors that deserve consideration in the country risk assessment, it may wish to implement a system for evaluating these factors and determining a country risk rating. Various techniques are available to achieve this objective. The following are some of the more popular techniques.

- Checklist approach
- Delphi technique
- Quantitative analysis
- Inspection visits
- Combination of techniques

Incorporating Country Risk in Capital Budgeting

If the risk rating of a country is in the tolerable range, any project related to that country deserves further consideration. Country risk can be incorporated in the capital budgeting analysis of a proposed project by adjusting the discount rate or by adjusting the estimated cash flows. Each method is discussed here.

ADJUSTMENT OF THE DISCOUNT RATE The discount rate of a proposed project is supposed to reflect the required rate of return on that project. Thus, the discount rate can be adjusted to account for the country risk. The lower the country risk rating, the higher the perceived risk and the higher the discount rate applied to the project's cash flows. This approach is convenient in that one adjustment to the capital budgeting analysis can capture country risk. However, there is no precise formula for adjusting the discount rate to incorporate country risk. The adjustment is somewhat arbitrary and may therefore cause feasible projects to be rejected or unfeasible projects to be accepted.

ADJUSTMENT OF THE ESTIMATED CASH FLOWS Perhaps the most appropriate method for incorporating forms of country risk in a capital budgeting analysis is to estimate how the cash flows would be affected by each form of risk. For example, if there is a 20% probability that the host government will temporarily block funds from the subsidiary to the parent, the MNC should estimate the project's net present value (*NPV*) under these circumstances, realizing that there is a 20% chance that this *NPV* will occur.

If there is a chance that the host government takeover will occur, the foreign project's *NPV* under these conditions should be estimated. Each possible form of risk has an estimated impact on the foreign project's cash flows and therefore on the project's *NPV*. By analyzing each possible impact, the MNC can determine the probability distribution of *NPV*s for the project. Its accept/reject decision on the project will be based on its assessment of the probability that the project will generate a positive *NPV*, as well as the size of possible *NPV* outcomes. Though this procedure may seem somewhat tedious, it directly incorporates forms of country risk into the cash flow estimates and explicitly illustrates the possible results from implementing the project. The more convenient method of adjusting the discount rate in accordance with the country risk rating does not indicate the probability distribution of possible outcomes.

Reducing Exposure to Host Government Takeovers

Although direct foreign investment offers several possible benefits, country risk can offset such benefits. The most severe country risk is a host government takeover. This type of takeover may result in major losses, especially when the MNC does not have any power to negotiate with the host government.

The following are the most common strategies used to reduce exposure to a host government takeover.

- Use a short-term horizon.
- Rely on unique supplies or technology.
- Hire local labor.
- Borrow local funds.
- Purchase insurance.

Use a Short-Term Horizon

An MNC may concentrate on recovering cash flow quickly so that in the event of expropriation, losses are minimized. An MNC would also exert only a minimum effort to replace worn-out equipment and machinery at the subsidiary. It may even phase out its overseas investment by selling off its assets to local investors or the government in stages over time.

Rely on Unique Supplies or Technology

If the subsidiary can bring in supplies from its headquarters (or a sister subsidiary) that cannot be duplicated locally, the host government will not be able to take over and operate the subsidiary without those supplies. Also the MNC can cut off the supplies if the subsidiary is treated unfairly.

If the subsidiary can hide the technology in its production process, a government takeover will be less likely. A takeover would be successful in this case only if the MNC would provide the necessary technology, and the MNC would do so only under conditions of a friendly takeover that would ensure that it received adequate compensation.

Hire Local Labor

If local employees of the subsidiary would be affected by the host government's takeover, they can pressure their government to avoid such action. However, the government could still keep those employees after taking over the subsidiary. Thus, this strategy has only limited effectiveness in avoiding or limiting a government takeover.

Borrow Local Funds

If the subsidiary borrows funds locally, local banks will be concerned about its future performance. If for any reason a government takeover would reduce the probability that the banks would receive their loan repayments promptly, they might attempt to prevent a takeover by the host government. However, the host government may guarantee repayment to the banks, so this strategy has only limited effectiveness. Nevertheless, it could still be preferable to a situation in which the MNC not only loses the subsidiary but also still owes home country creditors.

Purchase Insurance

Insurance can be purchased to cover the risk of expropriation. For example, the U.S. government provides insurance through the Overseas Private Investment Corporation (OPIC). The insurance premiums paid by a firm depend on the degree of insurance coverage and the risk associated with the firm. Yet, any insurance policy will typically cover only a portion of the company's total exposure to country risk.

Many home countries of MNCs have investment guarantee programs that insure to some extent the risks of expropriation, wars, or currency blockage. Some guarantee programs have a one-year waiting period or longer before compensation is paid on losses due to expropriation. Also, some insurance policies do not cover all forms of expropriation. Furthermore, to be eligible for such insurance, the subsidiary might be required by the country to concentrate on exporting rather than on local sales. Even if a subsidiary qualifies for insurance, there is a cost. Any insurance will typically cover only a portion of the assets and may specify a maximum duration of coverage, such as 15 or 20 years. A subsidiary must weigh the benefits of this insurance against the cost of the policy's premiums and potential losses in excess of coverage. The insurance can be helpful, but it does not by itself prevent losses due to expropriation.

In 1993, Russia established an insurance fund to protect MNCs against various forms of country risk. The Russian government took this action to encourage more direct foreign investment in Russia.

The World Bank has established an affiliate called the Multilateral Investment Guarantee Agency (MIGA) to provide political insurance for MNCs with direct foreign investment in less developed countries. MIGA offers insurance against expropriation, breach of contract, currency inconvertibility, war, and civil disturbances.

Impact of an MNC's Country Risk Analysis on Its Value

An MNC's country risk analysis can affect its value. The country risk analysis determines the expected cash flows derived from each foreign subsidiary in the future. A country risk analysis may also lead to a decision to divest a subsidiary, which means that the expected foreign currency cash flows generated by that subsidiary will terminate after that point. Thus, the expected foreign currency cash flows that will ultimately be remitted to the U.S. parent are influenced by the country risk analysis.

The parent's required rate of return on the funds it provides to support operations in foreign countries is also affected by its country risk analysis. During the Asian crisis, many MNCs revised their country risk assessment upward for Asian countries. Thus, the required rate of return for investment in Asian operations would have been revised upward even if no other factors changed, which reduced the value of the MNC.

Mergers, Acquisitions, and Business Valuations

Mergers and Acquisitions

The purpose of this section is to provide you with a general understanding of mergers, the motivations for mergers, and merger activity in the United States. Merger analysis, which is the evaluation of the attractiveness of a merger, should be conducted in the same manner as capital budgeting analysis. (If the present value of the cash flows expected to result from the merger exceeds the price that must be paid for the company being acquired, then the merger has a positive net present value and the acquiring firm should proceed with the acquisition.)

Rationale for Mergers

There are five principal reasons two or more firms are merged to form a single firm.

1. **Synergy.** The primary motivation for most mergers is to increase the value of the combined enterprise—the hope is that *synergy* exists so that the value of the company formed by the merger is greater than the sum of the values of the individual companies taken separately. Synergistic effects can arise from four sources: (a) *operating economies of scale* occur when cost reductions result from the combination of the companies; (b) *financial*

economies might include a higher price/earnings ratio, a lower cost of debt, or a greater debt capacity; (c) *differential management efficiency* generally results when one firm is relatively inefficient, so the merger improves the profitability of the acquired assets; and (d) *increased market power* occurs if reduced competition exists after the merger. Operating and financial economies are socially desirable, as are mergers that increase managerial efficiency; but mergers that reduce competition are both undesirable and often illegal.

In the 1880s and 1890s, many mergers occurred in the United States, and some of them clearly were directed toward gaining market power at the expense of competition rather than increasing operating efficiency. As a result, Congress passed a series of acts designed to ensure that mergers are not used as a method of reducing competition. Today, the principal acts include the Sherman Act (1890), the Clayton Act (1914), and the Celler-Kefauver Act (1950). These acts make it illegal for firms to combine in any manner if the combination will lessen competition. They are administered by the antitrust division of the Justice Department and by the Federal Trade Commission.

2. **Tax considerations.** Tax considerations have stimulated a number of mergers. For example, a firm that is highly profitable and in the highest corporate tax bracket could acquire a company with large accumulated tax losses, then use those losses to shelter its own income. Similarly, a company with large losses could acquire a profitable firm. Also, tax considerations could cause mergers to be a desirable use for excess cash. For example, if a firm has a shortage of internal investment opportunities compared to its cash flows, it will have excess cash, and its options for disposing of this excess cash are to (a) pay an extra dividend, (b) invest in marketable securities, (c) repurchase its own stock, or (d) purchase another firm. If the firm pays an extra dividend, its stockholders will have to pay taxes on the distribution. Marketable securities such as Treasury bonds provide a good temporary parking place for money, but the rate of return on such securities is less than that required by stockholders. A stock repurchase might result in a capital gain for the remaining stockholders, but it could be disadvantageous if the company has to pay a high price to acquire the stock, and, if the repurchase is designed solely to avoid paying dividends, it might be challenged by the IRS. However, using surplus cash to acquire another firm has no immediate tax consequences for either the acquiring firm or its stockholders, and this fact has motivated a number of mergers.

3. **Purchase of assets below their replacement cost.** Sometimes a firm will become an acquisition candidate because the replacement value of its assets is considerably higher than its market value. For example, in the 1980s oil companies could acquire reserves more cheaply by buying out other oil companies than by exploratory drilling. This factor was a motive in **Chevron's** acquisition of **Gulf Oil**. The acquisition of **Republic Steel** (the sixth largest steel company) by **LTV** (the fourth largest) provides another example of a firm being purchased because its purchase price was less than the replacement value of its assets. LTV found that it was less costly to purchase Republic Steel for $700 million than it would have been to construct a new steel mill. At the time, Republic's stock was selling for less than one-third of its book value. However, the merger did not help LTV's inefficient operations—ultimately, the company filed for bankruptcy.

4. **Diversification.** Managers often claim that diversification helps to stabilize the firm's earnings and thus reduces corporate risk. Therefore, diversification often is given as a reason for mergers. Stabilization of earnings certainly is beneficial to a firm's employees, suppliers, and customers, but its value to stockholders and debtholders is less clear. If an investor is worried about earnings variability, he or she probably could diversify through stock purchases (investment portfolio adjustment) more easily than the firm could through acquisitions.

5. **Maintaining control.** Some mergers and takeovers are considered *hostile* because the management of the acquired firm opposes the merger. One reason for the hostility is that the managers of the acquired companies generally lose their jobs, or at least their autonomy. Therefore, managers who own less than 50% plus one share of the stock in their firms look to devices that will lessen the chances of their firms' being taken over. Mergers can serve as such a device. For example, when **Enron** was under attack, it arranged to buy **Houston Natural Gas Company**, paying for Houston primarily with debt. That merger made Enron much larger and hence harder for any potential acquirer to "digest." Also, the much higher debt level resulting from the merger made it hard for any acquiring company to use debt to buy Enron. Such **defensive mergers** are difficult to defend on economic grounds. The managers involved invariably argue that synergy, not a desire to protect their own jobs, motivated the acquisition, but there can be no question that many mergers have been designed more for the benefit of managers than for stockholders.

Mergers undertaken only to use accumulated tax losses probably would be challenged by the IRS. However, because many factors are present in any given merger, it is hard to prove that a merger was motivated only, or even primarily, by tax considerations.

Types of Mergers

Economists classify mergers into four groups: (1) horizontal, (2) vertical, (3) congeneric, and (4) conglomerate. A **horizontal merger** occurs when one firm combines with another in its same line of business. For example, the acquisition of **Chrysler** by **Daimler-Benz AG** in 1998 was a horizontal merger because both firms are automobile manufacturers. An example of a **vertical merger** is a steel producer's acquisition of one of its own suppliers, such as an iron or coal mining firm. The 1993 merger of **Merck & Co.**, a manufacturer of health care products, and **Medco Containment**, the largest mail-order pharmacy service, is an example of a vertical merger. Congeneric means "allied in nature or action"; hence, a **congeneric merger** involves related enterprises but not producers of the same product (horizontal) or firms in a producer-supplier relationship (vertical). Examples of congeneric mergers include **Viacom's** acquisitions of **Paramount Communications** and **Blockbuster Entertainment** in 1994. Viacom owns several television stations and cable systems and distributes television programming, while Paramount produces movies and other entertainment shown both on television and in theaters, and Blockbuster's principal business is the rental of movies, most of which previously have been shown in theaters. A **conglomerate merger** occurs when unrelated enterprises combine, as illustrated by **Sears, Roebuck & Company** acquisitions of **Dean Witter Reynolds Organization Inc.**, a securities broker and investment banker, and **Coldwell Banker & Company**, a real estate firm, in 1981. (Sears has since divested itself of both firms.)

> Another type of merger is beachhead merger which is used to enter a new industry to exploit perceived opportunities.

Operating economies (and also anticompetitive effects) are dependent on the type of merger involved. Vertical and horizontal mergers generally provide the greatest synergistic operating benefits, but they also are the ones most likely to be attacked by the U.S. Department of Justice. In any event, it is useful to think of these economic classifications when analyzing the feasibility of a prospective merger.

Merger Activity

Four major "merger waves" have occurred in the United States. The first was in the late 1800s, when consolidations occurred in the oil, steel, tobacco, and other basic industries. The second was in the 1920s, when the stock market boom helped financial promoters consolidate firms in a number of industries, including utilities, communications, and autos. The third was in the 1960s, when conglomerate mergers were the rage, while the fourth began in the early 1980s, and it is still going strong. Many of the recent mergers have been horizontal mergers.

The current "merger mania" has been sparked by several factors: (1) at times, the depressed level of the dollar relative to Japanese and European currencies have made U.S. companies look cheap to foreign buyers; (2) the unprecedented level of inflation that existed during the 1970s and early 1980s, which increased the replacement value of firms' assets even while a weak stock market reduced their market values; (3) the general belief among the major natural resource companies that it is cheaper to "buy reserves on Wall Street" through mergers than to explore and find them in the field; (4) attempts to ward off raiders by use of defensive mergers; (5) the development of the junk bond market, which has made it possible to use far more debt in acquisitions than had been possible earlier; and (6) the increased globalization of business, which has led to increased economies of scale and to the formation of worldwide corporations.

Many of the mergers in 1998 and 1999 resulted either because the acquired firms were considered undervalued or because it was felt economies of scale could produce less costly combined operations. Increased global competition and governmental reforms were the major reasons for merger activities in the telecommunications and financial services industries, which accounted for the nearly 50% of the 1998 mergers. Experts expect these industries and other industries, such as defense, consumer products, and natural resources, to become significantly reshaped as merger activity continues in the future.

Leveraged Buyouts (LBOs)

With the extraordinary merger activity that took place in the 1980s, we witnessed a huge increase in the popularity of **leveraged buyouts,** or **LBOs.** The number and size of LBOs jumped significantly during this period. This development occurred for the same reasons that mergers and divestitures occurred—the existence of potential bargains, situations in which companies were using insufficient leverage, and the development of the junk bond market, which facilitated the use of leverage in takeovers.

LBOs can be initiated in one of two ways: (1) The firm's own managers can set up a new company whose equity comes from the managers themselves, plus some equity from pension funds and other institutions. This new company then arranges to borrow a large amount of money by selling junk bonds through an investment banking firm. With the financing arranged, the management group then makes an offer to purchase all the publicly owned shares through a tender offer. (2) A specialized LBO firm, with **Kohlberg Kravis Roberts (KKR)** being the best known, will identify a potential target company, go to the management, and suggest that an LBO deal be done. KKR and other LBO firms have billions of dollars of equity, most put up by pension funds and other large investors, available for the equity portion of the deals, and they arrange junk bond financing just as would a management-led group. Generally, the newly formed company will have at least 80% debt, and sometimes the debt ratio is as high as 98%. Thus, the term *leveraged* is most appropriate.

To illustrate an LBO, consider the $25 billion leveraged buyout of **RJR Nabisco** by KKR in 1989. RJR, a leading producer of tobacco and food products with such brands as Winston, Camel, Planters, Ritz, and Oreo, was trading at about $55 a share. Then F. Ross Johnson, RJR Nabisco's president and CEO at the time, announced a $75 per share, or $17.6 billion, offer to take the firm private. The day after the announcement, RJR's stock soared to $77.25, which indicated that investors thought that the final price would be even higher than Johnson's opening bid. A few days later, KKR offered $90 per share, or $20.6 billion, for the firm. The battle between the two bidders continued until late November, when RJR's board accepted a revised KKR bid of cash and securities worth about $109 per share, for a total value of about $25.1 billion.

Was RJR worth $25 billion, or did Henry Kravis and his partners let their egos govern their judgment? At the time the LBO was initiated, analysts believed that the deal was workable, but barely. Six years after the deal, KKR had disposed of all its interest in RJR Nabisco, and many experts called the biggest LBO of its time the biggest financial flop in history.

It is not clear if LBOs are, on balance, a good or a bad idea. Some government officials and others have stated a belief that the leverage involved might destabilize the economy. On the other hand, LBOs certainly have stimulated some lethargic managements, and that is good. Good or bad, though, LBOs have helped reshape the face of corporate America.

Business Valuations

The value of a firm is determined by its profitability and growth rates, which are influenced by its marketing and finance strategies.

Business valuation is valuing the worth of a business entity, whether in whole or part. The value of a business is derived from its ability to generate cash flows consistently period after period over the long term. Business valuation can be performed at various milestones such as new product introduction; mergers, acquisitions, divestitures, recapitalization, and stock repurchases; capital expenditures and improvements; joint venture agreements; and ongoing review of performance of business unit operations.

The corporate philosophy is that shareholders are the owners of the corporation, the board of directors acts as their representatives, and the corporation's objective is to maximize the shareholder value. A company management that focuses on building and enhancing shareholder value is creating more value for its shareholders. Companies with higher labor productivity are more likely to create more value than those with lower productivity, and companies that are able to create more value will be able to create more jobs. This solid value chain is shown here.

Higher labor productivity → Higher company value → More jobs creation

Shareholder value in the stock market is the ultimate output measure of a company's performance, and is based on discounted cash flow (DCF) techniques. Financial indicators such as growth rate and return on invested capital (ROIC), which are linked to free cash flows, are useful in assessing historical performance or in setting short-term targets. DCF, which is driven by growth rate and ROIC, is valuable for strategic analysis since its focus is on long-term.[7]

ROIC is calculated as follows.

ROIC = Net operating profit after taxes divided by invested capital, where invested capital is investment in net working capital plus investment in net fixed assets plus investment in other assets.

Growth rate is calculated as follows.

Growth rate = Return on new invested capital × investment rate, where investment rate is net investment divided by operating profit.

Free cash flows are computed according to equations presented in the DCF model.

Managers who use DCF approaches to business valuation, focusing on increasing long-term free cash flows, ultimately will be creating higher stock prices. Attention to accounting earnings can lead to value-decreasing decisions while attention to cash flows can lead to value-increasing decisions. This is because accounting earnings are static, historical in nature, different from cash flows, and do not deal with the time value of money.

> *Discounted cash flow techniques combine performance across time horizons into a single result.*

Business Valuation Models

A model is a representation of a real system. There are eleven models to help management in making sound decisions during valuation of a business opportunity. The output of these models will assist management in reaching a price to be paid or money to be invested. These models, in the order of importance and usefulness, include book value model, liquidation value model, replacement cost model, discounted abnormal earnings model, price multiples model, financial analysis model, economic-value added model, market value-added model, economic profit model, net present value model, and discounted cash flow model. In practice, a combination of models is recommended. For example, the economic-value added model should be combined with market-value added model and the net present value or DCF model. Each model will be discussed.

Book Value Model

The book value of a company's stock represents the total assets of the company less its liabilities. Other terms for book value are *net assets, shareholders' equity,* or *net worth*. The book value per share has no relation to market value per share, as book values are based on historical cost of assets, not at the current value at which they could be sold. Book values are not meaningful because they are distorted by inflation factors and different accounting assumptions used in valuing assets. One use of book value is to provide a floor value, with the true value of the company being some amount higher. The floor value is the normal minimum value that the company should command in the marketplace. Sales prices of companies are usually expressed as multiples of book values within each industry. If all firms in an industry are priced at five times the book value, and the target company involved in acquisition is only selling for two times the book value, this might be an indicator of an undervalued situation. Takeover experts look for firms that are undervalued. Industries that tend to have more liquid assets tend to have higher book values than others.

Book Value Versus Market Value

- When the book value of a firm is less than its industry average, the firm is undervalued. It is an indication of inefficient utilization of the firm's assets.
- When the book value of a firm is more than its industry average, the firm is overvalued. It is an indication of efficient utilization of the firm's assets.
- Book values have no relation to market values because book values are based on historical costs while current costs are used for market values. Earnings power and cash flows also drive the market values.

Determining the book per share is relatively easier if a company has only common stock outstanding; difficult when it has both preferred and common stock. When a company has both types of stock, the equity allocated to preferred stock is subtracted, including dividends in arrears from the total stockholders' equity, to determine the equity remaining to common shareholders. In computing the common shares outstanding, treasury stock is subtracted and the common stock distributable is included.

Example 2 *A firm has stockholders' equity of $1 million and treasury stock of 10,000 shares, and issued common stock of 110,000 shares. What is the book value per share of common stock?*

Outstanding common stock = Issued common stock − treasury stock = 110,000 − 10,000 = 100,000 shares
Book value per share of common stock = $1,000,000/100,000 = $10 per share

Example 3 *A firm has stockholders' equity of $2,565,000 and treasury stock of 10,000 shares, issued common stock of 110,000 shares, and preferred stock of 5,000 shares issued at $100 and callable at $105 per share, with 8% cumulative and one year of dividends in arrears. What is the book value per share of preferred stock and common stock?*

Equity allocated to preferred stockholders = (Number of shares x callable price) + dividends in arrears = (5,000 × $105) + ($500,000 × 0.08) = $525,000 + $40,00 = $565,000.

Equity remaining to common stockholders = Total stockholders' equity − Equity allocated to preferred stockholders = $2,565,000 − $565,000 = $2,000,000

Outstanding common stock = Issued common stock − treasury stock = 110,000 − 10,000 = 100,000 shares

Book value per share of preferred stock = $565,000/5,000 = $113 per share

Book value per share of common stock = $2,000,000/100,000 = $20.00 per share

Liquidation Value Model

Liquidation value of a firm is total assets minus all liabilities and preferred stock minus all liquidation costs incurred. Liquidation value may be a more realistic measure of a firm than its book value in that liquidation price reflects the current market value of the assets and liabilities if the firm is in a growing, profitable industry. Depending on the power of negotiations of the parties involved and the asset utilization rates of a firm, liquidation prices may be set at "fire sale" prices. Note that the liquidation value is not equal to true market value because the real market value depends on the earning power of the firm's assets and how efficiently these assets are utilized by management. Sometimes, liquidation value can act as a floor value.

Replacement Cost Model

The replacement cost model is based on the estimated cost to replace a company's assets, which include both tangible and intangible assets. The concern here is that only tangible assets such as plant, equipment, and buildings are replaceable. Intangible assets such as patents, copyrights, and human and organizational capital are not replaceable. This model ignores the value of intangible assets and hence is not a complete or useful model. Because of these concerns, the replacement cost of a company's assets understate the real market value of the company. Sometimes the replacement value of a firm's assets is higher than its market value.

Discounting Abnormal Earnings Model

If a firm can earn only a normal rate of return on its book value, then investors will pay no more than the book value. The deviation of a firm's market value from its book value depends on the firm's power to generate "abnormal earnings." We define abnormal earnings as follows.

Abnormal earnings = Total earnings − Normal earnings

Abnormal earnings = Total earnings − (cost of capital × beginning book value)

The estimated value of a firm's equity is the sum of the current book value plus the discounted future abnormal earnings.

Price Multiples Model

The value of a firm is based on price multiples of "comparable" firms in the industry. This model requires calculation of the desired price multiples and then applying the multiple to the firm being valued. Examples of price multiples include: price-to-earnings (P/E) ratio, price-to-book ratio, price-to-sales ratio, price-to-cash-flow ratio, and market-to-book ratio. Next each ratio is presented briefly.

PRICE-TO-EARNINGS RATIO This ratio should vary positively with differences in abnormal earnings and negatively with differences in discount rates (risk). It assumes that a firm will be worth some multiple of its future earnings.

PRICE-TO-BOOK RATIO   This ratio should vary across firms according to differences in their future return on equity (ROE), growth in book value, and differences in discount rates.

PRICE-TO-SALES RATIO   This ratio should vary with expected profit margins. This means firms with higher expected margins are worth more in dollar sales. This ratio is the product of price-earnings ratio and earnings-to-sales ratio.

PRICE-TO-CASH-FLOW RATIO   This ratio refers to a multiple of operating earnings before depreciation and interest, or some similar measure. The numerator in this ratio should not include the value of debt (i.e., unlevered), and the denominator should use operating earnings before interest, taxes, depreciation, and amortization (EBITDA).

MARKET-TO-BOOK RATIO   This ratio is similar to the price-to-earnings ratio. It assumes that a firm will be worth some multiple of its book value.

Financial Analysis Model

Financial analysis includes ratio analysis and cash flow analysis. The objective of ratio analysis is to evaluate the effectiveness of the firm's policies in operating, investment, and financing strategies. Effective ratio analysis involves relating the financial numbers to the underlying business factors and assumptions. While ratio analysis may not give an analyst all the answers regarding a firm's performance, it will help the analyst ask probing questions. The analyst uses income statements (net profit margin analysis) and balance sheets (asset turnover and financial leverage) for conducting the specific ratio analysis.

The target company in the merger and acquisition analysis should have a high liquidity, a low leverage, a low price earnings (P/E) ratio, increasing cash flows, and high earnings power.

In ratio analysis, the analyst can (1) compare ratios for a firm over several years (a time-series comparison), (2) compare ratios for the firm and other firms in the industry (cross-sectional comparison), and (3) compare ratios to some benchmark data. Two categories of ratios include profitability and solvency ratios. Examples of profitability ratios include gross margins, ratio of net sales to assets, return on total assets, return on equity (ROE), earnings per share (EPS), price-earnings (P/E) ratio, dividends per share, dividends yield (dividend payout ratio), and sustainable growth rate. Examples of solvency ratios include current ratio, quick ratio, accounts receivable turnover, inventory turnover, debt-to-equity ratio, and number of times interest charges are earned. These ratios were discussed in Module 600, Accounting, Section 620.

While ratio analysis focuses on analyzing a firm's income statement or its balance sheet, the cash flow analysis will focus on operating, investing, and financing policies of a firm by reviewing its statement of cash flows. Cash flow analysis also provides an indication of the quality of the information in the firm's income statement and balance sheet.

Recall that accounting-based net income differs from operating cash flows because revenues and expenses are measured on an accrual basis. There are two types of accruals included in net income. First, there are current accruals, such as credit sales and unpaid expenses. Current accruals result in changes in a firm's current assets (such as accounts receivable, inventory, and prepaid expenses), and current liabilities (such as accounts payable and accrued liabilities). The second type of accruals included in the income statement is noncurrent accruals, such as depreciation, deferred taxes, and equity income from unconsolidated subsidiaries. To derive cash flow from accounting-based net income, adjustments have to be made for both these types of accruals. In addition, adjustments have to be made for nonoperating gains and losses included in net income, such as profits from sales of assets. These adjustments were fully discussed in Module 600, Accounting, Section 620.

Economic-Value-Added Model

Economic-value-added (EVA) is operating profit minus a charge for the opportunity cost of capital. An advantage of the EVA method is its integration of revenues and costs of short-term decisions into long-term capital budgeting process. A disadvantage of EVA is that it focuses only on a single period and that it does not consider risk. The EVA model can be combined with market-valued-added model, which is described next, to address this disadvantage.

The formula for calculating the EVA follows.

$$EVA = \text{Operating Profit} - (\text{Weighted Average Cost of Capital} \times \text{Capital Invested})$$

Example 4 A company's financial data includes $40 million in revenues, $24 million in cost of goods sold, and $7.5 million in operating expenses. It invested $30 million in long-term capital and has a weighted-average cost of capital of 10%. What is the economic-value added for this company?

First, we need to compute the operating profit and then apply the EVA formula. Operating profit is revenues ($40 million) minus cost of goods sold ($24 million) minus operating expenses ($7.5 million), which is $8.5 million.

EVA = Operating profit − (weighted average cost of capital × capital invested)
EVA = $8,500,000 − (0.10 × $30,000,000) = $5,500,000

Market-Value-Added Model

Market-value-added (MVA) is the difference between the market value of a company's debt and equity and the amount of capital invested since its origin. The MVA measures the amount by which stock market capitalization increases in a period. Market capitalization is simply the number of shares outstanding multiplied by share price. Possible variations of the model include (1) the market-to-capital ratio which is market capitalization of a company's debt and equity divided by the amount of capital invested since its origin, (2) the market-to-book (M/B) ratio in that only the common stock is considered; that is, the market value of the common stock minus the capital invested since its origin. These are represented in terms of equation as follows:

Market-Value-Added = Present Value of Debt + Market Value of Equity − Capital Invested
Market-to-Capital Ratio = (Present Value of Debt + Market Value of Equity)/Capital Invested
Market-Value-Added = Market Value of Common Stock − Capital Invested

Example 5 A firm has 2 million common shares outstanding at a market price of $50 per share. Its debt is valued at $5 million and it employed a capital of $6 million. How much market-value is added to the firm?

Market value of equity = Number of common shares outstanding × market price per share = 2 million shares × $50 per share = $10 million
Market-value added = Present value of debt + market value of equity − capital invested
MVA = $5 million + $10 million − $6 million = $9 million

Economic Profit Model

According to the economic profit model, the value of a company equals the amount of capital invested plus a premium equal to the present value of the cash flows created each year.[8] Economic profit measures the value created in a company in a single period is calculated as follows.

Economic profit = Invested capital × (ROIC − WACC)

Where ROIC is return on invested capital and WACC is weighted average cost of capital. In other words, economic profit equals the difference between the return on invested capital and the weighted average cost of capital times the amount of invested capital. The economic profit is similar in concept to accounting profit, but it explicitly charges a firm for all its capital employed, not just the interest on its debt.

Two other related measures include present value of a firm's economic profit and free cash flows in perpetuity. These are calculated as follows.

Present value of a firm's economic profit in perpetuity = Economic profit per year/WACC
Present value of free cash flows in perpetuity = Free cash flows per year/WACC

Example 6 Firm A has invested a capital of $1 million, its return on invested capital is 12%, and the weighted average cost of capital is estimated at 10%. Its free cash flows per year are estimated at $100,000.

What is Firm A's economic profit per year?

Economic profit = Invested capital × (ROIC − WACC) = $1,000,000 × (0.12−0.10) = $20,000

What is Firm A's present value of economic profit in perpetuity?

Present value of economic profit = Economic profit per year/WACC = $20,000/0.10 = $200,000

What is Firm A's present value of free cash flows in perpetuity?

Present value of free cash flows = Free cash flows per year/WACC = $100,000/0.10 = $1,000,000

Net Present Value Model

Basically, the net present value (NPV) model compares the benefits of a proposed project or firm with the costs, including financing costs, and approves those projects or firms whose benefits exceed costs. The NPV model incorporates the time value of money and the riskiness of the cash flows, which are the vital elements of a valuation model. The approach is to calculate the NPV of each alternative and then select the alternative with the highest NPV. The calculation involves discounting all cash inflows (cash receipts) to the beginning of the base timeline (present), then subtracting the present value of the cash outflows (cash disbursements) from the present value of the cash inflows. The discounting is done using the cost of capital, which represents the riskiness of the cash flows. The cost of capital is called the *hurdle rate*.

Net present value (NPV) = Present value of all cash inflows − Present value of all cash outflows

If the resulting NPV is positive, the alternative is good; if negative, it is bad; if zero, it is indifferent.

Example 7 Firm A is considering the acquisition of Firm B, where the latter firm has a cash flow of $1 million per year. After acquisition, the cash flows for Firm B are expected to grow at 6% per year for 10 years. In order to achieve these cash flows, Firm A needs to invest $0.5 million annually. If the required rate of return is 12%, what is the maximum price Firm A should pay to acquire Firm B?

Year	Cash flows	Investment	Net cash flows	PV factor	PV of net cash flows
1	$1,060,000	$500,000	$ 560,000	0.8929	$ 500,024
2	1,123,600	500,000	623,600	0.7972	497,134
3	1,191,016	500,000	691,016	0.7118	491,865
4	1,262,477	500,000	762,477	0.6355	484,554
5	1,338,226	500,000	838,226	0.5674	475,609
6	1,418,519	500,000	918,519	0.5066	465,322
7	1,503,630	500,000	1,003,630	0.4523	453,942
8	1,593,848	500,000	1,093,848	0.4039	441,805
9	1,689,479	500,000	1,189,479	0.3606	428,926
10	1,790,848	500,000	1,290,848	0.3220	415,653
			Total present value		$4,654,834

The present value (PV) factor is taken from Table A-1 (Module 700 Appendix) at 12% required rate of return for each of the ten years. The maximum price that Firm A can pay to acquire Firm B is approximately $4.6 million.

Discounted Cash Flow Model

The total value of a firm is value of its debt plus value of its equity. The discounted cash flow (DCF) model goes beyond the NPV model and uses free cash flows. The economic profit model measures the value created in a company in a single period, while the DCF model measures the value over multiple periods due to its free cash flows. The DCF model focuses on discounting cash flows from operations after investment in working capital, less capital expenditures. The model does not consider interest expense and cash dividends.

The calculation involves the generation of detailed, multiple-year forecasts of cash flows available to all providers of capital (debt and equity). The forecasts are then discounted at the weighted cost of capital to arrive at an estimated present value of the firm. The value of debt is subtracted from the value of the firm to arrive at the value of equity. To accomplish this, four steps are suggested.[9]

STEP 1: Forecast free cash flows available to debt and equity holders over a finite forecast horizon (usually 5 to 10 years). The final year of the horizon is called the "terminal year." The computation of free cash flows is given below.

   Earnings before depreciation and deferred taxes
   plus depreciation (noncash charge)
   minus capital expenditures (fixed assets)
   plus deferred taxes
   minus investment in net working capital and other assets
   equals free cash flows

STEP 2: Forecast free cash flows beyond the terminal year, based on some simplifying assumption.

STEP 3: Discount free cash flows at the weighted average cost of capital, that is, the required return on the combination of debt and equity capital. The discounted amount represents the estimated present value of free cash flows available to debt and equity holders as a group.

$$\text{Present value of cash flows} = \text{Free cash flows}/(\text{cost of capital minus growth rate})$$

where growth rate represents both sales and earnings growth.

STEP 4: To arrive at the estimated value of currently outstanding equity, subtract from the discounted free cash flows the estimated present value of debt. If there are nonoperating assets held by the firm that have not been included in the previous cash flow forecasts (for example, marketable securities, real estate held for sale, or investments in unrelated, unconsolidated businesses), then add their value to the equity amount. Similarly, the expected cost of unrecorded liabilities (nonoperating liabilities), and the market value of options, warrants, and convertible securities are subtracted from the equity amount. The value of currently outstanding equity is calculated as follows.

   Present value of discounted free cash flows available to debt and equity holders
   minus present value of debt
   plus value of nonoperating assets
   minus expected cost of unrecorded liabilities
   minus market value of options, warrants, and convertible securities
   equals the value of currently outstanding equity

The value of currently outstanding equity can be divided by the number of outstanding common shares to arrive at an estimated per-share value of the common stock. The estimated per-share amount can be compared with the current market price per share.

Example 8 Firm A is planning to acquire Firm B. The forecast of financial data (in thousands) for Firm B is given below for years 2003 and 2004.

	2003	2004
Earnings before depreciation and deferred taxes	$1,100	$1,200
Depreciation	50	75
Capital expenditures	150	200
Deferred taxes	20	25
Investment in net working capital	200	100

What is the amount of free cash flows for the year 2003?

Free cash flows for year 2003 = 1,100 + 50 − 150 + 20 − 200 = $820

What is the free cash flow growth rate for the year 2004?

Free cash flows for year 2004 = $1,200 + 75 − 200 + 25 − 100 = $1,000
Free cash flow growth rate for the year 2004 = ($1,000 − $820)/$820 = 21.9%

Example 9 Firm X is planning to acquire Firm Y. The forecast of financial data (in thousands) for Firm Y is given below for the year 2003.

The discounted present value of free cash flows available to debt and equity holders	= $3,020
Present value of debt	= 120
Value of nonoperating assets	= 200
Market value of options	= 50

What is the value of currently outstanding equity for Firm Y?

Value of currently outstanding equity for Firm Y = $3,020 − 120 + 200 − 50 = $3,050

Operations, Marketing, and Finance

Relation Between Operations, Marketing, and Finance

The relation between operations, marketing, and finance functions is interesting and conflicting at times. It would be interesting if all three functions can work together; it would be conflicting otherwise. Goal conflict occurs when individual objectives differ from business objectives. Typical business objectives include (1) operations producing a product or providing a service, (2) marketing selling the product or service, and (3) finance funding the product or service. In order to achieve these objectives, marketing wants more inventory on hand, production wants more raw materials and labor on hand, and finance wants less inventory, raw materials, and labor on hand. Each function's objectives are right in their own way, but the method of achieving these objectives could require improvement. For example, marketing staff should coordinate with operations staff to ensure that production budget and sales budget are synchronized at the unit level, and that inventory budget meets the goals of marketing, operations, and finance. More specifically, operations and marketing should coordinate and communicate well during the following activities.

- Sales forecasting
- Production scheduling
- Shipping schedules
- Product design specifications
- Inventory levels

The best way to achieve common goals and objectives is to share information with common databases, frequent meetings with open communications, and close coordination with mutual trust and confidence.

The following information is supplied by marketing to finance.

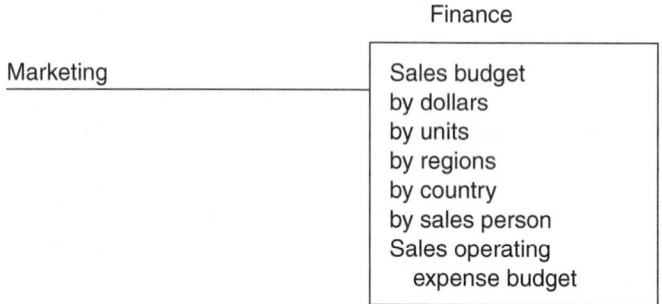

The following information is supplied by finance to marketing.

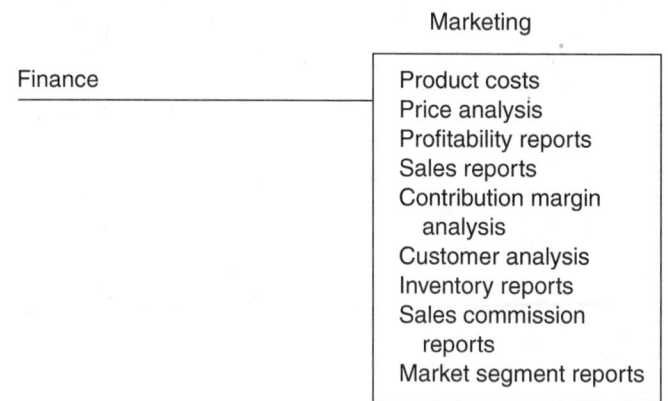

The following information is supplied by marketing to operations.

Marketing	Operations
	Sales budget
	by units
	by model
	by product
	by quarter
	Inventory budget

The following information is supplied by operations to marketing.

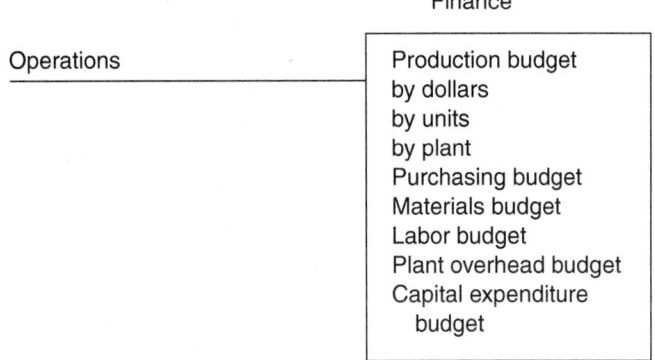

The following information is supplied by operations to finance.

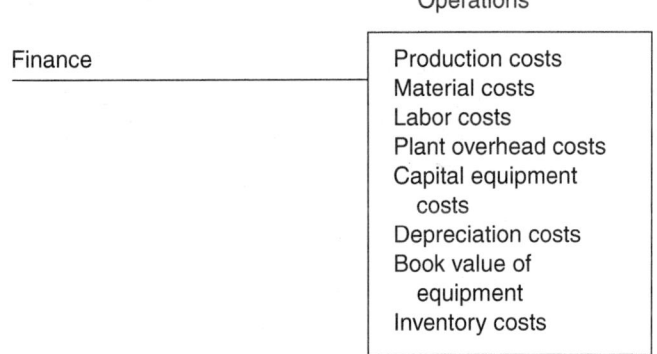

The following information is supplied by finance to operations.

```
                        Operations
                        ┌─────────────────────────┐
Finance                 │ Production costs        │
────────────            │ Material costs          │
                        │ Labor costs             │
                        │ Plant overhead costs    │
                        │ Capital equipment       │
                        │    costs                │
                        │ Depreciation costs      │
                        │ Book value of           │
                        │    equipment            │
                        │ Inventory costs         │
                        └─────────────────────────┘
```

Quantitative Techniques and Finance

In this section, we will present a variety of quantitative techniques used in the finance and accounting functions. These include cash management model; depreciation, depletion, and amortization methods; the time value of money; and basic valuation of assets.

770. QUANTITATIVE TECHNIQUES AND FINANCE   367

The Cash Management Model

The cash management model (Miller-Orr model) is used to monitor the cash position of a company, which is subject to fluctuations daily, weekly, or monthly. The management goal is to invest excess idle cash and to meet ongoing financial obligations. The model sets two control limits: the *lower control limit* (LCL), which is a minimum; and the *upper control limit* (UCL), which is a maximum, similar to statistical process control in a manufacturing quality control environment. As long as the target cash balance (TCB) is between LCL and UCL, no action needs to be taken. When the actual cash balance reaches the LCL (point X in Exhibit 700.48), investment securities worth of TCB-LCL are to be sold in order to return the cash balance to the target level. When the actual cash balance reaches the UCL (point Y in Exhibit 700.48), investment securities worth of UCL-TCB are to be bought in order to return the cash balance to the target level. Exhibit 700.48 shows a graph for the Miller-Orr model.

Management sets the lower control limit, which acts as a safety stock or a required compensating balance. The firm needs to calculate the standard deviation of monthly net cash flows, hence its variance, in order to compute the target cash balance. The upper control limit can be calculated as $(3 \times TCB) - (2 \times LCL)$ and the average cash balance (ACB) can be calculated as $(4 \times TCB - LCL)/3$.

Other Quantitative Methods

- *Simultaneous equations are used in allocating a production department's overhead costs to service departments in a manufacturing firm.*
- *A Markov chain analysis is used to identify changes in the customer's collection experience. The analysis is related to the uncollected receivable balance percentages.*

Example 10 Firm XYZ has established a minimum cash balance requirement of $100 and a target cash balance of $400. What is the maximum cash balance for firm XYZ?

$$UCL = (3 \times TCB) - (2 \times LCL) = (3 \times \$400) - (2 \times \$100) = \$1,000$$

What is the average cash balance for firm XYZ?

$$ACB = (4 \times TCB - LCL)/3 = (4 \times 400 - 100)/3 = \$500$$

How much securities can be bought if the cash balance reaches the maximum?

$$\text{Amount of securities to be bought} = UCL - TCB = \$1,000 - \$400 = \$600$$

Exhibit 700.48 *The Miller-Orr Model Graph*

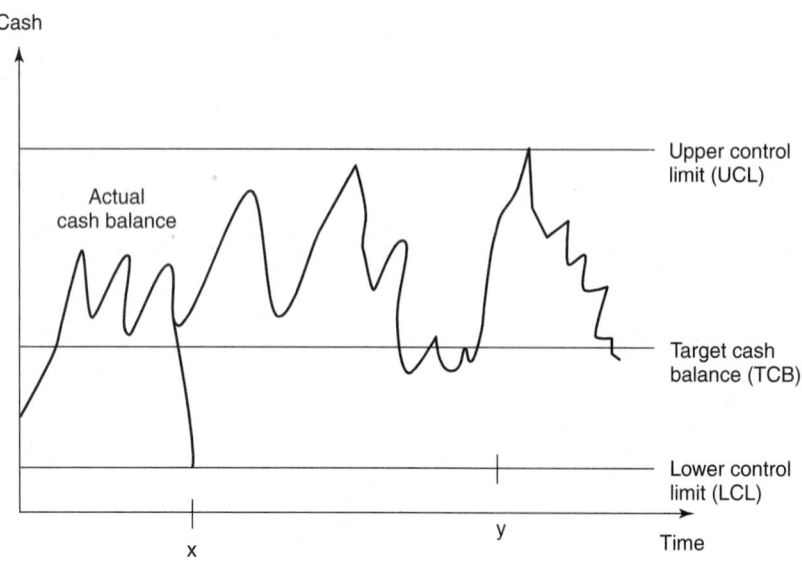

Depreciation, Depletion, and Amortization Methods

Simple ratios and basic math calculations are used in allocating costs of operational, long-term, fixed assets. Cost allocation for operational assets is known as depreciation for plant and equipment, depletion for natural resources such as coal and iron ore, and amortization for intangible assets such as patents and copyrights.

Higher depreciation expense results in lower taxes and higher cash flows.

Depreciation is a process of cost allocation, not valuation of assets. The depreciation expense for an asset, which is used to manufacture a product, is part of the overhead cost and is included in the cost of goods sold and cost of inventory. Because depreciation is a non-cash expense, the amount of depreciation is added back to the accounting net income to compute cash flows for the period.

Depreciation Methods

There are two specific methods for depreciation: the straight-line method for stockholder reporting ("book") purposes, and the accelerated cost recovery method (known as Modified Accelerated Cost Recovery System, MACRS) for tax purposes. The straight line method is simple and widely used, as an equal amount of depreciable base is allocated to each year of the asset's service life. The depreciable base, which is the original cost of the equipment minus the residual value, is divided by the number of years of the asset's service life. The book value of a machine is its original cost minus the accumulated depreciation expense. The MACRS method uses asset lives and recovery allowance percentages for personal property provided by tax authorities. The yearly recovery allowance for depreciation expense is determined by multiplying each asset's depreciable basis by the applicable recovery percentages. In the MACRS method, the entire cost of an asset is expensed over its depreciable life, unlike the straight line method. This means salvage value is ignored in the MACRS method, giving businesses larger tax deductions and thereby increasing their cash flows available for reinvestment.

Example 11 *A manufacturing company purchased a machine for $200,000. The company expects the service life of the machine to be five years. It is expected that the machine will produce 100,000 units during its life. The residual value is estimated at $50,000. What is the depreciation expense per year using the straight-line method?*

Depreciable base/number of years = ($200,000 − $50,000)/5 = $150,000/5 = $30,000 per year

Depletion Methods

The activity-based units-of-production method is widely used to calculate periodic depletion of natural resources such as coal and iron ore. Depletion base is cost less any anticipated residual value. The depletion rate per unit is multiplied with actual units extracted to obtain the total depletion expense.

Example 12 *The coal deposits for a firm are estimated at 1,000,000 tons with the capitalized costs of $700,000 and residual value of $100,000. The actual coal extracted in the month of January is 400,000 tons. What is the depletion expense for the month of January?*

Depletion rate per ton = Depletion base/estimated extractable tons
0.60/ton = ($700,000 − $100,000)/1,000,000
The depletion expense for the January month = extracted tons in January × depletion rate per ton
$240,000 = 400,000 × $0.60

Amortization Methods

The capitalized cost of an intangible asset must be allocated to the periods in which the asset is expected to contribute to the company's revenue generating activities. Intangible assets such as goodwill, patents, franchises, and copyrights have no residual value, so the amortization base is simply the original cost. GAAP states that the service life of most intangible assets should not exceed 40 years. In practice, goodwill is amortized over 20 years, patents are amortized over 17 years, franchise is amortized during the life of its agreement, and copyrights are amortized over 40 years, although the actual rights exceed 40 years allowed by GAAP. The straight-line method should be used to amortize the cost of intangible assets unless the company can show that another method is more appropriate.

The Time Value of Money

Financial decision making, whether from the perspective of firms or investors, is primarily concerned with determining how value will be affected by the expected outcomes (payoffs) associated with alternative choices. For example, if you have $5,500 to invest today, you must decide what to do with the money. If you have the opportunity to purchase an investment that will return $7,020 after five years or an investment that will return $8,126 after eight years, which should you choose? To answer this question, you must determine which investment alternative has greater value to you.

All else equal, a dollar received soon is worth more than a dollar expected in the distant future because the sooner a dollar is received the quicker it can be invested to earn a positive return. So does that mean the five-year investment is more valuable than the eight-year investment? Not necessarily, because the eight-year investment promises a higher dollar payoff than the five-year investment. To determine which investment is more valuable, the dollar payoffs for the investments need to be compared at the same point in time. Thus, for these two investments, we could determine the current values of both investments by restating, or revaluing, the payoffs expected at different times in the future (for example, $7,020 in five years and $8,126 in eight years) in terms of current (today's) dollars. The concept used to revalue payoffs such as those associated with these investments is termed the *time value of money*. It is essential that both financial managers and investors have a clear understanding of the time value of money and its impact on the value of an asset. We show how the timing of cash flows affects asset values and rates of return.

The principles of time value analysis that are developed in this section have many applications, ranging from setting up schedules for paying off loans to decisions about whether to acquire new equipment. *In fact, of all the techniques used in finance, none is more important than the concept of the time value of money (TVM).*

Cash Flow Timelines

One of the most important tools in time value of money analysis is the **cash flow timeline,** which is used to help us visualize when the cash flows associated with a particular situation occur.

Cash flows are placed directly below the tick marks, and interest rates are shown directly above the cash flow time line. Unknown cash flows, which we are trying to find in the analysis, are indicated by question marks. For example, consider the following timeline:

TIME: 0   5%   1   2   3
                                ├─────────┼───────┼───────┤
         Cash Flows: 2100   ?

Here the interest rate for each of the three periods is 5%; a single amount (or lump sum) cash **outflow** is made at Time 0; and the Time 3 value is an unknown **inflow.** Because the initial $100 is an outflow (an investment), it has a minus sign. Because the Period 3 amount is an inflow, it does not have a minus sign. Note that no cash flows occur at Time 1 and Time 2.

Future Value

A dollar in hand today is worth more than a dollar to be received in the future because, if you had it now, you could invest it, earn interest, and end up with more than one dollar in the future. The process of going from today's values, which are termed present values (PV), to future values (FV) is called **compounding.** To illustrate, suppose you deposited $100 in a bank account that paid 5% interest each year. How much would you have at the end of one year? To begin, we define the following terms.

- PV = Present value, or beginning amount, in your account. Here PV = $100.
- i = Interest rate the bank pays on the account per year. The interest earned is based on the balance in the account at the beginning of each year, and we assume that it is paid at the end of the year. Here i = 5%, or, expressed as a decimal, i = 0.05. Throughout this chapter, we designate the interest rate as i because that symbol is used on most financial calculators. Note, though, that in later chapters we use the symbol k to denote interest rates because k is used more often in the financial literature.
- INT = Dollars of interest you earn during the year 5 (Beginning of year amount) × i. Here INT = $100 × 0.05 = $5 in the first year.
- FV_n = Future value, or value of the account at the end of n periods (years in this case), after the interest earned has been added to the account.
- n = Number of periods interest is earned. Here n = 1.

In our example, n = 1, so FV_n can be calculated as follows:

$$FV_n = FV_1 = PV + INT$$
$$= PV + (PV \times i)$$
$$= PV(1 + i)$$
$$= \$100(1 + 0.05) = \$100(1.05) = \$105.$$

Thus, the **future value (FV)** at the end of one year, FV_1, equals the present value multiplied by 1.0 plus the interest rate. So you will have $105 in one year if you invest $100 today and 5% interest is paid at the end of the year.

In general, the future value of an initial sum at the end of n years can be found by applying Equation 7.51.

$$FV_n = PV(1 + i)^n \tag{7.51}$$

Equation 7.51 and most other time value of money problems can be solved in three ways: numerically with a regular calculator, with interest rate tables, or with a financial calculator. We choose the first two approaches in this section.

Numerical Solution

According to Equation 7.51, to compute the future value, FV, of an amount invested today (PV) we need to determine by what multiple the amount invested will increase in the future. As you can see, the multiple by which any amount will increase is based on the total dollar interest earned, which depends on both the interest rate and the length of time interest is earned. This multiple, termed the **future value interest factor for i and n ($FVIF_{i,n}$),** is defined as $(1 + i)^n$.

Interest Tables (Tabular Solution)

As we showed in the previous section, computing the values for $FVIF_{i,n}$ is not a very difficult task if you have a calculator handy. Exhibit 700.49 gives the future value interest factors for i values from 4% to 6% and n values from 1 to 6 periods, while Table A-3 in Module 700 Appendix contains $FVIF_{i,n}$ values for a wide range of i and n values.

Because $(1 + i)^n = FVIF_{i,n}$, Equation 7.51 can be rewritten as follows.

$$FV_n = PV(1 + i)^n = PV(FVIF_{i,n}) \tag{7.51a}$$

To illustrate, the FVIF for our five-year, 5% interest problem can be found in Exhibit 700.49 by looking down the first column to Period 5, and then looking across that row to the 5% column, where we see that $FVIF_{5\%,5} = 1.2763$. Then, the value of $100 after five years is found as follows.

$$FV_n = PV(FVIF_{i,n})$$
$$= \$100(FVIF_{5\%,5})$$

Exhibit 700.49 *Future Value Interest Factors:* $FVIF_{i,n} = (1+i)^n$

Period (N)	4%	5%	6%
1	1.0400	1.0500	1.0600
2	1.0816	1.1025	1.1236
3	1.1249	1.1576	1.1910
4	1.1699	1.2155	1.2625
5	1.2167	**1.2763**	1.3382
6	1.2653	1.3401	1.4185

Using the interest Table A-3 in Module 700 Appendix, the future value of $1 for five years at 5% interest rate is 1.2763. Then the value of $100 after five years is

$$= \$100(1.2763)$$
$$= \$127.63$$

Present Value

Suppose you have some extra cash, and you have a chance to buy a low-risk security that will pay $127.63 at the end of five years. Your local bank is currently offering 5% interest on five-year certificates of deposit, and you regard the security as being very safe. The 5% rate is called your **opportunity cost rate,** or the rate of return you could earn on alternative investments of *similar risk*. How much should you be willing to pay for the security?

From the future value example presented in the previous section, we saw that an initial amount of $100 invested at 5% per year would be worth $127.63 at the end of five years. As we will see in a moment, you should be indifferent to the choice between $100 today and $127.63 at the end of five years, and the $100 is defined as the **present value,** or **PV,** of $127.63 due in five years when the opportunity cost rate is 5%. If the price of the security is anything less than $100, you should definitely buy it because it would cost you exactly $100 to produce the $127.63 in five years if you earned a 5% return. Therefore, if you could find another investment with the same risk that would produce the same future amount ($127.63) but it cost less than $100 (say $95), then you could earn a return higher than 5% by purchasing that investment. Similarly, if the price of the security is greater than $100, you should not buy it because it would cost you only $100 to produce the same future amount at the given rate of return. If the price is exactly $100, then you could either buy it or turn it down because $100 is the security's fair value if it has a 5% expected return.

In general, *the present value of a cash flow due n years in the future is the amount that, if it were on hand today, would grow to equal the future amount.* Because $100 would grow to $127.63 in five years at a 5% interest rate, $100 is the present value of $127.63 due five years in the future when the opportunity cost rate is 5%. Finding present values is called **discounting,** and it simply is the reverse of compounding—if you know the PV, you can compound to find the FV, while if you know the FV, you can discount to find the PV. When discounting, you would follow these steps:

CASH FLOW TIMELINE:
```
        0    5%   1    2    3    4    5
        |─────────|────|────|────|────|
       PV 5 ?                      127.63
```

EQUATION:
To develop the present value, or discounting, equation, we begin with Equation 7.51a:

$$FV_n = PV(1+i)^n = PV(FVIF_{i,n}) \quad (7.51a)$$

and then solve for PV to yield

$$PV = \frac{FV_n}{(1+i)^n} = FV_n \left[\frac{1}{(1+i)^n}\right] = FV_n(PVIF_{i,n}) \quad (7.52)$$

The middle form and the last form of Equation 7.52 recognizes that the interest factor $PVIF_{i,n}$ is equal to

$$PVIF_{i,n} = \frac{1}{(1+i)^n} \quad (7.52a)$$

The term given in Equation 7.52a is called the **present value interest factor for i and n ($PVIF_{i,n}$).**

Tabular Solution:

Table A-1 in Module 700 Appendix contains present value interest factors for selected values of i and n, $PVIF_{i,n}$. The value of $PVIF_{i,n}$ for i = 5% and n = 5 periods is 0.7835, so the present value of $127.63 to be received after five years when the opportunity cost rate is 5% equals

$$\begin{aligned} PV &= \$127.63 \, (PVIF_{5\%,5}) \\ &= \$127.63(0.7835) \\ &= \$100 \end{aligned}$$

Future Value of an Annuity

An **annuity** is a series of equal payments made at fixed intervals for a specified number of periods. For example, $100 at the end of each of the next three years is a three-year annuity. The payments are given the symbol PMT, and they can occur at either the beginning or the end of each period. If the payments occur at the end of each period, as they typically do in business transactions, the annuity is called an **ordinary,** or **deferred, annuity.** If payments are made at the *beginning* of each period, the annuity is an **annuity due.** Because ordinary annuities are more common in finance, when the term *annuity* is used in this module, you should assume that the payments occur at the end of each period unless otherwise noted.

Ordinary Annuities

If you deposit $100 at the end of each year for three years in a savings account that pays 5% interest per year, how much will you have at the end of three years? To answer this question, we must find the future value of an ordinary annuity, FVA_n. Each payment is compounded out to the end of Period n, and the sum of the compounded payments is the future value of the annuity.

CASH FLOW TIMELINE:
Here we show the regular cash flow time line as the top portion of the diagram, but we also show how each cash flow is processed to produce the value FVA_n in the lower portion of the diagram.

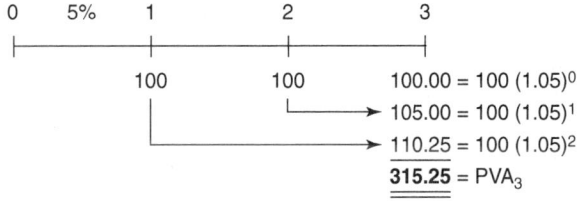

EQUATION:
The cash flow time line shows that we can compute the future value of the annuity simply by determining the future values of the individual payments and then summing the results. Thus, the equation for the future value of an ordinary annuity can be written as follows:

$$\begin{aligned} FVA_n &= PMT(1+i)^0 + PMT(1+i)^1 + PMT(1+i)^2 \\ &\quad + \ldots + PMT(1+i)^{n-1} \\ &= PMT \sum_{t=1}^{n} (1+i)^{n-t} = PMT \sum_{t=0}^{n-1} (1+i)^t \end{aligned} \qquad (7.53)$$

Note that the first line of Equation 7.53 presents the annuity payments in reverse order of payment, and the superscript in each term indicates the number of periods of interest each payment receives. In other words, because the first annuity payment was made at the end of Period 1, interest would be earned in Period 2 through Period n only; thus, compounding would be for n − 1 periods rather than n periods, compounding for the second annuity payment would be for Period 3 through Period n, or n − 2 periods, and so on. The last annuity payment is made at the same time the computation is made, so there is no time for interest to be earned; thus, the superscript 0 represents the fact that no interest is earned. Simplifying the first line produces the last line of Equation 7.53.

NUMERICAL SOLUTION The lower section of the cash flow time line shows the numerical solution. The future value, FV, of each cash flow is found, and those FVs are summed to find the FV of the annuity. This is a tedious process for long annuities.

The numerical solution is easier if we simplify Equation 7.53 as follows:[8]

$$FVA_n = PMT\left[\sum_{t=1}^{n}(1+i)^{n-t}\right] = PMT\left[\frac{(1+i)^n - 1}{i}\right] \quad (7.53a)$$

Using Equation 7.53a, the future value of $100 deposited at the end of each year for three years in a savings account that earns 5% interest per year is:

$$FVA_3 = \$100\left[\frac{(1.05)^3 - 1}{0.05}\right]$$
$$= \$100(3.1525)$$
$$= \$315.25$$

TABULAR SOLUTION The summation term in the brackets in Equation 7.53a is called the **future value interest factor for an annuity of n payments at i interest (FVIFA$_{i,n}$)**:

$$FVIFA_{i,n} = \sum_{t=1}^{n}(1+i)^{n-t} = \frac{(1+i)^n - 1}{i}$$

FVIFAs have been calculated for various combinations of i and n; Table A–4 in Module 700 Appendix contains a set of FVIFA factors. To find the answer to the three-year, $100 annuity problem, first refer to Table A–4 and look down the 5% column to the third period; the FVIFA is 3.1525. Thus, the future value of the $100 annuity is $315.25.

$$FVA_n = PMT(FVIFA_{i,n})$$
$$FVA_3 = \$100(FVIFA_{5\%,3})$$
$$= \$100(3.1525)$$
$$= \$315.25.$$

Annuities Due

Had the three $100 payments in the previous example been made at the *beginning* of each year, the annuity would have been an *annuity due*. In the cash flow time line, each payment would be shifted to the left one year; therefore, each payment would be *compounded for one extra year (period)*, which means each payment would earn interest for an additional year.

CASH FLOW TIMELINE:

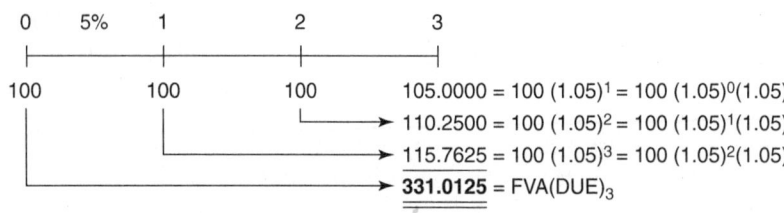

Again, the regular time line is shown at the top of the diagram, and the future value of each annuity payment at the end of Year 3 is shown in the Year 3 column, with the actual computations shown to the right.

NUMERICAL SOLUTION We can find the FV of each cash flow and then sum the results to find the FV of the annuity due, FVA(DUE)$_n$. This procedure is shown in the lower section of the cash flow time line. Note from the diagram that the difference between an ordinary annuity and an annuity due is that *each of the payments of the annuity due earns interest for one additional year*. So the numerical solution for an annuity due can also be found by adjusting Equations 7.53 and 7.53a to account for the fact that each annuity payment is able to earn an additional year's interest when compared to an ordinary annuity. The solution for FVA(DUE)$_n$ is

$$FVA(DUE)_n = PMT\left[\sum_{t=1}^{n}(1+i)^t\right] = PMT\left[\left\{\sum_{t=1}^{n}(1+i)^{n-t}\right\} \times (1+i)\right] \quad (7.53b)$$

$$= PMT\left[\left\{\frac{(1+i)^n - 1}{i}\right\} \times (1+i)\right]$$

The future value of the three $100 deposits made at the beginning of each year into a savings account that earns 5% annually is

$$FVA(DUE)_3 = \$100\left[\left\{\frac{(1.05)^3 - 1}{0.05}\right\} \times (1.05)\right]$$
$$= \$100[(3.1525) \times 1.05]$$
$$= \$331.0125$$

TABULAR SOLUTION As we have shown, for an annuity due, each payment is compounded for one additional period, so the future value interest factor for an *annuity due*, **FVIFA(DUE)$_{i,n}$**, is equal to the FVIFA$_{i,n}$ for an ordinary annuity compounded for one additional period. In other words,

$$FVIFA(DUE)_{i,n} = \left[\left\{\frac{(1+i)^n - 1}{i}\right\} \times (1+i)\right] \quad (7.53c)$$
$$= [(FVIFA_{i,n})(1+i)]$$

Here is the tabular solution for FVA(DUE)$_n$:

$$FVA(DUE)_n = PMT[FVIFA(DUE)_{i,n}]$$
$$= PMT[(FVIFA_{i,n})(1+i)]$$
$$FVA(DUE)_3 = \$100[(3.1525)(1.05)]$$
$$= \$331.0125$$

The payments occur earlier than for the ordinary annuity, so more interest is earned. Therefore, the future value of the annuity due is larger—$331.01 versus $315.25 for the ordinary annuity.

Present Value of an Annuity

Suppose you were offered the following alternatives: (1) a three-year annuity with payments of $100 at the end of each year or (2) a lump-sum payment today. You have no need for the money during the next three years, so if you accept the annuity, you would simply deposit the payments in a savings account that pays 5% interest per year. Similarly, the lump-sum payment would be deposited into the same account. How large must the lump-sum payment today be to make it equivalent to the annuity? To answer this question, we must find the present value of an ordinary annuity, **PVA$_n$**. Each payment is discounted, and the sum of the discounted payments is the present value of the annuity.

CASH FLOW TIMELINE:

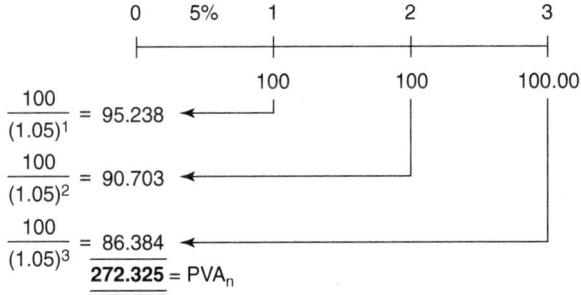

The regular cash flow time line is shown at the top of the diagram, and the numerical solution values are on the left. The PV of the annuity, PVA$_n$, is $272.325.

EQUATION:
As you can see from the cash flow time line, the present value of an annuity can be determined by computing the PV of the individual payments and summing the results. The general equation used to find the PV of an ordinary annuity is shown here:

$$PVA_n = PMT\left[\frac{1}{(1+i)^1}\right] + PMT\left[\frac{1}{(1+i)^2}\right] + \cdots + PMT\left[\frac{1}{(1+i)^n}\right]$$
$$= PMT\left[\sum_{t=1}^{n}\frac{1}{(1+i)^t}\right] \quad (7.54)$$

NUMERICAL SOLUTION   One method of determining the present value of the annuity is to compute the present value of each cash flow and then sum the result. This procedure is shown in the lower left section of the cash flow time line diagram, where we see that the PV of the annuity is $272.325. This approach can be tedious if the number of annuity payments is large.

The numerical solution is easier if we simplify Equation 7.54:[10]

$$PVA_n = PMT\left[\sum_{t=1}^{n}\frac{1}{(1+i)^t}\right] = PMT\left[\frac{1-\frac{1}{(1+i)^n}}{i}\right] \tag{7.54a}$$

Using Equation 7.54a, the PV of the three-year annuity with end-of-year payments of $100 is

$$PVA_n = \$100\left[\frac{1-\frac{1}{(1.05)^3}}{0.05}\right]$$
$$= \$100(2.72325)$$
$$= \$272.325$$

TABULAR SOLUTION   The summation term in the brackets in Equation 7.54 is called the **present value interest factor for an annuity of n payments at i interest (PVIFA$_{i,n}$)**.[11]

$$PVIFA_{i,n} = \sum_{t=1}^{n}\frac{1}{(1+i)^t} = \left[\frac{1-\frac{1}{(1+i)^n}}{i}\right]$$

The values for PVIFA at different values of i and n are shown in Table A-2 of Module 700 Appendix at the back of this module.

To find the answer to the three-year, $100 annuity problem, simply refer to Table A-2 and look down the 5% column to the third period. The PVIFA is 2.7232, so the present value of the $100 annuity is $272.32:

$$PVA_n = PMT(PVIFA_{i,n})$$
$$PVA_3 = \$100(PVIFA_{5\%,3})$$
$$= \$100(2.7232)$$
$$= \$272.32$$

Annuities Due

Had the three $100 payments in our earlier example been made at the *beginning* of each year, the annuity would have been an *annuity due*. On the cash flow time line, each payment would be shifted to the left one year, so each payment would be *discounted for one less year*. Here is the cash flow time line setup.

CASH FLOW TIMELINE:

```
                                    0     5%    1          2          3
                                    ├───────────┼──────────┼──────────┤
  100                  100
  ─────  × (1.05) =   ─────   = 100.000        100        100
  (1.05)¹              (1.05)⁰
  100                  100
  ─────  × (1.05) =   ─────   =  95.238  ◄──────┘
  (1.05)²              (1.05)¹
  100                  100
  ─────  × (1.05) =   ─────   =  90.703  ◄─────────────────┘
  (1.05)³              (1.05)²
                                 ───────
                                 285.941 = PVAₙ
```

NUMERICAL SOLUTION   Again, we can find the PV of each cash flow and then sum these PVs to find the PV of the annuity due, PVA(DUE)$_n$. This procedure is illustrated in the lower section of the time line diagram. Because the cash flows occur sooner, the PV of the annuity due exceeds that of the ordinary annuity—$285.94 versus $272.32.

The cash flow timeline shows that the difference between the PV of an annuity due and the PV of an ordinary annuity is that *each of the payments of the annuity due is discounted one less year*. So the numerical solution for an annuity due can also be found by adjusting Equations 7.54 and 7.54a to account for the fact each annuity payment will have the *opportunity* to earn an additional year's (period's) interest when compared with an ordinary annuity.

$$PVA(DUE)_n = \left[\sum_{t=0}^{n-1} \frac{1}{(1+i)^t}\right] = PMT\left[\left\{\sum_{t=1}^{n} \frac{1}{(1+i)^n}\right\} \times (1+i)\right]$$

$$= PMT\left[\left\{\frac{1 - \frac{1}{(1+i)^n}}{i}\right\} \times (1+i)\right] \tag{7.54b}$$

Therefore, if the three $100 payments were made at the beginning of the year, the PV of the annuity would be:

$$= PVA(DUE)_3 = \$100\left[\left\{\frac{1 - \frac{1}{(1.05)^3}}{0.05}\right\} \times (1.05)\right]$$

$$= \$100[(2.72325)(1.05)]$$
$$= \$100(2.85941)$$
$$= \$285.941$$

TABULAR SOLUTION We can use the PVIFAs given in Table A-2 of Module 700 Appendix, which are computed for ordinary annuities, if we adjust these values to account for the fact that the payments associated with an annuity due occur one period earlier than the payments associated with an ordinary annuity. As the cash flow time line and the numerical solution indicate, the adjustment is rather simple—just multiply the PVIFA for an ordinary annuity by $(1+i)$. So, the present value interest factor for an annuity due, **PVIFA(DUE)$_{i,n}$**, is:

$$= PVIFA(DUE)_{i,n} = \left[\left\{\frac{1 - \frac{1}{(1+i)^n}}{i}\right\} \times (1+i)\right] \tag{7.54c}$$

$$= [(PVIFA_{i,n})(1+i)]$$

The tabular solution for PVA(DUE)$_n$ is

$$PVA(DUE)_n = PMT[PVIFA(DUE)_{i,n}]$$
$$= PMT[(PVIFA_{i,n}) \times (1+i)]$$
$$PVA(DUE)_3 = \$100[(2.7232)(1.05)]$$
$$= \$100(2.85941)$$
$$= \$285.941$$

Amortized Loans

One of the most important applications of compound interest involves loans that are paid off in installments over time. Included are automobile loans, home mortgages, student loans, and most business debt other than very short-term loans and long-term bonds. If a loan is to be repaid in equal periodic amounts (monthly, quarterly, or annually), it is said to be an **amortized loan**. The word *amortized* comes from the Latin *mors*, meaning "death," so an amortized loan is one that is "killed off" over time.

To illustrate, suppose a firm borrows $15,000, and the loan is to be repaid in three equal payments at the end of each of the next three years. The lender is to receive 8% interest on the loan balance that is outstanding at the beginning of each year. The first task is to determine the amount the firm must repay each year, or the annual payment. To find this amount, recognize that the $15,000 represents the present value of an annuity of PMT dollars per year for three years, discounted at 8%.

CASH FLOW TIMELINE AND EQUATION:

```
0      8%     1           2           3
|-------------|-----------|-----------|
15,000       PMT         PMT         PMT
```

$$PVA_n = \frac{PMT}{(1+i)^1} + \frac{PMT}{(1+i)^2} + \frac{PMT}{(1+i)^3} = \sum_{t=1}^{3} \frac{PMT}{(1+i)^t}$$

$$\$15{,}000 = \sum_{t=1}^{3} \frac{PMT}{(1.08)^t}$$

Here we know everything except PMT, so we can solve the equation for PMT.

NUMERICAL SOLUTION You can solve for PMT as follows:

$$\$15{,}000 = \sum_{t=1}^{3} \frac{PMT}{(1.08)^t} = PMT\left[\sum_{t=1}^{3} \frac{1}{(1.08)^t}\right] = PMT\left[\frac{1 - \frac{1}{(1.08)^3}}{0.08}\right]$$

$$\$15{,}000 = PMT(2.2.5771)$$

$$PMT = \frac{\$15{,}000}{2.5771} = \$5{,}820.50$$

TABULAR SOLUTION Substitute in known values and look up PVIFA for I = 8% and n = 3 periods in Table A-2 of Module 700 Appendix.

$$PVA_n = PMT(PVIFA_{i,n})$$
$$\$15{,}000 = PMT(FVIFA_{8\%,3}) = PMT(2.5771)$$
$$PMT = \frac{\$15{,}000}{2.5771} = \$5{,}820.50$$

Comparison of Different Types of Interest Rates

Up to this point, we have discussed three different types of interest rates. If you will be working with relatively difficult time value problems, then it is useful to compare the three types and to know when each should be used, as we discuss next.

1. **Simple, or quoted, rate, i_{SIMPLE}.** This is the rate that is quoted by borrowers and lenders, and it is used to determine the rate earned per compounding period (periodic rate). Practitioners in the stock, bond, lending, banking, and other markets generally express financial contracts in terms of simple rates. So if you talk with a banker, broker, mortgage lender, auto finance company, or student loan officer about rates, the simple rate is the one he or she will normally quote you. However, to be meaningful, the simple rate quotation also must include the number of compounding periods per year. For example, a bank might offer 6.5%, compounded annually, on CDs, or a mutual fund might offer 6%, compounded monthly, on its money market account.

   Simple rates can be compared with one another, *but only if the instruments being compared use the same number of compounding periods per year.* Thus, to compare a 6.5% annual payment CD with a 6% monthly payment money market fund, we would need to put both instruments on an effective annual rate (EAR) basis.

   Note also that the simple rate never is shown on a time line, and it is never used as an input in a financial calculator unless compounding occurs only once a year (in which case i_{SIMPLE} = periodic rate = EAR). If more frequent compounding occurs, you must use either the periodic rate or the effective annual rate as discussed below.

2. **Periodic rate.** This is the rate charged by a lender or paid by a borrower *each interest period*. It can be a rate per year, per six-month period, per quarter, per month, per day, or per any other time interval (usually one year or less). For example, a bank might charge 1% per month on its credit card loans, or a finance company might charge 3% per quarter on consumer loans. We find the periodic rate as follows:

$$\text{Periodic rate} = \frac{i_{SIMPLE}}{m} \quad (7.55)$$

which implies that

$$i_{\text{SIMPLE}} = (\text{Periodic rate}) \times (m) = \text{APR} \qquad (7.56)$$

Here i_{SIMPLE} is the simple annual rate and m is the number of compounding periods per year. APR, which is the **annual percentage rate,** represents the periodic rate stated on an annual basis without considering interest compounding; it is i_{SIMPLE}. *The APR never is used in actual calculations; it is simply reported to borrowers.*

If there is one payment per year, or if interest is added only once a year, then m = 1 and the periodic rate is equal to the simple rate. *But, in all cases where interest is added or payments are made more frequently than annually, the periodic rate is less than the simple rate.*

The periodic rate is used for calculations in problems where two conditions hold: (a) payments occur on a regular basis more frequently than once a year, and (b) a payment is made on each compounding (or discounting) date. Thus, if you are dealing with an auto loan that requires monthly payments, with a semiannual payment bond, or with an education loan that calls for quarterly payments, then on your cash flow time line and in your calculations you would use the Periodic rate = $i_{\text{SIMPLE}} \div m$, and the appropriate number of periods would be n × m.

3. **Effective annual rate, EAR.** This is the rate with which, under annual compounding (m = 1), we would obtain the same result as if we had used a given periodic rate with m compounding periods per year. The EAR is found as follows.

$$\text{EAR} = \left(1 + \frac{i_{\text{SIMPLE}}}{m}\right)^m - 1.0$$
$$= (1 + \text{Periodic rate})^m - 1 \qquad (7.57)$$

To illustrate further, suppose you could borrow using either a credit card that charges 1% per month or a bank loan with a 12% quoted simple interest rate that is compounded quarterly. Which should you choose? To answer this question, the cost of each alternative must be expressed as an EAR.

$$\begin{aligned}
\text{Credit card loan: EAR} &= (1 + 0.01)^{12} - 1.0 \\
&= (1.01)^{12} - 1.0 \\
&= 1.126825 - 1.0 \\
&= 0.126825 = 12.6825\%. \\
\text{Bank loan: EAR} &= (1 + 0.03)^4 - 1.0 \\
&= (1.03)^4 - 1.0 \\
&= 1.125509 - 1.0 \\
&= 0.125509 = 12.5509\%.
\end{aligned}$$

Thus, the credit card loan costs a little more than the bank loan. This result should have been intuitive to you—both loans have the same 12% simple rate, yet you would have to make monthly payments on the credit card versus quarterly payments under the bank loan.

Summary of Time Value of Money Techniques

Financial decisions often involve situations in which someone pays money at one point in time and receives money at some other time. Dollars that are paid or received at two different points in time are different, and this difference is recognized and accounted for by time value of money (TVM) analysis. We next summarize the types of TVM analysis and the key concepts covered in this section, using the data shown in Exhibit 700.50 to illustrate the various points. Refer to the figure constantly, and try to find in it an example of the points covered as you go through this summary.

- **Compounding** is the process of determining the **future value (FV)** of a cash flow or a series of cash flows. The compounded amount, or future value, is equal to the beginning amount plus the interest earned.

$$\text{Future value (single payment): } FV_n = PV(1 + i)^n = PV(\text{FVIF}_{i,n})$$

Exhibit 700.50 *Illustration for Time Value of Money Summary*

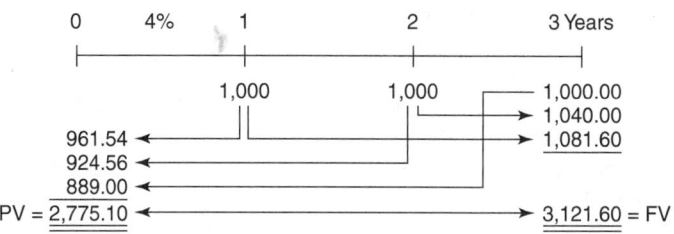

Example 13 *$924.56 compounded for two years at 4%:*

$$FV_2 = \$924.56(1.04)^2 = \$1,000$$

- **Discounting** is the process of finding the **present value (PV)** of a future cash flow or a series of cash flows; discounting is the reciprocal (inverse) of compounding.

Basic Valuation of Assets

The time value of money (TVM) concepts are used by managers and investors to establish the worth of any asset whose value is derived from future cash flows, including such assets as real estate, factories, machinery, oil wells, stocks, and bonds. Now, in this section, we use time value of money techniques to explain how the values of assets are determined. The material covered in the section obviously is important to investors who want to establish the values of their investments. But knowledge of valuation is equally important to financial managers because all important corporate decisions should be analyzed in terms of how they will affect the value of the firm. Remember that the goal of managerial finance is to maximize the value of the firm. Thus, it is critical that we understand the valuation process so we can determine what affects the value of the firm.

The *value* of anything, whether it is a financial asset like a stock or a bond or a real asset like a building or a piece of machinery, *is based on the present value of the cash flows the asset is expected to produce in the future*. On a cash flow timeline, value can be depicted as follows.

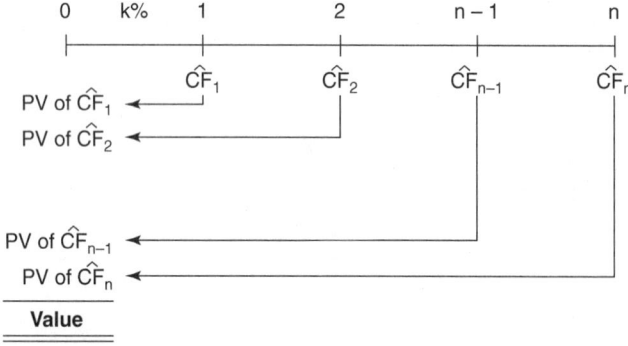

Therefore, the value of any asset can be expressed in general form as follows.

$$\text{Asset value} = V = \frac{\hat{CF}_1}{(1+k)^1} + \frac{\hat{CF}_2}{(1+k)^2} + \cdots + \frac{\hat{CF}_n}{(1+k)^n} \qquad (7.58)$$

Here

- $\hat{CF}_t$ = The cash flow expected to be generated by the asset in period t.
- k = The return investors consider appropriate for holding such an asset. This return is usually termed the *required return*, and is based on both economic conditions and the riskiness of the asset.

According to Equation 7.58, the value of an asset is affected by the cash flows it is expected to generate, $\hat{CF}$, and the return required by investors, k. As you can see, *the higher the expected cash flows, the greater the asset's value; also, the lower the required return, the greater the asset's value*.

Economics and Finance

The Relation Between Economics and Finance

Economics and finance are interconnected. Economics deals with interest rates (the cost of money), inflation, and trade balance. Finance deals with raising money, budgets, and business acquisition activity. The amount of money a firm can raise depends, in part, on the level of interest rates and the amount of inflation in the economy.

In this section, we will focus on interest rate levels, the determinants of market interest rates, the factors that influence interest rate levels, and how interest rates influence business decisions.

The Cost of Money

In a free economy, funds are allocated through the price system. *The interest rate is the price paid to borrow funds, whereas in the case of equity capital, investors expect to receive dividends and capital gains.* The factors that affect the supply of and demand for investment capital, and hence the cost of money, are discussed in this section.

The four most fundamental factors affecting the cost of money are (1) **production opportunities,** (2) **time preferences for consumption,** (3) **risk,** and (4) **inflation.**

Thus, we see that the interest rate paid to savers depends in a basic way on (1) the rate of return producers expect to earn on invested capital, (2) savers' time preferences for current versus future consumption, (3) the riskiness of the loan, and (4) the expected future rate of inflation. The returns borrowers expect to earn by investing the funds they borrow set an upper limit on how much they can pay for savings, while consumers' time preferences for consumption establish how much consumption they are willing to defer, hence how much they will save at different levels of interest offered by borrowers. Higher risk and higher inflation also lead to higher interest rates.

Interest Rate Levels

Funds are allocated among borrowers by interest rates. Firms with the most profitable investment opportunities are willing and able to pay the most for capital, so they tend to attract it away from less efficient firms or from those whose products are not in demand. Of course, our economy is not completely free in the sense of being influenced only by market forces—the federal government has agencies that help designated individuals or groups obtain credit on favorable terms, including small businesses, certain minorities, and firms willing to build plants in areas with high unemployment. Still, most capital in the U.S. economy is allocated through the price system.

Capital markets are interdependent and there are many capital markets in the United States. U.S. firms also invest and raise funds throughout the world, and foreigners both borrow and lend funds in the United States. There are markets in the United States for home loans, farm loans, business loans, government loans, and so forth. For each type of capital, there is a price, and these prices change over time as shifts occur in supply and demand conditions. Short-term rates are responsive to current economic conditions, whereas long-term rates primarily reflect long-run expectations for inflation. As a result, short-term rates are sometimes above and sometimes below long-term rates. The relationship between long-term and short-term rates is called the *term structure of interest rates.*

The Determinants of Market Interest Rates

In general, the quoted (or nominal) interest rate on a debt security, k, is composed of a real risk-free rate of interest, k^*, plus several premiums that reflect inflation, the riskiness of the security, and the security's marketability (or liquidity). This relationship can be expressed as follows.

$$\text{Quoted interest rate} = k = k^* + IP + DRP + LP + MRP \qquad (7.59)$$

In Equation 7.59 the variables are defined as follows.

- k = the quoted, or *nominal*, rate of interest on a given security. There are many different securities, hence many different quoted interest rates
- k* = the *real risk-free rate of interest*; k* is pronounced "k-star"
- IP = inflation premium
- DRP = default risk premium
- LP = liquidity, or marketability, premium
- MRP = maturity risk premium

We discuss the components whose sum makes up the quoted, or nominal, rate on a given security in the following sections. The term *nominal* as it is used here means the *stated* rate as opposed to the *real* rate, which is adjusted to remove the effects of inflation. If you bought a ten-year Treasury bond in March 1999, the quoted, or nominal, rate would be about 5.6%, but if inflation was expected to average 2.1% over the next ten years, the real rate would be about 5.6% − 2.1% = 3.5%.

The Real Risk-Free Rate of Interest, k*

The **real risk-free rate of interest, k*,** is defined as the interest rate that would exist on a security with a *guaranteed* payoff (termed a riskless, or risk-free, security) if inflation was expected to be zero during the investment period. It can be thought of as the rate of interest that would exist on short-term U.S. Treasury securities in an inflation-free world. The real risk-free rate changes over time depending on economic conditions, especially (1) on the rate of return corporations and other borrowers are willing to pay to borrow funds and (2) on people's time preferences for current versus future consumption. It is difficult to measure the real risk-free rate precisely, but most experts think that k* has fluctuated in the range of 1 to 4% in the United States in recent years.

The Nominal, or Quoted, Risk-Free Rate of Interest, k_{RF}

The **nominal, or quoted, risk-free rate, k_{RF},** is the *real risk-free rate plus a premium for expected inflation:* k_{RF} = k* + IP. If we combine k* + IP and let this sum equal k_{RF}, then Equation 7.59 becomes:

$$k = k_{RF} + DRP + LP + MRP \qquad (7.60)$$

Inflation Premium (IP)

Inflation has a major impact on interest rates because it erodes the purchasing power of the dollar and lowers the real rate of return on investments. Investors are well aware of all this, so when they lend money, they build in an **inflation premium (IP)** equal to the *average inflation rate expected over the life of the security*. Therefore, if the real risk-free rate of interest, k*, is 3%, and if inflation is expected to be 4% (IP = 4%) during the next year, then the quoted rate of interest on one-year T-bills would be 7%. In March of 1999, economists forecasted the one-year inflation rate to be between 1.5% and 2%, and, at the same time, the yield on one-year T-bills was about 4.7%. This implies that the real risk-free rate on short-term securities at that time was expected to be between 2.7% and 3.2%.

Default Risk Premium (DRP)

The risk that a borrower will *default* on a loan, which means not to pay the interest or the principal, also affects the market interest rate on a security: The greater the default risk, the higher the interest rate lenders charge (demand). Treasury securities have no default risk; thus, they generally carry the lowest interest rates on taxable securities in the United States. For corporate bonds, the better the bond's overall credit rating, the lower its default risk, and, consequently, the lower its interest rate. Note that bonds rated AAA are judged to have less default risk than bonds rated AA, AA bonds are less risky than A bonds, and so on. Ratings might also be designated AAA or Aaa, AA or Aa, and so forth, depending on the rating agency.

The difference between the quoted interest rate on a T-bond and that on a corporate bond with similar maturity, liquidity, and other features is the default risk premium (DRP).

Liquidity Premium (LP)

Liquidity generally is defined as the ability to convert an asset to cash on short notice and "reasonably" capture the amount initially invested. Of course, the most liquid asset of all is cash, and the more easily an asset can be converted to cash at a price that substantially recovers the initial amount invested, the more liquid it is considered. Consequently, financial assets are considered more liquid than real assets, such as land and equipment, and short-term financial assets generally are more liquid than long-term financial assets. Because liquidity is important, investors evaluate and include **liquidity premiums (LP)** when interest rates are established. Although it is very difficult to accurately measure liquidity premiums, a differential of at least two and probably four or five percentage points exists between the least liquid and the most liquid financial assets of similar default risk and maturity.

Maturity Risk Premium (MRP)

The prices of bonds decline whenever interest rates rise, and because interest rates can and do occasionally rise, all bonds, even Treasury bonds, have an element of risk called **interest rate risk.** As a general rule, the bonds of any organization, from the U.S. government to **General Motors**, have more interest rate risk the longer the maturity of the bond. Therefore, a **maturity risk premium (MRP),** which is higher the longer the years to maturity, must be included in the required interest rate. The effect of maturity risk premiums is to raise interest rates on long-term bonds relative to those on short-term bonds. This premium, like the others, is extremely difficult to measure, but (1) it seems to vary over time, rising when interest rates are more volatile and uncertain, then falling when interest rates are more stable, and (2) in recent years, the maturity risk premium on 30-year T-bonds appears to have generally been in the range of one or two percentage points.

We should mention that although long-term bonds are heavily exposed to maturity risk, short-term investments are heavily exposed to **reinvestment rate risk.** When short-term investments mature and the proceeds are reinvested, or "rolled over," a decline in interest rates would necessitate reinvestment at a lower rate and hence would lead to a decline in interest income. Thus, although "investing short" preserves one's principal, the interest income provided by short-term investments varies from year to year, depending on reinvestment rates.

Long-term bonds also have some reinvestment rate risk. To actually earn the quoted rate on a long-term bond, the interest payments must be reinvested at the quoted rate. However, if interest rates fall, the interest payments would be reinvested at a lower rate; thus, the realized return would be less than the quoted rate. Note, though, that the reinvestment rate risk is lower on a long-term bond than on a short-term bond because only the interest payments (rather than interest plus principal) on the long-term bond are exposed to reinvestment rate risk. Only zero coupon bonds are completely free of reinvestment rate risk.

The Term Structure of Interest Rates

The relationship between long- and short-term rates, which is known as the **term structure of interest rates,** is important to corporate treasurers, who must decide whether to borrow by issuing long- or short-term debt, and to investors, who must decide whether to buy long- or short-term bonds. Thus, it is important to understand (1) how long- and short-term rates are related to each other and (2) what causes shifts in their relative positions.

A **yield curve** shows the relationship between interest rates and maturities of securities. The yield curve changes both in position and in slope over time. It shows a downward slope when short-term interest rates are higher than long-term rates; an upward slope when short-term interest rates are lower than long-term rates.

Historically, long-term interest rates have been above short-term rates, so usually the yield curve has been upward sloping. For this reason, an upward-sloping curve is called a "normal" yield curve and a yield curve that slopes downward is called an inverted ("abnormal") yield curve.3

Term Structure Theories (Explanations)

Several theories have been proposed to explain the shape of the yield curve. The three major ones are (1) the expectations theory, (2) the liquidity preference theory, and (3) the market segmentation theory.

775. ECONOMICS AND FINANCE

EXPECTATIONS THEORY The **expectations theory** states that the yield curve depends on *expectations* concerning future inflation rates. Specifically, $k_{RF,t}$, the nominal interest rate on a U.S. Treasury bond that matures in t years, is found as follows under the expectations theory.

$$k_{RF,t} = k^* + IP_t$$

Here k^* is the real risk-free interest rate, and IP_t is an inflation premium, which is equal to the *average expected rate of inflation* over the t years until the bond matures. Under the expectations theory, the maturity risk premium (MRP) is assumed to be zero, and, for Treasury securities, the default risk premium (DRP) and liquidity premium (LP) also are zero.

LIQUIDITY PREFERENCE THEORY The **liquidity preference theory** states that long-term bonds normally yield more than short-term bonds for two reasons: (1) All else equal, investors generally prefer to hold short-term securities, because such securities are more liquid in the sense that they can be converted to cash with little danger of loss of principal. Investors will, therefore, generally accept lower yields on short-term securities, and this leads to relatively low short-term rates. (2) Borrowers, on the other hand, generally prefer long-term debt, because short-term debt exposes them to the risk of having to repay the debt under adverse conditions. Accordingly, borrowers want to "lock into" long-term funds, which means they are willing to pay a higher rate, other things held constant, for long-term funds than for short-term funds—this also leads to relatively low short-term rates. Thus, lender and borrower preferences both operate to cause short-term rates to be lower than long-term rates. Taken together, these two sets of preferences—and hence the liquidity preference theory—imply that under normal conditions, a positive maturity risk premium (MRP) exists, and the MRP increases with years to maturity, causing the yield curve to be upward sloping.

MARKET SEGMENTATION THEORY Briefly, the **market segmentation theory** states that each lender and each borrower has a preferred maturity. The thrust of the market segmentation theory is that the slope of the yield curve depends on supply/demand conditions in the long- and short-term markets. Thus, according to this theory, the yield curve could at any given time be either flat, upward sloping, or downward sloping. An upward-sloping yield curve would occur when there was a large supply of short-term funds relative to demand, but a shortage of long-term funds. Similarly, a downward-sloping curve would indicate relatively strong demand for funds in the short-term market compared to that in the long-term market. A flat curve would indicate balance between the two markets.

Various tests of the theories explaining the shape of the yield curve have been conducted, and these tests indicate that all three theories have some validity. Thus, the shape of the yield curve at any given time is affected (1) by expectations about future inflation, (2) by liquidity preferences, and (3) by supply/demand conditions in long- and short-term markets. One factor might dominate at one time, another at another time, but all three affect the term structure of interest rates.

Other Factors That Influence Interest Rate Levels

Factors other than those discussed in the previous section also influence both the general level of interest rates and the shape of the yield curve. The four most important factors are (1) Federal Reserve policy, (2) the level of the federal budget deficit, (3) the foreign trade balance, and (4) the level of business activity.

Federal Reserve Policy

As you probably learned in your economics courses, (1) the money supply has a major effect on both the level of economic activity and the rate of inflation, and (2) in the United States, the Federal Reserve Board controls the money supply. If the Fed wants to control growth in the economy, it slows growth in the money supply. The initial effect of such an action is to cause interest rates to increase and inflation to stabilize. The reverse holds if the Fed loosens the money supply.

During periods when the Fed is actively intervening in the markets, the yield curve will be distorted. Short-term rates will be temporarily "too low" if the Fed is easing credit, and "too high" if it is tightening credit. Long-term rates are not affected as much by Fed intervention because they represent averages of short-term expectations. The Fed deals primarily in the short-term end of the market.

Federal Budget Deficits

If the federal government spends more than it takes in from tax revenues, it runs a deficit, and that deficit must be covered either by borrowing or by printing money. If the government borrows, this added demand for funds pushes up interest rates. If it prints money, this increases expectations for future inflation, which also drives up interest rates. Thus, the larger the federal deficit, other things held constant, the higher the level of interest rates. Whether long- or short-term rates are more affected depends on how the deficit is financed, so we cannot state, in general, how deficits will affect the slope of the yield curve.

Foreign Trade Balance

Businesses and individuals in the United States buy from and sell to people and firms in other countries. If we buy more than we sell (that is, if we import more than we export), we are said to be running a foreign trade deficit. When trade deficits occur, they must be financed, and the main source of financing is debt. The deficit could also be financed by selling assets, including gold, corporate stocks, entire companies, and real estate. The United States has financed its massive trade deficits by all of these means at various times, but the primary method has been by borrowing. Therefore, the larger our trade deficit, the more we must borrow, and as we increase our borrowing, this drives up interest rates. Also, foreigners are willing to hold U.S. debt only if the interest rate on this debt is competitive with interest rates in other countries. Therefore, if the Federal Reserve attempts to lower interest rates in the United States, causing our rates to fall below rates abroad, then foreigners will sell U.S. bonds, which will depress bond prices and cause U.S. interest rates to increase. Thus, the existence of a deficit trade balance hinders the Fed's ability to combat a recession by lowering interest rates.

Level of Business Activity

Business conditions influence interest rates. Here are the key points.

1. Because inflation increased from the late 1960s to 1981, the general tendency during this period was toward higher interest rates. However, since the 1981 peak, the trend has generally been downward.
2. Until the mid-1960s, short-term rates were almost always below long-term rates. Thus, in those years the yield curve was almost always "normal" in the sense that it was upward sloping.
3. During recessions both the demand for money and the rate of inflation tend to fall, and, at the same time, the Federal Reserve tends to increase the money supply in an effort to stimulate the economy. As a result, there is a tendency for interest rates to decline during recessions.
4. During recessions, short-term rates decline more sharply than long-term rates. This occurs because (a) the Fed operates mainly in the short-term sector, so its intervention has the strongest effect here, and (b) long-term rates reflect the average expected inflation rate over the next 20 to 30 years, and this expectation generally does not change much, even when the current rate of inflation is low (or high).

Interest Rate Levels and Stock Prices

Interest rates have two effects on corporate profits. First, because interest is a cost, the higher the rate of interest, the lower a firm's profits, other things held constant. Second, interest rates affect the level of economic activity, and economic activity affects corporate profits. Interest rates obviously affect stock prices because of their effects on profits, but, perhaps even more important, they have an effect due to competition in the marketplace between stocks and bonds. If interest rates rise sharply, investors can get higher returns in the bond market, which induces them to sell stocks and to transfer funds from the stock market to the bond market. A massive sale of stocks in response to rising interest rates obviously would depress stock prices. Of course, the reverse occurs if interest rates decline. Indeed, the bull market of December 1991, when the Dow Jones Industrial Index rose 10% in less than a month, was caused almost entirely by the sharp drop in long-term interest rates. On the other hand, the poor performance exhibited by the stock market in 1994—common stocks declined in average by more than three percent—resulted from sharp increase in interest rates during that year. For the past several years, as interest rates have declined and remained at historically low levels, the stock market has been the "hot" investment.

Interest Rate Levels and Business Decisions

Financing decisions would be easy if we could develop accurate forecasts of future interest rates. Unfortunately, predicting future interest rates with consistent accuracy is somewhere between difficult and impossible—people who make a living by selling interest rate forecasts say it is difficult, but many others say it is impossible. But, even if it is difficult to predict future interest rate levels, it is easy to predict that interest rates will fluctuate—they always have, and they always will. This being the case, sound financial policy calls for using a mix of long- and short-term debt, as well as equity, in such a manner that the firm can survive in most interest-rate environments. Further, the optimal financial policy depends in an important way on the nature of the firm's assets—the easier it is to sell off assets and thus to pay off debts, the more feasible it is to use large amounts of short-term debt. This makes it more feasible to finance current assets than noncurrent (fixed) assets with short-term debt.

Accounting and Finance

The Relation Between Accounting and Finance

In their basic forms, *accounting* is data collection and *finance* is data analysis. The accounting function in any organization is responsible for recording, analyzing, and reporting the results of actions taken by managers in the organization. The accounting function is a scorekeeping or recordkeeping process, while the finance function is a decision-making process. The accounting function focuses solely on economic transactions that have already occurred, while finance focuses on future events such as raising money and spending money on capital equipment items, to name a few. Interestingly enough, the accounting and financial functions are closely related to each other, partly due to sharing of same transactions and data.

The accounting function is concerned with measuring the economic effects of exchange transactions undertaken by the organization. These economic transactions are classified according to their effect on the assets, liabilities, and owner's equity of the organization. The accounting equation has been defined in these three terms as follows.

$$\text{Assets} = \text{Liabilities} + \text{Owner's Equity}$$

The layout of the balance sheet is a rewrite of the accounting equation in that the left side of the balance sheet represents the total value of assets and the right side represents the total value of liabilities and shareholders' equity (owner's equity). The accounting function ensures the ongoing balance between the sources (liabilities and equity) and uses (assets) of the organization's funds. The right side of the accounting equation represents the sources of funds and the left side of the equation indicates how such sources are put to use, that is, how sources are transformed into current and noncurrent assets. The finance function ensures that adequate funds are available to run the business; if not, sources are found to meet the funding requirements. The sources include debt (liabilities) and equity (stocks) from outside the organization and retained earnings from inside the organization's operations.

The accounting function is constrained by external demands placed on it by the Financial Accounting Standards Board (FASB) and by the Securities and Exchange Commission (SEC) in terms of financial reporting regulations and disclosure requirements in an effort to protect the "informed investors." Because of theses constraints, the accounting function focuses on the past data while finance looks at the future data. If the accounting function is satisfying the needs of external parties such as investors, regulators, and creditors by issuing audited financial statements, the finance function should satisfy the needs of internal parties such as managers, directors, owners, and employees. The accounting function reports the historical data through financial statements while the finance function's approach should be strategic in helping the organization's management make sound financial decisions.

Whether it is an accounting report or a finance report, the numbers in these reports will affect managers' behavior throughout the organization. The reports make certain outcomes or processes more visible than others, thus drawing the attention of top management. These numbers can influence a manager's compensation, promotion potential, bonuses, or even future with the organization.

Both accounting and finance functions are service-oriented and staff-supported departments in the organization. Both functions are managed by a single person with the title of Chief Financial Officer (CFO). The CFO is being asked to join the top management decision-making team and to support ongoing efforts for continuous improvement throughout the organization. Senior management wants the accounting and finance functions to be a value-adding activity, moving away from the traditional "watchdog" role to a "team player" role.

Quality and Finance

Relation Between Quality and Finance

Earlier, we said that the accounting function provides information to external customers (for example, investors, regulators, and creditors), and its goal should be to provide an unbiased report of historical, economic events taking place within a firm. We also said that the finance function should create value through participating in management decision making and providing quality information to internal customers (for example, managers, owners, and employees). The value creation approach requires a proactive mind-set on the part of the finance manager, where the manager will (1) seek ways to enhance the service provided to the rest of the organization, (2) learn quality management tools for continuous improvement, and (3) adopt and adapt total quality management (TQM) principles and practices to the finance function. This means that the finance manager is a full-time team player in the company's constantly changing approach to managing the business. Traditionally, both the accounting and finance functions are seen as "custodial" roles while quality thinking requires a "partner" role.

Examples of how companies have implemented TQM principles within the finance and accounting function include the following.

1. Encouraging sales and marketing staff to perform credit analysis prior to developing customer prospects.
2. Helping the operations and marketing staff in capital and operating budget decisions and preparation activities by changing the finance and accounting roles from policing and judging to coaching and facilitating.
3. Transferring financial work from a centralized finance group to nonfinancial staff in the field. This requires training nonfinancial employees in the fundamentals of finance and accounting.
4. Changing the custodial role of the finance and accounting staff to partner role requires training of finance and accounting staff in "soft skills" (people skills). This includes communication, negotiation, and interpersonal skills.
5. Conducting surveys of internal and external customers, listening to the "voice of the customer," and practicing to exceed customer expectations.
6. Changing the company's reward system to recognize and support team-based as well as individual-based contributions.
7. Developing an error-free billing system and monitoring on-time payments and unpaid invoices with the use of statistical process control tools.
8. Developing error reports to show out-of-balance accounts (inter- or intracompany), out-of-period adjustments, the number of post-closing journal entries used, and unexplained account variances.
9. Developing standards for response time to customers' and suppliers' phone inquiries and correspondence.
10. Developing turnaround time standards for paying expense reports, processing check requests, and handling cash advance requests.
11. Processing payments to suppliers without delay or error.
12. Measuring performance of cash collection activities to increase cash inflows.
13. Integrating traditional finance tools such as capital budgeting, financial analysis, and risk management evaluations with TQM tools such as Pareto charts, bar charts, control charts, run charts, flow charts, scatter diagrams, and cause-and-effect diagrams.
14. Developing task forces, quality improvement teams, and quality councils within the finance and accounting functions to address quality-related problems.
15. Incorporating problem-solving tools such as brainstorming and imagineering into the accounting and finance functions. Brainstorming is a process for generating ideas, while imagineering is a process for describing a "perfect" function.
16. Implementing management-by-fact principles rather than management-by-opinion.
17. Benchmarking the finance, treasury, and accounting functions with Best-in-Class or World-Class finance, treasury, and accounting functions.

18. Redesigning the internal audit process to be faster, more accurate, less costly, and more beneficial to auditees.
19. Encouraging the local operations and marketing staff to conduct self-audits for problem identification and resolution without involving auditors from headquarters.
20. Discouraging an "earnings management" strategy, which can destroy the financial quality of a firm.

Law and Finance

Relation Between Law and Finance

Various laws impact the finance function in an effort to protect investors and creditors from misinformation and fraudulent activities. Topics such as bankruptcy, debt securities, sinking fund requirements, uniform commercial code, equity securities, stockholders' equity, and dividends are discussed in this section.

Bankruptcy

Organizations can go bankrupt when they have liquidity problems, meaning inability to meet financial obligations such as debt payments, wages, and taxes. When a business becomes insolvent (meaning having liquidity problems), it does not have enough cash to meet scheduled interest and principal payments; that is, the firm cannot service its debt obligations. A decision must be made whether to dissolve the firm through liquidation or to permit it to reorganize and thus continue. Chapter 7 of the Bankruptcy Act governs the liquidation issues while Chapter 11 of the Act addresses the reorganization issues. The final decision whether to liquidate or reorganize a firm is made by a federal bankruptcy court judge. This decision depends on whether the value of the reorganized firm is likely to be greater than the value of the firm's assets if they were sold off piecemeal.

Liquidation

Liquidation occurs if the firm is deemed to be too far gone to be saved—if it is "worth more dead than alive." If the bankruptcy court orders a liquidation, assets are distributed to secured creditors first, then wages and taxes are paid; the remaining proceeds are distributed to unsecured creditors, to preferred stockholders, and finally to common stockholders (if anything is left) in that order. The priority of claims established by federal bankruptcy statutes must be followed when distributing the proceeds from a liquidating firm.

Reorganization

In a reorganization, a committee of unsecured creditors is appointed by the court to negotiate with management on the terms of a potential reorganization. The reorganization plan might call for a restructuring of the firms' debt, in which case the interest rate might be reduced, the term to maturity lengthened, or some of the debt might be exchanged for equity. The point of the restructuring is to reduce the financial charges to a level that the firm's cash flows can support. Of course, the common stockholders also have to give up something—they normally see their position eroded as a result of additional shares of equity being given to debtholders in exchange for accepting a reduced amount of debt principal and interest. A trustee might be appointed by the court to oversee the reorganization, or the existing management might be allowed to retain control over the organization.

Debt Securities

Debt securities, which include bonds and notes, do not represent an ownership interest in the company. Rather, they create a debtor-creditor relationship between the corporation and the debtholder. The board of directors can issue bonds without the specific authorization or consent of the stockholders. A bond indenture is a form of contract between the bond issuers and the bondholders. Legal restrictions are designed to ensure that the company does nothing to cause the quality of bonds to deteriorate after they have been issued. The indenture is the legal document that spells out the rights of the bondholders and the corporation that issues the bonds.

Major funding sources of a corporation include debt securities, equity securities, and retained earnings.

Restrictive covenants cover such points as (1) early payoff of the bond, (2) maintenance of times-interest-earned ratio, (3) payment of dividends when earnings do not meet certain specifications, and (4) maintenance of current ratio and the debt ratios at specified levels. Indenture covenants not only influence a firm's financing decision, but also can force a company into bankruptcy if the covenants are violated.

Sinking Fund Requirements

Sinking fund is a required annual payment designed to amortize a bond or preferred stock issue. It is a legal provision that facilitates the orderly retirement of a bond issue. A failure to meet the sinking fund requirement causes the bond issue to become default, which might force the company into bankruptcy. In a way, the sinking fund was created to protect from possible bankruptcy.

Uniform Commercial Code

The uniform commercial code (UCC) is a system of standards that simplifies procedures for establishing short-term loan security. The heart of the UCC is the Security Agreement, a standardized document on which the specific pledged assets are listed. The assets can be items of equipment, accounts receivables, or inventory. For example, accounts receivables are either pledged or factored as security for short-term credit. Methods such as blanket liens, trust receipts, and warehouse receipts are used for inventory as security for short-term credit.

Equity Securities

Equity securities represent an ownership interest in the corporation and include both common and preferred stock. All states have statutes regulating the issuance and sale of corporate shares. **"Blue sky laws"** are statutes containing provisions prohibiting fraud in the sale of securities. In addition, a number of states require the registration of securities, and some states also regulate investment brokers, dealers, and others engaged in the selling and buying of securities. U.S. Federal statutes such as the Securities Act of 1933 and 1934 regulate the sale of securities through the use of the mails or otherwise engaged in interstate commerce.

Stockholders' Equity

A company's stockholders' equity section of the balance sheet contains three sections: contributed capital, retained earnings, and treasury stock.

- **Contributed capital** represents the investments made by the stockholders in the corporation. It includes (1) preferred stock with its par value and number of shares authorized, issued, and outstanding; (2) common stock with its par value and number of shares authorized, issued, and outstanding; and (3) paid-in capital in excess of par value. Outstanding shares that are still in circulation are equal to authorized shares minus issued shares minus treasury shares. Issued shares that are bought back and held by the firm are called *treasury shares*. Due to treasury shares, a firm can have more shares issued than are currently outstanding.

  Stockholders' equity is contributed capital plus retained earnings minus treasury stock.

- **Retained earnings** are earnings of the corporation, since its inception, less any losses and dividends, or transfers to contributed capital. They are not a pool of funds or cash to be distributed to the stockholders; instead, they

represent earnings reinvested in the corporation. They represent stockholders' claims to the assets of the company resulting from profitable operations. A part of the retained earnings can be restricted or reserved for special transactions.
- **Treasury stock** is capital stock, either common or preferred, that has been issued and later reacquired by the issuing company and has not subsequently been resold or retired. A company can buy its own stock back for strategic reasons by purchasing it from the open market like any other investor.

Par value or stated value is the amount of face value per share and make up the **legal (stated) capital** of the corporation. A company cannot declare a dividend that would cause stockholders' equity to fall below the legal capital of the firm. Therefore, the par value is an arbitrary figure or a minimum cushion of capital that protects creditors and owners.

Dividends

Corporate law does not require companies to pay dividends. It is the company's board of directors' decision whether to pay a dividend or not, and if decided to pay, how much to pay and when. When decided, the dividend should be paid to outstanding stockholders of record only. Usually, factors such as working capital requirements, stockholder expectations, tax consequences, and cash availability influence the board in forming a dividend distribution policy. The ex-dividend date is controlled by law, which is two business days before the holder-of-record date. Dividends are not expenses of a corporation, hence cannot be deducted from taxes. Instead, dividends are distribution of capital to investors and stockholders.

Most states do not allow the board of directors to declare a dividend that exceeds retained earnings. When a dividend exceeds retained earnings, it is called a *liquidating dividend*, and is usually paid when a company is going out of business or reducing its operations. It is the availability of cash, not the amount of retained earnings, that decides how much dividend to pay and when. Other forms of dividends include property dividends. Neither a stock dividend nor a stock split is a distribution of assets to the stockholders.

Two types of dividend tests include the cash flow test, required by all states, and the balance sheet test, required by some states.

There are two types of legal restrictions placed on dividends. One is based on cash flow test and the other one is based on balance sheet test. The cash flow test (also called *equity insolvency test*) prohibits the payment of any dividends when the corporation either is insolvent or would become so through the payment of the dividend. Insolvency is the inability to pay debts as they become due in the usual course of business. It can be translated into difficulty of cash flows.

The balance sheet test focuses on few specific tests: (1) all states prohibit dividends paid from capital surplus or stated (legal) capital; instead, they should be paid only from earned surplus; (2) less restrictive states permit dividends to be paid out of either earned surplus or capital surplus; and (3) net asset test, which permits a company to pay dividends as long as the total assets after dividends payment is more than its total liabilities plus payments to preferential stockholders.

Surplus is the amount by which the net assets of a corporation exceeds its stated capital. Net assets is total assets minus total debts. Earned surplus is the amount of undistributed net profits, income, gains, and losses, computed from the date of incorporation. Capital surplus is the amount of surplus other than the earned surplus.

Specific Legal Rules and Restrictions Related to Finance

- A corporation may not redeem or purchase its redeemable shares when insolvent or when such redemption or purchase would render it insolvent or would reduce its net assets below a certain level.
- A corporation may purchase its own shares only out of earned surplus or, if the articles of incorporation permit or if the stockholders approve, out of capital surplus. It cannot purchase when it is insolvent or when such purchase would make it insolvent.
- When there is an exchange of stock for noncash assets, the board of directors have the right to determine the fair market value of the property.
- A share of stock that originally was issued at par value or greater and fully paid for, and that then was reacquired as treasury stock, can be reissued at less than par value without any negative financial or legal consequences.

- If a corporation decides that it will not reissue stock it has purchased (treasury stock), it can retire the stock with the approval of its stockholders.
- Preferred stockholders have a priority over common stockholders in the event of liquidation of a firm.

Ethics and Finance

Business Ethics

The word *ethics* is defined in *Webster's dictionary* as "standards of conduct or moral behavior." Business ethics can be thought of as a company's attitude and conduct toward its employees, customers, community, and stockholders. High standards of ethical behavior demand that a firm treat each party it deals with in a fair and honest manner. A firm's commitment to business ethics can be measured by the tendency of the firm and its employees to adhere to laws and regulations relating to such factors as product safety and quality, fair employment practices, fair marketing and selling practices, the use of confidential information for personal gain, community involvement, bribery, and illegal payments to foreign governments to obtain business.

There are many instances of firms engaging in unethical behavior. For example, since 1985, the employees of several prominent Wall Street investment banking houses have been sentenced to prison for illegally using insider information on proposed mergers for their own personal gain, and **E. F. Hutton**, a large brokerage firm, lost its independence through a forced merger after it was convicted of cheating its banks out of millions of dollars in a check kiting scheme. **Drexel Burnham Lambert**, one of the largest investment banking firms, went bankrupt, and its "junk bond king," Michael Milken, who had earned $550 million in just one year, was sentenced to ten years in prison plus charged a huge fine for securities-law violations. Even more recently, **Salomon Brothers Inc**. was implicated in a Treasury-auction bidding scandal that resulted in the removal of key officers and a significant reorganization of the firm.

In spite of all this, the results of a recent study indicate that the executives of most major firms in the United States believe their firms should, and do, try to maintain high ethical standards in all of their business dealings. Further, most executives believe that there is a positive correlation between ethics and long-run profitability because ethical behavior (1) avoids fines and legal expenses, (2) builds public trust, (3) attracts business from customers who appreciate and support its policies, (4) attracts and keeps employees of the highest caliber, and (5) supports the economic viability of the communities in which it operates.

Most firms today have in place strong codes of ethical behavior, and they conduct training programs designed to ensure that all employees understand the correct behavior in different business situations. However, it is imperative that top management—the chairman, president, and vice presidents—be openly committed to ethical behavior and that they communicate this commitment through their own personal actions as well as through company policies, directives, and punishment/reward systems.

Specific Examples of Unethical Practices in Finance

The following is a list of specific examples of unethical practices in finance.

- Generally accepted accounting principles (GAAP) offer choices to firms in selecting accounting methods for valuing assets and liabilities. Different accounting methods can yield different asset and liability values, thus showing a different financial condition than what is in their firm's balance sheets. Similarly, revenue and expense items on income statements can be handled differently, thus showing a net income different than what it should be.
- Financial institutions and banks offer interest rates on savings and other deposits. The question is, are they offering the maximum interest rates allowed by law and at the maximum frequency of interest compounding? Improper practices can affect annual percentage rates and effective annual rates.
- Use of improper discount rate for computing a firm's unfunded pension liability to adjust earnings.

- Overstating savings and/or understating costs during preparation of capital expenditure project requests in order to obtain senior management or board of directors approvals.
- Use of "padding" techniques during operating budget preparation to increase required costs and decrease projected revenues in order to look good at the end of the year.
- The practice of allocating "hot" initial public offerings (IPOs) to the best customers and friends of the underwriter or syndicate member. Similarly, practice of "insider trading" in leaking information to friends and relatives or for personal gain about forthcoming mergers, acquisitions, and divestitures.
- Practice of dubious actions such as paying bills late and still taking discounts, setting invoice dates well before shipping dates, and imposing large delinquency charges for late payments.
- Practice of kiting procedures to conceal cash shortages.
- Practice of lapping procedures involving customer payments.
- Practice of skimming procedures involving removal of cash.
- Practice of check tampering schemes for employee's personal benefit.

International Issues

This section addresses a variety of topics such as international flow of funds, international financial markets, financing international trade, currency derivatives, short-term financing, international cash management, and long-term financing.

International Flow of Funds

International business is facilitated by markets that allow for the flow of funds between countries. The transactions arising from international business cause money flows from one country to another. The balance of payments is a measure of international money flows.

Financial managers of Multinational Coprorations (MNCs) monitor the balance of payments so that they can determine how the flow of international transactions is changing over time. The balance of payments can indicate the volume of transactions between specific countries and may even signal potential shifts in specific exchange rates.

International Trade Flows

Canada, France, Germany, and other European countries rely more heavily on trade than the United States does. Canada's trade volume of exports and imports per year is valued at more than 50% of its annual gross domestic product (GDP). The trade volume of European countries is typically between 30 and 40% of their respective GDPs. The trade volume of the United States and Japan is typically between 10 and 20% of their respective GDPs. Nevertheless, for all countries, the volume of trade has grown over time.

Factors Affecting International Trade Flows

Because international trade can significantly affect a country's economy, it is important to identify and monitor the factors that influence it. The most influential factors are

- Inflation
- National income
- Government restrictions
- Exchange rates

IMPACT OF INFLATION If a country's inflation rate increases relative to the countries with which it trades, its current account would be expected to decrease, other things being equal. Consumers and corporations in that country will most likely purchase more goods overseas (due to high local inflation), while the country's exports to other countries will decline.

IMPACT OF NATIONAL INCOME If a country's income level (national income) increases by a higher percentage than those of other countries, its current account is expected to decrease, other things being equal. As the real income level (adjusted for inflation) rises, so does consumption of goods. A percentage of that increase in consumption will most likely reflect an increased demand for foreign goods.

>**Example 14** *The removal of the Iron Curtain boosted Europe's economy in late 1989 and in 1990, which led to an increase in national income in Europe. Consequently, there was an increase in the demand for U.S. goods, which improved the U.S. balance of trade with Europe.*

Just as an increase in national income can increase the demand for imports, a reduction in national income may result in the reduction in the demand for imports.

>**Example 15** *During the 1997–1998 Asian crisis, the national income of Asian countries declined, causing a decline in the Asian demand for products imported from countries in other regions of the world. Thus, the amount of exports sold by the United States and some other countries to Asian countries declined as a result of the Asian crisis.*

IMPACT OF GOVERNMENT RESTRICTIONS A country's government can prevent or discourage imports from other countries. By imposing such restrictions, the government disrupts trade flows. Among the most commonly used trade restrictions are tariffs and quotas.

Tariffs and Quotas If a country's government imposes a tax on imported goods (often referred to as a **tariff**), the prices of foreign goods to consumers are effectively increased. Tariffs imposed by the U.S. government are on average lower than those imposed by other governments. Some industries, however, are more highly protected by tariffs than others. American apparel products and farm products have historically received more protection against foreign competition as a result of high tariffs on related imports.

In addition to tariffs, a government can reduce its country's imports by enforcing a **quota**, or a maximum limit that can be imported. Quotas have been commonly applied to a variety of goods imported by the United States and other countries.

Other Types of Restrictions Some trade restrictions may be imposed on products for health and safety reasons.

>**Example 16** *In 2001, an outbreak of foot-and-mouth disease occurred in the United Kingdom and eventually spread to several other European countries. This disease can spread by direct or indirect contact with infected animals. The U.S. government imposed trade restrictions on some products produced in the United Kingdom for health reasons. Consequently, U.K. exports to the United States declined abruptly.*

This example illustrates how uncontrollable factors besides inflation, national income, tariffs and quotas, and exchange rates can affect the balance of trade between two countries.

Impact on Jobs Trade restrictions may save jobs, but only at a cost. A study by the Institute for International Economics estimated the cost per job saved to be $705,000 for the U.S. automobile industry and $1 million for the specialty steel industry. Furthermore, trade restrictions tend to benefit some industries at the expense of others, as other countries retaliate by imposing their own trade restrictions.

IMPACT OF EXCHANGE RATES Each country's currency is valued in terms of other currencies through the use of exchange rates, so that currencies can be exchanged to facilitate international transactions. The values of most currencies can fluctuate over time because of market and government forces. If a country's currency begins to rise in value against other currencies, its current account balance should decrease, other things being equal. As the currency strengthens, goods exported by that country will become more expensive to the importing countries. As a consequence, the demand for such goods will decrease.

> **Example 17** *A tennis racket that sells in the United States for $100 will require a payment of C$125 by the Canadian importer if the Canadian dollar is valued at C$1 = $.80. If C$1 = $.70, it would require a payment of C$143, which might discourage the Canadian demand for U.S. tennis rackets. A strong local currency is expected to reduce the current account balance if the traded goods are **price-elastic** (sensitive to price changes).*

> **Example 18** *During the 1997–1998 Asian crisis, the exchange rates of Asian currencies declined substantially against the dollar, which caused the prices of Asian products to decline from the perspective of the United States and many other countries. Consequently, the demand for Asian products increased and sometimes replaced the demand for products of other countries. For example, the weakness of the Thai baht during this period caused an increase in the global demand for fish from Thailand and a decline in the demand for similar products from the United States (Seattle).*

Just as a strong dollar is expected to cause a lower (or more negative) U.S. balance of trade as explained above, a weak dollar is expected to cause a higher balance of trade. The dollar's weakness lowers the price paid for U.S. goods by foreign customers and can lead to an increase in the demand for U.S. products. A weak dollar also tends to increase the dollar price paid for foreign goods and thus reduces the U.S. demand for foreign goods.

INTERACTION OF FACTORS Because the factors that affect the balance of trade interact, their simultaneous influence on the balance of trade is complex. For example, as a high U.S. inflation rate reduces the current account, it places downward pressure on the value of the dollar. Because a weaker dollar can improve the current account, it may partially offset the impact of inflation on the current account.

Correcting a Balance of Trade Deficit

By reconsidering some of the factors that affect the balance of trade, it is possible to develop some common methods for correcting a deficit. Any policy that will increase foreign demand for the country's goods and services will improve its balance of trade position. Foreign demand may increase if export prices become more attractive. This can occur when the country's inflation is low or when its currency's value is reduced, thereby making the prices cheaper from a foreign perspective.

A floating exchange rate could possibly correct any international trade imbalances in the following way. A deficit in a country's balance of trade suggests that the country is spending more funds on foreign products than it is receiving from exports to foreign countries. Because it is selling its currency (to buy foreign goods) in greater volume than the foreign demand for its currency, the value of its currency should decrease. This decrease in value should encourage more foreign demand for its goods in the future.

While this theory seems rational, it does not always work as just described. It is possible that, instead, a country's currency will remain stable or appreciate even when it has a balance of trade deficit.

> **Example 19** *During the year 2000, the United States experienced a large balance of trade deficit, which should have placed downward pressure on the value of the dollar. Yet, during this same period, there*

was substantial investment in dollar-denominated securities by foreign investors. This foreign demand for the dollar placed upward pressure on its value, thereby offsetting the downward pressure caused by the trade imbalance. Consequently, a country cannot always rely on currency movements to correct a trade deficit.

WHY A WEAK HOME CURRENCY IS NOT A PERFECT SOLUTION Even if a country's home currency weakens, its balance of trade will not necessarily improve for the following reasons.

Counterpricing by Competitors When a country's currency weakens, its prices become more attractive to foreign customers, and many foreign companies lower their prices to remain competitive with the country's firms.

Impact of Other Weak Currencies The currency does not necessarily weaken against all currencies at the same time.

Example 20 *When the dollar weakens in Europe, the dollar's exchange rates with the currencies of Hong Kong, Singapore, South Korea, and Taiwan may remain more stable. As some U.S. firms terminate their demand for supplies produced in European countries, they tend to increase their demand for goods produced in Asian countries. Consequently, the dollar's weakness in European countries causes a change in international trade behavior but does not eliminate the U.S. trade deficit.*

Prearranged International Transactions Many international trade transactions are prearranged and cannot be immediately adjusted. Thus, non-U.S. importing companies may be attracted to U.S. firms as a result of a weaker dollar but cannot immediately sever their relationships with suppliers from other countries. Over time, they may begin to take advantage of the weaker dollar by purchasing U.S. imports, if they believe that the weakness will continue. The lag time between the dollar's weakness and the non-U.S. firms' increased demand for U.S. products has sometimes been estimated to be 18 months or even longer.

The U.S. balance of trade may actually deteriorate in the short run as a result of dollar depreciation. It only improves when U.S. and non-U.S. importers respond to the change in purchasing power that is caused by the weaker dollar. This pattern is called the **J-curve effect,** and it is illustrated in Exhibit 700.51. The further decline in the trade balance before a reversal creates a trend that can look like the letter J.

Exhibit 700.51 *J-Curve Effect*

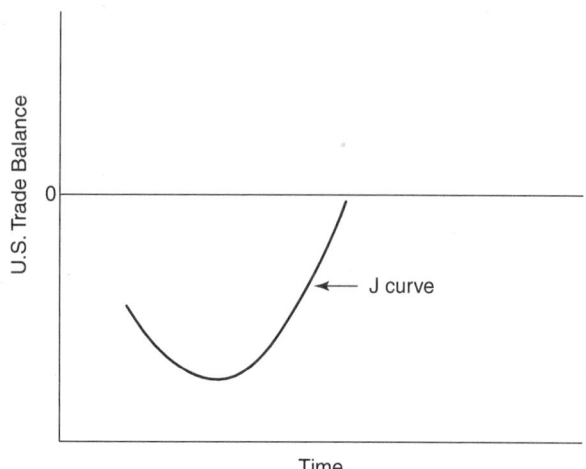

Intercompany Trade A fourth reason why a weak currency will not always improve a country's balance of trade is that importers and exporters that are under the same ownership have unique relationships. Many firms purchase products that are produced by their subsidiaries in what is referred to as **intracompany trade.** This type of trade makes up more than 50% of all international trade. The trade between the two parties will normally continue regardless of exchange rate movements. Thus, the impact of exchange rate movements on intracompany trade patterns is limited.

International Capital Flows

Capital flows usually represent direct foreign investment or portfolio investment. The direct foreign investment (DFI) positions inside and outside the United States have risen substantially over time, an indication of increasing globalization. Both DFI positions level off during recessionary periods (such as in the early 1980s and in the early 1990s) but increase during periods of strong economic growth.

Factors Affecting Direct Foreign Investment

Capital flows resulting from DFI change whenever conditions in a country change the desire of firms to conduct business operations there. Some of the more common factors that could affect a country's appeal for DFI are identified here.

CHANGES IN RESTRICTIONS Restrictions on DFI were lowered in many Eastern European countries during the mid-1990s and in Asian countries following the Asian crisis in the late 1990s. These changes allowed more DFI in these countries.

Globalization continues to increase in response to reductions in tariffs and other barriers imposed by governments. For example, when **PepsiCo, Inc.,** owner of **KFC, Pizza Hut,** and **Taco Bell** (subsequently spun off to **Tricon Global Restaurants**), the company entered various markets in the Caribbean and Asia that were previously restricted, in pursuit of its goal to be in any country where people desire chicken, pizza, or tacos. Many U.S.-based MNCs, including **Bausch & Lomb, Colgate-Palmolive,** and **General Electric**, have been penetrating less developed countries such as Argentina, Chile, Mexico, India, China, and Hungary. New opportunities in these countries have arisen from the removal of government barriers.

PRIVATIZATION Direct foreign investment has also been stimulated by the move toward free enterprise, as several national governments have sold some of their operations to corporations and other investors. This **privatization** has already taken place in some Latin American countries such as Brazil and Mexico, in Eastern European countries such as Poland and Hungary, and in such Caribbean territories as the Virgin Islands. Privatization allows for greater international business as foreign firms can acquire operations sold by national governments.

Governments' reasons for privatization vary. Privatization was used in Chile to prevent a few investors from controlling all the shares and in France to prevent a possible reversion to a more nationalized economy. In the United Kingdom, privatization was promoted to spread stock ownership across investors, which allowed more people to have a direct stake in the success of British industry.

The primary reason that the market value of a firm may increase in response to privatization is the anticipated improvement in managerial efficiency. Managers in a privately-owned firm can focus on the goal of maximizing shareholder wealth, whereas in a state-owned business, the state must consider the economic and social ramifications of any business decision. Also, managers of a privately-owned enterprise are more motivated to ensure profitability because their careers may depend on it. For these reasons, privatized firms will search for local and global opportunities that could enhance their value. The trend toward privatization will undoubtedly create a more competitive global marketplace.

POTENTIAL ECONOMIC GROWTH Countries that have more potential economic growth are more likely to attract DFI because firms recognize that they may be able to capitalize on that growth by establishing more business there. During the Asian crisis, expected economic growth was reduced, which limited the desire of MNCs to expand in that region (even though they were subject to fewer restrictions when acquiring Asian companies).

TAX RATES Countries that impose relatively low tax rates on corporate earnings are more likely to attract DFI. Firms estimate the after-tax cash flows that they would expect to earn when assessing the feasibility of DFI.

EXCHANGE RATES Firms typically prefer to direct DFI to countries where the local currency is strengthening against their own. Under these conditions, they can invest funds to establish their operations in a country while that country's currency is relatively cheap (weak). Then, earnings from the new operations can periodically be converted back to the firm's currency at a more favorable exchange rate.

Factors Affecting International Portfolio Investment

The desire by individual or institutional investors to direct international portfolio investment to a specific country is influenced by the following factors.

TAX RATES ON INTEREST OR DIVIDENDS Investors normally prefer to invest in a country where the taxes on interest or dividend income from investments are relatively low. Investors assess their potential after-tax earnings from investments in foreign securities.

INTEREST RATES Portfolio investment can also be affected by interest rates. Money tends to flow to countries with high interest rates, as long as the local currencies are not expected to weaken.

EXCHANGE RATES If a country's home currency is expected to strengthen, foreign investors may be willing to invest in the country's securities to benefit from the currency movement. Conversely, if a country's home currency is expected to weaken, foreign investors may decide to purchase securities in other countries.

Agencies That Facilitate International Flows

A variety of agencies have been established to facilitate international trade and financial transactions. These agencies often represent a collection of nations. A description of some of the more important agencies follows.

International Monetary Fund

The United Nations Monetary and Financial Conference held in Bretton Woods, New Hampshire, in July 1944, was called to develop a structured international monetary system. As a result of this conference, the **International Monetary Fund (IMF)** was formed. The major objectives of the IMF, as set by its charter, are to (1) promote cooperation among countries on international monetary issues, (2) promote stability in exchange rates, (3) provide temporary funds to member countries attempting to correct imbalances of international payments, (4) promote free mobility of capital funds across countries, and (5) promote free trade. It is clear from these objectives that the IMF's goals encourage increased internationalization of business.

World Bank

The **International Bank for Reconstruction and Development (IBRD),** also referred to as the **World Bank,** was established in 1944. Its primary objective is to make loans to countries to enhance economic development. For example, the World Bank recently extended a loan to Mexico for about $4 billion over a 10-year period for environmental projects to facilitate industrial development near the U.S. border. Its main source of funds is the sale of bonds and other debt instruments to private investors and governments. The World Bank has a profit-oriented philosophy. Therefore, its loans are not subsidized but are extended at market rates to governments (and their agencies) that are likely to repay them.

A key aspect of the World Bank's mission is the **Structural Adjustment Loan (SAL),** established in 1980. The SALs are intended to enhance a country's long-term economic growth. For example, SALs have been provided to Turkey and to some less developed countries that are attempting to improve their balance of trade.

Because the World Bank provides only a small portion of the financing needed by developing countries, it attempts to spread its funds by entering into **cofinancing agreements.**

The World Bank recently established the **Multilateral Investment Guarantee Agency (MIGA),** which offers various forms of political risk insurance. This is an additional means (along with its SALs) by which the World Bank can encourage the development of international trade and investment.

The World Bank is one of the largest borrowers in the world; its borrowings have amounted to the equivalent of $70 billion. Its loans are well diversified among numerous currencies and countries. It has received the highest credit rating (AAA) possible.

World Trade Organization

The **World Trade Organization (WTO)** was created as a result of the Uruguay Round of trade negotiations that led to the GATT accord in 1993. This organization was established to provide a forum for multilateral trade negotiations and to settle trade disputes related to the GATT accord. It began its operations in 1995 with 81 member countries, and more countries have joined since then. Member countries are given voting rights that are used to make judgments about trade disputes and other issues.

International Financial Corporation

In 1956 the **International Financial Corporation (IFC)** was established to promote private enterprise within countries. Composed of a number of member nations, the IFC works to promote economic development through the private rather than the government sector. It not only provides loans to corporations but also purchases stock, thereby becoming part owner in some cases rather than just a creditor. The IFC typically provides 10 to 15% of the necessary funds in the private enterprise projects in which it invests, and the remainder of the project must be financed through other sources. Thus, the IFC acts as a catalyst, as opposed to a sole supporter, for private enterprise development projects. It traditionally has obtained financing from the World Bank but can borrow in the international financial markets.

International Development Association

The **International Development Association (IDA)** was created in 1960 with country development objectives somewhat similar to those of the World Bank. Its loan policy is more appropriate for less prosperous nations, however. The IDA extends loans at low interest rates to poor nations that cannot qualify for loans from the World Bank.

Bank for International Settlements

The **Bank for International Settlements (BIS)** attempts to facilitate cooperation among countries with regard to international transactions. It also provides assistance to countries experiencing a financial crisis. The BIS is sometimes referred to as the "central banks' central bank" or the "lender of last resort." It played an important role in supporting some of the less developed countries during the international debt crisis in the early and mid-1980s. It commonly provides financing for central banks in Latin American and Eastern European countries.

Regional Development Agencies

Several other agencies have more regional (as opposed to global) objectives relating to economic development. These include, for example, the Inter-American Development Bank (focusing on the needs of Latin America), the Asian Development Bank (established to enhance social and economic development in Asia), and the African Development Bank (focusing on development in African countries).

In 1990, the European Bank for Reconstruction and Development was created to help the Eastern European countries adjust from communism to capitalism. Twelve Western European countries hold a 51% interest, while Eastern European countries hold a 13.5% interest. The United States is the biggest shareholder, with a 10% interest. There are 40 member countries in aggregate.

How International Trade Affects an MNC's Value

An MNC's value can be affected by international trade. The cash flows (and therefore the value) of an MNC's subsidiaries that export to a specific country are typically expected to increase in response to a higher inflation rate (causing local substitutes to be more expensive) or a higher national income (which increases the level of spending) in that country. The expected cash flows of the MNC's subsidiaries that export or import may increase as a result of country trade agreements that reduce tariffs or other trade barriers. The expected cash flows of some subsidiaries may be reduced if they now face increased competition from foreign exporters as a result of trade agreements.

Cash flows to a U.S.-based MNC that occur in the form of payments for exports manufactured in the United States are expected to increase as a result of a weaker dollar because the demand for its dollar-denominated exports should increase. However, cash flows of U.S.-based importers may be reduced by a weaker dollar because it will take more dollars (increased cash outflows) to purchase the imports. A stronger dollar will have the opposite effects on cash flows of U.S.-based MNCs involved in international trade.

International Financial Markets

As a result of growth in international business over the last 30 years, various international financial markets have been developed. Financial managers of MNCs must understand the various international financial markets that are available so that they can use those markets to facilitate their international business transactions.

The specific objectives of this section are to describe the background and corporate use of the following international financial markets.

- Foreign exchange market
- Eurocurrency market
- Eurocredit market
- Eurobond market
- International stock markets

Motives for Using International Financial Markets

Several barriers prevent the markets for real or financial assets from becoming completely integrated; these barriers include tax differentials, tariffs, quotas, labor immobility, cultural differences, financial reporting differences, and significant costs of communicating information across countries. Nevertheless, the barriers can also create unique opportunities for specific geographic markets that will attract foreign creditors and investors. For example, barriers such as tariffs, quotas, and labor immobility can cause a given country's economic conditions to be distinctly different from others. Investors and creditors may want to do business in that country to capitalize on favorable conditions unique to that country. The existence of imperfect markets has precipitated the internationalization of financial markets.

Motives for Investing in Foreign Markets

Investors invest in foreign markets for one or more of the following motives.

- *Economic conditions.* Investors may expect firms in a particular foreign country to achieve more favorable performance than those in the investor's home country. For example, the loosening of restrictions in Eastern European countries created favorable economic conditions there. Such conditions attracted foreign investors and creditors.
- *Exchange rate expectations.* Some investors purchase financial securities denominated in a currency that is expected to appreciate against their own. The performance of such an investment is highly dependent on the currency movement over the investment horizon.
- *International diversification.* Investors may achieve benefits from internationally diversifying their asset portfolio. When an investor's entire portfolio does not depend solely on a single country's economy, cross-border differences in economic conditions can allow for risk-reduction benefits. A stock portfolio representing firms across European countries is less risky than a stock portfolio representing firms in any single European country. Furthermore, access to foreign markets allows investors to spread their funds across a more diverse group of industries than may be available domestically. This is especially true for investors residing in countries where firms are concentrated in a relatively small number of industries.

Motives for Providing Credit in Foreign Markets

Creditors (including individual investors who purchase debt securities) have one or more of the following motives for providing credit in foreign markets.

- *High foreign interest rates.* Some countries experience a shortage of loanable funds, which can cause market interest rates to be relatively high, even after considering default risk. Foreign creditors may attempt to capitalize on the higher rates, thereby providing capital to overseas markets. Yet, relatively high interest rates are often perceived to reflect relatively high inflationary expectations in that country. To the extent that inflation can cause depreciation of the local currency against others, high interest rates in the country may be somewhat offset by a weakening of the local currency over the time period of concern. The relation between a country's expected inflation and its local currency movements is not precise, however, because several other factors can influence currency movements as well. Thus, some creditors may believe that the interest rate advantage in a particular country will not be offset by a local currency depreciation over the period of concern.

- *Exchange rate expectations.* Creditors may consider supplying capital to countries whose currencies are expected to appreciate against their own. Whether the form of the transaction is a bond or a loan, the creditor benefits when the currency of denomination appreciates against the creditor's home currency.
- *International diversification.* Creditors can benefit from international diversification, which may reduce the probability of simultaneous bankruptcy across borrowers. The effectiveness of such a strategy depends on the correlation between the economic conditions of countries. If the countries of concern tend to experience somewhat similar business cycles, diversification across countries will be less effective.

Motives for Borrowing in Foreign Markets

Borrowers may have one or more of the following motives for borrowing in foreign markets.

- *Low interest rates.* Some countries have a large supply of funds available compared to the demand for funds, which can cause relatively low interest rates. Borrowers may attempt to borrow funds from creditors in these countries because the interest rate charged is lower. A country with relatively low interest rates is often expected to have a relatively low rate of inflation, which can place upward pressure on the foreign currency's value and offset any advantage of lower interest rates. The relation between expected inflation differentials and currency movements is not precise, however, so some borrowers will choose to borrow from a market where nominal interest rates are low, since they do not expect an adverse currency movement to fully offset this advantage.
- *Exchange rate expectations.* When a foreign subsidiary of a U.S.-based MNC remits funds to its U.S. parent, the funds must be converted to dollars and are subject to exchange rate risk. The MNC will be adversely affected if the foreign currency depreciates at that time. If the MNC expects that the foreign currency may depreciate against the dollar, it can reduce the exchange rate risk by having the subsidiary borrow funds locally to support its business. The subsidiary will remit less funds to the parent if it must pay interest on local debt before remitting the funds. Thus, the amount of funds converted to dollars will be smaller, resulting in less exposure to exchange rate risk.

If the U.S. parent needs to borrow funds for its own purposes, it may pursue a more aggressive strategy and borrow a foreign currency that is expected to depreciate. In this case, the parent would borrow that currency and convert it to dollars for use. The value of the foreign currency when converted to dollars would exceed the value when the MNC repurchases the currency to repay the loan. The favorable currency effect can offset part or all of the interest owed on the funds borrowed. Such a strategy may be especially desirable if the foreign currency has a low interest rate compared to the U.S. interest rate.

Foreign Exchange Market

The **foreign exchange market** allows currencies to be exchanged in order to facilitate international trade or financial transactions. MNCs rely on the foreign exchange market to exchange their home currency for a foreign currency that they need to purchase imports or use for direct foreign investment. Alternatively, they may need the foreign exchange market to exchange a foreign currency that they receive into their home currency. The system for establishing exchange rates has changed over time.

Foreign Exchange Transactions

The "foreign exchange market" should not be thought of as a specific building or location where traders exchange currencies. Companies normally exchange one currency for another through a commercial bank over a telecommunications network. These include spot markets and forward transactions.

SPOT MARKET The most common type of foreign exchange transaction is for immediate exchange at the so-called **spot rate.** The market where these transactions occur is known as the **spot market.** The average daily foreign exchange trading by banks around the world now exceeds $1.5 trillion. The average daily foreign exchange trading in the United States alone exceeds $200 billion.

The U.S. dollar is not part of every transaction. Foreign currencies can be traded for each other. For example, a Japanese firm may need British pounds to pay for imports from the United Kingdom. Much of the foreign exchange trading is conducted by banks in London, New York, and Tokyo, the three largest foreign exchange trading centers.

Many foreign transactions do not require an exchange of currencies but allow a given currency to cross country borders. For example, the U.S. dollar is commonly accepted as a medium of exchange by merchants in many countries, especially in countries such as Bolivia, Brazil, China, Cuba, Indonesia, Russia, and Vietnam where the home currency is either weak or subject to foreign exchange restrictions. Many merchants accept U.S. dollars because they can use them to purchase goods from other countries. The U.S. dollar is the official currency of Liberia and Panama.

SPOT MARKET STRUCTURE Hundreds of banks facilitate foreign exchange transactions, but the top 20 handle about 50% of the transactions. **Deutsche Bank** (Germany), **Citibank** (subsidiary of Citigroup, U.S.), and **J.P. Morgan Chase** are the largest traders of foreign exchange. Some banks and other financial institutions have formed alliances (one example is FX Alliance LLC) to offer currency transactions over the Internet.

At any given point in time, the exchange rate between two currencies should be similar across the various banks that provide foreign exchange services. If there is a large discrepancy, customers or other banks will purchase large amounts of a currency from whatever bank quotes a relatively low price and immediately sell it to whatever bank quotes a relatively high price. Such actions cause adjustments in the exchange rate quotations that eliminate any discrepancy.

If a bank begins to experience a shortage in a particular foreign currency, it can purchase that currency from other banks. This trading between banks occurs in what is often referred to as the **interbank market.** Within this market, banks can obtain quotes, or they can contact brokers who sometimes act as intermediaries, matching one bank desiring to sell a given currency with another bank desiring to buy that currency. About 10 foreign exchange brokerage firms handle much of the interbank transaction volume.

Although foreign exchange trading is conducted only during normal business hours in a given location, these hours vary among locations due to different time zones. Thus, at any given time on a weekday, somewhere around the world a bank is open and ready to accommodate foreign exchange requests.

When the foreign exchange market opens in the United States each morning, the opening exchange rate quotations are based on the prevailing rates quoted by banks in London and other locations where the foreign exchange markets have opened earlier. Suppose the quoted spot rate of the British pound was $1.80 at the previous close of the U.S. foreign exchange market, but by the time the market opens the following day, the opening spot rate is $1.76. News occurring in the morning before the U.S. market opened could have changed the supply and demand conditions for British pounds in the London foreign exchange market, reducing the quoted price for the pound.

With the newest electronic devices, foreign currency trades are negotiated on computer terminals, and a push of a button confirms the trade. Traders now use electronic trading boards that allow them to instantly register transactions and check their bank's positions in various currencies. Also, several U.S. banks have established night trading desks. The largest banks initiated night trading to capitalize on foreign exchange movements at night and to accommodate corporate requests for currency trades. Even some medium-sized banks have begun to use night trading to accommodate corporate clients.

FORWARD TRANSACTIONS In addition to the spot market, a forward market for currencies enables an MNC to lock in the exchange rate (called a **forward rate**) at which it will buy or sell a currency. A **forward contract** specifies the amount of a particular currency that will be purchased or sold by the MNC at a specified future point in time and at a specified exchange rate. Commercial banks accommodate the MNCs that desire forward contracts. MNCs commonly use the forward market to hedge future payments that they expect to make or receive in a foreign currency. In this way, they do not have to worry about fluctuations in the spot rate until the time of their future payments.

ATTRIBUTES OF BANKS THAT PROVIDE FOREIGN EXCHANGE The following characteristics of banks are important to customers in need of foreign exchange.

1. *Competitiveness of quote.* A savings of 1¢ per unit on an order of one million units of currency is worth $10,000.
2. *Special relationship with the bank.* The bank may offer cash management services or be willing to make a special effort to obtain even hard-to-find foreign currencies for the corporation.
3. *Speed of execution.* Banks may vary in the efficiency with which they handle an order. A corporation needing the currency will prefer a bank that conducts the transaction promptly and handles any paperwork properly.

4. *Advice about current market conditions.* Some banks may provide assessments of foreign economies and relevant activities in the international financial environment that relate to corporate customers.
5. *Forecasting advice.* Some banks may provide forecasts of the future state of foreign economies, the future value of exchange rates, and so forth.

This list suggests that a corporation needing a foreign currency should not automatically choose a bank that will sell that currency at the lowest price. Most corporations that often need foreign currencies develop a close relationship with at least one major bank in case they ever need favors from a bank.

BID/ASK SPREAD OF BANKS   Commercial banks charge fees for conducting foreign exchange transactions. At any given point in time, a bank's **bid** (buy) quote for a foreign currency will be less than its ask (**sell**) quote. The **bid/ask spread** represents the differential between the bid and ask quotes, and is intended to cover the costs involved in accommodating requests to exchange currencies. The bid/ask spread is normally expressed as a percentage of the ask quote.

Example 21 *To understand how a bid/ask spread could affect you, assume you have $1,000 and plan to travel from the United States to the United Kingdom. Assume further that the bank's bid rate for the British pound is $1.52 and its ask rate is $1.60. Before leaving on your trip, you go to this bank to exchange dollars for pounds. Your $1,000 will be converted to 625 pounds (£), as follows:*

$$\frac{\text{Amount in U.S. dollars to be converted}}{\text{Bank's ask rate per pound}} = \frac{\$1,000}{\$1.60} = £625$$

Now suppose that because of an emergency you cannot take the trip, and you reconvert the £625 back to U.S. dollars, just after purchasing the pounds. If the exchange rate has not changed, you will receive

£625 × (Bank's bid rate of $1.52 per pound) = $950.

Due to the bid/ask spread, you have $50 (5%) less than what you started with. Obviously, the dollar amount of the loss would be larger if you originally converted more than $1,000 into pounds.

COMPARISON OF BID/ASK SPREAD AMONG CURRENCIES   The differential between a bid quote and an ask quote will look much smaller for currencies that have a smaller value. This differential can be standardized by measuring it as a percentage of the currency's spot rate.

Example 22 *Charlotte Bank quotes a bid price for yen of $.007 and an ask price of $.0074. In this case, the nominal bid/ask spread is $.0074 − $.007, or just four-hundredths of a penny. Yet, the bid/ask spread in percentage terms is actually slightly higher for the yen in this example than for the pound in the previous example. To prove this, consider a traveler who sells $1,000 for yen at the bank's ask price of $.0074. The traveler receives about ¥135,135 (computed as $1,000/$.0074). If the traveler cancels the trip and converts the yen back to dollars, then, assuming no changes in the bid/ask quotations, the bank will buy these yen back at the bank's bid price of $.007 for a total of about $946 (computed by ¥135,135 × $.007), $54 (or 5.4%) less than what the traveler started with. This spread exceeds that of the British pound (5% in the previous example).*

Exhibit 700.52 *Computation of the Bid/Ask Spread*

Currency	Bid Rate	Ask Rate	$\dfrac{\text{Ask Rate} - \text{Bid Rate}}{\text{Ask Rate}}$ =	Bid/Ask Percentage Spread
British pound	$1.52	$1.60	$\dfrac{\$1.60 - \$1.52}{\$1.60}$ =	.05 or 5%
Japanese yen	$.0070	$.0074	$\dfrac{\$.0074 - \$.007}{\$.0074}$ =	.054 or 5.4%

A common way to compute the bid/ask spread in percentage terms follows.

$$\text{Bid/ask spread} = \frac{\text{Ask rate} - \text{Bid rate}}{\text{Ask rate}}$$

Using this formula, the bid/ask spreads are computed in Exhibit 700.52 for both the British pound and the Japanese yen.

Notice that these numbers coincide with those derived earlier. Such spreads are common for so-called retail transactions serving consumers. For larger so-called wholesale transactions between banks or for large corporations, the spread will be much smaller. The spread is normally larger for currencies that are less frequently traded. Commercial banks are normally exposed to more exchange rate risk when maintaining these currencies.

The bid/ask spread as defined here represents the discount in the bid rate as a percentage of the ask rate. An alternative bid/ask spread uses the bid rate as the denominator instead of the ask rate and measures the percentage markup of the ask rate above the bid rate. The spread is slightly higher when using this formula because the bid rate used in the denominator is always less than the ask rate.

In the following discussion and in examples throughout much of this section, the bid/ask spread will be ignored. That is, only one price will be shown for a given currency to allow you to concentrate on understanding other relevant concepts. These examples depart slightly from reality because the bid and ask prices are, in a sense, assumed to be equal. Although the ask price will always exceed the bid price by a small amount in reality, the implications from examples should nevertheless hold, even though the bid/ask spreads are not accounted for. In particular examples where the bid/ask spread can contribute significantly to the concept, it will be accounted for.

IMPACT OF THE EURO ON FOREIGN EXCHANGE TRANSACTIONS   As a result of several European countries adopting the euro as their currency, many transactions within Europe no longer require conversion into a different currency. This is relevant for MNCs that conduct operations in Europe because they no longer incur a transaction cost from exchanging currencies and no longer need to worry about exchange rate fluctuations on most transactions within Europe.

Interpreting Foreign Exchange Quotations

Exchange rate quotations for widely traded currencies are provided in *The Wall Street Journal* and in business sections of many newspapers on a daily basis. With some exceptions, each country has its own currency. In 1999, several European countries (including Germany, France, and Italy) adopted the euro as their new currency for commercial transactions, replacing their own currencies. Their own currencies were phased out by the year 2002.

QUOTATIONS OF FORWARD RATES   Some quotations of exchange rates include forward rates for the most widely traded currencies. Other forward rates are not quoted in business newspapers but are quoted by the banks that offer forward contracts in various currencies.

DIRECT VERSUS INDIRECT QUOTATIONS   The quotations of exchange rates for currencies normally reflect the ask prices for large transactions. Since exchange rates change throughout the day, the exchange rates quoted in a newspaper reflect only one specific point in time during the day. Quotations that represent the value of a foreign currency in dollars (number of dollars per currency) are referred to as **direct quotations**. Conversely, quotations that represent the number of units of a foreign currency per dollar are referred to as **indirect quotations**. The indirect quotation is the reciprocal of the corresponding direct quotation.

Discussions of exchange rate movements can be confusing because some comments refer to direct quotations while others refer to indirect quotations. For consistency, this text uses direct quotations unless an example can be clarified by the use of indirect quotations. Direct quotations are easier to link with comments about any foreign currency.

CROSS EXCHANGE RATES Most tables of exchange rate quotation express currencies relative to the dollar, but in some instances, a firm will be concerned about the exchange rate between two nondollar currencies. For example, if a Canadian firm needs Mexican pesos to buy Mexican goods, it is concerned about the Mexican peso value relative to the Canadian dollar. The type of rate desired here is known as a **cross exchange rate**, because it reflects the amount of one foreign currency per unit of another foreign currency. Cross exchange rates can be easily determined with the use of foreign exchange quotations. The general formula follows.

$$\text{Value of 1 unit of Currency A in units of Currency B} = \frac{\text{Value of Currency A in \$}}{\text{Value of Currency B in \$}}$$

Example 23 If the peso is worth $.07, and the Canadian dollar is worth $.70, the value of the peso in Canadian dollars (C$) is calculated as follows:

$$\text{Value of peso in C\$} = \frac{\text{Value of peso in \$}}{\text{Value of C\$ in \$}} = \$.07/\$.70 = \text{C\$}.10$$

Thus, a Mexican peso is worth C$.10. The exchange rate can also be expressed as the number of pesos equal to one Canadian dollar. This figure can be computed by taking the reciprocal: .70/.07 = 10.0, which indicates that a Canadian dollar is worth about 10.0 pesos according to the information provided.

Currency Futures and Options Markets

A **currency futures contract** specifies a standard volume of a particular currency to be exchanged on a specific settlement date. Some MNCs involved in international trade use the currency futures markets to hedge their positions.

Example 24 Memphis Co. has ordered supplies from European countries that are denominated in euros. It expects the euro to increase in value over time and therefore desires to hedge its payables in euros. Memphis buys futures contracts on euros to lock in the price that it will pay for euros at a future point in time. Meanwhile, it will receive Mexican pesos in the future and wants to hedge these receivables. Memphis sells futures contracts on pesos to lock in the dollars that it will receive when it sells the pesos at a specified point in the future.

Futures contracts are somewhat similar to forward contracts except that they are sold on an exchange whereas forward contracts are offered by commercial banks. Additional details on futures contracts, including other differences from forward contracts, are provided later in this section.

Currency options contracts can be classified as calls or puts. A **currency call option** provides the right to buy a specific currency at a specific price (called the **strike price** or **exercise price**) within a specific period of time. It is used to hedge future payables. A **currency put option** provides the right to sell a specific currency at a specific price within a specific period of time. It is used to hedge future receivables.

Currency call and put options can be purchased on an exchange. They offer more flexibility than forward or futures contracts because they do not require any obligation. That is, the firm can elect not to exercise the option.

Currency options have become a popular means of hedging. The **Coca-Cola Co.** has replaced about 30 to 40% of its forward contracting with currency options. FMC, a U.S. manufacturer of chemicals and machinery, now hedges its foreign sales with currency options instead of forward contracts. A recent study by the **Whitney Group** found that 85% of U.S.-based MNCs use currency options. Additional details about currency options, including other differences from futures and forward contracts, are provided later in this section.

Eurocurrency Market

Financial markets exist in every country to ensure that funds are transferred efficiently from surplus units (savers) to deficit units (borrowers). These markets are overseen by various regulators that attempt to enhance the markets' safety and efficiency. The financial institutions that serve these financial markets exist primarily to provide information and expertise. The surplus units typically do not know who needs to borrow funds at any particular point in time. Furthermore, they often cannot adequately evaluate the credit risk of any potential borrowers or establish the documentation necessary when providing loans. Financial institutions specialize in collecting funds from surplus units and then repackaging and transferring the funds to deficit units.

Development of the Eurocurrency Market

Like domestic firms, MNCs sometimes obtain funding through short-term loans from local financial institutions or by issuing short-term securities such as commercial paper. However, they can also obtain funds from the financial institutions in foreign markets. International financial intermediation emerged in the 1960s and 1970s as MNCs expanded their operations. During this period, the Eurodollar market, or what is now referred to as the **Eurocurrency market**, grew to accommodate the increasing international business. The Eurodollar market was created as corporations in the United States deposited U.S. dollars in European banks. These European banks were willing to accept dollar deposits, since they could then lend dollars to corporate customers based in Europe.

Because the U.S. dollar is widely used even by foreign countries as a medium for international trade, there is a consistent need for dollars in Europe. U.S.-dollar deposits in banks located in Europe and on other continents as well became known as **Eurodollars.**

Composition of the Eurocurrency Market

The Eurocurrency market is composed of several large banks (referred to as **Eurobanks**) that accept deposits and provide loans in various currencies. Countries in the Organization of Petroleum Exporting Countries (OPEC) also use the Eurocurrency market to deposit a portion of their petroleum revenues. The deposits usually are denominated in U.S. dollars because OPEC generally requires payment for oil in dollars. The deposits are sometimes referred to as **petrodollars.** The Eurocurrency market has historically recycled the oil revenues from the oil-exporting countries to other countries. That is, oil revenues deposited in the Eurobanks are sometimes lent to oil-importing countries that are short of cash. As these countries purchase more oil, funds are again transferred to oil-exporting countries, which in turn results in new deposits. This recycling process has been an important source of funds for some countries.

The Eurocurrency market normally focuses on business transactions that involve large deposits and loans, often the equivalent of $1 million or more. Large financial transactions such as these can reduce a bank's operating expenses. This is another reason why Eurobanks can offer attractive rates on deposits and loans.

Syndicated Eurocurrency Loans

Although the Eurocurrency market concentrates on large-volume transactions, at times no single Eurobank may be willing to provide the amount needed by a particular corporation or government agency. In this case, a **syndicate** of Eurobanks may be organized. Each bank within the syndicate participates in the lending. A lead bank is responsible for negotiating terms with the borrower. Then the lead bank organizes a group of banks to underwrite the loans. The syndicate of banks is usually formed in about six weeks, or less if the borrower is well known because the credit evaluation can then be conducted more quickly.

Borrowers that receive a syndicated loan incur various fees besides the interest on the loan. Front-end management fees are paid to cover the costs of organizing the syndicate and underwriting the loan. In addition, a commitment fee of about .25% or .50% is charged annually on the unused portion of the available credit extended by the syndicate.

Syndicated loans can be denominated in a variety of currencies. The interest rate depends on the currency denominating the loan, the maturity of the loan, and the creditworthiness of the borrower. Interest rates on syndicated loans are commonly adjustable according to movements in an interbank lending rate, and the adjustment may occur every six months or every year.

Syndicated Eurocurrency loans not only reduce the default risk of a large loan to the degree of participation for each individual bank, but they can also add an extra incentive for the borrower to repay the loan. If a government defaults on a loan to a syndicate, word will quickly spread among banks, and the government will likely have difficulty obtaining future loans. Borrowers are therefore strongly encouraged to repay syndicated loans promptly. From the perspective of the banks, syndicated Eurocurrency loans increase the probability of prompt repayment.

Standardizing Bank Regulations Within the Eurocurrency Market

The trend toward globalization in the banking industry is attributed to the growing standardization of regulations around the world. Two of the more significant regulatory events allowing for a more competitive global playing field are (1) the Single European Act and (2) the Basel Accord, which are described next.

SINGLE EUROPEAN ACT One of the most significant events affecting international banking is the **Single European Act,** which was phased in by 1992 throughout the European Union (EU) countries. The following are some of the more relevant provisions of the Single European Act for the banking industry.

- Capital can flow freely throughout Europe.
- Banks can offer a wide variety of lending, leasing, and securities activities in the EU.
- Regulations regarding competition, mergers, and taxes are similar throughout the EU.
- A bank established in any one of the EU countries has the right to expand into any or all of the other EU countries.

As a result of this act, banks have expanded across European countries. Efficiency in the European banking markets has increased because banks can more easily cross countries without concern for country-specific regulations that prevailed in the past.

Another key provision of the act is that banks entering Europe receive the same banking powers as other banks there. Similar provisions apply to non-U.S. banks that enter the United States.

BASEL ACCORD Before 1987, capital standards imposed on banks varied across countries, which allowed some banks to have a comparative global advantage over others. As an example, suppose that a bank in the United States was subject to a 6% capital ratio, which was twice that of a foreign bank. The foreign bank could achieve the same return on equity as the U.S. bank by generating a return on assets that was only one-half that of the U.S. bank. In essence, the foreign bank's **equity multiplier** (assets divided by equity) was double that of the U.S. bank, which would offset the low return on assets. Given these conditions, foreign banks could accept lower profit margins while still achieving the same return on equity. This afforded them a stronger competitive position. In addition, they could grow more easily, as a relatively small amount of capital was needed to support an increase in assets.

Some analysts countered that these advantages were somewhat offset by the perception that banks with low capital ratios entailed higher risks. Nevertheless, because the governments in those countries were likely to back banks that experienced financial problems, the banks with low capital were not necessarily perceived as too risky. Therefore, some non-U.S. banks had globally competitive advantages over U.S. banks, without being subject to excessive risk. In December 1987, 12 major industrialized countries attempted to resolve the disparity by proposing uniform bank standards. In July 1988, in the **Basel Accord,** central bank governors of the 12 countries agreed on standardized guidelines. Capital was classified as either Tier 1 ("core") capital or Tier 2 ("supplemental") capital (Tier 1 capital being at least 4% of risk-weighted assets). The use of risk weightings on assets implicitly created a higher required capital ratio for riskier assets. Off-balance sheet items were also accounted for so that banks could not circumvent capital requirements by focusing on services (such as letters of credit and interest rate swaps) that are not explicitly shown on a balance sheet. The uniform capital requirements represent significant progress toward a more level global field.

Asian Dollar Market

Although the Eurocurrency market can be broadly defined to include banks in Asia that accept deposits and make loans in foreign currencies (mostly dollars), this market is sometimes referred to separately as the **Asian dollar market.** Most activity takes place in Hong Kong and Singapore. The only significant difference between the Asian market and the Eurocurrency market is location. Like the Eurocurrency market, the Asian dollar market grew to accommodate the needs of businesses that were using the U.S. dollar (and some other foreign currencies) as a medium of exchange for international trade. These businesses could not rely on banks in Europe because of the distance and different time zones.

The primary function of banks in the Asian dollar market is to channel funds from depositors to borrowers. The major sources of Asian dollar deposits are MNCs with excess cash and government agencies. Manufacturers are major borrowers in this market. Another function is interbank lending and borrowing. Banks that have more qualified loan applicants than they can accommodate use the interbank market to obtain additional funds. Banks in the Asian market commonly borrow from or lend to banks in the Eurocurrency market.

Eurocredit Market

Multinational corporations and domestic firms sometimes obtain medium-term funds through term loans from local financial institutions or through the issuance of notes (medium-term debt obligations) in their local markets. However, MNCs also have access to medium-term funds through Eurobanks located in foreign markets. Loans of one year or longer extended by Eurobanks to MNCs or government agencies are commonly called Eurocredits or **Eurocredit loans.** These loans are provided in the so-called **Eurocredit market.** The loans can be denominated in dollars or many other currencies and commonly have a maturity of five years.

Because Eurobanks accept short-term deposits and sometimes provide longer-term loans, their asset and liability maturities do not match. This can adversely affect a bank's performance during periods of rising interest rates, since the bank may have locked in a rate on its Eurocredit loans while the rate it pays on short-term deposits is rising over time. To avoid this risk, Eurobanks now commonly use floating rate Eurocredit loans. The loan rate floats in accordance with the movement of some market interest rate, such as the **London Interbank Offer Rate (LIBOR),** which is the rate commonly charged for loans between Eurobanks. For example, a Eurocredit loan may have a loan rate that adjusts every six months and is set at "LIBOR plus 3%." The premium paid above LIBOR will depend on the credit risk of the borrower.

Eurobond Market

MNCs, like domestic firms, can obtain long-term debt by issuing bonds in their local markets. MNCs can access long-term funds in foreign markets by issuing bonds in the international bond markets. International bonds are typically classified as either foreign bonds or Eurobonds. A **foreign bond** is issued by a borrower foreign to the country where the bond is placed. For example, a U.S. corporation may issue a bond denominated in Japanese yen, which is sold to investors in Japan. In some cases, a firm may issue a variety of bonds in various countries. The currency denominating each type of bond is determined by the country where it is sold. These foreign bonds are sometimes specifically referred to as **parallel bonds.**

Eurobonds are sold in countries other than the country represented by the currency denominating them. They have been very popular during the last decade as a means of attracting long-term funds. U.S.-based MNCs such as **McDonald's** and **Walt Disney** commonly use the Eurobond market. Non-U.S. firms such as **Guinness, Nestlé**, and **Volkswagen** also use this market as a source of funds.

In recent years, governments and corporations from emerging markets such as Croatia, Ukraine, Romania, and Hungary have frequently utilized the Eurobond market. New corporations that have been established in emerging markets rely on the Eurobond market to finance their growth. They have to pay a risk premium of at least three percentage points annually above the U.S. Treasury bond rate on dollar-denominated Eurobonds.

Underwriting Process

Eurobonds are underwritten by a multinational syndicate of investment banks and simultaneously placed in many countries, providing a wide spectrum of fund sources to tap. The underwriting process takes place in a sequence of steps. The multinational managing syndicate sells the bonds to a large underwriting crew. In many cases, a special distribution to regional underwriters is allocated before the bonds finally reach the bond purchasers. One problem with the distribution method is that the second- and third-stage underwriters do not always follow up on their promise to sell the bonds. The managing syndicate is therefore forced to redistribute the unsold bonds or to sell them directly, which creates "digestion" problems in the market and adds to the distribution cost. To avoid such problems, bonds are often distributed in higher volume to underwriters that have fulfilled their commitments in the past at the expense of those that have not. This has helped the Eurobond market maintain its desirability as a bond placement center.

Features

Eurobonds have several distinguishing features. They usually are issued in bearer form, and coupon payments are made yearly. Some Eurobonds carry a convertibility clause allowing them to be converted into a specified number of common stock shares. Eurobonds typically have few, if any, protective covenants, which is an advantage to the issuer. Also, even short-maturity Eurobonds include call provisions. Some Eurobonds, called **floating rate notes (FRNs),** have a variable rate provision that adjusts the coupon rate over time according to prevailing market rates.

International Stock Markets

MNCs and domestic firms commonly obtain long-term funding by issuing stock locally. Yet, MNCs can also attract funds from foreign investors by issuing stock in international markets. The stock offering may be more easily digested when it is issued in several markets. In addition, the issuance of stock in a foreign country can enhance the firm's image and name recognition there.

The recent conversion of many European countries to a single currency (the euro) has resulted in more stock offerings in Europe by U.S.- and European-based MNCs. In the past, an MNC needed a different currency in every country where it conducted business and therefore borrowed currencies from local banks in those countries. Now, it can use the euro to finance its operations across several European countries and may be able to obtain all the financing it needs with one stock offering in which the stock is denominated in euros. The MNCs can then use a portion of the revenue (in euros) to pay dividends to shareholders who have purchased the stock.

Issuance of Foreign Stock in the United States

Non-U.S. corporations or governments that need large amounts of funds sometimes issue the stock in the United States (these are called Yankee stock offerings) due to the liquidity of the new-issues market there. In other words, a foreign corporation or government may be more likely to sell an entire issue of stock in the U.S. market, whereas in other, smaller markets, the entire issue may not necessarily sell.

The U.S. investment banks commonly serve as underwriters of the stock targeted for the U.S. market and receive underwriting fees ranging from about 3 to 6% of the value of stock issued. Since many financial institutions in the United States purchase non-U.S. stocks as investments, non-U.S. firms may be able to place an entire stock offering within the United States.

Firms that issue stock in the United States typically are required to satisfy stringent disclosure rules on their financial condition. However, they are exempt from some of these rules when they qualify for a Securities and Exchange Commission guideline (called Rule 144a) through a direct placement of stock to institutional investors.

Many of the recent stock offerings in the United States by non-U.S. firms have resulted from privatization programs in Latin America and Europe, whereby businesses that were previously government owned are being sold to U.S. shareholders. Given the large size of some of these businesses, the local stock markets are not large enough to digest the stock offerings. Consequently, U.S. investors are financing many privatized businesses based in foreign countries.

When a non-U.S. firm issues stock in its own country, its shareholder base is quite limited, as a few large institutional investors may own most of the shares. By issuing stock in the United States, such a firm diversifies its shareholder base, which can reduce share price volatility caused when large investors sell shares.

Non-U.S. firms also obtain equity financing by using **American depository receipts (ADRs),** which are certificates representing bundles of stock. The use of ADRs circumvents some disclosure requirements imposed on stock offerings in the United States, yet enables non-U.S. firms to tap the U.S. market for funds. The ADR market grew after businesses were privatized in the early 1990s, as some of these businesses issued ADRs to obtain financing.

Issuance of Stock in Foreign Markets

Although the U.S. market offers an advantage for new stock issues due to its size, the registration requirements can sometimes cause delays in selling the new issues. For this reason, some U.S. firms have issued new stock in foreign markets in recent years. Other U.S. firms issue stock in foreign markets simply to enhance their global image. The existence of various markets for new issues provides corporations in need of equity with a choice. This competition among various new-issues markets should increase the efficiency of new issues.

The locations of an MNC's operations can influence the decision about where to place stock, as the MNC may desire a country where it is likely to generate enough future cash flows to cover dividend payments. The stocks of some U.S.-based MNCs are widely traded on numerous stock exchanges around the world. For example, the stock of **The Coca-Cola Co., IBM, TRW** and many other U.S.-based MNCs have their stock listed on several different stock exchanges overseas. When an MNC's stock is listed on foreign stock exchanges, it can easily be traded by foreign investors who have access to those exchanges.

Comparison of International Financial Markets

Exhibit 700.53 illustrates the foreign cash flow movements of a typical MNC. These cash flows can be classified into four corporate functions, all of which generally require use of the foreign exchange markets. The spot market, forward market, currency futures market, and currency options market are all classified as foreign exchange markets.

The first function is foreign trade with business clients. Exports generate foreign cash inflows, while imports require cash outflows. A second function is direct foreign investment, or the acquisition of foreign real assets. This function requires cash outflows but generates future inflows through remitted dividends back to the MNC parent or the sale of these foreign assets. A third function is short-term investment or financing in foreign securities. The Eurocurrency market is commonly used for this purpose. A fourth function is longer-term financing in the Eurocredit, Eurobond, or international stock markets.

Financing International Trade

The international trade activities of MNCs have grown in importance over time. This trend is attributable to the increased globalization of the world economies and the availability of trade finance from the international banking community. Although banks also finance domestic trade, their role in financing international trade is more critical due to the additional complications involved. First, the exporter might question the importer's ability to make payment. Second, even if the importer is creditworthy, the government might impose exchange controls that prevent payment to the

Exhibit 700.53   *Foreign Cash Flow Chart of an MNC*

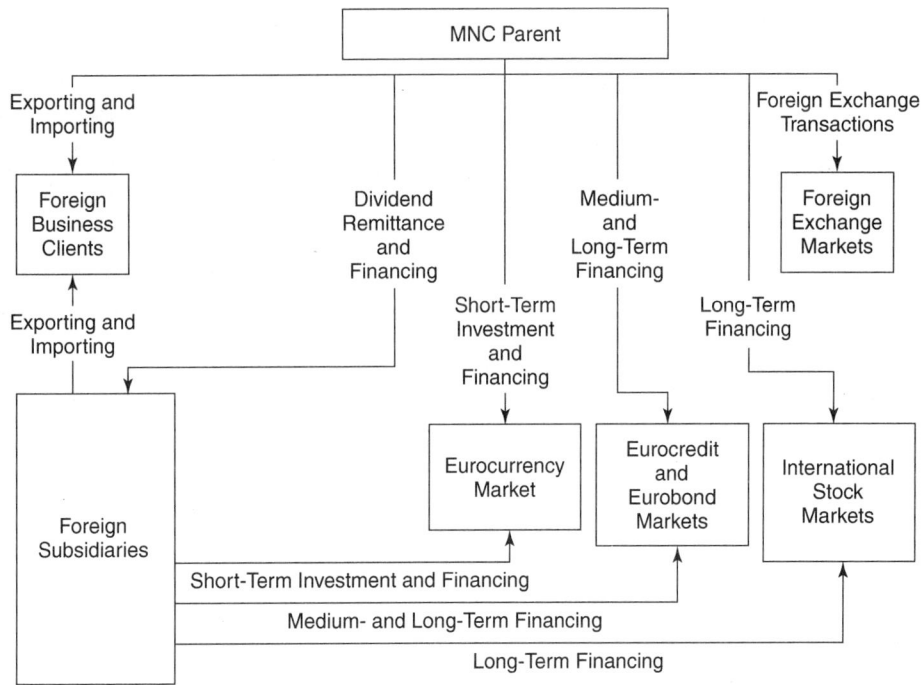

exporter. Third, the importer might not trust the exporter to ship the goods ordered. Fourth, even if the exporter does ship the goods, trade barriers or time lags in international transportation might delay arrival time. Financial managers must recognize methods that they can use to finance international trade so that they can conduct exporting or importing in a manner that maximizes the value of an MNC.

Payment Methods for International Trade

In any international trade transaction, credit is provided by either the supplier (exporter), the buyer (importer), one or more financial institutions, or any combination of these. The supplier may have sufficient cash flow to finance the entire trade cycle, beginning with the production of the product until payment is eventually made by the buyer. This form of credit is known as **supplier credit.** In some cases, the exporter may require bank financing to augment its cash flow. On the other hand, the supplier may not desire to provide financing, in which case the buyer will have to finance the transaction itself, either internally or externally, through its bank. Banks on both sides of the transaction can thus play an integral role in trade financing.

In general, five basic methods of payment are used to settle international transactions, each with a different degree of risk to the exporter and importer (Exhibit 700.54):

- Prepayment
- Letters of credit
- Drafts (sight/time)
- Consignment
- Open account

Prepayment

Under the **prepayment** method, the exporter will not ship the goods until the buyer has remitted payment to the exporter. Payment is usually made in the form of an international wire transfer to the exporter's bank account or foreign bank draft. As technology progresses, electronic commerce will allow firms engaged in international trade to make electronic credits and debits through an intermediary bank. This method affords the supplier the greatest degree of protection, and it is normally requested of first-time buyers whose creditworthiness is unknown or whose countries are in financial difficulty. Most buyers, however, are not willing to bear all the risk by prepaying an order.

Exhibit 700.54 *Comparison of International Payment Methods*

Method	Usual Time of Payment	Goods Available to Buyers	Risk to Exporter	Risk to Importer
Prepayment	Before shipment	After payment	None	Relies completely on exporter to ship goods as ordered
Letter of credit	When shipment is made	After payment	Very little or none, depending on credit terms	Assured shipment made, but relies on exporter to ship goods described in documents
Sight draft; documents against payment	On presentation of draft to buyer	After payment	If draft unpaid, must dispose of goods	Same as above unless importer can inspect goods before payment
Time draft; documents against acceptance	On maturity of drafts	Before payment	Relies on buyer to pay drafts	Same as above
Consignment	At time of sale by buyer	Before payment	Allows importer to sell inventory before paying exporter	None; improves cash flow of buyer
Open account	As agreed	Before payment	Relies completely on buyer to pay account as agreed	None

Letters of Credit (L/C)

A **letter of credit (L/C)** is an instrument issued by a bank on behalf of the importer (buyer) promising to pay the exporter (beneficiary) upon presentation of shipping documents in compliance with the terms stipulated therein. In effect, the bank is substituting its credit for that of the buyer. This method is a compromise between seller and buyer because it affords certain advantages to both parties. The exporter is assured of receiving payment from the issuing bank as long as it presents documents in accordance with the L/C. It is important to point out that the issuing bank is obligated to honor drawings under the L/C regardless of the buyer's ability or willingness to pay. On the other hand, the importer does not have to pay for the goods until shipment has been made and documents are presented in good order. However, the importer must still rely upon the exporter to ship the goods as described in the documents, since the L/C does not guarantee that the goods purchased will be those invoiced and shipped. Letters of credit will be described in greater detail later in this section.

Drafts

A **draft** (or **bill of exchange**) is an unconditional promise drawn by one party, usually the exporter, instructing the buyer to pay the face amount of the draft upon presentation. The draft represents the exporter's formal demand for payment from the buyer. A draft affords the exporter less protection than an L/C, since the banks are not obligated to honor payments on the buyer's behalf.

Most trade transactions handled on a draft basis are processed through banking channels. In banking terminology, these transactions are known as **documentary collections.** In a documentary collection transaction, banks on both ends act as intermediaries in the processing of shipping documents and the collection of payment. If shipment is made under a sight draft, the exporter is paid once shipment has been made and the draft is presented to the buyer for payment. The buyer's bank will not release the shipping documents to the buyer until the buyer has paid the draft. This is known as **documents against payment.** It provides the exporter with some protection, since the banks will release the shipping documents only according to the exporter's instructions. The buyer needs the shipping documents to pick up merchandise. The buyer does not have to pay for the merchandise until the draft has been presented.

If a shipment is made under a time draft, the exporter provides instructions to the buyer's bank to release the shipping documents against acceptance (signing) of the draft. This method of payment is sometimes referred to as **documents against acceptance.** By accepting the draft, the buyer is promising to pay the exporter at the specified future date. This accepted draft is also known as a **trade acceptance,** which is different from a banker's acceptance. In this type of transaction, the buyer is able to obtain the merchandise prior to paying for it.

The exporter is providing the financing and is dependent upon the buyer's financial integrity to pay the draft at maturity. Shipping on a time draft basis provides some added comfort in that banks at both ends are used as collection agents. In addition, a draft serves as a binding financial obligation in case the exporter wishes to pursue litigation on uncollected receivables. The added risk is that if the buyer fails to pay the draft at maturity, the bank is not obligated to honor payment. The exporter is assuming all the risk and must analyze the buyer accordingly.

Consignment

Under a **consignment** arrangement, the exporter ships the goods to the importer while still retaining actual title to the merchandise. The importer has access to the inventory but does not have to pay for the goods until they have been sold to a third party. The exporter is trusting the importer to remit payment for the goods sold at that time. If the importer fails to pay, the exporter has limited recourse because no draft is involved and the goods have already been sold. As a result of the high risk, consignments are seldom used except by affiliated and subsidiary companies trading with the parent company. Some equipment suppliers allow importers to hold some equipment on the sales floor as demonstrator models. Once the models are sold or after a specified period, payment is sent to the supplier.

Open Account

The opposite of prepayment is the **open account transaction** in which the exporter ships the merchandise and expects the buyer to remit payment according to the agreed-upon terms. The exporter is relying fully upon the financial creditworthiness, integrity, and reputation of the buyer. As might be expected, this method is used when seller and buyer have mutual trust and a great deal of experience with each other. Despite the risks, open account transactions are widely utilized, particularly among the industrialized countries in North America and Europe.

Trade Finance Methods

As mentioned in the previous section, banks on both sides of the transaction play a critical role in financing international trade. The following are some of the more popular methods of financing international trade.

- Accounts receivable financing
- Factoring
- Letters of credit (L/Cs)
- Banker's acceptances
- Working capital financing
- Medium-term capital goods financing (forfaiting)
- Countertrade

Each of these methods is described in turn.

Accounts Receivable Financing

In some cases, the exporter of goods may be willing to ship goods to the importer without an assurance of payment from a bank. This could take the form of an open account shipment or a time draft. Prior to shipment, the exporter should have conducted its own credit check on the importer to determine creditworthiness. If the exporter is willing to wait for payment, it will extend credit to the buyer.

If the exporter needs funds immediately, it may require financing from a bank. In what is referred to as **accounts receivable financing**, the bank will provide a loan to the exporter secured by an assignment of the account receivable. The bank's loan is made to the exporter based on its creditworthiness. In the event the buyer fails to pay the exporter for whatever reason, the exporter is still responsible for repaying the bank.

Accounts receivable financing involves additional risks, such as government restrictions and exchange controls, that may prevent the buyer from paying the exporter. As a result, the loan rate is often higher than domestic accounts receivable financing. The length of a financing term is usually one to six months. To mitigate the additional risk of a foreign receivable, exporters and banks often require export credit insurance before financing foreign receivables.

Factoring

When an exporter ships goods before receiving payment, the accounts receivable balance increases. Unless the exporter has received a loan from a bank, it is initially financing the transaction and must monitor the collections of receivables. Since there is a danger that the buyer will never pay at all, the exporting firm may consider selling the accounts receivable to a third party, known as a factor. In this type of financing, the exporter sells the accounts receivable without recourse. The factor then assumes all administrative responsibilities involved in collecting from the buyer and the associated credit exposure. The factor performs its own credit approval process on the foreign buyer before purchasing the receivable. For providing this service, the factor usually purchases the receivable at a discount and also receives a flat processing fee.

Factoring provides several benefits to the exporter. First, by selling the accounts receivable, the exporter does not have to worry about the administrative duties involved in maintaining and monitoring an accounts receivable accounting ledger. Second, the factor assumes the credit exposure to the buyer, so the exporter does not have to maintain personnel to assess the creditworthiness of foreign buyers. Finally, the sale of the receivable to the factor provides immediate payment and improves the exporter's cash flow.

Since it is the importer who must be creditworthy from a factor's point of view, **cross-border factoring** is often used. This involves a network of factors in various countries who assess credit risk. The exporter's factor contacts a correspondent factor in the buyer's country to assess the importer's creditworthiness and handle the collection of the receivable. Factoring services are usually provided by the factoring subsidiaries of commercial banks, commercial finance companies, and other specialized finance houses. Factors often utilize export credit insurance to mitigate the additional risk of a foreign receivable.

Letters of Credit (L/C)

Introduced earlier, the letter of credit (L/C) is one of the oldest forms of trade finance still in existence. Because of the protection and benefits it accords to both exporter and importer, it is a critical component of many international trade transactions. The L/C is an undertaking by a bank to make payments on behalf of a specified party to a beneficiary under specified conditions. The beneficiary (exporter) is paid upon presentation of the required documents in compliance with the terms of the L/C. The L/C process normally involves two banks, the exporter's bank and the importer's bank. The issuing bank is substituting its credit for that of the importer. It has essentially guaranteed payment to the exporter, provided the exporter complies with the terms and conditions of the L/C.

Sometimes the exporter is uncomfortable with the issuing bank's promise to pay because the bank is located in a foreign country. Even if the issuing bank is well known worldwide, the exporter may be concerned that the foreign government will impose exchange controls or other restrictions that would prevent payment by the issuing bank. For this reason, the exporter may request that a local bank confirm the L/C and thus assure that all the responsibilities of the issuing bank will be met. The confirming bank is obligated to honor drawings made by the beneficiary in compliance with the L/C regardless of the issuing bank's ability to make that payment. Consequently, the confirming bank is trusting that the foreign bank issuing the L/C is sound. The exporter, however, need worry only about the credibility of the confirming bank.

Trade-related letters of credit are known as **commercial letters of credit** or **import/export letters of credit.** There are basically two types: revocable and irrevocable. A **revocable letter of credit** can be canceled or revoked at any time without prior notification to the beneficiary, and it is seldom used. An **irrevocable letter of credit** cannot be canceled or amended without the beneficiary's consent. The bank issuing the letter of credit is known as the **"issuing" bank.** The correspondent bank in the beneficiary's country to which the issuing bank sends the L/C is commonly referred to as the **"advising" bank.** An irrevocable L/C obligates the issuing bank to honor all drawings presented in conformity with the terms of the L/C. Letters of credit are normally issued in accordance with the provisions contained in "Uniform Customs and Practice for Documentary Credits," published by the International Chamber of Commerce.

The bank issuing the L/C makes payment once the required documentation has been presented in accordance with the payment terms. The importer must pay the issuing bank the amount of the L/C plus accrued fees associated with obtaining the L/C. The importer usually has an account established at the issuing bank to be drawn upon for payment, so that the issuing bank does not tie up its own funds. However, if the importer does not have sufficient funds in its account, the issuing bank is still obligated to honor all valid drawings against the L/C. This is why the bank's decision to issue an L/C on behalf of an importer involves an analysis of the importer's creditworthiness and is analogous to the decision to make a loan. The documentary credit procedure is depicted in the flowchart in Exhibit 700.55. In what is commonly referred to as a *refinancing of a sight L/C,* the bank arranges to fund a loan to pay out the L/C instead of charging the importer's account immediately. The importer is responsible for repaying the bank both principal and interest at maturity. This is just another method of providing extended payment terms to a buyer when the exporter insists upon payment at sight.

The bank issuing the L/C makes payment to the beneficiary (exporter) upon presentation of documents that meet the conditions stipulated in the L/C. Letters of credit are payable either at sight (upon presentation of documents) or at a specified future date. The typical documentation required under an L/C includes a draft (sight or time), a commercial invoice, and a bill of lading. Depending upon the agreement, product, or country, other documents (such as a certificate of origin, inspection certificate, packing list, or insurance certificate) might be required. The three most common L/C documents include draft, bill of lading, and commercial invoice, which are discussed next.

DRAFT Also known as a **bill of exchange,** a draft (introduced earlier) is an unconditional promise drawn by one party, usually the exporter, requesting the importer to pay the face amount of the draft at sight or at a specified future date. If the draft is drawn at sight, it is payable upon presentation of documents. If it is payable at a specified future date (a time draft) and is accepted by the importer, it is known as a trade acceptance. A **banker's acceptance** is a time draft drawn on and accepted by a bank. When presented under a letter of credit, the draft represents the exporter's formal demand for payment. The time period, or **tenor,** of most time drafts is usually anywhere from 30 to 180 days.

Exhibit 700.55 *Documentary Credit Procedure for Letters of Credit*

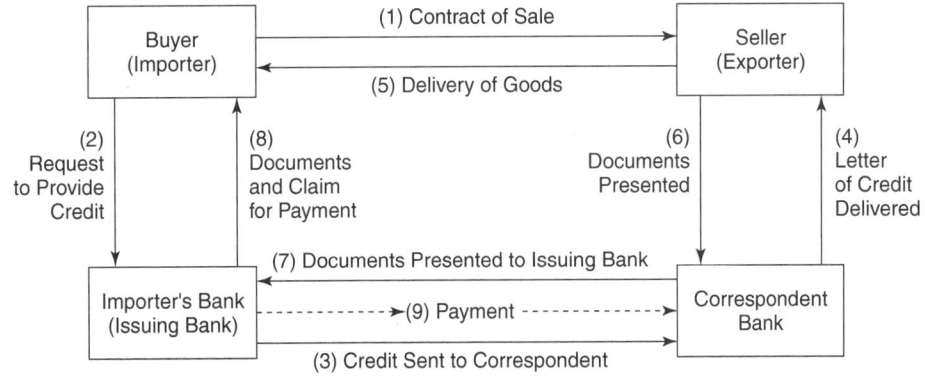

BILL OF LADING   The key document in an international shipment under an L/C is the **bill of lading (B/L).** It serves as a receipt for shipment and a summary of freight charges; most importantly, it conveys title to the merchandise. If the merchandise is to be shipped by boat, the carrier will issue what is known as an **ocean bill of lading.** When the merchandise is shipped by air, the carrier will issue an **airway bill.** The carrier presents the bill to the exporter (shipper), who in turn presents it to the bank along with the other required documents.

A significant feature of a B/L is its negotiability. A straight B/L is consigned directly to the importer. Since it does not represent title to the merchandise, the importer does not need it to pick up the merchandise. When a B/L is made out to order, however, it is said to be in negotiable form. The exporter normally endorses the B/L to the bank once payment is received from the bank.

The bank will not endorse the B/L over to the importer until payment has been made. The importer needs the original B/L to pick up the merchandise. With a **negotiable B/L,** title passes to the holder of the endorsed B/L. Because a negotiable B/L grants title to the holder, banks can take the merchandise as collateral. The usual provisions contained in a B/L include the following.

- A description of the merchandise
- Identification marks on the merchandise
- Evidence of loading (receiving) ports
- Name of the exporter (shipper)
- Name of the importer
- Status of freight charges (prepaid or collect)
- Date of shipment

COMMERCIAL INVOICE   The exporter's (seller's) description of the merchandise being sold to the buyer is the **commercial invoice,** which normally contains the following information.

- Name and address of seller
- Name and address of buyer
- Date
- Terms of payment
- Price, including freight, handling, and insurance if applicable
- Quantity, weight, packaging, and so on
- Shipping information

Under an L/C shipment, the description of the merchandise outlined in the invoice must correspond exactly to that contained in the L/C.

VARIATIONS OF THE L/C   There are several variations of the L/C that are useful in financing trade. A **standby letter of credit** can be used to guarantee invoice payments to a supplier. It promises to pay the beneficiary if the buyer fails to pay as agreed. Internationally, standby L/Cs often are used with government-related contracts and serve as bid bonds, performance bonds, or advance payment guarantees. In an international or domestic trade transaction, the seller will agree to ship to the buyer on standard open account terms as long as the buyer provides a standby L/C for a specified amount and term. As long as the buyer pays the seller as agreed, the standby L/C is never funded. However, if the buyer fails to pay, the exporter may present documents under the L/C and request payment from the bank. The buyer's bank is essentially guaranteeing that the buyer will make payment to the seller.

A **transferable letter of credit** is a variation of the standard commercial L/C that allows the first beneficiary to transfer all or a part of the original L/C to a third party. The new beneficiary has the same rights and protection as the original beneficiary. This type of L/C is used extensively by brokers, who are not the actual suppliers.

Example 25   *The broker asks the foreign buyer to issue an L/C for $100,000 in his favor. The L/C must contain a clause stating that the L/C is transferable. The broker has located an end supplier who will provide the product for $80,000, but requests payment in advance from the broker. With a transferable L/C, the broker can transfer $80,000 of the original L/C to the end supplier under the same terms* *and conditions, except for the amount, the latest shipment date, the invoice, and the period of validity. When the end supplier ships the product, it presents its documents to the bank. When the bank pays the L/C, $80,000 is paid to the end supplier and $20,000 goes to the broker. In effect, the broker has utilized the credit of the buyer to finance the entire transaction.*

Another type of L/C is the **assignment of proceeds**. In this case, the original beneficiary of the L/C pledges (or assigns) the proceeds under an L/C to the end supplier. The end supplier has assurance from the bank that if and when documents are presented in compliance with the terms of the L/C, the bank will pay the end supplier according to the assignment instructions. This assignment is valid only if the beneficiary presents documents that comply with the L/C. The end supplier must recognize that the issuing bank is under no obligation to pay the end supplier if the original beneficiary never ships the goods or fails to comply with the terms of the L/C.

Banker's Acceptance

Introduced earlier, a banker's acceptance is a bill of exchange, or time draft, drawn on and accepted by a bank. It is the accepting bank's obligation to pay the holder of the draft at maturity.

In the first step in creating a banker's acceptance, the importer orders goods from the exporter. The importer then requests its local bank to issue an L/C on its behalf. The L/C will allow the exporter to draw a time draft on the bank in payment for the exported goods. The exporter presents the time draft along with shipping documents to its local bank, and the exporter's bank sends the time draft along with shipping documents to the importer's bank. The importer's bank accepts the draft, thereby creating the banker's acceptance. If the exporter does not want to wait until the specified date to receive payment, it can request that the banker's acceptance be sold in the money market. By doing so, the exporter will receive less funds from the sale of the banker's acceptance than if it had waited to receive payment. This discount reflects the time value of money.

A money market investor may be willing to buy the banker's acceptance at a discount and hold it until payment is due. This investor will then receive full payment because the banker's acceptance represents a future claim on funds of the bank represented by the acceptance. The bank will make full payment at the date specified, since it expects to receive this amount plus an additional fee from the importer.

If the exporter holds the acceptance until maturity, it provides the financing for the importer as it does with accounts receivable financing. In this case, the key difference between a banker's acceptance and accounts receivable financing is that a banker's acceptance guarantees payment to the exporter by a bank. If the exporter sells the banker's acceptance in the secondary market, however, it is no longer providing the financing for the importer. The holder of the banker's acceptance is financing instead.

A banker's acceptance can be beneficial to the exporter, importer, and issuing bank. The exporter does not need to worry about the credit risk of the importer and can therefore penetrate new foreign markets without concern about the credit risk of potential customers. In addition, the exporter faces little exposure to political risk or to exchange controls imposed by a government because banks normally are allowed to meet their payment commitments even if controls are imposed. In contrast, controls could prevent an importer from paying, so without a banker's acceptance, an exporter might not receive payment even though the importer is willing to pay. Finally, the exporter can sell the banker's acceptance at a discount before payment is due and thus obtain funds up front from the issuing bank.

The importer benefits from a banker's acceptance by obtaining greater access to foreign markets when purchasing supplies and other products. Without banker's acceptances, exporters may be unwilling to accept the credit risk of importers. In addition, due to the documents presented along with the acceptance, the importer is assured that goods have been shipped. Even though the importer has not paid in advance, this assurance is valuable because it lets the importer know if and when supplies and other products will arrive. Finally, because the banker's acceptance allows the importer to pay at a later date, the importer's payment is financed until the maturity date of the banker's acceptance. Without an acceptance, the importer would likely be forced to pay in advance, thereby tying up funds.

The bank accepting the drafts benefits in that it earns a commission for creating an acceptance. The commission that the bank charges the customer reflects the customer's perceived creditworthiness. The interest rate charged the customer, commonly referred to as the **all-in-rate**, consists of the discount rate plus the acceptance commission. In general, the all-in-rate for acceptance financing is lower than prime-based borrowings, as shown in the following comparison, Exhibit 700.56.

Exhibit 700.56   Comparison Between a Traditional Loan and a Banker's Acceptance

	Traditional Loan	Banker's Acceptance
Amount:	$1,000,000	$1,000,000
Term:	180 days	180 days
Rate:	Prime + 1.5%	BA rate + 1.5%
	10.0% + 1.5% = 11.5%	7.60% + 1.5% = 9.10%
Interest cost:	$57,500	$45,500

In this case, the interest savings for a six-month period is $12,000. Since the banker's acceptance is a marketable instrument with an active secondary market, the rates on acceptances usually fall between the rates on short-term Treasury bills and the rates on commercial paper. Investors are usually willing to purchase acceptances as an investment because of their yield, safety, and liquidity. When a bank creates, accepts, and sells the acceptance, it is actually using the investor's money to finance the bank's customer. As a result, the bank has created an asset at one price, sold it at another, and retained a commission (spread) as its fee.

Banker's acceptance financing can also be arranged through the refinancing of a sight letter of credit. In this case, the beneficiary of the L/C (the exporter) may insist on payment at sight. The bank arranges to finance the payment of the sight L/C under a separate acceptance-financing agreement. The importer (borrower) simply draws drafts upon the bank, which in turn accepts and discounts the drafts. The proceeds are used to pay the exporter. At maturity, the importer is responsible for repayment to the bank.

Acceptance financing can also be arranged without the use of an L/C under a separate acceptance agreement. Similar to a regular loan agreement, it stipulates the terms and conditions under which the bank is prepared to finance the borrower using acceptances instead of promissory notes. As long as the acceptances meet one of the underlying transaction requirements, the bank and borrower can utilize banker's acceptances as an alternative financing mechanism.

Working Capital Financing

As just explained, a banker's acceptance can allow an exporter to receive funds immediately, yet allow an importer to delay its payment until a future date. The bank may even provide short-term loans beyond the banker's acceptance period. In the case of an importer, the purchase from overseas usually represents the acquisition of inventory. The loan finances the working capital cycle that begins with the purchase of inventory and continues with the sale of the goods, creation of an account receivable, and conversion to cash. With an exporter, the short-term loan might finance the manufacture of the merchandise destined for export (preexport financing) or the time period from when the sale is made until payment is received from the buyer. For example, the firm may have imported foreign beer, which it plans to distribute to grocery and liquor stores. The bank cannot only provide a letter of credit for trade finance, but it can also finance the importer's cost from the time of distribution and collection of payment.

Medium-Term Capital Goods Financing (Forfaiting)

Because capital goods are often quite expensive, an importer may not be able to make payment on the goods within a short time period. Thus, longer-term financing may be required here. The exporter might be able to provide financing for the importer but may not desire to do so, since the financing may extend over several years. In this case, a type of trade finance known as **forfaiting** could be used. Forfaiting refers to the purchase of financial obligations, such as bills of exchange or promissory notes, without recourse to the original holder, usually the exporter. In a forfait transaction, the importer issues a promissory note to pay the exporter for the imported goods over a period that generally ranges from three to seven years. The exporter then sells the notes, without recourse, to the forfaiting bank.

In some respects, forfaiting is similar to factoring, in that the forfaiter (or factor) assumes responsibility for the collection of payment from the buyer, the underlying credit risk, and the risk pertaining to the countries involved. Since the forfaiting bank assumes the risk of nonpayment, it should assess the creditworthiness of the importer as if it were extending a medium-term loan. Forfait transactions normally are collateralized by a bank guarantee or letter of credit issued by the importer's bank for the term of the transaction. Since financial information is usually difficult to obtain on the importer, the forfaiting bank places a great deal of reliance on the bank guarantee as the collateral in the event the buyer fails to pay as agreed. It is this guarantee backing the transaction that has fostered the growth of the forfait market, particularly in Europe, as a practical means of trade finance.

Forfaiting transactions are usually in excess of $500,000 and can be denominated in most currencies. For some larger transactions, more than one bank may be involved. In this case, a syndicate is formed wherein each participant assumes a proportionate share of the underlying risk and profit. A forfaiting firm may decide to sell the promissory notes of the importer to other financial institutions willing to purchase them. However, the forfaiting firm is still responsible for payment on the notes in the event the importer is unable to pay.

Countertrade

The term **countertrade** denotes all types of foreign trade transactions in which the sale of goods to one country is linked to the purchase or exchange of goods from that same country. Some types of countertrade, such as barter, have been in existence for thousands of years. Only recently, however, has countertrade gained popularity and importance. The growth in various types of countertrade has been fueled by large balance-of-payment disequilibriums, foreign currency shortages, the debt problems of less developed countries and stagnant worldwide demand. As a result, many MNCs have encountered countertrade opportunities, particularly in Asia, Latin America, and Eastern Europe. The most common types of countertrade include barter, compensation, and counterpurchase.

Barter is the exchange of goods between two parties without the use of any currency as a medium of exchange. Most barter arrangements are one-time transactions governed by one contract. An example would be the exchange of 100 tons of wheat from Canada for 20 tons of shrimp from Ecuador.

In a **compensation** or clearing-account arrangement, the delivery of goods to one party is compensated for by the seller's buying back a certain amount of the product from that same party. The transaction is governed by one contract, and the value of the goods is expressed in monetary terms. The buy-back arrangement could be for a fraction of the original sale (**partial compensation**) or more than 100% of the original sale (**full compensation**). An example of compensation would be the sale of phosphate from Morocco to France in exchange for purchasing a certain percentage of fertilizer. In some countries, this is also referred to as an industrial cooperation arrangement. Such arrangements often involve the construction of large projects, such as power plants, in exchange for the purchase of the project's output over an extended period of time. For example, Brazil sold a hydroelectric plant to Argentina and in exchange purchased a percentage of the plant's output under a long-term contract.

The term **counterpurchase** denotes the exchange of goods between two parties under two distinct contracts expressed in monetary terms. Delivery and payment of both goods are technically separate transactions.

Despite the economic inefficiencies of countertrade, it has become much more important in recent years. The primary participants are governments and MNCs, with assistance provided by specialists in the field, such as attorneys, financial institutions, and trading companies. The transactions are usually large and very complex. Many variations of countertrade exist, and the terminology used by the various market participants is still forming as the countertrade market continues to develop.

Agencies That Facilitate International Trade

Due to the inherent risks of international trade, government institutions and the private sector offer various forms of export credit, export finance, and guarantee programs to reduce risk and stimulate foreign trade.

Three prominent agencies provide these services in the United States.

- Export-Import Bank of the United States (Ex-Imbank)
- Private Export Funding Corporation (PEFCO)
- Overseas Private Investment Corporation (OPIC)

Currency Derivatives

Currency derivatives are often used by speculators interested in trading currencies simply to achieve profits but also used by firms to cover their foreign currency positions. Because MNCs commonly use currency derivatives, their managers must understand how these derivatives can be used to achieve corporate goals. Topics include forward market, currency futures market, and currency options market.

Forward Market

The forward market facilitates the trading of forward contracts on currencies. A **forward contract** is an agreement between a corporation and a commercial bank to exchange a specified amount of a currency at a specified exchange rate (called the **forward rate**) on a specified date in the future. When multinational corporations (MNCs) anticipate a future need for or future receipt of a foreign currency, they can set up forward contracts to lock in the rate at which they can purchase or sell a particular foreign currency. Virtually all large MNCs use forward contracts. Some MNCs, such as TRW, have forward contracts outstanding worth more than $100 million to hedge various positions.

Because forward contracts accommodate large corporations, the forward transaction will often be valued at $1 million or more. Forward contracts normally are not used by consumers or small firms. In cases when a bank does not know a corporation well or fully trust it, the bank may request that the corporation make an initial deposit to assure that it will fulfill its obligation.

The most common forward contracts are for 30, 60, 90, 180, and 360 days, although other periods (including longer periods) are available. The forward rate of a given currency will typically vary with the length (number of days) of the forward period.

How MNCs Use Forward Contracts

MNCs use forward contracts to hedge their imports. They can lock in the rate at which they obtain a currency needed to purchase imports.

> **Example 26** Turz, Inc., is an MNC based in Chicago that will need 1,000,000 Singapore dollars in 90 days to purchase Singapore imports. It can buy Singapore dollars for immediate delivery at the spot rate of $.50 per Singapore dollar (S$). At this spot rate, the firm would need $500,000 (computed as S$1,000,000 × $.50 per Singapore dollar). However, it does not have the funds right now to exchange for Singapore dollars. It could wait 90 days and then exchange dollars for Singapore dollars at the spot rate existing at that time. But, Turz does not know what the spot rate will be at that time. If the rate rises to $.60 by then, Turz will need $600,000 (computed as S$1,000,000 × $.60 per Singapore dollar), an additional outlay of S$100,000 due to the appreciation of the Singapore dollar.
>
> To avoid exposure to exchange rate risk, Turz can lock in the rate it will pay for Singapore dollars 90 days from now without having to exchange dollars for Singapore dollars immediately. Specifically, Turz can negotiate a forward contract with a bank to purchase S$1,000,000 90 days forward.

Corporations also use the forward market to lock in the rate at which they can sell foreign currencies. This strategy is used to hedge against the possibility of those currencies depreciating over time.

> **Example 27** Scanlon, Inc., based in Virginia, exports products to a French firm and will receive payment of (€)400,000 in four months. It can lock in the amount of dollars to be received from this transaction by selling euros forward. That is, Scanlon can negotiate a forward contract with a bank to sell the (€)400,000 for dollars at a specified forward rate today. Assume the prevailing four-month forward rate on euros is $.1.10. In four months, Scanlon will exchange its (€)400,000 for $440,000 (computed as (€)$400,000 × $1.10 = $440,000).

Exhibit 700.57 *Computation of Forward Rate Premiums or Discounts*

Type of Exchange Rate for £	Value	Maturity	Forward Rate Premium or Discount for £
Spot rate	$1.681		
30-day forward rate	$1.680	30 days	$\dfrac{\$1.680 - \$1.681}{\$1.681} \times \dfrac{360}{30} = -.71\%$
90-day forward rate	$1.677	90 days	$\dfrac{\$1.677 - \$1.681}{\$1.681} \times \dfrac{360}{90} = -.95\%$
180-day forward rate	$1.672	180 days	$\dfrac{\$1.672 - \$1.681}{\$1.681} \times \dfrac{360}{180} = -1.07\%$

BID/ASK SPREAD Like spot rates, forward rates have a bid/ask spread. For example, a bank may set up a contract with one firm agreeing to sell the firm Singapore dollars 90 days from now at $.510 per Singapore dollar. This represents the ask rate. At the same time, the firm may agree to purchase (bid) Singapore dollars 90 days from now from some other firm at $.505 per Singapore dollar.

The spread between the bid and ask prices is wider for forward rates of currencies of developing countries, such as Chile, Mexico, South Korea, Taiwan, and Thailand. Because these markets have relatively few orders for forward contracts, banks are less able to match up willing buyers and sellers. This lack of liquidity causes banks to widen the bid/ask spread when quoting forward contracts. The contracts in these countries are generally available only for short-term horizons.

PREMIUM OR DISCOUNT ON THE FORWARD RATE If the forward rate exceeds the existing spot rate, it contains a **premium.** If it is less than the existing spot rate, it contains a **discount.** This premium or discount is normally computed on an annual basis as shown in Exhibit 700.57. For example, assume the forward exchange rates shown in Column 2 of Exhibit 700.57 are quoted for the British pound. Based on those forward rates, the forward discount has been computed for each maturity. The forward discounts can first be computed in decimal form, which is easily converted into percentage form.

Forward rates typically differ from the spot rate for any given currency. If the forward rate were the same as the spot rate, and interest rates of the two countries differed, it would be possible for some investors (under certain assumptions) to use **arbitrage** to earn higher returns than would be possible domestically without incurring additional risk. Consequently, the forward rate usually contains a premium (or discount) that reflects the difference between the home interest rate and the foreign interest rate.

Nondeliverable Forward Contracts

A new type of forward contract called a **nondeliverable forward contract (NDF)** is frequently used for currencies in emerging markets. Like a regular forward contract, an NDF represents an agreement regarding a position in a specified amount of a specified currency, a specified exchange rate, and a specified future settlement date. However, an NDF does not result in an actual exchange of the currencies at the future date. That is, there is no delivery. Instead, one party to the agreement makes a payment to the other party based on the exchange rate at the future date.

Although an NDF does not involve delivery, it can effectively hedge future foreign currency payments that are anticipated by an MNC. Because an NDF can specify that any payments between the two parties be in dollars or some other available currency, firms can even use NDFs to hedge existing positions of foreign currencies that are not convertible. Consider an MNC that expects to receive payment in a foreign currency that cannot be converted into dollars. Though the MNC may use the currency to make purchases in the local country of concern, it still may desire to hedge against a decline in the value of the currency over the period before it receives payment. It takes a sell position in an NDF and uses the closing exchange rate of that currency as of the settlement date as the reference index. If the currency depreciates against the dollar over time, the firm will receive the difference between the dollar value of the position when the NDF contract was created and the dollar value of the position as of the settlement date. Thus, it will receive a payment in dollars from the NDF to offset any depreciation in the currency over the period of concern.

Currency Futures Market

Currency futures contracts are contracts specifying a standard volume of a particular currency to be exchanged on a specific settlement date. They are commonly used by MNCs to hedge their foreign currency positions. In addition, they are traded by speculators who hope to capitalize on their expectations of exchange rate movements. A buyer of a currency futures contract locks in the exchange rate to be paid for a foreign currency at a future point in time. Alternatively, a seller of a currency futures contract locks in the exchange rate at which a foreign currency can be exchanged for the home currency. In the United States, currency futures contracts are purchased to lock in the amount of dollars needed to obtain a specified amount of a particular foreign currency; they are sold to lock in the amount of dollars to be received from selling a specified amount of a particular foreign currency.

When participants in the currency futures market take a position, they need to establish an initial margin, which may represent as little as 10% of the contract value. The margin required is in the form of cash for small investors or Treasury securities for institutional investors. In addition to the initial margin, participants are subject to a variation margin, which is intended to accumulate a sufficient amount of funds to back the futures position. Full-service brokers typically charge a commission of about $50 for a round-trip trade in currency futures, while discount brokers charge a commission of about $20. Some Internet brokers also trade currency futures.

> **Example 28** Assume that as of February 10, a futures contract on 62,500 British pounds with a March settlement date is priced at $1.50 per pound. Consider the positions of two different firms on the opposite sides of this contract. The buyer of this currency futures contract will receive £62,500 on the March settlement date and will pay $93,750 for the pounds (computed as £62,500 × $1.50 per pound). The seller of this contract is obligated to sell £62,500 at a price of $1.50 per pound and therefore will receive $93,750 on the settlement date.

Comparison of Currency Futures and Forward Contracts

Currency futures contracts are similar to forward contracts in that they allow a customer to lock in the exchange rate at which a specific currency is purchased or sold for a specific date in the future. Nevertheless, there are some differences between currency futures contracts and forward contracts. Currency futures contracts are sold on an exchange, while each forward contract is negotiated between a firm and a commercial bank over a telecommunications network. Thus, forward contracts can be tailored to the needs of the firm, while the currency futures contracts are standardized.

Corporations that have established relationships with large banks tend to use forward contracts rather than futures contracts because forward contracts are tailored to the precise amount of currency to be purchased or sold in the future and the precise forward date that they prefer. Conversely, small firms and individuals who do not have established relationships with large banks or prefer to trade in smaller amounts tend to use currency futures contracts.

Currency Options Market

In late 1982, exchanges in Amsterdam, Montreal, and Philadelphia allowed trading in standardized foreign currency options. Since that time, options have been offered on the Chicago Mercantile Exchange and the Chicago Board Options Exchange. A currency option is an alternative type of contract that can be purchased or sold by speculators and firms. Currency options are currently available for many currencies, including the British pound, Canadian dollar, Japanese yen, euro, Swiss franc, and Australian dollar.

The options exchanges in the United States are regulated by the Securities and Exchange Commission (SEC). Options can be purchased or sold through brokers for a commission. The commission per transaction is commonly $30 to $60 for a single currency option, but it can be much lower per contract when the transaction involves multiple contracts. Brokers require that a margin be maintained during the life of the contract. The margin is increased for clients whose option positions have deteriorated. This protects against possible losses if the clients do not fulfill their obligations.

In addition to the exchanges where currency options are available, there is an over-the-counter market where currency options are offered by commercial banks and brokerage firms. Unlike the currency options traded on an exchange, currency options are tailored to the specific needs of the firm. Since these options are not standardized, all the terms must be specified in the contracts. The number of units, desired strike price, and expiration date can be tailored to the specific needs of the client. The minimum size of currency options offered by financial institutions is normally about $5 million. Since these transactions are conducted with a specific financial institution rather than an exchange, there are no credit guarantees. Thus, the agreement made is only as safe as the parties involved. For this reason, financial institutions may require some collateral from individuals or firms desiring to purchase or sell currency options. Currency options are classified as either **calls** or **puts,** as discussed in the next section.

Currency Call Options

A **currency call option** grants the right to buy a specific currency at a designated price within a specific period of time. The price at which the owner is allowed to buy that currency is known as the **exercise price** or **strike price,** and there are monthly expiration dates for each option.

Call options are desirable when one wishes to lock in a maximum price to be paid for a currency in the future. If the spot rate of the currency rises above the strike price, owners of call options can "exercise" their options by purchasing the currency at the strike price, which will be cheaper than the prevailing spot rate. This strategy is somewhat similar to that used by purchasers of futures contracts, but the futures contracts require an obligation, which the currency option does not. The owner can choose to let the option expire on the expiration date without ever exercising it. Owners of expired call options will have lost the premium they initially paid, but that is the most they can lose.

Currency options quotations are summarized each day in *The Wall Street Journal* and other business newspapers. Although currency options typically expire near the middle of the specified month, some of them expire at the end of the specific month and are designated as EOM. Some options are listed as "European Style," which means that they can be exercised only upon expiration.

A currency call option is said to be *in the money* when the present exchange rate exceeds the strike price, *at the money* when the present exchange rate equals the strike price, and *out of the money* when the present exchange rate is less than the strike price. For a given currency and expiration date, an in-the-money call option will require a higher premium than options that are at the money or out of the money.

FACTORS AFFECTING CURRENCY CALL OPTION PREMIUMS Premiums of call options vary due to three main factors.

- *Level of existing spot price relative to strike price.* The higher the spot rate relative to the strike price, the higher the option price will be. This is due to the higher probability of buying the currency at a substantially lower rate than what you could sell it for. This relationship can be verified by comparing premiums of options for a specified currency and expiration date that have different strike prices.

- *Length of time before the expiration date.* It is generally expected that the spot rate has a greater chance of rising high above the strike price if it has a longer period of time to do so. A settlement date in June allows two additional months beyond April for the spot rate to move above the strike price. This explains why June option prices exceed April option prices given a specific strike price. This relationship can be verified by comparing premiums of options for a specified currency and strike price that have different expiration dates.

- *Potential variability of currency.* The greater the variability of the currency, the higher the probability that the spot rate will be above the strike price. Thus, more volatile currencies have higher call option prices. For example, the Canadian dollar is more stable than most other currencies. If all other factors are similar, Canadian call options should be less expensive than call options on other foreign currencies.

The potential currency variability can also vary over time for a particular currency. For example, at the beginning of the Asian crisis in 1997, the Asian countries experienced financial problems, and their currency values were subject to much more uncertainty. Consequently, the premium on over-the-counter options of Asian currencies such as the Thai baht, Indonesian rupiah, and Korean won increased. The higher premium was necessary to compensate those who were willing to sell options in these currencies, as the risk to sellers had increased because the currencies had become more volatile.

HOW FIRMS USE CURRENCY CALL OPTIONS Corporations with open positions in foreign currencies can sometimes use currency call options to cover these positions.

Using Call Options to Hedge Payables MNCs can purchase call options on a currency to hedge future payables.

Example 29 When Pike Co. of Seattle orders Australian goods, it makes a payment in Australian dollars to the Australian exporter upon delivery. An Australian dollar call option locks in a maximum rate at which Pike can exchange dollars for Australian dollars. This exchange of currencies at the specified strike price on the call option contract can be executed at any time before the expiration date. In essence, the call option contract specifies the maximum price that Pike must pay to obtain these Australian dollars. If the Australian dollar's value remains below the strike price, Pike can purchase Australian dollars at the prevailing spot rate when it needs to pay for its imports and simply let its call option expire.

Options may be more appropriate than futures or forward contracts for some situations. **Intel Corp.** uses options to hedge its order backlog in semiconductors. If an order is canceled, it has the flexibility to let the option contract expire. With a forward contract, it would be obligated to fulfill its obligation even though the order was canceled.

Using Call Options to Hedge Project Bidding U.S.-based MNCs that bid for foreign projects may purchase call options to lock in the dollar cost of the potential expenses.

Example 30 Kelly Co. is an MNC based in Fort Lauderdale that has bid on a project sponsored by the Canadian government. If the bid is accepted, Kelly will need approximately C$500,000 to purchase Canadian materials and services. However, Kelly will not know whether the bid is accepted until three months from now. In this case, it can purchase call options with a three-month expiration date. Ten call option contracts will cover the entire amount of potential exposure. If the bid is accepted, Kelly can use the options to purchase the Canadian dollars needed. If the Canadian dollar has depreciated over time, Kelly will likely let the options expire.

Assume that the exercise price on Canadian dollars is $.70 and the call option premium is $.02 per unit. Kelly will pay $1,000 per option (since there are 50,000 units per Canadian dollar option), or $10,000 for the 10 option contracts. With the options, the maximum amount necessary to purchase the C$500,000 is $350,000 (computed as $.70 per Canadian dollar × C$500,000). The amount of U.S. dollars needed would be less if the Canadian dollar's spot rate were below the exercise price at the time the Canadian dollars were purchased.

Even if Kelly's bid is rejected, it will exercise the currency call option if the Canadian dollar's spot rate exceeds the exercise price before the option expires and sell the Canadian dollars in the spot market. Any gain from exercising may partially or even fully offset the premium paid for the options.

This type of example is quite common. **When Air Products and Chemicals, Inc.** was hired to perform some projects, it needed capital equipment from Germany. The purchase of equipment was contingent on whether the firm was hired for the projects. The company used options to hedge this possible future purchase.

Using Call Options to Hedge Target Bidding Firms can also use call options to hedge a possible acquisition.

Example 31 Morrison Co. is attempting to acquire a French firm and has submitted its bid in euros. Morrison has purchased call options on the euro because it will need euros to purchase the French company's stock. The call options hedge the U.S. firm against the potential appreciation of the euro by the time the acquisition occurs. If the acquisition does not occur and the spot rate of the euro remains below the strike price, Morrison Co. can let the call options expire. If the acquisition does not occur and the spot rate of the euro exceeds the strike price, Morrison Co. can exercise the options and sell the euros in the spot market. Alternatively, Morrison Co. can sell the call options it is holding. Either of these actions may offset part or all of the premium paid for the options.

SPECULATING WITH CURRENCY CALL OPTIONS The corporate use of currency options is more important than the speculative use. Speculative trading is discussed here in order to provide more background on the currency options market.

Individuals may speculate in the currency options market based on their expectation of the future movements in a particular currency. Speculators who expect that a foreign currency will appreciate can purchase call options on that currency. Once the spot rate of that currency appreciates, the speculators can exercise their options by purchasing that currency at the strike price and then sell the currency at the prevailing spot rate.

Just as with currency futures, for every buyer of a currency call option there must be a seller. A seller (sometimes called a **writer**) of a call option is obligated to sell a specified currency at a specified price (the strike price) up to a specified expiration date. Speculators may sometimes want to sell a currency call option on a currency that they expect will depreciate in the future. The only way a currency call option will be exercised is if the spot rate is higher than the strike price. Thus, a seller of a currency call option will receive the premium when the option is purchased and can keep the entire amount if the option is not exercised. When it appears that an option will be exercised, there will still be sellers of options. However, such options will sell for high premiums due to the high risk that the option will be exercised at some point.

The net profit to a speculator who purchases call options on a currency is based on a comparison of the selling price of the currency versus the exercise price paid for the currency and the premium paid for the call option.

Example 32 Jim is a speculator who buys a British pound call option with a strike price of $1.40 and a December settlement date. The current spot price as of that date is about $1.39. Jim pays a premium of $.012 per unit for the call option. Assume there are no brokerage fees. Just before the expiration date, the spot rate of the British pound reaches $1.41. At this time, Jim exercises the call option and then immediately sells the pounds at the spot rate to a bank. To determine Jim's profit or loss, first compute his revenues from selling the currency. Then, subtract from this amount the purchase price of pounds when exercising the option, and also subtract the purchase price of the option. The computations follow. Assume one option contract specifies 31,250 units.

	Per Unit	Per Contract
Selling price of £	$1.41	$44,063 ($1.41 × 31,250 units)
− Purchase price of £	−1.40	−43,750 ($1.40 × 31,250 units)
− Premium paid for option	−.012	−375 ($.012 × 31,250 units)
= Net profit	−$.002	−$62 (−$.002 × 31,250 units)

799. INTERNATIONAL ISSUES

423

Assume that Linda was the seller of the call option purchased by Jim. Also assume that Linda would purchase British pounds only if and when the option was exercised, at which time she must provide the pounds at the exercise price of $1.40. Using the information in this example, Linda's net profit from selling the call option is derived here.

	Per Unit	Per Contract
Selling price of £	$1.40	$43,750 ($1.40 × 31,250 units)
− Purchase price of £	−1.41	−44,063 ($1.41 × 31,250 units)
+ Premium received	+.012	+375 ($.012 × 31,250 units)
= Net profit	$.002	+$62 ($.002 × 31,250 units)

Example 33 *Assume the following information.*

- Call option premium on Canadian dollars (C$) = $.01 per unit.
- Strike price = $.70.
- One option contract represents C$50,000.

A speculator who had purchased this call option decided to exercise the option shortly before the expiration date, when the spot rate reached $.74. The speculator immediately sold the Canadian dollars in the spot market. Given this information, the net profit to the speculator is computed as follows.

	Per Unit	Per Contract
Selling price of C$	$.74	$37,000 ($.74 × 50,000 units)
− Purchase price of C$	−.70	−35,000 ($.70 × 50,000 units)
− Premium paid for option	−.01	−500 ($.01 × 50,000 units)
= Net profit	$.03	$1,500 ($.03 × 50,000 units)

If the seller of the call option did not obtain Canadian dollars until the option was about to be exercised, the net profit to the seller of the call option was

	Per Unit	Per Contract
Selling price of C$	$.70	$35,000 ($.70 × 50,000 units)
− Purchase price of C$	−.74	−37,000 ($.74 × 50,000 units)
+ Premium received	+.01	+500 ($.01 × 50,000 units)
= Net profit	−$.03	−$1,500 (−$.03 × 50,000 units)

When brokerage fees are ignored, the currency call purchaser's gain will be the seller's loss. The currency call purchaser's expenses represent the seller's revenues, and the purchaser's revenues represent the seller's expenses. Yet, because it is possible for purchasers and sellers of options to close out their positions, the relationship described here will not hold unless both parties begin and close out their positions at the same time.

An owner of a currency option may simply sell the option to someone else before the expiration date rather than exercising it. The owner can still earn profits, since the option premium changes over time, reflecting the probability that the option can be exercised and the potential profit from exercising it.

Break-Even Point From Speculation The purchaser of a call option will break even if the revenue from selling the currency equals the payments for (1) the currency (at the strike price) and (2) the option premium. In other words, regardless of the number of units in a contract, a purchaser will break even if the spot rate at which the currency is sold is equal to the strike price plus the option premium.

> **Example 34** Based on the information in the previous example, the strike price is $.70 and the option premium is $.01. Thus, for the purchaser to break even, the spot rate existing at the time the call is exercised must be $.71 ($.70 + $.01). Of course, speculators will not purchase a call option if they think the spot rate will only reach the break-even point and not go higher before the expiration date. Nevertheless, the computation of the break-even point is useful for a speculator deciding whether to purchase a currency call option.

Currency Put Options

The owner of a **currency put option** receives the right to sell a currency at a specified price (the strike price) within a specified period of time. As with currency call options, the owner of a put option is not obligated to exercise the option. Therefore, the maximum potential loss to the owner of the put option is the price (or premium) paid for the option contract. A currency put option is said to be *in the money* when the present exchange rate is less than the strike price, *at the money* when the present exchange rate equals the strike price, and *out of the money* when the present exchange rate exceeds the strike price. For a given currency and expiration date, an in-the-money put option will require a higher premium than options that are at the money or out of the money.

FACTORS AFFECTING CURRENCY PUT OPTION PREMIUMS The three main factors influencing call option premiums also influence put option premiums. First, the spot rate of a currency relative to the strike price is important. The lower the spot rate relative to the strike price, the more valuable the put option will be, because there is a higher probability that the option will be exercised. Recall that just the opposite relationship held for call options. A second factor influencing put option premium is the length of time until the expiration date. As with currency call options, the longer the time to expiration, the greater the put option premium will be. A longer period creates a higher probability that the currency will move into a range where it will be feasible to exercise the option (whether it is a put or a call). These relationships can be verified by assessing quotations of put option premiums for a specified currency. A third factor that influences the put option premium is the variability of a currency. As with currency call options, the greater the variability, the greater the put option premium will be, again reflecting a higher probability that the option may be exercised.

HEDGING WITH CURRENCY PUT OPTIONS Corporations with open positions in foreign currencies can use currency put options in some cases to cover these positions.

> **Example 35** Assume Duluth Co. has exported products to Canada and invoiced the products in Canadian dollars (at the request of the Canadian importers). Duluth is concerned that the Canadian dollars it is receiving will depreciate over time. To insulate itself against possible depreciation, Duluth purchases Canadian dollar put options, which entitle it to sell Canadian dollars at the specified strike price. In essence, Duluth locks in the minimum rate at which it can exchange Canadian dollars for U.S. dollars over a specified period of time. If the Canadian dollar appreciates over this time period, Duluth can let the put options expire and sell the Canadian dollars it receives at the prevailing spot rate.

SPECULATING WITH CURRENCY PUT OPTIONS Individuals may speculate with currency put options based on their expectations of the future movements in a particular currency. For example, speculators who expect that the British pound will depreciate can purchase British pound put options, which will entitle them to sell British pounds at a specified strike price. If the pound's spot rate depreciates as expected, the speculators can then purchase pounds at the spot rate and exercise their put options by selling these pounds at the strike price.

Speculators can also attempt to profit from selling currency put options. The seller of such options is obligated to purchase the specified currency at the strike price from the owner who exercises the put option. Speculators who believe the currency will appreciate (or at least will not depreciate) may sell a currency put option. If the currency appreciates over the entire period, the option will not be exercised. This is an ideal situation for put option sellers, since they keep the premiums received when selling the options and bear no cost.

The net profit to a speculator from purchasing put options on a currency is based on a comparison of the exercise price at which the currency can be sold versus the purchase price of the currency and the premium paid for the put option.

Example 36 *A put option contract on British pounds specifies the following information.*

- *Put option premium on British pound (£) = $.04 per unit.*
- *Strike price = $1.40.*
- *One option contract represents £31,250.*

A speculator who had purchased this put option decided to exercise the option shortly before the expiration date, when the spot rate of the pound was $1.30. The speculator purchased the pounds in the spot market at that time. Given this information, the net profit to the purchaser of the put option is calculated as follows.

	Per Unit	Per Contract
Selling price of £	$1.40	$43,750 ($1.40 × 31,250 units)
− Purchase price of £	−1.30	−40,625 ($1.30 × 31,250 units)
− Premium paid for option	−.04	−1,250 ($.04 × 31,250 units)
= Net profit	$.06	$1,875 ($.06 × 31,250 units)

Assuming that the seller of the put option sold the pounds received immediately after the option was exercised, the net profit to the seller of the put option is calculated as follows.

	Per Unit	Per Contract
Selling price of £	$1.30	$40,625 ($1.30 × 31,250 units)
− Purchase price of £	−1.40	−43,750 ($1.40 × 31,250 units)
+ Premium received	+.04	+1,250 ($.04 × 31,250 units)
= Net profit	−$.06	−$1,875 (−$.06 × 31,250 units)

The seller of the put options could simply refrain from selling the pounds (after being forced to buy them at $1.40 per pound) until the spot rate of the pound rose. However, there is no guarantee that the pound will reverse its direction and begin to appreciate. The seller's net loss could potentially be greater if the pound's spot rate continued to fall, unless the pounds were sold immediately.

Whatever an owner of a put option gains, the seller loses, and vice versa. This relationship would hold if brokerage costs did not exist and if the buyer and seller of options entered and closed their positions at the same time. Brokerage fees for currency options exist, however, and are very similar in magnitude to those of currency futures contracts.

Speculating With Combined Put and Call Options For volatile currencies, one possible speculative strategy is to create a **straddle**, which uses both a put option and a call option at the same exercise price. This may seem unusual because owning a put option is appropriate for expectations that the currency will depreciate while owning a call option is appropriate for expectations that the currency will appreciate. However, it is possible that the currency will depreciate (at which time the put is exercised) and then reverse direction and appreciate (allowing for profits when exercising the call).

Also, a speculator might anticipate that a currency will be substantially affected by current economic events yet be uncertain of the exact way it will be affected. By purchasing a put option and a call option, the speculator will gain if the currency moves substantially in either direction. Although two options are purchased and only one is exercised, the gains could more than offset the costs.

Short-Term Financing

All firms make short-term financing decisions periodically. Beyond the trade financing discussed earlier, MNCs obtain short-term financing to support other operations as well. Because MNCs have access to additional sources of funds, their short-term financing decisions are more complex than those of other companies. Financial managers must understand the possible advantages and disadvantages of short-term financing with foreign currencies so that they can make short-term financing decisions that maximize the value of the MNC.

Sources of Short-Term Financing

MNC parents and their subsidiaries typically use various methods of obtaining short-term funds to satisfy their liquidity needs. These include Euronotes, Euro-commercial paper, and Eurobank loans.

Euronotes

One method increasingly used in recent years is the issuing of Euronotes, or unsecured debt securities. The interest rates on these notes are based on LIBOR (the interest rate Eurobanks charge on interbank loans). Euronotes typically have maturities of one, three, or six months. Some MNCs continually roll them over as a form of intermediate-term financing. Commercial banks underwrite the notes for MNCs, and some commercial banks purchase them for their own investment portfolios.

Euro-Commercial Paper

In addition to Euronotes, MNCs also issue **Euro-commercial paper** to obtain short-term financing. Dealers issue this paper for MNCs without the backing of an underwriting syndicate, so a selling price is not guaranteed to the issuers. Maturities can be tailored to the issuer's preferences. Dealers make a secondary market by offering to repurchase Euro-commercial paper before maturity.

Eurobank Loans

Direct loans from Eurobanks, which are typically utilized to maintain a relationship with Eurobanks, are another popular source of short-term funds for MNCs. If other sources of short-term funds become unavailable, MNCs rely more heavily on direct loans from Eurobanks. Most MNCs maintain credit arrangements with various banks around the world. Some MNCs have credit arrangements with more than 100 foreign and domestic banks.

Criteria Considered for Foreign Financing

An MNC must consider various criteria in its international financing decision, including the following.

- Interest rate parity
- The forward rate as a forecast
- Exchange rate forecasts

These criteria can influence the MNC's decision regarding which currency or currencies to borrow. Each is discussed in turn.

Interest Rate Parity

Recall that covered interest arbitrage was described as a foreign short-term investment with a simultaneous forward sale of the foreign currency denominating the foreign investment. From a financing perspective, covered interest arbitrage can be conducted as follows. First, borrow a foreign currency and convert that currency to the home currency for use. Also, simultaneously purchase the foreign currency forward to lock in the exchange rate of the currency needed to pay off the loan. If the foreign currency's interest rate is low, this may appear to be a feasible strategy. However, such a currency normally will exhibit a forward premium that offsets the differential between its interest rate and the home interest rate.

This can be shown by recognizing that the financing firm no longer will be affected by the percentage change in exchange rates but instead by the percentage difference between the spot rate at which the foreign currency was converted to the local currency and the forward rate at which the foreign currency was repurchased. The difference reflects the forward premium (unannualized).

If interest rate parity exists, the attempt of covered interest arbitrage to finance with a low interest rate currency will result in an effective financing rate similar to the domestic interest rate.

Exhibit 700.58 summarizes the implications of a variety of scenarios relating to interest rate parity. Even if interest rate parity exists, financing with a foreign currency may still be feasible, but it would have to be conducted on an uncovered basis (without use of a forward hedge). In other words, foreign financing may result in a lower financing cost than domestic financing, but it cannot be guaranteed (unless the firm has receivables in that same currency).

The Forward Rate as a Forecast

Assume the forward rate (F) of the foreign currency borrowed is used by firms as a predictor of the spot rate that will exist at the end of the financing period. The expected effective financing rate from borrowing a foreign currency can be forecasted.

When interest rate parity exists here, the forward rate can be used as a break-even point to assess the financing decision. When a firm is financing with the foreign currency (and not covering the foreign currency position), the effective financing rate will be less than the domestic rate if the future spot rate of the foreign currency (spot rate at the time of loan repayment) is less than the forward rate (at the time the loan is granted). Conversely, the effective financing rate in a foreign loan will be greater than the domestic rate if the future spot rate of the foreign currency turns out to be greater than the forward rate.

If the forward rate is an unbiased predictor of the future spot rate, then the effective financing rate of a foreign currency will on average be equal to the domestic financing rate. In this case, firms that consistently borrow for-

Exhibit 700.58 *Implications of Interest Rate Parity for Short-Term Financing*

Scenario	Implications
1. Interest rate parity holds.	Foreign financing and a simultaneous hedge of that position in the forward market will result in financing costs similar to those in domestic financing.
2. Interest rate parity holds, and the forward rate is an accurate forecast of the future spot rate.	Uncovered foreign financing will result in financing costs similar to those in domestic financing.
3. Interest rate parity holds, and the forward rate is expected to overestimate the future spot rate.	Uncovered foreign financing is expected to result in lower financing costs than those in domestic financing.
4. Interest rate parity holds, and the forward rate is expected to underestimate the future spot rate.	Uncovered foreign financing is expected to result in higher financing costs than those in domestic financing.
5. Interest rate parity does not hold; the forward premium (discount) exceeds (is less than) the interest rate differential.	Foreign financing with a simultaneous hedge of that position in the forward market results in higher financing costs than those of domestic financing.
6. Interest rate parity does not hold; the forward premium (discount) is less than (exceeds) the interest rate differential.	Foreign financing with a simultaneous hedge of that position in the forward market results in lower financing costs than those of domestic financing.

eign currencies will not achieve lower financing costs. Although the effective financing rate may turn out to be lower than the domestic rate in some periods, it will be higher in other periods, causing an offsetting effect. Firms that believe the forward rate is an unbiased predictor of the future spot rate will prefer borrowing their home currency, where the financing rate is known with certainty and is not expected to be any higher on average than foreign financing.

Exchange Rate Forecasts

While the forecasting capabilities of firms are somewhat limited, some firms may make decisions based on cycles in currency movements. Firms may use the recent movements as a forecast of future movements to determine whether they should borrow a foreign currency. This strategy would have been successful on average if utilized in the past. It will be successful in the future if currency movements continue to move in one direction for long periods of time.

Once the firm develops a forecast for the exchange rate's percentage change over the financing period (e_f), it can use this forecast along with the foreign interest rate to forecast the effective financing rate of a foreign currency. The forecasted rate can then be compared to the domestic financing rate.

Financing With a Portfolio of Currencies

Although foreign financing can result in significantly lower financing costs, the variance in foreign financing costs over time is higher. MNCs may be able to achieve lower financing costs without excessive risk by financing with a portfolio of foreign currencies.

Portfolio Diversification Effects

When both foreign currencies are borrowed, the only way the portfolio will exhibit a higher effective financing rate than the domestic rate is for *both* currencies to experience their maximum possible level of appreciation. If only one does, the severity of its appreciation will be somewhat offset by the other currency's not appreciating to such a large extent. The probability of maximum appreciation is 20% for the Swiss franc and 25% for the Japanese yen. The joint probability of both of these events occurring simultaneously is (20%)(25%) = 5%. This is an advantage of financing in a portfolio of foreign currencies. Nevada, Inc., has a 95% chance of attaining lower costs with the foreign portfolio than with domestic financing.

The expected value of the effective financing rate for the portfolio can be determined by multiplying the percentage financed in each currency by the expected value of that currency's individual effective financing rate. Recall that the expected value was 11.888% for the Swiss franc and 11.834% for the Japanese yen. Thus, for a portfolio representing 50% of funds borrowed in each currency, the expected value of the effective financing rate is .5(11.888%) + .5(11.834%) = 11.861%. Based on an overall comparison, the expected value of the portfolio's effective financing rate is very similar to that from financing solely in either foreign currency. However, the risk (of incurring a higher effective financing rate than the domestic rate) when financing with the portfolio is substantially less.

In the example, the computation of joint probabilities requires the assumption that the two currencies move independently. If movements of the two currencies are actually highly positively correlated, then financing with a portfolio of currencies will not be as beneficial as demonstrated because there is a strong likelihood of both currencies experiencing a high level of appreciation simultaneously. If the two currencies are not highly correlated, they are less likely to simultaneously appreciate to such a degree. Thus, the chances that the portfolio's effective financing rate will exceed the U.S. rate are reduced when the currencies included in the portfolio are not highly positively correlated.

The example included only two currencies in the portfolio. Financing with a more diversified portfolio of additional currencies that exhibit low interest rates might increase the probability that foreign financing will be less costly than domestic financing; several currencies are unlikely to move in tandem and therefore unlikely to simultaneously appreciate enough to offset the advantage of their low interest rates. Again, the degree to which these currencies are correlated with each other is important. If all currencies are highly positively correlated with each other, financing with such a portfolio would not be very different from financing with a single foreign currency.

The assessment of a currency portfolio's effective financing rate and variance is not restricted to just two currencies. The mean effective financing rate for a currency portfolio of any size will be determined by totaling the respective individual effective financing rates weighted by the percentage of funds financed with each currency.

Impact of Short-Term Financing on the MNC's Value

Short-term financing can affect the value of an MNC. The cost of obtaining short-term funds reflects a financing expense for MNCs. To the extent that the MNC's parent can achieve short-term financing in currencies that will reduce its short-term financing expenses, it can maintain less cash to cover such expenses, which frees up additional cash flow and adds value to the MNC.

Short-term financing decisions by foreign subsidiaries also affect the valuation of MNCs because they can affect the timing and the amounts of the foreign currency cash flows that are ultimately remitted to the U.S. parent. For example, if a foreign subsidiary is able to obtain short-term financing at a very low interest rate, this will increase the amount of foreign currency cash flows that will ultimately be received by the U.S. parent and will therefore enhance the value of the MNC.

International Cash Management

The term **cash management** can be broadly defined to mean optimization of cash flows and investment of excess cash. From an international perspective, cash management is very complex because of different laws among countries that pertain to cross-border cash transfers. In addition, exchange rate fluctuations can affect the value of cross-border cash transfers. Financial managers need to understand the advantages and disadvantages of investing cash in foreign markets so that they can make international cash management decisions that maximize the value of the MNC.

Cash Flow Analysis: Subsidiary Perspective

The management of working capital (such as inventory, accounts receivable, and cash) has a direct influence on the amount and timing of cash flow. Working capital management and the management of cash flow are integrated. We discuss them here first before focusing on cash management.

Subsidiary Expenses

Begin with outflow payments by the subsidiary to purchase raw materials or supplies. The subsidiary will normally have a more difficult time forecasting future outflow payments if its purchases are international rather than domestic because of exchange rate fluctuations. In addition, there is a possibility that payments will be substantially higher due to appreciation of the invoice currency. Consequently, the firm may wish to maintain a large inventory of supplies and raw materials so that it can draw from its inventory and cut down on purchases if the invoice currency appreciates. Still another possibility is that imported goods from another country could be restricted by the host government (through quotas, and so on). In this event, a larger inventory would give a firm more time to search for alternative sources of supplies or raw materials. A subsidiary with domestic supply sources would not experience such a problem and therefore would not need such a large inventory.

Outflow payments for supplies will be influenced by future sales. If the sales volume is substantially influenced by exchange rate fluctuations, its future level becomes more uncertain, which makes outflow payments for supplies more uncertain. Such uncertainty may force the subsidiary to maintain larger cash balances to cover any unexpected increase in supply requirements.

Subsidiary Revenues

If subsidiaries export their products, their sales volume may be more volatile than if the goods were only sold domestically. This volatility could be due to the fluctuating exchange rate of the invoice currency. Importers' demand for these finished goods will most likely decrease if the invoice currency appreciates. The sales volume of exports is also susceptible to business cycles of the importing countries. If the goods were sold domestically, the exchange rate fluctuations would not have a direct impact on sales, although they would still have an indirect impact since the fluctuations would influence prices paid by local customers for imports from foreign competitors.

Sales can often be increased when credit standards are relaxed. However, it is important to focus on cash inflows due to sales rather than on sales themselves. Looser credit standards may cause a slowdown in cash inflows from sales, which could offset the benefits of increased sales. Accounts receivable management is an important part of the subsidiary's working capital management because of its potential impact on cash inflows.

Subsidiary Dividend Payments

The subsidiary may be expected to periodically send dividend payments and other fees to the parent. These fees could represent royalties or charges for overhead costs incurred by the parent that benefit the subsidiary. An example is research and development costs incurred by the parent, which would improve the quality of goods produced by the subsidiary. Whatever the reason, payments by the subsidiary to the parent are often necessary. When dividend payments and fees are known in advance and denominated in the subsidiary's currency, forecasting cash flows is easier for the subsidiary. The level of dividends paid by subsidiaries to the parent is dependent on liquidity needs of each subsidiary, potential uses of funds at various subsidiary locations, expected movements in the currencies of the subsidiaries, and regulations of the host country government.

Subsidiary Liquidity Management

After accounting for all outflow and inflow payments, the subsidiary will find itself with either excess or deficient cash. It uses liquidity management to either invest its excess cash or borrow to cover its cash deficiencies. If it anticipates a cash deficiency, short-term financing is necessary. If it anticipates excess cash, it must determine how the excess cash should be used. Investing in foreign currencies can sometimes be attractive, but exchange rate risk makes the effective yield uncertain.

Liquidity management is a crucial component of a subsidiary's working capital management. Subsidiaries commonly have access to numerous lines of credit and overdraft facilities in various currencies. Therefore, they may maintain adequate liquidity without substantial cash balances. While liquidity is important for the overall MNC, it cannot be properly measured by liquidity ratios. Potential access to funds is more relevant than cash on hand.

Centralized Cash Management

Each subsidiary should manage its working capital by simultaneously considering all of the points discussed thus far. Often, though, each subsidiary is more concerned with its own operations than with the overall operations of the MNC. Thus, a centralized **cash management group** may need to monitor, and possibly manage, the parent-subsidiary and intersubsidiary cash flows. This role is critical since it can often benefit individual subsidiaries in need of funds or overly exposed to exchange rate risk.

> **Example 37** *The treasury department of Kraft Foods is centralized to manage liquidity, funding, and foreign exchange requirements of its global operations. And Monsanto (part of Pharmacia Corp.) has a centralized system for pooling different currency balances from various subsidiaries in Asia that saves hundreds of thousands of dollars per year.*

Exhibit 700.59 is a complement to the following discussion of cash flow management. It is a simplified cash flow diagram for an MNC with two subsidiaries in different countries. Although each MNC may handle its payments in a different manner, Exhibit 700.59 is based on simplified assumptions that will help illustrate some key concepts of international cash management. The exhibit reflects the assumption that the two subsidiaries periodically send loan repayments and dividends to the parent or send excess cash to the parent (where the centralized cash management process is assumed to take place). These cash flows represent the incoming cash to the parent from the subsidiaries. The parent's cash outflows to the subsidiaries can include loans and the return of cash previously invested by the subsidiaries. The subsidiaries also have cash flows between themselves because they purchase supplies from each other.

While each subsidiary is managing its working capital, there is a need to monitor and manage the cash flows between the parent and the subsidiaries, as well as between the individual subsidiaries. This task of international cash management should be delegated to a centralized cash management group. International cash management can be segmented into two functions: (1) optimizing cash flow movements and (2) investing excess cash.

The centralized cash management division of an MNC cannot always accurately forecast events that affect parent-subsidiary or intersubsidiary cash flows. It should, however, be ready to react to any event by considering (1) any potential adverse impact on cash flows and (2) how to avoid such an adverse impact. If the cash flow situation between the parent and subsidiaries results in a cash squeeze on the parent, it should have sources of funds (credit

Exhibit 700.59 *Cash Flow of the Overall MNC*

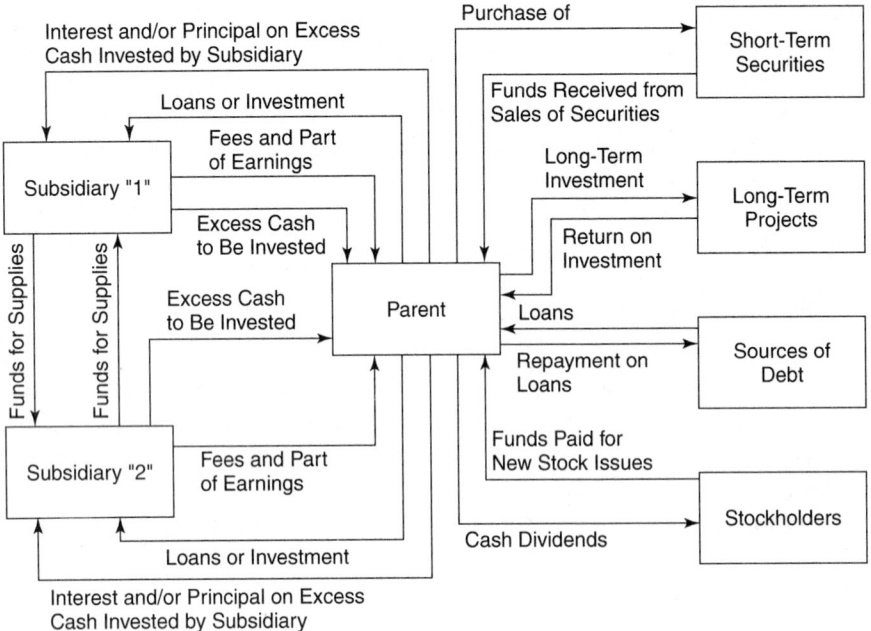

lines) available. On the other hand, if it has excess cash after considering all outflow payments, it must consider where to invest funds.

Techniques to Optimize International Cash Flows

International cash inflows can be optimized by the following techniques.

- Accelerating cash inflows
- Minimizing currency conversion costs
- Managing blocked funds
- Managing intersubsidiary cash transfers

Each of these techniques is discussed in turn.

Accelerating Cash Inflows

The first goal in international cash management is to accelerate cash inflows, as the more quickly the inflows are received, the more quickly they can be invested or used for other purposes. Several managerial practices are advocated for this endeavor, some of which may be implemented by the individual subsidiaries. First, a corporation may establish **lockboxes** around the world, which are post office boxes to which customers are instructed to send payment. When set up in appropriate locations, lockboxes can help reduce mailing time (**mail float**). A bank usually processes incoming checks at a lockbox on a daily basis. A second method for accelerating cash inflows is the **preauthorized payment**, which allows a corporation to charge a customer's bank account up to some limit. Both preauthorized payments and lockboxes are even used in a domestic setting. Because international transactions may have a relatively long mailing time, these methods of accelerating cash inflows can be quite valuable for an MNC.

Minimizing Currency Conversion Costs

Another technique for optimizing cash flow movements, **netting**, can be implemented with the joint effort of subsidiaries or by the centralized cash management group. This technique optimizes cash flow by reducing the administrative and transaction costs that result from currency conversion.

Example 38 Montana, Inc., has subsidiaries located in France and in Hungary. Whenever the French subsidiary needs to purchase supplies from the Hungarian subsidiary, it needs to convert euros into Hungary's currency (the forint) to make payment. Hungary's subsidiary must convert its forint into euros when purchasing supplies from the French subsidiary. Montana, Inc., has instructed both subsidiaries to net their transactions on a monthly basis so that only one net payment is made at the end of each month. By using this approach, both subsidiaries avoid (or at least reduce) the transaction costs of currency conversion.

Over time, netting has become increasingly popular because it offers several key benefits. First, it reduces the number of cross-border transactions between subsidiaries, thereby reducing the overall administrative cost of such cash transfers. Second, it reduces the need for foreign exchange conversion since transactions occur less frequently, thereby reducing the transaction costs associated with foreign exchange conversion. Third, the netting process imposes tight control over information on transactions between subsidiaries. Thus, all subsidiaries engage in a more coordinated effort to accurately report and settle their various accounts. Finally, cash flow forecasting is easier since only net cash transfers are made at the end of each period, rather than individual cash transfers throughout the period. Improved cash flow forecasting can enhance financing and investment decisions.

A **bilateral netting system** involves transactions between two units: between the parent and a subsidiary, or between two subsidiaries. A **multilateral netting system** usually involves a more complex interchange among the parent and several subsidiaries. For most large MNCs, a multilateral netting system would be necessary to effectively reduce administrative and currency conversion costs. Such a system is normally centralized so that all necessary information is consolidated. From the consolidated cash flow information, net cash flow positions for each pair of units (subsidiaries, or whatever) are determined, and the actual reconciliation at the end of each period can be dictated. The centralized group may even maintain inventories of various currencies so that currency conversions for the end-of-period net payments can be completed without significant transaction costs.

MNCs commonly monitor the cash flows between their subsidiaries with the use of an intersubsidiary payments matrix.

Example 39 Exhibit 700.60 is an example of an intersubsidiary payments matrix that totals each subsidiary's individual payments to each of the other subsidiaries. The first row indicates that the Canadian subsidiary owes the equivalent of $40,000 to the French subsidiary, the equivalent of $90,000 to the Japanese subsidiary, and so on. During this same period, these subsidiaries have also received goods from the Canadian subsidiary, for which payment is due. The second column (under Canada) shows that the Canadian subsidiary is owed the equivalent of $60,000 by the French subsidiary, the equivalent of $100,000 by the Japanese subsidiary, and so on.

Exhibit 700.60 *Intersubsidiary Payments Matrix*

Payments Owed by Subsidiary Located in:	\multicolumn{5}{c}{U.S. Dollar Value (in Thousands) Owed to Subsidiary Located in:}
	Canada	France	Japan	Switzerland	United States
Canada	—	40	90	20	40
France	60	—	30	60	50
Japan	100	30	—	20	30
Switzerland	10	50	10	—	50
United States	10	60	20	20	—

Because subsidiaries owe each other, currency conversion costs can be reduced by requiring that only the net payment be extended. Using the intersubsidiary table, the schedule of net payments is determined as shown in Exhibit 700.61. Because the Canadian subsidiary owes the French subsidiary the equivalent of $40,000 but is owed the equivalent of $60,000 by the French subsidiary, the net payment required is the equivalent of $20,000 from the French subsidiary to the Canadian subsidiary. Exhibits 700.60 and 700.61 convert all figures to U.S. dollar equivalents to allow for consolidating payments in both directions so the net payment can be determined.

Exhibit 700.61 *Netting Schedule*

Net Payments to Be Made by Subsidiary Located in:	Canada	France	Japan	Switzerland	United States
Canada	—	0	0	10	30
France	20	—	0	10	0
Japan	10	0	—	10	10
Switzerland	0	0	0	—	30
United States	0	10	0	0	—

Net U.S. Dollar Value (in thousands) Owed to Subsidiary Located in:

There can be some limitations to multilateral netting due to foreign exchange controls. Although the major industrialized countries typically do not impose such controls, some other countries do, and some countries prohibit netting altogether. Thus, an MNC with subsidiaries around the world may not be able to include all of its subsidiaries in its multilateral netting system. Obviously, this will limit the degree to which the netting system can reduce administration and transaction costs.

Managing Blocked Funds

Cash flows can also be affected by a host government's blockage of funds, which might occur if the government requires all funds to remain within the country in order to create jobs and reduce unemployment. To deal with funds blockage, the MNC may implement the same strategies used when a host country government imposes high taxes. To make efficient use of these funds, the MNC may instruct the subsidiary to set up a research and development division, which incurs costs and possibly generates revenues for other subsidiaries.

Another strategy is to use transfer pricing in a manner that will increase the expenses incurred by the subsidiary. A host country government is likely to be more lenient on funds sent to cover expenses than on earnings remitted to the parent.

When subsidiaries are restricted from transferring funds to the parent, the parent may instruct the subsidiary to obtain financing from a local bank rather than from the parent. By borrowing through a local intermediary, the subsidiary is assured that its earnings can be distributed to pay off previous financing. Overall, most methods of managing blocked funds are intended to make efficient use of the funds by using them to cover expenses that are transferred to that country.

Example 40 Wittenberg, Inc., a U.S.-based MNC, has a subsidiary in the Philippines. During a turbulent period, the subsidiary was prevented from exchanging its Philippine pesos into U.S. dollars to be sent home. Wittenberg held its corporate meeting in Manila so that it could use the pesos to pay the expenses of the meeting (hotel, food, etc.) in pesos. In this way, it was able to use local funds to cover an expense that it would have incurred anyway. Normally, its parent would have paid the expenses of the corporate meeting if it had been held in the parent's country.

Managing Intersubsidiary Cash Transfers

Proper management of cash flows can also be beneficial to a subsidiary in need of funds. The leading or lagging strategy can make efficient use of cash and therefore reduce debt. Some host governments prohibit the practice by requiring that a payment between subsidiaries occur at the time the goods are transferred. Thus, an MNC needs to be aware of any laws that restrict the use of this strategy.

> **Example 41** Texas, Inc., has two foreign subsidiaries called Short Sub and Long Sub. Short Sub needs funds, while Long Sub has excess funds. If Long Sub purchases supplies from Short Sub, it can provide financing by paying for its supplies earlier than necessary. This technique is often called **leading**. Alternatively, if Long Sub sells supplies to Short Sub, it can provide financing by allowing Short Sub to lag its payments. This technique is called **lagging**.

Complications in Optimizing International Cash Flow

Most complications encountered in optimizing international cash flow can be classified into three categories.

- Company-related characteristics
- Government restrictions
- Characteristics of banking systems

Each complication is discussed in turn.

Company-Related Characteristics

In some cases, optimizing cash flow can become complicated, due to characteristics of the MNC. If one of the subsidiaries delays payments to other subsidiaries for supplies received, the other subsidiaries may be forced to borrow until the payments arrive. A centralized approach that monitors all intersubsidiary payments should be able to minimize such problems.

Government Restrictions

The existence of government restrictions can disrupt a cash flow optimization policy. Some governments prohibit the use of a netting system, as noted earlier. In addition, some countries periodically prevent cash from leaving the country, thereby preventing net payments from being made. These problems can arise even for MNCs that do not experience any company-related problems. Countries in Latin America commonly impose restrictions that affect an MNC's cash flows.

Characteristics of Banking Systems

The abilities of banks to facilitate cash transfers for MNCs vary among countries. Banks in the United States are advanced in this field, but banks in some other countries do not offer services. MNCs prefer some form of zero-balance account, where excess funds can be used to make payments but earn interest until they are used. In addition, some MNCs benefit from the use of lockboxes. Such services are not available in some countries.

In addition, a bank may not update the MNC's bank account information sufficiently or provide a detailed breakdown of fees for banking services. Without full use of banking resources and information, international cash management is limited in its effectiveness. In addition, an MNC with subsidiaries in, say, eight different countries will typically be dealing with eight different banking systems. Much progress has been made in foreign banking systems in recent years. As time passes and a more uniform global banking system emerges, such problems may be alleviated.

Investing Excess Cash

Any remaining funds can be invested in domestic or foreign short-term securities. In some periods, foreign short-term securities will have higher interest rates than domestic interest rates. The differential can be substantial. However, firms must account for the possible exchange rate movements when assessing the potential yield on foreign investments.

How to Invest Excess Cash

International money markets have grown to accommodate corporate investments of excess cash. MNCs may use international money markets in an attempt to achieve higher returns than what they can achieve domestically.

One of the most commonly used international money market instruments is the Eurocurrency deposit, with the Eurodollar deposit being the most popular type of deposit. The dollar volume of Eurodollar deposits has more than doubled since 1980. Eurodollar deposits commonly offer MNCs a slightly higher yield than bank deposits in the United States. Many MNCs establish large deposits in various currencies in the Eurocurrency market. While Eurodollar deposits still dominate the market, the relative importance of nondollar currencies has increased over time.

In addition to using the Eurocurrency market, MNCs can also purchase foreign Treasury bills and commercial paper. Improved telecommunications systems have increased access to these securities in foreign markets and allow for a greater degree of integration among money markets in various countries.

Centralized Cash Management

An MNC's short-term investing policy can either maintain separate investments for all subsidiaries or employ a centralized approach. Recall that the function of optimizing cash flows can be improved by a centralized approach, since all subsidiary cash positions can be monitored simultaneously. With regard to the investing function, centralization allows for more efficient usage of funds and possibly higher returns. Here the term *centralized* means that excess cash from each subsidiary is pooled until it is needed by a particular subsidiary.

CENTRALIZATION WHEN SUBSIDIARIES USE THE SAME CURRENCY To understand the advantages of a centralized system, consider that the rates paid on short-term investments such as bank deposits are often higher for larger amounts. Thus, if two subsidiaries have excess cash of $50,000 each for one month, the rates on their individual bank deposits may be lower than the rate they could obtain if they pooled their funds into a single $100,000 bank deposit. In this manner, the centralized (pooling) approach generates a higher rate of return on excess cash. The centralized approach can also facilitate the transfer of funds from subsidiaries with excess funds to those that need funds.

> **Example 42** *Subsidiary A of Moorhead, Inc., has excess cash of $50,000 during the next month, while Subsidiary B of Moorhead, Inc., needs to borrow $50,000 for one month. If cash management is not centralized, Subsidiary A may use the $50,000 to purchase a one-month bank certificate earning, say, 10% (on an annualized basis). At the same time, Subsidiary B may borrow from a bank for one month at a rate of, say, 12%. The bank must charge a higher rate on loans than it offers on deposits. With a centralized approach, Subsidiary B can borrow Subsidiary A's excess funds, thereby reducing its financing costs.*

CENTRALIZED CASH MANAGEMENT OF MULTIPLE CURRENCIES Centralized cash management is more complicated when the MNC uses multiple currencies. All excess funds could be pooled and converted to a single currency for investment purposes. However, the advantage of pooling may be offset by the transaction costs incurred when converting to a single currency.

Centralized cash management can still be valuable, though. The short-term cash available among subsidiaries can be pooled together so that there is a separate pool for each currency. Then excess cash in a particular currency can still be used to satisfy other subsidiary deficiencies in that currency. In this way, funds can be transferred from one subsidiary to another without incurring transaction costs that banks charge for exchanging currencies. This strategy is especially feasible when all subsidiary funds are deposited in branches of a single bank so that the funds can easily be transferred among subsidiaries.

Another possible function of centralized cash management is to invest funds in securities denominated in the foreign currencies that will be needed by the subsidiaries in the future. MNCs can use excess cash to invest cash in international money market instruments so that they can cover any payables positions in specific foreign currencies. If they have payables in foreign currencies that are expected to appreciate, they can cover such positions by creating short-term deposits in those currencies. The maturity of a deposit would ideally coincide with the date at which the funds are needed.

IMPACT OF TECHNOLOGY ON CENTRALIZED CASH MANAGEMENT   International cash management requires timely information across subsidiaries regarding cash positions in each currency by each subsidiary, along with interest rate information about each currency. A centralized cash management system needs a continual flow of information about currency positions so that it can determine whether one subsidiary's shortage of cash can be covered by another subsidiary's excess cash in that currency. Given the major improvements in online technology in recent years, all MNCs can easily and efficiently create a multinational communications network among their subsidiaries to ensure that information about cash positions is continually updated.

Long-Term Financing

Multinational corporations (MNCs) typically use long-term sources of funds to finance long-term projects. They have access to domestic and foreign sources of funds. It is worthwhile for MNCs to consider all possible forms of financing before making their final decisions. Financial managers must be aware of their sources of long-term funds so that can finance international projects in a manner that maximizes the wealth of the MNC.

Long-Term Financing Decision

An MNC's long-term financing decision is commonly influenced by the different interest rates that exist among currencies. The actual cost of long-term financing is based on both the quoted interest rate and the percentage change in the exchange rate of the currency borrowed over the loan life. Just as interest rates on short-term bank loans vary among currencies, so do bond yields. The wide differentials in bond yields among countries reflect a different cost of debt financing for firms in different countries.

Because bonds denominated in foreign currencies sometimes have lower yields, U.S. corporations often consider issuing bonds denominated in those currencies. For example, **Hewlett-Packard, IBM, PepsiCo,** and **Walt Disney** recently issued bonds denominated in Japanese yen to capitalize on low Japanese interest rates. Since the actual financing cost to a U.S. corporation issuing a foreign currency-denominated bond is affected by that currency's value relative to the U.S. dollar during the financing period, there is no guarantee that the bond will be less costly than a U.S. dollar-denominated bond. The borrowing firm must make coupon payments in the currency denominating the bond. If this currency appreciates against the firm's home currency, more funds will be needed to make the coupon payments. For this reason, a firm will not always denominate debt in a currency that exhibits a low interest rate.

To make the long-term financing decision, the MNC must (1) determine the amount of funds needed, (2) forecast the price at which it can issue the bond, and (3) forecast periodic exchange rate values for the currency denominating the bond. This information can be used to determine the bond's financing costs, which can be compared with the financing costs the firm would incur using its home currency. Finally, the uncertainty of the actual financing costs to be incurred from foreign financing must be accounted for as well.

Measuring the Cost of Financing

From a U.S.-based MNC's perspective, the cost of financing in a foreign currency is influenced by the value of that currency when the MNC makes coupon payments to its bondholders and when it pays off the principal at the time the bond reaches maturity.

Normally, exchange rates are more difficult to predict over longer time horizons. Thus, the time when the principal is to be repaid may be so far away that it is virtually impossible to have a reliable estimate of the exchange rate at that time. For this reason, some firms may be uncomfortable issuing bonds denominated in foreign currencies.

IMPACT OF A STRONG CURRENCY ON FINANCING COSTS If the currency that was borrowed appreciates over time, an MNC will need more funds to cover the coupon or principal payments. This type of exchange rate movement increases the MNC's financing costs.

IMPACT OF A WEAK CURRENCY ON FINANCING COSTS Whereas an appreciating currency increases the periodic outflow payments of the bond issuer, a depreciating currency will reduce the issuer's outflow payments and therefore reduce its financing costs.

Assessing Exchange Rate Risk

Given the importance of the exchange rate when issuing bonds in a foreign currency, an MNC needs a reliable method to account for the potential impact of exchange rate fluctuations. It can use a point estimate exchange rate forecast of the currency used to denominate its bonds for each period in which an outflow payment will be provided to bondholders. However, a point estimate forecast does not account for uncertainty surrounding the forecast, which varies depending on the volatility of the currency. From a U.S. borrower's perspective, for example, a bond denominated in Canadian dollars is subject to less exchange rate risk than a bond denominated in most other foreign currencies (assuming the borrower has no offsetting position in these currencies). The Canadian dollar exhibits less variability against the U.S. dollar over time and therefore is less likely to deviate far from its projected future exchange rate. The uncertainty surrounding a point estimate forecast can be accounted for by using probabilities or simulation.

Reducing Exchange Rate Risk

The exchange rate risk from financing with bonds in foreign currencies can be reduced by using one of the alternative strategies described next. These include offsetting cash inflows, forward contracts, currency swaps, parallel loans, diversifying among currencies.

Offsetting Cash Inflows

Some firms may have inflow payments in particular currencies, which could offset their outflow payments related to bond financing. Thus, a firm may be able to finance with bonds denominated in a foreign currency that exhibits a lower coupon rate without becoming exposed to exchange rate risk. Nevertheless, it is unlikely that the firm would be able to perfectly match the timing and amount of the outflows in the foreign currency denominating the bond to the inflows in that currency. Therefore, some exposure to exchange rate fluctuations will exist. The exposure can be substantially reduced, though, if the firm receives inflows in the particular currency denominating the bond. This can help to stabilize the firm's cash flow.

Example 43 *Many MNCs, including* **Honeywell** *and* **The Coca-Cola Co.**, *issue bonds in some of the foreign currencies that they receive from operations.* **PepsiCo** *issues bonds in several foreign currencies and uses proceeds in those same currencies resulting from foreign operations to make interest and principal payments.* **TRW, Inc.** *typically borrows the equivalent of more than $100 million in foreign currencies and uses its foreign currency revenue to cover the debt payments.*

Forward Contracts

When a bond denominated in a foreign currency has a lower coupon rate than the firm's home currency, the firm may consider issuing bonds denominated in that currency and simultaneously hedging its exchange rate risk through the forward market. Because the forward market can sometimes accommodate requests of five years or longer, such an approach may be possible. The firm could arrange to purchase the foreign currency forward for each time at which payments are required. However, the forward rate for each horizon will most likely be above the spot rate. Consequently, hedging these future outflow payments may not be less costly than the outflow payments needed if a dollar-denominated bond were issued.

Currency Swaps

A currency swap enables firms to exchange currencies at periodic intervals. **Ford Motor Co., Johnson & Johnson, General Motors,** and many other MNCs use currency swaps.

Example 44 Miller Co., a U.S. firm, desires to issue a bond denominated in euros because it could make payments with euro inflows to be generated from existing operations. However, Miller Co. is not well known to investors who would consider purchasing euro-denominated bonds. Meanwhile Beck Co. of Germany desires to issue dollar-denominated bonds because its inflow payments are mostly in dollars. However, it is not well known to the investors who would purchase these bonds.

If Miller is known in the dollar-denominated market while Beck is known in the euro-denominated market, the following transactions are appropriate. Miller issues dollar-denominated bonds, while Beck issues euro-denominated bonds. Miller will provide euro payments to Beck in exchange for dollar payments. This swap of currencies allows the companies to make payments to their respective bondholders without concern about exchange rate risk. This type of currency swap is illustrated in Exhibit 700.62.

Exhibit 700.62   *Illustration of a Currency Swap*

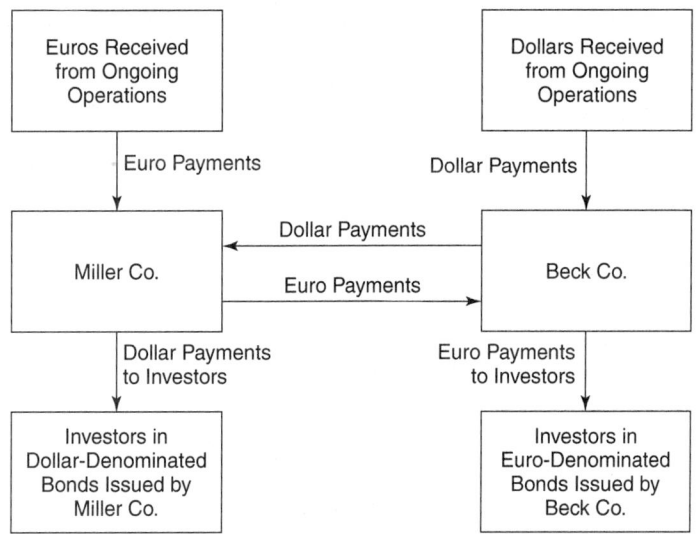

Many MNCs simultaneously swap interest payments and currencies. **The Gillette Co.** engaged in swap agreements that converted $500 million in fixed rate dollar-denominated debt into multiple currency variable rate debt. **PepsiCo** enters into interest rate swaps and currency swaps to reduce borrowing costs.

The large commercial banks that serve as financial intermediaries for currency swaps sometimes take positions. That is, they may agree to swap currencies with firms, rather than simply search for suitable swap candidates.

Parallel Loans

Firms can also obtain financing in a foreign currency through a parallel (or back-to-back) loan, which occurs when two parties provide simultaneous loans with an agreement to repay at a specified point in the future.

> **Example 45** The parent of **Ann Arbor Co.** desires to expand its British subsidiary, while the parent of a British-based MNC desires to expand its American subsidiary. The British parent provides pounds to the British subsidiary of Ann Arbor Co., while the parent of Ann Arbor Co. provides dollars to the American subsidiary of the British-based MNC (as shown in Exhibit 700.63). At the time specified by the loan contract, the loans are repaid. The British subsidiary of Ann Arbor Co. uses pound-denominated revenues to repay the British company that provided the loan. At the same time, the American subsidiary of the British-based MNC uses dollar-denominated revenues to repay the U.S. company that provided the loan.

Diversifying Among Currencies

A U.S. firm may denominate bonds in several foreign currencies, rather than a single foreign currency, so that substantial appreciation of any one currency will not drastically increase the number of dollars needed to cover the financing payments.

Exhibit 700.63 *Illustration of a Parallel Loan*

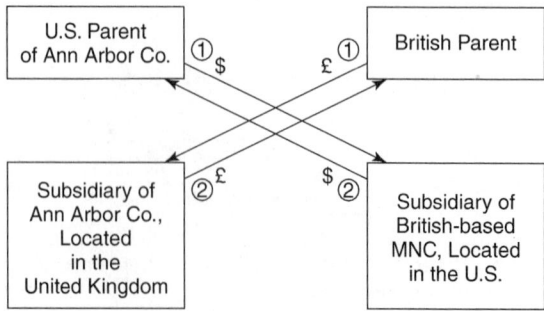

1. Loans are simultaneously provided by parent of each MNC to subsidiary of the other MNC.
2. At a specified time in the future, the loans are repaid in the same currency that was borrowed.

Example 46 *Nevada, Inc. a U.S.-based MNC, is considering four alternatives for issuing bonds to support its U.S. operations.*

1. *Issue bonds denominated in U.S. dollars.*
2. *Issue bonds denominated in Japanese yen.*
3. *Issue bonds denominated in Canadian dollars.*
4. *Issue some bonds denominated in Japanese yen and some bonds denominated in Canadian dollars.*

Nevada, Inc., has no net exposure in either Japanese yen or Canadian dollars. The coupon rate for a U.S. dollar-denominated bond is 14%, while for a yen- or Canadian dollar-denominated bond the coupon rate is 8%. It is expected that any of these bonds could be sold at par value.

If the Canadian dollar appreciates against the U.S. dollar, Nevada's actual financing cost from issuing Canadian dollar-denominated bonds may be higher than that of the U.S. dollar-denominated bonds. If the Japanese yen appreciates substantially against the U.S. dollar, Nevada's actual financing cost from issuing yen-denominated bonds may be higher than that of the U.S. dollar-denominated bonds. If the exchange rates of the Canadian dollar and Japanese yen move in opposite directions against the U.S. dollar, then both types of bonds could not simultaneously be more costly than U.S. dollar-denominated bonds, so financing with both types of bonds would almost ensure that the Nevada's overall financing cost would be less than the cost from issuing U.S. dollar-denominated bonds.

There is no guarantee that the exchange rates of the Canadian dollar and Japanese yen will move in opposite directions. The movements of these two currencies are not highly correlated, however, so it is unlikely that both currencies will simultaneously appreciate to an extent that will offset their lower coupon rate advantages. Therefore, financing in bonds denominated in more than one foreign currency can increase the probability that the overall cost of foreign financing will be less than that of financing with the dollars. Nevada decides to issue bonds denominated in Canadian dollars and in yen.

The preceding example involved only two foreign currencies. In reality, a firm may consider several currencies that exhibit lower interest rates and issue a portion of its bonds in each of these currencies. Such a strategy can increase the other costs (advertising, printing, and so on) of issuing bonds, but those costs may be offset by a reduction in cash outflows to bondholders.

CURRENCY COCKTAIL BONDS A firm can finance in several currencies without issuing various types of bonds (thus avoiding higher transaction costs) by developing a **currency cocktail bond,** denominated in not one, but a mixture (or "cocktail") of currencies. A currency cocktail simply reflects a multicurrency unit of account. Several currency cocktails have been developed to denominate international bonds, and some have already been used in this manner. One of the more popular currency cocktails is the **Special Drawing Right (SDR),** which was originally devised as an alternative foreign reserve asset but is now used to denominate bonds and bank deposits and to price various services. With the creation of the euro, the use of currency cocktail bonds in Europe is limited because one currency is now used by numerous European countries.

Module 700 Appendix

Mathematical Tables

Table A-1: *Present Value of $1 Due at the End of n Periods*

EQUATION:

$$PVIF_{i,n} = \frac{1}{(1+i)^n}$$

FINANCIAL CALCULATOR KEYS:

n [N]   i [I]   Table Value [PV]   0 [PMT]   1.0 [FV]

Period	1%	2%	3%	4%	5%	6%	7%	8%	9%	10%
1	.9901	.9804	.9709	.9615	.9524	.9434	.9346	.9259	.9174	.9091
2	.9803	.9612	.9426	.9246	.9070	.8900	.8734	.8573	.8417	.8264
3	.9706	.9423	.9151	.8890	.8638	.8396	.8163	.7938	.7722	.7513
4	.9610	.9238	.8885	.8548	.8227	.7921	.7629	.7350	.7084	.6830
5	.9515	.9057	.8626	.8219	.7835	.7473	.7130	.6806	.6499	.6209
6	.9420	.8880	.8375	.7903	.7462	.7050	.6663	.6302	.5963	.5645
7	.9327	.8706	.8131	.7599	.7107	.6651	.6227	.5835	.5470	.5132
8	.9235	.8535	.7894	.7307	.6768	.6274	.5820	.5403	.5019	.4665
9	.9143	.8368	.7664	.7026	.6446	.5919	.5439	.5002	.4604	.4241
10	.9053	.8203	.7441	.6756	.6139	.5584	.5083	.4632	.4224	.3855
11	.8963	.8043	.7224	.6496	.5847	.5268	.4751	.4289	.3875	.3505
12	.8874	.7885	.7014	.6246	.5568	.4970	.4440	.3971	.3555	.3186
13	.8787	.7730	.6810	.6006	.5303	.4688	.4150	.3677	.3262	.2897
14	.8700	.7579	.6611	.5775	.5051	.4423	.3878	.3405	.2992	.2633
15	.8613	7430	.6419	.5553	.4810	.4173	.3624	.3152	.2745	.2394
16	.8528	.7284	.6232	.5339	.4581	.3936	.3387	.2919	.2519	.2176
17	.8444	.7142	.6050	.5134	.4363	.3714	.3166	.2703	.2311	.1978
18	.8360	.7002	.5874	.4936	.4155	.3503	.2959	.2502	.2120	.1799
19	.8277	.6864	.5703	.4746	.3957	.3305	.2765	.2317	.1945	.1635
20	.8195	.6730	.5537	.4564	.3769	.3118	.2584	.2145	.1784	.1486
21	.8114	.6598	.5375	.4388	.3589	.2942	.2415	.1987	.1637	.1351
22	.8034	.6468	.5219	.4220	.3418	.2775	.2257	.1839	.1502	.1228
23	.7954	.6342	.5067	.4057	.3256	.2618	.2109	.1703	.1378	.1117
24	.7876	.6217	.4919	.3901	.3101	.2470	.1971	.1577	.1264	.1015
25	.7798	.6095	.4776	.3751	.2953	.2330	.1842	.1460	.1160	.0923
26	.7720	.5976	.4637	.3607	.2812	.2198	.1722	.1352	.1064	.0839
27	.7644	.5859	.4502	.3468	.2678	.2074	.1609	.1252	.0976	.0763
28	.7568	.5744	.4371	.3335	.2551	.1956	.1504	.1159	.0895	.0693
29	.7493	.5631	.4243	.3207	.2429	.1846	.1406	.1073	.0822	.0630
30	.7419	.5521	.4120	.3083	.2314	.1741	.1314	.0994	.0754	.0573
35	.7059	.5000	.3554	.2534	.1813	.1301	.0937	.0676	.0490	.0356
40	.6717	.4529	.3066	.2083	.1420	.0972	.0668	.0460	.0318	.0221
45	.6391	.4102	.2644	.1712	.1113	.0727	.0476	.0313	.0207	.0137
50	.6080	.3715	.2281	.1407	.0872	.0543	.0339	.0213	.0134	.0085
55	.5785	.3365	.1968	.1157	.0683	.0406	.0242	.0145	.0087	.0053

Table A-1 *Continued*

Period	12%	14%	15%	16%	18%	20%	24%	28%	32%	36%
1	.8929	.8772	.8696	.8621	.8475	.8333	.8065	.7813	.7576	.7353
2	.7972	.7695	.7561	.7432	.7182	.6944	.6504	.6104	.5739	.5407
3	.7118	.6750	.6575	.6407	.6086	.5787	.5245	.4768	.4348	.3975
4	.6355	.5921	.5718	.5523	.5158	.4823	.4230	.3725	.3294	.2923
5	.5674	.5194	.4972	.4761	.4371	.4019	.3411	.2910	.2495	.2149
6	.5066	.4556	.4323	.4104	.3704	.3349	.2751	.2274	.1890	.1580
7	.4523	.3996	.3759	.3538	.3139	.2791	.2218	.1776	.1432	.1162
8	.4039	.3506	.3269	.3050	.2660	.2326	.1789	.1388	.1085	.0854
9	.3606	.3075	.2843	.2630	.2255	.1938	.1443	.1084	.0822	.0628
10	.3220	.2697	.2472	.2267	.1911	.1615	.1164	.0847	.0623	.0462
11	.2875	.2366	.2149	.1954	.1619	.1346	.0938	.0662	.0472	.0340
12	.2567	.2076	.1869	.1685	.1372	.1122	.0757	.0517	.0357	.0250
13	.2292	.1821	.1625	.1452	.1163	.0935	.0610	.0404	.0271	.0184
14	.2046	.1597	.1413	.1252	.0985	.0779	.0492	.0316	.0205	.0135
15	.1827	.1401	.1229	.1079	.0835	.0649	.0397	.0247	.0155	.0099
16	.1631	.1229	.1069	.0930	.0708	.0541	.0320	.0193	.0118	.0073
17	.1456	.1078	.0929	.0802	.0600	.0451	.0258	.0150	.0089	.0054
18	.1300	.0946	.0808	.0691	.0508	.0376	.0208	.0118	.0068	.0039
19	.1161	.0829	.0703	.0596	.0431	.0313	.0168	.0092	.0051	.0029
20	.1037	.0728	.0611	.0514	.0365	.0261	.0135	.0072	.0039	.0021
21	.0926	.0638	.0531	.0443	.0309	.0217	.0109	.0056	.0029	.0016
22	.0826	.0560	.0462	.0382	.0262	.0181	.0088	.0044	.0022	.0012
23	.0738	.0491	.0402	.0329	.0222	.0151	.0071	.0034	.0017	.0008
24	.0659	.0431	.0349	.0284	.0188	.0126	.0057	.0027	.0013	.0006
25	.0588	.0378	.0304	.0245	.0160	.0105	.0046	.0021	.0010	.0005
26	.0525	.0331	.0264	.0211	.0135	.0087	.0037	.0016	.0007	.0003
27	.0469	.0291	.0230	.0182	.0115	.0073	.0030	.0013	.0006	.0002
28	.0419	.0255	.0200	.0157	.0097	.0061	.0024	.0010	.0004	.0002
29	.0374	.0224	.0174	.0135	.0082	.0051	.0020	.0008	.0003	.0001
30	.0334	.0196	.0151	.0116	.0070	.0042	.0016	.0006	.0002	.0001
35	.0189	.0102	.0075	.0055	.0030	.0017	.0005	.0002	.0001	*
40	.0107	.0053	.0037	.0026	.0013	.0007	.0002	.0001	*	*
45	.0061	.0027	.0019	.0013	.0006	.0003	.0001	*	*	*
50	.0035	.0014	.0009	.0006	.0003	.0001	*	*	*	*
55	.0020	.0007	.0005	.0003	.0001	*	*	*	*	*

*The factor is zero to four decimal places.

Table A-2 *Present Value of an Annuity of $1 per Period for n Periods*

EQUATION:	FINANCIAL CALCULATOR KEYS:

$$PVIFA_{i,n} = \sum_{t=1}^{N} \frac{1}{(1+i)^n} = \frac{1 - \frac{1}{(1+i)^n}}{i} = \frac{1}{i} = \frac{1}{i(1+i)^n}$$

Financial Calculator Keys: [N] n, [I] i, [PV] Table Value, [PMT] 1.0, [FV] 0

Number of Periods	1%	2%	3%	4%	5%	6%	7%	8%	9%
1	0.9901	0.9804	0.9709	0.9615	0.9524	0.9434	0.9346	0.9259	0.9174
2	1.9704	1.9416	1.9135	1.8861	1.8594	1.8334	1.8080	1.7833	1.7591
3	2.9410	2.8839	2.8286	2.7751	2.7232	2.6730	2.6243	2.5771	2.5313
4	3.9020	3.8077	3.7171	3.6299	3.5460	3.4651	3.3872	3.3121	3.2397
5	4.8534	4.7135	4.5797	4.4518	4.3295	4.2124	4.1002	3.9927	3.8897
6	5.7955	5.6014	5.4172	5.2421	5.0757	4.9173	4.7665	4.6229	4.4859
7	6.7282	6.4720	6.2303	6.0021	5.7864	5.5824	5.3893	5.2064	5.0330
8	7.6517	7.3255	7.0197	6.7327	6.4632	6.2098	5.9713	5.7466	5.5348
9	8.5660	8.1622	7.7861	7.4353	7.1078	6.8017	6.5152	6.2469	5.9952
10	9.4713	8.9826	8.5302	8.1109	7.7217	7.3601	7.0236	6.7101	6.4177
11	10.3676	9.7868	9.2526	8.7605	8.3064	7.8869	7.4987	7.1390	6.8052
12	11.2551	10.5753	9.9540	9.3851	8.8633	8.3838	7.9427	7.5361	7.1607
13	12.1337	11.3484	10.6350	9.9856	9.3936	8.8527	8.3577	7.9038	7.4869
14	13.0037	12.1062	11.2961	10.5631	9.8986	9.2950	8.7455	8.2442	7.7862
15	13.8651	12.8493	11.9379	11.1184	10.3797	9.7122	9.1079	8.5595	8.0607
16	14.7179	13.5777	12.5611	11.6523	10.8378	10.1059	9.4466	8.8514	8.3126
17	15.5623	14.2919	13.1661	12.1657	11.2741	10.4773	9.7632	9.1216	8.5436
18	16.3983	14.9920	13.7535	12.6593	11.6896	10.8276	10.0591	9.3719	8.7556
19	17.2260	15.6785	14.3238	13.1339	12.0853	11.1581	10.3356	9.6036	8.9501
20	18.0456	16.3514	14.8775	13.5903	12.4622	11.4699	10.5940	9.8181	9.1285
21	18.8570	17.0112	15.4150	14.0292	12.8212	11.7641	10.8355	10.0168	9.2922
22	19.6604	17.6580	15.9369	14.4511	13.1630	12.0416	11.0612	10.2007	9.4424
23	20.4558	18.2922	16.4436	14.8568	13.4886	12.3034	11.2722	10.3711	9.5802
24	21.2434	18.9139	16.9355	15.2470	13.7986	12.5504	11.4693	10.5288	9.7066
25	22.0232	19.5235	17.4131	15.6221	14.0939	12.7834	11.6536	10.6748	9.8226
26	22.7952	20.1210	17.8768	15.9828	14.3752	13.0032	11.8258	10.8100	9.9290
27	23.5596	20.7069	18.3270	16.3296	14.6430	13.2105	11.9867	10.9352	10.0266
28	24.3164	21.2813	18.7641	16.6631	14.8981	13.4062	12.1371	11.0511	10.1161
29	25.0658	21.8444	19.1885	16.9837	15.1411	13.5907	12.2777	11.1584	10.1983
30	25.8077	22.3965	19.6004	17.2920	15.3725	13.7648	12.4090	11.2578	10.2737
35	29.4086	24.9986	21.4872	18.6646	16.3742	14.4982	12.9477	11.6546	10.5668
40	32.8347	27.3555	23.1148	19.7928	17.1591	15.0463	13.3317	11.9246	10.7574
45	36.0945	29.4902	24.5187	20.7200	17.7741	15.4558	13.6055	12.1084	10.8812
50	39.1961	31.4236	25.7298	21.4822	18.2559	15.7619	13.8007	12.2335	10.9617
55	42.1472	33.1748	26.7744	22.1086	18.6335	15.9905	13.9399	12.3186	11.0140

Table A-2 *Continued*

Number of Periods	10%	12%	14%	15%	16%	18%	20%	24%	28%	32%
1	0.9091	0.8929	0.8772	0.8696	0.8621	0.8475	0.8333	0.8065	0.7813	0.7576
2	1.7355	1.6901	1.6467	1.6257	1.6052	1.5656	1.5278	1.4568	1.3916	1.3315
3	2.4869	2.4018	2.3216	2.2832	2.2459	2.1743	2.1065	1.9813	1.8684	1.7663
4	3.1699	3.0373	2.9137	2.8550	2.7982	2.6901	2.5887	2.4043	2.2410	2.0957
5	3.7908	3.6048	3.4331	3.3522	3.2743	3.1272	2.9906	2.7454	2.5320	2.3452
6	4.3553	4.1114	3.8887	3.7845	3.6847	3.4976	3.3255	3.0205	2.7594	2.5342
7	4.8684	4.5638	4.2883	4.1604	4.0386	3.8115	3.6046	3.2423	2.9370	2.6775
8	5.3349	4.9676	4.6389	4.4873	4.3436	4.0776	3.8372	3.4212	3.0758	2.7860
9	5.7590	5.3282	4.9464	4.7716	4.6065	4.3030	4.0310	3.5655	3.1842	2.8681
10	6.1446	5.6502	5.2161	5.0188	4.8332	4.4941	4.1925	3.6819	3.2689	2.9304
11	6.4951	5.9377	5.4527	5.2337	5.0286	4.6560	4.3271	3.7757	3.3351	2.9776
12	6.8137	6.1944	5.6603	5.4206	5.1971	4.7932	4.4392	3.8514	3.3868	3.0133
13	7.1034	6.4235	5.8424	5.5831	5.3423	4.9095	4.5327	3.9124	3.4272	3.0404
14	7.3667	6.6282	6.0021	5.7245	5.4675	5.0081	4.6106	3.9616	3.4587	3.0609
15	7.6061	6.8109	6.1422	5.8474	5.5755	5.0916	4.6755	4.0013	3.4834	3.0764
16	7.8237	6.9740	6.2651	5.9542	5.6685	5.1624	4.7296	4.0333	3.5026	3.0882
17	8.0216	7.1196	6.3729	6.0472	5.7487	5.2223	4.7746	4.0591	3.5177	3.0971
18	8.2014	7.2497	6.4674	6.1280	5.8178	5.2732	4.8122	4.0799	3.5294	3.1039
19	8.3649	7.3658	6.5504	6.1982	5.8775	5.3162	4.8435	4.0967	3.5386	3.1090
20	8.5136	7.4694	6.6231	6.2593	5.9288	5.3527	4.8696	4.1103	3.5458	3.1129
21	8.6487	7.5620	6.6870	6.3125	5.9731	5.3837	4.8913	4.1212	3.5514	3.1158
22	8.7715	7.6446	6.7429	6.3587	6.0113	5.4099	4.9094	4.1300	3.5558	3.1180
23	8.8832	7.7184	6.7921	6.3988	6.0442	5.4321	4.9245	4.1371	3.5592	3.1197
24	8.9847	7.7843	6.8351	6.4338	6.0726	5.4509	4.9371	4.1428	3.5619	3.1210
25	9.0770	7.8431	6.8729	6.4641	6.0971	5.4669	4.9476	4.1474	3.5640	3.1220
26	9.1609	7.8957	6.9061	6.4906	6.1182	5.4804	4.9563	4.1511	3.5656	3.1227
27	9.2372	7.9426	6.9352	6.5135	6.1364	5.4919	4.9636	4.1542	3.5669	3.1233
28	9.3066	7.9844	6.9607	6.5335	6.1520	5.5016	4.9697	4.1566	3.5679	3.1237
29	9.3696	8.0218	6.9830	6.5509	6.1656	5.5098	4.9747	4.1585	3.5687	3.1240
30	9.4269	8.0552	7.0027	6.5660	6.1772	5.5168	4.9789	4.1601	3.5693	3.1242
35	9.6442	8.1755	7.0700	6.6166	6.2153	5.5386	4.9915	4.1644	3.5708	3.1248
40	9.7791	8.2438	7.1050	6.6418	6.2335	5.5482	4.9966	4.1659	3.5712	3.1250
45	9.8628	8.2825	7.1232	6.6543	6.2421	5.5523	4.9986	4.1664	3.5714	3.1250
50	9.9148	8.3045	7.1327	6.6605	6.2463	5.5541	4.9995	4.1666	3.5714	3.1250
55	9.9471	8.3170	7.1376	6.6636	6.2482	5.5549	4.9998	4.1666	3.5714	3.1250

Table A-3 *Future Value of $1 at the End of n Periods*

EQUATION:	FINANCIAL CALCULATOR KEYS:
$FVIF_{i,n} = (1 + i)^n$	n, i, 0, 1.0 → N, I, PV, PMT, FV (Table Value)

Period	1%	2%	3%	4%	5%	6%	7%	8%	9%	10%
1	1.0100	1.0200	1.0300	1.0400	1.0500	1.0600	1.0700	1.0800	1.0900	1.1000
2	1.0201	1.0404	1.0609	1.0816	1.1025	1.1236	1.1449	1.1664	1.1881	1.2100
3	1.0303	1.0612	1.0927	1.1249	1.1576	1.1910	1.2250	1.2597	1.2950	1.3310
4	1.0406	1.0824	1.1255	1.1699	1.2155	1.2625	1.3108	1.3605	1.4116	1.4641
5	1.0510	1.1041	1.1593	1.2167	1.2763	1.3382	1.4026	1.4693	1.5386	1.6105
6	1.0615	1.1262	1.1941	1.2653	1.3401	1.4185	1.5007	1.5869	1.6771	1.7716
7	1.0721	1.1487	1.2299	1.3159	1.4071	1.5036	1.6058	1.7138	1.8280	1.9487
8	1.0829	1.1717	1.2668	1.3686	1.4775	1.5938	1.7182	1.8509	1.9926	2.1436
9	1.0937	1.1951	1.3048	1.4233	1.5513	1.6895	1.8385	1.9990	2.1719	2.3579
10	1.1046	1.2190	1.3439	1.4802	1.6289	1.7908	1.9672	2.1589	2.3674	2.5937
11	1.1157	1.2434	1.3842	1.5395	1.7103	1.8983	2.1049	2.3316	2.5804	2.8531
12	1.1268	1.2682	1.4258	1.6010	1.7959	2.0122	2.2522	2.5182	2.8127	3.1384
13	1.1381	1.2936	1.4685	1.6651	1.8856	2.1329	2.4098	2.7196	3.0658	3.4523
14	1.1495	1.3195	1.5126	1.7317	1.9799	2.2609	2.5785	2.9372	3.3417	3.7975
15	1.1610	1.3459	1.5580	1.8009	2.0789	2.3966	2.7590	3.1722	3.6425	4.1772
16	1.1726	1.3728	1.6047	1.8730	2.1829	2.5404	2.9522	3.4259	3.9703	4.5950
17	1.1843	1.4002	1.6528	1.9479	2.2920	2.6928	3.1588	3.7000	4.3276	5.0545
18	1.1961	1.4282	1.7024	2.0258	2.4066	2.8543	3.3799	3.9960	4.7171	5.5599
19	1.2081	1.4568	1.7535	2.1068	2.5270	3.0256	3.6165	4.3157	5.1417	6.1159
20	1.2202	1.4859	1.8061	2.1911	2.6533	3.2071	3.8697	4.6610	5.6044	6.7275
21	1.2324	1.5157	1.8603	2.2788	2.7860	3.3996	4.1406	5.0338	6.1088	7.4002
22	1.2447	1.5460	1.9161	2.3699	2.9253	3.6035	4.4304	5.4365	6.6586	8.1403
23	1.2572	1.5769	1.9736	2.4647	3.0715	3.8197	4.7405	5.8715	7.2579	8.9543
24	1.2697	1.6084	2.0328	2.5633	3.2251	4.0489	5.0724	6.3412	7.9111	9.8497
25	1.2824	1.6406	2.0938	2.6658	3.3864	4.2919	5.4274	6.8485	8.6231	10.835
26	1.2953	1.6734	2.1566	2.7725	3.5557	4.5494	5.8074	7.3964	9.3992	11.918
27	1.3082	1.7069	2.2213	2.8834	3.7335	4.8223	6.2139	7.9881	10.245	13.110
28	1.3213	1.7410	2.2879	2.9987	3.9201	5.1117	6.6488	8.6271	11.167	14.421
29	1.3345	1.7758	2.3566	3.1187	4.1161	5.4184	7.1143	9.3173	12.172	15.863
30	1.3478	1.8114	2.4273	3.2434	4.3219	5.7435	7.6123	10.063	13.268	17.449
40	1.4889	2.2080	3.2620	4.8010	7.0400	10.286	14.974	21.725	31.409	45.259
50	1.6446	2.6916	4.3839	7.1067	11.467	18.420	29.457	46.902	74.358	117.39
60	1.8167	3.2810	5.8916	10.520	18.679	32.988	57.946	101.26	176.03	304.48

Table A-3 *Continued*

Period	12%	14%	15%	16%	18%	20%	24%	28%	32%	36%
1	1.1200	1.1400	1.1500	1.1600	1.1800	1.2000	1.2400	1.2800	1.3200	1.3600
2	1.2544	1.2996	1.3225	1.3456	1.3924	1.4400	1.5376	1.6384	1.7424	1.8496
3	1.4049	1.4815	1.5209	1.5609	1.6430	1.7280	1.9066	2.0972	2.3000	2.5155
4	1.5735	1.6890	1.7490	1.8106	1.9388	2.0736	2.3642	2.6844	3.0360	3.4210
5	1.7623	1.9254	2.0114	2.1003	2.2878	2.4883	2.9316	3.4360	4.0075	4.6526
6	1.9738	2.1950	2.3131	2.4364	2.6996	2.9860	3.6352	4.3980	5.2899	6.3275
7	2.2107	2.5023	2.6600	2.8262	3.1855	3.5832	4.5077	5.6295	6.9826	8.6054
8	2.4760	2.8526	3.0590	3.2784	3.7589	4.2998	5.5895	7.2058	9.2170	11.703
9	2.7731	3.2519	3.5179	3.8030	4.4355	5.1598	6.9310	9.2234	12.166	15.917
10	3.1058	3.7072	4.0456	4.4114	5.2338	6.1917	8.5944	11.806	16.060	21.647
11	3.4785	4.2262	4.6524	5.1173	6.1759	7.4301	10.657	15.112	21.199	29.439
12	3.8960	4.8179	5.3503	5.9360	7.2876	8.9161	13.215	19.343	27.983	40.037
13	4.3635	5.4924	6.1528	6.8858	8.5994	10.699	16.386	24.759	36.937	54.451
14	4.8871	6.2613	7.0757	7.9875	10.147	12.839	20.319	31.691	48.757	74.053
15	5.4736	7.1379	8.1371	9.2655	11.974	15.407	25.196	40.565	64.359	100.71
16	6.1304	8.1372	9.3576	10.748	14.129	18.488	31.243	51.923	84.954	136.97
17	6.8660	9.2765	10.761	12.468	16.672	22.186	38.741	66.461	112.14	186.28
18	7.6900	10.575	12.375	14.463	19.673	26.623	48.039	85.071	148.02	253.34
19	8.6128	12.056	14.232	16.777	23.214	31.948	59.568	108.89	195.39	344.54
20	9.6463	13.743	16.367	19.461	27.393	38.338	73.864	139.38	257.92	468.57
21	10.804	15.668	18.822	22.574	32.324	46.005	91.592	178.41	340.45	637.26
22	12.100	17.861	21.645	26.186	38.142	55.206	113.57	228.36	449.39	866.67
23	13.552	20.362	24.891	30.376	45.008	66.247	140.83	292.30	593.20	1178.7
24	15.179	23.212	28.625	35.236	53.109	79.497	174.63	374.14	783.02	1603.0
25	17.000	26.462	32.919	40.874	62.669	95.396	216.54	478.90	1033.6	2180.1
26	19.040	30.167	37.857	47.414	73.949	114.48	268.51	613.00	1364.3	2964.9
27	21.325	34.390	43.535	55.000	87.260	137.37	332.95	784.64	1800.9	4032.3
28	23.884	39.204	50.066	63.800	102.97	164.84	412.86	1004.3	2377.2	5483.9
29	26.750	44.693	57.575	74.009	121.50	197.81	511.95	1285.6	3137.9	7458.1
30	29.960	50.950	66.212	85.850	143.37	237.38	634.82	1645.5	4142.1	10143.
40	93.051	188.88	267.86	378.72	750.38	1469.8	5455.9	19427.	66521.	*
50	289.00	700.23	1083.7	1670.7	3927.4	9100.4	46890.	*	*	*
60	897.60	2595.9	4384.0	7370.2	20555.	56348.	*	*	*	*

*FVIF > 99,999.

Table A-4 *Future Value of an Annuity of $1 per Period for n Periods*

EQUATION:

$$FVIFA_{i,n} = \sum_{t=1}^{n} (1+i)^{n-t} = \frac{(1+i)^n - 1}{i}$$

FINANCIAL CALCULATOR KEYS:

n	i	1.0	0	
N	I	PV	PMT	FV

Table Value

Number of Periods	1%	2%	3%	4%	5%	6%	7%	8%	9%	10%
1	1.0000	1.0000	1.0000	1.0000	1.0000	1.0000	1.0000	1.0000	1.0000	1.0000
2	2.0100	2.0200	2.0300	2.0400	2.0500	2.0600	2.0700	2.0800	2.0900	2.1000
3	3.0301	3.0604	3.0909	3.1216	3.1525	3.1836	3.2149	3.2464	3.2781	3.3100
4	4.0604	4.1216	4.1836	4.2465	4.3101	4.3746	4.4399	4.5061	4.5731	4.6410
5	5.1010	5.2040	5.3091	5.4163	5.5256	5.6371	5.7507	5.8666	5.9847	6.1051
6	6.1520	6.3081	6.4684	6.6330	6.8019	6.9753	7.1533	7.3359	7.5233	7.7156
7	7.2135	7.4343	7.6625	7.8983	8.1420	8.3938	8.6540	8.9228	9.2004	9.4872
8	8.2857	8.5830	8.8923	9.2142	9.5491	9.8975	10.260	10.637	11.028	11.436
9	9.3685	9.7546	10.159	10.583	11.027	11.491	11.978	12.488	13.021	13.579
10	10.462	10.950	11.464	12.006	12.578	13.181	13.816	14.487	15.193	15.937
11	11.567	12.169	12.808	13.486	14.207	14.972	15.784	16.645	17.560	18.531
12	12.683	13.412	14.192	15.026	15.917	16.870	17.888	18.977	20.141	21.384
13	13.809	14.680	15.618	16.627	17.713	18.882	20.141	21.495	22.953	24.523
14	14.947	15.974	17.086	18.292	19.599	21.015	22.550	24.215	26.019	27.975
15	16.097	17.293	18.599	20.024	21.579	23.276	25.129	27.152	29.361	31.772
16	17.258	18.639	20.157	21.825	23.657	25.673	27.888	30.324	33.003	35.950
17	18.430	20.012	21.762	23.698	25.840	28.213	30.840	33.750	36.974	40.545
18	19.615	21.412	23.414	25.645	28.132	30.906	33.999	37.450	41.301	45.599
19	20.811	22.841	25.117	27.671	30.539	33.760	37.379	41.446	46.018	51.159
20	22.019	24.297	26.870	29.778	33.066	36.786	40.995	45.762	51.160	57.275
21	23.239	25.783	28.676	31.969	35.719	39.993	44.865	50.423	56.765	64.002
22	24.472	27.299	30.537	34.248	38.505	43.392	49.006	55.457	62.873	71.403
23	25.716	28.845	32.453	36.618	41.430	46.996	53.436	60.893	69.532	79.543
24	26.973	30.422	34.426	39.083	44.502	50.816	58.177	66.765	76.790	88.497
25	28.243	32.030	36.459	41.646	47.727	54.865	63.249	73.106	84.701	98.347
26	29.526	33.671	38.553	44.312	51.113	59.156	68.676	79.954	93.324	109.18
27	30.821	35.344	40.710	47.084	54.669	63.706	74.484	87.351	102.72	121.10
28	32.129	37.051	42.931	49.968	58.403	68.528	80.698	95.339	112.97	134.21
29	33.450	38.792	45.219	52.966	62.323	73.640	87.347	103.97	124.14	148.63
30	34.785	40.568	47.575	56.085	66.439	79.058	94.461	113.28	136.31	164.49
40	48.886	60.402	75.401	95.026	120.80	154.76	199.64	259.06	337.88	442.59
50	64.463	84.579	112.80	152.67	209.35	290.34	406.53	573.77	815.08	1163.9
60	81.670	114.05	163.05	237.99	353.58	533.13	813.52	1253.2	1944.8	3034.8

Table A-4 Continued

Number of Periods	12%	14%	15%	16%	18%	20%	24%	28%	32%	36%
1	1.0000	1.0000	1.0000	1.0000	1.0000	1.0000	1.0000	1.0000	1.0000	1.0000
2	2.1200	2.1400	2.1500	2.1600	2.1800	2.2000	2.2400	2.2800	2.3200	2.3600
3	3.3744	3.4396	3.4725	3.5056	3.5724	3.6400	3.7776	3.9184	4.0624	4.2096
4	4.7793	4.9211	4.9934	5.0665	5.2154	5.3680	5.6842	6.0156	6.3624	6.7251
5	6.3528	6.6101	6.7424	6.8771	7.1542	7.4416	8.0484	8.6999	9.3983	10.146
6	8.1152	8.5355	8.7537	8.9775	9.4420	9.9299	10.980	12.136	13.406	14.799
7	10.089	10.730	11.067	11.414	12.142	12.916	14.615	16.534	18.696	21.126
8	12.300	13.233	13.727	14.240	15.327	16.499	19.123	22.163	25.678	29.732
9	14.776	16.085	16.786	17.519	19.086	20.799	24.712	29.369	34.895	41.435
10	17.549	19.337	20.304	21.321	23.521	25.959	31.643	38.593	47.062	57.352
11	20.655	23.045	24.349	25.733	28.755	32.150	40.238	50.398	63.122	78.998
12	24.133	27.271	29.002	30.850	34.931	39.581	50.895	65.510	84.320	108.44
13	28.029	32.089	34.352	36.786	42.219	48.497	64.110	84.853	112.30	148.47
14	32.393	37.581	40.505	43.672	50.818	59.196	80.496	109.61	149.24	202.93
15	37.280	43.842	47.580	51.660	60.965	72.035	100.82	141.30	198.00	276.98
16	42.753	50.980	55.717	60.925	72.939	87.442	126.01	181.87	262.36	377.69
17	48.884	59.118	65.075	71.673	87.068	105.93	157.25	233.79	347.31	514.66
18	55.750	68.394	75.836	84.141	103.74	128.12	195.99	300.25	459.45	700.94
19	63.440	78.969	88.212	98.603	123.41	154.74	244.03	385.32	607.47	954.28
20	72.052	91.025	102.44	115.38	146.63	186.69	303.60	494.21	802.86	1298.8
21	81.699	104.77	118.81	134.84	174.02	225.03	377.46	633.59	1060.8	1767.4
22	92.503	120.44	137.63	157.41	206.34	271.03	469.06	812.00	1401.2	2404.7
23	104.60	138.30	159.28	183.60	244.49	326.24	582.63	1040.4	1850.6	3271.3
24	118.16	158.66	184.17	213.98	289.49	392.48	723.46	1332.7	2443.8	4450.0
25	133.33	181.87	212.79	249.21	342.60	471.98	898.09	1706.8	3226.8	6053.0
26	150.33	208.33	245.71	290.09	405.27	567.38	1114.6	2185.7	4260.4	8233.1
27	169.37	238.50	283.57	337.50	479.22	681.85	1383.1	2798.7	5624.8	11198.0
28	190.70	272.89	327.10	392.50	566.48	819.22	1716.1	3583.3	7425.7	15230.3
29	214.58	312.09	377.17	456.30	669.45	984.07	2129.0	4587.7	9802.9	20714.2
30	241.33	356.79	434.75	530.31	790.95	1181.9	2640.9	5873.2	12941.	28172.3
40	767.09	1342.0	1779.1	2360.8	4163.2	7343.9	22729.	69377.	*	*
50	2400.0	4994.5	7217.7	10436.	21813.	45497.	*	*	*	*
60	7471.6	18535.	29220.	46058.	*	*	*	*	*	*

*FVIFA > 99,999.

Module 700 Glossary

A

Absolute form of purchasing power parity Also called the "law of one price," this theory suggests that prices of two products of different countries should be equal when measured by a common currency.

Account analysis statement Monthly listing that banks provide corporate customers indicating the services used and the charges assessed the company. The statement provides in-depth balance information, a 12-month balance history, a detailed listing and pricing of services used, and the degree to which the company's actual balances offset fees charged for the services used.

Accounting profit A firm's net income as reported on its income statement.

Account parameters and records Credit customer identifiers such as name, address, and the customer's bank transit routing number. These items are included in the customer's credit file.

Account reconciliation A disbursement-related service in which the bank develops a detailed report of checks paid as well as miscellaneous debits and stopped payments. In a full account reconciliation, the company also provides the bank with a record of checks drawn, and the bank informs the company of which checks remain outstanding.

Accounts payable A liability that is generated by purchasing a good or service on credit.

Accounts receivable financing Indirect financing provided by an exporter for an importer by exporting goods and allowing for payment to be made at a later date.

Accounts receivable turnover Computed by dividing days' sales outstanding into the number of days in the calculation period, which is usually 365. Indicates how many times per year the seller's investment in accounts receivable "turns over" into sales, which is an efficiency measure giving the same signal as days sales outstanding.

Accrual A liability account that results from expenses incurred during the operating process that are not yet paid.

Accruals Continually recurring short-term liabilities; liabilities such as wages and taxes that increase spontaneously with operations.

ACH credit Payment order transmitted through the automated clearing house system and originated by the payor. The routing bank (originating institution) in this case is the payor's disbursement bank.

ACH debit Payment order for payment through the automated clearing house system and originated by the payee, based on the prior authorization by the payor. This order is routed through the payee's bank (originating financial depository institution, or OFDI). Another name for an electronic depository transfer.

Active investment strategy An approach to investing which involves relatively more trading and active monitoring of the portfolio, and many times is motivated by a philosophy that the investor can "beat the market." Active strategy managers would rarely buy a security with the intention of holding it to maturity. For example, when an analyst forecasts a change in interest rates, trading strategies can be devised to enhance investment profits.

Actual (realized) rate of return, $\bar{k}_s$ The rate of return on a common stock actually received by stockholders. $\bar{k}_s$ may be greater than or less than $\hat{k}_s$ and/or k_s.

Additional funds needed (AFN) Funds that a firm must raise externally through borrowing or by selling new stock.

Additional paid-in capital Funds received in excess of par value when a firm issues new stock.

Add-on interest Interest that is calculated and then added to the amount borrowed to obtain the total dollar amount to be paid back in equal installments.

Adjustable-rate preferred stock (ARPS) Preferred stock on which the dividend is reset quarterly.

Adjusted r^2 A measure for a statistical model's goodness of fit which compensates for the upward bias in goodness-of-fit resulting from the inclusion of additional predictor variables.

Advised line A standard lending service used abroad, which is very similar to credit lines in the United States. The advised line involves unsecured lending of up to one year maturity, available on short notice to the borrower.

Advising bank Corresponding bank in the beneficiary's country to which the issuing bank sends the letter of credit.

Advisory services Include all specialized and general financial management consulting banks might provide to corporations.

After-tax cost of debt, k_{dT} The relevant cost of new debt, taking into account the tax deductibility of interest; used to calculate the WACC.

Agencies Securities issued by governmental agencies and several private financing institutions that have governmental backing.

Agency problem A potential conflict of interest between (1) the principals (outside shareholders) and the agent (manager) or (2) stockholders and creditors (debtholders).

Aggressive approach A policy where all of the fixed assets of a firm are financed with long-term capital, but *some* of the firm's permanent current assets are financed with short-term nonspontaneous sources of funds.

Aggressive strategy A strategy that minimizes the amount of long-term financing used. This strategy generally results in a lower current ratio and higher but more volatile profitability during periods of normal yield curves.

Aging schedule A report showing how long accounts receivable have been outstanding; the report divides receivables into specified periods, which provides information about the proportion of receivables that is current and the proportion that is past due for given lengths of time. Shows a percent breakdown of present receivables, with the categories shown typically as follows: current, 0–30 days past due, 31–60 days past due, and over 90 days past due.

Airway bill Receipt for a shipment by air, which includes freight charges and title to the merchandise.

All-in-rate Rate used in charging customers for accepting banker's acceptances, consisting of the discount interest rate plus the commission.

American depository receipts (ADRs) Certificates representing ownership in stocks of foreign companies, which are held in trust by a bank located in the country the stock is traded. ADRs are traded on stock exchanges in the United States.

Amortization schedule A schedule showing precisely how a loan will be repaid. It gives the required payment on each payment date and a breakdown of the payment, showing how much is interest and how much is repayment of principal.

Amortized loan A loan that is repaid in equal payments over its life.

Annual compounding The arithmetic process of determining the final value of a cash flow or series of cash flows when interest is added once a year.

Annual percentage rate (APR) The rate reported to borrowers—it is the periodic rate times the number of periods in the year; thus, interest compounding is not considered. The periodic rate × the number of periods per year.

Annual report A report issued annually by a corporation to its stockholders. It contains basic financial statements, as well as management's opinion of the past year's operations, and the firm's future prospects.

Annuity A series of payments of an equal amount at fixed intervals for a specified number of periods.

Annuity due An annuity whose payments occur at the beginning of each period.

ANSI The American National Standards Institute.

Anticipation This transfer rule initiates a cash transfer before the related deposit is made.

Appreciation Increase in the value of a currency.

Arbitrage Action to capitalize on a discrepancy in quoted prices; in many cases, there is no investment of funds tied up for any length of time.

Asian dollar market Market in Asia in which banks collect deposits and make loans denominated in U.S. dollars.

Ask price Price at which a trader of foreign exchange (typically a bank) is willing to sell a particular currency.

Asset-based lending A form of collateralized lending which has a claim on an asset or group of assets, ordinarily receivables or inventory, which could be easily sold if the borrower defaults on the loan.

Asset-based loans A source of financing obtained from a bank or commercial finance company secured by accounts receivable or inventory.

Asset management ratios A set of ratios that measures how effectively a firm is managing its assets.

Asset securitization Has become prevalent in the United States because of the need for banks to increase their capital-to-assets ratio.

Asset swap A swap created to hedge cash flows related to assets or investments.

Assignment of proceeds Arrangement which allows the original beneficiary of a letter of credit to pledge or assign proceeds to an end supplier.

Asymmetric information The situation in which managers have different (better) information about their firm's prospects than do outside investors.

Auction preferred stock (APS) Preferred stock on which the dividend is reset every 49 days through an auction bidding process.

Automated clearing house (ACH) A quick and relatively inexpensive means of electronically processing large numbers of routine transactions. This system is comprised of a loosely tied network of associations spread across the country. The electronic equivalent of the paper check clearing system.

Availability float The delay from the time a check is deposited and the time when funds are available to be spent. This time lag may not always coincide with the amount of time it takes the check to actually clear, but generally the two are closely linked. Delays in collecting checks caused by delays in the check clearing process after the check has been deposited.

Availability schedule Listing of how long after deposit checks will become "good funds" for spending by the depositor. Prior to recording available funds, the bank will credit the depositor's ledger balance, but the portion of the total deposit available as "good funds" ready to be spent varies according to the bank's schedule.

Average collection period How long the typical customer is taking to pay its bills. Alternately, how long, on average, the seller is taking to collect its receivables. It is computed by dividing accounts receivable by daily sales. Also known as days sales outstanding.

Average tax rate Taxes paid divided by taxable income.

Avoidance The pricing of invoices in the seller's currency.

B

Back value date The date that cleared checks are assigned and may cause funds to be drawn from an account before the check actually arrives at the drawee bank.

Balance fractions, inventory The percent of an inventory purchase order that remains as inventory over succeeding months.

Balance fractions, payables The dollar amount remaining to be paid in succeeding months as a percent of the original accounts payable balance.

Balance of payments Statement of inflow and outflow payments for a particular country.

Balance of trade Difference between the value of merchandise exports and merchandise imports.

Balance on goods and services Balance of trade, plus the net amount of payments of interest and dividends to foreign investors and from investment, as well as receipts and payments resulting from international tourism and other transactions.

Balance reporting services Means by which the treasurer may inquire by phone or PC hook-up about the balance positions in many different accounts and about transactions affecting the accounts.

Balance sheet A statement of the firm's financial position at a specific point in time.

Bank deposit notes Short-term debt securities issued by banks, which range from 9 months to 30 years in maturity, and have an active secondary market.

Banker's acceptance (BA) A corporate time draft drawn on the buyer, whose bank agrees to pay ("accepts") the amount if the buyer does not. Related to this, a short-term acceptance facility allows the selling firm to initiate drafts (called bills of exchange) against the buyer's bank instead of against the buyer, which can be discounted at the bank. A time draft drawn against a deposit in a commercial bank but with payment at maturity guaranteed by the bank.

Bank for International Settlements (BIS) Institution that facilitates cooperation among countries involved in international transactions and provides assistance to countries experiencing international payment problems.

Bank Holding Company Act of 1956 Prohibited further acquisitions by bank holding companies unless specifically allowed by state law in the state of the proposed acquisition.

Banking Act, 1991 Prohibited the FDIC from voluntarily covering a bank's uninsured depositors except when the Department of Treasury, the Federal Reserve Board, the FDIC, and the President all agree that the financial system would be endangered by the bank's closure.

Bank Letter of Credit Policy Policy that enables banks to confirm letters of credit by foreign banks supporting the purchase of U.S. exports.

Bank notes Technically not deposits, these bank debt obligations thereby avoid FDIC insurance premiums which also forfeits deposit insurance coverage.

Bank relationship policy Document that establishes the company's objectives, compensations, and review process for the banks with which it has a relationship.

Bank selection process Involves assembling a system of banks to serve all of a company's cash management and related needs.

Barter Exchange of goods between two parties without the use of any currency as a medium of exchange.

Base case An analysis in which all of the input variables are set at their most likely values.

Basel Accord Agreement among country representatives in 1988 to establish standardized risk-based capital requirements for banks across countries.

Best-case scenario An analysis in which all of the input variables are set at their best reasonably forecasted values.

Best efforts arrangement Agreement for the sale of securities in which the investment bank handling the transaction gives no guarantee that the securities will be sold.

Beta coefficient, β A measure of the extent to which the returns on a given stock move with the stock market.

Beta (market) risk That part of a project's risk that cannot be eliminated by diversification; it is measured by the project's beta coefficient.

Biased expectations hypothesis A theory of the term structure of interest rates in which market expectations are modified by some degree of liquidity preference.

Bid/ask spread Difference between the price at which a bank is willing to buy a currency and the price at which it will sell that currency.

Bid price Price that a trader of foreign exchange (typically a bank) is willing to pay for a particular currency.

Bilateral and multilateral netting systems Are centralized bookkeeping entries made to eliminate ("net out") offsetting amounts owed by divisions or subsidiaries within a company.

Bilateral netting system Netting method used for transactions between two units.

Bill of exchange (draft) Promise drawn by one party (usually an exporter) to pay a specified amount to another party at a specified future date, or upon presentation of the draft.

Bill of lading Document serving as a receipt for shipment and a summary of freight charges and conveying title to the merchandise.

Blue sky laws State laws that prevent the sale of securities that have little or no asset backing.

Board of Governors The main Federal Reserve System's policy-making body, which is comprised of seven members. Governors are appointed by the President and confirmed by the U.S. Senate. The Board of Governors supervises the district Federal Reserve banks, limiting to some extent the powers and privileges of their stockholders.

Bond A long-term debt instrument.

Bond anticipation notes Short-term debt instrument which provides working capital financing for states and localities as they await anticipated revenues from upcoming bond issuance.

Book value per share The accounting value of a share of common stock; equal to common equity (common stock plus additional paid-in capital plus retained earnings) divided by the number of shares outstanding.

Box-Jenkins model A type of time-series forecasting technique. Named after two pioneers in the field of time series modeling, this approach lets the data specify the best model.

Breadth Refers to the number and size of parties that are potential buyers of the instruments in a market.

Break point (BP) The dollar value of new capital that can be raised before an increase in the firm's weighted average cost of capital occurs.

Bretton Woods Agreement An agreement signed by the major trading countries following World War II which returned the world economy to a type of gold standard. The U.S. dollar was pegged to the dollar at $35 per ounce. Currencies of all other countries were then fixed in price to the dollar and the countries agreed to maintain the established exchange rate within 1 percent.

Brokers Middlemen which do not inventory the securities they arrange transactions for.

Business risk The possibility that a company will not be able to meet ongoing operating expenditures. The risk associated with projections of a firm's future returns on assets (ROA) or returns on equity (ROE) if the firm uses no debt.

Buy-and-hold strategy An approach to investing that involves holding until maturity securities purchased. Quite often, this is part of a "maturity matching" approach to investing that prescribes investing in a security that will mature at the end of the investment horizon.

Buy hedge A hedge created by purchasing a futures contract.

Bylaws A set of rules drawn up by the founders of the corporation that indicate how the company is to be governed; includes procedures for electing directors, whether the common stock has a preemptive right, and how to change the bylaws when necessary.

C

Call See *currency call option*.

Call option A contract that allows the owner to purchase the underlying asset at a specific price over a specific span of time. An option to buy, or "call," a share of stock at a certain price within a specified period.

Call option on real assets Project that contains an option of pursuing an additional venture.

Call premium The amount in excess of par value that a company must pay when it calls a security.

Call provision A provision in a bond contract that gives the issuer the right to redeem ("recall") the bonds under specified terms prior to the normal maturity date.

Capital account Account reflecting changes in country ownership of long-term and short-term financial assets.

Capital asset pricing model (CAPM) A model used to determine the required return on an asset, which is based on the proposition that any asset's return should be equal to the risk-free rate of return plus a risk premium that reflects the asset's nondiversifiable risk.

Capital budgeting The process of planning and evaluating expenditures on assets whose cash flows are expected to extend beyond one year.

Capital component One of the types of capital used by firms to raise money.

Capital gain (loss) The profit (loss) from the sale of a capital asset for more (less) than its purchase price.

Capital gains yield The change in price (capital gain) during a given year divided by the price at the beginning of the year.

Capital markets The financial markets for stocks and long-term debt (generally longer than one year).

Capital rationing A situation in which a constraint is placed on the total size of the firm's capital investment.

Capital structure The combination of debt and equity used to finance a firm.

Captive finance companies A financing subsidiary of a corporation that facilitates arranging financing for customers of the firm's products.

Captive finance subsidiary Separate entity within a company that provides financing for parent company or its customers, and which is thought to provide a marketing advantage or debt capacity advantage.

Carryforwards Tax losses that are applied in a future year to offset income in the future year.

Cash and securities mix decision The proportional breakdown of cash and securities held by a company as part of its current asset holdings.

Cash application Crediting the account upon payment for a credit sale, this process frees up that amount of the credit limit for additional orders from this customer.

Cash budget Forecast showing cash receipts and disbursements on a monthly basis for a minimum horizon of one year, typically assembled before the beginning of a new fiscal year.

Cash collection system A management-designed system that converts checks to cash and considers mail float, processing float, and availability float.

Cash concentration The process of moving dollar balances from deposit banks to concentration banks.

Cash conversion cycle The length of time from the payment for the purchase of raw materials to manufacture a product until the collection of accounts receivable associated with the sale of the product.

Cash conversion period A liquidity measure that takes a going-concern approach. It measures the difference in time from when cash is received from credit customers and when cash is paid to suppliers. The length of time from when cash is paid out for purchases and when cash is received from collections on credit sales.

Cash cycle The time that elapses from the purchase of raw materials until cash is received from the sale of the final product.

Cash discount The percentage amount that can be subtracted from the invoice if the customer pays within a stated period of time.

Cash flow The actual cash, as opposed to accounting net income, that a firm receives or pays during some specified period.

Cash flow cycle The way in which actual net cash, as opposed to accounting net income, flows into or out of the firm during some specified period.

Cash flow from operations One of the most direct measures of liquidity found by subtracting operating cash disbursements from operating cash receipts.

Cash flow timeline An important tool used in time value of money analysis; it is a graphical representation used to show the timing of cash flows.

Cash inflows The cash benefits arising from sources of cash increases.

Cash items Deposited checks given immediate, provisional credit by the bank.

Cash letter The accompanying listing of checks that are bundled by the deposit bank for routing through the check clearing process.

Cash management Optimization of cash flows and investment of excess cash.

Cash outflows Cash being disbursed.

Causal distributions A set of outcomes characterized by situations where a predictor variable has changed from what was expected, causing the forecast variable to deviate from what was expected.

Causal techniques Forecasting methods linking the forecast values of an effect variable to one or more hypothesized causes.

Central exchange rate Exchange rate established between two European currencies through the European Monetary System arrangement; the exchange rate between the two currencies is allowed to move within bands around that central exchange rate.

Centralized cash flow management Policy that consolidates cash management decisions for all MNC units, usually at the parent's location.

Centralized disbursing An organizational structure that disburses corporate cash from a central area, allowing the corporate headquarters' staff to check each disbursement and possibly initiate each payment as well.

Centralized processing system A cash collection system where corporate headquarters receives all customer remittances.

Centralized transfer initiation The timing and amount of the transfer is centered either at the concentration bank or corporate headquarters.

Certificate of deposit (CD) An interest-bearing account that evidences (certifies) that a certain amount of money has been deposited at the bank for a prespecified period of time, and that will be redeemed with interest at the end of that time (maturity).

Check processing float Delays in collecting cash caused by delays between the time a check is received and when it is deposited in the banking system.

Check truncation Involves expediting clearing by scanning the data on the check's MICR line, and then processing only that data back to the payee's bank.

CHIPS Short for Clearing House Interbank Payment System, the institution which was established in 1970 to handle interbank transactions needed to settle international transactions. CHIPS is a private association of banks that operates through the New York Clearinghouse Association.

Classified stock Common stock that is given a special designation, such as Class A, Class B, and so forth, to meet special needs of the company.

Clearing agent Often a Federal Reserve bank, branch or RCPC, an entity that uses the information printed at the bottom of the check to process the check.

Clearing bank(s) When checks are deposited, the bank(s) used for processing those checks into the clearing system. Sometimes called deposit bank(s).

Clearing float Sometimes called "availability float," the delay in availability incurred after deposit. The length of this component of float is linked to the bank's availability schedule in connection with the location of the payor's bank.

Clearing house A central location where representatives of area banks meet, and each bank settles its balances with one institution (the clearing house) instead of with each bank individually.

Clientele effect The tendency of a firm to attract the type of investor who likes its dividend policy.

Closely held corporation A corporation that is owned by a few individuals who are typically associated with the firm's management.

Coefficient of determination Measure of the percentage variation in the dependent variable that can be explained by the independent variables when using regression analysis.

Coefficient of variation (CV) Standardized measure of the risk per unit of return; calculated as the standard deviation divided by the expected return.

Cofinancing agreements Arrangement in which the World Bank participates along with other agencies or lenders in providing funds to developing countries.

Coin and currency services Procedures provided by banks that include receiving of bulk cash deposits sent by armed courier, sorting of deposit items, same day verification of the total deposit if received by the bank's cutoff time, and supply of coins and currency for the company's cash payment needs.

Collected balance Sometimes called the *available balance*, this amount represents how much of a deposit balance is immediately spendable. It may be somewhat less than the ledger balance because of availability delays applied to the checks by the bank.

Collection bank The bank of deposit that encodes the dollar amount of the check in magnetic ink on the bottom right side of the check and then routes the check through the clearing process.

Collection float The sum of the delays in collecting cash from customers caused by mail, process, and availability delays.

Collection policy The procedures followed by a firm to collect its accounts receivables.

Collection procedures Detailed statements regarding when and how the company will carry out collection of past due accounts. These policies specify how long the company will wait past the due date to initiate collection efforts, the method(s) of contact with delinquent customers and whether and at what point accounts will be referred to an outside collection agency.

Commercial invoice Exporter's description of merchandise being sold to the buyer.

Commercial letter of credit A guarantee of payment by an importer, made by its bank, that becomes binding when the shipping and other documents related to the goods sold are presented to the bank.

Commercial paper An unsecured IOU issued mainly by financial companies such as banks, their parent holding companies, and consumer or commercial finance companies. A short-term promissory note issued by a corporation for a fixed maturity generally in the 30 day range but can be as much as 270 days. Unsecured, short-term promissory notes issued by large, financially sound firms to raise funds.

Commitment fee A fee charged on the *unused* balance of a revolving credit agreement to compensate the bank for guaranteeing that the funds will be available when needed by the borrower; the fee normally is about 1/4 percent of the unused balance.

Committed facility Lending arrangement in which the bank charges a fee to compensate it for agreeing to lend upon request for a period of five to seven years.

Committed line A line of credit where the firm pays a commitment fee that obligates the bank to provide funding for the credit line with a formal written agreement.

Common equity The sum of the firm's common stock, paid-in capital, and retained earnings, which equals the common stockholders' total investment in the firm stated at book value.

Common stockholders' equity (net worth) The capital supplied by common stockholders—capital stock, paid-in capital, retained earnings, and, occasionally, certain reserves.

Company processing center An administrative office or area within the corporation that processes payments received from customers.

Comparative advantage Theory suggesting that specialization by countries can increase worldwide production.

Comparative ratio analysis An analysis based on a comparison of a firm's ratios with those of other firms in the same industry.

Compensating balance (CB) A minimum checking account balance that a firm must maintain with a bank to borrow funds—generally 10 to 20 percent of the amount of loans outstanding.

Compensation Arrangement in which the delivery of goods to a party is compensated for by buying back a certain amount of the product from that same party.

Compensatory Financing Facility (CFF) Facility that attempts to reduce the impact of export instability on country economies.

Competitive bids Offers to buy securities at a given price or yield. In the Treasury auctions, these are mainly entered by financial institutions, including dealers.

Competitive Equality Banking Act of 1987 Allows existing nonbank banks to continue to operate, but prohibits the establishment of new nonbank banks.

Complete enumeration A lockbox model that analyzes all possible lockbox sites to determine the optimal combination that maximizes shareholder wealth.

Compounded interest Interest earned on interest.

Compounding The process of determining the value of a cash flow or series of cash flows some time in the future when compound interest is applied.

Comprehensive payables Is the outsourcing of part or all of the accounts payable and/or disbursement functions.

Concentration account Deposit account into which funds are pooled at the endpoint(s) of a company's collection system.

Concentration bank A bank that receives balance transfers from several deposit or gathering banks.

Concentration banking A technique used to move funds from many bank accounts to a more central cash pool in order to more effectively manage cash.

Concentration services Closely linked to collection services, these services mobilize and pool collected cash in order to increase interest income and reduce interest expense.

Congeneric merger A merger of firms in the same general industry, but for which no customer or supplier relationship exists.

Conglomerate merger A merger of companies in totally different industries.

Conservative approach A policy where all of the fixed assets, all of the permanent current assets, and some of the temporary current assets of a firm are financed with long-term capital.

Conservative strategy A strategy that uses a majority of long-term sources to fulfill its financing needs. This strategy results in a higher current ratio but a lower level but more stable level of profitability during periods of normal yield curves.

Consignment An arrangement whereby a retailer obtains an inventory item without obligation. If not sold, the inventory can be returned.

Consol A perpetual bond issued by the British government to consolidate past debts; in general, any perpetual bond.

Constant growth model Also called the Gordon Model, it is used to find the value of a stock that is expected to experience constant growth.

Constant payout ratio Payment of a constant *percentage* of earnings as dividends each year.

Contingency graph Graph showing the net profit to a speculator in currency options under various exchange rate scenarios.

Contingency plans Actions that can be taken if and when necessitated by deteriorating conditions.

Continuous compounding A situation in which interest is added continuously rather than at discrete points in time.

Continuously compounding When compounding is done every moment.

Continuous probability distribution The number of possible outcomes is unlimited or infinite.

Contracting cost motive Theoretical motive for trade credit extension in which the buyers' sales contracting costs are reduced in that they can inspect the quantity and quality of the goods prior to payment due to the delayed payment offered.

Controlled disbursement accounts (CDA) Checking accounts in which funds are not deposited until checks are presented for payment, usually on a daily basis.

Control limits Trigger points that signal a purchase or sale of securities, and are part of the decision-making apparatus in the Miller-Orr cash management model.

Conversion ratio, CR The number of shares of common stock that can be obtained by converting a convertible bond or a share of convertible preferred stock.

Convertible bond A bond that is exchangeable, at the option of the holder, for common stock of the issuing firm.

Convertible security A security, usually a bond or preferred stock, that is exchangeable at the option of the holder for the common stock of the issuing firm.

Corporate agency services Security-related services, some of which are related to short-term borrowing and investing, offered by financial institutions to publicly held corporations.

Corporate charter A document filed with the secretary of the state in which the firm is incorporated that provides information about the company, including its name, address, directors, and amount of capital stock.

Corporate (within-firm) risk Risk that does not take into consideration the effects of stockholders' diversification; it is measured by a project's effect on the firm's earnings variability.

Corporation A legal entity created by a state, separate and distinct from its owners and managers, having unlimited life, easy transferability of ownership, and limited liability.

Correlation coefficient, r A measure of the degree of relationship between two variables.

Costly trade credit Credit taken in excess of "free" trade credit, whose cost is equal to the discount lost.

Cost of new common equity, k_e The cost of external equity; based on the cost of retained earnings, but increased for flotation costs.

Cost of preferred stock, k_{ps} The rate of return investors require on the firm's preferred stock. k_{ps} is calculated as the preferred dividend, D_{ps}, divided by the net issuing price, NP.

Cost of retained earnings, k_s The rate of return required by stockholders on a firm's existing common stock.

Counterpurchase Exchange of goods between two parties under two distinct contracts expressed in monetary terms.

Countertrade Sale of goods to one country which is linked to the purchase or exchange of goods from that same country.

Country risk Characteristics of the host country, including political and financial conditions, that can affect the MNC's cash flows. The possibility of loss of assets due to political, economic, or regulatory instability in a nation in which business is being conducted.

Coupon-equivalent yield Interest return figure calculated based on a 365-day year instead of 360 days. For a discount security maturing within one year, it is also adjusted to account for the fact that the price paid is less than the face value, which increases the true yield.

Coupon interest rate The stated annual rate of interest paid on a bond.

Coupon payment The specified number of dollars of interest paid each period, generally each six months, on a bond.

Coupon security One which pays interest periodically prior to maturity.

Covered interest arbitrage Investment in a foreign money market security with a simultaneous forward sale of the currency denominating that security.

Credit administration The establishment of credit policy and planning, organizing, directing, and controlling all aspects of the credit function.

Credit decision process Sequence beginning with the marketing contact with potential customers and ending with the credit extension decision. Includes credit investigation, customer information contacts, written document preparation, credit file establishment, and financial analysis.

Credit extension The decision to sell on credit to a customer.

Credit-granting decision Determination of whether and how much credit to give customers, a process which involves four distinct steps: development of credit standards, getting necessary information about customers, application of credit standards, and setting credit limits.

Credit interchange bureaus Departments of local credit associations that provide information on the credit history of local businesses and individuals.

Credit limit Where credit is extended, the maximum dollar amount that cumulative credit purchases can reach for a given customer. Also known as the credit line.

Credit period The length of time for which credit is granted; after that time, the credit account is considered delinquent.

Credit policy A set of decisions that includes a firm's credit standards, credit terms, methods used to collect credit accounts, and credit monitoring procedures.

Credit reporting agencies Sources of business credit information, such as Dun & Bradstreet.

Credit scoring models Evaluation approach that weights variables depending on their helpfulness in discriminating between "good" and "bad" applicants, based on past payment histories. These models are developed with the assistance of computerized statistical techniques such as multiple discriminant analysis.

Credit standards Standards that indicate the minimum financial strength a customer must have to be granted credit.

Credit terms Specification of when invoiced amounts are due and whether a cash discount can be taken for earlier payment.

Cross-border factoring Factoring by a network of factors across borders. The exporter's factor can contact correspondent factors in other countries to handle the collections of accounts receivable.

Cross exchange rate Exchange rate between currency A and currency B, given the values of currencies A and B with respect to a third currency.

Cross hedge A hedge that uses a futures contract that has a different underlying instrument from the cash market instrument being hedged.

Cross-hedging Hedging an open position in one currency with a hedge on another currency that is highly correlated with the first currency. This occurs when for some reason the common hedging techniques cannot be applied to the first currency. A cross-hedge is not a perfect hedge, but can substantially reduce the exposure.

Crossover rate The discount rate at which the NPV profiles of two projects cross and, thus, at which the projects' NPVs are equal.

Cross-sectional analysis Analysis of relationships among a cross-section of firms, countries, or some other variable at a given point in time.

Cumulative dividends A protective feature on preferred stock that requires preferred dividends previously not paid to be paid before any common dividends can be paid.

Currency Board System for maintaining the value of the local currency with respect to some other specified currency.

Currency call option Contract that grants the right to purchase a specific currency at a specific price (exchange rate) within a specific period of time.

Currency cocktail bond Bond denominated in a mixture (or cocktail) of currencies.

Currency diversification Process of using more than one currency as an investing or financing strategy. Exposure to a diversified currency portfolio typically results in less exchange rate risk than if all of the exposure was in a single foreign currency.

Currency futures contract Contract specifying a standard volume of a particular currency to be exchanged on a specific settlement date.

Currency put option Contract granting the right to sell a particular currency at a specified price (exchange rate) within a specified period of time.

Currency swap Agreement to exchange one currency for another at a specified exchange rate and date. Banks commonly serve as intermediaries between two parties who wish to engage in a currency swap.

Current account Broad measure of a country's international trade in goods and services.

Current liquidity index A cash coverage ratio found by adding beginning of period balance of cash assets and the cash flow from operations during the period and then dividing this sum by the sum of beginning of period notes payable and current maturing debt.

Current maturity The length of time remaining until a security matures. When first issued a five-year Treasury note has an original maturity of five years; one year later it has a current maturity of four years.

Current ratio This ratio is calculated by dividing current assets by current liabilities. It indicates the extent to which current liabilities are covered by assets expected to be converted into cash in the near future.

Current yield The annual interest payment on a bond divided by its current market value.

Custody account Specialized account in which financial institution holds securities, automatically reinvests interest and other investment-related cash receipts, transfers funds per corporate instructions, monitors issuers actions such as calls and refundings, and provides a monthly statement on all account transactions.

Cutoff time Deposit deadline for receiving a given day's stated availability.

D

Daily NPV Is the difference between the present value of a project's daily inflows and the present value of its daily outflows.

Daily transfer rule The simplest and most common transfer rule that initiates a daily transfer from the deposit bank to the concentration bank in the amount of the daily deposit.

Daylight overdrafts Bookkeeping negative account balances which occur when a bank's Federal Reserve account book balance is negative during the day or it sends more funds via Fedwire than it receives, prior to final end-of-day settlements. Many of the overdrafts occur because of international funds transfers of government securities transactions.

Days of cost of goods sold invested in inventory An inventory activity measure which indicates the average number of days it takes to sell inventory.

Days inventory held The average number of days a firm holds inventory found by dividing average daily cost of goods sold into the balance sheet inventory account.

Days payables outstanding The average number of days the firm takes to pay for its purchases found by dividing average daily purchases into the balance sheet accounts payable balance.

Days purchases outstanding The average number of days a firm takes to pay its payables.

Days sales outstanding (DSO) Measure of how long a company is taking to collect receivables. Also known as average collection period. It is computed by taking the latest period's accounts receivables and dividing it by daily credit sales. Daily credit sales, in turn, are computed by taking the period's sales and dividing by the number of days in the period—365 when computing DSO over a yearly period. The average number of days credit customers take to pay for their purchases found by dividing average daily sales into the accounts receivable balance.

Dealers Market participants which typically "take a position" in the security instrument(s) they trade, meaning they hold an inventory of securities.

Debenture A long-term bond that is not secured by a mortgage on specific property.

Debit cards Similar to credit cards except the transaction amount is immediately (or within two business days) charged against the user's checking account balance. These cards allow consumers to pay grocery and other bills through an electronic charge to their bank accounts.

Debt ratio The ratio of total debt to total assets. It is a measure of the percentage of funds provided by creditors.

Decentralized disbursing Corporate arrangement which allows payments to be made by divisional offices or individual stores, usually from accounts held at nearby banks.

Decentralized processing system A collection system that has the company's various field offices or stores receive payments from the company's customers.

Decentralized transfer initiation The cash transfer decision initiated by the field office manager.

Decomposition method Analysis of collection experience which involves segregating the period-to-period changes in receivables into three effects: the collection effect, the sales effect, and the interaction effect.

Default risk The possibility that the issuer will not meet contractual obligations to pay interest or repay principal or will violate a covenant in a debt agreement.

Default risk premium (DRP) The difference between the interest rate on a U.S. Treasury bond and a corporate bond of equal maturity and marketability.

Defensive merger A merger designed to make a company less vulnerable to a takeover.

Degree of financial leverage (DFL) The percentage change in earnings available to common stockholders associated with a given percentage change in earnings before interest and taxes.

Degree of operating leverage (DOL) The percentage change in operating income (EBIT) associated with a given percentage change in sales.

Degree of total leverage (DTL) The percentage change in EPS that results from a given percentage change in sales; DTL shows the effects of both operating leverage and financial leverage.

Delphi technique Collection of independent opinions without group discussion by the assessors who provide the opinions; used for various types of assessments (such as country risk assessment).

Demand deposit account (DDA) Noninterest bearing checking accounts. This account is the foundation for all other cash management services the bank might offer to the corporate client.

Demand flow An inventory system similar to the just-in-time system, but more encompassing.

Denomination Refers to a security's dollar amount or face value.

Dependent variable Term used in regression analysis to represent the variable that is dependent on one or more other variables.

Depository Institution Deregulation and Monetary Control Act of 1980 Landmark legislation which enabled savings and loans, mutual savings banks, and credit unions to operate more like commercial banks. Also established reserve requirement ranges for various deposit accounts.

Depository transfer checks (DTC) Nonnegotiable, unsigned checks used by firms to move funds from one account to another. They are often used to move (concentrate) monies collected in many different locations into a pooled account in a "concentration bank," where the money can be invested as a single large amount.

Deposit reconciliation One type of account reconciliation, this service minimizes the number of depository accounts a company must have while offering the added advantage of convenience.

Deposit reporting service Information on account balances offered by a bank or third-party vendor, which enables the treasury staff to know when and where the company's operations have deposited money into bank accounts.

Depreciation Decrease in the value of a currency.

Depth A characteristic of a market in which a very large dollar amount of securities can be easily absorbed without large changes in the market price.

Detachable warrant A warrant that can be detached from a bond and traded independently of it.

Deterministic model Data input for deterministic models are single point estimates.

Direct deposit Service in which the employer's bank automatically deposits employees' wages and salaries. The bank sorts out the on-us checks for employees having checking accounts at that bank, and credits their accounts. Employees banking elsewhere are paid through the local clearing house or ACH-initiated transactions. Direct deposit of payroll is easily the most popular electronic payment application.

Direct foreign investment (DFI) Investment in real assets (such as land, buildings, or even existing plants) in foreign countries.

Direct format One possible format allowed for presenting the Statement of Cash Flows that computes cash inflows and cash outflows directly, showing the major components of operating cash receipts and operating cash disbursements.

Direct hedge A hedge using a futures contract that is of the same type as the cash market instrument being hedged.

Direct Loan Program Program in which Ex-Im Bank offers fixed-rate loans directly to the foreign buyer to purchase U.S. capital equipment and services.

Direct presenting Situation in which checks are sent to the drawee bank or its local clearinghouse via courier. Direct presenting is mainly used for large checks.

Direct quotations Exchange rate quotations representing the value measured by number of dollars per unit.

Disbursement float The delay between the time when the company writes the check and the time when its bank charges the checking account for the amount of the check.

Disbursement policy Whether an informal strategy or a formal written document, specifies which payment mechanism to utilize for a given disbursement, when to pay a given invoice, and the setup of guidelines regarding the disbursement system (including which bank(s) might be involved).

Disbursements and receipts method (scheduling) The net cash flow is determined by estimating the cash disbursements and the cash receipts expected to be generated each period.

Disbursement system A company's payment methods, disbursement banks, and disbursing locations.

Disbursing bank Bank used to pay from.

Discount As related to forward rates, represents the percentage amount by which the forward rate is less than the spot rate.

Discount basis When the selling price of a financial instrument is less than its face value or value at maturity.

Discount bond A bond that sells below its par value; occurs whenever the going rate of interest rises above the coupon rate.

Discounted cash flow (DCF) techniques Methods of evaluating investment proposals that employ time value of money concepts; two of these are the net present value and the internal rate of return.

Discounted payback The length of time it takes for a project's *discounted* cash flows to repay the cost of the investment.

Discounting The process of finding the present value of a cash flow or a series of cash flows; the reverse of compounding.

Discount interest loan A loan in which the interest, which is calculated on the amount borrowed, is paid at the beginning of the loan period; interest is paid in advance.

Discount rate In a capital project evaluation it is the opportunity cost of the use of funds, which is used to determine the present value of cash flows.

Discount rate (Fed) The rate charged depository institutions when they borrow reserves from the Fed in order to meet their reserve requirements or meet unusual loan demand.

Discount security One which does not pay regular interest payments, but compensates the investor for implied interest by returning at maturity a principal amount greater than the purchase price.

Discount yield The difference between the maturity cash flow and the purchase price on a discount (noninterest bearing) security, expressed as a percentage of the purchase price.

Discrete probability distribution The number of possible outcomes is limited or finite.

Distribution method A regression-based cash forecasting approach which spreads, or "distributes," a monthly total across the weeks or days within that month. This method has also been used to model payroll-related cash disbursements by relating cash outflows to how many business days have elapsed since payroll checks have been issued.

Dividend capture strategy Corporate investment strategy involving buying a common or preferred stock shortly before it pays its dividend, or buying a preferred stock having an adjustable dividend payment. Because intercorporate dividends have been largely excludable for income tax purposes (presently there is a 70% exclusion), corporate investors buy stocks with high dividend yields, hold them at least 49 days (until the record date for payment), and then sell.

Dividend irrelevance theory The theory that a firm's dividend policy has no effect on either its value or its cost of capital.

Dividend policy decision The decision as to how much of current earnings to pay out as dividends rather than to retain for reinvestment in the firm.

Dividend reinvestment plan (DRIP) A plan that enables a stockholder to automatically reinvest dividends received back into the stock of the paying firm.

Dividend relevance theory The value of a firm is affected by its dividend policy—the optimal dividend policy is the one that maximizes the firm's value.

Dividend roll An investment approach that involves buying stocks with high dividend yields, holding them at least 49 days to collect the dividend, and then selling the stocks.

Dividends Distributions made to stockholders from the firm's earnings, whether those earnings were generated in the current period or in previous periods.

Dividend yield The expected dividend divided by the current price of a share of stock.

Documentary collections Trade transactions handled on a draft basis.

Documents against acceptance Situation in which the buyer's bank does not release shipping documents to the buyer until the buyer has accepted (signed) the draft.

Documents against payment Shipping documents that are released to the buyer once the buyer has paid for the draft.

Dollar-day float A measure of delay that considers both the dollar amount and the time lag.

Dominant Securities which provide a higher expected return for a given amount of risk than other securities.

Double counting This can either occur when a bank counts the same balances as compensation for a loan and as compensation for cash management services, or if the company has written a depository check for which it has been granted availability at the concentration bank, but has not had its checking account debited.

Double-entry bookkeeping Accounting method in which each transaction is recorded as both a credit and a debit.

Draft A written order to make payment to a third party, where the entity ordered to pay the draft is usually a bank. Any party holding a credit balance for the person writing the draft may have a draft drawn on it.

Draft (bill of exchange) Unconditional promise drawn by one party (usually the exporter) instructing the buyer to pay the face amount of the draft upon presentation.

Drawee bank The bank on which a check or draft was written ("drawn").

Driving variable A key variable in most financial planning models to which most relationships are tied. Sales is generally such a variable in many financial planning models.

Dual balance The same dollar balance that is temporarily on deposit at two different banks.

Dummy variables Variables included in the regression equation when modeling seasonal or monthly effects. The number included is one less than the number of seasons. Each dummy variable that is included as an independent variable takes on a value of 1 only when the season it represents is the season for which the forecast is being made, and 0 at all other times.

Dumping Selling products overseas at unfairly low prices (a practice perceived to result from subsidies provided to the firm by its government).

DuPont chart A chart designed to show the relationships among return on investment, asset turnover, the profit margin, and leverage.

DuPont equation A formula that gives the rate of return on assets by multiplying the profit margin by the total assets turnover.

Duration A tool for evaluating the interest rate risk of interest-bearing notes and bonds. It is defined as the weighted average time until the investor receives an investment's discounted cash flows.

Dynamic hedging Strategy of hedging in those periods when existing currency positions are expected to be adversely affected, and remaining unhedged in other periods when currency positions are expected to be favorably affected.

E

Earnings credit rate (ECR) A rate that banks credit collected balances with as compensation for leaving the balances in the account.

Earnings per share (EPS) Net income divided by the number of shares of common stock outstanding.

Economic exposure Refers to the possibility that the long-term net present value of a firm's expected cash flows will change due to unexpected changes in exchange rates.

Economic order quantity The order quantity that minimizes the total cost of managing inventory.

Economies of scale Achievement of lower average cost per unit by means of increased production.

ECU The outgrowth of the European Monetary System is a new currency, referred to as the ECU, which represents a basket of currencies of the members of the EEC.

EEC The European Economic Community.

Effective annual rate (EAR) The annual rate earned or paid considering interest compounding during the year (that is, the annual rate that equates to a given periodic rate compounded for m periods during the year).

Effective interest rate The rate of interest that is equal to or greater than the stated interest rate because of out-of-pocket expenses and usable funds that are less than the face value of the loan.

Effective yield Yield or return to an MNC on a short-term investment after adjustment for the change in exchange rates over the period of concern.

Efficient frontier Set of points reflecting risk-return combinations achieved by particular portfolios (so-called efficient portfolios) of assets.

Efficient markets Where prices change freely and instantly in response to supply and demand, and are not significantly affected by poor information or tax code barriers.

Efficient markets hypothesis (EMH) The hypothesis that securities are typically in equilibrium—that they are fairly priced in the sense that the price reflects all publicly available information on each security.

Electronic business data interchange (EBDI) The electronic movement of information such as invoices between corporate trading partners.

Electronic check presentment Is an arrangement in which the image of the MICR line of a check is presented to the paying back, instead of presenting the physical check, shortening clearance float.

Electronic corporate trade payment An arrangement between two corporations (a buyer and a seller) and the banks of the two parties so that payment is effected without a paper check being issued.

Electronic data interchange (EDI) The electronic transmission of purchase-related data such as orders, shipping notices, invoices, credits and other adjustments, and payment notices.

Electronic depository transfer (EDT) Payment process in which a local or regional account is debited electronically and the amount sent through an automated clearing house to the concentration bank account. Also known as an ACH debit, is an electronic equivalent to the paper DTC. The electronic transaction provides quicker availability in the concentration account for the company.

Electronic funds transfer (EFT) The actual electronic transfer of payments, or value, between trading partners.

Electronic lockbox Collection system offered by banks for companies to receive payments, via wire transfers or ACH, from customers.

EMS Members of the EEC created a subset of controlled exchange rates between their respective currencies which is referred to as the European Monetary System.

Enterprise resources planning (ERP) Accounting-oriented information systems used for identifying and planning the enterprise-wide resources needed to take, make, ship, and account for customer orders.

EPS indifference point The level of sales at which EPS will be the same whether the firm uses debt or common stock financing.

Equilibrium The condition under which the expected return on a security is just equal to its required return, $\hat{k} = k$, and the price is stable.

Equilibrium exchange rate Exchange rate at which demand for a currency is equal to the supply of the currency for sale.

Equity multiplier Assets divided by equity.

Equivalent annual annuity (EAA) method A method that calculates the annual payments a project would provide if it were an annuity. When comparing projects of unequal lives, the one with the higher equivalent annual annuity should be chosen.

Error distribution The shape or pattern of the array of forecast errors.

Euro A new currency that represents a basket of currencies of the participating countries in the European Monetary System.

Eurobanks Commercial banks that participate as financial intermediaries in the Eurocurrency market.

Eurobonds Bonds sold in countries other than the country represented by the currency denominating them.

Euro-clear Telecommunications network that informs all traders about outstanding issues of Eurobonds for sale.

Euro-commercial paper Debt securities issued by MNCs for short-term financing.

Euro cp Similar in concept to domestic commercial paper except issued in the Euro-market which has fewer restrictions, is unrated, and generally has a longer maturity averaging from 60 to 90 days.

Eurocredit loans Loans of one year or longer extended by Eurobanks.

Eurocredit market Collection of banks that accept deposits and provide loans in large denominations and in a variety of currencies. The banks that comprise this market are the same banks that comprise the Eurocurrency market; the difference is that the Eurocredit loans are longer term than so-called Eurocurrency loans.

Eurocurrency market Collection of banks that accept deposits and provide loans in large denominations and in a variety of currencies.

Eurodebt Debt sold in a country other than the one in whose currency the debt is denominated.

Eurodollar Term used to describe U.S. dollar deposits placed in banks located in Europe.

Eurodollar CDs Dollar-denominated deposits held in banks or bank branches outside the U.S. or in International Banking Facilities (IBFs, which can offer Eurodollar deposits only to non-U.S. residents) located within the United States.

Euronotes Unsecured debt securities issued by MNCs for short-term financing.

European Central Bank (ECB) Central bank created to conduct the monetary policy for the countries participating in the single European currency, the euro.

European Currency Unit (ECU) Unit of account representing a weighted average of exchange rates of member countries within the European Monetary System.

Evaluated receipt settlement An electronic payment process in which receipt of shipment (not receipt of invoice) triggers payment by the purchasing company.

Event risk Includes any security feature or possible event that subjects the investor to a disruption to or reduction in the expected yield.

Exchange Rate Mechanism Method of linking European currency values with the European Currency Unit (ECU).

Exchange rate risk The uncertainty associated with the price at which the currency from one country can be converted into the currency of another country. The risk that a firm faces when buying or selling in one or more currencies different from its domestic currency.

Ex-dividend date The date on which the right to the next dividend no longer accompanies a stock; it usually is two working days prior to the holder-of-record date.

Executive stock option A type of incentive plan that allows managers to purchase stock at some future time at a given price.

Exercise price (strike price) Price (exchange rate) at which the owner of a currency call option is allowed to buy a specified currency; or the price (exchange rate) at which the owner of a currency put option is allowed to sell a specified currency.

Expansion decisions Whether to purchase capital projects and add them to existing assets to *increase* existing operations.

Expansion project A project that is intended to increase sales.

Expectations theory The theory that the shape of the yield curve depends on investors' expectations about future inflation rates.

Expected rate of return, $\hat{k}_s$ The rate of return on a common stock that an individual stockholder expects to receive; equal to the expected dividend yield plus the expected capital gains yield.

Expected return on a portfolio, $\hat{k}_p$ The weighted average expected return on the stocks held in the portfolio.

Expedited check processing Speedier check clearing provided by the clearing bank if the depositor is willing to perform extra tasks or pay the bank the extra charge involved.

Expedited Funds Availability Act of 1987 Required that shorter availability schedules be put in place to reduce arbitrarily long holds on deposited checks.

Expert systems Computerized decision-making procedure based on a mimicking of what experienced human decision makers have done in many similar situations.

Exponential smoothing Statistical forecasting technique similar to a moving average, but overcoming the slowness of adaptation to changing patterns inherent in the moving average by allowing a greater weighting for more recent data.

Export-Import Bank (Ex-Im Bank) Bank that attempts to strengthen the competitiveness of U.S. industries involved in foreign trade.

Externalities The effect accepting a project will have on the cash flows in other parts (areas) of the firm.

Extra dividend A supplemental dividend paid in years when the firm does well, and excess funds are available for distribution.

F

Face value Investors holding an investment to maturity will receive this amount back from the issuer. Also called the investment's principal. The amount of the loan, or the amount borrowed; also called the principal amount of the loan.

Factor Firm specializing in collection on accounts receivable; exporters sometimes sell their accounts receivable to a factor at a discount.

Factoring Purchase of receivables of an exporter by a factor without recourse to the exporter. The outright sale of receivables.

FASB Statement 95 The accounting standard that created the Statement of Cash Flows.

Federal Advisory Council Is a group of prominent commercial bankers which gives input into Fed decision making.

Federal Deposit Insurance Corp. Improvement Act of 1991 Requires the FDIC to give acquiring banks the choice of whether to bid for all of a failed bank's deposits or just the insured deposits, signaling a reduction in coverage for uninsured deposits.

Federal Open Market Committee (FOMC) The seven members of the Board of Governors are also members of this group, which makes most of the monetary policy for the U.S. in its eight regularly scheduled meetings per year. The FOMC effects changes in the money supply by buying and selling Treasury securities (open market operations), which affects the reserve position of banks, and ultimately the money supply.

Federal Reserve Act (1913) Established the Federal Reserve System to oversee and regulate the national money and credit system.

Federal Reserve member banks See member banks.

Federal Reserve System (Fed) The nation's central bank, this organization oversees the national money and credit system by acting as lender of last resort, lending money to banks through the "discount window," and facilitating the payments mechanism, and is one of several national bodies that supervises and regulates banks.

Fed float Part of the clearing float for a mailed check, it arises because the Fed may grant availability to the clearing bank before it presents the check (and debits the account of) the payee's bank. Fed float has been greatly reduced since 1980, because the 1980 Monetary Control Act mandated that the Fed eliminate or charge for Fed float.

Fed funds rate The rate charged on reserve borrowings, mostly overnight, transacted between banks.

Fedwire A linked network of the twelve Fed district banks which transfers funds for banks (and by extension their customers) by debiting or crediting the banks' reserve accounts. It is a major part of the Federal Reserve System's payment system involvement.

Field warehouse agreement Inventories pledged as collateral and physically segregated from other inventory generally on the borrower's premises.

Financial Accounting Standards Board (FASB) Statement 95 Provides a set of guidelines to help classify cash receipts and disbursement according to type of activity.

Financial breakeven analysis Determining the operating income (EBIT) the firm needs to just cover all of its fixed financing costs and produce earnings per share equal to zero.

Financial break-even point The level of EBIT at which EPS equals zero.

Financial control The phase in which financial plans are implemented; control deals with the feedback and adjustment process required to ensure adherence to plans and modification of plans because of unforeseen changes.

Financial EDI (FEDI) The exchange of electronic business information such as lockbox information reports, daily balance reports, and monthly account analysis reports between a firm and its bank. In the context of payments, financial EDI refers to electronic data interchange combined with payment instructions. This allows customers to include invoice data and payment instructions in the same payment order.

Financial flexibility The ability of the firm to augment its future cash flows to cover any unforeseen needs or to take advantage of any unforeseen opportunities.

Financial Institution Buyer Credit Policy Policy that provides insurance coverage for loans by banks to foreign buyers of exports.

Financial Institutions Reform, Recovery and Enforcement Act (1989) Allowed bank holding companies to buy healthy savings and loan associations.

Financial intermediaries Specialized financial firms that facilitate the transfer of funds from savers to borrowers.

Financial lease A lease that does not provide for maintenance services, is not cancelable, and is fully amortized over its life; also called a *capital lease*.

Financial leverage The extent to which fixed-income securities (debt and preferred stock) are used in a firm's capital structure. The use of debt financing.

Financial markets "Mechanisms" by which borrowers and lenders get together.

Financial motive One of the theoretical motives for trade credit extension, applies where the seller has a lower cost of capital than the buyer and is able to pass along some of the difference.

Financial planning The projection of sales, income, and assets based on alternative production and marketing strategies, as well as the determination of the resources needed to achieve these projections.

Financial restructuring Situation in which the company changes it product lines or its relative use of assets with heavy fixed operating costs altering the company's business risk.

Financial risk The portion of stockholders' risk, over and above basic business risk, resulting from the manner in which the firm is financed. The possibility that a company will not be able to cover financing related expenditures such as lease payments, interest, principal repayment, and referred stock dividends.

Financial Services Modernization Act of 1999 Also known as the Gramm-Leach-Bliley Act, this law repealed the 1933 Glass-Steagall Act's prohibition on bank-investment company affiliations.

Financial statement approach Utilizes profitability analysis along with a balance sheet evaluation of what the effect of a proposed course of action would have on the company's liquidity and cash position. Approximate timing of financial effects can be seen through the use of pro forma, or projected, financial statements.

Financial swap An exchange of periodic cash flows between two parties.

Financing activities Defined as cash flows resulting from proceeds of issuance of securities, retirement of debt, and payments of dividends or other distributions to shareholders.

Financing feedbacks The effects on the income statement and balance sheet of actions taken to finance forecasted increases in assets.

Finished goods inventory Inventory of the finished product ready for sale.

Firm-specific, or diversifiable, risk That part of a security's risk associated with random outcomes generated by events, or behaviors, specific to the firm; it can be eliminated by proper diversification.

First differencing A means of correcting a data series for autocorrelation, which is accomplished by subtracting the previous value for the dependent variable from the current value, and then using the differences as the dependent variable (in lieu of the original values of the dependent variable).

Fisher effect Theory that nominal interest rates are composed of a real interest rate and anticipated inflation.

Five C's of credit Traditional means of evaluating a corporate credit applicant by investigating character, collateral, capacity, conditions, and capital. Character is thought to be the single most important aspect in this approach.

Fixed assets turnover ratio The ratio of sales to net fixed assets.

Fixed charge coverage ratio This ratio expands the TIE ratio to include the firm's annual long-term lease payments and sinking fund payments.

Fixed costs Expenses which do not change with changes in activity or sales volume, such as rent or insurance.

Fixed exchange rate system Monetary system in which exchange rates are either held constant or allowed to fluctuate only within very narrow boundaries.

Fixed-for-floating rate swap In this type of swap, Party A, with floating rate debt, agrees to pay Party B, who has fixed rate debt, a fixed-rate interest payment based on the notional dollar amount stated in the agreement, in exchange for receipt of a floating-rate interest payment.

Flat yield curve Horizontally shaped graph of the yields to maturity of securities with various maturities, implying a "no change" forecast of future interest rates.

Float The delay between the time a payment is initiated and the time when the payment is debited to the payor (disbursement float) or credited to the payee (collection float). Within ethical limits companies try to maximize it on payments or minimize it on collections, and float continues to be an important fact of life that must be coped with. The difference between the balance shown in a firm's (or individual's) checkbook and the balance on the bank's records.

Floating lien A financing arrangement where a borrower's inventory in general is pledged as collateral for a loan.

Floating rate bond A bond whose interest rate fluctuates with shifts in the general level of interest rates.

Floating-rate note Type of loan in which the interest rate is reset either daily, weekly, monthly, quarterly, or semi-annually.

Floating rate notes (FRNs) Provision of some Eurobonds, in which the coupon rate is adjusted over time according to prevailing market rates.

Floor planning The common name used for trust receipt loans made to automobile dealerships.

Flotation costs The costs associated with issuing new stocks or bonds.

Forecast bias Tendency for a forecasting model to systematically over- or under-predict the variable of interest. It can often be detected on a graph of forecast errors over time or across values of an important predictor variable.

Forecast horizon How far ahead the cash balance is being projected.

Forecast interval The units the horizon is segmented into, such as months in a year-ahead forecast.

Foreign bond Bond issued by a borrower foreign to the country where the bond is placed.

Foreign debt A debt instrument sold by a foreign borrower but denominated in the currency of the country in which it is sold.

Foreign exchange market Market composed primarily of banks, serving firms and consumers who wish to buy or sell various currencies.

Foreign exchange rate The price of one currency stated in relation to the price of another currency.

Foreign exchange risk The possibility that exchange rates will move adversely, causing results of foreign business activities to have a reduced value when converted into the company's home currency.

Foreign investment risk matrix (FIRM) Graph that displays financial and political risk by intervals, so that each country can be positioned according to its risk ratings.

Forfaiting Method of financing international trade of capital goods.

Forward contract Agreement between a commercial bank and a client about an exchange of two currencies to be made at a future point in time at a specified exchange rate.

Forward discount Percentage by which the forward rate is less than the spot rate; typically quoted on an annualized basis.

Forward premium Percentage by which the forward rate exceeds the spot rate; typically quoted on an annualized basis.

Forward rates Prices or yields which the market collectively forecasts today for future periods. In foreign exchange markets, forward rates refer to exchange rates between currencies which is contracted to exist at a future value date.

Forward value date The date that good funds will be credited to the account (similar to availability schedules in the United States).

Founders' shares Stock owned by the firm's founders who have sole voting rights; this type of stock generally has restricted dividends for a specified number of years.

Franchising Agreement by which a firm provides a specialized sales or service strategy, support assistance, and possibly an initial investment in the franchise in exchange for periodic fees.

Free cash flow hypothesis All else equal, firms that pay dividends from cash flows that cannot be reinvested in positive net present value projects, which are termed *free cash flows*, have higher values than firms that retain free cash flows.

Freely floating exchange rate system Monetary system in which exchange rates are allowed to move due to market forces without intervention by country governments.

"Free" trade credit Credit received during the discount period.

Full compensation An arrangement in which the delivery of goods to one party is fully compensated for by buying back more than 100% of the value that was originally sold.

Full reconciliation Service which provides detailed checks outstanding information along with the checks paid data from company-supplied check issue detail.

Fundamental forecasting Forecasting based on fundamental relationships between economic variables and exchange rates.

Funded debt Long-term debt; "funding" means replacing short-term debt with securities of longer maturity.

Futures contract A standardized contract that obligates the buyer (issuer) to purchase (sell) a specified amount of the item represented by the contract at a set price at the expiration of the contract.

Futures option An option contract that gives the buyer (issuer) the right to purchase (sell) the futures contract underlying the options contract.

Futures rates An exchange rate at which currencies can be traded at a future date. Futures differ from forwards in that the futures contract is standardized and traded on a national exchange.

Future value (FV) The amount to which a cash flow or series of cash flows will grow over a given period of time when compounded at a given interest rate.

Future value interest factor for an annuity (FVIFA$_{i,n}$) The future value interest factor for an annuity of n periods compounded at i percent.

Future value interest factor for i and n (FVIF$_{i,n}$) The future value of $1 left on deposit for n periods at a rate of i percent per period—the multiple by which an initial investment grows because of the interest earned.

FVA$_n$ The future value of an ordinary annuity over n periods.

FVIFA(DUE)$_{i,n}$ The future value interest factor for an annuity due—FVIFA(DUE)$_{i,n}$ = FVIFA$_{i,n}$ × (1 + i).

G

Garn-St. Germain Depository Institutions Act (1982) Enacted alterations allowing: (1) depository institutions to pay interest on money market deposit accounts in order to compete with money market mutual funds and (2) savings and loans associations to lend to businesses.

General Agreement on Tariffs and Trade (GATT) Agreement allowing for trade restrictions only in retaliation against illegal trade actions of other countries.

General obligation The banking for the interest principal payments of these securities is simply future general revenues and the issuer's capacity to raise taxes.

Giro acceptance Foreign payment method in which computer-processable stub card is signed by the customer, who then takes it to the post office. The bill mailed to the customer has a stub attached to it that includes the seller's bank and account number.

GIRO systems A collection system for consumer payments that is common place in Europe. Sellers send customers an invoice with a payment stub encoded with the seller's bank account number. The customer signs the stub and then takes it to a GIRO processor. The processor delivers the stubs to the nearest GIRO bank which then debits the customer's account and credits the seller's account.

Going public The act of selling stock to the public at large by a closely held corporation or its principal stockholders.

Gold standard Era in which each currency was convertible into gold at a specified rate, allowing the exchange rate between two currencies to be determined by their relative convertibility rates per ounce of gold.

Government warrant Essentially a payable-through-draft issued by a government agency.

Greenmail A situation in which a firm, trying to avoid a takeover, buys back stock at a price above the existing market price from the person(s) trying to gain control of the firm.

Growth rate, g The expected rate of change in dividends per share.

H

Hedge To insulate a firm from exposure to exchange rate fluctuations.

Hedger A person who has a cash position or an anticipated cash position that he or she is trying to protect from adverse interest rate movements.

High Dollar Group Sort A special expediting of large dollar amounts through the clearing system, with the Fed granting the depositing bank immediate credit if it deposits the check early in the morning.

High liquidity strategy Current asset allocation strategy which prescribes a high proportion of assets to be held in cash and securities in order to reduce the chance of running out of cash.

Historical yield spread analysis Study of risk-related and maturity-related interest rate differences, motivated by a desire to detect profitable trading strategies.

Holder-of-record date (date of record) The date the company opens the ownership books to determine who will receive the dividend; the stockholders of record on this date receive the dividend.

Holding costs The costs associated with the storage of inventory.

Horizontal merger A combination of two firms that produce the same type of good or service.

Hostile takeover The acquisition of a company over the opposition of its management.

I

Imaging Digitizing documents, such as invoices and checks.

Imperfect market The condition where, due to the costs to transfer labor and other resources used for production, firms may attempt to use foreign factors of production when they are less costly than local factors.

Import/export letters of credit Trade-related letters of credit.

Improper accumulation Retention of earnings by a business for the purpose of enabling stockholders to avoid personal income taxes.

Income bond A bond that pays interest to the holder only if the interest is earned by the firm.

Income statement A statement summarizing the firm's revenues and expenses over an accounting period, generally a quarter or a year.

Incremental cash flow The change in a firm's net cash flow attributable to an investment project.

Incremental operating cash flows The changes in day-to-day cash flows that result from the purchase of a capital project and continue until the firm disposes of the asset.

Indenture A formal agreement (contract) between the issuer of a bond and the bondholders.

Independent projects Projects whose cash flows are not affected by decisions made about other projects.

Independent variable Term used in regression analysis to represent the variable that is expected to influence another (so-called "dependent") variable.

Indexed (purchasing power) bond A bond that has interest payments based on an inflation index to protect the holder from inflation.

Index fund A managed portfolio assembled to mirror a particular financial market composite.

Indirect format One possible format allowed for presenting the Statement of Cash Flows that begins with net profit and then presents adjustments for items that do not results in current-period cash transactions including depreciation and changes in the various working capital accounts.

Indirect quotations Exchange rate quotations representing the value measured by number of units per dollar.

Inflation The tendency of prices to increase over time.

Inflation premium (IP) A premium for expected inflation that investors add to the real risk-free rate of return.

Inflow A receipt of cash from an investment, an employer, or other sources.

Information content (signaling) hypothesis The theory that investors regard dividend changes as signals of management's earnings forecasts.

Initial investment Expenses necessary to implement a capital budgeting proposal must be determined. This may include set-up costs, physical asset acquisition or disposition costs, permanent increases in the company's investment in cash, receivables, and inventories, and other cash outflows incurred at the time the project is initiated.

Initial investment outlay Includes the incremental cash flows associated with a project that will *occur only at the start of a project's life,* $\hat{CF}_0$.

Initial public offering (IPO) market The market consisting of stocks of companies that have just gone public.

In-sample validation Involves gauging forecast errors by using the data set on which the model is fitted. This gives an upward bias to forecast accuracy.

Insiders Officers, directors, major stockholders, or others who might have inside, or privileged, information on a company's operations.

Instrument A class of similar investments. Examples are agency notes, commercial paper, Treasury bills, certificates of deposit (CDs), banker's acceptances, and repurchase agreements.

Interbank market Market that facilitates the exchange of currencies between banks.

Interdistrict Transportation System Redesign of the Federal Reserve's routing modes and techniques to shorten delays and minimize system-wide float.

Interest-bearing When the interest paid is based on a quoted rate based on the face value of the financial instrument.

Interest Equalization Tax (IET) Tax imposed by the U.S. government in 1963 to discourage U.S. investors from investing in foreign securities.

Interest rate cap A financial contract which limits the rise in a selected interest rate.

Interest rate collar A financial contract which restricts the movement of a selected interest rate within a narrow band referred to as a collar. It is essentially a combination of an interest rate floor and cap.

Interest rate floor A financial contract which limits the decline in a selected interest rate.

Interest rate parity Theory specifying that the forward premium (or discount) is equal to the interest rate differential between the two currencies of concern.

Interest rate parity (IRP) line Diagonal line depicting all points on a four-quadrant graph that represent a state of interest rate parity.

Interest rate parity theory Theory suggesting that the forward rate differs from the spot rate by an amount that reflects the interest differential between two currencies.

Interest rate price risk The risk of changes in bond prices to which investors are exposed due to changing interest rates.

Interest rate reinvestment risk The risk that income from a bond portfolio will vary because cash flows have to be reinvested at current market rates.

Interest rate risk The possibility that interest rates will increase, causing the prices of existing fixed-income securities to drop.

Interest rate swap Agreement to swap interest payments, whereby interest payments based on a fixed interest rate are exchanged for interest payments based on a floating interest rate.

Internal rate of return (IRR) The discount rate that forces the PV of a project's expected cash flows to equal its initial cost. IRR is similar to the YTM on a bond.

International Bank for Reconstruction and Development (IBRD) Bank established in 1944 to enhance economic development by providing loans to countries. Also referred to as the World Bank.

International Development Association (IDA) Association established to stimulate country development; it was especially suited for less prosperous nations, since it provided loans at low interest rates.

International Financial Corporation (IFC) Firm established to promote private enterprise within countries; it can provide loans to and purchase stock of corporations.

International Fisher effect Theory specifying that a currency's exchange rate will depreciate against another currency when its interest rate (and therefore expected inflation rate) is higher than that of the other currency.

International Fisher Effect (IFE) line Diagonal line on a graph that reflects points at which the interest rate differential between two countries is equal to the percentage change in the exchange rate between their two respective currencies.

International Monetary Fund (IMF) Agency established in 1944 to promote and facilitate international trade and financing.

International mutual funds Mutual funds containing securities of foreign firms.

Interstate Banking and Branching Efficiency Act (1994) Permitted interstate bank acquisitions, mergers, and branching.

In-the-money option When it is beneficial financially for the option holder to exercise the option.

Intracompany trade International trade between subsidiaries that are under the same ownership.

Intrinsic value, $\hat{P}_0$ The value of an asset that in the mind of a particular investor is justified by the facts; $\hat{P}_0$ may be different from the asset's current market price, its book value, or both.

Inventory control systems An information system employed to help control inventory.

Inventory financing A very important component of the total financial plan of most corporations because inventory makes up a significant portion of total working capital.

Inventory turnover ratio A measure of inventory usage that is found by dividing cost of goods sold by either the year-end inventory balance or by the average inventory balance.

Inverted "abnormal" yield curve Downward-sloping graph of yields to maturity of securities with different maturities. Given the possibility to engage in arbitrage (simultaneously buy and sell otherwise identical securities having different maturities), this slope implies that the market collectively anticipates future shorter-term interest rates to decline.

Investing activities On the statement of cash flows items that are defined as receipts of cash from loans, sale of property, and cash disbursed for loans to other business entities and payments for property, plant, and equipment.

Investment banker An organization that underwrites and distributes new issues of securities; helps businesses and other entities obtain needed financing.

Investment grade bonds Bonds rated A or triple-B; many banks and other institutional investors are permitted by law to hold only investment-grade or better bonds.

Investment opportunity schedule (IOS) A graph of the firm's investment opportunities ranked in order of the projects' internal rates of return.

Investment policy Defines the company's posture toward risk and return and specifies how that posture is to be implemented.

Irrevocable letter of credit Letter of credit issued by a bank that cannot be cancelled or amended without the beneficiary's approval.

Issuing bank Bank that issues a letter of credit.

J

Jamaica Agreement As a result of the inflation and balance of payment problems after World War II, causing many countries great difficulty in maintaining their appropriate exchange rate, the major trading nations signed the Jamaica Agreement in 1976 to demonetize gold and create a system of floating exchange rates.

J-curve effect Effect of a weaker dollar on the U.S. trade balance, in which the trade balance initially deteriorates; it only improves once U.S. and non-U.S. importers respond to the change in purchasing power that is caused by the weaker dollar.

Joint venture Venture between two or more firms in which responsibilities and earnings are shared.

Judgmental approach Relies heavily on intuition to adjust what is known about upcoming cash flows to arrive at the cash forecast.

Junk bond A high-risk, high-yield bond used to finance mergers, leveraged buyouts, and troubled companies.

Just-in-time inventory system An inventory system designed to reduce the levels of inventory kept at the manufacturing site increasing quality in the production process and by shifting the inventory burden to the supplier.

L

Lagged regression analysis A quick and relatively inexpensive way of determining a company's collection experience by determining a mathematical equation relating cash collections to the sales that gave rise to them.

Lagging Strategy used by a firm to stall payments, normally in response to exchange rate projections. The practice of delaying collections or payments.

Lambda A liquidity measure from a function of the likelihood that a firm will exhaust its liquid reserve. The measure's numerator is the sum of the firm's initial liquid reserve and total anticipated net cash flow during the analysis horizon and denominator is the standard deviation of the net cash flow during the analysis horizon.

Leading Strategy used by a firm to accelerate payments, normally in response to exchange rate expectations. The practice of accelerating collections or payments.

Lead, or managing, underwriter The member of an underwriting syndicate that actually *manages* the distribution and sale of a new security offering.

Ledger balance Reflects all credits and debits posted to an account as of a certain time, but this balance may not be entirely spendable.

Lessee The party that uses, rather than the one who owns, the leased property.

Lessor The owner of the leased property.

Letter of credit (L/C) A promise by a bank to make payment to a party upon presentation of a draft provided that the party complies with certain documentary requirements. This guarantees the investor of principal repayment, and the use of backup bank financing allows the bank's credit rating to be substituted for the issuer's.

Leveraged buyout (LBO) A transaction in which a firm's publicly-owned stock is bought up in a mostly debt-financed tender offer, and a privately owned, highly leveraged firm results.

Liability swap A swap created to hedge cash flows related to liabilities.

LIBOR The London Interbank Offer Rate which is commonly used internationally as a reference rate for variable rate loans.

Licensing Arrangement in which a local firm in the host country produces goods in accordance with another firm's (the licensing firm's) specifications; as the goods are sold, the local firm can retain part of the earnings.

Line of credit An arrangement in which a bank agrees to lend up to a specified maximum amount of funds during a designated period. Short-term lending arrangement which allows the company to borrow up to a prearranged dollar amount during the one-year term.

Liquid asset An asset that can be easily converted into cash without significant loss of its original value.

Liquidity The ability to sell an asset quickly, at or very close to the present market price. For a company the ability of the firm to pay its bills on time.

Liquidity preference hypothesis Theoretical explanation for the term structure of interest rates that hypothesizes that higher yields will be necessary to induce investors to tie their funds up for long time periods (in other words, to be illiquid) in light of the increasing interest rate risk. Preference for liquidity is thought to characterize enough investors that the yield curve (in the absence of expectations or other influences on other than the shortest-term securities) should slope upward from left to right. The longer the maturity, the larger the liquidity premium must be to attract investors.

Liquidity preference theory The theory that, all else equal, lenders prefer to make short-term loans rather than long-term loans; hence, they will lend short-term funds at lower rates than long-term funds.

Liquidity premium (LP) A premium added to the rate on a security if the security cannot be converted to cash on short notice and at close to the original cost.

Liquidity ratios Ratios that show the relationship of a firm's cash and other current assets to its current liabilities.

Liquidity risk The inability to sell quickly at or very near the current market price, which is tied to the marketability of a security.

Loan participation After a bank or syndicate of banks arranges a large loan, part or all of the loan may be sold off to corporate or other institutional investors, as well as to other banks.

Locational arbitrage Action to capitalize on a discrepancy in quoted exchange rates between banks.

Lockbox A special post office box where customers are instructed to mail their remittances.

Lockbox arrangement A technique used to reduce float by having payments sent to post office boxes located near the customers.

Lockbox collection system A cash collection system that intercepts customer remittances close to the sending location and deposits the checks in the banking system prior to the company receiving notification.

Lockbox consortium A system composed of several independent banks operating under a contractual agreement to provide lockbox services for each other's customers.

Lockbox optimization model A set of variables, relationships, and rules that determine the optimal number of lockboxes, their locations, and the customer allocations to the selected lockbox sites.

Lockbox services A collection service offered by banks, with the emphasis being to reduce collection float. Banks receiving one million or more pieces of mail per year can have a unique zip code set up for them, saving one or more sorts by post office personnel.

Lockbox study A study usually conducted by a bank consulting group to help a corporation decide the structure of its collection system.

Log-linear regression Is an approach to estimating a variable's growth rate, which takes into account all of the variable's observed values.

London Interbank Offer Rate (LIBOR) The short-term interest rate at which banks offer Eurodollar loans to each other.

Long-term forward contracts Contracts that state any exchange rate at which a specified amount of a specified currency can be exchanged at a future date (more than one year from today). Also called long forwards.

Louvre Accord 1987 agreement between countries to attempt to stabilize the value of the U.S. dollar.

Low liquidity strategy Aggressive current asset allocation strategy which entails driving the company's investment in cash and securities to a minimum.

Lumpy assets Assets that cannot be acquired in small increments; instead, they must be obtained in large, discrete amounts.

M

Macroassessment Overall risk assessment of a country without considering the MNC's business.

Magnetic Ink Character Recognition (MICR) line The clearing agent, often a Federal Reserve bank, branch or RCPC, uses the information printed at the bottom of the check to process the check. This information can be read by scanning machines and indicates several items about the drawee bank.

Mail float The time that elapses from the point when the check is written until it is received by the payee. It may range from a day for local checks immediately mailed out to 10 days for a check sent to New York from Rome, Italy.

Maintenance margin The level that the margin account returns to after a margin call.

Managed float Exchange rate system in which currencies have no explicit boundaries, but central banks may intervene to influence exchange rate movements.

Managing about a target rule Rather than make daily transfers, this transfer rule makes only one transfer for several days of deposits and the amount transferred takes into consideration a desired target balance that is to be left at the deposit bank.

Manufacturing resource planning systems (MRP II) Systems that are made up of a variety of functions that are linked together including business planning, sales and operations planning, production planning, master production scheduling, material requirements planning, capacity requirements planning, and the execution support systems for capacity and materials.

Margin A small percentage of the contract price that is put up rather than paying the full price of the contract.

Margin call A call from a broker asking for more money to support a stock purchase loan.

Margin requirement Deposit placed on a contract (such as a currency futures contract) to cover the fluctuations in the value of that contract; this minimizes the risk of the contract to the counterparty.

Marginal cost of capital (MCC) The cost of obtaining another dollar of new capital; the weighted average cost of the last dollar of new capital raised.

Marginal tax rate The tax applicable to the last unit of income.

Marked-to-market When changes in the market price of the futures contract impact the margin account on a daily basis.

Market microstructure Consists of the participants and mechanics involved in making transactions.

Market price, P_0 The price at which a stock sells in the market.

Market risk premium, RP_M The additional return over the risk-free rate needed to compensate investors for assuming an average amount of risk.

Market segmentation hypothesis A theoretical explanation of the term structure of interest rates which contends that instead of being close substitutes, securities with short, medium, and long maturities are seen by investors (fund suppliers) and issuers (funds demanders) as quite different. Thus interest rates for securities with different maturities are set by diverse supply and demand conditions.

Market segmentation theory The theory that each borrower and lender has a preferred maturity and that the slope of the yield curve depends on the supply of and demand for funds in the long-term market relative to the short-term market.

Market value ratios A set of ratios that relate the firm's stock price to its earnings and book value per share.

Market, or nondiversifiable, risk That part of a security's risk that *cannot* be eliminated by diversification because it is associated with economic, or market, factors that systematically affect most firms.

Market/book (M/B) ratio The ratio of a stock's market price to its book value.

Marketable securities Securities that can be sold on short notice without loss of principal or original investment.

Market-based forecasting Use of a market-determined exchange rate (such as the spot rate or forward rate) to forecast the spot rate in the future.

Master note Open-ended commercial paper, which allow the investor to add or withdraw monies on a daily basis, up to a specified maximum amount.

Material requirements planning (MRP) An inventory planning system that focuses on the amount and timing of finished goods demanded and translates this into the derived demand for raw materials and subassemblies at various stages of production.

Maturity date A specified date on which the par value of a bond must be repaid.

Maturity extension swap Situation where a security is sold and replaced or exchanged with another security which will increase the yield or dollar return, while affecting credit risk minimally. The swap is executed when the manager wishes to ride the yield curve, but to make the investment he must liquidate another security.

Maturity matching, or "self-liquidating," approach A financing policy that matches asset and liability maturities. This would be considered a moderate current asset financing policy.

Maturity risk premium (MRP) A premium that reflects interest rate risk; bonds with longer maturities have greater interest rate risk.

McFadden Act (1927) Limited branch banking by national banks to the same areas in which state-chartered banks in that state were permitted to branch, effectively prohibiting interstate branching.

Mean absolute error (MAE) Measure of forecast error calculated by adding up the absolute values of the difference between forecasted and actual values, and then dividing by the number of forecasts.

Mean square error Weights large errors more than small ones, and thus favors forecasting models that rarely if ever miss by a large amount.

Medium-Term Guarantee Program Program conducted by Ex-Im Bank in which commercial lenders are encouraged to finance the sale of U.S. capital equipment and services to approved foreign buyers; Ex-Im Bank guarantees the loan's principal and interest on these loans.

Member banks Commercial banks which belong to the Federal Reserve System. Being a member of the Federal Reserve System has historically been a requirement of all national banks, and many state-chartered banks joined voluntarily. Subsequent to the 1980 Monetary Control Act membership has been much less important, in that all depository institutions must adhere to reserve requirements and can now borrow from the Fed.

Merger The combination of two or more firms to form a single firm.

Microassessment The risk assessment of a country as related to the MNC's type of business.

Mixed approach When applied to forecasting, involves the use of both quantitative and judgmental approaches.

Mixed forecasting Development of forecasts based on a mixture of forecasting techniques.

Mixed instruments Specialized investment instruments which offer tailoring to the specific desires of the investor.

Model audit The monitoring of an existing model to ensure its continued validity.

Model estimation Includes the selection of an appropriate forecasting technique and model calibration.

Modeling The process of establishing a relationship between a set of independent variables in order to produce an estimate of a dependent variable.

Moderate current asset investment policy A policy that is between the relaxed and restrictive policies.

Moderate liquidity strategy An approach to liquidity management which implies an intermediate concentration of current assets in the form of cash and securities, with corresponding intermediate levels of risk. This strategy falls between and should be contrasted with conservative and aggressive liquidity strategies.

Moderate strategy In short-term financing, a strategy that is a blend of the aggressive and conservative financing strategies.

Modified accrual technique Sometimes called the "accrual addback technique" or "adjusted net income technique," this cash forecasting approach begins with accounting reports or the operating budget and then adjusts these number to reflect the timing of cash flows related to these transactions.

Modified buy-and-hold strategy An approach to investing in which the investor plans to hold the security to maturity, but will selectively sell securities on which capital gains might be realized. This strategy might be utilized when the investor wishes to take advantage of anticipated favorable interest rate movements.

Modified IRR (MIRR) The discount rate at which the present value of a project's cost is equal to the present value of its terminal value, in which the terminal value is found as the sum of the future values of the cash inflows, compounded at the firm's required rate of return (cost of capital).

Money markets The financial markets in which funds are borrowed or loaned for short periods (generally one year or less).

Money market deposit accounts Savings accounts offered by depository institutions which pay interest. These were introduced to give depository institutions an account to compete with money market mutual funds.

Money market hedge Use of international money markets to match future cash inflows and outflows in a given currency.

Money market mutual fund A mutual fund that invests in short-term, low-risk securities and allows investors to write checks against their accounts.

Monte Carlo simulation A risk analysis technique in which probable future events are simulated on a computer, generating a probability distribution that indicates the most likely outcomes.

Mortgage bond A bond backed by fixed assets. First mortgage bonds are senior in priority to claims of second mortgage bonds.

Moving average Statistical forecasting technique which evens out temporary ups and downs by taking the mean of the most recent observations.

Multibuyer policy Policy administered by Ex-Im Bank that provides credit risk insurance on export sales to many different buyers.

Multicollinearity Presence of moderate or high correlation between predictor variables in a regression equation. This condition is a violation of one of the assumptions of ordinary least squares regression modeling, the most common form of regression analysis.

Multilateral Investment Guarantee Agency (MIGA) Agency established by the World Bank that offers various forms of political risk insurance to corporations.

Multilateral netting system Complex interchange for netting between a parent and several subsidiaries.

Multinational restructuring Restructuring of the composition of an MNC's assets or liabilities.

Multiple-drawee checks Negotiable payment order having more than one bank listed on the face of the check, with one of the banks being a bank located near the disbursing location, for which the check is an "on us" item.

Multiple IRRs The situation in which a project has two or more IRRs.

Multiple processing centers Processing centers established around the country to pick up lockbox mail and do the processing while the processed checks are deposited in accounts at correspondent banks in the company's name. Cash is then concentrated in the company's account at the lockbox bank's headquarters.

Multiple regression Statistical model incorporating two or more predictor variables to explain the movement in the variable of interest. The form of a multiple regression model having two predictor variables is generally of the form: $Y = a + b_1X_1 + b_2X_2$.

Multivariate models Description of the relationship between three or more variables, typically with one of the variables being explained as the influence of two or more predictor variables.

Municipal obligations Securities issued by governmental authorities, governments, or government-authorized entities at other than the federal level. These securities, sometimes called "munis," pay interest that is not taxable for federal income tax purposes and usually not taxable for state income tax purposes in the state in which the issuer is located. Examples of issuers would be states, counties, localities, and school districts.

Mutually exclusive projects A set of projects in which the acceptance of one project means the others cannot be accepted.

N

NACHA The National Automated Clearing House Association. NACHA has been involved in developing five format options that allow the movement of funds electronically, each with varying amounts of data.

Nearby contract The futures contract with a maturity date that occurs nearest to, but after, the date of the cash market transaction that is to be hedged.

Negotiable bill of lading Contract that grants title of merchandise to the holder, which allows banks to use the merchandise as collateral.

Negotiable certificate of deposit Bank deposits that come in $100,000 and larger denominations. Negotiability means the security can be legally sold and exchanged between investors, circumventing the early withdrawal penalty charged by the issuing bank. Only the first $100,000 is insured by the Federal Deposit Insurance Corporation, however.

Net float The difference between disbursement float and collections float; the difference between the balance shown in the checkbook and the balance shown on the bank's books.

Net liquid balance Cash and marketable securities less notes payable and current maturities of long-term debt.

Net operating loss carrybacks Practice of applying losses to offset earnings in previous years.

Net operating loss carryforwards Practice of applying losses to offset earnings in future years.

Net present value (NPV) A measure of the present dollar equivalent of all cash inflows and outflows flowing from a capital investment proposal. To compute net present value each cash inflow and outflow must be converted to its dollar value at a standard point in time. Calculation of NPV involves discounting all cash flows to the beginning of the cash flow timeline, then subtracting the present value of the outflows from the present value of the inflows.

Net present value (NPV) method A method of evaluating capital investment proposals by finding the present value of future net cash flows, discounted at the rate of return required by the firm.

Net present value (NPV) profile A curve showing the relationship between a project's NPV and various discount rates (required rates of return).

Net profit margin on sales This ratio measures net income per dollar of sales; it is calculated by dividing net income by sales.

Net transaction exposure Consideration of inflows and outflows in a given currency to determine the exposure after offsetting inflows against outflows.

Net working capital Current assets minus current liabilities—the amount of current assets financed by long-term liabilities.

Netting Combining of future cash receipts and payments to determine the net amount to be owed by one subsidiary to another.

Nominal interest rate The stated interest rate for an investment or borrowing opportunity, ignoring the effect of the frequency of compounding. In order to compare various investments, the nominal rate is usually converted to an effective annual rate.

Nominal (quoted) risk-free rate, k_{RF} The rate of interest on a security that is free of all risk; k_{RF} is proxied by the T-bill rate or the T-bond rate. k_{RF} includes an inflation premium.

Nonbank banks Make loans or accept deposits, but not both.

Noncallable A feature of a security which stipulates that the investor need not worry about a forced buyback of the security if interest rates fall subsequent to issuance. The absence of a call feature allows the issuer to pay a slightly lower interest rate due to the lower risk to the investor.

Noncompetitive bid Bids that are entered directly through a tender offer to the nearest Federal Reserve district bank, or through a broker or commercial bank. Investors willing to accept the average yield of all accepted competitive bids enter a noncompetitive bid.

Nonconstant growth The part of the life cycle of a firm in which growth either is much faster or much slower than that of the economy as a whole.

Nondeliverable Forward Contracts (NDFs) Like a forward contract, represents an agreement regarding a position in a specified currency, a specified exchange rate, and a specified future settlement date, but does not result in delivery of currencies. Instead, a payment is made by one party in the agreement to the other party based on the exchange rate at the future date.

Nonrecourse or without recourse When a factor buys receivables and the selling firm is not ultimately responsible for final payment.

Nonsterilized intervention Intervention in the foreign exchange market without adjusting for the change in money supply.

Normal (constant) growth Growth that is expected to continue into the foreseeable future at about the same rate as that of the economy as a whole; g is a constant.

Normal distributions In forecasting, an array of forecast errors which occur in seemingly random fashion above and below forecasted values and graph as a symmetrical, bell-shaped curve.

Normal profits/rates of return Those profits and rates of return that are close to the average for all firms and are just sufficient to attract capital.

Normal yield curve Upward-sloping graph of yields to maturity for securities with various maturities, with longer-term maturities yielding more than shorter-term.

Notional amount The agreed upon face amount of the swap contract which exchange rates or interest rates are to be applied to calculate the cash flows which are to be swapped.

Number of days of payables outstanding (DPO) A payables activity measure found by dividing the payables balance by average daily purchases (alternatively, average daily cost of goods sold can be used in the denominator).

O

Ocean bill of lading Receipt for a shipment by boat, which includes freight charges and title to the merchandise.

Off-balance-sheet financing Financing in which the assets and liabilities involved do not appear on the firm's balance sheet.

Offering price The price at which common stock is sold to the public.

Omitted variables Independent variables which should have been included in a regression model, and that could have helped the analyst predict the variable of interest. If important, omission may give rise to a violation of ordinary least squares assumption, a condition known as serial correlation.

Ongoing validation Involves continually checking a model's forecast accuracy by monitoring each period's forecast error and comparing it to past forecast errors.

On-us When the payee deposits the check in the bank on which it is drawn.

Open account (or open book account) Once approved for credit, a customer can make repeated purchases as long as the total amount owed at any one time is less than some predetermined ceiling.

Open account transaction Sale in which the exporter ships the merchandise and expects the buyer to remit payment according to agreed-upon terms.

Operating activities Those cash flows that are not classified as either investing or financing activities. Generally operating cash flows are related to cash collected from sales and cash disbursed to supplies, workers, management, and taxes.

Operating break-even analysis An analytical technique for studying the relationship between sales revenues, operating costs, and profits.

Operating break-even point Represents the level of production and sales at which operating income is zero; it is the point at which revenues from sales just equal total operating costs.

Operating cash flows Those cash flows that arise from normal operations; the difference between cash collections and cash expenses.

Operating cycle The process of funds flowing from inventory to receivables to payables.

Operating lease A lease under which the lessor maintains and finances the property; also called a *service lease.*

Operating leverage The existence of fixed operating costs, such that a change in sales will produce a larger change in operating income (EBIT).

Operating motive Theoretical motive for trade credit extension in which the seller responds to variable and uncertain demand by altering its trade credit availability.

Operational restructuring When a company changes its product lines or use of assets with heavy fixed operating costs and alters the company's business risk.

Opportunity cost The return on the best alternative use of an asset; the highest return that will not be earned if funds are invested in a particular project.

Opportunity cost rate The rate of return on the best available alternative investment of equal risk.

Optimal dividend policy The dividend policy that strikes a balance between current dividends and future growth and maximizes the firm's stock price.

Option A contract that gives the option holder the right to buy or sell an asset at some predetermined price within a specified period of time.

Order handling Disposition of orders that are within credit limits and handling of orders which violate limits.

Ordering costs Costs associated with the inventory ordering process.

Ordinary (deferred) annuity An annuity whose payments occur at the end of each period.

Organized security exchange A formal organization, having a tangible physical location, that facilitates trading in designated ("listed") securities. The two major national security exchanges in the United States are the New York Stock Exchange (NYSE) and the American Stock Exchange (AMEX).

Original maturity Length of time until principal is repaid, measured at the time the security is first sold.

Originating ACH The automated clearing house contacted by the bank initiating the transaction. The originating ACH must then transmit the payment order to the receiving institution's ACH (termed the receiving ACH).

Originating depository financial institution (ODFI) Bank that is contacted by the payment initiator.

Outflow A payment, or disbursement, of cash for expenses, investments, and so on.

Out of pocket expenses Financing expenses that include interest and bank commitment fees.

Out-of-sample validation Using a new data set to assess a forecasting model's forecast accuracy.

Out-of-the-money option When it is *not* beneficial financially for the option holder to exercise the option—a loss would be incurred if the option is exercised.

Outsourcing Is contracting with outside companies to conduct certain business functions, such as check issuance.

Overdraft credit lines Whether uncommitted or committed, have the added feature of being automatically drawn down whenever the company writes a check for which it does not have the sufficient funds to cover when it clears. Used extensively in foreign countries.

Overdraft facility A banking service that allows a firm to overdraw its account. The overdraft is then charged interest as if it were a loan.

Overhedging Hedging an amount in a currency larger than the actual transaction amount.

Over-the-counter (OTC) market A large collection of brokers and dealers, connected electronically by telephones and computers, that provides for trading in securities not listed on the organized exchanges.

P

Paid-only reconciliation Bank-provided demand deposit report which indicates all paid checks by check number, with check number, dollar amount, and date paid.

Parallel bonds Bonds placed in different countries and denominated in the respective currencies of the countries where they are placed.

Parallel loan Loan involving an exchange of currencies between two parties, with a promise to reexchange the currencies at a specified exchange rate and future date.

Partial compensation An arrangement in which the delivery of goods to one party is partially compensated for by buying back a certain amount of product from the same party.

Partnership An unincorporated business owned by two or more persons.

Par value The nominal or face value of a stock or bond.

Passive investment strategy Involves a minimal amount of oversight and very few transactions once the portfolio has been selected.

Payable through draft (PTD) Gives the payor 24 hours to decide whether to honor or refuse payment after it has been presented to the payor's bank. They are used for claim reimbursement by insurance companies, which use the 24 hour period to verify the signature and endorsements.

Payables turnover ratio Found by dividing purchases over a given time period by the year-end or average payables balance. Indicates the firm's payment behavior.

Payback period The length of time before the original cost of an investment is recovered from the expected cash flows.

Paying agent The bank performing this function makes interest and dividend payments to bondholders and shareholders, respectively, and repays the bond principal at maturity.

Payment (PMT) This term designates constant cash flows.

Payment date The date on which a firm actually mails dividend checks.

Pegged exchange rate Exchange rate whose value is pegged to another currency's value or to a unit of account.

Percent of sales Forecasting model in which an expense or balance sheet amount is expressed as some fraction of sales.

Perfect forecast line A 45-degree line on a graph that matches the forecast of an exchange rate with the actual exchange rate.

Performance shares A type of incentive plan in which managers are awarded shares of stock on the basis of the firm's performance over given intervals with respect to earnings per share or other measures.

Periodic rate The rate charged by a lender or paid by a borrower each interest period (for example, monthly, quarterly, annually, and so on).

Permanent current assets Current assets' balances that do not change due to seasonal or economic conditions; these balances exist even at the trough of a firm's business cycle. The minimum amount of funds that are invested in current assets over the firm's operating cycle.

Perpetuity A cash flow stream of equal dollar amounts that will last indefinitely into the future.

Petrodollars Deposits of dollars by countries which receive dollar revenues due to the sale of petroleum to other countries; the term commonly refers to OPEC deposits of dollars in the Eurocurrency market.

Piggyback Situation in which a bank is permitted to add a check or checks it is clearing and an accompanying listing to whatever checks the local Fed district bank is sending to the distant Fed office. This way the clearing bank can miss the local Fed's cutoff time but still meet the distant Fed's cutoff.

Plaza Accord Agreement among country representatives in 1985 to implement a coordinated program to weaken the dollar.

Pledging receivables A lender makes a loan protected by a lien placed on a certain portion of the firm's receivables. Using accounts receivable as collateral for a loan.

Poison pill An action taken by management to make a firm unattractive to potential buyers and thus to avoid a hostile takeover.

Political risk Political actions taken by the host government or the public that affect the MNC's cash flows. The risk of expropriation (seizure) of a foreign subsidiary's assets by the host country or of unanticipated restrictions on cash flows to the parent company.

Pooling A banking service offered by many banking systems outside the U.S. which allows a firm's excess balances spread across its bank branches to offset corporate deficit balances in other branches of the same bank.

Portfolio risk The risk associated with an investment when it is held in combination with other assets, not by itself.

Positive float The time period between receipt of the goods or services and the date on which cash payment is made.

Positive pay A company sends its daily check issue file to its disbursing bank. Before the bank honors incoming checks, it refers to the issue file to see if the payee and check amounts match up.

Post-audit A comparison of the actual and expected results for a given capital project.

Preauthorized debit system A system that allows a customer's bank to periodically transfer funds from its account to a selling firm's bank account for the payment of bills.

Preauthorized debits Arrangement in which a customer agrees to allow his bank to automatically charge his checking account balance to make a fixed or variable payment each month.

Preauthorized draft Payment order initiated by the payee, who has been authorized to draw against the payor's account. Banks sometimes collect mortgage payments this way, and most automobile dealerships now make payments to Ford, GM, and Chrysler by these drafts.

Preauthorized payment The seller and buyer agree to a payment date and the seller initiates a request to the buyer's bank for payment of the predetermined amount.

Precautionary balances A cash balance held in reserve for unforeseen fluctuations in cash flows.

Precautionary motive Additional inventory held as a cushion for an unexpected increase in demand.

Preemptive right A provision in the corporate charter or bylaws that gives common stockholders the right to purchase on a *pro rata* basis new issues of common stock (or convertible securities).

Premium As related to forward rates, represents the percentage amount by which the forward rate exceeds the spot rate. As related to currency options, represents the price of a currency option.

Premium bond A bond that sells above its par value; occurs whenever the going rate of interest falls below the coupon rate.

Prepayment Method which exporter uses to receive payment before shipping goods.

Present value (PV) The value today of a future cash flow or series of cash flows.

Present value interest factor for an annuity (PVIFA$_{i,n}$) The present value interest factor for an annuity of n periods discounted at i percent.

Present value interest factor for i and n (PVIF$_{i,n}$) The present value of $1 due n periods in the future discounted at i percent per period.

Presentment Step seven in the check clearing process, when the check is returned to the drawee bank for payment.

Price/earnings (P/E) ratio The ratio of the price per share to earnings per share; it shows the dollar amount investors will pay for $1 of current earnings.

Price-elastic Sensitive to price changes.

Pricing market Also called the original issue market, is centered in money centers such as New York City, London, Frankfurt, Singapore, and Hong Kong. Investors can access this "over-the-counter" market from anywhere, as the market consists of phone and computer hook-ups among all participating dealers and brokers.

Pricing motive Theoretical motive for trade credit extension in which sellers unable to change prices, perhaps due to market conditions or regulation, alter trade credit instead in order to charge varying amounts to buyers.

Primary market The market in which firms issue new securities to raise corporate capital.

Prime rate A published rate of interest charged by banks to short-term borrowers (usually large, financially secure corporations) with the best credit; rates on short-term loans generally are "pegged" to the prime rate.

Principal The original amount invested or borrowed.

Principal amount, face value, maturity value, par value The amount of money the firm borrows and promises to repay at some future date, often at maturity.

Private placement Security issuance transaction in which a large institution such as a retirement fund or insurance company buys the entire issue.

Privatization Conversion of government-owned businesses to ownership by shareholders or individuals.

Probability distribution A listing of all possible outcomes, or events, with a probability (chance of occurrence) assigned to each outcome.

Processing float The amount of time that transpires from the point of receipt of the check at a post office box or company mail room and the time when the check is deposited at the bank is termed processing float.

Product cycle theory Theory suggesting that a firm initially establish itself locally and expand into foreign markets in response to foreign demand for its product; over time, the MNC will grow in foreign markets; after some point, its foreign business may decline unless it can differentiate its product from competitors.

Production opportunities The returns available within an economy from investment in productive (cash-generating) assets.

Profitability ratios A group of ratios showing the effect of liquidity, asset management, and debt management on operating results.

Profit maximization The maximization of the firm's net income.

Pro forma balance sheet approach Method of generating a cash forecast which involves determination of the amount of cash and marketable securities by computing the difference between projected assets (excluding cash and marketable securities) and the sum of projected liabilities and owner's equity.

Project Finance Loan Program Program that allows banks, Ex-Im Bank, or a combination of both to extend long-term financing for capital equipment and related services for major projects.

Project required rate of return, k_{proj} The risk-adjusted required rate of return for an individual project.

Projected (pro forma) balance sheet method A method of forecasting financial requirements based on forecasted financial statements.

Promissory note A document specifying the terms and conditions of a loan, including the amount, interest rate, and repayment schedule.

Proprietorship An unincorporated business owned by one individual.

Prospectus A document describing a new security issue and the issuing company.

Prox Payment due on a specific day in the following month.

Proxy A document giving one person the authority to act for another, typically the power to vote shares of common stock.

Proxy fight An attempt by a person or group of people to gain control of a firm by getting its stockholders to grant that person or group the authority to vote their shares in order to elect a new management team.

Publicly-owned corporation A corporation that is owned by a relatively large number of individuals who are not actively involved in its management.

Purchase order with payment voucher attached A draft coupled with a purchase order, which eliminates the need for a supplier to issue an invoice and for a customer to process the invoice and issue a check.

Purchase terms Terms of credit offered by suppliers.

Purchasing cards Are credit cards used by businesses to make small dollar purchases of maintenance, repair, and operating supplies. Use of purchasing, or procurement, cards greatly reduces the number of purchase orders and invoices processed and payments made.

Purchasing Power Parity (PPP) line Diagonal line on a graph that reflects points at which the inflation differential between two countries is equal to the percentage change in the exchange rate between the two respective currencies.

Purchasing Power Parity (PPP) theory Theory suggesting that exchange rates will adjust over time to reflect the differential in inflation rates in the two countries; in this way, the purchasing power of consumers when purchasing domestic goods will be the same as that when they purchase foreign goods.

Purchasing power risk The possibility that an investment's proceeds will not be worth as much as anticipated due to general price level increases in the economy. Anticipated inflation is built into the risk-free interest rate, but investors are still vulnerable to losses in purchasing power from unanticipated inflation and will require a higher yield when price levels are volatile.

Pure play method An approach used for estimating the beta of a project in which a firm identifies companies whose only business is the product in question, determines the beta for each firm, and then averages the betas to find an approximation of its own project's beta.

Put See currency put option.

Putable bond A bond that can be redeemed at the bondholder's option.

Put option A contract that allows the owners to sell the underlying asset at a specific price over a specific span of time. The option to sell a specified number of shares of stock at a prespecified price during a particular period.

Put option on real assets Project that contains an option of divesting part or all of the project.

PVA_n The present value of an ordinary annuity with n payments.

$PVIFA(DUE)_{i,n}$ The present value interest factor for an annuity due—$PVIFA(DUE)_{i,n} = PVIFA_{i,n} \times (1 + i)$.

Q

Quantitative approach Any forecasting technique which involves the use of a numerical model to forecast; the technique is usually implemented on a computer.

Quantity discounts A reduction in the cost per order based on the quantity ordered.

Quick (acid test) ratio This ratio is calculated by deducting inventories from current assets and dividing the remainder by current liabilities. The quick ratio is a variation of the current ratio.

Quick ratio The ratio of current assets less inventory to current liabilities.

Quota Maximum limit imposed by the government on goods allowed to be imported into a country.

R

Range reconciliation Provides subtotals of all checks within a range of check serial numbers. This is especially useful for identifying disbursements from the same account but from several locations.

Raw material inventory Inventory of the raw material of production.

Real cost of hedging The additional cost of hedging when compared to not hedging (a negative real cost would imply that hedging was more favorable than not hedging).

Real interest rate Nominal (or quoted) interest rate minus the inflation rate.

Realized rate of return, $\bar{k}$ The return that is actually earned. The actual return ($\bar{k}$) is usually different from the expected return ($\hat{k}$).

Real options Implicit options on real assets.

Real risk-free rate of interest, k* The rate of interest that would exist on default-free U.S. Treasury securities if no inflation were expected.

Receipts and disbursements method A commonly used cash forecasting approach which involves determining upcoming sources of cash inflows and outflows, then laying these out on a schedule to see the aggregate effect.

Receivables control Procedures and methods for following up credit extensions, including monitoring and corrective actions.

Receivables monitoring The process of evaluating the credit policy to determine if a shift in the customers' payment patterns occurs.

Receiving depository financial institution (RDFI) ACH payee's bank in an ACH credit transaction.

Recourse The lender can seek payment from the borrowing firm when receivables' accounts used to secure a loan are uncollectible. When a factor buys receivables with recourse, the selling firm is ultimately responsible for payment if the customer defaults.

Recursive least squares (RLS) In the context of receivables monitoring, a regression model which allows the estimated receivables collection fractions (the regression coefficients) to change over time.

Refunding Retiring an existing bond issue with the proceeds of a newly issued bond.

Regional Check Processing Centers (RCPCs) Eleven Fed offices set up to help clear checks. Together the 12 district banks plus the 25 regional branches and 11 RCPCs gives the Fed a network of 48 offices to clear checks.

Registrar Bank which keeps records of the number of shares of stock authorized, issued, and redeemed, and ensures that the number of share issued does not exceed those authorized.

Registration statement A statement of facts filed with the SEC about a company that plans to issue securities.

Regression analysis Statistical technique used to measure the relationship between variables and the sensitivity of a variable to one or more other variables.

Regression coefficient Term measured by regression analysis to estimate the sensitivity of the dependent variable to a particular independent variable.

Regulation CC Effective September 1990, this ruling stipulates that from the day of deposit local checks must be given availability within two business days, and nonlocal checks within five days.

Regulation Q A Federal Reserve regulation that restricts banks from paying interest on demand deposit accounts.

Reinvestment rate assumption The assumption that cash flows from a project can be reinvested (1) at the cost of capital, if using the NPV method, or (2) at the internal rate of return, if using the IRR method.

Reinvestment rate risk The possibility that the investor will have to invest cash proceeds at a lower interest rate for the remainder of a predetermined investment horizon.

Reinvoicing center Facility that centralizes payments and charges subsidiaries fees for its function; this can effectively shift profits to subsidiaries where tax rates are low.

Relationship approach One view of the corporation's link to its banks, in which the corporation chooses its bank services primarily based on preexisting business dealings. Loyalty to prior arrangements is considered to be more important than price when selecting banks for cash management or lending services. Usually implies that credit and cash management services will both be handled by the same bank or network of banks.

Relative form of purchasing power parity Theory stating that the rate of change in the prices of products should be somewhat similar when measured in a common currency, as long as transportation costs and trade barriers are unchanged.

Relaxed current asset investment policy A policy under which relatively large amounts of cash and marketable securities and inventories are carried and under which sales are stimulated by a liberal credit policy that results in a high level of receivables.

Relevant cash flows The specific cash flows that should be considered in a capital budgeting decision.

Relevant risk The risk of a security that cannot be diversified away, or its market risk. This reflects a security's contribution to the risk of a portfolio.

Remittance advice A document that usually accompanies payment, indicating customer, account number, date, and invoice(s) being paid.

Reorder point The inventory level at which an order should be placed.

Repatriation of earnings The process of sending cash flows from a foreign subsidiary back to the parent company.

Replacement chain (common life) approach A method of comparing projects of unequal lives that assumes each project can be replicated as many times as necessary to reach a common life span; the NPVs over this life span are then compared, and the project with the higher common life NPV is chosen.

Replacement decisions Whether to purchase capital assets to take the place of existing assets to maintain or improve existing operations.

Repurchase agreement (RP) The sale of a portfolio of securities with a prearranged buyback one or several days later. A repurchase agreement, or "repo" as it is often called, involves the bank "selling" the investor a portfolio of securities, then agreeing to buy the securities back (repurchase) at an agreed-upon future date.

Required rate of return, k_s The minimum rate of return on a stock that stockholders consider acceptable.

Required rate of return, or hurdle rate The discount rate (cost of funds) that the IRR must exceed for a project to be considered acceptable.

Reserve borrowing capacity The ability to borrow money at a reasonable cost when good investment opportunities arise; firms often use less debt than specified by the MM optimal capital structure to ensure that they can obtain debt capital later if they need to.

Residual dividend policy A policy in which the dividend paid is set equal to the actual earnings minus the amount of retained earnings necessary to finance the firm's optimal capital budget.

Residual value The value of leased property at the end of the lease term.

Resiliency Condition of a market in which new orders enter when a temporary imbalance of buy or sell orders push the price away from its equilibrium level.

Restricted current asset investment policy A policy under which holdings of cash and marketable securities, inventories, and receivables are minimized.

Restrictive covenant A provision in a debt contract that constrains the actions of the borrower.

Retail lockbox Is set up for a business receiving a large volume of relatively small dollar checks. Processing costs must be considered here along with collection float, and optically scannable invoices are read by machine to minimize human processing.

Retail lockbox system A lockbox system structured to handle a large volume of standardized invoice materials where the remittance checks have a relatively low average dollar face value.

Retail market An exchange situation where the buyers and/or sellers are primarily small entities, especially individuals.

Retained earnings The balance sheet account that indicates the total amount of earnings the firm has not paid out as dividends throughout its history; these earnings have been reinvested in the firm.

Return items Checks that bounce, leading to their return to the bank of first deposit through each bank involved in the forward presentment.

Return on common equity (ROE) The ratio of net income to common equity; it measures the rate of return on common stockholders' investment.

Return on total assets (ROA) The ratio of net income to total assets; it provides an idea of the overall return on investment earned by the firm.

Revenue Anticipation Notes Short-term debt instruments that provide working capital financing for states and localities as they await anticipated revenues from other sources of revenue.

Revenue securities Issues which tie cash flows to pledged revenue from the facility(ies) being financed: rental revenue from a convention center, or tolls from a bridge or toll road.

Reverse positive pay The disbursing bank sends the check presentment file to the company to see if all the items should be honored.

Reverse repo The other side of a repurchase agreement. In this case a firm needing a temporary source of cash for a few days can negotiate with its bank to temporarily sell securities with an agreement to repurchase them at the end of the specified period.

Revocable letter of credit Letter of credit issued by a bank that can be cancelled at any time without prior notification to the beneficiary.

Revolving credit agreement Allows the borrower to continually borrow and repay amounts up to an agreed-upon limit. The agreement is annually renewable at a variable interest rate during an interim period of anywhere from one to five years.

Revolving (guaranteed) line of credit A formal, committed line of credit extended by a bank or other lending institution.

Riding the yield curve Investing strategy that involves buying securities with maturities longer than the investment horizon, fully intending to liquidate the position early.

Risk In a financial market context, the chance that a financial asset will not earn the return promised.

Risk-adjusted discount rate Higher (lower) interest rate used in present value calculations when the project is of greater (lesser) risk than the average capital budgeting project invested in by the company.

Risk aversion Risk-averse investors require higher rates of return to invest in higher-risk securities.

Risk classes An approach to risk adjusting potential capital projects by developing discount rates based on anticipated variability in the projects' cash flows. Proposals with longer time horizons, permanent effects on the firm's cash flows, or those with a short time horizon that might result in a very large range or standard deviation of outcomes would be assigned a higher discount rate.

Risk-free rate Is determined primarily by investors' collective time preferences, the rate of inflation expected over the maturity period, and demand-side influences such as economic productivity.

Risk premium, RP The portion of the expected return that can be attributed to the additional risk of an investment; it is the difference between the expected rate of return on a given risky asset and that on a less risky asset.

Risk spread The added yield necessary to compensate for risk factors other than maturity differences, such as default risk and liquidity risk.

Risk structure of interest rate Set of interest rate differences between various securities which arise due to any factor other than a different maturity. The main risk factors giving rise to this structure are default risk, reinvestment rate risk, and purchasing power risk.

Root mean square error Has become increasingly popular in business and economic applications. It simply involves taking the square root of the mean square error (MSE).

S

S corporation A small corporation which, under Subchapter S of the Internal Revenue Code, elects to be taxed as a proprietorship or a partnership yet retains limited liability and other benefits of the corporate form of organization.

Safety stock An extra inventory balance that acts as insurance against inventory stock outs.

Sale and leaseback An operation whereby a firm sells land, buildings, or equipment and simultaneously leases the property back for a specified period under specific terms.

Sales agents Dealers sometimes function as brokers in their role as for banks and other issuers of short-term securities. For a commission the agent will locate buyers for the institution's securities, again without risk because the agent does not have to buy and resell the securities.

Sales forecast A forecast of a firm's unit and dollar sales for some future period; generally based on recent sales trends plus forecasts of the economic prospects for the nation, region, industry, and so forth.

Same-Day Settlement Is presentment of a check to the paying bank by 8:00 A.M. local time, with payment of the check required by Fedwire by the close of business day. This Fed initiative was enacted to reduce arbitrary holds or fees used by disbursing banks to slow check clearing.

Scenario analysis A risk analysis technique in which "bad" and "good" sets of financial circumstances are compared with a most likely, or base case, situation.

Seasonal dating Allows customers to purchase inventory before the peak buying season and defer payment until after the peak season.

Secondary market The market in which "used" stocks are traded after they have been issued by corporations.

Secured loan A loan backed by collateral; for short-term loans, the collateral often is inventory, receivables, or both.

Securities and Exchange Commission (SEC) The U.S. government agency that regulates the issuance and trading of stocks and bonds.

Securitization Involves issuing debt securities collateralized by a pool of selected financial assets such a mortgages, auto loans or credit card receivables.

Security A specific investment offered by a given issuer.

Security market line (SML) The line that shows the relationship between risk as measured by beta and the required rate of return for individual securities.

Sell hedge A hedge created by selling a futures contract.

Selling group A group (network) of brokerage firms formed for the purpose of distributing a new issue of securities.

Semiannual compounding The arithmetic process of determining the final value of a cash flow or series of cash flows when interest is added twice a year.

Semistrong-form efficient Description of foreign exchange markets, implying that all relevant public information is already reflected in prevailing spot exchange rates.

Sensitivity analysis Means of incorporating risk in financial outcomes which involves varying key inputs, one at a time, and observing the effect on the decision variable(s). For example, the analyst might vary the sales level, and observe the effect on the company's cash forecast.

Serial correlation The existence of correlated errors in a regression model of a time series of data points.

Shareholder value maximization Presumed goal of publicly held companies, in which decisions are made which will lead to the greatest anticipated increase in the value of the financial claims on the company. In practice, the company's stock price is utilized as a measure of the value of all financial claims.

Shelf registration Securities are registered with the SEC for sale at a later date; the securities are held "on the shelf" until the sale.

Short-term credit Any liability originally scheduled for repayment within one year.

Sight draft A formal, written agreement whereby an importer (drawee) contracts to pay a certain amount on demand ("at sight") to the exporter. The bank is not extending credit, but simply helping in the payment process by receiving the draft and presenting it to the drawee. Sight drafts often must have documentation attached to verify that conditions for payment (receipt, or "sight" of goods) have been met.

Signal An action taken by a firm's management that provides clues to investors about how management views the firm's prospects.

Simple interest Arrangement in which interest is only added to the account at maturity. Because no compounding occurs, the nominal interest rate is also the annual effective rate.

Simple interest approximation formula Simple interest formula to approximate the present value effect of a financial decision. the simplicity of this approach makes its use desirable where the effect of ignoring cash flow compounding would not have a significant effect on the valuation of those flows.

Simple interest loan Both the amount borrowed and the interest charged on that amount are paid at the maturity of the loan; there are no payments made before maturity.

Simple (quoted) interest rate The contracted, or quoted, interest rate that is used to compute the interest paid per period.

Simple, or quoted, rate, i_{SIMPLE} The rate quoted by borrowers and lenders that is used to determine the rate earned per compounding period (periodic rate).

Simple regression A statistical model in which the equation used to predict the value of the variable of interest (dependent variable) involves just one predictor (independent) variable.

Simulation Technique for assessing the degree of uncertainty. Probability distributions are developed for the input variables; simulation uses this information to generate possible outcomes.

Single-Buyer policy Policy administered by Ex-Im Bank which allows the exporter to selectively insure certain transactions.

Single European Act Act intended to remove numerous barriers imposed on trade and capital flows between European countries.

Sinking fund A required annual payment designed to amortize a bond or preferred stock issue.

Small Business Policy Policy providing enhanced coverage to new exporters and small businesses.

Smithsonian Agreement Conference between nations in 1971 that resulted in a devaluation of the dollar against major currencies and a widening of boundaries (2 percent in either direction) around the newly established exchange rates.

Snake Arrangement established in 1972, whereby European currencies were tied to each other within specified limits.

Social responsibility The concept that businesses should be actively concerned with the welfare of society at large.

Solvency A firm is solvent when the dollar level of its assets exceed the dollar level of its liabilities.

Special Drawing Rights (SDRs) Reserves established by the International Monetary Fund; they are used only for intergovernment transactions; the SDR also serves as a unit of account (determined by the values of five major currencies) that is used to denominate some internationally traded goods and services, as well as some foreign bank deposits and loans.

Speculative balance A cash balance that is held to enable the firm to take advantage of any bargain purchases that might arise.

Speculative motive Additional inventory held to take advantage of unique business opportunities such as future shortages.

Speculator A person who has no operating cash flow position to protect and is trying to profit solely from interest rate movements.

Spontaneous financing Those financing sources such as accounts payables and accruals that are generated as a part of the operations of the firm.

Spontaneously generated funds Funds that are obtained from routine business transactions.

Spot market Market in which exchange transactions occur for immediate exchange.

Spot rates Existing prices or interest rates in today's markets. In foreign exchange, the spot rate is an exchange rate quote based on immediate deliver of the currency being traded.

Spurious correlation Chance association between two variables, which the analyst should watch for because it might account for a high coefficient of determination.

Stable distribution Pattern of outcomes which characterizes a variable with a well-defined, consistent trend or seasonal component.

Stable, predictable dividends Payment of a specific dollar dividend each year, or periodically increasing the dividend at a constant rate—the annual dollar dividend is relatively predictable by investors.

Stakeholders Individuals or entities that have an interest in the well-being of a firm—stockholders, creditors, employees, customers, suppliers, and so on.

Stand-alone risk The risk an asset would have if it were a firm's only asset; it is measured by the variability of the asset's expected returns.

Standard check processing When the deposit bank verifies the depositor's cash letter—which lists the checks and their amounts—and then encodes the dollar amount on the MICR line and sends the checks to a correspondent bank or the nearest Federal Reserve facility to be cleared back to the disbursing bank on which the check was written.

Standard deviation, σ A measure of the tightness, or variability, of a set of outcomes.

Standby letter of credit Document used to guarantee invoice payments to a supplier; it promises to pay the beneficiary if the buyer fails to pay.

Statement of cash flows A statement reporting the impact of a firm's operating, investing, and financing activities on cash flows over an accounting period.

Statement of retained earnings A statement reporting the change in the firm's retained earnings as a result of the income generated and retained during the year. The balance sheet figure for retained earnings is the sum of the earnings retained for each year the firm has been in business.

Statistical decomposition A complex forecasting technique which uses the past observations of a variable to forecast future values. Sometimes called Census X-11 decomposition (after the computer software developed by the Census Bureau), this approach is especially useful for forecasting variables which have trend, seasonal, and cyclical variations.

Stepped-up exercise price An exercise price that is specified to be higher if a warrant is exercised after a designated date.

Sterilized intervention Intervention by the Federal Reserve in the foreign exchange market, with simultaneous intervention in the Treasury securities markets to offset any effects on the dollar money supply; thus, the intervention in the foreign exchange market is achieved without affecting the existing dollar money supply.

Stochastic model Data input for stochastic models represent probability distributions for one or more of the variables.

Stock dividend A dividend paid in the form of additional shares of stock rather than cash.

Stockholder wealth maximization The appropriate goal for management decisions; considers the risk and timing associated with expected earnings per share in order to maximize the price of the firm's common stock.

Stock split An action taken by a firm to increase the number of shares outstanding, such as doubling the number of shares outstanding by giving each stockholder two new shares for each one formerly held.

Stone model Optimization process similar to Miller-Orr but allows the cash manager's knowledge of imminent cash flows to permit him to selectively override model directives.

Straddle Combination of a put option and a call option.

Stretching accounts payable The practice of deliberately paying accounts payable late.

Strike price See Exercise price.

Striking (exercise) price The price that must be paid (buying or selling) for a share of common stock when an option is exercised.

Strong-form efficient Description of foreign exchange markets, implying that all relevant public information and private information is already reflected in prevailing spot exchange rates.

Structural Adjustment Loan Facility (SAL) Facility established in 1980 by the World Bank to enhance a country's long-term economic growth through financing projects.

Subordinated debenture A bond having a claim on assets only after the senior debt has been paid off in the event of liquidation.

Sunk cost A cash outlay that already has been incurred and that cannot be recovered regardless of whether the project is accepted or rejected.

Super-NOW accounts While banks continue to set higher minimum balance requirements for NOW accounts, in 1986 regulators removed interest rate distinctions between the accounts by eliminating the maximum NOW rate of 5 1/4%.

Supplier credit Credit provided by the supplier to itself to fund its operations.

Supply chain management The process by which companies move materials and parts from suppliers through the production process and on to the consumers.

Sustainable growth The rate of sales growth that is compatible with a firm's established financial policies including asset turnover, net profit margin, dividend payout, and debt to equity ratio and assumes that new equity is derived only through retained earnings not new common stock.

Swap Exchange of securities between two parties, often with the assistance of an intermediary known as a swap dealer. In its simplest form, a company engaging in a swap exchanges a fixed interest rate obligation for one that has a variable, or floating interest rate.

Swap strategies See, for example, *maturity extension swap* and *yield spread swap*.

Sweep accounts Special accounts whereby excess funds are automatically or at the cash manager's request transferred ("swept") from the demand deposit account into an interest-bearing overnight investment.

SWIFT The Society of Worldwide Interbank Financial Telecommunications, is a communication network for relaying payment instructions for international transactions. It boasts roughly 1,500 member banks in 68 counties, and almost 3,000 banks are connected to the network.

Symmetric information The situation in which investors and managers have identical information about the firm's prospects.

Synchronized cash flows A situation in which cash inflows coincide with cash outflows, thereby permitting a firm to hold low transactions balances.

Syndicate Sometimes a group of investment banks works together on the marketing and shares the risk involved with bringing a new issue to market, which may or may not be acceptable at the predetermined price. This grouping is called a syndicate.

Syndicated Eurocredit loans Loans provided by a group (or syndicate) of banks in the Eurocredit market.

Synthetic composite An artificial security which is devised to mirror the portfolio's average coupon interest rate, maturity, and risk rating.

Systematic risk Is the degree of sensitivity of the company's stock returns to market-wide returns.

T

Takeover An action whereby a person or group succeeds in ousting a firm's management and taking control of the company.

Target (minimum) cash balance The minimum cash balance a firm desires to maintain in order to conduct business.

Target (optimal) capital structure The combination (percentages) of debt, preferred stock, and common equity that will maximize the price of the firm's stock.

Target zones Implicit boundaries established by central banks on exchange rates.

Tariff Tax imposed by a government on imported goods.

Tax Anticipation Notes Short-term debt instruments which provide working capital financing for states and localities as they await anticipated revenues from tax collections.

Taxable income Gross income minus exemptions and allowable deductions as set forth in the tax code.

Taxable instruments Security types that are not given preferential tax treatment, including commercial paper, domestic and Eurodollar certificates of deposit, banker's acceptances, repurchase agreements, and money market mutual funds invested in these instruments.

Taxable-equivalent yield The yield of a tax-exempt security on an after-tax basis, which facilitates comparison with the yield of taxable securities. The taxable-equivalent yield is the nominal (stated) yield divided by (1 − corporation's marginal tax rate).

Tax-advantaged instruments Those on which part or all of the income is exempted from taxation, or where the tax is deferred.

Tax-exempt commercial paper States and localities also issue some of these items. The risks are very similar to those of anticipation notes.

Tax loss carryback and carryover Losses that can be carried backward or forward in time to offset taxable income in a given year.

Technical forecasting Development of forecasts using historical prices or trends.

Temporary current assets Current assets that fluctuate with seasonal or cyclical variations in a firm's business. The accumulation of inventory in anticipation of the peak selling season and the resulting receivables generated by the increased sales. This bulge then subsides as the firm passes through its peak selling season.

Tenor Time period of drafts.

Term loan A loan made with an initial maturity of more than one year.

Term repos Repurchase agreement that is arranged with a maturity of several days to several weeks, making them well-suited for the investor having an investment horizon longer than one day.

Term spread The component of a security's return that is necessary to induce investors to bear risks linked to maturity.

Term structure of interest rates The relationship between yields and maturities of securities.

Terminal cash flow The *net* cash flow that occurs at the end of the life of a project, including the cash flows associated with (1) the final disposal of the project and (2) returning the firm's operations to where they were before the project was accepted.

Terminal value The future value of a cash flow stream.

Terminal warehouse agreement Inventories pledged as collateral are moved to a public warehouse that is physically separated from the borrower's premises.

Terms of credit The payment conditions offered to credit customers; the terms include the length of the credit period and any cash discounts offered.

Thin market One with little participation by buyers and/or sellers.

Third-party information vendor An information service that receives deposit information from field offices and transmits that information to the appropriate concentration banks and to corporate headquarters.

Tiered pricing The Fed has proposed this method where it reduces its charges to banks submitting large volumes of checks. This move to preserve its market share is seen as contradictory to the privatization initiative that the Fed officially espouses.

Time draft Involves a credit element, because the payment obligation agreed to by the drawee is designated as due at a specified future date. Time drafts are usually dated after verification of a shipment of goods.

Time preferences for consumption The preferences of consumers for current consumption as opposed to saving for future consumption.

Time-series analysis Analysis of relationships between two or more variables over periods of time.

Time series models Models that examine series of historical data; sometimes used as a means of technical forecasting, by examining moving averages.

Time series regression A naive modeling approach in the sense that the mere passage of time generally does not cause the variable to change in value.

Time-series techniques Forecasting methods which predict future movements in the forecast variable based on patterns revealed in historical movements of that same variable.

Times-interest-earned (TIE) ratio A ratio that measures the firm's ability to meet its annual interest obligations; calculated by dividing earnings before interest and taxes by interest charges.

Total assets turnover ratio The ratio calculated by dividing sales by total assets.

Trade acceptance Draft that allows the buyer to obtain merchandise prior to paying for it.

Trade credit Permission to delay payment which arises when goods are sold under delayed payment terms.

Trade discount Percent reduction to quoted price offered to all customers, and not linked to early payment. This discount is typically offered to all customers, and the seller expects all customers to pay at the discounted price within the agreed-upon period. One example is a quantity discount, a price break given for a large purchase.

Traders Market participants which try to profit on anticipated interest rate or currency movements. They hold securities not as intermediaries, but as investors attempting to gain profits for their company's own account.

Transaction approach An approach to bank selecting in which there is a decoupling or "unbundling" of services, meaning the company will not necessarily borrow from the bank(s) it utilizes for cash management services. Increasingly prevalent, in this approach the treasurer selects the bank(s) that can best provide a specific service or can provide it at the best price.

Transaction exposure Degree to which the value of future cash transactions can be affected by exchange rate fluctuations.

Transaction motive Inventory held in relation to the level of operating activity expected by the firm.

Transaction sets A set of standards for EDI information flows developed by the ANSI X12 committee to facilitate the electronic communication between trading patterns.

Transactions balance A cash balance necessary for day-to-day operations; the balance associated with routine payments and collections.

Transferable letter of credit Document that allows the first beneficiary on a standby letter of credit to transfer all or part of the original letter of credit to a third party.

Transfer agent The financial institution that takes care of updating the records for the corporation's stock and registered bonds.

Transfer items Checks drawn on banks that do not participate in a bank's local clearing house or exchange; these are sometimes called "out-of-town" checks.

Transfer pricing Policy for pricing goods sent by either the parent or a subsidiary to a subsidiary of an MNC.

Transit items Are checks drawn on banks that do not participate in a deposit bank's local clearinghouse or exchange.

Transit routing number Also called the FRD/ABA (Federal Reserve District/American Banker's Association) bank ID number, a number imprinted on checks which identifies the payee's bank. This number is used by the deposit bank to determine how best to clear the check.

Translation exposure Degree to which a firm's consolidated financial statements are exposed to fluctuations in exchange rates.

Treasury management workstation A computer system that provides a means for the treasury manager to efficiently manage cash concentration, account balances at banks, cash transfers, and the short-term investment and borrowing portfolio. These are sold by banks and some specialized vendors.

Trend analysis An analysis of a firm's financial ratios over time, used to determine the improvement or deterioration in its financial situation.

Triangular arbitrage Action to capitalize on a discrepancy where the quoted cross exchange rate is not equal to the rate that should exist at equilibrium.

Trust receipt loans A financing arrangement where the collateralized inventory items are noted by serial number or some other readily identifiable mark.

Trust services Safekeeping, record keeping, and perhaps investing of corporate or individual pension or profit-sharing plans. For a corporate pension, the trustee institution receives the payments, invests them, maintains record for each of the employees, and pays the pensioners after they retire.

Trustee An official who ensures that the bondholders' interests are protected and that the terms of the indenture are carried out.

Trustee under indenture The third-party financial institution charged by investors with the responsibility of monitoring the issuing corporation to ensure that it abides by all provisions of the bond agreement, called indenture.

U

Umbrella policy Policy issued to a bank or trading company to insure exports of an exporter and handle all administrative requirements.

Unbiased expectations hypothesis A theory of interest rate determination which posits that the prevailing yield curve is mathematically derived from the present short-term rate and expectations for rates that will exist at various points in time in the future.

Uncollected balance percentages A proportional breakdown of the present accounts receivable balance, with the proportions based on the month the credit sales originated. The pitfalls of DSO, accounts receivable turnover, and the aging schedule have led to the development of this improved measure, in which the receivables balance is broken down, and the monthly components are divided by the credit sales in the month in which the receivables originated. Sometimes called the "payments pattern approach," the uncollected balance percentages accurately depict a company's collection experience, even when sales are changing.

Uncommitted lines of credit Short-term lending agreements which are not technically binding on the bank, although they are almost always honored. Uncommitted lines are usually renewable annually if both parties are agreeable. A less formal agreement than a committed line and the availability of funds may be in question if the general economic or bank internal liquidity position slips.

Underwriter's spread The difference between the price at which the investment banking firm buys an issue from a company and the price at which the securities are sold in the primary market; it represents the investment banker's gross profit on the issue.

Underwriting syndicate A syndicate of investment firms formed to spread the risk associated with the purchase and distribution of a new issue of securities.

Underwritten arrangement Agreement for the sale of securities in which the investment bank guarantees the sale by purchasing the securities from the issuer, thus agreeing to bear any risks involved in the transaction.

Uneven cash flow stream A series of cash flows in which the amount varies from one period to the next.

Uniform commercial code A system of standards that simplifies procedures for establishing loan security.

Unilateral transfers Accounting for government and private gifts and grants.

Unique ZIP code Used by banks to increase the efficiency of their lockbox operations.

Unsecured Lending arrangement in which there is no collateral backing up the loan in the event of a default.

Upper control limit (UCL) Cash balance that triggers a purchase of securities large enough to reduce excess cash balances to a predetermined return point.

Usable funds The net proceeds the firm receives from the financing sources. This represents the amount borrowed less compensating balances, in the case of credit lines, and the bid-ask spread in the case of commercial paper.

Usage rate The daily rate of drawing down the inventory balance. Calculated by dividing the total inventory needs by the number of days in the production planning period.

V

Valuation The determination of the present dollar value of a series of cash flows.

Valuation approach Method of financial decision-making in which the anticipated shareholder value effect determines which alternative is chosen. The present values of cash inflows and outflows are compared for each alternative.

Value added network (VAN) A computer system that receives EDI information from one firm in one format and transmits to another firm or bank in a different format. The system transmits messages and data from point of origination to prespecified endpoints, and which may offer one or more auxiliary services.

Value dating Involves forward movement of the amount of a deposited check and back dating of a presented check. This is a common practice by some European banks.

Variable costs Expenses that increase or decrease with the level of production or sales, such as direct labor or raw materials.

Variable identification Involves determining what items need to be forecasted and how best to measure those items.

Variable rate demand notes Medium-term debt instruments issued by municipalities, which are found in some corporate short-term investments portfolios because their interest rates are periodically reset.

Variance, σ^2 The standard deviation squared. The amount by which the actual amount is over or under the forecasted or budgeted amount.

Variance analysis model Receivables control technique that builds on the decomposition model, and compares actual receivables performance to the budgeted amounts. If the budget captures the unique conditions and sales levels a company is experiencing, or is so adjusted after the period is over ("flexible budgeting") then one can discern the true reason(s) for changes in receivables levels.

Vertical merger A merger between a firm and one of its suppliers or customers.

W

Warrant A long-term option issued by a corporation to buy a stated number of shares of common stock at a specified price.

WCR/S Working capital requirements divided by sales.

Weak-form efficient Description of foreign exchange markets, implying that all historical and current exchange rate information is already reflected in prevailing spot exchange rates.

Weekend effect A concern in making cash transfers that takes into account weekend balances, since deposit accounts in the United States do not earn interest, and also considers weekend deposits that will be credited to the deposit account on Monday.

Weighted-average cost of capital (WACC) The summed product of the proportion of each type of capital used and the cost of that capital source, this "hurdle rate" for capital investments is usually based on a company's long-term financing sources.

Wholesale lockbox system Special arrangement for collecting mailed payments, established for collecting relatively few large dollar remittances. Because the dollar amounts per check are larger (perhaps $1 million or more), the received checks are processed more often and checks are processed for deposit more rapidly by bank than by company personnel.

Wholesale market Investment supply and demand interaction for large dollar transactions between large investors (such as the money market).

"Window dressing" techniques Techniques employed by firms to make their financial statements look better than they actually are.

Wire drawdowns Wire transfers that are initiated by the receiving party, instead of the sender or payor.

Wire transfers Are bookkeeping entries that simultaneously debit the payor's account and credit the payee's account. The best way to quickly move money from one place to another is with a wire transfer. A real-time transfer of account balances between banks.

With recourse When the factor can demand funds returned for uncollected receivables.

Without recourse The seller is not liable for uncollected receivables.

Working capital A firm's investment in short-term assets—cash, marketable securities, inventory, and accounts receivable.

Working capital cycle The continual flow of resources through the various working capital accounts such as cash, accounts receivables, inventory, and payables.

Working Capital Guarantee Program Program conducted by Ex-Im Bank which encourages commercial banks to extend short-term export financing to eligible exporters; Ex-Im Bank provides a guarantee in the loan's principal and interest.

Working capital investment decision The proportion of total assets held in current asset accounts, with the outcome usually linked closely to the company's risk posture.

Working capital management The management of short-term assets (investments) and liabilities (financing sources).

Working capital policy Decisions regarding (1) the target levels for each current asset account and (2) how current assets will be financed.

Working capital requirements The difference between current operating assets (receivables, inventory, and prepaids) and current operating liabilities (accounts payable and accruals).

Work in process inventory Inventory of items beyond the raw material stage but not yet at the completed product state.

World Bank Bank established in 1944 to enhance economic development by providing loans to countries.

World Trade Organization Organization established to provide a forum for multilateral trade negotiations and to settle trade disputes related to the GATT accord.

Worst-case scenario An analysis in which all of the input variables are set at their worst reasonably forecasted values.

Writer Seller of an option.

Y

Yankee stock offerings Offerings of stock by non-U.S. firms in the U.S. markets.

Yield curve A graph showing the relationship between yields and maturities of securities.

Yield spread The difference between two interest rates, expressed as a percentage difference.

Yield spread swap Exchange of one debt security for another, usually with the motivation of taking advantage of a mispriced security, based on the investor's study of historical interest rate differences.

Yield to maturity (YTM) The average rate of return earned on a bond if it is held to maturity.

Z

Zero-balance account (ZBA) A special checking account used for disbursements that has a balance equal to zero when there is no disbursement activity.

Zero coupon bond A bond that pays no annual interest but is sold at a discount below par, thus providing compensation to investors in the form of capital appreciation.

Zero-growth stock A common stock whose future dividends are not expected to grow at all; that is, $g = 0$, and $\hat{D}_1 = \hat{D}_2 = \ldots = \hat{D}_\infty$.

Module 700 Endnotes

1. See Verlyn Richards and Eugene Laughlin, "A Cash Conversion Cycle Approach to Liquidity Analysis," *Financial Management,* Spring 1980, 32–38.
2. Chun-Hao Chang, Krishnan Dandapani, and Arun J. Prakish, "Current Assets Policies of European Corporations: A Critical Examination," *Management International Review,* Special Issue 1995/2, 105–117.
3. See Eugene F. Brigham, Louis C. Gapenski, and Phillip R. Daves, *Intermediate Financial Management,* 6th ed. (Fort Worth, Tex.: The Dryden Press, 1999), Chapter 18, for a more complete discussion of the problems with the DSO and aging schedule and how to correct for them.
4. Franco Modigliani and Merton H. Miller, "The Cost of Capital, Corporation Finance, and the Theory of Investment," *American Economic Review,* June 1958, 261–297, and "Corporate Income Taxes and the Cost of Capital," *American Economic Review,* June 1963, 433–443. Modigliani and Miller both won Nobel Prizes for their work.
5. Myron J. Gordon "Optimal Investment and Financing Policy," *Journal of Finance,* May 1963, 264–272, and John Lintner, "Dividends, Earnings, Leverage, Stock Prices, and the Supply of Capital to Corporations," *Review of Economics and Statistics,* August 1962, 243–269.
6. Rafael La Porta, Florencio Lopez-de-Silanes, Andrei Shleifer, and Robert W. Vishny, "Agency Problems and Dividend Policies Around the World," unpublished manuscript, Harvard University, November 1997.
7. Copeland, Koller, and Murrin, *Valuation: Measuring and Managing the Value of Companies,* 3rd ed., John Wiley & Sons, Inc., 2000.
8. *Ibid.*
9. Palepu, Bernard, Healy, *Business Analysis and Valuation Using Financial Statements,* Cincinnati, OH: Southwestern Publishing Company, 1996.
10. Like Equation 7.54a, the simplification shown in Equation 7.55a is found by applying the algebra of geometric progressions. This equation is useful in situations in which the required values of i and n are not in the tables or when a financial calculator is not available.
11. It should be apparent from Equation 7.55 that, unlike the interest factors for the FV and PV of a lump-sum amount ($FVIF_{i,n}$ and $PVIF_{i,n}$, respectively), the interest factors for the FV and PV of an annuity ($FVIFA_{i,n}$ and $PVIFA_{i,n}$, respectively) are not reciprocals of each other. In other words, the inverse of the sum of a series of values does not equal the sum of the inverses of those same values—that is, $1/(2 + 3 + 4) = 1/9 \neq 1/2 + 1/3 + 1/4 = 13/12$.

MODULE

Information Technology

801 Information Technology Strategies, 481

803 Role of Information Technology and Chief Information Officer, 487

805 Information Systems Planning, 488

810 Information Technology Control and Governance, 496

815 Information Technology Risk Management, 497

820 Managing Information and Technology, 503

825 Decision Making and Information Technology, 511

830 Value Creation With Information Technology, 519

835 Quality and Information Technology, 525

840 Best Practices in Information Technology, 526

845 Data and Knowledge Management, 530

850 Systems Development and Acquisition, 551

855 Managing Information Technology Resources, 578

860 Telecommunications and Networks, 589

865 Business Information Systems, 608

870 Information Technology Security and Controls, 621

875 Electronic Commerce and Information Technology, 630

880 Information Technology Contingency Plans, 641

885 Auditing and Information Technology, 643

890 Ethics and Information Technology, 644

895 Law and Information Technology, 647

899 International Issues, 653

Module 800 Glossary, 659

Module 800 Endnotes, 673

Information Technology Strategies

Strategic Uses of Information Systems

Strategy and Strategic Moves

Although many information systems are built to solve problems, many others are built to seize opportunities. And, as anyone in business can tell you, identifying a problem is easier than creating an opportunity. Why? Because a problem already exists; it is an obstacle to a desired mode of operation and, as such, calls attention to itself. An opportunity, on the other hand, is less tangible. It takes a certain amount of vision to identify an opportunity, or to create one and seize it. Information systems that help seize opportunities are called **strategic information systems (SISs)**. They can be developed from scratch, or they can evolve from an organization's existing information systems (ISs).

The word *strategy* originates from the Greek word "*strategos*," meaning "general." In war, a strategy is a plan to gain advantage over the enemy. Other disciplines, especially business, have borrowed the term. As you know from media coverage, corporate executives often discuss actions in ways that make business competition sound like war. Businesspeople must devise decisive courses of action to win, just as generals do. In business, a strategy is a plan designed to help an organization outperform its competitors. However, business strategy, unlike battle plans, often takes the form of creating new opportunities rather than beating rivals.

In a free-market economy, it is difficult for a business to do well without some strategic planning. Although strategies vary, they tend to fall into some basic categories, such as developing a new product, identifying an unmet consumer need, changing a service to entice more customers or retain existing clients, or taking any other action that increases the organization's value through improved performance.

Many strategies do not, and cannot, involve information systems. But increasingly, corporations are able to implement certain strategies—such as maximizing sales and lowering costs—thanks to the innovative use of information systems. In other words, better information gives corporations a competitive advantage in the marketplace. A company achieves **strategic advantage** by using strategy to maximize its strengths, resulting in a **competitive advantage**. When a business uses a strategy intending to *create* a market for new products or services, it does not aim to compete with other organizations, because that market does not yet exist. Therefore, a strategic move is not always a competitive move. However, in a free-enterprise society, a market rarely remains the domain of one organization for long; thus, competition ensues almost immediately. So, we often use the terms "competitive advantage" and "strategic advantage" interchangeably.

You may have heard statements about using the World Wide Web ("the Web") strategically. Business competition is no longer limited to a particular country or even region of the world. To increase the sale of goods and services, companies must regard the entire world as their market. Because thousands of corporations and hundreds of millions of consumers have access to the Web, augmenting business via the Web has become strategic: many companies that utilized the Web early on have enjoyed greater market shares, greater experiences, and larger revenues than latecomers. Some companies developed information systems, or features of information systems, that are unique, such as "one click" purchase and reverse auctioning. Practically any Web-based system that gives a company competitive advantage is a strategic information system.

Achieving a Competitive Advantage

Let's consider competitive advantage in terms of a for-profit company, whose major goal is to maximize profits by lowering costs and increasing revenue. A for-profit company achieves competitive advantage when its profits increase significantly, most commonly through increased market share. Exhibit 800.1 lists eight basic initiatives that can be used to gain competitive advantage, including offering a product or service that competitors cannot provide or providing the same product or service more attractively to customers. It is important to understand that the eight listed are the most common, but not the only, types of business strategy an organization can pursue. The essence of strategy is innovation, so competitive advantage often occurs when an organization tries a strategy that no one has tried before.

Exhibit 800.1 *Eight Basic Initiatives to Competitive Advantage*

Initiative	Benefit
1. Reduce costs	A company can gain advantage if it can sell more units at a lower price while providing quality and maintaining or increasing its profit margin.
2. Raise barriers to market entrants	A company can gain advantage if it deters potential entrants into the market, enjoying less competition and more market potential.
3. Establish high switching costs	A company can gain advantage if it creates high switching costs, making it economically infeasible for customers to buy from competitors.
4. Create new products or services	A company can again advantage if it offers a unique product or service.
5. Differentiate products or services	A company can gain advantage if it can attract customers by convincing them its product differs from the competition's.
6. Enhance products or services	A company can gain advantage if its product or service is better than anyone else's.
7. Establish alliances	Companies from different industries can help each other gain advantage by offering combined packages of goods or services at special prices.
8. Lock in suppliers or buyers	A company can gain advantage if it can lock in either suppliers or buyers, making it economically impractical for suppliers or buyers to deal with competitors.

Exhibit 800.2 *Many Strategic Moves Can Work Together to Achieve a Competitive Advantage*

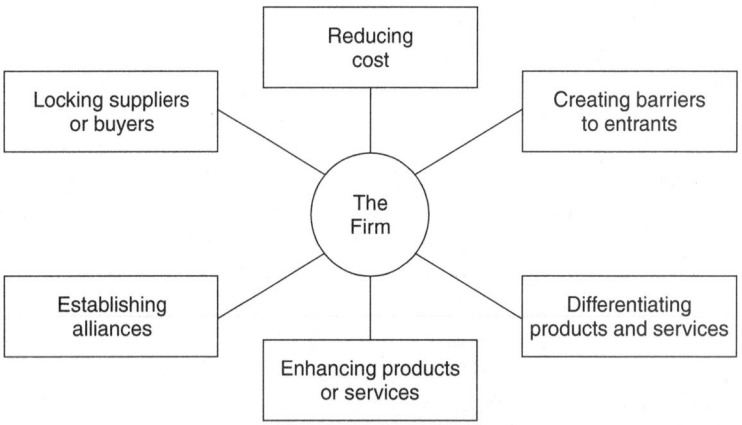

For example, **Dell** was the first PC manufacturer to use the Web to take customer orders. Competitors have long imitated the practice, but Dell, first to gain the Web-bound audience, gained more experience than other PC makers on this e-commerce vehicle and still sells more computers via the Web than its competitors. Exhibit 800.2 indicates that a company can use many strategies together to gain a competitive advantage.

Initiative #1: Reduce Costs

Customers like to pay as little as possible while still receiving the quality of service or product they need. One way to increase market share is to lower prices, and the best way to lower prices is to lower costs. For instance, if carried out successfully, massive automation of any business process gives an organization competitive advantage. The reason is simple: automation makes an organization more productive, and any cost savings can be transferred to customers through lower prices. We saw this happen in the auto industry. In the 1970s, Japanese automakers brought robots to their production and assembly lines and reduced costs—and subsequently prices—quickly and dramatically. The robots weld, paint, and assemble parts at a far lower cost than manual labor. Until their foreign competitors began to employ robots, the Japanese had a clear competitive advantage because they were able to sell high-quality cars for less than their competitors.

In the service sector, the Web has created an opportunity to automate what until recently was considered a "human-only" activity: customer service. An enormous trend toward automating online customer service began with companies like **FedEx**, which initially gave customers an opportunity to track their parcels' status by logging on to a dedicated, private network and database. The same approach is now implemented through the Web. Many sites today include answers to FAQs (frequently asked questions). Others have special programs that can actually respond to questions a caller poses. Other Web technologies enable customers to shop, receive information on products, select items, and pay without any need for human intervention by online retailers. Online service gives businesses two major benefits: it turns service from labor-intensive to technology-intensive, which is much less expensive; and it provides customers easy access to a service seven days a week, twenty-four hours a day (commonly called 24/7). It cuts costs not only of expensive human labor but also of telephone and mailing charges. Companies that are first to adopt advanced systems reducing labor enjoy competitive advantage for as long as their competitors lag behind.

Initiative #2: Raise Barriers to Market Entrants

The smaller the number of companies competing within an industry, the better off each company is. Therefore, an organization may gain competitive advantage by making it difficult, or impossible, for other organizations to produce the product or service it provides. Using expertise or technology that is unavailable to competitors or prohibitively expensive is one way to bar new entrants.

Companies raise **barriers to entrants** in a number of ways. Obtaining legal protection of intellectual property such as an invention or artistic work bars competitors from freely using it. **Microsoft** and other software powerhouses have gained tremendous strategic advantages by copyrighting and patenting software. On the Web, there are numerous examples of such protection. Consider **Amazon.com**, probably the largest online retailer. The company secured a patent for "one click" purchases, which enables customers to enter their details, including credit information, only once. From that moment on whenever they make a purchase at the site, they can click only once to buy an item. Amazon successfully sued **BarnesandNoble.com** when B&N implemented the same technology. **Priceline.com** holds a patent for online reverse ("Name your price") auctioning, which prevented competitors from entering its business space.

Another barrier to potential new market entrants is the high expense of entering that market. An example is the pension fund management industry. **State Street Corporation** is one of its most successful competitors. In the 1980s, State Street committed massive amounts of money to developing ISs that helped make the company a leader in managing pension funds and international bank accounts. The huge capital allocation required to build a system to compete successfully with State Street's keeps new entrants out of the market. Instead, other pension management corporations rent State Street's technology and expertise. In fact, State Street derives about 70% of its revenues from selling its IS services. This company is an interesting example of an entire business refocusing around its ISs.

Initiative #3: Establish High Switching Costs

Switching costs are expenses incurred when a customer stops buying a product or service from one business and starts buying it from another. Switching costs can be explicit (such as charges the seller explicitly levies on a customer for switching) or implicit (such as the indirect costs in time and money of adjusting to a new product that does the same job as the old).

Often, explicit switching costs are fixed, nonrecurring costs, such as a penalty a buyer must pay for terminating a deal early. In the cellular telephone service industry, you can usually get an attractive deal, but if you cancel the service before a full year has passed, you have to pay a hefty penalty. So although another company's service may be more attractive, you may decide to wait the full year because the penalty outweighs the benefits of the new company's service. When you do decide to switch, you will probably discover that the telephone is not suitable for service with any other telephone company. The cost of the telephone itself, then, is another disincentive to switch.

A perfect example of indirect switching expenses are those involved in the time and money required to adjust to new software. Once a company trains its personnel to use one word-processing or spreadsheet program, a competing software company must offer a very enticing deal to make switching worthwhile. The same principle holds for many other applications, such as database management systems and Web browsers. Consider Microsoft's popular Office suite; you can download free of charge Sun Microsystems' StarOffice, a software suite that is as good as MS Office. Yet, few organizations or consumers, who are so used to MS Office, are willing to switch to StarOffice.

Initiative #4: Create New Products or Services

Clearly, creating a new and unique product or service that many organizations and individuals need gives an organization great competitive advantage. Unfortunately, the advantage lasts only until other organizations in the industry start offering an identical or similar product or service for a comparable or lower price.

Examples of this scenario abound in the software industry. For instance, **Lotus Development Corporation** became the major player in the electronic spreadsheet market after it introduced its Lotus 1-2-3 program. When two competitors tried to market similar products, Lotus sued for copyright infringement and won the court case, sustaining its market dominance for several years. However, with time, Microsoft established its Excel spreadsheet application as the world leader, not only by aggressive marketing but also by including better features in its application.

Another example of a company creating a new service is FedEx, which created a market in the late 1970s by providing overnight delivery service. FedEx's market share slipped when the U.S. Postal Service, **United Parcel Service**, and other companies entered the same market several years later, providing virtually the same service at the same or lower prices. However, FedEx regained market share by providing the means for clients to log on to FedEx's IS to track their own packages, a service it now offers through the Web. Clients can connect to the system and receive real-time information about any item they send or are scheduled to receive. The extra service has been credited for attracting clients back to FedEx. Competitors have emulated this initiative, too. Evidently, strategic initiatives cannot be static; they must be dynamic for a business to maintain its advantage.

We have already mentioned Amazon.com's one-click service. This unique feature, in addition to brand-name recognition and excellent overall service, has given the company a competitive advantage in the online retail industry. While the technologies of online catalogs, search engines, payment processing, wish lists, and customer feedback have been adopted by many online retailers and are no longer of strategic importance, the one-click feature is still a strategic technology.

One recent example of how strategic advantage can be wiped out within just a few months is in the Internet arena. **Netscape Corporation** dominated the Web browser market, which was new in 1994. By allowing individual users to download its browser free, it cornered over 80% of the market. The wide use of the browser by individuals moved commercial organizations to purchase the product and other software compatible with the browser. Netscape's dominance quickly diminished when Microsoft aggressively marketed its own browser, which many perceived as at least as good as Netscape's. Microsoft provided Internet Explorer free of charge to anyone and then bundled it into the operating system software distributed with almost all PCs. Even after the court-ordered unbundling, its browser still dominates. Microsoft now has over 85% of the browser market, while Netscape's market share has slipped to 12%.

Initiative #5: Differentiate Products or Services

A company can achieve a competitive advantage by persuading consumers that its product or service is better than its competitors', even if it is not. Called product differentiation, this advantage is usually achieved through advertising. Brand name success is a perfect example of product differentiation. Think of Levi's Jeans, Chanel and Lucky perfumes, and Nautica clothes. The customer buys the brand-name product, perceiving it to be superior to similar products. In fact, some products *are* the same, but units sold under a prestigious brand name sell for higher prices. You often see this phenomenon in the food, clothing, drug, and cosmetics markets.

The advent of the Internet as a business tool gives companies an opportunity to render a great number of services through the Web and e-mail, from delivering new software applications to answering frequently asked questions to presenting information about huge selections of items on the Web in vivid color and animation. All are new services. While mimicking such services is easy, companies that offered them first often manage to maintain a measure of competitive advantage because the brand name they established keeps attracting customers. For example, Amazon.com established a name for itself as the predominant seller of books, music CDs, and small appliances on the Web. Although **Barnes & Noble**, the big "brick and mortar" bookstore chain, followed suit and established its own online store, it found luring customers away from Amazon difficult. Clearly its brand name gives Amazon its great market share. Marketing experts have acknowledged brand-name recognition as a key to success in retail on the Web. When consumers look to purchase an item, they tend first to visit the sites that are more familiar. Online businesses can increase brand-name recognition by inventing and implementing ISs that enhance the shopping experience and the speed at which orders are fulfilled. For example, wireless phone companies introducing the concept of "rollover" minutes is a value-adding and service differentiation initiative. This concept is facilitated by information technology.

Initiative #6: Enhance Products or Services

Instead of differentiating a product or service, an organization may actually add to it to enhance its value to the consumer, called *product* or *service enhancement*. For example, car manufacturers may entice customers by offering a longer warranty period for their cars, and real-estate agents may attract more business by providing useful financing information to potential buyers.

Since the Internet opened its doors to commercial enterprises in the early 1990s, an increasing number of companies have supplemented their products and services. Their Web sites provide up-to-date information that helps customers utilize their purchased products better or receive additional services. Companies that pioneered such Internet use reaped great rewards.

For example, **Charles Schwab** gained a huge competitive advantage over other, older brokerage companies such as **Merrill Lynch**, by opening a site for online stock transactions. Nearly half its revenue now comes from this site, while revenue from stock trading of "brick and mortar" brokers constantly diminishes.

Initiative #7: Establish Alliances

Companies can gain competitive advantage by combining services to make them more attractive (and usually less expensive) than purchasing services separately. These alliances provide two draws for customers: combined service is cheaper and one-stop shopping is more convenient. The travel industry is very aggressive in this area. For example, airlines collaborate with hotel chains and car-rental firms to offer travel and lodging packages and with credit-card companies that offer discount ticket purchases from particular airlines or the products of particular manufacturers. Credit-card companies commonly offer frequent flier miles for every dollar spent. In all these cases, alliances create competitive advantages.

As Exhibit 800.3 indicates, by creating an alliance, organizations enjoy synergy: the combined profit for the allies from the sales of a package of goods or services exceeds the profits earned when each acts individually. Sometimes, the alliances form more than two organizations. Consider the benefits **American Express** and its business partners offer. Clients who subscribe to a corporate charge card receive a quarterly management report summarizing expenses by category and by employee, a 10% discount on FedEx next-business-day delivery if they pay for shipping services with the American Express card, a 10% discount on **Kinko's** products and copying services, a 2% discount on **ExxonMobil** gasoline purchases, and travel and lodging discounts from **Hertz** and **Hilton** on car rentals and lodging, respectively.

Exhibit 800.3 *Strategic Alliances Combine Services to Create Synergies*

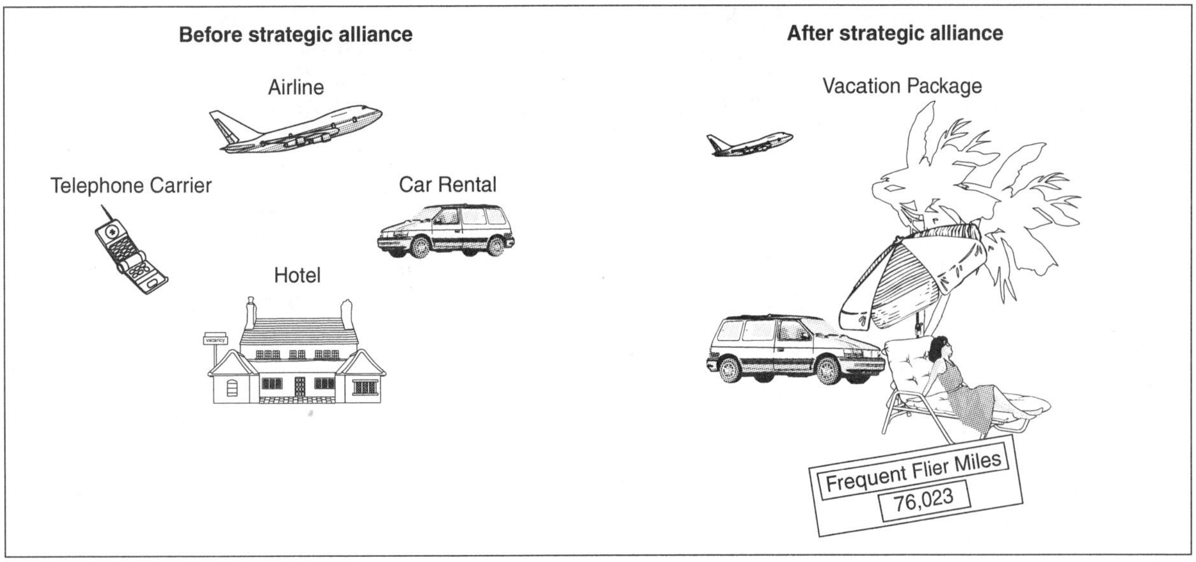

What is the common denominator of all these companies? An information system that tracks all these transactions and discounts. A package of attractive deals entices clients who need all these services (and most businesses do). Why purchase them without the discounts and other benefits? Would this offer be feasible without an IS to track transactions and discounts? Probably not.

Growing Web use for e-commerce has pushed organizations to create alliances that would be unimaginable a few years ago. Consider the alliance between **Hewlett-Packard** and FedEx. HP is a leading manufacturer of computers and computer equipment, known primarily for its excellent printers. FedEx, as we mentioned earlier, is a shipping company. HP maintains inventory of its products at FedEx facilities. When customers order items from HP via its Web site, HP routes the order, via the Web, to FedEx. FedEx packages the items and ships them to customers. This arrangement lets HP ship ordered items within hours rather than days. The alliance gives HP an advantage that other computer equipment makers do not share and gives HP a great volume of business from FedEx orders.

On the Web, the best examples of alliances are affiliate programs. Anyone who maintains a Web site can place links to commercial sites. Any purchase that results from clicking through to a commercial site rewards the first site's owner with a fee. Some online retailers have thousands of affiliates. The early adopters of such programs, Amazon.com, **Buy.com**, Priceline, and other large e-retailers, enjoyed a competitive advantage.

Initiative #8: Lock in Suppliers or Buyers

Organizations can achieve competitive advantage if they are powerful enough to lock either suppliers into their mode of operation or buyers to their product. Possessing bargaining power—the leverage to influence buyers and suppliers—is the key to this approach. As such, companies so large that suppliers and buyers must listen to their demands use this tactic nearly exclusively.

A firm gains bargaining power with a supplier either when the firm has few competitors or when the firm is a major competitor in its industry. In the former case, the fewer the companies that make up a supplier's customer base, the more important each company is to the supplier; in the latter case, the more important a specific company is to a supplier's success, the greater bargaining power that company has over that supplier.

The most common leverage in bargaining is purchase volume. Companies that spend millions of dollars purchasing parts and services have the power to force their suppliers to conform to their methods of operation, and even to shift some costs onto suppliers as part of the business arrangement. Consider **Wal-Mart**, the world's largest retailer. Not only does the company bring suppliers in for meetings in a warehouse where it badgers them to provide the lowest prices, but it also requires them to use information systems compatible with its own to automate processes.

One way to lock in *buyers* in a free market is to create the impression that an organization's product is significantly better than the competitors', or to enjoy a situation in which customers fear high switching costs. In the software arena, ERP (enterprise resource planning) applications are a good example. This type of software helps organizations manage a wide array of operations: purchasing, manufacturing, human resources, finance, and so forth. The software is expensive, costing hundreds of thousands or even millions of dollars. After a company purchases ERP software from a firm, it's locked to that firm's services: training, implementation, updates, and so forth. Thus, companies that sell ERP software, such as **SAP, Baan, PeopleSoft, J.D. Edwards**, and **Oracle**, make great efforts to improve both their software and support services to maintain leadership in this market.

Another way to lock in clients is by **creating a standard.** The software industry has pursued this strategy vigorously, especially in the Internet arena. For example, Microsoft's decision to give away its Web browser by letting both individuals and organizations download it free from its site was not altruistic. Microsoft executives knew that the greater the number of Internet Explorer users, the greater the user base. The greater the user base, the more likely organizations were to purchase Microsoft's proprietary software to help manage their Web sites. Also, once individual users committed to Internet Explorer as their main browser, they were likely to purchase Microsoft software that enhanced the browser's capabilities.

Similarly, **Adobe** gives away its Acrobat Reader software, an application that lets Web surfers open and manipulate documents created using different computers running different operating systems, such as IBM and Mac. When the Reader user base became large enough, organizations and individuals found it economically justifiable to purchase and use the writer application (the application used to create the documents) and related applications. Using this strategy put Adobe's PDF (portable data format) standard in an unrivaled position.

Role of Information Technology and Chief Information Officer

Roles and Responsibilities

The role of information technology (IT) in organizations is value creating and value enhancing. IT is a support function in helping senior management achieve their goals and objectives. The fact that a corporation has a position titled **chief information officer** (**CIO**) reflects the importance that the company places on ISs as a strategic resource. The CIO, who is responsible for all aspects of an organization's ISs, is often, but not always, a corporate vice president. In a centralized IS organization, the CIO supervises all IS professionals. In a distributed organization, this person supervises the corporate IS unit directly and the divisional IS personnel professionally. Some companies prefer to call this position **chief technology officer** (**CTO**). However, you may find organizations where there are both a CIO and a CTO and one reports to the other. There is no universal agreement of what the responsibility of each should be. Yet, in most cases when you encounter both positions in one organization, the CTO reports to the CIO.

A person who holds the position of CIO must have both technical understanding of current and developing information technologies and business knowledge. As Exhibit 800.4 shows, the CIO plays an important role in integrating the IS strategic plan into the organization's overall strategic plan. He or she must not only keep abreast of technical developments but also have a keen understanding of how different technologies can improve business processes or aid in the creation of new products and services.

The most important duties of a CIO are the following.

- Overseeing all IS research and development, including scouting new technologies that can be applied to emerging business needs and developing new products and services
- Overseeing the development of an IS infrastructure, including creating standard technologies and using organizational skills that will yield greater flexibility and shorter system development times

Exhibit 800.4 *The Traits of a Successful CIO*

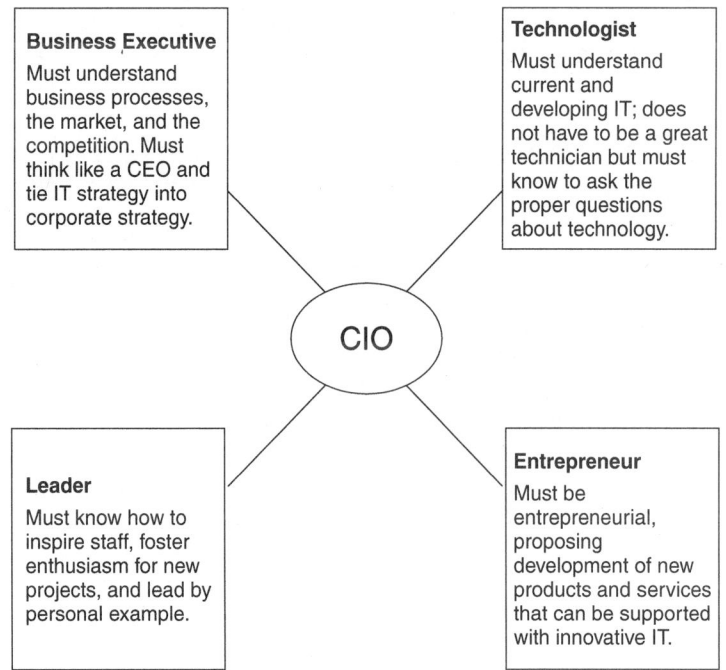

(Note that we use IT and IS interchangeably in this module.)

- Being the chief technologist, discovering how new technologies, such as data mining and virtual reality, can be applied to existing business needs
- Being the chief agent of change, using his or her companywide perspective, knowledge of technology, and change-management skills to lead or guide the redesign of business processes

The CIO position can be very demanding. Survey after survey shows that the turnover rate among North American CIOs is one of the highest among senior executives, usually around 20%. (That means that every year about one in five CIOs moves to another organization.) About 10% are promoted to another top management position within the organization.

The Chief Knowledge Officer

Chief knowledge officer (CKO) is a title that started to pop up in the mid-1990s. The position is most often found in large companies, especially in knowledge-intensive ones, such as consulting firms and companies that rely heavily on intellectual property. The CKO is responsible for coping with the daunting challenge of accumulating, organizing, and retrieving knowledge. While the CIO or CTO is responsible for the management of IT and the technical issues of ISs, the CKO is responsible for finding the appropriate knowledge resources that are strategically important for the organization, starting with the organization's own employees and also including databases, Web sites, and commercial data resources offered either online or on storage media such as compact discs. In service businesses, such as public accounting or management consulting firms, the CKO also devises methods to retain knowledge accumulated through interaction with clients. This resource reduces the need to reinvent the wheel with other clients who may need similar advice in the future. So, in general, the CKO builds the knowledge resources needed for an organization.

In some organizations, the CKO is also responsible for making the business a **learning organization.** Therefore, some organizations call this person a **chief learning officer.** This officer looks for ways to retain knowledge accumulated over time and ensure that managers and other professionals have access to information resources that help them learn how to perform their jobs better. When the CKO finds the resources, the CIO or CTO oversees the implementation of the knowledge dissemination through the firm's ISs. To succeed, the CKO must closely cooperate with the CIO or CTO.

Information Systems Planning

Key Steps in Information Systems Planning

Until the late 1970s, organizations planned without considering either the role IS professionals could take in the planning process or the planning that is necessary to create a productive IS department. Most companies called their IS units *data processing departments,* and data processing professionals were considered technicians who concentrated on automating processes rather than professionals who could help the organization achieve its goals. As indicated in several studies of the proliferation of IS use in corporate America in the 1970s, top management didn't realize for several years that the ISs themselves had to be planned, lest expenditures balloon uncontrollably. In the past, ISs were either not planned at all or planned bottom-up. Eventually, organizations recognized that the large amounts of time and money they spent on ISs required **IS planning**—for their deployment and for the resources needed to develop and maintain the systems. The modern approach to systems development is no longer based on reacting to emerging business needs, as it was earlier. Nowadays, ISs are often the core of business processes, and sometimes the generator of new revenue. Thus, IS managers are involved with short-range and long-range IS planning.

For example, because of their traditional focus, credit-card companies were accustomed to focusing on "processing data" and serving their existing customers well in that regard. Processing data was the main purpose of their ISs. Now, these same companies collect and use their data for many more reasons than just serving their customers' credit needs. The data are used in sophisticated data warehouses, data mining, and artificial intelligence techniques to gain more customers, create alliances with other organizations, and augment their market share by offering more services.

Exhibit 800.5 *Advances in Information Systems (IS) Planning Since the 1970s*

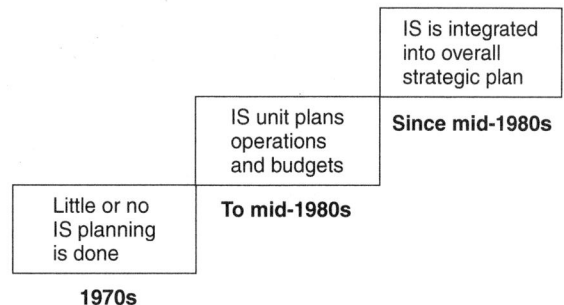

When the focus is only to automate business processes, not much planning is required; however, when ISs are to be used for strategic purposes, planning is essential.

Not only do IS managers have to plan their activities, but now many organizations integrate their IS planning into their overall organizational strategic planning. Top management acknowledges that IT plays a role in generating business, not just in improving it in small increments. For example consider **Pep Boys**, the American auto service chain. The operations of such an organization may seem simple enough not to warrant the integration of ISs into its business planning. However, management does consider ISs in its plans, which has resulted in the development of a data warehouse of close to 2 TB (terabytes), one of the country's largest data warehouses. This warehouse is a major part of the company's long-range business plan. Among other activities, top management can use the data warehouse to find out which services are most popular with customers—information that serves a strategic purpose. The company can also use the data warehouse to continue to minimize customer returns due to car problems that were not fixed well the first time.

Reaction to needs only satisfies the needs, while planning can create opportunities. As Exhibit 800.5 indicates, IS planning has evolved over the past three decades to become fully integrated into organizations' strategic planning.

IS planning includes a few key steps that are a part of any successful planning process:

- Creating a corporate and IS mission statement
- Articulating the vision for IT within the organization
- Creating IS strategic and tactical plans
- Creating a plan for operations to achieve the mission and vision
- Creating a budget to ensure that resources are available to achieve the mission and vision (see Exhibit 800.6)

Note that the broadest, most overarching statement of an organization's purpose is sometimes referred to as its *mission* and sometimes as its *vision,* terms that are often used interchangeably. For example: a university may have a mission to provide the highest-quality education it can at affordable tuition, while attracting students from a wide range of social and economic backgrounds. Some people differentiate mission and vision by saying that the mission is a declared overall long-term purpose of the organization, and the vision is the general manner in which the mission will be accomplished.

The increasing need to collaborate both with suppliers and customers in e-commerce increases the complexity of IT planning. Now CIOs and CTOs must not only plan their own company's ISs but also consider the ISs of their business partners. They must regard the systems of their suppliers, of their own company, and of their customers as if they were all one large system.

Prerequisites for Information Systems Planning

Several conditions must exist before effective IS planning can take place (see Exhibit 800.7), and the most important conditions relate to top management. First, top management must recognize that IT is an indispensable resource in all business activities. It must see that the impact IT has on an organization is at least as great as the impact of new manufacturing machinery and that it may significantly change the way an organization conducts its business. Without such recognition, senior managers may not agree to fund the acquisition of ISs.

Exhibit 800.6 *The Steps of Information Systems (IS) Planning*

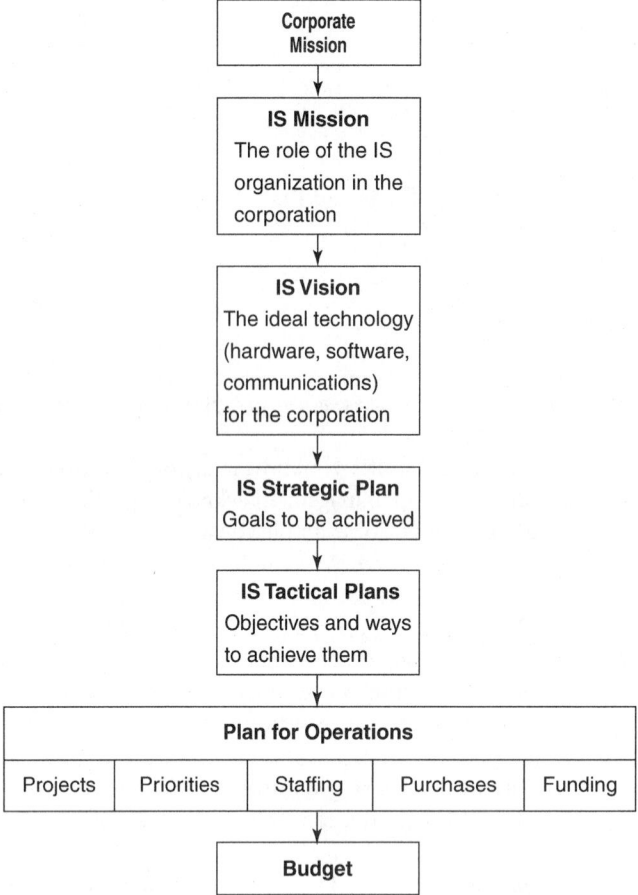

Exhibit 800.7 *Prerequisites for Effective IS Planning*

> **For IS planning to be successful, top management must:**
> - Recognize IT as an indispensable resource
> - Understand that IT is a complex resource
> - Regard IT as owned by the entire organization
> - Regard ISs as a source for gaining strategic goals
> - View ISs as a tool to control power

Second, top management must understand that the development and use of ISs must be planned like any other complex resource. Executives must be aware that ISs are more than just computers; they are hardware, software, telecommunications, people, procedures, and data. The interplay among these components must be planned to avoid waste. If the implementation is not planned well, the organization may end up with a hodgepodge of hardware and software that do not integrate well to serve the organization. While senior managers are rarely technical experts, they can always rely on internal and external advisors to explain issues such as hardware obsolescence and software incompatibility.

Third, top management must see IT as a resource owned by all members of the organization, not just the IS unit. Its development and use should be planned like human resources, manufacturing machinery, and finances.

Fourth, top management must realize that ISs are a source for achieving strategic goals, rather than merely for solving problems or supporting existing business processes. For example, top management is more likely to approve the acquisition of ISs that help augment the company's market share or sustain its position in a highly competitive market than the acquisition of computers that seemingly only make some employees happier.

Fifth, since information is power, ISs influence the distribution of power. Top management should be aware of how this power is granted or denied and should integrate that understanding into planning ISs. Top management's involvement in planning may help minimize political struggles while ensuring that employees are given appropriate access to IT resources.

When top managers recognize these realities, they ensure that ISs are planned and that IS plans become an integral part of the organizational plan.

The Corporate and IS Mission Statements

As we discussed, strategic planning starts with a corporate mission statement that details the purpose of the organization and its overall goals. These general goals provide a framework within which the organization's strategic goals will be formulated. For example, such a goal may be to become the nation's largest car-rental company. Once the corporate mission has been articulated, then each business function formulates its own mission, consistent with the organization's mission.

Although the organization's mission statement will usually not mention the IS function specifically, the IS mission statement reflects how the IS management sees its place in the organization and its responsibilities. The statement outlines the purpose of ISs in the organization. Note that the terms *IS* and *IT* are used interchangeably.

The IT Vision

As part of the mission statement, or as a separate document, the IS managers draft their vision paper. This draft is a wish list of what these professionals would like to see in terms of hardware, software, and communications, to contribute to the overall goals of the organization. For example, it may detail the following: (1) every knowledge worker who needs access to databases or business applications will have a desktop computer from which to access the resources, (2) all desktop computers will be connected by a local area network and the Internet to provide e-mail, Internet, intranet, and extranet services, (3) clients will be able to access some corporate databases through communications lines, if corporate strategy so requires, and so on. Obviously, the list may be changed as business needs change, or as new technology emerges.

Strategic and Tactical Information Systems Planning

The IS strategic plan, a part of the overall organizational strategic plan, is a more detailed extension of the IS vision paper, detailing *what* is to be achieved, with a list of specific goals. The IS tactical plan breaks down strategic goals into objectives that together describe *how* and *when* the strategic goals will be achieved. The strategic plan is established for the long run, such as three to five years, while the tactical plan usually covers one to three years. All tactical plans are subsections of the strategic plan.

For example, a strategic *goal* may be the desire to provide end users with more flexible access to databases and tools to develop their own database applications. This goal will be translated into the tactical plan of advancing toward a client/server architecture. Of course, there are different levels of client/server architecture, and different ways to achieve this goal, which would have to be itemized in the plan for operations.

Each objective has a plan for operations, detailing the tasks involved, the department that will carry out the assignment or assignments, and the time frame within which they will be accomplished. For each objective, the plan also provides a list of resources needed to achieve the objective: personnel, hardware, software, and purchased services.

What happens after the strategic plan is in place? Although strategic plans are made for the long run, they are usually not rigid (that is, unchanged for a long period of time). Most strategic plans are dynamic—they are examined and revised relatively frequently (see Exhibit 800.8). Many organizations, especially in industries characterized by frequent change, review their plans annually or biannually and change them if necessary. Dynamic strategic IS plans are more prevalent now than several years ago because of the tremendous developments in IT: hardware and software become obsolete faster than they used to; the variety of hardware and software is much greater; and there are many more types of telecommunications lines and services. The emergence of the Web as a major vehicle for e-commerce has also made IS planning more complex. Thus, many organizations prefer to update their strategic IS plans frequently.

To translate the IS tactical objectives into action, a plan for operations is created based on the tactical plan. At this stage, projects are defined and assigned resources, including staff and funds, for execution. As the personnel and funds are allocated, the IS budget is developed. Often, management lets the new project managers select their own staff.

Exhibit 800.8 *Rigid and Dynamic Planning*

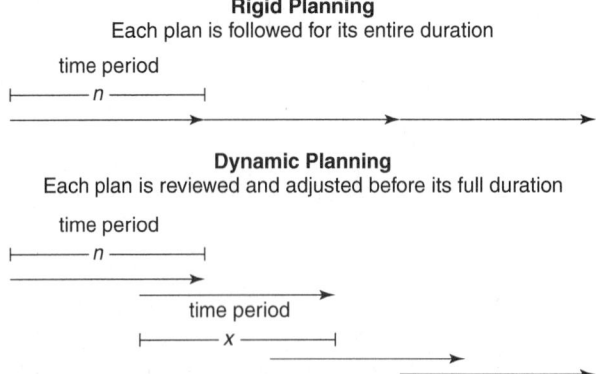

Large-scale projects are often lengthy and may take several years to complete. In such cases, an organization often refers to the project as an organizational unit, and the project manager is considered the head of that unit. Once the project is completed, the staff is disbanded and assigned to other projects. Realize, however, that many IS projects are not over when a new system is installed. The maintenance of a system is an ongoing effort for which dedicated professionals, sometimes working full-time, are required. It is not unusual for a project to last three or five years. Sometimes, the development team of an IS becomes a permanent organizational unit in charge of the maintenance and continual upgrading of the system. This was the case with SABRE, the pioneer airline reservation system at **American Airlines**. The project team was later spun off as a sister corporation to American Airlines, **Sabre Inc.**, and is the leading provider of technology for the travel industry.

Important Factors in IS Tactical Planning

Many IS issues are decided in the analysis and design phase of IS development, which usually follows the planning phase. However, some issues are not specific to individual systems, and they should be considered at the planning stage:

- *Flexibility.* Flexibility is the degree to which an organization can use the same hardware or software for different business functions, in different physical and logical environments, over time. Careful planning enables IS planners to designate which equipment and software may be used anywhere in an organization. Planning also allows an organization to select the best hardware and software for the long run, even if they may not be used at their optimal levels in the short run. Many companies that fail to consider flexibility of IS resources and their long-term implications find their resources are quickly obsolete. They then incur the extra costs involved in acquiring additional resources.
- *Compatibility.* Computers and peripheral equipment are not always compatible. Although different business units may prefer computers from different vendors, buying the same product for the entire enterprise may be necessary to ensure software, hardware, and telecommunications compatibility. Similarly, planners must consider how compatible software packages are, so that workers from different departments can import and share data. For example, if an organization is already committed to a certain database management system (DBMS) and is looking for a new electronic spreadsheet program, IS planners should develop a list of spreadsheet programs that are compatible with the DBMS. This way, workers will be able to import data from the database to their own spreadsheet and vice versa.
- *Connectivity.* IS planners, particularly those concerned with planning communications networks, should participate in the decision-making process for hardware and software to allow maximum connectivity among the organization's computers. Although Internet protocols and Web technologies have made it easier to link with other businesses and with consumers, some issues will need to be considered. For example, ActiveX applets run only on PCs that run Windows, and some Web pages look different when viewed with different browsers.
- *Scalability.* Scalability refers to how easy it is to augment hardware and software and their use as the business grows.

A small organization may have one person handle all accounting data entry and report generation. As an organization grows, clerks are added to form an accounts receivable department. At that point, several people may need to

Exhibit 800.9 *Hardware Planning*

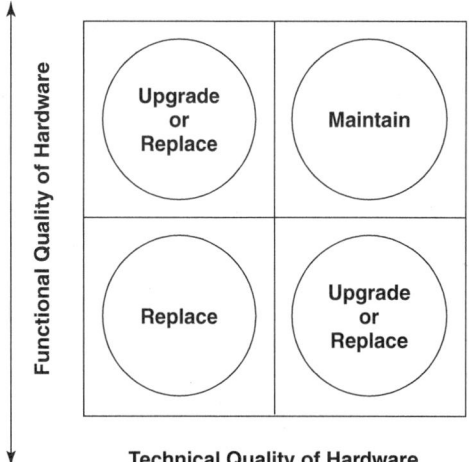

use the system from their PCs at the same time. As the organization continues to grow, the accounts receivable personnel may be divided geographically or by type of customer, with separate accounts receivable departments for each. Scalability allows an organization going through change to continue providing the same features and speed of processing as when the system was used by a single employee.

Scalability is extremely important for any organization that is engaged in e-commerce. Typically, business at a Web site starts slowly and grows in time. As the number of inquiries and transactions grows, the organization needs to add servers to handle the growing traffic. Forethought allows smooth growth of the hardware, software, and communications links by adding components instead of throwing away elements of the site and rebuilding it.

- *Standardization.* Many organizations have set standards requiring all business units to use certain hardware and software. IS managers must periodically evaluate the appropriateness of the standards and determine whether they should be maintained or updated. A grid of factors can be used to consider replacement or continuing maintenance of resources, according to the level of functional and technical quality of the resource. To assist in that type of decision, planners can map hardware pieces used by the organization in a two-dimensional diagram (see Exhibit 800.9). The two dimensions are the degree to which the hardware supports a business process (its functional quality) and the technical quality of the hardware in general. The assessment of technical quality is highly dependent on the introduction by manufacturers of similar equipment with higher quality (such as similar equipment that is more reliable, has easier-to-use features, offers faster performance, and the like). The decision may be to maintain the hardware, discard it (retire it), or upgrade or replace it.
- *Total cost of ownership.* Obviously, any planning decision must also include cost implications. In recent years, CIOs have started realizing that costs involved in the adoption of IT are not all apparent at a first glance—but they may be quite high. These hidden costs include time taken from employees' regular jobs for training in the use of new hardware or software, the time-prorated cost of software that cannot run on the new computers, the cost of help-desk time due to the adoption of new hardware or software, and others. Some research firms have concluded, for example, that the actual cost of a new PC purchased for an office worker may reach ten times the cost of the computer itself.

IS Planning Initiatives

Where do IS planners get information about new IS needs, problems, and opportunities within their organizations? Four groups of people within an organization can initiate consideration of new or improved ISs, each with a different perspective: top management, line managers, users, and IS professionals (see Exhibit 800.10). Typically, top managers are concerned with strategic information systems and enterprisewide applications because they consider the impact of such systems on the entire organization or on major parts of it. IS professionals usually draw attention to

Exhibit 800.10 *IS Planning Can Be Driven by a Variety of Sources*

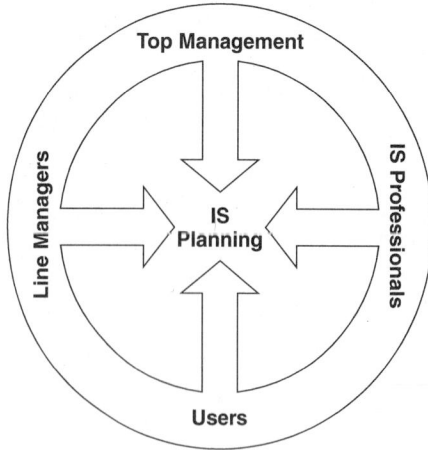

new technologies, hardware, software, and telecommunications and suggest ways to use them to improve business processes. Line managers may initiate consideration of new or improved ISs after they have talked to colleagues from other organizations or read an article in a trade journal. Users inquire how new or improved ISs can solve problems they encounter in their daily work.

Members of top management, such as a CIO, CTO, or another senior executive, typically consider new strategic ISs that can affect the entire organization. By comparison, line managers, who observe their staff daily, often recommend ISs that would improve business processes and staff performance. Users are most familiar with the strengths and weaknesses of existing systems and therefore are best qualified to recommend ways in which IS performance could be made more efficient and effective. Through discussions with their peers from competing organizations, these users also often bring ideas about better ISs to their own organizations.

Although modern IS planning and development holds that change initiatives should come from business managers, IS managers who are familiar with business processes can often see how a new technology could create a business opportunity. As a result, the initiative for IS planning and systems development may come from several sources. The results of one survey of CEOs and other executives indicates that business unit managers, IT managers, and top executives all initiate consideration of new IS development projects.

The Champion

Although a true business need usually spurs new system development, there may not be universal support from all members of an organization. For political or rational reasons, some managers may object to the development. In addition, top management is always wary of proposals that require a commitment of resources, and executives usually request substantive justification for the expense. A sound business and technical proposal for a new system is usually not enough for top management to endorse the new effort. The project needs a *champion:* a high-ranking officer who commands sufficient political clout to promote the idea that a new system is needed and—when the go-ahead is granted—to remove obstacles as the project progresses. The champion represents the top management interest in the new system. The most effective champions are executives who are not IS professionals. Their grounding in other business functions lends credence to their argument that the organization needs the system for a business operation, rather than just for the glory of the IS staff. It also conveys the impression that the champion is not influenced by narrow self-centered considerations.

A successful champion is a true leader who can do the following.

- Promote the vision of information technology in the organization
- Inspire top management and subordinates alike

- Remove barriers to realizing the vision
- Focus on both short-term and long-term objectives
- Be a torchbearer for making change happen
- Drive accountability to the lowest organizational level, so that all who are involved in the development of the new IS (1) feel responsible and therefore committed to succeeding in their roles and (2) are ready to report their progress at any time

Sometimes, the ideal champion is actually a pair of people: an IT manager as technical champion paired with a management champion. The technical manager takes responsibility for product evaluation, planning, and implementation, while the management champion helps deal with corporate culture, political issues, convincing top management of the return on investment (ROI), and the application of the new system to specific business problems.

Although champions often do not come from the ranks of IS professionals, practice shows that overall leadership skills coupled with IT knowledge create champions who drive their organizations to the forefront of business technology use. One of **Citicorp's** (now part of **Citigroup**) CEOs was the main reason the company became a leader in the use of ATMs and other advanced systems, which gave the corporation strategic advantages. The CEO of **Circuit City**, a former IS officer, championed the development and implementation of the most advanced IS in that company's market. Executives from competing electronic appliance chains admit that Circuit City's integrated inventory and customer service system is superior to theirs.

The Systems Analyst as an Agent of Change

Planning almost always deals with change: changing methods, changing the structure of business units, and changing the way workers receive, process, and communicate information. However, the physical law of inertia also applies to people. As objects will continue to move in the same direction unless their course is changed, so do people wish to continue to act in the same manner, unless they have to change. The changes created by new ISs force people to learn new procedures and use new technologies, which many people dislike, particularly if they have performed their jobs the same way for many years. Resistance to change is especially strong if the changes reward the organization but not the individual employee—the employee may perceive no tangible incentive to change.

When the change being addressed relates to developing or implementing a new IS, the systems analyst is often the agent of change who must not only explain how the system will improve business performance but also train individuals in the use of the new system (see Exhibit 800.11). To gain cooperation, the analyst must convince users that the new system will help them in their work. For instance, to clerical staff, the benefits of the new system may be a more relaxed working environment, the satisfaction of creating greater output with less effort, and, often, the satisfaction of learning how to operate a more sophisticated system and enhance work skills. The systems analyst must be a good listener. He or she must carefully listen to employees who will use the new system and to their managers, so that the features of the system can best fit their needs.

In the past, the popular view held that the implementation of a new IS would be handled almost exclusively by the systems analyst, who would communicate almost no information until the time came to train personnel to use the system. It is now recognized that (1) the changes involved in a new IS must be communicated to employees well before the new system is delivered to them and (2) education, not just training, is a key success factor. Much of this burden is on the shoulders of the systems analyst.

Exhibit 800.11 *The role of a system analyst*

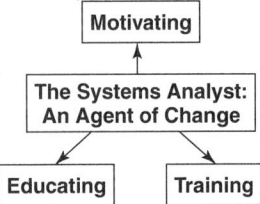

(Systems analysts facilitate change by motivating, educating, and training.)

Information Technology Control and Governance

IT Governance Definition

In the information economy, successful enterprises integrate IT and business strategies, culture, and ethics in order to attain business objectives, optimize information value, and capitalize on technologies. Extended enterprises, which incorporate customers, business partners, vendors, stakeholders, and constituents, rely on the efficient and effective sharing of information, including goals, expectations, status, and ultimately knowledge. Making this happen at all is mission-critical to most enterprises—and making it happen as it should happen requires IT governance [www.ITgovernance.org].

Effective enterprise governance focuses on individual and group expertise and experience in specific areas in which they can be most effective, monitors and measures performance, and provides assurance regarding critical issues. IT, long considered solely an enabler of an enterprise's strategy, is now regarded as an integral part of that strategy. CEOs, CFOs, and CIOs alike agree that strategic alignment between IT and enterprise objectives is a critical success factor.

IT governance helps ensure achievement of this critical success factor by efficiently and effectively deploying secure, reliable information and applied technology. IT governance is a structure of relationships and processes to direct and control the enterprise in order to achieve the enterprise's goals by adding value while balancing risk versus return over IT and its processes. The relationships are between management and its governing body. The processes cover setting objectives, giving direction on how to attain them, and measuring performance. Simply put, IT is so critical to the success of enterprises that it is an issue that cannot be relegated solely to management or IT specialists, but must instead receive the focused attention of both.

Relationship of Enterprise and IT Governance

Looking at the interplay of enterprise and IT governance processes in more detail, enterprise governance, the system by which entities are directed and controlled, drives and sets information and technology governance. At the same time, IT should provide critical input to and form an important component of strategic plans devised as a function of enterprise governance. IT may, in fact, influence strategic opportunities outlined by the enterprise.

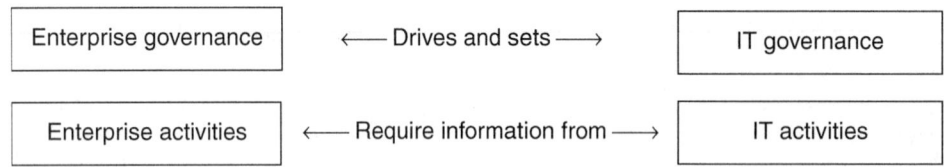

Enterprise activities require information from IT activities in order to meet business objectives. Successful organizations ensure interdependence between their strategic planning and their IT activities. IT must be aligned with and enable the enterprise to take full advantage of its information, thereby maximizing benefits, capitalizing on opportunities and gaining a competitive advantage.

How Enterprise and IT Governance Work

Enterprises set objectives, the assurance of which are governed by generally accepted good (or best) practices. From these objectives flow the organization's direction, which dictates certain enterprise activities using the enterprise's resources. The results of the enterprise activities are measured and reported on, providing input to the constant revision and maintenance of the controls, thus beginning the cycle again.

IT also sets objectives to ensure that the enterprise's information and related technology support its business objectives, its resources are used responsibly, and its risks are managed appropriately. These objectives form a basis for direction of IT activities, which can be characterized as planning and organizing, acquiring and implementing, delivering and supporting, and monitoring, for the dual purposes of managing risks (to gain security, reliability, and compliance), and realizing benefits (increasing effectiveness and efficiency). Reports are issued on the outcomes of IT activities, which are measured against the various practices and controls, and the cycle begins again.

"IT governance" is an inclusive term, which encompasses the following.

- Information systems, technology, and communication
- Business, legal, and other issues
- All concerned stakeholders, directors, senior management, process owners, IT suppliers, users, and auditors

How can IT governance, control, and assurance impact an enterprise's effectiveness?

- By addressing business issues, such as electronic commerce and enterprise resource planning (ERP)
- By assuring security, reliability, and integrity of strategic information
- By protecting the enterprise's investment in IT, including systems and networks
- By ensuring the appropriate management of an entity's information assets, which are often directly responsible for the success and survival of the entity itself

Simply put, IT governance is good business.

Information Technology Risk Management

Risks to Information Systems

While stories about damage caused to ISs by malicious Internet attacks are popular, the truth about risks to ISs is simpler: the number-one cause of systems downtime is hardware failure. The next two contributors are fire and theft. In recent years, especially because of the growth of online business, corporations have considered protection of their IS resources an increasingly important issue, for good reasons. Exhibit 800.12 provides a sample of average losses in some types of businesses when ISs go down. We discuss here the most pervasive risks to IS operations.

Exhibit 800.12 *Cost Per Hour of System Downtime*

Industry	Business Operation	Cost per Hour of Downtime
Financial	Brokerage	$6,450,000
Financial	Credit Card Authorization	$2,600,000
Financial	ATM Fees	$ 14,500
Retail	Home Catalog Sales	$ 90,000
Transportation	Airline Reservations	$ 89,500
Media	Ticket Sales	$ 69,000

Source: *Dataquest,* 2000.

Risks to Hardware

Risks to hardware involve physical damage to computers, peripheral equipment, and communications media. The major causes of such damage are natural disasters, blackouts and brownouts, and vandalism.

Natural Disasters

Natural disasters that pose a risk to ISs include fires, floods, earthquakes, hurricanes, tornadoes, and lightning, which can destroy hardware, software, or both, causing total or partial paralysis of systems or communications lines. Floodwater short-circuits and burns delicate components such as microchips. Lightning and voltage surges cause tiny wires to melt and destroy circuitry. Obviously, all data and programs stored in memory chips in a computer are lost when this happens. Water from floods and the heat created when circuits are shorted may also ruin the surface of storage media such as magnetic disks and tapes, thereby destroying data. In addition, wildlife and human error occasionally destroy communications lines; animals gnaw cables, and farmers occasionally cut wires inadvertently while tending their crops. The easiest way to protect against loss of data caused by natural disasters (but not only by natural disasters) is to automatically duplicate all data periodically and store the duplicate copy in a site many miles away from the office, as explained later.

Where natural damage is concerned, communications media are among the most vulnerable parts of a system because they run outside the confines of an organization's operation. Although they add significantly to the cost of communications hardware, thick protective sheaths made of special plastics protect communications cables and wires. But when lightning strikes a power line or telephone line to which a computer is connected, the computer is usually damaged. Surge protectors and similar devices that simply disconnect power to the machine rarely protect it from lightning.

Blackouts and Brownouts

Computers run on electricity. If power is disrupted, the computer and its peripheral devices cannot function, and the change in power supply can be very damaging to computer processes and storage. **Blackouts** are total losses of electrical power. In **brownouts**, the voltage of the power decreases, or there are very short interruptions in the flow of power. Power failure may not only disrupt operations but also cause irreparable damage to hardware. Occasional surges in voltage are equally harmful, because their impact on equipment is similar to that of lightning.

The popular way of handling brownouts is to connect a voltage regulator between computers and the electric network. A voltage regulator boosts or decreases voltage to smooth out drops or surges and maintains voltage within an acceptable tolerance.

To ensure against interruptions in power supply, organizations use **uninterruptible power supply (UPS) systems,** which provide an alternative power supply for a short time, as soon as a power network fails. The only practical measure against prolonged blackouts in a public electrical network is to buy and maintain a separate generator that uses gasoline or another fuel. Once the general power stops, the generator can kick in and produce the power needed for the computer system.

Vandalism

Vandalism occurs when human beings deliberately destroy computer systems. Bitter customers may damage ATMs, or disgruntled employees may destroy computer equipment out of fear that it will eliminate their jobs or simply to get even with their superiors. For instance, several years ago, postal service employees stuck paperclips in a new computer that sorted mail because they feared the new system would eliminate jobs.

It is difficult to defend computers against vandalism. ATMs and other equipment that are accessible to the public are often encased in metal boxes, but someone with persistence can still cause severe damage. In the workplace, the best measure against vandalism is to allow access only to those who have a real need for the system. Sensitive equipment, such as servers, should be locked in a special room.

Risks to Applications and Data

All computer systems are susceptible to disruption and damage. While the culprit in the destruction of hardware is often some natural disaster or power spike, the culprit in damage to software is almost always human. The major risks to software applications and data are theft of information; data alteration, destruction, and defacement; computer viruses and logic bombs; and nonmalicious mishaps.

Theft of Information

Before the advent of electronic computers, most businesses kept secret information in a safe. A thief had to physically tear a locking mechanism out or illegally obtain a key to the safe. Now even the most sensitive information is usually stored electronically somewhere on a company's information system. Today's electronic equivalent of the physical key is a code, a combination of characters that is needed to access secured data. Before the computer age, large amounts of data meant a lot of paper, which was awkward to steal and awkward to hide when stolen. These days, thousands of pages filled with information can be stored on a small magnetic disk, making information easier to steal (as the following story shows), and also easier to hide.

The leading causes of data loss are power failure/surge (45.3%), storm damage (9.4%), fire/explosion (8.2%), hardware/software error (8.2%), flood and water damage (6.7%), earthquake (5.5%), network outage (4.5%), human error/sabotage (3.2%), HVAC failure (2.3%), and miscellaneous (6.7%).

Source: Levine, D.E., "A Guide to UPS," Datamation, May 23, 2001, itmanagement.earthweb.com.

A young man worked in the research and development department of an international food company that had over 100 microcomputers in its headquarters. In 1985 he inserted his own disk into a computer that held the formulas for flavoring products of a successful food line; he made a copy of the information and sent the disk to a former manager, who worked for a competitor. Since the manager did not know how to print out the information from the disk, he gave it to a service company to do it for him. The service person noticed that the name of the manager's company was different from the company name appearing on the printout and notified the victim company. Managers at the company had been wondering how the competitor kept introducing similar products so soon after their own new products came on the market; now they understood.

Data Alteration, Data Destruction, and Defacement

Alteration or destruction of data is often an act of mischief (in which case it is called "data diddling"). In San Francisco, **United States Leasing International** found one morning that data in its files were replaced with curses and names that should not have been there. In this case, the damage was financial: employees spent time searching for all the changed records and correcting them. In other cases, however, computer pranks such as these can put people's lives at risk.

In 1983, a group of Milwaukee teenagers accessed a computer system at Sloan-Kettering Cancer Research Institute in New York via a modem and altered patients' records just for "fun." An alert nurse noticed a double—and lethal—dose of a medication in a patient's record and called a doctor. She saved the patient's life.

In a survey conducted by the American Bar Association's Task Force on Computer Crime, respondents ranked "destruction or alteration of data" as the most significant type of computer crime. A related crime, "destruction or alteration of software," was ranked second. These two crimes are the dreaded nightmares of chief information officers and database administrators. It is not only the effort to reinstate missing or altered records that causes financial damage. Even if the actual damage is not great, IS staff must spend a lot of time scanning the data pools to ascertain the integrity of the entire resource, and they must also figure out how the perpetrator managed to circumvent security controls. This activity itself wastes the time of high-salaried employees.

Since organizations started establishing Web sites, hackers—people who access information systems without permission—have had a new target: Web pages. Each day, some organizations find their Web sites have been defaced. In the best-case scenario, Web defacement is the cyber equivalent of street graffiti—someone adds offensive text or pictures to the page. In the worst-case scenario, pages are totally replaced with offensive content. Defacement causes several types of damage: first-time visitors are not likely to stay around long enough or revisit to learn about the true nature of the site, and they may associate the offensive material with the organization; frequent visitors may never come back; and shoppers who have had a good experience with the site may leave it forever because they no longer trust its security measures.

To deface a Web site, an intruder needs to know the site's access code or codes that enable the Webmaster and other authorized people to work on the site's server and update its pages. The intruder may either obtain the codes from someone who knows them or use special software that "tries and errs" until it succeeds in accessing the pages.

Sometimes hackers do not vandalize Web pages but replace them with their own pages to send a social or political message. On July 25, 2001, hackers paid a visit to the site of the official Palestinian news agency. A title in Hebrew was placed at the top of the homepage: "Crimes committed by the Palestinian Authority and Palestinian leaders." The new page showed 137 pictures of Israelis killed in the preceding 10 months of violence. Small images of memorial candles were placed between pictures. The director of the news agency accused Israeli hackers of the deed.

Attrition (www.attrition.org), a Web site that publishes statistics on computer security breaches, reported that in the period between August 1999 and January 2001, 8,071 different Web sites were broken into and subsequently defaced. The best measure against defacement, of course, is software that protects against unauthorized access. However, since such software may fail, the public damage may be minimized by ensuring that some members of the organization monitor the home page and other essential pages frequently. When the defacement is detected shortly after it occurs, the defaced pages can be replaced with the original ones before too many visitors have seen the rogue pages.

The cure to any unauthorized entry to an IS is to find the "hole" in its security software and fix it with the appropriate software. Such software is often called a "patch." Software companies that sell server management applications often produce patches and invite clients to download and install them.

Computer Viruses and Logic Bombs

A biological virus is a microorganism that attacks the living cells of a host, either a human being or another animal. It penetrates the cells, multiplies, and then causes the cells to burst, thereby destroying them. It is rapidly transmitted from one living creature to another. Computer viruses are usually a few lines of programming code that are inserted in a legitimate program that is later copied and activated by unwary users. **Computer viruses** are so named because they act on programs and data in a fashion similar to the way viruses act on living tissue: computer viruses easily spread from computer to computer. Since so many computers are now connected to one another, and since we share many of our files with other people, we unknowingly transmit to other computers viruses that have infected our own files. Once a virus reaches a computer, it damages applications and data files. In addition to destroying legitimate applications and data files, viruses may disrupt data communications: the presence of viruses causes data communications applications to process huge numbers of messages and files for no useful purpose, which detracts from the efficiency of transmitting and receiving legitimate messages and files.

Exhibit 800.13 shows the results of a survey of 745 respondents about the frequency of security breaches they experienced. The survey was completed by *Information Security Magazine* readers, a pool of respondents that includes administrators, managers, and executives in IT, security, networking, and data management. Evidently, more companies experienced viruses than any other threat to their information systems.

Viruses are spread by way of copying infected software from someone else's disk or by receiving infected software from another computer through a communications link. A virus that spreads through networks is also called a *worm*. Because millions of people use e-mail, computer networks, especially the Internet, make it easy to spread a computer virus. The worst viruses are those that attach themselves to operating systems. As you already know, the operating system is the large program that manages and controls all basic computer resources. Since the operating system interacts with every program and data file that is used in the computer, a virus in an operating system can damage every file used.

Almost all viruses are now spread through the Internet, and almost always by e-mail. The Melissa virus of 1999, the Love Bug of 2000, and the SirCam virus of 2001 demonstrated why you should be suspicious of e-mail messages even when they seemingly come from people or organizations you know.

Exhibit 800.13 *Frequency of Security Breaches in a 12-month Period Based on a Survey of 745 Professionals*

Type of Breach	Respondents Reporting Breach	% Responding
Viruses	573	77%
Employee access abuse	388	52%
Unauthorized access by outsiders	175	23%
Theft/destruction of computing resources	170	23%
Leak of proprietary information	137	18%
Theft/destruction of data	110	15%
Access abuse by nonemployee	101	14%
Hacking of phone/PBX/voice-mail system	86	12%
Other	37	5%

Source: Briney, A., "Got Security?" *Information Security Magazine*, 1999.

One way to protect against viruses is to use **antivirus software,** which is readily available on the market from companies that specialize in developing this kind of software. The problem with virus-detection software, however, is that it is usually designed to intercept only known viruses. If a new virus is designed to operate in a way not yet known, the software is unlikely to detect it. Sometimes the software can only detect a virus, but not destroy it. The user then must delete the suspect file. Most virus-detection applications allow the user to automatically, or selectively, destroy suspect programs.

Software firms that specialize in antivirus applications have also decided to fight viruses in more original ways. One method implemented by **Symantec** is the remote cure approach. A special application runs on the PCs of subscriber companies. The application periodically scans for unidentified viruses at the subscribers' sites. When a suspected virus is found, the application sends the infected file via the Internet to Symantec's labs, where the virus is tricked into believing that it is running on a desktop computer. Actually, it is running on a mainframe computer, and it is tricked into replicating (which is what viruses do). By tracking what the virus does, a special program tries to create a cure in the form of software fix. The "antidote" software is sent to the company's PC, again via the Internet.

As the Melissa, Love Bug, SirCam and similar viruses teach us, it is wise to reject e-mail messages even from known sources if the topic, timing, or circumstances are suspicious. It may also be prudent to use features such as macros judiciously. Many computer users are not aware that some documents contain macros. When you open a document that contains macros, your computer is at the mercy of the macro—that is, the person who wrote it. This sneak attack by something appearing to be innocent is the reason why viruses such as the Love Bug (also called Love Letter) are often called "Trojan horses." In their war against Troy, the Greeks pretended they were abandoning the city's outskirts and left behind a big wooden horse as a present. The Trojans pulled the horse into the city. When night fell, Greek soldiers hidden within the horse jumped out and opened the gates for thousands of their comrades, who by then had secretly landed back on the city's shores. They conquered the city. Similarly, electronic Trojan horses are accepted innocently and then wreak havoc.

Some rogue computer programs do not spread immediately like a virus but are often significantly more damaging to the individual organization that is victimized. A **logic bomb** is software that is programmed to cause damage at a specified time to specific applications and data files. It lies dormant until a certain event takes place in the computer or until the computer's inner clock reaches the specified time; the event or time triggers the virus to start causing damage. Logic bombs are usually planted by insiders, that is, employees of the victimized organization.

Nonmalicious Mishaps

Unintentional damage to software occurs because of (1) poor training, (2) lack of adherence to simple backup procedures, or (3) simple human error. Although unintentional damage rarely occurs in robust applications, poor training may result in inappropriate use of an application so that it ruins data, unbeknownst to the user. For instance, when faced with an instruction that may change or delete data, a robust application will pose a question such as: "Are you sure you want to delete the record?" or issue a warning such as "This may destroy the file." More common damage is caused by the failure to save all work and create a backup copy. Destruction of data often happens when using a word-processing program to create text files and when updating databases.

Accidental damage to computer systems also occurs through installation of unauthorized peripheral equipment and unauthorized downloading and installation of software. The latter has been made easy thanks to the ubiquitous links to the Internet. A survey of 1,897 IS professionals from different organizations found that 48% of all IS security breaches were accidental. The respondents were unsure about 35% of the incidents and said only 17% could be confirmed as deliberate.

Risks to Online Operations

The massive movement of operations to the Internet has attracted hackers who try to interrupt such operations daily. In addition to unauthorized access, data theft, and defacing of Web pages, there has been a surge in denial of service attacks. A more sophisticated but less frequent phenomenon is *spoofing*.

Denial of Service

One day in February 2000, traders at the stock brokerage firm **National Discount Brokers Group** noticed unusual activity at the firm's Web site. Customers who wanted to send buy and sell orders could not log on to the site, but the servers were experiencing heavy traffic. Many of the firm's 200,000 customers were unable to place stock orders through the firm's Web site, forcing them to relay orders on the telephone. Apparently, the site was experiencing a denial of service attack.

Denial of service (**DoS**) occurs when too many requests are received to log on to a Web site's pages. The intention of such log-in requests is to slow down legitimate traffic on the site's server, and business can slow down even to a halt. Multiple log-in requests may be perpetrated by a single person who uses specially designed software that automatically repeats requests for a long period of time. The server's or servers' frantic efforts to handle the massive amount of traffic denies legitimate visitors and business partners access to the site, and hence its name.

Such attacks can also be perpetrated from multiple computers, in which case they are called **distributed denial of service** (**DDoS**). DDoSs can be an orchestrated attack by people who have agreed to send multiple log-in requests to a site at the same time. However, most such attacks are more sophisticated; the perpetrator launches software that uses other people's computers for the attack—unbeknownst to them. Professionals call the computers used in these attacks *zombies* because of their mindless response to destructive commands. Zombie computers not only exacerbate the volume of calls but also make it impossible to track down the generator of the DDoS.

There is no apparent cure for a DoS attack, because it is impossible to stop anyone from trying to log on to a Web site. When managers realize that their site is being attacked, they usually shut it down for several hours, hoping that the attackers will get discouraged and go away. Network professionals can also try to detect the IP addresses from which a large number of requests are coming and program the server not to accept any requests from that particular server. However, blocking requests may also deny access to legitimate visitors, especially if the server is used by an ISP who provides Internet access to thousands of people and organizations. One way to mitigate DoS attacks is for an organization to use multiple servers, which is a good idea anyway to handle times of legitimate traffic increases.

No organization is immune to DDoS. Some of the most visible Web sites have been attacked, including those of **eBay**, **Amazon**, **CNN**, and the U.S. White House. All had to shut down their sites for several hours. eBay, Amazon, and other sites have lost revenue as a result. Even the CERT was forced to shut down its site in May 2001 for 30 hours. A DDoS attack sent information into its Web site at rates several hundred times higher than normal. A 2001 report from the University of California at San Diego reveals that there are 4,000 DDoS attacks somewhere in the world each week.

Spoofing

Imagine someone hung a sign above the entrance to your store in a busy mall telling shoppers the store was closed and sending them to a competing store. For several hours you are not aware of the sign. When the equivalent happens on the Web, the act is called *spoofing*. Spoofing on the Internet may mean satirizing a Web site. But in recent years **spoofing** has also come to mean deception for the purpose of gaining access, or deception of users to make them think they are logged on to a certain Web site while they actually are logged on to another.

Most spoofing attacks are designed to embarrass organizations, but security experts worry that spoofing techniques may take a more sinister angle: a serious spoofing attack may result in massive fraud. During spoofing, the perpetrator takes advantage of certain vulnerabilities in domain name system (DNS) software. When a user types a domain name into her browser, the local DNS server sends a query through the Internet's distributed hierarchical DNS to look up the matching IP address for that domain name. Spoofers manipulate the DNS software so that the path to the IP address is redirected; visitors believe they are connected to the requested server when in fact they are connected to another. This interception and redirection is akin to someone switching your name with someone else's in a telephone directory so you receive all that person's calls.

On June 21, 2000, a group of hackers calling themselves S-11 victimized the site of **Nike**, the athletic shoe manufacturer. They redirected traffic from www.nike.com to the servers of a Scotland-based ISP. The hijacking lasted 6 to 24 hours, depending on the schedules on which different ISPs reloaded the Nike Web site. People who tried to access Nike's site were instead sent to one that criticized the company and the World Economic Forum, a pro-capitalism group that includes Nike as a member. Nike's sales through its Web site did not suffer significantly, but the spoof caused much consternation among businesses. Spoofing requires knowledge and sophistication on the perpetrator's part, and it does not occur often. Experts are working on solutions to vulnerabilities of DNS software to such acts.

Managing Information and Technology

Managers and Information

Generally speaking, managers at different levels of an organizational hierarchy make different types of decisions, control different types of processes, and therefore have different information needs. While companies have many different organizational structures, in this section, we will discuss the most common: a generic pyramid-shaped hierarchy with a few leaders at the top and an increasing number of workers at each subsequent managerial and operational level. There has long been a fairly close correlation between the level of work a person does in an organization and the type of IS he or she uses. But today, with computers on every desk, that relationship is no longer as clear. The availability of increasingly flexible and powerful information systems throughout all organizational levels has had a profound effect on organizational structure. For instance, in the past, companies had specialized staff whose main task was to process data and generate information to meet managers' requests. Now, the ability to generate information has been placed directly in managers' hands, which has contributed to the downsizing of middle management. Technology aside, the politics of information within an organization can undermine optimal business decision making. Trying to retain power in their hands, and realizing that information is power, managers sometimes oppose the trend of making both data and processing tools available throughout a company. Problems often arise when the potential politics are not considered when developing systems and deciding how people will support those systems.

Characteristics of Information at Different Managerial Levels

People in different management levels have different information needs. As shown in Exhibit 800.14, the information needed by different managerial and operational levels varies in the time span covered, level of detail, source, and other characteristics over a broad spectrum. For instance, clerical workers need data that allow them to fulfill daily operations but not necessarily make decisions. To serve customers and other workers, they must have access to information such as how many units of a certain item are available for sale, how much a certain customer service costs, and how much overtime a certain employee worked last week. Usually, these people make ad hoc inquiries to satisfy immediate information needs.

On the other hand, most of the information that managers require is used to make decisions. Operational managers need information based on data that are generally narrow in scope, gathered over a short period of time, and useful for decisions that have an impact in the short run, that is, hours, days, and weeks. The decisions middle managers make affect a greater number of organizational units for longer periods of time, and they require information extracted from data that are broader in scope and time, and that information may come from outside their departments.

The decision-making process of middle managers and above is less structured than that of operational managers; despite the broader scope of the data—and sometimes *because* of it—there are no proven methods for selecting a course of action that guarantees a predicted outcome.

The decisions that senior managers make affect whole divisions or the entire organization and have long-standing impact. Their decision making is very unstructured. Senior managers need information gleaned from vast amounts of raw data that have been collected over long periods of time from many or all of an organization's units. The original data for the information come from internal organizational sources as well as external sources, such as the mass media, the Web, national and international trade bulletins, and consulting firms.

Exhibit 800.14 *Characteristics of Data and Information for Different Levels of Management*

Data Range	Time Span	Level of Detail	Source	Degree of Structure	Purpose
Wide (enterprise-wide)	**Long** • Months • Years • Far past • Long-term future (forecasts)	Summarized	Internal and External	Unstructured	Decision Making
Narrow (departmental)	**Short** • Hours • Days • Recent past • Near future	Detailed and Specific	Internal	Structured	Daily Operations

Data Range

Data range refers to the amount of data from which information is extracted, in terms of the number of organizational units supplying data or the length of time the data cover. For example, data gathered from just one department have a narrower range than data from every department of the organization. In addition, one department's data from several months have a broader range than the same department's data from one week.

Data range is different from level of detail. When a lot of data is summarized into a few figures, such as totals and averages, the level of detail is low; however, the data range may be high if the data are about numerous people, departments, or events. Data range refers to the number of individuals, departments, or events about which data were collected.

To make a strategic decision, top management may need a single figure that is calculated from a wide range of data, such as the average monthly expenditure on U.S. television advertising of sports shoes. The data are collected on as many sport shoe manufacturers as possible to produce information that reflects the entire industry, not a single company or a small number of companies. Although the information provided is a single figure, it is derived from vast amounts of data spanning a long time and many corporations. Therefore, the data range is wide. At the other extreme, the manager of a shop in a manufacturing plant may need only information that is extracted from data collected within that organizational unit. The data range is then narrow.

Time Span

The **time span** of data refers to how long a period of time the data cover. Data that cover hours or days (the time span usually needed by lower-level managers) are said to have a short time span relative to data that cover months, years, or decades, which are said to have a long time span. Senior managers typically use data that reach far into the past. They also make extrapolations based on the patterns of performance in the past to forecast what might happen in the future. Data warehouses, which accumulate historical data, are an excellent source for data collected over a long time span.

Level of Detail

The **level of detail** is the degree to which the information generated is specific. When a department manager looks at the number of shoes sold every day of the week broken down by style, the information is, obviously, very detailed. Operational managers usually consider highly detailed information. Senior managers, in contrast, typically consider information that is highly summarized. This type of information includes totals and averages for categories of products (rather than individual products) over long periods of time. These different levels of detail serve the different operational purposes. Operational managers typically examine actual facts relating to present events so they can control immediate situations, while senior managers are often interested in trends to formulate strategies. The difference can be compared to looking at only several pieces of a puzzle or looking at the entire picture the puzzle forms.

Usually, the more detailed the information, the closer it is to the data from which it is derived, and thus proportionately less processing is involved in generating it. Daily totals of sales in the shoe department are more detailed than an annual total for the entire chain of stores. The latter requires significantly more processing because it combines data from many sources.

Source: Internal Versus External

Internal data are collected within the organization, usually by transaction processing systems, but also through employee and customer surveys. **External data** are collected from a wide array of sources outside the organization, including mass communications media such as television, radio, and newspapers; specialized newsletters published by private organizations; government agencies; and the vast sources of news and statistics on the Web. For instance, to plan the expansion or contraction of a national supermarket chain, top managers cannot rely only on their organization's internal data. They must track national trends. Thus, they need information on national annual demographic changes. Without it, they may spend resources on increasing the number of stores only to find, a few years later, that their customer base has shrunk. Multinational corporations rely on even more external data; the data they use come from many different parts of the world, from many different sources, and often in many different formats. For example, they must rely on demographic and economic statistics of several nations rather than one.

In some industries, almost all the information comes from external sources. For example, managers of mutual funds and pension funds must track changes in the prices of stocks and other securities daily (sometimes even hourly) to be able to optimize the capital gains of the funds. The data they analyze come mainly from stock exchanges. Firms that operate Web sites that generate advertising revenues rely on data from companies that rate Web traffic.

Structured and Unstructured Data

Structured data are numbers and facts that can be conveniently stored and retrieved in an orderly manner for operations and decision making. The sources of such data are primarily internal files and databases that capture transactions. Data warehouses also provide highly structured data, such as numbers of units in inventory, number of units sold, and the like. Unstructured data are drawn from meeting discussions, private conversations, textual documents, graphical representations, and other "nonuniform" sources.

Structured data are used for daily operations and decisions that are relatively easy to make with the help of proven models. The higher a managerial position, the less structured decisions a manager faces; therefore, unstructured data are extremely valuable in managerial decision making, especially at the higher levels of an organization.

Many people speak of "management science." However, as you may have surmised, many managerial processes are more an art than a science.

The Web: The Great Equalizer

Much information that was previously hard to find or unavailable is now literally at the fingertips of anyone who needs it via the World Wide Web (the Web). Government agencies, industry associations, trade unions, consumer organizations, advocacy groups, many newspapers and magazines, and other organizations post useful information at their sites. Search engines take key words entered by a user and scour billions of Web pages at millions of Web sites for relevant content. Is your company considering applying for a patent on a new machine or method? Before your company spends millions of dollars on development and thousands of dollars on preparing the application, managers can log on to the Patent and Trademark Office's Web site and within minutes find out whether someone else has registered a patent on the same idea. Are you starting a small business to manage investments in a limited number of stocks for your friends? You do not have to pay for real-time quotes of the current prices of shares traded at some stock exchanges. You can get the information free on the Web. Are you a fleet manager considering purchasing new cars for your small company? Numerous sites on the Web provide you with expert advice and ratings of the performance and cost of a long list of vehicles. Everyone, from a one-person home-based business to a multinational company, has access to the same useful information.

Much of the information on the Web is free. Some of the information is offered in a format that looks exactly as it appears in the equivalent printed version.

Users may need special software to view certain data and information on the Web. For instance, a lot of sites have chosen to post previously published documents in PDF (portable document format), which can easily be read using Adobe's Acrobat Reader. PDF documents can be read or printed in their original forms regardless of the user's operating system. The special Reader software for PDF documents can be downloaded free of charge from Adobe's site.

Some sites allow "data shoppers" to download data in different formats, so that they can further process the data to fit their needs. Any text on Web pages can be copied into word-processable documents or spreadsheets for further "massaging." Text and numbers copied from Web sites can be integrated into reports and presentations (be sure to include appropriate credit for sources and make sure that reusing the material does not infringe on any copyrights). At some Web sites you may have seen the printer icon with the words "Friendly Printer Format" underneath. Also, it is very easy to attach whole Web pages to e-mail messages. This ease of access facilitates the transmission of external data and information in an organization.

Another method of receiving useful external information over the Web is by subscribing to online message services on highly focused topics. Many trade journals provide this service. You can choose to receive e-mail messages, either in text or Web-page format, on many topics. Some online magazines offer to send you any story that has your designated key words in it. This free service can save managers much time in screening information, because the site's software does the screening for them, and it allows managers to enjoy a wealth of information tailored to a specific business environment. Business research and consulting firms offer, for a fee, to e-mail organizations results of research and reports of trends and forecasts.

Characteristics of Effective Information

ISs can be designed to accommodate the different ways in which human beings process data. Some managers like their information in graphic format, some like it in text, some like tables, and some like to hear the information from their staff. Most people are comfortable with some form of visual data, such as diagrams and pictures.

Tabular and Graphical Representation

Studies have investigated the relationships between personal characteristics and data-representation preferences. One study found that when solving problems, engineering students performed better when the data were presented as tables of numbers, while business students solved problems more successfully when data were presented in graphs.

There are certain types of information that most people grasp more quickly when they are presented graphically (see Exhibit 800.15). For instance, trends are immediately recognized when presented as lines on graphs; distributions of data (such as percentages of respondents' responses) are easily comprehended when displayed in pie charts; and a comparison of performance is best displayed with bar charts. However, when solving complex problems, many people prefer tabular raw data so that they can extract the information *they* deem necessary. Many managers think that a graph renders only one interpretation of the data, possibly masking other meaningful relationships.

In the past, researchers found that information systems design should accommodate the psychological type of the intended user. However, such customization was always highly impractical or prohibitively expensive. Now, though, many applications provide a wide array of data display options, allowing users to select their preferences. In these systems, the users may display and examine raw data, selected from a database or a spreadsheet, in tables or graphs. Many applications allow users to display the same information in a number of different forms at the same time, such as in tables and graphs, or in graphs embedded in tables and vice versa. You may have noticed that many Web sites give you the option to display information in many different forms—tables, bar graphs, pie charts—and for different lengths of time—weekly, monthly, and annually. Thus, managers can, to some degree, tailor information presentation to their liking when using online resources.

Online Analytical Processing

Tables, even if joining data from several sources, limit the review of information to only two dimensions. Often, executives need to view information in three dimensions. For example, an executive may want to see a summary of the

Exhibit 800.15 *Tabular and Graphical Presentations*

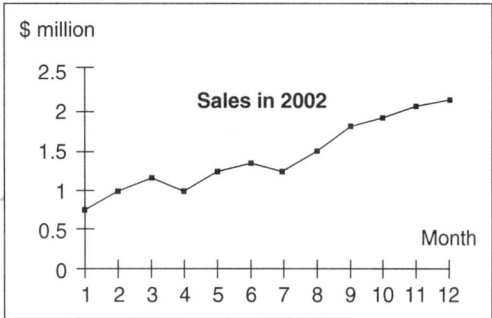

(The information in the two presentations is identical, but the trend is detected faster with the line graph.)

quantity of each product sold in each region. Then, she may want to view the total quantities of each product sold within each city of a region. And she may also want to view quantities sold of a specific product in all cities of all regions. Simple relational database processing applications (called online transaction processing, or OLTP, applications) cannot yield such tables. Another approach, called OLAP, is especially designed to answer queries such as these.

Online analytical processing (OLAP) applications are designed to let a user virtually rotate cubes of information, whereby each side of the cube provides another two dimensions of relevant information.

Managers and Their Information Systems

Employees at different levels in an organization must make decisions that vary in scope and type. Exhibit 800.16 shows the traditional view of the types of information systems needed for an organization's different operational and managerial levels. While these relationships generally hold true, information needs vary widely in practice. With ISs making information available throughout organizational hierarchies, these traditional correlations can become blurred.

Transaction Processing Systems

Workers at the bottom of the organizational hierarchy use point-of-sale (POS) terminals, order-entry systems, and other transaction processing systems (TPSs) to enter data at its source at the time transactions take place. These data are the raw materials for producing useful information. TPSs are linked to applications that provide clerical workers and operational managers with up-to-date information, such as the quantity-on-hand of a certain inventory item, the latest deposit in a customer's bank account, the shipping date and contents of a customer's order, or the latest prescription filled for a customer in a drugstore. Clerical workers use the systems to perform their routine responsibilities:

Exhibit 800.16 *Types of Information Systems Typically Used at Different Levels of an Organization's Hierarchy*

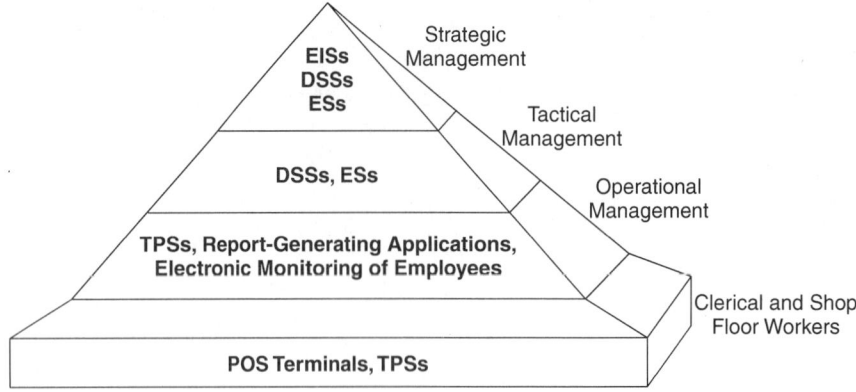

serving customers, placing purchase orders with suppliers, and providing information to other employees. TPSs are also used by operational managers, mainly to generate ad hoc reports, usually on-screen.

Decision Support Systems and Expert Systems

Middle managers must solve problems that are typically more complex and nonroutine than those faced by operational managers. Their decision-making tasks require significantly more data. Therefore, they use computer-based decision aids, including decision support systems (DSSs) and expert systems (ESs), to assist them.

Senior managers also use DSSs and ESs, although historically they have been more reluctant to use computers in their decision making. Until several years ago, it was rare to find a PC on the desk of a corporate president or vice president. This reluctance was partly because they perceived desktop computers to be more appropriate for lower-level managers and clerical staff. The sophistication and ease of use of such systems nowadays has probably contributed to the adoption of the systems by many high-ranking executives.

Executive Information Systems

In addition to the more traditional DSSs and ESs, executive information systems (EISs) provide managers with timely and concise information about the performance of their organization. EISs deliver summarized and concise information that helps managers quickly grasp business conditions. For instance, summary information (such as revenue per employee in a specific region) may attract the attention of a manager. Then, the manager can use an EIS to "drill down" and isolate the data that are related to the cause of a problem. Executives who use EISs can usually connect their computers (or have them permanently connected) to an OLAP server so they can view information in different combinations and receive such information fast.

Senior managers realize they need to use computerized decision aids to keep their companies competitive.

Many executives also have their microcomputers connected to external commercial services that provide business and general news, including economic indices, stock and commodity prices, and summaries of information sorted by industry on a regional, national, and international basis.

While there is a general correlation between managerial level and type of IS, it is important to note that nothing prevents any member of an organization from using any type of IS. Of course, management may not put an EIS at the routine discretion of a clerk, but clerks may use DSSs, ESs, and sometimes even EISs for their work. Also, while we discuss different types of ISs, many applications are actually combinations of several types of such ISs. For example, some decision support systems are combined with expert systems techniques and OLAP capabilities to serve as sophisticated EISs.

Customer Relationship Management Systems

Because an increasing number of transactions are executed through the Web, managers can use data that are already in electronic form to analyze and strategize. One type of system proven to be highly useful is a customer relationship management (CRM) system. CRM systems help collect data about customers and analyze the data into useful information to help serve customers better. They can also help managers find effective and efficient marketing strategies. The challenge is to address the right customer, at the right time, with the right offer, instead of spending millions of dollars in mass marketing or covering numerous Web sites with ads.

By compiling billions of consumer clickstream data and creating behavioral models, these companies can glean individual consumers' interests from the sites they visited (what do they like?), the frequency of visits (are they loyal?), the times they surf (are they at work or at home?), and the number of times they click on ads or complete a transaction. Then, sites can display ads that match the typical interests at sites where the likely customers tend to visit. They can use software that will change the ad for each visitor by detecting the computer (IP number) from which the individual visits.

Consider the challenge that was facing a Web-based drugstore. Management wanted to reach more customers who were likely to purchase its products, but they did not have the tools to know who those people were.

Information, Politics, and Power

We assume that employees make all their work-related decisions based on what is best for the company and its goals. However, human nature being what it is, employees—including managers—often consider their personal interests and their close peers' interests, even when they are making work-related decisions. Politics and power influence daily interactions in organizations. They are doubly important in the context of information systems, because information is often perceived to be a source of power.

Politics

Unfortunately, the process of developing and controlling ISs often involves problematic politics. Politics arise when an individual's or group's interests are put ahead of the organization's as a whole. In contrast, rational decisions are made to achieve organizational goals. Politics can affect ISs adversely in a number of different ways—for instance, when managers are motivated to control systems rather than to make them responsive to the corporation's needs or when managers refuse to use systems that are not designed specially for their organizational unit.

When the interests of individual managers are aligned with those of the organization, both benefit. This alignment of goals is often the case but not always. For example, a manager may resent other departments' access and use of information that his department creates and maintains because he believes it subjects him to scrutiny. Because of his fears, a manager may oppose expanded access to the information even though it would be in the best interests of the organization as a whole.

Politics also take the form of personal alliances among managers. The unspoken agreement between managers that they will help each other out is common in organizations but can sometimes undermine their success. For instance, if a senior manager in the IS department has an alliance with a manager in one of the other units, the IS manager may work on the information needs of his friend rather than the more urgent needs of other managers.

The negative impact of politics is also at play when a manager decides not to pull the plug on a development project to save face, even though he knows it will never work. Organizations invest billions of dollars in the development of new ISs, and about a third of these systems are never completed (for various reasons). However, millions of dollars could be saved if managers stopped them before the financial loss (and often loss of morale) grew. People do not like to admit failure because they fear it will tarnish their image. So, often managers decide to continue projects to save their own reputation, resulting in a decision that is out of sync with the good of the organization.

This happened at California's Department of Motor Vehicles in the 1980s and caused a $45 million loss. It also happened at the Oregon Department of Motor Vehicles. Its system was abandoned after a loss of $123 million. The U.S. federal government has reportedly lost an estimated $7.3 billion on abandoned IS projects. While some losses are unavoidable in any development project, observers say that significant portions of these losses could be prevented if high-ranking decision makers did not try to "save face."

Power

Anyone who has worked for an organization recognizes that having access to information is often the road to acquiring power. And power is something that people do not give away willingly. When management decides a new IS should be implemented, department managers usually concur on several issues. But often questions arise for senior executives. For instance:

- *Who owns the system?* Unfortunately, many managers make decisions based on wanting to look powerful, regardless of the consequences. They follow the rule that the more resources they control (people, machinery, funds, and so on), the more power they have. Building information system "empires" is just another way to look—and sometimes to be—powerful. Usually, the department that owns an information system also controls it. That department may have the final say in determining its features and in modifying it. When a system serves more than one department, managers often struggle for control, leading to a system that is not used properly or at all by those who have been denied ownership. Management is often forced to announce which unit owns the system and what rights other units have to it. To resolve disputes when a system serves more than one department equally, top managers sometimes say that they are the owner of the system. Making the proper decision and educating employees about sharing systems is especially important when enterprise applications such as ERP systems are being implemented.
- *Who pays for developing the system?* Everyone wants something for nothing, and managers are no different. So, when several units are going to share a new system, their managers often try to offload the cost of development and operation on each other. Top management's challenge is to allocate the development and operating costs fairly among departments, preferably based on the benefits each group will receive.
- *Who accesses what information?* As noted previously, many managers make decisions to gain power. Because information is power, these managers often try to gain access to as much of it as they can while denying access to as many other people as possible. Many managers don't like their information accessed by people from outside their departments. They dislike scrutiny and don't want to give outsiders an opportunity to judge and question their decisions. Also, many managers feel more powerful when others who need information turn to them first.
- *Who has update privileges?* Update privilege is the authority to modify information in files and databases. Some managers make some decisions based on data collected by departments they do not control. So, if you control the data, you can influence their decisions. Management should give "view access" on a "need to know" basis. Update access should be given only to users who must update data or applications as part of their jobs. Often, these employees are the database administrator or another high-ranking MIS officer and some of his or her staff. These decisions must be made carefully in order not to alienate other managers. The decisions must be explained satisfactorily to those who may not be given privileges they think they deserve.

Political struggles are especially harmful when several organizational units share systems. Some managers use subversive tactics to undermine the successful implementation of a system. Some managers insist on adding features for the sole purpose of giving themselves more control. Other managers may try to derail the implementation effort by not cooperating with the developers or consultants or by promoting an alternate system.

The Not-Invented-Here Phenomenon

Sometimes, managers do whatever they can to *not* use an IS. The reason is known as the not-invented-here phenomenon: Managers and their subordinates often believe that if the new system is the fruit of an outsider's idea, it will not serve them well. They may know this is not true, but they may still deny others credit for something they feel *they* should have invented. Again, managers may use a variety of tactics to undermine a new system in their department. They may try to convince top management that the system is not needed, or that it does not satisfy their "unique" business needs.

Top management must be aware of these issues and distinguish valid arguments from political ones. For instance, a manager may ask for IS systems or services that serve both his own interests and the organization's. Such requests are legitimate. But he could damage the organization if the request serves only his own goals, or the goals of his unit. Since an increasing number of ISs are not developed or implemented for individual departments, but for the entire organization, managers must be vigilant to the motives of staff members.

Decision Making and Information Technology

Decision Making in Business

The success of an organization largely depends on the quality of the decisions that its managers make. When decision making involves large amounts of information and a lot of processing, computer-based systems can make the process efficient and effective. Several types of information systems support decision making: decision-support systems, executive information systems, and expert systems. In recent years applications have been developed to combine several of the features and methods; thus, the distinction between decision-support systems, executive information systems, and other types of decision-support applications is no longer discernible in many of these applications. Also, many decision-support modules are often integrated into larger enterprise applications. For example, enterprise resource planning, (ERP) systems support decision making in such areas as inventory replenishment.

Decision-Support System Components

To save time and effort in their decision making, managers use several types of decision-support applications. One such type is decision-support systems. **Decision-support systems** (DSSs) are computer-based information systems designed to help managers select one of many alternative solutions to a problem. DSSs can help corporations increase market share, reduce costs, increase profitability, and enhance product quality. By automating some of the decision-making process, the systems give managers access to analyses that were previously unavailable. Technically, certain analyses could be performed by managers, but it would be prohibitively time-consuming and would render late, and therefore bad, decisions. DSSs provide sophisticated and fast analysis of vast amounts of data and information. Although the use of DSSs typically increases with the level of management, the systems are used at all levels, and often by nonmanagerial staff.

The traditional definition of a DSS has been changing over the years. In the following sections we discuss the components of "traditional" stand-alone DSSs: either self-contained applications or applications that were designed to address a rather narrow decision-making domain. Nowadays, many companies use software such as data-mining applications, which aid in decision making but often are not called DSSs. Also, you should realize that some components of a computer-based decision aid, such as a database, may already be in place when a new DSS is developed. Therefore, you should consider the following discussion a general framework and not a rigid recipe for the development of all DSSs.

The majority of DSSs comprise three major components: a data management module, a model management module, and a dialog module (see Exhibit 800.17). Together, these modules (1) help the user enter a request in a convenient manner, (2) search vast amounts of data to focus on the relevant facts, (3) process the data through desired models, and (4) present the results in one or several manners so the output can be easily understood.

The Data Management Module

A DSS's **data management module** is a database or data warehouse that allows a decision maker to conduct the intelligence phase of decision making. For example, an investment consultant always needs access to current stock prices and those from at least the preceding few years. A data management module accesses the data and provides a means for the DSS to select data according to certain criteria: type of stock, range of years, and so on.

A DSS may use a database created specially for that system, but DSSs are usually linked to databases used for other purposes as well, such as purchasing, shipping, billing, and other daily transactions. Companies that have built data warehouses often prefer their DSSs to access the data warehouse rather than the transactional database, to minimize interference with transactions and to provide substantially more historical data than transactional databases.

Many DSSs are now closely intertwined with other organizational systems, including data warehouses, data marts, and ERP systems, from which they draw relevant data.

Exhibit 800.17 *Components of a DSS and Their Interaction*

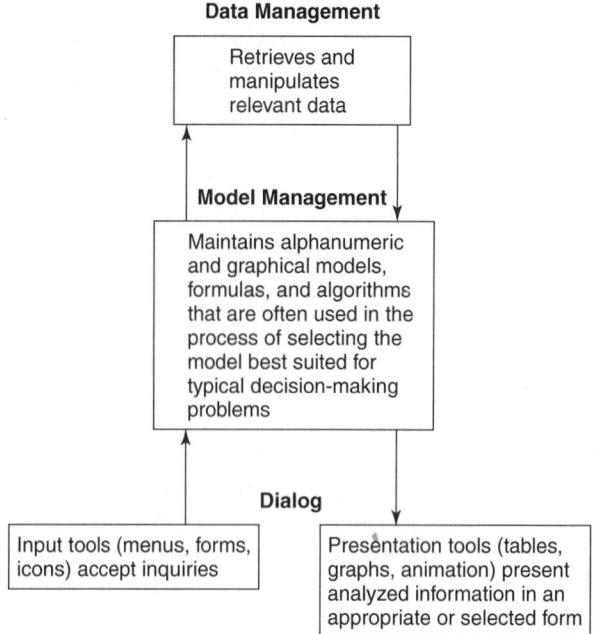

The Model Management Module

To turn data into useful information, the user selects a model from the **model management module,** which is a collection of models the DSS draws on to assist in decision making. A sequence of events or a pattern of behavior may become a useful model when the relationships among its inputs, outputs, and conditions can be established well enough that they can be used to analyze different parameters. Models are used to predict output on the basis of different input or different conditions or to estimate what combination of conditions and input might lead to a desired output. Models are often based on mathematical research or on experience. A model may be a widely used method to predict performance, such as "best-fit" linear analysis, or it may be built by the organization, using the experience that knowledge workers in the firm have accumulated over time. Many companies will not divulge details of the models they have programmed, because they view them as important trade secrets and as valuable assets that may give them competitive advantages. Patterns or models may be unique to a certain industry or even to an individual business. For example:

- In trying to serve customers better in a bank, operations research experts try to create a model that predicts the best positioning and scheduling of tellers.
- In the trucking business, models are developed to minimize the total mileage trucks must travel and maximize the trucks' load, while maintaining a satisfactory delivery time. Similar models are developed in the airline industry to maximize revenue.
- A model for revenue maximization in the airline industry will automatically price tickets according to the parameters the user enters: date of the flight, day of the week of the flight, departure and destination points, and the length of stay if the ticket is for a round-trip flight.
- Car rental companies use similar models to price their services by car class, rental period, and drop-off options in different countries.

Among the general statistical models, a linear regression model is the best-fit linear relationship between two variables, such as sales and the money spent on marketing. A private business may develop a linear regression model to estimate future sales based on past experience. For example, the marketing department of a shoe store chain may apply linear regression to the relationship between the dollar amount spent on television commercials and change in sales volume. This linear relationship can be translated into a program in a DSS. Then the user can enter the total amount to be spent on television commercials for the next year into the DSS, and the program will enter that figure into the model and find the estimated change in the sales volume. The relationship between the two variables can be plotted, as shown in Exhibit 800.18.

Exhibit 800.18 *A Linear Regression Model for Predicting Sales Volume as a Function of Dollars Spent on Advertising*

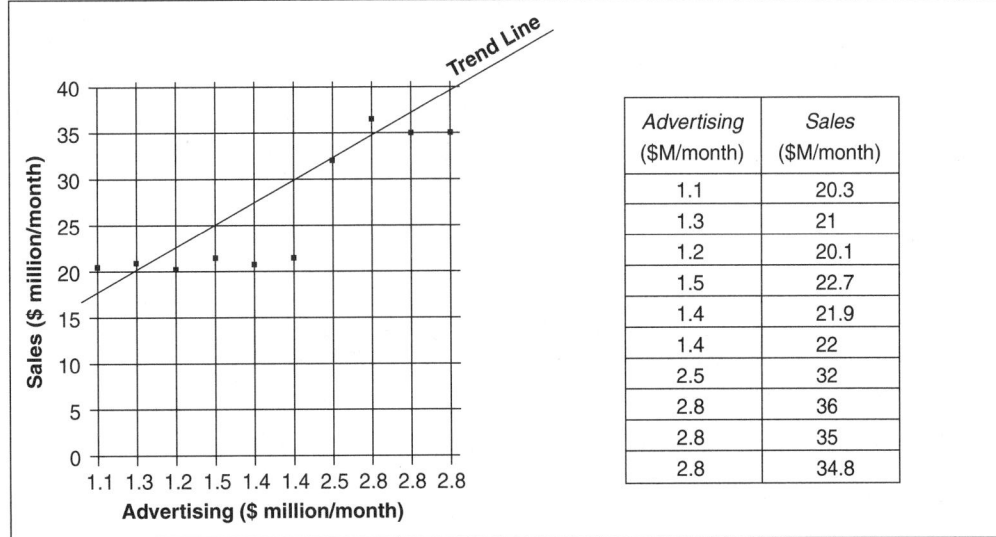

Note that the actual data points rarely lie on the regression line produced from the data. This illustrates the uncertainty involved in many models. For instance, in Exhibit 800.18, if the marketing managers tried to estimate the sales volume resulting from spending $1.4 million per month on advertising, their estimates for both months plotted on the graph would be more than the actual sales. In spite of these discrepancies, the regression line may be adequate in general for modeling, with the understanding that results are not necessarily precise. Also note that models often describe relationships among more than two variables and that some models can be expressed as a curve, rather than a straight line.

Usually, models are not so simple. In this advertising and sales example, for instance, many more factors may play a role: the number of salespeople, the location of the stores, the types of shoes offered for sale, the television programs in which the commercials are presented, and many more parameters. Therefore, before models are programmed to become part of a DSS, the environment in which the decision will be executed must be carefully considered.

Not all DSSs are business oriented. In some areas, especially engineering, models in DSSs may simulate physical environments rather than business environments. For example, aeronautical engineers build computer models of wind tunnels to view how an aircraft with a new wing design might behave. It is significantly less expensive to construct a software model than to build a physical model. The simulation provides valuable information on vibrations, drag, metal fatigue, and other factors, in relation to various speeds and weather conditions. The output, in the form of both animated pictures and numerical tables, enables engineers to make important decisions before spending huge amounts of money to actually build aircraft—decisions such as the angle in which the aircraft wings are swept, the shape of the hull's cross section, the spreading of weight over different parts of the plane, and so forth. When using this type of model, engineers base part of their decision on visual examination of the behavior of the simulation model.

The Dialog Module

For the user to interact with the DSS, the system must provide an easy way to interact with the program. The part of the DSS that allows the user to interact with it is called the **dialog module.** It prompts the user to select a model, allowing the user to access the database and select data for the decision process or to set criteria for selecting such data. It lets the user enter parameters and change them to see how the change affects the result of the analysis. The dialog may be in the form of commands, pull-down menus, icons, dialog boxes, or any other approach. In essence, the dialog module is not different from the user interfaces of other types of applications.

The dialog module is also responsible for displaying the results of the analysis. DSSs use various textual, tabular, and graphical displays from which the decision maker can choose. In disciplines that require decisions regarding the physical construction of objects, such as aircraft or buildings, the output is often animated. For example, an architect may want to test the strength of a new structure by creating a computer model of the building and subjecting the model to increasing pressures until the construction collapses. Decisions can then be based on the sequence of events that appears on the monitor, along with the display of textual and tabular data.

Different colors and patterns may also play an important role in DSS output, by quickly drawing attention to exceptional results that do not comply with certain rules of analysis. Take the previous advertising effort scenario, for example, where the company's marketing manager is trying to decide how to spend promotional dollars (see Exhibit 800.18). The dialog component of the DSS presents a menu allowing the marketing executive to select "TV advertising" from a variety of promotional choices and to choose the amount to be spent in that channel. Now the dialog module invokes the part of the database that holds current data on advertising expenditures and sales volumes for the corresponding months. At this point, the system may either present a list of models for analyzing the data from which the user can choose or, if it is sophisticated enough, select a model automatically, based on the problem at hand. The model projects sales figures based on the data from the database, and the dialog component presents the results of the analysis. The output helps the executive make a decision by answering the question: Will the proposed amount to be spent on television commercials yield a large enough boost in sales?

Types of Decision-Support Systems

The general structure of all DSSs is similar and comprises the components detailed in Exhibit 800.19, but DSSs may differ in their degree of sophistication and the manner in which they are used. DSSs can be categorized into two basic categories: personal DSSs and group DSSs. Usually, when people refer to DSSs they mean the former type. In this discussion we add the word *personal* to distinguish DSSs used by individuals from those used by groups.

Personal Decision-Support Systems

Personal DSSs are built for the individual knowledge worker to use in his or her daily work. Usually, they run on personal computers and often contain a single model for data processing. Personal DSSs are often developed with the participation of all prospective users or of those who are most experienced. However, many software companies develop

Exhibit 800.19 *A DSS Helps Marketers Make Decisions*

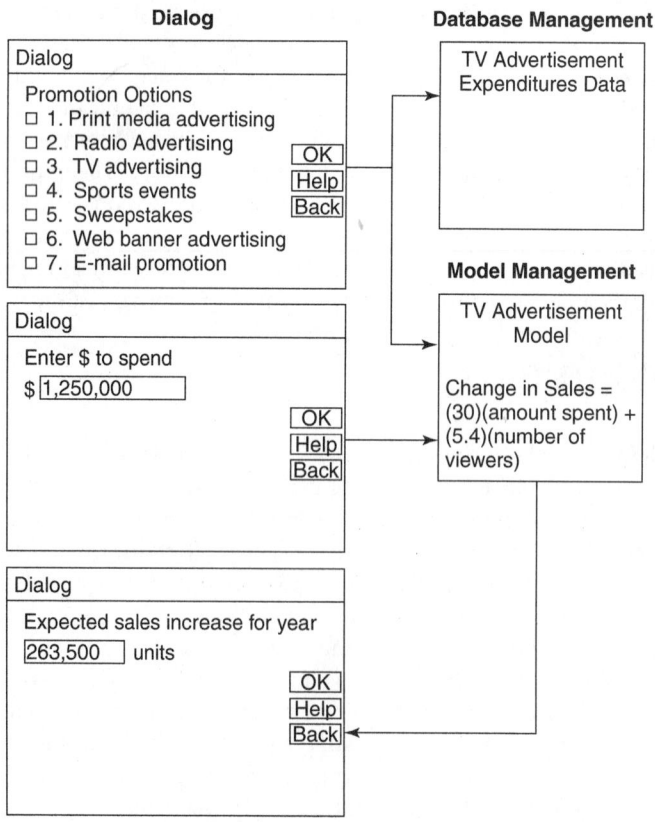

prepackaged DSSs for mass marketing based on a collaboration of specialized experts and programmers. An increasing number of personal DSSs are not tailor-made for a specific company.

With personal DSSs, raw data may be entered directly into a program by the user, or it may be drawn from a firm's database or data warehouse, from an external source, or from a combination of sources. Some companies using DSSs have policies saying that managers should act on the system's "decision." For example, **Mrs. Fields Cookies** provides store managers with DSSs that decide for the managers which types of cookies to make, what quantities of each type, and which ingredients to use, on the basis of the store's sales volumes and corporate-dictated baking instructions. In this case, the company has structured the business environment for the store managers. However, if users work in a highly unstructured environment, they must carefully examine output before acting on it or rejecting it.

The Canadian government has sponsored the development of a series of DSSs for farmers, one of which is Prairie Crop Protection Planner, a system that helps farmers plan protection of crops. When a farmer enters basic information about a particular crop and the pest problem he is experiencing—weeds, insects, or diseases—the Planner outlines options such as chemicals and ways to apply them. The farmer can describe his sprayer, the size of his field, and the current chemical prices from his local supplier, and the Prairie Crop Protection Planner calculates application rates, costs per acre, the amount of product the farmer will need to use in the sprayer's tank, and the amount of chemical he will need to spray on the entire field.

Not surprisingly, there are plenty of DSSs for investment managers, because there are many different variables to consider and complex models to use when planning portfolios for high return. Using the program, investors can create filters—that is, they can identify the criteria of the securities they are interested in by return on investment or by share price change over a particular period. Investors can also pick securities by name. Then, they can build a hypothetical portfolio, see a pie chart of the proportions of each security or type of security in the portfolio, and receive an estimated return on the investment. Investors can use the program to create multiple model portfolios and can then compare the portfolios' performances.

For several years companies have enabled employees to use a shared DSS, which is stored on a computer server and accessed through a LAN. Many companies now let employees from various sites access such DSSs using intranets. Some nonprofit organizations, such as governments and universities, provide online access to DSSs through the Web. For example, the University of Arizona placed a DSS online to help ranchers make cow-culling decisions.

Organizations can use the Internet to access data from several sites for DSS data analysis. For example, **Accrue Software** offers a DSS that uses the Internet to access data from several sources rather than just a local data warehouse. Regional managers can access information of individual stores, which was previously available only at headquarters. For example, they can access sales and inventory information for stores, by day or week for recent weeks, and compare it with data for the same period last year. The software lets them see which stores are underperforming in terms of profit. They can measure sales per square foot of selling space by stores and departments and evaluate store characteristics so the lessons learned can be applied to all the stores in the chain or region. Other applications can determine which items tend to be purchased together for better placement on shelves. Using statistical models, the DSS can provide accurate and timely sales forecasts by item and store for improved merchandise allocation and markdowns.

Group Decision-Support Systems

Often, business decisions are made by a group of managers rather than a single person. To facilitate such decision-making sessions, many organizations use group DSSs. *Group decision-support systems (GDSSs)* are usually installed in conference-room settings or through a group of networked computers. In recent years several software vendors have offered Internet-based GDSSs to accommodate users from several disparate locations. GDSSs are designed specifically to take input from multiple users interacting with the program simultaneously and converging on a decision together. Although personal DSSs can help groups make decisions, the nature of group decision making is different from that of a single individual. In individual decision making, the individual may share ideas with others, but he or she does not have to agree with any other person about the data collected, the ideas raised, or the decision made. A decision made by a group, on the other hand, can be the result of a consensus or majority vote. GDSSs are designed to provide methods such as weighing votes to overcome impasses.

Sensitivity Analysis

An outcome is almost always affected by more than one parameter; for instance, the sales volume of a product is affected by the number of salespeople, the number of regional sales representatives, the amount spent on national and local television advertising, price, competition, and so on. However, outcomes rarely respond in equal measure to changes in parameters. For instance, a small change in price per unit may result in a dramatic increase in sales, which means sales volume has a high sensitivity to product price. However, the same sales may increase only slightly in response to a huge investment in advertising dollars, which means that sales have a low sensitivity to advertising expenditure. It is important to pinpoint the parameters to which the outcome is highly sensitive, so that an organization can focus efforts where they will be most effective. Sometimes the parameters to which an outcome is most sensitive also affect other parameters, so these interactions must be carefully tracked as well.

If a company wishes to maximize profit, managers must find the optimal combination of many factors. To equip a DSS to help achieve this goal, an approximate mathematical formula that expresses the relationship between each factor and the total profit is built into the DSS. Then a **sensitivity analysis** is conducted to test the degree to which the total profit grows or shrinks if one or more of the factors is increased or decreased. The results indicate the relative sensitivity of the profit to the changes. If the outcome is affected significantly even when the parameter is changed only a little, then the sensitivity of the outcome to the parameter is said to be high. The opposite is also true: If the outcome is affected only a little even when the parameter is varied widely, the outcome is said to be insensitive to the parameter. For instance, a manager may ask, "What is the impact on total quarterly profits if television advertising is decreased by 10% and the number of commissioned sales representatives is increased by 5%?" Because questions typically are phrased in this format, sensitivity analysis is often referred to as **what if analysis.** Note that you can use a DSS to perform "what if" analyses on multiple parameters at the same time.

Executive Information Systems

Executive information systems (EISs) are decision aids specially designed for high-ranking managers, to provide them with the most essential information for running their organizations. EISs are useful in paring down information for executives, who almost always suffer from information overload. *Information overload* is a situation in which the very volume of information makes it impossible to sort through what is important. Any additional information only adds to the burden, rather than helping to solve problems and make decisions. Unlike other decision aids, EISs do not contain analytical models; rather, they consolidate and summarize data that are obtained both from within the organization and from outside sources.

You may recall that high-level managers make decisions based on highly summarized information. They review ratios such as sales per employee per quarter or per year, sales per region, return on investment, and inventory turnover for different items. EISs can display these data graphically so that exceptions can be easily spotted. Unlike regular DSSs, many EISs do not require a user to enter the values of parameters. The system is linked with the organization's databases and data warehouses and uses predetermined or selected models to respond to queries, displaying the results in the fashion requested.

The purpose of EISs is not so much to perform sophisticated analysis as it is to **drill down** in databases and data warehouses to find the most relevant information for executive decision making. Often, an executive first needs a general picture of a business situation, such as the ratio of research and development to revenue over the past three years or a ratio of inventory turnover. But more detailed (and less summarized) information may be needed to pinpoint a problem. For example, a low inventory turnover (which means that the company does not sell its inventory fast enough) may be caused by a single item that sells extremely slowly. By drilling down to more details, the executive may discover that fact, in which case the decision may be to simply stop producing the item. For this reason, many EISs are interfaced with online analytical processing (OLAP) applications.

Some vendors market EISs with a "what if" feature, which brings the system closer to the format and purpose of a DSS. This convergence demonstrates how meaningless the classification of computer-based decision aids is becoming.

An effective EIS has the following features.

- An easy-to-use and easy-to-learn graphical user interface
- On-request "drill down" capability that allows the executive to reach information in further detail
- On-demand financial and other ratios and indicators (such as sales per employee or ratio of divisional total actual expense to budgeted funds) that reflect organizational strengths and weaknesses
- Easy-to-use but sophisticated tools to allow navigation in databases and data warehouses
- Statistical analysis tools
- The ability to respond to ad hoc queries and sensitivity analyses
- Access to external data pools
- The ability to solve diverse business problems

Many full-blown DSSs are now sold by vendors under the label of *EIS,* probably because the term EIS is perceived as more sophisticated or more attractive to executives. The lines between DSSs and EISs have been blurred in recent years. When an organization purchases a system, management should look not at its label but at the features it offers.

Developing Decision-Support Systems

Although vendors now offer off-the-shelf DSSs, many organizations develop their own systems, especially if the systems deal with business problems that are unique to the organization. To make a wise choice, managers who consider the acquisition of a new DSS must understand what circumstances justify the investment in employee time and effort for a development project and when using an off-the-shelf DSS that serves a less specialized market is warranted, despite the compromises.

When Should a DSS Be Built?

Like investment in any information system, the investment in developing a DSS may be hundreds of thousands or even millions of dollars. Therefore, management must consider several factors before making a commitment. Following are questions that can help guide the decision.

- *What type of problem are we trying to address, and how structured is it?* Not every decision needs a DSS or EIS. In general, the less structured the problem, the more analysis it requires and the more likely it is that managers will benefit from a decision aid. But many decisions can be made with a quick look at the appropriate data. In fact, some analyses are so simple that they can be performed within seconds. Even some unstructured problems can be solved easily with common sense. But for solving highly unstructured problems, with many different models as possible analysis tools and many factors and parameters to be considered, even the most experienced managers can benefit from using a DSS.

    Highly unstructured problems are usually qualitative rather than quantitative. For instance, consider a purchasing manager for a software company deciding which supplier to use for blank recordable CDs. He or she must consider several factors, including the quality of the CDs, delivery time, price, payment terms, and warranty. If there are only two CD manufacturers, and the factors listed are similar for both, then the manager does not need a DSS to make a decision; he or she may simply negotiate a better price.

    However, if the company has many potential suppliers, the manager must consider many combinations of values, in which case a DSS could aid in the evaluation and selection of the best supplier. Similarly, if the firm tried many suppliers but found one to be more reliable in meeting delivery times and easier to work with, then the firm would most likely purchase from this supplier even if his prices were somewhat higher. Often, the business relationship is determined largely by trust: the purchasing officer simply trusts certain suppliers more than others to come through when needed. Such factors cannot be quantified and used as parameters in a DSS.
- *Are the data required for the analysis available in automated databases and data warehouses?* The accessibility of relevant data from existing internal and external databases, or from the creation of a combined new database, is an important consideration in the development of a DSS. A DSS designer may determine that an entire database needs to be maintained for the system, or that adequate interfaces can be developed for existing databases. In general, the higher the level of the managers who use decision aids, the greater the amount of external data required. Hence, DSS developers have the added challenge of effectively combining internal and external sources.
- *How often do managers encounter the problem?* The more frequently the problem occurs, the more justified the development of a DSS to solve it. If the problem is encountered rarely, the development cost will outweigh the benefits.
- *Who will use the system?* In general, the greater the number of prospective users and the higher the position of the users in the organization, the greater the positive impact a DSS will have. Depending on the level of management, if only one person, or a handful of people, will use the system, it may be more economical to have them develop their own individual systems using a fourth generation language (4GL) or spreadsheet. However, if the sole prospective user is the company's president, and this person will use it frequently, then the investment may be justified because of the great benefit the DSS might have for the entire organization.

- *Can the prospective users spare adequate time for the development process?* The development of automated decision aids requires much time and effort of the users, so management has to be willing to let workers take time from their regular duties to help in the development effort.

The Electronic Spreadsheet: A DSS Tool

If data must be drawn from external databases and decisions require complex, special calculations, a DSS may have to be programmed from scratch. But many DSSs can be developed using inexpensive off-the-shelf software referred to as DSS tools. A DSS tool is any application that lets you build models and access the proper data. The most widely used tools are electronic spreadsheets.

Geographic Information Systems

Many business decisions concern geographic locations—either as input, as output, or both. For example, consider the process of choosing the best locations for new stores or determining how to deploy police forces optimally. For map-related decisions, *geographic information systems (GISs)* are often the best decision aids to use. GISs are systems that process location data and provide output. For instance, a GIS could be used to help a housing developer determine where to invest by tracking and displaying population changes on a map, highlighting in color increases of more than 10% over the past three years. With this information, a developer could easily decide where to invest on the basis of population growth trends. Other examples include the following.

- Delivery managers looking for the shortest distance a truck can travel to deliver ordered goods at the lowest cost
- School-district officials looking for the most efficient routes for busing school children to and from their homes
- City planners looking to deploy services to better serve residents, which might include police officers deciding how to deploy their forces on the basis of precinct maps indicating levels of criminal activity
- Oil companies looking to determine drilling locations on the basis of geological tests
- Hunters, fishers, hikers, and other people who look for outdoor recreation can find suitable sites and trails for their activities based on their requirements, such as local fauna and trail length

A typical GIS consists of (1) a database of quantitative and qualitative data from which information is extracted for display, (2) a database of maps, and (3) a program that displays the information on the maps. The digitized maps are produced from satellite and aerial photography. Displays may be in the form of easily understood symbols and colors or even of moving images. For instance, an oil exploration map may show different concentrations of expected crude oil deposits in different hues of red. Or, population density may be similarly displayed on a map using different hues of blue. A more sophisticated GIS may display, in colors or icons, concentrations of specific consumer groups by age, income, and other characteristics.

Web technology helps promote the use of GISs by private organizations and governments alike. Intranets allow employees to bring up thousands of maps from a central repository on their own PCs. HTML and XML, the primary languages used to compose and retrieve Web pages, support the presentation of pictures with marked areas, which makes them ideal for retrieval of marked maps. Clicking different areas of a map can bring up related information in the form of other maps or in text, utilizing the multimedia capabilities of the Web to the fullest.

For example, sales managers can bring up maps of whole continents and see how past sales have "performed" over different territories. They can zoom in and zoom out on a territory. With the click of a mouse they can receive detailed information on who serves the territory and other pertinent information.

In government work a city clerk can bring up a map of the neighborhood of a resident, zoom in on the resident's house pictured on the map, click on the picture, and receive information such as real-estate taxes owed and paid over the past several years. Further information, such as whether a neighborhood uses septic tanks or a sewage system, may be rendered by different colors. The map can also show different zoning codes, such as land designated for residential, industrial, or commercial purposes.

Value Creation With Information Technology

Trends in Organizational Structure

Information technology (IT) is the most powerful tool available for increasing efficiency, solving problems, and making decisions in businesses today. Its impact contributed to vast organizational restructuring in the 1980s and 1990s, with a trend toward downsizing and "flattening," which often eliminated levels of management.

IT Flattens the Organization

Before the introduction of computers into business, lower-level managers spent much of their time processing data to produce useful information for their supervisors. Over the past two decades, many companies have used ISs to automate these activities, eliminating the need for several layers of middle managers. This shift has led to flatter organizational structures (as shown in Exhibit 800.20) and has been a major force behind the enormous downsizing in both the manufacturing and service sectors. In 1993, in the United States alone, some 450,000 middle managers lost their jobs. In 1994, more than a half million workers lost their jobs, almost all of them middle managers. There are signs the trend is continuing. And studies have been conducted showing that as IT proliferates, organizational staffing in general becomes leaner.

Strategic and operational managers have been affected much less by this trend. Strategic managers are still needed because of their responsibilities for setting the organizational course, and operational managers run the daily operations of the organization. Today, easy-to-use graphical user interfaces and affordable data communications allow senior managers to produce their own information and communicate directly with lower-level managers, who used to be at least two or three layers away. In many small organizations there are simply *no* middle managers at all between strategic managers and operational managers.

In some companies that make heavy use of the Internet for business, not only is the middle management layer "lean and mean," but the operational management and office worker layers are as well. For instance, when more and more consumers use corporate Web sites to purchase products and obtain customer service, there is less need for staff workers to help with these activities. Many organizations also claim that e-mail has flattened their structure because every employee can communicate with any other employee—including top executives. That ability does not necessarily flatten an organization, however. Top executives at **Mrs. Fields Cookies**, including the president and other executives, respond to all e-mail messages, which they can receive from any employee at any level. But this electronic correspondence does not affect the actual management of the company. If you take a look at the organizational structure, you will see a clear pyramid with several layers of management. It is not a flat organization.

The Matrix Structure

In the 1980s, the increasing power of information systems in organizations led to an organizational experiment: matrix management. **Matrix management** replaced a strict hierarchical structure with a flexible reporting structure, whereby

Exhibit 800.20 *Information Systems Flatten Managerial Layers*

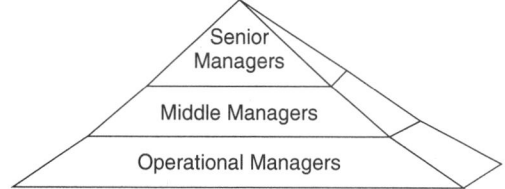

Exhibit 800.21 *An Example of Matrix Organization*

		Divisions		
		General Manager of Product A Division	General Manager of Product B Division	General Manager of Product C Division
Functions	V.P. of Marketing and Sales (M&S)	1. M&S personnel assigned to Division A	2. M&S personnel assigned to Division B	3. M&S personnel assigned to Division C
	V.P. of Manufacturing (Mfg.)	4. Mfg. personnel assigned to Division A	5. Mfg. personnel assigned to Division B	6. Mfg. personnel assigned to Division C
	V.P. of Engineering (Eng.)	7. Eng. personnel assigned to Division A	8. Eng. personnel assigned to Division B	9. Eng. personnel assigned to Division C

people reported to different supervisors, depending on the project, product, or location of the work. While this structure has been successful in some small entrepreneurial organizations that consist predominantly of knowledge workers (such as young high-tech companies), it was less successful in larger, non–high-tech organizations.

Exhibit 800.21 shows how a matrix organization might work, with the personnel of each unit reporting to both a divisional and a functional manager. The manager of the personnel in cell 1 reports to both the vice president of marketing and sales and the general manager of Division A. The vice president of marketing is responsible for the marketing of all the company's products and services. The general manager of Division A is responsible for all the activities related to Division A products and services, including engineering, manufacturing, *and* marketing. Technologically, IT supports a matrix structure, because both divisional and functional managers can have access to cross-sectional information. Following the example in Exhibit 800.21, the same database can provide executive information to the vice president of engineering for all three divisions and product information to a division general manager for marketing, manufacturing, and engineering activities related to the product.

The matrix structure came about because sometimes divisional supervision (by geography or product, for instance) and functional supervision are equally important. If so, then top management has to be composed of both divisional executives (such as general managers of the divisions and corporate vice presidents) and functional executives (such as vice presidents of finance, marketing, engineering, and the like).

Unfortunately, human nature sometimes stands in the way of ideas that look good on paper. Many problems arise when people report to more than one authority, especially when business is not going well or when an individual's performance is in question. Also, power plays may interfere with and undermine rational decision making. As a result, most of the organizations that tried matrix management abandoned it for the traditional pyramid, in which each manager reports to a single supervisor.

Still, a matrix structure facilitates flow of information because all employees have easier access to their managers. They do not need approval to pass information outside an organizational unit because the lines of reporting are more flexible than in a hierarchical structure. With more vertical and lateral lines of communication, there is less tendency to block access to information. The freer communication does have an impact on information needs, and thus on the design of ISs. To serve a matrix organization well, ISs must be integrated, and they must provide easy access to, and incorporation of, different databases and applications.

Strategic Information as a Competitive Weapon

Companies can take some of the strategic initiatives just described using information systems. A strategic information system (SIS) is any information system that can help an organization achieve a long-term competitive advantage. An SIS can be created from scratch, developed by modifying an existing system, or "discovered" by realizing that a system already in place can be used to strategic advantage. While companies continue to explore new ways of devising SISs, some successful SISs resulted from less lofty endeavors: the intention to improve mundane operations using IT yielded a system with strategic qualities.

Strategic information systems combine two types of ideas: ideas for making potentially winning business moves and ideas for harnessing information technology to implement the moves. For an information system to be an SIS, two conditions must exist. First, the information system must serve an organizational goal, rather than simply provide information; second, the IS unit must work with managers of other functional units (including marketing, finance, purchasing, human resources, and so on) to pursue the organizational goal.

Creating a Strategic Information System

To develop an SIS, top management must be involved from initial consideration through development and implementation. In other words, the SIS must be part of the overall organizational strategic plan. There is always the danger that a new SIS will be considered the IS unit's exclusive property. However, to succeed the project must be a corporate effort, involving all managers who will use the system.

Exhibit 800.22 presents questions that management should ask to determine whether to develop a new SIS. Executives meet to try to identify areas in which information can support a strategic goal. Only after completing the activities outlined in Exhibit 800.23 will management be able to conceptualize an SIS that seizes an opportunity. Exhibit 800.23 shows the steps involved in SIS planning. As you can see, activities involved in *planning* an SIS focus on education and brainstorming, not on technical details. Later, managers must consider technical details to decide whether the new SIS, like any system, is feasible.

A word of caution regarding Question 4 in Exhibit 800.22, the issue of economic justification of an SIS: an increasing number of researchers and practitioners conclude that estimating financial benefits of information systems is extremely difficult. This difficulty is especially true of SISs. The purpose of these systems is not simply to reduce cost or increase output per employee; many create a whole new service or product. Some completely change the way an organization does business. Because so many fundamental business changes are involved, measuring financial impact is difficult, if not impossible, even after implementation, let alone before. For example, if a bank is considering offering a full range of financial services via the Web, how can management know whether the move justifies the great cost of the special software? It is extremely difficult to estimate the success of such a bold approach in terms of how many new customers the bank would gain.

Exhibit 800.22 *Questions for Considering a New SIS*

1. What would be the most effective way to gain an advantage?
2. Would better (more accessible, accurate, timely) information help establish an advantage?
3. Can an information system be developed that will provide better information?
4. Will the development effort be economically justified?
   - Can existing competitors afford to fund the development of similar systems?
   - How long will it take the competitors to build their own, similar systems?
   - Can we make our system a moving target to the competition by constantly enhancing it, so that it always retains its superiority?
5. What is the risk of not developing an SIS?
6. Are alternative means of achieving the same goals available, and, if so, how do they compare with the advantages and disadvantages of a new SIS?

Exhibit 800.23 *Steps Involved in SIS Planning*

Step	Activity
1	Present potential strategic moves
2	Brainstorm different strategic moves
3	Select the most attractive move
4	Brainstorm ways to support the selected move with IT
5	Evaluate the viability of an SIS to support the move
6	List the general functions the SIS will fulfill
7	List the major features of the SIS

Reengineering and Organizational Change

Sometimes, to implement an SIS and achieve competitive advantage, organizations must rethink the entire way they operate. While brainstorming about strategic plans, management should ask: "If we established this business unit again, from scratch, what processes would we implement and how?" The answer to this question often leads to the decision to eliminate one set of operations and build others from the ground up. Management consultants call changes such as these **reengineering**. Reengineering often involves adoption of new machinery and elimination of management layers. Frequently, information technology plays an important role in this process.

Reengineering's goal is not to gain small incremental cost savings but to achieve great efficiency leaps—of 100% and even 1000%. With that degree of improvement, a company often gains competitive advantage. Interestingly, a company that undertakes reengineering along with implementing a new SIS cannot always tell whether the SIS was successful. The reengineering process makes it impossible to determine how much each change contributed to the organization's improved position.

Implementation of an SIS requires a business to revamp processes—to undergo organizational change—to gain an advantage. For example, when GM decided to manufacture a new car that would compete with Japanese cars, it chose a production process totally different from that of its other cars. Management first identified goals that could make the new car successful in terms of how to build it and also how to deliver and service it. Realizing that none of its existing divisions could meet these goals because of their organizational structure, their cultures, and their inadequate ISs, management established Saturn as an independent company with a completely separate operation.

Part of GM's initiative was recognizing the importance of Saturn dealerships in gaining competitive advantage. Through satellite communications, the new company gave dealers access to factory information. Clients could find out if, and exactly when, different cars with different features would be available.

Another feature of Saturn's SIS was improved customer service. Saturn embeds an electronic computer chip in the chassis of each car. The chip maintains a record of the car's technical details and the owner's name. When the car is serviced after the sale, new information is added to the chip. At their first service visit, many Saturn owners were surprised to be greeted by name as they rolled down their windows. While the quality of the car itself has been important to Saturn's success, the new SIS also played an important role.

Competitive Advantage as a Moving Target

As you may have guessed, competitive advantage is not long lasting. In time, competitors imitate the leader, and the advantage diminishes. So, the quest for innovative strategies must be dynamic. Corporations must continuously contemplate new ways to use information technology to their advantage. In a way, companies' jockeying for the latest competitive advantage is a lot like an arms race. Side A develops an advanced weapon, then side B develops a similar weapon that terminates the advantage of side A, and so on.

In an environment where most information technology is available to all, SISs originally developed to create a strategic advantage quickly become an expected standard business practice. A prime example is the banking industry, where surveys indicate that increased IS costs did not yield long-range strategic advantages. The few banks that provided services such as ATMs and banking by phone once had a powerful strategic advantage, but now almost every bank provides these services. Home banking, the popular name for banking from a home PC, provided some banks a moderate advantage but quickly became a staple for many banks. The next wave, Web-based banking, attracted Web-savvy clients to some banks but did not improve any particular bank's profit because the technology is immediately available to all.

A system can only help a company sustain competitive advantage if the company continuously modifies and enhances it, creating a moving target for competitors. **American Airlines'** SABRE—the online reservation system for travel agents—is a classic example. The innovative IS was designed in the late 1970s to expedite airline reservations and sell travel agencies a new service. But over the years, the company spun off an office automation package for travel agencies called Agency Data Systems. The reservation system now encompasses hotel reservations, car rentals, train schedules, theater tickets, and limousine rentals. It also provides a feature that lets travelers use SABRE from their own computers. The system has been so successful that in some years American earned more from it than from its airline operations. The organizational unit that developed and operated the software became a separate IT powerhouse at AMR, the parent company of American Airlines, and now operates as **Sabre Inc.**, an AMR subsidiary. It is the leading provider of technology for the travel industry. Chances are you are using its technology when you make airline reservations through the Web.

Another example is **Amazon.com**. Management believes that it must add new features to its Web site to attract buyers back over and over again. The company continuously improves its Web pages' look and the online services it provides. It moved from merely selling books through the Web to providing best-seller lists, readers' reviews, authors' interviews, consumer wish lists, product reviews by customers, and other "cool stuff."

Sources of Strategic Information Systems

Many strategic information systems are not the fruits of calculated plans or forethought. Usually, they evolve because managers recognize that they can use an existing system to create a strategic competitive advantage. Strategic information systems have evolved from systems designed for automation or from systems designed to provide a new service or enhance an existing service. For example, **State Street Bank** simply wanted to automate management of its pension funds and enhance its ISs over the years. However, because these systems were so advanced and because other pension-management institutions had no advanced ISs for this purpose, competitors started paying State Street for use of its ISs. These ISs became strategic weapons. SISs have also evolved from profitably using excess information that a company's existing IS collected, or from using customer data to expand an existing business into complementary businesses. For years, credit bureaus such as **Experian**, **TransUnion**, and **Equifax** have collected data to sell credit reports to financial institutions and other clients, but they also sell the data to any organization for purposes other than credit checks, such as target marketing.

Although many SISs are based on existing technology, sometimes an advance in technology creates an opportunity for an SIS. Technological advances in themselves do not guarantee strategic advantage, but smart use of technology can make the difference between leading and lagging behind. Often, the new idea gives the organization the competitive advantage.

From Automation to SISs

Many companies originally developed SISs to automate manual processes. Such is the case of ASAP, the information system that lets giant hospital supplier **Baxter International Inc.'s** customers place orders electronically and receive products more quickly than ever before. In 1978, **American Hospital Supply Corporation (AHS)**, now part of Baxter Healthcare Corporation and one of America's largest providers of medical supplies, decided that shortening the time between receiving and shipping an order would give it a competitive advantage. That year, the company installed ASAP (Analytic Systems Automatic Purchasing), a new information system, to help the company achieve its goal. The system integrated shipping, billing, invoicing, and inventory data and information, allowing the company to improve its service.

AHS took an innovative step to facilitate communication with customers: it offered to pay for and install terminals and software in its customers' hospital offices, so that hospital personnel could enter and transmit orders electronically. No more paperwork for the hospital, and immediate useful data for AHS. Pretty soon, the hospitals realized that they not only received their orders more quickly but also spent much less time placing orders. The hospitals eventually preferred working only with AHS for all items AHS could sell them. AHS enjoyed a 17% compound annual growth rate in sales. With accurate up-to-date order data available at any time, AHS reduced inventory and lowered sales costs, reaping a profit four times the industry average.

In time, other hospital suppliers adopted similar systems, but hospitals hooked into ASAP had every reason to stay with AHS. They already had hardware and software installed and personnel trained to use the system. Switching to another purchasing system would have been too costly. What started as an automation system turned into an SIS. AHS gained competitive advantage by providing enhanced services and incidentally creating high switching costs for its customers.

SISs From a New Service

Another famous example of an SIS is **Merrill Lynch's** Cash Management Account, or CMA account. In 1980 for the first time, clients could withdraw cash from their investments directly, rather than having to sell shares and wait for checks to clear before accessing their money. Merrill Lynch made this possible by establishing an alliance with a bank to provide a combined investment and banking service that was much more efficient for the customer. In the late 1970s, the concept of a central asset account (also called an asset management account) was revolutionary. Only a computer-based information system could promptly track every investment and withdrawal of millions of client dollars efficiently and effectively.

Before Merrill Lynch's CMA account, a customer needed two separate accounts to access the cash value of his or her stocks or mutual funds: one account with a stockbroker (to invest money in stock and other securities) and another with a bank (to maintain a checking account). The customer could access the cash value of the stock only by first selling some stock through the stock brokerage account, then depositing the sales proceeds in a checking account, and finally waiting for the deposit to clear before writing a check. The process was time-consuming and inefficient.

With Merrill Lynch's CMA service, every dollar that a customer deposits buys shares in a money-market fund. All the customer does to liquidate some of his or her account is write a check. Shares of the mutual fund are automatically redeemed. The customer does not need to wait to receive money from the broker and then deposit it in a checking account.

At the time, this service was revolutionary. Many corporations, small businesses, and individuals subscribed to the service. By the time other organizations followed suit, Merrill Lynch had captured the lion's share of the market.

SISs From New Technology

Often, the technology involved in an SIS has been around for some time, just waiting to be used strategically. Sometimes, however, a *new* technology sparks a major change in the way a firm does business. For instance, progress in telecommunications technology now lets organizations connect their branches across continents into one large network of offices. This network turns disparate sites into one large virtual site capable of providing information to any member of the organization and any customer, anywhere, at any time via dedicated lines or the Internet. A new technology may be available to anyone in the industry, but the company that figures out how to harness it gains competitive advantages.

SISs From Excess Information

Sometimes, the potential for a strategic move is in a firm's existing information system. In fact, many companies collect huge amounts of data that are not necessary for their own business, but they may put them to use in a new service or complementary product. For instance, Web-based content providers often request online subscribers to type in personal information that has nothing to do with operating the site. However, they sell the personal data to other organizations. The highly trafficked sites generate a significant portion of their revenue from such sales, which allows them to further invest in the site and attract more visitors.

The proliferation of the Web as a commercial vehicle has enhanced the ability to collect consumer and corporate data by anyone who maintains a Web site. Millions of consumers voluntarily provide personal information.

Looking for strategic use of its information, a company should ask these three questions.

1. What information that we generate, or could generate, from our databases could another company use? What would that company be willing to pay?
2. What information, or data-processing capacity, that we have can we use to start a new business?
3. Can we produce information that may help create new products (or services) related to our products (or services), or to other companies' products (or services)?

Modern approaches to data resources regard them as gold mines: the gold is there; it only needs to be mined. Similarly, data that can be used in one of the three situations listed may become a strategic resource. Searching for useful data in huge amounts of records, indeed, is called *data mining*.

SISs From Vertical Information

When you shop for a new car, dealers offer you two services. First, they offer to take your old car as a trade-in. Second, they offer to help you finance the purchase of the new car. Why do they offer these services? Because they understand that they solve the two main problems you are likely to have when shopping for a new car. Dealers stretch their business "backwardforward," an effort known as *vertical extension,* to enhance their chances of getting your business.

Consider real-estate agencies. Real-estate agents expand their services vertically to offer financing information you need *before* your purchase and relocation information that you need *after* your purchase. The agency can ask you for information that will help moving companies make you an offer as soon as you purchase your new home. Realtors who extend their services vertically are more appealing to some clients.

Attracting new customers and maintaining the ones you have is a constant challenge for online service providers. Therefore, they use software and links with other companies to offer additional services every few months. For example, brokerage sites offer financial advice such as investment portfolio allocation and retirement planning.

The Bleeding Edge

As you may often hear, huge rewards go to whomever first implements a new idea. Innovators may enjoy a strategic advantage until competitors discover the benefits of a new business idea or a new technology. In some cases, failure results from rushing implementation without adequately testing a market. But even with more careful planning, pioneers sometimes get burned.

For example, several supermarket chains tried self-check stations in the mid-1990s. Consumers were expected to ring up the items they purchased. By and large, investment in such devices failed not because the technology was bad, but because many consumers either preferred the human touch, or because they did not want to learn how to correct mistakes when the devices did not pick up the price of an item or picked it up twice.

While it is tempting to take the lead, the risk of business failure is quite high. Several organizations have experienced disasters with new business ideas, which are only magnified when implementing new technology. When failure occurs because an organization tries to be on the technological leading edge, observers call it the **bleeding edge.** The pioneering organization "bleeds" cash on a technology that increases costs instead of profits. Adopting a new technology involves great risk: there is no experience from which to learn, no guarantees that the technology will work well, and no certainty that customers and employees will welcome it.

Being on the bleeding edge often means that implementation costs are significantly more than anticipated, that the new technology does not work as well as expected, or that the parties who were supposed to benefit—employees, customers, or suppliers—do not like using it. Thus, instead of leading, the organization ends up "bleeding," that is, suffering from high cost and lost market share. For this reason, some organizations decide to let competitors test new technology before they adopt it. They risk losing the initial rewards they might reap, but if a competitor succeeds, they can quickly adopt the technology and even try to use it better than the pioneering organization.

Microsoft generally takes this approach. It seizes an existing idea, improves it, and promotes the result with its great marketing power. For instance, the company did not invent word processing, but its Word is the most popular word-processing application today. The company did not invent the electronic spreadsheet, but its Excel is the most popular spreadsheet application. And Microsoft was not the first to introduce a PC database management application, but it sells the highly popular Access, a PC database management application. The company joined the Internet rush late, but it developed and gave away Internet Explorer, a Web browser that competed with the highly popular Netscape Navigator and now dominates the market (in part because it was given free to everyone, including for-profit businesses). You may call this approach "competing by emulating and improving," rather than competing by being on the leading edge.

Quality and Information Technology

Relation Between Quality and IT

Similar to product quality in a manufacturing department, quality in information technology (IT) products and services is important to survival of a firm. The objective is to "build" controls into the systems before they are implemented instead of "adding on" such controls later. This measure is in keeping with a proactive management attitude. Establishing an IT quality assurance function is an important step in achieving the objective. The function should have a written charter describing its objectivity and independence from operations, performance levels expected, polices and procedures, and roles and responsibilities of the quality assurance staff.

IT Quality Assurance

Charter

A charter should be developed for the quality assurance function either separately or as a part of the IT charter. This charter should explain the authority, duties, and responsibilities of the people who are involved in the quality assurance function.

Independence

Independence and objectivity are important for the quality assurance function. Independence is partly achieved when the head of the quality assurance function reports to a high-level IT management or even to management outside the IT department. Independence is assumed to be lost when the head of the quality assurance function reports to IT software development and maintenance management because quality assurance reviews are performed in their areas. Objectivity requires that the quality assurance staff is unbiased in their reviews and conclusions.

Performance

Performance is critical for the quality assurance staff because their reviews will affect the way a software development and maintenance process works. Good performance leads to better development and maintenance process and vice versa. To deliver high levels of performance, the quality assurance staff should be composed of persons well-versed in systems development and maintenance, computer operations, telecommunications, and business functions. Membership in professional organizations and attendance at seminars and conferences are also encouraged.

Policies and Procedures

A policy statement from senior management addressing the need to establish a quality assurance function will add more credibility to the function. A detailed procedure will clarify the role of the quality assurance function and what to expect from it.

Roles and Responsibilities

The roles of the quality assurance staff are those of consultant and problem-solver. This is in keeping with the proactive attitude. Performance reviews will prevent problems before they occur. Responsibilities should be spelled out clearly to avoid employee misunderstanding and performance gaps.

Best Practices in Information Technology

Best Practices Defined

"Best practices" refers to the processes, practices, and systems identified in public and private organizations that performed exceptionally well and that are widely recognized as improving an organization's performance and efficiency in specific areas. Successfully identifying and applying best practices can reduce business expenses and improve organizational efficiency.

When Is a Best-Practices Approach Appropriate?

A best-practices review can be applied to a variety of processes such as payroll, travel administration, employee training, procurement, accounting, transportation and distribution, maintenance and repair services, and information technology. The decision to use a best-practices review should be made in a larger context that considers the strategic objectives of the organization and then looks at the processes and operating units that contribute to those objectives. An effective strategy asks questions like: (1) What drives the costs in a particular process? and (2) Is the process effective in achieving its goals?

An initial step is to determine all the variables that contribute to the expenditures associated with the area. Another early step is to start with the areas that the customers think are of major importance to the organization being reviewed.

Identifying the scope of the process to review is not always easy. It is not always clear where to start and where to stop. It is important that the entire process be considered, rather than just part of the process. At least initially, select a process that is ready to accept change.

Best-Practices Approach

The best-practices evaluation will look not only at quantitative data such as costs, but also at how other processes and aspects, such as organizational culture, might be affected by change. Any best-practices review can include the following six elements.

1. Gaining an understanding of and documenting the process for improvement
2. Researching industry trends and literature and speaking with consultants, academics, and interest-group officials about the subject
3. Selecting appropriate organizations for the review
4. Collecting data from these selected organizations
5. Identifying barriers to change
6. Comparing and contrasting processes to develop recommendations for improvement

In identifying best practices among organizations, the "benchmarking" technique is frequently used. In benchmarking with others, an organization (1) determines how leading organizations perform a specific process, (2) compares their methods to its own, and (3) uses the information to improve upon or completely change its process. Benchmarking is typically an internal process, performed by personnel within an organization who already have a thorough knowledge of the process under review.

Leading Best Practices in IT

Examples of Best Practices in IT Management Strategy

There are three key functions critical to building a modern IT management infrastructure: (1) deciding to work differently (that is, decide to change), (2) directing resources toward high-value uses (that is, direct change), and (3) supporting improvement with the right skills, roles, and responsibilities (that is, support change). These three key functions are expanded into 11 practices, described as follows [U.S. General Accounting Office, GAO].

Decide to Change	Initiate, mandate, and facilitate major changes in information management to improve performance.
Practice 1	Recognize and communicate the urgency to change information management practices.
Practice 2	Get line management involved and create ownership.
Practice 3	Take action and maintain momentum.
Direct Change	Establish an outcome-oriented, integrated strategic information-management process.
Practice 4	Anchor strategic planning in customer needs and mission goals.
Practice 5	Measure the performance of key mission delivery processes.
Practice 6	Focus on process improvement in the context of an architecture.
Practice 7	Manage IT projects as investments.
Practice 8	Integrate the planning, budgeting, and evaluation processes.

Support Change	Build organization-wide information management capabilities to address mission needs.
Practice 9	Establish customer/supplier relationships between line and information management professionals.
Practice 10	Position a chief information officer as a senior management partner.
Practice 11	Upgrade skills and knowledge of line and information management professionals.

Examples of Best Practices in IT Security Management

Many leading organizations, both public and private, have adopted the following five principles and have implemented the following 16 best practices in their risk management cycle in order to manage the information security function [U.S. General Accounting Office, GAO].

Principles
1. Assess risk and determine needs.
2. Establish a central management focal point.
3. Implement appropriate policies and related controls.
4. Promote awareness.
5. Monitor and evaluate policy and control effectiveness.

Best Practices to Implement Principle 1
1. Recognize information resources as essential organizational assets.
2. Develop practical risk-assessment procedures that link security to business needs.
3. Hold business and program managers accountable.
4. Manage risk on a continuing basis.

Best Practices to Implement Principle 2
5. Designate a central group to carry out key activities.
6. Provide the central group ready and independent access to senior executives.
7. Designate dedicated funding and staff.
8. Enhance staff professionalism and technical skills.

Best Practices to Implement Principle 3
9. Link policies to business risks.
10. Distinguish between policies and guidelines.
11. Support policies through a central-security group.

Best Practices to Implement Principle 4
12. Continually educate users and others on risks and related policies.
13. Use attention-getting and user-friendly techniques.

Best Practices to Implement Principle 5
14. Monitor factors that affect risk and indicate security effectiveness.
15. Use results to direct future efforts and hold managers accountable.
16. Be alert to new monitoring tools and techniques.

Examples of Best Practices in IT Investment Management

Integrated Approach for IT Investment Management

An IT investment management process is an integrated approach to managing IT investments that provides for the continuous identification, selection, control, life-cycle management, and evaluation of IT investments. This structured process provides a systematic method for organizations to minimize risks while maximizing the return on IT investments [U.S. General Accounting Office, GAO].

To be most successful, an IT investment management process should have elements of three essential phases: Control, Select, and Evaluate. However, each phase should not be viewed as a separate step. Rather, each is conducted as part of a continual, interdependent management effort. Information from one phase is used to support activities in the other two phases.

CONTROL VERSUS SELECT VERSUS EVALUATE

Control	What are you doing to ensure that the projects will deliver the benefits projected?
Select	How do you know you have selected the best projects?
Evaluate	Based on your evaluation, did the system deliver what you expected?

Critical Success Factors in IT Investment Management

To be successful, an organization's IT investment management processes should generally include the following elements or factors.

1. Key organizational decision makers are committed to the process and are involved throughout each project's life cycle.

    Projects are assessed jointly by operational, financial, and IT managers.

2. The investment management process is repeatable, efficient, and conducted uniformly and completely across the organization.

    The process includes provisions for continually selecting, managing, and evaluating projects in the investment portfolio.

3. Decisions are made consistently throughout the organization.

    Decisions at any level of the organization are made using uniform decision criteria.

    Decisions are driven by accurate and up-to-date cost, risk, and benefit information.

    Decisions are made from an overall mission focus. (There is an explicit link with the goals and objectives established in the organization's strategic plan or annual performance plans and with the organization's IT architecture.)

4. Accountability and learning from previous projects are reinforced.
5. The emphasis is on optimizing the portfolio mix in order to manage the risk and maximize the rate of return.
6. The process incorporates all IT investments but recognizes and allows for differences between various project types (mission-critical, administrative, infrastructure) and phases (proposed, under development, operational, etc.)

Data and Knowledge Management

Managing Digital Data

Businesses collect and dissect data for a multitude of purposes. Digital data can be stored in a variety of ways on different types of media. They can be stored in what we will call the traditional file format, in which the different pieces of information are not labeled and categorized but are stored as continuous strings of bytes. The chief advantage of this format is the efficient use of space, but the data are nonetheless difficult to locate and manipulate and are therefore of limited use. By contrast, the database format, in which each piece of data is labeled or categorized, provides a much more powerful information management tool. Data in this format can be easily accessed and manipulated in almost any way desired to create useful information and optimize productivity.

The impact of database technology on business cannot be overstated. Not only has it changed the way almost every industry conducts business, but it has also created an information industry with far-reaching effects on both our business and personal lives. Databases are behind the successful use of automated teller machines (ATMs), increased efficiency in retail stores, almost every marketing effort, and the numerous online search engines and electronic storefronts on the World Wide Web. Combined with interactive Web pages on the Internet, databases have made an immense contribution to e-commerce. Without them, there would be no online banking, no online consumer catalogs, no online stock brokerages, and no online chat rooms. Their impact on business has allowed fewer people to complete larger tasks, and their power has allowed organizations to learn more about us, as consumers, than we may realize. Imagine: every time you enter the URL (Web address) of a site, a special program tries to match your request with one of millions of URLs in a huge database. Every time you fill out an online form with details such as your address, phone number, Social Security number, or credit-card number, a program launches the data into a database, where each item is recorded for further use.

In virtually every type of business today, you must understand the power of databases. This section reviews the different approaches to organizing and manipulating data in databases and data warehouses.

The Traditional File Approach

We can roughly distinguish between two different approaches to maintaining data: traditional file organization—which has no mechanism for tagging, retrieving, and manipulating data—and the **database approach,** which does have that mechanism. To appreciate the benefits of the database approach, you must keep in mind the inconvenience involved in accessing and manipulating data in the **traditional file approach:** program/data dependency, high data redundancy, and low data integrity.

Database Approach

In the database approach, we maintain and manipulate data about entities. An **entity** is any object about which an organization chooses to collect data. It may be a student enrolled in a class, a sales transaction in a business, or a part in an inventory. In the context of data management, entity refers to all the occurrences sharing the same types of data. Therefore, it does not matter if we maintain a record of one class or many classes; the entity is "class." To understand how data are organized in a database, you must first understand the data hierarchy. The smallest piece of data is a **character** (a letter in a first or last name or address, and so on). Several characters make up data in a field (also called a *data item*), such as last name, first name, and the like. A **field** is one piece of information about an entity, such as the last name or first name of a student. Several fields related to the same entity make up a **record.** A collection of related records is called a **file.** Often, several related files must be kept together. A collection of such files is referred to as a database. However, the features of a database can be enjoyed by builders and users of databases even when a database consists of a single file.

Database fields are not limited to holding text and numbers. They can hold pictures, sounds, and video clips. Fields can hold any content that can be digitized. For example, when you shop online, you can search for a product by its product name or code, and then retrieve its picture or a video clip about the product.

Database Management Systems

While a database itself is a collection of several related *files,* the program used to build databases, populate them with data, and manipulate the data is called a **database management system** (**DBMS**). The files themselves *are* the database, but DBMSs do all the work—structuring files, storing data, and linking records. If you wanted to access data from files that were stored in a traditional file approach, the records would have to be organized in a very specific way, and you would have to know exactly how many characters were designated for each type of data. A DBMS, however, does much of this work (and a lot of other work) for you.

If you are using a database, you want to be able to move rapidly from one record to another, sorting by different criteria, creating different types of reports, and analyzing the data in different ways. Because of these demands, databases are stored on direct access storage devices (DASDs), such as CDs or magnetic disks, but cannot be stored on sequential storage devices such as magnetic or optical tapes because it would take too long to access different fields.

QUERIES Data are accessed in a database by sending messages called *queries,* which request data from specific fields and direct the computer to display the results on the monitor. Queries are also entered to manipulate data. Usually, the same software that is used to construct and populate the database, that is, the DBMS, is also used to present queries. Modern DBMS programs provide fairly user-friendly means of querying a database.

SECURITY The use of databases raises security and privacy issues. The fact that data are stored only once in a database does not mean that everyone with access to that database should have access to *all* the data in it. Restricting access is easily dealt with by customizing menus for different users and requiring users to enter codes that limit access to certain fields or records. As a result, users have different views of the database, as illustrated in Exhibit 800.24. The ability to limit users' views to only specific columns or records gives the database administrator (the person who plans the database and ensures that it is up and running) another advantage: the ability to implement security measures. The measures are implemented once for the database, rather than multiple times for different files. For instance, in the database in Exhibit 800.25, while a human resource manager has access to all fields of the employee file (represented by the top, middle, and lower parts of the figure), the payroll personnel have access only to four fields of the employee file (middle part of the figure), and a project manager has access only to the Name and Hours Worked fields. Views may be limited to certain fields in a database, or certain records, or a combination thereof.

Traditional Files Versus Databases: Pros and Cons

The advantages of storing data in database files far outweigh those of storing them in flat files. While there are some trade-offs, databases generally allow much greater flexibility, easier access by different applications, easier maintenance

Exhibit 800.24 *Different Database Views Reveal Different Combinations of Data*

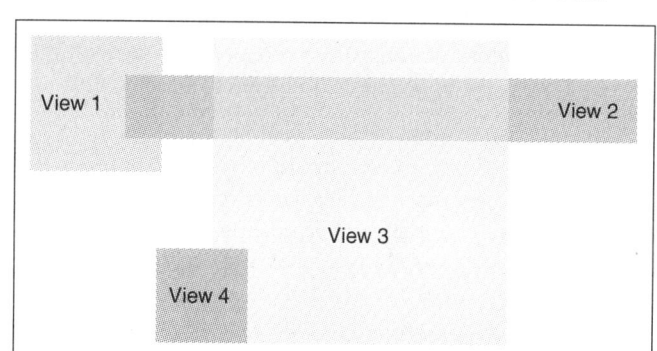

Exhibit 800.25 *Different Views of One Employee Database*

View of Human Resource Manager				
SSN	Name	D.O.B.	Hire Date	Marital Status

View of Payroll Personnel			
SSN	Hourly Rate	Benefits Code	Hours Worked

View of Project Manager	
Name	Hours Worked

of data currency and integrity, and savings in both cost and time, all of which make them far superior to disparate flat files. Database advantages include the following.

1. *Reduced data redundancy.* Although there may still be some redundancy in a database, it is significantly less than in the traditional file approach. This streamlining saves storage space.
2. *Application-data independence.* Writing an application to use data from a database is much simpler than writing one to use data from flat files. To access data in a database, a program can use field names and the names of the data sets in which the data exist, such as a list of patient records in a hospital. This programming efficiency saves programming time and allows users with limited knowledge to access data through queries or even to develop simple applications.
3. *Better control.* Since all data are concentrated in one place in a database, it is easier to control access and maintain data, and it is easier to get an overall view of data about an entity.
4. *Flexibility.* Modifying a database by adding new data related to entities is much simpler than adding data to flat files.

In general, the opposite of these database advantages are the disadvantages of using traditional files to store data. The traditional file approach creates data redundancy and application-data dependence. It does not support as tight control over data currency, accuracy, and integrity as the database approach, and it provides less flexibility in data maintenance. However, the traditional file approach does have some advantages, including the following.

1. *Efficiency.* Applications written for flat files run more efficiently than those written for databases because they do not use the additional CPU time and memory space required by preprogrammed functions that are a part of the DBMS. Often, the easier a program is to use, the more CPU time and memory space it needs.
2. *Simplicity.* Constructing a database can be very complex and time-consuming. Sometimes, it may be simpler to create simple files and to develop applications for them, especially when an application accesses just one flat file.
3. *Customization.* The preprogrammed features of a DBMS allow only certain relationships among data. However, using the more flexible procedural features of a third- or fourth-generation language to build files and to access them allows a tight tailoring of applications to business needs—more so than using only the preprogrammed features of a DBMS.

The overwhelming advantages of databases raise the question: Why use flat files at all? If you were starting with a clean slate, you probably wouldn't choose to use flat files. However, businesses have accumulated a considerable amount of historical data in flat file format that they will be dealing with for many years to come. Because considerable amounts of data in businesses are still stored in flat files and accessed through applications that were written with third-generation languages such as COBOL (which by their nature are designed to access flat files), it may be too costly to switch to databases. However, almost all new data banks are developed and maintained with the aid of DBMSs.

Exhibit 800.26 *Advantages and Disadvantages of Database Models*

	Database Model		
	Hierarchical	Network	Relational
Conceptualization	Moderately easy	Difficult	Easy
Ease of Design	Very difficult	Moderately difficult	Difficult
Ease of Maintenance	Difficult	Very difficult	Easy
Data Redundancy	High	Low	High
Ease of Use	Moderate	Low	High

Database Models

A **database model** is the general logical structure in which records are stored within a database. There are three different database models. They differ in the manner in which records are linked to each other. These differences, in turn, dictate the manner in which a user can navigate the database and retrieve desired records. As summarized in Exhibit 800.26, each model has advantages and disadvantages when compared with the other two.

Keys

To retrieve records from a relational database, or to sort them, you must use a key. A **key** is a field whose values identify records either for display or for processing. You may use any field as a key. A key is unique if the value (content) in that field appears only in one record. Sometimes a key is composed of several fields so that their combination provides a unique key.

Primary Key

Depending on the software you use, you may receive the first one that meets the condition, or a list of all the records with that value in the field. The only way to be sure you are retrieving the desired record is to use a unique key (such as a Social Security number). A unique key is called a **primary key.**

Usually, a table in a relational database must have a primary key, and most relational DBMSs enforce this rule; if the designer does not designate a field as a key, the DBMS creates its own serial number field as the primary key field for the table. Once the designer of the table determines the primary key when constructing the records' format, the DBMS will not allow a user to enter two records with the same value in that column. Note that there may be situations in which more than one field may be used as a primary key. Such is the case with motor vehicles, because both the vehicle identification number (VIN) and the license plate number uniquely identify a car. Thus, a database designer may establish either field as a primary key to retrieve records.

Many DBMSs will force you to designate a primary key in each table you construct. Usually, the software requires that the primary key be the leftmost field in the record. By default, many DBMSs automatically sort the records the user enters in ascending order of the primary key.

Some relational databases use **composite keys,** a combination of two or more fields that together serve as a primary key. An example: the last name, first name, and department in a table that holds professors' records could together be considered a primary key. Unless we expect two people with the same name to lecture for the same department, the combination will be a valid primary key.

Linking

To link records from one table with records of another table, the tables must have one field in common (that is, one column in each table must contain the same type of data), and that field must be a primary key field for one of the tables. We say that this repeated field is a primary key in one table, and a **foreign key** field in the other table.

As you can see, all database design requires careful forethought. The designer must include fields for foreign keys from other tables so that join tables can be created in the future. The inclusion of foreign keys may cause considerable data redundancy. This complexity has not diminished the popularity of relational databases, however. Since the relationships between tables are created as part of manipulating the table, the relational model supports both one-to-many (1:M) and many-to-many (M:M) relationships between records of different tables.

The Object-Oriented Structure

While the move from traditional file systems to databases was a leap forward in data management efficiency, recent years have seen a new development that may lead to even greater benefits: object-oriented databases. In object-oriented technology, an object consists of both data and the procedures that manipulate the data. So, in addition to the attributes of an entity, it also contains the relationships with other entities. The combined storage of both data and the procedures that manipulate them is referred to as "encapsulation." Thus, an object can be "planted" in different data sets. The ability in object-oriented structures to automatically create a new object by replicating all or some of the characteristics of a previously developed object (called the parent object) is called **inheritance.**

Entity-Relationship Diagrams

Many business databases consist of multiple files with relationships among them. For example, a hospital may use a database that has a file holding the records of all its physicians, another one with all its nurses, another one with all the current patients, and so on. The administrative staff must be able to create reports that link data from multiple files. Thus, the database must be carefully planned to allow useful data manipulation and report generation. The planning task often involves the creation of a conceptual blueprint of the database. This blueprint is called an **entity-relationship (ER) diagram.** An ER diagram is a graphical representation of all entity relationships.

Components of Database Management Systems

When designers have a clear understanding of how a database should be structured to accommodate the different data sets and the relationships among them, they select a DBMS to construct the new database. While DBMSs have different interfaces, they share similar components. These components allow the user to create sets of data about entities, define fields, organize record structures, populate the database with data, and manipulate the data in the different files, records, and fields. Simple databases can often be designed by lay users, but more complex databases usually require the involvement of an experienced database designer. The components of a DBMS are the data definition language (which enables the building of schemas and data dictionaries) and the data manipulation language (which allows the user to manipulate data).

Note the difference between a record structure and a record: a "*record structure*" is the general structure of a record, defining the types of fields that make it up; a "*record*" is the actual data that pertain to a specific instance. Therefore, for a file that holds the records of professors, we need to design a record structure that describes which fields will appear in *every* actual data record (for instance, ID number, last name, first name, department name, and telephone number). A record will be the row of data describing a specific professor in the professors' file (such as, 120-33-7685, Weinrib, Janet, English, 209-8256). That is, a record contains the actual data values.

The Schema

When building a new database, users must first build a schema (from the Greek word for "plan"). The **schema** describes the structure of the database being designed: the names and types of fields in each record type and the general relationships among different sets of records or files. It includes a description of the database's structure, the names and sizes of fields, and details such as which field is a primary key. The number of records is never specified because it may change, and the maximum number of records is determined by the capacity of the storage medium.

In a hierarchical DBMS, the schema includes the relationships between parent and child record structures. Similarly, relationships must be detailed in the schema of a network database. The schema of a relational database is simpler. It describes only the record structure of each table, namely, the fields of which each record in that table will consist.

The builder of a new database must also indicate which fields will be used as primary keys. Many DBMSs also allow a builder to indicate when a field is not unique, meaning that the value in that field may be the same for more than one record.

The Data Dictionary

All the information supplied by the database developer when constructing the schema is maintained in the data dictionary, which includes the file names, record names and types, field names and types, and, if applicable, the relationships among record types. In addition, the **data dictionary** contains the notation of who is responsible for updating each part of the database and descriptions (such as titles) or names of the people who are authorized to access the different parts of the database.

Data dictionaries are often referred to as *metadata,* meaning "data about the data." They are useful when trying to understand a database designed by someone else. Many PC DBMSs do not allow the users direct access to the data dictionary. The user can view, and to a certain extent change, only the schema. But some mainframe DBMSs provide users with a facility to add to the data dictionary information such as the name of the database designer, the date the database was built, the purpose of each field and its minimum and maximum values, the people who may make changes in the schema, the people who are authorized to access which data in the database, and other valuable information.

The Data Definition Language

Every DBMS must include a subprogram (in this case a language) called a **data definition language** (**DDL**) to construct the schema. This language has various commands and protocols the database designer uses to define and name the files, records, and fields in a database before beginning to populate them. In most PC DBMSs, the user interface of the DDL presents screens and prompts the designer to enter the appropriate parameters from a menu. These interfaces are intuitive and allow a database to be created by someone who may have relatively little development experience. In other DBMSs, the user must know the commands used in the DDL to construct the schema.

The Data Manipulation Language

Data manipulation language (**DML**) is the software that serves the user who is querying the database. Some DBMSs require the user to type in commands. For example, consider a database holding personnel data: ID, Last_Name, First_Name, Department, and Salary. Suppose you want a list showing the last names, department number, and salaries of employees whose department number is 4530 and whose salary is less than $25,000. It is the DML that allows such a query to be placed and executed.

Some DBMSs hide the DML from the user. Instead of statements, the user expresses a query by example (QBE). The user invokes the query module of the program, which displays the fields available, and then places check marks in the fields to be listed and conditions in the proper fields. Virtually all the popular PC relational DBMSs provide QBE dialog interfaces.

Many DBMSs are now part of fourth-generation languages (4GLs). 4GLs are flexible enough to allow programmers to use the language both to develop applications that retrieve and manipulate data from a database and also to perform tasks that have nothing to do with the database, all in the same application.

Database Architecture

Database architecture refers to both the physical and logical layouts of databases in an organization. In the past, most organizations' databases—data and programs alike—were centrally located on mainframes and accessed from remote locations throughout the company from dumb terminals. There have been significant changes in database architecture as both databases and the programs running them have moved from mainframes to PCs and from a centralized to a distributed model.

Distributed Databases

Many organizations operate through geographically remote sites. Still, much of the data used by one site is often also used by other sites. Of course, the organization can use a centrally located database and let the other sites use it through communications lines. A less expensive solution, however, is to distribute the database at different sites for all to use. This arrangement is called a *distributed database.* There are two distributed database models: replicated and fragmented.

The **database administrator** (**DBA**) can either replicate the database so there are exact copies in many locations, or fragment it, so that different parts of the database are maintained on different machines. **Replication** of the database means that a full copy of the entire database is stored at all the sites that need access to it. This approach is expensive and not conducive to data integrity, because all the updates must be performed at all the sites, and the chance of errors occurring due to delayed updates and copying errors is high.

Many organizations have opted for the other alternative: in a **fragmented** database, different parts of the database are stored in the locations where they are accessed most often, but they continue to be fully accessible to others through telecommunications. Together, all the parts make up the database. The result is just one copy of the database, distributed among the various sites by way of communications lines. Applications' use of remote fragments of the database is transparent to the users. The users do not know, and need not bother to know, which part of the database resides locally at their site and which is processed remotely. One advantage of a fragmented database is the lower communications costs. With only one copy of the database, another advantage is better data integrity. Many experts refer to fragmented databases as *distributed databases*. Note that the telecommunications lines through which data are accessed do not differ in these two approaches. Nowadays, many multisite companies enable employees and business partners to access databases through intranets and extranets using Web software.

Shared Resource and Client/Server Systems

Some organizations store their databases and the applications that run them on mainframes or on minicomputers accessible remotely from dumb terminals. Others distribute their database but leave the processing of the data centralized. Some experts refer to these arrangements as *shared resource architecture*. The central resource is used by remote terminals and PCs not only for the data in its databases, but also for the applications that process the data.

However, the increasing power of microcomputers and the great progress and declining cost of data communications are driving organizations to move to what is called *client/server architecture*. IS professionals use this term loosely to describe any distribution of data and applications between a server and its clients, including allowing users to access data remotely but process it locally (see Exhibit 800.27). The server is a computer, usually a powerful PC or a minicomputer, that serves the clients—the users' PCs—by storing databases and managing remote access communications. Users can use applications on their own PCs to process data copied from the server. (Note that sometimes the *applications* that are used on the PCs are also called clients. For example, you may have heard the term "e-mail client," which simply means e-mail application.)

In a client/server network, software may run not only on a host but wherever it makes most sense. In fact, software can process "cooperatively" on various computers across the network. It seems that the computer becomes the network, and the network becomes the computer in this scenario. Often, the physical location where the processing takes place is transparent to the user; that is, the user does not know where processing occurs, physically.

To use a human analogy, thoughts are processed throughout an office, not just in the mind of the boss. And thoughts are communicated as requirements of the collective process. In a client/server network, users may have much computing power at their local PC, where they can process data, produce information, and then decide what to save on the server and what to save locally in their own computers. This additional computing power is the reason that many experts say the client/server architecture empowers employees; it gives them more independence and the ability to make their own decisions regarding information.

Exhibit 800.27   *Shared Resource and Client/Server Architectures*

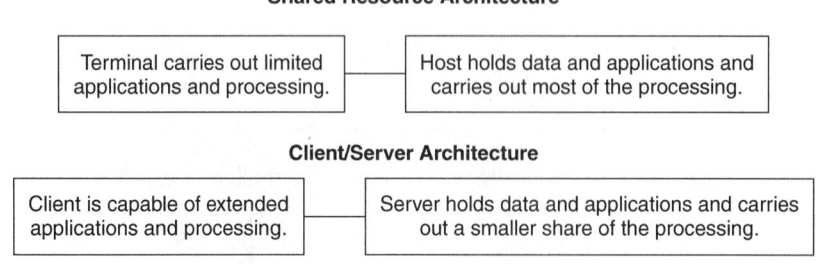

A client/server architecture can follow any of the following four basic models:

- Applications run at a server; PCs serve as terminals, primarily formatting and validating data.
- Applications run on local PCs; the database resides at the server; no significant part of the application runs on the server.
- Applications run on both local PCs and the server; the database resides at the server.
- Applications and key elements of the database are split between the local PCs and the server. Applications call data or other procedures at other locations.

Web Databases

The Internet and its user-friendly application, the Web, would be practically useless if people could not access databases online. The premise of the Web is that people can not only browse appealing Web pages but also search for and find information in databases. When a shopper accesses an online store, he or she can look for information about any of thousands or hundreds of thousands of items offered for sale. For example, when you access the site of **CDNow**, you can receive online information (such as an image of a CD's cover, its popularity ranking, price, and shipping time) for any of a half million music CDs. If you access **IBM's** site, you can retrieve information on each of thousands of products and services or select an article from a huge electronic library. In business-to-business e-commerce, wholesalers make their catalogs and special prices available to retailers online. Applications at auction sites receive inquiries by type of item, color, date, and other attributes and identify records of matching items, which often include pictures and detailed descriptions. Behind each of these sites is a database. The only way for organizations to conduct these Web-based businesses is to give people outside the organizations access to their databases. In other words, the organizations must link their databases to the Internet.

Databases on the Web

Databases on the Web are used in several ways.

- *Catalogs,* in both business-to-business and business-to-consumer e-commerce. Catalog databases allow browsers to search items by key words or combinations of key words. To do so, the site provides a local search engine that scours Web pages stored in its database.
- *Libraries* of books, articles, CDs, and movie clips. These sites also often include a local search engine that allows a user to search for the key words in a title, author name, or an entire article. University faculty, staff, and students often have access to such large databases through their schools. Most of these databases are not owned by the school but are operated by organizations that specialize in library databases such as **ABI/Inform** and **UMI**.
- *Directories,* which can include names, addresses, telephone numbers, and e-mail addresses. For instance, professional associations can provide members with access to membership lists.
- *Client lists and profiles.* Usually, individual users have access to these databases only for the purpose of inserting or updating their own records. A registered user name and password are usually required to gain access to these databases. For example, **ValuPage**, a Web site that provides supermarket coupons online, collects data on shoppers. To receive periodic e-mail messages with coupons that you can print out and use for supermarket discounts, you must first enter personal data, including your address, e-mail address, and shopping preferences. The data are sold for profit to other organizations.

From a technical point of view, online databases that are used with Web browsers are not different from other databases. However, an interface must be designed to work with the Web. The user must be given a form in which to enter queries or key words to obtain information from the site's database. The interface designers must provide a mechanism to figure out data that users insert in the online forms so that they can be placed in the proper fields in the database. The system also needs a mechanism to pass queries and key words from the user to the database. There are several such interface programs, including CGI (Common Gateway interface), API (application program interface), Java servlets, and active server pages.

845. DATA AND KNOWLEDGE MANAGEMENT

Points to Consider When Linking Databases

When linking a database to the Internet, IT professionals must consider several points.

- Which application to use
- How to ensure that online access by Web surfers does not interfere with database updates
- How to maintain security

A CGI is an application that enables a Web surfer to fill out an online form with data that is then used to update a database. As just mentioned, other applications can fulfill this function, and there are some trade-offs to consider. For example, both API interfaces and Java servlets run faster than conventional CGI applications, but they are more difficult to develop and implement.

To ensure that Web surfers do not interfere with their employees' work, organizations avoid linking their transactions databases to the Internet. They are also careful when linking a data warehouse to the Internet. Usually, companies use a mirror (a copy of the original database) stored on a dedicated server to link to the Web. That server is linked directly to the Web at one end and to the server with the original database at the other end. Special software blocks access of unauthorized Web users to the original database. The mirror database is updated at regular intervals.

Organizations must understand, however, that once a computer is linked to a public network, there is a risk of unauthorized access to it and any other computer that is linked to it. Thus, security measures are critical to prevent unauthorized access. People often gain unauthorized access to deface Web pages or even destroy data in databases. To screen and block access, a special type of software called a *firewall* is used on the server.

Data Warehousing

The great majority of data collections in business are used for daily transactions and operations: records of customers and their purchases and information on employees, patients, and other parties for monitoring, collection, payment, and other business or legal purposes. However, many organizations have found that if they archive transaction data, they can use them for important management decisions, such as researching market trends or tracking down fraud. The accumulated data are like a huge heap of dirt in which precious gems are hidden. If the data are organized well, and if proper tools are used to analyze the data, those gems may be found. Uncovering the gems is the purpose of data warehousing.

A **data warehouse** is a huge collection of data that supports management decision making (see Exhibit 800.28). It maintains snapshots of business conditions at predetermined points in time, such as the end of each business day or the first of every month. A data warehouse is a large—usually relational—database. The purpose of data warehouses is to let managers produce reports or analyze large amounts of archival data and make decisions. Data warehousing experts must be familiar with the types of business analyses that will be done with the data. They also have to design the data warehouse tables to be flexible enough for modifications in years to come, when business activities change or when different information must be extracted.

Exhibit 800.28 *Data Are Warehoused for Analysis and Reporting*

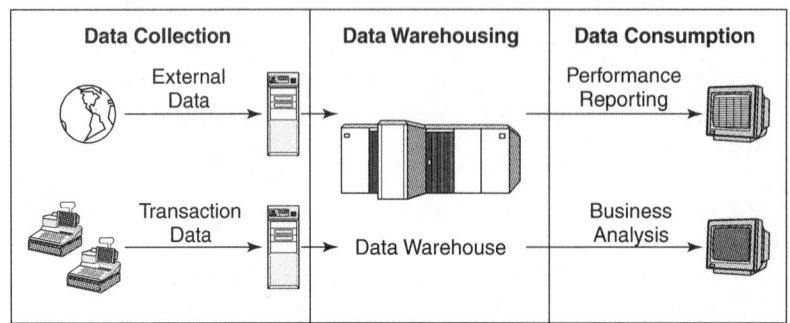

Data warehouses do not replace transactional databases, which are updated with daily transactions such as sales, billing, cash receipts, and returns. Instead, data warehouses are designed to record periodic "snapshots" of the transactional databases—"to provide pictures" of the different aspects of a business. This large archive contains valuable hidden information for the organization. For example, an insurance company may keep monthly tables of policy sales; it can then see trends in the types of policies customers prefer in general or by age group. Data from transactional databases are added to the data warehouse at the end of each business day, week, or month. While a transactional database contains current data, which is disposed of after some time, the data in data warehouses are accumulated and may reflect many years of business activities.

While a data warehouse combines data from databases across an entire organization, organizations also use **data marts,** smaller collections of data that focus on a particular subject or department. If a business maintains a data warehouse that consists of several data marts, they are called *dependent data marts*. If data are organized in data marts but need to be used as one large data warehouse, special software tools can unify data marts and make them appear as one large data warehouse. To uncover the valuable information contained in their data, organizations must use software that can effectively investigate data warehouses.

From Database to Data Warehouse

Unlike data warehouses, transactional databases are usually not suitable for business analysis because they contain current, not historical, data. Often, data in transactional databases are also scattered in different systems throughout an organization. The same data are often stored differently and under other names. For example, customer names may be recorded in a column called Name in one department's table and in two columns—First Name and Last Name—in another department's table. These discrepancies commonly occur when an organization uses both its own data and data it purchases from other organizations. Also, transactional systems were simply not designed for decision support. As such, they are often incompatible with computer-based decision aids such as decision support systems and executive support systems. When management decides to build a data warehouse, the IT staff must carefully consider the hardware, software, and data involved in the effort.

Hardware

The larger the data warehouse, the larger the storage capacity, the greater the memory, and the greater the processing power of the computer that is needed. Because of capacity needs, organizations often choose mainframe computers with multiple CPUs to store and manage data warehouses. The computer memory must be large enough to allow processing of huge amounts of data at once. The amount of storage space and the access speed of disks is also important. Processing millions of records may take a long time, and variations in disk speed may mean the difference between hours or minutes in processing time. And since a data warehouse is considered a highly valuable asset, all data must be automatically backed up. Keep in mind that data warehouses grow continually, because their very purpose is to hold historic records. Retail companies record millions of sales transactions daily, all of which are channeled into data warehouses. So do banks, credit-card issuers, and health-care organizations.

Data and Software

The data from which data warehouses are built usually come from within an organization, mainly from transactions, but they can also come from outside an organization. The latter may include national or regional demographic data, data from financial markets, and weather data. Data warehouse designers create metadata, that is, data about the data, including the following.

1. The source of the data, including contact information
2. Tables that are related to the data
3. Field and index information, such as the size and type of the field (whether it is text or numeric), and the ways the data are sorted
4. Programs and processes that use the data
5. Population rules: what is inserted, or updated, and how often

The designers must keep in mind scalability: the ability of the data warehouse to grow as the amount of the data and the processing needs grow. Future growth needs involve good planning in terms of both hardware and software.

Phases in Building a Data Warehouse

Once an organization has ensured that it has adequate hardware and software, it can begin building the data warehouse. Several phases are involved in building a data warehouse from transactional data: chiefly, the extraction, cleansing, and loading phases. In the **extraction phase,** the builders create the files from transactional databases and save them on the server that will hold the data warehouse.

In the **cleansing phase,** the builders modify the data into a form that allows insertion into the data warehouse. For example, they ascertain whether the data contain any spelling errors, and if there are any, they fix them. They make sure that all data are consistent. For instance, Pennsylvania may be denoted as Pa., PA, Penna, or Pennsylvania. Only one form would be used in a warehouse. Warehouse builders ensure that all addresses follow the same form, using upper- or lowercase letters consistently and defining fields uniformly (such as one field for the entire street address and a separate field for zip codes). All data that express the same type of quantities are "cleansed" to use the same measurement units.

In the **loading phase,** the builders transfer the cleansed files to the database that will serve as the data warehouse. They then compare the data in the data warehouses with the original data from the transactional database to ascertain completeness. They document the data for users, so the users know what they can find and analyze in the data warehouse.

The new data warehouse is then ready for use. It is a single source for all the data required for analysis, is accessible to more users than the transactional databases (whose access is limited only to those who record transactions), and provides a "one-stop shopping" place for data. In fact, it is not unusual for an organization to have one very large table of data with numerous fields.

Data Mining

One of the main purposes of maintaining a data warehouse is to be able to "mine" it for useful information. **Data mining** is the process of selecting, exploring, and modeling large amounts of data to discover previously unknown relationships. Data mining software searches through large amounts of data for meaningful patterns of information (see Exhibit 800.29). Data mining is most often used by marketing managers, who are constantly analyzing purchasing patterns, so that potential buyers can be targeted more efficiently through special sales, product displays, or direct mail and e-mail campaigns. Data mining is an especially powerful tool in an environment in which businesses are shifting from mass-marketing a product to targeting the individual consumer with a variety of products that are likely to satisfy him or her. Some observers call this approach "marketing to one."

Exhibit 800.29 *Potential Applications of Data Mining*

Data-Mining Application	Description
Consumer clustering	Identify the common characteristics of customers who tend to buy the same products and services from your company.
Customer churn	Identify the reason customers switch to competitors; predict which customers are likely to do so.
Fraud detection	Identify which characteristics of transactions are most likely to be fraudulent.
Direct marketing	Identify which prospective clients should be included in a mailing or e-mail list to obtain the highest response rate.
Interactive marketing	Predict what each individual accessing a Web site is most likely to be interested in seeing.
Market-based analysis	Understand what products or services are commonly purchased together, and on what days of the week.
Trend analysis	Reveal the difference between a typical customer this month and a typical customer last month.

However, data mining is also used in banking, where it is employed to find profitable customers and patterns of fraud. For example, when **Bank of America (BofA)** looked for new approaches to retain customers, it used data-mining techniques. It merged various behavior patterns into finely tuned customer profiles. The data were clustered into smaller groups of individuals who were using banking services that didn't best support their activities. Bank employees contacted these customers and offered advice on services that would serve them better. The result was greater customer loyalty (measured in fewer accounts closed and fewer moves to other banks). The people who were contacted thought that the bank was trying to take good care of their money.

To illustrate the difference between "traditional" queries and data-mining queries, consider the following examples. A typical "traditional" query would be: "Is there a relationship between the amount of product X and the amount of product Y that we sold over the past quarter?" A typical data-mining query would be: "Discover two products most likely to sell well together on a weekend." The latter query lets the software find patterns that would otherwise not be detected through observation. While we have traditionally used data to see whether this or that pattern existed, data mining allows us to ask *what* patterns exist. Thus, some experts say that in data mining we let the computer answer questions that we do not know to ask. The combination of data warehousing techniques and data-mining software makes it easier to predict future outcomes based on patterns discovered within historical data.

To analyze the data in data warehouses, organizations can use **online analytical processing** (**OLAP**) applications, or more sophisticated software. However, while OLAP tools help find relationships by running data through statistical models, they do not answer the question that more powerful data-mining tools can answer: "What are the relationships we do not yet know?" This is because the investigator must determine which relationship the software should look for in the first place. To answer this question, other techniques are used in data-mining, including artificial intelligence techniques.

Historically, banks were among the first to use data-mining techniques. **Chase Manhattan** continues to pursue the practice eagerly. The bank wanted to analyze the habits of its checking account customers for clues that might reveal how to set the minimum balance requirements. To many customers, the minimum balance requirement is a key criterion in choosing a bank. Management wanted to know whether business with these customers was profitable. If Chase was losing profitable customers because the minimum balance required was too high, that balance should be lowered; but if the bank was losing money on them, the balance should be left as is.

Management wanted answers to questions such as: How many checks do these customers write per month? Do they use ATMs or use teller service? What other accounts do they hold, and what other services do they use? Data-mining techniques provided answers. The bank found out who its profitable customers were. It lowered the minimum required balance, and the ratio of profitable customers to overall customers increased. A manager at Chase likened data mining to X-rays; a doctor can examine a patient by just looking at him or use X-rays to learn much more about the patient.

Knowledge Management

Knowledge management is the combination of activities involved in gathering, organizing, sharing, analyzing, and disseminating knowledge to improve an organization's performance.

Knowledge is usually perceived as "know-how," which is usually accumulated through experience combined with accumulating certain information or, at least, knowing where information can be found. Much knowledge is kept in people's minds, on paper notes, on discussion transcripts, and in other places that are not readily accessible to a company's employees. Therefore, knowledge management is a great challenge. Knowledge management is the attempt by organizations to put procedures and technologies in place to do the following.

- Transfer individual knowledge into databases
- Filter and separate the most relevant knowledge
- Organize that knowledge in databases that either
    (1) Allow other employees to easily access the knowledge or
    (2) "Push" specific knowledge to employees based on their prespecified needs

Lotus Development Corp., an **IBM** division, initiated a knowledge management project to better serve its customers. For a long time, customer support personnel logged help calls but did not record what they learned from customers about the software products the company sold. To change that, the IS department created an applet to capture this data. Now, a call to the support desk is not complete until the employee has entered the substance of the call into Lotus Notes, the software in which the applet was created. Identifying recurring problems allowed the company to enhance the training of its support desk staff in critical areas and resulted in greater customer satisfaction and more efficient response time.

KPMG, a big five accounting and management consulting firm, established a knowledge intranet called KWorld, available to the firm's more than 100,000 professionals in 160 different countries. In the past, consultants had to locate specialists' hard copy documents and read through dozens of documents to find the facts and expertise they were looking for. Now, through a single corporate Web portal, the system lets any member of the consulting staff tap information detailing the experiences of other consultants with a certain type of problem, software, or client. With KWorld, expert information is available through the consultants' PCs, anywhere, anytime, and the single repository of knowledge eliminates the phenomenon of redundant searches. The knowledge base is organized around product, industry, and geographic region. A KPMG consultant assigned to a new project can log on to the KWorld system and search for all consultants with expertise in a specific industry, technology, country, or all three elements. A consultant sitting in an office in New York can use a networked PC to receive expert information on an installation of an enterprise resource planning (ERP) system in the Netherlands. Consultants are required to submit their experience with every consulting project. Fifteen full-time "knowledge editors" in New York City maintain the knowledge repository. They capture not only internal knowledge but also external information, a daily lot of some 8,000 published papers, speeches, books, and magazine articles.

Artificial Intelligence in Business

Intelligence is the ability to acquire and apply knowledge, to think, and to reason. The better equipped a person is with mental tools to learn and apply new ideas, the higher his or her intelligence. Intelligence actually includes many abilities: making associations between a previous experience and a new situation, drawing systematic conclusions, quickly adopting new ways to solve problems, being able to separate what is important from what is not in solving a problem, and determining what tools can or cannot help in handling complex situations. **Artificial intelligence (AI)** researchers and developers try to emulate the human mind in machines. Efforts by nonacademic organizations have yielded many commercial products. One of the areas in which AI has had a positive impact is business. Combined with information systems and database management systems (DBMSs), programs that use the principles of artificial intelligence can provide outstanding support for high-level decision making in business. In this section, we describe the concepts involved in artificial intelligence and the way it has enhanced business.

Although AI may still have the aura of an esoteric research area, it has actually been implemented in numerous practical applications. For example, **Charles Schwab**, the largest online brokerage business, has added AI functions to its Web site to handle customers' questions better. In another area, a company called **Continental Divide Robotics (CDR)** has developed a system that combines AI, signals from the GPS (global positioning system) satellites above the earth, and telecommunications in robots for monitoring parolees. A special device is attached to the parolees. If parolees leave a certain area or go near a designated house, the CDR system in the device will decide whom it should contact.

AI efforts may be classified into several categories, as illustrated in Exhibit 800.30. While the research and development in some areas, such as robotics and artificial vision, involve hardware and software, the research and development in other areas involve only software.

Robotics

Robotics engineers build machines designed to perform useful work. Contrary to popular belief, the majority of **robots** in industrial use do not look like human beings. However, many are designed to do what human beings have long done, only more efficiently and effectively. In the auto industry, robots are used to weld, paint, and screw nuts. Much of the

Exhibit 800.30 *The Various Research Efforts in Artificial Intelligence*

Subfields of Artificial Intelligence			
Robotics	Artificial Vision	Natural Language Processing	Expert Systems
Neural Networks	Fuzzy Logic	Genetic Algorithms	Intelligent Agents

automotive and other manufacturing work done manually until the early 1980s is now done by robots. In many industries, only the research and development phase of making products is performed by human beings; the actual production is done by robots. For instance, the manufacture of microprocessors is almost completely automated with robots, which is the main reason that computer prices have dropped so sharply over the years. At **Lexmark**, an IBM subsidiary that manufactures printers, the use of smart robots reduced cycle time by 90%. A printer that once took four hours to assemble now takes only 24 minutes. Consequently, a Lexmark printer that used to cost $200 not long ago now costs only $50.

Robots are also extremely useful in environments where people can be easily and seriously injured. For example, police forces use remote control units and television monitors to guide robots to defuse bombs. Some sophisticated robots are even capable of detecting explosives by "smelling" objects suspected to be bombs (that is, sensing the molecular structure of certain elements in the air). Similar robots are used in nuclear power plants to perform duties that pose health hazards.

Some companies have developed robots that carry out household chores such as vacuuming, sweeping, and even removing dishes from tables and turning on appliances. Some companies developed commercial lawn-mowing robots.

All robots either contain a computer or are connected to one. In general, they need to sense their position and their surroundings, execute the functions they are programmed to perform, and provide feedback as needed. With the advancement of voice recognition, some robots are programmed to recognize and execute vocal commands.

Engineers who specialize in robotics are working on improving robot operation and mode of interaction. They program specially built machines with mechanical limbs to move, recognize their position in space, grab objects, lay them down, and so on.

Artificial Vision

Another important feature needed for robots to function successfully in their environments is artificial vision. **Artificial vision** is the ability of a machine to "see" its environment, to make choices about its actions based on what it sees, and to recognize visual input (such as handwriting) according to general patterns. For instance, robots must recognize their position in space so they do not bump into obstacles, and they must recognize their position relative to an object that they must act on, pick up, or push. Currently, trial devices are being used in the U.S. Postal Service to recognize handwriting, parse it correctly, and digitize the information so it can be used for sorting.

Natural Language Processing

Natural language processors (**NLPs**) are programs that are designed to take human language as input and translate it into a standard set of statements that a computer can execute. The programs work by parsing sentences and trying to eliminate ambiguity in a given context. The purpose of these sophisticated programs is to allow human beings to use their own natural language when interacting with programs such as database management systems (DBMSs) or decision-support systems (DSSs).

The goal of natural language processors is to eventually eliminate the need for people to learn programming languages or customized commands for computers to understand them. Their great advantage is in the way they can be combined with voice-recognition devices to allow the user to command computers to perform tasks without touching a keyboard or any other input device.

One of the greatest challenges in natural language processing is the completely different meanings the same combination of words may take on in different contexts. The challenge is to teach the machine to interpret the words correctly, according to their context.

In recent years, NLP applications have been developed for use in Web search engines and as the front end of data-mining software. AI-based search engines enable users to enter simple English questions or sentences from which they can understand which information to fetch from pages throughout the Web. The challenge is to make the applications understand what the user needs within a context, so that the engine does not fetch millions of irrelevant pages along with the few that are relevant. In data mining, the challenge is similar: to have the application understand what relationships among business variables exist within a context. Companies use data mining in data warehouses to find relationships that help in target marketing, fraud detection, and other areas.

Expert Systems

The purpose of *expert systems (ESs)* is to replicate the unstructured and undocumented knowledge of the few (the experts), and put it at the disposal of others. Because of the way ESs are formulated (based on the experience of experts), ESs cannot help users deal with events that are not considered by the experts during development. However, more advanced programs that include what are called "neural networks" can learn from new situations and formulate new rules in their knowledge bases to address events not originally considered in their development.

To build an ES, a specialist called a **knowledge engineer** questions experts and translates their knowledge into code. In most systems, the knowledge is represented in one of several forms. The most popular form is IF-THEN rules. For example: "If the patient is female, and if the patient's temperature is over 100°F, and if the patient has a rash (and so on), then the patient has disease X."

Two other methods used to represent knowledge in a computer program are semantic frames, which are tables that list entities and their attributes, and semantic networks, which are maps of entities and their related attributes, both of which are discussed later.

ES shells—programs designed to facilitate development of ESs with minimal programming—have facilitated the building of ESs. ES researchers continue to look for ways to better capture knowledge and represent it. They test the results of such efforts in highly unstructured problem-solving domains, including games. One such game, which has intrigued both researchers and laypeople, is chess. The game is a highly unstructured environment in which the number of possible moves is enormous, and hence, the player must be an expert to select the best move for every board configuration.

Some companies that specialize in building the systems stopped calling them expert systems and now prefer to call them *knowledge management systems* and *data miners,* especially when the systems are used to "mine" for unknown relationships in data warehouses.

Neural Networks

Rather than containing a set of IF-THEN rules (as explained later), more sophisticated ESs use programs called **neural networks,** which are designed to mimic the way a human brain operates—the way it links facts, draws conclusions, and uses experience to learn and to understand how new facts relate to each other. Neural networks enable machine learning, the ability of a system to update its knowledge dynamically from its own experiences and apply them to future sessions.

Neural networks are software applications programmed to simulate the "wiring" style of a human brain, whose software "cells," or nodes, are connected to other software "cells," or nodes, to form a network. The network consists of several layers of nodes and each layer is represented by a different color. The network of software nodes is programmed to mimic the physical network of neurons in our own, human brains. The software nodes are linked logically rather than physically and simulate brain activity by having different processes take place in different locations and assimilating them to create the output.

Unlike expert systems, a neural net system learns through trial and error. After an action, which is based on advice from the system, produces results, the knowledge engineer provides the results as feedback, which the system records. The system then changes the code to refine its decision rules. As the number of trials and amount of feedback increase, the system becomes more and more accurate in its evaluation and output. Many systems let the user view a graphical representation of the logical connections among the nodes on the computer monitor; these connections are sometimes called "wires." As the system learns, it starts to see the favored path to a solution, which the graphical representation indicates by color-coding.

The uncanny ability of neural networks to learn by themselves, without benefit of explicit software instructions, has been enticing scientists for several years. But implementation of the technology in the business world is progressing slowly, mainly because businesspeople find the technology difficult to understand. Many systems that are now marketed as ESs have neural net technology integrated into them. Sometimes they are called *neural net ESs.*

Business applications have increasingly used combined neural networks and ES technologies in software that monitors business processes and supply chain management.

Fuzzy Logic

Fuzzy logic is based on rules that do not have discrete boundaries but lie along a continuum, enabling a system to better deal with ambiguity. This reasoning process mirrors the way people tend to think, which is in relative, not absolute, terms. As a result, fuzzy logic allows computer applications to solve problems in a more humanlike manner. When fuzzy logic is incorporated into an ES, the result is a system that more closely mimics the natural manner in which a human expert would solve a problem.

Because fuzzy logic can support decisions in highly unstructured environments, it also has applicability in more information-oriented industries such as finance, insurance, and pharmaceuticals. A good example in the finance field is a system that combines neural networks and fuzzy logic to forecast convertible bond ratings.

Genetic Algorithms

Sometimes, scientists or engineers understand what occurs in a natural process, recognize that it would be helpful to adapt the process to occur in a program, and figure out how to artificially replicate the process in a program that is designed to solve problems. **Genetic algorithms** are mathematical functions that use Darwinian principles to improve an application. The functions are designed to simulate in the software environment, in minutes or seconds, what happens in natural environments over millions of years. In nature, living organisms improve through mutation and natural selection based on their success or failure surviving in the physical environment; with genetic algorithms, software mimics this process, within a very short time, to produce the "fittest," that is the optimal, computer program that can solve a problem.

The process starts with a large collection of functions, which are relatively small and well-defined computer programs designed to solve part of an overall problem. Each function is equivalent to a chromosome in nature. They are randomly combined into programs. The programs are run, and the results are tested to determine which programs give the best results in solving a problem. The best programs are kept (this is the "natural" selection), the others are mutated (broken up into functions that are recombined), and the new generation of programs is tested. The process is repeated until a clear best program emerges.

Unlike neural nets, which start work with a clean slate and learn patterns through analysis of feedback, genetic algorithms start their work with a large number of building blocks. Through an enormous number of trials and errors, they produce viable solutions that could take human beings years to reach.

Intelligent Agents

The latest development in AI is **intelligent agents,** computer programs that automatically wade through massive amounts of data and select and deliver the most suitable information for the user, according to contextual or specific requirements that automatically perform tasks for organizations or individuals based on certain conditions. Intelligent agents have been used most often on the Web. In addition to bringing useful information to the desktops of their "masters," advanced intelligent agents are also expected to execute some operations such as retrieving price lists of specified consumer goods, copying articles related to certain subjects, paying outstanding debts electronically, and purchasing goods and services. Note that intelligent agents are not expert systems, which are programmed to provide expert advice in a narrow field of expertise. The main purpose of intelligent agents is to carry out their assignments significantly faster, more frequently, and more effectively than human beings. Experts say that soon intelligent agents will automatically link your computer to your favorite sites, alert you when these sites have been updated, and tailor specific pages to suit your preferences.

As in the case of expert systems, one of the most difficult problems that researchers must overcome is how to install common sense in intelligent agent programs. In the future, the research is expected to address not only the technical challenges of developing agents but the social and ethical issues as well, such as who should have control (the human owner or the program) in which situations.

Contribution of Expert Systems

Expert Systems can make valuable contributions to organizations. Although the cost of developing some systems can reach seven figures or more, the benefits can outweigh the expense. The greatest benefit of ESs is their contribution to productivity—they perform some time-consuming tasks, freeing employees to focus on work only human beings can do. ESs have been applied to several areas.

1. *Planning.* ESs can use information from previous projects to improve subsequent plans, by cautioning the planner against pitfalls that may cause budget and time overruns, for example.
2. *Decision Making.* ESs can support decision making by bringing input from several experts, rather than from a single expert, thereby providing the organization with a true strategic weapon.
3. *Monitoring.* ESs can be used to monitor industrial processes, cash management, and employee activities, easily providing security against fraud by identifying aberrations in cash disbursement.
4. *Diagnosis.* ESs can provide valuable support in diagnosing different conditions: human diseases in medicine; malfunctioning equipment, products, or processes in industry; or hardware problems and their solutions in business. Major Swedish corporations such as **Volvo**, **Saab**, **Asea Brown Boveri**, and **Televerket** have developed ESs to solve control and processing problems in their plants. The British steel industry developed ESs that help in the production of stainless steel slabs.
5. *Training.* Many ESs contain an explanation facility that describes the logic being used to address the problem at hand. This feature makes AI techniques handy in producing ESs that are devoted to training. Training ESs teach users decision rules, which the user can then bring to his or her own work.
6. *Incidental Learning.* Studies have shown that while using an ES in the regular course of their work, people internalize how the system reaches decisions. This unplanned learning increases their own expertise and makes them better decision makers, even in times when an ES is not available.
7. *Replication of Expertise.* Once the expertise is captured in the system, it can easily and inexpensively be replicated and disseminated. Thus, many employees in various divisions and sites can enjoy the knowledge of the same experts.
8. *Timely Response.* Unlike human expert consultants, ESs are on call at all times to provide immediate support and to perform processes, in moments, that would be prohibitively time-consuming for human beings.
9. *Consistent Solutions.* Many organizations want their managers and employees to be consistent in their decision making. For example, a bank would not like its credit officers to evaluate creditworthiness following different guidelines. Since ESs are programmed to solve a certain problem in the same way every time they are queried, they provide the desired consistency.

Development of Expert Systems

Expert systems have caught the attention of knowledge workers in a wide variety of industries. Because they are designed for use in highly unstructured settings, such as investment in securities, tax planning, and financial analysts, accountants, and other professionals have recognized the potential of ESs to provide expert advice without the need for a human expert. However, development of ESs is usually a major undertaking. Thus, you should be familiar with the concept of expertise and the way it is translated into an ES.

What Is Expertise?

Consider what happens when your car malfunctions and emits a strange sound. You realize you do not have a clue how to diagnose the problem. When you take it to a repair shop, the mechanic listens to the noise, looks at something under the hood, and decides that the water pump is broken. Solving the problem seemed simple for this expert mechanic. However, gaining the expertise might have taken many years of work. Through years of dealing with this problem and this noise, the expert mechanic knows what is *not* the right diagnosis, and through many trials and errors, the mechanic has formulated rules that lead him or her to the diagnosis. These rules make up a mechanic's expertise in solving car problems.

Expertise is the skill and knowledge, primarily gained from experience, whose input into a process results in performance that is far above the norm. Expertise often consists of massive amounts of factual information, coupled with rules of thumb, simplifications, rare facts, and wise procedures, all compiled in a way that allows an expert to analyze specific problems efficiently. Some expertise can be acquired through formal education, but to a large extent, expertise is gained through trial and error. Such experience allows experts to skip options they know will not be fruitful and choose those that will. Most of the rules that experts accumulate over time are **heuristics** (from the Greek word *Heuristikein,* "to find"): rules that cannot be formulated as a result of ordinary, proven knowledge but only through experience. Heuristics are compiled hindsight, and they draw their power from the regularity and continuity in the world. They arise through specialization, generalization, and analogy.

Exhibit 800.31   *Components of an Expert System; Numbers Indicate the Order of the Processes*

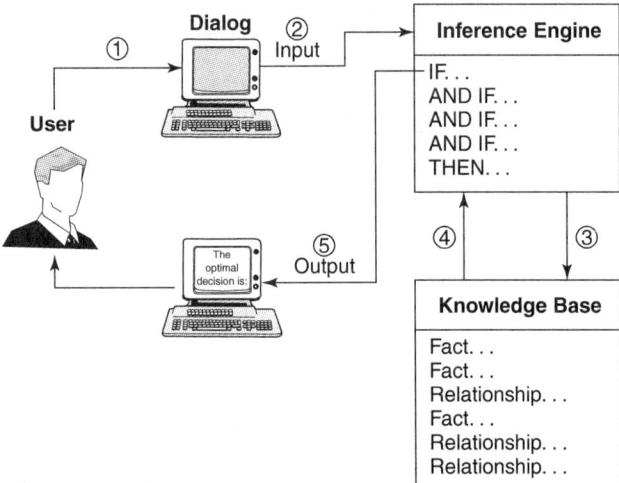

Components of Expert Systems

An Expert System consists of three components (see Exhibit 800.31): (1) The "interface," or **dialog,** program facilitates interaction between the user and the system. It is similar to the dialog program in a DSS. The dialog module prompts the user to enter parameters required to make a decision in an orderly manner. (2) The **knowledge base** is a set of facts and the relationships among the facts provided as input to the system. (3) The **inference engine** is a program that associates the user-supplied data with a set of rules to deduce solutions and explain how they were reached. The inference engine takes the input the user supplies through the dialog component and combines it with knowledge in the knowledge base to produce a solution to a problem: a decision or a diagnosis.

Construction of Expert Systems

While decision-support systems use databases and data warehouses as their information sources, ESs use knowledge bases. A knowledge base contains, in a computer-readable form, the facts, associations, relationships, and beliefs supplied by an expert. There are several methods used to organize knowledge in a knowledge base, such as IF-THEN rules, frames, and semantic nets. We then discuss details of expert system development, functioning, and rationale: knowledge engineering, chaining, and factors justifying acquisition of ESs.

IF-THEN Rules

IF-THEN rules, also called **production rules,** are by far the most popular method of knowledge representation, found in over 70% of all ESs. As a simple example, consider a knowledge base for classifying animals. The system holds the facts in the form of IF-THEN statements such as: "If it has *4 legs,* and if it has *a tail,* and if it *barks,* then it is *a dog.*" The knowledge base may contain hundreds or thousands of such rules.

Frames

Knowledge can also be organized as facts in tables, referred to as **frames,** where each table is devoted to one entity or occurrence and its attributes (see Exhibit 800.32). For instance, the frame for the entity *dog* would include the facts that it is a mammal, has fur, has four legs, barks, and so on. When queried, the inference engine searches the tables. Conditions are satisfied if the information is found in the frame relating to the event or entity.

Exhibit 800.32 *A Frame Describing a Dog*

Attribute	Value
Mammal	Yes
Fur	Yes
Sound	Barks
Legs	Four
Tail	Yes

Semantic Nets

When knowledge is stored in the form of objects and the relationships among them, it is said to be stored in **semantic nets** because, when graphed, the knowledge base looks like a network where the boxes contain objects, and the lines represent attributes and relationships. To reach a solution to a problem, the system navigates along the network according to the parameters supplied by the user until it finds a unique object that satisfies the parameters.

Knowledge Engineering

It takes more than a good programmer to construct an ES. A *knowledge engineer* is a programmer who specializes in developing ESs. He or she is skilled in asking experts the appropriate questions and translating the answers into a knowledge base that follows one of the preceding approaches. Interestingly, but not surprisingly, many successful knowledge engineers have a formal education in psychology. This background enables knowledge engineers to help people work cooperatively to provide all the information they can, which can be a process requiring excellent communications skills and great patience. For instance, imagine trying to get the mechanic described earlier to explain how she knows what is wrong with a car by listening to the motor. She may tell you she knows "from experience." But what does that mean? Is there a certain irregular sound coming from the motor? Is it always associated with the same malfunction? Is there a combination of factors that lead her to her diagnosis? Clearly, it is not easy to obtain a step-by-step explanation of facts and link them.

Expert System Shells

Early ESs were developed using programming languages that were invented especially for AI applications: LISP (LISt Processing), KEE (Knowledge Engineering Environment), Prolog, and others. While some ESs are still constructed using these languages, most knowledge engineers now use **expert system shells,** which are programs that provide an interface to assist the developer in creating an ES. The shell queries the developer for facts and the links among them, and enters the information into a knowledge base. Vendors now offer expert system shells that enable novice programmers to develop their own ESs.

Forward Chaining and Backward Chaining

An ES that takes certain values of parameters as input, runs them through an inference engine, and outputs the solution to the problem is said to be carrying out **forward chaining** (forward reasoning). That is, the system starts the process with facts and works its way to a result. Therefore, forward chaining is also referred to as a *result-driven* process. If the system is given a goal and asked to state the conditions that would bring about the desired outcome, then the process is **backward chaining** (backward reasoning), or a *goal-driven* process. For example, if an investor decides to invest $100,000 for one year in municipal bonds, forward chaining will predict an annual return of 3%. If the investor wants to earn at least a 20% annual return, backward chaining will lead to recommending an investment in technology stocks for more than two years.

While it may sound as if the system must be developed to do either forward chaining or backward chaining, this is not the case. Think of decision making as traversing a decision tree, where at each junction you must find the best path. The same decision tree can serve you to move from a set of givens to a result (forward chaining) or from a goal to the givens (backward chaining). Indeed, many ES shell programs accommodate the usage of the ES they help to build both in forward and backward chaining modes.

While a person can use an ES blindly, providing information as asked and letting the ES do the work, most people want to understand how the system is approaching a problem. So, if an ES requests certain data in the process of considering a problem, a user may ask to see the reasoning behind the request. In backward chaining, the system simply goes one step back, fetches the previous step's set of conditions, and presents them as an explanation. In many ESs the menu item or icon for this feature is "Why?" or "Explain."

Factors Justifying the Acquisition of Expert Systems

There are certain factors that should be considered before deciding to develop an ES, (see Exhibit 800.33). First, the problem to be solved should not be trivial. Trivial problems can be solved by novices without any aid. Second, the problem must be in a highly unstructured domain that requires the wisdom of an expert. Third, the problem should occur frequently. Fourth, an expert must be available for building the expert system. The development of an ES requires that an expert contribute much of his or her time in long sessions with a knowledge engineer. This time is expensive and not always available.

Expert Systems in Action

Expert Systems have been implemented to help professionals in many different industries, such as telecommunications, credit, tax, securities, mining, agriculture, and manufacturing. The following is a small sample.

Telephone Network Maintenance

Pacific Bell uses an ES to diagnose network failures and fix them. The system consists of three parts: Monitor, Consultant, and Forecaster. Monitor constantly monitors Pacific Bell's telephone network, checking for errors. When a problem is detected, the system uses a synthesized voice to warn network specialists, who can then use Consultant to walk them through recommended troubleshooting and repair procedures to correct the problem. Before the company started using the ES, a small number of highly trained specialists did the troubleshooting, which is now done by employees with less training. Forecaster, the third part of the ES, checks system files and notifies personnel of problems likely to occur, based on previous experience, allowing the staff to prevent problems from occurring.

Credit Evaluation

Holders of **American Express (AmEx)** charge cards can potentially charge the card for hundreds of thousands of dollars per purchase. Obviously, most retailers and restauranteurs will not process a charge before they contact AmEx for approval. The AmEx clerk who considers the request uses an ES. The system requests data such as account number, location of the establishment, and amount of the purchase. Coupled with information from a database that contains previous data on the account, and a knowledge base with criteria for approving or denying credit, the ES provides a response.

Another expert system called FAST (Financial Analysis Support Techniques) helps with credit analysis. The system is used by over 30 of the top 100 U.S. and Canadian banks as well as some of the largest industrial and financial

Exhibit 800.33 *Justifications Factors for the Acquisition of an Expert System*

- The problem must be nontrivial.
- The problem must occur in a highly unstructured setting.
- The problem must occur frequently.
- An expert must be available to develop the system.

companies in the world. It gives a credit analyst access to the expertise of more experienced advisors, accelerating the training process and increasing productivity.

The system provides complex analysis of the data contained in applicants' financial reports. The expert system not only provides English language interpretation of the historical financial output but also prepares the assumptions for annual projections and produces text output linkable to word processing software. It eliminates much of the tedious writing of analytical reports, producing standard financial statement reviews.

Loan officers periodically update the knowledge base to customize it for a bank's current loan policy, as well as national and local economic forecasts and interest rate projections. The system consistently and reliably interprets the relationship of these variable factors and the levels of sensitivity that the loan officers associate with a particular financial statement.

Tax Planning

Because federal and state tax laws are so complex, choosing business strategies to minimize tax payments requires expertise. Several tax ESs have been developed for this purpose. For instance, TaxAdvisor solves problems dealing with income and transfer tax planning for individuals. The system makes recommendations, based on projected events, for tax-related actions to maximize the wealth that an individual transfers at death.

Financial Advisor is used by tax consultants to get advice on projects, products, mergers, and acquisitions. A consultant provides information about a company, and the system evaluates how proposed transactions, changes in the tax law, or other factors affect the tax owed.

Detection of Insider Securities Trading

Like other similar institutions, the American Stock Exchange (AMEX) has a special department to prevent insider trading of the securities under its supervision. Insider trading is the trading of stocks based on information available only to those affiliated with a company, not to the general public. This practice is a serious breach of U.S. federal law. To detect insider trading, the department receives information, from several sources, on unusual trading activity and uses this information to identify a stock it may want to investigate. Using an ES, the department's analysts access a large database of the stock's history and choose a time period of interest. The system provides questions that the analysts can answer with the information they received from the database. The questions are formulated to reflect the experience of expert investigators. After the analysts finish answering all the questions, the system provides two numbers: the probability that a further investigation is warranted, and the probability that it is not.

Detection of Common Metals

Metallurgists are experts, and their time is expensive. Also, they usually work in laboratories, which are expensive, too. **General Electric Corp.** developed an expert system that helps nonexperts to identify common metals and alloys outside laboratories. The user provides information on density, color, and hardness of the metal and results of simple chemical tests that can be performed by novices outside the laboratory setting. If the user provides sufficient information, the system will positively identify the metal or alloy. If there is not sufficient information, the system will provide a list of possible metals in order of likelihood. Even such a list can be helpful in some situations, saving much time, labor cost, and the need to wait for lab testing.

Mineral Exploration

Another common application of ESs is in identifying whether drilling should continue during a mineral exploration. For instance, when prospecting for molybdenum, the composition of mud samples helps determine whether the likelihood of finding deposits is high enough to warrant continued drilling. Assessing the chances of hitting deposits requires the input of a highly experienced and expensive engineer. PROSPECTOR takes mud composition as input and provides the likelihood of finding deposits based on the knowledge base of experts. Using the program, less experienced and less expensive engineers can analyze the mud samples, and the ES does the expensive work.

Irrigation and Pest Management

Knowing the quantities of water and pesticides to use at different stages of peanut growing can save farmers millions of dollars. After much research, the U.S. Department of Agriculture developed an ES called EXNUT to help peanut growers make these decisions. Scientists produced a large knowledge base on plants, weather, soil, and other factors that affect the yield of peanut fields. Farmers feed EXNUT with data about the field throughout the growing season, and the program provides recommendations on irrigation, the application of fungicide, and the likelihood of pest conditions. It recommends that farmers withhold water during certain stages and that they use the highest and lowest soil temperatures as indicators of soil moisture and plant health.

By 1997, the system had been used by more than 50 farms in Georgia that cultivate about 10,000 acres. Farmers who are not considered experts were able to increase their yield to quantities greater than those harvested by expert farmers, while using less water and fungicide. Versions of EXNUT have been developed for many other states.

Predicting Failure of Diesel Engines

A reliable way to predict the failure of diesel locomotive engines is to examine the oil from the engine. Experienced technicians at **Canadian Pacific Railroad** took many years to develop this expertise, which involves a technician analyzing a sample of lubrication oil for metal impurities, and a mechanic analyzing the data. The process not only takes years to learn but is difficult to teach to novices, so Canadian Pacific decided to develop an ES for this purpose.

Limitations of Expert Systems

While the use of expert systems can save resources, the systems have their limitations. Time and research efforts will be needed to overcome the limitations that ESs still have, including the following.

- **ESs can handle only narrow domains.** Early attempts to create general problem solvers failed miserably. Current ESs perform well if the domain they handle is narrowly defined.
- **ESs do not possess common sense.** With all their sophistication, ESs cannot recognize problems that require common sense. The system will be able to solve only those problems it was specifically programmed to solve.
- **ESs have a limited ability to learn.** While neural network technology made great strides in the area of machine learning, the ability of computer-based programs to learn remains limited. Knowledge engineers must coach the systems and provide continual feedback for the systems to learn. It may take many years for scientists to produce an ES that can quickly learn and apply self-learned knowledge.

Systems Development and Acquisition

Systems Development

Why Develop an Information System?

As we have discussed, while some organizations develop their enterprisewide information systems (ISs) by combining many different smaller divisional or departmental systems, others create their ISs from the ground up. The process of developing ISs within a planned framework, which is the topic of this section, often creates the best systems and helps organizations avoid patching together a collection of incompatible ISs. Companies usually embark on a systematic development of ISs when they find they are losing competitive ground because they have either inefficient ISs or no ISs to support a business process. Developing an IS is not a trivial matter. It requires a thorough understanding of existing processes, a vision of how an organization should operate, discipline, knowledge, and excellent communication skills.

Three phenomena can trigger the development of a new IS: an opportunity, a problem, or a directive. In this context, an **opportunity** means a potential increase in revenue, reduction of costs, or gain in competitive advantage that can be achieved using an IS. A **problem** is any undesired situation. Many problems can be resolved by using an IS. For instance, an organization may realize that certain processes are too slow, cost too much, or produce products or services of inferior quality and that a new IS could solve the problem. Seeking an opportunity is considered proactive, while solving a problem is considered reactive. A **directive** is an order to take a certain action. In this context, an organization may need an IS to comply with a law or regulation. For example, a law may require that patient or financial records be recorded and maintained in a certain manner that can only be implemented with an IS.

The phase of planning an IS should always precede systems development. The IS plan provides a framework within which new ISs are acquired, either by purchasing them or by developing them.

Note that nowadays most organizations do not develop their ISs themselves unless they want the system to be proprietary, the system will be mission-critical, or they cannot find a commercial application that satisfies requirements. The great majority purchase ready-made applications or contract with firms that specialize in application development. Often, organizations adopt ready-made software and have IT professionals change elements of the software to tailor it to their business processes. Yet, many organizations use some phases of the systems development life cycle when considering and implementing a new IS. These phases include analysis of the current and proposed system and the method of conversion from an existing system to a new one, whether developed especially for the organization or purchased. This section discusses what happens when the decision is made to develop, rather than purchase, a new system. Once the decision is made, the systems development life cycle begins.

The Systems Development Life Cycle

Large ISs that address structured problems, such as accounting and payroll systems, are usually conceived, planned, developed, and maintained within a framework called the **systems development life cycle** (**SDLC**). The SDLC consists of several distinct phases that are followed methodically. While the SDLC is a powerful methodology for systems development, organizations are sometimes forced to take shortcuts, skipping a step here or there. Sometimes, time pressures, funding constraints, or other factors lead developers to use other types of systems development, such as outsourcing, purchased software, or end user systems.

The SDLC approach assumes that the life of an IS starts with a need, followed by an assessment of the functions that a system must have to fulfill that need, and ends when the benefits of the system no longer outweigh its maintenance costs, at which point the life of a new system begins. Hence, the process is called a *life cycle*. After the planning phase, the SDLC includes four major phases: analysis, design, implementation, and support. Exhibit 800.34 depicts the cycle and the conditions that may trigger the return to a previous phase. The analysis and design phases are broken down into several steps, as described in the following discussion.

Exhibit 800.34   *The Systems Development Life Cycle*

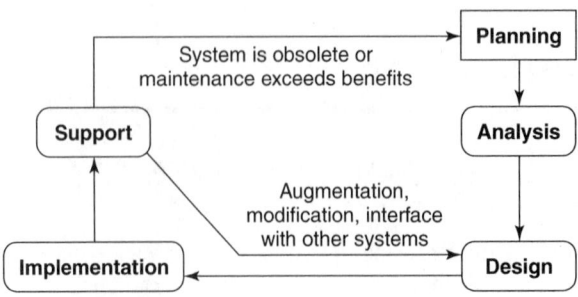

Exhibit 800.35 *Phases in Systems Analysis*

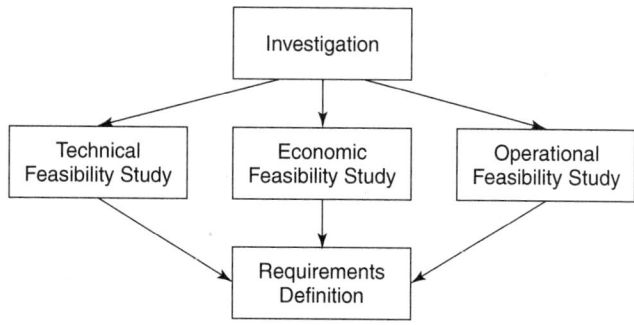

Analysis

The *systems analysis* phase is a five-step process (summarized in Exhibit 800.35) that is designed to answer these questions.

Investigation:

- How does the existing system work?
- What business opportunity do we want the system to seize, or what problems do we want it to solve, or what directive must we fulfill?

Technical Feasibility Study:

- Is there technology to create the system we want?

Economic Feasibility Study:

- What resources do we need to implement the system?
- Will the system's benefits outweigh its costs?

Operational Feasibility Study:

- Will the system be used appropriately by its intended users?
- Will the system be used to its full capacity?

Requirements Definition:

- What features do we want the system to have?
- What interfaces will the system have with other systems?

INVESTIGATION The first step in systems analysis is investigation, which determines whether there is a real need for a system and whether the system as conceived is feasible. Usually, a small ad hoc team—consisting of a representative of the sponsoring executive, one or two systems analysts, and representatives of business units that would use the new system or be affected by it—is put together to perform a quick preliminary investigation. The team may also be hired from a consulting firm.

The team interviews staff, spends time with employees at their workstations to learn first-hand about the way they currently carry out their duties, and interviews the workers about problems with the current system. This direct contact with users gives workers the opportunity to express their ideas about the way they would like a new IS to function to improve their work. The investigative team prepares a written report summarizing the information gathered. The team members also forward their own opinions on the need for a new system. They may or may not agree with the requesting managers that a new system is justified.

If the preliminary report concludes that the business situation warrants investment in a new IS, a more comprehensive investigation may be authorized. The sponsoring executive selects members for a larger analysis team. Usually, members of the original team are included in this augmented group. The objective of the larger investigation team is to determine whether the proposed system is feasible technically, economically, and operationally.

850. SYSTEMS DEVELOPMENT AND ACQUISITION

THE TECHNICAL FEASIBILITY STUDY In a **technical feasibility study,** a new IS is technically feasible if its components exist or can be developed with available tools. As we know by now, ISs consist of hardware, software, and, often, telecommunications equipment. The investigators use their own knowledge and information from trade journals and from hardware and software vendors to determine whether the proposed system can be built. Prospective users occasionally ask for technical features that cannot be developed.

The team must also consider the organization's existing commitments to hardware, software, and telecommunications equipment. For example, if the company recently purchased hundreds of units of a certain computer, it is unlikely that management will approve the purchase of computers of another model for a single new application. Thus, the investigators must find out whether the proposed system can run on existing hardware.

THE ECONOMIC FEASIBILITY STUDY Like any project, the development of a new IS must be economically justified, so organizations conduct an **economic feasibility study.** That is, over the life of the system, the benefits must outweigh the costs. To this end, the analysts prepare a **cost/benefit analysis,** which can be a spreadsheet showing all the costs incurred by the system and all the benefits that are expected from its operation (such as in Exhibit 800.36).

The most accurate method of economic analysis is **internal rate of return** (IRR), which is a calculation of the difference between the stream of benefits and the stream of costs over the life of the system, discounted by the applicable interest rate. To find the IRR, the net present value of the system is calculated by combining the net present value of the costs of the system with the net present value of the benefits of the system, using calculations based on annual costs and benefits and using the appropriate interest rate. If the IRR is positive, the system is economically feasible, or cost-justified. Remember that during the time the system is developed, which may be several years, there are no benefits, only development costs. Operational costs during the system's life include maintenance personnel, telecommunications, computer-related supplies (such as replacement of hardware during breakdowns, upgrading of software, and purchase of paper and toner), and power. If the system involves a Web site, the cost of revising and enhancing the site by Webmasters and other professionals must also be included. Usually, if the net present value is positive, the IRR will be positive too.

Exhibit 800.36 presents a simplified example of a cost/benefit spreadsheet and analysis for a small system. Because the net present value of the system is positive ($43,152), and therefore the benefits exceed the investment, the development effort is economically justified. In the figure, in the year 2005, the net present value starts to diminish. As this value continues to diminish, the organization should consider creating a new system. If the system is not replaced or significantly upgraded, the existing system will become a drain on the organization over time.

Often, it is difficult to justify the cost of a new IS because too many of the benefits are **intangible,** that is, they cannot be quantified in dollar terms. Improved customer service, better decision making, and the creation of a more enjoyable workplace are all benefits that might eventually increase profit but are very difficult to estimate in dollar amounts. This inability to measure benefits is especially true when the new IS is intended not merely to automate a manual process but to support a new business initiative or improve intellectual activities such as decision making. In addition, other benefits, although tangible, can sometimes be overlooked. Furthermore, often the mere fact that a com-

Exhibit 800.36 *Estimated Benefits and Costs of an IS ($000).*

Year	2002	2003	2004	2005	2006	2007
Benefits						
Increase in sales			56,000	45,000	30,000	10,000
Reduction in clerical staff			20,000	20,000	20,000	20,000
Total benefits	0	0	76,000	65,000	50,000	30,000
Costs						
Analysis	15,000					
Design	37,500					
Implementation	0	56,000				
Hardware	0	20,000				
Operation and maintenance	0	0	5,000	5,000	5,000	5,000
Total costs	52,000	76,000	5,000	5,000	5,000	5,000
Difference	(−52,000)	(−76,000)	71,000	60,000	45,000	25,000
Discounted at 5%	(−49,524)	(−68,934)	61,332	49,362	32,259	18,657
Net present value for six years	43,152					

pany does not install the latest ISs that competitors have installed may make it less competitive and push it out of business. Savings from staff reductions are probably the most common tangible benefit of new information systems such as client/server applications or sales force automation. But other tangible benefits from new technologies often go unrecognized in the standard IRR analyses used in most corporations, such as those listed in Exhibit 800.36, including the following.

- A new IS may help to turn over accounts receivable faster. If a new system can send invoices out just one day sooner, then annual cash flow may increase by 1/365. For a company with $365 million in sales, that translates into $1 million in increased cash flow per year. If the interest cost on $1 million is 5%, that translates into savings of $50,000 per year.
- A new IS may help shorten the monthly general ledger closing cycles, allowing managers to make better decisions based on analysis of more timely financial information.
- A new IS may allow managers to perform "what if" analyses in real time during the financial planning cycle, testing ideas that may improve business.
- A new client/server accounting IS may reduce system support costs for an existing mainframe-based IS.
- A new IS may improve efficiencies by reducing errors in billings.
- A new IS may reduce the time (and cost) of preparing budgets, business plans, and proposals by making business data increasingly available in real time.
- A new IS may make it possible to track, and therefore control, costs more closely.

These benefits are extremely important in business and must be considered, even if they are not quantifiable. To convince management that a new IS is needed, the system's champion and systems analysts must consider all the benefits and present them in a compelling manner. Yet, calculating IRR is extremely difficult, and many executives now understand that even the most experienced IS professionals cannot always quantify the benefits of new ISs. Perhaps the question that decision makers should ask themselves is not "What is the return on investment of this proposed IS?" but "Can we continue to be competitive without this proposed IS?"

THE OPERATIONAL FEASIBILITY STUDY   The purpose of the **operational feasibility study** is to determine whether the new system will be used as intended. More specifically, this analysis answers the following questions.

- Will the system fit into the culture of this organization?
- Will all the intended users use the system to its full capacity?
- Will the system interfere with company policies or statutory laws?

Organizational culture is an umbrella term referring to the general tone of the corporate environment. It includes issues such as the nature of relationships between supervisors and subordinates (casual or formal); the existence or lack of dress code; the use of or ban on flex time, which allows employees to start and stop work anytime within a range of hours as long as they work the required total; and acceptance or rejection of telecommuting, which allows employees to work at home. The development team must consider culture to ensure that the new system will fit the organization. For example, if the system will be used by telecommuters, it must be open to telecommunications from external telephone lines. The analysts must find out whether this need would compromise information security and confidentiality.

Another point the team considers is compliance with statutory regulations and company policy. For example, the recordkeeping system the staff wants to use may violate customer privacy or risk the confidentiality of government contracts with the company. If these issues cannot be overcome at the outset, then the proposed system is not operationally feasible.

REQUIREMENTS DEFINITION   When the analysts determine that the proposed system is feasible, the project team is installed. Management or the consulting firm nominates a project leader who puts together a project team that will develop the system until it is ready for delivery. The team includes systems analysts, programmers, and, often, representatives from the prospective group of users.

One of the first pieces of information the analysts need to know is the system requirements. **System requirements** are the functions that the system is expected to fulfill and the features through which it will perform its tasks. In other words, system requirements are what the system should be able to do and the means by which it will fulfill its stated goal. For example, the prospective users may want to be able to capture orders via a Web-based transaction system and have the system route some of the data into a file that can later be used for marketing. This need would be a system requirement. Definition of requirements is often also called *fact finding*. There are several ways to collect information for system requirements:

- *Interviews.* The analysts meet with prospective users and ask questions. The users are given an opportunity to discuss problems with the existing system and ways they would like these problems solved.

- *Questionnaires.* Employees involved in the business processes for which the system is to be developed fill out questionnaires. The analysts glean the information they need from the answers.
- *Examination of documents.* The employees give the analysts forms and other documents containing input data and output information involved in their work.
- *On-the-job observation.* The analysts spend time with employees while they carry out their normal work. The analysts follow the business process firsthand.

Once facts are gathered, they are organized into a document detailing the system requirements. The analysts then present the list to the users and their managers to confirm that they are the features they need. In many organizations, the project leader requests that the prospective owners of the system sign a requirements report indicating their agreement with its content. This formal sign-off is a crucial milestone in the analysis process; if the requirements are not well defined, resources will be wasted or underbudgeted, and the completion of the project will be delayed.

It is important to understand that the requirements report does not include any details of the hardware and software that will ultimately be used. For example, there is no mention at this point of the specific computer models that will be used or of the programming languages in which the software will be written. In fact, at this early stage, the analysts have not yet decided whether to develop the application in-house or purchase a ready-made software package.

For instance, the requirements report may say that the accounting department needs a new client/server IS that is capable of accepting bar-coded information entered by shipping personnel at shipping docks, automatically generating invoices, and allowing authorized users to generate financial reports from their PCs. The document would not say what type of computer or software the system would use to accomplish these goals.

Design

With a comprehensive list of requirements, the project team can begin the next step in systems development, designing the new system. **Systems design** is the evaluation of alternative solutions to a business problem and the specification of hardware, software, and communications technology for the selected solution. The purpose of this phase is to devise the means to meet all the business requirements detailed in the requirements report. As indicated in Exhibit 800.37, systems design comprises four steps, one that describes how the system will work logically, one that describes the physical layout, and others that deal with the construction and testing of the system.

LOGICAL DESIGN The **logical design,** which immediately precedes the physical design of the system, is a translation of the user requirements into detailed functions of the system. During the logical design phase, the designers determine the following components.

- *Input files:* the files that will be used to capture the input data.
- *Procedures:* the logical algorithms used to process the input. The procedures will later be transformed into code written in a programming language.
- *Output files:* the files that will be used to capture information that is the result of processing data, and the files that will record input by customers, employees, suppliers, job applicants, or other parties.

Exhibit 800.37 *Phases in Systems Design*

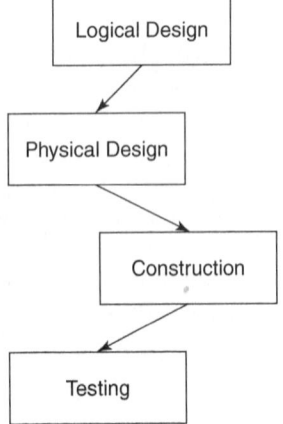

Exhibit 800.38 *Payroll System Development*

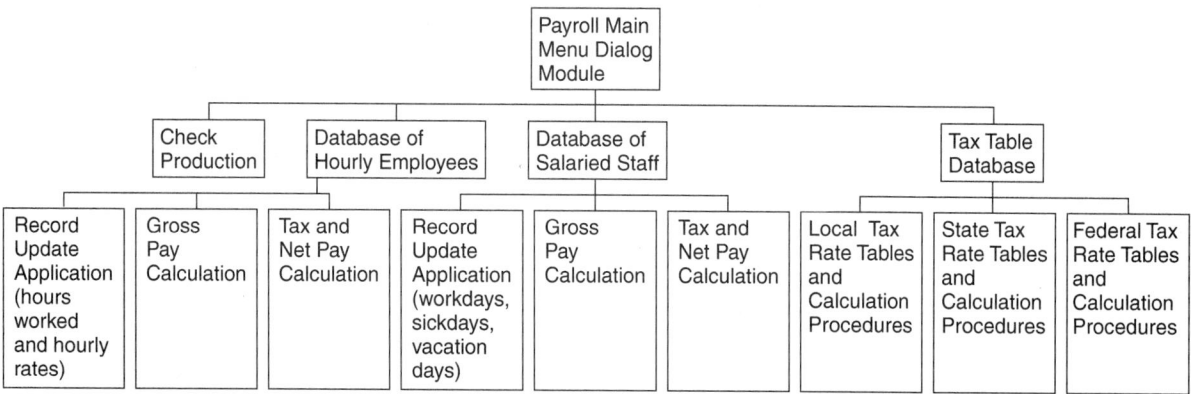

(Using the divide-and-conquer approach, the planned system is broken into hierarchical modules.)

- *User dialog:* the manner in which the users will interact with the system: windows, menus, icons, or provisions for query by example. Usually, creating an intuitive, easy-to-use graphical user interface (GUI) is emphasized.
- *Interfaces:* how the system will interact with other systems. Interface decisions include provisions for input of data and information from the files of other systems, lookups in other systems for decision making, retrieval of data from other systems, and output of data to other systems.

Neither the logical nor the physical design steps include any construction of real code. At this point, the analysts have not yet chosen the tools with which the application will be built, the programming languages that will be used, the DBMS that will be used to construct the databases, the Web page authoring tools to construct the Web site, or any similar tools.

Designing and constructing a new IS can be very complex and even complicated. The approach used most often by managers to simplify the task is "divide and conquer," that is, break the assignment down into small, hierarchical modules and assign one or several modules to each team. Dividing the system into modules isolates problems and delays to avoid hampering the progress of other modules.

Let us consider how the development of a payroll system might be managed in modules, as shown in Exhibit 800.38. One module would be the database of hourly employees, which includes the processes of collecting data about the number of hours worked and maintaining the correct hourly rates. Another module maintains the database of salaried staff. The third module, the tax table database, would be accessed by the first two modules for tax calculation. It includes tax rate tables and procedures for calculating tax amounts. The check production module receives the gross and net amounts to be paid from either of the first two modules for an employee, and the total tax from the tax table module, and then prints out the paycheck or activates an electronic funds transfer. The first three modules are further broken into smaller modules. The four major modules are linked to a dialog module, the payroll main menu, which provides the main menu for selection of the desired operation.

Although potential users may not bring up security issues, the project leader should raise them and propose alternative methods of addressing these potential problems. For instance, the system should be designed to minimize unauthorized access to procedures and files. This protection is especially important if the system will be connected to the Internet and be part of an intranet or an extranet or if the system will serve consumers.

Flowcharts **Flowcharts** use graphical symbols to illustrate a system's logical operations as well as the physical parts involved. For instance, there are symbols that represent different pieces of hardware, such as terminals, disks, and communications lines, and also logical operations such as the beginning and ending points of a process and points of decision making. Flowcharts used to be one of the most important tools in systems development, but they have largely been replaced with other tools, which are discussed later.

Exhibit 800.39 shows an example of a flowchart representing the following logic for giving salespeople bonuses: A salesperson with sales over $1 million will get a bonus of $1,000 plus 0.5% of sales; a salesperson with less than $1 million in sales will receive a bonus of 0.4% of the sales volume.

For over 50 years, systems analysts and programmers have used flowcharts as a language-independent means of describing a system's logical sequence. After detailing the logic of a process in a flowchart, programmers translate

Exhibit 800.39 *A Flowchart Describing a Sales Bonus System*

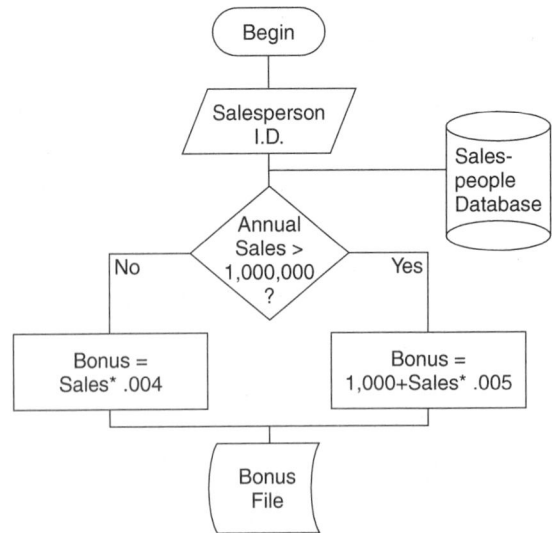

the logic into a computer program. There are more than 30 different symbols, each representing an event, a process, a hardware device, or a report type. While some symbols have been standardized by the American National Standards Institute (ANSI), others remain nonstandard. Occasionally, analysts may use the same symbol to represent different things. The multitude of symbols, the use of nonstandard symbols, and the use of symbols to represent too many things in the same chart (processes, hardware, and so on) have rendered flowcharting less and less popular in recent years. A simpler alternative to graphically representing ISs has been developed. This method is called *data flow diagrams*.

Software programs are used to create flowcharts, data flow diagrams, and other graphical renditions of ISs.

Data Flow Diagrams Data flow diagrams (**DFDs**) are used to describe the flow of data in a business operation, using only four symbols for these elements: external entities, processes, data stores, and the direction in which data flows (see Exhibit 800.40). **Entities** include individuals and groups of people that are external to the system, such as customers, employees, other departments in the organization, or other organizations. A **process** is any event or sequence of events in which data are either changed or acted on, such as the processing of data into information or the application of data to decision making. A **data store** is any form of data at rest, such as a filing cabinet or a database. Data flow from an entity to a process, from a process to a data store, from a data store to a process, and so on. Thus, a carefully drawn DFD can provide a useful representation of a system, whether existing or planned.

It is important to understand that DFDs describe only entities, processes, data stores, and data flows—nothing else. They are not meant to represent hardware devices or types of reports, nor are they meant to detail the logic of processes. The use of only four symbols and the simplicity of DFDs are their great advantage. They are easy to learn and use. Often, systems analysts produce three levels of a system's DFD. The first level contains the least number of symbols and is the least detailed. The second level is more detailed; what may be represented only as a general process in the first level is exploded into several subprocesses and several databases. The third level diagram explodes some processes further and is the most detailed; it shows every possible process, data store, and entity involved. Usually, the first and second level diagrams are presented to non-IS executives, and the third level DFD is considered by the IS professionals while they analyze or develop the system.

The DFD in Exhibit 800.41 shows the same process of calculating a sales bonus that Exhibit 800.39 showed using a flowchart. A sales clerk is an entity entering data (in this case, salespeople's ID numbers), which flow into a process, namely, the bonus calculation, which also receives data from the salespeople database (in this case, the dollar amount each salesperson sold over the past year). The result of the process is the bonus amount for each salesperson, information that flows into a bonus file. Later, the company's controller will use the information to generate bonus checks.

DFDs are used in both the analysis and design phases of systems development. In the analysis phase, they are used to describe and illustrate how the existing system operates. DFD symbols are suitable for describing any IS, even if it is not computer based. A DFD of the existing system helps pinpoint its weaknesses by describing data flow graphically

Exhibit 800.40 *Data Flow Diagram Symbols*

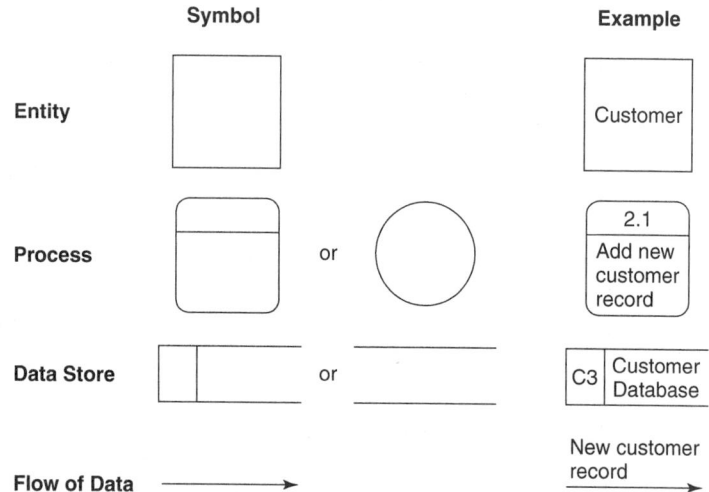

Exhibit 800.41 *A Data Flow Diagram Describing a Sales Bonus System*

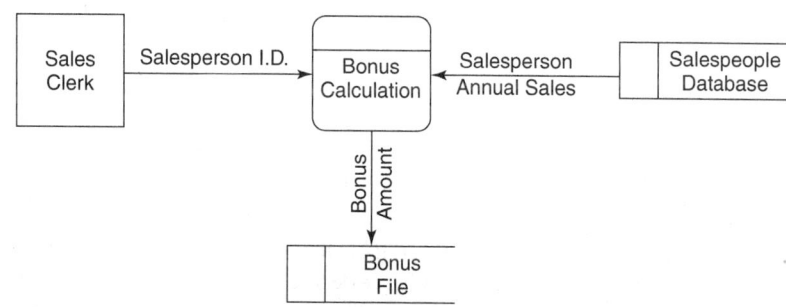

and allowing analysts to pinpoint which processes and databases can be automated, shared by different processes, or otherwise changed to strengthen the IS. If a new IS is needed, a DFD of the conceptualized new system is drawn to provide the logical blueprint for its construction.

PHYSICAL DESIGN   Once the logical blueprint for the new system is ready, the **physical design** begins. A system's physical design process includes specifying the necessary software and hardware needed to support it. Many organizations have hardware that is not being used to full capacity, in which case the project team designs software to fit the existing hardware. Of course, organizations usually look first for packaged software, and only if the appropriate system cannot be purchased off the shelf do companies develop systems from scratch.

If a program has to be developed in-house, the project leader will choose development tools (which the organization may already have) such as programming languages, database management systems for building databases, and special software tools to facilitate the development effort. As with hardware, if certain software development tools are the standard at the organization, only these tools will be used.

To ease maintenance of the new code, the programmers practice structured programming, in which the logical process is divided into small functional units, such as the modules described in the payroll system previously, which are programmed independently. Then each program unit is designed to be triggered from a controlling module. Such programs are often referred to as "GOTO-less" programs because they do not use GOTO statements. It is best to avoid too many GOTO commands because they create code that logically resembles spaghetti, which is difficult to follow. In structured programs in general, each logical unit starts with a comment, or nonexecutable remark in plain English, explaining each part of the code to any person who needs to debug or modify it.

CONSTRUCTION   Once the software development tools are chosen, the construction of the system begins. System construction is predominantly programming. Professional programmers translate input, output, and processes, as described in flowcharts and data flow diagrams, into programs. When a program module is completed, it is tested. Testing is performed by way of walk-through and simulation.

In a walk-through, the systems analysts and programmers follow the logic of the program, conduct processes that the system is programmed to execute when running, produce output, and compare output with what they know the results should be. In simulation, the team actually runs the program with these data. When all the modules of the application are completed and successfully tested, the modules are integrated into one coherent program.

TESTING Although simulation with each module provides some testing, it is important to test the entire integrated system. The system is checked against the system requirements originally defined in the analysis phase by running typical data through the system. The quality of the output is examined, and processing times are measured to ensure that the original requirements are met.

Testing should include attempts to get the system to fail, by violating processing and security controls. The testers should try to "outsmart" the system, entering unreasonable data and trying to access files that should not be accessed directly by some users or, under certain circumstances, by any user. This violation of typical operating rules is a crucial step in the development effort, because many unforeseen snags can be discovered and fixed before the system is introduced for daily use. If the new system passes the tests, it is ready for introduction in the business units that will use it.

Testing tends to be the least respected phase in systems development. Too often project managers who are under time pressure to deliver a new IS either hasten testing or forego it altogether. Since it is the last phase before delivery of the new system, it is the natural "victim" when time and budget have run out. This rush has caused many failures and, eventually, longer delays than if the system had undergone comprehensive testing. A thorough testing phase may delay delivery, but it drastically reduces the probability that flaws will be discovered only after the new system is delivered.

Implementation

The **implementation** of a new IS, also called *delivery,* consists of two steps: training and conversion. Although training usually precedes conversion, if training is done on the job it may occur after conversion.

TRAINING To operate the new IS, the staff must be trained. People can be trained in several ways. The most common methods are in classes or on the job. The main advantage of classes is the economical use of instructors, and the main disadvantage is that large classes are generally only suitable for general information and presentation of the major features of a new system. They are ineffective in teaching the detailed features and modes of operation. Because people learn by doing, on-the-job training, in which a trainer coaches a new user or a small group of users as they perform their jobs with the new system, is much more effective in teaching the day-to-day uses of a new system. Multimedia technology and other training software can also be used. This approach frees systems analysts to attend to other business while employees train themselves and also allows each trainee to learn the system at his or her own pace.

Several vendors of widely sold packaged programs such as word processors and spreadsheets now offer training software that employees can use individually for self-training. Large companies often develop their own multimedia programs to train employees to use tailor-made ISs.

CONVERSION **Conversion** takes place when an operation switches from using an old system to using a new system. Conversion can be a difficult time for an organization. Operators need time to get used to new systems, and although every effort may be made to thoroughly test systems, conversion can hold some unpleasant surprises if certain bugs or problems have not been discovered earlier. Services to other departments and to customers may be delayed, and data may be lost. There are four basic conversion strategies designed to manage the transition (see Exhibit 800.42). They include parallel, phased, cold turkey (cut over), and pilot conversions.

Parallel Conversion In **parallel conversion,** the old system is used along with the new system for a predetermined period of time. This duplication minimizes risk because if the new system fails, operations are not stopped and no damage is caused to the organization. However, parallel conversion is costly because of the expenses, especially labor costs, associated with running two systems.

Phased Conversion ISs, especially large ones, can often be broken into functional modules and phased into operation one at a time, a process called **phased conversion.** For example, conversion of an accounting IS can be phased, with the accounts receivable module converted first, then the accounts payable, then the general ledger, and so on. A supply chain management system may be implemented one module at a time: first, the customer order module, then the shipment module, then the inventory control module, and so on, up to the collection module. This phased approach also reduces risk, although the benefits of using the entire integrated system are delayed. Also, users can learn how to use one module at a time, which is easier than learning the entire system at once.

Exhibit 800.42 *Strategies Used to Convert From One Information System to Another*

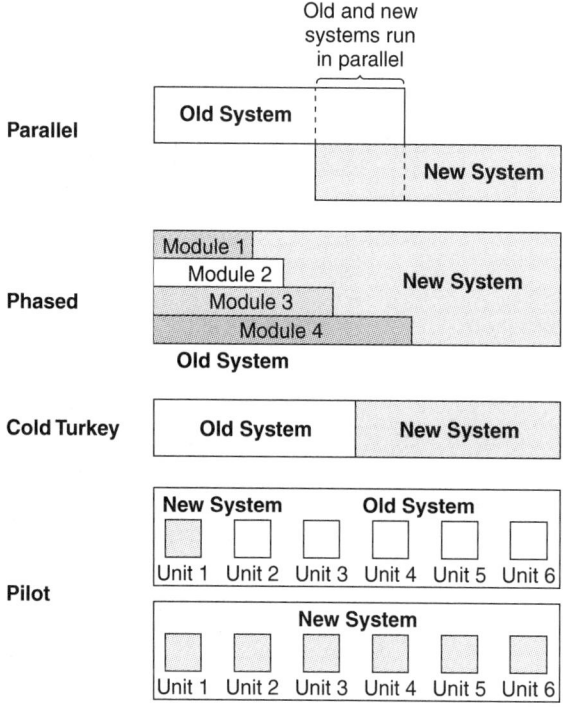

Cold Turkey Conversion In a "**cold turkey**," or "**cut over**," **conversion**, the old system is discarded, and the new one takes over the entire business operation for which it was developed. This strategy is highly risky, but it can be inexpensive, if successful, because no resources are spent on running two systems in parallel, and the benefits of the entire new system are immediately realized.

Pilot Conversion If the new system is to be used in more than one business unit, it may first be introduced, for a period of time in a single unit, where problems can be addressed and the system can be polished before implementing it in the other business units. This trial conversion is also possible for systems shared by many departments and disparate sites, as is increasingly the case due to the growing popularity of intranets and extranets. Obviously, **piloting** reduces risks because it confines any problems to fewer business units. It is especially useful for determining how comfortable staff members are with a new system, a lesson that can be applied to the later business units. As with the parallel strategy, the pilot strategy means that benefits of the full implementation of the system are delayed.

Support

The role of IS professionals does not end with the delivery of the new system. They must support it and ensure that it can be operated satisfactorily by users. **Support** includes two main responsibilities: maintenance and user help (see Exhibit 800.43). Maintenance consists of post-implementation debugging and updating (making changes and additions). Usually, updating is the greater effort.

Debugging is the correction in programs of bugs or problems that were not discovered during tests. Updating is revising the system to comply with changing business needs that occur after the implementation phase. For example, if a company collects personal data for market analysis, managers may want to use the new IS to collect more data, which may require new fields in the databases. Over the past few years, companies that use Web sites for e-commerce have updated both the sites' pages and the databases connected to them continually, as more sophisticated software became available. It is expected that once XML (Extensible Markup Language) standards are agreed on, many companies will move from traditional EDI (electronic data interchange) to Web-based EDI, requiring a major update effort.

Although maintenance is viewed by IS professionals as glamorless, it should not be taken lightly or left to less-experienced professionals. Although maintenance costs vary widely from system to system, company surveys show that up to 80% of IS budgets is spent on maintenance. The major reason for this huge sum is that support is the

Exhibit 800.43 *Activities in Information Systems Support*

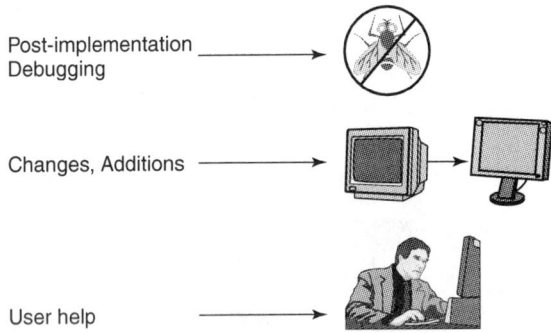

longest phase in a system's life cycle. While development takes several months to about three years, the system is expected to yield benefits over many years. Efficient and effective system maintenance is possible only if good documentation is written while the system is being developed, and if the code is written in a structured, easy-to-follow manner.

Documentation consists of three main types: paper books, electronic documents, and in-program documentation. The latter are nonexecutable comments in the code, seen only when reviewing the application's source code. You can see this type of documentation when you retrieve the source code of many Web pages. In-program documentation briefly describes what each module of the program does, and sometimes who developed it. Printed and electronic documentation is prepared both for programmers, who can better understand how to revise code, and for users who want to learn about the various features of the application.

Support also includes user help. The people who work at an organization's help desk must be familiar with the new system so that they can provide advice and guidance to users.

Prototyping

In prototyping, prospective users of an IS are involved in many steps of the development process.

While the traditional SDLC has its advantages for new-system development, it is a lengthy process and requires a rather inflexible and formal series of steps. To overcome these drawbacks, an increasing number of ISs are being developed under a looser approach called *prototyping*. In manufacturing, a prototype is an original machine or system that serves as a model for production of more machines or systems. So, in that context it is an actual physical product that is later mass-produced for marketing. IS **prototyping,** however, has a slightly different meaning, whereby systems are developed through an iterative rather than a systematic process: the developers and users are constantly interacting, revising, and testing the prototype system until it evolves into an acceptable application (see Exhibit 800.44). This process is unlike the traditional step-by-step analysis and development process used in the SDLC.

The purpose of prototyping is to develop a working model as quickly as possible, which can then be revised and tweaked as developers and users work together. Developers construct a "quick and dirty" model; the model is tested by the prospective users, who provide feedback; using the feedback, developers add some features, delete others, enhance input, output, and processes, and then submit the revised system for the users to test again. This iterative process goes on until the users are satisfied with the product. Then, the productive life of the system starts. While a prototype IS can be duplicated and introduced in many business units, the process is still called "prototyping" even if only one copy of the system will be used. A developer once described this process as a "two steps forward, one step back" procedure. Prototyping is commonly used to develop Web sites.

Several studies have shown that prototyping has become a popular approach to systems development, mainly because it requires fewer staff hours and usually leads to a new system more quickly than the SDLC. These studies have shown that the greatest cost component of systems development is personnel time and that prototyping can translate into cost savings of up to 85%, compared with full SDLC. Prototyping also significantly shortens systems development backlog, the time users have to wait for a response to their system requests because IS departments cannot respond to them in a timely fashion.

The benefits of prototyping do not come without risks, however. First, the analysis phase is reduced to a minimum or is sometimes eliminated completely. Reducing or skipping analysis increases the risk of incompatibilities and other

Exhibit 800.44 *The Meaning of IS Prototyping*

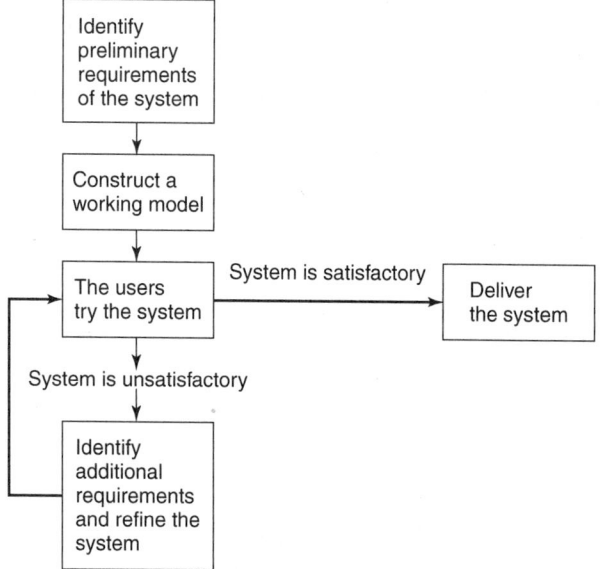

(In prototyping, refinement of the system continues until users are satisfied.)

Exhibit 800.45 *When to Prototype and When Not to Prototype*

When to prototype	When not to prototype
Small-scale systems	Large-scale systems
Systems solving unstructured problems	Complex systems
When it's difficult for user to specify system requirements	Systems with interfaces to other systems

unforeseen mishaps. Also, the developers devote most of their time to construction and hardly any time to documentation, so modification at a later date can be extremely time-consuming, if not impossible. Because of the inherent risks, there are times when prototyping is appropriate and others when it is not (see Exhibit 800.45).

When to Prototype

Prototyping is an efficient approach to development when a system is small, when it deals with unstructured problems, and when the users cannot specify all the requirements at the start of the project.

When a system to be developed is small in scale, the risk involved in the lack of thorough analysis is minimal, partly because the investment of resources is small. (A small system is one that serves one person or a small group of employees. A large system is one that serves many employees, who may be accessing the system via a network from different sites.) If the small-system development takes longer than planned, the overall cost is still likely to be smaller than if a full SDLC were performed.

Even if the IS is large, it is impractical to carry out a formal SDLC when the system is to function in an unstructured environment. With many decision support systems (DSSs) and expert systems (ESs), for example, developers must hold frequent sessions with the experts who provide the sequences of problem solving. This ongoing refinement leads to *de facto* prototyping. The developer interviews the experts, builds a crude system or part thereof, lets the experts try it, improves it, and so on until the system performs satisfactorily. Then it is delivered to its intended users.

When users cannot communicate their requirements, either because they are not familiar with technological developments or because they find it hard to conceptualize the system's input and output files, processes, and user interface, developers have no choice but to prototype. In this case the users are often able to communicate their requirements as the development proceeds. For example, it is easier for marketing personnel to evaluate Web pages designed for a new electronic catalog and promotion site than to describe in detail what they want before seeing anything. Without being shown actual examples, users often can offer little guidance beyond "I will know it when I see it." Similarly, a witness who remembers the face of a suspected criminal but cannot describe it may be able to recognize it when police show photos or illustrations. It is easier for future users to respond to screens, menus, procedures, and other features developed by IS professionals than to provide a list of requirements for them.

When Not to Prototype

Prototyping is not appropriate for all systems development. If a system is large or complex, or if it is designed to interface with other systems, prototyping may pose too great a risk because it skips some major phases of systems development, including the feasibility studies.

Prototyping is not recommended for large systems because they require a significant investment of resources; therefore, system failure could entail great financial loss. The systematic approach of the SDLC is also recommended if the system is complex and consists of many modules, because extra care must be applied in documenting requirements and the manner in which components will be integrated, to ensure smooth and successful development.

For the same reasons, prototyping should be avoided when a system is to be interfaced with other systems. The system requirements and integration must be analyzed carefully, documented, and carried out according to a plan agreed on by the users and developers before the design and construction phases start. This early consensus reduces the risk of incompatibility and damage to other, existing systems. Therefore, accounting ISs, large order-entry systems, and payroll systems as whole systems are rarely prototyped. However, prototyping is almost always used nowadays in the construction phase. Programmers use visual programming languages such as Visual Basic and object-oriented languages such as C++ and Java to quickly develop elements of the application and test them.

Computer-Aided Software Engineering

Computer-aided software engineering (**CASE**) **tools** ease and speed the analysis, design, and programming of new ISs. Systems analysts can use CASE tools to build data flow diagrams of a new IS and flowcharts for the different program modules. They can use CASE tools to plan data dictionaries and database schemas for ISs, which, once found to satisfy users' needs, become the basis of a DBMS.

CASE tools draw their users' attention to flaws in some logic processes and to violations of data flow rules. They also automate the documentation of all phases of systems analysis, design, and programming. Developers of such tools constantly add sophisticated features to shorten the time between conceptualization of an application and its programming and documentation. The ultimate CASE tool will be one that takes requirements as input and then generates the necessary software and documents it.

Project Management

Like any other organizational effort, **project management** is a critical part of systems development. When management decides to develop a system, it places the responsibility for the effort with a senior executive, often a vice president. The executive nominates a project manager, sometimes referred to as the project leader, who is responsible for the timely execution of the project within the budget's limits. Project management was fully discussed in Volume 1, Section 190.

To maximize the success of IS projects, organizations need not only good project managers but also involved top management. A 2001 study of 159 CIOs and their immediate subordinates revealed that the major reasons for failure are lack of communication between top management and project leaders. It also found that lack of clear goals and deliverables were a major factor in project failures.[1]

Systems Development Led by End Users

Before 1980, the users' role in systems development ended in the formulation of system requirements. At that point, the end users were practically disconnected from the development effort, which was carried out by IS professionals until the system was complete. In the 1980s, prototyping promised more user involvement because users were polled for their input throughout the project. But they still did not lead IS development projects.

In the 1990s, a new phenomenon started to take root: users assuming a greater role in *leading* organizational IS development projects. The projects they lead are not small systems developed by the users for their own work but large organizational systems for use across business units. **Systems development led by users** (**SDLU**) reflects the view that users, not systems analysts, programmers, or information service organizations, are responsible for their ISs. The concept reinforces the users' ownership of their new systems. SDLU's benefits are (1) better design, (2) an increased willingness by business units to use the system, and (3) a more favorable attitude toward computer-based systems in general. But SDLU requires that business leaders have at the very least a basic understanding of ISs.

A survey of IS managers and executives of 77 companies was conducted at Drake and Auburn Universities and reported in the August 1994 *Journal of Systems Management.* The results indicated that 59% of the companies studied granted users voting or leadership responsibilities during program development; one company in seven placed users in positions of leadership on the requirement team; and one in 11 placed users in positions of leadership on the program development team. The researchers were surprised by the high rate of SDLU.[2] It is doubtful that users will be leaders of many large-scale systems development projects, because they lack the technical expertise and because a smaller and smaller number of applications are developed in-house. But we may see a greater number of users on the leadership team.

JAD: An Example of User-Led Systems Development

In the 1980s, IBM developed **joint application development** (**JAD**), a method to be used in SDLU. The method is an alternative to the SDLC, but it doesn't skip thorough analysis, as prototyping often does. While the traditional SDLC is sequential and lengthy, JAD facilitates analysis and design by involving representatives of the prospective users in all of the phases (not only in the requirements definition step, as does the SDLC) and by using prototyping wherever possible. It is, however, more systematic than applying prototyping alone.

As shown in Exhibit 800.46 JAD uses a six-step process to take the team through the project's two phases: plan and design. Each of the two phases consists of three steps: customize, workshop, and wrap-up. In the first phase of JAD, management appoints a team to determine what the new system must do, what business processes to use in managing the new system, how big the new system should be, and what the overall time frame for the project is. The customer-led team creates specifications in a workshop setting with a facilitator. The team includes an executive sponsor who is often not an IS professional, a team leader, IS team members, customer team members who are usually cross-functional, experts who are part-time members as needed, a facilitator who is not necessarily an IS person, and a recording secretary, referred to as a *scribe*. Usually, this phase involves members of senior management who do not participate in subsequent phases.

The second phase, JAD design, determines how the system will work. These team sessions produce business flow diagrams, data elements in databases, data dictionaries, screens and reports, edit and validation criteria, interfaces, and processing routines. Since many members of the team are people who will actually use the new system, a strong emphasis is placed on developing a design that satisfies the specific requirements of the users. Prototyping is heavily used in designing the system, especially screens, forms, files, and the like, to provide the customer with an idea of how the system will "feel."

The following factors have been identified as critical to successful use of JAD.

- All participants must be committed to the JAD process.
- The customers and IS people must agree on the project's scope.
- The sponsor must be supportive and involved.
- JAD team members must be empowered decision makers.

Exhibit 800.46 *The Six Steps of Joint Application Development (JAD)*

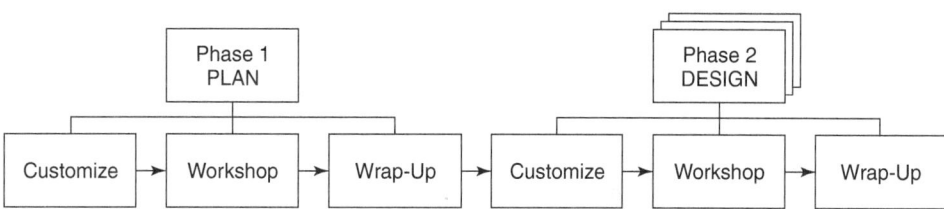

- Business objectives must be clearly defined.
- Business processes must be understood.
- Team members must be able to meet two or more days per week.
- Members must be committed to the team.

Proponents of the JAD method cite the following benefits.

- JAD speeds up the development process by shortening the time required to gather requirements and resolve business issues.
- JAD increases customer commitment, confidence, and involvement, while improving communication and design quality.
- There is increased commitment to the process because the IS unit and the customers are partners, each with a vested interest in the project.
- The resulting system costs less than one developed in a traditional SDLC.

While the method has few disadvantages, it does require participants to dedicate significant amounts of time, which are often difficult to schedule.

Systems Integration

Firms often must wrestle with highly distributed, heterogeneous environments populated with applications for special tasks, which cannot be accessed by systems used for other tasks. Often, the disparate systems cannot "talk to each other" because they run on different operating systems (or, as IS professionals say, on "different platforms").

Much of what systems analysts do is systems integration, rather than the more traditional analysis and development of a standalone IS. **Systems integration** takes a look at the information needs of an entire organization, or at least of a major division of it. The analysts consider the existing, but often disparate, ISs and then produce a plan to integrate them so that (1) data can flow more easily among different units of the organization, and (2) users can access different types of data via a single interface. Consequently, many IS service companies call themselves "systems integrators."

Systems integration is far more difficult than systems development. In fact, systems development is regarded as a subspecialty of systems integration because the integrator must develop systems with an understanding of how data maintained in disparate systems can be efficiently retrieved and used for effective business processes.

For example, marketing managers can have richer information for decision making if they have easy access to accounting and financial data through their own marketing IS. The better the integration, the better they can incorporate this information into their marketing information.

Systems integrators must also be well versed in hardware and software issues, because different ISs often use incompatible hardware and software. Often, overcoming incompatibility issues is one of the most difficult aspects of integration.

Systems integration has become increasingly complex because it now involves the ISs not only of a single organization but of several organizations. In the era of extranets, the challenge is many times more difficult because IT professionals must integrate systems of several different companies so that they can communicate and work well using telecommunications. Imagine how difficult it is to integrate existing, disparate, legacy systems of several companies. (*Legacy* in this context means "old.") For this reason, companies often contract with highly experienced experts or consultants for such projects.

Systems Acquisition

Sources of Information Systems

The past decade has seen the increasing use of several alternatives to traditional in-house development of information systems (see Exhibit 800.47). **Outsourcing**—trusting all or part of an organization's IS operation to an outside company—has become a popular way to manage IT. In addition, the proliferation of **prepackaged software** that satisfies increasingly specific business needs has resulted in suitable applications for many situations, and they are immediately available. A more recent alternative to IS acquisition is the ability to **rent applications.** One option is to rent software

Exhibit 800.47 *Alternatives to In-House Development of Information Systems*

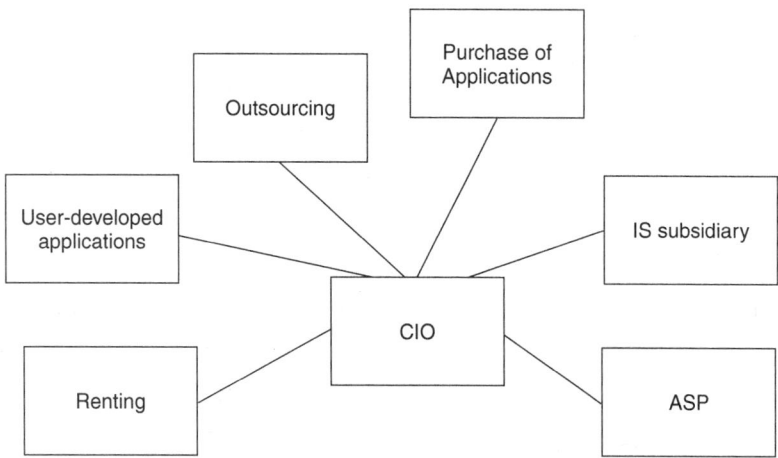

from a third party and install it on your hardware. Another option is to contract with an **application service provider, (ASP)** who lets your organization use applications via an Internet link. At some corporations, the IS units have grown so much that top management has turned them into **IS subsidiaries,** independent corporations that offer services not only to the parent company but also to other companies. And in many organizations the ever more sophisticated and easy-to-use development tools allow many computer-literate **users to develop their own applications.**

How do IS managers learn about these alternatives, find out who offers them, and determine which is best suited to their particular needs? The best initial source is paper and online trade journals.

If your company has decided to acquire a new IS, how should it choose which course to take: develop in-house or outsource the development? Purchase a packaged application or contract with an application service provider for its use? Or should it outsource the management of its ISs, including their acquisition, to another company? First, it's important to understand the pluses and minuses of each approach and then to analyze the needs specific to your company.

Managers' input into the process of deciding whether to develop a system in-house, purchase it off the shelf, outsource the development of part or all of IS services and products, or use the services of an ASP may have a tremendous effect on how managers and their subordinates will work for many years. Issues such as incompatibility of purchased software with existing applications, disclosure of strategic positioning when outsourcing, and possible poor performance of user-developed applications are the business not only of IS professionals but of every manager.

Outsourcing

A multitude of companies specializing in IS services provide expertise and economies of scale that no single organization can achieve. "Outsourcing" used to refer only to contracting with an IT company for the development of a system. However, in the 1990s the term has come to mean more than that. Currently, outsourcing often means that an organization trusts all the activities associated with its ISs, including development of new systems, to another company. A growing number of businesses turn to IS companies, not just for specific hardware or software purchases, but for long-term IS services: purchasing and maintenance of hardware; development, purchasing, and maintenance of software; installation and maintenance of communications networks; development, maintenance, and operation of Web sites; help desks, running of the IS daily operation, managing customer and supplier relations, and so on. An organization may use a combination of in-house and outsourced services. It may outsource the development of an IS but then put its own employees in charge of its operation, or it may outsource both the development and operation of the system to another company.

In considering whether to develop systems in-house or to outsource their development, top managers should ask the following questions.

1. What are our core business competencies? Of the business we conduct, what specialties should we continue to practice ourselves?
2. What do we do outside our specialties that could be done better for us by organizations that specialize in that area?

850. SYSTEMS DEVELOPMENT AND ACQUISITION

Exhibit 800.48 *Outsourced Information Systems (IS) Services*

- Application development and software maintenance
- Hardware purchasing and hardware maintenance
- Telecommunications installation and maintenance
- Help-desk services
- Web site design and maintenance
- Staff training

3. Which of our activities could be improved if we created an alliance with IS organizations?
4. Which of our activities should we work to improve internally?

Many companies have come to realize that IT is not their core competency and should not be a focus of their efforts. In addition, the fast pace of developments in IT require more and more expertise that is unavailable within many organizations.

Outsourcing has come to mean two different things: (1) a short-term contractual relationship with a service firm to develop a specific application for an organization and (2) a long-term contractual relationship with a service firm to take over all or some of an organization's IS functions (see Exhibit 800.48). We will use the term to mean the latter—that is, subcontracting all, or major segments of, IT services. Sometimes an organization hires the services of a consulting firm to satisfy its needs in only one specialized segment of IT, such as telecommunications. In other cases, a company outsources distinct segments of its IS needs to different providers, each specializing in its own segment. It is not uncommon for an organization to outsource help-desk services to one company and its hardware support to another.

Thus, when an organization decides to outsource IS services to another party, it does not have to outsource all of the services to a single company. Clients often outsource each type of service to an organization they consider best in the service.

There is a peculiar—and paradoxical—aspect to IT outsourcing. While contracts are signed for long periods of time, they typically involve rapidly changing technologies. As a result, clients sometimes find themselves bound by contracts that no longer satisfy their needs. They then try to renegotiate the contract.

Advantages of Outsourcing

Clients contract for IT services to offload in-house responsibility and to better manage risks. When a client outsources, management knows how much the outsourced services will cost; thus, the risk of miscalculation is eliminated. But there are additional advantages that make the option attractive.

- *Improved financial planning.* Outsourcing allows a client to know exactly what the cost of its IS functions will be over the period of the contract, which is usually several years. This certainty allows for better financial planning.
- *Reduced license and maintenance fees.* Professional IS firms often pay discounted prices for CASE tools and other resources, based on volume purchases; they can pass these savings on to their clients.
- *Increased attention to core business.* Letting outside experts manage IT frees executives from managing an IS business. They can thus concentrate on the company's core business—including developing and marketing new products.
- *Shorter implementation cycles.* IS vendors can usually complete a new application project in less time than an in-house development team can, thanks to their experience with development projects of similar systems for other clients.
- *Reduction of personnel and fixed costs.* In-house IS salaries and benefits and expensive capital expenditures for items such as CASE tools are paid whether or not the IS staff is productive. IS firms, on the other hand, spread their fixed and overhead costs (office space, furnishings, systems development software, and the like) over many projects and many clients, thereby decreasing the expense absorbed by any single client.
- *Increased access to highly qualified know-how.* Outsourcing allows clients to tap into one of the greatest assets of an IS vendor: experience gained through work with many clients in different environments.

- *Availability of ongoing consulting as part of standard support.* Most outsourcing contracts allow client companies to consult the vendor for all types of IT advice, which would otherwise be unavailable (or only available from a highly paid consultant). Such advice may include guidance on how to use a feature of a recently purchased application or on how to move data from one application to another.
- *Increased security.* An experienced IS vendor is more qualified to implement control and security measures than a client company.

As you can see, cost savings is only one reason to outsource IS functions. In fact, studies show that saving money is not the most common reason for seeking other companies' services. Other benefits, such as access to technological skills and industry expertise, are more important to IS executives than cost savings. The benefits that managers expect from outsourcing have not changed over the past decade.

Increasingly, companies purchase enterprise applications such as enterprise resource planning (ERP) and supply-chain management (SCM) systems, whose installation is very complex. Few companies have staffs that are qualified to install—and sometimes maintain—such systems. Often, the systems must be modified ("tweaked," in professional lingo) to fit idiosyncratic business needs, a process that requires highly experienced professionals. For these reasons, the vast majority of businesses outsource the selection, modification, installation, testing, and, often, maintenance of such systems to the vendors who sell the systems or to firms that can provide the necessary experienced staff. Often, these professionals are people who took courses and exams with the software vendors (such as SAP AG, Oracle, and PeopleSoft) and are certified by the companies. Even if management decides to have its own staff maintain the systems after installation and testing, the implementation project itself takes a long time, typically 6 to 24 months.

Risks of Outsourcing

Despite its popularity, outsourcing is not a panacea and should be considered carefully before it is adopted. There are conditions under which organizations should avoid outsourcing. The major risks are as follows.

- Loss of control.
- Loss of experienced employees.
- Risks of losing a competitive advantage.
- High price.

Outsourcing strategic or core business ISs incurs more risk than outsourcing the routine tasks of operational ISs such as payroll.

The most important element of an outsourcing agreement for both parties, but mostly for the client, is what professionals call **service level agreement.** The negotiators for the client must carefully list all the types of services expected of the vendor as well as the metrics that will be used to measure the degree to which the vendor has met the level of promised services. Clients should not expect vendors to list the service level and metrics; *the clients* must do it. It is in the client's interest to have as specific a contract as possible, because any service that is not included in the contract, or is mentioned only in general terms, leaves the door open for the vendor not to render it, or not to render it to a level expected by the client.

Purchased Applications (Prepackaged Software)

The last decade has seen a huge growth in high-quality packaged software, from office applications that fit on a CD to large enterprise applications. Therefore, purchasing prepackaged software should be the first alternative considered when a company needs to acquire a new system. Unless an IS must be tailored to uncommon needs in an organization, purchasing a prepackaged system may well be the best option. Software vendors now offer a huge variety of applications in business, often even those for highly specialized businesses.

Why Purchase?

When purchasing a software package, the buyer gains several benefits: immediate system availability, high quality, low price, and available support. Immediate availability helps shorten the software development backlog, the long list of applications waiting to be developed for a company's various business units. Purchasing software frees the company's IS professionals to develop the systems that must be specifically tailored to its business needs.

High-quality software is guaranteed through purchase partly because the software company specializes in developing its products and partly because its products would not survive on the market if they weren't strong. Often, large developers distribute prerelease versions, called beta versions, or simply betas, of software to be tested by companies (called beta sites) that agree to use the application with actual data for several months. The beta sites then report problems and propose improvements in return for receiving the fully developed software free. By the time the software is released to the general market, it has been well tested.

Because software companies spread product development costs over many units, the price to a single customer is a fraction of what it would cost to develop a similar application in-house or to hire an outside company to develop it. Also, instead of tying up its own personnel to maintain the software, the buyer can usually contract for long-term service and be notified of new, advanced versions of the application. Most software development companies provide a telephone number that users can call when they encounter a problem. Often, buyers enjoy a period of 3 to 12 months of free service.

There are many sources for packaged software, which is available for almost any imaginable application. Organizations cannot simply purchase the software and install it; they must employ professionals who specialize in the installation of the software, which may take months. Within limits, the providers of these large applications agree to customize part of the applications to the specific needs of a client. However, such customization is very expensive and is often risky; in some cases customization took significantly longer than planned and could not be done to the full satisfaction of the client.

Steps in Purchasing Prepackaged Software

Most people tend to think of ready-made or prepackaged software in terms of $200 word-processing or spreadsheet applications, but enterprise applications cost hundreds of thousands of dollars. Usually, the software's price is only a fraction of the price tag for acquiring the systems, because of the expense involved in hiring the specialists to install it. Thus, purchasing and installation often cost several million dollars.

When selecting a particular software package, companies invest a lot of money and make a long-term commitment to conducting their business in a particular manner. Factors such as the complexity of installation, cost of training, and quality and cost of after-sale service must be considered in addition to the demonstrable quality of the software. Once a company decides that it will purchase a ready-made application, a project management team is formed to oversee system implementation and handle all vendor contact. The project management team has the following responsibilities (see Exhibit 800.49).

- *Identifying the problem.* This step is similar to the initial inquiry and fact-finding step in the systems development life cycle (SDLC). The inquiry results in the identification of gross functional requirements and key integration points with other systems. The report generated often serves as a basis for a request for information from potential vendors.
- *Identifying potential vendors.* On the basis of information in trade journals (printed and on the Web) and previously received promotional material, as well as client references, vendors are identified who offer applications in the domain at hand. In addition to these sources, IS people may gather information at trade shows, from other organizations that have used similar technology, and from colleagues.
- *Soliciting vendor information.* The project manager sends a **request for information** (**RFI**) to the vendors identified, requesting general, somewhat informal, information about the product.
- *Defining system requirements.* The project manager lists a set of functional and technical requirements and identifies the functional and technical capabilities of all vendors, highlighting the items that are common to both lists,

Exhibit 800.49 *The Process of Choosing Prepackaged Software*

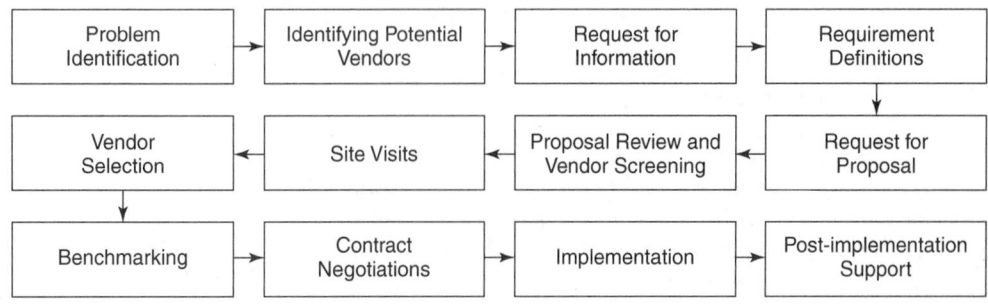

as well as those that are not. The project management team involves the users in defining system requirements to ensure that the chosen application will integrate with existing and planned systems.

- *Requesting vendor proposals.* The team prepares a **request for proposal (RFP),** a document specifying all the system requirements and soliciting a proposal from each vendor contacted. The response should include not only technical requirements but also a detailed description of the implementation process as well as a timetable and budget that can be easily transformed into a contractual agreement. The team should strive to provide enough detail and vision to limit the amount of precontract clarification and negotiation.
- *Reviewing proposals and screening vendors.* The team reviews the proposals and identifies the most qualified vendors. Vendor selection criteria include functionality, architectural fit, price, services, and support.
- *Visiting sites.* The complexity of the RFP responses may make evaluation impossible without a visit to a client site where a copy of the application is in use. The team should discuss with other clients the pros and cons of the application.
- *Selecting the vendor.* The team ranks the remaining vendors. The selection factors are weighted, and the vendor with the highest total points is chosen for contract negotiation. Sometimes make-or-break factors are identified early in the process, to eliminate vendors that cannot provide the essential service. By now, the team has gathered enough information on the functionality of the various systems.

> A system should be purchased only if all or most needs are met.

- *Benchmarking.* Before finalizing the purchasing decision, the system should be tested using **benchmarking,** which is a codified system for comparing actual performance against specific quantifiable criteria. If all other conditions are the same for all the bidders, the vendor whose application meets or exceeds the benchmarks best is selected.
- *Negotiating a contract.* The contract should clearly define performance expectations and include penalties if requirements are not met. Special attention should be given to schedule, budget, responsibility for system support, and support response times. Some clients include a clause on keeping the source code in escrow. If the vendor goes out of business, the client will receive the source code, without which the system cannot be maintained. The client should tie all payments to completion of milestones by the vendor and acceptance of deliverables.
- *Implementing the new system.* The new system is introduced in the business units it will serve. Training and conversion take place.
- *Managing post-implementation support.* Vendors expect buyers of their large applications to request extensive on-site post-implementation support. Unexpected lapses or unfamiliarity with the system may require fine-tuning, additional training, and modification of the software. It is best to develop an ongoing relationship with the vendor because a solid relationship will foster timely service and support.

When choosing a vendor, organizations look for the quality and reliability of the product, but there are additional factors, such as quality of service and support, vendor's support for industry standards, and vendor financial soundness, that are extremely important. In surveys, IS managers have almost invariably revealed the importance of factors considered in selecting a vendor as shown in Exhibit 800.50 (in descending order). Product quality and reliability stood well ahead of the price/performance ratio.

Exhibit 800.50 *How IS Managers Rank the Importance of Product Purchase Factors (in Descending Order)*

Factor
Product quality and reliability
Product performance
Quality of after-sale service and support
Trustworthiness of vendor
Price/performance ratio
Ease of doing business with vendor
Vendor's support for industry standards
Openness of future strategies and plans
Vendor financial stability

Benchmarking—An Evaluation and Testing Tool

In addition to being used in the evaluation process, benchmarking is a powerful testing tool when used as an ongoing check after a new system is implemented. This codified system of comparing one system's performance with another's uses general performance measurements, which are not specific to a particular system. For instance, one benchmark might be the average time required to train someone; another might be a more technical performance measurement, such as the rate of transactions per second, the speed of locating a record in a database, the speed of transferring a file from one computer to another, and the like.

When choosing which vendor to use, professionals in the client organization set certain minimum measurable levels for each performance criterion that the software must meet. The software should be temporarily installed in the organization's computers to be tested against the benchmark in a demonstration before finalizing the purchase, then retested continually after the purchase.

The key to meaningful benchmarking is to measure the identified criteria during typical daily operations, under a wide range of circumstances. This spectrum of testing will demonstrate how the system runs in extreme cases of work load and time pressure. For example, a new client/server system should be tested with the maximum number of users on the system to determine whether response time decreases to an unacceptable degree as more and more users log on.

There are many methods of benchmarking. But since applications are different, and organizations may even use the same application differently, the best benchmark is one that is tailored by the client organization.

Learning From Experience in Purchased Software

Learning from others' experience can save you time and headaches. After one large company purchased software that had been successfully implemented, its evaluation leader was asked what improvements he would make the next time. His answer could serve as a good checklist for all IS managers.

- Double the number of users on the evaluation team.
- Obtain more raw information from suppliers early in the process and force the vendors to give more details about their products, training, consulting services, financing options, and discounts.
- Hold all vendor demonstrations on the same day, at specific sites, for better comparison.
- Insist that vendors use scenarios and data supplied by the purchasing company, not by the vendors.
- Use consultants to help narrow the field to a list of finalist vendors in less time.
- Don't divulge to users which product has been selected before the contract is signed; the information may leak out and undermine the negotiations for better price and terms.
- Use more multiple-choice questions in the original customer survey to get more user responses and to make evaluating the responses easier.
- Ascertain that vendors know that their representatives will meet with real end users.
- Leverage existing relationships with vendors.

Risks in Purchased Software

Although purchasing a ready-made application is attractive, it has its risks.

- *Loose fit between needs and features.* Ready-made software is developed for the widest common denominator of potential user organizations. It may be useful to many, but it will be optimal for few. Companies must take extra care to ensure that ready-made software truly complies with company needs, including organizational culture. Obtaining input from many potential users in the selection process reduces this risk.
- *Bankruptcy of the vendor.* If the vendor goes out of business, the purchaser is left without support, maintenance service, and the opportunity to purchase upgrades to an application to which it is committed. Arranging for software escrow can reduce this risk.
- *High turnover of vendor personnel.* Turnover among IS professionals is significantly higher than in other occupations. If a substantial number of employees involved in application development and upgrading leave a vendor,

support is likely to deteriorate, and upgrades will be of poor quality. Developing an in-house support staff as backup personnel can reduce this risk.

Renting Software

The life expectancy of software, especially purchased software, has become shorter and shorter over the years. While in the past an organization could be on the cutting edge of technology for five or six years with the software it had, now some applications become obsolete within two or three years. If you want to use the most current applications, such as word processors and spreadsheets, you must pay several tens or hundreds of dollars to upgrade your version every two or three years. Now imagine how much money organizations have to pay for the same privilege for hundreds or thousands of employees. Worse, unlike households and small firms, many organizations spend millions of dollars on enterprisewide applications, such as SCM, ERP, and Web-based transaction systems only to find that two or three years later their version is old and lags behind the newer versions that their competitors use. Also, for small companies, the cost of even a single module of an enterprisewide system may be too high to purchase. They often cannot afford to pay a large sum for a new application. One solution to these challenges is renting.

Many IS executives would rather rent software for a limited period and pay less than own it for a much higher cost. To satisfy this need, many software vendors now offer rental programs. For example, many organizations rent antivirus software. **Network Associates**, the company that owns the popular McAfee antivirus software, offers rental contracts for limited periods, as short as one year. The company realized that since thousands of new computer viruses are launched every year, its customers prefer to rent a version for only one year and, when the next version is available, to rent the newer version to provide updated protection.

When a company rents software, the rental rate is determined by the number of users and the length of time. At the end of the rental period, the company must delete all copies of the software from its computers or renew the rental agreement. Thus, the only difference between owning and renting software is the period of use: in the former, it is unlimited; in the latter, it is limited.

The major advantage of renting is the flexibility of choice and the lower sums that need to be committed up front. At the end of the rental period, the company can either rent an advanced version of the application from the same vendor or opt to rent (or purchase) a different application from another vendor. There are no apparent risks in this approach.

Application Service Providers

The ability to rent and use software through the Web was introduced in 1999. An organization that offers the use of software through communication lines is called an *application service provider* (ASP).

An ASP does not install any software on a client's computers. Rather, the application is installed at the ASP's location, along with the databases and other files that the application processes for the client. However, clients can choose to save all the files produced by the application on their own local storage devices. The clients' employees access the application through the Web. They invoke the application, enter data, process the data, produce reports online and on paper, and in general use the application the same way they would had it been installed at their location.

ASPs do not necessarily rent their own software packages. They often rent software developed by other companies. For some small companies, renting enterprise applications through the Web is their only option, because they cannot afford to build their own, or even pay for the installation of a packaged application.

As Exhibit 800.51 shows, there are several benefits to renting and using software through the Web. As in any time-limited rental, the client does not have to commit large sums of money up front. No employees have to devote time to learning how to maintain the software, nor to maintaining it once it is installed. No storage hardware is required for the applications and associated data, because the vendor uses its own hardware. And the software is usually available significantly sooner than if installed at the client's location; while it may take years to install and test enterprise applications on-site, an online renter can use the same application three to six weeks after signing a contract. And even if an organization is willing to pay for the software, it may not find skilled personnel to install and maintain the software.

The obvious risk is that the client cedes control of the systems, the application—and its related data—to another party. Although some vendors are willing to make minor changes to suit the client's needs, they will not make all that are requested. Some experts argue that by renting, clients have less control over their systems and that it is better to

Exhibit 800.51 *Benefits and Risks of Application Service Provider (ASP) Services*

> **Benefits**
> - No need to learn to maintain the application
> - No need to maintain the application
> - No need to allocate hardware for the installation
> - No need to hire experts for installation and maintenance
> - Timely availability
>
> **Risks**
> - Possible long transaction response time on the Internet
> - Security risks, such as interception by competitors

retain the ability to modify applications in-house. Response time may become a problem as well, because neither the ASP nor the client have full control over traffic on the Internet. Also, as with all activities through a public network, there are security risks, such as interception of information by a competitor.

For this reason, some clients prefer to use a leased line rather than the Internet to connect to the ASP. Organizations should also consider the type of application and data their company is about to use. The application should not reveal any vital information to competitors.

The Application Service Provider (ASP) Industry

The ASP industry has been infamous for its instability. Many ASPs had short life spans. Others made promises to clients which they could not keep. Even with reputable providers, some clients were disappointed because the scope of services and level of reliability were not what they had expected when they signed the contract. Managers in organizations considering ASPs should heed the following commandments.

1. *Check the ASP's history.* Ask the provider for a list of references, and contact these customers to ask about their experience. Ask how soon the provider switched to a new version of the application they rented.
2. *Check the financial strength.* Request copies of the ASP's financial reports. Ensure that it has enough funds or secured funding to stay in business for the duration of your planned contract.
3. *Ensure you understand the price scheme.* Ask whether the price changes when you decide to switch to using another application. Ask whether the price includes help desk services.
4. *Get a list of the provider's infrastructure.* Ask to see a list of the ASP's hardware, software, and telecommunication facilities. Ask who the ASP's business partners are that provide hardware, software, and telecommunication services.
5. *Craft the service contract carefully.* Ensure that the contract includes penalties the ASP will pay if services are not rendered fully. Ensure that your organization will not have to pay penalties for early termination.

One important point to check when examining the list of ASP facilities is up time. **Up time** is the proportion of time that the ASP's systems and communication links are up. Since no provider can guarantee 100% up time, ASPs often promise 99.9% ("three nines," in professional lingo) up time, which sounds satisfactory, but it may not be. Three nines mean that down time may reach 500 minutes per year. This is usually acceptable for customer relationship management systems. Human resource managers or sales representatives, who typically use ISs less than 50 hours per week, may settle even for two nines (99% guaranteed up time). However, experts recommend that organizations look for ASPs that can guarantee five nines—99.999% up time. This high up-time ratio will ensure down time of no more than five minutes per year.

Who hires the services of ASPs? Although you will find a variety of companies among ASP clients, the majority of the clients fall into four categories.

1. Companies that are growing fast and rely on software for deployment of their operations
2. Small companies that do not have the cash to pay up front but must use office, telecommunications, and basic business operations applications

3. Midsize companies that need expensive software, such as enterprise applications for their operations, but cannot afford the immediate payment of large sums (examples are ERP applications from companies such as **SAP** and **PeopleSoft**)
4. Organizational units at geographical sites where it is difficult to obtain desired software or personnel to install and maintain the software. These sites are typically located far away from a regional headquarters in a less-developed country. The office at that site can then use applications from a more developed country.

A new type of service provider, similar to an ASP, started to catch the attention of businesses in need of IT services: the **storage service provider** (**SSP**). An SSP does not sell the use of software but of storage space. Instead of spending money on the purchase of magnetic disks, a company can contract with an SSP and have all or some of its files stored remotely on the SSP's storage devices. The storage and retrieval are executed through communication lines, in most cases the Internet.

The Information Systems Subsidiary

Some large companies—such as **Boeing**, **Dun & Bradstreet**, **Bell Atlantic**, and **Chevron**—own IS subsidiaries, so they have IS services at their disposal while avoiding the direct burden of maintaining an in-house IS organization. IS subsidiaries are IS vendors like any other IT consulting firm, except that they almost always have a primary client—the company that owns them. The main advantage of a parent company's having an IS subsidiary is that the parent company has priority over other clients, without having to carry all the overhead costs during its times of low IS demand. The other advantage is the subsidiary's potential to generate additional revenue for the parent. The creation of an IS subsidiary occurs in one of two ways.

Corporations that use a lot of IT often see their in-house IS organizations grow to levels where they can render services not only to the corporation but to outside parties as well. To optimize this overcapacity, management then incorporates the IS organization as an independent subsidiary authorized to render services to any organization.

User Application Development

If an adequate application is not available on the market, or if an organization does not wish to take the risks we discussed earlier with purchasing or renting, and if the application is not too complex, there is another alternative to software development: **user application development,** in which nonprogrammer users write their own business applications. Typically, user-developed software is fairly simple and limited in scope; it is unlikely that users could develop complex applications such as SCM and ERP systems. If end users do have the necessary skills, they should be allowed to develop small applications for immediate needs, and when they do, such applications can be maintained by the end users (see Exhibit 800.52). They should be encouraged to develop applications that will be used for a brief time and then discarded. End users should not develop large or complex applications, applications that interface with other systems, or applications that are vital for the survival of the organization. They should also be discouraged from developing applications that may survive their own tenure in the organization.

Until the early 1980s, computer programs were always developed by professional systems analysts and programmers, but now an increasing number of applications in organizations are developed by their own users. Usually, these are small-scale programs that fit the immediate needs of the individual user, or those of small groups of users.

Exhibit 800.52 *Guidelines for End-User Development of Applications*

End user should develop if . . .	End user should not develop if . . .
End users have the necessary skills.	The application is large or complex.
The application is small.	The application interfaces with other systems.
The application is needed immediately.	The application is vital for the organization's survival.
The application can be maintained by the users.	The application will survive the user's tenure.
The application will be used briefly and discarded.	

Factors Encouraging User Application Development

Several factors led to the shift of development efforts from specialized programmers to end-users themselves.

The Programming Backlog

Until the early 1980s, virtually all scientific and business applications were created by professional programmers. The increasing need for ISs caused a great backlog of programming assignments. In some companies, systems that had been approved for development had to wait two or more years before the professional programming staff started writing code. This lag put increasing pressure on business units to develop their own applications.

As higher-level programming languages (for example, 4GLs) emerged, business units in many organizations decided to allow their own staff to develop applications. With high-level visual programming languages, organizations find that they no longer have to employ professional programmers to develop every single application; they can quickly have nonprogrammers learn how to develop simple applications.

The Widespread Use of PCs

Highly centralized mainframe architectures did not offer business units easy access to computing resources. At best, procedures dictated a rigid schedule of use by business units other than the IS department. The IS staff did not encourage direct access to computing resources.

This situation changed with the proliferation of PCs in businesses. Users were no longer dependent on a mainframe but owned their own computing resource. This widespread access to PCs, coupled with friendlier software development tools, encouraged many lay users to experiment with application development.

The Emergence of 4GLs

The availability of PCs alone could not solve the programming backlog problem. Easy-to-use programs, such as electronic spreadsheets, encouraged users to do a little programming through the use of macros. User-friendly versions of third-generation languages, such as BASIC, also contributed to self-reliance. But the greatest encouragement came from fourth-generation languages (4GLs). These tools are easy to learn, and programming skills can be put to use within days.

Graphical 4GLs, such as Focus or Magic, may further augment the circle of end users who develop their own applications. With a graphical 4GL, the programmer uses icons rather than commands to create code. The program contains prebuilt modules and forms. It offers comprehensive data-modeling capabilities helping the developer to construct a database.

Increasing Popularity of Prototyping

The increasing use of prototyping (with software tools that support the approach), as well as the availability of graphical development tools and support from information centers, creates a convenient environment for the lay developer to become more self-sufficient. The new software eliminates much of the need to master any code-writing skills, and the end user requires less of IS professionals' time, leaving information center staff free to assist more users in their systems development efforts.

Increasing Popularity of Client/Server Architecture

A major purpose of the adoption of client/server architecture is to empower end users in their daily data processing. Therefore, most client/server environments make additional tools available to users for the development of applications on their own desktop computers.

Managing User-Developed Applications

The proliferation of user-developed applications poses challenges to managers, both in IS units and other business units. In addition to the guidelines outlined in Exhibit 800.52, management must cope with the following challenges.

- *Managing the reaction of IS professionals.* IS professionals often react negatively to user development because they perceive it as undermining their own duties and authority. To solve this problem, management must set clear guidelines delineating what types of applications end users may and may not develop.
- *Providing support.* To encourage users to develop applications, IS managers must designate a single technical contact for users. Usually, this resource is a function of the help desk in the information center.

    It is difficult to provide IS support for user-developed applications, because the IS staff members are usually unfamiliar with an application developed without their involvement. Yet, IS staff should help solve problems or enhance such applications when end users think their own skills are not adequate.
- *Compatibility.* To ensure compatibility with other applications within an organization, the organization's IS professionals should adopt and supply standard development tools to interested users. Users should not be allowed to use nonstandard tools. Note that compatibility in this context is for the purpose of transferring data among end users; interfacing user-developed applications with other organizational systems should be discouraged.
- *Managing access.* Sometimes, users need to copy data from organizational databases to their own developed spreadsheets or databases. If access to organizational databases is granted at all for such a purpose, access should be tightly controlled by the IS staff to maintain data integrity and security. Users should be forewarned not to rely on such access when developing their own applications if this is against the organization's policy.

Advantages and Risks in User-Developed Applications

There are several important advantages to user development of applications.

- *Shortened lead times.* Users almost always develop applications more quickly than IS personnel, because they are highly motivated (they will benefit from the new system); their systems are usually simpler in design; and they have a head start by being totally familiar with the business function for which they are developing the application.
- *Good fit to needs.* Nobody knows the users' specific business needs better than the users themselves. Thus, they are apt to develop an application that will satisfy all their needs.
- *Compliance with culture.* User-developed software closely conforms to an individual unit's subculture, which makes the transition to a new system easier for employees.
- *Efficient utilization of resources.* Developing software on computers that are already being used for many other purposes is an efficient use of IT resources.
- *Acquisition of skills.* The more employees who know how to develop applications, the greater an organization's skills inventory.
- *Free IS staff time.* User-developers free IS staff to develop and maintain an organization's more complex and sophisticated systems.

However, with all the pros, there are also cons to application development by users. They must be considered seriously. The risks are as follows.

- *Poorly developed applications.* User-developers are not as skilled as IS personnel. On average, the applications they develop are of lower quality than systems developed by professionals. Users are often tempted to develop applications that are too complex for their skills and tools, resulting in systems that are difficult to use and maintain.
- *Islands of information.* An organization that relies on user development runs the risk of creating islands of information and "private" databases not under the control of the organization's IS managers. This lack of control may make it difficult to achieve the benefits of integrated ISs.
- *Duplication.* User-developers often waste resources developing applications that are identical or similar to systems that already exist elsewhere within the organization.
- *Security problems.* Giving end users access to organizational databases for the purpose of creating systems may result in violations of security policies. This risk is especially true in client/server environments. The creation of "private databases" known only to the individual user is risky. The user may not be aware that the information he or she produces from the data is "classified" under an organization's policy.
- *Poor documentation.* Practically speaking, "poor documentation" may be a misnomer. Usually, users do not create any documentation at all because (1) they do not know how to write documentation and (2) they develop

the application on their own to have it ready as soon as possible, and they don't want to take the time to document it. Lack of documentation makes system maintenance difficult at best, and impossible at worst. Often, applications are patched together by new users, and pretty soon nobody knows how to correct errors or modify programs.

Managing Information Technology Resources

Information Systems Architecture and Management

Organizations have their own distinct managerial styles, most of which fall somewhere between two extremes on a spectrum. One extreme is centralized management, which designates staff positions and departments in a strict vertical hierarchy and places control of the organization in a few hands. The other is decentralized management, which delegates authority to lower-level managers. In most organizations, the management and structure of information systems follow the same pattern as the organization's overall management: centralized management tends to want centralized control over ISs; decentralized management is more likely to be comfortable with decentralized ISs.

If you pick up an IS trade journal, you are likely to come across two terms: *IS infrastructure* and *IS architecture*. **IS infrastructure** refers to the IS resources that an organization owns: hardware, software, telecommunications devices and lines, and other IS assets. **IS architecture** refers to the manner in which these assets are deployed and connected and the ways they interact with each other. Also, be aware that the term *enterprise* in IS lingo refers to any organization that uses ISs. (Thus, the term *enterprise applications* is used for organizationwide shared ISs.)

Because of the influence of an organization's overall management style on other systems, companies with centralized IS management tend to have centralized IS architecture, and companies with decentralized IS management tend to have decentralized IS architecture, although exceptions may be found. Remember that architecture does not strictly dictate how systems are managed (a decentralized architecture can be managed centrally, and a centralized architecture can be decentrally managed), but architecture always has an impact on the way access to data is controlled.

With the recent e-commerce boom, organizations have faced new challenges of managing their Web sites, including linking internal applications and databases to those sites. Large organizations especially have more than one server linked to the Internet. So, they must question whether individual organizational units should manage their own Web sites or whether the company should manage all Web activities through a single home page—essentially a central Web site. Different business functions can use the Web for different purposes. For instance, marketing and sales can promote products and services. Human resources can recruit employees, and finance can make electronic payments. Should the design and implementation of these various functions be the responsibilities of individual departments, or should they be cleared through a central department or manager? The challenge becomes even more complex for multinational organizations, with regional headquarters in different countries. Because many workers today can easily design and create Web pages for their departments, managers are often tempted to establish their own unit's Web site, independent of the central IS organization's priorities. Also, senior executives of some organizations have actually left the IS unit out of the loop when deciding on Web design and operational issues, not realizing that problems can arise later—when the Web site evolves from a mere presence to an important e-commerce vehicle involving many internal resources such as transactional databases and data warehouses. Thus, in many companies the issue of management of IS resources has become more complicated as technology advances.

Centralized Information Systems Architecture

For a long time, mainframes were the only computers available for business. By their nature, they dictated a **centralized architecture** because all applications and data were usually stored on a company's single mainframe. As an example, Exhibit 800.53 shows a typical physical layout of the centralized IS of a single-site company whose gen-

Exhibit 800.53 *Centralized IS Architecture*

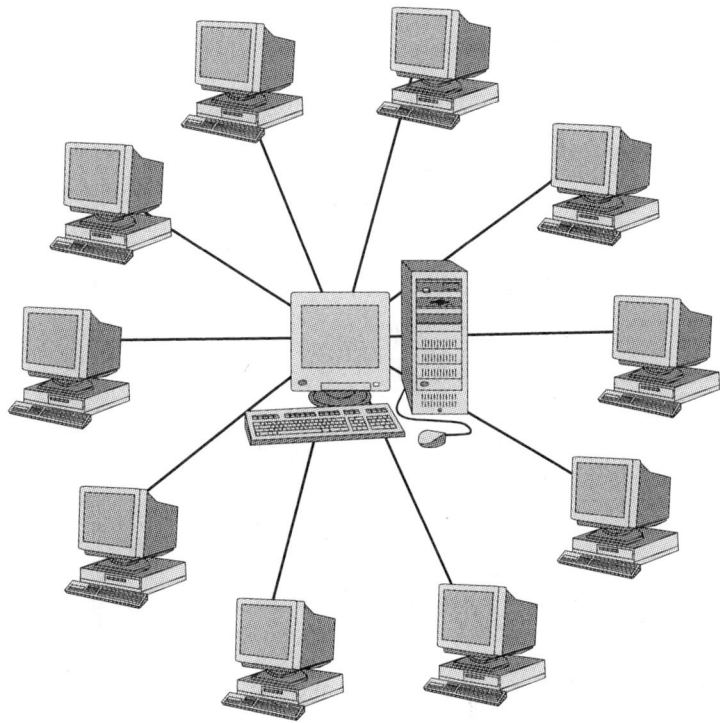

(In centralized IS architecture, information resources are maintained on one or several large computers that are centrally controlled.)

eral management philosophy advocates upper management's tight control of operations. A centralized IS is still favored in some organizations. However, with the introduction of inexpensive desktop computers and reliable data communications technology, many organizations moved to a decentralized or distributed architecture, which we discuss next.

The great advantage of a centralized architecture is that it allows top management and the IS department a high degree of control, making it easy to (1) maintain standards of hardware, software, procedures, and operations and (2) control access to information. The main disadvantage of a centralized system is its inflexibility. A centralized system is run so that it can be used by everyone, but that does not mean the system is optimal for everyone. Different departments and remote sites have different information needs; usually with a centralized system, everyone is served, but few are completely satisfied. These disadvantages are especially problematic when an organization consists of multiple remote sites.

Decentralized Information Systems Architecture

A **decentralized architecture** allows departments and remote sites a large degree of independence in organizing and utilizing their information systems (see Exhibit 800.54). In a decentralized model, each unit within an organization has its own local IS department to establish an infrastructure and to select hardware and software to satisfy the specific information needs of that unit, without necessarily considering other units. In fully decentralized architectures the systems of the independent units are not linked to each other or to the organization's headquarters. Nowadays, however, this situation is rare; even remote units that used to be decentralized are now linked, at least by the Internet.

The major disadvantage of decentralized ISs is that the variety of independent systems makes it difficult to share applications and data. It is also more expensive for an organization to establish maintenance and service contracts with many vendors than with just one or a few.

Exhibit 800.54 *Decentralized IS Architecture*

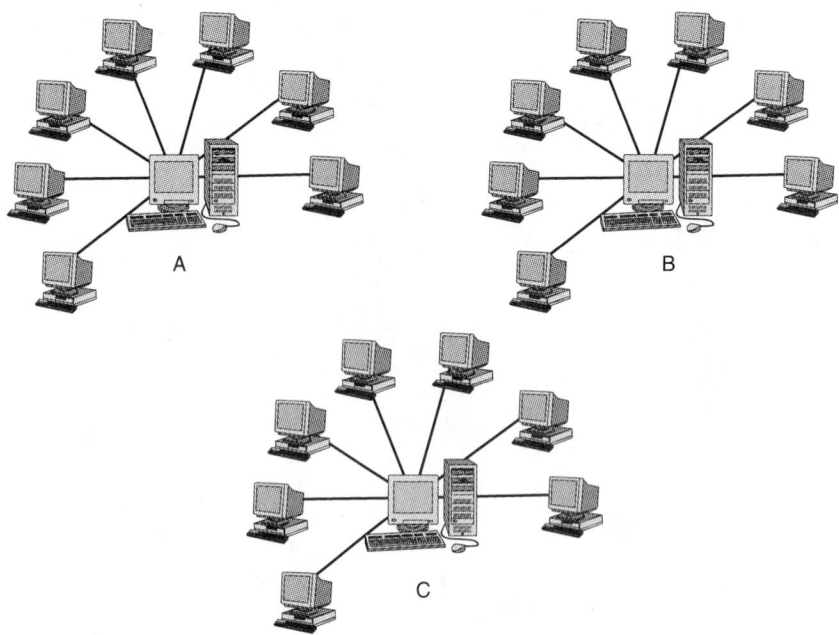

(In decentralized IS architecture, workers at different sites and departments (A, B, C) use information resources that are dedicated to their site or department.)

Distributed Information Systems

Organizations that wish to give their employees independence without losing centralized control of their ISs prefer to rely on what is called **distributed architecture.** With distributed architecture, an organization can enjoy the benefits of both decentralized and centralized architectures. Each unit enjoys sufficient independence in selecting and implementing its own system to optimize its operation, but it can also share resources remotely with other units through communications lines (see Exhibit 800.55).

The increasing reliability and affordability of data communications and PC technology have encouraged organizations to change from centralized and decentralized architectures to distributed architecture. Now, when IS professionals say "decentralized systems" they usually mean "distributed systems."

Centralized Versus Decentralized Information Systems: Advantages and Disadvantages

Thanks to telecommunications technology and the growing use of intranets, organizations can choose to manage any type of architecture centrally or locally. However, the different architectures make some operations easier to manage and others harder. In this discussion we use the terms *centralized* and *decentralized IS* to mean centralized and decentralized management of IS resources. As summarized in Exhibit 800.56, when choosing between more or less centralized IS management, organizations trade off different advantages and disadvantages in IS efficiency, ease of training, level of control, and other factors.

Advantages of Centralized IS Management

Centralized IS management, as illustrated in Exhibit 800.57, has several major advantages.

- ***Standardized hardware and software.*** Centralized ISs can establish corporate software and hardware standards, which saves time and money in purchasing and installation and simplifies interdepartmental sharing of data and information. Standardizing software is particularly important for facilitating data exchange and the sharing of applications.

Exhibit 800.55 *Distributed IS Architecture*

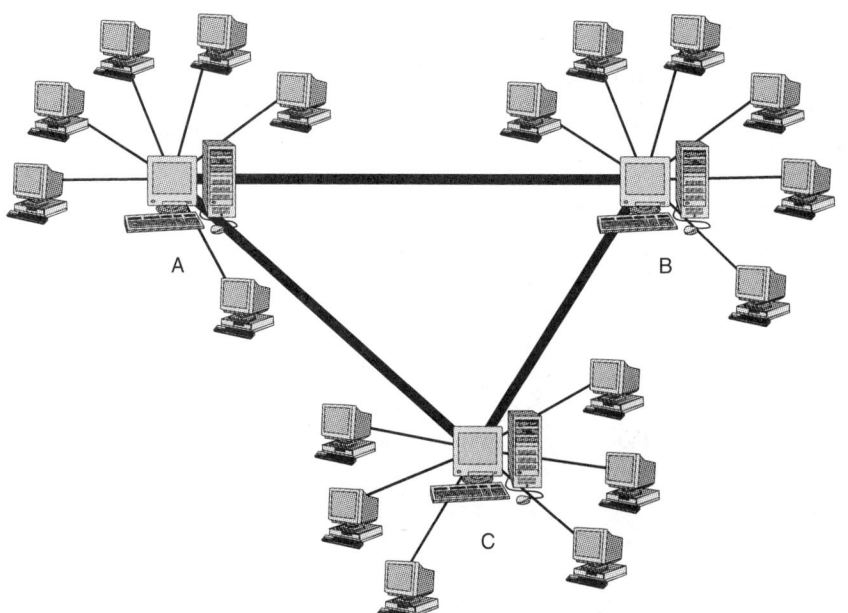

(In distributed IS architecture, workers use the information resources of their own site or department but can also use the resources of other sites or departments through communications lines.)

Exhibit 800.56 *Centralized Versus Decentralized IS Trade-offs*

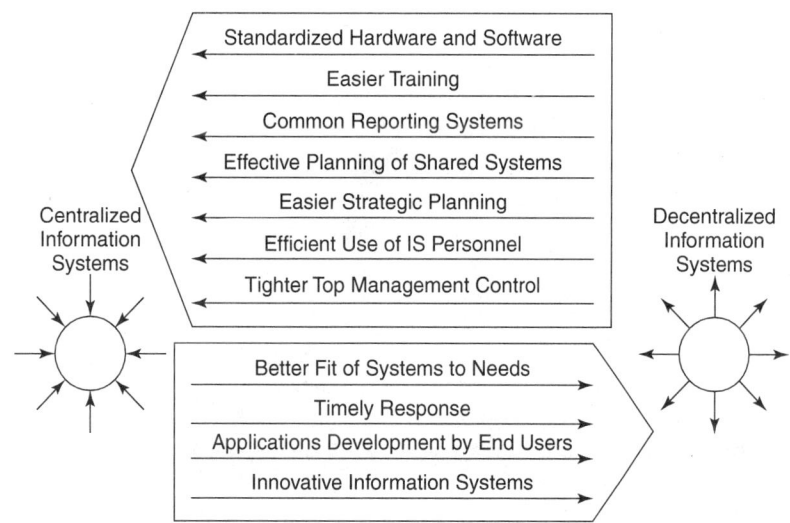

Exhibit 800.57 *Centralized Management of ISs*

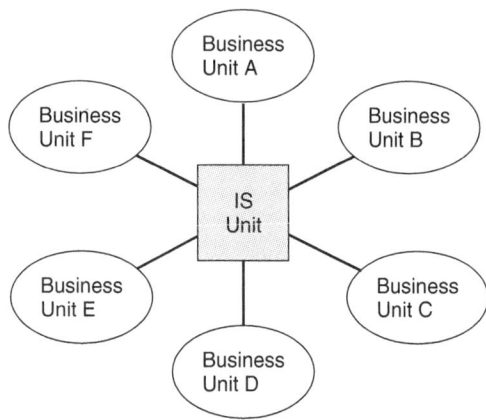

855. MANAGING INFORMATION TECHNOLOGY RESOURCES

- *Easier training.* Training, often a major expense in a company's budget, is much more efficient and less expensive when an organization uses standardized hardware and software. The training staff can do a better job when they can specialize in a small variety of hardware and software.
- *Common reporting systems.* Central IS management can easily standardize reporting systems and formats across departments, which many companies and some laws and regulations require for accounting or tax reporting. With standardized reporting, managers do not have to "re-map" the information they receive from one unit to a report with a different format used by another unit. This uniformity saves time and increases clarity. When reports need to be merged, it is easier to merge them (using spreadsheets, for instance) when they share the same format.
- *Effective planning of shared systems.* Large and complex systems that are shared by several organizational units can best be developed by a central IS department that knows the "big picture."
- *Easier strategic planning.* Strategic IS planning considers an organization's entire IS resources. It is easier to link an IS strategic plan to an organization's overall strategic plan when IS management is centralized.
- *Efficient use of IS personnel.* With a centralized IS department, an organization is more likely to employ highly specialized IS professionals who are better qualified to develop information systems, especially the larger and more complex ones, than are IS professionals who are dispersed in non-IS organizational units.
- *Tighter control by top management.* A centralized IS management allows top management to maintain control over the often vast resources spent on ISs.

Advantages of Decentralized IS Management

Historically, most organizations have moved from a centralized IS management to a decentralized management. Decentralized IS management, illustrated in Exhibit 800.58, has several advantages.

- *Better fit of ISs to business needs.* The individual IS units can use their familiarity with their departments' information needs to develop systems that fit those needs more closely.
- *Timely response of IS units to business demands.* Individual IS units can arrange IS development and maintenance to fit their business units' priorities. They can be more responsive because their responsibility is more focused.
- *End user development of applications.* In a decentralized setting, end users are usually encouraged to develop their own small applications to increase their productivity.
- *Innovative use of ISs.* Since a business IS unit knows its clients better than a centralized one, it has a better chance of devising innovative ISs.
- *Support for delegation of authority.* Decentralized IS management works best if top management wishes to delegate more authority to lower-level managers.

Although you will find many companies with centralized IS management, fully decentralized IS management is rare. Because telecommunications technology is so pervasive and there are so many advantages of sharing information, systems that may have started as separate ISs years ago are usually networked now. Relatively speaking, decen-

Exhibit 800.58 *Decentralized Management of ISs*

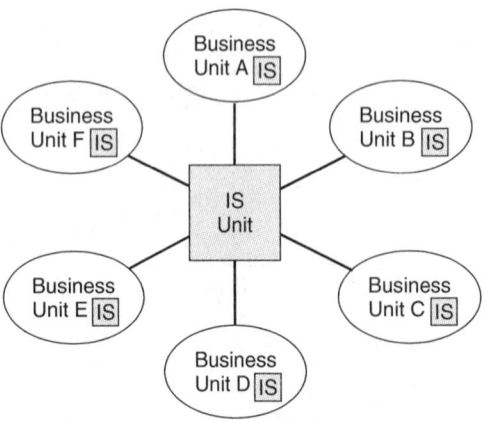

tralized management is more advantageous if an organization has divisions that produce completely different products and services. That way, each unit's information needs can be more closely served. Then, the decentralized units can share resources through networking. Some types of systems must be managed centrally even if they span many different business units, however. With enterprise applications, such as ERP systems, the one large integrated system must be managed by a single team.

Organizing the IS Staff

Now that we have addressed the advantages and disadvantages of centralized and decentralized IS management, we turn to the organization of the IS unit itself. There are various ways to deploy IS staff, even if an organization operates from a single site. In this section we discuss the two extremes of organizing IS professionals in an organization: central IS organization and functional IS organization. Not surprisingly, decentralized IS management often calls for functional organization of the IS staff.

In **central IS organization** there is a corporate IS team to whom all units turn with their IS needs. In **functional IS organization** there is a separate IS team for each business unit. Some arrangements combine elements of both. The approach selected has a direct effect on how IS professionals are positioned in the organizational structure of the business. But regardless of the structure, the goal of any IS organization is to optimize IS services to fit the organization's goals and culture.

Central IS Organization

A centrally organized IS department has what we will call an IS director, who may in fact be a member of top management or a high-level executive who reports to a vice president (usually of finance or operations). The highest-ranking IS officer in an organization is often given the title of chief information officer (CIO) or chief technology officer (CTO) and, in many organizations, that person is also a vice president.

As seen in Exhibit 800.59, the most common central IS unit organization has the IS director overseeing several departments. One department implements and maintains current systems. Another department runs the information center, whose function is to provide ad hoc advice about hardware and software to business units. The communications department develops and manages local area and wide area networks. And the data administration department develops and maintains corporate databases, data warehouses, and data management and analysis applications. In large organizations there may also be a research and development department, which keeps the IS unit abreast of technological advances and develops ideas for the strategic uses of ISs.

A central IS unit is usually involved in virtually every aspect of IT in an organization. It determines which computers and peripheral equipment are approved for purchasing; in some cases it is the only unit that is authorized to purchase hardware. It approves or rejects software purchases, is in charge of training new users, and (except for small and simple programs) is the only body that is authorized to develop ISs for business units.

Exhibit 800.59 *An Example of an IS Unit's Organization with Centrally Managed ISs*

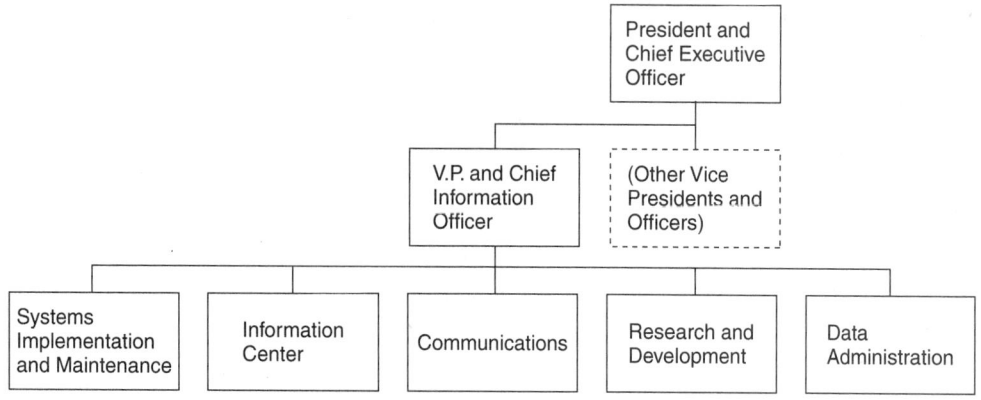

The advantages and disadvantages of a centrally organized IS unit are essentially the same as those for centralized IS management. When centrally managed, the IS unit ensures compatibility of hardware and software and provides the interface between different systems that must work together, such as purchasing and cost accounting; payroll, accounts payable, and cost accounting; and sales and accounts receivable. This approach helps all top managers share an organizational vision of how information technology will serve the corporation in the future.

Regardless of architecture, central IS management usually includes a **steering committee** with representatives from a variety of key business units. It establishes priorities for systems development and implementation of communications networks; it considers and prioritizes requests for new systems; and it commits funds to projects. It is the organizational institution in charge of the budgets for all or most of the IS services.

In recent years the great majority of organizations have adopted ready-made software such as ERP systems. Others have outsourced some or all of their IS functions. Some now use the services of application service providers. But, the central IS unit still oversees the implementation of ready-made software, outsourcing, and relationships with ASPs.

It is often easier to integrate an IS plan into an organization's overall strategic plan with centralized IS management rather than decentralized IS services. On the other hand, when only a central department is available, business units often find themselves overly dependent on—and at times resentful of—the department. The resentment often springs from the lack of control over the services the IS department renders as other units depend on it for their success. Under a centralized IS organization, business units must receive approval for almost anything they do with computers, software, and telecommunications—a situation that can discourage the development of applications by end users, even if they are technologically knowledgeable enough to do so.

Functional IS Organization

At the other end of the IS staffing spectrum is the approach whereby each unit fulfills its IS needs independently, deciding for itself which systems it needs and how to develop them (see Exhibit 800.60). There is usually still an IS unit at corporate headquarters, but it is relatively small and serves to coordinate IS needs for departments that cannot handle their own needs. Only large and complex systems, especially those that affect several departments, are implemented under the auspices of this unit.

Each business unit has one or several IS professionals who report to the unit's manager. These workers know their non-IS colleagues' daily operations well and understand their information needs better than central IS personnel do.

In a functional IS organization, funds for the development and maintenance of the unit's ISs always come from the unit's own budget, which is intended to optimize the use of resources. While the unit's IS professionals may seek input from their central IS colleagues, decisions are made by the units fairly independently. In this environment, IS professionals are often involved in many aspects of operations that do not necessarily involve IT, and they may be promoted from an IT position into another type of position within the business. Such a system enhances their chances of advancing up the organizational ladder to general managerial positions.

Exhibit 800.60 *An Example of IS Personnel Locations in an Organization With Functionally Managed ISs*

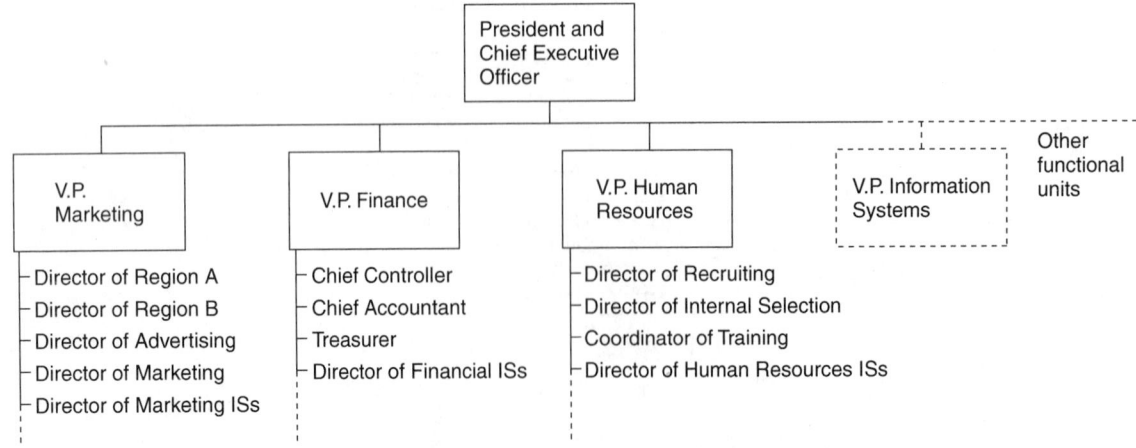

As Exhibit 800.60 indicates, an organization that chooses the functional IS staffing approach may still have a corporate IS director, possibly a vice president, who oversees a small central IS unit, consults with functional IS units, and concentrates on larger, more complex enterprisewide IS projects. However, the IS personnel of the various units do not report to the central IS unit.

The Best of Both Approaches

Small companies typically use the central approach to IS personnel because their IT staffs are small. Among mid-size and large companies, a purely central or functional IS organization is rare. Most of them use elements of both central and functional organization of IS personnel. For instance, a large corporate IS unit may have liaisons in the functional units who report to the corporate IS unit. **Gillette**, the world's largest supplier of shaving blades and other toiletry products, has established such an arrangement and found it very beneficial. A relatively large corporate IS unit coordinates intraorganizational systems, while the different sites (including international divisions) develop and maintain their own local systems. This approach helped the company remain on the leading edge of IT while maintaining a strong sense of ownership at the local sites.

In addition to their own personnel, in many organizations you will also find employees of other companies serving alongside the IS personnel. These professionals handle services that were outsourced by the company to an IS service firm. These people may work in a central IS unit or anywhere else in the organization, depending on the contact signed with the service firm. Many organizations also hire consultants for several weeks or months to help find and implement IT solutions to ad hoc problems or to seize opportunities. Again, these consultants work alongside the organization's employees as if they, too, were its employees. Senior consultants often take part in top management conferences.

Regardless of the approach to managing IS personnel and other resources, surveys show that IS implementation is handled differently according to the position of the highest IS officer in the organizational structure. If this person reports to the vice president of finance or another vice president, it is a sign that top management decided that IT can help automate processes but cannot change the company's strategic position significantly; the IS personnel then tend to provide mere technical solutions to business problems. However, if the highest-ranking IS executive reports to the CEO, it is a sign that top management consider IT as holding the potential to significantly change the organization's future; the IS professionals are then significantly more involved in strategic planning, and they also search for opportunities rather than just solve problems. The trend has been to upgrade the position from reporting to a vice president to reporting to the chief executive officer because of the importance of ISs to companies' survival.

Challenges for IS Managers and Line Managers

For ISs to be developed and maintained successfully, IS managers and line managers must understand what each party expects from the other and must find the best ways to respond to those expectations. By "line managers," we mean all managers in charge of areas other than ISs. What are the expectations?

Line Managers' Expectations of IS Managers

The first thing that line managers must remember is that they should have a continual dialog with the company's IS managers, to explore new ways to help their operations. Although line managers are not expected to be well versed in IT's cutting edge, they should collaborate with the IS manager to explore new technologies to support the work of their subordinates. Line managers need the following from the IS unit.

- *A broad understanding of the business activities.* IS professionals are expected to understand the nature of the activities of the business unit they support. Whom does the business unit serve? Where do its raw data come from? What information does it use? What systems do the business unit's systems interface with? Understanding the business helps IS professionals put themselves in the users' shoes and develop systems from the users' point of view.

- *Prompt response to the information needs of the business unit.* Line managers are often disappointed with the long time it takes IS units to react to business needs. A business unit that cannot elicit a prompt response from the IS staff may resort to finding haphazard—and ultimately problematic—solutions to its information needs.
- *A clear, jargon-free explanation of what the technology can and cannot do for the business unit.* To show off their expertise, IS professionals sometimes use technical jargon to communicate ideas. While use of technical terms facilitates communication among professionals, it may cause problems for lay users. Line managers and their employees may be reluctant to admit that they do not understand certain terms, so communication can break down, resulting in costly misunderstandings. If technical terms must be used, IS professionals should explain them.
- *Candid explanations of what information systems can and cannot do.* Line managers and their employees count on IS professionals to tell them not only what marvels a planned information system will accomplish but also what the system's limitations are. Outlining the limitations of a system will eliminate disappointment and ensure proper usage of the system.
- *Honest budgeting.* Line managers depend on IS managers for an honest, detailed assessment of the resources needed to develop a new IS and maintain an existing one. Time and budget overruns often occur in systems development projects. IS managers must detail the work that will be done, how much it will cost in terms of person hours and other resources, and how much time each project phase will take.
- *Single point of contact.* To serve the business units after an IS is installed or modified, IS managers should assign one contact person to respond to the business units' questions and problems.

> The dialogue between IS managers and general managers must be ongoing for an organization to take full advantage of IT to improve business operations.

In general, IS managers should treat line managers as clients, although they all work for the same organization. This approach has been adopted in an increasing number of companies. Some have taken the client/vendor model to such an extreme that line managers are allowed to use outside IS vendors if the internal IS unit cannot offer comparable service at comparable prices.

IS Managers' Expectations of Line Managers

IS managers are expected to keep themselves abreast of developments in the IT field, suggest adoption of new technologies, and make recommendations to improve business operations. To do this job well, IS managers also need clear communication from line managers in three basic areas: basic business planning, general systems planning, and specific systems development.

- *Basic business planning.* To plan ahead, IS managers need to know their own business, but they also need to know their clients' (the business units') plans and needs. For instance, if a business department is planning to hire ten new people to introduce a new product, the IS manager must be informed to budget for purchasing and installing new equipment, installing new software, and training the new employees to use it. Business plans for, say, three years into the future will become a part of the organization's overall IS plan, which in turn is a part of the organization's overall strategic plan.
- *General systems planning.* Once an IS unit is called on to develop a new system, it needs a clear explanation of business processes that need support. An IS manager can only develop an effective IS if line managers and their employees clearly communicate the exact processes they want automated.
- *Specific systems selection or development.* Once the general automation plan is agreed on, the IS manager needs to know what features the business manager wants in the new system. Although IS professionals are more familiar with IT than many users, they still need to know how a new system will be used in daily operations to design or install it correctly. The business manager is responsible for communicating what features are needed in a new system.

This information helps IS professionals include all input, processing, and output mechanisms, as well as user interfaces that are intuitive, easy to learn, and easy to use.

The Information Center

Users of IT in all organizations need professional help with hardware, software, and telecommunications in their daily work. To satisfy this need, organizations often establish a separate organizational unit for support. The unit may have many names, but we refer to it by the most common one: the **information center.** The need for such a unit is especially high if the company maintains a decentralized IS organization and, in particular, when management encourages the development of applications by non-IS employees (sometimes called *local systems development*). Local systems development can create problems, including incompatibility of data files and databases throughout the company, isolation of useful data in "private" databases that are not accessible to the rest of the company, and inability to control sensitive information. Also, individual users, even in organizations with functional IS management, find they need advice on new software and the compatibility of files and documents created with different software packages. Thus, a typical information center has two functions: coordination and control, and support.

Coordination and Control

One way to allow sufficient local independence in IS acquisition and use, while controlling the problems it can create, is to coordinate and control hardware and software purchases by end users through an information center. A user who needs a tailored application would contact the center to determine whether anyone else has already developed a similar application that could be replicated or adapted. The information center also notifies departments of new hardware or software that could be useful and may also determine which hardware or software to purchase for a department so that its system remains compatible with other departments.

The same approach applies to coordinating data collection among departments. A department that needs access to certain data can check with the information center to see whether someone else in the business has already organized a database that can satisfy its needs. Information center personnel may also determine which data may or may not be gathered and kept by individual departments.

Central coordination and control is especially a challenge when an organization is involved in mergers and acquisitions. When a company acquires other companies, top management must implement standards that mesh with corporate strategy.

Support Through Help Desk

Another important function of the information center is providing hardware and software support through both training and responding to ongoing requests for help. The latter is usually accomplished through a help desk. The **help desk** usually consists of small teams specializing in troubleshooting problems in different areas: hardware, software, communications, and so on. The success of the help desk depends largely on its ability to provide a single point of contact that can connect the user to the appropriate expert, on demand (see Exhibit 800.61).

Exhibit 800.61   *The Help Desk Is an Essential Resource for Information Systems (IS) Users*

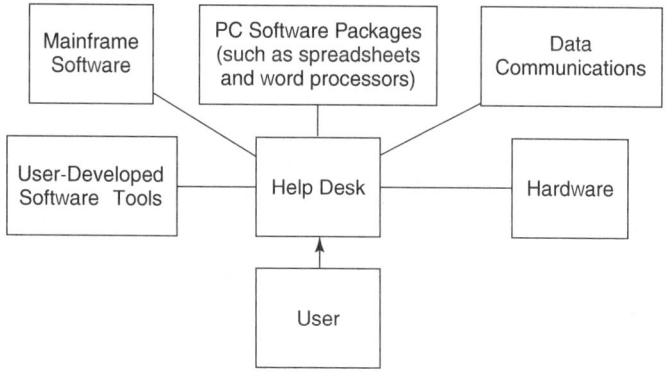

Charge-Back Methods

Some companies treat the cost of the IS function as a part of **overhead cost,** a general expense carried by all departments that is considered essential to running the company—like the lights or phone service. In companies such as these, business units don't purchase services from the IS departments, they simply call on IS services at will and receive them seemingly "free," that is, without a direct impact on their budgets. But this arrangement has a downside—IS services can be easily, if not intentionally, abused, mostly because departments are tempted to order many additional services because no cost is directly associated with them.

To mitigate this problem, many organizations have established charge-back systems. A **charge-back system** is a method by which organizational units pay for the services they receive, often referred to as *service charges*. Charge-back systems may reduce tension between providers and receivers of IS services, because the receivers know exactly what they are being charged for. It also makes the allocation of the services more efficient, because it encourages individual departments to use only those services that they really need for their operations.

Service Charges

Without a charge-back system, politics often prevail as the controlling factor in deciding who receives IS services. Even if top management limits IS services, business units with strong political clout tend to receive more service than other units that may, objectively, need it more. Politics becomes less of a problem as units start paying for their service, but other problems may appear.

For instance, although many users now know how to develop their own simple applications, they still count on a central IS unit to satisfy most of their information needs. When a functional unit depends on a central IS unit to provide a service, tensions may grow. The functional IS staff has only its department and commitments as a priority, but the central IS personnel must prioritize many requests from a corporate perspective. When a service is eventually delivered and charged, tension may build if the users do not understand what their department is being charged for, and by what criteria.

What Is Chargeable?

The items for which a functional unit may be charged fall into the following categories.

- *Personnel hours.* Usually, IS staff time is the largest part of the charge for systems development or systems maintenance. The IS unit charges either a fixed hourly rate or hourly rates that differ according to the level of expertise being provided.
- *Computer time.* This charge is normally billed to departments for the use of mainframe computers or computers on loan.
- *External storage space.* IS departments charge for storing data according to the amount stored. The charge is so many dollars per megabyte per month.
- *Number of input and output operations.* Some IS departments charge business departments for each log-on involving a shared computer.
- *Paper output.* Some IS departments charge business departments per page of paper printout.

Costs that cannot be definitely attributed to specific business units are generally not charged back. For example, the purchase price of any hardware or software that is to be shared by many departments cannot be charged directly to any one department.

Desirable Charge-Back Features

Charge-back methods are successful when they have the following features.

- *Accountability.* Every element of the IS service—including personnel time, computer time, and paper—must be accounted for and attributed to the manager who ordered it. If the cost of some services, such as intraorganizational communication time, cannot be accurately allocated to individual units, they are not charged to individual units. Such costs are considered overhead and are absorbed by divisional or corporate headquarters.

- *Controllability.* Managers who order services should be able to control what they purchase. The charge-back system should be designed so that business managers can determine the type and amount of service to purchase to best fit their specific information needs.
- *Timeliness.* The IS unit must bill managers periodically, with reasonable intervals between billings, so that the managers can track the IS costs they incur and change their request if they so wish.
- *Congruence with organizational goals.* Charge-back rates should be established to encourage business units to use resources that are in the interests of the corporation and to discourage business units from using services that are not in the corporation's overall interest. For example, a low hourly rate may be charged for time IS personnel spend on training employees to use their PC software to develop applications, if management wishes to encourage application development by users. A high per-page rate may be charged for the generation of paper reports if management wants to encourage online ad hoc reports and paperless operations.

Charge-Back Criticism

The charge-back approach is not without its critics. The major argument against charge-back systems is that the expense may discourage managers from exploring new IT opportunities for business activities. Because IS technology is adopted for current and future needs, there is an element of long-term investment. Managers who are focused on quick profitability may opt to spend their budgets on other resources that they believe will generate immediate benefits. Also, in many organizations managers and other employees are frustrated at the high rates their departments must pay for what they perceive as simple services. Disagreement over how much a job should cost may create friction rather than cooperation. The goal of charge-back systems is to increase efficiency in the allocation of IS services, but if IS charge backs are unreasonably priced, the system may create the opposite of its goal: managers may try to do by themselves what only professionals can do well, creating inefficiencies.

Overhead Expenditures

Some IS department expenses—such as research and development, and corporatewide data communications installation and maintenance—cannot be directly attributed to the services the IS department performs for business units. These costs are often treated as overhead expenses shared by the entire organization and are therefore excluded from the charge-back scheme. In many corporations, the cost of implementing systems that are used by a large number of organizational units, such as ERP systems, is treated as overhead expense. It is practically impossible to determine how much each unit will use the new system and therefore how much to charge. Another reason these systems are not charged back to business units is that their managers may elect not to have them installed. Since it is in corporate management's interest to install such systems, management takes away both the decision and the financial burden from the individual units.

Telecommunications and Networks

Telecommunications in Business

Telecommunications, which is essential to today's smooth business operations, is the transmittal of data and information from one point to another. Thus, telecommunications is communications over a distance. Telephone, fax, e-mail, the World Wide Web—none of these essential business services would be available without fast, reliable telecommunications. In fact, electronic commerce, popularly called *e-commerce*, would be impossible. This section will help you understand the technical foundations of telecommunications, an essential ingredient to managing its role in business. We will discuss the hardware and software needed for telecommunications, the cost/benefit trade-offs of different systems, and the technical trade-offs a successful manager needs to understand to participate in critical business decisions. It is equally, if not more, important to understand how telecommunications affects the way businesses run and how managers can use technology to do a better job. Telecommunications has brought four basic improvements to business processes.

- *Better business communication.* When no physical objects need to be transferred from one place to another, telecommunications technology can make geographical distance irrelevant. E-mail, voice mail, faxing, file transfer, cellular telephony, and teleconferencing enable detailed and instant communication, whether among managers, between managers and their staffs, or among different organizations. Telecommunications can also be used by one person to monitor another person's performance in real time. Telecommunications is used to communicate directions and receive feedback without requiring people to coordinate their schedules to hold a meeting. And the use of e-mail has brought some secondary benefits to business communications by establishing a permanent written record of, and accountability for, ideas. The result is more accurate business communications.
- *Higher efficiency.* Telecommunications has made business processes more efficient. Many business processes are serial in nature: one department must have the input of another department before acting and must then produce its own information, which in turn serves as input for a third department, and so on. For example, when the sales department receives a purchase order from a customer, it must communicate the order to the warehouse, which needs the information to prepare the package. The warehouse workers must then forward shipping documents to the accounts receivable department for billing. With telecommunications, all documents can be accessed electronically by many different departments at the same time. Furthermore, processes that used to take a long time for action and counter action by two or more parties can now be carried out in one session attended by all parties involved, through telecommunication lines.
- *Better distribution of data.* Organizations that can quickly transmit vital data from one computer to another no longer need centralized databases. Business units that need certain data frequently may store it locally, while others can access it remotely. Only fast, reliable transfer of data makes this efficient arrangement possible.
- *Instant transactions.* The availability of the Internet to millions of businesses and consumers has shifted a significant volume of business transactions to the Web. Both businesses and consumers can shop, purchase, and pay instantly online. In addition to commercial activities, people can use telecommunications for online education and entertainment.

As a manager, you will be responsible for ensuring that your organization maximizes its benefits from fast and reliable telecommunications. To do so, you may be involved in selecting a telecommunications system or in exploring the demands on your organization's system. To be a creative and productive contributor to these key decisions, it is essential that you grasp the basic technology behind telecommunications.

At the same time we enjoy the great opportunities created by telecommunications technology, we must recognize that it poses great risks as well. Once an organization connects its ISs to a public network, security issues become extremely important. Unauthorized access and data destruction are constant threats. Thus, organizations must establish proper security controls as preventive measures. Security issues have become especially important due to the popularity of the Internet and its growing accessibility.

Data Communications

Data communications is any transfer of data within a computer, between a computer and another device, or between two computers. For a computer to function, binary data in the form of electrical impulses must flow from one component to another, such as from the CPU to the primary memory, from the CPU to the monitor, or from the primary memory to the hard disk. This type of communication is done through the computer's bus. The bus is a system of wires, or strings of conductive material, soldered on the surface of a computer board. It is a communications channel that allows the transmission of a whole byte or more in one pass.

Telecommunications is communication of data and information between two devices over a distance. In our discussion, we will refer to telecommunication among computers or between computers and other digital devices. The data may represent any number of media, including voice, video, animation, or text. Once communications are transmitted *between* computer systems rather than *within* a single system, the rules of the communications game become more complex. A number of questions about how to manage communications arise, such as the following.

- What physical channels should be used to transmit and receive signals?
- How can we maximize communication speed per dollar spent on communication links?
- What is the best layout of the nodes in an internal network for our business?

Other issues must be taken into account when considering a telecommunications system. For instance, communications devices must be compatible. As always, the benefits of the telecommunications devices and software have to be weighed against their costs.

Types of Data Communications

Data can be transmitted in two basic modes: a whole byte at a time, which is feasible only over very short distances, or a single bit at a time, currently the only practical mode for communicating over long distances. Within the computer, and between the computer and its peripheral equipment (such as its printer and external hard disk), the transmission can take the form of parallel transmission. In **parallel transmission,** each byte is transmitted in its entirety. The electrical impulses representing the bits of a byte are transmitted along a bundle of parallel lines, one bit through each line. These lines are often called a "bus" (although the word *bus* is not reserved only for parallel transmission). In **serial transmission,** on the other hand, data are transmitted one bit at a time through a single line.

Parallel and serial data transmission require different types of wiring. In the back of a computer are several outlets for connecting different cables. An outlet that can accept multiwire cord to transmit in parallel is a **parallel port.** An outlet that accepts a cord for serial transmission is a **serial port.**

Rules must be set so that both the transmitting and the receiving devices can "understand" each other. For instance, in serial transmission, rules determine when each byte begins and ends. The transmitting and receiving ends must agree on details such as whether each byte is transmitted with bits indicating the start and stop of the byte, the number of bits to be transmitted per second, and other features. Without rules, the transmission may result in a long stream of meaningless bits. Sets of such rules are called **protocols.** We discuss protocols later in this section.

Why not transmit only in parallel? Because the public infrastructure that can accommodate parallel transmission is limited. The communications networks available to most people are the telephone network and the Internet, and these networks can accommodate only serial transmission of data.

Communication Direction

The three modes of communication between devices—simplex, half-duplex, and full-duplex—are distinguished by whether communication is one-way in one direction, one-way at a time in two directions, or two-way (see Exhibit 800.62).

Exhibit 800.62 *Simplex, Half-Duplex, and Full-Duplex Communication*

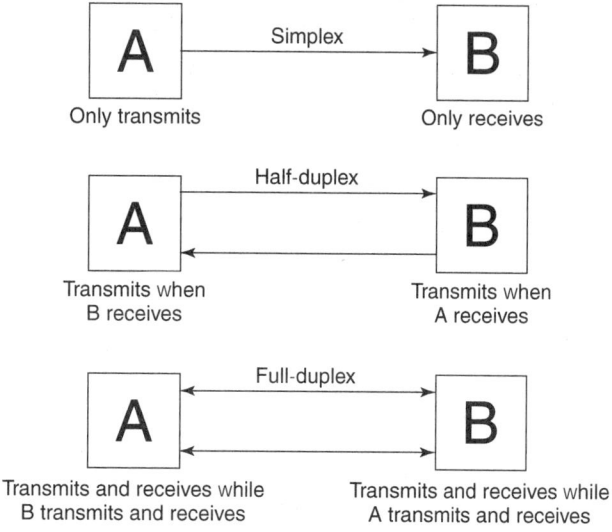

860. TELECOMMUNICATIONS AND NETWORKS

591

Simplex

In **simplex** communication, device A can transmit to device B, but device B cannot transmit to device A. An example of simplex communication is commercial radio transmission. Your car radio can receive signals from a radio station but cannot transmit back to it.

Half-Duplex

In **half-duplex** mode, device A can transmit to device B while device B receives the signal. Device B can transmit to device A while device A receives the signal. However, the two devices cannot transmit to each other simultaneously, and one device can transmit to the other only when the other device is in reception mode. One example of half-duplex is CB (citizens band) communication. Half-duplex may also take place when you use a computer terminal to communicate with a mainframe computer.

Full-Duplex

In **full-duplex** communication, either device can transmit to the other device while simultaneously receiving signals from the other device. That is, device A can transmit to B and receive from B at the same time, and vice versa. Telephony is an example of full-duplex: both parties can talk and listen at once (although this method is neither a practical nor a polite way to use the telephone). Full-duplex data communication is often used between computers.

Synchronization

Telecommunications can work only if the transmitting and receiving devices are synchronized, or "time-coordinated." Otherwise, the receiving device cannot correctly interpret the message encoded in the stream of bits it receives. There are two ways to synchronize communication: one is called *synchronous* and, despite the seeming contradiction in terminology, the other is called *asynchronous*.

Asynchronous Communication

In asynchronous transmission, the devices are not synchronized by timing aids as they are in synchronous communication. Rather, each character (that is, each byte) is transmitted along with additional special bits that tell the receiving device how to interpret the transmission. A start bit indicates the beginning of the byte, a stop bit indicates its end, and an additional bit may be added for error detection.

Regardless of transmission type, synchronous or asynchronous, to ensure accurate reception of a stream of bytes, the receiving end has to "sample the line" at the same rate the transmitting end is sending. Sampling means detecting the signal at preset time intervals. For example, if the transmitter sends at a rate of 56,000 bits per second, the receiver must sample the transmission once every 1/56,000 of a second. If the receiver samples at a different rate, after several thousand bits the reception will be out of sequence with the transmission; the receiver will misinterpret the location and meaning of bits.

The timing of communications devices—that is, the sampling rate—can vary slightly from one machine to another, throwing off the coordination between the transmitting and receiving devices. To overcome timing differences that may arise, a start bit (a 1) is added to the beginning of the transmittal of each byte, and a stop bit (a 0) is added at the end of each byte. The start-bit signal tells the receiver to realign with the transmitter. At worst, sampling rate differences between the parties will be very small, too small to disrupt smooth communication. Realigning at the beginning of each byte ensures that the sampling gap never becomes so large that the receiving device misses an entire bit. Still, we call this type of data communication **asynchronous,** because transmission and reception are synchronized only at the byte level, not for every single bit.

Sometimes, power brownouts or other mishaps may disrupt a connection, resulting in unintended addition or loss of bits. **Parity check** is an error-detection method used to assure that no bits are added or deleted during transmission. Parity checks eliminate a lot of errors in telecommunication but not all.

The advantage of asynchronous transmission is that it does not require sophisticated and expensive timing hardware. The disadvantage of asynchronous transmission is its high *overhead,* or time spent transmitting bits that are not a part of the primary data (the "start," "stop," and "parity check" bits).

Synchronous Communication

The use of timing devices in **synchronous** transmission allows several bytes to be transmitted without the great overhead of start, stop, and parity check bits for each byte. The basic unit transmitted is called a *packet*, rather than a single byte (see Exhibit 800.63). A **packet** is a group of bytes transmitted together with no overhead bits added between them, although some precede and follow the packet. As indicated in Exhibit 800.63, a single message consists of several streams of bits that make up synchronization bytes ("sync bytes," to announce the beginning and end of an entire packet), a packet, and error check bits. Each of the message's packets is passed from the source computer to the destination computer, often through intermediate nodes. (A node is a computer or a communications device in a communications network.) At each node, the entire packet is received, stored, and then passed on to the next node, until all packets, either kept together or reassembled, reach the destination. Because overhead bits only precede and trail each packet, the overall overhead in synchronous communication is significantly smaller than in asynchronous communication.

Channels and Media

A communications **channel** is the physical medium, such as telephone lines or television cables, through which data can be communicated. In our context, the term is synonymous with communications links and communications paths. The **capacity** of the channel is the speed at which data are communicated, which is also called the **transmission rate.** Capacity is measured in **bits per second** (**bps**); the greater the capacity, the faster the transmission. As is often the case, communications speed, also called *channel capacity* and *bandwidth*, is a limited resource. The greater the speed, the higher the cost of the communications line. Thus, determining the type of communications lines to install or subscribe to is an important business decision.

Channel Capacity

When the channel is of small capacity, it is said to be **narrow band.** (Media with the lowest capacity—such as copper telephone wires—are considered to have **baseband** capacity.) When a channel has great capacity and can carry several streams of data simultaneously, it is said to be **broadband.** For example, copper wire telephone lines are a baseband medium that cannot transmit effectively at speeds of more than 56,000 bps and, even at this speed, only for short distances, unless special software is used. Other specially treated, or "conditioned," telephone lines can handle greater capacities. Of course, you can force your computer to deliver signals into the line at a higher rate, but the destination will receive a garbled message.

Exhibit 800.63 *Synchronous Transmission*

| Sync Byte | Sync Byte | Error Check Bits | Packet | Sync Byte | Sync Byte | → |

Media

A channel is also called a **medium,** but not every medium requires a physical line. A medium is anything through which data are transmitted. In the examples of channel capacity, a *guided medium,* the hose, carried the first transmission. An *unguided medium,* air (which has no physical channel), carried the second transmission. Another example of unguided media is outer space. Unguided media allow wireless telecommunications, which is so important for businesspeople outside the office; however, as you will see later, it is also useful in computer networks inside offices.

Transmission Speeds

A medium's capacity is determined by the maximum number of bits per second that it can carry. You should remember, though, that the number of signals per second is not always equal to the number of bits per second. Sometimes one signal can represent two or more bits. The number of signals per second is called **baud.** If the baud rate is 28,800 and each signal represents two bits, then the bps rate is 57,600.

The bit rate of any communication should be chosen on the basis of the distance over which it must be carried, because the greater the distance, the less clear the signal. Therefore, the farther a signal must travel, the more slowly it must be transmitted in order to be received correctly. To illustrate, consider the flashlight example again. If your friend is standing nearby, she can easily detect the flashes of light. But if she is standing at a great distance, she cannot detect the bursts of light; the signals will blur. Even sending the bursts more slowly (at greater intervals) will not help. Signals become weaker as the distance they travel gets longer. The signals will be too weak to be perceived unless you use a repeater—such as a reflector—to capture the signal and retransmit it at its original strength. A **repeater** receives and strengthens signals and then sends them on the next leg of their journey.

The many different media—including twisted pair, coaxial cable, microwaves, and optical fibers—vary in a number of ways: how much information they can carry, what their vulnerability to corrupting interference is, what they cost, whether they guide the data, and how readily available they are (see Exhibit 800.64).

Twisted Pair

The most pervasive and commonly available communications network is the telephone network. Telephones are connected either directly to a local telephone company office or to a local **private branch exchange** (**PBX**), which is connected to a telephone company office. A traditional telephone line is made of a pair of twisted copper wires that acts as a single communications link. The wires are twisted to reduce electromagnetic interference (EMI), which can alter voice and data and make them unclear.

In much of the telephone network in the United States and many other countries, copper has been replaced with higher capacity media such as optical fibers; only the line from the telephone company's office to the home or office telephone jack is still made of copper. Although the line's length varies, we often refer to that distance as "the last mile," because this is the last part of the telephone network that is still made of copper wires, and probably will stay so for many years.

Exhibit 800.64 *Characteristics of Channel Media*

Medium	Capacity	Vulnerability to Electromagnetic Interference	Cost	Guided/ Unguided	Availability
Twisted Pair	Lower	High	Lower	Guided	Everywhere
Coaxial Cable	↑	Low	↑	Guided	Low
Microwave	↓	Low	↓	Unguided	High
Optical Fiber	Higher	Nonexistent	Higher	Guided	Most of United States and parts of other countries

The rate at which digital data completes its transmittal depends on the distance it travels. When twisted pair is used for local area networks supporting personal computers, the transmission rate may reach 100 Mbps (megabits per second, or one million bits per second). The "last mile" of copper wires can be enabled to transmit digital signals at speeds up to 8 Mbps with special equipment and software both at the telephone exchange (often called "central office") and at the subscriber's end. The service is called **digital subscriber line** (**DSL**) and is provided by telecommunication companies both to businesses and households in a growing number of regions in the United States and other countries. DSL enables high speed connection to the Internet.

Coaxial Cable

Coaxial cable is sometimes called *TV cable* because of its common use for cable television transmission. Like telephone lines, it is made of two conductors but is constructed differently to permit operation over a wider range of frequencies. It consists of a hollow outer conductor and an inner wire conductor, with an insulator between them, usually of wax or plastic. The outer conductor is covered with PVC, a special plastic.

- *Twisted pairs, previously the most common telecommunications medium, are being replaced by optical fibers.*
- *Coaxial cables are used primarily for television transmission but are also used for data communications.*

Coaxial cable is significantly more expensive than twisted pair, but its transmission rate is greater. Thanks to its shielded concentric construction, coaxial cable is much less susceptible to EMI. In voice communication, it is less prone to cross talk (the intrusion of a third party's conversation on your line) than twisted pair.

In recent years the use of coaxial cable for Internet connection has been popular among households. Companies that provide cable television service use their networks to link subscribers to the Internet.

Microwaves

Microwaves are high-frequency, short radio-frequency (RF) waves. Short radio-frequency waves can carry signals over long distances with high accuracy. RF uses different waves to represent bits. You have probably noticed the ubiquitous parabolic antennas on the roofs of buildings. They are so numerous because microwave communication is effective only if the line of sight between the transmitter and receiver is unobstructed. Microwave antennas are also often installed on high buildings and the tops of mountains to obtain a clear line of sight.

- *Microwave transceivers are used by many businesses to communicate data.*
- *Low earth orbit (LEO) satellites blanket the earth to provide uninterrupted communication.*
- *Large companies lease frequencies of telecommunications satellites to transmit data coast to coast and across national borders.*

Terrestrial Microwave

Microwave communication requires far fewer repeaters and amplifiers than coaxial cable and optical fibers, for the same distance. Terrestrial microwave communication—so-called because signals are sent from and received by stations on the ground—is good for long-distance telecommunications but can also be used in local area networks in and among buildings. It is commonly used for voice and television communications.

Satellite Microwave

Signals can also be transmitted using microwaves via satellite technology. There are two major types of satellites: geostationary, also called GEO, and low earth orbit, also called LEO. Both types serve as radio relay stations in orbit above the earth that receive, amplify, and redirect signals. Microwave **transceiver** (transmitter-receiver) dishes are aimed at the satellite, which has antennas, amplifiers, and transmitters. The satellite receives a signal, amplifies it, and retransmits it to the destination.

Communications satellites are launched not only by private enterprises but also by national governments. The satellites are used for television broadcasts, long-distance telephone transmissions, and private business networks. A satellite owner can divide the frequency (that is, the band) into several channels and lease different channels to different users. Large companies, such as **Kmart** and **Wal-Mart**, have leased satellite channels. They use the links to quickly transmit business data among stores and distribution centers.

Optical Fiber

Fiber-optic technology uses light instead of electricity to represent bits. Fiber-optic lines are made of thin fiberglass filaments. A transmitter sends bursts of light using a laser or a light-emitting diode device. The receiver detects the light and samples the line to receive the data bits. Optical-fiber systems operate in the infrared and visible light frequencies. Because light is not susceptible to EMI (electromagnetic interference) and RFI (radio-frequency interference), fiber-optic communication is much less error-prone than twisted pair and radio transmission.

Optical fibers compare favorably with coaxial cable networks in providing a fast, reliable medium for telecommunications. As a result, they are rapidly replacing both twisted-pair and coaxial cable telephone lines. **Sprint Communications**, a major telephone carrier, implemented its entire network using trunk lines of optical fibers, and other carriers have followed suit. In 1991, optical fibers surpassed satellites as the dominant means for global digital network communications. Expanding fiber-optic networks and their declining prices offer great opportunities for businesses.

Modulation

Until several years ago, the most widespread communications network was a huge web of twisted-pair telephone lines designed to carry voice communication. The majority of homes and many offices still have telephone hookups suitable only for voice communication. More recently, however, business demands and technological progress have required that the same lines be used to transmit data. Unfortunately, the type of signal used to transmit voice messages—called **analog**, or continuous, signals—is not well suited to the communication of digital signals, such as data communications.

Analog Versus Digital

Exhibit 800.65 graphically represents an analog signal as a continuous series of waves and a digital signal as a series of short lines of two different heights. Analog signals transmit voice communications well: these signals are not limited to one high pitch and one low pitch but can reproduce all variations of voice, with an infinite number of pitches and sound levels over a wide continuous range. Computer data, on the other hand, is **digital** because it consists of a series of discrete bits represented by only two different states and nothing in between. Ideally, we want to transmit

Exhibit 800.65 *Signal Modulation*

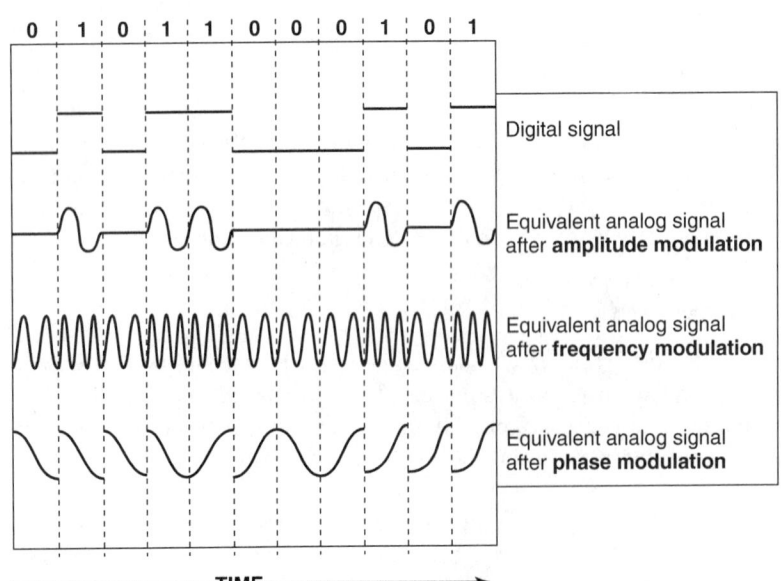

data communications over a line that can carry a digital signal. If the line can carry only analog signals, we must translate digital signals into equivalent analog signals as they pass from the computer to the analog line and then translate them back to the original digital signals just before they are transferred to the receiving computer. This modification of a digital signal (from the computer) into an analog signal (for the phone line to transmit) is called **modulation.** The transformation of an analog signal (from the phone line) into a digital signal (so the computer can understand it) is called **demodulation.** There are three different types of modulation: amplitude modulation, frequency modulation, and phase modulation.

Amplitude Modulation

An analog signal can be graphically represented as a continuous series of waves of different heights. The height of the wave is its amplitude. Amplitude modulation uses differences in amplitude to express digital signals. The 0 bits are transformed into an analog signal whose amplitude is either zero (flat) or very low. The 1 bits are transformed into a higher wave of a fixed amplitude. The two amplitudes represent the 0s and 1s of digital transmission.

Frequency Modulation

In frequency modulation, the amplitude of the wave remains constant, but variations in frequency are used to represent digital signals. Frequency is the number of waves per second. Whenever a 0 bit is transmitted, the frequency is low. Whenever a 1 bit is transmitted, the frequency is higher. The two frequencies represent the 0s and 1s.

Phase Modulation

In phase modulation, transmission always starts with a certain bit, 0 or 1. When the wave abruptly stops and immediately continues at another phase, it indicates a shift from the previously transmitted bit to the other bit, such as from 0 to 1 or from 1 to 0.

Modems

Because the telephone company's signaling is already set up for analog wave transmission, it is easier for the company to use analog rather than digital signals to send information back and forth between your telephone and the telephone company.

Much of the telephone networking in North America, Western Europe, and Japan is technically ready for digital transmission. However, modulation/demodulation devices are still needed, because the "last mile" between the telephone company's switching office and the home or office of the telephone user are made of copper wires (twisted pairs) set up for analog signals only, unless the household or business subscribes to DSL service.

A **modem**—a word contracted from *mod*ulator-*dem*odulator—is a device whose purpose is to modulate and demodulate communications signals. A modem can be internal (plugged into the computer's motherboard) or external (outside the computer, plugged into a serial port or a universal serial bus port). To use a modem, the user needs to attach it to a computer and use communications software, which is part of today's operating systems.

Modems are rated by their transmission for different speeds. Practically all new PCs come with an internal modem installed. If you want to use coaxial cable for telecommunications, you must use a cable modem (and subscribe to a cable service). Cable modems cost significantly more than standard modems because of their more sophisticated circuitry and the significantly smaller number of units sold. Subscription to DSL service requires a DSL modem, which is actually not a modem but a bridge. A **bridge** is a device that connects dissimilar networks into a seamless network. A DSL bridge enables the smooth flow of the digital signals between the computer and the "last mile" wires.

Set-Up

To set up a modem for transmission and reception, you must select the communication protocol, that is, the number of data bits in each byte, the number of start and stop bits, whether there is a parity check bit, and if so, whether it is odd or even. Operating systems contain help software, or "wizards," to help users set up their connections.

Fax/Voice

Nowadays, all PC modems are also fax-capable, that is, they allow the computer to be used as a fax machine. First the modem "digitizes" any page that needs to be faxed. Digitization is a way of "taking a picture" of a page and relaying it as an array of dots. Special software divides the page into many tiny areas. Each area is assigned a binary code that represents its location on the page and its color, or hue. This digital code is then transmitted as a stream of bits. The receiving device transforms the digitized stream and reconstructs the picture.

To receive a fax through a fax-modem, the receiving computer must be on. The received digitized page is saved in a file. Note that the fax is an *image* of the page. If a letter or other text is faxed, the digital file is *not* the ASCII code representing the characters; it is just a picture of the characters. As such, the file cannot be manipulated and edited with a word processor. Many modems also allow callers to leave voice messages, which are digitized and stored for later retrieval.

A fax-modem can transmit to a fax machine or another fax-modem only from a computer file. For example, you cannot transmit your picture via a fax-modem unless the picture is in digital form on the computer. However, you can use a scanner to scan the picture, store the scanned version in a file, and fax the file via the fax-modem.

Most modems are connected to telephone lines. More recently, cable modems have started to take advantage of the high transmission rates of coaxial cable. Cable modems are becoming increasingly popular as the use of coaxial cable for digital communication becomes more widespread, especially due to the popularity of the Web and the growing amount of data retrieved and transmitted through the Internet.

Multiplexers

Multiplexers are communications devices that allow several telephones or computers to transmit voice or digital data through a single line. Multiplexers sometimes incorporate modem technology, so the telephone line can be used to transmit data as well. The great advantage of multiplexers is cost savings. Instead of installing a line between a central computer and each terminal with which it communicates, terminals can be connected to one channel through a multiplexer (see Exhibit 800.66). Another multiplexer serves the host computer. There are two types of multiplexing: frequency division and time division.

Exhibit 800.66 *Multiplexing*

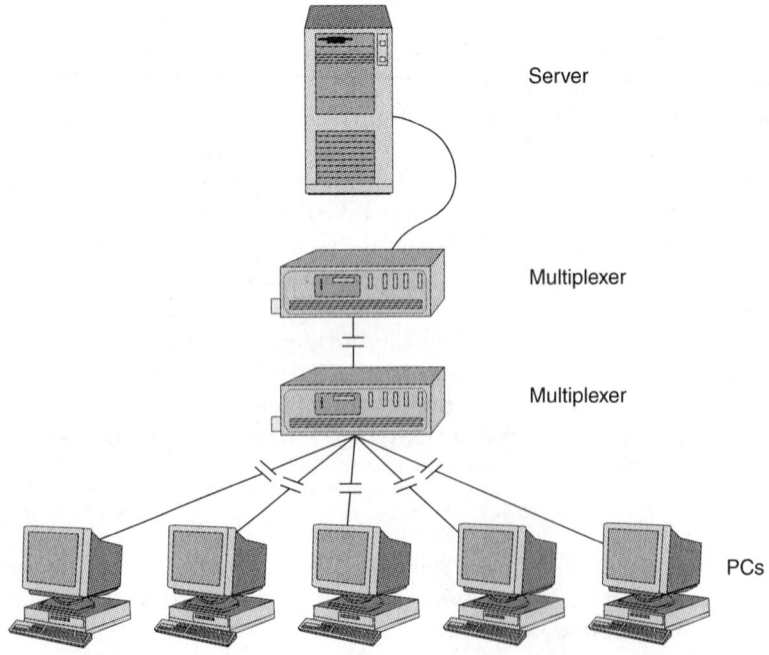

Frequency-Division Multiplexing

If the bandwidth of a carrier channel—that is, the range of frequencies it can carry—is large enough, it can be divided into several narrower bandwidths. This allows for *frequency-division multiplexing*, whereby several computers transmit data, each at its own assigned frequency, to the host computer. The multiplexer can literally transmit data from several computers at the same time. The multiplexer attached to the host computer identifies the source of the data according to its unique frequency.

Time-Division Multiplexing

Some multiplexers allocate specified equal amounts of time to each connected terminal, receiving a part of each terminal's signal at a time, in a round-robin fashion, and piecing the signals together again. This is called *time-division multiplexing* and is most commonly used by terminals interacting with a host computer.

In time-division multiplexing, each terminal is allotted its time slots whether it uses the time to communicate or not. Often, some terminals use their time slots less than others, which causes inefficient use of communication resources. A statistical multiplexer dynamically allocates time slots to those devices that need to transmit more frequently. This way, terminals that need the line more frequently can use time that would otherwise be automatically allocated to other terminals that don't need it.

Networks in Business

The key to fast and efficient telecommunications is networks. In the context of data communications, a **network** is a combination of devices (at least two computers) connected to each other through one of the communication channels just discussed. Networks in which a single host computer serves only dumb terminals (computers with no processing capability of their own) are becoming obsolete as prices of microcomputers are plummeting.

We usually refer to two types of networks: LANs (local area networks), which serve an office or several adjacent offices; and WANs (wide area networks), which are larger, national and global networks. Often, both types of networks use the same type of layout, also called **topology,** and the same types of protocols for signal transmission and reception. In such cases, the only difference between LANs and WANs is the distance between the networked computers.

Local Area Networks (LANs)

A computer network within a building, or among adjacent buildings, is called a **local area network,** or **LAN.** No specific distance classifies a network as local, but usually as long as it is confined to a radius of 3 to 4 miles, it is called a LAN. LANs, which can be hardwired or wireless, are the most common way to let users share software and hardware resources and to enhance communication among workers.

In LANs one computer is often used as a central repository of programs and files that all connected computers can use; this computer is called a server. Connected computers can store documents on their own disks or on the server, can share hardware such as printers, and can exchange e-mail.

When a LAN has a server, the server usually has centralized control of communications among the connected computers and between the computers and the server itself. Another computer or special communications device can also exercise this control. A **peer-to-peer LAN** is one in which no central device controls communications.

Although wireless LANs are still expensive, they offer significant benefits: installation is much easier because companies don't have to drill through walls to install wires, and they can move equipment wherever it is needed. Wireless networks offer significant savings in some environments. Wireless LANs are less costly to maintain when the network spans two or more buildings. They are also more scalable. **Scalability** is the ease of augmenting a system. It is relatively easy to add more nodes, or clients, to a wireless LAN. The installation of wireless LANs is expected to continue to grow significantly.

Wide Area Networks (WANs)

A network that crosses organizational boundaries or, in the case of a multisite organization, reaches outside the immediate environment of local offices and factory facilities is called a **wide area network** (**WAN**). WANs can be public or private. The Internet is an example of a public WAN. A private WAN may use either dedicated lines or very-small-aperture-terminal satellites (VSATs), which provide narrow bandwidths and are less expensive.

Many organizations cannot afford to maintain a private WAN. They pay to use existing networks, which are provided in two basic formats: common carriers or value-added networks.

A **common carrier** provides public telephone lines that anyone can access or dial up and leased lines, which are dedicated to the leasing organization's exclusive use. The user pays for public lines based on time used and distance called. **AT&T**, **WorldCom**, and **Sprint** are common carriers. Leased lines are dedicated to the lease-holder and have a lower error rate than dial-up lines, because they are not switched among many different subscribers.

Value-added networks (**VANs**) such as Tymnet and Sprintnet provide enhanced network services such as protocol conversion and error detection and correction. VANs fulfill organizational needs for reliable data communications while relieving the organization of providing its own network management and maintenance. Many businesses use VANs for their electronic data interchange (EDI) with other businesses, suppliers, and buyers. However, due to cost considerations, an increasing number of organizations prefer to conduct e-commerce via the Internet rather than through VANs. VAN services cost much more than those offered by Internet service providers.

As with LANs, **wireless communication** is being used more and more in WANs. Outfitted with a radio modem, which is a regular modem with an antenna for communicating radio signals, a user can send data on a radio frequency to a selected recipient or for Internet connection. There are no wires to connect and no telephone jacks to look for. The most visible use of wireless WANs may be with hand-held PDAs (personal digital assistants) such as Palm VII and several models of cellular phones that serve the dual purpose of a phone and an Internet-enabled PDA. Note, however, that the small screens of such units do not allow the same reception of Web pages as your PC does. The pages displayed on these devices are limited. The units are capable of sending and receiving e-mail, stock quotes, and other information, but graphic content is limited.

Network Topology

Network topology is the physical layout of nodes in a network, which often dictates the type of communications protocol used by the network. (For the sake of simplicity, we use the term *node* to denote any computer or communications device in a network.) In reality, only small LANs use a single topology. Larger networks are usually a combination of two or more different topologies. Exhibit 800.67 illustrates the main network topologies; we describe these topologies with their advantages and disadvantages.

Star

As illustrated in Exhibit 800.67, in a **star topology** all nodes connect to one central device. That device may be a file sever, a private branch exchange (PBX), or a network "hub." When the user of a node wants to transmit to another node, the communication is managed by, and transmitted through, the central device, which contains the communications software.

Star topology is the most popular network topology at present. The advantage of star topology is that it is easy to determine the source of a network problem, such as a cable failure. The main disadvantage of star topology is that if the central device is not working, the entire network is down. Another disadvantage is that adding computers can be costly, because each connected computer needs a cable to the central device. Star networks are considered more difficult to implement and maintain than the ring and bus topologies.

Ring

Exhibit 800.67 shows the **ring topology** employed in LANs. Every node connects to two other nodes through a single line: a twisted pair, coaxial cable, or optical fiber. No central computer manages communication. Usually one computer with a large storage capacity is used as a server; however, it does not control the network. Signals flow in the ring in one direction. Each node filters signals that are addressed to it from all signals. If a token ring protocol is employed, a token, which is a special byte, travels around the ring until a node wishing to send a message seizes it, launches the message to the token, and then releases the token back into the ring.

The major advantage of ring topology is its simplicity. Adding a new computer to the existing network is easy. Also, because each computer regenerates the messages that pass through it, ring networks can be deployed over larger areas than other topologies such as bus. The failure of a single node or a node connector does not affect the network. However, a failure (such as a break) of the ring cable affects the entire network.

Exhibit 800.67 *Network Topologies*

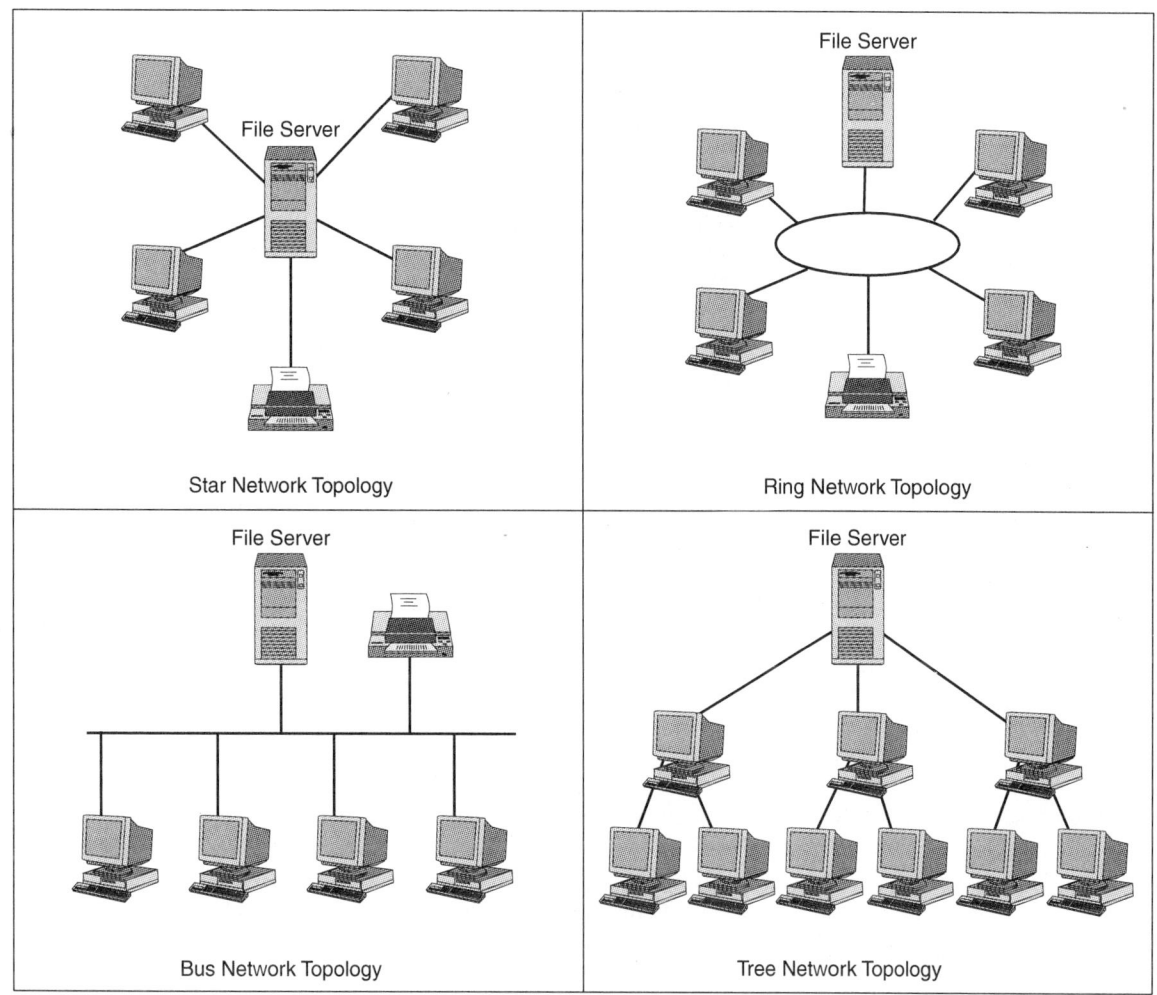

Bus

Bus topology is an open-ended ring. As Exhibit 800.67 shows, all devices connect to an open-ended line. A bus network is the simplest to design and easiest to wire. Individual nodes (such as PCs and printers) connect to a single cable using a network interface connector with a terminator at each end to prevent signal echo (signals bouncing back). When a computer transmits a signal, it is broadcast to every other node. A receiving node filters signals addressed to it from other signals. A file server is typically treated just as any other node. Individual nodes can be added. Also, branches, which are essentially also buses, can be connected to the single cable bus as long as each cable has a terminator at the end. Failure of a single node does not affect the network, but failure of the cable does affect the entire network. Bus networks do not handle high traffic as well as ring networks.

Tree

Tree topology—or hierarchical topology—consists of several stars connected to form a treelike structure. Exhibit 800.67 shows this configuration, which is typical of large computer networks. A tree lends itself to broadcasting messages in organizations because once the "root" computer launches a message, the message can be transmitted in parallel by the next layer of computers, each sending the message to several other computers. Parallel transmission is its main advantage. Its main disadvantage is that if the link of one star is disabled, all computers on that branch of the tree are disconnected from the rest of the network. The tree topology is more difficult to wire and configure than other topologies.

Virtual Private Networks (VPNs)

A LAN is a private network because it only provides access to members of an organization. When a firm leases lines, although it does not own them, the network of leased lines may be considered a private network because only members authorized by the organization can use it. In the Internet age, many companies that cannot afford a private network may create a virtual private network (VPN).

A VPN is a combination of public and private lines. To allow employees, customers, and suppliers access to its network, an organization can connect it to the largest of all public networks, the Internet. The Internet is accessible to any party. Thus, the organization need only create a link between its private network and the Internet to allow anyone it wishes to access its private network. The link between the Internet and the organization's network is often called a "tunnel," as if this is a tunnel through which travelers access the organization's territory. "Virtual" in VPN refers to the illusion that the user is accessing a private network directly, rather than through public lines. VPNs allow the use of intranets and extranets, which are discussed in the next chapter. An intranet is a network that uses Web technologies to serve an organization's employees who are located in several sites that are many miles apart from each other; an extranet also uses Web technologies but serves both the employees and other enterprises that do business with the organization. It is important to understand that once a LAN is linked to a public network, such as the Internet, technically anyone with access to the public network can obtain access to the LAN. Therefore, organizations that link their LANs to the Internet implement sophisticated security measures to control or totally deny such access.

Protocols

As discussed earlier, a communications protocol is a set of rules that govern communication between computers or between computers and other computer-related devices that exchange data. When these rules govern a network of devices, the rule set is often referred to as **network protocol**. If a device does not know what the network's agreed-upon protocol is, or cannot comply with it, that device cannot communicate on that network.

In a way, a protocol is like human language and basic understanding. Human beings make certain gestures when they start a conversation, and certain words signal its end. Each element of the language, be it English, French, or German, means the same thing to all parties who speak that language. Computers, too, need an agreed-upon set of rules to communicate.

A network protocol determines a number of factors, such as whether transmission is synchronous or asynchronous. If asynchronous, the protocol determines how many data bits and how many control bits (start bit, stop bit, and parity check bit) are transmitted at a time. Both transmitter and receiver must "understand" which stream of bits signals the beginning of the transmission and which signals the end. And, of course, both parties must transmit and receive at an agreed-upon speed. If the transmission is synchronous, a specified protocol determines for all parties features such as the number of bytes per packet and the specific header and trailer bytes.

Some communications software allows a user to establish protocols: bit rate, parity, number of data bits, stop bits, and a handshake procedure.

Before you log on to a network from your PC, you must ascertain that your communication software is set to conform with the corresponding elements of the network's protocol. If your computer is not instructed to follow the protocol, you cannot communicate on the network.

LAN Protocols

Before sending a message, a node must announce its intention and determine that the receiving node is ready. There are several methods for establishing this understanding before the actual transmission of data. The most popular methods are polling, contention, and token passing.

In **polling**, a communications processor—a special device or a host computer—conducts a continuous roll-call of the nodes. It sends an electrical pulse to each node in the network in a sequence. A node that has a message to send responds to the call. The communications processor then instructs the node to send the message. When the communication is over, polling resumes. This protocol is used in star networks.

In **contention,** each node has to contend for the line. When a node has a message to send, it checks the line. If the line is not in use, the message will be sent. Obviously, two or more nodes may start sending messages at the same time, and the messages could be garbled. To prevent this problem, a protocol called CSMA/CD (carrier sense multiple access with collision detection) is used. When a collision occurs, the communications processor stops both transmissions and forces the colliding nodes to wait for varying lengths of time. Then, the first node to seize the line transmits first.

The contention approach was first introduced by **Xerox** and subsequently adopted by **Digital Equipment Corporation** (now part of **Compaq**) and **Novell**. The design is usually referred to as **Ethernet,** the name given it by Xerox. It is typically used in bus networks.

Another popular access method is token passing. In **token passing,** a special signal is transmitted on the line by the communications processor. Usually, the signal—or token—is a byte that is not used for any other purpose. Token passing is used in both bus and ring LANs. The token may be "empty," or it may contain a message. If an empty token is received and the node wishes to transmit data, it holds the token and adds to it the destination address, its own address, and the message itself. The token is then passed on to the next node. Because the token is no longer marked as "empty," other computers cannot transmit messages at the same time. When the token is finally passed to the computer that has an address corresponding to the token's destination address, that station reads the message and then marks the token as having been read. The token is then passed on to the next node. In a ring, it continues to be passed until it completes a full circuit and reaches the originating node. At this point the message is erased, and the token is again marked as being "empty." The token then continues to travel until captured by another computer that wishes to send a message. In a bus, the procedure is similar, but the token is sent back and forth between the two farthest nodes.

WAN Protocols

Wide area network protocols are significantly more complex than LAN networks. WANs are often made up of incompatible lines, communications processors, and nodes. Also, because of the long distances between nodes, signals may deteriorate and become garbled. There are several WAN protocols. After many years of international negotiations, **Open Systems Interconnection** (**OSI**), developed by the International Standards Organization (ISO), has emerged as the dominant standard. Note that although OSI is often called a protocol, it is actually a general model for protocols.

As illustrated in Exhibit 800.68, OSI consists of seven layers. Conceptually, they operate in the following way: each computer need only concern itself with the message and identifying the receiver. The OSI views the telecommunication

Exhibit 800.68 *The Seven Layers of the OSI Model*

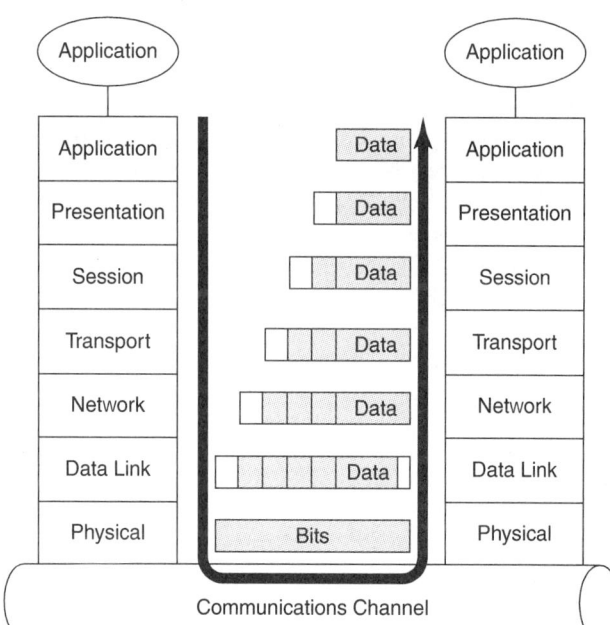

process as a layered activity, where each layer deals with another aspect of the process, and each must have a protocol in order for communication to take place. OSI establishes a protocol for each layer.

The *physical layer* protocols are concerned with the physical medium, or the channel, such as wires, radio waves, and optical fibers. This layer deals with the transmission of an unstructured stream of bits over the physical channel and the properties of the transmission. Included at this level is information about (1) the voltages used to represent a 1 and a 0, respectively, (2) the duration of bit transmission, and (3) the procedures used to maintain the channel.

The next OSI layer, the *data link layer,* takes a raw stream of bits and organizes it into frames by adding special header and trailer bits to indicate the boundaries of each frame. The data link layer transmits the message frames to the physical layer for actual transmittal over the line and provides error detection and control.

In the third layer, the *network layer,* the computer interacts with the network to specify the destination address and to request network facilities and priorities. The network layer is where switching and routing take place.

The *transport layer* provides a transparent transport of data from one computer to another, free of error or duplication. "Transparent" means that neither the user nor other layers need to be aware of error detection. This layer may also be concerned with optimizing the use of network services. At this layer, security measures are taken.

The *session layer* provides the mechanism for controlling the dialogue between the communicating systems. For example, in this layer the communication direction dialogue type is coordinated: half-duplex or full-duplex.

The *presentation layer* defines the format of the communicated data. For example, data encryption and data compression take place at this layer. Data **encryption** is the scrambling of data at the transmitting end to minimize the risk that an unauthorized party will understand it. The receiving end has the appropriate descrambling device or software. Data compression procedures allow the transmission of significantly fewer bits to convey a message. For example, instead of using five bytes for five spaces, the transmitter can send one byte for the number "five" and one byte for a "space."

The *application layer* contains management functions and useful mechanisms to support distributed applications such as file transfer, electronic mail, and node access to remote computers.

The sending and receiving ends transmit and receive data only. Senders do not have to concern themselves with anything except the message itself and the address to which they wish to send it. At each layer, special software adds a header to the message frame in the form of several special bytes. The next level adds its own header, while regarding the previous headers as part of the stream of bits. At the data link layer, in addition to a header, a trailer is added as a rear boundary of the frame. The physical layer regards the data bits, headers, and trailers as one long stream of bits. At the receiving end, each layer strips the frame off the corresponding header and trailer until the user receives a data-only message at the application layer. The other layers are transparent to users.

Switching Techniques

Imagine that your telephone could connect to only one other telephone. Of course, this limitation would render the telephone impractical. The same is true of communications when using computers. You want to be able to link your computer to every other computer on a network. Or, imagine that you can link to any other computer but you have to wait for a specific communications path to open to conduct a conversation; no other path is available to you. So you may wait a long time until no one is using any segment of that path to make your call. Obviously, this wait would be very inconvenient. To avoid such inconveniences, data communications must have mechanisms to allow your messages to be routed through any number of paths: if one is busy, then another can be used. These mechanisms, called **switching techniques,** provide answers to questions such as: Will the transmitter send its messages all at once, break them into a few large pieces, or divide them into many small pieces before sending them? Will the entire message travel the same path, or will different parts travel different paths? We examine the two major switching techniques—circuit switching and packet switching—next.

Circuit Switching

In **circuit switching,** a dedicated channel (a circuit) is established for the duration of the transmission. The sending node signals the receiving node that it is going to send a message. The receiver must acknowledge the signal. The receiving node then receives the entire message. Telephone communication is the most common type of circuit switching communication. The advantages of circuit switching are that data and voice can use the same line and that no special training or protocols are needed to handle data traffic. One disadvantage is the requirement that the communications devices be compatible at both ends.

Packet Switching

In **packet switching,** a message is divided into packets, each of which is a fixed number of bytes or a frame of a variable number of bytes. On their way to their final destination, the packets are transmitted separately to intermediate nodes. Different packets of the same message may be routed through different paths to minimize delay. This type of switching offers some advantages. Sending and receiving devices do not have to be data-rate compatible because buffers in the network may receive data at one rate and retransmit it at another. The lines are used on demand rather than being dedicated to a particular call. Packet switching lends the lines to multiplexing: a host computer can have simultaneous exchanges with several nodes over a single line. The main disadvantage of packet switching is its requirement for complex routing and control software. When the load is high, there are delays. When the network is used for voice communication, a conversation with long delays may sound unnatural, so voice communication in telephone systems uses circuit switching. The Internet is based on a packet-switching protocol called **TCP/IP** (**Transmission Control Protocol/Internet Protocol**), which is actually a set of related protocols.

Circuit switching is ideal for real-time communications, when the destination must receive the message without delay. Packet switching is more efficient, but it is suitable only if some delay in reception is acceptable. A high-level TCP/IP protocol, TCP, supports packet switching, but in a manner suitable for real-time communication: the protocol guarantees that the packets are delivered in the order they were sent and also handles differences in transmission and reception rates so that the destination receives a stream of packets without delay. This protocol, along with growing additions of high-speed media to the Internet, enables growing use of the Internet for packet-switching telephoning.

A Variety of Services

Both organizations and individuals can now choose from a variety of different options when subscribing to networking services. Technological improvements and new standards have enabled networking companies to provide high-speed lines. The proliferation of high-speed connection services, also called *broadband services*, is mainly the result of businesses' and individuals' rush to the Internet. Some of the services, such as ISDN, cable, DSL, and satellite links, are offered both to businesses and residences. Others, such as T1 and T3 lines, are offered only to businesses, largely because of their high cost. All the services except ISDN connect subscribers directly to the Internet.

Integrated Services Data Networks (ISDN)

ISDN lines transmit data at speeds up to 128 Kbps. They are available to millions of people in North America and other regions of the world. Years ago they were expected to support all the data, voice, and television communication we could possibly desire. However, as the richness and sophistication of data, voice, and television content increased, it became clear that such speeds cannot accommodate fast communication. The signals traveling in ISDN lines are digital, but the connection is circuit-switched. When using an ISDN line from home for data communications, you still need to use a modem because the "last mile" link is analog. Because of its relative slow speed now, most experts do not refer to ISDN as broadband.

Cable

Cable links are provided by television cable firms. The medium is the same as for television reception, but the firms connect the cable to an Internet server. At the subscriber's residence, the cable is split—one end is connected to the television set, and the other is connected to the computer via a bridge that is often called a cable modem. Both television transmission and data are transmitted through the same line. The cable link is always on, so the computer is constantly connected to the Internet. The subscriber does not have to dial up any telephone number. More than 90% of cable operators in the Unites States offer Internet access.

The major downside of cable is that cable nodes are shared by all the subscribers connected to the node. Therefore, at peak time, such as evening television prime time, communication speed slows down. The speed also slows down as more subscribers join the service in a given territory.

Digital Subscriber Line (DSL)

With normal telephone service, the telephone company filters information that arrives in digital form and then transforms it to analog form; thus, it requires a modem to transform the signal back to digital form. This conversion constrains the capacity of the link between your telephone (or computer) and the telephone company's switching center to a low speed of 56 Kbps (or 128 Kbps with ISDN service).

With DSL, digital data remain digital throughout their entire transmission; they are never transformed into analog signals. So, the telephone company can transmit to subscribers' computers at significantly higher speeds: up to 8 Mbps. To provide DSL service, the telecommunications company connects your telephone line to a DSL bridge (often called a DSL modem). At the telephone company's regional central office, DSL traffic is aggregated in a unit called the DSL Access Multiplexer (DSLAM) and forwarded to the Internet service provider (ISP) or data network provider with which the subscriber has a contract. As with cable connection, DSL connection is always on.

There are several types of DSL, but they can be generally placed in one of two categories: symmetric and asymmetric. *Asymmetric DSL* (*ADSL*) allows reception at a much faster rate than transmission, or in professional lingo they are faster "downstream" than "upstream." (Often, the respective terms *download* and *upload* are used.) The reason for the faster download is that home users and small businesses usually receive significantly more information (from the Web, for example) than they transmit. *Symmetric DSL* (*SDSL*) is designed for short distance connections that require high speed in both directions. Many ADSL technologies are actually RADSL (Rate Adjusted DSL) technologies; the speed is adjusted based on signal quality. Some ADSL technologies let subscribers use the same telephone lines for both Internet connection and analog voice telephone service. Symmetric DSL lines cannot share lines with telephones.

The bit rates of DSL lines are closely related to the distance of the subscriber's computer from the regional central office of the telephone company. Telecommunications companies may offer the service to subscribers as far as 20,000 feet from the central office, but the speed then is usually not faster than 144 Kbps. Some companies do not offer the service if the subscriber's address is not within 15,000 feet of the central office.

T1 and T3 Lines

A T1 line is a point-to-point dedicated digital circuit provided by telephone companies. It is made up of 24 channels (groups of wires) of 64 Kbps each. T3 lines are similar to T1 lines but made up of 672 channels of 64 Kbps. T1 and T3 lines are expensive. Therefore, only businesses that must rely on high speeds are willing to accept the high cost of subscribing to the service. Most universities use T1 lines for Internet connection.

Satellite

Households in rural areas and other regions that cannot obtain the preceding services may be able to obtain satellite services. In fact, satellite service providers target these households. The service provider installs a dish antenna that is tuned to a communications satellite. Satellite connection may reach a speed of 45 Mbps.

Fixed Wireless

Another alternative for households and small businesses that cannot obtain cable or DSL connections to the Internet is fixed wireless. Fixed wireless is point-to-point transmission between two stationary devices, as opposed to mobile wireless, in which people carry a mobile device. Companies such as **WorldCom**, **Sprint**, and **AT&T** offer the service. They install microwave transceivers on rooftops instead of laying physical wires and cables. Subscribers connect their computers to the rooftop transceiver. They can communicate at speeds up to 2 Mbps. Repeaters are installed close to each other to enhance the signal, which can deteriorate in the presence of buildings, trees, and foul weather. Transmission rates depend on the distance between the receiver and the base station. Up to nine miles from the base station, the speed is 100 Mbps; speeds drop to about 2 Mbps at 35 miles from the base.

Fixed wireless is highly modular—the telecommunications company can add as many transceivers as it needs to serve a growing number of subscribers. Unlike cable service, the company does not need franchise licenses. Only 3% of U.S. commercial buildings have a fiber-optic connection, but almost anybody in an area served by fixed wireless can install a transceiver on the roof. This potential attracts telecommunications companies to the fixed wireless market.

Gigabit Ethernet

The latest development in high-speed Internet access for businesses is gigabit Ethernet, a communications standard that until recently was used only for the backbones of networks, including the Internet and LANs. With this technology, the telecommunications company connects an existing office network directly to a fiber-optic line outside the office at a high speed of 1 Gbps. Because Ethernet technology has been around for many years, the hardware (such as routers and switches) is relatively inexpensive, and network administrators know how to maintain it. It may take several years, though, until gigabit Ethernet becomes a viable option.

The Changing Business Environment

In addition to understanding the technical foundations of telecommunications, you need to understand its continuing impact on business operations. The same technologies that have served us so well for voice and television communications also serve us for data communications. In fact, we no longer refer to telephone numbers for telephony only, nor do we use Internet links for data communications only. The lines of *uses* are blurred, and now we simply speak of telecommunications, regardless of form. But to get a comprehensive grasp of the effect of telecommunications on day-to-day business operations, we must include in our "portfolio" all technologies that facilitate telecommunications. Therefore, we now turn to a discussion of some of the technologies most commonly used in business today.

Cellular Phones

Cellular phones derive their name from the territories of service providers, which are divided into areas known as cells. Each cell has at its center a computerized *transceiver*, because it both transmits signals to another receiver and receives signals from another transmitter. When a call is placed on a cellular phone, the signal is first transmitted to the closest transceiver, which sends a signal that dials the desired phone number. If the receiving telephone is not in the same cell as the sending phone, a series of transceivers receive and retransmit the message until it reaches the destination phone. Communication takes place between the cellular phone and the receiving party through the transceivers. As the user moves from one area, or cell, to another, other transceivers pick up the transmission and receiving tasks.

Millions of people use cellular phones: as long as a cellular service is available, people can transmit and receive calls anywhere, freeing them from a fixed office location. Cellular phones can also be used for e-mail and faxing, and some are designed to enable use of the Web. "My car is my office" is a reality for many managers who spend much of their time traveling. As technology advances, we will soon be able to say "My pocket is my office."

Videoconferencing

Until recently, when managers from two remote sites wanted to confer in person, they had to travel to a meeting place. Now, people sitting in conference rooms thousands of miles apart are brought together by their transmitted images and speech in what is called videoconferencing.

Videoconferencing saves travel costs and the time of highly salaried employees, whether they work in different organizations or in different sites of the same organization. From national and global perspectives, videoconferencing also reduces traffic congestion and air pollution.

Voice Mail

Virtually every personal computer can be equipped with hardware and software that allows its user to transmit and receive voice mail. Many PCs are sold with the appropriate software already installed. Everyone is familiar with the basic idea of voice mail. With PC-based voice mail, a telephone line is connected to a modem, which in turn is connected to a PC. When a person calls the line and leaves a voice message, the message is translated into bytes and stored on the PC. Then, the voice-mail file can be retrieved and played through the PC's speakers. Alternatively, the voice-mail file can be accessed by calling the PC again and listening to the stored message over the phone. Voice mail has largely replaced answering machines in the business environment. Digitized messages are significantly clearer than those recorded on tape.

Facsimile

Facsimile (from the Latin word for duplicate), or fax, is the transmission and reception of images over telephone lines. As we discussed with fax/modems earlier in the chapter, a fax machine digitizes an image and transmits the representative bits to a receiving fax machine. The receiving machine converts the digitized codes back into an image. The great advantage of using fax machines is their ability to transmit original documents, both text and images, without first converting them into a computer file. Fax machines also provide an easy means of communicating graphical images. Virtually every modem offered on the market now is a fax/modem.

Web-Based Electronic Commerce

Fast digital communication enables millions of organizations to conduct business using the Web. Whole industries, such as online exchanges and auctions, have been created thanks to the Web. Some technologies, such as electronic data interchange, are migrating to the Web.

Business Information Systems

Information Systems in Business Functions

Effectiveness and Efficiency

The telephones at the offices of **Capital One Financial Corp.**, a leading credit-card issuer, ring more than a million times per week. Cardholders call to ask about their balance or to ensure that the company received their recent payment. While callers almost immediately hear a human voice at the other end, computers actually do the initial work. The computers use the caller's telephone number to search the company's huge databases. Inferring from previous calls and numerous recorded credit-card transactions of the caller, the computers predict the reason for calling. Based on the assumed reason, the computers channel the call to one of 50 employees who can best handle the situation. On the computer monitor of that employee, the computers bring up important information about the caller. Although callers usually do not contact the company to make purchases, the computer also brings up information about what the caller may want to purchase. As soon as the customer service representative provides the caller with satisfactory answers, he or she also offers the cardholder special sales. Many callers do indeed purchase the offered merchandise. All of these steps—accepting the call, reviewing and analyzing the data, routing the call, and recommending merchandise—take the computers a mere one tenth of a second.

It is often said that the use of information technology makes our work more effective, more efficient, or both. What do these terms mean? **Effectiveness** defines the degree to which a goal is achieved. Thus, a system is more or less effective depending upon (1) how much of its goal it achieves and (2) the degree to which it achieves better outcomes than other systems do.

Efficiency is determined by the relationship between resources expended and the benefits gained in achieving a goal. Expressed mathematically,

$$\text{Efficiency} = \frac{\text{Benefits}}{\text{Costs}}$$

Thus, one system is more efficient than another if its operating costs are lower for the same or better quality product, or if its product's quality is greater for the same or lower costs. The term productivity is commonly used

Exhibit 800.69 *Information Technology Supports a Variety of Business Functions*

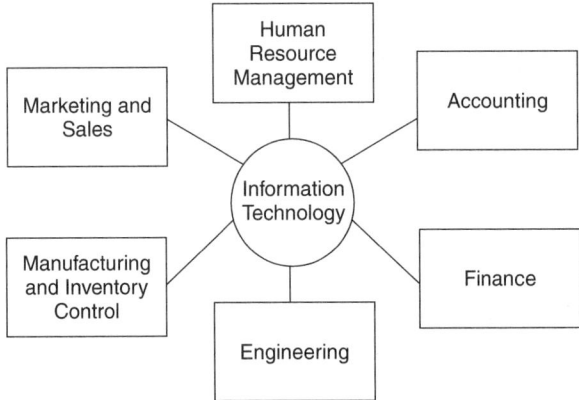

as a synonym for efficiency. However, **productivity** specifically refers to the efficiency of *human* resources. Productivity improves when fewer workers are required to produce the same amount of output, or, alternately, when the same number of workers produces a larger output. This is why IS professionals often speak of "productivity tools," which are software applications that help workers produce more in less time. The closer the result of an effort is to the ultimate goal, the more effective the effort. The fewer the resources spent on achieving a goal, the more efficient the effort.

Suppose your goal is to design a new car that reaches a speed of 60 miles per hour in 10 seconds. If you manage to build it, then you produce the product effectively. If the car does not meet the requirement, your effort is ineffective. If your competitor makes a car with the same features and performance but uses fewer people and fewer other resources, then your competitor is as effective but more efficient than you.

ISs contribute to both the effectiveness and efficiency of businesses, especially when positioned in specific business functions, such as accounting, finance, and engineering, and when used to help companies achieve their goals more quickly by facilitating collaborative work (see Exhibit 800.69). ISs can be used in a wide variety of applications. They can automate manual processes, such as painting cars; they can make innovative products and services accessible, such as Web-based customer service available 24 hours per day, 365 days per year; they can shorten routine processes, such as issuing purchase orders; and they can improve an organization's strategic position, such as establishing a Web site for selling products directly to consumers before the competition does.

This section discusses how ISs have changed the most common business functions. The discussion addresses the role of information systems, one business function at a time. Organizing the information this way does not take full advantage of IT, but most businesses do operate many ISs separately: one for engineering, one for marketing, one for finance, and so on. Usually, they do this because systems developed at different times for different business functions are often incompatible in hardware, software, data sharing, and the like. However, business functions do, in fact, have substantial information interdependencies. Systems thinking tells us that, ideally, ISs supporting different functions would connect so that information from one system flows into another accurately and without delay. For example, a business can develop information from market research to define design requirements for products, and the sales force can then use the information to sell the products.

Exhibit 800.70 illustrates how information systems commonly used in various business functions can be interdependent. Organizations that have the opportunity to create systems from the ground up try to implement this model. However, ISs have typically evolved independently for each business function in organizations. Companies whose systems have operated separately for years often opt to replace them with an integrated enterprisewide IS.

Accounting

The purpose of accounting is to track every financial transaction within a company, from dollar to multimillion dollar purchases, from salaries to benefits, to sales of every item. Without tracking the costs of labor, materials, and purchased services using a cost-accounting system, a company may discover too late that it sells products below what it costs to

Exhibit 800.70 *Information Systems in Different Business Functions Are Interdependent*

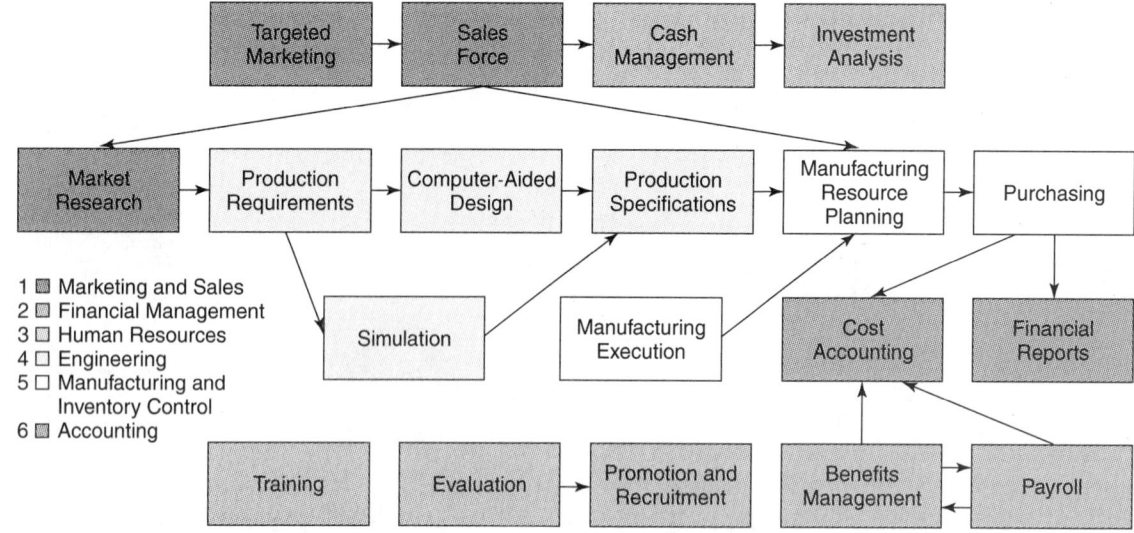

make them. Without a system of accounts receivable, managers may not know who owes the company how much money and when it is due. Without an accounts payable system, managers cannot know how much money the company owes each supplier and when payment is due. Without a system that records and helps plan cash flow, managers cannot keep enough cash in the bank to make payments on schedule. At the year's end, the company cannot present a picture of its financial situation—called a balance sheet—and an income statement, unless it maintains a general ledger to record every transaction with a financial impact.

Accounting was among the earliest business functions to embrace IT. Virtually all businesses in the industrialized world use IT for accounting. General ledger, accounts receivable, accounts payable, and cash-flow books conveniently lend themselves to computerization and can easily generate balance sheets and income statements from records. There are also systems to manage capital investments (see Exhibit 800.71).

Typically, accounting ISs receive records of routine business transactions—such as the purchase of raw materials or services, or the sale of manufactured goods—from transaction processing systems (TPSs). The system automatically routes every purchase of raw materials or services to the accounts payable system, which uses it to produce checks. Then a program reconciles checks against the company's bank account. Whenever a sale is recorded, the transaction is routed to the accounts receivable system (which generates invoices) and other destinations. Totals of accounts receivable and accounts payable can be automatically transferred to a balance sheet. Data from the general ledger can be automatically compiled to generate a cash-flow report or an income report for the past quarter or year. Accounting ISs can generate any of these reports on demand, as well as at scheduled times.

When a company develops and manufactures a new product that has never been available on the market, how can it determine a price that covers costs and generates a decent profit? It must maintain a system that tracks the costs of labor, materials, consulting fees, and every other expense related to the product's development and manufacture. Cost-accounting systems, used to accumulate data about costs involved in producing specific products, make excellent use of IT to compile pricing data. ISs also help allocate costs to specific work orders. A work order is an authorization to perform work for a specific purpose. When interfaced with payroll and purchasing ISs, a cost-accounting system automatically captures records of every penny spent (and originally recorded in the payroll and purchasing systems) and routes expenses to the appropriate work order. Because work orders are associated with specific products and services, the company now knows how much each product or service costs.

Accounting ISs are also used extensively for managerial purposes, assisting in organizing quarterly and annual budgets for departments, divisions, and entire corporations. The same systems help managers control their budgets by tracking income and expense in real time and comparing them with the amounts predicted in the budget.

Widespread use of accounting ISs placed new demands on auditors, certified public accountants hired by shareholders to verify that an organization's accounting books reflect true financial information. Electronic accounting systems created a new specialty called **information systems audit,** which ensures that electronic systems comply with standard regulations and acceptable rules, and that systems cannot be manipulated to circumvent these principles.

Exhibit 800.71 *Accounting Information Systems*

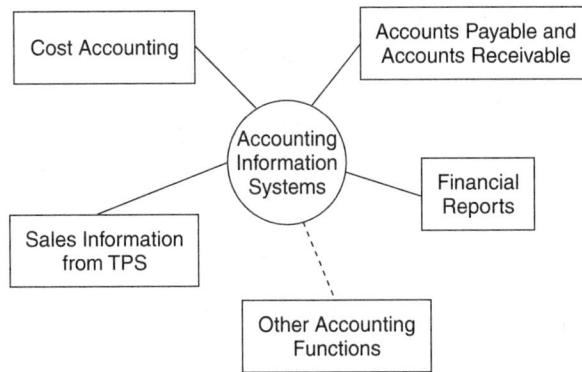

(Accounting information systems include features that reflect up-to-date performance of the organization in financial terms.)

Exhibit 800.72 *Financial Information Systems*

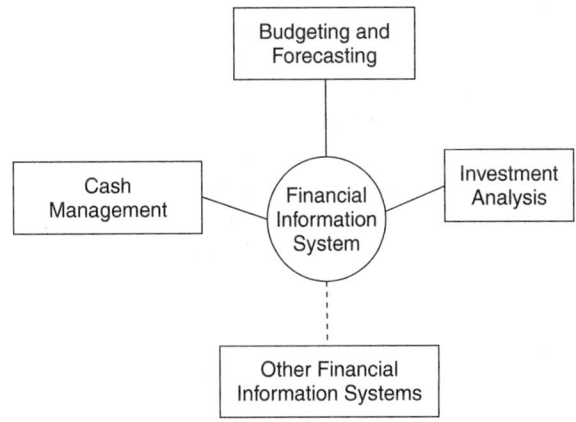

(Financial information systems help manage cash and investment portfolios.)

Finance

A firm's health is often measured by its finances, and ISs can significantly improve financial management (see Exhibit 800.72). The goal of financial managers, including controllers and treasurers, is to manage an organization's money as efficiently as possible. They achieve this goal by (1) collecting payables as soon as possible, (2) making payments at the latest time allowed by contract or law, (3) ensuring that sufficient funds are available for day-to-day operations, and (4) taking advantage of opportunities to accrue the highest yield on funds not used for current activities. These goals can be best met by careful cash management and investment analysis and service.

Cash Management

Financial information systems help managers track a company's finances. These systems record every payment and cash receipt to reflect cash movement, employ budgeting software to track plans for company finances, and include capital investment systems to manage investments, thus balancing the need to accrue interest on idle money against the need to have cash available. Systems that deal specifically with cash are often called **cash management systems** (**CMSs**). One common use for a CMS is to execute cash transactions in which financial institutions transfer huge amounts of money using **electronic funds transfer** (**EFT**). EFT is the electronic transfer of cash from an account in one bank to an account in another bank.

A growing number of companies (and individuals) do their banking through the Web: applying for credit, paying bills, transferring funds from one corporate account to another, and executing other common banking operations. Online banking saves time by reducing the time financial managers spend on the phone and in face-to-face visits with bank officers. Observers expect the number to grow in the near future.

Investment Analysis and Service

Every investor's goal is to buy an asset and later sell it for more than it cost. When investing in securities, such as stocks and bonds, it is important to know the prices of securities in real time, that is, "right now." The ability of financial ISs to record millions of security prices and their changes over long time periods, coupled with the ability to manipulate numbers using software, puts powerful analysis tools in investment managers' hands. Within seconds, an investment analyst can use a financial IS and chart prices of a specific stock or bond over a given period and then build models to estimate what may happen to stock prices in the future.

ISs can also be used to transmit buy and sell orders through communications lines in a matter of seconds. Even the smallest investment firm can inexpensively provide clients with detailed statements listing the stocks they own (called a portfolio), periodic yield, and the portfolio's current value, with the system performing all calculations. The Web allows brokerage houses and investment firms to let clients view their account positions and outstanding transaction orders directly online, which makes these companies' services not only better but also more efficient. Companies and individuals can conduct their own stock trading (buying and selling) via the Web, saving the time and money involved in using the telephone.

Some financial services would simply be impossible without IT. Consider the money-market accounts millions of businesses use to manage investments. These businesses can invest extra cash in securities only because all records are connected through an IS, so that any amount of investment can be liquidated by simply writing a check. The managing bank redeems an amount of securities held in the company's account to cover the check. The system can also automatically generate a combined statement of deposits, investments, and liquidations. Without ISs and telecommunications networks, this transaction would take days rather than seconds, as it indeed did until the late 1970s.

Within seconds, ISs now provide subscriber brokers with news, in addition to stock prices, commodity prices, and currency exchange rates from multiple locations across the world. Consider what happens when a foreign currency's exchange rate fluctuates a fraction of a percent. A brokerage house can make a profit of several thousand dollars within two minutes of buying and selling several million dollars' worth of the foreign currency. Information technology has enabled many smaller companies to enter the arena.

Managers at financial institutions can use three-dimensional graphs showing a "landscape" of risk, return, and liquidity of various potential investments. Managers can "fly" over the landscape and select the investment with the best trade-off of these three factors.

Financial managers need to consider many factors. In the past, evaluating more than one or two at a time was difficult. Now financial ISs provide new tools for visualizing decision-making factors in three-dimensional graphics. Managers at financial institutions such as insurance companies find these tools useful in managing their portfolios of stocks, bonds, and other commercial papers. Some of the most important factors these financiers must consider are (1) risk, measured as the variability (degree of change) of the paper's past yield, (2) expected return, and (3) liquidity, a measure of how fast an investment can be turned into cash. Special programs help calculate these factors and present the results either in tables or graphs.

Engineering

The time between generating an idea for a product and completing a prototype that can be mass-manufactured is devoted to engineering and is known as engineering lead time, or **time-to-market.** Engineering includes brainstorming, developing a concept, creating mock-ups, building prototypes, testing, and other activities that require investments of time, labor, and money. Minimizing this time is key to maintaining a competitive edge: it leaves competitors insufficient time to introduce their own products first. Changes over the past two decades in the automotive industry indicate how ISs can contribute significantly to this effort. Over the past decade, automakers have used ISs mostly in engineering to reduce the time from product concept to market from seven to two years.

Computer-aided design systems significantly shorten the time needed to produce drawings and complete the design of new products.

IT's greatest contribution to engineering is in the area of **computer-aided design** (**CAD**) and **rapid prototyping** (creating one-of-a-kind products to test design in three dimensions). Instead of using the traditional paper and pencil, engineers and technicians can use computers to quickly modify and store drawings electronically. With groupware software, they perform much of this process in collaboration: engineers can conduct remote conferences while viewing and developing plans and drawings together. Sophisticated systems then allow manufacturing departments to feed the data of the electronic drawings into **computerized numeric control** (**CNC**) machines that take the data and create instructions that tell robots how to manufacture and assemble prototypes. Ultimately, engineers can design the manufacturing process directly from the original drawings, a process that was enormously time-consuming in the past.

Manufacturing and Inventory Control

Manufacturing is the processing of raw materials into physical products. Manufacturing is more complex to manage than most services because, in addition to customers and personnel, it involves elements with which the service sector does not deal: purchasing and warehousing raw materials and running production and assembly lines. Probably the most important IT achievement in manufacturing is improved agility, which is a company's ability to adjust its manufacturing process in real time to meet both market and manufacturing demands. ISs have been instrumental in reducing manufacturing costs, including the costs of managing resources and controlling inventory (see Exhibit 800.73).

Information technology helps in the following manufacturing activities.

- Scheduling plant activities, optimizing the combined use of all resources: machines, personnel, tooling, and raw and interim materials
- Planning material requirements based on current and forecasted demand
- Reallocating material rapidly from one order to another, to satisfy due dates
- Letting users manage inventories in real time, taking into consideration demand and the responsiveness of all work centers
- Grouping work orders by "characteristics" of items ordered, such as color and width of products
- Considering the qualifications of each resource (such as qualified labor, set-up crews, and specialized tools) to accomplish its task

For instance, people and raw materials can be moved from one plant to another to respond to machine breakdown or customer emergency, and design changes can be implemented quickly to respond to changes in customer wishes.

Materials Requirement Planning

One area of manufacturing that has experienced the greatest improvement from IS is inventory control, or **materials requirement planning** (**MRP**). Traditional inventory control techniques operated according to the

> MRP systems help reduce inventory cost while ensuring availability.

Exhibit 800.73 *Manufacturing and Inventory Control Information Systems*

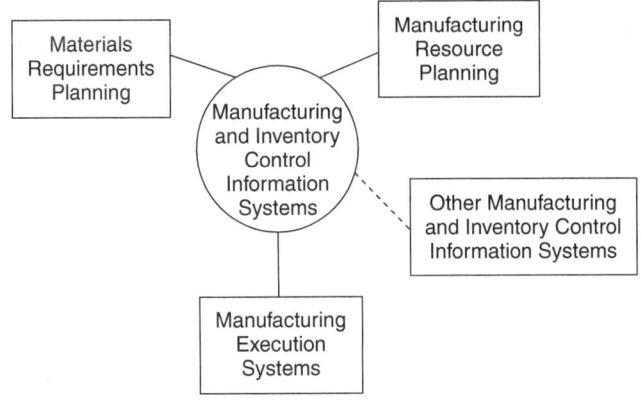

(Manufacturing and inventory control information systems help reduce cycle times and the cost of maintaining inventory.)

865. BUSINESS INFORMATION SYSTEMS

basic principle that future inventory needs are based on past use: once used up, inventory was replaced. By contrast, replenishment in MRP is based on future need, calculated by MRP software from demand forecasts. MRP programs take customer demand as their initial input. The main input to MRP programs is the number of product units needed and the time at which they are needed; the programs then work back to calculate the amounts of resources required to produce subparts and assemblies. The programs use long-range forecasts to put long-lead material on order.

Other important input to MRP applications includes a list of all raw materials and subcomponent demands (called the **bill of materials,** or **BOM**) and the economic order quantity of different raw materials. The **economic order quantity (EOQ)** of a specific raw material is the optimal quantity that allows a business to minimize overstocking and save cost, without risking understocking and missing production deadlines. A special program calculates EOQ. It considers several factors: the item's cost, the discount schedule for large quantities, the cost of warehousing ordered parts, the cost of alternate uses of the money (such as the interest the money could earn had it not been spent on inventory), and other factors affecting the cost of ordering the item. Some MRP applications are tied to a purchasing IS, to automatically produce purchase orders when the quantity on hand reaches a reorder level. The purchase order includes the economic order quantity.

Manufacturing Resource Planning

Manufacturing resource planning (**MRP II**) combines MRP with other manufacturing-related activities to plan the entire manufacturing process, not just inventory. MRP II systems can quickly modify schedules to accommodate orders, track production in real time, and fix quality slippage. The most important input of MRP II systems is the **master production schedule** (**MPS**), which specifies how production capacity will be used to meet customer demands and maintain inventories. Virtually every report an MRP II package generates starts with, or is based on, the MPS. Purchases of materials and internal control of manufacturing work flow, for example, start with the MPS, so the MPS directly affects operational costs and asset use.

MRP II systems help balance production economies, customer demands, manufacturing capacity, and inventory levels over a planning horizon of several months. Successful MRP II systems have made a significant contribution to **just-in-time** (**JIT**) manufacturing, where suppliers ship parts directly to assembly lines, saving the cost of warehousing raw materials, parts, and subassemblies.

MRP II systems help manage production and assembly lines and reduce manufacturing costs.

Ideally, the ISs of manufacturing organizations and their suppliers would link in a way that makes them subsystems of one large system. The MRP II application of an organization that manufactures a final product would plan and dictate the items required, their quantities, and the exact times they are needed at the assembly lines. Suppliers would ship items directly to assembly lines just before they are incorporated into the final product (hence the term *just-in-time manufacturing*). Manufacturing organizations have not yet reached the point where JIT is accomplished with every product, but they have made great progress toward this ideal.

Manufacturing Execution Systems

MRP and MRP II systems are designed to *plan* for manufacturing, not control it. That is, they are fed information on the current situation: expected demand, EOQs, and the production capacity of each machine in the production line. But some of the current situation can still be improved. The production manager should ask: Is the maximum capacity of Machine A really just x units per month? What are the bottlenecks in the line? **Manufacturing execution systems** help answer these questions. Their purpose is to track, schedule, and control manufacturing processes. These systems collect data such as the number of hours the machine operates every day of the month, the number of hours the machine lies idle, and the reasons. Analyzing this data can pinpoint problems that can sometimes be easily resolved.

Marketing, Sales, and Customer Service

No commercial organization can survive without selling its products or services. Thus, businesses seek to provide products that consumers want and to entice them to buy what they produce. They exert marketing efforts to pinpoint demographic groups that are most likely to buy products, to determine features that consumers desire most, and to provide the most efficient and effective ways to execute a sale when a consumer shows interest in the product or service. Because these efforts depend mainly on the analysis of huge amounts of data, ISs have become key tools to con-

Exhibit 800.74 *Marketing Information Systems*

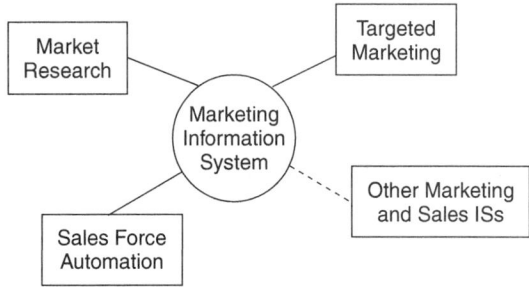

(Marketing and sales information systems help target potential buyers and serve clients.)

ceiving and executing marketing strategies. When marketing succeeds, ISs support the sales effort; to entice customers to continue to purchase, ISs support customer service (see Exhibit 800.74).

Market Research

Few organizations can sell their products and services without promotion; fewer still can promote successfully without market research. Market research systems help to find the populations and regions that are most likely to purchase a new product or service. They also help analyze how a new product fares in its first several months on the market.

Through interviews with consumers and retailers, market researchers collect information on what consumers like and dislike about products. When the researchers collect sufficient data, the marketing department uses statistical models to predict sales volumes of different products and of different designs of the same product. This critical information aids in planning manufacturing capacities and production lines. It is also extremely important for budgeting purposes.

Many companies have enthusiastically embraced the opportunity to collect consumer data via the Web. Consumers provide valuable personal data in return for Web-based services or participation in sweepstakes. Special software programs track and record the click stream (the sequence of mouse clicks a person executes when browsing a site) of online shoppers. The advantage of this data collection method is not only its low cost but also its electronic form. Records are automatically routed into databases, from which they are later retrieved for analysis.

Targeted Marketing

To save resources, businesses use IT to promote to people most likely to purchase their products (called **targeted marketing**). Great advances in database technology enable even the smallest and poorest business to use targeted marketing. The principle of targeted marketing is to define the prospective customer as accurately as possible and then to direct promotional dollars only to those people most likely to purchase your product. Perhaps the best evidence of how much companies use ISs for targeted marketing is the huge amount of promotional mail—usually called "junk mail"—we receive daily. While many people hate to receive junk mail, commercial organizations know that it is one of the least costly and most effective means to market their products and services. Many organizations also use the Internet for mass communication of their promotional e-mail, in a practice called "spamming." Many people loathe spamming, but it is certainly one of the least expensive methods of advertising.

To define their target, businesses collect data everywhere they can: from sales transactions and warranty cards, or by purchasing databases with information about organizations and individuals. Using database management systems (DBMSs), special programs to build and manipulate data pools, a company can sort and categorize names by age, gender, income, previous purchase of a related product, or any combination of these facts and other demographic information. The company then selects those whose characteristics match the company's customer profile and spends its promotional dollars to try to sell to those select customers.

The great amount of personal information that corporations collect and purchase lets them prepare electronic dossiers on the interests, tastes, and buying habits of individuals. The information they possess lets them target "a market of one," namely, an individual rather than a group. Some marketing experts like to call this 1:1 (one-to-one) marketing. Because obtaining and manipulating the information has become so inexpensive, and the marketing applications so affordable, targeting "a market of one" is now economical in some industries, especially financial services. In addition, software companies use information they collect from printed and online registration forms to create a profile of typical software each customer uses. They encourage customers to provide registration information to receive help, service, and, often, rebates. The vendor later sends promotional material via ground mail or e-mail only to those customers whose profiles indicate potential interest.

The Web has been used to hone this practice even further. Using special software, companies that offer shopping and related purchase services through their Web sites can track the click stream to compile a purchasing profile. Numerous online retailers use this technique to promote sales by sending e-mail to people whose shopping and purchasing profiles are a good match. Furthermore, special software presents lists of new items for sale that are generated specifically for an individual visiting the site.

Telemarketing (marketing over the telephone) makes much use of IT. The telemarketer uses a PC connected to a large database. The database contains records of potential or existing customers. With a retrieved record displayed on the screen, a marketer dials the number by pressing a single key or clicking the mouse. The telemarketer speaks to the potential buyer while looking at that person's purchasing record with the organization or even other organizations. Universities and charitable organizations use the same method to solicit donations. Although not targeted marketing, marketing via television also involves information technology. When you call to order an item that has just been advertised on your TV, a computer most likely takes your order. All you need to do is press keys on your phone, following the computer's instructions.

Computer telephony integration is a technique allowing a computer to use the digital signal coming through a telephone line as input in a computer system. It has been used often in both marketing, sales, and customer service. For example, some mail-order firms use caller ID to better serve their customers. Caller ID was originally intended to identify the telephone number from which a person calls, but mail-order businesses quickly found a new use for the gadget. They connect it to their customer database. When you call to order, a simple program searches for your number, retrieves your record, and displays it on a PC monitor. You may be surprised when the person who receives your call greets you by name and later asks if you want to use the same credit-card number you used in your last purchase.

The Computer as a Marketing and Selling Medium

For several decades, radio and television were marketing's only nonprint media. Now, the household computer has become a means of promoting products. In the mid-1980s, several companies, especially in the auto industry, started to develop disk programs with information on their products, usually called promotional disks. Companies sent the disks to previous buyers and other prospective customers to examine on their personal computers.

While some companies still mass-mail these disks, most now use the Internet for the same purpose. Users are attracted from one Web site to another through banners and icons that serve as links to other sites. E-mail messages containing attractive graphics and animations provide links to commercial Web sites. While a television commercial can keep a viewer's attention for an average of 30 seconds, Web sites keep visitors for several minutes. Also, a 30-second television commercial costs many times more than does an informative Web page laced with attractive graphics, animation, and online games.

Use of information technology for target marketing has taken the boldest forms on the Web. Special software on the servers of online retailers keeps track of every visit consumers make and captures their click streams and the amount of time they spend viewing each page. They combine this information with information from online purchases to personalize the pages whenever consumers revisit the site. The reconstructed page introduces information about the products that the individual visitor is most likely to purchase.

Another method to market online is expected to become commonplace once millions of people own devices that allow mobile Web browsing. Retailers located within your proximity may send a signal to your mobile device (which is likely to be a cellular phone that also serves as a handheld computer) and invite you to take advantage of a sales promotion.

Commercial announcements pervade the Web. Sites that have nothing to do with marketing often place advertisements for other companies for a fee. Web surfers who reach these sites cannot avoid seeing them. Interactive software lets surfers receive several levels of information on products and services and, if they wish, purchase them immediately. For a decade, PC sales have exceeded television sales and the average time spent online by Web users is increasing constantly. Marketing executives cannot ignore this great potential. The Web provides excellent marketing and sales opportunities.

Sales Force Automation

Sales force automation is equipping traveling salespeople with information technology to facilitate their productivity. Typically, salespeople are equipped with notebook computers that store promotional information for prospective customers, software for manipulating this in-

Sales force automation increases marketing and sales productivity.

formation, and computerized forms. In recent years, many salespeople started carrying handheld computers, also called palm computers. Sales force automation can increase sales productivity significantly, making sales presentations more efficient and letting field representatives close deals on the spot, using preformatted contracts and forms.

Information technology lets salespeople present different options for products and services on the computer, rather than asking prospective customers to wait until the main office faxes or mails the information. At the end of the day or the week, salespeople can upload sales information to a computer at the main office, where it is raw input to the order processing department, the manufacturing unit, or the shipping and invoicing departments. In the past, transmitting such information to the office required the use of dial-up through a physical telephone line. Now, many salespeople use wireless communication, which allows them to send the information from almost anywhere.

Using personal digital assistants (PDAs) that connect to the Internet wirelessly enables salespeople to check prices, check availability of the items in which a customer is interested, and place an order away from the office. The salespeople can then spend much more time on the road, increasing time spent with prospective customers, and they can place the order faster.

Customer Relationship Management

Corporations regard customer service as an important part of their overall marketing and sales effort. With growing competition and so many options available to consumers, keeping customers satisfied is extremely important. Many executives will tell you that their companies do not make money (and may even lose money) on a first sale to a new customer because of the great investment in marketing. Thus, they use customer service and other techniques to ensure repeat sales and to encourage customer loyalty.

To better serve customers and learn of their changing needs, companies use customer relationship management (CRM) applications. The applications help track past purchases and payments, update online answers to frequently asked questions (FAQs) about products and services, and analyze customers' contacts with the company to maintain and update an electronic customer profile. As the Web evolved into an important vehicle for commercial activity, companies have endeavored to automate much of the relationship with customers so that they can help themselves, save company resources, still receive accurate answers to their questions, and obtain faster service.

Web-based customer service provides automated customer support 24 hours per day, 365 days per year. At the same time, it saves companies the cost of labor required when humans provide the same service. Letting customers pay their bills electronically also saves (both customers and companies) the cost of postage and paper and saves the company time dealing with paper documents.

Human Resources

Human resource (HR) management has become more complex due to the fast growth in specialized occupations, the need to train and promote highly skilled employees, and the growing variety of benefits programs. Human resource management can be classified into five main activities: (1) employee record management, (2) promotion and recruitment, (3) training, (4) performance evaluation, and (5) compensation and benefits management (see Exhibit 800.75).

Employee Record Management

ISs easily facilitate employee record management. Human resource departments must keep personnel records to satisfy both external regulations (such as federal and state laws) and internal regulations, as well as for payroll and tax calculation and deposit, promotion consideration, and periodic reporting. Many HR ISs are now completely digitized

Exhibit 800.75 *Human Resource Information Systems*

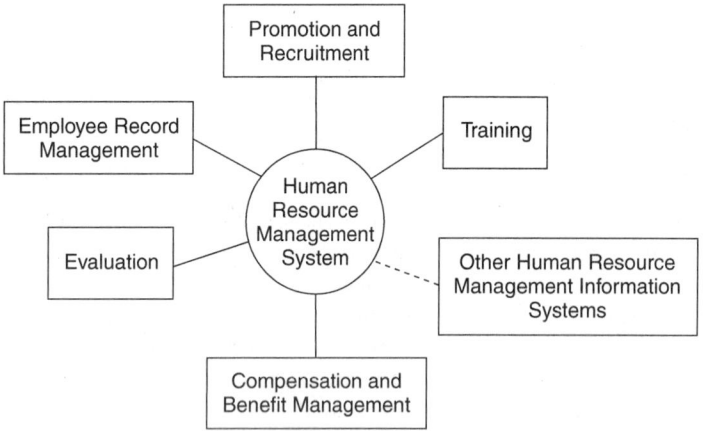

(Human resource management information systems help managers optimize the assignment of employees and provide payroll, benefits, and other employee-related services.)

(including employees' pictures), which dramatically reduces the space needed to store records, the time needed to retrieve them, and the costs of both.

Promotion and Recruitment

To select the best qualified person for a position, a human resource manager can search a database of applicants and existing employees' records for set criteria, such as a specific type and length of education, particular experience, specific talents, and required licenses or certifications. Automating the selection process significantly minimizes time and money spent on recruitment but does require that a current database be maintained.

Intranets (intraorganizational networks that support Web applications) help HR managers post position vacancy announcements for employees to peruse and consider from their own PCs. This system is especially efficient in large organizations that employ thousands of workers, and even more so at multisite organizations.

The more common way to recruit people for new positions is to communicate with the general population, for instance, through classified ads. The most dramatic development in this arena is recruiting on the Web. Search companies have set up Web sites that let potential candidates post their resumes in their databases. Using keywords, recruiting consultants can then use special software to scour the databases for the most qualified candidates. HR consultants say that this process reduces the time spent on a typical search from several hours to several minutes. The Web has prompted many companies to e-recruit, making much of the recruiting process electronic.

Training

One important function of human resource departments is improving employee skills. In both the manufacturing and service sectors, multimedia software training is rapidly replacing training programs involving classrooms and teachers. Such applications include interactive, three-dimensional simulated environments. Some applications contain full-blown virtual reality components. For example, one such application trains workers to make wrought-iron parts that must be hammered manually. The worker wears special goggles and holds a hammer in one hand and a piece of metal in the other, over an anvil. The worker "sees" the metal piece through the goggles, "hears" the hitting sound through earphones, and receives a programmed, realistic jolt every time he "hits" the metal. This safely prepares the worker for the dangerous work instead of putting him at risk for injury before he has enough experience to do the actual work. Although the initial investment in multimedia training systems may be high, human resource managers find the systems very effective.

Developments in IT enable organizations to dramatically reduce training costs.

Training software emulates situations in which an employee must act and includes tests and modules to evaluate a trainee's performance. In addition to savings in trainers' time, there are other benefits. The trainee is more comfortable because he or she controls the speed at which the sessions run. The software lets the trainee go back to a certain point in the session if a concept is missed. Also, the software can emulate hazardous situations, thereby testing employee performance in a safe environment. And if training in a real environment involves destruction of equipment or consumption of materials, virtual reality training applications accomplish the same results in skill enhancement without destruction or waste.

Performance Evaluation

One of the difficult, and often unpleasant, tasks of supervisors is the periodic evaluation of technical ability, communications skills, professional conduct, and general behavior of employees on the job. While objective factors are involved in evaluation—such as attendance rates and punctuality—employee evaluation is often very subjective. Assessing performance and effort levels, and their relative weights of importance, varies significantly, depending upon who is evaluating. A supervisor may forget to include some factors altogether or may inappropriately weigh a particular aspect of performance. Subjectivity is particularly problematic when several employees are being considered for a promotion, and their evaluations are compared to determine the strongest candidate. By helping to standardize the evaluation process across employees and departments, evaluation software adds a certain measure of objectivity and consistency.

Information systems help supervisors create accurate and thorough employee performance evaluations.

In an evaluation, a supervisor provides feedback to an employee, records the evaluation for official records and future comparison, and accepts input from the employee. Software helps managers standardize their employee evaluations by providing step-by-step guides to writing performance reviews, a checklist of performance areas to include in the evaluation (with the option to add or remove topics), scales to indicate how strong the employee is in each area, and the ability to select the relative importance each factor should hold in the overall evaluation. Performance areas include written and oral communication, job knowledge, and management skills, with each topic broken down into basic elements to assist the supervisor in creating an accurate evaluation. A typical application guides the user through all necessary factors and includes a help guide. When the evaluator finishes entering data, the application automatically computes a subtotal for each category and a weighted grade, which can then be electronically stored as part of the employee's record.

Compensation and Benefits Management

ISs help HR officers manage compensation (salaries, hourly pay, commissions, and bonuses) efficiently and effectively. Programs can easily calculate weekly, monthly, and hourly pay according to annual salaries and can include federal, state, and local tax tables to assist in complying with compensation regulations. This same system can also automatically generate paychecks or direct deposits, which are electronic transfers of funds from the firm's bank account to the employee's.

Special software helps the HR department manage benefits, such as health insurance, life insurance, retirement plans, and sick and leave days, which are determined by seniority, amounts individuals pay into programs, and other factors. To optimize benefits, some companies use special software, incorporating expert systems (ISs that emulate human expertise) that determine the optimal health and retirement plans for each employee based on factors such as marital status, age, occupation, and other data.

An employee uses an interactive benefits plan system to optimize the combination of benefits.

Using intranets, many organizations allow their employees to access the benefits database directly and make changes to their preferences, such as selecting another health-care insurance program, or adding a family member as a beneficiary in a life insurance plan. By making the changes directly from their PCs, employees reduce the amount of work of the HR staff and reduces the company's overhead costs.

Enterprise Resource Planning (ERP)

In recent years, many corporations have opted to replace their disparate ISs with a single integrated system. Rather than using an IS, or several ISs, in each business function, all business functions are served by one system that supports different activities for different departments. Such systems are often called **enterprise resource planning** (**ERP**) systems.

Although these systems do help in planning, their main focus is to help *run* the different functions. Therefore, their more accurate name is enterprise applications, but ERP is their more popular name.

Designers of ERP systems take a systems approach to an enterprise. They regard all business processes, such as purchasing, manufacturing, shipping, and billing, as a chain of main and supporting activities. The chain is often called a *supply chain*; therefore, ERP systems are said to support **supply chain management (SCM)**.

An ERP system helps manage an organization's data and information in multiple business functions.

ERP systems are quite complex. Because they are not tailored to the needs of specific clients, they often require adjustment and fine-tuning for specific businesses. Therefore, their installation and testing involve experts who are usually employees of the software vendor or professionals who are certified for such work by the vendor.

While a multimodule ERP application may cost several hundred thousand dollars, its installation and tweaking for a business's needs often costs several million dollars and takes many months to complete. Implementation of ERP systems can fail because of formidable challenges: the gap between system capabilities and business needs, lack of expertise on the consultant's part, and mismanagement of the implementation project. For example, **Hershey Foods**, the largest U.S. manufacturer of sweets, missed the great sales seasons of Halloween and Thanksgiving of 1999 because of time overruns in the implementation of a new ERP application.

Groupware and Collaborative Work

When people work together, either to provide a service or create a product, they often do so in sequence: one person provides his or her input to the project, then passes it along to another person, who does the same, and so on along a chain. A series of such repeated activities is called a **work cycle,** or simply **cycle.** Work cycles may take a long time to complete.

For instance, engineers developing a new car must wait for the body design so that they can figure how to fit in the engine and other mechanical items. Or, lawyers representing a buyer and a seller must wait for each other's modifications to a draft contract before agreeing on a final version. Almost without exception, across a full range of industries and business functions, IT can shorten cycle times and deliver products and services significantly sooner by allowing people to work together in real time rather than wait a long time for the result of their peers' work.

Software that lets users work together is called **groupware,** a term that refers to a broad and somewhat diverse collection of technologies, including group calendaring and scheduling, collaborative document handling, group application development tools, audio/video/desktop conferencing, group decision-support systems, electronic-meeting and voting systems, and work flow and group project management. ISs can help with three major types of collaborative work: document control, collaborative projects, and brainstorming.

Document Control

Business processes produce thousands of documents, many of which are repeatedly accessed worldwide and continually revised through collaborative efforts. Frequent revisions often create a problem: people inadvertently work with outdated information, unaware that revisions have been made. For instance, engineering design sheets and blueprints are updated so frequently that engineers often find themselves working with outdated plans because updated plans haven't been distributed or it's too costly to redistribute plans every time they're updated.

A project-management tool in groupware lets all connected users make changes to the same document simultaneously.

To help prevent these problems, programs like Notes and Sametime from Lotus Development let users distribute and track electronic documents containing text, graphics, and video or audio data. The latter software, available in 15 different languages, lets users chat via typed messages and share and collaborate on documents in real time. Shared documents are usually stored in a central location. Both these programs track annotations by time and source and immediately include the information in the electronic document, so that the document is current whenever accessed. This currency can be extremely important to accurate, efficient work, especially when it involves engineering.

Collaborative Projects

Managing a project—especially a large one involving many organizational units—and keeping on track requires enormous effort. Frequent phone calls must be made; a log must be kept to record progress and updates to specifications; meetings must be scheduled and decisions communicated; and documents need to be created and edited. When team members work in different locations, these tasks become even more complex, especially when architectural drawings or product specifications require approval from several team members.

Several groupware programs, such as MarkUp from Mainstay, let multiple users working on many different terminals coordinate their efforts on a single document. Keeping the original document intact, MarkUp lets workers use on-screen tools to change parts of drawings, add notes, and delete material. Another type of application maintains an unchanged original text document that each user can edit on his or her local PC. Authorized participants may permanently replace the master copy with one that includes the desired changes. Other users can then retrieve the updated document. Such applications prove extremely helpful in law offices, publishing houses, and other text-intensive environments.

Brainstorming

In business, brainstorming refers to the process of a group of colleagues meeting and working collaboratively to generate creative solutions and new ideas. Groupware software can facilitate this process and eliminate the expensive practice of bringing everyone to the same location. Groupware lets users type ideas on a "whiteboard," that is, a window that everyone can see on a monitor. People working in the same location can use the same technology as well: the "whiteboard" can be a large monitor, and participants may keep ideas and information they do not wish to share on their own computers.

Collaborative software enables two or more participants to see each other and make changes to the same text or pictures.

Ideas can be organized, reorganized, discussed, and then voted on. A major advantage of this process is that individual users can propose revolutionary ideas anonymously, motivating discussion without risking criticism. Some of the best ideas are generated using such groupware, thanks to the low-pressure environment it fosters.

Information Technology Security and Controls

Goals of Information Security

As you have already seen, the development, implementation, and maintenance of ISs constitute a large and growing part of the cost of doing business; protecting these resources is a primary concern. The increasing reliance on ISs, combined with their connection to the outside world in the form of the Internet, makes securing corporate ISs increasingly challenging. What would happen if an enterprisewide system were infected with a virus and ceased operating? What would happen if an errant employee accessed confidential data and sold them? How would illicit interception of information affect an organization that takes orders through the Internet? Needless to say, these questions highlight the potential for catastrophe if a system is not secure. The role of computer controls and security is to protect systems against these and many other mishaps, as well as to help organizations ensure that their IS operations comply with the law and with expectations of employees and customers for privacy. The major goals of information security follow.

- To reduce the risk of systems and organizations ceasing operations
- To maintain information confidentiality

Exhibit 800.76 *Common Controls to Protect Computer Systems from Risk*

- Program robustness and data entry controls
- Backup
- Access controls
- Atomic transactions
- Audit trail

- To ensure the integrity and reliability of data resources
- To ensure the uninterrupted availability of data resources and online operations
- To ensure compliance with national security laws and privacy policies and laws

These goals can be jeopardized in the ways indicated previously, perhaps most of all by the explosion of online activity over the Internet and the increasing use of intranets and extranets. To plan measures to support these goals, organizations first must be aware of the possible risks to their information resources, which include hardware, applications, data, and networks; then they must execute security measures (controls) to defend against those risks.

Controls

Controls are constraints and other restrictions imposed on a user or a system, and they can be used to secure systems against the risks just discussed or to reduce damage caused to systems, applications, and data. Exhibit 800.76 lists the most common controls.

Program Robustness and Data Entry Controls

A computer program is said to be *robust* if it is free of bugs and can handle unforeseen situations well. While programmers debate whether any software can be fully bug-free, they can develop it so that it does not lock up the computer, cause damage to files, or display dialog boxes that do not help the users fix the problem. Robust applications can resist inappropriate usage, such as incorrect data entry or processing. An application can be written with different levels of robustness, depending on the developers' expectations about the way the program will be used. The least robust program assumes that the user is experienced and will enter only parameters that are expected of him or her. The most robust program considers every possible misuse or abuse. A highly robust program includes code that promptly produces a clear message if a user either errs or tries to circumvent a process.

For example, a system programmed to accept telephone numbers may have a number of controls built into it. Let's say the phone numbers should be input only in a certain format, such as 10 digits (3-digit area code followed by 3-digit exchange and 4-digit phone number). If a user enters a 7- or 11-digit number, a system with data entry controls might display an error message, such as "You must enter a 10-digit number." The system might also be programmed to accept a record into a file only if the telephone number is included, rejecting any record that doesn't include a phone number or displaying a message if the user leaves a field empty or enters invalid data into a field.

Controls also translate business policies into system features. For example, **Blockbuster Video** used its IS to implement a policy limiting debt for each customer to a certain level. When a renter reaches the debt limit and tries to rent another tape, a message appears on the cash register screen: "Do not rent!" Thus, the policy is implemented by using a control at the point of sale.

Menus are useful control tools. Systems can be programmed so that different menu options are displayed, depending on a user's access authorization. By providing limited menus, a system forcibly restricts what users can do with the system.

Clear error messages are an important data entry control.

Another effective way to control system use, especially when dealing with a transaction-processing system (TPS), is to program limits on the numerical values that can be either entered into quantitative fields or output through processing. Upper limits are often set on quantities such as payments, salaries, number of units ordered, and lengths of time (such as the number of hours spent on a task). Systems often establish both a minimum and maximum that are reasonable in a particular type of transaction. For example, an organization may set a minimum for the sum paid for a purchase at zero and a maximum at $50,000, if that is the most expensive item the organization purchases. Another example: upper and lower limits for a field recording the daily number of hours worked by an individual would be 24 and zero, respectively.

Backup

Probably the easiest way to protect against loss of data caused by natural disasters, computer viruses, or human errors is to automatically duplicate all data periodically, a process referred to as data **backup**. Many systems have built-in automatic backup programs. The data may be duplicated on inexpensive storage devices such as magnetic tapes. Manufacturers of storage devices also offer redundant arrays of independent disks (RAID) for this purpose. A **RAID** is a set of disks that is programmed to redundantly store data to provide a higher degree of reliability.

Of course, backing up data is not enough. The disks or tapes with backed-up data must be routinely transported off-site, so that if a business site is damaged by a disaster, the remote storage can be used since it is likely to be spared. In the past, many companies had a truck haul backup disks and tapes to the storage location at the end of every business day, and some may still do so. However, due to the great developments in telecommunications in recent years, most corporations prefer to back up data at a remote site through communications lines. Often, the backup disks or tapes reside thousands of miles away from the organization's business offices. For additional protection, the disks or tapes are locked in safes that can withstand fire and floods.

Redundant arrays of independent disks (RAID) automatically backup transactions onto disks that can be removed and stored in a safe place.

Companies can also use the services of firms that specialize in providing backup facilities. The vendor maintains a site with huge amounts of disk space linked to the Internet. The company typically provides the client organizations with an application that copies designated files from the client's systems to the remote disks. For obvious reasons, some professionals call this type of service *e-vaulting*.

Access Controls

Unauthorized access to information systems, usually via public networks such as the Internet, does not always damage IT resources. However, it is regarded as one of the most serious threats to security because it is often the prelude to the destruction of Web sites, databases, and other resources.

Access controls are measures taken to ensure that only those who are authorized have access to a computer or network or to certain applications or data. One way to block access to a computer is by physically locking it in a facility to which only authorized users have a key or by locking the computer itself with a physical key. However, in the age of networked computers, this solution is often impractical. Organizations rightfully need to protect their systems from harm, but access controls are also being used by some governments to limit their citizens' access to information.

The most common way to control access is through the combination of an access code (also called a *user ID*) and a password. While access codes usually are not secret, passwords are. IS managers encourage users to change their passwords frequently, which most systems easily allow, so that others do not have time to figure them out. Some organizations have systems that force users to change their passwords at preset time intervals, such as once a month, once every three months, and the like. Some systems also prevent users from selecting a password that they have used in the past, to minimize the chance that someone else might guess it.

Passwords are by far the most widely used type of access control.

Access codes and their related passwords are maintained either in a special list that becomes part of the operating system or in a database that the system searches before allowing access, to determine whether a user is authorized to access the desired resource. In many business situations, employees or customers have "read" access (whereby they can view data) but not "write" or "update" access (which would allow them to change data). Apparently, many companies do a poor job maintaining their password lists, especially in times of high employee turnover. Research indicates that as many as 30% of a company's approved passwords are for employees who have left. In some cases, laid-off employees accessed their former employer's system to cause damage.

In recent years, some companies have adopted physical access controls called biometrics. A **biometric** is a unique physical, measurable characteristic of a human being that is used to identify a person. Characteristics such as fingerprints, retinal pictures, or voiceprints can be used as *biometrics*. When a fingerprint is used, the user presses a finger

Fingerprint readers have been adopted by an increasing number of organizations as biometric access controls.

on a scanner or puts it before a digital camera. The fingerprint is compared against a database of digitized fingerprints of people with authorized access. The procedure is similar when the image of a person's retina is scanned. With voice, the user is instructed to utter a word or several words. The intonation and accent are digitized and compared with a list of digitized voice samples.

For instance, **Compaq**, the giant PC maker, introduced a device called *Fingerprint Identification Technology* (FIT), which is the size of a deck of cards and is used to access personal computers. Instead of keying in a password, employees hold one of their fingers up to a camera that allows the system to compare the image to a database of fingerprints. Using biometric access devices is the best way not only to prevent unauthorized access to computers but also to reduce the workload of help-desk personnel. Up to 50% of the calls help-desk personnel receive come from employees who have forgotten their passwords.

Atomic Transactions

As you know, in an efficient IS, a user enters data only once, and the data are recorded in different files for different purposes, according to the system's programmed instructions. For instance, in a typical order system, a sale is recorded in several files: the shipping file (so that the warehouse knows what to pack and ship), the invoice file (to produce an invoice and keep a copy in the system), the accounts receivable file (for accounting purposes), and the commission file (so that the salesperson can be compensated with the appropriate commission fee at the end of the month). A system supports atomic transactions when its code will only allow the recording of data if they successfully reach all their many destinations. So using **atomic transactions** ensures that only full entry occurs in all the appropriate files.

Atomic transactions ensure updating of all appropriate files. Either all files are updated, or none is updated and the control produces an error message.

For instance, suppose the different files just mentioned reside on more than one disk, one of which is malfunctioning. When the clerk enters the sales transaction, the system tries to automatically record the appropriate data from the entry into each of the files. The shipping, accounts receivable, and invoice files are updated, but the malfunctioning commission file cannot accept the data. Without controls, the sale would be recorded, but unknown to anyone, the commission would not be updated, and the salesperson would be deprived of the commission on this deal. However, an atomic transactions control mechanism detects that not all four files have been updated with the transaction, and it doesn't update any of the files. The system may try to update again later, but if the update does not go through, the application will produce an appropriate error message for the clerk, and remedial action can be taken.

Note that this is a control not only against a malfunction but also against fraud. Suppose the salesperson collaborates with the clerk to enter the sale only in the commission file, so she can be rewarded for a sale that has never taken place—and then plans to split the fee with the clerk. The atomic transactions control would not let this happen.

Audit Trail

In spite of the many steps taken to prevent system abuse, it nonetheless occurs. Consequently, further steps are needed to track transactions so that (1) when abuses are found, they can be traced and (2) fear of detection will indirectly discourage abuse. One popular tracking tool is the **audit trail:** a series of documented facts that help detect who recorded which transactions, at what time, and under whose approval. Whenever an employee records a transaction, such a system prompts the employee to provide certain information: an invoice number, account number, salesperson ID number, and the like. Sometimes an audit trail is automatically created using data, such as the date and time of a transaction or the name or password of the user updating the file. These data are recorded directly from the computer—often unbeknownst to the user—and attached to the record of the transaction.

Audit trail information helps uncover undesirable acts, from innocent mistakes to premeditated fraud. The information helps determine who authorized and/or made the entries, the date and time of the transactions, and other identifying data that are essential in correcting mistakes or recovering losses. The audit trail is the most important tool of the **information systems auditor,** the professional whose job it is to find erroneous or fraudulent cases and investigate them.

Encryption

When communicating sensitive information via a public network such as the Internet, the parties must authenticate each other and keep the message secret. **Authentication** is the process of ensuring that the person who sends a message to or receives a message from you is indeed that person. Authentication can be accomplished by senders and receivers exchanging codes known only to them. Once authentication is established, keeping a message secret, too, can be accomplished by transforming it into a form that cannot be read by anyone who intercepts it. Coding a message into a form unreadable to an interceptor is called *encryption*.

Both authentication and secrecy are important when communicating confidential information such as financial and medical records. Authentication and secrecy are also essential when transacting business through a public network. For example, millions of people now buy and sell shares and other financial products on the Web, businesses and individuals make purchases through the Web and use credit-card account numbers for payment, and medical clinics use the Web to transmit patient records to insurance companies and prescriptions to pharmacies. All must authenticate the recipient and keep the entire communication confidential.

To authenticate the users and maintain secrecy, the parties can use encryption programs. Encryption programs scramble information transmitted over the network so that an interceptor will receive unintelligible data. The original message is called **plaintext**; the coded message is called **ciphertext**. Encryption uses a mathematical algorithm, which is a formula, and a key. The key is a combination of bits that must be used to figure out the formula. The receiving computer uses the key to activate the algorithm that translates the ciphertext back into plaintext.

Encrypting communications increases security.

Plain Text —— Encryption ——▶ Encrypted Message —— Decryption ——▶ Decrypted Message

Digital Signatures and Digital Certificates

With the increasing use of e-commerce for all types of business transactions came the pressure to allow legally binding transactions online as well. Some countries have now broken that barrier and recognized the legal validity of electronic signatures.

Electronic Signatures

In the information age, it was only a matter of time until electronic signatures would become legally binding in commercial transactions. As of October 2000, U.S. law recognizes such signatures. The Electronic Signatures in Global and National Commerce Act states that electronic contracts with electronic signatures have the same legal validity as paper contracts. The law defines the term *electronic signature* as "an electronic sound, symbol, or process attached to or logically associated with a contract or other record and executed or adopted by a person with the intent to sign the record." Other countries, including Ireland, Mexico, and Bermuda, have enacted similar laws.

Electronic signatures can take several forms. In one form, instead of signing on paper, the user signs with a stylus on a special clear plastic pad. The signature is recorded as a graphic. Along with it, some systems also record how quickly the signature is written and how much force the signer uses against the pad so that subsequent signatures can be compared with these characteristics for authentication. You may have already used this system when you signed an authorization to charge your credit card at **OfficeMax** or when you received a package delivered by **UPS**.

Another electronic signature method records a biometric of the signer. Remember that a biometric is a physical characteristic of a person, such as a fingerprint, retina pattern, or voice signature. A person's biometric is recorded once and then compared with subsequent signatures for authentication. For example, **Sony**, the electronics giant, offers a product that digitally records a user's fingerprints. The users can then access their electronic signature only after placing a finger or thumb on a scanner for comparison.

Electronic signatures alone do not provide any security when transmitted in a communication network. On the contrary, they raise the necessity to authenticate the signer. To ensure authenticity that the sender of a message is indeed who he or she claims to be, digital signatures can be used. Note that the term *digital certificate* has a special technical meaning in the context of the following discussion. A digital signature in the context of public key encryption is *not* simply any electronic signature.

Digital Signatures

Every electronic signature is digitized, or it could not be stored and processed by a computer. However, in the great majority of electronic signatures, no physical characteristics will be involved. Rather, people will use *digital signatures* instead. A **digital signature,** to differentiate it from an electronic signature, is an encrypted digest of the text that is sent along with a message, usually a text message, but possibly one that contains other types of information, such as pictures. A digital signature authenticates the identity of the sender of a message and also guarantees that no one has altered the sent document; it is as if the message were carried in an electronically sealed envelope.

When you send an encrypted message, two phases are involved in creating a digital signature. First, the encryption software uses a hashing algorithm (a mathematical formula) to create a message digest from the file you wish to transmit. A message digest is akin to the unique fingerprint of a file. Then, the software uses your private (secret) key to encrypt the message digest. The result is a digital signature for that specific file.

Digital Certificates

To authenticate a digital signature, both buyers and sellers must use digital certificates (also known as digital IDs). **Digital certificates** are computer files that serve as the equivalent of ID cards. Issuers of digital certificates are called certificate authorities, and therefore many of them have the letters CA as part of their names. Some are subsidiaries of banks and credit-card companies and others are independent. **American Express CA**, **Digital Signature Trust Co.**, **VeriSign Inc.**, and **GlobalSign Toot CA** are just a few of the numerous companies that sell digital certificates. (Certificate authorities also issue public and private keys, and they have arranged with financial corporations, such as credit-card issuers, to verify information that applicants provide for the certificates.)

A digital certificate contains its holder's name, a serial number, expiration dates, and a copy of the certificate holder's public key (used to encrypt messages and digital signatures). It also contains the digital signature of the certificate authority so that a recipient can verify that the certificate is real. To view the digital certificate of a secure online business, click on the lock icon at the bottom right corner of your browser. Click the Details tab to view the version, serial number, signature encryption method, issuer name, and other details of the certificate (right).

Digital certificates are the equivalent of tamper-proof photo identification cards. They are based on public key encryption techniques that verify the identities of the buyer and seller in electronic transactions and prevent documents from being altered after the transaction is completed. Consumers have their own digital certificates stored on their home computers' hard disks. In a transaction, a consumer uses one digital key attached to the certificate that he or she sends to the seller. The seller sends the certificate and his own digital key to a certificate authority, which then can determine the authenticity of the digital signature. Completed transaction documents are stored on a secure hard disk maintained by a trusted third party.

The recipient of an encrypted message uses the certificate authority's public key to decode the digital certificate attached to the message, verifies it as issued by the certificate authority, and then obtains the sender's public key and identification information held within the certificate. With this information, the recipient can send an encrypted reply.

When using the Web, encryption and authentication take place automatically and are transparent to the users. However, there is an indication in the browser's window if the communication is secure. In **Microsoft's** Internet Explorer, a small padlock appears in the lower-right corner. In **Netscape's** Communicator, an open padlock appears in the lower-left corner if the site you reached is not secure, and a closed padlock appears if it is secure. You may see these signs as soon as the page requiring your password appears in your browser. If you double-click on the padlock, a window will open with details on the digital certificate that the site uses, such as the certificate issuer's name, the date it was issued, and the date it will expire.

Firewalls

As we discussed earlier, the great increase in the number of people and organizations using the Internet, and especially Web sites, has provided fertile ground for unauthorized and destructive activity. The best defense against unauthorized access to systems over the Internet is a **firewall,** which is software whose purpose is to block access to computing resources. (Early firewalls used combinations of hardware and software.) Firewall software screens the activities of a person who logs on to a Web site; it allows retrieval and viewing of certain material but blocks at-

Exhibit 800.77 *A Firewall for Security*

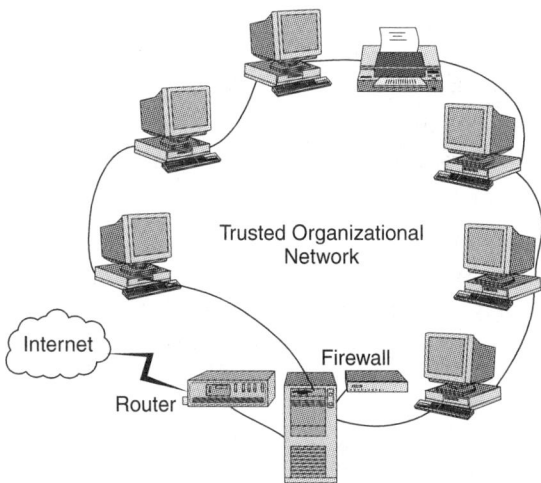

tempts to change the information or to access other resources that reside on the same computer or computers connected to it.

It is important to note that while firewalls are used to keep unauthorized users out, they are also used to keep unauthorized software or instructions away such as computer viruses and other rogue software. When an employee uses a company computer to access external Web sites, the firewall screens for viruses and active attempts to invade company resources through the open communications line. It may also be programmed to block employee access to sites that are suspected of launching rogue programs, or to sites that provide no useful resources. The firewall then prohibits the user from logging on to those sites.

As Exhibit 800.77 illustrates, a firewall controls communication between a trusted network and the "untrusted" Internet. The firewall is installed between the organization's internal network and a router. A router is a communication device that forwards communications data from one network to another, in this case from the organization's network to the Internet and vice versa. Network professionals use the firewall software to check which applications can access the Internet and which servers may be accessed from the organization's network.

To increase security, some companies implement the DMZ (DeMilitarized Zone) approach. The DMZ is a link between two servers, one of which is a proxy server. A proxy server "represents" another server for all information requests and acts as a buffer between internal and external networks. When a business hires the services of an ISP, the proxy server is often the one operated by an Internet Service Provider (ISP). The DMZ provides a barrier between the Internet and a company's organizational network, which is usually an intranet. Both the organizational network server and proxy server employ firewalls. In Exhibit 800.77, the firewalls would be installed on the gray server of the organizational network and the router. The router is often called a *boundary router*. The double firewall architecture adds an extra measure of security for the intranet.

Information Security Standards

Developers of ISs can use one of several sets of standards when integrating security measures into new systems. Some companies that specialize in development of enterprise applications have their own standards, but others usually follow well-established national or international standards, especially if the systems they develop are to be used by government agencies or contractors. There are two prominent standards, one developed by the U.S. government (The Orange Book) and the other developed by the International Standard Organization.

The Orange Book

Perhaps the best-known security standards are those detailed in *Trusted Computer System Evaluation Criteria (TCSEC)*, a book published by the National Computer Security Center (NCSC), an arm of the U.S. Department of Defense (DOD) and popularly known as The Orange Book because of the color of its cover. (The document is DOD

Standard 5200.28.) The book was originally written for military ISs, but it is now used by the IT industry as a guide. In it, NCSC defines four security levels, ranging from minimal protection, called Division D, to ultrasecurity called Division A.

1. Division A: Verified Protection (has only one class—A1)
2. Division B: Mandatory Protection (has three classes — B1, B2, and B3)
3. Division C: Discretionary Protection (has two classes—C1 and C2)
4. Division D: Minimal Protection (has only one class)

The four categories are further broken down into subclasses (seven in all) that represent, as the book itself puts it, "increasing desirability from a computer security point of view." These subclasses are numbered, with 1 indicating the lowest security within a class, and subsequent numerals indicating increasingly rigorous security.

Essentially, a level D classification means that a system is unrated, or that it has no inherent security. An example would be an out-of-the-box plain PC. Systems that merit a level B3 or A1 rating—the top two levels defined by the NCSC—are assumed to be "bulletproof" since they are designed from scratch to protect classified military information and government secrets.

Most commercial-grade systems, both hardware and software, fall into either the C1 or C2 rating. At this level, the owner of data can determine who has access to it. C1 indicates that a system employs user IDs; C2 indicates that a system employs a user ID and a password. The Orange Book says that a C1 system "satisfies discretionary security requirements" by providing separation of users and data. Essentially, C1 systems let users protect their data from the roaming hands of other users.

The more robust C2 rating "makes users individually accountable for their actions through log-in procedures, auditing of security-relevant events, and resources isolations," The Orange Book states. Practically speaking, a C2 rating means that the system automatically creates an audit trail, as explained before. Many commercial operating systems, such as **Microsoft Corporation's** Windows NT and Windows 2000, **Apple Computer Inc.'s** A/UX, and **IBM's** OS/2, meet the C2 requirement.

Levels B and A include mandatory access control, whereby access is based on standard Department of Defense (DOD) clearances. In A and B levels, each data structure contains a sensitivity level, such as top-secret, secret, or unclassified, and is available only to users with that level of clearance. B1 is DOD clearance levels. B2 provides that the system can be tested and that these clearances cannot be downgraded. A1, the highest security level, requires access methods that rely on a mathematical model whose robustness can be proven. This is the level used by U.S. military computers.

The European Information Technology Security Evaluation Criteria (ITSEC) issued by a European Community organization called SOG-IS (Senior Officials Groups—Information Systems Security) is similar to The Orange Book.

Critics of The Orange Book claim that it is fine for protection of secrecy but not for protection from other damage, such as monetary fraud. Because the emphasis is on secrecy, the only aspect considered is access. Critics also claim that The Orange Book does not address networking issues. All these concerns are addressed by the new ISO/IEC Standard.

The ISO Standard

In 1999, the ISO (International Organization for Standardization) and the IEC (International Electrotechnical Commission), which are international bodies, published ISO/IEC Standard 15408 titled *Information Technology-Security Techniques-Evaluation Criteria for IT Security*. The purpose of the document is to provide "a common set of requirements for the security functions of IT products and systems and for assurance measures applied to them during a security evaluation."

The organizations say that the standard permits comparability between the results of independent security evaluations and that it does so by providing common requirements for the security functions of IT products and systems and for assurance measures applied to them during a security evaluation. The evaluation may help consumers determine whether the IT product or system is secure enough for their intended application and whether the security risks implicit in its use are tolerable.

Experience shows that once a set of standards is established, it becomes a reference for many players in the industry, and manufacturers start incorporating the standards into their products. Makers of hardware and developers of software will no doubt take notice and soon adhere to the ISO/IEC standard.

The Downside of Security Controls

Security controls, especially passwords, encryption applications, and firewalls, have a price that relates to more than money: they slow down data communications, and they require user discipline, which is not always easy to maintain. Employees tend to forget their passwords, especially if they must replace them every 30 or 90 days. To remember their passwords, many employees write them on a piece of paper and keep them where they are most likely to need them: taped to their computers. Any office visitor can see many of these little notes on computers in cubicles.

Employees are especially annoyed when they have to use a different password for every system they use; in some companies, there may be four or five different systems, each with its own access control. A simpler solution is an approach called SSO (single sign-on). With SSO, users are required to identify themselves only once before accessing several different systems. However, SSO requires special software that interacts with all the systems in an organization, and the systems must be linked through a network. Not many organizations have installed such software.

Encryption slows down communication because the software must encrypt and decrypt every message. Remember that when you use a secure Web site, much of the information you view on your screen was encrypted by the software installed on the site's server and then decrypted by your browser. All this activity takes time, and the delay only exacerbates the Internet's low download speed during periods of heavy traffic. (Low download speed is also caused by the use of regular modems; high-speed links such as cable and DSL are still not widespread.)

Firewalls have the same slowing effect; screening every download takes time, which affects anyone trying to access information, including employees, business partners, and individual consumers. Customers may become frustrated if they have to wait too long for response from a Web site. They may turn away and decide to shop and buy at a competitor's site. Business partners may complain about inconvenience.

IT specialists must clearly explain to managers the implications of applying security measures, especially on systems connected to the Internet. The IT specialists and other managers must first determine which resource should be accessed only with passwords and which also require other screening methods, such as firewalls. They must tell employees what impact a new security measure will have on their daily work, and if the measure will adversely affect their work, the specialists must convince the employees that the inconvenience is the price for protecting data.

The Economic Aspect of Security Measures

A study by research firm GartnerGroup revealed that most companies spend less than 1% of their budgets on computer security; the firm says that the figure should be closer to 5 to 8% in light of the great risks resulting from the growing business activity on the Internet. Apparently, consulting firms spend the largest sums of money on IT security, followed by financial institutions and high-tech companies. In recent years, the largest portions of IT security budgets have been dedicated to firewalls. Budgets for encryption technologies have also been increasing. Both facts are a reflection of the growing use of the Internet in business and the commensurate concern for security.

From a pure cost point of view, how much should an organization spend on data security measures? There are two types of costs that must be considered to answer this question: the cost of the potential damage, and the cost of implementing a preventive measure. The cost of potential damage is the aggregate of all the cost of disruptions multiplied by their respective probabilities, as follows.

$$Cost\ of\ Potential\ Damage = \sum_{i=1}^{n} Cost\text{-}of\text{-}disruption_i \times Probability\text{-}of\text{-}disruption_i$$

Where i is a probable event, and n is the number of events.

Experts are usually employed to estimate the cost and probabilities of damages, as well as the cost of security measures. Obviously, the more extensive the preventive measures, the smaller the damage potential. So, as the cost of security measures goes up, the cost of potential damage goes down. Ideally, the enterprise will place itself at the optimum point, which is the point at which the total of the two costs is minimized, as Exhibit 800.78 illustrates.

When budgeting for IT security, managers need to define what they want to protect. They should focus on the assets they must protect, which in most cases is information, not applications. Copies of applications are usually kept in

Exhibit 800.78 *Cost of Security Measures*

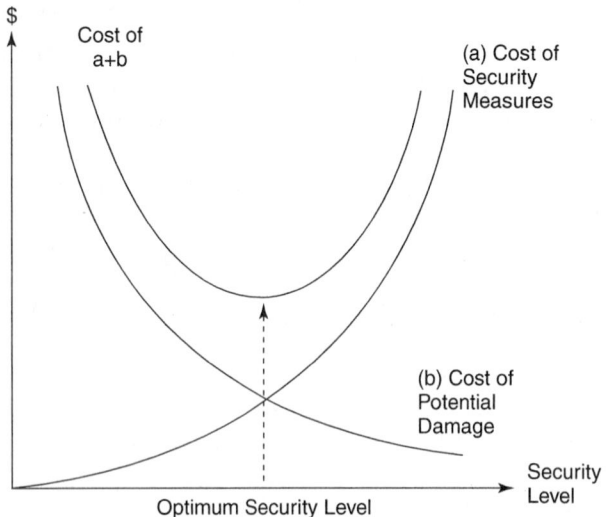

(The total cost to the enterprise is lowest at "optimum." No less, and no more, should be spent on information security measures.)

a safe place to replace those that get damaged. They should also estimate the loss of revenue from downtime. Then, they should budget sums that do not exceed the value of what the measures protect—information and potential revenues. Even the most ardent IT security advocates agree that there is no point spending $100,000 to protect information that is worth $10,000.

Electronic Commerce and Information Technology

What Are the Internet, Intranet, and Extranet?

Internet

The Development of the Internet

Today, the Internet is a network of networks, with millions of servers. Tens of millions of people take for granted that with a simple phone connection via their modems or permanent cable link, they can access a huge number of files from Internet servers, do research, participate in electronic discussions, shop, make purchases, and make payments. Just a few years ago, the picture was completely different.

What's on the Internet?

The Internet is a vast resource—much more than the multimedia world of the Web. One way to categorize the massive amount of information available via the Internet is to segment it by the manner in which it is organized, searched, and transmitted. Information is posted, retrieved, transmitted, and received differently, depending on the standards to which the different segments adhere. Accordingly, the applications that are used to post, retrieve, transmit, and receive it vary also. The most popular segment of the Internet is e-mail, consisting mainly of text. Other uses of the Internet include file transfer, news groups, Internet relay chat, and Internet telephoning.

Intranets and Extranets

Soon after the Web caught the interest of the corporate world, IS managers conceived a simple idea: if HTML can be used to communicate information effectively on the Internet, why not use the same technology for communications *within* an organization?

So a new concept was created: the **intranet**. An intranet is a computer network within an organization that uses Internet technologies, such as hypertext markup language (HTML) and extensible markup language (XML), to communicate. The designers use the same tools to build sites and pages, and the users can use the same browsers on their intranet sites as they use to access external sites. In fact, many of today's intranets did not require any additional hardware; the existing LANs and other intraorganizational networks already used for telecommunications were sufficient. Web applications, such as server programs and browsers, were simply added to these networks to allow access to all the advanced features that are available on the Web.

An intranet is a private network in the sense that its content is shared only by members of one organization. Intranets are often used in multisite organizations. They offer employees information, enable them to change benefits programs online, and help them access organizational databases for their daily work. This is accomplished through virtual private networks (VPNs). In order to give remote sites or traveling managers access, a "tunnel" is created between the Internet and intranet, which allows those outside an organization to use the Internet to access the intranet.

VPN technology is also used to establish extranets. An **extranet** is similar to an intranet, but its purpose is to facilitate communication and trade between an organization and its business partners, such as suppliers. It is not meant to serve consumers. Unlike an intranet, an extranet is not limited to employee use. It may be thought of as the part of an intranet that is extended to business partners. Exhibit 800.79 lists the potential of the Internet, intranets, and extranets to enhance productivity for a business. Doing business via the Internet, intranets, and extranets lowers the average cost of typical transactions compared to traditional systems.

Exhibit 800.79 *Internet, Intranet, and Extranet Potential for Productivity Enhancement*

An Internet Web site can enhance productivity through . . .
- Providing product information
- Sending and receiving external e-mail
- Accepting orders
- Processing orders and payment
- Conducting research

An Intranet can enhance productivity through . . .
- Sending and receiving internal e-mail
- Collaborative processing
- Allowing access to "organizational memory" residing in databases
- Order processing
- Providing personal Web pages
- Providing departmental Web pages
- Permitting group communications
- Permitting organizationwide communications
- Providing product and company information

An extranet can enhance productivity through . . .
- Implementing electronic data interchange (EDI) with suppliers and clients
- Collaborating with other organizations in development of new products and services
- Sharing product catalogs exclusively with wholesalers
- Sharing news and other information of shared interest exclusively with business partners

Establishing an E-Commerce Web Site

To establish a Web business, an organization must have access to an Internet server. Recall that an Internet server is a computer that is connected to the Internet backbone. Businesses have several options when establishing a Web site.

1. Installing their own server (i.e., a dedicated server)
2. Contracting with an ISP site
3. Contracting with a Web portal
4. Establishing an electronic storefront
5. Contracting with a Web hosting service
6. Using a virtual Web server
7. Setting up a subdomain

In the following sections, we discuss the benefits and disadvantages of each option for different types of businesses.

Dedicated Server

Installing and maintaining the business's own server is the most expensive option, but it gives the business the greatest degree of control. Setting up a server requires expertise, which may or may not be available within the business. The business must also employ specialists to maintain the server. In large organizations they may be employees of the company; in smaller ones, they may be consultants whose services the company hires. The specialists purchase a server (or several servers) for the company, connect it to the Internet through a dedicated line (such as a T1 line), and install the proper software for managing the server and creating Web pages. They "scale up" the server system when the business grows and handle issues such as load balancing to ensure quick response and to minimize the probability of site crashing. A site crashes when too many people try to log on and the software stops responding to anyone. **Load balancing** transfers visitor inquiries from a busy server to a less busy server.

ISP Site

Internet service providers (ISPs) offer low-fee or free space for individual or business Web sites. If the hosting ISP is named Oz and the business name is Great Stuff, a typical URL for a business of this sort would be *members.oz.com/greatstuff*. Some small businesses have chosen this option, but many others avoid it because it can give the appearance that such online businesses are ephemeral. Using an ISP's Web site service is probably more appropriate for individual Web sites than for business sites.

Web Portal

Large portals are another option. A **portal** is a site that enjoys heavy traffic and often offers a search engine and general information such as weather, news, and stock market quotations. Examples include *www.yahoo.com, www.lycos.com,* and *www.msn.com*. Most large portals offer free hosting of personal Web pages. Some allow small businesses to maintain their pages on the portal's servers. As with ISPs, this option is suitable only for small businesses. The space provided is usually limited, and the businesses must comply by using templates for their sites. Templates are set formats for Web pages.

Electronic Storefront

Some companies provide a **cybermall,** which is a virtual shopping mall on the Web. A cybermall hosts all the Web pages of a business that make up the business's site. The company offering the service develops the pages for the hosted businesses. This variation of Web hosting, also called an **electronic storefront,** can be quite expensive, and service quality varies widely. Yahoo! and Lycos are two of the major portals that offer storefront services. The service typically costs several hundred dollars per month. One of the benefits of posting a storefront with a large portal is the heavy traffic the business may enjoy. Portals are visited by millions of people daily.

Many local newspapers that maintain Web sites also offer electronic storefronts. On the Web home page of the newspaper, a list of participating local businesses appears, often with clickable logos. The target audience of newspaper cybermalls are residents of the newspaper's city and suburbs. The main purpose of the client business's site is to attract customers to the brick-and-mortar business. A client pays a fee of several thousand dollars to have the newspaper staff build its business's pages.

Web Hosting Service

Some companies specialize in offering Web hosting services for businesses. Most of them specifically target small businesses. The hosting companies offer space on their servers for hosting of Web sites. All provide templates for pages, and some provide software tools for more flexible page development. For an additional monthly fee, several of them offer transaction and payment software for use by the subscribing businesses' clients. For example, a company named Bigstep provides "wizards" that walk you through the otherwise time-consuming process of setting up catalogs and reports. Monthly fees are usually several tens of dollars. Due to the space and trading limits that these companies offer, hosting is appropriate for individuals and small businesses only.

Virtual Web Server

A virtual Web server creates the impression that it is owned by the business, but it is actually owned and operated by another business. To establish a virtual Web server, a business must have its own, registered domain name. Shoppers may assume that the business maintains its own server; in reality the domain name points to the server of another company. To arrange a virtual Web server, the business must ask the domain name registrar to associate the domain name with the other company's server. This arrangement is popular and usually more cost-effective for many companies than maintaining their own Web server or using a cybermall. The company owning the server provides all the maintenance services, such as running the server management software, adding servers when the business grows, and keeping and updating security measures. If the client business wishes to leave a service company and move to another, it can move the Web pages to a server of another company and ask the registrar to reassociate the domain name with the new server.

Subdomain

A business can also use a subdomain instead of registering its own domain name and use the services of a hosting company for hosting the Web pages. For example, if the business name is SmallBiz, and if Oz is the host company that owns the name ozhosting, it may host the site with the subdomain *smallbiz.ozhosting.net*. There are two disadvantages to this option: the business's domain name contains the name of another entity, and unlike with virtual Web servers, the business's online address (the URL) is associated with a single Web server. If the client business moves the Web pages to another server, it can no longer use this URL.

Considerations in Selection of a Web Service Provider

The majority of businesses do not maintain their own Web server; they use host services. When doing so, managers must consider several factors. Exhibit 800.80 lists the factors and provides a template where points can be logged for comparison. A simple evaluation method is for managers to compare each factor for the prospective companies, compare the total scores, and then make a decision. The evaluators may wish to assign different weights to the various items based on how important each item is to the business.

Technical support involves the quality of the equipment that the hosting company provides, security measures it maintains, the sophistication of server and load management, and the technical skill of its personnel. Companies should inquire about past down times and recovery time frames for the hosting company because they are such an important part of technical support.

In addition, if the client needs help in developing and updating Web pages, the evaluators should explore the appearance and functionality of current clients of the hosting company. They should also examine the credentials and experience of the Web page designers.

Setup and monthly fees are self-explanatory. Monthly fees can range from several dollars to several hundred dollars. Some hosting companies offer large discounts to clients that sign annual contracts.

Exhibit 800.80 *Factors to Consider in Web Service Providers*

Factor	Points	Hosting Company A	Hosting Company B
Quality of technical support			
Quality of content support			
Setup fee			
Monthly fee			
Amount of disk space			
Traffic limits and fees			
Availability of e-mail accounts and services			
Availability of FTP service			
CGI scripts			
Scalability			
Support of page design standards			

As the business grows and more information and services are provided, the number and complexity of Web pages also grows. So the business will need more disk space on the host's server. Therefore, it is advisable to contract with a host that is responsive to requests for additional disk space. Large hosting companies often provide only a limited amount of disk space, and any additional space may incur high costs. Smaller companies are usually more flexible and responsive to the individual needs of clients.

Some Web hosting companies charge extra fees if the site experiences activity above a predetermined amount of data that is downloaded from the site or number of visits from Web surfers. These visits are called *hits*. Usually, the first 5,000 hits per month are free, and there is a per-hit charge above this level. Web hosting companies price this way because the greater the number of hits, the more bandwidth they must allocate.

Most hosting companies provide e-mail services. The most popular type is a Post Office Protocol 3 (POP3) account. There is usually no extra charge for such accounts. Clients may want to inquire about additional services, such as mail forwarding (channeling e-mail messages to another e-mail address), auto-responding (automating e-mail reply), and access to mailing lists, and find out which e-mail services are free and which carry a charge.

For many online businesses it is important to have file transfer protocol (FTP) capabilities. FTP allows the site's owner to upload pages to the site and post downloadable files, as explained earlier. Uploading enables the site personnel to update the Web pages whenever they need to, which makes them independent of other companies, including the hosting firm. The ability to post uploadable files lets the business serve its customers better.

The availability of common gateway interface (CGI) scripts lets visitors interact with the site. CGI allows site visitors to use a local "find" mechanism to find products by name, manufacturer, or style within the client business pages; fill out forms and submit them; or change the appearance of pages they often access. Most Web hosting companies provide CGI scripts and data access applications. A good hosting company should have a large library of such scripts and allow you to add your own CGI scripts.

Scalability is the ability for a Web site to grow—an important factor for most businesses. It is best to select a hosting company that has the hardware, software, and expertise to accommodate varying traffic levels and that can demonstrate its site's ability to develop from a simple, static one to a heavily trafficked, interactive one.

The better hosting companies maintain software that supports a large variety of standards, so the client business can rest assured that all the features it develops for its pages can be supported by the hosting company's servers. For example, if there are ActiveX features in the business's Web pages, the host's server must support ActiveX. The same principle applies to features developed with the FrontPage design application. Some attractive features may not run properly unless the proper software is installed on the server to support FrontPage.

E-Commerce Practices on the Internet

The Internet offers not only a means for conducting existing day-to-day business but also opportunities for companies to generate revenue purely by establishing a whole new business on the Web. Web pages provide different types of interactivity. The simplest is publication of static company information on a home page, similar to a billboard advertisement. An increasing number of businesses do not settle for that, however; they have established Web sites that enable customers to search for specific items offered for sale, dropping items into a virtual shopping cart, and paying for the purchases.

Although electronic business, popularly called e-business, had been conducted before the advent of the Web, most of it is now conducted using Web technologies and the Internet. E-commerce is usually classified by the parties involved in the interaction: business-to-business (B2B) and business-to-consumer (B2C). Some people also add government-to-consumer, government-to-government, and government-to-business.

Examples of applications in B2B include electronic data interchange (EDI), exchanges and auctions, online business alliances, and application service providers (ASPs).

Examples of applications in B2C include advertising, e-retailing, auctions and reverse auctions, software sales, and stock trading.

Rules for Successful Online Business Transactions

Once an organization has a solid business plan for e-commerce, it should consider the manner in which it will conduct online business and try to exploit its site's potential. There are several elements to consider.

Target the Right Customers

Targeting the people who are most likely to need the products and services you offer has always been the most important effort in marketing, with or without the Web. On the Web targeting includes identifying the sites your audience frequently visits. For instance, a business that sells sporting goods should create clickable links at sites that cover sporting events and provide sports statistics. Banks that offer mortgage loans should create links at realtors' sites. And any business that targets its products to young people should do so at music sites.

Own the Customer's Total Experience

By using cookies and recording shoppers' movements, sophisticated customer relationship management (CRM) software can create electronic consumer profiles for each shopper and buyer. The shopper's experience with the site then becomes an asset of the business. Such marketing research fine-tunes the portfolio of products that the business offers and tailors Web pages for individual customers. It also can be used to "market to one" by e-mailing the shopper about special deals on items in which he or she showed interest.

Personalize the Service

A combination of CRM software and Web page customization software can be combined to enable *customers* to personalize the pages and the service they receive when they log on to the site. Online businesses should not force customization and promotions. They should allow customers the option to receive certain information through pop-up browser windows and e-mail messages. Most importantly, they must respect customers' privacy by letting customers opt in rather than opt out. Opting in means that the customer can actively check options to receive e-mail and other promotions, while opting out requires the customer to select *not* to receive such information—an annoyance to some customers. Some companies have created sites that enable customers to customize the products they purchase.

Shorten the Business Cycle

One of the reasons people like to do business on the Net is that it saves them time. Businesses should keep looking for opportunities to shorten the business cycle for their customers, from shopping to paying to receiving the items they ordered. **Fulfillment**, the activities taking place after customers place orders online, is one of the greatest challenges for online businesses. The **Boston Consulting Group** found that pure-play Internet retailers do poorly in comparison with traditional catalog-based retailers. The reason for this disappointing performance is that most online retailers underestimate the challenges of fulfillment.

Those who can ship the ordered products fastest are likely to sustain or increase their market shares. Some have decided to outsource the entire fulfillment task to organizations that specialize in fulfillment, such as **UPS's e-Logistics**, **FedEx's** Supply Chain Services, and **SubmitOrder.com**. E-Logistics, for example, offers to receive and store the business's merchandise in its warehouses, receive orders online, and then pick, pack, and ship them to the online business's customers. It also offers a product return service.

Let Customers Help Themselves

Customers often need information from an e-commerce organization. Such information includes the status of an order, the status of a shipped item, and after-the-sale information such as installation of add-on components and troubleshooting. Much of this information is still provided over the telephone, but customers prefer to have access to the information any time—not only on weekdays and during normal work hours—and they prefer not to wait for it.

Practically every online business now sends e-mail messages with the status of the order, a tracking number, and a link to the shipping company for checks on the shipping status. Hardware companies can post online assembly instructions for their "assembly required" products. In addition to including Frequently Asked Questions (FAQs) information, some companies have experimented with artificial intelligence software that can answer open-ended questions. Some sites provide a link to internet relay chat (IRC) or to Internet voice, software to enable shoppers to communicate with a salesperson rather than hear only inanimate textual information.

Be Proactive

Expecting customers to visit your Web site every time they need your service may not be enough in today's competitive marketplace. Customers now demand not only prompt replies via the Net but also proactive alerts. For example, Travelocity, a travel Web site, e-mails customers information on gate and time information if a customer's flight is delayed. Similarly, businesses should use customers' profiles (assembled through previous transactions and cookies) to e-mail them information on special sales and availability of new or previously unavailable items.

Successful Business Models

Although there are many successful online business models, among the most successful of them we find the following types.

1. *Niche retailing.* Niche retailers do not sell a large array of items. They specialize in a narrow selection of the best and most expensive items, which have a wide profit margin. All the items offered online are tightly related. For example, Waggin' Tails sells high-margin pet supplies and is profitable, unlike Pets.com, the large pet supplier that went bankrupt in 2000. Many small online suppliers of exotic dry and canned foods have been profitable as well, for the same reason: they specialize in a narrow range of high-margin products, many of which are not easy to find offline.

2. *Selling hard-to-obtain information.* The main reason organizations and individuals come to the Internet is to find information. Companies that sell useful information that is available only to them can make a profit from its sale. For example, Monster.com, a leading job-posting site, charges employers (but not job seekers) for the service and is profitable.

3. *Click-and-mortar retailing.* Traditional, brick-and-mortar retailers that extended their operations to the Web managed to generate new business and increase profits. **Staples**, **Sears**, and **Kmart** have all capitalized on their existing reputations as they moved online. Kmart has an online arm called BlueLight.com. The existing stores provide a means for consumers to return products with which they are not satisfied. The fact that the chain has been around for some time and has an established brand name helps attract consumers.

While entrepreneurs are looking for new business models, a developing technology may add an interesting twist to e-commerce: mobile commerce (m-commerce).

M-Commerce

As mobile devices proliferate, some people can already do what Internet prophets say will be the wave of the future: mobile commerce, popularly called **m-commerce**. Mobile devices already let users log on to the Internet, but they can also provide an additional benefit to businesses: the device can be located within several feet of a business, much like locating a cellular phone. As soon as you come within a few blocks of a store, your hand-held computer may beep and display a promotional message on its monitor.

Mobile devices need to use a special protocol to enable conversion of HTML (and XML and other Web standards) into formats that can be displayed on mobile devices. The most common protocol is Wireless Access Protocol (WAP).

Smart mobile devices may be helpful in sales force automation. Instead of connecting laptop computers to telephone jacks and modems or to cellular phones, traveling salespeople will be able to access data through the mobile device anywhere. They will be able to access corporate databases through their company's intranet.

Although the United States has usually been the leader in Internet technologies, mobile communication in general and m-commerce in particular seem to be developing faster in Europe and Japan. Mobile connections are still too slow to attract a large number of users, especially consumers. However, when mobile technologies mature, m-commerce may pick up speed. Experts opine that the most attractive mobile application may not be buying but the delivery of highly relevant information, custom-tailored to the user's current location and activity. Location services include downloading coupons at the store in which the consumer has just entered, finding out about nearby restaurants, or reading product reviews while shopping at an appliance store. Because location services need technology that locates the hand-held device more accurately than networks can currently, and because of privacy fears, such services may not emerge for several years.

Privacy proponents have already voiced concerns about m-commerce. Apparently, not many people are happy to find out that commercial organizations can track them down anytime as long as their mobile device is on. These devices will not only allow consumer profiling as is already practiced by many online retailers but also tell retailers and other organizations your exact location at any given time.

Sharing Information Systems: The Rise of E-Commerce

The future of many organizations depends on their ability to adopt an IS perspective that considers the organizations with which they interact. Large organizations have discovered the benefits of sharing their ISs with other organizations. Small organizations are slowly realizing that they must collaborate with their more powerful clients when flow of information is involved. One example is the numerous manufacturers of auto parts who must share ISs with **General Motors**, **Ford**, and **DaimlerChrysler** to survive, because the alternative would be being cut from these big companies' supplier lists. And in the global arena, the future of the world economy depends, to a large extent, on the flow of information across national borders. Many organizations now acknowledge that they are just links in a series of activities performed by a chain of players, as in a relay race. They do not just exchange goods and services for money; they also interchange information to facilitate their interactions.

From an interactive perspective, commercial organizations can be roughly classified into two categories: vertical markets and horizontal markets. A **vertical market** is one in which the goods of one business are used as raw materials or components in the production or sale process of another business: one business sells to another business until the final product is sold either to consumers or to a business that uses the product as a means of production, such as a machine. In a **horizontal market,** all players buy or sell the same products, so they are competitors. Nevertheless, they can share ISs to cooperate on certain elements of their activities or to exchange products through a bidding process. Obviously, a single business is in a vertical market with some businesses and in a horizontal market with others. Both vertical and horizontal markets have benefited greatly from Internet technologies. E-commerce has turned markets into electronic markets, in which significantly larger numbers of businesses can participate.

E-commerce has also brought many markets closer to perfect markets. In a perfect market, anyone can join or leave the market at any time; no seller or buyer is so powerful that it can influence prices; and all participants have access to the same information simultaneously. The latter condition has been chiefly aided by the growing accessibility to the Web and the advancement of its technologies.

Electronic Data Interchange

A significant portion of the cost of products and services can be attributed to the creation, handling, and storage of paper documents: requests for proposals, purchase orders, shipping documents, invoices, payment approvals, and checks, not to mention the equipment such as file cabinets and shelves to store the documents and the time spent preparing, processing, and shipping documents. The cost of handling a single paper transaction is estimated between tens and hundreds of dollars, depending on the industry. An increasing number of organizations

Suppliers, manufacturers, and retailers cooperate in some of the most successful applications of EDI.

Exhibit 800.81 *Benefits of Electronic Data Interchange (EDI)*

Cost savings	• Reduction of employee hours involved in creation and handling of paper documents • Reduction in the cost of funds transfer • Reduction in the cost of storage space • No mailing cost
Speed	• Faster forwarding of documents through a computer network than mail
Accuracy	• Rekeying of information minimized • Direct and easily verifiable communication • No loss of mail
Security	• Less susceptibility to interception and falsification of information
System integration	• Increasing interface of EDI software with internal systems so that incoming data trigger applications and further automation of data processing
Just-in-time support	• Increased communication speed enhances intercompany just-in-time operations, which significantly reduces inventory costs—vendor ships only the necessary items to arrive directly at the manufacturing or assembly line

that share information for their mutual benefit have replaced their paper-based transactions. Instead, they use interorganizational information systems that utilize telecommunications to exchange electronic data. This concept, called **electronic data interchange** (**EDI**), has been used in some industries since the early 1970s, but the popularity of EDI grew tremendously in the late 1980s and the 1990s. While technically EDI can be executed on any wide-area network, its popularity has grown in the late 1990s and early 2000s, thanks to the ability to implement the concept on the Internet.

As enumerated in Exhibit 800.81, tremendous benefits are being realized by companies that have adopted the EDI concept—especially manufacturing companies. By linking its vendors, customers, and subcontractors, a manufacturing firm can use EDI to quickly query raw or interim goods suppliers, who in turn can provide on-time delivery of the exact amount of resources needed. EDI technology also allows changes in production schedules to be communicated quickly both to suppliers and customers, minimizing the disruption in the plans of either the buying or supplying firm. Therefore, EDI is the underlying concept for interorganizational supply chain management, which we discuss later in the section.

An example of how EDI may work between two organizations is described next.

- First, the supplier's proposal is sent electronically to the purchasing organization.
- Next, an electronic contract is approved over the network, with both organizations maintaining a digital copy.
- The supplier manufactures and packages the goods, attaching to each box shipping data recorded on a bar code (including quantities packaged, date of shipment, means of shipment, and so on).
- Quantities shipped and their prices are entered into the system and flow automatically to an invoicing program; the shipping data documents and invoices are transmitted to the purchasing organization, so the receiving workers know what items they will receive.
- The manufacturer ships the order.
- When the packages are received at the purchasing organization, the bar codes are scanned, and the data are compared with both the data transmitted with the invoices and the actual items received.
- If there are no discrepancies, an approval for payment is transferred electronically by the purchaser to its accounts payable department, which instructs the bank to pay the supplier.
- Using EFT (electronic funds transfer), the bank reduces the purchasing organization's balance by the proper amount, and electronically transfers the sum to the supplier's account at its bank.

None of the documents involved in the process is on paper.

Most EDI users are in the health-care, insurance, and retailing industries. In health care, hospitals and private clinics use networks to transmit claim forms and disbursement approvals. Similarly, insurance companies accept electronic claims. Retailers accept paperless invoices and approve payment online. Other major industries that implemented EDI include finance and banking, automotive, petroleum and chemical, and transportation companies.

Consider the case of **Toys R Us**, the world's largest toy retailer. Annually, the company processes over half a million invoices electronically, dramatically reducing costs and improving the integrity and management of related information. Some of its most important suppliers even have direct access to point-of-sale information, to determine sales trends and generate purchase orders on behalf of Toys R Us.

Making electronic signatures legally binding fosters the proper legal environment for e-commerce in general and EDI in particular. An *electronic signature* is any signature made and kept digitally, such as a digitized written signature or a special code that uniquely identifies the signer. By 2001, the United States, Ireland, Mexico, and Bermuda had enacted electronic signature laws.

EDI is conducted in two major forms: value-added networks and the Web. We discuss both of these forms next.

Value Added Network EDI

The earliest form of EDI business partners used was subscription to the service with a **value-added network** (**VAN**) operator, also referred to simply as a VAN. We use the term VAN EDI for this service.

To use VAN EDI, business partners subscribe to the service and use the VAN's private communication lines, mailboxes, and special software. The VAN mediates all EDI communication between the companies with special software that translates business documents into EDI documents. It batches electronic documents several times per day and transmits them to the destination company. The software that translates business documents to and from EDI convention strictly conforms to EDI standards, the most prevalent of which are the United Nations–supported EDIFACT (EDI for Administration Commerce and Transport) and the American National Standards Institute's (ANSI) X12. Standards determine such conventions as codes for address lines and product prices and the length of text comments in an invoice. If the subscribers use two different standards, the VAN must use special software to transform the EDI document from one standard's conventions to the other's.

VAN EDI provides several advantages.

- *Transaction integrity.* The entire transaction must be communicated without interference. VAN EDI software is designed to ensure transaction integrity. If the software senses that there might be interference or that only a part of an electronic document reached the VAN's mailbox, it requests retransmission.
- *Privacy and security.* Business partners expect and need privacy for their transactions. Private networks are fully controlled by the VANs and are accessible only to subscribers of the EDI service, so their security is a plus. The VANs implement strict security measures that practically prevent any interception of electronic documents.
- *Nonrepudiation.* The parties involved in EDI need to be certain that transactions are verified. For example, if a purchasing officer launched a purchase order to a supplier, she should not be able to deny the fact later—the supplier must be certain transactions will proceed once initiated. A VAN's mailbox system ensures that the sender cannot repudiate sent documents, so both parties can feel secure that transactions requested will be fulfilled.
- *Solid standards.* EDI standards such as EDIFACT are solid and universally accepted for numerous industries, such as manufacturing, trucking, hospitals, and many others.

Web EDI

In 1997, about 95% of all EDI transactions took place through VAN lines. Because of the increasing popularity of the Web, the rate was expected to decrease to about 50%. Practically all new EDI implementations use Web technologies. The Internet is a natural vehicle for EDI because of its ease of access and inexpensive implementation. A huge global network has become available to even the smallest and poorest businesses. Recall that many trading partners now use extranets for transactions that have been executed on traditional EDI systems for decades. Many organizations that would balk at the cost of implementing EDI can now do it quite comfortably by using the Internet.

The success of Web EDI can largely be attributed to XML standards. Recall that XML (Extensible Markup Language) is a programming language for the Web, which is complementary to hypertext markup language (HTML). The important difference between HTML and XML is this: HTML tags around text, pictures, and other elements instruct a Web browser how to display the elements; XML tags around an element tell the browser the data content. As long as there is a universal agreement on such tags, they can be devised to communicate any business data, from company addresses to product specifications and prices to shipping dates. The universal agreement is what makes such tags a standard.

Extranet EDI offers several advantages over VAN EDI, including these.

- *Lower cost.* Compared with implementing VAN EDI, a business has to invest only modest amounts of money to implement extranet EDI. The network already exists, so there is no need to lease the services of VAN providers, which are quite expensive. A business just needs to pay the monthly ISP's fee, which is several tens of dollars per month per server. The cost of the software is modest, as well. The most common interface used with extranet EDI is a standard Web browser, which is free.

- *More familiar software.* Users are already familiar with Web browsers, which they have used for other purposes, such as surfing the Web at home. So, adding Web EDI functions includes very little training.
- *Worldwide connectivity.* In VAN EDI, partners have to coordinate connectivity and ensure compatibility of their telecommunications equipment and software. In contrast, access to the Web is available to almost every business in the world, which makes it relatively easy for any two businesses located thousands of miles apart to immediately implement EDI.
- *Fast communication.* By and large, the Internet backbone is made of communication lines capable of greater speeds than most VAN lines, which are generally older. Also, electronic documents on the Internet are not batched, as they are by the VAN, before they are launched from the mailbox to the recipient. Thus, transactions can be communicated faster on the Internet. However, VAN speeds are guaranteed, but Internet communication speed is not guaranteed because the network is shared by many parties, and communication can slow down when traffic is heavy.

With such cost and efficiency advantages, it is not surprising that Web EDI has grown so rapidly.

Supply Chain Management

The activities of commercial organizations, especially those that produce physical goods, fall into a general pattern. Each takes in input in the form of raw materials and parts, adds value to the parts by assembling or processing them, then delivers the output to another unit for further processing or to a customer. Eventually, one of the organizations in the sequence sells a final product to a customer, which may be a consumer or another business. This chain of purchase, process, and delivery is called a *supply chain*. Monitoring and controlling the supply chain is called *supply chain management (SCM)*, and ISs that support such management are called *supply chain management systems*.

Several enterprise applications, such as ERP systems, also serve as SCM systems. Many such systems enable managers not only to monitor what goes on at their own units or organization but also to follow what goes on at the facilities of their suppliers and contractors. For example, at any given point in time managers can know the status of the following: an order now being handled by a contractor, by order number; the phase of manufacturing the produced units have reached; and the date of delivery, including any delays and their length. When purchasing parts, managers use the systems for issuing electronic purchase orders, and they can follow the fulfillment process at the supplier's facilities, such as when the parts were packed, when they were loaded on trucks, and when they are estimated to arrive at the managers' floor or the floor of another business partner who needed the parts.

SCM applications streamline operations throughout the chain, from suppliers to customers, lowering inventories, decreasing production costs, and improving responsiveness to suppliers and clients. Now most such systems are designed to use the Internet. Harnessing the global network, managers can supervise an entire supply chain regardless of the location of the activity—at their own facilities or another organization's, at the same location or thousands of miles away. Older SCM systems connected two organizations. New ones connect several. For example, a distributor can reorder products from Organization A and simultaneously alert Organization B, the supplier of Organization A. The systems let all parties—suppliers, manufacturers, distributors, and customers—see the same information. A change made by any organization that affects an order can effect a corresponding change in scheduling and operations in the other organization's activities.

Companies that have adopted SCM systems have seen improvement in three major areas: reduction in inventory, reduction in cycle time, and, as a result, reduction in production cost. (Cycle time is the time it takes to complete a business process, such as purchasing or production. Every hour that a plant can gain from reducing its production cycle saves labor and allows the company to deliver and collect payment earlier.) Companies can reduce their inventory by communicating to their suppliers through a shared SCM system the exact number of units of each item they need and the exact time they need them. In ideal situations, they do not need to stockpile any inventory, saving warehouse costs.

Similar to ready-made ERP applications, SCM applications can also be purchased packaged. Experts usually praise the software for its benefits and ease of use, but there are some implementation challenges. The greatest obstacle to successful implementation is planning and training. The move to the systems must be well planned, and the systems must be fully tested before they are put into use. Employees must also be educated about the changes that come with such systems and be well trained to use the system's features.

Information Technology Contingency Plans

Recovery Measures

In 1998, although the company had not experienced any server overload, **Schwab's** chief information officer decided to play it safe and double the number of servers that route and process customer inquiries and transactions. The extra servers turned out to be a good investment. Despite occasional attacks by hackers and viruses, the firm has never experienced any downtime, and clients have never complained about slow response. On the other hand, the world's largest auction site, **eBay**, and many other online merchants have had to apologize to clients several times for long hours of no response—from unforeseen load or because of denial of service (DoS) attacks.

Security measures may reduce undesirable mishaps, but nobody can control all disasters. To be prepared for disasters when they do occur, organizations must have recovery measures in place. Organizations that depend heavily on ISs for their daily business often use redundancy; that is, they run all systems and transactions on two computers in parallel to protect against loss of data and business. If one computer is down, the work can continue on the other computer. Redundancy makes the system fault tolerant. However, in distributed systems, doubling every computing resource is extremely expensive, so other measures must be taken.

To prepare for mishaps, either natural or malicious, many organizations have well-thought-out programs in place, called **business recovery plans** or **business continuity plans.** The plans detail what should be done and by whom, if critical ISs go down or if IS operations become untrustworthy. Business recovery plans deal mostly with steps to take when ISs are incapacitated.

The Business Recovery Plan

Concern about disaster recovery has spread beyond banks, insurance companies, and data centers, the traditional disaster recovery fanatics. Many customer service and retail firms realize that they can easily lose customers if they don't deliver services and products in a timely manner, which is why the term *business recovery* or *business resumption* has caught on in some circles. In interactive-computing environments, when business systems are idle, so are the people who bring in revenue. In addition, companies' reputations can be harmed, and competitive advantage and market share lost.

Experts propose nine steps for the development of a business recovery plan.

1. **Obtain management's commitment to the plan.** Development of a recovery plan requires substantial resources. Top management must be convinced of the potential damages that paralysis of information systems may cause. Once management is committed, it should appoint a business recovery coordinator who will develop the plan and execute it if disaster occurs.
2. **Establish a planning committee.** The coordinator establishes a planning committee comprising representatives from all business units that are dependent on computer-based ISs. The members serve as liaisons between the coordinator and their unit managers. The managers are authorized to establish emergency procedures for their own departments.
3. **Perform risk assessment and impact analysis.** The committee assesses which operations would be hurt by disasters, and how long the organization could continue to operate without the damaged resources. This analysis is carried out through interviews with managers of functional business areas. The committee compiles information regarding maximum allowable down time, required backup information, and the financial, operational, and legal consequences of extended down time.
4. **Prioritize recovery needs.** The disaster recovery coordinator ranks each IS application according to its effect on an organization's ability to achieve its mission. **Mission-critical applications,** those without which the

business cannot conduct its operations, are given the highest priority. The largest or most widely used system may not be the most critical. Applications may be categorized into several classes, such as:

- 4.1 *Critical.* Applications that cannot be replaced with manual systems under any circumstances
- 4.2 *Vital.* Applications that can be replaced with manual systems for a brief period, such as several days
- 4.3 *Sensitive.* Applications that can be replaced with acceptable manual systems for an extended period of time, though at great cost
- 4.4 *Noncritical.* Applications that can be interrupted for an extended period of time at little or no cost to the organization

5. **Select a recovery plan.** Recovery plan alternatives are evaluated by considering advantages and disadvantages in terms of risk reduction, cost, and the speed at which employees can adjust to the alternative system.
6. **Select vendors.** If it is determined that an external vendor can better respond to a disaster than in-house staff and provide a better alternate system, then the external vendor that will be most cost-effective is selected. Factors considered should include the vendor's ability to provide telecommunications alternatives, experience, and capacity to support current applications.
7. **Develop and implement the plan.** The plan includes organizational and vendor responsibilities and the sequence of events that will take place. Each business unit is informed of its responsibilities, key contacts in each department, and training programs for personnel.
8. **Test the plan.** Testing includes a walk-through with each business unit, simulations as if a real disaster had occurred, and (if no damage will be caused) a deliberate interruption of the system and implementation of the plan. In mock disasters, the coordinator measures the time it takes to implement the plan and its effectiveness.
9. **Continually test and evaluate.** The staff must be aware of the plan at all times. Therefore, the plan must be tested periodically. It should be evaluated in light of new business practices and the addition of new applications. If necessary, the plan should be modified to accommodate these changes.

The plan should include the key personnel and their responsibilities, as well as a procedure to reinstitute interactions with outside business partners and suppliers. Because an organization's priorities and environment change over time, the plan must be examined periodically and updated if necessary. There will be new business processes or changes in the relative importance of existing processes or tasks, new or different application software, changes in hardware, and new or different IS and end-user personnel. The plan must be modified to reflect the new environment, and the changes must be thoroughly tested. A copy of the plan should be kept off-site, because if a disaster occurs, an on-site copy may not be available.

Consider the effort **Kodak Corporation** exerted to protect its ISs. With $14 billion in annual sales, the company has a detailed business recovery plan. Executives from every division agreed on a nine-step restoration sequence: First priority goes to order-entry systems, second priority is attached to inventory control, then come systems that support manufacturing processes, purchasing systems, warehouse control systems, payroll and accounting, and then quality assurance and master data. Not only does the list help the IS professionals to prioritize their response in case of a natural disaster or another mishap, but the sequence allows members of each business unit to understand their importance in the company. The firm's CIO said that the existence of the plan helps managers in every facility of this multisite international company know what they are to do when ISs go down; there are no questions about where to start, what to do, whom to call, and how to be involved. To shorten the restoration time of its ERP system, the company can use an ERP system at a standby site. Moving operations to that system now takes fewer than eight hours.

CIOs often find the tasks of earmarking funds for disaster recovery programs difficult because they cannot show the return on investment (ROI) of such "investment." Most companies institute recovery programs only after a disaster or near disaster occurs. Usually, the larger companies have such programs. **Gratner Group** found that 85% of Fortune 1000 companies have such programs. However, of these companies, 80% have only programs to rescue corporate centers, 50% of the plans cover networks, and fewer than 35% protect data that reside on networked PCs.

Outsourcing the Recovery Plan

Companies that choose not to develop their own recovery plan can outsource it to companies that specialize in recovery. The major companies in this industry include **IBM**, **SunGard**, and **Strohl Systems**. Another industry leader, **Comdisco**, sold its business continuity services division to **Hewlett-Packard** in 2001. These services include an all-encompassing system called GroundZero, which addresses every aspect of disaster preparedness. Small companies that cannot afford an expensive recovery plan can opt for Web-based services such as EmergencyPlan.com and Evergreen Data Continuity, Inc. In case of a natural disaster or another mishap, employees can access business data remotely.

Usually, a company that outsources its recovery plan uses a remote link to storage devices at the vendor's site to periodically store all its essential data files. It may also save a copy of unique applications there. If the client cannot use its own system for any reason—a natural disaster or a crippling hacker attack—the client's employees can either physically move to the vendor's facility or move to an office that provides Internet links. The latter option is becoming highly popular because it does not require relocation of employees during the recovery period. Employees simply move to an office located close to the organization's office and use the applications and data files remotely. Vendors usually have widely used applications (such as the MS Office suite) and proper use licenses available to clients.

Auditing and Information Technology

Auditing the information technology (IT) function is similar to auditing any business function in the organization. Auditors, both internal and external, are required to review the adequacy, effectiveness, and efficiency of controls over the IT systems and resources. Auditors review control objectives, practices, and procedures of an organization prior to making their opinion on the adequacy, effectiveness, and efficiency of controls.

Control Objectives, Control Practices, and Control Procedures

Control, in general, is any action taken by management that would result in accomplishment of the organization's goals, objectives, and mission. Control objectives are management's intentions of what controls should be accomplished to achieve organizational goals. Control practices and procedures help to achieve the desired control objectives, which are aimed to prevent, detect, and correct errors, irregularities, and omissions occurring in IT areas and functional business areas.

Control practices can also help the auditor in understanding the control concerns and estimating the consequences of a lack of adequate controls. This awareness can provide the basis for recommendations to management in strengthening overall internal controls. The auditor will note that a single control practice or procedure may affect more than one control objective.

Information Systems Control Objectives

There are several detailed information systems control objectives that an internal control structure must meet to prevent, detect, and correct errors, omissions, irregularities, and computer intrusions such as viruses and worms, and to recover from such activities to ensure continuity of business operations. Here, the term *system* includes hardware, data, software, people, documentation, and the associated procedures, whether manual or automated.

Information systems control objectives include the following.

- **System assets are safeguarded.** An organization's technology assets and resources, such as computer facilities, computer equipment, people, programs, and data, are to be safeguarded at all times to minimize waste and loss.
- **System functionality is assured.** The computer-based application system supports business needs and the system's requirements for the maintenance of data confidentiality, integrity, and availability.
- **System assurance is provided.** The computer system provides confidence to the user/customer of the system as to how well the functionality has been implemented. Assurance is a combination of correctness and effectiveness of the system functions.
- **Software safety is guaranteed.** The objective is to develop and maintain the software correctly to protect against failure of the software. The software must have provisions to mitigate the consequences of its failure. The goal is to protect human life and prevent bodily injuries.

- **System reliability is assured.** The objective is to ensure that the hardware, software, and data are stable and that people can be trusted to carry out the organization's mission.
- **System serviceability is provided.** The objective is to correct hardware and software problems in a timely manner to meet service-level guidelines and agreements.
- **System security is assured.** An organization's assets and information resources are to be protected from unauthorized access and use.
- **Data integrity is maintained.** Integrity deals with controls over how data are entered, communicated, processed, stored, and reported. The objective is to ensure that data are authorized, complete, accurate, consistent, and timely.
- **System availability is assured.** The objective is to ensure that the system (hardware, software, data) and its components are available when they are needed, where they are needed, and for whom they are needed.
- **System confidentiality is assured.** The objective is to ensure that sensitive data are disclosed only to authorized people.
- **System controllability is maintained.** Adequate manual and automated controls and procedures regarding hardware, software, data, and people should be available.
- **System maintainability is assured.** The system, which includes hardware and software, should be maintained with existing resources at minimum cost and time.
- **System auditability is provided.** The objective is to develop a chronological record of system activities that is sufficient to enable the reconstruction, reviewing, and examination of the sequence of activities.
- **System usability is assured.** For example, the application system is appropriately user-friendly, or the system design invites rather than inhibits the authorized user.
- **System effectiveness is ensured.** For example, system effectiveness is measured by determining that the system performs the intended functions and that users get the information they need, in the right form and in a timely fashion.
- **System economy and efficiency are maintained.** An economical and efficient system uses the minimum number of information resources to achieve the output level the system's users require. Economy and efficiency must always be considered in the context of system effectiveness.
- **System quality is maintained.** This is an overall goal. In addition to the above, the computer system should have built-in quality-related features such as testability, portability, convertability, modifiability, readability, reliability, reusability, structuredness, consistency, understandability, and, above all, adequate documentation.

Ethics and Information Technology

Codes of Ethics for IT Professionals

IS/IT professionals have a huge impact on planning, building, and maintaining ISs. Their decisions commit organizations to large investments and may radically change the way in which the organizations operate. Yet, unlike doctors, lawyers, public accountants, and other professionals, they do not have obligatory codes of ethics and professional standards.

Like other professionals, IS professionals must protect the interests of different constituencies: society at large, their employers, the employers' clients, and their own colleagues. Often, IT professionals find themselves in situations where the interests of two, or even three, of these constituencies collide. While some organizations have professional codes of conduct addressing many aspects of the IS profession, most do not provide guidelines for resolving conflicts-of-interest situations.

Consider this conflict. A programmer working for a consulting firm is involved in a large project for a client. The programmer comes to realize that the software has security holes. When she approaches her supervisor at the consulting firm, her boss demands that she ignore these holes and not alert the client because, "we are doing everything according to the contract." Her obligation to her employer is to follow his instructions. However, her obligation to the client is to inform him about the incompatibility. The programmer is faced with an ethical dilemma.

As another example, what would you do in the following situation? You are an independent database expert involved in the upgrading of a database for a large bank. Your contact at the bank is one of its senior vice presidents, who hired you and approved the payment for your consulting fees. While analyzing the database, you discover that the vice president has been involved in embezzlement. The victims are some bank clients (that is, the public) and, of course, the bank. What should you do? Is it your obligation to inform the bank's management? Should you inform the public by contacting a reporter? Or should you simply go on with the work for which you were hired, and for which you are being paid?

Although ethical conflicts are not less frequent in other professions, the ethical codes of other professions provide clearer decision rules than those of IT professionals. For example, a lawyer's first obligation is always to his client. The same principle applies to physicians. The ethical code of journalism is to strictly obey the rule of not exposing a source without the source's consent. Journalists have protected their sources to the point of obstructing justice; that is, they have honored the source's interests over the public's interests. An architect who learns that a building may not meet safety standards is expected to halt his work to protect the public, even though this may conflict with his obligations to an employer or client. Unlike physicians, attorneys, certified public accountants, and many other professionals, IT professionals must resolve their ethical dilemmas by themselves.

Information Ethical Standards

The information technology (IT) manager needs to understand what motivates people to behave in an unethical manner in the information age and in an environment conducive to computer crime, misuse, and fraud. A good manager can create an environment that will discourage computer abuse and promote ethical behavior.

Computer hardware and software vendors, service contractors, systems developers and maintainers, system managers, and system users all have an **equal role** in sharing ethical responsibilities. The key issues involved in information ethics are:

1. Software piracy
2. Data security and individual privacy
3. Data integrity
4. Human/product safety
5. Fairness, honesty, and loyalty

Each issue is discussed here briefly.

Software Piracy

Software piracy conveys that the creative and intellectual work of the author has been used or duplicated without permission, compensation, or payment of royalty to the author. Software piracy is an act of infringement on ownership rights, and the person who violates it could be sued civilly for damages, criminally prosecuted, or both. Software piracy is the most difficult act to control and enforce. Self-monitoring and honesty are the best controls.

The vast majority of the software involved in software piracy legal cases is off-the-shelf, PC software, such as word processing, spreadsheets, graphics, and databases. The issue is illegal use, copy, and distribution of software both inside and outside the organization. Here, *illegal* means a user has not paid for the software.

What Can Go Wrong in Software Use?

- *User organizations can be sued by software vendors or copyrighted owners for using their software illegally.*
- *Disgruntled employees are the major source of reporting illegal use of software to owners, followed by consultants.*
- *Most often, employees inherit their computers and are not aware of illegal software on the hard disk their predecessors left behind.*
- *In addition to actual users, software dealers and hard disk loaders are equally guilty of pirated software. They are also subject to legal suits.*

Software piracy policies are needed to protect the organization from legal suits by owners. The policy should do the following.

- Prohibit illegal copy and use of software.
- Develop a software inventory management system that includes a list of popular application programs. This list can be compared to the organization's purchase orders, original software diskettes, or original documentation manual.
- Periodically check the hard disks for illegally copied software.
- Make illegal copying of software grounds for employee dismissal.
- Require all employees to sign a statement pledging not to use illegal software at work and not to use illegal software taken from work to home.
- Prohibit copying of internally developed software.
- Prohibit pirated, externally developed software from being brought into the organization.
- Monitor all sensitive programs to prevent illegal copying.

Data Security and Individual Privacy

Data security and individual privacy includes all the controls and procedures developed to protect against unauthorized individuals accessing the computer system, disclosing confidential data, and denying essential computer services to those who need them the most. Specifically, it requires the careful protection of personal records such as medical reports and credit reports. Privacy issues raise questions such as (1) Who is collecting the data? (2) For what use is the data being collected? and (3) For what purpose will the data be disseminated? Education and training programs should help the employee treat data as resources and respect their confidentiality.

The objective is to eliminate or minimize emotional, financial, or other damage to the owners of the data due to disclosure and misuse of inaccurate and/or incomplete data.

Data Integrity

Data integrity requires that personal data contained in certain documents such as credit reports, medical reports, police reports, debt default notices, and insurance reports be absolutely accurate, complete, up-to-date, relevant, and timely. Because these reports are automated, it puts more responsibility on information systems professionals and auditors to ensure data integrity.

Human/Product Safety

Software developers and maintainers and hardware manufacturers could be liable if their products and devices cause physical, financial, or other damage to the users. It could even cost human loss due to erroneous system design or incorrect data in the system. Other considerations include exposure to radiation and eye strain resulting from computer terminals, personal computers, workstations, or workbenches.

A risk is that people can die or become seriously ill based on output results from computer software or hardware. For example, a medical doctor could prescribe a medicine based on diagnostic results from an erroneously designed or incompletely tested expert-knowledge-based computer system.

Fairness, Honesty, and Loyalty

Fairness depends on the relationship between parties such as computer vendors and customers, their relative power structure, and the size and nature of the business transaction. Unfair practices toward employees can encourage fraudulent activities. Honesty deals with truthful representations between sellers and buyers of information technology products, devices, and services. Product advertising and labeling and contract negotiations are some areas where honesty is important. Loyalty is supposed to be a two-way street between employees and employers, between buyers and sellers, and between manufacturers and suppliers of information technology products, devices, and services. The relationship between the affected parties should be based on mutual trust, confidence, and faith instead of solely on paycheck, price, commission, and profits.

Legal Issues in Information Ethics

- Entrapment is useful for making computers more secure. Entrapment of hackers is permitted because they have no right to attack an organization. It is best to try preventive controls first and detective controls next. When these controls do not work, entrapment should begin. Entrapment is a controversial issue.
- Prelogging questionnaires are legally appropriate. Prelogging questionnaires include ascertaining whether users are authorized to use the computer and making sure that they access only the data and system to which they are entitled. Post-logging questionnaires are used after the fact and are not of much use.
- Both welcome and unwelcome screens make the computer installation and the organization name known to the public. Legal issues may arise from these screens.
- A "no trespassing" notice at a computer system's initial logon screen is an all-inclusive warning to confront potential system intruders. It is a deterrent tactic to scare system intruders. Placing this notice is legal.
- Use of pirated (bootleg) software can lead to legal problems because it allows users to obtain software from unauthorized sources (e.g., Internet). It can also introduce some risks such as computer viruses and infringement of freeware copyrights. Freeware is software that is made available to the public at no cost. The author retains copyrights and can place restrictions on how the program is used and distributed.
- An effective way to prevent software piracy is to use a dongle device. A dongle is a small hardware device that is shipped with some software packages. The dongle is hard-coded with a unique serial number that corresponds to the software. When the program runs, it checks for the presence of the device. If the device is not plugged in, the program will not run.

Law and Information Technology

Laws, directives, and regulations exist to protect consumers, industries, and the society as a whole. They do not normally provide detailed instructions for protecting computer-related assets (e.g., hardware, software, and data). Instead, they specify requirements such as restricting the availability of personal data to authorized users. Handbooks or manuals are needed to provide detailed instructions, in developing an effective, overall security approach, and in selecting cost-effective controls to meet such requirements. Following are some examples of laws, directives, and regulations.

The Clinger-Cohen Act of 1996

The Clinger-Cohen Act of 1996 is intended to improve the productivity, efficiency, and effectiveness of U.S. federal programs through the improved acquisition, use, and disposal of information technology (IT) resources. Among other provisions, the law (1) encourages federal agencies to evaluate and adopt best management and acquisition practices used by both private and public sector organizations; (2) requires agencies to base decisions about IT investments on quantitative and qualitative factors associated with the costs, benefits, and risks of those investments and to use performance data to demonstrate how well the IT expenditures support improvements to agency programs through measurements such as reduced costs, improved employee productivity, and higher customer satisfaction; and (3) requires executive agencies to appoint CIOs to carry out the IT management provisions of the act and the broader information resources management requirements of the Paperwork Reduction Act. The Clinger-Cohen Act also streamlines the IT acquisition process by eliminating the General Services Administration's central acquisition authority, placing procurement responsibility directly with federal agencies and encouraging the adoption of smaller, modular IT acquisition projects.

U.S. Computer Security Act of 1987

The U.S. Computer Security Act of 1987 requires federal agencies to identify sensitive systems, conduct computer security training, and develop computer security plans. The Act, which focuses on protecting computer-related assets, does the following.

- It requires federal agencies to identify existing systems and new systems under development that contain sensitive information.
- It requires development of a security plan for each identified sensitive computer system.
- It requires mandatory periodic training in computer security awareness and accepted computer security practice of all employees involved with the management, use, or operation of federal computer systems within or under the supervision of a federal agency.

The Computer Security Act of 1987 addresses the importance of ensuring and improving the security and privacy of sensitive information in the U.S. federal computer systems. The act requires that the National Institute of Standards and Technology (NIST) develop standards and guidelines for computer systems to control loss and unauthorized modification or disclosure of sensitive information and to prevent computer-related fraud and misuse. The act also requires that all operators of federal computer systems, including both federal agencies and their contractors, establish security plans.

U.S. Privacy Act of 1974

This law was enacted to provide for the protection of information related to individuals maintained in federal information systems and to grant access to such information by the individual. The law establishes criteria for maintaining the confidentiality of sensitive data and guidelines for determining which data are covered.

The Act imposes numerous requirements upon federal agencies to prevent the misuse of data about individuals, to respect its confidentiality, and to preserve its integrity. Federal agencies can meet these requirements by the application of selected managerial, operational, and technical control procedures that, in combination, achieve the objectives of the Act.

The major provisions of the Act (1) limit disclosure of personal information to authorized persons and agencies; (2) require accuracy, relevance, timeliness, and completeness of records; and (3) require the use of safeguards to ensure the confidentiality and security of records.

Although the Act sets up legislative prohibitions against abuses, technical and related procedural safeguards are required in order to establish a reasonable confidence that compliance is indeed achieved. It is thus necessary to provide a reasonable degree of protection against unauthorized disclosure, destruction, or modification of personal data, whether intentionally caused or resulting from accident or carelessness.

The Privacy Act of 1974 protects the privacy of individuals identified in IS maintained by U.S. federal agencies by regulating the collection, maintenance, use, and dissemination of information by such agencies.

U.S. OMB Circular A-130, Management of Federal Information Resources

Office of Management and Budget (OMB) Circular A-130, Appendix III, Security of Federal Automated Information Systems, has specific requirements for establishing the agency computer security program. The program should include application security, personnel security, information technology installation security, and security awareness and training programs. Federal agencies are required to address security in their annual internal control report required under OMB Circular A-123.

U.S. OMB Circular A-123, Internal Control Systems

Office of Management and Budget (OMB) Circular A-123 has specific policies and standards for federal agencies for establishing and maintaining internal controls in their programs and administration activities. This includes requirements for vulnerability assessments and internal control reviews. The main provisions of A-123 became law through the enactment of the Federal Manager's Financial Integrity Act of 1982.

U.S. Federal Managers' Financial Integrity Act of 1982

This law enacted the main provisions of OMB Circular A-123. Its purpose is to ensure that agencies maintain effective systems of accounting and administrative controls against fraud, waste, and abuse.

U.S. OMB Circular A-127, Financial Management Systems

OMB Circular A-127 has specific policies and standards for federal agencies for establishing and maintaining internal controls in financial management systems. This includes requirements for annual reviews of agency financial systems that build on reviews required by OMB Circular A-123.

Paperwork Reduction Act

The Paperwork Reduction Act (PRA) of 1995 applied life-cycle management principles to information management and focused on reducing the U.S. government's information collection burden. To this end, PRA designated senior information-resources manager positions in the major departments and agencies with responsibility for a wide range of functions. PRA also created the Office of Information and Regulatory Affairs within the OMB to provide central oversight of information management activities across the federal government.

U.S. Freedom of Information Act

The Freedom of Information Act of 1966 has established the right of public access to government information by requiring U.S. federal agencies to make information accessible to the public, either through automatic disclosure or upon specific request, subject to specified exemptions.

This law makes federal information readily available to the public. It also establishes the conditions under which information may be withheld from the public to ensure that certain information such as trade secrets be protected.

Security and Freedom Through Encryption (SAFE) Act

The SAFE Act, which was approved in May 1997, guarantees the rights of all U.S. citizens and residents to use or sell any encryption technology. The purpose is to relax export controls on encryption. The bill specifically makes it legal for any person to use encryption, regardless of encryption algorithm, key length, or implementation technique; makes it legal for any person to sell encryption software, regardless of encryption algorithm, key length, or implementation technique; and prohibits the state and federal governments from requiring anyone to surrender control of an encryption key. Note that the bill specifies legal, not illegal, usage of encryption.

The Act, for example, potentially escalates a minor crime to felony status if the person committing the minor crime used encryption in carrying it out. The Act allows the U.S. software industry to provide the data security features that consumers require to protect their data. In the past, government restrictions on encryption prevented this opportunity. The Act gives the American software users the freedom to use software with unlimited encryption strengths, prohibits mandatory key escrow requirements, and allows for export of encryption software.

Electronic Communications Privacy Act (ECPA)

The Electronic Communications Privacy Act (ECPA) governs how investigators can obtain stored account records and contents from network service providers, including Internet service providers (ISPs), telephone companies, cell phone service providers, and satellite services. ECPA issues arise often in cases involving the Internet: any time investigators seek stored information concerning Internet accounts from providers of Internet service, they must comply with the statute.

The Promotion of Commerce Online in the Digital Era Act and the Encryption Communications Privacy Act

Both Acts significantly liberalized export restrictions on software with strong encryption and seek to protect both privacy and security on the Internet. Both bills give software users the freedom to use data security software with no government intervention.

The Economic Espionage and Protection of Proprietary Economic Information Act of 1996

The Act addresses the problem of industrial and corporate espionage work. The law allows the Federal Bureau of Investigation (FBI) to investigate cases in which a foreign intelligence service attacks American firms to gather proprietary information to benefit companies in their own countries. High-technology and defense industries are the primary targets. The Act redefines *stolen property* to include proprietary economic information.

The Act supplements state trade secret laws and defines a trade secret to be financial, technical, business, engineering, scientific, or economic information, whether tangible or intangible and regardless of how it is stored. In addition, the Act specifies that the owner must take "reasonable measures" to keep the information secret.

Penalties under the Act are up to $500,000 and 15 years in prison (10 years if a foreign government's interest is not involved). The Act also gives the government the right to seize any proceeds from the sale of trade secrets or property obtained as a result of espionage.

U.S. Federal Sentencing Guidelines

The U.S. federal sentencing guidelines for organizational defendants became effective in November of 1991. These guidelines provide judges with a compacted formula for sentencing business organizations for various white collar crimes. Included are federal securities, antitrust, and employment and contract laws as well as the crimes of mail and wire fraud, kickbacks and bribery, and money laundering.

Specific Federal Sentencing Guidelines

The federal sentencing guidelines represent a unique "carrot-and-stick" approach calling for business organizations found guilty of crimes to face sanctions reaching potentially hundreds of millions of dollars (the "stick"). Organizations may be given offsetting credits against these penalties if they can demonstrate that (a) they exercised due diligence (reasonable care) prior to the offense, (b) the wrongdoing was investigated, and (c) they cooperated with government investigators (the "carrot"). *The fines and penalties are adjusted depending upon whether an organization has an effective program to prevent or detect violations of law.*

An organization is well advised to be able to demonstrate, prior to the accusation of any offense, that it exercised **due diligence** in seeking to prevent and detect criminal conduct by its agents. Due diligence requires that the organization has taken, at a minimum, the following seven steps.

1. Established compliance policies that define standards and procedures.
2. Assigned specific high-level responsibility to ensure compliance with these standards and procedures.
3. Used **due care** in not delegating substantial discretionary authority to individuals who could engage in illegal activities.
4. Communicated standards and procedures to all employees (by requiring participation in training programs and disseminating publications).
5. Took reasonable steps to achieve compliance with standards (by utilizing monitoring and auditing systems including a system, for employees to report violations without fear of reprisal).
6. Consistently enforced standards through appropriate disciplinary mechanisms.
7. Took all reasonable steps to prevent future similar offenses.

The federal sentencing guidelines are equally applicable to computers and information systems security function of a business organization by requiring security plans, policies, procedures, and standards developed and implemented. It is important to ensure that these policies and procedures reflect the actual controls and practices being used and enforced.

Right to Financial Privacy Act of 1978 (U.S.)

Few countries require banks and financial institutions to *report* currency transactions that exceed a specified amount. However, many other countries require banks to *record* transactions over some specified threshold. These records can then be made available to law enforcement officials under the terms of that country's bank secrecy laws.

Many countries also either require or encourage financial institutions to report those transactions considered to be suspicious or indicative of criminal activity. However, certain provisions in the Right to Financial Privacy Act of 1978 generated questions in the banking community about the type of customer information that could be disclosed in reporting a suspicious transaction, as well as concerns of potential liability for such disclosure. Subsequent legislation provided certain protections against civil liability for institutions reporting suspicious transactions.

The Money Laundering Control Act of 1986 (U.S.)

What Is Money Laundering?

To launder money is to disguise the origin or ownership of illegally gained funds to make them appear legitimate. Hiding legitimately acquired money to avoid taxation also qualifies as money laundering. It is not limited to drug trafficking. It is associated with nearly all kinds of "crimes for profit," such as real estate fraud and savings and loan abuses.

Law enforcement officials describe three steps in money laundering.

1. *Placement*—introducing cash into the banking system or into legitimate commerce
2. *Layering*—separating the money from its criminal origins by passing it through several financial transactions, for example, transferring it into and then out of several bank accounts or exchanging it for travelers' checks or a cashier's check
3. *Integration*—aggregating the funds with legitimately obtained money or providing a plausible explanation for its ownership

The Money Laundering Control Act of 1986 amended the Right to Financial Privacy Act to explicitly define the specific types of account information that financial institutions could disclose without customer permission, subpoena, summons, or search warrant. The intent was to strike a balance between the privacy rights of customers while allowing financial institutions to give government investigators enough information about the nature of possible violations in order for such investigators to determine whether there was a basis to proceed with a summons, subpoena, or search warrant for additional information. The 1986 amendments also established a limited "good faith" defense whereby financial institutions and their employees, when making a disclosure of certain specified information, would be shielded from a civil liability to the customer for such disclosure or for any failure to notify the customer of such disclosure. Despite this provision, many banks were concerned that they might still be liable under the Right to Financial Privacy Act for disclosures made on a voluntary basis.

The Racketeer Influenced and Corrupt Organization Act (U.S.)

In 1970, the U.S. Congress enacted the Racketeer Influenced and Corrupt Organization Act (RICO) as a weapon against mobsters and racketeers who were influencing legitimate business. The Act defines the term "racketeering activities" to include crimes such as mail fraud and fraud of the sale and purchase of securities.

The RICO Act can bring civil or criminal cases, where the former can include treble damages. For civil cases, the standard of proof requires a "preponderance of evidence." The plaintiff must prove that the defendant (1) employed any device to defraud, (2) made untrue statement of material fact or omitted material fact, and (3) engaged in act, practice, or course of business to commit fraud or deceit in connection with purchase or sale of securities. The plaintiff must also prove damages sustained, material misstatement or omission, reliance, and a scienter.

For criminal cases, the standard of proof is "beyond a reasonable doubt." Section 32(a) of the Act establishes criminal liability for "willfully" and "knowingly" making false or misleading statements in reports under the 1934 Security Exchange Act. This section provided for criminal penalties consisting of fines of not more than $100,000 or imprisonment of not more than five years or both.

In summary, the computer is used as a tool or media to perpetrate fraudulent activities. The information system security management must develop policies, procedures, and standards to prevent and/or detect these fraudulent activities. To this end, security plans and programs must be effective and efficient.

Organization for Economic Cooperation and Development (OECD)

OECD developed "Guidelines for the Security of Information Systems" in 1980 covering data collection limitations, quality of data, limitations on data use, IS security safeguards, and accountability of the data controller.

Computer Fraud and Abuse Act (U.S.)

The Act, amended in 1996, deals with computers used in interstate commerce and makes it a crime to alter, damage, or destroy information, to steal passwords, or to introduce viruses or worms. It covers classified defense or foreign relations information, records of financial institutions or credit reporting agencies, and government computers. Unauthorized access or access in excess of authorization became a felony for classified information and a misdemeanor for financial information. The Act provides for limited imprisonment for the unintentional damage to one year and civil penalties in terms of compensatory damages or other relief.

The Foreign Corrupt Practices Act of 1974 (U.S.)

The Foreign Corrupt Practices Act of 1974, among other things, requires certain procedures for a public corporation to preserve its records. A vital records program must be initiated considering legal, regulatory, and business requirements. Internal accounting controls of a corporation should provide reasonable, cost-effective safeguards against the unauthorized use or disposition of company assets. This requires executives of public companies to preserve computer records, which requires disaster recovery planning. Hefty penalties can be assessed against executives found to be negligent in this area.

Health Insurance Portability and Accountability Act (HIPAA)

Purpose

The U.S. Congress recognized the need for national patient record privacy standards in 1996 when they enacted the Health Insurance Portability and Accountability Act (HIPAA) of 1996. The law includes provisions designed to save money for health care businesses by encouraging electronic transactions, but it also required new safeguards to protect the security and confidentiality of that information.

Accountability for Medical Records Use and Release

In HIPAA, Congress provided penalties for covered entities that misuse personal health information.

CIVIL PENALTIES Health planners, providers, and clearinghouses that violate these standards will be subject to civil liability. Civil money penalties are $100 per violation, up to $25,000 per person, per year for each requirement or prohibition violated.

CRIMINAL PENALTIES Criminal penalties are up to $50,000 and one year in prison for obtaining or disclosing protected health information; up to $100,000 and up to five years in prison for obtaining protected health information under "false pretenses;" and up to $250,000 and up to ten years in prison for obtaining or disclosing protected health information with the intent to sell, transfer, or use it for commercial advantage, personal gain, or malicious harm.

British Computer Act

The British Standard 7799 (BS7799) is a comprehensive set of controls addressing information security. It is intended to serve as a single reference point for identifying controls needed for most situations where information systems are used in industry and commerce for large, medium, and small organizations. The standard has three major components: confidentiality, integrity, and availability.

The standard points out how organizations are dependent on information systems and technologies, and the need to comply with laws and contractual terms. It makes the point that the use and advances in information technology increased the range of possible threats to information security, including such things as fraud, unauthorized access, damage, and system failures.

The standard recommends the following controls at the system specification and design stages.

1. Information security policy document
2. Allocation of security responsibilities
3. Information security education and training
4. Reporting of security incidents
5. Virus controls (prevention, detection, and correction)
6. Business continuity planning process
7. Control of intellectual property
8. Safeguarding of company records and equipment
9. Compliance with data protection laws and regulations
10. Compliance with organization's security policy

U.S. Computer Software Piracy

The purpose of the U.S. Executive Order on computer software piracy (intellectual property) is to prevent and combat computer software piracy by observing the relevant provisions of international agreements in effect in the United States, including applicable provisions of the World Trade Organization Agreement on Trade-Related Aspects of Intellectual Property Rights, the Berne Convention for the Protection of Literary and Artistic Works, and relevant provisions of U.S. Federal law, including the Copyright Act.

International Issues

International and Multinational Organizations

An increasing number of the world's corporations have branched into countries all over the globe, becoming true multinationals. While they may have headquarters in a single country, they operate divisions and subsidiaries in different countries to take advantage of local benefits. For instance, a company might establish engineering facilities in countries that offer large pools of qualified engineers, build production lines in countries that can supply inexpensive labor, and open sales offices in countries that are strategically situated for effective marketing.

Because of spread of operations, a company's nationality is not always clear. For example, consider **IBM** and **Philips**. While IBM is known as an "American" corporation because its headquarters and most of its research activities are in the

United States, the company has numerous subsidiaries in other countries. These subsidiaries are registered and operate under the laws of the respective countries, and they employ local workers. Likewise, not many Americans realize that Philips's headquarters is in the Netherlands and that it owns one of the largest U.S. sellers of electric razors, **Norelco**. Similarly, **Intel**, an American company, has major research and development facilities in Israel, where some of its latest microprocessors have been developed.

One hundred of the 500 largest Canadian companies have majority U.S. ownership, and 90% of U.S. multinational companies have Canadian offices. Japanese companies own whole U.S. subsidiaries in every imaginable industry. British companies have the largest foreign investment in the United States. Thanks to the North American Free Trade Agreement (NAFTA) and agreements between the United States and the European Union, we may witness the internationalization of many more American, Canadian, Mexican, and European corporations.

Networks link businesses and individuals across the country and worldwide.

To effectively manage an international corporation, executives need a free flow of information among divisions across national borders—as among departments within a company operating in a single location. A number of surveys reflect the fact that IS managers are giving increasing attention to international integration of their ISs.

Using the Web for International Commerce

The emergence of the Web as a global medium for information exchange has made it an important vehicle for both business-to-business (B2B) and business-to-consumer (B2C) commerce. In the future, English is expected to be the language of fewer than one-third of Internet users worldwide, and the ratio of non-English speakers to English speakers will continue to grow.

The spread of Internet usage opens great opportunities for businesses the world over. The opportunities are especially great because some of the countries with low participation rates currently have the greatest potential, such as China. Only about 3.2 million Chinese logged on in 2000, but more than a billion Chinese may do so in the future.

The Web offers opportunities not only to increase revenue, but also to save on costs. Consider, for example, how much money could be saved if, instead of printing product and service manuals on paper and shipping them to customers, companies published them on the Web, ready to be downloaded at a user's convenience. Furthermore, imagine the convenience if the manuals were prepared using hypertext, graphics, and animation for easier and more informative use.

Nortel Networks did exactly that. It converted all its product documentation to the Web. The company sells telecommunications hardware to customers in numerous countries from its base in Nashville, Tennessee. Before moving its documentation to the Web, Nortel had a large customer-service unit that responded to customer queries and complaints. Now, customers serve themselves through Nortel's online information, and the customer-service unit is significantly smaller. The company also translated the documentation into the languages of its customers, who can now access the documents on the Web and read them in their native languages. (The translation was performed by commercially available software.) As a result, the company cut its customer service costs by 50%.

Businesses that cater to international audiences must "glocalize" their Web sites.

Organizations that wish to do business globally through their Web sites must be sensitive to local audiences. Thus, Web sites should be tailored to the audiences they are meant to reach. For example, while English is still the single most posted language on the Web, the majority of Web surfers are no longer native English speakers. As Exhibit 800.82 shows, organizations must plan and carefully design their global sites so that they also cater to local needs and preferences, a process sometimes called **glocalization**.

Challenges to Global Information Systems

While the Web offers great opportunities for establishing international ISs, global ISs are not without their problems, both for B2B and B2C e-commerce. Some of the challenges that businesses must address are technological barriers, electronic payment mechanisms, different languages and cultures of the audiences, economic and political considerations, lack of standardized business practices, and legal barriers. We discuss these challenges in the following sections.

Exhibit 800.82 *Imperatives to Heed When Designing Web Sites for an International Audience*

Plan	Plan the site before you develop it. An international audience requires more planning than a national site.
Know the Audience	Learn the cultural preferences, convention differences, and legal issues, or use experts who know these preferences. Tailor each local site (or the local section of your site) to the way in which the local people prefer to shop, buy, and pay.
Translate Properly	Use local interpreters to translate content for local audiences. Do not use software or other automated methods, unless humans review the translated material. Experienced translators are attentive to contemporary nuances and connotations.
Be Egalitarian	Do not let any audience feel as if it is less important than other audiences. Keep all local sections of your site updated and with the same level of information and services.
Avoid Cultural Imperialism	If the local language or culture has a word or picture for communicating an idea, use it; do not use those of your own country. Give the local audience a homey experience.

Technological Challenges

Not all countries have adequate information technology infrastructures to allow resident companies to build international ISs. International ISs, especially those using the Web, often incorporate graphics to convey technical or business information, and those applications, as well as interactive software, require increasingly fast (wide bandwidth) communication lines. The bandwidth of some countries' lines, such as China's, is too narrow for high-volume transmission of the graphically rich Web pages and applets. Thus, companies may have to offer two versions of their sites, one for wide-bandwidth and another for narrow-bandwidth lines. Other technological challenges include language conversion and telephone number lengths.

Differences in Payment Mechanisms

One of the greatest expectations of e-commerce is easy payment methods for what we buy. Credit cards are very common in North America and are the way businesses prefer to be paid. However, this practice is not widespread in other regions of the world. The high rate of stolen credit cards, especially in Eastern Europe, attaches risk to such payments and deters potential online customers. Also, most Europeans prefer to use debit cards rather than credit cards. (The holder of a debit card must maintain a bank account from which the purchase is immediately deducted; the holder of a credit card receives a grace period of up to a month and pays the credit-card issuer in any way he or she prefers.) Americans are more willing to give credit-card details via the Web than any other nation. Until citizens of other countries become as willing to do so, payment through the Web, and therefore B2C trade, will not reach its full potential.

Language Differences

To communicate internationally, parties must agree on one acceptable language, and that can create problems. For instance, data may not be transmittable internationally in real time because the information must first be translated (usually by human beings). Although some computer applications can translate "on the fly," they are far from perfect. Another hurdle is that national laws usually forbid businesses to run accounting and other systems in a foreign language, leading to an awkward and expensive solution: running these systems in two languages, the local one and English, which is the *de facto* international language.

Companies that are in the forefront of Web-based e-commerce have translated their original Web sites into local languages. They localize their sites by creating a dedicated site for each national audience. But translation may be tricky. For instance, the Taiwanese use the traditional set of Chinese characters, but people in the People's Republic of China prefer the simplified character set. **Cisco Systems**, a communications hardware leader, discovered that there is one Spanish word for "router" (a device that routes packets of electronic communication) in Spain and another in Latin America. Because the company wanted to use one Spanish-language site, it had a problem. The Spanish representatives insisted on "their" word, while the Latin American representatives insisted on theirs—in fact, Latin Americans did not even know the term the Spaniards used for "router."

Cultural Differences

Cultural differences refer in general to the many ways in which people from different countries vary in their tastes, gestures, preferred colors, treatment of people of certain gender or age, attitudes about work, opinions about different ethical issues, and the like. ISs may challenge cultural traditions by imposing the culture of one nation upon another. Conservative groups in some countries have complained about the "Americanization" of their young generations. Governments may be inclined to forbid the reception of some information for reasons of undesirable cultural influence. An example of such fear is the French directive against use of foreign words in government-supported mass media and official communications. A similar example is the ban by the Canadian province of Quebec on the use of non-French words in business signs. These fears have intensified with growth of the Internet and use of the Web. Because the Web was invented in the United States and is still used by Americans more than by any other single nation, its predominant culture is American.

Some nations are afraid that cross-border information flow promotes cultural imperialism.

As we mentioned previously, companies that use the Web for business must learn cultural differences and design their sites accordingly. **Lycos**, the company running one of the Web's predominant search engines and portals, launched a Korean version of its portal site in March 1999. The company uses a golden retriever mascot that looks attractive to Americans. But the company discovered that the dog meant something completely different to Koreans: food. Europeans did not like the mascot either.

Here are some other examples of cultural differences that Web site designers need to keep in mind: black has sinister connotations in Europe, Asia, and Latin America; the index-finger-to-thumb sign of approval is a rude gesture meaning "jackass" in Brazil; the thumbs-up sign is a rude gesture in Latin America, as is the waving hand in Arab countries; and pictures of women with exposed arms or legs are offensive in many Muslim countries.

Conflicting Economic, Scientific, and Security Interests

The goal of corporate management is to seize a large market share and maximize its organization's profits. The goal of a national government is to protect the economic, scientific, and security interests of its people. Scientific information is both an important national resource for a country and a great source of income for corporations, so occasionally those interests conflict.

For instance, companies that design and manufacture weapons have technical drawings and specifications that are financially valuable to the company but also valuable to the security of their country. Hence, many governments, including the U.S. federal government, do not allow the exchange of weapon designs. Transfer of military information to another country, even if the receiving party is part of an American business, is prohibited. Often, products whose purpose has nothing to do with the military are included in the list of prohibited trade items, because of the fear that they could be converted for use against the country of origin. In recent years, the list has included many software packages. The result is that, although American divisions of a company may use such software, their sister divisions in other countries cannot.

Governments prohibit the sharing of sensitive information with other countries, especially if the information can compromise national security.

Consider some of the free encryption applications offered for downloading by American software developers, particularly PGP (Pretty Good Privacy). The developer, Phil Zimmerman, was faced with federal criminal charges and severe penalties because he offered his excellent encryption software on the Web. His purpose was to allow individuals and companies to scramble their communications via computer networks. Companies use such software to protect corporate information. However, encryption methods are on the U.S. federal government's list of restricted exports because, like weapons, they could compromise America's national security. Since the incident, the government has relaxed its rules but still reviews export of some types of encryption software.

Another problem that arises with international information interchange is that countries treat trade secrets, patents, and copyrights differently. Sometimes business partners are reluctant to transfer documents when one partner is in a country that restricts intellectual property rights, while another is in a country that has more relaxed laws to protect intellectual property. On the other hand, the employees of a division of a multinational corporation may be able to divulge information locally with impunity. Intellectual property is tightly protected in the United States, and American trade negotiators and diplomats have pressured some countries to pass and enforce similar laws. Reportedly, the legislatures of several Asian nations have passed such laws or revised existing laws in response to American pressure.

Political Challenges

Information is power. And some countries fear that a policy of free access to all information may threaten their sovereignty. For instance, a nation's government may believe that access to certain data, such as the location and quantity of natural resources, may give other nations an opportunity to control an indigenous resource, thereby gaining a business advantage that would adversely affect the resource-rich country's political interests.

Governments are also increasingly recognizing software as an important economic resource, leading some countries to dictate that companies operating within their borders must purchase software from within their borders. For example, until 1997, Brazil's authorities allowed local businesses to purchase software from other countries only after demonstrating that the software was not available domestically. The rule was enforced even if the business was owned by a foreign company. Similar laws regulate the purchase and installation of telecommunications hardware and software. These policies can hinder standardization and compatibility of international ISs by preventing use of the same software throughout a multinational corporation.

Lack of Standards

Differences in standards must be considered when integrating ISs internationally, even within the same company. Because nations use different standards and rules in their daily business operations, sometimes records within one company are incompatible. For instance, the bookkeeping records of one division of a multinational company may be incompatible with the records of other divisions and headquarters. As another example, the United States still uses the English system of weights and measures (inches, feet, miles, quarts, pounds, and so on), while the rest of the world (including England) officially uses the metric system (centimeters, meters, liters, kilograms, and the like). There are also different standards for communicating dates, times, temperatures, and addresses. The United States uses the format of month, day, year, while the rest of the world records dates in the format of day, month, year. A date recorded as 10/12/03 may be misinterpreted. The United States uses a 12-number time notation with the addition of a.m. or p.m., while the rest of the world uses a 24-number notation (called "military time" in the United States because the U.S. military does use this notation). America uses Fahrenheit temperatures, while other countries use Celsius temperatures. Americans communicate addresses in the format of street number, street name, and city name. Citizens of some other countries communicate addresses in the format of street name, street number, and city name.

Differences in standards pose a challenge to companies that wish to integrate their information system across national borders.

The damage that different standards can cause may be extremely costly. In 1999 NASA lost track of a spacecraft that it sent to Mars. An investigation found that an error in a transfer of information between the Mars Climate Orbiter team in Colorado and the mission navigation team in California led to the spacecraft's loss. Apparently, one team used English units, and the other used metric units for a key spacecraft operation. The information was critical to the maneuvers required to place the spacecraft in the proper Mars orbit. The cost to U.S. taxpayers was $165 million.

Legal Barriers

Although many of the challenges involved in cross-border data transfer have been resolved through international agreements, one remains unresolved: respect for individual privacy in the conduct of international business. Interestingly, despite the importance we attach to privacy, that value is not even mentioned in the constitutions of the United States and many other countries. Nonetheless, a majority of the democratic nations try to protect individual privacy.

Countries differ in their approaches to the issue of privacy, as reflected in their laws. Some are willing to forego some privacy for the sake of a freer flow of information and better marketing. Others restrict any collection of personal data without the consent of the individual.

Data protection laws from various countries can be generally described by three different criteria.

1. Whether the law applies to the collection and treatment of data by the private sector (companies), the public sector (governments), or by both

2. Whether the laws apply to manual data, to automated data, or to both
3. Whether data protected under the law are only those concerning human beings or those concerning both human and "legal" entities (that is, organizations)

Except for the American and Canadian privacy acts, privacy laws apply to both the public and private sectors; that is, government and private organizations are subject to the same regulation of collection, maintenance, and disclosure of personal data. Over half the laws (including U.S. federal statutes) encompass manual and computerized record-keeping systems. A minority of the laws apply to legal persons. Denmark, Austria, and Luxembourg are among the countries that protect the privacy of some types of corporations.

Countries that support protection of corporate data argue that it is difficult to separate data about individuals from data on business activities involving or performed by individuals, especially with small businesses. For example, the financial information of a small business also reveals financial information about the people involved with and/or running the business. Furthermore, a large corporation may unfairly compete against a smaller firm if it has access to the smaller firm's data.

The most important development regarding privacy in recent years was the 1998 adoption of the Directive on Data Privacy by the European Union (EU). The EU defines personal data as "any information relating to an identified or identifiable natural person; an identifiable person is one who can be identified, directly or indirectly, in particular by reference to an identification number or to one or more factors specific to his physical, physiological, mental, economic, cultural or social identity."

Some of the principles of the directive are in stark conflict to the practices of U.S. businesses and therefore severely limit the free flow of personal data between the United States and the EU. For example, consider the following provisions and how they conflict with U.S. practices.

Two Approaches to E-Commerce Jurisdiction As we have seen, the issue of e-commerce jurisdiction is broad. The U.S. Federal Trade Commission and European government organizations have examined the issue in an attempt to reach an international agreement such as the one reached within the EU.

There are two approaches to such agreement. One approach is the *country of origin* principle, whereby all legal matters are confined to the country from which the site operates. Under this principle, the laws of that country apply to the operations and conduct of the site and whoever interacts with the site, regardless of their own location. Therefore, a lawsuit could be brought only in the country of the Web site and would be adjudicated according to that country's laws. Under this principle it is likely many firms would opt to establish Web sites in countries with lax consumer protection laws.

The other approach is the *country of destination*, whereby the laws of the country to which the site caters apply regarding dealings with the site, regardless of the site's country. The EU adopted this approach within its territory. It may take several years until we see an international agreement on e-commerce jurisdiction.

- Personal data can be collected only for specified, explicit, and legitimate purposes and not further processed in a way incompatible with those purposes. However, in the United States, businesses often collect data from people without telling them how the data will be used. Many U.S. corporations use personal data for purposes other than the original one, and many organizations purchase personal data from other organizations, so subjects do not even know that the data are used, let alone for what purpose. Obviously, these activities would not be allowed under the EU directive.
- Personal data may be processed only if the subject has given unambiguous consent or under other specific circumstances that the directive provides. Such circumstances are not required by American laws. In the United States, private organizations are allowed to process personal data without the subject's consent, and for practically any purpose.
- Individuals or organizations that receive personal data (the directive calls them "controllers") not directly from the subject must identify themselves to the subject. In the United States, many organizations purchase personal data from third parties and never notify the subject.
- People have the right to obtain from data controllers "without constraint at reasonable intervals and without excessive delay or expense" confirmation that data about them are processed, to whom the data are disclosed, and the source that provided the data. They are also entitled to receive information on the "logic involved in any automatic processing of data concerning" them at least in the case of automated decision making. Decision making, practically speaking, means using decision-support systems and expert systems to make decisions on hiring, credit extension, admittance to educational institutions, and so forth. None of these rights is mandated by any U.S. law.

- People have the right to object, "on request and free of charge," to the processing of personal data for the purpose of direct marketing, or to be informed before personal data are disclosed for the first time to third parties or used for direct marketing. Furthermore, data controllers must expressly offer the right to object free of charge to disclosure of personal data to others. American companies use personal data *especially* for direct marketing, never tell subjects that they obtain data about them from third parties, and rarely offer subjects the right to object to disclosure of such data to other parties.

American companies are very busy collecting, buying, and selling personal data for decision-making and marketing purposes. The American view is that such practices are essential to efficient business operations, especially in marketing and extension of credit. Thus, this huge discrepancy between the European and American approaches does not allow unrestricted flow of information.

The directive is only a framework within which member states may maintain their own, more restrictive, laws. Consider, for example, the French law, which states: "An individual shall not be subject to an administrative or private decision involving an assessment of conduct which has, as its sole basis, the automatic processing of personal data defining his profile or personality." This provision limits the use of a computer as a decision aid in certain circumstances. For instance, this law forbids automatic decisions for credit applications or admittance to a college. While the latter decision is often accompanied by human intervention, the former is often automated in the United States and other countries.

The EU directive recognizes that countries outside the EU use personal data that are transferred from the EU. It therefore provides that when a "third country does not ensure an adequate level of protection within the meaning of [the directive], member states shall take the measures necessary to prevent any transfer of data of the same type to the third country." This provision has created a strange situation: representatives of the EU arrive at least monthly in the United States to monitor American companies that process personal data of European citizens to ensure that the EU Directive on Data Protection is obeyed regarding these citizens. These representatives monitor the ISs of companies such as Visa, MasterCard, American Express, and other credit-card issuers. Companies that want to do business in EU member states must accept the restrictions of the directive on their practices. Business leaders on both continents hope that a way can be found to bridge the gap between the two approaches to data privacy, but it seems that a legal solution will not come before a change in culture. The EU did agree that the U.S. government establish a "safe harbor," a list of U.S. companies that have agreed to comply with the EU directive so that European companies can trade with them without fear of violating the directive. The U.S. Federal Trade Commission maintains the list.

Module 800 Glossary

A

Access control Hardware and software measures, such as user IDs and passwords, used to control access to information systems.

ActiveX A Microsoft scripting language for small applications for specific tasks.

Ad hoc reports Unplanned, special reports designed to help solve specific problems; also called *on-demand reports*.

ADSL (Asynchronous DSL) DSL Technology in which the downstream communication (to the subscriber) is several times greater than the upstream communication (from the subscriber). *See* DSL.

Agent of change Any person (such as an employee, a consultant, or a board member) whose work results in significant changes in the way workers perform their jobs. Often, systems analysts are agents of change because they drive companies to take fuller advantage of information technology.

Algorithm A sequence of steps one takes to solve a problem. Often, these steps are expressed as mathematical formulas.

Analog signal A continuous signal, for example a human voice or the movement of the hands in an analog watch, that represents different degrees of mechanical or electrical power.

Antecedent The *if* component of an *if-then* rule knowledge representation.

Antivirus software Software designed to detect and intercept computer viruses.

Applet A small software application, usually written in Java or another programming language for the Web.

Application A computer program that addresses a general or specific business or scientific need. General applications include electronic spreadsheets and word processors. Specific applications are written especially for a business unit to accommodate special activities.

Application/Data independence A situation in which an application can be developed to manipulate data without regard to the physical organization of the data in the files. This is achieved in the database approach to data management.

Application generator A software tool that expedites the application development process. Often, the term is synonymous with fourth generation language. Modern application generators include graphical user interfaces.

Application service provider (ASP) A firm that rents the use of software applications through an Internet link.

Application-specific software A collective term for all computer programs that are designed specifically to address certain business problems, such as a program specifically written to deal with a company's market research effort.

Arithmetic logic unit (ALU) The electronic circuitry in the central processing unit of a computer responsible for arithmetic and logic operations.

Artificial intelligence The study and creation of computer programs that mimic human behavior. This discipline combines the interests of computer science, cognitive science, linguistics, and management information systems. The main subfields of AI are: robotics, artificial vision, natural language processors, and expert systems.

Artificial vision A subfield of artificial intelligence devoted to the development of hardware and software that can mimic human vision.

ASCII (pronounced: AS-kee) American Standard Code for Information Interchange, a computer encoding scheme whereby each group of 8 bits (a byte) uniquely represents a character.

ASP *See* Application Service Provider.

Assembler A compiler for an assembly language.

Assembly languages Second-generation programming languages that assemble several bytes into groups of characters that are human-readable, to expedite programming tasks.

Asymmetric key encryption Encryption technology in which a message is encrypted with one key and decrypted with another.

Asynchronous communications Data communications whereby the communications devices must synchronize the transmission and reception after the transmission of each byte. Each byte is accompanied by synchronization bits, such as start and stop bits.

Atomic transaction A transaction whose entry is not complete until all entries into the appropriate files have been successfully completed. A data entry control.

Audit trails Names, dates, and other references in computer files that can help an auditor track down the person who used an IS for a transaction, legal or illegal.

Authentication The process of ensuring that the person who sends a message to or receives a message from another party is indeed that person.

B

Backbone The network of copper lines, optical fibers, and radio satellites that supports the Internet.

Backup Periodic duplication of data in order to guard against loss.

Backward chaining (backward reasoning) The processes in which an expert system searches the conditions that would bring about the achievement of a specified goal. For example, an ES uses backward chaining to determine how long to invest how much money in which stocks to achieve a specified yield.

Bandwidth The capacity of the communications channel; the number of signal streams the channel can support. A greater bandwidth also supports a greater bit rate, that is, transmission speed.

Banners Advertisements that appear on a Web page.

Bar code A series of wide and narrow lines that represents data. Usually printed on product tags for ease of data entry and the recording of shipment and sales by a specific machine used to read the code.

Barriers to entrants Any and all of the measures that a business can take to prevent potential competitors from entering the market.

Baseband link A communications channel that allows only a very low bit rate in telecommunications, such as unconditioned telephone twisted pair cables.

Batch processing A mode of transaction processing in which all the transactions of the same type for a given period of time are collected, and then entered into a computer system together and processed.

Baud After J.M. Emile Baudot, a French scientist; the number of signals per second that a communications channel can support.

Benchmarking The measurement of time intervals and other important characteristics of hardware and software, usually when testing them before a decision to purchase or reject.

Beta site An organization that agrees to use a new application for a specific period and report errors and unsatisfactory features to the developer in return for free use and support.

Bill of materials A list showing an explosion of the materials that go into the production of an item. Used in planning the purchase of raw materials.

Bill presentation Sending a bill (especially for telephone use, electricity, and similar services) via e-mail; usually with an option to pay online by credit card or bank transfer.

Binary number system A number system in which 2 is the base (rather than 10, which is the normal base human beings use in everyday counting). Used in computers.

Biometric A unique, measurable characteristic or trait of a human being used for automatically authenticating a person's identity. Biometrics include digitized fingerprints, retinal pictures, and voice. Used with special hardware to uniquely identify a person who tries to access a facility or an IS, instead of a password.

Bit Binary digit; either a zero or a one. The smallest unit of information used in computing.

Bit map The arrangement of bits representing an image for display on a computer monitor or a paper printout.

Bits per second (bps) The measurement of the capacity (or transmission rate) of a communications channel.

Blackouts and brownouts Periods of power loss or a significant fall in power. Such events may cause computers to stop working, or even damage them. Computers can be protected against these events by using proper equipment, such as UPS (uninterruptible power supply) systems.

Bleeding edge The situation in which a business fails because it tries to be on the technological leading edge.

Bottom-up planning An approach to planning based on satisfying the needs of individual business units. Reactive in nature.

Brainstorming The process of a group collaboratively generating new ideas and creative solutions to problems.

Bridge A device connecting two communications networks that use similar hardware.

Broadband link A communications channel that supports high-speed communication.

Browsers Special software designed to search the Web for specific sites and retrieve information in the form of text, pictures, sound, and animation.

Browsing Using a special application called a Web browser to move from one Web site to another.

Bug An error in a computer program. Despite a famous story about a real insect that interrupted the work of a 1940s computer, the word "bug" had been used for "error" a long time before the advent of computers, and has nothing to do with that event.

Bus The set of wires or soldered conductors in the computer through which the different components (such as the CPU and RAM) communicate. It also refers to a data communications topology whereby communicating devices are connected to a single, open-ended medium.

Business continuity plan Organizational plan that prepares for disruption in information systems, detailing what should be done and by whom, if critical information systems fail or become untrustworthy; also called *business recovery plan* and *disaster recovery plan*.

Business model The manner in which businesses generate income.

Business planning The general idea or explicit statement of where an organization wishes to be at some time in the future.

Business Recovery Plan (BRP) *See* Business Continuity Plan.

Buzzword A new or existing word that takes on a very specific meaning when used in a particular context. Buzzwords are usually used to impress someone with new jargon or to promote a product, service, or idea.

Byte A standard group of bits. In ASCII, a byte comprises 7 bits. In ASCII-8 and EBCDIC, a byte comprises 8 bits.

C

Cache From French, pronounced "cash." A part of RAM devoted to the most frequently used instructions and data of a program for faster retrieval.

Callback A telecommunications security measure whereby the communications device at the destination end disconnects and calls the user back at the user-provided telephone number, to ensure the authenticity of the caller.

CASE (Computer-Aided Software Engineering) Software tools that expedite systems development. The tools provide a 4GL or application generator for fast code writing, facilities for flowcharting or data-flow diagramming, data-dictionary facility, word-processing capability, and other features required to develop and document the new software. Modern CASE is often called I-CASE (integrated CASE).

Cash Management Systems Information systems that help reduce the interest and fees that organizations have to pay when borrowing money, and increase the yield that organizations can receive on unused funds.

Cathode-ray tube A display (for a computer or television set) that uses an electronic gun to draw and paint on the screen by bombarding pixels on the internal side of the screen.

CD-ROM (Compact Disc Read-Only Memory) A compact disc whose data were recorded by the manufacturer and cannot be changed.

Central IS organization Organizational structure that includes a corporate information systems team to whom all units turn with their information systems needs.

Centralized architecture Information systems architecture in which all applications and data are stored in a single mainframe.

Central Processing Unit (CPU) The circuitry of a computer microprocessor that fetches instructions and data from the primary memory and executes the instructions. The CPU is the most important electronic unit of the computer.

Champion An executive with much clout who supports a project and endeavors to muster support from top management. A champion is important for the success of a project, such as developing a new information system.

Channel (link, path) The guiding or nonguiding environment in which communications signals are transmitted.

Character The smallest piece of data in the data hierarchy.

Chargeback A method used to manage the expenses involved in rendering information system services. The greater part of the expense is charged to the budget of the business unit that ordered it.

Chief Executive Officer (CEO) The top leader in an organization, to whom a small group of executives reports.

Chief Learning Officer *See* CKO.

Children The data records linked to a parent record.

Chip A flat piece of silicon in which electronic circuitry is integrated.

CIO (Chief Information Officer) The highest-ranking IS officer in the organization, usually a vice president, who oversees the planning, development, and implementation of IS and serves as leader to all IS professionals in the organization.

Ciphertext A coded message designed to authenticate users and maintain secrecy.

Circuit switching A communication process in which a dedicated channel (circuit) is established for the duration of a transmission; the sending node signals the receiving node; the receiver acknowledges the signal and then receives the entire message.

CKO (Chief Knowledge Officer) A relatively new position in some large organizations. The CKO is responsible for garnering knowledge and making it available for future operations in which employees can learn from previous experience. The CKO works closely with the CIO, who is in charge of the technical means for garnering the necessary information. In some firms, the position is called chief learning officer.

Cleansing phase The stage at which database builders modify data into a form that allows insertion into the data warehouse.

Client/server An information system arrangement in which one large computer holds large databases that are tapped by the users of smaller local microcomputers, but much discretion and the creation of the applications that manipulate the data are in the hands of the users. The larger computer is the server, while the local computers are the clients.

Clock rate The rate of repetitive machine cycles that a computer can perform; also called *frequency*.

Closed system A system that stands alone, with no connection to another system.

Coaxial cable A transmission medium consisting of thick copper wire insulated and shielded by a special sheath of meshed wires to prevent electromagnetic interference. Supports high-speed telecommunication.

Cold turkey conversion A swift switch from an old information system to the new; also called *cut-over conversion*.

Common Gateway Interface (CGI) Special software used in Internet servers that allows the capture of data from a form displayed on a page and the storage of the data in a database.

Communications channel Any medium that supports the transmission and reception of data and information. May be a guided channel, such as wires, or an unguided channel, such as the atmosphere or space. Also called *communications link* and *communications path*.

Communications protocol The set of rules that govern data communications. When more than two parties participate in the communication, it is also called *network protocol*.

Compact disc (CD) A plastic disk in which pits and flat areas represent bits. A laser beam "reads" the data. Also called "optical disc" and "laser disc." CDs have a storage capacity 100-150 times that of regular magnetic disks. Used as the predominant medium for storing musical works and archival data.

Competitive advantage A position in which one dominates a market; also called *strategic advantage*.

Compiler A program whose purpose is to translate code written in a high-level programming language into the equivalent code in machine language for execution by the computer.

Composite key In a data file, a combination of two fields that can serve as a unique key to locate specific records.

Compression (data compression) The restorage or communication of data, using special software techniques, so that the new file takes up significantly less space on the storage medium, or takes less time to communicate over a channel.

Computer-aided design (CAD) Special software used by engineers and designers that facilitates engineering and design work.

Computerized numeric control (CNC) Control by computers that take data and create instructions that tell robots how to manufacture and assemble parts and products.

Computer virus (virus) Destructive software that propagates and is activated by unwary users; a virus usually damages applications and data files or disrupts communications.

Conclusion The *then* component of an *if-then* rule in knowledge representation.

Consumer profiling The collection of information about individual shoppers in order to know and serve consumers better.

Controls Constraints applied to a system to ensure proper use and security standards.

Control unit The circuitry in the CPU that fetches instructions and data from the primary memory, decodes the instructions, passes them to the ALU for execution, and stores the results in the primary memory.

Conversion The process of abandoning an old information system and implementing a new one.

Cookie A small file that a Web site places on a visitor's hard disk so that the Web site can remember something about the visitor later, such as an ID number or user name.

Cost/benefit analysis An evaluation of the costs incurred by an information system and the benefits gained by the system.

Critical success factors Processes and their results that are critical to the success of business units. One approach to defining requirements for information systems is the outlining of CSFs by managers.

Cultural differences The many ways in which people from different countries vary in their tastes, gestures, treatment of others, attitudes, and opinions.

Custom-designed software Software designed to meet the specific needs of a particular organization or department; also called *tailored software*.

Customer Relationship Management (CRM) A set of applications designed to gather and analyze information about customers.

Customized application A computer program designed especially for an organization, to satisfy particular business needs.

Cybermall A virtual shopping mall on the Web.

D

DASD (Direct Access Storage Device) An external storage medium that allows direct storage and retrieval of records from stored files. Example: magnetic disks and optical discs.

Data Facts about people, other subjects, and events. May be manipulated and processed to produce information.

Database A collection of shared, interrelated records, usually in more than one file. An approach to data management that facilitates data entry, update, and manipulation.

Database administrator (DBA) The individual in charge of organizational databases.

Database approach An approach to maintaining data that contains a mechanism for tagging, retrieving, and manipulating data.

Database model The general logical structure in which records are stored within a database.

Data communication The transmission and reception of digitized data in the computer, between the computer and its peripheral devices, and between computers. Data communication over a distance is called *telecommunication*.

Data definition language The part of the database management system that allows the builder of a database to define the characteristics of fields and records, and the relationships among records.

Data dictionary The part of the database that contains information about the different sets of records and fields.

Data entry control Software controls whose purpose is to minimize errors in data entry, such as rejecting a Social Security number with more or fewer than nine digits.

Data flow diagram A convention of four symbols used to describe external entities, data stores, processes, and direction of data flow in an information system.

Data management module In a decision support system, a database or data warehouse that allows a decision maker to conduct the intelligence phase of decision making.

Data manipulation language The part of a database management system that allows the user to enter commands to retrieve, update, and manipulate data in a database.

Data mining Using a special application that scours large databases for relationships among business events, such as items typically purchased together on a certain day of the week, or machinery failures that occur along with a specific use mode of a machine. Instead of the user querying the databases, the application dynamically looks for such relationships.

Data processing The operation of changing and manipulating data.

Data range The amount of data from which information is extracted, in terms of the number of organizational units supplying data or the length of time the data cover.

Data redundancy The existence of the same data in more than one place in a computer system. Although some data redundancy is unavoidable, efforts should be made to minimize it.

Data store Any form of data at rest, such as a filing cabinet or a database.

Data warehouse A huge collection of data that supports management decision making.

Data warehousing Techniques to store very large amounts of data in databases, especially for data mining.

DBA (Database administrator) The IS professional in charge of building and maintaining the organization's databases.

DBMS (Database Management System) A computer program that allows the user to construct a database, populate it with data, and manipulate the data.

Debugging The process of finding and correcting errors in software programs.

Decision A choice that must be made from between two or more alternatives.

Decision support systems Information systems that aid managers in making decisions based on built-in models. DSSs comprise three modules: data management, model management, and dialog management.

Demodulation The transformation of an analog signal (from a phone line) into a digital signal (so a computer can understand it).

Denial of service (DoS) The inability of legitimate visitors to log on to a Web site when too many malicious requests are launched by an attacker.

Desktop publishing Using word processing programs and high-quality printers to prepare books and pamphlets for publication.

DFD (Data Flow Diagram) A graphical method to communicate the data flow in a business unit. Usually serves as a blueprint for a new information system in the development process. The DFD uses four symbols, for entity, process, data store, and data flow.

Dialog module The part of a decision-support system, or any other system, that allows the user to interact with it.

Digital certificates Computer files that serve as the equivalent of ID cards.

Digital signal An expression of discrete, noncontinuous signals produced by electrical or electromagnetic bursts of different power levels. Only a digital signal can represent bits, and therefore be processed by a computer.

Digital signature An encrypted digest of the text that is sent along with a message, that authenticates the identity of the sender and guarantees that no one has altered the sent document.

Digital Subscriber Line (DSL) Technology that relieves individual subscribers of the need for the conversion of digital signals into analog signals between the telephone exchange and the subscriber jack. DSL lines are linked to the Internet on a permanent basis and support bit rates significantly greater than a normal telephone line between the subscriber's jack and the telephone exchange. The service is not offered everywhere.

Direct access The manner in which a record is retrieved from a storage device, without the need to seek it sequentially. The record's address is calculated from the value in its logical key field.

Directive An order to take a certain action.

Disaster Recovery Plan *See* Business Continuity Plan.

Distributed Denial of Service (DDoS) Multiple log-in requests from many computers to the same Web site, so that the Web site is jammed with requests and cannot accept inquiries of legitimate visitors.

Domain name The name assigned to an Internet server.

Dot-matrix printer A printer on which the print head consists of a matrix of little pins; thus, each printed character is made up of tiny dots.

Downloading The copying of data or applications from a computer to your computer, for example from a mainframe computer to a notebook computer. The term has come to mean the copying from another computer to your own computer, regardless of computer size.

Drill down The process of finding the most relevant information for executive decision making within a database or data warehouse.

Driver The software that enables an operating system to control a device, such as an optical disc drive or joystick.

DVD (Digital Video Disc) A collective term for several types of high-capacity storage optical discs, used for data storage and motion pictures.

Dynamic IP number The IP number assigned to a computer that is connected to the Internet intermittently for the duration of the computer's connection.

E

EBCDIC (Extended Binary Coded Decimal Interchange Code) A binary computer encoding scheme devised by IBM. Consists of 8 bits per byte, each byte uniquely representing a character.

E-commerce Business activity that is electronically executed between parties, such as between two businesses or between a business and a consumer.

Economic feasibility study An evaluation of whether the benefits outweigh the costs of a proposed information system over the life of the system.

Economic Order Quantity (EOQ) The optimal quantity of a specific raw material that allows a business to minimize overstocking and save cost without risking understocking and missing production deadlines.

Effectiveness The measure of how well a job is performed.

Efficiency The ratio of output to input; the greater the ratio, the greater the efficiency.

Electronic agent A computer program that searches Internet sites and other resources in a telecommunications network to respond to a request made by its user.

Electronic Data Interchange (EDI) A set of software, standards, and telecommunications technology designed to support the interchange of electronic documents between organizations.

Electronic Funds Transfer (EFT) The electronic transfer of cash from an account in one bank to an account in another bank.

Electronic Superhighway The Internet. Often called *the information superhighway*.

E-mail (electronic mail) The exchange of messages between computers either in the same building or over great distances.

Encoding scheme A convention of representing characters with another, small, set of characters or special marks. Morse code, EBCDIC, and ASCII are encoding schemes.

Encryption The conversion of plaintext to an unreadable stream of characters, especially to prevent a party that intercepts telecommunicated messages from reading them. Special encryption software is used by the sending party to encrypt messages, and by the receiving party to decipher them.

Enterprise Application Systems Information systems that fulfill a number of functions together, such as inventory planning, purchasing, payment, and billing.

Enterprise Resource Planning (ERP) An information system that supports different activities for different departments, assisting executives with planning and running different functions.

Entity Any object about which an organization chooses to collect data.

Entity relationship diagram One of several conventions for graphical rendition of the data elements involved in business processes and the logical relationships among the elements.

Ergonomics The science of designing and modifying machines to better suit people's health and comfort.

Ethernet The design, introduced and named by Xerox, for the contention data communications protocol.

Exception reports Periodic or ad hoc reports that flag facts or numbers that deviate from preset standards.

Execution error A program error in which a certain operation cannot be carried out, such as division by zero.

Executive information system An information system that extracts high-level organization-wide information from large amounts of data stored in the business' databases. Typically, an EIS presents information graphically as charts and diagrams, allowing for a quick grasp of patterns and trends. Also called *executive support system*.

Expert System (ES) A computer program that mimics the decision process of a human expert in providing a solution to a problem. Current expert systems deal with problems and diagnostics in narrow domains. An ES consists of a knowledge base, an inference engine, and a dialog management module.

Expert system shell An expert system without a knowledge base. A tool that eases the building of an expert system by prompting the designer for facts and relationships among the facts that are built into the shell as a knowledge base.

Expertise The skill and knowledge, primarily gained from experience, whose input into a process results in performance that is far above the norm.

Extensible Markup Language (XML) A programming language that tags data elements in order to indicate what the data mean.

External data Data that are collected from a wide array of sources outside the organization, including mass communications media, specialized newsletters, government agencies, and the Web.

Extraction phase The stage of data warehouse building in which the builders create the files from transactional databases and save them on the server that will hold the data warehouse.

Extranet A network, part of which is the Internet, whose purpose is to facilitate communication and trade between an organization and its business partners.

F

Fault-tolerant computer system A computer system that has extra hardware, software, and power lines that guarantee that the system will continue running even when a mishap occurs.

Feasibility studies A series of studies conducted to determine if a proposed information system can be built, and whether or not it will benefit the business; the series includes technical, economic, and operational feasibility studies.

Field A data element in a record, describing one aspect of an entity or event.

File A collection of records of the same type, for different entities or events.

File transfer protocol (ftp) Software that allows the transfer of files over communications lines.

Firewall Hardware and software designed to control access by Internet surfers to an information system, and access to Internet sites by organizational users.

First generation languages Machine languages.

Flash memory A memory chip that can be rewritten and hold its content without electric power.

Flowchart A graphical method used to describe an information system, including hardware pieces and logical processes. Over 30 symbols represent various types of operations, processes, input and output devices, and communication.

Foreign key In a relational database: a field in a file that is a primary key in another file. Foreign keys allow association of data between the two files.

Forward chaining (forward reasoning) The process in which an expert system looks for an outcome under the constraints of given conditions. Example: A medical ES accepts the conditions (age, temperature, and so on) of a patient and provides a diagnosis of the patient's disease.

Fourth-generation languages (4GLs) High-level programming languages that allow the programmer to concentrate on what the program should do, rather than on how it should do it. 4GLs contain many preprogrammed functions to expedite code writing. Sometimes called *application generators*.

Fulfillment Picking, packing, and shipping after a customer places an order online.

Full-duplex Telecommunications whereby a party can transmit and receive data at the same time while the other party also transmits and receives.

Fuzzy logic A rule-based method used in artificial intelligence to solve problems with imprecise conditions. The method uses membership functions to characterize a situation.

G

Gantt chart A list of organizational activities, along with their start and completion times.

Gateway A device that connects two communications networks, each consisting of different hardware devices, for example an IBM- and a Macintosh-based network.

General purpose application software Programs that serve varied purposes, such as developing decision-making tools or creating documents; examples include spreadsheets and word processors.

Genetic algorithms Sets of algorithms used in artificial intelligence to solve complex problems for which the number of models for a solution is huge. The algorithms are either eliminated or combined with other algorithms to eventually produce the one that can solve the problem optimally. Called *genetic algorithms* because the method mimics the evolution of species over millions of years through changes in their genetic codes.

Geographic Information Systems (GIS) Information systems that exhibit information visually on a computer monitor with local, regional, national, or international maps, so that the information can easily be related to locations or routes on the map. GISs are used, for example, in the planning of transportation and product distribution, or the examination of government resources distributed over an area.

Global village A term used to refer to our world in the age of information and telecommunications because people are highly accessible to each other.

Glocalization The planning and designing of global Web sites so that they also cater to local needs and preferences.

Graphical User Interface (GUI) Icons, frames, scroll bars, and other graphical means that make software easy and intuitive to learn and use.

Group decision support system A set of personal computers and one large screen with special software that facilitates brainstorming, the examination of ideas, voting, and reaching a decision by a group of decision makers.

Groupware Any of several types of software that enable users of computers in remote locations to work together on the same project. The users can create and change documents and graphic designs on the same monitor.

H

Hacker A person who accesses a computer system without permission.

Half-duplex Telecommunications whereby the receiving party must wait until the transmitting party finishes, before transmitting to the party. A party cannot receive while transmitting or transmit while receiving.

Hand-held computers Computers that are small enough to fit in the palm of a person's hand; also called *palm computers* or *personal digital assistants* (PDAs).

Hard disk A stack of several rigid aluminum platters usually installed in the same box that holds the CPU and other computer components; may be portable.

Help desk The group of small teams who specialize in troubleshooting problems in different areas of an information system—hardware, software, communications, and so forth.

Heuristics Rules that cannot be formulated as a result of ordinary, proven knowledge but only through experience.

Hierarchical database A database model that generally follows an upside-down tree structure, in which each record can have only one parent record.

Holistic planning Organizational planning that focuses on the big picture, including objectives and goals; also called *top-down planning*.

Home page The opening page of a Web site.

Horizontal information interchange The sharing of information by organizations in a horizontal market.

Horizontal market A market in which all players buy or sell the same type of product, making them competitors.

Hypermedia Perhaps the Web's most essential ingredient, this feature enables a computer user to access additional information by clicking on selected text or graphics displayed on-screen.

Hypertext Computer-generated text that allows the reader to click designated words (typically colored or boldfaced) to open a linked file that elaborates on the topic, or to invoke images or sound associated with the topic.

Hypertext Markup Language (HTML) A programming language for Web pages and Web browsers.

Hypertext Transfer Protocol (HTTP) Software that allows browsers to log on to Web sites.

I

If-then rules A method of knowledge representation that holds the facts in the form of *if-then* statements; also called *production rules*.

Imaging The transformation of text and graphical documents into digitized files. The document can be electronically retrieved and printed to reconstruct a copy of the original. Imaging has saved much space and expense in paper-intensive business areas.

Impact printer A printer that reproduces an image on a page using mechanical impact.

Implementation The phase of implementing a new information system that includes training and conversion; also called *delivery*.

Indexed file A data file that contains an index, a directory-like table that indicates where each record physically resides on the storage medium by the value of its key field. The records are usually organized sequentially, so that retrieval can be carried out either sequentially, without using the index, or through the index. To retrieve a record, a lookup is performed to find the record's location.

Indexed sequential organization A method of file organization that allows direct access to specific records in a sequential file by using an index of key fields.

Inference engine The part of an expert system that links facts and relationships in the knowledge base to reach a solution to a problem.

Information The product of processing data so that they can be used in a context by human beings.

Information center The unit within an organization that provides coordination, control, and support for all aspects of the organization's information systems and its users.

Information map The description of data and information flow within an organization set out in a visual chart or map.

Information overload A situation in which people have too much information from which to choose for their problem solving and decision making.

Information system (IS) A computer-based set of hardware, software, and telecommunications components, supported by people and procedures, to process data and turn them into useful information.

Information systems auditor The information systems professional whose job is to find erroneous or fraudulent transactions and investigate them; auditing.

Information Technology (IT) Refers to all technologies that collectively facilitate construction and maintenance of information systems.

Ink-jet printer Inexpensive type of printer that sprays ink to create the printed text or pictures of a computer-generated document.

Input Raw data entered into a computer for processing.

Input device A tool, such as a keyboard or voice recognition system, used to enter data into an information system.

Insourcing Assigning an IS service function to the organization's own IS unit. The term was invented to emphasize a decision not to outsource.

Instant messaging The capability for several online computer users to share messages in real time; also called *chatting online*.

Integrated circuits Electronic semiconductors within computers that integrate a large number of circuits into one silicon chip.

Intelligence (1) The ability to learn, think, and deduce; (2) The first phase in the decision-making process: gathering relevant data.

Intelligent agent A sophisticated program that can be instructed to perform services for human beings, especially on the Internet.

Interface The connection of two systems to establish interaction.

Internal data Data that are collected within the organization, usually by transaction processing systems but also through employee and customer surveys.

Internal memory The memory circuitry inside the computer, communicating directly with the CPU. Consists of RAM and ROM.

Internet An international network of networks providing millions of people with access to rich information resources.

Internet domain The part of an Internet address, such as .com, .edu, or .gov, that is shared by many users and indicates the particular community of their owners.

Internet Protocol (IP) number A unique number assigned to a server or another device that is connected to the Internet, for identification purposes consists of 32 bits.

Internet Relay Chat (IRC) Internet software that allows remote users to correspond in real time.

Internet servers The computers that are linked directly to the Internet backbone and carry the files accessed over the Internet.

Internet Service Provider (ISP) An individual or organization that provides Internet connection, and sometimes other related services, to subscribers.

Interorganizational information systems Systems that are shared by two or more organizations to transfer data electronically.

Interpreter A programming language translator that translates the source code, one statement at a time, and executes it. If the instruction is erroneous, the interpreter produces an appropriate error message.

Intranet A network using Web browsing software, that serves employees within an organization.

IS architecture The manner in which an organization's IS assets are deployed and connected.

IS infrastructure The IS resources that an organization owns, including hardware, software, and telecommunications devices and lines.

IS planning Planning for the deployment and for the resources needed to develop and maintain information systems.

IS subsidiaries Independent corporations that offer services not only to the parent company but also to other companies.

ISDN (Integrated Services Digital Network) A set of hardware and software standards that support the transmission of text, images, and sounds through the same communications channel. ISDN will result in the combination of the telephone, fax, computer, and television into one device.

J

Java Object-oriented programming language that allows Web browsers to download applets that can run on any computer with any operating system.

Join The joining of data from multiple tables.

Joint Application Development (JAD) A method of systems development that facilitates analysis and design by involving representatives of the prospective users in all of the phases and by using prototyping wherever possible.

Just In Time (JIT) The manufacturing strategy in which suppliers ship parts directly to assembly lines, saving the cost of warehousing raw materials, parts, and subassemblies.

K

Key A field in a database table whose values identify records either for display or for processing. Typical keys are part number (in an inventory file) and Social Security number (in a human resources file).

Knowledge base The collection of facts and the relationships among them that mimic the decision-making process in an expert's mind and constitute a major component of an expert system.

Knowledge engineer A programmer whose expertise is the extraction of knowledge from a domain expert and the transformation of the knowledge into code, that is, into the knowledge base of an expert system. Knowledge engineers construct expert systems.

Knowledge management The combination of activities involved in gathering, sharing, analyzing, and disseminating knowledge to improve an organization's performance.

Knowledge worker Any worker who produces information. The term roughly overlaps with "professional."

L

LAN (Local Area Network) A computer network confined to a building or a group of adjacent buildings, as opposed to a wide area network.

Laser printer A nonimpact printer that uses laser beams to produce high-quality printouts.

Learning organization The concept of an organization that accumulates knowledge through the experiences of its employees. Information systems facilitate learning by organizations.

Leaves The lowest-level records in a hierarchical database.

Legacy system An old information system still in use. Usually, the term is used when contrasting such a system with a new information system, or a new type of information system.

Level of detail The degree to which the information generated is specific.

Liquid crystal display (LCD) A flat-panel computer monitor in which a conductive-film-covered screen is filled with a liquid crystal whose molecules can align in different planes when charged with certain electrical voltage, which either blocks light or allows it to pass through the liquid. The combination of light and dark produces images of characters and pictures.

Load balancing The transfer of visitor inquiries from a busy server to a less busy server.

Logic bomb A destructive computer program that is inactive until it is triggered by an event taking place in the computer, such as the deletion of a certain record from a file.

When the event is the occurrence of a particular time, the logic bomb is referred to as a *time bomb*.

Logic error A program error that occurs when the logic of the program does not achieve its goals.

Logical design A translation of user requirements into detailed functions of a proposed information system.

M

Machine cycle The four steps that the CPU follows repeatedly: fetch an instruction, decode the instruction, execute the instruction, and store the result.

Machine language Binary programming language that is specific to a computer. A computer can execute a program only after the program's source code is translated to object code expressed in the computer's machine language.

MacOS The family of Macintosh operating systems.

Magnetic disk A disk, or set of disks sharing a spindle, coated with an easily magnetized substance to record data in the form of tiny magnetic fields.

Magnetic-ink character recognition (MICR) A technology that allows a special electronic device to read data printed with special magnetic ink. The data are later processed by a computer. MICR is widely used in banking. The bank code, account number, and the amount of a check are printed on the bottom of checks.

Magnetic tape Coated polyester tape used to store computer data; similar to tape recorder or VCR tape.

Mainframe A computer larger than a midrange computer, but smaller than a supercomputer.

Maintenance Ironing out bugs that went undetected in the final testing of a program and modifying a program to meet new business needs.

Management by exception An approach for reducing the amount of information that managers must consume that allows managers to review only exceptions from expected results that are of a certain size or type.

Management Information System (MIS) A computer-based information system used for planning, control, decision making, or problem solving.

Manufacturing execution system An information system that helps pinpoint bottlenecks in production lines.

Manufacturing Resource Planning (MRP II) The combination of MRP with other manufacturing-related activities to plan the entire manufacturing process, not just inventory.

Master Production Schedule (MPS) The component of an MRP II system that specifies production capacity to meet customer demands and maintain inventories.

Materials Requirement Planning (MRP) Inventory control that includes a calculation of future need.

Matrix organization An organization in which managers report to both a divisional executive and a functional executive. For instance, the marketing manager of the Manufacturing Division reports both to the division's president and to the corporate vice president of marketing.

M-commerce Mobile commerce, spawned by advances in technology for mobile communications devices.

Medium Anything through which data are transmitted; may be guided or unguided.

Microcomputer The smallest type of computer; includes desktop, laptop, and hand-held computers. The term is used less and less. Trade journals now use the terms *PC* and *PDA*.

Microprocessor An electronic chip that contains the circuitry of either a CPU or a processor with a dedicated and limited purpose, for example a communications processor.

Midrange computer A computer larger than a microcomputer but smaller than a mainframe.

Migration The move from old hardware or software to new hardware or software.

MIPS Millions of instructions per second.

Mirror An Internet server that holds the same software and data as another server, which may be located thousands of miles away.

Mission-critical applications Applications without which a business cannot conduct its operations.

Mission-critical hardware or software Hardware or software without which the business cannot operate and survive.

Model A representation of reality.

Model management module A collection of models that a decision-support system draws on to assist in decision making.

Modem (modulator/demodulator) A communications device that transforms digital signals to analog telephone signals, and vice versa, for data communications over voice telephone lines. Almost all of the commercial modems currently offered on the market also serve as fax devices, and are, therefore, called fax/modems. ("Fax" comes from the Latin words *fac simile*, "make alike" or "copy.")

Modulation The modification of a digital signal (from a computer) into an analog signal (for a phone line to transmit).

Multimedia Computer-based technology that provides information comprising text, images, motion pictures, and sound from the same source.

Multiplexer A device that allows a single channel to communicate data from multiple sources simultaneously.

Multiprocessing The mode in which a computer uses more than one processing unit simultaneously to process data.

Multiprogramming The capacity to allow several people to use the same computer simultaneously via different terminals.

Multitasking The ability of a computer to run more than one program seemingly at the same time; it enables the notion of windows in which different programs are represented.

N

Name-your-price auction An online auction in which participants post the prices they are willing to pay for certain goods or services and sellers are given the opportunity to meet the terms; also called a *reverse auction*.

Narrow band A small-capacity communications channel.

Native application A computer program originally written for the specific type of computer that is running it. As opposed to a native application, a cross-system application is one that was originally written for one type of machine, but then adapted for a newer computer. Usually, a cross-system application exhibits slow or poor performance.

Natural Language Processors (NLPs) Programs that are designed to take human language input and translate it into a standard set of statements that a computer can execute.

Network A combination of a communications device and a computer, or several computers, or two or more computers and terminals, so that the various devices can send and receive text or audiovisual information.

Network model A type of database that has the ability to store a record only once in the entire database, while creating links that establish relationships with several records of another type of entity.

Network protocol The set of rules that governs a network of communications devices.

Neural net An artificial intelligence computer program that emulates the way in which the human brain operates, especially its ability to learn.

Newsgroup A group of people who share questions, opinions, and information about a specific subject at a specific site.

Nonimpact printer A printer that creates an image on a page without pressing any mechanism against the paper; includes laser, ink-jet, electrostatic, and electrothermal printers.

Nonvolatile memory Storage media that keep data and programs unchanged because they do not need electric power to maintain the stored material. Examples: ROM chips and magnetic disks.

Notebook computer A computer as small as a book, yet with computing power similar to that of a desktop microcomputer.

O

Object code Program code in machine language, immediately processable by the computer.

Object linking and embedding (OLE) The linking of different applications to the same software so that it can be addressed and used by any of these applications. The object may be text, graphic, or audiovisual material.

Object-oriented programming (OOP) A programming method that combines data and the procedures that process the data into a single unit called an "object," which can be invoked from different programs.

OLAP (online analytical processing) A type of application that operates on data stored in databases and data warehouses to produce summary tables with multiple combinations of dimensions. An OLAP server is connected to the database or data warehouse server at one end, and to the user's computer at the other.

Online processing Using a computer while in current interaction with the CPU, so that the data are processed as they are entered, as opposed to batch processing.

Open source software Software whose source code can be accessed by the general public.

Open system A system that interfaces and interacts with other systems.

Open Systems Interconnection (OSI) The dominant standard that works as a general model for wide area network protocols.

Operating system System software that supports the running of applications developed to utilize its features and controls peripheral equipment.

Operational feasibility study An evaluation made to determine whether a new information system will be used as intended.

Operational managers Individuals who are in charge of small groups of workers.

Opportunity A potential increase in revenue, reduction of costs, or gain in competitive advantage that can be achieved using an information system.

Optical character recognition (OCR) A way of capturing data from source documents, in which scanning devices read characters and transform them into digital data processable by the computer.

Optical disc A disc on which data are recorded by treating the disc surface so it reflects light in different ways; also called a *compact disc* (CD).

Optical fiber A thin fiberglass filament used as a medium for transmitting bursts of light that represent bits. The most advanced physical communications channel, now in use for data, voice, and image telecommunication.

Optical tape A storage device that uses the same principles as a compact disc.

Organizational culture An umbrella term referring to the general tone of a corporate environment.

Output The result of processing data by the computer; usually, information.

Output device A device, usually a monitor or printer, that delivers information from a computer to a person.

Outsourcing Buying the services of an information service firm that undertakes some or all of the organization's IS operations.

Overhead cost A general expense carried by all departments that is considered essential to running a company.

P

Packaged software General purpose applications that come ready to install from a magnetic disk, CD, or file downloaded from a vendor's Web site.

Packet Several bytes that make up a part of a telecommunicated message.

Packet Switching A telecommunications method whereby messages are broken into groups of fixed amounts of bytes, and each group (packet) is transmitted through the shortest route available. The packets are assembled at the destination into the original message.

Palm computer A computer that is small enough to be held in a person's palm; also called a *hand-held computer* or *personal digital assistant* (PDA).

Parallel conversion Using an old information system along with a new system for a predetermined period of time before relying only on the new one.

Parallel processing The capacity for several CPUs in one computer to process different data at the same time.

Parallel transmission Transmission of more than one bit at a time; usually the transmission of one byte at a time via parallel channels. Such transmission can take place only inside the computer or between the computer and its physically close peripheral equipment, such as a printer.

Parameters The categories that are considered when following a sequence of steps in problem solving.

Parent In a hierarchical database, the data record to which several records of a lower level are linked.

Parity check A method to reduce errors in data communication both inside the computer and among remote communications devices. An extra bit is added to each transmitted byte to ascertain that the number of 1s is odd (in an odd parity check) or even (if an even parity check).

Peer-to-peer LAN A local area network (LAN) in which no central device controls communications.

Peripheral equipment The additional equipment, such as a printer and keyboard, connected to a computer.

Personal decision-support system A decision-support system that is built for the individual knowledge worker to use in his or her daily work.

Personal digital assistant (PDA) A small handheld computer. Many PDAs require the use of a special stylus to enter handwritten information that is recognized by the computer.

PERT chart A chart showing events, the activities required to reach the events, and the interdependencies among activities. The events are usually completion milestones.

Phased conversion Implementing a new information system one module at a time.

Physical design The process of information system design that includes specifying the necessary software and hardware needed to support it.

Piloting A trial conversion in which a new information system is introduced in one business unit before introducing it in others.

Pipelining A technique in which one part of a CPU can do its job while others do theirs, allowing faster processing.

Pixel (picture element) A phosphor dot on the inside of a cathode-ray tube monitor. In a color monitor a triad of red, green, and blue dots is used. When the pixels are bombarded by electrons shot from the tube's electron gun, they emit light, thereby creating an image on the screen. The larger the number of pixels on the screen, the better the resolution.

Plaintext An original message, before encryption.

Planning Focusing on shaping the future as well as monitoring and controlling processes within an organization.

Platform Either the standard hardware or the standard operating system that the organization uses. The term has been used differently in different contexts by IS professionals and trade journals.

Plug-and-play The ability of an operating system to recognize a new attachment and its function without a user's intervention.

Point of presence (POP) A telephone number that a user can dial to log on to a server even if the server is many miles away, to save the user long-distance call charges.

Point to point protocol (PPP) A protocol for communication between two computers (as opposed to a network).

Polling A protocol in which a communications processor conducts a continuous roll-call of the nodes.

Port A socket on a computer to which external devices, such as printers, keyboards, and scanners, can be connected.

Portal A site that offers a search engine and general information such as weather, news, and stock market quotations; Yahoo! is one example.

Primary key In a file, a field that holds values that are unique to each record. Only a primary key can be used to uniquely identify and retrieve a record.

Primary memory (primary storage, main memory, main storage) The built-in memory chips in the computer, made of transistors. The majority of the memory is of the RAM type, and the rest is of the ROM type.

Privacy The ability to control information about ourselves. In a larger sense, "the right to be left alone." Information technology has made invasion of privacy a major issue in our society, due to its ability to collect, maintain, store, and manipulate huge amounts of personal information.

Private Branch Exchange (PBX) A computer-based digital switching device that simultaneously handles communications of internal voice telephones, computers, and the external telephone network.

Problem Any undesirable situation.

Process Any manipulation of data, usually with the goal of producing information.

Production rules A method of knowledge representation that holds the facts in the form of *if-then* statements; also called if-then *rules*.

Productivity Efficiency, when the input is labor. The fewer labor hours needed to perform a job, the greater the productivity.

Program A set of instructions to a computer.

Programmable problem A problem that can be solved by a computer program.

Programming The process of writing software.

Programming languages Sets of syntax for abbreviated forms of instructions that special programs can translate into machine language so a computer can understand the instructions.

Project The selection of certain columns from a table.

Project management The set of activities that is performed to ensure the timely and successful completion of a project within the budget. Project management includes planning activities, hiring and managing personnel, budgeting, conducting meetings, and tracking technical and financial performance. Project management software applications facilitate these activities.

Protocol A standard set of rules that governs telecommunication between two communications devices or in a network.

Prototyping An approach to the development of information systems in which several analysis steps are skipped, to accelerate the development process. A "quick and dirty" model is developed and continually improved until the prospective users are satisfied.

Public-key encryption Encryption technology in which a public key is used to encrypt and a private key is used to decrypt.

Pyramid model A management structure in which the CEO is at the top, a small group of senior managers are one level down, a larger number of middle managers are the next level down, and so forth.

Q

Query An instruction to a database management system to retrieve records that meet certain conditions.

R

RAID (Redundant Array of Independent Disks) A set of magnetic disk packs maintained for backup purposes. Sometimes RAIDs are used for storing large databases.

Random Access Memory (RAM) The major part of a computer's internal memory. RAM is volatile; that is, software is held in it temporarily and disappears when the machine is unplugged or turned off, or it may disappear when operations are interrupted or new software is installed or activated. RAM is made of microchips containing transistors. Many computers have free sockets that allow the expansion of RAM.

Rapid Application Development (RAD) Methods using I-CASE tools and 4GLs to quickly prototype an information system. Often, software is reused in RAD.

Rapid prototyping Using software and special output devices to create prototypes to test design in three dimensions.

Reach percentage The percentage of Web users who have visited a site in the past month, or the ratio of visitors to the total Web population.

Read-Only Memory (ROM) The minor part of a computer's internal memory. ROM is loaded by the manufacturer with software that cannot be changed. Usually, ROM holds very basic system software, but sometimes also applications. Like RAM, ROM consists of microchips containing transistors.

Record A set of standard field types. All the fields of a record contain data about a certain entity or event.

Reengineering (also: business process engineering) The process by which an organization takes a fresh look at a business process and reorganizes it to attain efficiency. Almost always, reengineering includes the integration of a new or improved information system.

Register A fast memory location in the CPU, made of special semiconductors and circuitry.

Relational database A database in which the records are organized in individual tables (called "relations"). In order for data from different tables to be related, tables must contain foreign keys, which are primary keys in other tables in the database. The ease of building and maintaining a relational database has made it more popular than the hierarchical and network models.

Relational operation An operation that creates a temporary table that is a subset of the original table or tables in a relational database.

Repeater A device that strengthens signals and then sends them on their next leg toward their next destination.

Replication A process in which a full copy of an entire database is stored at all the sites that need access to it.

Request for information (RFI) A request to vendors for general, somewhat informal, information about their products.

Request for proposal (RFP) A document specifying all the system requirements and soliciting a proposal from vendors who might want to bid on a project or service.

Resolution The degree to which the image on a computer monitor is sharp. Higher resolution means a sharper image. Resolution depends on the number of pixels on the screen and the dot pitch.

Return on investment (ROI) A calculation of the difference between the stream of benefits and the stream of costs over the life of an information system.

Reverse auction An online auction in which participants post the price they want to pay for a good or service, and retailers compete to make the sale; also called a name-your-price auction.

Ring A communications network topology in which each computer (or other communications device) is connected to two other computers.

RISC (Reduced Instruction Set Computer) A computer whose CPU includes only the most commonly used functions. A reduced instruction set makes the computer significantly faster than the same computer with a full instruction set in its CPU.

Robotics The science and specialty of developing machines that can mimic human movement. Robots are highly automated machines controlled by computers.

S

Sales force automation Equipping traveling salespeople with notebook computers, PDAs, telecommunications devices, and other devices that allow them to communicate with the home office, retrieve and store information from and to other computers remotely, and fax information.

Scalability The ability to adapt applications as business needs grow.

Scanner A device that scans pictures and text and transforms them into digitized files.

Schema The structure of a database, detailing the names and types of fields in each set of records, and the relationships among sets of records.

Second generation languages Assembly languages.

Security measures Systems or application programs that provide such services as tracking account numbers and passwords, and controlling access to files and programs.

Select In a relational database, the selection of records that meet certain conditions.

Semantic nets A method of representing knowledge where-by facts are linked by relationships. The links create a "net."

Semistructured problem An unstructured problem with which the decision maker may have had some experience. Requires expertise to resolve.

Sensitivity analysis Using a model to determine the extent to which a change in a factor affects an outcome. The analysis is done by repeating *if-then* calculations.

Sequential access A file organization for sequential record entry and retrieval. The records are organized as a list that follows a logical order, such as ascending order of ID numbers, or descending order of part numbers. To retrieve a record, the application must start the search at the first record and retrieve every record, sequentially, until the desired record is encountered.

Serial port An outlet that accepts a cord for serial transmission.

Serial transmission Transmission of streams of bits one after another. This is the only kind of transmission possible in telecommunications.

Server A computer connected to several less powerful computers that can utilize its databases and applications.

Service level agreement (SLA) A document that lists all the types of services expected of an outsourcing vendor as well as the metrics that will be used to measure the degree to which the vendor has met the level of promised services. Usually, the client makes the list.

Simplex Transmission from a device that can only transmit, to devices that can only receive. Example: radio and television broadcasts.

Snail mail Regular mail handled by the Postal Service (as opposed to e-mail).

Software Sets of instructions that control the operations of a computer.

Software piracy The phenomenon of copying software illegally.

SOHO (Small Office/Home Office) The fastest growing type of business, thanks to the availability of inexpensive microcomputers and fax/modems. Also called TOHO (Tiny Office/Home Office).

Source code An application's code written in the original high-level programming language.

Speech recognition The process of translating human speech into computer-readable data and instructions.

Speech synthesizing Technology that allows machines to create sounds emulating a human voice.

Spoofing Deception for the purpose of gaining access to a Web site, or deception of users to make them think they are logged on to a certain Web site when they are actually logged on to another.

SQL (Structured Query Language) A data manipulation language for relational database management systems that has become a de facto business standard.

Star A network topology in which many computers are linked to a single computer through which all messages must be passed.

Static IP number An Internet Protocol number permanently associated with a device.

Steering committee A group of representatives from a variety of key business units that establishes priorities for systems development and implementation of communications networks, prioritizes requests for new systems, and commits funds to projects.

Storage The operation of storing data and information in an information system.

Storage service provider (SSP) A firm that rents storage space for software through an Internet link.

Strategic advantage A position in which one dominates a market; also called competitive advantage.

Strategic information system Any information system that gives its owner a competitive advantage.

Strategic managers Individuals who make decisions that affect an entire organization, or large parts of it, and leave an impact in the long run.

Structured data Numbers and facts that can be conveniently stored and retrieved in an orderly manner for operations and decision making.

Structured problem A problem for whose solution there is a known set of steps to follow. Also called a *programmable problem*.

Structured Query Language (SQL) The data definition and manipulation language of choice for many developers of relational database management systems.

Stylus A penlike marking device used to enter commands and data on a computer screen.

Subsystem A component of a larger system.

Suite A group of general software applications that are often used in the same environment. The strengths of the different applications can be used to build a single powerful document. Current suites are usually a combination of a spreadsheet, a word processor, and a database management system.

Supercomputer The most powerful class of computers, used by large organizations, research institutions, and universities for complex scientific computations and the manipulation of very large databases.

Supply chain management (SCM) The coordination of purchasing, manufacturing, shipping, and billing operations, often supported by an enterprise resource planning system.

Support The maintenance and provision for user help on an information system.

Surfers Computer users who have dial-up or faster access to the Internet and who visit Web sites.

Switching costs Expenses that are incurred when a customer stops buying a product or service from one business and starts buying it from another.

Switching techniques Data communications mechanisms that allow messages to be routed through a variety of paths; if one is busy, another can be used.

Symmetric encryption Encryption technology in which both the sender and recipient of a message use the same key for encryption and decryption.

Synergy From Greek "to work together." The attainment of output, when two factors work together, that is greater or better than the sum of their products when they work separately.

Syntax error A program error that is equivalent to a typo in regular written language.

System An array of components that work together to achieve a common goal or multiple goals.

System clock Special circuitry within the computer control unit that synchronizes all tasks.

System requirements The functions that an information system is expected to fulfill and the features through which it will perform its tasks.

System software Software that executes routine tasks. System software includes operating systems, language translators, and communications software. Also called *support software*.

Systems analysis The early steps in the systems development process, to define the requirements of the proposed system and determine its feasibility.

Systems design The evaluation of alternative solutions to a business problem and the specification of hardware, software, and communications technology for the selection solution.

Systems development led by users (SDLU) An approach to systems development that reflects the view that users, not information systems professionals, are responsible for their information systems.

Systems development life cycle (SDLC) The oldest method of developing an information system, consisting of several phases of analysis and design, which must be followed sequentially.

Systems integration Interfacing several information systems.

Systems integrator An individual or an organization that specializes in integrating several different hardware items and software applications for business operations. Often, the system integrator integrates one new information system into the existing information resources of the business.

Systems thinking The approach of thinking of an organization in terms of its suborganizations or systems; a framework for problem solving and decision making.

T

Tablet computer A full-power personal computer in the form of a thick writing tablet.

Tactical managers Individuals who receive general directions and goals from their superiors and, within those guidelines, make decisions for their subordinates; also called middle managers.

Target marketing Promoting products and services to the people who are most likely to purchase them.

TCP/IP (Transmission Control Protocol/Internet Protocol) A packet-switching protocol that is actually a set of related protocols that can guarantee packets are delivered in the correct order and can handle differences in transmission and reception rates.

Technical feasibility study An evaluation of whether the components of a proposed information system exist or can be developed with available tools.

Telecommunications Communications over a long distance, as opposed to communication within a computer, or between adjacent hardware pieces.

Telecommunications manager The individual who is responsible for the acquisition, implementation, management, maintenance, and troubleshooting of computer networks throughout the organization.

Telecommuting The phenomenon of working from home with the help of information technology, rather than performing the same tasks in the office.

Teleconferencing The ability to hold conferences with a number of other people who are all geographically remote from one another, via telecommunications devices.

Thin client A computer without an external storage device.

Third-generation languages (3GLs) Higher-level programming languages that let the programmer focus on a problem without being concerned with how the hardware will execute the program; but they require the programmer to detail a logical procedure to solve the problem.

Time bomb Rogue code that is installed in a computer system and starts destroying data files and applications at a pre-set time.

Time span The period of time that a set of data covers.

Time to market The time between generating an idea for a product and completing a prototype that can be mass-manufactured; also called *engineering lead time*.

Token passing A telecommunications method whereby a computer that needs to send a message captures a "token," consisting of a small group of bytes, and releases the token with the message.

Top-down planning Planning that begins at the top level of an organization and focuses on clear objectives for the entire organization; also called *holistic planning*.

Topology The physical layout of a network.

Touch screen A computer monitor that serves both as input and output device. The user touches the areas of a certain menu item to select options, and the screen senses the selection at the point of the touch.

Track pad A device used for clicking, logging, and dragging displayed information; the cursor is controlled by moving one's finger along a touch-sensitive pad.

Trackball A device similar to a mouse, used for clicking, locking, and dragging displayed information; in this case, the ball moves within the device rather than over a surface.

Transaction A business event. In an IS context, the record of a business event.

Transaction Processing System (TPS) Any system, whether on paper or via computer, that records transactions.

Transceiver A communications device that can receive messages, amplify them, and retransmit them to their destination. Transceivers are used when the distance is long, and the signal may weaken on its way to the destination.

Transmission Rate The speed at which data are communicated over a channel.

Transparency A desired environment for the use of applications and telecommunication whereby the user is not exposed to the inner workings of the software or to the fact that information may actually come from different sources.

Tree A network topology in which each computer (or other communications device) is connected to several other computers in a shape that resembles the breaches of a tree.

Twisted-pair-cable Traditional telephone wires, twisted in pairs to reduce electromagnetic interference.

U

Uniform Resource Locator (URL) The address of a Web site. Always starts with *http://*

Uninterruptible power supply (UPS) A system that provides an alternative power supply as soon as a power network fails.

Unique visitor pages The number of different pages at a Web site that a single visitor accesses.

Unique visitors per month The number of people who visit a Web site each month; each person is counted only once, even if that person visits the site more than once during the month.

UNIX A popular operating system, versions of which run on machines from different manufacturers, and therefore make the software almost machine-independent.

Unstructured problem A problem for whose solution there is no pretested set of steps, and with which the solver is not familiar—or is only slightly familiar—from previous experience.

Uploading Copying from one computer onto another computer.

Utilities Programs that provide help in routine user operations.

V

Value-added network (VAN) A telecommunications network owned and managed by a vendor that charges clients periodic fees for network management services.

Vertical market A market in which the goods of one business are used as raw materials or components in the production or sale process of another business.

Videoconferencing A telecommunication system that allows people who are in different locations to meet via transmitted images and speech.

Virtual memory Storage space on a disk that is treated by the operating system as if it were part of the computer's RAM.

Virtual organization An organization that requires very little office space. Its employees telecommute, and services to customers are provided through telecommunications lines.

Virtual reality A set of hardware and software that creates images, sounds, and possibly the sensation of touch that give the user the feeling of a real environment and experience. In advanced VR systems, the user wears special goggles and gloves.

Virtual Reality Modeling Language (VRML) A standard programming language that supports three-dimensional presentation on the Web.

Virus (computer virus) A rogue computer program that infects any computers it is entered into. It spreads in computers like a biological virus.

Voice recognition Technology that enables computers to recognize human voice, translate it into program code, and act upon the voiced commands.

Volatile memory Computer memory that cannot hold the original data when the machine is unplugged. Example: RAM.

W

Wait states The clock-beat intervals during which a CPU sits idle.

WAN (Wide Area Network) A network of computers and other communications devices that extends over a large area, possibly comprising national territories. Example: the Internet.

Web page A screenful of text, pictures, sounds, and animation that the user encounters when using a Web browser.

Web page authoring tools Software tools that make Web page composition easier and faster than writing code by providing icons and menus.

Web site The electronic presence of an organization or individual on the World Wide Web. The site is composed of Web pages and either shares a server with other sites or has a dedicated server.

Webmaster The person who is in charge of constructing and maintaining the organization's Web site.

What-if analysis An analysis that is conducted to test the degree to which one variable affects another; also called *sensitivity analysis*.

Wireless access protocol (WAP) A protocol used in mobile communication (M-commerce).

Wireless communication Transmission of data as radio signals without wires or telephone jacks.

Wireless LAN A local area network that uses electromagnetic waves (radio or infrared light) as the medium of communication.

Word (data word) The number of bits that the control unit of a computer fetches from the primary memory in one machine cycle. The larger the word, the faster the computer.

Work cycle A series of sequentially repeated activities involved in providing a service or creating a product.

Workstation A powerful microcomputer providing high-speed processing and high-resolution graphics. Used primarily for scientific and engineering assignments.

World Wide Web (Web, WWW) The application of the Internet that allows the posting and retrieval of text, pictures, sounds, and motion pictures. "Surfing" the Web is done by way of clicking on marked text and pictures to move to other pages at the same site or to a different site.

Worm A rogue code that spreads in a computer network.

WORM (Write Once, Read Many) A storage medium that is loaded with software by the manufacturer, and can never be overwritten. Example: CD-ROM.

Module 800 Endnotes

1. Oz, E. and Sosik, J.J., "Why Information Systems Projects are Abandoned: A Leadership and Communication Theory and Exploratory Study," *Journal of Computer Information Systems,* Fall 2000, Vol. 41, No. 1, pp. 66–78.
2. Dodd, J.L. and Houston, H.C., "Systems Development Led by End-users: An Assessment of End-user Involvement in Information Systems Development," *Journal of Systems Management,* August 1994, p. 34.

MODULE 900

Corporate Control and Governance

901 Corporate Control Strategies, 675

910 Internal Control Framework and Control Models, 677

920 Best Practices in Internal Control, 684

930 Corporate Fraud, 685

940 Corporate Risk Management, 726

950 Corporate Citizenship and Accountability, 745

960 Corporate Public Policy and Affairs, 756

970 Issues Management and Crisis Management, 761

980 Corporate Ethics and Management Assurance, 771

990 Corporate Governance, 782

999 International Issues, 792

Module 900 Glossary, 802

Module 900 Endnotes, 810

Corporate Control Strategies

Control strategies should be linked to business strategies in that controls and the control environment in an organization should facilitate the achievement of business objectives. Here, controls are labeled into three categories such as management control, operational control, and internal control.

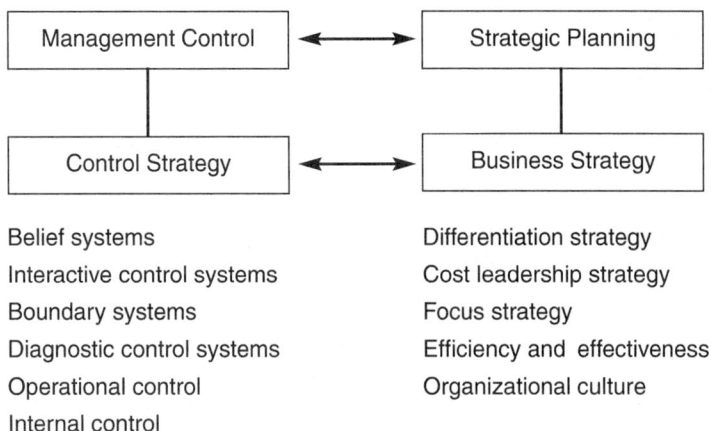

Belief systems
Interactive control systems
Boundary systems
Diagnostic control systems
Operational control
Internal control

Differentiation strategy
Cost leadership strategy
Focus strategy
Efficiency and effectiveness
Organizational culture

Management Control

Management control is the process by which managers assure that resources are obtained and used effectively and efficiently in the accomplishment of the organization's objectives.[1] Management control is a process carried on within the framework established by strategic planning. Decisions about next year's budget, for example, are constrained within policies and guidelines prescribed by top management. The management control process is intended to make possible the achievement of planned objectives as effectively and efficiently as possible within these givens.

The purpose of a management control system is to encourage managers to take actions that are in the best interests of the company. Technically, this purpose can be described as *goal congruence*. Ordinarily, a management control system is a total system in the sense that it embraces all aspects of the company's operations.

The management control process tends to be rhythmic; it follows a definite pattern and timetable, month after month and year after year. The management control system is a single system consisting of interlocking subsystems that are highly coordinated and integrated. Above all, line managers, not the staff, are the focal points in management control.

Examples of activities for which management control is necessary are the total operations in manufacturing activities consisting of plant inputs such as materials, direct and indirect labor, employee safety and training programs; marketing activities dealing with advertising, sales promotions, pricing, and selling decisions; human resource activities to select and recruit employees; financing activities to raise money; research and development activities to bring out new products; and the activities of top management such as strategic planning, implementation, and control.

Strategic Planning

Strategic planning is the process of deciding on the objectives of the organization, on changes in these objectives, on the resources used to attain these objectives, and on the policies that are to govern the acquisition, use, and disposition of these resources.

Business Strategy

Business strategy is derived from the strategic planning process. We defined how one model (Volume 1, Section 101), Porter's competitive strategy, can be used to affect organization design. Porter's strategy emphasizes three items:

(1) product or service differentiation, (2) low-cost leadership, and (3) focus on a specific market or customer group. Porter's strategic model should be combined with organizational culture to achieve effectiveness and efficiency of operations.

Control Strategy

Robert Simons, of Harvard Business School, in his book *Levers of Control,* describes four control levers for an effective implementation of business strategy.[2] The first two levers include belief systems and interactive control systems, which create positive and inspirational forces. The last two levers include boundary systems and diagnostic control systems, which create negative forces such as constraints for compliance with policies and rules. More specifically, the four levers of control include the following.

1. **Belief systems** are used to inspire, empower, and direct the search for new opportunities.
2. **Interactive control systems** are used to stimulate and expand organizational learning and to guide the emergence of new ideas and strategies.
3. **Boundary systems** are used to set limits or rules on opportunity-seeking behavior.
4. **Diagnostic control systems** are used to motivate, monitor, and reward achievement of specified goals and objectives. These systems focus attention on the implementation of intended strategies.

These four levers of control, working together, can help in the achievement of intended strategies. They provide the motivation, measurement, learning, and control that allow efficient goal achievement, creative adaptation, and profitable growth.

Operational Control

Operational control is the process of assuring that specific tasks are carried out effectively and efficiently. The focus of operational control is on individual tasks or transactions, scheduling and controlling individual jobs through a production shop, procuring specific items for inventory, and specific personnel actions and rules.

Examples of activities that are susceptible to operational control are automated plants for power and cement production, production scheduling operations, inventory control systems, order processing systems, billing systems, payroll accounting, human resource administration tasks, and other routine functions.

Comparison of Management Control With Operational Control

Management control covers the whole of an organization. Each operational control procedure is restricted to a subunit, often a narrow activity. Just as management control occurs within a set of policies derived from strategic planning, so operational control occurs within a set of well-defined procedures and rules derived from management control.

Control is more difficult in management control than in operational control because of the absence of a scientific standard with which actual performance can be compared. A good operational control system can provide a much higher degree of assurance that actions are proceeding as desired than can a management control system.

An operational control system is a rational system; that is, the action to be taken is decided by a set of logical rules programmed into a computer. In management control, psychological considerations are dominant in that it requires management's action or intervention.

The management control system is ordinarily built around a financial structure, whereas operational control data are often nonfinancial in nature. Data in an operational control system are often in real time and relate to individual events, whereas data in a management control system are often retrospective and summarize many separate events.

Similarly, operational control uses exact data, whereas management control needs only approximations. Material is ordered and scheduled in specific quantities and employees are paid the exact amount due them in operational control systems. An operational control system requires a mathematical model of the operation. Models are not so important in management control.

The success or failure of the management control system depends on the personal characteristics of the manager—his or her judgment, knowledge, and ability to influence others. An operational control system states what action should be taken; it makes the decisions.

In general, the degree of management involvement in operational control is small, whereas in management control it is large. As new techniques are developed, there is a tendency for more and more business activities to become susceptible to operational control. This includes manufacturing, marketing, human resources, finance, and other functions.

Internal Control

The scope of internal controls is broad in nature in that it consists of organizational structure that creates a division of responsibilities among employees, management authorization of business transactions, communication programs explaining the company's policies and standards to all employees, and selection and training of qualified and competent managers. The scope also includes procedural checks and balances that safeguard assets and assure integrity of data. Without basic internal controls, the risks of significant control failure become unacceptably high. Internal control is fully discussed in Section 910.

Internal Control Framework and Control Models

Internal Control Framework

The committee of sponsoring organizations (COSO) of the Treadway Commission in the United States published an internal control-integrated framework to guide management in 1992.[3] Senior executives have long sought ways to better control the enterprises they run. Internal controls are put in place to keep the company on course toward profitability goals and achievement of its mission, and to minimize surprises along the way. They enable management to deal with rapidly changing economic and competitive environments, shifting customer demands and priorities, and restructuring for future growth. Internal controls promote efficiency, reduce risk of asset loss, and help ensure the reliability of financial statements and compliance with laws and regulations.

Internal Control Definition and Objectives

Internal control is broadly defined as a process, effected by an entity's board of directors, management, and other personnel, designed to provide reasonable assurance regarding the achievement of objectives in the following three categories.

1. Effectiveness and efficiency of operations
2. Reliability of financial reporting
3. Compliance with applicable laws and regulations

The first category addresses an entity's basic business objectives, including performance and profitability goals and safeguarding of resources. The second category relates to the preparation of reliable published financial statements, including interim and condensed financial statements and selected financial data derived from such statements, such as earnings releases, reported publicly. The third category deals with complying with those laws and regulations to which the entity is subject. These distinct but overlapping categories address different needs and allow a directed focus to meet the separate needs.

Internal control systems operate at different levels of effectiveness. Internal control can be judged effective in each of the three categories, respectively, if the board of directors and management have reasonable assurance that:

- They understand the extent to which the entity's operations objectives are being achieved.
- Published financial statements are being prepared reliably.
- Applicable laws and regulations are being complied with.

While internal control is a process, its effectiveness is a state or condition of the process at one or more points in time.

Components of Internal Control

According to the COSO report, internal control consists of five interrelated components. These are derived from the way management runs a business, and are integrated with the management process.

1. **Control Environment.** The core of any business is its people—their individual attributes, including integrity, ethical values, and competence—and the environment in which they operate. They are the engine that drives the entity and the foundation on which everything rests. An entity's objectives and the way they are achieved are based on preferences, value judgments, and management styles. There often is a trade-off between competence and cost and between the extent of supervision and the requisite competence level of the individual. Companies can operate in a formal or informal mode. Formal documentation is not always necessary for a policy to be in place and operating effectively. A more formally managed company may rely more on written policies, performance indicators, and exception reports.

2. **Risk Assessment.** The entity must be aware of and deal with the risks it faces. It must set objectives that are integrated with the sales, production, marketing, financial, and other activities so that the organization is operating in concert. It also must establish mechanisms to identify, analyze, and manage the related risks.

    Objective setting is a precondition to risk assessment. There must first be objectives before management can identify risks to their achievement and take necessary actions to manage the risks. Objective setting, then, is a key part of the management process. While not an internal control component, it is a prerequisite to and an enabler of internal control.

3. **Control Activities.** Control policies and procedures must be established and executed to help ensure that the actions identified by management as necessary to address risks to achievement of the entity's objectives are effectively carried out. Examples of control activities include approvals, authorizations, verifications, reconciliations, reviews of operating performance, security of assets, and segregation of duties. Types of control activities can include preventive controls, detective controls, manual controls, computer controls, and management controls. Regardless of whether a policy is written, it must be implemented thoughtfully, conscientiously, and consistently. Controls are also classified into two categories: hard controls and soft controls. Hard controls are formal, tangible, and easier to measure and evaluate. Examples of hard controls include budgets, dual controls, written approvals, reconciliations, authorization levels, verifications, and segregation of duties. On the other hand, soft controls are informal, intangible, and difficult to measure and evaluate. Examples of soft controls include ethics, integrity, values, culture, vision, commitment to competence, management philosophy, level of understanding and commitment, and communication. Tools to evaluate hard controls include flowcharts, system narratives, testing, and counting. Tools to evaluate soft controls include self-assessments, questionnaires, interviews, and workshops. Generally speaking, senior managers most often use soft skills and soft controls to achieve their objectives while other managers most often use hard skills and hard controls. Soft skills include people skills such as interpersonal skills, motivation, leadership, and communications skills. Hard skills include technical skills such as functional skills, problem identification and solving skills, and decision-making skills.

4. **Information and Communication.** Surrounding these activities are information and communication systems. These enable the entity's people to capture and exchange the information needed to conduct, manage, and control its operations. Reliable internal financial measurements are also essential to planning, budgeting, pricing, evaluating vendor performance, and evaluating joint ventures and other alliances. Information can be obtained through questionnaires, interviews, broad-based market demand studies, or targeted focus groups. Information systems must provide the right information on time and at the right place. Because of these requirements, information systems must be controlled due to their influence on control.

5. **Monitoring.** The entire process must be monitored, and modifications must be made as necessary. In this way, the system can react dynamically, changing as conditions warrant. Monitoring is not a precondition to internal control because it is a part of internal control. Monitoring activities include management or supervisory

Exhibit 900.1 *Relationship of Internal Control Objectives and Components*

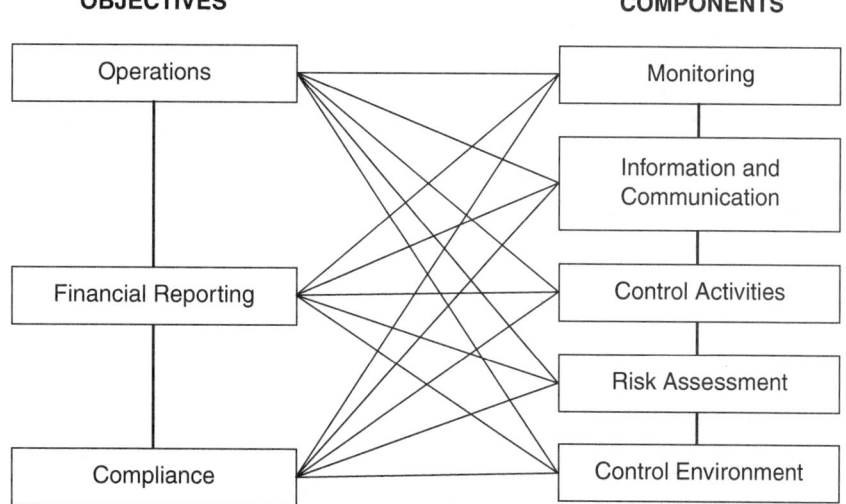

reviews, comparisons, and reconciliations. Emphasis should be put on "building in" rather than "adding on" controls. Monitoring can be done in two ways: through ongoing activities or through separate evaluations. Usually, some combination of ongoing monitoring and separate evaluations will ensure that the internal control system maintains its effectiveness over time.

The internal control definition—with its underlying fundamental concepts of a process, effected by people, providing reasonable assurance—together with the categorization of objectives and the components and criteria for effectiveness, and the associated discussions, constitute this internal control framework.

There is a direct relationship between the three categories of objectives, which are what an entity strives to achieve, and components, which represent what is needed to achieve the objectives. All components are relevant to each objectives category. When looking at any one category—the effectiveness and efficiency of operations, for instance—all five components must be present and functioning effectively to conclude that internal control over operations is effective. See Exhibit 900.1 for the relationship between internal control objectives and components.

What an Internal Control Can and Cannot Do

Internal control can help an entity achieve its performance and profitability targets and prevent loss of resources. It can help ensure reliable financial reporting. And it can help ensure that the enterprise complies with laws and regulations, avoiding damage to its reputation and other consequences. In sum, internal control can help an entity get to where it wants to go, while avoiding pitfalls and surprises along the way.

What internal control cannot do is (1) ensure an entity's success or survival or (2) ensure the reliability of financial reporting and compliance with laws and regulations.

Internal controls promote efficiency, reduce risk of asset loss, and help ensure the reliability of financial statements and compliance with laws and regulations.

Internal Control Is a Process

Internal control is not one event or circumstance, but a series of actions that permeate an entity's activities. These actions are pervasive and are inherent in the way management runs the business. Internal controls are most effective when they are built into the entity's infrastructure and are part of the essence of the enterprise. Controls should be "built in" rather than "built on." "Building in" controls can directly affect an entity's ability to reach its goals, and supports a business's quality initiatives. In fact, internal control not only is integrated with quality programs, it is usually critical to their success.

Internal Control Is People

Internal control is effected by a board of directors, management, and other personnel in an entity. It is accomplished by the people of an organization, by what they do and say. People establish the entity's objectives and put control mechanisms in place.

Similarly, internal control affects people's actions. Internal control recognizes that people do not always understand, communicate, or perform consistently. Each individual brings to the workplace a unique background and technical ability, and each has different needs and priorities.

The Limitations of Internal Control

No two entities will or should have the same internal control system. Companies and their internal control needs differ dramatically by industry and size and by culture and management philosophy. Internal control has been viewed by some observers as ensuring that an entity will not fail—that is, the entity will always achieve its operations, financial reporting, and compliance objectives. In this sense, internal control sometimes is looked upon as a cure-all for all real and potential business ills. This view is misguided. Internal control is not a panacea.

Even effective internal control operates at different levels with respect to different objectives. Also, internal control sometimes cannot provide reasonable assurance, due to differences in judgment, breakdowns in controls, management overrides, collusion, and problems in cost/benefit measurements.

Roles and Responsibilities in Internal Control

Everyone in an organization has responsibility for internal control. We will discuss briefly the responsibility of management, board of directors, auditors, and employees.

Management

The chief executive officer is ultimately responsible and should assume "ownership" of the internal control system. More than any other individual, the chief executive sets the "tone at the top" that affects integrity and ethics and other factors of a positive control environment. In a large company, the chief executive fulfills this duty by providing leadership and direction to senior managers and reviewing the way they are controlling the business. Senior managers, in turn, assign responsibility for establishment of more specific internal control policies and procedures to personnel responsible for the business unit's functions. In a smaller entity, the influence of the chief executive, often an owner-manager, is usually more direct. In any event, in a cascading responsibility, a manager is effectively a chief executive of his or her sphere of responsibility. Of particular significance are financial officers and their staffs, whose control activities cut across, as well as up and down, the operating and other units of an enterprise.

Board of Directors

Management is accountable to the board of directors, which provides corporate governance, guidance, and oversight. Effective board members are objective, capable, and inquisitive. They also have a knowledge of the entity's activities and environment, and commit the time necessary to fulfill their broad responsibilities. Management may be in a position to override controls and ignore or stifle communications from subordinates, enabling a dishonest management which intentionally misrepresents results to cover its tracks. A strong, active board, particularly when coupled with effective upward communication channels and capable financial, legal, and internal audit functions, is often best able to identify and correct such a problem.

In 1978, the Securities and Exchange Commission (SEC) proposed a list of eight "customary functions" of audit committees. The audit committee consists of board members and is similar to other committees such as compensation, standing, or legal committees. The "customary functions" of the audit committees include the following.

1. Recommend engagement or discharge of the independent auditors
2. Direct and supervise investigations into matters within the scope of its duties
3. Review with the independent auditors the plan and results of the auditing engagement

4. Review the scope and results of internal auditing activities
5. Approve each professional service provided by the independent auditor prior to its performance
6. Review the independence of the independent auditors
7. Consider the range of audit and non-audit fees
8. Review the adequacy of the systems of internal controls

Auditors

Both internal and external auditors are committed to improving internal controls. Internal auditors play an important role in evaluating the effectiveness of the control system and contribute to ongoing effectiveness. Because of organizational position and authority in an entity, an internal audit function often plays a significant monitoring role. External auditors, bringing an independent and objective view, contribute directly through the financial statement audit and indirectly by providing information useful to management and the board in carrying out their responsibilities.

Employees

Virtually all employees produce information used in the internal control system or take other actions needed to effect control. Also, all employees should be responsible for communicating upward problems in operations, noncompliance with the code of conduct, or other policy violations or illegal actions.

Control Models

In this section, we will discuss several control models for effective functioning of internal control systems. These include the COSO model, the CoCo model, the Control Self-Assessment model, the Turnbull model, the King model, the KonTraG model, the COBIT model, and the CONCT model.

The COSO Model in the United States

The COSO model was discussed earlier in this section.

The CoCo Model in Canada

The Canadian Institute of Chartered Accountants (CICA) has issued twenty "criteria of control" (CoCo) as a framework for making judgments about control. The term *control* has a broader meaning than internal control over financial reporting. CoCo defines control as "those elements of an organization (including its resources, systems, processes, culture, structure, and tasks) that, taken together, support people in the achievement of the organization's objectives." It defines three categories of objectives:

- Effectiveness and efficiency of operations
- Reliability of internal external reporting
- Compliance with applicable laws, regulations, and internal policies

The criteria of control are the basis for understanding control in an organization and for making judgments about the effectiveness of control. The criteria are formulated to be broadly applicable. The effectiveness of control in any organization, regardless of the objective it serves, can be assessed using these criteria. The criteria are phrased as goals to be worked toward over time; they are not minimum requirements to be passed or failed.

CoCo defines four types of criteria: purpose, commitment, capability, and monitoring and learning. The *purpose* type groups criteria that provide a sense of the organization's direction and address objectives (including mission, vision, and strategy); risks (and opportunities); policies; planning; and performance targets and indicators. The *commitment* type groups criteria that provide a sense of the organization's identity and values and address ethical values, including integrity, human resource policies, authority, responsibility, accountability, and mutual trust. The *capability* type groups criteria that provide a sense of the organization's competence and address knowledge, skills, and tools; communication processes; information; coordination; and control activities. The *monitoring and learning* type groups criteria that provide a sense of the organization's evolution and address monitoring internal and external environment, monitoring performance, challenging assumptions, reassessing information needs and information systems, follow-up procedures, and assessing the effectiveness of control.

The Control Self-Assessment Model

Overview

Control self-assessment (CSA) deals with evaluating the system of internal control in any organization. CSA is a shared responsibility among all employees in the organization, not just internal auditing or senior management. The examination of the internal control environment is conducted within a structured, documented, and repetitive process. The formal assessment approach takes place in workshop sessions with business users as participants (process owners) and internal auditors as facilitators (subject matter experts) and as nonfacilitators (note takers). The purpose of the sessions is conversation and mutual discovery and information sharing.

Definition of CSA

CSA has five elements: (1) up-front planning and preliminary audit work, (2) the gathering of process owners with a meeting facilitator, (3) a structured agenda to examine the process's risks and controls, (4) a note taker and electronic voting technology to input comments and opinions, and (5) reporting the results and the development of corrective action plans.

Scope of CSA

CSA can be done either as a stand-alone project or as a supplement to traditional audit work. CSA is not suitable to situations such as (1) finding fraud, (2) compliance reviews (for example, regulatory audits), or (3) when participants have conflicting objectives, as in third-party contracts. CSA can be applied to numerous situations, business issues, and industries, regardless of size. It is a management tool that has equal application to horizontal (organization-wide), vertical (single department), or diagonal (process inquiries) issues.

Effect on Auditors

CSA can be used to assess business and financial statement risks, control activities, ethical values, and control effectiveness; the controls that mitigate those risks; and overall compliance with policies and procedures.

During the assessment process, there is a constant interactive dialogue between the auditor and the auditee, as well as between the auditees. This interaction increases communication and builds trust and confidence between each party. At the same time, it is educational to both parties because there is a knowledge transfer between the auditor and the auditee. The auditors will have a greater knowledge of business functions, while the auditees will have a better understanding of and appreciation for controls and the business process of which they are a part.

The increased communication and the knowledge transfer adds value to the organization in the following ways.

- Auditors accomplish control assessment.
- Auditees understand the purpose of controls.
- Management takes responsibility for the development and maintenance of the control environment.
- Process improvement issues are identified and resolved (that is, implemented or deferred).

Interrelationships Between CSA, CoCo, and COSO

CSA can be an effective tool for accomplishing the objectives of both CoCo and COSO. CSA acts as a link to the CoCo and COSO.

The CSA audit can address the four elements of the CoCo framework (that is, purpose, commitment, capability, and monitoring and learning). Both commitment and capability are examples of soft controls (for example, risk assessment, the achievement of business objectives and goals, and the attitude of people toward controls).

Conclusions for CSA

CSA is a dynamic business process improvement and control-enhancing technique. The CSA in relation to internal auditing is like total quality management and continuous process improvement techniques in relation to other parts of the organization. The only difference is how the CSA program is implemented in each organization, but the benefits are real and long-lasting.

The Turnbull Model in the United Kingdom

In 1998, the London Stock Exchange developed a Combined Code for corporate governance. The Code requires that company directors should, at least annually, conduct a review of the effectiveness of the system of internal control and should report to shareholders that they have reviewed the effectiveness of all three types of controls, including financial, operational, and compliance control.

The King Model in South Africa

The Institute of Directors in Southern Africa has established the King Committee on Corporate Governance that produced the King Report in 1994. The Committee has developed a Code of Corporate Practices and Conduct, and compliance with the Code is a requirement to be listed in the JSE Securities Exchange in South Africa.

The KonTraG Model in Germany

In 1998, the German government proposed changes for the reform of corporate governance. The model affects control and transparency in business. Specifically, it impacts the board of directors, supervisory board, corporate capitalization principles, authorization of no-par-value shares, small nonlisted stock corporations, banks investing in industrial companies, and the acceptance of internationally recognized accounting standards.

The COBIT Model

Control objectives for information and related technology (COBIT), issued by the Information Systems Audit and Control Foundation (ISACF), are aimed at addressing business objectives. The control objectives make a clear and distinct link to business objectives in order to support significant use outside the audit community. Control objectives are defined in a process-oriented manner following the principle of business reengineering [ISACF].

The COBIT framework includes (1) the classification of domains where high-level control objectives apply (domains and processes), (2) an indication of the business requirements for information in that domain, and (3) the IT resources primarily impacted by control objectives. The framework is based on research activities that have identified 34 high-level control objectives and 318 detailed control objectives. In establishing the list of business requirements, COBIT combines the principles embedded in existing and known reference models.

1. Quality requirements cover quality, cost, and delivery.
2. Fiduciary requirements (COSO report) cover effectiveness and efficiency of operations, reliability of information, and compliance with laws and regulations.
3. Security requirements cover confidentiality, integrity, and availability.

The COBIT framework consists of high-level control objectives and an overall structure for their classification. The underlying theory of the classification is that there are, in essence, three levels of IT efforts when considering the management of IT resources. Starting at the bottom, there are activities and tasks needed to achieve a measurable result. Activities have a life-cycle concept while tasks are more discrete. The life-cycle concept has typical control requirements that are different from discrete activities. Processes are then defined one layer up as a series of joined activities or tasks with natural (control) breaks. At the highest level, processes are naturally grouped together into domains.

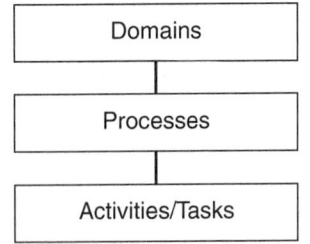

The conceptual framework can be approached from three vantage points: (1) information criteria, (2) IT resources, and (3) IT processes. Four domains were identified: planning and organization, acquisition and implementation, delivery and support, and monitoring.

In summary, in order to provide the information that the organization needs to achieve its objectives, IT governance must be exercised by the organization to ensure that IT resources are managed by a set of naturally grouped IT processes.

The CONCT Model

Control objectives for net centric technology (CONCT), issued by the ISACF, focus on the following activities: intranet, extranet, internet; data warehouses; and online transaction processing systems. CONCT provides well-structured ways of understanding and assessing the very complex centric technology environment that exists.

The IT governance model for the centric technology has three dimensions. They are: IT control objectives for information services, IT activities, and the IT resources required for the accomplishment of these activities.

Best Practices in Internal Control

We defined internal control as a process effected by an entity's board of directors, management, and other personnel that is designed to provide reasonable assurance regarding the achievement of objectives such as (1) effectiveness and efficiency of operations, (2) reliability of financial reporting, and (3) compliance with applicable laws and regulations.

Best practices refer to the approaches that produce exceptional results. Next, we introduce objectives and tools as examples of best practices in internal control in the following areas: Operations, Marketing and Sales, Service, and Financial and Operational Reporting.[4]

Operations

1. Schedule operations to minimize inventory and to ensure sufficient availability of completed products in a timely manner.
2. Minimize production downtime.
3. Produce products in appropriate quantities and in accordance with specifications and production schedules.
4. Comply with applicable laws and regulations during production of goods.
5. Produce products in accordance with quality control standards.

Marketing and Sales

1. Design marketing strategies giving consideration to competitive, regulatory, and business environments, or other factors that may influence the entity's marketing activities and potential changes in those factors.
2. Identify potential and existing customers, and develop marketing strategies to influence those parties to purchase the entity's products or services.
3. Maintain delivery capabilities for delivery of products to customers on a timely basis at the least distribution cost.
4. Address market needs for product, including introduction of new products, and continuance, changes to, or discontinuance of existing products.
5. Implement marketing strategies effectively to manage sales activities.
6. Meet or exceed sales targets in an efficient manner.
7. Forward all sales orders to outbound activities (for example, shipping) and service in a timely manner.

Service

1. Handle customer inquiries expeditiously and efficiently.
2. Satisfy customer service needs so as to further sales and marketing objectives.
3. Make authorized installations correctly, efficiently, and on a timely basis.
4. Ensure that warranty policies are consistent with marketing and financial strategies.
5. Investigate and respond to requests for service on a timely basis and in accordance with warranties.
6. Ensure that customer service representatives use up-to-date pricing and other product information to assist customers.
7. Investigate and respond to requests for services in the most efficient manner and on a timely basis.

Financial and Operational Reporting

1. Provide timely and accurate information needed by management and others to discharge their responsibility.
2. Prepare external financial reports (for example, balance sheet, income statement, cash flow statements) on a timely basis and in compliance with applicable laws, regulations, rules, or contractual agreements.
3. Prepare internal operational reports (product line profitability analysis, turnover and utilization statistics) on a timely basis and in compliance with management needs and schedules.
4. Maintain confidentiality of financial and operational information.

Corporate Fraud

The Nature of Fraud

Seriousness of the Fraud Problem

Although most people and even researchers believe that fraud is increasing both in size and frequency, it is very difficult to know for sure. First, it is impossible to know what percentage of fraud *perpetrators* are caught. Are there perfect frauds that are never discovered, or are all frauds eventually discovered? In addition, many frauds that are discovered are handled quietly within the victim organization and never made public. In many cases, companies merely hide the frauds and quietly terminate or transfer perpetrators rather than make them public.

Statistics on how much fraud is occurring, whether it is increasing or decreasing, and how much the average fraud costs come from four basic sources.

1. **Government agencies.** Agencies such as the FBI or various health agencies publish fraud statistics from time to time, but only those statistics related to their *jurisdiction*. Generally, their statistics are not complete, are not collected randomly, and do not provide a total picture even of all the fraud in the areas for which they have responsibility.
2. **Researchers.** Researchers often conduct studies about particular types of fraud in particular industrial sectors. Unfortunately, data on actual frauds is difficult to get and, as a result, most research studies only provide small insights into the magnitude of the problem, even in the specific area being studied. Comprehensive research on the occurrence of fraud is rare and is not always based on sound scientific approaches.
3. **Insurance companies.** Insurance companies often provide fidelity bonding or other types of coverage against employee and other fraud. When fraud occurs, they undertake investigations and, as a result, have collected some fraud statistics. Generally, however, their statistics relate only to actual cases where they provided employee bonding or other insurance. At best, their look at the problem is incomplete.
4. **Victims of fraud.** Sometimes we learn about fraud from those who have been *victims*. In almost all industries, there is no organized way for victims to report fraud and, even if there were, many companies would choose not to make their fraud losses public.

Even with the difficulties in measuring fraud, most people believe that fraud is a growing problem. Both the numbers of frauds committed and the total dollar amounts lost from fraud seem to be increasing. Because fraud affects how much we pay for goods and services, each of us pays not only a portion of the fraud bill but also for the detection and investigation of fraud. It is almost impossible to read a newspaper or business magazine without coming across multiple incidents of fraud.

Even more alarming than the increased number of fraud cases is the size of discovered frauds. In earlier times, if a thief wanted to steal from his or her employer, the perpetrator had to physically remove the assets from the business premises. Because of fear of being caught with the goods, frauds tended to be small. With the advent of computers, the Internet, and complex accounting systems, employees now need only make a telephone call, misdirect purchase invoices, bribe a supplier, manipulate a computer program, or simply push a key on the keyboard to misplace company assets. Because physical possession of stolen property is no longer required and because it is just as easy to program a computer to misdirect $100,000 as it is $1,000, the size and number of frauds have increased tremendously.

To understand how costly fraud is to organizations, consider what happens when fraud is committed against a company. Losses incurred from fraud reduce a firm's income on a dollar-for-dollar basis. This means that for every $1 of fraud, *net income* is reduced by $1. Because fraud reduces net income, it takes significantly more *revenue* to recover the effect of the fraud on net income. To illustrate, consider the $436 million fraud loss that a U.S. automobile manufacturer experienced a few years ago.[5] If the automobile manufacturer's *profit margin* (net income divided by revenues) at the time was 10%, the company would have to generate up to $4.36 billion in additional revenue (or 10 times the amount of the fraud) to recover the effect on net income. If we assume an average selling price of $20,000 per car, the company must make and sell an additional 218,000 cars. Considered this way, fighting fraud is a serious business. The automobile company can spend its efforts manufacturing and marketing additional new cars, or trying to reduce fraud, or a combination of both.

As another example, a large bank was the victim of a fraud that totaled $100 million in one year. With a profit margin of 5%, and assuming that the bank made $100 per year per checking account, how many new checking accounts must the bank generate to compensate for the fraud losses? The answer, of course, is up to 20 million new checking accounts ($100 million fraud loss ÷ 0.05 = $2 billion in additional revenues; $2 billion ÷ $100 per account = 20 million new accounts).

Because of different cost/revenue structures, the amount of additional revenues a firm must generate to recover fraud losses varies from firm to firm. It is easy to see that in order to maximize profits eliminating fraud should be a key goal of every business. The best way to minimize fraud is to prevent it from occurring.

What Is Fraud?

There are two principal methods of getting something from others illegally. Either you physically force someone to give you what you want, or you trick them out of their assets. The first type of theft we call robbery, and the second type we call *fraud*. Robbery is generally more violent and more traumatic than fraud and attracts much more media attention, but losses from fraud far exceed losses from robbery. Fraud always involves deception, confidence, and trickery.

Although there are many definitions of fraud, probably the most common is the following.

Fraud is a generic term, and embraces all the multifarious means which human ingenuity can devise, which are resorted to by one individual, to get an advantage over another by false representations. No definite and invariable rule can be laid down as a general proposition in defining fraud, as it includes surprise, trickery, cunning and unfair ways by which another is cheated. The only boundaries defining it are those which limit human knavery.[6]

Fraud is deception that includes the following elements.

1. A *representation*
2. About a *material* point
3. Which is *false*
4. And *intentionally or recklessly* so
5. Which is *believed*
6. And *acted upon* by the victim
7. To the victim's *damage*

Fraud is different from unintentional error. If, for example, someone mistakenly enters incorrect numbers on a *financial statement,* is this fraud? No, it is not fraud because it was not done with intent or for the purpose of gaining advantage over another through false pretense. But, if in the same situation, someone purposely enters incorrect numbers on a financial statement to trick investors, then it *is* fraud!

Types of Fraud

The most common way to classify fraud is to divide frauds into those committed *against* an organization and those committed *on behalf* of an organization.

In occupational fraud—fraud committed against an organization—the victim of the fraud is the employee's organization. The Association of Certified Fraud Examiners (ACFE) defines this type of fraud as, *"The use of one's occupation for personal enrichment through the deliberate misuse or misapplication of the employing organization's resources or assets."*[7] Occupational fraud results from the misconduct of employees, managers, or executives. Occupational fraud can be anything from lunch break abuses to high-tech schemes. *The Report to the Nation on Occupation Fraud and Abuse* by the ACFE states that, "The key to occupational fraud is that the activity (1) is clandestine, (2) violates the employee's fiduciary duties to the organization, (3) is committed for the purpose of direct or indirect financial benefit to the employee, and (4) costs the employing organization assets, revenues, or reserves."[8]

The most common fraud committed on behalf of an organization—usually through actions of the top management—is fraudulent financial reporting. These frauds are committed to make reported earnings look better or to increase a company's stock price. Sometimes, executives misstate earnings in order to ensure a larger year-end bonus. Financial statement fraud often occurs in companies that are experiencing net losses or have profits much less than expectations. See Exhibit 900.2 for types of fraud.

Exhibit 900.2   *Types of Fraud*

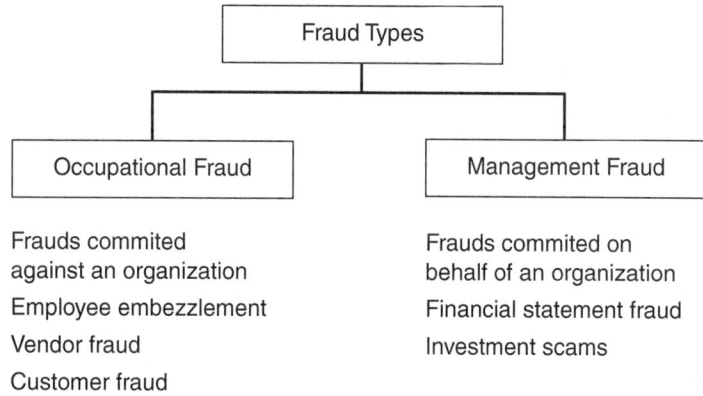

930. CORPORATE FRAUD

Exhibit 900.3 *Summary of Fraud Types*

Type of Fraud	Victim	Perpetrator	Explanation
1. Employee embezzlement or occupational fraud	Employers	Employees	Employees directly or indirectly steal from their employers.
2. Management fraud	Stockholders, lenders, and others who rely on financial statements	Top management	Top management provides misrepresentation, usually in financial information.
3. Investment scams	Investors	Individuals	Individuals trick investors into putting money into fraudulent investments.
4. Vendor fraud	Organizations that buy goods or services	Organizations or individuals that sell goods or services	Organizations overcharge for goods or services or nonshipment of goods, even though payment is made.
5. Customer fraud	Organizations that sell goods or services	Customers	Customers deceive sellers into giving customers something they should not have or charging them less than they should.

In June, 2001, a "Big 5" CPA firm and three of its partners were fined by the Securities and Exchange Commission for allowing a client to engage in a series of improper accounting practices that inflated its earnings for several years. The fine against the CPA firm and its partners totaled $7 million. The firm agreed to pay the fine and settle the case, although it would not admit to or deny the allegations. The fines against specific partners were the first since the mid-1980s and were imposed by the SEC because it is trying to curb what it sees as a growing problem of accounting fraud.[9]

A more inclusive classification scheme divides fraud into the following six types.

1. employee embezzlement
2. management fraud
3. investment scams
4. vendor fraud
5. customer fraud
6. miscellaneous fraud

Fraud that does not fall into one of the first five types and that may have been committed for reasons other than financial gain is simply labeled *miscellaneous fraud*. The other five types of fraud are summarized in Exhibit 900.3 and are discussed in the paragraphs that follow.

Employee Embezzlement

Employee embezzlement is another name for occupational fraud. In this type of fraud, employees deceive their employers by taking company assets. Embezzlement can be either direct or indirect. Direct fraud occurs when an employee steals company cash, inventory, tools, supplies, or other assets. It also occurs when employees establish dummy companies and have their employers pay for goods that are not actually delivered. With direct fraud, company assets go directly into the perpetrator's pockets without the involvement of third parties. Indirect employee fraud, on the other hand, occurs when employees take bribes or kickbacks from vendors, customers, or others outside the company to allow for lower sales prices, higher purchase prices, nondelivery of goods, or the delivery of inferior goods. In these cases, payment to employees is usually made by organizations that deal with the perpetrator's employer, not by the employer itself.

One example of direct employee fraud is the fraud perpetrated against **Liahona Construction**, which was in the home repair business. What management did not know was, so was one of their employees. The employee used $25,000 of the company's supplies and equipment to do his own remodeling jobs, pocketing the profits himself.

Here is an example of indirect employee fraud. Mark, who worked for **"Big D" Advertising** as purchase agent, paid a company in New York City nearly $100,000 for contracted work that should have cost about $50,000. The contractor then paid Mark a kickback of nearly $30,000. Only after someone noticed that the quality of work performed by the New York contractor decreased substantially was the fraud suspected and detected.

Management Fraud

As stated previously, *management fraud* is distinguished from other types of fraud both by the nature of the perpetrators and by the method of deception. In its most common form, management fraud involves top management's deceptive manipulation of financial statements. Well-known examples of alleged management fraud in recent years include **Phar-Mor** and **Crazy Eddie, Inc.**, both of which supposedly overstated inventories on financial statements; and **ZZZZ Best**, **ESM Government Securities**, **Regina Vacuum Company**, and **MiniScribe Corporation**, all of which supposedly overstated revenues and/or receivables. In all these cases, management wanted stockholders to believe that the companies' financial positions were better than they really were.

To illustrate management fraud, consider John Blue, the CEO for a fast-growing music store chain. The company was opening new stores almost monthly. The fast-growing music chain had lots of business and was famous for its low prices. When the company went public, shares of the stock soared. Here is what the shareholders didn't know: The chain was selling the music below cost—it was *losing* money on each item sold. John and his CFO hid the losses by inflating inventories and recording fictitious revenues. The scam eventually unraveled when a top accountant reported the fraud. When word leaked out, shares of the company's stock became worthless overnight.

Investment Scams

Closely related to management fraud are *investment scams*. In these scams, fraudulent and usually worthless investments are sold to unsuspecting investors. Perpetrators trick individuals into putting their money in fake investments. Telemarketing fraud usually falls into this category, as does the selling of worthless partnership interests and other investment opportunities. Charles Ponzi is regarded as the father of investment scams. Unfortunately, he has not lacked for imitators. His form of deception is extremely common today, with one estimate being that one of every three Americans will fall prey to this type of fraud sometime during his or her lifetime.

Vendor Fraud

Vendor fraud has been in the news time and again over the years because of significant overcharges by major vendors on defense and other government contracts. Vendor fraud, which is extremely common in the United States, comes in two main varieties: (1) fraud perpetrated by vendors acting alone and (2) fraud perpetrated through collusion between buyers and vendors. Vendor fraud usually results in either an overcharge for purchased goods, the shipment of inferior goods, or the nonshipment of goods even though payment was made.

Customer Fraud

In *customer fraud*, customers either do not pay for goods purchased, or they get something for nothing, or they deceive organizations into giving them something they should not have. For example, consider the bank customer who walked into a branch of a large bank one Saturday morning and convinced the branch manager to give her a $525,000 cashier's check, even though she had only $13,000 in her bank account. The manager believed she was a very wealthy customer and did not want to lose her business. Unfortunately for the bank, she was a white-collar thief, and she proceeded to defraud the bank of over $500,000. In another customer fraud, six individuals sitting in a downtown Chicago hotel room pretended to be representatives of large corporate customers, made three calls to a Chicago bank, and had the bank transfer nearly $70 million to their accounts in another financial institution in New Jersey. Once the money was transferred to New Jersey, it was quickly transferred to Switzerland, withdrawn, and used to purchase Russian diamonds.

Criminal and Civil Prosecution of Fraud

When people commit fraud, they can be prosecuted criminally and/or civilly. To succeed in a criminal or civil prosecution, it is usually necessary to show that the perpetrator acted with *intent* to defraud the victim. This is best accomplished by gathering evidential matter. *Evidential matter* consists of the underlying data and all corroborating information available. More is said later.

Who Commits Fraud and Why

Who Commits Fraud

Past research has shown that anyone can commit fraud.[10] Fraud perpetrators usually cannot be distinguished from other people by demographic or psychological characteristics. Most fraud perpetrators have profiles that look like those of other honest people.

It is important to understand the characteristics of fraud perpetrators because they appear to be very much like people who have traits that organizations look for in hiring employees, seeking out customers and clients, and selecting vendors. This knowledge helps us to understand that (1) most employees, customers, vendors, and business associates and partners fit the profile of fraud perpetrators and are probably capable of committing fraud, and (2) it is impossible to predict in advance which employees, vendors, clients, and customers will become dishonest. In fact, when fraud does occur, the most common reaction by those around the fraud is denial. Victims cannot believe that individuals who look and behave much like them and who are usually well trusted can behave dishonestly.

Why People Commit Fraud

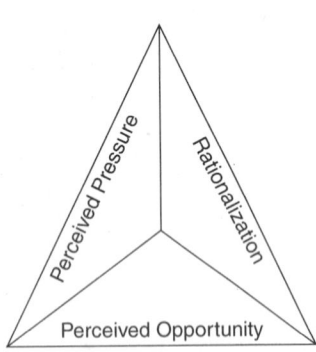

Although there are thousands of ways to perpetrate fraud, three key elements are common to all of them. Fraud includes: (1) a perceived pressure, (2) a perceived opportunity, and (3) some way to rationalize the fraud as acceptable. These three elements make up what we call the *fraud triangle*.

Perceived pressure, perceived opportunity, and rationalization are common to every fraud. Whether the fraud is one that benefits the perpetrators directly, such as employee fraud, or one that benefits the perpetrator's organization, such as management fraud, the three elements are always present. In the case of management fraud, for example, the pressure may be the need to make earnings look better to meet debt covenants, the opportunity may be a weak audit committee, and the rationalization may be that "we'll only cook the books until we can get over this temporary hump."

Fraud resembles fire in many ways. For a fire to occur, three elements are necessary: (1) oxygen, (2) fuel, and (3) heat. These three elements make up the "fire triangle." When all three elements come together, there is fire.

Firefighters know that a fire can be extinguished by eliminating any one of the three elements. Oxygen is often eliminated by smothering, by using chemicals, or by causing explosions, as is the case in oil well fires. Heat is most commonly eliminated by pouring water on fires. Fuel is removed by building fire lines or fire breaks or by shutting off the source of the fuel.

As with the elements in the fire triangle, the three elements in the fraud triangle are also interactive. With fire, the more flammable the fuel, the less oxygen and heat it takes to ignite. Similarly, the purer the oxygen, the less flammable the fuel needs to be to ignite. With fraud, the greater the perceived opportunity or the more intense the pressure, the less rationalization it takes to motivate someone to commit fraud. Likewise, the more dishonest a perpetrator is, the less opportunity and/or pressure it takes to motivate fraud.

People who try to prevent fraud usually work on only one of the three elements of the fraud triangle: opportunity. Because fraud-fighters generally believe that opportunities can be eliminated by having good internal controls, they focus all or most of their preventive efforts on implementing controls and ensuring adherence to them. Rarely do they focus on the pressures motivating fraud or on the rationalizations of perpetrators.

It is interesting to note that almost every study of honesty reveals that levels of honesty are decreasing.[11] Given the interactive nature of the elements in the fraud triangle, society's retreat from this value presents a scary future for companies combatting fraud. Less honesty makes it easier to rationalize, thus requiring less perceived opportunity and/or pressure for fraud to occur.

The First Element of Fraud: Perceived Pressure

Fraud is perpetrated to benefit oneself or to benefit an organization, or both. Employee fraud, in which individuals embezzle from their employers, usually benefits the perpetrator. Management fraud, in which an organization's officers deceive investors and creditors (usually by manipulating financial statements), is most often perpetrated to benefit an organization and its officers. In this section we will discuss the different pressures that motivate individuals to perpetrate fraud on their own behalf. Most experts on fraud believe these pressures can be divided into four types: (1) financial pressures, (2) vices, (3) work-related pressures, and (4) other pressures.

Financial Pressures

Studies conducted by Steven Albrecht show that approximately 95% of all frauds involve either financial or vice-related pressures.[12] Here are the common financial pressures associated with fraud that benefits perpetrators directly.

1. Greed
2. Living beyond one's means
3. High bills or personal debt
4. Poor credit
5. Personal financial losses
6. Unexpected financial needs

This list is not exhaustive, and these pressures are not mutually exclusive. However, each pressure in this list has been associated with numerous frauds. We know of individuals who committed fraud because they were destitute. We know of perpetrators who were living lifestyles far beyond that of their peers.

Financial pressures can occur suddenly or can be long term. Unfortunately, very few fraud perpetrators inform others when they are having financial problems.

Financial pressure is the most common pressure that drives people to commit fraud. Usually when management fraud occurs, companies overstate assets on the balance sheet and net income on the income statement. They usually feel pressured to do so because of a poor cash position, receivables that aren't collectible, a loss of customers, obsolete inventory, a declining market, or restrictive loan covenants that the company is violating. **Regina Vacuum's** management committed massive financial statement fraud. The main pressure that drove them to fraud was that their vacuum cleaners were defective—parts melted—and thousands were being returned. The large number of returns reduced revenues significantly and created such income pressures that management intentionally understated sales returns and overstated sales.[13]

Vices

Closely related to financial pressures are *vices*—addictions such as gambling, drugs, and alcohol—and expensive extramarital relationships.

Vices are the worst kind of pressure—out-of-control lifestyles are frequently cited as the trigger that drives previously honest people to commit fraud. We know of female employees who embezzled because their children were on drugs and they could not stand to see them go through withdrawal pains. We also know of "successful" managers who, in addition to embezzling from their companies, burglarized homes and engaged in other types of theft to support their drug habits.

Work-Related Pressures

Whereas financial pressures and vices motivate most frauds, some people commit fraud to get even with their employer. Factors such as not enough recognition for job performance, dissatisfaction with the job, fear of losing one's job, being overlooked for a promotion, and feeling underpaid motivate many frauds.

Other Pressures

Once in a while, fraud is motivated by other pressures, such as a spouse who insists on an improved lifestyle or a desire to beat the system.

All of us face pressures in our lives. We have legitimate financial needs, we make foolish or speculative investments, we are possessed by addictive vices, we feel overworked and/or underpaid, or we simply want more than we have. We sometimes have a difficult time distinguishing between wants and needs. Indeed, the objective of most people in capitalistic societies is to obtain wealth. We often measure success by how much money or wealth a person has. If you say you have a very successful relative, you probably mean that he or she lives in a big house, has a cabin or a condominium, drives expensive automobiles, and has money to do whatever he wants. But most of us don't put our success ahead of our honesty and integrity.

To some people, however, being successful is more important than being honest. If they were to rank the personal characteristics they value most in their lives, success would rank higher than integrity. Psychologists tell us that most people have a price at which they will be dishonest. Individuals with high integrity and low opportunity need high pressure to be dishonest.

Most of us can think of scenarios in which we, too, might commit fraud. If for example, we were starving, and we worked in an environment where cash was abundant and not accounted for, and we really believed that we would repay the money taken to feed ourselves, we might commit fraud. The U.S. president most famous for his honesty, Abraham Lincoln, once threw a man out of his office, angrily turning down a substantial bribe. When someone asked why he was so angry, he said, "Every man has his price, and he was getting close to mine."[14] One thing is for certain—eliminating pressures in the fraud triangle has an effect similar to removing heat from the fire triangle. Without some kind of pressure, fraud rarely occurs.

The Second Element of Fraud: Perceived Opportunity

A perceived opportunity to commit fraud, to conceal it, or to avoid being punished is the second element in the fraud triangle. At least six major factors increase opportunities for individuals to commit fraud in organizations. The following list is not exhaustive, but it does show system weaknesses that create opportunity.

1. Lack of or circumvention of controls that prevent and/or detect fraudulent behavior
2. Inability to judge quality of performance
3. Failure to discipline fraud perpetrators
4. Lack of access to information
5. Ignorance, apathy, and incapacity
6. Lack of an audit trail

The Third Element of Fraud: Rationalization

Nearly every fraud involves rationalization. Most perpetrators are first-time offenders who would not commit other crimes. Rationalizing helps them hide from the dishonesty of their acts. Here are some common rationalizations used by fraudsters.

- The organization owes it to me.
- I am only borrowing the money—I will pay it back.
- Nobody will get hurt.
- I deserve more.
- It's for a good purpose.
- We'll fix the books as soon as we get over this financial difficulty.
- Something has to be sacrificed—my integrity or my reputation. (If I don't embezzle to cover my inability to pay, people will know I can't meet my obligations and that will be embarrassing because I'm a professional.)

Certainly, there are countless other rationalizations. These, however, are representative and serve as an adequate basis to discuss the role rationalization plays in fraud.

It is important to recognize that there are very few, if any, people who do not rationalize. We rationalize being overweight. We rationalize not exercising enough. We rationalize spending more than we should. Most of us rationalize being dishonest.

We rationalize dishonesty by our desire to make other people feel good. The same sort of rationalization often enables fraud to be perpetrated. Sometimes, one lies to oneself; sometimes one lies to others.

Control Factors: Controls That Prevent and Detect Fraud

Having an effective control structure is probably the single most important step organizations can take to prevent and detect employee fraud. There are three components in a company's control structure: (1) the control environment, (2) the accounting system, and (3) control activities or procedures. The accounting profession and the Committee of

Sponsoring Organizations (COSO) have defined these components; here we discuss only those components that are most effective in deterring fraud.

The Control Environment

Taken together, the five elements—(1) proper management modeling, (2) good communication or labeling, (3) effective hiring procedures, (4) clear organizational structure and assigned responsibilities, and (5) an effective internal audit department and security function—create an atmosphere in which fraud opportunities are decreased because employees see that fraud is neither acceptable nor tolerated. Relaxing any one of these elements increases opportunities for committing fraud.

The Accounting System

The second component of the control structure is a good *accounting system*. Every fraud is comprised of three elements: (1) the theft, in which assets are taken; (2) concealment, which is the attempt to hide the fraud from others; and (3) conversion, in which the perpetrator spends the money or converts the stolen assets to cash and then spends the money. An effective accounting system provides an *audit trail* that allows frauds to be discovered and makes concealment difficult. Unlike bank robbery, in which there is usually no effort to conceal the theft, concealment is a distinguishing element of fraud.

Frauds are often concealed in the accounting records. Accounting records are based on transaction documents, either paper or electronic. To cover up a fraud, paper or electronic documentation must be altered or misplaced. Frauds can be discovered in the accounting records by examining transaction entries that have no support or by probing financial statement amounts that are not reasonable. Without a good accounting system, distinguishing between actual fraud and unintentional errors is often difficult. A good accounting system ensures that recorded transactions are (1) valid, (2) properly authorized, (3) complete, (4) properly classified, (5) reported in the proper period, (6) properly valued, and (7) summarized correctly.

Control Activities (Procedures)

The third component of the control structure is good *control activities* (or *procedures*). Individuals who own their own businesses and are the sole "employee" probably do not need many control procedures. Although these people may have ample opportunity to defraud their own business, they have no incentive to do so. They would not steal from themselves, and they would never want to treat customers poorly. However, organizations that involve many employees must have control procedures so that the actions of employees are congruent with the goals of management or the owners. In addition, with control procedures, opportunities to commit and/or conceal frauds are eliminated or minimized. No matter what the business is, whether it is the business of operating a financial institution, a grocery store, or a Fortune 500 company, or the business of investing personal assets, there are five primary control procedures or activities.

1. Segregation of duties or dual custody
2. System of authorizations
3. Independent checks
4. Physical safeguards
5. Documents and records

Although there are thousands of control activities used by businesses, they are basically all variations of these five basic procedures. Good fraud detection and prevention efforts involve matching the most effective control procedures with the various risks of fraud.

SEGREGATION OF DUTIES OR DUAL CUSTODY Activities can usually be better controlled by invoking either *segregation of duties* or dual-custody control. Segregation of duties involves dividing a task into two parts, so that one person does not have complete control of the task. Dual custody requires two individuals to work together at the same task. Either way, it takes two people to do one job. This control, like most preventive controls, is most often used when cash is involved. For example, the opening of incoming cash in a business is usually done by two people or by segregating duties. The accounting for, and the handling of, cash are separated so that one person does not have access to both.

There are at least three critical functions that even small business owners should either set up as segregated duties or always do themselves: (1) writing checks, (2) making bank deposits, and (3) reconciling bank statements.

Because two individuals are involved, dual custody or segregation of duties is usually the most expensive of all controls. Labor costs are high, and hiring two people to complete one job is a luxury that most businesses do not believe they can afford. This control always involves a trade-off between higher labor cost and less opportunity for error and fraud. Besides being expensive, good dual custody is often difficult to enforce. When two individuals are working on the same task, they shouldn't take their eyes or their minds off the task to answer telephones, use the restroom, respond to a question, or even sneeze.

SYSTEM OF AUTHORIZATIONS   The second internal control procedure is a proper system of authorizations. Authorization control procedures take many forms. Passwords authorize individuals to use computers and to access certain databases. Signature cards authorize individuals to enter safe deposit boxes, to cash checks, and to perform other functions at financial institutions. Spending limits authorize individuals to spend only what is in their budget or approved level.

When people are not authorized to perform an activity, the opportunity to commit fraud is reduced. For example, when individuals are not authorized to enter safe deposit boxes, they cannot enter and steal the contents of someone else's box. When individuals are not authorized to approve purchases, they cannot order items for personal use and have their companies pay for the goods.

INDEPENDENT CHECKS   The theory behind *independent checks* is that if people know their work or activities are monitored by others, the opportunity to commit and conceal a fraud is reduced. There are many varieties of independent checks. The Office of the Controller of the Currency (OCC) requires that every bank employee in the United States take one week's vacation (five consecutive days) each year. While employees are gone, others are supposed to perform their work. If an employee's work piles up while he or she is out for the week, this "mandatory vacation" control is not working as it should and the opportunity to commit fraud is not eliminated.

Periodic job rotations, cash counts or certifications, supervisor reviews, employee hotlines, and the use of auditors are other forms of independent checks. One large department store in Europe has a complete extra staff of employees for its chain of department stores. This staff goes to a store and works while everyone who is employed there goes on vacation for a month. While they are gone, the transient staff operates the store. One purpose of this program is to provide complete, independent checks on the activities of store employees. If someone who is committing fraud is forced to leave for a month, the illegal activity is often discovered.

PHYSICAL SAFEGUARDS   Physical safeguards protect assets from theft by fraud or other means. *Physical safeguards,* such as vaults, safes, fences, locks, and keys, take away opportunities to commit fraud by making it difficult for people to access assets. Money locked in a vault, for example, cannot be stolen unless someone gains unauthorized access or unless someone who has access violates the trust. Physical controls also protect inventory by storing it in locked cages or warehouses; small assets such as tools or supplies by locking them in cabinets; and cash by locking it in vaults or safes.

DOCUMENTS AND RECORDS   The fifth control procedure involves using *documents or records* to create a record of transactions and an audit trail. Documents rarely serve as preventive controls, but they do provide excellent detective tools. Banks, for example, prepare kiting-suspect reports as well as reports of employee bank account activity to detect abuse by employees or customers. Most companies require a customer order to initiate a sales transaction. In a sense, the entire accounting system serves as a documentary control. Without documents, no accountability exists. Without accountability, it is much easier to perpetrate fraud and not get caught.

Summary of the Controls That Prevent or Detect Fraud

The control environment, the accounting system, and the many variations of the five control activities work together to eliminate or reduce the opportunity for employees and others to commit fraud. A good control environment establishes an atmosphere in which proper behavior is modeled and labeled, honest employees are hired, and all employees understand their job responsibilities. The accounting system provides records that make it difficult for perpetrators to gain access to assets, to conceal frauds, and to convert stolen assets without being discovered. Together, these three components make up the control structure of an organization. Exhibit 900.4 summarizes these components and their elements.

Unfortunately, many frauds are perpetrated in environments in which controls that are supposed to be in place are not being followed. Indeed, it is the overriding and ignoring of existing controls, not the lack of controls, that allow most frauds to be perpetrated. Next, we will discuss noncontrol factors influencing fraud.

Exhibit 900.4 *Summary of Internal Control Structure*

Control Environment	Accounting System	Control Activities
1. Management philosophy and operating style, modeling	1. Valid transactions	1. Segregation of duties
2. Effective hiring procedures	2. Properly authorized	2. Proper procedures for authorization
3. Clear organizational structure of proper modeling and labeling	3. Completeness	3. Independent checks on performance
4. Effective internal audit department	4. Proper classification	4. Physical control over assets and records
	5. Proper timing	5. Adequate documents and records
	6. Proper valuation	
	7. Correct summarization	

Noncontrol Factors Influencing Fraud

Noncontrol Factor: Inability to Judge the Quality of Performance

If you pay someone to construct a fence, you can examine the completed job and determine whether or not the quality of work meets your specifications and is consistent with the agreed contract. If, however, you hire a lawyer, a doctor, a dentist, an accountant, an engineer, or an auto mechanic, it is often difficult to know whether you are paying an excessive amount or receiving inferior service or products. With these kinds of contracts, it is easy to overcharge, perform work not needed, provide inferior service, or charge for work not performed.

Noncontrol Factor: Failure to Discipline Fraud Perpetrators

Fraudsters are repeat offenders who are neither prosecuted nor disciplined. An individual who commits fraud and is not punished or is merely terminated suffers no significant penalty and often resumes the fraudulent behavior.

Fraud perpetrators often command respect in their jobs, communities, churches, and families. If they are marginally sanctioned or terminated, they rarely inform their families and others of the real reason for their termination or punishment. On the other hand, if they are prosecuted, they usually suffer significant embarrassment when family, friends, and business associates find out about their offenses. Indeed, humiliation is often the strongest factor in deterring future fraud activity.

Because of the expense and time involved in prosecuting, many organizations simply dismiss dishonest employees, hoping to rid themselves of the problem. What these organizations fail to realize is that such action is shortsighted. They may rid themselves of one fraudster, but they have also sent a message to others in the organization that perpetrators will not suffer significant consequences for their actions. Indeed, lack of prosecution gives others "perceived opportunity" that, when combined with pressure and rationalization, can result in additional frauds in the organization. Perceived opportunity is removed when employees understand that perpetrators will be punished according to the law, not merely terminated.

In a society in which workers are mobile and often move from job to job, termination often helps perpetrators build an attractive resume, but it does not deter future fraud.

Noncontrol Factor: Lack of Access to Information

Many frauds occur because victims don't have access to information possessed by the perpetrators. This is especially prevalent in large management frauds that are perpetrated against stockholders, investors, and debt holders.

Most investment scams and management frauds depend on their ability to withhold information from victims. Individuals can attempt to protect themselves against such scams by insisting on full disclosure, including audited financial statements, a business history, and other information that could reveal the fraudulent nature of such organizations.

Noncontrol Factor: Ignorance, Apathy, and Incapacity

Older people, individuals with language difficulties, and other vulnerable citizens are often victims of fraud because perpetrators know that such individuals may not have the capacity or the knowledge to detect their illegal acts. Vulnerable people are, unfortunately, easier to deceive.

930. CORPORATE FRAUD

Noncontrol Factor: Lack of an Audit Trail

Organizations go to great lengths to create documents that provide an audit trail so that transactions can be reconstructed and understood at a later time. Many frauds, however, involve cash payments or manipulation of records that cannot be followed. Smart perpetrators understand that their frauds must be concealed. They also know that such concealment usually involves manipulation of financial records. When faced with a decision about which financial record to manipulate, perpetrators almost always manipulate the income statement, because they understand that the audit trail will quickly be erased. This is because income statement accounts start with zero every year.

Fighting Fraud: An Overview

The four activities toward fighting include (1) fraud prevention, (2) fraud detection, (3) fraud investigation, and (4) fraud resolution (follow-up legal action). Comprehensive fraud programs focus on all four. Investigation and resolution are the least effective and most expensive fraud-fighting efforts.

Fraud Prevention

Preventing fraud is the most cost-effective way to reduce losses from fraud. Once a fraud has been committed, there are no winners. Perpetrators lose—they suffer humiliation and legal consequences. They must make tax and restitution payments, and they also face financial penalties and other consequences. Victims lose—assets have been stolen and they must now incur legal fees, lost time, negative publicity, and other adverse consequences. Organizations and individuals that install proactive fraud prevention measures find that the measures pay big dividends. Because investigating fraud can be very expensive, *preventing* it is crucial.

As we noted earlier, people commit fraud because of three factors: (1) perceived pressure, (2) perceived opportunity, and (3) some way to rationalize the fraud as acceptable. When perceived pressures and opportunities are high, a person needs less rationalization to commit fraud. When perceived pressures and opportunities are low, a person needs more rationalization. Unfortunately, sometimes pressures and/or the ability to rationalize are so high that, no matter how hard an organization tries to prevent fraud, theft still occurs. Indeed, fraud is often impossible to prevent, especially in a cost-effective way. The best an organization can hope for is to minimize the costs of fraud.

Certain organizations have significantly higher levels of employee fraud and are more susceptible to fraudulent financial reporting. Research consistently shows that almost all organizations have fraud of one type or another.[15] Only those organizations that carefully examine their risk for fraud and take proactive steps to create the right kind of environment succeed in preventing fraud.

Fraud prevention involves two fundamental activities: (1) creating and maintaining a culture of honesty and integrity and (2) assessing and mitigating the risk of fraud and developing concrete responses to minimize risk and eliminate opportunity.

Creating and Maintaining a Culture of Honesty and Integrity

There are several ways to create such a culture: (1) insist that top management model appropriate behavior, (2) hire the right kind of employees, (3) communicate expectations throughout the organization and require periodic written confirmation of acceptance of those expectations, (4) create a positive work environment, and (5) develop and maintain effective policies for punishing perpetrators once fraud occurs.

Research in moral development strongly suggests that honesty is reinforced when proper examples are set—sometimes referred to as "the tone at the top."[16] Management cannot act one way and expect others in the organization to behave differently. Management must reinforce through its own actions that dishonest, questionable, or unethical behavior will not be tolerated.

The second element is hiring the right employees. People are not equally honest, nor do they embrace equally well-developed personal codes of ethics. In fact, research indicates that many people, when faced with significant pressure and opportunity, will behave dishonestly rather than face the "negative consequences" of honest behavior (for example, loss of reputation or esteem, failure to meet quotas or expectations, exposure of inadequate performance, inability to pay debts, and so on). If an organization is to be successful in preventing fraud, it must have effective hiring policies that distinguish between marginal and highly ethical individuals, especially when they recruit for high-risk positions. Proactive hiring procedures include such things as conducting background investigations on prospective employees, thoroughly checking references and learning how to interpret responses to inquiries about candidates, and testing for honesty and other attributes.

The third critical element—communicating expectations—includes (1) identifying appropriate values and ethics, (2) fraud awareness training that helps employees understand potential problems they may encounter and how to resolve or report them, and (3) communicating consistent punishment of violators. For codes of conduct to be effective, they must be written and communicated to employees, vendors, and customers. They must also be developed in such a manner that management and employees "own" them. Requiring employees to confirm in writing that they understand the organization's expectations goes a long way toward creating a culture of honesty. In fact, many organizations have found that annual written confirmations are very effective in both preventing frauds and detecting them before they become large. The punishment for fraud must be clearly communicated by top management throughout the organization. For example, a strong statement from management that dishonest actions will not be tolerated and that violators will be terminated and prosecuted to the fullest extent of the law do help prevent fraud.

The fourth element in creating an honesty-driven culture involves developing a positive work environment. Research indicates that fraud occurs less frequently when employees have feelings of ownership toward their organization than when they feel abused, threatened, or ignored by it.[17] Factors associated with high levels of fraud that detract from a positive work environment include the following.

1. Top management does not care about or pay attention to appropriate behavior.
2. Negative feedback and lack of recognition of job performance are present.
3. Perceived inequities exist in the organization.
4. Autocratic rather than participative management is present.
5. There is low organizational loyalty.
6. Budget expectations are perceived as unreasonable.
7. Pay is unrealistically low.
8. Poor training and promotion opportunities are present.
9. There are high turnover and/or absenteeism.
10. Organizational responsibilities are unclear.
11. There are poor communication practices within the organization.

The last critical element is the organization's policy for handling fraud once it occurs. No matter how well developed the culture of honesty and integrity in an organization, it is still likely to experience some fraud. How the organization reacts to incidents of fraud sends a strong signal that affects the rate at which future incidents occur. An effective policy for handling fraud assures that the facts are investigated thoroughly, firm and consistent actions are taken against perpetrators, risks and controls are assessed and improved, and communication and training are ongoing.

Assessing and Mitigating the Risk of Fraud

Neither fraud committed by top management on behalf of an organization nor fraud committed against an organization can occur without opportunity. Organizations can eliminate opportunity by (1) accurately identifying sources and measuring risks; (2) implementing appropriate preventative and detective controls; (3) creating widespread monitoring by employees; and (4) installing independent checks, including an effective audit function.

Identifying sources and measuring risk means that an organization needs a process in place that both defines areas of greatest risk and evaluates and tests controls that minimize those risks. In identifying risk, organizations should consider organizational, industry, and country-specific characteristics that encourage and discourage fraud.

Risks that are inherent in the environment of an organization can be addressed with an appropriate system of control. Once risks have been assessed, the organization can identify processes, controls, and other procedures that can minimize risks. Appropriate internal systems include well-developed control environments, effective accounting systems, and appropriate control procedures.

Research has shown that employees and managers—not auditors—detect most frauds.[18] Therefore, employees and managers must be taught how to watch for and recognize fraud. To involve employees in the all-important monitoring process, provide a protocol for communication. Such protocol details to whom employees should report suspected fraud and what form their communication should take. The protocol should assure confidentiality and stress that retribution will not be tolerated. Organizations that are serious about fraud prevention must make it easy for employees and managers to come forward and must reward (not punish) them for doing so.

Fraud Detection

Most frauds start small and, if not detected, continue to get larger and larger. Events that scare or threaten the perpetrator result in discontinuance of the theft, which is then resumed when the threats pass. Because those that commit fraud increase the amounts they steal, in most cases, amounts taken just before discovery far exceed those taken earlier. In one case, the amounts taken *quadrupled* every month during the period of the fraud! Indeed, small frauds are just large frauds that got caught early. And, in cases where top management or owners are perpetrating the fraud, prevention is difficult, so early detection is critical.

When fraud is committed by owners of small organizations, who perform the accounting tasks themselves, fraud is not preventable. If owners commit fraud, there is nothing anyone can do to stop them. Rather, the emphasis in these situations must be on detecting the fraud.

Because most frauds increase dramatically over time, it is extremely important that frauds, when they occur, be detected early. Detection, of course, involves steps and actions taken to uncover a fraud. It does not include investigations taken to determine motives, extent, method of embezzlement, or other elements of the theft. Fraud is unlike other crimes in which the occurrence of the crime is easily recognized. Because fraud is rarely obvious, one of the most difficult tasks is determining whether one has actually occurred.

Detection usually begins when employees, managers, or victims notice "red flags," symptoms such as disturbing trends in numbers, or missing assets that indicate something is awry. Unfortunately, red flags don't always mean that fraud is occurring. There are two primary ways to detect fraud: (1) by chance and (2) by proactively searching for and encouraging early recognition of symptoms. In the past, most frauds were detected by accident. Unfortunately, by the time detection occurred, the frauds had been going on for some time and the losses were large. In most cases, individuals in the victim organizations suspected that fraud was occurring but did not come forward because they weren't sure, didn't want to wrongly accuse someone, didn't know how to report the fraud, or were fearful of being branded a whistle-blower.

In recent years, organizations have implemented a number of initiatives to better detect fraud. Probably the most common detection initiative has been hotlines whereby employees, co-workers, and others can phone in anonymous tips. Some hotlines are maintained within the company, and others are outsourced to independent organizations. Organizations that have installed hotlines now detect many frauds that would previously have gone undetected, but they also pay a price for doing so. Not surprisingly, many calls do not involve fraud at all. Some are hoaxes; some are motivated by grudges, anger, or a desire to do harm to an organization or individual; and some are about reasonable red flags that are caused by factors other than fraud.

Except for hotlines, organizations have only recently undertaken other serious proactive detection efforts. Advances in technology now allow organizations to analyze and mine databases to search for red flags. Banks, for example, use software that identifies suspected kiting. These programs draw the bank's attention to customers who have high volumes of bank transactions in short periods of time. Insurance companies use programs that examine claims within a short time after purchasing insurance. Some programs systematically identify the kinds of frauds that may be occurring by cataloging the various symptoms those frauds generate, and then building real-time queries into their computer systems to search for these symptoms.

Fraud Investigation

Investigation should be based on a "predication of fraud." *Predication* refers to circumstances that, taken as a whole, would lead a reasonable, prudent professional to believe a fraud has occurred, is occurring, or will occur. Fraud investigations should not be conducted without predication. A specific allegation of fraud against another party is not necessary, but there must be some reasonable basis for concern that fraud may be occurring. Once predication is present, an investigation is usually undertaken to determine whether or not fraud is occurring, as well as the who, why, how, when, and where elements of the fraud. The purpose of an investigation is to find the truth—to determine whether the symptoms actually represent fraud or whether they represent unintentional errors or other factors. Fraud investigation is a complex and sensitive matter. If investigations are not properly conducted, the reputations of innocent individuals can be irreparably injured, guilty parties can go undetected and be free to repeat the act, and the offended entity may not have information to use in preventing and detecting similar incidents or in recovering damages.

Approaches to Fraud Investigation

Investigations must have management's approval. Because they can be quite expensive, investigations should be pursued only when there is reason to believe that fraud has occurred (when predication is present). Investigative approaches vary, although most investigators rely heavily on interviews.

Fraud investigations can be classified by the types of evidence produced or by the elements of fraud. Using the first approach, the *evidence square* below shows the four classifications of evidence.

The four types of evidence that can be collected in fraud investigations are as follows.

1. *Testimonial evidence,* which is gathered from individuals. Specific investigative techniques used to gather testimonial evidence include interviewing, interrogation, and honesty tests.
2. *Documentary evidence,* which is gathered from paper, computers, and other written or printed sources. Some of the most common techniques for gathering this evidence include document examination, public records searches, audits, computer searches, net worth calculations, and financial statement analysis.
3. *Physical evidence* includes fingerprints, tire marks, weapons, stolen property, identification numbers or marks on stolen objects, and other tangible evidence that can be associated with the act. The gathering of physical evidence often involves forensic analysis by experts.
4. *Personal observation* involves evidence that is collected by the investigators themselves, including *invigilation,* surveillance, and covert operations, among others.

Many professionals prefer to classify investigative approaches according to the three elements of fraud, as shown in the triangle.

Investigation of the theft involves efforts to catch the perpetrator(s) in the act itself and information-gathering efforts. Investigation of the concealment focuses on records, documents, computer programs and servers, and other places where perpetrators might try to conceal or hide their deceit. Investigation of the conversion involves searching out the ways in which perpetrators have spent the stolen assets. A fourth set of investigative techniques, *inquiry methods,* has to do with the overall approach as it applies to all these elements. Thus, this approach to classifying investigative techniques is called the *fraud triangle plus inquiry approach.*

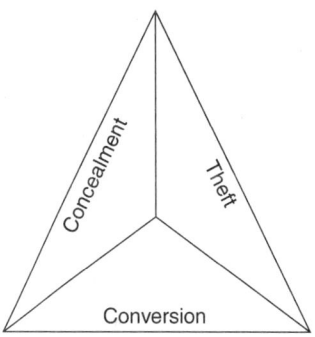

Conducting a Fraud Investigation

For now, it is important to know that fraud investigators need some way to coordinate the investigation. Some investigations are very large and conducting investigative steps in the wrong order or doing them inappropriately can lead to a failed investigation and other problems. In fact, it is extremely important that you understand the significant risks that investigators face.

You must also remember that investigating a fraud is a traumatic experience for everyone involved, including the perpetrators. As we stated previously, most fraud perpetrators are first-time offenders who have pristine reputations at work, and in their community, family, and church. Sometimes, admitting that they are being investigated for fraud or have committed fraud is more than they can take.

Maintaining high ethics in conducting investigations is also important. As a minimum, investigations of fraud must proceed as follows.

1. They must be undertaken only to "establish the truth of a matter under question."
2. The individuals who conduct the investigation must be experienced and objective. If such individuals do not exercise care in choosing words to describe the incident or do not maintain a neutral perspective, their objectivity immediately becomes suspect in the eyes of management and employees. Investigators should never jump to conclusions.
3. Any hypothesis investigators have about whether or not someone committed fraud should be closely guarded when discussing the progress of an investigation with others. Even though good investigators often form preliminary opinions or impressions, they must objectively weigh every bit of information against known facts and evidence and must always protect the confidentiality of the investigation.

4. Investigators must ensure that those who have a need to know (for example, management) are kept apprised of investigation activities and agree to the investigation and techniques employed.
5. Good investigators must ensure that all information collected during an inquiry is independently corroborated and determined to be factually correct. Failure to corroborate evidence is a common mistake of inexperienced investigators.
6. Investigators must exercise care to avoid questionable investigative techniques. Experienced investigators make sure that the techniques used are scientifically and legally sound and fair. Thoroughness and dogged tenacity, not questionable techniques, lead to successful conclusions.
7. Investigators must report all facts fairly and objectively. Communications throughout the term of an investigation, from preliminary stage to final report, should be carefully controlled to avoid obscuring facts and opinions. Communications, including investigative reports, must not only include information obtained that points to guilt, but must also include facts and information that may exonerate. Ignoring and failing to document information is a serious investigative flaw, with potential for serious consequences.

Fraud Resolution

One of the major decisions a company, stockholders, and others must make when fraud is committed is what kind of follow-up action should be taken. Why the fraud occurred should always be determined, and controls or other measures to prevent or deter its reoccurrence should be implemented. The bigger and often troubling question that must then be addressed is what legal action should be taken with respect to the perpetrators.

Most organizations and other victims of fraud usually make one of three choices: (1) take no legal action; (2) pursue civil remedies; and/or (3) pursue criminal action against the perpetrators, which is sometimes done for them by law enforcement agencies.

Take No Legal Action

Research shows that legal action is taken against perpetrators in less than half of all fraud cases.[19] Management often wants only to get the fraud behind it as quickly as possible. They understand that pursuing legal action is expensive, time-consuming, sometimes embarrassing, and is often *considered* an unproductive use of time. Thus, management most often terminates perpetrators, but sometimes it doesn't even go that far. Unfortunately, when organizations do not pursue legal action, the word spreads quickly that "nothing serious will happen if you steal from the company." Employees who receive this message are more likely to steal than are employees who understand that punishment "to the letter of the law" will follow for all dishonest acts. When one Fortune 500 company changed its stance on fraud from "the CEO is to be informed when someone is prosecuted for fraud" to "the CEO is to be informed when someone who commits fraud is not prosecuted," the number of frauds in the company decreased significantly.

Pursue Civil Action

The purpose of a civil action is to recover money or other assets from the perpetrators and others associated with the fraud. Civil actions are quite rare in cases of employee fraud (because perpetrators have usually spent the money), but are much more common when frauds involve other organizations. Vendors who pay kickbacks to company employees often find themselves the target of civil actions by victim companies, especially if losses are high. Likewise, stockholders and creditors who suffer losses from management fraud almost always sue not only the perpetrators, but usually the auditors and others associated with the company as well. The plaintiff's lawyers are usually more than willing to represent shareholders in a class-action, contingent fee lawsuit.[20]

Pursue Criminal Action

Criminal action can only be brought by law enforcement or statutory agencies. Organizations that decide to pursue criminal action against perpetrators must work with local, state, or federal agencies to get their employees or other perpetrators prosecuted. Criminal penalties involve fines, prison terms, or both. Perpetrators may be required to enter into restitution agreements to pay back stolen funds over a period of time. Pursuing criminal penalties for fraud is becoming more and more common. Corporate executives who commit fraud are often given 10-year jail sentences and are ordered to pay fines equal to the amounts they embezzled. However, it is much more difficult to get a criminal conviction than it is to get a judgment in a civil case. Whereas only a preponderance of the evidence (more than 50%) is necessary to win a civil case, convictions are only successful if there is proof "beyond a reasonable doubt" that the perpetrator "intentionally" stole money or other assets.

Fraud Against Organizations (Occupational Fraud)

In this section, we look at how employees, customers, and vendors perpetuate fraud against organizations. This fraud is sometimes called *occupational fraud*, and we focus on two aspects of it: asset misappropriation and corruption. As you think about the various types of fraud, always remember that fraud perpetrators are creative, and they come up with new schemes every day.

Asset Misappropriations

Dishonest employees, vendors, and customers have three opportunities to steal assets: They can (1) steal *receipts* of cash and other assets as they come into the organization, (2) steal cash and other assets that are *on hand,* or (3) commit *disbursement fraud* (the organization pays for something it shouldn't pay for or pays too much for purchases). With each type of fraud, perpetrators can act alone or in collusion with others. The following diagram outlines possible ways to misappropriate funds.

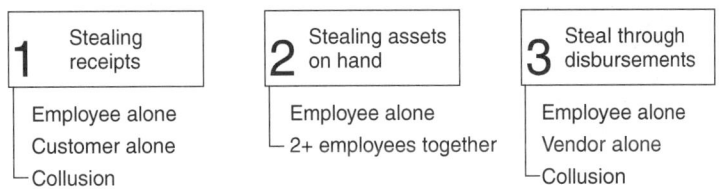

The fraud taxonomy developed by Wells[21] of ACFE is more complicated and detailed than the one we show. He divides asset misappropriations into two major categories: (1) thefts of cash and (2) thefts of inventory and other assets. Thefts of cash he further subdivides as follows: (1) larceny (intentionally taking an organization's cash without its consent and against its will), (2) skimming (removing cash prior to its entry into the accounting system), and (3) fraudulent disbursements. Thefts of inventory and other assets he also divides into two groups: (1) larceny and (2) misuse. We will discuss the misappropriation of assets using Wells's classification scheme.

Theft of Cash Through Larceny

In larceny, cash is stolen by employees or others after it has been recorded in the company's accounting system. As a result, larceny is easier to detect than skimming and is far less common.

Cash larcenies take place in situations in which perpetrators have access to cash. Commonly, perpetrators take cash or currency on hand (in cash registers or cash boxes) or from bank deposits. Cash larcenies are most successful when they involve relatively small amounts over extended periods of time. With such thefts, businesses often write the small missing amounts off as "shorts" or "miscounts," rather than as thefts. For example, in one bank, annual cash shortages by tellers exceed $3 million per year. Some of this teller shortage is no doubt truly miscounting, and certainly customers are more likely to inform their teller when they are given too little cash than when they are given too much cash. However, a significant portion of the shortage is also caused by larceny.

Theft of Cash Through Skimming

Complicated skimming schemes occur when employees (1) understate sales and collections by recording false or larger-than-reality sales discounts; (2) misappropriate customer payments and write off the receivable as "uncollectible"; (3) embezzle a first customer's payment and then credit that customer's account when a second customer pays (a delayed recognition of payment, called *lapping*); or (4) collude with customers so they either pay later than required or less than required. As an example of this latter scheme, consider the $2.2 million fraud perpetrated on a Fortune 500 company. An employee who collected receivables gave a high-volume customer extra time to pay receivables without reporting them as delinquent. As a result of this fraud, the dishonest customer earned interest on cash that should have been used to pay the accounts payable; the interest exceeded $2 million. The money was then split with the accounts receivable manager, who worked for the victim company. The victim company lost (1) the interest they should have been earning on the receivables and (2) the interest they had to pay out on loans to cover the shortfall. This fraud encompassed both skimming and corruption.

Theft of Cash Through Fraudulent Disbursements

The ACFE research project found that fraudulent disbursements comprise by far the highest percentage of asset misappropriations. In fact, based on the sample studied, fraudulent disbursements represent 67% of all cases, more than double the total of skimming (38.9% of all misappropriations) and larceny (4.1% of all cases).

The ACFE divides fraudulent disbursements into six major types: (1) check tampering, (2) register-disbursement schemes, (3) billing schemes, (4) expense schemes, (5) payroll schemes, and (6) others. In terms of frequency and amount of losses, billing schemes are the largest, as shown below.

Type of Disbursements Fraud	Percent of Total Cases	Percent of Total Losses
Billing schemes	33.3%	51.6%
Check tampering	24.5%	13.2%
Payroll schemes	16.5%	10.7%
Expense schemes	14.9%	4.0%
Other fraudulent disbursements	8.1%	0.1%
Register-disbursement schemes	2.7%	20.4%

Theft of Inventory and Other Assets

Fraudsters misappropriate company assets other than cash in one of two ways. They misuse (or "borrow") the asset or they steal it. Simple misuse is obviously the less egregious of the two types of fraud. Assets that are misused but not "technically" stolen include company vehicles, company supplies, computers, and other office equipment. These assets are also used by perpetrators to conduct personal work on company time. In many instances, the side businesses are of the same nature as the employer's business, so the fraudster is essentially competing with the employer and using the employer's equipment to do it.

Although the misuse of company property is a problem, the theft of company property is a much greater problem. Losses from inventory theft run into the millions of dollars. The means employed to steal company property range from simple larceny—walking off with company property—to more complicated schemes that involve falsifying company documents and records. Larceny usually involves taking inventory or other assets from the company premises, without attempting to conceal it in the books and records or "justify" its absence. Most noncash larceny schemes are not very complicated. They are typically committed by employees (such as warehouse personnel, inventory clerks, and shipping clerks) who have access to inventory and other assets.

Another common noncash asset theft is the use of asset requisitions and other forms that allow assets to be moved from one location in a company to another location. Often, perpetrators use internal documents to gain access to merchandise that they otherwise might not be able to handle without raising suspicion. Transfer documents allow them to move assets from one location to another and ultimately take the merchandise for themselves. The most basic scheme occurs when fraudsters requisition materials to complete a work-related project and then steal the materials. In more extreme cases, perpetrators completely fabricate a project that necessitates the use of the assets that they want to steal.

A third noncash asset theft uses a company's purchasing and receiving functions. In purchasing-scheme frauds, perpetrators use company funds to purchase items for their personal use. In noncash asset frauds, assets are intentionally purchased by the company and then misappropriated by perpetrators. In these schemes, victim companies lose three ways. The company is deprived not only of the cash it paid for the merchandise, but also of the merchandise itself. And, because the organization doesn't have as much inventory on hand as it thinks it has, stock-outs and unhappy customers often result.

Corruption

Perpetrators also commit fraud against organizations through corruption. Corruption and embezzlement are the oldest white-collar crimes. "Paying off" officials, both public and private, for preferential treatment is rooted in our crudest business systems.

Corruption breaks down into four types: (1) bribery, (2) conflicts of interest, (3) economic extortion, and (4) illegal gratuities. By far the largest of these is bribery, which accounts for 89.2% of all corruption losses, compared to 9% for conflicts of interest, 1.6% for extortion, and 0.2% for illegal gratuities. Although bribery is not as common as some types of fraud, the median loss from bribery is by far the highest of any of the schemes discussed in this section—over $500,000 per incident.

Bribery

Bribery involves offering, giving, receiving, or soliciting anything of value in order to influence an official act. The term "official act" means that traditional bribery involves payments made to influence the decisions of government agents or employees.

A lot of corruption involves commercial bribery, in which something of value is offered to influence a business decision (rather than an official act of government). In commercial bribery, payment is received by corrupt employees without the employer's consent. That is, they accept under-the-table payments in return for influence over a business transaction.

Bribery generally falls into two broad categories: kickbacks and bid-rigging schemes. Kickbacks are undisclosed payments made by vendors to employees of the purchasing companies. The purpose is to enlist the corrupt employee in an overbilling scheme. Sometimes vendors pay kickbacks simply to get extra business from the victim company. Unfortunately, once vendors pay kickbacks, the control of purchasing transactions transfers from the buyer to the vendor. When corrupt vendors are in control of purchasing transactions, goods are sold at higher prices, and their quality can deteriorate substantially.

Bid-rigging schemes occur when corrupt employees help vendors falsely win a contract through "competitive" bidding. This process, in which suppliers or contractors vie for contracts in what can be cutthroat environments, is tailor-made for bribery. Any advantage a vendor gains over competitors in this arena is extremely valuable. The benefit of "inside influence" can ensure that a vendor wins a sought-after contract. Many vendors are willing to pay for this influence. How the bidding is rigged depends largely on the level of influence of the corrupt employee. The more power a person has over the bidding process, the more likely they can influence the selection process. Therefore, employees who participate in bid-rigging schemes (like those in kickback schemes) often have a good measure of influence over the bidding process, or access to influence. Potential targets for bribes include buyers, contracting officials, engineers and technical representatives, quality or product assurance representatives, subcontractor liaison employees—in short, anyone with authority over the awarding of contracts.

Conflicts of Interest

A conflict of interest occurs when an employee, manager, or executive has an undisclosed economic or personal interest in a transaction that adversely affects the company. As with other corruption schemes, conflicts of interest involve corrupt employees exerting influence to the detriment of their company. Conflicts usually involve self-dealing by these employees. In some cases, their act benefits a friend or relative, even though they receive no financial benefit themselves.

To be classified as a conflict of interest scheme, the employee's interest in a transaction must be undisclosed. The essential element in conflict cases is that perpetrators take advantage of their employers: the victim company is unaware that its employee has divided loyalties. If an employer *knows* of the employee's interest in a business deal or negotiation, there can be no conflict of interest, no matter how favorable the arrangement is for the employee.

Conflict schemes fall into one of two categories: purchase schemes and sales schemes. In purchase schemes, corrupt employees (or a friend or relative of the employee) have some kind of undisclosed ownership or employment interest in the vendor that submits the invoice. The bill must originate from a real company in which the perpetrator has an economic or personal interest, and the perpetrator's interest in the company must be undisclosed to the victim company.

In common sales schemes, corrupt employees with a hidden interest have the victim company sell its goods or services below fair market value, which results in a lower profit margin or even a loss on the sale for the company. As an example, a few years ago a large U.S. paper-and-pulp company uncovered a major sales fraud. To get wood for making paper, the company owns its own forests and purchases lumber from others. One of the vendors providing lumber to the company turned out to be a group of its own employees who cut timber on the company's own forest reserves and then sold the timber back to the company. In this case, the company lost twice—it paid for lumber it already owned, and had less of its own lumber to process.

Economic Extortion and Illegal Gratuities

Compared to bribery and conflicts of interests, economic extortion and illegal gratuities occur relatively infrequently and are usually quite small. Economic extortion is basically the flip side of bribery. Instead of a vendor *offering* payments for influence, corrupt employees *demand* payments from vendors for deciding in the vendors' favor. Thus, situations that are ripe for bribery are also ripe for extortion. Illegal gratuities is really a subcategory of bribery; here corrupt employees are rewarded for making favorable decisions. Illegal gratuities are made after deals are approved.

Summary of Occupational Fraud

The following graphic summarizes the taxonomy used to describe asset misappropriation and corruption schemes presented in this section. This classification scheme was developed by Joe Wells, of ACFE.

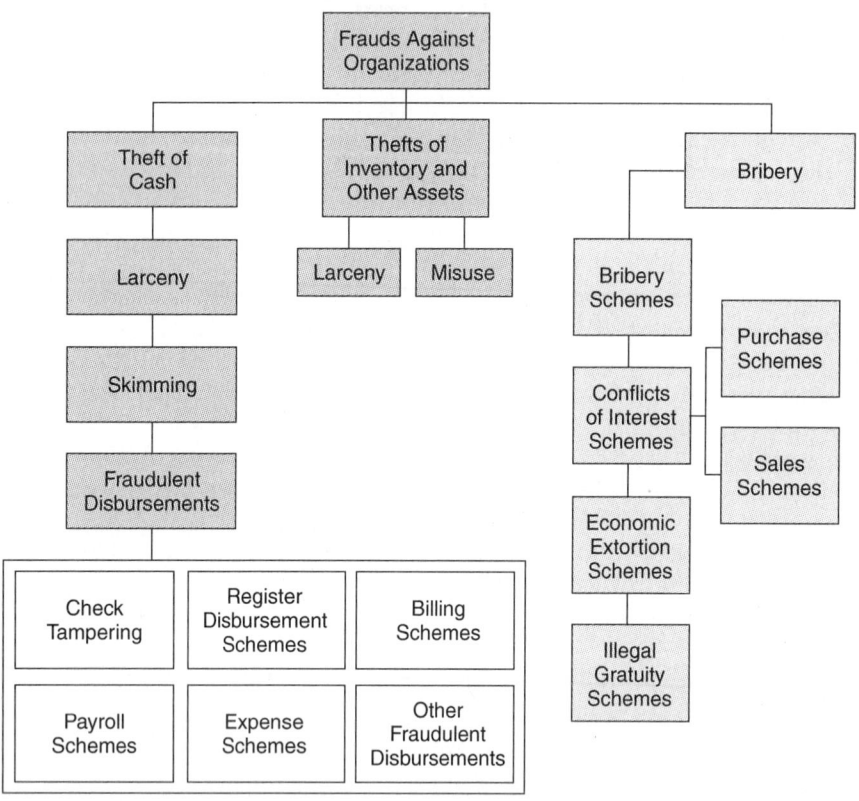

Financial Statement Fraud (Management Fraud)

The Growing Problem of Financial Statement Fraud

The capital markets of the United States are the envy of the world. The efficiency, liquidity, and resiliency of our markets stand second to none. We cannot overstate the important role that financial statements play in keeping U.S. markets efficient. Financial statements are—normally—meaningful disclosures of where a company has been, where it is currently, and where it is going. Most statements present a fair representation of the financial position of the organization issuing them, and are prepared using GAAP (generally accepted accounting principles), which guide how transactions are to be accounted for. Although GAAP does allow some flexibility, standards of objectivity, integrity, and judgment are supposed to prevail.

Unfortunately, financial statements sometimes misrepresent an organization's financial position and results. The misstatement of financial statements happens because accounting records are manipulated, falsified, or altered. Misleading statements cause serious problems in the markets and in the economy. They result in large losses for investors, a break in the trust in our system, and litigation and embarrassment for individuals and organizations associated with the fraud.

The Nature of Financial Statement Fraud

Financial statement fraud, like other frauds, involves intentional deceit and attempted concealment. Financial statement fraud may be concealed through falsified documentation, including forgery, and through collusion by management, employees, or third parties. Unfortunately, like other fraud, financial statement fraud is rarely visible. Rather, symptoms of fraud—red flags—are observed. Because symptoms can be caused by legitimate factors, the presence of symptoms does not always mean that fraud exists. Documents are sometimes legitimately lost, the general ledger can be out of balance because of an unintentional (and real) accounting error, and unexpected analytical relationships can be the result of unrecognized changes in underlying economic factors. Caution must be used even when fraud tips come in, because the person may be mistaken or may be intentionally making false allegations.

Fraud symptoms cannot easily be ranked in order of importance, nor can they be combined into effective predictive models. Their significance varies widely. Some factors will be present when no fraud exists, and only a small number of symptoms may present themselves when fraud is occurring. Many times, the fraud is difficult to prove. Without a confession, obviously forged documents, or a number of repeated, similar thefts (so a pattern of fraud can be inferred), convicting someone of fraud is difficult. Because of the difficulty of detecting and proving fraud, always exercise extreme care when you conduct fraud examinations, quantify fraud, or perform other investigation activities.

Motivations Behind Financial Statement Fraud

The motivations behind fraudulent financial statements vary. Sometimes, perpetrators want to support a high stock price or a bond or stock offering. Sometimes they want to increase the company's stock price. Other times, top executives own large amounts of company stock, and a decrease in the stock price would significantly decrease their personal net worth.

Managers sometimes overstate financial results to meet Wall Street's expectations. Pressure to perform is high, and when faced with the choice between failure and cheating, some people choose cheating. In the **Phar-Mor** case, Monus wanted his company to grow quickly, so he lowered prices on 300 "price-sensitive" items. Prices were cut so much that items sold below cost—each sale resulted in a loss. The strategy may have helped Phar-Mor win new customers and open dozens of new stores each year, but it also resulted in huge losses for the company. Rather than admitting that the company was facing losses, Monus hid the drain and made Phar-Mor appear more profitable. The motivations for financial statement fraud differ, but the results are always the same—adverse consequences for the company, its principals, and its investors.

A Framework for Detecting Financial Statement Fraud

Identifying fraud exposures or opportunities for fraud is one of the most difficult steps in detecting financial statement fraud. To correctly identify exposures, you must clearly understand the operations and the nature of the organization you are examining as well as the industry and its competitors. You must understand the organization's management and what motivates them. You must also understand how the company is organized and be aware of the company's relationships with other parties and the influence that each party has on your client and its officers.

Financial statement frauds are rarely detected by analyzing financial statements alone. Rather, these frauds are detected by comparing financial statement numbers with real-world numbers. The context in which management is operating and by which they are being motivated must be understood. Changes in reported assets, liabilities, revenues, and expenses from period to period are examined. Company performance is compared to industry norms.

The fraud exposure rectangle shown below is useful in identifying management fraud. Although auditors traditionally focus almost entirely on the financial statements and results of operations in their endeavors to detect financial fraud, all four "corners" present fraud exposures that must be examined.

1 Management and Directors	2 Company's Relationship with Other Entities
3 The Organization and Its Industry	4 Financial Results and Operating Characteristics

930. CORPORATE FRAUD

Management and the Board of Directors

Top management is almost always involved in financial statement fraud. Unlike embezzlement and misappropriation, financial statement fraud requires the involvement of individuals high up in an organization, and most often *on behalf* of the organization as opposed to *against* the organization. Because of this, management and the directors must be investigated to determine their exposure to, and motivation for, committing fraud. Gaining an understanding of management and what motivates them is crucial. In particular, three aspects of management should be investigated.

1. Their backgrounds
2. Their motivations
3. Their influence in organizational decision making

With respect to backgrounds, you need to understand what organizations and situations management and directors have been associated with in the past.

You need to know what motivates directors and management. Is their personal worth tied up in the organization? Are they under pressure to deliver unrealistic results? Is their compensation primarily performance-based? Must debt covenants or other financial measures be met? Are managers' jobs at risk? These questions—and others of similar ilk—must be asked and answered in order to properly understand management's motivations. Many financial statement frauds are perpetrated because management is under pressure to report positive or high income to support stock prices, or to show positive earnings for a public stock or debt offering, or to report profits to meet regulatory or loan restrictions.

Management's ability to influence organizational decisions is also important to understand because perpetrating fraud is much easier when only a few individuals have primary decision-making power. In organizations with democratic leadership, fraud is much harder to perpetrate. Most people who commit management fraud are first-time offenders, and their "first time" is tough on them. Things get even more difficult when the fraud requires two people to simultaneously be dishonest or three people to simultaneously be dishonest. When decision making is spread among several individuals, or when the board of directors takes an active role in the organization, fraud becomes very difficult to perpetrate. Because of this, most financial statement frauds do not occur in large, historically profitable organizations. Rather, they occur in smaller organizations where one or two individuals have almost total control over decision making, and where the board of directors and the audit committee are inactive. An active board of directors or an audit committee that is involved in major decisions does much to deter management fraud.

Here are some key questions that fraud examiners ask about management and the directors.

Understanding Management and Director Backgrounds

1. Have key executives or board members been associated with other organizations in the past, and what was the nature of those relationships?
2. Are key members of management promoted from within the organization or recruited from outside?
3. Do key members of management have past regulatory or legal problems, either personally or with prior organizations?
4. Have there been significant changes in the makeup of management or the board of directors?
5. Has there been a high turnover of management and/or board members?
6. Do any managers or board members have criminal backgrounds?
7. Are there other issues regarding the backgrounds of management and the board of directors?

Understanding What Motivates Management and the Board of Directors

1. Is key executives' personal worth tied up in the organization?
2. Is management under pressure to meet earnings or other financial expectations, or does management commit to achieving what appear to be unduly aggressive forecasts?
3. Is management's compensation primarily performance-based (bonuses, stock options, and so on)?
4. Must management meet significant debt covenants or other financial restrictions?
5. Is the job security of key members of management at serious risk?
6. Is the organization's reported performance decreasing?
7. Is management excessively interested in maintaining or increasing the entity's stock price?

(continued)

8. Does management have an incentive to use inappropriate means to minimize reported earnings for tax reasons?
9. Are there any other significant issues regarding motivations of management and board members?

Understanding the Scope of Influence of Management and the Board of Directors

1. Who among management or the board of directors has the most influence?
2. Do one or two people have dominant influence in the organization?
3. Is the management style autocratic or democratic?
4. Is management centralized or decentralized?
5. Does management effectively communicate and support the entity's values and ethics, or do they communicate inappropriate values or ethics?
6. Does management fail to correct known reportable conditions in internal control on a timely basis?
7. Does management set unduly aggressive financial targets and expenditures for operating personnel?
8. Does management have too much involvement in, or influence over, the selection of accounting principles or the determination of significant estimates?
9. Are there other significant issues regarding the influence of management and/or the board of directors?

Companies' Relationships With Other Entities

Financial statement fraud is often perpetrated with the help of other real or fictitious organizations. **Lincoln Savings and Loan**, for example, structured sham transactions with "straw buyers" to make its negative performance appear profitable. A real estate limited partnership, the **DuVall Limited Real Estate Partnerships**, structured fraudulent transactions with bankers to hide mortgages on their holdings. Relationships with related parties are problematic because they often allow for other than arms-length transactions. The management of **ESM Government Securities**, for example, hid a $400 million financial statement fraud by creating a large receivable from a nonconsolidated entity.

Although relationships with all parties should be examined to determine if they present opportunities for management fraud, relationships with financial institutions, related organizations and individuals, external auditors, lawyers, investors, and regulators should be carefully scrutinized. Relationships with financial institutions and bondholders are important because they indicate the extent to which the company is leveraged. Here are typical questions to ask about debt relationships.

- How leveraged is the company, with which financial institutions, and is it in line with the industry?
- What assets has the organization pledged as collateral?
- What debt or other restrictive covenants must be met?
- Do the banking relationships appear normal, or are there strange relationships with financial institutions, such as using institutions in unusual geographical locations?
- Are there relationships between the officers of the financial institutions and your client organization?

In the DuVall Limited Real Estate Partnerships referred to earlier, a Wisconsin company took out unauthorized loans from a bank located in another state, where it had no business operations. The partnership was used because the client company's CEO had a relationship with the bank president, who later falsified an audit confirmation. The loans were discovered when auditors performed a lien search on properties owned. The bank president denied the existence of the loans, so liabilities were significantly understated on the balance sheet.

Related organizations and individuals (related parties) should be examined because structuring improper and unrealistic transactions with related organizations and individuals is an easy way to perpetrate financial statement fraud. These symptoms are identified by examining large and/or unusual transactions, especially those that occur at strategic times (such as at the end of an accounting period) to make the financial statements look better. Here are transactions events that should be carefully examined.

- Large transactions that result in revenues and/or income for the organization
- Sales and/or purchases of assets between related entities
- Transactions that result in goodwill or other tangible assets being recognized in the financial statements
- Loans and other financing transactions between related entities
- Transactions that appear to be unusual or questionable for the organization, especially unrealistically large ones

A company's relationship with its auditors is important to analyze for several reasons. If there has been a recent change in auditors, there is probably a good reason for the change. Auditing firms do not easily give up clients, and the termination of an auditor-auditee relationship is often caused by (1) failure of the client to pay, (2) an auditor-auditee disagreement, (3) the auditor's suspicion of fraud or other problems, or (4) the auditee's view that the auditor's fees are too high. Although high fees don't usually signal fraud, the other three reasons can. The fact that an auditor was dismissed or resigned, together with the difficulties that first-year auditors will encounter in discovering financial statement fraud, is cause for concern.

Relationships with lawyers pose an even greater risk. Auditors are supposed to be independent and are obliged to resign if they suspect inaccurate or inappropriate financial results. However, lawyers act as advocates for their clients, and therefore tend to follow and support their clients until it is extremely obvious that fraud has occurred. In addition, lawyers are often privy to information about a client's legal difficulties, regulatory problems, and other significant occurrences. Like auditors, lawyers rarely give up a profitable client unless something is very wrong. Thus a change in legal firms can be cause for concern. And, unlike changing auditors, where publicly held companies have to file a 10-K, changing lawyers entails no such reporting requirement.

Relationships with investors are important because financial statement fraud is often motivated by wanting to promote a debt or equity offering to investors. In addition, a knowledge of the number and types of investors (public versus private company, major exchange versus small exchange, and so on) often indicates the level of pressure and public scrutiny management faces in its performance. If an organization is publicly held, investor groups and investment analysts are following the company very closely and can often provide information that something is wrong. For example, "short" investors are always looking for bad news that makes a stock go down. If they suspect something awry, they may contact management, the media, or even the auditors to vent their concerns. Investor groups focus on information very different from that used by auditors, and sometimes fraud symptoms are more obvious to them.

Finally, understanding the client's relationship with regulators is important. If your client company is publicly held, you need to know whether the SEC has ever issued an enforcement release against them. You also need to know whether annual, quarterly, and other reports are filed on a timely basis. If the client is in a regulated industry, such as banking, you need to know what their relationship is with appropriate regulatory bodies. Are there significant issues raised by those bodies? Does the organization owe back taxes to the federal or state government or to other taxing districts? Because of the recourses and sanctions available to taxing authorities, organizations don't fall behind on their payments unless something is very wrong or they are having serious cash flow problems. These are typical questions to ask about a company's relationships.

Relationships With Financial Institutions

1. With what financial institution does the organization maintain significant relationships?
2. How leveraged is the organization through its bank or other loans?
3. Do loan or debt covenants or restrictions pose significant problems for the organization?
4. Do banking relationships appear normal, or are there unusual attributes about the relationships (strange geographical locations, too many banks, and so on)?
5. Do members of management or the board have personal or other close relationships with officers of the company's major banks?
6. Have there been significant changes in the financial institutions the company uses? If so, why?
7. Are there significant bank accounts or subsidiary or branch operations in tax havens for which there appears to be no clear business justification?
8. Have critical assets of the company been pledged as collateral on risky loans?
9. Are there other questionable financial institution relationships?

Relationships With Related Parties

1. Are there significant transactions with related parties not in the ordinary course of business or with related parties that have not been audited or that were audited by another firm?
2. Are there large and/or unusual transactions at or near the end of a period that significantly improve the company's reported financial performance?
3. Are there significant receivables and/or payables between related parties?

(continued)

4. Is a significant amount of the organization's revenues and/or income derived from related-party transactions?
5. Is a significant part of the company's income or revenues derived from one or two large transactions?
6. Are there any other questionable related-party relationships?

Relationships With Auditors

1. Have there been frequent disputes with current or preceding auditors on accounting, auditing, or reporting matters?
2. Has management placed unreasonable demands on its auditors, including unreasonable time constraints?
3. Has the company placed formal or informal restrictions on auditors that inappropriately limit their access to people or information or limit their ability to communicate effectively with the board of directors or the audit committee?
4. Is management behavior toward auditors domineering? Has management attempted to influence the scope of the auditor's work?
5. Has there been a change in auditors, and if so, for what reason?
6. Are there other questionable auditor relationships?

Relationships With Lawyers

1. Has there been significant litigation involving the company in matters that could severely and adversely affect its performance?
2. Has there been an attempt to hide litigation from auditors or others?
3. Has there been a change in outside counsel, and if so, for what reason?
4. Are there other questionable lawyer relationships?

Relationships With Investors

1. Is the organization in the process of issuing an initial or secondary public debt or equity offering?
2. Are there investor-related lawsuits?
3. Are there problematic or questionable relationships with investment bankers, stock analysts, or others?
4. Has there been significant "short selling" of the company's stock, and if so, for what reasons?
5. Are there questionable investor relationships?

Relationships With Regulatory Bodies

1. Does management disregard regulatory authorities?
2. Have there been claims against the entity or its senior management that allege fraud or violations of securities laws?
3. Have 8-Ks been filed with the SEC, and if so, for what reasons?[22]
4. Are there any new accounting, statutory, or regulatory requirements that could impair the financial stability or profitability of the entity?
5. Are there significant tax disputes with the IRS or other taxing authorities?
6. Is the company current on paying its payroll taxes and other payroll-related expenses, and is the company current on paying other liabilities?
7. Are there other questionable relationships with regulatory bodies?

The Organization and Its Industry

Perpetrators sometimes mask financial statement fraud by creating an organizational structure in which hiding fraud is easy. For example, **Enron** used complicated and even off-book organizational structures to mask problems such as large liabilities. Several Enron transactions, such as the famous Chewco and LMJ1 transactions, were hidden in off-balance-sheet partnerships. Another example is **Lincoln Savings and Loan**, a subsidiary of **American National**, which had over 50 other subsidiaries and related companies. Lincoln Savings and Loan also had several subsidiaries, some with no apparent business purpose. A significant part of the fraud involved the structuring of supposedly "profitable" transactions near the end of each quarter by selling land to "straw buyers."[23] To entice buyers to participate, perpetrators often made the down payment themselves by having Lincoln Savings and Loan simultaneously loan the straw buyers the same amount of money (or more) that they needed for the down payments. The simultaneous transactions were not easily identifiable because Lincoln Savings and Loan sold the land themselves but had another entity make the loan. The complexity functioned as "smoke" to hide illicit transactions. The same was true of ESM. In that case, organizations were established solely to make it look like receivables were due them when, in fact, they were not audited and could not have been paid even a small portion of what they were owed.

Organizational attributes that typically suggest potential frauds include unduly complex organizational structures, lack of an internal audit department, a board of directors with few outsiders, control of related parties by a small group of individuals, offshore affiliates with no apparent business purpose, or new subsidiaries with no apparent business purpose. Investigators must understand exactly who owns the organization. Sometimes silent or hidden owners use organizations in questionable activities.

The COSO-sponsored study of the attributes of firms that commit financial statement fraud concluded the following.

The relatively small size of fraud companies suggests that the inability or even unwillingness to implement cost-effective internal controls may be a factor affecting the likelihood of financial statement fraud (for example, override of controls is easier). Smaller companies may be unable or unwilling to employ senior executives with sufficient financial reporting knowledge and experience.

The concentration of fraud among companies with under $50 million in revenues and with generally weak audit committees highlights the importance of rigorous audit committee practices even for smaller organizations. In particular, the number of audit committee meetings per year and the financial expertise of the audit committee members may deserve closer attention. Investors should be aware of the possible complications arising from family relationships and from individuals (founders, CEO/board chairs, etc.) who hold significant power or incompatible job functions.[24]

The industry of your client organization must also be carefully examined. Some industries are riskier than others. In addition, the organization's performance relative to that of similar organizations in the industry should be examined. These are typical questions you should ask about organizational structure and industry attributes.

1. Does the company have an overly complex organizational structure; that is, does it have legal entities, managerial lines of authority, or contractual arrangements without apparent business purpose?
2. Is there a legitimate business purpose for each separate entity of the business?
3. Is the board of directors comprised primarily of officers of the company or other related individuals?
4. Is the board of directors passive, or active and independent?
5. Is the audit committee comprised primarily of insiders or outsiders?
6. Is the audit committee passive, or active and independent?
7. Is the internal audit department independent and active?
8. Does the organization have offshore activities without an apparent business purpose?
9. Is the organization a new entity without a proven history?
10. Have there been significant recent changes in the nature of the organization?
11. Is there adequate monitoring of controls?
12. Is there an effective accounting and information technology staff?
13. Does the organization face stiff competition or market saturation for its products, accompanied by declining margins?
14. Is the client's industry declining; that is, is it experiencing increasing business failures and significant decreases in customer demand?
15. Is the industry subject to rapidly changing technology or rapid product obsolescence?
16. Is the company's performance similar or contrary to other firms in the industry?
17. Are there other significant issues about the organization and the industry?

Financial Results and Operating Characteristics

Much can be learned about exposure to financial statement fraud by closely examining management and the board of directors, relationships with others, and the nature of the organization, and looking at those three elements is always a good idea. In examining financial statements to assess a company's exposure to fraud, effective investigators take a nontraditional approach to financial statements. As we noted earlier, fraud symptoms often exhibit themselves through changes in the financial statements. **Footnotes** are another key item to examine; in fact, understanding what they are *really* saying is very important. Many times, footnotes strongly hint that fraud is occurring, but auditors and others miss it.

When investigators use a company's financial statements and its operating characteristics to determine whether fraud is occurring, they compare the statement balances with those of similar organizations in the industry, and they also check to see whether the real-world numbers match the statement numbers. That is, the $2 million inventory on a statement has to be located somewhere, and it will require space to store it, forklifts and other equipment to move it, and people to manage it. Investigators therefore ask, are the statement numbers realistic, given the inventory that is on hand?

In order to use financial statements in this manner, you must understand the nature of the client's business, the types of accounts that should be included in the statements, the types of fraud that the organization is particularly vulnerable to, and the symptoms these frauds generate. For example, the activities of a manufacturing company typically divide into sales and collections, acquisition and payment, financing, payroll, and inventory and warehousing. To identify fraud, you would break an organization down into activities like these and then identify the functions performed in each activity, the inherent risk in each function, the abuses and frauds that can occur, and the symptoms these frauds generate. You can then use detection techniques to determine whether fraud is occurring in these activities. Here are critical questions to ask about financial statement relationships and operating results.

1. Are the changes in financial statement account balances unrealistic?
2. Are the account balances themselves realistic given the nature, age, and size of the company?
3. Do actual physical assets exist in the amounts and values reported in the statements?
4. Have there been significant changes in the nature of the organization's revenues or expenses?
5. Do one or a few large transactions account for a significant portion of an account balance or amount?
6. Are there significant end-of-period transactions that positively impact results, especially ones that are unusual or complex or that pose "substance over form" questions?
7. Do financial results appear consistent on a quarter-by-quarter or month-by-month basis, or are there unrealistic amounts in a subperiod?
8. Is the organization reporting earnings and earnings growth, yet having trouble generating cash flow?
9. Is the organization continually having to obtain additional capital to stay competitive?
10. Are reported assets, liabilities, revenues, or expenses based on estimates that involve unusually subjective judgments or uncertainties or that are subject to potential significant change in the near term in a manner that may have a financially disruptive effect on the entity—such as ultimate collectibility of receivables, timing of revenue recognition, realizability of financial instruments based on the highly subjective valuation of collateral or difficult-to-assess repayment sources, or significant deferral of costs?
11. Is profitability growing at an unusually rapid pace, especially compared with other companies in the industry?
12. Is the organization particularly vulnerable to changes in the interest rates?
13. Are sales or profitability incentive programs unrealistically aggressive?
14. Does the organization face imminent bankruptcy or foreclosure? Is it threatened by a hostile takeover?
15. Are adverse consequences probable on pending transactions, such as a business combination or contract award, if poor financial results are reported?
16. Is there a poor or deteriorating financial position in which management has personally guaranteed significant debts of the entity?
17. Does the firm continuously operate in "crisis" mode or without a careful budgeting and planning process?
18. Does the organization have difficulty collecting receivables? Does it have other cash flow problems?
19. Does the organization's success depend on one or two key products or services? Can these products or services quickly become obsolete? Do its competitors adapt better to market swings?
20. Do statement footnotes contain information about difficult-to-understand issues?
21. Are there adequate disclosures in the footnotes?
22. Are there questionable or suspicious aspects in the financial results or operating characteristics?

Revenue and Inventory Frauds

Revenue Fraud

By far, the most common accounts manipulated when financial statement fraud is perpetrated are revenues and/or accounts receivable. A study by the Committee of Sponsoring Organizations (COSO) found that over half of all financial statement frauds involve revenues and/or accounts receivable.[25] The COSO study also found that the most common way to manipulate revenue accounts is by recording fictitious revenues and the second most common is by recording revenues prematurely.

Revenue frauds are common for two reasons. First, there are acceptable alternatives for recognizing revenue, and each approach can be interpreted and applied in situation-specific ways. Just as organizations differ, the types of revenues they generate also differ, and each revenue type requires specific recognition and reporting methods. A company that collects cash before delivering goods or performing services, such as a franchiser, for example, recognizes revenue differently than a company that collects cash after the delivery of goods or the performance of a service, such as a manufacturing firm. A company that has long-term, construction-type contracts uses different revenue recognition criteria than one whose revenue is based on small, discrete work tasks. In many cases, identifying the most significant events that should control the timing of revenue recognition is difficult.

REVENUE FRAUD SCHEMES As you will see, various schemes are used to misstate financial statements. One of the best ways to understand how financial statement frauds are perpetrated using revenue is to first identify the various types of transactions that bring in revenue. Diagrams of the various transactions between an organization and its customers are really helpful here to analyze accounts involved in each transaction, and to determine how misstatements can occur. As a fraud examiner, you might diagram a company's revenue-related transactions as follows.

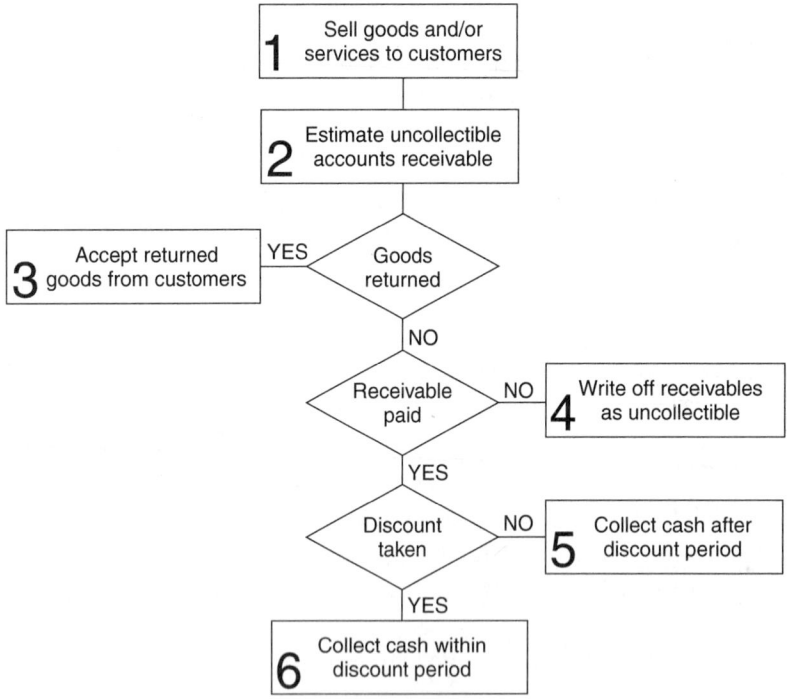

Once you have diagrammed the company's revenue transactions, a good way to determine possible avenues for financial statement fraud is to correlate the accounts involved in each transaction with typical manipulation. The following table uses numbers from the preceding diagram to identify likely transactions.

As you have no doubt noticed, all 11 schemes result in overstated revenues and overstated net income. Of course, companies can also commit fraud by understating revenues and net income. However, such frauds are extremely rare and usually occur only when a company wants to pay lower income taxes.

Once you have identified the various schemes that are possible, you can then list scheme-specific symptoms of fraud, proceed with proactive auditing and/or investigation, and follow up on observed symptoms to determine whether fraud exists.

Transaction	Revenue Fraud Accounts Involved	Possible Fraud Schemes
1. Sell goods and/or services to customers	Accounts receivable, revenues (for example, sales revenue)	1. Record fictitious sales (related parties, sham sales, sales with conditions, consignment sales, and so on) 2. Recognize revenues too early (improper cut-off, percentage of completion, and so on) 3. Overstate real sales (alter contracts, inflate amounts, and so on)
2. Estimate uncollectible accounts receivable	Bad debt expense, allowance for doubtful accounts	4. Understate allowance for doubtful accounts, thus overstating receivables
3. Accept returned goods from customers	Sales returns, accounts receivable	5. Don't record returned goods from customers 6. Record returned goods after the end of the period
4. Write off receivables as uncollectible	Allowance for doubtful accounts, accounts receivable	7. Don't write off uncollectible receivables 8. Write off uncollectible receivables in a later period
5. Collect cash after discount period	Cash, accounts receivable	9. Record bank transfers as cash received from customers 10. Manipulate cash received from related parties
6. Collect cash within discount period	Cash, sales discounts, accounts receivable	11. Don't record discounts given to customers

REVENUE-RELATED FRAUD SYMPTOMS Fraud is rarely observed directly. Instead, employees, customers, auditors, and fraud examiners observe only symptoms, or red flags. To detect fraud, you must be able to identify something as a symptom. We divide fraud symptoms (for all types of fraud) into six categories: analytical symptoms, accounting or documentary symptoms, control symptoms, behavioral or verbal symptoms, lifestyle symptoms, and tips and complaints.

Revenue-Related Fraud Symptoms

Analytical Symptoms

1. Reported revenue or sales account balances appear too high.
2. Reported sales discounts account balances appear too low.
3. Reported sales returns account balances appear too low.
4. Reported bad debt expense account balances appear too low.
5. Reported accounts receivable account balances appear too high or are increasing too fast.
6. Reported allowance for doubtful accounts account balances appear too low.
7. Too little cash is collected from reported revenues.

Accounting or Documentary Symptoms

1. Revenue-related transactions are not recorded in a complete or timely manner or are improperly recorded as to amount, accounting period, classification, or entity policy.
2. Balances are unsupported, or transactions are unauthorized.
3. Last-minute revenue adjustments significantly improve financial results.
4. Documents in the revenue cycle are missing.
5. Original documents are unavailable; only photocopies are used to support transactions.

(continued)

> **Accounting or Documentary Symptoms** (continued)
> 6. Significant items on bank and other reconciliations are not explained.
> 7. Revenue-related ledgers (sales, cash receipts, and so on) do not balance.
> 8. Unusual discrepancies exist between revenue-related records and corroborating evidence (such as accounts receivable confirmation replies).
>
> **Control Symptoms**
> 1. Management overrides significant internal control activities related to the revenue cycle.
> 2. New, unusual, or large customers do not appear to have gone through the customer-approval process.
>
> **Behavioral or Verbal Symptoms**
> 1. Responses from management or employees about revenue or analytical procedures are inconsistent, vague, or implausible.
> 2. Auditors are denied access to facilities, employees, records, customers, vendors, or others from whom revenue-related audit evidence might be sought.
> 3. Undue time pressures are imposed by management to resolve complex revenue-related issues.
> 4. Unusual delays occur in providing requested information.
> 5. Responses to auditors' queries are untrue.
> 6. Behavior of management when asked about revenue-related transactions or accounts is suspicious.
>
> **Lifestyle Symptoms**
> Managers and other company officers live lavish lifestyles.
>
> **Tips and Complaints**
> There is an uptick in tips or complaints about revenue-related fraud.

Inventory and Cost of Goods Sold Frauds

After revenue frauds, the next most common financial statement fraud is the manipulation of inventory and/or cost of goods sold (COGS) accounts. Many high-profile financial statement frauds involve overstating inventory. **Phar-Mor**, for example, significantly overstated the value of its inventory, and then moved inventory back and forth between stores, so that it could be counted multiple times.

To understand why inventory and/or cost of goods sold frauds are so common, you need to understand the income statement. The format for a typical income statement is shown in Exhibit 900.5.

From this format, you can see that if inventory is overstated, cost of goods sold is understated, and net income is overstated by an equal amount (less the tax effect). To better understand the effect of cost of goods sold on inventory, consider how the cost of sold account balance is calculated (Exhibit 900.6).

This calculation shows how cost of goods sold can be understated—by understating purchases or by overstating inventory. (It can also be understated by overstating purchase returns or purchase discounts.) Of these alternatives, overstating the end-of-period inventory tends to be the "fraud of choice" because it not only increases net income, it also increases recorded assets and makes the balance sheet look better.

Exhibit 900.5   *Income Statement*

Income Statement	Overstated Inventory
Gross revenues (sales)	No effect
− Sales returns	No effect
− Sales discounts	No effect
Net revenues (sales)	No effect
− Cost of goods sold	Understated
Gross margin	Overstated
− Expenses	No effect
Net income	Overstated

Exhibit 900.6 *Cost of Goods Sold*

Cost of Goods Sold	Overstated Ending Inventory	Understated Purchases
Beginning Inventory	No effect	No effect
+ Purchases of inventory	No effect	Understated
− Returns of inventory to vendor	No effect	No effect
− Purchase discounts on inventory purchases	No effect	No effect
Goods available for sale	No effect	Understated
− Ending Inventory	Overstated	No effect
Cost of goods sold	Understated	Understated

IDENTIFYING INVENTORY/COST OF GOODS SOLD FRAUDS As with revenue frauds, an easy way to identify financial statement frauds is to diagram the various types of inventory transactions that occur in an organization. For many companies, that diagram might appear as follows for inventory cycle transactions.

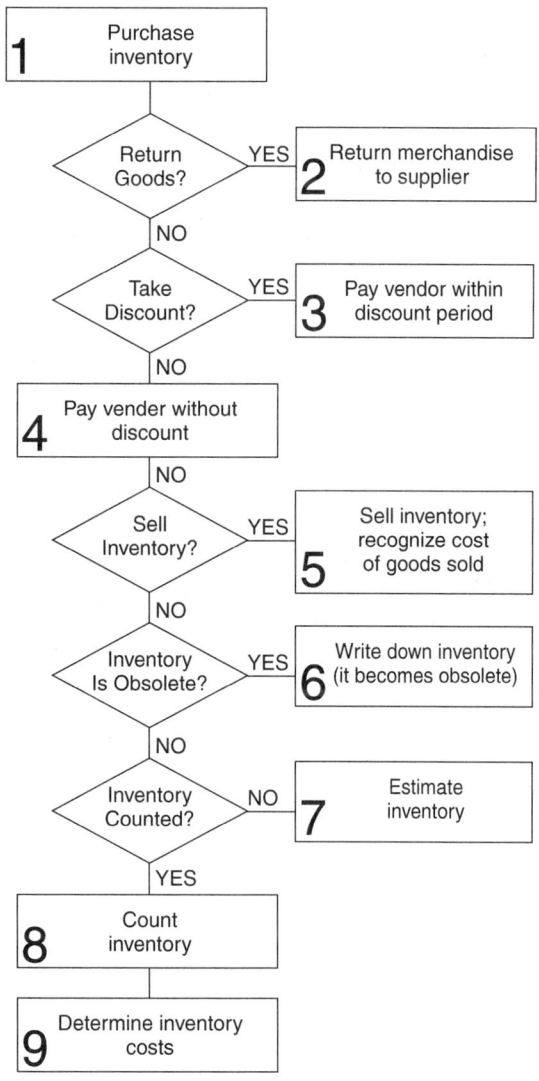

930. CORPORATE FRAUD

As you can see from this diagram, nine different transactions and counts are involved in accounting for inventories and the cost of goods sold. The following table shows the accounts involved in each transaction and common fraud schemes. You can use this table to determine vulnerabilities in situations you are investigating or analyzing. The effect on cost of goods sold and potential fraud schemes are the same under the perpetual and periodic inventory systems.

As you can see, by focusing on transactions and inventory counts, we have identified 17 schemes for overstating inventory and/or understating cost of goods sold. Obviously, some of these schemes are more common than others, but all are used to manipulate inventory and cost of goods sold on financial statements. And, as with revenue frauds, these schemes all have the effect of increasing net income. (Obviously, although rare, it is also possible to commit inventory fraud by understating inventory and net income if, for example, a company wanted to pay less taxes.)

Inventory and Cost of Goods Sold Frauds

Transaction	Accounts Involved	Possible Fraud Schemes
1. Purchase inventory	Inventory, accounts payable	1. Underrecord purchases 2. Record purchases too late (cut-off problem) 3. Not record purchases
2. Return merchandise to supplier	Accounts payable, inventory	4. Overstate returns 5. Record returns in an earlier period (cut-off problem)
3. Pay vendor within discount period	Accounts payable, inventory, cash	6. Overstate discounts 7. Don't reduce inventory cost
4. Pay vendor without discount	Accounts payable, cash	8. Don't reduce inventory cost 9. Record purchase and payment in a later period
5. Sell inventory; recognize cost of goods sold	Cost of goods sold, inventory	10. Record at too low an amount 11. Don't record cost of goods sold or reduce inventory
6. Write down inventory (it becomes obsolete)	Loss on write-down of inventory, inventory	12. Don't write off or write down obsolete inventory
7. Estimate inventory	Inventory shrinkage, inventory	13. Overestimate inventory (use incorrect ratio, and so on)
8. Count inventory	Inventory shrinkage, inventory	14. Overcount inventory (double counting, and so on)
9. Determine inventory costs	Inventory, cost of goods sold	15. Use incorrect costs 16. Make incorrect extensions 17. Record fictitious inventory

Inventory overstatement frauds present a more difficult challenge to perpetrators than do revenue frauds. With revenue frauds, reported revenues are overstated in the current period, and accounts receivable are overstated on the balance sheet. Thus, a compounding effect does not occur in the subsequent period. With inventory frauds, however, the "overstated ending inventory" of one period becomes the "overstated beginning inventory" of the next period and causes net income to be understated in the second period. Thus, if management wants to continue the fraud and overstate net income in the ensuing periods (and most frauds are multiple-period frauds), it must not only offset the overstated beginning inventory, it must then increase net income over and above the offsetting manipulation. The results are ever larger misstatements of inventory, which rapidly becomes easy to detect. Fortunately, most financial statement frauds are perpetrated out of desperation, and perpetrators are focused on how they can overstate income in the current period, with no thought to the accounting problems facing them in subsequent periods.

IDENTIFYING INVENTORY/COST OF GOODS SOLD FRAUD SYMPTOMS Once again, the six categories of fraud symptoms also apply to inventory and cost of goods sold frauds. The most common symptoms with these frauds are listed below.

Inventory Cost of Goods Sold Fraud Symptoms

Analytical Symptoms

1. Reported Inventory balances appear too high or are increasing too fast.
2. Reported Cost of Goods Sold balances appear too low or are decreasing too fast.
3. Reported "Purchase Returns" appear too high or are increasing too rapidly.
4. Reported "Purchase Discounts" appear too high or are increasing too rapidly.
5. Reported "Purchases" appear too low for inventory levels.

Accounting or Documentary Symptoms

1. Inventory and/or cost of goods sold transactions are not recorded in a complete or timely manner or are improperly recorded as to amount, accounting period, classification, or entity.
2. Inventory/cost of goods sold–related transactions are unsupported or unauthorized.
3. End-of-period inventory and/or cost of goods sold adjustments significantly affect the entity's financial results.
4. Inventory and/or cost of goods sold documents are missing.
5. Original documents to support inventory and/or cost of goods sold transactions are unavailable; only photocopies are presented.
6. Cost of goods sold–related accounting records (purchases, sales, cash payments, and so on) do not balance.
7. Unusual discrepancies exist between the entity's inventory and/or cost of goods sold records and corroborating evidence (such as inventory counts).
8. Inventory counts and inventory records differ systematically.
9. Receiving reports and inventory actually received differ.
10. Purchase orders, purchase invoices, receiving records, and inventory records differ.
11. Purchases from suppliers are not approved on vendor lists.
12. Inventory is missing.
13. Purchase orders or invoice numbers are duplicated.
14. Vendors are not listed in Dun & Bradstreet or telephone directories.

Control Symptoms

1. Management overrides significant internal control activities related to purchases, inventory, and/or cost of goods sold.
2. New or unusual vendors do not go through the regular vendor-approval process.
3. Weaknesses in the inventory counting process exist.

Behavioral or Verbal Symptoms

1. Management or employees give inconsistent, vague, or implausible responses to inventory, purchase, or cost of goods sold–related inquiries or analytical procedures.
2. Auditors/investigators are denied access to facilities, employees, records, customers, vendors, or others from whom evidence might be sought.
3. Undue time pressures are imposed by management to resolve contentious or complex inventory and/or cost of goods sold–related issues.
4. Unusual delays occur in providing requested inventory and/or cost of goods sold–related information.
5. Management responses to inventory and/or cost of goods sold or other queries made by auditors are untrue or questionable.
6. The behavior or responses of management are suspicious when they are asked about inventory and/or cost of goods sold–related transactions, vendors, or accounts.

(continued)

> **Lifestyle Symptoms**
> 1. As with revenue frauds, lifestyle symptoms are often not particularly relevant to inventory frauds involving large organizations. In smaller companies, however, where officers can benefit personally from higher stock prices or from obtaining bank loans, they can be relevant.
>
> **Tips and Complaints**
> 1. Tips or complaints suggest that inventory, purchase, and/or cost of goods sold fraud (any of the schemes discussed earlier) might be occurring.

Obviously these lists are not exhaustive. Rather, they represent common symptoms of inventory and/or cost of goods sold–related fraud.

Liability, Asset, and Disclosure Frauds

The revenue and inventory frauds discussed so far are the most common financial statement frauds. However, three other financial statement frauds occur frequently: (1) understating liabilities, (2) overstating assets, and (3) inadequate disclosure.

Liability Fraud

Frauds that entail understating liabilities are difficult for auditors to detect. In fact, all financial statement frauds fall on a continuum of "easy to detect/should be detected" to "difficult to detect/cannot be detected" by auditors performing a Generally Accepted Auditing Standards (GAAS) audit. The following are some of the factors that make frauds difficult to detect.

- Collusion with outsiders
- Forgery, which GAAS auditors are not trained to detect
- Complex audit trails or frauds that are mainly revealed on internal reports that are not reviewed in financial statement audits
- Lying by management and other key people
- Frauds that mimic normal transactions (in other words, are not unusual)
- Silence by individuals "in the know"
- Off-book frauds (no records on the company's books are fraudulent)
- Misleading documentation
- Small frauds relative to financial statement balances

IDENTIFYING LIABILITY FRAUDS As with revenue and inventory frauds, the first step in uncovering liability frauds is to identify transactions that involve liabilities and that can be understated. To do this, you must understand what type of organization you are dealing with, because different types of companies have different liabilities and perpetrate different liability frauds. The following table lists the six transactions that can create liabilities for retail or wholesale companies. When you analyze the accounts involved in these transactions, you will note at least 19 different ways (some are similar) to understate liabilities in financial statements.

SYMPTOMS OF LIABILITY FRAUD In our discussion on detecting liability frauds, we consider only analytical symptoms and accounting/documentary symptoms.

Analytical Symptoms In accounts payable understatements, one analytical symptom is balances that appear too low. Other symptoms include purchase or cost of goods sold numbers that appear too low, or purchase returns or purchase discounts that appear too high. In unearned revenues, symptoms are reported payroll, payroll tax, rent, interest, utility, or other accrued liabilities that appear too low. To determine whether these balances are "too low," you must compare recorded amounts to balances in past periods, relationships with other accounts, and to equivalent balances in similar companies. Analytical symptoms for premature recognition of unearned revenues involve unearned liability account

Transaction	Liability Fraud Accounts Involved	Possible Fraud Schemes
1. Purchase inventory	Inventory, Accounts payable	1. Record payables in subsequent period 2. Don't record purchases 3. Overstate purchase returns and purchase discounts 4. Record payments made in later periods as paid in earlier periods 5. Fraudulent recording of payments (for example, kiting)
2. Incur payroll and other accrued liabilities	Payroll tax expense, Salary expense, Various expenses, Salaries payable, Payroll taxes payable, Various accrued liabilities	6. Don't record accrued liabilities 7. Record accruals in later period
3. Sell products purchased	Accounts receivable, Sales revenue, Unearned revenue	8. Record unearned revenues as earned revenues
4. Service products sold, repay deposits, or repurchase something in the future (future commitments)	Warranty (service) expense, Warranty or service liability	9. Don't record warranty (service) liabilities 10. Underrecord liabilities 11. Record deposits as revenues 12. Don't record repurchase agreements and commitments
5. Borrow money	Cash, Notes payable, Mortgages payable, and so on	13. Borrow from related parties at less than arms-length transactions 14. Don't record liabilities 15. Borrow against equities in assets 16. Write off liabilities as forgiven 17. Claim liabilities as personal debt rather than as debt of the entity
6. Incur contingent liabilities	Loss from contingencies, Losses payable	18. Don't record contingent liabilities that are probable 19. Record contingent liabilities at too low an amount

balances that appear too low and revenue accounts that appear too high. Significant judgment is needed, in most cases, to determine whether revenues are being recognized before they are earned; this often means examining terms of contracts, sales agreements, and other revenue-related documentation. Analytical symptoms for the under- and non-recording of service warranties or other future commitments include balances in warranty, repurchases, or deposits that appear too low. In many cases, investigators compare them with other accounts—for example, they compare warranties with sales—to make the determination.

Analytical symptoms for unrecorded notes and mortgages payable involve unreasonable relationships between interest expense and recorded liabilities; significant decreases in recorded debt; significant purchases of assets with no recorded debt; and recorded amounts of notes payable, mortgages payable, lease liabilities, pension liabilities, and other debts that appear to be too low. Finally, analytical symptoms are not especially helpful in discovering contingent liabilities that should be recorded because it is difficult to determine whether a contingent liability should be recorded and, if so, for how much. Frequently, the past amounts needed for the comparisons do not exist, and identifying an expectation against which the amount of a contingent liability should be recorded is difficult.

Accounting or Documentary Symptoms Symptoms of fraud show up in documentation as vendor statements received with no liability recorded; large purchases recorded at the beginning of a period; large payments made in subsequent periods, backdated to the current period; receiving reports with no recorded liability; and errors in cut-off tests. The following are documentary symptoms for liability frauds.

- Photocopied purchase records where originals should exist
- Unusual discrepancies between the entity's records and confirmation replies
- Transactions not recorded in a complete or timely manner or improperly recorded as to amount

- Accounting period, classification, or entity policy; unsupported or unauthorized balances or transactions
- Last-minute adjustments by the entity that significantly affect financial results
- Missing documents; significant unexplained items on reconciliations
- Denied access to records, facilities, certain employees, customers, vendors, or others from whom audit evidence might be sought

Specific accounts can show symptoms of fraudulent documentation. With payroll, for example, the red flags will be employees with no withholdings, lack of payments to governmental entities, no accruals at year-end, payroll tax rates that are too low, fewer employees paid than are listed on the payroll records, and capitalization of employee wages as start-up or other deferred costs when they should be expensed. If interest is understated, you may find notes payable with no interest expense, bank confirmations of notes that are not recorded by the company, and interest expense deducted on tax returns but not recorded on the financial statements. Other symptoms include inconsistencies between revenue recognition criteria and the timing specified in contracts and sales agreements, the method and timing with which revenues are recognized, large reclassification entries near the end of a period that increase revenues and lower liabilities, differences between confirmation balances and revenue recognized by the company, no shipping documentation for recorded revenues, revenues recognized before customers are billed, and inconsistencies in the timing or method of recording unrecorded liabilities.

Symptoms for frauds perpetrated by under- or nonrecording of service or other future obligations take the form of differences between amounts expensed as warranty or service costs and amounts that should be expensed, based on sales contracts or sales agreements; improper treatment of deposits; differences between confirmations of repurchase agreements, deposits, or other confirmed amounts and balances reported on the financial statements; and differences between what contracts say should be recorded as liabilities and what the company is doing. When liabilities are underrecorded or not recorded, you will find bank confirmations of liabilities that are not recorded by the company, unrecorded liens, differences between contract amounts and recorded loans, interest expense with no recorded debt, liabilities written off without payment, significant purchases of assets without a comparable decrease in cash or increase in liabilities, and significant repayment of debt immediately prior to year-end, with new borrowing immediately after year-end.

Documentary symptoms are the best way to find underrecorded contingent liabilities. These symptoms include identification of lawsuits by attorneys; payments to attorneys without acknowledged litigation; litigation mentioned in corporate minutes; correspondence with governmental agencies, such as the Environmental Protection Agency (EPA), or the Securities and Exchange Commission (SEC); significant payments to plaintiffs and others; filing of an 8-K with the SEC;[26] withdrawal or issuance of less-than-clean audit opinion by previous auditors; and correspondence from previous auditors, bankers, regulators, and others.

Asset Fraud

Identifying Asset Fraud Most organizations show different types of assets on their balance sheets. Usually, management overstated assets by improperly deferring costs. As was the case with liabilities, different assets are overstated in different ways. The following exhibit identifies five types of assets that are commonly overstated.

Overstated Assets	
Type 1	• Cash • Short-term investments • Marketable securities
Type 2	• Receivables • Inventory
Type 3	• Fixed assets
Type 4	• Mergers and acquisitions • Intercompany accounts and/or transactions
Type 5	• Intangible assets • Deferred assets

Improper Capitalizing or Expensing Even though most financial statement frauds occur in smaller, less established companies, CPAs must also be alert to the fraud symptoms when they audit large, well-established companies. Remember that any company can encounter problems with profitability, and financial statement fraud is a quick fix during trying times. To make their financial statements look better, start-up companies often overstate assets by capitalizing as intangible assets such things as start-up or preoperation costs, advertising costs, research and development, marketing costs, and certain salaries, and other initial costs. Management often argues that they are in the start-up or development phase and therefore these costs must be capitalized as deferred charges and written off against future profitable operations. In some cases, the deferred charges are justified; in other cases, they are clearly fraudulent. The question of whether these costs should be capitalized is one of whether the costs being incurred will truly generate future revenues and whether the future revenues will be sufficient to cover the costs.

In most cases, fraudulent capitalization of deferred charges does not occur all at once. Rather, it starts by capitalizing borderline (or questionable) deferred charges and progresses to management routinely capitalizing costs that are not even remotely appropriate. Many times, capitalizing deferred charges, like other financial statement frauds, becomes the proverbial slippery slope: It is hard to stop once it starts, especially if the organization is experiencing profit pressures, and justifying it becomes easier and easier.

Capitalizing costs that should be expensed increases net income by the same amount of the capitalized costs. Why? Because expenses that should be deducted from revenues are not deducted until future periods when they are amortized. In many cases, these illicit capitalizations are not written off for many years.

Inflating Assets in Mergers, Acquisitions, and Restructurings There have been several financial statement frauds where companies involved in mergers or acquisitions overstated their assets by either (1) using market values instead of book values, (2) having the wrong entity act as purchaser, or (3) improperly allocating book values to assets (assigning higher book values to assets that will be amortized or depreciated over longer periods or not depreciated at all, and lower values to assets that will be amortized or depreciated over shorter periods).

In one case, the asset in the merger was written up by having the wrong entity act as the purchaser. In other cases, companies overstate assets in mergers by using market values instead of book values.

Cases show that whenever assets are revaluated or two companies merge there is an opportunity to use inappropriate values. This is especially true when the merging companies are related parties, when companies are struggling, or when they have a strong incentive to report profits. Fraud is also perpetrated by manipulating intercompany accounts and/or transactions.

Overstating Fixed Assets Fixed assets (property, plant, and equipment) can be overstated in many ways. The most common ways leave worthless or expired assets on the books (not writing them off), underreport depreciation expense, overstate residual values, record fixed assets at inflated values (sometimes through sham or related-party purchases), or simply fabricate fixed assets for the financial statements. One company recorded assets on its balance sheet at their "estimated fair market value" when, in fact, the assets had been fully depreciated in prior years.

Finally, fixed assets can be overstated by underrecording depreciation expense. To do this, companies use asset lives that are too long; allocate too much cost in a basket purchase of land and building to land that is not depreciated; use salvage values that are too high; or fail to make the accrual entries for depreciation.

Overstating Cash and Marketable Securities There are several famous cases where marketable securities were materially overstated, but it is difficult to overstate cash because cash balances can be easily confirmed with banks and other financial institutions. What does happen with cash is employees or vendors steal cash in magnitudes significant enough to result in misstated financial statements (without management's knowledge). Consider these three cases: a small thrift institution where a vice president embezzled several million dollars over a period of 16 years; a small, five-branch bank where a proof operator embezzled $7 million over eight years; and **General Motors**, where one car dealer embezzled $436 million. These large cash thefts resulted in financial statement fraud of a different type than we have been discussing in this section—financial statement misstatement without management's knowledge.

It is much easier to perpetrate asset fraud by overstating marketable securities, especially when the securities in question are not widely traded. What many people don't realize is that the term "publicly traded" means much more than "companies whose securities are traded on the New York Stock Exchange, the American Stock Exchange, and NASDAQ." Many smaller, over-the-counter stocks are traded only rarely and are not actively listed by even over-the-counter stock exchanges, but whose stock prices are circulated among brokers via "pink sheets." These pink sheets are distributed daily to brokers and listing dealers who might be willing to buy and sell through other methods. Assigning market values to many of these securities is often problematic (and placing market values on securities that are not publicly traded is even more difficult), and once in a while, management commits fraud by materially overstating their values. One well-known fraud (**Lincoln Savings and Loan**) involved sham transactions between the company and related parties, and materially overvalued securities were listed as current assets on the balance sheet. Another case involved a minority investment in another company that was carried at several million dollars when, in fact, the company had negative stockholders' equity and losses of several million dollars in each of the preceding five years. The securities should have been written off because the investment was basically worthless.

Overstating Accounts Receivable or Inventory We discussed how accounts receivable are inflated by recording fictitious revenues and how inventory is overstated and cost of goods sold understated. Accounts receivable and inventory are also overstated in order to overstate assets and cover thefts of cash. That is what happened in the ESM fraud where management stole $350 million and covered the theft by creating a fictitious receivable from a related entity. In the **Phar-Mor** fraud, inventory was overstated to offset cash that Monus took out of the business to support his World Basketball League.

Summary of Asset Fraud   It behooves us to summarize the various asset fraud schemes we have discussed thus far. Although not exhaustive, the following table lists the most common schemes.

Asset Fraud

Transaction	Accounts Involved	Possible Fraud Schemes
By improper capitalizing costs as assets that should be expensed	Various deferred charge and intangible assets accounts	1. Inappropriately capitalizing assets as: • start-up costs expensed • marketing costs • salaries • R&D costs • other such expenditures
• Through mergers, acquisitions, and restructuring • Through manipulating inter-company accounts and/or transactions	Any asset account	2. Using market values rather than book values to record assets 3. Having wrong entity be "purchaser" 4. Allocating costs among assets in inappropriate ways 5. Recording fictitious assets or inflating the value of assets in intercompany accounts or transactions
By overstating fixed assets	• Land, Buildings • Equipment • Leasehold Improvements	6. Sham purchases and sales of assets using "straw buyers" 7. Overstating asset costs with related parties 8. Not recording depreciation 9. Collusion with outside parties to overstate assets (for example, allocating inventory costs to fixed assets)
By overstating cash marketable securities	• Cash • Marketable Securities • Other Short-Term Assets	10. Misstating marketable securities using related parties
By overstating accounts receivable and/or inventory to hide thefts of cash by management	• Accounts Receivable • Inventory	11. Covering thefts of cash or other assets by overstating receivables or inventory

SYMPTOMS OF ASSET FRAUD   Symptoms that indicate assets are overstated closely parallel those that indicate understated liabilities. Thus, often just one or two large fictitious accounting entries, rather than a series of smaller entries, result in asset overstatement. In some ways, however, asset overstatements are easier to detect than other financial statement frauds because the overstated assets are always included on the balance sheet, whereas understated liabilities do not show up on the financial statements. Fraud investigators search for symptoms by examining the actual assets that make up the reported amounts, to make sure they really exist and to verify that they are listed in appropriate amounts.

Disclosure Fraud

The final financial statement fraud we discuss is disclosure fraud. In inadequate disclosures, fraudulent or misleading statements or press releases are issued without line-item effects. That is, somewhere in its annual report or through press releases or other media, management makes statements that are wrong but which do not impact the statement numbers. Disclosure fraud can also be perpetrated by *omission*—statements that should have been but were not made by management (that is, they mislead because of what they *don't* say).

Because inadequate disclosure does not impact the financial statements, analytical symptoms do not exist. However, there may or may not be documentary symptoms, depending on the type of misstatement.

Disclosure frauds are a different "animal" than liability and asset fraud. Misleading disclosures can be made about anything; therefore, symptoms vary from fraud to fraud. As a result, generalizing symptoms is difficult.

One thing you should remember is that fraud vulnerability are particularly relevant to disclosure frauds. Management rarely makes willful misstatements if there are no significant pressures or opportunities to do so. Therefore, when you observe management, organizational structure, relationships with other parties, and operating characteristic vulnerability, keep your level of skepticism higher than normal, not only about statement numbers, but also about management disclosures and representations made in annual reports and in other information distributed by the company.

TYPES OF DISCLOSURE FRAUD   Disclosure frauds misrepresent:

1. The nature of the company or its products, through news reports, interviews, annual reports, and elsewhere
2. The company's performance in management discussions and in annual reports, 10-Ks, 10-Qs, and other reports
3. Unusual business dealings in footnotes to the financial statements

IDENTIFYING DISCLOSURE FRAUD   Identifying disclosure fraud is harder than other frauds. In fact, without a tip or complaint, it is difficult to know that disclosure fraud is even occurring. Misleading disclosures are easier to detect than missing disclosures. Also, the symptoms differ, depending on which type of disclosure fraud is occurring. In overall misrepresentations of a company or its products, for example, symptoms will relate to the nature of the company, its assets and organization, its management, and its operating characteristics.

Misleading Financial Reports and Statement Footnotes   Several fraud investigation techniques can be used to identify inadequate disclosures. First, look for inconsistencies between disclosures and information in the financial statements and other information you are aware of. Second, make inquiries of management and other personnel concerning related-party transactions, contingent liabilities, and contractual obligations. Make these inquiries at several levels of management and do them separately and judiciously. Inquiries should also be made about different accounting policies that management is aware of. Even though some of these inquiries may be routine or involve basic questions, differences in responses may tip you off that management is engaging in fraudulent activities.

Another way to identify inadequate disclosures, especially those concerning related parties, is to review the company's files and records with the SEC and other regulatory agencies. Check for names of officers and directors who occupy management or directorship positions in other companies. It is also possible, given the number and variety of databases available today, to search for common ownership and directorship interests. If you suspect something awry, use databases such as Lexis/Nexis to perform background searches on key individuals. Other good places to look for inadequate disclosures are the board of director minutes, correspondence and invoices from attorneys, confirmations with banks and others, contracts, loan agreements, loan guarantees, leases, correspondence from taxing and regulatory authorities, pension plan documents, sales agreements, and any type of legal document.

In many disclosure frauds, financial statement auditors actually "get their hands on the fraud" but don't recognize it for what it is. To identify disclosure fraud and other financial statement frauds, auditors and others must realize that such things as inconsistencies between financial statements and other information often represent fraud symptoms and not merely mistakes. If something doesn't look right, is not consistent with GAAP, or has other characteristics that make you uncomfortable, do not let management explain away the problem. Detecting fraud requires you to look beyond transactions, documents, and other information and to ask what possible explanations exist for its occurrence or for it being reported or represented in the way it is. These days, acquiring answers to questions you have about business relationships, management backgrounds, and other information from publicly available sources is not difficult. If something looks suspicious or questionable, research the issue or gather independent evidence, rather than merely accepting management representations. If management can commit financial statement fraud, they can certainly lie to you.

Summary of Management Fraud

In this section, we covered the first steps in detecting financial statement fraud. Four areas must be examined: (1) management and directors, (2) relationships with others, (3) the organization and its industry, and (4) financial results and operating characteristics. Perpetrators choose fraud schemes as much for their "ease to commit and conceal" than for any other factor. Most fraud symptoms, especially those that show up in the financial results and the organization's operating characteristics, are scheme-specific. We also discussed understatement of liability frauds, overstatement of asset frauds, and inadequate disclosure frauds. For each type of scheme, we also discussed which symptoms indicate that fraud may be occurring, ways to search for fraud symptoms, and ways to determine whether observed symptoms are occurring because of fraud or because of some other reason.

Looking for fraud is not unlike hiking in a forest. Perpetrators stand camouflaged and motionless as they try to conceal themselves and their fraud. Many people walk right by deer or elk in the forest; they do not see the animal unless they look for movement, changes in color or shadows, or changes in shapes, or the animal is pointed out to them. Likewise, to discover fraud, we look for analytical symptoms (movements), accounting or documentary symptoms (changes in color), behavioral and lifestyle symptoms (changes in shapes), control symptoms (changes in shadows), and tips and complaints (the evidence that is pointed out).

Financial Shenanigans

What Are Financial Shenanigans?

Financial fraud causes great harm to individuals, to companies, and to society at large. Financial shenanigans (a form of financial fraud) are actions or omissions intended to hide or distort the real financial performance or financial condition of a business entity. They range from minor deceptions (such as failing to segregate operating gains and losses from nonoperating gains and losses) to more serious misapplication of accounting principles (such as failing to write off worthless assets), and outright fraudulent behavior (such as the recording of fictitious revenue to overstate an entity's real financial performance).[27]

Why Do Shenanigans Exist?

There are three general reasons for shenanigans: (1) it pays to do it, (2) it is easy to do it, and (3) it is unlikely that perpetrators will get caught (at least in the short term).

1. *It pays to do it.* When a bonus plan encourages managers to post higher sales and profits (with no questions asked about how those gains were achieved), it may create an incentive for using shenanigans. Misguided incentive plans should be revisited.
2. *It is easy to do it.* Honest managers select accounting methods from a variety of acceptable choices to portray fairly the company's financial performance. Unscrupulous managers use the flexibility offered in generally accepted accounting principles (GAAP) to distort financial reports.
3. *It is unlikely that perpetrators will get caught.* Companies may use accounting tricks because they believe that they will not get caught by auditors or regulators. Consider that only the annual financial statements of publicly held companies are audited by an independent, certified public accountant. Privately held companies are not required to be audited.

The Seven Shenanigans

Companies with a weak "control environment"—those that lack independent members of the board, a competent independent auditor, or an adequate internal audit function—have a greater tendency toward committing shenanigans than others.

Financial shenanigans, which permit companies to manipulate net income, may be separated into seven broad categories. The first five boost current-year profits; the last two shift current-year profits to the future.

1. Recording revenue too soon to show more sales
2. Recording bogus revenue to show more income
3. Boosting income with one-time gains to show more income
4. Shifting current expenses to a later period to show more income

5. Failing to record or disclose all liabilities to show more assets
6. Shifting current income to a later period to minimize taxes
7. Shifting future expenses to the current period to show less income

Shenanigans Prevention Techniques

The primary shenanigan prevention strategies available to board of directors are to improve the company's incentive structure (to motivate) and to strengthen its control environment (to monitor). Specific prevention techniques include the following.

1. Structure managers' incentives to reward honest financial reporting and to punish any activities that might constitute or contribute to financial shenanigans.
2. Establish and encourage managers to adopt conservative accounting principles and policies.
3. Appoint outside board members as watchdogs over senior management and corporate officers, with wide-ranging and early access to corporate financial data.
4. Appoint both internal auditors and independent auditors and assign them the mission of preventing and detecting shenanigans. Grant internal auditors both the power and the security to communicate directly with outside board members about their findings.
5. Establish a senior-level audit committee with the same mission of preventing and detecting shenanigans.

Shenanigans Detection Techniques

Sometimes, even the best intentions and the most comprehensive preventive measures fail, and gimmicks begin to spread. Shenanigan detection approaches include both general attention to certain "red flags" and detailed review of particular data from the company's financial statements.

At a general level, warning signs of a financially troubled business that might be resorting to financial shenanigans or prone to committing them include the following.

1. Weak internal control environment
2. Inadequate outside checks and balances
3. Vulnerability to external influences
4. Poor organizational culture
5. Convoluted financial, legal, and organizational structure
6. Shortage of "free" cash flows from operations
7. Unusually low or high operating revenues
8. Profits out of line with current sales and with previous quarters and years
9. Inventories and receivables out of balance with sales
10. Too many "irregular" events

Role of Directors in Controlling Corporate Fraud

Corporate directors have a direct liability in fraudulent activities perpetrated against a corporation. They have the power to control fraud with their position in the company. They should look for early warning signs from financial statements such as uncollectibility of receivables, inadequate salability of inventory, improper valuation of investments, obsolescence of fixed assets, overstatement of intangibles, and unreported or underreported liabilities. By taking proper steps to prevent and detect shenanigans, the board of directors can not only shield themselves from undue liability but contribute toward a more ethical corporate world.

Corporate Risk Management

Introduction to Risk

Risk, which is often used to mean "uncertainty," creates both problems and opportunities for businesses and individuals in nearly every walk of life. Executives, employees, investors, students, householders, travelers, and farmers all confront risk and deal with it in various ways. Sometimes a particular risk is consciously analyzed and managed; other times risk is simply ignored, perhaps out of lack of knowledge of its consequences.

Risk regarding the possibility of loss can be especially problematical. If a loss is certain to occur, it may be planned for in advance and treated as a definite, known expense. It is when there is uncertainty about the occurrence of a loss that risk becomes an important problem. Thus, if a store owner knows for sure that a certain amount of shoplifting will occur, this loss may be recovered by marking up all goods by the necessary percentage. There is little or no risk involved unless actual shoplifting is greater than normal. The store is more concerned about the risk of abnormal shoplifting losses than about those viewed as normal or expected.

The Burden of Risk

The idea of risk bearing can be tantalizing. After all, it is a well-known investment principle that the largest potential returns are associated with the riskiest ventures. There are some risks, however, that involve only the possibility of loss. For example, businesses located near the Mississippi River confront the possibility of periodic flooding. When a flood occurs, loss caused by property damage and lost revenues is likely. On the other hand, no gain is expected merely because in some years a flood does not occur.

The risk surrounding potential losses creates significant economic burdens for businesses, government, and individuals. Billions of dollars are spent each year on strategies for financing potential losses. But when losses are not planned for in advance, they may cost even more. For example, a multimillion dollar adverse liability judgment may reduce a business's profitability, lower its credit ratings, cause a loss of customers, and perhaps result in bankruptcy if the firm has not made adequate plans to pay for the loss.

Risk of loss may also deprive society of services judged to be too risky, such as medicine and law. Similarly, businesses of all types may be reluctant to engage in projects that are otherwise strategically attractive if the potential losses appear to be unmanageable.

Businesses, as well as individuals, may try either to avoid risk of loss as much as possible or to reduce its negative consequences. Overall, an entity's **cost of risk** is the sum of: (1) expenses of strategies to finance potential losses, (2) the cost of unreimbursed losses, (3) outlays to reduce risks, and (4) the opportunity cost of activities forgone due to risk considerations. For a particular firm, the first two components of the cost of risk are often the easiest to measure. To minimize the cost of risk efficiently, one must study the subject of risk, learn more about the different types of risk, and find ways to deal with risk more effectively.

Definitions of Risk

Thus far, the terms *risk* and *uncertainty* have been used interchangeably. However, many forms of uncertainty exist and, in a comprehensive study of risk, it is helpful to define the concept more precisely. Three common groups to classify risk are described in this section. As illustrated in Exhibit 900.7, these groupings are not mutually exclusive. Rather, risks can be categorized simultaneously according to all three types of classifications.

Pure Versus Speculative Risk

An important classification of risk involves the concepts of pure risk and speculative risk. **Pure risk** exists when there is uncertainty as to whether loss will occur. No possibility of gain is presented by pure risk—only the potential for loss. Examples of pure risk include the uncertainty of damage to property by fire or flood or the prospect of premature death caused by accident or illness. In contrast to pure risk, **speculative risk** exists when there is uncertainty about an

Exhibit 900.7 *Types of Risk*

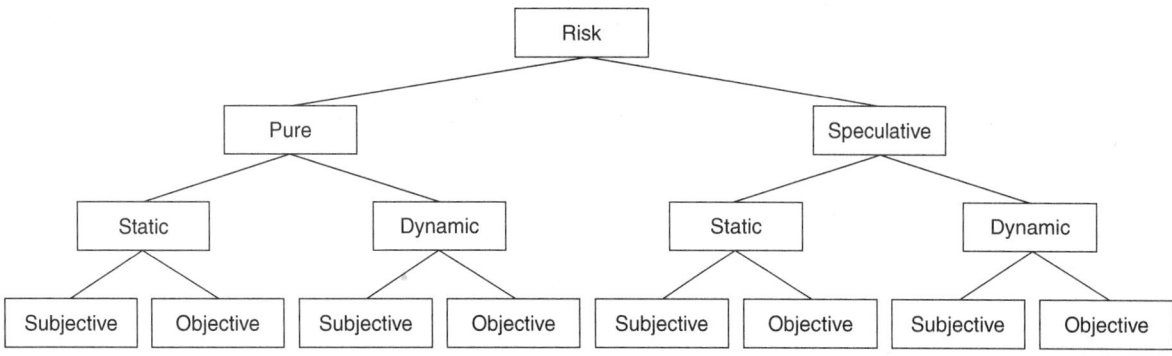

event that could produce either a profit or a loss. Business ventures and investment decisions are examples of situations involving speculative risk. Gains as well as losses may occur, changing the nature of the uncertainty that is present.

Both pure and speculative risks may be present in some situations. It is important to recognize that many profit-motivated, speculative-risk decisions made by individuals and firms can have an impact on pure risk exposures. For example, a firm purchasing land for development is making a decision that entails speculative risk. However, if after the purchase it discovers that the land contains a latent pollution problem, the firm would then face a new pure risk. Another example is the decision that a firm makes to introduce a new product. This decision may represent primarily a speculative risk. But as has been seen for products like asbestos and silicon breast implants, this decision also is accompanied by the pure risk associated with potential product liability. Failure to consider the overlapping effects of these two types of risk can lead to decisions that overstate the potential benefits to the firm.

Static Versus Dynamic Risk

Another way of classifying risk involves the extent to which uncertainty changes over time. **Static risks,** which can be either pure or speculative, stem from an unchanging society that is in stable equilibrium. Examples of pure static risks include the uncertainties due to such random events as lightning, windstorms, and death. Business undertakings in a stable economy illustrate the concept of speculative static risk. In contrast, **dynamic risks** are produced because of changes in society. Dynamic risks also can be either pure or speculative. Examples of sources of dynamic risk include urban unrest, increasingly complex technology, and changing attitudes of legislatures and courts about a variety of issues.

Static and dynamic risks are not independent; greater dynamic risks may increase some types of static risks. An example involves uncertainty due to weather-related losses. This risk is usually considered to be static. However, recent evidence suggests that environmental pollution caused by increased industrialization may be affecting global weather patterns and thereby increasing this source of static risk.

Subjective Versus Objective Risk

A third way to classify risk is by whether it is objective or subjective. **Subjective risk** refers to the mental state of an individual who experiences doubt or worry as to the outcome of a given event. In addition to being subjective, a particular risk may also be either pure or speculative and either static or dynamic. Subjective risk is essentially the psychological uncertainty that arises from an individual's mental attitude or state of mind. **Objective risk** differs from subjective risk primarily in the sense that it is more precisely observable and therefore measurable. In general, objective risk is the probable variation of actual from expected experience. This term is most often used in connection with pure static risks, although it can also be applied to the other types of uncertainties. Details regarding measurement of objective risk are included later in this section.

The concept of subjective risk is especially important because it provides a way to interpret the behavior of individuals faced with seemingly identical situations yet arriving at different decisions. For example, one person may be ultraconservative and tend always to take the "safe way" out, even in cases that may seem quite risk-free to other decision makers. Objective risk may actually be the same in two cases but may be viewed very differently by those examining this risk from their own perspectives. Thus, it is not enough to know only the degree of objective risk; the attitude toward risk of the person who will act on the basis of this knowledge must also be known.

Sources of Risk

The emphasis of this section is on pure risks. The array of pure risks encountered is vast. Some of these risks are static, while many others are extremely dynamic. This section briefly describes the common sources of pure risks, which include **property risks; liability risks;** and **life, health, and loss of income risks,** with some consideration also given to financial risks of a speculative nature.

Property Risks

All businesses and individuals that own, rent, or use property are exposed to the risk that the property may be damaged, destroyed, or stolen. For example, lightning may strike a building, causing a fire that destroys the structure and the inventory, supplies, and equipment inside. Property owned or used outside of the building may also be susceptible to loss. Typical examples include trucks, automobiles, and mobile equipment. To fully analyze property risk exposures, businesses must consider both the types of property susceptible to loss and the potential sources of such risk. Sources include not only fire and lightning but also theft, tornadoes, hurricanes, explosions, riots, collisions, falling objects, floods, earthquakes, and freezing, to name only a few.

If property damage is extensive, a business may be forced to shut down temporarily, thereby incurring a loss of income in addition to the expense of replacing the damaged property. But in some instances involving severe property damage, management may decide that temporarily closing the business is not a viable option. For example, Rocky Mountain Bank likely would never regain its customers if it were to close for several months following a fire and not allow its customers to transact necessary banking business. In this situation, the bank would probably incur the extra expenses necessary to continue operations from a different location while repairs were made to its own premises.

In addition to risks arising out of property they own and/or use, businesses also are exposed to risks associated with property owned or used by other firms. Another illustration of losses to one business affecting another business involves companies selling primarily over the Internet. Such firms typically utilize others to make deliveries to their customers and could suffer significant losses if the delivery firms were unable to perform.

Liability Risks

A second major category of risks is liability exposure. U.S. society has become increasingly litigious in recent years, with businesses and individuals often held financially liable for damages resulting from a vast and expanding array of situations. Liability judgments may result in payments made to compensate injured parties as well as to punish those responsible for the injuries, with multimillion dollar awards no longer rare. Even when an individual is eventually absolved of liability, the expenses involved in defending a case often prove to be substantial. Consequently, both individuals and businesses must be careful to identify all sources of liability risk that may affect them and then make suitable arrangements for dealing with such exposures to loss.

Life, Health, and Loss of Income Risks

Potential losses associated with the health and well-being of individuals make up the third and final category of sources of risk. The possibility of the untimely death of a star salesperson exposes the person's employer to potential loss if a replacement with the same skills and experience is not readily available. Even if the salesperson could be easily replaced, in many cases employee deaths are disruptive for other workers and may result in temporarily reduced productivity. This phenomenon is especially true if the death is due to job-related conditions.

Businesses and individuals also face risks associated with health problems. Persons who become ill or who are injured in accidents will incur expenses for medical treatment, and the cost of such treatment is becoming increasingly expensive. Sometimes businesses arrange to pay some or all of such expenses for their employees, regardless of whether a sickness or injury is job related. As medical costs increase, however, more and more individuals (whether employed or not) must pay substantial sums each year for medical care for themselves and their families. In addition to these expenses, there is another potential loss associated with sickness and accidents. If a previously employed individual is severely injured or gravely ill, that person may be unable to work for several months or even years. The resultant loss of income can have serious repercussions on the financial stability of the person and family involved.

Other risks that confront an employed individual are those associated with unemployment and retirement. Both events result in the loss of an income source that previously existed. A significant difference, however, relates to timing. Retirement usually is not a surprise and therefore presents many options for advance planning. In contrast, abrupt layoffs often are not expected and are therefore harder to plan for ahead of time. Through pension and other retirement benefits, as well as unemployment insurance provided in each state, businesses are also affected by these risks that their employees face.

Financial Risk

Although the major emphasis of this section is on pure risks, it is increasingly important that risks from other sources be considered as well. A variety of **financial risks,** which often are speculative in nature, can impact on a firm's earnings. Examples of these financial risks include credit risk, foreign exchange risk, commodity risk, and interest rate risk. Although most of these financial risks tend to have the characteristics of speculative risks, they still present the firm with some of the same problems associated with pure risks. Although the techniques used to manage these risks may be very different from those used to manage pure risks, it remains critical that these risks be identified and assessed in order for the firm to achieve its business goals.

Measurement of Risk

Once risk sources have been identified, it is often helpful to measure the extent of the risk that exists. As noted above, risks that are classified as subjective cannot be precisely measured. In contrast, the amount of objective risk is often more readily observable. Several important concepts related to the measurement of objective risk are discussed in this section.

Chance of Loss

The long-term chance of occurrence, or relative frequency of loss, is defined to be the **chance of loss.** The concept has little meaning if applied to the chance of occurrence of a single event. Rather, it is meaningful primarily when applied to the chance of a loss occurring among a large number of possible events. Thus, chance of loss is expressed as the ratio of the number of losses that are likely to occur compared to the larger number of possible losses in a given group. For example, suppose 1,000 buildings in a particular city are considered to be susceptible to the risk of loss due to a tornado. If past experience indicates that 20 of these buildings are likely to be damaged by a tornado during a given time period, then the chance of loss due to a tornado is 2%. This number is determined by dividing the probable number of losses (20) by the number of buildings exposed to loss (1,000).

In making chance of loss calculations, it is common practice to perform separate computations for different causes of loss. In this sense, the term **peril** is used to describe a specific contingency that may cause a loss. For example, one of the perils that can cause loss to an automobile is collision. Other perils are illustrated by considering ways in which a building can be damaged; examples include fires, tornadoes, and explosions. Sometimes conditions exist that either increase the chance of loss from particular perils or tend to make the loss more severe once the peril has occurred. Such conditions are known as **hazards** and can be classified in the following three ways.

PHYSICAL HAZARD   A **physical hazard** is a condition stemming from the material characteristics of an object. Consider the peril of collision, which may cause loss to an automobile. A physical condition that makes the occurrence of collision more likely is an icy street. The icy street is the hazard, and the collision is the peril. The chance of loss due to collision may be higher in winter than at other times of the year because of the greater incidence of the physical hazard of icy streets.

Physical hazards include such phenomena as the existence of dry forests (a hazard affecting the peril of fire), earth faults (a hazard for earthquakes), and the existence of oily rags in a firm's storage closet (a hazard for fire). Such hazards may or may not be within human control. For example, the oily rag hazard can easily be eliminated. Other physical hazards, such as weather conditions, usually cannot be controlled, although their existence often may be observed.

MORALE HAZARD   The mental attitude of a careless or accident-prone person is known as **morale hazard.** Sometimes a subconscious desire for a loss may exist, even though the individual is not fully aware of this desire. In other cases, circumstances may cause someone to be indifferent to the possibility of a loss, thus causing that person to behave in a careless manner. For example, suppose the managers of ABC Company believe the federal government will provide disaster assistance that will fully compensate ABC for all earthquake losses it may incur. In making plans for a new building near a major fault line, ABC's management may be tempted to ignore more expensive construction designs and procedures that can lessen damage from earthquakes. In essence, ABC's assumption regarding the potential for federal disaster aid makes its management indifferent to the prospect of loss and, therefore, more prone to make unmindful decisions.

MORAL HAZARD The condition known as **moral hazard** also stems from an individual's mental attitude. It is associated with intentional actions designed either to cause a loss or to increase its severity. Moral hazards often are typified by individuals with known records of dishonesty. In addition, the existence of insurance may sometimes exacerbate the existence of moral hazard. For example, managers who purchase fire insurance on a factory full of unprofitable, out-of-date equipment may feel an incentive to "sell the building to the insurance company" by arranging for a fire to destroy the property. Moral hazard also describes the change in attitude that can occur when insurance is available to pay for loss, such as the tendency for individuals to consume more health care if the costs are covered by insurance.

Other examples of moral hazards involve accidents and sicknesses, especially where an employer provides generous income replacement during the time an employee is unable to work. In these situations, workers who are not pleased with their jobs or who fear being laid off in the future may be inclined to suffer an "accident" or contract an "illness." Closely related to this are cases where the original accident or illness is indeed legitimate but the recovery period is intentionally extended by the injured or sick person. Reasons for such behavior include the lack of a sufficient financial incentive to return to work and the psychological satisfaction some sick persons experience from the attention and concern given to them by their family and friends.

Degree of Risk

The amount of objective risk present in a situation, sometimes referred to as the **degree of risk,** is the relative variation of actual from expected losses. More precisely, the degree of risk is the range of variability around the expected losses, which are calculated using the chance of loss concept by means of the following formula.

$$\text{Objective risk} = \frac{\text{Probable variation of actual from expected losses}}{\text{Expected losses}}$$

Consider the possibility of fire losses to buildings in Acworth and Branson. There are 100,000 buildings in each city and, on average, each city has 100 fire losses per year. By looking at historical data, statisticians are able to estimate that the actual number of fire losses in Acworth during the next year will very likely range from 95 to 105. In Branson, however, the range probably will be greater, with at least 80 fire losses expected and possibly as many as 120. The degree of risk for each city is computed as follows.

$$\text{Risk}_{\text{Acworth}} = (105 - 95) / 100 = 10\%$$
$$\text{Risk}_{\text{Branson}} = (120 - 80) / 100 = 40\%$$

As shown, the degree of risk for Branson is four times that for Acworth, even though the chances of loss are the same.

A few other observations are important regarding degree of risk and chance of loss. If a loss has already occurred, the probable variation of actual from expected losses in that particular situation is zero and, therefore, the degree of risk is zero. At the opposite extreme, if it is impossible for a loss to occur, the probable variation also is zero and the degree of risk is zero as well. Finally, in measuring the degree of risk, results are meaningful only in terms of a group large enough to analyze statistically. If the numbers involved are very small, then the range of probable variation may be so large as to seem virtually infinite when viewed in a relative sense.

To illustrate this latter point, consider the Online Action Corporation, which is concerned about the possible death of Barbara Thomas, a valuable, highly paid 24-year-old worker in its product development department. Online Action has been informed that Barbara's probability of dying during the next year is 0.3%. Or, using the terminology introduced in this section, the chance of loss due to the peril of death is 0.003. The degree of risk is not particularly meaningful, however, when applied only to Barbara's life. Either Barbara will die or she will not, making the relative variation of actual from expected losses extremely large.

$$\frac{(1 - 0)}{0.003} = 333.33 = 33{,}333\,\%$$

Management of Risk

In the previous sections, several types of risk that affect individuals and businesses were introduced, together with ways to measure the amount of objective risk present. After sources of risk are identified and measured, a decision can be made as to how the risk should be handled. A pure risk that is not identified does not disappear; the business or individual merely loses the opportunity to consciously decide on the best technique for dealing with that risk. The process used to systematically manage risk exposures is known as **risk management.**

Some persons use the term *risk management* only in connection with businesses, and often the term refers only to the management of pure risks. In this sense, the traditional risk-management goal has been to minimize the cost of pure risk to the company. But as firms broaden the ways that they view and manage many different types of risk, the need for new terminology has become apparent. The terms **integrated risk management** and **enterprise risk management** reflect the intent to manage all forms of risk, regardless of type.

Many businesses have a special department charged with overseeing the firm's risk-management activities; the head of such a department often has the title of **risk manager.** The traditional type of risk manager may be charged with minimizing the adverse impact of losses on the achievement of the company's goals. In implementing the more integrated approach to risk management, however, some firms have formed risk-management committees. Others have created a new position of **chief risk officer** (CRO) to coordinate the firm's risk-management activities, regardless of the source of the risk. As part of his or her duties, the risk manager and/or CRO is likely to be involved in many aspects of a firm's activities. Examples may include developing employee safety programs, examining planned mergers and acquisitions, analyzing investment opportunities, purchasing insurance to protect against some types of risk, and setting up pension and health plans for employees. The evolution of integrated risk management reflects a realization of the importance of coordinating the many risk-management activities of the firm in order to meet its strategic goals.

Whether the concern is with a business or an individual situation, the same general steps can be used to systematically analyze and deal with risk. Known as the **risk-management process,** these steps form the basis for the remainder of discussion. At this point they can be summarized as follows.

1. *Identify risks.* There are many potential risks that confront individuals and businesses. Therefore, the first step in the risk-management process is to identify relevant exposures to risks. This step is important not only for traditional risk management, which focuses on pure risks, but also for enterprise risk management, where much of the focus is on identifying the firm's exposures from a variety of sources, including operational, financial, and strategic activities. Objectives should be determined prior to identifying risks.

2. *Evaluate risks.* For each source of risk that is identified, an evaluation should be performed. At this stage, pure risks can be categorized as to how often associated losses are likely to occur. In addition to this evaluation of loss **frequency,** an analysis of the size, or **severity,** of the loss is helpful. Consideration should be given both to the most probable size of any losses that may occur and to the maximum possible losses that might happen. As part of the overall risk evaluation, in some situations it may be possible to measure the degree of risk in a meaningful way. In other cases, especially those involving individuals, computation of the degree of risk may not yield helpful information.

3. *Select risk-management techniques.* The results of the analyses in step 2 are used as the basis for decisions regarding ways to handle existing risks. In some situations, the best plan may be to do nothing. In other cases, sophisticated ways to finance potential losses may be arranged. The available techniques for managing risks are discussed later, together with consideration of when each technique is appropriate.

4. *Implement and review decisions.* Following a decision about the optimal methods for handling identified risks, the business or individual must implement the techniques selected. However, risk management should be an ongoing process in which prior decisions are reviewed regularly. Sometimes new risk exposures arise or significant changes in expected loss frequency or severity occur. As noted in this section, even pure risks are not necessarily static; the dynamic nature of many risks requires a continual scrutiny of past analyses and decisions.

Risk Identification and Evaluation

Risk Identification

The identification of risks and exposures to loss is perhaps the most important element of the risk-management process. Unless the sources of possible losses are recognized, it is impossible to consciously choose appropriate, efficient methods for dealing with those losses should they occur.

A **loss exposure** is a potential loss that may be associated with a specific type of risk. Loss exposures are typically classified as to whether they result from property, liability, life, health, and loss of income or financial risks.

Approaches used by many risk managers involve loss exposure checklists, financial statement analysis, flowcharts, contract analysis, on-site inspections, and statistical analysis of past losses.

Loss Exposure Checklists

One risk-identification tool that can be used both by businesses and by individuals is a **loss exposure checklist,** which specifies numerous potential sources of loss from the destruction of assets and from legal liability. For each item on the checklist, the user asks the question, "Is this a potential source of loss to me or my firm?" In this way, the systematic use of loss exposure checklists reduces the likelihood of overlooking important sources of risk. Also, checklists can be helpful not only in risk identification but also in compiling information necessary for an in-depth evaluation of risks that are identified.

Financial Statement Analysis

Another approach that can be used by businesses to identify risks is **financial statement analysis.** Using this method, all items on a firm's balance sheet and income statement are analyzed in regard to risks that may be present. By including budgets, long-range forecasts, and written strategic plans in the analysis, this method can also help identify possible future risks that may not currently exist.

To illustrate this method of risk identification, consider the asset categories included on the balance sheets of business entities. Buildings owned by a firm are usually noted on its balance sheet, and leased buildings may be noted in footnotes to the financial statements. Future building acquisitions may be noted in budgets and strategic plans. Once such present and future buildings are identified, potential losses associated with them can then be considered. The loss exposures associated with building damage may include repair costs, the value of inventories and equipment inside, loss of income while the building cannot be used, and injuries to employees and customers inside the building. If a building is leased, relevant concerns would also include the disposition of the lease if the building is destroyed, including cost estimates of alternative facilities. This example does not begin to exhaust the range of possible losses that might result from damage to a building. It does, however, illustrate the thought process that is essential to the financial statement analysis method of risk identification.

Flowcharts

A third tool—the **flowchart**—is especially useful for businesses in identifying sources of risk in their production processes. The simplified flowchart in Exhibit 900.8 illustrates how they can pinpoint areas of potential losses. The question may be asked, "What events could disrupt the even and uninterrupted flow of parts to the final assembly floor, on which the whole production process depends?" For example, where are paints and solvents kept for the activities undertaken at Stage 3 in the figure? Are appropriate steps being taken to safeguard these materials from fire? Are floors kept clean and free of grease that might cause spills? Are any particular dangers threatening the storage of finished products that may require special protection? If the finished products are fragile, are appropriate protective measures being taken in loading and unloading?

Only through careful inspection of the entire production process can the full range of loss exposures be identified. And for some firms, even that may not be sufficient. It may be important, for example, to expand the flowchart to include the suppliers of parts and materials, particularly if a firm's production process is dependent on only a few suppliers. Thus, if there is only one possible supplier of a crucial part, a complete risk analysis will include identification

Exhibit 900.8 *Flowchart for a Production Process*

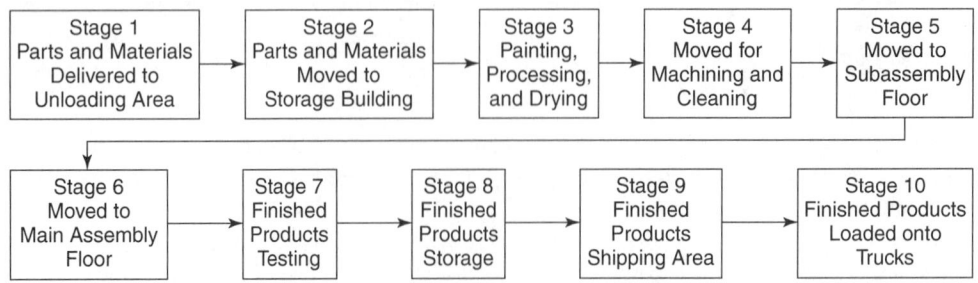

of potential losses to that supplier as well as to the firm itself. Similar situations may arise if a firm manufactures products that are purchased by only a few customers. In this case, expansion of the flowchart to include customers will help identify risks that might otherwise be overlooked.

Contract Analysis

The analysis of contracts into which the firm enters is another method for identifying potential exposures to risk. It is not unusual for contracts to state that some losses, if they occur, are to be borne by specific parties. For example, a company may require building contractors that it hires to bear the cost of any liability suits arising out of the builder's construction operations. In this way, suits that might otherwise be directed against the hiring firm will be directed against the builder.

This type of **contractual liability** may be found not only in construction contracts but also in sales contracts and lease agreements. For example, a property owner with a superior bargaining position may require her tenants to be responsible for all injuries that occur on the leased premises, even if caused by the property owner's own negligence. In other situations, she might agree to bear the liability arising out of a tenant's negligence. Ideally, the specification of who is to pay for various losses should be a conscious decision that is made as part of the overall contract negotiation process. But even where that ideal is not possible, it is important to examine all contracts so that important sources of risk are identified prior to the occurrence of any losses.

On-Site Inspections

Because some risks may exist that are not readily identifiable with the tools discussed thus far, it is important for business risk managers to visit periodically the various locations and departments within the firm. During these visits, it can be especially helpful to talk with department managers and other employees regarding their activities. Through this type of personal interaction, the risk manager can become better informed about current exposures to risk as well as potential future exposures that may arise.

Statistical Analysis of Past Losses

A final risk-identification tool that may be helpful for very large firms is that of statistical analysis of past losses. A **risk-management information system (RMIS)** is a computer software program that assists in performing this task. Some characteristics of past losses that may prove to be important in this regard include the cause of loss, the particular employees (if any) involved, where the loss occurred, and the total dollar amount of the loss.

To illustrate how these factors can prove important, suppose a trucking company experiences several vehicle accidents involving the same driver. Upon further investigation, the firm may discover that it has several problem drivers because it is not adequately checking the driving records of its employment applicants. Similarly, a restaurant chain that experiences a large number of employee injuries at its Dallas location may have safety hazards present that warrant additional investigation. As risk-management information systems become increasingly sophisticated and user-friendly, it is anticipated that more businesses will be able to effectively use statistical analysis in their risk-management activities.

Risk Evaluation

Once a risk is identified, the next step in the risk-management process is to estimate both the frequency and severity of potential losses. In this way, the risk manager obtains information that is helpful in determining the relative importance of identified risks and in selecting particular techniques for managing those risks.

In some cases, no particular problem would arise even if losses were incurred regularly, because the potential size of each loss is small. Thus, the daily occurrence of some inventory breakage may be an expected part of some businesses and would warrant only minimal attention from the risk manager. But other losses that occur infrequently yet are relatively large when they do occur (such as accidental deaths or destruction by a large fire) may be treated entirely differently. Such losses might cause bankruptcy if they were to happen with no means in place to counteract the resulting adverse financial effects for the firm.

One complicating factor in evaluating exposures is that many losses do not result in complete destruction of the asset involved. For example, if David Sommer's business is struck by lightning, the building will not necessarily burn to the ground. In evaluating the risk of loss from this peril, David should consider three things: (1) the frequency with which lightning may strike his building, (2) the **maximum probable loss** that would likely result if lightning did strike, and (3) the **maximum possible loss** if the building were completely destroyed. The difference between these last two factors is that the maximum probable loss is an estimate of the likely severity of losses that occur, whereas the maximum possible loss is an estimate of the catastrophe potential associated with a particular exposure to risk. In other words, what is the worst possible loss that might result from a given occurrence? To assess that potential, David needs to consider not only the loss of the building itself but also the destruction of inventory and equipment located inside. Furthermore, if David would seek to operate his business from another location in the event of loss, then his estimate of maximum possible loss should also include the cost of such temporary facilities.

The actual estimation of the frequency and severity of losses may be done in various ways. Some risk managers consider these concepts informally in evaluating identified risks. They may broadly classify the frequency of various losses into categories such as "slight," "moderate," and "certain," and may have similarly broad estimates for loss severity. Even this type of informal evaluation is better than none at all. But as risk management becomes increasingly sophisticated, most large firms attempt to be more precise in evaluating risks. It is now common to use probability distributions and statistical techniques in estimating both loss frequency and severity.

Risk Mapping or Profiling

With the evolution of integrated or enterprise risk management, alternative methods of risk identification and assessment have emerged. One such method is **risk mapping,** sometimes referred to as **risk profiling.** Because integrated risk management is based on identifying all the risks facing the firm, it is not unusual for a firm to identify in excess of 100 risks when using this approach. Cataloguing and making sense of so many risks requires a structured process. Risk mapping or profiling involves arraying these risks in a matrix, with one dimension being the frequency of events and the other being the severity. Each risk is then marked to indicate whether it is covered by insurance or not. By considering the likelihood and severity of each of the risks in this matrix, as well as the extent to which insurance protection is already available, it becomes possible for the firm to identify the risks that are most likely to seriously affect the firm's ability to achieve its goals.

Risk-Management Techniques

After identifying and evaluating exposures to risk, systematic consideration can be given to alternative techniques for managing each exposure. Techniques for managing exposures include (1) risk avoidance, (2) loss control, (3) risk retention, and (4) risk transfer. Broadly speaking, techniques 1 and 2 can be classified as risk control methods, while techniques 3 and 4 can be classified as risk financing methods.

Risk Avoidance

Risk avoidance is a conscious decision not to expose oneself or one's firm to a particular risk of loss. In this way, risk avoidance can be said to decrease one's chance of loss to zero. For example, the eccentric chief executive of a multibillion dollar firm may decide not to fly to avoid the risk of dying in an airplane crash. Dr. Gary Luke may decide to leave the practice of medicine rather than contend with the risk of malpractice liability losses. Similarly, firms may decide not to enter the pharmaceutical line of business to avoid costly product liability suits. Yet another example of risk avoidance is to delay taking responsibility for goods during transportation. A customer presented with a choice of terms of sale may have the seller assume all risks of loss until the goods arrive at the buyer's warehouse. In this way the buyer avoids the risk of loss to the property until delivery has actually occurred.

Risk avoidance is common, particularly among those with a strong aversion to risk. However, avoidance is not always feasible and may not be desirable even when it is possible. Risk managers must always weigh the relative costs and benefits associated with activities that give rise to risks. When a risk is avoided, the potential benefits, as well as costs, are given up. For example, the doctor who quits practicing medicine avoids future liability risks but also forfeits the income and other forms of satisfaction that may be associated with a career in medicine. The firm that avoids manufacturing pharmaceuticals relinquishes potential profits as well as liability risks. And if a business is to operate at all, certain risks are nearly impossible to avoid. An example is the liability risk of owning or leasing premises from which the business is conducted.

Loss Control (Risk Reduction or Mitigation)

When particular risks cannot be avoided, actions may often be taken to reduce the losses associated with them. This method of dealing with risk is known as **loss control.** It is different than risk avoidance, because the firm or individual is still engaging in operations that give rise to particular risks. Rather than abandoning specific activities, loss control involves making conscious decisions regarding the manner in which those activities will be conducted. Common goals are either to reduce the probability of losses or to decrease the cost of losses that do occur.

Risk Retention

A third technique for managing risk, known as **risk retention,** involves the assumption of risk. That is, if a loss occurs, an individual or firm will pay for it out of whatever funds are available at the time. Retention can be planned or unplanned, and losses that occur can either be funded or unfunded in advance.

Planned Versus Unplanned Retention

Planned retention involves a conscious and deliberate assumption of recognized risk. Sometimes planned retention occurs because it is the most convenient risk treatment technique or because there are simply no alternatives available short of ceasing operations. At other times, a risk manager has thoroughly analyzed all of the alternative methods of treating an existing risk and has decided that retention is the most appropriate technique.

When a firm or individual does not recognize that a risk exists and unwittingly believes that no loss could occur, risk retention also is under way—albeit **unplanned retention.** Sometimes unplanned retention occurs even when the existence of a risk is acknowledged. This result can ensue if the maximum possible loss associated with a recognized risk is significantly underestimated. For example, a manufacturer of kitchen appliances may recognize the potential for product liability suits. But the potential size of adverse liability judgments may be much greater than the manufacturer anticipates. Thus, even though the exposure is recognized, the firm is engaging in unplanned retention of losses that exceed its estimate of the maximum possible loss.

Funded Versus Unfunded Retention

Many risk-retention strategies involve the intention to pay for losses as they occur, without making any funding arrangements in advance of a loss. If a loss happens, it is paid for from the firm's current revenues. For example, a convenience food store may decide to absorb the expense of shoplifting losses as they occur, rather than making any special advance arrangements to pay for them. This **unfunded retention** makes sense in this situation because some level of shoplifting losses is often viewed as part of the overall cost of doing business. Glass breakage is another exposure that many firms manage using unfunded retention. In general, unfunded retention should be used with caution, because financial difficulties may arise if the actual total losses are considerably greater than what was expected. In contrast to unfunded retention, a firm or individual may decide to practice **funded retention** by making various preloss arrangements to ensure that money is readily available to pay for losses that occur.

CREDIT The use of credit may provide some limited opportunities to fund losses that result from retained risks. It is usually not a viable source of funds for the payment of large losses, however. Further, unless the risk manager has already established a line of credit prior to the loss, the very fact that the loss has occurred may make it impossible to obtain credit when needed. For example, creditors may be unwilling to loan money to replace destroyed assets if those are the very assets that normally would have been used as collateral for the loan. For these reasons, credit tends not to be a major source of financial resources for most firms' funded retention programs.

RESERVE FUNDS Sometimes a reserve fund is established to pay for losses arising out of risks a firm has decided to retain. If the maximum possible loss due to a particular risk is relatively small, the existence of a reserve fund may be an efficient means of managing risk. For example, a firm may set aside $5,000 in liquid assets to pay for periodic repair or replacement of office equipment. Thus, when a fax machine or computer breaks down, the firm has funds readily available for the repair bill, which likely will be considerably less than the total reserve fund.

When the maximum possible loss is quite large, however, a reserve fund may not be appropriate. If a small employer plans for a $50,000 reserve fund to pay for any hospital costs its employees incur, it has no way of knowing whether or not this fund is adequate. A single period of hospitalization could easily exhaust the savings, and a second period of hospitalization might occur before the fund could be restored. For this type of exposure, alternative risk-management techniques probably would be more appropriate than risk retention, especially for a small firm.

SELF-INSURANCE If a firm has a group of exposure units large enough to reduce risk and thereby predict losses, the establishment of a fund to pay for those losses is a special form of planned, funded retention known as **self-insurance.**

Some people object to this particular term, because the word *insurance* usually implies that a risk is transferred to another party. Obviously, self-insurance will not involve a transfer of risk in this sense. In spite of such objections, the term *self-insurance* continues to be used to describe some special situations in which risk retention has been consciously selected as an appropriate risk-management technique. The mere establishment of a reserve fund is not self-insurance. There are two necessary elements of self-insurance: (1) existence of a group of exposure units that is sufficiently large to enable accurate loss prediction and (2) prefunding of expected losses through a fund specifically designed for that purpose.

CAPTIVE INSURERS   One final form of funded risk retention is the establishment of a **captive insurer,** which combines the techniques of risk retention and risk transfer.

Decisions Regarding Retention

In any given situation, there are several factors to consider in assessing retention as a potential risk-management technique. These factors include financial resources, ability to predict losses, and feasibility of establishing retention programs.

FINANCIAL RESOURCES   A large business can often use risk retention to a greater extent than can a small firm or an individual, in part because of the large firm's greater financial resources. Thus, losses due to many risks may merely be absorbed by such a firm as the losses occur, without much advance planning. Some risks are recognized and their retention is planned, but in many cases no attempt is made to prefund those losses because their potential size would not cause undue financial hardship. Examples for some businesses might include pilferage of office supplies, breakage of windows, and burglary of vending machines.

In the case of funded retention, large firms also are often better able to utilize the retention technique than are small firms. For a given size, firms that are financially healthy will be better able to retain risk than those that are not. The following elements from a firm's financial statements should be considered when choosing possible retention levels.

1. Total assets
2. Total revenues
3. Asset liquidity
4. Ratio of revenues to net worth
5. Retained earnings
6. Ratio of total debt to net worth

For all of these items except the last one, the greater the number, the greater is the firm's ability to retain risk. In the case of the ratio of total debt to net worth, firms with lower ratios are in a better position to fund risk retention than are those with higher ratios.

ABILITY TO PREDICT LOSSES   Another important consideration in evaluating the desirability of risk retention is the degree to which losses may or may not be predictable. Although a firm may be able to retain the maximum probable loss associated with a particular risk, problems may result if there is considerable variability in the range of possible losses. The ability to predict losses is enhanced when a firm has a large enough group of items exposed to the same risk to enable it to accurately predict loss experience.

Thus, if **RWT Company** employs 30,000 workers nationwide, it should be able to accurately predict its likely costs associated with work-related injuries. It can then make careful estimates of the funds needed to meet these losses and decide if it wants to pay for them as they are incurred or set aside money ahead of time. In the latter case, RWT probably can set up a fund with relative certainty that, within some margin for error, the fund will actually equal the losses incurred.

FEASIBILITY OF ESTABLISHING THE RETENTION PROGRAM   If the decision to retain losses involves advance funding, administrative issues may need to be considered. Similarly, if the risk is likely to result in several losses over time, there will be administrative expenses associated with investigating and paying for those losses. An example is a decision by **MWT Corporation** to retain expenses arising from injuries to its employees. Because many relatively small losses can be expected over time, MWT must prepare for the administrative issues that will arise in its retention program. Administrative issues are of particular concern when a firm decides to set up a self-insurance or captive insurer arrangement.

Risk Transfer

The final risk-management tool is **risk transfer,** which involves payment by one party (the **transferor**) to another (the **transferee,** or risk bearer). The transferee agrees to assume a risk that the transferor desires to escape. Sometimes the degree of risk is reduced through the transfer process, because the transferee may be in a better position to use the law of large numbers to predict losses. In other cases the degree of risk remains the same and is merely shifted from the transferor to the transferee for a price. Risk sharing can be viewed as a special case of risk transfer. Note that risk retention is mutually exclusive with risk transfer. Five forms of risk transfer are hold-harmless agreements, incorporation, diversification, hedging, and insurance.

Hold-Harmless Agreements

Provisions inserted into many different kinds of contracts can transfer responsibility for some types of losses to a party different than the one that would otherwise bear it. Such provisions are called **hold-harmless agreements,** or sometimes **indemnity agreements.** The intent of these contractual clauses is to specify the party that will be responsible for paying for various losses. Usually, no dollar limit is stated. Thus, the transferee must pay for all losses covered by the agreement, regardless of size.

An example of a hold-harmless agreement is that of a landlord who includes a clause in his apartment leases making tenants responsible for all injuries that guests may suffer while on the leased premises. This transfer entails a shift in responsibility for paying for losses, but there is no actual reduction in the original risk because the tenants' ability to predict losses is no greater than that of the landlord.

FORMS OF HOLD-HARMLESS AGREEMENTS Hold-harmless agreements differ in the extent to which risk is transferred. The **limited form** merely clarifies that all parties are responsible for liabilities arising from their own actions. A second type of hold-harmless agreement is the **intermediate form,** in which the transferee agrees to pay for any losses in which both the transferee and transferor are jointly liable. The **broad form** is the third type of hold-harmless agreement. It requires the transferee to be responsible for all losses arising out of particular situations, regardless of fault.

ENFORCEMENT OF HOLD-HARMLESS AGREEMENTS Hold-harmless agreements are not always legally enforceable. If the transferor is in a superior position to the transferee with respect to either bargaining power or knowledge of the factual situation, an attempt to transfer risk through a hold-harmless agreement may not be upheld by the courts. This result is particularly true of broad-form hold-harmless agreements.

Incorporation

Another way for a business to transfer risk is to incorporate. In this way, the most that an incorporated firm can ever lose is the total amount of its assets. Personal assets of the owners cannot be attached to help pay for business losses, as can be the case with sole proprietorships and partnerships. Through this act of incorporation, a firm transfers to its creditors the risk that it might not have sufficient assets to pay for losses and other debts.

Diversification

While risk management might not be the primary motivation, many of the production decisions that a firm makes can serve to transfer risk. **Diversification** across various businesses or geographic locations, while frequently justified by business synergies or economies of scale, also results in the transfer of risk across business units. Additionally, this combining of businesses or geographic locations in one firm can even result in a reduction in total risk through the portfolio effect of pooling individual risks that have different correlations. For example, a firm with two production facilities may sustain windstorm damages to its facility in Nebraska resulting from a tornado. However, it is unlikely that the same storm would cause damage to its facility in Georgia.

Hedging

Hedging involves the transfer of a speculative risk. It is a business transaction in which the risk of price fluctuations is transferred to a third party, which can be either a **speculator** or another **hedger.** In addition to futures contracts, forwards, swaps, and options are other commonly used tools for hedging speculative risk.

Insurance

The most widely used form of risk transfer is insurance.

The Value of Risk Management

Some elements of risk management, such as loss control decisions, can be viewed as positive net present value projects. If the expected gains from an investment in loss control exceed the expected costs associated with that investment, the project should increase the value of the firm.

However, shareholders in a publicly-traded corporation can eliminate firm-specific risk by holding a diversified portfolio of different company stocks. As a result, the shareholder would appear to care little about the management of nonsystematic or firm-specific risk, risk that the shareholder can eliminate through portfolio diversification. This would appear to make many risk-management activities, such as various forms of risk transfer, negative net present value projects. Nevertheless, corporations do engage in a number of activities directed at managing firm-specific risk, including the use of risk transfer. Why is this economically justified?

When evaluating risk management from the perspective of its impact on the value of the corporation, the source of the risk is less important than its effect on volatility. Regardless of whether the reduction in earnings comes from fire damage to the corporation's property, or from an increase in commodity prices, the financial impact on the shareholders is the same. This broader view of risk underpins the movement toward **enterprise-wide risk management**. Additionally, this holistic view reflects the realization that appropriate risk management must consider the fact that the corporation faces a portfolio of risks. And just as investment theory suggests that diversification can reduce the risk associated with a portfolio of securities, diversification within the portfolio of risks facing the corporation can alter the firm's risk profile. Ignoring these diversification effects by managing the firm's many risks independently can lead to inefficient use of the corporation's resources.

Selecting and Implementing Risk-Management Techniques

The selection of appropriate risk-management techniques is a dynamic problem. The best method for handling a particular exposure today may not be the best method a year from now because so many relevant factors change regularly. For example, the nature of an exposure may shift over time. Or the expected frequency and severity of losses may vary, causing estimates for the maximum possible loss and maximum probable loss to fluctuate. Finally, the cost and availability of different risk-management tools cannot be assumed to remain constant. Thus a risk-management plan that seems to be both effective and efficient one year may not make as much sense in the next.

All of these factors make it clear that the risk-management process should be an ongoing one rather than an exercise that is performed once and then forgotten. As exposures to risk are identified and analyzed, available risk-management tools and techniques must be considered. The steps for selecting among available risk-management techniques for a given situation may be summarized as follows.

1. Avoid risks if possible.
2. Implement appropriate loss control measures.
3. Select the optimal mix of risk retention and risk transfer.

Avoid Risks If Possible

Risks that can be eliminated without an adverse effect on the goals of an individual or business probably should be avoided. Without a systematic identification of pure risk exposures, however, some risks that easily could be avoided may inadvertently be retained.

Implement Appropriate Loss Control Measures

For risks that a business or individual cannot or does not wish to avoid, consideration should be given to available loss control measures. In analyzing the likely costs and benefits of loss control alternatives, it should be recognized that loss control will always be used in conjunction with either risk retention or risk transfer. That is, even if substantial funds are spent to reduce loss frequency and severity, some risk will still be present. In fact, objective risk may actually increase when actions are taken that decrease the chance of loss. Thus, either the remaining risk will be retained or it will be transferred to another party. This phenomenon is true whether it is specifically planned or happens by default.

Therefore, part of the cost/benefit analysis regarding potential loss control is recognition of the likely effects on the transfer or retention of the risk existing after loss control measures are implemented.

The selection between risk retention and risk transfer as the optimal risk-management technique may change after loss control expenditures are made. It may involve purchasing less insurance and engaging in relatively more risk retention following the loss control measures.

Analyzing Loss Control Decisions

Fortunately, the techniques used in making capital budgeting decisions in finance and accounting can be applied to risk-management decisions regarding loss control. Consider Cole Department Store, which has been experiencing both substantial shoplifting losses as well as occasional vandalism to its building. Cole is considering hiring 24-hour security guards in an attempt to decrease both the frequency and severity of these losses. The estimated annual cost of this 24-hour protection is $60,000, which will cover salaries and employee benefits for the guards. By analyzing the pattern of past losses, Cole estimates that the presence of security guards will decrease shoplifting losses by $30,000 and vandalism losses by $20,000. In addition, Cole's property insurance premiums are expected to decrease by $5,000. Should the guards be hired?

An answer based only on these financial considerations can be obtained by comparing the size of the savings with the amount of cash outlay required to hire the guards. The estimated savings are:

$30,000	Decreased shoplifting losses
20,000	Decreased vandalism losses
5,000	Lower insurance premium
$55,000	Estimated savings from hiring guards

Because the $55,000 in savings is less than the $60,000 cost of hiring the guards, Cole may conclude that the potential savings do not justify the loss control expense. Before making a final decision, however, Cole should review both the estimated costs and savings. Cole should also consider whether there are any additional relevant factors that may have been overlooked. For example, would the presence of a security guard make employees feel safer? Would this intangible consideration make it possible to hire better employees? What about customer relations? Would they be enhanced by the presence of a guard? The financial calculations provide a good starting point for decision making, but the final decision often will be made in light of additional, less quantifiable, nonfinancial considerations.

Select the Optimal Mix of Risk Retention and Risk Transfer

As previously stated, loss control decisions should be made as part of an overall risk-management plan that also considers the techniques of risk retention and risk transfer. To further complicate the decision-making process, risk retention and risk transfer often will both be used, with the relevant question being, "What is the appropriate mix between these two techniques?" Usually a loss control or loss prevention decision makes sense for losses that have a low expected frequency and low expected severity.

General Guidelines

As a rule, risk retention is optimal for losses that have a low expected severity, with the rule becoming especially appropriate when expected frequency is high. Physical damage losses to the cars within a large fleet driven by thousands of salespersons working for the same firm may fall into this category. Thus, no attempt may be made to transfer this risk to a third party;

Exhibit 900.9 *Guidelines for Using Different Risk-Management Techniques*

Expected Frequency	Expected Severity	Technique*
Low	Low	Retention
High	Low	Retention
Low	High	Transfer
High	High	Avoidance

*Loss control also should be considered in conjunction with each technique.

rather, the risk is retained, and an extra amount is added to the price of the product being sold to pay for expected losses due to collision and other damages to the cars. Of course, loss control measures such as safety instruction may be implemented as well. But due to the nature of the risk, retention likely will make sense. At some point, however, the company may also want insurance to protect against the possibility that the total of the losses could be greater than expected. Management must decide how to distinguish between losses that are to be retained and those that are to be transferred to a third party.

Another general guideline applies to risks that have a low expected frequency but a high potential severity. In this situation, risk transfer often is the optimal choice. Small business owner Michael is concerned about possible tornado losses. He knows that it is quite possible his firm will never be damaged by a tornado. If he does have such a loss, though, Michael also knows that his building and all its contents could be completely destroyed. Because his firm would not be able to pay for such a large loss from either current income or accumulated savings, the appropriate decision for Michael is to transfer this risk to a third party, probably an insurance company. As part of this decision, Michael may decide to retain part of the exposure and only buy insurance for losses that exceed a specified level.

Finally, when losses have both high expected severity and high expected frequency, it is likely that risk transfer, risk retention, and loss control all will need to be used in varying degrees. Such a situation is, of course, not a desirable one to be in and should probably be accompanied by a reexamination of overall goals and priorities. Thus, some doctors in medical specialties that are frequent targets of large malpractice suits have decided either to change specialties or to leave the practice of medicine altogether. In the latter case, risk avoidance is seen as a rational response to potential losses that have high frequency as well as high potential severity.

What constitutes "high" and "low" loss frequency and severity in applying the preceding guidelines must be established on an individual basis. What is low loss severity for a multimillion dollar company may be quite high for a small firm or an individual. In this regard, concepts such as total assets, net worth, and expected future income all are relevant. Subjective risk considerations also are important, as persons with a different tolerance for risk will often classify situations differently. A summary of the guidelines discussed in this section is provided in Exhibit 900.9.

Selecting Retention Amounts

Because in many situations both risk retention and risk transfer will be used in varying degrees, it is important to determine the appropriate mix of these two risk-management techniques. Both capital budgeting methods and statistical procedures may be used in selecting an appropriate retention level, with insurance purchased for losses in excess of that level.

But because the price of insurance does not necessarily vary proportionately with different levels of retention, the appropriate mix between retention and transfer is not an exact science. In general, decision makers try to minimize their total costs, considering not only the losses that are retained but also the premiums that must be paid for insurance that is purchased. Only at the end of the year (or other relevant time period) will it be known what the optimal decision at the beginning of the year would have been.

THE DEDUCTIBLE DECISION Selecting a particular deductible level is one way of mixing risk retention and risk transfer. Deductibles help lower the cost of insurance as well as increase its availability. They may also make management more loss conscious, because a firm must absorb losses within the deductible level. However, as a general rule, risk managers do not accept a deductible unless (1) the firm can afford the associated losses and (2) sufficient premium savings will result.

For example, the risk manager of Alliance Corporation is faced with the following choices in purchasing automobile insurance for the company-owned cars used by the Alliance sales force. As the deductible increases, the premium decreases. But the amount of premium savings is not in direct proportion to the size of the deductible. Thus, $300 in premium savings results by increasing the deductible from $100 to $250. But only $100 in savings results from increasing the

Deductible per Car ($)	Annual Premium per Car ($)
100	2,000
250	1,700
500	1,500
1,000	1,400

deductible from $500 to $1,000. The risk manager may decide that the additional premium savings from a $1,000 deductible does not sufficiently justify the associated increase in risk retention.

THE SELF-INSURANCE DECISION   The possibility of self-insurance is another way of mixing risk retention and risk transfer. For example, suppose past loss data for a large fleet of automobiles owned by BNM Corporation indicate a 95% probability that total annual collision losses for BNM will be less than $50,000. BNM may then decide to self-insure losses up to this level and purchase insurance that will pay only if total losses for the year exceed $50,000. In this way, BNM realizes some of the advantages of self-insurance while still maintaining adequate protection if losses are greater than expected. The most important element in the previous example, of course, is the specific dollar amount of losses that should be retained. The same statistical techniques used to select deductibles can be used in choosing a retention level for a self-insurance program.

The cash flow advantage of funds set aside in a reserve fund is an additional factor that must be considered in assessing the value of self-insurance as a way of handling risk. Because losses are not always paid out in the year in which the event producing them occurs, a company has the use of self-insurance funds for varying periods and may earn interest on them until such time as the losses are actually paid. The concept of present value methods can be helpful in analyzing self-insurance funding decisions.

Even though it may be clear that a firm can save money in the long run with self-insurance, management may prefer stable, predictable insurance premiums each year. Further, some companies prefer to avoid the details of managing self-insurance programs and instead to concentrate on their main operations. The following conditions are suggestive of the types of situations where self-insurance by a business is both possible and feasible.

1. The firm should have a sufficient number of objects so situated that they are not subject to simultaneous destruction. The objects also should be reasonably similar in nature and value so that calculations of probable losses will be accurate within a narrow range.
2. The firm must have accurate records or have access to satisfactory statistics to enable it to make good estimates of expected losses. To increase the accuracy of the calculations, it may be wise to use data that cover a long period of time. If outside data are used, caution must be employed to assure that the data are applicable to the firm's own experience.
3. The firm must make arrangements for administering the plan and managing the self-insurance fund. Someone must pay claims, inspect exposures, implement appropriate loss control measures, keep necessary records, and take care of the many administrative details. If the necessary specialized executive talent is not available within the firm, it may be possible to contract for these services to be done by an independent **third-party administrator.** However, if management does not appreciate the necessity of paying continuing attention to numerous details in some manner, then the self-insurance arrangement will not be a satisfactory risk-management solution.
4. The general financial condition of the firm should be satisfactory, and the firm's management must be willing and able to deal with large and unusual losses. If management is unwilling to set up adequate reserves for funding the optimal retention level, then insurance may be used to a greater extent than might be indicated by mathematical analyses.

Implementing Risk-Management Decisions

After the decision has been made regarding the appropriate mix of various risk-management techniques, the decision must be implemented. This step in the risk-management process may involve considerable interaction among risk managers, insurance agents, brokers, and insurance carriers. Several of the considerations involved in this process are discussed in this section.

Risk Manager Versus Insurance Agent

Do business firms need a risk manager to handle loss exposures when similar services are offered by a commercial insurance agent or broker? First, the risk manager and the insurance agent or broker do *not* perform identical functions; the job of the risk manager is considerably broader in scope than merely buying insurance. Second, firms have often found from experience that it is difficult to coordinate insurance programs without having someone from inside the firm primarily responsible—an outside broker cannot have the degree of familiarity with internal business affairs necessary to best perform the insurance-buying function. Third, the firm needs someone with primary concern for the needs of the firm. A broker receives compensation only if the firm purchases insurance or pays for a service provided by a broker. With a risk manager making the decisions, the firm's interest comes first. Fourth, the responsibility for the protection of corporate property is often considered too important to place in the hands of an outsider. One of the basic duties of a corporate director is to exercise due care in protecting corporate assets against impairment. To expose these assets to loss through failure to supervise effectively their proper insurance might expose the directors to legal liability to the stockholders. If corporate officers do not directly supervise the insurance, they must delegate the authority to another—and this person is increasingly being recognized as a full-time employee, the risk manager of the company.

In summary, risk management supplements and complements, but does not necessarily duplicate or replace, the functions performed by insurance agents and brokers. Both functions are needed, especially in large firms where risk management is a vital and complex function.

Organization for Risk Management

Exhibit 900.10 depicts an organizational chart for the risk-management function in a large firm. Note that in this firm the risk manager supervises all kinds of insurance, including self-insurance programs, foreign risks, and safety administration. Claims and loss records are also under the risk manager's control. The risk manager is only two levels beneath the president of the firm and may have 5 to 10 professional employees to assist in administering risk-management function. The duties and responsibilities of the risk manager tend to increase with the size of the firm. A risk manager's compensation also tends to increase with the size of the firm.

Commercial Risk Management

One of the first actions a risk manager should take when developing a program is to develop a risk-management policy statement to guide the decision-making efforts of the risk-management department; this statement is normally ex-

Exhibit 900.10 *Organization for Risk-Management Function*

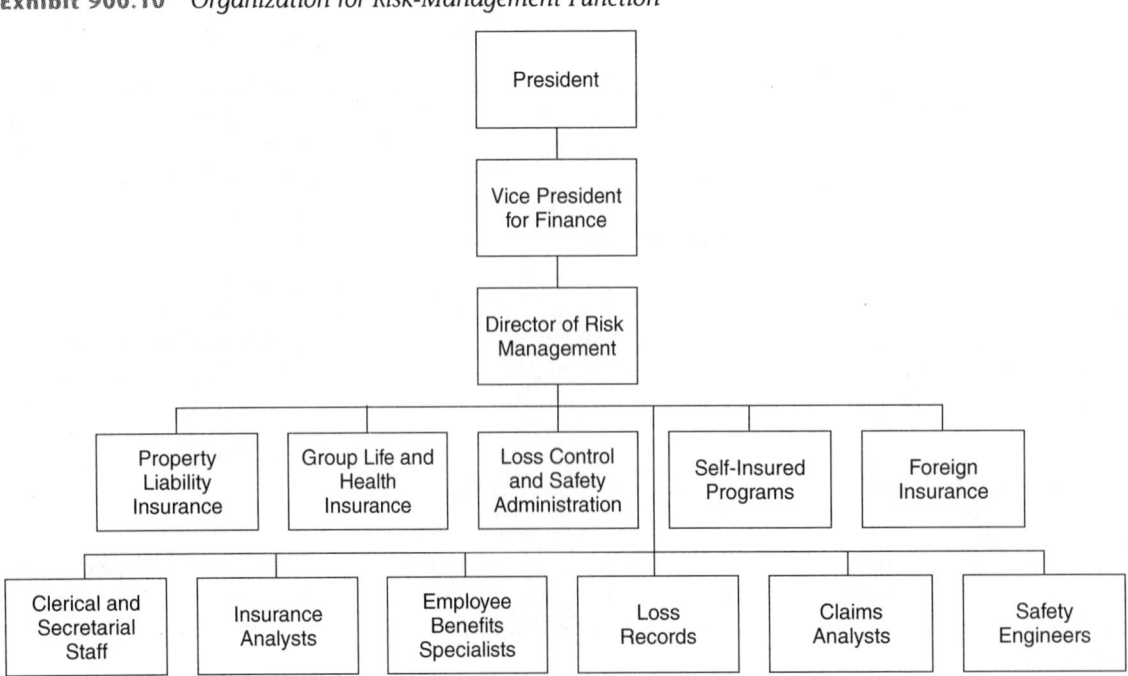

pressed in general terms. The firm will also have numerous minor policies that are quite specific to certain tasks, such as "It will be the policy of the firm to have at least a $50,000 deductible on all insurance contracts."

A **risk-management policy** is a plan, procedure, or rule of action followed for the purpose of securing consistent action over a period of time. The advantage of having definite policies to guide risk managers is that, once the rule is adopted, executives do not have to restudy recurring problems before making decisions.

Managing a Risk-Management Program

In managing a risk-management program, a person has many duties to perform.

1. First, the loss exposures must be identified and measured with respect to size and frequency. Then an analysis must be made to determine how to treat the loss exposure: retain, avoid, prevent, or transfer. Once these items are determined, the risk-management plan must be put into action.
2. When putting the plan into action, the risk manager must decide who is to do the work. That is, will in-house staff be employed, or will the work be given to people outside the firm (outsourcing)? Often, large national brokers or service vendors are retained by the risk manager. It is not uncommon for a risk manager to use an insurance company for a firm's risk-management information system (RMIS) and a broker for loss prevention services. Both these functions can be performed by persons other than employees of the firm. For example, electric utility companies often use a combination of such services.
3. When a risk manager is building the insurance side of a risk-management program, specifications for coverages must be developed, and several brokers will bid for the account. During this process, the risk manager is not only creating the insurance program but also choosing a broker. Most risk managers take their program to the market at least once every three years. The broker may not change that often, but the insurers can. The broker plays a role as advisor as well as the person who provides access to insurance markets.
4. In addition to managing risk, the risk manager must manage a department within a firm. Reports have to be written for management and information provided to the operating units so that they will know their cost of risk as well as information on losses—how to reduce them, and procedures to follow after they have occurred. Most large corporations have a detailed plan for situations when a major loss occurs. For instance, when North Carolina periodically is hit by hurricanes and tornados, employers once again discover how difficult it is for employees to get to work when the roads are blocked. On such occasions, one firm employs a tree service firm from Atlanta to go to North Carolina and clean up employees' yards so the employees are more able to come to work.
5. Another important task for the risk manager is to negotiate and settle claims with insurers and/or claimants. When major losses create claims of millions of dollars, much attention must be given to the process of proving the claims. Risk managers may retain persons that are experts in handling certain claims, such as business income losses. Of course, when the firm is being sued, the risk manager must work with the legal department to ensure that the claim is handled in the correct manner and that the interests of the firm are protected. One large manufacturer was engaged in so much litigation that it actually built an information system on many of the courts in which it had suits. The system contained information on awards, judge's personality, the attitude of juries, and other pertinent information with regard to having a trial in that jurisdiction.
6. With the development of relatively low-cost local area networks, risk managers need to be able to develop RMIS. The information contained in these systems should be organized in such a manner that timely and accurate reports can be made for management, insurers, outside vendors, and others in the firm who need information. By developing a RMIS, a risk manager can reduce the department's dependence on the firm's IT department and design a system that is tailored for the needs of a risk-management department.

Subjective Risk Management

Because objective and subjective risks are often both present in the same situation, some consideration must also be given to managing subjective risk. In one sense, the techniques applied to objective risk should also affect subjective risk. If risks have been systematically identified and analyzed, and if decisions have been made regarding the appropriate methods for dealing with those risks, then in most cases subjective risk can be expected to decrease. In addition, two other specific ways to deal with the existence of subjective risk are obtaining more information and group discussion.

Obtaining More Information

Perhaps the best way of handling subjective risk is by adding knowledge through research, training, or education. A risk averter may be more willing to accept risk once there is a better understanding of the uncertainties. With better knowledge, one is likely to perceive less risk in a given situation. Similarly, a risk taker may be willing to assume even greater risks as knowledge increases.

Group Discussion

It has been demonstrated that perceived subjective risk declines after group discussion of the problem. This fact suggests that an effective way to reduce subjective risk is to set up discussion groups, focus groups, committees, or seminars before decisions are made. In this way, bolder and quicker action may result, and indecision may be reduced.

Enterprise Risk Management and Alternative Risk Transfer

Firms increasingly are broadening their perspective of risk. Enterprise risk management, rather than focusing solely on pure or hazard risks, seeks to consider all exposures that could negatively affect the firm's ability to achieve its strategic goals. Russ Banham, in the April 1999 issue of *CFO Magazine*, states that the goal of enterprise risk management is to identify, analyze, quantify, and compare all of a firm's exposures stemming from operational, financial, and strategic activities. The exposures in this enterprisewide view of risk include traditional insurable risks such as liability, as well as financial, commodity, legal, environmental, and other less-tangible exposures such as reputational effects and reduction in brand image.

Traditionally, the risk-management tools—avoidance, loss control, retention, and transfer—have been applied primarily to the pure or hazard risks facing a firm. Further, even when similar risk-management techniques have been applied to other categories of risk, the risk-management activities of the firm have remained compartmentalized and relatively uncoordinated. Evan R. Busman, in the January 1998 issue of *risk-management*, observes that risk management for many firms has been performed by different individuals with narrowly defined specialties. The traditional risk manager handles pure or hazard risk; the treasurer focuses on credit and financial risk; strategic business units develop controls for operational and commodity risk; and marketing and public relations staff focus on reputational risk.

In addition to the organizational segmentation of risk management within the firm, risk-management tools that are used to manage risks in these separate categories often differ. The techniques of insurance and self-insurance are commonly limited to the treatment of pure risks, such as fire, product liability, and workers' compensation. However, futures, options, swaps, and other derivatives contracts are typically applied to the management of financial risks, such as foreign exchange, commodity price, and interest rate risk.

The traditional method of assigning the risk-management process to different functional areas, using what has been called a "silo" approach, can lead to a less efficient management of risk for the firm as a whole. Many types of risks may be relatively uncorrelated with each other. As a result, combining these risks produces a form of "natural" hedging. As an example, earthquake damage to a multinational firm's property in one part of the world would be unlikely to have any correlation with its exposure to foreign exchange risk in another part of the world. The combination of these risks within the same firm reduces the level of risk. The traditional silo approach could actually reduce the overall efficiency of the firm's risk-management activities by destroying the natural hedging that exists at the enterprisewide level.

As the enterprisewide view of risk management has progressed, the role of the traditional risk manager and risk-management tools also have been evolving. Indicative of their changing role, traditional risk managers are increasingly being called on to become involved in the management of various nonhazard or financial risks facing their firms.

Alternative Risk-Transfer Tools

A growing array of alternative risk-transfer tools have been introduced since the mid-1990s (*alternative* here means an option to traditional insurance). Although the market shares of some of the alternative risk-transfer tools are relatively small, the pace of innovation and new product development has been very brisk. A sampling of alternative risk-transfer tools includes the following.

- **Captives.** An insurer owned by a noninsurance firm or organization for the purpose of accepting the risks of the parent firm. Although captives were originally conceived as an alternative to traditional insurance, they provide firms with a potentially effective vehicle for assuming the broader risks involved in enterprise risk management.
- **Finite risk or financial insurance.** Risk transfer contracts which are based on the concept of spreading risk over time, as opposed to across a pool of similar exposures. Generally, these contracts involve a limit on the extent of risk ultimately transferred by the insured. The primary focus is on smoothing losses during the period of the contract, usually 5 to 10 years. Further, these contracts usually involve a sharing of the investment returns between the insurer and the insured.
- **Multiline/multiyear insurance.** Insurance contracts that combine a broad array of risks (multiline) into a contract with a policy period that extends over multiple years (multiyear). The combination of risks might be limited to pure risks, such as a blending of liability, workers' compensation, auto, and property risks into one policy with common limits and deductibles. Alternatively, the contract might involve a blending of insurance risks with financial risks such as commodity, credit, or currency risks.
- **Multiple-trigger policies.** These contracts reflect the notion that to the shareholders of the firm, the source of the risk is not as important as the impact of the risk on the earnings of the firm. These contracts pool risks that in combination could have a very serious impact on the value of the firm. Most of the multiple-trigger policies issued thus far have combined a pure risk with a financial risk. The policy is "triggered," and payment is made, only upon the occurrence of an adverse event in each risk category. For example, a power company might buy a policy that is triggered if it experiences an unscheduled outage at one of its power plants, the first risk, during a period of extreme price volatility for electricity, the second risk.
- **Securitization.** The creation of securities such as bonds or derivatives contracts, options, swaps, futures, that have a payout or price movement that is linked to an insurance risk. Examples include catastrophe options, earthquake bonds, catastrophe bonds, and catastrophe equity puts. The driving motivation behind many of the securitized contracts is the interest in tapping the extensive risk transfer potential available in the capital markets. USAA and Tokyo Fire and Marine are two insurers that have used such tools to transfer hurricane and earthquake risks, respectively. Additionally, Tokyo Disneyland was purported to be the first noninsurer to use earthquake bonds to transfer risk to the capital markets, without the involvement of any insurer.

The risk managers forecast an almost fourfold increase in their use of the vehicles that involve the highest degree of risk integration, pure and financial risk integrated contracts, and securitization.

Corporate Citizenship and Accountability

The Scope of Corporate Citizenship

The scope of corporate citizenship includes corporate social responsibility, corporate social responsiveness, and corporate social performance. Each one is described next.

Corporate Social Responsibility

Raymond Bauer presented an early view of corporate social responsibility (CSR) as follows: "Corporate social responsibility is seriously considering the impact of the company's actions on society."[28] Another definition that may be helpful is "The idea of social responsibility ... requires the individual to consider his [or her] acts in terms of a whole social system, and holds him [or her] responsible for the effects of his [or her] acts anywhere in that system."[29]

Both of these definitions provide preliminary insights into the idea of social responsibility. Exhibit 900.11 illustrates the business criticism/social response cycle, depicting how the concept of CSR grew out of business criticism

Exhibit 900.11 *Business Criticism/Social Response Cycle*

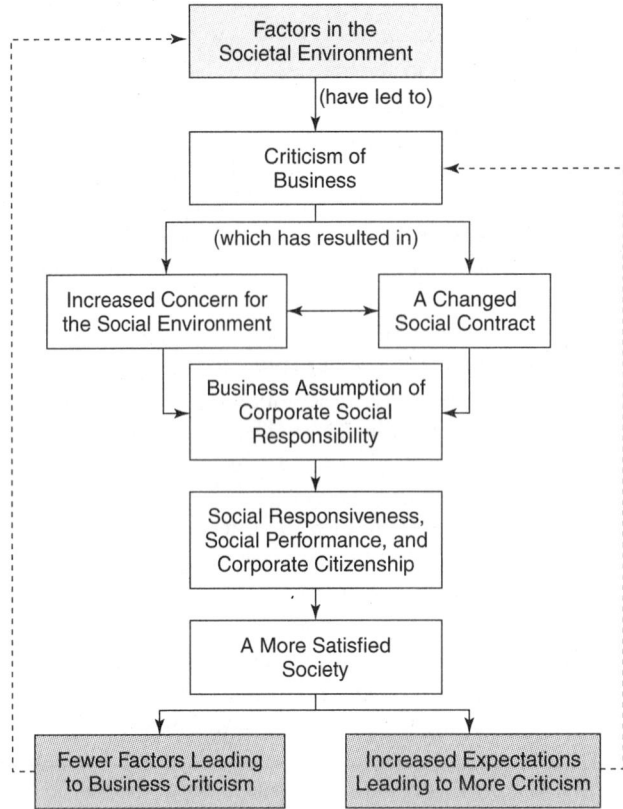

and the increased concern for the social environment and the changed social contract. We see also in Exhibit 900.11 that the commitment to social responsibility by businesses has led to increased corporate responsiveness to stakeholders and improved social (stakeholder) performance.

As we will discuss later, some observers today prefer the language of "corporate citizenship" to collectively embrace the host of concepts related to CSR.

CORPORATE CITIZENSHIP CONCEPTS

Corporate social *responsibility*—emphasizes obligation, accountability.
↓
Corporate social *responsiveness*—emphasizes action, activity.
↓
Corporate social *performance*—emphasizes outcomes, results.

The growth of these ideas has brought about a society more satisfied with business. However, this satisfaction, although it has reduced the number of factors leading to business criticism, has at the same time led to increased expectations that may result in more criticism; this double effect is indicated in Exhibit 900.11. The net result is that the overall levels of business performance and societal satisfaction should increase with time in spite of this interplay of positive and negative factors. Should business not be responsive to societal expectations, it could conceivably enter a downward spiral, resulting in significant changes in the business/society relationship.

Carroll's Four-Part Definition of Corporate Social Responsibility (CSR)

We would like to present Archie Carroll's four-part definition of corporate social responsibility (CSR) that focuses on the types of social responsibilities it might be argued that business has. Carroll's definition helps us to understand the component parts that make up CSR:

> The social responsibility of business encompasses the economic, legal, ethical, and discretionary (philanthropic) expectations that society has of organizations at a given point in time.[30]

Carroll's four-part definition attempts to place economic and legal expectations of business in context by relating them to more socially-oriented concerns. These social concerns include ethical responsibilities and philanthropic (voluntary/discretionary) responsibilities. This definition, which includes four kinds of responsibilities, elaborates and builds upon the definition proposed by McGuire.

ECONOMIC RESPONSIBILITIES First, there are business's **economic responsibilities**. It may seem odd to call an economic responsibility a social responsibility, but, in effect, this is what it is. First and foremost, the American social system calls for business to be an economic institution. That is, it should be an institution whose orientation is to produce goods and services that society wants and to sell them at fair prices—prices that society thinks represent the true values of the goods and services delivered and that provide business with profits adequate to ensure its perpetuation and growth and to reward its investors. While thinking about its economic responsibilities, business employs many management concepts that are directed toward financial effectiveness—attention to revenues, costs, strategic decision making, and the host of business concepts focused on maximizing the long-term financial performance of the organization.

LEGAL RESPONSIBILITIES Second, there are business's **legal responsibilities.** Just as society has sanctioned our economic system by permitting business to assume the productive role mentioned earlier, as a partial fulfillment of the social contract, it has also laid down the ground rules—the laws—under which business is expected to operate. Legal responsibilities reflect society's view of "codified ethics" in the sense that they embody basic notions of fair practices as established by our lawmakers. It is business's responsibility to society to comply with these laws. If business does not agree with laws that have been passed or are about to be passed, our society has provided a mechanism by which dissenters can be heard through the political process. In the past 30 years, our society has witnessed a proliferation of laws and regulations striving to control business behavior.

As important as legal responsibilities are, legal responsibilities do not cover the full range of behaviors expected of business by society. The law is inadequate for at least three reasons. First, the law cannot possibly address all the topics, areas, or issues that business may face. New topics continually emerge such as Internet-based business (e-commerce) and genetically-engineered foods. Second, the law often lags behind more recent concepts of what is considered appropriate behavior. For example, as technology permits more exact measurements of environmental contamination, laws based on measures made by obsolete equipment become outdated but not frequently changed. Third, laws are made by lawmakers and may reflect the personal interests and political motivations of legislators rather than appropriate ethical justifications. A wise sage once said: "Never go to see how sausages or laws are made." It may not be a pretty picture.

ETHICAL RESPONSIBILITIES Because laws are important but not adequate, **ethical responsibilities** embrace those activities and practices that are expected or prohibited by societal members even though they are not codified into law. Ethical responsibilities embody the full scope of norms, standards, and expectations that reflect a belief of what consumers, employees, shareholders, and the community regard as fair, just, and in keeping with the respect for or protection of stakeholders' moral rights.[31]

In one sense, changes in ethics or values precede the establishment of laws because they become the driving forces behind the initial creation of laws and regulations. For example, the civil rights, environmental, and consumer movements reflected basic alterations in societal values and thus may be seen as ethical bellwethers foreshadowing and leading to later legislation. In another sense, ethical responsibilities may be seen as embracing and reflecting newly emerging values and norms that society expects business to meet, even though they may reflect a higher standard of performance than that currently required by law. Ethical responsibilities in this sense are often ill defined or continually under public scrutiny and debate as to their legitimacy and thus are frequently difficult for business to agree upon. Regardless, business is expected to be responsive to newly emerging concepts of what constitutes ethical practices.

Superimposed on these ethical expectations emanating from societal and stakeholder groups are the implied levels of ethical performance suggested by a consideration of the great ethical principles of moral philosophy, such as justice, rights, and utilitarianism.[32]

For the moment, let us think of ethical responsibilities as encompassing those areas in which society expects certain levels of moral or principled performance but for which it has not yet articulated or codified into law.

PHILANTHROPIC RESPONSIBILITIES Fourth, there are business's voluntary/discretionary or **philanthropic responsibilities.** These are viewed as responsibilities because they reflect current expectations of business by the public.

Exhibit 900.12 *Understanding the Four Components of Corporate Social Responsibility*

Type of Responsibility	Societal Expectation	Examples
Economic	REQUIRED of business by society	Be profitable. Maximize sales, minimize costs. Make sound strategic decisions. Be attentive to dividend policy.
Legal	REQUIRED of business by society	Obey all laws, adhere to all regulations. Environmental and consumer laws. Laws protecting employees. Obey Foreign Corrupt Practices Act. Fulfill all contractual obligations. Honor warranties and guarantees.
Ethical	EXPECTED of business by society	Avoid questionable practices. Respond to spirit as well as letter of law. Assume law is a floor on behavior, operate above minimum required. Do what is right, fair, and just. Assert ethical leadership.
Philanthropic	DESIRED of business by society	Be a good corporate citizen. Make corporate contributions. Provide programs supporting community—education, health/human services, culture and arts, civic. Provide for community betterment. Engage in volunteerism.

These activities are voluntary, guided only by business's desire to engage in social activities that are not mandated, not required by law, and not generally expected of business in an ethical sense. Nevertheless, the public has an expectation that business will engage in philanthropy and thus this category has become a part of the social contract between business and society. Such activities might include corporate giving, product and service donations, volunteerism, partnerships with local government and other organizations, and any other kind of voluntary involvement of the organization and its employees with the community or other stakeholders.

The distinction between ethical responsibilities and philanthropic responsibilities is that the latter typically are not expected in a moral or an ethical sense. Communities desire and expect business to contribute its money, facilities, and employee time to humanitarian programs or purposes, but they do not regard firms as unethical if they do not provide these services at the desired levels. Therefore, these responsibilities are more discretionary, or voluntary, on business's part, although the societal expectation that they be provided is always present. This category of responsibilities is often referred to as good "corporate citizenship."

In essence, then, our definition forms a four-part conceptualization of corporate social responsibility that encompasses the economic, legal, ethical, and philanthropic expectations placed on organizations by society at a given point in time. Exhibit 900.12 summarizes the four components, society's expectation regarding each component, and examples. The implication is that business has accountability for these areas of responsibility and performance. This four-part definition provides us with categories within which to place the various expectations that society has of business. With each of these categories considered as indispensable facets of the total social responsibility of business, we have a conceptual model that more completely describes the kinds of expectations that society expects of business. One advantage of this model is that it can accommodate those who have argued against CSR by characterizing an economic emphasis as separate from a social emphasis. This model offers these two facets along with others that collectively make up corporate social responsibility.

THE PYRAMID OF CORPORATE SOCIAL RESPONSIBILITY A helpful way of graphically depicting the four-part definition is envisioning a pyramid composed of four layers. The pyramid portrays the four components of CSR, beginning with the basic building block of economic performance (making a profit), at the base. At the same time, business is expected to obey the law, because the law is society's codification of acceptable and unacceptable behavior. Next is business's responsibility to be ethical. At its most basic level, this is the obligation to do what is right, just, and fair and to avoid or minimize harm to stakeholders (employees, consumers, the environment, and others). Finally, business is expected to be a good corpo-

A socially responsible firm should strive to:
- *Make a profit.*
- *Obey the law.*
- *Be ethical.*
- *Be a good corporate citizen.*

rate citizen—to fulfill its voluntary/discretionary or philanthropic responsibility to contribute financial and human resources to the community and to improve the quality of life.

The most critical tensions, of course, are those between economic and legal, economic and ethical, and economic and philanthropic. The traditionalist might see this as a conflict between a firm's "concern for profits" and its "concern for society," but it is suggested here that this is an oversimplification. A CSR or stakeholder perspective would recognize these tensions as organizational realities but would focus on the total pyramid as a unified whole and on how the firm might engage in decisions, actions, policies, and practices that simultaneously fulfill all its component parts. This pyramid should not be interpreted to mean that business is expected to fulfill its social responsibilities in some sequential fashion, starting at the base. Rather, business is expected to fulfill all its responsibilities simultaneously.

In summary, the total social responsibility of business entails the concurrent fulfillment of the firm's economic, legal, ethical, and philanthropic responsibilities. In equation form, this might be expressed as follows.

$$\text{Economic Responsibilities} + \text{Legal Responsibilities} + \text{Ethical Responsibilities} \\ + \text{Philanthropic Responsibilities} \\ = \text{Total Corporate Social Responsibility}$$

Arguments Against and for Corporate Social Responsibility

In an effort to provide a balanced view of CSR, we will consider the arguments that traditionally have been raised against and for it. We should state clearly at the outset, however, that those who argue against corporate social responsibility are not using in their considerations the comprehensive CSR definition and model presented in Exhibit 900.12.

Rather, it appears that the critics are viewing CSR more narrowly—as only the efforts of the organization to pursue social, noneconomic/nonlegal goals (our ethical and philanthropic categories). Some critics equate CSR with only the philanthropic category. We should also state that only a very few businesspeople and academics continue to argue against the fundamental notion of CSR today. The debate among businesspeople more often centers on the kinds and degrees of CSR and on subtle ethical questions, rather than on the basic question of whether or not business should be socially responsible. Among academics, economists and finance professors are probably the easiest groups to single out as being against the pursuit of corporate social goals. But even some of them no longer resist CSR on the grounds of economic theory.

Arguments Against Corporate Social Responsibility

Let us first look at the arguments that have surfaced over the years from the anti-CSR school of thought. Most notable has been the classical economic argument. This traditional view holds that management has one responsibility: to maximize the profits of its owners or shareholders. This classical economic school, led by economist Milton Friedman, argues that social issues are not the concern of businesspeople and that these problems should be resolved by the unfettered workings of the free market system.[33] Further, this view holds that if the free market cannot solve the social problem, then it falls upon government and legislation to do the job. Friedman softens his argument somewhat by his assertion that management is "to make as much money as possible while conforming to the basic rules of society, both those embodied in the law and those embodied in ethical customs."[34] When Friedman's entire statement is considered, it appears that he accepts three of the four categories of the four-part model—economic, legal, and ethical. The only item not specifically embraced in his quote is the voluntary or philanthropic category. In any event, it is clear that the economic argument views corporate social responsibility more narrowly than we have in our conceptual model.

A second major objection to CSR has been that business is not equipped to handle social activities. This position holds that managers are oriented toward finance and operations and do not have the necessary expertise (social skills) to make social decisions.[35] Although this may have been true at one point in time, it is less true today. Closely related to this argument is a third: If managers were to pursue corporate social responsibility vigorously, it would tend to dilute the business's primary purpose.[36] The objection here is that CSR would put business into fields not related, as F. A. Hayek has stated, to their "proper aim."[37]

A fourth argument against CSR is that business already has enough power—economic, environmental, and technological—and so why should we place in its hands the opportunity to wield additional power?[38] In reality, today, business has this social power regardless of the argument. Further, this view tends to ignore the potential use of business's social power for the public good.

One other argument that merits mention is that by encouraging business to assume social responsibilities we might be placing it in a deleterious position in terms of the international balance of payments. One consequence of being socially responsible is that business must internalize costs that it formerly passed on to society in the form of dirty air, unsafe products, consequences of discrimination, and so on. The increase in the costs of products caused by including social considerations in the price structure would necessitate raising the prices of products, making them less competitive in international markets. The net effect might be to dissipate the country's advantages gained previously through technological advances. This argument weakens somewhat when we consider the reality that social responsibility is quickly becoming a global concern, not one restricted to U.S. firms and operations.

The arguments presented here constitute the principal claims made by those who oppose the CSR concept, as it once was narrowly conceived. Many of the reasons given appear quite rational. Value choices as to the type of society the citizenry would like to have, at some point, become part of the total social responsibility question. Whereas some of these objections might have had validity at one point in time, it is doubtful that they carry much weight today.

Arguments for Corporate Social Responsibility

Thomas Petit's perspective is useful as our point of departure in discussing support of the CSR doctrine. He says that authorities have agreed upon two fundamental points: "(1) Industrial society faces serious human and social problems brought on largely by the rise of the large corporations, and (2) managers must conduct the affairs of the corporation in ways to solve or at least ameliorate these problems."[39]

This generalized justification of corporate social responsibility is appealing. It actually comes close to what we might suggest as a first argument for CSR—namely, that it is in business's long-range self-interest to be socially responsible. Petit's argument provides an additional dimension by suggesting that it was partially business's fault that many of today's social problems arose in the first place and, consequently, that business should assume a role in remedying these problems. It may be inferred from this that deterioration of the social condition must be halted if business is to survive and prosper in the future.

The long-range self-interest view holds that if business is to have a healthy climate in which to exist in the future, it must take actions now that will ensure its long-term viability. Perhaps the reasoning behind this view is that society's expectations are such that if business does not respond on its own, its role in society may be altered by the public—for example, through government regulation or, more dramatically, through alternative economic systems for the production and distribution of goods and services.

It is sometimes difficult for managers who have a short-term orientation to appreciate that their rights and roles in the economic system are determined by society. Business must be responsive to society's expectations over the long term if it is to survive in its current form or in a less restrained form.

One of the most practical reasons for business to be socially responsible is to ward off future government intervention and regulation. Today there are numerous areas in which government intrudes with an expensive, elaborate regulatory apparatus to fill a void left by business's inaction. To the extent that business polices itself with self-disciplined standards and guidelines, future government intervention can be somewhat forestalled. Later, we will discuss some areas in which business could have prevented intervention and simultaneously ensured greater freedom in decision making had it imposed higher standards of behavior on itself.

Keith Davis has presented two additional supporting arguments that deserve mention together: "Business has the resources" and "Let business try."[40] These two views maintain that because business has a reservoir of management talent, functional expertise, and capital, and because so many others have tried and failed to solve general social problems, business should be given a chance. These arguments have some merit, because there are some social problems that can be handled, in the final analysis, only by business. Examples include a fair workplace, providing safe products, and engaging in fair advertising. Admittedly, government can and does assume a role in these areas, but business must make the final decisions.

Another argument is that "proacting is better than reacting." This position holds that proacting (anticipating and initiating) is more practical and less costly than simply reacting to problems once they have developed. Environmental pollution is a good example, particularly business's experience with attempting to clean up rivers, lakes, and other waterways that were neglected for years. In the long run, it would have been wiser to have prevented the environmental deterioration from occurring in the first place. A final argument in favor of CSR is that the public strongly supports it. A 2000 *Business Week*/Harris poll revealed that, with a stunning 95% majority, the public believes that companies should not only focus on profits for shareholders but that companies should be responsible to their workers and communities, even if making things better for workers and communities requires companies to sacrifice some profits.[41]

Millennium Poll on Corporate Social Responsibility

The Conference Board Survey in 1999 suggests that CSR is fast becoming a global expectation that requires a comprehensive strategic response. Ethics and CSR need to be made a core business value integrated into all aspects of the firm.

In the twenty-first century, major companies will be expected to do all the following.

- Demonstrate their commitment to society's values and their contribution to society's social, environmental, and economic goals through actions.
- Fully insulate society from the negative impacts of company operations and its products and services.
- Share the benefits of company activities with key stakeholders as well as with shareholders.
- Demonstrate that the company can make more money by doing the right thing, in some cases reinventing its business strategy. This "doing well by doing good" will reassure stakeholders that the new behavior will outlast good intentions.

Corporate Social Responsiveness

We have discussed the evolution of corporate social responsibility, a model for viewing social responsibility, and the arguments for and against it. It is now important to address a concept that has arisen over the use of the terms *responsibility* and *responsiveness*. We will consider the views of several writers to develop the idea of **corporate social responsiveness**—the action-oriented variant of corporate social responsibility (CSR).

Ackerman and Bauer's Action View

A general argument that has generated much discussion over the past several decades holds that the term *responsibility* is too suggestive of efforts to pinpoint accountability or obligation. Therefore, it is not dynamic enough to fully describe business's willingness and activity—apart from obligation—to respond to social demands. For example, Robert Ackerman and Raymond Bauer criticized the CSR term by stating, "The connotation of 'responsibility' is that of the process of assuming an obligation. It places an emphasis on motivation rather than on performance." They go on to say, "Responding to social demands is much more than deciding what to do. There remains the management task of doing what one has decided to do, and this task is far from trivial."[42] They argue that "social responsiveness" is a more apt description of what is essential in the social arena.

Their point was well made, especially when it was first set forth. *Responsibility*, taken quite literally, does imply more of a state or condition of having assumed an obligation, whereas *responsiveness* connotes a dynamic, action-oriented condition. We should not overlook, however, that much of what business has done and is doing has resulted from a particular motivation—an assumption of obligation—whether assigned by government, forced by special-interest groups, or voluntarily assumed. Perhaps business, in some instances, has failed to accept and internalize the obligation, and thus it may seem odd to refer to it as a responsibility. Nevertheless, some motivation that led to social responsiveness had to be there, even though in some cases it was not articulated to be a responsibility or an obligation.

Sethi's Three-Stage Schema

S. Prakash Sethi takes a slightly different, but related, path in getting from social responsibility to social responsiveness. He proposes a three-stage schema for classifying corporate behavior in responding to social or societal needs: social obligation, social responsibility, and social responsiveness.

Social obligation, Sethi argues, is corporate behavior in response to market forces or legal constraints. Corporate legitimacy is very narrow here and is based on legal and economic criteria only. *Social responsibility*, Sethi suggests, "implies bringing corporate behavior up to a level where it is congruent with the prevailing social norms, values, and expectations."[43] He argues that whereas the concept of social obligation is proscriptive in nature, social responsibility is prescriptive in nature. *Social responsiveness*, the third stage in his schema, suggests that what is important is "not how corporations should respond to social pressure but what should be their long-run role in a dynamic social system."[44] He suggests that here business is expected to be "anticipatory" and "preventive." Note that his obligation and responsibility categories embody essentially the same message we were attempting to convey with our four-part conceptual definition of CSR.

950. CORPORATE CITIZENSHIP AND ACCOUNTABILITY

Frederick's CSR1, CSR2, and CSR3

William Frederick has distinguished between corporate social responsibility, which he calls CSR_1, and corporate social responsiveness, which he terms CSR_2, in the following way:

> Corporate social responsiveness refers to the capacity of a corporation to respond to social pressures. The literal act of responding, or of achieving a generally responsive posture, to society is the focus.... One searches the organization for mechanisms, procedures, arrangements, and behavioral patterns that, taken collectively, would mark the organization as more or less capable of responding to social pressures.[45]

Frederick further argued that advocates of social responsiveness (CSR_2) "have urged corporations to eschew philosophic questions of social responsibility and to concentrate on the more pragmatic matter of responding effectively to environmental pressures." He later articulated an idea known as CSR_3—corporate social rectitude—which addressed the moral correctness of actions taken and policies formulated.[46] However, we would argue that the moral dimension is implicit in CSR, as we included it in our basic four-part definition.

Epstein's Process View of Social Responsiveness

Edwin Epstein discusses corporate social responsiveness within the context of a broader concept that he calls the corporate social policy process. In this context, Epstein emphasizes the *process* aspect of social responsiveness. He asserts that corporate social responsiveness focuses on the individual and organizational processes "for determining, implementing, and evaluating the firm's capacity to anticipate, respond to, and manage the issues and problems arising from the diverse claims and expectations of internal and external stakeholders."[47]

Other Views of Social Responsiveness

Several other writers have provided conceptual schemes that describe the responsiveness facet. Ian Wilson, for example, asserts that there are four possible business strategies: reaction, defense, accommodation, and proaction.[48] Terry McAdam has likewise described four social responsibility philosophies that mesh well with Wilson's and describe the managerial approach that would characterize the range of the responsiveness dimension: "Fight all the way," "Do only what is required," "Be progressive," and "Lead the industry."[49] Davis and Blomstrom describe alternative responses to societal pressures as follows: withdrawal, public relations approach, legal approach, bargaining, and problem solving.[50] Finally, James Post has articulated three major social responsiveness categories: adaptive, proactive, and interactive.[51]

Thus, the corporate social responsiveness dimension that has been discussed by some as an alternative focus to that of social responsibility is, in actuality, an action phase of management's response in the social sphere. In a sense, the responsiveness orientation enables organizations to rationalize and operationalize their social responsibilities without getting bogged down in the quagmire of definition problems, which can so easily occur if organizations try to get an exact determination of what their true responsibilities are before they take any action.

In an interesting study of social responsiveness among Canadian and Finnish forestry firms, researchers concluded that the social responsiveness of a corporation will proceed through a predictable series of phases and that managers will tend to respond to the most powerful stakeholders.[52] This study demonstrates that social responsiveness is a process and that stakeholder power, in addition to a sense of responsibility, may sometimes drive the process.

Corporate Social Performance

For the past few decades, there has been a trend toward making the concern for social and ethical issues more and more pragmatic. The responsiveness thrust that we just discussed was a part of this trend. It is possible to integrate some of the concerns into a model of corporate social performance (CSP). The performance focus is intended to suggest that what really matters is what companies are able to accomplish—the results of their acceptance of social responsibility and adoption of a responsiveness philosophy. In developing a conceptual framework for CSP, we not only have to specify the nature (economic, legal, ethical, philanthropic) of the responsibility, but we also need to identify a particular philosophy, pattern, or mode of responsiveness. Finally, we need to identify the stakeholder issues or topical areas to which these responsibilities are manifested. One need not ponder the stakeholder issues that have evolved under the rubric of social responsibility to recognize how they have changed over time. The issues, and especially the degree of organizational interest in the issues, are always in a state of flux. As the times change, so does the emphasis on the range of social issues that business must address.

Also of interest is the fact that particular issues are of varying concern to businesses, depending on the industry in which they exist as well as other factors. A bank, for example, is not as pressed on environmental issues as a manufacturer. Likewise, a manufacturer is considerably more absorbed with the issue of environmental protection than is an insurance company.

Carroll's Corporate Social Performance (CSP) Model

Carroll's **corporate social performance (CSP) model** brings together the three major dimensions we have discussed.

1. Social responsibility categories—economic, legal, ethical, and (philanthropic) discretionary
2. Philosophy (or mode) of social responsiveness—for example, reaction, defense, accommodation, and proaction
3. Social (or stakeholder) issues involved—consumerism, environment, discrimination, and so on)[53]

One dimension of this model pertains to all that is included in our definition of social responsibility—the economic, legal, ethical, and (philanthropic) discretionary components. Second, there is a social responsiveness continuum. Although some writers have suggested that this is the preferable focus when one considers social responsibility, the model in Carroll's suggests that responsiveness is but one additional aspect to be addressed if CSP is to be achieved. The third dimension concerns the scope of social or stakeholder issues (for example, consumerism, environment, and discrimination) that management must address.

Usefulness of the CSP Model to Academics and Managers

The corporate social performance model is intended to be useful to both academics and managers. For academics, the model is primarily a conceptual aid to perceiving the distinction among the concepts of corporate social responsibility that have appeared in the literature. What previously have been regarded as separate definitions of CSR are treated here as three separate aspects pertaining to CSP. The model's major use to the academic, therefore, is in helping to systematize the important concepts that must be taught and understood in an effort to clarify the CSR concept. The model is not the ultimate conceptualization. It is, rather, a modest but necessary step toward understanding the major facets of CSP.

The conceptual model can assist managers in understanding that social responsibility is not separate and distinct from economic performance. The model integrates economic concerns into a social performance framework. In addition, it places ethical and philanthropic expectations into a rational economic and legal framework. The model can help the manager systematically think through major stakeholder issues. Although it does not provide the answer to how far the organization should go, it does provide a conceptualization that could lead to better-managed social performance. Moreover, the model could be used as a planning tool and as a diagnostic problem-solving tool. The model can assist the manager by identifying categories within which the organization can be situated.

Corporate Citizenship

Corporate citizenship has been described by some as a broad, encompassing term that basically embraces all that is implied in the concepts of social responsibility, responsiveness, and performance. Graves, Waddock, and Kelly, for example, define good corporate citizenship as "serving a variety of stakeholders well."[54] Fombrun also proposes a broad conception. He holds that corporate citizenship is composed of a three-part view that encompasses (1) a reflection of shared moral and ethical principles, (2) a vehicle for integrating individuals into the communities in which they work, and (3) a form of enlightened self-interest that balances all stakeholders' claims and enhances a company's long-term value.[55]

Davenport's research also resulted in a broad definition of corporate citizenship that includes a commitment to ethical business behavior, and balancing the needs of stakeholders, while working to protect the environment.[56] Finally, Carroll has recast his four categories of corporate social responsibility as embracing the "four faces of corporate citizenship,"—economic, legal, ethical, and philanthropic. Each face, aspect, or responsibility reveals an important facet that contributes to the whole. He poses that "just as private citizens are expected to fulfill these responsibilities, companies are as well."[57]

At the narrow end of the spectrum, Altman speaks of corporate citizenship in terms of corporate community relations. In this view, it embraces the functions through which business intentionally interacts with nonprofit organizations, citizen groups, and other stakeholders at the community level.[58] Other definitions of corporate citizenship fall in between these broad and narrow perspectives, and some refer to global corporate citizenship as well, as increasingly companies are expected to conduct themselves appropriately wherever they are doing business.

The benefits of good corporate citizenship to stakeholders is fairly apparent. But, what are the benefits of good corporate citizenship to business itself? A literature review of studies attempting to discern the benefits to companies of corporate citizenship, defined broadly, revealed empirical and anecdotal evidence supporting the following:[59]

- Improved employee relations (for example, improves employee recruitment, retention, morale, loyalty, motivation, and productivity)
- Improved customer relationships (for example, increased customer loyalty, acts as a tiebreaker for consumer purchasing, enhances brand image)
- Improved business performance (for example, positively impacts bottom-line returns, increases competitive advantage, encourages cross-functional integration)
- Enhanced company's marketing efforts (for example, helps create a positive company image, helps a company manage its reputation, supports higher prestige pricing, and enhances government affairs activities)

The terminology of corporate citizenship is especially attractive because it resonates so well with the business community's attempts to describe their own socially responsive activities and practices. Therefore, we can expect that this concept will be around for some years to come. Generally speaking, as we refer to CSR, social responsiveness, and social performance, we are also embracing activities that would typically fall under the purview of a firm's corporate citizenship.[60]

Social Performance and Financial Performance

One issue that comes up frequently in considerations of corporate social performance is whether or not there is a demonstrable relationship between a firm's social responsibility or performance and its financial performance. Unfortunately, attempts to measure this relationship are typically hampered by measurement problems. The appropriate performance criteria for measuring financial performance and social responsibility are subject to debate. Furthermore, the measurement of social responsibility is fraught with definitional problems. Even if a definition of CSR could be agreed on, there still would remain the complex task of operationalizing the definition. Exhibit 900.13 presents three perspectives.

A Multiple Bottom-Line Perspective

A basic premise of all these perspectives is that there is only one "bottom line"—a corporate bottom line that addresses primarily the stockholders', or owners', investments in the firm. An alternative view is that the firm has "multiple bottom lines" that benefit from corporate social performance. This stakeholder-bottom-line perspective argues that the impacts or benefits of CSP cannot be fully measured or appreciated by considering only the impact of the firm's financial bottom line.

To truly operate with a stakeholder perspective, companies need to accept the multiple-bottom-line view. Thus, CSP cannot be fully comprehended unless we also consider that its impacts on stakeholders, such as consumers, employees, the community, and other stakeholder groups, are noted, measured, and considered. Research may never conclusively demonstrate a relationship between CSP and financial performance. If a stakeholder perspective is taken, however, it may be more straightforward to assess the impact of CSP on multiple stakeholders' bottom lines. This model of CSP and stakeholders' bottom lines might be depicted as shown in Exhibit 900.14.

Socially Conscious or Ethical Investing

Special-interest groups, the media, and academics are not alone in their interest in business's social performance. Investors are also interested. The **socially conscious or ethical investing** movement arrived on the scene in the 1970s and has continued to grow and prosper. By the early 2000s, social investing had matured into a comprehensive investing approach complete with social and environmental screens, shareholder activism, and community investment, accounting for over $2 trillion of investments in the United States, according to the Social Investment Forum.[61]

The concept of *"social screening"* is the backbone of the socially conscious investing movement. Investors seeking to put their money into socially responsible firms want to screen out those firms they consider to be socially irresponsible or to actively invest in those firms they think of as being socially responsible. Thus, there are negative social screens and positive social screens. Some of the negative social screens that have been used in recent years include the avoidance of investing in tobacco manufacturers, gambling casino operators, and defense or weapons contractors.

Exhibit 900.13 *Relationships Among Corporate Social Performance (CSP), Corporate Financial Performance (CFP), and Corporate Reputation (CR)*

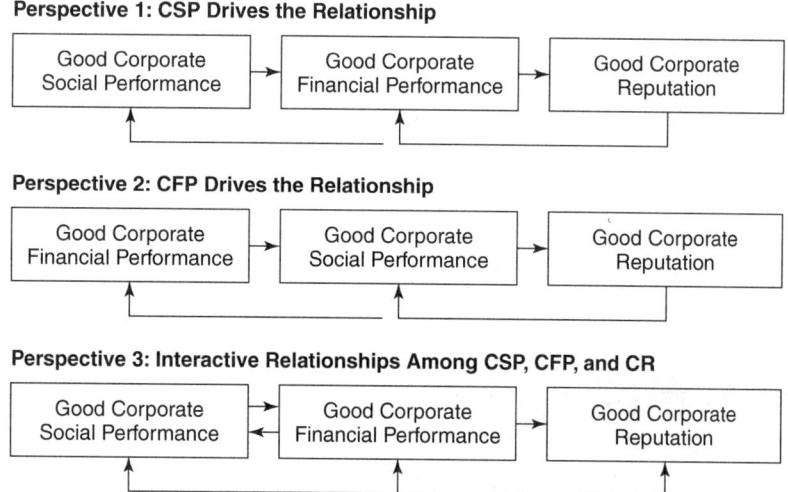

Exhibit 900.14 *Relationship Between Corporate Social Performance (CSP) and Stakeholders' "Multiple Bottom Lines"*

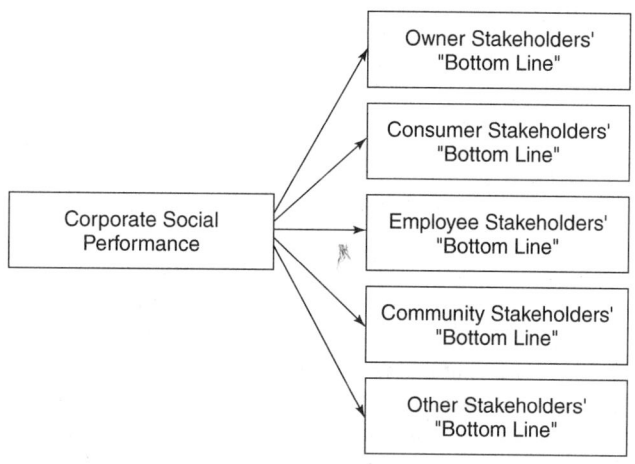

It is more difficult, and thus more challenging, to implement positive social screens, because they require the potential investor to make judgment calls as to what constitutes an acceptable or a good level of social performance on social investment criteria. Criteria that may be used as either positive or negative screens, depending on the firm's performance, might include the firm's record on issues such as equal employment opportunity and affirmative action, environmental protection, treatment of employees, corporate citizenship (broadly defined), and treatment of animals.

The financial performance of socially conscious funds shows that investors do not have to sacrifice profitability for principles. Recent evidence suggests that investors expect and receive competitive returns from social investments.[62]

It should be added, however, that there is no clear and consistent evidence that returns from socially conscious funds will equal or exceed the returns from funds that are not so carefully screened. Therefore, socially conscious funds are valued most highly by those investors who really care about the social performance of companies in their portfolios and are willing to put their money at some risk. A recent study concluded that there is no penalty for improved CSP in terms of institutional ownership and that high CSP tends in fact to lead to an increase in the number of institutional investors holding a given stock.[63]

The Council on Economic Priorities has suggested that there are at least three reasons why there has been an upsurge in socially conscious or ethical investing:[64]

1. There is more reliable and sophisticated research on corporate social performance than in the past.

950. CORPORATE CITIZENSHIP AND ACCOUNTABILITY

2. Investment firms using social criteria have established a solid track record, and investors do not have to sacrifice gains for principles.
3. The socially conscious 1960s generation is now making investment decisions.

In recent years, as more and more citizen employees are in charge of their own IRAs and 401(k)s, people have become much more sophisticated about making investment decisions than in the past. Further, more people are seeing social investments as a way in which they can exert their priorities concerning the balance of financial and social concerns.

Corporate Public Policy and Affairs

Corporate Public Policy

The impact of the social-ethical-public-stakeholder environment on business organizations is becoming more pronounced each year. It is an understatement to suggest that this multifaceted environment has become tumultuous, and brief reminders of a few actual cases point out the validity of this claim quite dramatically. **Procter & Gamble** and its Rely Tampon recall, **Firestone** and its radial tire debacle, **Ford Motor Company** and its disastrous Pinto gas tank problem, and **Johnson & Johnson** and its tainted Tylenol capsules are *classic* reminders of how social issues can directly affect a firm's product offerings. In addition, there are many examples in which social issues have had major impacts on firms at the general management level. **Exxon's** catastrophic *Valdez* oil spill, **Dow Corning's** ill-fated silicone breast implants, and the tobacco industry's battles with the federal and state government over the dangers of its product are all examples of the impacts of top-level decisions that entail ethical ramifications. More recently, **Coca-Cola's** disastrous and massive recall of soft drinks in Belgium and France and **Bridgestone-Firestone's** tire tread separations in a number of countries of the world and the United States provide examples of ethical issues that have dramatic implications for top executive decision makers.

What started as an awareness of social issues and social responsibility matured into a focus on the management of social responsiveness and performance. Today, the trend reflects a preoccupation with ethics, stakeholders, and corporate citizenship as we navigate the first decade of the new millennium. The term *corporate public policy* is an outgrowth of an earlier term, *corporate social policy*, which had been in general usage for over 20 years. The two concepts have essentially the same meaning, but we will use "corporate public policy" because it is more in keeping with terminology more recently used in business. Much of what takes place under the banner of corporate public policy is also referred to as corporate citizenship by businesses today.

What is meant by corporate public policy? **Corporate public policy** is a firm's posture, stance, strategy, or position regarding the public, social, and ethical aspects of stakeholders and corporate functioning. We will discuss how businesses formalize this concern under the rubric of corporate public affairs, or public affairs management. Businesses encounter many situations in their daily operations that involve highly visible public and ethical issues. Some of these issues are subject to intensive public debate for specific periods of time before they become institutionalized. Examples of such issues include sexual harassment, AIDS in the workplace, affirmative action, product safety, and employee privacy. Other issues are more basic, more enduring, and more philosophical. These issues might include the broad role of business in society, the corporate governance question, and the relative balance of business versus government direction that is best for our society.

The idea behind corporate public policy is that a firm must give specific attention to issues in which basic questions of right, wrong, justice, fairness, or public policy reside. The dynamic stakeholder environment of the past 40 years has necessitated that management apply a policy perspective to these issues. At one time, the social environment was thought to be a relatively constant backdrop against which the real work of business took place. Today these issues are center stage, and managers at all levels must address them. Corporate public policy is the process by which management addresses these significant concerns.

Public Policy as a Part of Strategic Management

Where does corporate public policy fit into strategic management? First, let us briefly discuss strategic management. **Strategic management** refers to the overall management process that focuses on positioning a firm relative to its environment. A basic way in which the firm relates to its environment is through the products and services it produces and the markets it chooses to address. Strategic management is also thought of as a kind of overall or comprehensive organizational management by the firm's top-level executives. In this sense, it represents the overall executive leadership function in which the sense of direction of the organization is decided upon and implemented.

Top management teams must address many issues as a firm is positioning itself relative to its environment. The more traditional issues involve product/market decisions—the principal decision thrust of most organizations. Other decisions relate to marketing, finance, accounting, information systems, human resources, operations, research and development, competition, and so on. Corporate public policy is that part of the overall strategic management of the organization that focuses specifically on the public, ethical, and stakeholder issues that are embedded in the functioning and decision processes of the firm. Therefore, just as a firm needs to develop policy on human resources, operations, marketing, or finance, it also must develop corporate public policy to proactively address the host of issues it is facing.

Relationship of Public Policy to Strategic Management

Although a consideration of ethics is implicit in corporate public policy discussions, it is useful to make this relationship more explicit. The concept of corporate public policy and the linkage between ethics and strategy are better understood when we think about (1) the four key levels at which strategy decisions arise and (2) the steps in the strategic management process.

Four Key Strategy Levels

Because organizations are hierarchical, it is not surprising to find that strategic management is hierarchical, too. That is, there are several different levels in the firm at which strategic decisions are made or the strategy process occurs. These levels range from the broadest or highest levels (where missions, visions, goals, decisions, and policies entail higher risks and are characterized by longer time horizons, more subjective values, and greater uncertainty) to the lowest levels (where planning is done for specific functional areas, where time horizons are shorter, where information needs are less complex, and where there is less uncertainty). Four key strategy levels have been recognized and are important to consider: enterprise-level strategy, corporate-level strategy, business-level strategy, and functional-level strategy.

The broadest level of strategic management is known as *societal-level strategy* or *enterprise-level strategy*, as it has come to be known. **Enterprise-level strategy** is the overarching strategy level that poses the basic questions, "What is the role of the organization in society?" and "What do we stand for?" Enterprise-level strategy encompasses the development and articulation of corporate public policy. It may be considered the first and most important level at which ethics and strategy are linked. Until fairly recently, corporate-level strategy was thought to be the broadest strategy level. In a limited, traditional sense, this is true, because **corporate-level strategy** addresses what is often posed as the most defining question for a firm, "What business(es) are we in or should we be in?" It is easy to see how **business-level strategy** is a natural follow-on because this strategy level is concerned with the question, "How should we compete in a given business or industry?" Thus, a company whose products or services take it into many different businesses or industries might need a business-level strategy to define its competitive posture in each of them. A competitive strategy might be based on low cost or a differentiated product. Finally, **functional-level strategy** addresses the question, "How should a firm integrate its various subfunctional activities and how should these activities be related to changes taking place in the various functional areas (finance, marketing, operations)?"[65]

The purpose of identifying the four strategy levels is to clarify that corporate public policy is primarily a part of enterprise-level strategy, which, in turn, is but one level of strategic decision making that occurs in organizations. Exhibit 900.15 illustrates that enterprise-level strategy is the broadest level and that the other levels are narrower concepts that cascade from it.

Another major indicator of enterprise-level strategic thinking is the extent to which the firm attempts to identify social or public issues, analyze them, and integrate them into its strategic management processes. We will now discuss how corporate public policy is integrated into the strategic management process.

The Steps in the Strategic Management Process

To understand how corporate public policy is but one part of the larger system of management decision making, it is useful to provide an overview of the major steps that make up the strategic management process. There are several acceptable ways to conceptualize this process, but we will use the six-step process identified by Hofer and Schendel. These

Exhibit 900.15 *The Hierarchy of Strategy Levels*

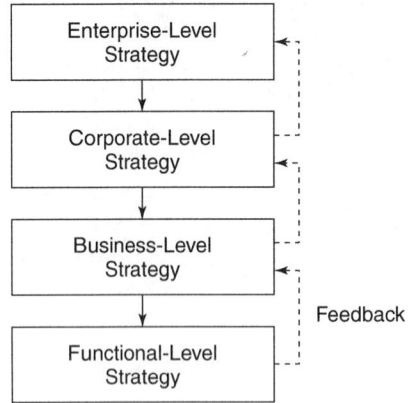

Exhibit 900.16 *The Strategic Management Process and Corporate Public Policy*

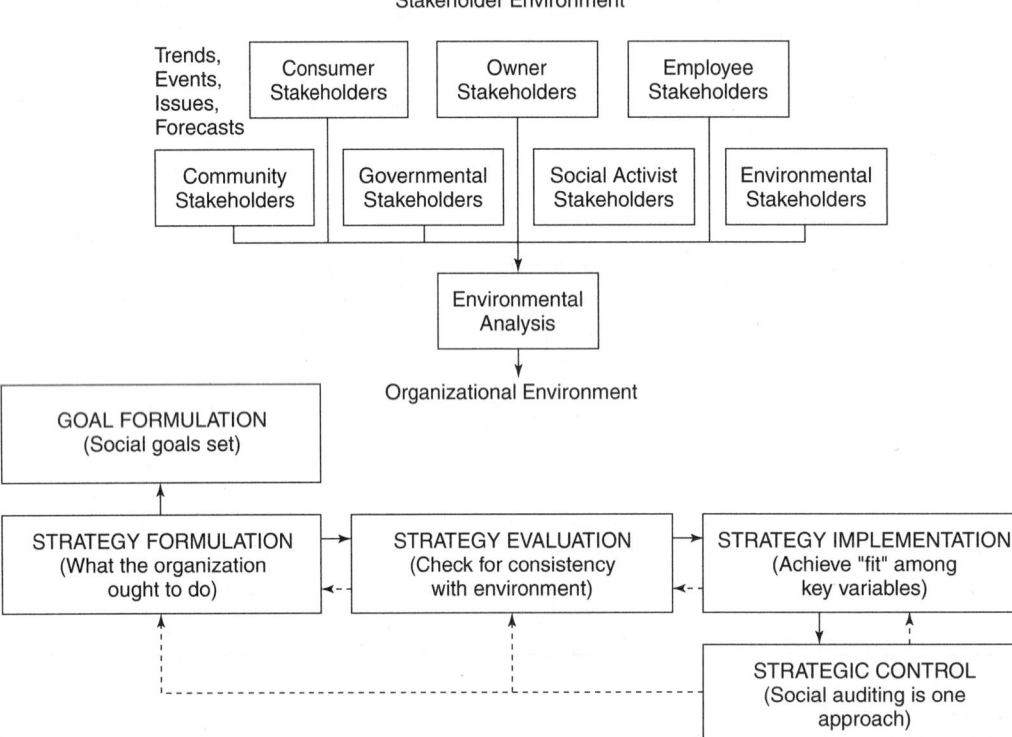

six steps are (1) goal formulation, (2) strategy formulation, (3) strategy evaluation, (4) strategy implementation, (5) strategic control, and (6) environmental analysis.[66] Exhibit 900.16 graphically portrays an expanded view of this process.

Narayanan and Fahey's conceptualization of the environmental analysis stage in the strategic management process is useful. They suggest that the process consists of four analytical stages.

1. *Scanning* the environment to detect warning signals
2. *Monitoring* specific environmental trends
3. *Forecasting* the future directions of environmental changes
4. *Assessing* current and future environmental changes for their organizational implications[67]

Note that the environmental analysis component collects information on trends, events, and issues that are occurring in the stakeholder environment and that this information is then fed into the other steps of the process. Note that these six steps are interactive and nonlinear.

Corporate Public Affairs

Corporate public affairs and **public affairs management** are umbrella terms used by companies to describe the management processes that focus on the formalization and institutionalization of corporate public policy. The public affairs function is a logical and increasingly prevalent component of the overall strategic management process. As an overall concept, public affairs management embraces corporate public policy, along with **issues management** and **crisis management.** Indeed, many issues management and crisis management programs are housed in public affairs departments or intimately involve public affairs professionals. Corporate public affairs also embraces the broad areas of governmental relations and corporate communications.

Public Affairs as a Part of Strategic Management

In a comprehensive management system, the overall flow of activity would be as follows. A firm engages in strategic management, part of which includes the development of enterprise-level strategy, which poses the question, "What do we stand for?" The answers to this question should help the organization to form a corporate public policy, which is a more specific posture on the public, social, or stakeholder environment or specific issues within this environment. Some firms call this a public affairs strategy. Two important planning approaches in corporate public policy are issues management and, often, crisis management. These two planning aspects frequently derive from or are related to environmental analysis, which we discussed earlier. Some companies embrace these processes as part of the corporate public affairs function. These processes are typically housed, from a departmental perspective, in a **public affairs department.** *Public affairs management* is a term that often describes all these components. Exhibit 900.17 helps illustrate likely relationships among these processes.

We will now consider how the public affairs function has evolved in business firms, what issues public affairs departments currently face, and how public affairs thinking might be incorporated into the operating manager's job. This last issue is crucial, because public affairs management, to be most effective, is best thought of as an indispensable part of every manager's job, not as an isolated function or department that alone is responsible for the public issues and stakeholder environment of the firm.

Public Affairs Strategy

We will not discuss the issue of public affairs strategy extensively, but we want to report the findings of a major research project that was undertaken by Robert H. Miles and resulted in a book entitled *Managing the Corporate Social Environment: A Grounded Theory.* Because very little work has been done on public affairs strategy, Miles's work deserves reference even though we cannot do it complete justice here. Miles's study focused on the insurance industry, but many of his findings may be applicable to other businesses.[68]

Exhibit 900.17 *Relationships Among Key Corporate Public Affairs Concepts*

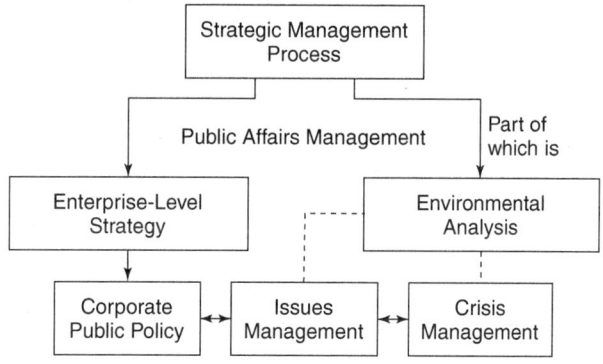

960. CORPORATE PUBLIC POLICY AND AFFAIRS

Design of the Corporate External Affairs Function and Corporate Social Performance

Miles studied the external affairs strategies (also called public affairs strategies) of major insurance firms in an effort to see what relationships existed between the strategy and design of the corporate external affairs function and corporate social performance. He found that the companies that ranked best in corporate social performance had top management philosophies that were *institution oriented*. That is, top management saw the corporation as a social institution that had a duty to adapt to a changing society and thus needed a collaborative/problem-solving external affairs strategy. The **collaborative/problem-solving strategy** was one in which firms emphasized long-term relationships with a variety of external constituencies and broad problem-solving perspectives on the resolution of social issues affecting their businesses and industries.[69]

Miles also found that the companies with the worst social performance records employed top management philosophies based on operation of the company as an independent economic franchise. Such philosophies were in sharp contrast with the institution-oriented perspectives of the best social performers. In addition, Miles found that these worst social performers employed an **individual/adversarial external affairs strategy.** In this posture, the executives denied the legitimacy of social claims on their businesses and minimized the significance of challenges they received from external critics. Therefore, they tended to be adversarial and legalistic.[70]

Business Exposure and External Affairs Design

On the subject of the external affairs units within firms, Miles found that a contingency relationship existed between what he called business exposure to the social environment and four dimensions of the external affairs design: breadth, depth, influence, and integration. High business exposure to the social environment means that the firm produces products that move them into the public arena because of such issues as their availability, affordability, reliability, and safety. In general, consumer products tend to be more exposed to the social environment than do commercial or industrial products.[71]

Breadth, depth, influence, and integration refer to dimensions of the external affairs unit that provide a measure of sophistication versus simplicity. Units that are high on these dimensions are sophisticated, whereas units low on these dimensions are simple. Miles found that firms with high business exposure to the social environment require more sophisticated units, whereas firms with low business exposure to the social environment could manage reasonably well with simple units.[72]

It is tempting to overgeneralize Miles's study, but we must note it as a significant advance in the realm of public affairs strategy and organizational design research. The important conclusion seems to be that a firm's corporate social performance (as well as its industry legitimacy and viability and economic performance) is a function of business exposure, top management philosophy, external affairs strategy, and external affairs design.

Other initiatives in public relations strategy include integrating public affairs into corporate strategic planning, using strategic management audits for public affairs, building a balanced performance scorecard for public affairs, managing the corporation's reputation, and using core competencies to manage performance.[73]

Incorporate Public Affairs Thinking Into Managers' Jobs

In today's highly specialized business world, it is easy for operating managers to let public affairs (PA) departments worry about government affairs, community relations, issues management, or any of the numerous other PA functions. David H. Blake has taken the position that organizations ought to incorporate public affairs, or what we would call *public affairs thinking,* into every operating manager's job. He argues that operating managers are vital to a successful PA function, especially if they can identify the public affairs consequences of their actions, be sensitive to the concerns of external groups, act to defuse or avoid crisis situations, and know well in advance when to seek the help of the PA experts. There are no simple ways to achieve these goals, but Blake proposes four specific strategies that may be helpful: (1) make public affairs truly relevant, (2) develop a sense of ownership of success, (3) make it easy for operating managers, and (4) show how public affairs makes a difference.[74]

Issues Management and Crisis Management

Managerial decision-making processes known as issues management and crisis management are two major ways by which business has responded to these situations. These two approaches symbolize the extent to which the environment has become turbulent and the public has become sensitized to business's responses to the issues that have emerged from this turbulence. In the ideal situation, issues management and crisis management might be seen as the natural and logical byproducts of a firm's development of enterprise-level strategy and overall corporate public policy, but this has not always been the case. Some firms have not thought seriously about public and ethical issues; for them, these approaches represent first attempts to come to grips with the practical reality of a threatening social environment.

Examples of issues include employee rights, sexual harassment, product safety, workplace safety, sweatshops, bribery and corruption, smoking in the workplace, affirmative action, and deceptive advertising.

Like all planning processes, issues management and crisis management have many characteristics in common. They also have differences and we have chosen to treat them separately for discussion purposes. One common thread that should be mentioned at the outset is that both processes are focused on improving stakeholder management and enabling the organization to be more ethically responsive to stakeholders' expectations. Issues and crisis management, to be effective, must have as their ultimate objective an increase in the organization's social responsiveness to its stakeholders. They are also related to the extent that effective issues management may enable managements to engage in more effective crisis management. That is, some crises may be anticipated and avoided through a carefully implemented issues management initiative.

Issues Management

Issues management is a process by which organizations identify issues in the stakeholder environment, analyze and prioritize those issues in terms of their relevance to the organization, plan responses to the issues, and then evaluate and monitor the results. It is helpful to think of issues management in connection with concepts such as the strategic management process, enterprise-level strategy, corporate public policy, and environmental analysis. The process of strategic management and environmental analysis requires an overall way of managerial thinking that includes economic, technological, social, and political issues. Enterprise-level strategy and corporate public policy, on the other hand, focus on public or ethical issues. Issues management, then, devolves from these broader concepts.

Two Approaches to Issues Management

Thinking about the concepts mentioned here requires us to make some distinctions. A central consideration seems to be that issues management has been thought of in two major ways: (1) narrowly, in which public, or social, issues are the primary focus; and (2) broadly, in which strategic issues and the strategic management process are the focus of attention. Liam Fahey provides a useful distinction between these two approaches. He refers to (1) the conventional approach and (2) the strategic management approach.[75] The **conventional approach** (narrowly focused) **to issues management** has the following characteristics.[76]

- Issues fall within the domain of public policy or public affairs management.
- Issues typically have a public policy/public affairs orientation or flavor.
- An issue is any trend, event, controversy, or public policy development that might affect the corporation.
- Issues originate in social/political/regulatory/judicial environments.

The **strategic management approach** (broadly inclusive) **to issues management** has evolved in a small number of companies and is typified by the following:[77]

- Issues management is typically the responsibility of senior line management or strategic planning staff.
- Issues identification is more important than it is in the conventional approach.
- Issues management is seen as an approach to the anticipation and management of external and internal challenges to the company's strategies, plans, and assumptions.

At the risk of oversimplification, we will consider the principal distinction between the two perspectives on issues management to be that the conventional approach focuses on public/social issues, whereas the strategic approach is broadly inclusive of all issues. In addition, the conventional approach can be used as a "stand alone" decision-making process, whereas the strategic approach is intimately interconnected with the strategic management process as a whole. Another difference may be whether operating managers/strategic planners or public affairs staff members are implementing the system. Beyond these distinctions, the two approaches have much in common.

The Changing Issue Mix

The emergence in the past two decades of new "company issues management groups" and "issues managers" has been a direct outgrowth of the changing mix of issues that managers have had to handle. Economic and financial issues have always been an inherent part of the business process, although their complexity seems to have increased as international markets have broadened and competitiveness has become such an important issue. The growth of technology, especially the Internet, has presented business with other issues that need to be addressed. The most dramatic growth has been in social, ethical, and political issues—all public issues that have high visibility, media appeal, and interest among special-interest stakeholder groups. We should further observe that these issues become more interrelated over time.

For most firms, social, ethical, political, and technological issues are at the same time economic issues, because firms' success in handling them frequently has a direct bearing on their financial statuses and well-being. Over time, there is a changing mix of issues and an escalating challenge that management groups face as these issues create a cumulative effect.

Issue Definition and the Issues Management Process

Before describing the issues management process, we should briefly discuss what constitutes an issue and what assumptions we are making about issues management. An issue may be thought of as a matter that is in dispute between two or more parties. The dispute typically evokes debate, controversy, or differences of opinion that need to be resolved. At some point, the organization needs to make a decision on the unresolved matter, but such a decision does not mean that the issue is resolved. Once an issue becomes public and subject to public debate and high-profile media exposure, its resolution becomes increasingly difficult. One of the features of issues, particularly those arising in the social or ethical realm, is that they are ongoing and therefore require ongoing responses.

Model of the Issues Management Process

Exhibit 900.18 presents a model of the issues management process. It contains planning aspects (identification, analysis, ranking/prioritization of issues, and formulation of responses) and implementation aspects (implementation of responses and evaluation, monitoring, and control of results). Although we will discuss the stages in the issues management process as though they were discrete, we should recognize that in reality they may be interrelated and overlap one another.

Identification of Issues

Many names have been given to the process of issue identification. At various times, the terms *social forecasting, futures research, environmental scanning,* and *public issues scanning* have been used. Similarly, many techniques have been employed. All of these approaches/techniques are similar, but each has its own unique characteristics. Common to all of them, however, is the need to scan the environment and to identify emerging issues or trends that might later be determined to have some relevance to or impact on the organization.

Issue identification, in its most rudimentary form, involves the assignment to some individual in the organization the tasks of continuously scanning a variety of publications—newspapers, magazines, specialty publications, the World

Exhibit 900.18 *A Model of the Issues Management Process*

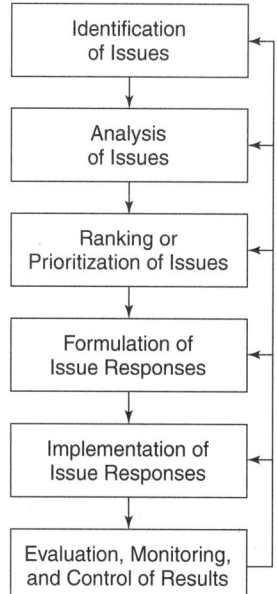

Wide Web—and developing a comprehensive list of issues. Often this same person, or group, is instructed to review public documents, records of congressional hearings, and other such sources of information. One result of this scanning is an internal report or a newsletter that is circulated throughout the organization. The next step in this evolution may be for the company to subscribe to a trend information service or newsletter that is prepared and published by a private individual or consulting firm that specializes in environmental or issue scanning.[78]

Analysis of Issues

The next two steps (analysis and ranking of issues) are closely related. To analyze an issue means to carefully study, dissect, break down, group, or engage in any specific process that helps you better understand the nature or characteristics of the issue. An analysis requires that you look beyond the obvious manifestations of the issue and strive to learn more of its history, development, current nature, and potential for future relevance to the organization. William King proposed a series of key questions that focus on stakeholder groups in attempting to analyze issues.[79]

- Who (which stakeholders) are affected by the issue?
- Who has an interest in the issue?
- Who is in a position to exert influence on the issue?
- Who has expressed opinions on the issue?
- Who ought to care about the issue?

In addition to these questions, a consulting firm—Human Resources Network—proposed the following key questions to help with issue analysis:[80]

- Who started the ball rolling? (Historical view)
- Who is now involved? (Contemporary view)
- Who will get involved? (Future view)

Answers to these questions place management in a better position to rank or prioritize the issues so that it will have a better sense of the urgency with which the issues need to be addressed.

Ranking or Prioritization of Issues

Once issues have been carefully analyzed and are well understood, it is necessary to rank them in some form of a hierarchy of importance or relevance to the organization. We should note that some issues management systems place this step before analysis. This is done especially when it is desired to screen out those issues that are obviously not relevant and deserving of further analysis.

The prioritization stage may range from a simple grouping of issues into categories of urgency to a more elaborate or sophisticated scoring system. Two examples will serve to illustrate the grouping technique. **Xerox** has used a process of categorizing issues into three classifications: (1) *high priority* (issues on which management must be well informed), (2) *nice to know* (issues that are interesting but not critical or urgent), and (3) *questionable* (issues that may not be issues at all unless something else happens). **PPG Industries** has grouped issues into three priorities: *Priority A* (critical issues that warrant executive action and review), *Priority B* (issues that warrant surveillance by the division general manager or staff), and *Priority C* (issues that have only potential impact and warrant monitoring by the public affairs department).[81]

A somewhat more sophisticated approach uses a **probability-impact matrix** requiring management to assess the *probability of occurrence of an issue* (high, medium, or low) on one dimension and its *impact on the company* (high, medium, or low) on the other dimension. In using such an approach, management would place each issue in the appropriate cell of the matrix, and the completed matrix would then serve as an aid to prioritization. As a variation on this theme, management could rank issues by considering the mathematical product of each issue's impact (for example, on a scale from 1 to 10) and probability of occurrence (on a scale from 0 to 10).

William R. King has provided a somewhat more elaborate issues-ranking scheme. He recommends that issues be screened on five filter criteria: strategy, relevance, actionability, criticality, and urgency.[82] Once each issue has been scored on a 10-point scale on each criterion, issues are then ranked according to their resulting point totals. In addition to this filtering/ranking process, other techniques that have been used in issues identification, analysis, and prioritization include polls/surveys, expert panels, content analysis, the Delphi technique, trend extrapolation, scenario building, and the use of precursor events or bellwethers.[83]

Earlier we described a simple issues identification process as involving an individual in the organization or a subscription to a newsletter or trend-spotting service. The analysis and ranking stages could be done by an individual, but more often the company has moved up to a next stage of formalization. This next stage involves assignment of the issues management function to a team, often as part of a public affairs department, which begins to specialize in the issues management function. This group of specialists can provide a wide range of issues management activities, depending on the commitment of the company to the process.

Formulation and Implementation of Responses to Issues

We should observe that the formulation and implementation stages in the issues management process are quite similar to the corresponding stages pertained to the strategic management process as a whole.

Formulation in this case refers to the response design process. Based on the analysis conducted, companies can then identify options that might be pursued in dealing with the issues, in making decisions, and in implementing those decisions. Strategy formulation refers not only to the formulation of the actions that the firm intends to take but also to the creation of the overall strategy, or degree of aggressiveness, employed in carrying out those actions. Options might include aggressive pursuit, gradual pursuit, or selective pursuit of goals, plans, processes, or programs.[84] All of these more detailed plans are part of the strategy formulation process.

Once plans for dealing with issues have been formulated, implementation becomes the focus. There are many organizational aspects that need to be addressed in the implementation process. Some of these include the clarity of the plan itself, resources needed to implement the plan, top management support, organizational structure, technical competence, and timing.[85]

Social Audit Versus Stakeholder Audit

- The social audit is a systematic attempt to identify, measure, monitor, and evaluate an organization's performance with respect to its social efforts, goals, and programs.

- The stakeholder audit is a systematic attempt to identify and measure an organization's stakeholder's issues and measure and evaluate their opinions with respect to its effective resolution.

Evaluation, Monitoring, and Control of Issues

These recognizable steps in the issues management process were also treated as steps in the strategic management process. In the present context, they mean that companies should continually evaluate the results of their responses to the issues and ensure that these actions are kept on track. In particular, this stage requires careful monitoring of stakeholders' opinions. A form of stakeholder audit—something derivative of the social audit—might be used. The information that is gathered during this final stage in the issues management process is then fed back to the earlier stages in the process so that changes or adjustments might be made as needed. Evaluation information may be useful at each stage in the process.

We have presented the issues management process as a complete system. In actual practice, companies apply the stages in various degrees of formality or informality as needed or desired. For example, because issues management is more important in some situations than in others, some stages of the process may be truncated to meet the needs of different firms in different industries. In addition, some firms are more committed to issues management than others.

Issues Development Process

A vital attribute of issues management is that issues tend to develop according to an evolutionary pattern. This pattern might be thought of as a developmental or growth process or, as some have called it, a life cycle. It is important for managers to have some appreciation of this **issues development process** so that they can recognize when an event or trend is becoming an issue and also because it might affect the strategy that the firm employs in dealing with the issue. Companies may take a variety of courses of action depending on the stage of the issue in the process. Exhibit 900.19 presents a simplified view of the issue development life cycle process.

We should note that the stages in the process, especially the early stages, might occur in a different sequence or in an iterative pattern. Further, not all issues complete the process; some are resolved before they reach the stage of legislation or regulation.

Finally, we are reminded by Bigelow, Fahey, and Mahon that "issues do not necessarily follow a linear, sequential path, but instead follow paths that reflect the intensity and diversity of the values and interests stakeholders bring to an issue and the complexity of the interaction among . . ." all the variables.[86] This should serve as a warning not to oversimplify the issues development process.

Issues Management in Practice

Issues management in practice today has very much become a subset of activities performed by the public affairs departments of major corporations. A late 1990s survey of corporate public affairs officers of major corporations revealed that 67% engage in issues management functions. Furthermore, the survey revealed that there is now greater use of interdepartmental issues teams, with the public affairs department serving as coordinator and strategist but with appropriate line and staff executives charged with ultimate accountability for implementation. In practice, there-

Exhibit 900.19 *Issue Development Life Cycle Process*

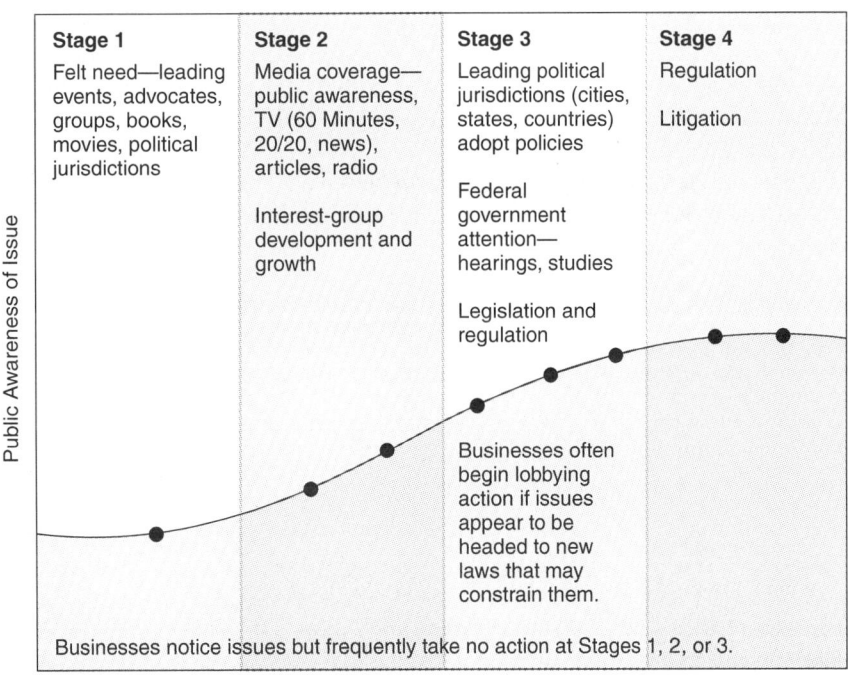

fore, it can be seen that issues management does not function as a stand alone activity but has been subsumed into a host of functions for which modern public affairs departments take responsibility.[87]

Issues management faces a serious challenge in business today. From the standpoint of the turbulence in the stakeholder environment, issues management may be needed. To become a permanent part of the organization, however, issues management will have to continuously prove itself. We can talk conceptually about the process with ease, but the field still remains somewhat nebulous even though it is struggling to become more scientific and legitimate. Managers in the real world want results, and if issues management cannot deliver those results, it will be destined to failure as a management process.

Issues Management Is a Bridge to Crisis Management

Ideally, firms use issues management to assist them in planning for and preventing crises that then require crisis management. Issues management represents careful planning that may head off impending crises. This is because many crises are embedded in issues or erupt from issues that could have been anticipated and studied in carefully designed issues management processes. Issues management can be seen as a form of precrisis planning. It is intended to help organizations anticipate and plan for possible crisis eruptions. Not all crises can be planned for, of course, but many can be anticipated through effective issues management programs. It has been suggested by Kate Miller that one of the most effective ways for keeping a crisis plan "living" is issues management.[88] Thus, we can see how issues and crisis management are different, but related.

Crisis Management

Issues typically evolve gradually over a period of time. Issues management is a process of identifying and preparing to respond to potential issues. Crises, on the other hand, occur abruptly. They cannot always be anticipated or forecast. Some crises occur within an issue category considered; many do not. Issues and crisis management are related, however, in that they both are concerned about organizations becoming prepared for uncertainty in the stakeholder environment.

The Nature of Crises

There are many kinds of crises. Hurt or killed customers, hurt employees, injured stockholders, and unfair practices are the concerns of modern crisis management. Not all crises involve such public or ethical issues, but these kinds of crises almost always ensure front-page status. Major companies can be seriously damaged by such episodes, especially if the episodes are poorly handled. Very quickly, they achieve a high-visibility status.

What is a crisis? Dictionaries state that a crisis is a "turning point for better or worse," an "emotionally significant event," or a "decisive moment." We all think of crises as being emotion charged, but we do not always think of them as turning points for better or for worse. The implication here is that a crisis is a decisive moment that, if managed one way, could make things worse but, if managed another way, could make things better. Choice is present, and how the crisis is managed can make a difference.

From a managerial point of view, a line needs to be drawn between a problem and a crisis. Problems, of course, are common in business. A crisis, however, is not as common. A useful way to think about a **crisis** is with a definition set forth by Laurence Barton:

> A crisis is a major, unpredictable event that has potentially negative results. The event and its aftermath may significantly damage an organization and its employees, products, services, financial condition, and reputation.[89]

Another definition set forth by Pearson and Clair is also helpful in understanding the critical aspects of a crisis:

> An organizational crisis is a low-probability, high-impact event that threatens the viability of the organization and is characterized by ambiguity of cause, effect, and means of resolution, as well as by a belief that decisions must be made swiftly.[90]

Types of Crises

Situations in which the executives surveyed by Steven Fink felt they were vulnerable to crises included industrial accidents, environmental problems, union problems/strikes, product recalls, investor relations, hostile takeovers, proxy fights, rumors/media leaks, government regulatory problems, acts of terrorism, and embezzlement.[91] Other common crises include product tampering, executive kidnapping, work-related homicides, malicious rumors, terrorism, and natural disasters that destroy corporate offices or information bases.[92]

Mitroff and Anagnos (2001) have suggested that crises may be categorized according to the following types of crises.[93]

Economic. Labor strikes, market crashes, major declines in earnings

Informational. Loss of proprietary information, false information, tampering with computer records

Human resource. Loss of key executives, personnel or workplace violence

Reputational. Slander, tampering with corporate logos

Psychopathic. Product tampering, kidnapping, hostage taking

Natural. Earthquakes, fire, tornadoes

Of the major crises that have recently occurred, the majority of the companies reported the following outcomes: The crises escalated in intensity, were subjected to media and government scrutiny, interfered with normal business operations, and damaged the company's bottom line.

Four Crisis Stages

There are a number of ways we could categorize the stages through which a crisis may progress. According to Steven Fink, a crisis may consist of as many as four distinct stages: (1) a **prodromal crisis stage,** (2) an **acute crisis stage,** (3) a **chronic crisis stage,** and (4) a **crisis resolution stage.**[94]

Prodromal Crisis Stage. This is the warning stage. ("Prodromal" is a medical term that refers to a previous notice or warning.) This warning stage could also be thought of as a symptom stage. Although it could be called a "precrisis" stage, this presupposes that one knows that a crisis is coming. According to Mitroff and Anagnos, crises "send out a repeated trail of early warning signals" that managers can learn to recognize.[95] Perhaps management should adopt this perspective: Watch each situation with the thought that it could be a crisis in the making. Early symptoms may be quite obvious, such as in the case where a social activist group tells management it will boycott the company if a certain problem is not addressed. On the other hand, symptoms may be more subtle, as in the case where defect rates for a particular product a company makes start edging up over time.

Acute Crisis Stage. This is the stage at which the crisis actually occurs. There is no turning back; the incident has occurred. Damage has been done at this point, and it is now up to management to handle or contain the damage. If the prodromal stage is the precrisis stage, the acute stage is the actual crisis stage. The crucial decision point at which things may get worse or better has been reached.

Chronic Crisis Stage. This is the lingering period. It may be the period of investigations, audits, or in-depth news stories. Management may see it as a period of recovery, self-analysis, or self-doubt. In Fink's survey of major companies, he found that crises tended to linger as much as two and a half times longer in firms without crisis management plans than in firms with such plans.

Crisis Resolution Stage. This is the final stage—the goal of all crisis management efforts. Fink argues that when an early warning sign of a crisis is noted, the manager should seize control swiftly and determine the most direct and expedient route to resolution. If the warning signs are missed in the first stage, the goal is to speed up all phases and reach the final stage as soon as possible.

Exhibit 900.20 presents one way in which these four stages might be depicted. It should be noted that the phases may overlap and that each phase varies in intensity and duration. It is hoped that management will learn from the crisis and thus will be better prepared for, and better able to handle, any future crisis.

Other views of crises and crisis management may be taken. Gerald C. Meyers, former chairman of **American Motors Corporation** and a consultant on crisis management, and others lay out the scenario for a *poorly managed crisis,* which typically follows a predictable pattern.[96] The pattern is as follows.

- Early indications that trouble is brewing occur.
- Warnings are ignored/played down.
- Warnings build to a climax.
- Pressure mounts.

Exhibit 900.20   *Fink's Four Stages in a Management Crisis*

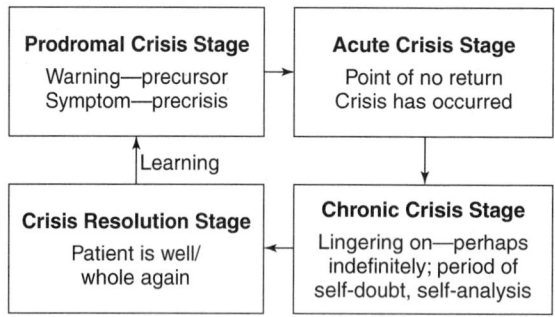

- Executives are often overwhelmed or can't cope effectively.
- Quick-fix alternatives look appealing. Hasty moves create trouble.
- Clamming-up versus opening-up options present themselves.
- Most firms choose the former.
- A siege mentality prevails.

Visualizing the attributes or pattern of a poorly managed crisis is valuable because it illustrates how not to do it—a lesson that many managers may find quite valuable.

Managing Business Crises

Business Week's Five Practical Steps in Managing Crises

A more complete view of crisis management holds that a series of five steps must be taken. These five steps, synthesized by *Business Week* magazine from the actual experiences of companies experiencing crises, are discussed next and are summarized in Exhibit 900.21.[97]

FIRST: IDENTIFYING AREAS OF VULNERABILITY   In this first step, some areas of vulnerability are obvious, such as potential chemical spills, whereas others are more subtle. The key seems to be in developing a greater consciousness of how things can go wrong and get out of hand. At **Heinz**, after the "Tunagate" incident, a vice president set up brainstorming sessions. He said, "We're brainstorming about how we would be affected by everything from a competitor who had a serious quality problem to a scandal involving a Heinz executive."[98]

SECOND: DEVELOPING A PLAN FOR DEALING WITH THREATS   A plan for dealing with the most serious crisis threats is a logical next step. One of the most crucial issues is communications planning. After a **Dow Chemical** railroad car derailed near Toronto, forcing the evacuation of 250,000 people, Dow Canada prepared information kits on the hazards of its products so that executives would be knowledgeable enough to respond properly if a similar crisis were to arise in the future. Dow Canada also trained executives in interviewing techniques. This effort paid off several years later when an accident caused a chemical spill into a river that supplied drinking water for several nearby towns. The company's emergency response team arrived at the site almost immediately and established a press center that distributed information about the chemicals. In addition, the company recruited a neutral expert to speak on the hazards and how to deal with them. Officials praised Dow for its handling of this crisis.[99]

Richard J. Mahoney, former CEO of **Monsanto Company**, has offered the following *ten "Rs" for the effective handling of public policy crises*. He recommends these steps as part of an overall crisis plan.[100]

- Respond early.
- Recruit a credible spokesperson.
- Reply truthfully.
- Respect the opposition's concerns.
- Revisit the issue with follow-up.
- Retreat early if it's a loser.

Exhibit 900.21 *Business Week's Five Steps in Crisis Management*

1. Identifying areas of vulnerability
   A. Obvious areas
   B. Subtle areas
2. Developing a plan for dealing with threats
   A. Communications planning is vital
   B. Training executives in product dangers and dealing with media
3. Forming crisis teams
   A. Vital to successful crisis management
   B. Identifying executives who can work well under stress
4. Simulating crisis drills
   A. Experience/practice is helpful
   B. "War rooms" serve as gathering places for team members
5. Learning from experience
   A. Assess effectiveness of crisis strategies
   B. Move from reaction to proaction

- Redouble efforts early if it's a critical company issue.
- Reply with visible top management.
- Refuse to press for what is not good public policy.
- Repeat the prior statement regularly.

Some of these steps may not apply to every crisis situation, but many may be useful as part of a crisis management plan. Mahoney notes that getting an entire organization trained to deal with crises is difficult and expensive, but he paraphrases what a car repairman said in a TV commercial: "You can pay now or pay a lot more later." Mahoney thinks that now is infinitely better for everyone.[101]

THIRD: FORMING CRISIS TEAMS   Another step that can be taken as part of an overall planning effort is the formation of **crisis teams.** Such teams have played key roles in many well-managed disasters. A good example is the team formed at **Procter & Gamble** when its Rely tampon products were linked with the dreaded disease toxic shock syndrome. The team was quickly assembled, a vice president was appointed to head it, and after one week the decision was made to remove Rely from marketplace shelves. The quick action earned the firm praise, and it paid off for P&G in the long run.

Another task in assembling crisis teams is identifying managers who can cope effectively with stress. Not every executive can handle the fast-moving, high-pressured, ambiguous decision environment that is created by a crisis, and early identification of executives who can is important. We should also note that it is not always the CEO who can best perform in such a crisis atmosphere.

Despite the careful use of crisis teams, crises can often overwhelm a carefully constructed plan. When **ValuJet's** Flight 592 crashed in the Florida Everglades in 1996, for example, ValuJet flawlessly executed a three-pronged, team-based crisis management plan calling for the company to (1) show compassion, (2) take responsibility, and (3) demonstrate that the airline learned from the crisis. Experts have said that the company handled the crisis well. However, a close look at the tragedy revealed that a series of complicating factors turned the crisis into something even more difficult than a well-scripted, perfectly executed crisis management plan could handle.[102]

FOURTH: SIMULATING CRISIS DRILLS   Some companies have gone so far as to run crisis drills in which highly stressful situations are simulated so that managers can "practice" what they might do in a real crisis. As a basis for conducting crisis drills and experiential exercises, a number of companies have adopted a software package known as Crisis Plan wRiter. This software allows companies to centralize and maintain up-to-date crisis management information and allows company leaders to assign responsibilities to their crisis team, target key audiences, identify and monitor potential issues, and create crisis-response processes.[103]

FIFTH: LEARNING FROM EXPERIENCE   The final stage in crisis management is learning from experience. At this point, managers need to ask themselves exactly what they have learned from past crises and how that knowledge can be used to advantage in the future. Part of this stage entails an assessment of the effectiveness of the firm's crisis-handling strategies and identification of areas where improvements in capabilities need to be made. Without a crisis management system of some kind in place, the organization will find itself reacting to crises after they have occurred. If learning and preparation for the future are occurring, however, the firm may engage in more proactive behavior.[104]

Augustine's Six Stages of Crisis Management

As an alternative to the previous steps in crisis management, Norman Augustine, former president of Lockheed Martin Corporation, distinguished among six stages of crisis management. To some extent, these overlap and embrace the steps, but it is useful to see an alternative conceptualization of the steps that should be taken in crisis management. Augustine's list begins with the idea that the crisis should be avoided.[105]

- Stage 1: Avoiding the Crisis
- Stage 2: Preparing to Manage the Crisis
- Stage 3: Recognizing the Crisis
- Stage 4: Containing the Crisis
- Stage 5: Resolving the Crisis
- Stage 6: Profiting from the Crisis

We should note that Pearson and Mitroff have accurately observed that effective crisis management requires a program that is tailored to a firm's specific industry, business environment, and crisis management experience. Effective crisis managers will understand that there are major crisis management factors that may vary from situation to situation, such as the type of crisis (for example, natural disaster or human induced), the phase of the crisis, the systems affected (for example, humans, technology, culture), and the stakeholders affected. Managers cannot eliminate crises. However, they can become keenly aware of their vulnerabilities and make concerted efforts to understand and reduce these vulnerabilities through continuous crisis management programs.[106]

Crisis Communications

An illustration of crisis management without effective communications occurred during the **Jack in the Box** hamburger disaster of 1993. There was an outbreak of E. coli bacteria in the Pacific Northwest area, resulting in the deaths of four children. Following this crisis, the parent company, San Diego-based **Foodmaker**, entered a downward spiral after lawsuits by the families of victims enraged the public and franchises. Foodmaker did most of the right things and did them quickly. The company immediately suspended hamburger sales, recalled suspect meat from its distribution system, increased cooking time for all foods, pledged to pay for all the medical costs related to the disaster, and hired a food safety expert to design a new food-handling system. But, it forgot to do one thing: communicate with the public, including its own employees.[107]

The company's **crisis communications** efforts were inept. It waited a week before accepting any responsibility for the tragedy, preferring to point fingers at its meat supplier and even the Washington state health officials for not explaining the state's new guidelines for cooking hamburgers at higher temperatures. The media pounced on the company. The company was blasted for years even though within the company it was taking the proper steps to correct the problem. The company suffered severe financial losses, and it took at least six years before the company really felt it was on the road to recovery. "The crisis," as it is still called around company headquarters, taught the firm an important lesson. CEO Robert Nugent was quoted as saying in 1999, "Nobody wants to deal with their worst nightmare, but we should have recognized you've got to communicate."[108]

Virtually all crisis management plans call for effective crisis communications. There are a number of different stakeholder groups with whom effective communications are critical, especially the media and those immediately affected by the crisis. Many companies have failed to successfully manage their crises because of inadequate or failed communications with key stakeholder groups. Successful communications efforts are crucial to effective crisis management. It is axiomatic that *prepared* communications will be more helpful than *reactive* communications. Jonathan L. Bernstein has offered **ten steps of crisis communication** that are worth summarizing.[109]

1. Identify your crisis communications team.
2. Identify key spokespersons who will be authorized to speak for the organization.
3. Train your spokespersons.
4. Establish communications protocols.
5. Identify and know your audience.
6. Anticipate crises.
7. Assess the crisis situation.
8. Identify key messages you will communicate to key groups.

9. Decide on communications methods.
10. Be prepared to ride out the storm.

A brief elaboration on the importance of identifying key messages that will be communicated to key groups is useful (point 8). It is important that you communicate with your *internal stakeholders* first because rumors are often started there, and uninformed employees can do great damage to a successful crisis management effort. Internal stakeholders are your best advocates and can be supportive during a crisis. Prepare news releases that contain as much information as possible and get this information out to all *media outlets* at the same time. Communicate with *others in the community* who have a need to know, such as public officials, disaster coordinators, stakeholders and others. *Uniformity of response* is of vital importance during a crisis. Finally, have a designated "release authority" for information (point 2). The first 24 hours of a crisis can make or break the organization, and how these key spokespersons work is of vital importance to handling the crisis.[110]

Mitroff and Anagnos have stressed the importance of "telling the truth" in effective crisis communications. They argue that there are no secrets in today's society and that eventually the truth will get out. Therefore, from a practical point of view, the question is not whether the truth will be revealed but rather when that truth will become public and under what circumstances.[111] From both an ethical and a practical perspective, truth-telling is an important facet of crisis communications.

Corporate Ethics and Management Assurance

The scope of corporate ethics includes business ethics and management ethics.

Business Ethics

To understand business ethics, it is useful to comment on the relationship between ethics and morality. **Ethics** is the discipline that deals with what is good and bad and with moral duty and obligation. Ethics can also be regarded as a set of moral principles or values. **Morality** is a doctrine or system of moral conduct. Moral conduct refers to that which relates to principles of right and wrong in behavior. For the most part, then, we can think of ethics and morality as being so similar to one another that we may use the terms interchangeably to refer to the study of fairness, justice, and right and wrong behavior in business.

Business ethics, therefore, is concerned with good and bad or right and wrong behavior and practices that take place within a business context. Concepts of right and wrong are increasingly being interpreted today to include the more difficult and subtle questions of fairness, justice, and equity.

Two key branches of moral philosophy, or ethics, are descriptive ethics and normative ethics. It is important to distinguish between the two because they each take a different perspective. **Descriptive ethics** is concerned with describing, characterizing, and studying the morality of a people, a culture, or a society. It also compares and contrasts different moral codes, systems, practices, beliefs, and values.[112] In descriptive business ethics, therefore, our focus is on learning what is occurring in the realm of behavior, actions, decisions, policies, and practices of business firms, managers, or, perhaps, specific industries. The public opinion polls give us glimpses of descriptive ethics—what people believe to be going on based on their perceptions and understandings. Descriptive ethics focuses on "what is" the prevailing set of ethical standards in the business community, specific organizations, or on the part of specific managers. A real danger in limiting our attention to descriptive ethics is that some people may adopt the view that "if everyone is doing it," it must be acceptable. For example, if a survey reveals that 70% of employees are padding their expense accounts, this describes what is taking place but it does not describe what *should* be taking place. Just because many are participating in this questionable activity doesn't make it an appropriate practice. This is why normative ethics is important.

Normative ethics, by contrast, is concerned with supplying and justifying a coherent moral system of thinking and judging. Normative ethics seeks to uncover, develop, and justify basic moral principles that are intended to guide behavior, actions, and decisions.[113] Normative business ethics, therefore, seeks to propose some principle or principles for distinguishing ethical from unethical in the business context. It deals more with "what ought to be" or "what ought not to be" in terms of business practices. Normative ethics is concerned with establishing norms or standards by which business practices might be guided or judged.

In our study of business ethics, we need to be ever mindful of this distinction between descriptive and normative perspectives. It is tempting to observe the prevalence of a particular practice in business (for example, discrimination or deceptive advertising) and conclude that because so many are doing it (descriptive ethics), it must be acceptable behavior. Normative ethics would insist that a practice be justified on the basis of some ethical principle, argument, or rationale before being considered acceptable. Normative ethics demands a more meaningful moral anchor than just "everyone is doing it." Normative ethics is our primary frame of reference in this discussion, though we will frequently compare "what ought to be" with "what is (going on in the real world)."

We will introduce three major approaches to thinking about business ethics.

1. Conventional approach
2. Principles approach
3. Ethical tests approach

We will focus on the conventional approach to business ethics in this section and the other two approaches are briefly mentioned here.

The principles approach to ethics or ethical decision making is based on the idea that managers may desire to anchor their decisions on a more solid foundation than the conventional approach to ethics. A principle of business ethics is a concept, guideline, or rule that, if applied when faced with an ethical dilemma, will assist an individual in making an ethical decision. The principles approach augments the conventional approach. Examples of major principles include utilitarianism, rights, justice, caring, virtue ethics, servant leadership, and the golden rule.

The ethical tests approach is based on practice while the principles approach is based on philosophy. No single test is recommended as a universal answer; instead a combination will be useful. Examples of tests include common sense, one's best self, making something public, ventilation, purified idea, and gag test.

The Conventional Approach to Business Ethics

The **conventional approach to business ethics** is essentially an approach whereby we compare a decision or practice with prevailing norms of acceptability. We call it the conventional approach because it is believed that this is the way that general society thinks. The major challenge of this approach is answering the questions "Whose norms do we use?" in making the judgment, and "What norms are prevailing?" This approach may be depicted by highlighting the major variables to be compared with one another:

Decision or Practice ↔ Prevailing Norms of Acceptability

There is considerable room for variability on both of these issues. With respect to whose norms are used as the basis for ethical judgments, the conventional approach would consider as legitimate those norms emanating from family, friends, religious beliefs, the local community, one's employer, law, the profession, and so on. In addition, one's conscience, or the individual, would be seen by many as a legitimate source of ethical norms.

Exhibit 900.22 illustrates some of the sources of norms that come to bear on the individual and that might be used in various circumstances, and over time, under the conventional approach. These sources compete in their influence on what constitutes the "prevailing norms of acceptability" for today.

Exhibit 900.22 *Sources of Ethical Norms Communicated to Individuals*

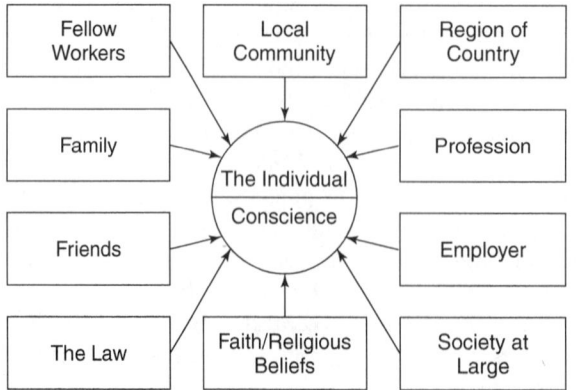

In many circumstances, the conventional approach to ethics may be useful and applicable. What does a person do, however, if norms from one source conflict with norms from another source? Also, how can we be sure that societal norms are really appropriate or defensible? Our society's culture sends us many and often conflicting messages about what is appropriate behavior. We get these messages from television, movies, music, and other sources in the culture.

Ethics and the Law

We have made various references to ethics and the law. We said that ethical behavior is typically thought to reside above behavior required by the law. This is the generally accepted view of ethics. We should make it clear, however, that in many respects the law and ethics overlap. To appreciate this, you need to recognize that the law embodies notions of ethics. That is, the law may be seen as a reflection of what society thinks are minimal standards of conduct and behavior. Both law and ethics have to do with what is deemed appropriate or acceptable, but law reflects society's *codified* ethics. Therefore, if a person breaks a law or violates a regulation, she or he is also behaving unethically. In spite of this overlap, we continue to talk about desirable ethical behavior as behavior that extends beyond what is required by law. Viewed from the standpoint of minimums, we would certainly say that obedience to the law is generally regarded to be a minimum standard of behavior.

In addition, we should make note of the fact that the law does not address all realms in which ethical questions might be raised. Thus, there are clear roles for both law and ethics to play. It should be noted that research on illegal corporate behavior has been conducted for some time. Illegal corporate behavior, of course, comprises business practices that are in direct defiance of law or public policy. Research has focused on two dominant questions: (1) Why do firms behave illegally or what leads them to engage in illegal activities, and (2) what are the consequences of behaving illegally?[114]

Making Ethical Judgments

When a decision is made about what is ethical (right, just, fair) using the conventional approach, there is room for variability on several counts (see Exhibit 900.23). Three key elements compose such a decision. First, we observe the *decision, action,* or *practice* that has been committed. Second, we *compare the practice with prevailing norms of acceptability*—that is, society's or some other standard of what is acceptable or unacceptable. Third, *we must recognize that value judgments are being made* by someone as to what really occurred (the actual behavior) and what the prevailing norms of acceptability really are. This means that two different people could look at the same behavior, compare it with their concepts of what the prevailing norms are, and reach different conclusions as to whether the behavior was ethical or not. This becomes quite complex as perceptions of what is ethical inevitably lead to the difficult task of ranking different values against one another.

If we can put aside for a moment the fact that perceptual differences about an incident do exist, and the fact that we differ among ourselves because of our personal values and philosophies of right and wrong, we are still left with the problematic task of determining society's prevailing norms of acceptability of business behavior. As a whole, members of society generally agree at a very high level of abstraction that certain behaviors are wrong. However, the consensus tends to disintegrate as we move from the general to specific situations.

The conventional approach to business ethics can be valuable, because we all need to be aware of and sensitive to the total environment in which we exist. We need to be aware of how society regards ethical issues. It has limitations, however, and we need to be cognizant of these as well. The most serious danger is that of falling into an **ethical relativism** where we pick and choose which source of norms we wish to use based on what will justify our current actions or maximize our freedom.

Exhibit 900.23 *Making Ethical Judgments*

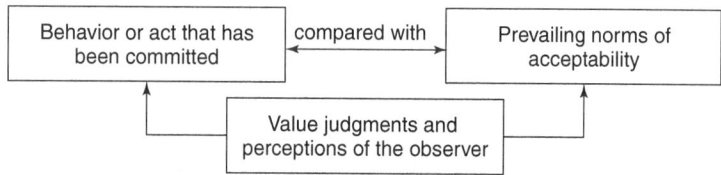

Exhibit 900.24 *A Venn Diagram Model for Ethical Decision Making*

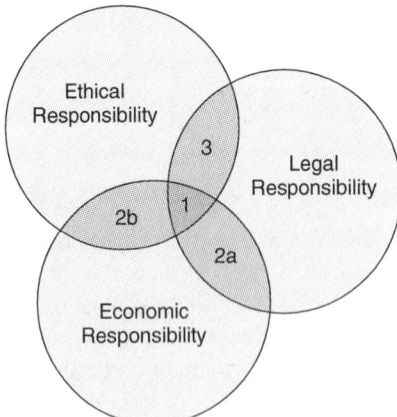

Area 1 —
Profitable, legal, ethical:
Go for it!

Area 2a —
Profitable and legal.
Proceed cautiously.

Area 2b —
Profitable and ethical. Probably legal, too.
Proceed cautiously.

Area 3 —
Legal and ethical but
not profitable. Find ways
to seek profitability.

Ethics, Economics, and Law: A Venn Diagram Model

When we focus on ethics and ethical decision making, it is useful to consider the primary forces that come into tension while making ethical judgments. When we are discussing a firm's corporate social responsibility (CSR), philanthropy definitely enters the discussion. This is because philanthropic initiatives are the primary way many companies display their CSR in the community—through good and charitable works. In ethical decision making, however, we tend to set aside philanthropic expectations and focus on ethical expectations and, especially, those forces that primarily come into tension with ethics—economics (the quest for profits) and law. Thus, in most decision-making situations, ethics, economics, and law become the central expectations that must be considered and balanced against each other in the quest to make wise decisions.

A firm's economic, legal, and ethical responsibilities can be depicted in a Venn diagram model illustrating how certain actions, decisions, or policies fulfill one, two, or three of these responsibility categories. Exhibit 900.24 presents this Venn diagram model, illustrating the overlapping potential of these responsibility categories.

In Area 1, where the decision, action, or practice fulfills all three responsibilities, the management prescription is to "go for it." That is, the action is profitable, in compliance with the law, and represents ethical behavior. In Area 2a, the action under consideration is profitable and legal, but its ethical status may be uncertain. The guideline here is to "proceed cautiously." In these kinds of situations, the ethics of the action needs to be carefully considered. In Area 2b, the action is profitable and ethical, but perhaps the law does not clearly address the issue or is ambiguous. If it is ethical, there is a good chance it is also legal, but the guideline again is to proceed cautiously. In Area 3, the action is legal and ethical but not profitable. Therefore, the strategy here would be to avoid this action or find ways to make it profitable. However, there may be a compelling case to take the action if it is legal and ethical and, thus, represents the right thing to do. Mark Schwartz has agreed that the four-part CSR model can appropriately be recast into a Venn model, especially for ethical analysis.[115]

By taking philanthropy out of the picture, the ethics Venn model serves as a useful template for thinking about the more immediate expectations that society has on business in a situation in which the ethical dimension plays an important role.

Four Important Ethics Questions

It is also useful to provide some additional "big picture" perspectives that could legitimately be asked of ethics, in general, or of business ethics, in particular. Philosophers have concepts and terminology that are more academic, but let us approach this broad perspective, as Otto Bremer has done,[116] by starting with four apparently simple but really different kinds of questions:

1. What really is?
2. What ought to be?
3. How do we get from what is to what ought to be?
4. What is our motivation in all this?

These four questions capture the core of what ethics is all about. They force an examination of *what really is* (descriptive ethics) going on in a business situation, *what ought to be* (normative ethics), how we *close the gap* between what is and what ought to be (practical question), and what our *motivation* is for doing all this.

Before we discuss each question briefly, let us suggest that these four questions may be asked at five different levels: the level of the individual (the personal level), the level of the organization, the level of the industry or profession, the societal level, and the global or international level. By asking and then answering these questions, a greater understanding of a business ethics dilemma may be achieved.

What Really Is?

The "what really is?" question forces us to face the reality of what is actually going on in an ethical sense in business or in a specific decision or practice. Ideally it is a factual, scientific, or descriptive question. Its purpose is to help us understand the reality of the ethical behavior we find before us in the business environment. As we discussed earlier when we were describing the nature of making ethical judgments, it is not always simple to state exactly what the "real" situation is. This is because we are humans and thus make mistakes when we "sense" what is happening. Also, we are conditioned by our personal beliefs, values, and biases, and these factors affect what we see or sense. Or, we may perceive real conditions for what they are but fail to think in terms of alternatives or in terms of "what ought to be." Think of the difficulty you might have in attempting to describe "what really is" with respect to business ethics at the personal, organizational, industry/professional, societal, or global levels. The questions then become:

- What are your personal ethics?
- What are your organization's ethics?
- What are the ethics of your industry or profession?
- What are society's ethics?
- What are global ethics?

What Ought to Be?

This second question is quite different from the first question. It is normative rather than descriptive. It is certainly not a scientific question. The "what ought to be?" question seldom gets answered directly, particularly in a managerial setting. Managers are used to identifying alternatives and choosing the best one, but seldom is this done with questions that entail moral content or the "rightness, fairness, or justice" of a decision. The "ought to be" question is often viewed in terms of what management *should* do (in an ethical sense) in a given situation. Examples of this question in a business setting might be the following.

- How *ought* we treat our aging employees whose productivity is declining?
- How safe *ought* we make this product, knowing full well we cannot pass all the costs on to the consumer?
- How clean an environment *should* we aim for?
- How *should* we treat long-time employees when the company is downsizing or moving the plant to a foreign country?

How Do We Get From What Is to What Ought to Be?

This third question represents the challenge of bridging the gap between where we are and where we ought to be with respect to ethical practices. Therefore, it represents an action dimension. We may discuss endlessly where we "ought" to be in terms of our own personal ethics or the ethics of our firm, of our industry, or of society. As we move further away from the individual level, we have less control or influence over the "ought to be" question.

When faced with these ideas as depicted by our "ought to be" questions, we may find that from a practical point of view we cannot achieve our ideals. This does not mean we should not have asked the question in the first place. Our "ought to be" questions become goals or objectives for our ethical practices. They form the normative core of business ethics. They become moral benchmarks that help us to measure progress.

This is also the stage at which managerial decision making and strategy come into play. The first step in managerial problem solving is identifying the problem (what "is"). Next comes identifying where we want to be (the "ought" question). Then comes the managerial challenge of closing the gap. "Gap analysis" sets the stage for concrete business action.

What Is Our Motivation in All This?

Pragmatic businesspeople do not like to dwell on this fourth question, which addresses the motivation for being ethical, because sometimes it reveals some manipulative or self-centered motive. At one level, is it perhaps not desirable to discuss motivation, because isn't it really actions that count?

Although we would like to believe that managers are appropriately motivated in their quest for ethical business behavior and that motivations are important, we must continue to understand and accept Andrew Stark's observation that we live in a "messy world of mixed motives." Therefore, managers do not typically have the luxury of making abstract distinctions between altruism and self-interest but must get on with the task of designing structures, systems, incentives, and processes that accommodate the "whole" employee, regardless of motivations.[117]

Management Ethics

Three Models of Management Ethics

In attempting to understand the basic concepts of business ethics, it is useful to think in terms of key ethical models that might describe different types of management ethics found in the organizational world.[118] These models should provide some useful base points for discussion and comparison. The media have focused so much on immoral or unethical business behavior that it is easy to forget or not think about the possibility of other ethical styles or types. For example, scant attention has been given to the distinction that may be made between those activities that are *immoral* and those that are *amoral;* similarly, little attention has been given to contrasting these two forms of behavior with ethical or *moral* management.

Believing that there is value in developing descriptive models for purposes of clearer understanding, here we will describe, compare, and contrast three models or types of ethical management.

1. Immoral management
2. Moral management
3. Amoral management

Let us consider the two extremes first—immoral and moral management—and then amoral management, as depicted below.

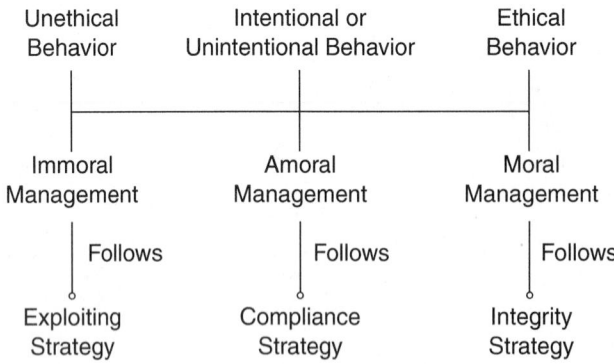

Immoral Management

Using *immoral* and *unethical* as synonyms, **immoral management** is defined as a posture that not only is devoid of ethical principles or precepts but also implies a positive and active opposition to what is ethical. Immoral management decisions, behaviors, actions, and practices are discordant with ethical principles. This model holds that management's motives are selfish and that it cares only or principally about its own or its company's gains. If management's activity is actively opposed to what is regarded as ethical, this suggests that management knows right from wrong and yet chooses to do wrong. Thus, its motives are deemed greedy or selfish. According to this model, management's goals are profitability and organizational success at virtually any price. Management does not care about others' claims to be treated fairly or justly.

What about management's orientation toward the law, considering that law is often regarded as an embodiment of minimal ethics? Immoral management regards legal standards as barriers that management must avoid or overcome in order to accomplish what it wants. Immoral management would just as soon engage in illegal activity as in immoral or unethical activity.

OPERATING STRATEGY OF IMMORAL MANAGEMENT The operating strategy of immoral management is focused on exploiting opportunities for corporate or personal gain. An active opposition to what is moral would suggest that managers cut corners anywhere and everywhere it appears useful. Thus, the key operating question guiding immoral management is, "Can we make money with this action, decision, or behavior, *regardless of what it takes?*" Implicit in this question is that nothing else matters, at least not very much. We can call this "exploiting strategy."

Moral Management

At the opposite extreme from immoral management is **moral management.** Moral management conforms to the highest standards of ethical behavior or professional standards of conduct. Although it is not always crystal clear what level of ethical standards prevail, moral management strives to be ethical in terms of its focus on high ethical norms and professional standards of conduct, motives, goals, orientation toward the law, and general operating strategy.

In contrast to the selfish motives in immoral management, moral management aspires to succeed, but only within the confines of sound ethical precepts—that is, standards predicated on such norms as fairness, justice, respect for rights, and due process. Moral management's motives, therefore, likely would be termed fair, balanced, or unselfish. Organizational goals continue to stress profitability, but only within the confines of legal obedience and sensitivity to and responsiveness to ethical standards. Moral management pursues its objectives of profitability, legality, and ethics as both required and desirable. Moral management would not pursue profits at the expense of the law and sound ethics. Indeed, the focus here would be not only on the letter of the law but on the spirit of the law as well. The law would be viewed as a minimal standard of ethical behavior, because moral management strives to operate at a level above what the law mandates.

OPERATING STRATEGY OF MORAL MANAGEMENT The operating strategy of moral management is to live by sound ethical standards, seeking out only those economic opportunities that the organization or management can pursue within the confines of ethical behavior. The organization assumes a leadership position when ethical dilemmas arise. The central question guiding moral management's actions, decisions, and behaviors is, "Will this action, decision, behavior, or practice be fair to all stakeholders involved as well as to the organization?"

Lynn Sharp Paine has set forth what she calls an "integrity strategy" that closely resembles the moral management model.[119] The **integrity strategy** is characterized by a conception of ethics as the driving force of an organization. Ethical values shape management's search for opportunities, the design of organizational systems, and the decision-making process. Ethical values in the integrity strategy provide a common frame of reference and serve to unify different functions, lines of business, and employee groups. Organizational ethics, in this view, helps to define what an organization is and what it stands for. Some common features of an integrity strategy include the following,[120] which are all consistent with the moral management model.

- Guiding values and commitments make sense and are clearly communicated.
- Company leaders are personally committed, credible, and willing to take action on the values they espouse.
- Espoused values are integrated into the normal channels of management decision making.
- The organization's systems and structures support and reinforce its values.
- All managers have the skills, knowledge, and competencies to make ethically sound decisions on a daily basis.

Amoral Management

Amoral management is not just a middle position on a continuum between immoral and moral management. Conceptually it has been positioned between the other two, but it is different in kind from both. There are two kinds of **amoral management.** First, there is **intentional amoral management.** Amoral managers of this type do not factor ethical considerations into their decisions, actions, and behaviors because they believe business activity resides outside the sphere to which moral judgments apply. These managers are neither moral nor immoral. They simply think that different rules apply in business than in other realms of life. Intentionally amoral managers are in a distinct minority today. At one time, however, as managers first began to think about reconciling business practices with sound ethics, some managers adopted this stance. A few intentionally amoral managers are still around, but they are a vanishing breed in today's ethically conscious world.

Second, there is **unintentional amoral management.** Like intentionally amoral managers, unintentionally amoral managers do not think about business activity in ethical terms. These managers are simply casual about, careless about, or inattentive to the fact that their decisions and actions may have negative or deleterious effects on others. These managers lack ethical perception and moral awareness; that is, they blithely go through their organizational lives not thinking that what they are doing has an ethical dimension or facet. These managers are well intentioned but are either too insensitive or too self-absorbed to consider the effects of their behavior on others.

Amoral management pursues profitability as its goal but does not cognitively attend to moral issues that may be intertwined with that pursuit. If there is an ethical guide to amoral management, it would be the marketplace as constrained by law—the letter of the law, not the spirit. The amoral manager sees the law as the parameters within which business pursuits take place.

OPERATING STRATEGY OF AMORAL MANAGEMENT The operating strategy of amoral management is not to bridle managers with excessive ethical structure but to permit free rein within the unspoken but understood tenets of the free enterprise system. Personal ethics may periodically or unintentionally enter into managerial decisions, but it does not preoccupy management. Furthermore, the impact of decisions on others is an afterthought, if it ever gets considered at all. Amoral management represents a model of decision making in which the managers' ethical mental gears, to the extent that they are present, are stuck in neutral. The key management question guiding decision making is, "Can we make money with this action, decision, or behavior?" Note that the question does not imply an active or implicit intent to be either moral or immoral.

Paine has articulated a "compliance strategy" that is consistent with amoral management. The **compliance strategy,** as contrasted with her integrity strategy, is more focused on obedience to the law as its driving force. The compliance strategy is legally driven and is oriented not toward ethics or integrity but more toward compliance with existing regulatory and criminal law. The compliance approach uses deterrence as its underlying assumption. This approach envisions managers as rational maximizers of self-interest, responsive to the personal costs and benefits of their choices, yet indifferent to the moral legitimacy of those choices.[121]

Making Moral Management Actionable

The characteristics of immoral, moral, and amoral management discussed should provide some useful benchmarks for managerial self-analysis, because self-analysis and introspection will ultimately be the way in which managers will recognize the need to move from the immoral or amoral ethic to the moral ethic. Numerous others have suggested management training for business ethics; therefore, this prescription will not be further developed here, although it has great potential. However, until senior management fully embraces the concepts of moral management, the transformation in organizational culture that is so essential for moral management to blossom, thrive, and flourish will not take place. Ultimately, senior management has the leadership responsibility to show the way to an ethical organizational climate by leading the transition from amoral to moral management, whether this is done by business ethics training and workshops, codes of conduct, mission/vision statements, ethics officers, tighter financial controls, more ethically sensitive decision-making processes, or leadership by example.

Underlying all these efforts, however, needs to be the fundamental recognition that amoral management exists and that it is an undesirable condition that can be certainly, if not easily, remedied. Most notably, organizational leaders must acknowledge that amoral management is a morally vacuous condition that can be quite easily disguised as just an innocent, practical, bottom-line philosophy—something to take pride in. Amoral management is, however, and will continue to be, the bane of American management until it is recognized for what it really is and until managers take steps to overcome it. American managers are not all "bad guys," as they so frequently are portrayed, but the idea that managerial decision making can be ethically neutral is bankrupt and no longer tenable in the society of the new millennium.[122]

Elements of Moral Judgment

For growth in moral judgment to take place, it is useful to appreciate the key elements involved in making moral judgments. This is a notion central to the transition from the amoral management state to the moral management state. Charles Powers and David Vogel suggest that there are six major elements or capacities that are essential to making moral judgments: (1) moral imagination, (2) moral identification and ordering, (3) moral evaluation, (4) tolerance of moral disagreement and ambiguity, (5) integration of managerial and moral competence, and (6) a sense of moral obligation and integrity.[123] Each reveals an essential ingredient in developing moral judgment.

Moral Imagination

Moral imagination refers to the ability to perceive that a web of competing economic relationships is, at the same time, a web of moral or ethical relationships. Developing moral imagination means not only becoming sensitive to ethical issues in business decision making but also developing the perspective of searching out subtle places where people are likely to be detrimentally affected by decision making or behaviors of managers. This is a necessary first step but is extremely challenging because of prevailing methods of evaluating managers on bottom-line results. It is essential before anything else can happen, however.

Moral Identification and Ordering

Moral identification and ordering refers to the ability to discern the relevance or nonrelevance of moral factors that are introduced into a decision-making situation. Are the moral issues real or just rhetorical? The ability to see moral issues as issues that can be dealt with is at stake here. Once moral issues have been identified, they must be ranked, or ordered, just as economic or technological issues are prioritized during the decision-making process. A manager must not only develop this skill through experience but also finely hone it through repetition. It is only through repetition that this skill can be developed.

Moral Evaluation

Once issues have been identified and ordered, evaluations must be made. *Moral evaluation* is the practical phase of moral judgment and entails essential skills, such as coherence and consistency, that have proved to be effective principles in other contexts. What managers need to do here is to understand the importance of clear principles, develop processes for weighing ethical factors, and develop the ability to identify what the likely moral as well as economic outcomes of a decision will be.

The real challenge in moral evaluation is to integrate the concern for others into organizational goals, purposes, and legitimacy. In the final analysis, though, the manager may not know the "right" answer or solution, although moral sensitivity has been introduced into the process. The important point is that amorality has not prevailed or driven the decision process.

Tolerance of Moral Disagreement and Ambiguity

An objection managers often have to ethics discussions is the amount of disagreement generated and the volume of ambiguity that must be tolerated in thinking ethically. This must be accepted, however, because it is a natural part of ethics discussions. To be sure, managers need closure and precision in their decisions. But the situation is seldom clear in moral discussions, just as it is in many traditional and more familiar decision contexts of managers, such as introducing a new product based on limited test marketing, choosing a new executive for a key position, deciding which of a number of excellent computer systems to install, or making a strategic decision based on instincts. All of these are precarious decisions, but managers have become accustomed to making them in spite of the disagreements and ambiguity that prevail among those involved in the decision or within the individual.

In a real sense, the *tolerance of moral disagreement and ambiguity* is simply an extension of a managerial talent or facility that is present in practically all decision-making situations managers face. But managers are more unfamiliar with this special kind of decision making because of a lack of practice.

Integration of Managerial and Moral Competence

The *integration of managerial and moral competence* underlies all that we have been discussing. Moral issues in management do not arise in isolation from traditional business decision making but right smack in the middle of it. The scandals that major corporations face today did not occur independently of the companies' economic activities but were embedded in a series of decisions that were made at various points in time and culminated from those earlier decisions. Therefore, moral competence is an integral part of managerial competence. Managers are learning—some the hard way—that there is a significant corporate, and in many instances personal, price to pay for their amorality. The amoral manager sees ethical decisions as isolated and independent of managerial decisions and competence, but the moral manager sees every evolving decision as one in which an ethical perspective must be integrated. This kind of future-looking view is an essential executive skill.

A Sense of Moral Obligation and Integrity

The foundation for all the capacities we have discussed is a *sense of moral obligation* and integrity. This sense is the key to the process but is the most difficult to acquire. This sense requires the intuitive or learned understanding that moral fibers—a concern for fairness, justice, and due process to people, groups, and communities—are woven into the fabric of managerial decision making and are the integral components that hold systems together.

These qualities are perfectly consistent with, and indeed are essential prerequisites to, the free-enterprise system as we know it today. One can go back in history to Adam Smith and the foundation tenets of the free-enterprise system and not find references to immoral or unethical practices as being elements that are needed for the system to work. Milton Friedman, our modern-day Adam Smith, even alluded to the importance of ethics when he stated that the purpose of business is "to make as much money as possible while conforming to the basic rules of society, both those embodied in the law and those embodied in ethical custom."[124] The moral manager, then, has a sense of moral obligation and integrity that is the glue that holds together the decision-making process in which human welfare is inevitably at stake. Exhibit 900.25 presents a brief sketch of some ethical principles for a business manager.

Exhibit 900.25 *A Brief Sketch of Some Ethical Principles*

- **THE CATEGORICAL IMPERATIVE:** Act only according to that maxim by which you can at the same time "will" that it should become a universal law. In other words, one should not adopt principles of action unless they can, without inconsistency, be adopted by everyone else.
- **THE CONVENTIONALIST ETHIC:** Individuals should act to further their self-interests so long as they do not violate the law. It is allowed, under this principle, to bluff (lie) and to take advantage of all legal opportunities and widespread practices and customs.
- **THE DISCLOSURE RULE:** If the full glare of examination by associates, friends, family, newspapers, television, and so on, were to focus on your decision, would you remain comfortable with it? If you think you would, it probably is the right decision.
- **THE GOLDEN RULE:** Do unto others as you would have them do unto you. It includes not knowingly doing harm to others.
- **THE HEDONISTIC ETHIC:** Virtue is embodied in what each individual finds meaningful. There are no universal or absolute moral principles. If it feels good, do it.
- **THE INTUITION ETHIC:** People are endowed with a kind of moral sense with which they can apprehend right and wrong. The solution to moral problems lies simply in what you feel or understand to be right in a given situation. You have a "gut feeling" and "fly by the seat of your pants."
- **THE MARKET ETHIC:** Selfish actions in the marketplace are virtuous because they contribute to efficient operation of the economy. Decision makers may take selfish actions and be motivated by personal gain in their business dealings. They should ask whether their actions in the market further financial self-interest. If so, the actions are ethical.
- **THE MEANS-ENDS ETHIC:** Worthwhile ends justify efficient means—that is, when ends are of overriding importance or virtue, unscrupulous means may be employed to reach them.
- **THE MIGHT-EQUALS-RIGHT ETHIC:** Justice is defined as the interest of the stronger. What is ethical is what an individual has the strength and power to accomplish. Seize what advantage you are strong enough to take without respect to ordinary social conventions and laws.
- **THE ORGANIZATION ETHIC:** The wills and needs of individuals should be subordinated to the greater good of the organization (be it church, state, business, military, or university). An individual should ask whether actions are consistent with organizational goals and what is good for the organization.
- **THE PROFESSIONAL ETHIC:** You should do only that which can be explained before a committee of your peers.
- **THE PROPORTIONALITY PRINCIPLE:** I am responsible for whatever I "will" as a means or an end. If both the means and the end are good in and of themselves, I may ethically permit or risk the foreseen but unwilled side effects if, and only if, I have a proportionate reason for doing so.
- **THE REVELATION ETHIC:** Through prayer or other appeal to transcendent beings and forces, answers are given to individual minds. The decision makers pray, meditate, or otherwise commune with a superior force or being. They are then apprised of which actions are just and unjust.
- **THE UTILITARIAN ETHIC:** The greatest good for the greatest number. Determine whether the harm in an action is outweighed by the good. If the action maximizes benefit, it is the optimum course to take among alternatives that provide less benefit.

Source: T. K. Das, "Ethical Preferences Among Business Students: A Comparative Study of Fourteen Ethical Principles," *Southern Management Association* (November 13–16, 1985), 11–12. For further discussion, see T. K. Das, "Ethical Principles in Business: An Empirical Study of Preferential Rankings," *International Journal of Management* (Vol. 9, No. 4, December, 1992), 462–472.

Management Assurance

Management Discussion and Analysis

Management of an organization is responsible for preparing the financial statements and the external auditor is responsible for expressing an opinion on them. The fact that the auditor assists the management in the preparation of financial statements does not relieve management from their responsibility. Ultimately, management is responsible for all decisions concerning the form and content of the financial statements.

Many companies include a management responsibility report titled "Management Discussion and Analysis" in their annual reports to stockholders. In this report, management assures stockholders of the following.

- The company maintains a system of internal controls that are continuously reviewed by both internal and external auditors for their adequacy and effectiveness.
- The company's financial statements are prepared in accordance with generally accepted accounting principles (GAAP).
- The company's assets (for example, inventory, equipment, and machinery) are properly accounted for and safeguarded against loss from unauthorized use.
- Both the internal and external auditors have unrestricted and unlimited access to the board of directors and the audit committee.
- The board of directors fulfills their responsibility in financial statements through its audit committee, which consists solely of directors who are neither officers nor employees of the company. The audit committee meets periodically with independent public accountants, internal auditors, and representatives of company management to discuss internal control, auditing, and financial reporting matters.

The auditor should maintain professional skepticism toward management's assertions. This means that the auditor should neither disbelieve management's assertions nor blindly accept them without concern for their truthfulness. Rather, the auditor recognizes the need to objectively verify data, evaluate conditions observed, and evidence gathered during the audit.

Accounting Reform Legislation

As a result of recent corporate scandals resulting from management's "lack of integrity," management fraud, accounting firms' negligence, and use of earnings management techniques, both investors and creditors have lost confidence in corporate America. In light of this financial crisis, the U.S. Congress passed new legislation entitled Sarbanes-Oxley Act of 2002 to reform the accounting profession and corporate management.

Essentially, the Act creates a five-member Public Company Accounting Oversight Board, which has the authority to set and enforce auditing, attestation, quality control, and ethics (including independence) standards for auditors of public companies. It also is empowered to inspect the auditing operations of public accounting firms that audit public companies as well as impose disciplinary and remedial sanctions for violations of the board's rules, securities laws, and professional auditing and accounting standards.

Other provisions affecting the accounting profession include requiring the rotation of the lead audit partner and reviewing audit partner every five years, and extending the statute of limitations for the discovery of fraud to two years from the date of discovery and five years after the act. The law restricts the consulting work public company auditors can perform for their publicly traded audit clients and establishes harsh penalties for securities law violations, corporate fraud, and document shredding. Regarding sanctions, fines range from $100,000 for individual negligent conduct to $15 million to a firm for knowing or intentional conduct, including recklessness and repeated acts of negligence.

The Act also requires CEOs and CFOs to certify their company's financial statements as part of the annual report to stockholders. They also have a greater duty to communicate and coordinate with corporate audit committees who are now responsible for hiring, compensating, and overseeing the independent auditors. There are new requirements regarding enhanced financial disclosures as well.

Corporate Governance

Owner Stakeholders and Corporate Governance

Throughout the 1980s and 1990s, there was rampant shareholder unrest. Shareholder groups became increasingly critical of how management groups and boards of directors ran their firms. They complained about management's lack of accountability, ineffective and complacent boards, excessive managerial compensation, and a general lack of focus on the importance of shareholders relative to management. Today the evidence suggests that their complaints were heard. Although problems certainly remain, the state of corporate governance in the United States has never been stronger.

In this section, we will explore corporate governance and the ways in which it has evolved. First, we will examine the concept of legitimacy and the part that corporate governance plays in establishing the legitimacy of the firm. We will explore how good corporate governance can mitigate the problems created by the separation of ownership and control and examine some of the specific challenges facing board members today.

Legitimacy and Corporate Governance

To understand corporate governance, it is useful to understand the idea of **legitimacy**. Legitimacy is a somewhat abstract concept, but it is vital in that it helps explain the importance of the relative roles of a corporation's charter, shareholders, board of directors, management, and employees—all of which are components of the modern corporate governance system.

Let us start with a slightly modified version of Talcott Parsons's definition of legitimacy. He argued that "organizations are legitimate to the extent that their activities are congruent with the goals and values of the social system within which they function."[125] From this definition, we may see legitimacy as a condition that prevails when there is a congruence between the organization's activities and society's expectations. Thus, whereas legitimacy is a condition, **legitimation** is a dynamic process by which business seeks to perpetuate its acceptance. The dynamic process aspect should be emphasized, because society's norms and values change, and business must change if its legitimacy is to continue. It is also useful to consider legitimacy at both the micro, or company, level and the macro, or business institution, level.

At the *micro level of legitimacy*, we refer to individual business firms achieving and maintaining legitimacy by conforming with societal expectations. According to Epstein and Votaw, companies seek legitimacy in several ways. First, a company may adapt its methods of operating to conform to what it perceives to be the prevailing standard. For example, a company may discontinue door-to-door selling if that marketing approach comes to be viewed in the public mind as a shoddy sales technique,[126] or a pharmaceutical company may discontinue offering free drug samples to medical students if this practice begins to take on the aura of a bribe. Second, a company may try to change the public's values and norms to conform to its own practices by advertising and other techniques.[127] **Amazon.com** was successful at this when it began marketing through the Internet.

Finally, an organization may seek to enhance its legitimacy by identifying itself with other organizations, people, values, or symbols that have a powerful legitimate base in society.[128] This occurs at several levels. At the national level, companies proudly announce appointments of celebrities, former politicians, or other famous people to managerial positions or board directorships. At the community level, the winning local football coach may be asked to endorse a company by sitting on its board or promoting its products.[129]

The *macro level of legitimacy* is the level with which we are most concerned in this section. The macro level refers to the corporate system—the totality of business enterprises. It is difficult to talk about the legitimacy of business in pragmatic terms at this level. American business is such a potpourri of institutions of different shapes, sizes, and industries that saying anything conclusive about it is difficult. Yet this is an important level at which business needs to be concerned about its legitimacy. What is at stake is the existence, acceptance, and form of business as an institution in our society. William Dill has suggested that business's social (or societal) legitimacy is a fragile thing.

> Business has evolved by initiative and experiment. It never had an overwhelmingly clear endorsement as a social institution [emphasis added]. The idea of allowing individuals to joust with one another in pursuit of personal profit was an exciting and romantic one when it was first proposed as a way of correcting other problems in society; but over time, its ugly side and potential for abuse became apparent.[130]

Quite a bit of the excitement and romanticism has long since worn off; business must accept that it has a fragile mandate.[131] It must realize that its legitimacy is constantly subject to ratification. And it must realize that it has no inherent right to exist—it exists solely because society has given it that right.[132]

In comparing the micro view of legitimacy with the macro view, one may observe that, although specific business organizations try to perpetuate their own legitimacy, the corporate or business system as a whole rarely addresses the issue at all. This is unfortunate because the spectrum of powerful issues regarding business conduct clearly indicates that such institutional introspection is needed if business is to survive and prosper. If business is to continue to justify its right to exist, the question of legitimacy and its operational ramifications must be remembered.

The Issue of Corporate Governance

The issue of corporate governance is a direct outgrowth of the question of legitimacy. For business to be legitimate and to maintain its legitimacy in the eyes of the public, its governance must correspond to the will of the people.

Corporate governance refers to the method by which a firm is being governed, directed, administered, or controlled and to the goals for which it is being governed. Corporate governance is concerned with the relative roles, rights, and accountability of such stakeholder groups as owners, boards of directors, managers, employees, and others who assert to be stakeholders.

Components of Corporate Governance

To appreciate fully the legitimacy and corporate governance issues, it is important that we understand the major groups that make up the corporate form of business organization, because it is only by so doing that we can appreciate how the system has failed to work according to its intended design.

Roles of Four Major Groups

The four major groups we need to mention in setting the stage are the shareholders (owners/stakeholders), the board of directors, the managers, and the employees. Overarching these groups is the **charter** issued by the state, giving the corporation the right to exist and stipulating the basic terms of its existence. Exhibit 900.26 presents these four groups, along with the state charter, in a hierarchy of corporate governance authority.

Under American corporate law, **shareholders** are the owners of a corporation. As owners, they should have ultimate control over the corporation. This control is manifested primarily in the right to select the board of directors of the company. Generally, the degree of each shareholder's right is determined by the number of shares of stock owned. The individual who owns 100 shares of **Apple Computer**, for example, has 100 "votes" when electing the board of directors. By contrast, the large public pension fund that owns 10 million shares has 10 million "votes."

Exhibit 900.26 *The Corporation's Hierarchy of Authority*

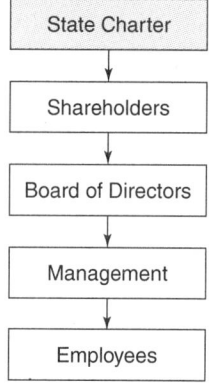

990. CORPORATE GOVERNANCE

783

Because large organizations may have hundreds of thousands of shareholders, they elect a smaller group, known as the **board of directors,** to govern and oversee the management of the business. The board is responsible for ascertaining that the manager puts the interests of the owners (that is, shareholders) first. The third major group in the authority hierarchy is **management**—the group of individuals hired by the board to run the company and manage it on a daily basis. Along with the board, top management establishes overall policy. Middle- and lower-level managers carry out this policy and conduct the daily supervision of the operative employees. **Employees** are those hired by the company to perform the actual operational work. Managers are employees, too, but in this discussion we use the term *employees* to refer to nonmanagerial employees.

Separation of Ownership From Control

The social and ethical issues that have evolved in recent years focus on the *intended* versus *actual* roles, rights, responsibilities, and accountability of these four major groups. The major condition embedded in the structure of modern corporations that has contributed to the corporate governance problem has been the **separation of ownership from control.** In the precorporate period, owners were typically the managers themselves. Thus, the system worked the way it was intended; the owners also controlled the business. Even when firms grew larger and managers were hired, the owners often were on the scene to hold the management group accountable.

As the public corporation grew and stock ownership became widely dispersed, a separation of ownership from control became the prevalent condition. Exhibit 900.27 illustrates the precorporate and corporate periods. The dispersion of ownership into hundreds of thousands or millions of shares meant that essentially no one or no one group owned enough shares to exercise control. This being the case, the most effective control that owners could exercise was the election of the board of directors to serve as their representative and watch over management.

The problem with this evolution was that authority, power, and control rested with the group that had the most concentrated interest at stake—management. The corporation did not function according to its designed plan with effective authority, power, and control flowing downward from the owners. The shareholders were owners in a technical sense, but most of them perceived themselves as investors rather than owners. If you owned 100 shares of **Walt Disney Co.** and there were 10 million shares outstanding, you likely would see yourself as an investor rather than an owner. With just a telephone call issuing a sell order to your stockbroker, your "ownership" stake could be gone. Furthermore, with stock ownership so dispersed, no conscious, intended supervision of corporate boards was possible.

The other factors that added to management's power were the corporate laws and traditions that gave the management group control over the **proxy process**—the method by which the shareholders elected boards of directors. Over time, it was not difficult for management groups to create boards of directors of like-minded executives who would simply collect their fees and defer to management on whatever it wanted. The result of this process was that power, authority, and control began to flow upward from management rather than downward from the shareholders

Exhibit 900.27 *Precorporate Versus Corporate Ownership and Control*

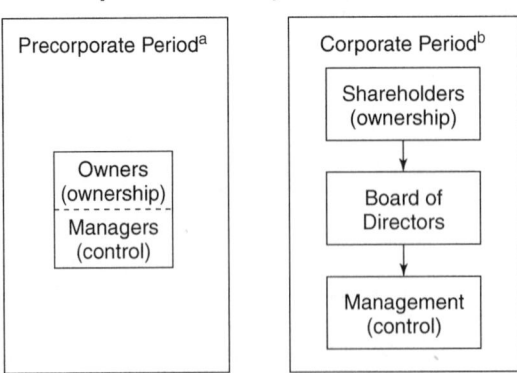

[a] In the precorporate period, the owners were also the managers, and therefore ownership and control were combined. Later, large companies hired managers, but the owners were always there to exercise control.

[b] In the corporate period, ownership was separated from control by the intervention of a board of directors. Theoretically, the board should have kept control on behalf of owners, but it did not always turn out that way.

(owners). **Agency problems** developed when the interests of the shareholders were not aligned with the interests of the manager, and the manager (who is simply a hired *agent* with the responsibility of representing the owner's best interest) began to pursue self-interest instead.

The Role of the Board of Directors

It is clear from the preceding discussion that a potential governance problem is built into the corporate system because of the separation of ownership from control. It is equally clear that the board of directors is intended to oversee management on behalf of the shareholders. However, this is where the system had once broken down. For corporate governance to function as it was originally intended, the board of directors must be an effective, potent body carrying out its roles and responsibilities in ascertaining that management pursue the shareholders' best interests.

Are boards doing what they are supposed to be doing? Problems in some corporations remain. In March 2001, *Business Week* characterized the board of **Xerox** as being "asleep at the wheel" with a "host of governance problems."[133] The board had too many members with ties to the firm, board members sat on too many other boards, and the directors owned little equity in the firm.[134]

In spite of the problems that remain, most of the corporate governance news is decidedly good. In its annual report on the "Best and Worst Corporate Boards in America," *Business Week* offered the following assessment of the trend in corporate governance:

> The governance revolution that swept through Corporate America's boardrooms in the 1990s has led to far more active oversight. Composed largely of independent directors, boards are more accountable than ever. Directors who rarely if ever bought a single share of their company's stock in the past are often significantly invested today. And in the face of shareholder dissatisfaction they are more likely to demand change. "All of the rhetorical battles are over," comments James E. Heard, chairman of Proxy Monitor and a longtime player in governance circles. "With the exception of a few rogues, most boards are doing the job they are supposed to do."[135]

Credit for the turnaround in corporate governance goes to several sources. Robert Lear and Boris Yavitz credit Arthur Levitt and the SEC for the changes in proxy statements. Information on executive and director compensation is much more clearly presented than it was in the 1980s and early 1990s. They also credit "enlightened CEOs and directors" who didn't wait for regulatory reforms but put changes through voluntarily.[136]

Although the governance battle has been won at large U.S. companies, the war is not over. Midsize and smaller companies, and overseas boards, still do not often follow the guidelines for good governance. Dotcoms in particular have tended to have boards dominated by insiders, a combination of current management and others with connections to the company.[137] Europe too is just entering the corporate governance battle. Mass stock ownership is a new phenomenon but investors who feel stung by steep price drops are taking action. European shareholders are going to court and showing up en masse at annual meetings.[138]

The Need for Board Independence

Board independence from management is a crucial aspect of good governance. It is here that the difference between **inside directors** and **outside directors** becomes most pronounced. Outside directors are independent from the firm and its top managers. In contrast, inside directors have some sort of ties to the firm. Sometimes they are top managers in the firm; other times, insiders are family members or others with close ties to the CEO. To varying degrees, each of these parties is "beholden" to the CEO and, therefore, might be hesitant to speak out when necessary. Courtney Brown, an experienced director who served on many boards, said that he never saw a subordinate officer serving on a board dissent from the position taken by the CEO.[139] Insiders might also be professionals such as lawyers under contract to the firm or bankers whose bank does business with the firm: This can create conflict-of-interest situations.[140] For example, a commercial banker/director may expect the company on whose board she or he is serving to restrict itself to using the services of her or his own firm and be willing to support the CEO in return for the business provided.

Another problem is managerial control of the board processes. CEOs often can control board perks such as director compensation and committee assignments. Board members who rock the boat may find they are left out in the cold. As one corporate board member told *Fortune*, under conditions of anonymity, "This stuff is wrong.... What people understand they have to do is go along with management, because if they don't they won't be part of the club.... What it comes down to is that directors aren't really independent. CEOs don't want independent directors."[141]

Issues Surrounding Compensation

CEO Compensation

The issue of executive pay was a lightning rod for the concern that managers place their own interests over those of their shareholders. Two issues are at the heart of the CEO pay controversy: (1) the extent to which CEO pay is tied to firm performance and (2) the overall level of CEO pay.

The move to tie CEO pay more closely to firm performance grew in momentum when shareholders observed CEO pay rising as firm performance fell. Many executives had gotten staggering salaries, even while profits were falling, workers were being laid off, and shareholder return was dropping. Shareholders were assisted in their effort to monitor CEO pay by stricter disclosure requirements from the Securities and Exchange Commission (SEC). The revised compensation disclosure rule, adopted by the SEC in 1992, was designed to provide shareholders with more information about the relationship between firm performance and CEO compensation.[142] According to the results of one study, it seems to have worked. Since the rule's implementation, compensation committees have met more frequently, lessened the number of insiders as members, and become more moderate in size. More importantly, largely through the use of stock options, CEO pay has become more closely aligned with accounting and market performance measures than it was before the rule's implementation.[143] There is some evidence that boards of directors are becoming the watchdogs they are always supposed to be.[144]

Outside Director Compensation

It was suggested earlier that there may be some link between CEO and executive compensation and board members. Therefore, it should not be surprising that directors' pay is becoming an issue, too. According to a survey by *Executive Compensation Reports*, the average annual compensation for a 1996 nonexecutive board member was $73,473, with an additional fee of $1,284 for each meeting attended. In addition, 94% of the companies surveyed gave their directors stock.[145] Paying board members is a relatively recent idea. Eighty years ago, it was illegal to pay nonexecutive board members. The logic was that because board members represented the shareholders, paying them out of the company's (that is, shareholders') funds would be self-dealing.[146] A 1992 Korn/Ferry survey showed that board members typically spent 95 hours a year on the board. By 2000, that figure had increased to 173 hours. The average director received a 23% increase in pay for the 82% increase in time spent on the job.[147]

Consequences of the Merger, Acquisition, and Takeover Wave

Mergers and acquisitions are another form of corporate governance, one that comes from outside the corporation. The expectation is that the threat of a possible takeover will motivate top managers to pursue shareholder, rather than self, interest. The merger, acquisition, and hostile takeover wave of the 1980s brought out many new issues related to corporate governance. The economic prosperity of the 1980s, coupled with the rise of junk bonds and other creative methods of financing, made it possible for small firms and individuals to buy large corporations. Many corporate CEOs and boards went to great lengths to protect themselves from these takeovers. A major criticism of CEOs and boards during this period was that they were overly obsessed with self-preservation rather than making optimal decisions on behalf of their owners/stakeholders. Three of the most questionable top management practices to emerge from the hostile takeover wave were greenmail, poison pills, and golden parachutes. We will briefly consider each of these and see how they fit into the corporate governance problem we have been discussing. Then, we will examine the issue of insider trading.

Greenmail

Named after blackmail, **greenmail** is the repurchase of stock from an unwanted suitor at a higher-than-market price. Companies pay the greenmail to end the threat of a takeover.[148] For example, assume that Corporate Raider A quietly purchases a 5% stake in the ABC Corporation. It threatens to launch an all-out hostile takeover of ABC. ABC's management sees this as a threat to their jobs and agrees to pay greenmail for (buy back) the shares from Corporate Raider A at a premium price. This example is somewhat simplified, but it basically describes the process. With greenmail, the potential acquirer wins big, and management gets to keep its jobs and perks. The losers are the shareholders of the target company who are left sitting with shares whose underlying value has been eroded.[149] Some companies have passed corporate bylaws that prohibit greenmail. In addition, the courts now limit the tax deductibility of greenmail payments.[150]

Poison Pill

A **poison pill** is a shareholder rights plan aimed at discouraging or preventing a hostile takeover. Typically, the poison pill provides that when a hostile suitor acquires more than a certain percentage of a company's stock, other shareholders receive share purchase rights designed to dilute the suitor's holdings and make the acquisition prohibitively expensive. Some poison pills adopted by companies have been ruled illegal by the courts.[151] However, efforts to adopt poison pills continue. In 2001, **Yahoo!'s** board of directors adopted a poison pill that would make a hostile takeover prohibitively expensive. The plan gives Yahoo! shareholders the right to buy one unit of a share of preferred stock for $250 if a person or group acquires at least 15% of Yahoo!'s stock. According to the company, the poison pill was not instituted in response to any specific acquisition threat but instead to "deter coercive takeover tactics."[152]

Golden Parachutes

A **golden parachute** is a contract in which a corporation agrees to make payments to key officers in the event of a change in the control of the corporation.[153] The original intent of golden parachutes was to prevent top executives involved in takeover battles from putting themselves before their shareholders. However, in a study of over 400 tender offers (that is, takeover attempts in which the acquirers offered shareholders premiums to sell their shares), golden parachutes showed no effect on takeover resistance. Neither the existence of the parachute, nor the magnitude of the potential parachute payout, influenced CEO reactions to takeover attempts.[154]

Cochran and Wartick offer several arguments against golden parachutes. They argue that executives are already being paid well to represent their companies and that their getting additional rewards constitutes "double dipping." They also argue that these executives are, in essence, being rewarded for failure. The logic here is that if the executives have managed their companies in such a way that the companies' stock prices are low enough to make the firms attractive to takeover specialists, the executives are being rewarded for failure. Another argument is that executives, to the extent that they control their own boards, are giving themselves the golden parachutes. This represents a conflict of interest.[155]

Insider Trading Scandals

Insider trading is the practice of obtaining critical information from inside a company and then using that information for one's own personal financial gain. A scandal began in 1986 when the Securities and Exchange Commission (SEC) filed a civil complaint against Dennis B. Levine, a former managing partner of the **Drexel Burnham Lambert** investment banking firm, and charged him with illegally trading in 54 stocks. Levine then pleaded guilty to four criminal charges and gave up $10.6 million in illegal profits—the biggest insider trading penalty up to that point.[156] He also spent 17 months in prison.

Levine's downfall set off a chain reaction on Wall Street. His testimony led directly to the SEC's $100 million judgment against Ivan Boesky, one of Wall Street's most frenetically active individual speculators. In a consent decree, Boesky agreed to pay $100 million, which was then described as by far the largest settlement ever obtained by the SEC in an insider trading case. Boesky, it turns out, had made a career of the high-rolling financial game known as **risk arbitrage**—the opportunistic buying and selling of companies that appear on the verge of being taken over by other firms.[157] The Boesky settlement set off a flurry of litigation as dozens of private and corporate lawsuits were filed in response to these disclosures.[158]

Ivan Boesky then fingered Martin Siegel, one of America's most respected investment bankers, at **Kidder Peabody**. Apparently Siegel and Boesky began conspiring in 1982, and over the next 2 years Siegel leaked information about upcoming takeovers to Boesky in exchange for $700,000 cash. Siegel pleaded guilty and began cooperating with investigators, and then he himself proceeded to finger two former executives at Kidder Peabody and one at **Goldman Sachs**.[159]

The insider trading scandals rocked Wall Street as accusations reached the upper levels of the financial industry's power and salary structure. New arrests seemed to occur weekly, and one of the most frequently asked questions was "Who's next?"[160] In 1987, Ivan Boesky was sentenced to 3 years in prison. However, Boesky helped prosecutors reel in the biggest fish of all—junk bond king Michael Milkin. The Securities and Exchange Commission accused Milkin and his employer, Drexel Burnham, of insider trading, stock manipulation, and other violations of federal securities laws. Drexel Burnham agreed in 1988 to plead guilty to six felonies, settle SEC charges, and pay a record fine of $650 million. A year later, the junk bond market crashed and Drexel Burnham filed for bankruptcy. In 1990, Milkin agreed to plead guilty to six felony counts of securities fraud, market manipulation, and tax fraud. He agreed to pay a personal fine of $600 million and later was sentenced to 10 years in prison.[161] He served only 2 years in prison before being released.

Although insider trading scandals of this magnitude have not recurred, the revelations and repercussions of the Wall Street scandal will be with us for years. Unfortunately, the scandal gave the financial industry on Wall Street the biggest "black eye" it has had in over 50 years. Not only are shareholders suspicious of what has been going on unbeknownst to them, but small investors and the general public have lost faith in what they thought was the stable and secure financial industry. In 2001, the SEC instituted new disclosure rules designed to aid the small investor who historically has not had access to the information large investors hold. Regulation FD (fair disclosure) set limits on the common company practice of selective disclosure. When companies disclose meaningful information to shareholders and securities professionals, they must now do so publicly so that small investors can enjoy a more level playing field.[162]

Board Member Liability

In the mid to late 1980s, not many individuals wanted board director positions. Concerned about increasing legal hassles emanating from stockholder, customer, and employee lawsuits, directors were quitting such positions or refusing to accept them in the first place. Although courts rarely hold directors personally liable in the hundreds of shareholder suits filed every year, over the past several years there have been a few cases in which directors have been held personally and financially liable for their decisions. The **Trans Union Corporation** case involved an agreement among the directors to sell the company for a price the owners later decided was too low. A suit was filed, and the court ordered that the board members be held personally responsible for the difference between the price the company was sold for and a later-determined "fair value" for the deal.[163] In addition to the Trans Union case, **Cincinnati Gas and Electric** reached a $14 million settlement in a shareholder suit that charged directors and officers with improper disclosure concerning a nuclear power plant.[164]

The recent **Caremark** case further heightened directors' concerns about **personal liability.** Caremark, a home health care company, paid substantial civil and criminal fines for submitting false claims and making illegal payments to doctors and other health care providers. The Caremark board of directors was then sued for breach of fiduciary duties because the board members had failed in their responsibility to monitor effectively the Caremark employees who violated various state and federal laws. In late 1996, the Delaware Chancery Court ruled that it is the duty of the board of directors to ensure that a company has an effective reporting and monitoring system in place. If the board fails to do this, individual directors can be held personally liable for losses that are caused by their failure to meet appropriate standards.[165]

Improving Corporate Governance

Efforts to improve corporate governance may be classified into two major categories for discussion purposes. First, changes could be made in the composition, structure, and functioning of boards of directors. Second, shareholders—on their own initiative or on the initiative of management or the board—could assume a more active role in governance. Each of these possibilities deserves closer examination.

Changes in Boards of Directors

In the past decade or so, changes have begun to be made in boards of directors. These changes have occurred because of the growing belief that CEOs and executive teams need to be made more accountable to shareholders and other stakeholders. Here we will discuss several of these changes and some other recommendations that have been set forth for improving board functioning.

COMPOSITION OF THE BOARD Prior to the 1960s, boards were composed primarily of white, male inside directors. It was not until the 1960s that pressure from Washington, Wall Street, and various stakeholder groups began to emphasize the concept of board diversity. By 2000, their efforts were beginning to pay off: 78% of U.S. board members were outsiders.[166] Of the S&P 500 companies, 93% had at least one woman director in 2000. Although most firms still only have one token woman director, the tide seems to be shifting. In 2000, 21% of new board members were women, and 25% of the nation's largest companies had more than one female director.[167] Ethnic minorities are making inroads, too. Sixty percent of U.S. corporate boards now have ethnic minority directors, with African-Americans comprising 39%, Latinos comprising 12%, and Asians comprising 9% of the positions. The world seems to be awakening to the importance of diverse and independent boards. The problem is that good candidates are increasingly hard to find.[168]

Part of the problem is an increase in demand for good independent directors. Institutional investors value good corporate governance so highly that they are willing to pay a premium for firms with outside directors. A 2000 study by the McKinsey Company found that the premium was as high as 28% in Venezuela. Although it varied, each country's premium was well above 15%.[169] South Korea passed a law requiring that outside directors occupy at least one-fourth of the positions on large company boards.[170] This increase in demand for outside directors is part of the reason they are in increasingly short supply.

Another factor limiting the supply of directors is the greater level of expectations placed on board members. Board committees and subcommittees are now given more to do than ever before. Furthermore, the globalization of business has placed new demands on board members for travel. Last, firms realize the time demands placed on outside directors and so they limit the number of outside boards on which their own executives may sit. For example, former GE CEO Jack Welch would not allow his senior managers to sit on the boards of other companies.[171]

The difficulty in finding outside board members is exacerbated when searching for members of minority groups or women to bring diversity to the board. In the past, many candidates were excluded because they never had the title of CEO. A new trend in board recruitment, focusing more on experience than title, is helping to bring more independence and diversity to the boardroom. This broadens the pool of candidates available.[172]

Today, advocates of strong, independent, and diverse boards have largely succeeded in convincing corporations of the importance of board composition. The difficulty now is in putting those recommendations into effect.

USE OF BOARD COMMITTEES   The **audit committee** is typically responsible for assessing the adequacy of internal control systems and the integrity of financial statements. Recent scandals, like the revelation that **Cendant Corporation** booked almost $300 million in fake revenues, underscore the importance of a strong audit committee. Commenting on the Cendant Corporation situation, *The Wall Street Journal* opined, "Too many audit committees are turning out to be toothless tigers."[173] To lessen the occurrence of such scandals, the Securities and Exchange Commission has placed much emphasis on audit committees, and the New York Stock Exchange mandates such committees, composed of independent outside directors, for the firms listed with it. Charles Anderson and Robert Anthony, authors of *The New Corporate Directors: Insights for Board Members and Executives*,[174] argue that the principal responsibilities of an audit committee are as follows.

1. To ensure that published financial statements are not misleading
2. To ensure that internal controls are adequate
3. To follow up on allegations of material, financial, ethical, and legal irregularities
4. To ratify the selection of the external auditor

According to Arjay Miller, a board member and former president of **Ford Motor Company**, there should be at least one meeting per year between the audit committee and the firm's internal auditor.[175] The internal auditor should be scheduled to meet alone with the committee and always be instructed to speak out whenever she or he believes something should be brought to the committee's attention. The committee should also meet with the outside auditor in a setting in which members of management are not present. Three major questions should be asked of the outside auditor by the audit committee.

1. Is there anything more that you think we should know?
2. What is your biggest area of concern?
3. In what area did you have the largest difference of opinion with company accounting personnel?

The **nominating committee,** which should be composed of outside directors, or at least a majority of outside directors, has the responsibility of ensuring that competent, objective board members are selected. The American Assembly recommended that this committee be composed entirely of independent outside directors. The function of the nominating committee is to nominate candidates for the board and for senior management positions. In spite of the suggested role and responsibility of this committee, in most companies the CEO continues to exercise a powerful role in the selection of board members.

The **compensation committee** has the responsibility of evaluating executive performance and recommending terms and conditions of employment. This committee should be composed of outside directors. Although most large companies have compensation committees, one might ask how objective these board members are when the CEO has played a significant role in their being elected to the board.

Finally, each board has a **public issues committee,** or **public policy committee.** Although it is recognized that most management structures have some sort of formal mechanism for responding to public or social issues, this area is important enough to warrant a board committee that would become sensitive to these issues, provide policy leadership, and monitor management's performance on these issues. Most major companies today have public issues committees that typically deal with such issues as affirmative action, equal employment opportunity, environmental affairs, employee health and safety, consumer affairs, political action, and other areas in which public or ethical issues are present. Debate continues over the extent to which large firms really use such committees, but the fact that they have institutionalized such concerns by way of formal corporate committees is encouraging. The American Assembly recommends that firms develop evaluation systems to help them monitor the social performance of their corporate executives, but the evidence does not show that companies are doing this.[176]

Recently, the National Association of Corporate Directors (NACD) issued a director's handbook titled *The Governance Committee*. Its purpose is to raise the bar of board performance through effective oversight of the board's governance practices, use of ethics, and the process for director recruitment and retention. It is hoped that this handbook will improve the corporate governance process through the **governance committee**.

GETTING TOUGH WITH CEOS It has always been a major responsibility of board directors to monitor CEO performance and to get tough if the situation dictates. Historically, chief executives were protected from the axe that hit other employees when times got rough. Changes are now occurring that are resulting in CEOs being taken to task, or even fired, for reasons that heretofore did not create a stir in the boardroom. These changes include the tough, competitive economic times, the rising vigilance of outside directors, and the increasing power of large institutional investors.

Other suggestions have been proposed for creating effective boards of directors and for improving board members' abilities to monitor executive teams to ensure that crises do not occur undetected. Exhibit 900.28 summarizes some of these recommendations.

Increased Role of Shareholders

Prior to the 1980s, civil rights activists, consumer groups, and other social activist pressure groups insisted that companies join their causes. Today, companies are increasingly understanding the stakeholder perspective. However, it has created a new dilemma for companies as they deal with two broad types of shareholders. First, there are the traditional shareholder groups that are primarily interested in the firm's financial performance. Examples of such groups include the large institutional investors, such as pension funds. Second, there are growing numbers of social activist shareholders. These groups are typically pressuring firms to adopt their desired postures on social causes, such as Third World employment practices, animal testing, affirmative action, and environmental protection.

Exhibit 900.28 *Recommendations for Improving Boards and Board Members*

BUILDING A BETTER BOARD[a]
- Don't overload it with too many members.
- Don't meet too often.
- Don't think you need high-profile CEOs or famous academics.
- Keep directors on for at least 5 years.
- Encourage directors to buy large quantities of stock.
- Pay directors with stock options, not with restricted stock.

SHARPENING THE BOARD'S SENSORS[b]
- Insist that board members become educated about their company.
- Insist that information-gathering systems deliver quickly the right information from the bottom to the top.
- Insist that board members understand board decision-making processes and not operate by consensus.
- Insist that the company undergo periodic audits of corporate activities and results.

BOARD ACTIONS[c]
- Directors should evaluate regularly the CEO's performance against established goals and strategies.
- Evaluations of the CEO should be done by "outside directors."
- Outside directors should meet alone at least once a year.
- Directors should set qualifications for board members and communicate these expectations to shareholders.
- Outside directors should screen and recommend board candidates who meet the established qualifications.

KEEP DIRECTORS' EYES ON CEO[d]
- CEOs need written job descriptions and annual report cards.
- Boards should measure their own performance as well as assess individual members.
- Board nominating committees should exclude the company's major suppliers, officials of nonprofit organizations that receive substantial donations from the corporation, and the CEO's close friends.
- A chief executive should hold only one outside board seat.

Sources: [a]Graef S. Crystal, "Do Directors Earn Their Keep?" *Fortune* (May 6, 1991), 79. [b]Richard O. Jacobs, "Why Boards Miss Black Holes," *Across the Board* (June 1991), 54. [c]The Working Group on Corporate Governance, "A New Compact for Owners and Directors," *Harvard Business Review* (July–August 1991), 142–143. [d]Joann S. Lublin, "How to Keep Directors' Eyes on the CEO," *The Wall Street Journal* (July 20, 1994), B1.

A major problem seems to be that both groups of shareholders feel like neglected constituencies. They are attempting to rectify this condition through a variety of means. They are demanding effective power. They want to hold management groups accountable. They want to make changes, including changes in management if necessary. Like companies' earlier responses to other stakeholder activist groups, many managements are resisting. The result is a battle between managers and shareholders for corporate control.[177]

Our discussion of an increased role for shareholders centers around two perspectives: (1) the perspective of shareholders themselves asserting their rights on their own initiative and (2) initiatives being taken by companies to make shareholders a true constituency. The shareholder initiatives will dominate our discussion, because they clearly constitute the bulk of the activity underway.

SHAREHOLDER INITIATIVES   These initiatives may be classified into three major, overlapping areas: (1) the rise of shareholder activist groups, (2) the filing of shareholder resolutions and activism at annual meetings, and (3) the filing of shareholder lawsuits.

Rise of Shareholder Activist Groups   One major reason that relations between management groups and shareholders have heated up is that shareholders have discovered the benefits of organizing and wielding power. **Shareholder activism** is not a new phenomenon. It goes back over 60 years to 1932, when Lewis Gilbert, then a young owner of 10 shares, was appalled by the absence of communication between New York–based **Consolidated Gas Company's** management and its owners. Supported by a family inheritance, Gilbert decided to quit his job as a newspaper reporter and "fight this silent dictatorship over other people's money." He resolved to devote himself "to the cause of the public shareholder."[178]

Filing of Shareholder Resolutions and Activism at Annual Meetings   One of the major vehicles by which shareholder activists communicate their concerns to management groups is through the filing of **shareholder resolutions,** or shareholder proposals. An example of such a resolution is, "The company should name women and minorities to the board of directors." To file a resolution, a shareholder or a shareholder group must obtain a stated number of signatures to require management to place the resolution on the proxy statement so that it can be voted on by all the shareholders. Resolutions that are defeated (fail to get majority votes) may be resubmitted provided that they meet certain SEC requirements for such resubmission.

Because most shareholder resolutions never pass, one might ask why groups pursue them. The main reason is that they gain national publicity, which is part of what protesting groups are out to achieve. Increasingly, companies are negotiating with groups to settle issues before resolutions ever come up for a vote.

Closely related to the surge in shareholder resolutions has been the increased activism at corporate annual meetings in the past decade. Professional "corporate gadflies" purchase small numbers of shares of a company's stock and then attend its annual meetings to put pressure on managers to explain themselves. An example of the kind of social activism that can occur during an annual meeting was the case in which **GM** shareholders sought explanations for a series of embarrassing controversies surrounding the automaker. Some shareholders wanted to know why the company substituted Chevrolet engines in cars sold by some of its other divisions, a move that infuriated many consumers who were not notified of the changes.[179] More recently, corporate executives have been asked to explain high executive compensation packages, positions on hostile takeover attempts, plant closings, greenmail, golden parachutes, and environmental issues.

The motives for bringing up these issues at annual meetings are similar to those for filing shareholder resolutions: to put management on the spot and publicly demand some explanation or corrective action. Activism at annual meetings is one of the few methods shareholders have of demanding explanations and obtaining accountability from top management.

Defending a company at annual meetings has become such an important task of top management that several consulting firms now publish annual booklets of shareholder questions that are likely to be asked. These booklets are intended to help management and directors anticipate and plan for what they might be quizzed on at annual meetings.

Filing of Shareholder Lawsuits   We earlier made reference to the **Trans Union** case wherein shareholders sued the board of directors for approving a buyout offer that the shareholders argued should have had a higher price tag. Their suit charged that the directors had been negligent in failing to secure a third-party opinion from experienced investment bankers. The case went to trial and resulted in a $23.5 million judgment against the directors.[180] The Trans Union case may be one of the largest successful shareholder suits, but it does not stand alone. One estimate was that the number of **shareholder lawsuits** quadrupled over the decade from 1977 to 1987.[181] The large number of shareholder suits being filed today makes one think that almost every decision a company makes is subject to a shareholder suit. As these suits proliferate, many wonder whose interests are really being served. Quite often, the shareholders' attorneys walk away with more money than the protesting shareholders receive.

Shareholder suits are easy to file but difficult to defend. One study estimated that 70% of the suits are settled out of court. Therefore, charges of corporate wrongdoing are seldom resolved. Quite often, these lawsuits are seen as legitimate protests by shareholders against management actions, and the threat of litigation does deter corporate misbehavior. From the company's viewpoint, however, such lawsuits are an expensive nuisance. Some experts argue that management's quick willingness to settle before going to trial invites more suits. In spite of this, companies give in because the downside risks of trials and adverse publicity are too great.[182]

In 1995, Congress sought to stem the growing tide of shareholder lawsuits by passing the **Private Securities Litigation Reform Act of 1995.** The law made it more difficult for companies to bring class-action lawsuits to federal court.[183] However, rather than stemming the tide of lawsuits, the act simply prompted shareholders to change their venue. Suits filed in federal court decreased, while suits filed in state courts increased. The Securities Litigation Uniform Standards Act of 1998 was designed to plug that loophole. It says that "Any covered class action brought into any state courts shall be removable to the federal district courts for the district in which the action is pending."[184]

COMPANY INITIATIVES The need for companies to reestablish a relationship with their owners/stakeholders is somewhat akin to parents having to reestablish relations with their children once the children have grown up. Over the years, the evidence suggests that corporate managements have neglected their owners rather than making them a genuine part of the family. As share ownership has dispersed, there are several legitimate reasons why this separation has taken place. But there is also evidence that management groups have been too preoccupied with their own self-interests. In either case, corporations are beginning to realize that they have a responsibility to their shareholders that cannot be further neglected. Owners are demanding accountability, and it appears that they will be tenacious until they get it.

Public corporations have obligations to their shareholders and to potential shareholders. **Full disclosure** is one of these responsibilities. Disclosure should be made at regular and frequent intervals and should contain information that might affect the investment decisions of shareholders. This information might include the nature and activities of the business, financial and policy matters, tender offers, and special problems and opportunities in the near future and in the longer term.[185] Of paramount importance are the interests of the investing public, not the interests of the incumbent management team. Board members should avoid conflicts between personal interests and the interests of shareholders. Company executives and directors have an obligation to avoid taking personal advantage of information that is not disclosed to the investing public and to avoid any personal use of corporation assets and influence.

With regard to corporate takeovers, fair treatment of shareholders necessitates special safeguards, including (1) candor in public statements on the offer made, (2) full disclosure of all information, (3) absence of undue pressure, and (4) sufficient time for shareholders to make considered decisions. A constructive purpose, not a predatory one, should be served by takeovers. The firm's major stakeholders are its owners. They are interdependent with other stakeholders, and, therefore, management should carry out its obligations to other constituency groups within the context of shareholder concern.[186]

Shareholder programs are not a substitute for keeping shareholders foremost in the minds of managements and boards when economic decisions are being made. However, they do demonstrate an attempt by managements to give serious consideration to corporate/shareholder relations. These types of programs help the corporate governance problem because they show the shareholders that they matter and that they are important to the firm.

International Issues

Ethical Issues in the Global Business Environment

For many companies, most of the ethical problems that arise in the international environment are in the same categories as those that arise in their domestic environments. These ethical issues reside in all of the functional areas of business: production/operations, marketing, finance, and management. These issues concern the fair treatment of stakeholders—employees, customers, the community, and competitors. These issues involve product safety, plant safety, advertising practices, human resource management, environmental problems, and so on.

The ethical problems seem to be somewhat fewer in developed countries, but they exist there as well. The ethical difficulties seem to be worse in underdeveloped countries, less developed countries (LDCs), or developing countries because these countries are at earlier stages of economic development. This situation creates an environment in which there is a temptation to adhere to lower standards, or perhaps no standards, because few government regulations or activist groups exist to protect the stakeholders' interests. In the LDCs, the opportunities for business exploitation and the engagement in questionable (by developed countries' standards) practices are abundant.

We will illustrate some prominent examples of ethical problems in the multinational sphere to provide some appreciation of the development of these kinds of issues for business. We will discuss two classic ethical issues that have arisen with regard to questionable marketing and safety practices. Next, will discuss the issue of "sweatshops" (the use of cheap labor in developing countries)—a topic that has dominated international business in the decade of the 1990s and carries forward into the new millennium. Then, we will consider the special problems of corruption, bribery, and questionable payments, which have been ethical issues in the United States for over 30 years. From these examples, we should be able to develop an appreciation of the ethical challenges that confront MNCs and others doing business globally.

Questionable Marketing and Plant Safety Practices

A classic example of a questionable marketing practice is the now infamous infant formula controversy that spanned most of the 1970s, continued into the 1980s and 1990s, and remains an issue today. The plant safety issue is best illustrated by examining the **Union Carbide** Bhopal crisis that began in late 1984 and continued into the 1990s and is not completely resolved today.

Questionable Marketing: The Infant Formula Controversy

The **infant formula controversy** is a classic in illustrating the ethical questions that can arise while doing business abroad. We will briefly refer to James Post's observations about this now-classic case.[187] For decades, physicians working in tropical lands (many of which were LDCs) realized that there were severe health risks posed to infants from bottle feeding as opposed to breast feeding. Such countries typically had neither refrigeration nor sanitary conditions. Water supplies were not pure, and, therefore, infant formula mixed with this water contained bacteria that would likely lead to disease and diarrhea in the bottle-fed infant. Because these LDCs are typically poor, this condition encourages mothers to overdilute powdered formula, thus diminishing significantly the amount of nutrition the infant receives. Once a mother begins bottle feeding, her capacity for breast feeding quickly diminishes. Poverty also leads the mother to put in the bottle less expensive substitute products. These products, such as powdered whole milk and corn starch, are not acceptable substitutes. They are nutritionally inadequate and unsatisfactory for the baby's digestive system.

By the late 1960s, it was apparent that in the LDCs there was increased bottle feeding, decreased breast feeding, and a dramatic increase in the numbers of malnourished and sick babies. Bottle feeding was cited as one of the major reasons. The ethical debate began when it was noted that several of the infant formula companies, aware of the environment just described, were promoting their products and, therefore, promoting bottle feeding in an intense way. Such marketing practices as mass advertising, billboards, radio jingles, and free samples became commonplace. These promotional devices typically portrayed the infants who used their products as healthy and robust, in sharp contrast with the reality that was brought about by the conditions mentioned.

One of the worst marketing practices entailed the use of "milk nurses"—women dressed in nurses' uniforms who walked the halls of maternity wards urging mothers to get their babies started on formula. In reality, these women were sales representatives employed by the companies on a commission basis. Once the infants began bottle feeding, the mothers' capacity to breast feed diminished.[188]

Plant Safety and the Bhopal Tragedy

The Union Carbide **Bhopal tragedy** in India in late 1984 brings into sharp focus the dilemma of multinationals operating in a foreign, particularly less-developed, environment. At this writing, the legal issues surrounding this event have not been totally resolved and may not be for years to come. On December 3, 1984, a leak of methyl isocyanate gas caused what many have termed the "worst industrial accident in history." The gas leak killed more than 2,000 people and injured 200,000 others. The tragedy has raised numerous legal, ethical, social, and technical questions for MNCs.[189] Observers who have studied this tragedy say the death toll and destruction are many times greater than the "official" numbers indicate.

Interviews with experts just after the accident revealed a belief that the responsibility for the accident had to be shared by the company and the Indian government. According to Union Carbide's own inspector, the Bhopal plant did not meet U.S. standards and had not been inspected in over 2 years. The Indian government allowed thousands of people to live very near the plant, and there were no evacuation procedures.[190]

Many different questions have been raised by the Bhopal disaster. Among the more important of these issues are the following.[191]

1. To what extent should MNCs maintain identical standards at home and abroad regardless of how lax laws are in the host country?
2. How advisable is it to locate a complex and dangerous plant in an area where the entire workforce is basically unskilled and where the populace is ignorant of the inherent risks posed by such plants?
3. How wise are laws that require plants to be staffed entirely by local employees?
4. What is the responsibility of corporations and governments in allowing the use of otherwise safe products that become dangerous because of local conditions? (This question applies to the infant formula controversy also.)
5. After reviewing all the problems, should certain kinds of plants be located in developing nations?

The lessons from the Bhopal disaster are many and will continue to be debated. In companies around the globe, the Bhopal disaster has sparked continued enthusiasm in the debate about operating abroad. To be sure, ethical and legal issues are central to the discussions. What is at stake, however, is not just the practices of businesses abroad but also the very question of the presence of businesses abroad. Depending on the final outcome of the Union Carbide debacle, MNCs may decide that the risk of doing business abroad is too great.

Sweatshops and Labor Abuses

No issue has been more prominent since the early 1990s in the global business ethics debate than MNCs' use and abuse of women and children in cheap-labor factories in developing countries. The major players in this controversy, large corporations, have highly recognizable names—**Nike**, **Wal-Mart**, **Kmart**, **Reebok**, **J.C.Penney**, and **Disney**—to name a few. The countries and regions of the world that have been involved are also recognizable—Southeast Asia, Pakistan, Indonesia, Honduras, Dominican Republic, Thailand, the Philippines, and Vietnam. Sweatshops have not been eliminated in the United States either.[192]

Though **sweatshops,** characterized by child labor, low pay, poor working conditions, worker abuse, and health and safety violations, have existed for decades, they have grown in number in the past few years as global competition has heated up and corporations have gone to the far reaches of the world to lower their costs and increase their productivity. A landmark event that brought the sweatshop issue into sharp focus was the 1996 revelation by labor rights activists that part of Wal-Mart's Kathie Lee Collection, a line of clothes endorsed by prominent U.S. talk-show host Kathie Lee Gifford, was made in Honduras by seamstresses slaving 20 hours a day for 31 cents an hour. The revelation helped turn Gifford, who was unaware of where the clothes were being made or under what conditions, into an antisweatshop activist.[193] The Nike Corporation has also become a lightning rod for social activists concerned about overseas manufacturing conditions, standards, and ethics. A major reason for this is the company's high visibility, extensive advertising, and expensive shoes, as well as the stark contrast between the tens of millions of dollars Nike icon Michael Jordan earned and the $2.23 daily wage rate the company's subcontractors paid their Indonesian workers.[194]

Critics of MNC labor practices, including social activist groups and grassroots organizations, have been speaking out, criticizing business abusers and raising public awareness. These critics claim certain businesses are exploiting children and women by paying them poverty wages, working them to exhaustion, punishing them for minor violations, violating health and safety standards with them, and tearing apart their families. Many of these companies counter that they offer the children and women workers a superior alternative. They say that, although their wage rates are embarrassing by developed-world standards, those rates frequently equal or exceed local legal minimum wages, or average wages. They further say that, because so many workers in LDCs work in agriculture and farming, where they make less than the average wage, the low but legal minimums in many countries put sweatshop workers among the higher-paid workers in their areas.[195]

The sweatshop issue has been so prominent in the past few years that, to improve their situations or images, many criticized companies have begun working to improve working conditions, further joint initiatives, establish codes of conduct or standards for themselves and their subcontractors, conduct social or ethical audits, or take other steps.

A new proposal should also help eliminate sweatshops. This proposal calls for clothing firms and their contractors to impose a code of conduct that would prohibit child labor, forced labor, and worker abuse; establish health and safety regulations; recognize workers' right to join a union; limit the workweek to 60 hours (except in exceptional business circumstances); and insist that workers be paid at least the legal minimum wage (or the "prevailing industry wage") in every country in which garments are made. Under this proposal, the garment industry would also create an association to police the agreement.[196]

Sweatshops and labor abuses sharply contrast the "haves" and the "have-nots" of the world's nations. Consumers in developed countries have benefited greatly by the lower prices made possible by cheap labor. It remains to be seen how supportive those consumers will be if prices rise because MNCs improve wage rates and conditions in LDCs. The MNCs face a new and volatile ethical issue that is not likely to go away. Their profits, public image, and reputations may hinge on how well they respond. The MNCs must handle a new dimension in their age-old quest to balance shareholder profits with the desires of expanded, global stakeholders who want better corporate social performance.

Corruption, Bribery, and Questionable Payments

Corruption, bribes, and questionable payments occurred for decades prior to the 1970s. It was in the mid-1970s, however, that evidence of widespread questionable corporate payments to foreign government officials, political parties, and other influential persons became widely known.

Corruption in international business continues to be a major problem. It starts with outright bribery of government officials and the giving of questionable political contributions. Beyond these there are many other activities that are corrupt: the misuse of company assets for political favors, kickbacks and protection money for police, free junkets for government officials, secret price-fixing agreements, and insider dealing, just to mention a few. All of these activities have one thing in common. They are attempts to influence the outcomes of decisions wherein the nature and extent of the influence are not made public. In essence, these activities are abuses of power.[197] Bribes, more than any other form of corruption, have been the subject of continuing debate, and they merit closer examination.

Arguments for and Against Bribery

Arguments typically given in favor of permitting bribery include the following: (1) they are necessary for profits in order to do business; (2) everybody does it—it will happen anyway; (3) it is accepted practice in many countries—it is normal and expected; and (4) bribes are forms of commissions, taxes, or compensation for conducting business between cultures.

Arguments frequently cited against giving bribes include (1) bribes are inherently wrong and cannot be accepted under any circumstances; (2) bribes are illegal in the United States and, therefore, unfair elsewhere; (3) one should not compromise her or his own beliefs; (4) managers should not deal with corrupt governments; (5) such demands, once started, never stop; (6) one should take a stand for honesty, morality, and ethics; (7) those receiving bribes are the only ones who benefit; (8) bribes create dependence on corrupt individuals and countries; and (9) bribes deceive stockholders and pass on costs to customers.[198]

The costs of bribes and other forms of corruption are seldom fully understood or described. Several studies suggest the economic costs of such corrupt activities. When government officials accept "speed" money or "grease payments" to issue licenses, the economic cost is 3 to 10% above the licensing fee. When tax collectors permit underreporting of income in exchange for a bribe, income tax revenues may be reduced by up to 50%. When government officials take kickbacks, goods and services may be priced 20 to 100% higher to them. In addition to these direct economic costs, there are many indirect costs—demoralization and cynicism and moral revulsion against politicians and the political system. Due to bribery and corruption, politicians have been swept from office in Brazil, Italy, Japan, and Korea.[199]

The Foreign Corrupt Practices Act

Many of the payments and bribes made by U.S.–based MNCs were not illegal prior to the passage of the 1977 Foreign Corrupt Practices Act (FCPA). Even so, firms could have been engaging in illegal activities depending on whether and how the payments were reported to the Internal Revenue Service (IRS). With the passage of the FCPA, however, it became a criminal offense for a representative of an American corporation to offer or give payments to the officials of other governments for the purpose of getting or maintaining business. The FCPA specifies a series of fines and prison terms that can result if a company or management is found guilty of a violation.[200] The legislation was passed not only for ethical reasons but also out of a concern for the image of the United States abroad.

Over its history, the FCPA has been controversial. The law does not prohibit so-called **grease payments,** or minor, facilitating payments to officials, for the primary purpose of getting them to do whatever they are supposed to do anyway. Such payments are commonplace in many countries. The real problem is that some forms of payments are prohibited (for example, bribes), but other payments (for example, grease payments) are not prohibited. The law is sometimes ambiguous on the distinctions between the two.[201] To violate the FCPA, payments (other than grease payments) must be made corruptly to obtain business. This suggests some kind of *quid pro quo.* The idea of a corrupt *quid pro quo* payment to a foreign official may seem clear in the abstract, but the circumstances of the payment

Exhibit 900.29 *Key Features of the Antibribery Provisions of the Foreign Corrupt Practices Act (FCPA)*

- In general, the FCPA prohibits American companies from making corrupt payments to foreign officials for the purpose of obtaining or keeping business.
- The Department of Justice is the chief enforcement agency, with a coordinate role played by the Securities and Exchange Commission (SEC).
- The FCPA's antibribery provisions extend to two types of behavior: (1) making bribes directly and (2) making bribes through intermediaries.
- Applies to any individual firm, officer, director, employee, or agent of the firm and any stockholder acting on behalf of the firm.
- The person making or authorizing the payment must have a corrupt intent, and the payment must be intended to induce the recipient to misuse his official position to order wrongfully to direct business to the payor. The corrupt act does not need to succeed in its purpose to be illegal.
- Prohibits paying, offering, promising to pay, or authorizing to pay or offer, money or anything of value.
- The prohibition extends only to corrupt payments to a foreign official, a foreign political party or party official, or any candidate for foreign political office, or anyone acting in an official capacity.
- Prohibits corrupt payments through intermediaries.
- An explicit exception is made to the bribery provisions for "facilitating payments" for "routine governmental action."
- The following criminal penalties may be imposed: firms are subject to a fine of up to $2 million; officers, directors, stockholders, employees and agents are subject to a fine of up to $100,000 and imprisonment for up to five years. Fines imposed on individuals may not be paid by the firm.

Source: "Foreign Corrupt Practices Act Antibribery Provisions," U.S. Department of Justice, http://www.ita.doc.gov/legal/fcparev.html.

Exhibit 900.30 *Bribes Versus Grease Payments*

Definitions	Examples
Grease Payments (Not Prohibited)	
Relatively small sums of money given for the purpose of getting minor officials to: • Do what they are supposed to be doing • Do what they are supposed to be doing faster or sooner • Do what they are supposed to be doing better than they would otherwise	Money given to minor officials (clerks, attendants, customs inspectors) for the purpose of expediting. This form of payment helps get goods or services through red tape or administrative bureaucracies.
Bribes (Prohibited)	
Relatively large amounts of money given for the purpose of influencing officials to make decisions or take actions that they otherwise might not take. If the officials considered the merits of the situation only, they might take some other action.	Money given, often to high-ranking officials. Purpose is often to get these people to purchase goods or services from the bribing firm. May also be used to avoid taxes, forestall unfavorable government intervention, secure favorable treatment, and so on.

may easily blur the distinction between what is acceptable "grease" (for example, payments to expedite mail pickup or delivery, to obtain a work permit, to process paperwork) and what is illegal bribery. The safest strategy for managers to take is to be careful and to seek a legal opinion when questions arise.

Exhibit 900.29 summarizes some of the key features of the antibribery provisions of the FCPA. Exhibit 900.30 presents a basic distinction with examples between bribes (which are prohibited) and grease (or facilitating) payments (which are not prohibited) based on the FCPA.

Bribery Trends: The Growing Anticorruption Movement

As we usher in the first decade of the new millennium, corruption and bribery in international business continue to be popular topics. With significant increases in global competition, free markets, and democracy over the past decade, this comes as no surprise. Two developments in the past decade are worthy of mention. Both have contributed to what some have called a growing **anticorruption movement**.

TRANSPARENCY INTERNATIONAL First, a new special-interest group was founded in Berlin in 1993—Transparency International (TI)—modeled after the human rights group Amnesty International. TI has established itself as the world's foremost anticorruption lobby. It maintains over 70 national chapters run by local activists and compiles an annual corruption rating using surveys of businesspeople, political analysts, and the general public.

Using various color shades to represent labels varying from "least corrupt" to "most corrupt" on a map of the world, TI's "Corruption Perception Index" depicts countries in various ways. In the Corruption Perception Index of 2001, the least corrupt countries were identified as Finland, Denmark, New Zealand, Iceland, Singapore, and Sweden. Out of the 91 countries ranked, the United States was ranked 16th least corrupt. The most corrupt nations, according to the CPI, were Indonesia, Uganda, Nigeria, and Bangladesh.[202] Undoubtedly, TI hopes and expects that public exposure to its corruption ratings will bring pressure to bear on countries and companies.

OECD ANTIBRIBERY INITIATIVES A second development in the growing anticorruption movement is a new antibribery treaty and initiatives that the 29 industrialized nations of the Organization for Economic Cooperation and Development (OECD) and five other countries agreed to in late 1997.[203] The OECD member nations agreed to ban international bribery and to ask each member to introduce laws patterned after the U.S. FCPA in its country. The main thrust of the treaty was to criminalize bribes to foreign officials who have sway over everything from government procurement contracts and infrastructure projects to privatization tenders.

The OECD Convention to combat bribery went into effect on February 15, 1999. The Convention makes it a crime to offer, promise, or give a bribe to a foreign public official in order to obtain or retain international business deals. A related text effectively puts an end to the practice of according tax deductibility for bribe payments made to foreign officials. However, the OECD represents a significant initiative in the global battle to eliminate corruption from commercial transactions.

In addition to OECD antibribery initiatives, some individual countries have begun antibribery campaigns on their own.

The best way to deal with bribes seems to be to stem the practice before it starts. A major paradox is that the very people who often benefit from illicit payments—the politicians—are the ones who must pass the laws and set the standards against bribes and corruption in the first place. Another factor is that bribes and corruption, whenever possible, need to be exposed. Public exposure, more than anything else, has the potential to bring questionable payments under control. This means that practices and channels of accountability need to be made public.[204] Beyond these steps, managers need to be able to see that such activities are no longer in their best interests. Not only do bribes corrupt the economic system, but they corrupt business relationships as well and cause business decisions to be made on the basis of factors that ultimately destroy all the institutions involved. In a sense, the new OECD treaty indicates that member nations now understand this important point. It will not eliminate bribery, but it does represent a significant step toward reducing bribery and bringing it under control.

We have by no means covered all the areas in which ethical problems reside in the global business environment. The topics treated have been major ones subjected to extensive public discussion. Examples of other issues that have become important recently and will probably increase in importance include the issues of international competitiveness, protectionism, industrial policy, political risk analysis, and antiterrorism. These issues are of paramount significance in discussions of business's relations with international stakeholders. Other issues that include an ethical dimension are national security versus profit interests, the use of internal transfer prices to evade high taxes in a country, mining of the ocean floor, and harboring of terrorists.

Improving Global Business Ethics

The most obvious conclusion to extract from the discussion up to this point is that business ethics is more complex at the global level than at the domestic level. The complexity arises from the fact that a wide variety of value systems, stakeholders, cultures, forms of government, socioeconomic conditions, and standards of ethical behavior exists throughout the world. Recognition of diverse standards of ethical behavior is important, but if we assume that U.S. firms should operate in closer accordance with U.S. standards than with foreign standards, the strategy of ethical leadership in the world is indeed a challenging one. Because the United States, and hence U.S.–based MNCs, have played such a leadership role in world affairs—usually espousing fairness and human rights—U.S. firms have a heavy responsibility, particularly in underdeveloped countries and LDCs. The power-responsibility equation also argues that U.S. firms have a serious ethical responsibility in global markets. That is, our larger sense of ethical behavior and social responsiveness derives from the enormous amount of power we have.

Exhibit 900.31   *Ethical Choices in Home versus Host Country Situations*

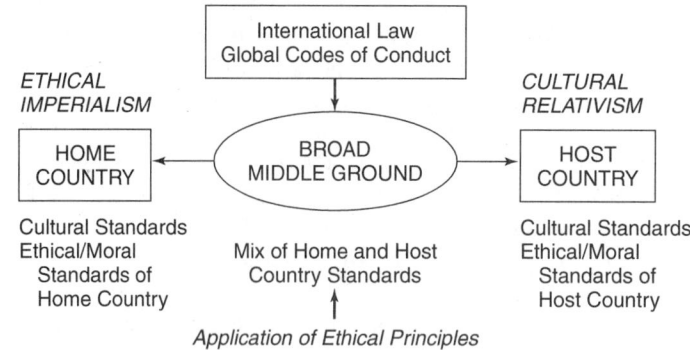

Balancing and Reconciling the Business Ethics Traditions of Home and Host Countries

Perhaps one of the greatest challenges that face businesses operating in foreign countries is achieving some kind of reconciliation and balance in honoring both the cultural and moral standards of their home and host countries. Should a business adhere to its home country's ethical standards for business practices or to the host country's ethical standards? There is no simple answer to this question. The diagram presented in Exhibit 900.31 frames the extreme decision choices businesses face when they consider operating globally.

At one extreme is a position some might call "ethical imperialism." This position argues that the MNC should continue to follow its home country's ethical standards even while operating in another country. Because U.S. standards for treating employees, consumers, and the natural environment are quite high relative to the standards in many other less-developed countries, it is easy to see how managers might find this posture appealing.

As reliance on foreign factories has soared in recent years and harsh conditions have been documented by the media, an increasing number of companies, such as **Levi Strauss**, **Nordstrom, Inc.**, **Wal-Mart**, and **Reebok**, have espoused higher standards for foreign factories that cover such issues as wages, safety, and workers' rights to organize.[205] These standards more nearly approximate U.S. views on how such stakeholders ought to be treated than some host country's views. Such higher standards could be seen by foreign countries, however, as the United States attempting to impose its standards on the host country—thus the name "ethical imperialism" for one end of the continuum.

At the other extreme in Exhibit 900.31 is a position often called "cultural relativism." This position is characterized by foreign direct investors such as MNCs following the host country's ethical standards. This is the posture reflected in the well-known saying, "When in Rome, do as the Romans." This position would argue that the investing MNC should set aside its home country's ethical standards and adopt the ethical standards of the host country. For example, if Saudi Arabia holds that it is illegal to hire women for most managerial positions, the investing MNC would accept and adopt this standard, even if it counters its home country's standards. Or, if the host country has no environmental protection laws, this position would argue that the MNC need not be sensitive to environmental standards.

As Tom Donaldson has argued, cultural relativism holds that no culture's ethics are better than any other's and that there are, therefore, no international rights or wrongs. If Thailand tolerates the bribery of government officials, then Thai tolerance is no worse than Japanese or German intolerance. If Switzerland does not find insider trading morally repugnant, then Swiss liberality is no worse than American restrictiveness.[206] Most ethicists find cultural relativism to be a case of moral or ethical relativism and, therefore, an unacceptable posture for MNCs to take.

A Typology of Global Types

George Enderle, an international business expert, has observed and categorized at least four different types of global firms with respect to their use of home versus host country ethical standards.[207]

- Foreign country type
- Empire type
- Interconnection type
- Global type

FOREIGN COUNTRY TYPE This type of firm conforms to local customs and ethics, assuming that the ethical standards of the host country are adequate and appropriate. This approach represents moral or cultural relativism.

EMPIRE TYPE This type of company applies its domestic or home country standards without making any serious adaptations to the host country. These companies export their values in a wholesale fashion, often disregarding the consequences. An example would be Great Britain in India and elsewhere prior to 1947. This approach represents moral imperialism.

INTERCONNECTION TYPE These companies regard the international sphere as differing significantly from the domestic sphere in that their interconnectedness transcends national identities. An example of this would be the United States engaging in commercial business in the European Union or NAFTA. In this type, the entire concept of national interests is blurred. Companies do not try to project a national identity.

GLOBAL TYPE This type of business firm abstracts from all regional differences. These firms view the domestic or home standards as not relevant or applicable. With this type, the nation-state may be seen as vanishing as only global citizenry applies.

The purpose of identifying each of these types is to illustrate the various mixtures or combinations of home and host country standards that a business operating in the global sphere might adopt.

INTEGRATIVE SOCIAL CONTRACT THEORY (ISCT) Donaldson and Dunfee (1999) have presented Integrative Social Contract Theory (ISCT) as an approach to navigating cross-national cultural differences.[208] Two key concepts in their theory are the notions of *hypernorms* and *moral free space*. They explain these two concepts by depicting a series of concentric circles representing the core norms held by corporations, industries, or economic cultures. At the center are **hypernorms**, which are transcultural values. They include, for example, fundamental human rights or basic prescriptions common to most major religions. The values they represent are by definition acceptable to all cultures and all organizations.

Moving out from the center of the concentric circles, next would be **consistent norms**. These values are more culturally specific than those in the center, but are consistent with hypernorms and other legitimate norms. The next circle is **moral free space.** Here, one finds norms that are inconsistent with at least some other legitimate norms existing in other economic cultures. These norms could be in mild tension with hypernorms, though they may be compatible with them. These are strongly held cultural beliefs in particular countries. Finally, in the outer circle are **illegitimate norms**. These are norms that are incompatible with hypernorms. An example of this might be the practice of exposing workers to unacceptable levels of carcinogens.

Donaldson and Dunfee then use these different levels of norms to comment on Enderle's four types of corporations. Regarding the foreign country type, they say that nothing limits the free moral space of the host country. Thus, if a host country accepts government corruption and environmental degradation, then so much the worse for honest people and environmental integrity. Both the global and empire types succeed in avoiding the fierce relativism of the foreign country type, but may fall prey to the opposite problem. Because each of these has its own set blueprint of right and wrong, each may suffocate the host country's moral free space and leave no room for legitimate local norms. The empire type exhibits a version of moral imperialism; the global type may impose its home country morality on a host culture, thus imposing its version of a global morality on the host country.[209]

According to Donaldson and Dunfee, only the interconnection type satisfies ISCT by acknowledging both universal moral limits (hypernorms) and the ability of communities to set moral standards of their own (moral free space). This type balances better than the others a need to retain local identity with the acknowledgment of values that transcend individual communities; thus, it manages to balance moral principles with moral free space in a more convincing way than in the other three models.[210]

In summary, ISCT uses the principles of moral free space and adherence to hypernorms as a balanced approach to navigating global international waters. While honoring hypernorms, companies do not have to simply adopt a "do in Rome as the Romans do" philosophy. But, they do need to be sensitive to the transcultural value implications of their actions. In turn, the concept of moral free space makes them ever vigilant of the need to precede judgment with an attempt to understand the local host country culture. The result, of course, is the very real probability that moral tension will be an everyday part of doing business in the global sphere.[211]

It may sound like a simplistic solution to say that the MNC needs to operate in some broad middle ground where a mix of home and host country ethical standards may be used. The challenge for managers will be to determine what mix of ethical standards should be used and how this decision should be made. Managers will need to ask themselves which moral standards are applicable in the situations they face. Use of ethical principles such as those articulated in the previous sections—rights, justice, utilitarianism, and the Golden Rule—still apply. Managers will need to decide which ethical standards should transcend national boundaries and thus represent hypernorms: safety? health? discrimination? freedom? Managers will need to decide what will represent their moral minimums with respect to these and other issues. It would be nice to think that international laws and global codes of conduct will make these decisions easier. Though some are available, it is doubtful that such guidelines will be easily applicable. In the interim, managers will need to be guided by the ethical concepts at their disposal, possibly with help from some of the approaches to which we now turn.

Four Actions for Improving International Business Ethics

Laczniak and Naor have set forth four actions that would help MNCs conduct international business while maintaining an ethical sensitivity in their practices and decision making. We will now discuss these and use them to help organize suggested actions that have been made by a number of experts. Global codes of conduct is one of the four actions.

Ethics and Global Strategy

The major recommendation here is that the ethical dimensions of multinational corporate activity should be considered as significant inputs into top-level strategy formulation and implementation.[212] Carroll, Hoy, and Hall have argued even more broadly that corporate social policy should be integrated into strategic management.[213] At the top level of decision making in the firm, corporate strategy is established. At this level, commitments are made that will define the underlying character and identity that the organization will have. The overall moral tone of the organization and all decision making and behaviors are set at the strategic level, and management needs to ensure that social and ethical factors do not get lost in the preoccupation with market opportunities and competitive factors.

If ethics does not get factored in at the strategic formulation level, it is doubtful that ethics will be considered at the level of operations where strategy is being implemented. Unfortunately, much current practice has tended to treat ethics and social responsibility as residual factors. A more proactive stance is needed for dealing with ethical issues at the global level. Strategic decisions that may be influenced by ethical considerations in the global sphere include, but are not limited to, product/service decisions, plant location, manufacturing policy, marketing policy and practices, and human resources management policies.

Suspension of Activities by MNC

An MNC may sometimes encounter unbridgeable gaps between the ethical values of its home country and those of its host country. When this occurs, and reconciliation does not appear to be in sight, the MNC should consider suspending activities in the host country. For example, years ago **IBM** and **Coca-Cola** suspended their activities in India because of that country's position on the extent of national ownership and control.[214]

Also, **Levi Strauss** undertook a phased withdrawal from China, largely in response to human rights concerns and suspended sourcing in Peru because of concerns about employee safety. It later lifted the suspension because conditions had improved.[215] More recently, companies have pulled out of Burma due to human rights violations.

Suspension of business in a foreign country is not a decision that can or should be taken precipitously, but it must be regarded as a viable option for those firms that desire to travel on the higher moral road. Each country is at liberty to have its own standards, but this does not mean that U.S. firms must do business in that country. What does ethical leadership mean if it is not backed up by a willingness and an ability to take a moral stand when the occasion merits?

Ethical Impact Statements

MNCs should be constantly aware of the impacts they are having on society, particularly foreign societies. One way to do this is to periodically assess the company's impacts. Companies have a variety of impacts on foreign cultures, and ethical impacts represent only a few of these. The impact statement idea probably derived, in part, from the practice of environmental impact statements that the U.S. Environmental Protection Agency pioneered in the early 1970s. These statements are similar to the corporate social audit. *Social auditing* is "a systematic attempt to identify, analyze, measure (if possible), evaluate, and monitor the effect of an organization's operations on society (that is, specific social groups) and on the public well-being."[216] **Ethical impact statements** would be an attempt to assess the underlying moral justifications for corporate actions and the consequent results of those actions. The information derived from these actions would permit the MNCs to modify or change their business practices if the impact statement suggested that such changes would be necessary or desirable.

One form of ethical impact assessment is some firms' attempts to monitor their compliance with their companies' global ethics codes. For example, **Mattel** developed an independent audit and monitoring system for its code. Mattel's monitoring program is headed by an independent panel of commissioners who select a percentage of the company's manufacturing facilities for annual audits. In one audit, for example, Mattel terminated its relationship with three contractor facilities—one in Indonesia for its inability to confirm the age of its employees and two in China for refusing to meet company-mandated safety procedures.[217] Such audits conducted for monitoring compliance are not as comprehensive as ethical impact statements, but they serve similar purposes.

Fundamental International Rights for MNCs

One major approach to doing business ethically in the global sphere has been for companies to adhere to various sets of international rights or moral guidelines. Thomas Donaldson set forth ten fundamental international rights that he argues should be honored and respected by all international actors, including nation-states, individuals, and corporations. He argues that these rights serve to establish a "moral minimum" for the behavior of all international economic agents. Donaldson's ten fundamental rights are as follows.[218]

1. The right to freedom of physical movement
2. The right to ownership of property
3. The right to freedom from torture
4. The right to a fair trial
5. The right to nondiscriminatory treatment (freedom from discrimination on the basis of such characteristics as race and gender)
6. The right to physical security
7. The right to freedom of speech and association
8. The right to minimal education
9. The right to political participation
10. The right to subsistence

Such a list of rights is somewhat general and still leaves considerable room for interpretation. However, the list serves to establish a beginning point for MNCs as they contemplate what responsibilities they have in international markets. These rights are similar to hypernorms.

Seven Moral Guidelines to Improve MNC Operations

Another way of looking at what MNCs should be doing in the global sphere is the recommendation that they follow certain moral guidelines in their operations. According to Richard DeGeorge, MNCs should apply seven moral guidelines in their international operations.[219] Some of these are rather straightforward and general, but they do summarize a useful perspective that might well improve MNC operations in the global sphere. Like the principles of rights stated earlier, these moral guidelines are similar to the hypernorms discussed earlier.

1. MNCs should do no intentional, direct harm.
2. MNCs should produce more good than bad for the host country.

3. MNCs should contribute by their activities to the host country's development.
4. MNCs should respect the human rights of their employees.
5. MNCs should pay their fair share of taxes.
6. To the extent that local culture does not violate moral norms, MNCs should respect the local culture and work with it, not against it.
7. MNCs should cooperate with the local government in the development and enforcement of just background institutions (for example, the tax system and health and safety standards).

DeGeorge does not present these seven guidelines as a panacea. He does suggest that if they were brought to bear on the dilemmas that MNCs face, the companies could avoid the moral stings of their critics. The spirit of these seven guidelines, if adopted, would go a long way toward improving MNC–host country relations.

Like the other lists presented, these guidelines can serve only as general principles for managers who are aspiring to make ethical decisions in the global arena. They do, however, provide the consensus thinking of a host of stakeholder representatives as to the responsibilities of international corporations.

Module 900 Glossary

8-K Monthly report to the SEC when significant events occur.

10-K Annual report filed by publicly traded companies to the SEC.

10-Q Quarterly report filed by publicly traded companies to the SEC.

A

Accounting and Auditing Enforcement Release (AAER) Public document released by the SEC when a company commits financial statement fraud or other inappropriate activities.

Accounting anomalies Inaccuracies in source documents, journal entries, ledgers, or financial statements.

Accounting cycle Procedures for analyzing, recording, classifying, summarizing, and reporting the transactions of a business.

Accounting system Policies and procedures for recording economic transactions in an organized manner.

Accounts receivable turnover ratio The rate at which a company collects its receivables; computed by dividing sales by average accounts receivable.

Accounts receivable turnover Sales divided by average accounts receivable; a measure of the efficiency with which receivables are being collected.

Accrued liability Liabilities arising from end-of-period adjustments, not from specific transactions.

Acquisition The purchase of something, such as the purchase of one company by another company.

Acute crisis stage The stage at which a crisis actually occurs.

Affidavit Written statement or declaration given under oath.

Agency problems May develop when the interests of the shareholders are not aligned with the interests of the manager.

Allowance for doubtful accounts A contra-asset (receivable) account representing the amount of receivables that are estimated to be uncollectible.

Allowance for uncollectible assets as a percentage of receivables Allowance for doubtful accounts divided by accounts receivable; a measure of the percentage of receivables estimated to be uncollectible.

Analytical anomalies Relationships, procedures, or events that do not make sense.

Appellate Court Review court to which participants in lower court cases can have their cases reviewed or retried if they are unhappy with the outcome.

Application controls Programmed procedures in application software and related manual procedures, designed to help ensure the completeness and accuracy of information processing. Examples include computerized edit checks of input data, and numerical sequence checks and manual procedures to follow up on items listed in exception reports.

Arraignment Court hearing where charges against the defendant are read. At the arraignment, the defendants may plead guilty, not guilty, or nolo contendere.

Asset fraud Financial statement fraud in which assets are recorded at higher amounts than they should be.

Asset misappropriations Theft that is committed by stealing receipts, stealing assets on hand, or by committing some type of disbursement fraud.

Asset turnover Total sales divided by average total assets; a measure of the amount of sales revenue generated with each dollar of assets.

Association of Certified Fraud Examiners (ACFE) An international organization, based in Austin, Texas, dedicated to fighting fraud and white-collar crime.

Audit command language (ACL) Popular commercial data-mining software; helps investigators detect fraud.

Audit committee Responsible for assessing the adequacy of internal control systems and the integrity of financial statements.

Audit trail Documents and records that can be used to trace transactions.

Autocratic management Management conducted by a few key people who do not accept advice or participation from other employees.

B

Bad debt expense An expense representing receivables and/or revenues that are presumed not to be collectible.

Balance sheet Financial statement that reports a company's assets, liabilities, and owner's equity as of a particular date.

Bankruptcy A legal process that either allows a debtor to work out an orderly plan to settle debts or to liquidate a debtor's assets and distribute them to creditors.

Bankruptcy Code Title 11 of the U.S. Code—the federal statute that governs the bankruptcy process.

Bankruptcy Courts Federal courts that hear only bankruptcy cases.

Benchmarking An ongoing, systematic approach by which a public affairs unit measures and compares itself with higher performing and world-class units in order to generate knowledge and action about public affairs roles, practices, processes, products, services, and strategic issues that will lead to improvement in performance. Originated in the Total Quality Management (TQM) movement.

Bid-rigging scheme Collusive fraud wherein an employee helps a vendor illegally obtain a contract that was supposed to involve competitive bidding.

Billing scheme Submission of a false or altered invoice that causes an employer to willingly issue a check.

Biometrics Using unique features of the human body (for example, retinal scans) to create secure access controls.

Bribery The offering, giving, receiving, or soliciting anything of value to influence an official act.

Business ethics Concerned with good and bad or right and wrong behavior and practices that take place within a business context.

Business-level strategy Is concerned with the question, "How should we compete in a given business or industry?"

Bustout A planned bankruptcy.

C

Capitalization Recording expenditures as assets rather than as expenses. (For example, start-up costs that are "capitalized" are recorded as assets and amortized.)

Captive insurer A type of insurer that is generally formed and owned by potential insureds to meet their own distinctive needs.

Chain of custody Maintaining detailed records about documents from the time they are received in the investigation process until the trial is completed. Helps to substantiate that documents have not been altered or manipulated since coming into the investigator's hands.

Chapter 11 bankruptcy Bankruptcy that allows the bankrupt entity time to reorganize its operational and financial affairs, settle its debts, and continue to operate in a reorganized fashion.

Chapter 7 bankruptcy Complete liquidation or "shutting down of a business" and distribution of any proceeds to creditors.

Check tampering Scheme in which dishonest employees (1) prepare fraudulent checks for their own benefit or (2) intercept checks intended for a third party and convert the checks for their own benefit.

Chronic crisis stage The lingering period of a crisis; may involve investigations, audits, or in-depth news stories.

Civil law Body of law that provides remedies for violation of private rights-deals with rights and duties between individuals.

Collaborative problem-solving strategy Firms emphasize long-term relationships with a variety of external constituencies and broad problem-solving perspectives on the resolution of social issues affecting their businesses and industries.

Collusion Fraud perpetrated by two or more employees or others, each of whose job responsibilities is necessary to complete the fraud.

Commercial data-mining software Commercial software packages that use query techniques to detect patterns and anomalies in data that may suggest fraud.

Committee of Sponsoring Organizations (COSO) Organization made up of representatives from major accounting firms that focus on internal controls and financial statement fraud.

Common-size financial statements Financial statements that have been converted to percentages.

Compensation committee Has the responsibility of evaluating executive performance and recommending terms and conditions of employment.

Complaint Request filed by a plaintiff to request civil proceedings against someone—usually to seek damages.

Compliance strategy Is focused on obedience to the law as its driving force.

Components of internal control The internal control components are the control environment, risk assessment, control activities, information and communication, and monitoring.

Computer controls (1) Controls performed by a computer, that is, controls programmed into computer software (contrast with manual controls). (2) Controls over computer processing of information, consisting of general controls and application controls (both programmed and manual).

Concealment investigative methods Investigating a fraud by focusing on the cover-up efforts, such as the manipulation of source documents.

Consistent norms Values that are more culturally specific, but that are consistent with hypernorms and other legitimate norms.

Contingent liability A possible liability. If the likelihood of payment is "probable," the contingent liability must be reported as a liability on the financial statements; if likelihood of payment is reasonably possible, it must be disclosed in the footnotes to the financial statements; if likelihood of payment is remote, no mention of the possible liability needs to be made.

Control A policy or procedure that is part of internal control.

Control activities or procedures Specific error-checking routines performed by company personnel.

Control environment The actions, policies, and procedures that reflect the overall attitudes of top management, the directors, and the owners about control and its importance to the entity.

Corporate citizenship Includes corporate social responsiveness and corporate social performance.

Corporate governance The method by which a firm is being governed, directed, administered, or controlled and to the goals for which it is being governed. Corporate governance is concerned with the relative roles, rights, and accountability of such stakeholder groups as owners, boards of directors, managers, employees, and others who assert to be stakeholders.

Corporate-level strategy Addresses what is often posed as the most defining question for a firm: "What business(es) are we in or should we be in?"

Corporate public affairs and public affairs management The management processes that focus on the formalization and institutionalization of corporate public policy. The public affairs function is a logical and increasingly prevalent component of the overall strategic management process.

Corporate public policy A firm's posture, stance, strategy, or position regarding the public, social, and ethical aspects of stakeholders and corporate functioning.

Corporate social performance model Includes social responsibility categories, philosophy (or mode) of social responsiveness, and social (or stakeholder) issues involved.

Corporate social responsiveness The action-oriented variant of corporate social responsibility.

Corrective control An action or procedure that will ensure the correction of an error or omission.

Corruption Dishonesty that involves the following schemes: (1) bribery, (2) conflicts of interest, (3) economic extortion, and (4) illegal gratuities.

Cost of goods sold The cost of goods sold to customers; calculated by subtracting ending inventory from the sum of beginning inventory plus purchases.

Cost of risk The sum of (1) outlays to reduce risks, (2) the opportunity cost of activities forgone due to risk considerations, (3) expenses of strategies to finance potential losses, and (4) the cost of reimbursed losses.

Covert operations Placing an agent in an undercover role in order to observe the suspect.

Creditor A person or entity owed money by a debtor.

Criminal law Branch of law that deals with offenses of a public nature or against society.

Crisis A major, unpredictable event that has potentially negative results. The event and its aftermath may significantly damage an organization and its employees, products, services, financial condition, and reputation.

Crisis resolution stage The final stage of a crisis and the goal of all crisis management efforts.

Criteria A set of standards against which an internal control system can be measured in determining its effectiveness.

Current ratio Measure of the liquidity of a business; equal to current assets divided by current liabilities.

Customer fraud Customers not paying for goods purchased, getting something for nothing, or deceiving organizations into giving them something they should not have.

D

Database Set of interrelated, centrally controlled data files that are stored with as little redundancy as possible. A database consolidates many records previously stored in separate files into a common pool of data and serves a variety of users and data processing applications.

Data theft Theft of data or personal information through such means as sniffing, spoofing, and customer impersonation.

Debtor A person or entity declaring bankruptcy.

Debt-to-equity ratio The number of dollars of borrowed funds for every dollar invested by owners; computed as total liabilities divided by total equity.

Deductive fraud detection Determining the types of frauds that can occur and then using query techniques and other methods to determine if those frauds may actually exist.

Deferred asset Expenditure that has been capitalized to be expensed in the future.

Deficiency A perceived, potential, or real internal control shortcoming, or an opportunity to strengthen the internal control system to provide a greater likelihood that the entity's objectives will be achieved.

Deposition Sworn testimony taken before a trial begins. At depositions, the opposing side's attorneys ask questions of witnesses.

Descriptive ethics Concerned with describing, characterizing, and studying the morality of a people, a culture, or a society.

Detective control A control designed to discover an unintended event or undesirable result that has been detected.

Digital signatures and certificates A signature sent over the Internet.

Disbursement fraud Having an organization pay for something it shouldn't pay for or pay too much for something it purchases.

Disclosure fraud The issuance of fraudulent or misleading statements or press releases without financial statement line-item effect or the lack of appropriate disclosures that should have been, but were not, made by management.

Discovery Legal process by which each party's attorneys try to find all information about the other side's case before a trial begins.

Discovery sampling Sampling used in fraud detection that assumes a zero expected error rate. The methodology allows an auditor to determine confidence levels and make inferences from the sample to the population.

Diversification Process of spreading risk through a firm's involvement in various businesses or through the location of its operations in different geographic areas.

Divorce The legal separation of two married partners resulting in the dissolution of their marriage.

Documentary evidence Evidence gathered from paper, documents, computer records, and other written, printed, or electronic sources.

Document examiner Specialized investigator who applies forensic chemistry, microscopy, photography, and other scientific methods to determine whether documents or other evidence are genuine, forged, counterfeit, or fraudulent.

Documents and records Documentation of all transactions in order to create an audit trail.

Dummy or shell company Fictitious entity created for the sole purpose of committing fraud; usually involves an employee making fraudulent payments to the dummy company.

Dynamic risks Uncertainties, either pure or speculative, that are produced because of societal changes.

E

Earnings per share Net income divided by the number of shares of stock outstanding; a measure of profitability.

E-Business The use of information technology and electronic communication networks to exchange business information and conduct transactions in electronic, paperless form.

Economic extortion scheme Involves an employee demanding payment from a vendor in order to make or influence a decision in that vendor's favor.

Effective internal control This reflects a state or condition of internal control. While internal control is a process, its effectiveness is a state or condition of the process at a point in time.

Electronic surveillance Using video, e-mail, wiretapping, and so on to watch fraud suspects.

Elements of fraud The theft act, concealment, and conversion that are present in every fraud.

Embezzlement Theft or fraudulent appropriation of money through deception; often used interchangeably with the term fraud.

Employee embezzlement Employees deceiving their employers by taking company assets.

Enterprise-level strategy The overarching strategy level that poses the basic questions, "What is the role of the organization in society?" and "What do we stand for?"

Enterprise risk-management Approach for managing both pure and speculative risks together; another name for *integrated risk-management*.

Environmental monitoring stage Focuses on the tracking of specific trends and events with an eye toward confirming or disconfirming trends or patterns.

Environmental scanning stage Focuses on identification of precursors or indicators of potential environmental changes and issues.

Ethical impact statement An attempt to assess the underlying moral justifications for corporate actions and the consequent results of those actions.

Ethical relativism Picking and choosing which source of norms to use based on what will justify current actions or maximize freedom.

Ethical responsibilities Those activities and practices that are expected or prohibited by societal members even though they are not codified into law.

Ethical values Moral values that enable a decision maker to determine an appropriate course of behavior; these values should be based on what is "right," which may go beyond what is "legal."

Ethics The discipline that deals with what is good and bad and with moral duty and obligation.

Evidence square A categorization of fraud investigative procedures that includes testimonial evidence, documentary evidence, physical evidence, and personal observation.

Evidential matter The underlying data and all corroborating information available about a fraud.

Expense scheme Scheme in which perpetrators produce false documents to claim false expenses.

Expert witness Trial witness who can offer opinions about a matter, based on unique experience, education, or training.

F

Falsified identity (customer impersonation) Pretending to be someone you're not—a major problem in e-business transactions.

Federal Courts Courts established by the federal government to enforce federal laws and statutes.

Financial risks Risk involving credit, foreign exchange, commodity trading, and interest rate; may involve chance for gain as well as loss.

Financial shenanigans Actions or omissions intended to hide or distort the real financial performance or financial condition of a business entity.

Financial statement fraud Intentional misstatement of financial statements by omitting critical facts or disclosures, misstating amounts, or misapplying GAAP.

Financial statements Financial reports such as the balance sheet, income statement, and statement of cash flows that summarize the profitability and cash flows of an entity for a specific period and the financial position of the entity as of a specific date.

Fixed assets Property, plant, and equipment assets of an organization; also called *long-term and noncurrent assets*.

Fixed point surveillance Watching a fraud suspect from a fixed point, such as a restaurant, office, or other set location.

Footnotes Information that accompanies a company's financial statements and that provides interpretive guidance to the financial statements or includes related information that must be disclosed.

Fraud "A generic term that embraces all the multifarious means which human ingenuity can devise, which are resorted to by one individual, to get an advantage over another by false representations. No definite and invariable rule can be laid down as a general proposition in defining fraud, as it includes surprise, trickery, cunning and unfair ways by which another is cheated. The only boundaries defining it are those which limit human knavery."

Full disclosure One of the responsibilities of a public corporation to its shareholders and potential shareholders.

Functional-level strategy Addresses the question, "How should a firm integrate its various subfunctional activities and how should these activities be related to changes taking place in the various functional areas?"

G

General controls Policies and procedures that help ensure the continued, proper operation of computer information systems. They include controls over data center operations, system software acquisition and maintenance, access security, and application system development and maintenance. General controls support the functioning of programmed application controls. Other terms sometimes used to describe general controls are general computer controls and information technology controls.

Global Reporting Initiative An international, multistakeholder effort to create a common framework for voluntary reporting of the economic, environmental, and social impact of organization-level activity.

Globalization Refers to the global economic integration of many formerly national economies into one global economy.

Golden parachute A contract in which a corporation agrees to make payments to key officers in control of the corporation.

Gramm-Leach Bliley Act Passed in 1999, this law prohibits the use of false pretenses to access the personal information of others. It does allow banks and other financial institutions to share or sell customer information, unless customers proactively "opt out" and asks that their information not be shared.

Grand jury Body of 4 to 23 individuals who deliberate in secret to decide whether there is sufficient evidence to charge someone in a preliminary hearing.

Grease payments Minor, facilitating payments to officials for the primary purpose getting them to do whatever they are supposed to do anyway.

Greenmail The repurchase of stock from an unwanted suitor at a higher-than-market price.

Gross profit margin Gross profit margin divided by net sales; a measure of markup.

H

Hard controls Based on objective evidence, hard controls are formal and tangible, and easier to measure and evaluate. An example is budget.

Hard skills Include technical skills such as functional skills, problem-solving and decision-making skills. In a way hard skills are acquired.

Hedging A transfer of risk from one party to another; similar to speculation and may be used to handle risks not subject to insurance, such as price fluctuations.

Higher trial courts State courts that try felony (larger crimes) and civil cases above a predetermined amount.

Horizontal analysis Tool that determines the percentage change in balance sheet and income statement numbers from one period to the next.

Hypernorms Transcultural values, including fundamental human rights.

I

Illegal gratuities Similar to bribery, except that there is no intent to influence a particular business decision, but rather to reward someone for making a favorable decision.

Illegitimate norms Norms that are incompatible with hypernorms (for example, exposing employees to unacceptable levels of carcinogens.

Immoral management A posture that is devoid of ethical principles or precepts and that implies a positive and active opposition to what is ethical.

Income statement Financial statement that reports the amount of net income earned by a company during a specified period.

Independent checks Procedures for verifying and monitoring other controls.

Individual/adversarial external affairs strategy Executives deny the legitimacy of social claims on their businesses and minimize the significance of challenges they receive from external critics.

Inductive fraud detection Proactively searching for fraud by identifying anomalies or unusual or unexpected patterns and/or relationships, without determining in advance the kinds of fraud for which you are looking.

Inherent limitations The limitations that apply to all internal control systems. The limitations relate to the limits of human judgment, resource constraints and the need to consider the cost of controls in relation to expected benefits, the reality that breakdowns can occur, and the possibility of management override and collusion.

Inherent risks A business's susceptibility to fraud, assuming that appropriate controls are not in place.

Initial pleading Complaint filed by a plaintiff to request legal proceedings against someone.

Inside directors Persons with some sort of ties to the firm.

Insider trading The practice of obtaining critical information inside a company and then using that information for one's own personal financial gain.

Intangible asset An asset that has no tangible existence (for example, goodwill).

Integrated risk management Approach for managing both pure and speculative risks together; another name for *enterprise risk management*.

Integrity strategy Is driven by ethical values that provide a common frame of reference and that serve to unify different functions, lines of business, and employee groups.

Integrity The quality or state of being of sound moral principle; uprightness, honesty, and sincerity; the desire to do the right thing and to profess and live up to a set of values and expectations.

Intentional amoral management Does not factor ethical considerations into decisions, actions, and behaviors because of the belief that business activity resides outside the sphere to which moral judgments apply.

Internal control A process effected by an entity's board of directors, management, and other personnel that is designed to provide reasonable assurance regarding the achievement of objectives such as (1) effectiveness and efficiency of operations, (2) reliability of financial reporting, and (3) compliance with applicable laws and regulations.

Internal control structure Specific policies and procedures designed to provide management with reasonable assurance that the goals and objectives it believes important to the entity will be met.

Internal control weakness Weakness in the control environment, accounting system, or the control activities or procedures.

Internationalization A process by which firms increase their awareness of the influence of international activities on their future and establish and conduct transactions with firms from other countries.

Interrogatory A series of written questions that specifically identify information needed from the opposing party.

Inventory turnover ratio Measure of the efficiency with which inventory is managed; computed by dividing cost of goods sold by average inventory for a period.

Investment scams The selling of fraudulent and worthless investments to unsuspecting investors.

Invigilation Imposing strict temporary controls on an activity so that, during the observation period, fraud is virtually impossible. Involves keeping detailed records before, during, and after the invigilation period and comparing suspicious activity during the three periods to obtain evidence about whether fraud is occurring.

Issues management and crisis management Two major ways by which business has responded to critical situations.

J

Jurisdiction The limit or territory over which an organization has authority.

K

Kickback fraud Fraud perpetrated by an employee and the employee's vendor or customer. Usually involves the employee buying goods or services from the vendor at an overstated price or giving the customer a lower-than-normal price, and in return the vendor or customer pays the employee a "kickback."

Kiting Fraud that conceals cash shortages by (1) transferring funds from one bank to another and (2) recording the receipt on or before the balance sheet date and the disbursement after the balance sheet date.

L

Labeling Teaching and training.

Lapping Fraud that involves stealing one customer's payment and then crediting that customer's account when a subsequent customer pays.

Larceny Intentionally taking an employer's cash or other assets without the consent and against the will of the employer, after it has been recorded in the company's accounting system.

Lease Obligation to make periodic payments over a specified period for use or "rent" of an asset; does not involve ownership of the asset.

Legitimation Dynamic process by which a business seeks to perpetuate its acceptance.

Less-developed countries (LDCs) Emerging or developing nations.

Liability frauds Financial statement fraud in which liabilities (amounts owed to others) are understated.

Lien Claim on property for the satisfaction of just debt.

Loss control Actions taken to reduce the frequency and/or severity of losses (risk reduction or mitigation).

Loss exposure A potential loss that may be associated with a specific type of risk.

Loss exposure checklist A risk identification tool used by businesses and individuals that lists many different potential losses. The user can determine which of the potential losses is relevant.

Lower trial courts State courts that try misdemeanors (small crimes) and pretrial issues.

M

Management controls Controls performed by one or more managers at any level in an organization.

Management fraud Deception perpetrated by an organization's top management through the manipulation of financial statement amounts or disclosures.

Management intervention Management's actions to overrule prescribed policies or procedures for legitimate purposes; management intervention is usually necessary to deal with nonrecurring and nonstandard transactions or events that otherwise might be handled inappropriately by the system.

Management override Management's overruling of prescribed policies or procedures for illegitimate purposes with the intent of personal gain or an enhanced presentation of an entity's financial condition or compliance status.

Management process The series of actions taken by management to run an entity. An internal control system is a part of and integrated with the management process.

Marketable securities Stocks, bonds, and other noncash assets; sometimes called short-term investments.

Marking the evidence Placing unique identification tags or descriptions on documents when they are received, so that they can be identified during the investigation and trial process.

Merger Combining of two organizations into one business entity.

Miscellaneous fraud Deception that doesn't fall into any of the other five categories of fraud.

Mobile observation Another term for *tailing*.

Modeling Setting an example.

Moral free space Norms that are inconsistent with at least some legitimate norms existing in other economic cultures.

Moral management Conforms to the highest standards of ethical behavior or professional standards of conduct; strives to be ethical in terms of its focus on high ethical norms and professional standards of conduct, motives, goals, orientation toward the law, and general operating strategy.

Mortgage Long-term loan secured by property, such as a home mortgage.

Motion Response to a complaint or pleading by the defendant. Sometimes "motion" refers to any request made to the judge for a ruling in a case by either party.

Motion for dismissal Request to the judge to dismiss a claim because there is no genuine issue of a material fact.

Moving surveillance Another term for tailing; involves following suspects wherever they go (within limits) and observing or recording their activities.

N

National Crime Information Center (NCIC) The major criminal database maintained by the FBI. This database contains information on stolen vehicles, securities, boats, missing persons, and other information helpful in fraud investigations.

Net income An overall measure of the performance of a company; equal to revenues minus expenses for the period.

Net worth method Analytical method that estimates a suspect's unexplained income. Liabilities are subtracted from assets to give net worth, then the previous year's net worth is subtracted to find the increase in net worth. Living expenses are then added to the change in net worth to determine a person's total income, and finally known income is subtracted from total income to determine the unknown income.

Nolo contendere Plea by a defendant that does not contest the charges but does not admit guilt.

Nominating committee Has the responsibility of ensuring that competent, objective board members are selected; usually composed of outside directors.

Nonsampling risk Risk that a sample will be examined and the characteristics of the sample will be misinterpreted.

Normative ethics Concerned with supplying and justifying a coherent moral system of thinking and judging.

Number of days in receivables 365 (number of days in a year) divided by accounts receivable turnover; a measure of how long it takes to collect receivables.

O

Objective risk The probable variation of actual from expected experience.

Operating performance ratio Net income divided by total sales; a measure of the percentage of revenues that become profits.

Operations Used with "objectives" or "controls" and having to do with the effectiveness and efficiency of an entity's operations, including performance and profitability goals, and safeguarding resources.

Opting-out right Right of customers to give written notice to financial institutions that prohibits the institution from sharing or selling customer's personal information.

Outside directors Persons who are independent of the firm and its top managers.

P

Participative management Management style that expects everyone in the organization to take ownership and responsibility for their conduct and responsibilities and that allows input into decisions.

Passwords Secret codes or names that allow users to access networks and other computer systems.

Payroll fraud scheme Using the payroll function to commit fraud, such as creating ghost employees or overpaying wages.

Pension Postretirement cash benefits paid to former employees.

Perceived opportunity A situation where people believe they have a favorable or promising combination of circumstances to commit fraud and not be detected.

Perceived pressure A situation where people perceive they have a need to commit fraud; a constraining influence on the will or mind, as a moral force.

Perpetrator A person who has committed a fraud.

Personal observation evidence Evidence that is sensed (seen, heard, felt, and so on) by investigators.

Philanthropic responsibilities Responsibilities viewed as such because they reflect current expectations of business by the public.

Philanthropy Contributions to charity and other worthy causes.

Physical evidence Evidence of a tangible nature—includes fingerprints, tire marks, weapons, stolen property, identification numbers or marks on stolen objects, and so on—that can be used in an investigation to provide information about a fraud or other crime.

Physical safeguards Vaults, fences, locks, and so on that protect assets from theft.

Poison pill A shareholder rights plan aimed at discouraging or preventing a hostile takeover.

Policy Management's dictate of what should be done to effect control. A policy serves as the basis for procedures for its implementation.

Population Collection of all units with similar characteristics from which samples are drawn.

Postal inspectors Inspectors or investigators hired by the U.S. Postal Service to handle major fraud cases that are perpetrated through the U.S. mail system.

Predication Circumstances that, taken as a whole, would lead a reasonable, prudent professional to believe that a fraud has occurred, is occurring, or will occur.

Preliminary hearing Pretrial hearing to determine whether there is "probable cause" to charge the defendant with a crime.

Preloss activities Loss control methods implemented before any losses occur. All measures with a frequency-reduction focus, as well as some based on severity reduction, are of this type.

Preventive control A control designed to avoid an unintended event or result.

Private Securities Litigation Reform Act of 1995 Law that made it more difficult for companies to bring class-action lawsuits to federal court.

Probability-impact matrix Assesses the probability of occurrence of an issue on one dimension and its impact on the company on the other dimension.

Procedure An action that implements a policy.

Process *See* Management process.

Prodromal crisis stage Warning or symptom stage of a crisis.

Profit margin Measure of the profit generated from each dollar of revenue; calculated by dividing net income by revenue. Also known as return on sales, profit margin percentage, profit margin ratio, or operating performance ratio.

Proxy process The method by which shareholders elect boards of directors.

Psychopath A person with a personality disorder, especially one manifested in aggressively antisocial behavior.

Public issues committee (public policy committee) A firm's mechanism for responding to public or social issues.

Public relations (PR)/Public affairs (PA) Principal distinctions are that, whereas PR deals with government as one of many publics, PA professionals are experts on government, and that whereas PR has many communication responsibilities, PA deals with issues management and serves as a corporate conscience.

Pure risk Uncertainty as to whether a loss will occur.

Q

Quick (acid-test) ratio Measure of a firm's ability to meet current liabilities, computed by dividing net quick assets (all current assets, except inventories and prepaid expenses) by current liabilities.

R

Rationalization Self-satisfying but incorrect reasons for one's behavior.

Reasonable assurance The concept that internal control, no matter how well designed and operated, cannot guarantee that an entity's objectives will be met. This is because of inherent limitations in all internal control systems.

Register disbursement scheme Scheme that involves false refunds or false voids.

Remedy Judgments asked for in civil cases (what it would take to right a private wrong).

Reportable condition An internal control deficiency related to financial reporting; it is a significant deficiency in the design or operation of the internal control system that could adversely affect the entity's ability to record, process, summarize, and report financial data consistent with the assertions of management in the financial statements.

Repurchase agreements Agreement to buy back something previously sold.

Request for admission Request that the opposing party admit designated facts relevant to litigation.

Restructuring Reevaluation of a company's assets because of impairment of value or for other reasons. Restructured companies usually have lower amounts of assets and look quite different than before the restructuring.

Return on equity Measure of the profit earned per dollar of investment; computed by dividing net income by equity.

Revenue Increases in a company's resources from the sale of goods or services.

Revenue recognition Determining that revenues have been earned and are collectible and thus should be reported on the income statement.

Risk Uncertainty as to economic loss.

Risk-adjusted return on capital (RAROC) Assesses how much capital would be required by the organization's various activities (such as products, projects, loans, and so on) to keep the probability of bankruptcy below a specified probability level.

Risk arbitrage The opportunistic buying and selling of companies that appear on the verge of being taken over by other firms.

Risk assessment The identification, analysis, and management of risk, such as the risk associated with the possibility of fraud.

Risk avoidance A conscious decision not to expose oneself or one's firm to a particular risk of loss.

Risk management The process used to systematically manage pure risk exposures.

Risk-management information system (RMIS) A computer software program that assists in tracking and statistical analysis of past losses.

Risk-management policy A plan, procedure, or rule of action followed for the purpose of securing consistent action over a period of time.

Risk-management process (1) Identify risks, (2) evaluate risks as to frequency and severity, (3) select risk-management techniques, and (4) implement and review decisions.

Risk manager An individual charged with minimizing the adverse impact of losses on the achievement of a company's goals.

Risk mapping (risk profiling) Method of risk identification and assessment by arranging all risks in a matrix reflecting frequency, severity, and existing insurance coverage.

Risk reduction A decrease in the total amount of uncertainty present in a particular situation.

Risk retention Handling risk by bearing the results of risk, rather than employing other methods of handling it, such as transfer or avoidance.

Risk transfer A risk-management technique whereby one party (transferor) pays another (transferee) to assume a risk that the transferor desires to escape.

S

Sales return percentage (ratio) Sales returns divided by total sales; a measure of the percentage of sales being returned by customers.

Sales returns (sales returns and allowances) Sold merchandise that is returned by customers and/or damaged, or other sold merchandise for which credit is given.

Sample Portion of the population that is examined in order to draw inferences about the population.

Sampling risk Risk that a sample is not representative of the population.

Search warrant Order issued by a judge that gives the investigator consent to search a suspect's personal information, such as bank records, tax returns, or their premises.

Securities and Exchange Commission (SEC) Government body responsible for regulating stock trading and the financial statements and reports of public companies.

Segregation of duties Division of tasks into two parts, so one person does not have complete control of the task.

Settlement Negotiated pretrial agreement between the parties to resolve a legal dispute.

Skimming Removal of cash from a victim organization prior to its entry in an accounting system.

Sniffing Illegal or unauthorized viewing of information as it passes along a network communication channel.

Social audit A systematic attempt to identify, measure, monitor, and evaluate an organization's performance with respect to its social efforts, goals, and programs.

Socially conscious (or ethical investing) movement A comprehensive investing approach complete with social and environmental screens, shareholder activism, and community investment.

Soft controls Based on subjective evidence, soft controls are informal and intangible, and difficult to measure and evaluate. An example is ethical behavior.

Soft skills Include interpersonal skills, motivation, leadership, and communication skills. Also known as people skills. In a way soft skills are innate.

Speculative risk The uncertainty of an event that could produce either a profit or a loss, such as a business venture or a gambling transaction.

Spoofing Changing the information in an e-mail header or an IP address used to hide identities.

Stakeholder audit A systematic attempt to identify and measure an organization's stakeholders' issues and measure and evaluate their opinions with respect to its effective resolution.

Stakeholder environment Composed of trends, events, issues, expectations, and forecasts that may have a bearing on the strategic management process and the development of corporate public policy.

Statement of cash flows Financial statement that reports an entity's cash inflows (receipts) and outflows (payments) during an accounting period.

Static surveillance Another term for fixed-point surveillance.

Stationary surveillance Locating a scene to be observed, anticipating the actions that are most likely to occur at the scene, and keeping detailed notes on tape or film on all activities involving the suspect.

Statistical analysis The use of statistics and number patterns to discover relationships in certain data, such as Benford's law.

Statute A law or regulation; a law enacted by the legislative branch of a government.

Strategic management The overall management process that focuses on positioning a firm relative to its environment.

Subjective risk The risk based on the mental state of an individual who experiences uncertainty or doubt as to the outcome of a given event.

Subpoena (subpoena duces tecum) Order issued by a court or a grand jury to produce documents or requiring a witness to submit to a deposition, give testimony at trial, or report to an administrative body.

Surveillance Investigation technique that relies on the senses, especially hearing and seeing.

Sweatshops Businesses characterized by child labor, low pay, poor working conditions, worker abuse, and health and safety violations.

System of authorizations A system of limits on who can and cannot perform certain functions.

T

Tailing Secretly following a fraud suspect in an attempt to gain additional information; another name for moving surveillance.

Tax courts Federal courts that hear only tax cases.

Testimonial evidence Evidence based on querying techniques, such as interviewing, interrogation, and honesty testing.

Theft investigation methods Investigation methods that focus on the actual transfer of assets from the victim to the perpetrator; helps determine how the theft was committed and often includes methods such as surveillance and covert operations, invigilation, and the obtaining of physical evidence.

Trash investigation Searching through a person's trash for possible evidence in an investigation.

Treadway Commission National Commission on Fraudulent Financial Reporting that made recommendations on financial statement fraud and other matters in 1987.

Trustee Individual or firm who collects a debtor's assets and distributes them to creditors.

U

Unearned revenues Amounts that have been received from customers but for which performance of a service or sale of a product has not yet been made.

Unintentional amoral management Results when managers are casual about, careless about, or inattentive to the fact that their decisions and actions may have negative or deleterious effects on others.

V

Value at risk (VAR) Estimate of the risk of loss at various probability levels.

Value chain Activities in an organization are related to what is sometimes referred to as the *value chain:* inbound (receiving), operations (production or service), outbound (shipping), marketing, sales, and service.

Vendor fraud An overcharge for purchased goods, the shipment of inferior goods, or the nonshipment of goods even though payment is made.

Vertical analysis Tool that converts financial statement numbers to percentages so that they are easy to understand and analyze.

Victim The person or organization deceived by the perpetrator.

Voir dire Legal process of qualifying an expert witness.

Vulnerability chart Tool that coordinates the various elements of a fraud investigation to help identify possible suspects.

W

Warrant Order issued by a judge to arrest someone.

Warranty liabilities Obligation to perform service and repair items sold within a specific period of time and/or use after sale.

Web-visit hijacking Mimicking another, similarly named Web site in order to trick or confuse e-mail and e-business users into sending information to a business other than the intended one.

Working capital turnover ratio Sales divided by average working capital; a measure of the amount of working capital used to generate revenues.

Module 900 Endnotes

1. William E. Thomas, Jr., *Readings in Cost Accounting, Budgeting, and Control,* 4th ed., Cincinnati, OH: Southwestern Publishing, 1973.
2. Robert Simons, *Levers of Control: How Managers Use Innovative Control Systems to Drive Strategic Renewal,* Boston, MA: President and Fellows of Harvard College, 1995.
3. Committee of Sponsoring Organizations of the Treadway Commission, *Internal Control-Integrated Framework,* Jersey City, New Jersey: American Institute of Certified Public Accountants, 1994.
4. Ibid.
5. "McNamara's Money Game," *Newsday: The Long Island Newspaper,* April 16, 1992, pp. 4–5.
6. *Webster's New World Dictionary, College Edition.* 1964. Cleveland and New York: World, p. 380.
7. The Association of Certified Fraud Examiners. 1996. *The Report to the Nation on Occupation Fraud and Abuse,* Austin, TX: ACFE, p. 4.
8. Ibid., p. 9.
9. U.S. Securities and Exchange Commission, Litigation Release No. 17039, June 19, 2001 (http://www.sec.gov).
10. See, for example, W. S. Albrecht, D. Cherrington, R. Payne, A. Roe, and M. Romney, How to Detect and Prevent Business Fraud, Prentice-Hall, 1981.
11. For example, several studies on retail theft over time by Richard C. Hollinger (University of Florida) and others have shown that a higher percentage of employees were dishonest in later years than in earlier years. Other studies have found similar results.
12. See *How to Detect and Prevent Business Fraud,* op. cit.
13. http://www.better-investing.org.
14. From speech by Lynn Turner, former chief accountant of U.S. Securities and Exchange Commission, given at the 39th Annual Corporate Counsel Institute, Northwestern University School of Law, October 12, 2000.
15. Almost every year, KPMG Forensic and Investigative Services conducts a fraud survey. These surveys show that almost all companies surveyed have major frauds. For more information about the surveys, contact Michael D. Carey, NY (212-872-6825).
16. For example, read the research of the Social and Moral Research Group, University of Maryland (http://www.education.umd.edu/Depts/EDHD/faculty/killen/SMDRG).

17. See, for example, *Theory O: Creating an Ownership Style of Management,* discussed at http://www.nceo.org/pubs/theoryo.html.
18. See, for example, *2002 Report to the Nation: Occupational Fraud and Abuse,* Association of Certified Fraud Examiners, Austin, Texas, 2002.
19. See, for example, *Deterring Fraud: The Internal Auditor's Perspective,* W. Steve Albrecht, K. Howe, and M. Romney, The Institute of Internal Auditors, Altamonte Spring, Florida, 1984.
20. Class-action lawsuits are permitted under federal law and some state rules of court procedure in the United States. In a class-action suit, a relatively small number of aggrieved plaintiffs with small individual claims can bring suit for large damages in the name of an extended class. After a fraud, for example, 40 bondholders who lost $40,000 might decide to sue, and they can sue on behalf of the entire class of bondholders for all their alleged losses (say $50 million). Lawyers are more than happy to take such suits on a contingency fee basis (a percentage of the judgment, if any).
21. Material from *Occupational Fraud and Abuse,* published by Obsidian Publishing Company, Inc., in 1997 (800 West Avenue, Austin, Texas 78701), is used with permission. After working for the FBI, Joe Wells started Wells & Associates, a group of consulting criminologists that concentrates on white-collar crime prevention, detection, and education. That venture led to the formation of the Association of Certified Fraud Examiners, a professional organization of fraud professionals that now has approximately 25,000 members. Since its inception, Joe Wells has been the Chairman of the Board of Directors and CEO.
22. Form 8–K is the SEC report filed at the end of any month in which significant events have occurred that are of interest to public investors. Such events include the acquisition or sale of a subsidiary, a change in officers or directors, an addition of a new product line, or a change in auditors.
23. A straw buyer helps someone commit fraud by pretending to buy the property at an inflated price. A straw buyer is an "unreal" buyer that is being represented as buying something, when in reality he or she is only helping the perpetrator commit fraud. In Lincoln's case, straw buyers (friends of Keating) were told that if they would "park" the properties on their financial statements for a time, Keating would assume all the risk and even take the properties back.
24. *Fraudulent Financial Reporting: 1987–1997: An Analysis of U.S. Public Companies,* op. cit., p. 80.
25. M. S. Beasley, J. V. Carcello, and D. R. Hermanson, 1999, *Fraudulent Financial Reporting: 1987–1997: An Analysis of U.S. Public Companies,* Committee of Sponsoring Organizations (COSO).
26. Form 8–K is the report filed at the end of any month in which significant events have occurred that are of interest to public investors. Such events include the acquisition or sale of a subsidiary, a change in officers or directors, an addition of a new product line, or a change in auditors.
27. Howard M. Schilit, *What Directors Can Do to Prevent and Detect Financial Shenanigans,* Washington DC: National Association of Corporate Directors (NACD), 1994.
28. Quoted in John L. Paluszek, *Business and Society: 1976–2000* (New York: AMACOM, 1976), 1.
29. Keith Davis, "Understanding the Social Responsibility Puzzle," *Business Horizon* (Winter 1967), 45–50.
30. Archie B. Carroll, "A Three-Dimensional Conceptual Model of Corporate Social Performance," *Academy of Management Review* (Vol. 4, No. 4, 1979), 497–505.
31. Archie B. Carroll, "The Pyramid of Corporate Social Responsibility: Toward the Moral Management of Organizational Stakeholders," *Business Horizons* (July-August 1991), 39–48. Also see Archie B. Carroll, "The Four Faces of Corporate Citizenship," *Business and Society Review* (Vol. 100–101, 1998), 1–7.
32. Ibid.
33. Milton Friedman, "The Social Responsibility of Business Is to Increase Its Profits," *New York Times* (September 1962), 126.
34. Ibid., 33 (emphasis added).
35. Christopher D. Stone, *Where the Law Ends* (New York: Harper Colophon Books, 1975), 77.
36. Keith Davis, "The Case For and Against Business Assumption of Social Responsibilities," *Academy of Management Journal* (June 1973), 312–322.
37. F. A. Hayek, "The Corporation in a Democratic Society: In Whose Interest Ought It and Will It Be Run?" in H. Ansoff (ed.), *Business Strategy* (Middlesex: Penguin, 1969), 225.
38. Davis, 320.
39. Thomas A. Petit, *The Moral Crisis in Management* (New York: McGraw-Hill, 1967), 58.
40. Davis, 316.
41. Cited in Aaron Bernstein, "Too Much Corporate Power," *Business Week* (September 11, 2000), 149.
42. Robert Ackerman and Raymond Bauer, *Corporate Social Responsiveness: The Modern Dilemma* (Reston, VA: Reston Publishing Company, 1976), 6.
43. S. Prakash Sethi, "Dimensions of Corporate Social Performance: An Analytical Framework," *California Management Review* (Spring 1975), 58–64.
44. Ibid., 62–63.
45. William C. Frederick, "From CSR_1 to CSR_2: The Maturing of Business-and-Society Thought," Working Paper No. 279 (Graduate School of Business, University of Pittsburgh, 1978), 6. See also *Business and Society* (Vol. 33, No. 2, August 1994), 150–164.

46. William C. Frederick, "Toward CSR$_3$: Why Ethical Analysis Is Indispensable and Unavoidable in Corporate Affairs," *California Management Review* (Winter 1986), 131.
47. Epstein, 107.
48. Ian Wilson, "What One Company Is Doing About Today's Demands on Business," in G.A. Steiner (ed.), *Changing Business-Society Interrelationships* (UCLA, 1975).
49. T. W. McAdam, "How to Put Corporate Responsibility into Practice," *Business and Society Review/Innovation* (Summer 1973), 8–16.
50. Davis and Blomstrom, 85–86.
51. James E. Post, *Corporate Behavior and Social Change* (Reston, VA: Reston Publishing Co., 1978), 39.
52. Juha Näsi, Salme Näsi, Nelson Phillips, and Stelios Zyglidopoulos, "The Evolution of Corporate Responsiveness," *Business and Society* (Vol. 36, No. 3, September 1997), 296–321.
53. Carroll, 1979, 502–504.
54. Samuel P. Graves, Sandra Waddock, and Marjorie Kelly, "How Do You Measure Corporate Citizenship?" *Business Ethics*, March/April 2001, 17.
55. Charles J. Fombrum, "Three Pillars of Corporate Citizenship," in Noel Tichy, Andrew McGill, and Lynda St. Clair (eds.), *Corporate Global Citizenship* (San Francisco: The New Lexington Press), 27–61.
56. Kimberly S. Davenport, "Corporate Citizenship: A Stakeholder Approach for Defining Corporate Social Performance and Identifying Measures for Assessing It," doctoral dissertation, The Fielding Institute, Santa Barbara, CA.
57. Archie B. Carroll, "The Four Faces of Corporate Citizenship," *Business and Society Review*, 100/101, 1998, 1–7.
58. Barbara W. Altman, *Corporate Community Relations in the 1990s: A Study in Transformation,* Unpublished doctoral dissertation, Boston University.
59. Archie B. Carroll, Kim Davenport, and Doug Grisaffe, "Appraising the Business Value of Corporate Citizenship: What Does the Literature Say?" Proceedings of the International Association for Business and Society, Essex Junction, VT, 2000.
60. For more on corporate citizenship, see the special issue "Corporate Citizenship," *Business and Society Review*, 105:1, Spring 2000, edited by Barbara W. Altman and Deborah Vidaver-Cohen; also see Jorg Andriof and Malcolm McIntosh (eds.) *Perspectives on Corporate Citizenship* (London: Greenleaf Publishing, 2001). Also see, Isabelle Maignan, O. C. Ferrell, and G. Tomas M. Hult, "Corporate Citizenship: Cultural Antecedents and Business Benefits," *Journal of the Academy of Marketing Science* (Vol. 27, No. 4, Fall 1999), 455–469. Also see Malcolm McIntosh, Deborah Leipziger, Keith Jones, and Gill Coleman, *Corporate Citizenship: Successful Strategies for Responsible Companies* (London: Financial Times/ Pitman Publishing), 1998.
61. Philip Johansson, "Social Investing Turns 30," *Business Ethics* (January-February 2001), 12–16.
62. "Good Works and Great Profits," *Business Week* (February 16, 1998), 8.
63. Samuel B. Graves and Sandra A. Waddock, "Institutional Owners and Corporate Social Performance," *Academy of Management Journal* (Vol. 37, No. 4, August 1994), 1034–1046.
64. Ibid.
65. Charles W. Hofer, Edwin A. Murray, Jr., Ram Charan, and Robert A. Pitts, *Strategic Management: A Casebook in Policy and Planning*, 2d ed. (St. Paul, MN: West Publishing Co., 1984), 27–29. Also see Gary Hamel and C. K. Prahalad, *Competing for the Future* (Boston: Harvard Business School Press, 1994).
66. C. W. Hofer and D. E. Schendel, *Strategy Formulation: Analytial Concepts* (St. Paul: West, 1978), 52–55. Also see J. David Hunger and Thomas L. Wheelen, *Essentials of Strategic Management* (Reading, MA: Addison-Wesley, 2000).
67. V. K. Narayanan and Liam Fahey, "Environmental Analysis for Strategy Formulation," in William R. King and David I. Cleland (eds.) *Strategic Planning and Management Handbook* (New York: Van Nostrand Reinhold, 1987), 156.
68. Robert H. Miles, *Managing the Corporate Social Environment: A Grounded Theory* (Englewood Cliffs, NJ: Prentice-Hall, Inc., 1987).
69. Ibid., 8.
70. Ibid., 9–10, 111.
71. Ibid., 2–3.
72. Ibid., 11, 113.
73. Fleisher (ed.), 1997, 139–196.
74. David H. Blake, "How to Incorporate Public Affairs into the Operating Manager's Job," *Public Affairs Review* (1984), 35.
75. Liam Fahey, "Issues Management: Two Approaches," *Strategic Planning Management* (November 1986), 81, 85–96.
76. Ibid., 81.
77. Ibid., 86.
78. Ibid., 32.
79. William R. King, "Strategic Issue Management," in William R. King and David I. Cleland (eds.) *Strategic Planning and Management Handbook* (New York: Van Nostrand Reinhold, 1987), 257.

80. James K. Brown, *This Business of Issues: Coping with the Company's Environment* (New York: The Conference Board, 1979), 45.
81. Ibid., 33.
82. King, 257.
83. Joseph F. Coates, Vary T. Coates, Jennifer Jarratt, and Lisa Heinz, *Issues Management* (Mt. Airy, MD: Lomond Publications, 1986), p. 46.
84. I. C. MacMillan and P. E. Jones, "Designing Organizations to Compete," *Journal of Business Strategy* (Vol. 4, No. 4, Spring 1984), 13.
85. Roy Wernham, "Implementation: The Things That Matter," in King and Cleland, 453.
86. Barbara Bigelow, Liam Fahey, and John Mahon, "A Typology of Issue Evolution," *Business & Society* (Spring 1993), 28. For another useful perspective, see John F. Mahon and Sandra A. Waddock, "Strategic Issues Management: An Integration of Issue Life Cycle Perspectives," *Business & Society* (Spring 1992), 19–32. Also see Steven L. Wartick and Robert E. Rude, "Issues Management: Fad or Function," *California Management Review* (Fall 1986), 134–140.
87. Public Affairs Council, "Public Affairs: Its Origins, Its Present, and Its Trends," http://www.pac.org/whatis/index.htm; 2001.
88. Kate Miller, "Issues Management: The Link Between Organization Reality and Public Perception," *Public Relations Quarterly* (Vol. 44, No. 2, Summer 1999), 5–11.
89. Laurence Barton, *Crisis in Organizations: Managing and Communicating in the Heat of Chaos* (Cincinnati: South-Western Publishing Co., 1993), 2.
90. Christine M. Pearson and Judith Clair, "Reframing Crisis Management," *Academy of Management Review* (Vol. 23, No. 1, 1998), 60.
91. Steven Fink, *Crisis Management: Planning for the Inevitable* (New York: Amacom, 1986), p. 68. For further discussion of types of crises, see Ian Mitroff, "Crisis Management and Environmentalism: A Natural Fit," *California Management Review* (Winter 1994), 101–113.
92. Pearson and Clair, 60.
93. Ian Mitroff, with Gus Anagnos, *Managing Crises Before They Happen: What Every Executive and Manager Needs to Know about Crisis Management,* New York: AMACOM, 2001, Chapter 3.
94. Fink, 20.
95. Mitroff and Anagnos, 2001.
96. "How Companies Are Learning to Prepare for the Worst," *Business Week* (December 23, 1985), 74–75.
97. "How Companies Are Learning to Prepare for the Worst," *Business Week* (December 23, 1985), 76.
98. Ibid.
99. Ibid.
100. Richard J. Mahoney, "The Anatomy of a Public Policy Crisis," *The CEO Series,* Center for the Study of American Business (May 1996), 7.
101. Ibid.
102. Greg Jaffe, "How Florida Crash Overwhelmed ValuJet's Skillful Crisis Control," *The Wall Street Journal* (June 5, 1996), S1.
103. Melissa Master, "Keyword: Crisis," *Across the Board* (September 1998), 62.
104. Ian Mitroff, Paul Shrivastava, and Firdaus Udwadia, "Effective Crisis Management," *Academy of Management Executive* (November 1987), 285.
105. Norman R. Augustine, "Managing the Crisis You Tried to Prevent," *Harvard Business Review* (November-December 1995), 147–158.
106. Christine M. Pearson and Ian I. Mitroff, "From Crisis Prone to Crisis Prepared: A Framework for Crisis Management," *Academy of Management Executive* (Vol. VII, No. 1, February 1993), 58–59. Also see Ian Mitroff, Christine M. Pearson, and L. Katherine Harrington, *The Essential Guide to Managing Corporate Crises* (New York: Oxford University Press, 1996).
107. Robert Goff, "Coming Clean," Forbes (May 17, 1999), 156–160.
108. Ibid.
109. Johnathan L. Bernstein, "The Ten Steps of Crisis Communications," June 4, 2001, Internet source: http://www.crisisnavigator.org.
110. Richard Wm. Brundage, "Crisis Management—An Outline for Survival." June 4, 2001, Internet source: http://www.crisisnavigator.org.
111. Mitroff and Anagnos, 2001.
112. Richard T. DeGeorge, *Business Ethics,* 4th ed. (New York: Prentice Hall, 1995), 20–21; See also Rogene A. Buchholz and Sandra B. Rosenthal, *Business Ethics* (Upper Saddle River, NJ: Prentice Hall, 1998), 3.
113. DeGeorge, op. cit.15.
114. See, for example, Melissa Baucus and Janet Near, "Can Illegal Corporate Behavior Be Predicted? An Event History Analysis," *Academy of Management Journal* (Vol. 34, No. 1, 1991), 9–36; and P. L. Cochran and D. Nigh, "Illegal Corporate Behavior and the Question of Moral Agency," in William C. Frederick (ed.), *Research in Corporate Social Performance and Policy,* Vol. 9 (Greenwich, CT: JAI Press, 1987), 73–91.

115. For examples that may fit in the various portions of the model, see Mark Schwartz, "Developing Portraits of Corporate Social Responsibility," 1995, unpublished manuscript; See also Mark Schwartz, "Carroll's Pyramid of Corporate Social Responsibility: A New Approach," IABS Proceedings, 1997, 236–241.
116. Otto A. Bremer, "An Approach to Questions of Ethics in Business," *Audenshaw Document No. 116* (North Hinksey, Oxford: The Hinksey Centre, Westminster College, 1983), 1–12.
117. Andrew Stark, "What's the Matter with Business Ethics?" *Harvard Business Review* (May-June, 1993), 7.
118. Most of the material in this section comes from Archie B. Carroll, "In Search of the Moral Manager," *Business Horizons* (March/April 1987), 7–15; See also Archie B. Carroll, "Models of Management Morality for the New Millennium," *Business Ethics Quarterly,* Vol. 11, Issue 2, April 2001, 365–371.
119. Lynn Sharp Paine, "Managing for Organizational Integrity," *Harvard Business Review* (March-April, 1994), 106–117.
120. Ibid., 111–112.
121. Paine, 109–113.
122. Carroll, 1987, 7–15.
123. Charles W. Powers and David Vogel, *Ethics in the Education of Business Managers* (Hastings-on-Hudson, NY: The Hastings Center, 1980), 40–45. Also see Patricia H. Werhane, Moral Imagination and Management Decision Making, New York: Oxford University Press, 1999.
124. Milton Friedman, "The Social Responsibility of Business Is to Increase Its Profits," *The New York Times* (September, 1962), 126 (italics added).
125. Cited in Edwin M. Epstein and Dow Votaw (eds.) *Rationality, Legitimacy, Responsibility: Search for New Directions in Business and Society* (Santa Monica, CA: Goodyear Publishing Co., 1978), 72.
126. Ibid., 73.
127. Ibid.
128. Ibid.
129. Ibid.
130. William R. Dill (ed.) *Running the American Corporation* (Englewood Cliffs, NJ: Prentice-Hall, 1978), 11.
131. Ibid.
132. Ibid.
133. Louis Lavelle, "Shhh, You'll Wake the Board," *Business Week* (March 5, 2001), 92.
134. Ibid.
135. John A. Byrne, "The Best and Worst Boards," *Business Week* (January 24, 2000), 142.
136. Robert W. Lear and Boris Yavitz, "Boards on Trial," *Chief Executive* (October 2000), 40–48.
137. "The Fading Appeal of the Boardroom," *The Economist* (February 10, 2001), 67–69.
138. "Europe's Shareholders to the Barricades," *Business Week* (March 19, 2001).
139. Murray L. Weidenbaum, *Strengthening the Corporate Board: A Constructive Response to Hostile Takeovers* (St. Louis: Washington University, Center for the Study of American Business, September 1985), 4–5.
140. Linda Himelstein, "Boardrooms: The Ties That Blind," *Business Week* (May 2, 1994), 112–114.
141. Carol J. Loomis, "This Stuff Is Wrong," *Fortune* (June 25, 2001), 72–84.
142. John A. Byrne, "Executive Pay: Deliver-Or Else," *Business Week* (March 27, 1995), 36–38.
143. Nikos Vafeas and Zaharoulla Afxentiou, "The Association Between the SEC's 1992 Compensation Disclosure Rule and Executive Compensation Policy Changes," *Journal of Accounting and Public Policy* (Spring 1998), 27–54.
144. Ann Buchholtz, Michael Young, and Gary Powell, "Are Board Members Pawns or Watchdogs? The Link Between CEO Pay and Firm Performance," *Group and Organization Management* (March 1998), 6–26.
145. Tracey Grant, "Big Bucks on Board," *The Washington Post* (September 29, 1997), F3.
146. Geoffrey Colvin, "Is the Board Too Cushy?" *Director* (February 1997), 64–65.
147. "The Fading Appeal of the Boardroom," *The Economist* (February 10, 2001), 67.
148. Ed Leefeldt, "Greenmail, Far from Disappearing, Is Doing Quite Well in Disguised Forms," *The Wall Street Journal* (December 4, 1984), 15.
149. Ruth Simon, "Needed: A Generic Remedy," *Forbes* (November 5, 1984), 40.
150. Craig W. Friedrich, "Recent Developments," *Journal of Corporate Taxation* (Winter 1998), 422–425.
151. Ibid.
152. Verne Kopytoff, "Yahoo's Not an Attractive Target for a Takeover, Analysts Say," *San Francisco Chronicle* (March 3, 2001), D1.
153. Philip L. Cochran and Steven L. Wartick, "Golden Parachutes: Good for Management and Society?" in S. Prakash Sethi and Cecilia M. Falbe (eds.) *Business and Society: Dimensions of Conflict and Cooperation* (Lexington, MA: Lexington Books, 1987), 321.

154. Ann K. Buchholtz and Barbara A. Ribbens, "Role of Chief Executive Officers in Takeover Resistance: Effects of CEO Incentives and Individual Characteristics," *Academy of Management Journal* (June 1994), 554–579.
155. Cochran and Wartick, 325–326.
156. George Russell, "The Fall of a Wall Street Superstar," *Time* (November 24, 1986), 71.
157. Ibid.
158. Donald Baer, "Getting Even with Ivan and Company," *U.S. News & World Report* (March 2, 1987), 46.
159. Anthony Bianco and Gary Weiss, "Suddenly the Fish Get Bigger," *Business Week* (March 2, 1987), 29–30.
160. "New Arrests on Wall Street: Who's Next in the Insider Trading Scandal?" *Newsweek* (February 23, 1987), 48–50.
161. James B. Stewart, "Scenes from a Scandal: The Secret World of Michael Milkin and Ivan Boesky," *The Wall Street Journal* (October 2, 1991), B1.
162. Christopher H. Schmitt, "The SEC Lifts the Curtain on Company Info," *Business Week* (August 11, 2000).
163. "A Landmark Ruling That Puts Board Members in Peril," *Business Week* (March 18, 1985), 56–57.
164. Laurie Baum and John A. Byrne, "The Job Nobody Wants: Outside Directors Find That the Risks and Hassles Just Aren't Worth It," *Business Week* (September 8, 1986), 57.
165. Paul E. Fiorella, "Why Comply? Directors Face Heightened Personal Liability After Caremark," *Business Horizons* (July/August 1998), 49–52.
166. "The Fading Appeal of the Boardroom," *The Economist* (February 10, 2001), 67.
167. Toddi Gutner, "Wanted: More Diverse Directors," *Business Week* (April 30, 2001), 134.
168. "Board Diversity Increases," *Association Management* (January 2000), 25.
169. Paul Coombes and Mark Watson, "Three Surveys on Corporate Governance," *McKinsey Quarterly* (2000, No. 4), cited in "The Fading Appeal of the Boardroom," *The Economist* (February 10, 2001), 67–69.
170. "The Fading Appeal of the Boardroom," *The Economist* (February 10, 2001), 67.
171. Ibid.
172. Gutner, 134.
173. Joann S. Lublin and Elizabeth MacDonald, "Scandals Signal Laxity of Audit Panels," *The Wall Street Journal* (July 17, 1998), B1.
174. Charles A. Anderson and Robert N. Anthony, *The New Corporate Directors: Insights for Board Members and Executives* (New York: John Wiley & Sons, 1986), 141.
175. Arjay Miller, "A Director's Questions," *The Wall Street Journal* (August 18, 1980), 10.
176. Donald E. Schwartz, "Corporate Governance," in Thorton Bradshaw and David Vogel (eds.) *Corporations and Their Critics* (New York: McGraw-Hill, 1981), 227–228.
177. Bruce Nussbaum and Judith Dobrzynski, "The Battle for Corporate Control," *Business Week* (May 18, 1987), 102–109.
178. Lauren Tainer, *The Origins of Shareholder Activism* (Washington, DC: Investor Responsibility Research Center, July 1983), 2.
179. Leonard Apcar and Terry Brown, "GM Reputation Is Defended by Chairman Under Barrage of Shareholder Questions," *The Wall Street Journal* (May 23, 1977), 17.
180. Thomas J. Neff, "Liability Panic in the Board Room," *The Wall Street Journal* (November 10, 1986), 22.
181. Julie Amparano, "A Lawyer Flourishes by Suing Corporations for Their Shareholders," *The Wall Street Journal* (April 28, 1987), 1.
182. Richard B. Schmitt, "Attorneys Are Often Big Winners When Shareholders Sue Companies," *The Wall Street Journal* (June 12, 1986), 31.
183. Steven M. Schatz and Douglas J. Clark, "Securities Litigation," *International Financial Law Review* (June 1998), 27.
184. "Securities Litigation Reore Revisited," *Journal of Accountancy* (January 1999), 20–21.
185. "The Responsibility of a Corporation to Its Shareholders," *Criteria for Decision Making* (C.W. Post Center, Long Island University, 1979), 14.
186. Ibid., 14–15.
187. James E. Post, "Assessing the Nestlé Boycott: Corporate Accountability and Human Rights," *California Management Review* (Winter 1985), 115–116.
188. Ibid., 116–117.
189. Stuart Diamond, "The Disaster in Bhopal: Lessons for the Future," *The New York Times* (February 5, 1985), 1; See also Russell Mokhiber, "Bhopal," *Corporate Crime and Violence* (San Francisco: Sierra Club Books, 1988), 86–96.
190. Stuart Diamond, "Disaster in India Sharpens Debate on Doing Business in Third World," *The New York Times* (December 16, 1984), 1.
191. Ibid., 1.
192. Mark Clifford, Michael Shari, and Linda Himelstein, "Pangs of Conscience: Sweatshops Haunt U.S. Consumers," *Business Week* (July 29, 1996), 46–47; See also Keith B. Richburg and Anne Swardson, "Sweatshops or Economic Development?" The *Washington Post National Weekly Edition* (August 5–11, 1996), 19.

193. "Stamping Out Sweatshops," *The Economist* (April 19, 1997), 28–29.
194. Clifford, Shari, and Himelstein, 46.
195. Andrew Young, "A Debate over Child Labor: The World's Next Moral Crusade," *The Atlanta Journal* (March 9, 1997), R2.
196. *The Economist* (April 19, 1997), 28.
197. Bruce Lloyd, "Bribery, Corruption and Accountability," *Insights on Global Ethics* (Vol. 4, No. 8, September 1994), 5.
198. Ian I. Mitroff and Ralph H. Kilmann, "Teaching Managers to Do Policy Analysis: The Case of Corporate Bribery," *California Management Review* (Fall 1977), 50–52.
199. "The Destructive Costs of Greasing Palms," *Business Week* (December 6, 1993), 133–138; See also Henry W. Lane and Donald G. Simpson, "Bribery in International Business: Whose Problem Is It?" (Reading 12) in H. W. Lane, J. J. DiStefano, and M. L. Maznevski (eds.), *International Management Behavior*, 4th ed., (Oxford: Blackwell Publishers, 2000), 469–487.
200. Dwight R. Ladd, "The Bribery Business," in Tom L. Beauchamp (ed.), *Case Studies in Business, Society and Ethics* (Englewood Cliffs, NJ: Prentice Hall, 1983), 256.
201. John Garland and Richard H. Farmer, *International Dimensions of Business Policy and Strategy* (Boston: Kent Publishing Company, 1986), 183.
202. Transparency International, "2001 Corruption Perception Index," http://www.transparency.org.
203. Paul Deveney, "34 Nations Sign Accord to End Bribery in Deals," *The Wall Street Journal* (December 18, 1997), A16.
204. Lloyd, 5.
205. G. Pascal Zachary, "Levi Tries to Make Sure Contract Plants in Asia Treat People Well," *The Wall Street Journal* (July 28, 1994), A1.
206. Tom Donaldson, "Global Business Must Mind Its Morals," *The New York Times* (February 13, 1994), F-11; See also Tom Donaldson, "Ethics Away from Home," *Harvard Business Review* (September-October, 1996).
207. George Enderle, "What Is International? A Typology of International Spheres and Its Relevance for Business Ethics," paper presented at annual meeting of International Association for Business and Society, Vienna, Austria, 1995, as quoted and described in Tom Donaldson and Thomas W. Dunfee, "When Ethics Travel: The Promise and Peril of Global Business Ethics," *California Management Review*, Vol 41, No. 4 (Summer 1999), 48–49.
208. Donaldson and Dunfee, op. cit.
209. Ibid.
210. Ibid.
211. Ibid.
212. Gene R. Laczniak and Jacob Naor, "Global Ethics: Wrestling with the Corporate Conscience," *Business* (July–September 1985), 7–8.
213. Archie B. Carroll, Frank Hoy, and John Hall, "The Integration of Corporate Social Policy into Strategic Management," in S. Prakash Sethi and Cecilia M. Falbe (eds.), *Business and Society: Dimensions of Conflict and Cooperation* (Lexington, MA: Lexington Books, 1987), 449–470.
214. Laczniak and Naor, 8.
215. Robert D. Haas, "Ethics in the Trenches," *Across the Board* (May 1994), 12.
216. David H. Blake, William C. Frederick, and Mildred S. Myers, *Social Auditing: Evaluating the Impact of Corporate Programs* (New York: Praeger, 1976), 3.
217. Mattel press release, November 20, 1997.
218. Thomas Donaldson, *The Ethics of International Business* (New York: Oxford University Press, 1989), 81.
219. Richard T. DeGeorge, "Ethical Dilemmas for Multinational Enterprise: A Philosophical Overview," in Hoffman, Lange, and Fedo (eds.), 39–46; See also Richard T. DeGeorge, *Business Ethics*, 5th ed. (Englewood Cliffs, NJ: Prentice Hall, 1999), Chapters 18–20; and Richard T. DeGeorge, *Competing with Integrity in International Business* (New York: Oxford University Press, 1993).

MODULE 1000

International Business

1001 Global Business Strategies, 818

1010 Forms of International Business and Marketing Strategies, 823

1020 International Risks, 836

1030 Global Organization Structure and Control, 838

1040 International Trade and Investment, 855

1050 International Payments, 866

1060 International Cultures and Protocols, 871

1070 Economics and International Business, 880

1075 International Banking, 901

1080 Law and International Business, 908

1090 Ethics and International Business, 919

1099 International Issues, 924

Module 1000 Glossary, 931

Module 1000 Endnotes, 948

Global Business Strategies

Why Firms Internationalize Their Operations

Historically, domestic enterprises have **internationalized their business operations** either to seize **opportunities** or to deal with **threats,** or both.[1] For example, the European Union's (EU) current efforts to become more unified are expected to present both opportunities and threats for non-EU business enterprises. The advent of the Internet as a means of conducting international business also presents opportunities and threats. The ensuing sections discuss the opportunities and threats that cause domestic enterprises to internationalize their operations.

Opportunity Reasons

The opportunity reasons for internationalizing operations include greater profits, appearance of new markets, faster growth in new markets, obtaining new products for the domestic market, and globalization of financial markets.

Greater Profits

Many domestic firms have internationalized their operations because their managers saw the opportunity to earn greater profits by charging higher prices in a higher per capita income foreign country where a high demand for the product or service existed or where there was less competition. Enterprises have also internationalized their operations because their managers determined that they could earn higher profits by attaining greater *economies of scale* with foreign expansion. Additionally, many enterprises have been able to earn greater profits by producing in a country where labor was cheaper and/or where materials cost less than at home.

Appearance of New Markets

Population expansion, income growth, and technological advancements around the globe have created **new markets** and demands and thus new business opportunities. Many domestic firms have internationalized their operations to meet those new demands.

Faster Growth in New Markets

Many domestic organizations have a strong growth orientation. These firms often enter foreign markets because they can grow at a faster rate there than they can in the established domestic market.

Obtaining New Products for the Domestic Market

Many individuals from the home market travel abroad and develop a desire for a product that they would like to have available in their home market. For example, English ales, German beers, and French wines sell well in the U.S. market. Domestic enterprises therefore internationalize their operations to obtain products for domestic consumers. If they do not, their competitors will.

Globalization of Financial Markets

In recent decades, there has been an expansion in the ways in which international business can be financed. This growth in **financial options** has been the catalyst for the expansion of international business. These new tools include the International Monetary Fund, created in 1945 by the United Nations to encourage and aid world trade, and the World Bank, created by the United Nations for the purpose of encouraging the extension of loans to less-developed countries. Banks such as **Citicorp**, **Dai-ichiKangyo Bank**, and **Bank Nationale de Paris** have grown into international organizations that draw on a variety of investors from many parts of the world.[2]

Threat Reasons

The threat reasons for internationalizing operations include protection from declining demand in the home market, acquisition of raw materials, acquisition of managerial know-how and capital, protection of the home market, and protection from imports.

Protection From Declining Demand in Home Market

Demand for a firm's product or service may be low in the home market due to recessionary conditions, a saturated market, or a declining product life cycle. Many firms have been able to hedge against recessions at home and maintain their growth by expanding into foreign markets.

Acquisition of Raw Materials

Many domestic manufacturers depend on and import raw materials available in foreign countries. To be assured of the necessary raw materials, numerous enterprises have set up operations overseas. For example, rubber, which is required by numerous U.S. manufacturers, is not available in the continental United States. Tire-producing firms must acquire rubber from other countries—those in Southeast Asia, for instance. Likewise, oil companies search the world for new petroleum reserves.

Acquisition of Managerial Know-How and Capital

Enterprises sometimes must go abroad to obtain the managerial know-how and capital that they lack but need to improve their operations. For example, in recent years, there has been a booming demand for travel in Russia. The Russian airline, **Aeroflot**, was one of the least efficient airlines in the world. To deal with this problem, the Russian carrier's management shopped around for Western partners who could bring the managerial know-how and capital it needed to meet its expansion demands.[3]

Protection of Home Market

Many firms have internationalized their operations to protect their home market. For example, a firm services a domestic manufacturer which, for its own reasons, decides to set up subsidiary operations abroad. The service enterprise would be wise to follow and provide the services required by the manufacturer's foreign subsidiaries. Otherwise, an aggressive competitor that gets its "foot in the door" through the manufacturer's foreign subsidiary may soon take over the service activities in the domestic market as well.

Protection From Imports

Foreign competitors often hold an advantage over domestic firms because they have access to cheaper labor and/or materials in a foreign country. To remain competitive, domestic firms must often transfer their production activities to a foreign country to obtain the same cost advantages the foreign competitors enjoy. For example, many of the parts used to manufacture U.S.-produced automobiles are actually manufactured abroad.

The Internal Review

Environmental changes, which are detected through an **external review** of the global environment, often require that firms develop international strategies. To help them develop effective international strategies, along with total familiarity with the external environment, managers must examine their enterprises' internal conditions; they must conduct an internal review to become familiar with the company's internal situation. Knowledge of their firm's internal factors will help its managers develop wise strategies for penetrating a foreign market or for coping with environmental changes. Basically, managers need to determine how much money the firm has access to, including cash on hand, borrowing power, and ability to sell stock, which can be used to finance the strategy; the nature of its physical assets; its personnel capabilities; and its strengths.

Foreign Sources of Finance

Even if an enterprise has access to the funds required to finance the expansion, managers should inquire about the availability of **financial assistance in the foreign market.** The governments of many foreign countries make special concessions to foreign firms that bring them the technologies they believe will aid their nations' development efforts. For example, the government of Morocco was actively seeking foreign investment in its tourism sector. To attract investment, it offered several incentives, such as the possibility of 100% foreign ownership; tax exemptions of up to ten years, depending on the location of investment; and the availability of long-term, low-interest financing.[4]

Nature of the Firm's Physical Assets and Personnel Competencies

Managers also need to obtain information about the enterprise's physical assets and their current state. Is their manufacturing capacity capable of producing for the foreign market? Or are new manufacturing means needed? Furthermore, managers must obtain information about their firm's **personnel competencies** in relation to the company's international strategy. Does the enterprise have the personnel capable of producing for the foreign market(s)? Does it have personnel with the ability to manage the international operations? Again, the governments of many foreign countries will help foreign firms finance machinery and factories and will provide trained personnel, or assist in training personnel, as a means of attracting technologies to aid in accomplishing the nation's developmental objectives.

The firm's internal conditions also affect how it enters a foreign market. Two fundamental approaches to conducting business abroad are by exporting to it or by manufacturing in it. Exporting involves manufacturing at home and shipping the goods to the foreign market. Exporting generally requires less investment than manufacturing abroad. If the firm is cash-short, has idle equipment, and its personnel is not highly competent in international business, the firm may prefer to export. However, by producing abroad, the company can often save on transportation, labor, and materials costs, as well as on tariffs. Therefore, if an enterprise has adequate cash to invest, has international managerial know-how, the foreign demand justifies the investment, and the foreign environment is conducive to the investment, it may want to produce abroad.

Lead From Strength

The internal review should also include an assessment of the enterprise's strengths. A business should always "**lead from strength**"; that is, it should focus on doing what it can do better than its competitors. For example, a firm's strength may be engineering and design. Instead of manufacturing, it may be more efficient for the firm to farm it out to a company whose strength is manufacturing.

Furthermore, a firm may be strong in production, but weak in conducting foreign business. This firm may therefore have to form a joint venture or enter into a strategic alliance with an enterprise that is strong in conducting foreign business. Basically, organizations enter into joint ventures or strategic alliances to share costs and risks, to gain additional technical and market knowledge, to complement each other, to serve an international market, to strengthen themselves against other competitors, and to develop industry standards together.[5] Managers should be aware, however, that joint ventures and strategic alliances can backfire, especially when one of the partners becomes stronger by learning more than the other(s). The stronger partner may break up the alliance and go on its own, which may harm the weaker partner.

It should be noted that foreign countries' environments generally have an effect on a firm's strengths and weaknesses. For example, an organization may possess a strong ability to distribute a product in one nation because it is capable of dealing with that country's distribution laws and practices. At the same time it may possess a weak capability to distribute in another country because it lacks the ability to deal with that nation's distribution laws and practices. For instance, international business transactions are either in cash or in barter trade. Many enterprises have experience in cash transactions but not in barter trade transactions. In the latter case, if the enterprise wishes to penetrate a foreign market where barter trade is required, it may have to form a partnership with a firm that has experience in barter trade.

Also, an enterprise may possess the ability to differentiate a product to fit the needs of a specific country's culture, and at the same time lack the ability to differentiate to fit another country's cultural needs. U.S. car manufacturers, for example, have historically possessed the capability of differentiating their automobiles to fit the needs of many countries, but not the needs of some countries, such as England, where the steering wheel is located on the right-hand side of the automobile. In this case, if a U.S. car manufacturer wanted to penetrate the British car market, it might have to form a partnership with a car manufacturer that has the capability of producing cars with the steering wheel on the right-hand side.

Types of International Strategies

International firms typically develop their core strategy for the home country first. Subsequently, they internationalize their core strategy through international expansion of activities and through adaptation. Eventually, they globalize their strategy by integrating operations across nations.[6] These steps translate into four distinct types of strategies applied by international enterprises: ethnocentric, multidomestic, global, and transnational.

Ethnocentric Strategy

Following World War II, U.S. enterprises operated mainly from an **ethnocentric** perspective. These companies produced unique goods and services, which they offered primarily to the domestic market. The lack of international competition offset their need to be sensitive to cultural differences. When these firms exported goods, they did not alter them for foreign consumption—the costs of alterations for cultural differences were assumed by the foreign buyers. In effect, this type of company has one strategy for all markets.

Multidomestic Strategy

The multidomestic firm has a different strategy for each of its foreign markets. In this type of strategy, "a company's management tries to operate effectively across a series of worldwide positions with diverse product requirements, growth rates, competitive environments, and political risks. The company prefers that local managers do what is necessary to succeed in R&D, production, marketing, and distribution, but holds them responsible for results."[7] In essence, this type of corporation competes with local competitors on a market-by-market basis. A multitude of American corporations use this strategy, for example, **Procter & Gamble** in household products, **Honeywell** in controls, **Alcoa** in aluminum, and **General Foods** in consumer goods. Japanese car manufacturer **Toyota** also follows this strategy.

Global Strategy

The **global corporation** uses all of its resources against its competition in a very integrated fashion. All of its foreign subsidiaries and divisions are highly interdependent in both operations and strategy. As Thomas Hout, et al., said:

> In a global business, management competes worldwide against a small number of other multinationals in the world market. Strategy is centralized, and various aspects of operations are decentralized or centralized as economics and effectiveness dictate. The company seeks to respond to particular local market needs, while avoiding a compromise of efficiency of the overall global system.[8]

Therefore, whereas in a multidomestic strategy the managers in each country react to competition without considering what is taking place in other countries, in a global strategy, competitive moves are integrated across nations. The same kind of move is made in different countries at the same time or in a systematic fashion. For example, a competitor is attacked in one nation in order to exhaust its resources for another country, or a competitive attack in one nation is countered in a different country—for instance, the counterattack in a competitor's home market as a parry to an attack on one's home market.[9]

Advantages and Disadvantages of the Global Strategy

Outlined below are the advantages and disadvantages of the global strategy.[10] The advantages of the global strategy would negate the disadvantages of the multidomestic strategy, and the disadvantages of the global strategy would be negated by the advantages of the multidomestic strategy.

Advantages of the Global Strategy (Multidomestic strategy does not provide these advantages.)

- By pooling production or other activities for two or more nations, a firm can increase the benefits derived from economies of scale.
- A company can cut costs by moving manufacturing or other activities to low-cost countries.
- A firm that is able to switch production among different nations can reduce costs by increasing its bargaining power over suppliers, workers, and host governments.
- By focusing on a smaller number of products and programs than under a multidomestic strategy, a corporation is able to improve both product and program quality.

- Worldwide availability, serviceability, and recognition can increase preference through reinforcement.
- The company is provided with more points from which to attack and counterattack competition.

Disadvantages of the Global Strategy (Multidomestic strategy can reduce these disadvantages.)

- Through increased coordination, reporting requirements, and added staff, substantial management costs can be incurred.
- Overcentralization can harm local motivation and morale, therefore reducing the firm's effectiveness.
- Standardization can result in a product that does not totally satisfy any customers.
- Incurring costs and revenues in multiple countries increases currency risk.
- Integrated competitive moves can lead to the sacrificing of revenues, profits, or competitive positions in individual countries—especially when the subsidiary in one country is told to attack a global competitor in order to convey a signal or divert that competitor's resources from another nation.

Transnational Strategy

The **transnational strategy** provides for global coordination (like the global strategy) and at the same time it allows local autonomy (like the multidomestic strategy). **Nestlé**, the world's largest food company, headquartered in Switzerland, follows this strategy.[11] The challenges managers of transnational corporations face are to identify and exploit cross-border synergies and to balance local demands with the global vision for the corporation. Building an effective transnational organization requires a corporate culture that values global dissimilarities across cultures and markets.[12]

International Strategic and Tactical Objectives

Organizations generally establish two kinds of measurable objectives: strategic and tactical. **Strategic objectives,** which are guided by the enterprise's mission or purpose and deal with long-term issues, associate the enterprise to its external environment and provide management with a basis for comparing performance with that of its competitors and in relation to environmental demands. Examples of strategic objectives include to increase sales, to increase market share, to increase profits, and to lower prices by becoming an international firm. **Tactical objectives,** which are guided by the enterprise's strategic objectives and deal with shorter term issues, identify the key result areas in which specific performance is essential for the success of the enterprise and aim to attain internal efficiency. They identify specifically how, for example, to lower costs, to lower prices, to increase output, to capture a larger portion of the market, and to penetrate an international market.

Technology and Global Strategy

Technology has been the root of the most dramatic changes occurring in commerce today. It now enables organizations to integrate their systems, where changes in one part ripple throughout the system, causing shifts in the other parts. Therefore, no strategy has been left untouched. It has leveled the playing field for small firms, allowing them to compete successfully with large corporations in the same markets. With e-mail, teleconferencing, multimedia CD-ROMs, and networked databases, small businesses can emulate the marketing tactics of much larger companies—they can set up a home page on the World Wide Web right next door to **Wal-Mart**. And electronic networks and the Internet have enabled organizations to decentralize business activities and to outsource activities to other organizations.

From a strategic viewpoint, technology impacted international strategy in several ways.[13]

- Emphasis has moved from products to information and solutions.
- Products can be launched from commercialization tactics based on identifying specific customer needs.
- Relationships with customers have been made easier, which enhances product acceptance and minimizes costs due to redesign.
- Firms can now target specific products and services to specific customers.
- Technology supports the integration of engineering and commercialization to get the product to the customer in the least amount of time.
- Technology helps prevent midcourse corrections in product design, which usually result in higher costs and longer time to commercialize.

From a tactical viewpoint, current technology aids businesses in the commercialization of their products and services in numerous ways.

- E-mail enables firms to communicate rapidly and easily with customers, strategic partners, suppliers, distributors, and others around the globe. This lowers the costs of travel and speeds up response time.
- Teleconferencing allows enterprises to hold international strategic meetings without getting on an airplane.
- Networked databases provide organizations with online access to research and development information existing around the globe.
- Modems and laptop computers let employees work from virtually anywhere in the world, increasing efficiency and bringing the organization closer to the customer.
- Voice mail lets organizations record telephone messages when no one is available to receive them.
- Satellite systems, which a firm can lease from a provider, allow organizations to receive broadcast messages from chain manufacturers that help move the product.
- Laser color printers let enterprises quickly produce signs, banners, cards, price tags, and so on, that look as good as those printed by a professional.
- Some industries have CD-ROM services that businesses can tie into on a regular basis to receive updated information of things such as equipment and supplies. This also makes it easier for a firm to quickly locate customer items that it normally does not carry in stock.
- The World Wide Web as a commercial tool is enabling smaller businesses to be on the same playing field as larger businesses.
- Online databases have put information at the hands of anyone who chooses to access them.

One must bear in mind that **technology is a tool used by strategists to improve business activities**. It is not intended to replace personal contact with the customer, nor is it intended to replace a manager's unique ability to take vast amounts of information and make sense of it in terms of strategy for the organization. It does make it easier for the manager to integrate all activities of the firm, to automate routine tasks, and generally free up more time to focus on the firm's strategy.

Forms of International Business and Marketing Strategies

Forms of International Business

We classify international business into three categories: (1) trade, (2) intellectual property rights (trademarks, patents, and copyrights) and international licensing agreements, and (3) foreign direct investment. To the marketer, these broad categories describe three important methods for entering a foreign market. To the lawyer, they also represent the form of doing business in a foreign country and the legal relationship between parties to a business transaction. Each method brings a different set of problems to the firm because the level of **foreign penetration** and entanglement in that country is different. Trade usually represents the least entanglement, and thus, the least political, economic, and legal risk, especially if the exporting firm is not soliciting business overseas or maintaining sales agents or inventories there. An investment in a plant and operations overseas usually represents the greatest market penetration and thus, the greatest risk to the firm.

Considerable overlap occurs among these different forms of doing business. A business plan for the production and marketing of a single product may contain elements of each form. To illustrate, a U.S. firm might purchase the rights to a trademark for use on an article of high-fashion clothing made from fabric exported from China and assembled in offshore plants in the Caribbean for shipment to the United States and Europe. Here, a business strategy encompasses elements of trade, licensing, and investment. For firms just entering a new foreign market, the method of entry might depend on a host of considerations, including the sophistication of the firm, its overseas experience, the nature of its product or services, its commitment of capital resources, and the amount of risk it is willing to bear.

Trade

Trade consists of the import and export of goods and services. *Exporting* is the term generally used to refer to the process of sending goods out of a country, and *importing* is used to denote when goods are brought into a country. However, a more accurate definition is that *exporting is the shipment of goods or the rendering of services to a foreign buyer located in a foreign country. Importing* is then defined as *the process of buying goods from a foreign supplier and entering them into the customs territory of a different country.* Every export entails an import, and vice versa.

Exporting

Trade is often a firm's first step into international business. Compared to the other forms of international business (licensing and investment), trade is relatively uncomplicated. It provides the inexperienced or smaller firm with an opportunity to penetrate a new market, or at least to explore foreign market potential, without significant capital investment and the risks of becoming a full-fledged player (that is, citizen) in the foreign country. For many larger firms, including multinational corporations, exporting may be an important portion of their business operations. The U.S. aircraft industry, for example, relies heavily on exports for significant revenues.

Firms that have not done business overseas before should first prepare an export plan, which may mean assembling an export team, composed possibly of management and outside advisors and trade specialists. Their plan should include the assessment of the firm's readiness for exporting, the export potential of its products or services, the firm's willingness to allocate resources (including financial, production output, and human resources), and the selection of its channels of distribution. The firm may need to modify products, design new packaging and foreign language labeling, and meet foreign standards for product performance or quality assurance. The firm must also gauge the extent to which it can perform export functions in-house or whether these functions should best be handled indirectly through an independent export company. Export functions include foreign marketing, sales and distribution, shipping, and handling international transfers of money.

Firms accept varying levels of responsibility for moving goods and money and for other export functions. The more experienced exporters can take greater responsibility for themselves and are more likely to export directly to their foreign customers. Firms that choose to accept less responsibility in dealing with foreign customers, or in making arrangements for shipping, for example, must delegate many export functions to someone else. As such, exporting is generally divided into two types: direct and indirect.

DIRECT EXPORTING At first glance, **direct exporting** seems similar to selling goods to a domestic buyer. A prospective foreign customer may have seen a firm's products at a trade show, located a particular company in an industrial directory, or been recommended by another customer. A firm that receives a request for product and pricing information from a foreign customer may be able to handle it routinely and export directly to the buyer. With some assistance, a firm can overcome most hurdles, get the goods properly packaged and shipped, and receive payment as anticipated. Although many of these one-time sales are turned into long-term business success stories, many more are not. A firm hopes to develop a regular business relationship with its new foreign customer. However, the problems that can be encountered even in direct exporting are considerable.

Many firms engaged in direct exporting on a regular basis reach the point at which they must hire their own full-time export managers and international sales specialists. These people participate in making export marketing decisions, including product development, pricing, packaging, and labeling for export. They should take primary responsibility for dealing with foreign buyers, for attending foreign trade shows, for complying with government export and import regulations, for shipping, and for handling the movement of goods and money in the transaction. Direct exporting is often done through **foreign sales agents** who work on commission. It also can be done by selling directly to **foreign distributors**. Foreign distributors are independent firms, usually located in the country to which a firm is exporting, that purchase goods for resale to their customers. They assume the risks of buying and warehousing goods in their market and provide additional product support services. The distributor usually services the products they sell, thus, relieving the exporter of that responsibility. They often train end users to use the product, extend credit to their customers, and bear responsibility for local advertising and promotion.

INDIRECT EXPORTING **Indirect exporting** is used by companies seeking to minimize their involvement abroad. Lacking experience, personnel, or capital, they may be unable to locate foreign buyers or are not yet ready to be handling the mechanics of a transaction on their own. There are several different types of indirect exporting. **Export trading companies**, commonly called ETCs, are companies that market the products of several manufacturers in foreign markets. They have extensive sales contacts overseas and experience in air and sea shipping. They often operate with the assistance and financial backing of large banks, thus making the resources and international contacts of the bank's foreign branches available to the manufacturers whose products they market. ETCs are licensed to operate under the U.S. antitrust laws.

Export management companies (EMC)s, on the other hand, are really consultants that advise manufacturers and other exporters. They are used by firms that cannot justify their own in-house export managers. They engage in foreign market research, identify overseas sales agents, exhibit goods at foreign trade shows, prepare documentation for export, and handle language translations and shipping arrangements. As in direct exporting, all forms of indirect exporting can involve sales through agents or to distributors.

Importing and Global Sourcing

Here, importing is presented from the perspective of the global firm for which importing is a regular and necessary part of their business. **Global sourcing** is the term commonly used to describe the process by which a firm attempts to locate and purchase goods or services on a worldwide basis. These goods may include, for example, raw materials for manufacturing, component parts for assembly operations, commodities such as agricultural products or minerals, or merchandise for resale.

Government Controls Over Trade: Tariffs and Nontariff Barriers

Both importing and exporting are governed by the laws and regulations of the countries through which goods or services pass. Nations regulate trade in many ways. The most common methods are **tariffs** and **nontariff barriers**. Tariffs are import duties or taxes imposed on goods entering the customs territory of a nation. Tariffs are imposed for many reasons, including (1) the collection of revenue, (2) the protection of domestic industries from foreign competition, and (3) political control (for example, to provide incentives to import products from politically friendly countries and to discourage importing products from unfriendly countries).

NONTARIFF BARRIERS TO TRADE Nontariff barriers are *all barriers to importing or exporting other than tariffs*. Nontariff barriers are generally a greater barrier to trade than are tariffs because they are more insidious. Unlike tariffs, which are published and easily understood, nontariff barriers are often disguised in the form of government rules or industry regulations and are often not understood by foreign companies. Countries impose nontariff barriers to protect their national economic, social, and political interests. Imports might be banned for health and safety reasons. Imported goods usually have to be marked with the country-of-origin and labeled in the local language so that consumers know what they are buying. One form of nontariff barrier is the **technical barrier to trade**, or **product standard**. Examples of product standards include safety standards, electrical standards, and environmental standards (for example, German cars meeting U.S. emission standards not mandated in Europe). A **quota** is a restriction imposed by law on the numbers or quantities of goods, or of a particular type of good, allowed to be imported. Unlike tariffs, quotas are not internationally accepted as a lawful means of regulating trade except in some special cases. An **embargo** is a total or near total ban on trade with a particular country, sometimes enforced by military action and usually imposed for political purposes. An internationally orchestrated embargo was used against Iraq after its invasion of Kuwait in 1990. A **boycott** is a refusal to trade or do business with certain firms, usually from a particular country, on political or other grounds.

Tariffs and nontariff barriers have a tremendous influence on how firms make their trade and investment decisions. These decisions, in turn, are reflected in the patterns of world trade and the flows of investment capital.

TRADE LIBERALIZATION AND THE WORLD TRADE ORGANIZATION **Trade liberalization** refers to the efforts of governments to reduce tariffs and nontariff barriers to trade. In the twentieth century, the most important effort to liberalize trade came with the international acceptance of the **General Agreement on Tariffs and Trade (GATT)**. This is an agreement between nations, first signed in 1947, and continually expanded since that time, that sets the rules for how nations will regulate international trade in goods and services. In 1995, the Geneva-based **World Trade Organization (WTO)**, was created to administer the rules and to assist in settling trade disputes between its member nations. All WTO nations are entitled to **normal trade relations** with one another. This is referred to as **Most Favored Nation (MFN)** trading status. This means that a member country must charge the same tariff on imported goods, and not a higher one, as that charged on the same goods coming from other WTO member countries. Trade liberalization has led to increased economic development and an improved quality of life around the world.

EXPORT CONTROLS Another type of restriction over trade is export control. An **export control** limits the type of product that may be shipped to any particular country. They are usually imposed for economic or political purposes and are used by all nations of the world. For instance, high-tech computers might not be allowed to be shipped from the United States or Canada to another country without a license from the U.S. or Canadian government. Before signing a contract for the sale of certain products or technical know-how to a foreign customer, U.S. exporters must consider whether they will be able to obtain U.S. licensing for the shipment.

Intellectual Property Rights and International Licensing Agreements

Intellectual property rights are a grant from a government to an individual or firm of the exclusive legal right to use a copyright, patent, or trademark for a specified time. **Copyrights** are legal rights to artistic or written works, including books, software, films, music, or to such works as the layout design of a computer chip. **Trademarks** include the legal right to use a name or symbol that identifies a firm or its product. **Patents** are governmental grants to inventors assuring them of the exclusive legal right to produce and sell their inventions for a period of years. Copyrights, trademarks, and patents compose substantial assets of many domestic and international firms. As valuable assets, intellectual property can be sold or licensed for use to others through a licensing agreement.

International licensing agreements are contracts by which the holder of intellectual property will grant certain rights in that property to a foreign firm under specified conditions and for a specified time. Licensing agreements represent an important foreign market entry method for firms with marketable intellectual property. For example, a firm might license the right to manufacture and distribute a certain type of computer chip or the right to use a trademark on apparel such as bluejeans or designer clothing. It might license the right to distribute Hollywood movies or to reproduce and market word-processing software in a foreign market, or it might license its patent rights to produce and sell a high-tech product or pharmaceutical. United States firms have extensively licensed their property around the world, and in recent years have purchased the technology rights of Japanese and other foreign firms.

A firm may choose licensing as its market entry method because licensing can provide a greater entrée to the foreign market than is possible through exporting. A firm may realize many advantages in having a foreign company produce and sell products based on its intellectual property instead of simply shipping finished goods to that market. When exporting to a foreign market, the firm must overcome obstacles such as long-distance shipping and the resulting delay in filling orders. Exporting requires a familiarity with the local culture. Redesign of products or technology for the foreign market may be necessary. Importantly, an exporter may have to overcome trade restrictions, such as quotas or tariffs, set by the foreign government. Licensing to a foreign firm allows the licensor to circumvent trade restrictions by having the products produced locally, and it allows entrance to the foreign market with minimal initial start-up costs. In return, the licensor might choose to receive a guaranteed return based on a percentage of gross revenues. This arrangement ensures payment to the licensor whether or not the licensee earns a profit. Even though licensing agreements give the licensor some control over how the licensee utilizes its intellectual property, problems can arise. For instance, the licensor may find that it cannot police the licensee's manufacturing or quality control process. Protecting itself from the unauthorized use or "piracy" of its copyrights, patents, or trademarks by unscrupulous persons not party to the licensing agreement is also a serious concern for the licensor.

Protecting Intellectual Property Rights

Rights in property can be rendered worthless if those rights cannot be protected by law. The protection of intellectual property is a matter of national law (as in the United States where it is protected primarily under federal statutes). However, intellectual property rights granted in one nation are not legally recognized and enforceable in another, unless the owner takes certain legal steps to protect those rights under the laws of that foreign country. Most developed countries, such as Canada, Western Europe, and Japan, have laws that protect the owners of intellectual property, and they enforce those laws. However, copyrights, patents, and trademarks are widely pirated in the developing countries of Asia, Latin America, Africa, Russia, Eastern Europe, and the Middle East, whose protection laws are either nonexistent or not enforced. Indeed, some developing countries encourage piracy because of the perceived financial gains to their economies. Some products deemed indispensable to the public, such as pharmaceuticals and chemicals, are often not covered by patent laws at all in these countries.

Lost profits and lost royalties to U.S. firms now amount to billions of dollars each year in counterfeited goods sold overseas. But international efforts are being made to rectify the problem. At the behest of U.S. movie and record producers, pharmaceutical manufacturers, software makers, and publishers, the United States has encouraged these countries to pass legislation protecting intellectual property and to ensure the enforcement of these laws. For instance, in 1991, the People's Republic of China acted to avert a trade war with the United States by agreeing to bring its intellectual property laws in line with those in other developing countries. The United States had been losing an estimated $700 million per year in China due to piracy. The United States threatened to impose punitive tariffs on Chinese goods (toys, games, footwear, clothing, and textiles). China announced stricter enforcement efforts and a new copyright law, and a major trade war was averted. Today, the protection of property rights abroad is a principal objective of U.S. trade policy.

Technology Transfer

The exchange of technology and manufacturing know-how between firms in different countries through arrangements such as licensing agreements is known as **technology transfer**. Transfers of technology and know-how are regulated by government control in some countries. This control is common when the licensor is from a highly industrialized country such as the United States and the licensee is located in a developing country such as those in Latin America, the Middle East, or Asia. In their efforts to industrialize, modernize, and develop a self-sufficiency in technology and production methods, these countries often restrict the terms of licensing agreements in a manner benefiting their own country. For instance, government regulation might require that the licensor introduce its most modern technology to the developing countries or train workers in its use.

International Franchising

Franchising is a form of licensing that is gaining in popularity worldwide. The most common form of franchising is known as a **business operations franchise**, usually used in retailing. Under a typical franchising agreement, the franchisee is allowed to use a trade name or trademark in offering goods or services to the public in return for a royalty based on a percentage of sales or other fee structure. The franchisee will usually obtain the franchiser's know-how in operating and managing a profitable business and its other "secrets of success" (ranging from a "secret recipe" to store design to accounting methods). Franchising in the United States accounts for a large proportion of total retail sales. In foreign markets as well, franchising has been successful in fast-food retailing, hotels, video rentals, convenience stores, photocopying services, and real estate services, to name but a few. U.S. firms have excelled in franchising overseas, making up the majority of new franchise operations worldwide. The prospects for future growth in foreign markets are enormous, especially in developing countries such as in Latin America. For instance, American fast-food and retail franchises are common throughout Mexico City, Brazil, Eastern Europe, and the former Soviet Union.

Some Legal Aspects of Franchising

Franchising is a good vehicle for entering a foreign market because the local franchisee provides capital investment, entrepreneurial commitment, and on-site management to deal with local customs and labor problems. However, many legal requirements affect franchising. Franchising in the United States is regulated primarily by the Federal Trade Commission at the federal level. The agency requires the filing of extensive disclosure statements to protect prospective investors. Other countries have also enacted new franchise disclosure laws. Some developing countries have restrictions on the amount of money that can be removed from the country by the franchiser. Moreover, some countries, such as China, also require government approval for franchise operations. Other countries might have restrictions on importing supplies (ketchup, bed linens, paper products, or whatever) for the operation of the business to protect local companies. However, more progressive developing countries are now abandoning these strict regulations because they want to welcome franchisers, their high quality consumer products, and their managerial talent to their markets. Because of this more receptive attitude toward foreign firms, Mexico and Brazil have become home to many profitable new franchise operations.

Foreign Direct Investment

The term **foreign investment**, or **foreign direct investment**, refers to the ownership and active control of ongoing business concerns, including investment in manufacturing, mining, farming, assembly operations, and other facilities of production. A distinction is made between the home and host countries of the firms involved. The **home country** refers to that country under whose laws the investing corporation was created or is headquartered. For example, the United States is home to multinational corporations such as **Ford**, **Exxon**, and **IBM**, to name a few, but they operate in **host countries** throughout every region of the world. Of the three forms of international business, foreign investment provides the firm with the most involvement, and perhaps the greatest risk, abroad. Investment in a foreign plant is often a result of having had successful experiences in exporting or licensing, and of the search for ways to overcome the disadvantages of those other entry methods. For example, by producing its product in a foreign country, instead of exporting, a firm can avoid quotas and tariffs on imported goods, avoid currency fluctuations on the traded goods, provide better product service and spare parts, and more quickly adapt products to local tastes and market trends. Manufacturing overseas for foreign markets can mean taking advantage of local natural resources, labor, and manufacturing economies of scale. Foreign investment in the United States is often called reverse investment. Most of the foreign investment in the United States has come from the United Kingdom.

Multinational Corporations

Multinational corporations (**MNCs**) are firms with significant foreign direct investment assets. They are characterized by their ability to derive and transfer capital resources worldwide and to operate facilities of production and penetrate markets in more than one country, usually on a global scale. Over the past twenty years, many writers have argued over the best name to use in referring to these companies. **Multinational enterprise** (**MNE**) has been a popular term because it reflects the fact that many global firms are not, technically speaking, "corporations." The terms **transnational corporation** and **supranational corporation** are often used within the United Nations system, in which many internationalists argue that the operations and interests of the modern corporation "transcend" national boundaries.

One significant trend in business during the last half of the twentieth century has been the globalization of multinational corporations. At one time, multinational corporations were simply large domestic companies with foreign operations. Today, they are global companies. They typically make decisions and enter strategic alliances with each other without regard to national boundaries. They move factories, technology, and capital to those countries with the most hospitable laws, the lowest tax rates, the most qualified workforce, or abundant natural resources. They see market share and company performance in global terms. Foreign sales and operations are extremely profitable for many multinationals. As an example, **Gillette**, **Colgate**, **IBM**, **Coca-Cola**, and many of the five hundred largest U.S. corporations collected over 50% of their revenues from products sold outside the United States. Switzerland's **Nestlé Corporation** garnered over 95% of its revenues from outside Switzerland.

Subsidiaries, Joint Ventures, Mergers, and Acquisitions

Multinational corporations wishing to enter a foreign market through direct investment can structure their business arrangements in many different ways. Their options and eventual course of action may depend on many factors, including industry and market conditions, capitalization of the firm and financing, and legal considerations. Some of these options include the start-up of a new foreign subsidiary company, the formation of a joint venture with an existing foreign company, or the acquisition of an existing foreign company by stock purchase. For now, keep in mind that multinational corporations are usually not a single legal entity. They are global enterprises that consist of any number of interrelated corporate entities, connected through extremely complex chains of stock ownership. Stock ownership gives the investing corporation tremendous flexibility when investing abroad.

The **wholly owned foreign subsidiary** is a "foreign" corporation organized under the laws of a foreign host country, but owned and controlled by the parent corporation in the home country. Because the parent company controls all of the stock in the subsidiary, it can control management and financial decision making.

The **joint venture** is a cooperative business arrangement between two or more companies for profit. A joint venture may take the form of a partnership or corporation. Typically, one party will contribute expertise and another the capital, each bringing its own special resources to the venture. Joint ventures exist in all regions of the world and in all types of industries. Where the laws of a host country require local ownership or that investing foreign firms have a local partner, the joint venture is an appropriate investment vehicle. **Local participation** refers to the requirement that a share of the business be owned by nationals of the host country. These requirements are gradually being reduced in most countries that, in an effort to attract more investment, are permitting wholly owned subsidiaries. Many American companies do not favor the joint venture as an investment vehicle because they do not want to share technology, expertise, and profits with another company.

Another method of investing abroad is for two companies to **merge** or for one company to acquire another ongoing firm. This option has appeal because it requires less know-how than does a new start-up and can be concluded without disruption of business activity.

International Marketing Strategies

To remain competitive and to increase their opportunities, domestic enterprises will need to develop strategies for entering the international business arena. Effective internationalization of business operations marketing relies on managers' ability to develop international product/service, place/entry, price, and promotion strategies. We discuss each of these in turn.

International Product/Service Strategy

In developing **product/service strategy,** managers are typically concerned with what the product or service should look like and what it should be able to do. In conducting this assessment for foreign markets, managers must overcome the *self-reference criterion* (SRC). They must determine whether their product or service can be sold in standard form or whether it must be customized to fit differing foreign market needs. They must understand that many products or services do not immediately sell well in foreign markets but that they must undergo a diffusion process.

The Self-Reference Criterion (SRC)

The **self-reference criterion** (SRC) is the unconscious reference to one's own cultural values. This unconscious reference is the root of many international business problems.[14] Huge problems can occur when the SRC leads a manager to assume that a product or service that sells well in the home market will sell well in foreign markets. In many cases it does not because the needs for products and services differ among societies. Managers can eliminate the SRC by first defining the problem in terms of the home society's cultural traits, values, habits, and norms, and then redefining the problem, without value judgments, in terms of the foreign market's cultural traits, values, habits, and norms. The difference represents the cultural influence on the problem. The manager subsequently restates and solves the problem in the context of both cultures.

It should be noted that the assessment may sometimes reveal that the firm's product or service, because of cultural or other factors, cannot be customized for a foreign market. Therefore, international strategists should seek answers to four basic questions.[15]

1. *Who in the foreign market uses the product?* In what way(s) are the targeted foreign buyers similar to or different from domestic buyers? How can this product be incorporated into foreign market's lifestyle?
2. *What are the values of the people in the foreign market?* Is their value based on timeliness, quality, service, or price? What changes in the products/services need to be made to meet the foreign customers' needs?
3. *What are the signals that indicate change in the market?* Does the market accept foreign ideas? Are there cross-cultural trends?
4. *How can the firm increase market share?* Who are the local competitors? Who are the foreign competitors? How much disposable income do consumers have?

Next, we present separate strategies for products and services.

Product Strategy

CUSTOMIZATION VERSUS STANDARDIZATION Fundamentally, there are three viable alternatives when entering a foreign market: (1) market the same product everywhere (**standardization**), (2) adapt the product for foreign markets (**customization**), and (3) develop a totally new product. By combining these three alternatives with promotional efforts, five different product strategies can be developed.[16]

1. **Standardize product/standardize message.** Using this strategy, a firm sells the same product and uses the same promotional appeals in all markets. In other words, product and promotional appeals are globally standardized. **Coca-Cola, Pepsi-Cola, Avon, McDonald's, Sony Walkman, Levi's,** and **Maidenform** follow this strategy.
2. **Standardize product/customize message.** Enterprises using this approach customize only the promotional message. For example, a bicycle may be sold in the U.S. market as a pleasure vehicle. In an economically poor country, however, the promotional message may have to be customized to stress economy; that is, the bicycle would be promoted as a means of relatively inexpensive basic transportation.
3. **Customize product/standardize message.** Using this strategy, the company customizes the product to meet the needs of the specific foreign market, but promotes the same use as it does in the domestic market. For example, electric sewing machines manufactured for the U.S. market would not sell well in a market where few

residents have access to electricity. The manufacturer could, however, customize the machine to sell in that market by producing hand- or foot-cranked sewing machines. The hand- or foot-cranked machine would be promoted in the foreign market in the same way it is in the U.S. market—to sew clothes.

4. **Customize product/customize message.** Manufacturers applying this strategy customize the product to meet different use patterns in the foreign market and customize the promotional message attached to it as well. For example, bicycles in the United States are usually lightweight and are generally promoted for use in leisure activities. In many less-developed countries, however, because of rough roads, the need may be for a stronger bicycle, and the bicycle is often used as a major form of transportation. China is one example of a country where bicycles are heavyweight and are used as a major means of transportation.

5. **Different product.** Using this approach, rather than adapting an existing product, the manufacturer invests in the development of a totally new one to fit the needs of specific foreign markets. For example, Coca-Cola's and Pepsi's diet sodas do not sell well in Asia and Europe because consumers there prefer the creamy sweetness of regular Coke or Pepsi and consider sugar-free sodas as drinks of diabetics and the obese, not of the young and vital. To deal with this problem, Pepsi designed a new diet cola, called Pepsi Max, specifically for these and other markets. Pepsi Max uses a sweetener that makes it close to the regular colas in taste.[17]

American marketing professor Theodore Levitt contends that in an era of global competition, the product strategy of successful firms is evolving from offering customized products (a multidomestic strategy) to offering globally standardized ones (a global strategy). Such a product strategy requires the development of universal products or products that require no more than a cosmetic change for adaptation to different local needs and use conditions.[18] Japanese automobile manufacturer **Honda** has a strategy to build a global car. The strategy entails using a new standardized manufacturing system with flexibility to build cars customized to fit specific market needs. Using this new manufacturing system, the costs of customization are far lower than when using the older systems.

Service Strategy

As indicated above, a dilemma in global strategy for manufacturing businesses is the need to balance standardization with local customization. In contrast, in service delivery, in many cases, standardization and customization is equally feasible. There are three broad service categories: people-processing, possession-processing, and information-based services.[19]

PEOPLE-PROCESSING SERVICES In these services, customers become part of the production process. Such services include passenger transportation, health care, food services, and lodging services. The customer is present during the service. For example, **Disney** provides entertainment services in theme parks in Paris, France, and in Tokyo, Japan. (Of course, Disney also provides these services for foreign customers in California and Florida.) London hospitals maintain a lucrative business caring for wealthy Middle Eastern patients, as do Miami, Florida, hospitals caring for patients from Latin America.

POSSESSION-PROCESSING SERVICES Services of this nature involve tangible actions to tangible objects to enhance their value to customers. The customer need not be present. These services include transporting freight, installing equipment, and maintenance. For example, an American living near the Canadian border could go into Canada to have his or her car serviced because of lower costs resulting from favorable exchanges rates. For instance, if it costs $300 in both countries to have a car tuned-up, and the exchange rate is U.S. $1 equals Canadian $1.50, the American who goes into Canada for the service would save U.S. $100, less the expense of driving across the border. An international corporation might provide such services as bridge repair services or elevator repair services throughout the world.

INFORMATION-BASED SERVICES The provision of these services involves collecting, manipulating, interpreting, and transmitting data to create value. Examples include such services as accounting, banking, consulting, education, insurance, legal services, and news. For instance, **CNN** provides news service in most countries. **Prudential** provides insurance services in many countries. **Citicorp** provides banking services in many parts of the world. Many American colleges and universities service a multitude of students from foreign countries around the globe in the United States, and a number of them (American University in Cairo, Egypt, for example) have established satellites in foreign countries to service students abroad. Many American students are now pursuing college degrees in Canadian universities because the cost of tuition there is much lower than at home.[20]

INFORMATION TECHNOLOGY AND SERVICE STRATEGY For all three types of services described above, use of current information technology, such as the Internet, may enable businesses to benefit from favorable labor costs or exchange rates by consolidating operations of supplementary services (such as reservations) or certain office functions (such as accounting) in just one or a few countries.

International Place/Entry Strategy

Managers of business enterprises must determine how their products or services will reach the consumer—the **place/entry strategy.** Distribution methods generally require variations from country to country as well as within each country. Generally, the methods are shaped by the size of the market, by the scope and quality of the competition, by the available distribution channels, and by the firm's resources. Distribution methods are also shaped by the laws of the country (the laws of some countries require foreign companies to use local distribution systems) and by the firm's entry strategy.

Basically, manufacturing enterprises can enter a foreign country by:

1. Manufacturing the product at home and exporting it to the foreign country for distribution in the local market.
2. Manufacturing parts at home and exporting them to the foreign country for assembly, for distribution in the local market, and/or for export to other markets (including back to the home market).
3. Manufacturing the product in the foreign country for distribution in the local market and/or for export to other markets (including back to the home market).

With respect to service enterprises,

1. Some, such as consulting companies, can provide the services from their home country or they can set up subsidiaries in the foreign country.
2. Others, such as insurance and banking companies, generally must establish subsidiaries in the foreign country.

The above suggests that firms enter a foreign market either by **exporting to it or setting up manufacturing facilities in it.**

International Pricing Strategy

Operating in foreign markets brings new price strategy challenges as there are new market variables to consider. For example, the attitudes of foreign governments are an important and serious problem that differs from one country to another. Sometimes foreign governments act as price arbiters. Therefore, effective price setting consists of much more than mechanically adding a standard markup to cost. International pricing strategy is much more complex than domestic pricing strategy.

International pricing strategy is made complex by monetary exchange factors as well as by firms often being required to countertrade; that is, to trade by barter or a similar system. Pricing policy is also affected by the commercial practices of the country in which the firm is doing business, by the type of product being merchandised, and by existing competitive conditions. In establishing pricing policy, some firms are influenced by the view that pricing is an **active tool** by which to accomplish their marketing objectives, and some are influenced by the belief that price is a **static element** in business decisions. Furthermore, some firms emphasize control over final prices and some over the net price received by the enterprise.

Pricing as an Active Tool

Utilizing the view that pricing is an active tool, the firm uses pricing to accomplish its objective relative to a target return from its overseas operations or to accomplish a target volume of market share.

Pricing as a Static Element

If a firm follows the view that **pricing is a static element,** it will most likely be content to sell what it can overseas and consider it to be a bonus value. Pricing as an active tool is more closely allied with firms that make direct investment in the foreign country, whereas pricing as a static element is more closely allied with firms that export.

Control Over Final Prices

To achieve a desired level of foreign market penetration, a firm must have the ability to control the end price. Enterprises with the desire to attain a high level of market penetration therefore attempt to obtain all possible **control over the final price.** These firms are more likely to view pricing as an active tool than as a static element.

Net Price Received

Firms using this approach do not attempt to control the price at which the product is finally sold. The enterprise's main concern is with the **net price it receives.** This type of firm most likely shares the view of pricing as a static element more than as an active tool.

Foreign National Pricing and International Pricing

Pricing for foreign markets is further complicated by managers' having to be concerned with two types of pricing: foreign national pricing and international pricing. Basically, the former is pricing for selling in another country and the latter is pricing in another country for export.

Foreign National Pricing

A firm's **foreign national pricing** is influenced by its international pricing strategy as well as by foreign governments. A government can influence its nation's prices by taking various actions. It can institute **national price controls.** These controls may encompass all products sold within the nation's borders or impose them on only specific products. Some governments influence prices on foreign imports by levying higher import duties or subsidizing local industries. Governments can also affect prices by applying legislation relative to labor costs.

The product life cycle in a specific market also influences the price. If it is a new product and there is a demand for it, a higher price can often be charged. On the other hand, to achieve market penetration where the product is in a late life cycle stage, a firm may have to charge a lower price.

International Pricing

International pricing basically relates to the managerial decision of what to charge for goods produced in one nation and sold in another. A common practice of global corporations to establish a strong position in global markets is intracorporate sales. In applying this practice, a global corporation attempts to rationalize production by requiring subsidiaries to specialize in the manufacture of some items while importing others. The subsidiaries' imports may consist of components assembled into the end product, or they may be finished products imported to complement their product mix. This import-export practice among subsidiaries located in different countries enables the global corporation to control and transfer prices and to control the profits and losses of its subsidiaries. These corporations will realize no profits in a country where, for reasons discussed below, it is not beneficial to do so, and will realize them in a country where it is beneficial.

REASON 1. AVOIDING A COUNTRY'S HIGH TAX RATE Both foreign and domestic governments are interested in profits and the role of transfer prices in their attainment. This is because of the consequences profits have on the amount of taxes paid. Because of the differences in tax structures among nations, global corporations can often obtain significant profits by instructing a subsidiary in a country that has a **high corporate tax rate** to sell the product at cost to another subsidiary in a country where taxes are lower. The profit is thereby earned in the country where taxes are lower.

REASON 2. AVOIDING A COUNTRY'S CURRENCY RESTRICTIONS Transfer pricing may also be used to get around **currency restrictions.** For example, a nation suffering from a lack of foreign exchange may impose controls that limit the amount of profit that can be repatriated, that is, profits that can be transferred back to the corporation's home base. For instance, suppose nation X imposes controls on the amount of profits that can be repatriated and that there is trade with country Y, which does not have such controls. The corporation at home could instruct the subsidiary in country X to sell its product to a subsidiary in country Y at cost. This would transfer X's profit to Y, from where the global corporation can repatriate profits.

REASON 3. AVOIDING CURRENCY DEVALUATIONS, HAVING TO REDUCE PRICES, AND HAVING TO INCREASE WAGES   The international pricing approach could also be employed by global corporations when a foreign nation's **currency is devaluated,** when there is government pressure in the foreign country to **reduce prices** because of excessive profits, and when labor in the foreign country demands **higher wages** because of high profits earned.

REASON 4. ARMS-LENGTH PRICING   Because of these manipulative practices, many governments insist on **arms-length pricing;** that is, the price charged to company affiliates must be the same as that paid by unrelated customers. For example, under section 482 of the U.S. Internal Revenue Code, U.S. tax authorities have the authority to reconstruct an intracorporate transfer price. When they suspect that low prices were set to avoid taxes, the tax authorities may recalculate the tax. It should be noted that many U.S. executives prefer the arms-length approach because it enables them to properly monitor and evaluate foreign managements.[21] They also tend to prefer it because the transfers can demoralize the management of the foreign subsidiaries that do not show positive results—they were transferred to another subsidiary.

Fluctuating Exchange Rates and Costs

Fluctuating exchange rates force periodic adjustments in price. The same principle applies to fluctuating costs, including costs of raw materials and supplies, inflation, and interest rates. When a firm enters into a long-term contract at a fixed rate, shifts can prove disastrous if the firm cannot adjust its prices in some way. The lesson is that in international pricing, a firm must develop strong international money management skills.

Countertrade

Pricing strategies are further complicated by the fact that not all foreign transactions can be in cash. For example, sales to communist countries and to Third World countries with "soft currency," currency that is not readily accepted in international transactions, often take place in the form countertrade, which fundamentally means the buyer of a product pays the seller with another product that has the equivalent monetary value. The pricing problem derives from the difficulty of assessing the value of the product received in exchange. A miscalculation could lead to financial disaster. There are four basic types of countertrade transactions: barter, compensation, switch, and counterpurchase.[22]

BARTER   **Barter** is an arrangement in which the exporter sells goods to a foreign importer without the exchange of cash. That is, specified goods are sold to the importer for other specified goods.

COMPENSATION   Using the **compensation** procedure, the exporter sells technology and equipment to an importer in the foreign market. The importer pays the exporter with goods produced with the imported technology or equipment.

SWITCH   In the **switch** procedure, the exporter transfers the commitment to a third party who may be an end user of the product received by the exporter or to a trading house employed to dispose of the product. An advantage here is that the third party can be highly effective in selling the product. A disadvantage is that the third party often seeks to obtain the product at a bargain price, therefore lessening profit and complicating negotiations.

COUNTERPURCHASE   Under a **counterpurchase** agreement, two parties agree to sell each other products or services with some balancing of values. The exporter sells goods, technology, or services to the foreign importer for cash, but agrees to purchase goods with the cash equivalent from the importer within a specified period—the goods are selected from a list that usually excludes those items produced by the technology being imported. An advantage of this approach is that the exporter has use of the cash for the specified period.

Exporters entering into countertrade agreements must often use a trading firm to market the goods they purchase. However, the goods purchased can often be distributed or used by a subsidiary of the exporter. For example, **PepsiCo** has been selling to Russia the concentrate for a drink to be bottled and sold in Russia. In return, PepsiCo has been paid with vodka, which it has distributed through a subsidiary. Often, exporters receive raw materials or parts that can be used in their production process.

In general, the major problem in countertrade is determining the value and the potential demand of the goods offered by the other firm, and it is time consuming. Firms, however, are motivated to participate in countertrade for various reasons, including to make sales in nonmarket nations and in many less-developed countries and to adjust their accounting records to enable them to pay lower taxes and tariffs. This occurs when both parties underestimate the value of the goods.

International Promotion Strategy

In general, problems related to international promotion strategy include the legal aspects of the country, tax considerations, language complexities, cultural diversity, media limitations, credibility of advertising, and degree of illiteracy. Some governments regulate advertising more closely than others. Laws in some nations restrict the amount of money that may be spent on advertising, the media utilized, the type of product advertised, the methods used in advertising, and the way in which the price is advertised. Some nations have special taxes on advertisements. Language translation presents many barriers. For example, translation of semantic and idiomatic meanings across cultures are difficult to make, which presents huge impediments to communication.

Why International Promotional Strategies Fail

There are numerous reasons international promotional strategies fail. The reasons include insufficient research, overstandardization, poor follow-up, narrow vision, and rigid implementation.[23]

INSUFFICIENT RESEARCH **Insufficient research** prior to making international strategic decisions generally leads to failure. For example, **Lego A/S**, the Danish toy company, had improved its penetration in the American market by offering "bonus" packs and gift promotion. Encouraged by its success in the United States, Lego decided to apply the same approaches, unaltered, to other markets, including Japan, where penetration had been lagging. The Japanese customers were not attracted to those tactics. A later investigation revealed that Japanese consumers viewed the promotions as wasteful, expensive, and not too appealing. The results were similar in other countries as well.

OVERSTANDARDIZATION Some commodities, such as Coca-Cola, have a global appeal. In this situation, the message to be communicated can be much the same throughout the world. Many products, however, do not have universal appeal.[24] The message to be communicated must therefore be tied to individual motivation; the promotional campaign, instead of being **overstandardized,** must reflect local tastes. The foreign environment thus has a significant effect on promotional strategy. Failure to adapt promotional strategy to the foreign environment inevitably creates difficulties. Managers therefore need to determine whether or not a promotional message is appropriate for the foreign culture, and if not, what adoptions must be made.

POOR FOLLOW-UP Failure to monitor the promotional campaign for problems and solve them as they arise will contribute to failure. For instance, a U.S.-based computer company implemented a software house cooperation program in Europe to help penetrate the small- and medium-sized accounts market segment, where it was weak. The program needed a large change in sales force operation. The sales force, no longer in control of the hardware and software package, had to determine its content together with a software house that had access to the smaller accounts. The success of the new program depended on how effectively the sales force carried out its new assignments as well as on central coordination and attention, which it never got. Lacking central coordination and **follow-up,** there was no communication channel for sharing and building on the experiences of subsidiaries.

NARROW VISION An enterprise may centralize promotional strategic decision making or it may decentralize it to its local managers. Both approaches have pros and cons. The centralized approach can be effective by providing an overall global perspective, but it can be ineffective because decision making is not close to the market. The decentralized approach may be effective since decision making is close to the market; however, it may be ineffective because it does not provide a global perspective.

RIGID IMPLEMENTATION High-level managers sometimes ignore local managers' reservations about **rigidly implementing** a standardized promotional program and force compliance, which usually leads to failure. This is so because local managers' reservations are often based on a solid understanding of local conditions. Top management may also become inflexible to changing market conditions.

Developing an Effective International Promotional Strategy

To develop an effective international promotional strategy, strategists must determine (a) the promotional mix—the blend of advertising, personal selling, and sales promotions—needed for each market; (b) the extent of worldwide promotional standardization; (c) the most effective message; (d) the most effective medium; and (e) the necessary controls to aid in assessing whether or not the potential objectives are being met.[25]

Factors to Consider When Doing Business Abroad

This section presents some questions that the strategist should answer, or factors that should be considered, to be successful doing business abroad.

- Does your firm have a mission statement? That is, do you know why the company exists and what it plans to do? If you don't, you won't have a sense of direction.
- Why do you want to go international? Is it for opportunity or threat reasons or both? Or is it because it is currently fashionable to internationalize? If it is the latter, you might not apply the intensity needed to be successful abroad.
- Are you ready to go abroad? Will going abroad really solve your problems? How long has the company been in business? Is it stable enough (financially and psychologically) to endure the initial hardship of internationalization? Does it have a national reputation? Being successful at home will help mitigate the internationalization hardship?
- Have you done your homework? That is, have you ascertained where there may be a demand for your product/service? Are you totally familiar with domestic and international environments? Have you thoroughly familiarized yourself with the potential market's cultural, economic, legal, political, competitive, trade and monetary barriers, and labor relations factors? That is, are you thoroughly familiar with the challenge you will be facing in internationalizing?
- Are you thoroughly familiar with your strengths and weaknesses? That is, do you have a thorough understanding of your international management capabilities? Do you have a clear understanding of the nature of your product/service? Do you know how to capitalize on your product's/service's strengths, how to minimize its weaknesses, how to correct its shortcomings, and how to customize it to fit the needs of the foreign market? How strong or weak is your firm with respect to e-commerce?
- Have you developed viable product/service, place/entry, pricing, and promotion strategies that are based on the answers to the questions posed above.

In essence, the above means that, to be successful in internationalizing a business, the strategist must do his or her homework. Those who do their homework will have a far greater chance of succeeding abroad than those who do not.

International Risks

Two types of risks related to international business are discussed in this section. These include political risk and economic risk.

Political Risk

Politics and laws of a host country affect international business operations in a variety of ways. The good manager will understand these dimensions of the countries in which the firm operates so that he or she can work within existing parameters and can anticipate and plan for changes that may occur.

Firms usually prefer to conduct business in a country with a stable and friendly government, but such governments are not always easy to find. Managers must therefore continually monitor the government, its policies, and its stability to determine the potential for political change that could adversely affect corporate operations.

There is **political risk** in every nation, but the range of risks varies widely from country to country. In general, political risk is lowest in countries that have a history of stability and consistency. Political risk tends to be highest in nations that do not have this sort of history. In a number of countries, however, consistency and stability that were apparent on the surface have been quickly swept away by major popular movements that drew on the bottled-up frustrations of the population. Three major types of political risk can be encountered: **ownership risk,** which exposes property and life; **operating risk,** which refers to interference with the ongoing operations of a firm; and **transfer risk,** which is mainly encountered when attempts are made to shift funds between countries. Firms can be exposed to political risk due to government actions or even actions outside the control of governments.

Transfer Risks Versus Operating Risks Versus Ownership Risks

- *Political risks can be broken down into transfer risks, operating risks, and ownership risks. Transfer risk stem from government policies that limit the transfer of capital, payments, production, people, and technology in or out of a country. Examples of transfer risks include tariffs on exports and imports, restrictions on exports, dividend remittance, and capital repatriation.*

- *Operating risks stem from government policies and procedures that directly constrain the international management and performance of local business activities. Examples of operating risks include price controls, financing restrictions, export commitments, taxes, and local-sourcing requirements.*

- *Ownership risks are brought about by govenment policies or actions that inhibit ownership or control of local operations. Pressure for local participation, confiscation, expropriation, and abrogation of property rights are examples of ownership risks.*

A major political risk in many countries is that of conflict and violent change. A manager will want to think twice before conducting business in a country in which the likelihood of such change is high. To begin with, if conflict breaks out, violence directed toward the firm's property and employees is a strong possibility. Guerrilla warfare, civil disturbances, and terrorism often take an anti-industry bent, making companies and their employees potential targets. International corporations are often subject to major threats, even in countries that boast great political stability. Sometimes the sole fact that a firm is market oriented is sufficient to attract the wrath of terrorists.

Less drastic, but still worrisome, are changes in government policies that are not caused by changes in the government itself. These occur when, for one reason or another, a government feels pressured to change its policies toward foreign businesses. The pressure may be the result of nationalist or religious factions or widespread anti-Western feeling.

A broad range of policy changes is possible as a result of political unrest. All of the changes can affect the company's international operations, but not all of them are equal in weight. Except for extreme cases, companies do not usually have to fear violence against their employees, although violence against company property is quite common. Also common are changes in policy that result from a new government or a strong new stance that is nationalist and opposed to foreign investment. The most drastic public steps resulting from such policy changes are usually expropriation and confiscation.

Expropriation is the transfer of ownership by the host government to a domestic entity with payment of compensation. Expropriation was an appealing action to many countries because it demonstrated their nationalism and transferred a certain amount of wealth and resources from foreign companies to the host country immediately. It did have costs to the host country, however, to the extent that it made other firms more hesitant to invest there. Expropriation does not relieve the host government of providing compensation to the former owners. However, these compensation negotiations are often protracted and frequently result in settlements that are unsatisfactory to the owners. For example, governments may offer compensation in the form of local, nontransferable currency or may base compensation on the book value of the firm. Even though firms that are expropriated may deplore the low levels of payment obtained, they frequently accept them in the absence of better alternatives.

The use of expropriation as a policy tool has sharply decreased over time. In the mid-1970s, more than 83 expropriations took place in a single year. By the turn of the century, the annual average had declined to fewer than 3. Apparently, governments have come to recognize that the damage they inflict on themselves through expropriation exceeds the benefits they receive.

Confiscation is similar to expropriation in that it results in a transfer of ownership from the firm to the host country. It differs in that it does not involve compensation for the firm. Some industries are more vulnerable than others to confiscation and expropriation because of their importance to the host country's economy and their lack of ability to shift operations. For this reason, such sectors as mining, energy, public utilities, and banking have frequently been targets of such government actions.

Confiscation and expropriation constitute major political risk for foreign investors. Other government actions, however, are equally detrimental to foreign firms. Many countries are turning from confiscation and expropriation to more subtle forms of control, such as **domestication.** The goal of domestication is the same—that is, to gain control over foreign investment—but the method is different. Through domestication, the government demands transfer of ownership and management responsibility. It can impose **local content** regulations to ensure that a large share of the product is locally produced or demand that a larger share of the profit is retained in the country. Changes in labor laws, patent protection, and tax regulations are also used for purposes of domestication.

Domestication can have profound effects on an international business operation for a number of reasons. If a firm is forced to hire nationals as managers, poor cooperation and communication can result. If domestication is imposed within a very short time span, corporate operations overseas may have to be headed by poorly trained and inexperienced local managers. Domestic content requirements may force a firm to purchase its supplies and parts locally. This can result in increased costs, less efficiency, and lower-quality products. Export requirements imposed on companies may create havoc for their international distribution plans and force them to change or even shut down operations in third countries.

Finally, domestication usually will shield an industry within one country from foreign competition. As a result, inefficiencies will be allowed to thrive due to a lack of market discipline. This will affect the long-run international competitiveness of an operation abroad and may turn into a major problem when, years later, domestication is discontinued by the government.

If government action consists of weakening or not enforcing **intellectual property right** protection, companies run the risk of losing their core competitive edge. Such steps may temporarily permit domestic firms to become quick imitators. Yet, in the longer term, they will not only discourage the ongoing transfer of technology and knowledge by multinational firms, but also reduce the incentive for local firms to invest in innovation and progress.

One might ask why companies would choose to do business in risky markets. However, as with anything international (or any business for that matter), the issue is not whether there is any risk but rather the degree of risk that exists. Key links to risk are the dimension of reward. With appropriate rewards, many risks become more tolerable.

Economic Risk

Most businesses operating abroad face a number of other risks that are less dangerous, but probably more common, than the drastic ones already described. A host government's political situation or desires may lead it to impose economic regulations or laws to restrict or control the international activities of firms.

Nations that face a shortage of foreign currency will sometimes impose controls on the movement of capital into and out of the country. Such controls may make it difficult for a firm to remove its profits or investments from the host country. Sometimes **exchange controls** are also levied selectively against certain products or companies in an effort to reduce the importation of goods that are considered to be luxuries or to be sufficiently available through domestic production. Such regulations often affect the importation of parts, components, or supplies that are vital to production operations in the country. They may force a firm either to alter its production program or, worse yet, to shut down its entire plant. Prolonged negotiations with government officials may be necessary to reach a compromise on what constitutes a "valid" expenditure of foreign currency resources. Because the goals of government officials and corporate managers are often quite different, such compromises, even when they can be reached, may result in substantial damage to the international operations of the firm.

Countries may also use **tax policy** toward foreign investors in an effort to control multinational corporations and their capital. Tax increases may raise much-needed revenue for the host country, but they can severely damage the operations of foreign investors. This damage, in turn, will frequently result in decreased income for the host country in the long run. The raising of tax rates needs to be carefully differentiated from increased tax scrutiny of foreign investors. Many governments believe that multinational firms may be tempted to shift tax burdens to lower-tax countries by using artificial pricing schemes between subsidiaries. In such instances, governments are likely to take measures to obtain their fair contribution from multinational operations. In the United States, for example, increased focus on the taxation of multinational firms has resulted in various back-tax payments by foreign firms and the development of corporate pricing policies in collaboration with the Internal Revenue Service.[26]

The international executive also has to worry about **price controls.** In many countries, domestic political pressures can force governments to control the prices of imported products or services, particularly in sectors considered highly sensitive from a political perspective, such as food or health care. A foreign firm involved in these areas is vulnerable to price controls because the government can play on citizens' nationalistic tendencies to enforce the controls. Particularly in countries that suffer from high inflation, frequent devaluations, or sharply rising costs, the international executive may be forced to choose between shutting down the operation or continuing production at a loss in the hope of recouping profits when the government loosens or removes its price restrictions. Price controls can also be administered to prevent prices from being too low. Governments have enacted antidumping laws, which prevent foreign competitors from pricing their imports unfairly low in order to drive domestic competitors out of the market. Since dumping charges depend heavily on the definition of "fair" price, a firm can sometimes become the target of such accusations quite unexpectedly. Proving that no dumping took place can become quite onerous in terms of time, money, and information disclosure.

Managing the International Risk

Managers face the risk of confiscation, expropriation, domestication, or other government interference whenever they conduct business overseas, but ways exist to lessen the risk. Obviously, if a new government comes into power and is dedicated to the removal of all foreign influences, there is little a firm can do. In less extreme cases, however, managers can take actions that will reduce the risk, provided they understand the root causes of the host country's policies.

Adverse governmental actions are usually the result of nationalism, the deterioration of political relations between home and host country, the desire for independence, or opposition to colonial remnants. If a host country's citizens feel exploited by foreign investors, government officials are more likely to take antiforeign action. To reduce the risk of government intervention, the international firm needs to demonstrate that it is concerned with the host country's society and that it considers itself an integral part of the host country, rather than simply an exploitative foreign corporation. Ways of doing this include intensive local hiring and training practices, better pay, contributions to charity, and societally useful investments. In addition, the company can form joint ventures with local partners to demonstrate that it is willing to share its gains with nationals. Although such actions will not guarantee freedom from political risk, they will certainly lessen the exposure.

Another action that can be taken by corporations to protect against political risk is the close monitoring of political developments. Increasingly, private sector firms offer such monitoring assistance, permitting the overseas corporation to discover potential trouble spots as early as possible and to react quickly to prevent major losses.

Firms can also take out insurance to cover losses due to political and economic risk. Most industrialized countries offer insurance programs for their firms doing business abroad. In Germany, for example, Hermes Kreditanstalt (**www.hermes.de**) provides exporters with insurance. In the United States, the Overseas Private Investment Corporation (OPIC) (**www.opic.gov**) can cover three types of risk insurance: currency inconvertibility insurance, which covers the inability to convert profits, debt service, and other remittances from local currency into U.S. dollars; expropriation insurance, which covers the loss of an investment due to expropriation, nationalization, or confiscation by a foreign government; and political violence insurance, which covers the loss of assets or income due to war, revolution, insurrection, or politically motivated civil strife, terrorism, and sabotage. The cost of coverage varies by country and type of activity, but for manufacturers it averages $0.30 for $100 of coverage per year to protect against inconvertibility, $0.60 to protect against expropriation, and $1.05 to compensate for damage to business income and assets from political violence.[27] Usually the policies do not cover commercial risks and, in the event of a claim, cover only the actual loss—not lost profits. In the event of a major political upheaval, however, risk insurance can be critical to a firm's survival.

The discussion to this point has focused primarily on the political and economic environment. Laws have been mentioned only as they appear to be the direct result of political change. However, the laws of host countries need to be considered on their own to some extent, for the basic system of law is important to the conduct of international business.

Global Organization Structure and Control

As companies evolve from purely domestic to multinational, their organizational structure and control systems must change to reflect new strategies. With growth comes diversity in terms of products and services, geographic markets, and people in the company itself, bringing along a set of challenges for the company. Two critical issues are basic to all of these challenges: (1) the type of organization that provides the best framework for developing worldwide strategies while at the same time maintaining flexibility in implementation with respect to individual markets and operations and (2) the type and degree of control to be exercised from headquarters to maximize total effort. Organizational structures, organizations' abilities to implement strategies, and control systems have to be adjusted as market conditions change.

This section will focus on the advantages and disadvantages of various organizational structures, as well as their appropriateness at different stages of internationalization. A determining factor is where decision-making authority within the organizational structure will be placed. The roles of the different entities that make up the organization need to be defined, including how to achieve collaboration among the units for the benefit of the entire network. The section will also outline the need for devising a control system to oversee the international operations of the company, emphasizing the additional control instruments needed beyond those used in domestic business and the control strategies of multinational corporations. The appropriateness and eventual cost of the various control approaches will vary as the firm expands its international operations. The overall objective of the section is to study the intraorganizational relationships critical to the firm's attempt to optimize its competitiveness.

Organizational Structure

The basic functions of an organization are to provide: (1) a route and locus of decision making and coordination and (2) a system for reporting and communications. Authority and communication networks are typically depicted in the organizational chart.

Organizational Designs

The basic configurations of international organizations correspond to those of purely domestic ones; the greater the degree of internalization, the more complex the structures can become. The types of structures that companies use to manage foreign activities can be divided into three categories, based on the degree of internationalization.

1. *Little or no formal organizational recognition of international activities of the firm.* This category ranges from domestic operations handling an occasional international transaction on an ad hoc basis to firms with separate export departments.
2. *International division.* Firms in this category recognize the ever-growing importance of the international involvement.
3. *Global organizations.* These can be structured by product, area, function, process, or customer, but ignore the traditional domestic-international split.

Hybrid structures may exist as well, in which one market may be structured by product, another by areas. Matrix organizations have merged in large multinational corporations to combine product-specific, regional, and functional expertise. As worldwide competition has increased dramatically in many industries, the latest organizational response is networked global organizations in which heavy flows of hardware, software, and personnel take place between strategically interdependent units to establish greater global integration. The ability to identify and disseminate best practices throughout the organization is an important competitive advantage for global companies. For example, a U.S. automaker found that in the face of distinctive challenges presented by the local environment, Brazilian engineers developed superior seals, which the company then incorporated in all its models worldwide.[28]

Little or No Formal Organization

In the very early stages of international involvement, domestic operations assume responsibility for international activities. The role of international activities in the sales and profits of the corporation is initially so minor that no organizational adjustment takes place. No consolidation of information or authority over international sales is undertaken or is necessary. Transactions are conducted on a case-by-case basis, either by the resident expert or quite often with the help of facilitating agents, such as freight forwarders.

As demand from the international marketplace grows and interest within the firm expands, the organizational structure will reflect it. As shown in Exhibit 1000.1 an export department appears as a separate entity. This may be an outside export management company—that is, an independent company that becomes the de facto export department

Exhibit 1000.1 *The Export Department Structure*

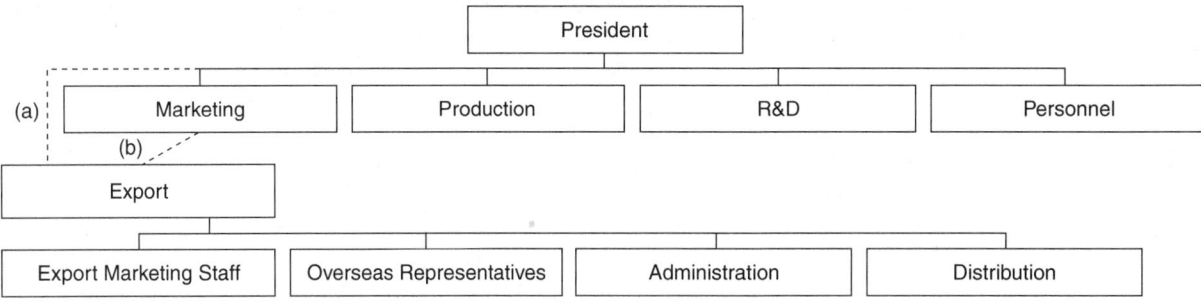

of the firm. This is an indirect approach to international involvement in that very little experience is accumulated within the firm itself. Alternatively, a firm may establish its own export department, hiring a few seasoned individuals to take responsibility for international activities. Organizationally, the department may be a subdepartment of marketing (alternative b in Exhibit 1000.1) or may have equal ranking with the various functional departments (alternative a). The choice will depend on the importance assigned to overseas activities by the firm. The export department is the first real step toward internationalizing the organizational structures. It should be a full-fledged marketing organization and not merely a sales organization; that is, it should have the resources for market research and market-development activities (such as trade show participation).

Licensing as an international entry mode may be assigned to the R&D function despite its importance to the overall international strategy of the firm. A formal liaison among the export, marketing, production, and R&D functions has to be formed for the maximum utilization of licensing.[29] If licensing indeed becomes a major activity for the firm, a separate manager should be appointed.

The more the firm becomes involved in foreign markets, the more quickly the export department structure will become obsolete. For example, the firm may undertake joint ventures or direct foreign investment, which require those involved to have functional experience. The firm therefore typically establishes an international division.

Some firms that acquire foreign production facilities pass through an additional stage in which foreign subsidiaries report directly to the president or to a manager specifically assigned the duty.[30] However, the amount of coordination and control that are required quickly establish the need for a more formal international organization in the firm.

The International Division

The international division centralizes in one entity, with or without separate incorporation, all of the responsibility for international activities, as illustrated in Exhibit 1000.2. The approach aims to eliminate a possible bias against international operations that may exist if domestic divisions are allowed to serve international customers independently. In some cases, international markets have been treated as secondary to domestic markets. The international division concentrates international expertise, information flows concerning foreign market opportunities, and authority over international activities. However, manufacturing and other related functions remain with the domestic divisions to take advantage of economies of scale.

To avoid putting the international division at a disadvantage in competing for products, personnel, and corporate services, coordination between domestic and international operations is necessary. Coordination can be achieved through a joint staff or by requiring domestic and international divisions to interact in strategic planning and to submit the plans to headquarters. Further, many corporations require and encourage frequent interaction between domestic and international personnel to discuss common problems in areas such as product planning. Coordination is also important because domestic operations are typically organized along product or functional lines, whereas international divisions are geographically oriented.

International divisions best serve firms with few products that do not vary significantly in terms of their environmental sensitivity and with international sales and profits that are still quite insignificant compared with those of the domestic divisions.[31] Companies may outgrow their international divisions as their sales outside of the domestic market grow in significance, diversity, and complexity. European companies have traditionally used international divisions far less than their U.S. counterparts due to the relatively small size of their domestic markets. **Philips, Nestlé**, or **Nokia**, for example, would have never grown to their current prominence by relying on their home markets alone. While international divisions were popular among U.S. companies in the 1970s and 1980s, globalization of markets

Exhibit 1000.2 *The International Division Structure*

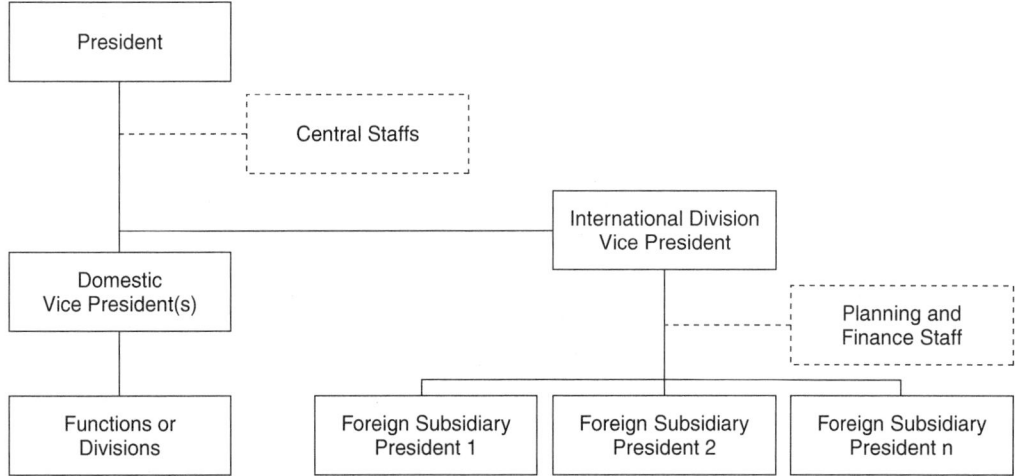

and the increased share of overseas sales have made international divisions less suitable in favor of global structures.[32] For example, **Loctite**, a leading marketer of sealants, adhesives and coatings, moved from an international division to a global structure by which the company is managed by market channel (for example, industrial automotive and electronics industry) to enable **Loctite** employees to synergize efforts and expertise worldwide.[33]

Global Organizational Structures

Global structures have grown out of competitive necessity. In many industries, competition is on a global basis, with a result that companies must have a high degree of reactive capability.

Six basic types of global structures are available.

1. Global product structure, in which product divisions are responsible for all manufacture and marketing worldwide
2. Global area structure, in which geographic divisions are responsible for all manufacture and marketing in their respective areas
3. Global functional structures, in which functional areas (such as production, marketing, finance, and personnel) are responsible for the worldwide operations of their own functional area
4. Global customer structures, in which operations are structured based on distinct worldwide customer groups
5. Mixed—or hybrid—structures, which may combine the other alternatives
6. Matrix structures, in which operations have reporting responsibility to more than one group (typically, product, functions, or area)

PRODUCT STRUCTURE The **product structure** is the form most often used by multinational corporations.[34] The approach gives worldwide responsibility to strategic business units for the marketing of their product lines, as shown in Exhibit 1000.3. Most consumer-product firms use some form of this approach, mainly because of the diversity of their products. One of the major benefits of the approach is improved cost efficiency through centralization of manufacturing facilities. This is crucial in industries in which competitive position is determined by world market share, which in turn is often determined by the degree to which manufacturing is rationalized.[35] Adaptation to this approach may cause problems because it is usually accompanied by consolidation of operations and plant closings. A good example is **Black & Decker**, which rationalized many of its operations in its worldwide competitive effort against **Makita**, the Japanese power tool manufacturer. Similarly, **Goodyear** reorganized itself into a single global organization with a complete business-team approach for tires and general products. The move was largely prompted by tightening worldwide competition.[36] In a similar move, **Ford** merged its large and culturally distinct European and North American auto operations by vehicle platform type to make more efficient use of its engineering and product development resources against rapidly globalizing rivals.[37] The Ford Focus, Ford's compact car introduced in 1999, was designed by one team of engineers for worldwide markets.

Exhibit 1000.3 *The Global Product Structure*

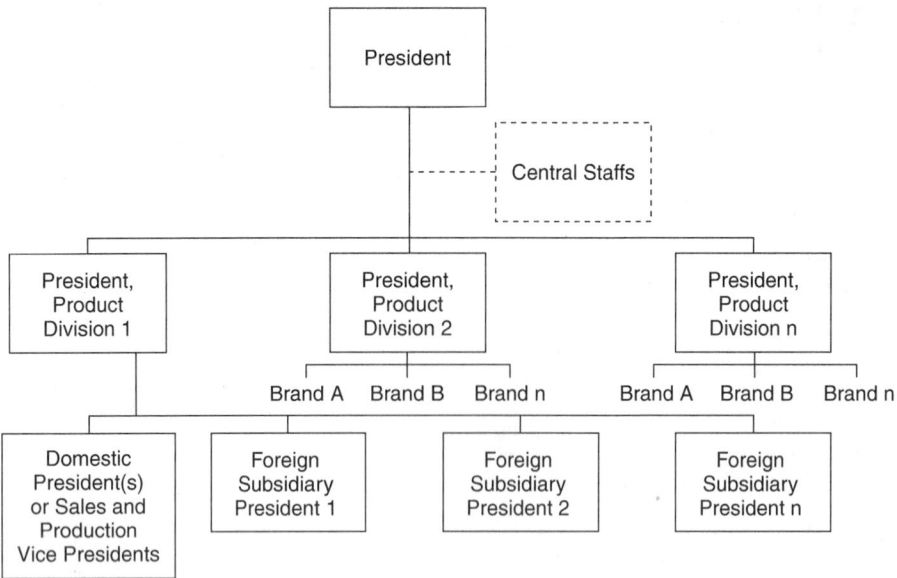

Other benefits of the product structure are the ability to balance the functional inputs needed for a product and the ability to react quickly to product-specific problems in the marketplace. Even smaller brands receive individual attention. Product-specific attention is important because products vary in terms of the adaptation they need for different foreign markets. All in all, the product approach is ideally suited to the development of a global strategic focus in response to global competition.

At the same time, the product structure fragments international expertise within the firm because a central pool of international experience no longer exists. The structure assumes that managers will have adequate regional experience or advice to allow them to make balanced decisions. Coordination of activities among the various product groups operating in the same markets is crucial to avoid unnecessary duplication of basic tasks. For some of these tasks, such as market research, special staff functions may be created and then filled by the product divisions when needed. If they lack an appreciation for the international dimension, product managers may focus their attention only on the larger markets or only on the domestic, and fail to take the long-term view.

AREA STRUCTURE The second most used approach is the **area structure,** illustrated in Exhibit 1000.4. Such firms are organized on the basis of geographical areas; for example, operations may be divided into those dealing with North America, the Far East, Latin America, and Europe. Ideally, no special preference is given to the region in which the headquarters is located—for example, North America or Europe. Central staffs are responsible for providing coordination support for worldwide planning and control activities performed at headquarters.

Regional integration is playing a major role in area structuring; for example, many multinational corporations have located their European headquarters in Brussels, where the EU has its headquarters. In some U.S. companies, North American integration led to the development of a North American division, which replaced the U.S. operation as the power center of the company. The driver of structural choices may also be cultural similarity, such as in the case of Asia, or historic connections between countries, such as in the case of combining Europe with the Middle East and Africa.

The area approach follows the marketing concept most closely because individual areas and markets are given concentrated attention. If market conditions with respect to product acceptance and operating conditions vary dramatically, the area approach is the one to choose. Companies opting for this alternative typically have relatively narrow product lines with similar end uses and end users. However, expertise is needed in adapting the product and its marketing to local market conditions. Once again, to avoid duplication of effort in product management and in functional areas, staff specialists—for product categories, for example—may be used.

Without appropriate coordination from the staff, essential information and experience may not be transferred from one regional entity to another. Also, if the company expands its product lines and if end markets begin to diversify, the area structure may become inappropriate.

Some managers may feel that going into a global product structure may be too much, too quickly, and opt, therefore, to have a regional organization for planning and reporting purposes. The objective may also be to keep profit or sales cen-

Exhibit 1000.4 *The Global Area Structure*

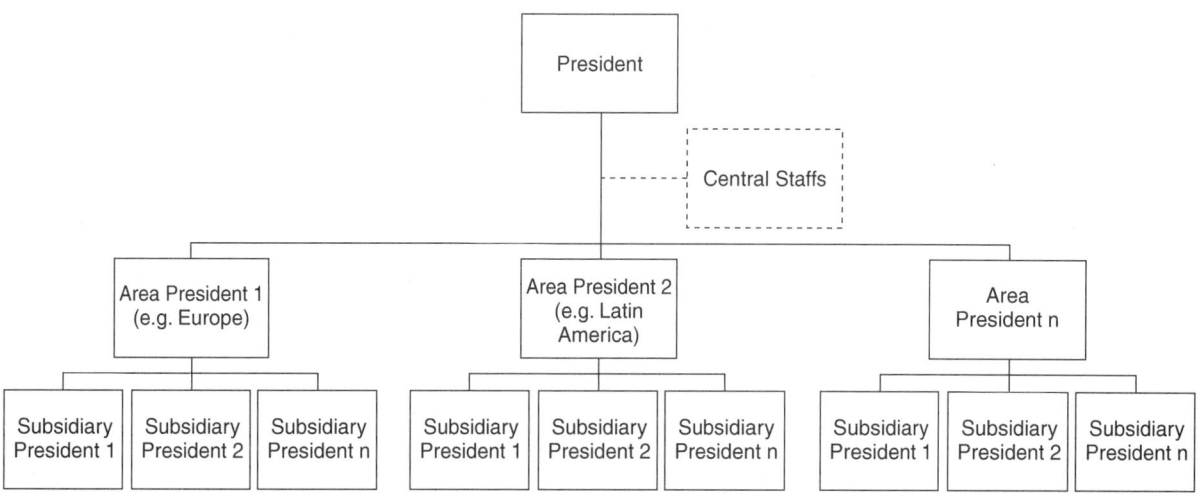

ters of similar size at similar levels in the corporate hierarchy. If a group of countries has small sales as compared with other country operations, they may be consolidated into a region. The benefit of a regional operation and regional headquarters would be the more efficient coordination of programs across the region (as opposed to globally), a more sensitized management to country-market operations in the region, and the ability to have the region's voice heard more clearly at global headquarters (as compared to what an individual, especially smaller, country operation could achieve).[38]

FUNCTIONAL STRUCTURE Of all the approaches, the **functional structure** is the simplest from the administrative viewpoint because it emphasizes the basic tasks of the firm—for example, manufacturing, sales, and research and development. The approach, illustrated in Exhibit 1000.5, works best when both products and customers are relatively few and similar in nature. Coordination is typically the key problem, therefore, staff functions have been created to interact between the functional areas. Otherwise, the company's marketing and regional expertise may not be exploited to the fullest extent possible.

A variation of the functional approach is one that uses processes as a basis for structure. The **process structure** is common in the energy and mining industries, where one corporate entity may be in charge of exploration worldwide and another may be responsible for the actual mining operations.

CUSTOMER STRUCTURE Firms may also organize their operations using the **customer structure,** especially if the customer groups they serve are dramatically different—for example, consumers and businesses and governments. Catering to such diverse groups may require concentrating specialists in particular divisions. The product may be the same, but the buying processes of the various customer groups may differ. Governmental buying is characterized by bidding, in which price plays a larger role than when businesses are the buyers.

MIXED STRUCTURE In some cases, mixed, or hybrid, organizations exist. A **mixed structure** combines two or more organizational dimensions simultaneously. It permits adequate attention to product, area, or functional needs as is needed by the company. The approach may only be a result of a transitional period after a merger or an acquisition, or it may come about due to unique market characteristics or product line. It may also provide a useful structure before the implementation of a worldwide matrix structure.[39]

Naturally, organizational structures are never as clear-cut and simple as presented here. Whatever the basic format, product, functional, and area inputs are needed. Alternatives could include an initial product structure that would subsequently have regional groupings or an initial regional structure with subsequent product groupings. However, in the long term, coordination and control across such structures become tedious.

MATRIX STRUCTURE Many multinational corporations, in an attempt to facilitate planning for, organizing, and controlling interdependent businesses, critical resources, strategies, and geographic regions, have adopted the **matrix structure.**[40] **Eastman Kodak** shifted from a functional organization to a matrix system based on business units. Business is driven by a worldwide business unit (for example, photographic products or commercial and information systems)

Exhibit 1000.5 *The Global Functional Structure*

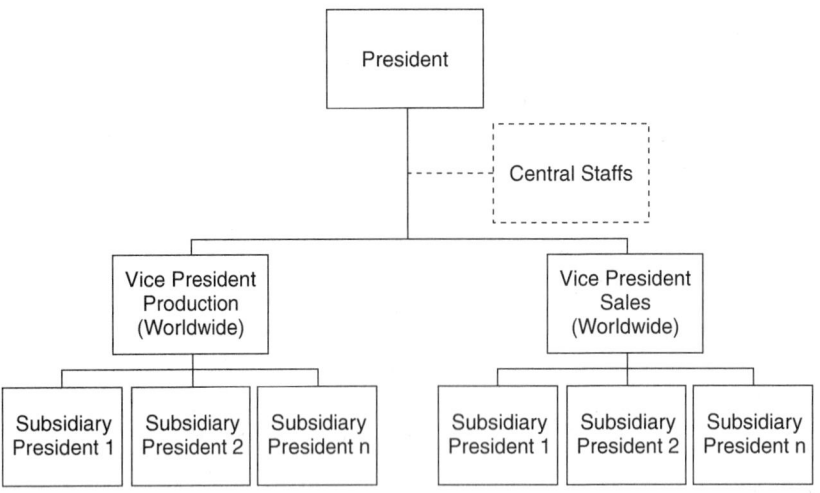

Exhibit 1000.6 *The Global Matrix Structure at Philips*

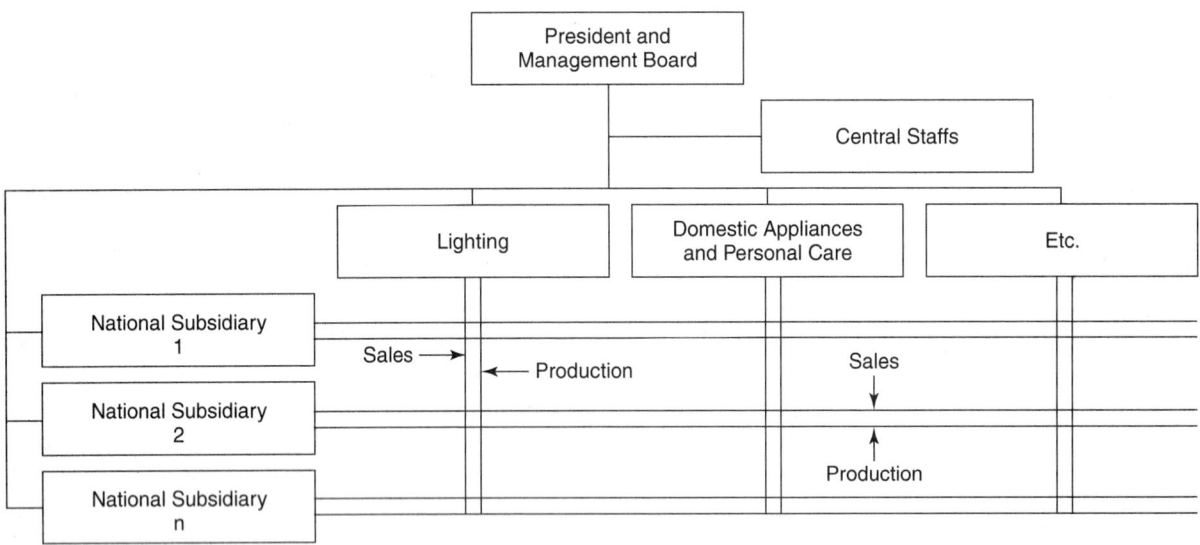

and implemented by a geographic unit (for example, Europe or Latin America). The geographical units, as well as their country subsidiaries, serve as the "glue" between autonomous product operations.[41]

Organizational matrices integrate the various approaches already discussed, as the **Philips** example in Exhibit 1000.6 illustrates. The 7 product divisions (which are then divided into 60 product groups) have rationalized manufacturing to provide products for continentwide markets rather than lines of products for individual markets.[42] Philips has three general types of country organizations. In "key" markets, such as the United States, France, and Japan, product divisions manage their own marketing as well as manufacturing. In "local business" countries, such as Nigeria and Peru, the organizations function as importers from product divisions, and if manufacturing occurs, it is purely for the local market. In "large" markets, such as Brazil, Spain, and Taiwan, a hybrid arrangement is used, depending on the size and situation. The product divisions and the national subsidiaries interact in a matrixlike configuration, with the product divisions responsible for the globalization dimension and the national subsidiaries responsible for local representation and coordination of common areas of interest, such as recruiting.

Matrices vary in terms of their number of dimensions. For example, **Dow Chemical's** three-dimensional matrix consists of five geographic areas, three major functions (marketing, manufacturing, and research), and more than 70 products. The matrix approach helps cut through enormous organizational complexities in making business managers, functional managers, and strategy managers cooperate. However, the matrix requires sensitive, well-trained middle managers who can cope with problems that arise from reporting to two bosses—for example, a product-line manager and an area manager. For example, every management unit may have a multidimensional reporting relationship, which may cross functional, regional, or operational lines. On a regional basis, group managers in Europe for example, report administratively to a vice president of operations for Europe, but report functionally to group vice presidents at global headquarters.

Most companies have found the matrix arrangement problematic.[43] The dual reporting channel easily causes conflict, complex issues are forced into a two-dimensional decision framework, and even minor issues may have to be solved through committee discussion. Ideally, managers should solve the problems themselves through formal and informal communication; however, physical and psychic distance often make that impossible. The matrix structure, with its inherent complexity, may actually increase the reaction time of a company, a potentially serious problem when competitive conditions require quick responses. As a result, the authority has started to shift in many organizations from area to product, although the matrix still may officially be used.

Evolution of Organizational Structures

Companies have been shown to develop new structures in a pattern of stages as their products diversify and share of foreign sales increases.[44] At the first stage of autonomous subsidiaries reporting directly to top management, the establishment of an international division follows. As product diversity and the importance of the foreign marketplace increase, companies develop global structures to coordinate subsidiary operations and to rationalize worldwide production. As multinational corporations have been faced with simultaneous pressures to adapt to local market conditions and to rationalize production and globalize competitive reactions, many have opted for the matrix structure.[45] The matrix structure probably allows a corporation to best meet the challenges of global markets (to be global and local, big and small, decentralized with centralized reporting) by allowing the optimizing of businesses globally and maximizing performance in every country of operation.[46]

Implementation

Organizational structures provide the frameworks for carrying out decision-making processes. However, for that decision making to be effective, a series of organizational initiatives are needed to develop strategy to its full potential, that is, to secure implementation both at the national level and across markets.[47]

Locus of Decision Making

Organizational structures themselves do not indicate where the authority for decision making and control rests within the organization nor will it reveal the level of coordination between the units. The different levels of coordination between country units are summarized in Exhibit 1000.7. Once a suitable structure is found, it has to be made to work.

If subsidiaries are granted a high degree of autonomy, the system is called **decentralization.** In decentralized systems, controls are relatively loose and simple, and the flows between headquarters and subsidiaries are mainly financial; that is, each subsidiary operates as a profit center. On the other hand, if controls are tight and the strategic

Exhibit 1000.7 *Levels of Coordination*

Level	Description
5. Central control	No national structures
4. Central direction	Central functional heads have line authority over national functions
3. Central coordination	Central staff functions in coordinating role
2. Coordinating mechanisms	Formal committees and systems
1. Informal cooperation	Functional meetings: exchange of information
0. National autonomy	No coordination between decentralized units, which may even compete in export markets

Level 5 = highest; Level 0 = lowest. Most commonly found levels are 1–4.

Source: Norman Blackwell, Jean-Pierre Bizet, Peter Child, and David Hensley. "Creating European Organizations that Work," *The McKinsey Quarterly* 27, 2(1991): 376.

decision making is concentrated at headquarters, the system is described as **centralization.** Firms are typically neither completely centralized nor decentralized; for example, some functions of the firm—such as finance—lend themselves to more centralized decision making; others—such as promotional decisions—do so far less. Research and development in organizations is typically centralized, especially in cases of basic research work. Some companies have, partly due to governmental pressures, added R&D functions on a regional or local basis. In many cases, however, variations are product and market based; for example, **Corning Incorporated's** TV tube marketing strategy requires global decision making for pricing and local decision making for service and delivery.

The basic advantage of allowing maximum flexibility at the country-market level is that subsidiary management knows its market and can react to changes more quickly. Problems of motivation and acceptance are avoided when decision makers are also the implementors of the strategy. On the other hand, many multinationals faced with global competitive threats and opportunities have adopted global strategy formulation, which by definition requires a higher degree of centralization. What has emerged as a result can be called **coordinated decentralization.** This means that overall corporate strategy is provided from headquarters, while subsidiaries are free to implement it within the range agreed on in consultation between headquarters and the subsidiaries.

However, companies moving into this new mode may face significant challenges. Among these systemic difficulties are a lack of widespread commitment to dismantling traditional national structures, driven by an inadequate understanding of the larger, global forces at work. Power barriers from perceived threats to the personal roles of national managers, especially if their tasks are under the threat of being consolidated into regional organizations, can lead to proposals being challenged without valid reason. Finally, some organizationally initiatives (such as multicultural teams or corporate chat rooms) may be jeopardized by the fact the people do not have the necessary skills (for example, language ability) or that an infrastructure (for example, intranet) may not exist in an appropriate format.[48]

One particular case is of special interest. Organizationally, the forces of globalization are changing the country manager's role significantly. With profit-and-loss responsibility, oversight of multiple functions, and the benefit of distance from headquarters, country managers enjoyed considerable decision-making autonomy as well as entrepreneurial initiative when country operations were largely stand-alone. Today, however, many companies have to emphasize global and regional priorities, which means that the power has to shift at least to some extent from the country manager to worldwide strategic business unit and product-line managers. Many of the local decisions are now subordinated to global strategic moves. Therefore, the future country manager will have to wear many hats in balancing the needs of the operation for which the manager is directly responsible with those of the entire region or strategic business unit.[49] To emphasize the importance of the global/regional dimension in the country manager's portfolio, many companies have tied the country manager's compensation to how the company performs globally or regionally, not just in the market for which the manager is responsible.

Factors Affecting Structure and Decision Making

The organizational structure and locus of decision making in a multinational corporation are determined by a number of factors, such as: (1) its degree of involvement in international operations, (2) the products the firm markets, (3) the size and importance of the firm's markets, and (4) the human resource capability of the firm.[50]

The effect of the degree of involvement on structure and decision making was discussed earlier in the chapter. With low degrees of involvement, subsidiaries can enjoy high degrees of autonomy as long as they meet their profit targets. The same situation can occur even with the most globally oriented companies, but within a different framework. Consider, for example, **Philips USA** which generates 20% of the company's worldwide sales. Even more important it serves as a market that is on the leading edge of digital media development. Therefore, it enjoys independent status in terms of local policy setting and managerial practices but is still, nevertheless, within the parent company's planning and control system.

The firm's country of origin and the political history of the area can also affect organizational structure and decision making. For example, Swiss-based **Nestlé**, with only 3 to 4% of its sales from its small domestic market, has traditionally had a highly decentralized organization. Moreover, European history for the past 80 years—particularly the two world wars—has often forced subsidiaries of European-based companies to act independently to survive.

The type and variety of products marketed will affect organizational decisions. Companies that market consumer products typically have product organizations with high degrees of decentralization, allowing for maximum local flexibility. On the other hand, companies that market technologically sophisticated products—such as **GE**, which markets turbines—display centralized organizations with worldwide product responsibilities. Even within matrix organizations, one of the dimensions may be granted more say in decisions; for example, at **Dow Chemical**, geographical managers have been granted more authority than other managers.

Going global has recently meant transferring world headquarters of important business units abroad. For example, Philips has moved headquarters of several of its global business units to the United States, including its Digital Video Group, Optimal Storage, and Flat Panel Display activities to Silicon Valley.

The human factor in any organization is critical. Managers at both headquarters and the country organizations must bridge the physical and cultural distances separating them. If country organizations have competent managers who rarely need to consult headquarters about their challenges, they may be granted high degrees of autonomy. In the case of global organizations, local management must understand overall corporate goals in that decisions that meet the long-term objectives may not be optimal for the individual local market.

The Networked Global Organization

No international structure is ideal and some have challenged the wisdom of even looking for one. They have recommended attention to new processes that would, in a given structure, help to develop new perspectives and attitudes that reflect and respond to the complex, opposing demands of global integration and local responsiveness.[51] The question thus changes from which structural alternative is best to how the different perspectives of various corporate entities can better be taken into account when making decisions. In structural terms, nothing may change. As a matter of fact, Philips has not changed its basic matrix structure, yet major changes have occurred in internal relations. The basic change was from a decentralized federation model to a networked global organization. The term **glocal** has been coined to describe this approach.[52]

Companies that have adopted the approach have incorporated the following three dimensions into their organizations: (1) the development and communication of a clear corporate vision, (2) the effective management of human resource tools to broaden individual perspectives and develop identification with corporate goals, and (3) the integration of individual thinking and activities into the broad corporate agenda.[53] The first dimension relates to a clear and consistent long-term corporate mission that guides individuals wherever they work in the organization. Examples of this are **Johnson & Johnson's** corporate credo of customer focus and NEC's C&C (computers and communications). The second relates both to the development of global managers who can find opportunities in spite of environmental challenges as well as creating a global perspective among country managers. The last dimension relates to the development of a cooperative mind-set among country organizations to ensure effective implementation of global strategies. Managers may believe that global strategies are intrusions on their operations if they do not have an understanding of the corporate vision, if they have not contributed to the global corporate agenda, or if they are not given direct responsibility for its implementation. Defensive, territorial attitudes can lead to the emergence of the "not-invented-here" syndrome, that is, country organizations objecting to or rejecting an otherwise sound strategy.

The network avoids the problems of effort duplication, inefficiency and resistance to ideas developed elsewhere by giving subsidiaries the latitude, encouragement, and tools to pursue local business development within the framework of the global strategy. Headquarters considers each unit a source of ideas, skills, capabilities, and knowledge that can be utilized for the benefit of the entire organization. This means that subsidiaries must be upgraded from mere implementors and adaptors to contributors and partners in the development and execution of worldwide strategies. Efficient plants may be converted into international production centers, innovative R&D units converted into centers of excellence (and thus role models), and leading subsidiary groups given the leadership role in developing new strategies for the entire corporation.

Promoting Internal Cooperation

The global business entity in today's environment can only be successful if is able to move intellectual capital within the organization; that is, take ideas and move them around faster and faster.[54] One of the tools is teaching.

Another method to promote internal cooperation for global strategy implementation is the use of international teams or councils. In the case of a new product or program an international team of managers may be assembled to develop strategy. While final direction may come from headquarters, it has been informed of local conditions, and implementation of the strategy is enhanced since local-country managers were involved in its development. The approach has worked even in cases involving seemingly impossible market differences.

The term *network* also implies two-way communications between headquarters and subsidiaries and between subsidiaries themselves. While this communication can take the form of newsletters or regular and periodic meetings of appropriate personnel, new technologies are allowing businesses to link far-flung entities and eliminate the traditional barriers of time and distance. **Intranets** integrate a company's information assets into a single accessible system using Internet-based technologies such as e-mail, news groups, and the World Wide Web. In effect, the formation of **virtual teams** becomes a reality.

The benefits of intranet are: (1) increased productivity in that there is no longer a time lag between an idea and the information needed to assess and implement it; (2) enhanced knowledge capital, which is constantly updated and upgraded; (3) facilitated teamwork enabling online communication at insignificant expense; and (4) incorporation of best practice at a moment's notice by allowing managers and functional-area personnel to make to-the-minute decisions anywhere in the world.

As can be seen from the discussion, the networked approach is not a structural adaptation but a procedural one, calling for a change in management mentality. It requires adjustment mainly in the coordination and control functions of the firm. Of the many initiatives developed to enhance the workings of a networked global organization, such as cross-border task forces and establishment of centers of excellence, the most significant was the use of electronic networking capabilities.[55]

Further adjustment in organizational approaches is required as businesses face new challenges such as emerging markets, global accounts, and the digitization of business.[56] Emerging markets present the company with unique challenges such as product counterfeiters and informal competitors who ignore local labor and tax laws. How these issues are addressed may require organizational rethinking. **Colgate-Palmolive**, for example, grouped its geographies under two different organizations: one responsible for mature, developed economies and the other for high-growth, emerging markets.[57] Global account managers need to have skills and the empowerment to work across functional areas and borders to deliver quality service to the company's largest clients. Finally, digital business, such as business-to-business and business-to-consumer Internet-based activities, need to be brought into the mainstay of the businesses activities and structures and not seen as a separate activity.

The Role of Country Organizations

Country organizations should be treated as a source of supply as much as a source of demand. Quite often, however, headquarters managers see their role as the coordinators of key decisions and controllers of resources and perceive subsidiaries as implementors and adaptors of global strategy in their respective local markets. Furthermore, they may see all country organizations as the same. This view severely limits utilization of the firm's resources and deprives country managers of the opportunity to exercise their creativity.[58]

The role that a particular country organization can play naturally depends on that market's overall strategic importance as well as its organizational competence. Using these criteria, four different roles emerge: strategic leader, contributor, implementor, and black hole.

The role of a **strategic leader** can be played by a highly competent national subsidiary located in a strategically critical market. Such a country organization serves as a partner of headquarters in developing and implementing strategy.

A **contributor** is a country organization with a distinctive competence, such as product development. Increasingly, country organizations are the source of new products.

Implementors provide the critical mass for the global effort. These country organizations may exist in smaller, less-developed countries in which there is less corporate commitment for market development. Although most entities are given this role, it should not be slighted, since the implementors provide the opportunity to capture economies of scale and scope that are the basis of a global strategy.

The **black hole** situation is one in which the international company has a low-competence country organization—or no organization at all—in a highly strategic market. In strategically important markets such as the European Union, a local presence is necessary to maintain the company's global position and, in some cases, to protect others. One of the major ways of remedying the black hole situation is to enter into strategic alliances. In some cases, firms may use their presence in a major market as an observation post to keep up with developments before a major thrust for entry is executed.

Depending on the role of the country organization, its relationship with headquarters will vary from loose control based mostly on support to tighter control to ensure that strategies get implemented appropriately. Yet, in each of these cases, it is imperative that country organizations have enough operating independence to cater to local needs and to provide motivation to country managers. For example, an implementor's ideas concerning the development of a regional or global strategy or program should be heard. Country organization initiative is the principal means by which global companies can tap into new opportunities in markets around the world.[59] For example, customers' unmet demands in a given market may result not only in the launch of a local product but subsequently in its roll-out

Organizational Controls

The function of the organizational structure is to provide a framework in which objectives can be met. A set of instruments and processes is needed, however, to influence the performance of organizational members so as to meet the goals. Controls focus on means to verify and correct actions that differ from established plans. Compliance needs to be secured from subordinates through different means of coordinating specialized and interdependent parts of the organization.[60] Within an organization, control serves as an integrating mechanism. Controls are designed to reduce uncertainty, increase predictability, and ensure that behaviors originating in separate parts of the organization are compatible and in support of common organizational goals despite physical, psychic, and temporal distances.[61]

The critical issue here is the same as with organizational structure: What is the ideal amount of control? On the one hand, headquarters needs controls to ensure that international activities contribute the greatest benefit to the overall organization. On the other hand, they should not be construed as a code of laws and subsequently allowed to stifle local initiative.

This section will focus on the design and functions of control instruments available for international business operations, along with an assessment of their appropriateness. Emphasis will be placed on the degree of formality of controls used by firms.

Types of Controls

Most organizations display some administrative flexibility, as demonstrated by variations in how they apply management directives, corporate objectives, or measurement systems. A distinction should be made, however, between variations that have emerged by design and those that are the result of autonomy. The first are the result of a management decision, whereas the second typically have grown without central direction and are based on emerging practices. In both instances, some type of control will be exercised. Controls that result from headquarters initiative rather than those that are the consequences of tolerated practices will be discussed here. Firms that wait for self-emerging controls often experience rapid international growth but subsequent problems in product-line performance, program coordination, and strategic planning.[62]

Whatever the system, it is important in today's competitive environment to have internal benchmarking. This relates to organizational learning and sharing of best practices throughout the corporate system to avoid the costs of reinventing solutions that have already been discovered. Three critical features are necessary in sharing best practice. First, there needs to be a device for organizational memory. For example, at **Xerox**, contributors to solutions can send their ideas to an electronic library where they are indexed and provided to potential adopters in the corporate family. Second, best practice must be updated and adjusted to new situations. For example, best practice adopted by a company's China office will be modified and customized, and this learning should then become part of the database. Finally, best practice must be legitimized. This calls for a shared understanding that exchanging knowledge across units is organizationally valued and that these systems are important mechanisms for knowledge exchange. Use can be encouraged by including an assessment in employee performance evaluations of how effectively employees share information with colleagues and utilize the databases.

In the design of the control systems, a major decision concerns the object of control. Two major objects are typically identified: output and behavior.[63] Output controls include balance sheets, sales data, production data, product-line growth, and performance reviews of personnel. Measures of output are accumulated at regular intervals and forwarded from the foreign locale to headquarters, where they are evaluated and critiqued based on comparisons to the plan or budget. Behavioral controls require the exertion of influence over behavior after—or, ideally, before—it leads to action. Behavioral controls can be achieved through the preparation of manuals on such topics as sales techniques to be made available to subsidiary personnel or through efforts to fit new employees into the corporate culture.

To institute either of these measures, instruments of control have to be decided upon. The general alternatives are either bureaucratic/formalized control or cultural control.[64] Bureaucratic controls consist of a limited and explicit set of regulations and rules that outline the desired levels of performance. Cultural controls, on the other hand, are much less formal and are the result of shared beliefs and expectations among the members of an organization. Exhibit 1000.8 provides a schematic explanation of the types of controls and their objectives.

Exhibit 1000.8 *Comparison of Bureaucratic and Cultural Control Mechanisms*

	Type of Control	
Object of Control	Pure Bureaucratic/Formalized Control	Pure Cultural Control
Output	Formal performance reports	Shared norms of performance
Behavior	Company policies, manuals	Shared philosophy of management

Source: B. R. Baliga and Alfred M. Jaeger, "Multinational Corporations: Control Systems and Delegation Issues," *Journal of International Business Studies* 15 (Fall 1984): 25–40.

Bureaucratic/Formalized Control

The elements of a bureaucratic/formalized control system are: (1) an international budget and planning system, (2) the functional reporting system, and (3) policy manuals used to direct functional performance.

Budgets refers to shorter term guidelines regarding investment, cash, and personnel policies, while *plans* refers to formalized plans with more than a one-year horizon. The budget and planning process is the major control instrument in headquarters-subsidiary relationships. Although systems and their execution vary, the objective is to achieve as good a fit as possible with the objectives and characteristics of the firm and its environment.

The budgetary period is typically one year, since it is tied to the accounting systems of the multinational. The budget system is used for four main purposes: (1) allocation of funds among subsidiaries; (2) planning and coordination of global production capacity and supplies; (3) evaluation of subsidiary performance; and (4) communication and information exchange among subsidiaries, product organizations, and corporate headquarters.[65] Long-range plans vary dramatically, ranging from two years to ten years in length, and are more qualitative and judgmental in nature. However, shorter periods such as two years are the norm, considering the added uncertainty of diverse foreign environments.

Although firms strive for uniformity, achieving it may be as difficult as trying to design a suit to fit the average person. The processes themselves are very formalized in terms of the schedules to be followed.

Functional reports are another control instrument used by headquarters in managing subsidiary relations. Examples of functional reports include balance sheet, income statement, production output, market share, and sales per product. These vary in number, complexity, and frequency. The structure and elements of the reports are typically highly standardized to allow for consolidation in the headquarters level.

Since the frequency of reports required from subsidiaries is likely to increase due to globalization, it is essential that subsidiaries see the rationale for the often time consuming exercise. Two approaches, used in tandem, can facilitate the process: participation and feedback. The first refers to avoiding the perception at subsidiary levels that reports are "art for art's sake" by involving the preparers in the actual use of the reports. When this is not possible, feedback about their consequences is warranted. Through this process, communication is enhanced as well.

On the behavioral front, headquarters may want to guide the way in which subsidiaries make decisions and implement agreed-upon strategies. U.S.-based multinationals tend to be far more formalized than their Japanese and European counterparts, with a heavy reliance on manuals for all major functions.[66] The manuals discuss such items as recruitment, training, motivation, and dismissal policies. The use of manuals is in direct correlation with the required level of reports from subsidiaries.

Cultural Control

As seen from the country comparisons, less emphasis is placed outside the United States on formal controls, as they are viewed as too rigid and too quantitatively oriented. Rather, MNCs in other countries emphasize corporate values and culture, and evaluations are based on the extent to which an individual or entity fits in with the norms. Cultural controls require an extensive socialization process to which informal, personal interaction is central. Substantial resources have to be spent to train the individual to share the corporate cultures, or "the way things are done at the company."[67] To build common vision and values, managers spend a substantial share of their first months at Matsushita in what the company calls "cultural and spiritual training." They study the company credo, the "Seven Spirits of Matsushita," and the philosophy of the founder, Konosuke Matsushita and learn how to translate the internalized lessons into daily behavior and operational decisions. Although more prevalent in Japanese organizations, many Western entities have similar programs, such as **Philips's** "organization cohesion training" and **Unilever's** "indoctrination."[68] This corporate acculturation will be critical to achieve the acceptance of possible transfers of best practice within the organization.[69]

The primary instruments of cultural control are the careful selection and training of corporate personnel and the institution of self-control. The choice of cultural controls can be justified if the company enjoys a low turnover rate; they are thus applied when companies can offer and expect lifetime or long-term employment, as many firms do in Japan.

In selecting home-country nationals and, to some extent, third-country nationals, MNCs are exercising cultural control. The assumption is that the managers have already internalized the norms and values of the company and they tend to run a country organization with a more global view. In some cases, the use of headquarters personnel to ensure uniformity in decision making may be advisable; for example, **Volvo** uses a home-country national for the position of chief financial officer. Expatriates are used in subsidiaries not only for control purposes but also to effect change processes. Companies control the efforts of management specifically through compensation and promotion policies, as well as through policies concerning replacement.

When the expatriate corps is small, headquarters can still exercise its control through other means. Management training programs for overseas managers as well as time at headquarters will indoctrinate individuals to the company's ways of doing things. Similarly, formal visits by headquarters teams (for example, for a strategy audit) or informal visits (perhaps to launch a new product) will enhance the feeling of belonging to the same corporate family. Some of the innovative global companies assemble temporary teams of their best talent to build local skills. **IBM**, for example, drafted 50 engineers from its facilities in Italy, Japan, New York, and North Carolina to run three-week to six-month training courses on all operations carried on at its Shenzhen facility in China. After the trainers left the country, they stayed in touch by e-mail, so whenever the Chinese managers have a problem, they know they can reach someone for help. The continuation of the support has been as important as the training itself.[70]

Corporations rarely use one pure control mechanism. Rather, most use both quantitative and qualitative measures. Corporations are likely, however, to place different levels of emphasis on different types of performance measures and on how they are derived.

Exercising Controls

Within most corporations, different functional areas are subject to different guidelines because they are subject to different constraints. For example, the marketing function has traditionally been seen as incorporating many more behavioral dimensions than manufacturing or finance. As a result, many multinational corporations employ control systems that are responsive to the needs of the function. Yet such differentiation is sometimes based less on appropriateness than on personalities. It has been hypothesized that manufacturing subsidiaries are controlled more intensively than sales subsidiaries because production more readily lends itself to centralized direction, and technicians and engineers adhere more firmly to standards and regulations than do salespeople.[71]

In their international operations, U.S.-based multinationals place major emphasis on obtaining quantitative data. Although this allows for good centralized comparisons against standards and benchmarks or cross-comparisons among different corporate units, it entails several drawbacks. In the international environment, new dimensions—such as inflation, differing rates of taxation, and exchange rate fluctuations—may distort the performance evaluation of any given individual or organizational unit. For the global corporation, measurement of whether a business unit in a particular country is earning a superior return on investment relative to risk may be irrelevant to the contribution an investment may make worldwide or to the long-term results of the firm. In the short term, the return may even be negative.[72] Therefore, the control mechanism may quite inappropriately indicate reward or punishment. Standardizing the information received may be difficult if the various environments involved fluctuate and require frequent and major adaptations. Further complicating the issue is the fact that although quantitative information may be collected monthly, or at least quarterly, environmental data may be acquired annually or "now and then," especially when a crisis seems to loom on the horizon. To design a control system that is acceptable not only to headquarters but also to the organization and individuals abroad, great care must be taken to use only relevant data. Major concerns, therefore, are the data collection process and the analysis and utilization of data. Evaluators need management information systems that provide for greater comparability and equity in administering controls. The more behaviorally based and culture-oriented controls are, the more care needs to be taken.[73]

In designing a control system, management must consider the costs of establishing and maintaining it versus the benefits to be gained. Any control system will require investment in a management structure and in systems design. Consider, for example, costs associated with cultural controls: personal interaction, use of expatriates, and training programs are all quite expensive. Yet these expenses may be justified by cost savings through lower employee turnover, an extensive worldwide information system, and an improved control system.[74] Moreover, the impact goes beyond the administrative component. If controls are misguided or too time-consuming, they can slow or undermine the strategy implementation process and thus the overall capability of the firm. The result will be lost opportunities or, worse yet, increased threats. In addition, time spent on reporting takes time from everything else, and if the exercise is seen as mundane, it results in lowered motivation. A parsimonious design is therefore imperative. The control system should collect all the information required and trigger all the intervention necessary; however, it should not lead to the pulling of strings by a puppeteer.

The impact of the environment has to be taken into account, as well, in two ways. First, the control system must measure only those dimensions over which the organization has actual control. Rewards or sanctions make little sense if they are based on dimensions that may be relevant to overall corporate performance but over which no influence can be exerted, such as price controls. Neglecting the factor of individual performance capability would send wrong signals and severely harm motivation. Second, control systems have to be in harmony with local regulations and customs. In some cases, however, corporate behavioral controls have to be exercised against local customs even though overall operations may be affected negatively. This type of situation occurs, for example, when a subsidiary operates in markets in which unauthorized facilitating payments are a common business practice.

Corporations are faced with major challenges in appropriate and adequate control systems in today's business environment. Given increased local government demands for a share in companies established, controls can become tedious, especially if the MNC is a minority partner. Even if the new entity is a result of two companies' joining forces through a merger—such as the one between **Ciba** and **Sandoz** to create **Novartis**—or two companies joining forces to form a new entity—such as **Siecor** established by **Siemens AG** and **Corning Incorporated**—the backgrounds of the partners may be different enough to cause problems in devising the required controls.

Export Controls

Many nations have **export-control systems,** which are designed to deny or at least delay the acquisition of strategically important goods by adversaries. The legal basis for export controls varies in nations. For example, in Germany, armament exports are covered in the so-called War Weapons list which is a part of the War Weapons Control Law. The exports of other goods are covered by the German Export List. **Dual use items,** which are goods useful for both military and civilian purposes, are then controlled by the Joint List of the European Union.[75] In the United States, the export control system is based on the Export Administration Act and the Munitions Control Act. These laws control all export of goods, services, and ideas from the United States. The determinants for controls are national security, foreign policy, short supply, and nuclear nonproliferation.

Export licenses are issued by the Department of Commerce, which administers the Export Administration Act.[76] In consultation with other government agencies—particularly the Departments of State, Defense, and Energy—the Commerce Department has drawn up a list of commodities whose export is considered particularly sensitive. In addition, a list of countries differentiates nations according to their political relationship with the United States. Finally, a list of individual firms that are considered to be unreliable trading partners because of past trade-diversion activities exists for each country.

After an export license application has been filed, specialists in the Department of Commerce match the commodity to be exported with the **critical commodities list,** a file containing information about products that are either particularly sensitive to national security or controlled for other purposes. The product is then matched with the country of destination and the recipient company. If no concerns regarding any of the three exist, an export license is issued. Control determinants and the steps in the decision process are summarized in Exhibit 1000.9

The international business repercussions of export controls are important. It is one thing to design an export control system that is effective and that restricts those international business activities subject to important national concerns. It is, however, quite another when controls lose their effectiveness and when one country's firms are placed at a competitive disadvantage with firms in other countries whose control systems are less extensive or even nonexistent.

Exhibit 1000.9 *U.S. Export Control System*

Determinants of Export Controls
- National Security
- Foreign Policy
- Short Supply
- Nuclear Nonproliferation

Decision Steps in the Export Licensing Process

Should a Given Product Be Exported?
↓
To a Given Country?
↓
For Use by a Given Firm?

Export Control Problems and Conflicts

There are several key export control problem areas for firms and policymakers. First is the continuing debate about what constitutes military-use products, civilian-use products, and **dual-use items.** Increasingly, goods are of a dual-use nature, typically commercial products that have potential military applications. The classic example is a pesticide factory that, some years later, is revealed to be a poison gas factory.[77] It is difficult enough to clearly define weapons. It is even more problematic to achieve consensus among nations regarding dual-use goods. For example, what about quite harmless screws if they are to be installed in rockets or telecommunications equipment used by the military? The problem becomes even greater with attempts to classify and list subcomponents and regulate their exportation. Individual country lists will lead to a distortion of competition if they deviate markedly from each other. The very task of drawing up any list is itself fraught with difficulty when it comes to components that are assembled. For example, the Patriot missile, which was deployed in the Persian Gulf War, consists, according to German law, only of simple parts whose individual export is permissible.

Even if governments were to agree on lists and continuously updated them, the resulting control aspects would be difficult to implement. Controlling the transfer of components within and among companies across economic areas such as NAFTA or the European Union (EU) would significantly slow down business. Even more importantly, to subject only the export of physical goods to surveillance is insufficient. The transfer of knowledge and technology is of equal or greater importance. Weapons relevant information easily can be exported via books, periodicals, and disks, therefore their content also would have to be controlled. Foreigners would need to be prevented from gaining access to such sources during visits or from making use of data networks across borders. Attendance at conferences and symposia would have to be regulated, the flow of data across national borders would have to be controlled, and today's communication systems and highways such as the Internet would have to be scrutinized. All these concerns have lead to the emergence of controls of **deemed exports.** These controls address people rather than products in those instances where knowledge transfer could lead to a breach of export restrictions.

Conflicts also result from the desire of nations to safeguard their own economic interests. Due to different industrial structures, these interests vary between nations. For example, Germany, with a strong world market position in machine tools, motors, and chemical raw materials, will think differently about manufacturing equipment controls than a country such as the United States, which sees computers as an area of its competitive advantage.

These problems and conflicts seem to ensure that dissent and disagreement in the export control field are unlikely to decrease, but rather will multiply in the future. As long as regulations are not harmonized internationally, firms will need to be highly sensitive to different and perhaps rapidly changing export control regimens.

Regulating International Business Behavior

Home countries may implement special laws and regulations to ensure that the international business behavior of firms headquartered in them is conducted within moral and ethical boundaries considered appropriate. The definition of appropriateness may vary from country to country and from government to government. Therefore, the content, enforcement, and impact of such regulations on firms may vary substantially among nations. As a result, the international manager must walk a careful line, balancing the expectations held in different countries.

One major area in which nations attempt to govern international business activities involves **boycotts.** Caught in a web of governmental activity, firms may be forced either to lose business or to pay substantial fines. This is especially true if the firm's products are competitive yet not unique, so that the supplier can opt to purchase them elsewhere. The heightening of such conflict can sometimes force companies to search for new, and possibly risky ways to circumvent the law or to totally withdraw operations from a country.

Another area of regulatory activity affecting the international business efforts of firms is **antitrust laws.** These laws often apply to international operations as well as to domestic business. In many countries, antitrust agencies watch closely when a firm buys a company, engages in a joint venture with a foreign firm, or makes an agreement abroad with a competing firm in order to ensure that the action does not result in restraint of competition.

Given the increase in worldwide cooperation among companies, however, the wisdom of extending antitrust legislation to international activities is being questioned. Some limitations to these tough antitrust provisions were already implemented decades ago. For example, in the United States the **Webb-Pomerene Act** of 1918 excludes from antitrust prosecution firms cooperating to develop foreign markets. This law was passed as part of an effort to aid export efforts in the face of strong foreign competition by oligopolies and monopolies. The exclusion of international activities from antitrust regulation was further enhanced by the Export Trading Company Act of 1982, which ensures that cooperating firms are not exposed to the threat of treble damages. Further steps to loosen the application of antitrust laws to international business are under consideration because of increased competition from strategic alliances and global megacorporations.

Firms operating abroad are also affected by laws against **bribery** and **corruption.** In many countries, payments or favors are a way of life, and "a greasing of the wheels" is expected in return for government services. As a result, many companies doing business internationally routinely are forced to pay bribes or do favors for foreign officials in order to gain contracts. Even in the late 1990s, the British Chamber of Commerce reported that bribery and corruption was a problem for 14% of exporters.[78] In the 1970s, a major national debate erupted in the United States about these business practices, led by arguments that U.S. firms have an ethical and moral leadership obligation and that contracts won through bribes do not reflect competitive market activity. As a result, the **Foreign Corrupt Practices Act** was passed in 1977, making it a crime for U.S. executives of publicly traded firms to bribe a foreign official in order to obtain business.

A number of U.S. firms have complained about the act, arguing that it hinders their efforts to compete internationally against companies whose home countries have no such antibribery laws. The problem is one of ethics versus practical needs and, to some extent, of the amounts involved. For example, it may be hard to draw the line between providing a generous tip and paying a bribe in order to speed up a business transaction. Many business executives believe that the United States should not apply its moral principles to other societies and cultures in which bribery and corruption are endemic. To compete internationally, executives argue, they must be free to use the most common methods of competition in the host country.

On the other hand, applying different standards to executives and firms based on whether they do business abroad or domestically is difficult to do. Also, bribes may open the way for shoddy performance and loose moral standards among executives and employees and may result in a spreading of general unethical business practices. Unrestricted bribery could result in firms concentrating on how to bribe best rather than on how to best produce and market their products. Typically, international businesses that use bribery fall into three categories: those who bribe to counterbalance the poor quality of their products or their high price; those who bribe to create a market for their unneeded goods; and, in the bulk of cases, those who bribe to stay competitive with other firms that bribe.[79] In all three of these instances, the customer is served poorly, the prices increase, and the transaction does not reflect economic competitiveness.

The international business manager must carefully distinguish between reasonable ways of doing business internationally—that is, complying with foreign expectations—and outright bribery and corruption. To assist the manager in this task, the 1988 Trade Act clarifies the applicability of the Foreign Corrupt Practices legislation. The revisions outline when a manager is expected to know about violation of the act, and they draw a distinction between the facilitation of routine governmental actions and governmental policy decisions. Routine actions concern issues such as the obtaining of permits and licenses, the processing of governmental papers (such as visas and work orders), the providing of mail and phone service, and the loading and unloading of cargo. Policy decisions refer mainly to situations in which the obtaining or retaining of a contract is at stake. While the facilitation of routine actions is not prohibited, the illegal influencing of policy decisions can result in the imposition of severe fines and penalties. The risks inherent in bribery have grown since 1999, when the Organization for Economic Cooperation and Development (OECD) adopted a treaty criminalizing the bribery of foreign public officials, moving well beyond its previous discussions, which only sought to outlaw the tax deductibility of improper payments. The Organization of American States (OAS) has also officially condemned bribery. Similarly, the World Trade Organization (WTO) has decided to consider placing bribery rules on its agenda. In addition, nongovernmental organizations such as Transparency International are conducting widely publicized efforts to highlight corruption and bribery and even to rank countries on a Corruption Perceptions Index.

These issues place managers in the position of having to choose between home-country regulations and foreign business practices. This choice is made even more difficult because diverging standards of behavior are applied to businesses in different countries. However, the gradually emerging consensus among international organizations may eventually level the playing field.

A final, major issue that is critical for international business managers is that of general standards of behavior and ethics. Increasingly, public concerns are raised about such issues as environmental protection, global warming, pollution, and moral behavior. However, these issues are not of the same importance in every country. What may be frowned upon or even illegal in one nation may be customary or at least acceptable in others. For example, the cutting down of the Brazilian rain forest may be acceptable to the government of Brazil, but scientists and concerned consumers may object vehemently because of the effect on global warming and other climatic changes. The export of U.S. tobacco products may be legal but results in accusations of exporting death to developing nations. China may use prison labor in producing products for export, but U.S. law prohibits the importation of such products. Mexico may permit the use of low safety standards for workers, but the buyers of Mexican products may object to the resulting dangers.

International firms must understand the conflicts in standards and should assert leadership in implementing change. Not everything that is legally possible should be exploited for profit. By acting on existing, leading-edge knowledge and standards, firms will be able to benefit in the long term through consumer goodwill and the avoidance of later recriminations.

International Trade and Investment

The Theory of International Trade

Topics include classical trade theory, factor proportions trade theory, product ranges theory, product cycle theory, and the new trade theory.

Classical Trade Theory

International trade is expected to improve the productivity of industry and the welfare of consumers. The question of why countries trade has proven difficult to answer. Since the second half of the eighteenth century, academicians have tried to understand not only the motivations and benefits of international trade, but also why some countries grow faster and wealthier than others through trade. Exhibit 1000.10 provides an overview of the evolutionary path of trade theory since the fall of mercantilism. Although somewhat simplified, it shows the line of development of the major theories put forward over the past two centuries. It also serves as an early indication of the path of modern theory: the shifting focus from the country to the firm, from cost of production to the market as a whole, and from the perfect to the imperfect market.

The Theory of Absolute Advantage

Generally considered the father of economics, Adam Smith published *The Wealth of Nations* in 1776 in London. In this book, Smith attempted to explain the process by which markets and production actually operate in society. Smith's two main areas of contribution, *absolute advantage* and the *division of labor* were fundamental to trade theory.

Production, the creation of a product for exchange, always requires the use of society's primary element of value, human labor. Smith noted that some countries, owing to the skills of their workers or the quality of their natural resources, could produce the same products as others with fewer labor-hours. He termed this efficiency **absolute advantage.**

Adam Smith observed the production processes of the early stages of the Industrial Revolution in England and recognized the fundamental changes that were occurring in production. In previous states of society, a worker performed all stages of a production process, with resulting output that was little more than sufficient for the worker's own needs. The factories of the industrializing world were, however, separating the production process into distinct stages, in which each stage would be performed exclusively by one individual, the **division of labor.** This specialization increased the production of workers and industries.

Adam Smith then extended his division of labor in the production process to a division of labor and specialized product across countries. Each country would specialize in a product for which it was uniquely suited. More would be produced for less. Thus, by each country, specializing in products for which it possessed absolute advantage, countries could produce more in total and exchange products—trade—for goods that were cheaper in price than those produced at home.

The Theory of Comparative Advantage

Although Smith's work was instrumental in the development of economic theories about trade and production, it did not answer some fundamental questions about trade. First, Smith's trade relied on a country possessing absolute advantage in production, but did not explain what gave rise to the production advantages. Second, if a country did not possess absolute advantage in any product, could it (or would it) trade?

Exhibit 1000.10 *The Evolution of Trade Theory*

The Theory of Absolute Advantage
Adam Smith

Each country should specialize in the production and export of that good which it produces most efficiently, that is, with the fewest labor-hours.

The Theory of Comparative Advantage
David Ricardo

Even if one country was most efficient in the production of two products, it must be relatively more efficient in the production of one good. It should then specialize in the production and export of that good in exchange for the importation of the other good.

The Theory of Factor Proportions
Eli Heckscher and Bertil Ohlin

A country that is relatively labor abundant (capital abundant) should specialize in the production and export of that product which is relatively labor intensive (capital intensive).

The Leontief Paradox
Wassily Leontief

The test of the factor proportions theory which resulted in the unexpected finding that the United States was actually exporting products that were relatively labor intensive, rather than the capital intensive products that a relatively capital abundant country should according to the theory.

Overlapping Product Ranges Theory
Staffan Burenstam Linder

The type, complexity, and diversity of product demands of a country increase as the country's income increases. International trade patterns would follow this principle, so that countries of similar income per capita levels will trade most intensively having overlapping product demands.

Product Cycle Theory
Raymond Vernon

The country that possesses comparative advantage in the production and export of an individual product changes over time as the technology of the product's manufacture matures.

Imperfect Market and Trade Theory
Paul Krugman

Theories that explain changing trade patterns, including intra-industry trade, based on the imperfection of both factor markets and product markets.

The Competitive Advantage of Nations
Michael Porter

A nation's competitiveness depends on the capacity of its industry to innovate and upgrade. Companies gain competitive advantage because of pressure and challenge. Companies benefit from having strong domestic rivals, aggressive home-based suppliers, and demanding local customers.

David Ricardo, in his 1819 work entitled *On the Principles of Political Economy and Taxation,* sought to take the basic ideas set down by Smith a few steps further. Ricardo noted that even if a country possessed absolute advantage in the production of two products, it still must be relatively more efficient than the other country in one good's production than the other. Ricardo termed this the **comparative advantage.** Each country would then possess comparative advantage in the production of one of the two products, and both countries would then benefit by specializing completely in one product and trading for the other.

A Numerical Example of Classical Trade Theory

To fully understand the theories of absolute advantage and comparative advantage, consider the following example. Two countries, France and England, produce only two products, wheat and cloth (or beer and pizza, guns and butter, and so forth). The relative efficiency of each country in the production of the two products is measured by comparing the number of labor-hours needed to produce one unit of each product. Exhibit 1000.11 provides an efficiency comparison of the two countries.

Exhibit 1000.11 *Absolute Advantage and Comparative Advantage**

Country	Wheat	Cloth
England	2	4
France	4	2

- England has absolute advantage in the production of wheat. It requires fewer labor-hours (2 being less than 4) for England to produce one unit of wheat.
- France has absolute advantage in the production of cloth. It requires fewer labor-hours (2 being less than 4) for France to produce one unit of cloth.
- England has comparative advantage in the production of wheat. If England produces one unit of wheat, it is forgoing the production of 2/4 (0.50) of a unit of cloth. If France produces one unit of wheat, it is forgoing the production of 4/2 (2.00) of a unit of cloth. England therefore has the lower opportunity cost of producing wheat.
- France has comparative advantage in the production of cloth. If England produces one unit of cloth, it is forgoing the production of 4/2 (2.00) of a unit of wheat. If France produces one unit of cloth, it is forgoing the production of 2/4 (0.50) of a unit of wheat. France therefore has the lower opportunity cost of producing cloth.

*Labor-hours per unit of output.

England is obviously more efficient in the production of wheat. Whereas it takes France four labor-hours to produce one unit of wheat, it takes England only two hours to produce the same unit of wheat. France takes twice as many labor-hours to produce the same output. England has absolute advantage in the production of wheat. France needs two labor-hours to produce a unit of cloth that it takes England four labor-hours to produce. England therefore requires two more labor-hours than France to produce the same unit of cloth. France has absolute advantage in the production of cloth. The two countries are exactly opposite in relative efficiency of production.

David Ricardo took the logic of absolute advantages in production one step further to explain how countries could exploit their own advantages and gain from international trade. Comparative advantage, according to Ricardo, was based on what was given up or traded off in producing one product instead of the other. In this numerical example England needs only two-fourths as many labor-hours to produce a unit of wheat as France, while France needs only two-fourths as many labor-hours to produce a unit of cloth. England therefore has comparative advantage in the production of wheat, while France has comparative advantage in the production of cloth. A country cannot possess comparative advantage in the production of both products, so each country has an economic role to play in international trade.

Concluding Points About Classical Trade Theory

Classical trade theory contributed much to the understanding of how production and trade operates in the world economy. Although like all economic theories they are often criticized for being unrealistic or out of date, the purpose of a theory is to simplify reality so that the basic elements of the logic can be seen. Several of these simplifications have continued to provide insight in understanding international business.

- **Division of labor.** Adam Smith's explanation of how industrial societies can increase output using the same labor-hours as in preindustrial society is fundamental to our thinking even today. Smith extended this specialization of the efforts of a worker to the specialization of a nation.
- **Comparative advantage.** David Ricardo's extension of Smith's work explained for the first time how countries that seemingly had no obvious reason for trade could individually specialize in producing what they did best and trade for products they did not produce.
- **Gains from trade.** The theory of comparative advantage argued that nations could improve the welfare of their populations through international trade. A nation could actually achieve consumption levels beyond what it could produce by itself. To this day this is one of the fundamental principles underlying the arguments for all countries to strive to expand and "free" world trade.

Factor Proportions Trade Theory

Trade theory changed drastically in the first half of the twentieth century. The theory developed by the Swedish economist Eli Heckscher and later expanded by his former student Bertil Ohlin formed the theory of international trade that is still widely accepted today, **factor proportions theory.**

Exhibit 1000.12 *Factor Proportions in Production*

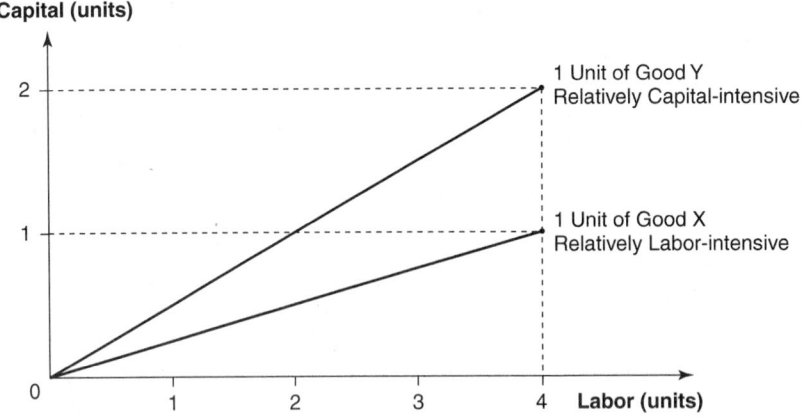

Factor Intensity in Production

The Heckscher-Ohlin theory considered two **factors of production,** labor and capital. Technology determines the way they combine to form a good. Different goods required different proportions of the two factors of production.

Exhibit 1000.12 illustrates what it means to describe a good by its factor proportions. The production of one unit of good X requires 4 units of labor and 1 unit of capital. At the same time, to produce 1 unit of good Y requires 4 units of labor and 2 units of capital. Good X therefore requires more units of labor per unit of capital (4 to 1) relative to Y (4 to 2). X is therefore classified as a relatively labor-intensive product, and Y is relatively capital intensive. These **factor intensities,** or **proportions,** are truly relative and are determined only on the basis of what product X requires relative to product Y and not to the specific numbers of labor to capital.

It is easy to see how the factor proportions of production differ substantially across goods. For example, the manufacturing of leather footwear is still a relatively labor-intensive process, even with the most sophisticated leather treatment and patterning machinery. Other goods, such as computer memory chips, however, although requiring some highly skilled labor, require massive quantities of capital for production. These large capital requirements include the enormous sums needed for research and development and the manufacturing facilities needed for clean production to ensure the extremely high quality demanded in the industry.

According to factor proportions theory, factor intensities depend on the state of technology—the current method of manufacturing a good. The theory assumed that the same technology of production would be used for the same goods in all countries. It is not, therefore, differences in the efficiency of production that will determine trade between countries as it did in classical theory. Classical theory implicitly assumed that technology or the productivity of labor is different across countries. Otherwise, there would be no logical explanation why one country requires more units of labor to produce a unit of output than another country. Factor proportions theory assumes no such productivity differences.

Factor Endowments, Factor Prices, and Comparative Advantage

If there is no difference in technology or productivity of factors across countries, what then determines comparative advantage in production and export? The answer is that factor prices determine cost differences. And these prices are determined by the endowments of labor and capital the country possesses. The theory assumes that labor and capital are immobile; factors cannot move across borders. Therefore, the country's endowment determines the relative costs of labor and capital as compared with other countries.

Using these assumptions, factor proportions theory stated that a country should specialize in the production and export of those products that use intensively its relatively abundant factor.

- A country that is relatively labor abundant should specialize in the production of relatively labor-intensive goods. It should then export those labor-intensive goods in exchange for capital-intensive goods.
- A country that is relatively capital abundant should specialize in the production of relatively capital-intensive goods. It should then export those capital-intensive goods in exchange for labor-intensive goods.

The Leontief Paradox

One of the most famous tests of any economic or business theory occurred in 1950, when economist Wassily Leontief tested whether the factor proportions theory could be used to explain the types of goods the United States imported and exported. Leontief's premise was the following.

> A widely shared view on the nature of the trade between the United States and the rest of the world is derived from what appears to be a common sense assumption that this country has a comparative advantage in the production of commodities which require for their manufacture large quantities of capital and relatively small amounts of labor. Our economic relationships with other countries are supposed to be based mainly on the export of such "capital intensive" goods in exchange for forgoing products which—if we were to make them at home—would require little capital but large quantities of American labor. Since the United States possesses a relatively large amount of capital—so goes this oft-repeated argument—and a comparatively small amount of labor, direct domestic production of such "labor intensive" products would be uneconomical; we can much more advantageously obtain them from abroad in exchange for our capital intensive products.[80]

Leontief first had to devise a method to determine the relative amounts of labor and capital in a good. His solution, known as **input-output analysis,** was an accomplishment on its own. Input-output analysis is a technique of decomposing a good into the values and quantities of the labor, capital, and other potential factors employed in the good's manufacture. Leontief then used this methodology to analyze the labor and capital content of all U.S. merchandise imports and exports. The hypothesis was relatively straightforward: U.S. exports should be relatively capital intensive (use more units of capital relative to labor) than U.S. imports. Leontief's results were, however, a bit of a shock.

Leontief found that the products that U.S. firms exported were relatively more labor intensive than the products the United States imported.[81] It seemed that if the factor proportions theory was true, the United States is a relatively labor-abundant country! Alternatively, the theory could be wrong. Neither interpretation of the results was acceptable to many in the field of international trade.

A variety of explanations and continuing studies have attempted to solve what has become known as the **Leontief Paradox.** At first, it was thought to have been simply a result of the specific year (1947) of the data. However, the same results were found with different years and data sets. Second, it was noted that Leontief did not really analyze the labor and capital contents of imports but rather the labor and capital contents of the domestic equivalents of these imports. It was possible that the United States was actually producing the products in a more capital-intensive fashion than were the countries from which it also imported the manufactured goods.[82] Finally, the debate turned to the need to distinguish different types of labor and capital. For example, several studies attempted to separate labor factors into skilled labor and unskilled labor. These studies have continued to show results more consistent with what the factor proportions theory would predict for country trade patterns.

Linder's Overlapping Product Ranges Theory

The difficulties in empirically validating the factor proportions theory led many in the 1960s and 1970s to search for new explanations of the determinants of trade between countries. The work of Staffan Burenstam Linder focused, not on the production or supply side, but instead on the preferences of consumers—the demand side. Linder acknowledged that in the natural resource–based industries, trade was indeed determined by relative costs of production and factor endowments.

However, Linder argued, trade in manufactured goods was dictated not by cost concerns but rather by the similarity in product demands across countries. Linder's was a significant departure from previous theory and was based on two principles.

1. As income, or more precisely per-capita income, rises, the complexity and quality level of the products demanded by the country's residents also rises. The total range of product sophistication demanded by a country's residents is largely determined by its level of income.

2. The entrepreneurs directing the firms that produce society's needs are more knowledgeable about their own domestic market than about foreign markets. An entrepreneur could not be expected to effectively serve a foreign market that is significantly different from the domestic market because competitiveness comes from experience. A logical pattern would be for an entrepreneur to gain success and market share at home first then expand to foreign markets that are similar in their demands or tastes.

1040. INTERNATIONAL TRADE AND INVESTMENT

International trade in manufactured goods would then be influenced by similarity of demands. The countries that would see the most intensive trade are those with similar per-capita income levels, for they would possess a greater likelihood of overlapping product demands.

So where does trade come in? According to Linder, the overlapping ranges of product sophistication represent the products that entrepreneurs would know well from their home markets and could therefore potentially export and compete with in foreign markets. For example, the United States and Canada have almost parallel sophistication ranges, implying they would have a lot of common ground, overlapping product ranges, for intensive international trade and competition. They are quite similar in their per-capita income levels. But Mexico and the United States, or Mexico and Canada, would not. Mexico has a significantly different product sophistication range as a result of a different per-capita income level.

The overlapping product ranges described by Linder would today be termed **market segments.** Not only was Linder's work instrumental in extending trade theory beyond cost considerations, but it also found a place in the field of international marketing.

International Investment and Product Cycle Theory

A very different path was taken by Raymond Vernon in 1966 concerning what is now termed **product cycle theory.** Diverging significantly from traditional approaches, Vernon focused on the product (rather than the country and the technology of its manufacture), not its factor proportions. Most striking was the appreciation of the role of information, knowledge, and the costs and power that go hand in hand with knowledge.

> . . . we abandon the powerful simplifying notion that knowledge is a universal free good, and introduce it as an independent variable in the decision to trade or to invest.

Using many of the same basic tools and assumptions of factor proportions theory, Vernon added two technology-based premises to the factor-cost emphasis of existing theory.

1. Technical innovations leading to new and profitable products require large quantities of capital and highly skilled labor. These factors of production are predominantly available in highly industrialized capital-intensive countries.
2. These same technical innovations, both the product itself and more importantly the methods for its manufacture, go through three stages of maturation as the product becomes increasingly commercialized. As the manufacturing process becomes more standardized and low-skill labor-intensive, the comparative advantage in its production and export shifts across countries.

The Stages of the Product Cycle

Product cycle theory is both supply-side (cost of production) and demand-side (income levels of consumers) in its orientation. Each of these three stages that Vernon described combines differing elements of each.

STAGE I: THE NEW PRODUCT Innovation requires highly skilled labor and large quantities of capital for research and development. The product will normally be most effectively designed and initially manufactured near the parent firm and therefore in a highly industrialized market due to the need for proximity to information and the need for communication among the many different skilled-labor components required.

In this development stage, the product is nonstandardized. The production process requires a high degree of flexibility (meaning continued use of highly skilled labor). Costs of production are therefore quite high. The innovator at this stage is a monopolist and therefore enjoys all of the benefits of monopoly power, including the high profit margins required to repay the high development costs and expensive production process. Price elasticity of demand at this stage is low; high-income consumers buy it regardless of cost.

STAGE II: THE MATURING PRODUCT As production expands, its process becomes increasingly standardized. The need for flexibility in design and manufacturing declines, and therefore the demand for highly skilled labor declines. The innovating country increases its sales to other countries. Competitors with slight variations develop, putting downward pressure on prices and profit margins. Production costs are an increasing concern.

As competitors increase, as well as their pressures on price, the innovating firm faces critical decisions on how to maintain market share. Vernon argues that the firm faces a critical decision at this stage, either to lose market share to foreign-based manufacturers using lower-cost labor or to invest abroad to maintain its market share by exploiting the comparative advantages of factor costs in other countries. This is one of the first theoretical explanations of how trade and investment become increasingly intertwined.

STAGE III: THE STANDARDIZED PRODUCT In this final stage, the product is completely standardized in its manufacture. Thus, with access to capital on world capital markets, the country of production is simply the one with the cheapest unskilled labor. Profit margins are thin, and competition is fierce. The product has largely run its course in terms of profitability for the innovating firm.

The country of comparative advantage has therefore shifted as the technology of the product's manufacture has matured. The same product shifts in its location of production. The country possessing the product during that stage enjoys the benefits of net trade surpluses. But such advantages are fleeting, according to Vernon. As knowledge and technology continually change, so does the country of that product's comparative advantage.

Trade Implications of the Product Cycle

Product cycle theory shows how specific products were first produced and exported from one country but, through product and competitive evolution, shifted their location of production and export to other countries over time. As the product and the market for the product mature and change, the countries of its production and export shift.

The Contributions of Product Cycle Theory

Although interesting in its own right for increasing emphasis on technology's impact on product costs, product cycle theory was most important because it explained international investment. Not only did the theory recognize the mobility of capital across countries (breaking the traditional assumption of factor immobility), it shifted the focus from the country to the product. This made it important to match the product by its maturity stage with its production location to examine competitiveness.

Product cycle theory has many limitations. It is obviously most appropriate for technology-based products. These are the products that are most likely to experience the changes in production process as they grow and mature. Other products, either resource-based (such as minerals and other commodities) or services (which employ capital but mostly in the form of human capital), are not so easily characterized by stages of maturity. And product cycle theory is most relevant to products that eventually fall victim to mass production and therefore cheap labor forces. But, all things considered, product cycle theory served to breach a wide gap between the trade theories of old and the intellectual challenges of a new, more globally competitive market in which capital, technology, information, and firms themselves were more mobile.

Imperfect Markets and the New Trade Theory

Global trade developments in the 1980s and 1990s led to much criticism of the existing theories of trade. First, although there was rapid growth in trade, much of it was not explained by current theory. Secondly, the massive size of the merchandise trade deficit of the United States—and the associated decline of many U.S. firms in terms of international competitiveness—served as something of a country-sized lab experiment demonstrating what some critics termed the "bankruptcy of trade theory." Academics and policymakers alike looked for new explanations.

Two new contributions to trade theory were met with great interest. Paul Krugman, along with several colleagues, developed a theory of how trade is altered when markets are not perfectly competitive, or when production of specific products possess economies of scale. A second and very influential development was the growing work of Michael Porter, who examined the competitiveness of industries on a global basis, rather than relying on country-specific factors to determine competitiveness.

Economies of Scale and Imperfect Competition

Paul Krugman's theoretical developments once again focused on cost of production and how cost and price drive international trade. Using theoretical developments from microeconomics and market structure analysis, Krugman focused on two types of economics of scale, *internal economies of scale* and *external economies of scale*.[83]

INTERNAL ECONOMIES OF SCALE When the cost per unit of output depends on the size of an individual firm, the larger the firm the greater the scale benefits, and the lower the cost per unit. A firm possessing internal economies of scale could potentially monopolize an industry (creating an *imperfect market*), both domestically and internationally. If it produces more, lowering the cost per unit, it can lower the market price and sell more products, because it *sets* market prices.

The link between dominating a domestic industry and influencing international trade comes from taking this assumption of imperfect markets back to the original concept of comparative advantage. For this firm to expand sufficiently to enjoy its economies of scale, it must take resources away from other domestic industries in order to expand. A country then sees its own range of products in which it specializes narrowing, providing an opportunity for other countries to specialize in these so-called **abandoned product ranges.** Countries again search out and exploit comparative advantage.

A particularly powerful implication of internal economies of scale is that it provides an explanation of intra-industry trade, one area in which traditional trade theory had indeed seemed bankrupt. **Intra-industry trade (IIT)** is when a country seemingly imports and exports the same product, an idea that is obviously inconsistent with any of the trade theories put forward in the past three centuries. According to Krugman, internal economies of scale may lead a firm to specialize in a narrow product line (to produce the volume necessary for economies of scale cost benefits); other firms in other countries may produce products that are similarly narrow, yet extremely similar: product differentiation. If consumers in either country wish to buy both products, they will be importing and exporting products that are, for all intents and purposes, the same.[84]

Intra-industry trade has been studied in detail in the past decade. Intra-industry trade is measured with the Grubel-Lloyd Index, the ratio of imports and exports of the same product occurring between two trading nations. It is calculated as follows:

$$\text{Intra-Industry Trade Index}_i = \frac{|X_i - M_i|}{(X_i + M_i)}$$

where i is the product category and $|X - M|$ is the absolute value of net exports of that product (exports − imports). For example, if Sweden imports 100 heavy machines for its forest products industry from Finland, and at the same time exports to Finland 80 of the same type of equipment, IIT index would be:

$$\text{IIT Index} = \frac{|80 - 100|}{(80 + 100)} = 1 - 0.1111 = .89$$

The closer the index value to 1, the higher the level of intra-industry trade in that product category. The closer the index is to 0, the more one-way the trade between the countries exists, as traditional trade theory would predict.

Intra-industry trade is now thought to compose roughly 25% of global trade. And to its credit, intra-industry trade is increasingly viewed as having additive benefits to the fundamental benefits of comparative advantage. Intra-industry trade does allow some industrial segments in some countries to deepen their specialization while simultaneously allowing greater breadth of choices and commensurate benefits to consumers. Of course, one potentially disturbing characteristic of the growth in intra-industry trade is the potential for trade of all kinds to continue to expand in breadth and depth between the most industrialized countries (those producing the majority of the more complex manufactured goods) while those less industrialized nations do not see this added boost to trade growth.

EXTERNAL ECONOMIES OF SCALE When the cost per unit of output depends on the size of an industry, not the size of the individual firm, the industry of that country may produce at lower costs than the same industry that is smaller in size in other countries. A country can potentially dominate world markets in a particular product, not because it has one massive firm producing enormous quantities (for example, **Boeing**), but rather because it has many small firms that interact to create a large, competitive, critical mass (for example, semiconductors in Penang, Malaysia). No one firm need be all that large, but several small firms in total may create such a competitive industry that firms in other countries cannot ever break into the industry on a competitive basis.[85]

Unlike internal economies of scale, external economies of scale may not necessarily lead to imperfect markets, but they may result in an industry maintaining its dominance in its field in world markets. This provides an explanation as to why all industries do not necessarily always move to the country with the lowest-cost energy, resources, or labor. What gives rise to this critical mass of small firms and their interrelationships is a much more complex question. The work of Michael Porter provides a partial explanation of how these critical masses are sustained.

The Competitive Advantage of Nations

The focus of early trade theory was on the country or nation and its inherent, natural, or endowment characteristics that might give rise to increasing competitiveness. As trade theory evolved, it shifted its focus to the industry and product level, leaving the national-level competitiveness question somewhat behind. Recently, many have turned their attention to the question of how countries, governments, and even private industry can alter the conditions within a country to aid the competitiveness of its firms.

The leader in this area of research has been Michael Porter of Harvard. Porter argued innovation is what drives and sustains competitiveness. A firm must avail itself of all dimensions of competition, which he categorized into four major components of "the diamond of national advantage."

1. *Factor conditions.* The appropriateness of the nation's factors of production to compete successfully in a specific industry. Porter notes that although these factor conditions are very important in the determination of trade, they are not the only source of competitiveness as suggested by the classical, or factor proportions, theories of trade. Most importantly for Porter, it is the ability of a nation to continually create, upgrade, and deploy its factors (such as skilled labor) that is important, not the initial endowment.

2. *Demand conditions.* The degree of health and competition the firm must face in its original home market. Firms that can survive and flourish in highly competitive and demanding local markets are much more likely to gain the competitive edge. Porter notes that it is the character of the market, not its size, that is paramount in promoting the continual competitiveness of the firm. And Porter translates *character* as demanding customers.

3. *Related and supporting industries.* The competitiveness of all related industries and suppliers to the firm. A firm that is operating within a mass of related firms and industries gains and maintains advantages through close working relationships, proximity to suppliers, and timeliness of product and information flows. The constant and close interaction is successful if it occurs not only in terms of physical proximity but also through the willingness of firms to work at it.

4. *Firm strategy, structure, and rivalry.* The conditions in the home-nation that either hinder or aid in the firm's creation and sustaining of international competitiveness. Porter notes that no one managerial, ownership, or operational strategy is universally appropriate. It depends on the fit and flexibility of what works for that industry in that country at that time.

These four points, as illustrated in Exhibit 1000.13 constitute what nations and firms must strive to "create and sustain through a highly localized process" to ensure their success.

Porter's emphasis on innovation as the source of competitiveness reflects an increased focus on the industry and product that we have seen in the past three decades. The acknowledgment that the nation is "more, not less, important" is to many eyes a welcome return to a positive role for government and even national-level private industry in encouraging international competitiveness. Including factor conditions as a cost component, demand conditions as a

Exhibit 1000.13 *Determinants of National Competitive Advantage: Porter's Diamond*

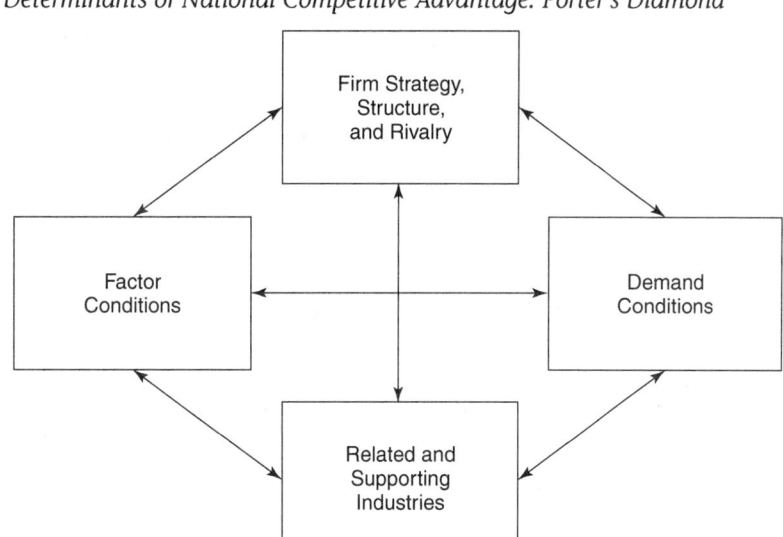

motivator of firm actions, and competitiveness all combine to include the elements of classical, factor proportions, product cycle, and imperfect competition theories in a pragmatic approach to the challenges that the global markets of the twenty-first century present to the firms of today.

The Theory of International Investment

Trade is the production of a good or service in one country and its sale to a buyer in another country. In fact, it is a firm (not a country) and a buyer (not a country) that are the subjects of trade, domestically or internationally. A firm is therefore attempting to access a market and its buyers. The producing firm wants to utilize its competitive advantage for growth and profit and can also reach this goal by international investment.[86]

Although this sounds easy enough, consider any of the following potholes on the road to investment success. Any of the following potholes may be avoided by producing within another country.

- Sales to some countries are difficult because of tariffs imposed on your good when it is entering. If you were producing within the country, your good would no longer be an import.
- Your good requires natural resources that are available only in certain areas of the world. It is therefore imperative that you have access to the natural resources. You can buy them from that country and bring them to your production process (import) or simply take the production to them.
- Competition is constantly pushing you to improve efficiency and decrease the costs of producing your good. You therefore may want to produce where it will be cheaper—cheaper capital, cheaper energy, cheaper natural resources, or cheaper labor. Many of these factors are still not mobile, and therefore you will go to them instead of bringing them to you.

There are thousands of reasons why a firm may want to produce in another country, and not necessarily in the country that is cheapest for production or the country where the final good is sold.

The subject of international investment arises from one basic idea: the mobility of capital. Although many of the traditional trade theories assumed the immobility of the factors of production, it is the movement of capital that has allowed **foreign direct investments** across the globe. If there is a competitive advantage to be gained, capital can and will get there.

The Theory of Foreign Direct Investment

What motivates a firm to go beyond exporting or licensing? What benefits does the multinational firm expect to achieve by establishing a physical presence in other countries? These are the questions that the theory of foreign direct investment has sought to answer. As with trade theory, the questions have remained largely the same over time, while the answers have continued to change. With hundreds of countries, thousands of firms, and millions of products and services, there is no question that the answer to such an enormous question will likely get messy.

The following overview of investment theory has many similarities to the preceding discussion of international trade. The theme is a global business environment that attempts to satisfy increasingly sophisticated consumer demands, while the means of production, resources, skills, and technology needed become more complex and competitive.

Firms as Seekers

A firm that expands across borders may be seeking any of a number of specific sources of profit or opportunity.

1. *Seeking resources.* There is no question that much of the initial foreign direct investment of the eighteenth and nineteenth centuries was the result of firms seeking unique and valuable natural resources for their products. Whether it be the copper resources of Chile, the linseed oils of Indonesia, or the petroleum resources spanning the Middle East, firms establishing permanent presences around the world are seeking access to the resources at the core of their business.

2. *Seeking factor advantages.* The resources needed for production are often combined with other advantages that are inherent in the country of production. The same low-cost labor at the heart of classical trade theory provides incentives for firms to move production to countries possessing these factor advantages. As noted by Vernon's Product Cycle, the same firms may move their own production to locations of factor advantages as the products and markets mature.
3. *Seeking knowledge.* Firms may attempt to acquire other firms in other countries for the technical or competitive skills they possess. Alternatively, companies may locate in and around centers of industrial enterprise unique to their specific industry, such as the footwear industry of Milan or the semiconductor industry of the Silicon Valley of California.
4. *Seeking security.* Firms continue to move internationally as they seek political stability or security. For example, Mexico has experienced a significant increase in foreign direct investment as a result of the tacit support of the United States, Canada, and Mexico itself as reflected by the North American Free Trade Agreement.
5. *Seeking markets.* Not the least of the motivations, the ability to gain and maintain access to markets is of paramount importance to multinational firms. Whether following the principles of Linder, in which firms learn from their domestic market and use that information to go international, or the principles of Porter, which emphasize the character of the domestic market as dictating international competitiveness, foreign market access is necessary.

Firms as Exploiters of Imperfections

Much of the investment theory developed in the past three decades has focused on the efforts of multinational firms to exploit the imperfections in factor and product markets created by governments. The work of Hymer, Kindleberger, and Caves noted that many of the policies of governments create imperfections. These market imperfections cover the entire range of supply and demand of the market: trade policy (tariffs and quotas), tax policies and incentives, preferential purchasing arrangements established by governments themselves, and financial restrictions on the access of foreign firms to domestic capital markets.

1. *Imperfections in access.* Many of the world's developing countries have long sought to create domestic industry by restricting imports of competitive products in order to allow smaller, less competitive domestic firms to grow and prosper—so-called **import substitution** policies. Multinational firms have sought to maintain their access to these markets by establishing their own productive presence within the country, effectively bypassing the tariff restriction.
2. *Imperfections in factor mobility.* Other multinational firms have exploited the same sources of comparative advantage identified throughout this chapter—the low-cost resources or factors often located in less-developed countries or countries with restrictions on the mobility of labor and capital. However, combining the mobility of capital with the immobility of low-cost labor has characterized much of the foreign direct investment seen throughout the developing world over the past 50 years.
3. *Imperfections in management.* The ability of multinational firms to successfully exploit or at least manage these imperfections still relies on their ability to gain an "advantage." Market advantages or powers are seen in international markets as in domestic markets: cost advantages, economies of scale and scope, product differentiation, managerial or marketing technique and knowledge, financial resources and strength.

All these imperfections are the things of which competitive dreams are made. The multinational firm needs to find these in some form or another to justify the added complexities and costs of international investments.

Firms as Internalizers

The question that has plagued the field of foreign direct investment is, Why can't all of the advantages and imperfections mentioned be achieved through management contracts or licensing agreements? Why is it necessary for *the firm itself* to establish a physical presence in the country? What pushes the multinational firm further down the investment decision tree?

The research of Buckley and Casson and Dunning has attempted to answer these questions by focusing on non-transferable sources of competitive advantage—proprietary information possessed by the firm and its people. Many advantages firms possess center around their hands-on knowledge of producing a good or providing a service. By establishing their own multinational operations they can internalize the production, thus keeping confidential the information that is at the core of the firm's competitiveness. **Internalization** is preferable to the use of arms-length arrangements such as management contracts or licensing agreements. They either do not allow the effective transmission of the knowledge or represent too serious a threat to the loss of the knowledge to allow the firm to successfully achieve the hoped-for benefits of international investment.

International Payments

Balance of Payments

International business transactions occur in many different forms over the course of a year. The measurement of all international economic transactions between the residents of a country and foreign residents is called the **balance of payments (BOP)**.[87] Government policymakers need such measures of economic activity to evaluate the general competitiveness of domestic industry, to set exchange-rate or interest-rate policies or goals, and for many other purposes. Individuals and businesses use various BOP measures to gauge the growth and health of specific types of trade or financial transactions by country and regions of the world against the home country.

International transactions take many forms. Each of the following examples is an international economic transaction that is counted and captured in the U.S. balance of payments.

- U.S. imports of **Honda** automobiles, which are manufactured in Japan.
- A U.S.-based firm, **Bechtel**, is hired to manage the construction of a major water-treatment facility in the Middle East.
- The U.S. subsidiary of a French firm, **Saint Gobain**, pays profits (dividends) back to the parent firm in Paris.
- **Daimler-Benz**, the well-known German automobile manufacturer, purchases a small automotive parts manufacturer outside Chicago, Illinois.
- An American tourist purchases a hand-blown glass figurine in Venice, Italy.
- The U.S. government provides grant financing of military equipment for its NATO (North Atlantic Treaty Organization) military ally, Turkey.
- A Canadian dentist purchases a U.S. Treasury bill through an investment broker in Cleveland, Ohio.

These are just a small sample of the hundreds of thousands of international transactions that occur each year. The balance of payments provides a systematic method for the classification of all of these transactions. There is one rule of thumb that will always aid in the understanding of BOP accounting: watch the direction of the movement of money.

The balance of payments is composed of a number of subaccounts that are watched quite closely by groups as diverse as investors on Wall Street, farmers in Iowa, politicians on Capitol Hill, and in boardrooms across America. These groups track and analyze the two major subaccounts, the **current account** and the **capital/financial account**, on a continuing basis. Before describing these two subaccounts and the balance of payments as a whole, it is necessary to understand the rather unusual features of how balance of payments accounting is conducted.

Fundamentals of Balance of Payments Accounting

The balance of payments must balance. If it does not, something has either not been counted or counted properly. It is therefore improper to state that the BOP is in disequilibrium. It cannot be. The supply and demand for a country's currency may be imbalanced, but that is not the same thing. Subaccounts of the BOP, such as the merchandise trade balance, may be imbalanced, but the entire BOP of a single country is always balanced.

There are three main elements to the process of measuring international economic activity: (1) identifying what is and is not an international economic transaction; (2) understanding how the flow of goods, services, assets, and money creates debits and credits to the overall BOP; and (3) understanding the bookkeeping procedures for BOP accounting, called double entry.

Defining International Economic Transactions

Identifying international transactions is ordinarily not difficult. The export of merchandise, goods such as trucks, machinery, computers, telecommunications equipment, and so forth, is obviously an international transaction. Imports such as French wine, Japanese cameras, and German automobiles are also clearly international transactions. But this merchandise trade is only a portion of the thousands of different international transactions that occur in the United States or any other country each year.

Many other international transactions are not so obvious. The purchase of a glass figure in Venice, Italy, by an American tourist is classified as a U.S. merchandise import. In fact, all expenditures made by American tourists around the globe that are for goods or services (meals, hotel accommodations, and so forth) are recorded in the U.S. balance of payments as imports of travel services in the current account. The purchase of a U.S. Treasury bill by a foreign resident is an international financial transaction and is dutifully recorded in the capital account of the U.S. balance of payments.

The BOP as a Flow Statement

The BOP is often misunderstood because many people believe it to be a balance sheet, rather than a cash flow statement. By recording all international transactions over a period of time, it is tracking the continuing flow of purchases and payments between a country and all other countries. It does not add up the value of all assets and liabilities of a country like a balance sheet does for an individual firm.

Two types of business transactions dominate the balance of payments.

1. *Real Assets.* The exchange of goods (for example, automobiles, computers, watches, textiles) and services (for example, banking services, consulting services, travel services) for other goods and services (barter) or for the more common type of payment, money.
2. *Financial Assets.* The exchange of financial claims (for example, stocks, bonds, loans, purchases or sales of companies) in exchange for other financial claims or money.

Although assets can be separated as to whether they are real or financial, it is often easier to simply think of all assets as being goods that can be bought and sold. An American tourist's purchase of a handwoven area rug in a shop in Bangkok is not all that different from a Wall Street banker buying a British government bond for investment purposes.

BOP Accounting: Double-Entry Bookkeeping

The balance of payments employs an accounting technique called **double-entry bookkeeping.** Double-entry bookkeeping is the age-old method of accounting in which every transaction produces a debit and a credit of the same amount. Simultaneously. It has to. A debit is created whenever an asset is increased, a liability is decreased, or an expense is increased. Similarly, a credit is created whenever an asset is decreased, a liability is increased, or an expense is decreased.

An example clarifies this process. A U.S. retail store imports from Japan $2 million worth of consumer electronics. A negative entry is made in the merchandise-import subcategory of the current account in the amount of $2 million. Simultaneously, a positive entry of the same $2 million is made in the capital account for the transfer of a $2 million bank account to the Japanese manufacturer. Obviously, the result of hundreds of thousands of such transactions and entries should theoretically result in a perfect balance.

The Accounts of the Balance of Payments

The balance of payments is composed of two primary subaccounts, the *Current Account* and the *Capital/Financial Account*. In addition, the *Official Reserves Account* tracks government currency transactions, and a fourth statistical subaccount, the *Net Errors and Omissions Account,* is produced to preserve the balance in the BOP.

The Current Account

The *Current Account* includes all international economic transactions with income or payment flows occurring within the year, the *current* period. The *Current Account* consists of four subcategories.

1. *Goods trade.* This is the export and import of goods. Merchandise trade is the oldest and most traditional form of international economic activity. Although many countries depend on imports of many goods (as they should according to the theory of comparative advantage), they also normally work to preserve either a balance of goods trade or even a surplus.
2. *Services Trade.* This is the export and import of services. Some common international services are financial services provided by banks to foreign importers and exporters, travel services of airlines, and construction services of domestic firms in other countries. For the major industrial countries, this subaccount has shown the fastest growth in the past decade.
3. *Income.* This category is predominantly *current income* associated with investments that were made in previous periods. If a U.S. firm created a subsidiary in South Korea to produce metal parts in a previous year, the proportion of net income that is paid back to the parent company in the current year (the dividend) constitutes current investment income. Additionally, wages and salaries paid to nonresident workers is also included in this category.
4. *Current Transfers.* Transfers are the financial settlements associated with the change in ownership of real resources or financial items. Any transfer between countries that is one-way, a gift, or a grant, is termed a *current transfer.* A common example of a current transfer would be funds provided by the United States government to aid in the development of a less-developed nation. Transfers associated with the transfer of fixed assets are included in a new separate account, the Capital Account, which now follows the Current Account. The contents of what previously had been called the capital account are now included within the *Financial Account.*

All countries possess some amount of trade, most of which is merchandise. Many smaller and less-developed countries have little in the way of service trade, or items that fall under the income or transfers subaccounts.

The Current Account is typically dominated by the first component described—the export and import of merchandise. For this reason, the *Balance on Trade* (BOT), which is so widely quoted in the business press in most countries, refers specifically to the balance of exports and imports of goods trade only. For a larger industrialized country, however, the BOT is somewhat misleading because service trade is not included; it may be opposite in sign on net, and it may actually be fairly large as well.

Exhibit 1000.14 summarizes the Current Account and its components for the United States for the 1996–1999 period. As illustrated, the U.S. goods trade balance has consistently been negative, but has been partially offset by the continuing surplus in services trade.

The Capital and Financial Account

The *Capital and Financial Account* of the balance of payments measures all international economic transactions of financial assets. It is divided into two major components, the *Capital Account* and the *Financial Account.*

- **The Capital Account.** The Capital Account is made up of transfers of financial assets and the acquisition and disposal of nonproduced/nonfinancial assets. The magnitude of capital transactions covered is of relatively minor amount, and will be included in principle in all of the following discussions of the financial account.
- **The Financial Account.** The Financial Account consists of three components: *direct investment, portfolio investment,* and *other asset investment.* Financial assets can be classified in a number of different ways including the length of the life of the asset (its maturity) and by the nature of the ownership (public or private). The Financial Account, however, uses a third way. It is classified by the degree of control over the assets or operations the claim

Exhibit 1000.14 *The U.S. Current Account, 1996–1999 (billions of U.S. dollars)*

	1996	1997	1998	1999
Goods exports	614	682	672	687
Goods imports	−803	−876	−917	−1030
Goods trade balance (BOT)	−189	−195	−245	−343
Services trade credits	238	255	261	270
Services trade debits	−151	−167	−183	−191
Services trade balance	87	89	78	78
Income receipts	224	257	258	276
Income payments	−205	−251	−265	−295
Income balance	19	6	−6	−18
Current transfers, credits	9	8	9	9
Current transfers, debits	−49	−49	−53	−57
Net transfers	−40	−41	−44	−48
Current Account Balance	−123	−141	−217	−331

Source: Derived from International Monetary Fund's *Balance of Payments Statistics Yearbook 2000.*

Exhibit 1000.15 *The U.S. Financial Account and Components, 1996–1999 (billions of U.S. dollars)*

	1996	1997	1998	1999
Direct Investment				
Direct investment abroad	−92	−105	−146	−151
Direct investment in the United States	87	106	186	276
Net direct investment	−5	1	40	125
Portfolio Investment				
Assets, net	−150	−119	−136	−129
Liabilities, net	368	386	269	342
Net portfolio investment	218	267	133	214
Other Investment				
Other investment assets	−179	−264	−47	−159
Other investment liabilities	117	265	27	136
Net other investment	−61	1	−20	−24
Net Financial Account Balance	151	269	154	315

Source: Derived from International Monetary Fund's *Balance of Payments Statistics Yearbook 2000.*

represents: *portfolio investment*, where the investor has no control, or *direct investment*, where the investor exerts some explicit degree of control over the assets. (The contents of the Financial Account are for all intents and purposes the same as those of the Capital Account under the IMF's BOP accounting framework used prior to 1996.)

Exhibit 1000.15 shows the major subcategories of the U.S. Financial Account balance from 1996–1999, *direct investment, portfolio investment,* and *other investments.*

1. *Direct investment.* This is the net balance of capital dispersed out of and into the United States for the purpose of exerting control over assets. For example, if a U.S. firm either builds a new automotive parts facility in another country or actually purchases a company in another country, this would fall under *direct investment* in the U.S. balance of payments accounts. When the capital flows out of the United States, it enters the balance of payments as a negative cash flow. If, however, foreign firms purchase firms in the United States (for example, **Sony** of Japan purchased **Columbia Pictures** in 1989) it is a capital inflow and enters the balance of payments positively. Whenever 10% or more of the voting shares in a U.S. company is held by foreign investors, the company is classified as the U.S. affiliate of a foreign company, and a *foreign direct investment.* Similarly, if U.S. investors hold 10% or more of the control in a company outside the United States, that company is considered the foreign affiliate of a U.S. company.

2. *Portfolio investment.* This is net balance of capital that flows in and out of the United States, but does not reach the 10% ownership threshold of direct investment. If a U.S. resident purchases shares in a Japanese firm, but does not attain the 10% threshold, it is considered a *portfolio investment* (and in this case an outflow of capital). The purchase or sale of debt securities (like U.S. Treasury bills) across borders is also classified as *portfolio investment* because debt securities by definition do not provide the buyer with ownership or control.
3. *Other investment assets/liabilities.* This final category consists of various short-term and long-term trade credits, cross-border loans from all types of financial institutions, currency deposits and bank deposits, and other accounts receivable and payable related to cross-border trade.

Current and Financial Account Balance Relationships

One of the basic economic and accounting relationships of the balance of payments is *the inverse relationship between the Current and Financial Accounts.* This inverse relationship is not accidental. The methodology of the balance of payments, double-entry bookkeeping, requires that the Current and Financial Accounts be offsetting. Countries experiencing large current account deficits "finance" these purchases through equally large surpluses in the Financial Account and vice versa.

Official Reserves Account

The **official reserves account** is the total currency and metallic reserves held by official monetary authorities within the country. These reserves are normally composed of the major currencies used in international trade and financial transactions (so-called "hard currencies" like the U.S. dollar, German mark, and Japanese yen) and gold. Note that the official reserve account should offset the total of current account, capital account, financial account, and net errors and omissions account. If the total of these four accounts is negative (deficit), the reserve account should be positive (surplus), and vice versa.

The significance of official reserves depends generally on whether the country is operating under a **fixed exchange rate** regime or a **floating exchange rate** system. If a country's currency is fixed, this means that the government of the country officially declares that the currency is convertible into a fixed amount of some other currency. For example, for many years the South Korean won was fixed to the U.S. dollar at 484 won equal to 1 U.S. dollar. It is the government's responsibility to maintain this fixed rate (also called *parity rate*). If for some reason there is an excess supply of Korean won on the currency market, to prevent the value of the won from falling, the South Korean government must support the won's value by purchasing won on the open market (by spending its hard currency reserves, its *official reserves*) until the excess supply is eliminated. Under a floating rate system, the government possesses no such responsibility and the role of official reserves is diminished.

Net Errors and Omissions Account

As noted before, because Current Account and Financial Account entries are collected and recorded separately, errors or statistical discrepancies will occur. The **net errors and omissions account** (this is the title used by the International Monetary Fund) makes sure that the BOP actually balances.

The Balance of Payments and Economic Crises

The sum of cross-border international economic activity—the balance of payments—can be used by international managers to forecast economic conditions and, in some cases, the likelihood of economic crises. The mechanics of international economic crisis often follow a similar path of development.

1. A country that experiences rapidly expanding current account deficits will simultaneously build financial account surpluses (note the inverse relationship).
2. The capital that flows into a country, giving rise to the financial account surplus, acts as the "financing" for the growing merchandise/services deficits—the constituent components of the current account deficit.

3. Some event, whether it be a report, a speech, an action by a government or business inside or outside the country, raises the question of the country's economic stability. Investors of many kinds, portfolio and direct investors in the country, fearing economic problems in the near future, withdraw capital from the country rapidly to avoid any exposure to this risk. This is prudent for the individual, but catastrophic for the whole if all individuals move similarly.
4. The rapid withdrawal of capital from the country, so-called "capital flight," results in the loss of the financial account surplus, creating a severe deficit in the country's overall balance of payments. This is typically accompanied by rapid currency depreciation (if a floating-rate currency) or currency devaluation (if a fixed-rate currency).

International debt and economic crises have occurred for as long as there have been international trade and commerce. And they will occur again. Each crisis has its own unique characteristics, but all follow the economic fundamentals described above (the one additional factor which differentiates many of the crises is whether inflation is a component). The recent Asian economic crisis was a devastating reminder of the tenuousness of international economic relationships.

International Cultures and Protocols

The Cross-Cultural Communication Process

Effective communication across nations/cultures can take place only when the sender encodes the message using language, idioms, norms and values, and so on that are familiar to the receiver or when the receiver (or receivers) is familiar with the language, idioms, and so on used by the sender. Attaining familiarity with language, slang, norms and values, and so on across nations/cultures is by no means an easy task because words and concepts are often not easily translatable (and sometimes not translatable at all) from one culture to another. For example, the concept of "self-fulfillment" is well understood in the American culture, but such a concept is not translatable to many cultures throughout the world, who understand better the concept of "group-fulfillment." Furthermore, words often have different meanings when translated into another language. For instance, U.S. manufacturer **General Motors Corporation** advertised on many of the automobiles it produced that the body was made by Fisher ("Body by Fisher"). The Flemish interpreted it to mean "Corpse by Fisher." The above suggests that communication is bound to create many problems for people conducting international/cross-cultural business. And international managers cannot generally be effective if they do not possess strong cross-cultural communication skills.

Expressions and Nonverbal Communication

Expressions and nonverbal communication play an important role in cross-cultural encoding. For example, U.S. movie-making firms export movies and television programs made for American audiences. Usually, these must be modified by dubbing in the local language. Accurate language translation is therefore essential. But what is also important is the nonverbal communication contained in the films. For example, the ways of depicting affection in American-made movies and television programs are viewed by some cultures as being offensive. Gestures are widely used as a means of communication in films and television programs, and the same sign has different meanings across different cultures. Some gestures may offend many foreign viewers and must therefore be edited out or somehow isolated before the film is distributed in the foreign culture. For example, Americans form a circle with their index finger and thumb to communicate that something is "OK." Imagine the embarrassment of a former U.S. president who visited Brazil, stepped out of the airplane, and made that gesture to a waiting crowd of Brazilians. The same sign in Brazil means that one is interested in having sex. The same OK sign means zero in France and is a symbol for money in Japan. In many cultures, including those of the United States and China, pointing one's thumb up is a gesture meaning "good" or "great," but in Australia it is a crude gesture.

The Role of Formality and Informality in Communication

Cultures vary in their **requirements for formality and informality,** and these variations also affect cross-cultural communication encoding. Some cultures, especially American and Australian, value informality in communication, but most cultures throughout the world value formality.[88] Individuals in cultures that value informality place low importance on the use of rank, status, and position in communication and often use first names when communicating with each other, even in business settings. On the other hand, individuals in cultures that value formality place high importance on the use of last names, titles, and other indications of rank and status in communication.

In many cultures rank and status are shown by seating arrangements, by the way individuals enter a room, and by who speaks first. In Japan, for instance, the oldest male is normally the most senior, and he must not be the first to enter a room; he is preceded by his assistants, and followed by other assistants, and he sits in the middle. Correspondence to people of higher status must be written individually, and mass mailings are often disliked because they emphasize efficiency over the honoring of individuals' rank and position. People in cultures that value informality, such as Americans, often become frustrated when forced to pay deference to someone simply because of his or her status (family ties, schooling, age, and so on), and not because of the person's accomplishments.

How Much Information Is Needed?

Individuals in some cultures, such as Japan, France, and Germany, can be generally categorized or risk-avoidant. These individuals make decisions slowly, avoid risks, and dislike ambiguity. (Conditions of uncertainty and ambiguity make them feel uncomfortable.) They therefore have a strong need for much detail and information. On the other hand, people in some cultures, such as Singapore, the United States, and Australia, feel relatively more comfortable with risk and ambiguity, make decisions more quickly, and require less detail and information.[89]

Language Translation

The above suggests that cross-cultural, cross-national communicators, to communicate effectively, must make certain that the language used, including the words, symbols, slang, formal and informal behaviors, as well as nonverbal behaviors, is the one that will be understood by the receiver(s). In conducting global business, businesspeople often do not the possess the command of the language necessary to communicate effectively with foreign associates. These senders therefore have to find a way to convert the language they understand into the language understood by the foreign associates (the receivers).

Translating one language into another is a huge problem confronting cross-cultural, cross-national communicators. To overcome translation problems of written communications, international businesspeople often use the **dual-translation** approach. This involves having a translator in the home country interpret and convert the message into the foreign language, and before the message is communicated, having another translator in the foreign country interpret and convert the message back into the home country's language. For example, a communicator transmitting a message from the United States to Angola, where Portuguese is spoken, first has a translator of English to Portuguese in the United States interpret the message from English to Portuguese. The translated message is then sent to a translator of Portuguese to English in Angola to be interpreted back to English. The sender will transmit the message after he or she has been assured that the translated message will be understood by the receiver(s) as intended.

The Effective Translator

It is obvious that the lack of an effective translator will lead to problems. Several factors help define the **effective translator.**[90] These factors include characteristics of the message itself (both implicit and explicit content), characteristics of the language involved (job titles, first-name basis), the interpreter's relationship with the client, the interpreter's skills (listening skills), context, characteristics of the parties, and cultural norms and values. The last three factors are discussed next.

Context

The time, place, and purpose of the meeting affect a translator's ability. High-stakes negotiations that take place in a hostile environment and that must be accomplished in a short period of time create stress for the translator and for the communicator, reducing their effectiveness. Negotiations should therefore be arranged to cause minimum stress for the translator and the communicator.

Characteristics of the Parties

The translator is familiar with the personal styles, idiosyncrasies, and communication strengths, including encoding and decoding abilities, of the parties for whom he or she is interpreting.

Cultural Norms and Values

The effective translator is familiar with the cultural norms and values of both cultures. For example, some cultures are high context and some are low context. When conducting business, people in **high-context cultures,** including the Chinese, Korean, Japanese, Vietnamese, Arab, Greek, and Spanish cultures, (1) establish social trust first, (2) value personal relations and goodwill, (3) make agreements on the basis of general trust, and (4) like to conduct slow and ritualistic negotiations.[91] People in these cultures prefer that messages not be structured directly, that they do not get right to the point and state conclusions or bottom lines first. Instead, they prefer that a message be indirect, building up to the point and stating conclusions or bottom lines last.[92] On the other hand, individuals in **low-context cultures,** including the Italian, English, North American, Scandinavian, Swiss, and German cultures, (1) get down to business first; (2) value expertise and performance; (3) like agreement by specific, legalistic contract; and (4) like to conduct negotiations as efficiently as possible.[93] Individuals in these cultures prefer that messages be structured directly, that they get immediately to the point and state conclusions or bottom lines first.[94]

The translator can guide the communication flow accordingly, and when the parties for whom he or she is acting as intermediary are opposites (one is high context and the other low context), the translator educates his or her clients accordingly and applies the most viable communication customs. For instance, if a Japanese businessperson is competing with other companies to obtain a contract from a German company, the German customs are likely to be the most applicable. If, however, a German businessperson is competing with other companies to obtain a contract from a Japanese company, the Japanese customs are likely to be the most applicable.

Identifying the Right Transmission Channel Stage

A message is typically transmitted in writing, orally, and nonverbally (body/facial expressions). Ongoing advancements in communications technologies present new means of transmitting messages. Written messages can now be transmitted via mail, computer, fax, and e-mail. Oral messages can be transmitted via meetings, telephone, and videoconferencing. Nonverbal messages can be sent via videoconferencing. Some of these communication channels are not available in many countries, especially in the less-developed countries.

Written or Spoken Message?

Regardless of the channels available, the sender must decide whether to transmit the message orally or in writing. Cultural norms affect the decision. Some cultures prefer written messages and others prefer spoken messages. Individuals in high-context cultures, which value trust, tend to prefer spoken communication and agreements; confirming an idea in writing may be taken as an indication that you think their word is no good. On the other hand, people in low-context cultures, which value efficiency, tend to prefer written communication and agreements.[95] Also, as indicated earlier, many people who understand English as a second or third language learned it by reading and listening, and have not developed a strong command of the language. These receivers may therefore feel more comfortable with written communication than with oral communication, because written communication gives them more time to understand the message. The literacy level of the audience also affects the decision. If the illiteracy rate is high, oral messages would be more effective than written messages.

Body Language

Body language, including eye contact, physical distance and touching, hand movements, pointing, and facial expressions, which vary across cultures,[96] also affects the transmission of a message.

EYE CONTACT   **Eye contact** between superiors and subordinates is avoided in many Southeast Asian cultures because it is a sign of disrespect. On the other hand, in Western cultures avoiding eye contact is a sign of disrespect. Therefore, an American and a Malaysian subordinate may very well view each other as being disrespectful when the American attempts to make eye contact and the Malaysian avoids it. Both are correct in their own cultures.

PHYSICAL DISTANCE AND TOUCHING   In Asia, once a relationship is established between individuals, **physical distance** is placed between them, and touching or display of emotions are substantially reduced. On the other hand, in Latin America, once a relationship is established between individuals, physical distance between them is reduced, and touching and display of emotions are increased.

HAND MOVEMENTS   Some cultures make greater use of **hand movements** when communicating than others. For example, Italians tend to use their hands extensively, while Americans make limited use of hand movements—they believe that too much hand movement while communicating orally distracts the receiver(s).

POINTING   **Pointing** with the index finger is rude in some cultures, including those of Sudan, Venezuela, and Sri Lanka. Pointing your index finger toward yourself is insulting in Germany, the Netherlands, and Switzerland.

FACIAL EXPRESSIONS   Russians do not use **facial expressions** very much and Scandinavians do not use many gestures. This does not mean that they are not enthusiastic.[97]

Transmission of Messages Through Mediators

Messages (written, spoken, and nonverbal) are typically sent directly to the receiver(s). In some situations in some cultures, it is not wise to send messages directly to the receiver(s); it is wise to use a **mediator**—the encoder sends the message to a mediator (a third party), who in turn conveys it to the receiver(s). For example, sincere Americans are often factually blunt and frank, even if it upsets the listeners.[98] The Japanese, however, culturally neither practice nor accept overt criticism and bluntness well. In Japan, to be sincere means having concern for the emotional, not the factual. In fact, to avoid being offensive (a concern for the emotional), a Japanese receiver may not even say "no" to a request from a sender with which he or she does not want to comply; instead, he or she would respond "maybe" (which really means "no" in Japan). Therefore, when a message being transmitted to a Japanese receiver must contain critical and blunt facts, it is better to submit it through a mediator. The bluntness is mitigated because the message was only indirectly passed from the sender to the receiver.

In Japan, when use of a mediator or message is too impractical, the Japanese use **informal get-togethers** to discuss formal matters. At the informal meeting's setting (often after work hours in bars, nightclubs, and restaurants), serious matters can be obscured as entertainment. Discussions in such settings can be semi-serious and hint of disagreements (the message can be blunt, but not too blunt) that would be unwelcome in formal settings.

To communicate effectively across cultures also requires good listening skills. One must be able to listen to spoken as well as to nonverbal (such as facial expressions) messages. An impatient American who constantly looks at his or her watch is not likely to communicate effectively across cultures.

Developing Cross-Cultural Communication Competence

Professor Linda Beamer of California State University, Los Angeles, has developed a model for the purpose of describing the process of **developing cross-cultural communication competence.**[99] The model proposes five levels of learning: acknowledgment of diversity, organizing information according to stereotypes, posing questions to challenge the stereotypes, analyzing communication episodes, and generating "other culture" messages. The intent of the learning process, according to Beamer, "is to develop the ability to decode effectively signs that come from members of other cultures, within a business context, and to encode messages using signs that carry the encoder's intended meaning to members of other cultures."[100] The five levels do not cease to exist once attained; they are continually revisited in the process of learning. This means that newer differences in a culture are constantly being discovered.

Cross-Cultural Business Practices

As corporations become increasingly international and competition for global markets increases, business managers who are not attentive to cultural differences will not be able to function in foreign markets effectively—they will make their companies less competitive. Effective international managers have learned how varying cultural practices across societies affect business and management practices and how to adapt to the differences. Learning something about the culture of a country before transacting business there shows respect, and those who understand the culture are more likely to develop successful, long-term business relationships than those who do not.[101]

Approaches to conducting business vary from culture to culture, making the practice of business at the international level much more complex than in the home market. Some factors that affect **cross-cultural business** include time, thought patterns, personal space, material possessions, family roles and relationships, competitiveness and individuality, and social behavior[102] as well as whether a culture is high-context or low-context.

People transacting business across cultures must be sensitive to the above dynamics, as well as to varying business customs. Culture affects business behavior and customs. Business customs from around the world that differ from country to country are presented in Exhibit 1000.16. Note that the descriptions in Exhibit 1000.16 are generalizations. Not all residents of a country necessarily adhere to those customs—especially the immigrants in a country. For example, many people in Australia are from other countries, such as China and Italy. These people may adhere to the customs of their country of birth.

Cross-Cultural Negotiations

Negotiating across cultures is far more complex than negotiating within a culture because foreign negotiators have to deal with differing negotiating styles and cultural variables simultaneously. In other words, the negotiating styles that work at home generally do not work in other cultures. As a result, cross-cultural business negotiators have one of the most complicated business roles to play in organizations. They are often thrust into a foreign society consisting of what appears to be "hostile" strangers. They are put in the position of negotiating profitable business relationships with these people or suffering the negative consequences of failure. And quite often they find themselves at a loss as to why their best efforts and intentions have failed them.

How to Avoid Failure in International Negotiations

Negotiators in a foreign country often fail because the local counterparts have taken more time to learn how to overcome the obstacles normally associated with international/cross-cultural negotiations. Failure may occur because of time and/or cost constraints. For example, a negotiator may be given too a short period of time to obtain better contract terms than were originally agreed to in a country where negotiations typically take a long time. A negotiator may think that "what works in the home country is good enough for the rest of the world," which is far from the truth. In fact, strategies that fail to take into account cultural factors are usually naive or misconceived. Typically, the obstacles to overcome include

- **Learning the local language,** or at least being able to select and use an effective language translator.
- **Learning the local culture,** including how the culture handles conflict, its business practices, and its business ethics, or at least being able to select and use an effective cultural translator.
- **Becoming well-prepared for the negotiations,** that is, along with the above, the negotiator must have a thorough knowledge of the subject matter being negotiated.

Effective cross-cultural negotiators understand the cultural differences existing between all parties involved; and they know that failure to understand the differences serves only to destroy potential business success.[103]

How Much Must One Know About the Foreign Culture?

Realistically, it is nearly impossible to learn everything about another culture, although it may be possible if one lives in the culture for several years. The reason for this is that each culture has developed, over time, multifaceted structures that are much too complex for any foreigner to understand totally. Therefore, foreign negotiators need not have total awareness of the foreign culture; they do not need to know as much about the foreign culture as the locals, whose frames of reference

Exhibit 1000.16 *Business Customs Around the World*

Australia	Business is almost always conducted over drinks, and it is considered rude to buy out of turn. Australians like to be addressed by their titles.
Austria	Austrians prefer to be addressed by their titles and consider it rude if a business associate tries to pick up the tab for a lunch or dinner they have initiated. They enjoy discussing art and music as well as skiing.
Belgium	Belgians like to get down to business immediately and are very conservative and efficient in their approach to business meetings. One must address French-speaking Belgians as "monsieur" or "madame," while Dutch-speaking Belgians must be addressed as "Mr." or "Mrs."
Egypt	Egypt is dominated by the Muslim faith, and their business customs reflect this. Business is slow-paced and the red tape is limitless. Egyptians take offense at refusals and at the use of direct negatives.
France	Conducting business in France in August is difficult because most people are on vacation. The French use titles until use of first names is proposed. In negotiations, they like to debate issues; they like to show their intellect and to challenge your intellect. To successfully sell the French requires convincing them of the merits of the product/service through intellectual debate, not through flashy, high-powered presentations. They use sophisticated table manners.
Germany	One should expect much handshaking, but in order of the person's importance in the enterprise. Germans insist on using titles, seldom use first names, use surname preceded by title, dislike small talk, and are very punctual. Germans are competitive negotiators who get straight to the point and leave little room for debate. German executives tend to have an engineering and science background, and one must therefore appeal to their technical tastes—glitzy presentations are likely to fail. They do not strongly emphasize the development of personal relationships with business associates—they value their privacy and keep business and private matters separate.
Greece	The Greeks are famous for their extensive bargaining and for never discussing business without a cup of coffee. Building a personal rapport with Greeks is important. Business entertaining normally takes place in the evening at a local tavern, and spouses are often included. It is important that a business relationship be built on trust. Government plays an important role in business, which means that one must work through bureaucracy. Business is highly personalized—family connections, political connections, and business connections. How one connects is often more important than the quality of the product/service. In Greece, negotiations are not finished even after the contract has been awarded—a contract is viewed as an evolving document of agreement.
Guatemala	A luncheon set for a specific time means that some guests may arrive 10 minutes early, while others may be 45 minutes late.
India	Business is conducted at an extremely leisurely pace; therefore, Indians are very patient, unlike their American counterparts. When invited to dinner, one should accept and pass the food with the right hand only and expect to be asked many personal questions—which Indians see as a sign of politeness. Indians avoid discussing political issues with their business contacts.
Ireland, Republic of	Do not confuse it with Northern Ireland or the United Kingdom—it is politically and culturally distinct from both.
Italy	Italians use a handshake for greetings and goodbyes. Unlike in the United States, men do not stand when a woman enters or leaves a room, and they do not kiss a woman's hand—this is reserved for royalty. Appearance and style are very important to Italian businesspeople. The appeal and polish of a presentation reflect the quality of the product/service or the firm itself. Italian businesspeople are confident, shrewd, and competent negotiators, and they tend to rely mainly on their instincts and not as much on the advice of specialists.
Malaysia	Most Malaysians are Muslims, so they do not eat pork, drink alcohol, or party on Friday night, the eve of the Muslim sabbath. They are very status- and role-conscious, and therefore do not readily mingle at social gatherings, particularly if men and women are together at the same gathering.
Mexico	Local contacts (connections) are required prior to arrival in Mexico. It is impolite to make extended eye contact with Mexicans. Timeliness is not important—it is OK for your host to keep you waiting. Don't say "America" to mean the U.S.A. because Mexicans are Americans too, and don't say "the United States" to mean the U.S.A. because Mexico is a United States too—the United States of Mexico. Don't get down to business right away. First get to know your prospective Mexican clients and their families by socializing.
Netherlands	The Dutch are competitive negotiators who get straight to the point and normally have little conflict or debate.
Nigeria	Business is slow-paced and never conducted over the telephone.

Exhibit 1000.16 *(continued)*

Pakistan	The Islamic faith is a dominant factor in Pakistani life and in business as well. It is a male-dominated country where women are largely confined to the domestic sphere; hence Pakistani men are uncomfortable or may even refuse to transact business with a woman. They refuse alcohol, cigarettes, and pork. One should never try to take a picture of a Pakistani without his or her permission.
Portugal	One must take the time to establish a rapport with Portuguese business associates.
Saudi Arabia	Business is informal, slow paced, and male-dominated. The Saudies are insulted if forced to deal with a representative rather than with the main person. When invited to a Saudi home, never bring flowers or gifts to the lady of the house, never eat or drink with the left hand, and never praise the house furnishings unless you would like to receive them as a gift the following day.
South Africa	Businesspeople like to discuss politics with their peers, and they are generally ultraconservative.
Spain	The Spanish work long days and break appointments often. The business lunch is an important part of conducting business in Spain, and great ceremony is applied in lunch meetings. Lunches stretch from 2:30 P.M. to 5:00 P.M.; then work goes on until 8:30 P.M. or 9:00 P.M. These lunches are used to develop the relationship required before business can be conducted.
Thailand	Thailand's traditional greeting is the *wai*, which is made by the placement of both hands together in a prayer-like position at the chin and bowing slightly. The gesture means "thank you" and "I am sorry" as well as "hello." The higher the hands, the more respect is symbolized. The fingertips, however, should never be raised above the eye level. Failure to return a *wai* is equivalent to refusing to shake hands in the West. In Thailand it is considered offensive to place one's arm over the back of the chair in which another person is sitting, and men and women should not show affection in public. First names are used, and last names are reserved for very formal occasions or in writing.
United Kingdom	In the United Kingdom, never sit with the ankle resting on the knee; one should instead cross his or her legs with one knee on top of the other. Avoid backslapping and putting an arm around a new acquaintance. Use titles until use of first names is suggested. Gift-giving is not a normal custom in the United Kingdom The British are very civil and reserved, they do not admire overt ambition and aggressiveness, and are offended by hard-sell tactics. They do not brag about their finances or positions. And they are good negotiators, but do not have a high regard for bargaining in general.
United States	Americans often feel that the European practice of meticulously cultivating personal relationships with business associates slows the expedient conduct of business; they agree that time is money, and the Europeans waste time. Business comes first, and friendship or pleasure comes later, if at all.

Source: Excerpted from David Altany, "It Takes Cultural Savvy," *Industry Week* (October 2, 1989); M. Katherine Glover, "Do's and Taboos: Cultural Aspects of International Business," *Business America* (August 13, 1990): 3; Dean Foster, "Business Across Borders: International Etiquette for the Effective Secretary," *The Secretary* (October 1992): 23; and excerpted from Valeria Frazee, "Getting Started in Mexico," *Workforce* 2, no. 1 (January 1997): 16, 17.

were shaped by that culture. However, they will need to know enough about the culture and about the locals' negotiating styles to avoid being uncomfortable during (and after) negotiations.[104] Besides knowing enough to not fail, they also need to know enough to win. For example, in negotiations between Japanese and American businesspeople, Japanese negotiators have sometimes used their knowledge that Americans have a low tolerance for silence to their advantage.

In other words, for negotiation to take place, the foreigner must at least recognize those ideas and behaviors that the locals intentionally put forward as part of the negotiation process—and the locals must do the same for the foreigners. Both sides must be capable of interpreting these behaviors sufficiently to distinguish common from conflicting positions, to spot movement from positions, and to respond in ways that sustain communication. Ultimately, cross-cultural negotiators must determine their counterparts' personal motivations and agendas and adapt the negotiation style to them.

The purpose of the previous discussion is to develop a cross-cultural negotiations process. The process includes both strategy and tactics. **Strategy** refers to a long-term plan, and **tactics** refers to the actual means used to implement the strategy.[105]

Strategic Planning for International Negotiations

Strategic planning for international negotiations involves several stages: preparation for face-to-face negotiations, determining settlement range, determining where the negotiations should take place, deciding whether to use an individual or a group of individuals in the negotiations, and learning about the country's views on agreements/ contracts.

Preparation for Face-to-Face Negotiations

Generally, at the preparation stage, the issues to be identified are common interests, desired outcomes, possible conflicts (and tactics for handling them), participants' abilities and limitations, business markets, financial status, participants' reputation, and similar products/services.[106] Typically, the negotiating strategy that is effective in the home market will have to be modified for negotiating with foreign businesses; as indicated above, cultural factors, business customs, and ethical standards of the foreign country must be considered.[107] For instance, in negotiating with the Chinese, Americans want to agree on specific terms first while the Chinese want to determine general principles (the "spirit of the contract") and then discuss specifics. In other words, Americans tend to be concerned with short-term goals, such as profits, while the Chinese are more concerned with long-term interests, such as the procurement of American technology and business techniques.[108]

Determining a Settlement Range

At this phase, a negotiation or **settlement range** (all possible settlements a negotiator would be willing to make) must be established. The "least acceptable result" and a "maximum supportable position" must be identified. In this respect, the Japanese have a saying, "*Banana no tataki uri,*" which means "ask outrageous prices and lower them when faced with buyer objections."[109] Establishing a range provides negotiators the ability to make concessions and therefore more flexibility in the negotiations. Some cultures, Russia, for example, view concessions as a sign of weakness, not gestures of goodwill or flexibility. To be able to establish a reasonable negotiating range, an accurate analysis of the nature of all relevant markets must be conducted.[110] If there are other options, that is, if either the seller or the buyer has other forms of leverage or enticement, he or she may not need to make as many concessions or may not need to make any concessions at all.

Where Should Negotiations Take Place?

Negotiations can take place in the home country, in the counterpart's home country, or at a neutral site. Most negotiators would prefer that negotiations take place on their home turf. Familiar surroundings and easy access to information provide more leverage; fatigue and stress associated with foreign travel are not experienced; and, of course, lower travel costs are incurred.[111] On the other hand, negotiating in the foreign country does have its advantages, such as sometimes receiving certain concessions because you have endured the burdens of traveling. And quite often it is a good idea to base decisions on site observations—for example, it is a good idea to see the plant where your product is going to be manufactured. A neutral site that is equally advantageous to both parties is often ideal. For example, an American executive from Park Avenue in New York City may not adapt well in a Brazilian village in the Amazon, and an executive from this village may not adapt well in New York City. A negotiating site that falls between the two extremes may be the most viable.

Individual or Team Negotiations?

An organization can assign one individual or a group of individuals to conduct the negotiations. The obvious advantages of using **one person** are that it is cheaper and a decision can be made quickly. An obvious disadvantage is that one person may not have sufficient ability to deal with the other side, which typically consists of a group of experts and negotiating specialists—an advantage of the group approach. Furthermore, in Japan, for instance, not using a group may be interpreted to mean that you are not very serious about the negotiation or the business deal. Also, the individual negotiator often finds himself or herself pressed to make a decision when it is not the right time to do so. In a group, the members can always take a break to confer, therefore "buying time" to assess the situation and develop new strategies and tactics. (The Japanese typically use this method because their decisions usually require group consensus.) Thus, in negotiating situations where the cost and speed of a decision are more important than the other factors, use one negotiator; otherwise, use a group of experts and negotiating specialists.

To speed up decision making a bit and still have access to expert input, a **team of negotiators** can be used, but one member is given full negotiating authority (Americans generally use this approach). Of course, the other side may know this. And in the negotiations game, for tactical reasons, both parties try to learn who the decision maker is. In this respect, American decision makers usually reveal themselves quickly because they tend to be very active in the negotiations. On the other hand, Japanese decision makers are usually not very active in the negotiations—they simply remain silent and listen. It should also be noted that the Japanese tend to include several young executives in the negotiations team simply for exposure and on-site development purposes.[112]

What Are the Country's Views on Agreements/Contracts?

Countries existing on a high commercial level have generally developed a working base on which agreements can rest. The base may be on one or a combination of three types.[113]

1. Rules that are spelled out technically as laws or regulations.
2. Moral practices mutually agreed upon and taught to the young as a set of principles.
3. Information customs to which everyone conforms without being able to state the exact rules.

Some cultures favor one type, and some another. Americans, for example, rely heavily on written contracts, and they tend to consider the negotiations ended when the contract is signed. Many societies, however, do not place much importance on written contracts; they rely more on the development of a social relationship. And in many countries, Greece, for instance, a signed contract is simply a starting point for negotiations, which end only when the project is completed—the clauses in the contract are subject to renegotiation. Thus, the international negotiator must understand the nature of the other country's views and practices relating to agreements and contracts.

Tactical Planning for International Negotiations

Tactical planning for international negotiations involves determining how to obtain leverage, use delay tactics, and deal with emotions.

Leverage

In negotiations, it is generally accepted that the more options you have, the more leverage you have, and the more concessions your opponents may be willing to make. For example, if you are negotiating with the Argentinean government to establish a manufacturing subsidiary in Argentina, and the Argentinean negotiators know that their site is the only viable one you have, they will not make any concessions, and are likely to ask you for some concessions. But if the Argentinean negotiators believe that you can just as easily set up the subsidiary in Peru or Brazil, and they need the technology—as most less-developed nations do—they are likely to be willing to make concessions.

Less-developed countries appear to have leverage over multinational corporations because they control access to their own territory, including markets, local labor supplies, investment opportunities, sources of raw materials, and other resources that multinational corporations need or desire. China, for instance, is developing economically rather quickly these days. Its more than one billion prospective customers, along with its relatively inexpensive cost of labor, make China an attractive place for many foreign companies to establish operations. This, it seems, would give Chinese negotiators considerable leverage, and concessions would often have to be made by foreign negotiators. This may be true in some cases, but in many instances, multinational corporations have negotiating advantages because they possess the capital, technology, managerial skills, access to global markets, and other resources that governments in less-developed countries need for economic development.[114]

Delay

Applying **delay tactics** is another form of leverage. If you walk away from the negotiations and your opponents become overly anxious, they may be willing to make some concessions. On the other hand, if you become anxious before your opponent does, you may have to make some concessions. Furthermore, the pause in the negotiations enables you to rest and recuperate, assess progress, obtain other information, and reformulate strategy.[115] In this context, patience is generally recognized as being a key personal attribute in negotiators. Americans tend to be low on patience, while the Japanese tend to be high.

Emotions

Even though behavior in negotiations is mainly intuitive, it should never be judgmental. To be able to listen to other negotiators, one should exclude his or her subjective opinions, preconceptions, and emotional filters. By becoming aware of your **emotions,** you can learn to change your reactions and avoid being manipulated by others or by the emotions themselves—you prevent emotion from controlling a negotiation. On the other hand, if you negotiate solely on the basis of logic, you will miss emotional signals sent out by the other negotiator. Thus, the key to negotiations is to be perceptive of feelings (your and theirs) without being reactive.[116]

Ethical Constraints

Business ethics and corporate social responsibility place constraints on negotiators. For example, a negotiator's ethical concerns for honesty and fair dealings, regardless of the power status of negotiating parties, will affect the outcome. There is no global standard or view of what is ethical or unethical behavior in business transactions—what is viewed as unethical behavior in one culture may be viewed as ethical in another culture, and vice versa. For instance, if a negotiator on one side "pays off" an influential decision maker on the other side to obtain a favorable decision, it would be an unethical business practice in some cultures (and illegal in the United States), but it would be quite acceptable in other cultures.

Economics and International Business

Macroeconomic Policy in an Open Economy

A nation with a closed economy can select its economic policies in view of its own goals. In an open world economy, however, consequences of a nation's activities are felt by its trading partners. The result has been efforts among nations to coordinate their economic policies.

Economic Policy in an Open Economy

International economic policy refers to activities of national governments that affect the movement of trade and factor inputs among nations. Included are not only the obvious measures such as import tariffs and quotas, but also domestic measures such as monetary policy and fiscal policy. Policies that are undertaken to improve the conditions of one sector in a nation tend to have repercussions that spill over into other sectors. Because an economy's *internal* (domestic) sector is tied to its *external* (foreign) sector, one cannot designate economic policies as purely domestic or purely foreign. Rather, the effects of economic policy should be viewed as being located on a continuum between two poles—an internal-effects pole and an external-effects pole. Although the primary impact of an import restriction is on a nation's trade balance, for example, there are secondary effects on national output, employment, and income. Most economic policies are located between the external and internal poles rather than falling directly on either one.

Economic Objectives of Nations

What are the basic objectives of economic policies? Since the Great Depression of the 1930s, governments have actively pursued the goal of economic stability at full employment. Known as **internal balance,** this objective has two dimensions: (1) a fully employed economy, and (2) no inflation—or, more realistically, a reasonable amount of inflation. Nations traditionally have considered internal balance to be of primary importance and have formulated economic policies to attain this goal.

Policy makers are also aware of a nation's balance-of-payments (BOP) position. A nation is said to be in **external balance** when it realizes neither BOP deficits nor BOP surpluses. In practice, policy makers usually express external balance in terms of a BOP subaccount, such as the current account. In this context, external balance occurs when the current account is neither so deeply in deficit that the home nation is incapable of repaying its foreign debts in the future nor so strongly in surplus that foreign nations cannot repay their debts to it. Although nations usually consider internal balance to be the highest priority, they are sometimes forced to modify priorities when confronted with large and persistent external imbalances.

Nations have economic targets other than internal balance and external balance, such as long-run economic development and a reasonably equitable distribution of national income. Although these and other commitments may influence international economic policies, the discussion in this section is confined to the pursuit of internal balance and external balance.

Policy Instruments

To attain the objectives of external balance and internal balance, policy makers enact expenditure-changing policies, expenditure-switching policies, and direct controls. **Expenditure-changing policies** alter the level of aggregate demand for goods and services, including those produced domestically and those imported. They include **fiscal policy,** which refers to changes in government spending and taxes, and **monetary policy,** which refers to changes in the money supply by a nation's central bank (such as the Federal Reserve). Depending on the direction of change, expenditure-changing policies are either expenditure increasing or expenditure reducing.

If *inflation* is a problem, it is likely to be because the level of aggregate demand (total spending) is too high for the level of output that can be sustained by the nation's resources at constant prices. The standard recommendation in this case is for policy makers to reduce aggregate demand by implementing *expenditure-decreasing policies* such as reductions in government expenditures, tax increases, or decreases in the money supply; these policies offset the upward pressure on prices resulting from excess aggregate demand. If *unemployment* is excessive, the standard recommendation is for policy makers to increase aggregate demand for goods and services by initiating *expenditure-increasing policies.*

Expenditure-switching policies modify the direction of demand, shifting it between domestic output and imports. Under a system of fixed exchange rates, a trade-deficit nation could devalue its currency to increase the international competitiveness of its industries, thus diverting spending from foreign goods to domestic goods. To increase its competitiveness under a managed floating exchange-rate system, the nation could purchase other currencies with its currency, thereby causing the exchange value of its currency to depreciate. The success of these policies in promoting trade balance largely depends on switching demand in the proper direction and amount, as well as on the capacity of the home economy to meet the additional demand by supplying more goods. Exchange-rate adjustments are general switching policies that influence the balance of payments indirectly, through their effects on the price mechanism and national income.

Direct controls consist of government restrictions on the market economy. They are selective expenditure-switching policies whose objective is to control particular items in the balance of payments. Direct controls, such as automobile tariffs and dairy quotas, are levied on imports in an attempt to switch domestic spending away from foreign goods to domestic goods. Similarly, the object of an export subsidy is to enhance exports by switching foreign spending to domestic output. When a government wishes to limit the volume of its overseas sales, it may impose an export quota (such as Japan's automobile export quotas of the 1980s). Direct controls may also be levied on capital flows so as to either restrain excessive capital outflows or stimulate capital inflows.

Economic policy formation is subject to **institutional constraints** that involve considerations of fairness and equity.[117] Policy makers are aware of the needs of groups they represent, such as labor and business, especially when pursuing conflicting economic objectives. For example, to what extent are policy makers willing to permit reductions in national income, output, and employment at the cost of restoring BOP equilibrium? The outcry of adversely affected groups within the nation may be more than sufficient to convince policy makers not to pursue external balance as a goal. During election years, government officials tend to be especially sensitive to domestic economic problems. Reflecting perceptions of fairness and equity, policy formation tends to be characterized by negotiation and compromise.

Inflation With Unemployment

The analysis so far has looked at internal balance under special circumstances. It has been assumed that as the economy advances to full employment, domestic prices remain unchanged until full employment is reached. Once the nation's capacity to produce has been achieved, further increases in aggregate demand pull prices upward. This type of inflation is known as **demand-pull inflation.** Under these conditions, internal balance (full employment with stable prices) can be viewed as a single target that requires but one policy instrument: reductions in aggregate demand via monetary policy or fiscal policy.

A more troublesome problem is the appropriate policy to implement when a nation experiences *inflation with unemployment.* Here the problem is that internal balance cannot be achieved just by manipulating aggregate demand. To decrease inflation, a reduction in aggregate demand is required; to decrease unemployment, an expansion in aggregate demand is required. Thus, the objectives of full employment and stable prices cannot be considered as one and the same target; rather, they are two independent targets, requiring two distinct policy instruments.

Achieving overall balance thus involves three separate targets: (1) BOP equilibrium, (2) full employment, and (3) price stability. To ensure that all three objectives can be achieved simultaneously, monetary/fiscal policies and exchange-rate adjustments may not be enough; direct controls may also be needed.

Inflation with unemployment has been a problem for the United States. In 1971, for example, the U.S. economy experienced *inflation with recession and BOP deficit.* Increasing aggregate demand to achieve full employment would presumably intensify inflationary pressures. The President therefore implemented a comprehensive system of **wage and price controls** to remove the inflationary constraint. Later the same year, the United States entered into exchange-rate realignments that resulted in a depreciation of the dollar's exchange value by 12% against the trade-weighted value of other major currencies. The dollar depreciation was intended to help the United States reverse its BOP deficit. In short, it was the President's view that the internal and external problems of the United States could not be eliminated through expenditure-changing policies alone.

International Economic-Policy Coordination

Policy makers have long been aware that the welfare of their economies is linked to that of the world economy. Because of the international mobility of goods, services, capital, and labor, economic policies of one nation have spillover effects on others. This spillover is especially true for the larger industrial economies, but even here, the linkages are stronger among some nations, such as those within Western Europe, than for others. Recognizing these spillover effects, governments have often made attempts to coordinate their economic policies.

International Equilibrium

We have emphasized the role of international differences in the cost of producing tradable goods as the main determinant of international trade patterns. By considering only supply-side factors, however, we could not determine (1) the equilibrium point on each nation's production possibilities schedule, (2) the equilibrium value of the international terms of trade, or (3) the equilibrium consumption point of each nation under free trade. Let us now include the role of demand conditions in our trade model so that we can determine the magnitude of these items.

Indifference Curves

Modern trade theory contends that the pattern of world trade is governed by international differences in *supply conditions* and *demand conditions.* Therefore, the role of demand must be developed and introduced into the trade model. Economic theory reasons that an individual's demand curve is based on several underlying determinants, among them (1) the level of disposable income and (2) personal tastes and preferences. Here we consider the role of personal tastes and preferences in demand analysis.

The role of tastes and preferences can be illustrated graphically by a consumer's indifference curve. An **indifference curve** depicts the various combinations of two commodities that are equally preferred in the eyes of the consumer—that is, yield the same level of satisfaction. The term *indifference curve* stems from the idea that the consumer is indifferent among the many possible commodity combinations that provide identical amounts of satisfaction. Exhibit 1000.17 illustrates a consumer's **indifference map,** which consists of a set of indifference curves. Referring to indifference curve I, a consumer is just as happy consuming, say, 6 bushels of wheat and 1 auto at point *A* as consuming 3 bushels of wheat and 2 autos at point *B*. All combination points along an indifference curve are equally desirable because they yield the same level of satisfaction. Besides this fundamental characteristic, indifference curves have several other features.

Inspection of Exhibit 1000.17 reveals that an indifference curve tends to be negatively sloped—that is, sloped downward to the right. This is assured by the assumption that a consumer always desires more of a commodity than less of it. Because each combination of goods along an indifference curve provides the same level of satisfaction, it follows that a consumer who increases auto holdings must decrease wheat intake by some amount if the initial level of satisfaction is to be maintained. If the wheat holdings are not decreased, the new market basket would include more of the combined amount of both commodities, resulting in a higher level of satisfaction. Because changes in the consumption of one commodity are inversely related to changes in the amount consumed of another for a given level of satisfaction to be maintained, it follows that an indifference curve slopes downward to the right.

Indifference curves are also generally convex (bowed in) to the diagram's origin. The negative slope of an indifference curve indicates that, for any given level of satisfaction, some amount of one good must be sacrificed if more of another is to be acquired. The rate at which the substitution occurs is called the **marginal rate of substitution (MRS).** In terms of Exhibit 1000.17, the marginal rate of substitution indicates the extent to which a consumer is will-

Exhibit 1000.17 *A Consumer's Indifference Map*

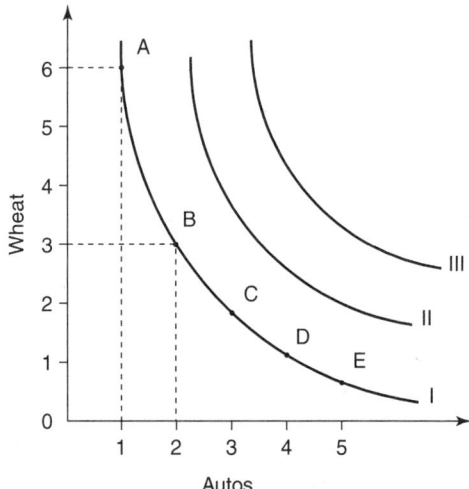

An indifference map is a graph that illustrates an entire set of indifference curves. Each higher indifference curve represents a greater level of satisfaction for the consumer. A community indifference curve denotes various combinations of two goods that yield equal amounts of satisfaction to the nation as a whole.

ing to substitute autos for wheat (or vice versa) while maintaining a given level of satisfaction. The marginal rate of substitution of autos for wheat is expressed algebraically as

$$MRS = \frac{\Delta Wheat}{\Delta Autos}$$

The marginal rate of substitution is equal to an indifference curve's absolute slope. As we move downward along the indifference curve, autos become relatively plentiful while wheat becomes relatively scarce. With less wheat and more autos, each additional auto becomes less valuable to the consumer. For each additional auto consumed, the consumer is willing to sacrifice smaller amounts of wheat. This means that the marginal rate of substitution of autos for wheat decreases as more autos are consumed—hence, the convex nature of an indifference curve.

The indifference map in Exhibit 1000.17 shows several of the consumer's indifference curves. Those indifference curves lying farther from the origin (the "higher" curves) represent greater levels of satisfaction. This is because any point on a higher indifference curve suggests at least the same amount of one commodity plus more of another commodity. Although the figure contains only three indifference curves, an infinite number can be drawn.

Having developed an indifference curve for one individual, can we assume that the preferences of all consumers in the entire nation could be added up and summarized by a **community indifference curve?** Strictly speaking, the answer is no, because it is impossible to make interpersonal comparisons of satisfaction. For example, person A may prefer a lot of coffee and little sugar, whereas person B prefers the opposite. The dissimilar nature of individuals' indifference curves results in their being noncomparable. Despite these theoretical problems, a community indifference curve can be used as a pedagogical device that depicts the role of consumer preferences in international trade.

Equilibrium in the Absence of Trade

Beginning once again with the assumption of isolation, what is the optimal level of production and consumption for a nation? In other words, *at what point on its production possibilities schedule will a nation choose to locate in the absence of trade?*

Assuming that a nation wishes to maximize satisfaction, it will attempt to consume some combination of goods on the highest indifference curve that it can reach. But an indifference curve only tells what a nation would like to do. Given the availability and quality of resources and the level of technology, there is a constraint on how many goods will actually be available to consume. For a nation, this production constraint is represented by its production possibilities schedule. A nation in the absence of trade will maximize satisfaction if it can reach the highest attainable indifference curve, given the production constraint of its production possibilities schedule. This will occur when the production possibilities schedule is *tangent* to an indifference curve.

Exhibit 1000.18 *Indifference Map and Production Possibilities Schedule*

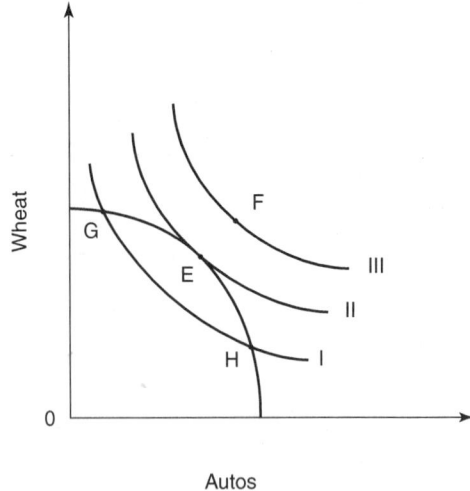

In the absence of trade, a nation achieves equilibrium at the point where its community indifference curve is tangent to its production possibilities schedule. At this point, the nation experiences the highest attainable level of satisfaction given the constraint of its production possibilities schedule, which limits the amount of goods available for consumption.

Exhibit 1000.18 illustrates the production possibilities schedule and indifference map for a single nation. In the absence of trade, the nation will maximize satisfaction if it produces and consumes at point E, where indifference curve II is tangent to its production possibilities schedule. Any point on a higher indifference curve—say, F—is unattainable because it is beyond the economy's capacity to produce. Any point on a lower indifference curve, such as G or H, does not represent maximum satisfaction. This is because a higher indifference curve can be reached with the existing production possibilities schedule. Point E, then, represents the equilibrium of production and consumption in the absence of trade.

A Restatement: Basis for Trade, Gains From Trade

Using indifference curves, let us now develop a trade example to restate the basis-for-trade and the gains-from-trade issues. Exhibit 1000.19 depicts the trading position of the United States. Assuming that the United States attempts to maximize satisfaction, its location of production and consumption will be at point A, where the U.S. production possibilities schedule is just tangent to indifference curve I. At point A, the U.S. relative price ratio is denoted by line $t_{U.S.}$ which equals the absolute slope of the production possibilities curve at that point.

Suppose that the United States has a comparative advantage vis-à-vis Canada in the production of autos. The United States will find it advantageous to specialize in auto production until the two countries' relative prices of autos equalize. Suppose this occurs at production point B (24 autos and 240 bushels of wheat), where the U.S. price rises to Canada's price, depicted by line *tt*. Also suppose that *tt* becomes the international terms-of-trade line. Starting at production point B, the United States will export autos and import wheat, trading along line *tt*. The immediate problem the United States faces is to determine the *level of trade that will maximize its welfare*.

Suppose that the United States exchanges 6 (24−6=18) autos for 50 (240+50=290) bushels of wheat at terms-of-trade *tt*. This would shift the United States from production point B to posttrade consumption point D. But the United States would be no better off with trade than it was in the absence of trade. This is because in both cases the consumption points are located along indifference curve I. Trade volume of 6 autos and 50 bushels of wheat thus represents the *minimum* acceptable volume of trade for the United States. Any smaller volume would force the United States to locate on a lower indifference curve.

Suppose instead that the United States decides to trade 22 (24−22=2) autos for 183 (240+183=423) bushels of wheat. The United States would move from production point B to post-trade consumption point E. With trade, the United States would again locate on indifference curve I, resulting in no gains from trade. From the U.S. viewpoint, trade volume of 22 autos and 183 bushels of wheat therefore represents the *maximum* acceptable volume of trade. Any greater volume would find the United States moving to a lower indifference curve.

Exhibit 1000.19 *Basis for Trade, Gains From Trade*

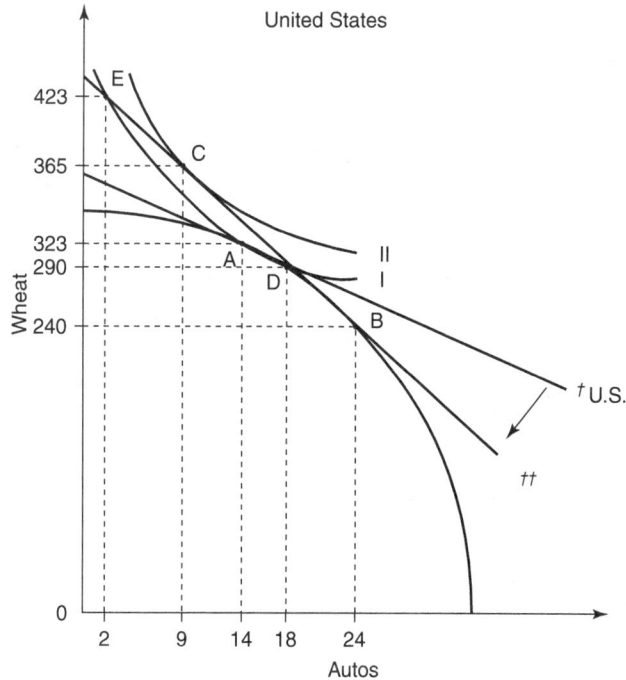

A nation benefits from international trade if it can achieve a higher level of satisfaction (indifference curve) than it can attain in the absence of trade. Maximum gains from trade occur at the point where the international terms-of-trade line is tangent to a community indifference curve.

Trading along terms-of-trade line *tt*, the United States can achieve *maximum welfare* if it exports 15 (24−15=9) autos and imports 125 (240+125=365) bushels of wheat. The U.S. post-trade consumption location would be at point *C* along indifference curve II, the highest attainable level of satisfaction. Comparing point *A* and point *C* reveals that with trade the United States consumes more wheat, but fewer autos, than it does in the absence of trade. Yet point *C* is clearly a preferable consumption location. This is because under indifference-curve analysis, the gains from trade are measured in terms of total satisfaction rather than in terms of number of goods consumed.

Terms-of-Trade Estimates

The gains a nation enjoys from its foreign trade consist of a larger income owing to a wider range of goods available to consumers and the favorable influence trade has on productivity levels. Estimating these gains at a particular time would be extremely difficult, for it would require knowledge of what a nation's imports would cost if it produced them itself instead of purchasing them from a less expensive foreign source. Instead, economists have attempted to measure the direction of these gains over time. This is accomplished by calculating changes in the terms of trade.

The **commodity terms of trade** (also referred to as the *barter terms of trade*) is the most frequently used measure of the direction of trade gains. It measures the relationship between the prices a nation gets for its exports and the prices it pays for its imports. This is calculated by dividing a nation's export price index by its import price index, multiplied by 100 to express the terms of trade in percentages.

$$\text{Terms of Trade} = \frac{\text{Export Price Index}}{\text{Import Price Index}} \times 100$$

An *improvement* in a nation's terms of trade requires that the prices of its exports rise relative to the prices of its imports over the given time period. A smaller quantity of export goods sold abroad is required to obtain a given quantity of imports. Conversely, a *deterioration* in a nation's terms of trade is due to a rise in its import prices relative to its export prices over a time period. The purchase of a given quantity of imports would require the sacrifice of a greater quantity of exports.

Tariffs

The conclusion of the trade models presented so far is that free trade leads to the most efficient use of world resources. When nations specialize according to the comparative-advantage principle, the level of world output is maximized. Not only does free trade enhance world welfare, but it can also benefit each participating nation. Every nation can overcome the limitations of its own productive capacity to consume a combination of goods that exceeds the best it can produce in isolation.

Despite the power of the free-trade argument, however, free-trade policies meet major resistance among those companies and workers who face losses in income and jobs because of import competition. Policy makers are torn between the appeal of greater global efficiency made possible by free trade and the needs of the voting public whose main desire is to preserve short-run interests such as employment and income. The benefits of free trade may take years to achieve and are spread out over wide segments of society, whereas the costs of free trade are immediate and fall on specific groups (for example, workers in the import-competing industry).

In today's world, restrictions on the flow of goods and services in international trade are widespread. This section considers one type of restriction, tariffs, and their impact on trade.

The Tariff Concept

A **tariff** is simply a tax (duty) levied on a product when it crosses national boundaries. The most widespread tariff is the *import tariff*, which is a tax levied on an imported product. A less common tariff is an *export tariff*, which is a tax imposed on an exported product. Export tariffs have often been used by developing nations. For example, cocoa exports have been taxed by Ghana, and oil exports have been taxed by the Organization of Petroleum Exporting Countries (OPEC) in order to raise revenue or promote scarcity in global markets and hence increase the world price.

Did you know that the United States cannot levy export tariffs? When the U.S. Constitution was written, southern cotton-producing states feared that northern textile-manufacturing states would pressure the federal government into levying export tariffs to depress the price of cotton. An export duty would lead to decreased exports and thus a fall in the price of cotton within the United States. As the result of negotiations, the Constitution was worded so as to prevent export taxes: "No tax or duty shall be laid on articles exported from any state."

Tariffs may be imposed for protection or revenue purposes. A **protective tariff** is designed to insulate import-competing producers from foreign competition. Although a protective tariff generally is not intended to totally prohibit imports from entering the country, it does place foreign producers at a competitive disadvantage when selling in the domestic market. A **revenue tariff** is imposed for the purpose of generating tax revenues and may be placed on either exports or imports.

Over time, tariff revenues have decreased as a source of government revenue for industrial nations, including the United States. In 1900, tariff revenues constituted more than 41% of U.S. government receipts; by 1998, the figure stood at 1%. However, many developing nations currently rely on tariffs as a major source of government revenue.

Types of Tariffs

Tariffs can be specific, ad valorem, or compound. A **specific tariff** is expressed in terms of a fixed amount of money per physical unit of the imported product. For example, a U.S. importer of a German computer may be required to pay a duty to the U.S. government of $100 per computer, regardless of the computer's price. An **ad valorem tariff,** much like a sales tax, is expressed as a fixed percentage of the value of the imported product. Suppose that an ad valorem duty of 15% is levied on imported trucks. A U.S. importer of a Japanese truck valued at $20,000 would be required to pay a duty of $3,000 to the government ($20,000 × 15% = $3,000). A **compound tariff** is a combination of specific and ad valorem tariffs. For example, a U.S. importer of a television might be required to pay a duty of $20 plus 5% of the value of the television.

Effective Rate of Protection

A main objective of an import tariff is to protect domestic producers from foreign competition. By increasing the domestic price of an import, a tariff serves to make home-produced goods more attractive to resident consumers. Output in the import-competing industry can thus expand beyond what would exist in the absence of a tariff. The degree of protection afforded by a tariff reflects the extent to which domestic prices can rise above foreign prices before the home producers are priced out of the market.

The **nominal tariff rate** published in a country's tariff schedule gives us a general idea of the level of protection afforded the home industry. But it may not always truly indicate the actual, or effective, protection given. For example, it is not necessarily true that a 25% import tariff on an automobile provides the domestic auto industry a protective margin of 25% against foreign producers. This is because the nominal tariff rates apply only to the total value of the final import product. But in the production process, the home import-competing industry may use imported material inputs or intermediate products that are subject to a different tariff than that on the final product; in this case, the **effective tariff rate** will differ from the nominal tariff rate. The effective tariff is a measure that applies to a single nation. In a world of floating exchange rates, if all nominal or effective tariff rates rose, the effect would be offset by a change in the exchange rate.

The effective tariff rate is an indicator of the actual level of protection that a nominal tariff rate provides the domestic import-competing producers. It signifies *the total increase in domestic productive activities (value added) that an existing tariff structure makes possible,* compared with what would occur under free-trade conditions. The effective rate tells us how much more expensive domestic production can be relative to foreign production and still compete in the market.

Assume that the domestic radio industry adds value to imported inputs by assembling component radio parts imported from abroad. Suppose the imported components can enter the home country on a duty-free basis. Suppose also that 20% of a radio's final value can be attributed to domestic assembly activities (value added), the remaining 80% reflecting the value of the imported components. Furthermore, let the cost of the radio components be the same for both the domestic country and the foreign country. Finally, assume that the foreign country can produce a radio for $100.

Suppose the home country imposes a nominal tariff of 10% on finished radios, so that the domestic import price rises from $100 to $110 per unit (see Exhibit 1000.20). Does this mean that home producers are afforded an effective rate of protection equal to 10%? Certainly not! The imported component parts enter the country duty-free (at a nominal tariff rate less than that on the finished import product), so the effective rate of protection is 50%. Compared with what would exist under free trade, domestic radio producers can be 50% more costly in their assembly activities and still be competitive!

Exhibit 1000.20 shows the figures in detail. Under free trade (zero tariff), a foreign radio could be imported for $100. To meet this price, domestic producers would have to hold their assembly costs down to $20. But under the protective umbrella of the tariff, domestic producers can afford to pay up to $30 for assembly and still meet the $110 domestic price of imported radios. The result is that domestic assembly costs could rise to a level of 50% above what would exist under free-trade conditions: ($30 − $20) / $20 = 0.5.

In general, the effective tariff rate is given by the following formula.

$$e = \frac{(n - ab)}{(1 - a)}$$

where

$e =$ the effective rate of protection
$n =$ the nominal tariff rate on the final product
$a =$ the ratio of the value of the imported input to the value of the final product
$b =$ the nominal tariff rate on the imported input

When the values from the radio example are plugged into this formula, we obtain

$$e = \frac{0.1 - 0.8\,(0)}{1 - 0.8}$$

$$e = 0.5.$$

Exhibit 1000.20 *The Effective Rate of Protection*

Foreign Radio Import	Cost	Domestic Competing Radio	Cost
Component parts	$ 80	Component parts	$ 80
Assembly activity (value added)	20	Assembly activity (value added)	30 (?)
Nominal tariff	10	Domestic price	$110
Import price	$110		

The nominal tariff rate of 10% levied on the final import product thus affords domestic production activities an effective degree of protection equal to 50%—five times the nominal rate.

Two consequences of the effective-rate calculation are worthy of mention. First, the degree of effective protection increases as the value added by domestic producers declines (the ratio of the value of the imported input to the value of the final product increases). In the formula, the higher the value of a, the greater the effective-protection rate for any given nominal tariff rate on the final product. Second, a tariff on imports used in the production process reduces the level of effective protection. The higher the value of b, the lower the effective-protection rate for any given nominal tariff on the final product. In the formula, as b rises, the numerator of the formula decreases and hence e decreases. Note that is possible for the effective-tariff rate to assume a negative value, depending on the values of the components in the formula for the calculation of the effective-tariff rate.

Generalizing from this analysis, *when material inputs or intermediate products enter a country at a very low duty while the final imported commodity is protected by a high duty, the result tends to be a high protection rate for the domestic producers.* The nominal-tariff rate on finished goods thus understates the effective rate of protection. But should a tariff be imposed on imported inputs that exceeds that on the finished good, the nominal-tariff rate on the finished product would tend to overstate its protective effect. Such a situation might occur if the home government desired to protect suppliers of raw materials more than domestic manufacturers.

Tariff Escalation

In many industrialized nations the effective rate of protection is more than twice the nominal rate. An apparently low nominal tariff on a final import product may thus understate the effective rate of protection, which takes into account the effects of tariffs levied on raw materials and intermediate goods. In addition, the tariff structures of industrialized nations have generally been characterized by rising rates that give greater protection to intermediate and finished products than to primary commodities. This is commonly referred to as **tariff escalation.** Although raw materials are often imported at zero or low tariff rates, the nominal and effective protection increases at each stage of production. Many industrialized nations afford a relatively high degree of protection to their manufacturing sector.

The tariff structures of the industrialized nations may indeed discourage the growth of processing and manufacturing industries in the less-developed nations. The industrialized nations' low tariffs on primary commodities encourage the developing nations to expand operations in these sectors, while the high protective rates levied on manufactured goods pose a significant entry barrier for any developing nation wishing to compete in this area. From the point of view of the less-developed nations, it may be in their best interest to discourage disproportionate tariff reductions on raw materials. The effect of these tariff reductions is to magnify the discrepancy between the nominal and effective tariffs of the industrialized nations, worsening the potential competitive position of the less-developed nations in the manufacturing and processing sectors.

Who Pays for Import Restrictions?

Empirical studies often maintain that the total cost of trade restrictions can be high. Trade restrictions also affect the distribution of income within a society. A legitimate concern of government officials is whether the welfare costs of protectionism are shared uniformly by all people in a country, or whether some income groups absorb a disproportionate share of the costs.

How a Tariff Burdens Exporters

The benefits and costs of protecting domestic producers from foreign competition are based on the direct effects of an import tariff. Import-competing businesses and workers can benefit from tariffs through increases in output, profits, jobs, and compensation. A tariff imposes costs on domestic consumers in the form of higher prices of protected products and reductions in consumer surplus. There is also a net welfare loss for the economy because not all of the loss of consumer surplus is transferred as gains to domestic producers and the government (the protective effect and consumption effect).

A tariff carries additional burdens. In protecting import-competing producers, a tariff leads indirectly to a reduction in domestic exports. The net result of protectionism is to move the economy toward greater self-sufficiency, with lower imports and exports. For domestic workers, the protection of jobs in import-competing industries comes at the expense of jobs in other sectors of the economy, including exports. Although a tariff is intended to help domestic producers, the economy-wide implications of a tariff are adverse for the export sector. The welfare losses due to restrictions in output and employment in the economy's export industry may offset the welfare gains enjoyed by import-competing producers.

Because a tariff is a tax on imports, the burden of a tariff falls initially on importers, who must pay duties to the domestic government. However, importers generally try to shift increased costs to buyers through price increases. There are at least three ways in which the resulting higher prices of imports injure domestic exporters.

First, exporters often purchase imported inputs subject to tariffs that *increase the cost of inputs*. Because exporters tend to sell in competitive markets where they have little ability to dictate the prices they receive, they generally cannot pass on a tariff-induced increase in cost to their buyers. Higher export costs thus lead to higher prices and reduced overseas sales.

Tariffs also *raise the cost of living* by increasing the price of imports. Workers thus have the incentive to demand correspondingly higher wages, resulting in higher production costs. Tariffs lead to expanding output for import-competing companies that in turn bid for workers, causing money wages to rise. As these higher wages pass through the economy, export industries ultimately face higher wages and production costs, which lessen their competitive position in international markets.

Finally, import tariffs have *international repercussions* that lead to reductions in domestic exports. Tariffs cause the quantity of imports to decrease, which in turn decreases other nations' export revenues and ability to import. The decline in foreign export revenues results in a smaller demand for a nation's exports and leads to falling output and employment in its export industries.

If domestic export companies are damaged by import tariffs, why don't they protest such policies more vigorously? One problem is that tariff-induced increases in costs for export companies are subtle and invisible. Many exporters may not be aware of their existence. Also, the tariff-induced cost increases may be of such magnitude that some potential export companies are incapable of developing and have no tangible basis for political resistance.

Arguments for Trade Restrictions

The **free-trade argument** is, in principle, persuasive. It states that if each nation produces what it does best and permits trade, over the long run all will enjoy lower prices and higher levels of output, income, and consumption than could be achieved in isolation. In a dynamic world, comparative advantage is constantly changing owing to shifts in technologies, input productivities, and wages, as well as tastes and preferences. A free market compels adjustment to take place. Either the efficiency of an industry must improve, or else resources will flow from low-productivity uses to those with high productivity. Tariffs and other trade barriers are viewed as tools that prevent the economy from undergoing adjustment, resulting in economic stagnation.

Virtually all nations have imposed restrictions on the international flow of goods, services, and capital. Often, proponents of protectionism say that free trade is fine in theory, but that it does not apply in the real world. Modern trade theory assumes perfectly competitive markets whose characteristics do not reflect real-world market conditions. Moreover, even though protectionists may concede that economic losses occur with tariffs and other restrictions, they often argue that noneconomic benefits such as national security more than offset the economic losses. In seeking protection from imports, domestic industries and labor unions attempt to secure their economic welfare. Over the years, a number of arguments have been advanced to pressure the U.S. President and Congress to enact restrictive measures.

These arguments include job protection, protection against cheap foreign labor, fairness in trade (a level playing field), maintenance of the domestic standard of living, equalization of production costs, infant-industry argument, and noneconomic arguments such as national security and cultural and sociological considerations.

Nontariff Trade Barriers

This section considers policies other than tariffs that restrict international trade. Referred to as **nontariff trade barriers (NTBs),** such measures have been on the rise since the 1960s and have become the most widely discussed topics at recent rounds of international trade negotiations. Indeed, the post–World War II success in international negotiations for the reduction of tariffs has made remaining NTBs even more visible.

NTBs encompass a variety of measures. Some have unimportant trade consequences; for example, labeling and packaging requirements can restrict trade, but generally only marginally. Other NTBs significantly affect trade patterns;

examples include import quotas, domestic content requirements, and subsidies. These NTBs are intended to reduce imports and thus benefit domestic producers.

Import Quotas

An **import quota** is a physical restriction on the quantity of goods that may be imported during a specific time period; the quota generally limits imports to a level below that which would occur under free-trade conditions.

Quotas Versus Tariffs

Besides differing in their revenue effects and restrictive impacts on the volume of trade, tariffs and quotas have several other notable differences. Quotas are administratively easier to manage than tariffs, but they normally do not provide government tax revenues. Quotas are relatively easy to enact for emergency purposes, whereas enactment of tariffs is a time-consuming process requiring Congress to enact legislation.

Tariff-Rate Quota: A Two-Tier Tariff

Another restriction used to insulate a domestic industry from foreign competition is the **tariff-rate quota.** The U.S. government has imposed tariff-rate quotas on imports such as stainless steel flatware, brooms, cattle, fish, sugar, and milk.

As its name suggests, a tariff-rate quota displays both tariff-like and quota-like characteristics. This device allows a specified number of goods to be imported at one tariff rate (the *within-quota rate*), whereas any imports above this level face a higher tariff rate (the *over-quota rate*). A tariff-rate quota is thus a *two-tier tariff.*

Domestic Content Requirements

Today, many products, such as autos and aircraft, embody worldwide production. Domestic manufacturers of these products purchase resources or perform assembly functions outside the home country, a practice known as **foreign sourcing** (outsourcing) or production sharing. For example, **General Motors** has obtained engines from its subsidiaries in Mexico, **DaimlerChrysler** has purchased ball joints from Japanese producers, and **Ford** has acquired cylinder heads from European companies. Firms have used foreign sourcing to take advantage of lower production costs overseas, including lower wage rates. Domestic workers often challenge this practice, maintaining that foreign sourcing means that cheap foreign labor takes away their jobs and imposes downward pressure on the wages of those workers who are able to keep their jobs.

To limit the practice of foreign sourcing, organized labor has lobbied for the use of **domestic content requirements.** These requirements stipulate the minimum percentage of a product's total value that must be produced domestically. The effect of content requirements is to force both domestic and foreign firms who sell products in the home country to use domestic inputs (workers) in the production of those products. The demand for domestic inputs thus increases, contributing to higher input prices. Manufacturers generally lobby against domestic content requirements, because they prevent manufacturers from obtaining inputs at the lowest cost, thus contributing to higher product prices and loss of competitiveness.

Worldwide, local content requirements have received most attention in the automobile industry. Developing countries have often used content requirements to foster domestic automobile production.

Subsidies

National governments sometimes grant **subsidies** to domestic producers to help improve their trade position. Such devices are an indirect form of protection provided to home businesses, whether they be import-competing producers or exporters. By providing domestic firms a cost advantage, a subsidy allows them to market their products at prices lower than warranted by their actual cost or profit considerations. Governments wanting to see certain domestic industries expand may provide subsidies to encourage their development. Governmental subsidies assume a variety of forms, including outright cash disbursements, tax concessions, insurance arrangements, and loans at below-market interest rates. Exhibit 1000.21 provides examples of governmental subsidies for several nations.

For purposes of our discussion, two types of subsidies can be distinguished: a **domestic subsidy,** which is sometimes granted to producers of import-competing goods, and an **export subsidy,** which goes to producers of goods

Exhibit 1000.21 *Examples of Governmental Subsidies*

Country	Subsidy Policy
Australia	Export market development grants extended to Australian exporters to seek out and develop overseas markets.
Canada	Rail transportation subsidies granted to Canadian exporters of wheat, barley, oats, and alfalfa.
European Union	Export subsidies provided to many agricultural products such as wheat, beef, poultry, fruits, and dairy products. Financial assistance extended to Airbus.
Japan	Financial assistance extended to Japanese aerospace producers, including loans at low interest rates and assistance with R&D costs.
United States	Export subsidies provided to U.S. producers of agricultural and manufactured goods through the Commodity Credit Corporation and the Export Import Bank

Source: Office of the U.S. Trade Representative, *Foreign Trade Barriers,* Washington, DC, U.S. Government Printing Office, various issues.

that are to be sold overseas. In both cases, the recipient producer views the subsidy as tantamount to a negative tax: the government adds an amount to the price the purchaser pays rather than subtracting from it. The net price actually received by the producer equals the price paid by the purchaser plus the subsidy. The subsidized producer is thus able to supply a greater quantity at each consumer's price.

Dumping

The case for protecting import-competing producers from foreign competition is bolstered by the antidumping argument. **Dumping** is recognized as a form of international price discrimination. It occurs when foreign buyers are charged lower prices than domestic buyers for an identical product, after allowing for transportation costs and tariff duties. Selling in foreign markets at a price below the cost of production is also considered dumping.

Forms of Dumping

Commercial dumping is generally viewed as sporadic, predatory, or persistent in nature. Each type is practiced under different circumstances.

Sporadic dumping (distress dumping) occurs when a firm disposes of excess inventories on foreign markets by selling abroad at lower prices than at home. This form of dumping may be the result of misfortune or poor planning by foreign producers. Unforeseen changes in supply and demand conditions can result in excess inventories and thus in dumping. Although sporadic dumping may be beneficial to importing consumers, it can be quite disruptive to import-competing producers, who face falling sales and short-run losses. Temporary tariff duties can be levied to protect home producers, but because sporadic dumping has minor effects on international trade, governments are reluctant to grant tariff protection under these circumstances.

Predatory dumping occurs when a producer temporarily reduces the prices charged abroad to drive foreign competitors out of business. When the producer succeeds in acquiring a monopoly position, prices are then raised commensurate with its market power. The new price level must be sufficiently high to offset any losses that occurred during the period of cutthroat pricing. The firm would presumably be confident in its ability to prevent the entry of potential competitors long enough for it to enjoy economic profits. To be successful, predatory dumping would have to be practiced on a massive basis to provide consumers with sufficient opportunity for bargain shopping. Home governments are generally concerned about predatory pricing for monopolizing purposes and may retaliate with antidumping duties that eliminate the price differential. Although predatory dumping is a theoretical possibility, economists have not found empirical evidence that supports its existence.

Persistent dumping, as its name suggests, goes on indefinitely. In an effort to maximize economic profits, a producer may consistently sell abroad at lower prices than at home. The rationale underlying persistent dumping is excess capacity.

International Price Discrimination

Consider the case of a domestic seller that enjoys market power as a result of barriers that restrict competition at home. Suppose this firm sells in foreign markets that are highly competitive. This means that the domestic consumer response to a change in price is less than that abroad; the home demand is less elastic than the foreign demand. A profit-maximizing firm would benefit from international price discrimination, charging a higher price at home, where competition is weak and demand is less elastic, and a lower price for the same product in foreign markets to meet competition. The practice of identifying separate groups of buyers of a product and charging different prices to these groups results in increased revenues and profits for the firm as compared to what would occur in the absence of price discrimination.

Excess Capacity

Another reason for sporadic or distress dumping is that producers sometimes face reductions in demand that leave them with idle productive capacity. This *excess capacity* is of particular concern to a nation such as Japan, which has guaranteed lifetime employment to much of its industrial labor force. For many Japanese companies, therefore, labor comes close to being a fixed cost because wages must be paid regardless of the company's production, sales, or profitability. Management thus has the incentive to compete vigorously for sales and to keep output high to generate revenues.

Should a firm find that its productive capacity exceeds the requirements of the domestic market, it may consider it more profitable to use the capacity to fulfill export orders at low prices rather than to allow the capacity to go idle. If necessary to keep exports high, a firm may be willing to sell abroad at a loss. Any profits generated by higher-priced domestic sales can help subsidize the goods that are dumped in foreign markets.

Antidumping Regulations

Despite the benefits that dumping may offer to importing consumers, governments have often levied stiff penalty duties against commodities they believe are being dumped into their markets from abroad. U.S. antidumping law is designed to prevent price discrimination and below-cost sales that injure U.S. industries. Under U.S. law, an **antidumping duty** is levied when the U.S. Department of Commerce determines a class or kind of foreign merchandise is being sold at *less than fair value* (LTFV) and the U.S. International Trade Commission (ITC) determines that LTFV imports are causing or threatening material injury (such as unemployment and lost sales and profits) to a U.S. industry. Such antidumping duties are imposed in addition to the normal tariff in order to neutralize the effects of price discrimination or below-cost sales.

The **margin of dumping** is calculated as the amount by which the foreign market value exceeds the U.S. price. Foreign market value is defined in one of two ways. According to the **priced-based definition,** dumping occurs whenever a foreign company sells a product in the U.S. market at a price below that for which the same product sells in the home market. When a home-nation price of the good is not available (for example, if the good is produced only for export and is not sold domestically), an effort is made to determine the price of the good in a third market.

In cases where the price-based definition cannot be applied, a **cost-based definition** of foreign market value is permitted. Under this approach, the Commerce Department "constructs" a foreign market value equal to the sum of (1) the cost of manufacturing the merchandise, (2) general expenses, (3) profit on home-market sales, and (4) the cost of packaging the merchandise for shipment to the United States. The amount for general expenses must equal at least 10% of the cost of manufacturing, and the amount for profit must equal at least 8% of the manufacturing cost plus general expenses.

Other Nontariff Trade Barriers

Other NTBs consist of governmental codes of conduct applied to imports. Even though such provisions are often well disguised, they remain important sources of commercial policy. Let's consider three such barriers: government procurement policies, social regulations, and sea transport and freight restrictions.

Government Procurement Policies

Because government agencies are large buyers of goods and services, they are attractive customers for foreign suppliers. If governments purchased goods and services only from the lowest-cost suppliers, the pattern of trade would not differ significantly from that which occurs in a competitive market. Most governments, however, favor domestic suppliers over foreign ones in the procurement of materials and products. This is evidenced by the fact that the ratio of imports to total purchases in the public sector is much smaller than in the private sector.

Governments often extend preferences to domestic suppliers in the form of **buy-national policies.** The U.S. government, through explicit laws, openly discriminates against foreign suppliers in its purchasing decisions. Although most other governments do not have formally legislated preferences for domestic suppliers, they often discriminate against foreign suppliers through hidden administrative rules and practices. Such governments utilize closed bidding systems that restrict the number of companies allowed to bid on sales, or they may publicize government contracts in such a way as to make it difficult for foreign suppliers to make a bid.

Social Regulations

Since the 1950s, nations have assumed an ever-increasing role in regulating the quality of life for society. **Social regulation** attempts to correct a variety of undesirable side effects in an economy that relate to health, safety, and the environment—effects that markets, left to themselves, often ignore. Social regulation applies to a particular issue, say environmental quality, and affects the behavior of firms in many industries such as automobiles, steel, and chemicals.

Sea Transport and Freight Restrictions

During the 1990s, U.S. shipping companies serving Japanese ports complained of a highly restrictive system of port services. They contended that Japan's association of stevedore companies (companies that unload cargo from ships) used a system of prior consultations to control competition, allocate harbor work among themselves, and frustrate the implementation of any cost cutting by shipping companies.

In particular, shipping companies contended that they were forced to negotiate with the Japanese stevedore-company association on everything from arrival times to choice of stevedores and warehouses. Because port services were controlled by the stevedore-company association, foreign shippers could not negotiate with individual stevedore companies about prices and schedules. Moreover, U.S. shippers maintained that the Japanese government approved these restrictive practices by refusing to license new entrants into the port service business and by supporting the requirement that foreign shippers negotiate with Japan's stevedore-company association.

Exchange-Rate Systems

In choosing an exchange-rate system, a nation must decide whether to allow its currency to be determined by free-market forces (floating rate) or to be fixed (pegged) against some standard of value. If a nation adopts floating rates, it must decide whether to float independently, to float in unison with a group of other currencies, or to crawl according to a predetermined formula such as relative inflation rates. The decision to peg a currency includes the options of pegging to a single currency, to a basket of currencies, or to gold. Since 1971, however, the technique of expressing official exchange rates in terms of gold has not been used; gold has been phased out of the international monetary system.

Members of the International Monetary Fund (IMF) have been free to follow any exchange-rate policy that conforms to three principles: (1) exchange rates should not be manipulated to prevent effective balance-of-payments adjustments or to gain unfair competitive advantage over other members, (2) members should act to counter short-term disorderly conditions in exchange markets, and (3) when members intervene in exchange markets, they should take into account the interests of other members. Exhibit 1000.22 summarizes the exchange-rate practices of IMF member countries as of 1999; Exhibit 1000.23 highlights some of the factors that affect the choice of an exchange-rate system.

Fixed (pegged) **exchange rates** are used primarily by small, developing nations that maintain pegs to a **key currency,** such as the U.S. dollar or the French franc. A key currency is widely traded on world money markets, has demonstrated relatively stable values over time, and has been widely accepted as a means of international settlement.

One reason why developing nations choose to tie their currencies to a key currency is that it is used as a means of international settlement. Consider a Norwegian importer who wants to purchase Argentinean beef over the next year. If the Argentine exporter is unsure of what the Norwegian krone will purchase in one year, he might reject the krone in settlement. Similarly, the Norwegian importer might doubt the value of Argentina's peso. One solution is for the contract to be written in terms of a key currency such as the U.S. dollar. Generally speaking, smaller nations with relatively undiversified economies and large foreign-trade sectors have been inclined to peg their currencies to one of the key currencies.

Maintaining pegs to a key currency provides several benefits for developing nations. First, the prices of the traded products of many developing nations are determined primarily in the markets of industrialized nations such as the United States; by pegging, say, to the dollar, these nations can stabilize the domestic-currency prices of their imports and exports. Second, many nations with high inflation have pegged to the dollar (the United States has relatively low inflation) in order to exert restraint on domestic policies and reduce inflation. By making the commitment to stabilize their exchange rates against the dollar, governments hope to convince their citizens that they are

Exhibit 1000.22 *Exchange-Rate Arrangements of IMF Members, 1999*

Exchange Rate Arrangement	Number of Countries
Exchange arrangements with no separate legal tender*	37
Currency board arrangements	8
Conventional pegged (fixed) exchange rates	44
Pegged exchange rates within horizontal bands	8
Crawling pegged exchange rates	6
Exchange rates within crawling bands	9
Managed floating exchange rates	25
Independently floating exchange rates	48
	185

*The currency of another country circulates as the sole legal tender, or the member belongs to a monetary or currency union in which the same legal tender is shared by the members of the union.
Source: International Financial Statistics, June 2000, p. 2.

Exhibit 1000.23 *Factors for Choosing an Exchange-Rate System*

Characteristics of Economy	Implication for the Desired Degree of Exchange-Rate Flexibility
Size and openness of the economy	If trade is a large share of national output, then the costs of currency fluctuations can be high. This suggests that small, open economies may best be served by fixed exchange rates.
Inflation rate	If a country has much higher inflation than its trading partners, its exchange rate needs to be flexible to prevent its goods from becoming uncompetitive in world markets. If inflation differentials are more modest, a fixed rate is less troublesome.
Labor-market flexibility	The more rigid wages are, the greater the need for a flexible exchange rate to help the economy respond to an external shock.
Degree of financial development	In developing countries with immature financial markets, a freely floating exchange rate may not be sensible because a small number of foreign-exchange trades can cause big swings in currencies.
Credibility of policy makers	The weaker the reputation of the central bank, the stronger the case for pegging the exchange rate to build confidence that inflation will be controlled.
Capital mobility	The more open an economy to international capital, the harder it is to sustain a fixed rate.

Source: International Monetary Fund, *World Economic Outlook,* October 1997, p. 83.

willing to adopt the responsible monetary policies necessary to achieve low inflation. Pegging the exchange rate may thus lessen inflationary expectations, leading to lower interest rates, a lessening of the loss of output due to disinflation, and a moderation of price pressures.

In maintaining fixed exchange rates, nations must decide whether to peg their currencies to another currency or to a currency basket. Pegging to a *single currency* is generally done by developing nations whose trade and financial relationships are mainly with a single industrial-country partner. For example, Ivory Coast, which trades primarily with France, pegs its currency to the French franc.

Developing nations with more than one major trading partner often peg their currencies to a group or *basket of currencies*. The basket is composed of prescribed quantities of foreign currencies in proportion to the amount of trade done with the nation pegging its currency. Once the basket has been selected, the currency value of the nation is computed using the exchange rates of the foreign currencies in the basket. Pegging the domestic-currency value of the basket enables a nation to average out fluctuations in export or import prices caused by exchange-rate movements. The effects of exchange-rate changes on the domestic economy are thus reduced.

Rather than constructing their own currency basket, many nations peg the value of their currencies to the **special drawing right (SDR),** a basket of five currencies established by the IMF. The IMF requires that the valuation of the SDR basket be reviewed every five years; the basket is to include, in proportional amounts, the currencies of the members having the largest exports of goods and services during the previous five years. The currencies comprising the basket as of 1999, along with their amounts and percentage weights, are listed in Exhibit 1000.24.

Exhibit 1000.24 *Special Drawing Right (SDR) Basket of Currencies*

Currency	Amount
U.S. dollar	0.5821
Euro (Germany)	0.2280
Japanese yen	27.2000
Euro (France)	0.1239
Pound sterling	0.1050

Source: International Monetary Fund, *Annual Report*, 1999, p. 109.

The idea behind the SDR basket valuation is to make the SDR's value more stable than the foreign-currency value of any single national currency. The SDR is valued according to an index based on the moving average of those currencies in the basket. Should the values of the basket currencies either depreciate or appreciate against one another, the SDR's value would remain in the center. The SDR would depreciate against those currencies that are rising in value and appreciate against currencies whose values are falling. Nations desiring exchange-rate stability are attracted to the SDR as a currency basket against which to peg their currency values.

Fixed Exchange-Rate System

Few nations have allowed their currencies' exchange values to be determined solely by the forces of supply and demand in a free market. Until the industrialized nations adopted managed floating exchange rates in the 1970s, the practice generally was to maintain a pattern of relatively fixed (pegged) exchange rates among national currencies. Changes in national exchange rates presumably were to be initiated by domestic monetary authorities when long-term market forces warranted it.

Par Value and Official Exchange Rate

Under a fixed exchange-rate system, governments assign their currencies a **par value** in terms of gold or other key currencies. By comparing the par values of two currencies, we can determine their **official exchange rate.** For example, the official exchange rate between the U.S. dollar and the British pound was $2.80 = £1 as long as the United States bought and sold gold at a fixed price of $35 per ounce and Britain bought and sold gold at £12.50 per ounce (35.00 / 12.50 = 2.80). The major industrial nations set their currencies' par values in terms of gold until gold was phased out of the international monetary system in the early 1970s.

Today, many developing nations choose to define their par values in terms of certain key currencies, such as the U.S. dollar. Under this arrangement, the monetary authority first defines its official exchange rate in terms of the key currency. It then defends the fixed parity by purchasing and selling its currency for the key currency at that rate. Assume, for example, that Bolivian central bankers fix their peso at 20 pesos = US$1, whereas Ecuador's sucre is set at 10 sucres = US$1. The official exchange rate between the peso and sucre becomes 1 peso = 0.5 sucre.

Exchange-Rate Stabilization

A first requirement for a nation participating in a fixed exchange-rate system is to determine an official exchange rate for its currency. The next step is to set up an **exchange-stabilization fund** to defend the official rate. Through purchases and sales of foreign currencies, the exchange-stabilization fund attempts to ensure that the market exchange rate does not move above or below the official exchange rate.

Devaluation and Revaluation

Under a fixed exchange-rate system, a nation's monetary authority may decide to pursue balance-of-payments equilibrium by devaluing or revaluing its currency. The purpose of **devaluation** is to cause the home currency's exchange value to *depreciate,* thus counteracting a payments *deficit.* The purpose of currency **revaluation** is to cause the home currency's exchange value to *appreciate,* thus counteracting a payments *surplus.*

The terms *devaluation* and *revaluation* refer to a legal redefinition of a currency's par value under a system of fixed exchange rates. The terms *depreciation* and *appreciation* refer to the actual impact on the market exchange rate caused by a redefinition of a par value or to changes in an exchange rate stemming from changes in the supply of or demand for foreign exchange.

Devaluation and revaluation policies are considered to be *expenditure-switching* instruments because they work on relative prices to divert domestic and foreign expenditures between domestic and foreign goods. By raising the home price of the foreign currency, a devaluation makes the home country's exports cheaper to foreigners in terms of the foreign currency, while making the home country's imports more expensive in terms of the home currency. Expenditures are diverted from foreign to home goods as home exports rise and imports fall. In like manner, a revaluation discourages the home country's exports and encourages its imports, diverting expenditures from home goods to foreign goods.

Before implementing a devaluation or revaluation, the monetary authority must decide (1) if an adjustment in the official exchange rate is necessary to correct a payments disequilibrium, (2) when the adjustment will occur, and (3) how large the adjustment should be. Exchange-rate decisions of government officials may be incorrect—that is, ill timed and of improper magnitude.

In making the decision to undergo a devaluation or revaluation, monetary authorities generally attempt to hide behind a veil of secrecy. Just hours before the decision is to become effective, public denials of any such policies by official government representatives are common. This is to discourage currency speculators, who try to profit by shifting funds from a currency falling in value to one rising in value. Given the destabilizing impact that massive speculation can exert on financial markets, it is hard to criticize monetary authorities for being secretive in their actions. However, the need for devaluation tends to be obvious to outsiders as well as to government officials and in the past has nearly always resulted in heavy speculative pressures.

Legal Versus Economic Implications

Currency devaluations and revaluations are used in conjunction with a *fixed* exchange-rate system. The monetary authority changes a currency's exchange rate by decree, usually by a sizable amount at one time. How is such a policy implemented?

Recall that under a fixed exchange-rate system, the home currency is assigned a par value by the nation's monetary authorities. The par value is the amount of a nation's currency that is required to purchase a fixed amount of gold, a key currency, or the special drawing right. These assets represent the legal *numeraire*, or the unit of contractual obligations. By comparing various national currency prices of the numeraire, monetary authorities determine the official rate of exchange for the currencies.

In the *legal* sense, a devaluation or revaluation occurs when the home country redefines its currency price of the official numeraire, changing the par value. The *economic* effect of the par value's redefinition is the impact on the market rate of exchange. Assuming that other trading nations retain their existing par values, one would expect (1) a devaluation to result in a depreciation in the currency's exchange value, or (2) a revaluation to result in an appreciation in the currency's exchange value.

Stabilizing Currencies of Developing Countries: Currency Boards Versus Dollarization

In recent years, stabilization of the beleaguered currencies of the developing countries has been a hotly debated topic. Rather than relying on a central bank's exchange-stabilization fund, developing countries have increasingly resorted to currency boards and dollarization as stabilization devices. Let us examine these techniques.

Currency Board

A **currency board** is a monetary authority that issues notes and coins convertible into a foreign anchor currency at a *fixed exchange rate*. The anchor currency is a currency chosen for its expected stability and international acceptability. For most currency boards, the U.S. dollar or British pound has been the anchor currency. Also, a few currency boards have used gold as the anchor. Usually, the fixed exchange rate is set by law, making changes to the exchange rate very costly for governments. Put simply, currency boards offer the strongest form of a fixed exchange rate that is possible short of full currency union.

Dollarization

Instead of using a currency board to promote a stable currency, why not "dollarize" an economy? This is what several Latin American countries, such as Argentina and Mexico, were considering at the turn of the millennium.

Dollarization occurs when residents of, say, Argentina, use the U.S. dollar alongside or instead of the peso. *Unofficial dollarization* (partial dollarization) occurs when Argentines hold dollar-denominated bank deposits or Federal Reserve notes to protect against high inflation in the peso. Unofficial dollarization has existed for years in many Latin American and Caribbean countries, where the United States is a major trading partner and a major source of foreign investment.

Official dollarization (full dollarization) means the elimination of the Argentine peso, and its complete replacement with the U.S. dollar. The monetary base of Argentina, which initially consists entirely of peso-denominated currency, would be converted into U.S. Federal Reserve notes. To replace its currency, Argentina would sell foreign reserves (mostly U.S. Treasury securities) to buy dollars and exchange all outstanding peso notes for dollar notes. The U.S. dollar would be the sole legal tender and sole unit of account in Argentina. As of 2000, there were 13 officially dollarized countries in Latin America and the Caribbean.

Floating Exchange Rates

Instead of utilizing fixed exchange rates, some nations allow their currencies to float in the foreign-exchange market. By **floating** (or flexible) **exchange rates,** we mean currency prices that are established daily in the foreign-exchange market, without restrictions imposed by government policy on the extent to which the prices can move. With floating rates, there is an equilibrium exchange rate that equates the demand for and supply of the home currency. Any other rate can create either a surplus or shortage of currency. Changes in the exchange rate will ideally correct a payments imbalance by bringing about shifts in imports and exports of goods, services, and short-term capital movements. The exchange rate depends on relative money supplies, income levels, interest rates, prices, and other factors.

Unlike fixed exchange rates, floating exchange rates are not characterized by par values and official exchange rates; they are determined by market supply and demand conditions rather than central bankers. Although floating rates do not have an exchange-stabilization fund to maintain existing rates, it does not necessarily follow that floating rates must fluctuate erratically. They will do so if the underlying market forces become unstable. Because there is no exchange-stabilization fund under floating rates, any holdings of international reserves serve as working balances rather than to maintain a given exchange rate for any currency.

Arguments for and Against Floating Rates

One advantage claimed for floating rates is their simplicity. Floating rates allegedly respond quickly to changing supply and demand conditions, clearing the market of shortages or surpluses of a given currency. Instead of having formal rules of conduct among central bankers governing exchange-rate movements, floating rates are market determined. They operate under simplified institutional arrangements that are relatively easy to enact.

Because floating rates fluctuate throughout the day, they permit continuous adjustment in the balance of payments. The adverse effects of prolonged disequilibriums that tend to occur under fixed exchange rates are minimized under floating rates. It is also argued that floating rates partially insulate the home economy from external forces. This means that governments will not have to restore payments equilibrium through painful inflationary or deflationary adjustment policies. Switching to floating rates frees a nation from having to adopt policies that perpetuate domestic disequilibrium as the price of maintaining a satisfactory balance-of-payments position. Nations thus have greater freedom to pursue policies that promote domestic balance than they do under fixed exchange rates.

Although there are strong arguments in favor of floating exchange rates, this system is often considered to be of limited usefulness for bankers and businesspeople. Critics of floating rates maintain that an unregulated market may lead to wide fluctuations in currency values, discouraging foreign trade and investment. Although traders and investors may be able to hedge exchange-rate risk by dealing in the forward market, the cost of hedging may become prohibitively high.

Floating rates in theory are supposed to allow governments to set independent monetary and fiscal policies. But this flexibility may cause a problem of another sort: *inflationary bias.* Under a system of floating rates, monetary authorities may lack the financial discipline required by a fixed exchange-rate system. Suppose a nation faces relatively high rates of inflation compared with the rest of the world. This domestic inflation will have no negative impact on the nation's trade balance under floating rates because its currency will automatically depreciate in the exchange market. However, a protracted depreciation of the currency would result in persistently increasing import prices and a rising price level, making inflation self-perpetuating and the depreciation continuous. Because there is greater freedom for domestic financial management under floating rates, there may be less resistance to overspending and to its subsequent pressure on wages and prices.

Adjustable Pegged Rates

Rather than maintaining completely fixed exchange rates or allowing the exchange rate to be determined by the free-market forces of supply and demand, nations have often pursued limited exchange-rate flexibility. Such is the case of the adjustable pegged-rate system.

In 1944, delegates from 44 member nations of the United Nations met at Bretton Woods, New Hampshire, to create a new international monetary system. They were aware of the unsatisfactory monetary experience of the 1930s, during which the international gold standard collapsed as the result of the economic and financial crises of the Great Depression and nations experimented unsuccessfully with floating exchange rates and exchange controls. The delegates wanted to establish international monetary order and avoid the instability and nationalistic practices that had been in effect until 1944.

The international monetary system that was created became known as the **Bretton Woods system.** The founders felt that neither completely fixed exchange rates nor floating rates were optimal; instead, they adopted a kind of managed exchange-rate system known as **adjustable pegged exchange rates.** The Bretton Woods system lasted from 1946 until 1973.

The main feature of the adjustable peg system is that currencies are tied to each other to provide stable exchange rates for commercial and financial transactions. When the balance of payments moves away from its long-run equilibrium position, however, a nation can repeg its exchange rate via devaluation or revaluation policies. Member nations agreed in principle to defend existing par values as long as possible in times of balance-of-payments disequilibrium. They were expected to use fiscal and monetary policies first to correct payments imbalances. But if reversing a persistent payments imbalance would mean severe disruption to the domestic economy in terms of inflation or unemployment, member nations could correct this *fundamental disequilibrium* by repegging their currencies up to 10% without permission from the International Monetary Fund and by greater than 10% with the Fund's permission.

Although adjustable pegged rates are intended to promote a viable balance-of-payments adjustment mechanism, they have been plagued with operational problems. In the Bretton Woods system, adjustments in prices and incomes often conflicted with domestic-stabilization objectives. Also, currency devaluation was considered undesirable because it seemed to indicate a failure of domestic policies and a loss of international prestige. Conversely, revaluations were unacceptable to exporters, whose livelihoods were vulnerable to such policies. Repegging exchange rates only as a last resort often meant that when adjustments did occur, they were sizable. Moreover, adjustable pegged rates posed difficulties in estimating the equilibrium rate to which a currency should be repegged. Finally, once the market exchange rate reached the margin of the permissible band around parity, it in effect became a rigid fixed rate that presented speculators with a one-way bet. Given persistent weakening pressure, for example, at the band's outer limit, speculators had the incentive to move out of a weakening currency that was expected to depreciate further in value as the result of official devaluation.

Managed Floating Rates

In 1973, a **managed floating system** was adopted, under which informal guidelines were established by the IMF for coordination of national exchange-rate policies.

The motivation for the formulation of guidelines for floating arose from two concerns. The first was that nations might intervene in the exchange markets to avoid exchange-rate alterations that would weaken their competitive position. When the United States suspended its gold-convertibility pledge and allowed its overvalued dollar to float in the exchange markets, it hoped that a free-market adjustment would result in a depreciation of the dollar against other, undervalued currencies. Rather than permitting a **clean float** (a free-market solution) to occur, foreign central banks refused to permit the dollar depreciation by intervening in the exchange market. The United States considered this a **dirty float,** because the free-market forces of supply and demand were not allowed to achieve their equilibrating role. A second motivation for floating guidelines was the concern that free floats over time might lead to disorderly markets with erratic fluctuations in exchange rates. Such destabilizing activity could create an uncertain business climate and reduce the level of world trade.

Under managed floating, a nation can alter the degree to which it intervenes on the foreign-exchange market. Heavier intervention moves the nation nearer the fixed exchange-rate case, whereas less intervention moves the nation nearer the floating exchange-rate case. Concerning day-to-day and week-to-week exchange-rate movements, a main objective of the floating guidelines has been to prevent the emergence of erratic fluctuations. Member nations should intervene on the foreign-exchange market as necessary to prevent sharp and disruptive exchange-rate fluctuations from day to day and week to week. Such a policy is known as **leaning against the wind**—intervening to reduce short-term fluctuations in exchange rates without attempting to adhere to any particular rate over the long run. Members should also not act aggressively with respect to their currency exchange rates; that is, they should not enhance the value when it is appreciating or depress the value when it is depreciating.

Under the managed float, some nations choose target exchange rates and intervene to support them. Target exchange rates are intended to reflect long-term economic forces that underlie exchange-rate movements. One way for managed floaters to estimate a target exchange rate is to follow statistical indicators that respond to the same economic forces as the exchange-rate trend. Then, when the values of indicators change, the exchange-rate target can be adjusted accordingly. Among these indicators are rates of inflation in different nations, levels of official foreign reserves, and persistent imbalances in international payments accounts. In practice, defining a target exchange rate can be difficult in a market based on volatile economic conditions.

Managed Floating Rates in the Short Run and Long Run

Managed floating exchange rates attempt to combine market-determined exchange rates with foreign-exchange market intervention in order to take advantage of the best features of floating exchange rates and fixed exchange rates. Under a managed float, market intervention is used to stabilize exchange rates in the short run; in the long run, a managed float allows market forces to determine exchange rates.

The Crawling Peg

Since 1968, the Brazilian government has announced a change in the par value of the cruzeiro several times a year. The frequent adjustments in Brazil's exchange rate occur in response to the following indicators: (1) the movement in prices in Brazil relative to those of its main trading partners, (2) the level of foreign-exchange reserves, (3) export performance, and (4) the position of the current account of the balance of payments. These exchange-rate adjustments are an application of a mechanism dubbed the **crawling peg.** Not only has Brazil adopted this system, but it also has been used by Argentina, Chile, Israel, and Peru.

The crawling-peg system, a compromise between fixed and floating rates, means that a nation makes small, frequent changes in the par value of its currency to correct balance-of-payments disequilibriums. Deficit and surplus nations both keep adjusting until the desired exchange-rate level is attained. The term *crawling peg* implies that par-value changes are implemented in a large number of small steps, making the process of exchange-rate adjustment continuous for all practical purposes. The peg thus crawls from one par value to another.

The crawling-peg mechanism has been used primarily by nations with high inflation rates. Some developing nations, mostly South American, have recognized that a pegging system can operate in an inflationary environment only if there is provision for frequent changes in the par values. Associating national inflation rates with international competitiveness, these nations have generally used price indicators as a basis for adjusting crawling pegged rates. In these nations, the primary concern is the criterion that governs exchange-rate movements, rather than the currency or basket of currencies against which the peg is defined.

The crawling peg differs from the system of adjustable pegged rates. Under the adjustable peg, currencies are tied to a par value that changes infrequently (perhaps once every several years) but suddenly, usually in large jumps. The idea behind the crawling peg is that a nation can make small, frequent changes in par values, perhaps several times a year, so that they creep along slowly in response to evolving market conditions.

Supporters of the crawling peg argue that the system combines the flexibility of floating rates with the stability usually associated with fixed rates. They contend that a system providing continuous, steady adjustments is more responsive to changing competitive conditions and avoids a main problem of adjustable pegged rates—that changes in par values are frequently wide of the mark. Moreover, small, frequent changes in par values made at random intervals frustrate speculators with their irregularity.

In recent years, the crawling-peg formula has been used by developing nations facing rapid and persistent inflation. But the IMF has generally contended that such a system would not be in the best interests of nations such as the United States or Germany, which bear the responsibility for international currency levels. The IMF has felt that it would be hard to apply such a system to the industrialized nations, whose currencies serve as a source of international liquidity. Although even the most ardent proponents of the crawling peg admit that the time for its widespread adoption has not yet come, the debate over its potential merits is bound to continue.

Exchange Controls

The exchange-rate mechanisms discussed so far all have one important characteristic in common: all are based on the principle of a free exchange market and automatic market forces. It is true that monetary authorities may modify the exchange-rate outcome by purchasing and selling national currencies, but the foreign-exchange transactions conducted among private exporters and importers are free from government regulation. A private foreign-exchange market thus exists.

A government that does not wish to permit a free foreign-exchange market can set up a system of exchange measures to keep its balance of payments under control when the exchange rate moves away from its equilibrium level. Among the devices that have been used to achieve this objective are direct control over balance-of-payments transactions and multiple exchange rates.

Exchange controls achieved prominence during the economic crises of the late 1930s and immediately after World War II. It was not until the late 1950s that the industrialized nations of Western Europe considered themselves financially stable enough so that most controls could be dismantled and a high degree of freedom provided for many international transactions. Exchange controls are still widespread today in the less developed nations of Africa, South America, and the Far East.

At one extreme, a government may seek to gain control over its payments position by directly circumventing market forces through the imposition of direct controls on international transactions. For example, a government that has a virtual monopoly over foreign-exchange dealings may require that all foreign-exchange earnings be turned over to authorized dealers. The government then allocates foreign exchange among domestic traders and investors at government-set prices.

The advantage of such a system is that the government can influence its payments position by regulating the amount of foreign exchange allocated to imports or capital outflows, limiting the extent of these transactions. Exchange controls also permit the government to encourage or discourage certain transactions by offering different rates for foreign currency for different purposes. Furthermore, exchange controls can give domestic monetary and fiscal policies greater freedom in their stabilization roles. By controlling the balance of payments through exchange controls, a government can pursue its domestic economic policies without fear of balance-of-payments repercussions.

A related method of gaining control of the balance of payments is the practice of **multiple exchange rates.** Used primarily by the developing nations, multiple exchange rates attempt to ensure that necessary goods are imported and less essential goods are discouraged. Essential imports, such as raw materials or capital goods, are subsidized when the government sets a low exchange rate for these commodities, resulting in lower prices to domestic buyers. For less desirable imports, such as luxury products, a higher price will be set when the government makes foreign exchange available only at a high rate. Multiple exchange rates can thus be used to subsidize or tax import purchases so that a nation's scarce supply of foreign exchange will be rationed among only the most essential commodities. Obviously, the implementation of such a mechanism requires an elaborate classification system, as well as strict penalties against smuggling.

Nations have also used **dual** (*two-tier*) **exchange rates** to cope with destabilizing international capital flows. Short-term capital tends to move across national borders in response to anticipated changes in exchange rates and interest-rate differentials. Such movements may prevent monetary authorities from pursuing policies insulated from balance-of-payments considerations or even from defending official exchange rates.

Dual exchange rates attempt to insulate a nation from the balance-of-payments effects of capital flows while providing a stable business climate for commercial (current account) transactions involving merchandise trade and services. This is accomplished by having separate exchange rates for commercial and capital transactions. *Commercial* transactions must be conducted in a market where exchange rates are officially *pegged* by national monetary authorities, whereas *capital* transactions occur in a financial market in which exchange rates are *floating*. Although history gives no example of a dual exchange-rate system in which complete segregation of commercial and capital transactions has been achieved, the experiences of Belgium, France, and Italy have approximated such a mechanism.

International Banking

International Banking: Reserves, Debt, and Risk

The world's banking system plays a vital role in facilitating international transactions and maintaining economic prosperity. Commercial banks, such as **Citicorp**, help finance trade and investment and provide loans to international borrowers. Central banks, such as the Federal Reserve, serve as a lender of last resort to commercial banks and sometimes intervene in foreign-currency markets to stabilize currency values. Finally, the International Monetary Fund (IMF) serves as a lender to nations having long-term deficits in their balance of payments. This section concentrates on the role that banks play in world financial markets, the risks associated with international banking, and strategies employed to deal with these risks.

We'll begin with an investigation of the nature of international reserves and their importance for the world financial system. This is followed by a discussion of banks as international lenders and the problems associated with international debt.

Nature of International Reserves

The need of a central bank, such as the Bank of England, for international reserves is similar to an individual's desire to hold cash balances (currency and checkable deposits). At both levels, monetary reserves are intended to bridge the gap between monetary receipts and monetary payments.

Suppose that an individual receives income in equal installments every minute of the day and that expenditures for goods and services are likewise evenly spaced over time. The individual will require only a minimum cash reserve to finance purchases, because no significant imbalances between cash receipts and cash disbursements will arise. In reality, however, individuals purchase goods and services on a fairly regular basis from day to day, but receive paychecks only at weekly or longer intervals. A certain amount of cash is therefore required to finance the discrepancy that arises between monetary receipts and payments.

When an individual initially receives a paycheck, cash balances are high. But as time progresses, these holdings of cash may fall to virtually zero just before the next paycheck is received. Individuals are thus concerned with the amount of cash balances that, on average, are necessary to keep them going until the next paycheck arrives.

Although individuals desire cash balances primarily to fill the gap between monetary receipts and payments, this desire is influenced by a number of other factors. The need for cash balances may become more acute if the absolute dollar volume of transactions increases, because larger imbalances may result between receipts and payments. Conversely, to the extent that individuals can finance their transactions on credit, they require less cash in hand.

Just as an individual desires to hold cash balances, national governments have a need for **international reserves**. The chief purpose of international reserves is to enable nations to finance disequilibriums in their balance-of-payments positions. When a nation finds its monetary receipts falling short of its monetary payments, the deficit is settled with international reserves. Eventually, the deficit must be eliminated, because central banks tend to have limited stocks of reserves.

From a policy perspective, the advantage of international reserves is that they enable nations to sustain temporary balance-of-payments deficits until acceptable adjustment measures can operate to correct the disequilibrium. Holdings of international reserves facilitate effective policy formation because corrective adjustment measures need not be implemented prematurely. Should a deficit nation possess abundant stocks of reserve balances, however, it may be able to resist unpopular adjustment measures, making eventual adjustments even more troublesome.

Demand for International Reserves

When a nation's international monetary payments exceed its international monetary receipts, some means of settlement is required to finance its payments deficit. Settlement ultimately consists of transfers of international reserves among nations. Both the magnitude and the longevity of a balance-of-payments deficit that can be sustained in the absence of equilibrating adjustments are limited by a nation's stock of international reserves.

On a global basis, the **demand for international reserves** depends on two related factors: (1) the monetary value of international transactions and (2) the disequilibrium that can arise in balance-of-payments positions. The demand for international reserves is also contingent on such things as the speed and strength of the balance-of-payments adjustment mechanism and the overall institutional framework of the world economy.

Exchange-Rate Flexibility

One determinant of the demand for international reserves is the *degree of exchange-rate flexibility* of the international monetary system. This is because exchange-rate flexibility in part underlies the efficiency of the balance-of-payments adjustment process.

If exchange rates are fixed or pegged by the monetary authorities, international reserves play a crucial role in the exchange-rate stabilization process. If the U.S. dollar is not to depreciate beyond the pegged rate, the monetary authorities—that is, the Federal Reserve—must enter the market to supply pounds, in exchange for dollars, in the amount necessary to eliminate the disequilibrium.

Rather than operating under a rigidly pegged system, suppose a nation makes an agreement to foster some automatic adjustments by allowing market rates to float within a narrow band around the official exchange rate. This limited exchange-rate flexibility would be aimed at correcting minor payments imbalances, whereas large and persistent disequilibriums would require other adjustment measures.

A fundamental purpose of international reserves is to facilitate government intervention in exchange markets to stabilize currency values. The more active a government's stabilization activities, the greater is the need for reserves. Most exchange-rate standards today involve some stabilization operations and require international reserves. However, if exchange rates were allowed to float freely without government interference, theoretically there would be no need for reserves. This is because a floating rate would serve to eliminate an incipient payments imbalance, negating the need for stabilization operations.

Other Determinants

Changes in the degree of exchange-rate flexibility are inversely related to changes in the quantity of international reserves demanded. In other words, a monetary system characterized by more rapid and flexible exchange-rate adjustments requires smaller reserves, and vice versa.

In addition to the degree of exchange-rate flexibility, several other factors underlie the demand for international reserves, including (1) automatic adjustment mechanisms that respond to payments disequilibriums, (2) economic policies used to bring about payments equilibrium, and (3) the international coordination of economic policies.

Analysis has shown that adjustment mechanisms involving prices, interest rates, incomes, and monetary flows automatically tend to correct balance-of-payments disequilibriums. A payments deficit or surplus initiates changes in each of these variables. The more efficient each of these adjustment mechanisms is, the smaller and more short-lived market imbalances will be and the fewer reserves will be needed. The demand for international reserves therefore tends to be smaller with speedier and more complete automatic adjustment mechanisms.

The demand for international reserves is also influenced by the choice and effectiveness of government policies adopted to correct payments imbalances. Unlike automatic adjustment mechanisms, which rely on the free market to identify industries and labor groups that must bear the adjustment burden, the use of government policies involves political decisions. All else being equal, the greater a nation's propensity to apply commercial policies (including tariffs, quotas, and subsidies) to key sectors, the less will be its need for international reserves. This assumes, of course, that the policies are effective in reducing payments disequilibriums. Because of uncertainties about the nature and timing of payments disturbances, however, nations are often slow to initiate such trade policies and find themselves requiring international reserves to weather periods of payments disequilibriums.

The international coordination of economic policies is another determinant of the demand for international reserves. A primary goal of economic cooperation among finance ministers is to reduce the frequency and extent of payments imbalances and hence the demand for international reserves. Since the end of World War II, nations have moved toward the harmonization of national economic objectives by establishing programs through such organizations as the International Monetary Fund and the Organization of Economic Cooperation and Development. Another example of international economic organization has been the European Union, whose goal is to achieve a common macroeconomic policy and full monetary union. By reducing the intensity of disturbances to payments balance, such policy coordination reduces the need for international reserves.

Other factors influence the demand for international reserves. The quantity demanded is positively related to the level of world prices and income. One would expect rising price levels to inflate the market value of international transactions and, therefore, to increase the potential demand for reserves. The need for reserves would also tend to rise with the level of global income and trade activity.

In summary, central banks need international reserves to cover possible or expected excess payments to other nations at some future time. The quantity of international reserves demanded is directly related to the size and duration of these payment gaps. If a nation with a payments deficit is willing and able to initiate quick actions to increase receipts or decrease payments, the amount of reserves needed will be relatively small. Conversely, the demand for reserves will be relatively large if nations initiate no actions to correct payments imbalances or adopt policies that prolong such disequilibriums.

Supply of International Reserves

The analysis so far has emphasized the demand for international reserves. But what about the **supply of international reserves?** The total supply of international reserves consists of two distinct categories: *owned reserves* and *borrowed reserves*. Reserve assets such as acceptable nationalsw (foreign) currencies, gold, and special drawing rights (SDRs) are generally considered to be directly owned by the holding nations. But if nations with payments deficits find their stocks of owned reserves falling to unacceptably low levels, they may be able to borrow international reserves as a cushioning device. Lenders may be foreign nations with excess reserves, foreign financial institutions, or international agencies such as the IMF.

Owned Reserves: National (Foreign) Currencies

International reserves are a means of payment used in financing foreign transactions. One such asset is holdings of *national currencies* (foreign currencies) such as pounds and dollars. Using the dollar as a reserve currency meant that the supply of international reserves varied with the payments position of the United States. During the 1960s, this situation gave rise to the so-called **liquidity problem.** To preserve confidence in the dollar as a reserve currency, the United States had to strengthen its payments position by eliminating its deficits. But correction of the U.S. deficits would mean elimination of additional dollars as a source of reserves for the international monetary system. The creation in 1970 of SDRs as reserve assets and their subsequent allocations have been intended as a solution for this problem.

Owned Reserves: Gold

The historical importance of gold as an international reserve asset should not be underemphasized. At one time, gold served as the key monetary asset of the international payments mechanism; it also constituted the basis of the money supplies of many nations.

As an international money, gold fulfilled several important functions. Under the historic **gold standard,** gold served directly as an international means of payments. It also provided a unit of account against which commodity prices as well as the parities of national currencies were quoted. Although gold holdings do not yield interest income, gold has generally served as a viable store of value despite inflation, wars, and revolutions. Perhaps the greatest advantage of gold as a monetary asset is its overall acceptability, especially when compared with other forms of international monies.

Today, the role of gold as an international reserve asset has declined. Over the past 30 years, gold has fallen from nearly 70% to less than 3% of world reserves. Private individuals rarely use gold as a medium of payment and virtually never as a unit of account. Nor do central banks currently use gold as an official unit of account for stating the parities of national currencies. The monetary role of gold is currently recognized by only a few nations, mostly in the Middle East. In most nations outside the United States, private residents have long been able to buy and sell gold as they would any other commodity.

Owned Reserves: Special Drawing Rights

The liquidity and confidence problems of the gold exchange standard that resulted from reliance on the dollar and gold as international monies led in 1970 to the creation by the IMF of a new reserve asset, termed **special drawing rights (SDRs).** The objective was to introduce into the payments mechanism a new reserve asset, in addition to the dollar and gold, that could be transferred among participating nations in settlement of payments deficits. With the IMF managing the stock of SDRs, world reserves would presumably grow in line with world commerce.

SDRs are unconditional rights to draw currencies of other nations. When the fund creates a certain number of SDRs, they are allocated to the member nations in proportion to the relative size of their fund quotas. Nations can then draw on their SDR balances in financing their payments deficits. The key point is that certain surplus nations are designated by the fund to trade their currencies for an equivalent amount in SDRs to deficit nations in need of foreign-exchange reserves. Nations whose currencies are acquired as foreign exchange are not required to accept more than three times their initial SDR allotments.

SDRs pay interest to surplus nations on their net holdings (the amount by which a nation's SDR balance exceeds its allocation as determined by its fund quota). Interest payments come from deficit nations that draw their SDR balances below their original allotments. The SDR interest rate is adjusted periodically in line with the short-term interest rates in world money markets. It is reviewed quarterly and adjusted on the basis of a formula that takes into account the short-term interest rates of the United States, the United Kingdom, Germany, France, and Japan.

When the SDR was initially adopted, it was agreed that its value should be maintained at a fixed tie to the U.S. dollar's par value, which was then expressed in terms of gold. The value of the SDR was originally set at US $1. After several monetary developments, this linkage became unacceptable. With the suspension of U.S. gold convertibility in 1971, it was doubted whether the gold value of the dollar should serve as the official unit of account for international transactions. The United States was making it known that it wished to phase out gold as an international monetary instrument. Furthermore, the dollar's exchange rate against gold fell twice as the result of U.S. devaluations in 1971 and 1973. Finally, under the system of managed floating exchange rates, adopted by the industrialized nations in 1973, it became possible for the SDR's value to fluctuate against other currencies while still bearing a fixed tie to the dollar's value. In view of these problems, in 1974, a new method of SDR valuation was initiated—the **basket valuation.**

Basket valuation is intended to provide stability for the SDR's value under a system of fluctuating exchange rates, making the SDR more attractive as an international reserve asset. The SDR is called a basket currency because it is based on the value of five currencies: the U.S. dollar, German mark, Japanese yen, French franc, and British pound. An appreciation, or increase in value, of any one currency in the basket in terms of all other currencies will raise the value of the SDR in terms of each of the other currencies. Conversely, a depreciation, or decline in value, of any one currency will lower the value of the SDR in terms of each other currency. Because the movements of some currencies can be offset or moderated by the movements of other currencies, the value of the SDR in terms of a group of currencies is likely to be relatively stable.

Besides helping nations finance balance-of-payments deficits, SDRs have a number of other uses. Some of the fund's member nations peg their currency values to the SDR. The SDR is the unit of account for IMF transactions and is used as a unit of account for individuals (such as exporters, importers, or investors) who desire protection against the risk of fluctuating exchange rates.

For example, several major banks in London offer certificates of deposit (CDs) denominated in SDRs. The major attraction of SDR-denominated CDs is that they offer investors a financial instrument that is less susceptible to exchange-rate fluctuations than financial assets denominated in any single currency. Although the SDR-denominated CDs are sold for and repaid in dollars, their dollar value at, or any time before, maturity depends on the dollar/SDR exchange rate. Because the dollar/SDR rate is a weighted average of the dollar exchange rates relative to other currencies in the SDR basket, the exchange-rate gains or losses over the term of the deposit will be less than those for any one of the currencies making up the SDR. Therefore, by purchasing SDR-indexed CDs, investors can reduce their overall exchange-rate risk, because losses on one currency may be offset by gains on another in the SDR basket.

Facilities for Borrowing Reserves

The discussion so far has considered the different types of *owned reserves*—national currencies, gold, and SDRs. Various facilities for *borrowing reserves* have also been implemented for nations with weak balance-of-payments positions. Borrowed reserves do not eliminate the need for owned reserves, but they do add to the flexibility of the international monetary system by increasing the time available for nations to correct payments disequilibriums. Let's examine the major forms of international credit for borrowing reserves.

IMF Drawings

One of the original purposes of the IMF was to help member nations finance balance-of-payments deficits. The fund has furnished a pool of revolving credit for nations in need of reserves. Temporary loans of foreign currency are made to deficit nations, which are expected to repay them within a stipulated time. The transactions by which the fund makes foreign-currency loans available are called **IMF drawings.**

Deficit nations do not borrow from the fund. Instead they purchase with their own currency the foreign currency required to help finance deficits. When the nation's balance-of-payments position improves, it is expected to reverse the transaction and make repayment by repurchasing its currency from the fund. The fund currently allows members to purchase other currencies at their own option up to the first 50% of their fund quotas, which are based on the nation's economic size. Special permission must be granted by the fund if a nation is to purchase foreign currencies in excess of this figure. The fund extends such permission once it is convinced that the deficit nation has enacted reasonable measures to restore payments equilibrium.

Since the early 1950s, the fund has also fostered liberal exchange-rate policies by entering into *standby arrangements* with interested member nations. These agreements guarantee that a member nation may draw specified amounts of foreign currencies from the fund over given time periods. The advantage is that participating nations can count on credit from the fund should it be needed. It also saves the drawing nation from administrative time delays when the loans are actually made.

General Arrangements to Borrow

The General Arrangements to Borrow do not provide a permanent increase in the supply of world reserves once the loans are repaid and world reserves revert back to their original levels. However, these arrangements have made world reserves more flexible and adaptable to the needs of deficit nations.

Swap Arrangements

During the early 1960s, there occurred a wave of speculative attacks against the U.S. dollar, based on expectations that it would be devalued in terms of other currencies. To help offset the flow of short-term capital out of the dollar into stronger foreign currencies, the U.S. Federal Reserve agreed with several central banks in 1962 to initiate reciprocal currency arrangements, commonly referred to as **swap arrangements.** Today, the swap network on which the United States depends to finance its interventions in the foreign-exchange market includes the central banks of Canada and Mexico.

Swap arrangements are bilateral agreements between central banks. Each government provides for an exchange, or swap, of currencies to help finance temporary payments disequilibriums. If Mexico, for example, is short of dollars, it can ask the Federal Reserve to supply them in exchange for pesos. A drawing on the swap network is usually initiated by telephone, followed by an exchange of wire messages specifying terms and conditions. The actual swap is in the form of a foreign-exchange contract calling for the sale of dollars by the Federal Reserve for the currency of a foreign central bank. The nation requesting the swap is expected to use the funds to help ease its payments deficits and discourage speculative capital outflows. Swaps are to be repaid (reversed) within a stipulated period of time, normally within 3 to 12 months.

International Lending Risk

In many respects, the principles that apply to international lending are similar to those of domestic lending: the lender needs to determine the credit risk that the borrower will default. When making international loans, however, bankers face two additional risks: country risk and currency risk.

Credit risk is financial and refers to the probability that part or all of the interest or principal of a loan will not be repaid. The larger the potential for default on a loan, the higher the interest rate that the bank must charge the borrower.

Assessing credit risk on international loans tends to be more difficult than on domestic loans. U.S. banks are often less familiar with foreign business practices and economic conditions than those in the United States. Obtaining reliable information to evaluate foreign credit risk can be time-consuming and costly. Many U.S. banks, therefore, confine their international lending to major multinational corporations and financial institutions. To attract lending by U.S. banks, a foreign government may provide assurances against default by a local private borrower, thus reducing the credit risk of the loan.

Country risk is political and is closely related to political developments in a country, especially the government's views concerning international investments and loans. Some governments encourage the inflow of foreign funds to foster domestic economic development. Fearing loss of national sovereignty, other governments may discourage such inflows by enacting additional taxes, profit restrictions, and wage/price controls that can hinder the ability of local borrowers to repay loans. In the extreme, foreign governments can expropriate the assets of foreign investors or make foreign loan repayments illegal.

Currency risk is economic and is associated with currency depreciations and appreciations as well as exchange controls. Some loans of U.S. banks are denominated in foreign currency instead of dollars. If the currency in which the loan is made depreciates against the dollar during the period of the loan, the repayment will be worth fewer dollars. If the foreign currency has a well-developed forward market, the loan may be hedged. But many foreign currencies, especially of the developing nations, do not have such markets, and loans denominated in these currencies cannot always be hedged to decrease this type of currency risk. Another type of currency risk arises from exchange controls, which are common in developing nations. Exchange controls restrict the movement of funds across national borders or limit a currency's convertibility into dollars for repayment, thus adding to the risk of international lenders.

When lending overseas, bankers must evaluate credit risk, country risk, and currency risk. Evaluating risks in foreign lending often results in detailed analyses, compiled by a bank's research department, that are based on a nation's financial, economic, and political conditions. When international lenders consider detailed analyses too expensive, they often use reports and statistical indicators to help them determine the risk of lending.

The Problem of International Debt

Much concern has been voiced over the volume of international lending in recent years. At times, the concern has been that international lending was insufficient. Such was the case after the oil shocks in 1974–1975 and 1979–1980, when it was feared that some oil-importing developing nations might not be able to obtain loans to finance trade deficits resulting from the huge increases in the price of oil. It so happened that many oil-importing nations were able to borrow dollars from commercial banks. They paid the dollars to OPEC nations, who redeposited the money in commercial banks, which then re-lent the money to oil importers, and so on. In the 1970s, the banks were part of the solution; if they had not lent large sums to the developing nations, the oil shocks would have done far more damage to the world economy.

Reducing Bank Exposure to Developing-Nation Debt

When developing nations cannot meet their debt obligations to foreign banks, the stability of the international financial system is threatened. Banks may react to this threat by increasing their capital base, setting aside reserves to cover losses, and reducing new loans to debtor nations.

Banks have additional means to improve their financial position. One method is to liquidate developing-nation debt by engaging in outright *loan sales* to other banks in the secondary market. But if there occurs an unexpected increase in the default risk of such loans, their market value will be less than their face value. The selling bank thus absorbs costs because its loans must be sold at a discount. Following the sale, the bank must adjust its balance sheet to take account of any previously unrecorded difference between the face value of the loans and their market value. Many small and medium-sized U.S. banks, eager to dump their bad loans in the 1980s, were willing to sell them in the secondary market at discounts as high as 70%, or 30 cents on the dollar. But many banks could not afford such huge discounts. Even worse, if the banks all rushed to sell bad loans at once, prices would fall further. Sales of loans in the secondary market were often viewed as a last-resort measure.

Another debt-reduction technique is the *debt buyback*, in which the government of the debtor nation buys the loans from the commercial bank at a discount. Banks have also engaged in *debt-for-debt swaps*, in which a bank exchanges its loans for securities issued by the debtor nation's government at a lower interest rate or discount.

Cutting losses on developing-nation loans has sometimes involved banks in **debt/equity swaps.** Under this approach, a commercial bank sells its loans at a discount to the developing-nation government for local currency, which it then uses to finance an equity investment in the debtor nation. In the late 1980s, **Citicorp** converted some of its Chilean loans into pesos, which were used to purchase ownership shares in Chilean gold mines and pulp mills. Citicorp maintained that it could get better value by selling and swapping the loans without using the secondary market. In Chile, Citicorp typically converted debt at about 87 cents worth of local currency for each $1 of debt. Although debt/equity swaps enhance a bank's chances of selling developing-nation debt, they do not necessarily decrease its risk. Some equity investments in developing nations may be just as risky as the loans that were swapped for local factories or land. Moreover, banks that acquire an equity interest in developing-nation assets may not have the knowledge to manage those assets. Debtor nations also worry that debt/equity swaps will allow major companies to fall into foreign hands.

Debt Reduction and Debt Forgiveness

Another method of coping with developing-nation debt involves programs enacted for debt reduction and debt forgiveness. **Debt reduction** refers to any voluntary scheme that lessens the burden on the debtor nation to service its external debt. Debt reduction is accomplished through two main approaches. The first is the use of negotiated modifications in the terms and conditions of the contracted debt, such as debt reschedulings, retiming of interest payments, and improved borrowing terms. Debt reduction may also be achieved through measures such as debt/equity swaps and debt buybacks. The purpose of debt reduction is to foster comprehensive policies for economic growth by easing the ability of the debtor nation to service its debt, thus freeing resources that will be used for investment.

Some proponents of debt relief maintain that the lending nations should permit **debt forgiveness.** Debt forgiveness refers to any arrangement that reduces the value of contractual obligations of the debtor nation; it includes schemes such as markdowns or write-offs of developing-nation debt or the abrogation of existing obligations to pay interest.

Debt-forgiveness advocates maintain that the most heavily indebted developing nations are unable to service their external debt and maintain an acceptable rate of per capita income growth because their debt burden is overwhelming. They contend that if some of this debt were forgiven, a debtor nation could use the freed-up foreign-exchange resources to increase its imports and invest domestically, thus increasing domestic economic growth rates. The release of the limitation on foreign exchange would provide the debtor nation additional incentive to invest because it would not have to share as much of the benefits of its increased growth and investment with its creditors in the form of interest payments. Moreover, debt forgiveness would allow the debtor nation to service its debt more easily; this would reduce the debt-load burden of a debtor nation and could potentially lead to greater inflows of foreign investment.

Debt-forgiveness critics question whether the amount of debt is a major limitation on developing-nation growth and whether that growth would in fact resume if a large portion of that debt were forgiven. They contend that nations such as Indonesia and South Korea have experienced large amounts of external debt relative to national output but have not faced debt-servicing problems. Also, debt forgiveness does not guarantee that the freed-up foreign-exchange resources will be used productively—that is, invested in sectors that will ultimately generate additional foreign exchange.

The Eurocurrency Market

One of the most widely misunderstood topics in international banking is the nature and operation of the **Eurocurrency market.** This market operates as a financial intermediary, bringing together lenders and borrowers. It serves as one of the most important tools for moving short-term funds across national borders. When the Eurocurrency market first came into existence in the 1950s, its volume was estimated to be approximately $1 billion. The size of the Eurocurrency market in the mid-1990s was estimated to be more than $5 trillion.

Eurocurrencies are deposits, denominated and payable in dollars and other foreign currencies—such as the Swiss franc—in banks outside the United States, primarily in London, the market's center. The term *Eurocurrency market* is something of a misnomer because much Eurocurrency trading occurs in non-European centers, such as Hong Kong and Singapore. Dollar deposits located in banks outside the United States are known as *Eurodollars,* and banks that conduct trading in the markets for Eurocurrencies (including the dollar) are designated *Eurobanks.*

Eurocurrency depositors may be foreign exporters who have sold products in the United States and have received dollars in payment. They may also be U.S. residents who have withdrawn funds from their accounts in the United States and put them in a bank overseas. Foreign-currency deposits in overseas banks are generally for a specified time period and bear a stated yield, because most Eurocurrency deposits are held for investment rather than as transaction balances.

Borrowers go to Eurocurrency banks for a variety of purposes. When the market was first developed, borrowers were primarily corporations that required financing for international trade. But other lending opportunities have evolved with the market's development. Borrowers currently include the British government and U.S. banks.

Development of the Eurocurrency Market

Although several hundred banks currently issue Eurocurrency deposits on investor demand, it was not until the late 1950s and early 1960s that the market began to gain prominence as a major source of short-term capital. Several factors contributed to the Eurocurrency market's growth.

One factor was fear that deposits held in the United States would be frozen by the government in the event of an international conflict. The Eastern European countries, notably Russia, were among the first depositors of dollars in

European banks, because during World War II the United States had impounded Russian dollar holdings located in U.S. banks. Russia was thus motivated to maintain dollar holdings free from U.S. regulation.

Ceilings on interest rates that U.S. banks could pay on savings deposits provided another reason for the Eurocurrency market's growth. These ceilings limited the U.S. banks in competing with foreign banks for deposits. During the 1930s, the Federal Reserve system under Regulation Q established ceiling rates to prevent banks from paying excessive interest rates on savings accounts and thus being forced to make risky loans to generate high earnings. By the late 1950s, when London was paying interest rates on dollar deposits that exceeded the levels set by Regulation Q, it was profitable for U.S. residents and foreigners to transfer their dollar balances to London. Large U.S. banks directed their foreign branches to bid for dollars by offering higher interest rates than those allowed in the United States. The parent offices then borrowed the money from their overseas branches. To limit such activity, the Federal Reserve in 1969 established high reserve requirements on head-office borrowings from abroad. In 1973, the Federal Reserve system made large-denomination certificates of deposit exempt from Regulation Q ceilings, further reducing the incentive to borrow funds from overseas branches.

Throughout the 1970s, 1980s, and 1990s, the Eurocurrency market has continued to grow. A major factor behind the sustained high growth of the market has been the risk-adjusted interest-rate advantage of Eurocurrency deposits relative to domestic deposits, reflecting increases in the level of dollar interest rates and reductions in the perceived riskiness of Euromarket deposits.

Financial Implications

Eurocurrencies have significant implications for international finance. By increasing the financial interdependence of nations involved in the market, Eurocurrencies facilitate the financing of international trade and investment. They may also reduce the need for official reserve financing, because a given quantity of dollars can support a large volume of international transactions. On the other hand, it is argued that Eurocurrencies may undermine a nation's efforts to implement its monetary policy. Volatile movements of these balances into and out of a nation's banking system complicate a central bank's attempt to hit a monetary target.

Another concern is that the Eurocurrency market does not face the same financial regulations as do the domestic banking systems of most industrialized nations. Should the Eurocurrency banks not maintain sound reserve requirements or enact responsible policies, the pyramid of Eurocurrency credit might collapse. Such fears became widespread in 1974 with the failure of the Franklin National Bank in the United States and the Bankus Herstatt of Germany, both of which lost huge sums speculating in the foreign-exchange market.

1080 Law and International Business

International Laws and Politics

Legal Differences and Restraints

Countries differ in their laws as well as in their use of the law. For example, over the past decade the United States has become an increasingly litigious society in which institutions and individuals are quick to initiate lawsuits. Court battles are often protracted and costly, and even the threat of a court case can reduce business opportunities. In contrast, Japan's tradition tends to minimize the role of the law and of lawyers. On a per capita basis, Japan has only about 5% of the number of lawyers that the United States has.[118] Whether the number of lawyers is cause or effect, the Japanese tend not to litigate. Litigation in Japan means that the parties have failed to compromise, which is contrary to Japanese tradition and results in loss of face. A cultural predisposition therefore exists to settle conflicts outside the court system.

While legal systems are important to society, from an international business perspective, the two major legal systems worldwide can be categorized into common law and code law. **Common law** is based on tradition and depends less on written statutes and codes than on precedent and custom. Common law originated in England and is the system of law in the United States. **Code law** on the other hand, is based on a comprehensive set of written statutes. Countries with code law try to spell out all possible legal rules explicitly. Code law is based on Roman law and is found in the majority of the nations of the world.

In general, countries with the code law system have much more rigid laws than those with the common law system. In the latter, courts adopt precedents and customs to fit cases, allowing a better idea of basic judgment likely to be rendered in new situations. The differences between code law and common law and their impact on international business, while wide in theory, are not as broad in practice. One reason is that many common-law countries, including the United States, have adopted commercial codes to govern the conduct of business.

Host countries may adopt a number of laws that affect the firm's ability to do business. Tariffs and quotas, for example, can affect the entry of goods. Special licenses for foreign goods may be required.

Other laws may restrict entrepreneurial activities. In Argentina, for example, pharmacies must be owned by the pharmacist. This legislation prevents an ambitious businessperson from hiring druggists and starting a pharmacy chain. Similarly, the law prevents the addition of a drug counter to an existing business such as a supermarket and thus the broadening of the product offering to consumers.

Specific legislation may also exist regulating what does and does not constitute deceptive advertising. Many countries prohibit specific claims that compare products to the competition, or they restrict the use of promotional devices. Even when no laws exist, regulations may hamper business operations. For example, in some countries, firms are required to join the local chamber of commerce or become a member of the national trade association. These institutions in turn may have internal sets of rules that specify standards for the conduct of business that may be quite confining.

Seemingly innocuous local regulations that may easily be overlooked can have a major impact on the international firm's success. For example, Japan had an intricate process regulating the building of new department stores or supermarkets. The government's desire to protect smaller merchants brought the opening of new, large stores to a virtual standstill. Since department stores and supermarkets serve as the major conduit for the sale of imported consumer products, the lack of new stores severely affected opportunities for market penetration of imported merchandise.[119] Only after intense pressure from the outside did the Japanese government decide to reconsider the regulations. Another example concerns the growing global controversy that surrounds the use of genetic technology. Governments increasingly devise new rules that affect trade in genetically modified products. Australia introduced a mandatory standard for foods produced using biotechnology, which prohibits the sale of such products unless the food has been assessed by the Australia New Zealand Food Authority.

Other laws may be designed to protect domestic industries and reduce imports. For example, Russia charges a 20% value-added tax (VAT) on most imported goods, assesses high excise taxes on goods such as cigarettes, automobiles, and alcoholic beverages, and provides a burdensome import licensing regime for alcohol to depress Russian demand for imports.[120]

Finally, the interpretation and enforcement of laws and regulations may have a major effect on international business activities. For example, in deciding what product can be called a "Swiss" Army knife or "French" wine, the interpretation given by courts to the meaning of a name can affect consumer perceptions and sales of products.

The Influencing of Politics and Laws

To succeed in a market, the international business manager needs much more than business know-how. He or she must also deal with the intricacies of national politics and laws. Although to fully understand another country's legal political system will rarely be possible, the good manager will be aware of its importance and will work with people who do understand how to operate within the system.

Many areas of politics and law are not immutable. Viewpoints can be modified or even reversed, and new laws can supersede old ones. Therefore, existing political and legal restraints do not always need to be accepted. To achieve change, however, some impetus for it—such as the clamors of a constituency—must occur. Otherwise, systemic inertia is likely to allow the status quo to prevail.

The international business manager has various options. One is to simply ignore prevailing rules and expect to get away with it. Pursuing this option is a high-risk strategy because the possibility of objection and even prosecution exists. A second, traditional, option is to provide input to trade negotiators and expect any problem areas to be resolved in multilateral negotiations. The drawbacks to this option are, of course, the quite time-consuming process involved and the lack of control by the firm.

A third option involves the development of coalitions and constituencies that can motivate legislators and politicians to consider and ultimately implement change. This option can be pursued in various ways. One direction can be the recasting or redefinition of issues. Often, specific terminology leads to conditioned, though inappropriate responses. For example, in the United States, the trade status accorded to the People's Republic of China has been controversial for many years. The U.S. Congress had to decide annually whether or not to grant "Most Favored Nation" (MFN) status to China. The debate on this decision was always very contentious and acerbic, and often framed around the question as to why China deserved to be treated the "most favored way." Lost in the debate was often the fact that the term "most favored" was simply taken from WTO terminology, and only indicated that trade with China would be treated like that with any other country. Only in late 1999 was the terminology changed from MFN to NTR or "normal trade relations." Even though there was still considerable debate regarding China, at least the controversy about special treatment had been avoided.[121]

Beyond terminology, firms can also highlight the direct links and their costs and benefits to legislators and politicians. For example, a manager can explain the employment and economic effects of certain laws and regulations and demonstrate the benefits of change. The picture can be enlarged by including indirect links. For example, suppliers, customers, and distributors can be asked to help explain to decision makers the benefit of change. In addition, the public at large can be involved through public statements or advertisements.

Developing such coalitions is not an easy task. Companies often seek assistance in effectively influencing the government decision-making process. Such assistance is particularly beneficial when narrow economic objectives or single-issue campaigns are involved. Typically, **lobbyists** provide this assistance. Usually, there are well-connected individuals and firms that can provide access to policymakers and legislators in order to communicate new and pertinent information.

Many U.S. firms have representatives in Washington, DC, as well as in state capitals and are quite successful at influencing domestic policies. Often, however, they are less adept at ensuring proper representation abroad even though, for example, the European Commission in Brussels wields far-reaching economic power. For example, a survey of U.S. international marketing executives found that knowledge and information about foreign trade and government officials was ranked lowest among critical international business information needs. This low ranking appears to reflect the fact that many U.S. firms are far less successful in their interactions with governments abroad and far less intensive in their lobbying efforts than are foreign entities in the United States.[122]

Many countries and companies have been effective in their lobbying in the United States. As an example, Brazil has retained nearly a dozen U.S. firms to cover and influence trade issues. Brazilian citrus exporters and computer manufacturers have hired U.S. legal and public relations firms to provide them with information on relevant U.S. legislative activity. The Banco do Brasil also successfully lobbied for the restructuring of Brazilian debt and favorable U.S. banking regulations.

Although representation of the firm's interests to government decision makers and legislators is entirely appropriate, the international business manager must also consider any potential side effects. Major questions can be raised if such representation becomes very overt. Short-term gains may be far outweighed by long-term negative repercussions if the international firm is perceived as exerting too much political influence.

International Relations and Laws

In addition to understanding the politics and laws of both home and host countries, the international business manager must also consider the overall international political and legal environment. This is important because policies and events occurring among countries can have a profound impact on firms trying to do business internationally.

International Politics

The effect of politics on international business is determined by both the bilateral political relations between home and host countries and by multilateral agreements governing the relations among groups of countries.

The government-to-government relationship can have a profound influence in a number of ways, particularly if it becomes hostile. President Bush's characterization in February 2002 of Iran, Iraq, and North Korea as an "axis of evil" aggravated already unstable political relationships and threatened to set back negotiations by U.S. companies to secure lucrative oil deals.[123] In another example, although the internal political changes in the aftermath of the Iranian revolution certainly would have affected any foreign firm doing business in Iran, the deterioration in U.S.–Iranian political relations that resulted had a significant additional impact on U.S. firms, which were injured not only by the physical damage caused by the violence, but also by the anti-American feelings of the Iranian people and their government. The resulting clashes between the two governments subsequently destroyed business relationships, regardless of corporate feelings or agreements on either side.

International political relations do not always have harmful effects. If bilateral political relations between countries improve, business can benefit. One example is the improvement in Western relations with Central Europe following the official end of the Cold War. The political warming opened the potentially lucrative former Eastern bloc markets to Western firms.

The overall international political environment has effects, whether good or bad, on international business. For this reason, the good manager will strive to remain aware of political currents and relations worldwide and will attempt to anticipate changes in the international political environment so that his or her firm can plan for them.

International Law

International law plays an important role in the conduct of international business. Although no enforceable body of international law exists, certain treaties and agreements are respected by a number of countries and profoundly influence international business operations. For example, the World Trade Organization (WTO) defines internationally acceptable economic practices for its member nations. Although it does not directly deal with individual firms, it does affect them indirectly by providing some predictability in the international environment.

The **Patent Cooperation Treaty (PCT)** provides procedures for filing one international application designating countries in which a patent is sought, which has the same effect as filing national applications in each of those countries. Similarly, the European Patent Office examines applications and issues national patents in any of its member countries. Other regional offices include the African Industrial Property Office (ARIPO), the French-speaking African Intellectual Property Organization (OAPI), and one in Saudi Arabia for six countries in the Gulf region.

International organizations such as the United Nations and the Organization for Economic Cooperation and Development (OECD) have also undertaken efforts to develop codes and guidelines that affect international business. These include the Code on International Marketing of Breast-milk Substitutes, which was developed by the World Health Organization (WHO), and the UN Code of Conduct for Transnational Corporations. Even though there are 34 such codes in existence, the lack of enforcement ability hampers their full implementation.

In addition to multilateral agreements, firms are affected by bilateral treaties and conventions between the countries in which they do business. For example, a number of countries have signed bilateral Treaties of Friendship, Commerce, and Navigation (FCN). The agreements generally define the rights of firms doing business in the host country. They normally guarantee that firms will be treated by the host country in the same manner in which domestic firms are treated. While these treaties provide for some sort of stability, they can also be canceled when relations worsen.

The international legal environment also affects the manager to the extent that firms must concern themselves with jurisdictional disputes. Because no single body of international law exists, firms usually are restricted by both home and host country laws. If a conflict occurs between contracting parties in two different countries, a question arises concerning which country's laws are to be used and in which court the dispute is to be settled. Sometimes the contract will contain a jurisdictional clause, which settles the matter with little problem. If the contract does not contain such a clause, however, the parties to the dispute have a few choices. They can settle the dispute by following the laws of the country in which the agreement was made, or they can resolve it by obeying the laws of the country in which the contract will have to be fulfilled. Which laws to use and in which location to settle the dispute are two different decisions. As a result, a dispute between a U.S. exporter and a French importer could be resolved in Paris but be based on New York State law. The importance of such provisions was highlighted by the lengthy jurisdictional disputes surrounding the Bhopal incident in India.

In cases of disagreement, the parties can choose either arbitration or litigation. **Litigation** is usually avoided for several reasons. It often involves extensive delays and is very costly. In addition, firms may fear discrimination in foreign countries. Therefore, companies tend to prefer conciliation and **arbitration,** because they result in much quicker decisions. Arbitration procedures are often spelled out in the original contract and usually provide for an intermediary who is judged to be impartial by both parties. Intermediaries can be representatives of chambers of commerce, trade associations, or third-country institutions. One key nongovernmental organization handling international commercial disputes is the International Court of Arbitration, founded in 1923 by the International Chamber of Commerce (ICC). Each year it handles arbitrations in some 48 different countries with arbitrators of some 57 different nationalities. Arbitration usually is faster and less expensive than litigation in the courts. In addition, the limited judicial recourse available against arbitral awards, as compared with court judgments, offers a clear advantage. Parties that use arbitration rather than litigation know that they will not have to face a prolonged and costly series of appeals. Finally, arbitration offers the parties the flexibility to set up a proceeding that can be conducted as quickly and economically as the circumstances allow. For example, a multimillion dollar ICC arbitration was completed in just over two months.[124]

International Business Law

Today every aspect of business, including business law, requires some understanding of international business practices. Since World War II, the global economy has become increasingly interconnected. Many U.S. corporations now have investments or manufacturing facilities in other countries; simultaneously, the number of foreign corporations with business operations in the United States has increased dramatically. Furthermore, whether a domestic corporation exports goods or not, it competes with imports from many other countries. For example, U.S. firms face competition from Japanese electronics and automobiles, French wines and fashions, German machinery, and Taiwanese textiles. In order to compete effectively, U.S. firms need to be aware of international business practices and developments.

Laws vary greatly from country to country: what one nation requires by law, another may forbid. To complicate matters, there is no single authority in international law that can compel countries to act. When the laws of two or more nations conflict, or when one party has violated an agreement and the other party wishes to enforce it or to recover damages, establishing who will adjudicate the matter, which laws will be applied, what remedies will be available, or where the matter should be decided often is very confusing. Nonetheless, given the growing impact of the global economy, a basic understanding of international business law is essential.

The International Environment

International law deals with the conduct and relations between nation-states and international organizations, as well as some of their relations with persons. Unlike domestic law, international law generally cannot be enforced. Consequently, international courts do not have compulsory jurisdiction, though they do have authority to resolve an international dispute if the parties to the dispute accept the court's jurisdiction over the matter. Furthermore, a sovereign nation that has adopted an international law will enforce that law to the same extent as all of its domestic laws. In this section, we will examine some of the sources and institutions of international law.

International Court of Justice

The United Nations, which is probably the most famous international organization, has a judiciary branch called the **International Court of Justice (ICJ)**. The ICJ consists of fifteen judges, no two of whom may be from the same sovereign state, elected for nine-year terms by a majority of both the U.N. General Assembly and the U.N. Security Council. The usefulness of the ICJ is limited, however, because only nations (not private individuals or corporations) may be parties to an action before the court. Furthermore, the ICJ has contentious jurisdiction only over nation-parties who agree both to allow the ICJ to decide the case and to be bound by its decision. Moreover, because the ICJ cannot enforce its rulings, countries displeased with an ICJ decision may simply ignore it. Consequently, few nations submit their disputes to the ICJ.

The ICJ also has advisory jurisdiction if requested by a U.N. organ or specialized U.N. agency. Neither sovereign states nor individuals may request an advisory opinion. These opinions are nonbinding, and the U.N. agency requesting the opinion usually votes to decide whether to follow it.

International law Includes law that deals with the conduct and relations of nation-states and international organizations as well as some of their relations with persons; such law is enforceable by the courts of a nation that has adopted the international law as domestic law.

International Court of Justice Judicial branch of the United Nations having voluntary jurisdiction over nations.

Regional trade communities International organizations, conferences, and treaties focusing on business and trade regulations; the EU (European Union) is the most prominent of these.

Regional Trade Communities

Of much greater significance are international organizations, conferences, and treaties that focus on business and trade regulation. **Regional trade communities**, such as the European Union (EU), promote common trade policies among member nations. Other important regional trade communities include the Central American Common Market (CACM), the Caribbean Community Market (CARICOM), the Association of South East Asian Nations (ASEAN), the Andean Common Market (ANCOM), the Common Market for Eastern and Southern Africa (COMESA), the Asian Pacific Economic Cooperation (APEC), Mercado Comun del Cono Sur (Latin American Trading Group, MERCO-SUR), and the Economic Community of West African States (ECOWAS).

EUROPEAN UNION (EU) The European Community (EC), the predecessor to the European Union, was formed in 1967 through a merger between the European Economic Community (better known as the Common Market), the European Coal and Steel Community, and the European Atomic Energy Community (Euratom). The EC worked to remove trade barriers between its member nations and to unify their economic policies. The EC had the power to make rules that bound member nations and that preempted its members' domestic laws.

In 1993 the Treaty on European Union (popularly called the Maastricht Treaty) took effect. It changed the name of the EC to the European Union and stated the Union's objectives to include (1) promoting economic and social progress by creating an area without internal borders and by establishing an economic and monetary union, (2) asserting its identity on the international scene by implementing a common foreign and security policy, (3) strengthening the protection of the rights and interests of citizens of its member states, and (4) developing close cooperation on justice and home affairs. The EU currently has fifteen full members: Austria, Belgium, Denmark, Finland, France, Germany, Greece, Ireland, Italy, Luxembourg, the Netherlands, Portugal, Spain, Sweden, and the United Kingdom.

NAFTA The North American Free Trade Agreement, which took effect in 1994, established a free trade area among the United States, Canada, and Mexico. Its objectives are to (1) eliminate trade barriers to the movement of goods and services across the borders, (2) promote conditions of fair competition in the free trade area, (3) increase investment opportunities in the area, and (4) provide adequate and effective enforcement of intellectual property rights. Over fifteen years, the treaty will gradually eliminate all tariffs between the three countries.

International Treaties

A treaty is an agreement between or among independent nations. The U.S. Constitution authorizes the president to enter into treaties with the advice and consent of the Senate "providing two-thirds of the Senators present concur." The U.S. Constitution provides that all valid treaties are "the law of the land," having the legal force of a federal statute.

Nations have entered into bilateral and multilateral treaties in order to facilitate and regulate trade and to protect their national interests. In addition, treaties have been used to serve as constitutions of international organizations, to establish general international law, to transfer territory, to settle disputes, to secure human rights, and to protect investments. The Treaty Section of the Office of Legal Affairs within the United Nations Secretariat is responsible for registering and publishing treaties and agreements among member nations. Since its inception in 1946, the U.N. Secretariat has registered and published more than 30,000 treaties that expressly or indirectly concern international business.

International treaties
Agreements between or among independent nations, such as the General Agreement on Tariffs and Trade (GATT), now called the World Trade Organization (WTO).

Probably the most important multilateral trade treaty is the General Agreement on Tariffs and Trade (GATT). The basic purpose of GATT (now called the World Trade Organization with more than 130 members) is to facilitate the flow of trade by establishing agreements on potential trade barriers such as import quotas, customs, export regulations, antidumping restrictions (the prohibition against selling goods for less than their fair market value), subsidies, and import fees. Such agreements arise under GATT's *most favored nation provision,* which states that all signatories must treat each other as favorably as they treat any other country. Thus, any privilege, immunity, or favor given to one country must be given to all. Nevertheless, nations may give preferential treatment to developing nations and may enter into free trade areas with one or more other nations. A free trade area permits countries to discriminate in favor of their free trade partners, provided that the agreement covers substantially all trade among the partners. A second important principle adopted by GATT is that the protection offered domestic industries should take the form of customs tariffs, rather than other, more trade-inhibiting measures.

The most recent set of accords, adopted in 1994, included agreements on such matters as agricultural products, textiles and clothing, technical barriers to trade, trade-related investment measures, customs valuation, subsidies and countervailing measures, trade in services, antidumping measures, and protection of intellectual property rights. It also created the Dispute Settlement Body and increased the scope of GATT's dispute resolution process.

Jurisdiction Over Actions of Foreign Governments

In this section, we will focus on a sovereign nation's power—and the factors limiting that nation's power—to exercise jurisdiction over a foreign nation or to take over property owned by foreign citizens. More specifically, we will examine state immunities (the principle of sovereign immunity and the act of state doctrine) and the power of a state to take foreign investment property.

Sovereign Immunity

One of the oldest concepts in international law is that each nation has absolute and total authority over the events occurring within its territory. It has also been long recognized, however, that in order to maintain international relations and trade, a host country must refrain from imposing its laws on a foreign sovereign nation present within its borders. This absolute immunity from the courts of a host country is known as **sovereign immunity.** Originally, all acts of a foreign sovereign nation within a host country were considered immune from the host country's laws. In modern times, however, international law distinguishes between a foreign nation's public acts and its commercial ones. Only public acts, such as those concerning diplomatic activity, internal administration, or armed forces, will be granted sovereign immunity. By engaging in trade or commercial activities, a foreign nation subjects itself to the jurisdiction of its host country's courts with respect to any disputes that arise out of those commercial activities.

Sovereign immunity Foreign country's freedom from a host country's laws.

In 1976, Congress enacted the Foreign Sovereign Immunities Act in order to establish exactly the circumstances under which the United States would extend immunity to foreign nations. The act specifically provides that a foreign state shall be immune from neither federal nor state court jurisdiction if the suit is based upon (1) a commercial activity conducted in the United States by the foreign state, (2) an act that the foreign state performed in the United States in connection with a commercial activity it conducted elsewhere, or (3) a commercial activity performed outside the United States that nonetheless directly affects the United States. If an activity is one that a private party could normally carry on, it is commercial and a foreign government engaging in that activity is not immune. On the other hand, if the activity is one that only governments can undertake, it is noncommercial under the act. Examples of commercial activities include a contract by a foreign government to buy provisions or equipment for its armed forces; a foreign government's contract to construct or repair a government building; and a foreign government's sale of a service or a product or its leasing of property, borrowing of money, or investing in a security of a U.S. corporation. Examples of public (noncommercial) activities to which sovereign immunity would extend include nationalizing a corporation, determining limitations upon the use of the foreign state's natural resources, and the granting of licenses to export a natural resource.

Act of State Doctrine

Act of state doctrine Rule that a court should not question the validity of actions taken by a foreign government in its own country.

Expropriation Governmental taking of foreign-owned property for a public purpose and with payment of just compensation.

Confiscation Governmental taking of foreign-owned property without payment (or for a highly inadequate payment) or for a nonpublic purpose.

The **act of state doctrine** provides that a nation's judicial branch should not question the validity of the actions a foreign government takes within that foreign sovereign's own borders. In 1897, the U.S. Supreme Court described the act of state doctrine in terms that remain valid today: "Every sovereign State is bound to respect the independence of every other sovereign State, and the courts of one country will not sit in judgment on the acts of the government of another done within its own territory."

In the United States, there are several possible exceptions to the act of state doctrine. Some courts hold (1) that a sovereign may waive its right to raise the act of state defense and (2) that the doctrine may be inapplicable to commercial activities of a foreign sovereign. In addition, by federal statute, courts will not apply the act of state doctrine to a claim to specific property located in the United States when such a claim is based on the assertion that a foreign state confiscated the property in violation of international law, unless the President of the United States determines that the doctrine should be applied to that particular case.

Taking of Foreign Investment Property

Investing in foreign states involves the risk that the host nation's government may take the investment property. An **expropriation** or nationalization occurs when a government seizes foreign-owned property or assets for a public purpose and pays the owner just compensation for what is taken. In contrast, **confiscation** occurs when a government offers no payment (or a highly inadequate payment) in exchange for seized property, or seizes it for a nonpublic purpose. Confiscations violate generally observed principles of international law, whereas expropriations do not. In either case, few remedies are available to injured parties.

The World Bank established the Multilateral Investment Guarantee Agency (MIGA) to encourage increased investment in developing nations. The MIGA Convention has been signed by more than 150 nations. It offers foreign investment risk insurance for noncommercial risks including deprivation of ownership or control by governmental actions, breach of contract by a government when there is no judicial recourse, and loss from military action or civil disturbance.

> *If you invest in foreign states, consider obtaining expropriation insurance from a private insurer or from the Overseas Private Investment Corporation (OPIC), an agency of the U.S. government.*

Transacting Business Abroad

Transacting business abroad may involve activities such as selling goods, information, or services; investing capital; or arranging for the movement of labor. Because these transactions may affect the national security, economy, foreign policy, and interests of both the exporting and importing countries, nations have imposed measures to restrict or encourage such transactions. In this section, we will examine the legal controls imposed upon the flow of trade, labor, and capital across national borders. International contracts, antitrust laws, securities regulation, and intellectual property are also discussed.

Flow of Trade

Advances in modern technology, communication, transportation, and production methods have swelled the flow of goods across national boundaries. The governments within each country thereby face a dilemma. On the one hand, they wish to protect and stimulate domestic industry. On the other hand, they want to provide their citizens with the best quality goods at the lowest possible prices and to encourage exports from their own countries.

Governments have used a variety of trade barriers to protect domestic businesses. A frequently applied device is the **tariff,** which is a duty or tax imposed on goods moving into or out of a country. Tariffs raise the price of imported goods, prompting some consumers to purchase less expensive, domestically produced items. Governments can also use **nontariff barriers** to give local industries a competitive advantage. Examples of nontariff barriers include unilateral or bilateral import quotas, import bans, overly restrictive safety, health, or manufacturing standards, environmental laws, complicated and time-consuming customs procedures, and subsidies to local industry.

Dumping is the sale of exported goods from one country to another country at less than normal value. Under the WTO's Antidumping Code, "normal value" is the price that would be charged for the same or a similar product in the ordinary course of trade for domestic consumption in the exporting country. Dumping violates the GATT "if it causes or threatens material injury to an established industry in the territory of a contracting party or materially retards the establishment of a domestic industry."

Governments also control the flow of goods out of their countries by imposing quotas, tariffs, or total prohibitions. **Export controls** or restrictions usually result from important policy considerations, such as national defense, foreign policy, or the protection of scarce national resources. For example, the United States passed the Export Administration Act of 1979, which, as amended in 1985 and 1988, restricts the flow of technologically advanced goods and data from the United States to other countries. Nonetheless, in order to assist domestic businesses, countries generally encourage exports through the use of *export incentives* and *export subsidies.*

> **Flow of trade** Controlled by trade barriers on imports and exports.
>
> **Tariff** Duty or tax imposed on goods moving into or out of a country.
>
> **Nontariff barriers** Include quotas, bans, safety standards, and subsidies.

> *If you export goods, be sure to determine whether you must obtain an export license from the U.S. government and what import barriers, such as tariffs, you must satisfy in the countries to which you are sending the goods.*

Flow of Labor

The **flow of labor** across national borders generates policy questions concerning the employment needs of local workers. Each country has its own immigration policies and regulations. Almost all countries require that foreigners obtain valid passports before entering their borders; citizens, in turn, often must have passports in order to leave or reenter the country. In addition, a country may issue foreign citizens visas that permit them to enter the country for identified purposes or for specific periods of time. For example, the U.S. Immigration and Naturalization Service issues various types of visas to persons who are temporarily visiting the

> **Flow of labor** Controlled through passport, visa, and immigration regulations.

United States for pleasure or business, to persons who enter the United States to perform services that the unemployed in this country cannot perform, and to persons who are transferred to the United States by their employers.

Flow of Capital

Multinational businesses frequently need to transfer funds to, and receive money from, operations in other countries. Because there is no international currency, nations have sought to ease the **flow of capital** among themselves. In 1945, the International Monetary Fund (IMF) was established to facilitate the expansion and balanced growth of international trade, to assist in the elimination of foreign exchange restrictions that hamper such growth, and to shorten the duration and ease the disequilibrium in the international balance of payments between the members of the fund. Currently, more than 150 countries are members of the IMF.

Flow of capital International Monetary Fund facilitates the expansion and balanced growth of international trade, assists in eliminating foreign exchange restrictions, and smooths the international balance of payments.

Many nations have laws regulating foreign investment. Restrictions on the establishment of foreign investment tend to limit the amount of equity and the amount of control allowed to foreign investors. They may also restrict the way in which the investment is created, such as limiting or prohibiting investment by acquiring an existing locally owned business. Approximately 100 nations have become parties to the Convention on the Settlement of Investment Disputes Between States and Nationals of Other States. The Convention created the International Centre for the Settlement of Investment Disputes, which offers a form of arbitration for investment disputes.

Nations also have cooperated in forming international and regional banks to facilitate the flow of capital and trade. Such banks include the International Bank for Reconstruction and Development (part of the World Bank), the African Development Bank, the Asian Development Bank, the European Investment Bank, and the Inter-American Development Bank.

International Contracts

The legal issues inherent in domestic commercial contracts also arise in international contracts. Moreover, additional issues, such as differences in language, customs, legal systems, and currency, are peculiar to international contracts. Such a contract should specify its official language and include definitions for all the significant legal terms used in it. In addition, it should specify the acceptable currency (or currencies) and payment method. The contract should include a choice of law clause designating what law will govern any breach or dispute regarding the contract, and a choice of forum clause designating whether the parties will resolve disputes through one nation's court system or through third-party arbitration. Finally, the contract should include a force majeure (unavoidable superior force) clause apportioning the parties' liabilities and responsibilities in the event of an unforeseeable occurrence, such as a typhoon, tornado, flood, earthquake, war, or nuclear disaster.

International contracts Involve additional issues beyond those in domestic contracts, such as differences in language, legal systems, and currency.

When you enter into international contracts, be sure that your contracts include provisions for payment, including acceptable currencies, choice of law, choice of forum, and force majeure (acts of God).

CISG United Nations Convention on Contracts for the International Sales of Goods (CISG) governs all contracts for international sales of goods between parties located in different nations that have ratified the CISG.

CISG The United Nations Convention on Contracts for the International Sales of Goods (**CISG**), which has been ratified by the United States and more than forty other countries, governs all contracts for the international sales of goods between parties located in different nations that have ratified the CISG. Because treaties are federal law, the CISG supersedes the Uniform Commercial Code in any situation to which either could apply. The CISG includes provisions dealing with interpretation, trade usage, contract formation, obligations and remedies of sellers and buyers, and risk of loss. Parties to an international sales contract may, however, expressly exclude CISG governance from their contract. The CISG specifically excludes sales of (1) goods bought for personal, family, or household use; (2) ships or aircraft; and (3) electricity. In addition, it does not apply to contracts in which the primary obligation of the party furnishing the goods consists of supplying labor or services.

LETTERS OF CREDIT International trade involves a number of risks not usually encountered in domestic trade, most notably governmental controls over the export or import of goods and currency. The most effective means of managing these risks—as well as the ordinary trade risks of nonperformance by seller and buyer—is the irrevocable documentary letter of credit. Most international letters of credit are governed by the Uniform Customs and Practices for Documentary Credits, a document drafted by commercial law experts from many countries and adopted by the International Chamber of Commerce. A **letter of credit** is a promise by a buyer's bank to pay the seller, provided certain conditions are met. The letter of credit transaction involves three or four different parties and three underlying contracts. To illustrate: a U.S. business wishes to sell computers to a Belgian company. The U.S. and Belgian firms enter into a sales agreement that includes details such as the number of computers, the features they will have, and the date they will be shipped. The buyer then enters into a second contract with a local bank, called an *issuer,* committing the bank to pay the agreed price upon receiving specified documents. These documents normally include a bill of lading (proving that the seller has delivered the goods for shipment), a commercial invoice listing the purchase terms, proof of insurance, and a customs certificate indicating that customs officials have cleared the goods for export. The buyer's bank's commitment to pay is the irrevocable letter of credit. Typically, a *correspondent* or *paying bank* located in the seller's country makes payment to the seller. Here, the Belgian issuing bank arranges to pay the U.S. correspondent bank the agreed sum of money in exchange for the documents. The issuer then sends the U.S. computer firm the letter of credit. When the U.S. firm obtains all the necessary documents, it presents them to the U.S. correspondent bank, which verifies the documents, pays the computer company in U.S. dollars, and sends the documents to the Belgian issuing bank. Upon receiving the required documents, the issuing bank pays the correspondent bank and then presents the documents to the buyer. In our example, the Belgian buyer pays the issuing bank in Belgian francs for the letter of credit when the buyer receives the specified documents from the bank.

> **Letter of credit** Bank's promise to pay the seller, provided certain conditions are met; used to manage the payment risks in international trade.

Antitrust Laws

Section 1 of the Sherman Act provides that U.S. **antitrust laws** shall have a broad, extraterritorial reach. Contracts, combinations, or conspiracies that restrain trade with foreign nations, as well as among the domestic states, are deemed illegal. Therefore, agreements among competitors to increase the cost of imports, as well as arrangements to exclude imports from U.S. domestic markets in exchange for agreements not to compete in other countries, clearly violate U.S. antitrust laws. The antitrust provisions are also designed to protect U.S. exports when privately imposed restrictions seek to exclude U.S. competitors from foreign markets. Amendments to the Sherman Act and the Federal Trade Commission Act limit their application to unfair methods of competition that have a direct, substantial, and reasonably foreseeable effect on U.S. domestic commerce, U.S. import commerce, or U.S. export commerce.

> **Antitrust laws** Apply to unfair methods of competition that have a direct, substantial, and reasonably foreseeable effect on the domestic, import, or export commerce of the United States.

Securities Regulation

The securities markets have become increasingly internationalized, thereby raising questions regarding which country's law governs a particular transaction in securities. Foreign issuers who issue securities in the United States must register them under the 1933 Act unless an exemption is available. Foreign issuers whose securities are sold in the secondary market in the United States must register under the 1934 Act unless the issuer is exempt. Some nonexempt foreign issuers may avoid registration under the 1934 Act by providing the SEC with copies of all information material to investors that they have made public in their home country. Regulation S provides a **safe harbor** from the 1933 Act registration requirements for offshore sales of equity securities of U.S. issuers. The antifraud provisions of the U.S. securities laws apply to securities sold by the use of any means or instrumentality of interstate commerce. In determining the extraterritorial application

> **Securities regulation** Foreign issuers who issue securities, or whose securities are sold in the secondary market in the United States, must register them unless an exemption is available; the antifraud provisions apply where there is either conduct or effects in the United States relating to a violation of the federal securities laws.

of these provisions, the courts have generally found jurisdiction where there is either *conduct* or *effects* in the United States relating to a violation of the federal securities laws.

Protection of Intellectual Property

Protection of intellectual property The owner of an intellectual property right must comply with each country's requirements to obtain from that country whatever protection is available.

The U.S. laws protecting intellectual property do not apply to transactions in other countries. Generally, the owner of an intellectual property right must comply with each country's requirements to obtain from that country whatever protection is available. The requirements vary substantially from country to country, as does the degree of protection. The United States belongs to multinational treaties that try to coordinate the application of member nations' intellectual property laws. The principal treaties for patent protection are the Paris Convention for the Protection of Industrial Property and the Patent Cooperation Treaty. International treaties protecting trademarks are the Paris Convention, the Arrangement of Nice Concerning the International Classification of Goods and Services, and the Vienna Trademark Registration Treaty. Copyrights are covered by the Universal Copyright Convention and the Berne Convention for the Protection of Literary and Artistic Works. The Trade-Related Aspects of Intellectual Property Rights portion of the World Trade Organization Agreement covers the range of intellectual property.

Foreign Corrupt Practices Act

In 1977, Congress enacted the **Foreign Corrupt Practices Act (FCPA)** prohibiting all domestic concerns from bribing foreign governmental or political officials. The FCPA makes it unlawful for any domestic concern or any of its officers, directors, employees, or agents to offer or give anything of value directly or indirectly to any foreign official, political party, or political official for the purpose of (1) influencing any act or decision of that person or party in his or its official capacity, (2) inducing an act or omission in violation of his or its lawful duty, or (3) inducing such person or party to use his or its influence to affect a decision of a foreign government in order to assist the domestic concern in obtaining or retaining business. An offer or promise to make a prohibited payment is a violation even if the offer is not accepted or the promise is not performed. The 1988 amendments to the FCPA explicitly excluded routine governmental actions not involving the discretion of the official, such as obtaining permits or processing applications. This exclusion does *not* cover any decision by a foreign official whether, or on what terms, to award new business or to continue business with a particular party. The amendments also added an affirmative defense for payments that are lawful under the written laws or regulations of the foreign official's country.

Foreign Corrupt Practices Act Prohibits all U.S. companies from bribing foreign governmental or political officials.

Violations can result in fines of up to $2 million for companies; individuals may be fined a maximum of $100,000 or imprisoned up to five years, or both. Fines imposed upon individuals may not be paid directly or indirectly by the domestic concern on whose behalf they acted. In addition, the courts may impose civil penalties of up to $11,000.

In 1997 the United States and thirty-three other nations signed the Organization for Economic Cooperation and Development Convention on Combating Bribery of Foreign Public Officials in International Business Transactions (OECD Convention). In 1998 Congress enacted the International Anti-Bribery and Fair Competition Act of 1998 to conform the FCPA to the Convention. The 1998 Act expands the FCPA to include (1) payments made to "secure any improper advantage" from foreign officials, (2) all foreign persons who commit an act in furtherance of a foreign bribe while in the United States, (3) officials of public international organizations within the definition of a "foreign official." A public international organization is defined as either an organization designated by executive order pursuant to the International Organizations Immunities Act or any other international organization designated by executive order of the president.

Employment Discrimination

Title VII of the Civil Rights Act of 1964, the Americans with Disabilities Act, and the Age Discrimination in Employment Act apply to U.S. citizens employed abroad by U.S. employers or by foreign companies controlled by U.S. employers. Employers, however, are not required to comply with these employment discrimination laws if compliance would violate the law of the foreign country in which the workplace is located.

> *Take care to instruct your employees and agents not to bribe foreign officials, political parties, or political officials. Moreover, train them to distinguish between bribes, which are prohibited, and nondiscretionary facilitating (grease) payments, which are permitted.*

Ethics and International Business

Cross-National Ethics

Some businesspeople believe that what is **ethical** or **unethical** is governed by the legality of the situation and by the social aspects of the situation (what members of the society generally accept as being "right" or "wrong"). For example, if it is illegal to practice the act of bribery in a country and a firm's manager bribes someone there to obtain a favor, it would be unethical, and the violator could be prosecuted under the law. And if **bribery** is not illegal in a country, but it is known to be generally **socially unacceptable,** it would be unethical to practice it; the violator would be punished not by formal law but by informal means, such as by negative publicity and/or by customers boycotting the firm's product or service.

Regarding the social aspects of the situation, many cultures establish informal ethical principles or moral standards that define "right" and "wrong" conduct. However, what is right or wrong is difficult to define conclusively and agree upon in any culture. For example, in the United States, some Americans believe legal abortion is right; others think it is wrong. And what is right or wrong is far more difficult to define conclusively and agree upon among the different cultural environments around the globe. This is because different societies are confronted with different opportunities and constraints, and to cope, each society develops a unique culture and standard of ethics. As a result, what is right and wrong may differ dramatically from one culture to another. This means that managers of MNCs will often find themselves with **conflicting ethical responsibilities;** that is, one's own nation's standard of ethics often collides with those of other nations. For example, the practice of bribery in business transactions is acceptable in Thailand but not in the United States. An American executive transacting business in Thailand would thus be confronted with conflicting ethical responsibilities.

In part because of these conflicting ethical responsibilities, the actions of many U.S. MNCs have been subjected to considerable criticism, which in turn has led to a wide range of negative consequences, such as bad publicity, consumer boycotts, lawsuits, and government intervention, such as the passage of the Foreign Corrupt Practices Act.

Bribery and Payoffs Abroad

Forms of Bribery

Basically, a **bribe** can be defined as *a payment in any form (cash or gift) for the purpose of influencing action by a government official in order to obtain or retain business.* Bribes can be classified as "whitemail bribes" or as "lubrication bribes."

WHITEMAIL BRIBES **Whitemail bribery** refers to payments made to induce an official in a position of power to give favorable treatment where such treatment is either illegal or not warranted on an efficiency, economic benefit scale. Fundamentally, a key point in this type of bribery is that the payment be intended to induce the official "to do or omit doing something in violation of his lawful duty, or to exercise his [or her] discretion in favor of the payor's request for a contract, concession, or privilege on some basis other than merit."[125] These payments, when exposed, can lead to scandals, fines, and so on. Payments of this nature have historically been "buried" in the books of MNCs or concealed in some other way.

LUBRICATION BRIBES   This type of bribe is typically described as payment to facilitate, expedite, or speed up routine government approvals or other actions to which the firm would legally be entitled. Such payments are generally made to minor officials like custom agents or licensing clerks. Another trait of **lubrication bribes** is that the amounts are generally smaller than whitemail bribes although there have been cases where large lubrication-type payments were made. The number and acceptability of the practice of lubrication bribes is much greater than that of whitemail bribes. Officials in many Third World countries are especially noted for requiring "grease" to make their political and administrative wheels turn. Somewhat similar to waiters or waitresses in the United States who receive a low salary and rely on customers' tips to supplement their income, in many countries, numerous officials receive a low salary and rely on "grease" payments to supplement their income.

Extortion

A distinction can be made between bribery and extortion. Bribery is offered by an individual or a corporation seeking an unlawful advantage, while extortion is force exerted in the other direction—an official seeking payment from an individual or corporation for an action to which the individual or corporation may lawfully be entitled. **Gulf Oil's** dilemma in South Korea is an example of extortion.

To Bribe or Not to Bribe?

Bribery and corruption top the list of global ethics issues. Thus, when a manager crosses a nation's borders to conduct or negotiate business, he or she will sometimes be confronted with the need to decide whether or not to practice the act of bribery.

The U.S. Foreign Corrupt Practices Act of 1977

The revelations by the SEC and Senate Foreign Relations subcommittee investigations of U.S. MNCs' "whitemail bribery" practices abroad, and the concern for the negative image such practices generated for the United States, helped plant the seed that eventually produced U.S. Senate Bill 305, the **Foreign Corrupt Practices Act (FCPA)**. The FCPA was passed and signed into law in 1977. Its purpose was twofold:

1. to establish a worldwide code of conduct for any kind of payment by United States businesses to foreign government officials, political parties, and political candidates;
2. to require appropriate accounting controls for full disclosure of firms' transactions

The law applies even if such payments are common practice (viewed as an ethical practice) in the country where they are made. Some of the basic provisions of the FCPA are as follows.

- It is a criminal offense for a firm to make payments to a foreign government official, political party, party official, or candidate for political office in order to secure or retain business in another nation.
- Sales commissions to independent agents are illegal if the business has knowledge that any part of the commission is being passed to foreign officials.
- Government employees whose duties are essentially ministerial or clerical are excluded, so expediting payments to persons such as customs agents and bureaucrats are permitted. (Thus, the FCPA does not apply to small "lubrication" bribes.)
- In addition to the antibribery provisions that apply to all businesses, all publicly held corporations that are subject to the SEC are required to establish internal accounting controls to ensure that all payments abroad are authorized and properly recorded.[126]

The penalty levied on the business enterprise for not complying with the FCPA was set at $1 million for each count. The penalty levied on individual members of the corporation found guilty of making the illegal payment is a fine of up to a $10,000 and/or five years imprisonment, with the added provision that the firm may not pay or reimburse the employees for the fines levied on them. Thus, the FCPA calls for both civil and criminal penalties.

Enforcement of the FCPA was assigned to two federal agencies: the SEC and the Department of Justice. The SEC's responsibility included enforcement of the record keeping and accounting control provisions of the FCPA and civil authority to enforce the prohibitions against foreign bribery by U.S. publicly held corporations. The Department of Justice was given the responsibility to enforce the criminal penalties for corporate bribery of foreign officials and the authority to bring civil actions against domestic concerns whose securities are not registered with the SEC.

COMPLAINTS FROM MNCs OVER THE FCPA   The major areas of concern communicated by U.S. multinational corporations over the FCPA were as follows.

- The FCPA placed them at a competitive disadvantage because companies from other countries, as well as from the host country, were not bound by the FCPA laws and could continue making whitemail payments to secure business, thus putting them at a competitive advantage.
- The accounting burden of internal controls, along with the vagueness of this section of the law, makes the MNCs' duty and liability difficult to assess.
- MNCs complain that the FCPA forces them to become political tools of the U.S. government because they have to exert its will in the world through their economic power.

1988 AMENDMENTS TO THE FCPA   In early 1981 and again in early 1983, the U.S. Senate attempted to repair some of the uncertainties associated with the FCPA. The Senate's proposed amendments were rejected by the House of Representatives. The amendment finally passed as a section of the Omnibus Trade and Competitiveness Act of 1988. The amendment clarifies various provisions of the FCPA, consolidates most of the enforcement responsibilities for bribery violations into the U.S. Department of Justice, and increases the civil and criminal penalties for violating the FCPA. Relative to the accounting aspects of the FCPA, the amendment limits future criminal liability to intentional actions to circumvent the internal accounting control system or falsify the corporation's books. With respect to payments made through third parties, the amendment eliminates the "reason to know" standard and modified the "knowing" standard. Under the act, "knowing" is defined to entail the substantial certainty or conscious disregard of a high probability that the third-party payment will become a bribe.[127]

Relative to enforcement of the FCPA, the amendment increased the civil and criminal penalties for violations. Criminal penalties were increased from $1 million to $2 million for corporations and from $10,000 to $100,000 for individuals. The maximum imprisonment remained five years. A civil penalty of $10,000 for individuals was established and may not be paid by the corporation. All jurisdictions for enforcing the antibribery provisions of the FCPA were consolidated within the Department of Justice. The SEC remained responsible for civil enforcement of the records and internal accounting control provisions of the FCPA.[128]

An Alternative Payoff Approach

Many international executives do not view the FCPA as hindering their competitiveness in the global marketplace. These executives enhance their competitiveness by improving their enterprises' technical expertise, their customer service, and their responsibility to the customer through quality. Furthermore, there are indications that the practice of bribery is not as widespread as it once was; it seems to be waning. And when these executives must make some sort of payment to obtain a favor, they do not pay "private individuals"; instead, they make payments to institutions, such as contributions to build schools, hospitals, medical clinics, or agricultural projects.[129] Payments of this nature obtain favors and goodwill for the MNC; they also improve the local situation, such as by increasing local employment. This payment approach, thus, does not improve only one person's bank account; instead, the payment is shared with the community.

Cross-National Social Responsibility

Social responsibility has been defined as "the notion that corporations have an obligation to constituent groups in society other than stockholders and beyond that prescribed by law or union contract."[130] Corporate social responsibility therefore means that a firm's actions must take into account not only the well-being of the stockholders but also the well-being of the community, the employees, and the customers. With respect to MNCs' **cross-national social responsibility,** many international business executives condone the concept of cultural relativism, while others condone the concept of universalism.

The Concept of Cultural Relativism

Cultural relativism holds that "no culture's ethics are any better than any other's."[131] Under this standard there are no international "rights" or "wrongs." Thus, if Thailand tolerates the bribery of public officials, then Thai tolerance is no worse than American or German intolerance. If Switzerland is liberal with respect to insider trading, then Swiss liberalism is no worse than American restrictiveness.[132] These executives would therefore not support the FCPA.

But the concept of cultural relativism can backfire. For example, suppose a U.S. corporation invents a product and patents it. Patent piracy is wrong (and illegal) in the United States, but it is not wrong in some nations (and if it is illegal, culturally, it is not enforced). What if a company in one of these countries pirated the patent? Would the executives in the company from which the patent was pirated simply write the loss off as, "Oh well, that's culture"? As illustration, some enterprises in China readily pirate U.S. firms' copyrighted computer software, movies, and music and put phony American labels on consumer products. If the American pirated firms' executives adhered to the cultural relativism concept, they would not complain about the Chinese firms' pirating practices because they are not viewed as being unethical in China. However, U.S. trade representatives are currently applying strong pressure on Chinese government officials to implement and enforce policies that preclude Chinese enterprises from undertaking such activities.[133] Suppose also that a U.S. MNC is manufacturing in Bangladesh using cheap child labor. Use of child labor in such a way is not tolerable in the United States, but it is tolerable in Bangladesh. What happens to the MNC when the U.S. press gets hold of the information and promulgates it among the U.S. public? Will it result in a boycott? It therefore seems that the concept of cultural relativism is often not very practical.

The Concept of Universalism

On the other hand, the concept of **universalism,** a rigid global yardstick by which to measure all moral issues (for example, the FCPA), is often not very practical either. This is because its application would show disrespect for valid cultural differences and different economic needs. For example, people in the United States do not tolerate manufacturing facilities that disperse health-damaging smog. Under the concept of universalism, it would be unethical to transfer such manufacturing facilities to another country. But in countries where people are starving, economic development may be more important than health, and such manufacturing facilities would thus be welcome. A manager guided by the cultural relativism view would export such manufacturing facilities to the starving country. But, as mentioned above, it is likely to backfire.

Thus, developing, implementing, and controlling cross-cultural business ethics and social responsibility programs is an enormous challenge confronting the managers of MNCs. The problem is enlarged by the press sometimes persuading MNCs to impose their social responsibility on their manufacturing subcontractors. For example, **Starbucks Coffee** has agreed to adopt a "code of conduct" that must be adhered to by its coffee suppliers and may help workers in Guatemala and other Third World nations. Starbucks' management made the decision after stores in British Columbia, Canada, and the U.S. were targeted in a February 1995 leafletting blitz. The protesters were concerned about "harsh working conditions, paltry pay, and human rights violations on Guatemalan coffee plantations."[134] The press therefore often asks MNCs to reject the concept of cultural relativism and apply the concept of universalism.

Toward the Globalization of Business Ethics

The U.S. approach to business ethics is unique. In comparison with other capitalistic societies, it is more individualistic, legalistic, and universalistic.[135] In other words, issues of business ethics are far more visible in the United States than they are in other capitalistic societies. This may be because there are far more laws regulating business in the United States than there are in other capitalistic countries. Therefore, the American public reads and hears far more about business misconduct than do people in other countries. Hence, the "**ethics gap**" between the United States and the rest of the developed world is considerably large.[136]

The Impact of Culture on the Business Ethics Visibility Gap

The United States is one of the most individualistic cultures in the world. People's decisions in individualistic cultures tend to be guided by self-interests, as opposed to group interests. On the other hand, managers in group-oriented cultures tend to reflect less their personal moral guidance and more their shared understanding of the nature and scope of the corporation's responsibilities—and the enterprise's moral expectations are shaped by the norms of the community, not the personal values and reflections of the individual.[137] This helps explain why there are far more laws regulating business in the United States than there are in other advanced nations, and it helps explain why there is such a large business ethics gap between the United States and other nations.

This suggests that globalization of business ethics (application of the concept of universalism) is distant and that the concept of cultural relativism still prevails. Thus, as the integration of the global economy increases, effective international managers develop a "better appreciation of the differences in the legal and cultural context of business ethics between the United States and other capitalist nations and between Western and Asian economies as well."[138]

Business Ethics and the Internet

The **World Wide Web,** an area of the Internet, is a virtual, global, open-ended organization of interconnected information sources. It is now a quick way for companies, large or small, to market products or services globally to people who access the Internet. However, managers of such a global network are faced with the challenge of addressing the concerns of its constituents with respect to confidentiality, authenticity, and integrity, balancing security against responsiveness and performance. The system needs to be secure against malicious use, misuse, and data corruption while protecting the privacy of its users and the intellectual property of the vendors. For example, providing copyright protection for knowledge providers on the Internet is quite different from providing it to their counterparts in hardcopy publication. However, hardcopy publications do not have much protection in numerous countries. The Internet may thus be a great challenge in this respect.[139]

Ethical Issues in International Business

Just as laws differ from country to country, so does the definition of ethical behavior. In international business, "*the law is a floor for our behavior, but ethical codes and personal values call on us to exceed that which is required by law.*" When called on to evaluate a course of action according to a code of ethics or personal value system, one must consider the decision in the cultural context. In other words, what is considered appropriate behavior in one culture may not be so in another. Managers often must evaluate their actions according to ethical codes or personal values that may or may not be commonly accepted in the country in which they are operating. The following examples serve as preparation for the consideration of ethical issues:

Example 1   You have been negotiating with a representative of the Portuguese government to sell products to them for a new state building project. He arrives at your company's offices with a blank purchase order in hand. After negotiating a fixed price and delivery, he "suggests" that you prepare a price quotation on a "pro forma invoice"—at double the negotiated price. His government will pay the full amount shown on the invoice through a Portuguese bank, and your firm will pay him the difference as a "commission" in U.S. dollars deposited to his bank account in New York. He convincingly argues that this practice is customary in his country. The temptation for you might be great; the deal would be a profitable one. But would it be legal or ethical? Certainly, laws and ethical standards vary from country to country. In this example, you would have to consider the laws and ethical codes of both Portugal and the United States. Even though bribery is more common in certain other countries, this transaction would clearly be illegal under U.S. law, and you would be subject to criminal prosecution, fines, and possible imprisonment.

Example 2   Imagine that your firm enters into a contract to sell drilling equipment to a Korean company. The contract is closed while the Korean company president is visiting the U.S. plant. After closing, the Korean executive points out that all imports to Korea must be channeled through a registered "local agent." He quickly suggests that a wholly owned trading company *that he owns* could handle all of the paperwork—for a fee. Compare this with the first example. Should you comply with his request? Is it legal? If it is, is it ethical? The prudent manager will avoid potential legal liability and will also attempt to conform to what he or she deems to be ethical.

Example 3   Your company intends to locate a plant in Mexico for the assembly of automobile engines. If the plant were in the United States, the laws require considerable expenditures for environmental controls such as antipollution equipment. United States law also mandates expensive safeguards to protect the health and safety of U.S. workers, as well as the added cost of minimum wage rules, social security contributions, health care, and other employee benefits. Assume that Mexican law is not so strict and that operating costs there are less as a result. To what extent should you conform to the legal standards applicable in the United States? Is it ethical not to? Indeed, should any firm operating in a host country carry with it the ethical codes of its home country? How does the international manager justify decisions in cross-cultural situations?

Example 4   You are an international manager for a U.S. apparel designer that sells to major U.S. department stores and retailers. Several years ago your firm decided to have clothing sewn in India and Pakistan, which resulted in tremendous cost savings as opposed to having the work done in the United States. In making the decision, the firm considered its impact on U.S. families who depend on the income from these jobs. It opted for the cost savings, seeing its responsibility to produce a profit for shareholders as more important than providing jobs in the United States. Now, however, it finds that its contractor in India is overworking and abusing child labor in violation of internationally accepted standards for the treatment of children in the workplace. The Indian government shows little interest in policing its own labor practices. The sad story of the Indian children is run on national television and appears in the national press. If you decide to discontinue working with sewing contractors in India, would you do so to protect Indian children or because of the adverse publicity in the United States, or both? Consider the company's course of action and how you should react now.

International Issues

The International Business Environment

This section analyzes the international business environment by looking at political, financial, societal, and technological conditions of change and providing a glimpse of possible future developments as envisioned by an international panel of experts.[140] The impact of these factors on doing business abroad, on international trade relations, and on government policy is of particular interest to the international business manager.

The Political Environment

The international political environment is undergoing a substantial transformation characterized by the reshaping of existing political blocks, the formation of new groupings, and the breakup of old coalitions.

Planned Versus Market Economies

The second half of the last century was shaped by the political, economic, and military competition between the United States and the Soviet Union which resulted in the creation of two virtually separate economic systems. This key adversarial posture has now largely disappeared, with market-based economic thinking emerging as the frontrunner. Virtually all of the former centrally planned economies are undergoing a transition with the goal of becoming market oriented.

International business has made important contributions to this transition process. Trade and investment have offered the populace in these nations a new perspective, new choices, new jobs, and new alternatives for marketing their products and services. At the same time, the bringing together of two separate economic and business systems has resulted in new, and sometimes devastating competition, a loss of government-ordained trade relationships, and substantial dislocations and pain during the adjustment process.

Over the next five years the countries of Eastern and Central Europe will continue to be attractive for international investment due to relatively low labor cost, low-priced input factors, and large unused production capacities. This attractiveness, however, will translate mainly into growing investment from Western Europe for reasons of geographic proximity and attractive outsourcing opportunities.[141] Even these investment flows, however, are likely to take place only selectively, resulting in very unbalanced economic conditions in the region. Firms and governments outside of Western Europe are likely to be much more reluctant to invest in Eastern Europe. This aversion is not so much driven by caution about a potential resurgence of Communism or fear of economic and political instability, but mainly due to attractive investment alternatives elsewhere.

Russia and the other nations of the former Soviet Union are seen as facing great difficulty. The collapse of the ruble and repeated setbacks in economic development have led to a paradox faced by Russia and the world. Russia today is the world's sixth most populous country, a key nuclear power, and the holder of a permanent seat on the U.N. Security Council. Its economic health and creditworthiness, however, place it in the same tier of global powers as the Sudan and Afghanistan. Economic recovery and participation in world trade are likely to be very gradual. In part, the slowness is a function of self-imposed constraints due to domestic fears of outsiders. In addition, if financial inflows into the region are to make a difference, governments need to find market-oriented ways to reduce the flight of capital abroad.

Overall, many business activities will be subject to regional economic and political instability, increasing the risk of international business partners. Progress toward the institution of market-based economies may be halted or even reversed as large population segments are exposed to growing hardship during the transformation process. It will be important to develop institutions and processes internally which assure domestic and foreign investors that there will be protection from public and private corruption and respect for property rights and contractual arrangements.

Emerging Markets

Much of the growth of the global economy will be fueled by the emerging markets of Latin America and the Asia Pacific region. In Latin America, the international business climate will improve due to economic integration, market liberalization, and privatization. In spite of some inefficiencies, Mercosur continues to bring countries closer together and encourages their collaboration. There is also the increasing likelihood of a Free Trade Arrangement of the Americas, which will align the common economic interests of countries in South, Central, and North America. Due to substantial natural resources and relatively low cost of production, an increased flow of foreign direct investment and trade activity is forecast, emanating not only from the United States, but also from Europe and Japan.

The Asia Pacific region is likely to regain its growth in the next decade. For the industrialized nations, this development will offer a significant opportunity for exports and investment, but it will also diminish, in the longer term, the basis for their status and influence in the world economy. While the nations in the region are likely to collaborate, they are not expected to form a bloc of the same type as the European Union or NAFTA. Rather, their relationship is likely to be defined in terms of trade and investment flows (for example, Japan) and social contacts (for example, the Chinese business community). A cohesive bloc may only emerge as a reaction to a perceived threat by other major blocs.

China's emergence is likely to be the economic event of the decade. Despite innumerable risks, experts see Chinese pragmatism prevailing. Companies already present in the market and those willing to make significant investments are likely to be the main beneficiaries of growth. Long-term commitment, willingness to transfer technology, and an ability to partner either with local firms through joint ventures or with overseas Chinese-run firms are considered crucial for success. The strategic impact of Chinese trade participation is also likely to change. With membership in the World Trade Organization, the recipients of Chinese goods will be much less able to exclude them with higher tariffs or nontariff barriers. China, in turn, is likely to assume a much higher profile in its trading activities. For example, rather than be the supplier of goods which are then marketed internationally under a Japanese or U.S. label, Chinese firms will increasingly develop their own brand names and fight for their own name recognition, customer loyalty, and market share.[142]

Among the other promising emerging markets are Korea and India. Korea could emerge as a participant in worldwide competition, while India is considered more important for the size of its potential market. Korean firms must still improve their ability to adopt a global mindset. Some experts are also concerned about the chaebols status as the Korean economy becomes democratized. In addition, the possible impact of the reunification of the Korean peninsula on the country's globalization efforts must be taken into account.

With the considerable liberalization that took place in India during the 1990s, many expect it to offer major international marketing opportunities due to its size, its significant natural wealth, and its large, highly educated middle class. While many experts believe that political conflict, both domestic and regional, nationalism, and class structure may temper the ability of Indian companies to emerge as a worldwide competitive force, there is strong agreement that India's disproportionately large and specialized workforce in engineering and computer sciences makes the nation a power to be reckoned with.

Overall, the growth potential of these emerging economies may be threatened by uncertainty in terms of international relations and domestic policies, as well as social and political dimensions, particularly those pertaining to income distribution. Concerns also exist about infrastructural inadequacies, both physical—such as transportation—and societal—such as legal systems. The consensus of experts is, however, that growth in these countries will be significant.

A Divergence of Values

It might well be that different nations or cultures become increasingly disparate in terms of values and priorities. For example, in some countries, the aim for financial progress and an improved quantitative standard of living may well give way to priorities based on religion or the environment. Even if nations share similar values, their priorities among these values may differ strongly. For example, within a market-oriented system, some countries may prioritize profits and efficiency, while others may place social harmony first, even at the cost of maintaining inefficient industries.

Such a divergence of values will require a major readjustment of the activities of the international corporation. A continuous scanning of newly emerging national values thus becomes imperative for the international executive.

The International Financial Environment

Debt constraints and low commodity prices create slow growth prospects for many developing countries. They will be forced to reduce their levels of imports and to exert more pressure on industrialized nations to open up their markets. Even if the markets are opened, however, demand for most primary products will be far lower than supply. Ensuing competition for market share will therefore continue to depress prices.

Developed nations have a strong incentive to help the debtor nations. The incentive consists of the market opportunities that economically healthy developing countries can offer and of national security concerns. As a result, industrialized nations may very well find that funds transfers to debtor nations, accompanied by debt-relief measures such as debt forgiveness, are necessary to achieve economic stimulation at home.

The dollar will remain one of the major international currencies with little probability of gold returning to its former status in the near future. However, some international transaction volume in both trade and finance is increasingly likely to be denominated in nondollar terms, using particularly the euro. The system of floating currencies will likely continue, with occasional attempts by nations to manage exchange rate relationships or at least reduce the volatility of swings in currency values. However, given the vast flows of financial resources across borders, it would appear that market forces rather than government action will be the key determinant of a currency's value. Factors such as investor trust, economic conditions, earnings perceptions, and political stability are therefore likely to have a much greater effect on the international value of currencies than domestic monetary and fiscal experimentation.

Given the close links among financial markets, shocks in one market will quickly translate into rapid shifts in others and easily overpower the financial resources of individual governments. Even if there should be a decision by governments to pursue closely coordinated fiscal and monetary policies, they are unlikely to be able to negate long-term market effects in response to changes in economic fundamentals.

Since foreign creditors expect a return on their investment, a substantial portion of future U.S. international trade activity will have to be devoted to generating sufficient funds for such repayment. For example, at an assumed interest rate or rate of return of 10%, the international U.S. debt level—without any growth—would require the annual payment of $200 billion, which amounts to almost 20% of current U.S. exports. Therefore, it seems highly likely that international business will become a greater priority than it is today and will serve as a source of major economic growth for firms in the United States.

To some degree, foreign holders of dollars may also choose to convert their financial holdings into real property and investments in the United States. This will result in an entirely new pluralism in U.S. society. It will become increasingly difficult and, perhaps, even unnecessary to distinguish between domestic and foreign products—as is already the case with Hondas made in Ohio. Senators and members of Congress, governors, municipalities, and unions will gradually be faced with conflicting concerns in trying to develop a national consensus on international trade and investment. National security issues may also be raised as major industries become majority owned by foreign firms.

Industrialized countries are likely to attempt to narrow the domestic gap between savings and investments through fiscal policies. Without concurrent restrictions on international capital flows, such policies are likely to meet with only limited success. Lending institutions can be expected to become more conservative in their financing, a move that may hit smaller firms and developing countries the hardest. At the same time, the entire financial sector is likely to face continuous integration, ongoing bank acquisitions, and a reduction in financial intermediaries. Customers will be able to assert their independence by increasingly being able to present their financial needs globally and directly to financial markets, and thus obtaining better access to financial products and providers.

The Effects of Population Shifts

The population discrepancy between less-developed nations and the industrialized countries will continue to increase. In the industrialized world, a **population increase** will become a national priority, given the fact that in many countries, particularly in Western Europe, the population is shrinking. The shrinkage may lead to labor shortages and to major societal difficulties when a shrinking number of workers has to provide for a growing elderly population.

In the developing world, **population stabilization** will continue to be one of the major challenges of governmental policy. In spite of well-intentioned economic planning, continued rapid increases in population will make it more difficult to ensure that the pace of economic development exceeds population growth. If the standard of living of a nation is determined by dividing the GNP by its population, any increase in the denominator will require equal increases in the numerator to maintain the standard of living. With an annual increase in the world population of 100 million people, the task is daunting. It becomes even more complex when one considers that within countries with high population increases, large migration flows take place from rural to urban areas. As a result, by the end of this decade, most of the world's ten largest metropolitan areas will be in the developing world.[143]

The Technological Environment

The concept of the global village is commonly accepted today and indicates the importance of communication. For both consumer services and business-to-business relations, the Internet is democratizing global business. It has made it easier for new global retail brands—like **amazon.com** and **CDnow**—to emerge. The Internet is also helping specialists like Australia's high sensitivity hearing aids manufacturer **Cochlear** to reach target customers around the world without having to invest in a distribution network in each country. The ability to reach a worldwide audience economically via the Internet spells success for niche marketers who could never make money by just servicing their niches in the domestic market. The Internet also allows customers, especially those in emerging markets, to access global brands at more competitive prices than those offered by exclusive national distributors.[144]

Starting a new business will be much easier, allowing a far greater number of suppliers to enter a market. Small- and medium-sized enterprises, as well as large multinational corporations, will now be full participants in the global marketplace. Businesses in developing countries can now overcome many of the obstacles of infrastructure and transport that limited their economic potential in the past. The global services economy will be a knowledge-based economy and its most precious resource will be information and ideas. Unlike the classical factors of production—land, labor, and capital—information and knowledge are not bound to any region or country but are almost infinitely mobile and infinitely capable of expansion.[145] This wide availability, of course, also brings new risks to firms. For example, unlike the past, today one complaint can easily be developed into millions of complaints by e-mail.[146] In consequence, firms are subject to much more scrutiny and customer response on an international level.

Overall, these new technologies, in turn, offer exciting new opportunities to conduct international business. High technology will also be one of the more volatile and controversial areas of economic activity internationally. Developments in biotechnology are already transforming agriculture, medicine, and chemistry. Chemically engineered foods, patient-specific pharmaceuticals, gene therapy, and even genetically engineered organs are on the horizon. Innovations such as these will change what we eat, how we treat illness, and how we evolve as a civilization.[147] However, skepticism of such technological innovations is rampant. In many instances, people are opposed to such changes due to religious or cultural reasons, or simply because they do not want to be exposed to such "artificial" products. Achieving agreement on what constitutes safe products and procedures, of defining the border between what is natural and what is not, will constitute one of the great areas of debate in the years to come. Firms and their managers must remain keenly aware of popular perceptions and misperceptions and of government regulations in order to remain successful participants in markets.

Even firms and countries that are at the leading edge of technology will find it increasingly difficult to marshal the funds necessary for further advancements. For example, investments in semiconductor technology are measured in billions rather than millions of dollars and do not bring any assurance of success. Not to engage in the race, however, will mean falling behind quickly in all areas of manufacturing when virtually every industrial and consumer product is "smart" due to its chip technology.

The Effects of Changes in Trade Relations

The formation of the World Trade Organization (WTO) has brought to conclusion a lengthy and sometimes acrimonious round of global trade negotiations. However, key disagreements among major trading partners are likely to persist. Ongoing major imbalances in trade flows will tempt nations to apply their own national trade remedies, particularly in the antidumping field. Even though WTO rules permit for a retaliation against unfair trade practices, such actions would only result in an ever-increasing spiral of adverse trade relations.

A key question will be whether nations are willing to abrogate some of their sovereignty even during difficult economic times. An affirmative answer will strengthen the multilateral trade system and enhance the flow of trade. However, if key trading nations resort to the development of insidious nontariff barriers, unilateral actions, and bilateral negotiations, protectionism will increase on a global scale and the volume of international trade is likely to decline. The danger is real. Popular support for international trade agreements appears to be on the wane.

International trade relations also will be shaped by new participants whose market entry will restructure the composition of global trade. For example, new players with exceptionally large productive potential, such as the People's Republic of China and Central Europe will substantially alter world trade flows. And while both governments and firms will be required to change many trading policies and practices as a result, they will also benefit in terms of market opportunities and sourcing alternatives.

Finally, the efforts of governments to achieve self-sufficiency in economic sectors, particularly in agriculture and heavy industries, have ensured the creation of long-term, worldwide oversupply of some commodities and products, many of which historically had been traded widely. As a result, after some period of intense market share competition aided by subsidies and governmental support, a gradual and painful restructuring of these economic sectors will have to take place. This will be particularly true for agricultural cash crops such as wheat, corn, and dairy products and industrial products such as steel, chemicals, and automobiles.

Government Policy

International trade activity now affects domestic policy more than ever. For example, trade flows can cause major structural shifts in employment. Links between industries spread these effects throughout the economy. Fewer domestically produced automobiles will affect the activities of the steel industry. Shifts in the sourcing of textiles will affect the cotton industry. Global productivity gains and competitive pressures will force many industries to restructure their activities. In such circumstances, industries are likely to ask their governments to help in their restructuring efforts. Often, such assistance includes a built-in tendency toward protectionist action.

Governmental policymakers must take into account the international repercussions of domestic legislation. For example, in imposing a special surcharge tax on the chemical industry designed to provide for the cleanup of toxic waste products, they need to consider its repercussions on the international competitiveness of the chemical industry. Similarly, current laws such as antitrust legislation need to be reviewed if the laws hinder the international competitiveness of domestic firms.

Policymakers also need a better understanding of the nature of the international trade issues confronting them. Most countries today face both short-term and long-term trade problems. Trade balance issues, for example, are short term in nature, while competitiveness issues are much more long term. All too often, however, short-term issues are attacked with long-term **trade policy measures,** and vice versa. In the United States, for example, the desire to "level the international playing field" with mechanisms such as vigorous implementation of import restrictions or voluntary restraint agreements may serve long-term competitiveness well, but it does little to alleviate the publicly perceived problem of the trade deficit. Similarly, a further opening of Japan's market to foreign corporations will have only a minor immediate effect on that country's trade surplus or the trading partners' deficit. Yet it is the expectation and hope of many in both the public and the private sectors that such instant changes will occur.[148] For the sake of the credibility of policymakers, it therefore becomes imperative to precisely identify the nature of the problem and to design and use policy measures that are appropriate for its resolution.

In the years to come, governments will be faced with an accelerating technological race and with emerging problems that seem insurmountable by individual firms alone, such as pollution of the environment and global warming. As market gaps emerge and time becomes crucial, both governments and the private sector will find that even if the private sector knows that a lighthouse is needed, it may still be difficult, time-consuming, and maybe even impossible to build one with private funds alone. As a result, it becomes increasingly important for government to work closely with the business sector to identify market gaps and to devise market-oriented ways of filling them. The international business manager in turn will have to spend more time and effort dealing with governments and with macro rather than micro issues.

The Future of International Business Management

Global change results in an increase in risk. One shortsighted alternative for risk-averse managers would be the termination of international activities altogether. However, businesses will not achieve long-term success by engaging only in risk-free actions. Further, other factors make the pursuit of international business mandatory.

International markets remain a source of high profits, as a quick look at a list of multinational firms would show.[149] International activities help cushion slack in domestic sales resulting from recessionary or adverse domestic conditions and may be crucial to the very survival of the firm. International markets also provide firms with foreign experience that helps them compete more successfully with foreign firms in the domestic market.

International Planning and Research

Firms must continue to serve customers well to be active participants in the international marketplace. One major change that will come about is that the international manager will need to respond to general governmental concerns to a greater degree when planning a business strategy. Further, societal concern about macro problems needs to be taken into account directly and quickly because societies have come to expect more social responsibility from corporations. Taking on a leadership role regarding social causes may also benefit corporations' bottom lines, since consumers appear more willing than ever to act as significant pressure points for policy changes and to pay for their social concerns. Therefore, reputation management, or the art of building reputation as a corporate asset, is likely to gain prominence in the years ahead as the pressure on corporations to be good corporate citizens grows.[150]

Increased competition in international markets will create a need for more niches in which firms can create a distinct international competence. As a result, increased specialization and segmentation will let firms fill very narrow and specific demands or resolve very specific problems for their international customers. Identifying and filling the niches will be easier in the future because of the greater availability of international research tools and information. The key challenge to global firms will be to build and manage decision-making processes that allow quick responses to multiple changing environmental demands. This capability is important since firms face a growing need for worldwide coordination and integration of internal activities, such as logistics and operations, while being confronted with the need for greater national differentiation and responsiveness at the customer level.[151]

In spite of the frequent short-term orientation by corporations and investors, companies will need to learn to prepare for long-term horizons. Particularly in an environment of heated competition and technological battles, of large projects and slow payoffs, companies, their stakeholders, and governments will need to find avenues that not only permit but encourage the development of strategic perspectives.

Governments both at home and abroad will demand that private business practices not increase public costs and that businesses serve customers equally and nondiscriminately. The concept directly counters the desire to serve first the markets that are most profitable and least costly. International executives will therefore be torn in two directions. To provide results acceptable to governments, customers, and to the societies they serve, they must walk a fine line, balancing the public and the private good.

International Product Policy

One key issue affecting product planning will be environmental concern. Major growth in public attention paid to the natural environment, environmental pollution, and global warming will provide many new product opportunities and affect existing products to a large degree. For example, manufacturers will increasingly be expected to take responsibility for their products from cradle to grave, and be intimately involved in product disposal and recycling.

Firms will therefore have to plan for a final stage in the product life cycle, the "postmortem" stage, during which a firm continues to expend further corporate investment and management attention, even though the product may have been terminated some time ago.[152]

Although some consumers show a growing interest in truly "natural" products, even if they are less convenient, consumers in most industrialized nations will require products that are environmentally friendly but at the same time do not require too much compromise on performance and value.

Worldwide introduction of products will occur much more rapidly in the future. Already, international product life cycles have accelerated substantially. Whereas product introduction could previously be spread out over several years, firms now must prepare for product life cycles that can be measured in months or even weeks.[153] As a result, firms must design products and plan even their domestic marketing strategies with the international product cycle in mind. Product introduction will grow more complex, more expensive, and more risky, yet the rewards to be reaped from a successful product will have to be accumulated more quickly.

Early incorporation of the global dimension into product planning, however, does not point toward increased standardization. On the contrary, companies will have to be ready to deliver more mass customization. Customers are no longer satisfied with simply having a product: they want it to precisely meet their needs and preferences. **Mass customization** requires working with existing product technology, often in modular form, to create specific product bundles for a particular customer, resulting in tailor-made jeans or a customized car.

Factor endowment advantages have a significant impact on the decisions of international executives. Nations with low production costs will be able to replicate products more quickly and cheaply. Countries such as China, India, Israel, and the Philippines offer large pools of skilled people at labor rates much lower than in Europe, Japan, or the United States. All this talent also results in a much wider dissemination of technological creativity, a factor that will affect the innovative capability of firms. For example, in 2000, almost half of all the patents in the United States were granted to foreign entities.

This indicates that firms need to make nondomestic know-how part of their production strategies, or they need to develop consistent comparative advantages in production technology in order to stay ahead of the game. Similarly, workers engaged in the productive process must attempt, through training and skill enhancement, to stay ahead of foreign workers who are willing to charge less for their time.

An increase will occur in the trend toward strategic alliances, or partnerings, permitting the formation of collaborative arrangements between firms. These alliances will enable firms to take risks that they could not afford to take alone, facilitate technological advancement, and ensure continued international market access. These partners do not need to be large in order to make a major contribution. Depending on the type of product, even small firms can serve as coordinating subcontractors and collaborate in product and service development, production, and distribution.

International Communications

The advances made in international communications will also have a profound impact on international management. Entire industries are becoming more footloose in their operations; that is, they are less tied to their current location in their interaction with markets. Most affected by communications advances will be members of the services sector. For example, **Best Western Hotels** in the United States has channeled its entire reservation system through a toll-free number that is being serviced out of the prison system in Utah. Companies could even concentrate their communications activities in other countries. Communications for worldwide operations, for example, could easily be located in Africa or Asia without impairing international corporate activities.

For manufacturers, staff in different countries can not only talk together but can also share pictures and data on their computer screens. These simultaneous interactions with different parts of the world will strengthen research and development efforts. Faster knowledge transfer will allow for the concentration of product expertise, increased division of labor, and a proliferation of global operations.

International Distribution

Innovative distribution approaches will determine new ways of serving markets. For example, television, through QVC, has already created a shopping mall available in more than 60 million homes. The use of the Internet offers new distribution alternatives. For example, self-sustaining consumer distributor relationships emerge through, say, refrigerators that report directly to grocery store computers that they are running low on supplies and require a home delivery billed to the customer's account. Firms that are not part of such a system will simply not be able to have their offer considered for the transaction.

The link to distribution systems will also be crucial to international firms on the business-to-business level. As large retailers develop sophisticated inventory tracking and reordering systems, only the firms able to interact with such systems will remain eligible suppliers. Therefore, firms need to create their own distribution systems that are able to respond to just-in-time (JIT) and direct-order entry requirements around the globe.

More sophisticated distribution systems will, at the same time, introduce new uncertainties and fragilities into corporate planning. For example, the development of just-in-time delivery systems makes firms more efficient yet, on an international basis, also exposes them to more risk due to distribution interruptions. A strike in a faraway country may therefore be newly significant for a company that depends on the timely delivery of supplies.

International Pricing

International price competition will become increasingly heated. As their distribution spreads throughout the world, many products will take on commodity characteristics, as semiconductors did in the 1980s. Therefore, small price differentials per unit may become crucial in making an international sale. However, since many new products and technologies will address completely new needs, **forward pricing,** which distributes development expenses over the planned or anticipated volume of sales, will become increasingly difficult and controversial as demand levels are impossible to predict with any kind of accuracy.

Even for consumer products, price competition will be substantial. Because of the increased dissemination of technology, the firm that introduces a product will no longer be able to justify higher prices for long; domestically produced products will soon be of similar quality. As a result, exchange rate movements may play more significant roles in maintaining the competitiveness of the international firm. Firms can be expected to prevail on their government to manage the country's currency to maintain a favorable exchange rate. Technology also allows much closer interaction on pricing between producer and customer. The success of electronic commerce providers such as **e-bay** (www.ebay.com) or www.priceline.com demonstrates how auctioning and bidding, alone or in competition with others, offers new perspectives on the global price mechanism.

Through subsidization, targeting, government contracts, or other hidden forms of support, nations will attempt to stimulate their international competitiveness. Due to the price sensitivity of many products, the international business manager will be forced to identify such unfair practices quickly, communicate them to his or her government, and insist on either similar benefits or government action to create an internationally level playing field.

At the same time, many firms will work hard to reduce the price sensitivity of their customers. By developing relationships with their markets rather than just carrying out transactions, other dimensions such as loyalty, consistency, the cost of shifting suppliers, and responsiveness to client needs may become much more important than price in future competition.

Module 1000 Glossary

A

Abandoned product ranges The outcome of a firm narrowing its range of products to obtain economies of scale, which provides opportunities for other firms to enter the markets for the abandoned products.

Absolute advantage The ability to produce a good or service more cheaply than it can be produced elsewhere.

Accounting diversity The range of differences in national accounting practices.

Acculturation The process of adjusting and adapting to a specific culture other than one's own.

Act of state doctrine Rule that a court should not question the validity of actions taken by a foreign government in its own country.

Ad hoc groups Problem-specific teams or groups consisting of individuals who possess the relevant knowledge to address a particular organizational problem.

Adaptability screening A selection procedure that usually involves interviewing both the candidate for an overseas assignment and his or her family members to determine how well they are likely to adapt to another culture.

Adaptable management A firm's management is able to adapt managerial techniques to the unique needs of specific countries.

Adaptation Refers to the stage in the expatriation process in which the expatriate must learn to cope with cultures, laws, political systems, legal processes, and other subtleties that are different from his or her own.

Adaptation problems Difficulties that arise for expatriates during the adaptation process. They are especially common when the physical and sociocultural environments are at odds with the expatriate's own value system and living habits.

Adaptive transformative innovations Modify and adjust existing modern technologies (for example, in farming, a modern, more efficient tractor replaces an older, less efficient model).

Agent A representative or intermediary for the firm that works to develop business and sales strategies and that develops contacts.

Airfreight Transport of goods by air; accounts for less than one percent of the total volume of international shipments, but more than 20% of value.

Alliances Firms with unique strengths that join to be more effective and efficient than their competitors.

Allocation mentality The tradition of acquiring resources based not on what is needed but on what is available.

American-based leadership and motivation theories Traditionally, these theories advance the notion that participative leadership behavior is more effective than authoritative leadership behavior. Popular theories include McGregor's *Theory X and Theory Y Managers* and Likert's *System 4 Management*.

American terms Quoting a currency rate as the U.S. dollar against a country's currency (for example, U.S. dollars/yen).

Analogy A method for estimating market potential when data for the particular market do not exist.

Antidumping Laws that many countries use to impose tariffs on foreign imports. They are designed to help domestic industries that are injured by unfair competition from abroad due to imported products being sold at less than fair market value.

Antiplanning Belief that any attempt to lay out specific and "rational" plans is either foolish or dangerous and downright evil. Correct approach is to live in existing systems, react in terms of one's own experience, and not try to change them by means of some grandiose scheme or mathematical model.

Antitrust laws Laws that prohibit monopolies, restraint of trade, and conspiracies to inhibit competition. Apply to unfair methods of competition that have a direct, substantial, and reasonably foreseeable effect on the domestic, import, or export commerce of the United States.

Arbitration The procedure for settling a dispute in which an objective third party hears both sides and makes a decision; a procedure for resolving conflict in the international business arena through the use of intermediaries such as representatives of chambers of commerce, trade associations, or third-country institutions.

Area expertise A knowledge of the basic systems in a particular region or market.

Area structure An organizational structure in which geographic divisions are responsible for all manufacturing and marketing in their respective areas.

Area studies Training programs that provide factual preparation prior to an overseas assignment.

Arm's-length price A price that unrelated parties would have reached.

Autarky Self-sufficiency: a country that is not participating in international trade.

Authoritative decision making Refers to a style of decision making in which the leader simply makes a decision and instructs followers what to do without consulting or involving them in the decision-making process.

Average cost method An accounting principle by which the value of inventory is estimated as the average cost of the items in inventory.

B

Backtranslation The retranslation of text to the original language by a different person than the one who made the first translation. Useful to find translation errors.

Backward innovation The development of a drastically simplified version of a product.

Badwill What international corporations create when they exploit foreign markets without sharing benefits with locals.

Balance of payments (BOP) A statement of all transactions between one country and the rest of the world during a given period; a record of flows of goods, services, and investments across borders.

Bank draft A financial withdrawal document drawn against a bank.

Barriers Elements that inhibit the implementation and maintenance of various business programs and strategies.

Barter A direct exchange of goods of approximately equal value, with no money involved.

Base salary Salary not including special payments such as allowances paid during overseas assignments.

Bearer bond A bond owned officially by whoever is holding it.

Bilateral negotiations Negotiations carried out between two nations focusing only on their interests.

Bill of lading A contract between an exporter and a carrier indicating that the carrier has accepted responsibility for the goods and will provide transportation in return for payment.

Black hole The situation that arises when an international marketer has a low-competence subsidiary—or none at all—in a highly strategic market.

Body language Includes eye contact, physical distance and touching, hand movements, pointing, and facial expressions.

Boycott An organized effort to refrain from conducting business with a particular seller of goods or services; used in the international arena for political or economic reasons.

Brain drain A migration of professional people from one country to another, usually for the purpose of improving their incomes or living conditions.

Bretton Woods Agreement An agreement reached in 1944 among finance ministers of 45 Western nations to establish a system of fixed exchange rates.

Bribery The use of payments or favors to obtain some right or benefit to which the briber has no legal right; a criminal offense in the United States but a way of life in many countries.

Buffer stock Stock of a commodity kept on hand to prevent a shortage in times of unexpectedly great demand; under international commodity and price agreements, the stock controlled by an elected or appointed manager for the purpose of managing the price of the commodity.

Bulk service Ocean shipping provided on contract either for individual voyages or for prolonged periods of time.

Business ethics gap Compared with other capitalistic societies, the approach to ethics is more individualistic, legalistic, and universalistic in the United States.

Business ethics visibility gap The people of the United States read and hear far more about business misconduct than people in other countries.

Bustarella Italian term for bribery/payoffs.

Buy-back A refinement of simple barter with one party supplying technology or equipment that enables the other party to produce goods, which are then used to pay for the technology or equipment that was supplied.

C

Capital account An account in the BOP statement that records transactions involving borrowing, lending, and investing across borders. It is also called financial account.

Capital budget The financial evaluation of a proposed investment to determine whether the expected returns are sufficient to justify the investment expenses.

Capital flight The flow of private funds abroad because investors believe that the return on investment or the safety of capital is not sufficiently ensured in their own countries.

Caribbean Basin Initiative (CBI) Extended trade preferences to Caribbean countries and granted them special access to the markets of the United States.

Carriage and insurance paid to (CIP) The price quoted by an exporter for shipments not involving waterway transport, including insurance.

Carriage paid to (CPT) The price quoted by an exporter for shipments not involving waterway transport, not including insurance.

Cartels Groups of private businesses that agree to set prices, share markets, and control production. An association of producers of a particular good, consisting either of private firms or of nations, formed for the purpose of suppressing the market forces affecting prices.

Cash pooling Used by multinational firms to centralize individual units' cash flows, resulting in less spending or foregone interest unnecessary cash balances.

Center of excellence The location of product development outside the home country because of an advantage of skills.

Centralization The concentrating of control and strategic decision making at headquarters. Most of the important decisions relative to local matters are made by headquarters management rather than by managers in the local subsidiary.

Central plan The economic plan for the nation devised by the government of a socialist state; often a five-year plan that stipulated the quantities of industrial goods to be produced.

Change agent A person or institution who facilitates change in a firm or in a host country.

Channel design The length and width of the distribution channel.

Chief learning officer Responsible for developing on a worldwide scale the organization's human talent and for using the human knowledge present in the organization.

Circular cultures Belief that since individuals can see what has happened in the past, their past is ahead of them, and since they cannot see into the future, their future is behind them.

CISG United Nations Convention on Contracts for the International Sales of Goods governs all contracts for international sales of goods between parties located in different nations that have ratified the CISG.

Clusters Geographic concentrations of interconnected companies and institutions in a particular field.

Code law Law based on a comprehensive set of written statutes.

Codetermination A management approach in which employees are represented on supervisory boards to facilitate communication and collaboration between management and labor.

Collective In stage six of the social interaction paradigm, leaders look for opportunities that benefit the group as a whole.

Commercial invoice A bill for transported goods that describes the merchandise and its total cost and lists the addresses of the shipper and seller and delivery and payment terms.

Commercial Service A department of the U.S. Department of Commerce that gathers information and assists business executives in business abroad.

Commitment An important reciprocal relationship in which the employee is committed to the organization and its goals and is matched by the employer's commitment to the employee's welfare.

Committee on Foreign Investments in the United States (CFIUS) A federal committee, chaired by the U.S. Treasury, with the responsibility to review major foreign investments to determine whether national security or related concerns are at stake.

Commodity price agreement An agreement involving both buyers and sellers to manage the price of a particular commodity, but often only when the price moves outside a predetermined range.

Common agricultural policy (CAP) An integrated system of subsidies and rebates applied to agricultural interests in the European Union.

Common law Law based on tradition and depending less on written statutes and codes than on precedent and custom—used in the United States.

Common market A group of countries that agree to remove all barriers to trade among members, to establish a common trade policy with respect to nonmembers, and also to allow mobility for factors of production—labor, capital, and technology.

Communication services Services that are provided in the areas of videotext, home banking, and home shopping, among others.

Comparative advantage The ability to produce a good or service more cheaply, relative to other goods and services, than is possible in other countries.

Competitive advantage The ability to produce a good or service more cheaply than other countries due to favorable factor conditions and demand conditions, strong related and supporting industries, and favorable firm strategy, structure, and rivalry conditions.

Competitive assessment A research process that consists of matching markets to corporate strengths and providing an analysis of the best potential for specific offerings.

Competitive environment This environment is affected by bribery and the existence of cartels.

Composition of trade The ratio of primary commodities to manufactured goods in a country's trade.

Concentration strategy The market expansion policy that involves concentrating on a small number of markets.

Confiscation Governmental taking of foreign-owned property without payment (or for a highly inadequate payment) or for a nonpublic purpose.

Confucianism A system of practical ethics based on a set of pragmatic rules for daily life derived from experience.

Consensus Employed in choice and implementation tactics within collectivist cultures to maintain harmony and unity.

Consulting services Services that are provided in the areas of management expertise on such issues as transportation and logistics.

Container ships Ships designed to carry standardized containers, which greatly facilitate loading and unloading as well as intermodal transfers.

Contingency decision making A style of decision making committed to recognizing the uniqueness of different situations and therefore using different approaches when confronting varying situations, cultures, and so on.

Contract enforcement Usually, a contract entered into by firms from different nations stipulates whose law is applied in the event of default. However, some countries' legal systems mandate that the laws of the nation where the contract was signed shall be applied. Other legal systems mandate that the laws of the country where the contract was executed shall be applied.

Contract manufacturing Outsourcing the actual production of goods so that the corporation can focus on research, development, and marketing.

Contractual alliances Many enterprises enter foreign markets via non–equity-based joint ventures, often referred to as contractual alliances or strategic alliances.

Contractual hedging A multinational firm's use of contracts to minimize its transaction exposure.

Contributor A national subsidiary with a distinctive competence, such as product development.

Control Refers to restrictions on what a foreign investor may own or control in another country.

Conversational principles Those principles governing verbal and nonverbal communication applicable in all aspects of cross-cultural communication.

Coordinated decentralization The providing of overall corporate strategy by headquarters while granting subsidiaries the freedom to implement it within established ranges.

Coordinated intervention A currency value management method whereby the central banks of the major nations simultaneously intervene in the currency markets, hoping to change a currency's value.

Corporate culture Refers to an organization's practice, such as its symbols, heroes, and rituals, and its values, such as its employees' perception of good/evil, beautiful/ugly, normal/abnormal, and rational/irrational. The practice aspects differ from corporation to corporation within a national culture, and the value aspects vary from country to country.

Corporate income tax A tax applied to all residual earnings, regardless of what is retained or what is distributed as dividends.

Corporate social responsibility An objective to respond appropriately everywhere possible to societal expectations and environmental needs.

Correspondent banks Banks located in different countries and unrelated by ownership that have a reciprocal agreement to provide services to each other's customers.

Corruption Payments or favors made to officials in return for services.

Cost and freight (CFR) Seller quotes a price for the goods, including the cost of transportation to the named port of debarkation. Cost and choice of insurance are left to the buyer.

Cost, insurance, and freight (CIF) Seller quotes a price including insurance, all transportation, and miscellaneous charges to the point of debarkation from the vessel or aircraft.

Cost leadership A pricing tactic where a company offers an identical product or service at a lower cost than the competition.

Cost of communication The cost of communicating electronically or by telephone with other locations. These costs have been drastically reduced through the use of fiber-optic cables.

Cost of living allowance (COLA) An allowance paid during assignment overseas to enable the employee to maintain the same standard of living as at home.

Cost-plus method A pricing policy in which there is a full allocation of foreign and domestic costs to the product.

Counterpurchase A refinement of simple barter that unlinks the timing of the two transactions.

Countertrade A buyer of a product pays the seller with another product of the equivalent monetary value.

Country-related cultural factors framework Identifies certain national cultural dimensions and their impact on decision-making behavior.

Coups d'état A forced change in a country's government, often resulting in attacks of foreign firms and policy changes by the new government.

Critical commodities list A U.S. Department of Commerce file containing information about products that are either particularly sensitive to national security or controlled for other purposes.

Cross-cultural communication Effective communication across nations/cultures can only take place when the sender encodes the message using language, idioms, norms and values, and so on, that are familiar to the receiver or when the receiver is familiar with the language, idioms, and so on, used by the sender. Also, the sender and receiver must be aware of both his or her own and the other's environmental, cultural, sociocultural, and psychocultural contexts.

Cross-cultural message adjustment The process of adjusting and adapting incoming signifiers to the existing repository of signs, and of adapting and adjusting the repository of signifieds to create new signs.

Cross-cultural research Conducted by researchers from one culture to ascertain how people in one or more other cultures behave—usually to identify the similarities and differences existing among the cultures.

Cross-cultural social responsibility A firm's actions must take into account not only the well-being of stockholders, but also the well-being of the community, the employees, and the customers.

Cross-marketing activities A reciprocal arrangement whereby each partner provides the other access to its markets for a product.

Cross rates Exchange rate quotations which do not include the U.S. dollar as one of the two currencies quoted.

Cross-subsidization The use of resources accumulated in one part of the world to fight a competitive battle in another.

Cultural assimilator A program in which trainees for overseas assignments must respond to scenarios of specific situations in a particular country.

Cultural barriers Business behavior in one culture does not transfer well to another culture due to cultural differences. For example, Americans' "spirit of competitiveness" culture does not transfer well to "spirit of cooperation" cultures, such as Japan.

Cultural briefing Predeparture education and orientation of the expatriate and his or her family about the foreign country. The briefing includes the country's cultural traditions, history, government, economy, living conditions, and so on.

Cultural contexts See *Cross-cultural communication*.

Cultural convergence Increasing similarity among cultures accelerated by technological advances.

Cultural environment To develop an effective international business strategy, the critical aspects of culture must be identified.

Cultural fluency A strong command of not only the language of a foreign country, but also its culture. This is required for effective cross-cultural communication.

Cultural imperialism Criticism by some that the United States is forcing its products and culture on other cultures through technological advances and the globalization of business.

Cultural relativism The belief that no culture's ethics are any better than any other's.

Cultural risk The risk of business blunders, poor customer relations, and wasted negotiations that results when firms fail to understand and adapt to the differences between their own and host countries' cultures.

Cultural-toughness dimension Through a battery of tests, an assessor determines if an applicant for an expatriate assignment has the ability to adapt to the "toughness" of a specific culture.

Cultural universals Manifestations of the total way of life of any group of people.

Culture Comprises an entire set of social norms and responses that condition people's behavior; it is acquired and inculcated, a set of rules and behavior patterns that an individual learns but does not inherit at birth.

Culture-free A theory proposing that managerial behavior is affected by specific situations in all cultures.

Culture shock The more pronounced reactions to the psychological disorientation that most people feel when they move for an extended period of time in to a markedly different culture. What expatriates experience after the novelty of living in a new culture wears out.

Culture shock phase The third phase in the expatriation process usually begins two months into the disillusionment phase. After two months of day-to-day confusion, the expatriate faces culture shock and wishes to go back to his or her old, familiar environment.

Culture-specific A theory proposing that managerial behavior is affected by a nation's culture.

Cumulative transaction adjustment (CTA) A balance sheet account created to maintain a balanced translation for the purchase of a subsidiary; the CTA has no effect on the firm until the subsidiary is either sold or liquidated.

Currency exchange rates Countries' currency exchange rates fluctuate. Fluctuations can be dirty or clean. Dirty fluctuations result when a government adjusts the exchange rate up or down. Clean fluctuations are the result of supply and demand.

Currency flows The movement of currency from nation to nation, which in turn determine exchange rates.

Currency swap An agreement by which a firm exchanges or swaps its debt service payments in one currency for debt service payments in a different currency. The equivalent of the interest rate swap, only the currency of denomination of the debt is different.

Current account An account in the BOP statement that records the results of transactions involving merchandise, services, and unilateral transfers between countries.

Current transfer A current account on the Balance of Payments statement that records gifts from the residents of one country to the residents of another.

Customer involvement The active participation of customers; a characteristic of services in that customers often are actively involved in the provision of services they consume.

Customer satisfaction An important measure of quality.

Customer service A total corporate effort aimed at customer satisfaction; customer service levels in terms of responsiveness that inventory policies permit for a given situation.

Customer structure An organizational structure in which divisions are formed on the basis of customer groups.

Customization Products are modified to fit the needs of specific markets.

Customs union Collaboration among trading countries in which members dismantle barriers to trade in goods and services and also establish a common trade policy with respect to nonmembers.

Cybernetic system A system that enables corporations to monitor and coordinate the activities of its subsidiaries around the globe.

D

Data privacy Electronic information security that restricts secondary use of data according to laws and preferences of the subjects.

Decentralization Managers at the subsidiary are given the autonomy to make most of the important decisions relative to local matters.

Deemed exports Addresses people rather than products where knowledge transfer could lead to a breach of export restrictions.

Delay tactics Another form of leverage. A pause, or delay, by one party during a negotiation may make the other party overly anxious, causing them to make concessions. A delay tactic also allows a negotiator time to rest, recuperate, assess progress, obtain other information, and reformulate strategy.

Delivery duty paid (DDP) Seller delivers the goods, with import duties paid, including inland transportation from import point to the buyer's premises.

Delivery duty unpaid (DDU) Only the destination customs duty and taxes are paid by the consignee.

Delphi studies A research tool using a group of participants with expertise in the area of concern to state and rank major future developments.

Density Weight-to-volume ratio; often used to determine shipping rates.

Deregulation Removal of government regulation.

Differentiation Takes advantage of the company's real or perceived uniqueness on elements such as design or after-sales service.

Diffusion of innovation The process by which innovation is communicated through certain channels over time among members of a social system.

Direct exporting The firm produces at home and creates a division to export to foreign markets.

Direct export sales Seller contracts directly with the buyer in the other country.

Direct intervention The process governments used in the 1970s if they wished to alter the current value of their currency. It was done by simply buying or selling their own currency in the market using their reserves of other major currencies.

Direct investment account An account in the BOP statement that records investments with an expected maturity of more than one year and an investor's ownership position of at least 10%.

Direct involvement Participation by a firm in international business in which the firm works with foreign customers or markets to establish a relationship.

Direct quotation A foreign exchange quotation that specifies the amount of home country currency needed to purchase one unit of foreign currency.

Direct taxes Taxes applied directly to income.

Discriminatory regulations Regulations that impose larger operating costs on foreign service providers than on local competitors, that provide subsidies to local firms only, or that deny competitive opportunities to foreign suppliers.

Disillusionment phase Beginning two months into the expatriation process, the novelty of the new culture wears out, and day-to-day inconveniences caused by different practices in the local culture along with the inability to communicate effectively create disillusionment for the expatriate.

Distributed earnings The proportion of a firm's net income after taxes which is paid out or distributed to the stockholders of the firm.

Distributor A representative or intermediary for the firm that purchases products from the firm, takes title, and assumes the selling risk.

Distributorship MNE sells to a foreign distributor who takes title to the merchandise.

Diversification A market expansion policy characterized by growth in a relatively large number of markets or market segments.

Division of labor The premise of modern industrial production where each stage in the production of a good is performed by one individual separately, rather than one individual being responsible for the entire production of the good.

Domestic enterprises Companies that derive all of their revenues from their home market.

Domestic environment Home country factors, including the political, competitive, economic, and legal and governmental climates, affect the enterprise.

Domestication Government demand for partial transfer of ownership and management responsibility from a foreign company to local entities, with or without compensation.

Double taxation The situation in which an expatriate is taxed by both the home-country and host-country governments. In some cases the firm will pay for the over-taxation.

Double-entry bookkeeping Accounting methodology where each transaction gives rise to both a debit and a credit of the same currency amount. It is used in the construction of the Balance of Payments.

Dual pricing Price-setting strategy in which the export price may be based on marginal cost pricing, resulting in a lower export price than domestic price; may open the company to dumping charges.

Dual translation Using an interpreter in a country to translate a sender's message into a foreign language and then using an interpreter in the foreign country to translate the message back into the sender's language.

Dual use items Goods and services that are useful for both military and civilian purposes.

Dumping The practice by an MNC of selling a product in a foreign market at a price lower than the price for which it sells the product in its own market and/or below production cost with the intent to eliminate its competition.

E

E-commerce The ability to offer goods and services over the Web.

Economic and monetary union (EMU) The ideal among European leaders that economic integration should move beyond the four freedoms; specifically, it entails (1) closer coordination of economic policies to promote exchange rate stability and convergence of inflation rates and growth rates, (2) creation of a European central bank, and (3) replacement of national monetary authorities by the European Central Bank and adoption of the euro as the European currency.

Economic environment The way in which people of a society manage their material wealth and the results of their management.

Economic exposure The potential for long-term effects on a firm's value as the result of changing currency values.

Economic infrastructure The transportation, energy, and communication systems in a country.

Economic security Perception of a business activity as having an effect on a country's financial resources, often used to restrict competition from firms outside the country.

Economic union A union among trading countries that has the characteristics of a common market and also harmonizes monetary policies, taxation, and government spending and uses a common currency.

Economies of scale Production economies made possible by the output of larger quantities.

Education allowance Reimbursement by company for dependent educational expenses incurred while a parent is assigned overseas.

Effective tax rate Actual total tax burden after including all applicable tax liabilities and credits.

Embargo A governmental action, usually prohibiting trade entirely, for a decidedly adversarial or political rather than economic purpose.

Emotions Even though behavior in business and negotiations is mainly intuitive, it should never be judgmental. To be able to listen to other negotiators, one should exclude his or her subjective opinions, preconceptions, or emotional filters. It is important to prevent emotions from controlling negotiations.

Empowerment Giving individuals or groups in the organization the decision-making power necessary to make effective and efficient decisions in their respective units.

Engineering services Services that are provided in the areas of construction, design, and engineering.

Environmental contexts See *Cross-cultural communication.*

Environmental protection Actions taken by governments to protect the environment and resources of a country.

Environmental scanning Obtaining ongoing data about a country.

Ethical What members of a given society generally accept as being "right."

Ethnocentric Tending to regard one's own culture as superior; tending to be home-market oriented.

Ethnocentric staffing outlook The belief that key positions in foreign subsidiaries should be staffed by citizens from the parent company's home country.

Ethnocentric strategy Companies produce unique goods and services that they offer primarily to their domestic market, and when they export, they do not modify the product or service for foreign consumption.

Ethnocentrism The regarding of one's own culture as superior to others'.

Euro A single currency proposed for use by the European Union that will eventually replace all the individual currencies of the participating member states.

Eurobond A bond that is denominated in a currency other than the currency of the country in which the bond is sold.

Eurocurrency A bank deposit in a currency other than the currency of the country where the bank is located; not confined to banks in Europe.

Eurodollars U.S. dollars deposited in banks outside the United States; not confined to banks in Europe.

Euromarkets Money and capital markets in which transactions are denominated in a currency other than that of the place of the transaction; not confined to Europe.

European Monetary System (EMS) An organization formed in 1979 by eight EC members committed to maintaining the values of their currencies within a 2 1/4% of each other's.

European terms Quoting a currency rate as a country's currency against the U.S. dollar (for example, yen/U.S. dollars).

European Union The January 1, 1994, organization created by the 12 member countries of the European Community (now 15 members).

Exchange controls Controls on the movement of capital in and out of a country, sometimes imposed when the country faces a shortage of foreign currency.

Exchange rate mechanism (ERM) The acceptance of responsibility by a European Monetary System member to actively maintain its own currency within agreed-upon limits versus other member currencies established by the European Monetary System.

Expatriate A home-country national, usually an employee of the firm, who is sent abroad to manage a foreign subsidiary.

Expatriation program Takes place while the expatriate is working in the foreign operations; certain delivery and communications programs are required.

Experiential knowledge Knowledge acquired through involvement (as opposed to information, which is obtained through communication, research, and education).

Experimentation A research tool to determine the effects of a variable on an operation.

Export complaint systems Allow customers to contact the original supplier of a product in order to inquire about products, make suggestions, or present complaints.

Export-control system A system designed to deny or at least delay the acquisition of strategically important goods to adversaries; in the United States, based on the Export Administration Act and the Munitions Control Act.

Export license A license obtainable from the U.S. Department of Commerce Bureau of Export Administration, which is responsible for administering the Export Administration Act.

Export management companies (EMCs) Domestic firms that specialize in performing international business services as commission representatives or as distributors.

Export trading company (ETC) The result of 1982 legislation to improve the export performance of small- and medium-sized firms, the export trading company allows businesses to band together to export or offer export services. Additionally, the law permits bank participation in trading companies and relaxes antitrust provisions.

Expropriation The government takeover of a company with compensation frequently at a level lower than the investment value of the company's assets.

External collaboration See *External cooperation*.

External cooperation To be more effective and efficient, a firm focuses on what it can do best, and forms an alliance with other firms to obtain the additional organizational capabilities needed to be more effective and efficient than their competitors.

External economies of scale Lower production costs resulting from the free mobility of factors of production in a common market.

External review A company's management becoming familiar with the domestic, international, and foreign factors that affect its business activities.

Extortion An official in a foreign country in a position of power seeking payment from an individual or corporation for an action to which the individual or corporation may be lawfully entitled.

Extraterritoriality An exemption from rules and regulations of one country that may challenge the national sovereignty of another. The application of one country's rules and regulations abroad.

Ex-works (EXW) Price quotes that apply only at the point of origin; the seller agrees to place the goods at the disposal of the buyer at the specified place on a date or within a fixed period.

F

Factor intensities The proportion of capital input to labor input used in the production of a good.

Factor mobility The ability to freely move factors of production across borders, as among common market countries.

Factor proportions theory Systematic explanation of the source of comparative advantage.

Factors of production All inputs into the production process, including capital, labor, land, and technology.

Factual cultural knowledge Knowledge obtainable from specific country studies published by governments, private companies, and universities and also available in the form of background information from facilitating agencies such as banks, advertising agencies, and transportation companies.

Fatalism A view that individuals cannot control their destiny, that God has predetermined the course of their life.

Field experience Experience acquired in actual rather than laboratory settings; training that exposes a corporate manager to a different cultural environment for a limited amount of time.

FIFO Method of valuation of inventories for accounting purposes, meaning First-In-First-Out. The principle rests on the assumption that costs should be charged against revenue in the order in which they occur.

Financial incentives Monetary offers intended to motivate; special funding designed to attract foreign direct investors that may take the form of land or building, loans, or loan guarantees.

Financial infrastructure Facilitating financial agencies in a country; for example, banks.

Financing cash flows The cash flows arising from the firms funding activities.

Fiscal incentives Incentives used to attract foreign direct investment that provide specific tax measures to attract the investor.

Five stages of national economic development A theory proposing that nations advance from an agricultural economy to an advanced industrial economy in five stages.

Fixed exchange rate The government of a country officially declares that its currency is convertible into a fixed amount of some other currency.

Flat structures Structures should be as flat as possible. That is, they should have fewer managerial layers than traditional hierarchical organizations.

Flextime A modification of work scheduling that allows workers to determine their own starting and ending times within a broad range of available hours.

Floating exchange rate Under this system, the government possesses no responsibility to declare that its currency is convertible into a fixed amount of some other currency; this diminishes the role of official reserves.

Flow of capital International Monetary Fund facilitates the expansion and balanced growth of international trade, assists in eliminating foreign exchange restrictions, and smoothes the international balance of payments.

Flow of labor Controlled through passport, visa, and immigration regulations.

Flow of trade Controlled by trade barriers on imports and exports.

Focus group A research technique in which representatives of a proposed target audience contribute to market research by participating in an unstructured discussion.

Foreign agents A local agent in the host country is used to provide limited involvement for an MNE.

Foreign availability The ability of a firm's products to be obtained in markets outside the firm's home country.

Foreign bond Bonds that are issued by a country's borrowers in other countries, subject to the same restrictions as bonds issued by domestic borrowers.

The Foreign Corrupt Practices Act An established U.S. code of conduct making it illegal for United States businesses to bribe foreign government officials, political parties, and political candidates, even if it is an acceptable practice in the foreign country; requires appropriate accounting controls for full disclosure of firms' foreign transactions.

Foreign direct investment The establishment or expansion of operations of a firm in a foreign country. Like all investments, it assumes a transfer of capital.

Foreign environment Refers to factors in a country that affect international business, including the country's cultural, legal, political, competitive, economic, and technological systems.

Foreign investment Many countries' laws dictate that foreign investments in their nation must be in the form of a joint venture with local partners and that the local partners must be majority owners.

Foreign market opportunity analysis Broad-based research to obtain information about the general variables of a target market outside a firm's home country.

Foreign policy The area of public policy concerned with relationships with other countries.

Foreign service premium A financial incentive to accept an assignment overseas, usually paid as a percentage of the base salary.

Foreign subsidiary An international firm's operating unit established in foreign countries. It typically has its own management structure.

Foreign tax credit Credit applied to home-country tax payments due for taxes paid abroad.

Foreign trade zones Special areas where foreign goods may be held or processed without incurring duties and taxes.

Formalization Represents decision making through bureaucratic mechanisms such as formal systems, established rules, and prescribed procedures.

Fortress Europe Suspicion raised by trading partners of Western Europe, claiming that the integration of the European Union may result in increased restrictions on trade and investment by outsiders.

Forward contracts Agreements between firms and banks which permit the firm to either sell or buy a specific foreign currency at a future date at a known price.

Forward pricing Setting the price of a product based on its anticipated demand before it has been introduced to the market.

Forward rates Contracts that provide for two parties to exchange currencies on a future date at an agreed-upon exchange rate.

Franchising A form of licensing that allows a distributor or retailer exclusive rights to sell a product or service in a specified area.

Free alongside ship (FAS) Exporter quotes a price for the goods, including charges for delivery of the goods alongside a vessel at a port. Seller handles cost of unloading and wharfage; loading, ocean transportation, and insurance are left to the buyer.

Free carrier (FCA) Applies only at a designated inland shipping point. Seller is responsible for loading goods into the means of transportation; buyer is responsible for all subsequent expenses.

Free on board (FOB) Applies only to vessel shipments. Seller quotes a price covering all expenses up to and including delivery of goods on an overseas vessel provided by or for the buyer.

Free trade area An area in which all barriers to trade among member countries are removed, although sometimes only for certain goods or services.

Free Trade Area of the Americas (FTAA) A hemispheric trade zone covering all of the Americas. Organizers hope for it to be operational by 2005.

Freight forwarders Specialists in handling international transportation by contracting with carriers on behalf of shippers.

Functional structure An organizational structure in which departments are formed on the basis of functional areas such as production, marketing, and finance.

G

Gap analysis Analysis of the difference between market potential and actual sales.

General Agreement on Tariffs and Trade (GATT), now called World Trade Organization (WTO) A 124-nation organization that provides the conditions under which a nation can impose trade barriers such as tariffs. The new World Trade Organization was created to settle trade disputes.

General Agreement on Trade in Services (GATS) A legally enforceable pact among GATT participants that covers trade and investments in the services sector.

Geocentric staffing outlook Holds that nationality should not make any difference in the assignment of key positions anywhere (local subsidiary, regional headquarters, or central headquarters); that competence should be the prime criterion for selecting managerial staff.

Glasnost The Soviet policy of encouraging the free exchange of ideas and discussion of problems, pluralistic participation in decision making, and increased availability of information.

Global Worldwide interdependencies of financial markets, technology, and living standards.

Global account management Global customers of a company may be provided with special services including a single point of contact for domestic and international operations and consistent worldwide service.

Global corporate culture Corporate core values that cut across all of a firm's subsidiaries located around the globe.

Global corporations International businesses that view the world as their marketplace.

Global manager An international executive with the ability to manage enterprises in diverse cultures.

Global mind-set In today's global environment, even for employees who may not go abroad, it is necessary to constantly sensitize everyone to the notion that the company is in a global business.

Global strategy A corporation using this strategy uses all of its resources against its competition in a very integrated fashion—all of its foreign subsidiaries and divisions are highly interdependent in both operations and strategy.

Globalization The notion that in the future more and more companies will have to conduct their business activities in a highly interconnected world, thus presenting their managements with the challenge of re-engineering their systems to cope with this new environment. Awareness, understanding, and response to global developments as they affect a company.

Glocalization A term coined to describe the networked global organization approach to an organizational structure.

Gold standard A standard for international currencies in which currency values were stated in terms of gold.

Goods trade An account of the BOP statement that records funds used for merchandise imports and funds obtained from merchandise exports.

Goodwill What international corporations create when they share with locals the benefits derived from the markets they exploit.

Government policies Extreme social and economic conditions may sometimes force a political party into radical policy changes. Generally, however, governments change their policies gradually; they implement new policies to attract the foreign investments needed by the nation to attain its economic development objectives.

Government regulation Interference in the marketplace by governments.

Gray market A market entered in a way not intended by the manufacturer of the goods.

H

Hard currencies Money that is readily acceptable as payment in international business transactions—usually the currencies of industrially advanced countries (for example, dollars and pounds).

Hardship allowance An allowance paid during an assignment to an overseas area that requires major adaptation.

Hedge To counterbalance a present sale or purchase with a sale or purchase for future delivery as a way to minimize loss due to price fluctuations; to make counterbalancing sales or purchases in the international market as protection against adverse movements in the exchange rate.

High-context cultures Cultures in which behavioral and environmental nuances are an important means of conveying information. In the course of business, participants establish social trust first, value personal relations and goodwill, make agreements on the basis of general trust, and like to conduct slow and ritualistic business negotiations.

Horizontal promotions Instead of slowly climbing the organizational ladder, workers and managers make lateral movements, acquiring expertise in different functions such as marketing or manufacturing.

Host-country national A resident of the country where the firm's subsidiary is located, or will be located, employed to manage the operations.

Housing allowance An allowance paid during assignment overseas to provide living quarters.

I

Implementor A type of leader who takes a newly initiated vision and systematically puts into operation the desired changes. The typical subsidiary role, which involves implementing strategy that originates with headquarters.

Import substitution A policy for economic growth adopted by many developing countries that involves the systematic encouragement of domestic production of goods formerly imported.

Income elasticity of demand A means of describing change in demand in relative response to a change in income.

Incoterms International Commerce Terms. Widely accepted terms used in quoting export prices.

Indirect exporting The firm manufactures at home and employs a middle person to export its product(s) to foreign markets.

Indirect involvement Participation by a firm in international business through an intermediary, in which the firm does not deal with foreign customers or firms.

Indirect quotation Foreign exchange quotation that specifies the units of foreign currency that could be purchased with one unit of the home currency.

Indirect taxes Taxes applied to nonincome items, such as value-added taxes, excise taxes, tariffs, and so on.

Individualism Refers to the degree to which people in a society look after primarily their own interests or belong to and depend on "in-groups."

Informal integration Allowing a foreign subsidiary to adopt the corporation's global vision, core values, and cultural principles in its own way. That is, the corporation's central management does not formally force these on the foreign subsidiaries; rather it listens to people at the local level and communicates with them.

Information-based services The provision of these services involves collecting, manipulating, interpreting, and transmitting data to create value. Examples include such services as accounting, banking, consulting, education, insurance, legal services, and news.

Information system Can provide the decision maker with basic data for most ongoing decisions.

Infrastructure shortages Problems in a country's underlying physical structure, such as transportation, utilities, and so on.

Inhwa Influences South Korean business behavior; stresses harmony; links people who are unequal in rank, prestige, and power; and stresses loyalty to hierarchical rankings and superiors' concern for the well-being of subordinates.

Initial phase The first phase in the expatriation process. When the expatriate transfers to the foreign assignment, the newness of the culture creates a great deal of excitement for him or her.

Innovator A type of leader who identifies new ideas and visions and "sells" them to the institution.

Input-output analysis A method for estimating market activities and potential that measures the factor inflows into production and the resultant outflow of products.

Insurance services Services that are provided in underwriting, risk evaluation, and operations.

Intangibility The inability to be seen, tasted, or touched in a conventional sense; the characteristic of services that most strongly differentiates them from products.

Intellectual property right Legal right resulting from industrial, scientific, literary, or artistic activity.

Interbank interest rates The interest rate charged by banks to banks in the major international financial centers.

Interest rate swap A firm uses its credit standing to borrow capital at low fixed rates and exchange its interest payments with a slightly lower credit-rated borrower who has debt service payments at floating rates.

Intermodal movements The transfer of freight from one mode or type of transportation to another.

Internal bank A multinational firm's financial management tool that actually acts as a bank to coordinate finances among its units.

Internal collaboration See *Internal cooperation.*

Internal cooperation The organization develops an internal environment where there is downward, upward, and horizontal communication, as well as a focal point to coordinate the communication, for the purpose of making effective and efficient decisions.

Internal economies of scale Lower production costs resulting from greater production for an enlarged market.

Internal review A company's management becoming familiar with the firm's ability to implement a strategy aimed at coping with external demands.

Internalization Occurs when a firm establishes its own multinational operation, keeping information that is at the core of its competitiveness within the firm.

International bond Bond issued in domestic capital markets by foreign borrowers (foreign bonds) or issued in the Eurocurrency markets in currency different from that of the home currency of the borrower (Eurobonds).

International competitiveness The ability of a firm, an industry, or a country to compete in the international marketplace at a stable or rising standard of living.

International contracts Involve additional issues beyond those in domestic contracts, such as differences in language, legal systems, and currency.

International corporations International businesses that produce products in their home country and export to other countries.

International Court of Justice Judicial branch of the United Nations having voluntary jurisdiction over nations.

International debt load Total accumulated negative net investment of a nation.

International division A unit established to supervise a firm's exports, foreign distribution agreements, foreign sales forces, foreign sales branches, and foreign subsidiaries.

International environment Refers to groupings of nations (such as the European Union), worldwide bodies (such as the World Bank), and organizations of nations by industry (such as the Organization of Petroleum Exporting Countries).

International human resource management function Consists of interplay among three dimensions: the broad function, country categories, and types of employees.

International labor relations The management of an MNC interacting with organized labor units in each country.

International law Includes law that deals with the conduct and relations of nation-states and international organizations as well as some of their relations with persons; such law is enforceable by the courts of a nation that has adopted the international law as domestic law.

International Monetary Fund (IMF) A specialized agency of the United Nations established in 1944. An international financial institution for dealing with Balance of Payment problems; the first international monetary authority with at least some degree of power over national authorities.

International organizational structures The firm's organizational structure is its "skeleton"; it provides support and ties together disparate functions.

International pricing A managerial decision about what to charge for goods produced in one nation and sold in another.

International product life cycle (IPLC) A theory that many products that are exported to foreign countries are eventually produced abroad, and that foreign producers subsequently obtain a competitive edge over the original producers, forcing them to either create a new product or go out of business.

International relocation and orientation The making of arrangements for predeparture training, immigration and travel details, and finalizing compensation details between the expatriate and the home country.

International Trade Organization (ITO) A forward-looking approach to international trade and investment embodied in the 1948 Havana Charter; due to disagreements among sponsoring nations, its provisions were never ratified.

International treaties Agreements between or among independent nations, such as the General Agreement on Tariffs and Trade (GATT), now called the World Trade Organization.

Interpretive knowledge An acquired ability to understand and appreciate the nuances of foreign cultural traits and patterns.

Interviews A face-to-face research tool to obtain in-depth information.

Intra-industry trade The simultaneous export and import of the same good by a country. It is of interest due to the traditional theory that a country will either export or import a good, but not do both at the same time.

Intranet A process that integrates a company's information assets into a single accessible system using Internet-based technologies such as e-mail, news groups, and the World Wide Web.

Inventory Materials on hand for use in the production process; also finished goods on hand.

Inventory carrying costs The expense of maintaining inventories.

Investment income The proportion of net income that is paid back to a parent company.

ISO 9000 Requires each enterprise to define and document its own quality process and provide evidence of their implementation. ISO stands for International Organization for Standardization.

J

Joint occurrence Occurrence of a phenomenon affecting the business environment in several locations simultaneously.

Joint Research and Development Act A 1984 act that allows both domestic and foreign firms to participate in joint basic-research efforts without fear of U.S. antitrust action.

Joint ventures Two or more firms that band together to establish operations in foreign markets in order to capitalize on each other's resources and reduce risk. They share profits, liabilities, and duties.

Just-in-time inventory Materials scheduled to arrive precisely when they are needed on a production line.

K

Keiretsu Japanese giant industrial groups linked by cross-ownership.

L

Labor laws Laws in many countries provide extensive security for workers and make it extremely expensive to terminate an employee.

Lags Paying a debt late to take advantage of exchange rates.

Land bridge Transfer of ocean freight on land among various modes of transportation.

Language translator Fluent in both languages being used in a cross-cultural communication, translators help eliminate the verbal and nonverbal communication barriers.

Law of One Price The theory that the relative prices of any single good between countries, expressed in each country's currency, is representative of the proper or appropriate exchange rate value.

Leads Paying a debt early to take advantage of exchange rates.

Legal environment Includes rules of competition, packaging laws, patents, trademarks, copyright laws and practices, labor laws, and contract enforcement.

Leontief Paradox Wassily Leontief's studies of U.S. trade indicated that the United States was a labor-abundant country, exporting labor-intensive products. This was a paradox because of the general belief that the United States was a capital-abundant country which should be exporting capital-intensive products.

Less-developed country (LDC) A country with a less diversified economy, a lower than average gross national product, and a lower than average per capita income.

Letter of credit Bank's promise to pay the seller, provided certain conditions are met; used to manage the payment risks in international trade.

Leverage Generally refers to the power you have in a negotiation. In negotiations, the more leverage (options) you have, the more concessions your opponent will have to make.

LIBOR The London InterBank Offer Rate. The rate of interest charged by top-quality international banks on loans to similar quality banks in London. This interest rate is often used in both domestic and international markets as the rate of interest on loans and other financial agreements.

Licensing MNE sells a foreign company the right to use technology or information. A firm gives a license to another firm to produce or package its product.

Licensing agreement An agreement in which one firm permits another to use its intellectual property in exchange for compensation.

LIFO Method of valuation of inventories for accounting purposes, meaning Last-In-First-Out. The principle rests on the practice of recording inventory by "layer" of the cost at which it was incurred.

Linear cultures View the past as being behind them and the future in front of them; they view change as good and attempt to take advantage of business opportunities that they foresee.

Liner service Ocean shipping characterized by regularly scheduled passage on established routes.

Lingua franca The language habitually used among people of diverse speech to facilitate communication.

Lobbyist Typically, a well-connected person or firm that is hired by a business to influence the decision making of policymakers and legislators.

Local content Regulations to gain control over foreign investment by ensuring that a large share of the product is locally produced or a larger share of the profit is retained in the country.

Location decision A decision concerning the number of facilities to establish and where they should be situated.

Logistics platform Vital to a firm's competitive position, it is determined by a location's ease and convenience of market reach under favorable cost circumstances.

Longitudinal analysis A method of estimating market demand by factoring in the time lag of demand patterns.

Low-context cultures Cultures in which most information is conveyed explicitly rather than through behavioral and environmental nuances. In the conduct of business, participants get down to business quickly, value expertise and performance, like agreement by specific, legalistic contract, and like to conduct business negotiations as efficiently as possible.

Lubrication bribes A payment made to an official to facilitate, expedite, and speed up routine government approvals or other actions to which the firm would be legally entitled. They are also called *grease payments*.

M

Maastricht Treaty The agreement signed in December 1991 in Maastricht, the Netherlands, in which European Community members agreed to a specific timetable and set of necessary conditions to create a single currency for the EU countries.

Macroeconomic level Level at which trading relationships affect individual markets.

Management contract An international business alternative in which the firm sells its expertise in running a company while avoiding the risk or benefit of ownership.

Managerial commitment The desire and drive on the part of management to act on an idea and to support it in the long run.

Maquiladoras Mexican border plants that make goods and parts or process food for export back to the United States. They benefit from lower labor costs.

Marginal cost method This method considers the direct costs of producing and selling goods for export as the floor beneath which prices cannot be set.

Market audit A method of estimating market size by adding together local production and imports, with exports subtracted from the total.

Market-differentiated pricing Price-setting strategy based on demand rather than cost.

Marketing infrastructure Facilitating marketing agencies in a country; for example, market research firms, channel members.

Market segment Overlapping ranges of trade targets with common ground and levels of sophistication.

Market transparency Availability of full disclosure and information about key market factors such as supply, demand, quality, service, and prices.

Masculinity Refers to the degree to which people in a society stress material success and assertiveness and assign different roles to males and females.

Mass customization Working with existing product technology to create specific product bundles, resulting in a customized product for a particular customer.

Master of destiny A view that individuals can substantially influence their future, that they control their destiny, and through hard work they can make things happen.

Material possessions Individuals in some cultures equate success with material wealth. However, individuals in many cultures place relatively little importance on material possessions and view the flaunting of wealth as disrespectful.

Materials management The timely movement of raw materials, parts, and supplies into and through the firm.

Matrix structure An organizational structure that uses functional and divisional structures simultaneously. This structure is strongly decentralized: it allows local subsidiaries to develop products that fit into local markets. And yet at its core, it is very centralized; it allows companies to coordinate activities across the globe and capitalize on synergies and economies of scale.

Maximization of shareholder value The ultimate goal of the management of a multinational firm is to increase the value of the shareholder's investment as much as possible.

MBO In this approach, the manager and subordinate meet, and together set objectives for the subordinate.

Mechanistic organization Roles and objectives are clearly and rigidly outlined for employees—managers and subordinates are allowed little or no discretion. Historically, large organizations have tended to adopt the mechanistic form.

Media strategy Strategy applied to the selection of media vehicles and the development of a media schedule.

Mediators In some situations within cultures, it is not wise to send messages directly to the receiver(s); it is wise to use a mediator. The encoder sends the message to a mediator (a third party), who in turn conveys it to the receiver(s).

Mercantilism Political and economic policy in the seventeenth and early eighteenth centuries aimed at increasing a nation's wealth and power by encouraging the export of goods in return for gold.

Microeconomic level Level of business concerns that affect an individual firm or industry.

Mininationals Newer companies with sales between $200 million and $1 billion that are able to serve the world from a handful of manufacturing bases.

Minority participation Participation by a group having less than the number of votes necessary for control.

Mixed aid credits Credits at rates composed partially of commercial interest rates and partially of highly subsidized developmental aid interest rates.

Mixed structure An organizational structure that combines two or more organizational dimensions; for example, products, areas, or functions.

Monetary barriers Sometimes employed by governments to restrict trade, reduce competition, or encourage certain imports. Monetary barriers occur when governments sell foreign currencies needed to pay for undesired imports at a higher rate than the one charged for currencies needed to pay for desired imports.

Most-Favored Nation (MFN) A term describing a GATT/WTO clause that calls for member countries to grant other member countries the same most favorable treatment they accord any country concerning imports and exports.

Multicultural centers Some countries, such as the United States, are multicultural centers. These countries' residents came from many parts of the world and maintain much of their former country's culture.

Multicultural team Teams whose members represent diverse views and come from varied cultures.

Multidimensional development The ninth stage in the social interaction paradigm is characterized by "stepping aside," that is, leaving an important position and distributing political and economic power across private and public sectors.

Multidomestic strategy A business strategy where each individual country organization is operated as a profit center.

Multilateral negotiations Trade negotiations among more than two parties; the intricate relationships among trading countries.

Multinational corporations (MNCs) Companies that invest in countries around the globe. International businesses that establish subsidiaries in foreign markets.

Multinational enterprise (MNE) Any business that engages in transactions involving the movement of goods, information, money, people, or services across national borders.

N

National-culture scheme Proposes that HSRs are affected by national cultural dimensions.

National security The ability of a nation to protect its internal values from external threats.

National sovereignty The supreme right of nations to determine national policies; freedom from external control.

Nationalization Occurs when a government takes over private property—reasonable compensation is usually paid by the government.

Natural hedging The structuring of a firm's operations so that cash flows by currency, inflows against outflows, are matched.

Nemawashi A Japanese term borrowed from gardening. In business terms, it means many private or semiprivate meetings in which true opinions are shared before a major decision-making meeting takes place.

Net errors and omissions account Makes sure the balance of payments (BOP) actually balances.

Net present value (NPV) The sum of the present values of all cash inflows and outflows from an investment project discounted at the cost of capital.

Netting Cash flow coordination between a corporation's global units so that only one smaller cash transfer must be made.

Network A system in which everyone is linked and interconnected and where there is a free exchange of ideas and data.

Networks Similar to the contractual alliance arrangement, a corporation subcontracts its manufacturing functions to other companies.

Nonfinancial incentives Nonmonetary offers intended to motivate; special offers designed to attract foreign direct investors that may take the form of guaranteed government purchases, special protection from competition, or improved infrastructure facilities.

Nonprogrammed decision making Entails analyzing current data and information, which was obtained through a systematic investigation of the current environment, for the purpose of identifying and solving a problem.

Nontariff barriers Include quotas, bans, safety standards, and subsidies. Sometimes employed by governments to restrict trade or reduce competition. Nontariff barriers occur when governments impose restrictive and costly administrative and legal requirements on imports.

Normative integration The headquarters-foreign subsidiary control relationship relies neither on direct headquarters involvement nor on impersonal rules but on the socialization of managers into a set of shared goals, values, and beliefs that then shape their perspectives and behavior.

Not-invented-here syndrome A defensive, territorial attitude that, if held by managers, can frustrate effective implementation of global strategies.

O

Observation A research tool where the subjects' activity and behavior are observed.

Ocean shipping The forwarding of freight by ocean carrier.

Official reserves account An account in the BOP statement that shows (1) the change in the amount of funds immediately available to a country for making international payments and (2) the borrowing and lending that has taken place between the monetary authorities of different countries either directly or through the International Monetary Fund.

Offshore banking The use of banks or bank branches located in low-tax countries, often Caribbean islands, to raise and hold capital for multinational operations.

One-stop logistics Allows shippers to buy all the transportation modes and functional services from a single carrier.

Open criticism A style of Chinese management in which the practice of public scolding (*ma ren*) is used frequently. Represents the Chinese view that the practice of quiet, subtle criticism is sneaky and therefore all communication, including criticism, should take place in the open.

Operating cash flows The cash flows arising from the firm's everyday business activities.

Operating or service lease A lease that transfers most but not all benefits and costs inherent in the ownership of the property to the lessee. Payments do not fully cover the cost of purchasing the asset or incurring the liability.

Operating risk The danger of interference by governments or other groups in one's corporate operations abroad.

Opportunity cost Cost incurred by a firm as the result of foreclosure of other sources of profit; for example, for the licenser in a licensing agreement, the cost of forgoing alternatives such as exports or direct investment.

Order cycle time The total time that passes between the placement of an order and the receipt of the merchandise.

Organic organization Allows employees considerable discretion in defining their roles and the organization's objectives. Historically, small organizations have tended to adopt the organic form.

Organizational culture The pattern of basic assumptions that a given group has invented, discovered, or developed in learning to cope with its problems of external adaptation and internal integration; having worked well enough to be considered valid, the pattern may therefore be taught to new members as the correct way to perceive, think, and feel in relation to those problems.

Orientation program A program that familiarizes new workers with their roles; the preparation of employees for assignment overseas.

Overcentralization Expatriates are unable to establish and maintain an effective relationship with local associates because their authority is constrained by headquarters management overcentralizing decision making.

Ownership risk The risk inherent in maintaining ownership of property abroad. The exposure of foreign owned assets to governmental intervention.

P

Pacifier-oriented leader The type of leader needed in an organization that has achieved a certain level of stability and in which daily operations are running smoothly.

Participation Involving employees in the decision-making process.

Participative decision making Refers to making decisions after consulting others. This style of decision making is perceived negatively in many cultures and causes the decision maker to lose credibility in the eyes of subordinates.

Patent Cooperations Treaty (PCT) An agreement that outlines procedures for filing one international patent application rather than individual national applications.

Pax Americana An American peace between 1945 through 1990 that led to increased international business transactions.

Payoffs Illegal payments made abroad by MNCs to foreign government officials and politicians in the course of conducting business.

Pension liabilities The accumulating obligations of employers to fund the retirement or pension plans of employees.

People-processing services In these services, customers become part of the production process. Such services include passenger transportation, health care, food services, and lodging services.

Performance-based pay Pay related to and directly derived from performance.

Perishability Susceptibility to deterioration; the characteristic of services that makes them difficult to store.

Personnel competencies The ability of a firm's personnel to implement its strategy to internationalize its operations.

Physical distribution The movement of finished products from suppliers to customers.

Place/entry strategy Managers of business enterprises must determine how their products or services will reach the consumer. Distribution methods generally require variations from country to country as well as within each country.

Plaza Agreement An accord reached in 1985 by the Group of Five that held that the major nations should join in a coordinated effort to bring down the value of the U.S. dollar.

PM theory of leadership A Japanese leadership theory; the P stands for showing a concern for subordinates and leadership that is oriented toward forming and reaching group goals; the M stands for leadership that is oriented toward preserving group stability.

Political environment A nation's political system, government policies, attitude toward the product, and management of scarce foreign exchange.

Political risk The risk of loss by an international corporation of assets, earning power, or managerial control as a result of political actions by the host country.

Political systems The types of political system—one-party, two-party, or multiparty—affects the level of stability and consistency in governmental policies as it relates to business.

Political union A group of countries that have common foreign policy and security policy and that share judicial cooperation.

Polycentric staffing outlook The belief that key positions in foreign subsidiaries should be staffed by host-country nationals (locals).

Population increase The effect of changes in countries' populations on economic matters.

Population stabilization An attempt to control rapid increases in population and ensure that economic development exceeds population growth.

Portfolio investment account An account in the BOP statement that records investments in assets with an original maturity of more than one year and where an investor's ownership position is less than 10%.

Portfolio models Tools that have been proposed for use in market and competitive analysis. They typically involve two measures—internal strength and external attractiveness.

Ports Harbor towns or cities where ships may take on or discharge cargo; the lack of ports and port services is the greatest constraint in ocean shipping.

Positioning The perception by consumers of a firm's product in relation to competitors' products.

Positive adjustment phase Beginning at about month four of the expatriation phase, the expatriate begins to adapt, and by about month six of the assignment, the expatriate feels more positive about the foreign environment; in this phase, he or she will attain neither the "high" of the first phase nor the "low" of the second or third phases.

Possession-processing services Services of this nature involve tangible actions to tangible objects to enhance their value to customers. The customer may not be present. These services include transporting freight and installing and maintaining equipment.

Power distance Refers to the degree to which people in a society accept centralized power and depend on superiors for structure and direction.

Practices Cultural foundations of organizational behavior, including symbols, heroes, and rituals, and values.

Pre-expatriation program Once the expatriate has been selected for the foreign assignment, but before leaving the home country, he or she is involved in certain training to prepare for what will be encountered in the foreign country.

Preferential policies Government policies that favor certain (usually domestic) firms; for example, the use of national carriers for the transport of government freight even when more economical alternatives exist.

Presentation principles Those principles governing verbal and nonverbal communication that are applicable when making a presentation to a foreign audience.

Price controls Government regulation of the prices of goods and services; control of the prices of imported goods or services as a result of domestic political pressures.

Price escalation The establishing of export prices far in excess of domestic prices—often due to a long distribution channel and frequent markups.

Price strategy Some firms are influenced by the view that pricing is an active tool by which to accomplish their marketing objectives, while some are influenced by the belief that price is a static element in business decisions.

Primary audience In the communication process, those who receive a message directly.

Primary data Data obtained directly for a specific research purpose through interviews, focus groups, surveys, observation, or experimentation.

Primary research To secure first-hand information about the environment.

Private placement The sale of debt securities to private or institutional investors without going through a public issuance like that of a bond issue or equity issue.

Privatization A policy of shifting government operations to privately owned enterprises to cut budget costs and ensure more efficient services.

Process structure A variation of the functional structure in which departments are formed on the basis of production processes.

Product cycle theory A theory that views products as passing through four stages: introduction, growth, maturity, decline; during which the location of production moves from industrialized to lower-cost developing nations.

Product differentiation The effort to build unique differences or improvements into products.

Product division structure Each of the enterprise's product divisions is responsible for the sale and profits of its product.

Product/service strategy Managers are typically concerned with what the product or service should look like and what it should be able to do. In foreign markets, they must determine whether their product or service can be sold in standard form or be customized to fit differing foreign market needs.

Product structure An organizational structure in which product divisions are responsible for all manufacturing and marketing.

Production possibilities frontier A theoretical method of representing the total productive capabilities of a nation used in the formulation of classical and modern trade theory.

Programmed decision making Making decisions based on precedent, custom, policies and procedures, and on training and development.

Promotion strategy Problems related to international promotion strategy include the legal aspects of the country, tax considerations, language complexities, cultural diversity, media limitations, credibility of advertising, and degree of illiteracy.

Promotional message The content of an advertisement or a publicity release.

Protection of intellectual property The owner of an intellectual property right must comply with each country's requirements to obtain from that country whatever protection is available.

Protectionistic legislation A trade policy that restricts trade to or from one country to another country.

Proxy information Data used as a substitute for more desirable data that are unobtainable.

Psychocultural contexts See *Cross-cultural communication*.

Punitive tariff A tax on an imported good or service intended to punish a trading partner.

Purchasing power parity (PPP) A theory that the prices of tradable goods will tend to equalize across countries.

Q

Qualitative information Data that have been analyzed to provide a better understanding, description, or prediction of given situations, behavioral patterns, or underlying dimensions.

Quality Refers to products/services that meet or exceed consumers' expectations at the lowest cost possible.

Quality circles Groups of workers who meet regularly to discuss issues related to productivity.

Quality of life The standard of living combined with environmental factors, it determines the level of well-being of individuals.

Quality of work life Various corporate efforts in the areas of personal and professional development undertaken with the objectives of increasing employee satisfaction and increasing productivity.

Quotas Legal restrictions on the import quantity of particular goods, imposed by governments as barriers to trade.

R

Reference groups Groups such as the family, coworkers, and professional and trade associations that provide the values and attitudes that influence and shape behavior, including consumer behavior.

Regiocentric staffing outlook The belief that key positions at the regional headquarters should be staffed by individuals from one of the region's countries.

Regional structure An international corporate structure wherein regional heads are made responsible for specific territories, usually consisting of multiple countries, such as Europe, East Asia, and South America.

Regional trade communities International organizations, conferences, and treaties focusing on business and trade regulations; the EU (European Union) is the most prominent of these.

Reinvoicing The policy of buying goods from one unit and selling them to a second unit and reinvoicing the sale to the next unit, to take advantage of favorable exchange rates.

Reliability Dependability; the predictability of the outcome of an action. For example, the reliability of arrival time for ocean freight or airfreight.

Religion Different societies develop different religious systems, which are major causes of cultural differences in many societies. Religious systems provide motivation and meaning beyond the material aspects of life.

Repatriation Reassigning the expatriate to his or her home.

Repatriation program Programs that assist the returning expatriate in readjusting to the home country's environment. Attempts to alleviate the effects of reverse culture shock.

Representative office An office of an international bank established in a foreign country to serve the bank's customers in the area in an advisory capacity; does not take deposits or make loans.

Respect-oriented leadership Prevalent in China, Japan, Korea, Singapore, and Turkey; characterized by avoiding confrontation, displaying patience, listening to others, and avoiding losing face.

Reverse culture shock What expatriates experience upon returning home after a long assignment in a foreign country.

Reverse distribution A system responding to environmental concerns that ensures a firm can retrieve a product from the market for subsequent use, recycling, or disposal.

Reverse engineering Learning to reproduce technology by taking it apart to determine how it works and then copying it.

Ringi A group-oriented participative decision-making technique used in many Japanese organizations.

Risk exposure Possible terrorism in a foreign country, especially in countries where some groups hold hostile feelings toward "capitalists," or where there is a high possibility of the expatriate being kidnapped for ransom.

Roll-on-roll-off (RORO) Transportation vessels built to accommodate trucks, which can drive on in one port and drive off at their destinations.

Royalty The compensation paid by one firm to another under an agreement.

S

Sanction A governmental action, usually consisting of a specific coercive trade measure, that distorts the free flow of trade for an adversarial or political purpose rather than an economic one.

Scanning system A system that enables corporations to monitor the activities taking place in markets around the globe for the purpose of responding to changing market needs.

Scenario building The identification of crucial variables and determining their effects on different cases or approaches.

Sea bridge The transfer of freight among various modes of transportation at sea.

Secondary audience In the communication process, those who do not receive a message directly, but who will hear about the message, need to participate in the decision-making, or are affected by the message.

Secondary data Data originally collected to serve another purpose than the one in which the researcher is currently interested.

Secondary research Uses information that was gathered through primary research by other organizations.

Securities regulation Foreign issuers who issue securities, or whose securities are sold in the secondary market in the United States, must register them unless an exemption is available; the antifraud provisions apply where there is either *conduct* or *effects* in the United States relating to a violation of the federal securities laws.

Self-management Independent decision making; a high degree of worker involvement in corporate decision making.

Self-reference criterion (SRC) The unconscious reference to one's own cultural values.

Selling forward A market transaction in which the seller promises to sell currency at a certain future date at a pre-specified price.

Sensitivity training Training in human relations that focuses on personal and interpersonal interactions; training that focuses on enhancing an expatriate's flexibility in situations quite different from those at home.

Sequential oral interpreters Used by clients involved in cross-language business negotiations and social functions. Unlike simultaneous oral interpreters, they translate both language and culture.

Service capacity The maximum level at which a service provider is able to provide services to customers.

Service consistency Uniform quality of service.

Service heterogeneity The difference from one delivery of a product to another delivery of the same product as a result of the inability to control the production and quality of the process.

Services trade The international exchange of personal or professional services, such as financial and banking services, construction, and tourism.

Settlement range A phase of strategic planning in which a negotiation range (all possible settlements that a negotiator would be willing to take) must be established. During this phase, the LAR (least acceptable result) and MSP (most supportable position) must be identified.

Shipper's order A negotiable bill of lading that can be bought, sold, or traded while the subject goods are still in transit and that is used for letter of credit transactions.

Sign A signal that is recognized, structured into a category, and assigned meaning.

Signal Transmitted by a sender to a receiver; the receiver must decode and try to understand the signal.

Signified The meaning attached to the signifier.

Signifier The sound or shape of the signal that is sensorially perceived without meaning yet attached to it.

Simultaneous oral interpreters Used by speakers in formal situations such as conferences, where the audience and the speaker communicate using different languages.

Single European Act The legislative basis for the European Integration.

Situational scheme Proposes that certain situational factors influence the HSR in all countries.

Smoot-Hawley Act A 1930 act that raised import duties to the highest rates ever imposed by the United States; designed to promote domestic production, it resulted in the downfall of the world trading system.

Social altruism An individual's major concern is the functioning of society. He or she acts to generate vital long-term benefits for others without the want or need to acquire rewards for him or herself.

Social awareness Understanding human/societal needs outside one's own individual-based ends furnishes a base for interorganizational cooperative behavior and for molding effective strategies to merge human endeavors to solve difficult problems.

Social contribution Refers to the mixture of striving to fulfill other people's needs while simultaneously pursuing one's own growth and social power.

Social infrastructure The housing, health, educational, and other social systems in a country.

Social interaction paradigm Used to explain the inherent cooperative culture behind the economic success of the Pacific Rim economies; extends the hierarchy of needs beyond the self-actualization model.

Social responsibility The notion that corporations have an obligation to constituent groups in society other than stockholders and beyond that prescribed by law or union contract.

Social stratification The division of a particular population into classes.

Socially unacceptable and unacceptable Standards or practices determined by each individual culture such that what is acceptable in one culture might be unacceptable in another.

Sociocultural contexts See *Cross-cultural communication*.

Soft currencies Refers to money that is not readily acceptable in international business transactions—usually the currencies of industrially less-advanced countries and of communist countries.

Southeast Asian management The basis of an opposing theory to Theory X and Y known as Theory T and T+, representing two styles and attitudes found to be prevalent in Southeast Asian countries.

Sovereign immunity Foreign country's freedom from a host country's laws.

Special economic zones Areas created by a country to attract foreign investors, in which there are no tariffs, substantial tax incentives, and low prices for land and labor.

Specie Gold and silver.

Spot rates Contracts that provide for two parties to exchange currencies with delivery in two business days.

Stage of subsidiary development Traditionally, MNCs have staffed foreign subsidiaries with expatriates in the early stages of establishing operations in the foreign country. In the later stages, at least at the lower levels, host-country nationals are employed.

Standardization Products sold unchanged or only slightly changed in all markets.

Standard of living The level of material affluence of a group or nation, measured as a composite of quantities and qualities of goods.

Standard worldwide pricing Price-setting strategy based on average unit costs of fixed, variable, and export-related costs.

State-owned enterprise A corporate form that has emerged in non-Communist countries, primarily for reasons of national security and economic security.

Stereotypes Generalizations about a particular culture and its members. Normally simple or brief, these are statements that characterize an entire group, culture, or its members. For example, "Americans are efficiency-oriented" or "The French are rude to non–French-speaking visitors."

Straight bill of lading A nonnegotiable bill of lading usually used in prepaid transactions in which the transported goods involved are delivered to a specific individual or company.

Strategic alliance Two or more companies band together to attain efficiency (see *joint venture*).

Strategic leader A highly competent firm located in a strategically critical market.

Strategic objectives Guided by the enterprise's mission or purpose, they associate the enterprise with its external environment and provide management with a basis for comparing performance with that of its competitors, in relation to environmental demands.

Subsidiary A subunit of a business entity established in a foreign country for the purpose of serving that market or other markets, including the business entity's home-country market.

Supply-chain management Results where a series of value-adding activities connect a company's supply side with its demand side.

Surveys Typically, the use of questionnaires to obtain quantifiable research information.

Systems concept A concept of logistics based on the notion that materials-flow activities are so complex that they can be considered only in the context of their interaction.

T

Tactical objectives Guided by the enterprise's strategic objectives, they identify the key result areas in which specific performance is essential for the success of the enterprise, and aim to attain internal efficiency.

Tariffs Duties or taxes on imported goods and services, instituted by governments as a means to raise revenue and as barriers to trade.

Tariffs and quotas Often employed by governments to restrict trade or reduce competition. Tariffs are a form of tax imposed on incoming goods, and quotas specify the number of foreign units that can be imported.

Tax equalization Reimbursement by the company when an employee in an overseas assignment pays taxes at a higher rate than if he or she were at home.

Tax policy A means by which countries may control foreign investors.

Teaching services Services that are provided in the areas of training and motivating as well as in teaching of operational, managerial, and theoretical issues.

Team building A process that enhances the cohesiveness of a department or group by helping members learn how to organize their work and assume responsibility for it.

Team culture See *culture*, as it pertains to teams.

Teams Many organizations manage themselves through empowered self-managed teams.

Technology transfer The transfer of systematic knowledge for the manufacture of a product, the application of a process, or the rendering of a service.

"Tentative U.S. tax" The calculation of U.S. taxes on foreign source incomes to estimate U.S. tax payments.

Terrorism Illegal and violent acts toward property and people.

Theocracy A legal perspective based on religious practices and interpretations.

Theory T and Theory T+ Complementary theories based on Southeast Asian assumptions that work is a necessity but not a goal itself, people should find their rightful place in peace and harmony with their environment; absolute objectives exist only with God; in the world, persons in authority positions represent God, so their objectives should be followed; and people behave as members of a family and/or group, and those who do not are rejected by society.

Third-country national A resident of a country other than the home-country or host-country assigned to manage a firm's foreign subsidiary.

Time equals money The perception of people in some cultures that time is a commodity and an asset and high importance is placed on it.

Total cost concept A decision concept that uses cost as a basis for measurement in order to evaluate and optimize logistical activities.

Total quality management (TQM) A style of management with a long-term commitment to the ongoing improvement of quality throughout the whole system.

Tourism The economic benefit of money spent in a country or region by travelers from outside the area.

Tracking The capability of a shipper to track goods at any point during the shipment.

Trade barriers Imposed by nations to limit or restrict competition.

Trade creation A benefit of economic integration; the benefit to a particular country when a group of countries trade a product freely among themselves but maintain common barriers to trade with nonmembers.

Trade diversion A cost of economic integration; the cost to a particular country when a group of countries trade a product freely among themselves but maintain common barriers to trade with nonmembers.

Trade draft A withdrawal document drawn against a company.

Trade-off concept A decision concept that recognizes linkages within the decision system.

Trade policy measures Mechanisms used to influence and alter trade relationships.

Trade promotion authority The right to negotiate, accept, or reject trade treaties and agreements with minimal amendments by other parties.

Trading blocs Formed by agreements among countries to establish links through movement of goods, services, capital, and labor across borders.

Tramp service Ocean shipping via irregular routes, scheduled only on demand.

Transaction exposure The potential for losses or gains when a firm is engaged in a transaction denominated in a foreign currency.

Transfer prices The prices at which a firm sells its products to its own subsidiaries and affiliates.

Transfer risk The danger of having one's ability to transfer profits or products in and out of a country inhibited by governmental rules and regulations.

Transformative technological innovations Replace traditional technologies (in farming, a tractor replaces the plow).

Transit time The period between departure and arrival of a carrier.

Translation exposure The potential effect on a firm's financial statements of a change in currency values.

Transnational strategy See *global strategy*.

Triangular arbitrage The exchange of one currency for a second currency, the second for a third, and the third for the first in order to make a profit.

Trigger mechanisms Specific acts or stimuli that set off reactions.

Turnkey operation A specialized form of management contract between a customer and an organization to provide a complete operational system together with the skills needed for unassisted maintenance and operation.

U

Ubuntu An African thought system that stresses a high degree of harmony and emphasizes unity of the whole, rather than its distinct parts.

Uncertainty avoidance The extent to which people in a society tolerate uncertainty and ambiguity.

Undistributed earnings The proportion of a firm's net income after taxes which is retained within the firm for internal purposes.

Unethical What members of the society generally accept as being "wrong."

United States Foreign Corrupt Practices Act (FCPA) Makes it illegal for U.S. citizens and businesses to practice bribery in the conduct of business not only in the United States but in other countries as well, even when it is an acceptable or expected business practice there.

Universal factors framework Identifies various universal situations and their impact on decision-making behavior.

Universalism A rigid global yardstick by which to measure all moral issues.

Unsolicited order An unplanned business opportunity that arises as a result of other activities.

Unstructured data Information collected for analysis with open-ended questions.

V

Value Refers to the usefulness, desirability, and worth of a product, object, or thing.

Value-added tax (VAT) A tax on the value added at each stage of the production and distribution process; a tax assessed in most European countries and also common among Latin American countries.

Values A company's vision, objective, and philosophy as communicated to employees and the public worldwide. National values include good/evil, beautiful/ugly, normal/abnormal, and rational/irrational. Values vary from corporation to corporation, and national values vary from country to country.

Virtual teams Groups of geographically and/or organizationally dispersed co-workers who are assembled using a combination of telecommunications and information technologies to accomplish an organizational task.

Visible pay inequity Visible pay inequity between the expatriates and their local peers could demoralize the foreign subsidiary's staff.

Voluntary restraint agreements Trade-restraint agreements resulting in self-imposed restrictions not covered by the GATT rules; used to manage or distort trade flows. For example, Japanese restraints on the export of cars to the United States.

W

Wa A Japanese concept that necessitates that members of a group, be it in a work team, or a company, or a nation, co-operate with and trust each other.

Webb-Pomerene Act A 1918 statute that excludes from antitrust prosecution U.S. firms cooperating to develop foreign markets.

Whitemail bribery Payments made to induce an official in a foreign country who is in a position of power to give favorable treatment where such treatment is either illegal or not warranted on an efficiency or economic benefit scale.

Wholly-owned subsidiary Enables an MNE to retain control and authority over all phases of operation. The firm establishes a subsidiary in a foreign country maintaining 100% ownership; unlike joint ventures, risks are not shared.

Withholding taxes Taxes applied to the payment of dividends, interest, or royalties by firms.

Work redesign programs Programs that alter jobs to both the quality of the work experience and productivity.

Work scheduling Preparing schedules of when and how long workers are at the workplace.

Working capital management The management of a firm's current assets (cash, accounts receivable, inventories) and current liabilities (accounts payable, short-term debt).

Works council Councils that provide labor a say in corporate decision making through a representative body that may consist entirely of workers or of a combination of managers and workers.

World Bank An international financial institution created to facilitate trade.

World-class competitors Multinational firms that can compete globally with domestic products.

World Trade Organization (WTO) The institution that supplanted GATT in 1995 to administer international trade and investment accords.

Written principles Those principles governing language and behavior that must be transmitted when sending a written message across cultures.

Module 1000 Endnotes

1. Part of this discussion draws from S. Rose, "Why the Multinational Is Ebbing," *Fortune* (August 1977): 111–120. Rose uses the labels "aggressive" and "defensive" reasons.
2. D. C. Shanks, "Strategic Planning for Global Competition," *Journal of Business Strategy 5*, no. 3 (Winter 1985): 80.
3. R. Brady, M. Maremont, and P. Galuszka, "Aeroflot Takes Off for Joint-Ventureland," *Business Week* (October 30, 1989): 48–49.
4. Frank E. Bair, (Ed.) *International Marketing Handbook* 2nd Edition (Detroit: Michigan: Gale Research Company, 1985), p. 1582.
5. J. G. Wissema and L. Euser, "Successful Innovation Through Inter-Company Networks," *Long-Range Planning 24* (December 1991): 33–39.
6. Thomas Hout, Michael E. Porter, and Eileen Rudden, "How Global Companies Win Out," *Harvard Business Review* (September–October 1982): 103.
7. Ibid.
8. Ibid.
9. George S. Yip, "Global Strategy . . . in a World of Nations?" *Sloan Management Review* (Fall 1989): 29.
10. Ibid.
11. Nestlé Home Page, February 8, 1998 (http://www.nestle.com).
12. M. A. Hitt, B. W. Keats, and S. M. DeMario, "Navigating in the New Competitive Landscape: Building Strategic Flexibility and Competitive Advantage in the 21st Century," *Academy of Management Executive 12*, no. 4 (November 1998): 23.
13. Charles K. Kao, *A Choice Fulfilled: The Business of High Technology* (New York: St. Martin's Press, 1991).
14. James E. Lee, "Cultural Analysis in Overseas Operations," *Harvard Business Review* (March–April 1966): 106–114.
15. Adapted from Allison Lucas, "Market Researchers Study Abroad," *Sales and Marketing Management* (February 1996): 13.
16. Warren J. Keegan, "Multinational Product Planning: Strategic Alternatives," *Journal of Marketing* (January 1969): 58–62.
17. Laurie M. Grossman, "PepsiCo Plans Big Overseas Expansion in Diet Cola Wars with Its Pepsi Max," *The Wall Street Journal*, April 4, 1994, p. B6.
18. Theodore Levitt, "The Globalization of Markets," *Harvard Business Review 61* (May–June 1983): 92–102.
19. This discussion draws from C.H. Lovelock and G.S. Yip, "Developing Global Strategies for Service Businesses," *California Management Review 38*, no. 2 (Winter 1996): 64–86.
20. William M. Bulkeley, "Having High-Tuition Blues? Look North," *The Wall Street Journal*, November 26, 1997, pp. C1, C19.
21. J. Greene and M. Duerr, *International Transactions in the Multinational Firm* (New York: The Conference Board, 1970), p. 8.
22. This discussion draws from P. Maher, "The Countertrade Boom," *Business Marketing* (January 1984): 50–52; and "Countertrade Without Cash?" *Finance and Development* (December 1983): 14.

23. The following discussion is adopted from Kamran Kashiani, "Beware the Pitfalls of Global Marketing," *Harvard Business Review* (September–October 1989): 91–98.
24. "Global Messages for the Global Village Are Here," *Business World* (Autumn 1983): 51.
25. Adapted from Cateora and Hess, *International Marketing*, p. 417.
26. Paul Blustein, "Kawasaki to Pay Additional Taxes to U.S.," *The Washington Post,* December 11, 1992, D1.
27. www.opic.gov, Washington, DC: Overseas Private Investment Corporation, May 2, 2001.
28. Robert J. Flanagan, "Knowledge Management in the Global Organization in the 21st Century," *HR Magazine* 44, 11 (1999): 54–55.
29. Michael Z. Brooke, *International Management: A Review of Strategies and Operations* (London: Hutchinson, 1986); 173–174.
30. Stefan Robock and Kenneth Simmonds, *International Business and Multinational Enterprises* (Homewood, IL: Richard D. Irwin, 1973), 429.
31. Richard D. Robinson, *Internationalization of Business: An Introduction* (Hinsdale, IL: The Dryden Press, 1984).
32. William H. Davidson and Philippe Haspeslagh, "Shaping a Global Product Organization," *Harvard Business Review* 59 (March/April 1982): 69–76.
33. See http://www.loctite.com/about/global_reach.html, and "How Loctite Prospers with 3-Man Global HQ, Strong Country Managers," *Business International,* May 2, 1988, 129–130.
34. See Joan P. Curhan, William H. Davidson, and Suri Rajan, *Tracing the Multinationals* (Cambridge, MA: Ballinger, 1977); M. E. Wicks, *A Comparative Analysis of the Foreign Investment Evaluation Practices of U.S.-based Multinational Corporations* (New York: McKinsey & Co., 1980); and Lawrence G. Franko, "Organizational Structures and Multinational Strategies of Continental European Enterprises," in *European Research in International Business.* eds. Michel Ghertman and James Leontiades (Amsterdam, Holland: North Holland Publishing Co., 1977).
35. Davidson and Haspeslagh, "Shaping a Global Product Organization."
36. "How Goodyear Sharpened Organization and Production for a Tough World Market," *Business International* (January 16, 1989): 11–14.
37. "Red Alert at Ford," *Business Week,* December 2, 1996, 38–39.
38. John D. Daniels, "Bridging National and Global Marketing Strategies Through Regional Operations," *International Marketing Review* 4 (autumn 1987): 29–44; and Philippe Lasserre, "Regional Headquarters: The Spearhead for Asia Pacific Markets," *Long Range Planning* 29 (February, 1996): 30–37.
39. Daniel Robey, *Designing Organizations: A Macro Perspective* (Homewood, IL: Richard D. Irwin, 1982), 327.
40. Thomas H. Naylor, "International Strategy Matrix," *Columbia Journal of World Business* 20 (summer 1985): 11–19.
41. "Kodak's Matrix System Focuses on Product Business Units," *Business International* (July 18, 1988): 221–223.
42. See http://www.philips.com/finance/investor/divstruc.html.
43. Thomas J. Peters, "Beyond the Matrix Organization," *Business Horizons* 22 (October 1979): 15–27.
44. See John M. Stopford and Louis T. Wells, *Managing the Multinational Enterprise* (New York: Basic Books, 1972); also A. D. Chandler, *Strategy and Structure* (Cambridge, MA: MIT Press, 1962); and B. R. Scott, *Stages of Corporate Development* (Boston: ICCH, 1971).
45. Stanley M. Davis, "Trends in the Organization of Multinational Corporations," *Columbia Journal of World Business* 11 (summer 1976): 59–71.
46. William Taylor, "The Logic of Global Business," *Harvard Business Review* 68 (March–April 1990): 91–105.
47. Ilkka A. Ronkainen, "Thinking Globally, Implementing Successfully," *International Marketing Review* 13, 3 (1996): 4–6.
48. Norman Blackwell, Jean-Pierre Bizet, Peter Child, and David Hensley, "Creating European Organizations that Work," *The McKinsey Quarterly* 27, 2 (1991): 376–385.
49. John A. Quelch and Helen Bloom, "The Return of the Country Manager," *International Marketing Review* 13, 3 (1996): 31–43.
50. Rodman Drake and Lee M. Caudill, "Management of the Large Multinational: Trends and Future Challenges," *Business Horizons* 24 (May–June 1981): 83–91.
51. Christopher Bartlett, "MNCs: Get off the Reorganization Merry-Go-Round," *Harvard Business Review* 60 (March/April 1983): 138–146.
52. Thomas Gross, Ernie Turner, and Lars Cederholm, "Building Teams for Global Operations" *Management Review* (June 1987): 32–36.
53. Christopher A. Bartlett and Sumantra Ghoshal, "Matrix Management: Not a Structure, a Frame of Mind," *Harvard Business Review* 68 (July–August 1990): 138–145.
54. "See Jack. See Jack Run Europe," *Fortune,* September 27, 1999, 127–136.
55. Ingo Theuerkauf, David Ernst, and Amir Mahini, "Think Local, Organize...." *International Marketing Review* 13, 3 (1996): 7–12.
56. C.K. Prahalad, "Globalization, Digitization, and the Multinational Enterprise," paper presented at the Annual Meetings of the Academy of International Business, November, 1999.
57. James A. Gingrich, "Five Rules for Winning Emerging Market Consumers," *Strategy & Business* (second quarter, 1999): 19–33.

58. Christopher A. Bartlett and Sumantra Ghoshal, "Tap Your Subsidiaries for Global Reach," *Harvard Business Review* 64 (November–December 1986): 87–94.
59. Julian Birkinshaw and Nick Fry, "Subsidiary Initiatives to Develop New Markets," *Sloan Management Review* 19 (spring 1998): 51–61.
60. Amitai Etzioni, *A Comparative Analysis of Complex Organizations* (Glencoe, England: Free Press, 1961).
61. William G. Egelhoff, "Patterns of Control in U.S., U.K., and European Multinational Corporations," *Journal of International Business Studies* 15 (fall 1984): 73–83.
62. William H. Davidson, "Administrative Orientation and International Performance," *Journal of International Business Studies* 15 (Fall 1984): 11–23.
63. William G. Ouchi, "The Relationship Between Organizational Structure and Organizational Control," *Administrative Science Quarterly* 22 (March 1977): 95–112.
64. B. R. Baliga and Alfred M. Jaeger, "Multinational Corporations: Control Systems and Delegation Issues," *Journal of International Business Studies* 15 (fall 1984): 25–40.
65. Laurent Leksell, *Headquarters-Subsidiary Relationships in Multinational Corporations* (Stockholm, Sweden: Stockholm School of Economics, 1981), Chapter 5.
66. Anant R. Negandhi and Martin Welge, *Beyond Theory Z* (Greenwich, CT: JAI Press, 1984), 16.
67. Richard Pascale, "Fitting New Employees into the Company Culture," *Fortune* (May 28, 1984): 28–40.
68. Bartlett and Ghoshal, "Matrix Management: Not a Structure, a Frame of Mind."
69. Michael R. Czinkota and Ilkka A. Ronkainen, "International Business and Trade in the Next Decade: Report from a Delphi Study," *Journal of International Business Studies* 28, 4 (1997): 676–694.
70. Tsun-Yuan Hsieh, Johanne La Voie, and Robert A. P. Samek, "Think Global, Hire Local," *The McKinsey Quarterly* 35, 4 (1999): 92–101.
71. R. J. Alsegg, *Control Relationships Between American Corporations and Their European Subsidiaries*, AMA Research Study No. 107 (New York: American Management Association, 1971), 7.
72. John J. Dyment, "Strategies and Management Controls for Global Corporations," *Journal of Business Strategy* 7 (spring 1987): 20–26.
73. Hans Schoellhammer, "Decision-Making and Intra-organizational Conflicts in Multinational Companies," presentation at the Symposium on Management of Headquarter-Subsidiary Relationships in Transnational Corporations, Stockholm School of Economics, June 2–4, 1980.
74. Alfred M. Jaeger, "The Transfer of Organizational Culture Overseas: An Approach to Control in the Multinational Corporation," *Journal of International Business Studies* 14 (fall 1983): 91–106.
75. Michael R. Czinkota and Erwin Dichtl, "Export Controls and Global Changes," *der markt*, 35, 3, 1996: 148–155.
76. Robert M. Springer, Jr., "New Export Law an Aid to International Marketers," *Marketing News*, January 3, 1986, 10, 67.
77. E. M. Hucko, *Aussenwirtschaftsrecht-Kriegswaffenkontrollrecht, Textsammlung mit Einführung*, 4th ed. (Cologne, 1993).
78. "Bribery a Problem with Overseas Customers," *Management Accounting* 75, 6 (June 1997): 61.
79. George Moody, *Grand Corruption: How Business Bribes Damage Developing Countries* (Oxford: World View Publishing, 1997): 23.
80. Wassily Leontief, "Domestic Production and Foreign Trade: the American Capital Position Re-Examined," *Proceedings of the American Philosophical Society*, 97, no. 4 (September 1953), as reprinted in Wassily Leontief, *Input-Output Economics* (New York: Oxford University Press, 1966), 69–70.
81. In Leontief's own words: "These figures show that an average million dollars' worth of our exports embodies considerably less capital and somewhat more labor than would be required to replace from domestic production an equivalent amount of our competitive imports.... The widely held opinion that—as compared with the rest of the world—the United States' economy is characterized by a relative surplus of capital and a relative shortage of labor proves to be wrong. As a matter of fact, the opposite is true." Leontief, 1953, 86.
82. If this were true, if would defy one of the basic assumptions of the factor proportions theory, that all products are manufactured with the same technology (and therefore same proportions of labor and capital) across countries. However, continuing studies have found this to be quite possible in our imperfect world.
83. For a detailed description of these theories see Elhanan Helpman and Paul Krugman, *Market Structure and Foreign Trade* (Cambridge: MIT Press, 1985).
84. This leads to the obvious debate as to what constitutes a "different product" and what is simply a cosmetic difference. The most obvious answer is found in the field of marketing: If the consumer believes the products are different, then they are different.
85. There are a variety of potential outcomes from external economies of scale. For additional details see Paul R. Krugman and Maurice Obstfeld, *International Economics: Theory and Policy*, 3rd ed. (Harper-Collins, 1994).
86. The term *international investment* will be used in this chapter to refer to all nonfinancial investment. International financial investment includes a number of forms beyond the concerns of this chapter, such as the purchase of bonds, stocks, or other securities issued outside the domestic economy.

127. Andrew W. Singer, "Ethics: Are Standards Lower Overseas?" *Across the Board* (September 1991): 15–16.
128. Ibid., p. 16.
129. Kent Hodgson, "Adapting Ethical Decisions to a Marketplace," *Management Review* (May 1992): 56–57.
130. Donna J. Wood, "Corporate Social Performance Revisited," *Academy of Management Review* 16 (October 1991): 691–718.
131. Thomas Donaldson, "Values in Tension: Ethics Away from Home," *Harvard Business Review* (September–October 1996): 48–62.
132. Donaldson, "Global Business Must Mind Its Morals."
133. David E. Rosenbaum, "China Trade Rift with U.S. Deepens," *The New York Times,* January 29, 1995, p. 1.
134. Sarah Cox, "Starbucks Pours One for Coffee Workers," *Monday Magazine* (Victoria, B.C.) (March 16–22, 1995): 6
135. David Vogel, "The Globalization of Business Ethics: Why America Remains Distinctive," *California Management Review 35*, no. 1 (Fall 1992): 30.
136. Ibid., pp. 35–37.
137. Ibid., pp. 46–47.
138. Ibid., p. 49.
139. N. A. Adam, B. Slonim, J. Wagner, P. Yesha, Yelena, "Globalizing Business, Education, Culture, Through the Internet," *Communications of the ACM 40,* no. 2 (February 1997): 115–121.
140. The information presented here is based largely on an original Delphi study by Michael R. Czinkota and Ilkka A. Ronkainen utilizing an international panel of experts. More details can be found in: M. R. Czinkota and I. A. Ronkainen, "International Business and Trade in the Next Decade: Report from a Delphi Study," *Journal of International Business Studies* 28, 4 (Fourth Quarter 1997): 827–844.
141. Reiner Springer, and Michael R. Czinkota, "Marketing's Contribution to the Transformation of Central and Eastern Europe," *Thunderbird International Business Review*, 41, 1 (1999): 29–48.
142. John Pomfret, "Chinese Industry Races to Make Global Name for Itself," *The Washington Post*, April 23, 2000, H1.
143. Murray Weidenbaum, "All the World's a Stage," *Management Review*, October 1999. 147–48.
144. John Ouelch, "Global Village People," *Worldlink Magazine*, January/February 1999, www.worldlink.co.uk.
145. Renato Ruggiero, "The New Frontier," *WorldLink*, January/ February 1998, www.worldlink.co.uk.
146. Minoru Makihara, Co-Chairman of the Annual Meeting of the World Economic Forum, Davos 2001, www.worldeconomicforum.org.
147. Polly Campbell, "Trend Watch 2001," *The Edward Lowe Report*, January 2001, 1–3.
148. Michael R. Czinkota and Masaaki Kotabe, "The Role of Japanese Distribution Strategies," *Japanese Distribution Strategy*, M. R. Czinkota and M. Kotabe, eds. (London: Business Press, 2000): 6–16.
149. *U.S. Manufacturers in the Global Marketplace* (New York: The Conference Board, 1994).
150. "The Corporation and the Public: Open for Inspection," World Economic Forum, www.worldeconomicforum.org, February 2, 2001.
151. Benn R. Konsynski and Jahangir Karimi, "On the Design of Global Information Systems," in *Globalization, Technology, and Competition: The Fusion of Computers and Telecommunications in the 1990s*, ed. S. Bradley, J. Hausman, and R. Nolan (Boston: 1993): 81–108.
152. Michael R. Czinkota and Masaaki Kotabe, *Marketing Management* 2d ed., (Cincinnati: South-Western College Publishing, 2001), 234–235.
153. Michael R. Czinkota and Masaaki Kotabe, "Product Development the Japanese Way," in *Trends in International Business: Critical Perspectives,* ed. M. Czinkota and M. Kotabe (Oxford: Blackwell Publishing 1998), 153–158.

87. The official terminology used throughout this chapter, unless otherwise noted, is that of the International Monetary Fund (IMF). Since the IMF is the primary source of similar statistics for balance of payments and economic performance worldwide, it is more general than other terminology forms, such as that employed by the U.S. Department of Commerce.
88. This discussion draws from Dean Foster, "Business Across Borders: International Etiquette for the Effective Global Secretary," *The Secretary* (October 1992): 20–24.
89. Ibid., p. 24.
90. Lyle Sussman and Denise M. Johnson, "The Interpreted Executive: Theory, Models, and Implications," *The Journal of Business Communication, 30,* no. 4 (1993): 419–420.
91. Edward T. Hall, "How Cultures Collide," *Psychology Today* (July 1976): 67–74.
92. Mary Munter, "Cross-Cultural Communication for Managers," *Business Horizons* (May–June 1993): p. 74.
93. Hall, "How Cultures Collide," pp. 67–74.
94. Ibid., p. 74.
95. Munter, "Cross-Cultural Communication for Managers," p. 74.
96. Ibid., p. 75.
97. Ibid., p. 76.
98. This discussion draws from Jon P. Alston, "Wa, Guanxi, and Inhwa: Managerial Principles in Japan, China, and Korea," *Business Horizons* 32, no. 2 (March–April 1989): 27–28.
99. Linda Beamer, "Learning Intercultural Communication Competence," *The Journal of Business Communication 29,* no. 3 (1992), 291–301.
100. Ibid., p. 291.
101. M. Katherine Glover, "Do's and Taboos: Cultural Aspects of International Business," *Business America* (August 13, 1990): 3.
102. Adapted from R. Knotts, "Cross-Cultural Management: Transformations and Adaptations," *Business Horizons* (January–February 1989): 29–33.
103. Dean Allan Foster, *Bargaining Across Borders* (New York: McGraw-Hill, 1992), p. 5.
104. Ibid.
105. Hokey Min and William Galle, "International Negotiation Strategies of U.S. Purchasing Professionals," *International Journal of Purchasing and Materials Management* (Summer 1993): 43.
106. Trenholme J. Griffin and W. Russell Daggatt, *The Global Negotiator* (New York: Harper Business Publishers, 1990, p. 74.
107. Min and Galle, "International Negotiation Strategies," p. 42.
108. Robert O. Joy, "Cultural and Procedural Differences That Influence Business Strategies and Operations in the People's Republic of China," *SAM Advanced Management Journal* (Summer 1989): 31.
109. Griffin and Daggatt, *The Global Negotiator,* p. 77.
110. Min and Galle, "International Negotiation Strategies," p. 43.
111. Ibid., pp. 43–44.
112. Ibid., p. 44.
113. Edward T. Hall, "The Silent Language in Overseas Business," *Harvard Business Review* (May–June 1960): 93.
114. Shah M. Tarzi, "Third World Governments and Multinational Corporations: Dynamics of Host's Bargaining Power" (n.d., n.p.), p. 237.
115. Griffin and Daggatt, *The Global Negotiator,* p. 120.
116. Ibid., p. 106.
117. See A. C. Day, "Institutional Constraints and the International Monetary System," in R. Mundell and A. Swoboda, eds., *Monetary Problems of the International Economy* (Chicago: University of Chicago Press, 1969), pp. 333–342.
118. Federal News Service, *Hearing of the House Judiciary Committee,* April 23, 1997.
119. Michael R. Czinkota and Jon Woronoff, *Unlocking Japan's Market* (Chicago: Probus Publishing, 1991).
120. *National Trade Estimate Report on Foreign Trade Barriers,* Washington, DC office of the United States Trade Representative, 2000, www.ustr.gov.
121. Michael R. Czinkota, "The Policy Gap in International Marketing," *Journal of International Marketing, 8,* 1, 2000: 99–111.
122. Michael R. Czinkota, "International Information Needs for U.S. Competitiveness," *Business Horizons* 34, 6 (November/December 1991): 86-91.
123. Najmeh Bozorgmehr and Stefan Wagstyl, "European Business Sees New Area of Potential," *Financial Times,* February 6, 2002. www.ft.com.
124. *International Court of Arbitration: 1999 Statistical Report* (Paris: International Chamber of Commerce, 2001).
125. W. A. Label and J. Kaikati, "Foreign Antibribery Law: Friend or Foe?" *Columbia Journal of World Business* (Spring 1980): 46.
126. O. Ronald Gray, "The Foreign Corrupt Practices Act: Revisited and Amended," *Business and Society* (Spring 1990): 14.

Subject Index

A

Abandoned product ranges, 862, 931
Absence of trade, equilibrium in, 883–884
Absolute advantages, 855, 857, 931
Absolute form of purchasing power parity, 450
Absorption costing, 112, 172
   income analysis under, 113–114
   income statement under, 112–113
   management's use of, 114–120
Accelerated cost recovery method, 369
Accelerated depreciation method, 172
Accelerating cash inflows, 432
Access controls, 623–624, 659
Account, 172
   open, 411
Account analysis method, 46
Account analysis statement, 450
Accountants, ethics for, 141
Account distribution, 132
Account form, 17, 172
Accounting, 1–172, 609–611
   accrual, 3–4
   aggressive, 141
   anomalies in, 802
   assets, liabilities and owners' equity in, 9–26
   auditing and, 123–127
   balance of payments, 866–870
   in business, 3–4
   control and, 127–140
   controller and, 3–8
   cost, 4
   cost behavior, control and decision making in, 43–57
   creative practices in, 141
   cultural influences on, 143–149
   decision making and, 98–120
   decision models in, 98–111
   defined, 3
   economics and, 142
   environmental, 4
   ethics and, 140–141
   financial, 6
   financial statements in, 27–43
   information systems and, 122–123
   international, 4, 143–172

law and, 142–143
   managerial, 4, 6
   not-for-profit, 4
   operating budgets and performance evaluation in, 68–97
   private, 4
   product and service costs in, 57–68
   public, 4
   relation between finance and, 386
   reporting and, 120–122
   responsibility, 85
   social, 4
   strategies in, 2–3
   tax, 4
Accounting and Auditing Enforcement Release (AAER), 802
Accounting costs, economic costs versus, 142
Accounting cycle, 8, 172, 802
Accounting diversity, 931
Accounting equation, 9, 172
   business transactions and, 9–13
Accounting exposures, 172
Accounting function, 2–3
   primary qualities, 2
   secondary qualities, 3
Accounting growth, economic growth versus, 142
Accounting income
   cash flow versus, 325–326
   economic income versus, 142
Accounting information, 151–152
   qualities of, 2–3
Accounting measurements and disclosures, 149–157
   costs versus benefits criterion, 151–152
   disclosure issues for multinationals, 155–156
   evolving disclosure process, 150
   reasons for financial reporting disclosures, 150–151
   reporting approaches of multinational companies, 154–155
   social impact disclosure practices, 156–157
   worldwide diversity in measurement and reporting, 152–154
Accounting period concept, 172
Accounting principles. *See* Accounting standards

Accounting Principles Board Opinion No. 15, 172
Accounting process, 8–9
Accounting profession, 151
Accounting profits, 450
   economic profits versus, 142
Accounting rate of return (ARR) method, 323
Accounting reform legislation, 781
Accounting reports, 3, 4
   managerial, 6
Accounting standards, 125, 167, 172
   prudence concept in, 153
   in selected countries, 158–164
Accounting Standards Executive Committee (AcSEC), 162
Accounting systems, 4, 122–123, 172, 802
   in prevention and detection of fraud, 693
Account parameters and records, 450
Account reconciliation, 450
Accounts payable, 11, 172, 221–222, 450
Accounts receivable, 11, 17, 172
   analysis of, 34–35
   factoring, 225–226
   financing, 225–227, 412, 450
   overstating, 721–722
   pledging, 225
   turnover, 450
Accounts receivable turnover, 34–35, 172, 450, 802
Accounts receivable turnover ratio, 802
Accrual(s), 220–221, 450
Accrual accounting, 3–4
Accrual accounting rate of return (AARR) method, 172
Accrual basis, 172
Accrued expenses, 172
Accrued liability, 802
Accrued revenues, 172
Acculturation, 931
Accumulated depreciation account, 172
ACH credit, 450
ACH debit, 450
Acid-test ratio, 33–34, 172, 471, 808
Acquisitions, 355, 802, 828–829
   consequences of, in corporate governance, 786–788
   inflating assets in, 721
Active investment strategy, 219, 450

Active tool, 831
ActiveX, 659
Activity analysis, 172
Activity-based costing, 61, 110, 172
Activity-based management (ABM), 173
Activity-based units-of-production method, 369
Activity bases, 44, 60, 88, 172, 173
Activity cost pools, 173
Activity drivers, 44, 60
Activity rates, 173
Activity ratios. *See* Efficiency ratios
Act of state doctrine, 914, 931
Actual rate of return, 260, 450
Acute crisis stage, 767, 802
Adaptability screening, 931
Adaptable management, 931
Adaptation, 931
Adaptation problems, 931
Adaptive transformative innovations, 931
Additional funds needed (AFN), 267, 269, 450
Additional paid-in capital, 233, 450
Add-on interest, 450
Ad hoc groups, 931
Ad hoc reports, 659
Adjustable pegged exchange rates, 898
Adjustable-rate preferred stock (ARPS), 450
Adjusted r^2, 450
Adjusted trial balance, 173
Adjusting entries, 173
Adjusting process, 173
Administrative expenses, 62, 173
ADSL (Asynchronous DST), 606, 659
Ad valorem tariff, 886
Advanced determination ruling (ADR), 173
Advance pricing agreement, 173
Adverse opinion, 124
Advised line, 450
Advising bank, 413, 450
Advisory services, 450
Affidavit, 802
Affiliate programs, 486
African Development Bank, 398, 916
African Industrial Property Office (ARIPO), 911
African Intellectual Property Organization (OAPI), 911
After-tax cost of debt, k_{dT}, 450
Age Discrimination in Employment Act, 918–919
Agencies, 450
Agency problems, 193, 450, 785, 802
Agency relationships, 193–195
Agent, 931
Agent of change, 659
  systems analyst as, 495

Aggregate investment in cash and securities, 219–220
Aggressive accounting, 141
Aggressive approach, 206–207, 450
Aggressive financing strategy, 230, 450
Aging schedule, 214–215, 450
Aging the receivables, 173
Airfreight, 931
Airway bill, 414, 450
Algorithm, 659
Alliances, 931
  establishing, 485–486
All-in-rate, 415, 450
Allocation base, 60
Allocation mentality, 931
Allowance method, 173
Allowances
  for deferred income tax assets, 173
  for doubtful accounts, 802
  for uncollectible assets as a percentage of receivables, 802
Alternative risk transfer tools, 744–745
American-based leadership and motivation theories, 931
American depository receipts (ADRs), 342–343, 408, 451
American Institute Certified Public Accountants (AICPA), 121, 162, 171, 173
  Auditing Standards Board of, 170
American Stock Exchange (AMEX), 339
Americans with Disabilities Act, 918
American terms, 931
Amoral management, 777–778
Amortization, 173
  methods of, 370
Amortization schedule, 451
Amortized loans, 377–378, 451
Amplitude modulation, 597
Analogy, 931
Analog signals, 596–597, 659
Analysis, 123
Analytical anomalies, 802
Analytical procedures in financial statement analysis, 27–32
  common-size statements, 30–31
  horizontal analysis, 27–29, 31
  vertical analysis, 29–30, 31
Andean Common Market (ANCOM), 912
Annual compounding, 451
Annual percentage rate (APR), 379, 451
Annual reports, 451
  corporate, 120–121
Annuities, 173, 451
  future value of, 373–375
  ordinary, 373
  present value of, 375–377
Annuities due, 373, 374–375, 376–377, 451
ANSI, 451

Antecedent, 659
Anticipation, 451
Anticorruption movement, 796–797
Antidumping, 931
Antidumping duty, 892
Antidumping regulations, 892
Antiplanning, 931
Antitrust laws, 853, 917, 931
Antivirus software, 501, 659
Apathy, 695
Appellate Court, 802
Applet, 659
Application, 659
Application controls, 802
Application/data independence, 659
Application generator, 660
Application service provider (ASP), 567, 573–575, 635, 660
Application service provider industry, 574–575
Application-specific software, 660
Appraisal costs, 173
Appreciation, 451
Appropriation, 173
Arbitrage, 173, 419, 451
Arbitration, 911, 931
Area expertise, 931
Area structure, 842–843, 931
Area studies, 931
Arithmetic logic unit (ALU), 660
Arms-length price, 833, 932
Arraignment, 802
Arrangement of Nice Concerning the International Classification of Goods and Services, 918
Artificial intelligence, 660
  in business, 542–545
Artificial vision, 543, 660
ASCII, 660
Asian Development Bank, 398, 916
Asian dollar market, 406–407, 451
Asia-Pacific Economic Cooperation (APEC), 173, 912
Ask price, 451
ASP. *See* Application service provider
Assembler, 660
Assembly languages, 660
Asset-and liability approach, 173
Asset-based lending, 451
Asset-based loans, 451
Asset fraud, 720–722, 802
  identifying, 720–722
  symptoms of, 722
Asset management ratios, 451
Assets, 9, 17, 173
  basic valuation of, 380
  current, 17
  financial, 867
  fixed, 17, 36, 138–139
  inflating, in mergers, acquisitions and restructuring, 721

954   SUBJECT INDEX

long-term, 17
misappropriations, 701–702, 802
net, 390
plant, 17
quick, 34
rate earned on total, 38–39
rate of return on, 90
ratio of net sales to, 38
real, 867
requisitions, 702
theft of other, 702
Asset securitization, 451
Asset swap, 451
Asset turnover, 802
Asset valuation, similarities between capital budgeting and, 317
Assignment of proceeds, 415, 451
Associated firms. See Representative firms
Association of Certified Fraud Examiners (ACFE), 687, 802
Association of Southeast Asian Nations (ASEAN), 173, 912
Asymmetric DSL (ADSL), 606, 659
Asymmetric information, 308, 451
Asymmetric key encryption, 660
Asynchronous communication, 592–593, 660
Atomic transactions, 624, 660
Auction markets, 340
Auction preferred stock (APS), 451
Auctions, 635
Audit(s)
    Generally Accepted Auditing Standards (GAAS), 718
    information systems, 610
    model, 467
    post, 324–325, 470
    social, 801
    social versus stakeholder, 764
    types of, 126–127
Audit command language (ACL), 802
Audit committee, 789, 802
Auditing
    accounting and, 123–127
    compliance, 127
    external, 124–125, 167–172
    financial, 126
    information technology, 127
    internal, 126, 165–167
    issues in, for global operations, 165–172
    nature of, 123–124
    operational, 127
    performance, 127
    program, 127
Auditing standards, 168

Auditing Standards Board of the American Institute of Certified Public Accountants, 170
Auditors, in internal control, 681
Auditor's report, 124, 173
    opinions based on another, 171
    standard, 124
Audit trails, 624, 660, 802
    lack of, 696
Autarky, 932
Authentication, 625, 660
Authoritative decision making, 932
Autocratic management, 802
Automated clearing house (ACH), 451
Availability float, 451
Availability schedule, 451
Available-for-sale security, 173
Average collection period, 451
Average cost method, 173, 932
Average rate of return, 173
Average tax rate, 451
Avoidance, 451

B

Backbone, 660
Backtranslation, 932
Backup, 623, 660
Back value date, 451
Backward chaining, 548–549, 660
Backward innovation, 932
Backward reasoning, 660
Bad debt expense, 803
Badwill, 932
Balanced scorecard, 94–95, 173
Balance fractions
    inventory, 451
    payables, 451
Balance of payments (BOP), 451, 866, 880, 932
    accounts of, 868–870
    economic crises and, 870–871
    as flow statement, 867
Balance of payments accounting, 866–870
Balance of payments deficit, 173
Balance of payments surplus, 173
Balance of the account, 173
Balance of trade, 451
    correcting deficit in, 394–396
Balance on goods and services, 451
Balance reporting services, 451
Balance sheet, 8, 9, 17–18, 173, 451, 610, 803
    budgeted, 73, 83
    emphasis on, versus income statement, 158
    presentation of cash on, 135
    pro forma, 210
Balance sheet budgets, 80–83
Balance sheet effects, 314

Balance sheet recognition, 154, 173
Balance sheet test, 390
Balassa-Samuelson theory, 173
Bandwidth, 593, 660
Bank(s)
    accounts in, as cash control, 132–134
    advising, 413, 450
    attributes of, that provide foreign exchange, 401–402
    bid/ask spread of, 402
    cash deposit in, 131
    clearing, 454
    collection, 454
    commercial, 337–338
    concentration, 454
    disbursing, 457
    drawee, 458
    issuing, 464
    member, 460, 466
    nonbank, 468
    selection process, 452
Bank deposit notes, 451
Bank draft, 932
Banker's acceptance, 224, 413, 415–416, 451
Bankers' ratio, 33
Bank exposure, reducing, to developing-nation debt, 906
Bank for International Settlements (BIS), 398, 451
Bank Holding Company Act (1956), 452
Banking
    concentration, 211, 454
    international, 901–908
    investment, 343–346
Banking Act, 1991, 452
Banking systems, characteristics of, 435
Bank Letter of Credit Policy, 452
Bank loans, cost of, 224
Bank Nationale de Paris, 818
Bank notes, 452
Bank reconciliation, 134–135, 173
Bank relationship policy, 452
Bankruptcy, 388, 803
    Chapter 7, 388, 803
    Chapter 11, 388, 803
Bankruptcy Code, 803
Bankruptcy Courts, 803
Bank statement, 133
Banners, 660
Bar charts, 387
Bar code, 660
Barriers, 932
    cultural, 934
    to entrants, 483, 660
    monetary, 942
    nontariff trade, 825, 889–893, 915, 942
    tariff, 825
    technical, to trade, 825
    trade, 947

Barter, 417, 452, 833, 885, 932
Baseband link, 593, 660
Base case, 331, 452
Basel Accord, 406, 452
Base salary, 932
Basis for trade, 884–885
Basket of currencies, 894
Basket valuation, 904
Batch processing, 660
Baud, 594, 660
Beachhead merger, 357
Bearer bond, 932
Behavioral controls, 849
Belief systems, 676
Benchmarking, 571, 572, 660, 803
    internal, 849
Benefits management, 619
Berne Convention for the Protection of Literary and Artistic Works, 653, 918
Best-case scenario, 331, 452
Best efforts arrangement, 344, 452
Best-fit linear analysis, 512
Best practices
    in information technology, 526–529
    in internal control, 684–685
        financial and operations reporting, 685
        marketing and sales, 685
        operations, 684
        service, 685
Beta, concept of, 350
Beta coefficient, β, 350, 452
Beta risk, 329, 332–333, 452
Beta sites, 570, 660
Betterment, 173
Bhopal tragedy, plant safety and the, 793–794
Bias, inflationary, 897
Biased expectations hypothesis, 452
Bid/ask spread, 419, 452
    among currencies, 402–403
    of banks, 402
Bid price, 452
Bid-rigging scheme, 703, 803
Big Five, 174
Bilan Social (social report), 156, 174
Bilateral advance pricing agreement, 174
Bilateral negotiations, 932
Bilateral netting system, 433, 452
Billing scheme, 803
Bill of exchange, 411, 413, 452
Bill of lading, 414, 452, 932
Bill of materials, 614, 660
Bill presentation, 660
Binary number system, 660
Biometrics, 623–624, 660, 803
Bit, 660
Bit map, 660
Bits per second, 593, 660

Black hole, 848, 932
Blackouts, 498, 660
Blanket liens, 227
Bleeding edge, 660
Blocked funds, managing, 434
Blue sky laws, 342, 452
Board of directors
    changes in, in improving corporate governance, 788–790
    in controlling corporate fraud, 725
    in corporate governance, 784, 785, 788
    in internal control, 680
    involvement of, in fraud, 706–707
    need for independence, 785
Board of Governors, 452
Body language, 874, 932
Bond(s), 174, 236–237, 452
    bulldog, 245
    convertible, 237
    finding interest rate on, 257–258
    floating rate, 240
    foreign, 245, 407
    income, 237
    indexed, 237
    investment grade, 241
    junk, 240
    mortgage, 237
    parallel, 407
    purchasing power, 237
    putable, 237
    Samurai, 245
    valuation of, 255–258
    Yankee, 245
    zero (or very low) coupon, 239–240
Bond anticipation notes, 452
Bond indentures, 174, 238
Bond ratings, 240–241
    criteria for, 241
Bond refunding, 238, 244–245
Bond valuation model, 256
Bond-yield-plus-risk-premium approach, 295
Bookkeeping, double-entry, 867
Book value, 17, 174
    of the asset, 174
    market value versus, 359
    model for, 359–360
    per share, 233, 452
Boot, 174
Borrowing, motives for, in foreign markets, 400
Bottom-up planning, 660
Boundary systems, 676
Box-Jenkins model, 452
Boycotts, 825, 853, 932
Brain drain, 932
Brainstorming, 621, 660

Brazil
    accounting standards and financial reporting in, 158–159
    independent auditing environment in, 168–169
Breadth, 452
Breakeven analysis
    financial, 279–281
    operating, 273
Breakeven chart, 274
Breakeven computation, 274–275, 281
Breakeven graph, 280
Break-even point, 50–53, 174
    effects of changes on, 53
    from speculation, 425
Break point, 299, 452
Bretton Woods, 452, 898, 932
Bribery, 703, 795, 803, 854, 919, 932
    arguments for and against, 795
    forms of, 919–920
    lubrication, 920
    trends in, 796–797
    whitemail, 919
Bridge, 597, 660
British Computer Act, 653
Broadband link, 593, 660
Broad form of hold-harmless agreements, 737
Brokerage departments, 339
Brokers, 452
Brownouts, 498, 660
Browsers, 661
Browsing, 661
Budget(s), 69, 174, 315, 850
    balance sheet, 80–83
    capital expenditures, 82–83
    cash, 80–82, 209–210
    cost of goods sold, 78
    direct labor cost, 77–78
    direct materials purchases, 76
    factory overhead cost, 78
    flexible, 72
    income statement, 74–80
    master, 73
    operating, 68–69
    production, 75
    sales, 74–75
    selling and administrative expenses, 78
    setting goals, 70–71
    static, 71–72
Budgetary slack, 70
Budgeted balance sheet, 73, 83
Budgeting
    computerized systems, 73
    continuous, 71
    human behavior and, 70–71
    objectives of, 69–70
    zero-based, 71
Budgeting income statement, 73, 78–80
Budgeting systems, 71–73
Budget performance report, 174

Buffer stock, 932
Bug, 661
Bulk service, 932
Bulldog bonds, 245
Bureaucratic controls, 849
Bureaucratic/formalized control, 850
Bureaucratic hurdles, 146
Bus, 661
Business, 174
    artificial intelligence in, 542–545
    controller in, 7–8
    cross-cultural practices in, 875
    decision making in, 511
    level of activity in, 385
    managing crises in, 768–770
    networks in, 599–604
    role of accounting in, 3–4
    telecommunications in, 589–590
Business bank accounts, 133
Business continuity plans, 641, 661, 663
Business decisions, interest rate levels and, 385–386
Business entity concept, 5, 174
Business ethics, 140, 149, 391, 771–772, 803
    balancing and reconciling traditions of home and host countries, 798–800
    conventional approach to, 772–773
    globalization of, 922–923
    Internet and, 923
Business ethics gap, 932
Business ethics visibility gap, 932
Business exposure, 760
Business information systems, 608–621
Business-level strategy, 757, 803
Business models, 636, 661
Business operations franchise, 827
Business organization, alternative forms of, 197–199
Business planning, 661
Business process engineering, 670
Business recovery plans (BRP), 641–642, 661
Business report, 161–162, 174
Business risk, 350, 351, 452
Business stakeholder, 174
Business strategy, 481, 675–676
Business-to-business (B2B), 635
Business-to-consumer (B2C), 635
Business transactions, 174
    accounting equation and, 9–13
    online, 635–636
Business valuation, 358–365
    models for, 359–365
Bustarella, 932
Bus topology, 601
Buy-and-hold strategy, 219, 452
Buy-back, 932
Buyers, locking in, 486
Buy hedge, 452

Buy-national policies, 892–893
Buy orders, 340
Buzzword, 661
Bylaws, 199, 452
Byte, 661

C

Cable links, 605
Cache, 661
Callback, 661
Call options, 251, 452
    currency, 404, 421–425
    on real assets, 452
Call premium, 452
Call provisions, 238, 247–248, 255, 452
Calls, 421
Canada, CoCo model in, 681–682
Canadian Institute of Chartered Accountants (CICA), 681
Capacity, 593
Capital, 293
    acquisition of, 819
    additional paid-in, 233, 450
    contributed, 389
    cost of, 292–293, 297–301
    flow of, 916
    gross working, 200
    legal, 390
    marginal cost of, 297–301, 466
    net working, 200, 468
    weighted average cost of, 292, 297, 362, 478
    working, 200, 201, 478
Capital account, 452, 868–870, 932
Capital Asset Pricing Model (CAPM), 263, 294–295, 350, 453
Capital budget, 932
Capital budgeting, 174, 315–335, 453
    decision methods in, 323–324
    evaluation techniques in, 317–325
    importance of, 315–316
    incorporating country risk in, 353–354
    project risk in decisions in, 333–334
    similarities between asset valuation and, 317
Capital budgeting analysis, 355
    evaluation methods used in, 323
    incorporating risk in, 329–333
Capital components, 293, 453
Capital expenditures, 174
Capital expenditures budget, 82–83, 174
Capital/financial account, 866
Capital flight, 871, 932
Capital flows, international, 396–397
Capital gain, 453
Capital gains yield, 259, 453
Capital investment analysis, 174
Capitalization, 803
    improper, 720–721

Capital lease, 174, 249
Capital loss, 453
Capital management, working, 199–204
Capital markets, 336, 453
Capital projects, generating ideas for, 316
Capital rationing, 174, 334–335, 453
Capital stock, 10, 174
Capital structure, 301–308, 453
    determining optimal, 302–303
    liquidity and, 307
    target, 301–302
    theory of, 307–308
Capital structure ratios. *See* Coverage ratios
Captive finance companies, 453
Captive finance subsidiary, 453
Captive insurers, 736, 803
Captives, 745
Caribbean Basin Initiative (CBI), 932
Caribbean Community Market (CARI-COM), 912
Carriage and Insurance paid to (CIP), 932
Carriage paid to (CPT), 932
Carroll's four-part definition, of corporate social responsibility, 746–749
Carryforwards, 453
Carrying amount, 174
Cartels, 932
CASE (Computer-Aided Software Engineering), 661
Cash, 174
    aggregate investment in, 219–220
    bank accounts as control over, 132–134
    controlling mail-receipt of, 131
    deposit of, in bank, 131
    nature of, and the importance of controls over, 130–135
    overstating, 721
    presentation of, on balance sheet, 135
    sources and used of, 24–26
    theft of
        through fraudulent disbursement, 702
        through larceny, 701
        through skimming, 701–702
Cash and cash equivalents, 135
Cash and securities mix decision, 453
Cash application, 453
Cash basis, 174
Cash before delivery (CBD), 213
Cash budget, 80–82, 174, 209–210, 453
Cash collection system, 453
Cash concentration, 453
Cash conversion cycle, 201–204, 453
Cash conversion period, 453
Cash cycle, 453
Cash discounts, 213, 453

Cash dividend, 174
Cash equivalents, 135, 174
Cash flow, 325, 453
    accounting income versus, 325–326
    analysis of, 430–431
    complications in optimizing, 435
    estimation and risks, 325–333
    from financial activities, 18, 21–22, 174
    forecasting monthly, 286–292
    free, 22–23
    incremental, 326–327, 327–328
    incremental operating, 328
    from investing activities, 18, 21, 174
    from operating activities, 18, 20–21, 174
    from operations, 453
    per share, 22
    relevant, 325–327
    techniques to optimize, 432–435
    terminal, 328
    time line in, 370, 373–374, 453
Cash flow cycle, 453
Cash flow synchronization, 210
Cash flow test, 390
Cash forecasting, 286
Cash inflows, 453
    offsetting, 438
Cash items, 453
Cash letter, 453
Cash management, 209, 217, 453, 611
    centralized, 431–432, 436–437
    international, 430–437
    model, 368
    techniques in, 210–212
Cash management systems (CMSs), 611, 661
Cash on delivery (COD), 213
Cash outflows, 453
Cash payback period, 174
Cash payments
    estimated, 81–82
    internal controls of, 132
Cash pooling, 932
Cash receipts
    control of, 130–131
    estimated, 80–81
Cash sales, controlling cash received from, 130–131
Cash short and over account, 174
Categorical imperative, 780
Cathode-ray tube, 661
Causal distributions, 453
Causal techniques, 453
Cause-and-effect diagrams, 387
CD-ROM (Compact Disc Read-Only Memory), 661
Celler-Kefauver Act (1950), 356
Cellular phones, 607
Center of excellence, 932

Central American Common Market (CACM), 912
Central exchange rate, 453
Central IS organization, 583, 661
Centralization, 846, 932
Centralized architecture, 578–579, 661
Centralized business, 84
Centralized cash flow management, 431–432, 436–437, 453
Centralized disbursing, 453
Centralized information systems, 661
    advantages of, 580–583
    architecture, 578–579, 661
    decentralized information systems versus, 580–583
    disadvantages of, 580–583
Centralized internal audit model, 174
Centralized multinational organizations, 174
Centralized processing system, 453
Centralized transfer initiation, 453
Central plan, 932
Central Processing Unit (CPU), 661
CEO. *See* Chief executive officers (CEOs)
Certificate of deposit (CD), 453
Certified internal auditor (CIA), 174
Certified public accountant (CPA), 121, 171, 174
CFO. *See* Chief financial officer (CFO)
Chain of custody, 803
Champion, 494–495, 661
Chance of loss, 729–730
Change agent, 932
Change fund, 130–131
Channel (link, path), 661
    communications, 593
Channel capacity, 593
Channel design, 932
Chapter 7 bankruptcy, 388, 803
Chapter 11 bankruptcy, 288, 803
Character, 530, 661
Chargeback, 588–589, 661
Charter, 783
Chart of accounts, 174
Check, 133
Check-clearing process, 210
Check processing float, 453
Check tampering, 803
Check truncation, 453
Chicago Board Option Exchange (CBOE), 250–251, 420
Chicago Mercantile Exchange, 420
Chief executive officers (CEOs), 7–8, 661
    compensation for, 786
Chief financial officer (CFO), 7–8, 386
Chief information officer (CIO), 487, 494, 661
    roles and responsibilities of, 487

Chief knowledge officer (CKO), 488, 661
    roles and responsibilities of, 488
Chief learning officer, 488, 932
Chief risk officer (CRO), 731
Chief technology officer (CTO), 494
    roles and responsibilities of, 487–488
Child labor, 794
Children, 661
Chip, 661
CHIPS, 453
Chronic crisis stage, 767, 803
CIO. *See* Chief information officer (CIO)
Ciphertext, 625, 661
Circuit switching, 604, 661
Circular cultures, 932
CISG, 932–933
Citicorp, 818
Civil action, pursuit of, in fraud resolution, 700
Civil law, 803
Civil prosecution, of fraud, 689
Civil Rights Act (1964), 918
CKO. *See* Chief knowledge officer (CKO)
Classical trade theory, 855–857
    concluding points about, 857
    numerical example of, 856–857
Classic system, 174
Classified stock, 234, 453
Clayton Act (1914), 356
Clean float, 898
Cleansing phase, 540, 661
Clearing agent, 454
Clearing banks, 454
Clearing float, 454
Clearing house, 454
Click-and-mortar retailing, 636
Clientele effect, 309–310, 454
Client/server architecture, 536–537, 661
    increasing popularity of, 576
Clinger-Cohen Act (1996), 647
CLO. *See* Chief learning officer
Clock rate, 661
Closed system, 661
Closely held corporations, 340, 454
Closely held stock, 340
Closing entries, 174
Clusters, 933
Coaxial cable, 595, 661
Code law, 909, 933
Code of ethics, 141
Code on International Marketing of Breast-milk Substitutes, 911
Codetermination, 933
Coefficient of determination, 454
Coefficient of variation, 348, 454
Cofinancing agreements, 397, 454
Coin and currency services, 454
Cold turkey conversion, 561, 661

Collaborative problem-solving strategy, 760, 803
Collaborative projects, 621
Collaborative software, 621
Collaborative work, 620–621
Collateral, availability of, 244
Collected balance, 454
Collection bank, 454
Collection float, 454
Collection policy, 214, 454
Collection procedures, 454
Collective, 933
Collectivism, 175
Collusion, 803
Comarketing agreement, 175
Commercial banks, 337–338
Commercial data-mining software, 803
Commercial invoice, 414, 454, 933
Commercial letters of credit, 413, 454
Commercial paper, 135, 223, 454
　effective cost of, 231–232
Commercial risk management, 742–743
Commercial Service, 933
Commitment, 933
Commitment fee, 223, 454
Committed facility, 454
Committed line, 454
Committee of Sponsoring Organizations (COSO), 165–166, 681, 692–693, 803
　interrelationships with CSA and CoCo, 682–683
　on revenue fraud, 712
　in the United States, 677
Committee on Foreign Investments in the United States (CFIUS), 933
Commodity price agreement, 933
Commodity terms of trade, 885
Common agricultural policy (CAP), 933
Common carrier, 600
Common equity, 232, 454
Common Gateway Interface (CGI), 634, 662
Common law, 908–909, 933
Common life approach, 472
Common market, 913, 933
Common market for Eastern and Southern Africa (COMESA), 912
Common shareholders, legal rights and privileges of, 233–234
Common-size financial statements, 30–31, 175, 803
Common stock, 175, 258
　balance sheet accounts and definitions, 232–233
　cost of newly issued, 296
　earnings per share on, 40
　evaluation of, as source of funds, 234–235
　market for, 340–342
　types of, 234

Common stockholders' equity (net worth), 454
Communication
　asynchronous, 592–593
　cross-cultural, 871–874
　data, 590–591, 662
　expressions, 871
　full-duplex, 592, 664
　half-duplex, 592, 665
　information and, 129
　nonverbal, 871
　role of formality and informality in, 872
　simplex, 592, 670
　synchronous, 593
　wireless, 600, 673
Communication direction, 591–593
Communications, 678
　crisis, 770–771
Communications channel, 593, 662
Communication services, 933
Communications protocol, 662
Community indifference curve, 883
Compact disc (CD), 662
Company initiatives, in corporate governance, 792
Company processing center, 454
Company property, misuse of, 702
Comparability of accounting information, 3
Comparative advantage, 454, 856, 857, 858, 933
　theory of, 855–856
Comparative ratio analysis, 454
Compensating balance, 135
Compensating balances, 209, 223, 454
Compensation, 417, 454, 619, 833
　CEO, 786
　outside director, 786
Compensation committee, 789, 803
Compensatory Financing Facility (CFF), 454
Competition-based pricing, 105
Competitive advantage, 152, 481, 662, 863–864, 933
　achieving, 481–486
　as moving target, 522–523
Competitive assessment, 933
Competitive bids, 454
Competitive environment, 933
Competitive Equality Banking Act (1987), 454
Competitive weapon, strategic information as, 520–524
Compiler, 662
Complaint, 803
Complete enumeration, 454
Compliance auditing, 127
Compliance strategy, 778, 803
Components of internal control, 803

Composite keys, 533, 662
Composition of trade, 933
Compounded interest, 454
Compounding, 371, 379–380, 454
Compound tariff, 886
Comprehensive income, 175
Comprehensive payables, 454
Compression (data compression), 662
Computer-aided design (CAD), 612, 662
Computer-aided software engineering, 564
Computer controls, 803
Computer Fraud and Abuse Act (1996), 652
Computerized budgeting systems, 73
Computerized numeric control (CNC), 613, 662
Computers
　handheld, 665
　as marketing and selling medium, 616
　micro, 667
　midrange, 667
　notebook, 668
　palm, 668
　personal, 576
　super, 671
　tablet, 671
　use of, in cost-volume-profit analysis, 54
Computer Security Act (1987), 648
Computer software piracy, 645–646, 653, 670
Computer telephony integration, 616
Computer virus, 500–501, 662
Concealment investigative methods, 803
Concentration account, 454
Concentration bank, 454
Concentration banking, 211, 454
Concentration services, 455
Concentration strategy, 933
Conclusion, 662
Confiscation, 836–837, 914, 933
Conflicting ethical responsibilities, 919
Conflicts of interest, 703–704
Confucianism, 933
Congeneric merger, 357, 455
Conglomerate merger, 357, 455
Consensus, 933
Conservative approach, 207, 455
Conservative financing strategy, 230–231, 455
Consignment, 411, 455
Consistency of accounting information, 3
Consistency principle, 175
Consistent norms, 799, 803
Consol, 455
Consolidated financial statements, 163, 175
Consolidation, 175

SUBJECT INDEX

959

Constant dollar accounting. *See*
  Constant monetary unit
  restatement
Constant growth model, 262, 455
  DCF approach to, 295–296
Constant growth stock
  expected rate of return on, 262–263
  valuing, 261–263
Constant monetary unit restatement, 175
Constant payout ratio, 311, 455
Constraints, 110
Consulting services, 933
Consumer profiling, 662
Container ships, 933
Contention, 603
Contingency decision making, 933
Contingency graph, 455
Contingency plans, 455
Contingent liability, 803
Continuous budgeting, 71, 175
Continuous compounding, 455
Continuously compounding, 455
Continuous probability distribution, 455
Contra accounts, 175
Contra asset, 175
Contract analysis, 733
Contract enforcement, 933
Contracting cost motive, 455
Contract manufacturing, 933
Contract rate, 175
Contracts, international, 916–917
Contractual alliances, 933
Contractual hedging, 933
Contributed capital, 389
Contribution margin, 48–50, 175, 275
Contribution margin analysis,
  118–120, 175
Contribution margin ratio, 49, 175
Contributor, 848, 933
Control(s), 126, 622–624, 662, 678, 803,
  849–852, 933. *See also* Internal
  control(s)
  access, 623–624, 659
  accounting and, 127–140
  activities or procedures in, 803
  behavioral, 849
  bureaucratic, 849
  bureaucratic/formalized, 850
  of cash receipts, 130–131
  corrective, 804
  cultural, 849, 850–851
  data entry, 622–623, 662
  detective, 130
  document, 620
  exercising, 851–852
  export, 852–855
  hard, 678
  importance of, over cash, 130–135
  manufacturing and inventory,
    613–614
  output, 849

  in the prevention and detection of
    fraud, 692–696
  preventive, 130
  procedures in, 127–130
  security, 629
  separation of ownership from,
    784–785
  soft, 678
  types of, 849–851
  using leverage and forecasting for,
    283–284
Control charts, 387
Control environment, 678, 803
Controllable costs, 114–115, 175
Controllable expenses, 87, 175
Controllable revenues, 87
Controllable variance, 175
Controlled disbursement accounts,
  212, 455
Controller, 7–8, 175
Control limits, 455
Controlling account, 175
Control models, 681–684
Control objectives for information and
  related technology (COBIT),
  683–684
Control objectives for net centric
  technology (CONCT) model, 684
Control over the final price, 832
Control procedures, 127–130
Control self-assessment (CSA),
  682–683
  conclusions of, 683
  definition of, 682
  effect on auditors, 682
  interrelationships with CoCo and
    COSO, 682–683
  scope of, 682
Control strategy, 676
Control system, 148, 175
  cultural considerations in, 148–149
Control unit, 662
Convenience translation, 175
Conventional approach
  to business ethics, 772–773
  to issues management, 761
Conventionalist ethic, 780
Conversational principles, 933
Conversion, 560, 662
Conversion costs, 59, 175
Conversion price, 253–254
Conversion ratio, 253–254, 455
Conversion value, 175
Convertibility, 247
Convertible bonds, 237, 455
Convertibles, 253–254
  in financing, 254
  reporting earnings when, are
    outstanding, 255
Convertible security, 455
Cookie, 662

Coordinated decentralization, 846, 933
Coordinated intervention, 933
Copromotion agreement, 175
Copyright, 175, 369, 656, 823, 826, 918
Copyright Act, 653
Corporate agency services, 455
Corporate annual reports, 120–121
  financial highlights, 121
  historical summary, 121
  independent auditors' report, 121
  management discussion and
    analysis, 121
  president's letter to stockholders, 121
Corporate charter, 199, 455
Corporate citizenship, 753–754, 803
  scope of, 745–756
Corporate control and governance,
  674–816
  best practices in internal control in,
    684–685
  corporate citizenship and
    accountability in, 745–756
  corporate ethics and management
    assurance in, 771–781
  corporate fraud in, 685–725
  corporate governance in, 782–792
  corporate public policy and affairs in,
    756–760
  corporate risk management in,
    726–745
  internal control framework in,
    677–684
  international issues in, 792–802
  issues management and crisis
    management in, 761–771
  strategies in, 675–677
Corporate control strategies, 675–677
  business strategy, 675–676
  comparison of management control
    with operational control, 676–677
  control strategy, 676
  internal control, 677
  management control, 675
  operational control, 676
  strategic planning, 675
Corporate culture, 933
Corporate fraud, 685–725
  control environment, 693–696
  defined, 686–687
  perpetrators of, 690
  role of directors in controlling, 725
  seriousness of, 685–686
  types of, 687–689
Corporate governance, 782–792,
  803–804
  board member liability, 788
  compensation and, 786
  components of, 783–784
  consequences of merger, acquisition
    and takeover, 786–788
  defined, 783

improving, 788–792
increased role of shareholders, 790–792
issue of, 783
legitimacy and, 782–783
owner stakeholders and, 782–792
role of board of directors, 785
Corporate income tax, 933
Corporate-level strategy, 757, 804
Corporate public affairs, 759, 804
Corporate public policy, 756–760, 804
Corporate risk, 329, 332, 455
Corporate risk management, 726–745
avoidance, if possible, 738
burden of, 726
cost of, 726
definitions of, 726
degree of risk, 730
implementing appropriate loss control measures, 739
implementing decisions, 741–743
loss control, 734–735
management of risk, 730
measurement of risk, 729–730
pure versus speculative risk, 726–727
risk avoidance, 734
risk evaluation, 733–734
risk identification, 731–733
risk mapping or profiling, 734
risk retention, 735–736
risk transfer, 737–738
selecting and implementing risk-management techniques, 738
selecting the optimal mix of risk retention and risk transfer, 739–741
sources of, 728–729
static versus dynamic risk, 727
subjective versus objective risk, 727
Corporate social performance model, 752–753, 753, 804
usefulness of, to academics and managers, 753
Corporate social responsibility, 745–751, 933
arguments against, 749–750
arguments for, 750
Carroll's four-part definition of, 746–749
millennium poll on, 751
pyramid of, 748–749
Corporate social responsiveness, 751–752, 804
Ackerman and Bauer's action view, 751
Epstein's process view of social responsiveness, 752
Frederick's CSR1, CSR2, and CSR3, 752
other views, 752
Sethi's three-stage schema, 751

Corporations, 175, 198–199, 390, 455
goals of, 191–192
Corrective control, 804
Correlation coefficient, 455
Correspondent banks, 917, 933
Correspondent firms. *See* Representative firms
Corruption, 703–704, 795, 804, 854, 933
judicial, 147
political, 146
Corruption Perception Index, 854
COSO. *See* Committee of Sponsoring Organizations (COSO)
Cost(s), 57, 175
controlling, 114–115
conversion, 59
direct labor, 58
fixed, 45–46
flotation, 344
issuance, 344
marginal, 115
mixed, 46–47
of money, 381
opportunity, 103, 327
overhead, 588, 668
product, 59
reducing, 482–483
semivariable, 46
shipping and installation, 327
sunk, 326–327
switching, 483–484, 671
variable, 44–45
Cost, insurance, and freight (CIF), 934
Cost accounting, 4, 59, 175
Cost allocation, 60, 175
Cost and freight (CFR), 934
Cost-based definition, 892
Cost-based transfer pricing, 175
Cost behavior, 43–48, 175
Cost/benefit analysis, 554, 662
Cost centers, 175
responsibility accounting for, 85–86
Cost concept, 5, 175
Cost distortion, 175
Cost driver, 175
Cost flows, for process manufacturer, 65
Cost leadership, 934
Costly trade credit, 455
Cost method, 175
Cost object, 175
Cost of capital, 292
marginal, 297–301
weighted average, 292, 297
Cost of communication, 934
Cost of debt, 293
Cost of goods sold, 60, 61–62, 175, 804
Cost of goods sold budget, 78, 175
Cost of living allowance (COLA), 934
Cost of merchandise sold, 60, 175
Cost of new common equity, 455
Cost of preferred stock, 293–294, 455

Cost of production report, 66, 175
for decision making, 66–67
Cost of quality, 176
Cost of quality report, 176
Cost of retained earnings, 294–296, 455
Cost of risk, 804
Cost of trade credit, 221–222
Cost per equivalent unit, 176
Cost-plus approach cost concept, 109–110
Cost-plus method, 934
Cost price approach, 97, 176
Costs versus benefits criterion, 151–152
Cost variance, 176
Cost-volume-profit analysis, 48–57, 176
assumptions of, 57
mathematical approach to, 50–54
relationships in, 48–50, 55–57
use of computers in, 54
Cost-volume-profit chart, 176
Council on Economic Priorities, 755–756
Counterpurchase, 417, 455, 834, 934
Countertrade, 417, 455, 833, 934
Country of destination principle, 658
Country of origin principle, 658
Country organizations, role of, 848–849
Country-related cultural factors framework, 934
Country risk, 350, 351–354, 455, 905
assessment of, 352–353
incorporating, in capital budgeting, 353–354
Coupon-equivalent yield, 455
Coupon interest rate, 255, 455
Coupon payment, 255, 455
Coupon security, 455
Coups d'état, 934
Coverage ratios, 176
Covered interest arbitrage, 455
Covered options, 251
Covert operations, 804
Crawling peg, 899–900
Creating standard, 486
Credit, 176, 735
motives for providing in foreign markets, 399–400
supplier, 410
Credit administration, 455
Credit decision process, 455
Credit evaluation, 549–550
Credit extension, 455
Credit-granting decision, 455
Credit interchange bureaus, 455
Credit limit, 455
Credit management, 213, 218
Credit memorandum, 133, 176
Creditor, 804
Creditors, stockholders versus, 194–195
Credit period, 213, 456

SUBJECT INDEX 961

Credit policy, 213–214, 456
   analyzing proposed changes in, 215–217
Credit reporting agencies, 456
Credit risk, 905
Credit scoring models, 456
Credit standards, 213, 456
Credit terms, 456
Credit unions, 338
Crimes, white-collar, 703
Criminal action, pursuit of, in fraud resolution, 700–701
Criminal law, 804
Criminal prosecution, of fraud, 689
Crisis
   defined, 766, 804
   managing business, 768–770
   stages in, 767–768
   types of, 766–767
Crisis communications, 770–771
Crisis management, 759, 766–771, 806
   Augustine's six stages of, 770
   issues management as bridge to, 766
   nature of crises, 766–767
Crisis resolution stage, 767, 804
Crisis teams, 769
Criteria, 804
Criteria of control model in Canada, 681–682
   interrelationships with CSA and COSO, 682–683
Critical commodities list, 852, 934
Critical success factors, 662
Cross-border factoring, 412, 456
Cross-cultural business practices, 875
Cross-cultural communication, 871–874, 934
   developing competence in, 874–875
Cross-cultural message adjustment, 934
Cross-cultural negotiations, 875–880
Cross-cultural research, 934
Cross-cultural social responsibility, 934
Cross-currency swap, 176
Cross exchange rates, 404, 456
Cross hedge, 456
Cross-hedging, 456
Cross-marketing activities, 934
Cross-national ethics, 919–921
Cross-national social responsibility, 921–923
Crossover rate, 322, 456
Cross rates, 934
Cross-sectional analysis, 456
Cross-subsidization, 934
CSMA/CD (carrier sense multiple access with collision detection), 603
CTO. *See* Chief technology officer (CTO)
Cultural assimilator, 934
Cultural barriers, 934
Cultural briefing, 934
Cultural contexts, 934

Cultural controls, 849, 850–851
Cultural convergence, 934
Cultural differences, 656, 662
Cultural environment, 934
Cultural fluency, 934
Cultural imperialism, 934
Cultural relativism, 798–799, 921–922, 934
Cultural risk, 934
Cultural-toughness dimension, 934
Cultural universals, 934
Culture(s), 934
   high-context, 873
   impact of
      on the business ethics visibility gap, 922–923
      on financial reporting, 148
   influence on accounting, 143–149
   low-context, 873
   needed knowledge about foreign, 875–879
   organizational, 555
   policy formulation and, 149
Culture-free, 934
Culture shock phase, 934
Culture-specific, 934
Cumulative dividends, 247, 456
Cumulative preferred stock, 176
Cumulative transaction adjustment (CTA), 934
Currencies
   bid/ask spread among, 402–403
   diversification among, 440–441
   financing with portfolio of, 429
   foreign, 903
   stabilizing, of developing countries, 896–897
Currency Board, 456, 896
Currency call options, 404, 421–425, 452, 456
   factors affecting premiums, 421
   speculating with, 423–425
   use of, 421–422
Currency cocktail bonds, 441, 456
Currency conversion costs, minimizing, 432–434
Currency derivatives, 417–427
Currency devaluation, avoiding, 833
Currency diversification, 456
Currency exchange rates, 176, 934
Currency flows, 934
Currency futures
   comparison of forward contracts and, 420
   options markets and, 404–405
Currency futures contract, 456
Currency futures market, 420
Currency options contract, 176
Currency options market, 420–427
Currency put options, 404, 425–427, 456, 471

   factors affecting premiums, 425
   hedging with, 425
   speculating with, 426
Currency restrictions, avoiding, 833
Currency risk, 906
Currency swaps, 176, 439–440, 456, 935
Current account, 456, 866, 868, 935
Current asset financing policies, 205–207
Current asset investment policies, 204–205
Current assets, 17, 176
Current cost accounting. *See* Current value accounting
Current exchange rate, 176
Current liabilities, 17, 176
Current liquidity index, 456
Currently attainable standards, 176
Current maturity, 456
Current-noncurrent method, 176
Current position analysis, 33–34
Current purchasing power accounting, 176
Current rate method, 176
Current ratio, 33, 176, 456, 804
Current transfers, 868, 935
Current value accounting, 176
Current yield, 456
Custody account, 456
Custom-designed software, 662
Customer-centric companies, 176
Customer fraud, 689, 804
Customer impersonation, 805
Customer involvement, 935
Customer relationship management, 509, 617, 662
Customer satisfaction, 935
Customer service, 935
Customer structure, 843, 935
Customization, 830, 935
   mass, 929
Customized application, 662
Customs union, 935
Cutoff time, 456
Cut over conversions, 561
Cybermall, 632, 662
Cybernetic system, 935
Cycle, 620

D

Dai-ichiKangyo Bank, 818
Daily NPV, 456
Daily transfer rule, 456
DASD (direct access storage device), 662
Data, 662
   alteration of, 499–500
   external, 505
   internal, 505
   management of, 530–551

structured, 505
unstructured, 505
Data backup, 623
Database, 662, 804
    traditional files versus, 531–533
    on the Web, 537
Database administrator (DBA), 536, 662
Database approach, 530–531, 662
Database architecture, 535
Database management systems
    (DMSs), 531, 543, 615, 663
    components of, 534–535
Database models, 533–534, 662
Data communications, 590–591, 662
    types of, 591
Data definition language, 535, 662
Data destruction, 499–500
Data dictionary, 535, 662
Data encryption, 604
Data entry controls, 622–623, 662
Data flow diagrams, 558–559, 662
Data integrity, 646
Data management module, 511–512, 662
Data manipulation language, 535, 662
Data marts, 539
Data mining, 540–541, 662
Data privacy, 935
Data processing, 662
Data protection laws, 657–658
Data range, 504, 662
Data redundancy, 663
Data security, 646
Data store, 558, 663
Data theft, 804
Data warehouses, 541, 663
    phases in building, 540
Data warehousing, 538–540, 663
Date of record, 312
Daylight overdrafts, 456
Days inventory held, 456
Days of cost of goods sold invested in
    inventory, 456
Days payables outstanding, 456
Days purchases outstanding, 456
Days sales outstanding (DSO), 214, 456
DBA (database administrator), 663
DBMS (database management
    system), 663
Dealers, 457
Debentures, 237, 457
    subordinated, 237
Debit, 176
Debit cards, 457
Debit memorandum, 133, 176
Debt
    cost of, 293
    floating rate, 240
Debt capital, 176
Debt contracts
    features of, 238–239
    restrictions in existing, 244

Debt/equity swaps, 906
Debt forgiveness, 907
Debt instruments, traditional, 236–237
Debt markets, 335
Debtor, 804
Debt ratio, 457
Debt reduction, 907
Debt securities, 388–389
Debt-to-equity ratio, 804
Debugging, 561, 663
Decentralization, 84, 176, 845, 935
    advantages of, 84
    coordinated, 846
    disadvantages of, 84–85
Decentralized disbursing, 457
Decentralized information systems
    advantages of, 580–583
    architecture, 579
    centralized information systems
        versus, 580–583
    disadvantages of, 580–583
Decentralized internal audit model, 176
Decentralized multinational
    organizations, 176
Decentralized processing system, 457
Decentralized transfer initiation, 457
Decision, 663
Decision making
    accounting and, 98–120
    in business, 511
    factors affecting, 846–847
    income models and, 112–120
    information technology and, 511–518
    job order costing for, 62–63
    locus of, 845–846
    reporting variable and fixed costs
        for, 48
    using the cost of production report
        for, 66–67
Decision models in accounting, 98–111
Decision-support systems (DSSs), 508,
    543, 563, 663
    components of, 511–514
    developing, 517–518
    types of, 514–515
Declaration date, 312
Declining-balance depreciation
    method, 176
Decomposition method, 457
Dedicated server, 632
Deductive fraud detection, 804
Deemed exports, 853, 935
Defacement, 499–500
Default risk, 457
Default risk premium (DRP), 382, 457
Defensive mergers, 356, 457
Deferred annuity, 373, 469
Deferred asset, 804
Deferred expenses, 176
Deferred income tax asset, 176
Deferred income tax liability, 176

Deferred revenues, 176
Deficiency, 804
Defined benefit plan, 176
Defined contribution plan, 176
Degree of financial leverage (DFL), 281,
    305–306, 457
Degree of operating leverage (DOL),
    276, 305, 457
Degree of total leverage (DTL),
    306–307, 457
Delay tactics, 879, 935
Delivery duty paid (DDP), 935
Delivery duty unpaid (DDU), 935
Delphi studies, 935
Delphi technique, 457
Demand-based pricing, 105
Demand deposit account (DDA), 457
Demand flow, 457
Demand-pull inflation, 881
Demodulation, 597, 663
Denial of service (DoS), 501–502, 663
Denomination, 457
Density, 935
Dependent variable, 457
Depletion, 139, 176
Depletion methods, 369
Deposition, 804
Depository Institution Deregulation
    and Monetary Control Act
    (1980), 457
Depository transfer check (DTC), 457
Deposit reconciliation, 457
Deposit reporting service, 457
Deposit ticket, 133
Depreciation, 17, 176, 369, 457
Depreciation expense, 176
Depth, 457
Deregulation, 935
Derivative, 176
Derivative securities, 251
Descriptive ethics, 771, 804
Design, 123
Desktop publishing, 663
Detachable warrants, 253, 457
Detection of fraud, 698
Detective control, 804
Detective controls, 130
Deterministic model, 457
Devaluation, 895–896
Developing countries, stabilizing
    currencies of, 896–897
Developing-nation debt, reducing bank
    exposure to, 906
DFD (data flow diagram), 663
Diagnostic control systems, 676
Dialog, 547
Dialog module, 513–514, 663
Diesel engines, predicting failure of, 551
Differential analysis, 98–105, 177
Differential cost, 98, 177
Differential income or loss, 98

SUBJECT INDEX   963

Differential revenue, 98, 177
Differentiation, 935
Diffusion of innovation, 935
Digital certificates, 626, 663
Digital data, managing, 530–551
Digital signals, 596–597, 663
Digital signatures, 626, 663
Digital signatures and certificates, 804
Digital subscriber line (DSL), 595, 606, 663
Direct access, 663
Direct access storage device (DASD), 662
Direct controls, 881
Direct costing, 48, 112
Direct deposit, 457
Direct exporting, 824, 935
Direct export sales, 935
Direct-financing lease, 177
Direct foreign investment, 457
  factors affecting, 396–397
Direct format, 457
Direct fraud, 688
Direct hedge, 457
Direct intervention, 935
Direct investment, 177
Direct investment account, 869, 935
Direct involvement, 935
Directive, 552, 663
Direct labor cost, 58, 177
Direct labor cost budget, 77–78
Direct labor rate variance, 177
Direct labor time variance, 177
Direct Loan Program, 457
Direct materials costs, 58, 177
Direct materials price variance, 177
Direct materials purchases budget, 76
Direct materials quantity variance, 177
Direct method, 20, 177
Direct-order entry requirements, 930
Directors. *See* Board of directors
Direct presenting, 457
Direct quotations, 403, 457, 935
Direct taxes, 935
Direct transfer of money and securities, 336
Direct write-off method, 177
Dirty float, 898
Disaster recovery plan. See Business Continuity Plans
Disbursement and receipts method (scheduling), 457
Disbursement control, 211–212
Disbursement float, 211, 457
Disbursement fraud, 804
Disbursement policy, 457
Disbursement system, 457
Disbursing bank, 457
Disclaimer of opinion, 124
Disclosure fraud, 722–723, 804
  identifying, 723
  types of, 723

Disclosure rule, 780
Disclosures, 149, 177
  evolving process of, 150
  as issue for multinationals, 155–156
  perceptions based on method of, 154
  social impact practices, 155–157
  voluntary, 151
  worldwide, 157–165
Discontinued operations, 177
Discount, 177, 458
Discount basis, 458
Discount bond, 458
Discounted cash flow (DCF) model, 364–365
Discounted cash flow (DCF) techniques, 319, 358, 458
  constant growth model using, 295–296
Discounted payback, 320, 458
Discounting, 372, 380, 458
Discounting abnormal earnings model, 360
Discount interest loan, 458
Discount rate, 177, 458
  adjustment of, 353
Discount security, 458
Discount yield, 458
Discovery, 804
Discovery sampling, 804
Discrete probability distribution, 458
Discrimination
  age, 918–919
  employment, 918–919
  international price, 891–892
Discriminatory regulations, 935
Dishonored note receivable, 177
Disillusionment phase, 935
Distributed architecture, 580
Distributed databases, 535–536
Distributed denial of service (DDoS), 502, 663
Distributed earnings, 935
Distributed information systems, 580
Distribution method, 458
Distribution strategies, 930
Distributor, 935
Distributorship, 935
Diversifiable risk, 350
Diversification, 737, 804, 935
  among currencies, 440–441
Diversity, worldwide, in measurement and reporting, 152–154
Divided irrelevance theory, 309
Dividend capture strategy, 458
Dividend irrelevance theory, 458
Dividend payments
  constraints on, 312
  subsidiary, 431
  types of, 310–311
Dividend policies, 308–315
  around the world, 315

decision on, 193, 458
  factors influencing, 312–313
  investors and, 309–310
  in practice, 310–312
  stock value and, 309
Dividend reinvestment plan (DRIP), 458
Dividend relevance theory, 309, 458
Dividend roll, 458
Dividends, 177, 308, 390, 458
  expected, as basis for stock values, 260–261
  extra, 311
  liquidating, 390
  property, 390
  stock, 313–314
Dividends per share, 41, 177
Dividend yield, 41–42, 177, 458
Division of labor, 855, 857, 935
Divisions, 84, 177
Divorce, 804
Documentary collections, 411, 458
Documentary evidence, 804
  in fraud investigation, 699
Document control, 620
Document examiner, 804
Documents and records, 804
  against acceptance, 411, 458
  against payment, 411, 458
  in preventing and detection of fraud, 694
Dollar-day float, 458
Dollarization, 897
Domain name, 663
Domain name system (DNS) software, 502
Domestication, 837, 935
Domestic content requirements, 890
Domestic enterprises, 935
Domestic environment, 935
Domestic market, obtaining new products for, 818
Domestic subsidy, 890–891
Dominant, 458
Doomsday ratio, 177
Dot-matrix printer, 663
Double counting, 458
Double-entry accounting, 177
Double-entry bookkeeping, 458, 867, 935
Double taxation, 935
Downloading, 663
Downsizing, 177
Draft, 411, 413, 458
Drawee, 133
Drawee bank, 458
Drawer, 133
Drill down, 516, 663
Driver, 663
Driving variable, 458
DSL Access Multiplexer (DSLAM), 606
Dual balance, 458
Dual exchange rates, 900

Dual pricing, 935
Dual translation, 872, 936
Dual-use items, 852, 853, 936
Due care, 650
Due diligence, 650
Dummy or shell company, 804
Dummy variables, 458
Dumping, 458, 891–892, 915, 936
   margin of, 892
   persistent, 891
   predatory, 891
   sporadic, 891
DuPont chart, 458
DuPont equation, 458
Duration, 458
DVD (Digital Video Disc), 663
Dynamic hedging, 458
Dynamic IP number, 663
Dynamic risks, 727, 804

E

Earned surplus, 390
Earnings, retained, 389–390
Earnings before interest and taxes (EBIT), 267
Earnings credit rate (ECR), 459
Earnings flexibility. *See* Income smoothing
Earnings management, 3, 141
Earnings per share (EPS), 192, 255, 459, 804
   on common stock, 40, 177
Earnings per share (EPS) indifference analysis, 303
EBCDIC (Extended Binary Coded Decimal Interchange Code), 663
EBIT/EPS analysis, of effects of financial leverage, 302–303
E-Business, 804
E-commerce, 663, 936
   establishing web site, 632
   information technology and, 630–640
   on Internet, 634–635
   rise of, 637
Economic and monetary union (EMU), 936
Economic Community of West African Sales (ECOWAS), 912
Economic costs, accounting costs versus, 142
Economic crises, balance of payments and, 870–871
Economic environment, 936
Economic Espionage and Protection of Proprietary Economic Information Act (1996), 650
Economic exposure, 177, 459, 936
Economic extortion, 704, 804
Economic feasibility study, 554–555, 663

Economic growth
   accounting growth versus, 142
   potential, 396
Economic income, accounting income versus, 142
Economic infrastructure, 936
Economic objectives, of nations, 880
Economic order quantity (EOQ), 459, 614, 663
Economic policy in open economy, 880
Economic profit model, 362–363
Economic profits, accounting profits verus, 142
Economic responsibilities in corporate social responsibility, 747
Economic risk, 177, 837–838
Economic risk exposure, economic stability and, 145
Economics
   accounting and, 142
   ethics, law and, 774
   international business and, 880–900
   relations between finance and, 381–388
Economic security, 936
Economic stability
   economic risk exposure and, 145
   political stability and, 145–146
Economic system, as cultural influence on accounting, 144–145
Economic union, 936
Economic-value-added (EVA) model, 361–362
Economies of scale, 272, 459, 818, 936
   imperfect competition and, 861
ECU. *See* European Currency Unit (ECU)
Education allowance, 936
Educational system as cultural influence on accounting, 147
Effective annual rate (EAR), 379, 459
Effective interest rate, 177, 231, 232, 459
Effective internal control, 805
Effectiveness, 608, 663
Effective rate of interest, 177
Effective tariff rate, 887
Effective tax rate, 936
Effective translator, 872–873
Effective yield, 459
Efficiency, 608, 663
Efficiency ratios, 177
Efficient frontier, 459
Efficient markets, 459
Efficient markets hypothesis (EMH), 265, 459
   semistrong form of, 265
   strong form of, 265
   weak form of, 265
Electromagnetic interference (EMI), 594
Electronic agent, 663

Electronic business data interchange (EBDI), 459
Electronic check presentment, 459
Electronic Communications Privacy Act (ECPA), 649
Electronic corporate trade payment, 459
Electronic data interchange (EDI), 177, 459, 561, 600, 635, 637–640, 663
   value added network, 639
   Web, 639–640
Electronic depository transfer (EDT), 459
Electronic funds transfer (EFT), 132, 177, 459, 611, 663
Electronic lockbox, 459
Electronic signatures, 625, 639
Electronic Signatures in Global and National Commerce Act (2000), 625
Electronic spreadsheet, 518
Electronic storefront, 632–633
Electronic superhighway, 663
Electronic surveillance, 805
Elements of fraud, 805
Elements of internal control, 177
E-mail (electronic mail), 663
Embargo, 825, 936
Embezzlement, 703, 805
   employee, 688–689
Emerging markets, 925
Emotions, 879, 936
Empire type business firm, 799
Employee fraud, 177
Employee involvement, 177
Employee record management, 617–618
Employees
   earnings record of, 177
   embezzlement by, 688–689, 805
   in internal control, 681
   social impact disclosure practices and, 156
Employment discrimination, 918–919
Empowerment, 936
Encoding scheme, 663
Encryption, 625, 629, 663
Encryption Communications Privacy Act, 650
End users, systems development led by, 564–565
Engineering, 612–613
Engineering change order, 177
Engineering method, 46
Engineering services, 936
Enterprise application systems, 664
Enterprise governance, 496–497
Enterprise-level strategy, 757, 805
Enterprise resource planning (ERP), 459, 569, 619–620, 664
   software for, 73
Enterprise risk management, 731, 744–745, 805

SUBJECT INDEX   965

Enterprise-wide risk management, 738
Entities, 530, 558, 664
Entity-relationship diagrams, 534, 664
Environmental accounting, 4
Environmental contexts, 936
Environmental monitoring stage, 805
Environmental performance, 156–157
Environmental protection, 936
Environmental scanning, 805, 936
Environment-specific, 177
EPS indifference point, 459
Equal roles, 645
Equilibrium, 264, 459
   in absence of trade, 883–884
   international, 882–885
Equilibrium exchange rate, 459
Equity, valuation of, 258–265
Equity capital, 177
Equity insolvency test, 390
Equity markets, 335
Equity method, 177
Equity multiplier, 406, 459
Equity reserves, 154, 177
Equity securities, 177, 389
Equivalent annual annuity (EAA) method, 459
Equivalent units of production, 177
Ergonomics, 664
Error distribution, 459
Estimated cash flows, adjustment of, 353
Estimated cash payments, 81–82
Estimated cash receipts, 80–81
Ethernet, 603, 664
Ethical constraints on negotiations, 880
Ethical impact statements, 801, 805
Ethical imperialism, 798
Ethical investing movement, 754–756, 809
Ethical judgments, making, 773–774
Ethical relativism, 773, 805
Ethical responsibilities, 805
   in corporate social responsibility, 747
Ethical values, 805
Ethics, 178, 771, 805, 936
   accounting and, 140–141
   business, 149, 771–772
      conventional approach to, 772–773
   conventionalist, 780
   cross-national, 919–921
   descriptive, 771
   economics, law and, 774
   finance and, 391–392
   global business, 797–800
   in global business environment, 792–802
   global strategy and, 800
   hedonistic, 780
   important questions on, 774–776
   information technology and, 644–647
   in international business, 923–924
   intuition, 780
   law and, 773
   management, 776–780
   for management, 141
   market, 780
   means-ends, 780
   might-equals-right, 780
   normative, 771
   organization, 780
   professional, 780
   relationship of, to strategic management, 757–758
   revelation, 780
   utilitarian, 780
Ethnocentric, 936
Ethnocentric staffing outlook, 936
Ethnocentric strategy, 821, 936
Ethnocentrism, 936
Euro, 459, 936
   impact of, on foreign exchange transactions, 403
Eurobank loans, 427
Eurobanks, 405, 459, 907
Eurobond market, 407–408
Eurobonds, 245, 407, 459, 936
Euro-clear, 459
Euro-commercial paper (Euro-CP), 246, 427, 459
Euro cp, 459
Eurocredit loans, 459
Eurocredit market, 407, 459
Eurocredits, 246
Eurocurrencies, 907, 908, 936
Eurocurrency market, 405–407, 459, 907–908
   composition of, 405
   development of, 405, 907–908
   standardizing bank regulations within, 406
Eurodebt, 245, 459
Eurodollar CDs, 459
Eurodollars, 405, 459, 907, 936
Euromarkets, 936
Euronotes, 246, 427, 459
European Atomic Energy Community, 913
European Bank for Reconstruction and Development, 398
European Central Bank (ECB), 460
European Coal and Steel Community, 913
European Community, 913
European Confederation of Institutes of Internal Auditing, 178
European Currency Unit (ECU), 460
European Economic Community (EEC), 459, 913
European Investment Bank, 916
European Monetary System (EMS), 459, 936

European terms, 936
European Union (EU), 157, 178, 659, 853, 912, 913, 936
   Directive on Data Protection, 659
European Union directives, 178
   Eighth Directive, 186
   Fourth Directive, 156, 186
   Seventh Directive, 156, 186
Evaluated receipt settlement, 460
Event risk, 460
Evidence square, 805
Evidential matter, 689, 805
Examination of documents, 556
Exception reports, 664
Excess capacity, 270, 272, 892
Excess cash, investing, 436–437
Exchange controls, 837, 900, 936
Exchange price, 5
Exchange-rate flexibility, 902
Exchange rate forecasts, 429
Exchange rate mechanisms, 460, 936
Exchange rate risk, 460
   assessing, 438
   reducing, 438–441
Exchange rates, 178
   adjustable pegged, 898
   dual (two-tier), 900
   floating, 897–898
   impact on trade, 394
   multiple, 900
Exchange-rate stabilization, 895
Exchange-rate systems, 893–895
   fixed, 895–896
Exchanges, 635
Ex-dividend date, 312, 460
Execution error, 664
Executive information systems (EISs), 508, 516–517, 664
Executive stock options, 194, 460
Exercise price, 250, 404, 421, 460, 475
Exit measurement. *See* Output price measurement
Expansion decisions, 316, 460
Expansion project, 460
Expatriate, 936
Expatriation program, 936
Expectations theory, 384, 460
Expected rate of return, 260, 261, 460
   on constant growth stock, 262–263
Expected return on a portfolio, 460
Expedited check processing, 460
Expedited Funds Availability Act (1987), 460
Expenditure-changing policies, 881
Expenditure-switching policies, 881
Expense liability reserves, 154, 178
Expenses, 11, 178
   administrative, 62
   controllable, 87
   prepaid, 11

selling, 62
subsidiary, 430
Expense scheme, 805
Expensing, improper, 720–721
Experiential knowledge, 936
Experimentation, 936
Expertise, 546, 664
Expert systems (ES), 460, 508, 544, 563, 664
    in action, 549–551
    components of, 547
    construction of, 547
    contribution of, 545–546
    development of, 546–547
    factors justifying acquisition of, 549
    limitations of, 551
Expert system shells, 548, 664
Expert witness, 805
Exponential smoothing, 460
Export Administration Act, 852
Export complaint systems, 936
Export controls, 826, 852–855, 915, 936
    problems and conflicts in, 853
Exporters, tariffs as builder on, 888–889
Export-Import Bank (Ex-ImBank), 417, 460
Exporting, 824–825
    direct, 824
    indirect, 825
Export licenses, 852, 936–937
Export management companies, 825, 937
Exports, deemed, 853
Export subsidies, 890–891, 915
Export trading companies (ETC), 825, 937
Expression communication, 871
Expropriation, 836, 837, 914, 937
Extensible Markup Language (XML), 561, 631, 639, 664
External affairs design, 760
External auditing, 124–125, 167–172
    comparison of financial accounting and, 125
    in the international environment, 168
External audit objective, 167–168
External audits, coordination of, with internal audits, 167
External balance, 880
External collaboration, 937
External cooperation, 937
External data, 505, 664
External economies of scale, 861, 862, 937
External environment, 195–196
External equity, 296
External failure costs, 178
Externalities, 327, 460
External review, 819, 937
Extortion, 920, 937
    economic, 704, 804
Extraction phase, 540, 664

Extra dividend, 311, 460
Extranet, 631, 664
Extraordinary items, 178
Extraordinary repair, 178
Extraterritoriality, 937
Ex-works (EXW), 937
Eye contact, 874

F

Face-to-face negotiations, 878
Face value, 255, 460, 470
Facial expressions, 874
Facilitating payments, 178
Facsimile, 608
Fact finding, 555
Factor, 460
Factor endowments, 858
Factoring, 225, 412, 460
    cross-border, 412
Factor intensities, 937
    in production, 858
Factor mobility, 937
Factor prices, 858
Factor proportions theory, 857–858, 937
Factors of production, 178, 858, 937
Factory burden, 59
Factory labor, 58–59
Factory overhead, allocating, 60
Factory overhead balance, disposal of, 61
Factory overhead cost budget, 78
Factory overhead costs, 59, 178
Factory overhear rate, predetermined, 60–61
Factual cultural knowledge, 937
Falsified identity (customer impersonation), 805
Fatalism, 937
Fault-tolerant computer system, 664
Fax/voice, 598
Feasibility studies, 664
Federal Advisory Council, 460
Federal budget deficits, 384–385
Federal Courts, 805
Federal Deposit Insurance Corp. Improvement Act (1991), 460
Federal Managers' Financial Integrity Act (1982), 649
Federal Open Market Committee (FOMC), 460
Federal Reserve Act (1913), 460
Federal Reserve policy, 384
Federal Reserve System, 460
    under Regulation Q, 472, 908
Federal Sentencing Guidelines, 142, 143, 650–651
Federal Trade Commission (FTC), 659, 827
Federal Trade Commission Act, 917
Fed float, 460
Fedwire, 460

Feedback, 123
Feedback value of accounting information, 2, 70
Fees earned, 11
Femininity, 178
Fiber optic technology, 596
FICA tax, 178
Field, 530, 664
Field experience, 937
Field warehouse agreement, 460
FIFO, 937
File, 530, 664
File transfer protocol (FTP), 634, 664
Finance, 190–449, 611–612
    accounting and, 386
    capital budgeting in, 315–335
    cost of capital, capital structure and dividend policy in, 292–315
    economics and, 381–388
    ethics and, 391–392
    financial markets, instruments, and institutions in, 335–346
    forecasting, planning, and control in, 266–292
    foreign sources of, 820
    international issues in, 392–441
    law and, 388–391
    long-term financing in, 232–266
    mathematical tables in, 442–449
    mergers, acquisitions, and business valuations in, 355–367
    operations, marketing and, 365–366
    in organizational structure of firm, 196–197
    quality and, 387–388
    quantitative techniques in, 367–380
    risk management in, 346–355
    role of finance and chief financial officer in, 196–199
    short-term assets in, 208–220
    short-term financing in, 220–232
    specific legal rules and restrictions related to, 390–391
    strategies in, 191–196
    unethical practices in, 391–392
    working capital policy in, 199–208
Finance lease. *See* Capital lease
Finance strategies, 191–196
Financial account, 868–870
Financial accounting, 6, 178
    comparison of external auditing and, 125
Financial Accounting Standards Board (FASB), 5, 129, 158, 162, 178, 386
    Statement 13, 250
    Statement 95, 460
Financial activities, cash flows from, 18, 21–22
Financial analysis model, 361
Financial Analysis Support Techniques (FAST), 549–550

Financial assets, 867
　valuation of
　　bonds, 255–258
　　stock, 258–265
Financial assistance in foreign markets, 820
Financial auditing, 126
Financial breakeven analysis, 279–281, 461
　using, 281
Financial breakeven point, 280, 461
Financial control, 267, 273–284, 461
Financial EDI (FEDI), 461
Financial environment, 335–346
Financial flexibility, 461
Financial forecasting, 266–292
Financial implications, 908
Financial incentives, 937
Financial infrastructure, 937
Financial Institution Buyer Credit Policy, 461
Financial institutions, 336–339
Financial Institutions Reform, Recovery and Enforcement Act (1989), 461
Financial instruments in international markets, 342–343
Financial insurance, 745
Financial intermediaries, 336, 337, 461
Financial leases, 249, 461
Financial leverage, 281–282, 351, 461
　combining operating leverage and, 282–283
　degree of, 305–306
　EBIT/EPS analysis of effects of, 302–303
Financial manager, responsibilities of, 196
Financial markets, 335–336, 461
　globalization of, 818
　internationalization of, 150
Financial motive, 461
Financial options, 818
Financial performance, and social performance, 754
Financial planning, 266–292, 461
　control and, 266–267, 266–292
　forecasting and, 267–272
　model for, 285–286
　short-term, 284–286
Financial pressures, fraud and, 691
Financial quality, 122
Financial ratio analysis, 178
Financial reporting
　fraudulent, 141
　impact of culture on, 148
　in internal control, 685
　in selected countries, 158–164
Financial reporting disclosures, 149, 178
　costs of, 152
　reasons for, 150–151

Financial reports
　fraudulent, 687
　misleading, 723
Financial resources, 736
Financial restructuring, 461
Financial risk, 350, 351, 461, 729, 805
　factors in, 352
Financial risk management, 346–355
Financial Services Modernization Act (1999), 461
Financial shenanigans, 724–725, 805
　defined, 724
　detection techniques, 725
　identifying specific, 724–725
　prevention techniques, 725
　reasons for existence of, 724
Financial statement(s), 8, 13–14, 805
　analysis of, 732
　balance sheet, 8, 9, 17–18
　consolidated, 163
　effect of inventory errors on, 137–138
　effects of leases, 249–250
　footnotes to, 711
　income statement, 8, 9, 14
　prepared for use in other countries, 171
　projected (pro forma), 267–270
　retained earning statement, 8, 14–15
　statement of cash flows, 8, 14, 18–26
Financial statement analysis, 27, 178
　analytical procedures in, 27–32
　profitability analysis, 37–42
　solvency analysis, 32–37
Financial statement approach, 461
Financial statement audit
　benefits of, 125
　limitations of, 125
　need for, 124–125
Financial statement fraud, 687, 704–724, 805
　framework for detecting, 705–711
　growing problem of, 704–705
　motivations behind, 705
　nature of, 705
Financial swap, 461
Financing
　accounts receivable, 412
　convertibles in, 254
　long-term, 232–266, 437–441
　short-term, 427–430
　warrants in, 252–253
Financing activities, 461
Financing cash flows, 937
Financing feedbacks, 270, 461
Financing policies, working capital investment and, 204–207
Financing strategies, short-term, 228–231
Fingerprint Identification Technology (FIT), 624

Finished goods ledger, 178
Finished goods inventory, 60, 178, 461
Finite risk insurance, 745
Firewalls, 626–627, 629, 664
Firing, threat of, 193
Firms
　current and forecasted financial conditions, 243–244
　as exploiters of imperfections, 865
　as internalizers, 865–866
　nature of physical assets and personnel competencies, 820
　as seekers, 864–865
Firm-specific risk, 350, 461
　market risk versus, 349–350
First differencing, 461
First Flight Associates case, 826
First generation languages, 664
First-in, first-out (FIFO) method, 61, 65–66, 153, 178, 937
Fiscal incentives, 937
Fiscal policy, 881
Fiscal year, 8–9, 178
Fisher effect, 461
Five C's of credit, 461
Five stages of national economic development, 937
Fixed assets, 17, 178, 805
　internal control of, 138–139
　overstating, 721
　ratio of, to long-term liabilities, 36
Fixed assets turnover ratio, 461
Fixed charge coverage ratio, 461
Fixed costs, 45–46, 178, 461
　effect of changes in, 51
　reporting, for decision making, 48
Fixed exchange rates, 870, 893, 937
Fixed exchange-rate system, 461, 895–896, 896
Fixed-for-floating rate swap, 461
Fixed point surveillance, 805
Fixed rate currency, 178
Fixed wireless, 606
Flash memory, 664
Flat structures, 937
Flat yield curve, 461
Flexible budget, 72, 178
Flextime, 937
Float, 210–211, 461
Floating exchange rates, 870, 897–898, 937
　managed, 898–899
　in short run and long run, 899
Floating lien, 461
Floating rate bond, 240, 461
Floating rate currency, 178
Floating rate debt, 240
Floating rate notes (FRNs), 408, 461
Floor planning, 462
Flotation costs, 296, 344, 462

Flowcharts, 387, 557–558, 664
  in risk management, 732–733
Flow of capital, 916, 937
Flow of funds, international, 392
Flow of labor, 915–916, 937
Flow of trade, 915, 937
Flow statement, balance of payments as, 867
Fluctuating exchange rates and costs, 833
FOB (free on board) destination, 137, 178
FOB (free on board) shipping point, 137, 178
Focus group, 937
Follow-up, 835
Footnote disclosure, 154, 178
Footnotes to financial statements, 711, 805
Forecast, forward rate as, 428–429
Forecast bias, 462
Forecast horizon, 462
Forecasting
  monthly cash flows, 286–292
  using, for control, 283–284
Forecast interval, 462
Foreign agents, 937
Foreign availability, 937
Foreign bonds, 245, 407, 462, 937
Foreign Corrupt Practices Act (FCPA) (1977), 142, 143, 165, 178, 652, 795–796, 854, 918, 920–921, 937, 946–947, 947
Foreign country business firm, 799
Foreign currencies, 903
Foreign currency forward contract, 178
Foreign currency transactions, 178
Foreign currency translation, 178
Foreign debt, 245, 462
  instruments in, 245–246
Foreign direct investment, 823, 828–829, 937
  theory of, 864
Foreign distributors, 824
Foreign environment, 937
Foreign equity instruments, 343
Foreign exchange, attributes of banks that provide, 401–402
Foreign exchange market, 400–404, 400–405, 462
Foreign exchange quotations, interpreting, 403–404
Foreign exchange rate, 462
Foreign exchange risk, 462
Foreign exchange risk management, 178
Foreign exchange transactions, 400–404
Foreign financing, criteria considered for, 427–429
Foreign governments, jurisdiction over actions of, 913–915
Foreign investment, 937

Foreign investment property, taking of, 914–915
Foreign investment risk matrix (FIRM), 462
Foreign key, 533, 664
Foreign market opportunity analysis, 938
Foreign markets, issuance of stock in, 408–409
Foreign national pricing, 832
Foreign penetration, 823
Foreign policy, 938
Foreign sales agents, 824
Foreign service premium, 938
Foreign sources, of finance, 820
Foreign stock, issuance of, in United States, 408
Foreign subsidiary, 938
Foreign tax credit, 938
Foreign trade balance, 385
Foreign trade zones, 938
Forfeiting, 416, 462
Formalization, 938
Fortress Europe, 938
Forward chaining (forward reasoning), 548–549, 664
Forward contracts, 401, 418, 439, 462, 938
  comparison of currency futures and, 420
  non-deliverable, 419
  use of, by multinational corporations (MNCs), 418–419
Forward discount, 462
Forward exchange contract, 178
Forward market, 418
Forward premium, 462
Forward pricing, 930, 938
Forward rates, 178, 401, 403, 418, 462, 938
  as forecast, 428–429
  premium or discount on, 419
Forward reasoning, 664
Forward transactions, 401
Forward value date, 462
Founders' shares, 234, 462
Fourth-generation languages (4GLs), 535, 664
  emergence of, 576
Fragmented database, 536
Frames, 547
Franchising, 462, 938
  international, 827
  legal aspects of, 827–828
Fraud, 805
  assessing and mitigating the risk of, 697
  asset, 720–722
  controls that prevent and detect, 692–696
  corruption in, 703–704
  criminal and civil prosecution of, 689

  customer, 689
  detection of, 698
  direct, 688
  disclosure, 722–723
  fighting, 696–701
  financial statement, 704–724
  inventory and cost of goods sold, 714–718
  investigation of, 698–700
  liability, 718–720
  management, 689
  occupational, 687, 701–704
  perceived opportunity and, 692
  perceived pressure and, 690–692
  prevention of, 696–697
  purchasing-scheme, 702
  rationalization of, 692
  resolution of, 700–701
  revenue, 712–714
  vendor, 689
Fraud perpetrators, failure to discipline, 695
Fraud triangle, 690
Fraudulent disbursements, theft of cash through, 702
Fraudulent financial reporting, 141, 687
Free alongside ship (FAS), 938
Free carrier (FCA), 938
Free cash flow, 22–23, 178
Free cash flow hypothesis, 310, 462
Freedom of Information Act (1966), 649
Freely floating exchange rate system, 462
Free market economic system, 178
Free on board (FOB), 938
Free Trade Area for the Americas (FTAA), 938
Free trade area, 938
Free-trade argument, 889
Free trade credit, 462
Freight forwarders, 938
Frequency-division multiplexing, 599
Frequency modulation, 597
Frequently asked questions (FAQs), 617
Fringe benefits, 179
Fulfillment, 635, 664
Full compensation, 417, 462
Full disclosure, 792, 805
Full-duplex communication, 592, 664
Full reconciliation, 462
Fully diluted earnings per share (EPS), 255
Functional currency, 179
Functional information systems (IS) organization, 583, 584–585
Functional-level strategy, 757, 805
Functional structure, 843, 938
Functions, 84
Fundamental forecasting, 462
Funded debt, 235–236, 462
Funded retention, 735

SUBJECT INDEX 969

Funds, evaluation of common stock as source of, 234–235
Futures contract, 462
Futures markets, 336
Futures option, 462
Futures rates, 462
Future value (FV), 179, 371–372, 379, 462
Future value interest factor for an annuity (FVIFA$_{i,n}$), 462
Future value interest factor for i and n (FVIF$_{i,n}$), 371, 462
Future value of annuity, 373–375, 448–449
Future value of $1 at the end of n periods, 446–447
Fuzzy logic, 544–545, 664
FVA$_n$, 462
FVIFA(DUE)$_{i,n}$, 462

G

GAAP. *See* Generally accepted accounting principles (GAAP)
Gains from trade, 857, 884–885
Gantt chart, 664
Gap analysis, 938
Garn-St. Germain Depository Institutions Act (1982), 462
Gateway, 664
Gearing adjustment, 179
General Agreement on Tariffs and Trade (GATT), 462, 826, 913, 938
General Agreement on Trade in Services (GATS), 938
General controls, 805
General expenses, 173
General ledger, 179
Generally accepted accounting principles (GAAP), 5, 6, 155, 162, 179, 370, 391
  business entity concept, 5
  cost concept, 5
  fraud and, 704
  matching concept, 5, 14
  objectivity concept, 5
  unit of measure concept, 5
Generally Accepted Auditing Standards (GAAS) audit, 718
General obligation, 462
General price index, 179
General price-level accounting, 179
General purpose application software, 664
General reserve, 154, 179
Genetic algorithms, 545, 664
Geocentric staffing outlook, 938
Geographic information systems (GIS), 518, 665
Germany
  accounting standards and financial reporting in, 160–161
  independent auditing environment in, 169
  KonTraG model in, 683
Gestures, 871
Gigabit Ethernet, 607
Giro acceptance, 462
GIRO systems, 462
Glasnost, 938
Glass-Steagall Act (1933), 338
Global, 179, 938
Global account management, 938
Global account managers, 848
Global business ethics, 792–802
  improving, 797–800
Global business firm, 799
Global business strategies, 818–823
Global capital markets, 179
Global corporate culture, 938
Global corporations, 821, 938
Global information systems, challenges to, 654–655
Globalization, 805, 938
  of financial markets, 818
Global manager, 938
Global mind-set, 938
Global operations, auditing issues for, 165–172
Global organizations, 839, 841–845
  networked, 847
Global organization structure and control, 838–855
  controls, 849–852
  export controls, 852–855
  implementation, 845–849
  organizational structure, 839–845
Global Reporting Initiative, 805
Global sourcing, importing and, 825
Global strategy, 821, 938
  advantages and disadvantages of, 821
  ethics and, 800
  technology and, 822–823
Global village, 665
Globalization, 665, 847, 938
Goal conflict, 70, 179, 365
Goal congruence, 675
Going concern concept, 179
Going public, 462
Gold, 903
Golden parachute, 787, 805
Golden rule, 780
Gold standard, 463, 903, 938
Goods trade, 868, 938
Goodwill, 179, 938
Governance, 126
Government agencies, fraud and, 686
Governmental Accounting Standards Board (GASB), 162
Government Auditing Standards, 127
Government controls, over trade, 825
Government policies, 928, 938
Government procurement policies, 892–893
Government regulation, 938
Government restrictions, impact on trade, 393
Government takeovers, reducing exposure to host, 354–355
Government warrant, 463
Gramm-Leach Bliley Act, 805
Grand jury, 805
Graphical representation, 506
Graphical user Interface (GUI), 665
Gratuities, illegal, 704
Gray market, 938
Grease payments, 795, 805
Greenmail, 194, 463, 786, 806
Gross pay, 179
Gross profit, 179
Gross profit margin, 275, 806
Gross profit method, 179
Gross working capital, 200
Group decision-support systems, 515, 665
Groupware, 613, 620–621, 621, 665
Growth rate, 259, 358, 463
Grubel-Lloyd Index, 862

H

Hacker, 665
Half-duplex communication, 592, 665
Hand-held computers, 665
Hand movements, 874
Hard controls, 678, 806
Hard currencies, 939
Hard disk, 665
Hardship allowance, 939
Hard skills, 806
Hardware, mission-critical, 667
Harmonization, 165, 179
  standardization versus, 164–165
Hazards, 729
  moral, 730
  morale, 729
  physical, 729
Health Insurance Portability and Accountability Act (HIPAA) (1996), 652–653
Hedge, 463, 939
Hedger, 463, 737
Hedging, 179, 737, 806
  with currency put options, 425
  project bidding, 422
  target bidding, 422–423
Hedonistic ethic, 780
Held-to-maturity securities, 179
Help desk, 587, 665
Heuristics, 546, 665
Hierarchical database, 665
High-context cultures, 873, 939
High corporate tax rate, 832

High Dollar Group Sort, 463
Higher trial courts, 806
High-liquidity strategy, 220, 463
High-low method, 46, 179
High power distance culture, 179
Historical cost convention, 179
Historical yield spread analysis, 219, 463
Holder-of-record date, 312, 463
Hold-harmless agreements, 737
Holding costs, 463
Holistic planning, 665
Home market
   protection from declining demand
      in, 819
   protection of, 819
Home page, 665
Honesty, creating and maintaining a
      culture of, 696–697
Horizontal analysis, 27–29, 31, 179, 806
Horizontal information interchange, 665
Horizontal market, 637, 665
Horizontal merger, 357, 463
Horizontal promotions, 939
Host-country national, 939
Hostile takeovers, 194, 463
Housing allowance, 939
Human behavior, budgeting and, 70–71
Human/product safety, 646
Human resources, 617–619
Hurdle rates, 321, 363, 472
Hybrid structures, 839
Hypermedia, 665
Hypernorms, 799, 806
Hypertext, 665
Hypertext Markup Language (HTML),
      631, 639, 665
Hypertext Transfer Protocol (HTTP), 665

I

Idle capacity, 179
If-then rules, 544, 547, 665
Ignorance, 695
Illegal gratuities, 704, 806
Illegitimate norms, 799, 806
Imaging, 463, 665
Immoral management, 776–777, 806
Impact printer, 665
Impairment of capital rule, 312
Imperfect competition, economies of
      scale and, 861
Imperfections
   in access, 865
   in factor mobility, 865
   firms as exploiters of, 865
   in management, 865
Imperfect markets, 179, 463
   new trade theory and, 861–864
Imperfect market theory, 179
Imperialism, ethical, 798
Implementation, 123, 665

Implementors, 848, 939
Import/export letters of credit, 413, 463
Importing, 824
   global sourcing and, 825
Import quotas, 890
Import restrictions, 888
Imports, protection from, 819
Import substitution, 865, 939
Import tariff, 886
Improper accumulation, 463
Incapacity, 695
Income, 868
   residual, 93
Income analysis, under variable costing
      and absorption costing, 113–114
Income bonds, 237, 463
Income elasticity of demand, 939
Income from operations, 89, 179
Income leveling, 154, 179
Income models, decision making and,
      112–120
Income smoothing, 141, 154, 179
Income statement, 8, 9, 14, 179,
      463, 806
   budgeted, 73, 78–80
   emphasis on balance sheet versus, 158
   under variable costing and
      absorption costing, 112–113
Income statement budgets, 74–80
Income summary, 179
Incorporation, 737
Incoterms, 939
Incremental cash flows, 326–327, 463
   identifying, 327–328
Incremental operating cash flows,
      328, 463
Indemnity agreements, 737
Indenture, 463
Independent auditing environment in
      selected countries, 168–172
Independent auditors' report, 121
Independent checks, 806
   in preventing and detection
      of fraud, 694
Independent projects, 316, 322, 463
Independent variable, 463
Indexed bonds, 237, 463
Indexed file, 665
Indexed sequential organization, 665
Index fund, 463
Indifference curves, 882–884
Indifference map, 882
Indirect exporting, 825, 939
Indirect format, 463
Indirect investment, 179
Indirect involvement, 939
Indirect labor, 59
Indirect materials, 58
Indirect method, 20, 179
Indirect quotations, 403, 463, 939
Indirect taxes, 939

Individual/adversarial external affairs
      strategy, 760, 806
Individualism, 179, 939
Individual privacy, 646
Inductive fraud detection, 806
Inference engine, 547, 665
Inflation, 179, 327, 381, 463
   impact on trade, 392
   with unemployment, 881–882
Inflation accounting, 179
Inflationary bias, 897
Inflation premium, 382, 463
Inflow, 463
Influence peddling, 179
Influential special interest groups, 151
Informal get-togethers, 874
Informal integration, 939
Information, 665, 678
   asymmetric, 308
   characteristics of, at different
      managerial levels, 503–505
   characteristics of effective, 506–507
   communication and, 129
   lack of access to, 695
   managers and, 503
   need for, in communication, 872
   selling hard-to-obtain, 636
   symmetric, 308
   theft of, 499
Information-based services, 831, 939
Information center, 587, 665
Information content hypothesis,
      309, 463
Information ethics
   legal issues in, 647
   standards for, 645
Information map, 665
Information overload, 516, 665
Information security
   goals of, 621–622
   standards for, 627–629
Information systems (IS), 665, 939
   accounting and, 122–123
   architecture of, 578–583, 666
   business, 608–621
   corporate mission statement for, 491
   infrastructure in, 578, 666
   management of, 578–583
   of managers, 507–509
   planning, 666
   reasons for developing, 551–552
   risks to, 497–501
   sharing, 637
   sources of, 566–567
   staff in, 583–585
   strategic uses of, 481–486
   subsidiaries in, 567, 575, 666
   tactical planning in, 492–493
Information systems audit, 610
Information Systems Audit and Control
      Foundation (ISACF), 683

Information systems auditor, 624, 665
Information systems managers, expectations of line managers, 586
Information systems organization, central, 583–584
Information systems planning, 488
  initiatives in, 493–494
  key steps in, 488–489
  prerequisites for, 489–491
  strategic and tactical, 491–492
Information technology (IT), 480–659, 665
  best practices in, 526–529
  business information systems in, 608–621
  chief information officer in, 487–488
  contingency plans in, 641–644
  control in, 496–497
  data and knowledge management in, 530–551
  decision making and, 511–518
  electronic commerce and, 630–640
  ethics and, 644–647
  governance in, 496–497
  information systems planning in, 488–495
  international issues in, 653–659
  law and, 647–653
  managing, 503–510
  quality and, 525–526
  quality assurance in, 525–526
  resource management in, 578–589
  risk management, 497–502
  risk management in, 497–502
  security and controls in, 621–630
  strategies in, 481–486
  systems development and acquisition in, 551–578
  telecommunications and networks in, 589–608
  value creation with, 519–525
  vision, 491
Information technology and service strategy, 831
Information technology auditing, 127
Information technology investment management
  critical success factors in, 529
  integrated approach for, 529
Infrastructure shortages, 939
Inherent limitations, 806
Inherent risks, 806
Inhwa, 939
Initial investment, 463
Initial investment outlay, 328, 463
Initial phase, 939
Initial pleading, 806
Initial public offering (IPO) market, 341, 463
Ink-jet printer, 665
Innovator, 939

Input, 665
Input device, 665
Input files, 556
Input-output analysis, 859, 939
Input price measurement, 179
In-sample validation, 463
Inside directors, 785, 806
Insiders, 342, 463
Insider securities trading, detection of, 550
Insider trading, 787–788, 806
Insourcing, 665
Instant messaging, 666
Institute of Internal Auditors (IIA), 126, 179
Institutional constraints, 881
Instrument, 463
Insufficient research, 834
Insurance, 738
  financial, 745
  finite risk, 745
  multi-line-multi-year, 745
  self-, 735–736, 741
Insurance agent, versus risk manager, 742
Insurance companies, fraud and, 686
Insurance services, 939
Intangibility, 939
Intangible assets, 180, 806
Intangible benefits, 554
Integrated circuits, 666
Integrated international operation, 180
Integrated risk-management, 731, 806
Integrated services digital network (ISDN), 605
Integrated system, 180
Integrative Social Contract Theory (ISCT), 799–800
Integrity, 806
  creating and maintaining a culture of, 696–697
Integrity strategy, 777, 806
Intellectual property, 826–828, 837, 939
  protection of, 827, 918
Intelligence, 666
Intelligent agents, 545, 666
Intentional amoral management, 777–778, 806
Interactive control systems, 676
Inter-American Development Bank, 398, 916
Interbank interest rates, 939
Interbank market, 401, 463
Interconnection business firm, 799
Interdistrict Transportation System, 463
Interest-bearing, 463
Interest Equalization Tax (IET), 463
Interest rate cap, 463
Interest rate collar, 463
Interest rate floor, 464
Interest rate levels, 243, 381
  business decisions and, 385–386

  stock prices and, 385
Interest rate parity, 428, 464
Interest rate parity line, 464
Interest rate parity theory, 464
Interest rate price risk, 464
Interest rate reinvestment risk, 464
Interest rate risk, 464
Interest rates
  comparison of different types of, 378–380
  expectations about future, 243
  factors that influence levels of, 384–385
  finding, on a bond, 257–258
  market, 381–383
  term structure of, 383–384
Interest rate swap, 464, 939
Interest revenue, 11
Interfaces, 557, 666
Intermediate form, of hold-harmless agreements, 737
Intermodal movements, 939
Internal auditing, 126, 165–167, 180
  global trends in, 165–166
  in the international environment, 166–167
Internal audits, coordination of, with external audits, 167
Internal balance, 880
Internal bank, 939
Internal benchmarking, 849
Internal collaboration, 939
Internal control(s), 123, 180, 677, 806. See also Control(s)
  achievements of, 679
  best practices in, 684–685
  of cash payments, 132
  components of, 678–679
  definition and objectives, 677–678
  of fixed assets, 138–139
  framework, 677–681
  of inventories, 136–138
  limitations of, 680
  of payroll systems, 139–140
  people and, 680
  as process, 679
  of receivables, 135–136
  roles and responsibilities in, 680–681
  structure, 806
  weakness, 806
Internal cooperation, 939
  promoting, 847–848
Internal data, 505, 666
Internal economies of scale, 861, 862, 939
Internal failure costs, 180
Internalization, 866, 939
Internalizers, firms as, 865–866
Internal memory, 666

Internal rate of return (IRR), 180, 320–321, 464, 554
   comparison of net present value and, 322–323
   multiple, 323
   rationale for, 321
Internal review, 819–820, 939
International. *See* Global
International accounting, 4, 180
International Accounting Standard (IAS), 180
International Anti-Bribery and Fair Competition Act (1998), 918
International Bank for Reconstruction and Development (IBRD), 397, 464, 916
International banking, 901–908
International bond, 939
International business, 817–952
   environment in, 924–931
   ethical issues in, 923–924
   factors to consider in, 835
   forms of, 823–835
   regulating behavior, 853–855
International business law, 912–919
International business management, future of, 928–931
International capital flows, 396–397
International cash management, 430–437
International Chamber of Commerce (ICC), 911
International commerce, using the Web for, 654
International communications, 930
International competitiveness, 940
International contracts, 916–917, 940
International corporations, 180, 940
International Court of Arbitration, 911
International Court of Justice (ICJ), 912, 940
International cultures and protocols, 871–880
International debt, problem of, 906
International debt load, 940
International Development Association (IDA), 398, 464
International division, 839, 840–841, 940
International economic-policy coordination, 882
International economic transactions, 867
International environment, 940
   external auditing in, 168
   internal auditing in, 166–167
International equilibrium, 882–885
International Federation of Accountants (IFAC), 167, 180
   International Standards on Auditing, 172
International Financial Corporation (IFC), 398, 464

International financial environment, 926
International financial markets, 399–409
   comparison of, 409
   Eurobond, 407–408
   Eurocredit, 407
   Eurocurrency, 405–407
   financing trade, 409–417
   foreign exchange, 400–405
   motives for borrowing in, 400
   motives for investing in, 399
   motives for providing credit in, 399–400
   motives for using, 399–400
   stock markets, 408–409
International Fisher effect, 464
International Fisher effect (IFE) line, 464
International flow of funds, 392
International flows, agencies that facilitate, 397–398
International franchising, 827
International human resource management function, 940
International investment
   product cycle theory and, 860–861
   theory of, 864–866
Internationalization, 806
Internationalized their business operations, 818–819
International labor relations, 940
International law, 911, 940
International laws and politics, 908–919
   influencing of, 909–910
   legal differences and restraints, 908–909
International lending risk, 905–906
International licensing, 823
International licensing agreements, 826–828
International marketing strategies, 829–835
International markets, financial instruments in, 342–343
International Monetary Fund (IMF), 397, 464, 818, 893, 902, 916, 940
International Monetary Fund (IMF) drawings, 904–905
International mutual funds, 464
International negotiations
   strategic planning for, 877–879
   tactical planning for, 879–880
International organizational structures, 940
International Organization of Securities Commission (IOSCO), 180
International organizations, 653–659
International payments, 866–871
   balance of, 866
   fundamentals of balance of accounting, 866–870
International place/entry strategy, 831

International planning and research, 929
International politics, 910–911
International portfolio investment, factors affecting, 397
International price discrimination, 891–892
International pricing, 832–833, 930–931, 940
International pricing strategy, 831–834
International product life cycle (IPLC), 940
International product policy, 929–930
International product/service strategy, 829–831
International promotion strategy, 834–835
International relocation and orientation, 940
International reserves
   demand for, 901–903
   facilities for borrowing, 904–905
   nature of, 901
   supply of, 903
International risks, 836–838
   economic risk, 837–838
   managing, 838
   political risk, 836–837
International Standards on Auditing (ISA), 180
International Standards Organization (ISO), 603, 628
International stock markets, 408–409
International strategic and tactical objectives, 822
International strategies, types of, 821–822
International teams, 847
International trade
   agencies that motivate, 417
   currency futures market, 420
   currency options market, 420–427
   effect of, on multinational corporation (MNC) value, 398
   financing, 409–417
   payment methods for, 410–411
   theory of, 855–864
International trade and investment, 855–866
International trade flows, 392–396
International Trade Organization (ITO), 940
International treaties, 913, 940
Internet, 630–631, 666
   development of, 630
   e-commerce practices on, 634–635
Internet domain, 666
Internet Protocol (IP) number, 666
Internet Relay Chat (IRC), 666
Internet servers, 666
Internet service provider (ISP), 632, 666

Interorganizational information systems, 666
Interpretations, 5
Interpreter, 666
Interpretive knowledge, 940
Interrogatory, 806
Interstate Banking and Branching Efficiency Act (1994), 464
Intersubsidiary cash transfers, managing, 435
Intervention, 180
Interviews, 555, 940
In-the-money option, 251, 464
Intracompany trade, 396, 464
Intra-industry, 862
Intra-industry trade, 862, 940
Intranets, 518, 631, 666, 848, 940
Intrinsic value, 259, 464
Intuition ethic, 780
Inventories, 136, 940
    effect of errors in, on financial statements, 137–138
    internal control of, 136–138
    overstating, 721–722
    physical, 137, 138–139
    theft of, 702
Inventory analysis, 35–36
Inventory and cost of goods sold frauds, 714–718
    identifying, 715–716
    symptoms, 716–718
Inventory blanket lien, 227
Inventory carrying costs, 940
Inventory control systems, 464
Inventory financing, 227–228, 464
    evaluation of, 228
Inventory ledger, 137
Inventory management, 218
Inventory overstatement frauds, 716
Inventory shrinkage, 180
Inventory turnover, 35–36, 180
Inventory turnover ratio, 464, 806
Inverted yield curve, 464
Investigation
    of fraud, 698–700
    in systems analysis, 553
Investing activities, 464
    cash flows from, 18, 21
Investment(s), 180
    direct, 869
    motives for, in foreign markets, 399
    portfolio, 870
    rate of return on, 90–93
Investment analysis and service, 612
Investment banker, 337, 464
Investment banking, 343–346
Investment banking house, 336
Investment carrying costs, 940
Investment centers, 90, 180
    responsibility accounting for, 90–95
Investment grade bonds, 241, 464

Investment income, 940
Investment opportunities, 312
Investment opportunity schedule (IOS), 464
Investment policy, 464
Investment risk, 346–350
Investment scams, 689, 806
Investment turnover, 91, 180
Investors, dividend policy and, 309–310
Invigilation, 806
Invoice, 180
    commercial, 414
Irrevocable letter of credit, 413, 464
Irrigation and pest management, 551
IS architecture, 666
IS infrastructure, 666
IS planning, 666
IS subsidiaries, 666
ISDN (Integrated Services Digital Network), 666
ISO 9000, 940
Issuance costs, 344
Issuer, 917
Issues
    analysis of, 763
    development of, 765
    evaluation, monitoring and control of, 764–765
    formulation and implementation of responses to, 764
    identification of, 762–763
    ranking or prioritization of, 763–764
Issues management, 759, 761–766, 806
    as bridge to crisis management, 766
    changing issue mix, 762
    conventional approach to, 761
    issue definition and, 762–765
    issues development process, 765
    in practice, 765–766
    strategic management approach to, 762
Issuing bank, 413, 464

J

Jamaica Agreement, 464
Japan
    accounting standards and financial reporting in, 161–162
    independent auditing environment in, 169–170
Java, 666
J-curve effect, 395, 464
Job, 59
Job cost sheet, 180
Job order costing
    comparing process costing and, 64–65
    for decision making, 62–63
    for professional service businesses, 63
Job order cost system, 59, 180
    for manufacturing business, 60–62
Job shops, 59

Join, 666
Joint application development (JAD), 565–566, 666
Joint List of the European Union, 852
Joint occurrence, 940
Joint Research and Development Act, 940
Joint ventures, 464, 828–829, 940
Journal, 180
Journal entry, 180
Journalizing, 180
Judgmental approach, 464
Judgments, making ethical, 773–774
Judicial corruption, 147
Junk bonds, 240, 464
Jurisdiction, 806
Just-in-time (JIT), 614, 666
Just-in-time distribution, 930
Just-in-time inventory, 464, 940
Just-in-time manufacturing, 180, 614
Just-in-time processing, 67–68, 180

K

Kanbans, 68
Keiretsu, 940
Key currency, 893
Keys, 533, 666
    composite, 533
    foreign, 533
    primary, 533
Kickback fraud, 806
Kickbacks, 703
King model in South Africa, 683
Kiting, 806
Knowledge, management of, 530–551, 541–542, 666
Knowledge base, 547, 666
Knowledge engineer, 544, 548, 666
Knowledge engineering, 548
Knowledge management, 666
Knowledge worker, 666
KonTraG model in Germany, 683

L

Labeling, 807
Labor, flow of, 915–916
Labor abuses, 794–795
Labor laws, 940
Labor productivity, 180
Lagged regression analysis, 464–465
Lagging, 465
Lags, 940
Lambda, 465
LAN (Local Area Network), 666
Land bridge, 940
Language translation, 872
Language translator, 940
Lapping, 701, 807
Larceny, 702, 807
    theft of cash through, 701

Large power distance culture, 180
Laser printer, 666
Last-in, first-out (LIFO) method, 61, 180, 941
Law
    accounting and, 142–143
    code, 909
    common, 908–909
    ethics, economics and, 774
    ethics and the, 773
    information technology and, 647–653
    international, 911
    international business, 912–919
    relation between finance and, 388–391
Law of One Price, 940
Lead from strength, 820
Leading, 465
Leads, 940
Lead time, 180
Lead underwriter, 345, 465
Leaning against the wind, 899
Learning organization, 488, 666
Leases, 180, 248–250, 807
    capital, 249
    financial, 249, 461
    financial statement effects of, 249–250
    operating, 249, 469
    service, 249
    types of, 248–249
Least squares method, 46
Leaves, 666
Ledger, 180
Ledger balance, 465
Legacy system, 666
Legal capital, 390
Legal environment, 940
Legal reserve, 154
Legal responsibilities, in corporate social responsibility, 747
Legal system as cultural influence on accounting, 146–147
Legitimacy, and corporate governance, 782–783
Legitimation, 782, 807
Lending risk, international, 905–906
Leontief Paradox, 859, 940–941
Less-developed countries (LDCs), 807, 941
Lessee, 248, 465
Lessor, 248, 465
Letters of credit, 223, 411, 412–415, 465, 917, 941
Level of detail, 504–505, 666
Leverage, 39, 180–181, 879, 941
    degree of, 303–307
    financial, 351
    using, for control, 283–284
Leveraged buyouts (LBOs), 357–358, 465
Leverage ratios, 180
Liabilities, 9, 17–18, 180
    ratio of, to stockholders' equity, 36–37

Liability frauds, 718–720, 807
    identifying, 718
    symptoms of, 718–720
Liability risks, 728
Liability swap, 465
LIBOR. *See* London Interbank Offer Rate (LIBOR)
Licenses, export, 852
Licensing, 465, 826, 840, 941
Licensing agreement, 941
Licensing program, 180
Lien, 807
Life, health, and loss of income risks, 728–729
Life insurance companies, 339
LIFO, 941
Limited form, of hold-harmless agreements, 737
Linder's overlapping product ranges theory, 859–860
Linear cultures, 941
Line department, 7
Line managers, expectations of information systems unit, 585–586
Line of credit, 223, 465
Liner service, 941
Lingua franca, 941
Linking, 533–534
Liquid asset, 465
Liquidating dividend, 390
Liquidation, 388
Liquidation value model, 360
Liquid crystal display (LCD), 666
Liquidity, 213, 465
    capital structure and, 307
Liquidity management, subsidiary, 431
Liquidity preference theory, 384, 465
Liquidity premium, 383, 465
Liquidity problem, 903
Liquidity ratios, 181, 465
Liquidity risk, 465
Litigation, 911
Load balancing, 632, 666
Loading phase, 540
Loan participation, 465
Loans
    amortized, 377–378
    asset-based, 451
    bank, 224
    discount interest, 458
    Eurobank, 427
    Eurocredit, 459
    parallel, 469
    secured, 224, 473
    short-term bank, 222–223
    structural adjustment, 397
    syndicated Eurocredit, 475
    syndicated Eurocurrency, 405–406
    term, 236, 476
    trust receipt, 477
Lobbyists, 910, 941

Local area networks (LANs), 599, 602
    protocols, 602–603
Local content, 837, 941
Localization, 665
Local participation, 829
Locational arbitrage, 465
Location decision, 941
Lockbox, 432, 465
Lockbox arrangement, 211, 465
Lockbox collection system, 465
Lockbox consortium, 465
Lockbox optimization model, 465
Lockbox services, 465
Lockbox study, 465
Locus of decision making, 845–846
Logic bombs, 500–501, 666–667
Logic error, 667
Logical design, 556–559, 667
Logistics platform, 941
Log-linear regression, 465
London Interbank Offer Rate (LIBOR), 236, 246, 407, 465, 941
Longitudinal analysis, 941
Long-term assets, 17
Long-term debt, 235–242
    cost of, versus short-term debt, 207
    risk of, versus short-term debt, 208
Long-term financing, 232–266, 437–441
    assessing exchange rate risk, 438
    decision, 437–438
    factors influencing decisions in, 242
    measuring cost of, 438
    reducing exchange rate risk, 438–441
Long-term forward contracts, 465
Long-term liabilities, 18, 181
    ratio of fixed assets to, 36
Long-term orientation, 181
Loss control, 734–735, 807
    analyzing decisions in, 739
Losses, ability to predict, 736
Loss exposure, 731–732, 807
Loss exposure checklist, 732, 807
Loss frequency, 731
Loss from operations, 181
Louvre Accord, 465
Love Bug virus, 501
Low-context cultures, 873, 941
Lower control limit (LCL), 368
Lower-of-cost-or-market (LCM) method, 181
Lower trial courts, 807
Low-liquidity strategy, 219, 465
Low power distance culture, 181
Lubrication bribes, 920, 941
Lumpy assets, 272, 465

M

Maastricht Treaty, 913, 941
MACHA, 467
Machine cycle, 667

SUBJECT INDEX   975

Machine language, 667
MacOS, 667
Macroassessment, 352, 353, 465
Macroeconomic level, 941
Macroeconomic policy in open economy, 880–882
Macro level of legitimacy, 782
Magnetic disk, 667
Magnetic-ink character recognition (MICR), 466, 667
Magnetic tape, 667
Mail, controlling cash received in, 131
Mail float, 432, 466
Mainframe, 667
Maintenance, 667
Maintenance margin, 466
Managed earnings, 154. *See also* Income smoothing
Managed floating rates, 898–899
Management
　amoral, 777–778
　in corporate governance, 784
　ethics for, 141
　immoral, 776–777
　in internal control, 680
　involvement of, in fraud, 706–707
　moral, 777
　use of variable costing and absorption costing, 114–120
Management accountant in organization, 7–8
Management accounting, 4, 181
Management assurance, 781
Management by exception, 667
Management by objectives (MBO), 941
Management contract, 941
Management controls, 675, 807
　comparison of, with operational control, 676–677
Management discussion and analysis, 121, 181
Management ethics, 776–780
　models of, 776–778
Management fraud, 689, 704–724, 807
Management Information System (MIS), 667
Management intervention, 807
Management override, 807
Management process, 807
Managerial accounting, 4, 6, 181
Managerial actions to maximize shareholder wealth, 192–193
Managerial commitment, 941
Managerial compensation plans, 194
Managerial competence, integration of moral competence and, 779
Managerial incentives to maximize shareholder wealth, 191
Managerial know-how, acquisition of, 819

Managers, 181
　information and, 503
　information systems of, 507–509
　stockholders versus, 193–194
Managing about a target rule, 466
Managing underwriter, 345
Manufacturing and inventory control, 613–614
Manufacturing business, 57–58, 181
　job-order cost systems for, 60–62
Manufacturing cells, 67–68, 181
Manufacturing execution systems, 614, 667
Manufacturing margin, 181
Manufacturing overhead, 59
Manufacturing resource planning, 614
Manufacturing resource planning systems (MRP II), 466, 667
Maquiladoras, 941
Margin, 466
Marginal cost method, 941
Marginal cost of capital, 297–301, 466
Marginal costs, 115
Marginal rate of substitution (MRS), 882–883
Marginal tax rate, 466
Margin calls, 342, 466
Margin of safety, 55, 181
Margin requirements, 342, 466
Marketable securities, 212–213, 466, 807
　characteristics of, 212–213
　overstating, 721
　rationale for holding, 212
Market audit, 941
Market-based forecasting, 466
Market-based transfer pricing, 181
Market/book ratio, 466
Market-differentiated pricing, 941
Market economies, planned economies versus, 924–925
Market entrants, raising barriers to, 483
Market ethic, 780
Marketing
　in internal control, 685
　questionable, 793
　relations between operations, finance and, 365–366
　targeted, 615–616
Marketing infrastructure, 941
Marketing strategies, international, 829–835
Market interest rates, determinants of, 381–383
Market microstructure, 466
Market price, 96, 181, 259, 466
Market research, 615
Market risk, 329, 332–333, 350, 452, 466
　firm-specific risk versus, 349–350
Market risk premium, 466
Market segmentation theory, 384, 466

Market segments, 116, 181, 860, 941
　analyzing, 116–118
Market share, reducing costs in increasing, 482–483
Market-to-book ratio, 361
Market-to-market, 466
Market transparency, 941
Market value, book value versus, 359
Market value added (MVA) model, 362
Market value ratios, 466
Marking the evidence, 807
Markov chain analysis, 368
Markup, 105, 181
Masculinity, 181, 941
Mass customization, 929, 941
Master budget, 73, 181
Master note, 466
Master of destiny, 941
Master operating budget, 181
Master production schedule (MPS), 614, 667
Matching concept, 5, 14, 181
Materiality concept, 181
Material possessions, 941
Material requirement planning (MRP), 466, 613–614, 667
Materials, 58
Materials inventory, 60, 181
Materials ledger, 181
Materials management, 941
Materials requisitions, 181
Mathematical approach to cost-volume-profit analysis, 50–54
Matrix organization, 667
Matrix structure, 519–520, 843–845, 941
Maturing product, 860–861
Maturity, 212, 222, 248
Maturity date, 255, 466
Maturity extension swap, 466, 475
Maturity matching, 205–206, 242–243, 466
Maturity risk premium (MRP), 383, 466
Maturity value, 181, 255, 470
Maximization of shareholder value, 941
Maximum possible loss, 733–734
Maximum probable loss, 733–734
MBO, 941
McFadden Act (1927), 466
M-commerce, 636–637, 667
Mean absolute error (MAE), 466
Means-ends ethic, 780
Mean square error, 466
Measurement, 149, 181
Mechanistic organization, 941
Media, 594
Media strategy, 942
Mediators, 874, 942
　transmission of messages through, 874
Medical records use and release, accountability for, 652–653
Medium, 594, 667

Medium-term capital goods financing, 416–417
Medium-Term Guarantee Program, 466
Melissa virus, 501
Member banks, 460, 466
Mercado Commun del Cono Sur (Latin American Trading Group, MERCO-SUR), 912
Mercantilism, 942
Merchandise inventory, 181
Merchandising businesses, 181
Mergers, 181, 355, 357, 466, 807, 828–829
   analysis of, 355
   beachhead, 357
   congeneric, 357
   conglomerate, 357
   consequences of, in corporate governance, 786–788
   defensive, 356
   horizontal, 357
   inflating assets in, 721
   rationale for, 355–356
   vertical, 357
Metadata, 535
Metals, detection of common, 550
Microassessment, 352, 353, 466
Microcomputer, 667
Microeconomic level, 942
Microeconomic theory, 115
Micro level of legitimacy, 782
Microprocessor, 667
Microwaves, 595–596
Midrange computer, 667
Might-equals-right ethic, 780
Migration, 667
Mineral exploration, 550
Mininationals, 942
Minority interest, 181
Minority participation, 942
MIPS, 667
Mirror, 667
Miscellaneous fraud, 807
Mission-critical applications, 641–642, 667
Mission-critical hardware or software, 667
Mission statements
   corporate, 491
   information systems (IS), 491
Mixed aid credits, 942
Mixed approach, 467
Mixed costs, 46–47, 181
Mixed forecasting, 467
Mixed instruments, 467
Mixed structure, 843, 942
Mobile observation, 807
Model, 667
Model audit, 467
Model estimation, 467
Modeling, 467, 807

Model management module, 512–513, 667
Modem (modulator/demodulator), 597–598, 667
Moderate current asset investment policy, 204, 467
Moderate financing strategy, 231, 467
Moderate-liquidity strategy, 220, 467
Modified Accelerated Cost Recovery System (MACRS), 369
Modified accrual method, 289–290, 467
Modified buy-and-hold strategy, 219, 467
Modified IRR (MIRR), 467
Modulation, 596–599, 597, 667
   amplitude, 597
   frequency, 597
   phase, 597
Monetary barriers, 942
Monetary items, 181
Monetary-nonmonetary method, 181
Monetary policy, 881
Money, cost of, 381
Money Laundering Control Act (1986), 651
Money market deposit accounts, 467
Money market funds, 339
Money market hedge, 467
Money market mutual fund, 467
Money markets, 336, 467
Monitoring, 129, 678–679
Monte Carlo simulation, 331–332, 467
Moral competence, integration of managerial and, 779
Moral disagreement and ambiguity, tolerance of, 779
Morale hazard, 729
Moral evaluation, 779
Moral free space, 799, 807
Moral guidelines in improving MNC operations, 801–802
Moral hazards, 730
Moral identification and ordering, 779
Moral imagination, 779
Morality, 771
Moral judgment, elements of, 778–780
Moral management, 777, 807
   making, actionable, 778
Moral obligation and integrity, 779–780
Mortgage, 807
Mortgage bonds, 237, 467
Mortgage markets, 336
Mortgage note payable, 18
Mortgage payable, 18
Most-favored nation (MFN), 826, 910, 913, 942
Motion, 807
   for dismissal, 807
Motivation, cultural considerations for, 148–149
Moving average, 467
Moving surveillance, 807

Multibuyer policy, 467
Multicollinearity, 467
Multicultural centers, 942
Multicultural team, 942
Multidimensional development, 942
Multidomestic strategy, 821, 942
Multilateral Investment Guarantee Agency (MIGA), 397, 467, 914
Multilateral negotiations, 942
Multilateral netting systems, 433, 452, 467
Multilateral strategy, 942
Multi-line-multi-year insurance, 745
Multimedia, 667
Multinational agreements, 911
Multinational corporations (MNCs), 181, 828, 942
   country risk analysis, 355
   disclosure issues for, 155–156
   effect of international trade on value of, 398
   fundamental international rights for, 801
   impact of short-term financing on value of, 430
   moral guidelines to improve, 801–802
   reporting approaches of, 154–155
   suspension of activities by, 800
   use of forward contracts by, 418–419
Multinational enterprise (MNE), 181, 828, 942
Multinational organizations, 653–659
Multinational restructuring, 467
Multinational working capital management, 208, 217–218
Multiple-drawee checks, 467
Multiple exchange rates, 900
Multiple internal rate of return (IRR), 323, 467
Multiple processing centers, 467
Multiple production department factory overhead rate method, 181
Multiple regression, 467
Multiple-step income statement, 181
Multiple-trigger policies, 745
Multiplexers, 598–599, 667
Multiprocessing, 667
Multiprogramming, 667
Multitasking, 667
Multivariate models, 467
Municipal obligations, 467
Munitions Control Act, 852
Mutual funds, 339
Mutually exclusive projects, 316, 322–323, 467

N

Name-your-price auction, 667
NACHA, 467
Narrow band, 593, 667

Nasdaq-Amex Market Group, 340
National Association of Corporate Directors (NACD), 789–790
National Association of Securities Dealers (NASD), 340, 342
National Association of Securities Dealers Automated Quotations (NASDAQ), 165, 340
National Computer Security Center (NCSC), 627–628
National Counter-Corruption Commission, 146
National Crime Information Center (NCIC), 807
National-culture scheme, 942
National income, impact on trade, 393
National Institute of Standards and Technology (NIST), 648
Nationalization, 942
National price controls, 832
National security, 942
National sovereignty, 942
Nations, economic objectives of, 880
Native application, 667
Natural business year, 8, 181
Natural disasters, 498
Natural hedging, 942
Natural language processors (NLPs), 543, 667
Natural resources, 139
Nearby contract, 467
Negative exposure, 181
Negotiable bill of lading, 414, 467
Negotiable certificate of deposit, 467–468
Negotiated price approach, 96–97, 181
Negotiated transfer pricing, 182
Negotiations
 avoiding failure in international, 875
 cross-cultural, 875–880
 ethical constraints on, 880
 face-to-face, 878
 strategic planning for international, 877–879
 tactical planning for, 879–880
 team, 878
Nemawashi, 942
Nepotism, 182
Net assets, 359, 390
Net cash flow
 provided by financing activities, 21
 provided by investing activities, 21
 used for financing activities, 21
 used for investing activities, 21
Net errors and omissions account, 870, 942
Net float, 211, 468
Netherlands
 accounting standards and financial reporting in, 159–160
 independent auditing environment in, 169

Net income, 14, 182, 807
Net liquid balance, 468
Net loss, 14, 182
Net operating income (NOI), 273
Net operating loss carrybacks, 468
Net operating loss carryforwards, 468
Net pay, 182
Net present value (NPV), 182, 319–320, 468, 942
 comparison of internal rate of return (IRR) method and, 322–323
 rationale for, 320
Net present value (NPV) model, 363
Net present value (NPV) profile, 322, 468
Net price received, 832
Net profit, 14
Net profit margin on sales, 468
Net realizable value, 182
Netting, 468, 942
Net transaction exposure, 468
Networked global organization, 847
Net working capital, 200, 468
Network model, 668
Network protocol, 602, 668
Networks, 599, 667, 942
 in business, 599–604
Network topology, 600–601
Net worth, 359, 454
Net worth method, 807
Neural net, 668
Neural net expert systems, 544
Neural networks, 544
Neutrality of accounting information, 2
Newawashi, 942
New business reporting model, 121
New economy, 182
New markets
 appearance of, 818
 faster growth in, 818
New products, 860
 obtaining, for domestic market, 818
Newsgroup, 668
New trade theory, imperfect markets and, 861–864
New York Stock Exchange (NYSE), 165, 339
Nolo contendere, 807
Nominal interest rate, 468
Nominal risk-free rate of interest, 382, 468
Nominal tariff rate, 887
Nominating committee, 789, 807
Nonbank banks, 468
Noncallable, 468
Noncash investing and financing activities, 22
Noncompetitive bid, 468
Nonconstant growth, 468
Nonconstant growth firms, 263
Noncontrollable costs, 114–115, 182

Non-deliverable forward contracts (NDF), 419, 468
Nondiversifiable risk, 350, 466
Nonfinancial incentives, 942
Nonfinancial measure, 182
Nonimpact printer, 668
Nonmalicious mishaps, 501
Nonmonetary item, 182
Nonparticipating preferred stock, 182
Nonprogrammed decision making, 942
Nonrecourse or without recourse, 468
Nonroutine reports, 182
Nonsampling risk, 807
Nonsterilized intervention, 468
Nontariff trade barriers, 825, 889–893, 915, 942
Nonvalue-added activities, 182
Nonvalue-added lead time, 182
Nonverbal communication, 871
Nonvolatile memory, 668
Normal distributions, 468
Normal (constant) growth, 468
Normal profits/rates of return, 468
Normal yield curve, 468
Normative ethics, 771, 807
Normative integration, 942
Norms
 consistent, 799
 illegitimate, 799
North American Free Trade Agreement (NAFTA), 157, 182, 654, 853, 865, 913
Notebook computer, 668
Notes receivable, 17, 182
Not-for-profit accounting, 4
Not-invented-here syndrome, 510, 942
Notional amount, 468
Not-sufficient-funds (NSF) check, 135
Number of days of payables outstanding (DPO), 468
Number of days' sales in inventory, 36, 182
Number of days' sales in receivables, 35, 182, 807
Number of times interest charges are earned, 37, 182
Number of times preferred dividends are earned, 37

O

Object code, 668
Objective risk, 727, 807
Objectivity concept, 5, 182
Object linking and embedding (OLE), 668
Object-oriented programming (OOP), 668
Object-oriented structure, 534
Observation, 942
Occupational fraud, 687, 701–704

Ocean bill of lading, 414, 468
Ocean shipping, 942
Off-balance-sheet financing, 249, 468
Offering price, 344, 468
Office of Management and Budget, United States (OMB)
  Circular A-123, Internal Control Systems, 648
  Circular A-127, Financial Management Systems, 649
  Circular A-130, Management of Federal Information Resources, 648
Official exchange rate, 895
Official reserves account, 870, 942
Offshore banking, 942
OLAP. *See* Online analytical processing (OLAP)
Omitted variables, 468
One-stop logistics, 942
One-transaction approach, 182
Ongoing validation, 468
Online analytical processing (OLAP), 506–507, 668
  applications, 516, 541
Online business alliances, 635
Online business transactions, 635–636
Online operations, risks to, 501–502
Online processing, 668
Online transaction processing (OLTP), 507
On-site inspections, 733
On-the-job observation, 556
On-us, 468
Open account, 411, 468
Open account transaction, 411, 468
Open criticism, 943
Open economy
  economic policy in, 880
  macroeconomic policy in, 880–882
Open regionalism, 182
Open source software, 668
Open system, 668
Open Systems Interconnection (OSI), 603, 668
Operating activities, 468
  cash flows from, 18, 20–21
Operating breakeven
  analysis of, 273, 276, 468
  operating leverage and, 278–279
Operating breakeven point, 274, 469
Operating budgets, 68–69
Operating cash flows, 469, 943
Operating cycle, 469
Operating income, 179
Operating leases, 182, 249, 469, 943
Operating leverage, 56–57, 182, 276–278, 469
  combining financial leverage and, 282–283
  degree of, 305
  operating breakeven and, 278–279

Operating motive, 469
Operating performance ratio, 807
Operating risk, 836, 943
Operating system, 668
Operational auditing, 127
Operational control, 676
Operational feasibility study, 555–556, 668
Operational managers, 668
Operational plans, 182
Operational restructuring, 469
Operations, 807
  in internal control, 684
  reasons for internationalizing, 818–819
  relations between marketing, finance and, 365–366
Operations reporting in internal control, 685
Opportunity, 552, 668, 818
Opportunity costs, 103, 182, 327, 372, 469, 943
Opportunity costs per unit, 182
Optical character recognition (OCR), 668
Optical disc, 668
Optical fiber, 596, 668
Optical tape, 668
Optimal dividend policy, 308, 469
Opting-out right, 807
Options, 250–252, 469
Options markets, currency futures and, 404–405
Options trading, 251
Orange Book, 627–628
Order cycle time, 943
Order handling, 469
Ordering costs, 469
Ordinary annuities, 373, 469
Organic organization, 943
Organizational change, 522
Organizational culture, 555, 668, 943
Organizational designs, 839–845
Organizational structure
  finance in, 196–197
  trends in, 519–520
Organizational structures, 839–845
  evolution of, 845
  factors affecting, 846–847
  global, 841–845
Organization ethic, 780
Organization for Economic Cooperation and Development (OECD), 182, 652, 854, 902, 911
  antibribery iniatives, 797
Organization for Economic Cooperation and Development Convention on Combating Bribery of Foreign Public Officials in International Business Transactions (OECD Convention), 918

Organization of American States (OAS), 854
Organization of Petroleum Exporting Countries (OPEC), 405, 886
Organized security exchanges, 339, 469
Orientation program, 943
Original maturity, 255, 469
Originating ACH, 469
Originating depository financial institution (ODFI), 469
Other expenses, 182
Other income, 182
Other investment assets/liabilities, 870
Outflow, 469
Out-of-money option, 251
Out-of-pocket costs, 231
Out-of-pocket expenses, 231, 469
Out-of-sample validation, 469
Out-of-the-money option, 469
Output, 668
Output controls, 849
Output device, 668
Output files, 556
Output price measurement, 182
Outside directors, 785, 807
  compensation for, 786
Outsourcing, 469, 566, 567–569, 668
  advantages of, 568–569
  recovery plan, 642–643
  risks of, 569
Outstanding stock, 182
Overabsorbed factory overhead, 61
Overapplied factory overhead, 61, 182
Overcentralization, 943
Overdraft credit lines, 469
Overdraft facility, 469
Overhead cost, 588, 668
Overhedging, 469
Overseas Private Investment Corporation (OPIC), 354–355, 417, 838
Overstandardization, 834
Overstating
  accounts receivable, 721–722
  cash, 721
  fixed assets, 721
  inventory, 721–722
  marketable securities, 721
Over-the-counter (OTC) market, 340, 469
Owner's equity, 9, 14, 182
Ownership, separation of control from, 784–785
Ownership risk, 836, 943
Owner stakeholders, and corporate governance, 782–792

P

Pacifier-oriented leader, 943
Packaged software, 668
Packet, 593, 668

Packet switching, 605, 668
Paid-only reconciliation, 469
Palm computer, 668
Paperwork Reduction Act (1995), 649
Par, 182
Parallel bonds, 407, 469
Parallel conversion, 560, 668
Parallel loans, 440, 469
Parallel port, 591
Parallel processing, 668
Parallel transmission, 591, 668
Parameters, 668
Parent, 182, 668
Parent company, 182
Parent/subsidiary relationship, 182
Pareto charts, 182, 387
Paris Convention for the Protection of Industrial Property, 918
Parity check, 593, 668
Parity rate, 870
Partial compensation, 417, 469
Participating preferred stocks, 247
Participation, 943
Participative decision making, 943
Participative management, 807
Participatory design approach, 182
Partnership, 182, 198, 469
Par value, 232, 247, 255, 469, 470, 895
Passive investment strategy, 218, 219, 469
Passwords, 808
Patent Cooperation Treaty (PCT), 911, 918, 943
Patents, 182, 369, 656, 823, 826, 918
Pax Americana, 943
Payables concentration, 211
Payables turnover ratio, 469
Payable through draft, 469
Payback period, 318–319, 469
Payback period method, 182
Payee, 133
Paying agent, 469
Paying bank, 917
Payment, 469
Payment date, 312, 469
Payment procedures, 312
Payoffs, 943
Payroll, 183
Payroll fraud scheme, 808
Payroll register, 183
Payroll systems, internal controls for, 139–140
Peer-to-peer LAN, 599, 668
Pegged exchange rates, 469, 893
Pension, 808
Pension funds, 338
Pension liabilities, 943
People-processing services, 830, 943
Perceived opportunity, 808
    fraud and, 692
Perceived pressure, 808
    fraud and, 690–692

Percent-of-sales forecasting model, 284–285, 469
Perfect forecast line, 469
Performance auditing, 127
Performance-based pay, 943
Performance evaluation, 84–85, 619
Performance report, 183
Performance shares, 194, 469
Peril, 729
Period costs, 62, 183
Periodic inventory system, 183
Periodic rate, 470
Peripheral equipment, 668
Perishability, 943
Permanent current assets, 205, 229, 470
Permanent differences, 183
Perpetrator, 808
Perpetual inventory system, 183
Perpetuity, 261, 470
Persistent dumping, 891
Personal computers, widespread use of, 576
Personal decision-support systems, 514–515, 668
Personal digital assistant (PDA), 617, 669
Personal liability, 788
Personal observation
    evidence of, 808
    in fraud investigation, 699
Personnel competencies, 820, 943
PERT chart, 669
Petrodollars, 405, 470
Petty cash fund, 183
Phased conversion, 560, 669
Phase modulation, 597
Philanthropic responsibilities, 808
    in corporate social responsibility, 747–748
Philanthropy, 808
Physical design, 559, 669
Physical distance, 874
Physical distribution, 943
Physical evidence, 808
    in fraud investigation, 699
Physical flows, for process manufacturer, 65
Physical hazard, 729
Physical inventory, 137, 138–139, 183
Physical safeguards, 808
    in preventing and detection of fraud, 694
Piggyback, 470
Pilot conversion, 561
Piloting, 561, 669
Pipelining, 669
Piracy, computer software, 645–646, 653, 670
Pixel (picture element), 669
Place/entry strategy, 943
    international, 831

Plaintext, 625, 669
Planned economies, market economies versus, 924–925
Planned retention, 735
Planning, 669
Plant assets, 17
Plant safety, and the Bhopal tragedy, 793–794
Platform, 669
Plaza Accord, 470
Plaza Agreement, 943
Pledging, 225
Pledging receivables, 470
Plug-and-play, 669
PM theory of leadership, 943
Pointing, 874
Point of presence (POP), 669
Point to point protocol (PPP), 669
Poison pill, 194, 470, 787, 808
Policy, 808
Policy formulation, culture and, 149
Policy instruments, 881
Political corruption, 146
Political environment, 924, 943
Political risk, 183, 352, 470, 836–837, 943
Political stability, economic stability and, 145–146
Political systems, 943
    as cultural influence on accounting, 145–146
Political union, 943
Politics, 509
    international, 910–911
Polling, 602, 669
Polycentric staffing outlook, 943
Pooling, 470
Pooling-of-interests method, 183
Population, 808
Population increase, 926, 943
Population shifts, effects of, 926–927
Population stabilization, 926–927, 943
Port, 669
Portal, 632, 669
Porter's competitive strategy, 675–676
Portfolio approach, 183
Portfolio diversification, 429
Portfolio investment account, 870, 943
Portfolio models, 943
Portfolio returns, 348–349
Portfolio risk, 347, 470
    measuring, 348–349
Ports, 943
Positioning, 943
Positive adjustment phase, 943
Positive exposure, 183
Positive float, 470
Positive pay, 470
Possession-processing services, 830–831, 943–944
Postal inspectors, 808
Post-audit, 324–325, 470

Post-closing trial balance, 183
Posting, 183
Post Office Protocol (POP3), 634
Post-retirement benefits, 183
Potential economic growth, 396
Power, 510
Power distance, 183, 944
Practices, 944
Preauthorized debits, 211, 470
Preauthorized debit system, 470
Preauthorized draft, 470
Preauthorized payments, 432, 470
Precautionary balances, 209, 470
Precautionary motive, 470
Predatory dumping, 891
Predetermined factory overhead rate, 60–61, 183
Predication, 808
Predictive value of accounting information, 2
Preemptive right, 234, 470
Pre-expatriation program, 944
Preferential policies, 944
Preferred dividends, 246
Preferred stock, 183, 246–248, 258
  cost of, 293–294
  major provisions of issues, 247–248
  pros and cons of, 248
Preliminary hearing, 808
Preloss activities, 808
Premium, 183, 470
Premium bond, 470
Prepackaged software, 566, 569–573
  steps in purchasing, 570–571
Prepaid expenses, 11, 183
Prepayment, 470
Prepayment method, 410
Presentation principles, 944
Presentment, 470
Present value, 183, 372–373, 470
Present value concept, 183
Present value index, 183
Present value interest factor for an annuity, 470
Present value interest factor for i and n (PVIF$_{i,n}$), 372, 470
Present value of an annuity, 183, 375–377, 444–445
Present value of $1 due at the end of *n* periods, 442–443
Pretty Good Privacy (PGP), 656
Prevention costs, 183
Preventive controls, 130, 808
Price controls, 837–838, 944
Priced-based definition, 892
Price discrimination, international, 891–892
Price/earnings (P/E) ratio, 41, 183, 470
Price effects, 315
Price-elastic, 470
Price escalation, 944

Price factor, 183
Price multiples model, 360–361
Prices
  exchange, 5
  setting normal product selling, 105–110
  transfer, 95
Price strategy, 944
  international, 831–834
Price-to-book ratio, 361
Price-to-cash-flow ratio, 361
Price-to-earnings ratio, 360
Price-to-sales ratio, 361
Pricing
  as an active tool, 832
  arms-length, 833
  of products, 115
  as static element, 832
  transfer, 95–97
Pricing market, 470
Pricing motive, 470
Primary audience, 944
Primary data, 944
Primary earnings per share (EPS), 255
Primary key, 533, 669
Primary markets, 336, 341, 470
Primary memory (primary storage, main memory, main storage), 669
Primary research, 944
Prime rate, 224, 470
Principal, 470
Principal amount, 255, 470
Prior-period adjustments, 183
Privacy, 669
Privacy Act (1974), 648
Private accounting, 4
Private branch exchange (PBX), 594, 669
Private Export Funding Corporation (PEFCO), 417
Private placement, 470, 944
Private Securities Litigation Reform Act (1995), 142, 143, 792, 808
Privatization, 183, 396, 470, 944
Probability distribution, 470
Probability-impact matrix, 764, 808
Problem, 552, 669
Procedures, 556, 808
Proceeds, 183
Process, 558, 669, 808
Process cost system, 59, 64–68, 183
  comparing job order costing and, 64–65
Processing float, 470
Processing methods, 123
Process manufacturers, 64, 183
  physical flows and cost flows for, 65
Process-oriented layout, 183
Process structure, 843, 944
Prodromal crisis stage, 767, 808
Product costing, 183
Product costs, 57–59, 107–108, 183

Product cost concept, 183
Product cycle
  stages of, 860–861
  trade implications of, 861
Product cycle theory, 183, 470–471, 944
  contributions of, 861
  international investment and, 860–861
Product differentiation, 944
Product division structure, 944
Production
  factor intensity in, 858
  planning, 115–116
Production bottlenecks, 183
  product pricing under, 111
  product profitability under, 110–111
Production budget, 75, 183
Production opportunities, 381, 471
Production possibilities frontier, 944
Production rules, 547, 669
Productivity, 183, 609, 669
Product mix, 117
Product-oriented layout, 183
Product pricing, under production bottlenecks, 111
Product profitability, under production bottlenecks, 110–111
Product profitability analysis, 117–118
Products, 84
  creating new, 484
  differentiating, 484–485
  enhancing, 485
  maturing, 860–861
  new, 860
  pricing, 115
  standardized, 861
Product selling prices, setting, 105–110
Product/service strategy, 944
Product standard, 825
Product strategy, 829–830
Product structure, 841–842, 944
Professional ethic, 780
Professional service businesses, job order cost systems for, 63
Profitability, 32, 183
Profitability analysis, 37–42
  dividends per share, 41
  dividend yields, 41–42
  earnings per share on common stock, 40
  price-earnings ratio, 41
  product, 117–118
  rate earned on common stockholders' equity, 39–40
  rate earned on total assets, 38–39
  rate earned on total stockholders' equity, 39
  ratio of net sales to assets, 38
  salesperson, 118
  sales territory, 116–117
Profitability index method, 323

SUBJECT INDEX 981

Profitability ratios, 183, 471
Profit centers, 183
    reporting by, 89–90
    responsibility accounting for, 86–90
Profit margin, 91, 184, 808
Profit maximization, 192–193, 471
Profits, 191
Profit-volume chart, 184
Profit-volume ratio, 49
Pro forma balance sheet, 210, 291–292, 470
Program, 669
Program auditing, 127
Programmable problem, 669
Programmed decision making, 944
Programming, 669
Programming backlog, 576
Programming languages, 669
Program robustness, 622–623
Project, 669
Project bidding, using call options to hedge, 422
Projected balance sheet method, 471
Projected earnings per share, 193
Projected financial statements, 267–270
Project Finance Loan Program, 471
Project management, 564, 669
Project required rate of return, k_{proj}, 471
Project risk, in capital budgeting decisions, 333–334
Promissory note, 184, 222, 471
Promotion, 618
Promotional message, 944
Promotion of Commerce Online in the Digital Era Act, 650
Promotion strategy, 944
    international, 834–835
Proofs, 129
Property, plant, and equipment, 17
Property dividends, 390
Property risk, 728
Proportionality principle, 780
Proportions, 858
Proposal for appropriation of retained earnings, 162, 184
Proprietorship, 184, 197, 471
Prospectus, 341–342, 471
Protectionistic legislation, 944
Protection of intellectual property, 944
Protective tariff, 886
Protocols, 591, 602–604, 669
    network, 602
    wide area network (WAN), 603–604
Prototyping, 562–564, 669
    popularity of, 576
Proxy, 233, 471
Proxy fight, 233, 471
Proxy information, 944
Proxy process, 784–785, 808
Prudence concept, 153, 184
Psychocultural contexts, 944

Psychopath, 808
Public accounting, 4
Public affairs, 808
    corporate, 759
    as part of strategic management, 759–760
Public affairs department, 759
Public affairs management, 759, 804
Public affairs strategy, 759–760
Public affairs thinking, incorporate, into managers' jobs, 760
Public Company Accounting Oversight Board, 781
Public issues committee, 789, 808
Public-key encryption, 669
Publicly held stock, 340
Publicly owned corporations, 340, 471
Public policy
    corporate, 756–760
    as a part of strategic management, 756–757
Public policy committee, 789, 808
Public relations (PR)/Public affairs (PA), 808
Pull manufacturing, 184
Punitive tariff, 944
Purchased applications, 569–573
Purchased software
    learning from experience in, 572
    risks in, 572–573
Purchase method, 184
Purchase order with payment voucher attached, 471
Purchase schemes, conflicts of interest and, 703
Purchases discounts, 184
Purchases returns and allowances, 184
Purchase terms, 471
Purchasing cards, 471
Purchasing power bonds, 237
Purchasing power gain, 184
Purchasing power loss, 184
Purchasing power parity (PPP), 944
Purchasing Power Parity (PPP) line, 471
Purchasing Power Parity (PPP) theory, 471
Purchasing power risk, 471
Purchasing-scheme frauds, 702
Pure play method, 333, 471
Pure risk, 726–727, 808
Push manufacturing, 184
Putable bonds, 237, 471
Put option, 251, 471
    currency, 404
    on real assets, 471
Puts, 421
PVA_n, 471
$PVIFA(DUE)_{i,n}$, 471
Pyramid model, 669

Q

Qualified opinion, 124
Qualitative information, 944
Quality, 944
    information technology and, 525–526
    relation between finance and, 387–388
Quality assurance, information technology (IT), 525–526
Quality circles, 944
Quality of life, 944
Quality of work life, 944
Quantitative techniques and finance, 367–380, 471
    amortization methods, 370
    amortized loans, 377–378
    cash flow time lines, 370
    cash management model, 368
    comparison of different types of interest rates, 378–380
    depletion methods, 369
    depreciation methods, 369
    future value, 371–372
    future value of annuity, 373–375
    present value, 372–373
    present value of annuity, 375–377
    time value of money, 370
Quantity discounts, 471
Quantity factor, 119, 184
Query, 669
Query by example (QBE), 535
Questionable marketing, 793
Questionable payments, 795
Questionnaires, 556
Quick assets, 34, 184
Quick ratio, 34, 184, 471, 808
Quotas, 393, 471, 825, 944
    import, 890
    tariffs versus, 890, 946
Quoted risk-free rate of interest, 382, 468

R

Racketeer Influenced and Corrupt Organization Act (1970), 651–652
RAID (Redundant Array of Independent Disks), 669
Random Access Memory (RAM), 669
Range reconciliation, 471
Rapid Application Development (RAD), 669
Rapid prototyping, 612, 669
Rate earned
    on common stockholders' equity, 39–40, 184
    on stockholders' equity, 184

on total assets, 38–39, 184
on total stockholders' equity, 39
Rate of income from operations to total assets, 39
Rate of return
  on assets, 90
  on investment, 90–93, 184, 191
Rationalization, 808
  fraud and, 692
Ratio of fixed assets to long-term liabilities, 184
Ratio of liabilities to stockholders' equity, 184
Ratio of net sales to assets, 38, 184
Raw and in process inventory, 184
Raw materials, acquisition of, 819
Raw materials inventory, 60, 471
Reach percentage, 669
Read-only memory (ROM), 669–670
Real accounts, 184
Real assets, 867
  valuation of, 265–266
Real cost of hedging, 471
Real interest rate, 471
Realized gains, 184
Realized losses, 184
Realized rates of return, 260, 349, 471
Real options, 471
Real risk-free rate of interest, 382, 471
Reasonable assurance, 808
Receipts, acceleration of, 211
Receipts and disbursements method, 286–289, 471–472
Receivable control, 472
Receivable monitoring, 214–215, 472
Receivables, 184
  internal control of, 123
Receivables financing
  cost of, 226
  evaluation of, 226
  future use of, 226–227
Receiving depository financial institution (RDFI), 472
Receiving report, 184
Records, 530, 670, 804
  in preventing and detection of fraud, 694
Recourse, 225, 472
Recovery plan, outsourcing, 642–643
Recruitment, 618
Recursive least squares (RLS), 472
Redundant arrays of independent disks (RAID), 623
Reengineering, 184, 522, 670
Reevaluation reserve, 154
Reference groups, 944
Refunding, 472
Regiocentric staffing outlook, 944
Regional audit staff internal audit model, 184

Regional Check Processing Centers (RCPCs), 472
Regional structure, 944
Regional trade communities, 912–913, 944
Register, 670
Register disbursement scheme, 808
Registrar, 472
Registration statement, 341, 472
Regression analysis, 472
Regression coefficient, 472
Regular reports, 184
Regulation CC, 472
Regulation Q, 472, 908
Reinvestment rate assumption, 323, 472
Reinvestment rate risk, 383, 472
Reinvoicing, 945
Reinvoicing center, 472
Relational database, 670
Relational operation, 670
Relationship approach, 472
Relative form of purchasing power parity, 472
Relativism, cultural, 798–799, 921–922
Relaxed current asset investment, 204, 472
Relevance of accounting information, 2
Relevant cash flows, 325–327, 472
Relevant range, 44, 184
Relevant risk, 350, 472
Reliability, 945
Reliability of accounting information, 2
Religion, 945
  as cultural influence on accounting, 147
Remedy, 808
Remittance advice, 131, 133, 472
Rental, 184
Rent applications, 566
Rent revenue, 11
Reorder point, 472
Reorganization, 388
Repatriation, 945
Repatriation of earnings, 472
Repatriation program, 945
Repeater, 594, 670
Replacement chain approach, 472
Replacement cost, 184, 360
Replacement decisions, 316, 472
Replication, 670
  of database, 536
Reportable condition, 808
Report form, 17, 184
Reporting, accounting and, 120–122
Representational faithfulness of accounting information, 2
Representative firms, 184
Representative office, 945
Repurchase agreement, 472
Repurchase agreements, 808
Request for admission, 808

Request for information (RFI), 570, 670
Request for proposal (RFP), 571, 670
Required rate of return, 259, 321, 472
Research and development (R&D), 94, 95, 184
Research collaboration, 184
Researchers, fraud and, 686
Reserve borrowing capacity, 308, 472
Reserve funds, 735
Reserves, role of, 153–154
Resident staff and central reviewers internal audit model, 184
Resident staff and regional and central reviewers internal auditing model, 184
Resident staff and regional reviewers internal audit model, 185
Residual dividend policy, 310–311, 472
Residual income, 93, 185
Residual value, 185, 472
Resiliency, 472
Resolution, 670
Respect-oriented leadership, 945
Responsibility accounting, 85, 185
  for cost centers, 85–86
  for investment centers, 90–95
  for profit centers, 86–90
Responsibility centers, 69, 85, 185
Restricted current asset investment, 204, 472
Restrictive covenants, 238, 472
Restructuring, 808
  inflating assets in, 721
Retail inventory method, 185
Retail lockbox, 472, 473
Retail market, 473
Retained earnings, 11, 185, 232, 389–390, 473
  cost of, 294–296
Retained earnings statement, 8, 14–15, 185
Retention
  decisions regarding, 736
  funded, 735
  planned, 735
  selecting, amounts, 740–741
  unfunded, 735
  unplanned, 735
Return (yield), 213
Return items, 473
Return on assets (ROA), 185
Return on common equity (ROE), 473
Return on equity, 808
Return on invested capital (ROIC), 358
Return on investment (ROI), 185, 670
Return on total assets (ROA), 473
Revaluation, 895–896
Revaluation reserve, 185
Revelation ethic, 780
Revenue, 808
  subsidiary, 430

SUBJECT INDEX   983

Revenue Anticipation Notes, 473
Revenue center, 185
Revenue expenditures, 185
Revenue fraud, 712–714
Revenue recognition, 808
Revenue recognition concept, 185
Revenues, 11, 185
   controllable, 87
   differential, 98
   interest, 11
   rent, 11
Revenue securities, 473
Revenue tariff, 886
Reverse auction, 670
Reverse culture shock, 945
Reverse distribution, 945
Reverse engineering, 945
Reverse positive pay, 473
Reverse repo, 473
Reverse repurchase agreement, 224
Reverse splits, 313
Revocable letter of credit, 413, 473
Revolving credit agreement, 223, 473
Revolving line of credit, 473
Riding the yield curve, 219, 473
Rightsizing. *See* Downsizing
Right to Financial Privacy Act (1978), 651
Rigid implementation, 835
Ring, 670
Ringi, 945
Ring topology, 600, 671
RISC (Reduced Instruction Set Computer), 670
Risk(s), 212, 381, 473, 808
   business, 350, 351
   country, 350, 351–354, 905
   credit, 905
   currency, 906
   defined, 726
   defining and measuring, 346–347
   financial, 350, 351
   firm-specific, 349–350
   incorporating, in capital budgeting analysis, 329–333
   investment, 346–350
   market, 349–350
   portfolio, 348–349
   stand-alone, 347–348
   types of, 350–354
Risk-adjusted discount rate, 334, 473
Risk-adjusted return on capital (RAROC), 808
Risk arbitrage, 787, 808
Risk assessment, 678, 809
Risk aversion, 473
Risk avoidance, 734, 809
Risk classes, 473
Risk exposure, 945
Risk-free rate, 473
Risk management, 126, 185, 731, 809
   commercial, 742–743
   enterprise, 744–745
   managing program in, 743
   organization for, 742
   subjective, 743–744
   value of, 738
Risk-management information system (RMIS), 733, 809
Risk-management policy, 743, 809
Risk-management process, 809
Risk manager, 731, 809
   versus insurance agent, 742
Risk mapping (risk profiling), 734, 809
Risk of fraud, assessing and mitigating, 697
Risk premium, RP, 473
Risk profiling, 734, 809
Risk reduction, 809
Risk retention, 735–736, 809
   selecting optimal mix of, 739–741
Risk spread, 473
Risk structure of interest rate, 473
Risk transfer, 737–738, 809
   selecting optimal mix of, 739–741
Robinson-Patman Act, 105
Robotics, 542–543, 670
Roll-on-roll-off (RORO), 945
Root mean square error, 473
Routing reporting, 185
Royalty, 945
Rules of Professional Conduct, 185
Run charts, 387

S

Safety stocks, 205, 473
Sale and leaseback, 248, 473
Sales, 11
   in internal control, 685
Sales agents, 473
Sales budget, 74–75, 185
Sales discounts, 185
Sales force automation, 617, 670
Sales forecasts, 267, 473
Sales mix, 54–55, 117, 185
Salesperson profitability analysis, 118
Sales return percentage (ratio), 809
Sales returns and allowances, 185, 809
Sales schemes, conflicts of interest and, 703
Sales territory profitability analysis, 116–117
Sales-type lease, 185
Same-Day Settlement, 473
Sample, 809
Sampling risk, 809
Samurai bonds, 245
Sanction, 945
Sarbanes-Oxley Act (2002), 781
Satellite microwave, 595–596, 606
Savings and loan associations (S&Ls), 338
Scalability, 599, 634, 670
Scams, investment, 689
Scanner, 670
Scanning system, 945
Scatter diagrams, 387
Scattergraph method, 46
Scenario analysis, 330–331, 473
Scenario building, 945
Schema, 534, 670
S corporation, 473
SDSL (symmetric DSL), 606
Sea bridge, 945
Search warrant, 809
Seasonal dating, 473
Sea transport and freight restrictions, 893
Secondary audience, 945
Secondary data, 945
Secondary markets, 336, 341, 473
   maintenance of, 346
Secondary research, 945
Secondary statements, 155, 185
Second generation languages, 670
Secured loans, 224, 473
Securities, 473
   aggregate investment in, 219–220
   rationale for using different types of, 241–242
   use of, in short-term financing, 224–225
Securities and Exchange Commission (SEC), 157, 170, 341–342, 386, 420, 473, 809
   audit considerations for, 172
   customary functions of audit committees, 680–681
Securities markets, regulation of, 341–342
Securities regulation, 917–918, 945
Securitization, 473, 745
Security and Freedom Through Encryption (SAFE) Act (1997), 649
Security controls, downside of, 629
Security market line (SML), 263, 474
Security measures, 129, 670
   economic aspect of, 629–630
Seekers, firms as, 864–865
Segment reporting, 163
Segregation of duties, 809
   in preventing and detection of fraud, 693–694
Select, 670
Selective restatements, 155, 185
Self-insurance, 735–736
   decision on, 741
Self-liquidating approach, 205–206, 466
Self-management, 945
Self-reference criterion (SRC), 829, 945

Self-sustaining international operation, 185
Sell hedge, 474
Selling accounts receivable, 225
Selling and administrative expenses budget, 78
Selling expenses, 62, 185
Selling forward, 945
Selling group, 345, 474
Sell orders, 340
Sell quote, 402
Semantic nets, 548, 670
Semiannual compounding, 474
Semistrong-form efficient, 474
Semistructured problem, 670
Semivariable costs, 46
Sensitivity analysis, 54, 330, 474, 515–516, 670
Sensitivity training, 945
Separation of ownership and control, 784–785
Sequential access, 670
Sequential oral interpreters, 945
Serial correlation, 474
Serial port, 591, 670
Serial transmission, 591, 670
Server, 670
  dedicated, 632
Service(s)
  creating new, 484
  differentiating, 484–485
  enhancing, 485
  in internal control, 685
Service capacity, 945
Service charges, 588
Service consistency, 945
Service costs, manufacturing cost terms, 57–59
Service departments, 87
  charges by, 87–89, 185
Service heterogeneity, 945
Service leases, 249, 943
Service level agreement (SLA), 569, 670
Services businesses, 185
Services trade, 868, 945
Service strategy, 830–831
Settlement, 809
Settlement date, 185
Settlement range, 878, 945
Setup, 185
Severity of the loss, 731
Shared resource architecture, 536–537
Shareholder activism, 791
Shareholder lawsuits, 791–792
Shareholder resolutions, 791
Shareholders
  in corporate governance, 783
  increased role of, in corporate governance, 790–792
Shareholders' equity, 359
Shareholder value maximization, 474

Shareholder wealth
  managerial actions to maximize, 192–193
  managerial incentives to maximize, 191
Shelf registrations, 345, 474
Shell company, 804
Sherman Act (1890), 356, 917
Shipper's order, 945
Shipping and installation costs, 327
Short-term assets, managing, 208–220
Short-term bank loans, 222–223
Short-term credit, 220, 474
Short-term debt
  cost of, versus long-term debt, 207
  risk of, versus long-term debt, 208
Short-term financial planning, 284–286
Short-term financing, 427–430
  advantages and disadvantages of, 207–208
  effective cost of, 231
  impact of, on multinational corporations (MNCs) value, 430
  managing, 220–232
  sources of, 220–224, 427
  strategies in, 228–231
  use of security in, 224–225
Short-term horizon, 354
Short-term investment strategies, 218–219
Short-term liabilities, managing, 220
Short-term orientation, 185
Sight draft, 474
Sign, 945
Signal, 308, 474, 945
Signaling hypothesis, 309, 463
Signaling theory, 308
Signature card, 133
Signified, 945
Signifier, 945
Simple earnings per share (EPS), 255
Simple interest, 474
Simple interest approximation formula, 474
Simple interest loan, 474
Simple interest rate, 474
Simple regression, 474
Simplex communication, 592, 670
Simulation, 474
Simultaneous equations, 368
Simultaneous oral interpreters, 945
Single-Buyer policy, 474
Single European Act (1992), 406, 474, 945
Single plantwide factory overhead rate method, 185
Single-step income statement, 185
Sinking funds, 185, 239, 247, 389, 474
SirCam virus, 501
Situational scheme, 945
Six sigma quality, 185

Skimming, 809
  theft of cash through, 701–702
Slide, 185
Small Business Policy, 474
Small power distance culture, 185
Smithsonian Agreement, 474
Smoot-Hawley Act, 945
Snail mail, 670
Snake, 474
Sniffing, 809
Social accounting, 4
Social altruism, 945
Social audit, 809
  versus stakeholder audit, 764
Social auditing, 801
Social awareness, 946
Social contribution, 946
Social impact disclosure practices, 155–157
Social infrastructure, 946
Social interaction paradigm, 946
Socially conscious investing, 754–756, 809
Socially unacceptable and unacceptable, 946
Social performance
  corporate, 752–753
  financial performance and, 754
Social regulation, 893
Social responsibility, 191–192, 474, 946
  corporate, 745–751
  cross-national, 921–923
Social screening, 754
Social stratification, 946
Social welfare, stock price maximization and, 192
Sociocultural contexts, 946
Soft controls, 678, 809
Soft currencies, 946
Soft skills, 809
Software, 670
  antivirus, 501, 659
  application-specific, 660
  collaborative, 621
  custom-designed, 662
  domain name system, 502
  general purpose application, 664
  groupware, 613, 621
  mission-critical, 667
  open source, 668
  packaged, 668
  prepackaged, 566, 569–573
  purchased, 572–573
  renting, 573
  system, 671
Software piracy, 645–646, 653, 670
SOHO (Small Office/Home Office), 670
Solvency, 32, 185, 474

Solvency analysis, 32–37
   accounts receivable analysis, 34–35
   current position analysis, 33–34
   inventory analysis, 35–36
   number of times interest charges are earned, 37
   ratio of fixed assets to long-term liabilities, 36
   ratio of liabilities to stockholders' equity, 36–37
Solvency ratios. *See* Liquidity ratios
Source code, 670
South Africa, King model in, 683
Southeast Asian management, 946
Sovereign immunity, 914, 946
Special drawing right (SDR), 441, 474, 894–895, 903–904
Special economic zones, 946
Special interest groups, influential, 151
Special reports, 185
Specie, 946
Specific price index, 185
Specific tariff, 886
Speculation, break-even point from, 425
Speculative balances, 209, 474
Speculative motive, 474
Speculative risk, 726–727, 809
Speculator, 474, 737
Speech recognition, 670
Speech synthesizing, 670
Spontaneous financing, 474
Spontaneously generated funds, 268, 474
Spoofing, 502, 670, 809
Sporadic dumping, 891
Spot markets, 336, 400–401, 474
Spot rates, 185, 474, 946
Spurious correlation, 474
SQL (Structured Query Language), 670
Stable, predictable dividends, 311, 474
Stable distribution, 474
Staff department, 7
Stage of subsidiary development, 946
Stakeholder audit, 809
   versus social audit, 764
Stakeholder environment, 809
Stakeholders, 150, 185, 195, 474
Stand-alone risk, 329–332, 475
   measuring, 347–348
Standard audit report, 124
   departures from, 124
Standard check processing, 475
Standard cost, 185
Standard cost systems, 185
Standard deviation, 347–348, 475
Standardization, 165, 186, 829–830, 946
   harmonization versus, 164–165
Standardized product, 861
Standard of living, 946
Standard worldwide pricing, 946
Standby letter of credit, 414, 475
Star topology, 600, 671

Stated value, 186
Statement footnotes, misleading, 723
Statement of account, 133
Statement of cash flows, 8, 14, 18, 186, 475, 809
   general model for, 24–26
   purpose of, 18–23
Statement of Financial Accounting Standards No. 52, 186
Statement of retained earnings, 475
Statement of stockholders' equity, 186
Statements of Financial Accounting Concepts, 162
Statements of Financial Accounting Standards, 5, 162
Statements of Position, 162
Statements on Auditing Standards (SASs), 170, 186
State-owned enterprise, 946
Static budget, 71–72, 186
Static element, 831
Static IP number, 671
Static risks, 727
Static surveillance, 809
Stationary surveillance, 809
Statistical analysis, 809
   of past losses, 733
Statistical decomposition, 475
Statute, 809
Statutory merger, 186
Statutory reserve, 186
Steering committee, 584, 671
Stepped-up exercise prices, 253, 475
Stereotypes, 946
Sterilized intervention, 475
Stochastic model, 475
Stock dividends, 186, 313–314, 475
Stock exchanges, 339–340
Stockholders, 186
   creditors versus, 194–195
   managers versus, 193–194
Stockholders' equity, 18, 389–390
   rate earned on common, 39–40
   rate earned on total, 39
   ratio of liabilities to, 36–37
Stockholder wealth maximization, 191, 475
Stock market, 339–340
   types of transactions, 341
Stock market equilibrium, 263–265
Stock price maximization, social welfare and, 192
Stock prices, interest rate levels and, 385
Stocks, 186
   decision to list, 341
   valuation of, 258–265
      with constant growth, 261–263
      with zero growth, 261
Stock splits, 186, 313, 475
Stock valuation models, terms used in, 259–260

Stock values
   dividend policy and, 309
   expected dividends as basis for, 260–261
Stone model, 475
Storage, 671
Storage service provider (SSP), 575, 671
Straddle, 427, 475
Straight bill of lading, 946
Straight-line depreciation method, 186
Straight-line method, 369
Strategic advantage, 481, 671
Strategic alliance, 186, 946
Strategic information, as competitive weapon, 520–524
Strategic information systems (SISs), 481, 491–492, 671
   creating, 521
   sources of, 523–524
Strategic leader, 848, 946
Strategic management, 809
   in issues management, 762
   public affairs as part of, 759–760
   public policy as part of, 756–757
   relationship of ethics to, 757–758
   steps in, 757–758
Strategic managers, 671
Strategic objectives, 822, 946
Strategic plan, 186
Strategic planning, 186, 481, 675
   for international negotiations, 877–879
Strategy, 877
Stretching accounts payable, 222, 475
Strike price, 404, 421, 460
Striking price, 250, 475
Strong-form efficient, 475
Structural Adjustment Loan Facility (SAL), 397, 475
Structured data, 505, 671
Structured problem, 671
Structured Query Language (SQL), 671
Stylus, 671
Subdomain, 633
Subjective risk, 727, 809
Subjective risk management, 743–744
Subordinated debentures, 237, 475
Subpoena (subpoena duces tecum), 809
Subsidiaries, 186, 828–829, 946
Subsidiary company, 186
Subsidiary dividend payments, 431
Subsidiary expenses, 430
Subsidiary ledger, 186
Subsidiary liquidity management, 431
Subsidiary revenue, 430
Subsidy, 890–891
   domestic, 890–891
   export, 890–891
Subsystem, 671
Suite, 671

Sum-of-the-years-digits depreciation method, 186
Sunk costs, 98, 186, 326–327, 475
Supercomputer, 671
Super-NOW accounts, 475
Supplier credit, 410, 475
Supplier partnering, 186
Suppliers, locking in, 486
Supply chain, 640
Supply-chain management, 475
Supply-chain management (SCM), 569, 620, 640, 671, 946
Supply of international reserves, 903
Support, 561–562, 671
Supranational corporation, 828
Surfers, 671
Surplus, 390
   earned, 390
Surveillance, 809
Surveys, 946
Sustainable growth, 475
Swap, 475
Swap arrangements, 905
Sweatshops, 794–795, 809
Sweep accounts, 475
SWIFT, 475
Switch, 833
Switching
   costs of, 483–484, 671
   techniques, 604–605, 671
Symmetric DSL (SDSL), 606
Symmetric encryption, 671
Symmetric information, 308, 475
Synchronization, 592–593
Synchronized cash flows, 210, 475
Synchronous communication, 593
Syndicate, 475
Syndicated Eurocredit loans, 475
Syndicated Eurocurrency loans, 405–406
Syndicate of Eurobanks, 405
Synergy, 671
Syntax error, 671
Synthetic composite, 475
System, 671
Systematic risk, 475
System clock, 671
System of authorizations, 809
   in preventing and detection of fraud, 694
System requirements, 555, 671
Systems acquisition, 551–578, 566–567
Systems analysis, 553–556, 671
Systems analyst, as agent of change, 495
Systems concept, 946
Systems design, 556, 671
Systems development, 551–578
   led by end users, 564–565, 671
Systems development life cycle (SDLC), 552–562, 563, 671
   analysis, 553–556

   design, 556–560
   implementation, 560–561
   support, 561–562
Systems integration, 566, 671
Systems integrator, 671
System software, 671
Systems thinking, 671
System testing, 560

T

Tablet computer, 671
Tabular representation, 506
T account, 186
Tactical information systems planning, 491–492
Tactical managers, 671
Tactical objectives, 822, 946
Tactical planning for international negotiations, 879–880
Tactics, 877
Tailing, 809
Takeover, 475
   consequences of, in corporate governance, 786–788
Tangible assets, valuation of, 265–266
Target bidding, using call options to hedge, 422–423
Target capital structure, 242, 297, 301–302, 476
Target cash balance, 475
Target cost concept, 110, 186
Target costing, 186
Target marketing, 615–616, 671
Target profit, 53–54
Target zones, 476
Tariff barriers, 825
Tariff escalation, 888
Tariff-rate quota, 890
Tariffs, 393, 476, 886–889, 915, 946
   ad valorem, 886
   as burden on exporters, 888–889
   compound, 886
   import, 886
   protective, 886
   quotas versus, 890, 946
   revenue, 886
   specific, 886
   types of, 886
Taxable-equivalent yield, 476
Taxable income, 186, 476
Taxable instruments, 476
Tax accounting, 4
Tax-advantaged instruments, 476
Tax Anticipation Notes, 476
Tax benefit/bankruptcy cost trade-off theory, 307–308
Tax courts, 809
Tax credit, 186
Tax equalization, 946
Tax-exempt commercial paper, 476

Tax holiday, 186
Tax loss carryback and carryover, 476
Tax planning, 550
Tax policy, 837, 946
TCP/IP (Transmission Control Protocol/Internet Protocol), 605, 671
Teaching services, 946
Team building, 946
Team culture, 946
Team negotiations, 878
Team of negotiators, 878
Teams, 946
Technical feasibility study, 554, 671
Technical forecasting, 476
Technical innovations, 860
Technological environment, 927
Technology
   global strategy and, 822–823
   impact of, on centralized cash management, 437
Technology transfer, 827, 946
Telecommunications, 590, 671
   in business, 589–590
Telecommunications manager, 671–672
Telecommuting, 672
Teleconferencing, 672
Telemarketing, 616
Telephone network maintenance, 549
Telephones, cellular, 607
Temporal method, 186
Temporary accounts, 186
Temporary current assets, 205, 229, 476
Temporary differences, 186
Temporary investments, 186
10-K, 802
Tenor, 413, 476
10-Q, 802
Ten steps of crisis communication, 770–771
Tentative U.S. tax, 946
Terminal cash flow, 328, 476
Terminal value, 476
Terminal warehouse agreement, 476
Terminal warehousing, 227
Term loans, 236, 476
Term repos, 476
Terms of credit, 213, 476
Terms-of-trade estimates, 885
Term spread, 476
Term structure of interest rates, 383–384, 476
Term structure theories, 383–384
Terrestrial microwave, 595
Territorial approach, 186
Terrorism, 836, 946
Testimonial evidence, 809
   in fraud investigation, 699

Theft
  of cash through fraudulent disbursement, 702
  through larceny, 701
  through skimming, 701–702
  of inventory, 702
  investigation methods for, 809
  of other assets, 702
Theocracy, 946
Theoretical standards, 186
Theory of comparative advantage, 186
Theory of constraints (TOC), 110, 186
Theory T and Theory T+, 946–947
Thin capitalization, 186
Thin client, 672
Thin market, 476
Third-country national, 947
Third generation languages (3GLS), 672
Third-party administrator, 741
Third-party information vendor, 476
Threats, 818
Tiered pricing, 476
Time bomb, 672
Time-division multiplexing, 599
Time draft, 476
Time equals money, 947
Timeliness of accounting information, 2
Time preferences for consumption, 381, 476
Time-series analysis, 476
Time series models, 476
Time series regression, 476
Time-series techniques, 476
Times-interest-earned (TIE) ratio, 307, 476
Time span, 504, 672
Time tickets, 186
Time to market, 672
Time value of money, 370, 379–380
Time value of money concept, 186
T1 line, 606
T3 line, 606
Token passing, 603, 672
Top-down planning, 672
Topology, 599, 672
Total assets turnover ratio, 476
Total costs, 105–107, 186, 947
Total leverage, degree of, 306–307
Total quality management (TQM), 387, 947
Touching, 874
Touch screen, 672
Tourism, 947
Trackball, 672
Tracking, 947
Track pad, 672
Trade, 823, 824
  basis for, 884–885
  equilibrium in absence of, 883–884
  flow of, 915
  gains from, 884–885
  government controls over, 825
  nontariff barriers to, 825
Trade acceptance, 411, 476
Trade Act (1988), 854
Trade barriers, 947
Trade creation, 947
Trade credit, 221–222, 476
Trade discounts, 187, 476
Trade diversion, 947
Trade draft, 947
Trade finance methods, 412–417
Trade flows, international, 392–396
Trade implications, of product cycle, 861
Trade-in allowance, 187
Trade liberalization, 826
Trademarks, 187, 823, 826
Trade-off concept, 947
Trade policy measures, 928, 947
Trade promotion authority, 947
Trade relations, changes in, 927–928
Trade restrictions, 392–394
  arguments for, 889
Traders, 476
Trade secrets, 656
Trading blocs, 187, 947
Trading security, 187
Traditional files, 530
  databases versus, 531–533
Training, 618–619
Tramp service, 947
Transaction, 672
Transaction approach, 476
Transaction exposure, 476, 947
Transaction motive, 476
Transaction-processing system (TPS), 507–508, 622, 672
Transaction register, 133
Transaction risk exposure, 187
Transactions balance, 209, 477
Transaction sets, 476
Transceiver, 672
  microwave, 595
Transferable letter of credit, 414–415, 477
Transfer agent, 477
Transfer items, 477
Transfer prices, 95, 187, 947
Transfer pricing, 95–97, 477
Transfer risk, 836, 947
Transformative technological innovations, 947
Transit items, 477
Transit routing number, 477
Transit time, 947
Translation exposure, 477, 947
Transmission channel stage, identifying right, 873–874
Transmission Control Protocol/Internet Protocol (TCP/IP), 605, 671
Transmission rate, 593, 672
Transmission speeds, 594
Transnational corporations, 187, 828
Transnational strategy, 822, 947
Transparency, 672
Transparency International, 797, 854
Transposition, 187
Trash investigation, 810
Treadway Commission, 810
Treasury management workstation, 477
Treasury shares, 389
Treasury stock, 187, 390
Treaties of Friendship, Commerce, and Navigation, 911
Treaty on European Union (1993), 913
Tree topology, 601, 672
Trend analysis, 187, 477
Trial balance, 187
Triangular arbitrage, 477, 947
Trigger mechanisms, 947
True and fair view, 187
Trustee, 238, 810
Trustee under indenture, 477
Trust receipt loans, 477
Trust receipts, 227
Trust services, 477
Turnbull model in United Kingdom, 683
Turnkey operation, 947
Turnover ratios. *See* Efficiency ratios
Twisted-pair-cable, 594–595, 672
Two-column journal, 187
Two-tier exchange rates, 900
Two-transaction approach, 187

U

Ubuntu, 947
Umbrella policy, 477
Unbiased expectations hypothesis, 477
Uncertainty acceptance, 187
Uncertainty avoidance, 187, 947
Uncollected balance percentages, 477
Uncollectible accounts expense, 187
Uncommitted lines of credit, 477
Underapplied factory overhead, 187
Underlying stock, 251
Underwriter's spread, 344, 477
Underwriting process, 407–408
Underwriting syndicate, 345, 477
Underwritten arrangement, 344, 477
Undistributed earnings, 947
Unearned revenues, 187, 810
Unemployment, inflation with, 881–882
Unethical, 947
Uneven cash flow stream, 477
Unfunded retention, 735
Uniform Commercial Code (UCC), 225, 389, 477
Uniform Resource Locator (URL), 672
Unilateral transfers, 477
Unintentional amoral management, 778, 810

Uninterruptible power supply (UPS), 498, 672
Unique visitor pages, 672
Unique visitors per month, 672
Unique ZIP code, 477
Unit contribution margin, 49–50, 187
Unit cost factor, 119
United Kingdom, Turnbull model in, 683
United Nations (UN), 156, 187, 818, 911
    Code of Conduct for Transnational Corporation, 911
    Convention on Contracts for the International Sales of Goods (CISG), 916
United States
    accounting standards and financial reporting in, 162–164
    independent auditing environment in, 170–172
United States Foreign Corrupt Practices Act (FCPA), 947
Unit of measure concept, 5, 187
Unit price factor, 119
Unit selling price, effect of changes in, 52–53
Units-of-production depreciation method, 187
Universal. *See* Global
Universal Copyright Convention, 918
Universal factors framework, 947
Universalism, 922, 947
UNIX, 672
Unplanned retention, 735
Unrealized (holding) gains, 187
Unrealized holding gain or loss, 187
Unrealized (holding) losses, 187
Unsecured, 477
Unsolicited order, 947
Unstructured data, 505, 947
Unstructured problem, 672
Update privilege, 510
Uploading, 672
Upper control limit (UCL), 368, 477
Up time, 574
Usable funds, 231, 232, 477
Usage rate, 477
User application development, 575–578
    factors encouraging, 576
User-developed applications
    advantages and risks in, 577–578
    managing, 576–577
User dialog, 557
Utilitarian ethic, 780
Utilities, 672

V

Valuation, 477
Value added, 187
Value-added activities, 187
Value-added lead time, 187

Value-added networks (VANs), 600, 672
    electronic data interchange, 639
Value-added statements, 156, 187
Value-added tax (VAT), 187, 947
Value at risk (VAR), 810
Value chain, 810
Value creation, with information technology, 519–525
Value dating, 477
Value, 947
Values, 947
Vandalism, 498
Variable costing, 48, 112, 187
    income analysis under, 113–114
    income statement under, 112–113
    management's use of, 114–120
Variable costs, 44–45, 108–109, 187, 478
Variable cost concept, 187
    effect of changes in, 51–52
    reporting, for decision making, 48
Variable identification, 478
Variables rate demand notes, 478
Variance, 187, 348, 478
Variance analysis model, 478
Variation, coefficient of, 348
VAT concept, 187
Vendor fraud, 689, 810
Vertical analysis, 29–30, 31, 187, 810
Vertical market, 637, 672
Vertical merger, 357, 478
Vices, fraud and, 691
Victim, 810
Victims, of fraud, 686
Videoconferencing, 607, 672
Vienna Trademark Registration Treaty, 918
Virtual memory, 672
Virtual organization, 672
Virtual private networks (VPNs), 602, 631
Virtual reality, 672
Virtual Reality Modeling Language (VRML), 672
Virtual teams, 848, 947
Virtual Web server, 633
Virus (computer virus), 672
Visible pay inequity, 947
Voice mail, 607
Voice recognition, 672
Voir dire, 810
Volatile memory, 672
Volume variance, 187
Voluntary disclosures, 151
Voluntary restraint agreements, 947
Voting rights, 247
Voucher, 132, 187
Voucher system, 132, 187
Vulnerability chart, 810

W

Wa, 948
Wage and price controls, 882, 948
Wait states, 672
WAN (Wide Area Network), 673
Warehouse receipts, 227–228
Warrants, 237, 252–253, 478, 810
    reporting earnings when, are outstanding, 255
    use of, in financing, 252–253
Warranty liabilities, 810
War Weapons Control Law, 852
War Weapons list, 852
WCR/S, 478
Weak-form efficient, 478
Web
    databases on, 537
    using, for international commerce, 654
Web-based electronic commerce, 608
Webb-Pomerene Act (1918), 853–854, 948
Web databases, 537–538
Web electronic data interchange, 639–640
Web hosting service, 633
Webmaster, 673
Web page, 673
    authoring tools for, 673
Web portal, 632
Web server, virtual, 633
Web service provider, selection of, 633–634
Web site, 673
Web-visit hijacking, 810
Weekend effect, 478
Weighted average cost of capital (WACC), 292, 297, 362, 478
What-if analysis, 54, 516, 673
White-collar crimes, 703
Whitemail bribery, 919, 948
Wholesale lockbox system, 478
Wholesale market, 478
Wholly owned foreign subsidiary, 828
Wholly-owned subsidiary, 948
Wide area networks (WANs), 599–600
    protocols, 603–604
Window dressing techniques, 478
Wire drawdowns, 478
Wireless access protocol, 636, 673
Wireless communication, 600, 673
Wireless LAN, 673
Wire transfers, 478
Withholding taxes, 948
Within-firm risk, 329, 332
Without recourse, 478
With recourse, 478
Word (data word), 673
Work cycle, 620, 673

Working capital, 33, 187, 200, 478
　requirement for external financing, 201
Working capital cycle, 478
Working capital financing, 416
Working Capital Guarantee Program, 478
Working capital investment, 478
　financing policies and, 204–207
Working capital management, 199–204, 478, 948
　policies on, 208–213
Working capital policy, 199–208, 200, 478
Working capital ratio, 33
Working capital requirements, 478
Working capital terminology, 200–201
Working capital turnover ratio, 810
Work in process inventory, 60, 188
Work-in-process inventory, 478
Work redesign programs, 948
Work-related pressures, fraud and, 691

Work scheduling, 948
Works council, 948
Work sheet, 188
Workstation, 673
World Bank, 397, 478, 818, 948
World-class competitors, 948
World Health Organization (WHO), 911
World Trade Organization (WTO), 398, 478, 826, 854, 910, 911, 913, 927, 938, 948
　Agreement on Trade-Related Aspects of Intellectual Property Rights, 653
Worldwide approach, 188
Worldwide disclosures diversity and harmonization, 157–165
　accounting standard setting and financial reporting, 158–164
　disclosure diversity, 158
　standardization versus harmonization, 164–165
Worldwide diversity in measurement and reporting, 152–154

World Wide Web (WWW), 481, 505–506, 673
Worm, 673
WORM (Write Once, Read Many), 673
Worst-case scenario, 331, 478
Writer, 423
Written principles, 948

Y

Yankee bonds, 245
Yankee stock offerings, 478
Yield, 67, 188
Yield curve, 478
Yield spread, 478
Yield spread swap, 475, 478
Yield to maturity (YTM), 257–258, 478

Z

Zero-balance accounts, 211, 478
Zero-based budgeting, 71, 188
Zero coupon bonds, 239–240, 478
Zero-growth stock, 478
　valuing, 261